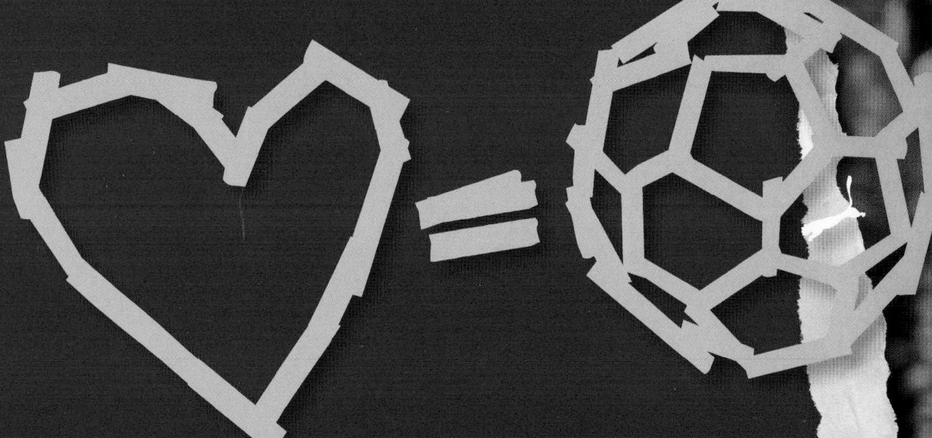

PUMA®

FA PREMIER LEAGUE

CHAMPIONSHIP LEAGUE

LEAGUE ONE

LEAGUE TWO

SCOTTISH PREMIER LEAGUE

SCOTTISH LOWER LEAGUE

IRISH LEAGUE

PUMA FOOTBALL

Since its founding, PUMA has been active as an international football sponsor and equipment supplier to players and teams.

The brand sponsors international football federations including 2006 World Champions Italy and 2011 Copa América Champions Uruguay, and other prominent footballing nations including The Czech Republic, Switzerland and Chile. PUMA is renowned for its sponsorship of many African teams including reigning African Cup of Nations Champions Egypt, Cameroon, Ghana, Ivory Coast and South Africa.

PUMA sponsors a number of club sides across Europe including Bordeaux, Stade Rennais, Sporting Lisbon, Lazio, Feyenoord, Club Brugge, VfB Stuttgart, Hoffenheim, AEK Athens and Olympiacos. Domestically PUMA is the biggest supplier of kit in English professional football sponsoring Premier League teams Newcastle United and Tottenham Hotspur and supporting teams such as Burnley, Cardiff City, Coventry City, Hibernian, Motherwell, Preston North End, Reading and Sheffield Wednesday.

PUMA also sponsors leading players including Nemanja Vidic, Michael Carrick, Phil Jones, Mikel Atreta, Shay Given, Kevin Doyle, Bacary Sagna, Johan Djourou, Matthew Etherington, Steven Pienaar and Peter Crouch.

PUMA TEAMWEAR AVAILABLE AT:
WWW.GENESISSPORTS.CO.UK
CALL: 0845 680 1204
(8AM TO 5PM WEEKDAYS)
OR EMAIL:
SALES@GENESISSPORTS.CO.UK

PUMA TEAMWEAR

Football is love.

This is why we play it anywhere, why we can't sleep before a match day, why we paint our faces and sing our hearts out. It is true for everyone of us whether we are a player or a fan, a child or a grown-up. Whether we support Ghana or Switzerland. Whether we call it Soccer, Calcio, Futbol or ... football. There's no time to think. The moment is all about spontaneity. Aim where your guts point. Do what your heart tells you – and don't argue. Let your personal performance refl ect your love for the game – and shine through for the good of the team.

When in a single moment, everything comes together and each player feels the instinctual rhythm that connects a team, magic happens.

That's how PUMA Teamsport works. It's fast and decisive, believing that joy and performances coming from the heart, from all ages on all levels together form success on the pitch.

For more than 60 years, we have celebrated numerous "once in a lifetime" moments with our players and multiple victories with our teams.

We have successfully merged sports and lifestyle and we will continue to go down that road. Our love for the game, coupled with our constant quest for innovative, performance-enhancing product solutions benefit footballers, cricketers, rugby and indoor sports players all over the world.

"Enjoy the game."

size
5
IMS
INTERNATIONAL
MATCHBALL
STANDARD

BRINGS
US TOGETHER.
=
SPEED UP YOUR GAME IN
THE NEW v1.11
PUMA
puma.com

NON-LEAGUE CLUB DIRECTORY 2012

(34th Edition)

EDITORS
MIKE WILLIAMS & TONY WILLIAMS

ASSISTANT EDITORS
JAMES WRIGHT
CRAIG POTTAGE

NON-LEAGUE CLUB DIRECTORY 2012
ISBN 978-1-869833-70-1

Copyright
Tony Williams Publications Ltd. All rights reserved.
No part of this publication may be reproduced, stored in a retrieval system or transmitted, in any form or by any means, electronic material, photocopying, recording or otherwise, without the permission of the copyright holder.

Editors
Mike Williams
(Tel: 01548 531 339)
tw.publications@btinternet.com)
Tony Williams
(Tel: 01823 490 684)
Email: t.williams320@btinternet.com
James Wright
6 Harp Chase, Taunton, Somerset TA1 3RY
(Tel: 07786 636659 Fax: 0800 048 8641)
Email: james@nlnewsdesk.co.uk

Published by Tony Williams Publications Ltd
(Tel: 01548 531 339)
Email: tw.publications@btinternet.com

Printed by Polestar Wheatons (Exeter, Devon)

Sales & Distribution
T.W. Publications (01548 531 339)

Front Cover: (Main Picture) Nantwich Town's Ash Carter (in green) in action - Carter clocked up his 200th appearance for Nantwich at the end of the 2010/11 season.
Inset Pictures (L-R): Goalmouth action from the FA Vase Final. Photo: Roger Turner.
A training session underway at Wealdstone FC. Photo: Alan Coomes.
Dover's Adam Birchal (white strip) challenges for the ball against Aldershot in the 2nd Round of the FA Cup. Photo: Eric Marsh

foreword....

Creating a comprehensive field guide for non-league football has, and always will be, a major undertaking. This edition, the 34th, is no exception and would not have been possible without the extensive research by Tony and Mike Williams and their valuable contributors.

The Annual Directories are to be kept but especially they are books to be read and read again, and then possibly re-read for each of the volumes over the years in their own special way has a vital quality in information and knowledge, valued by players, officials and fans.

There is always something uniquely exciting about the start of the season, expectations are high without anyone questioning anything but success. Dreams we can never replace.

Over the last years we have seen a number of important key changes and additions, non more than the restructuring of the National League System. Bringing together the majority of the leagues within the Football Pyramid significantly increasing the standards and sporting participation, revitalising the football landscape.

It has become more and more difficult by changes in the market place, peoples lives brought about by the advances in technology and the challenges facing us all today in the economic climate, never-the-less we are survivors, but the message is clear, don't reach out beyond that you can afford. Don't throw away your very existence.

Its a challenge worth winning.

Enjoy your packed Directory and best wishes for a successful 2011/ 2012 Season.

Dave Henson.
Football Association
Life Vice President.

Soccer Books Limited

72 ST. PETERS AVENUE (Dept. NLD)
CLEETHORPES
N.E. LINCOLNSHIRE
DN35 8HU
ENGLAND

Tel. 01472 696226 Fax 01472 698546

Web site www.soccer-books.co.uk
e-mail info@soccer-books.co.uk

Established in 1982, Soccer Books Limited has one of the largest ranges of English-Language soccer books available. We continue to expand our stocks even further to include many new titles including German, French, Spanish, Italian and other foreign-language books.

With well over 100,000 satisfied customers already, we supply books to virtually every country in the world but have maintained the friendliness and accessibility associated with a small family-run business. The range of titles we sell includes:

Yearbooks – All major yearbooks including many editions of the Sky Sports Football Yearbook (previously Rothmans), Supporters' Guides, Playfair Annuals, European Football Yearbooks and Asian, African and North, Central and South American yearbooks.

Club Histories – Complete Statistical Records, Official Histories, Definitive Histories plus many more.

World Football – World Cup books, International Line-up & Statistics Series, European Championships History, International and European Club Cup competition Statistical Histories and much more.

Biographies & Who's Whos – of managers and players plus Who's Whos etc.

Encyclopedias & General Titles – Books on stadia, hooligan and sociological studies, histories and hundreds of others, including the weird and wonderful!

DVDs – Season's highlights, histories, big games, World Cup matches, player profiles, a selection of over 40 F.A. Cup Finals with many more titles becoming available all the time.

For a current printed listing containing a selection of our titles, please contact us using the details at the top of this page. Alternatively, our web site offers a secure ordering system for credit and debit card holders and lists our full range of over 1,900 books and 400 DVDs.

CONTENTS

THE DIRECTORY'S 'TEAM SHEET'

TONY WILLIAMS
Editor

Educated at Malvern College, one of the country's best football schools in the late sixties, he represented England Under 18 against Scotland at Celtic Park before serving as an administrative officer in the Royal Air Force for five years.

He was on Reading's books from the age of 16 to 22, but also represented F.A. Amateur XI's and the R.A.F. while playing mainly in the old Isthmian League for Corinthian Casuals, Dulwich Hamlet and Kingstonian and joining Hereford United and Grantham during R.A.F. postings.

After taking an F.A. Coaching badge he coached at Harrow Borough, Epsom & Ewell and Hungerford Town and was asked to edit Jimmy Hill's Football Weekly after initial experience with the Amateur Footballer. Monthly Soccer and Sportsweek followed before he had the idea for a football Wisden and was helped by The Bagnall Harvey Agency to find a suitable generous sponsor in Rothmans.

After launching the Rothmans Football Yearbook in 1970 as its founder and co-compiler with Roy Peskett, he was asked to join Rothmans (although a non-smoker!) in the company's public relations department and was soon able to persuade the Marketing Director that Rothmans should become the first ever sponsor of a football league.

After a season's trial sponsoring the Hellenic and Isthmian Leagues, it was decided to go national with the Northern and Western Leagues and for four years he looked after the football department at Rothmans, with Jimmy Hill and Doug Insole presenting a brilliant sponsorship package which amongst many other innovations included three points for a win and goal difference.

So Non-League football led the way with league sponsorship and two, now well accepted, innovations.

Sportsmanship and goals were also rewarded in a sponsorship that proved a great success for football and for Rothmans. Indeed the sportsmanship incentives could be of great value to-day in the Football Association's bid to improve the game's image by ridding the game of dissent and cheating.

After the cigarette company pulled out of their sports sponsorship Tony produced the first Non-League Annual and later The Football League Club Directory, launching 'Non-League Football' magazine with "The Mail on Sunday" and then "Team Talk."

After his ten years with Hungerford Town, he moved West and served Yeovil Town as a Director for seven years but was thrilled when David Emery's plans for the exciting Non-League Media emerged and came into reality, thus giving the grass roots of the game the publicity and promotion that he and his team had been attempting to set up since the Annual (now Directory) was launched in 1978.

The aim of the company has always been to promote the non-league 'family,' its spirit and its general development. So a plaque from The Football Association inscribed 'To Tony Williams for his continued promotion of all that's good in football' was greatly appreciated as was the trophy to commemorate the thirtieth edition of the Directory and the recent GLS "Lifetime Award' for promoting non-league football.

MIKE WILLIAMS
Editorial Manager

What started out as a holiday job in 1988 helping put together (literally in those days) the Non-League Club Directory and League Club Directory, in the end forged a career which saw him work for Coventry City Football Club, e-comsport in London and finally return to TW Publications in 2003.

During his eight year spell with TW Publications he learned the ropes of all aspects of publishing culminating in the roll of production manager for the Non-League Club Directory, Team Talk Magazine, the League Club Directory and many more publications published by the company.

1995 saw the opportunity to take up the post of Publications Manager at Coventry City Football Club, and the transfer was made in the April of that year. Sky Blue Publications was formed and the League Club Directory became their leading title. Re-branded as the Ultimate Football Guide he was to deal with all aspects of the book, from design to sales and was also put on a steep learning curve into the world of Premiership programme production. The three years spent at the Midland's club gave him a great insight into all departments of a Premiership club, having produced publications for them all.

Leaving Coventry F.C. in 1998, and after a spell working on a world wide football player database for e-comsport in London, he returned to the West Country in 2001 to set up his own design/publishing company, which incorporated working on the Directory again. 2009 saw the full time switch to TW Publications and the responsibilities of publishing the Directory.

Having gone to a rugby school his football playing career was delayed. However, becoming the youngest player to have played for the First XV and representing Torbay Athletics club at 100 and 200m proved his sporting background. At the age of 20 he begun his football career which, at it's height, saw him playing for Chard Town in the Western League Premier Division.

As club secretary for South Devon League side Loddiswell Athletic, he has worked hard on and off the pitch to help bring success to the club, and last season history was made when 'Lodds' lifted the Division One title and won the Devon County Senior Cup. He is now looking forward to the club's inaugural season in the Premier Division.

JAMES WRIGHT
Assistant Editor

James Wright, brought up on the tiny island of St Agnes on the Isles of Scilly and, like his Midlands parents, a life-long Wolves fan, began his career in non-League journalism when joining Tony Williams's editorial staff at the Mail on Sunday Non-League Football magazine in August 1990. James soon assumed from Tony responsibility for the compilation of the Non-League Club Directory and edited the 1992, 1993, 1994 and 1995 editions of the best-selling annual. During this period, James was a founder member of the editorial team of Team Talk magazine, the top non-League periodical of the 1990s, and collated the acclaimed FA Cup Post War Club-by-Club Records. In 1995 James launched Non-League Newsdesk, a newsletter carrying up-to-date league tables and the week's results.

Over the six seasons James published the title, Newsdesk became an immensely popular, no frills, weekly. However, the 2000 launch of The Non-League Paper coupled with the proliferation of information on the internet saw Newsdesk sales dwindle. James decided to team up with the Paper, and for the past ten seasons has collected and collated the four or five pages of minor results and tables that appear each Sunday. The challenge has proved immensely enjoyable despite the fact that it prevents James from following his beloved Taunton Town on away days.

But James regards the highlight of his career to date as the 2000 launch of the Non-League Newsdesk Annual. During his years compiling the Directory he recognised the need for a much smaller publication to be available much earlier, i.e. in pre-season. The first edition of the Non-League Newsdesk Annual filled this void and was an immediate success outselling Alex Ferguson's official autobiography in the Sunday Times chart in its first week. The 2002 edition surpassed all others by reaching the number one slot - staying there for a further week.

The merger of the Non-League Directory and the Newsdesk Annual saw James return to his journalistic roots. After publishing nine editions of the Annual independently, he is relishing the challenge of implementing some of the popular features of the Annual into the Directory.

James attends 100+ matches each season, and covers Taunton Town for the Somerset County Gazette. Outside football he is a qualified marine cartographer, and a keen long distance runner and local league tennis player. He also enjoys fishing, boating and gigging. He lives in the West Country with long-time partner Karen and eleven year old daughter Rosie.

CRAIG POTTAGE
Assistant Editor

Craig has been a football aficionado since an early age and has always had an interest in players' careers. Craig has kept detailed records of non league players for the last few years and this is his sixth year involved in this publication.

Started work in Golf Course Design and Project Management for John Jacobs Golf Associates, doing design work on projects in the UK, France, China and Tenerife plus Project Management work in the UK and Tenerife.

Moved onto his present career in Business Development and Project Management for an IT Facilitation Company in Stevenage fourteen years ago, where he has been involved with many projects in varying roles.

Craig lives in the town with his wife and daughter.

Used to help run a Sunday League Side a few years ago but has put his management career on hold for now. He has been an Arsenal season ticket holder for over twenty years and also goes to watch Stevenage Borough when time allows. Also enjoys a beer or two.

ACKNOWLEDGMENTS

As a club secretary of my local side, Loddiswell Athletic, I know that without the help of others our success last season - history was made when we won the South Devon Football League Division One title and the Devon County Senior Cup - would not have been possible.

It's much the same with the Directory. Without the support of the Football Association, club secretaries, programme editors, league officials, contributors and photographers it would not be possible to publish the Directory each year. I haven't got room to personally thank everyone who has helped along the way but in particular I'd like to thank:

'OUR TEAM' OF PHOTOGRAPHERS

Peter Barnes, Graham Brown, Keith Clayton, Alan Coomes, Jonathan Holloway, 'Uncle Eric' Marsh, Roger Turner, Bill Wheatcroft and Gordon Whittington.

FA COMPETITIONS DEPARTMENT

Steve Clark, Chris Darnell and Scott Bolton

CONTRIBUTORS

Dennis Strudwick (Football Conference)

Alan Allcock (Northern Premier League). Bruce Badcock (Isthmian League).

Jason Mills (Southern League)

Arthur Evans (Photographer & reports).

Bill Mitchell & Stewart Davidson (Scottish Scene).

John Harman (Blue Square Players records).

Dr. Andrew Sarnecki (Pecking Order). Mike Simmonds (Schools).

And not forgetting Dad, James and Craig

Thank you, Mike Williams.

James Wright is grateful to the following (and many) others for their help in compiling this current edition: Richard Rundle, Nick House, Rowland Lyons, Rosie Wright, Karen Broom, John Shenton, Jane Phillips, John Shaw, Rob Errington, Margaret Errington, Jeremy Biggs, Jim Bean, Paul Rivers, Mrs S Moore, Graham Down, Ken Clarke, Brian King, Andrew Moffat, Phil Hiscox, Mike Sampson, Dave Lumley, Nigel Wood, Neil Juggins, Frank Harwood, Peter Francis, John Nisbet, Phil Mitcham, Arthur Green, Ann Bullock, Stephen Hosmer, Brian & Hilary Redmond, Steve Gilbert, Paul Redgate, Dave Braithwaite, Gary Berwick, Chris McCullough, Jim Wicks, Mary Ablett, Trevor Scorah, David Jarrett, Phil Annets, Roy Ainge, Bill Gardner, Jim Thorn, Peter Godfrey, John Thomas, Mark Rozzier, Dave Sponder, Ann Camm, Michael Stokes, Mike Hemmings, Ron Holpin, David Ward, Malcolm Pratt, Colin Goodwin, Rod Sutherland, Phil Potter, Dennis Johnson, Dave Marsay, Paul Birkitt, Kevin Bray, Mike Harvey, Dave Munday, Janet Hunt, Danny Braddock, Norman Pryce, Fiona Mitchell, Graham Thornton, Philip Rhodes, Jim Milner, Neville Butt, Dave Rattigan, David Wilcox, Rolant Ellis, Chas Rowland, R Griffiths, Ron Bridges, Tony Griffiths, Phil Woosnam, Alan Foulkes, William Davies, Glynn Jones, Trevor Syms, Martin Bryant, John Doe, Mike Markham, Sam Giles, David Holland, Les Bullock, Robin Goodwin-Davey, Elaine Waulmsley, Richard Mason, Peter Toft, Philip Coulthard, Geoff Jenkins, George McKitterick, Kevin Wilkinson, Richard Durrant, James Herbert, Alan Watkins.

AND A SPECIAL THANK YOU TO OUR MAIN SPONSOR
Who continue to show their support towards grass roots football.

Why not show your appreciation to Puma by checking out their website: www.**genesis**sports.co.uk

and see for yourself the great football kits, training gear and footballs on offer.

Do you still love the game?

Most of us who have been involved with Association Football all our lives, began by kicking a ball on the village sports field, in a garden or a street. We just loved kicking a ball around and when we eventually discovered eleven-a-side football we adopted our own heroes and built our own ambitions regarding 'our game'. When my mother actually bought some football kit for me at the age of seven I put it on and wouldn't take it off all day until I could show my Dad when he came home from work.

From that day onwards I have been in love with the game and I have no idea why, as I hadn't seen football played at that time. My father had been an all round sportsman so was happy to encourage my enthusiasm and I grew more and more involved with the game, probably to the detriment of my studies. That love has lasted a lifetime and I have been incredibly lucky to have spent my whole very happy life involved in the game as player, coach, manager, director, sponsor, journalist and publisher.

There are many reasons why this love story has lasted such a long time. The fun of playing cannot ever be bettered and if one is lucky, the thrill of belonging to a good side playing good football and being successful is a massive bonus. The comradeship, team spirit and dressing room banter within a successful club cannot ever be forgotten along with any successes your team or club achieve. Whether you are involved with the playing side, the administration or are supporting a club, your involvement is special and your loyalty to your colleagues, your club and the game itself, is extremely important.

That loyalty and lifetime love of the game has been severely tested in recent seasons, as, at all levels of the game, we sense different standards are being adopted.

A sense of fairplay, honesty and sportsmanship no longer appears to be respected by everyone.

'this culture of cheating to help your club appears to be accepted'

To obtain an advantage such as a free kick for your team or get an opposing player cautioned or sent off by clever cheating and simulation, can be considered a skill used to help your side to win.

At corner kicks we regularly see defenders, with their back to the ball, holding their attacking opponents causing more anger and retaliation, which the referees often use to get out of an awkward situation and give the defending side a free kick!

All over the country, thanks to the examples of many of our televised top clubs, this culture of cheating to help your club appears to be accepted, as success and the money involved in winning, has become so important to owners, management, supporters and consequently players. Thanks to the brilliant coverage the game gets on television, the rest of the football world is tempted to copy their heroes, so wherever you watch football these days you will see the sordid cheating being copied.

I know long term season ticket holders at top clubs who are not renewing next season 'because we are being asked to pay more to see more cheating'. I know parents who are not taking their young children to watch non-league games 'as the language and constant arguing on the field and the bench are not what I want my children involved with'. I know ex- players who get exasperated by referees allowing players to get away with consistent fouling and abusive attitudes.

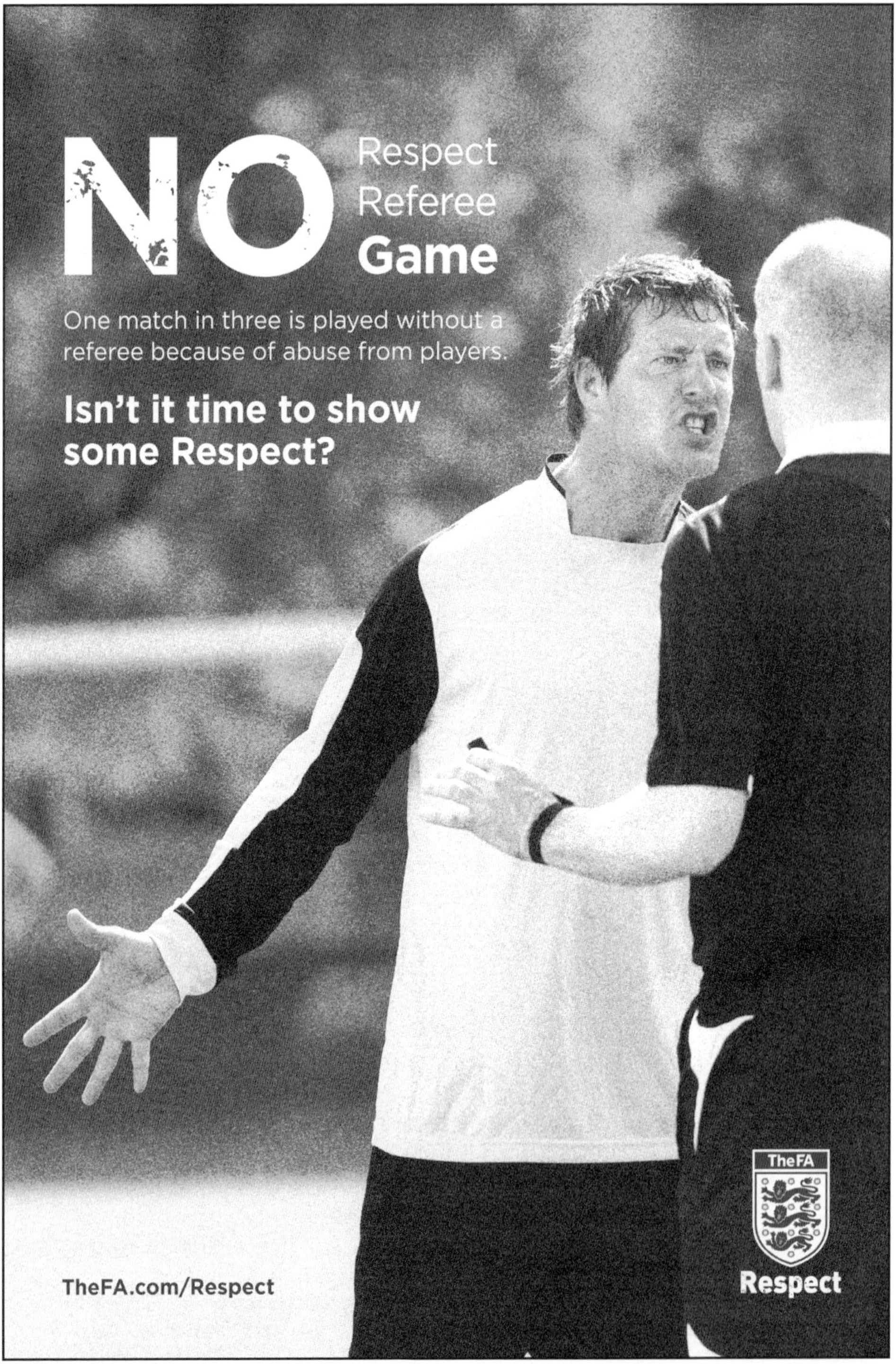

NO Respect
Referee
Game

One match in three is played without a referee because of abuse from players.

Isn't it time to show some Respect?

TheFA.com/Respect

TheFA
Respect

Why do we accept this in the game we love?

Why do we hear the excuse from referees and television pundits? 'If yellow cards were given every time the players swore at the referee or every time the defender held the opponent at a corner, we wouldn't finish with enough players on the field as everybody does it!

I'm quite sure if the referees all agreed to send players off for those offences, management would very soon ensure their players behaved. Surely the game needs the backing of the media who could do so much to ridicule the pathetic divers and cheats and could help the referees by highlighting the sad efforts of the simulators. We often hear the pundit condone the foul 'he had to do it for his team.'

I'm sure the vast majority of genuine 'football people' do still love the game and also respect sportsmanship, but surely we should be standing up for our sport not just joining the bandwagon and criticizing everyone else. The fact that there is every incentive to win football matches is not all bad. Surely in its own way there have always been great incentives to win promotion, championships and cups but you don't have to cheat to win them.

We all looked forward to The European Final between Barcelona and Manchester United but after the horrific semi-final between Barcelona and Real Madrid we dreaded another appalling display that would bring football's world wide image possibly even lower than it had sunk after the recent World Cup competition.

'We needn't have worried, both sides were magnificent'

We needn't have worried, both sides were magnificent at Wembley in their play and their spirit - just imagine how popular and enjoyable the game would be if we all attempted to copy those skills and attitudes!

So how about It? Why can't Non-League Clubs set a really good example? Wouldn't it be great if everyone visiting your club either as a player or a spectator, would leave knowing they had been involved in a sporting game of quality football, contested in the right spirit on and off the field and would look forward to a return visit to a real home of football - 'the beautiful game'.

I know - we're all human - and it's not possible all the time, but how about trying?

Having read these comments you may have views of your own regarding the reputation and image of your favourite sport. Non-League Football has its own weekly publication, so why not make your feelings known by contacting The Non-League Paper. Stand up for the game you love, whether you see some really encouraging signs that we do still love 'our game,' or perhaps offer some constructive help to improve its image. In this way, the world of non-league football can prove it cares and can certainly set an example to the national game.

Tony Williams

NON LEAGUE FOOTBALLER OF THE YEAR

MATT TUBBS

(Crawley Town)

When a club enjoys the success achieved by Crawley Town last season, their top scorer will most definitely have celebrated a memorable campaign. Matt Tubbs scored forty of his clubs 109 goals, featuring amongst his clubs' scorers in twenty six of their matches and registered hat tricks against Altrincham, Wrexham and Rushden & Diamonds. With Crawley's dominance over most opposition, it wasn't surprising that, as the club penalty taker, eleven goals were scored from the spot. Having proved his quality against Swindon Town, Derby County, Torquay United and Manchester United last season, Crawley's ace marksman will surely be looking forward to a successful season amongst the League Two clubs.

PAST WINNERS

2009-10	Dale Roberts (Rushden & Diamonds)
2008-09	Aaron Webster (Burton Albion)
2007-08	Sean Canham (Team Bath)
2006-07	Jon Main (Tonbridge Angels)
2005-06	Stuart Thurgood (Grays Athletic)
2004-05	Terry Fearns (Southport)
2003-04	Andrew Forbes (Winchester City)
2002-03	Darren Way (Yeovil Town)
2001-02	Daryl Clare (Boston United)
2000-01	Ray Warburton (Rushden & Dia)
1999-00	Gary Abbott (Aldershot Town)
1998-99	Neil Grayson (Cheltenham Town)
1997-98	Phil Everett (Tiverton Town)
1996-97	Howard Forinton (Yeovil Town)
1995-96	Barry Hayles (Stevenage Boro)
1994-95	Kevan Brown (Woking)
1993-94	Chris Brindley (Kidderminster H.)
1992-93	Steve Guppy (Wycombe Wndrs)
1991-92	Tommy Killick (Wimborne Town)
1990-91	Mark West (Wycombe Wndrs)
1989-90	Phil Gridelet (Barnet)
1988-89	Steve Butler (Maidstone Utd)
1987-88	David Howell (Enfield)
1986-87	Mark Carter (Runcorn)
1985-86	Jeff Johnson (Altrincham)
1984-85	Alan Cordice (Wealdstone)
1983-84	Brian Thompson (Maidstone Utd)

NON LEAGUE MANAGER OF THE YEAR

IAN CHANDLER

(Whitley Bay)

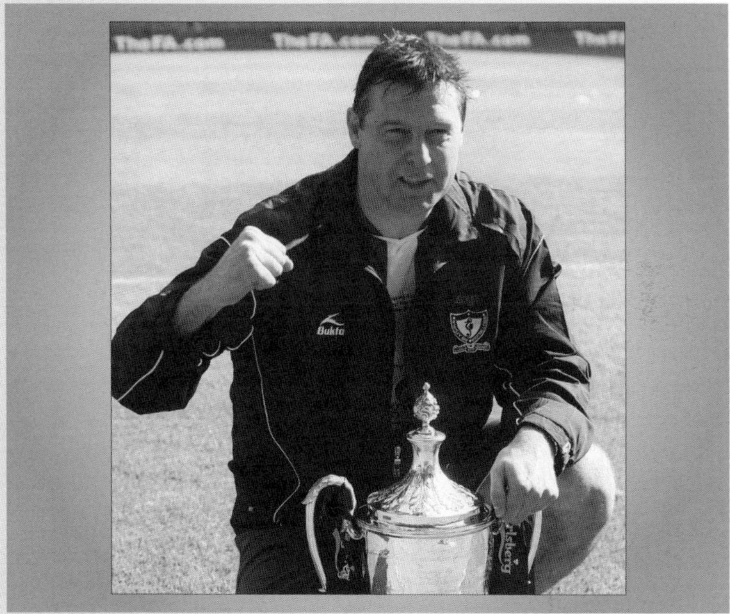

To be Manager of a club that wins the FA Vase at Wembley is special enough but to return to complete a hat trick of triumphs is bordering on the miraculous. Ian Chandler had enjoyed the winning feeling in the competition as a player but that had been in 2002 at Villa Park. For North Eastern clubs, a trip to Wembley Stadium has always been particularly special, but to mastermind three consecutive trips to the F.A. Vase Final and to actually win all three was surely only expected to be found in story books. After rather an easy victory in 2010, manager Chandler and his squad could have been forgiven for over confidence but against a very positive and hard working opposition in Coalville Town, Whitley Bay had to call on all their experience, quality and determination to earn a fabulous third Vase triumph. All credit to a very special Manager.

PAST WINNERS

2009-10	Graham Westley (Stevenage Boro)	2000-01	Jeff King (Canvey Island)
2008-09	Steve Fallon (Histon)	1999-00	Jan Molby (Kidderminster Harr.)
2007-08	Tony Greenwood (Fleetwood Town)	1998-99	Brendan Phillips (Nuneaton Boro')
2006-07	John Still (Dagenham & Redbridge)	1997-98	Steve Cotterill (Cheltenham Town)
2005-06	Steve Burr (Northwich Victoria)	1996-97	Paul Futcher (Southport)
2004-05	Paul Fairclough (Barnet)	1995-96	Paul Fairclough (Stevenage Boro)
2003-04	Graham Turner (Hereford United)	1994-95	Sammy McIlroy (Macclesfield T.)
2002-03	Gary Johnson (Yeovil Town)	1993-94	Bill Punton (Diss Town)
2001-02	Nigel Clough (Burton Albion)	1992-93	Martin O'Neill (Wycombe Wndrs)

Follow us on Twitter
or Facebook
twitter
f
For news about the
Directory.
Updates from around
the Non-League world.
Latest news from all
FA Competitions.
Plus have your say on
anything Football related.
LOG ON TO: www.non-leagueclubdirectory.co.uk
and join in today!

PECKING ORDER 2010-2011 by A J Sarnecki

Position in Season 07-08	08-09	09-10	10-11	Step	League	FA Cup ent	FA Cup xmt	FA Cup won	FA Trophy ent	FA Trophy xmt	FA Trophy won	FA Vase ent	FA Vase xmt	FA Vase won	C pts	T pts	V pts	Total pts
						1		1	3	2/8		1	4/6					
1	1	1	1	1	FOOTBALL CONFERENCE Premier	24	240	24	24	192	28				288	292		580
3	2	2	2	2	FOOTBALL CONFERENCE South	22	132	43	22	132	20				197	218		415
2	3	3	3	2	FOOTBALL CONFERENCE North	22	132	30	22	132	32				184	230		414
4	6	4	4	3	ISTHMIAN Premier	22	88	28	22	44	27				138	137		275
6	5	5	5	3	NORTHERN PREMIER Premier	22	88	24	22	44	28				134	138		272
5	4	6	6	3	SOUTHERN Premier	21	84	21	22	44	26				126	136		262
8	11	12	7	4	ISTHMIAN First North	21	44	24	21	2	22				87	87		176
11	9	7	8	4	NORTHERN PREMIER First North	22	44	21	22	0	22				87	88		175
12=	12	11	9	4	NORTHERN PREMIER First South	22	44	29	22	0	13				95	79		174
9	10	9	10	4	SOUTHERN First South & West	22	44	25	22	0	15				91	81		172
7	7	8	11	4	SOUTHERN First Central	22	44	17	22	0	21				89	87		170
10	8	10	12	4	ISTHMIAN First South	22	44	25	22	0	11				91	77		168
12=	13	13	13	5	NORTHERN First	22	0	31				22	26	44	53		92	145
14=	14	14	14	5	MIDLAND ALLIANCE	23	0	29				23	24	34	52		81	133
14=	19	21	15	5	WESSEX Premier	21	0	25				21	14	32	46		67	113
19	18	18	16	5	SPARTAN SOUTH MIDLANDS Premier	22	0	14				23	24	28	36		75	111
16	15	17	17	5	EASTERN COUNTIES Premier	18	0	19				20	20	25	37		65	102
17	20	19	18	5	WESTERN Premier	18	0	20				19	26	17	38		62	100
22=	23	23=	19	5	HELLENIC Premier	17	0	17				21	24	20	34		65	99
18	16	15	20=	5	UNITED COUNTIES Premier	18	0	16				20	20	24	34		64	98
24	17	16	20=	5	NORTH WEST COUNTIES Premier	21	0	17				22	20	18	38		60	98
21	21	23=	20=	5	NORTHERN COUNTIES EAST Premier	19	0	18				19	20	22	37		61	98
20	22	22	23	5	COMBINED COUNTIES Premier	20	0	13				21	20	23	33		64	97
25	25	26	24	5	KENT Premier	13	0	21				15	16	24	34		55	89
22=	24	20	25	5	SUSSEX COUNTY First	19	0	10				20	12	17	29		49	78
26	28	25	26	5	ESSEX SENIOR	16	0	9				17	16	19	25		52	77
new	34	27=	27	6	EAST MIDLAND COUNTIES	13	0	11				20	6	21	24		47	71
31	29=	29	28	6	WEST MIDLAND REGIONAL Premier	8	0	5				20	0	23	13		43	56
28	32	34	29	6	NORTHERN COUNTIES EAST First	10	0	8				19	0	18	18		37	55
29	27	27=	30=	6	NORTHERN Second	14	0	9				20	6	5	23		31	54
34	35	32	30=	6	SOUTH WEST PENINSULA Premier	8	0	5				15	6	20	13		41	54
27	29=	35=	32	6	NORTH WEST COUNTIES First	13	0	8				16	0	16	21		32	53
32	29=	31	33	6	MIDLAND COMBINATION Premier	12	0	9				17	0	13	21		30	51
33	33	33	34	6	WESTERN First	11	0	3				17	0	18	14		35	49
30	26	30	35	6	EASTERN COUNTIES First	9	0	5				15	0	14	14		29	43
41	38	37	36	6	WESSEX First	7	0	2				17	0	8	9		25	34
35	37	35=	37	6	SPARTAN SOUTH MIDLANDS First	7	0	5				13	0	8	12		21	33
42=	40	40	38	6	COMBINED COUNTIES First	5	0	6				12	0	3	11		15	26
36	36	38	39	6	SUSSEX COUNTY Second	7	0	2				8	0	8	9		16	25
39	39	39	40	6	UNITED COUNTIES First	3	0	2				9	0	2	5		11	16
44	41	43	41	6	HELLENIC First West	4	0	1				6	0	3	5		9	14
37	42	42	42	7	CENTRAL MIDLANDS Supreme	0	0	0				8	0	4	0		12	12
40	43	41	43	6	HELLENIC First East	2	0	0				3	0	3	2		6	8
38	44=	44=	44=	7	LEICESTERSHIRE SENIOR Premier	0	0	0				3	0	2	0		5	5
49=	49=	47=	44=	7	WEARSIDE	0	0	0				3	0	2	0		5	5
42=	44=	44=	46=	7	SOUTH WEST PENINSULA First West	0	0	0				2	0	2	0		4	4
48=	49=	47=	46=	7	HERTS SENIOR COUNTY Premier	0	0	0				2	0	2	0		4	4
			46=	--	NOTTS SENIOR Premier	0	0	0				1	0	3	0		4	4
46	52=	50=	49	7	SOUTH WEST PENINSULA First East	0	0	0				2	0	1	0		3	3
47	46=	46	50=	7	SUSSEX COUNTY Third	0	0	0				2	0	0	0		2	2
52	46=	47=	50=	7	WEST MIDLAND REGIONAL First	0	0	0				2	0	0	0		2	2
	52=	50=	50=	7	NORTH BERKSHIRE First	0	0	0				1	0	1	0		2	2
	52=	50=	50=	7	ESSEX OLYMPIAN Premier	0	0	0				2	0	0	0		2	2
			50=	7	SUFFOLK & IPSWICH Premier	0	0	0				1	0	1	0		2	2
48		50=	55=	7	DORSET PREMIER	0	0	0				1	0	0	0		1	1
		50=	55=	7	SPARTAN SOUTH MIDLANDS Second	0	0	0				1	0	0	0		1	1
			55=	7	SOMERSET SENIOR Premier	0	0	0				1	0	0	0		1	1
			55=	7	BEDFORDSHIRE Premier	0	0	0				1	0	0	0		1	1
			55=	8	CENTRAL MIDLANDS Premier	0	0	0				1	0	0	0		1	1

Points are given for status (acceptance into each of the three competitions), for prestige (exemption from early rounds) and performance (number of wins, however achieved, even by walkover). Entry to the Vase is valued at one point, that to the Trophy at 3. Cup entry gives a further bonus of one point. The number of entries from each league is shown in the appropriate column. Points for exemptions are valued at two for each round missed. The entry in the table is of the total points so gained by the given league, not the number of teams given exemptions. Finally, all wins are valued at one point, regardless of opposition: giving extra points for defeating 'stronger' opponents would be too arbitrary. After all, if they lost then they were not stronger on the day!

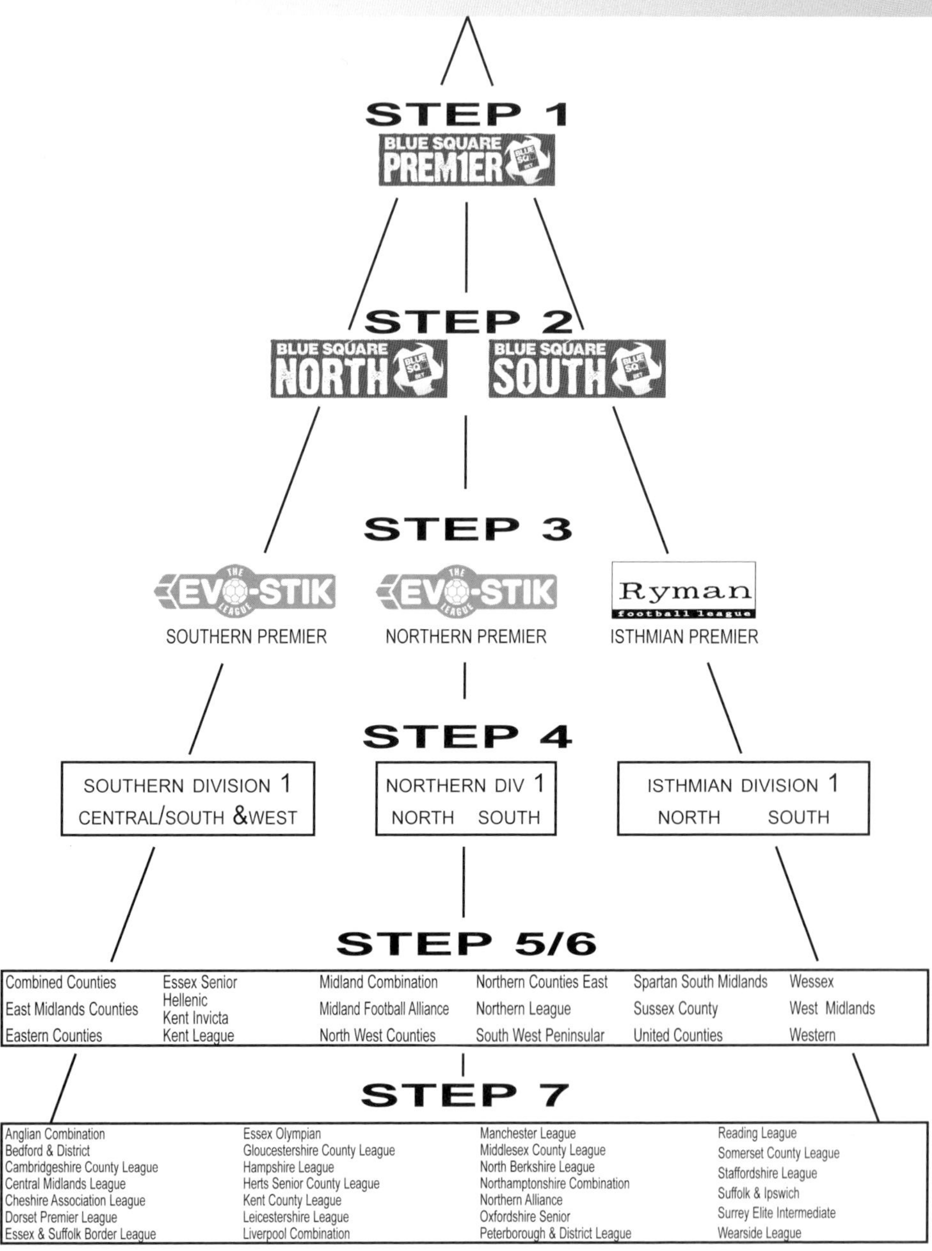

FOOTBALL LEAGUE
STEP 1
BLUE SQUARE PREM1ER
STEP 2
BLUE SQUARE NORTH
BLUE SQUARE SOUTH
STEP 3
EVO-STIK THE LEAGUE
SOUTHERN PREMIER
EVO-STIK THE LEAGUE
NORTHERN PREMIER
Ryman football league
ISTHMIAN PREMIER
STEP 4
SOUTHERN DIVISION 1
CENTRAL/SOUTH &WEST
NORTHERN DIV 1
NORTH SOUTH
ISTHMIAN DIVISION 1
NORTH SOUTH
STEP 5/6
Combined Counties
East Midlands Counties
Eastern Counties
Essex Senior
Hellenic
Kent Invicta
Kent League
Midland Combination
Midland Football Alliance
North West Counties
Northern Counties East
Northern League
South West Peninsular
Spartan South Midlands
Sussex County
United Counties
Wessex
West Midlands
Western
STEP 7
Anglian Combination
Bedford & District
Cambridgeshire County League
Central Midlands League
Cheshire Association League
Dorset Premier League
Essex & Suffolk Border League
Essex Olympian
Gloucestershire County League
Hampshire League
Herts Senior County League
Kent County League
Leicestershire League
Liverpool Combination
Manchester League
Middlesex County League
North Berkshire League
Northamptonshire Combination
Northern Alliance
Oxfordshire Senior
Peterborough & District League
Reading League
Somerset County League
Staffordshire League
Suffolk & Ipswich
Surrey Elite Intermediate
Wearside League

		P	W	D	L	F	A	Pts
1	Crawley Town	46	31	12	3	93	30	105
2	AFC Wimbledon	46	27	9	10	83	47	90
3	Luton Town	46	23	15	8	85	37	84
4	Wrexham	46	22	15	9	66	49	81
5	Fleetwood Town	46	22	12	12	68	42	78
6	Kidderminster Harriers (-5)	46	20	17	9	74	60	72
7	Darlington	46	18	17	11	61	42	71
8	York City	46	19	14	13	55	50	71
9	Newport County	46	18	15	13	78	60	69
10	Bath City	46	16	15	15	64	68	63
11	Grimsby Town	46	15	17	14	72	62	62
12	Rushden & Diamonds	46	16	14	16	65	62	62
13	Mansfield Town	46	17	10	19	73	75	61
14	Kettering Town	46	15	13	18	64	75	58
15	Gateshead	46	14	15	17	65	68	57
16	Hayes & Yeading United	46	15	6	25	57	81	51
17	Cambridge United	46	11	17	18	53	61	50
18	Barrow	46	12	14	20	52	67	50
19	Tamworth	46	12	13	21	62	83	49
20	Forest Green Rovers	46	10	16	20	53	72	46
21	Southport	46	11	13	22	56	77	46
22	Altrincham	46	11	11	24	47	87	44
23	Eastbourne Borough	46	10	9	27	62	104	39
24	Histon (-5)	46	8	9	29	41	90	28

PLAY-OFFS

Semi-Finals

Fleetwood Town 0-2 AFC Wimbledon / AFC Wimbledon 6-1 Fleetwood Town

Wrexham 0-3 Luton Town / Luton Town 2-1 Wrexham

Final (@ Manchester City, 21/5/11)

AFC Wimbledon 0-0 Luton Town (AFC Wimbledon won 4-3 on penalties)

	1	2	3	4	5	6	7	8	9	10	11	12	13	14	15	16	17	18	19	20	21	22	23	24
1 A F C Wimbledon		4–1	2–0	4–0	3–0	2–1	0–2	3–0	1–0	1–1	1–0	2–1	3–1	2–0	3–2	1–2	0–0	2–1	2–2	1–0	5–0	3–0	0–1	1–0
2 Altrincham	0–2		2–0	0–3	2–2	0–1	2–2	3–4	1–0	2–1	1–1	2–2	4–2	0–3	3–2	1–2	0–1	0–4	1–3	2–2	1–1	2–0	0–0	0–0
3 Barrow	2–0	1–0		0–1	1–2	1–1	1–1	4–0	0–2	3–0	1–3	0–2	2–0	1–1	5–0	2–1	0–1	2–2	2–1	2–0	1–1	0–2	0–1	0–0
4 Bath City	2–2	2–2	1–1		4–0	0–2	2–2	1–1	1–1	2–4	1–0	2–1	3–1	2–1	1–1	2–0	0–0	2–0	2–2	2–1	2–1	2–0	0–2	2–2
5 Cambridge United	1–2	4–0	3–1	1–2		2–2	0–1	2–0	0–1	1–1	5–0	1–1	1–0	0–0	3–0	1–2	0–0	1–5	0–1	0–2	0–0	3–3	1–3	2–1
6 Crawley Town	3–1	7–0	3–2	2–1	3–0		1–0	3–1	1–1	1–0	2–1	0–1	5–2	5–0	2–1	2–0	1–1	2–0	2–3	4–0	1–0	3–1	3–2	1–1
7 Darlington	0–0	0–1	3–1	3–1	1–0	1–1		6–1	4–0	3–0	2–0	0–1	0–1	3–1	1–1	1–1	2–2	0–0	1–0	2–0	1–0	1–0	0–1	2–1
8 Eastbourne Boro'	2–3	5–0	0–2	2–0	0–2	1–2	1–1		0–6	0–0	0–3	2–3	5–0	2–2	1–3	1–1	2–4	1–3	0–0	0–2	4–1	1–4	4–3	2–1
9 Fleetwood Town	1–1	3–1	1–0	2–1	2–2	1–2	1–0	0–1		2–0	0–0	3–0	1–1	1–1	4–1	1–1	0–3	3–0	1–1	1–1	2–0	2–1	1–0	2–1
10 Forest Green Rov'	0–0	1–0	2–3	0–0	1–1	0–3	1–1	3–4	1–0		1–1	3–3	1–0	0–1	0–2	1–1	0–1	2–1	0–0	2–2	0–0	4–0	3–0	2–1
11 Gateshead	0–2	2–0	3–0	1–1	2–3	0–0	2–2	3–0	0–2	1–1		0–0	1–0	2–0	0–0	2–2	1–0	1–1	1–7	2–2	1–0	3–1	0–1	0–3
12 Grimsby Town	2–1	0–1	1–1	2–2	1–1	0–0	0–1	2–2	1–2	1–1	2–2		1–2	2–1	2–1	3–3	2–0	7–2	2–0	1–1	1–1	2–2	2–1	0–0
13 Hayes & Yeading U	0–0	0–1	2–0	2–1	2–0	0–3	3–2	2–1	1–2	3–4	3–1	0–3		1–2	3–2	0–4	0–1	4–0	1–2	3–3	1–0	2–1	0–3	1–2
14 Histon	0–4	3–0	3–1	1–2	0–2	0–2	0–1	1–1	1–0	0–3	1–3	1–6	0–1		0–3	0–1	0–4	2–3	0–0	0–2	2–1	1–2	1–1	1–2
15 Kettering Town	1–2	3–3	1–1	2–1	2–2	0–0	0–0	3–0	2–1	2–1	1–4	1–2	2–1	4–3		1–1	1–3	0–2	2–0	0–1	3–1	0–1	1–1	1–1
16 Kidderminster H.	2–0	2–1	2–0	1–0	0–0	0–0	1–2	2–1	2–1	1–0	2–1	3–2	3–1	2–2	4–1		3–3	1–3	2–3	1–0	3–4	2–2	1–0	0–0
17 Luton Town	3–0	2–1	0–0	3–1	2–0	1–2	4–0	3–0	1–3	6–1	2–2	1–0	1–1	5–1	2–2	1–1		2–0	1–1	3–0	6–0	2–0	1–1	5–0
18 Mansfield Town	2–5	0–1	1–1	2–0	1–0	1–4	1–1	4–0	2–5	3–1	3–2	0–2	3–2	1–0	1–1	1–2	0–0		3–3	2–1	2–2	0–1	2–3	5–0
19 Newport County	3–3	2–1	5–0	1–2	1–1	0–1	2–1	3–3	1–3	3–1	2–1	2–1	2–1	2–2	1–2	3–0	1–1	1–0		1–3	2–0	1–1	1–1	4–0
20 Rushden & Dia'	1–0	1–2	5–0	5–1	2–1	0–1	2–1	2–0	1–1	2–2	0–2	4–1	1–1	2–0	1–2	2–1	0–1	1–0	0–1		2–2	1–1	2–2	0–4
21 Southport	0–1	1–0	2–4	2–3	1–1	0–4	1–1	1–3	1–0	4–0	5–1	2–2	0–0	3–1	1–2	2–2	2–1	1–2	2–1	2–2		2–1	0–1	4–0
22 Tamworth	2–5	1–0	2–2	2–2	1–1	0–3	1–1	4–2	0–2	2–1	1–1	2–1	2–3	0–1	3–1	2–2	3–1	0–2	3–2	1–2	0–1		1–1	1–3
23 Wrexham	1–2	2–1	1–1	2–0	1–0	0–0	2–1	2–1	0–0	2–1	2–7	2–0	0–2	4–0	2–0	2–2	1–0	1–1	1–0	1–1	2–1	4–2		1–1
24 York City	4–1	3–0	0–0	1–1	0–0	1–1	0–0	1–0	1–0	2–1	2–1	1–0	2–0	1–0	0–1	1–2	1–0	2–1	2–1	2–0	2–0	1–2	1–1	

		P	W	D	L	F	A	Pts
1	Alfreton Town	40	29	5	6	97	33	92
2	AFC Telford United	40	23	13	4	71	29	82
3	Boston United	40	23	10	7	72	33	79
4	Eastwood Town	40	22	7	11	82	50	73
5	Guiseley	40	20	13	7	56	41	73
6	Nuneaton Town	40	21	9	10	66	44	72
7	Solihull Moors	40	18	10	12	66	49	64
8	Droylsden	40	17	9	14	69	67	60
9	Blyth Spartans	40	16	10	14	61	54	58
10	Stalybridge Celtic	40	16	9	15	64	55	57
11	Workington	40	16	6	18	52	60	54
12	Harrogate Town	40	13	11	16	53	66	50
13	Corby Town	40	13	10	17	58	80	49
14	Gloucester City	40	14	5	21	49	63	47
15	Hinckley United	40	13	7	20	76	76	46
16	Worcester City	40	12	10	18	49	55	46
17	Vauxhall Motors	40	12	9	19	52	71	45
18	Gainsborough Trinity	40	12	5	23	50	74	41
19	Hyde	40	10	6	24	44	73	36
20	Stafford Rangers	40	8	8	24	39	78	32
21	Redditch United (-5)	40	2	8	30	30	105	9
	Ilkeston Town - record expunged							

PLAY-OFFS

Semi-Finals

Guiseley 1-0 Boston United / Boston United 3-2 Guiseley (Guiseley won 3-2 on penalties)

Nuneaton Town 1-1 AFC Telford United / AFC Telford United 2-1 Nuneaton Town

Final (@ AFC Telford United, 15/5/11)

AFC Telford United 3-2 Guiseley

Eastwood Town were ineligible for the play-offs due to their ground not meeting the required criteria.

	1	2	3	4	5	6	7	8	9	10	11	12	13	14	15	16	17	18	19	20	21
1 AFC Telford United		2–1	1–1	0–1	5–0	1–1	2–2	2–1	2–0	1–0	3–0	2–2	5–0	4–1	3–1	2–4	0–0	1–0	4–1	1–1	1–0
2 Alfreton Town	0–0		2–1	0–1	6–0	4–0	2–2	2–1	4–0	6–0	6–0	1–0	0–0	3–2	4–0	2–0	2–0	5–3	2–0	2–1	2–0
3 Blyth Spartans	3–0	1–4		0–0	1–1	2–4	0–0	1–3	0–2	0–0	1–0	4–0	3–0	1–0	2–0	0–1	3–2	1–2	2–2	3–0	2–1
4 Boston United	0–1	3–2	5–0		1–0	2–0	1–0	1–3	1–0	1–1	2–2	3–0	2–2	1–2	1–0	1–1	1–0	1–0	2–0	1–0	4–0
5 Corby Town	0–0	0–1	3–4	0–0		1–0	1–6	3–1	0–2	2–2	2–1	2–0	1–2	2–3	3–2	0–2	1–3	2–2	3–1	1–1	1–0
6 Droylsden	2–4	2–1	0–3	4–0	1–1		4–2	1–1	2–4	0–3	5–1	3–2	3–1	1–0	3–0	0–5	2–0	2–2	1–3	2–1	3–0
7 Eastwood Town	3–0	4–2	0–2	2–2	2–1	2–0		2–0	1–2	0–1	2–0	6–2	1–0	2–1	2–1	2–1	3–0	1–1	3–1	2–4	0–2
8 Gainsborough Trinity	0–5	0–3	0–2	0–3	3–1	0–3	1–3		2–0	1–3	1–3	0–1	2–1	1–2	3–0	1–1	2–2	1–3	1–1	0–2	1–1
9 Gloucester City	2–2	2–1	1–2	0–1	0–2	1–1	1–3	0–2		1–2	3–2	2–1	1–0	0–3	5–0	2–4	1–2	0–2	1–0	1–1	2–0
10 Guiseley	0–3	1–2	0–0	0–0	4–0	2–1	2–2	2–0	1–1		1–0	3–2	1–0	1–2	3–1	1–0	1–1	3–1	1–2	0–1	2–2
11 Harrogate Town	0–0	1–1	2–2	3–6	0–1	3–3	2–1	3–1	3–0	0–0		2–2	1–3	1–2	3–0	2–0	3–2	2–0	0–0	1–0	2–0
12 Hinckley United	1–1	1–3	5–1	0–1	3–3	1–1	2–3	3–1	3–0	1–2	4–0		2–0	0–3	4–0	2–2	4–0	5–2	2–3	3–1	1–2
13 Hyde	0–3	1–5	0–2	0–3	2–1	1–1	1–2	1–1	1–3	0–1	1–0	3–0		1–1	1–4	1–2	1–0	0–2	1–2	0–2	2–3
14 Nuneaton Town	0–0	1–3	3–2	1–1	2–3	1–1	2–1	1–2	0–0	0–1	3–0	2–0	1–2		1–1	2–1	1–0	2–1	3–0	2–1	2–1
15 Redditch United	1–1	1–5	2–1	0–9	2–2	1–3	0–6	1–4	0–1	2–3	0–1	2–3	0–1	0–5		0–0	0–1	1–3	2–2	0–0	1–1
16 Solihull Moors	0–1	0–1	2–0	1–0	7–2	2–2	2–0	0–2	2–1	0–1	2–2	2–7	3–2	1–1	3–0		1–1	3–1	1–0	2–0	2–0
17 Stafford Rangers	0–2	0–1	2–1	0–4	3–5	1–5	0–2	3–1	0–2	2–2	1–1	1–3	0–5	1–2	2–1	1–0		1–3	1–0	1–1	0–2
18 Stalybridge Celtic	0–1	1–2	0–0	3–1	1–1	4–0	2–1	2–0	4–3	0–0	0–1	1–1	1–2	0–2	2–0	1–1	3–2		1–3	0–0	2–1
19 Vauxhall Motors	0–1	0–2	2–6	0–0	3–2	0–1	1–2	1–0	2–1	2–2	1–1	2–0	3–2	1–1	2–1	3–3	2–1	0–3		2–3	1–2
20 Worcester City	0–3	1–2	1–0	2–0	0–2	0–1	1–1	1–2	2–0	1–2	2–3	3–2	4–2	2–2	1–1	0–1	2–2	1–0	4–1		1–2
21 Workington	0–1	0–0	1–1	3–5	1–2	2–0	0–3	4–2	2–1	0–1	2–1	3–1	1–1	0–1	5–1	2–1	2–0	0–5	2–1	2–0	

		P	W	D	L	F	A	Pts
1	Braintree Town	42	27	8	7	78	33	89
2	Farnborough	42	25	7	10	83	47	82
3	Ebbsfleet United	42	22	12	8	75	51	78
4	Chelmsford City	42	23	8	11	82	50	77
5	Woking	42	22	10	10	62	42	76
6	Welling United (-5)	42	24	8	10	81	47	75
7	Dover Athletic	42	22	8	12	80	51	74
8	Eastleigh	42	22	6	14	74	53	72
9	Havant & Waterlooville	42	16	10	16	56	51	58
10	Dartford	42	15	12	15	60	60	57
11	Bromley	42	15	12	15	49	61	57
12	Weston super Mare	42	15	8	19	56	67	53
13	Basingstoke Town	42	13	10	19	50	63	49
14	Boreham Wood	42	12	11	19	56	67	47
15	Staines Town	42	11	14	17	48	63	47
16	Bishop's Stortford	42	13	6	23	48	79	45
17	Dorchester Town	42	10	14	18	49	59	44
18	Hampton & Richmond Borough	42	9	15	18	43	60	42
19	Maidenhead United	42	10	10	22	43	70	40
20	Thurrock	42	8	13	21	50	77	37
21	Lewes	42	9	9	24	34	70	36
22	St Albans City (-10)	42	7	13	22	39	75	24

PLAY-OFFS

Semi-Finals

Woking 0-1 Farnborough / Farnborough 1-1 Woking

Chelmsford City 1-4 Ebbsfleet United / Ebbsfleet United 2-1 Chelmsford City

Final (@ Farnborough, 15/5/11)

Farnborough 2-4 Ebbsfleet United

	1	2	3	4	5	6	7	8	9	10	11	12	13	14	15	16	17	18	19	20	21	22
1 Basingstoke Town		0–1	1–0	0–2	4–1	2–3	2–2	1–0	3–2	1–2	1–2	1–0	4–0	0–2	1–1	3–4	0–2	4–1	2–2	1–3	2–2	1–0
2 Bishop's Stortford	0–2		2–0	1–2	0–1	2–2	0–1	2–1	1–4	0–1	0–3	1–4	0–2	1–5	1–0	0–0	4–0	2–1	1–0	0–4	1–1	0–4
3 Boreham Wood	1–0	1–2		0–2	2–4	2–0	3–1	0–0	2–3	2–1	0–1	2–4	2–2	1–0	3–0	4–2	0–3	2–2	2–2	0–1	6–3	0–0
4 Braintree Town	5–2	3–1	3–2		0–2	3–0	1–1	1–1	1–2	1–0	4–1	3–0	3–1	2–0	1–0	3–1	1–1	0–0	1–0	3–1	4–0	2–0
5 Bromley	0–1	4–3	1–1	0–3		0–3	4–1	2–1	0–2	0–2	1–1	0–0	1–2	1–0	1–1	0–2	1–1	0–1	1–0	2–1	3–2	2–2
6 Chelmsford City	4–0	4–1	3–1	0–0	2–0		2–0	2–0	2–2	3–0	2–3	0–1	3–1	1–2	4–0	2–0	1–1	3–1	6–1	0–2	1–0	3–0
7 Dartford	1–0	3–0	1–4	1–0	2–2	1–2		0–4	4–0	0–0	1–1	4–1	0–4	2–2	3–0	3–0	2–2	1–1	0–1	1–1	4–1	3–2
8 Dorchester Town	0–1	0–0	3–1	1–0	0–0	1–1	0–2		0–0	0–4	1–2	2–1	2–2	0–0	0–0	1–2	1–3	3–3	3–1	3–3	1–0	1–2
9 Dover Athletic	3–0	2–0	1–0	1–2	1–1	2–3	0–2	2–1		0–1	1–3	6–3	1–0	0–0	4–0	2–2	4–1	1–1	1–0	2–2	0–1	2–2
10 Eastleigh	0–1	1–2	3–0	0–2	1–0	2–1	3–0	3–0	0–2		0–3	0–3	3–0	4–2	2–1	3–0	4–2	1–4	3–1	1–4	1–1	4–1
11 Ebbsfleet United	3–1	0–0	2–2	0–0	1–2	1–3	2–1	3–2	0–2	2–2		0–3	1–0	2–1	1–0	1–2	4–0	1–1	2–2	4–0	3–1	1–1
12 Farnborough	1–1	3–2	0–1	2–1	2–2	3–1	2–1	0–0	4–1	1–2	1–2		2–0	2–0	1–0	2–2	1–0	0–0	3–2	2–2	2–0	1–2
13 Hampton & Richmond Bor	2–2	0–3	0–0	0–1	1–2	3–0	1–0	2–2	3–2	2–2	2–4	0–4		0–1	1–2	1–1	0–0	0–0	0–0	0–1	0–1	1–2
14 Havant & Waterlooville	2–0	4–1	2–1	1–2	2–0	1–2	1–0	3–1	0–0	2–2	2–3	0–3	1–2		1–2	2–1	0–1	1–1	4–1	1–3	0–0	1–1
15 Lewes	0–0	1–2	2–2	2–1	0–0	0–1	1–1	0–2	0–3	1–4	0–3	1–5	1–2	2–1		1–0	3–1	0–1	2–1	1–3	1–1	0–4
16 Maidenhead United	1–1	2–2	1–1	0–3	0–2	1–2	2–3	1–1	0–1	1–0	1–1	0–3	0–0	0–1	0–2		2–1	2–3	1–3	0–3	1–0	0–1
17 St Albans City	0–0	1–4	0–1	0–0	1–1	0–2	1–2	1–4	1–5	0–1	1–2	0–2	1–1	1–1	0–0	1–0		2–0	0–2	1–0	3–4	0–1
18 Staines Town	1–1	3–0	0–0	4–4	0–2	2–1	2–0	1–2	1–0	0–5	0–2	1–2	1–2	0–1	1–0	1–2	2–2		1–1	1–2	2–1	1–0
19 Thurrock	0–3	1–3	1–3	0–3	1–2	1–1	1–1	1–1	2–7	2–1	0–0	2–4	2–2	1–1	3–1	1–2	2–2	2–1		2–1	3–0	0–1
20 Welling United	4–0	3–1	3–1	1–3	3–1	3–2	2–1	1–2	0–1	4–2	1–1	1–0	0–0	0–2	2–1	2–1	6–0	4–0	1–1		1–0	2–0
21 Weston super Mare	1–0	3–1	2–0	2–1	7–0	2–2	0–1	1–0	1–4	0–2	3–2	0–2	0–0	1–1	0–3	3–1	2–1	2–1	2–1	2–0		0–1
22 Woking	2–0	2–0	3–0	0–1	1–0	2–2	2–2	2–1	0–1	1–1	3–0	1–1	2–1	3–1	2–1	0–2	2–0	2–0	1–0	0–0	4–3	

NATIONAL STRIKE FORCE (20 OR MORE GOALS)

Name	Club	Pens	C.S.M	T.S.M.	Hat tricks	Lge	F.A.C	F.A.T	Tot.
Adam Birchall	Dover Ath.	8	10	29	3 v Farnborough	34	11		45
					3 v Bishop's St'd				
					5 v Thurrock (a)				
Ross Hannah	Matlock Town	3	4	26	7 v BedworthU(FAT)	34	1	9	44
					3 v Nantwich T (a)				
					3 v Marine (a)				
					3 v Buxton (a)				
Matt Tubbs	Crawley Town	11	4	26	3 v Altrincham	37	3		40
					3 v Wrexham				
					3 v Rushden & D				
Craig Hammond	Cambridge C	5		24	4 v Halesowen T	29	1	3	33
Liam Hearn	Alfreton Town	2	4	22	3v Guiseley	30	1	1	32
Mike Norton	F.C. United	1	6	23		24	6	2	32
Jamie Rainford	Marine		6	21	4 v Stocksbridge	28		4	32
					3 v Northwich V				
Lee Stevenson	Eastwood Town		3	23	3v Hinckley Utd	23	5	4	32
James Walshaw	Guiseley	5	3	23	3v Redditch Utd	24+1	3	4	32
Alan Connell	Grimsby Town	4	4	23		25	1	3	29
Michael Lennon	Nantwich Town		3	20	4v Prescot Cables	20	1	7	28
Rocky Baptiste	Harrow Boro	4	2	19	3 v Horsham (a)	20+2	5		27
					4 v Horsham (h)				
Ciaran Kilheeney	Droylsden	3	3	22	4 v Stafford R (a)	20	6	1	27
Bobby Traynor	Kingstonian	8	4	21	3 v Billericay Town	23	2	2	27
Paul Brayson	Blyth Spartans	5	5	19	3v Vauxhall M(a)	23		3	26
Danny Kedwell	AFC Wimbledon	6	4	18	3 v Altrincham	23+1		2	26
Ben Tomlinson	Worksop Town	1	6	19	3 v Ashton United	22		4	26
Jamie Vardy	F.C.Halifax Town		3	15	3 v Chasetown	24	1	1	26
					3 v Kendal Town				
Callum Willock	Ebbsfleet Utd		3	22		19+1	3	3	26
Aaron Burns	Ashton United	6	6	16	3v Ossett T (a)	22		3	25
Jamie Slabber	Eastleigh	3	5	18	3 v Dorchester T(a)	21	2	2	25
					3 v Stanes Town (a)				
Phil Marsh	Stalybridge C	2	3	17	4 v Workington(A)	20	3	1	24
Gary Bradshaw	North Ferriby U	1	6	20		23			23
Keiran Lugsden	Buxton	1	3	16	3 v Retford United	20	3		23
Sean Marks	Braintree Town		4	19	3 v Weston-s-Mare	22	1		23
Matt Smith	Redditch United	1	2	7	3 v Hyde United (a)	9	1	1	23
	Solihull Moors		4	9		12			
Michael West	Ebbsfleet United		3	15	3 v Bomley (FAT)	13+6	1	3	23
Graeme Armstrong	Harrogate T	11	4	20		21	1		22
Warren Byerley	Weymouth	6	3	19		20	2		22
Denis Fenemore	Hemel Hem'd	4	2	15		20		2	22
Laurent Hamici	Cray Wanderers	1	5	16	3 v Harrow Boro	20	2		22
					3 v Tonbridge A (a)				
Ryan Rowe	Stourbridge		6	21		18	2	2	22
Magno Vieira	Fleetwood T	2	2	17	3 v Mansfield T (A)	22			22
					3 v Wrexham (a)				
Mark Reed	Buxton		4	3	17 3 v Retford U	18	3		21
Jon Shaw	Gateshead		3	15	3 v Hampton & R (T)	17		4	21
					3 v Wrexham (a)				
Tony Stokes	Concord Rangers	1	5	20		19	2		21
Jody Bevan	Cirencester T	1	2	15	3 v Bedford Town	17	1	2	20
					3 v Halesowen Town				
Bradley Bubb	Farnborough		8	15	3v Dover Athletic	17	3		20
Frannie Collin	Tonbridge Ang's	2	4	15	3 v AFC Hornchurch	18		2	20
					3v Maidstone U (a)				
Peter Dean	Wealdstone	2	3	15		16	2	2	20
Charlie Sheringham	Dartford	2	3	18		18		2	20

C.S.M. - Consecutive Scoring Matches T.S.M.- Total number of Scoring Matches

A.F.C. TELFORD UNITED

Chairman: Lee Carter
Secretary: Mrs Sharon Bowyer **(T)** 07970 040 106 **(E)** sharon.bowyer@telfordutd.co.uk
Additional Committee Members:
Win Pryce, Ian Tyrer, Lee Carter, Win Pryce, David Topping, Ian Dosser

Manager: Andy Sinton
Programme Editor: James Baylis **(E)** james.baylis@ppmedia.co.uk

Back row from left to right: Derek Wellings (Kit manager), Shane Killock, Liam Murray, Sean Newton, Phil Trainer, Karl Broadhurst and Ruddy Farquharson (physio). Middle row, left to right: Darryl Smith (Goalkeeper coach), Danny Carey-Bertram, Ashley Woolliscroft, Will Richards, Daniel Platt, Steve Abbott, Ryan Young, Carl Rodgers, Stuart Whitehead, Andy Brown and John Psaras (First Team Coach). Front row left to right: Tyree Clarke, Martyn Naylor, Richard Davies, Darren Reid (Assistant Manager), Andy Sinton (Manager), Jon Adams, Sean Evans and Paul Harrison.

Club Factfile

Founded: 2004 **Nickname:** The Bucks
Previous Names: AFC Telford United was formed when Telford United folded in May 2004
Previous Leagues: As AFC Telford United: Northern Premier 2004-06
As Telford United: Southern 1969-79. Alliance/Conference 1979-2004

Club Colours (change): White/black/black (Yellow/black/black)

Ground: New Bucks Head Stadium, Watling Street, Wellington, Telford TF1 2TU **(T)** 01952 640 064
Capacity: 6,380 **Seats:** 2,004 **Covered:** 5,000 **Clubhouse:** Yes **Shop:** Yes

Directions (Sat Nav follow TF1 2NW into Haybridge Road) From M54 Junction 6, A5223 towards Wellington, straight over first roundabout (retail park). Straight over second roundabout (B5067). Left at third roundabout (Furrows garage). Continue over railway bridge and follow road round to the right, then turn left into AFC Telford United Car Park.

Previous Grounds:

Record Attendance: 4,215 v Kendal Town - Northern Premier League play-off final
Record Victory: 7-0 v Runcorn (A) - Northern Premier League Division One 2005-06
Record Defeat: 3-6 v Bradford P.A. (H) - Northern Premier League Division One 2005-06
Record Goalscorer: Kyle Perry - 32 (2004-06)
Record Appearances: Stuart Brock - 132 (2004-09)
Additional Records: Paid £5,000 to Tamworth for Lee Moore 08/12/06
Received £33,000 from Burnley for Duane Courtney 31/08/05

Senior Honours: Northern Premier League Division 1 Play-off 2004-05, Premier Division Play-off 2006-07. Conference League Cup 2008-09.

10 YEAR RECORD

01-02	02-03	03-04	04-05	05-06	06-07	07-08	08-09	09-10	10-11
Conf 9	Conf 15	Conf 12	NP 1 3	NP P 10	NP P 3	Conf N 2	Conf N 4	Conf N 11	Conf N 2

AFC TELFORD

No.	Date	Comp	H/A	Opponents	Att:	Result	Goalscorers	Pos
1	Sat-14-Aug	BSN	H	Eastwood Town	372	W 4-2	Lloyd 23, Kilheeney 34, Holden 51, Brown 70	2
2	Tue-17-Aug	BSN	A	Harrogate Town	296	D 3-3	Lloyd 18, Kilheeney pen 57, McNiven 90	7
3	Sat-21-Aug	BSN	A	Nuneaton Town	902	D 1-1	Kerr 73	8
4	Wed-25-Aug	BSN	H	Hyde FC	433	W 3-1	McNiven 37, Kilheeney 55, Halford 60	7
5	Sat-28-Aug	BSN	A	Hinckley United	336	D 1-1	Holden 67	8
6	Mon-30-Aug	BSN	H	Blyth Spartans	418	L 0-3		10
7	Sat-04-Sep	BSN	H	Stafford Rangers	385	W 2-0	Kilheeney 9, Brown 77	7
8	Sat-11-Sep	BSN	A	Gainsborough Trinity	297	W 3-0	Holden 31, Kilheeney 2 (69, 77)	5
9	Sat-02-Oct	BSN	A	Gloucester City	304	D 1-1	McNiven 30	7
10	Sat-16-Oct	BSN	H	Redditch United	284	W 3-0	Banim 23, Brown 48, Kilheeney pen 62	7
11	Sat-30-Oct	BSN	H	Workington	358	W 3-0	Connors 16, Holden 48, Kerr 78	6
12	Mon-08-Nov	BSN	H	AFC Telford	391	L 2-4	Banim 60, Smith 75	6
13	Sat-13-Nov	BSN	H	Boston United	364	W 4-0	Connors 39, Byron 53, McNiven 79, Kilheeney 89	7
14	Tue-16-Nov	BSN	A	Stalybridge Celtic	626	L 0-4		7
15	Tue-23-Nov	BSN	A	Guiseley	338	L 1-2	Kilheeney 35	7
16	Sat-01-Jan	BSN	H	Vauxhall Motors	223	L 1-3	Brownhill 22	9
17	Mon-03-Jan	BSN	A	Blyth Spartans	517	W 4-2	Og (Morris) 23, McNiven 2 (24, 82), Gardner 90	7
18	Sat-08-Jan	BSN	H	Worcester City	264	W 2-1	Cryan 54, McNiven 90	6
19	Tue-18-Jan	BSN	A	Solihull Moors	209	D 2-2	Kilheeney 10, Banim 84	7
20	Mon-24-Jan	BSN	H	Stalybridge Celtic	476	D 2-2	Holden 25, Banim 87	7
21	Tue-01-Feb	BSN	A	Vauxhall Motors	187	W 1-0	McNiven 50	8
22	Sat-12-Feb	BSN	H	Nuneaton Town	320	W 1-0	Killeen 31	8
23	Mon-21-Feb	BSN	H	Hinckley United	192	W 3-2	Kilheeney 2 (48, 60), Rouse 82	8
24	Sat-26-Feb	BSN	H	Gainsborough Trinity	272	L 1-3	Banim 40	8
25	Tue-01-Mar	BSN	A	AFC Telford	1432	D 1-1	McNiven 82	8
26	Sat-05-Mar	BSN	A	Boston United	1139	L 0-2		8
27	Mon-07-Mar	BSN	H	Solihull Moors	204	L 0-5		8
28	Sat-12-Mar	BSN	A	Workington	389	L 0-2		8
29	Tue-15-Mar	BSN	A	Redditch United	70	W 3-1	Jones 48, Kilheeney 52, Miles 61	8
30	Sat-19-Mar	BSN	H	Alfreton Town	349	W 2-1	Kilheeney 3, McEvilly 45	8
31	Mon-21-Mar	BSN	A	Worcester City	500	W 1-0	McEvilly 26	6
32	Sat-02-Apr	BSN	A	Alfreton Town	707	L 0-4		9
33	Wed-06-Apr	BSN	A	Eastwood Town	340	L 0-2		9
34	Sat-09-Apr	BSN	H	Corby Town	200	D 1-1	McEvilly 49	9
35	Mon-11-Apr	BSN	H	Guiseley	244	L 0-3		9
36	Sat-16-Apr	BSN	A	Stafford Rangers	405	W 5-1	Kilheeney 4 (9, 44, 46, pen 55), Rouse 69	9
37	Wed-20-Apr	BSN	A	Corby Town	203	L 0-1		9
38	Sat-23-Apr	BSN	H	Harrogate Town	206	W 5-1	Kilheeney 32, Rouse 38, Chalmers 51, Connor 59, Miles 68	8
39	Mon-25-Apr	BSN	A	Hyde FC	472	D 1-1	Holden 16	8
40	Sat-30-Apr	BSN	H	Gloucester City	352	L 2-4	Kilheeney 5, Rose 20	8

CUPS

No.	Date	Comp	H/A	Opponents	Att:	Result	Goalscorers
1	Sat-25-Sep	FAC 2Q	A	Hyde FC	375	D 0-0	
2	Mon-27-Sep	FAC 2QR	H	Hyde FC	354	W 3-1	Kilheeney 5, Beck 40, Gardner 90
3	Sat-09-Oct	FAC 3Q	A	Ashington	543	W 4-1	Kilheeney 24, Beck 28, Banim 85, Brownhill 89
4	Sat-23-Oct	FAC 4Q	H	Barwell	411	W 3-0	Connors 24, McNiven 60, Kilheeney 88
5	Sat-06-Nov	FAC 1	A	Havant & Waterlooville	1102	W 2-0	Hardiker 57, Kilheeney 89
6	Sat-20-Nov	FAT 3Q	H	Stourbridge	246	W 3-2	Connors 12, Banim 18, Smith 49
7	Mon-29-Nov	FAC 2	H	Leyton Orient	1762	D 1-1	Kilheeney 24
8	Tue-07-Dec	FAC 2R	A	Leyton Orient	1345	L 2-8 (aet)	Kilheeney 6, Brown 54
9	Sat-11-Dec	FAT 1	H	Hinckley United	175	W 4-3	Hardiker 45, Banim 48, Holden 59, Gardner 79
10	Sat-15-Jan	FAT 2	H	Ebbsfleet United	336	W 1-0	Banim 35
11	Sat-05-Feb	FAT 3	A	Blyth Spartans	708	D 2-2	Boyd 30, Kilheeney 81
12	Mon-07-Feb	FAT 3R	H	Blyth Spartans	229	L 0-4	

League
Starts
Substitute
Unused Sub

Cups
Starts
Substitute
Unused Sub

Goals (Lg)
Goals (Cup)

PHILLIPS	VAUGHAN	BROWNHILL	KERR	HALFORD	BROWN	LLOYD	GARDNER	KILHEENEY	KILLEEN	HOLDEN	WHALLEY	CRYAN	BOOTH	ROCHE	TOWNS	BECK	MCNIVEN	ROUSE	HARDIKER	BYRON	CONNORS	SMITH	BANIM	LOWRY	TANDY	BOYD	CONNOR	BURGESS	WORSNOP	HANLEY	STOCKLEY	WALKER	HUNT	JONES	MCEVILLY	LAKE	MILES	CHALMERS	LOGAN
X	X	X	X	X	X	X	X	X	X	X	S	S	S	U	U																								
X	X	X	X	X	X	X	S	X	X	X		U	S	U		X	S																						
X	U	X	X	U	X	X	X	X	X	X		X	S	X		S	S																						
X	X	X	X	X	X		S	X	X	X			S	U		X	X	S	U																				
X	X	X	X	X	X	X	U		X	X			S	S		X	X	U	U																				
X	U	X	X	S		X	X	X	X	X			X	X	U		S		X	S																			
X		X	X		X	S	U	X	X	X				X	U	X	X	S	X	S																			
X	U	X	U		X		S	X	X	X				X	U		X	U	X	X	X																		
X		X			S			X	X	X		U		X	U	X	X		X	X	X	S	S																
X		X	X		X		S	X	X	X				X	U		S		X	U	X	S	X																
X	X	X	X		X		U	X	X	X							S	S	X	U	X	S	X																
X	U	X	X		X		S	X	X					X			X	S	X	U	X	S	X																
X	X	X	U		X		S	X	X	X		U					S	S	X	X	X		X																
X		X	S		X		U	X	X	X		U		X			X	S	X	X	X		S																
X	X	X			X		U	X	X	X		U		U			X		X	X	X	U	U																
X	X	X					X	X	X	X		X			U		S	U	X				X		S	X	S												
X	X	X					X	U	X	X		X			U		X	S	X				X		U	U	X												
X	X	X					X	S	X	X		X			U		X	S	X				X		U	X	S												
	X	X	X				S	X	X	X		U			X		X	S	X				X			X	U	S											
X	X	X					S	X	X	X		X		S			X	U	X				X			X	S		U										
X	X	X					X	X	X	X		X		S			S	U	X				X				X		U	S									
X	X	X	U				S		X	X		X		U			X	S	X				X			X	X				U								
X	X				U		S	X	X	X		X					X	S	X				X			X	X			U	S								
X	X						X	X	X	X		X					S	X	X				X			X	S			U		S	U						
X	X						S	X	X	U		X					S		X				X			X	X					S	U	X	X				
X		X					X	X	X	S		U					S		X				X			X	S					X	U	X	X				
X	U	X					X	S	X								X	S	X				X			X	U					X		X	X	U			
X	X	X	X				S	X	X	X		U											X			X	S					U		X		U	X		
X	X	X	X				X	X	X	X		U						S								X						S		X	S	U	X		
X	X	X	X					X	X	X		U						S								X						U		X	X	U	X	S	
X	X	X	X				X	X	X			U						S								X	S							X	X	U	X	S	
X	X	X	X				X	X	X			U						S								X	X							X	X	U		S	S
X	X	X	X				S	X	X	X		U						S								X								X	X	U	S	X	
X	X	X			S		X	X	X	X		U						S	X							X								X	X		S	U	
X	U	X	X		S		S	X		X		X						X								X	X								S		X	X	U
X	X	X			S			X	U	X		U						X								X	X								X	S	X	X	S
U	X	X	U		S		U	X		X								X								X	X								X	X	X	X	U
X	X	X	X		U		S	X	S	X								X								X	X								X	U	X	S	
X	X	X			X		S	X	U	X								X									X							S	X	U	X	X	S
X	X	X	U		S		S	X		X								X								X	X								X	U	X	X	S
X		X	U		X		S	X	X	X		U		X	U	S	S		X	X	X	X	U																
X		X	U		U		S	X	X	X		U		X	U	X	S		X	X	X	X	S																
X	U	X	X		S		S	X	X	X		U		X	U	X	X		X		X	U	S																
X	U	X	X		X		S	X	X	X		U		X	U		S		X	U	X	S	X																
X	U	X	X		X		S	X	X			U		X	U		X	S	X	U	X	S	X																
X	X	X			X		X	U	S	X		X		U			X			X	X	S	X		S														
X	U	X	X		X		S	X	X	X		U		X	U		S	S	X		X	U	X																
X	U	X	X		X		X	X	X			S		X	U		X	S	X	S		U	X																
X	X	X	X				S	X	X	X		U			U				X		X	S	X	X	S														
X	X	X	U				S	X	X	X		X		U	S		X	S	X				X			X													
X	X	X	S				S	X	X	X		X		U			X	S	X				X			X				U									
X	U	X	X		U		X		X	X				X	U		X	S	X				X			X				S									
38	29	37	19	4	14	5	14	35	34	34	0	11	1	8	1	5	15	7	23	5	8	0	17	0	0	22	12	0	0	0	0	2	0	10	13	1	10	6	0
0	0	0	1	1	6	1	17	2	1	1	1	1	5	3	0	1	11	18	0	2	0	4	2	0	1	0	7	1	0	1	1	3	0	1	2	1	2	4	4
1	6	0	5	1	2	0	6	1	2	1	0	15	0	5	9	0	0	5	2	3	0	1	1	0	2	1	2	0	2	2	1	2	3	0	0	10	0	1	2
12	4	12	7	0	6	0	3	10	11	10	0	3	0	8	0	2	7	0	11	3	8	2	9	1	0	3	0	0	0	0	0	0	0	0	0	0	0	0	0
0	0	0	1	0	1	0	9	0	1	0	0	1	0	0	1	1	4	6	0	1	0	4	2	0	2	0	0	0	0	1	0	0	0	0	0	0	0	0	0
0	6	0	3	0	2	0	0	1	0	0	0	7	0	3	9	0	0	0	0	2	0	3	1	0	0	0	0	0	0	1	0	0	0	0	0	0	0	0	0
0	0	1	2	1	4	2	1	20	1	6	0	1	0	0	0	0	9	3	0	1	2	1	5	0	0	0	1	0	0	0	0	0	0	1	3	0	2	1	0
0	0	1	0	0	2	0	2	7	0	1	0	0	0	0	0	2	1	0	2	0	2	1	4	0	0	1	0	0	0	0	0	0	0	0	0	0	0	0	0

PLAYING SQUAD

Existing Players		SN	HT	WT	DOB	AGE	POB	Career	Apps	Goals
GOALKEEPERS										
Lee	Evans	13			24/05/1983	28	Sutton Coldfield	Ilkeston, Stourport 6/03, Willenhall, Bedworth 8/04, Bromsgrove c/s 05, Chasetown 5/06, Gresley R (L) 10/08, Stafford R 6/09		
Ryan	Young	1			25/12/1979	31	Birmingham	Plymouth (Trainee), Chasetown, Nuneaton, Halesowen T (L) 10/01, Hucknall T 2/02, Hednesford 5/03, Redditch 6/05, AFC Telford 9/05, Kettering 2/06, Willenhall 3/06, Hednesford 6/06, AFC Telford 5/07	35	0
DEFENDERS										
Shane	Killock	6	6'00"	12 04	12/03/1989	22	Huddersfield	Ossett A (Yth), Huddersfield, Hyde U (SL) 2/08, Harrogate T (L) 9/08, Oxford U (L) 1/09 Perm 2/09, AFC Telford (2ML) 8/09 Perm 10/09	40	3
Sean	Newton	3	6'02"	13 00	23/09/1988	22	Liverpool	Chester, Southport (3ML) 8/07, Droylsden (SL) 2/08, Droylsden 8/08, Barrow 7/09, AFC Telford (2ML) 8/09 Perm 10/09	39	5
Dan	Preston	16	5'11"	12 04	26/09/1991	19	Birmingham	Birmingham Rel c/s 11, Hereford (L) 2/10, Hereford (3ML) 1/11, AFC Telford 7/11		
Will	Salmon	2			25/11/1986	24	Basingstoke	Aldershot Rel c/s 07, Fleet T (SL) c/s 05, Fleet T (SL) 8/06, AFC Wimbledon 6/07 Rel 5/08, Fleet T (L) 2/08, Fleet T c/s 08, Ebbsfleet 8/09, AFC Telford 8/10	40	0
Dwayne	Samuels	12	5'08"	11 00	11/10/1990	20	Wolverhampton	West Brom, Grimsby 8/10 Rel 6/11, Redditch (L) 1/11, AFC Telford 7/11		
Ryan	Valentine	23	5'11"	11 11	19/08/1982	29	Wrexham	Everton Rel c/s 02, Oxford U (Trial) 4/02, Darlington 8/02 Rel c/s 06, Wrexham 8/06, Darlington 1/08, Hereford 5/09 Rel c/s 11, AFC Telford 6/11		
Stuart	Whitehead	5	6'00"	12 02	17/07/1976	35	Bromsgrove	Bromsgrove, Bolton 9/95 Rel c/s 98, Carlisle 7/98, Darlington 10/02, Telford 6/03, Shrewsbury 6/04, Kidderminster 5/06, AFC Telford 1/08	25	0
Robbie	Williams	14	6'05"		06/07/1987	24	Blackpool	TNS/The New Saints Rel c/s 09, Newtown (3ML) 11/06, Caersws (4ML) 9/08, Altrincham 7/09, AFC Telford 6/11		
MIDFIELDERS										
Jon	Adams	11			08/01/1985	26		Leamington, AFC Telford c/s 07	38	2
Richard	Davies	20	5'11"	11 05	15/05/1990	21	Willenhall	Walsall Rel c/s 10, Solihull Moors (L) 12/09, AFC Telford 8/10, Chasetown (3ML) 11/10, Chasetown (Dual) 2/11	2	0
Jordan	Johnson	21						Port Vale (Yth), Man City (Trainee), Leek T c/s 03, Stone Dominoes (L) 12/05, Warrington 12/07, Congleton 1/08, Newcastle T 7/08, AFC Telford 7/11		
Greg	Mills		6'02"	13 01	18/09/1990	20	Derby	Derby Rel c/s 11, Solihull Moors (L) 9/09, Solihull Moors (6WL) 11/09, Macclesfield (L) 1/10, AFC Telford (5ML) 8/10, AFC Telford (SL) 1/11, AFC Telford 8/11	36	8
Courtney	Pitt	22	5'07"	10 08	17/12/1981	29	Paddington	Chelsea, Portsmouth £200,000 7/01, Luton (3ML) 8/03, Coventry (L) 12/03, Oxford U 3/04 Rel c/s 04, Luton (Trial) 7/04, Boston U 8/04 Rel c/s 05, Colchester (Trial) 7/05, Port Vale (Trial) 8/05, Cambridge U 9/05 Rel 4/10, CRC (L) 10/08, York C (SL) 1/10, Weymouth c/s 10, AFC Telford 11/10	6	0
James	Reid	7	5'10"	11 04	28/02/1990	21	Nottingham	Notts Forest Rel 1/10, Rushden & D (6ML) 7/09, Lincoln C NC 3/10, Hinckley U 8/10, AFC Telford 6/11		
Carl	Rodgers	4			26/03/1983	28	Chester	Chester (Yth), Caernarfon c/s 02, TNS 3/04, Colwyn Bay 5/04, AFC Telford 5/06	39	5
Nathan	Rooney	15	6'00"	11 11	02/10/1992	18	Telford	Wolves Rel 3/11, Shrewsbury (Trial) 3/11, AFC Telford 7/11		
Phil	Trainer	8	6'00"	12 00	03/07/1981	30	Wolverhampton	Crewe Rel c/s 02, Hyde (3ML) 12/00, Hednesford (3ML) 11/01, Stalybridge (L) 3/02, Northwich 8/02, Kidsgrove 9/02, Halesowen 12/02, Tamworth 8/03, Stourport S (L) 9/03, Moor Green/Solihull Moors (L) 10/03 Perm 11/03, Oxford U 7/07 Rel 4/09, AFC Telford (SL) 1/09, AFC Telford 5/09	38	10
FORWARDS										
Andy	Brown	10			03/03/1986	25	Lincoln	Scunthorpe (Scholar), Harrogate T (L) 3/05, Hinckley 5/05, Nuneaton 7/07, AFC Telford 6/08	33	14
Craig	Farrell	19	6'00"	12 11	05/12/1982	28	Middlesbrough	Leeds, Carlisle (2ML) 10/02 (Undisc) 12/02 Rel 5/05, Exeter c/s 05 Rel 5/06, York C 6/06, Oxford U (SL) 1/09, Rushden & D P/E 6/09, AFC Telford 6/11		
Craig	King	17	5'11"	11 12	06/10/1990	20	Chesterfield	Leicester Rel c/s 11, Hereford (SL) 9/09, Northampton (3ML) 11/10, AFC Telford 7/11		
James	Lawrie	18	6'00"	12 05	18/12/1990	20	Belfast	Port Vale Rel c/s 10, Kidderminster (SL) 2/10 (09/10 10,1), Exeter (Trial) 7/10, Stevenage (Trial) 7/10, Morecambe (Trial) 7/10, AFC Telford 8/10	21	4

		SN	HT	WT	DOB	AGE	POB	From - To	APPS	GOA
Alex	Meechan	9	5'08"	10 10	29/01/1980	31	Plymouth	Swindon, Bristol C 7/98, Forest Green (2ML) 8/00, Yeovil (L) 11/00, Forest Green NC 12/00, Dag & Red 6/03, Forest Green (3ML) 11/03 Perm 2/04 Rel 6/04, Luton (Trial) 7/04, Leigh RMI 8/04 Rel 11/04, Halifax 11/04 Rel 4/05, Forest Green 7/05 Rel 1/07, Chester 1/07 Rel c/s 07, York C 7/07, Stalybridge 11/07, Altrincham 6/08 Rel 3/09, Stalybridge (L) 1/09, Stalybridge 3/09, Droylsden 7/09, AFC Telford 7/10	27	4
Adam	Proudlock	31	6'00"	13 07	09/05/1981	30	Wellington	Wolves, Clyde (L) 8/00, Notts Forest (L) 3/02, Tranmere (L) 10/02, Sheff Wed (L) 12/02, Sheff Wed £150,000 9/03 Rel 9/05, Ipswich 10/05 Rel c/s 06, Walsall (Trial) 7/06, Stockport 8/06 Rel c/s 08, Darlington 7/08, Grimsby (2ML) 11/08 Perm 1/09 Rel c/s 10, Kidderminster (Trial) 8/10, AFC Telford 9/10	25	6

Loanees		**SN**	**HT**	**WT**	**DOB**	**AGE**	**POB**	**From - To**	**APPS**	**GOA**
(F)Lee	Smith				08/09/1983	27	Coney Hill	Forest Green 1/11 - Chippenham (L) 2/11, Weymouth (SL) 3/11, Rel 5/11, Nuneaton T 7/11	4	0
(M)Sam	Gwynne		5'09"	11 11	17/12/1987	23	Hereford	Hereford (SL) 1/11 - Rel 5/11	16	0
(D)Mark	Preece		6'02"	13 07	03/06/1987	24	Bristol	Mansfield 2/11 - Rel 5/11, Bath C 8/11	3	0
(G)Aaron	McCarey				14/01/1992	19	Monaghan	Wolves 2/11 -	4	0
(M)Aidan	Thomas				16/11/1991	19		Hereford (SL) 3/11 - Rel 5/11		

Departures		**SN**	**HT**	**WT**	**DOB**	**AGE**	**POB**	**From - To**	**APPS**	**GOA**
(F)Dave	Howarth				19/12/1991	19		Yth - Rel c/s 10		
(F)Steve	Thompson		5'07"	11 01	15/04/1989	22	Peterlee	Port Vale 10/09 - Rel c/s 10		
(M)Matt	Blair				21/06/1989	22		Redditch 3/10 - Kidderminster 8/10, York C 6/11		
(D)Karl	Broadhurst		6'00"	11 07	18/03/1980	31	Portsmouth	Crawley 8/10 - Rel 8/10, Solihull Moors 8/11		
(M)Tyree	Clarke				03/01/1992	19		Norwich - Rel 8/10, Stafford R 8/10		
(M)Aaron	Dillon				02/09/1991	19		Derby (Scholar) - Rel 8/10		
(D)Jacob	Rowe				09/12/1990	20		Birmingham 8/10 - Redditch 10/10, Worcester 6/11		
(D)Martin	Naylor				02/08/1977	34		The New Saints 8/10 - Stafford R 11/10	0	0
(D)Netan	Sansara		6'00"	12 00	03/08/1989	22	Darlaston	Dundee 10/10 - Rel 12/10, Corby T 12/10 Rel 6/11		
(D)Ashley	Wooliscroft		5'10"	11 02	28/12/1979	31	Stoke	Stafford R 6/10 - Rel 1/11, Stafford R (L) 9/10, Hednesford (L) 11/10, Stafford R 2/11, Ball Haye Green, Leek T 7/11	0	0
(M)Carlos	Logan		5'07"	11 00	07/11/1985	25	Wythenshawe	ex Hyde FC 12/10 - Northwich 1/11, Droylsden 3/11		
(D)Sam	Stockley		6'00"	12 08	05/09/1977	33	Tiverton	Ferencvaros (Hun) 1/11 - Droylsden 2/11, FC New York (USA) (G)		
Daniel	Platt				05/09/1991	19		Vauxhall Motors 8/10 - Nantwich 3/11	2	0
(M)Stefan	Bailey		5'11"	12 08	10/11/1987	23	Brent	Ebbsfleet 9/10 - Kettering 3/11	5	0
(F)Danny	Carey-Bertram		5'11"	13 00	14/06/1984	27	Birmingham	Bath C 10/08 - Rel 5/11, Hednesford (L) 10/10, Worcester 6/11	8	0
(D)Liam	Murray		6'03"	11 00	01/08/1985	26	Stafford	Solihull Moors 6/10 - Rel 5/11, Australia	17	1
(M)Steve	Abbott				31/07/1982	29	Whiston	Wrexham 6/10 - Chorley (L) 11/10, Chasetown (L) 2/11, Northwich 6/11	12	3
(M)Will	Richards				18/12/1991	19		Shrewsbury 8/10 - Market Drayton (L) 9/10, Redditch (L) 2/11, Solihull Moors 8/11		
(G)Dan	East		6'01"	13 02	18/03/1993	18		Wolves (Scholar) Rel 3/11, AFC Telford 3/11	0	0
(G)Ryan	Jones				02/09/1992	18		AFC Telford	0	0
(M)Sean	Evans		5'09"	11 00	25/09/1987	23	Ludlow	Stourbridge 11/09 -		
(M)Paul	Harrison				01/01/1985	26		Galicia (Spa) 7/10 - Witton (L) 8/10		
(M)Philip	John				18/08/1985	26		Fleet T 8/10 - Hayes & Yeading (Trial) 8/11	14	1
(M)Josh	Johnson		5'05"	10 07	16/04/1981	30	Carenage, Trin	Airbus UK 9/10 -		
(M)Danny	Williams				02/03/1981	30		RRFC Montegnee (Bel) 3/11 -	6	0
(F)Yannick	Salem		5'10"	11 06	29/03/1983	28	Amiens, Fra	Stockport 3/11 -	9	2

Caught in action....

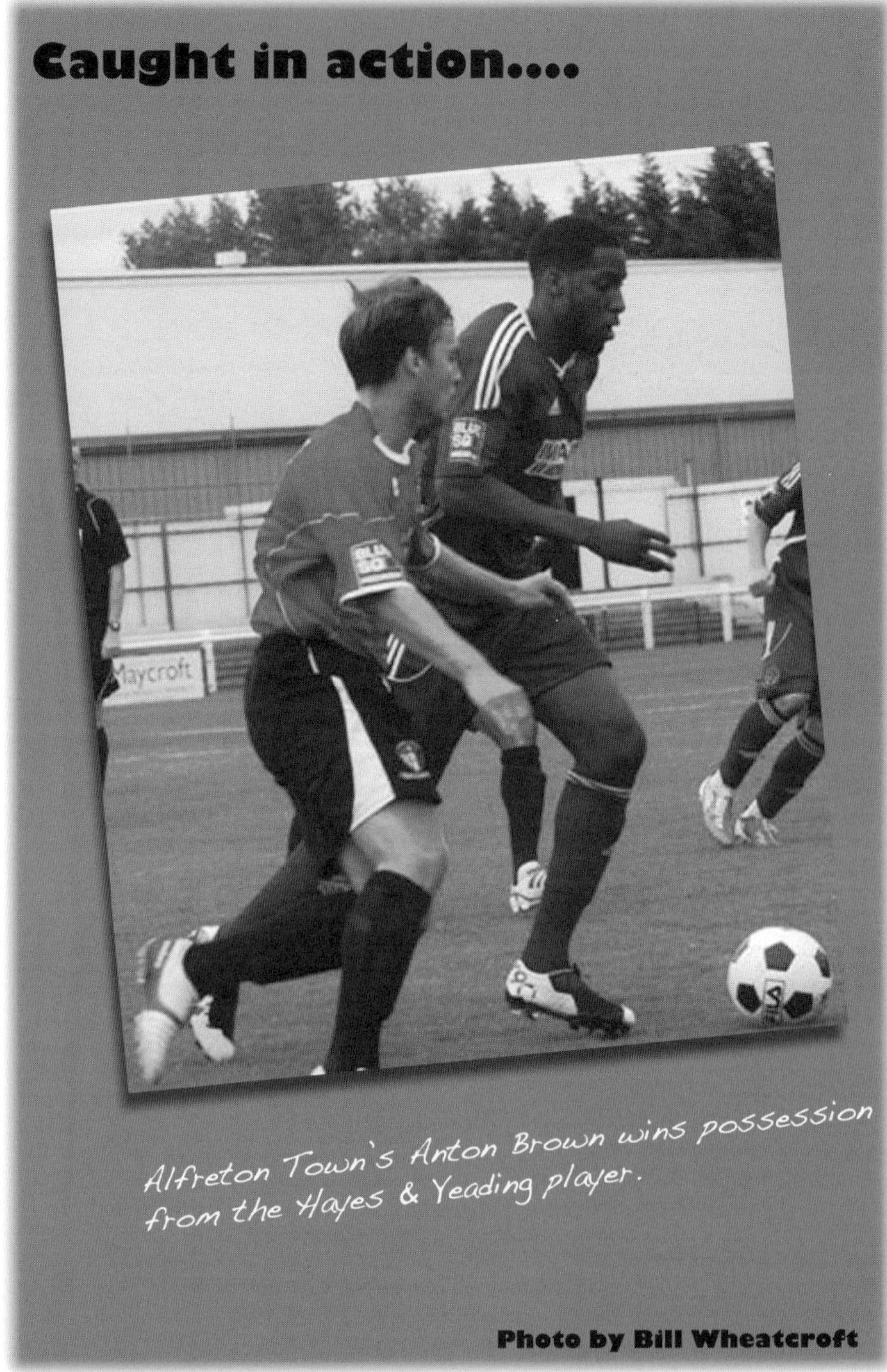

Alfreton Town's Anton Brown wins possession from the Hayes & Yeading player.

Photo by Bill Wheatcroft

ALFRETON TOWN

Chairman: Wayne Bradley
Secretary: Bryan Rudkin (T) 07710 444 195 (E) bryanrudkin@hotmail.com
Additional Committee Members:
Sean Egan, Dave Gregory, Ken Rae.

Manager: Nicky Law
Programme Editor: Chris Tacey (E) ctacey5087@aol.com

Back Row (L-R): Nicky Law (manager), Darren Stride, Aden Flint, Anton Brown, Matt Wilson, Ross Turner, Paddy Gamble, Anthony Wilson, Jake Moult, Anthony Howell, Paul Clayton,Paul Madin (physiotherapist), Russ O'Neill (assistant manager). Front row: Kyle McFadzean (now Crawley Town), Jordan Hall, Ian Ross, Liam Hearn, Chris Hall, Nathan Arnold, Chris Shaw, Josh Law.

Club Factfile

Founded: 1959 **Nickname:** The Reds
Previous Names: None
Previous Leagues: Central Alliance (pre reformation 1921-25) 59-61. Midland Combination 1925-27, 61-82. Northern Counties East 1982-87. Northern Premier 1987-99.
Club Colours (change): All red (All blue)

Ground: Impact Arena, North Street, Alfreton, Derbyshire DE55 7FZ (T) 01773 830 277
Capacity: 3,600 **Seats:** 1,500 **Covered:** 2,600 **Clubhouse:** Yes **Shop:** Yes

Directions
From M1 Junction 28 Take A38 towards Derby for 2 miles.
Then take slip road onto B600 Turn right at Tjunction towards town centre.
At pedestrian crossing turn left into North Street and the ground is on the right hand side.

Previous Grounds: Not known

Record Attendance: 5,023 v Matlock Town - Central Alliance 1960
Record Victory: 15-0 v Loughbrough Midland League 1969-70
Record Defeat: 1-9 v Solihull - FAT 1997. 0-8 v Bridlington - 1992
Record Goalscorer: J Harrison - 303
Record Appearances: J Harrison - 560+
Additional Records: Paid £2,000 to Worksop Town for Mick Goddard
Received £7,000 from Ilkeston Town for Paul Eshelby
Senior Honours: Northern Counties East 1984-85, 2001-02. Northern Premier League Division 1 2002-03.
Conference North 2010-11.
Derbyshire Senior Cup x7

10 YEAR RECORD

01-02	02-03	03-04	04-05	05-06	06-07	07-08	08-09	09-10	10-11
NCEP 1	NP 1 1	NP P 4	Conf N 14	Conf N 17	Conf N 14	Conf N 16	Conf N 3	Conf N 3	Conf N 1

ALFRETON TOWN

No.	Date	Comp	H/A	Opponents	Att:	Result	Goalscorers	Pos
1	Sat-14-Aug	BSN	H	Hinckley United	516	W 1-0	Moult 55	10
2	Tue-17-Aug	BSN	A	Redditch United	287	W 5-1	A Wilson 26, Arnold 43, Clayton 2 (67, 76), Moult 70	2
3	Sat-21-Aug	BSN	A	Hyde FC	396	W 5-1	Shaw 5, Flint 8, A Wilson 2 (83, 85), Hearn 88	3
4	Tue-24-Aug	BSN	H	Gainsborough Trinity	542	W 2-1	Og (Hume) 53, Clayton 73	2
5	Sat-28-Aug	BSN	A	Blyth Spartans	462	W 4-1	Moult 2 (3, pen 55), Og (Tait) 26, Hearn pen 76	1
6	Mon-30-Aug	BSN	H	Stafford Rangers	744	W 2-0	Clayton 22, Hearn pen 89	1
7	Sat-04-Sep	BSN	H	Vauxhall Motors	603	W 2-0	Franklin 57, Arnold 83	1
8	Sat-11-Sep	BSN	A	Nuneaton Town	1138	W 3-1	Arnold 38, Hearn 55, Brown 66	1
9	Sat-18-Sep	BSN	H	Boston United	1309	L 0-1		1
10	Sat-02-Oct	BSN	A	Stalybridge Celtic	1336	W 2-1	Hearn 2 (15, 68)	1
11	Sat-16-Oct	BSN	H	AFC Telford	1168	D 0-0		2
12	Sat-30-Oct	BSN	H	Worcester City	657	W 2-1	Hearn 29, A Wilson 79	1
13	Sat-06-Nov	BSN	A	Hinckley United	514	W 3-1	Hearn 71, Ross 78, L Wilson 90	1
14	Sat-13-Nov	BSN	H	Harrogate Town	662	W 6-0	M Wilson 3, Law 28, C Hall 33, Flint 58, Hearn 69, Ross 90	1
15	Sat-01-Jan	BSN	H	Eastwood Town	914	D 2-2	Hearn 51, Howell 90	3
16	Mon-03-Jan	BSN	A	Stafford Rangers	544	W 1-0	Hearn 52	2
17	Sat-08-Jan	BSN	H	Stalybridge Celtic	653	W 5-3	Clayton 22, Hearn 37, Franklin 42, Howell 46, Arnold 90	1
18	Tue-11-Jan	BSN	H	Workington	440	W 2-0	Flint 11, Clayton 51	1
19	Sat-12-Feb	BSN	A	Workington	348	D 0-0		3
20	Tue-15-Feb	BSN	H	Blyth Spartans	499	W 2-1	Howell 22, Og (White) 82	2
21	Tue-22-Feb	BSN	A	AFC Telford	2062	L 1-2	Garner 90	4
22	Tue-01-Mar	BSN	H	Gloucester City	418	W 4-0	Clare 16, Hearn 2 (19, 65), A Wilson 87	2
23	Sat-05-Mar	BSN	A	Vauxhall Motors	263	W 2-0	Ross 2, Arnold 90	2
24	Mon-07-Mar	BSN	A	Worcester City	579	W 2-1	Clare pen 35, Hearn 44	2
25	Sat-12-Mar	BSN	H	Corby Town	705	W 6-0	M Wilson 35, Hearn 2 (38, 67), Clare 51, Clayton 78, Arnold 83	2
26	Tue-15-Mar	BSN	A	Boston United	1503	L 2-3	Brown 20, Hearn 42	3
27	Sat-19-Mar	BSN	A	Droylsden	349	L 1-2	Clare 25	4
28	Tue-22-Mar	BSN	A	Guiseley	458	W 2-1	Clayton 21, Arnold 30	2
29	Sat-26-Mar	BSN	H	Hyde FC	643	D 0-0		2
30	Mon-28-Mar	BSN	H	Solihull Moors	791	W 2-0	Law 2 (18, pen 48)	1
31	Wed-30-Mar	BSN	A	Corby Town	323	W 1-0	Clayton 45	1
32	Sat-02-Apr	BSN	H	Droylsden	707	W 4-0	Clayton 19, Hearn 2 (53, 54), M Wilson 90	1
33	Tue-05-Apr	BSN	H	Guiseley	750	W 6-0	Arnold 1, Law pen 19, Hearn 3 (44, 45, 47), Jarman 67	1
34	Sat-09-Apr	BSN	A	Solihull Moors	459	W 1-0	Law pen 69	1
35	Tue-12-Apr	BSN	A	Eastwood Town	1112	L 2-4	Hearn 14, A Wilson 84	1
36	Sat-16-Apr	BSN	A	Gloucester City	375	L 1-2	Clayton 61	1
37	Tue-19-Apr	BSN	A	Harrogate Town	456	D 1-1	A Wilson 26	1
38	Sat-23-Apr	BSN	H	Redditch United	1364	W 4-0	Clayton 2 (9, 26), Hearn 2 (49, 77)	1 Champions
39	Mon-25-Apr	BSN	A	Gainsborough Trinity	474	W 3-0	A Wilson 2 (26, 41), Moult 65	1
40	Sat-30-Apr	BSN	H	Nuneaton Town	1123	W 3-2	Flint 8, Hearn 2 (52, pen 69)	1

CUPS

No.	Date	Comp	H/A	Opponents	Att:	Result	Goalscorers
1	Sat-25-Sep	FAC 2Q	A	Stalybridge Celtic	373	D 1-1	A Wilson 22
2	Tue-28-Sep	FAC 2QR	H	Stalybridge Celtic	387	L 1-2 aet	Hearn 80
3	Sat-20-Nov	FAT 3Q	H	Kendal Town	399	W 4-0	Howell 18, Clayton 73, Hearn 82, Arnold 88
4	Tue-14-Dec	FAT 1	H	Hyde FC	254	W 3-0	M Wilson 37, L Wilson 45, Clayton 90
5	Sat-15-Jan	FAT 2	H	Cambridge United	929	D 3-3	J Hall 53, L Wilson 60, Flint 73
6	Tue-18-Jan	FAT 2R	A	Cambridge United	1098	W 6-3 (aet)	Law pen 22, Clayton 3 (77, 96, 118), Brown 83, L Wilson 112
7	Sat-05-Feb	FAT 3	A	Mansfield Town	3408	D 1-1	Arnold 45
8	Tue-08-Feb	FAT 3R	H	Mansfield Town	2131	L 1-2	M Wilson 16

League
Starts
Substitute
Unused Sub

Cups
Starts
Substitute
Unused Sub

Goals (Lg)
Goals (Cup)

GAMBLE	LAW	SHAW	FLINT	MCFADZEAN	STRIDE	MOULT	BROWN	ARNOLD	CLAYTON	HEARN	J HALL	ROSS	M WILSON	C HALL	TURNER	A WILSON	FRANKLIN	HOWELL	L WILSON	NAYLOR	DILLON	LISTER	KEANE	MACKENZIE	STREETE	GARNER	CLARE	JARMAN
X	X	X	X	X	X	X	X	X	X	X	S	S	U	U	U													
X	X	X	X	X	X	X	X	X	X		S	S	U	S	U	X												
X	X	X	X		X	X	X	X	X	S	U	U	X	S	U	X												
X	X	X	X		X	X	X	X	X	U	U	U	X	U	U	X												
X	X	X	X		X	X	X	S	X	S	S	U	X	U		X	X											
X	X	X	X		X		X	S	X	X	U	U	X	S	U	X	X											
X	X	X	X		X		X	S	X	X	U	S	X	S	U	X	X											
	X	X	X		X		X	X	X	S	U	U	X	S	X	X	X											
X	X	X	X		X		X	X	X	S	U	S	X		U	X	X	S										
X	X	S	X				X	U	S	X	X	X		S	U	X	X	X	X									
X	X						X	S	S	X	X	U	X	U		X	X	X	X	X	U							
X	X		X		X	S	S	X		X	X			U		S	X	X	X	X	U							
X	X		X		X	U	S	X		X	X	S	X			U	X	X	X		U							
X	X		X				X	U		X	S	S	X	X		U	X	X	X	X	S							
X	X		X		U	S	X	S	X	X		S	X	U			X	X	X			X						
X	X		X		S	S		U	S	X	X	X		U		X	X	X	X			X						
	X		X		X	U		S	X	X	X	X		U	X	U	X	X	X		S							
X	X		X		X	U		X	X		X	X	S	U		S	X	X	X		S							
						X	X	X	X	S	S	S	X		U		X	X	X			U		X	X	X		
						X		X	S	X	X	U	X		U		X	X	X		U	U		X	X	X		
						X	U	X	S	X	X	S			U		X	X	X		S	X		X	X	X		
	X					U	X	S	S	X		X	X			S	X	X	U					X	X	X	X	
	X				U		X	S	S	X		X	X			S	X	X	U					X	X	X	X	
	X				S	U	X	U	S	X		X	X				X	X	U					X	X	X	X	
	X					S	X	S	S	X	U	X	X				X	X	U					X	X	X	X	
	X						X	S	S	X	U	X	X				X	X	U					X	X	X	X	S
					U	S	X	X	S		X	X	X				X	S	U					X	X	X	X	X
	X		X			U	U	X	X			U	X		X	S	X	X	X						X		X	S
	X		X			S	X	S	X			X	S			U	X	X	U					X	X		X	X
	X		X			U	S	X	X			U	X			X	X	X	X					X	X		U	U
	X		X			U	S	X	X			U	X			X	X	X	X					X	X		S	U
	X		X			U	S	X	X	X		U	X				X	X	X					X	X		S	S
	X		X				S	X	X	X		S	X			U	X	X	X					X	X		U	S
	X		X			U	U	X	X	X		U	X				X	X	X					X	X		S	S
	X		X				U	X	X	X		S	X			S	X	X	X					X	X		S	U
	X		X				U	X	X	X		S	X			S	X	X	X					X	X		S	U
	X		X				X	S	S	X	U	X	X		X	X	X		X						X		U	U
	X		X				X	X	X	X	U	S	X		X	U	X		X						X		S	S
			X		X	X	X	S	S	S	X	X	U			X			U					X	X		X	X
	X		X				X	X	S	X	S	U	X			X	X		U					X	X		S	X
X	X	X	X		X		X	S	X	X	U	S	X	U	U	X	X	S										
X	X	X	X				X	X	X	X	S	X		S	U	S	X	X										
X			X		X		X	S	S	X	X	S	X	X		U	X	X	X		U							
X	X		X		X			S	S	X	X	S	X	X	U	U	X	X	X									
X	X		X		X	U		X	X		X	X	S	U		U	X	X	X		U							
X	X		X		X	S	S	X	S		X	X	X	X		U	X		X		U							
	U				X	S	X	X	X	X	X	X	X		X		X		X		S		U					
	U				X	S	X	X	X	X	X	S	X		X		X	X	X		S		U					
16	35	9	30	2	14	9	25	23	23	26	11	13	30	1	5	16	35	26	22	3	0	3	0	19	22	9	9	4
0	0	1	0	0	2	6	6	13	14	6	6	13	2	6	0	7	0	2	0	0	4	0	0	0	0	0	7	6
0	0	0	0	0	3	10	5	4	0	1	10	13	3	9	11	6	0	0	9	0	4	2	0	0	0	0	3	5
6	5	2	6	0	7	0	5	5	5	6	6	4	6	3	2	1	8	5	6	0	0	0	0	0	0	0	0	0
0	0	0	0	0	0	3	1	3	3	0	1	4	1	1	0	1	0	1	0	0	2	0	0	0	0	0	0	0
0	2	0	0	0	0	1	0	0	0	0	1	0	0	2	3	4	0	0	0	0	3	0	2	0	0	0	0	0
0	5	1	4	0	0	5	2	8	13	28	0	3	3	1	0	9	2	3	1	0	0	0	0	0	0	1	4	1
0	1	0	1	0	0	0	1	2	5	2	1	0	2	0	0	1	0	1	3	0	0	0	0	0	0	0	0	0

PLAYING SQUAD

Existing Players		SN	HT	WT	DOB	AGE	POB	Career	Apps	Goals
GOALKEEPERS										
Paddy	Gamble		5'10"	10 12	01/09/1988	22	Bulwell	Notts Forest Rel 5/09, York C (2ML) 3/07, Stalybridge (SL) 7/07, Mansfield (5ML) 8/08, Alfreton 8/09	16	0
Dan	Lowson	1	6'01"		04/02/1988	23	Whitley Bay	Gretna, Newcastle Blue Star, Ilkeston 7/09 Rel 9/10, Darlington 10/10 Rel 11/10, Luton (Trial) 10/10, Blyth 1/11, Alfreton 6/11		
Ross	Turner	18	5'11"	12 00	17/06/1979	32	Sheffield	Parkgate, Stocksbridge PS 8/99, Worsborough Bridge, Scunthorpe 3/00 Rel c/s 00, Stocksbridge PS, Alfreton 11/01 Rel c/s 02, Worksop 6/02, Bradford PA (L) 8/02, Bradford PA (L) 3/03, Ilkeston 11/03, Buxton 2/06, Sheffield 3/07, Retford U 1/08, Eastwood T 8/09, Retford U 11/09, Alfreton 3/10	5	0
DEFENDERS										
Anton	Brown	7	6'01"		03/07/1987	24		Mansfield (Scholar), Greenwood Meadows, Alfreton 7/06	31	2
Connor	Franklin	3	5'09"		01/09/1987	23	Leicester	Leicester (Trainee), Nuneaton 11/06, Hinckley U 6/08, Lincoln C (Trial) 2/10, Coventry (Trial) 3/10, Burton (Trial) 7/10, Kidderminster (Trial) 8/10, Alfreton 8/10	35	2
Leigh	Franks	12	5'11"	12 00	07/03/1991	20	Scarborough	Scarborough (Yth), Bridlington T (Yth), Huddersfield (Scholar) 7/07 Pro 7/09 Rel c/s 11, Fleetwood (L) 1/10, Oxford U (6ML) 7/10, Alfreton 6/11		
Adrian	Hawes	20	6'03"		23/11/1987	23		Heanor T, Hucknall 2/09, Motherwell (Trial), 8/09, Dag & Red (Trial) 10/09, Eastwood T 5/10, Frickley (L) 11/10, Alfreton Undisc 7/11		
Theo	Streete	4	6'01"	12 06	23/11/1987	23	Birmingham	Walsall NC, Solihull College, Derby 7/06, Doncaster (4ML) 9/06, Bristol R (Trial) 1/07, Grimsby (Trial) 1/07, Rotherham 1/07, Solihull Moors 6/07, Alfreton Undisc 2/11	22	0
Greg	Young	5	6'02"	12 03	24/04/1983	28	Doncaster	Sheff Wed (Scholar), Shrewsbury (Trial) 3/02, Grimsby 7/02, Northwich (L) 10/04, Northwich (L) 12/04, Halifax 2/05, Northwich (L) 11/06, Alfreton (L) 8/07, Altrincham 1/08, York C 5/10, Altrincham (SL) 2/11, Alfreton 6/11		
MIDFIELDERS										
Nathan	Arnold	11	5'08"	10 07	26/07/1987	24	Mansfield	Mansfield Rel c/s 09, Grimsby (Trial) c/s 09, Hyde U 8/09, Alfreton 6/10	36	8
Jordan	Hall	14	5'08"	11 13	07/05/1984	27	Chesterfield	Chesterfield Rel 3/03, Staveley MW, Hucknall, Buxton c/s 05, Hucknall (2ML) 1/08, Alfreton 3/08, Belper (L) 1/10, Matlock (L) 2/10	17	0
Josh	Law	2	5'11"	11 06	19/08/1989	22	Nottingham	Chesterfield Rel c/s 08, Alfreton (SL) 10/07, Alfreton 5/08	35	5
Levi	Mackin	17	6'01"	12 00	04/04/1986	25	Chester	Wrexham Rel 5/09, Droylsden (3ML) 1/08, York C (SL) 1/09, York C 5/09 Rel 6/11, Alfreton 7/11		
Jake	Moult	8	5'10"	10 05	10/02/1989	22	Stoke	Port Vale (Scholar), Plymouth 7/07 Rel c/s 08, Kidderminster (SL) 3/08, Leek T 8/08, Stafford R 10/08, Alfreton 1/10, Hednesford (L) 11/10	15	5
Jamie	Mullan	19	5'06"	11 13	10/02/1988	23	Nottingham	Notts County (Yth), Man Utd Rel c/s 07, Leeds (Trial) 5/07, Huddersfield (Trial) 8/07, Carlisle (Trial) 9/07, Rochdale 11/07, Northwich 1/08, Fleetwood £5,000 5/09, Alfreton 7/11		
Matt	Wilson	6	6'02"		10/03/1987	24		Darlington (Yth), Mackinlay Park, Sheffield Hallam Univ, Diddington T, Grantham 3/07, Alfreton 8/07, Worksop (3ML) 8/08	32	3

FORWARDS										
Paul	Clayton	9	5'10"		31/08/1984	27		Barnsley (Scholar), Parkgate, Gainsborough 7/07, Alfreton 12/07	37	13
Nathan	Jarman	16	5'11"	11 03	19/09/1986	24	Scunthorpe	Barnsley Rel c/s 07, Bury (L) 1/06, Worksop (SL) 2/07, Grimsby (Trial) 7/07, Grimsby 9/07 Rel c/s 10, Harrogate T (Trial) c/s 10, Corby T 8/10, Alfreton Undisc 3/11	10	1
Chris	Senior	10	5'06"	9 01	18/11/1981	29	Huddersfield	Huddersfield, Wakefield-Emley 7/02, Scarborough 8/03 OOC 5/05, Halifax 8/05 Rel 5/07, Altrincham (SL) 1/07, Altrincham 7/07, Darlington 5/10 Rel 5/11, Alfreton 6/11		
Anthony	Wilson	15			25/08/1987	24		Hallam, Belper 8/07, Alfreton 5/10, Matlock (L) 1/11	23	9

Loanees		SN	HT	WT	DOB	AGE	POB	From - To	APPS	GOA
(M)Tom	Naylor		5'11"	11 04	28/06/1991	20	Sutton-in-Ashfield	Mansfield 10/10 -	3	0
(G)Richard	O'Donnell		6'02"	13 05	12/09/1988	22	Sheffield	Sheff Wed (2ML) 1/11 -		
(D)Scott	Garner		6'02"	13 02	20/09/1989	21	Coventry	Grimsby (2ML) 2/11 -	9	1
(F)Daryl	Clare		5'09"	11 00	01/08/1978	33	Jersey	Cambridge U (SL) 2/11 -	16	4
(G)Alessandro	Barcherini		6'03"					Belper T (Dual) 3/11 - Mickleover Sports 7/11		

Departures		SN	HT	WT	DOB	AGE	POB	From - To	APPS	GOA
(D)Kyle	McFadzean		6'01"	13 04	20/02/1987	24	Sheffield	Sheff Utd 6/07 - Crawley Undisc 8/10	2	0
(D)Chris	Shaw				18/12/1983	27		Corby T 12/09 - Eastwood T 11/10, Hednesford 6/11	10	1
(D)Aden	Flint		6'06"		11/07/1989	22		Pinxton FC (L) 10/08 Undisc 11/08 -Swindon £150,000 1/11, Alfreton (SL) 3/11	30	4
(G)James	McKeown		6'01"	13 07	24/07/1989	22	Sutton Coldfield	Peterborough 1/11 - RKSV Leonidas (Holl) 1/11, Grimsby 7/11 (M)		
Kallum	Keane							Derby 2/11 - Belper (Dual) 2/11, Exeter NC 3/11	0	0
(M)Ian	Ross		5'10"	11 00	23/01/1986	25	Sheffield	Gainsborough 3/09 - Rel 5/11, Harrogate T 5/11	26	3
(M)Laurie	Wilson		5'10"	11 03	05/12/1984	26	Brighton	Staveley Miners Welfare 10/10 - Harrogate T 5/11	22	1
(D)Paul	Lister				03/12/1989	21	Sheffield	Hinckley U 12/10 - Rel 5/11, Frickley (2ML) 3/11, Hinckley U 5/11	3	0
(D)Darren	Stride		6'00"	13 05	28/09/1975	35	Burton	Burton 8/10 - Rel 5/11, Chasetown 6/11	16	0
(M)Chris	Hall				03/03/1983	28	Lincoln	Gainsborough 2/10 - Rel 5/11, Stocksbridge PS (L) 1/11, Stocksbridge PS (SL) 3/11, Boston U 6/11	7	1
(F)Anthony	Howell				27/05/1986	25		Mansfield 5/09 - Mansfield 6/11	28	3
(F)Liam	Hearn		5'10"		27/08/1985	26		Quorn 9/08 - Grimsby Undisc 6/11	32	28
(M)Dan	Dillon		5'09"	10 07	06/09/1986	24	Huntingdon	Hinckley U 10/10 - Stocksbridge (Dual) 10/10, Workington 6/11	4	0
(G)Chris	Mackenzie		6'00"	12 09	14/05/1972	39	Northampton	Corby T Undisc 2/11 - Rel 7/11, Corby T 7/11	19	0

Caught in action....
Nathan Jarman
Alfreton Town FC
Photo by Bill Wheatcroft

BARROW

Chairman: Brian Keen
Secretary: Russell Dodd **(T)** 07789 757 639 **(E)** secbafc@aol.com
Additional Committee Members:
Neil McDonald, Dave Ingham, Keith Allen, Neil Chalker, Russell Dodd, Maurice Duffy, Brian Keen, Tony Keen, Dave Ryder, Martin Lewis.
Manager: Dave Bayliss and Darren Sheridan
Programme Editor: Bob Herbert **(E)** robertbobherb@aol.com

Club Factfile

Founded: 1901 **Nickname:** Bluebirds
Previous Names: None
Previous Leagues: Lancashire Combination 1901-21. Football League 1921-72. Northern Premier 1972-79, 83-84, 86-89, 92-98, 99-04. Conference 1979-83, 84-86, 89-92, 98-99.
Club Colours (change): White/blue/white (All sky blue)

Ground: Holker Street Stadium, Wilkie Road, Barrow-in-Furness LA14 5UW **(T)** 01299 823 061
Capacity: 4,500 **Seats:** 1,000 **Covered:** 2,200 **Clubhouse:** Yes **Shop:** Yes

Directions
M6 Junction 36, onto A590 signposted Barrow. Follow A590 all the way to the outskirts of Barrow (approx. 27 miles) entering via Industrial route. In a further 2 miles you pass the Fire Station on the right hand side, take next left into Wilkie Road, the ground is on the right.

Previous Grounds: Strawberry & Little Park, Roose.

Record Attendance: 16,854 v Swansea Town - FA Cup 3rd Round 1954
Record Victory: 12-0 v Cleator - FA Cup 1920
Record Defeat: 1-10 v Hartlepool United - Football League Division 4 1959
Record Goalscorer: Colin Cowperthwaite - 282 (December 1977 - December 1992)
Record Appearances: Colin Cowperthwaite - 704
Additional Records: Paid £9,000 to Ashton United for Andy Whittaker (07/94)
Received £40,000 from Barnet for Kenny Lowe (01/91)

Senior Honours: Lancashire Senior Cup 1954-55. Lancashire Challenge Trophy 1980-81. Northern Premier League 1983-84, 88-89, 97-98. FA Trophy 1989-90, 2009-10.

10 YEAR RECORD

01-02	02-03	03-04	04-05	05-06	06-07	07-08	08-09	09-10	10-11
NP P 8	NP P 2	NP P 3	Conf N 16	Conf N 14	Conf N 16	Conf N 5	Conf 20	Conf 15	Conf 18

BARROW

No.	Date	Comp	H/A	Opponents	Att:	Result	Goalscorers	Pos
1	Sat-14-Aug	BSP	A	Histon	533	L 1-2	Og (Clerima) 12	23
2	Tue-17-Aug	BSP	H	Gateshead	1440	L 1-3	Boyd 30	24
3	Sat-21-Aug	BSP	H	Rushden & Diamonds	1145	W 2-0	Walker 2 (69, pen 76)	17
4	Tue-24-Aug	BSP	A	York City	2212	D 0-0		17
5	Sat-28-Aug	BSP	A	Wrexham	2525	D 1-1	Walker 23	18
6	Mon-30-Aug	BSP	H	Darlington	1718	D 1-1	Walker pen 73	19
7	Sat-04-Sep	BSP	A	Bath City	875	D 1-1	M Pearson 32	19
8	Sat-11-Sep	BSP	H	Eastbourne Borough	1092	W 4-0	Walker 3 (41, 61, pen 73), Forrest 70	14
9	Sat-18-Sep	BSP	H	Forest Green Rovers	1246	W 3-0	Walker 11, Wiles 2 (22, 48)	9
10	Tue-21-Sep	BSP	A	Altrincham	1042	L 0-2		14
11	Sat-25-Sep	BSP	A	Hayes & Yeading United	340	L 0-2		16
12	Tue-28-Sep	BSP	H	Fleetwood Town	1634	L 0-2		17
13	Sat-02-Oct	BSP	H	Luton Town	1416	L 0-1		20
14	Tue-05-Oct	BSP	A	Tamworth	779	D 2-2	Og (Wylde) 13, Walker pen 75	18
15	Sat-09-Oct	BSP	H	Crawley Town	1155	D 1-1	Walker pen 59	19
16	Sat-16-Oct	BSP	A	Cambridge United	2726	L 1-3	Owen 79	22
17	Sat-30-Oct	BSP	A	Rushden & Diamonds	1107	L 0-5		22
18	Sat-06-Nov	BSP	H	Newport County	1089	W 2-1	Walker 55, Chadwick 69	20
19	Sat-13-Nov	BSP	H	AFC Wimbledon	1375	W 2-0	Owen 43, Goodfellow 77	17
20	Sat-20-Nov	BSP	A	Grimsby Town	3225	D 1-1	Chadwick 61	18
21	Sat-01-Jan	BSP	H	Southport	1339	D 1-1	Spender pen 84	18
22	Mon-03-Jan	BSP	A	Darlington	1407	L 1-3	Almond 59	18
23	Sat-08-Jan	BSP	H	Cambridge United	1015	L 1-2	Almond 90	20
24	Sat-15-Jan	BSP	H	Kidderminster Harriers	906	W 2-1	Almond 2 (17, 54)	17
25	Tue-18-Jan	BSP	A	Gateshead	518	L 0-3		18
26	Sat-22-Jan	BSP	A	Kidderminster Harriers	1232	L 0-2		18
27	Tue-25-Jan	BSP	H	Histon	883	D 1-1	Rutherford 75	18
28	Sat-05-Feb	BSP	H	Wrexham	1318	L 0-1		20
29	Sat-12-Feb	BSP	A	Kettering Town	1410	D 1-1	Chadwick 18	20
30	Sat-19-Feb	BSP	H	Mansfield Town	1130	D 2-2	Rutherford 30, Og (Connor) 54	21
31	Tue-22-Feb	BSP	H	Tamworth	874	L 0-2		21
32	Sat-26-Feb	BSP	A	Crawley Town	3941	L 2-3	Cook 19, Rutherford 42	21
33	Sat-05-Mar	BSP	H	York City	1342	D 0-0		21
34	Tue-08-Mar	BSP	H	Altrincham	953	W 1-0	Rutherford 46	20
35	Sat-12-Mar	BSP	A	Forest Green Rovers	757	W 3-2	M Pearson 2, Baker 48, Curtis 83	19
36	Tue-15-Mar	BSP	A	Southport	889	W 4-2	Baker 17, Ferrell 68, Almond 2 (84, pen 90)	18
37	Sat-19-Mar	BSP	A	Eastbourne Borough	1041	W 2-0	Baker 49, Ferrell 87	17
38	Sat-26-Mar	BSP	H	Bath City	1121	L 0-1		17
39	Tue-29-Mar	BSP	A	Luton Town	5528	D 0-0		17
40	Sat-02-Apr	BSP	A	AFC Wimbledon	3264	L 0-2		17
41	Sat-09-Apr	BSP	H	Kettering Town	1015	W 5-0	Rutherford 3 (54, 85, 90), P Smith 2 (59, 66)	16
42	Tue-12-Apr	BSP	A	Mansfield Town	1253	D 1-1	Forrest 78	16
43	Sat-16-Apr	BSP	A	Newport County	1331	L 0-5		17
44	Sat-23-Apr	BSP	H	Grimsby Town	1274	L 0-2		18
45	Mon-25-Apr	BSP	A	Fleetwood Town	2788	L 0-1		18
46	Sat-30-Apr	BSP	H	Hayes & Yeading United	1445	W 2-0	Baker 2 (52, 61)	18

CUPS

No.	Date	Comp	H/A	Opponents	Att:	Result	Goalscorers	Pos
1	Sun-24-Oct	FAC 4Q	A	FC United of Manchester	3263	L 0-1		
2	Sat-11-Dec	FAT 1	H	Guiseley	923	L 2-3	Blundell 2 (47, 77)	

League
Starts
Substitute
Unused Sub

Cups
Starts
Substitute
Unused Sub

Goals (Lg)
Goals (Cup)

MARTIN	SPENDER	BOLLAND	NICHOLAS	MILNE	BOYD	GOODFELLOW	OWEN	WILES	BLUNDELL	WALKER	COOK	M PEARSON	FORREST	S PEARSON	SHERIDAN	RUTHERFORD	JONES	EDWARDS	HULBERT	DONNELLY	WAINWRIGHT	CHADWICK	BAYLISS	CLAY	DARIKWA	MASTERS	HALSTEAD	GRANT	ALMOND	C SMITH	CURTIS	BAKER	TONER	FERRELL	P SMITH	
21	2	5	22	23	8	11	17	18	12	9	20	3	15	1	14	7	4	24	6	19	25	10	16	26	27	21	21	28	26	23	9	27	19	8	23	
X	X	X	X	X	X	X	X	X	X	X	S	S	S	U	U																					
X	X	X	X	X	X		X	X		X	X	U		U	U	X	U																			
X	X	X		U	X	X	X	S		X	S	U	S		X	X	X	X																		
X	X	X		U	X	X	X	S		X	U	S	U		X	X	X	X																		
X	X	X	U		X		X	X		X	U	S	X	U	S		X	X	X																	
X	X	X	U		X		X	X		X	S	S	X	U	U		X	X	X																	
	X	X	U		X		X	X	U	X	S	X	U	X	U			X	X	X																
X	X	X	U		X		S	X		X	S	X	X	U		X		X	X	S																
X	X	X			X		U	X	S	X	S	X	X	U		X		X	X	S																
X	X	X			X		U	X	S	X	S	X	X	U		X		X	X	S																
X	X	X			X		X		X	X	S	X	U	U		X	U	X	X	S																
X	X			U	U		X		U	X	S	X	X	U		X	X	X	X		X															
X	X	U			U		X		U	X	X	X	S	U		X	X	X	X		X															
	X	U			U		X		U	X		X	U	X	X	X	X	X	X	S	X															
	X				S		X		U	X		X	U	X	X	X	X	X	X	S	X	U														
	X				U		X		U	X		X	U	X	X	X	X	X		X	X	S														
	X	X			U	S	X		U	X		X		X		S	X			X	X	S		X	X											
	X	X				X	X		U	X		X		U		X	U	X	X			X		U	U	X										
	X	X			U	X	X		X			X		U	U	X	U	X	X	S		X					X									
	X	X			S	X	X		X			X		U	X	X	U	X		S		X				X		S								
X	X	X				X	X		X			X		U	U	X	U	X	X				U					X	S							
X	X	X				S	X		X			X		U	X	X	U	X		U			U					X	X							
	X	X				S	X		X			X		U		X	S	X		X						X		X	X							
	X	X				X	X				S	X		U		X	U	X		S		X				X		U	X	X						
	X	X				X	X				S	X		U		X	U	X		S		X				X		S	X	X						
	X	X				U	X				S	X		S		X	U	X		X		X				X		U	X	X						
	X	X				S	X				S	X		X	U	X	U	X		X		X						U	X	X						
	X					U	X		U		X	X		U	U	X	X	X	X			S				X			X		X					
	X	X				U			U		S	X		U	U	X	X	X	X			X				X			X	X						
	X	X	U			S			U		S	X		U	X	X	X	X				X				X			X			X				
	S	X	X			U			U		S	X		U		X	X	X	X			X				X			X			X				
	X	X	U			S					X	X		U	X	X	U	X								X			X		X	X	U			
	X	X	U			U					X	X		U	X	X		X								X			S		X	X	U	X		
	X	X	U			U					X	X		U	X	X		X								X			S		X	X	U	X		
	X	X	S			U					S	X		U	X	X		X								X			X		X	X	U	X		
	X	X	S			U					S	X		U	X	X		X								X			X		X	X	U	X		
	X	X	S			S			U		S	X		U	X	X		X								X			X		X	X		X		
	X	X	U			S			U		S	X		U	X	X		X								X			X		X	X		X		
	X	X	S			U			U		U	X		U	X	X		X								X			X		X			X	X	
	X	X	S			S			U		S	X		U	X	X		X								X			X		X			X	X	
	X	X	S			U	X				S	X	X	U	X	X		X	S							X					X				X	
	X	X	U				X				S	X	X	U	X	X		X	S							X					X	S			X	
	X	X	U				X				S	X	X	U	X	X		X	S							X					X	S			X	
	X	X	U			S	S				S	X	X	U	X	X		X								X					X	X			X	
	X	X	S			U	X				X	X		U	X	X		X				S				X						X			X	
	X	X	U				X				S	X		U	X	X	S	X				S				X					X	X			X	
	X	X			X	S			U	X		X	S	X	X	S	X	X	U	X		X	U													
X	X	X			U	X	X		X			X		U		X	U	X	X	S		X						S								
14	45	40	3	2	11	9	30	8	7	18	7	40	10	6	23	41	14	43	17	6	6	10	0	1	1	25	1	3	17	5	15	12	0	8	8	0
0	1	0	7	0	2	10	2	2	2	0	26	4	3	1	1	1	2	0	3	10	0	5	0	0	0	0	0	2	3	0	0	2	0	0	0	0
0	0	2	13	3	6	11	2	0	16	0	3	2	6	37	9	0	12	0	0	1	0	1	2	1	1	0	0	3	0	0	0	0	5	0	0	0
1	2	2	0	0	1	1	1	0	1	1	0	2	0	1	1	1	1	2	1	1	0	2	0	0	0	0	0	0	0	0	0	0	0	0	0	0
0	0	0	0	0	0	1	0	0	0	0	0	0	1	0	0	1	0	0	0	1	0	0	0	0	0	0	0	1	0	0	0	0	0	0	0	0
0	0	0	0	0	1	0	0	0	1	0	0	0	0	1	0	0	1	0	1	0	0	0	1	0	0	0	0	0	0	0	0	0	0	0	0	0
0	1	0	0	0	1	1	2	2	0	11	1	2	2	0	0	7	0	0	0	0	0	3	0	0	0	0	0	0	6	0	1	5	0	2	2	0
0	0	0	0	0	0	0	0	0	2	0	0	0	0	0	0	0	0	0	0	0	0	0	0	0	0	0	0	0	0	0	0	0	0	0	0	0

PLAYING SQUAD

Existing Players		SN	HT	WT	DOB	AGE	POB	Career	Apps	Goals
GOALKEEPERS										
Danny	Hurst	1			14/11/1980	30		Cheadle, Radcliffe 7/00, Sheff Wed (Trial) 2/03, Fleetwood 5 fig 1/07 Rel 5/11, Barrow 7/11		
Shaun	Pearson	21			16/08/1990	21	Bangor	Llangefni T, Barrow 8/10	7	0
DEFENDERS										
Dave	Bayliss		6'00"	12 11	08/06/1976	35	Liverpool	Rochdale, Luton 12/01 Rel c/s 05, Chester (2ML) 12/04, Bristol R (Trial) 4/05, Oxford U (Trial) 5/05, Wrexham 7/05 Rel c/s 06, Rochdale (L) 2/06, Lancaster 7/06, Barrow 11/06 Joint Man	0	0
Phil	Bolland	5	6'02"	13 08	26/08/1976	35	Liverpool	Altrincham, Salford C 10/95, Trafford 3/96, Knowsley U 8/96, Southport c/s 97, Oxford U 7/01, Chester (2ML) 1/02 £15,000 3/02, Peterborough 1/06 Rel c/s 06, Chester 6/06, Wrexham 1/08, Cambridge U 7/08 Rel 6/09, Barrow 7/09	40	0
Kelvin	Lomax	19	5'11"	12 03	12/11/1986	24	Bury	Oldham, Rochdale (2ML) 9/07, Chesterfield (5WL) 11/10, Shrewsbury 1/11 Rel c/s 11, Barrow 8/11		
Andy	Nicholas	4	6'02"	12 08	10/10/1983	27	Liverpool	Liverpool (Scholar) Rel c/s 03, Swindon 7/03 Rel 6/08, Chester (L) 3/05, Rotherham 8/08 Rel c/s 10, Mansfield (SL) 2/10, Barrow 8/10, Vauxhall Motors (3ML) 10/10	10	0
Michael	Pearson	2	5'11"	11 01	19/01/1988	23	Bangor	Liverpool (Sch), Oldham Rel c/s 08, Farsley Celtic (2ML) 10/07, Barrow 7/08	44	2
Adam	Quinn	17	6'02"	13 00	02/06/1983	28	Sheffield	Sheff Wed, Carlisle (Trial) 3/02, Halifax 8/02, Crawley 8/08, Forest Green (2ML) 11/10, Darlington £25,000 1/11, Barrow (3ML) 8/11		
Gavin	Skelton	3	5'10"	11 00	27/03/1981	30	Carlisle	Carlisle, Workington 10/00, Stoke (Trial) 11/00, Gretna 10/01 Rel c/s 08, Kilmarnock 6/08 Rel c/s 10, Hamilton 6/10 Rel c/s 11, Barrow 7/11		
MIDFIELDERS										
Richie	Baker	8	5'10"	11 05	29/12/1987	23	Burnley	Man Utd (Yth), Preston (Scholar), Bury 7/06 Rel c/s 10, Oxford U 7/10 Rel 1/11, Barrow 2/11	14	5
Andy	Ferrell	10	5'08"	11 05	09/01/1984	27	Newcastle	Newcastle Rel c/s 04, Watford 7/04 Rel c/s 05, Hereford 8/05 Rel 5/07, Kidderminster (L) 3/07, Kidderminster 6/07, York C 5/09, Gateshead 2/10 Rel 5/11, Barrow (L) 2/11, Barrow 6/11	8	2
Robin	Hulbert	6	5'10"	12 02	14/03/1980	31	Plymouth	Swindon, Newcastle (SL) 2/98, Bristol C £25,000 3/00, Shrewsbury (SL) 3/03, Telford 11/03, Port Vale 7/04 Rel c/s 08, Darlington 8/08 Rel c/s 09, Barrow 6/09	20	0
Jack	Mackreth	16	5'09"		13/04/1992	19	Liverpool	Tranmere Rel c/s 11, Burscough (2ML) 9/10, Colwyn Bay (L) 12/10, Hyde FC (L) 2/11, Chester FC (L) 3/11, Barrow 7/11		
James	Owen	12	5'09"	10 07	14/01/1991	20	Caernarfon	Chester Rel 1/10, Barrow 3/10	32	2
Paul	Rutherford	7	5'08"	10 11	10/07/1987	24	Moreton	Liverpool (Yth), Greenleas, Chester 10/05 Rel c/s 09, Bournemouth (Trial) 7/08, Barrow 7/09	42	7
Darren	Sheridan	14	5'05"	11 05	08/12/1967	43	Manchester	Leeds U (Trainee) Rel c/s 86, Local, Maine Road, Mossley, Curzon Ashton, Winsford, Barnsley £10,000 8/93, Wigan 7/99 Rel c/s 01, Oldham 7/01 Rel c/s 04, Clyde 6/04, St Johnstone 7/05, Barrow 1/07 Joint Man	24	0
Paul	Smith	15	5'09"	11 09	17/11/1991	19	Liverpool	Chester, Rhyl 8/09 Rel 1/10, Droylsden 3/10 Rel 8/10, Aigburth Peoples Hall, Barrow 3/11	8	2
FORWARDS										
Louis	Almond	18	5'11"	12 00	15/08/1990	21	Blackburn	Blackpool, Cheltenham (SL) 3/10, Barrow (3ML) 1/11, Barrow (6ML) 8/11	20	6
Adam	Boyes	11	6'02"		01/11/1990	20	Lingdale	York C, Man Utd (Trial) 6/08, Scunthorpe Undisc 7/09 Rel 1/11, York C (L) 10/09, Kidderminster (L) 2/10, Boston U 1/11 Rel 5/11, Barrow 7/11		
Andy	Cook	9	6'01"	11 04	18/10/1990	20	Bishop Auckland	Carlisle, Workington (2ML) 2/09, Workington (L) 8/09, Barrow (3ML) 10/09, Barrow (2ML) 8/10, Barrow 1/11	33	1

Loanees		SN	HT	WT	DOB	AGE	POB	From - To	APPS	GOA
(G)Alan	Martin		6'02"	11 11	01/01/1989	23	Glasgow	Leeds (5ML) 8/10 - Rel c/s 11, Crewe 7/11	14	0
(M)Neil	Wainwright		6'00"	12 00	04/11/1977	33	Warrington	Morecambe 9/10 - Rel c/s 11	6	0
(M)Craig	Clay		5'10"	11 06	05/05/1992	19	Nottingham	Chesterfield 10/10 -	1	0
(M)Tendayi	Darikwa				13/12/1991	19	Nottingham	Chesterfield 10/10 -	1	0
(G)Mark	Halstead		6'03"	14 00	01/01/1990	21	Blackpool	Blackpool 11/10 - Kettering (L) 1/11	1	0
(D)Christian	Smith		6'02"	13 02	10/12/1987	23	Crewe	Wrexham 1/11 - Tamworth (6WL) 3/11, Chester FC 8/11	5	0
(F)Wayne	Curtis		6'00"	12 00	06/03/1980	31	Barrow	Fleetwood (SL) 1/11 - Rel 5/11	15	1

Departures		SN	HT	WT	DOB	AGE	POB	From - To	APPS	GOA
(D)Matt	Heywood				26/08/1979	32		Grimsby 8/10 - Rel 10/10, Buxton 10/10		
(F)Jason	Walker		6'02"	14 04	21/03/1984	27	Barrow	Morecambe 3/07 - Luton (6WL) 11/10 Undisc 1/11, York C £60,000 6/11	18	11
(D)Andrew	Milne		5'11"	11 08	30/09/1990	20	Leeds	Leeds 8/10 - Rel 1/11, Gainsborough (L) 8/10, Altrincham (3ML) 10/10, FC Halifax 1/11 Rel 5/11	2	0
(M)Marc	Boyd		5'10"	12 04	22/10/1981	29	Carlisle	Sligo R 1/08 - Droylsden (L) 1/11 Perm 1/11, Workington 6/11	13	1
(M)Ciaren	Donnelly		5'08"	11 08	02/04/1984	27	Blackpool	AFC Blackpool 7/10 - Rel 1/11, Kendal T 2/11	16	0
(F)John	Grant		6'00"	12 08	09/08/1981	30	Manchester	ex Aldershot 11/10 - Rel 1/11, Macclesfield 8/11	5	0
(D)Paul	Jones		6'01"	11 09	03/06/1978	33	Liverpool	Hyde 6/06 - Rel 5/11, Droylsden (2ML) 2/11, Altrincham 7/11	16	0
(F)Danny	Forrest		5'10"	11 07	23/10/1984	26	Keighley	Crawley 6/10 - Rel 5/11, Guiseley (3ML) 1/11, Guiseley 5/11	13	2
(M)Marc	Goodfellow		5'08"	10 00	20/09/1981	29	Burton	Burton 8/10 - Rel 5/11, Gresley FC 8/11	19	1
(G)Clark	Masters		6'03"	13 12	31/05/1987	24	Hastings	Hastings U 11/10 - Rel 5/11, Eastbourne B 6/11	25	0
(D)Simon	Spender		5'11"	11 00	15/11/1985	25	Mold	Wrexham (SL) 3/09 Perm 5/09 - The New Saints 5/11	46	1
(F)Nick	Chadwick		6'00"	12 08	26/10/1982	28	Market Drayton	Chester 1/10 - Rel 5/11, Altrincham (Trial) 7/11, Stockport 7/11	15	3
(F)Gregg	Blundell		5'11"	12 03	03/10/1977	33	Liverpool	Chester (5WL) 11/09 Perm 1/10 - Rel c/s 11	9	0
(D)Paul	Edwards		5'11"	10 12	01/01/1980	31	Manchester	ex Port Vale 3/10 - Rel 6/10, Inverness Caledonian (Trial) c/s 10, Barrow 8/10, Fleetwood 6/11	43	0
(M)Simon	Wiles		5'11"	11 04	22/04/1985	26	Preston	USA 1/10 - Retired 8/11	10	2
(D)Shaun	Pejic	17	6'00"	12 01	16/11/1982	28	Hereford	Crystal Palace Baltimore (USA) 8/11 -Bangor C 8/11		
(M)Eddie	Toner							Yth -	0	0

Caught in action....

Alex Lawless, Luton, controls the ball as Mansfield's Ashley Cain closes in during the FA Trophy.

Photo by Bill Wheatcroft

BATH CITY

Chairman: TBC
Secretary: Quentin Edwards **(T)** 07785 795 532 **(E)** qcath@blueyonder.co.uk
Additional Committee Members:
John Reynolds, Paul Williams, Geoff Todd, Adie Britton, Andrew Jones, Andrew Pierce, Andy Weeks, Phil Weaver, Pete Sellwood.
Manager: Adie Britton
Programme Editor: TBC **(E)**

Back row (L-R): Dave Lukins (physio), John Freegard (coach), Luke Ruddick, Matt Coupe, Jake Reid, Gethin Jones, Danny Webb, Ryan Robinson, Gordon Rieck, Sekani Simpson, Sido Jombati, Adie Britton (manager), Vicky Gardiner (physio)
Front Row: Scott Murray, Joe Burnell, Hector Mackie, Mark Badman, Darren Edwards, Kaid Mohamed, Adam Connolly, Jim Rollo, Lewis Hogg, Adie Harris, Lee Phillips, Marc Canham.

Club Factfile

Founded: 1889 **Nickname:** The Romans
Previous Names: Bath AFC 1889-92. Bath Railway FC 1902-05. Bath Amateurs 1913-23 (Reserve side)
Previous Leagues: Western 1908-21. Southern 1921-79, 88-90, 97-2007. Alliance/Conference 1979-88, 90-97.

Club Colours (change): Black & white/black/black (Red/white/red)

Ground: Twerton Park, Twerton, Bath, Somerset BA2 1DB **(T)** 01225 423 087
Capacity: 8,840 **Seats:** 1,017 **Covered:** 4,800 **Clubhouse:** Yes **Shop:** Yes

Directions
Take Junction 18 off M4. 3rd exit off roundabout and follow A46 (10 miles) to Bath City Centre. Along Pulteney Road then right into Claverton Street and then follow A36 Lower Bristol Road (1.5 miles). Left under Railway bridge (signs Bath City FC) into Twerton High Street and ground is 2nd turning on left.

Previous Grounds: The Belvoir Ground 1889-92 & 1902-15. Lambridge Show Ground 1919-32.

Record Attendance: 18,020 v Brighton & Hove Albion - FA Cup
Record Victory: 8-0 v Boston United - 1998-99
Record Defeat: 0-9 v Yeovil Town - 1946-47
Record Goalscorer: Paul Randall - 106
Record Appearances: David Mogg - 530
Additional Records: Paid £15,000 to Bristol City for Micky Tanner. Received £80,000 from Southampton for Jason Dodd.

Senior Honours: Southern Lge Western Div.2 1928-29. Southern Lge Western Division 1933-34. Southern League 1959-60, 77-78, 2006-07. Southern League Cup 1978-79. Somerset Premier Cup 1951-52, 52-53, 57-58, 59-60, 65-66, 67-68, 69-70, 77-78, 80-81, 81-82, 83-84, 84-85, 85-86, 88-89, 89-90, 93-94, 94-95, 2007-08.

10 YEAR RECORD

01-02	02-03	03-04	04-05	05-06	06-07	07-08	08-09	09-10	10-11
SthP 17	SthP 14	SthP 16	SthP 6	SthP 2	SthP 1	Conf S 8	Conf S 8	Conf S 4	Conf 10

BATH CITY

No.	Date	Comp	H/A	Opponents	Att:	Result	Goalscorers	Pos
1	Sat-14-Aug	BSP	A	Hayes & Yeading United	328	L 1-2	Jones 90	16
2	Tue-17-Aug	BSP	H	Rushden & Diamonds	876	W 2-1	Connolly 46, D Edwards 58	12
3	Sat-21-Aug	BSP	H	York City	1066	D 2-2	Harris 38, Phillips 66	9
4	Tue-24-Aug	BSP	A	Crawley Town	1252	L 1-2	Webb 75	15
5	Sat-28-Aug	BSP	A	Forest Green Rovers	1464	D 0-0		17
6	Mon-30-Aug	BSP	H	Wrexham	1262	L 0-2		21
7	Sat-04-Sep	BSP	H	Barrow	875	D 1-1	D Edwards 77	22
8	Sat-11-Sep	BSP	A	AFC Wimbledon	3300	L 0-4		23
9	Sat-18-Sep	BSP	H	Darlington	951	D 2-2	Hogg 90, Mackie 90	22
10	Tue-21-Sep	BSP	A	Tamworth	920	D 2-2	Mohamed 19, Connolly 33	20
11	Sat-25-Sep	BSP	A	Fleetwood Town	1481	L 1-2	Mohamed pen 87	22
12	Tue-28-Sep	BSP	H	Kidderminster Harriers	742	W 2-0	Mohamed pen 16, Russell 45	20
13	Sat-02-Oct	BSP	A	Cambridge United	2670	W 2-1	Canham 28, Mohamed 90	18
14	Sat-09-Oct	BSP	H	Eastbourne Borough	1074	D 1-1	Mohamed 27	20
15	Sat-16-Oct	BSP	A	York City	2331	D 1-1	Russell 63	21
16	Sat-30-Oct	BSP	A	Luton Town	7003	L 1-3	Phillips 65	21
17	Sat-06-Nov	BSP	H	Altrincham	794	D 2-2	Phillips 2 (63, 74)	21
18	Tue-09-Nov	BSP	H	Hayes & Yeading United	532	W 3-1	Mohamed 20, Jones 87, Phillips 90	16
19	Sat-13-Nov	BSP	A	Southport	947	W 3-2	Mohamed 49, Webb 78, Phillips 85	14
20	Sat-20-Nov	BSP	H	Fleetwood Town	905	D 1-1	Canham 16	14
21	Thu-25-Nov	BSP	A	Histon	470	W 2-1	Jombarti 45, Phillips 55	12
22	Tue-28-Dec	BSP	H	Forest Green Rovers	1222	L 2-4	Mohamed pen 26, Phillips 68	12
23	Sat-01-Jan	BSP	A	Newport County	2903	W 2-1	Mohamed 57, Jones 90	11
24	Mon-03-Jan	BSP	A	Wrexham	2602	L 0-2		13
25	Sat-08-Jan	BSP	H	Luton Town	2301	D 0-0		13
26	Tue-18-Jan	BSP	H	Crawley Town	836	L 0-2		14
27	Sat-22-Jan	BSP	A	Altrincham	831	W 3-0	Phillips 2 (36, 88), Mohamed 81	13
28	Tue-25-Jan	BSP	H	AFC Wimbledon	1135	D 2-2	Canham 52, Phillips 85	13
29	Sat-29-Jan	BSP	H	Cambridge United	1338	W 4-0	Canham 47, Mohamed 2 (pen 78, pen 88), Murray 83	10
30	Sat-05-Feb	BSP	A	Kidderminster Harriers	1500	L 0-1		12
31	Sat-12-Feb	BSP	H	Tamworth	899	W 2-0	Watson 80, Murray 90	11
32	Tue-15-Feb	BSP	A	Kettering Town	796	L 1-2	Jombarti 31	13
33	Tue-22-Feb	BSP	H	Newport County	1551	D 2-2	Murray 9, Phillips 23	14
34	Sat-26-Feb	BSP	H	Southport	792	W 2-1	Og (Lever) 33, Phillips 53	12
35	Tue-01-Mar	BSP	A	Rushden & Diamonds	804	L 1-5	Murray pen 15	13
36	Sat-05-Mar	BSP	H	Kettering Town	890	D 1-1	Mohamed 90	14
37	Sat-19-Mar	BSP	H	Grimsby Town	1808	W 2-1	Watkins 32, Mackie 85	12
38	Sat-26-Mar	BSP	A	Barrow	1121	W 1-0	Phillips 6	11
39	Sat-02-Apr	BSP	H	Gateshead	952	W 1-0	Phillips 47	10
40	Mon-04-Apr	BSP	A	Gateshead	522	D 1-1	Clough 88	9
41	Sat-09-Apr	BSP	A	Darlington	1752	L 1-3	Phillips 75	11
42	Thu-14-Apr	BSP	A	Mansfield Town	2026	L 0-2		13
43	Sat-16-Apr	BSP	A	Grimsby Town	2389	D 2-2	Murray 80, Clough 90	13
44	Sat-23-Apr	BSP	H	Histon	754	W 2-1	Watkins 8, Hogg 74	11
45	Mon-25-Apr	BSP	A	Eastbourne Borough	1014	L 0-2		13
46	Sat-30-Apr	BSP	H	Mansfield Town	1051	W 2-0	Watkins 52, Murray 75	10

CUPS

No.	Date	Comp	H/A	Opponents	Att:	Result	Goalscorers
1	Sat-23-Oct	FAC 4Q	A	Swindon Supermarine	551	D 0-0	
2	Tue-26-Oct	FAC 4QR	H	Swindon Supermarine	665	L 3-4	Jombarti 5, Connolly 21, Mackie 33
3	Sat-11-Dec	FAT 1	A	Histon	263	W 3-2	Russell 2 (67, 90), Murray 70
4	Sat-15-Jan	FAT 2	A	Darlington	926	L 1-4	Connolly 58

League
Starts
Substitute
Unused Sub

Cups
Starts
Substitute
Unused Sub

Goals (Lge)
Goals (Cup)

ROBINSON	SIMPSON	JONES	WEBB	RUDDICK	HARRIS	MURRAY	CONNOLLY	HOGG	CANHAM	PHILLIPS	ROLLO	MOHAMED	MACKIE	COUPE	D EDWARDS	JOMBARTI	REID	HART	BORHY	BADMAN	J EDWARDS	WATKINS	RUSSELL	BURNELL	PENTNEY	JEANNE	WATSON	BROWN	HENRY	CLOUGH	LENNOX	EGAN												
1	2	5	14	15	6	7	8	11	16	10	3	23	12	4	9	20	18	22	17	21	25	27	28	19	29	30	31	32	9	22	4	25												
X	X	X	X	X	X	X	X	X	X	X	S	S	S	U	U																													
X	X	X	X		X		X	X	X	X	S		U	U	X	X	S	U																										
X	X	X	X		X		X	X	X	X	S	S	S	U	X	X	U																											
	X	X	X		X		X	X	S	X	U	X	S	X	S	X	U		X																									
X	X	X	X		X		X	X	X	X	U	X	S	U	U	X	S																											
X	X	X	X		X		X		X	X	U	S	X	U	X	X	S			U																								
X	X	X	X		X		X		X	S	X	X	X	U	X		S	U		S																								
X	X	X	X		X		X		X	X	S	S	S		X	X	U	U			X																							
X	X	X	X		U		X	X	X	X	S	X	S		S	X		U			X																							
X	X		X		S		X	X	X	X	X	X	U		S	X		U		U	X																							
X	X		X		X		X		X	X	X	X	U		S	X		S	U		X	S																						
X	S		X		S		X		X	X	X	X	U		S	X		U			X	X	X																					
X	X		X		X				X	X	X	X	S		S	X		U	U			X	X																					
X	X	U	X		X	S	S		X	X	X	X			S	X			U			X	X																					
X	X	X			U	S	X		X	X	X	X	U		S	X					S	X	X																					
X		X	X		U	S	X		X	S	X	X			U	X					X	X	X	S																				
		U	X		U	S	X		X	X	X	X			U	X			U		X		X	X	X																			
		S	X		S	X	X		X	X	X	X			U	X			U		S		X	X	X																			
U		X	X		S	S	X		X	X	X	X			U	X					X		X	S	X																			
		X	X	U	X	S	S		X	X	X	X			U	X		S					X	X	X																			
U		X	X	X	S	S	X		X	X	S	X				X		U					X	X	X																			
	X	X	X	X	U	S	X	X	X	X	U	X											X	S	X	S																		
	X	X	S		X	S	X	X	U	X	U	X				X							X	X	X	S																		
U	X	X	U		X	S	X	S	X	X	X	X				X								X	X	S																		
U	X	X	S		X	S	X		X	X	X	X				X		U						X	X	U																		
U	U	X	X	X	X	S	X	S	X		X	X				X		U							X		X																	
U	U	X	X	X	S	S	X	U	X	X	X	X				X									X		X																	
U	U	S	X	X	X	S	X	S	X	X	X	X				X									X		X																	
U	U	S	X	X		S	X	S	X	X	X	X				X								X	X		X																	
X	X	X		U		X	X	S	X	X	X	X				X		U				S		X			S																	
X	X	X		U		S	X	S	X	X	X	X				X		U				X		X			S																	
X	X	X		X		S	X	S	X	U	U	X				X			U			X		X			X																	
X	X	X		X		X	X	S	X	X	X					X		U	U			X						S	U															
X	X	X				X	X		X	X	X	S	U			X		X	U			X						S	S															
X	X	X				X	X		X	X	X	S	S			X		U				X				U			U	X														
X	X	X				X	X		X		S	X	S			X			U			X		X				U	U	X														
X	X	X				X	X		X	X	S	U	S			X			U			X		X					U	X														
X	X	X				X	X		X	X	S		S			X			U			X		X					U	X	S													
X	X	X				X	X		X	X	S		S			X			U			X		X					U	X	S													
X	X	X				S	X		X	X	X		S			X			U			X		X					X	S	U													
X	X		U			S	X		X	X	X		U			X			U			X		X					X	X	U													
X	X	X	U		S	S	X		X	X			X			X						X		X					U	X	S													
X	X	X	U		U	X	X		X	X	S		S			X						X		X						X	U													
X	X	X	U			X	X	S	X	X	U		S			X						X		X						X		S												
U	X	X	X				X	X	X	X	X		S			X			X					S					X	S		U												
X	X	X	X		S	X	X	S	X	X	S		U			X						X		X					U															
X		X	U		U	X	X	U	X	X	X	X	S		S	X		U	U		X		X																					
X		X	S		X	X	X		S	S	X		X		X	X		U	U		X		X	U																				
		X	X	X	U	S	X	S	X	X	U	X				X						X	X		X	S																		
U	X	X	X	X	X	S	X		X	U	X	X				X		U							X	S																		
31	35	36	27	9	17	13	43	10	44	41	26	28	3	1	5	43	0	1	2	0	8	20	12	21	13	0	5	0	3	9	0	0	0	0	0	0	0	0	0	0	0	0	0	0
0	1	3	2	0	8	20	2	10	1	2	12	6	16	0	8	0	4	2	0	1	2	2	0	4	0	3	2	2	1	2	3	1	0	0	0	0	0	0	0	0	0	0	0	0
9	4	2	5	3	6	0	0	1	1	1	7	1	8	6	7	0	3	14	14	2	0	0	0	0	0	2	0	1	8	0	3	1	0	0	0	0	0	0	0	0	0	0	0	0
2	1	4	2	2	2	2	4	0	3	2	3	3	1	0	1	4	0	0	0	0	2	1	3	0	2	0	0	0	0	0	0	0	0	0	0	0	0	0	0	0	0	0	0	0
0	0	0	1	0	0	2	0	1	1	1	0	0	1	0	1	0	0	0	0	0	0	0	0	0	0	2	0	0	0	0	0	0	0	0	0	0	0	0	0	0	0	0	0	0
1	0	0	1	0	2	0	0	1	0	1	1	0	0	0	0	0	0	3	2	0	0	0	0	1	0	0	0	0	0	0	0	0	0	0	0	0	0	0	0	0	0	0	0	0
0	0	3	2	0	1	6	2	2	4	16	0	13	2	0	2	2	0	0	0	0	0	3	2	0	0	0	1	0	0	2	0	0	0	0	0	0	0	0	0	0	0	0	0	0
0	0	0	0	0	0	1	2	0	0	0	0	0	1	0	0	1	0	0	0	0	0	0	2	0	0	0	0	0	0	0	0	0	0	0	0	0	0	0	0	0	0	0	0	0

PLAYING SQUAD

Existing Players		SN	HT	WT	DOB	AGE	POB	Career	Apps	Goals
GOALKEEPERS										
Glyn	Garner	1	6'02"	13 11	09/12/1976	34	Pontypool	Cwmbran, Llanelli, Bury 7/00, L.Orient 5/05 Rel c/s 07, Shrewsbury 8/07, Rel 1/10, Grays 2/10 Rel 5/10, Newport C 7/10, Bath C 5/11		
Jason	Matthews	17	6'00"	12 02	15/03/1975	36	Paulton	Mangotsfield, Welton R, Westbury, Bath C, Paulton, Nuneaton, Taunton 8/98, Exeter 8/99 Rel c/s 00, Aberystwyth c/s 00, Cleveden 6/01, Weymouth 8/02, Eastleigh 3/08 Rel 5/11, Bath C 6/11		
DEFENDERS										
Gethin	Jones	5	5'11"	12 04	08/08/1981	29	Llanbyther	Carmarthen, Cardiff 8/00 Rel c/s 03, Weymouth (L) 9/02, Bath C (Trial) c/s 03, Merthyr 8/03, Bath C 6/05	39	3
Mark	Preece	15	6'02"	13 07	03/06/1987	24	Bristol	Bristol R Rel c/s 06, Gloucester (SL) 1/06, Kidderminster (Trial) 7/06, Forest Green 7/06, Weston-super-Mare (L) 1/07, Mansfield 7/10 Rel 5/11, Eastwood T (L) 9/10, AFC Telford (L) 2/11, Bath C 8/11		
Jim	Rollo	4	6'00"	11 00	22/05/1976	35	Wisbech	Walsall Rel c/s 96, Yate T 4/96, Cardiff 8/96 Rel c/s 98, Bath C (L) 1/97, Ebbw Vale (L) 3/98, Yate T (Trial) c/s 98 Forest Green 6/98 Rel c/s 99, Cirencester (L) 10/98, Bath C (L) 1/99, Clevedon 8/99, Merthyr 6/01, Bath C 5/02	38	0
Danny	Rosser							Bath C		
Sekani	Simpson	2	5'10"	11 10	11/03/1984	27	Bristol	Bristol C Rel c/s 05, Forest Green (L) 3/04, Tamworth (SL) 9/04, Forest Green 7/05 Rel 5/06, Weston-Super-Mare 8/06 Rel 9/06 Bath C 10/06	36	0
Paul	Stonehouse	3	5'07"	11 03	13/07/1987	24	Wegburg	Forest Green, Yate T (2ML) 10/05, Cinderford (L) 1/06, Gloucester (7WL) 2/06, Gloucester (L) 1/07, Mansfield Undisc 6/10 Rel 5/11, Bath C 5/11		
Danny	Webb	14	6'01"	11 08	02/07/1983	28	Poole	Southampton (Scholar), Southend 12/00, Brighton (SL) 12/01, Brighton (L) 11/02, Hull C 12/02, Lincoln C (L) 3/03, Cambridge U (2ML) 12/03 Perm 2/04 Rel c/s 05, Weymouth 6/05, Yeovil 12/05, Rushden & D (L) 1/07, Woking (L) 3/07, Marsaxlokk (Mal) 7/07, AFC Wimbledon 7/07 Rel 5/08, Chelmsford 7/08 Rel 9/08, Havant & W 10/08, Salisbury 11/08, Bath C 5/10	29	2
MIDFIELDERS										
Joe	Burnell	19	5'10"	11 01	10/10/1980	30	Bristol	Bristol C, Wycombe 7/04 Rel c/s 06, Northampton 8/06 Rel c/s 08, Oxford U 7/08 Rel 7/09, Exeter 7/09 Rel c/s 10, Bath C 7/10	25	0
Marc	Canham	16	5'11"	12 03	11/09/1982	28	Wegburg, Ger	Colchester Rel 6/03, Bournemouth (Trial) c/s 03, Team Bath 8/03, Yeovil (Trial) 2/05, Hayes & Yeading 7/09 Rel 5/10, Bath C 6/10	45	4
Danny	Collins							Bath C		
Adam	Connolly	8	5'09"	12 04	10/04/1986	25	Manchester	Cheltenham Rel c/s 08, Newport C (Trial) 7/08, Hednesford 8/08, Bath C 9/08	45	2
Lewis	Hogg	11	5'09"	11 11	13/09/1982	28	Bristol	Bristol R Rel c/s 03, Barnet 8/03, Weston-s-Mare 12/03, Bath C 5/06	20	2
Gary	Mills	6	5'09"	11 06	20/05/1981	30	Sheppey	Rushden & D, Yeovil (Trial) 6/06, Crawley 8/06, Rushden & D 1/07 Rel 5/07, Tamworth 6/07, Kettering 10/07, Stevenage 5/08, Mansfield 6/09 Rel 1/11, Forest Green (L) 10/10, Rushden & D 1/11, Bath C 5/11		
Scott	Murray	7	5'10"	11 06	26/05/1974	37	Aberdeen	Fraserburgh, Aston Villa £35,000 3/94, Bristol C £150,000 12/97, Reading £650,000 7/03, Bristol C £500,000 3/04 Rel c/s 09, Cheltenham (3ML) 9/08, Yeovil 7/09 Rel c/s 10, Bath C 7/10	33	6
Alex	Russell	21	5'10"	11 07	17/03/1973	38	Crosby	Liverpool (Scholar), Stockport, Morecambe, Burscough, Rochdale £4,000 7/94 Rel c/s 98, Glenavon (L) 11/95, Cambridge U 8/98 Rel c/s 01, Torquay 8/01, Bristol C 7/05 Rel c/s 08, Northampton (3ML) 8/07, Cheltenham (SL) 1/08, Cheltenham 6/08, Exeter (SL) 2/09, Exeter 7/09 Rel c/s 10, Bath C NC 9/10, Yeovil 1/11 Rel c/s 11, Bath C 7/11	12	2
Marley	Watkins	18	5'10"	10 04	17/10/1990	20	London	Swansea (Yth), Cheltenham Rel 1/11, Bath C (3ML) 9/10, Bath C 1/11	22	3

FORWARDS										
Jamie	Cook	9	5'10"	10 09	02/09/1979	31	Oxford	Oxford U Rel 1/01, Darlington (Trial) 1/01, Boston U 2/01, Stevenage 2/03, Bath C (3ML) 2/04, Maidenhead 7/04, Witney U 9/05, Rushden & D (NC) 1/07, Havant & W 3/07, Crawley 7/07, Oxford U Undisc 9/09, Crawley 6/10 Rel 5/11, Bath C 5/11		
Lee	Phillips	10	5'10"	12 00	16/09/1980	30	Penzance	Plymouth, Weymouth (3ML) 12/00 Perm 3/01, Exeter 2/05, Torquay £17,500 6/07, Rushden & D Undisc 5/08, Weymouth 1/09 Rel 2/09, Cambridge U 3/09 Rel 4/10, Bath C 7/10	43	16
Lee	Howells							Bath C (Ass Man)		

Loanees		SN	HT	WT	DOB	AGE	POB	From - To	APPS	GOA
(D)Joe	Edwards		5'08"	11 07	31/10/1990	20	Gloucester	Bristol C (3ML) 9/10 -	10	0
(G)Carl	Pentney		6'00"	12 00	03/02/1989	22	Leicester	Colchester (3ML) 11/10 - Chelmsford (SL) 3/11	13	0
(F)Ben	Watson		5'10"	11 02	06/12/1985	25	Shoreham	Exeter 1/11 - Rel 5/11, Eastbourne B 6/11	7	1
(F)Charlie	Clough		6'02"	12 08	04/09/1990	20	Taunton	Bristol R (2ML) 2/11 -	11	2
(M)Joe	Lennox				22/11/1991	19		Bristol C 3/11 -	3	0

Departures		SN	HT	WT	DOB	AGE	POB	From - To	APPS	GOA
(M)Ben	Lacey				30/05/1991	20		Paulton c/s 10 - Paulton (Dual)		
(D)Matt	Coupe				07/10/1978	32	St Asaph	Forest Green 2/03 - Rel 9/10, Gloucester 9/10	1	0
(F)Jake	Reid				22/06/1987	24	London	Salisbury 7/10 - Rel 9/10, Salisbury 9/10	4	0
(M)Mark	Badman				21/12/1979	31	Bath	Chippenham 8/08 - Rel 9/10	1	0
(F)Darren	Edwards				04/08/1980	31	Bristol	Yate T 12/06 - Rel 11/10, Cinderford (L) 11/10, Gloucester 11/10	13	2
(F)Albjon	Blloku				29/07/1983	28	Albania	KF Kamza (Alb) 1/11 - Walton & H, Hendon 3/11		
(D)Callum	Hart		6'00"	11 00	21/12/1985	25	Cardiff	Weston-Super-Mare c/s 10 - Paulton R (Dual) 9/10, Salisbury 3/11	3	0
(M)Josh	Egan							Cheltenham (Scholar) 3/11 - Blackpool 5/11	1	0
(G)Giancarlo	Borhy		6'02"	14 02	31/03/1988	23		Somma (Ita) 8/10 - Rel 5/11, Chippenham (Dual) 12/10, Paulton R (L) 1/11	2	0
(G)Ryan	Robinson		6'02"	13 02	13/10/1982	28	Tebay	Forest Green 5/09 - Rel 5/11	31	0
(D)Leigh	Henry				29/09/1986	24	Swindon	Swindon Supermarine 2/11 - Rel 5/11, Swindon Supermarine (Dual) 3/11, Maidenhead 6/11	4	0
(M)Adie	Harris				21/02/1981	30	Cardiff	Weston-Super-Mare 1/10 - Neath 6/11	25	1
(F)Kaid	Mohamed		5'11"		23/07/1984	27	Cardiff	Forest Green 8/09 - AFC Wimbledon (SL) 3/11, Cheltenham 6/11	34	13
(M)Sido	Jombarti				20/08/1987	24	Portugal	Basingstoke 5/09 - Cheltenham Undisc 7/11	43	2
(F)Jonathan	Brown		5'11"	11 04	17/04/1990	21	Bridgend	Central Coast Mariners (Aust) 1/11 - Southport 7/11	2	0
(D)Luke	Ruddick	20	6'00"		03/03/1990	21	Ashford	Salisbury 6/10 - Salisbury 8/11	9	0
(M)Leon	Jeanne		5'08"	11 01	17/11/1980	30	Cardiff	Cardiff Corinthians 11/10 - Cinderford (Dual) 1/11, Afan Lido 8/11	3	0
(D)Gordon	Rieck		6'03"		22/09/1989	21		St Pauli II (Ger) 7/10 -		
(F)Hector	Mackie				10/05/1988	23	Inverness	Gloucester 2/11 -	19	2
Lee	Collier							3/11		

Come On Wombles....

....but can you spot a 'genuine' Womble!!!

Photo by Peter Barnes

BRAINTREE TOWN

Chairman: Lee Harding
Secretary: Tom Woodley **(T)** 07950 537 179 **(E)** tawoodley@talktalk.net
Additional Committee Members:
Barry Shepherd, Bird Luckin, Lee Harding, Barry Shepherd, Kim Cowell, Vic Dixon, Alan Stuckey, Terry Thorogood, Christine Thorogood.
Manager: Alan Devonshire
Programme Editor: Lee Harding **(E)** braintreetfc@aol.com

Club Factfile

Founded: 1898 **Nickname:** The Iron
Previous Names: Crittall Athletic > 1968, Braintree and Crittall Athletic > 1981, Braintree > 1983
Previous Leagues: N.Essex 1898-1925, Essex & Suffolk Border 1925-29, 55-64, Spartan 1928-35, Eastern Co. 1935-37, 38-39, 52-55, 70-91, Essex Co. 1937-38, London 1945-52, Gt London 1964-66, Met 1966-70, Southern 1991-96, Isthmian 1996-2006

Club Colours (change): Orange/royal blue/orange (All silver)

Ground: The Cressing Road Stadium, Clockhouse Way, Braintree CM7 3RD **(T)** 01376 345 617
Capacity: 4,000 **Seats:** 550 **Covered:** 1,769 **Clubhouse:** Yes **Shop:** Yes

Directions
Leave M11 at junction 8A (for Stansted Airport) and follow A120 towards Braintree and Colchester for 17 miles. At Gallows Corner roundabout (with WestDrive Kia on your right) take first exit into Cressing Road. Clockhouse Way and the entrance to the ground are three quarters of a mile on the left and are clearly sign-posted.

Previous Grounds: The Fiar Field 1898-1903, Spalding Meadow and Panfield Lane

Record Attendance: 4,000 v Tottenham Hotspur - Testimonial May 1952
Record Victory: 12-0 v Thetford - Eastern Counties League 1935-36
Record Defeat: 0-14 v Chelmsford City (A) - North Essex League 1923
Record Goalscorer: Chris Guy - 211 (1963-90)
Record Appearances: Paul Young - 524 (1966-77)
Additional Records: Gary Bennett scored 57 goals during season 1997-98
Received £10,000 from Brentford for Matt Metcalf and from Colchester United for John Cheesewright

Senior Honours: Eastern Counties League 1983-84, 84-85, Essex Senior Cup 1995-96. Isthmian League Premier Division 2005-06.
Conference South Champions 2010-11.
East Anglian Cup x3

10 YEAR RECORD

01-02	02-03	03-04	04-05	05-06	06-07	07-08	08-09	09-10	10-11
Isth P 4	Isth P 16	Isth P 23	Isth P 4	Isth P 1	Conf S 3	Conf S 5	Conf S 14	Conf S 7	Conf S 1

BRAINTREE TOWN

No.	Date	Comp	H/A	Opponents	Att:	Result	Goalscorers	Pos
1	Sat-14-Aug	BSS	H	Farnborough	501	W 3-0	Bailey-Dennis 4, Marks 27, Lechmere 43	1
2	Tue-17-Aug	BSS	A	Maidenhead United	262	W 3-0	Lechmere 27, Davis 61, Marks 68	1
3	Sat-21-Aug	BSS	A	St Albans City	330	D 0-0		3
4	Tue-24-Aug	BSS	H	Boreham Wood	438	W 3-2	Jones 2 (18, 33), Guy pen 88	2
5	Sat-28-Aug	BSS	H	Chelmsford City	1265	W 3-0	Marks 2 (33, 70), Bailey-Dennis 89	2
6	Mon-30-Aug	BSS	A	Ebbsfleet United	786	D 0-0		2
7	Sat-04-Sep	BSS	A	Basingstoke Town	405	W 2-0	Marks 17, Guy 43	2
8	Sat-11-Sep	BSS	H	Dover Athletic	561	L 1-2	Marks 81	2
9	Sat-18-Sep	BSS	H	Eastleigh	499	W 1-0	Marks 80	2
10	Sat-02-Oct	BSS	A	Woking	1056	W 1-0	Guy 48	2
11	Sat-16-Oct	BSS	H	Thurrock	455	W 1-0	Bailey-Dennis 25	1
12	Sat-23-Oct	BSS	A	Dorchester Town	584	L 0-1		1
13	Sat-30-Oct	BSS	H	Weston-Super-Mare	471	W 4-0	Marks 3 (47, pen 74, 83), Shulton 50	1
14	Sat-06-Nov	BSS	A	Thurrock	305	W 3-0	Marks 67, Lechmere 83, Paine 90	1
15	Sat-13-Nov	BSS	H	Bromley	772	L 0-2		2
16	Sat-27-Nov	BSS	A	Staines Town	248	D 4-4	Guy 4, Marks 2 (34, 76), Og (Wells) 74	1
17	Sat-01-Jan	BSS	A	Bishops Stortford	621	W 2-1	Guy 50, Marks 55	1
18	Mon-03-Jan	BSS	H	Ebbsfleet United	881	W 4-2	Guy pen 3, Reason 34, Bryant 43, Symons 47	1
19	Sat-15-Jan	BSS	H	Lewes	535	W 1-0	Marks 47	1
20	Sat-22-Jan	BSS	H	Hampton & Richmond Borough	506	W 3-1	Bryant 15, Marks 48, Reason 52	1
21	Tue-25-Jan	BSS	H	Bishops Stortford	507	W 3-1	Marks 21, Guy 35, Paine 47	1
22	Sat-29-Jan	BSS	H	Woking	713	W 2-0	Guy 45, Reason 48	1
23	Tue-01-Feb	BSS	A	Dartford	841	L 0-1		1
24	Sat-05-Feb	BSS	A	Welling United	622	W 3-1	Poole 2 (39, 74), Guy 44	1
25	Tue-08-Feb	BSS	A	Dover Athletic	720	W 2-1	Marks 2 (25, 34)	1
26	Sat-12-Feb	BSS	H	Dartford	771	D 1-1	Og (Burgess) 5	1
27	Sat-19-Feb	BSS	A	Eastleigh	628	W 2-0	Reason 2 (42, pen 90)	1
28	Tue-22-Feb	BSS	H	Basingstoke Town	513	W 5-2	Marks 40, Payne 3 (42, 52, 63), Lechmere 53	1
29	Mon-28-Feb	BSS	A	Chelmsford City	1710	D 0-0		1
30	Sat-05-Mar	BSS	H	Staines Town	581	D 0-0		1
31	Sat-12-Mar	BSS	A	Farnborough	942	L 1-2	Lechmere 50	1
32	Mon-14-Mar	BSS	A	Havant & Waterlooville	582	W 2-1	Akurang 70, Shulton 74	1
33	Sat-19-Mar	BSS	H	St Albans City	578	D 1-1	Pinney 13	1
34	Wed-23-Mar	BSS	A	Lewes	359	L 1-2	Akurang 65	1
35	Sat-26-Mar	BSS	H	Maidenhead United	442	W 3-1	Akurang 39, Pinney 59, Davis 81	1
36	Sat-02-Apr	BSS	H	Dorchester Town	561	D 1-1	Akurang 20	1
37	Tue-05-Apr	BSS	A	Boreham Wood	227	W 2-0	Marks pen 48, Quinton pen 54	1
38	Sat-09-Apr	BSS	A	Bromley	507	W 3-0	Davis 58, Akurang 68, Reason pen 89	1
39	Sat-16-Apr	BSS	H	Havant & Waterlooville	693	W 2-0	Davis 5, Marks 16	1
40	Fri-22-Apr	BSS	A	Hampton & Richmond Borough	607	W 1-0	Poole 75	1
41	Mon-25-Apr	BSS	H	Welling United	1645	W 3-1	Akurang 2 (10, 23), Reason pen 90	Champions 1
42	Sat-30-Apr	BSS	A	Weston-Super-Mare	355	L 1-2	Gallen 53	1

CUPS

No.	Date	Comp	H/A	Opponents	Att:	Result	Goalscorers
1	Sat-25-Sep	FAC 2Q	H	Welling United	433	W 2-0	Marks 28, Guy 80
2	Sat-09-Oct	FAC 3Q	A	Carshalton Athletic	490	L 1-4	Quinton pen 5
3	Sat-20-Nov	FAT 3Q	H	Farnborough	255	W 2-0	Reason 60, Symons 65
4	Sat-11-Dec	FAT 1	A	AFC Wimbledon	1201	L 0-3	

League
Starts
Substitute
Unused Sub

Cups
Starts
Substitute
Unused Sub

Goals (Lg)
Goals (Cup)

MCDONALD	STARKEY	JONES	BAILEY-DENNIS	PAINE	LECHMERE	QUINTON	SYMONS	DAVIS	GREEN	MARKS	GUY	BRYANT	CLARK	ALAILE	BRUNO	HOLLOWAY	HARRIS	PETERS	REASON	SHULTON	DOBSON	BENTLEY	POOLE	THORNE	PAYNE	AKURANG	CALVER	PINNEY	SULLIVAN	JAMES-LEWIS	FRANCIS	GALLEN
X	X	X	X	X	X	X	X	X	X	X	S	S	S	U	U																	
X	X	X	X	X	X	X	X	X	X	X	S	S	S	U	U																	
X	X	X	X	X	X	X	X	X	X	X	S	S		U	U	U																
X	X	X	X	X	X	X	X	X	X	X	S	S		U	S	U																
X	X	X	X	X	S	X	X	X	S	X	X	X		U	S	U																
X	X	X	X	X	X		X	X	X	X	S	S	U	U	X	U																
X	X	X		X	U		X	X	S	X	X	X	U	X	X	U	U															
X	X	X	X	X	X		X	X	S	X	X	S	U	U	X	U																
X	X	X	X	X	X	X		X		X	X	X	S	U	U	U		S														
X	X	X	X	X		X	S	X		X	X	X	U	U			S	U	X													
X	U	X	X	X	X		X	X		X	X	S	S	U	U			X	X													
X	U	X	X	X	X		X	X		S	X	X	X	U				X	S	S												
X	X	X	X	X	X		X	X		X	S	S	U	S				U	X	X												
X	X		X	X	X		X	X		X	S	S	S	U		X		U	X	X												
X	X		X	X	X		X	X		X	X	S	U	U		X		S	X	S												
X	X	X	X	X	S	S	X	X		X	X	S	U	U				X	X													
X	X	X	X	X	X		X	X		X	X	U			U		S	S	X	U												
X	X	U	X	X	S		X	X			X	X		U	S		S	X	X	X												
X	X	S	X	X	X		X	X		X	S	X						X	X		S											
X	X	X	X	X	U	S	X	X		X	S	X						U	X	S	X											
X	X	X	X	X	X		X	X		X	X	S			U			U	X	S	S											
X	X	X	X	X	S	S	X	X		X	X	X						U	X	U	S											
X	X	X	X	X	U	S	X	X		X	S	X						U	X	S	X											
	X	X	X	X	X	S	U	X		X	X	U						S	X	S		X	X									
	X	S	X	X	U	X	X	X		X	S	U						X	X	S		X	X									
X	X	U	X	X	S	X	U	X		U	X	X						X	X	S			X									
X	X	X	X		U	X	X	X		S	X							U	X	S			U	X	X							
X	S	X	X		X	S	X	U		X				U				X	X	S			X	X	X							
X	X	X	X	X	U	X	X	X		X									X	U			U	U	X	S						
X	X	X	X	X	X	X	U	X										U	X	S			X	S	S	X						
X	X	X	S	X	S	X	X	X										U	X	U			S	X	X	X						
X	X	X	X	X	X	S	X	X										U	X	S			X	U		X	S					
X		X	X	X		U	X	X										X	X	X			U	S		X	S	X	S			
X		X	X	X		X	X	X										X	X	S			S	U		X	S	X	U			
X	X		X	X	X	X		X										X		S			X			X	S	X	S	U	U	
X	X		X	X	S	X	S	X		U								X	X	U			X			X		S				X
X	X		X	X	U	X	U	X		X								X	X	S			X			X		S				S
X	X		X	X	S	X	U	X		X								X	X	U			X			X		S				S
X	X		X	X	S	X	U	X		X								X	X	S			X			X		U				U
X	X		X	X	S	X	U	X		X								X	X	U			X			X		S				U
X	X	X	X	X	X	X	U	X		U								U	X	U			X			X						U
X	X	S	X	X	S	X	X	X		U								X	X	U			S			X						X
X	X	X	X	X	U	X	U	X		X	X	X	S	U	U	U		S	X													
X	X	X	X	X	S	X	S	X		X	X	X	U	U	U		S	U	X													
X	X	X	X	X	X	S	X	X		X	X	U	U	U					X	U												
X	X	X	X		S	X	X	X		X	S	U	U	X				S	X	X												
40	37	29	40	40	21	22	30	41	5	29	16	11	1	1	3	2	0	17	31	4	2	2	13	3	4	13	0	3	0	0	0	2
0	1	3	1	0	11	7	2	0	3	2	11	12	5	1	3	0	3	4	1	16	3	0	3	2	1	1	4	4	2	0	0	2
0	2	2	0	0	7	1	8	1	0	4	0	3	7	16	7	7	1	12	0	9	0	0	3	3	0	0	0	1	1	1	1	3
4	4	4	4	3	1	3	2	4	0	4	3	2	0	1	0	0	0	0	4	1	0	0	0	0	0	0	0	0	0	0	0	0
0	0	0	0	0	2	1	1	0	0	0	1	0	1	0	0	0	1	2	0	0	0	0	0	0	0	0	0	0	0	0	0	0
0	0	0	0	0	1	0	1	0	0	0	0	2	3	3	2	1	0	1	0	1	0	0	0	0	0	0	0	0	0	0	0	0
0	0	2	3	2	5	1	1	4	0	22	9	2	0	0	0	0	0	0	7	2	0	0	3	0	3	7	0	2	0	0	0	1
0	0	0	0	0	0	1	1	0	0	1	1	0	0	0	0	0	0	0	1	0	0	0	0	0	0	0	0	0	0	0	0	0

PLAYING SQUAD

Existing Players		SN	HT	WT	DOB	AGE	POB	Career	Apps	Goals
GOALKEEPERS										
Ashlee	Jones	22	6'01"	12 05	04/08/1987	24	Walthamstowe	Southampton (Yth), Rushden & D, Basingstoke 8/06, Harrow (L) 3/07, Potters Bar c/s 07, Crawley 10/08, Fisher 11/08, Wycombe NC 3/09, Gillingham Reserves c/s 09, Kingstonian 9/09, Darlington 11/09 Rel 2/10, Kingstonian 2/10, Billericay 3/10 Rel 9/10, C.Palace (Trial) 5/10, Crawley (Trial) 9/10, Boreham Wood 9/10 Rel 1/11, Billericay 1/11		
Nathan	McDonald	1	6'00"	14 00	16/05/1991	20	Stevenage	Southend (Scholar) Rel c/s 09, Braintree c/s 09, AFC Sudbury (Dual) 3/10	40	0
DEFENDERS										
Adam	Bailey-Dennis	4			18/09/1990	20		Colchester, Felixstowe & W (WE) 1/09, Braintree 5/09, Billericay (L) 11/09, Great Wakering (L) 1/10, Aveley (L) 3/10	41	3
Kenny	Davis	8	5'07"	11 02	17/04/1988	23	London	Chelsea (Yth), Redbridge 3/05, Harlow c/s 05, Grays 8/08, Braintree 6/10	41	4
(D)Sean	Francis				14/06/1984	27		Aveley, Braintree, Aveley (L)	0	0
Mark	Jones	12			06/08/1979	32		Burnham Ramblers, Billericay Rel 8/99, Romford 8/99, Braintree 2/00	32	2
Pat	O'Connor	16	6'01"	13 00	05/09/1990	20	Croydon	Millwall Rel c/s 11, Tooting & M (L) 9/10, Hampton & R (10WL) 11/10, Hampton & R (6WL) 2/11, Lewes (SL) 3/11, Braintree 8/11		
Matthew	Paine	5	6'01"	12 12	22/12/1987	23	Bexley	Colchester Rel c/s 07, Staines (SL) 2/06, Thurrock (SL) 1/07, Thurrock c/s 07, Braintree 6/10	40	2
Ryan	Peters	2			21/08/1987	24		Brentford (Sch), Windsor & E (2ML) 9/04, Gravesend (L) 12/04, Crawley (L) 11/06, AFC Wimbledon (L) 3/07, Margate 1/08, Braintree 5/09, Staines 6/10 Rel 8/10, Braintree 9/1021		0
David	Stevens				17/07/1987	24		Bracknell, Uxbridge 10/09, Hampton & R 8/10, Luton (Trial) c/s 11, Braintree 7/11		
Aswad	Thomas	3	5'10"	11 06	09/08/1989	22	Westminster	Charlton Rel c/s 09, Accrington (SL) 1/08, Barnet (L) 8/08, Lewes (3ML) 9/08, Woking 6/09, Braintree 6/11		
MIDFIELDERS										
Sam	Lechmere				03/12/1990	20		Thurrock, West Ham (Trial) 11/08, Aveley 7/09, Yeovil 12/09 Rel 2/10, Grays 2/10, Braintree 7/10	32	5
Merrick	James-Lewis23				21/05/1992	19	Southend	Southend, Tooting & M (L) 11/10, Braintree (SL) 3/11, Braintree (3ML) 8/11	0	0
Kevin	McLeod		5'11"	11 03	12/09/1980	30	Liverpool	Everton, QPR (SL) 3/03, QPR (L) 8/03 Undisc 8/03, Swansea 2/05, Colchester 8/06 Rel c/s 08, Brighton 7/08, Wycombe 2/10 Rel c/s 10, Aldershot T (Trial) 7/10, Port Vale (Trial) 8/10, St Mirren (Trial) 8/10, Redbridge 9/10, Braintree 8/11		
Matt	Pooley	25						Dag & Red Rel c/s 11, Braintree 8/11		
Bradley	Quinton	15			07/09/1978	32		Tottenham (Jun), Hornchurch, Aveley, Romford c/s 98, Bishops Stortford 1/99, Braintree 1/00 Temp Man 10/07	29	1
Jai	Reason	6	5'11"	13 01	09/01/1990	21	Southend	Ipswich Rel 5/09, Cambridge U (SL) 2/09, Cambridge U 7/09 Rel 4/10, Crawley 8/10 Rel 9/10, Braintree 9/10	32	7
Nicky	Symons	7			27/06/1984	27		Maldon T, Tilbury 11/06, Maldon T c/s 07, Redbridge 10/07, Brentwood c/s 08, Aveley c/s 09, Braintree 6/10	32	1
Andy	Yiadom	17			02/12/1991	19		Watford (Scholar) Rel c/s 10, Hayes & Yeading 8/10 Rel c/s 11, Braintree 8/11		
FORWARDS										
Chibuzor	Chilaka	19	5'08"	13 00	21/10/1986	24	Nigeria	Rushden & D (Yth), Notts County Rel c/s 06, Hinckley U (6WL) 12/05, Grimsby (Trial) 7/06, Hull University, Hull C (Trial) 7/07, Bridlington T c/s 08, Leeds Carnegie 7/09, Guiseley (Trial) 7/10, Bradford C 8/10 Rel c/ 11, Bradford PA (L) 11/10, Harrogate T (6WL) 2/11, Braintree 8/11		
Leon	Constantine	18	6'02"	11 11	24/02/1978	33	Hackney	Edgware T, Millwall 8/00 Rel c/s 02, L.Orient (2ML) 8/01, Partick (L) 1/02, Brentford 8/02 Rel c/s 03, Oxford U (Trial) 7/03, Southend 8/03, Peterborough 7/04, Torquay (L) 10/04, Torquay £75,000 12/04, Port Vale (2ML) 11/05 £20,000 1/06 Rel c/s 07, Leeds 8/07, Oldham (L) 3/08, Northampton 7/08 Rel c/s 09, Cheltenham (L) 3/09, Hereford 7/09 Rel c/s 10, York C 9/10, Barnet (Trial) 7/11, Braintree 8/11		
Jamie	Guy		6'01"	13 00	01/08/1987	24	Barking	Colchester, Gravesend (L) 10/05, Staines (2ML) 10/05, Staines (L) 1/06, Cambridge U (SL) 2/06, Oxford U (SL) 7/08, Dag & Red (L) 3/09, Port Vale (L) 10/09, Grays 1/10 Rel 5/10, Braintree 7/10	27	9

		SN	HT	WT	DOB	AGE	POB	From - To	APPS	GOA
Sean	Marks	9			25/11/1985	25	Essex	Heybridge, Braintree £1,000 5/08	31	22
Ben	Wright	10	6'02"	13 05	10/08/1988	23	Basingstoke	Basingstoke, Winchester (L) 12/06, Andover (L) 1/07, Carshalton (Dual) 10/07 Perm, Andover (Dual) 2/08, Fleet 3/08, Hampton & R 8/08, Peterborough £50,000 1/09, Kettering (6WL) 3/09, Luton (L) 9/09, Grimsby (2ML) 11/09, Barnet (L) 3/10, Hayes & Yeading (L) 8/10, Crawley Undisc 8/10, Newport C (2ML) 11/10, Hayes & Yeading (SL) 1/11, Braintree 6/11		
Bradley	Simpson							Braintree		
Lewis	Amos							Braintree		

Loanees		SN	HT	WT	DOB	AGE	POB	From - To	APPS	GOA
(M)Danny (DJ)		Green			04/08/1990			21 Red 8/10 - Chelmsford (L) 11/10, Boreham Wood (L) 12/10	8	Dag & 0
(G)Daniel	Bentley				13/07/1993	18		Southend 2/11 -	2	0
(F)Stefan	Payne				10/08/1991	20	London	Gillingham 2/11 -	5	3
(F)Craig	Calver		5'10"		20/01/1991	20	Cambridge	Yeovil 3/11 - Bishops Stortford 8/11	4	0
(F)Nathaniel	Pinney		6'00"	12 05	16/11/1990	20	South Norwood	C.Palace (SL) 3/11 -	7	2
(M)James	Stevens				10/10/1992	18		Southend (SL) 3/11 - Great Wakering (L) 8/11		

Departures		SN	HT	WT	DOB	AGE	POB	From - To	APPS	GOA
(F)Martin	Tuohy				04/05/1984	27		Aveley 6/10 - Rel 7/10, AFC Hornchurch 8/10		
(M)Robbie	Martin				29/12/1984	26		Havant & W 2/10 - Rel 8/10, St Albans 8/10 Rel 11/10, AFC		
Sudbury 3/11										
(D)Ryan	Doyle		6'02"		22/12/1985	25		Aveley 6/10 - Rel 7/10, Brentwood 8/10		
(F)Louis	Riddle		5'11"	12 00	29/08/1982	29	Harlow	Bishops Stortford 6/10 - Rel 7/10, Harlow		
(G)Ollie	Morris-Sanders		6'04"		01/06/1980	31		Aveley 6/10 - AFC Hornchurch (L) 8/10, Heybridge 9/10 Retired 5/11		
(F)Michael	Power				08/01/1983	28	Kent	Cray W 10/09 - Thurrock 11/10		
(D)Bradley	Thomas		6'02"	13 00	29/03/1984	27	Forest Gate	Hendon 7/10 - Concord R (L) 8/10, Grays (L) 11/10 Perm	(D)	
Sam	Holloway				17/09/1987	23		Aveley 6/10 - Billericay (L) 9/10, AFC Hornchurch (SL) 12/10, Concord R 6/11	2	0
(M)Jack	Clark		6'00"	09 12	21/02/1991	20	Sidcup	Charlton 8/10 - Rel 1/11, Cray W 1/11, Dartford (L) 1/11	6	0
(M)Craig	Dobson		5'07"	10 06	23/01/1984	27	Chingford	Barnet 1/11 - Rel 2/11, Woking 2/11, Kettering 7/11	5	0
(F)David	Bryant				09/06/1982	29		Thurrock 8/10 - Rel 2/11, Boreham Wood 2/11	23	2
(D)Louis	Lavers				29/09/1990	20		Wealdstone 2/11 - North Greenford		
(F)Chris	Sullivan				26/09/1987	23		Billericay 3/11 - Aveley 3/11, AFC Sudbury 6/11	2	0
(D)Phil	Starkey		6'00"	12 06	10/09/1987	23	Dartford	Tonbridge A 8/09 - Dover 6/11	38	0
(D)Oliver	Thorne		6'03"	14 06	23/01/1990	21	Gravesend	Kidderminster 2/11 - Corby T 6/11, Hednesford 7/11	5	0
(F)Cliff	Akurang		6'02"	12 03	27/02/1981	30	Ghana	Maidenhead 2/11 - Chelmsford 6/11	14	7
(M)Glenn	Poole		5'07"	11 04	03/02/1981	30	Barking	Barnet 2/11 - Thurrock 7/11	16	3
(F)Roy	Essandoh		6'00"	12 04	17/02/1976	35	Belfast	St Neots 3/11 - Bury T 8/11		
(D)Michael	Alaile		6'00"	12 09	23/11/1988	22		Aveley 6/10 - Canvey Island (Dual) 2/11 Perm	2	0
(M)Tom	Bruno				09/06/1992	19		Harlow 8/09 - Harlow (L) 11/10, Concord R (SL) 2/11	6	0
(M)Reece	Harris				12/02/1991	20		Heybridge 12/09 - Concord R (L) 11/10, Thurrock (L) 2/11	3	0
(F)Kevin	Gallen		5'11"	12 10	21/09/1975	35	Chiswick	Luton 3/11 -	4	1
(F)Justin	Hazell		5'09"	11 06	15/01/1992	19	Leigh-on-Sea	Southend 6/10 -		
(F)Duane	Ofori-Acheampong							Southend 3/11 -		
(M)Scott	Shulton				31/01/1990	21		Bishops Stortford 10/10 - Bishops Stortford 8/11	20	2

Caught in action....

Michael Gash
Cambridge United / England 'C' International

Photo by Keith Clayton

CAMBRIDGE UNITED

Chairman: Paul Barry
Secretary: Claire Osbourn **(T)** 07769 217 872 **(E)** claire.osbourn@cambridge-united.co.uk
Additional Committee Members:
Renford Sargent, Robert Smith, Greg Mould, Jez George, Colin Proctor, Adrian Hanauer.

Manager: Jez George
Programme Editor: Mark Johnson **(E)** mark.johnson.6@btinternet.com

Club Factfile

Founded: 1912 **Nickname:** The U's
Previous Names: Abbey United 1919-51.
Previous Leagues: United Counties. Eastern Counties 1951-58. Southern 1958-70. Football League 1970-2005.

Club Colours (change): Amber/black/black (All sky blue)

Ground: The R Costings Abbey Stadium, Newmarket Road, Cambridge CB5 8LN **(T)** 01223 566 500
Capacity: 9,217 **Seats:** 2,500 **Covered:** 5,000 **Clubhouse:** Yes **Shop:** Yes

Directions
A14 towards Cambridge and Newmarket, leave A14 at Junction with B1047. Turn right at top of slip road, follow road through Fen Ditton to TJunction and traffic lights. Turn right at lights, and go straight over at roundabout. Ground is on left hand side approximately 1/2 mile from roundabout.

Previous Grounds: Not known

Record Attendance: 14,000 v Chelsea - Friendly 01/05/1970
Record Victory: 5-1 v Bristol City - FA Cup 5th Round 1989-90
Record Defeat: 0-7 v Sunderland - League Cup 2nd Round 2002-03
Record Goalscorer: John Taylor - 86 (1988-92, 96-2001)
Record Appearances: Steve Spriggs - 416 (1975-87
Additional Records: Paid £192,000 to Luton Town for Steve Claridge 11/92. Received £1m from Manchester United for Dion Dublin 08/92 and from Leicester City for Trevor Benjamin 07/2000

Senior Honours: Football League Division Division Four 1976-77. Three 1990-91.

10 YEAR RECORD

01-02	02-03	03-04	04-05	05-06	06-07	07-08	08-09	09-10	10-11
FL 2 24	FL 3 12	FL 3 13	FL 2 24	Conf 12	Conf 17	Conf 2	Conf 2	Conf 10	Conf 17

CAMBRIDGE UNITED

No.	Date	Comp	H/A	Opponents	Att:	Result	Goalscorers	Pos
1	Sat-14-Aug	BSP	A	Wrexham	4040	L 0-1		18
2	Tue-17-Aug	BSP	H	Crawley Town	2558	D 2-2	Russell 18, Saah 29	18
3	Sat-21-Aug	BSP	H	Southport	2506	D 0-0		21
4	Tue-24-Aug	BSP	A	Tamworth	863	D 1-1	Wright 54	21
5	Sat-28-Aug	BSP	A	Mansfield Town	2257	L 0-1		23
6	Mon-30-Aug	BSP	H	Eastbourne Borough	2465	W 2-0	Coulson 7, Jennings 43	17
7	Sat-04-Sep	BSP	H	Gateshead	2637	W 5-0	Wright 28, Clare 53, Russell 74, Saah 76, Gray 82	11
8	Sat-11-Sep	BSP	A	Luton Town	6691	L 0-2		17
9	Sat-18-Sep	BSP	A	Kidderminster Harriers	1291	D 0-0		18
10	Tue-21-Sep	BSP	H	Kettering Town	2646	W 3-0	Gray 71, Willmott 80, Wright 82	13
11	Sat-25-Sep	BSP	H	Newport County	2648	L 0-1		15
12	Wed-29-Sep	BSP	A	AFC Wimbledon	3119	L 0-3		16
13	Sat-02-Oct	BSP	H	Bath City	2670	L 1-2	Russell 5	19
14	Tue-05-Oct	BSP	A	Hayes & Yeading United	362	L 0-2		21
15	Sun-10-Oct	BSP	A	Fleetwood Town	2380	D 2-2	Willmott 2 (8, pen 81)	22
16	Sat-16-Oct	BSP	H	Barrow	2726	W 3-1	Russell 14, Og (M Pearson) 45, Coulson 89	18
17	Sat-30-Oct	BSP	A	Gateshead	1083	W 3-2	Coulson 28, Gray 31, Russell 45	14
18	Tue-09-Nov	BSP	H	Grimsby Town	2303	D 1-1	Wright 22	14
19	Sat-13-Nov	BSP	A	Kettering Town	1959	D 2-2	Willmott 2 (38, 45)	15
20	Sat-20-Nov	BSP	H	Tamworth	2809	D 3-3	Willmott pen 68, Patrick 75, Marriott 77	15
21	Sat-27-Nov	BSP	H	Altrincham	2123	W 4-0	Wright 2 (15, 65), Gray 2 (23, 56)	13
22	Tue-28-Dec	BSP	H	Mansfield Town	2505	L 1-5	Willmott 66	13
23	Sat-01-Jan	BSP	H	Histon	3225	D 0-0		14
24	Mon-03-Jan	BSP	A	Eastbourne Borough	983	W 2-0	Willmott 3, Gray 32	12
25	Sat-08-Jan	BSP	A	Barrow	1015	W 2-1	Willmott 18, Gray 54	10
26	Sat-22-Jan	BSP	H	Wrexham	2469	L 1-3	Willmott 59	14
27	Tue-25-Jan	BSP	A	Crawley Town	3241	L 0-3		16
28	Sat-29-Jan	BSP	A	Bath City	1338	L 0-4		16
29	Tue-01-Feb	BSP	A	Rushden & Diamonds	1279	L 1-2	Wright 3	16
30	Sat-05-Feb	BSP	H	Rushden & Diamonds	2366	L 0-2		17
31	Sat-12-Feb	BSP	A	Grimsby Town	3142	D 1-1	Coulson 61	17
32	Tue-15-Feb	BSP	H	Darlington	1635	L 0-1		17
33	Fri-18-Feb	BSP	H	Kidderminster Harriers	1869	L 1-2	Marriott 90	17
34	Tue-22-Feb	BSP	A	Histon	1903	W 2-0	Wright 44, Marriott 50	17
35	Tue-01-Mar	BSP	A	Newport County	1360	D 1-1	Russell 9	16
36	Sat-05-Mar	BSP	A	Darlington	2080	L 0-1		17
37	Sat-12-Mar	BSP	A	Southport	1107	D 1-1	Berry 90	17
38	Tue-15-Mar	BSP	H	Luton Town	2831	D 0-0		17
39	Sat-19-Mar	BSP	H	York City	2474	W 2-1	Hughes 19, Wright 78	16
40	Sat-26-Mar	BSP	H	Forest Green Rovers	2086	D 1-1	Bentley 43	16
41	Sat-02-Apr	BSP	A	Altrincham	1161	D 2-2	Hughes 39, Saah 59	16
42	Sat-09-Apr	BSP	H	AFC Wimbledon	2907	L 1-2	Wright 82	17
43	Sat-16-Apr	BSP	A	Forest Green Rovers	1092	D 1-1	Sinclair 45	18
44	Sat-23-Apr	BSP	H	Hayes & Yeading United	2619	W 1-0	Patrick 76	17
45	Mon-25-Apr	BSP	A	York City	2939	D 0-0		17
46	Sat-30-Apr	BSP	H	Fleetwood Town	2745	L 0-1		17

CUPS

No.	Date	Comp	H/A	Opponents	Att:	Result	Goalscorers
1	Sat-23-Oct	FAC 4Q	H	Lewes	1626	W 3-0	Gray 22, Wright 36, Russell 49
2	Sat-06-Nov	FAC 1	H	Huddersfield Town	3127	D 0-0	
3	Tue-16-Nov	FAC 1R	A	Huddersfield Town	3766	L 1-2	McAuley 53
4	Sat-11-Dec	FAT 1	H	Forest Green Rovers	1045	W 2-1	Partridge 58, Roberts 90
5	Sat-15-Jan	FAT 2	A	Alfreton Town	929	D 3-3	Russell 40, Saah 66, Marriott 88
6	Tue-18-Jan	FAT 2R	H	Alfreton Town	1098	L 3-6 (aet)	Saah 38, Wright 69, Jennings 89

League
Starts
Substitute
Unused Sub

Cups
Starts
Substitute
Unused Sub

Goals (Lg)
Goals (Cup)

BROWN	ROBERTS	JENNINGS	SAAH	PARTRIDGE	RUSSELL	WILLMOTT	MILLER	CARDEN	PLATT	WRIGHT	COULSON	MARRIOTT	GRAY	NAISBITT	IVES	THORPE	CLARE	COAKLEY	MCAULEY	BERRY	STAVRINOU	PATRICK	HUGHES	BRIGHTON	EADES	WELLARD	WALKER	JEFFERS	BENTLEY	HUDSON	HERBERT	SINCLAIR											
30	2	3	5	6	7	11	8	15	14	9	4	19	16	1	17	31	10	18	12	27	21	20	29	33	28	16	11	22	21	26	15	24											
X	X	X	X	X	X	X	X	X	X	X	S	S	S	U	U																												
X	X	X	X		X	X	X	X	X	X	X	S	U	U	U	U																											
X	X	X	X	U	X	X		X	X	X	X	X	S	U	S		S																										
X	X		X	X	X	X	X	X	X	X	X	S		U	U		S	U																									
X	X	X	X		X	X	X	X	X	X	X		U	U	S		S	S																									
X		X	X		X	S	X	X	X	X	X	S	S	U			X	U	X																								
X		X	X	U	X	X		X	X	X	X	S	S	U	S		X		X																								
X		X	X	U	X	X		X	X	X	X	S	S	U	S		X		X																								
X		X	X	X	X	X		X		X	X	S	S	U	S		X	U	X																								
X	X	U	X	X	X	X		X		X	X	S	S	U	S		X		X																								
X	X		X	X	X	X		X		X	X	S	X	U	U		S	U	X																								
X	X	U	X	X	X	X		X		X	X	S	X	U	U		S		X																								
X	X	X	X	S	X	X		X		X	X	S	S	U	U		X		X																								
X		X	X	S	X	X				X	X	X	S	U	X	X	S		X	U																							
X		X	X		X	X		X		X	X		X	U	U	U	S		X		X	S																					
U	S	X	X		X	X		X	S	X	X		X	X			U		X		X	U																					
U	X	X	X		X	X			S	X	X		X	X	U				X		X	U	U																				
U	X	X			X	X			X	X	X		X	X	U	U			X		X	S	S																				
U	X	X		X	X	X				X	X	U	X	X	U				X		X	S	S																				
U	X	X		X	X	X			U	X	X	S	X	X	U				X		X	S																					
U	X	X		X	X	X		X	S	X	X	S	X	X					S		U	X																					
U	X	X	S	X	X	X			U	X	X	S	X	X					X		X	S																					
U	X	X	U	X	X	X		X		X	X	S	X	X			S		X			S																					
U	X	X	X	X	X	X		X	U	X	X	U	X	X			S		U																								
U	X	X	X	X	X	X		X	U	X	X	U	X	X			S		S																								
U		X	X	X	X	X		X	S		X	S	X	X			X		X			U	S																				
X	X	X		X	X	X		X	S	X	X	S		U	U		X		X				S																				
X	X	X			X			X	X	X	X	S		U	U	X	X		X			S	S																				
X	X	X			X			X	X	X	X	U			X		U	S	X	S		X	S																				
X	U		X	X				X	X	X	X	S			S		X		X	X		X	U	U																			
X	X		S	X						X	X	U		U	S			X	X	X		X	X	S		X																	
X	X		X						S	X	X	S		U	U			X	X	X		X	X	U		X																	
X	X	X	X	U					X	X	X	X		U						X		S	S			X	X	S															
X	X	X	X	X	X				U	X		X		U	U	S				X		S				X	X																
X	X	X	X	X	X					X		X		U		U			S	X		S				X	X	U															
X	X	X	X	X						X		X		U	X	S			U	X		S				X	X	S															
X	X	X	X	X					U	X		X		U					S	X		X				X	S		X	S													
X	X	X	X	X					S	X				U					U	X		X	X			X		U	X	S													
X	X	X	X	X					S	X				U					S	X		X	X			X	S		X	U													
X	X	X	X	X					X	X	U			U	S	S			X			X	X						X		U												
X	X	X	X	X					X	X	U	S		U					S			X	X						X		S	X											
X	X	X	X	X					X	X	S	S		U					U	S		X	X						X			X											
X	X	X	X	X					S	X	S	X		U					X	X		X	X								U	S											
U	X	X	X						X	X	X	S		X	X				S	X		S	X							U		X											
U	X	X	X						X	X	X	S		X	S			U	X			X	X							U		X											
U	X		X						X	X	X	X		X	S			X	X			X	S		S					U		X											
U	X	X	X		X	X		X	S	X	X		X	X	U		S		X			S	U																				
U	X	X		X	X	X		X	U	X	X		X	X	U	U			X			U	U	U																			
U	X	X		X	X	X		X		X	X	U	X	X	U			U	X			U	U		U																		
U	X	X		X	X	X		X	S	X	X	S	X	X					U		U	X																					
U	X		X	X	X	X		X	S	X	X	S	X	X			S	X	U																								
U	X	X	X	X	X	X		X	S	S	X	S	X	X			X		U																								
32	37	38	36	27	31	26	5	24	19	45	35	9	14	14	4	2	10	3	28	12	7	14	10	0	0	9	4	0	6	0	0	5	0	0	0	0	0	0	0	0	0	0	0
0	1	0	2	2	0	1	0	0	9	0	3	24	9	0	11	3	10	2	7	2	0	12	8	1	1	0	2	2	0	2	1	1	0	0	0	0	0	0	0	0	0	0	0
14	1	2	1	4	0	0	0	0	6	0	2	5	2	30	15	4	2	5	4	1	1	3	2	2	0	0	0	2	0	4	2	0	0	0	0	0	0	0	0	0	0	0	0
0	6	5	3	5	6	6	0	6	0	5	6	0	6	6	0	0	1	1	3	0	0	1	0	0	0	0	0	0	0	0	0	0	0	0	0	0	0	0	0	0	0	0	0
0	0	0	0	0	0	0	0	0	4	1	0	3	0	0	0	0	2	0	0	0	0	1	0	0	0	0	0	0	0	0	0	0	0	0	0	0	0	0	0	0	0	0	0
6	0	0	0	0	0	0	0	0	1	0	0	1	0	0	3	1	0	1	3	0	1	2	3	1	1	0	0	0	0	0	0	0	0	0	0	0	0	0	0	0	0	0	0
0	0	1	3	0	6	10	0	0	0	10	4	3	7	0	0	0	1	0	0	1	0	2	2	0	0	0	0	0	1	0	0	1	0	0	0	0	0	0	0	0	0	0	0
0	1	1	2	1	2	0	0	0	0	2	0	1	1	0	0	0	0	0	1	0	0	0	0	0	0	0	0	0	0	0	0	0	0	0	0	0	0	0	0	0	0	0	0

PLAYING SQUAD

Existing Players		SN	HT	WT	DOB	AGE	POB	Career	Apps	Goals
GOALKEEPERS										
Simon	Brown	30	6'02"	15 00	03/12/1976	34	Chelmsford	Tottenham Rel c/s 99, Lincoln C (L) 12/97, Fulham (L) 8/98, Kingstonian (3ML) 9/98, Aylesbury (SL) 2/99, Colchester 7/99 Rel c/s 04, Hibernian 7/04, Brentford 6/07 Rel c/s 09, Darlington (5ML) 8/08, Northampton 9/09 Rel 1/10, Cambridge U 2/10	32	0
Danny	Naisbitt	1	6'01"	11 12	25/11/1978	32	Bishop Auckland	Middlesbrough (Trainee), Walsall, Bromsgrove (Trial) c/s 99, Barnet 8/99 Rel 9/03, Carlisle (L) 8/02, Southend (Trial), Harlow 9/03, Brentford 10/03, Cambridge C 11/03, Dag & Red 12/03 Rel 2/04, Peterborough 3/04, Hendon 3/04, Welling 3/04, AFC Wimbledon 6/04, Grimsby (Trial) 3/05, Lewes (L) 3/05, Cambridge C 9/05, Histon 5/07, Brighton (L) 3/10, Cambridge U 5/10	14	0
DEFENDERS										
James	Brighton	29					Bromsgrove	Birmingham C (Yth), Cambridge U 11/10	1	0
Josh	Coulson	4	6'03"	11 11	28/01/1989	22	Cambridge	Cambridge C (Yth), Cambridge U c/s 06	38	4
Harrison	Dunk	11			25/10/1990	20		Fulham (Yth), Millfield School, Bromley c/s 09, Cambridge U 6/11		
Blaine	Hudson	25			28/10/1991	19	Gorleston	Norwich (Yth), Cambridge U 5/08	2	0
James	Jennings	3	5'10"	11 02	02/09/1987	23	Manchester	Macclesfield, Altrincham (2ML) 1/08, Kettering 7/09, Cambridge U Undisc 5/10	38	1
Steve	Kinniburgh	15	6'00"	11 02	13/06/1989	22	Glasgow	Rangers, Queen of the South (5WL) 11/08, St Johnstone (SL) 3/09, Oxford U (SL) 8/09, Oxford U 6/10, Cambridge U (L) 8/11		
Kevin	Roberts	2	6'02"	14 00	10/03/1987	24	Liverpool	Chester Rel 2/10, Cambridge U 2/10	38	0
Jonathon	Thorpe	27			12/02/1993	18		Cambridge U	5	0
Michael	Wylde	5	6'02"	13 02	06/01/1987	24	Birmingham	Cheltenham Rel c/s 08, Cirencester (WE) 12/05, Kidderminster (SL) 3/08, Tamworth 7/08, Cambridge U 5/11		
MIDFIELDERS										
Luke	Allen	28						Cambridge U		
Luke	Berry	18			12/07/1992	19		Cambridge U	14	1
Ashley	Carew	10	6'00"	11 00	17/12/1985	25	Lambeth	Gillingham (Jun), Welling (L) 9/04, Maidstone (L) 10/04, Worthing (L) 11/04, Aveley (L) 8/05, Bromley 12/05 Rel 1/06, Sutton U 2/06, Beckenham 7/06, Fisher 1/07, Beckenham (Dual) 2/07, Barnet 5/07 Rel 3/09, Eastleigh (2ML) 1/09, Eastleigh 3/09, Bromley 6/09, Ebbsfleet 8/10, Cambridge U 7/11		
Jack	Eades	26			30/10/1991	19		Notts Forest (Scholar), Cambridge U (CRC) c/s 08, Needham Market (L) 2/11	1	0
Liam	Hughes	17			10/08/1992	19		Scunthorpe (Yth), Cambridge U (CRC) c/s 08	18	2
Rossi	Jarvis	16	6'00"	11 02	11/03/1988	23	Fakenham	Norwich Rel c/s 08, Torquay (L) 1/07, Rotherham (SL) 3/07, Luton 8/08 Rel 5/10, Barnet 7/10 Rel c/s 11, Cambridge U 8/11		
Rory	McAuley	12	5'10"	12 06	16/10/1989	21	Blackpool	Cambridge U	35	0
Adam	Miller		5'11"	11 06	19/02/1982	29	H. Hempstead	Ipswich (Scholar), Southend (Trial) 8/00, Canvey Island 10/00, Southend (Trial), Grays PE 8/02, Gravesend 9/03, Aldershot 10/03, QPR £50,000 11/04, Peterborough (L) 9/05, Stevenage 1/06, Gillingham (6WL) 11/07 Undisc 1/08 Rel c/s 10, Dag & Red (2ML) 11/09, Cambridge U 6/10	5	0
Kieran	Murtagh	8	6'00"	12 00	29/10/1988	22	Wapping	Charlton (Scholar) Rel c/s 07, Fisher 10/07, Fulham (Trial) 5/08, Yeovil 6/08, Wycombe 7/10 Rel c/s 11, Woking (2ML) 1/11, Cambridge U 6/11		
Jordan	Patrick	20			03/02/1991	20	Honolulu	Cambridge C (Yth), Cambridge U (Yth) c/s 06 Pro c/s 09	26	2
Tom	Shaw	6	6'00"	12 00	01/12/1986	24	Nottingham	Notts Forest (Jun), Rushden & D (7/04) Rel 7/08, Mansfield 8/08 Rel 10/08, Tamworth 10/08, Kidderminster 6/10, Cambridge U 5/11		

FORWARDS

		No	HT	WT	DOB	AGE	POB	From - To	APPS	GOA
Ryan	Charles	7	6'00"	11 13	30/09/1989	21	Enfield	Luton Rel 5/10, Hitchin (SL) 3/07, Hinckley U (WE) 12/07, Kettering (L) 3/09, Kidderminster (5WL) 11/09, Rushden & D 6/10, Cambridge U 6/11		
Daryl	Clare		5'09"	11 00	01/08/1978	33	Jersey	Grimsby Rel c/s 01, Northampton (3ML) 11/99, Northampton (L) 11/00, Cheltenham (L) 12/00, Boston U 7/01, Chester £25,000 10/02, Boston U Undisc 11/04, Crawley 8/05 £60,000, Burton 3/06, Rushden & D 5/08, Mansfield (SL) 3/09, Mansfield 5/09, Gateshead (3ML) 10/09 Perm 1/10, Cambridge U £10,000 6/10, Alfreton (SL) 2/11, Gainsborough (L) 8/11	20	1
Michael	Gash	9	5'09"	12 01	03/09/1986	24	Cambridge	Cambridge C, Cambridge U 6/06, Cambridge C (L) 1/07, Cambridge C 5/07, Ebbsfleet £20,000 7/08, York C £55,000 7/09 Rel c/s 11, Rushden & D (SL) 1/11, Cambridge U 6/11		
Adam	Marriott	19			14/04/1991	20	Brandon	Norwich (Yth), Cambridge C (Yth), Cambridge U (Yth) c/s 06 Pro c/s 09	33	3
Conal	Platt	14	5'09"	10 10	14/10/1986	24	Preston	Liverpool, Bournemouth 5/06 Rel c/s 07, Morecambe (L) 11/06, Weymouth (SL) 2/07, Weymouth 8/07, Rushden & D (SL) 2/08, Forest Green 5/08, Cambridge U 6/10	28	0

Loanees		HT	WT	DOB	AGE	POB	From - To	APPS	GOA
(M)Alex	Stavrinou	5'09"	11 12	13/09/1990	20	Harlow	Charlton (3ML) 10/10 - Rel 5/11, Ebbsfleet 8/11	7	0
(M)Ricky	Wellard	5'11"	09 12	09/05/1988	23	Hammersmith	AFC Wimbledon (2ML) 2/11 -	9	0
(F)Shaun	Jeffers	6'01"	11 03	14/04/1992	19	Bedford	Coventry 2/11 -	2	0
(F)Dan	Walker			27/04/1990	21		Luton 2/11 -	6	0
(M)Mark	Bentley	6'02"	13 04	07/01/1978	33	Hertford	Gillingham 3/11 - Rel 5/11, Hayes & Yeading 8/11	6	1
(F)Courtney	Herbert	6'02"	12 08	25/10/1988	22	Northampton	Northampton 3/11 - Rel 5/11, Daventry T 6/11??, Corby T 6/11 Rel 7/11	1	0
(M)Dean	Sinclair	5'10"	11 03	17/12/1984	26	St Albans	Grimsby (SL) 3/11 - Rel 5/11	6	1

Departures		HT	WT	DOB	AGE	POB	From - To	APPS	GOA
(M)Robbie	Willmott	5'09"	12 01	16/05/1990	21	Harlow	Yth - Luton £50,000 1/11	27	10
(F)Wayne	Gray	5'10"	11 05	07/11/1980	30	Dulwich	Grays 8/10 - Rel 1/11, Chelmsford 1/11, Woking 7/11	23	7
(M)George	O'Callaghan	6'01"	10 11	05/09/1979	31	Cork	Cork C 3/11 - Rel 3/11		
(D)David	Partridge	6'00"	13 05	26/11/1978	32	Westminster	St Patricks 1/10 - Rel 5/11	29	0
(M)Sam	Ives			24/06/1991	20	Cambridge	Cambridge C (Yth) - Rel 5/11, Bury T (L) 12/10, Corby T 6/11	15	0
(D)Darryl	Coakley			09/02/1991	20	Bury St Edmunds	Ipswich(Yth) Pro c/s 09 - Rel 5/11, Cambridge C (L) 1/11, Bury T 7/11	5	0
(F)Danny	Wright	6'02"	13 08	10/09/1984	26	Southampton	Histon 5/10 - Wrexham Undisc 6/11	45	10
(M)Paul	Carden	5'09"	11 10	29/03/1979	32	Liverpool	Accrington (SL) 1/08 Perm 5/08 - Rel 6/11, Luton (SL) 2/11	24	0
(D)Brian	Saah	6'03"	12 03	16/12/1986	24	Rush Green	L.Orient 8/09 - Torquay 7/11	38	3
(M)Simon	Russell	5'07"	10 06	19/03/1985	26	Hull	York C (SL) 1/10 Perm 5/10 - Lincoln C 7/11	31	6
(M)Steve	Connors			05/01/1986	25	Liverpool	Fleetwood 6/11 - Rel 7/11		

Darlington's Hatch and Arnison protect the ball from Mansfield's Nix during the FA Trophy Final at Wembley.

Photo by Keith Clayton

DARLINGTON

Chairman: Raj Singh
Secretary: Colin Galloway (T) 0755 741 6012 (E) cgalloway@darlington-fc.net
Additional Committee Members:
Graham Fordy, Andy Wilson, Alan Murray.

Manager: Mark Cooper
Programme Editor: Martin Walker (E) martin.walker50@hotmail.com

Back Row: Aaron Brown, Liam Hatch, Ryan Bowman, Chris Atkinson, Sam Russell, Graeme Lee, Ben Purkiss, Tommy Wright.
Middle Row: Tony Elliot (GK Coach), Jamie Chandler, John McReady, James Walshaw, Greg Taylor, Phil Gray, Adam Rundle, John Campbell, Craig Liddle (Head of Youth).
Front Row: Andrew Thompson(Kit Manager), Marc Bridge-Wilkinson, Ian Miller (Club Captain), Mark Cooper (Manager), Graham Fordy (Managing Director), Raj Singh(Chairman), Andy Wilson (Financial Director), Richard Dryden (Assistant Manager), Kris Taylor, Paul Arnison, Alistair Logan (Sports Therapist).

Club Factfile

Founded: 1883 **Nickname:** The Quakers
Previous Names: None
Previous Leagues: Northern League 1883-1908, North Eastern 1908-21, Football League 1921-89, 91-2010, Conference 1989-90

Club Colours (change): White & black & gold/white/white (All green fluorescent)

Ground: Darlington Arena, Neasham Road DL2 1DL (T) 01325 387 000
Capacity: 25,000 **Seats:** 25,000 **Covered:** 25,000 **Clubhouse:** Yes **Shop:** Yes

Directions Leave the A1(m) at junction 57 for Darlington. Follow road to roundabout. From here take the first exit off and follow road to second roundabout (Reg Vardy on right). Head straight over and follow signs for Teesside until you reach next roundabout. Turn left here and stadium is on right hand side.

Previous Grounds: Feethams > 2003, Reynolds Arena, Hurworth Moor

Record Attendance: 21,023 v Bolton Wanderers - League Cup 3rd Round 14/11/1960
Record Victory: 9-2 v Lincoln City - Division 3 North 07/01/1928
Record Defeat: 0-10 v Doncaster Rovers - Division 4 25/01/1964
Record Goalscorer: Alan Walsh - 100, Jerry Best - 80
Record Appearances: Ron Greener - 490, John Peverell - 465, Brian Henderson - 463
Additional Records: Paid £95,000 to Motherwell for Nick Cusack January 1992.
Received £400,000 from Dundee United for Jason Devos October 1998

Senior Honours: Northern League 1895-96, 99-1900. North Eastern League 1912-13, 20-21.
Football League Division 3 1924-25, Division 4 1990-91, Division 3 North Cup 1933-34.
Durham Senior Cup 1919-20. FA Trophy 2010-11.

10 YEAR RECORD

01-02	02-03	03-04	04-05	05-06	06-07	07-08	08-09	09-10	10-11
FL 3 15	FL 3 14	FL 3 18	FL 2 8	FL 2 8	FL 2 11	FL 2 6	FL 2 12	FL 2 24	Conf 7

DARLINGTON

No.	Date	Comp	H/A	Opponents	Att:	Result	Goalscorers	Pos
1	Sat-14-Aug	BSP	H	Newport County	2597	W 1-0	Hatch 4	8
2	Tue-17-Aug	BSP	A	Altrincham	1099	D 2-2	Og (Coburn) 82, Wright 90	6
3	Sat-21-Aug	BSP	A	Kettering Town	1350	D 0-0		7
4	Tue-24-Aug	BSP	H	Grimsby Town	1993	L 0-1		12
5	Sat-28-Aug	BSP	H	Gateshead	2233	W 2-0	Terry 45, Clarke 54	7
6	Mon-30-Aug	BSP	A	Barrow	1718	D 1-1	Terry 62	9
7	Sat-04-Sep	BSP	A	Eastbourne Borough	1464	D 1-1	Senior 43	9
8	Sat-11-Sep	BSP	H	Forest Green Rovers	1520	W 3-0	Senior 3, Og (Caines) 10, Chandler 83	7
9	Sat-18-Sep	BSP	A	Bath City	951	D 2-2	Senior 25, Hatch 69	7
10	Tue-21-Sep	BSP	H	Luton Town	1664	D 2-2	Hatch 26, Brown 73	8
11	Sat-25-Sep	BSP	H	Southport	1633	W 1-0	McReady 90	8
12	Mon-27-Sep	BSP	A	York City	3176	D 0-0		6
13	Sat-02-Oct	BSP	H	Wrexham	1690	L 0-1		9
14	Tue-05-Oct	BSP	A	Rushden & Diamonds	1034	L 1-2	Powell 14	11
15	Sat-09-Oct	BSP	H	Hayes & Yeading United	1536	L 0-1		13
16	Sat-16-Oct	BSP	A	Mansfield Town	2234	D 1-1	Wright 90	13
17	Sat-30-Oct	BSP	A	AFC Wimbledon	3952	W 2-0	Senior 14, Bridge-Wilkinson 62	12
18	Tue-09-Nov	BSP	H	Tamworth	2625	W 1-0	Hone 35	9
19	Sat-13-Nov	BSP	H	Crawley Town	2012	D 1-1	Bridge-Wilkinson 21	11
20	Sat-20-Nov	BSP	A	Wrexham	2619	L 1-2	Hatch 58	11
21	Sat-01-Jan	BSP	A	Fleetwood Town	1432	L 0-1		13
22	Mon-03-Jan	BSP	H	Barrow	1407	W 3-1	M Smith 12, Bridge-Wilkinson 33, Brown 61	11
23	Sat-08-Jan	BSP	H	AFC Wimbledon	2046	D 0-0		12
24	Tue-11-Jan	BSP	H	Histon	1725	W 3-1	Verma 42, Arnison 52, Hatch 86	10
25	Sat-22-Jan	BSP	A	Tamworth	1034	D 1-1	Hatch 64	12
26	Tue-25-Jan	BSP	H	Mansfield Town	1614	D 0-0		11
27	Tue-01-Feb	BSP	A	Luton Town	5770	L 0-4		13
28	Sat-12-Feb	BSP	H	Eastbourne Borough	1660	W 6-1	Bridge-Wilkinson 3 (19, pen 29, pen 33), Hatch 34, Campbell 37, Verma 58	13
29	Tue-15-Feb	BSP	A	Cambridge United	1635	W 1-0	G Smith 50	11
30	Sat-19-Feb	BSP	A	Forest Green Rovers	851	D 1-1	M Smith 66	10
31	Tue-22-Feb	BSP	H	Kidderminster Harriers	1615	D 1-1	M Smith 63	12
32	Tue-01-Mar	BSP	H	Fleetwood Town	1446	W 4-0	Miller 2, Bridge-Wilkinson 2 (pen 14, 49), M Smith 83	9
33	Sat-05-Mar	BSP	H	Cambridge United	2080	W 1-0	Hatch 67	8
34	Tue-08-Mar	BSP	A	Gateshead	1204	D 2-2	Miller 44, Bridge-Wilkinson 45	8
35	Tue-22-Mar	BSP	H	Kettering Town	1829	D 1-1	M Smith 2	9
36	Sat-26-Mar	BSP	H	Altrincham	1967	L 0-1		10
37	Tue-29-Mar	BSP	A	Grimsby Town	2642	W 1-0	Hatch 21	8
38	Sat-02-Apr	BSP	A	Crawley Town	3554	L 0-1		9
39	Tue-05-Apr	BSP	A	Newport County	1300	L 1-2	Verma 68	11
40	Sat-09-Apr	BSP	H	Bath City	1752	W 3-1	Hatch 2 (1, 16), Campbell 36	9
41	Tue-12-Apr	BSP	A	Histon	277	W 1-0	Campbell 81	8
42	Sat-16-Apr	BSP	A	Hayes & Yeading United	432	L 2-3	Og (Bygrave) 66, Taylor 69	9
43	Tue-19-Apr	BSP	A	Kidderminster Harriers	1626	W 2-1	Chandler 66, Moore 76	8
44	Sat-23-Apr	BSP	H	York City	2966	W 2-1	Wright 54, Miller 56	8
45	Mon-25-Apr	BSP	A	Southport	1866	D 1-1	Verma 72	8
46	Sat-30-Apr	BSP	H	Rushden & Diamonds	2009	W 2-0	Wright 64, Campbell 86	7
CUPS								
1	Sat-23-Oct	FAC 4Q	A	Mossley	619	W 6-2	Wright pen 25, Bridge-Wilkinson 31, Senior 2 (48, 85), Austin 61, G Smith 80	
2	Sat-06-Nov	FAC 1	H	Bristol Rovers	1602	W 2-1	Brough 14, G Smith 57	
3	Sat-27-Nov	FAC 2	H	York City	2500	L 0-2		
4	Tue-14-Dec	FAT 1	H	Tamworth	477	W 3-2	Main 2 (47, 67), Verma 78	
5	Sat-15-Jan	FAT 2	H	Bath City	926	W 4-1	Arnison 45, Hatch 2 (47, 75), Verma 61	
6	Sat-05-Feb	FAT 3	A	AFC Telford	1505	W 3-0	G Smith 2, Verma 74, Modest 90	
7	Sat-26-Feb	FAT 4	H	Salisbury City	1864	W 2-1	G Smith 71, Hatch 75	
8	Sat-12-Mar	FAT SF 1	H	Gateshead	4243	W 3-2	Bridge-Wilkinson 55, Hatch 2 (76, 83)	
9	Sat-19-Mar	FAT SF 2	A	Gateshead	5156	D 0-0	(W 3-2 agg)	
10	Sat-07-May	FAT Final	N	Mansfield Town	24668	W 1-0 aet	Senior 120 - Played at Wembley	
								League
								Starts
								Substitute
								Unused Sub
								Cups
								Starts
								Substitute
								Unused Sub
								Goals (Lg)
								Goals (Cup)

RUSSELL	ARNISON	MILLER	HONE	AUSTIN	CHANDLER	G SMITH	TERRY	HATCH	SENIOR	OFFIONG	MOORE	WRIGHT	M SMITH	JACK	CLARKE	J GRAY	BROWN	MCREADY	MAIN	P GRAY	THOMPSON	BARTON	POWELL	LOWSON	WAITE	LOUIS	BRIDGE-WILKINSON	BROUGH	OLDFIELD	GILLESPIE	VERMA	BERTRAM	BURN	QUINN	TAYLOR	MODEST	BARNES	CAMPBELL	ST LOUIS HAMILTON				
23	2	6	18	19	4	20	21	7	10	22	11	9	17	1	24	14	25	16	12	26	27	22	28	29	8	30	31	5	32	28	29	40	3	28	18	30	15	32	33				
X	X	X	X	X	X	X	X	X	X	X	S	S	S	U	U																												
X	X	X	X	X	X	X	X	X	X	X		S	U	U	S	S																											
X	X	X	X		X	X	X	X	S	S		X		U	U	X	X	S																									
X	X	X	X		U	X	X	X	S	X			S	U	S	X	X	X																									
X	X		X		X	X	X	X	S			X	X	U	X	S	X		S	U																								
X	X		X		X	X	X		X	S		X	X	U	X	S	X		U	U																								
X	X		X	X	X	X	X	X	X	S			X		X	S	U	S	U																									
X	X		X	X	S	X	X	X	X		U		X		X	U	X	S	S																									
X	X		X	X	X	X	X	X	X				X		U	S	X	U	S		U																							
X	X		X	X	S	X	X	X	X				X	U	X	S	X	U			U																						
X	X		X	X	U	X	X	X	X				X	U	X		X	S	S	U																								
X	X		X	X	S	X	X	X	X				S	U	X		X	S	X	U																								
X		X	X	X	S	X	X	X	X				S		S		X	X	U				X	U																				
X	X	X	X	X	X		X		X			S	X		U		X			U			X	U	S																			
X	X	X	X	X		X	X		S			S				U	X	X					X	U	S	X																		
X		X	X	X				X	S		X	X			U	S	X						S	U	X	X	X																	
X		X	X	U		X		X	X		X	X					X						S		S	S	X	X	U														
X	S	X	X			X		X	X		X	X				U	X		S						U	S	X	X															
X	U	X	X			X		X	X		X	U				S	X		S						S	X	X	X															
X	U	X	X	X		U		X	U		X	S				S			X								X	X		X	X												
X	U	X	X		U	X		X			X	S				S	X		S							X	X	X			X												
X	X	X			X	X		X			U	S	X			U	X		X						U	X				X		S										
X	X	X			X	X		X			U	S				U	X		X							X				X		U	X	U								
X	X	X			X	X		X			S	X				U	X		S	U											X		U	X	X								
X	X	X			X	X		X			U	S				U	X		S							X				X			X	S	X							
X	U	X			X	X		X			S		S			U	X		S							X				X			X	X	X							
X	X	X			X			X			S		U				X		U							X				X			X	X	S		X	U				
X	X	X			X	X		X	S								X											X				X		X	U	S	S		X	U				
X	X	X				X		X	U				S			X	U									X				X		X	U	X	X			U				
X	X	X			S	X			S				X			X	U	S								X				X			X	X	X			U				
X	X	X			X	X			U			S	X			X	U	X	U							X				X			X					U				
X	X	X			X			X	S			S	X			X	X		U							X				X		X	U					U				
X	X	X			X	X		X	S			U	X			X	U									X				X		X	U					U				
X	X	X			X	X		X	U			U	X			X	U									X				X			X	U				U				
X	X	X				X	U	X	S				X			X	X									X				X		X	U				S	U				
X	X	X			X	X	S	X	S				X			X										X				X		X	U				S	U				
X	U	X				X	S	X	U								X	X													X		X	X	X	S		X	U				
X	X	X				X	X	X	U				S			X	S									X							X		X	S		X	U				
X	U	X				X	S		X				X			X	U									X				X		X	X	X	S			U				
X	X	X					X	X	S								X	S		U							X				X			X	X	U		X	U				
U	S	X				X	U	X	S				X					X		X											X			X	X	X		S	X				
X	X	X					X		X				S			X	U		S							X				X			X	X	S		X	U				
U	X	X			X		X				S	S	X			X			S							X				X				X	U		X	X				
X	X	X			X		X	X			X	X	S			X			S							X				S				X			U	U				
U	S						X	U				X	S	X			X		X		X											X			X	X	X		S	X				
X	X	X			X	X	S	X			X	X					X			U							X				X				U	S		S					
X		X	X	X	U	X			X		X	X	U		S	S	X	U							U		X	X	U															
X	U	X	X	U	U	X		X	X		X	X				S	X		S		U				U		X	X																
X	S	X	X			U		X	X		S	X				U	X		U	U							X	X		X	X	U												
X		X	X	U	U	S				X	S					X		X	S						X	X	X		X	X													
X	X	X		U	X	X		X			U						U	X		X	U											X		X			X	U						
X	X	X			X	X		X	U		S						X		U								X				X		X			S		X	U				
X	X	X			X	X		X	S		U	X					X		U	S							X				X		X						U				
X	X	X			X			X	X			S	X						S	U							X	X			X		X			S			U				
X	X	X			X	X		X	U			U					X			U							X					X			S		X	U					
X	X	X			X	X	S	X	S		X	X					X			U							X				S							X	U				
43	34	37	21	13	23	37	20	37	16	3	9	9	20	0	7	3	40	8	5	2	0	0	3	0	1	4	27	5	0	1	25	0	9	14	14	6	0	7	3	0	0	0	0
0	3	0	0	0	5	0	4	0	13	3	5	13	9	0	3	10	0	7	11	3	0	0	2	0	4	2	0	0	0	0	1	0	1	0	2	7	0	5	0	0	0	0	0
3	6	0	0	1	3	1	3	0	6	0	4	3	2	9	5	8	1	9	4	10	1	1	0	4	1	1	0	0	1	0	0	0	2	6	3	2	0	1	16	0	0	0	0
10	6	10	4	1	6	7	0	8	4	0	4	5	1	0	0	0	9	0	2	0	0	0	0	0	0	1	9	5	0	2	7	0	5	0	0	1	0	3	0	0	0	0	0
0	1	0	0	0	0	1	1	0	2	0	2	2	0	0	1	2	0	0	2	2	0	0	0	0	0	0	0	0	0	0	1	0	0	0	0	3	0	0	0	0	0	0	0
0	1	0	0	3	3	1	0	0	2	0	2	1	1	0	0	2	0	1	3	5	1	0	0	0	2	0	0	0	1	0	0	1	0	0	0	0	1	0	5	0	0	0	0
0	1	3	1	0	2	1	2	11	4	0	1	4	5	0	1	0	2	1	0	0	0	0	1	0	0	0	9	0	0	0	4	0	0	0	1	0	0	4	0	0	0	0	0
0	1	0	0	1	0	4	0	5	3	0	0	1	0	0	0	0	0	0	2	0	0	0	0	0	0	0	2	1	0	0	3	0	0	0	0	1	0	0	0	0	0	0	0

PLAYING SQUAD

Existing Players		SN	HT	WT	DOB	AGE	POB	Career	Apps	Goals
GOALKEEPERS										
Scott	Pocklington	24	6'02"	13 00	18/09/1990	20	Newton Aycliffe	Darlington (Scholar) Rel c/s 09, Newcastle Benfield, Newton Aycliffe 3/10, Darlington 8/11		
Sam	Russell	23	6'00"	10 13	04/10/1982	28	Middlesbrough	Middlesbrough Rel c/s 04, Gateshead (SL) 2/02, Darlington (L) 12/02, Scunthorpe (3ML) 8/03, Darlington 8/04 Rel c/s 07, MK Dons (Trial) 7/07, Rochdale 8/07 Rel c/s 09, Wrexham 8/09, Darlington 5/10	43	0
DEFENDERS										
Paul	Arnison	2	5'10"	11 12	18/09/1977	33	Hartlepool	Newcastle, Hartlepool (L) 3/00 Perm 3/00, Carlisle (3ML) 10/03, Carlisle 2/04 Rel c/s 08, Bradford C 7/08, Darlington 7/09	37	1
Aaron	Brown	3	5'10"	11 11	14/03/1980	31	Bristol	Bristol C Rel c/s 04, Exeter (L) 1/00, QPR (Trial) c/s 04, QPR 1/05, Torquay (L) 3/05, Cheltenham (L) 9/05, Barnsley (Trial) 11/05, Swindon (2ML) 11/05 Perm 1/06 Rel c/s 07, Doncaster (Trial) 7/06 Gillingham 7/07, Lincoln C (Trial) 2/08, Lincoln C 6/08 Rel 2/10, Wrexham 3/10, Darlington 8/10	40	2
Phil	Gray	15			11/08/1993	18	South Shields	Darlington	5	0
Graeme	Lee	18	6'02"	13 07	31/05/1978	33	Middlesbrough	Hartlepool, Sheff Wed 7/03, Doncaster £50,000 1/06 Rel c/s 08, Hartlepool (L) 2/08, Shrewsbury (L) 3/08, Bradford C 8/08, Notts County 7/09 Rel c/s 11, Darlington 7/11		
Ian	Miller	6	6'02"	12 01	23/11/1983	27	Colchester	Bury T, Ipswich 9/06, Boston U (2ML) 11/06, Darlington (2ML) 2/07, Darlington (6ML) 7/07 Perm 1/08	37	3
Ben	Purkiss	22	6'00"	12 12	01/04/1984	27	Sheffield	Sheff Utd Rel c/s 03, Gainsborough 8/03, York C (SL) 3/07, York C 8/07, Oxford U 5/10, Darlington (L) 8/11		
Adam	Quinn	21	6'02"	13 00	02/06/1983	28	Sheffield	Sheff Wed, Carlisle (Trial) 3/02, Halifax 8/02, Crawley 8/08, Forest Green (2ML) 11/10, Darlington £25,000 1/11, Barrow (3ML) 8/11	14	0
Greg	Taylor	5	6'01"	12 01	15/01/1990	21	Bedford	Rushden & D (Yth), Northampton Rel c/s 09, Kettering 6/09, Darlington Undisc 1/11	16	1
MIDFIELDERS										
Chris	Atkinson	14	6'01"	11 13	13/02/1992	19	Huddersfield	Huddersfield, Darlington (6ML) 7/11		
Marc	Bridge-Wilkinson	31	5'06"	11 00	16/03/1979	32	Coventry	Derby Rel c/s 00, Carlisle (L) 3/99, Port Vale 7/00 Rel c/s 04, Stockport 8/04, Bradford C (L) 2/05 Perm 3/05 Rel c/s 07, Carlisle 7/07, Darlington (3ML) 10/10, Darlington 1/11	27	9
Michael	Brough		5'09"	11 07	01/08/1981	29	Nottingham	Notts County Rel 1/04, Spalding (L) 1/00, Macclesfield (Trial) 1/04, Lincoln C (Trial) 2/04, Stevenage 3/04, Forest Green 1/06, Torquay 5/08, Salisbury (SL) 2/09, Stevenage (L) 9/09, Mansfield (5WL) 11/09 Perm 1/10 Rel 5/10, Darlington 7/10	5	0
Jamie	Chandler	4	5'07"	11 02	24/03/1989	22	South Shields	Sunderland, Darlington (4ML) 8/09, Darlington 7/10	28	2
John	McReady	16	5'10"	11 06	12/05/1992	19	South Shields	Darlington, Billingham T (L) 1/10, Whitby (L) 11/10	15	1
Adam	Rundle	20	5'08"	11 02	08/07/1984	27	Durham	Darlington, Middlesbrough (Trial) 8/02, Fulham (Trial) 9/02, Carlisle £40,000 12/02, Dublin C (Ire) 8/04, Mansfield 1/05 Rel c/s 06, Rochdale 7/06, Rotherham (L) 11/09, Chesterfield 2/10, Morecambe 7/10, Gateshead (SL) 3/11, Darlington 7/11		
Gary	Smith		5'08"	10 10	30/01/1984	27	Middlesbrough	Middlesbrough Rel c/s 04, Colchester (Trial) 11/03 Wimbledon (SL) 3/04, MK Dons 8/04 Rel c/s 07, Brentford 8/07 Rel c/s 09, Darlington 7/09	37	1
Kris	Taylor	8	5'09"	13 05	12/01/1984	27	Stafford	Wolves (Yth), Man Utd, Walsall 2/03 Rel c/s 07, Burton (L) 12/04, Burton (3ML) 1/06, Hereford 8/07 Rel c/s 09, Port Vale 8/09 Rel c/s 11, Darlington 6/11		
FORWARDS										
Ryan	Bowman	12	6'02"	11 13	30/11/1991	19	Carlisle	Carlisle Rel c/s 11, Workington (WE) 2/10, Workington (L) 10/10, Darlington 8/11		
John	Campbell	11			23/11/1988	22		Man C (Scholar), Gateshead 3/07, Walker Central, Morpeth, Walker Central 11/09, Newcastle Benfield, Swindon (Trial) 10/10, L.Orient (Trial) 12/10, Darlington 1/11	12	4
Liam	Hatch	7	6'02"	12 03	03/04/1982	29	Hitchin	Herne Bay, Gravesend 6/01, Ashford T (L) 2/02, Barnet £23,000 7/03, Peterborough £150,000 1/08, Darlington (SL) 8/08, Luton (SL) 6/09, Darlington (6ML) 7/10 Perm 1/11	37	11
Michael	Smith	17	5'11"	11 03	17/10/1991	19	Wallsend	Darlington, Workington (L) 10/10	29	5
James	Walshaw	10			12/02/1984	27	Dewsbury	Thornhill, Ossett T, Lincoln C (Trial) 11/05, Bradford PA 3/07, Ossett T, Leek T 3/08 Farsley Celtic 7/08, Wakefield 11/08, Guiseley 3/09, Darlington 5/11		
Tommy	Wright	9	6'00"	11 12	28/09/1984	26	Kirby Muxloe	Leicester, Brentford (10WL) 9/03, Brentford (4ML) 12/03, Blackpool (4ML) 8/05, Barnsley £50,000 1/06, Walsall (7WL) 11/06, Darlington (L) 1/07 Undisc 1/07, Aberdeen £75,000 8/08 Rel 1/10, Grimsby 1/10, Darlington 5/10	22	4

Loanees	SN	HT	WT	DOB	AGE	POB	From - To	APPS	GOA
(D)Danny Hone		6'02"	12 00	15/09/1989	21	Croydon	Lincoln C (6ML) 7/10 -	21	1
(F)Richard Offiong		5'11"	12 02	17/12/1983	27	South Shields	Carlisle 8/10 - Gateshead 3/11 Rel 5/11	6	0
(F)Daniel Powell		5'11"	13 03	12/03/1991	20	Luton	MK Dons 9/10 -	5	1
(F)Jefferson Louis		6'02"	13 02	22/02/1979	31	Harrow	Gainsborough (3ML) 10/10 - Rel 1/11, Hayes & Yeading 1/11, Maidenhead 3/11	6	0
(M)Aman Verma		6'01"	13 00	03/01/1987	24	Birmingham	Leicester (SL) 11/10 - Rel 5/11, Kettering 7/11	26	4
(F)Nathan Modest		5'09"	12 02	29/09/1991	19	Sheffield	Sheff Wed (SL) 1/11 -	13	0

Departures	SN	HT	WT	DOB	AGE	POB	From - To	APPS	GOA
(M)Dominik Werling		5'08"	12 03	13/12/1982	28	Ludwigshafen, Ger	ex Huddersfield 4/10 - Hereford 8/10		
(G)Dan Lowson				04/02/1988	23	Whitley Bay	Ilkeston 10/10 - Rel 11/10, Luton (Trial) 10/10, Blyth 1/11, Alfreton 6/11	0	0
(G)Chris Oldfield				14/01/1991	20	Liverpool	Chester FC NC 10/10 - Rel 11/10, Rochdale 11/10, Bangor C 1/11	0	0
(M)Keith Gillespie		5'10"	11 02	18/02/1975	36	Larne	ex Glentoran 11/10 - Rel 12/10, Longford T 3/11	1	0
(G)Kelvin Jack		6'03"	16 00	29/04/1976	35	Arima, Trin & Tob	Southend 5/10 - Rel 1/11, Kettering (3ML) 10/10	0	0
(M)Joe Clarke				28/07/1988	23		Sollihull Moors 8/10 - Rel 2/11, Solihull Moors (2ML) 12/10, Solihull Moors 2/11, Wrexham 8/11	10	1
(D)Dan Burn		6'05"	13 00	09/05/1992	19	Blyth	Yth - Fulham Undisc 5/10	10	0
(F)Corey Barnes		5'08"	10 08	01/01/1992	19	Sunderland	Yth - Rel 4/11, Whitby (L) 9/10, Spennymoor 7/11	0	0
(F)Curtis Main		5'10"	10 07	20/06/1992	19	South Shields	Yth - Rel 4/11. Middlesbrough 5/11	16	0
(F)Chris Senior		5'06"	9 01	18/11/1981	29	Huddersfield	Altrincham 5/10 - Rel 5/11, Alfreton 6/11	29	4
(M)Chris Moore		5'08"	11 13	17/01/1984	27	Newcastle	Whitley Bay 3/10 - Rel 5/11, Spennymoor (L) 9/10, Gateshead 7/11	14	1
(M)Josh Gray		6'00"	11 11	22/07/1991	20	South Shields	Yth - Rel 5/11, Blyth (L) 2/11, Newton Aycliffe 8/11	13	0
(D)Kevin Austin		6'00"	14 08	12/02/1973	38	Hackney	Chesterfield 8/10 - Rel 5/11, Boston U (SL) 2/11, Boston U 6/11	13	0
(M)Gareth Waite		6'00"	13 00	16/02/1986	25	Stockton	Spennymoor 1/10 - Rel 5/11, Spennymoor 6/11	5	0
(G)Danzelle St Louis-Hamilton		6'05"	14 00	07/05/1990	21	Stevenage	Stoke 1/11 - Fleetwood 6/11	3	0
(M)Paul Terry		5'10"	12 06	03/04/1979	32	Barking	Rushden & D 7/10 - Thurrock 8/11	24	2
(G)Michael Bertram				13/11/1992	18	Hexham	Yth -	0	0
(G)Nick Thompson				21/09/1992	18	Newcastle	Yth -	0	0
(M)Jamie Barton				26/11/1993	17	Stockton	Yth -	0	0

Caught in action....

Senior shields the ball from Mansfield's Silk at Wembley stadium.

Photo by Keith Clayton

EBBSFLEET UNITED

Chairman: Philip Sonsara
Secretary: Peter Danzey **(T)** 07403 285 385 **(E)** peter@eufc.co.uk
Additional Committee Members:
Duncan Holt, Cheryl Wanless, Jessica McQueen, Spenser Lane.

Manager: Liam Daish
Programme Editor: Ian Dickety **(E)** ian@eufc.co.uk

Club Factfile

Founded: 1946 **Nickname:** The Fleet
Previous Names: Gravesend United and Northfleet United merged in 1946 to form Gravesend and Northfleet > 2007
Previous Leagues: Southern 1946-79, 80-96. Alliance 1979-80, Isthmian 1997-2001

Club Colours (change): Red/white/red (All purple)

Ground: Stonebridge Road, Northfleet, Kent DA11 9GN **(T)** 01474 533 796
Capacity: 4,184 **Seats:** 500 **Covered:** 3,000 **Clubhouse:** Yes **Shop:** Yes

Directions
A2 to Ebbsfleet/Eurostar International Junction.
Follow Brown signs to 'The Fleet'.

Previous Grounds: Gravesend United: Central Avenue

Record Attendance: 12,036 v Sunderland - FA Cup 4th Round 12/02/1963
Record Victory: 8-1 v Clacton Town - Southern League 1962-63
Record Defeat: 0-9 v Trowbridge Town - Southern League Premier DIvision 1991-92
Record Goalscorer: Steve Portway - 152 (1992-94, 97-2001)
Record Appearances: Ken Burrett - 537
Additional Records: Paid £8,000 to Wokingham Town for Richard Newbery 1996 and to Tonbridge for Craig Williams 1997
Received £35,000 from West Ham United for Jimmy Bullard 1998

Senior Honours: Southern League 1956-57, Division 1 South 1974-75, Southern Division 1994-95. Isthmian League Premier 2001-02.
FA Trophy 2007-08. Kent Senior Cup 1948-49, 52-53, 80-81, 99-00, 00-01, 01-02.

10 YEAR RECORD

01-02	02-03	03-04	04-05	05-06	06-07	07-08	08-09	09-10	10-11
Isth P 1	Conf 17	Conf 11	Conf 14	Conf 16	Conf 7	Conf 11	Conf 14	Conf 22	Conf S 3

EBBSFLEET UNITED

No.	Date	Comp	H/A	Opponents	Att:	Result	Goalscorers	Pos
1	Sat-14-Aug	BSS	H	Maidenhead United	790	L 1-2	Willock 63	18
2	Tue-17-Aug	BSS	A	Farnborough	663	W 2-1	Willock 37, West 90	9
3	Sat-21-Aug	BSS	A	Bishops Stortford	525	W 3-0	West 2 (11, 63), Marwa 32	4
4	Tue-24-Aug	BSS	H	Dover Athletic	1139	L 0-2		7
5	Sat-28-Aug	BSS	A	Dartford	2781	D 1-1	West 61	10
6	Mon-30-Aug	BSS	H	Braintree Town	786	D 0-0		9
7	Sat-04-Sep	BSS	H	Staines Town	832	D 1-1	Willock 12	11
8	Sat-11-Sep	BSS	A	Dorchester Town	473	W 2-1	Phipp 18, Stone 82	9
9	Sat-18-Sep	BSS	H	Weston-Super-Mare	911	W 3-1	Willock 2 (49, 90), West 79	6
10	Sat-02-Oct	BSS	A	Bromley	1010	D 1-1	Phipp 16	6
11	Sat-16-Oct	BSS	A	Boreham Wood	265	W 1-0	West 39	5
12	Sat-30-Oct	BSS	A	St Albans City	472	W 2-1	Willock 18, Phipp 43	6
13	Tue-09-Nov	BSS	H	Welling United	942	W 4-0	West 2 (24, 34), Willock 44, Howe 81	5
14	Sat-13-Nov	BSS	A	Maidenhead United	325	D 1-1	Carew 36	7
15	Tue-28-Dec	BSS	H	Dartford	2435	W 2-1	Duncan 10, Willock 32	5
16	Sat-01-Jan	BSS	H	Lewes	1187	W 1-0	Ginty 88	3
17	Mon-03-Jan	BSS	A	Braintree Town	881	L 2-4	Phipp 7, Lorraine 80	7
18	Sat-08-Jan	BSS	H	Dorchester Town	786	W 3-2	Phipp 2 (5, 14), West 24	6
19	Tue-11-Jan	BSS	H	Hampton & Richmond Borough	679	W 1-0	Willock 52	3
20	Sat-22-Jan	BSS	H	Bromley	1095	L 1-2	West 61	6
21	Tue-25-Jan	BSS	H	Thurrock	656	D 2-2	Lorraine 1, Phipp 47	7
22	Sat-29-Jan	BSS	A	Dover Athletic	1210	W 3-1	Phipp 12, Carew 18, Willock 56	5
23	Tue-01-Feb	BSS	A	Hampton & Richmond Borough	295	W 4-2	Willock 33, Okus pen 47, Shakes 2 (49, pen 87)	2
24	Sat-05-Feb	BSS	H	Farnborough	990	L 0-3		3
25	Tue-08-Feb	BSS	H	Eastleigh	695	D 2-2	Willock 14, Carew pen 45	4
26	Sat-12-Feb	BSS	A	Havant & Waterlooville	857	W 3-2	Carew 4, Lorraine 64, Shakes 81	4
27	Sat-19-Feb	BSS	H	Basingstoke Town	777	W 3-1	West 4, Carew pen 62, Willock 80	4
28	Wed-23-Feb	BSS	A	Lewes	593	W 3-0	Carew 2 (37, 90), Willock 86	2
29	Sat-26-Feb	BSS	A	Chelmsford City	931	W 3-2	Duncan 27, Carew 2 (78, 85)	2
30	Tue-01-Mar	BSS	A	Woking	1005	L 0-3		2
31	Sat-05-Mar	BSS	H	Boreham Wood	800	D 2-2	Erskine 8, Phipp 20	2
32	Sat-12-Mar	BSS	H	Havant & Waterlooville	879	W 2-1	Willock 2 (26, 61)	2
33	Sat-19-Mar	BSS	A	Weston-Super-Mare	366	L 2-3	Willock 2 (16, 87)	4
34	Tue-22-Mar	BSS	A	Welling United	1010	D 1-1	Carew 7	3
35	Sat-26-Mar	BSS	H	Bishops Stortford	824	D 0-0		4
36	Sat-02-Apr	BSS	A	Basingstoke Town	407	W 2-1	Shakes 2 (33, 75)	4
37	Tue-05-Apr	BSS	A	Staines Town	251	W 2-0	West 48, Phipp 71	3
38	Sat-09-Apr	BSS	H	St Albans City	840	W 4-0	Willock 26, Marwa 30, West 73, Ginty 84	3
39	Sat-16-Apr	BSS	A	Eastleigh	583	W 3-0	Carew 2 (14, 46), Shakes 42	3
40	Fri-22-Apr	BSS	H	Chelmsford City	1368	L 1-3	Phipp 17	3
41	Mon-25-Apr	BSS	A	Thurrock	647	D 0-0		3
42	Sat-30-Apr	BSS	H	Woking	1721	D 1-1	Carew pen 51	3

CUPS

No.	Date	Comp	H/A	Opponents	Att:	Result	Goalscorers
1	Sat-25-Sep	FAC 2Q	A	Cray Wanderers	408	D 2-2	Lorraine 21, Willock 81
2	Tue-28-Sep	FAC 2QR	H	Cray Wanderers	535	W 4-2	G Williams 4, West 13, Willock 80, Shakes 90
3	Sat-09-Oct	FAC 3Q	A	Needham Market	573	W 1-0	Phipp 57
4	Sat-23-Oct	FAC 4Q	H	Boreham Wood	1005	W 3-0	Lorraine 27, Shakes 45, Willock 62
5	Sat-06-Nov	FAC 1	A	AFC Wimbledon	3219	D 0-0	
6	Thu-18-Nov	FAC 1R	H	AFC Wimbledon	2306	L 2-3 aet	Carew 2 (pen 12, 18)
7	Tue-23-Nov	FAT 3Q	H	Bromley	611	W 4-0	West 3 (25, 37, 70), Willock 86
8	Sat-11-Dec	FAT 1	H	Hayes & Yeading United	614	W 3-1	Howe 30, Willock 2 (34, 86)
9	Sat-15-Jan	FAT 2	A	Droylsden	336	L 0-1	
10	Tue-03-May	PO SF 1	A	Chelmsford City	1701	W 4-1	West 2 (22, 26), Shakes 2 (78, 88)
11	Sun-08-May	PO SF 2	H	Chelmsford City	1538	W 2-1	West 2 (27, 35)
12	Sun-15-May	PO Final	A	Farnborough	4267	W 4-2	West 2 (29, 74), Shakes 53, Willock 91

League
Starts
Substitute
Unused Sub

Cups
Starts
Substitute
Unused Sub

Goals (Lg)
Goals (Cup)

EDWARDS	EASTON	LORRAINE	POOLEY	HENRY	DUNCAN	MARWA	CAREW	WEST	GINTY	WILLOCK	SEALEY	STONE	BENJAMIN	SHERLOCK	PHIPP	HAGAN	UDOJI	SHAKES	G WILLIAMS	MCCARTHY	HOWE	OKUS	BLAKE	A WILLIAMS	HAWKES	ERSKINE	FAKINOS	BANIM
X	X	X	X	X	X	X	X	X	X	X	S	S	S	U	U													
X		X	X	X	X	X	X	X	X	X	U	S	X	U	S	U												
X		X	X	X	X	X	X	X	X	X	S	S	S	U	X	U												
X		X	X	X	X	X	X	X		X	X	S	S	S	X	U												
X	S	X	X	X	X	X	X	X		X	U	X	S	U	X	U												
X	S	X	X	X	X	X	X	X		X	S	X	U	U	X	U												
X		X	X	X		X	X	X		X	S	X	U	U	X	U	X	S										
X	S	X	X	X	X	X		X		X	S	X			X	U	U	X	S									
X	X	X	X	X	S	X	U	X		X		X			S	U	U	X	X									
X	X	X	X	U		X	X	X		X	S	X			X	U	U	S	X									
X	X	X	U	U	X	X	X	X		X		X			X	U		X	S		U							
X	X	X	U	S	X	X	X	X		X		X			X	U		X	S		S							
X	X	X	S	U	X	X	X	X		X		X			X	U		X	S		S							
X	X	X	U	U		X	X	X	S	X		X			X	U		X	S		X							
X	X	X	U	U	X	X		X	S	X		X			X	U		S	X		X							
X		X	X	U	X	X	S	X	S	X		X			X	U		S	X		X							
X		X	X	S	X	X	S	X	S	X		X			X	U			X		X							
X	X	X	U			X	S	X	X	X		X			X	U		S	S		X	X						
X	X	X	U	U			S	X		X		X			X	U		X	U		X	X	X					
X	X	X	S			X	X	X		X		X			X	U		X	S		S	U	X					
X		X	X		S	X	X	X		X		X			X	U		X			S	S	X	U				
X		X	X		S	X	X			X		X			X	U		X	S		S	X	X	U				
X		X	X		U	X	X	S		X		X			X	U		X	S		S	X	X					
X	X	X	U		S	X	X	S		X		X			X			X	S		U	X	X					
X	X	X	U		X	X	X	X		X		U			X	U		X	S		X	U						
X	X	X	U			X	X	X		X		X			X	U		S	U		S	X	X					
	X	X	U			X	X	X		X		X		U	X			S	S		X	S	X		X			
X	X	X			X	X	X			X				U	S			X	X		X	X		U	U	S		
X	X	X	U		X	X	X			X				U	S			X	X		X	X			U	S		
X	X	X	S		X	X	X			X					X			X	X		X	S		U	U	S		
X		X	X		X	X	X			X				U	X			S	S		X	X		U	U	X		
X		X	X		X	X	X	X		X				U	X			S	U		X			U	U	X		
X	U	X	X		X	X	X		U	X		X			X			S	S		X				U	X		
X	X	X	U		X	X	X	X	S	X		X			X				S		S				U	X		
X	X	X	U		X	X	X	X		X		X			X			S	S		U					X	U	
X	X	X				X	X	X	U	X		X			X			X	U		U		X			S	S	
X	X	X				X	X	S	U			X			X			X			S		X		U	X	X	S
X	X	X				X	X	X	S	X		X						X			S		X		U	U	X	S
X	X	X			X	X	X	X	U	X		X			X			X			S					S	S	U
X	X	X			X	X	X	X	S	X		X			X			X	U		S					S	U	
X	X	X			X	X	X	X	S	X		X			X			X			S				S	U	U	
	U	X	X		X		X	X	X			X		U				S	S		X				X	X	X	U
X	X	X	X	X		X	S	X		X	U	X		U	S	U	U	X	X	U								
X	X	X	X	U		X	X	X		X	S	X		U	X	U	U	S	X	U								
X	X	X		U	X	X	X	X		X	S	X		U	X	U	U	X										
X	X	X	S	U	X	X	X	X		X		X		U	X	U		X	S		S							
X	X	X	U	U	X	X	X	X		X		X		U	X	U		X	S		S							
X	X	X	U	U	X	X	X	X	S	X		X		U	X	U		X	S		S							
X	X	X	S	S	X	X		X	U	X		X			X	U		S	X		X							
X	X	X	U		X	X	S	X	S	X		X			X	U		S	X		X							
X	X	X	U			X	S	X		X		X			S	U		X	S		X	X	X					
	X	X	U		X	X	X	X	U	X		X			X			X			S				X	S	S	
	X	X	U		X	X		X	S	X		X			X			X	U		S				X	S	X	
X	X	X	S			X		X	U	X		X			X			X	U		X				U	U	X	
40	26	42	19	9	26	40	35	33	5	40	1	32	1	0	35	0	1	22	8	0	15	9	11	0	2	7	3	0
0	3	0	3	2	4	0	4	3	8	0	6	4	4	1	4	0	0	12	17	0	13	3	0	0	1	6	2	2
0	2	0	13	7	1	0	1	0	4	0	2	1	2	12	1	24	3	0	5	0	4	2	0	6	9	2	3	2
10	12	12	2	1	8	12	6	12	0	12	0	12	0	0	10	0	0	9	4	0	4	1	1	0	2	0	2	0
0	0	0	3	1	0	0	3	0	3	0	2	0	0	0	2	0	0	3	4	0	5	0	0	0	0	2	1	0
0	0	0	6	5	0	0	0	0	3	0	1	0	0	6	0	9	3	0	2	2	0	0	0	0	1	1	0	0
0	0	3	0	0	2	2	13	13	2	19	0	1	0	0	11	0	0	6	0	0	1	1	0	0	0	1	0	0
0	0	2	0	0	0	0	2	10	0	7	0	0	0	0	1	0	0	5	1	0	1	0	0	0	0	0	0	0

PLAYING SQUAD

Existing Players		SN	HT	WT	DOB	AGE	POB	Career	Apps	Goals
GOALKEEPERS										
Preston	Edwards	1	6'00"	12 07	05/09/1989	21	Edmonton	Millwall Rel c/s 09, Dover (SL) 1/09, Grays 8/09 Rel 5/10, Ebbsfleet 8/10	40	0
Joe	Welch	17	6'02"	12 12	29/11/1988	22	Welwyn Garden	Southend Rel c/s 07, Diss T (L) 3/07, Bishops Stortford c/s 07 Rel 8/08, Cheshunt 8/08, Histon 10/08, Weymouth (2ML) 2/10, Stevenage (SL) 3/11, Ebbsfleet 7/11		
DEFENDERS										
John	Herd	3	5'09"	12 00	03/10/1989	21	Huntingdon	Southend Rel c/s 11, Ebbsfleet 8/11		
Joe	Howe	14	6'00"	11 04	21/01/1988	23	Sidcup	MK Dons Rel c/s 07, Walton & H (L) 8/06, Gravesend (WE) 1/07, Northampton 7/07 Rel 8/07, Kettering 8/07 Rel 12/07, Welling 12/07 Rel 7/08, Fisher 8/08, Croydon Ath 2/09, Ebbsfleet 10/10	28	1
Paul	Lorraine	6			12/10/1983	27		Welling, Dartford (L) 1/03, Erith & B 3/04, Braintree 5/04, Fisher 5/06, AFC Wimbledon (L) 12/06, Perm 1/07, Woking 5/07, AFC Wimbledon 5/09 Rel 4/10, Ebbsfleet 6/10	42	3
Paul	McCarthy		5'10"	13 10	04/08/1971	40	Cork	Brighton, Wycombe £100,000 7/96 Rel c/s 03, Oxford U (SL) 3/03, Oxford U 7/03, Rel c/s 04, Hornchurch 6/04, Gravesend/ Ebbsfleet 11/04	0	0
Ian	Simpemba	16	6'02"	12 08	28/03/1983	28	Dublin	Wycombe, Woking (3ML) 10/02, Woking (L) 9/03, Crawley Undisc 7/04, Aldershot (SL) 3/06, Lewes 6/06, Havant & W 5/08, Ebbsfleet 7/11		
MIDFIELDERS										
Lance	Azeez	18			07/01/1993	18		Ebbsfleet		
Clint	Easton	5	5'11"	11 00	01/10/1977	33	Barking	Watford, Norwich £200,000 6/01 Rel c/s 04, Wycombe 7/04, Gillingham 7/06 Rel c/s 07, Hereford 7/07 Rel 4/09, Mansfield (Trial) 4/09, Ebbsfleet 10/09	29	0
Giannoulis	Fakinos	4	5'08"		09/07/1989	22		Korinida FC Galatsi (Gre) (Yth), Olympiakos (Gre), Panionios (Gre) 1/08, GS Ilioupoli (Gre) 1/09, Apollon Smyrni (Gre) 8/09 Rel c/s 10, Ebbsfleet 3/11	5	0
Rambir	Marwa	8			10/01/1980	31	Barkingside	L.Orient (Trainee), Erith & B 2/00, Ilford 7/00, Erith & B 1/01, Australia, L.Orient (Trial) 6/03, Grays 8/03, St Albans 8/04, Dag & Red 5/05, St Albans (L) 1/06 (Perm) 3/06, Hayes & Yeading (L) 11/07 Perm 12/07 Rel 5/10, Ebbsfleet 7/10	40	2
Tom	Phipp	11			03/08/1992	19		Ebbsfleet	39	11
Ricky	Shakes	10	5'10"	12 00	26/01/1985	26	Brixton	Bolton Rel c/s 05, Bristol R (L) 2/05, Bury (SL) 3/05, Swindon 8/05 Rel c/s 07, Brentford (Trial) 7/07, Brentford 8/07 Rel 5/08, Ebbsfleet 7/08	34	6
Alex	Stavrinou	20	5'09"	11 12	13/09/1990	21	Harlow	Charlton Rel c/s 11, Ebbsfleet (SL) 11/09, Cambridge U (L) 10/10, Aldershot T (Trial) 5/11, Ebbsfleet 8/11		
Craig	Stone	2	6'00"	10 05	29/12/1988	22	Strood	Gillingham Rel 5/08, Brentford (2ML) 1/08, Ebbsfleet 6/08, Maidstone 3/10, Ebbsfleet 8/10	36	1
Michael	West	7			09/02/1991	20		Ebbsfleet	36	13

FORWARDS										
Liam	Enver-Marum	15	6'03"	12 00	17/11/1987	23	London	Reading (Scholar) Rel c/s 06, Brighton (Trial) 7/06, Cambridge U 8/06, Woking 1/07 Rel 5/09, Eastbourne B 5/09 Rel 5/10, Crawley 6/10 Rel 12/10, Hayes & Yeading (L) 9/10, Forest Green (L) 10/10, Forest Green 1/11, Ebbsfleet 7/11		
Scott	Ginty	12	5'08"	11 11	17/05/1991	20		Peterborough (Scholar) Rel c/s 09, Stamford (WE) 3/09, Ebbsfleet 8/09	13	2
Adam	Williams	19						Ebbsfleet	0	0
Callum	Willock	9	6'01"	12 08	29/10/1981	29	Waterloo	ADT College, Fulham 7/00, QPR (L) 11/02, Bristol R (L) 8/03, Peterborough (2ML) 10/03 £25,000 12/03, Brentford £50,000 1/06 Rel c/s 07, Port Vale 8/07 Rel 12/07, Stevenage 1/08 Rel 5/09, AFC Wimbledon (Trial) 7/09, Crawley 9/09 Rel 2/10, Cambridge U NC 2/10 Rel 4/10, Ebbsfleet 7/10	40	19

Loanees		HT	WT	DOB	AGE	POB	From - To	APPS	GOA
(M)Conor	Okus			15/09/1991	19		Dag & Red (2ML) 1/11 -	12	1
(D)Ryan	Blake	5'10"	10 10	08/12/1991	19	Kingston	Brentford (3ML) 1/11 -	11	0
(G)Darren	Hawkes			24/06/1993	18		Gillingham 2/11 - Hastings (L) 8/11	3	0

Departures		HT	WT	DOB	AGE	POB	From - To	APPS	GOA
(M)Stefan	Bailey	5'11"	12 08	10/11/1987	23	Brent	Grays 8/09 - Rel c/s 10, AFC Telford 9/10, Kettering 3/11		
(F)Joe	Benjamin	5'10"	11 04	08/10/1990	20	Woodford	Northampton 8/10 - Rel 9/10, Boreham Wood 9/10, AFC Hornchurch 11/10, Wealdstone 3/11, Chelmsford 7/11	5	0
(F)Tyron	Sealey			27/01/1989	22		Slough 8/10 - Rel 10/10, Tooting & M 10/10	7	0
(D)Emmanuel (Udo)	Udoji	6'00"	13 05	09/01/1989	22		Aveley 8/10 - Rel 10/10, Havant & W 11/10, Aveley, Bromley 3/11	1	0
(M)Chris	Henry			17/05/1991	20		Yth - Rel 2/11	11	0
(G)Joseph	Hagan			08/11/1991	19		Yth - Rel 2/11, Tonbridge A 3/11	0	0
(D)Dean	Pooley	6'01"	11 02	10/09/1986	24	Sidcup	ex Ballymena 8/08 - Rel 6/11, Margate 6/11	22	0
(F)Gareth A	Williams	5'10"	11 13	10/09/1982	28	Germiston	Croydon Ath 9/10 - Rel 6/11	25	0
(M)Aidan	Sherlock			18/02/1992	19		Ebbsfleet Rel 5/11, Maidstone (L) 12/10, Margate c/s 11, Sevenoaks T (Dual) 8/11	1	0
(M)Ashley	Carew	6'00"	11 00	17/12/1985	25	Lambeth	Bromley 8/10 - Cambridge U 7/11	39	13
(D)Derek	Duncan	5'10"	10 11	23/04/1987	24	Newham	AFC Wimbledon 7/10 - Woking 7/11	30	2
(F)Jacob	Erskine	6'01"	14 00	13/01/1989	22	Lambeth	Forest Green 2/11 - Bromley (Trial) 7/11, Hampton & R 8/11	13	1
(F)Jody	Banim	5'08"	13 01	01/04/1978	33	Manchester	Droylsden 3/11 -	2	0

Caught in action....

Fleetwood Town & England International, Geroge Donnelly, races Portugal's Daniel Carrico during the Inter Challenge Trophy final.

Photo by Keith Clayton

FLEETWOOD TOWN

Chairman: Andy Pilley
Secretary: Steve Edwards (T) 07894 526 810 (E) secretary@fleetwoodtownfc.com
Additional Committee Members:
Phil Brown, Steve Curwood.

Manager: Mickey Mellon
Programme Editor: Derick Thomas (E) press@fleetwoodtownfc.com

Club Factfile

Founded: 1908 **Nickname:** The Fishermen
Previous Names: Fleetwood 1908, Fleetwood Wanderers 1997 then in the same year reverted to Fleetwood Freeport > 2002
Previous Leagues: Lancashire Combination 1908-68. Northern Premier 1968-76, 87-96, 2005-08, Cheshire 1977-82, North West Counties 1982-87, 97-2005.

Club Colours (change): Red/white/red (Yellow & black/yellow/yellow)

Ground: Highbury Stadium, Park Avenue, Fleetwood, Lancashire FY7 6TX (T) 01253 770 702
Capacity: 3,000 **Seats:** 250 **Covered:** 1,200 **Clubhouse:** Yes **Shop:** Yes

Directions
Leave M6 J32 signposted M55. Leave M55 at J3. Take 3rd exit signposted Fleetwood. Stay on A585 for approx. 11.5 miles. At Eros Statue roundabout take 1st exit. At next roundabout take 6th exit onto Hatfield Avenue. Take 4th road on the left (Highbury Avenue). The entrance is on the right hand side between houses no. 65 & 67.

Previous Grounds: Two locations before moving to Highbury in 1939

Record Attendance: 7,900 v Liverpool - 12/08/2003
Record Victory: Not known
Record Defeat: Not known
Record Goalscorer: Not known
Record Appearances: Not known
Additional Records:

Senior Honours: North West Counties Division Two 1998-99, Division One 2004-05. Northern Premier League Cup 2006-07.

10 YEAR RECORD

01-02	02-03	03-04	04-05	05-06	06-07	07-08	08-09	09-10	10-11
NWC1 14	NWC1 10	NWC1 3	NWC1 1	NP 1 2	NP P 8	NP P 1	Conf N 8	Conf N 2	Conf 5

FLEETWOOD TOWN

No.	Date	Comp	H/A	Opponents	Att:	Result	Goalscorers	Pos
1	Sat-14-Aug	BSP	A	Rushden & Diamonds	1248	D 1-1	Vieira 23	11
2	Tue-17-Aug	BSP	H	Mansfield Town	1849	W 3-0	Curtis 6, Vieira 2 (19, 34)	3
3	Sat-21-Aug	BSP	H	Luton Town	2831	L 0-3		11
4	Tue-24-Aug	BSP	A	Gateshead	623	W 2-0	Vieira 35, McGuire 44	5
5	Sat-28-Aug	BSP	A	Southport	1546	L 0-1		11
6	Mon-30-Aug	BSP	H	York City	2020	W 2-1	Seddon 7, Vieira 83	5
7	Sat-04-Sep	BSP	A	Crawley Town	1637	D 1-1	Vieira 25	7
8	Sat-11-Sep	BSP	H	Kettering Town	1602	W 4-1	Craney 2 (45, 58), Vieira 2 (48, 81)	5
9	Sat-18-Sep	BSP	A	Grimsby Town	3099	W 2-1	Seddon 44, Pond 59	5
10	Tue-21-Sep	BSP	H	Kidderminster Harriers	1411	D 1-1	Craney 20	6
11	Sat-25-Sep	BSP	H	Bath City	1481	W 2-1	Vieira 31, Wright 58	3
12	Tue-28-Sep	BSP	A	Barrow	1634	W 2-0	Curtis 2 (19, 22)	1
13	Sat-02-Oct	BSP	H	Histon	1458	D 1-1	Vieira 63	3
14	Tue-05-Oct	BSP	A	Wrexham	2689	D 0-0		3
15	Sun-10-Oct	BSP	H	Cambridge United	2380	D 2-2	Vieira 7, McNulty 54	4
16	Sat-16-Oct	BSP	A	Altrincham	1106	L 0-1		5
17	Sat-30-Oct	BSP	A	Tamworth	946	W 2-0	Beeley 21, Vieira 51	6
18	Tue-09-Nov	BSP	H	Gateshead	1011	D 0-0		4
19	Sat-13-Nov	BSP	H	Rushden & Diamonds	1429	D 1-1	Barry 8	4
20	Sat-20-Nov	BSP	A	Bath City	905	D 1-1	Rogan 65	5
21	Sat-18-Dec	BSP	H	Newport County	1142	D 1-1	Vieira 21	5
22	Tue-28-Dec	BSP	H	Southport	2051	W 2-0	Og (Marsh-Evans) 27, Beeley 77	5
23	Sat-01-Jan	BSP	H	Darlington	1432	W 1-0	Seddon 20	5
24	Sat-08-Jan	BSP	A	Forest Green Rovers	762	L 0-1		6
25	Tue-11-Jan	BSP	A	Mansfield Town	1725	W 5-2	Vieira 3 (45, 57, 59), Seddon 48, McGuire 62	4
26	Tue-18-Jan	BSP	H	AFC Wimbledon	1808	D 1-1	Vieira 45	4
27	Sat-22-Jan	BSP	H	Hayes & Yeading United	1281	D 1-1	McGuire 30	5
28	Tue-25-Jan	BSP	A	Kettering Town	798	L 1-2	McGuire 90	5
29	Sat-29-Jan	BSP	H	Forest Green Rovers	1335	W 2-0	Brown 56, Clancy 80	5
30	Tue-01-Feb	BSP	A	Histon	255	L 0-1		5
31	Sat-05-Feb	BSP	A	AFC Wimbledon	3298	L 0-1		5
32	Sat-12-Feb	BSP	A	Luton Town	6227	W 3-1	Seddon 2 (9, 55), Barry 53	5
33	Tue-15-Feb	BSP	A	York City	2220	L 0-1		5
34	Sat-19-Feb	BSP	H	Grimsby Town	2004	W 3-0	Vieira 43, Seddon 78, Parker 90	5
35	Tue-22-Feb	BSP	H	Eastbourne Borough	1222	L 0-1		6
36	Tue-01-Mar	BSP	A	Darlington	1446	L 0-4		6
37	Sat-05-Mar	BSP	A	Newport County	1716	W 3-1	Seddon 2 (pen 34, 84), Donnelly 90	6
38	Sat-12-Mar	BSP	H	Crawley Town	2027	L 1-2	Donnelly 63	6
39	Sat-19-Mar	BSP	H	Wrexham	2207	W 1-0	Clancy 48	6
40	Sat-26-Mar	BSP	A	Hayes & Yeading United	303	W 2-1	Pond 12, Brown 45	6
41	Sat-02-Apr	BSP	H	Tamworth	1580	W 2-1	McGuire 34, Vieira pen 87	5
42	Sat-09-Apr	BSP	A	Eastbourne Borough	864	W 6-0	Parker 35, Vieira 2 (pen 45, 53), McGuire 57, Og (Jenkins) 59, Donnelly 73	5
43	Sat-16-Apr	BSP	H	Altrincham	1966	W 3-1	Clancy 37, Seddon 44, Donnelly 90	5
44	Fri-22-Apr	BSP	A	Kidderminster Harriers	2738	L 1-2	Mullan 39	5
45	Mon-25-Apr	BSP	H	Barrow	2788	W 1-0	Vieira 45	5
46	Sat-30-Apr	BSP	A	Cambridge United	2745	W 1-0	Harvey 77	5

CUPS

No.	Date	Comp	H/A	Opponents	Att:	Result	Goalscorers
1	Sat-23-Oct	FAC 4Q	H	Buxton	1181	W 2-1	Warlow 50, Seddon 90
2	Sat-06-Nov	FAC 1	H	Walsall	2319	D 1-1	Mullan 50
3	Tue-16-Nov	FAC 1R	A	Walsall	2056	L 0-2	
4	Tue-14-Dec	FAT 1	A	Blyth Spartans	354	L 0-2	
5	Fri-06-May	PO SF 1	H	AFC Wimbledon	4112	L 0-2	
6	Wed-11-May	PO SF 2	A	AFC Wimbledon	4538	L 1-6	Seddon 48

League
Starts
Substitute
Unused Sub

Cups
Starts
Substitute
Unused Sub

Goals (Lg)
Goals (Cup)

HURST	BEELEY	MCNULTY	GRAND	LINWOOD	POND	BARRY	CRANEY	MCGUIRE	VIEIRA	CURTIS	BEESLEY	THORPE	DAVIES	SEDDON	CAVANAGH	MILES	CONNORS	BROWN	MULLAN	CLANCY	DOOTSON	WRIGHT	ROGAN	GREGAN	WARLOW	HORNE	COUGHLIN	WORTHINGTON	MILLIGAN	ROWE	DONNELLY	HAINING	PARKER	HARVEY	CAMOZZI				
1	2	5	13	20	6	4	8	18	10	25	27	15	16	19	26	17	14	12	11	7	28	3	9	29	24	30	32	31	36	30	27	28	24	8	23				
X	X	X	X	X	X	X	X	X	X	X	S	U	U	U	U																								
X	X	X	X	X	X	X	X	U	X	X	U	S	U	S		X																							
X	X	X	X	X	X	X	X	S	X	X	U	S	U		U	X																							
X	X	X				X	X	X	X	X	X	X	U	S	X	U	S	U																					
X	X	X		X	X	U	X	S	X	X	S	X	U	S	X		X																						
X	X	X		X	U	X	X	X	X	X	U		U	X	X		S		S																				
X	X	X	U	X	S	X	X	X	X	X	U	S	S	X				X																					
	X	X		X	S	X	X	X	X	X	U		X	X				X	U	S	U																		
	X	X		X	X	X	X		X	X	S	S	X	X					U	S	U	X																	
	X	X	X		X	X	X	U	X		S	X	X	X	X				S	S	U																		
	X	X		X	X	X	X	S	X	X		U	X	X					S	S	U	X																	
	X	X		X	X	X	X	S	X	X		U	X	U					X	S	U	X																	
	X	X		X	X	X	X	S	X	X		U	X						X	U	U	X	S																
	X	X		X	X	X	X		X	X		S	X	U	U				X	U	U	X																	
	X	X		X	X	X	X		X	S		U	X	X		U			X	S	U	X																	
	X	X		X	X	X	X		X	X		U	X	S	X	U			S	X	U																		
	X	X				X	X	X	X			U	X	X		X			S		U	X		X	S	U													
	X	X			X	X	X			S		U	X	X	X	S			X	S	U			X	X														
		X			S	X		X		X		S	X		X	X			X	X	U		U	X	S	X													
	X	X				X		X		X		S	X	X	X	X			S	X	U	U	S	X															
	X	X				X		U	X			S	X	X				S				X	X	X			U	X	X	U									
U	X			X		X		S	X	X		S	X	X			S	X				U		X				X	X										
U	X			X		X		S	X	X		S	X	X			S	X				U		X				X	X										
U	X	X				X	X	X	X			S	X	X		S	U	X				S		X							X								
U	X	X			U	X		X	X			U	X	X			S			X		X		X						S	X								
U	X	X			U	X		X	X			U	X	X			U	X	S	X				X							X								
U	X	X			S	X		X	X			U	X	X				X	S	X				X					S		X								
U		X				X		X	X			S	X	X	X		U	X		X				X					S	U	X								
U		X				X		X	X			U	X	S	X		X	X		S									X	S	X	X							
U		X				X		X	S				X	X	X	U	S	X		X		S							X	X		X							
U	X				U	X		X	X				X	X		X		X	S	X				X					U	U		X							
U	X				S	X		X	X				X	X					X	X		X		X					U	U	S	X							
U	X				U	X		X	X			S	X						X	X		X		X					S	S	X	X							
U	X				U	X		X	X				X	X					X	S		X		X					X		S	X	S						
U	X				U	X		X	X				X	X					S	S		X		X					X		S	X	X						
U	X	X			S	X		X	X			S	X						S	U		X		X					X		X		X						
X		X		X	S	X		X	X				U	X	X			X	X	X									U		S		S						
X		X			U	X		X	X				U	X	X			X	X	X				X					S		S		S						
X	X	X			X	X		X	U				U					X	S	X				X					U	U	X		X						
X	X	X			X	X		X	U				U		U			X	X	X				X							X		S	S					
X	X	X			X	X		X	S				U		U			X	S	X				X							X		X	S					
X	X	X				X		X	X				U	X	S			X	U	X				X							S		X	S					
X	X	X				X		X	X				U	X	U			X	S	X				X							S		X	U					
X	X	X				X		X				S	U	X	U			X	X	X				X							X		S	U					
X		X				X		X	X				U	X	X			X	X	X		S		X						U			S	U					
U				X				U	X			X	X	U	X				U	S		X								X	X		X	X	X				
	X	X		U		X	X		X	X		S	X	X	X	X			S	U	U			X	S	U													
	X	X		U	X	X	X					S	X	X	X	X			S	U	U		U	X	X	S													
	X	X		X	U	X		X			U	X	X	X	X	X			S	X	U	U	U			U													
	X	X				X		X	X			S	X	S		X			X	U		X	X	X			U	U											
X	X	X				X		X	X				S	X	U			X	X	X				X							U		S	S					
X		X		S		X		X	X				U	X	X			X	U	S				X							X		U	X					
16	38	38	4	18	16	44	19	30	38	18	1	4	30	29	15	6	2	20	14	20	0	15	1	26	1	1	0	3	8	2	13	7	7	1	1	0	0	0	0
0	0	0	0	0	7	0	0	7	2	2	4	15	1	5	1	2	6	1	14	11	0	3	2	0	2	0	0	0	4	3	7	0	6	3	0	0	0	0	0
16	0	0	1	0	8	1	0	4	2	0	5	12	15	4	7	4	3	1	4	3	13	3	1	0	0	1	1	0	4	6	0	0	0	3	0	0	0	0	0
2	5	6	0	1	1	6	2	4	4	1	0	1	4	5	4	4	0	2	2	2	0	1	1	5	1	0	0	0	0	0	1	0	0	1	0	0	0	0	0
0	0	0	0	1	0	0	0	0	0	0	0	3	1	1	0	0	0	0	3	1	0	0	0	0	1	1	0	0	0	0	0	0	1	1	0	0	0	0	0
0	0	0	0	2	1	0	0	0	0	0	1	0	1	0	1	0	0	0	1	3	3	1	2	0	0	2	1	1	0	0	1	0	1	0	0	0	0	0	0
0	2	1	0	0	2	2	3	6	22	3	0	0	0	10	0	0	0	2	1	3	0	1	1	0	0	0	0	0	0	0	4	0	2	1	0	0	0	0	0
0	0	0	0	0	0	0	0	0	0	0	0	0	0	2	0	0	0	0	1	0	0	0	0	0	1	0	0	0	0	0	0	0	0	0	0	0	0	0	0

PLAYING SQUAD

Existing Players		SN	HT	WT	DOB	AGE	POB	Career	Apps	Goals
GOALKEEPERS										
Scott	Davies	1	6'00"	11 00	27/02/1987	24	Blackpool	Morecambe Rel 6/10, Leek T (L) 3/06, Leek T (L) 8/06, Gillingham (Trial) 7/07, Fleetwood 6/10	31	0
Danzelle	St Louis-Hamilton	16	6'05"	14 00	07/05/1990	21	Stevenage	Watford (Yth), Stoke Rel 1/11, Bristol R (3ML) 2/09, Vauxhall Motors (5ML) 7/09, Worcester (L) 2/10, Darlington 1/11, Fleetwood 6/11		
DEFENDERS										
Robert	Atkinson	25	6'01"	12 00	29/04/1987	24	North Ferriby	Barnsley, Scarborough (2ML) 11/05 (SL) 1/06, Halifax (L) 11/06, Rochdale (L) 10/07, Grimsby (SL) 11/07, Grimsby (2ML) 10/08, Grimsby 1/09 Rel 5/11, Fleetwood 6/11		
Shaun	Beeley	2	5'10"	11 04	21/11/1988	22	Stockport	Oldham (Scholar) Rel c/s 07, Southport 8/07, Fleetwood 11/07, Salford C (L) 1/09	38	2
Junior	Brown	12	5'09"	10 12	07/05/1989	22	Crewe	Crewe (5/07) Rel c/s 08, Kidsgrove (2ML) 12/07, Witton (L) 3/08, FC Halifax 8/08, Northwich 8/09, Fleetwood 6/10	21	2
Joe	Camozzi	23			10/07/1992	19		Fleetwood	1	0
Peter	Cavanagh	26	5'09"	11 09	14/10/1981	29	Bootle	Liverpool (Scholar), Accrington 9/01 Rel 8/09, Banned, Fleetwood 3/10	16	0
Jack	Duggan	21			03/01/1993	18		Fleetwood, Clitheroe (L) 8/10, Lancaster (L) 3/11		
Paul	Edwards	3	5'11"	10 12	01/01/1980	31	Manchester	Man C (Ass Sch), Crewe (Yth), Ashton U, Doncaster 2/98 Rel c/s 98, Knutsford, Altrincham 3/01, Leigh RMI (Trial) c/s 01, Swindon 8/01, Wrexham 7/02, Blackpool 7/04 Rel c/s 05, Oldham 8/05, Port Vale 7/07 Rel c/s 09, Wrexham (Trial), Barrow 3/10 Rel 6/10, Inverness Caledonian (Trial) c/s 10, Barrow 8/10, Fleetwood 6/11		
Matty	Flynn	28	6'00"	11 08	10/05/1989	22	Preston	Warrington (Yth), Macclesfield 5/07, Warrington (L) 11/07, Ashton U (L) 2/08, Rochdale (2WL) 8/09 Nominal 8/09 Rel c/s 11, Fleetwood 8/11		
Alan	Goodall	13	5'07"	11 08	02/12/1981	29	Birkenhead	Tranmere (Yth), Cammell Laird, Tranmere (Trial) c/s 01, Bangor C c/s 01, Wrexham (Trial), Rochdale 7/04, Luton 7/07 Rel c/s 08, Chesterfield 8/08 Rel c/s 10, Rochdale 7/10, Newport C (2ML) 11/10, Stockport 1/11 Rel 5/11, Fleetwood 7/11		
Matty	Hughes	24	6'00"		01/04/1992	19	Salford	Rochdale (Scholar), Liverpool (Trial) 1/08, Celtic Undisc 7/08, Fleetwood 7/11		
Paul	Linwood	20	6'02"	12 08	24/10/1983	27	Birkenhead	Tranmere, Wrexham (2ML) 8/05, Chester £15,000 8/06 Rel 5/09, Grimsby 7/09, Fleetwood 6/10	18	0
Steve	McNulty	5	6'01"	13 12	26/09/1983	27	Liverpool	Liverpool Rel 6/03, Chester (Trial) 3/03, Blackpool (Trial) 7/03, Burscough c/s 03, Vauxhall Motors £3,500 2/05, Barrow 6/07, Fleetwood £17,000 6/09	38	1
Liam	Wyn	22						Fleetwood, Lancaster (L) 2/11		
MIDFIELDERS										
Anthony	Barry	4	5'07"	10 00	29/05/1986	25	Liverpool	Everton (Trainee), Coventry, Accrington 4/05, Yeovil Undisc 1/06 Rel c/s 08, Chester 7/08 Rel 1/10, Wrexham 1/10, Fleetwood 1/10	44	2
Keith	Briggs	15	5'10"	11 06	11/12/1981	29	Glossop	Stockport, Norwich £65,000 1/03, Crewe (L) 8/04, Stockport 1/05 Rel 1/08, Shrewsbury 1/08 Rel 1/08, Mansfield 2/08 Rel c/s 08, Stalybridge 7/08, Kidderminster 5/10, Fleetwood £5,000+ 5/11		
Scott	Brown	29	5'07"	10 03	08/05/1985	26	Chester	Everton Rel c/s 04, Port Vale (Trial) 7/04, Bristol C 8/04, Cheltenham (L) 1/07 Perm 1/07, Port Vale (6WL) 11/08 Perm 1/09 Rel c/s 09, Injured, Cheltenham 3/10 Rel c/s 10, Grimsby (Trial) 7/10, Morecambe 9/10 Rel c/s 11, Fleetwood 7/11		
Sean	Clancy	7	5'08"	09 12	16/09/1987	23	Liverpool	Blackpool, Southport 8/06, Burscough (L) 3/07, USA, Shrewsbury NC 8/07, Altrincham 8/07 Rel 9/07, Burscough 9/07, Fleetwood Undisc 3/09	31	3
Stefan	Cox	17						Luton (Yth), Lewes 1/08, Horsham (L) 2/08, C,Palace (Trainee) 7/09, Dulwich 8/09, Sutton U 9/09, Carshalton 11/09, Leyton c/s 10, Dulwich H 1/11, Horsham YMCA 3/11, Tooting & M 7/11, Fleetwood 8/11		
Alex-Ray	Harvey	31	5'07"	10 09	04/04/1990	21	Burnley	Burnley, Fleetwood (SL) 3/11, Fleetwood (L) 8/11	4	1
Jamie	McGuire	18	5'07"	11 01	13/11/1983	27	Birkenhead	Tranmere Rel c/s 04, Northwich (L) 3/03, Northwich (2ML) 11/03, Cammell Laird c/s 04, Stockport (Trial) c/s 06, Droylsden 7/07, Fleetwood 5/09	37	6
Jamie	Milligan	8	5'06"	09 12	03/01/1980	31	Blackpool	Everton, Blackpool 3/01 cc c/s 03, Macclesfield 8/03 Rel 9/03, Leigh RMI 9/03, Droylsden 9/03, Hyde 12/03, Fleetwood 12/05, AFC Fylde 8/10, Fleetwood 11/10	12	0
Nathan	Pond	6			05/01/1985	26		Lancaster, Fleetwood, Bamber Bridge (Trial) 7/05, Kendal T (L) 12/10	23	2

		SN	HT	WT	DOB	AGE	POB	From - To	APPS	GOA
Peter	Till	11	5'11"	11 04	07/09/1985	25	Walsall	Birmingham, Scunthorpe (3ML) 10/05, Boston U (SL) 1/06, L.Orient (L) 10/06, Grimsby (3ML) 11/06 Perm 1/07 Rel c/s 09, Chesterfield (SL) 1/09, Walsall 7/09 Rel c/s 10, York C 6/10, Fleetwood 7/11		
FORWARDS										
Richard	Brodie	9	6'02"	12 13	08/07/1987	24	Gateshead	Whickham, Bolton (Trial), Newcastle Benfield c/s 06, York C 2/07, Barrow (L) 10/08, Crawley 8/10, Fleetwood (SL) 5/11		
George	Donnelly	27	6'02"	13 03	28/05/1988	23	Kirkby	Liverpool (Yth), Skelmersdale, Plymouth Undisc 3/09, Luton (L) 8/09, Stockport (SL) 1/10, Stockport (6ML) 7/10, Fleetwood Undisc 1/11	20	4
Andrew	Mangan	14	5'09"	10 03	30/08/1986	25	Liverpool	Blackpool Rel c/s 05, Hyde U (SL) 3/05, Accrington 8/05 Rel c/s 07, Bury 7/07 Rel c/s 08, Accrington (L) 2/08, Forest Green 5/08, Wrexham Undisc 1/10, Fleetwood 7/11		
Danny	Rowe	30						Preston (Yth), Man Utd (Yth) Undisc, Kendal T c/s 08, Fleetwood 12/10, Droylsden (L) 8/11	5	0
Gareth	Seddon	19	5'11"	12 00	23/05/1980	31	Burnley	Accrington, Atherstone, RAF Codsall, Everton (Trial), Bury 8/01 Rel c/s 04, Northwich (L) 1/03, Rushden & D 5/04 Retired 1/05, Padiham 8/05, Worcester 3/06, Hyde 6/06, Kettering Undisc 7/08, Fleetwood Undisc 9/09	34	10
Magno	Vieira	10	5'09"	11 07	13/02/1985	26	Bahia, Bra	Wigan Rel c/s 05, Northampton (2ML) 1/04, Carlisle (SL) 8/04, Year out, Barnet 7/06 Rel c/s 07, Crawley 6/07 Rel 5/08, Cambridge U (SL) 3/08, Wycombe 6/08 Rel c/s 09, Ebbsfleet 8/09, Fleetwood 7/10	40	22

Loanees		**SN**	**HT**	**WT**	**DOB**	**AGE**	**POB**	**From - To**	**APPS**	**GOA**
(G)Craig	Dootson		6'04"	14 02	23/05/1979	32	Preston	Harrogate T (3ML) 9/10 - Altrincham 1/11 Rel c/s 11, Kendal T 6/11	0	0
(M)Louis	Horne		6'02"	12 07	28/05/1991	20	Bradford	Bradford C 10/10 - FC Halifax (L) 11/10, Rel c/s 11, Hinckley U 8/11	1	0
(M)Jon	Worthington		5'09"	11 05	16/04/1983	28	Dewsbury	Oldham 11/10 - Bradford C 1/11 Rel c/s 11, Mansfield 6/11	3	0
(G)Andy	Coughlin		6'03"	14 02	31/01/1993	18		Tranmere 11/10 -	0	0
(D)Will	Haining		6'00"	11 02	02/10/1982	28	Glasgow	Morecambe 1/11 - Rel c/s 11	7	0
(F)Keigan	Parker		5'07"	10 05	08/06/1982	28	Livingston	Mansfield (SL) 2/11 - Rel c/s 11, Stockport 8/11	13	2

Departures		**SN**	**HT**	**WT**	**DOB**	**AGE**	**POB**	**From - To**	**APPS**	**GOA**
(M)Andy	Burgess		6'02"	11 11	10/08/1981	29	Bedford	Chester FC 10/10 - Corby T 11/10 Rel 1/11, Droylsden 1/11, Woking 3/11, Corby T (Pl/Coach) 5/11		
(F)Mark	Beesley		5'10"	11 10	10/11/1981	29	Burscough	Cambridge U 7/10 - York C (L) 10/10, Altrincham (6WL) 11/10 Perm 1/11 Rel c/s 11, Burscough 7/11	5	0
(M)Ian	Craney		5'10"	12 07	21/07/1982	29	Liverpool	Huddersfield 5/10 - Rel 1/11, Accrington (6WL) 11/10, Accrington 1/11	19	3
(F)Adam	Warlow		6'02"	12 08	03/02/1987	24	Southport	Witton 6/08 - Rel 2/11	3	0
(G)Danny	Hurst				14/11/1980	30		Radcliffe 5 fig 1/07 - Rel 5/11, Barrow 7/11	16	0
(F)Lee	Thorpe		6'00"	11 06	14/12/1975	35	Wolverhampton	Darlington 3/10 - Rel 5/11, AFC Fylde 7/11	19	0
(D)Alan	Wright		5'05"	10 02	28/09/1971	39	Ashton-under-Lyne	Cheltenham 7/09 - Rel 5/11	18	1
(M)John	Miles		5'10"	12 09	28/09/1981	29	Bootle	Accrington 6/10 - Rel 5/11, Droylsden (SL) 3/11, Stockport 7/11	8	0
(M)Simon	Grand		6'00"	10 03	23/02/1984	27	Chorley	Northwich 3/10 - Rel 5/11, Mansfield (3ML) 10/10, Aldershot (SL) 1/11, Southport 6/11	4	0
(D)Sean	Gregan		6'02"	14 00	29/03/1974	37	Guisborough	Oldham (3ML) 10/10 Perm 1/11 - Rel 5/11, Kendal (Trial) 7/11	26	0
(M)Steve	Connors				05/01/1986	25	Liverpool	Witton, Bradford PA 2/09 - Rel 5/11, Droylsden (3ML) 9/10, Altrincham (SL) 2/11, Cambridge U 6/11 Rel 7/11	8	0
(F)Wayne	Curtis		6'00"	12 00	06/03/1980	31	Barrow	Morecambe 7/10 - Rel 5/11, Barrow (SL) 1/11	20	3
(F)Nick	Rogan		5'10"	12 12	15/10/1983	27	Blackpool	Barrow 6/09 - Rel 5/11, Chester FC (L) 8/10, Workington (3ML) 1/11, Altrincham (Trial) 7/11, Corby T 7/11	3	1
(D)Adam	Sumner				04/12/1991	19		Yth - Northwich (3ML) 8/10, Kendal T (SL) 1/11, Northwich 7/11		
(M)Jamie	Mullan		5'06"	11 13	10/02/1988	23	Nottingham	Northwich £5,000 5/09 - Alfreton 7/11	28	1

Caught in action....

Matt Sommer scores one of Forest Green Rovers goals in the game that kept them up last season.

Photo by Bill Wheatcroft

FOREST GREEN ROVERS

Chairman: Dale Vince
Secretary: Colin Peake (T) 07763 831 070 (E) colin.peake@forestgreenroversfc.com
Additional Committee Members:
David Drew, Trevor Horlsey, Philip Catherall, Mike Bullingham, Paul Wheatcroft, Chris Wintle.

Manager: David Hockaday
Programme Editor: Terry Brumpton (E) terrybrumpton@yahoo.co.uk

Back Row (L-R): James Baldwin, Ollie Cleaver, Luke Jones, Reece Styche, Ian Herring, Ross Dyer, Yan Klukowski
Middle: Mick Byrne (Coach), Ian Wrixon (Kit Manager), Callum Henry, Zak Jones, James Bittner, Jon Else, Tim Griggs (Therapist), Kevin Phillips (Coach)
Front Row: Scott Bartlett, Lee Smith, Lee Fowler, Jared Hodgkiss, David Hockaday (Manager), Mike Fowler, Steve Davies, James Norwood

Club Factfile

Founded: 1890 **Nickname:** Rovers
Previous Names: None
Previous Leagues: Stroud & District 1890-1922, Gloucestershire Northern Senior 1922-67, Gloucestershire Senior 1967-73, Hellenic 1973-82, Southern 1982-89.
Club Colours (change): Black & white stripes/black/black (All red)

Ground: The New Lawn, Smiths Way, Nailsworth, Gloucestershire GL6 0FG (T) 01453 834 860
Capacity: 5,141 **Seats:** 2,000 **Covered:** 1,000 **Clubhouse:** Yes **Shop:** Yes

Directions
Nailsworth is on the A46 between Stroud and Bath. At mini roundabout in town turn up Spring Hill towards Forest Green (signposted) and the stadium is at the top of the hill after the second roundabout.
Satnav users should enter GL6 0ET and not the mail post code. Please note on Matchdays there is a Temporary Traffic Order in place on the highway around the stadium. Car parking is available inside the stadium at £3 per vehicle.

Previous Grounds:

Record Attendance: 4,836 v Derby County - FA Cup 3rd Round 03/01/2009
Record Victory: 8-0 v Fareham Town - Southern League Southern Division 1996-97
Record Defeat: 0-7 v Moor Green - Southern League Midland Division 1985-86
Record Goalscorer: Karl Bayliss
Record Appearances: Alex Sykes
Additional Records: Paid £20,000 to Salisbury City for Adrian Randall. Received £35,000 from Nuneaton Borough for Marc McGregor and from Oxford United for Wayne Hatswell.
Senior Honours: FA Vase 1981-82. Hellenic League 1981-82. Gloucestershire Senior Cup 1984-85, 85-86, 86-87. Gloucestershire Senior Professional Cup 1984-85, 86-86, 87-87.

10 YEAR RECORD

01-02	02-03	03-04	04-05	05-06	06-07	07-08	08-09	09-10	10-11
Conf 18	Conf 9	Conf 18	Conf 20	Conf 19	Conf 14	Conf 8	Conf 18	Conf 21	Conf 20

FOREST GREEN ROVERS

No.	Date	Comp	H/A	Opponents	Att:	Result	Goalscorers	Pos
1	Sat-14-Aug	BSP	A	Mansfield Town	2474	L 1-3	Caines 52	24
2	Tue-17-Aug	BSP	H	Wrexham	1216	W 3-0	Styche 20, L Jones 75, Klukowski 80	9
3	Sat-21-Aug	BSP	H	Gateshead	882	D 1-1	Styche 10	8
4	Tue-24-Aug	BSP	A	Hayes & Yeading United	286	W 4-3	Styche 28, Og (Harrison) 47, McDonald 63, Else 90	4
5	Sat-28-Aug	BSP	H	Bath City	1464	D 0-0		6
6	Mon-30-Aug	BSP	A	Crawley Town	1458	L 0-1		11
7	Sat-04-Sep	BSP	H	Southport	1064	D 0-0		13
8	Sat-11-Sep	BSP	A	Darlington	1520	L 0-3		18
9	Sat-18-Sep	BSP	A	Barrow	1246	L 0-3		19
10	Tue-21-Sep	BSP	H	Eastbourne Borough	709	L 3-4	Klukowski 35, Norwood 38, Herring pen 45	19
11	Sat-25-Sep	BSP	H	Kettering Town	779	L 0-2		21
12	Tue-28-Sep	BSP	A	Newport County	2677	L 1-3	Klukowski 15	22
13	Sat-02-Oct	BSP	A	AFC Wimbledon	3204	D 1-1	Watson 5	22
14	Thu-07-Oct	BSP	H	Grimsby Town	1007	D 3-3	Styche 12, Norwood 18, Klukowski 52	23
15	Sat-16-Oct	BSP	H	Histon	741	L 0-1		23
16	Tue-19-Oct	BSP	A	Luton Town	5704	L 1-6	Styche 39	23
17	Sat-30-Oct	BSP	H	York City	792	W 2-1	Caines 4, Styche 58	23
18	Tue-09-Nov	BSP	A	Eastbourne Borough	722	D 0-0		23
19	Sat-13-Nov	BSP	H	Mansfield Town	767	W 2-1	Klukowski pen 9, Styche 49	22
20	Sat-20-Nov	BSP	A	Gateshead	601	D 1-1	Styche 69	20
21	Sat-27-Nov	BSP	H	Rushden & Diamonds	642	D 2-2	McDonald 2 (20, 25)	20
22	Tue-28-Dec	BSP	A	Bath City	1222	W 4-2	Quinn 3, L Jones 37, Styche 45, Dyer 77	17
23	Sat-01-Jan	BSP	A	Kidderminster Harriers	1370	L 0-1		19
24	Mon-03-Jan	BSP	H	Crawley Town	1027	L 0-3		19
25	Sat-08-Jan	BSP	H	Fleetwood Town	762	W 1-0	Guinan 77	18
26	Sat-22-Jan	BSP	A	York City	2468	L 1-2	Styche pen 76	19
27	Tue-25-Jan	BSP	H	Kidderminster Harriers	687	D 1-1	Guinan 20	19
28	Sat-29-Jan	BSP	A	Fleetwood Town	1335	L 0-2		20
29	Sat-05-Feb	BSP	H	Hayes & Yeading United	787	W 1-0	Klukowski pen 47	18
30	Sat-12-Feb	BSP	A	Southport	1006	L 0-4		19
31	Sat-19-Feb	BSP	H	Darlington	851	D 1-1	Guinan 90	19
32	Tue-22-Feb	BSP	A	Grimsby Town	2401	D 1-1	Styche 36	19
33	Sat-26-Feb	BSP	H	Tamworth	681	W 4-0	Guinan 25, Dyer 2 (54, 89), Styche 78	18
34	Tue-01-Mar	BSP	H	Luton Town	1015	L 0-1		19
35	Sat-05-Mar	BSP	A	Wrexham	3386	L 1-2	Dyer 66	19
36	Tue-08-Mar	BSP	A	Rushden & Diamonds	759	D 2-2	Styche 79, Davies 88	18
37	Sat-12-Mar	BSP	H	Barrow	757	L 2-3	Caines 34, Klukowski 63	20
38	Tue-15-Mar	BSP	A	Altrincham	598	L 1-2	Styche 27	20
39	Sat-19-Mar	BSP	H	Newport County	1362	D 0-0		21
40	Sat-26-Mar	BSP	A	Cambridge United	2086	D 1-1	Forbes 81	22
41	Sat-02-Apr	BSP	A	Histon	426	W 3-0	Guinan 20, Dyer 80, Styche 86	21
42	Sat-09-Apr	BSP	H	Altrincham	937	W 1-0	McDonald 71	19
43	Sat-16-Apr	BSP	H	Cambridge United	1092	D 1-1	Matthews 45	20
44	Sat-23-Apr	BSP	A	Kettering Town	891	L 1-2	Forbes 61	20
45	Mon-25-Apr	BSP	H	AFC Wimbledon	1824	D 0-0		19
46	Sat-30-Apr	BSP	A	Tamworth	1717	L 1-2	Somner 52	20

CUPS

No.	Date	Comp	H/A	Opponents	Att:	Result	Goalscorers	Pos
1	Sat-23-Oct	FAC 4Q	H	Maidenhead United	580	W 1-0	Styche 45	
2	Sat-06-Nov	FAC 1	H	Northampton Town	1479	L 0-3		
3	Sat-11-Dec	FAT 1	A	Cambridge United	1045	L 1-2	Klukowski pen 85	
4								

League
Starts
Substitute
Unused Sub

Cups
Starts
Substitute
Unused Sub

Goals (Lg)
Goals (Cup)

BITTNER	L JONES	ARMSTRONG	SMITH	BALDWIN	CAINES	GRIMES	L FOWLER	KLUKOWSKI	STYCHE	NORWOOD	M FOWLER	ELSE	CLEAVER	HERRING	Z JONES	DAVIES	DYER	MCDONALD	BARTLETT	GILL	WATSON	HODGKISS	FLOOD	HEAD	MILLS	ENVER-MARUM	KAMARA	TURK	QUINN	STOKES	GUINAN	GRAY	FORBES	HENRY	ALLEN	HALL	SOMNER	IMUDIA	YOUNG	MATTHEWS				
1	5	6	7	14	20	22	16	19	9	18	8	17	12	4	21	11	10	23	3	24	25	2	26	22	27	29	24	25	28	18	26	22	27	15	30	16	28	23	12	31				
X	X	X	X	X	X	X	X	X	X	X	S	S	S	U	U																													
X	X	X	X	U	X	U	X	X	X	X	X	S		X	U	S																												
X	X	X	X	U	X		X	X	X	X	X	S		X	U	U	U																											
X	X	X	X	S	X	U	X	X	X	X		S		X	U	S		X																										
X	X	U	X	S	X	U	X	X	X		X	X		X		S		X	U																									
X	X	X	S		X	U	X	X	X		X	X		X	U	S		S	X																									
X	X	U	S	U		X	X	X	X		X	X		X	U	S		X		X																								
X	X	U	S		X	U	X	X	X		X	X		X			S	X	S	X																								
X	X	X	X		X	U		X		X	X	S		X		S		U	X	U	X																							
X	X		U		X	S		X	X	X	X	U		X		U		X	X	U	X																							
X	X		S			X		X	X		X	X		X				X	X	S	X	S																						
X	X				S	X	X	X	X	X	X			U	U			X		U	S	X	X																					
X	X			S	X	U	X		X	X	X	S		S	U			X			X	X	X																					
X	X				X	U	X	S	X	X	X	S		S	U			X			X	X	X																					
X	X	U			X			X	X	X	X	S		S	U			X			X	X	X	S																				
X	X	U			X			X	X	X	S				U			X				X	X	S	X	X	S																	
X	X	X			X			X	X		X				U		S		U			X		S	S	X	X	X																
X	X	X			S			X	X		X	S			U		X	X	U			X				S		X	X															
X	X	X			S			X	X		X	S					X	X	U			X		U		S		X	X															
X	X	X			S			X	X		X	U					X	X	U			X		S				X	X	U														
X	X	X			S			X			X	U					X	X	U			X				X		X	X	U	S													
X	X	X			X			X	X			S					X		U			X						X	X	U		X	S	U										
X	X	X			X			X	X								X		U			X						X	X	U	S	X	S		U									
X	X	X			X			X	X						U		S		S			X						X			X	S	X	U	X									
X	X	X			X			S	X								S		U			X						X		U	X	X	X		S	X								
X	X	X			X			X	S						U		X		U			X				S		X			X		X		U	X								
X	X	X			S			X	X						U		X		U			X				S		X			X		X		U	X								
X	X	X			X			X	X								X		U			X				S		X			S	S	X		U	X								
X	X	X			U			X	X								S		U			X				S		X			X	S	X			X	X							
X	X	X			S			U	U								X		S			X				X		X			X	S	X			X	X							
X	X				X			X	X			S			U		X									X				X	S		X	U	S	X	X							
X	X	U			X			X	X						U		X									X		S		X	S	U	X			X	X							
X	X	U			X			S	X						U		X									X		S		X	X	S	X			X	X							
X	X	U			X			X	X								X									S		X		X	S	U	X			X	X	U						
X	X	U			X			S	X								X									S		X		X	X	U	X	S		X	X							
X	X	U			X			X	X						U	S	X		S							S		X		X			X			X	X							
X	X	U			X			S	X							X	X		X							S		U		X			X			S	X		X					
X	X	X			X			U	X							S	X		X									X		X			X			U	X	S	U					
X		X			X				X			U				S	X	24										X		X	X	U	X	U	U	X	X							
X	X	U			X			S	X								X	X										U		X	S	S	X			X	X			X				
X	X	U			X			S	S								X	X										X		X	X	S	X			X	U			X				
X	X	U			X				X								X	X										X		X	U	X	X			X	S	U		S				
X	X	U			X				X						U		X	X										X		X	U	S	X				U	X		X				
X	X	U			X				X								X	X				S				S		X		X	U		X				S	X		X				
X	X	X			X				X			U					X	X				X				U					U	S	X		X		X			S				
X	X	X			X				X								X	X				X				U		U			S	U	X		X		X			S				
U	X	X			X			X	X		X	S		U	X		U		U			X		S	X	X	X	S																
X	X	X			U			X	X		X			U	U		X	U	U			X		S		X	S	X	X															
X	X	X		U	X			X				S		S	U		X		X			X						X	X		X													
46	45	24	6	1	36	4	11	30	41	11	18	5	0	10	0	1	26	22	6	2	6	21	5	0	1	7	1	23	6	14	10	4	23	0	3	16	14	2	1	4	0	0	0	0
0	0	0	4	3	7	1	0	7	2	0	2	12	1	3	0	9	5	1	4	1	1	2	0	4	1	11	1	2	0	0	8	9	2	1	2	1	2	1	0	3	0	0	0	0
0	0	16	1	3	1	8	0	2	1	0	0	5	0	2	21	2	1	1	13	3	0	0	0	1	0	2	0	3	0	5	4	5	0	4	5	1	2	2	1	0	0	0	0	0
2	3	3	0	0	2	0	0	3	2	0	2	0	0	0	1	0	2	0	1	0	0	3	0	0	1	2	1	2	2	0	1	0	0	0	0	0	0	0	0	0	0	0	0	0
0	0	0	0	0	0	0	0	0	0	0	0	2	0	1	0	0	0	0	0	0	0	0	0	2	0	0	1	1	0	0	0	0	0	0	0	0	0	0	0	0	0	0	0	0
1	0	0	0	1	1	0	0	0	0	0	0	0	0	2	2	0	1	1	2	0	0	0	0	0	0	0	0	0	0	0	0	0	0	0	0	0	0	0	0	0	0	0	0	0
0	2	0	0	0	3	0	0	7	15	2	0	1	0	1	0	1	5	4	0	0	1	0	0	0	0	0	0	0	1	0	5	0	2	0	0	0	1	0	0	1	0	0	0	0
0	0	0	0	0	0	0	0	1	1	0	0	0	0	0	0	0	0	0	0	0	0	0	0	0	0	0	0	0	0	0	0	0	0	0	0	0	0	0	0	0	0	0	0	0

PLAYING SQUAD

Existing Players		SN	HT	WT	DOB	AGE	POB	Career	Apps	Goals
GOALKEEPERS										
James	Bittner	1	6'02"	13 01	02/02/1982	29	Devizes	Swindon (Trainee), Fulham 7/00, Salisbury 11/01, Bournemouth 3/02, Torquay (Trial) 7/02, Cheltenham (Trial) 7/02, Chippenham 8/02, Southend (Trial) 7/03, Exeter 8/03 Rel 4/05, Torquay 6/05 Rel 5/06, Woking 12/06 Rel 5/07, Salisbury 6/07, Chippenham (L) 11/07, Forest Green 6/10	46	0
Matt	Bulman	13	6'00"	11 05	14/10/1986	24	Swindon	Swindon Rel 6/06, Salisbury 8/06, Cirencester 7/07, Swindon Supermarine 5/08, Cirencester 6/10, Forest Green 5/11		
DEFENDERS										
Luke	Graham	16	6'03"	12 07	27/04/1986	25	Kettering	Northampton, Aylesbury (L) 12/04, Kettering (2ML) 2/05, Forest Green (SL) 8/05, Kettering 5/06, Kings Lynn (SL) 10/08, Mansfield 5/09, York C (2ML) 11/09 Perm 1/10, Kettering 6/10, Luton (SL) 1/11, Forest Green 7/11		
Callum	Henry	15	6'00"	12 10	10/06/1991	20	Cheltenham	Forest Green, Frome T (L) 9/09, Frome T (L) 8/10, Cirencester (3ML) 9/10, Cirencester (L) 1/11	1	0
Jeffrey	Imudia	12			19/04/1990	21		Arsenal (Yth), Everton (Scholar), Watford (Trial), Southampton, Bournemouth (Trial), Swindon (Trial), Forest Green 9/09 Rel, Injured, Forest Green 2/11, Cirencester (Dual) 3/11	3	0
Chris	Stokes	3	5'07"	10 02	08/03/1991	20	Trowbridge	Bolton Rel c/s 10, Crewe (L) 3/10, Crewe (Trial) 7/10, Walsall (Trial) 7/10, Swindon Supermarine 10/10, Forest Green 11/10	14	0
Chris	Todd	6	6'01"	11 09	22/08/1981	30	Exeter	Swansea Rel c/s 02, Drogheda 8/02, Exeter 1/03, Torquay £7,000 6/07 Rel 5/10, Salisbury (L) 2/09, Salisbury (5WL) 11/09, Newport C (SL) 1/10, Newport C 5/10, Forest Green 5/11		
Jamie	Turley	5	6'01"	14 00	07/04/1990	21		Wycombe Rel c/s 09, Hitchin (L) 2/08, Hendon (2ML) 11/08, Salisbury 7/09, Forest Green 6/11		
MIDFIELDERS										
Chris	Allen	18	5'11"	11 10	03/01/1989	22	Bristol	Swindon Rel c/s 09, Exeter (Trial) c/s 09, Weymouth NC 8/09 Rel 2/10, Swindon Supermarine 2/10, Forest Green (Dual) 12/10 Perm 6/11	5	0
Ali	Bangura	20	5'08"	10 07	24/01/1988	23	Freetown, S Leone	Chertsey (Yth), Watford Rel c/s 09, Brighton (L) 3/09, Blackpool 8/09 Rel c/s 10, Mersin Idmanyurdu (Tur) 7/10, FC Gabala (Azer) 1/11, Forest Green 7/11		
Kieran	Forbes	11	5'04"	11 02	17/08/1990	21	Brent	Watford (Scholar) Rel c/s 08, Wealdstone 8/08, Forest Green 1/11	25	2
Jared	Hodgkiss	2	5'06"	11 02	15/11/1986	24	Stafford	West Brom Rel c/s 09, Aberdeen (5ML) 8/08, Northampton (SL) 3/09, Market Drayton 8/09, Forest Green 10/09	23	0
Curtis	McDonald	17	5'10"	10 08	24/03/1988	23	Cardiff	Cardiff Rel c/s 07, Accrington (L) 11/06, Hereford (Trial) 7/07, Carmarthen 8/07, MKS Swit (Pol) 10/07, Forest Green (Reserves) 11/07, Forest Green 8/08, Newport C 1/11, Forest Green (SL) 3/11, Forest Green 5/11	23	4
James	Rowe	19	5'11"		21/10/1991	19	Oxford	Southampton (Yth), Reading Rel c/s 11, Basingstoke (WE) 10/09, Oxford C (L) 2/10, Lewes (L) 1/11, Forest Green 8/11		
Wayne	Turk	4			21/01/1981	30	Swindon	Oxford U (Trainee), Cirencester, Salisbury 7/00, Newport C (SL) 11/08 Perm 4/09, Forest Green (2ML) 10/10 Perm 1/11	25	0
FORWARDS										
Charlie	Griffin	10	6'00"	12 07	25/06/1979	32	Bath	Bristol R (Ass Sch), Melksham, Chippenham T 7/98, Swindon £10,000 1/99, Yeovil (L) 10/99, Woking (L) 10/00 £15,000 11/00, Havant (L) 11/01, Chippenham T (L) 2/02, Chippenham 9/02, Forest Green 5/04, Wycombe 5/05, Forest Green (5ML) 7/06, Newport C 2/07 Rel 6/08, Salisbury NC 8/08, Stevenage 5/09 Rel c/s 11, Newport C (SL) 1/11, Forest Green 6/11		
Yan	Klukowski	8	6'00"	14 02	01/01/1987	24	Chippenham	Chippenham (Yth), Bath C, Reading (Trial) 4/05, Central Connecticut State University (USA) 8/05, Chippenham (L) 12/06, Ottawa Fury (Can), Cape Cod Crusaders (USA), Western Mass Pioneers (USA) 4/09, Carlisle (Trial) 7/09, Swindon (Trial) 8/09, Chippenham 8/09, Larkhall Ath, Forest Green 8/10	37	7
Robbie	Matthews	21			02/03/1982	29	Wiltshire	Bournemouth (Yth), Swindon (Yth), Salisbury, Bemerton Heath Harlequins 11/01, Eastleigh c/s 02, Southampton (Trial), Bristol R (Trial) 2/03, Salisbury 9/04, Havant & W (6WL) 11/08, Crawley (SL) 1/09, Kidderminster 8/09 Rel 7/10, Newport C 7/10, Forest Green (SL) 3/11, Forest Green (L) 8/11	7	1
James	Norwood	7	5'09"	11 04	05/09/1990	20	Eastbourne	Brighton (Yth), C. Palace (Yth), Eastbourne T 7/08, Exeter 7/09 Rel c/s 11, Sutton U (2ML) 11/09, Forest Green (2ML) 8/10, Eastbourne B (L) 1/11, Forest Green 6/11	11	2
Reece	Styche	9	6'01"	12 12	03/05/1989	22	Birmingham	Hednesford, Bromsgrove (L) 9/08, Chasetown 10/09, Forest Green 1/10	43	15

Loanees			HT	WT	DOB	AGE	POB	From - To	APPS	GOA
(D)Jamie	Grimes		6'02"	13 00	22/12/1990	20	Nottingham	Swansea (2ML) 8/10 - Rel c/s 11	5	0
(F)Ben	Watson		5'10"	11 02	06/12/1985	25	Shoreham	Exeter 9/10 - Bath C (L) 1/11, Rel 5/11, Eastbourne B 6/11	7	1
(M)Chris	Flood		5'10"		28/11/1989	21		Crawley 9/10 - Dorchester (L) 1/11 Perm 2/11	5	0
(F)Liam	Head		6'01"	13 05	26/01/1992	19	Bovey	Plymouth 10/10 - Rel c/s 11	4	0
(M)Gary	Mills		5'09"	11 06	20/05/1981	30	Sheppey	Mansfield 10/10 - Rel 1/11, Rushden & D 1/11, Bath C 5/11	2	0
(D)Adam	Quinn		6'02"	13 00	02/06/1983	28	Sheffield	Crawley (2ML) 11/10 - Darlington £25,000 1/11, Barrow (3ML) 8/11	6	1
(D)Danny	Hall		6'02"	12 07	14/11/1983	27	Ashton-under-Lyne	Crawley (2ML) 1/11 - Rel 5/11, Stockport 8/11	17	0
(M)Lewis	Young		5'10"	11 02	27/09/1989	21	Stevenage	Burton 3/11 - Rel 5/11, Northampton 7/11	1	0

Departures			HT	WT	DOB	AGE	POB	From - To	APPS	GOA
(D)Lee	Ayres		6'02"	12 06	28/08/1982	29	Birmingham	Redditch 12/08 - Halesowen T 8/10, Redditch 10/10, Solihull Moors 2/11		
(M)Ben	Gill		6'00"	11 11	09/10/1987	23	Harrow	Interblock 9/10 - Rel 10/10, Wealdstone 11/10	3	0
(D)James	Baldwin		6'00"	13 05	14/05/1989	22	York	Gloucester 8/10 - Cinderford (L) 11/10 Perm	4	0
(M)Malvin	Kamara		5'11"	13 00	17/11/1983	27	Southwark	ex Ossett T 10/10 - Rel 12/10, Stafford R 12/10, Tamworth 1/11 Rel 3/11, Farnborough 3/11	2	0
(M)Lee	Fowler		5'07"	10 00	10/06/1983	28	Cardiff	Halesowen T 6/10 - Rel 12/10, Wrexham 1/11	11	0
(M)Michael	Fowler		5'11"	11 13	22/08/1981	29	Cardiff	Salisbury 7/09 - Newport C 1/11, Weymouth NC 3/11	20	0
(F)Jacob	Erskine		6'01"	14 00	13/01/1989	22	Lambeth	Concord R 1/11 - Swindon Supermarine (L) 1/11, Ebbsfleet 2/11, Bromley (Trial) 7/11, Hampton & R 8/11		
(M)Ollie	Cleaver		6'00"	13 00	25/01/1992	19	Enfield	Cheshunt 8/10 - Rel, Histon 3/11	1	0
(M)Ian	Herring		6'01"	11 12	14/02/1984	27	Swindon	Northwich 6/10 - Eastleigh (L) 2/11 Perm 3/11 Rel 5/11	13	1
(M)Craig	Armstrong		5'11"	12 09	23/05/1975	36	South Shields	Mansfield (SL) 2/10, (Pl/Coach) 6/10 - Rel 5/11, Eastwood T (Jt Pl/Man) 5/11	24	0
(F)Stephen	Guinan		6'01"	13 02	24/12/1975	35	Birmingham	Northampton (6WL) 11/10 Perm 1/11 - Rel 5/11, Kidderminster 5/11	18	5
(M)Steve	Davies		5'09"	12 03	27/04/1989	22	Swansea	Cirencester 7/09 - Rel 5/11, Gloucester (3ML) 9/10, Gloucester 5/11	10	1
(G)Zak	Jones		5'10"	12 08	24/11/1988	22	Darwen	Blackburn 8/10 - Rel 5/11	0	0
(D)Jon	Else		5'10"	10 11	08/06/1989	22	Blackpool	Clevedon T - Rel 5/11, Stourport (L) 3/09, Highworth T 7/11	17	1
(F)Lee	Smith		5'06"	13 02	08/09/1983	27	Coney Hill	Gloucester 6/10 - Rel 5/11, Gloucester (3ML) 9/10, AFC Telford (L) 1/11, Chippenham (L) 2/11, Weymouth (SL) 3/11, Nuneaton T 7/11	10	0
(D)Luke	Jones		5'09"	11 09	10/04/1987	24	Blackburn	Mansfield 6/10 - Kidderminster 5/11	45	2
(D)Gavin	Caines		6'01"	12 00	20/09/1983	27	Birmingham	Kidderminster - 8/10 Rel 6/11, Eastwood T 8/11	43	3
(F)Ross	Dyer				12/05/1988	23	Stafford	Hednesford 5/10 - Mansfield 6/11	31	5
(M)Matt	Somner		6'00"	13 02	08/12/1982	28	Isleworth	Mansfield 1/11 - Lewes 7/11	16	1
(F)Liam	Enver-Marum		6'03"	12 00	17/11/1987	24	London	Crawley (L) 10/10 Perm 1/11 - Ebbsfleet 7/11	18	0
(F)Bradley	Gray		5'11"	11 07	05/07/1990	21	Swindon	Salisbury NC 12/10 - Swindon Supermarine 7/11	13	0
(D)Scott	Bartlett	14	5'10"	11 00	30/05/1979	31	Salisbury	Bath C 6/10 - Retired 8/11	10	0

Caught in action....

The celebrations begin, Forest Green maintain their Premier Division status for another year!

Photo by Bill Wheatcroft

GATESHEAD

Chairman: Graham Wood
Secretary: Mike Coulson (T) 07912 869 943 (E) mike.coulson@gateshead-fc.com
Additional Committee Members:
Brian Waites, Graham Wood.

Manager: Ian Bogie
Programme Editor: Jeff Bowron (E) jeffbowron@blueyonder.co.uk

Club Factfile

Founded: 1930 **Nickname:** Tynesiders, The Heed
Previous Names: Gateshead Town, Gateshead United.
Previous Leagues: Football League 1930-60, Northern Counties east 1960-62, North Regional 1962-68, Northern Premier 1968-70, 73-83, 85-86, 87-90, Wearside 1970-71, Midland 1971-72, Alliance/Conf 1983-85, 86-87, 90-98
Club Colours (change): White/black/black & white (Maroon/maroon/maroon & sky blue)

Ground: International Stadium, Neilson Road, Gateshead NE10 0EF (T) 0191 478 3883
Capacity: 11,795 **Seats:** 11,795 **Covered:** 3,300 **Clubhouse:** Yes **Shop:** Yes

Directions
A1(M) to Washington Services, then A194(M) to first roundabout.
Turn left onto A184 and the ground is situated approximately 3 miles on the left.

Previous Grounds: Redheugh Park 1930-71

Record Attendance: 11,750 v Newcastle United - Friendly 07/08/95
Record Victory: 8-0 v Netherfield - Northern Premier League
Record Defeat: 0-9 v Sutton United - Conference 22/09/90
Record Goalscorer: Paul Thompson - 130
Record Appearances: Simon Smith - 501 (1985-94)
Additional Records: Record transfer fee paid; £9,000 - Paul Cavell, Dagenham & Redbridge 1994
Record transfer fee received; £150,000 Lee Novak, Huddersfield Town 2009
Senior Honours: Northern Premier League 1982-83, 85-86, Northern Premier League play-off 2007-8, Conference North play-off 2008-9, Durham Challenge Cup 2010-11

10 YEAR RECORD

01-02	02-03	03-04	04-05	05-06	06-07	07-08	08-09	09-10	10-11
NP P 14	NP P 21	NP P 6	NP P 17	NP P 17	NP P 9	NP P 3	Conf N 2	Conf 20	Conf 15

GATESHEAD

No.	Date	Comp	H/A	Opponents	Att:	Result	Goalscorers	Pos
1	Sat-14-Aug	BSP	H	Kettering Town	639	D 0-0		13
2	Tue-17-Aug	BSP	A	Barrow	1440	W 3-1	Brittain 2 (34, pen 83), Turnbull 70	5
3	Sat-21-Aug	BSP	A	Forest Green Rovers	882	D 1-1	Mulligan 66	6
4	Tue-24-Aug	BSP	H	Fleetwood Town	623	L 0-2		13
5	Sat-28-Aug	BSP	A	Darlington	2233	L 0-2		19
6	Sat-04-Sep	BSP	A	Cambridge United	2637	L 0-5		23
7	Tue-07-Sep	BSP	H	Southport	471	W 1-0	Nelthorpe 90	19
8	Sat-11-Sep	BSP	H	Altrincham	539	W 2-0	Gate 38, Shaw 82	12
9	Sat-18-Sep	BSP	A	Crawley Town	1412	L 1-2	Shaw 51	17
10	Tue-21-Sep	BSP	H	Grimsby Town	863	D 0-0		18
11	Sat-25-Sep	BSP	H	Luton Town	1075	W 1-0	Shaw 7	12
12	Tue-28-Sep	BSP	A	Histon	285	W 3-1	Mulligan 7, Nelthorpe 2 (35, 89)	10
13	Sat-02-Oct	BSP	H	Mansfield Town	1046	D 1-1	Kay 80	11
14	Tue-05-Oct	BSP	A	Kidderminster Harriers	937	L 1-2	Brittain pen 8	13
15	Sat-09-Oct	BSP	H	Tamworth	807	W 3-1	Shaw 38, Gate 39, Ferrell 90	9
16	Sat-16-Oct	BSP	A	AFC Wimbledon	3330	L 0-1		11
17	Sat-30-Oct	BSP	H	Cambridge United	1083	L 2-3	Shaw 2 (29, 54)	13
18	Tue-09-Nov	BSP	A	Fleetwood Town	1011	D 0-0		13
19	Sat-13-Nov	BSP	A	Tamworth	802	D 1-1	Mulligan 63	13
20	Sat-20-Nov	BSP	H	Forest Green Rovers	601	D 1-1	Mulligan 28	13
21	Sat-01-Jan	BSP	H	York City	1231	L 0-3		17
22	Mon-03-Jan	BSP	A	Southport	904	L 1-5	Brittain 45	17
23	Sat-08-Jan	BSP	H	Kidderminster Harriers	508	D 2-2	Liddle 16, Shaw 73	17
24	Tue-18-Jan	BSP	H	Barrow	518	W 3-0	Shaw 22, Brittain pen 75, Fisher 90	16
25	Sat-22-Jan	BSP	A	Luton Town	5958	D 2-2	Gate 10, Og (Howells) 16	17
26	Fri-28-Jan	BSP	H	AFC Wimbledon	922	L 0-2		17
27	Tue-01-Feb	BSP	A	Eastbourne Borough	612	W 3-0	Brittain 2 (15, 17), Fisher 82	17
28	Sat-12-Feb	BSP	A	Rushden & Diamonds	874	W 2-0	Og (Prosser) 30, Shaw 87	14
29	Tue-15-Feb	BSP	H	Hayes & Yeading United	463	W 1-0	Fisher 31	14
30	Sat-19-Feb	BSP	A	Wrexham	3078	W 7-2	Shaw 3 (1, 72, 77), Fisher 2 (14, 33), Brittain pen 18, Nelthorpe 43	13
31	Tue-22-Feb	BSP	A	Kettering Town	812	W 4-1	Turnbull 44, Shaw 2 (45, 53), Clark 77	10
32	Tue-01-Mar	BSP	A	York City	2290	L 1-2	Curtis 50	12
33	Sat-05-Mar	BSP	A	Altrincham	765	D 1-1	Winn 57	13
34	Tue-08-Mar	BSP	H	Darlington	1204	D 2-2	Brittain pen 71, Clark 90	12
35	Tue-22-Mar	BSP	A	Grimsby Town	2517	D 2-2	Offiong 86, Fisher 90	14
36	Sat-26-Mar	BSP	H	Crawley Town	751	D 0-0		15
37	Tue-29-Mar	BSP	A	Newport County	1027	L 1-2	Fisher 69	15
38	Sat-02-Apr	BSP	A	Bath City	952	L 0-1		15
39	Mon-04-Apr	BSP	H	Bath City	522	D 1-1	Fisher 14	15
40	Sat-09-Apr	BSP	H	Histon	567	W 2-0	Gillies 2, Shaw 73	13
41	Tue-12-Apr	BSP	H	Eastbourne Borough	617	W 3-0	Shaw 51, Ferrell 2 (59, 90)	11
42	Sat-16-Apr	BSP	H	Rushden & Diamonds	701	D 2-2	Fisher 33, Shaw 42	12
43	Tue-19-Apr	BSP	A	Hayes & Yeading United	502	L 1-3	Winn 50	13
44	Sat-23-Apr	BSP	H	Wrexham	743	L 0-1		14
45	Mon-25-Apr	BSP	A	Mansfield Town	1749	L 2-3	Mulligan 2 (19, 40)	14
46	Sat-30-Apr	BSP	H	Newport County	824	L 1-7	Mulligan 24	15

CUPS

No.	Date	Comp	H/A	Opponents	Att:	Result	Goalscorers
1	Sat-23-Oct	FAC 4Q	A	Altrincham	797	W 2-0	Fisher 76, Turnbull 87
2	Sat-06-Nov	FAC 1	A	Notts County	3235	L 0-2	
3	Tue-14-Dec	FAT 1	H	Southport	233	D 2-2	Shaw 71, White 74
4	Sat-15-Jan	FAT 2	H	Hampton & Richmond Borough	336	W 6-0	Shaw 3 (37, 48, 61), Fisher 75, Edmundsson 87, Wake 89
5	Sat-05-Feb	FAT 3	H	Dartford	501	W 3-0	Turnbull 42, Wake 86, Gate 90
6	Sat-26-Feb	FAT 4	A	Blyth Spartans	2719	W 2-0	Og (Swailes) 14, Curtis 19
7	Sat-12-Mar	FAT SF 1	A	Darlington	4243	L 2-3	Fisher 20, Rundle 44
8	Sat-19-Mar	FAT SF 2	H	Darlington	5156	D 0-0	

League
Starts
Substitute
Unused Sub

Cups
Starts
Substitute
Unused Sub
Goals (Lg)
Goals (Cup)

DEASY	BAXTER	HECKINGBOTTOM	CLARK	JONES	GATE	BRITTAIN	TURNBULL	FERRELL	MARWOOD	MULLIGAN	NELTHORPE	FISHER	ALLAN	COOK	BROWN	FRANCIS	WAKE	CURTIS	SHAW	GILLIES	KAY	CLARKE	FARMAN	WINN	PORTER	WHITE	TAVERNIER	LIDDLE	EDMUNDSSON	RUNDLE	OFFIONG	BAPTISTE	BALL												
1	2	3	6	15	4	7	8	12	21	19	11	18	10	20	23	14	17	5	9	22	24	25	13	14	20	25	27	24	26	23	25	16													
X	X	X	X	X	X	X	X	X	X	X	S	S	U	U	U																														
X	X	X	X	X	X	X	X	X	X	X	S	S	S	U	U																														
X	X	X	X	X	X	X	X	X	X	X	S	S		U	U	U																													
X	X	X	X	X	X	S	X	U	X	X	X	S		U	U	X																													
X	X	X	X	X	X	X	X	S	X	X	S	X		U	U		S																												
X	X	X	X	U	X	X	X	X			X	S		U			S	X	X	S																									
X	S	X	X	X	X	X	X	U			X	X		U			S	X	X	S																									
X	U	X	X	X	X	X	X	S		X	X	S		U				X	X	S																									
X	U	X	X	X	X	X	X	S		X	X	S		U				X	X	S																									
X	U	X	X	X	X	X	X	U	S	X	X	S		U				X	X																										
X	S	X	X	X	X	X	X	S		X	X			U			S	X	X	U																									
X	X	X	X		X	X	X	U	U	X	X	S		U	U			X	X																										
X	U	X	X		X	X	X	U	U	X	X	U		U				X	X		X																								
X	U	X	X		X	X	X	S	S	X	X	S		U				X	X		X																								
X	U	X	X		X	X	X	X	S		X			U			U	X	X	U	X																								
X	U	X	X		X	X	X	X			X	S		U				X	X	S	X	S																							
X	X		X	U	X	X	X	U	S	X	X	S						X	X		X		U																						
X	X		X	U	X	X	X	U		S	X	S						X	X		X		S	X																					
	X		X	S	X	X	X	U		S	X						S	X	X		X		X	X	U																				
	X		X	U	X	S	X	U		X	X						U		X		X		X	X	U	X																			
U	X	X	X	U		X	X	S		X	X	S	S						X				X	X		X																			
U	X		X	X	X	X	X	S	X	X		S					S	X	X				X			U																			
X	U		X		X	X	X		S	S		U						X	X				U			X	X	X	X																
X	U		X		X	X	X			X		S					U	X	X	S			U				X	X	X																
X	S		X		X	X	X			X		S					S	X	X	U			U				X	X	X																
X	U			X	X	X	X			X	S	S						X	X	U			U				X	X	X																
X	U		X		X	X	X			X	S	S						X	X	S			U				X	X	X																
X	U		X	S	X	X	X				X	X					S	X	X	S			U				X	X																	
X	U		X		X	X	X				X	X					S	X	X	S			U	U			X	X																	
X	U		X		X	X	X				X	X					S	X	X	S			U	S			X	X																	
X	S		X		X	X	X				X	X					S	X	X	S			U	U			X	X																	
X	U		X		X		X				X	X					S	X	X	U			U	S			X	X		X															
X	U		X			X	X				S	S						X	X	S			U	X			X	X		X	X														
X	U		X	X		X	X		S			X								U			U	X			X	X		X	X	S													
X			X	U	X	X	X		S		S	X						X	X				U				X	X		X	S														
X	X		X	S	X	X	X		X	S		X						X	X				U					X		U	S														
X	X		X	X	X	U	X		X	X	S	S							S				U					X		X	X														
X	X	X	X	U		X	X		X			X	U						X	X			U					X			S	S													
X	X	X	X	U		X	X	X	S			X	U						X	S			U					X			X														
X	X	U	X			X	X	X	S			X						X	X	X			U	S				X			S														
X	X	U	X				X	X	X	S		X						X	X	X			U	S				X		U															
X	X	U	X			X	X	X	U	S		X						X	X				U	S				X		X															
X	X	U	X				X	X	S	S		X						X	X	S			U	X				X			X														
X	X	U	X				X	U	S	X	X	X						X					U	X				X		X	S														
U	X	X	X	S		X	X	X		X	X	X						X		S			X							U	S														
X	X	X		S		X	X	X		X	S	X	S					X		X				U				X		U															
X	X		X		X	X	X	X	S	X	X	S		U	U		U	X		U	X	U																							
X	X		X	U	X	X		X	U	X	X	S			U		U	X	X		X		U	S																					
U	X	X	X	S	X	X	X	X		X	S		U				U		X				X			X																			
X	S		X		X	X	X		U			X					S	X	X	S			U				X	X	X																
X	U		X		X	X	X			X	X	S					S	X	X	S			U				X	X																	
X	S		X		X	X	X			X	X						S	X	X	U			U	S			X	X																	
	U		X	X	X	X	X		S		S	X							X				X				X	X		X	S		U												
X			X	U	X	X	X		S		S	X						X	X				U				X	X		X	U														
41	24	21	44	14	34	39	46	13	10	24	24	19	0	0	0	1	0	35	36	4	8	0	5	8	0	3	13	23	5	7	5	0	0	0	0	0	0	0	0	0	0	0	0	0	0
0	4	0	0	5	0	2	0	7	11	7	10	21	3	0	0	0	12	0	1	15	0	1	1	5	0	0	0	0	0	0	6	2	0	0	0	0	0	0	0	0	0	0	0	0	0
3	17	5	0	8	0	1	0	10	3	0	0	2	3	16	6	1	3	0	0	6	0	0	23	3	2	1	0	0	0	4	0	0	0	0	0	0	0	0	0	0	0	0	0	0	0
6	3	1	8	1	8	8	7	3	0	3	4	5	0	0	0	0	0	6	7	0	2	0	2	0	0	1	5	5	1	2	0	0	0	0	0	0	0	0	0	0	0	0	0	0	0
0	2	0	0	1	0	0	0	0	3	0	3	2	1	0	0	0	3	0	0	2	0	0	0	2	0	0	0	0	0	0	1	0	0	0	0	0	0	0	0	0	0	0	0	0	0
1	2	0	0	2	0	0	0	0	2	0	0	0	1	1	2	0	3	0	0	2	0	1	5	0	0	0	0	0	0	0	1	0	1	0	0	0	0	0	0	0	0	0	0	0	0
0	0	0	2	0	3	9	2	3	0	7	4	9	0	0	0	0	0	1	17	1	1	0	0	2	0	0	0	1	0	0	1	0	0	0	0	0	0	0	0	0	0	0	0	0	0
0	0	0	0	0	1	0	2	0	0	0	0	3	0	0	0	0	2	1	4	0	0	0	0	0	0	1	0	0	1	1	0	0	0	0	0	0	0	0	0	0	0	0	0	0	0

PLAYING SQUAD

Existing Players		SN	HT	WT	DOB	AGE	POB	Career	Apps	Goals
GOALKEEPERS										
Tim	Deasy	1	6'01"	13 05	01/10/1985	25	Salford	Macclesfield Rel c/s 06, Stockport 8/06 Rel c/s 07, Barrow 8/07 Rel 5/10, Gateshead 8/10	41	0
Paul	Farman	13			02/11/1989	21	North Shields	Newcastle (Scholar). Blyth c/s 08, Mansfield (Trial) 1/09, Newcastle Blue Star (Dual) 1/09, Gateshead 6/09	6	0
DEFENDERS										
Craig	Baxter	14	5'10"	09 10	27/09/1986	24	Newcastle	Newcastle Rel c/s 06, Gateshead c/s 06	28	0
Chris	Carruthers	20	5'10"	12 03	19/08/1983	28	Kettering	Northampton, Hornchurch (L) 11/04, Kettering (L) 1/05, Bristol R (SL) 3/05, Bristol R Undisc 7/05 Rel c/s 08, Oxford U 7/08 Rel 1/10, Crawley (L) 8/09, York C (3ML) 9/09, York C 1/10 Rel 6/11, Gateshead 7/11		
Ben	Clark	6	6'02"	13 00	24/01/1983	28	Consett	Man Utd (Trainee), Sunderland, Hartlepool Undisc 10/04 Rel c/s 10, Gateshead 7/10	44	2
James	Curtis	5	6'5"	13.04	13/04/1982	29	Sunderland	Kenneck Ryhope CA, Washington, Gateshead 6/03	35	1
Ewan	Moyes	21			30/03/1990	21		Hibernian Rel c/s 11, Livingston (4ML) 8/09, Arbroath (SL) 1/10, Brechin (SL) 8/10, Crewe (Trial) 4/11 Gateshead 7/11		
Eddie Odhiambo (Was Anaclet)		2	5'09"	10 00	31/08/1985	26	Arusha, Tanzania	Southampton Rel 5/06, Chester (L) 12/04, Tamworth (3ML) 11/05, Oxford U 7/06, Stevenage 7/08, Newport C 7/10 Rel c/s 11, Gateshead 6/11 Sam		
Rents	3		5'09" 11 0322/06/1987 24			Brighton		Brighton Rel 5/08, Worthing (L) 11/05, Crawley 5/08 Rel 5/11, Hayes & Yeading (SL) 3/11, Gateshead 5/11		
MIDFIELDERS										
Rob	Briggs	22			29/12/1991	19		Gateshead		
Martin	Brittain	7	5'08"	10 07	29/12/1984	26	Newcastle	Newcastle Rel c/s 06, Hull C (Trial) 7/06, Brighton (Trial) 7/06, Kilmarnock (Trial) 8/06, Ipswich 8/06 Rel c/s 07, Yeovil (2ML) 10/06, Yeovil (SL) 1/07, Carlisle 8/07 Rel 8/07, Scunthorpe 12/07 Rel 12/07, Walsall 1/08 Rel c/s 08, Toronto FC (Trial) 3/08, Kidderminster 8/08 Rel 5/09, Gateshead 6/09	41	9
Michael	Cummins	11	6'00"	12 06	01/06/1978	33	Dublin	Middlesbrough, Port Vale 3/00 Rel c/s 06, Darlington 7/06 Rel c/s 08, Rotherham 5/08 Rel c/s 10, Grimsby 6/10 Rel 5/11, Gateshead 5/11		
Kris	Gate	4	5'07"	10 03	01/01/1985	26	Newcastle	Newcastle Rel c/s 07, Grimsby (Trial) 11/05, Gateshead 9/07	34	3
Josh	Gilles	16	5'10"	11.6	12/06/1990	21	Sunderland	Sunderland Nissan, Newcastle Blue Star 1/09, Blyth 7/09, Whitley Bay 3/10, Gateshead 6/10	19	1
James	Marwood	17	5'09"	11 05	21/05/1990	21	St Albans	Newcastle (Scholar) Rel c/s 09, Carlisle (Trial) 7/09, Blyth 11/09, Team Northumbria 2/10, Gateshead 6/10	21	0
Chris	Moore	19	5'08"	11 13	17/01/1984	27	Newcastle	Newcastle (Jun), Bishop Auckland c/s 03, Whitley Bay 12/04 Rel c/s 05, Working Abroad, Whitley Bay 1/08, Darlington 3/10 Rel 5/11, Spennymoor (L) 9/10, Gateshead 7/11		
Kyle	Nix	18	5'06"	09 10	21/01/1986	25	Sydney, Aust	Man Utd (Trainee), Aston Villa 7/02 Rel c/s 05, Sheff Utd 7/05 Rel c/s 06, Barnsley (SL) 2/06, Scunthorpe (Trial) 7/06, Buxton 11/06, Parkgate Rel c/s 07, Bradford C 7/07 Rel c/s 09, Mansfield 7/09 Rel 5/11, Sparta Rotterdam (Holl) (Trial) 7/10, Gateshead 7/11		
Phil	Turnbull	8	5'11"	11 08	07/01/1987	24	South Shields	Hartlepool Rel c/s 07, Gateshead (L) 12/05, Blyth (L) 3/07, York 7/07, Gateshead 2/08	46	2

FORWARDS		SN	HT	WT	DOB	AGE	POB	From - To	APPS	GOA
Nathan	Fisher	12	5'10"	11.07	06/07/1989	22	Northallerton	Middlesbrough (Scholar), Gretna Rel c/s 08, York C (Trial) 7/08, Durham C, Chester-le-Street 12/08, Consett c/s 09, Chester-le-Street, Gateshead 6/10	40	9
Gary	Mulligan	15	6'01"	12 03	23/04/1985	26	Dublin	Wolves, Rushden & D (3ML) 10/04, Sheff Utd 7/05 Rel c/s 06, Port Vale (3ML) 9/05, Gillingham (L) 1/06, Gillingham (SL) 3/06, Gillingham 7/06 Rel c/s 09, Northampton 7/09 Rel c/s 10, Cheltenham (Trial) 7/10, Gateshead 8/10	31	7
Yemi	Odubade	10	5'07"	11 07	04/07/1984	27	Lagos	Eastbourne T, Yeovil 7/04, Eastbourne B 2/05, Oxford U 1/06 Rel 4/09, Stevenage 5/09 Rel c/s 11, Newport C (SL) 1/11, Gateshead 6/11		
Jon	Shaw	9	6'00"	13 01	10/11/1983	27	Sheffield	Sheff Wed Rel 11/04, York (2ML) 11/03, Burton 11/04, Cheltenham (Trial) 11/04, Halifax 8/07, Rochdale £60,000 7/08 Rel 1/10, Crawley (SL) 1/09, Barrow (3ML) 8/09, Gateshead (5WL) 11/09, Mansfield 1/10 Rel 5/10, Gateshead 5/10	37	17

Loanees		SN	HT	WT	DOB	AGE	POB	From - To	APPS	GOA
(D)Michael	Kay		6'00"	11 05	12/09/1989	21	Consett	Sunderland (2ML) 9/10 - Tranmere (SL) 1/11	8	1
(D)Michael	Liddle		5'08"	11 00	25/12/1989	21	London	Sunderland (SL) 1/11 -	23	1
(D)James	Tavernier		5'09"	11 00	31/10/1991	19	Bradford	Newcastle (2ML) 1/11 - Carlisle (L) 8/11	13	0
(F)Joan Simun	Edmundsson				26/07/1991	20	Toftir, Faroes	Newcastle 1/11 -	5	0
(M)Adam	Rundle		5'08"	11 02	08/07/1984	27	Durham	Morecambe (SL) 2/11 - Darlington 7/11	7	0

Departures		SN	HT	WT	DOB	AGE	POB	From - To	APPS	GOA
(M)Alex	Francis		6'02"	12 08	07/01/1990	21	Gateshead	Newcastle (Scholar) 6/08 - Rel 10/10, Spennymoor 10/10	1	0
(G)Mark	Cook		6'00"	12 01	07/09/1988	22	North Shields	Hartlepool 8/10 - Harrogate T 10/10	0	0
(M)Shane	Clarke		6'01"	13 03	07/11/1987	23	Lincoln	ex Lincoln C 10/10 - Rel 11/10, Boston U 11/10, Chicago Fire (USA) (Trial) 2/11, Gainsborough 6/11	1	0
(D)David	Brown		5'08"		19/02/1991	20		Sunderland 8/10 - Rel 2/11	0	0
(D)Alan	White		6'01"	13 02	22/03/1976	35	Darlington	Stalybridge 11/10 - Rel 2/11, Blyth 2/11 Rel c/s 11	3	0
(F)Brian	Wake		6'00"	11 02	13/08/1982	29	Stockton	Greenock Morton 1/10 - Ostersunds FK (Swe) 3/11	12	0
(D)Paul	Heckingbottom		6'00"	12 05	17/07/1977	34	Barnsley	Mansfield (SL) 2/10 - Perm 5/10 Rel 5/11, Harrogate T 6/11	21	0
(D)Carl	Jones		6'01"	12 02	03/09/1986	24	Sunderland	York C (L) 1/08 Perm 1/08 - Rel 5/11, Blyth 6/11	19	0
(M)Steve	Baptiste				12/10/1990	20		Birtley T 2/09 - Rel 5/11, Bedlington (L) 1/11, Shildon 6/11	2	0
(M)Andy	Ferrell		5'08"	11 05	09/01/1984	27	Newcastle	York C 2/10 - Rel 5/11, Barrow (L) 2/11, Barrow 6/11	20	3
(M)Craig	Nelthorpe		5'10"	11 00	10/06/1987	24	Doncaster	York C 6/10 - Rel 5/11, Gainsborough 6/11	34	4
(F)Jonny	Allan		6'00"	11 03	24/05/1983	28	Penrith	Northwich 5/10 - Rel 5/11, Harrogate T 5/11	3	0
(F)Richard	Offiong		5'11"	12 02	17/12/1983	27	South Shields	Carlisle 3/11 - Rel 5/11	11	1
(G)Chris	Porter	20	6'02"	12 03	10/11/1979	31	Middlesbrough	Billingham Syn 11/10 - Rel c/s 11	0	0
(M)Ashley	Winn	18	5'11"	11 02	01/12/1985	25	Stockton	Southport (2ML) 11/10 £2,500 1/11 - Farnborough 7/11	13	2
(G)Jon	Ball				03/12/1992	18	Whitley Bay	Carlisle (Scholar) 3/11 -	0	0

Caught in action....

Lee Ridley in possession during Grimsby's FA Trophy Second Round tie.

Photo by Bill Wheatcroft

GRIMSBY TOWN

Chairman: John Fenty
Secretary: Ian Fleming (T) 07711 188 542 (E) ian@gtfc.co.uk
Additional Committee Members:
John Elsom, Mike Chapman.

Manager: Paul Hurst & Rob Scott
Programme Editor: Lucie Ramsden (E) lucie@gtfc.co.uk

Club Factfile

Founded: 1878 **Nickname:** The Mariners
Previous Names: Grimsby Pelham 1878-79
Previous Leagues: Football League 1892-2010

Club Colours (change): Black & white stripes/black/red (All white)

Ground: Blundell Park, Cleethorpes, North East Lincolnshire DN35 7PY (T) 01472 605 050
Capacity: 10,033 **Seats:** Yes **Covered:** Yes **Clubhouse:** Yes **Shop:** Yes

Directions
From the North/West All routes follow M180 onto the A180 to Grimsby. At first roundabout go straight on then follow signs for Cleethorpes (A180) onto Grimsby Road. Blundell Park is situated behind the Drive Thru' McDonalds. From the South A46 (Lincoln) Follow A46 into Grimsby, go straight on at roundabout after dual carriageway, following signs to Cleethorpes. At the 'Grimsby Institute' get in the right hand lane and keep following signs for Cleethorpes. At Isaac's Hill roundabout turn left onto Grimsby Road, the ground is on the right hand side behind the Drive Thru' at McDonalds.

Previous Grounds: Clee Park, Abbey Park

Record Attendance: 31,657 v Wolverhampton Wanderers - FA Cup 5th Round 20/02/1937
Record Victory: 9-2 v Darwen - Division 2 15/04/1899
Record Defeat: 1-9 v Arsenal - Division 1 28/01/1931
Record Goalscorer: Pat Glover - 180 (1930-39)
Record Appearances: John McDermott - 754 (1987-2007)
Additional Records: Paid £500,000 to Preston North End for Lee Ashcroft 11/08/1998
Received £1.5m from Everton for John Oster July 1997

Senior Honours: Football League Division 2 1900-01, 33-34, Division 3 North 1925-26, 55-56, Division 3 1979-80, Division 4 1971-72.
Division 2 Play-offs 1997-98.
League Group Cup 1982. Auto Windscreen Shield 1998.

10 YEAR RECORD

01-02	02-03	03-04	04-05	05-06	06-07	07-08	08-09	09-10	10-11
FL 1 19	FL 1 24	FL 2 21	FL 2 18	FL 2 4	FL 2 15	FL 2 16	FL 2 22	FL 2 23	Conf 11

GRIMSBY TOWN

No.	Date	Comp	H/A	Opponents	Att:	Result	Goalscorers	Pos
1	Sat-14-Aug	BSP	A	Crawley Town	2428	W 1-0	Peacock 39	9
2	Tue-17-Aug	BSP	H	York City	5037	D 0-0		7
3	Sat-21-Aug	BSP	H	Hayes & Yeading United	3405	L 1-2	Connell 90	14
4	Tue-24-Aug	BSP	A	Darlington	1993	W 1-0	Watt 48	9
5	Sat-28-Aug	BSP	A	Rushden & Diamonds	1575	L 1-4	Hudson 47	12
6	Mon-30-Aug	BSP	H	Histon	2925	W 2-1	Connell 2 (pen 39, 85)	8
7	Sat-04-Sep	BSP	H	Luton Town	3822	W 2-0	Connell pen 30, Cummins 71	4
8	Sat-11-Sep	BSP	A	Tamworth	1616	L 1-2	Connell 69	8
9	Sat-18-Sep	BSP	H	Fleetwood Town	3099	L 1-2	Connell 67	11
10	Tue-21-Sep	BSP	A	Gateshead	863	D 0-0		12
11	Sat-25-Sep	BSP	A	Altrincham	1364	D 2-2	Bore 28, Connell 77	11
12	Tue-28-Sep	BSP	H	Wrexham	2532	W 2-1	Watt 17, Connell 65	9
13	Sat-02-Oct	BSP	H	Newport County	3246	W 2-0	Connell 2 (30, 50)	7
14	Thu-07-Oct	BSP	A	Forest Green Rovers	1007	D 3-3	Eagle 2 (20, 68), Wright 65	7
15	Sun-10-Oct	BSP	A	Kidderminster Harriers	1587	L 2-3	Eagle 31, Connell 70	8
16	Sat-16-Oct	BSP	H	Southport	3101	D 1-1	Connell 73	9
17	Sat-30-Oct	BSP	H	Eastbourne Borough	2894	D 2-2	Coulson 40, Connell pen 78	9
18	Tue-09-Nov	BSP	A	Cambridge United	2303	D 1-1	Eagle 41	11
19	Sat-13-Nov	BSP	A	Hayes & Yeading United	551	W 3-0	Hudson 14, Eagle 44, Connell pen 90	9
20	Sat-20-Nov	BSP	H	Barrow	3225	D 1-1	Atkinson 66	10
21	Sat-01-Jan	BSP	H	Mansfield Town	3654	W 7-2	Bore 3 (5, 51, 89), Coulson 7, Connell 2 (56, 81), Kempson 69	9
22	Mon-03-Jan	BSP	A	Histon	1122	W 6-1	Ademeno 2 (21, 49), Sinclair 65, Hudson 80, Peacock 84, Eagle 90	8
23	Sat-08-Jan	BSP	A	Wrexham	3013	L 0-2		9
24	Tue-11-Jan	BSP	A	York City	3028	L 0-1		9
25	Tue-18-Jan	BSP	H	Kettering Town	2291	W 2-1	Atkinson 45, Eagle 65	7
26	Sat-22-Jan	BSP	H	Crawley Town	3382	D 0-0		9
27	Tue-25-Jan	BSP	A	Luton Town	5609	L 0-1		9
28	Sat-29-Jan	BSP	A	Eastbourne Borough	1002	W 3-2	Duffy 1, Connell 2 (75, 84)	8
29	Tue-01-Feb	BSP	A	Southport	853	D 2-2	Duffy 74, Atkinson 84	7
30	Sat-12-Feb	BSP	H	Cambridge United	3142	D 1-1	Sinclair 8	7
31	Sat-19-Feb	BSP	A	Fleetwood Town	2004	L 0-3		8
32	Tue-22-Feb	BSP	H	Forest Green Rovers	2401	D 1-1	Coulson 8	9
33	Sat-05-Mar	BSP	H	AFC Wimbledon	3182	W 2-1	Coulson 2 (37, 53)	10
34	Sat-12-Mar	BSP	A	Kettering Town	1403	W 2-1	Connell 80, Sinclair 82	10
35	Sat-19-Mar	BSP	A	Bath City	1808	L 1-2	Coulson 60	10
36	Tue-22-Mar	BSP	H	Gateshead	2517	D 2-2	Connell 10, Eagle 34	10
37	Sat-26-Mar	BSP	H	Tamworth	3002	D 2-2	Eagle 15, Hudson 48	8
38	Tue-29-Mar	BSP	H	Darlington	2642	L 0-1		10
39	Sat-02-Apr	BSP	A	Newport County	1506	L 1-2	Coulson 52	11
40	Sat-09-Apr	BSP	H	Kidderminster Harriers	2402	D 3-3	Hudson 24, Connell 56, Peacock 63	12
41	Wed-13-Apr	BSP	H	Rushden & Diamonds	2071	D 1-1	Atkinson 28	13
42	Sat-16-Apr	BSP	H	Bath City	2389	D 2-2	Connell 2 (12, 23)	14
43	Tue-19-Apr	BSP	A	Mansfield Town	1787	W 2-0	Coulson 43, I'Anson 83	10
44	Sat-23-Apr	BSP	A	Barrow	1274	W 2-0	Connell 55, Leary 73	10
45	Mon-25-Apr	BSP	H	Altrincham	4311	L 0-1		10
46	Sat-30-Apr	BSP	A	AFC Wimbledon	3752	L 1-2	Connell 39	11

CUPS

No.	Date	Comp	H/A	Opponents	Att:	Result	Goalscorers
1	Sat-23-Oct	FAC 4Q	A	Tamworth	928	D 1-1	Connell 90
2	Tue-26-Oct	FAC 4QR	H	Tamworth	1612	L 0-1	
3	Sat-11-Dec	FAT 1	H	Redditch United	1116	W 3-0	Coulson 15, Connell 2 (25, 70)
4	Sat-15-Jan	FAT 2	A	Chasetown	1012	L 1-2	Connell 79

League
Starts
Substitute
Unused Sub

Cups
Starts
Substitute
Unused Sub

Goals (Lg)
Goals (Cup)

ARTHUR	RIDLEY	KEMPSON	WATT	BORE	HUDSON	LEARY	WOOD	PEACOCK	COULSON	CONNELL	EAGLE	DIXON	GARNER	CUMMINS	SAMUELS	ADEMENO	CORNER	GOBERN	FULLER	THANOJ	CROUDSON	PEET	STOCKDALE	O'DONNELL	CARLTON	WRIGHT	ATKINSON	SINCLAIR	MAKOFO	DUFFY	HUGHES	GRAY	I'ANSON	SOUTHWELL	MULREADY									
1	3	5	16	2	4	14	19	10	11	17	29	24	6	8	15	9	23	7	20	21	30	40	39	38	18	28	25	22	18	12	7	27	33	32	31									
X	X	X	X	X	X	X	X	X	X	X	S	S	U	U	U																													
X	X	X	X	X	X	X	U	X	X	X	X	U	U	U	U																													
X	X	X	X	X	X	X	U		X	X	X		U	S	X	S	S																											
X	X	X	X	X	X		S	S		X	X		U	X	U	S	X	X																										
X		X	X		X		X	X		X	X		U	X	X	S	S	X	U	U																								
		X	X		X		X	X		X	S		U	X	X	X	S	X			X	U	U																					
	X	X	X	X	X		X	X		X	S		U	X	U		S	X			U			X																				
	X	X	X	X	X	U	X	X		X	S		S	X			S	X			U			X																				
X	X		X	X	X	U	S	S	X	X	X		X	X			X	S						U																				
	X	X	X	X	S	X	X	X		X	S		U	X			U	X			U			X																				
	X	X	X	X	X		X			X				X				X						X	X																			
	X	X	X	X	S		X	S		X	X		S	X				U			U			X	X	X																		
	X	X		X	S		X	S		X	X		X	X	S						U			X	X	X	U																	
	X	X	X	X	U		X	S		X	X		U	X	S						U			X	X	X																		
	U	X	X	X	S	S	X			X	X		S	X	X						U			X	X	X																		
	X	X		X	S	U	X	S		X			U	X	X						U			X	X	X	X																	
U	X	U		X	S		S	X	X	X	X		X	X		S								X		X	X																	
	X	X			X		S		X	X	X		X	U		X	S	S			X	U				X	X																	
	X	X			X	S	X		X	X	X			S	U	X	S				X	U				X	X																	
X	X	X		S	X		X		X	X	X		U	U		X	S				U					X	X																	
X	X	X		X	S		X	S	X	X	S		U	X		X					U						X	X																
X	X	X		X	S	U	X	S	X	X	S			X		X					U						X	X																
X	X	X		X	S		X	X	X	X	S	S	U	X							U						X	X																
X	X	X		X	S		X	S	X	X	X		U	X	U						U						X	X																
X		X	S	X	S	S	X	X		X	X			X			U				U		X				X	X																
X		X	X	X	S	S	X			X	X		U	X			U				U						X	X	X															
X		X	X	X	S	X	X			X	X		S	X			U				U						X	S	X															
X		X	S	X	S	U	X			X	X			X			S				U						X	X	X	X														
X		X	X	X	S		X	S		X	X			X							U						X	U	S	X	X													
X	X	X	U		X	U	X	S	X	X	X										U						X	X	S	X														
X	X	X	S	X	X	S	U	S	X	X				X							U						X		X	X														
X	X	X	X	S	X	S	X		X	X	X										U						U	X	S	X														
	X	X	S	X	X	X	S	S	X	X	X										X	U					X		U	X														
	X	X	U	X		X	X	S	X	X	X										X	U					X	S	S	X														
U	X		X			X	X	S	X	X	X									U	X						X	X	U	X		U												
X	X		X	X		S	S	S	X	X	X			X		U				X	U						X			X														
X	X		X	X	X		S	S	X	X	X			X		S				U	U						X			X														
X					X		X	U	X	X	X		X	X	X	S				S							X		S	X		U												
X					X		X	S	X	X	X		X		X		U			U							X		S	X	X	U												
X		X		S	X	X	X	X	X	X	S		X	S	X												U			U	X													
U		X		X	X	X	X	X	X	X	U		X	X						S	X						S			S														
U	X		U	X	X		X	X	X	X	X		X	S						S	X						X			S														
X			U	X	U	X	X	X	X	X			X	X						X							U						X	S	U									
X				X	S	X	X	S	X	X			X	X						X							U			X			X	S	U									
X					X	X	X	X	X	X	S		X	X	X												U			S			X	U	S									
X			U	X	U		X	S	X	X	U		X	X						X										X			X	S	X									
	X	U		X	X	S	X	X	S	X	S		X	X			X				X	U					X																	
	X	U		X	S	U	X	X	X	X	X		X	X	U		S		S		X	U					X																	
X	X	X		X	S		X	S	X	X	S		U	X		X					U						X	X																
X	X		S	X	X	U	X	S	X	X	U		X	X			X				U						X																	
28	30	34	21	34	24	13	36	15	29	46	29	0	13	32	9	6	2	7	0	4	8	0	1	10	6	9	24	10	4	14	3	0	4	0	1	0	0	0	0	0	0	0	0	0
0	0	0	4	3	16	7	7	20	0	0	10	2	4	4	2	6	9	2	0	3	0	0	0	0	0	0	1	2	6	3	0	0	0	3	1	0	0	0	0	0	0	0	0	0
4	1	1	5	0	3	6	3	1	0	0	2	1	15	4	6	1	5	1	1	4	23	5	1	1	0	0	6	1	2	1	0	3	0	1	2	0	0	0	0	0	0	0	0	0
2	4	1	0	4	2	0	4	2	3	4	1	0	3	4	0	1	2	0	0	0	2	0	0	0	0	0	4	1	0	0	0	0	0	0	0	0	0	0	0	0	0	0	0	0
0	0	0	1	0	2	1	0	2	1	0	2	0	0	0	0	0	1	0	1	0	0	0	0	0	0	0	0	0	0	0	0	0	0	0	0	0	0	0	0	0	0	0	0	0
0	0	2	0	0	0	2	0	0	0	0	1	0	1	0	1	0	0	0	0	0	2	2	0	0	0	0	0	0	0	0	0	0	0	0	0	0	0	0	0	0	0	0	0	0
0	0	1	2	4	5	1	0	3	8	25	9	0	0	1	0	2	0	0	0	0	0	0	0	0	0	1	4	3	0	2	0	0	1	0	0	0	0	0	0	0	0	0	0	0
0	0	0	0	0	0	0	0	0	1	4	0	0	0	0	0	0	0	0	0	0	0	0	0	0	0	0	0	0	0	0	0	0	0	0	0	0	0	0	0	0	0	0	0	0

PLAYING SQUAD

Existing Players		SN	HT	WT	DOB	AGE	POB	Career	Apps	Goals
GOALKEEPERS										
Kenny	Arthur	1	6'04"	13 08	02/12/1978	32	Bellshill	Possil YMCA, Partick 6/97 Rel 5/07, Accrington 6/07, Rochdale 7/09 Rel c/s 10, Grimsby 6/10	28	0
Steve	Croudson		6'00"	11 13	24/11/1980	30	Grimsby	Grimsby, Scunthorpe (L) 8/01, York C (Trial) 7/03, Boston U 8/03 Rel c/s 04, Grimsby (Trial) 7/04, Stevenage NC 8/04, Kettering 12/04, Halifax 3/05 Rel 4/05, Bangor C 8/05, Rhyl 12/06, Cammell Laird 7/07, Grimsby (Pl/Gk Coach)	8	0
James	McKeown	13	6'01"	13 07	24/07/1989	22	Sutton Coldfield	Coventry (Yth), Walsall Rel c/s 07, Peterborough 7/07 Rel 1/11, Kettering (L) 8/07, Worcester (L) 10/07, Boston (5ML) 8/10, Alfreton 1/11, RKSV Leonidas (Holl) 1/11, Grimsby 7/11		
DEFENDERS										
Scott	Garner	6	6'02"	13 02	20/09/1989	21	Coventry	Leicester, Ilkeston (L) 10/08, Mansfield 1/09, Grimsby 7/10, Alfreton (2ML) 2/11	17	0
Darran	Kempson	5	6'02"	12 13	06/12/1984	26	Blackpool	Preston (Sch), Accrington (L) 2/04, Morecambe (3ML) 12/04 Perm 3/05, Crewe 7/06 Rel 5/07, Bury (SL) 2/07, Shrewsbury 7/07, Accrington (L) 2/08, Wrexham 7/08, Forest Green (2ML) 11/08, Accrington 7/09, Grimsby 6/10	34	1
Charlie	I'Anson	26			01/07/1993	18		Grimsby	4	1
Shaun	Pearson	15			28/04/1989	21	York	Spalding U, Stamford 6/08, Boston U 8/09, Grimsby 6/11		
Lee	Ridley	3	5'10"	12 10	05/12/1981	29	Scunthorpe	Scunthorpe Rel c/s 07, Cheltenham 7/07 Rel c/s 10, Darlington (6WL) 11/07, Lincoln C (SL) 1/08, Grimsby 6/10	30	0
Gary	Silk	2	5'09"	13 07	13/09/1984	26	Newport, IOW	Portsmouth Rel c/s 06, Barnet (L) 12/03, Wycombe (8ML) 7/04, Boston U (SL) 1/06, Notts County 7/06 Rel c/s 08, Mansfield 7/08, Grimsby 6/11		
Robbie	Stockdale		5'11"	11 03	30/11/1979	31	Middlesbrough	Middlesbrough, Sheff Wed (L) 9/00, West Ham (3ML) 10/03, Rotherham (SL) 2/04, Rotherham 7/04, Hull C 1/05 Rel c/s 06, Darlington (L) 2/06, Tranmere 7/06 Rel c/s 08, Grimsby 7/08 (Pl/Yth Dev Officer) 6/10	1	0
Bradley	Wood	19	5'08"	11 00	02/09/1991	19	Leicester	Grimsby	43	0
MIDFIELDERS										
Frankie	Artus	11	6'00"	12 10	27/09/1988	22	Bristol	Bristol C, Exeter (2ML) 8/07, Brentford (2ML) 8/08, Kettering (L) 1/09, Cheltenham (SL) 3/09, Cheltenham (L) 8/09, Cheltenham (L) 10/09, Chesterfield (6WL) 1/10, Cheltenham 7/10 Rel c/s 11, Grimsby 7/11		
Anthony	Church	4			29/03/1987	24	Newham	Dag & Red (Yth), Ilford c/s 06, Redbridge, Newport C 7/08, Ilkeston 10/08, Boston U 7/09 Rel 6/11, Grimsby 7/11		
Michael	Coulson	7	5'10"	10 00	04/04/1988	23	Scarborough	Scarborough, Barnsley 7/06 Rel c/s 10, Northwich (L) 8/07, Chester (L) 10/09, Grimsby (SL) 11/09, Grimsby 5/10	29	8
Craig	Disley	8	5'10	11 00	24/08/1981	30	Worksop	Mansfield, Bristol R 7/04 Rel c/s 09, Shrewsbury 7/09 Rel c/s 11, Grimsby 6/11		
Robert	Eagle	29	5'08"	11 08	23/02/1987	24	Leiston	Ipswich (Yth), Norwich Rel 4/09, Stevenage (Trial) 3/09, Inverness Caledonian 7/09, L.Orient (Trial) 7/10, Grimsby 8/10	39	9
Andi	Thanoj	21			19/12/1992	18		Grimsby	7	0
Tyrone	Thompson	16	5'09"	11 02	08/05/1981	30	Sheffield	Sheff Utd Rel c/s 03, Halifax (Trial) 9/01, Lincoln C (L) 10/02, Doncaster (L) 3/03, Huddersfield 8/03 Rel 4/04, Scarborough 6/04, Halifax 8/05, Crawley 6/07, Torquay 5/08 Rel c/s 10, Mansfield 7/10 Rel 5/11, Grimsby 8/11		
FORWARDS										
Robert	Duffy	12	6'01"	12 04	02/12/1982	28	Swansea	Rushden & D Rel c/s 05, Stamford (L) 1/05, Peterborough (Trial) 7/05, Cambridge U 8/05, Kettering 9/05, Gainsborough 1/06, Stevenage 3/06 Rel 5/06, Oxford U 8/06 Rel 4/08, Wrexham (SL) 1/08, Mansfield (Trial) c/s 07, Newport C 7/08, Mansfield 1/09, Grimsby Undisc 1/11	17	2
Anthony	Elding	39	6'01"	13 10	16/04/1982	29	Boston	Notts Forest (Yth), Lincoln C (Yth), Grimsby (Yth), Boston U, Bedford T (L) 9/01, Tottenham (Trial) 1/02, Bolton (Trial) 1/02, Gainsborough (L) 2/03, Stevenage 2/03, Kettering £20,000 + 1/06, Boston U 5/06, Stockport Undisc 1/07, Leeds Undisc 1/08, Crewe £175,000 7/08, Lincoln C (3ML) 1/09, Kettering (2ML) 11/09 (09/10 8,3), Ferncvaros (Hun) 1/10, Rochdale 7/10, Stockport (SL) 1/11, Grimsby Undisc 7/11		
Liam	Hearn	10	5'10"		27/08/1985	26		Santos, Hucknall c/s 06, Eastwood T 10/07, Chasetown 1/08, Quorn 1/08, Alfreton 9/08, Grimsby Undisc 6/11		
Serge	Makofo	18	5'10"	12 05	22/10/1986	24	Kinshasa	Wimbledon/MK Dons, Kettering Undisc 3/06 Rel 5/07, Maidenhead 8/07, Halesowen T 3/08, Dorchester (Trial) 3/08, Potters Bar 3/08, Croydon Ath 12/08, Grays 6/09 Rel 8/09, Leyton 8/09, Burton 9/09 Rel 1/10, Billericay (Trial) 8/10, Kettering 8/10 Rel 1/11, Grimsby 1/11	10	0

		SN	HT	WT	DOB	AGE	POB	From - To	APPS	GOA
Sam	Mulready	14			06/05/1993	18	Kings Lynn	Grimsby	2	0
Dayle	Southwell				20/10/1993	17		Grimsby	3	0
Damian	Spencer	9	6'01"	14 05	19/09/1981	29	Ascot	Bristol C Rel c/s 02, Exeter (2ML) 3/01, Cheltenham 8/02 Rel c/s 09, Brentford (L) 3/09, Kettering 7/09, Kidderminster (9WL) 11/09, Aldershot (SL) 2/10, Aldershot 7/10, Eastbourne B (L) 1/11, Grimsby 6/11		

Loanees		SN	HT	WT	DOB	AGE	POB	From - To	APPS	GOA
(G)Richard	O'Donnell		6'02"	13 05	12/09/1988	22	Sheffield	Sheff Wed (2ML) 8/10 - Alfreton (2ML) 1/11	10	0
(F)Danny	Carlton		5'11"	12 04	22/12/1983	27	Bury	Bury 9/10 - Morecambe 2/11	6	0
(M)Andrew	Wright		6'01"	13 07	15/01/1985	26	Southport	Scunthorpe (2ML) 9/10 -	9	1

Departures		SN	HT	WT	DOB	AGE	POB	From - To	APPS	GOA
(F)Chris	Jones		5'07"	10 00	12/09/1989	21	Swansea	Swansea 7/09 - Rel 7/10, Neath (SL) 1/10, Neath 8/10		
(M)Nick	Hegarty		5'10"	11 00	25/06/1986	25	Hemsworth	Sheff Wed (Jun) - Rel 8/10, St Mirren 8/10		
(M)Adrian	Forbes		5'08"	11 10	23/01/1979	32	Greenford	Millwall (SL) 2/09 Perm 7/09 - Rel 9/10, Lowestoft T 9/10		(M)
Drew	Rhodes				05/12/1990	20		Grimsby Rel 9/10		
(G)Nick	Colgan		6'01"	12 00	19/09/1973	27	Drogheda	Sunderland 7/09 - Rel 1/11, Huddersfield (L) 10/10, Huddersfield 1/11		
(M)Lewis	Gobern		5'10"	11 07	28/01/1985	26	Birmingham	MK Dons 7/10 - Rel 1/11, Notts County 1/11 Rel 4/11	9	0
(D)Mark	Gray				19/12/1991	19	Grimsby	Yth - Rel 4/11, Spalding U (2ML) 10/10, Gainsborough 6/11	0	0
(F)Tom	Corner				14/07/1992	19	York	Yth - Rel 4/11	11	0
(F)Nathan	Dixon		5'09"	11 07	15/04/1992	19		Yth - Rel 4/11, Spalding U (L) 10/10	2	0
(M)Josh	Fuller		5'09"	10 12	09/02/1992	19	Grimsby	Yth - Rel c/s 11, Spalding U (L) 11/10	0	0
(M)Michael	Leary		5'11"	12 03	17/04/1983	28	Ealing	Barnet 7/09 - Rel 5/11, Gainsborough 7/11	20	1
(F)Lee	Peacock		6'00"	12 08	09/10/1976	34	Paisley	Swindon 1/10 - Rel 5/11, Havant & W 6/11	35	3
(M)Peter	Bore		6'00"	12 02	04/11/1987	23	Grimsby	Yth - Rel 5/11, Harrogate T 8/11	37	4
(D)Robert	Atkinson		6'01"	12 00	29/04/1987	24	North Ferriby	Barnsley (2ML) 11/08 Perm 1/09 - Rel 5/11, Fleetwood 6/11	25	4
(M)Mark	Hudson		5'10"	11 03	24/10/1980	30	Bishop Auckland	Gainsborough 11/09 - Rel 5/11, Worksop 8/11	40	5
(M)Michael	Cummins		6'00"	12 06	01/06/1978	33	Dublin	Rotherham 6/10 - Rel 5/11, Gateshead 5/11	36	1
(D)Steven	Watt		6'03"	14 00	01/05/1985	26	Aberdeen	Ross County 8/10 - Rel 5/11, Dover 7/11	25	2
(M)Bryan	Hughes		5'10"	11 08	19/06/1976	35	Liverpool	Burton 1/11 - Rel 5/11, IBV (Ice) 5/11	3	0
(M)Dean	Sinclair		5'10"	11 03	17/12/1984	26	St Albans	Charlton 12/10 - Rel 5/11, Cambridge U (SL) 3/11	12	3
(D)Dwayne	Samuels		5'08"	11 00	11/10/1990	20	Wolverhampton	West Brom 8/10 - Rel 6/11, Redditch (L) 1/11, AFC Telford 7/11	11	0
(F)Charles	Ademeno		5'10"	11 13	12/12/1988	22	Milton Keynes	Crawley £10,000 7/10 - Rel 6/11, AFC Wimbledon 6/11	12	2
(F)Alan	Connell		5'11"	10 08	15/02/1983	28	Enfield	Bournemouth 7/10 - Swindon Undisc 7/11	46	25
(G)Rob	Peet		6'02"		11/10/1992	18	Melton Mowbray	Leicester 8/10 - Man Utd (Trial) 2/11	0	0

Caught in action....

Hayes & Yeading skipper shapes to cross the ball during his side's Premier match v Alfreton.

Photo by Bill Wheatcroft

HAYES & YEADING

Chairman: Derek Goodall
Secretary: Bill Gritt (T) 07710 102 004 (E) secretary@handyutd.com
Additional Committee Members:
Trevor Griffiths, John Bond, Derrick Matthews, Derek Goodall, Nick Griffith, Dean Goodall, Trevor Gorman, Colin Hanlon, Avril Radford, Simon East, Eric Stevens.
Manager: Nas Bashir
Programme Editor: Andy Corbett (E) programme@handyutd.com

Club Factfile

Founded: 2007 **Nickname:**
Previous Names: Hayes - Botwell Mission 1909-29. Hayes and Yeading merged to form today's club in 2007
Previous Leagues: Isthmian

Club Colours (change): Red/black/black (Blue/white/white)

Ground: Beaconsfield Road, Hayes, Middlesex UB4 0SL (T) 0208 573 2075
Capacity: **Seats:** **Covered:** **Clubhouse:** Yes **Shop:** Yes

Directions
Exit M25 Junction 10 and follow A3 towards Guildford. Leave at next junction onto B2215 through Ripley and join A247 to Woking.
Alternatively exit M25 Junction 11 and follow A320 to Woking Town Centre.
The ground is on the outskirts of Woking opposite to the Leisure Centre.

Previous Grounds:

Record Attendance: 1,881 v Luton Town - Conference Premier 06/03/2010
Record Victory: 8-2 v Hillingdon Borough (A) - Middlesex Senior Cup 11/11/08
Record Defeat: 0-8 v Luton Town (A) - Conference Premier 27/03/10
Record Goalscorer: Josh Scott - 40 (2007-09)
Record Appearances: James Mulley - 137 (2007-10)
Additional Records:

Senior Honours: Conference South Play-offs 2008-09

10 YEAR RECORD

01-02	02-03	03-04	04-05	05-06	06-07	07-08	08-09	09-10	10-11
Conf 20	Isth P 7	Isth P 8	Conf S 12	Conf S 20	Conf S 16	Conf S 13	Conf S 4	Conf 17	Conf 16

HAYES & YEADING UNITED

No.	Date	Comp	H/A	Opponents	Att:	Result	Goalscorers	Pos
1	Sat-14-Aug	BSP	H	Bath City	328	W 2-1	Wright 2 (47, 83)	4
2	Tue-17-Aug	BSP	A	Eastbourne Borough	902	L 0-5		16
3	Sat-21-Aug	BSP	A	Grimsby Town	3405	W 2-1	Hand 19, Pritchard 69	5
4	Tue-24-Aug	BSP	H	Forest Green Rovers	286	L 3-4	Wright 3 (pen 39, 55, 69)	10
5	Sat-28-Aug	BSP	H	Crawley Town	320	L 0-3		16
6	Mon-30-Aug	BSP	A	Luton Town	6354	D 1-1	Pritchard 54	15
7	Sat-04-Sep	BSP	H	Histon	359	L 1-2	Buchanan 15	20
8	Sat-11-Sep	BSP	A	Kidderminster Harriers	1102	L 1-3	Patulea 28	21
9	Sat-18-Sep	BSP	A	York City	2252	L 0-2		23
10	Tue-21-Sep	BSP	H	Newport County	478	L 1-2	Malcolm 39	23
11	Sat-25-Sep	BSP	H	Barrow	340	W 2-0	Enver-Marum 45, Pritchard 64	20
12	Tue-28-Sep	BSP	A	Southport	753	D 0-0		21
13	Sat-02-Oct	BSP	A	Kettering Town	1391	L 1-2	Holmes 45	21
14	Tue-05-Oct	BSP	H	Cambridge United	362	W 2-0	Malcolm 11, Pritchard 71	20
15	Sat-09-Oct	BSP	A	Darlington	1536	W 1-0	Patulea 49	17
16	Sat-16-Oct	BSP	H	Wrexham	417	L 0-3		20
17	Sat-30-Oct	BSP	H	Altrincham	274	L 0-1		20
18	Tue-09-Nov	BSP	A	Bath City	532	L 1-3	Deen 82	22
19	Sat-13-Nov	BSP	H	Grimsby Town	551	L 0-3		23
20	Sat-20-Nov	BSP	A	Mansfield Town	2019	L 2-3	Hyde 2, Ferrell 28	23
21	Sat-27-Nov	BSP	A	Newport County	1601	L 1-2	Pritchard 90	23
22	Tue-07-Dec	BSP	H	Eastbourne Borough	190	W 2-1	Patulea pen 17, Cadmore 23	21
23	Sat-01-Jan	BSP	A	AFC Wimbledon	3176	L 1-3	Hyde 73	22
24	Tue-04-Jan	BSP	H	Luton Town	801	L 0-1		23
25	Sat-08-Jan	BSP	H	Tamworth	249	W 2-1	Buchanan 2 (39, 58)	21
26	Tue-18-Jan	BSP	H	Rushden & Diamonds	307	D 3-3	Buchanan 3 (5, 43, 58)	21
27	Sat-22-Jan	BSP	A	Fleetwood Town	1281	D 1-1	Pritchard 4	21
28	Tue-25-Jan	BSP	A	Altrincham	558	L 2-4	Louis 12, Pritchard 90	21
29	Sat-29-Jan	BSP	H	Kidderminster Harriers	288	L 0-4		21
30	Sat-05-Feb	BSP	A	Forest Green Rovers	787	L 0-1		21
31	Sat-12-Feb	BSP	A	Histon	463	W 1-0	Holmes 40	21
32	Tue-15-Feb	BSP	A	Gateshead	463	L 0-1		21
33	Sat-19-Feb	BSP	H	Southport	303	W 1-0	Pritchard 34	20
34	Sat-26-Feb	BSP	H	York City	458	L 1-2	Holmes 75	20
35	Tue-01-Mar	BSP	H	AFC Wimbledon	708	D 0-0		20
36	Sat-05-Mar	BSP	A	Rushden & Diamonds	1129	D 1-1	Yiadom 36	20
37	Sat-12-Mar	BSP	A	Tamworth	1171	W 3-2	Pritchard 14, Brown pen 52, Buchanan 76	21
38	Tue-15-Mar	BSP	A	Crawley Town	2236	L 2-5	Buchanan 2, Pritchard 45	21
39	Sat-19-Mar	BSP	H	Kettering Town	305	W 3-2	Cadmore 17, Brown pen 25, Buchanan 73	19
40	Sat-26-Mar	BSP	H	Fleetwood Town	303	L 1-2	Masterton 50	20
41	Sat-02-Apr	BSP	A	Wrexham	3207	W 2-0	Hand 7, Pritchard 30	19
42	Sat-09-Apr	BSP	H	Mansfield Town	316	W 4-0	Pritchard 12, Buchanan 2 (20, 25), Og (Thompson) 81	18
43	Sat-16-Apr	BSP	H	Darlington	432	W 3-2	Pritchard 10, Buchanan 28, Rents 53	16
44	Tue-19-Apr	BSP	H	Gateshead	502	W 3-1	Pritchard 10, Wright 71, Brown pen 90	16
45	Sat-23-Apr	BSP	A	Cambridge United	2619	L 0-1		16
46	Sat-30-Apr	BSP	A	Barrow	1445	L 0-2		16

CUPS

No.	Date	Comp	H/A	Opponents	Att:	Result	Goalscorers
1	Sat-23-Oct	FAC 4Q	A	Poole Town	1219	W 3-1	Brown 2 (36, pen 90), McLean 90
2	Sat-06-Nov	FAC 1	H	Wycombe Wanderers	1426	L 1-2	Holmes 70
3	Sat-11-Dec	FAT 1	A	Ebbsfleet United	614	L 1-3	Holmes 24

League
Starts
Substitute
Unused Sub

Cups
Starts
Substitute
Unused Sub

Goals (Lg)
Goals (Cup)

HARRISON	FERRELL	GREEN	CADMORE	BYGRAVE	DEEN	MULLEY	HOLMES	PRITCHARD	WRIGHT	BUCHANAN	YIADOM	MCLEAN	APPIAH	LENNIE	WEBB	WASSMER	HAND	WISHART	MALCOLM	BROWN	PATULEA	ENVER-MARUM	HYDE	BULMER	MONTGOMERY	PATTISON	PREDDIE	LOUIS	JOSEPH-DUBOIS	RENTS	MASTERTON	MCWEENEY												
1	2	3	4	6	11	7	8	15	9	12	17	18	19	21	33	22	14	27	9	23	10	24	25	21	26	16	21	10	26	5	7	22
X	X	X	X	X	X	X	X	X	X	X	S	U	U	U	U
X	X	X	X	X	X	X	X	X	X	X	S	S	U	U		S
X	X	X		X	X	X	X	X	X	S	S	U		U	U	X	X
X	X	X		X	X	S	X	X	X	X	S			U	U	X	X	S
	X	X	X	X	X	X	X	X		X	S		U	X	S	U	X	S
X	X	X	X	X		X	X	X		S	X			S	U	U	X	U	X
	X	X	X	X		X	X	X		X	S	U	U	X	U		X	S	X
	X		X	X	X	S	X	X		S	U		U	X			X	S	X	X	X
X	X		X	X	X	S	X	X		S	X		U	U			X		S	X		X
X	X		X		X	X	X	X		S	U		U	U			X	S	X	X		X
X	X		X	X	S	X	X	X		S	U		U	U			X		X	X		X
X	X		X	X	S	X	X	X		U	U			S			X		X	X	X	S
	X		X	X	U	X	X	X		U	S		U	X			X		X	X	X	S
	X		X	X	U	U	X	X		U	X		U	X			X		X	X	X	S
	X		X	X		U	X	X		U	X		U	X		S	X		X	X	X	S
U	X		X	X	U		X	X		S	X		S	X			X		X	X	X	S
X	X		X	X	U		X	X			X	S			U	U	X		X	X			X	U
	U	X	X	X	S		X	X		S	X	S	U		X		X		X				X	X
	U	X		X	S		X	X		S	X	U			X	X	X		X		X		S	X
	X	X	X	X	S		X	X			S		U			U	X		X				X	X	X	U
	X	X	X	X	U		X	X		U	U		S				X		X		S		X	X	X
U		X	X		S		X	X			X	U	S		X	X		S			X		X	X	X
X	X	X	X	X	U		X	X		X	X	S	S			U	X	S					X
X	X	X	X	X	U		X	X		X	X	S	S			X		S					X			U
X	S	X	X	X			X	X	X	X	U		S		X	X	X						U				U
X	X	X	X	X			X	X	X	X	U		S		U	X	X						S				U
X	X	X	X	X				X	X		S		X		U	X	X	S								U	U	X
U	X	X	X	X				X	X		S		X		S	X	X	S								U	X	X
X		U		X			X	X	X	X	U		S		X	X	X	S		X							U	X
X	U	X	X	X			X	X	S		X				S	X	X	U		X							U	X
X	U	U	X	X			X	X	X	X					S	X	X	U		X							U	X
		X	X	X			X	X	X	S	S				S	X	X	U		X						U	X	X
U			X	X			X	X	S	X	S		U		X	X	X	U		X							X	X
U	U		X	X			X	X	S	X	S		S		X	X	X			X							X	X
U	U	X		X			X	X	S	S	X		U		X	X	X			X							X	X
U	S	X		X			X	X	U	S	X		S		X	X	X			X							X	X
U	U	X	X	X			X	X	X	S	X		S		X		X	S		X							X
S	U		X	X			X	X		X	X		X		X		X	S		X						U	X		S
X	X		X	X			X	X	X	X	S		S		U			U		X									U	X	X
X	X	U	X	X			X	X	X	X	S		U							X									S	X	X	U
X	X	S	X	X			X	X	U	X			S				X			X									S	X	X	U
	X	U	X	X			X	X	U	X	S		S				X			X									S	X	X	X
X	X	U	X	X			X	X	S	X	S		S				X			X										X	X	U
X	X	U	X	X			X	X	S	X	S		S				X			X										X	X	U
X	X		X	X			X	X	S	X	S		S		U		X			X										X	X	U
X	X		X	X			X	X	X	S	S		S		U		X			X										X	X	U
X	X	U	X	X	U		X	X		S	X	S			U		X		X	X			X
X	U	U	X	X	S		X	X		S	X	U	U		X		X		X	X			X	S
X	X	X	X	U	X		X			U	X	S	S		X		X						X	U	X
25	32	23	40	44	8	10	44	46	15	21	16	0	3	7	11	17	40	0	15	28	8	3	7	5	3	0	8	10	0	8	8	1	0	0	0	0	0	0	0	0	0	0	0	0
1	2	1	0	0	6	3	0	0	7	14	20	5	18	2	5	2	0	13	1	0	1	5	2	0	0	0	0	0	4	0	0	0	0	0	0	0	0	0	0	0	0	0	0	0
8	8	6	0	0	7	2	0	0	3	5	8	5	16	7	11	5	0	6	0	0	0	0	1	1	0	6	6	0	1	0	0	6	0	0	0	0	0	0	0	0	0	0	0	0
3	2	1	3	2	1	0	3	2	0	0	3	0	0	0	2	0	3	0	2	2	0	0	3	0	1	0	0	0	0	0	0	0	0	0	0	0	0	0	0	0	0	0	0	0
0	0	0	0	0	1	0	0	0	0	2	0	2	1	0	0	0	0	0	0	0	0	0	0	1	0	0	0	0	0	0	0	0	0	0	0	0	0	0	0	0	0	0	0	0
0	1	2	0	1	1	0	0	0	0	1	0	1	1	0	1	0	0	0	0	0	0	0	0	1	0	0	0	0	0	0	0	0	0	0	0	0	0	0	0	0	0	0	0	0
0	1	0	2	0	1	0	3	14	6	12	1	0	0	0	0	0	2	0	2	3	3	1	2	0	0	0	0	1	0	1	1	0	0	0	0	0	0	0	0	0	0	0	0	0
0	0	0	0	0	0	0	2	0	0	0	0	1	0	0	0	0	0	0	0	2	0	0	0	0	0	0	0	0	0	0	0	0	0	0	0	0	0	0	0	0	0	0	0	0

PLAYING SQUAD

Existing Players		SN	HT	WT	DOB	AGE	POB	Career	Apps	Goals
GOALKEEPERS										
Steve	Arnold	1	6'01"	13 09	22/08/1989	22	Welham Green	Arsenal (Yth), Boreham Wood (Yth), Norwich (Yth 8/05) Rel 5/08, Grays 6/08 Rel c/s 09, Eastleigh 11/09, Wycombe (Trial) 12/09, Wycombe 1/10, Hayes & Yeading (L) 8/11		
Delroy	Preddie	21	6'00"		14/07/1976	35	Berkshire	Northampton (Trainee), Slough c/s 94, Walton & H (L) 3/96, Walton & H 8/96, Chesham 7/99, Yeading 5/03, Maidenhead 11/06, Staines 8/07, Hayes & Yeading 8/07 Rel 9/09, Walton & H 10/09, Windsor & E 8/10, Godalming 12/10, Hayes & Yeading 1/11	8	0
DEFENDERS										
Sam	Argent	2	5'11"	11 11	09/10/1991	19	Basingstoke	Southampton Rel c/s 11, Hayes & Yeading 8/11		
Tom	Cadmore	5	6'00"	13 01	26/01/1988	23	Rickmansworth	Watford (Yth), Wycombe Rel 5/08, Yeading (3ML) 8/07, Hayes & Yeading 7/08	40	2
Joe	Gritt	32						Hayes & Yeading (Yth), Wealdstone, Beaconsfield SYCOB, Hayes & Yeading 8/11		
Diak	John	3			08/10/1986	24		Fleet T, Wrightchoice CSA, Henley T, Reading T 7/10, Hungerford 10/10, Hayes & Yeading 8/11		
Jack	Saville	6	6'03"	12 00	02/04/1991	20	Frimley	Reading (Yth), Chelsea (Scholar), Southampton, Stockport (L) 11/10, Hayes & Yeading (L) 8/11		
Louis	Soares	7	5'11"	13 05	08/01/1985	26	Reading	Reading Rel c/s 05, Tamworth (2ML) 2/05, Bristol R (L) 5/05, Barnet 8/05 Rel 5/06, Aldershot 5/06, Southend 7/10 Rel c/s 11, Hayes & Yeading 8/11		
Curtis	Ujah	24	6'00"		22/07/1988	23	Sheffield	Reading, Slough (L) 9/06, Tamworth 3/07, Yeovil 7/07 Rel 12/07, Crawley (L) 8/07, Weston-Super-Mare 12/07 Rel 5/08, Dag & Red (Trial) c/s 08, Halesowen T 9/08 Rel 9/08, Dover (Trial), Hednesford 10/08, Boreham Wood 2/09, Tonbridge A 12/10, Exeter (Trial), Hayes & Yeading 8/11		
MIDFIELDERS										
Harrison	Bayley	22	5'10"	12 03	17/11/1989	21		Reading (Scholar), Glen Hoddle Academy c/s 08, KN Onisillos Sotiras (Cyp) 10/09, Hayes & Yeading 8/11		
Mark	Bentley	12	6'02"	13 04	07/01/1978	33	Hertford	Enfield, Aveley, Enfield, Aldershot 8/99, Southampton (Trial) 9/99, Crewe (Trial) 3/00, Gravesend 5/02, Dag & Red 6/03, Southend Undisc 1/04, Gillingham 5/06 Rel c/s 11, Cambridge U (L) 3/11, Hayes & Yeading 8/11		
Ryan	Crockford	8			03/12/1986	24	Reading	Reading, Aldershot (SL) 3/06 (05/06 6,0), Sutton U 7/06, Thatcham 11/06, Didcot T c/s 07, Reading T 12/07, Jail 4/08, Andover 3/10, Hungerford 6/10, Oxford U (Trial) 7/10, Hayes & Yeading 7/11		
Jerome	Federico	17			14/05/1992	19	Watford	Wycombe Rel c/s 11, Woking (L) 11/10, Wealdstone (L) 1/11, Maidenhead (L) 3/11, Hayes & Yeading 8/11		
Ben	Gladwin	19			08/06/1992	19		Wycombe (Yth), Nike Academy, AFC Wallingford, Salisbury 11/10, Windsor & E 1/11, Burnham 2/11, Hayes & Yeading 8/11		
Jamie	Hand	4	6'00"	11 08	07/02/1984	27	Uxbridge	Watford, Oxford U (2ML) 8/04, Livingston (3ML) 1/05, Peterborough (3ML) 9/05, Fisher 1/06, Northampton (SL) 2/06, Chester 7/06, Lincoln C 8/07 Rel 5/08, Oxford U (SL) 2/08, Ebbsfleet 8/08 Rel 2/09, Chelmsford 2/09 Rel 9/09, Woking 9/09 Rel 5/10, Hemel Hempstead (L) 3/10, Hayes & Yeading 8/10	40	2
Isaac	Osei-Tutu	18						Aldershot T, FC Beaconsfield, AFC Wallingford, Hayes & Yeading 8/11		
Luke	Williams	10						Reading (Scholar), Woodley T, Binfield 2/11, Hayes & Yeading 7/11		
FORWARDS										
Nathan	Elder	16	6'01"	13 12	05/04/1985	26	Hornchurch	Hornchurch, Ford U, Tilbury 9/03, Aveley 10/03, Billericay 12/04, Northampton (Trial) 11/05, Brighton Undisc 12/06, Brentford £35,000 1/08, Shrewsbury Undisc 8/09 Rel c/s 11, AFC Wimbledon (SL) 1/10, Hayes & Yeading 8/11		
Pierre	Joseph-Dubois	9			12/02/1988	23	Paris, Fra	Reading, Tooting & Mitcham (L) 8/06, Grays 1/07, Crawley 8/07 Rel 5/08, Weymouth 5/08 Rel 2/09, Histon NC 9/09 Rel 10/09, Weymouth 12/09, Hayes & Yeading (Trial) c/s 10, Hayes & Yeading 3/11	4	0
Matt	McClure	15			17/11/1991	19	Slough	C.Palace (Yth), Wycombe (Pro 7/10), Burnham (WE) 12/09, Wealdstone (L) 3/10, Hayes & Yeading (L) 8/11		
Richard	Pacquette	14	6'00"	12 06	23/01/1983	28	Paddington	QPR Rel 6/04, Stevenage (L) 10/02, Dag & Red (L) 12/03, Mansfield (L) 2/04, MK Dons 9/04 Rel 11/04, Fisher 11/04, Brentford 11/04, Farnborough 12/04 Rel 1/05, Stevenage 1/05 Rel 1/05, Grimsby (Trial) 1/05, St Albans 2/05, Hemel Hempstead 3/05, Hampton & R 3/05, Worthing 7/05, Thurrock (L) 2/06, Havant & W 3/06, Maidenhead 3/08, Histon (L) 2/09, York C 7/09 Rel 5/10, Eastbourne B 6/10 Rel c/s 11, Hayes & Yeeading 8/11		
Daniel	Wishart	11			28/05/1992	19		Hayes & Yeading, Hendon (2ML) 10/10	13	0

Loanees		SN	HT	WT	DOB	AGE	POB	From - To	APPS	GOA
(F)Ben	Wright		6'02"	13 05	10/08/1988	23	Basingstoke	Peterborough 8/10 - Crawley Undisc 8/10, Newport C (L) 11/10, Hayes & Yeading (SL) 1/11 Rel 5/11, Braintree 6/11	22	6
(F)Michael	Malcolm		5'10"	11 07	13/10/1985	25	Harrow	Crawley (3ML) 8/10 - Rel 12/10, Farnborough 12/10, Lewes 7/11	16	2
(M)Lee	Brown		6'00"	12 06	10/08/1990	21	Farnborough	QPR (2ML) 9/10, (SL) 1/11 - Rel c/s 11, Bristol R 7/11	28	3
(F)Adrian	Patulea		5'10"	11 04	10/11/1984	26	Targoviste, Rom	L.Orient (3ML) 9/10 - Rel 1/11, Hereford 3/11 Rel 5/11	9	3
(F)Liam	Enver-Marum		6'03"	12 00	17/11/1987	23	London	Crawley 9/10 - Forest Green (L) 10/10, Rel 12/10, Forest Green 1/11, Ebbsfleet 7/11	8	1
(G)Niki-Lee	Bulmer		5'11"		06/09/1991	19	Chester	QPR (2ML) 10/10 - Rel 12/10, Airbus UK 2/11	5	0
(M)Graeme	Montogomery		6'01"	12 00	03/03/1988	23	Dagenham	Dag & Red 11/10 - Newport C (SL) 1/11, Rel 5/11, Aldershot T 8/11	3	0
(D)Sam	Rents		5'09"	11 03	22/06/1987	24	Brighton	Crawley (SL) 3/11 - Rel 5/11, Gateshead 5/11	8	1
(M)Steve	Masterton		6'00"	13 05	02/01/1985	26	Irvine	Crawley (SL) 3/11 - Rel 5/11	8	1

Departures		SN	HT	WT	DOB	AGE	POB	From - To	APPS	GOA
(D)Matt	Ruby				18/03/1986	25	Chertsey	Woking 8/08 - Havant & W 8/10 Rel 10/10, Kingstonian 10/10		
(M)Toby	Little				19/02/1989	22		Yth - Woking NC 8/10, Staines 2/11, Basingstoke 7/11		
(M)James	Mulley				30/09/1988	22		Yth - Rel 10/10, Charlton (Trial) 7/10, Dag & Red (Trial) 8/10, Chelmsford 10/10 Rel 12/10, AFC Wimbledon 1/11	13	0
(G)Josh	Lennie		1.85	84	26/03/1986	25	Greenford	Dorking Wan 8/10 - Rel 10/10, Skelmersdale 10/10, Chester FC 3/11	9	0
(M)Ahmed	Deen		5'09"	11 05	30/06/1985	26	Freetown	Barnet 8/10 - Rel 2/11	14	1
(F)Jake	Hyde		6'01"	12 02	01/07/1990	21	Maidenhead	ex Barnet 10/10 - Rel 1/11, Lochee U 3/11, Dundee 3/11	9	2
(D)Charlie	Wassmer				21/03/1991	20		Yth - Crawley (SL) 3/11 Undisc 6/11	19	0
(F)Jefferson	Louis		6'02"	13 02	22/02/1979	32	Harrow	Gainsborough 1/11 - Maidenhead 3/11	10	1
(G)Lee	Harrison		6'02"	12 07	12/09/1971	39	Billericay	Barnet 7/10 - Retired 5/11, Newport C (Ass Coach) 5/11	26	0
(M)Bradley	Pritchard				19/12/1985	25	Zimbabwe	C.Palace, Carshalton 12/04, Nuneaton B, Tamworth 7/10 - Charlton 5/11	46	14
(D)Adam	Green		5'11"	10 11	12/01/1984	27	Hillingdon	ex Woking 7/09 - Dartford 6/11	24	0
(D)Adam	Bygrave		5'09"	12 02	24/02/1989	22	Walthamstow	Histon 8/10 - Farnborough 6/11	44	0
(D)Esmond	James				04/02/1990	21		Yth - Farnborough 6/11		
(F)Elliott	Buchanan		5'11"		17/07/1989	22		Slough 8/10 - Newport C 7/11	35	12
(M)Phil	Appiah				25/10/1989	21	Toronto, Can	ex Preston 8/10 - Hemel Hempstead (Dual) 10/10, Farnborough 7/11	21	0
(D)Lewis	Ferrell		6'00"	10 07	08/03/1991	20		Brentford 8/10 - Hampton & R 7/11	34	1
(M)Andy	Yiadom				02/12/1991	19		Watford 8/10 - Braintree 8/11	36	1
(M)Nathan	Webb				05/06/1992	19		Yth - Rel 8/11, Farnborough 8/11	16	0
(G)Shane	McWeeney		6'00"	13 00	14/10/1989	21	Cricklewood	Potters Bar 3/11 -	1	0
(D)Jack	Pattison				11/01/1991	20		Exeter 8/10 - Burnham (Dual) 2/11	0	0
(M)Peter	Holmes		5'11"	11 13	18/11/1980	30	Bishop Auckland	Ebbsfleet 8/10 - Braintree (Trial) 7/11	44	3
Darryl	McLean				04/05/1992	19		Southampton 8/10 -	5	0

Caught in action....

Marcus Kelly meets this cross well, but sees his effort go wide for Kettering in the FA Trophy against Chasetown.

Photo by Bill Wheatcroft

KETTERING TOWN

Chairman: Imraan Ladak
Secretary: Justin Boyd-Navazo **(T)** 07506 464 222 **(E)** info@ketteringtownfc.co.uk
Additional Committee Members:
Ken Samuel, Lee Thorn

Manager: Morell Maison
Programme Editor: TBC **(E)**

KETTERING TOWN FOOTBALL CLUB 2010-2011

Back Row:Patrick Noubissie,Luke Graham,Ian Roper,Nathan Abbey,Niall Cooper,John Dempster,Greg Taylor,Andre Boucaud
Middle Row:James Davidson(Physio),Marcus Kelly,Darren Wrack,SergeMakofo,Enzo Carrillo,Iyseden Christie,Mark Pryor,Brett Solkhon,James Dance,Sol Davis,Martin Harris,
Front Row:Jean Paul Marna,Ashley Westwood,Tommy Jaszczun(Coach),Lee Harper(Manager),Paul Furlong,Moses Ashikodi

Club Factfile

Founded: 1872 **Nickname:** The Poppies
Previous Names: Kettering > 1924
Previous Leagues: Midland 1892-1900, also had a team in United Counties 1896-99, Southern 1900-30, 1950-79, 2001-02, Birmingham 1930-50, Alliance/Conference 1979-2001, 02-03, Isthmian 2003-04

Club Colours (change): Red & black/black/black (Yellow & green/blue/white)

Ground: Nene Park, Irthingborough, Northants NN9 5QF **(T)** 01536 483 028
Capacity: 6,635 **Seats:** Yes **Covered:** All **Clubhouse:** Yes **Shop:** Yes

Directions
Nene Park is situated three quarters of a mile north of the A45/A6 junction.

Previous Grounds: North Park, Green Lane, Rockingham Road > 2011.

Record Attendance: 11,536 v Peterborough - FA Cup 1st Round replay 1958-59
Record Victory: 16-0 v Higham YMCI - FA Cup 1909
Record Defeat: 0-13 v Mardy - Southern League Division Two 1911-12
Record Goalscorer: Roy Clayton - 171 (1972-81)
Record Appearances: Roger Ashby
Additional Records: Paid £25,000 to Macclesfield for Carl Alford 1994. Recieved £150,000 from Newcastle United for Andy Hunt

Senior Honours: Southern League 1927-28, 56-57, 72-73, 2001-02. Conference North 2007-08.

10 YEAR RECORD

01-02	02-03	03-04	04-05	05-06	06-07	07-08	08-09	09-10	10-11
SthP 1	Conf 22	Isth P 9	Conf N 4	Conf N 6	Conf N 2	Conf N 1	Conf 8	Conf 6	Conf 14

KETTERING TOWN

No.	Date	Comp	H/A	Opponents	Att:	Result	Goalscorers	Pos
1	Sat-14-Aug	BSP	A	Gateshead	639	D 0-0		14
2	Tue-17-Aug	BSP	H	Luton Town	2906	L 1-3	Christie 32	23
3	Sat-21-Aug	BSP	H	Darlington	1350	D 0-0		22
4	Tue-24-Aug	BSP	A	Mansfield Town	2089	D 1-1	Ashikodi 87	23
5	Sat-28-Aug	BSP	A	Histon	681	W 3-0	Marna pen 4, Makofo 54, Kelly 87	15
6	Mon-30-Aug	BSP	H	Rushden & Diamonds	2313	L 0-1		18
7	Sat-04-Sep	BSP	H	AFC Wimbledon	1727	L 1-2	Marna 19	21
8	Sat-11-Sep	BSP	A	Fleetwood Town	1602	L 1-4	Christie 43	22
9	Sat-18-Sep	BSP	H	Wrexham	1533	D 1-1	Marna pen 85	21
10	Tue-21-Sep	BSP	A	Cambridge United	2646	L 0-3		22
11	Sat-25-Sep	BSP	A	Forest Green Rovers	779	W 2-0	Marna pen 45, Christie 69	19
12	Tue-28-Sep	BSP	H	Altrincham	1194	D 3-3	Marna 3 (12, 20, 71)	19
13	Sat-02-Oct	BSP	H	Hayes & Yeading United	1391	W 2-1	Makofo 5, Dance 49	17
14	Tue-05-Oct	BSP	A	York City	1978	W 1-0	Dempster 51	16
15	Sat-09-Oct	BSP	A	Southport	1117	W 2-1	Dance 39, Marna 45	11
16	Sat-16-Oct	BSP	H	Kidderminster Harriers	1650	D 1-1	Solkhon 4	12
17	Sat-30-Oct	BSP	A	Newport County	2230	W 2-1	Dance 2 (11, 70)	10
18	Tue-09-Nov	BSP	H	Mansfield Town	1270	L 0-2		12
19	Sat-13-Nov	BSP	H	Cambridge United	1959	D 2-2	Green 66, Furlong 70	12
20	Mon-21-Nov	BSP	A	AFC Wimbledon	3114	L 2-3	Solkhon 53, Furlong 80	13
21	Sat-01-Jan	BSP	H	Tamworth	1164	L 0-1		15
22	Mon-03-Jan	BSP	A	Rushden & Diamonds	2216	W 2-1	Christie 2 (7, 79)	15
23	Tue-11-Jan	BSP	A	Kidderminster Harriers	1036	L 1-4	Solkhon 59	16
24	Sat-15-Jan	BSP	A	Crawley Town	1812	L 1-2	Marna pen 15	16
25	Tue-18-Jan	BSP	A	Grimsby Town	2291	L 1-2	T Flanagan 3	17
26	Sat-22-Jan	BSP	H	Eastbourne Borough	1146	W 3-0	Furlong 2 (17, 86), Solkhon 61	16
27	Tue-25-Jan	BSP	H	Fleetwood Town	798	W 2-1	Solkhon 54, Christie 90	15
28	Thu-03-Feb	BSP	H	Crawley Town	1216	D 0-0		15
29	Sat-12-Feb	BSP	H	Barrow	1410	D 1-1	O'Neill 64	15
30	Tue-15-Feb	BSP	H	Bath City	796	W 2-1	Marna pen 12, Mills 89	15
31	Sat-19-Feb	BSP	A	Altrincham	752	L 2-3	Marna 2 (41, 44)	15
32	Tue-22-Feb	BSP	H	Gateshead	812	L 1-4	Marna 28	15
33	Sat-26-Feb	BSP	H	Newport County	1056	W 2-0	Marna 8, Og (Warren) 10	15
34	Wed-02-Mar	BSP	A	Tamworth	609	L 1-3	Mills 83	15
35	Sat-05-Mar	BSP	A	Bath City	890	D 1-1	Marna 29	15
36	Sat-12-Mar	BSP	H	Grimsby Town	1403	L 1-2	Marna 19	15
37	Tue-15-Mar	BSP	H	Histon	782	W 4-3	Mills 2 (19, 90), McKoy 78, Wilson 85	15
38	Sat-19-Mar	BSP	A	Hayes & Yeading United	305	L 2-3	McKoy 3, Marna 81	15
39	Tue-22-Mar	BSP	A	Darlington	1829	D 1-1	Marna 7	15
40	Sat-26-Mar	BSP	A	Eastbourne Borough	673	W 3-1	Solkhon 7, McKoy 70, Kelly 74	13
41	Sat-02-Apr	BSP	H	York City	1365	D 1-1	St Aimie 73	14
42	Tue-05-Apr	BSP	A	Luton Town	5715	D 2-2	Solkhon 49, Mills 90	14
43	Sat-09-Apr	BSP	A	Barrow	1015	L 0-5		15
44	Sat-16-Apr	BSP	A	Wrexham	3662	L 0-2		15
45	Sat-23-Apr	BSP	H	Forest Green Rovers	891	W 2-1	Marna pen 48, Mills 55	15
46	Sat-30-Apr	BSP	H	Southport	1403	W 3-1	Cunnington 25, O'Neill 87, Challinor 90	14

CUPS

No.	Date	Comp	H/A	Opponents	Att:	Result	Goalscorers
1	Sat-23-Oct	FAC 4Q	H	Rushden & Diamonds	2792	L 1-2	Furlong 64
2	Sat-11-Dec	FAT 1	A	Chasetown	444	D 3-3	Solkon 32, Furlong 71, Roper 89
3	Tue-14-Dec	FAT 1R	H	Chasetown	581	L 1-2 aet	Furlong 92

League
Starts
Substitute
Unused Sub

Cups
Starts
Substitute
Unused Sub

Goals (Lg)
Goals (Cup)

HARPER	GRAHAM	DAVIS	WESTWOOD	DEMPSTER	TAYLOR	DANCE	O'LEARY	BOUCAUD	FURLONG	CHRISTIE	MARNA	NOUBISSIE	ROPER	COOPER	ABBEY	MAKOFO	SOLKHON	ASHIKODI	SMITH	JASZCZUN	KELLY	PRYOR	HARDING	JACK	MCKOY	GREEN	HOBAN	TOWERS	MCDONALD	BUSSEY	T FLANAGAN	COLLINS	WILSON	HALSTEAD	CHALLINOR	GUERET	O'NEILL	JOHN	RAYNER	MCCRAE	MILLS	C FLANAGAN	CUNNINGTON	ST AIMIE
1	2	3	4	6	12	14	17	8	9	20	10	23	5	13	27	18	19	7	25	15	11	26	17	1	22	16	24	27	8	1	21	29	15	12	17	1	12	16	25	29	18	6	14	28
X	X	X	X	X	X	X	X	X	X	X	S	S	S	U																														
	X	X	X		U	X		X	S	X	X	X	X	U	X	X	S																											
U	X		X	X	X	X		X	X		X	X			X	X	S	S	S	U																								
	X		X	X	X	X		X	X		X	X	U	U	X	X	S	S																										
	X		X	X	X	X		X	S		X	X	U	U	X	X	S	X			S																							
	X	U	X	X	X	X		X		S	X	X		U	X	X	S	X			S																							
	X	U	X	X	X	X		X		X	X	X		U	X	S	S	S			X																							
	X	X	X	S	X	X		X		X	X	X		U	X	S	U	S			X																							
	S		X	X		X		X	S	X	X	U	X	U	X	S	X			X	X																							
	X		X	X		X		X	S	X	X	X	X	U	X	S	X				U	U																						
	X	X		X		X		X	U	X	X	X	S	U	X	X	X				S		U																					
	X			X	X	X		X	U	X	X	X	S	U	X	X	X				S		U																					
	X			X	X	X		X	U	X	X	X	U	U		X	X				S	U		X																				
	X		U	X	X	X		X	X		X	X	U	U		X	X				S			X	S																			
	X		X		X	X		X	S		X	X	X	U		X	X				S	U		X	S																			
	X	U		X	X	X		X	U		X	X	U	U		X	X				S			X	X																			
	X	X		X	X	X		X	X		X	X	S	U		S	X			U	S			X																				
	X	X		X		X		S	S		X	X	X	U		S	X				X	U		X		X																		
	X	X		X		X		X	S		X	X	U			X	S			U	X			X	S	X																		
	X	X		X		X		X	X		S	X	U	U		X	S				X			X	S	X																		
	X		X			X			X	S	S	X	U			X	X				X			X	X	X		S	U															
	U					S				X	X	X	X			X	X				X				X	X		U	S	X	X	S												
	S								S	X	X	X	X			X	X				X	U			X				X	X	X	S												
	S								S		X	X	X			X	X				X	U			X				S	X	X	X	X											
	U								S	S	X	X	X				X				X				X				X		X	X	X	X	S									
	X								S	X	X	U	X				X				X	U			X				X		X	X		X	S									
	X								X	S	X		X				X				X	U			X				X		X		X	X	S									
									X	S	X	S	X				X				X	U			X		U		X		X		X		U	X	X							
		S							S		X	S	X				X				X				X				X		X		X		U	X	X	X	U					
		S							X		X	U	X				X				X				X				X				X		U	X	X	X		S	S			
		X							S		X	X	X				X				X				X				S				X		U	X	X	U		S	X			
		X							S		X	X					X								X				S				X		S	X	X	X	U		X	X		
		U									X		X				X				X				X				X	31			X		S	X	X	U	S		S	X	X	
		S							S		X		X				X				X				X				X				X		U		X		X	U	S	X	X	
		S							U		X		S				X				X				X				S	X					X		X	U		X	X	X	X	
		U							S		X		S				X				X				X					X			S		X		X		U	X	X	X	X	
		S								U	X		S				X				X				X					U			X		X	X	X			X	X	X	S	
		X							S		X	U	X				X				X				X								X		X	X	S			S	X	U	X	
		X								S	X	X	X				U				S				X				X				X		U	X	X				S	X	X	
		X								S	X	U	X				X				X				X				U				X		S	X	X				S	X	X	
		X									X	X					S				X				X				X				X		U	X	X			U	S	X	X	S
		X									X	U	X				X				S				X				U				X			X	X				X	X	S	X
		S									X						X				X				X				X	U					S	X	X			S	X	X	X	X
		X									X	X	X				X				U				X										U	X	X				X	X	U	X
		U									X	X	X				X				X								X	X					S		X			S	X	X	X	S
		U									X	X	X				X				X				S				X	X					S		X			U	X	X	X	S
	X	X		X	X	X		X	S		X	X	U	U		S	S				X			X	X																			
	U		X	U	X	X			X		X	X	X				X				X	U		X	S	X	U																	
	U		X	X	X	X			X		X	X	U			S	S				X	U		X	X	X																		
1	22	16	12	17	13	21	1	19	10	12	43	30	24	0	11	17	34	2	0	1	28	0	0	9	25	5	0	0	14	7	8	3	16	3	4	14	18	3	1	3	11	14	11	3
0	3	6	0	1	0	1	0	1	17	7	3	3	7	0	0	6	9	4	1	0	11	0	0	0	5	0	0	1	5	0	0	2	1	0	9	0	1	0	1	5	6	0	2	3
1	2	7	1	0	1	0	0	0	5	1	0	6	8	18	0	0	2	0	0	3	2	9	2	0	0	0	1	1	3	2	0	0	0	0	8	0	0	3	3	3	0	1	1	0
0	1	1	2	2	3	3	0	1	2	0	3	3	1	0	0	0	1	0	0	0	3	0	0	3	2	2	0	0	0	0	0	0	0	0	0	0	0	0	0	0	0	0	0	0
0	0	0	0	0	0	0	0	0	1	0	0	0	0	0	0	2	2	0	0	0	0	0	0	0	1	0	0	0	0	0	0	0	0	0	0	0	0	0	0	0	0	0	0	0
0	2	0	0	1	0	0	0	0	0	0	0	0	2	1	0	0	0	0	0	0	0	2	0	0	0	0	1	0	0	0	0	0	0	0	0	0	0	0	0	0	0	0	0	0
0	0	0	0	1	0	4	0	0	4	6	19	0	0	0	0	2	7	1	0	0	2	0	0	0	3	1	0	0	0	0	1	0	1	0	1	0	2	0	0	0	6	0	1	1
0	0	0	0	0	0	0	0	0	3	0	0	0	1	0	0	0	0	0	0	0	0	0	0	0	0	0	0	0	0	0	0	0	0	0	0	0	0	0	0	0	0	0	0	0

ALSO PLAYED: WRACK (16) U (1,2,4). BLYTHE (30) U (26,27). BAILEY (21) U(42,43).

PLAYING SQUAD

Existing Players		SN	HT	WT	DOB	AGE	POB	Career	Apps	Goals
GOALKEEPERS										
Aldi	Haxhia	31	6'00"		22/12/1991	19	Mitrovica, Kos	Chelsea Rel c/s 10, Aston Villa (Academy L), Bristol C (Academy L), Birmingham (Academy L), Hayes & Yeading 7/10, Kettering 8/11		
Laurie	Walker	12	6'05"	11 09	08/02/1990	21	Bedford	MK Dons (Scholar), Millwall 7/08 Rel c/s 09, Tooting & M (L) 8/08, Harrow (L) 1/09, Cambridge U 7/09 (09/10 1,0), Morecambe 8/10 Rel c/s 11, Kettering 7/11		
DEFENDERS										
Sol	Davis	3	5'07"	12 04	04/09/1979	31	Cheltenham	Swindon, Luton £600,000 8/02 Rel c/s 09, Peterborough (2ML) 9/07, Grimsby (Trial) 7/09, MK Dons 8/09 Rel c/s 10, Kettering (5WL) 11/09, Kettering 5/10	22	0
Jerel	Ifil	6	6'01"	12 11	27/06/1982	29	Wembley	Watford, Huddersfield (L) 3/02, Swindon (2ML) 1/03, Swindon (L) 9/03, Swindon (2ML) 11/03, Swindon £70,000 7/04, Aberdeen 8/09 Rel 1/11, Bristol R 2/11 Rel c/s 11, Kettering 7/11		
Phil	Ifil	2	5'10"	12 02	18/11/1986	24	Willesden	Tottenham, Millwall (3ML) 9/05, Millwall (L) 1/06, Southampton (3ML) 9/07, Colchester Undisc 1/08 Rel c/s 10, Dag & Red 9/10 Rel c/s 11, Kettering 8/11		
Nathan	Koo-Boothe	21	6'05"	13 11	18/07/1985	26	Westminster	Hayes, Watford 2/03 Rel c/s 04, MK Dons 7/04 Rel 2/06, Grays (L) 11/05, Rushden & D (Trial) 1/06, Kettering 2/06 Rel 5/07, Dundee (Trial) 8/07, Aldershot (Trial) 10/07, Aldershot 12/07 Rel 3/08, Portmore U (Jam) c/s 08, Crewe (Trial) c/s 09, Mosta (Mal), Kaizer Chiefs (SA) (Trial), Kettering 3/11		
Jaime	Navarro	22	6'00"	11 04	03/02/1991	20	Madrid, Spa	Real Madrid C, Bolton (Trial), Kettering 8/11		
Andy	Parry	28			13/09/1991	19		Blackburn Rel c/s 11, Hartlepool (Trial) 4/11 Kettering 8/11		
Djoumin	Sangare	5	6'00"	12 08	16/12/1983	27	Dunkerque	Wasquehal (Fra), Redbridge 9/04, Chelmsford 1/05, Redbridge 1/05, Lewes, St Albans (L) 8/05, Grays 8/06 Rel 5/07, St Albans (SL) 1/07, Stafford R 7/07, Salisbury 7/08, York C 7/09 Rel 12/10, Lincoln C (Trial), Oxford U 1/11 Rel 5/11, Kettering 7/11		
George	Taft	18	6'03"		29/07/1993	18	Leicester	Leicester, Kettering (L) 8/11		
MIDFIELDERS										
Stefan	Bailey	30	5'11"	12 08	10/11/1987	23	Brent	QPR Rel 5/08, Oxford (L) 10/07, Grays 6/08, Farnborough (L) 2/09, Ebbsfleet 8/09 Rel c/s 10, AFC Telford 9/10, Kettering 3/11, Banbury U (Trial) 7/11	0	0
David	Bridges	20	6'00"	12 00	22/09/1982	28	Huntingdon	Cambridge U, New England Rev (USA) (Trial) c/s 04, Chesterfield (Trial) 7/04, Northampton (Trial) 8/04, Latvia c/s 04, Braintree 1/05, Rushden & D 2/05, Histon 3/05, Cambridge U 8/05 Rel 5/07, Kettering 7/07, Stevenage 5/08, Kettering 8/11		
Jon	Challinor	17	5'11"	11 11	02/12/1980	30	Northampton	Rushden & D, Stamford 4/99, Cambridge C 2/01 , Kalamazoo Kingdom (USA), St Albans 5/02, Aldershot 8/03 Rel 5/05, Exeter 5/05, Rushden & D 5/07, Cambridge U £15,000 8/08, Forest Green (L) 8/09, Mansfield (6WL) 11/09 Perm 1/10 Rel 4/10, Brackley 8/10, Newport C 10/10 Rel 12/10, Kettering 1/11	13	1
Craig	Dobson	9	5'07"	10 06	23/01/1984	27	Chingford	C.Palace (Scholar), Cheltenham 7/03 Rel 5/04, Brentford (Trial), Barnet 8/04, Waltham Forest 11/04, Lewes 12/04, Cambridge C 7/05, Stevenage 4 fig 7/06, MK Dons Undisc 1/08 Rel 1/09, Wycombe (L) 11/08, Brentford 3/09 Rel c/s 09, Shrewsbury (Trial) 7/09, Port Vale (Trial) 9/09, Mansfield 10/09 Rel 1/10, Kettering (5WL) 11/09, Farnborough 1/10 Rel 3/10, Sutton U 3/10, L.Orient (Trial), Thurrock 10/10, Barnet 11/10 Rel 1/11, Thurrock (L) 11/10, Braintree 1/11 Rel 2/11, Woking 2/11, Kettering 7/11		
Marcus	Kelly	11	5'07"	10 00	16/03/1986	25	Kettering	Rushden & D, Oxford U 5/09, Kettering (6WL) 11/09, Perm 1/10	39	2
Steven	Meechan	16	5'11"	11 08	30/03/1991	20	Glasgow	Motherwell Rel c/s 11, Albion R (6ML) 8/10, Kettering 7/11		
Patrick	Noubissie	23	5'10"	11 04	25/06/1983	28	Bois-Colombes (Fra)	CS Brétigny-sur-Orge (Fra), Le Mée-sur-Seine SF (Fra), CS Sedan Ardennes (Fra), US Roye Foot Picardie 80 (Fra), Sporting Toulon (Fra) 7/05, Crewe 11/06 Rel 1/07, Swindon 1/07 Rel c/s 07, Hibernian 8/07 Rel c/s 08, Livingston (3ML) 8/07, Dundee (L) 3/08, Ayia Napa (Cyp) 7/08, Kettering 8/09	33	0
Jake	Thomson	15	5'11"	11 05	12/05/1989	22	Southsea	Southampton, Bournemouth (5WL) 1/09, Torquay (SL) 10/09, Exeter 7/10 Rel c/s 11, Cheltenham (L) 2/11, Southend (Trial) 7/11, Kettering 8/11Aman		
Verma		8	6'01"	13 00	03/01/1987	24	Birmingham	Leicester (Yth), FC Khalsa, Ellistown, Bedworth c/s 07, Redditch 8/08, Leicester 12/08 Rel 5/11, Crewe (3ML) 8/09, Histon (L) 3/10, Kidderminster (L) 8/10, Darlington (SL) 11/10, Kettering 7/11		

FORWARDS

Moses	Ashikodi	7	6'00"	11 09	27/06/1987	24	Lagos, Nigeria	Millwall Rel 5/04, West Ham 8/04 Rel 1/06, Rushden & D (Trial) 7/05, Gillingham (3ML) 8/05, Rangers 1/06, Watford Undisc 1/07 Rel 2/09, Bradford C (SL) 3/07, Swindon (SL) 1/08, Hereford (5ML) 5/08, Luton (Trial) 2/09, Shrewsbury 2/09 Rel c/s 09, Kettering 9/09 Rel 12/09, Ebbsfleet 1/10, Kettering 6/10	6	1
Adam	Cunnington	24			07/10/1987	23	Leighton Buzzard	Coventry (Yth), Barton R, Leighton T, Hitchin 3/07, Aylesbury 10/07, Barton R 11/07, Rothwell T 2/08, Stamford 7/08, Barwell (L), Barwell c/s 09, Solihull Moors 7/10, Kettering Undisc 1/11	13	1
Jean-Paul	Marna	10	6'03"	13 09	21/02/1981	30	Cannes, Fra	Paris St Germain (Fra), Berkhamstead, Kettering 7/06	46	19
Leon	McKenzie	14	5'11"	12 11	17/05/1978	33	Croydon	C.Palace, Fulham (L) 10/97, Peterborough (L) 8/98, Peterborough (2ML) 10/98, Peterborough 10/00, Norwich 12/03, Coventry £600,000 8/06, Charlton 9/09 Rel c/s 10, Northampton 9/10 Rel c/s 11, Luton (Trial) 7/11, Kettering 8/11		
Jordan	Patrick	29	5'08"	11 00	14/01/1992	19	Luton	Luton Rel c/s 11, Spalding U (WE) 11/09, Hitchin (L) 2/11, Kettering 8/11		

Loanees		SN	HT	WT	DOB	AGE	POB	From - To	APPS	GOA
(M)Harry	Harding				06/12/1991	19		Reading 9/10 - Croydon Ath (L) 10/10, Bromley (SL) 10/10 Rel c/s 11, Bromley 7/11	0	0
(G)Kelvin	Jack		6'03"	16 00	29/04/1976	35	Arima, Trin & Tob	Darlington (3ML) 10/10 - Rel 1/11	9	0
(D)Tom	Flanagan		6'02"	11 05	21/10/1991	19	Hammersmith	MK Dons (2ML) 1/11 -	8	1
(F)Charlie	Collins		6'00"	11 11	22/11/1991	19	Hammersmith	MK Dons 1/11 -	5	0
(F)Callum	Wilson		5'11"	10 06	27/02/1992	19	Coventry	Coventry (3ML) 1/11 -	17	1
(G)Mark	Halstead		6'03"	14 00	01/01/1990	21	Blackpool	Blackpool 1/11 -	3	0
(D)Luke	O'Neill		6'00"	11 04	20/08/1991	20	Slough	Leicester (SL) 1/11 - Rel 5/11, Mansfield 6/11	19	2
(M)Jorrin	John		5'10"	11 04	06/11/1990	20		Leicester 2/11 - Rel 5/11	3	0
(F)Romone	McCrae		6'01"	12 07	01/08/1990	21	Southwark	Peterborough (SL) 2/11 - Rel c/s 11, Sutton U 7/11	8	0
(F)Danny	Mills		6'04"	13 00	27/11/1991	19	Peterborough	Peterborough (SL) 2/11 -	17	6
(D)Calum	Flanagan				30/12/1991	19	Birmingham	Aston Villa (SL) 2/11 -	14	0

Departures		SN	HT	WT	DOB	AGE	POB	From - To	APPS	GOA
(F)Martin	Smith		5'10"	11 13	13/11/1974	36	Sunderland	Retirement 8/10 - Rel 8/10	1	0
(M)Darren	Wrack		5'09"	12 10	05/05/1976	35	Cleethorpes	Walsall 7/08 - Rel 9/10, Stafford R NC 9/10 Rel 12/10	0	0
(G)Lee	Harper		6'01"	14 06	30/09/1971	39	Chelsea	MK Dons 8/07 (Pl/Man) 11/09 - Rel 9/10	1	0
(M)Stephen	O'Leary		5'10"	11 08	02/02/1985	26	London	Bradford C 8/10 - Rel 8/10, Personal Trainer, Boreham Wood 8/11	1	0
(G)Nathan	Abbey		6'01"	11 13	11/07/1978	33	Islington	Rushden & D 1/10 - Rel 11/10	11	0
(D)Tommy	Jaszczun		5'11"	11 02	16/09/1977	33	Kettering	Corby T as (Pl/Ass Man) 5/10 - Rel 12/10, Corby T 1/11 Rel 2/11, Corby T 3/11 Rel 5/11	1	0
(D)John	Dempster		6'00"	11 07	01/04/1983	28	Kettering	Oxford U 3/07 - Crawley Undisc 1/11	18	1
(D)Greg	Taylor		6'01"	12 01	15/01/1990	21	Bedford	Northampton 6/09 - Darlington Undisc 1/11	13	0
(M)Andre	Boucaud		5'10"	10 02	09/10/1984	26	Enfield	Wycombe 8/08 - York C (6WL) 11/10 Perm 1/11	20	0
(M)James	Dance				15/03/1987	24	Coleshill	Redditch 11/09 - Crawley Undisc 1/11, Luton Undisc 7/11	22	4
(M)Jamie	Towers							Barwell 12/10 - Barwell 1/11	1	0
(D)Nick	Green				01/01/1986	25		Barwell 11/10 - Solihull Moors 1/11, Barwell 7/11	5	1
(F)Serge	Makofo		5'10"	12 05	22/10/1986	24	Kinshasa	Billericay 8/10 - Rel 1/11, Grimsby 1/11	23	2
(D)Ashley	Westwood		5'11"	11 02	31/08/1976	35	Bridgnorth	Wrexham 7/10 - Rel 1/11, Crewe (Trial) 2/11, Crewe 3/11, Northampton 8/11	12	0
(M)Claudiu	Hoban		5'08"	11 04	23/11/1991	19		Northampton Spencer 11/10 - Rugby T, Daventry T 7/11	0	0
(F)Iyseden	Christie		5'10"	12 02	14/11/1976	34	Coventry	Tamworth 5/10 - Rel 5/11, Nuneaton T (SL) 3/11, Tamworth 8/11	19	6
(G)Niall	Cooper				22/05/1991	20		Sileby R 7/09 - Rel c/s 11, Romulus (SL) 1/11, Sutton Coldfield 6/11	0	0
(F)Kieron	St Aimie		6'01"	13 00	04/05/1989	22	Brent	AFC Hornchurch 3/11 - Tamworth 6/11	6	1
(M)Nick	McKoy		6'00"	12 04	03/09/1986	24	Newham	ex Sutton U 10/10 - Rel c/s 11, Northampton 7/11	30	3
(D)Luke	Graham		6'03"	12 07	27/04/1986	25	Kettering	York C 6/10 - Luton (SL) 1/11, Forest Green 7/11	25	0
(M)Brett	Solkhon		5'11"	12 06	12/09/1982	28	Canvey Island	Brackley 7/10 - Brackley 7/11	43	7
(D)Ian	Roper		6'03"	13 04	20/06/1977	34	Nuneaton	Luton 7/09 - Rel c/s 11, Bedworth 8/11	31	0
(F)Paul	Furlong		6'00"	13 08	01/10/1968	42	Wood Green	Barnet (Pl/Coach) 7/10 - St Albans 8/11	27	4
(G)Nick	Bussey				21/09/1984	26		Halesowen T 1/11 - Rel 1/11, Kettering 3/11, Maidenhead 8/11	7	0
(M)Liam	McDonald				19/02/1985	26		Stafford R 11/10 - Tamworth 8/11	19	0
(G)Willie	Gueret		6'00"	13 02	03/08/1973	38	St Claude (Fra)	Swansea 1/11 -	14	0
(G)Ryan	Rayner				25/05/1990	21		Godmanchester 2/11 -	2	0
(M)Mark	Pryor				21/08/1992	19		Yth -	0	0
(M)Richard	Blythe				04/09/1991	19		Rushall O 1/11 -	0	0

Caught in action....

Kettering's Marcus Kelly prepares to cross the ball into the Chasetown box during this FA Trophy match.

Photo by Bill Wheatcroft

KIDDERMINSTER HARRIERS

Chairman: Mark Serrell
Secretary: Russell Moore (T) 01562 823 931 (E) russell.moore@harriers.co.uk
Additional Committee Members:
Wayne Allen, JRuth Serrell, Andrew Maidstone, Keith Chandler, Joe Hancox.

Manager: Steve Burr
Programme Editor: Matt Wall (E) matt.wall@harriers.co.uk

Back row (L-R): Matty Blair, Callum Gittings, Nick Wright, Dave Hankin, Tom Shaw, Mark Albrighton, Mike Willams
Middle row: Graham Devenport (Kit Manager), Gavin Crowe (Physio), Michael Briscoe, Andrew Stevens, Chris McPhee, Daniel Lewis, Tom Sharpe, Ade Ganderton (Backroom staff), Scott Mason (Backroom staff).
Front row: Lee Vaughan, Jack Byrne, Aaron Griffiths, Steve Burr (Manager), Keith Briggs (Captain), Gary Whild (Assistant Manager), John Finnigan (Player/coach), Kyle Hadley, Lee Morris.

Club Factfile

Founded: 1886 **Nickname:** Harriers
Previous Names: Kidderminster > 1891
Previous Leagues: Birmingham 1889-90, 91-1939, 47-48, 60-62. Midland 1890-91. Southern 1939-45, 48-60, 72-83. Birmingham Comb. 1945-47. West Midlands 1962-72. Conference 1983-2000. Football League 2000-05.

Club Colours (change): Red & white/red/red (Navy & gold/navy/navy)

Ground: Aggborough Stadium, Hoo Road, Kidderminster DY10 1NB (T) 01562 823 931
Capacity: 6,419 **Seats:** 3.175 **Covered:** 3,062 **Clubhouse:** Yes **Shop:** Yes

Directions
From North M5 Junc 3 onto A456 to Kidderminster, From South M5 Junc 6 onto A449 to Kidderminster. Alternatively M40/42 Junc 1 onto A38 to Bromsgrove/A448 to Kidderminster. (All routes follow Brown signs to (SVR) Steam Railway then follow signs to Aggborough). Aggborough is signposted at either end of Hoo Road.

Previous Grounds:

Record Attendance: 9,155 v Hereford United - 27/11/48
Record Victory: 25-0 v Hereford (H) - Birmingham Senior Cup 12/10/1889
Record Defeat: 0-13 v Darwen (A) - FA Cup 1st Round 24/01/1891
Record Goalscorer: Peter Wassell - 432 (1963-74)
Record Appearances: Brendan Wassell - 686 (1962-74)
Additional Records: Paid £80,000 to Nuneaton Borough for Andy Ducros July 2000
Recieved £380,000 from W.B.A. for Lee Hughes July 1997

Senior Honours: FA Trophy 1986-87. Conference 1993-94, 1999-2000.

10 YEAR RECORD

01-02	02-03	03-04	04-05	05-06	06-07	07-08	08-09	09-10	10-11
FL 3 10	FL 3 11	FL 3 16	FL 3 23	Conf 15	Conf 10	Conf 13	Conf 6	Conf 13	Conf 6

KIDDERMINSTER HARRIERS

No.	Date	Comp	H/A	Opponents	Att:	Result	Goalscorers	Pos
								- 5 points Jan
1	Sat-14-Aug	BSP	A	York City	2682	W 2-1	Gittings 10, Shaw pen 89	5
2	Tue-17-Aug	BSP	H	Southport	1417	L 3-4	Briscoe 5, Wright 58, Marc Williams 88	10
3	Sat-21-Aug	BSP	H	Mansfield Town	1487	L 1-3	Shaw pen 8	16
4	Tue-24-Aug	BSP	A	Wrexham	2477	D 2-2	Wright 2 (45, 52)	16
5	Sat-28-Aug	BSP	A	Newport County	2026	L 0-3		22
6	Mon-30-Aug	BSP	H	Tamworth	1271	D 2-2	Briggs 43, Byrne 90	23
7	Sat-04-Sep	BSP	A	Altrincham	929	W 2-1	Gittings 72, McPhee pen 80	17
8	Sat-11-Sep	BSP	H	Hayes & Yeading United	1102	W 3-1	Wright 15, McPhee 72, Gittings 90	11
9	Sat-18-Sep	BSP	H	Cambridge United	1291	D 0-0		13
10	Tue-21-Sep	BSP	A	Fleetwood Town	1411	D 1-1	Byrne 79	16
11	Sun-26-Sep	BSP	H	AFC Wimbledon	1565	W 2-0	McPhee 44, Mike Williams 83	11
12	Tue-28-Sep	BSP	A	Bath City	742	L 0-2		13
13	Sat-02-Oct	BSP	A	Crawley Town	1483	L 0-2		16
14	Tue-05-Oct	BSP	H	Gateshead	937	W 2-1	Byrne 53, Blair 75	12
15	Sun-10-Oct	BSP	H	Grimsby Town	1587	W 3-2	McPhee 5, Blair 2 (11, 35)	10
16	Sat-16-Oct	BSP	A	Kettering Town	1650	D 1-1	McPhee 84	10
17	Fri-29-Oct	BSP	A	Southport	1447	D 2-2	Morris 52, McPhee pen 58	11
18	Tue-09-Nov	BSP	H	Rushden & Diamonds	1225	W 1-0	McPhee pen 16	8
19	Sat-13-Nov	BSP	A	Histon	571	W 1-0	McPhee 34	7
20	Sat-20-Nov	BSP	H	Eastbourne Borough	1271	W 2-1	Morris 9, Marc Williams 67	6
21	Tue-30-Nov	BSP	H	York City	1066	D 0-0		5
22	Tue-28-Dec	BSP	H	Newport County	1757	L 2-3	Blair 61, Matt 64	7
23	Sat-01-Jan	BSP	H	Forest Green Rovers	1370	W 1-0	McPhee pen 90	6
24	Mon-03-Jan	BSP	A	Tamworth	1183	D 2-2	Wright 3, Blair 25	6
25	Sat-08-Jan	BSP	A	Gateshead	508	D 2-2	Blair 22, Wright 24	7
26	Tue-11-Jan	BSP	H	Kettering Town	1036	W 4-1	Morris 11, Blair 50, Briggs 66, Gittings 90	6
27	Sat-15-Jan	BSP	A	Barrow	906	L 1-2	Wright 79	8
28	Sat-22-Jan	BSP	H	Barrow	1232	W 2-0	Morris 40, McPhee pen 85	8
29	Tue-25-Jan	BSP	A	Forest Green Rovers	687	D 1-1	McPhee 82	8
30	Sat-29-Jan	BSP	A	Hayes & Yeading United	288	W 4-0	Shaw 32, McPhee 2 (65, 78), Byrne 87	6
31	Sat-05-Feb	BSP	H	Bath City	1500	W 1-0	Shaw 34	6
32	Sat-12-Feb	BSP	H	Altrincham	2930	W 2-1	Byrne 24, Wright 37	6
33	Fri-18-Feb	BSP	A	Cambridge United	1869	W 2-1	Canham 41, Matt 90	5
34	Tue-22-Feb	BSP	A	Darlington	1615	D 1-1	Briggs 14	6
35	Sat-26-Feb	BSP	H	Wrexham	3028	W 1-0	McPhee pen 37	5
36	Sat-05-Mar	BSP	A	Luton Town	6108	D 1-1	McPhee 52	5
37	Tue-08-Mar	BSP	H	Crawley Town	1816	D 0-0		5
38	Sat-12-Mar	BSP	A	AFC Wimbledon	3517	W 2-1	Canham 42, Matt 74	5
39	Sat-26-Mar	BSP	A	Mansfield Town	2079	W 2-1	McPhee 15, Briggs 63	5
40	Sat-02-Apr	BSP	H	Luton Town	2756	D 3-3	McPhee pen 25, Morris 86, Mike Williams 90	6
41	Sat-09-Apr	BSP	A	Grimsby Town	2402	D 3-3	Blair 3 (33, 44, 83)	6
42	Sat-16-Apr	BSP	A	Eastbourne Borough	688	D 1-1	Shaw 76	6
43	Tue-19-Apr	BSP	H	Darlington	1626	L 1-2	Briggs 30	7
44	Fri-22-Apr	BSP	H	Fleetwood Town	2738	W 2-1	Byrne 2 (53, 57)	6
45	Mon-25-Apr	BSP	A	Rushden & Diamonds	1569	L 1-2	McPhee 85	6
46	Sat-30-Apr	BSP	H	Histon	1496	D 2-2	Blair 80, Briggs 80	6

CUPS

No.	Date	Comp	H/A	Opponents	Att:	Result	Goalscorers	Pos
1	Sat-23-Oct	FAC 4Q	H	York City	1123	L 0-2		
2	Sat-11-Dec	FAT 1	A	Wrexham	1122	L 0-2		

League
Starts
Substitute
Unused Sub

Cups
Starts
Substitute
Unused Sub

Goals (Lg)
Goals (Cup)

LEWIS	MIKE WILLIAMS	ALBRIGHTON	BRISCOE	SHAW	HANKIN	BRIGGS	MCPHEE	BYRNE	GITTINGS	MORRIS	WRIGHT	BLAIR	GRIFFITHS	STEVENS	SHARPE	MARC WILLIAMS	HADLEY	VAUGHAN	VERMA	THORNE	THOMPSON-BROWN	MATT	MCPIKE	LINDFIELD	CANHAM	LOWE	TAYLOR
1	3	6	16	5	7	8	10	11	18	9	14	17	13	33	15	29	19	2	21	22	30	20	31	21	23	4	21
X	X	X	X	X	X	X	X	X	X	X	S	S	S	U	U												
X	X	X	X	X	X	X	X	X	X		X	S	U	U	U	S											
X	X	X	X	X	X	X	X	X	X		X	S	U	U	U	S											
X	X		X	X	X	X	S	X	X	X	X	S	U	U	X		S										
X	X		X	X	X	X	S	S		S	X	U		U	X	X		X	X								
X	X	X	S	X	S	X	X	X		X	X	S		U		X		X	U								
X	X		X	X	S	X	X	X	S	X	X	S		U	U			X		X							
X	X	S	X	U	X	X	X	X	X		X	S		U		S		X		X							
X	X	U	X	S		X	X	X	X	X	X	S		U		S		X		X							
X	X	U	X	S	X	X	X	X	X	X		S		U		S		X		X							
X	X	U	X	S	X	X	X	X	X	X		S		U		S		X		X							
X	X	U	X	S	X	X	X	X	X	X	S			U		S		X		X							
X	X	U	X	S		X	X	X	X	X	S	X		U		S		X		X							
X	X	S	X	S		X	X	X	X	U	S	X		U		X		X		X							
X	X	X	X	S		X	X	X	X	X	S	X		U	U	S		X									
X		X	X	S		X	X	X	S	X	X	X	X	U		S		X		U							
X	X	X	X	X	S		X	X	X	S	U	X		U	U	X		X									
X	X		X	S	X	X	X		S	X	S	X		U	X	X		X			U						
X	X		X	S	X	X	X		S	X	U	X		U	X	X		X				S					
X	X		X	S	X	X	X		S	X	U	X		U	X	X		X				S					
X		U	X		X	X	X	X	S	X		X	X	U	X			X					S	S			
X		U	X	X	U	X		X	X	X	S	X		U	X					X		X	S				
X		X	X	X	X	X	X	X	S		S	X	U	U				X		U		X					
X	S	X	X	X	S	X	X	X	X		X	X	S	U				X		U							
X	X		X	X	S	X	X	X	X	U	X	X	U	U	X							S					
X	X			X	S	X	X	X	S	X	X	X	S	U	X							X					
X	X	X	S	X	U	X	X	X	S	X	S	X		U	X							X					
X	X	X	X	S	S	X	X	X	S	X	X	X		U				X				U					
X	X	X	X	U	X	X	X	S	X	X	S	S		U				X				X					
X	X	X	X	X	X	X	X	S	S		X	X		U	U			X				S					
X	X	X	X	X		X	X	X	X		X		U	U	U			X				S					
X	X	X	X	X		X	X	X	S		X	S		U	U			X				S			X		
X	X	X	X	X		X	X	X	S		X	S		U	U			X				S			X		
X	X	X	X	S	U	X	X	X	S		X	X		U	X							S			X		
X	X	X	X	X	S	X	X		S	U	X	X		U	X							S			X		
X	X	X	X	X		X	X		X	S	U	X		U	X			U				S			X		
X	X	X	X	X	S		X		X	X	S	X	U	U	X			S				X					
X	X		X	X	S	X	X		X	U	X	X						X				S			X	U	
X	X	X	X	X		X	X	U	S	S	X	X		U				X				U			X		
X	X	X	X		U	X	X	S	X	S	X	X		U				X				S			X		
X	X	X	X	X	U		X	X	S		X	X		U				X				S			X	U	
X	X	X	X	S	U	X	X	X	S		X	X		U				X				S			X		
X	X	X	X	X		X	X	S	X	U	S	X		U				X				X			S		
X	X	X	X	S		X	X	X	X	X	S	X		U				X				U			U		
X	X	X	X	S		X	X	X	X	X	S	X		U				X				U			S		
X	X	X	X	X	X	X	X		S	X	S	X		U							S					X	U
X	X	X	X	X	S	X	X		X	X	S	X		U	U			X		S	U						
X		U	X		X	X	X	X	X	X		S	X	U	X			X					S	S			
46	41	28	43	26	17	43	43	32	25	24	24	30	2	0	14	7	0	33	1	9	0	7	0	0	10	1	0
0	1	2	2	16	10	0	2	5	19	5	15	13	3	0	0	10	1	1	0	0	1	14	2	1	2	0	0
0	0	7	0	2	6	0	0	1	0	5	4	1	7	45	10	0	0	1	1	3	1	4	0	0	1	2	1
2	1	1	2	1	1	2	2	1	2	2	0	1	1	0	1	0	0	2	0	0	0	0	0	0	0	0	0
0	0	0	0	0	1	0	0	0	0	0	1	1	0	0	0	0	0	0	0	1	0	0	1	1	0	0	0
0	0	1	0	0	0	0	0	0	0	0	0	0	0	2	1	0	0	0	0	0	1	0	0	0	0	0	0
0	2	0	1	5	0	6	18	7	4	5	8	11	0	0	0	2	0	0	0	0	0	3	0	0	2	0	0
0	0	0	0	0	0	0	0	0	0	0	0	0	0	0	0	0	0	0	0	0	0	0	0	0	0	0	0

PLAYING SQUAD

Existing Players		SN	HT	WT	DOB	AGE	POB	Career	Apps	Goals
GOALKEEPERS										
Danny	Lewis	1	6'01"	14 00	18/06/1982	29	Redditch	Alvechurch (Yth), Garringtons, Studley c/s 02, Kidderminster 5/04 Rel 5/06, Moor Green 6/06, Redditch 6/07, Kidderminster 5/10	46	0
Dean	Lyness	21	6'03"	12 00	20/07/1991	20	Halesowen	Birmingham (Scholar), Hearts 7/09 Rel c/s 11, East Fife (SL) 1/11, Kidderminster 6/11		
DEFENDERS										
Michael	Briscoe	16	5'11"	12 00	04/07/1983	28	Northampton	Harpole, Coventry 4/03 Rel c/s 04, Macclesfield 7/04 Rel 5/06, Burton (SL) 3/05, Kettering (Trial) c/s 06, Hucknall 9/06, Tamworth (L) 2/07, Tamworth 5/07, Halesowen T 8/08, Redditch 2/09, Tamworth 6/09, Kidderminster 7/10	45	1
Micky	Demetriou	22			12/03/1990	21	Durrington	Worthing, Leicester (Trial) 3/09, Bognor 8/09, Glen Hoddle Academy (Spa) 8/10, Eastbourne B 1/11, Kidderminster 6/11		
Luke	Jones	4	5'09"	11 09	10/04/1987	24	Blackburn	Blackburn Rel c/s 06, Cercle Brugge (SL) c/s 05, Ashton U 9/06, Shrewsbury 11/06 Rel 4/08, Kidderminster (2ML) 1/08, Kidderminster 5/08 Rel 5/09, Mansfield 5/09 Rel 4/10, Forest Green 6/10, Kidderminster 5/11		
Tom	Marshall	6	6'04"		16/11/1987	23	Lichfield	Hednesford, Eastwood T 5/09, Chasetown (L) 10/09, Tamworth 6/10 Rel 5/11, Kidderminster 6/11		
Tom	Sharpe	15	6'02"	13 04	12/10/1988	22	Nottingham	Notts Forest Rel 5/09, Bury (6WL) 11/07, Halifax (L) 1/08, Stalybridge (3ML) 9/08, Kidderminster 7/09	14	0
Lee	Vaughan	2	5'07"	11 00	15/07/1986	25	Birmingham	Birmingham C (Yth), Portsmouth (Yth), Walsall 2/05, Willenhall (2ML) 8/05, AFC Telford 2/06, Kidderminster 5/10	34	0
Mike	Williams	3	5'11"	12 00	27/10/1986	24	Rhos-on-Sea	Wrexham Rel 4/10, Kidderminster 7/10	42	1
MIDFIELDERS										
Jack	Byrne	11			20/07/1989	22		Moor Green (Yth), Solihull B (Yth), Stratford T, Redditch 1/09, Kidderminster 3/10	37	7
Jack	Cresswell	19	5'10"		18/11/1992	18	Redditch	Man Utd (Yth), Walsall (Scholar) Rel 5/11, Kidderminster NC 5/11		
Callum	Gittings	18			19/11/1985	25		Wolves (Yth), Redditch, Alvechurch (L) 12/03, Cinderford (L) 3/04, Cinderford 7/04, Stourport 10/04, Tividale, Boldmere St Michaels 8/05, Alvechurch 3/06, Kidderminster 8/10	44	4
Dave	Hankin	7	6'03"		25/03/1985	26	Preston	Preston (Yth), Bamber Bridge, Squires Gate, Clitheroe 2/08, Stalybridge 6/09 Rel 4/10, Kidderminster 6/10	27	0
Scott	Phelan	5	5'07"	10 07	13/03/1988	23	Liverpool	Everton Rel c/s 07, Bradford C Rel c/s 08, FC Halifax 9/08, Kidderminster 5/11		
Kyle	Storer	24			30/04/1987	24	Nuneaton	Leicester (Jun), Bedworth 7/02, Tamworth 6/04, Hinckley U (L) 1/06, Hinckley U 9/07, Atherstone 8/08, Nuneaton T 2/09, Kidderminster £5,000 7/11		
James	Vincent	8	5'11"	11 05	27/09/1989	21	Glossop	Stockport Rel c/s 11, Kidderminster 6/11		
FORWARDS										
Stephen	Guinan	9	6'01"	13 02	24/12/1975	35	Birmingham	N.Forest, Greensboro Dynamo (L), Darlington (L) 12/95, Burnley (L) 3/97, Crewe (L) 3/98, Halifax (3ML) 10/98, Plymouth (SL) 3/99, Scunthorpe (L) 9/99, Cambridge U 12/99, Plymouth 3/00, Exeter (Trial) 2/02, Chester (Trial) 3/02, Shrewbury 3/02 Rel c/s 02, Hereford 8/02, Cheltenham 5/04, Hereford (3ML) 1/07, Hereford 7/07 Rel c/s 09, Northampton 7/09, Forest Green (6WL) 11/10 Perm 1/11 (10/11 18,5) Rel 5/11, Kidderminster 5/11		
Jamille	Matt	20			20/10/1989	21		Sutton Coldfield, Kidderminster 11/10	21	3
Luke	Medley	17	6'01"	13 03	21/06/1989	22	Greenwich	Welwyn Garden, Barnet (Protec), Tottenham (Scholar) Rel c/s 07, Bradford C 7/07 Rel c/s 08, Cambridge C (L) 1/08, Barnet 7/08 Rel c/s 10, Havant & W (SL) 3/09, Woking (6ML) 7/09, Havant & W (SL) 2/10, Mansfield 8/10, Aldershot T (L) 2/11, Kidderminster 6/11		
Robert	Thompson-Brown	13			07/08/1992	19		Kidderminster (Yth), Redditch 8/10, Stratford T 9/10, Kidderminster 10/10	1	0
Marc	Williams	10	5'09"	11 02	27/07/1988	23	Colwyn Bay	Wrexham Rel 5/11, Kidderminster (3ML) 8/10, Kidderminster 5/11	17	3
Nick	Wright	14	6'02"	12 00	25/11/1987	23	Birmingham	Birmingham, Tamworth (L) 1/06, Bristol C (L) 10/06, Northampton (6WL) 11/06, Ashford T (L) 3/07, Halesowen T 8/07, Tamworth 10/07, Kidderminster 7/10	39	8

Loanees		HT	WT	DOB	AGE	POB	From - To	APPS	GOA
(M)Aman	Verma	6'01"	13 00	03/01/1987	24	Birmingham	Leicester 8/10 - Darlington (SL) 11/10, Rel 5/11, Kettering 7/11	1	0
(F)Craig	Lindfield	6'00"	10 05	07/09/1988	22	Wirral	Accrington 11/10 - Rel c/s 11	1	0
(M)Mitchell	McPike	5'10"	12 01	21/09/1991	19	Birmingham	Birmingham (5WL) 11/10 -	2	0
(F)Sean	Canham	6'01"	13 01	26/09/1984	26	Exeter	Hereford (SL) 2/11 - Rel 5/11	12	2
(D)Matthew	Lowe	5'08"	10 12	20/10/1990	20	Stoke	Macclesfield (SL) 3/11 - Rel c/s 11, Nantwich T 6/11	1	0

Departures		HT	WT	DOB	AGE	POB	From - To	APPS	GOA
(M)Nathan	Hayward	5'08"	12 01	08/11/1991	19	Kidderminster	Birmingham (Yth) - Rel c/s 10, Stourport 1/11		
(D)Gavin	Caines	6'01"	12 00	20/09/1983	27	Birmingham	Cheltenham 8/09 - Forest Green 8/10		
(M)John	Finnigan	5'08"	10 11	29/03/1976	35	Wakefield	Cheltenham 7/09 (Temp Pl/Man) 12/09 (Pl/Ass Man) 1/10 - Rel 10/10, Bishops Cleeve 12/10		
(F)Kyle	Hadley	5'08"	11 07	27/11/1986	24		Stourbridge 7/09 - Rel 2/11, Harrogate T (3ML) 10/10, Belper 2/11, Harrogate T 2/11, North Ferriby 3/11, Buxton 7/11	1	0
(D)Oliver	Thorne	6'03"	14 06	23/01/1990	21	Gravesend	Newport C 8/10 - Rushden & D (L) 1/11, Braintree 2/11, Corby T 6/11, Hednesford 7/11	9	0
(G)Andrew	Stevens			19/04/1987	24		Rugby T 6/10 - Rel 5/11	0	0
(D)Aaron	Griffiths	5'06"		05/02/1990	21		Halesowen T 7/10 - Rel 5/11, Stourbridge (L) 3/11, Stourbridge 6/11	5	0
(M)Tom	Shaw	6'00"	12 00	01/12/1986	24	Nottingham	Tamworth 6/10 - Cambridge U 5/11	42	5
(D)Mark	Albrighton	6'01"	12 07	06/03/1976	35	Nuneaton	Stevenage 6/10 - Nuneaton T 5/11	30	0
(M)Keith	Briggs	5'10"	11 06	11/12/1981	29	Glossop	Stalybridge 5/10 - Fleetwood £5,000+ 5/11	43	6
(M)Matt	Blair			21/06/1989	22		AFC Telford 8/10 - York C 6/11	43	11
(F)Chris	McPhee	5'11"	11 09	20/03/1983	28	Eastbourne	Weymouth 2/09 - Torquay 6/11	45	18
(M)Lee	Morris	5'10"	11 07	30/04/1980	31	Blackpool	Hereford 7/10 - Eastwood T (Pl/Coach) 7/11	29	5
(M)Dan	Taylor						Yth -	0	0

Caption competition....

Send in your suggestions to tw.publications@btinternet.com and you could win a copy of the 2013 edition of the Directory...

Photo by Keith Clayton

LINCOLN CITY

Chairman: Bob Dorrian
Secretary: Fran Martin **(T)** 07880 705 741 **(E)** fran.martin@redimps.com
Additional Committee Members:
Jane Powell, Steve Prescott, Stuart Tindall, Kevin Cooke, David Beck, Jean Foster, Roger Bates, Dave Leonard.
Manager: Steve Tilson
Programme Editor: John Vickers **(E)** jv@redimps.com

Back: Tony Sinclair, Adam Watts, Josh O'Keefe, Kyle Perry, Danny Hone, Sam Smith, Francis Laurent.
Centre: John Nutter, Simon Russell, Andy Hutchinson, Joe Anyon, Josh Gowling, Doug Lindberg, Nicky Nicolau, James Wilson, Bradley Barraclough.
Front: Matt Carmichael (Kit Manager), Gavin McCallum, Jamie Taylor, Steve Tilson (Manager), Paul Brush (Assistant Manager), Alan Power, Ali Fuseini, Sam Rees (Physiotherapist).

Club Factfile

Founded: 1884 **Nickname:** Imps
Previous Names: None
Previous Leagues: Midland (Founder Member) 1889-91, 1908-09, 1911-12, 1920-21, Football Alliance 1891-92, Football League (Founder Member) 1892-1908, 1909-11, 1912-20, 1921-86, 1988-2011, Conference 1986-88.

Club Colours (change): Red & white stripes/black/red (Green & white hoops/green/green)

Ground: Sincil Bank Stadium, Lincoln LN5 8LD **(T)** 01522 880 011
Capacity: 9,800 **Seats:** Yes **Covered:** Yes **Clubhouse:** **Shop:** Yes

Directions
From South: Exit A1 at s/p 'Lincoln A46, Sleaford A17' onto the A46. At roundabout after 9.4 mile take 3rd exit (s/p Lincoln South A1434). Keep on A1434, following 'Lincoln and City Centre' signs for 4.3 miles. Then get into inside lane (s/p City Centre, Worksop A7) and go straight on (1st exit) at r'about into the High St. After 0.5 miles get in outside lane, and go straight on at lights (s/p City Ctre, Worksop A57). After 0.1 miles turn right into Scorer Street. **From North:** Exit A1(M) at the r'about after the Fina and Shell garages (s'p Lincoln A57, E. Markham) onto the A57. At junc. after 9.9 miles turn right (s/p Lincoln A57), remaining on A57 which here runs alongside the Foss Dyke. At r'about after 5.9 miles turn right (Lincoln South, Newark A46, Grantham A1) onto the A46. Straight on at r'about after 1.8 miles. At next r'about after 1.6 miles (by BP station) turn left (s/p) Lincoln South B1190, Doddington Ind.Est., into Doddington Rd, Sraight on for 2 miles to T-junction. Here, turn left (no signpost) onto Newark Rd A1434. Keep on A1434 following City Centre signs. Go straight on (1st exit) at r'about into the High St. After (0.5 miles get in outside lane, and go straight on at lights (s/p City Ctre, Worksop A57). After 0.1 miles turn right into Scorer St. Tip: Have some change ready for a small toll bridge (Dunham) en route.
Previous Grounds: John O'Gaunt's 1883-94.

Record Attendance: 23,196 v Derby County, League Cup 4th Round 15/11/1967
Record Victory: 11-1 v Crewe Alexandra, Division Three North 29/09/1951.
Record Defeat: 3-11 v Manchester City, Division Two 23/03/1895.
Record Goalscorer: (League) Andy Graver - 143, 1950-55, 58-61.
Record Appearances: (League) Grant Brown - 407, 1989-2002.
Additional Records: Paid, £75,000 for Tony Battersby from Bury, 08/1998.
Received, £500,000 for Gareth Anisworth from Port Vale, 09/1997.

Senior Honours: Midland League 1908-09, 20-21. Football League Division Three North 1931-32, 47-48, Division Four 1975-76. Football Conference 1987-88.

10 YEAR RECORD

01-02	02-03	03-04	04-05	05-06	06-07	07-08	08-09	09-10	10-11
FL 3 22	FL 3 6	FL 3 7	FL 2 6	FL 2 7	FL 2 5	FL 2 15	FL 2 13	FL 2 20	FL 2 23

LINCOLN CITY

No.	Date	Comp	H/A	Opponents	Att:	Result	
1	Sat 7 Aug	FL2	A	Rotherham	3,772	L	1-2
2	**Tue 10 Aug**	**LGC 1**	**A**	**Leeds United**	**12,602**	**L**	**0-4**
3	Sat 14 Aug	FL2	H	Torquay United	3,033	L	0-2
4	Sat 21 Aug	FL2	A	Gillingham	4,838	W	1-0
5	Sat 28 Aug	FL2	H	Crewe	3,024	D	1-1
6	**Tue 31 Aug**	**JPT (N)**	**A**	**Rotherham**	**1,677**	**L**	**0-1**
7	Sat 4 Sep	FL2	A	Chesterfield	6,429	L	1-2
8	Sat 11 Spe	FL2	H	Barnet	2,884	W	1-0
9	Fri 17 Sep	FL2	A	Accrington	1,844	L	0-3
10	Sat 25 Sep	FL2	H	Stevenage	3,215	L	0-1
11	Tue 29 Sep	FL2	H	Burton	2,510	D	0-0
12	Sat 2 Oct	FL2	A	Southend	5,154	L	0-1
13	Sat 9 Oct	FL2	H	Macclesfield	3,047	W	2-1
14	Sat 16 Oct	FL2	A	Shrewsbury	5,453	L	0-2
15	Sat 23 Oct	FL2	H	Stockport	4,809	D	0-0
16	Sat 30 Oct	FL2	A	Wycombe	4,325	D	2-2
17	Tue 2 Nov	FL2	H	Northampton	4,459	L	0-2
18	**Sat 6 Nov**	**FAC 1**	**H**	**Nuneaton Town**	**3,084**	**W**	**1-0**
19	Sat 13 Nov	FL2	A	Morecambe	2,085	W	2-1
20	Sat 20 Nov	FL2	H	Hereford	3,888	W	3-1
21	Tue 23 Nov	FL2	H	Bury	3,659	L	0-5
22	**Sat 27 Nov**	**FAC 2**	**A**	**Hereford**	**1,803**	**D**	**2-2**
23	Sat 1 Jan	FL2	H	Bradford City	3,225	L	1-2
24	Mon 3 Jan	FL2	A	Northampton	4,112	L	1-2
25	**Sat 8 Jan**	**FAC 3**	**H**	**Hereford**	**1,794**	**L**	**3-4**
26	Sat 15 Jan	FL2	H	Wycombe	2,890	L	1-2
27	Sat 22 Jan	FL2	A	Stockport	4,348	W	4-3
28	Tue 25 Jan	FL2	A	Cheltenham	2,292	W	2-1
29	Sat 29 Jan	FL2	H	Port Vale	3,370	W	1-0
30	Tue 1 Feb	FL2	A	Bradford City	10,543	W	2-1
31	Sat 5 Feb	FL2	A	Hereford	2,776	W	1-0
32	Tue 8 Feb	FL2	H	Shrewsbury	3,202	L	1-5
33	Sat 12 Feb	FL2	H	Morecambe	2,884	W	2-0
34	Tue 15 Feb	FL2	A	Aldershot Town	1,847	D	2-2
35	Sat 19 Feb	FL2	H	Chesterfield	4,172	L	0-2
36	Sat 26 Feb	FL2	A	Barnet	2,226	L	2-4
37	Tue 1 Mar	FL2	H	Oxford United	2,261	W	3-1
38	Sat 5 Mar	FL2	H	Accrington	2,868	D	0-0
39	Tue 8 Mar	FL2	A	Burton	2,051	L	1-3
40	Sat 12 Mar	FL2	H	Southend	3,560	W	2-1
41	Tue 15 Mar	FL2	A	Macclesfield	1,067	D	1-1
42	Sat 19 Mar	FL2	A	Stevenage	2,732	L	1-2
43	Fru 25 Mar	FL2	H	Rotherham	3,766	L	0-6
44	Tue 29 Mar	FL2	A	Port Vale	4,636	L	1-2
45	Sat 2 Apr	FL2	A	Torquay United	2,751	L	0-2
46	Sat 9 Apr	FL2	H	Gillingham	3,022	L	0-4
47	Sat 16 Apr	FL2	A	Crewe	3,731	D	1-1
48	Fri 22 Apr	FL2	A	Bury	4,248	L	0-1
49	Mon 25 Apr	FL2	H	Cheltenham	3,007	L	0-2
50	Sat 30 Apr	FL2	A	Oxford United	7,485	L	1-2
51	Sat 7 May	FL2	H	Aldershot Town	7,932	L	0-3

PLAYING SQUAD 2011-12

Existing Players		SN	HT	WT	DOB	AGE	POB	Career	Apps	Goals
GOALKEEPERS										
Joe	Anyon	1	6'02"	12 03	29/12/1986	24	Poulton-le-Fylde	Blackburn (Yth), Port Vale Rel c/s 10, Stafford R (L) 3/05, Stafford R (L) 8/05, Harrogate (L) 11/05, Harrogate (SL) 2/06, Lincoln C 7/10, Morecambe (L) 3/11		
DEFENDERS										
Josh	Gowling	5	6'03"	12 08	29/11/1983	27	Coventry	West Brom (Scholar) Rel c/s 03, Herfølge Boldklub (Den) 7/03 Rel c/s 05, Bournemouth 8/05, Carlisle 7/08, Hereford (SL) 11/08, Gillingham (5WL) 7/09 Perm 8/09, Rel c/s 11, Lincoln C (L) 10/10, Crewe (Trial) 7/11, Lincoln C 7/11		
Danny	Hone	6	6'02"	12 00	15/09/1989	20	Croydon	Lincoln C, Darlington (6ML) 7/10		
John	Nutter	3	6'02"	12 10	13/06/1982	29	Burnham	Blackburn (Sch), Wycombe Rel c/s 01, Aldershot 5/01, St Albans (L) 2/02, Gravesend (L) 11/02, Grays (L) 1/03, Grays 6/04, Stevenage 5/06, Gillingham (2ML) 11/07 Undisc 1/08 Rel c/s 11, Lincoln C 7/11		
Tony	Sinclair	13			05/03/1985	26		Gillingham (Yth), Beckenham, Maidstone 8/06 Rel 8/06, Beckenham, Fisher 3/07 Rel 5/07, Welling 8/07, Woking 6/09, Gillingham 7/10 Rel c/s 11, Lincoln C 7/11		
Adam	Watts	4	6'01"	11 09	04/03/1988	23	London	Fulham, MK Dons (L) 3/07, Northampton (SL) 3/09, Lincoln C (3ML) 10/09 Undisc 1/10		
MIDFIELDERS										
Jean-Francois	Christophe		6'01"	13 00	13/06/1982	29	Creil, Fra	Lens (Fra), Portsmouth 8/07, Bournemouth (6ML) 8/07, Yeovil (L) 3/08, Southend (3ML) 9/08, Southend 1/09 Rel c/s 10, Oldham 9/10, AFC Compiegne (Fra) 11/10, Lincoln C 8/11		
Ali	Fuseini	10	5'06"	09 10	07/12/1988	22	Accra, Ghana	Millwall Rel c/s 10, Leeds (Trial) 7/10, C.Palace (Trial) 7/10, L.Orient (Trial) 9/10, Lewes 1/11, Lincoln C 1/11		
Francis	Laurent	11	6'02"	13 13	06/01/1986	25	Paris, Fra	Sochaux Montbeliard (Fra), SV Eintracht Trier (Ger) 7/06, FSV Mainz 05 (Ger) 7/07, Barnet (Trial) c/s 08, Southend 8/08 Rel 7/10, Coventry (Trial) 7/10, Sheff Utd (Trial) 8/10, Cardiff (Trial) 8/10, AFC Compiègne (Fra) 10/10, Northampton 1/11 Rel c/s 11, Lincoln C 7/11		
Nicky	Nicolau	17	5'08"	10 03	12/10/1983	26	Camden	Arsenal Rel c/s 04, Southend (SL) 3/04, Southend 5/04 Rel c/s 05, Swindon 7/05 Rel 5/06, Hereford (3ML) 1/06, Barnet 7/06 Rel c/s 08, Weymouth (Trial) 7/08, Brighton (Trial) 7/08, Grimsby (Trial) 8/08, Barnet 9/08 Rel c/s 09, Maidenhead 8/09, Woking 9/09, Dover 8/10, Boreham Wood 12/10, Lincoln C 7/11		
Josh	O'Keefe	23	6'01"	11 05	22/12/1988	23	Whalley	Blackburn Rel c/s 09, Walsall 7/09 Rel c/s 10, Lincoln C 7/10		
Alan	Power	8	5'07"	11 06	23/01/1988	22	Dublin	Notts Forest Rel 5/08, Grays (3ML) 11/07, Hartlepool 7/08 Rel c/s 10, Rushden & D 6/10, Lincoln C 7/11		
Simon	Russell	15	5'07"	10 06	19/03/1985	25	Hull	Hull C, Kidderminster 7/04, York C 8/08 Rel 5/10, Tamworth (3ML) 9/09, Cambridge U (SL) 1/10, Cambridge U 5/10, Lincoln C 7/11		
FORWARDS										
Bradley	Barraclough	19			26/05/1989	22	Nuneaton	Bellarmine University Knights (USA), Cincinatti Knights (USA), Lincoln C 8/11		
Andy	Hutchinson	22	5'10"	10 07	10/03/1992	18	Lincoln	Lincoln C (Pro 7/10), Hinckley U (WE) 12/09, Harrogate T (L) 1/11, Lewes (SL) 3/11		
Gavin	McCallum	30	5'09"	12 00	24/08/1987	24	Mississauga, Can	Oakville YC (Can), Yeovil 1/06 Rel c/s 07, Tamworth (2ML) 8/06, Recalled 10/06, (L) 10/06, Crawley (L) 11/06, Dorchester (SL) 3/07, Weymouth 8/07, Havant & W 2/08 Rel 5/08, Sutton U 8/08, Hereford 8/09, Lincoln C 7/10		
Kyle	Perry	9	6'04"	14 05	05/03/1986	24	Birmingham	Walsall Rel c/s 05, Moor Green (L) 8/04, AFC Telford (SL) 9/04, AFC Telford c/s 05 Rel 7/06, Hednesford 7/06, Willenhall 9/06, Chasetown 6/07, Port Vale (Nominal) 1/08 Rel c/s 09, Northwich (L) 3/09, Mansfield 7/09, Tamworth 7/10, Lincoln C 7/11		
Sam	Smith	14			20/05/1990	20	Corby	Corby (Yth), Rushden & D 2/07, Corby T (L) 10/09, Hinckley U (L) 12/09, Lincoln C 7/11		
Jamie	Taylor	7	5'07"	11 11	16/12/1982	27	Crawley	Broadbridge H, Horsham c/s 01, Aldershot 8/02 Rel 2/04, Horsham (L) 2/03, Carshalton (L) 12/03, Oakwood 2/04, AFC Wimbledon 3/04, Horsham 10/04, Woking 12/06, Dag & Red 3/07, Grays (SL) 2/08, Grays 5/08, Eastbourne B 7/09, Lincoln C 6/11		
James	Wilson	24					Lincoln	Lincoln C		

Caught in action....

Alex Lawless on the ball for Luton during the play-off final against AFC Wimbledon.

Photo by Peter Barnes

LUTON TOWN

LUTON TOWN EST 1885 FOOTBALL CLUB

Chairman: Nick Owen
Secretary: Kevan Platt **(T)** 01582 411 622 **(E)** kevan.platt@lutontown.co.uk
Additional Committee Members:
Gary Sweet, Stephen Browne, Andrew Cook, Bob Curson,
David Wilkinson, Mick Pattinson, Paul Ballantyne, Dave Hoskins, Andrew Barringer
Manager: Gary Brabin
Programme Editor: Andrew Barringer **(E)** andrew.barringer@lutontown.co.uk

Club Factfile

Founded: 1885 **Nickname:** The Hatters
Previous Names: None
Previous Leagues: Football League 1897-1900, 1920-2009. Southern 1900-20.

Club Colours (change): Orange/navy/white (White/orange/white)

Ground: Kenilworth Stadium, 1 Maple Road, Luton LU4 8AW **(T)** 01582 411 622
Capacity: 10,226 **Seats:** 10,226 **Covered:** All **Clubhouse:** Yes **Shop:** Yes

Directions From the North: Exit the M1 at Junction 11, and join the A505 towards Luton. Follow the A505 for approximately 1.5 miles and Kenilworth Road is on your right as you leave the one-way system along Dunstable Road. To park, follow the one-way around, turning left, right and right again all in about 100 yards so that you do a complete U-turn and then take the second left into Ash Road. Continue down to the bottom, turn left at the end and the club is in front of you. Continue straight past the club and the road bends immediately over a dual carriageway bridge. Beyond this is plenty of street parking (and a great fish shop) if you are early. From the South: You can join the M1 from the M25 at Junction 21A, which is Junction 6 of the M1. Exit at Junction 11 and follow directions above in From the North. From the East: If you are on the A1, leave at Junction 8 of the A1(M) and take the A602 towards Hitchin, then follow the signs to Luton along the A505. When you come into Luton, head for the City Centre and once you reach the one-way system, follow signs to Dunstable and you will see Kenilworth Road on your left. From the West: Come in on the A505 and follow the directions above in From the North.

Previous Grounds: Excelsior, Dallow Lane 1885-97, Dunstable Road 1897-1905

Record Attendance: 30,069 v Blackpool - FA Cup 6th Round Replay 04/03/59
Record Victory: 12-0 v Bristol Rovers - Division 3 South 13/04/36
Record Defeat: 0-9 v Small Heath - Division Two 12/11/1898
Record Goalscorer: Gordon Turner - 243 (1949-64)
Record Appearances: Bob Morton - 495 (1948-64)
Additional Records: Paid £850,000 to Odense for Lars Elstrup
Recieved £2,500,000 from Arsenal for John Hartson

Senior Honours: Football League Division 3 South 1936-37, Division 4 1967-68, Division 2 1981-82, Division 1 2004-05. League Cup 1988. League Trophy 2008-09

10 YEAR RECORD

01-02	02-03	03-04	04-05	05-06	06-07	07-08	08-09	09-10	10-11
FL 3 2	FL 2 9	FL 2 10	FL 1 1	FLCh 10	FLCh 23	FL 1 24	FL 2 24	Conf 2	Conf 3

LUTON TOWN

No.	Date	Comp	H/A	Opponents	Att:	Result	Goalscorers	Pos
1	Sat-14-Aug	BSP	H	Altrincham	6665	W 2-1	Kroca 22, Barnes-Homer 88	6
2	Tue-17-Aug	BSP	A	Kettering Town	2906	W 3-1	Barnes-Homer 3 (pen 25, 73, pen 84)	1
3	Sat-21-Aug	BSP	A	Fleetwood Town	2831	W 3-0	Barnes-Homer 14, Gnapka 22, Craddock 88	1
4	Tue-24-Aug	BSP	H	Newport County	6945	D 1-1	Kroca 31	1
5	Sat-28-Aug	BSP	A	Tamworth	1694	L 1-3	Craddock 48	2
6	Mon-30-Aug	BSP	H	Hayes & Yeading United	6354	D 1-1	Drury 60	4
7	Sat-04-Sep	BSP	A	Grimsby Town	3822	L 0-2		6
8	Sat-11-Sep	BSP	H	Cambridge United	6691	W 2-0	Drury 34, G Pilkington 45	6
9	Fri-17-Sep	BSP	H	AFC Wimbledon	7283	W 3-0	G Pilkington 23, Kroca 38, Barnes-Homer 49	2
10	Tue-21-Sep	BSP	A	Darlington	1664	D 2-2	Gnapka 14, Howells 80	5
11	Sat-25-Sep	BSP	A	Gateshead	1075	L 0-1		7
12	Tue-28-Sep	BSP	H	Mansfield Town	6024	W 2-0	Crow 51, Morgan-Smith 54	6
13	Sat-02-Oct	BSP	A	Barrow	1416	W 1-0	Barnes-Homer 37	4
14	Tue-05-Oct	BSP	H	Crawley Town	6895	L 1-2	Drury pen 65	4
15	Sat-16-Oct	BSP	A	Eastbourne Borough	2518	W 4-2	G Pilkington 18, Barnes-Homer 63, Crow 2 (72, pen 76)	4
16	Tue-19-Oct	BSP	H	Forest Green Rovers	5704	W 6-1	Drury 6, Morgan-Smith 14, Crow 2 (34, 49), Barnes-Homer 81,D Walker 90	3
17	Sat-30-Oct	BSP	H	Bath City	7003	W 3-1	Crow 16, G Pilkington 28, Atieno 34	3
18	Thu-11-Nov	BSP	A	Wrexham	2733	L 0-1		3
19	Sat-13-Nov	BSP	A	Altrincham	1416	W 1-0	Lawless 47	3
20	Sat-20-Nov	BSP	H	Histon	5963	W 5-1	Gnapka 7, Howells 19, J Walker 39, Drury pen 69, Atieno 78	2
21	Sat-01-Jan	BSP	H	Rushden & Diamonds	6928	W 3-0	Barnes-Homer 2 (44, 51), Gnapka 75	3
22	Tue-04-Jan	BSP	A	Hayes & Yeading United	801	W 1-0	Gnapka 75	3
23	Sat-08-Jan	BSP	A	Bath City	2301	D 0-0		3
24	Wed-12-Jan	BSP	A	AFC Wimbledon	4287	D 0-0		2
25	Tue-18-Jan	BSP	H	York City	5997	W 5-0	Drury 18, Gnapka 31, Owusu 36, Kroca 45, Atieno 66	3
26	Sat-22-Jan	BSP	H	Gateshead	5958	D 2-2	Crow 27, Gnapka 37	3
27	Tue-25-Jan	BSP	H	Grimsby Town	5609	W 1-0	Gnapka 25	3
28	Tue-01-Feb	BSP	H	Darlington	5770	W 4-0	Gnapka 68, Owusu 2 (74, 82), Lawless 90	2
29	Sat-12-Feb	BSP	H	Fleetwood Town	6227	L 1-3	Owusu 7	3
30	Fri-18-Feb	BSP	A	Newport County	2834	D 1-1	Willmott 18	3
31	Tue-01-Mar	BSP	A	Forest Green Rovers	1015	W 1-0	Owusu 38	3
32	Sat-05-Mar	BSP	H	Kidderminster Harriers	6108	D 1-1	Barnes-Homer 27	3
33	Tue-08-Mar	BSP	H	Tamworth	5737	W 2-0	Owusu 38, Barnes-Homer 60	3
34	Tue-15-Mar	BSP	A	Cambridge United	2831	D 0-0		3
35	Tue-22-Mar	BSP	A	Rushden & Diamonds	2459	W 1-0	Willmott 11	3
36	Sat-26-Mar	BSP	A	Southport	1695	L 1-2	Barnes-Homer 74	3
37	Tue-29-Mar	BSP	H	Barrow	5528	D 0-0		3
38	Sat-02-Apr	BSP	A	Kidderminster Harriers	2756	D 3-3	Willmott 57, Gnapka 80, J Walker 90	3
39	Tue-05-Apr	BSP	H	Kettering Town	5715	D 2-2	Howells 40, Morgan-Smith 54	3
40	Sat-09-Apr	BSP	H	Southport	5844	W 6-0	Morgan-Smith 22, Willmott 39, F Murray 84, J Walker 88, Gnapka 90, Kroca 90	3
41	Tue-12-Apr	BSP	A	Crawley Town	3326	D 1-1	Lawless 29	3
42	Sat-16-Apr	BSP	A	Mansfield Town	2203	D 0-0		3
43	Tue-19-Apr	BSP	A	York City	2955	L 0-1		3
44	Sat-23-Apr	BSP	H	Eastbourne Borough	6171	W 3-0	Willmott 2 (18, 77), Gnapka 65	3
45	Mon-25-Apr	BSP	A	Histon	1159	W 4-0	Morgan-Smith 12, Barnes-Homer 2 (34, 90), Gnapka 47	3
46	Sat-30-Apr	BSP	H	Wrexham	6443	D 1-1	J Walker pen 88	3

CUPS

No.	Date	Comp	H/A	Opponents	Att:	Result	Goalscorers
1	Sat-23-Oct	FAC 4Q	H	St Albans City	4144	W 4-0	Morgan-Smith 3 (23, 38, 84), Crow 32
2	Sat-06-Nov	FAC 1	A	Corby Town	1750	D 1-1	Barnes-Homer 83
3	Wed-17-Nov	FAC 1R	H	Corby Town	3050	W 4-2	Barnes-Homer 5, Atieno 2 (29, 62), Gnapka 81
4	Sat-27-Nov	FAC 2	A	Charlton Athletic	8682	D 2-2	Drury 2 (30, 83)
5	Thu-09-Dec	FAC 2R	H	Charlton Athletic	5914	L 1-3	Kroca 38
6	Sun-12-Dec	FAT 1	H	Welling United	1639	D 0-0	
7	Tue-14-Dec	FAT 1R	A	Welling United	404	W 2-1	J Walker 82, Lawless 90
8	Sat-15-Jan	FAT 2	H	Uxbridge	1958	W 4-0	Atieno 2 (18, 78), Watkins 2 (pen 68, 80)
9	Fri-04-Feb	FAT 3	H	Gloucester City	2212	W 1-0	Graham 84
10	Sat-26-Feb	FAT 4	A	Guiseley	1152	W 1-0	Barnes-Homer 50
11	Sun-13-Mar	FAT SF 1	A	Mansfield Town	3208	L 0-1	
12	Sat-19-Mar	FAT SF 2	H	Mansfield Town	6133	D 1-1 aet	Owusu 46
13	Thu-05-May	PO SF 1	A	Wrexham	7211	W 3-0	Lawless 16, Gnapka 28, Asafu-Adjaye 36
14	Tue-10-May	PO SF 2	H	Wrexham	9078	W 2-	Kroca 29, J Walker 81
15	Sat-21-May	PO Final	N	AFC Wimbledon	18195	D 0-0	(L 3-4 pens) Played at Eastlands

League
Starts
Substitute
Unused Sub
Cups
Starts
Substitute
Unused Sub

Goals (Lg)
Goals (Cup)

TYLER	GLEESON	G PILKINGTON	F MURRAY	KEANE	KROCA	HOWELLS	DRURY	A MURRAY	BARNES-HOMER	GALLEN	CROW	GNAPKA	CRADDOCK	BLACKETT	K PILKINGTON	BESTA	NEWTON	ATIENO	D WALKER	ASAFU-ADJAYE	POKU	MORGAN-SMITH	WATKINS	KIDD	LACEY	PATRICK	WOODROW	O'DONNELL	LAWLESS	J WALKER	HINTON	CARNEY	TAVERNIER	ANN	CAIN	OWUSU	WILLMOTT	GRAHAM	CARDEN
1	2	6	3	4	13	15	11	14	9	20	19	18	10	12	30	17	7	10	29	16	25	8	28	31	24	32	33	26	14	23	5	34	35	37	38	34	11	5	17
X	X	X	X	X	X	X	X	X	X	X	S	S	S	U	U																								
U	X	X	X	X	X	S	X	X	X	X	S	X			X	S	U																						
X	X	X	X	X	X	S	X	U	X		X	X	S		U	X	U																						
X	X	X	X	X	X	S	X		X	X	S	X	S		U	X	U																						
U	X	X	X		X	S	X	X	X	S		X	X	U	X	X	S																						
X	X	X		X	X	X	X	X	X	S	X	S	U	X	U		U																						
X	X	X		X	X	U		X	X	X	S	X		X	U	S	X	S																					
X	X	X	X		X	S	X	X	X		S	X		X	U	U	S	X																					
X		X	X		X	X	X	U	X		U	X		X	U		X	X	S	U																		
X	S	X	X		X	X	X		X		S	X		X	U		X	X	U		U																	
X	X	X	X	X	X	S			X		S	X		X	U	U	X	X	S																				
X	X	X	X	X	X	X		S	X		X	X		U	U		S	S				X																		
X	X	X	X	X	X	X	X		X		X	X		U	U			S			S	S																		
X	X	X	X	X	X	U	X		X		S	X		X	U			X		U		U																		
X	X	X	X	X	X	X	X		X		X				U				S	U	S	X	U																
X	X	X	X	X	X	X	X		X		X	S			U				S	U	S	X																	
X	X	X	X	X	X	X	X		X		X					S		X	S	U			U	U															
X	X	X	X	X	X	X	X		X			X						S	S	U	U			U					X										
X	X	X	X	X	X	S	X		X		X	X				U		U	S	U										X										
X		X	X	X	X	X	X		X			X		S				S	U	S	U								X	X									
X	X	X		X	X	X	X		X		X	X								U	S	X								S	S	U							
X	X	X		X	X	X	X		X		X	X								U	U	X								S	S	U							
X	X	X		X	X	X	X		X		X	X								U	U	X			U				S	S								
X	X	X		X	X	X	X		X		X	X								U	U	X			U				S	S								
X	X	X		X	X	X	X		X		S	X				U		S		U	X		S													X			
X		X		X	X	X			X		X	X						S		X	S		S	U				U	X							X			
X	X	X		X	X	X	X		X		U	X								U	U		U						X	S					X			
X	X	X		X	X	X			X			X			U					U	X						X	S					X	S	S	
X	X	X		X	X	X			X		U	X			U					S	X						X	S					X		S	
X	X	X	X	X	X	S					U	X			U														U	X						X	X	S	X
X		X	X	X	X	X			X		S	X			U						U	U														X	X	X	S
X	X	X	X	X	X	X			X		U	X			U						U	S														X		U	X
X	X	X	X	X	X	X			X			X			U								S						X	S					X		U	U
X		X		X	X	X			S		X	S			U		X													S	U					X	X	X	X
X		X		X	X	X			X		X				U		X		U		S	X								S							X	U	X
X		X		X	X	X			X		S	X			U		X		S		U	S														X		X	X
X		X	X	X	X	X			X		X	S			U		X				U														U	X	U	X
X	X	X	X	X	X	X			X		X	S			U		S												X	S							X	U	
X		X		X	X	X			S			X			U		X				X						X	X					U	X	S	S
X		X	X	X	X	X			S			S			U		X				X						X	X						X	U	U
X	U	X	X		X	X			S			X			U		X				S						X	X						X	U	X
X	X	X	X	X	X	X			S			X			U		U				X						X	X						S		U
X	X	X	X	X		X			X			S			U		X		S		U	X								X						S	X	
X	X	X		X	X	X			U			X			U		S		S	S									X	X					X	X		
U	X				X				X			S			X		X		S	X	U	X						X	S						X	X	X
X		X			X				X						U		X		X	X	X		S		S			U		S					X	X	X	
X	X	X	X	X	X	X			X		X	X		U	U	U		U	S	S	S	X																		
X	X	X	X	X		X			X			X				U		X	X	X	S			U	U	U	U	U												
X	X	X	X	X		X	X		X			X				U		X	S	X	S			U	U	U		S												
X	X	X		X	X	X	X		X		X	X				U		S	S	U	U	X		U						U									
X	X	X		X	X	X	X		X		X	X				U		S	U		S	X		U	U							U									
X	U					X			U		U	U				X		X	X	X	X				X			S	X	X	X									
X															X		X	X	X	X			U	X	S	S	X	X	X	X	S	U						
X															X		X		X	X		X		X	U	S	X	X	X		S	X	S	U				
U		U			X	X				X	X			X				S	X	X	X	S				S	X		X								X	
U		X	X	X	X	X			X		S	S			X						S	X						U	X	X								X	
U		X	X	X	X	X			X		S	X			X					U	S	S							X							X		X	
U		X		X	X	X			X		S	X			X		X				U	S							X	S						X		X	
X	X	X		X	X	X			S			X			U		U			X									X	X						U	X	U	
X	X	X		X	X	X			S			X			U		S			X									X	X						U	X	U	
	X	X	X		X	X	X			S		U	X			U		S			X								X	X						X	U
43	33	45	28	39	45	34	23	6	39	4	17	33	1	7	3	3	14	6	1	3	2	15	0	0	0	0	0	0	15	8	0	0	0	0	0	13	12	6	8
0	1	0	0	0	0	8	0	1	5	2	11	9	3	1	0	3	5	7	11	2	7	5	3	0	1	0	0	0	5	12	0	0	0	0	0	0	3	4	2
3	1	0	0	0	0	2	0	2	1	0	5	0	1	4	32	4	5	1	3	13	13	3	3	3	2	0	0	2	1	1	2	0	0	0	0	2	0	7	3
11	8	11	5	11	10	13	3	0	8	0	4	11	0	0	4	3	1	5	3	9	4	5	1	0	3	0	0	3	9	8	2	0	1	0	0	2	3	4	0
0	0	0	0	0	0	0	0	0	3	0	3	1	0	0	0	0	2	2	4	1	6	2	1	0	0	1	3	2	0	1	0	2	0	1	0	0	0	0	0
4	1	1	0	0	0	0	0	0	1	0	2	1	0	1	4	5	1	1	1	2	2	0	0	5	3	3	1	2	0	0	2	0	1	0	1	2	0	3	0
0	0	4	1	0	5	3	6	0	16	0	7	13	2	0	0	0	0	3	1	0	0	5	0	0	0	0	0	0	3	4	0	0	0	0	0	6	6	0	0
0	0	0	0	0	2	0	1	0	3	0	1	2	0	0	0	0	0	4	0	1	0	3	2	0	0	0	0	0	2	2	0	0	0	0	0	1	0	1	0

PLAYING SQUAD

Existing Players		SN	HT	WT	DOB	AGE	POB	Career	Apps	Goals
GOALKEEPERS										
Lewis	Kidd	31			28/10/1992	18		Luton	0	0
Kevin	Pilkington	30	6'01"	13 00	08/03/1974	37	Hitchin	Man Utd Rel c/s 98, Rochdale (L) 2/96, Rotherham (3ML) 1/97, Celtic (SL) 3/98, Port Vale 7/98 Rel c/s 00, Macclesfield (Trial) 7/00, Wigan 8/00, Aberystwyth 9/00, Mansfield 9/00 Rel c/s 05, Notts County 7/05 Rel 5/10, Luton (2ML) 11/09, Luton 5/10, Mansfield (3ML) 10/10	3	0
Mark	Tyler	1	6'00"	12 09	02/04/1977	34	Norwich	Peterborough, Billericay (3ML) 1/96, Yeovil (L) 11/96, Hull C (L) 1/08, Watford (2ML) 9/08, Bury (2ML) 1/09, Luton 6/09	43	0
DEFENDERS										
Will	Antwi	17	6'02"	12 08	19/10/1982	28	Ashford, Kent	C.Palace Rel c/s 03, QPR (Trial) 5/03, Wycombe (Trial) 7/03, Ljungskile (Swe) 7/03, Aldershot 12/03, Wycombe 6/05 Rel 5/09, Northwich (L) 11/08, Dag & Red 7/09 Rel c/s 11, Luton 7/11		
Ed	Asafu-Adjaye	16	5'11"	12 04	22/12/1988	22	Southwark	Luton, Walton & H (L) 3/07, Salisbury (3ML) 1/08, Histon (L) 3/11	5	0
Dean	Beckwith	5	6'03"	13 02	18/09/1983	27	Southwark	Gillingham Rel c/s 05, Tonbridge A (L) 8/02, Dag & Red (L) 10/03, Margate (L) 9/04, Hereford 7/05 Rel c/s 09, Northampton 7/09 Rel 5/11, Luton 6/11		
Shane	Blackett	12	6'00"	12 11	03/10/1982	28	Luton	Dunstable, Arlesey 8/03, Dag & Red 5/04, Peterborough Undisc 1/07, Luton 7/09	8	0
Michael	Cain							Luton	0	0
Ashley	Deeney	32			25/11/1991	19	Milton Keynes	Luton, Leighton T (WE) 2/10, Arlesey (WE) 10/10, Bedford T (WE) 11/10		
Dan	Gleeson	2	6'03"	13 02	17/02/1985	26	Cambridge	Cambridge U Rel 5/06, Welling (L) 9/03, Notts County 7/06, Cambridge U (SL) 3/07, Cambridge U 5/07, Luton 5/10	34	0
Alex	Lacey	24			31/05/1993	28		Luton, Cambridge C (L) 8/11	1	0
Alex	Lawless	7	5'11"	10 08	05/02/1983	28	Llwynupion	Fulham, Torquay 7/05 Rel 5/06, Forest Green 8/06, York C 6/09, Luton (2ML) 11/10 Undisc 1/11	20	3
Fred	Murray	3	5'10"	11 12	22/05/1982	29	Clonmel	Blackburn, Cambridge (3ML) 12/01 Perm 3/02, Northampton 7/04 Rel c/s 07, L.Orient (Trial) 7/07, Stafford R 8/07, Stevenage 1/08 Rel c/s 08, Exeter 9/08 Rel c/s 09, Grays 8/09, Luton (6ML) 8/09 Perm 1/10	28	1
Curtis	Osano	18	5'11"	11 04	08/03/1987	24	Nakuru, Kenya	Reading Rel c/s 08, Aldershot T (3ML) 10/06, Woking (SL) 1/07, Rushden & D (SL) 7/07, Rushden & D 7/08, Luton 7/11		
George	Pilkington	6	5'11"	11 06	07/11/1981	29	Rugeley	Everton Rel c/s 03, Exeter (2ML) 11/02, Port Vale 7/03 Rel c/s 08, Luton 8/08	45	4
MIDFIELDERS										
Alasan	Ann							Luton	0	0
Newman	Carney		5'10"		23/03/1994	17		Luton	0	0
James	Dance	19			15/03/1987	24	Coleshill	Birmingham (Yth), Cheltenham (Scholar), Coleshill, Rushall O 6/09, Redditch 8/09, Kettering 11/09, Crawley Undisc 1/11, Luton Undisc 7/11		
Ryan	Dasilva							Luton		
Jake	Howells	15	5'09"	11 08	18/04/1991	20	St Albans	Luton	42	3
Keith	Keane	4	5'09"	11 01	20/11/1986	24	Luton	Luton	39	0
Jonathan	O'Donnell	26			29/10/1991	19		Watford (Yth), MK Dons (Yth), Hemel Hempstead, St Albans 7/09, Luton (Trial) 12/09, Luton 1/10, St Albans (L) 1/10, St Albans (L) 3/11, Cambridge C (L) 8/11	0	0
Godfrey	Poku	25			22/07/1990	21		Redbridge College, St Albans 8/09, Luton (Trial) 12/09, Luton 1/10, St Albans (L) 1/10	9	0
Christian	Tavernier	36						Luton	0	0
Adam	Watkins	28			08/09/1991	19	Luton	Luton, Arlesey T (WE) 2/10, Arlesey T (L) 9/10, Arlesey T (L) 12/10, Harrow (L) 3/11	3	0
Robbie	Willmott	11	5'09"	12 01	16/05/1990	21	Harlow	Cambridge U, Luton £50,000 1/11	15	6

FORWARDS										
Matthew	Barnes-Homer	9	5'11"	12 05	25/01/1986	25	Dudley	Wolves (Sch) Rel c/s 04, Aldershot 9/04 Rel 11/04, Hednesford 2/05, Bromsgrove 3/05, Sracuse (USA), Virginia Beach Mariners (USA), Tividale 7/06, Willenhall 8/06, Wycombe 3/07 Rel 5/07, Kidderminster 7/07, Luton (5WL) 11/09 £75,000 1/10	44	16
Danny	Crow	10	5'10"	11 00	26/01/1986	25	Great Yarmouth	Norwich, Northampton (2ML) 2/05, Peterborough 8/05 Rel 9/08, Notts County (L) 10/08, Notts County (SL) 2/09, Cambridge U 9/08, Luton 5/10	28	7
Charlie	Henry	21			01/07/1987	24	Stevenage	Luton (Yth), Buntingford, Arlesey, Wycombe 11/05, Grays 3/06 Rel c/s 06, Haverhill R 7/06, Cambridge C 10/06, Dorchester 6/07, Havant & W 11/07, Newport C 6/09, Luton (5WL) 11/10 Undisc 1/11		
Amari	Morgan-Smith	8	6'00"	13 06	03/04/1989	22	Wolverhampton	Wolves (Yth), Crewe (Scholar), Alsager T (WE) 3/07, Stockport 8/07 Rel c/s 08, Ilkeston 6/08 Rel 9/10, Derby (Trial) 7/10, Carlisle (Trial) 9/10, Luton 9/10	20	5
Aaron	O'Connor	14	5'10"	12 00	09/08/1983	28	Nottingham	Ilkeston, Scunthorpe 12/02 Rel 2/03, Ilkeston 3/03, Nuneaton c/s 03, Ilkeston, Gresley R 7/04, Rushden & D (Trial) 6/06 Grays 1/07, Mansfield 8/08, Rushden & D 6/09, Luton 6/11		
Dan	Walker	29			27/04/1990	21		Stony Stratford, Bedford T, Leighton T (SL) 10/09, Luton 8/10, Eastbourne B (L) 1/11, Cambridge U (L) 2/11	12	1

Loanees		SN	HT	WT	DOB	AGE	POB	From - To	APPS	GOA
(D)Craig	Hinton		6'00"	12 00	26/11/1977	33	Wolverhampton	Northampton (6WL) 11/10 - Rel c/s 11, Solihull Moors 8/11	0	0
(D)Luke	Graham		6'03"	12 07	27/04/1986	25	Kettering	Kettering (SL) 1/11 - Forest Green 7/11	10	0
(M)Paul	Carden		5'09"	11 10	29/03/1979	32	Liverpool	Cambridge U (SL) 2/11 - Rel 6/11	10	0

Departures		SN	HT	WT	DOB	AGE	POB	From - To	APPS	GOA
(M)Sam	Barker				29/05/1992	19	St Albans	Yth - St Albans 8/10		
(D)Alan	White		6'01"	13 02	22/03/1976	35	Darlington	Darlington 7/09 - Rel 8/10, Stalybridge 10/10, Gateshead 11/10 Rel 2/11, Blyth 2/11 Rel c/s 11		
(M)Kevin	Nicholls		6'00"	11 00	02/01/1979	32	Newham	Preston 8/08 - Rel 8/10		
(F)Tom	Craddock		5'11"	11 10	14/10/1986	24	Darlington	Middlesbrough (3ML) 10/08 £80,000 1/09 - Oxford U Undisc 8/10	4	2
(M)Adam	Murray		5'09"	10 00	30/09/1981	29	Birmingham	Oxford U 7/10 - Mansfield (3ML) 10/10 Perm 1/11	7	0
(M)Andy	Drury		5'11"	12 08	28/11/1983	27	Kent	Stevenage 5/10 - Ipswich Undisc 1/11	23	6
(F)Kevin	Gallen		5'11"	12 10	21/09/1975	35	Chiswick	MK Dons (2ML) 11/08 Perm 1/09 - Rel 1/11, Barnet (3ML) 10/10, Braintree 3/11	6	0
(F)Taiwo	Atieno		6'02"	12 12	06/08/1985	26	Brixton	USA 3/10 - Rel 1/11, Stevenage 2/11 Rel 5/11, Torquay 7/11	13	3
(D)Pavel	Besta		6'00"	11 13	02/09/1982	28	Ostrava	Ruzomberok (Slo) 8/10 - Rel 1/11	6	0
(M)Taylor	Nathaniel				16/01/1992	19	London	Yth - Rel 1/11		
(F)Cauley	Woodrow				12/11/1994	16		Yth - Fulham Undisc 3/11	0	0
(F)Lloyd	Owusu		6'02"	14 00	12/12/1976	34	Slough	Adelaide U (Aust) 1/11 - Rel c/s 11	13	6
(M)Adam	Newton		5'10"	11 06	04/12/1980	30	Grays	Brentford 7/09 - Rel c/s 11, Woking 6/11	19	0
(F)Jason	Walker		6'02"	14 04	21/03/1984	27	Barrow	Barrow (6WL) 11/10 Undisc 1/11 - York C £60,000 6/11	20	4
(M)Claude	Gnapka		6'02"	13 05	09/06/1983	28	Marseille, Fra	Peterborough 8/08 - Walsall 7/11	42	13
(D)Zdeněk	Kroča		6'05"	14 00	29/09/1980	30	Zlín	Tescoma Zlín (Cze) 8/10 - Kilmarnock 7/11	45	5
(F)Jordan	Patrick		5'08"	11 00	14/01/1992	19	Luton	Luton Rel c/s 11 - Hitchin (L) 2/11, Kettering 8/11	0	0

Caught in action....

Mansfield's Silk looks set to make a challenge on Darlington's Senior during the FA Trophy final.

Photo by Keith Clayton

MANSFIELD TOWN

Chairman: John Radford
Secretary: Catherine Hannant **(T)** 01623 482 482 **(E)** info@mansfieldtown.net
Additional Committee Members:
Steve Hymas, Steve Middleton, Andrew Saunders, Mark Stevenson, Darren Bland, Mark Hawkins.
Manager: Paul Cox
Programme Editor: Mark Stevenson **(E)** mark.Stevenson@mansfieldtown.net

Club Factfile

Founded: 1897 **Nickname:** The Stagds
Previous Names: Mansfield Wesleyans 1897-1906, Mansfield Wesley 1906-10
Previous Leagues: Mansfield & District Am. 1902-06, Notts & Dist. 1906-11, Central Alliance 1911-14, 15-21, Notts & Derbys' 1914-15, Midland 1921-26, Midland Combination 1926-31, Football League 1931-2008
Club Colours (change): Amber & blue/blue/blue (All navy)

Ground: Field Mill Stadium, Quarry Lane, Mansfield NG18 5DA **(T)** 01623 482 482
Capacity: 10000 **Seats:** **Covered:** All **Clubhouse:** Yes **Shop:** Yes

Directions
From the North: Take the M1 exiting at junction 29, then join the A617 to Mansfield, after around 6 miles turn right into Rosemary Street, then proceed to Quarry Lane where you should turn right to the ground. From the South: Take the M1 exiting at junction 28, then take the A38 to Mansfield, after around 6 miles turn right into Belvedere Street (at crossroads), then after a quarter of a mile turn right into Quarry Lane. From the East: Take the A617 to Rainworth, at the crossroads turn left, after 3 miles turn right into Nottingham Road, a left turn will take you into Quarry Lane where you find the ground. From the West: Take the M1 exiting at junction 28, then take the A38 to Mansfield, after around 6 miles turn right into Belvedere Street (at crossroads), then after a quarter of a mile turn right into Quarry Lane.

Previous Grounds: West Field Lane 1897-99, Ratcliffe Gate 1899-1901, 12-16, Newgate Lane 1901-12.

Record Attendance: 24,467 v Nottingham Forest - FA Cup 3rd Round 10/01/53
Record Victory: 9-2 v Rotherham United - Division 3 South 29/08/31
Record Defeat: 1-8 v Walsall - Division 3 North 19/01/33
Record Goalscorer: Harry Johnson - 104 (1931-36)
Record Appearances: Ron Arnold - 440 (1970-83)
Additional Records: Paid £150,000 to Carlisle United for Lee Peacock
Received £655,000 from Tottenham Hotspur for Colin Calderwood

Senior Honours: Football Division 4 1974-75, Division 3 1976-77. League Trophy 1987

10 YEAR RECORD

01-02		02-03		03-04		04-05		05-06		06-07		07-08		08-09		09-10		10-11	
FL 3	3	FL 3	23	FL 3	5	FL 2	13	FL 2	16	FL 2	17	FL 2	23	Conf	12	Conf	9	Conf	13

MANSFIELD TOWN

No.	Date	Comp	H/A	Opponents	Att:	Result	Goalscorers	Pos
1	Sat-14-Aug	BSP	H	Forest Green Rovers	2474	W 3-1	Connor 2 (47, 72), Mills 57	3
2	Tue-17-Aug	BSP	A	Fleetwood Town	1849	L 0-3		14
3	Sat-21-Aug	BSP	A	Kidderminster Harriers	1487	W 3-1	Medley 54, Connor 57, Duffy 90	4
4	Tue-24-Aug	BSP	H	Kettering Town	2089	D 1-1	Sandwith 20	6
5	Sat-28-Aug	BSP	H	Cambridge United	2257	W 1-0	Parker pen 62	4
6	Mon-30-Aug	BSP	A	Altrincham	1261	W 4-0	Connor 11, A Smith 18, Parker 2 (81, pen 90)	1
7	Sat-04-Sep	BSP	H	Tamworth	2516	L 0-1		3
8	Sat-11-Sep	BSP	A	Southport	1289	W 2-1	Istead 18, Gregory 40	3
9	Sat-18-Sep	BSP	A	Newport County	2713	L 0-1		6
10	Tue-21-Sep	BSP	H	York City	2202	W 5-0	A Smith 22, Duffy 55, Connor 64, Nix 89, Medley 90	2
11	Sat-25-Sep	BSP	H	Eastbourne Borough	2312	W 4-0	C Smith 43, Duffy pen 45, Medley 2 (74, 79)	1
12	Tue-28-Sep	BSP	A	Luton Town	6024	L 0-2		4
13	Sat-02-Oct	BSP	A	Gateshead	1046	D 1-1	Connor 29	5
14	Tue-05-Oct	BSP	H	AFC Wimbledon	2699	L 2-5	Connor 34, Briscoe 83	6
15	Sat-09-Oct	BSP	A	Rushden & Diamonds	1480	L 0-1		7
16	Sat-16-Oct	BSP	H	Darlington	2234	D 1-1	Connor 9	7
17	Sat-30-Oct	BSP	H	Crawley Town	2615	L 1-4	Parker pen 42	8
18	Tue-09-Nov	BSP	A	Kettering Town	1270	W 2-0	Og (Jack) 59, Briscoe 90	7
19	Sat-13-Nov	BSP	A	Forest Green Rovers	767	L 1-2	Mitchley 74	10
20	Sat-20-Nov	BSP	H	Hayes & Yeading United	2019	W 3-2	A Smith 3, Connor 78, Medley 82	9
21	Sat-27-Nov	BSP	A	Wrexham	2505	D 1-1	Connor 19	9
22	Tue-28-Dec	BSP	A	Cambridge United	2505	W 5-1	Murray 33, A Smith 37, Duffy 73, Og (Coulson) 90, Mitchley 90	6
23	Sat-01-Jan	BSP	A	Grimsby Town	3654	L 2-7	Duffy 44, Briscoe 57	8
24	Mon-03-Jan	BSP	H	Altrincham	2229	L 0-1		9
25	Sat-08-Jan	BSP	A	Eastbourne Borough	903	W 3-1	Nix 22, Murray 76, Parker 90	8
26	Tue-11-Jan	BSP	H	Fleetwood Town	1725	L 2-5	Murray 38, Foster 73	8
27	Sat-22-Jan	BSP	H	Histon	1880	W 1-0	Connor 90	7
28	Tue-25-Jan	BSP	A	Darlington	1614	D 0-0		7
29	Sat-29-Jan	BSP	H	Wrexham	3266	L 2-3	Briscoe 39, Thompson 45	9
30	Sat-12-Feb	BSP	H	Newport County	1986	D 3-3	Moult 2 (31, 45), Briscoe pen 35	10
31	Sat-19-Feb	BSP	A	Barrow	1130	D 2-2	A Smith 2 (73, 86)	11
32	Sat-05-Mar	BSP	A	Tamworth	1162	W 2-0	Cain 65, Briscoe 69	12
33	Tue-15-Mar	BSP	A	York City	2261	L 1-2	Naylor 28	13
34	Tue-22-Mar	BSP	A	Histon	380	W 3-2	Briscoe 3 (49, 68, 80)	12
35	Sat-26-Mar	BSP	H	Kidderminster Harriers	2079	L 1-2	Murray 79	14
36	Tue-29-Mar	BSP	A	Crawley Town	3162	L 0-2		14
37	Sat-02-Apr	BSP	H	Rushden & Diamonds	1758	W 2-1	Medley 29, Briscoe 90	13
38	Tue-05-Apr	BSP	H	Southport	1467	D 2-2	Higginson 30, Briscoe 44	13
39	Sat-09-Apr	BSP	A	Hayes & Yeading United	316	L 0-4		14
40	Tue-12-Apr	BSP	H	Barrow	1253	D 1-1	Briscoe 63	14
41	Thu-14-Apr	BSP	H	Bath City	2026	W 2-0	Higginson 62, Nix 74	11
42	Sat-16-Apr	BSP	H	Luton Town	2203	D 0-0		11
43	Tue-19-Apr	BSP	H	Grimsby Town	1787	L 0-2		12
44	Fri-22-Apr	BSP	A	AFC Wimbledon	3613	L 1-2	Thompson 14	12
45	Mon-25-Apr	BSP	H	Gateshead	1749	W 3-2	Murray 2 (75, 89), Briscoe 90	12
46	Sat-30-Apr	BSP	A	Bath City	1051	L 0-2		13
CUPS								
1	Sat-23-Oct	FAC 4Q	A	FC Halifax	2986	W 1-0	Briscoe 6	
2	Sat-06-Nov	FAC 1	H	Torquay United	2179	L 0-1		
3	Tue-14-Dec	FAT 1	A	Worksop Town	682	W 5-0	Parker pen 16, Briscoe 45, Duffy 51, Grand 65, Medley pen 90	
4	Sat-15-Jan	FAT 2	H	Newport County	1137	W 4-2	Connor 2 (16, 18), Parker 41, Briscoe 47	
5	Sat-05-Feb	FAT 3	H	Alfreton Town	3408	D 1-1	Connor 48	
6	Tue-08-Feb	FAT 3R	A	Alfreton Town	2131	W 2-1	Connor 60, Parker 77	
7	Tue-01-Mar	FAT 4	A	Chasetown	2000	D 2-2	Connor 35, Briscoe 74	
8	Tue-08-Mar	FAT 4R	H	Chasetown	2295	W 3-1	Murray 36, Briscoe 54, Mitchley 75	
9	Sun-13-Mar	FAT SF 1	H	Luton Town	3208	W 1-0	Mitchley 62	
10	Sat-19-Mar	FAT SF 2	A	Luton Town	6133	D 1-1 aet	Briscoe 118	
11	Sat-07-May	FAT Final	N	Darlington	24668	L 0-1 aet	Played at Wembley	
							League	
							Starts	
							Substitute	
							Unused Sub	
							Cups	
							Starts	
							Substitute	
							Unused Sub	
							Goals (Lg)	
							Goals (Cup)	

MARRIOTT	SILK	FOSTER	C SMITH	MILLS	THOMPSON	STONEHOUSE	A SMITH	BRISCOE	PARKER	CONNOR	MEDLEY	CAIN	ISTEAD	SANDWITH	COLLETT	NAYLOR	DUFFY	NIX	GREGORY	MURRAY	AKSALU	DAY	GRAND	COOK	PILKINGTON	VINCENTI	MITCHLEY	WILLIAMS	MOULT	GROF	SPENCE	PREECE	O'RAFFERTY	HIGGINSON	HALL
1	2	5	6	4	8	17	11	7	21	23	22	26	19	3	25	16	9	10	20	29	32	33	31	34	30	6	35	15	14	30	20	18	27	24	31
X	X	X	X	X	X	X	X	X	X	X	S	S	S	U	U																				
X	X	X	X	X	X	X	X	X	X	X	S		S	U	U	U																			
X	X	X	X	X	X	X	X	X	X	X	S			S	U	U	S																		
X	X	X	X	X	X		X	X	S	X	X			X	U	U	S	S																	
X	X	X	X	X	X		X	X	X	X	S			X	U	U	S	S																	
X	X	X	X	X	X		X	X	X	X	S			X	U	U	S	S																	
X	X	X	X	X	X		X	X	X	X	S			X	U	U	S	S																	
X	X	X	X	X					U	X	X	S	X	X	U	U	S	X	X																
X	X	X	X	X			X	S	S	X			X	X	U	U	S	X	X																
X	X	X	X	X		S	X	S		X	S		X	X	U	U	X	X																	
X	X	X	X	X		S	X	S		X	S		X	X	U	U	X	X																	
X	X	X	X	X		U	X	S		X	S		X	X	U	S	X	X																	
X	X		X	X		S	X	X		X	S		S	X	U	X	U	X		X															
X	X	X	X	X		U		X		X	S	X		X	S	U	S	X		X															
	X	X	X	X		U		X	S	X	X	X	S	X	U		S			X	X														
	X	X			X	X		X	S	X	S	X	S		U			X		X	X	X	U												
	S	X			X	X	X	X	S	X					U		S	U		X		X		X	X	X									
		X			X	U	X	X	X	S			S	X	U					X			X	X	X	X	S								
		X			X	U	X	X	X	S			S	X	U					X			X	X	X	X	S								
					X	U	X	X		X	S		X	X	U	U				X		X	X	X	X		S								
						U	X	X		X	S		X	X	U	U	S			X		X	X	X	X		X								
				S			X	X	X		S		X	X	U	U	X			X		X	X	X	X		S								
				U			X	X	X	S			X	X	U	U	X			X		X	X	X	X		S								
	X			S			X	X	S	X	S		X	X	U	U	X			X		X		X	X										
	X	X		S		U			X	S	S	X		X	U	X	X	X		X					X			X							
	X	X				U			X	S	S	X	S	X	U	X	X	X		X					X			X							
	X	X			X	X		X	X	X		X	U	X	X	U		S		X					U		S								
	X	X			X	X		X		X	S	X	S	X	X	U		S		X					U		X								
	X	X			X	X	S	X		X	U	X	U	X	X	U		U		X							X								
	X				X		U	X	S	X		X		X	X	X		U		X		X							X	U	U				
	X	U			X	X	S	X		X		X	U	X		X		S		X							S		X	X					
U	X	U			X		U	X		X		X		X		X		U		X							S		X	X	X				
U		X				X	X			S		X	X	U		X		S		X							X			X	X	S	X		
U		U			X	X	X	X		X			U	X		X				X							X			X	X	U	S		
U	X	U			X	X	X	X		X			S	X		X		S		X										X		U	X		
U	X	U			X	X		X		X	X		X	X		X				X										X		U			
X		X			X	X		X		X	X		X	U		X				X										S		U	S	X	U
		X			X	X		X		X	X		X	U	U	X				X										X		U	S	X	S
	U	X			X		S	X		X	X		X	X	U	X		S		X							S			X				X	
	X	U				X	U	X			X	X	U	X	U	X		X		X							X			X				S	
	X	X				X	U	X			X	X	U		U	X		X		X							X			X		U		S	
	X	X			U	X	S	X				X	X		U	X		X									X			X	U	S		X	
	X	X				X	X	X		X	S		U		U			X		X							U			X	U	X		X	
	X	X			X		X	S		X	X	X	S		X			U		X										U	X	X		S	
X	X	X			X		X	X				S	X		U	U		U		X											X	X	X		S
X	U	X			S	X	X	U			X	X	X		U			X													X	X	X		S
	U	U			S	X	X	X		X	S		U		U		X	X	S	X	X	X	X	X											
	X	S			S	X	X	X	X		U		U	U	U		S	X		X			X	X	X	X									
	X			S	X	U	X	X	X	X	S			X	X	U	S			X			X	X											
	X	X			X	X	U	X	X	X	U	X		X	X			S		X							U	U							
	X	X			X	X		X	S	X		X		X	X	S		U		X							U		X	U					
	X				X			X	S	X		X			X	X		U		X		X					U		X	U	X	U			
U	X	S			X	X	S	X		X		X		X		X		S		X							U		X	X					
U	X	U			X		U	X		X		X	U	X		X		U		X							X			X	X				
U	X	U			X	U	S	X		X		X	S	X		X		X									X			X	X				
U	X	U			X	U	S	X		X		X	S	X		X		X									X			X	X				
	X	X	X			X	U	X	X		X		S			U	X		X		X							S				X			
17	33	33	15	15	26	20	27	36	13	34	11	17	18	32	5	16	8	15	2	32	2	8	6	8	10	3	8	2	3	12	6	4	4	5	0
0	1	0	0	3	1	3	4	5	7	6	20	3	11	1	1	1	11	10	0	0	0	0	0	0	0	0	9	0	0	1	0	2	3	3	3
5	2	6	0	1	1	9	4	1	1	0	1	0	7	5	33	20	1	6	0	0	0	0	1	0	2	0	1	0	0	2	3	6	0	0	1
1	10	3	0	0	9	5	4	11	3	10	0	7	0	7	4	6	1	5	0	9	1	2	3	3	1	1	3	0	3	4	5	0	0	0	0
0	0	2	0	1	2	0	3	0	2	0	2	1	2	0	0	1	2	2	1	0	0	0	0	0	0	0	1	0	0	0	0	0	0	0	0
4	1	4	0	0	0	4	2	0	0	0	2	0	3	1	3	1	0	3	0	0	0	0	0	0	0	0	4	1	0	2	0	1	0	0	0
0	0	1	1	1	2	0	6	13	5	11	6	1	1	1	0	1	5	3	1	6	0	0	0	0	0	0	2	0	2	0	0	0	0	2	0
0	0	0	0	0	0	0	0	6	3	5	1	0	0	0	0	0	1	0	0	1	0	0	1	0	0	0	2	0	0	0	0	0	0	0	0

PLAYING SQUAD

Existing Players		SN	HT	WT	DOB	AGE	POB	Career	Apps	Goals
GOALKEEPERS										
Neil	Collett				02/10/1989	21	Coventry	Coventry Rel c/s 09, Nuneaton T 5/09, Mansfield 1/10, Nuneaton T (L) 7/11	6	0
Alan	Marriott	1	6'01"	12 05	03/09/1978	32	Bedford	Tottenham Rel c/s 99, Lincoln C 8/99 Rel c/s 08, Rushden & D 7/08, Mansfield 1/09	17	0
Shane	Redmond	23	6'02"	12 10	23/03/1989	22	Rathcole	Cherry Orchard (Ire) (Yth), Notts Forest Rel c/s 10, Eastwood T (SL) 9/08, Burton (6ML) 7/09, Darlington (3ML) 1/10, Chesterfield 8/10, Mansfield 7/11		
DEFENDERS										
Matt	Bell	18	5'10"	11 03	03/01/1992	19	Stoke	Port Vale Rel c/s 11, Newcastle T (L) 8/10, Newcastle T (SL) 3/11, Mansfield 6/11		
Rhys	Day	22	6'02"	13 06	31/08/1982	29	Bridgend	Man City, Blackpool (3ML) 12/01, Cambridge U (L) 9/02, Mansfield (2ML) 11/02 Perm 1/03 Rel c/s 05, Aldershot 7/06 Rel c/s 09, Oxford U 7/09, Mansfield (3ML) 10/10 Perm 1/11	8	0
Ben	Futcher	26	6'07"	12 05	20/02/1981	30	Manchester	Oldham Rel 1/02, Stalybridge (3ML) 8/01, Stalybridge 1/02, Doncaster 3/02, Lincoln C 5/02 Rel c/s 05, Boston U 7/05, Grimsby 1/06, Peterborough Undisc 8/06, Bury 6/07, Oxford U (2ML) 11/10, Mansfield (L) 8/11		
Joe	Kendrick	3	6'00"	11 04	26/06/1983	28	Dublin	St Josephs Boys (Ire), Newcastle Rel c/s 03, TSV 1860 Munich (Ger) 7/03, Darlington 8/04 Rel 5/06, Torquay 8/06 Rel 8/06, Tamworth 9/06, Workington 1/07, Newcastle Blue Star 11/07, Drogheda (Ire) 1/08, PFC Neftchi Baku (Aze) 1/09, Sligo R (Ire) 7/09, Drogheda (Ire) 1/10 Rel 7/10, Bray W (Ire) 1/11, Mansfield 7/11		
Tom	Naylor	2	5'11"	11 04	28/06/1991	20	Sutton-in-Ashfield	Mansfield, Belper (SL) 8/09, Alfreton (L) 10/10	17	1
Luke	O'Neill	16	6'00"	11 04	20/08/1991	20	Slough	Leicester Rel 5/11, Tranmere (L) 2/10, Kettering (SL) 1/11, Mansfield 7/11		
Martin	Riley	6	6'00	12 01	05/12/1986	24	Wolverhampton	Wolves Rel 12/07, Shrewsbury 3/08 Rel c/s 08, Kidderminster 8/08 Rel 7/10, Cheltenham 7/10 Rel c/s 11, Mansfield 7/11		
Ritchie	Sutton	17	6'00	11 04	29/04/1986	25	Stoke	Crewe Rel 5/07, Leek T (2ML) 11/05, Stafford R (L) 3/06, Stafford R (SL) 8/06, Stafford R 7/07, Northwich 5/08, FC Halifax (L) 12/08 Perm 1/09, Nantwich 6/09, Port Vale 7/10, Mansfield 6/11		
John	Thompson	5	6'00"	11 11	12/10/1981	29	Dublin	River Valley Rangers (Yth), Home Farm (Yth), Notts Forest Rel c/s 07, Tranmere (6WL) 10/06, Tranmere (SL) 1/07, Oldham 7/07, Notts County (10WL) 10/08 Perm 1/09 Rel c/s 11, Mansfield 7/11		
Nick	Wood	25	6'01"	12 02	09/11/1990	20	Ossett	Sheff Wed, Sheffield FC (L) 12/09, Tranmere 7/10 Rel c/s 11, Mansfield 8/11		
MIDFIELDERS										
Paul	Bolland	14	6'00"	12 06	23/12/1979	31	Bradford	Bradford C, Notts County (L) 1/99 £75,000 4/99 Rel c/s 05, Grimsby 8/05 Rel c/s 09, Macclesfield 7/09, Mansfield 6/11		
Adam	Murray	11	5'09"	10 00	30/09/1981	29	Birmingham	Derby, Mansfield (SL) 2/02, Kidderminster (L) 8/03, Solihull 11/03, Burton 11/03, Notts County 11/03, Kidderminster 1/04, Mansfield 6/04, Carlisle Nominal 3/05, Torquay £10,000 8/06, Macclesfield £17,500 1/07, Oxford U Undisc 1/08, Luton 7/10, Mansfield (3ML) 10/10 Perm 1/11	32	6
Lee	Stevenson	8	5'10"		01/06/1984	27	Sheffield	Sheff Wed (Scholar), Kings Lynn 3/03, Belper 11/06, Eastwood T 5/10, Mansfield Undisc 5/11		
Andy	Todd	20	6'00"	11 03	22/02/1979	32	Nottingham	Eastwood T, N.Forest 2/96, Scarborough 2/99, Eastwood T 5/99, Ilkeston 3/00, Eastwood T 7/01, Worksop 10/01, Hucknall 12/03, Burton 7/05, Accrington (SL) 1/06, Accrington Undisc 6/06, Rotherham 8/07 Rel c/s 09, Accrington (SL) 1/08, Eastwood T (SL) 10/08, Alfreton 8/09, Eastwood T 5/10, Mansfield (Pl/Coach) 6/11		
Jon	Worthington	4	5'09"	11 05	16/04/1983	28	Dewsbury	Huddersfield Rel c/s 09, Yeovil (2ML) 1/09, Oldham 7/09, Fleetwood (L) 11/10, Bradford C 1/11, Mansfield 6/11		
FORWARDS										
Louis	Briscoe	7	6'00"	11 13	02/04/1988	23	Burton	Port Vale Rel 1/07, Stafford R (Trial), Moor Green 3/07, Leek T 7/07, Huston Dynamoes (USA) (Trial) 3/08, Hednesford 6/08, Gresley R 9/08, Stafford R 11/08, Ilkeston 12/08, Mansfield 1/09	41	13
Paul	Connor	9	6'02"	11 08	12/01/1979	32	Bishop Auckland	Middlesbrough Rel c/s 99, Gateshead (L) 8/97, Hartlepool (L) 2/98, Stoke (SL) 3/99, Stoke 5/99, Cambridge U (3ML) 11/00, Rochdale £100,000 3/01, Swansea £35,000 3/04, L.Orient £40,000 1/06, Cheltenham £25,000 1/07 Rel c/s 09, Lincoln C 7/09 Rel c/s 10, Mansfield 7/10	40	11
Ross	Dyer	15	6'02"	13 02	12/05/1988	23	Stafford	Hednesford, Forest Green 5/10, Mansfield 6/11		
Matt	Green	10	5'08"	10 05	02/01/1987	24	Bath	Bristol C (Yth), Cirencester, Newport C 6/05, Cardiff C £10,000 1/07 Rel 5/08, Darlington (L) 10/07, Oxford U (L) 11/07, Oxford U (SL) 1/08, Torquay 5/08, Oxford U (SL) 6/09, Oxford U Undisc 6/10, Cheltenham (SL) 1/11, Mansfield (6ML) 7/11		

		SN	HT	WT	DOB	AGE	POB	From - To	APPS	GOA
Anthony	Howell	21			27/05/1986	25	Nottingham	Carlton T, Shepshed D 9/05, Carlton T 11/06, Grantham 3/07, Notts County (Trial) c/s 07, Eastwood T 6/07, Worksop 9/07, Eastwood (L) 1/08 Perm, Ilkeston 8/08, Mansfield 1/09 Rel 5/09, Alfreton (SL) 3/09, Alfreton 5/09, Mansfield 6/11		
Lindon	Meikle	24			21/03/1988	23	Nottingham	Vernon Colts, Eastwood T 7/04, Mansfield Undisc 5/11		
Adam	Smith	19	5'11"	12 00	20/02/1985	26	Huddersfield	Chesterfield Rel 6/08, Lincoln C (L) 1/08, Gainsborough 8/08, York C (2ML) 11/08, York C Undisc 1/09, Mansfield 5/10	31	6

Loanees		**SN**	**HT**	**WT**	**DOB**	**AGE**	**POB**	**From - To**	**APPS**	**GOA**
(G)Mihkel	Aksalu		6'03"	12 05	07/11/1984	26	Kuressaare (Est)	Sheff Utd (2ML) 10/10 -	2	0
(M)Simon	Grand		6'00"	10 03	23/02/1984	27	Chorley	Fleetwood (3ML) 10/10 - Aldershot (SL) 1/11, Rel 5/11, Southport 6/11	6	0
(D)Steve	Cook		6'01"	12 13	19/04/1991	20	Hastings	Brighton (3ML) 10/10 -	8	0
(F)Peter	Vincenti		6'02"	11 13	07/07/1986	25	Jersey	Stevenage (3ML) 10/10 - Aldershot Undisc 1/11	3	0
(G)Kevin	Pilkington		6'01"	13 00	08/03/1974	37	Hitchin	Luton (3ML) 10/10 -	10	0
(F)Louis	Moult		6'00"	13 05	14/05/1992	19	Stoke	Stoke (2ML) 1/11 -	3	2
(G)David	Grof		6'03"	14 02	17/04/1989	22	Budapest, Hun	Notts County (SL) 1/11 - Rel 5/11, Walsall 7/11	13	0

Departures		**SN**	**HT**	**WT**	**DOB**	**AGE**	**POB**	**From - To**	**APPS**	**GOA**
(D)Jason	Ventrella				22/04/1992	19		Yth - Rel 8/10, Hucknall 9/10		
(D)Julian	Cherel		6'05"	13 05	08/03/1983	28	Caen, Fra	Hartlepool 10/10 - Northwich 10/10		
(F)Lee	Gregory				26/08/1988	23	Sheffield	Staveley MW 9/09 - FC Halifax 12/10	2	1
(D)Chris	Smith		5'11"	11 06	30/06/1981	30	Derby	Tamworth 7/10 - York C (3ML) 10/10 Perm 1/11	15	1
(M)Gary	Mills		5'09"	11 06	20/05/1981	30	Sheppey	Stevenage 6/09 - Rel 1/11, Forest Green (L) 10/10, Rushden & D 1/11, Bath C 5/11	18	1
(F)Robert	Duffy		6'01"	12 04	02/12/1982	28	Swansea	Newport C 1/09 - Grimsby Undisc 1/11	19	5
(M)Matt	Somner		6'00"	13 02	08/12/1982	28	Isleworth	Notts County 7/08 - Rel 1/11, Altrincham (3ML) 10/10, Forest Green 1/11, Lewes 7/11		
(M)Ryan	Williams		5'04"	11 02	31/08/1978	33	Chesterfield	Weymouth 2/09 - Rel 1/11, Gainsborough (2ML) 10/10, Gainsborough 1/11	2	0
(D)Paul	Stonehouse		5'07"	11 03	13/07/1987	24	Wegburg	Forest Green Undisc 6/10 - Rel 5/11, Bath C 5/11	23	0
(D)Mark	Preece		6'02"	13 07	03/06/1987	24	Bristol	Forest Green 7/10 - Rel 5/11, Eastwood T (L) 9/10, AFC Telford (L) 2/11, Bath C 8/11	6	0
(M)Kyle	Nix		5'06"	09 10	21/01/1986	25	Sydney, Aust	Bradford C 7/09 - Rel 5/11, Gateshead 7/11	25	3
(F)Niall	O'Rafferty				02/07/1992	19	Nottingham	Yth - Rel 5/11	7	0
(M)Tyrone	Thompson		5'09"	11 02	08/05/1981	30	Sheffield	Torquay 7/10 - Rel 5/11, Grimsby 8/11	27	2
(F)Danny	Mitchley		5'10"	10 08	07/10/1989	21	Liverpool	Burscough NC 11/10 - Rel 5/11	17	2
(D)Steve	Foster		6'01"	13 00	03/12/74	36	Mansfield	Blyth 5/10 - Rel 5/11, Spennymoor 7/11	33	1
(D)Kevin	Sandwith		5'11"	13 06	30/04/1978	33	Workington	Oxford U 5/10 - Rel 5/11, Gainsborough 8/11	33	1
(D)Daniel	Spence		5'10"	12 06	22/10/1989	21		Glen Hoddle Football Academy 1/11 - Rel 5/11	6	0
(D)Ben	Turner		6'01"	10 09	22/09/1991	19	Worksop	Yth - Rel 5/11, North Ferriby (SL) 1/11		
(M)Ashley	Cain		6'02"	12 06	27/09/1990	20	Nuneaton	Coventry 7/10 - Rel 5/11, Tamworth 6/11	20	1
(M)Steven	Istead		5'08"	11 04	23/04/1986	25	South Shields	Ilkeston 6/09 - Rel 5/11, Eastwood T 6/11	29	1
(F)Luke	Medley		6'01"	13 03	21/06/1989	22	Greenwich	Barnet 8/10 - Rel 5/11, Aldershot (L) 2/11, Kidderminster 6/11	31	6
(D)Gary	Silk		5'09"	13 07	13/09/1984	26	Newport, IOW	Notts County 7/08 - Grimsby 6/11	34	0
(M)Paul	Hall		5'08"	11 04	03/07/1972	39	Manchester	Mansfield (Ass Man), Temp Man 5/11 - Rel 6/11	3	0
(M)Conor	Higginson		5'08"	10 09	27/01/1992	19	Ollerton	Yth - Rel c/s 11, Sheffield FC 7/11	8	2
(F)Keigan	Parker		5'07"	10 05	08/06/1982	29	Livingston	Oldham 7/10 - Rel c/s 11, Fleetwood (SL) 2/11, Stockport 8/11	20	5

Caught in action....

Ashley Cain has his clearance blocked by Luton's Jake Howells during Mansfield's first leg tie in the Semi Final of the FA Trophy.

Photo by Bill Wheatcroft

NEWPORT COUNTY

Chairman: Chris Blight
Secretary: Mike Everett (T) 07889 359 100 (E) mike.everett3@googlemail.com
Additional Committee Members:
John Allison, John Bowkett, Howard Greenhaf, Nick McDonald, Phil Morgan.

Manager: Anthony Hudson
Programme Editor: Ray Taylor (E) rayncafc@aol.com

Back Row : Jonny Evans (Ass Physio), Wayne Turk, Lee Baker, Craig Reid, Giuseppe Sole, Andrew Hughes, Jake Harris, Scott Rogers, Tony Taggart, John Fitzgerald (Physio)
Centre Row : Bobby Morris (Staff), Chris Todd, Jamie Collins, Oliver Thorne, Glyn Thompson, Gary Warren (C), Glyn Garner, Robbie Matthews, Sam Foley, Paul Bignot, Tony Gilbert (Kit Manager)
Front Row : Darryl Knights, Eddie Odhiambo, Matthew Bishop (Coach), Fraser Skimming (Assistant Manager), Chris Blight (Chairman), Dean Holdsworth (Manager), John Bowkett (Director), Tim Harris (Director of Football), Ian Harris (Goalkeeping Coach), Danny Rose, Charlie Henry

Club Factfile

Founded: 1998 **Nickname:** The Exiles
Previous Names: Newport AFC after demise of Newport County in 1988-89, changed back again in 1999
Previous Leagues: Hellenic 1989-90, Southern 1990-2004

Club Colours (change): Amber/black/black (All white)

Ground: Newport Stadium, Langland Way, Newport, South Wales NP19 4PT **(T)** 01633 662 262
Capacity: 4,300 **Seats:** 1,236 **Covered:** 3,236 **Clubhouse:** Yes **Shop:** Yes

Directions
From M4 Junction 24: Follow A48 (Signposted City Centre, Newport International Sports Village) For 2.5 Miles.
Turn left into Langland Way (adjacent to Carcraft).
Take first left after BOC depot.

Previous Grounds:

Record Attendance: 4,616 v Swansea City - FA Cup 1st Round 11/11/2006
Record Victory: 9-0 v Pontlottyn Blast Furnace (A) - Welsh Cup 01/09/90
Record Defeat: 1-6 v Stafford Rangers (A) - 06/01/96
Record Goalscorer: Chris Lillygreen - 93
Record Appearances: Mark Price - 275
Additional Records: Paid £5,000 to Forest Green Rovers for Shaun Chapple
Received £5,000 from Merthyr Tydfil for Craig Lima

Senior Honours: Hellenic League 1989-90. League Cup 1989-90. Gloucestershire Senior Cup 1993-94.
Southern League Midland Division 1994-95. Gwent FA Senior Cup 1996-97, 97-98, 99-2000, 00-01, 01-02, 03-04, 04-05.
Conference South 2009-10.

10 YEAR RECORD

01-02	02-03	03-04	04-05	05-06	06-07	07-08	08-09	09-10	10-11
SthP 5	SthP 10	SthP 7	Conf S 18	Conf S 18	Conf S 6	Conf S 9	Conf S 10	Conf S 1	Conf 9

NEWPORT COUNTY

No.	Date	Comp	H/A	Opponents	Att:	Result	Goalscorers	Pos
1	Sat-14-Aug	BSP	A	Darlington	2597	L 0-1		20
2	Tue-17-Aug	BSP	H	Tamworth	2217	D 1-1	Reid pen 71	21
3	Sat-21-Aug	BSP	H	Histon	1927	D 2-2	Rose 6, Matthews 18	19
4	Tue-24-Aug	BSP	A	Luton Town	6945	D 1-1	Henry 26	20
5	Sat-28-Aug	BSP	H	Kidderminster Harriers	2026	W 3-0	Matthews 35, Reid 2 (pen 44, pen 53)	13
6	Mon-30-Aug	BSP	A	AFC Wimbledon	3828	D 2-2	Reid 2 (pen 25, 79)	13
7	Sun-05-Sep	BSP	H	Wrexham	3206	D 1-1	Knights 89	15
8	Sat-11-Sep	BSP	A	Rushden & Diamonds	1351	W 1-0	Reid 33	9
9	Sat-18-Sep	BSP	H	Mansfield Town	2713	W 1-0	Rose 60	8
10	Tue-21-Sep	BSP	A	Hayes & Yeading United	478	W 2-1	Reid 47, Warren 55	7
11	Sat-25-Sep	BSP	A	Cambridge United	2648	W 1-0	Collins 3	5
12	Tue-28-Sep	BSP	H	Forest Green Rovers	2677	W 3-1	Foley 18, Reid 2 (34, 74)	2
13	Sat-02-Oct	BSP	A	Grimsby Town	3246	L 0-2		6
14	Tue-05-Oct	BSP	H	Eastbourne Borough	2403	D 3-3	Matthews 3, Collins 18, Rogers 80	5
15	Sat-09-Oct	BSP	H	York City	2802	W 4-0	Foley 2 (6, 27), Reid 2 (62, 70)	3
16	Sat-16-Oct	BSP	A	Crawley Town	2566	W 3-2	Rose 25, Reid 42, Knights 47	3
17	Sat-30-Oct	BSP	H	Kettering Town	2230	L 1-2	Henry 4	4
18	Sat-06-Nov	BSP	A	Barrow	1089	L 1-2	Warren 42	6
19	Sat-13-Nov	BSP	A	Eastbourne Borough	1065	D 0-0		5
20	Sat-20-Nov	BSP	H	Southport	1867	W 2-0	Wright 53, Reid 66	4
21	Sat-27-Nov	BSP	H	Hayes & Yeading United	1601	W 2-1	Knights 5, Reid pen 67	4
22	Sat-18-Dec	BSP	A	Fleetwood Town	1142	D 1-1	Matthews 76	4
23	Tue-28-Dec	BSP	A	Kidderminster Harriers	1757	W 3-2	Reid 29, Og (Shaw) 37, Bignot 82	2
24	Sat-01-Jan	BSP	H	Bath City	2903	L 1-2	Reid 83	4
25	Mon-03-Jan	BSP	H	AFC Wimbledon	3462	D 3-3	Todd 10, Collins 2 (18, 36)	4
26	Sat-08-Jan	BSP	A	Southport	1032	L 1-2	Todd 43	4
27	Tue-11-Jan	BSP	A	Tamworth	803	L 2-3	Reid 2 (10, 66)	5
28	Sat-22-Jan	BSP	H	Rushden & Diamonds	1743	L 1-3	Rose 26	6
29	Sat-29-Jan	BSP	A	Histon	452	D 0-0		7
30	Sat-12-Feb	BSP	A	Mansfield Town	1986	D 3-3	Matthews 1, Griffin 2, Rose 28	8
31	Fri-18-Feb	BSP	H	Luton Town	2834	D 1-1	Collins pen 90	7
32	Tue-22-Feb	BSP	A	Bath City	1551	D 2-2	Odubade 14, Hatswell 21	7
33	Sat-26-Feb	BSP	A	Kettering Town	1056	L 0-2		8
34	Tue-01-Mar	BSP	H	Cambridge United	1360	D 1-1	Collins pen 52	10
35	Sat-05-Mar	BSP	H	Fleetwood Town	1716	L 1-3	Warren 74	11
36	Sat-12-Mar	BSP	H	Altrincham	1201	W 2-1	Og (Piergianni), Warren 70	11
37	Sat-19-Mar	BSP	A	Forest Green Rovers	1362	D 0-0		11
38	Sun-27-Mar	BSP	A	Wrexham	3685	L 0-1		12
39	Tue-29-Mar	BSP	H	Gateshead	1027	W 2-1	Todd 8, Hughes 58	9
40	Sat-02-Apr	BSP	H	Grimsby Town	1506	W 2-1	Knights 59, Todd 72	8
41	Tue-05-Apr	BSP	H	Darlington	1300	W 2-1	Griffin 20, Knights 37	8
42	Sat-09-Apr	BSP	A	York City	2565	L 1-2	Collins 90	8
43	Sat-16-Apr	BSP	H	Barrow	1331	W 5-0	Warren 8, Knights 2 (15, 31), Foley 24, Morgan 56	8
44	Sat-23-Apr	BSP	A	Altrincham	963	W 3-1	Warren 7, Collins 32, Foley 60	9
45	Mon-25-Apr	BSP	H	Crawley Town	2026	L 0-1		9
46	Sat-30-Apr	BSP	A	Gateshead	824	W 7-1	Collins 2 (pen 35, 45), Todd 61, Miller 72, Rose 73, Baker 87, Griffin 88	9

CUPS

No.	Date	Comp	H/A	Opponents	Att:	Result	Goalscorers
1	Sat-23-Oct	FAC 4Q	H	Crawley Town	2247	L 0-1	
2	Sat-11-Dec	FAT 1	H	Wealdstone	1070	D 0-0	
3	Mon-13-Dec	FAT 1R	A	Wealdstone	324	W 1-0 aet	Challinor 119
4	Sat-15-Jan	FAT 2	A	Mansfield Town	1137	L 2-4	Og (Silk) 61, Matthews 70

League
Starts
Substitute
Unused Sub

Cups
Starts
Substitute
Unused Sub

Goals (Lg)
Goals (Cup)

THOMPSON	BIGNOT	WARREN	TODD	ODHIAMBO	COLLINS	ROSE	ROGERS	HENRY	REID	MATTHEWS	FOLEY	SOLE	KNIGHTS	THORNE	GARNER	MORGAN	TAGGART	JOHN	CLOUGH	PROCTOR	BAKER	CHALLINOR	GOODALL	WRIGHT	GREENING	DEERING	SMITH	HUGHES	MONTGOMERY	MCDONALD	FOWLER	LEAHY	HATSWELL	BURNS	MILLER	GRIFFIN	ODUBADE	LENNON
1	2	5	6	16	4	7	8	11	9	19	10	12	20	15	21	29	17	22	23	25	3	24	34	25	31	35	36	18	40	39	38	32	37	41	42	43	44	45
X	X	X	X	X	X	X	X	X	X	X	S	S	S	U	U																							
X	X	X	X	X	X	X	S	X	X	S	X	X	U	U	U																							
X	X	X	X	X	X	X	X	X	X	X	S		S	U	U	S																						
X	X	X	X	X	X	X	S	X	X	X	S		S	U	U	X																						
X	X	X	X	X	X	X	S	X	X	X	S		X	U	U	S																						
X	X	X	X	X	X	X	S	X	X	X			S	U	U	X	S																					
X	X	X	X	X	X	X	U	X	X	X	S		S		U	X	S																					
X	X	X	X	X	X	X	U	X	X	X	S		S		U	U		X																				
X	X	X	X	S	X	X	U	X	X	S	X		S		U	X		X																				
X		X	X	X	X	X	S	X	X	X	X		U		U	S	S	X																				
X	X	X		X	X	X	S	X	X	X	S		X		U	S	U	X																				
X	X	X	S	X	X	X	U	X	X	X	X				S	S		X	U																			
	X	X	X	X	X	X		X	X	S	X		S		X	U		X	S	U																		
		X	X	X	X	X	S	S	X	X	X		X		X	U		X	S	U																		
U	X		X	X	X	X	S	S	X	X	X		X		X	S		X	U																			
U	X	X	X	X	X	X		S	X	X	X		X		X	U		U	U																			
X	X	X	X	X	X	X		X	X	S	X		U		U	S		X				S																
X	X	X	X	U	X	X		X	X	X	S		X		U	S							X	S														
X	X		X	X	X	X		X	X		S		S		U	X						S	X	X	U													
X	X	S	X	X	X	X			X	S	S		X		U	X							X	X		U												
X	X	S	X	X	X	X			X	S			X		U	U							X	X		X	S											
X	X	X	X	X	X	X			X	S			X		U							S	X	U		X	U											
X	X	X	X	X	X	X			X	S	S		X		U	S							X	U		X												
X	X	X	X	X	X	X			X	S	X		X		U								X	S					S	U								
X	X	X	X	S	X	X			X	X	S		X		U								X	U					X	S								
X	X	X	X	S	X	X	U		X		X		X		U													U	X	X	S							
X	X	X	X	U	X	X	S		X	S	X		X		U														X	X	S							
X	X		X	S	X	X			X	X	X		X		U	S												X	S	U	X							
U	X		X	S		X			X	S	X		X		X	S													X	U			X	X	X			
U	X		X	X	X	X				X	S		X		X	S																	X	U	X	X	S	
X	X	X			X	X				X	U		X		U	S												X	S				X		X	X	S	
X	X	X			X	X				S			X		U	S												X	X				X		S	X	X	U
X	X	X			X	X				S	X		X		U	S												X					X		S	X	X	U
X	X	X	X		X	X				S	X		U		U	X														S					X	X	X	U
X	X	X	X	X	X	X				X	X		S		U	X																	U		X	U		S
X	X	X	X	X	X	X	X			S	X		S		U	X																	X			U		S
X	X	X	X		X	X	X			S	X		S		U	X																	X			S	X	U
X	X	X	X		X	X	X				S		S		U	X								U				X								X	S	X
X	X	X	X		X	X	X				S		X		U	U												X							U	X	S	X
X	X	X	X	S	X	X					S		X		U	X												X					U		S	X		X
X	X	X	X	S	X	X	S				U		X		U	X												X							S	X		X
X	X	X	X		X	X	U				S		X		U	X												X							U	X	S	X
X	X	X	X		S	X	X				X		X		U	S																	X		X	X	S	U
X		X	U	S	X	X	X				X		X		U	S												X					X		X	X		S
X		X	X		X	X	X				S		X		U	S					U												X		X	X	S	X
		X	X	X	X	X	X				X		S		X	X					S							U					X		X	S	U	
X	X	X	X	X	X	X	U	S	X	X	X		X		U	S			S		U																	
X		X	X	X	X	X			X	S	S		X			S						U	X	X		X		U										
X		X	X	X	X	X			X	X	X		X		U							S	X	S		S		U										
X	X		X	X		X	S		X	X	X		S		U	X												S		X	X	U						
39	41	39	40	26	44	46	10	16	29	19	22	1	27	0	7	15	0	9	0	0	0	0	8	3	0	3	0	10	5	2	1	0	11	1	9	13	4	6
0	0	2	1	8	1	0	10	3	0	16	18	1	14	0	1	18	3	0	2	0	1	3	0	2	0	0	1	0	3	2	2	0	0	0	4	2	7	3
4	0	0	1	2	0	0	6	0	0	0	2	0	4	6	38	6	1	1	3	2	1	0	0	3	2	1	1	2	0	3	0	0	2	1	2	2	1	5
4	2	3	4	4	3	4	0	0	4	3	3	0	3	0	0	1	0	0	0	0	0	0	2	1	0	1	0	0	0	1	1	0	0	0	0	0	0	0
0	0	0	0	0	0	0	1	1	0	1	1	0	1	0	0	2	0	0	1	0	0	1	0	1	0	1	0	1	0	0	0	0	0	0	0	0	0	0
0	0	0	0	0	0	0	1	0	0	0	0	0	0	0	3	0	0	0	0	0	1	1	0	0	0	0	0	2	0	0	0	1	0	0	0	0	0	0
0	1	6	5	0	10	6	1	2	18	5	5	0	7	0	0	1	0	0	0	0	1	0	0	1	0	0	0	1	0	0	0	0	1	0	1	3	1	0
0	0	0	0	0	0	0	0	0	0	1	0	0	0	0	0	0	0	0	0	0	0	1	0	0	0	0	0	0	0	0	0	0	0	0	0	0	0	0

PLAYING SQUAD

Existing Players		SN	HT	WT	DOB	AGE	POB	Career	Apps	Goals
GOALKEEPERS										
Lee	Harrison	40	6'02"	12 07	12/09/1971	39	Billericay	L.Orient (Sch), Charlton Rel c/s 93, Fulham (L) 11/91, Gillingham (SL) 3/92, Fulham (SL) 12/92, Fulham c/s 93 Rel c/s 96, Barnet 7/96, Peterborough (3ML) 12/02 L.Orient (L) 3/03 £10,000 4/03 Rel 6/05, Peterborough 7/05 Rel 5/06, Barnet 7/06 Rel c/s 10, Hayes & Yeading 7/10, Retired 5/11, Newport C (Ass Coach) 5/11		
Danny	Potter	1	5'11"	13 00	18/03/1979	32	Ipswich	Chelsea (Trainee), Colchester 10/97 Rel c/s 98, Exeter 8/98 Rel c/s 00, Weymouth (L) 11,99, Salisbury (L) 1/00, Weymouth 6/00, Chelmsford 2/02, Canvey Island 8/02, Stevenage 6/06, Cambridge U 5/07 Rel 4/10, Torquay 5/10, Newport C 5/11		
Glyn	Thompson	18	6'02"	13 01	24/02/1981	30	Telford	Shrewsbury, Fulham £50,000 10/99, Mansfield (3ML) 1/00, Shrewsbury (L) 1/01, Northampton (2ML) 11/02, Northampton 3/03 Rel c/s 04, Walsall 8/04, Koge (Den), Rushden & D (Trial) 2/05, Waterford U (Trial) 2/05, Stafford R 1/05, Chesterfield 3/05 Rel c/s 05, Shrewsbury 7/05 Rel 5/06, Koje Boldklub (Den), Hereford 6/06 Rel c/s 07, Newport C 7/0739		0
DEFENDERS										
Lee	Baker	3	5'10"	12 01	20/01/1989	22	Redditch	West Brom, Kidderminster (5ML) 8/08, Kidderminster 1/09, Newport C 6/10	1	1
Wayne	Hatswell	17	6'00"	13 10	08/02/1975	36	Swindon	Cinderford T, Witney T, Cinderford, Forest Green 7/99, Oxford U £35,000 12/00 Rel 4/02, Chester Free 5/02, Kidderminster £15,000 10/03, Rushden & D 1/06, Cambridge U Undisc 1/08, Dundalk (Pl/Coach) 1/10, Newport C (Pl/Coach) 1/11	11	1
Andrew	Hughes	16			05/06/1992	19	Cardiff	Cardiff (Yth), Newport C, Mangotsfield (2ML) 10/10	10	1
Paul	Robson	2	5'08"	11 05	04/08/1983	28	Hull	Doncaster (Scholar), Charlton Rel c/s 03, Bridlington T 8/04, Long Island Rough Riders (USA) 7/05, Crystal Palace Baltimore (USA) 2/08, C.Palace (Trial) 1/09, Newport C 7/11		
Paul	Rodgers	25	5'10"	10 10	06/10/1989	21	Edmonton	Arsenal Rel c/s 09, Northampton (SL) 1/09, Northampton 7/09 Rel c/s 11, Newport C 8/11		
Gary	Warren	5			16/04/1984	27	Bristol	Mangotsfield, Bristol R (Trial) 7/06, Team Bath 6/07, Newport C 5/09	41	6
Ismael	Yakabu	6	6'01"	12 09	05/04/1985	26	Kano, Nig	Barnet Rel c/s 10, AFC Wimbledon 7/10 Rel 5/11, Newport C 6/11		
MIDFIELDERS										
Tommy	Doherty	14	5'08"	09 13	17/03/1979	32	Bristol	Bristol C, QPR Undisc 7/05, Yeovil (L) 3/06, Wycombe (3ML) 9/06, Wycombe (SL) 1/07, Wycombe (3ML) 10/07 Perm 1/08 Rel 1/10, Ferencvaros (Hun) 1/10, Bradford C 7/10, Rel c/s 11, Newport C 6/11Sam		
Foley	10	6'00" 10 0817/10/198624				Upton		Cheltenham Rel c/s 08, Bath C (L) 3/08, Kidderminster 8/08, Redditch (2ML) 10/08, Newport C (SL) 2/09, Newport C 7/09	40	5
Ryan	Gilligan	12	5'10"	11 07	18/01/1987	24	Swindon	Watford (Scholar) Rel c/s 05, Northampton 8/05, Torquay (L) 2/11, Newport C (6ML) 8/11		
Troy	Greening	24			17/04/1993	18		Newport C	0	0
Tom	Miller	4			29/06/1990	21	Ely	Littleport (Yth), Ipswich (Yth), Norwich (Scholar) Rel c/s 4/08, Rangers 4/08, Brechin (L) 12/09, Dundalk 2/10, Newport C 1/11	13	1
Scott	Rogers	8	5'11"	11 00	23/05/1979	32	Bristol	Twyford Spartans (Yth), Exeter (Jun), Bristol C (Trainee), Tiverton 7/97, Forest Green 8/03, Weston-super-Mare (L) 11/05, Bath C 3/06, Newport C (L) 1/09, Newport C 4/09, Weymouth (L) 1/11	20	1
Daniel	Rose	7	5'07"	10 01	21/02/1988	23	Bristol	Man Utd, Oxford U (SL) 1/07, Oxford U 8/07 Rel 4/08, Newport C 7/08	46	6
Guillaume	Velez	29	5'10"	11 06	13/05/1991	20	Toulouse, Fra	Toulouse, Newport C 8/11		
FORWARDS										
Elliott	Buchanan	26	5'11"		17/07/1989	22		Northwood, Stevenage 1/08 Rel 5/09, AFC Wimbledon (SL) 3/08, Boreham Wood (L) 8/08, Concord R (SL) 1/09, Slough 9/09 Rel c/s 10, Hayes & Yeading 8/10, Newport C 7/11		
Jake	Harris	23			28/10/1990	20	Weston-Super-Mare	Weston-Super-Mare, Newport C 7/10, Gloucester (SL) 8/10		
Felino	Jardim	27	5'09"	11 08	10/08/1985	26	Rotterdam	Feyenoord (Holl), RKC Waalwijk 7/05 Rel c/s 06, Sparta Rotterdam (Holl) Rel c/s 08, Bedford T (Trial) c/s 08, Barnet (Trial) c/s 08, Cambridge U 8/08 Rel 2/09, RBC Roosendaal (Holl) 7/09, Newport 7/11		
Darryl	Knights	11	5'07"	10 01	01/05/1988	23	Ipswich	Ipswich Rel c/s 07, L.Orient (Trial) 1/07, Yeovil (SL) 2/07, Yeovil 7/07 Rel 5/08, Cambridge U (2ML) 10/07, Kidderminster (SL) 1/08, Kidderminster 5/08 Rel 7/10, Newport C 7/10	41	7

Robbie	Matthews	21			02/03/1982	29	Wiltshire	Bournemouth (Yth), Swindon (Yth), Salisbury, Bemerton Heath Harlequins 11/01, Eastleigh c/s 02, Southampton (Trial), Bristol R (Trial) 2/03, Salisbury 9/04, Havant & W (6WL) 11/08, Crawley (SL) 1/09, Kidderminster 8/09 Rel 7/10, Newport C 7/10, Forest Green (SL) 3/11, Forest Green (L) 8/11	35	5
Craig	McAllister	9	6'01"	12 07	28/06/1980	31	Glasgow	Eastleigh, Basingstoke 3/02, Stevenage 5/04 Rel 6/05, Gravesend (L) 12/04, Eastleigh (3ML) 2/05, Woking 7/05, Grays 5/07, Rushden & D (L) 10/07, Rushden & D (2ML) 11/07, Oxford U 1/08 Rel 4/08, Exeter 5/08 Rel c/s 10, Barnet (5WL) 11/09, Rotherham (SL) 3/10, Crawley 6/10 Rel 5/11, Newport C 5/11		

Loanees		**SN**	**HT**	**WT**	**DOB**	**AGE**	**POB**	**From - To**	**APPS**	**GOA**
(F)Kerry	Morgan		5'10"	11 03	31/10/1988	22	Merthyr	Swansea (5ML) 8/10, (SL) 1/11 - Neath Ath 5/11	33	1
(D)Martin	John				01/08/1988	23	London	Cardiff (3ML) 9/10 - Rel c/s 11	9	0
(F)Charlie	Clough		6'02"	12 08	04/09/1990	20	Taunton	Bristol R 9/10 - Weymouth (L) 1/11, Bath C (SL) 2/11	2	0
(F)Ben	Wright		6'02"	13 05	10/08/1988	23	Basingstoke	Crawley (2ML) 11/10 - Hayes & Yeading (SL) 1/11, Rel 5/11, Braintree 6/11	5	1
(D)Alan	Goodall		5'07"	11 08	02/12/1981	29	Birkenhead	Rochdale (2ML) 11/10 - Stockport 1/11 Rel 5/11, Fleetwood 7/11	8	0
(M)Sam	Deering		5'05"	11 00	26/02/1991	20	London	Oxford U (2ML) 11/10 - Barnet (SL) 2/11, Barnet 5/11	3	0
(D)Christian	Smith		6'02"	13 02	10/12/1987	23	Crewe	Wrexham 11/10 - Barrow (L) 1/11, Tamworth (6WL) 3/11, Chester FC 8/11	1	0
(M)Graeme	Montogomery		6'01"	12 00	03/03/1988	23	Dagenham	Dag & Red (SL) 1/11 - Rel 5/11, Aldershot T 8/11	8	0
(F)Charlie	Griffin		6'00"	12 07	25/06/1979	31	Bath	Stevenage (SL) 1/11 - Rel c/s 11, Forest Green 6/11	15	3
(F)Yemi	Odubade		5'07"	11 07	04/07/1984	27	Lagos	Stevenage (SL) 1/11 - Gateshead 6/11	11	1

Departures		**SN**	**HT**	**WT**	**DOB**	**AGE**	**POB**	**From - To**	**APPS**	**GOA**
(D)Oliver	Thorne		6'03"	14 06	23/01/1990	21	Gravesend	Forest Green 5/10 - Kidderminster 8/10, Rushden & D (L) 1/11, Braintree 2/11, Corby T 6/11, Hednesford 7/11	0	0
(M)Tony	Taggart		5'10"	11 02	07/10/1981	29	London	Eastleigh 5/10 - Eastleigh (2ML) 10/10 Perm 12/10, Sutton U 5/11	3	0
(F)Charlie	Henry				01/07/1987	24	Stevenage	Havant & W 6/09 - Luton (5WL) 11/10 Undisc 1/11	19	2
(M)Wayne	Turk				21/01/1981	30	Swindon	Salisbury (SL) 11/08 Perm 4/09 - Forest Green (2ML) 10/10 Perm 1/11(M)		
Jon	Challinor		5'11"	11 11	02/12/1980	30	Northampton	Brackley 10/10 - Rel 12/10, Kettering 1/11	3	0
(F)Giuseppe	Sole				08/01/1988	23	Woking	Woking 5/10 - Dorchester (L) 9/10, Havant & W (3ML) 10/10 Perm 1/11 Rel c/s 11, Woking 6/11	2	0
(F)Craig	Reid		5'10"	11 10	17/12/1988	22	Coventry	Grays (3ML) 9/08 Perm 12/08 - Stevenage Undisc 1/11	29	18
(D)Michael	Burns		5'10"	11 07	04/10/1988	22	Huyton	Runcorn Linnets 1/11 - Rel 2/11, Guiseley 6/11	1	0
(M)Michael	Fowler		5'11"	11 13	22/08/1981	30	Cardiff	Forest Green 1/11 - Weymouth NC 3/11	3	0
(G)Glyn	Garner		6'02"	13 11	09/12/1976	34	Pontypool	Grays 7/10 - Bath C 5/11	8	0
(D)Chris	Todd		6'01"	11 09	22/08/1981	30	Exeter	Torquay (SL) 1/10 Perm 5/10 - Forest Green 5/11	41	5
(M)Curtis	McDonald		5'10"	10 08	24/03/1988	23	Cardiff	Forest Green 1/11 - Forest Green (SL) 3/11, Forest Green 5/11	4	0
(M)Jamie	Collins		6'03"	12 00	28/09/1984	26	Barking	Hampton & R 10/09 - Aldershot 6/11	45	10
(M)Eddie	Odhiambo (Was Anaclet)		5'09"	10 00	31/08/1985	26	Arusha, Tanzania	Stevenage 7/10 - Rel c/s 11, Gateshead 6/11	34	0
(D)Paul	Bignot	2	6'01"	12 03	14/02/1986	25	Birmingham	Kidderminster 2/09 - Blackpool Undisc 7/11	41	1
(G)Kieron	Blackburn		6'00"	12 01	24/06/1988	23	Newport	Ton Pentre 1/09 -		
(G)Jamie	Proctor							Yth -	0	0
(F)Joe	Leahy				26/10/1992	18		Yth -	0	0
(F)Steve	Lennon		5'06"	09 08	20/01/1988	23	Irvine	Dundalk 2/11 -	9	0

Caught in action....

An aerial challenge between the Southport defence and Alfreton attack.

Photo by Bill Wheatcroft

SOUTHPORT

Chairman: Charles Clapham
Secretary: Ken Hilton (T) 07802 661 906 (E) secretary@southportfc.net
Additional Committee Members:
Sam Shrouder, Andrew Pope, Tim Medcroft, Stephen Porter, Gordon Medcroft, Wes Hall, Hayden Preece.
Manager: Liam Watson
Programme Editor: Rob Urwin (E) programme@southportfc.net

Back Row L to R: Chris Lever, Andy Owens, Matt Nemes, Earl Davis, Tony McMillan, Simon Grand, Steve Akrigg
Middle Row L to R: Russell Benjamin, Kevin Lee, Steve Daly, Jon Brown, Karl Ledsham, Aaron Turner, Shaun Whalley, Adam Carden
Front Row L to R: Michael Ordish, John Paul Kissock, James Smith, Chris Roberts (Physio), Liam Watson (Manager), Dominic Morley (Coach), Alan Moogan (Captain), Matty McGinn, Tony Gray

Club Factfile

Founded: 1881 **Nickname:** The Sandgrounders
Previous Names: Southport Central, Southport Vulcan
Previous Leagues: Preston & District, Lancashire 1889-1903, Lancashire comb. 1903-11, Central 1911-21, Football League 1921-78, Northern Premier 1978-93, 2003-04, Conference 1993-2003

Club Colours (change): Yellow & black/yellow/yellow (White/black/white)

Ground: Haig Avenue, Southport, Merseyside PR8 6JZ (T) 01704 533 422
Capacity: 6,008 **Seats:** 1,660 **Covered:** 2,760 **Clubhouse:** Yes **Shop:** Yes

Directions
Leave M6 at junction 26. Join M58 to junction 3. Join A570 signposted Southport, follow A570 through Ormskirk Town Centre following signs for Southport. At the big roundabout (McDonalds is on the left) take the fourth exit. Proceed along this road until you reach the 2nd set of pedstrian lights and take the next left into Haig Avenue.

Previous Grounds: Sussex Road Sports Ground, Scarisbrick New Road, Ash Lane (later named Haig Avenue)

Record Attendance: 20,010 v Newcastle United - FA Cup 1932
Record Victory: 8-1 v Nelson - 01/01/31
Record Defeat: 0-11 v Oldham Athletic - 26/12/62
Record Goalscorer: Alan Spence - 98
Record Appearances: Arthur Peat - 401 (1962-72)
Additional Records: Paid £20,000 to Macclesfield Town for Martin McDonald

Senior Honours: Lancashire Senior Cup 1904-05. Liverpool Senior Cup 1930-31, 31-32, 43-44, 62-63, 74-75, 90-91, 92-93, 98-99, Shared 57-58, 63-64. Football League Division 4 1972-73. Northern Premier League Challenge Cup 1990-91. Northern Premier League Premier Division 1992-93. Conference North 2004-05, 2009-10.

10 YEAR RECORD

01-02	02-03	03-04	04-05	05-06	06-07	07-08	08-09	09-10	10-11
Conf 15	Conf 21	NP P 6	Conf N 10	Conf 18	Conf 23	Conf N 4	Conf N 5	Conf N 1	Conf 21

SOUTHPORT

No.	Date	Comp	H/A	Opponents	Att:	Result	Goalscorers	Pos
1	Sat-14-Aug	BSP	H	AFC Wimbledon	1802	L 0-1		21
2	Tue-17-Aug	BSP	A	Kidderminster Harriers	1417	W 4-3	McNeil 2 (34, 48), McGinn 2 (74, pen 85)	11
3	Sat-21-Aug	BSP	A	Cambridge United	2506	D 0-0		12
4	Tue-24-Aug	BSP	H	Altrincham	1088	W 1-0	T Gray 82	8
5	Sat-28-Aug	BSP	H	Fleetwood Town	1546	W 1-0	Davis 31	5
6	Sat-04-Sep	BSP	A	Forest Green Rovers	1064	D 0-0		8
7	Tue-07-Sep	BSP	A	Gateshead	471	L 0-1		8
8	Sat-11-Sep	BSP	H	Mansfield Town	1289	L 1-2	Daly 80	10
9	Sat-18-Sep	BSP	H	Rushden & Diamonds	876	D 2-2	McGinn pen 6, Blakeman 67	12
10	Tue-21-Sep	BSP	A	Wrexham	2221	L 1-2	Daly 63	17
11	Sat-25-Sep	BSP	A	Darlington	1633	L 0-1		18
12	Tue-28-Sep	BSP	H	Hayes & Yeading United	753	D 0-0		18
13	Sat-02-Oct	BSP	H	Tamworth	966	W 2-1	McNeil 30, Daly 36	15
14	Tue-05-Oct	BSP	A	Histon	368	L 1-2	S Gray 34	17
15	Sat-09-Oct	BSP	H	Kettering Town	1117	L 1-2	Barratt 83	18
16	Sat-16-Oct	BSP	A	Grimsby Town	3101	D 1-1	Blakeman 25	19
17	Fri-29-Oct	BSP	H	Kidderminster Harriers	1447	D 2-2	Simm 17, Marsh-Evans 40	16
18	Sat-13-Nov	BSP	H	Bath City	947	L 2-3	Barratt 17, Powell 25	20
19	Sat-20-Nov	BSP	A	Newport County	1867	L 0-2		22
20	Tue-23-Nov	BSP	A	York City	2104	L 0-2		22
21	Tue-28-Dec	BSP	A	Fleetwood Town	2051	L 0-2		23
22	Sat-01-Jan	BSP	A	Barrow	1339	D 1-1	McNeil 81	23
23	Mon-03-Jan	BSP	H	Gateshead	904	W 5-1	Barratt 50, Ledsham 58, Kissock 67, McNeil 87, Powell 90	20
24	Sat-08-Jan	BSP	H	Newport County	1032	W 2-1	Lee 87, T Gray pen 90	19
25	Tue-18-Jan	BSP	H	Wrexham	1464	L 0-1		20
26	Sat-22-Jan	BSP	A	AFC Wimbledon	3408	L 0-5		20
27	Sat-29-Jan	BSP	H	York City	1308	W 4-0	Lever pen 3, Whalley 2 (4, 51), Lee 21	18
28	Tue-01-Feb	BSP	H	Grimsby Town	853	D 2-2	Whalley 8, Davis 29	18
29	Sat-12-Feb	BSP	H	Forest Green Rovers	1006	W 4-0	Ledsham 2 (7, 23), Marsh-Evans 18, Lee 53	18
30	Sat-19-Feb	BSP	A	Hayes & Yeading United	303	L 0-1		18
31	Tue-22-Feb	BSP	A	Crawley Town	3765	L 0-1		18
32	Sat-26-Feb	BSP	A	Bath City	792	L 1-2	Lee 44	19
33	Tue-01-Mar	BSP	H	Histon	652	W 3-1	Whalley 47, Ledsham 52, T Gray 80	18
34	Sat-05-Mar	BSP	A	Eastbourne Borough	1004	L 1-4	Whalley pen 33	18
35	Sat-12-Mar	BSP	H	Cambridge United	1107	D 1-1	Kissock 55	18
36	Tue-15-Mar	BSP	H	Barrow	889	L 2-4	Marsh-Evans 57, Whalley 86	19
37	Sat-19-Mar	BSP	A	Rushden & Diamonds	1061	D 2-2	McGinn pen 37, Whalley 55	20
38	Sat-26-Mar	BSP	H	Luton Town	1695	W 2-1	Moogan 82, Lee 88	19
39	Tue-29-Mar	BSP	A	Altrincham	1210	D 1-1	Daly 61	19
40	Sat-02-Apr	BSP	H	Eastbourne Borough	923	L 1-3	Daly 90	20
41	Tue-05-Apr	BSP	A	Mansfield Town	1467	D 2-2	Turner 57, McGinn pen 83	19
42	Sat-09-Apr	BSP	A	Luton Town	5844	L 0-6		21
43	Sat-16-Apr	BSP	H	Crawley Town	1011	L 0-4		21
44	Sat-23-Apr	BSP	A	Tamworth	944	W 1-0	Daly 63	21
45	Mon-25-Apr	BSP	H	Darlington	1866	D 1-1	Kissock 13	20
46	Sat-30-Apr	BSP	A	Kettering Town	1403	L 1-3	Whalley 63	21

CUPS

No.	Date	Comp	H/A	Opponents	Att:	Result	Goalscorers
1	Sat-23-Oct	FAC 4Q	A	Wrexham	2052	W 2-1	Og 2 (Blackburn 4, 70)
2	Sun-07-Nov	FAC 1	H	Sheffield Wednesday	4490	L 2-5	Barratt 52, McGinn 58
3	Tue-14-Dec	FAT 1	A	Gateshead	233	D 2-2	Daly 56, McGinn pen 83

League
Starts
Substitute
Unused Sub

Cups
Starts
Substitute
Unused Sub

Goals (Lg)
Goals (Cup)

MCMILLAN	LEVER	FLYNN	DAVIS	POWELL	MCGINN	WINN	MOOGAN	WILLIAMS	T GRAY	MCNEIL	COLLINS	BLAKEMAN	BARRATT	LEE	DICKINSON	DALY	S GRAY	SIMM	MORLEY	MARSH-EVANS	FITZPATRICK	LLOYD-MCGOLDRICK	LEDSHAM	KISSOCK	WHALLEY	TURNER
1	3	4	5	6	11	7	8	15	10	16	23	17	14	2	22	9	12	21	18	13	24	19	25	26	7	21
X	X	X	X	X	X	X	X	X	X	X	S	S	S	U	U											
X	X		X	X	X	X	X	X	X	X	U	S	S	X	U	S										
X	X	S	X	X	X	X	X	X	X	X		S	S	X	U	U										
X	X	S	X	U	X	X	X	X	X	X		X	S	X	U	S										
X		X	X	X	X	X	X	X	X	X		U	S	X	U	S	U									
X		X	X	S	X	X	X	X			S	X	X	X	U		U	X	S							
X		X	X	X	X	X	X	X			S	X	S	X	U		U	X	U							
X	X	X	X		X	X	X	S		X	U	X	S	X	U	X	S									
X		X	X		X	X	X	X	X	X	S	X	S	X	U	S	U									
X		X	X	X		X	X	X	X		S	X	S	S	U	X	X		U							
X		X	X	X	S	X	S	X	X		U	U	X	X	U	X	X									
X	U	X	X	S	X	X	X	X	X		U	X	X		U	X			U							
X	X	X	X	S	X	S	X	X	S	X	U	X	X		U	X										
X	X		X	X	S	X	X	X	X	X	U	U	S		U	X	X									
X	X	X	X	S	X	U	X	U	X		S	X	X	X	U	X										
X	X	X		S	S		X	X	S	X		X	X	X	U	U		X		X						
X	X	X	X	X	X			U	S	X		U	X	X	S	U		X		X						
X	X	X	X	X	X			U	U	X		S	X	X	U	S		X		X						
X	U		X	X	X		X	X	S	X		U	X	X		X		S		X		S				
U	X	S	X	U			X		X			X	X	X	X	X		X	U	X		S				
X		X	S	X	X		X	S	X	X		U	S	X	U					X			X	X		
X	X	X	X	X	S		X	X	X	S		U		X	U			X		S				X		
X	X	X	S	S				X	S	X		X	X	X	U			U		X			X	X		
X	U	X	X	S			X	X	S	X		X	X	X	U					S			X	X		
X	U	X	X	S	S		X	X	S	X		X	X		U					X			X	X		
X	S		X	S	X		X	X	U	X		X	S	X	U					X			X	X		
X	X	X		S			X	S	S	X		X	U	X	U					X			X	X	X	
X	X		X	S			X	X	X			U	U	X	U	S							X	X	X	X
X	X		X				X		X	X			S	X	U	S			U	X		S	X	X		X
X	X		X	U			X		X	X			S	X	U	S				X		S	X	X		X
X	X	U	X	S			X		X	U			S	X	U	X				X			X	X		X
X	X	X	X	S					U	X			S	X	U	S				X			X	X	X	X
X	S	U	X	X					S	X			X	X	U	S				X			X	X	X	X
X	X	X	S	U			X		S	X			X	X	U	S				X			X		X	X
X	X		X				X	U	S	X		U	S	X	U					X			X	X	X	X
X	U	X	X		X		X		S			U	X		U	X				X			X	X	S	X
X	X		X		X		X	X	X	S		U			U	X				X			S	S	X	X
X			X		X		X	U	S	X		U	S	X	U					X			X	X	X	X
X	X		X		X		X	S	X	S				X	U	X				X			S	U	X	X
X			X		X		X	X	S	X		U	S		U	S				X			X	X	X	X
X		S	X		X		X	X	U	X		U			U	X				X			X	X	S	X
X		S	X		X		X	X	S	S		U	X		U	X				X				X	X	X
X	S				X		X	X	U	X			S	X	U	S				X			X	X	X	X
X	X				X		X	X	S			S	S		U	X			U	X			X	X	X	X
X	X		X		X		X	X	S	X		S	S		U	U							X	X	X	X
X	X		X		X		X	X	U	X			U	X	U	X							S	S	X	X
X	X	X	X	S	S	U	X	X	U	X		X	X	X	U	U		X	U							
	X	X	X	S	S		X	X	S	X		X	X	X	X	U	U	X	U		U					
X		X	X	X	X		X	X	U	X			X	X	U	X	S	S	U							
45	27	23	39	14	28	13	40	29	20	31	0	16	17	33	1	17	3	7	0	26	0	0	21	22	15	19
0	3	5	3	13	5	1	1	4	17	4	6	6	22	1	1	13	1	1	1	2	0	4	3	2	2	0
1	5	2	0	4	0	1	0	5	6	1	6	15	3	1	43	4	4	1	6	0	0	0	0	1	0	0
2	2	3	3	1	1	0	3	3	0	3	0	2	3	3	1	1	0	2	0	0	0	0	0	0	0	0
0	0	0	0	2	2	0	0	0	1	0	0	0	0	0	0	0	1	1	0	0	0	0	0	0	0	0
0	0	0	0	0	0	1	0	0	2	0	0	0	0	0	2	2	1	0	3	0	1	0	0	0	0	0
0	1	0	2	2	5	0	1	0	3	5	0	2	3	5	0	6	1	1	0	3	0	0	4	3	8	1
0	0	0	0	0	2	0	0	0	0	0	0	0	1	0	0	1	0	0	0	0	0	0	0	0	0	0

PLAYING SQUAD

Existing Players		SN	HT	WT	DOB	AGE	POB	Career	Apps	Goals
GOALKEEPERS										
Anthony	McMillan	1			19/02/1982	29	Wigan	Preston (Scholar), Wigan, Runcorn, Lancaster 3/05, Burscough 6/06, Lancaster (2ML) 11/06, Ashton U (L) 2/07, Colwyn Bay (L) 3/07, Southport 7/08	45	0
Matthew	Nemes	13	5'10"	12 01	02/04/1987	24	Sydney	Central Coast Mariners (Aus), Spirit FC (Aust), Blacktown City (Aust), Trafford 3/11, AFC Telford (Trial) 3/11, Southport 8/11		
DEFENDERS										
Steve	Akrigg	4			02/01/1987	24	Liverpool	Warrington, Skelmersdale 1/07, Southport 5/11		
Earl	Davis	5	6'01"	13 02	17/05/1983	28	Manchester	Burnley, Southport (SL) 3/03, Southport 12/03, Swansea NC 1/04 Rel 2/04, Southport 2/04, Hyde U c/s 06, Burscough (3ML) 11/07 Perm 2/08, Southport 7/08	42	2
Simon	Grand	6	6'00"	10 03	23/02/1984	27	Chorley	Rochdale Rel c/s 04, Carlisle 8/04, Grimsby (L) 1/07 Undisc 1/07 Rel c/s 07, Morecambe 8/07 Rel c/s 08, Northwich 9/08, Chester (Trial) 9/08, Fleetwood 3/10 Rel 5/11, Mansfield (3ML) 10/10, Aldershot (SL) 1/11, Southport 6/11		
Kevin	Lee	2	6'00"	11 10	04/11/1985	25	Liverpool	Wigan, Accrington (L) 10/05, Blackpool (L) 3/06, Southport 7/06	34	5
Chris	Lever	3	5'10"	11 02	13/02/1987	24	Oldham	Oldham Rel c/s 07, Stalybridge (SL) 3/07, Southport c/s 07	30	1
Andy	Owens	15	6'03"	13 05	15/10/1989	21	Liverpool	Liverpool (Yth), Stoke (Scholar) Rel c/s 08, Leek T (WE) 2/08, Glen Hoddle Soccer Academy, Stafford R 8/09, Altrincham 11/09 Rel 1/10, Rhyl 1/10, Accrington 8/10, Northwich (L) 3/11, Southport 7/11		
James	Smith	14	5'10"	11 08	17/10/1985	25	Liverpool	Everton (Sch), Liverpool, Ross County (3ML) 1/07, Stockport (3ML) 8/07 Stockport 1/08, Altrincham (Trial) 9/08, Vauxhall Motors 10/08, Altrincham 11/08 Rel c/s 11, Southport 7/11		
MIDFIELDERS										
Russell	Benjamin	20			20/10/1991	19	Liverpool	Rochdale (Scholar) Rel c/s 11, Southport (WE) 2/09, Southport 8/11 Adam		
Carden	23			24/07/1985	26	Southport		Southport, Man City (Trial), Runcorn 8/03, Witton 3/04, Accrington, Prescot Cables 8/05, Radcliffe B 12/05 Rel 1/06, Burscough c/s 06, Warrington (L) 2/07, FCUM 9/07, Altrincham 12/09 Rel 8/10, Northwich 9/10 Rel 11/10, Kendal T 2/11, Southport 7/11		
Karl	Ledsham	17	6'03"		17/11/1987	23	Huyton	St Helens, Skelmersdale 9/09, Southport (6WL) 11/10 Perm 1/11	24	4
Matty	McGinn	11			27/06/1983	28	Fazackerley	Southport, Runcorn 8/02, Southport 7/05 Rel 9/06, Burscough 9/06, Southport 7/08, Skelmersdale (L) 2/11, Chester FC (L) 8/11	33	5
Alan	Moogan	8	5'10"	11 04	22/02/1984	27	Liverpool	Everton Rel c/s 04, Injured, Burscough c/s 06, Southport 7/08, Skelmersdale (Dual) 3/11	41	1
Dominic	Morley				07/06/1977	34	Liverpool	Liverpool (Trainee), Witton 7/95, Knowsley 8/96, Droylsden 4 fig 7/97, Southport c/s 99, Droylsden 8/00, Runcorn 10/01, Southport 5/04, Burscough 6/06 (Pl/Ass Man) 10/08, Southport (Pl/Coach) 5/10	1	0
Michael	Ordish	22			03/12/1992	18	Liverpool	Stockport (Scholar), Celtic 8/09 Rel c/s 11, Southport 8/11		
Aaron	Turner	16			05/05/1984	27	Rotherham	Ashton T, Skelmersdale c/s 06, Southport 1/11	19	1

FORWARDS										
Jonathan	Brown	12	5'11"	11 04	17/04/1990	21	Bridgend	Cardiff Rel c/s 09, Wrexham (SL) 11/08, L.Orient (Trial), Bryntirion Ath 8/09 Rel 11/09, Central Coast Mariners (Aust) 12/09 Rel c/s 10, Bath C 1/11 (10/11 2,0), Southport 7/11		
Steve	Daly	9			10/12/1981	29	Fazackerley	Wigan (Yth), Local, Runcorn 6/03, Southport 10/03, Droylsden 8/06, Burscough 5/08, Southport 7/08	30	6
Tony	Gray	10			06/04/1984	27	Liverpool	Newton, Bangor C 9/04, Burscough 7/05, Southport 6/06, Droylsden 12/08, Southport 5/10	37	3
Jon-Paul	Kissock	21	5'05"	10 09	02/12/1989	21	Liverpool	Everton Rel c/s 09, Gretna (SL) 1/08, Accrington (L) 1/09, Hamilton 8/09 Rel 12/09, Brighton (Trial) c/s 10, MK Dons (Trial) c/s 10, Newton 8/10, Formby 10/10, Southport 12/10	24	3
Leon	Osborne	18	5'10"	10 10	28/10/1989	21	Doncaster	Bradford C, Southport (L) 8/11		
Shaun	Whalley	7	5'09"	10 07	07/08/1987	24	Prescot	Southport, Chester 9/04 Rel c/s 05, Runcorn Halton 8/05, Witton 3/06, Accrington (2ML) 11/06 Perm 1/07 Rel c/s 08, Wrexham 6/08 Rel 5/09, Southport (SL) 2/09, Droylsden 8/09, Hyde FC 8/10, Southport 1/11, Skelmersdale (Dual) 3/11	17	8

Departures		HT	WT	DOB	AGE	POB	From - To	APPS	GOA
(G)Alan	Fitzpatrick					Kilkenny	Skelmersdale 11/10 - Rel	0	0
(M)Ashley	Winn	5'11"	11 02	01/12/1985	25	Stockton	Barrow 1/09 - Gateshead (2ML) 11/10 £2,500 1/11	14	0
(F)Chris	Simm	6'00"	12 08	10/04/1984	27	Wigan	Hyde 5/09 - Chorley (L) 9/10, Chester FC 1/11	8	1
(D)Shaun	Gray			28/01/1987	24	Ormskirk	Burscough 7/08 - Kendal T (L) 1/11 Perm	4	1
(M)Mike	Powell			11/09/1985	25	Ormskirk	Yth - Chester FC 3/11	27	2
(D)Adam	Flynn			12/10/1984	26	Whiston	Burscough 7/08 - Rel 4/11, Altrincham 6/11	28	0
(D)Paul	Barratt	5'10"	11 04	15/09/1987	23	Manchester	Northwich 5/09 - Rel 5/11	39	3
(F)Matty	McNeil	6'05"	14 03	14/07/1976	35	Manchester	Stockport 5/10 - Rel 5/11, Chester FC 6/11	35	5
(D)Robert	Marsh-Evans	6'03"	12 08	13/10/1986	24	Abergele	Vauxhall Motors 5/09 - Vauxhall Motors (2ML) 8/10, Chester FC 6/11	28	3
(M)Liam	Blakeman			06/09/1982	28	Southport	AFC Telford 6/10 - Rel c/s 11, Hednesford (L) 2/11, Kendal T (Trial) 7/11, Burscough 8/11	22	2
(D)Kenny	Strickland			10/10/1990	20		Skelmersdale 3/11 - Skelmersdale 6/11		
(G)Steve	Dickinson			01/12/1973	37	Leeds	Bradford PA 5/10 - Kendal T (Dual) 2/11, Skelmersdale (Dual) 3/11	2	0
(D)Lewis	Field			03/11/1989	21		Burscough 3/11 -		
(D)Dave	Roberts						Burscough 3/11 - Skelmersdale (L) 3/11		
(D)Robbie	Williams	5'10"	12 00	12/04/1979	32	Liverpool	ex Accrington 3/10 -	33	0
(M)Dan	Lloyd-McGoldrick			03/12/1991	19	Liverpool	Yth - Skelmersdale (3ML) 8/10, Skelmersdale (SL) 12/10	4	0
(F)Alan	Collins			07/02/1990	21	Fazackerley	??? 8/10 - Warrington (L)	6	0
(F)Jake	Ellis			09/01/1992	19	Braintree	Yth -		

Caught in action....

Seb Brown just gets his hand to the ball to deny Luton's Jason Walker in the Premier Divison Play-off.

Photo by Keith Clayton

STOCKPORT COUNTY

Chairman: Lord Peter Snape

Secretary: Tony Whiteside **(T)** 0161 286 8888 x257 **(E)** tony.whiteside@stockportcounty.com

Additional Committee Members:
Graham Shaw, Kevan Taylor, Ken Graham, Mike Clark, Rob Clare, Phil Brennan.

Manager: Dietmar Hamann

Programme Editor: Phil Brennan **(E)** phil.brennan@stockportcounty.com

Back Row: Richard Landon (kit man) Rodger Wylde (physio) John Miles, Ryan McCann, Andy Halls, Luke Ashworth, Danny O'Donnell, Matt Glennon, Martin Gritton, Nick Chadwick, Matty Mainwaring, Sean McConville, Sam Sheridan, Will McCutcheon (fitness coach).
Front Row: Danny Hall, Jon Nolan, Jon Routledge, Ryan Fraughan, Willie McStay (assistant manager) Dietmar Hamann (manager), Alan Lord (development officer), Danny Rowe, Mark Lynch, Euan Holden, Cameron Darkwah.

Club Factfile

Founded: 1883 **Nickname:** County or Hatters

Previous Names: Heaton Norris Rovers 1883-88, Heaton Norris 1888-90.

Previous Leagues: Football League 1900-2011.

Club Colours (change): Blue & white/blue/white (White/blue/white)

Ground: Edgeley Park, Hardcastle Road, Stockport SK3 9DD **(T)** 0161 286 8903

Capacity: 10,800 **Seats:** Yes **Covered:** Yes **Clubhouse:** **Shop:** Yes

Directions
From The South (M6): Exit the M6 at Junction 19 (sign-posted 'Manchester Airport, Stockport A55, M56 East') and at the r'about turn right onto the A556. At the Bowden r'about after 4.2 miles, turn right (sign-posted 'Manchester M56) onto the M56. Exit the M56 after 6.9 miles (sign-posted 'Stockport M60, Sheffield M67') onto the M60. Exit the M60 at Junction 1 ('sign-posted 'Stockport Town Centre and West'). At the r'about turn right and continue through to the second set of lights and turn left (ignoring the sign directing you to Stockport Co.) and follow the road to the left, which is Chestergate. At the lights turn right up King Street, past the fire station on the right to the top of the hill, turn right at the r'about signed Edgeley. Continue down Hardcastle street turning left after the bus stop signed Caroline Street. **From the North** (M62 from Leeds): Follow the M62 onto the M60 and continue south. Exit the M60 at Junction 1 ('sign-posted Stockport Town centre') At the roundabout turn right and continue through to the second set of lights and turn left (ignoring the sign directing you to Stockport Co.) and follow the road to the left, which is Chestergate. At the traffic lights turn right up King Street, past the fire station on the right to the top of the hill, turn right at the roundabout signed Edgeley. Continue down Hardcastle street turning left after the bus stop signed Caroline Street. At the end of Caroline St turn right where you will see the main car park on the left. (not available on Match Days)

Previous Grounds: Nursery Inn, Green Lane 1889-1902.

Record Attendance: 27,833 v Liverpool, FA Cup 5th Round 11/02/1950.

Record Victory: 13-0 v Halifax Town, Division Three North 06/01/1934.

Record Defeat: 1-8 v Chesterfield, Division Two 19/04/1902.

Record Goalscorer: (League) Jack Connor - 132, 1951-56.

Record Appearances: (League) Andy Thorpe - 489, 1978-86, 88-92.

Additional Records: Paid, £800,000 for Ian Moore from Nottingham Forest, 07/1998.
Received, £1,600,000 for Alun Armstrong from Middlesbrough, 02/1998.

Senior Honours: League Division Three North 1921-22, 36-37, Division Four 1966-67.

10 YEAR RECORD

01-02	02-03	03-04	04-05	05-06	06-07	07-08	08-09	09-10	10-11
FL 1 24	FL 2 14	FL 2 19	FL 1 24	FL 2 22	FL 2 8	FL 2 4	FL 1 18	FL 1 24	FL 2 24

STOCKPORT COUNTY

No.	Date	Comp	H/A	Opponents	Att:	Result	
1	Sat 7 Aug	FL2	A	Southend	5,589	D	1-1
2	**Tue 10 Aug**	**LGC 1**	**H**	**Preston**	**3,724**	**L**	**0-5**
3	Sat 14 Aug	FL2	H	Wycombe	3,837	D	0-0
4	Sat 21 Aug	FL2	A	Stevenage	2,726	L	1-3
5	Sat 28 Aug	FL2	H	Shrewsbury	4,350	L	0-4
6	Sat 4 Sep	FL2	A	Macclesfield	3,683	W	2-0
7	Sat 11 Sep	FL2	H	Bradford City	4,277	D	1-1
8	Sat 18 Sep	FL2	A	Oxford United	7,033	W	1-0
9	Sat 25 Sep	FL2	H	Aldershot Town	4,231	D	2-2
10	Tue 28 Sep	FL2	H	Accrington	3,584	D	2-2
11	Sat 2 Oct	FL2	A	Burton	3,107	L	1-2
12	Sat 9 Oct	FL2	A	Gillingham	4,755	L	1-2
13	Sat 16 Oct	FL2	H	Barnet	4,177	W	2-1
14	Sat 23 Oct	FL2	A	Lincoln City	4,809	D	0-0
15	**Tue 26 Oct**	**JPT (N)**	**A**	**Tranmere**	**2,223**	**L**	**0-0 (aet 3-4 on pens)**
16	Sat 30 Oct	FL2	H	Hereford	4,017	L	0-5
17	Tue 2 Nov	FL2	A	Morecambe	2,005	L	0-5
18	**Sat 6 Nov**	**FAC 1**	**H**	**Peterborough**	**2,001**	**D**	**1-1**
19	Sat 13 Nov	FL2	A	Bury	4,244	W	1-0
20	**Tue 16 Nov**	**FAC 1r**	**A**	**Peterborough**	**2,312**	**L**	**1-4**
21	Sat 20 Nov	FL2	H	Torquay United	3,772	D	1-1
22	Tue 23 Nov	FL2	H	Port Vale	4,571	L	0-5
23	Sat 4 Dec	FL2	A	Northampton	4,088	L	0-2
24	Sat 11 Dec	FL2	H	Crewe	4,036	D	3-3
25	Tue 28 Dec	FL2	A	Barnet	2,045	W	3-1
26	Sat 1 Jan	FL2	A	Chesterfield	7,542	L	1-4
27	Mon 3 Jan	FL2	H	Morecambe	3,890	L	0-2
28	Sat 8 Jan	FL2	H	Gillingham	3,573	L	1-5
29	Tue 11 Jan	FL2	H	Rotherham	3,612	D	3-3
30	Sat 15 Jan	FL2	A	Hereford	3,154	L	0-3
31	Sat 22 Jan	FL2	H	Lincoln City	4,348	L	3-4
32	Sat 29 Jan	FL2	A	Rotherham	4,876	L	0-4
33	Tue 1 Feb	FL2	H	Chesterfield	4,092	D	1-1
34	Sat 5 Feb	FL2	A	Torquay United	1,954	L	0-2
35	Sat 12 Feb	FL2	H	Bury	4,903	W	2-1
36	Sat 19 Feb	FL2	H	Macclesfield	5,470	L	1-3
37	Sat 26 Feb	FL2	A	Bradford City	15,332	L	2-3
38	Tue 1 Mar	FL2	A	Cheltenham	2,191	L	1-2
39	Sat 5 Mar	FL2	H	Oxford United	4,119	W	2-1
40	Tue 8 Mar	FL2	A	Accrington	1,831	L	0-3
41	Sat 12 Mar	FL2	H	Burton	4,278	D	0-0
42	Sat 19 Mar	FL2	A	Aldershot Town	2,263	L	0-1
43	Sat 26 Mar	FL2	H	Southend	3,335	W	2-1
44	Sat 2 Apr	FL2	A	Wycombe	6,836	L	0-2
45	Sat 9 Apr	FL2	H	Stevenage	3,449	D	2-2
46	Sat 16 Apr	FL2	A	Shrewsbury	5,711	L	0-2
47	Sat 23 Apr	FL2	A	Port Vale	5,334	W	2-1
48	Mon 25 Apr	FL2	H	Northampton	4,807	D	2-2
49	Sat 30 Apr	FL2	A	Crewe	4,799	L	0-2
50	Sat 7 May	FL2	H	Cheltenham	5,027	D	1-1

PLAYING SQUAD 2011-12

Existing Players		SN	HT	WT	DOB	AGE	POB	Career	Apps	Goals
GOALKEEPERS										
Matt	Glennon	1	6'02"	14 09	08/10/1978	32	Stockport	Bolton, Port Vale (2ML) 9/99, Stockport (L) 1/00, Bristol R (L) 9/00, Carlisle (SL) 11/00, Hull £50,000 6/01, Carlisle 10/02 Rel c/s 05, Falkirk 7/05, St Johnstone 1/06 Rel c/s 06, Huddersfield 6/06, Bradford C 1/10 Rel c/s 10, Stockport 9/10		
Ian	Ormson	12			16/05/1994	17	Liverpool	Stockport		
DEFENDERS										
Danny	Hall	6	6'02"	12 07	14/11/1983	27	Ashton-under-Lyne	Oldham Rel c/s 06, Scarborough (L) 2/03, Shrewsbury 5/06, Gretna 1/08 Rel 5/08, Chesterfield 7/08 Rel c/s 10, Darlington (L) 11/09, Crawley 5/10 Rel 5/11, Forest Green (3ML) 1/11, Stockport 8/11		
Andy	Halls	17	6'00"	12 01	20/04/1992	19	Urmston	Stockport		
Euann	Holden	3	6'00"	12 01	02/02/1988	23	Aberdeen	Aberdeen (Yth), Conneticut Huskies (USA), New Mexico Lobos (USA), Austin Aztec (USA), Vejle BK (Den) 1/10 Rel 6/10, Crewe (Trial) 9/10, Derby (Trial) 10/10, Oldham (Trial) 2/11, FC Hjorring (Den) 4/11, Stockport 7/11		
Mark	Lynch	2	5'11"	11 03	02/09/1981	29	Manchester	Man Utd, St Johnstone (SL) 10/01, Sunderland Undisc 7/04, Hull C 6/05, Yeovil (L) 8/06 Perm 8/06 Rel c/s 08, Rotherham 7/08, Stockport 7/10		
Daniel	O'Donnell	5	6'02"	11 11	10/03/1986	25	Liverpool	Liverpool, Crewe (SL) 8/06, Crewe Undisc 6/07 Rel c/s 10, Rochdale (Trial) 7/10, Shrewsbury 8/10 Rel 12/10, Stockport 1/11		
Carl	Piergianni	22			03/05/1992	19	Peterborough	Peterborough, Spalding U (WE) 12/09, Altrincham (SL) 1/11, Stockport 8/11		
MIDFIELDERS										
Nabil	Brahim-Bounab	21	6'00"	11 11	28/04/1988	23	Frejus, Fra	Hyeres (Fra), Frejus St-Raphael (Fra), Stockport 8/11		
Elliott	Chamberlain	24			29/04/1992	19	Paget, Ber	Leicester, Stockport (L) 8/11		
Cameron	Darkwah	13	5'09"		02/09/1992	18	Manchester	Stockport		
Ryan	Fraughan	11	5'06"	11 02	11/02/1991	20	Liverpool	Tranmere Rel c/s 11, Aberystwyth (SL) 1/10, Stockport 7/11		
Matty	Mainwaring	15	5'11"	12 02	28/03/1990	21	Salford	Preston (Scholar), Stockport 6/08		
Ryan	McCann	16	5'08"	11 02	21/09/1981	29	Bellshil	Celtic Rel c/s 03, St Johnstone (6ML) 7/02, Hartlepool 8/03, St Johnstone 9/04 Rel c/s 06, Clyde 8/06 Rel c/s 07, Bohemians 8/07 Rel 11/07, Queen of the South 12/07 Rel c/s 08, Morecambe 6/08, Queen of the South 1/09 Rel c/s 09, Airdrie 9/09, Ayr 6/10 Rel c/s 11, Stockport 7/11		
John	Nolan	8			22/04/1992	19	Huyton	Everton Rel c/s 11, Watford (Trial) 4/10, Stockport 7/11		
Jon	Routledge	4	6'00"	13 07	23/11/1989	21	Liverpool	Liverpool (Scholar) Rel 5/07, Wigan, Ostersunds FK (Swe) (3ML) 4/10, Hamilton (6ML) 8/10 Perm 1/11 Rel c/s 11, Stockport 8/11		
Danny	Rowe	18	6'00"	11 11	09/03/1992	19	Wythenshawe	Bolton (Yth), Stockport, Northwich (L) 11/10		
Sam	Sheridan	14			30/11/1989	21	Trafford	Bolton Rel c/s 11, Altrincham (L) 9/09, Stockport 7/11		
FORWARDS										
Nick	Chadwick	19	6'00"	12 08	26/10/1982	28	Market Drayton	Everton, Derby (L) 2/03, Millwall (6WL) 11/03, Millwall (SL) 3/04, Plymouth £250,000 2/05 Rel 6/08, Cheltenham (Trial) 9/08, Hereford 9/08, Shrewsbury 1/09 Rel c/s 09, Darlington (Trial) 7/09, Chester 8/09, Barrow 1/10 Rel 5/11, Altrincham (Trial) 7/11, Stockport 7/11		
Tom	Elliott	20	5'10"	11 00	09/09/1989	21	Leeds	Leeds, Macclesfield (L) 1/09, Bury (SL) 9/09, Rotherham (6ML) 7/10, Hamilton 1/11 Rel c/s 11, Bradford C (Trial) 6/11, Stockport 8/11		
Martin	Gritton	9	6'00"	12 05	01/06/1978	33	Glasgow	Porthleven, Plymouth 8/98, Yeovil (L) 2/01, Shelbourne (3ML) 11/01, Torquay (L) 8/02 Perm 9/02, Grimsby £5,000 12/04, Lincoln C 1/06 Rel c/s 07, Mansfield (SL) 1/07, Macclesfield 7/07, Chesterfield £40,000 1/09 Rel 1/11, Torquay (6ML) 7/10, Chester FC 2/11, Yeovil 3/11, Stockport 7/11		
Sean	McConville	7	5'10"	11 08	06/03/1989	22	Burscough	Burscough, Skelmersdale 7/07, Stockport (Trial) 1/09, Accrington Undisc 2/09 Rel c/s 11, Stockport 7/11		
John	Miles	10	5'10"	12 09	28/09/1981	29	Bootle	Liverpool, Port Vale (Trial) 3/02, Stoke 3/02, Crewe 8/02, Macclesfield (SL) 3/03, Macclesfield Undisc 5/03, Accrington 7/07, MK Dons (SL) 1/08, Fleetwood 6/10 Rel 5/11, Droylsden (SL) 3/11, Stockport 7/11		
Keigan	Parker	23	5'07"	10 05	08/06/1982	29	Livingston	St Johnstone Rel c/s 04, Blackpool 7/04, Huddersfield 7/08, Hartlepool (2ML) 3/09, Oldham 7/09 Rel c/s 10, Bury (L) 3/10, Mansfield 7/10 Rel c/s 11, Fleetwood (SL) 2/11, Stockport 8/11		

Caught in action....

The Tamworth defence jump highest to clear this Forest Green Rovers' attack.

Photo by Bill Wheatcroft

TAMWORTH

Chairman: Bob Andrews
Secretary: Rod Hadley **(T)** 01827 657 98 **(E)** clubsec@thelambs.co.uk
Additional Committee Members:
Stephen Lathbury, Brian Whitehouse, John Holcroft, Martin Newbold, Nick, Lunn, Dave Clayton.
Manager: Marcus Law
Programme Editor: Terry Brumpton **(E)** terrybrumpton@yahoo.co.uk

Back Row (L-R): Patrick Kanyuka, Liam Francis, Danny Mills, Joe Collister, Jonathan Hedge, Sam Andrew, Francino Francis, Callum Reynolds, Daniel Bradley, Rico Taylor.
Middle Row: Dale Belford (Goalkeeper Coach) Buster Belford (Kit Manager), Nabil Shariff, Samuel Habergham, Liam McDonald, Kieron St.Aimie, Richard Tait, Scott Barrow, Lee Weemes, Kyle Patterson, Paul O'Brian (Coach), Huseyin Torgut (Therapist).
Front Row: Danny Thomas, Ashley Cain, Connor Gudger, Paul Green, Marcus law (Manager), Duane Courtney, Jay Smith, Iyseden Christie, Troy Wallen

Club Factfile

Founded: 1933 **Nickname:** The Lambs
Previous Names: None
Previous Leagues: Birmingham Combination 1933-54, West Midlands (originally Birmingham League) 1954-72, 84-88, Southern 1972-79, 83-84, 89-2003, Northern Premier 1979-83
Club Colours (change): Red/black/red (All white)

Ground: The Lamb Ground, Kettlebrook, Tamworth, Staffordshire B77 1AA **(T)** 01827 657 98
Capacity: 4,100 **Seats:** 518 **Covered:** 1,191 **Clubhouse:** Yes **Shop:** Yes
Directions M42 Junction 10. Take A5/A51 to Town centre, then follow the signs for Kettlebrook and Tamworth FC.

Previous Grounds: Jolly Sailor Ground 1933-34

Record Attendance: 5,500 v Torquay United - FA Cup 1st Round 15/11/69
Record Victory: 14-4 v Holbrook Institue (H) - Bass Vase 1934
Record Defeat: 0-11 v Solihull (A) - Birmingham Combination 1940
Record Goalscorer: Graham Jessop - 195
Record Appearances: Dave Seedhouse - 869
Additional Records: Paid £7,500 to Ilkeston Town for David Hemmings December 2000
Received £7,500 from Telford United for Martin Myers 1990

Senior Honours: Birmingham Senior Cup 1960-61, 65-66, 68-69. West Midlands League 1964-65, 65-66, 71-72, 87-88. FA Vase 1988-89. Southern League Premier Division 2002-03. Conference North 2008-09.

10 YEAR RECORD

01-02	02-03	03-04	04-05	05-06	06-07	07-08	08-09	09-10	10-11
SthP 2	SthP 1	Conf 17	Conf 15	Conf 20	Conf 22	Conf N 15	Conf N 1	Conf 16	Conf 19

TAMWORTH

No.	Date	Comp	H/A	Opponents	Att:	Result	Goalscorers	Pos
1	Sat-14-Aug	BSP	H	Eastbourne Borough	723	W 4-2	Perry 11, Marshall 29, D Bradley 30, Rodman 67	1
2	Tue-17-Aug	BSP	A	Newport County	2217	D 1-1	Wylde 3	4
3	Sat-21-Aug	BSP	A	AFC Wimbledon	3144	L 0-3		15
4	Tue-24-Aug	BSP	H	Cambridge United	863	D 1-1	D Bradley 82	14
5	Sat-28-Aug	BSP	H	Luton Town	1694	W 3-1	Perry 11, Thomas 78, D Bradley 90	8
6	Mon-30-Aug	BSP	A	Kidderminster Harriers	1271	D 2-2	Perry 2 (45, 79)	10
7	Sat-04-Sep	BSP	A	Mansfield Town	2516	W 1-0	Wilkinson 30	5
8	Sat-11-Sep	BSP	H	Grimsby Town	1616	W 2-1	Rodman 14, Perry 38	4
9	Sat-18-Sep	BSP	A	Histon	653	W 2-1	Perry pen 66, Barrow 89	3
10	Tue-21-Sep	BSP	H	Bath City	920	D 2-2	Rodman 38, J Smith 68	4
11	Sat-25-Sep	BSP	H	York City	1282	L 1-3	Barrow 81	6
12	Wed-29-Sep	BSP	A	Crawley Town	1355	L 1-3	Wylde 40	8
13	Sat-02-Oct	BSP	A	Southport	966	L 1-2	Lake-Gaskin 45	10
14	Tue-05-Oct	BSP	H	Barrow	779	D 2-2	Rodman 2 (19, pen 90)	10
15	Sat-09-Oct	BSP	A	Gateshead	807	L 1-3	Rodman 17	12
16	Sat-16-Oct	BSP	H	Rushden & Diamonds	1002	L 1-2	Perry 11	14
17	Sat-30-Oct	BSP	H	Fleetwood Town	946	L 0-2		16
18	Tue-09-Nov	BSP	A	Darlington	2625	L 0-1		17
19	Sat-13-Nov	BSP	H	Gateshead	802	D 1-1	J Smith 44	18
20	Sat-20-Nov	BSP	A	Cambridge United	2809	D 3-3	Thomas 2 (20, 58), Perry 32	19
21	Sat-01-Jan	BSP	A	Kettering Town	1164	W 1-0	Og (Furlong) 57	16
22	Mon-03-Jan	BSP	H	Kidderminster Harriers	1183	D 2-2	Og (Vaughan) 12, Yussuf 17	16
23	Sat-08-Jan	BSP	A	Hayes & Yeading United	249	L 1-2	Marshall 90	16
24	Tue-11-Jan	BSP	H	Newport County	803	W 3-2	Rodman 3 (47, pen 76, 90)	15
25	Tue-18-Jan	BSP	H	Altrincham	795	D 1-1	Perry 79	15
26	Sat-22-Jan	BSP	H	Darlington	1034	D 1-1	Wylde 90	15
27	Tue-25-Jan	BSP	A	Eastbourne Borough	798	W 4-1	Thomas 36, J Bradley 62, Perry pen 68, Yussuf 89	14
28	Sat-29-Jan	BSP	A	Rushden & Diamonds	1216	D 1-1	Mackenzie 75	14
29	Sat-05-Feb	BSP	H	Histon	885	L 0-1		14
30	Sat-12-Feb	BSP	A	Bath City	899	L 0-2		16
31	Sat-19-Feb	BSP	H	AFC Wimbledon	1496	L 2-5	Wylde 51, D Bradley 65	16
32	Tue-22-Feb	BSP	A	Barrow	874	W 2-0	Thomas 42, Perry 54	16
33	Sat-26-Feb	BSP	A	Forest Green Rovers	681	L 0-4		16
34	Wed-02-Mar	BSP	H	Kettering Town	609	W 3-1	Tait 3, D Bradley 16, Perry 43	16
35	Sat-05-Mar	BSP	H	Mansfield Town	1162	L 0-2		16
36	Tue-08-Mar	BSP	A	Luton Town	5737	L 0-2		16
37	Sat-12-Mar	BSP	H	Hayes & Yeading United	1171	L 2-3	Perry 2 (34, 90)	16
38	Sat-19-Mar	BSP	A	Altrincham	895	L 0-2		18
39	Sat-26-Mar	BSP	A	Grimsby Town	3002	D 2-2	Perry 71, Marshall 80	18
40	Tue-29-Mar	BSP	H	Wrexham	1082	D 1-1	J Bradley 69	18
41	Sat-02-Apr	BSP	A	Fleetwood Town	1580	L 1-2	Thomas 66	18
42	Sat-09-Apr	BSP	H	Crawley Town	1569	L 0-3		20
43	Sat-16-Apr	BSP	A	York City	2484	W 2-1	Wilkinson 26, Perry 74	19
44	Sat-23-Apr	BSP	H	Southport	944	L 0-1		19
45	Mon-25-Apr	BSP	A	Wrexham	4330	L 2-4	Barrow 57, Perry 81	21
46	Sat-30-Apr	BSP	H	Forest Green Rovers	1717	W 2-1	C Smith 3, Sheridan 77	19

CUPS

No.	Date	Comp	H/A	Opponents	Att:	Result	Goalscorers
1	Sat-23-Oct	FAC 4Q	H	Grimsby Town	928	D 1-1	Mackenzie 72
2	Tue-26-Oct	FAC 4QR	A	Grimsby Town	1612	W 1-0	Perry 41
3	Sat-06-Nov	FAC 1	H	Crewe Alexandra	1776	W 2-1	Rodman 15, Thomas 55
4	Sat-27-Nov	FAC 2	A	Carlisle United	3599	L 2-3	Marshall 30, Thomas 75
5	Tue-14-Dec	FAT 1	A	Darlington	477	L 2-3	Rodman 58, Sheridan 70

League
Starts
Substitute
Unused Sub

Cups
Starts
Substitute
Unused Sub

Goals (Lg)
Goals (Cup)

ATKINS	RODMAN	MARSHALL	D BRADLEY	TAIT	J SMITH	MACKENZIE	THOMAS	WYLDE	PERRY	BARROW	OAKES	SHERIDAN	FARRELL	A MITCHELL	LYTTLE	LAKE-GASKIN	WILKINSON	CONNOR	MILLS	SEVERN	WALLEN	ELLIOTT	BOJANG	YUSSUF	J BRADLEY	KAMARA	CHRISTIE	COURTNEY	L MITCHELL	WARD	HENDRIE	C SMITH	BELFORD
1	10	3	17	2	7	8	11	5	9	19	4	14	16	6	15	12	20	21	18	1	18	16	23	24	16	25	10	4	1	28	27	18	13
X	X	X	X	X	X	X	X	X	X	X	S	S	S	U	U																		
X	X	X	X	X	X	X	X	X	X	X	S	S	U	U	U																		
X	X	X	X	X	X	X	X	X	X		S	U	S	X	U	S																	
X	X	X	X	X	X	X	X	X	X	X	S	S	U	U	U																		
X	X	X	X	X	X	U	X	X	X	X		S		U	U	U	X																
X	X	X	X	X	X	S	X	X	X	X		S		U	U	U	X																
X	X	X	X	X	X	U	X	X	X	X		S		U	U	U	X																
X	X	X		X	X	S	X	X	X	X	U	X		U	U	U	X																
X	X	X	S	X	X	U	X	X	X	X		X		U	U	S	X																
X	X	X	X	X	X	U	X	X	X	X		U		U	U	S	X																
X	X	X	S	X	X	U	X	X	X	X		X		S	U	S	X																
X	X	X	X	X	X	U	X	X	X	X		X		S	U	S	S																
X	X	X	S	X	X		X	X	X	X				S	X	X	U	U	U														
X	X	X	S	X	X	U	X	X	X	X	S			U	X	X	S																
X	X	X	X	X	X	S	X	X	S	X	S			U	U	X	X																
	X	X	X	X	X	S	X	X	X	X	U			U		X	S	U		X													
	X	S	S	X	X	X	X	X	X	X	S			X	U	X		U		X													
	X	U	X		X	X	X	X	X	X	X	S		X		S	S	U		X													
X	X	U	X	X	X	X	X	X		X	X	U		X		S	U	U															
X		U	X	X	X	X	X	X	X	X	X	U		X		U	S						S										
X	X	X	X	X	X	S	X			X		X		X		U	X	U					U	S									
X	X	X	X	X	X	S	X					X		X	U	S	X	U					S	X									
X	X	X	X	X		S	X	U		X		X		X		S	X	U					U	X									
X	X	X	X	X		X	X		S	X		X		X		S	U	U					U	X									
X	X	X	X	X		X	X	X	S	X		X		U		U								X	S	S							
X	X	X	X	X		X	X	X	X	X		U		U		U								S	X	S							
X		X	X	X		X	X	X	X	X		X		S			U	U						S	X	S							
X		X	X	X		X	X	X	X	X		X		S			U							S	X	S	U						
X		X	X	X		X	X	X	X	X		X		U				U						X		S	S	S					
X		X	X	X	S	X	X	X	X	X		S		U										X		S	U	X					
X		X	X	X	U	X	X	X	X	X		S	S	X			U									S		X					
X		X	X		X	U	X	X	X	X		X		U			X	U								U	S	X					
		X	X		X	U	X	X	X	X		X		U			X	U							S	S		X	X				
			X	X	X	S	X	X	X	X		X		S			X								S	U	U	X	X				
			X	X	X	U	X	X	X	X		X		U			X								S	S	U	X	X				
		S	X	X	X	U	X	X	X	X		X		U		S	X								S			X	X				
		U	X	X	X		X	X	X	X		X		U		S	U								S			X		X	X		
		U	X	X			X	X	X	X		S	S			X	U								S			X	X		X	X	
		X	X	X				X		X		U	X	U		X	U								X			X	X			X	
		X	X	X			X	X	S	U		S	X	U		X	X								X			X	X		U		
		X	X	X			X	X		U		S	X	U		X	S								X			X	X		S	X	
		X		X			X	X		S		S	X	U		X	X								X		U	X	X		S	X	
		X		X			X	S	X	X		X	S	U		X	X	U							S			X	X			X	
		X	S	X			X	S	X	X		X	U			X	X	U							S			X	X			X	
		X	X			S	X		X	X		X	S	X		U	X	X							X		U	X					S
		X	X		U	S			X	X		X	S			X	X	X							X		U	X				X	U
	X	U		X	X	X	X	X	X	X	S			X	U	X	S	U		X	U												
	X	S	S	X	X	X	X	X	X	X	S			X	U	X		U		X	U	U											
	X	S	X	X		X	X	X	X	X	X	U		X	U	S	S	U		X	U												
X	X	X	X	X	X	U	X	X	X	X	X	S		U		S	U	U					S										
X	X	X		X		X	X		X	X	X	S		X	U	S	X	U					S										
29	25	37	37	41	28	16	44	38	35	41	3	22	4	11	2	13	22	2	0	3	0	0	0	6	9	0	0	17	11	1	2	7	0
0	0	2	6	0	1	10	0	2	4	1	7	13	7	6	0	12	6	0	0	0	0	0	2	4	9	9	2	1	0	0	2	0	1
0	0	5	0	0	2	11	0	1	0	2	2	6	3	26	15	9	9	15	1	0	0	0	3	0	0	2	7	0	0	0	1	0	1
2	5	2	2	5	3	4	5	4	5	5	3	0	0	4	0	2	1	0	0	3	0	0	0	0	0	0	0	0	0	0	0	0	0
0	0	2	1	0	0	0	0	0	0	0	2	2	0	0	0	3	2	0	0	0	0	0	2	0	0	0	0	0	0	0	0	0	0
0	0	1	0	0	0	1	0	0	0	0	0	1	0	1	4	0	1	5	0	0	3	1	0	0	0	0	0	0	0	0	0	0	0
0	9	3	5	1	2	1	6	4	17	3	0	1	0	0	0	1	2	0	0	0	0	0	0	2	2	0	0	0	0	0	0	1	0
0	2	1	0	0	0	1	2	0	1	0	0	1	0	0	0	0	0	0	0	0	0	0	0	0	0	0	0	0	0	0	0	0	0

PLAYING SQUAD

Existing Players		SN	HT	WT	DOB	AGE	POB	Career	Apps	Goals
GOALKEEPERS										
Sam	Andrew	13			07/01/1993	18	Barnsley	Sheff Utd (Scholar) Rel 3/11, Tamworth 8/11		
Joe	Collister	21	6'00"	13 10	15/12/1991	19	Holyoak	Tranmere Rel c/s 11, Tamworth 8/11		
Jonathan	Hedge	1	6'02"	13 00	19/07/1988	23	Rotherham	Rotherham Rel c/s 06, Halifax 4/07 Rel 5/07, Queensland Roar (Aust) c/s 07, Harrogate T 7/08, FC Halifax 7/09, Tamworth 7/11		
DEFENDERS										
Scott	Barrow	19	5'08"	11 00	19/10/1988	22	Swansea	Swansea (Yth), Briton Ferry, Port Talbot 8/06, Tamworth 8/10	42	3
Duane	Courtney	4	5'11"	11 03	07/01/1985	26	Oldbury	Derby (Yth), Birmingham (Scholar) Rel c/s 04, AFC Telford 9/04, Burnley £25,000 8/05 Rel 8/06, The New Saints 9/06 Rel c/s 09, Kidderminster 7/09, York C 5/10 Rel 1/11, Tamworth 2/11	18	0
Francino	Francis	5	6'03"	14 02	18/01/1987	24	Kingston, Jam	Stoke (Scholar), Watford (Scholar) 7/05 Rel c/s 06, Kidderminster (2M) 1/06, Wealdstone (SL) 3/06, Redditch 6/06, Quorn 3/07, Rushall O 11/07, Halesowen T 12/07, Willenhall 1/08, Coalville, Barwell 3/08, Redditch 8/09, Barwell 8/09, Tamworth 6/11		
Liam	Francis	6	6'03"	11 04	27/09/1989	19	Birmingham	Coventry (Scholar), Stratford T 3/09, Redditch 8/09, Hednesford 2/10, Hinckley U (Trial) 7/10, Tamworth 6/11		
Paul	Green	16	5'08"	10 04	15/04/1987	24	Birmingham	Aston Villa, Lincoln C 1/07 Rel c/s 11, Tamworth 8/11		
Samuel	Habergham	3	6'00"	11 06	20/02/1992	19	Rotherham	Norwich Rel c/s 11, Lincoln C (Trial) 4/11, Tamworth 7/11		
Patrick	Kanyuka	24	6'00"	12 06	19/07/1987	24	Kinshasa, Con	L.Orient (Yth), QPR, Swindon 1/08 Rel c/s 09, Motherwell (Trial) 7/09, Northampton 10/09 Rel 12/09, CFR Cluj (Rom) 1/10 Rel 12/10, Unirea Alba Iulia (SL) 3/10, Lincoln C 1/11 Rel c/s 11, Tamworth 8/11		
Callum	Reynolds	20			10/11/1989	21		Rushden & D, Rugby T (WE) 3/07, Portsmouth 7/07, Basingstoke (L) 3/09, Luton (6ML) 7/09, Basingstoke 10/10, Tamworth 8/11		
Richard	Tait	2	5'11"	11 13	02/12/1989	21	Galashiels	Curzon Ashton, Notts Forest 12/07 Rel 5/09, Tamworth (L) 3/09 Tamworth 5/09	41	1
MIDFIELDERS										
Daniel	Bradley	18	6'00"		13/05/1991	20	Stafford	Aston Villa (Scholar) Rel c/s 10, Atherstone T (L) 2/10, Tamworth 8/10	43	5
Ashley	Cain	8	6'02"	12 06	27/09/1990	20	Nuneaton	Coventry Rel 4/10, Luton (L) 11/09, Oxford U (L) 2/10, Port Vale (Trial) 4/10, Mansfield 7/10, Tamworth 6/11		
Conor	Gudger	17	5'08"		23/09/1992	18	Nuneaton	Coventry Rel c/s 11, Hinckley U (SL) 1/11, Hinckley U 5/11, Tamworth 7/11		
Liam	McDonald	12			19/02/1985	26		Worcester, Bromsgrove 3/06, Evesham 3/07, Halesowen T 7/07, Sutton Coldfield 12/07, Cradley T 2/08, Hednesford 2/08, Evesham 7/08, Cradley T 8/08, Barwell 6/09, Stafford R NC 10/10, Kettering 12/10, Tamworth 8/11		
Kyle	Patterson	14	5'08"	10 00	06/01/1986	25	Birmingham	West Brom (Scholar), TP-47 Torino (Fin) 1/05, Saint Louis Lions (USA) 7/05, LA Galaxy (USA) 7/08 Rel 11/09, GAIS (Swe) 2/10, Hednesford 8/10, Tamworth 6/11		
Jay	Smith	7	5'07"	12 00	24/09/1981	29	Lambeth	Aston Villa, Southend (3ML) 8/02, Southend 11/02 Rel 1/07, Oxford U (SL) 3/06, Notts County (3ML) 11/06 Perm 1/07 Rel 1/09, Wigan (Trial), Eastwood T 12/09, Tamworth 1/10	29	2
Rico	Taylor	26			16/04/1994	17	Birmingham	Aston Villa (Yth), Birmingham (Yth), Boldmere St Michaels, Torquay (Scholar) 7/10, Sutton Coldfield 2/11, Tamworth 7/11		
Danny	Thomas	11	5'07"	11 05	01/05/1981	30	Leamington Spa	Notts Forest (Trainee), Leicester 5/98, Bournemouth (L) 2/02 Undisc 2/02, Notts County (Trial) 3/04, Boston U 3/04 Rel c/s 06, Grimsby (Trial) 8/06, Cheltenham (Trial) 9/06, Shrewsbury 11/06, Hereford 1/07 Rel c/s 07, Macclesfield 7/07 Rel c/s 09, Kettering 8/09, Tamworth 6/10	44	6
FORWARDS										
Iyseden	Christie	23	5'10"	12 02	14/11/1976	34	Coventry	Coventry Rel c/s 97, Bournemouth (L) 11/96, Mansfield (2ML) 2/97, Mansfield 6/97, L.Orient £40,000 7/99 Rel c/s 02, Rushden & D (Trial) 7/02, Mansfield 8/02 Rel c/s 04, Kidderminster 8/04, Rochdale £17,500 1/06, Kidderminster (4ML) 8/06 Perm 1/07, Stevenage 7/08 Rel 1/09, Kettering (4ML) 9/08, Torquay 2/09 Rel 5/09, Hibernians (Mal) (Trial) c/s 09, Kings Lynn 8/09, AFC Telford 9/09 Rel 10/09, Farnborough 10/09, Tamworth 11/09, Kettering 5/10 Rel 5/11, Nuneaton T (SL) 3/11, Tamworth 8/11		
Danny	Mills	9	6'04"	13 00	27/11/1991	19	Peterborough	Crawley, Peterborough Undisc 7/09, Torquay (L) 9/09, Rushden & D (L) 10/09, Histon (5ML) 7/10, Kettering (SL) 2/11, Tamworth (5ML) 8/11		
Nabil	Shariff	22			19/04/1992	19	Milton Keynes	Rushden & D, Newport Pagnell (L) 9/09, Banbury U (WE) 11/09, Banbury U (L) 8/10, Nuneaton T (2ML) 11/10, Tamworth 7/11		
Kieron	St Aimie	10	6'01"	13 00	04/05/1989	22	Brent	QPR Rel 1/08, Oxford U (L) 10/07, Barnet 1/08 Rel 2/09, Grays (L) 9/08, Stevenage (L) 11/08, Lewes (L) 1/09, St Albans (Trial), Thurrock 3/09, Hitchin 3/09, Maidenhead 8/09 Rel 3/11, Lewes 3/11, AFC Hornchurch 3/11, Kettering 3/11, Tamworth 6/11		
Troy	Wallen	27			18/11/1992	18	Birmingham	Tamworth, Dudley T (L) 11/10	0	0
Lee	Weemes	29			14/10/1992	18		Charlton (Yth), Wycombe (Scholar) Rel c/s 11, Tamworth 8/11		

Loanees		HT	WT	DOB	AGE	POB	From - To	APPS	GOA
(G)David	Grof	6'03"	14 02	17/04/1989	22	Budapest, Hun	Notts County 8/10 - Mansfield (SL) 1/11, Rel 5/11, Walsall 7/11		
(G)Ross	Atkins	6'00"	13 00	03/11/1989	21	Derby	Derby (2ML) 8/10, (SL) 11/10 - Recalled 2/11	29	0
(G)James	Severn	6'04"	14 11	10/10/1991	19	Nottingham	Derby 10/10 - Eastwood T (5ML) 8/11	3	0
(F)Abdillahie	Yussuf			03/10/1992	18		Leicester (6WL) 1/11 - Rel 5/11	10	2
(G)Liam	Mitchell			18/09/1992	18		Notts County (SL) 2/11 -	11	0
(G)Danny	Ward			22/06/1993	18	Wrexham	Wrexham 3/11 -	1	0
(F)Stuart	Hendrie	5'09"	11 00	01/11/1989	21	Solihull	Morecambe 3/11 - Rel c/s 11	4	0
(D)Christian	Smith	6'02"	13 02	10/12/1987	23	Crewe	Wrexham (6WL) 3/11 - Chester FC 8/11	7	1

Departures		HT	WT	DOB	AGE	POB	From - To	APPS	GOA
(F)Nick	Wright	6'02"	12 00	25/11/1987	23	Birmingham	Halesowen T 10/07 - Kidderminster 7/10		
(G)Danny	Alcock	5'11"	11 03	15/02/1984	27	Salford	Stafford R 12/08 - Nuneaton T 8/10		
(D)Gavin	Hurren	5'08"	13 07	22/10/1985	25	Birmingham	Crawley 6/09 - Sunshine George Cross (Aust), Halesowen T (Trial) 7/10, Eastwood T 9/10, Hednesford 10/10, Redditch 12/10, Worcester 2/11 (M)		
Gary	Mills	5'11"	11 09	11/11/1961	49	Northampton	Alfreton (Pl/Man) 1/07 - Rel 10/10, York C (Man) 10/10	0	0
(G)Shaun	Markie			29/07/1985	26		Wellingborough 8/10 - Wellingborough		
(F)Bakary	Bojang	5'10"	11 00	10/05/1986	25	Bakoteh, Gambia	Horden CW 11/10 - Rel 1/11	2	0
(M)Stefan	Oakes	5'10"	12 03	06/09/1978	32	Leicester	Lincoln C 8/10 - New York (Trial) 1/11	10	0
(M)Daniel	Elliott			18/08/1991	20	Gedling	Notts Forest - Rel, Hucknall 6/11	0	0
(F)Alex	Rodman	6'00"		15/12/1987	23	Sutton Coldfield	Nuneaton 5/08 - Aldershot 1/11	25	9
(F)Alando	Lewis						Yth - Rel 3/11, Dudley T (L) 11/10		
(M)Malvin	Kamara	5'11"	13 00	17/11/1983	27	Southwark	Stafford R 1/11 - Rel 3/11, Farnborough 3/11	9	0
(D)Des	Lyttle	5'09"	12 13	24/09/1971	39	Wolverhampton	Worcester 8/07 (Temp Man) 10/10 Perm Man 11/10 - Rel 4/11	2	0
(G)Louie	Connor			11/06/1992	19	Bristol	Yth - Rel c/s 11, Barwell (L) 3/11, Nuneaton (Trial) 7/11	2	0
(D)Tom	Marshall	6'04"		16/11/1987	23	Lichfield	Eastwood T 6/10 - Rel 5/11, Kidderminster 6/11	39	3
(D)Michael	Wylde	6'02"	13 02	06/01/1987	24	Birmingham	Cheltenham 7/08 - Cambridge U 5/11	40	4
(D)Aaron	Mitchell	6'05"	11 02	05/02/1990	21	Nottingham	Hucknall 3/10 - Eastwood T 6/11	17	0
(F)Jason	Bradley	6'03"	13 00	16/03/1989	22	Sheffield	Brackley T 1/11 - Eastwood T 6/11	18	2
(F)Kyle	Perry	6'04"	14 05	05/03/1986	25	Birmingham	Mansfield 7/10 - Lincoln C 7/11	39	17
(M)Neil	Mackenzie	6'02"	12 05	15/04/1976	35	Birmingham	Mansfield 6/09 - St Neots 7/11	26	1
(F)Jevais	Christie			11/06/1992	19		Arnold T 1/11 - Eastwood T 7/11	2	0
(M)Ben	Wilkinson	5'11"	12 01	25/04/1987	24	Sheffield	ex Chester 8/10 - Southport (Trial) 7/11, Boston U 7/11	28	2
(G)Dale	Belford	5'10"	13 00	11/07/1967	44	Tamworth	Tamworth NC 3/11 Temp Man 4/11 - Tamworth Coach	1	0
(M)Seb	Lake-Gaskin	5'09"	12 01	24/02/1991	20	Birmingham	West Brom (Scholar) 8/09 - Rel c/s 11, Leamington (L) 1/11	25	1
(M)Jake	Sheridan	5'09"	11 06	08/07/1986	25	Nottingham	Notts County 7/07 - Rel c/s 11, Eastwood T (Trial) 7/11	35	1
(F)Aaron	Farrell	6'00"	12 06	24/04/1986	25		Sollihull Moors 8/10 - Rel 8/10, Romulus 9/10, Sutton Coldfield 11/10, Tamworth 2/11 Rel c/s 11	11	0

Caught in action....

Tamworth's Rodman takes on, and goes past, Crewe's Ada during the Blue Square Premier side's FA Cup tie last season.

Photo by Keith Clayton

WREXHAM

Chairman: Ian Roberts
Secretary: Geraint Parry (T) 07801 749 021 (E)
Additional Committee Members:
Geoff Moss, Jon Harris

Manager: Dean Saunders
Programme Editor: Terry Brumpton (E)

Club Factfile

Founded: 1872 **Nickname:** The Robins
Previous Names: Wrexham Athletic for the 1882-83 season only
Previous Leagues: The Combination 1890-94, 1896-1906, Welsh League 1894-96, Birmingham & District 1906-21, Football League 1921-2008

Club Colours (change): All red (All green)

Ground: Racecourse Ground, Mold road, Wrexham LL11 2AH (T) 01978 262 129
Capacity: 15,500 **Seats:** 10,100 **Covered:** 15,500 **Clubhouse:** Yes **Shop:** Yes

Directions
From Wrexham by-pass (A483) exit at Mold junction (A451).
Follow signs for Town Centre and football ground is half a mile on the left hand side.

Previous Grounds: Rhosddu Recreation Ground during the 1881-82 and 1882-83 seasons.

Record Attendance: 34,445 v Manchester United - FA Cup 4th Round 26/01/57
Record Victory: 10-1 v Hartlepool United - Division Four 03/03/62
Record Defeat: 0-9 v v Brentford - Division Three
Record Goalscorer: Tommy Bamford - 201 (1928-34)
Record Appearances: Arfon Griffiths - 592 (1959-79)
Additional Records: Paid £800,000 to Birmingham City for Bryan Hughes March 1997
Received £210,000 from Liverpool for Joey Jones October 1978

Senior Honours: Welsh FA Cup 1877-78, 81-82, 92-93, 96-97, 1902-03, 04-05, 08-09, 09-10, 10-11, 13-14, 14-15, 20-21, 23-24, 24-25, 30-31, 56-57, 57-58, 59-60, 71-72, 74-75, 77-78, 85-86, 94-95. Welsh Lge 1894-95, 95-96. Combination 1900-01, 01-02, 02-03, 04-05. Football Lge Div. 3 1977-78. FAW Prem. Cup 1997-98, 99-2000, 00-01, 02-03, 03-04. F. Lge Trophy 2004-05

10 YEAR RECORD

01-02	02-03	03-04	04-05	05-06	06-07	07-08	08-09	09-10	10-11
FL 2 23	FL 3 3	FL 2 13	FL 1 22	FL 2 13	FL 2 19	FL 2 24	Conf 10	Conf 11	Conf 4

WREXHAM

No.	Date	Comp	H/A	Opponents	Att:	Result	Goalscorers	Pos
1	Sat-14-Aug	BSP	H	Cambridge United	4040	W 1-0	Morrell 25	10
2	Tue-17-Aug	BSP	A	Forest Green Rovers	1216	L 0-3		15
3	Sat-21-Aug	BSP	A	Eastbourne Borough	1055	L 3-4	Smith 2 (15, 76), Andrews 20	18
4	Tue-24-Aug	BSP	H	Kidderminster Harriers	2477	D 2-2	Brown 4, Keates 6	19
5	Sat-28-Aug	BSP	H	Barrow	2525	D 1-1	Og (M Pearson) 90	20
6	Mon-30-Aug	BSP	A	Bath City	1262	W 2-0	Morrell 28, Smith 58	12
7	Sun-05-Sep	BSP	A	Newport County	3206	D 1-1	Morrell 23	14
8	Sat-11-Sep	BSP	H	York City	2446	D 1-1	Morrell 8	15
9	Sat-18-Sep	BSP	A	Kettering Town	1533	D 1-1	Keates 43	15
10	Tue-21-Sep	BSP	H	Southport	2221	W 2-1	Taylor 27, Harris 41	11
11	Sat-25-Sep	BSP	H	Histon	2376	W 4-0	Tolley 11, Keates 18, Taylor 38, Knight-Percival 79	9
12	Tue-28-Sep	BSP	A	Grimsby Town	2532	L 1-2	Knight-Percival 90	11
13	Sat-02-Oct	BSP	A	Darlington	1690	W 1-0	Knight-Percival 87	8
14	Tue-05-Oct	BSP	H	Fleetwood Town	2689	D 0-0		7
15	Sat-09-Oct	BSP	H	AFC Wimbledon	3277	L 1-2	Mangan 27	10
16	Sat-16-Oct	BSP	A	Hayes & Yeading United	417	W 3-0	Harris 61, Cieslewicz 85, Taylor 90	8
17	Sat-30-Oct	BSP	A	Histon	914	D 1-1	Taylor 90	7
18	Thu-11-Nov	BSP	H	Luton Town	2733	W 1-0	Mangan 5	7
19	Sun-14-Nov	BSP	A	York City	2601	D 1-1	Tolley 13	8
20	Sat-20-Nov	BSP	H	Darlington	2619	W 2-1	Mangan 2 (10, 90)	7
21	Sat-27-Nov	BSP	H	Mansfield Town	2505	D 1-1	Andrews 37	6
22	Sat-01-Jan	BSP	A	Altrincham	1982	D 0-0		7
23	Mon-03-Jan	BSP	H	Bath City	2602	W 2-0	Taylor pen 34, Pogba 86	7
24	Sat-08-Jan	BSP	H	Grimsby Town	3013	W 2-0	Harris 70, Morrell 76	5
25	Tue-18-Jan	BSP	A	Southport	1464	W 1-0	Morrell 25	5
26	Sat-22-Jan	BSP	A	Cambridge United	2469	W 3-1	Mangan 2, Pogba 14, Blackburn 20	4
27	Sat-29-Jan	BSP	A	Mansfield Town	3266	W 3-2	Pogba 8, Morrell 72, Harris 90	4
28	Tue-01-Feb	BSP	H	Altrincham	3300	W 2-1	Morrell 43, Cieslewicz 85	4
29	Sat-05-Feb	BSP	A	Barrow	1318	W 1-0	Mangan pen 83	4
30	Sat-12-Feb	BSP	A	Crawley Town	3331	L 2-3	Mangan 2 (8, 31)	4
31	Tue-15-Feb	BSP	H	Crawley Town	4630	D 0-0		4
32	Sat-19-Feb	BSP	H	Gateshead	3078	L 2-7	Morrell 12, Tolley 64	4
33	Tue-22-Feb	BSP	A	AFC Wimbledon	3486	W 1-0	Pogba 76	3
34	Sat-26-Feb	BSP	A	Kidderminster Harriers	3028	L 0-1		3
35	Sat-05-Mar	BSP	H	Forest Green Rovers	3386	W 2-1	Mangan 5, Morrell 36	4
36	Tue-08-Mar	BSP	H	Eastbourne Borough	2410	W 2-1	Fowler 27, Tolley 44	4
37	Sat-12-Mar	BSP	H	Rushden & Diamonds	3187	D 1-1	Mangan 14	3
38	Sat-19-Mar	BSP	A	Fleetwood Town	2207	L 0-1		4
39	Sun-27-Mar	BSP	H	Newport County	3685	W 1-0	Mangan 74	4
40	Tue-29-Mar	BSP	A	Tamworth	1082	D 1-1	Keates 82	4
41	Sat-02-Apr	BSP	H	Hayes & Yeading United	3207	L 0-2		4
42	Sat-09-Apr	BSP	A	Rushden & Diamonds	1181	D 2-2	Mangan 2 (30, 52)	4
43	Sat-16-Apr	BSP	H	Kettering Town	3662	W 2-0	Mangan 56, Keates 88	4
44	Sat-23-Apr	BSP	A	Gateshead	743	W 1-0	Keates 48	4
45	Mon-25-Apr	BSP	H	Tamworth	4330	W 4-2	Obeng 10, Knight-Percival 53, Mangan 68, Taylor 79	4
46	Sat-30-Apr	BSP	A	Luton Town	6443	D 1-1	Moss 12	4

CUPS

No.	Date	Comp	H/A	Opponents	Att:	Result	Goalscorers
1	Sat-23-Oct	FAC 4Q	H	Southport	2052	L 1-2	Tolley 78
2	Sat-11-Dec	FAT 1	H	Kidderminster Harriers	1122	W 2-0	Harris 29, Brown 34
3	Sat-15-Jan	FAT 2	A	Salisbury City	1032	L 0-1	
4	Thu-05-May	PO SF 1	H	Luton Town	7211	L 0-3	
5	Tue-10-May	PO SF 2	A	Luton Town	9078	L 1-2	Mangan 8

League
Starts
Substitute
Unused Sub

Cups
Starts
Substitute
Unused Sub

Goals (Lg)
Goals (Cup)

SHEARER	ASHTON	BLACKBURN	SINCLAIR	WALKER	HARRIS	KEATES	KNIGHT-PERCIVAL	BROWN	MANGAN	MORRELL	TOLLEY	GALL	TAYLOR	MAXWELL	SMITH	ANDREWS	CIESLEWICZ	OBENG	HUNT	POGBA	CREIGHTON	WILLIAMS	MAYEBI	EDWARDS	FOWLER	MOSS	PENK	MCMILLAN	TOMASSEN	STEPHENS	SALATHIEL	COLBECK	OWEN	ANORUO
1	3	5	15	22	6	12	20	8	9	11	18	19	7	21	14	4	17	2	16	24	23	10	25	26	27	30	29	19	32	37	36	35	34	31
X	X	X	X	X	X	X	X	X	X	X	S	S	U	U	U																			
X	X	X	X	X	X	X	X	X	X	X	S	U	S	U		U																		
X	X	X	X	S	X	X	X	S	X	X	U	U	S		X	X																		
X	X	X		X	S	X	X	X	X	X	U	U	S		X	X	S																	
X	X	X		X	X	X	X	X	X	X	U	S	S		U	X	U																	
X	X	X		U	X	X	X	U		X	S	X	S		X	X	S	X																
X	X	X	X	U	X	X	X	U	S	X	U	X	U		X			X																
X		X	X	U	X	X	X	U	S	X	S	X	S		X			X	X															
X	X	X	X		X	X	S	U	X	X	X	U	X		S	X		S																
	X	X	X		X	X	U	U	X	X	X		X	X	U	X	S	U																
	X	X	X		X	X	S	S	X	X	X		X	X	U	X	S	U																
	X	X	X		X	X	S	U	X	X	X		X	X		X	S	S		U														
	X	X	X			X	X	U	X		X	U	X	X	U	X	U	X	S															
	X	X	X		S	X	X	U	X		X		X	X	U	X	U	X		S														
U	X	X	X		X	X		U	X	X	S		X	X		X	U	X		S														
	X	X	X		X	X	S	U	X	X	U		X	X		X	S	X		U														
	X	X	X	U	X	X	S	S	X	X	X		X	X	U	X				S														
	X	X			X	X	S	U	X	X	X		X	X	U	X	U	X		S														
		X			X	X	X	U	X	S	X		X	X		X	S	X	U	U	X													
		X	U		X	X	S	U	X	X	X		X	X		X	S	X		S	X													
		X	X			X	S	U	X	X	X		X	X		X	U	X		S	X	U												
	X	X	S		X	X	U	X		X			X	X		X	X			S	X	S	U											
	X	X	X		X	X	S	U		X	U		X	X			X	X		S	X	U												
	X	X	X		X	X	S	U	X	X	S			X			U	X		X	X	S												
	X	X	X		X	X	S	U	X	X	U			X			U	X		X	X	U												
	X	X	X		X	X	S	U	X	X	U			X		U	U	X		X	X													
	X	X	X		X	X	S	U	X	X	U			X		S	U	X		X	X													
	X	X	X		X	X	S	U	X	X	U			X		S	S	X		X	X													
	X	X	X		X	X	U	U	X	X	S			X		S	S	X		X	X													
	X	X	X		X	X	S		X	X	U		S	X		S	U	X		X	X													
	X	X	X			X	S		X	X	X		S	X		U	S			X	X		U					X						
	X	X	S		X	X	U		X	X	S		S	X		X	U			X	X							X						
	X	X	X		X		S		X		U		X	X		S	S	X		X	X				X			U						
	X	X	X		X		S		X	X	S		X	X		U		X		S	X				X			U						
	X	X	X		X				X	X	U		S	X		U	S	X		X	X				X			U						
	X		X		X		S		X	X	X		U	X		S	S	X		X	X				X			U						
	X		X				U		X	X	X		U	X		U	U	X		X	X		U		X			X						
	X	X	X			X			X	X			S	X		U	S	X		X	X	S			X			U						
	X	X	X		X	X			X	X			U	X		S	S	X		X	X				U			S						
	X	X	X		X	X			X	X			S	X		U	U	X		X	X				S			U						
	X	X	X		X	X			X	X			S	X		U	S	X		X	X				S			U						
	X	X	X		X	X	S		X	X			U	X		S	U	X		X	X				S									
	X	X	X		X	X	U		X	X			X	X		U	U	X			X	U			U									
	X	X	X		X	X	U		X	X			X	X		U		X		S	X		U		S									
	X	X	X		X	X	S		X		U		X	X		S		X		X	X		U		S									
				X				X			X					X	X		X			X	X		X	X		X	S	S	S	U	U	
U	X	X	X		X	X	U	U	X	X	S		X	X		X	S	X	U	S														
U	X	X	S		X		S	X		U				X		X	X	X	S	X	X	X												
	U						X	X	S		X			X			X	X	X	X		X	U	X	X	U	U							
	X	X	X		X	X	X		X		S		X	X		U		X			X		U		S									S
	X		X		X	X	U		X		S		X	X		S	X	X			X		U		X									S
9	41	43	37	5	38	40	11	6	40	40	15	3	20	36	5	20	3	32	2	19	27	1	1	0	7	1	0	4	0	0	0	0	0	0
0	0	0	2	1	2	0	21	3	2	1	9	2	13	0	1	9	17	2	1	10	0	3	0	0	5	0	0	1	1	1	1	0	0	0
1	0	0	1	4	0	0	7	21	0	0	14	5	6	2	8	11	16	2	1	3	0	4	5	0	2	0	0	7	0	0	0	1	1	0
0	4	3	3	0	4	3	2	2	3	1	1	0	3	5	0	2	3	5	1	2	3	2	0	1	2	0	0	0	0	0	0	0	0	0
0	0	0	1	0	0	0	1	0	1	0	3	0	0	0	0	1	1	0	1	1	0	0	0	0	1	0	0	0	0	0	0	0	0	2
2	1	0	0	0	0	0	2	1	0	1	0	0	0	0	0	1	0	0	1	0	0	0	3	0	0	1	1	0	0	0	0	0	0	0
0	0	1	0	0	4	6	0	1	15	10	4	0	6	0	3	2	2	1	0	4	0	0	0	0	1	1	0	0	0	0	0	0	0	0
0	0	0	0	0	1	0	0	1	1	0	1	0	0	0	0	0	0	0	0	0	0	0	0	0	0	0	0	0	0	0	0	0	0	0

PLAYING SQUAD

Existing Players		SN	HT	WT	DOB	AGE	POB	Career	Apps	Goals
GOALKEEPERS										
Chris	Maxwell	21			30/07/1990	21	Wrexham	Wrexham, Connahs Quay (6ML) 8/08	36	0
Joslain Leon	Mayebi	25	6'02"	14 02	14/10/1986	24	Douala, Cam	FC Metz (Fra), AEK Larnaca (Cyp) 7/08, Hakoah Ramat Gan (Isr) 1/09, Beitar Jerusalem (Isr) (5ML) 7/09, Maccabi Ahi Nazareth (SL) 1/10, Dinamo Bucharest II (Rom) 7/10, Preston (Trial) 12/10, Wrexham 1/11	1	0
Danny	Ward	13			22/06/1993	18	Wrexham	Wrexham, Tamworth (L) 3/11		
DEFENDERS										
Neil	Ashton	3	5'08"	12 06	15/01/1985	26	Liverpool	Tranmere, Shrewsbury (SL) 12/04, Shrewsbury 6/05 Rel c/s 09, Macclesfield (SL) 1/08, Chester 7/09 Rel 2/10, Wrexham 6/10	41	0
Chris	Blackburn	5	5'07"	10 06	02/08/1982	29	Crewe	Chester Rel c/s 03, Northwich 8/03, Morecambe 2/04, Swindon 7/07 Rel 5/08, Weymouth (SL) 3/08 (07/08 13,2), Aldershot 5/08, Wrexham 5/10	43	1
Leon	Clowes		5'10"	11 13	27/02/1992	19	Chester	Wrexham, Technogroup Welshpool (L) 8/09, Airbus UK (SL) 8/10		
Mark	Creighton	4	6'04"	12 01	08/10/1981	29	Birmingham	Kidderminster (Yth), Moor Green, Paget R, Halesowen T, Redditch, Bromsgrove, Willenhall 1/02, Redditch 8/05, Kidderminster 6/06, Oxford U Small Fee 5/09, Wrexham (2ML) 11/10 Perm 1/11	27	0
Johnny	Hunt	16	5'10"	10 03	23/08/1990	21	Liverpool	Wrexham, Droylsden (L) 2/11	3	0
Curtis	Obeng	2	5'09"	11 00	14/02/1989	22	Manchester	Man City Rel c/s 09, Wigan (Trial) 7/09, Wrexham 8/09	34	1
Matty	Owen				23/06/1994	17		Wrexham	0	0
Max	Penk				17/02/1993	18	Tarporley	Wrexham	0	0
Anthony	Stephens				21/01/1994	17		Wrexham	1	0
Steve	Tomassen				03/09/1993	17		Wrexham	1	0
Declan	Walker	22	5'10"	10 05	01/03/1992	18	Warrington	Wrexham, Droylsden (L) 2/11	6	0
Chris	Westwood	23	6'00"	12 02	13/02/1977	34	Dudley	Wolves Rel c/s 98, Injured, Reading (Trial), Telford (Trial), Hartlepool 3/99, Walsall 7/05 Rel c/s 07, Peterborough 5/07 Rel c/s 09, Cheltenham (2ML) 1/09, Wycombe 7/09 Rel c/s 11, Wrexham 6/11		
MIDFIELDERS										
Adrian	Cieslewicz	7	5'10"		16/11/1990	19		Man City, Wrexham 6/09	20	2
Joe	Clarke	26			28/07/1988	23		Redditch, Sollihull Moors 7/10, Darlington 8/10 Rel 2/11, Solihull Moors (2ML) 12/10, Solihull Moors 2/11, Wrexham 8/11		
Lee	Fowler	8	5'07"	10 00	10/06/1983	28	Cardiff	Coventry, Cardiff (L) 3/03, Huddersfield (3ML) 8/03 (Perm) 11/03, Grimsby (Trial) 7/05, Scarboough (2ML) 11/05 (Perm) 1/06 Rel c/s 06, Burton 5/06, Newport C (SL) 3/07, Newport C 5/07, Forest Green 6/08 Rel 5/09, Kettering 6/09 Rel 12/09, Oxford U 12/09 Rel 3/10, Cirencester 3/10, Halesowen T 3/10 Rel 5/10, Forest Green 6/10 Rel 12/10, Wrexham 1/11	12	1
Jay	Harris	6	5'07"	11 06	15/04/1987	24	Liverpool	Everton Rel c/s 06, Accrington 8/06 Rel c/s 08, Chester 7/08 Rel 8/09, Banned, Wrexham 7/10	40	4
Dean	Keates	12	5'06"	10 10	30/06/1978	33	Walsall	Walsall Rel c/s 02, Hull C 8/02, Kidderminster Undisc 2/04 Rel c/s 05, Lincoln C 8/05, Walsall 1/06 Rel c/s 07, Peterborough 7/07 Rel 12/09, Wycombe 1/10 Rel c/s 10. Wrexham 7/10	40	6
Nathaniel	Knight-Percival	20	6'00"	11 07	31/03/1987	24	Cambridge	Histon, Wrexham 6/10	32	0
Glen	Little	15	6'03"	13 00	15/10/1975	35	Wimbledon	C.Palace, Derry (L) 11/94, Glentoran 11/94, Burnley 11/96, Reading (SL) 3/03, Bolton (2ML) 9/03, Reading 7/04, Portsmouth 7/08 Rel c/s 09, Reading (SL) 3/09, Sheff Utd 8/09 Rel c/s 10, Aldershot T 7/10 Rel 1/11, Wrexham (Trial) 3/11, Wrexham 8/11		
Jamie	Morton				03/11/1993	17	Liverpool	Wrexham		
Louie	Moss				23/10/1993	17	Chester	Wrexham	1	1
Jamie	Tolley	18	6'00"	11 02	12/05/1983	28	Ludlow	Shrewsbury Rel c/s 06, Macclesfield 8/06 Rel c/s 09, Hereford 7/09 Rel 3/10, Wrexham 8/10	24	4

FORWARDS										
Obi	Anoruo	19	5'10"	11 06	28/08/1991	20	Nigeria	Wrexham, Newtown (4ML) 8/09, Vauxhall Motors (SL) 8/10	0	0
James	Colbeck				05/08/1993	18		Wrexham	0	0
Max	Fargin							Wrexham		
Andy	Morrell	11	5'11"	12 00	28/09/1974	36	Doncaster	Newcastle Blue Star, Wrexham 12/98, Coventry 7/03, Blackpool 8/06 Rel c/s 08, Bury 8/08, Wrexham 6/10	41	10
Mathias	Pogba	24	6'02"	13 09	19/08/1990	21		Celta Viga (Spa) (Yth), FC Quimper (Gui) 7/09, Wrexham 9/1029		4
Rob	Salathiel				28/08/1994	17		Wrexham	1	0
Jake	Speight	10	5'07"	11 02	28/09/1985	25	Sheffield	Sheff Utd, Leigh RMI (L) 3/05, Bury (Trial) c/s 05, Scarborough (L) 8/05 Perm 9/05, Bury (6WL) 12/05 Nominal 1/06 Rel 4/07, Northwich 6/07 Rel 5/08, Farsley Celtic 9/08, Droylsden 2/09, Mansfield 5/09, Bradford C £25,000 6/10, Port Vale (2ML) 10/10, Wrexham Undisc 7/11		
Gareth	Taylor	14	6'02"	13 08	25/02/1973	38	Weston-Super-Mare	Southampton (Trainee), Bristol R 7/91, C.Palace £750,000 9/95, Sheff Utd P/E 3/96, Man City £400,000 11/98 Rel c/s 01, Port Vale (L) 1/00, QPR (2ML) 3/00, Burnley (SL) 2/01, Burnley 6/01, Notts Forest £500,000 8/03 Rel c/s 06, Crewe (SL) 1/06, Tranmere 7/06, Doncaster (L) 1/08 Undisc 2/08 Rel c/s 09, Carlisle (L) 3/09, Wrexham 6/09	33	6
Danny	Wright	9	6'02"	13 08	10/09/1984	26	Southampton	Attleborough, Dereham c/s 05, Grimsby (Trial) 12/05, Histon 3/07 Rel 4/10, Peterborough (Trial) 11/09, Cambridge U 5/10, Wrexham Undisc 6/11		

Loanees		SN	HT	WT	DOB	AGE	POB	From - To	APPS	GOA
(D)Jordan	McMillan		5'10"	09 12	16/10/1988	22	Glasgow	Rangers (SL) 1/11 -	5	0

Departures		SN	HT	WT	DOB	AGE	POB	From - To	APPS	GOA
(G)Scott	Shearer		6'03"	11 08	15/02/1981	30	Glasgow	Wycombe 7/10 - Crawley 1/11	9	0
(F)Kevin	Gall		5'08"	11 00	04/02/1982	29	Merthyr	York C 7/10 - Rel 1/11, Altrincham (Trial) 7/11	5	0
(F)Marc	Williams		5'09"	11 02	27/07/1988	23	Colwyn Bay	Yth - Rel 5/11, Kidderminster (3ML) 8/10, Kidderminster 5/11	4	0
(F)David	Brown		5'10"	12 06	02/10/1978	32	Bolton	Forest Green 7/10 - Rel c/s 11	9	1
(F)Andrew	Mangan		5'09"	10 03	30/08/1986	25	Liverpool	Forest Green Undisc 1/10 - Fleetwood 7/11	42	15
(F)Wes	Baynes		5'11"	10 10	12/10/1988	22	Chester	Yth - Altrincham (SL) 10/10, Chester FC 6/11		
(D)Kai	Edwards		6'00"	12 02	29/01/1991	20		Yth - Prestatyn (5ML) 8/10, Prestatyn (SL) 1/11, Neath 7/11	0	0
(M)Christian	Smith		6'02"	13 02	10/12/1987	23	Crewe	York C 8/09 - Newport C (L) 11/10, Barrow (L) 1/11, Tamworth (6WL) 3/11, Chester FC 8/11	6	3
(D)Frank	Sinclair		5'08"	12 09	03/12/1971	39	Lambeth	Lincoln C 8/09 - Rel c/s 11	39	0
(D)Marvin	Andrews		6'01"	13 00	22/12/1975	35	San Juan	Queen of the South 8/10 -	29	2

Caption competition....

Send in your suggestions to tw.publications@btinternet.com and you could win a copy of the 2013 edition of the Directory...

Photo by Keith Clayton

YORK CITY

Chairman: Jason McGill
Secretary: Lisa Charlton **(T)** 07921 070 969 **(E)** lisa.charlton@ycfc.net
Additional Committee Members:
Sophie Hicks, Ian McAndrew, Rob McGill, Ross Porter

Manager: Gary Mills
Programme Editor: Mark Comer **(E)** mark.comer@themaxdp.co.uk

Back row (left to right): Andre Boucaud, Jamie Reed, Daniel Parslow, David McGurk, Jamal Fyfield, Liam Henderson.
Middle row: Rob Batty (kit), Adriano Moke, George Purcell (no longer with the club), Lanre Oyebanjo, Paul Musselwhite, Michael Ingham, James Meredith, Patrick McLaughlin, Michael Potts, Jeff Miller (physio).
Front row: David McDermott, Matty Blair, Scott Reed, Darron Gee (assistant manager), Gary Mills (manager), Chris Smith, Jason Walker, Ashley Chambers.

Club Factfile

Founded: 1922 **Nickname:** Minstermen
Previous Names: None
Previous Leagues: Football League

Club Colours (change): Red/blue/red (All sky blue)

Ground: Bootham Crescent, York YO30 7AQ **(T)** 01904 624 447
Capacity: 9,496 **Seats:** 1,844 **Covered:** 7,000 **Clubhouse:** Yes **Shop:** Yes

Directions
From Tadcaster (A64) take left turning onto A1237 (Outer Ringroad) continue for approx 5 miles to A19 and then turn right into York. Continue for just over 1 mile and turn left into Bootham Crescent opposite Grange Hotel.

Previous Grounds: Fulfordgate 1922-32

Record Attendance: 28,123 v Huddersfield Town - FA Cup 6th Round 1938
Record Victory: 9-1 v Southport - Division 3 North 1957
Record Defeat: 0-12 v Chester City - Division 3 North 1936
Record Goalscorer: Norman Wilkinson - 125 League (1954-66)
Record Appearances: Barry Jackson - 481 League (1958-70)
Additional Records: Paid £140,000 to Burnley for Adrian Randall December 1995
Received £1,000,000 from Manchester United for Jonathan Greening March 1998

Senior Honours: Football League Division 3 1983-84

10 YEAR RECORD

01-02	02-03	03-04	04-05	05-06	06-07	07-08	08-09	09-10	10-11
FL 3 14	FL 3 10	FL 3 24	Conf 17	Conf 8	Conf 4	Conf 14	Conf 17	Conf 5	Conf 8

YORK CITY

No.	Date	Comp	H/A	Opponents	Att:	Result	Goalscorers	Pos
1	Sat-14-Aug	BSP	H	Kidderminster Harriers	2682	L 1-2	Rankine pen 86	17
2	Tue-17-Aug	BSP	A	Grimsby Town	5037	D 0-0		22
3	Sat-21-Aug	BSP	A	Bath City	1066	D 2-2	Gash 43, Till 81	20
4	Tue-24-Aug	BSP	H	Barrow	2212	D 0-0		22
5	Sat-28-Aug	BSP	H	Altrincham	2095	W 3-0	Rankine 2 (70, 90), Brodie pen 75	14
6	Mon-30-Aug	BSP	A	Fleetwood Town	2020	L 1-2	Young 87	16
7	Sat-04-Sep	BSP	H	Rushden & Diamonds	2306	W 2-0	Till 76, Constantine 78	12
8	Sat-11-Sep	BSP	A	Wrexham	2446	D 1-1	Till 19	13
9	Sat-18-Sep	BSP	H	Hayes & Yeading United	2252	W 2-0	Rankine 56, Constantine 73	10
10	Tue-21-Sep	BSP	A	Mansfield Town	2202	L 0-5		15
11	Sat-25-Sep	BSP	A	Tamworth	1282	W 3-1	Rankine pen 27, Lawless 58, Fyfield 72	10
12	Mon-27-Sep	BSP	H	Darlington	3176	D 0-0		10
13	Sat-02-Oct	BSP	A	Eastbourne Borough	1104	L 1-2	Lawless 68	13
14	Tue-05-Oct	BSP	H	Kettering Town	1978	L 0-1		15
15	Sat-09-Oct	BSP	A	Newport County	2802	L 0-4		16
16	Sat-16-Oct	BSP	H	Bath City	2331	D 1-1	Rankine pen 30	16
17	Sat-30-Oct	BSP	A	Forest Green Rovers	792	L 1-2	Lawless 72	19
18	Sun-14-Nov	BSP	H	Wrexham	2601	D 1-1	Rankine pen 79	20
19	Sat-20-Nov	BSP	A	Rushden & Diamonds	1132	W 4-0	Racchi 8, Rankine 24, Chambers 36, Barrett 86	16
20	Tue-23-Nov	BSP	H	Southport	2104	W 2-0	Constantine pen 88, McDermott 90	12
21	Tue-30-Nov	BSP	A	Kidderminster Harriers	1066	D 0-0		14
22	Sat-01-Jan	BSP	A	Gateshead	1231	W 3-0	J Smith 61, Barrett 66, Constantine 89	12
23	Tue-11-Jan	BSP	H	Grimsby Town	3028	W 1-0	Constantine 19	12
24	Sat-15-Jan	BSP	A	Histon	578	W 2-1	Constantine 76, Till 86	10
25	Tue-18-Jan	BSP	A	Luton Town	5997	L 0-5		10
26	Sat-22-Jan	BSP	H	Forest Green Rovers	2468	W 2-1	Reed 56, Mackin 85	10
27	Sat-29-Jan	BSP	A	Southport	1308	L 0-4		11
28	Tue-01-Feb	BSP	H	AFC Wimbledon	2438	W 4-1	Parslow 16, Meredith 45, Rankine 70, Chambers 84	10
29	Sat-12-Feb	BSP	A	AFC Wimbledon	3532	L 0-1		12
30	Tue-15-Feb	BSP	H	Fleetwood Town	2220	W 1-0	Reed 48	9
31	Tue-22-Feb	BSP	A	Altrincham	1143	D 0-0		11
32	Sat-26-Feb	BSP	A	Hayes & Yeading United	458	W 2-1	J Smith 23, Rankine 80	7
33	Tue-01-Mar	BSP	H	Gateshead	2290	W 2-1	J Smith 8, Constantine pen 63	7
34	Sat-05-Mar	BSP	A	Barrow	1342	D 0-0		7
35	Sat-12-Mar	BSP	H	Eastbourne Borough	2357	W 1-0	Rankine 16	7
36	Tue-15-Mar	BSP	H	Mansfield Town	2261	W 2-1	Reed 2 (59, 69)	6
37	Sat-19-Mar	BSP	A	Cambridge United	2474	L 1-2	Reed 24	7
38	Sat-26-Mar	BSP	H	Histon	2364	W 1-0	Reed 48	7
39	Sat-02-Apr	BSP	A	Kettering Town	1365	D 1-1	Reed 8	7
40	Tue-05-Apr	BSP	H	Crawley Town	3060	D 1-1	J Smith 14	7
41	Sat-09-Apr	BSP	H	Newport County	2565	W 2-1	Rankine pen 50, Reed 70	7
42	Sat-16-Apr	BSP	H	Tamworth	2484	L 1-2	Constantine 89	7
43	Tue-19-Apr	BSP	H	Luton Town	2955	W 1-0	Reed 65	6
44	Sat-23-Apr	BSP	A	Darlington	2966	L 1-2	Carruthers 87	7
45	Mon-25-Apr	BSP	H	Cambridge United	2939	D 0-0		7
46	Sat-30-Apr	BSP	A	Crawley Town	2945	D 1-1	Og (Hunt) 5	8

CUPS

No.	Date	Comp	H/A	Opponents	Att:	Result	Goalscorers	Pos
1	Sat-23-Oct	FAC 4Q	A	Kidderminster Harriers	1123	W 2-0	Racchi 25, J Smith 54	
2	Sat-06-Nov	FAC 1	A	Rotherham United	3227	D 0-0		
3	Wed-17-Nov	FAC 1R	H	Rotherham United	2644	W 3-0	C Smith 66, Rankine 2 (pen 71, 79)	
4	Sat-27-Nov	FAC 2	A	Darlington	2500	W 2-0	Sangare 44, Chambers 90	
5	Sat-11-Dec	FAT 1	H	Boston United	1318	L 0-1		
6	Sat-08-Jan	FAC 3	A	Bolton Wanderers	13120	L 0-2		
7								

League
Starts
Substitute
Unused Sub

Cups
Starts
Substitute
Unused Sub

Goals (Lg)
Goals (Cup)

INGHAM	MCGURK	MEREDITH	PARSLOW	CARRUTHERS	SANGARE	J SMITH	LAWLESS	MACKIN	BRODIE	GASH	TILL	RANKINE	COURTNEY	PURCELL	BARRETT	MCDERMOTT	YOUNG	KNIGHT	CONSTANTINE	RICHARDSON	RACCHI	FYFIELD	DOWSON	BEESLEY	C SMITH	WEIR	CHAMBERS	BOUCAUD	REED	HATFIELD	DAFVILLE	KERR
24	5	3	6	11	12	4	7	17	16	9	8	15	2	10	14	22	18	1	25	23	27	16	28	29	30	21	19	28	7	20	2	29
X	X	X	X	X	X	X	X	X	X	X	S	S	S	U	U																	
X	X	X	X	X	X	S	X		X	X	U	X	U	S	X	U																
X	X	X	X	X	X	S	X		X	X	S	X	U		X	S	U															
X	X	X	X	X	X	X	X		X	X	S	S	U		X	S	U															
X	X	X	X	X	X	S	X		X	X	X	S	U		X	U	U															
X	X	X	X		S	X	X		X	X	S	X	U		X	S	X	U														
X	X	X	X		X	X	X			X	X	X	S		X	U	U	U	S													
X	X	X	X	X		X	X			X	X	X			X	U	S	U	S	U												
X	X	X	X			S	X			S	X	X	X		X	U	U	U	X		X											
X	X	X	X			X	X			S	X	X	X		X	S	U	U	X		U											
X	X	X	X				X			X	U	X	S		X		X	U	U		X	X	S									
X	X	X	X			S				X	X	X	U		X		X	U	S		X	X	S									
X	X	X	X			S	X			X	X	X	U		X		X	U	S			X	S									
X	X	X	X			S	X			S	X		U		X		X	U	X			X	S	X								
X	X	X	X			U	X			S	S				X		X	U	X		X	X	S	X								
X	X	X	X		U	X	X			X	X	X	X		S				U		X	S		S								
X	X	X	X	S		X	X				S	X			S	X	U		X		X	U			X							
X	X	X	X	S	X					S		X			U	X	X		U		X	U				X	X					
X	X	X	X	U	X						S	X			S	X			S		X	U			X	X	X					
X	X	X	X		U	X					X	X			U	S			S		X	S			X	X	X					
X	X	X	X		X						S	X			U	S	X		U		X	X				X	X	S				
X	X	X	X	X		X						X			X	S	U		S		U				X	X	X	S				
X	X	S	X	X		X		S			X					S	U		X		X	U			X			X	X			
X		U	X	X		X		U			X	S				U	X		X		X				X		S	X	X			
X	X	S	X	X		X		X			X	X					S		U		S				X		X	X	U			
	X	X	X	S				S			X	X				X	U	X	U		X				X		X	X	S			
X	X	X	X	X				X			X	X				U	S		U						X		X	X	S	S		
X		X	X	S		X		X			X	X					U		S						X		X	U	S		X	X
X	X	X	X	U		X					X	X			X				S						X		X	S	S		U	X
X	X	X	U	X		X					X	X			U				S						X		X	S	S		X	X
X	X	X	S	U		S					X	X							U		X				X		X	X	S		X	X
X		X	X	S		X						S			U	U			X						X		X	S	X	X	X	X
X		X	X	S		X					X	X			U				X						X		X	S	S	U	X	X
X	U	X	X			X					X	X							X		S				X		X	U	S	U	X	X
X	U	X	X			X					X	X				X			U						X		X	S	S	S	X	X
X	U	X	X			X					X	X				X			U		X				X			S	S	S	X	X
X	X	X	X	S		X					X	X				X		U	S									U	X	U	X	X
X	X	X	X	S		X					X	X			U	X			U								S	U	X		X	X
X	X	X	X			X		X			X	S			U	S			U						X		X	X	X		U	
X	X	X	X	S		X		U			X	X							S						X		S	U	X		X	X
X	X	X	X	S		X		S			X	X							U						X		S	U	X		X	X
X		X	X	S		X		U			X	X							S			U			X		X	S	X		X	X
X		X	X	S		X		S			S	U			X				X						X		X	U	X		X	X
X		X		X		X		S			S	S			X		U		X			X					X	X	X	U	X	
X		X		X		X		S			S	S			X		U		X			X					X	X	X	U	X	
X		X		X		S		X			S	X			U		U					X			X		X	X	S		X	X
X	X	X	X	S	U	X	X			S		X				X	U	U	X		X	U		U	X							
X	X	X	X	U	X	X	X				X	X			U	X	U	U	U		S	S			X							
X	X	X	X	X	X	X		S		U		X			S	X	U	U	U		X	S			X							
X	X	X		U	X	X					X	X			S	U	U	U	S		X	S			X	X	X					
X	X	X	X		S						U	X			U	X			S		X	U			X	X	X	X				
X	X	X	X	X		X		U			S	X			X		U	U	U		S				X	X	X		S			
45	34	43	41	15	9	30	16	6	6	12	29	34	3	0	19	8	9	1	13	0	15	9	0	2	24	5	22	10	12	1	17	16
0	0	2	1	12	1	9	0	6	0	5	12	8	3	1	3	9	3	0	13	0	2	2	5	1	0	0	4	9	11	3	0	0
0	3	1	1	3	2	1	0	3	0	0	2	1	8	1	10	8	14	11	13	1	2	5	0	0	0	0	0	7	1	5	2	0
6	6	6	5	2	3	5	2	0	0	0	2	6	0	0	1	4	0	0	1	0	4	0	0	0	6	3	3	1	0	0	0	0
0	0	0	0	1	1	0	0	1	0	1	1	0	0	0	2	0	0	0	2	0	2	3	0	0	0	0	0	0	1	0	0	0
0	0	0	0	2	1	0	0	1	0	1	1	0	0	0	2	1	5	5	3	0	0	2	0	1	0	0	0	0	0	0	0	0
0	0	1	1	1	0	4	3	1	1	1	4	12	0	0	2	1	1	0	8	0	1	1	0	0	0	0	2	0	9	0	0	0
0	0	0	0	0	1	1	0	0	0	0	0	2	0	0	0	0	0	0	0	0	1	0	0	0	1	0	1	0	0	0	0	0

PLAYING SQUAD

Existing Players		SN	HT	WT	DOB	AGE	POB	Career	Apps	Goals
GOALKEEPERS										
Michael	Ingham	24	6'04"	13 12	07/09/1980	30	Preston	Malachians, Cliftonville 7/98, Sunderland £30,000 7/99, Carlisle (2ML) 10/99, Cliftonville (3ML) 8/00, Stoke (L) 12/01, Stockport (2ML) 8/02, Darlington (L) 11/02, York C (SL) 1/03, Wrexham (SL) 3/04, Doncaster (L) 11/04, Wrexham 7/05 Rel c/s 07, Hereford 8/07 Rel c/s 08, York C 5/08	45	0
Paul	Musselwhite	1	6'02"	14 02	22/12/1968	42	Portsmouth	Portsmouth, Scunthorpe 3/88, Port Vale £20,000 7/92 Rel c/s 00, Chester (Trial) 7/00, Scunthorpe (Trial) 7/00, Darlington (Trial) 7/00, Sheff Wed 8/00, Hull C 9/00 Rel c/s 04, Scunthorpe 8/04 Rel c/s 06, Eastleigh 5/06 Rel 9/06, Kettering 11/06 Rel 11/06, Buxton 12/06, Port Vale 1/07, Harrogate T 6/07, Gateshead (L) 11/07, Gateshead 1/08 Retired c/s 09, Lincoln C (Pl/Coach) c/s 09, York C (Pl/Coach) 6/11		
DEFENDERS										
Jamal	Fyfield	16			17/03/1989	22		L.Orient, Maidenhead 8/07, York C 9/10, Maidenhead (L) 1/11	11	1
David	McGurk	5	6'00"	11 10	30/09/1982	28	Middlesbrough	Darlington, Bishop Auckland (L) 8/04, York (L) 9/04, York (6ML) 8/05, York (SL) 1/06, York 6/06	34	0
James	Meredith	3	6'00"	11 09	04/04/1988	23	Albury, Aust	Derby Rel c/s 07, Cambridge U (L) 10/06, Chesterfield (L) 2/07, Sligo R 8/07 Rel 12/07, Shrewsbury 1/08 Rel 6/09, AFC Telford (SL) 10/08, York C 7/09	45	1
Lanre	Oyebanjo	2	6'01"	11 04	24/04/1990	21	London	Brentford Rel c/s 08, Histon 7/08 Rel 6/11, Peterborough (Trial) 10/09, York C 6/11		
Daniel	Parslow	6	5'11"	12 05	11/09/1985	25	Rhymney Valley	Cardiff Rel c/s 06, Swansea (Trial) 3/06, York C 8/06	42	1
Chris	Smith	4	5'11"	11 06	30/06/1981	30	Derby	Leeds (Yth), Reading Rel c/s 01, Hayes (L) 12/99, York (Trial) 3/01, Kidderminster (Trial) 4/01, York C 5/01 Rel c/s 04, Stafford R 8/04 Rel c/s 05, Worcester 7/05, Tamworth 5/08, Mansfield 7/10, York C (3ML) 10/10 Perm 1/11	24	0
MIDFIELDERS										
Matt	Blair	17			21/06/1989	22	Warwick	RC Warwick, Stratford T 7/08, Bedworth 6/09, Redditch 11/09, AFC Telford 3/10, Kidderminster 8/10, York C 6/11		
Andre	Boucaud	15	5'10"	10 02	09/10/1984	26	Enfield	Reading Rel c/s 04, Peterborough (SL) 3/03, Peterborough (2ML) 8/03, Walsall (Trial) 2/04, Peterborough 7/04, Aldershot (3ML) 9/05, Kettering 5/06, Wycombe 8/07 Rel c/s 08, Kettering 8/08, York C (6WL) 11/10 Perm 1/11	19	0
Scott	Kerr	8	5'08"	12 10	11/12/1981	29	Leeds	Bradford C, Hull Undisc 6/01, Frickley (L) 9/02 Scarborough 3/03 Rel c/s 05, Lincoln C 7/05 Rel 1/11, York C 1/11	16	0
David	McDermott	19	5'05"	10 00	06/02/1988	23	Stourbridge	Walsall Rel c/s 08, Halesowen T (L) 1/07, Kidderminster 8/08 Rel 7/10, Halesowen T (L) 2/10, York C 7/10 Rel 10/10, York C 10/10	17	1
Patrick	McLaughlin	26	6'02"	11 08	14/01/1991	20	Larne, NI	Newcastle Rel c/s 11, York C 6/11		
Adriano	Moke	18	5'09"	10 00	11/01/1990	21		Man Utd (Yth), Barnsley (Yth), Leeds (Yth), Notts Forest (Scholar), Glen Hoddle Academy 3/10, Sheff Wed (Trial) 7/10, Jerez Industrial (Spa), York C 6/11		
Michael	Potts	14			26/11/1991	19		Man Utd (Yth), Blackburn (Scholar) 7/08 Pro 11/08 Rel c/s 11, York C 6/11		
Tom	Richardson				10/06/1993	18	York	York C	0	0
FORWARDS										
Ashley	Chambers	10	5'10"	11 06	01/03/1990	21	Leicester	Leicester Rel c/s 11, Wycombe (3ML) 8/09, Grimsby (SL) 1/10, Bournemouth (Trial) 9/10, York C (SL) 11/10, York C 7/11	26	2
Liam	Henderson	11	6'02"	12 02	28/12/1989	21	Gateshead	Hartlepool (Yth), Gateshead Redheugh, Watford Rel c/s 11, Wealdstone (SL) 2/08, Hartlepool (2ML) 1/09, Colchester (4ML) 9/10, Aldershot (L) 1/11, Rotherham (SL) 2/11, York C 7/11		
Danny	Pilkington		5'09"	11 08	25/05/1990	21	Blackburn	Myerscough College, Atherton Coll (Yth), Kendal T, Chorley, Stockport 7/08 Rel 1/11, Chesterfield (Trial) 7/11, York C 8/11		
Jamie	Reed	7	5'11"	11 07	13/08/1987	23	Deeside	Glentoran (Yth), Wrexham, Glentoran (SL) 1/06, Colwyn Bay (L) 10/06, Aberystwyth (5ML) 8/07, Tamworth (L) 1/08, Rhyl 7/08 Rel c/s 09, Bangor C 8/09, Dandedong Thunder (3ML) 5/10, York C 1/11	23	9
Jason	Walker	9	6'02"	14 04	21/03/1984	27	Barrow	Dundee, Morton 7/04, Morecambe 1/07, Barrow 3/07, Doncaster (Trial) 7/09, Luton (6WL) 11/10 Undisc 1/11, York C £60,000 6/11		

Loanees		HT	WT	DOB	AGE	POB	From - To	APPS	GOA
(G)David	Knight	6'00"	11 07	15/01/1987	24	Houghton-le-Spring	Histon (SL) 7/10 - Rel c/s 11	1	0
(F)Mark	Beesley	5'10"	11 10	10/11/1981	29	Burscough	Fleetwood 10/10 - Altrincham (6WL) 11/10 Perm 1/11 Rel c/s 11, Burscough 7/11	3	0
(M)Robbie	Weir	5'09"	11 07	12/12/1988	22	Belfast	Sunderland (2ML) 11/10 - Tranmere (SL) 2/11	5	0
(M)Will	Hatfield			10/10/1991	19		Leeds (SL) 1/11 -	4	0
(D)Aiden	Chippendale	5'08"	10 09	24/05/1992	19		Huddersfield 3/11 -		

Departures		HT	WT	DOB	AGE	POB	From - To	APPS	GOA
(F)Richard	Brodie	6'02"	12 13	08/07/1987	24	Gateshead	Newcastle Benfield 2/07 - Crawley 8/10, Fleetwood (SL) 5/11	6	1
(F)David	Dowson	5'10"	11 08	12/09/1988	22	Bishop Auckland	ex Gateshead 9/10 - Rel 10/10, Durham C 10/10	5	0
(D)Dean	Lisles	6'02"		05/05/1992	19	York	Yth - Rel 10/10, Ossett T 10/10		
(M)Jamie	Hopcutt	5'10"		23/06/1992	19	York	Yth - Rel 10/10, Ossett T 10/10		
(D)Alex	Lawless	5'11"	10 08	05/02/1983	28	Llwynupion	Forest Green 6/09 - Luton (2ML) 11/10 Undisc 1/11	16	3
(D)Djoumin	Sangare	6'00"	12 08	16/12/1983	27	Dunkerque	Salisbury 7/09 - Rel 12/10, Lincoln C (Trial), Oxford U 1/11 Rel 5/11, Kettering 7/11	10	0
(D)Duane	Courtney	5'11"	11 03	07/01/1985	26	Oldbury	Kidderminster 5/10 - Rel 1/11, Tamworth 2/11	6	0
(D)Danny	Racchi	5'08"	10 04	22/11/1987	23	Halifax	Bury 9/10 - Rel 4/11, Kilmarnock 6/11	17	1
(F)Michael	Rankine	6'01"	14 12	15/01/1985	26	Doncaster	Rushden & D £10,000 + P/E 6/09 - Aldershot T 5/11	42	12
(D)Greg	Young	6'02"	12 03	24/04/1983	28	Doncaster	Altrincham 5/10 - Altrincham (SL) 2/11, Alfreton 6/11	12	1
(D)Andy	McWilliams	5'08"		05/11/1989	21	Stockton	Yth - Stalybridge (SL) 8/10, Stalybridge 6/11		
(M)Peter	Till	5'11"	11 04	07/09/1985	25	Walsall	Walsall 6/10 - Fleetwood 7/11	41	4
(M)Jonathan	Smith	6'03"	11 02	17/10/1986	24	Preston	Forest Green 6/10 - Swindon £30,000 6/11	39	4
(D)Chris	Carruthers	5'10"	12 03	19/08/1983	28	Kettering	Oxford U 1/10 - Rel 6/11, Gateshead 7/11	27	1
(D)Liam	Darville			26/10/1990	20		Leeds 1/11 - Rel 6/11	17	0
(F)Leon	Constantine	6'02"	11 11	24/02/1978	33	Hackney	Hereford 9/10 - Rel 6/11, Braintree 7/11	26	8
(M)Neil	Barrett	5'10"	11 00	24/12/1981	29	Tooting	Ebbsfleet Undisc 6/09 - Rel 6/11	22	2
(M)Levi	Mackin	6'01"	12 00	04/04/1986	25	Chester	Wrexham (SL) 1/09 Perm 5/09 - Rel 6/11, Alfreton 7/11	12	1
(F)Michael	Gash	5'09"	12 01	03/09/1986	24	Cambridge	Ebbsfleet 7/09 - Rel c/s 11, Rushden & D (SL) 1/11, Cambridge U 6/11	17	1
(F)George	Purcell	5'11"	11 09	08/04/1988	23	Gravesend	Braintree Undisc 7/10 - Dartford (L) 11/10, Eastbourne B (SL) 1/11, Dover Undisc 7/11	1	0
(M)Papa	Agyemang	5'10"		25/04/1984	27		ex Motherwell 3/11 -		

CRAWLEY TOWN - BLUE SQUARE PREMIER CHAMPIONS

No.	Date	Comp	H/A	Opponents	Att:	Result	Goalscorers	Pos
1	Sat-14-Aug	BSP	H	Grimsby Town	2428	L 0-1		19
2	Tue-17-Aug	BSP	A	Cambridge United	2558	D 2-2	Tubbs 2 (5, 8)	19
3	Sat-21-Aug	BSP	A	Altrincham	776	W 1-0	Masterton 62	13
4	Tue-24-Aug	BSP	H	Bath City	1252	W 2-1	Tubbs 20, McAllister pen 42	7
5	Sat-28-Aug	BSP	A	Hayes & Yeading United	320	W 3-0	McAllister 2 (17, 26), Torres 71	3
6	Mon-30-Aug	BSP	H	Forest Green Rovers	1458	W 1-0	Tubbs pen 74	3
7	Sat-04-Sep	BSP	H	Fleetwood Town	1637	D 1-1	McAllister 8	2
8	Sat-11-Sep	BSP	A	Histon	497	W 2-0	McFadzean 20, Brodie 39	2
9	Sat-18-Sep	BSP	H	Gateshead	1412	W 2-1	Tubbs 2 (pen 47, 90)	1
10	Thu-23-Sep	BSP	A	AFC Wimbledon	4018	L 1-2	Tubbs 43	2
11	Sun-26-Sep	BSP	A	Rushden & Diamonds	1162	W 1-0	Tubbs 45	1
12	Wed-29-Sep	BSP	H	Tamworth	1355	W 3-1	Tubbs 2 (41, 76), Smith 47	1
13	Sat-02-Oct	BSP	H	Kidderminster Harriers	1483	W 2-0	Neilson 68, McAllister 76	1
14	Tue-05-Oct	BSP	A	Luton Town	6895	W 2-1	Brodie 80, McAllister 90	1
15	Sat-09-Oct	BSP	A	Barrow	1155	D 1-1	Tubbs 42	1
16	Sat-16-Oct	BSP	H	Newport County	2566	L 2-3	Brodie 32, Neilson 38	2
17	Sat-30-Oct	BSP	A	Mansfield Town	2615	W 4-1	Bulman 21, McAllister 2 (70, 90), Tubbs 87	1
18	Sat-13-Nov	BSP	A	Darlington	2012	D 1-1	Neilson 37	2
19	Sat-20-Nov	BSP	H	Altrincham	1331	W 7-0	Tubbs 3 (pen 2, 35, pen 38), Neilson 8, Torres 87, Brodie 2 (90, 90)	1
20	Sat-01-Jan	BSP	H	Eastbourne Borough	1894	W 3-1	Smith 13, Tubbs 2 (28, pen 61)	2
21	Mon-03-Jan	BSP	A	Forest Green Rovers	1027	W 3-0	McAllister 4, Tubbs 2 (63, 66)	2
22	Sat-15-Jan	BSP	H	Kettering Town	1812	W 2-1	Brodie 60, Tubbs pen 62	2
23	Tue-18-Jan	BSP	A	Bath City	836	W 2-0	Tubbs 2 (10, 83)	1
24	Sat-22-Jan	BSP	A	Grimsby Town	3382	D 0-0		2
25	Tue-25-Jan	BSP	H	Cambridge United	3241	W 3-0	McAllister 2 (61, 85), Cook 89	1
26	Thu-03-Feb	BSP	A	Kettering Town	1216	D 0-0		2
27	Sat-12-Feb	BSP	H	Wrexham	3331	W 3-2	Tubbs 3 (50, 82, pen 86)	2
28	Tue-15-Feb	BSP	A	Wrexham	4630	D 0-0		2
29	Tue-22-Feb	BSP	H	Southport	3765	W 1-0	Mills 75	2
30	Sat-26-Feb	BSP	H	Barrow	3941	W 3-2	McAllister 5, Brodie pen 28, Mills 86	2
31	Sat-05-Mar	BSP	H	Histon	3031	W 5-0	Tubbs pen 21, Smith 45, Simpson 77, Hunt 82, Gibson 89	2
32	Tue-08-Mar	BSP	A	Kidderminster Harriers	1816	D 0-0		1
33	Sat-12-Mar	BSP	A	Fleetwood Town	2027	W 2-1	Tubbs pen 32, Brodie 49	1
34	Tue-15-Mar	BSP	H	Hayes & Yeading United	2236	W 5-2	Dempster 25, Simpson 38, Tubbs 2 (58, 75), Mills 90	1
35	Fri-18-Mar	BSP	H	AFC Wimbledon	4054	W 3-1	Tubbs 5, McFadzean 8, Dance 53	1
36	Tue-22-Mar	BSP	A	Eastbourne Borough	2054	W 2-1	Wassmer 25, Torres 57	1
37	Sat-26-Mar	BSP	A	Gateshead	751	D 0-0		1
38	Tue-29-Mar	BSP	H	Mansfield Town	3162	W 2-0	McFadzean 13, Tubbs 82	1
39	Sat-02-Apr	BSP	H	Darlington	3554	W 1-0	Smith 67	1
40	Tue-05-Apr	BSP	A	York City	3060	D 1-1	Torres 49	1
41	Sat-09-Apr	BSP	A	Tamworth	1569	W 3-0	Tubbs 2 (26, pen 59), Wassmer 84	1 Champions
42	Tue-12-Apr	BSP	H	Luton Town	3326	D 1-1	Brodie 2	1
43	Sat-16-Apr	BSP	A	Southport	1011	W 4-0	Brodie 2 (7, 20), Neilson 57, Simpson 76	1
44	Fri-22-Apr	BSP	H	Rushden & Diamonds	3083	W 4-0	Tubbs 3 (34, 68, 82), Cook 90	1
45	Mon-25-Apr	BSP	A	Newport County	2026	W 1-0	Howell 68	1
46	Sat-30-Apr	BSP	H	York City	2945	D 1-1	Tubbs pen 69	1

CUPS

No.	Date	Comp	H/A	Opponents	Att:	Result	Goalscorers
1	Sat-23-Oct	FAC 4Q	A	Newport County	2247	W 1-0	McAllister 77
2	Sat-06-Nov	FAC 1	A	Guiseley	1609	W 5-0	Tubbs 15, Neilson 36, Hall56, Brodie 72, Torres 75
3	Sat-27-Nov	FAC 2	H	Swindon Town	3895	D 1-1	Tubbs 76
4	Tue-07-Dec	FAC 2R	A	Swindon Town	2955	W 3-2 (aet)	Smith 2 (16, 118), Og (Rose) 69
5	Sat-11-Dec	FAT 1	H	Dartford	1031	D 3-3	Brodie 55, McAllister pen 80, Howell 89
6	Tue-14-Dec	FAT 1R	A	Dartford	605	L 0-1	
7	Mon-10-Jan	FAC 3	H	Derby County	4145	W 2-1	McAllister 30, Torres 90
8	Sat-29-Jan	FAC 4	A	Torquay United	5065	W 1-0	Tubbs 39
9	Sat-19-Feb	FAC 5	A	Manchester United	74778	L 0-1	

League
Starts
Substitute
Unused Sub

Cups
Starts
Substitute
Unused Sub

Goals (Lg)
Goals (Cup)

KUIPERS	QUINN	HALL	WILSON	MILLS	RUSK	TORRES	MASTERTON	COGAN	TUBBS	MCALLISTER	JORDAN	ENVER-MARUM	MALCOLM	SMITH	REASON	NEILSON	FLOOD	MCFADZEAN	WRIGHT	HUTCHINSON	BRODIE	MARTIN	HOWELL	BULMAN	RENTS	COOK	BELL-BAGGIE	HUNT	SIMPSON	SHEARER	NAPPER	DANCE	DEMPSTER	GIBSON	WASSMER			
1	5	6	16	22	2	8	11	17	9	14	12	10	19	7	24	26	20	27	28	4	29	30	23	15	3	18	17	4	10	30	21	19	5	17	20			
X	X	X	X	X	X	X	X	X	X	X	S	S	S	U	U																							
	X	X	X	X	X	X	X	S	X	X	X	S	S		U	X	U																					
X	X	X	X	X	X	X	X	U	X	S	U	X			S	X		S																				
X	X	X	X	X	X	X	X	U	X	X	U		S		S	X		S																				
X	X	X	X	X	X	X	X		X	X	U				S	X	S	S	U																			
X	X	X	X	X	X	X			X	X	S				U	X	U	X	S	S																		
	X	X	X	X	X	X	X		X	X	X			U	S	X			S		S	U																
	X		X	X	X	X	X		X	S	X			U		X	S	X	S		X	U																
	X		X	X	X	X	X	X	X	S	X			S		S		X	U		X	U																
	X	U	X	X		X	X		X	S	X			S		X		X	U		X	U	X															
X		S	X	X		X	U		X	S	U			X		X		X	S		X		X	X														
X		S	X	X		X	U		X	S	U			X		X		X	S		X		X	X														
X		S	X	X		X	U		X	X	U			X		X		X	S		S			X	X													
X		S	X	X		X	U		X	S	U			X		X		X	S		X		X	X														
X		U	X	X		S	U		X	X	U			X		X		X	S		X		X	X														
X	X	U	X			X	S		X	S	U			X		X		X	S		X		X	X														
X		S	X	X		S	X		S	X	U					X		X	U		X		X	X	X													
X		X	U	X		S	X			X	U					X	S	X			X		X	X	X	S												
X		X	X	X		X	X		X	S	U			U		X					S		X	X	S	X												
X			X	X		X			X	X				X		X		X			S		X	X		U		S	S	U								
X			S	X		X			X	X				U		X		X			S		X	X		S		X	X	U								
X			X	X					X	S						X		X			X		X	X		U		X	X	U		S	U					
X				X		X			X	X				X		S		X			X		X	X				X	S	U		S	U					
X			X	X		X			X	X				S				X			S		X	X				S	X	U		X	U					
X			U	X		X				X				X				X			X		X	X		S		X	S	U		X	S					
X				X		S			S	X				X				X			X			X	X	X		X	X	U			U	S				
X			X			X			X	X				X				X			S		X	X		U		S	S	U			X	X				
U			X			S			X	S				U				X			X		X	X		S		X	X	X			X	X				
X				X	S				X	S				X				X			X		X	X		X		X	X	U			U	S				
U			X	X		X			S	X								X			X		X	X		S		X	U	X		U		X				
X			S			X			X	X				X				X			S		X	X				X	S	U		U	X	X				
X			S		S	X			X					U				X			S		X	X		X		X	X	U				X	X			
X			S	X	S	X			X					U				X			X		X	X		U		X	X	S				X				
			X	X		X			X		U			S							X		X	X		S		U	X	X		S	X	X				
				X		X			X	U	U			X				X			X		X	X		S		X	X	X		S			S			
			X	X	S	X			X	X	U			X									X			S		X	X	X		S	U		X			
			X	X	S	X			X	X	U			X									X			S		X	X	X			S	U	X			
			X		S	X			X	X	U			X				X			S		X			S		X	X	X				U	X			
			S			X			X	X	U			X				X			S		X	X		S		X	X	X				U	X			
			X		S	X				X	U			X				X			X		X	X		S		U	S	X				X	X			
			S			X			X	X	U			S				X			S		X	X		U		X	X	X				X	X			
			S		U					X	U			X		X		X			X		X	X		S		X	X	X				S	X			
			X						U	U	U			S		S		X			X		X	X		X		X	X	X			X	X				
U			U						X	X				X		X		X			S		X	X		S		X	X	X			X		S			
U			X						X	S				X		S					X		X			X		X	X	X	U		X	U	X			
U			X						X	S				S		X					X		X			S		X	X	X	U		X	X	X			
X		S	X	X		S	U	U	X	X	U			X		X		X					X	X	X	S												
X		X		X		S	X	U	X	X	U			U		X	U	X			S		X	X	X	S												
X		U	X	X		X	X		X	S	U			S		X		X			X		X	X	U	U	S											
	X		U	X	X		X	U		X	X	U			X		X		X			S		X	X	U	S	U										
U		X	X	X		S	X		U	S	X						X				X		S	X	X	X	X											
X		X	X			X	X		X	X	U					S	U	X			U		X		X	U	X											
X			X	X		X			X	X				X		X		X			S		X	X	U	S		S			U	U							
X			X	X	U	X			X	X				X				X			S		X	X	S	X		S			U	U							
X			U	X	S	X			X	X				X				X			S		X	X	U	S		X			U	U			X				
26	11	9	32	32	9	34	12	2	38	27	5	1	0	22	0	23	0	34	0	0	25	0	35	31	4	6	0	22	20	15	0	2	8	11	10	0	0	0
0	0	5	7	0	7	5	1	1	3	14	2	2	3	7	4	4	3	3	9	1	13	0	0	0	1	15	0	3	6	1	0	5	2	3	2	0	0	0
5	0	3	3	0	1	0	5	2	1	2	22	0	0	8	3	0	2	0	4	0	0	4	0	0	0	5	0	2	1	11	2	2	6	4	0	0	0	0
8	0	3	7	8	0	6	4	0	8	7	1	0	0	5	0	5	1	8	0	0	2	0	8	8	4	2	2	1	0	0	0	0	0	1	0	0	0	0
0	0	1	0	0	1	3	0	0	0	2	0	0	0	1	0	1	0	0	0	0	5	0	1	0	1	5	1	2	0	0	0	0	0	0	0	0	0	0
1	0	2	1	0	1	0	2	2	1	0	5	0	0	1	0	0	2	0	0	0	1	0	0	0	4	2	1	0	0	3	3	0	0	0	0	0	0	0
0	0	0	0	3	0	4	1	0	37	12	0	0	0	4	0	5	0	3	0	0	11	0	1	1	0	2	0	1	3	0	0	1	1	1	2	0	0	0
0	0	1	0	0	0	2	0	0	3	3	0	0	0	2	0	1	0	0	0	0	2	0	1	0	0	0	0	0	0	0	0	0	0	0	0	0	0	0

AFC WIMBLEDON - BLUE SQUARE PLAY-OFF WINNERS

No.	Date	Comp	H/A	Opponents	Att:	Result	Goalscorers	Pos
1	Sat-14-Aug	BSP	A	Southport	1802	W 1-0	Jolley 72	7
2	Tue-17-Aug	BSP	H	Histon	3126	W 2-0	Kedwell pen 90, Wellard 90	2
3	Sat-21-Aug	BSP	H	Tamworth	3144	W 3-0	S Moore 37, Kedwell 2 (60, 79)	2
4	Tue-24-Aug	BSP	A	Rushden & Diamonds	1365	L 0-1		2
5	Sat-28-Aug	BSP	A	Eastbourne Borough	2485	W 3-2	Kedwell 2 (31, 90), Minshull 55	1
6	Mon-30-Aug	BSP	H	Newport County	3828	D 2-2	Kedwell pen 16, Jolley 56	2
7	Sat-04-Sep	BSP	A	Kettering Town	1727	W 2-1	Hatton 14, Kedwell 57	1
8	Sat-11-Sep	BSP	H	Bath City	3300	W 4-0	S Moore 18, Yakabu 36, Jolley 65, Kedwell 68	1
9	Fri-17-Sep	BSP	A	Luton Town	7283	L 0-3		1
10	Thu-23-Sep	BSP	H	Crawley Town	4018	W 2-1	Hatton 77, Kedwell 80	1
11	Sun-26-Sep	BSP	A	Kidderminster Harriers	1565	L 0-2		3
12	Wed-29-Sep	BSP	H	Cambridge United	3119	W 3-0	Franks 2 (69, 90), Jolley 75	2
13	Sat-02-Oct	BSP	H	Forest Green Rovers	3204	D 1-1	Jolley 68	2
14	Tue-05-Oct	BSP	A	Mansfield Town	2699	W 5-2	S Moore 2 (1, 74), Jolley 9, Kedwell 43, Jackson 60	2
15	Sat-09-Oct	BSP	A	Wrexham	3277	W 2-1	Jolley 47, Yussuff 84	2
16	Sat-16-Oct	BSP	H	Gateshead	3330	W 1-0	Yakabu 72	1
17	Sat-30-Oct	BSP	H	Darlington	3952	L 0-2		2
18	Tue-09-Nov	BSP	A	Altrincham	901	W 2-0	Kedwell 2 (1, 45)	1
19	Sat-13-Nov	BSP	A	Barrow	1375	L 0-2		1
20	Sun-21-Nov	BSP	H	Kettering Town	3114	W 3-2	L Moore 2 (11, pen 18), Jolley 35	1
21	Tue-28-Dec	BSP	H	Eastbourne Borough	3364	W 3-0	Nwokeji 45, Wellard 80, Yussuff 89	1
22	Sat-01-Jan	BSP	H	Hayes & Yeading United	3176	W 3-1	Jackson 49, Mulley 51, L Moore 83	1
23	Mon-03-Jan	BSP	A	Newport County	3462	D 3-3	Mulley 28, Hatton 47, Yussuff 82	1
24	Sat-08-Jan	BSP	A	Darlington	2046	D 0-0		1
25	Wed-12-Jan	BSP	H	Luton Town	4287	D 0-0		1
26	Tue-18-Jan	BSP	A	Fleetwood Town	1808	D 1-1	Kedwell 16	2
27	Sat-22-Jan	BSP	H	Southport	3408	W 5-0	Mulley 2 (20, 90), L Moore 50, S Moore 56, Hatton pen 87	1
28	Tue-25-Jan	BSP	A	Bath City	1135	D 2-2	Kedwell pen 32, Hudson 45	2
29	Fri-28-Jan	BSP	A	Gateshead	922	W 2-0	Jolley 46, Kedwell 76	1
30	Tue-01-Feb	BSP	A	York City	2438	L 1-4	Jolley 63	1
31	Sat-05-Feb	BSP	H	Fleetwood Town	3298	W 1-0	Jolley 84	1
32	Sat-12-Feb	BSP	H	York City	3532	W 1-0	Hatton 20	1
33	Sat-19-Feb	BSP	A	Tamworth	1496	W 5-2	Mulley 18, Kedwell 2 (50, pen 89), Broughton 75, Yussuff 90	1
34	Tue-22-Feb	BSP	H	Wrexham	3486	L 0-1		1
35	Sat-26-Feb	BSP	H	Altrincham	3078	W 4-1	Kedwell 3 (37, 45, 60), Broughton 81	1
36	Tue-01-Mar	BSP	A	Hayes & Yeading United	708	D 0-0		1
37	Sat-05-Mar	BSP	A	Grimsby Town	3182	L 1-2	Yussuff 24	1
38	Sat-12-Mar	BSP	H	Kidderminster Harriers	3517	L 1-2	Minshull 82	2
39	Fri-18-Mar	BSP	A	Crawley Town	4054	L 1-3	Johnson 38	2
40	Sat-26-Mar	BSP	H	Rushden & Diamonds	3069	W 1-0	Kedwell pen 29	2
41	Sat-02-Apr	BSP	H	Barrow	3264	W 2-0	Johnson 32, Yussuff 83	2
42	Sat-09-Apr	BSP	A	Cambridge United	2907	W 2-1	Johnson 11, Mohamed 32	2
43	Sat-16-Apr	BSP	A	Histon	750	W 4-0	Kedwell 2 (13, 67), L Moore 2 (63, 64)	2
44	Fri-22-Apr	BSP	H	Mansfield Town	3613	W 2-1	Stuart 68, Jolley 86	2
45	Mon-25-Apr	BSP	A	Forest Green Rovers	1824	D 0-0		2
46	Sat-30-Apr	BSP	H	Grimsby Town	3752	W 2-1	L Moore 7, Johnson 51	2
CUPS								
1	Sat-23-Oct	FAC 4Q	A	Basingstoke Town	1750	W 1-0	Harris 71	
2	Sat-06-Nov	FAC 1	H	Ebbsfleet United	3219	D 0-0		
3	Thu-18-Nov	FAC 1R	A	Ebbsfleet United	2306	W 3-2 aet	Nwokeji 9, S Moore 2 (90, 120)	
4	Sat-27-Nov	FAC 2	H	Stevenage Borough	3633	L 0-2		
5	Sat-11-Dec	FAT 1	H	Braintree Town	1201	W 3-0	Jolley 8, Nwokeji 86, Kedwell 88	
6	Sat-15-Jan	FAT 2	H	Woking	2265	L 2-3	Nwokeji 32, Kedwell pen 65	
7	Fri-06-May	PO SF 1	A	Fleetwood Town	4112	W 2-0	L Moore 38, Mohamed 50	
8	Wed-11-May	PO SF 2	H	Fleetwood Town	4538	W 6-1	Mohamed 3 (1, 35, 63), Kedwell 28, Jolley 67, Mulley 80	
9	Sat-21-May	PO Final	N	Luton Town	18195	D 0-0	(W4-3 pens) - Played at Eastlands	
								League
								Starts
								Substitute
								Unused Sub
								Cups
								Starts
								Substitute
								Unused Sub
								Goals (Lg)
								Goals (Cup)

S BROWN	BLACKMAN	JOHNSON	YAKABU	HATTON	WELLARD	S MOORE	GREGORY	MAIN	L MOORE	KEDWELL	JACKSON	JOLLEY	MINSHULL	HARRIS	TURNER	YUSSUFF	JONES	FRANKS	NWOKEJI	BUSH	J BROWN	MULLEY	HUDSON	STUART	GWILLIM	KIERNAN	BROUGHTON	MOHAMED																
1	3	6	5	7	8	15	4	10	11	9	2	12	14	18	20	23	21	16	17	22	24	26	25	28	29	27	31	39																
X	X	X	X	X	X	X	X	X	X	X	S	S	S	U	U																													
X	X	X	X	X	X	X	X	X	X	X	S	S		U	U	S																												
X	X	X	X	X	X	X	X	X	X	X	S	S		U	U	S																												
X	X	X	X	X		X	X	X	X	X	S	S			U	X	S	U																										
X	X	X	X	X		X	X	U	X	X	S	X	X	U	U	S																												
X	X	X	X	X	X	X	X	X	S	X	U	X	S		U	S																												
X	X		X	X	S	X	X		S	X	X	X	X	X	U	U		S																										
X	X		X	X	U	X	X	S		X	X	X	X	X	U	S			S																									
X	X		X	X	S	X	X	S		X	X	X	X	X	U	S			U																									
X				X	X	X	X	X		X	X			X	U	S	U	X	S	X	U																							
X	S			X	S	X	X	S		X	X			X	U	X	U	X	X	X																								
X	X		X	X	X	X	X	U	S	X	X	X		X	U			S		S																								
X	X			X	X	X	X	S	S	X	X	X		X	U	S		X		U																								
X			X	X	X	X	X	S	S	X	X	X		X	U	U		S		X																								
X			X	X	X	X	X	U	S	X	X	X		X	U	S		U		X																								
X	U		X	X	X	X	X	S	S	X	X	X		X	U	S				X																								
X	U		X	X	U	X	X	S	S	X	X	X		X	U	X				X																								
X	X			X	X		X	X	S	X	X		S	X	U	X		X	S	U																								
X	U		X	X	X	X	S		S	X	X		S		U	X		X	X	X																								
X			X	X	X	X		U	X	S	S	X		X	U	X		S	X	X																								
X				X	X		X	S		X	X		X		U	X	S	X	X	X																								
X			X		X	X			S	X	X	U		S	U	X		X	X	X		X	S																					
X				X		U	X		X	X	X	S		X	U	S		X	S	X		X	X																					
X				X		X	X		S	X	X	X		U	U			X	S	X		X		X																				
X			X	X		X	X		X	X	S	S			U	S		X	U			X	X	X																				
X			X	X		X	X		S	X	X				U	S		U	S			X	X	X	X																			
X				X		X	X		X	X		S		U	U	S		X	S			X	X	X	X																			
X				X		X	X		X	X	S			U	U	S		X	S			X	X	X	X																			
X			X	X			X		X	X	S	X			U	X		S	S			X		X	X																			
X		S		X	X		X			X	X	X		U	U			X	S			X		X	X																			
X		X		X		X	X			X	X	X			U	S		U	U			X		X	X	U																		
X		X	U	X			X		X	X	S	X			U	X		S	U			X		X	X																			
X		X		X			X			X	U	X		U	U	X		S				X	X	X	X		S																	
X		X	U	X			X			X	S	X			U	X		S				X	X	X	X		S																	
X		X	S	X			X			X	U	X			U	X		S				X	X	X	X		S																	
X		X					X			X	S	S		U	U	X	U	X				X	X	X	X		X																	
X		X				S	X			X	S	X	S	U	U	X		X				X		X	X		X																	
X		X				X	X		X	X	S		S	U	U	X						X	X	X	X		S																	
X		X					X		X		X		S	X	U	X	U					X	S	X	X	S	X																	
X		X	X	X	X		X		S	X	X		S		U	X							U		X		S	X																
X		X	X	X	X		X		X	X	U		S		U	X			S					S	X			X																
X		X	X	X	X		X		X	X	U		X		U				S				S	S	X			X																
X		X	X		X		X		X	X		S	X		U	S						S	X	U	X			X																
U		X		X			X		X	X		S	S		X	X	X					S		X	X	U		X																
X		S	X		X					S	X	X	X		U	U			X			X	X	X		X		S																
X		X	X	X	X			S	X	X		U	X		U	X						S		S	X			X																
X	X		X	X	X	X	X	U	S	X	X	X		X	U	S		S	U																									
X	X		X	X	S	S	X	U	X	X	X	X		X	U	X		U	S																									
X	X	S	X	X	S	X	X	U	S	X	X			U	U	X		X	X																									
X			X	X	X	X	X	S	X	X	U	X	U	X	U	S		U	U	X																								
X	U		X	X	X		X		X	X	S	X			U	X	U	X	S	X																								
X				X	X	S			X	S	U	X		X	U	S		X	X			X	X		X																			
X		X	S	X	X		X		X	X		S	S		U	X						U		X	X			X																
X		X	S	X	X		X		X	X		S	U		U	X						S		X	X			X																
	X		X	S	X	X		X		X	X		U	S		U	X						S		X	X			X															
45	12	21	26	39	22	27	41	7	19	43	23	22	9	15	1	21	1	15	6	12	0	19	12	18	20	1	3	6	0	0	0	0	0	0	0	0	0	0	0	0	0	0	0	0
0	1	2	1	0	3	1	1	9	14	2	14	10	10	1	0	17	2	9	12	1	0	3	3	3	0	1	5	1	0	0	0	0	0	0	0	0	0	0	0	0	0	0	0	0
1	3	0	2	0	2	1	0	4	0	0	5	2	0	12	45	3	4	4	4	2	1	0	1	1	0	2	0	0	0	0	0	0	0	0	0	0	0	0	0	0	0	0	0	0
9	3	3	5	9	7	3	8	0	7	8	3	5	0	4	0	6	0	3	2	2	0	1	1	3	4	0	0	3	0	0	0	0	0	0	0	0	0	0	0	0	0	0	0	0
0	0	1	3	0	2	2	0	1	2	1	1	2	2	0	0	3	0	1	2	0	0	2	0	0	0	0	0	0	0	0	0	0	0	0	0	0	0	0	0	0	0	0	0	0
0	1	0	0	0	0	0	0	3	0	0	2	1	2	1	9	0	1	2	2	0	0	1	0	0	0	0	0	0	0	0	0	0	0	0	0	0	0	0	0	0	0	0	0	0
0	0	4	2	5	2	5	0	0	7	23	2	12	2	0	0	6	0	2	1	0	0	5	1	1	0	0	2	1	0	0	0	0	0	0	0	0	0	0	0	0	0	0	0	0
0	0	0	0	0	0	2	0	0	1	3	0	2	0	1	0	0	0	0	3	0	0	1	0	0	0	0	0	4	0	0	0	0	0	0	0	0	0	0	0	0	0	0	0	0

RUSHDEN & DIAMONDS - CLUB FOLDED SUMMER 2011

No.	Date	Comp	H/A	Opponents	Att:	Result	Goalscorers	Pos
1	Sat-14-Aug	BSP	H	Fleetwood Town	1248	D 1-1	Corcoran 90	12
2	Tue-17-Aug	BSP	A	Bath City	876	L 1-2	Porter 6	20
3	Sat-21-Aug	BSP	A	Barrow	1145	L 0-1		24
4	Tue-24-Aug	BSP	H	AFC Wimbledon	1365	W 1-0	Howe 64	18
5	Sat-28-Aug	BSP	H	Grimsby Town	1575	W 4-1	Miller 41, Charles 59, Howe 60, Porter 66	10
6	Mon-30-Aug	BSP	A	Kettering Town	2313	W 1-0	Og (Westwood) 32	6
7	Sat-04-Sep	BSP	A	York City	2306	L 0-2		10
8	Sat-11-Sep	BSP	H	Newport County	1351	L 0-1		16
9	Sat-18-Sep	BSP	A	Southport	876	D 2-2	O'Connor 57, Johnson 86	16
10	Tue-21-Sep	BSP	H	Histon	926	W 2-0	Miller 50, O'Connor 67	10
11	Sun-26-Sep	BSP	H	Crawley Town	1162	L 0-1		14
12	Wed-29-Sep	BSP	A	Eastbourne Borough	802	W 2-0	Howe 27, Miller 36	13
13	Sat-02-Oct	BSP	A	Altrincham	897	D 2-2	Howe pen 15, O'Connor 73	12
14	Tue-05-Oct	BSP	H	Darlington	1034	W 2-1	Howe 65, O'Connor 71	8
15	Sat-09-Oct	BSP	H	Mansfield Town	1480	W 1-0	Sills 8	6
16	Sat-16-Oct	BSP	A	Tamworth	1002	W 2-1	Howe 10, Power 90	6
17	Sat-30-Oct	BSP	H	Barrow	1107	W 5-0	Charles 2 (8, 45), O'Connor 23, Porter 58, Corcoran 65	5
18	Tue-09-Nov	BSP	A	Kidderminster Harriers	1225	L 0-1		6
19	Sat-13-Nov	BSP	A	Fleetwood Town	1429	D 1-1	O'Connor 73	6
20	Sat-20-Nov	BSP	H	York City	1132	L 0-4		8
21	Sat-27-Nov	BSP	A	Forest Green Rovers	642	D 2-2	Power pen 51, O'Connor 90	8
22	Sat-01-Jan	BSP	A	Luton Town	6928	L 0-3		10
23	Mon-03-Jan	BSP	H	Kettering Town	2216	L 1-2	Stuart 66	10
24	Sat-08-Jan	BSP	H	Altrincham	1024	L 1-2	O'Connor 22	11
25	Tue-18-Jan	BSP	A	Hayes & Yeading United	307	D 3-3	Smith 2 (68, 78), Prosser 85	13
26	Sat-22-Jan	BSP	A	Newport County	1743	W 3-1	Gash 19, O'Connor 40, Johnson 89	11
27	Sat-29-Jan	BSP	H	Tamworth	1216	D 1-1	Power 68	12
28	Tue-01-Feb	BSP	H	Cambridge United	1279	W 2-1	Smith 74, Farrell 89	11
29	Sat-05-Feb	BSP	A	Cambridge United	2366	W 2-0	O'Connor 14, Jamie Day 21	9
30	Sat-12-Feb	BSP	H	Gateshead	874	L 0-2		9
31	Tue-22-Feb	BSP	H	Eastbourne Borough	905	W 2-0	Cowan-Hall 22, Oshodi 90	8
32	Tue-01-Mar	BSP	H	Bath City	804	W 5-1	Gash 4 (9, 26, 44, 73), Charles 40	8
33	Sat-05-Mar	BSP	H	Hayes & Yeading United	1129	D 1-1	Gash 45	9
34	Tue-08-Mar	BSP	H	Forest Green Rovers	759	D 2-2	Charles 2 (31, 51)	9
35	Sat-12-Mar	BSP	A	Wrexham	3187	D 1-1	Huke 52	8
36	Sat-19-Mar	BSP	H	Southport	1061	D 2-2	Johnson 28, Porter 77	8
37	Tue-22-Mar	BSP	H	Luton Town	2459	L 0-1		8
38	Sat-26-Mar	BSP	A	AFC Wimbledon	3069	L 0-1		9
39	Sat-02-Apr	BSP	A	Mansfield Town	1758	L 1-2	O'Connor 15	12
40	Tue-05-Apr	BSP	A	Histon	363	W 2-0	O'Connor pen 59, Huke 83	9
41	Sat-09-Apr	BSP	H	Wrexham	1181	D 2-2	Shariff 79, O'Connor 90	10
42	Wed-13-Apr	BSP	A	Grimsby Town	2071	D 1-1	Shariff 38	10
43	Sat-16-Apr	BSP	A	Gateshead	701	D 2-2	Shariff 2 (18, 55)	10
44	Fri-22-Apr	BSP	A	Crawley Town	3083	L 0-4		11
45	Mon-25-Apr	BSP	H	Kidderminster Harriers	1569	W 2-1	O'Connor 49, Charles 90	11
46	Sat-30-Apr	BSP	A	Darlington	2009	L 0-2		12

CUPS

No.	Date	Comp	H/A	Opponents	Att:	Result	Goalscorers
1	Sat-23-Oct	FAC 4Q	A	Kettering Town	2792	W 2-1	Spence 17, Howe pen 23
2	Sat-06-Nov	FAC 1	H	Yeovil Town	1666	L 0-1	
3	Sat-11-Dec	FAT 1	H	Eastwood Town	657	D 1-1	Howe 38

League
Starts
Substitute
Unused Sub

Cups
Starts
Substitute
Unused Sub

Goals (Lg)
Goals (Cup)

ROBERTS	MILLER	STUART	OSANO	CORCORAN	PORTER	POWER	SPENCE	SIMMONDS	FARRELL	HOWE	CHARLES	HUKE	JOHNSON	ROBINSON	JOE DAY	GREEN	KORANTENG	JAMIE DAY	KEEHAN	O'CONNOR	KEY	SILLS	SMITH	KING	GASH	THORNE	PROSSER	BROADBENT	MILLS	EVANS	OSHODI	SHARIFF	COWAN-HALL	WOOLLEY	PHILLIPS	COUSINS
1	2	5	6	16	4	14	24	7	9	10	19	20	18	3	13	25	26	11	15	8	27	7	17	28	30	25	5	29	7	32	3	22	10	25	31	12
X	X	X	X	X	X	X	X	X	X	X	S	S	S	U	U																					
X	X	X	X	X	X	X	X		X	X	S	U	S	S	U	X																				
X	U	X	X	X	X	X	S	S		X	X	S	X	X	U	X																				
X	S		X	X	X	X	S			X	X	X	X	X	U	X	S	U																		
X	X	X	X		X	X	S			X	X		X	X	U	X	S	S	U																	
X	X	X	X		X	X	S			X	X		X	X	U	X	S	S	U																	
X		X	X		X	X	X			X	X		X	X	U	X	S	S	U	S																
X	X	X	X		X	X	S		S	X	X		S	U	U	X		X		X																
	X	X	X		X	X			X	X	S	X	S	U	X	U		X		X	U															
	X	X	X		X	X	U		X		X	X	S	S	X	S		X		X	U															
	X	X	X		X	X				X	S	X	S	U	X	S		X		X	U	X														
	X	X	X		X		S			X	S	X	X	S	X	U		X		X	U	X														
	X	X	X		X	U	S			X	S	X	X	U	X			X		X	U	X														
	X	X	X		X	U	U			X	S	X	X	S	X			X		X	U	X														
		X	X	U	X	X	S			X	S	X	X	S	X			X		X	U	X														
U		X	X	S	X	X	S			X	S	X	X	U	X			X		X		X														
U	S		X	X	X	X			S		X	X	X	S	X			X	U	X		X														
U	U	X	X	X	X	X	X		S	X	S		S		X			X		X		X														
U		X	X	X	X	X	S		U	X	S		X		X			X	X	X		S														
		X	X	X	X	X	U		S	X	X	X	S		X			X		X	U	S														
U	X	X			X	X	X		X		S	X	S	X	X				U	X		X	S													
	X	X	X	S		X			U	S	X	X	X		X					X	U		X	S	X											
	X	X	X	X	X	X	U		S		X		U		X			X		X	U			U	X											
	S		X	X	X	X			X		S		S		X			X		X				U	X	X	X	U								
			X	X	X	X			U		X		S		X			X		X			S		X	X	X		S	U						
			X	X	X	X			S		X		S		X			X		X			S		X	U	X		X	U						
			X	X	X	X			U		X		S		X			X		X			S		X		X		X	U	S					
	S		X	X	X	X			S		S		U		X			X		X			X		X				X	U	X					
			X	X	X	X			S		S		S		X			X		X			X		X		X		X	U	U					
			X	X	X	X			X		S		S		X			X		X					X		X	U	X		U	S				
	U		X	U	X	X			S			X	S		X			X		X					X				X	U	X		X			
	X		X	U	X	X			S		X	X	S		X					X					X				X	U	X	S				
	X		X	S	U	X			S		X	X	X		X					X					X				X	U	X	U				
	X		X	U	X	S			S		X	X	X		X			S		X					X				X	U	X					
	X				X	X			S		X	X	S		X			X	U						X				X	U	X	U	X			
	X			S	X	X			X			X	X		X			X	U						X				X	U	X	S		U		
				X	X	X			U		X	X	X		X			X	U						X				X	U	X	S			U	
	S			X	X	X			S		X	X	X		X			X	S						X				X	U	X	U				
	X		S	X	X	X			S		X	X	S		X			X	U	X					X				X	U						
	X		U	X	X	X			X			X	X		X			X	S	X									X	U		S		S		
	X		X		X	X			X			X	X					X	S	X								U	X	X		S			U	S
	X		X	U	X				X			X	S					X	X	X				U				U	X	X		X				S
	X		X	S	X						X	X	S					X	X	X								U	X	X		X	U			S
	X		X	U	X	X						X	X					X	U	X								U	X	X		X	S			S
	X		X	X		X			U		S	X	X					X	U	X								U		X	X	X				S
	X		X	X	X	X			S		U	X	S					X		X								U		X	X	X				S
U	S	X	X		X	X	X		U	X	S	X	X	S	X		U	X	U	X																
U	S		X	X	X	X	X		S	X	X	X	U	S	X	U		X	U	X																
U	X	X	X			X	X		X	X	S		X	X	X					X		U	S	U												
8	27	21	39	22	43	40	5	1	11	18	22	29	22	6	32	7	0	34	3	35	0	9	3	0	18	2	6	0	19	6	11	5	2	0	0	0
0	5	0	1	5	0	1	10	1	16	1	17	2	22	6	0	2	4	4	3	1	0	2	4	1	0	0	0	0	1	0	1	6	1	1	0	6
5	3	0	1	6	1	2	4	0	6	0	1	1	2	6	8	2	0	1	11	0	10	0	0	3	0	1	0	8	0	15	2	3	1	1	2	0
0	1	2	3	1	2	3	3	0	1	3	1	2	2	1	3	0	0	2	0	3	0	0	0	0	0	0	0	0	0	0	0	0	0	0	0	0
0	2	0	0	0	0	0	0	0	1	0	2	0	0	2	0	0	0	0	0	0	0	0	1	0	0	0	0	0	0	0	0	0	0	0	0	0
3	0	0	0	0	0	0	0	0	1	0	0	0	1	0	0	1	1	0	2	0	0	1	0	1	0	0	0	0	0	0	0	0	0	0	0	0
0	3	1	0	2	4	3	0	0	1	6	7	2	3	0	0	0	0	1	0	14	0	1	3	0	6	0	1	0	0	0	1	4	1	0	0	0
0	0	0	0	0	0	0	1	0	0	2	0	0	0	0	0	0	0	0	0	0	0	0	0	0	0	0	0	0	0	0	0	0	0	0	0	0

Blue Square North v Blue Square South Challenge
A comparison of The Positive Statistics from The 2010-2011 Season

1 Top Scoring Club in all Three Competitions
North: Alfreton Town 116
South: Ebbsfleet United 104

2 Highest aggregate of goals in their matches
North: Droylsden 174
South: Chelmsford City 170

3 Clubs Most Consecutive scoring games
North: Solihull Moors 23
South: Eastleigh 23

4 Top Individual Goalscorer
North: Liam Hearn (Alfreton Town) 32
South: Adam Birchall (Dover Athletic) 45

5 Player who scored in Most Games
North: Lee Stevenson (Eastwood Town) 23 games
South: Adam Birchall (Dover Athletic) 29 games

6 Best Individual Consecutive scoring run
North: Paul Brayson (Blyth Spartans) 5 games 6 goals
South: Adam Birchall (Dover A) 10 games 17 goals

7 Most Individual Goalscorers
North: Corby Town 23+ 4 ogs
South: Boreham Wood 23+ 4 ogs

8 Clubs with most hat tricks
North: 3 Eastwood Town: Lee Stevenson 2 Peter Knox
South: 3 Dover Athletic: Adam Birchall 3

9 Club with most players scoring 10+
North: 4 Alfreton Town: Liam Hearn 32 Paul Clayton 18
Laurie Wilson 18, Nathan Arnold 10
South: 5 Ebbsfleet United: Callum Willock 26, Michael West 23., Ashley Carew 14, Tom Phipp 12 & Ricky Shakes 11

10 Most Penalties scored by a club
North: Harrogate Town 11
South: Chelmsford City 15

11 Most Penalties scored by an individual
North: Graeme Armstrong (Harrogate Town) 11
South: David Rainford (Chelmsford City) 12

12 Least Goals conceded in the League Season
North: AFC Telford United 29
South: Braintree Town 33

13 Clubs failing to score on least occasions
North: Alfreton Town 4 times in 52 games
South: Chelmsford City 7 times in 51 games

14 Most Clean Sheets (games without conceding a goal)
North: Boston United 25
South: . Braintree Town 22

15 Most Consecutive 'Clean Sheets'
North: Alfreton Town and Boston United 6
South: Woking 5

16 Most Consecutive Victories
North: Alfreton Town 8
(first eight games of the season)
South: Bromley 7

17 Best Unbeaten Run
North: Eastwood Town 18
South: Ebbsfleet United 15

18 Best League Attendance
North: AFC Telford United 2508
South: Dartford 2781

19 Best Average League Attendance
North: AFC Telford United 1757
South: Dartford 1169

20 Most League attendances over 1,000
North: 53: AFC Telford United 20, Boston United 18, Nuneaton Town 5, Alfreton Town 4, Worcester City 3, Eastwood Town 2, Hinckley United and Stalybridge Celtic 1 each
South: 55: Woking 15, Dartford 14, Dover Athletic 7, Ebbsfleet United 6, Chelmsford City & Farnborough 3, Braintree Town 2, Welling United 2, Bromley, Lewes and Havant & Waterlooville 1 each

21 Most clubs qualifying for The FA Cup competition Proper
(i.e survived the qualifying rounds)
North: 6: 2nd Round: Droylsden
1st Round: Corby Town, Eastwood Town, Guiseley Nuneaton Town and Vauxhall Motors
South: 6: 3rd Round: Dover Athletic
2nd Round: Chelmsford City
1st Round: Dartford, Ebbsfleet United, Havant & Waterlooville, Woking

22 Club with the best F.A. Cup run:
North: Droylsden 2nd Round; Clubs beaten: Havant & Waterlooville
South: Dover Athletic 3rd Round. Clubs beaten: Gillingham and Aldershot Town

23 Most Clubs qualifying for The FA Challenge Trophy competition Proper.
North: 14: 4th Round: Blyth Spartans and Guiseley
3rd Round: AFC Telford United, Alfreton Town, Droylsden, Gloucester City
2nd Round: Boston United, Eastwood Town, Stalybridge Celtic and Worcester City
1st Round: Harrogate Town, Hinckley United, Hyde United Redditch United
South: 11: 3rd Round: Dartford, Eastleigh, Woking
2nd Round: Dorchester Town, Ebbsfleet Town
1st Round: Basingstoke Town, Boreham Wood , Braintree Town, Hampton & Richmond, St Albans City and Welling United

24 Clubs with best F.A. Challenge Trophy run:
North: Blyth Spartans.
4th Round. Clubs Beaten: Fleetwood Town, Altrincham and Droylsden.
Guiseley. 4th Round. Clubs Beaten: Barrow, Stalybridge Celtic and Eastbourne Borough.
South: Dartford. 3rd Round. Clubs Beaten: Crawley Town and Ashford Town (Middlesex).
Eastleigh. 3rd Round. Clubs Beaten: Sutton United and Worcester City
Woking. 3rd Round. Clubs Beaten: Harlow Town and AFC Wimbledon

FINAL RESULT:

Blue Square North	**11**
Blue Square South	**9**
Tied	**4**

ALTRINCHAM

Chairman: Grahame Rowley
Secretary: Derek Wilshaw **(T)** 07833 636 381 **(E)** dwilshaw@altrinchamfootball.co.uk
Additional Committee Members:
George Heslop, Andrew Shaw, Paul Daine, Brian Flynn.

Manager: Lee Sinnott
Programme Editor: Grahame Rowley. **(E)** altrinchamprog@yahoo.co.uk

Altrincham Football Club
2011/2012 Players & Staff

Club Factfile

Founded: 1903 **Nickname:** The Robins
Previous Names: Broadheath FC 1893-1903.
Previous Leagues: Manchester 1903-11. Lancashire C. 1911-19. Cheshire C. 1919-68. Northern Premier 1968-79,97-99. Conference 1979-97, 99-
Club Colours (change): Red & white stripes/black/red. (Yellow/blue/yellow)

Ground: Moss Lane, Altrincham, Cheshire WA15 8AP **(T)** 0161 928 1045
Capacity: 6,085 **Seats:** 1,154 **Covered:** Yes **Clubhouse:** Yes **Shop:** Yes

Directions
From M6 junction19, turn right towards Altrincham into town centre (approx 15 minutes). Turn down Lloyd Street, past Sainsburys on the right. Tesco Extra on left. Then follow signs for Altrincham F.C.

Previous Grounds: Pollitts Field 1903-10.

Record Attendance: 10,275 - Altrincham Boys v Sunderland Boys English Schools Shield 1925.
Record Victory: 9-2 v Merthyr Tydfil - Conference 1990-91.
Record Defeat: 1-13 v Stretford (H) - 04.11.1893.
Record Goalscorer: Jack Swindells - 252 (1965-71).
Record Appearances: John Davison - 677 (1971-86).
Additional Records: Transfer fee paid - £15k to Blackpool for Keith Russell. Received - £50k from Leicester for Kevin Ellison.

Senior Honours: Cheshire Senior Cup Winners 1904-05, 33-34, 66-67, 81-82. F.A. Trophy Winners 1977-78, 85-86.
Football Alliance Champions 1979-80, 80-81. N.P.L. Premier Champions 1998-99.
Conference North & South Play-off Winners 2004-05.

10 YEAR RECORD

01-02	02-03	03-04	04-05	05-06	06-07	07-08	08-09	09-10	10-11
NP P 9	NP P 14	NP P 12	Conf N 5	Conf 22	Conf 21	Conf 21	Conf 15	Conf 14	Conf 22

ALTRINCHAM

No.	Date	Comp	H/A	Opponents	Att:	Result	Goalscorers	Pos
1	Sat-14-Aug	BSP	A	Luton Town	6665	L 1-2	Reeves 70	15
2	Tue-17-Aug	BSP	H	Darlington	1099	D 2-2	Denham 51, Johnson 78	17
3	Sat-21-Aug	BSP	H	Crawley Town	776	L 0-1		23
4	Tue-24-Aug	BSP	A	Southport	1088	L 0-1		24
5	Sat-28-Aug	BSP	A	York City	2095	L 0-3		24
6	Mon-30-Aug	BSP	H	Mansfield Town	1261	L 0-4		24
7	Sat-04-Sep	BSP	H	Kidderminster Harriers	929	L 1-2	Reeves 75	24
8	Sat-11-Sep	BSP	A	Gateshead	539	L 0-2		24
9	Sat-18-Sep	BSP	A	Eastbourne Borough	1117	L 0-5		24
10	Tue-21-Sep	BSP	H	Barrow	1042	W 2-0	Densmore pen 55, Reeves 74	24
11	Sat-25-Sep	BSP	H	Grimsby Town	1364	D 2-2	Denham 53, Densmore 90	24
12	Tue-28-Sep	BSP	A	Kettering Town	1194	D 3-3	Denham 19, Reeves 30, Hewson 81	24
13	Sat-02-Oct	BSP	H	Rushden & Diamonds	897	D 2-2	Reeves 8, Williams 89	24
14	Sat-09-Oct	BSP	A	Histon	655	L 0-3		24
15	Sat-16-Oct	BSP	H	Fleetwood Town	1106	W 1-0	Twiss 60	24
16	Sat-30-Oct	BSP	A	Hayes & Yeading United	274	W 1-0	Densmore pen 81	24
17	Sat-06-Nov	BSP	A	Bath City	794	D 2-2	Clee 38, Twiss 47	24
18	Tue-09-Nov	BSP	H	AFC Wimbledon	901	L 0-2		24
19	Sat-13-Nov	BSP	H	Luton Town	1416	L 0-1		24
20	Sat-20-Nov	BSP	A	Crawley Town	1331	L 0-7		24
21	Sat-27-Nov	BSP	A	Cambridge United	2123	L 0-4		24
22	Sat-01-Jan	BSP	H	Wrexham	1982	D 0-0		24
23	Mon-03-Jan	BSP	A	Mansfield Town	2229	W 1-0	Reeves 59	24
24	Sat-08-Jan	BSP	A	Rushden & Diamonds	1024	W 2-1	Reeves 40, Milne 55	23
25	Tue-18-Jan	BSP	A	Tamworth	795	D 1-1	Reeves 7	23
26	Sat-22-Jan	BSP	H	Bath City	831	L 0-3		23
27	Tue-25-Jan	BSP	H	Hayes & Yeading United	558	W 4-2	Wedgbury 45, Clee 53, Reeves 72, Twiss 79	22
28	Tue-01-Feb	BSP	A	Wrexham	3300	L 1-2	Clee 87	22
29	Sat-12-Feb	BSP	A	Kidderminster Harriers	2930	L 1-2	Baynes 43	22
30	Tue-15-Feb	BSP	H	Histon	621	L 0-3		23
31	Sat-19-Feb	BSP	H	Kettering Town	752	W 3-2	Reeves pen 22, Baynes 64, Young 88	22
32	Tue-22-Feb	BSP	H	York City	1143	D 0-0		22
33	Sat-26-Feb	BSP	A	AFC Wimbledon	3078	L 1-4	Joseph 69	22
34	Sat-05-Mar	BSP	H	Gateshead	765	D 1-1	Joseph 88	22
35	Tue-08-Mar	BSP	A	Barrow	953	L 0-1		22
36	Sat-12-Mar	BSP	A	Newport County	1201	L 1-2	Reeves 1	22
37	Tue-15-Mar	BSP	H	Forest Green Rovers	598	W 2-1	Joseph 57, Twiss 59	22
38	Sat-19-Mar	BSP	H	Tamworth	895	W 2-0	Reeves 36, Johnson 60	22
39	Sat-26-Mar	BSP	A	Darlington	1967	W 1-0	Reeves 86	21
40	Tue-29-Mar	BSP	H	Southport	1210	D 1-1	Reeves pen 20	20
41	Sat-02-Apr	BSP	H	Cambridge United	1161	D 2-2	Lawton 27, Reeves pen 34	22
42	Sat-09-Apr	BSP	A	Forest Green Rovers	937	L 0-1		22
43	Sat-16-Apr	BSP	A	Fleetwood Town	1966	L 1-3	Johnson 90	22
44	Sat-23-Apr	BSP	H	Newport County	963	L 1-3	Johnson 90	22
45	Mon-25-Apr	BSP	A	Grimsby Town	4311	W 1-0	Joseph 52	22
46	Sat-30-Apr	BSP	H	Eastbourne Borough	1649	L 3-4	Beesley 2 (60, 82), Clee 76	22 Relegated

CUPS

No.	Date	Comp	H/A	Opponents	Att:	Result	Goalscorers
1	Sat-23-Oct	FAC 4Q	H	Gateshead	797	L 0-2	
2	Tue-14-Dec	FAT 1	A	Curzon Ashton	268	W 2-0	Williams 84, Denham pen 90
3	Sat-15-Jan	FAT 2	A	Blyth Spartans	620	L 1-2	Reeves 85

League
Starts
Substitute
Unused Sub

Cups
Starts
Substitute
Unused Sub

Goals (Lg)
Goals (Cup)

COBURN	JOSEPH	SMITH	WILLIAMS	BROWN	LAWTON	DENSMORE	CLEE	DANLYK	REEVES	JOHNSON	HOLMES	DENHAM	WELCH	MCCREADY	COATES	HOLSGROVE	TWISS	CROWELL	MCCARTHY	HEWSON	JONES	MILNE	SOMNER	BAYNES	BEESLEY	PIERGIANNI	DOOTSON	WEDGBURY	FOSTER	COLY	YOUNG	CONNORS	BATESON	KIDD	WOODS	SMART	LANGFORD	
1	4	2	5	15	7	6	11	16	8	14	19	10	22	17	21	12	9	18	23	20	14	27	25	17	19	26	30	28	14	29	22	18	3	23	31	27	25	
X	X	X	X	X	X	X	X	X	X	X	S	S	S	U	U																							
X	X	X	X	X	X	X	X	X	X	S	S	X	U		U	S																						
X	X	X	X	X		X	X	X	X	S	S	X	X	U	U	S																						
X	X	X	X	X	U		X		S	X	X	X	X	S	U	X	U																					
X	X	X	X	X		X		X	X	S	U		X	S	U	X	S	X																				
X	X	X	X	X		X	X	S	X		X		U		U	X	S	X	S																			
U	S	X	X	X	X	X		X	S			X	X		X		U	X	X	S																		
U	U	X	X	X	X	X	X	S	S				X		X		S	X	X	X																		
U	X	X	X	X	X	X	X	U	X				S		X	S		X	X	S																		
U	X	X	X	X	X	X		X	S		U	X	X		X	S			X	U																		
U	X	X	X	X	X	X		X	S			X	X		X	U		S	X	S																		
U	X	X	X		X	X	X	X	X			X			X	S		S	U	S	X																	
U	X	X	X		X	X	X	X	X			X			X	S		X	S	S	U																	
U	U	X	X	X	X	X	S	X	X			X	X		X	S	S	X																				
X	X	X	X	S	S	X	X		U						U	X	X		S	X		X	X															
X	X		X	X	S	X	X	S	S				U		U		X			X		X	X	X														
X	X		X	X	X	X	X	S	S				U		U		X			U		X	X	X														
X	X		X	X	X	X	X	U	U			S			U		X			S		X	X	X														
X	U	X	X	X	U	X	X	X	S			S			U		X					X	X	X														
X	X		X	X	X	X	S	U	S			X			U		X			S		X	X	X														
X	X	X	X	X		X	X	U				S			U	S	X					X	X	X	S													
X	X	X	X		U	X		X	S			X			U	U	X			S			X		X	X												
X	X		X	X	X	X	X	S	X				U		U	S				X		X		X	S													
X	X		X	X	X	X			X				S		U		S			S		X	X	X	X													
U	X	X	X	S	X	X	S	S	X			U			X		X			X				X	X													
X		X	X	U	X	X	S	U	X			S					X			X				X	X	X	U											
X		X	X	S	X	X	X	U	X								S			X					X	X	U	X	S									
X		X	X	U	X	X	X	U	X								S			X					X	X	U	X		U								
U	S	X	X		X	X	X		X								S			U				X	S	X	X	X			X							
U	X		X	S	X		X	U	X								X			X				X	S		X	X			X							
U	X		X	U	X		X	S	X								S							S	X	X	X	X			X	X						
U	X	X	X	U	X		X	U	X								S							S	X	X	X	X				X						
U	X	X	X	U	X		X	S	X								S							X	S	X	X				X	X						
U	X		X	S	X		X	S	X								S			X				X		X	X				X		X					
U	X		X	S	X		X	S	X								S							X		X	X				X	X	X					
U	X	U	X	X	X			S	X								X							X		X	X					X	X	U	U			
X	X	X	X	S	X		X	S	X								X							X	U	X	U					X	U					
X	X	X	X	X	X			S	X	S							X							X	U	X	U					X	S					
X	X	X	X		X		S	X	X	S							X							U		X	U				X	X	S					
X	X	X		U	X		X	X	X	X							U							S		X	U				X	X	S					
X	X		X	U	X		X		X	X							S							S	S	X	U				X	X	X					
X	X		X	U	X	U	X	X	X								X							S	S	X	U				X		X					
U	X	X	S	S	X	X	X		X	S														X	U	X	X				X		X					
U	X	U	X	S	X	X	X		X	X							S							X	S	X	X					X						
	X	X	X	X	X	X	X		X	X							S							S	S	X	X									U	U	
U	X	X	X	X	X	X	X		X	X							U							U	S	X	X									U		
X	X	X	X	S	U	X	X	U	S				S		U	U	X			X		X	X	X														
X	X	X	X			X	X	X				X			U	U	X			U		U	X	U	X													
X	X	X	X	X	X	X	U	X	X						U	S	S			S				X	X													
25	38	32	44	24	37	32	33	15	33	7	2	11	8	0	9	4	16	7	5	10	1	9	9	20	8	21	12	6	0	0	11	11	6	0	0	0	0	0
0	2	0	1	9	2	0	5	13	10	6	3	5	3	2	0	9	16	2	3	9	0	0	0	6	10	0	0	0	1	0	0	0	3	0	0	0	0	0
20	3	2	0	8	3	1	0	9	2	0	2	1	5	2	16	2	4	0	1	3	1	0	0	2	3	0	9	0	0	1	0	0	1	1	1	2	1	0
3	3	3	3	1	1	3	2	2	1	0	0	1	0	0	0	0	2	0	0	1	0	1	2	2	2	0	0	0	0	0	0	0	0	0	0	0	0	0
0	0	0	0	1	0	0	0	0	1	0	0	0	1	0	0	1	1	0	0	1	0	0	0	0	0	0	0	0	0	0	0	0	0	0	0	0	0	0
0	0	0	0	0	1	0	1	1	0	0	0	0	0	0	3	2	0	0	0	1	0	1	0	1	0	0	0	0	0	0	0	0	0	0	0	0	0	0
0	4	0	1	0	1	3	4	0	15	4	0	3	0	0	0	0	4	0	0	1	0	1	0	2	2	0	0	1	0	0	1	0	0	0	0	0	0	0
0	0	0	1	0	0	0	0	0	1	0	0	1	0	0	0	0	0	0	0	0	0	0	0	0	0	0	0	0	0	0	0	0	0	0	0	0	0	0

PLAYING SQUAD 2011/12

Existing Players		SN	HT	WT	DOB	AGE	POB	Career	Apps	Goals
GOALKEEPERS										
Stuart	Coburn		6'01"	14 00	05/05/1975	36	Manchester	Maine Road, Irlam, Trafford 94/95, Altrincham 3/97, Leigh RMI 5/02, Altrincham 10/03	25	0
Josh	Ollerenshaw		6'05"	12 10	05/10/1990	20	Manchester	Oldham Rel c/s 11, Silsden (L) 2/10, Mossley (L) 10/10, Altrincham 8/11		
Adam	Reid				29/06/1994	17		Altrincham		
DEFENDERS										
Ryan	Brown		5'10"	11 02	15/03/1985	26	Stoke	Port Vale Rel c/s 05, Leek T 8/05, Northwich 6/06, Altrincham (SL) 2/10, Altrincham 5/10	33	0
Joe	Coombs				12/01/1994	17		Altrincham		
Matthew	Fearon				07/09/1993	17		Altrincham		
Adam	Flynn				12/10/1984	26	Whiston	Liverpool (Scholar), Prescot Cables 8/04, Burscough 6/07, Southport 7/08 Rel 4/11, Altrincham 6/11		
Paul	Jones		6'01"	11 09	03/06/1978	33	Liverpool	Tranmere Rel c/s 97, Blackpool (L) 2/97, Barrow 8/97, Leigh RMI 8/99, Oldham 11/99 Rel c/s 02, Colwyn Bay 8/02 Rel 8/02, Hyde 3/03, Barrow 6/06 Rel 5/11, Droylsden (2ML) 2/11, Altrincham 7/11		
Mark	Lees				23/07/1988	23		Mossley (Yth), Curzon Ashton (Yth), Stalybridge (Yth), New Mills, Buxton 1/08, Ashton U 2/09, Hyde U/FC 7/09, Altrincham 6/11		
Christopher	Lynch		5'10"		29/12/1984	26	Manchester	Wigan (Scholar) Rel c/s 04, Hyde U c/s 04, Altrincham 6/11		
MIDFIELDERS										
Nicky	Clee				30/08/1983	28	Huddersfield	Local, Ossett A 12/02, Ashton U 8/04, Hyde U 6/05, Altrincham 7/09	38	4
Anthony	Danlyk		5'08"	11 08	01/02/1983	28	Stoke	Stoke (Jun), Stone Dominoes, Leek T 3/02, Belper 8/04, Leek T 6/05, Witton 5/07, Leek T 9/07, Altrincham 6/08	28	0
Shaun	Densmore		6'03"	14 09	11/11/1988	22	Liverpool	Everton Rel c/s 08, Bradford C (Trial) 7/08, Altrincham 9/08	32	3
Robbie	Lawton		6'00"	11 08	14/06/1979	32	Liverpool	Marine, Vauxhall Motors, Caernarfon, Vauxhall Motors 7/99, Altrincham 6/06	39	1
Simon	Richman		5'11"	11 12	02/06/1990	21	Ormskirk	Bolton (Yth), Port Vale Rel c/s 10, Southport (Trial) 7/10, Worcester 8/10, Altrincham 5/11		
Brian	Summerskill				10/09/1991	19		Crewe (Yth), The New Saints (Yth), Wrexham, Northwich 11/10, Altrincham 6/11		
FORWARDS										
Ashley	Mulholland				19/01/1988	23		Altrincham (Yth), Abbey Hey, Ashton U, Flixton, Altrincham 8/11		
Damien	Reeves		5'09"	11 10	18/12/1985	25	Doncaster	Leeds Rel c/s 05, Scarborough (Trial) c/s 05, Barnsley (Trial) 9/05, Wakefield & Emley 10/05, Farsley Celtic 1/06, Histon 6/08, Northwich 1/09, Farsley Celtic 3/09, Alfreton 7/09, Guiseley (L) 9/09, AFC Telford 11/09, Bradford PA 3/10, Altrincham 6/10	43	15
Neil	Tolson		6'02"	12 04	25/10/1973	37	Wordsley	Walsall, Oldham £150,000 3/92, Bradford C £50,000 12/93, Chester (L) 1/95, York £60,000 7/96 Rel c/s 99, Southend 7/99 Rel c/s 01, Retired, Leigh RMI 10/02, Kettering 1/03 Rel 1/03, Halifax 3/03, Hyde 7/03 Pl/Ass Man c/s 07 Rel 4/11, Radcliffe B (L) 2/06, Altrincham (Ass Man) 6/11		
Michael	Twiss		5'11"	13 03	28/12/1977	33	Salford	Man Utd Rel c/s 00, Sheff Utd (SL) 8/98, Norwich (Trial) 2/00, Preston (Trial) 3/00, Tranmere (Trial) 3/00, Port Vale 7/00 Rel c/s 01, Chesterfield (Trial) 7/01, Leigh RMI 8/01, Chester 5/02, Morecambe 5/04 Rel 3/10, Stalybridge 3/10 Rel 4/10, Altrincham 5/10	32	4

BISHOP'S STORTFORD

Chairman: Luigu Del Basso
Secretary: Ian Kettridge **(T)** 07904 169 017 **(E)** ianket@aol.com
Additional Committee Members:
Franco Del Basso, John Turner, Graeme Auger.

Manager: Ian Walker
Programme Editor: John Allington **(E)** j.allington@bsfc.co.uk

Club Factfile

Founded: 1874 **Nickname:** Blues or Bishops
Previous Names:
Previous Leagues: East Herts 1896-97, 1902-06, 19-21, Stansted & District 1906-19, Herts County 1921-25, 27-29, Herts & Essex Border 1925-27, Spartan 1929-51, Delphian 1951-63, Athenian 1963-73, Isthmian 1974-2004

Club Colours (change): Blue with white trim/blue/blue (All red)

Ground: Woodside Park, Dunmow Road, Bishop's Stortford, Herts CM23 5RG **(T)** 01279 306 456
Capacity: 4,000 **Seats:** 298 **Covered:** 700 **Clubhouse:** Yes **Shop:** Yes

Directions
Woodside Park is situated 1/4 mile from Junction 8 of M11.
Follow A1250 towards Bishop's Stortford Town Centre, entrance to ground is signposted through Woodside Park Industrial Estate.

Previous Grounds:

Record Attendance: 6,000 v Peterborough Town - FA Cup 2nd Round 1972-73 and v Middlesbrough - FA Cup 3rd Round replay 1982-83
Record Victory: 11-0 v Nettleswell & Buntwill - Herts Junior Cup 1911
Record Defeat: 0-13 v Cheshunt (H) - Herts Senior Cup 1926
Record Goalscorer: Post 1929 Jimmy Badcock - 123
Record Appearances: Phil Hopkins - 543
Additional Records:

Senior Honours: Athenian League 1969-70. FA Amateur Cup 1973-74. Isthmian League Division 1 1980-81. FA Trophy 1980-81. London Senior Cup 1973-74. Premier Inter League Cup 1989-90. Herts Senior Cup x9.

10 YEAR RECORD

01-02	02-03	03-04	04-05	05-06	06-07	07-08	08-09	09-10	10-11
Isth1 2	Isth P 13	Isth P 11	Conf S 10	Conf S 15	Conf S 5	Conf S 10	Conf S 9	Conf S 18	Conf S 16

BISHOP STORTFORD

No.	Date	Comp	H/A	Opponents	Att:	Result	Goalscorers	Pos
1	Sat-14-Aug	BSS	A	Eastleigh	428	W 2-1	Jackman 58, Prestedge 62	4
2	Tue-17-Aug	BSS	H	Staines Town	381	W 2-1	Prestedge 4, Ming 53	4
3	Sat-21-Aug	BSS	H	Ebbsfleet United	525	L 0-3		5
4	Tue-24-Aug	BSS	A	Dartford	882	L 0-3		10
5	Sat-28-Aug	BSS	A	Thurrock	248	W 3-1	Ming 42, Prestedge 2 (50, pen 88)	5
6	Mon-30-Aug	BSS	H	Bromley	464	L 0-1		7
7	Sat-04-Sep	BSS	H	Farnborough	465	L 1-4	Prestedge pen 90	12
8	Sat-11-Sep	BSS	A	Boreham Wood	202	W 2-1	Ming 38, Jackman 40	10
9	Sat-18-Sep	BSS	H	Hampton & Richmond Borough	349	L 0-2		11
10	Sat-02-Oct	BSS	A	St Albans City	354	W 4-1	Shulton 30, D Morgan 75, Jackman 82, Vernazza 87	8
11	Sat-16-Oct	BSS	H	Havant & Waterlooville	571	L 1-5	Duncan 7	13
12	Sat-23-Oct	BSS	A	Welling United	515	L 1-3	Arthur 24	13
13	Sat-30-Oct	BSS	H	Dover Athletic	490	L 1-4	Bakare 74	15
14	Sat-06-Nov	BSS	A	Dorchester Town	563	D 0-0		14
15	Tue-09-Nov	BSS	H	Lewes	264	W 1-0	Jackman 70	10
16	Sat-13-Nov	BSS	A	Basingstoke Town	358	W 1-0	Antoine 72	8
17	Sat-27-Nov	BSS	H	Maidenhead United	259	D 0-0		8
18	Sat-11-Dec	BSS	H	Thurrock	251	W 1-0	Prestedge 48	8
19	Sat-01-Jan	BSS	H	Braintree Town	621	L 1-2	O'Cearuill 28	10
20	Mon-03-Jan	BSS	A	Bromley	645	L 3-4	McNaughton 9, Ming 68, Bowditch 90	11
21	Sat-08-Jan	BSS	H	Boreham Wood	311	W 2-0	Norville 14, Hahn 62	10
22	Tue-11-Jan	BSS	H	Weston-Super-Mare	217	D 1-1	Ming 14	10
23	Sat-15-Jan	BSS	A	Staines Town	251	L 0-3		10
24	Wed-19-Jan	BSS	A	Farnborough	438	L 2-3	Norville 47, Ming pen 59	10
25	Sat-22-Jan	BSS	A	Chelmsford City	883	L 1-4	McNaughton 90	10
26	Tue-25-Jan	BSS	A	Braintree Town	507	L 1-3	Gaisie 5	10
27	Sat-29-Jan	BSS	H	Dartford	627	L 0-1		11
28	Sat-05-Feb	BSS	A	Maidenhead United	232	D 2-2	Prestedge 39, Ming pen 78	14
29	Sat-12-Feb	BSS	H	Woking	422	L 0-4		14
30	Sat-19-Feb	BSS	A	Weston-Super-Mare	191	L 1-3	Dean 45	14
31	Sat-05-Mar	BSS	H	Welling United	401	L 0-4		15
32	Sat-12-Mar	BSS	H	Eastleigh	305	L 0-1		18
33	Sat-19-Mar	BSS	A	Havant & Waterlooville	752	L 1-4	Habu 53	18
34	Tue-22-Mar	BSS	H	Chelmsford City	648	D 2-2	Ming 84, Adesayoi 90	18
35	Sat-26-Mar	BSS	A	Ebbsfleet United	824	D 0-0		18
36	Sat-02-Apr	BSS	A	Dover Athletic	784	L 0-2		19
37	Tue-05-Apr	BSS	A	Hampton & Richmond Borough	261	W 3-0	Bakare 2 (8, 44), Gaisie 88	17
38	Sat-09-Apr	BSS	H	Basingstoke Town	338	L 0-2		18
39	Sat-16-Apr	BSS	A	Woking	1281	L 0-2		19
40	Sat-23-Apr	BSS	H	St Albans City	401	W 4-0	Gaisie 7, Palmer 33, Rance 36, D Morgan 81	19
41	Mon-25-Apr	BSS	A	Lewes	835	W 2-1	Bakare 43, Rance 85	18
42	Sat-30-Apr	BSS	H	Dorchester Town	372	W 2-1	Bakare 2, Rance 75	16

CUPS

No.	Date	Comp	H/A	Opponents	Att:	Result	Goalscorers	Pos
1	Sat-25-Sep	FAC 2Q	H	Bromley	357	D 2-2	Palmer 24, Jackman 42	
2	Tue-28-Sep	FAC 2QR	A	Bromley	347	L 1-2	Prestedge 30	
3	Sat-20-Nov	FAT 3Q	H	Ashford Town (Middx)	226	L 1-2	Arthur 53	

League
Starts
Substitute
Unused Sub

Cups
Starts
Substitute
Unused Sub

Goals (Lg)
Goals (Cup)

N MORGAN	M JONES	PALMER	LETTEJALLOW	DUNCAN	ANGUS	MING	PRESTEDGE	JACKMAN	JUDGE	SHULTON	ANTOINE	ABDULLAHI	ARABA	R JONES	MASON	DALY	EYRE	LLEWELLYN	D MORGAN	O'CEARUILL	VERNAZZA	ARTHUR	DAWSON	GREENWOOD	BOWDITCH	EBERENDU	BAKARE	KITTERIDGE	ESSAM	HAHN	GAISIE	MCNAUGHTON	MATATA	NORVILLE	WHITE	HABU	FRANCIS	QUERRY	ADESAYOI	DEAN	GARROD	ANDERSON	MORRIS	RANCE
X	X	X	X	X	X	X	X	X	X	X	S	S	S	U	U																													
X	X	X	X	X	X	X	X	X			S	X	X	U	S																													
X	X	X	X	X	X		X	X	U	X	X	X	S	S	S	U																												
X	X	X	X	X	X	X	X	X	X	X		U		U	S	S																												
X	X	X	S	X	X	X	X	X	X	X		U	S	U	X	U																												
X	X	X	U	X	X	X	X	X	S	X		U	X	U	X	S																												
		X	S	X	X	X	X	X	S	X		U	X		X	S	X																											
	X	X		X	X	X	X	X		X		X	S	U	U	U	X	X	S																									
	X	X		X	X	X	X		X	X	S	X		U	S		X	X	S	U																								
	X	X		X	X	X	X	X		X				U	U			S	S		X	X		X	S																			
	X	X		X		X	X	X				X		U				S	S	X	X	X		X	S	U																		
	X	X		X	U	X	X	X						S				S	S	X	X	X		X	X		U																	
	X	X		X			X	X			S			S					X		X	X		U	X		S	X	X															
	X	X		X			X				X			X					X	U	X	S			X	S	U	X	X	S														
	X	X		X			X	X			X			X					S	U	X				X	U	S	X	X	S														
	X			X			X	X			X			X					X	S		X			X	S	U	X	X	S														
	X				U	X	X				X			X	S				X	X	S				X	X	U	X	X	U														
	X			X		X	X								S				X	X	X				X	X	S	X		S	X													
				U		X	X	X						X	U				X	X	S				X		X	X		S	X	X	S											
	X			S		X	X	X											U	X	S				X	X	X	X		U	X	X	S											
	X			U		S	X								S										X	X	X	X	X	X	S	X	U	X	X									
	X			U		X	X	X							S				S							X	X	X	X	X	U	X	S		X									
	X			X		X	X	X						S	S					U					X	S	X	X			U	X		X	X									
				U		X	X							X	X					U					X		X	X	X	S	X	X	U	X	S									
				U		X	X	S						X	X					X					X	X		X	X	X	U	S		X	S									
				U		S	X							X	U					X					X	X		X	X	X	X	X	U	X	S									
				U		X	X	S						X	S					X		X			X	U	X	X		X	X	X		S										
				X		X	X							X	S										X	X	X	X		X	X		S			X	S	U	U					
		S		X		X	X							X	U										X		X	X		X	S		S			X	U			X	X			
		X		X		X	X							U	S					X					X		X	X		S	S		X				U			X	X			
		X	X			X	X							S	U					X					X		X	X		X	S					X	S	U			X			
		X	X			X	X								S					X			U		X		X	X		U	S					X					S	X	X	
		X	X			X	X								S					X			U				X	X		X	S					X	U		S			X	X	
		X	X			X	X																U		X		X	X		X	S					X	U	S	S			X	X	
		X	X			X	X								S								U		X			X		X	S					X		X	U			X	X	
		X	X			X	X								S								U		X			X		X	S					S		U		X		X	X	X
		X	X			X	U																U		U		X	X		S	X					X				X		X	X	X
		X	X			X	U												S	X			U		S		X	X		S										X		X	X	X
		S	X			X	S								U		X						U		X		X			X	X					X				X		X	S	X
		X	X			X	X										X		S						X		S	U		U	X					X	S			X		X		X
		X	X			X	X										X		U						X		X	U		U						X	U	U		X		X		X
		X	X			X	X								U		X								X		X	U								X	U	S		X		X	U	X
	X	X		U	X	X	X	X				X		U	U		X	S	S	X	X	X	U																					
	X	X		X	X	X	X		U		S	X		U	S			X	U		X	X	U	X																				
	X				U		X				S							X	X	X	S	X			X	X	U	X	X	X														
6	21	27	16	21	10	35	39	18	4	9	5	5	3	11	5	0	7	2	6	14	7	6	0	3	27	8	19	26	10	13	10	8	1	5	3	12	0	1	0	9	3	11	7	7
0	0	2	2	1	0	2	1	2	2	0	4	1	4	5	16	3	0	3	9	1	3	1	0	0	3	3	4	0	0	9	9	1	5	1	3	1	3	2	2	0	1	0	1	0
0	0	0	1	7	2	0	2	0	1	0	0	4	0	10	9	3	0	0	2	5	0	0	8	1	1	3	4	3	0	5	3	0	3	0	0	0	6	4	2	0	0	0	1	0
0	3	2	0	1	2	2	3	1	0	0	0	2	0	0	0	0	1	2	1	2	2	3	0	1	1	1	0	1	1	1	0	0	0	0	0	0	0	0	0	0	0	0	0	0
0	0	0	0	0	0	0	0	0	0	0	2	0	0	0	1	0	0	1	1	0	1	0	0	0	0	0	0	0	0	0	0	0	0	0	0	0	0	0	0	0	0	0	0	0
0	0	0	0	1	1	0	0	0	1	0	0	0	0	2	1	0	0	0	1	0	0	0	2	0	0	0	1	0	0	0	0	0	0	0	0	0	0	0	0	0	0	0	0	0
0	0	1	0	1	0	8	7	4	0	1	1	0	0	0	0	0	0	0	2	1	1	1	0	0	1	0	5	0	0	1	3	2	0	2	0	1	0	0	1	1	0	0	0	3
0	0	1	0	0	0	0	1	1	0	0	0	0	0	0	0	0	0	0	0	0	0	1	0	0	0	0	0	0	0	0	0	0	0	0	0	0	0	0	0	0	0	0	0	0

PLAYING SQUAD 2011/12

Existing Players		SN	HT	WT	DOB	AGE	POB	Career	Apps	Goals
GOALKEEPERS										
George	Dawson							Bishops Stortford	0	0
Nick	Eyre		5'10"	10 10	07/09/1985	25	Braintree	Tottenham Rel c/s 05, Grays (L) 10/04, Grays 7/05 Rel 7/06, Rushden & D 8/06 Rel 12/06, Histon (Trial), Dag & Red 2/07, St Albans 7/07, Grays (L) 3/08, Bishops Stortford 7/08 Rel 3/10, Chelmsford 3/10 Rel 8/10, Bishops Stortford 9/10, AFC Sudbury (Dual) 10/10, Chelmsford 5/11 Rel 7/11, Bishops Stortford 7/11	7	0
Arnold	Gudalevic							FRK Atletas (Lit), Bishops Stortford 8/11		
Joe	Wright							Bishops Stortford		
DEFENDERS										
Phil	Anderson				01/03/1987	24		Southend, Aldershot 7/06 Rel 5/07, Thurrock c/s 07, Billericay 1/11, Bishops Stortford 3/11	11	0
Blue	Braithwaite							Bishops Stortford		
Connor	Essam				09/07/1992	19		Gillingham, Bishops Stortford (L) 10/10, Bishops Stortford (L) 1/11, Dover (SL) 3/11, Bishops Stortford (L) 8/11	10	0
Mohammed	Habu				26/05/1990	21		Redbridge, Leyton 3/10, Bishops Stortford 2/11	13	1
Jack	Jeffries							West Ham (Yth), Dag & Red (Scholar), Bishops Stortford 8/11		
Ritchie	Jones				06/03/1990	21		Northampton Rel 11/08, Cheshunt 12/08, Gillingham (Trial) 3/09, Dag & Red (Trial), Bishops Stortford 3/09	16	0
MIDFIELDERS										
Ali	Abdullahi				19/05/1991	20		Dulwich H, Bishops Stortford 11/09	6	0
Michael	Bakare				01/12/1986	24		Waltham Forest, Haringey, Hertford 10/06, Edgware, Welwyn Garden, Leyton 11/08, Maidenhead (Trial) 2/09, Welling 9/09, Thurrock 8/10, Bishops Stortford 10/10	23	5
Ade	Cole							Waltham Forest 8/08, Redbridge, Ware 3/10, Waltham Forest, Harrow 2/11, Bishops Stortford 8/11		
Ben	Davison							Bishops Stortford		
Danny	Francis							Arsenal (Yth), L.Orient (Yth), Enfield T, Aveley, Waltham Forest, Canvey Island 7/07, Harlow, Cheshunt 10/08, Potters Bar 11/08, Dulwich Hamlet 1/09, Walton & H, Leyton 11/09, Bishops Stortford 1/11	3	0
Mitch	Hahn				09/07/1986	25		Bolton (Yth), Southend (Yth), Wealdstone 3/04, Redbridge, Enfield T 6/08, Aveley 12/08, Brentwood (L) 1/09, Bishops Stortford 12/09, Waltham Abbey (L) 9/10, Waltham Forest (L) 10/10	22	1
Baimass	Lettejallow		5'09"	10 12	16/04/1984	26	London	Barnet, Braintree 10/03, Harlow 1/04, Dag & Red 1/05, Aveley (L) 2/07, Thurrock (SL) 9/07, Thurrock (3ML) 8/08, Bishops Stortford (SL) 1/09, Bishops Stortford c/s 09, Thurrock 9/10, Hampton & R 11/10, Bishops Stortford 3/11	18	0
Reece	Prestedge				25/12/1985	25		Bishops Stortford, Dag & Red, Brimsdown, Cheshunt 6/08, Bishops Stortford 2/09, Thurrock 10/09, AFC Hornchurch 10/09, Billericay 12/09, Bishops Stortford 3/10	40	7
Dean	Rance				14/05/1991	20	Maidstone	Gillingham, Maidstone (L) 3/10, Maidstone (L) 1/11, Bishops Stortford (SL) 3/11, Bishops Stortford (L) 8/11	7	3
Scott	Shulton				31/01/1990	21		Watford (Yth), Wycombe Rel 5/09, Hendon (WE) 11/07, Basingstoke (L) 9/08, Hendon (L) 12/08, Ebbsfleet 8/09, Bishops Stortford (L) 10/09 Perm 11/09, Southampton (Trial) 7/10, Braintree 10/10, Bishops Stortford 8/11	9	1
Les	Thompson		5'10"	11 06	03/10/1988	22	Newham	Bolton Rel c/s 08, Stockport (L) 10/07, Torquay (L) 1/08 (07/08 1,0), Gillingham (Trial) 7/08, Yeovil (Trial) 8/08, Thurrock 9/09 Rel 2/10, Croydon Ath 2/10, Concord R 9/10, Aveley 12/10, Bishops Stortford 8/11		
FORWARDS										
Craig	Calver		5'10"	12 00	20/01/1991	20	Cambridge	Cambridge C (Yth), Ipswich (Scholar) Rel 3/08, Southend Rel c/s 10, Harlow (L) 12/08, St Albans (L) 8/09, Braintree (L) 2/10, AFC Sudbury (L) 3/10, Yeovil 7/10, Braintree (L) 3/11, Histon (Trial) 6/11, Bishops Stortford 8/11		
Junior	Dadson				03/11/1988	22		Blackburn, Halifax 9/07 Rel 10/07, Potters Bar 10/07, Aveley 10/08, Boreham Wood 8/10, Billericay 10/10, Aveley 1/11, Bishops Stortford 7/11		
Dwight	Gayle							Arsenal (Yth), Stansted, Dag & Red 8/11, Bishops Stortford (SL) 8/11		
Alex	Read				17/05/1988	23		MK Dons, Leyton, Eaton Manor, Thurrock c/s 07, Enfield T 3/09, Redbridge, Romford 10/10, Bishops Stortford 8/11		

BLYTH SPARTANS

Chairman: Tony Platten
Secretary: Ian Evans (T) 0790 598 4308 (E) generalmanager@blythspartans.
Additional Committee Members:
Kevin Scott, Colin Baxter, Ian Evans, Andrew Dodds,
A Bowron, S Ord, S Frake, Ms J Freeman.
Manager: Steve Cuggy
Programme Editor: Glen Maxwell (E) glen_maxwell@live.co.uk

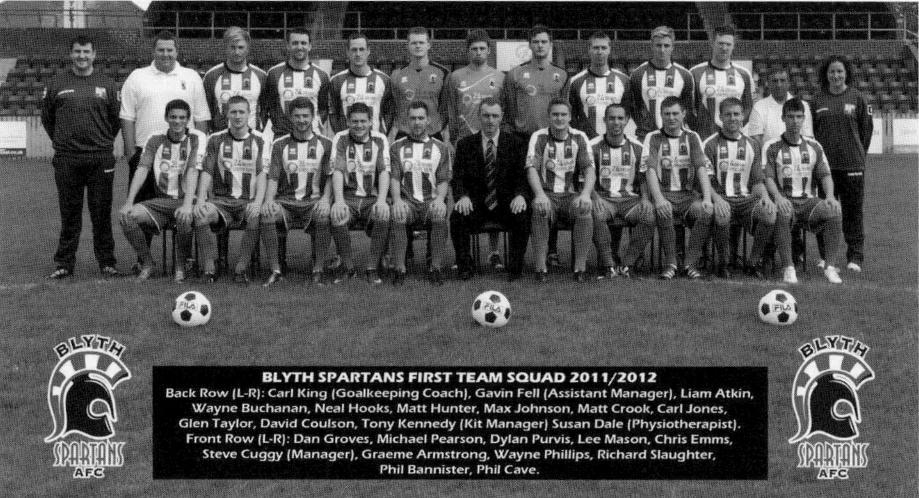

BLYTH SPARTANS FIRST TEAM SQUAD 2011/2012
Back Row (L-R): Carl King (Goalkeeping Coach), Gavin Fell (Assistant Manager), Liam Atkin, Wayne Buchanan, Neal Hooks, Matt Hunter, Max Johnson, Matt Crook, Carl Jones, Glen Taylor, David Coulson, Tony Kennedy (Kit Manager) Susan Dale (Physiotherapist).
Front Row (L-R): Dan Groves, Michael Pearson, Dylan Purvis, Lee Mason, Chris Emms, Steve Cuggy (Manager), Graeme Armstrong, Wayne Phillips, Richard Slaughter, Phil Bannister, Phil Cave.

Club Factfile

Founded: 1899 **Nickname:** Spartans
Previous Names: Not known.
Previous Leagues: Northumberland 1901-07, Northern All. 1907-13, 46-47, North Eastern 1913-39, Northern Com. 1945-46, Midland 1958-60, Northern Counties 1960-62, Northern 1962-94, Northern Premier 1994-2006

Club Colours (change): Green & white stripes/green/green (White & red/white/red)

Ground: Croft Park, Blyth, Northumberland NE24 3JE (T) 01670 352 373
Capacity: 4,435 **Seats:** 563 **Covered:** 1,000 **Clubhouse:** Yes **Shop:** Yes

Directions
From the Tyne Tunnel, take the A19 signposted MORPETH. At second roundabout take the A189 signposted ASHINGTON. From A189 take A1061 signposted BLYTH. At 1st roundabout follow signs A1061 to BLYTH. Go straight across next two roundabouts following TOWN CENTRE/SOUTH BEECH. At next roundabout turn left onto A193 go straight across next roundabout, and at the next turn right into Plessey Rd and the ground is situated on your left. Team coach should the turn left into William St (3rd left) and reverse up Bishopton St to the designated parking spot.

Previous Grounds: Not known.

Record Attendance: 10,186 v Hartlepool United - FA Cup 08/12/1956
Record Victory: 18-0 v Gateshead Town - Northern Alliance 28/12/1907
Record Defeat: 0-10 v Darlington - North Eastern League 12/12/1914
Record Goalscorer: Not known.
Record Appearances: Eddie Alder - 605 (1965-68)
Additional Records: Received £30,000 from Hull City for Les Mutrie

Senior Honours: North Eastern League 1935-36. Northern League 1972-73, 74-75, 75-76, 79-80, 80-81, 81-82, 82-83, 83-84, 86-87, 87-88. Northern League Division 1 1994-95. Northern Premier League Premier Division 2005-06.

10 YEAR RECORD

01-02	02-03	03-04	04-05	05-06	06-07	07-08	08-09	09-10	10-11
NP P 12	NP P 19	NP P 21	NP P 12	NP P 1	Conf N 7	Conf N 18	Conf N 15	Conf N 13	Conf N 9

BLYTH SPARTANS

No.	Date	Comp	H/A	Opponents	Att:	Result	Goalscorers	Pos
1	Sat-14-Aug	BSN	A	Solihull Moors	242	L 0-2		20
2	Tue-17-Aug	BSN	H	Stalybridge Celtic	443	L 1-2	Dale 7	19
3	Sat-21-Aug	BSN	H	Corby Town	406	D 1-1	Turnbull 88	18
4	Tue-24-Aug	BSN	A	Guiseley	342	D 0-0		19
5	Sat-28-Aug	BSN	H	Alfreton Town	462	L 1-4	Og (Flint) 29	20
6	Mon-30-Aug	BSN	A	Droylsden	418	W 3-0	Turnbull 2 (61, 90), Brayson 90	16
7	Sat-04-Sep	BSN	A	AFC Telford	2005	D 1-1	Brayson 32	16
8	Sat-11-Sep	BSN	H	Worcester City	397	W 3-0	Brayson 32, Tait 42, Deverdics 70	13
9	Sat-18-Sep	BSN	H	Vauxhall Motors	437	D 2-2	Brayson 2 (pen 45, 81)	12
10	Sat-02-Oct	BSN	A	Redditch United	254	L 1-2	Brayson pen 42	13
11	Sat-09-Oct	BSN	H	Gainsborough Trinity	427	L 1-3	Brayson 74	13
12	Sat-16-Oct	BSN	A	Eastwood Town	483	W 2-0	Brayson 2 (pen 26, 83)	12
13	Sat-23-Oct	BSN	H	Hyde FC	362	W 3-0	Og (Whalley) 49, Swailes 66, Brayson 82	10
14	Sat-30-Oct	BSN	A	Corby Town	641	W 4-3	Cave 30, Alexander 41, Hooks 45, Brayson 71	8
15	Sat-06-Nov	BSN	H	Boston United	558	D 0-0		9
16	Tue-09-Nov	BSN	H	Harrogate Town	370	W 1-0	Brayson pen 51	6
17	Sat-13-Nov	BSN	A	Gloucester City	305	W 2-1	Swailes 5, Turnbull 24	6
18	Sat-01-Jan	BSN	A	Workington	385	D 1-1	Tait 3	7
19	Mon-03-Jan	BSN	H	Droylsden	517	L 2-4	Brayson 25, Tait 58	8
20	Sat-08-Jan	BSN	A	Nuneaton Town	833	L 2-3	Tait 28, Brayson 47	8
21	Tue-18-Jan	BSN	H	AFC Telford	424	W 3-0	Brayson 2 (26, 39), Tait 65	8
22	Sat-22-Jan	BSN	A	Hyde FC	303	W 2-0	Deverdics 31, Hooks 66	7
23	Tue-25-Jan	BSN	A	Gainsborough Trinity	264	W 2-0	Brayson 24, Hooks 61	7
24	Sat-29-Jan	BSN	H	Stafford Rangers	501	W 3-2	Hooks 17, Tait 27, Dale 63	7
25	Sat-12-Feb	BSN	H	Eastwood Town	502	D 0-0		7
26	Tue-15-Feb	BSN	A	Alfreton Town	499	L 1-2	Brayson pen 58	7
27	Sat-19-Feb	BSN	H	Hinckley United	463	W 4-0	Alexander 46, Groves 65, Dale 69, Tait 72	7
28	Tue-22-Feb	BSN	H	Redditch United	528	W 2-0	Brayson 2 (2, 36)	6
29	Sat-05-Mar	BSN	H	Solihull Moors	420	L 0-1		7
30	Tue-08-Mar	BSN	A	Harrogate Town	225	D 2-2	Turnbull 16, White 56	7
31	Sat-12-Mar	BSN	A	Stafford Rangers	334	L 1-2	Turnbull 32	7
32	Sat-19-Mar	BSN	H	Nuneaton Town	496	W 1-0	Og (Dean) 46	7
33	Tue-22-Mar	BSN	H	Workington	408	W 2-1	Hooks 3, Deverdics 18	6
34	Sat-26-Mar	BSN	A	Vauxhall Motors	159	W 6-2	Alexander 45, Turnbull 48, Brayson 3 (57, 58, 75), White 77	6
35	Sat-02-Apr	BSN	A	Hinckley United	424	L 1-5	White 36	7
36	Tue-05-Apr	BSN	A	Stalybridge Celtic	366	D 0-0		8
37	Sat-09-Apr	BSN	H	Gloucester City	414	L 0-2		8
38	Sat-23-Apr	BSN	A	Boston United	1316	L 0-5		9
39	Mon-25-Apr	BSN	H	Guiseley	459	D 0-0		9
40	Sat-30-Apr	BSN	A	Worcester City	509	L 0-1		9

CUPS

No.	Date	Comp	H/A	Opponents	Att:	Result	Goalscorers
1	Sat-25-Sep	FAC 2Q	A	Vauxhall Motors	216	L 1-5	Turnbull 50
2	Sat-20-Nov	FAT 3Q	H	Stafford Rangers	391	W 1-0	Hooks 85
3	Tue-14-Dec	FAT 1	H	Fleetwood Town	354	W 2-0	Turnbull 10, Alexander 74
4	Sat-15-Jan	FAT 2	H	Altrincham	620	W 2-1	Brayson 2 (43, 78)
5	Sat-05-Feb	FAT 3	H	Droylsden	708	D 2-2	Brayson pen 52, Dale 77
6	Mon-07-Feb	FAT 3R	A	Droylsden	229	W 4-0	Tait 2 (7, 80), Groves 77, O'Mahoney 85
7	Sat-26-Feb	FAT 4	H	Gateshead	2719	L 0-2	

League
Starts
Substitute
Unused Sub

Cups
Starts
Substitute
Unused Sub

Goals (Lg)
Goals (Cup)

GRIEVESON	HARRISON	CAVE	TAIT	SWAILES	BUCHANAN	HOOKS	C SMITH	ALEXANDER	BRAYSON	DALE	GRAHAM	DEVERDICS	O'MAHONEY	CUNNINGHAM	MORRIS	TURNBULL	GROVES	GILLESPIE	RIDLEY	WILKINSON	LOWSON	WRIGHT	GRAY	WHITE	B SMITH
X	X	X	X	X	X	X	X	X	X	X	S	S	S	U	U										
X	X	X	X	X	X	X	X	S	X	X	U	S		U	U	X									
	X	X	X	X	X		X	S	X	X	U	X	S	X	U	X	S								
	X	X	X	X	X		X	U	X	X	X	U	U	X	U	X	U								
	X	X	X	X	X		X	S	X	X	X	S	S	X	U	X	U								
	X	X	X	X	X	X	U	U	X	X	X	S	U	X	U	X									
	X	X	X	X	X	X	U	U	X	X	U	X		X	U	X	U								
	X	X	X	X	X	X	S	U	X	X	S	X		X	S	X	U								
	X	X	X	X	X	X	U	U	X	X	S	X		X	U	X	U								
X	X			X	X	X	X	U	X	X	S	X	U		X	X	U								
		X	U	X	X	X		X	X	S	U	X	X	X	X	X	U								
		X	X	X	X	X		X	X	S		U	X	U		X	X	X	U						
		X	X	X	X	X		X	X	X		U	U	U	U	X	X	X	U						
		X		X	X	X		X	X	X		X	S	U	U	X	X	X	U						
		X	U	X	X	X		X	X	U		X	X	U	S	X	X	X	U						
		X	U	X	X	X		X	X	U		X	X	U	U	X	X	X	U						
		X	U	X	X	X		X	X	S		X	X	U	U	X	X	X	U						
		X	X	X	X	X		X	S	X		X	U	U	U	X	X	X	U						
			X	X	X	U		X	X	X		X	U	U	X	X	X	X	U	U					
		X	X	X	X	X		U	X	X		X	U	U	U	X	X	X							
		X	X	X	X	X		U	X	X		X	U	U		X	X		U		X				
		X	X	X	X	X		U	X	X		X	U	U		X	X		U		X				
		X	X	X	X	X			X	X		X	U	U		X	X		U		X				
		X	X	X	X	X			X	X		X	U	U		X	X		U		X	U			
		X	X	X	X	X		U	X	S		X	X	U		X	X				X		S	S	
		X	X	X	U	X		U	X	U		X	X	U		X	X				X		S	X	
		X	X	X	X	X		X		X		X	S	U		X	X		U		X		S	U	
		X		X		X		X	X	S		X	X	U		S	X		U		X	U	X	X	
		X	X	X	U	X		U	X	X		X	U	U		X	X				X		S	X	
		X		X	U	X		U	X	X		X		U		X	X		U		X		X	X	
		X		X	U	X		S	X	X		X	U	U		X	X		U		X		X	X	
		X	X	X	U	X		U	X	X		X	U	U		X	X		U		X			X	
		X	X	X	U	X		S	X	X		X	S	U		X	X				X			X	
		X	X	X	X	X		S	X	X		X	S	U		X	U		U		X			X	
		U	X	X	X	X		S	X	X		X	S	X		X	X				U			X	
		X	X	U	X			U	X	X		X	X	U		X	X		U		X			X	
		X	X	S	X			X	X	X		X		U		X	X		U		X			X	
		X	X	U	X	X		S	X	X		X		U		X	X				X			X	
		X	X	X	X	X		U	X	U		X	X	U		X	U		U		X			X	
		U	X	X	X	X		S	X	X			X	U		X	X				X			X	
U	X	X	X	X	X	X	S	S	X	X	S	X	U	X	U	X	U								
		X	X	X	X	X		X		X		X	X	U	S		X	X	U	S					
		X	X	X	X	X		X		X		X	U	U	U	X	X	X	U	U					
		X	X	X	X	X		U	X	X		X	U	U	U	X	X	X	U						
		X	X	X	X	X		U	X	X		X	S	U		X	X		U		X	U			
		X	X	X	X	X		U	X			X	X	U		X	X		U		X	U			
		X		X	X	X		X	X	X		X	S	U		X	X			U	X	U			U
3	10	36	31	37	33	34	6	13	38	31	3	32	11	9	3	38	27	9	0	0	19	0	3	14	0
0	0	0	0	1	0	0	1	9	1	5	4	4	8	0	2	1	1	0	0	0	0	0	4	1	0
0	0	2	4	2	6	1	3	16	0	4	4	3	14	30	14	0	9	0	21	1	1	2	0	1	0
0	1	7	6	7	7	7	0	3	5	6	0	7	2	1	0	6	6	3	0	0	3	0	0	0	0
0	0	0	0	0	0	0	1	1	0	0	1	0	2	0	1	0	0	0	0	1	0	0	0	0	0
1	0	0	0	0	0	0	0	3	0	0	0	0	3	6	3	0	1	0	5	2	0	3	0	0	1
0	0	1	7	2	0	5	0	3	23	3	0	3	0	0	0	7	1	0	0	0	0	0	0	3	0
0	0	0	2	0	0	1	0	1	3	1	0	0	1	0	0	2	1	0	0	0	0	0	0	0	0

PLAYING SQUAD 2011/12

Existing Players		SN	HT	WT	DOB	AGE	POB	Career	Apps	Goals
GOALKEEPERS										
Kyle	Barlow							Chester-le-Street (Jun), Seaham, Chester-le-Street c/s 10, Blyth (Dual) 8/11		
Matthew	Crook							Bedlington, Whitley Bay 12/09, Blyth 7/11		
Matty	Hunter				30/06/1993	18		Monkseaton College, Blyth 6/11		
Max	Johnson				21/05/1991	20		Burnley (Yth), Bury (Scholar), Newcastle (Scholar) 10/07 Rel c/s 10, Inverness Caledonian 7/10, Colorado Rapids (USA) (Trial), Blyth 8/11		
Tom	Kindley		6'03"		08/04/1991	20		Whitley Bay, Blyth 6/11		
DEFENDERS										
Liam	Atkin		6'02"	12 00	12/12/1986	24	Ashington	Newcastle, Carlisle 1/07 Rel c/s 07, Queen of the South 7/07, Newcastle Blue Star 9/07, Blyth 10/07, Gateshead 11/07 Rel 12/07, Ashington 12/07, Newcastle Blue Star 3/08, Airdrie (Trial) 7/08, Cheltenham (Trial) 8/08, West Allotment, Ashington 5/09, Blyth 6/11		
Wayne	Buchanan		6'02"	13 03	12/01/1982	29	Bambridge	Bolton Rel 1/03, Chesterfield (L) 3/02, Lisburn Distillery 1/03, Gold Coast United (Aus) (Trial) c/s 09, Gateshead 2/10 (09/10 2,0) Rel 5/10, Blyth 8/10	33	0
Phil	Cave				12/05/1987	24	Newcastle	Newcastle (Scholar), Gateshead 8/07, Livingston 7/08, Gateshead (SL) 2/09, Gateshead 8/09 Rel 5/10, Blyth 7/10	36	1
David	Coulson		6'01"	12 10	21/03/1984	27	Durham	Sunderland (Yth), Barnsley Rel c/s 02, Lincoln C c/s 02 Rel 1/04, Ilkeston (L) 10/03, Gateshead 1/04, Happy Valley (HK), Spennymoor 8/04, Whitley Bay 4/05, Blyth 6/11		
Carl	Jones		6'01"	12 02	03/09/1986	24	Sunderland	Chester-le-Street, Hartlepool 9/04 Rel c/s 07, York C 8/07 Rel 1/08, Gateshead (L) 11/07, Gateshead (L) 1/08 Perm 1/08 Rel 5/11, Blyth 6/11		
Michael	Pearson		5'11"		11/11/1992	18	Sunderland	Hartlepool (Scholar) Rel c/s 11, Blyth 7/11		
Dylan	Purvis				18/12/1991	19	Sunderland	Hartlepool Rel c/s 11, Blyth 7/11		
Richie	Slaughter				04/08/1990	21		West Allotment Celtic, Tow Law 10/09, Blyth 3/10, Conneticut State University (USA), Consett 1/11, Blyth 7/11		
Darren	Timmons		6'01"	11 02	03/02/1980	31	North Shields	Hartlepool Rel c/s 99, Tow Law, North Shields, Ashington, Whitley Bay 6/06 Rel c/s 07, Travelling, Whitley Bay 5/08, Blyth (Dual) 6/11		
MIDFIELDERS										
Chris	Emms				23/07/1984	27		Middlesbrough (Scholar), Peterlee, Gateshead 11/04, Peterlee 12/04, Billingham T 6/05, Durham, Newcastle Blue Star, ECU Joondaloop (Aust) 4/09, Harrogate T 7/09, Spennymoor, Blyth 6/11		
Adam	Forster				08/01/1993	18		Monkseaton Academy, Blyth 6/11		
Daniel	Groves				10/12/1990	20		Blyth	28	1
Neal	Hooks				03/07/1987	24	Hexham	Ross C, Elgin (SL) 1/07, Newcastle Blue Star 7/07, Ilkeston 9/08, Sunshine George Cross (Aust) 2/09, Ilkeston 9/09, Blyth 2/10	34	5
Wayne	Phillips				29/08/1985	26	South Shields	Newcastle (Yth), Sunderland (Yth), Peterlee Newtown, Blyth 3/03 Rel 1/05, Whitley Bay 1/05, Gateshead 7/07 Rel 5/10, Harrogate T 7/10, Blyth 6/11		
Shaun	Vipond		5'11"	11 04	25/12/1988	22	Hexham	Carlisle, Workington (3ML) 8/08 Perm 11/08, Hamilton (Trial) 1/09, Ostersund FK (Swe) 3/09 Rel 5/09, Workington 8/09, Blyth 6/11		
FORWARDS										
Graeme	Armstrong		6'00"	12 08	28/06/1983	28	Hexham	Haltwhistle U, Queen of the South 7/00, Annan Ath, Dunston Fed c/s 04, Gateshead £5,000 6/07 Rel 5/10, Harrogate T 5/10, Blyth 5/11		
Phil	Bannister				03/10/1988	22		Monkseaton College, Loyola Uni (USA), Colorado Rapids 1/11, Blyth 8/11		
Lee	Mason				04/02/1991	20	North Shields	Hartlepool (Scholar), Garforth (WE) 2/10, Unik FK (Swe), Whitley Bay 11/10, Blyth 7/11		
Glen	Taylor				11/05/1990	21		West Allotment Celtic, Ashington 5/09, North Shields 10/09, Ashington 1/10, Blyth 8/11		

BOSTON UNITED

Chairman: David Newton
Secretary: John Blackwell (T) 07860 663 299 (E) admin@bufc.co.uk
Additional Committee Members:
Neil Kempster, Chris Cook, John Blackwell, Craig Singleton.

Manager: Jason Lee and Lee Canoville
Programme Editor: Craig Singleton (E) craig.singleton@bufc.co.uk

Back (L to R): Ben Wilkinson, Kevin Holsgrove, Mikel Suarez, Tom Ward, Mickey Stones, Liam Parker, Kevin Austin.
Middle: Jason Hatfield (kit man), Adam Millson, Marc Newsham, Paul Bastock, Ryan Semple, Ricky Drury, Chris Hall, Harry Deane, Katie Cooper (sports therapist).
Front: Julian Joachim, Ben Milnes, Jason Lee (manager), Gareth Jelleyman (captain), Lee Canoville (manager), Liam Ogden, Jordan Fairclough.

Club Factfile

Founded: 1933 **Nickname:** The Pilgrims
Previous Names: Reformed as Boston United when Boston Town folded in 1933
Previous Leagues: Midland 1933-58, 62-64, Southern 1958-62, 98-2000, United Counties 1965-66, West Midlands 1966-68, Northern Premier 1968-79, 93-98, 2008-10, Alliance/Conference 1979-93, 2000-02, 07-08, Football League 2002-07

Club Colours (change): Amber and black/black/black (White & blue/blue/blue)

Ground: Jakemans Stadium, York Street, Boston PE21 6JN (T) 01205 364 406
Capacity: 6,645 **Seats:** 1,323 **Covered:** 6,645 **Clubhouse:** Yes **Shop:** Yes

Directions: A1 to A17 Sleaford to Boston-Over Boston Railway Station crossing, bear right at the Eagle Public House-To light over Haven Bridge-straight along John Adams Way(Dual Carriageway) -Turn right at traffic lights into main ridge, then right again into York Street (This is opposite Eagle Fisheries)-Ground is signposted after Railway crossing.

Previous Grounds:

Record Attendance: 10,086 v Corby Town - Floodlights inauguration 1955
Record Victory: 12-0 v Spilsby Town - Grace Swan Cup 1992-93
Record Defeat: Not known.
Record Goalscorer: Chris Cook - 181
Record Appearances: Billy Howells - 500+
Additional Records: Paid £30,000 to Scarborough for Paul Ellender, 08/2001
Received £50,000 from Bolton Wanderers for David Norris 2000

Senior Honours: Central Alliance League 1961-62. United Counties League 1965-66. West Midlands League 1966-67, 67-68. Northern Premier League 1972-73, 73-74, 76-77, 77-78, League Cup 1973-74, 75-76. Southern League 1999-2000. Conference 2001-02.

10 YEAR RECORD

01-02	02-03	03-04	04-05	05-06	06-07	07-08	08-09	09-10	10-11
Conf 1	FL 3 15	FL 3 11	FL 2 16	FL 2 11	FL 2 23	Conf N 10	NP P 16	NP P 3	Conf N 3

BOSTON UNITED

No.	Date	Comp	H/A	Opponents	Att:	Result	Goalscorers	Pos
1	Sat-14-Aug	BSN	H	Stafford Rangers	1604	W 1-0	Church 31	11
2	Mon-16-Aug	BSN	A	Hinckley United	615	W 1-0	Church 59	2
3	Sat-21-Aug	BSN	A	Redditch United	456	W 9-0	Davidson 2 (4, 85), Pearson 2 (16, 22), Church 2 (32, 49), Hunter 43, Weir-Daley 57, Semple 89	2
4	Tue-24-Aug	BSN	H	Nuneaton Town	1681	L 1-2	Hunter 85	4
5	Sat-28-Aug	BSN	A	Harrogate Town	447	W 6-3	Pearson 13, Og (Pell) 19, Yates 21, Church 25, Weir-Daley 33, Semple 45	4
6	Mon-30-Aug	BSN	H	Eastwood Town	1579	W 1-0	Pearson 28	4
7	Sat-04-Sep	BSN	A	Corby Town	907	D 0-0		4
8	Sat-11-Sep	BSN	H	Workington	1556	W 4-0	Davidson 41, Weir-Daley 2 (50, 53), Pearson 67	3
9	Sat-18-Sep	BSN	A	Alfreton Town	1309	W 1-0	Sleath 70	2
10	Sat-02-Oct	BSN	A	Vauxhall Motors	227	D 0-0		2
11	Sat-09-Oct	BSN	A	Hyde FC	479	W 3-0	Newsham 36, Weir-Daley 71, Sleath 90	2
12	Sat-16-Oct	BSN	H	Stalybridge Celtic	1602	W 1-0	Yates 39	1
13	Tue-02-Nov	BSN	A	Guiseley	432	D 0-0		2
14	Sat-06-Nov	BSN	A	Blyth Spartans	558	D 0-0		2
15	Tue-09-Nov	BSN	H	Corby Town	1279	W 1-0	Hunter 71	1
16	Sat-13-Nov	BSN	A	Droylsden	364	L 0-4		2
17	Sat-01-Jan	BSN	H	Gainsborough Trinity	1559	L 1-3	Weir-Daley 45	5
18	Mon-03-Jan	BSN	A	Eastwood Town	675	D 2-2	Weir-Daley 15, Suarez 89	5
19	Sat-08-Jan	BSN	A	Gloucester City	385	W 1-0	Weir-Daley 22	5
20	Tue-11-Jan	BSN	H	Hinckley United	955	W 3-0	Og (Burgess) 9, Suarez 31, Weir-Daley 61	5
21	Sat-22-Jan	BSN	H	Guiseley	1354	D 1-1	Sleath 69	5
22	Tue-25-Jan	BSN	H	Redditch United	994	W 1-0	Weir-Daley 16	4
23	Sat-05-Feb	BSN	A	Worcester City	637	L 0-2		5
24	Tue-08-Feb	BSN	A	Gainsborough Trinity	648	W 3-0	Boyes 2 (6, 70), Sleath 43	2
25	Sat-12-Feb	BSN	H	AFC Telford	1610	L 0-1		4
26	Tue-15-Feb	BSN	A	Stalybridge Celtic	331	L 1-3	Church 22	4
27	Sat-19-Feb	BSN	A	Workington	379	W 5-3	Boyes 2 (19, 32), Newsham 2 (79, 83), Semple 90	3
28	Tue-22-Feb	BSN	H	Solihull Moors	1042	D 1-1	Davidson 80	3
29	Sat-05-Mar	BSN	H	Droylsden	1139	W 2-0	Semple 27, Boyes 59	4
30	Tue-08-Mar	BSN	A	Stafford Rangers	260	W 4-0	Green 1, Church 28, Hunter 31, Pearson 41	4
31	Sat-12-Mar	BSN	H	Gloucester City	1377	W 1-0	Pearson 80	3
32	Tue-15-Mar	BSN	H	Alfreton Town	1503	W 3-2	Newsham 50, Sleath 68, Pearson 83	2
33	Sat-19-Mar	BSN	H	Harrogate Town	1369	D 2-2	Weir-Daley 2 (66, 90)	2
34	Sat-26-Mar	BSN	A	Solihull Moors	512	L 0-1		3
35	Sat-02-Apr	BSN	H	Worcester City	1352	W 1-0	Pearson 54	3
36	Sat-09-Apr	BSN	A	AFC Telford	2124	W 1-0	Pearson 31	3
37	Sat-16-Apr	BSN	H	Hyde FC	1536	D 2-2	Canoville 6, Church pen 28	3
38	Sat-23-Apr	BSN	H	Blyth Spartans	1316	W 5-0	Semple 32, Dudfield 37, Church 45, Clarke 86, Boyes 90	3
39	Mon-25-Apr	BSN	A	Nuneaton Town	1525	D 1-1	Canoville 61	3
40	Sat-30-Apr	BSN	H	Vauxhall Motors	1610	W 2-0	Stones 4, Church 40	3

CUPS

No.	Date	Comp	H/A	Opponents	Att:	Result	Goalscorers
1	Sat-25-Sep	FAC 2Q	H	Worcester City	1352	L 2-3	Newsham 54, Yates 75
2	Sat-20-Nov	FAT 3Q	H	Gainsborough Trinity	1136	W 2-1	Newsham pen 56, Og (Peat) 63
3	Sat-11-Dec	FAT 1	A	York City	1318	W 1-0	Weir-Daley 30
4	Sat-15-Jan	FAT 2	H	Gloucester City	1110	L 0-1	
5	Tue-03-May	PO SF 1	A	Guiseley	1022	L 0-1	
6	Sun-08-May	PO SF 2	H	Guiseley	2640	W 3-2 aet (L 2-3 pens)	Pearson 10, Church 79, Davidson 113

League
Starts
Substitute
Unused Sub

Cups
Starts
Substitute
Unused Sub

Goals (Lg)
Goals (Cup)

MCKEOWN	CANOVILLE	JELLEYMAN	CHURCH	PEARSON	MURPHY	YATES	SLEATH	NEWSHAM	WEIR-DALEY	SEMPLE	DAVIDSON	HUNTER	CULLINGWORTH	DEANE	BUTCHER	ASHTON	CLANCY	DAVIES	PARKER	WARD	HEWITT	LEE	SUAREZ	BURGE	MONTGOMERY	CLARKE	J WILLIAMS	HAYSTEAD	KORANTENG	NYONI	COLEMAN	BOYES	ROBINSON	D WILLIAMS	AUSTIN	GREEN	DARLEY	DRURY	BASTOCK	DUDFIELD	FROST	STONES
X	X	X	X	X	X	X	X	X	X	X	S	S	S	U	U																											
X	X	X	X	X	X	X	X			X	X	X	S	U	U	U	U																									
X	X	X	X	X	X	X	X		S	X	X	X	S	S	U	U																										
X	X	X	X	X	X	X	X		X	X	X	S	S	U	U	U																										
X	X	X	X	X	X	X	X	S	X	X	X		U	U	U			S																								
X	X	X	X	X	X	X	X	S	X	X	X		S		U		U	U																								
X	X	X	X	X	X	X	X	S	X	X	X	S	U					U	U																							
X	X	X	X	X	X	X	X	S	X	X	X	S	U		U			S																								
X	X	X	X	X	X	X	X	S	X	X	X	U	S					U	U																							
X	X	X	X	X	X	X	X	X	S	X		S	U		U			U				X																				
X	X	X	X	X	X	S	X	X	X	X		S	U	S				U				X																				
X	X	X	X	X	X	X	X	X	X	S		S	U	U								X	S																			
X	X	X	X	X	X	X	X		X	X	X	S	U	S									S	U																		
X	X	X	X	X	X	X	X	X	S	X	X	S	U										S	U																		
X	X	X	X	X	X	U	X	X	X	X	X	S	S										S	U																		
X		X	X	X	X	S	X	U	X	X	S	S	X							U			X	X																		
X	X	X	X	X	U	X	S	X	X	X	S	S	X													X		U														
	X	X	X		X	U	U	X	X	S	X	S	X										S			X		X	X													
	X	X	X				S	U	X	X	S	S	X			U							X			X		X	X	X												
	X		X			X	S	U	X	X	U	S	X										X			X		X	S	X	X											
	X	X	X	X		U	S	U	X	X	X		X										S			S		X		X	X											
		X	X			S	X	S	X	X	X	S	X			X				U						X		X	U		X											
	X	X	X	X		X	X	U	X	S	S	U	X													S		X			X	X										
	X	X	X	X		X	X	S	X		S	U	X	S												X		X			U	X										
	X	X	X	X		X	X	U	X	S	S	S	X													X		X			U	X										
	X		X	X		X	X	X	S	X	S		X	U														X	U			X	X	S								
	X		X	S		U	X	X	X	S	U	S	X															X				X	X	X	X							
			X	X			X	X	U	S	S	S	U															X				X	X	X	X	X	X					
		X	X	X		S	X	U	S	X		X	X															X				X		U	X	X	S					
		X	X	X		S	X	U	S	X		X	X															X				X		U	X	X	S					
		X	X	X		S	X	U	S	X		X	X															X				X			X	X	S	U				
	X		X	X		X	X	X	S	U	S	U	X															X				X			X	X	S					
	X		X	X		X	X	X	S	S	U	U	X																			X			X	X	S	X				
	U	X	X	X		X	X	U	X	X	S	U	X													U						X			X				X			
	X	X	X	X		X	X	S	X	X	S		U													S						X			X				X	U		
	X	X	X	X		X	X	U	X	X	S		U													U									X				X	X	U	
	X	X	X			X	X	X	X		U		X							U						U						S			X				X		X	U
	X	X	X			X	X	S	X	X			S							U						X						S			X				X	X		U
	X	X	X			X	X	X	S	X			U													X						X			X				X	S	U	U
	X	X	X	X		X	S		U				X									S				X						S			U				X	X	X	X
	X	X	X	X	X	X	S	X	S	S	X	U	X	U	X			X		U	U																					
	X	X	X		X	X	U	X	X	X		S	X	U									S		X	X	S															
X	X	X	X	X		X	S	X	X	X	S	U	X	U												X	S															
X	X		X			X	X	X	X	S	S	U	X							U			X			X			S		X											
	X	X	X		S	X	X		X	X			U									S				X						X			X				X		U	U
	X	X	X	X	X	X	X		X		S		U													S						S							X	X		U
17	33	34	40	32	17	28	34	15	27	29	14	5	20	0	0	1	0	0	0	0	0	3	3	1	0	10	0	15	2	3	4	14	3	2	13	6	1	1	7	3	2	1
0	0	0	0	1	0	6	5	9	10	7	13	19	8	4	0	0	0	2	0	0	0	1	6	0	0	3	0	0	1	0	0	3	0	1	0	0	5	0	0	1	0	0
0	1	0	0	0	1	4	1	11	2	1	4	6	12	6	8	4	2	5	2	4	0	0	0	3	0	3	0	1	2	0	2	0	0	2	1	0	0	1	0	1	2	3
2	6	5	6	3	3	6	3	4	5	3	1	0	4	0	1	0	0	1	0	0	0	0	1	0	1	4	0	0	0	0	1	1	0	0	1	0	0	0	2	1	0	0
0	0	0	0	0	1	0	2	0	1	2	3	1	0	0	0	0	0	0	0	0	0	1	1	0	0	1	2	0	1	0	0	1	0	0	0	0	0	0	0	0	0	0
0	0	0	0	0	0	0	1	0	0	0	0	3	2	3	0	0	0	0	0	2	1	0	0	0	0	0	0	0	0	0	0	0	0	0	0	0	0	0	0	0	1	2
0	2	0	10	10	0	2	5	4	12	5	4	4	0	0	0	0	0	0	0	0	0	0	2	0	0	1	0	0	0	0	0	6	0	0	0	1	0	0	0	1	0	1
0	0	0	1	1	0	1	0	2	1	0	1	0	0	0	0	0	0	0	0	0	0	0	0	0	0	0	0	0	0	0	0	0	0	0	0	0	0	0	0	0	0	0

PLAYING SQUAD 2011/12

Existing Players		SN	HT	WT	DOB	AGE	POB	Career	Apps	Goals
GOALKEEPERS										
Paul	Bastock		5'11"	14 00	19/05/1970	41	Leamington Spa	Coventry (Trainee), Cambridge Utd 3/88, Sabah (Mal) c/s 89, Kettering (L) 3/90, Kettering 7/90, Fisher (L), Boston Utd 8/92, Scarborough 10/04, Dag & Red 10/04, St Albans 11/04 Rel 5/07, Rushden & D 5/07 Rel 2/08, St Albans 2/08, Boston U 3/11		
Ricky	Drury				30/10/1989	21		Boston U (Yth), Sleaford, Boston U 7/10	1	0
Andy	Hewitt				18/09/1992	18		Boston U	0	0
DEFENDERS										
Kevin	Austin		6'00"	14 08	12/02/1973	38	Hackney	Saffron Walden, L.Orient 8/93, Lincoln C £30,000 7/96, Barnsley 7/99, Brentford (L) 10/00, Cambridge U 11/01 Rel 3/02, Kettering 3/02, Bristol R 7/02, Swansea 7/04, Chesterfield 8/08 Rel c/s 10, Darlington 8/10 Rel 5/11, Boston U (SL) 2/11, Boston U 6/11	13	0
Lee	Canoville		6'01"	11 03	14/03/1981	30	Ealing	Millwall (Ass Sch), Arsenal Rel c/s 01, Northampton (L) 1/01, Torquay 9/01 Rel c/s 05, Boston U 8/05 Rel c/s 07, Shrewsbury (SL) 1/07, Bournemouth (Trial) c/s 07, Notts County 7/07 Rel c/s 08, Grays 9/08 Rel 10/08, Halesowen T 10/08, Gainsborough (SL) 2/09, Boston U 7/09 Jt Coach 3/11 Pl/Man 5/11	33	2
Jordan	Fairclough		6'01"	11 08	08/05/1991	20	Leeds	Notts Forest Rel c/s 10, Burton (Trial) 7/10, Shepshed D 8/10, Corby T 3/11, Boston U 6/11		
Gareth	Jelleyman		5'10"	10 06	14/11/1980	30	Holywell	Norwich (Yth), Peterborough, Boston U (L) 12/98, Boston U (L) 8/04, Mansfield (L) 1/05 Perm 1/05, Rushden & D 7/08 Rel 5/09, Barrow (SL) 3/09, AFC Telford NC 7/09, Barrow 8/09 Rel 5/10, Boston U 7/10	34	0
Liam	Parker		6'01"	12 05	22/02/1986	25	Boston	Grimsby Rel c/s 05, Boston T, Boston U 7/08 Rel 9/10, Stamford 3/11, Boston U 7/11	0	0
Tom	Ward				30/08/1990	21		Sleaford T, Boston U c/s 10	0	0
MIDFIELDERS										
Harry	Deane				28/09/1991	19	Lincoln	Grimsby (Scholar), Boston U 8/10, Spalding U (L) 1/11, Stamford (L) 3/11	4	0
Chris	Hall				03/03/1983	28	Lincoln	Lincoln U, Burton 5/04, Gainsborough 6/07 Rel 2/10, York C (SL) 3/08, Alfreton 2/10 Rel 5/11, Stocksbridge PS (L) 1/11, Stocksbridge PS (SL) 3/11, Boston U 6/11		
Kevin	Holsgrove				09/01/1988	23		Everton (Yth), NEWI Cefn Druids 8/07, Colwyn Bay 8/09, Hyde U 9/09, Kidderminster (Trial) 7/10, Altrincham 8/10, Hyde FC (L) 10/10, Hyde FC (3ML) 1/11, Boston U 7/11		
Adam	Millsom				28/02/1990	21		Boston U Rel c/s 10, Spalding U (L) 12/09, Grantham 8/10, Kings Lynn T 11/10 Rel 11/10, Stamford 12/10, Boston U 8/11		
Ben	Milnes				12/09/1991	19		Leicester Rel c/s 11, Boston U 7/11		
Liam	Ogden				22/09/1989	21		Boston U		
Ryan	Semple		5'11"	10 11	04/07/1985	26	Belfast	Peterborough, Man Utd (Trial) 2/03, Farnborough (3ML) 11/03, Lincoln C 7/06 Rel 1/08, Chester (6WL) 11/06, Rushden & D (L) 8/07, Oxford U NC 2/08, Brackley T 3/08, Boston U (Trial) c/s 08, Deeping R 8/08, Haverhill R (Dual) 3/09, Gainsborough 6/09, Boston U 3/10	36	5
Danny	Sleath		5'08"	11 05	14/12/1986	24	Matlock	Mansfield Rel 5/08, Gresley (L) 10/06, Alfreton (L) 2/07, Boston U (L) 11/07, Gainsborough (SL) 3/08, Eastwood T 9/08, Ilkeston 3/09, Boston U 7/09	39	5
Ben	Wilkinson		5'11"	12 01	25/04/1987	23	Sheffield	Sheff Wed (Yth), Sheff Utd (Yth), Derby (Scholar), Hull C, Harrogate T (L) 12/06, York C (Trial) 1/08, Gretna (SL) 1/08, York C 6/08 Rel 7/09, Altrincham (SL) 3/09, Chester 7/09 Rel 2/10, Tamworth 8/10, Southport (Trial) 7/11, Boston U 7/11		
FORWARDS										
Lawrie	Dudfield		6'01"	13 09	07/05/1980	31	Southwark	Kettering, Leicester 6/97, Lincoln C (L) 9/00, Chesterfield (3ML) 12/00, Hull C £210,000 7/01, Northampton (L) 3/03 Perm 3/03, Southend (L) 2/04 Per 3/04, Northampton 8/05, Boston U 8/05 Rel 5/06, Notts County 6/06 Rel c/s 08, Cork City 8/08, Chelmsford 1/09 Rel 5/09, Corby C 5/09 Rel 7/09, Notts Forest Community Manager, Boston U 3/11 Rel 5/11, Boston U 8/11	4	1
Julian	Joachim		5'06"	12 02	20/09/1974	36	Boston	Leicester, Aston Villa £1.5 mill 2/96, Coventry P/E 7/01 Rel c/s 04, Leeds U 7/04, Walsall (SL) 3/05, Boston U 7/05, Darlington £100,000 8/06 Rel c/s 08, Kings Lynn 7/08, Thurmaston T 7/09, Quorn 8/09, Hinckley U 3/10, Holbeach 8/10, Boston U 7/11		
Jason	Lee		6'03"	13 08	09/05/1971	40	Forest Gate	Charlton, Fisher (L) 8/89, Stockport (L) 2/91, Lincoln C £35,000 3/91, Southend (L) 8/93 £150,000 9/93, N.Forest £200,000 3/94, Charlton (2ML) 2/97, Grimsby (L) 3/97, Watford £200,000 6/97, Chesterfield £250,000 8/98, Peterborough (2ML) 1/00 £50,000 3/00 Rel c/s 03, Scarborough (Trial) 7/03, Falkirk 8/03, Boston U 8/04, Northampton 1/06 Rel c/s 06, Notts County 6/06 Rel c/s 08, Mansfield 7/08, Kettering 1/09, Corby 3/09, Ilkeston 3/10, Boston U 9/10 Retired 11/10, Arnold T 3/11, Boston U (Jt Coach) 3/11 Pl/Man 5/11	4	0
Marc	Newsham		5'10"	09 11	24/03/1987	24	Hatfield, Yor	Rotherham Rel c/s 09, Gainsborough (L) 10/08, Sheffield FC (L) 12/08, Ilkeston (SL) 1/09, Boston U 6/09	24	4
Mickey	Stones				08/08/1984	27		Horncastle, Sleaford, Boston U 8/07, Sleaford, Boston U c/s 10	1	1
Mikel	Suarez				28/09/1986	24	Bilbao, Spa	Loughborough University, Nuneaton T (Trial) 7/09, Boston U 7/09, Worksop 1/11, Boston U 6/11	9	2

COLWYN BAY

Chairman: Robert Paton
Secretary: Grant McIndoe (T) 07769 538 012 (E) egmcindoe@yahoo.co.uk
Additional Committee Members:
Roger Skinner, Mark Williams, Connor Wakeham, Tim Channon.

Manager: David Challinor
Programme Editor: Mark Williams (E) mark_williams_cbfc@hotmail.co.uk

Club Factfile

Founded: 1885 **Nickname:** Seagulls
Previous Names:
Previous Leagues: North Wales Coast 1901-21, 33-35, Welsh National 1921-30, North Wales Combination 1930-31, Welsh League (North) 1945-84, North West Counties 1984-91
Club Colours (change): Sky blue and claret/claret/sky blue (White & claret/white/white)

Ground: Llanelian Road, Old Colwyn, North Wales LL29 8UN **(T)** 01492 514 581
Capacity: 2,500 **Seats:** 250 **Covered:** 700 **Clubhouse:** Yes **Shop:** Yes

Directions
From Queensferry take the A55 and exit at Junction 22 signposted Old Colwyn at end of slip road turn left, up the hill to the mini roundabout, straight across onto Llanelian Road, ground is approx half mile on the right.

Previous Grounds: Eirias Park

Record Attendance: 5,000 v Borough United at Eirias Park 1964
Record Victory: Not known
Record Defeat: Not known
Record Goalscorer: Peter Donnelly
Record Appearances: Bryn A Jones
Additional Records:

Senior Honours: Northern League Division 1 1991-92, Division 1 Play-off 2009-10

10 YEAR RECORD

01-02	02-03	03-04	04-05	05-06	06-07	07-08	08-09	09-10	10-11
NP P 20	NP P 22	NP 1 16	NP 1 13	NP 1 12	NP 1 5	NP1S 7	NP1N 4	NP1N 4	NP P 2

COLWYN BAY

No.	Date	Comp	H/A	Opponents	Att:	Result	Goalscorers	Pos
1	Aug-02	NPL P	A	North Ferriby United	158	W 3 - 1	Allen 9 Newby 38 86	1
2	24		H	Ashton United	393	L 0 - 3		
3	28		H	Bradford P.A.	440	D 2 - 2	Sheridan 31 Noon 44	13
4	30		A	F.C.Halifax Town	1561	D 1 - 1	Grannon 78	
5	Sept 4		H	Hucknall Town	323	W 2 - 0	Sheridan 38 Noon 45	9
6	7		A	Kendal Town	167	W 4 - 1	Grannon 22 Newby 43 Moran (og) 46 Sheridan 57	
7	**11**	**FAC 1Q**	**A**	**Marine**	**312**	**D 1 - 1**	**Lathem 3 (og)**	
8	**14**	**FAC 1Qr**	**H**	**Marine**	**234**	**W 2 - 0**	**Evans 33 Sheridan 70**	
9	18		H	Mickleover Sports	350	D 1 - 1	Newby 51	7
10	22		A	Chasetown	406	D 2 - 2	McGraa 57 Bailey 71	
11	**25**	**FAC 2Q**	**H**	**Guiseley**	**457**	**D 1 - 1**	**McGraa 41**	
12	**28**	**FACQ2r**	**A**	**Guiseley**	**256**	**L 0 - 3**		
13	Oct 2		A	Whitby Town	248	D 2 - 2	Bailey 63 Evans 90	12
14	5		A	Marine	321	W 3 - 1	Noon 31 89 Sheehan 66	
15	9		H	Northwich Victoria	558	L 0 - 6		10
16	12		H	Burscough	206	W 2 - 1	Sheridan 28 Newby 78	
17	**16**	**FAT 1Q**	**H**	**Bradford P.A.**	**337**	**W 2 - 0**	**Newby 17 Allen 67**	
18	23		A	Retford United	152	W 5 - 3	Challinor 13 Allen 24 Noon 35 51 Evans 49	4
19	26		H	Marine	283	L 0 - 3		
20	**30**	**FAT 2Q**	**A**	**F.C.United**	**1259**	**L 1 - 2**	**Grannon 66**	
21	Nov 6		A	Stocksbridge Park Steels	180	W 1 - 0	Newby 76	6
22	9		A	Burscough	147	D 0 - 0		
23	13		H	Buxton	376	W 2 - 1	Grannon 57 Newby 80	4
24	16		H	F.C.United	1003	W 3 - 1	Newby 62 Allen 67 Noon 73	
25	20		A	Matlock Town	309	L 0 - 3		2
26	27		H	Ossett Town	233	W 3 - 1	Newby1 Noon 36 McLachlan 85	
27	Dec 11		A	Mickleover Sports	175	L 0 - 3		2
28	Jan 1		A	Ashton United	154	L 0 - 3		
29	3		H	F.C.Halifax Town	827	W 2 - 1	Allen 63 Grannon 77	2
30	8		H	Kendal Town	309	L 1 - 2	Grannon 89	2
31	15		A	Bradford P.A.	281	W 4 - 1	HOPLEY 3 (6 29 82) Newby 59	2
32	Feb 2		A	F.C.United	1560	W 1 - 0	Newby 28	
33	12		A	Frickley Athletic	193	W 1 - 0	Noon 64	2
34	19		H	Chasetown	485	W 1 - 0	Hopley 49	
35	22		H	Matlock Town	371	L 0 - 1		3
36	26		H	North Ferriby United	377	L 0 - 2		4
37	March 5		H	Whitby Town	347	W 2 - 0	McLachan 70 Allen 72	
38	8		A	Northwich Victoria	322	W 1 - 0	Hopley 10	2
39	12		A	Ossett Town	107	W 3 - 2	McLachlan 13 McCarthy 45 72	
40	15		H	Worksop Town	269	W 2 - 1	Hopley 27 41	2
41	19		H	Frickley Athletic	288	W 4 - 0	Grannon 10 McLachlan 23 Titchiner 45 Hopley 57	
42	22		A	Nantwich Town	240	L 1 - 2	Sheehan 36	2
43	26		A	Worksop Town	275	W 1 - 0	Hopley 69	2
44	April 2		H	Retford United	631	W 1 - 0	Titchener 87	2
45	9		A	Buxton	408	D 0 - 0		2
46	16		H	Stocksbridge Park Steels	496	L 3 - 4	Allen 6 85 Denson 10	3
47	23		A	Hucknall Town	185	W 1 - 0	Newby 48	2
48	25		H	Nantwich Town	748	W 2 - 0	Hopley 57 Noon 75	
49	**28**	**P-OFF SF**	**H**	**North Ferriby Uited**	**861**	**W 2 - 0**	**Hopley 9 McCarthy 45**	
50	**May 2**	**P-Off Final**	**H**	**F.C.United**	**2000**	**W 1 - 0**	**Newby 68**	

PLAYING SQUAD 2011/12

Existing Players		SN	HT	WT	DOB	AGE	POB	Career	Apps	Goals
GOALKEEPERS										
Chris	Sanna				02/07/1987	24		Stoke, Watford (L) 10/05, Wrexham (Trial), Shrewsbury (Trial), Colwyn Bay 1/07, Stamford 2/07, Nuneaton (Trial) 7/07, Worcester (SL) 3/08, Halesowen T c/s 08, Colwyn Bay 12/08, Chester FC 11/10, Colwyn Bay 1/11		
Simon	Williams			11 11	28/06/1991	20	Prestatyn	Chester, The New Saints 6/09, Prestatyn (SL) 2/10, Prestatyn (SL) 9/10, Colwyn Bay 8/11		
DEFENDERS										
Luke	Denson		6'00"	11 00	26/02/1991	20	Wirral	Tranmere (Scholar) Rel c/s 09, Colwyn Bay 7/09		
Rodney	McDonald		6'03"		11/04/1992	19		Stoke, Nantwich (WE) 11/09, Oldham 8/10 Rel c/s 11, Stafford R (L) 10/10, Nantwich (SL) 2/11, Colwyn Bay 7/11		
Joe	McMahon				01/09/1983	27	Wales	Crewe (Jun), Colwyn Bay 7/01, Lancaster c/s 04, Fleetwood Undisc 6/06 Rel 11/06, Vauxhall Motors 11/06, Cammell Laird (L) 1/08, Marine 8/08, Colwyn Bay 10/10		
Danny	Meadowcroft		6'04"	12 05	22/05/1985	26	Macclesfield	Stockport, Mossley (L) 10/04 Perm 11/04, Morecambe 7/06 Rel 5/07, Mossley (L) 11/06, Bradford PA 7/07, Ossett T 10/07, Northwich 1/08 Rel 5/08, Droylsden c/s 08, FC Halifax 10/08, Northwich 3/09, Salford C (L) 12/09, Colwyn Bay (L) 1/10, Chester FC 5/10, Bamber Bridge (L) 10/10, Colwyn Bay 1/11		
MIDFIELDERS										
Damien	Allen		5'11"	11 04	01/08/1986	25	Cheadle	Man Utd (Yth), Stockport Rel c/s 07, Royal Antwerp (Bel) (SL) 1/07, Morecambe 8/07 Rel c/s 08, Droylsden 9/08, Flixton (Dual) 10/08, FC Halifax 10/08, Bury 7/09, Colwyn Bay 7/10		
Sean	Doherty		5'08"	10 06	10/05/1985	26	Basingstoke	Everton (Jun), Fulham, Blackpool (L) 9/03 Rel c/s 05, Den Haag 7/05, Port Vale 1/06 Rel c/s 06, Accrington 5/06 Rel c/s 07, Southport (6WL) 11/06 (06/07 6,1), Royal Antwerp (Bel) 7/07, Sligo R (Ire) 1/08 Rel 7/09, Witton 1/10, Marine 2/10, Colwyn Bay 7/11		
Gareth	Evans				29/04/1987	24		Chester (Yth), Bangor C, Mochdre, Llandudno, Colwyn Bay 9/10		
Mike	Lea		6'00"	12 00	04/11/1987	23	Salford	Man Utd, Royal Antwerp (4ML) 8/07, Scunthorpe Undisc 7/08, Chester 7/09 (09/10 19,0) Rel 3/10, Hyde U 3/10, Rochdale 3/10 Rel c/s 10, Hyde FC 7/10, Colwyn Bay 8/10		
Dan	Lloyd-McGoldrick				03/12/1991	19	Liverpool	Southport, Marine (Dual) 9/09, Chorley (SL) 11/09, Skelmersdale (3ML) 8/10, Skelmersdale (3ML) 12/10, Chasetown (L) 3/11, Colwyn Bay 8/11		
John	McKenna				15/05/1990	21		The New Saints Rel c/s 11, Ipswich (Trial) 1/08, Preston (Trial), Newtown (5ML) 8/10, AFC Telford (Trial) 7/11, Colwyn Bay 8/11		
Fraser	McLachlan		5'11"	12 07	09/11/1982	28	Knutsford	Stockport, Northwich (L) 8/04, Mansfield (2ML) 11/04 Undisc 1/05 Rel 5/06, Morecambe (SL) 3/06, Morecambe 7/06 Rel c/s 10, Colwyn Bay 8/10		
Anthony	Sheehan				16/08/1982	29		Rhyl, Poulton Vics 10/01, Cammell Laird, Colwyn Bay 6/09, Chester FC 6/10, Colwyn Bay 9/10		
Ryan	Williams				18/04/1991	20		Chester, Colwyn Bay 10/09		
FORWARDS										
Lee	Davey				20/02/1987	24		Heswall, Colwyn Bay 11/08, Buckley Ath (L) 11/09		
Rob	Hopley		6'04"		02/01/1985	26		Macclesfield (Yth), Winsford 12/04, Leek T 7/07, Colwyn Bay 6/08, Chester FC 5/10, Colwyn Bay (L) 12/10, Colwyn Bay 3/11		
Jon	Newby		6'00"	12 04	28/11/1978	32	Warrington	Liverpool, Carlisle (L) 12/99, Crewe (2ML) 3/00, Sheff Utd (3ML) 8/00, Bury (2ML) 2/01 £100,000 3/01 Rel c/s 03, Huddersfield 8/03, York C (L) 3/04, Bury 8/04 Rel 5/06, Kidderminster (L) 3/06, Wrexham 8/06 Rel 12/06, Southport 1/07 Rel 5/07, Morecambe 8/07 Rel c/s 08, Morton c/s 08 Rel 5/09, Burton (SL) 9/08, Northwich 7/09, Colwyn Bay 7/10		
Karl	Noon				15/09/1986	24		Tranmere (Yth), Liverpool (Scholar) Rel c/s 05, Prescot Cables c/s 05, Chester (Trial) 10/05, Bamber Bridge c/s 06, Marine 12/06, Southport c/s 07, Bangor C (L) 1/08 Perm, Vauxhall Motors 8/08, Colwyn Bay 8/10		

Caught in action....

Corby' keeper Aaron Butcher grabs the ball as Alfreton's Anthony Howell prepares to head.

Photo by Bill Wheatcroft

CORBY TOWN

Chairman: Peter Mallinger
Secretary: Graham Starmer **(T)** 07747 011 057 **(E)** gstarmer@footballcv.com
Additional Committee Members:
Ian Hopewell, Chris Rivett

Manager: Graham Drury
Programme Editor: Chris Rivett **(E)** hello9@finalthird.co.uk

Back row, left to right:- Glenn Walker, Chris Mackenzie, Tom Cross, Jack Drury, Michael Frew, Phil Gulliver.
Middle row, left to right:- Adam Webster, Andy Gooding, Danny Pitham, Simon Brown, Steve Towers, Asa Charlton, Liam Dolman, Chris Hope, Ben Mackey, Phil Watt, Steve Diggin, Ian Jackson (coach).
Front row, left to right:- Richard Lavery, Nathan Jarman, Danny Nicholls (assistant manager), Graham Drury (manager), Kevin Grundy (physio), Dean West, Andy Hall. Photo by David Tilley.

Club Factfile

Founded: 1947 **Nickname:** The Steelmen
Previous Names: Stewart & Lloyds (Corby) > 1947
Previous Leagues: United Counties 1935-52. Midland 1952-58. Southern 1958-2009

Club Colours (change): White/black/black (All maroon)

Ground: Rockingham Triangle Stadium, Rockingham Road, Corby NN17 2AE **(T)** 01536 406 640
Capacity: 6,000 **Seats:** 300 **Covered:** 1,000 **Clubhouse:** Yes **Shop:** Yes

Directions
From A14, Exit at Jnc 7, Keep left, at first roundabout take A6003 Oakham/Uppingham stay on this road for approx. 7 miles (ignore signs for Corby to your right en route) straight over two roundabouts at second B.P. petrol station on right. at next roundabout approx 1 mile Ahead turn right onto A6116 for 300 yards entrance to Ground between Rugby Club and Rockingham Forest Hotel (Great Western).

Previous Grounds: Not known.

Record Attendance: 2,240 v Watford - Friendly 1986-87
Record Victory: Not known
Record Defeat: Not known
Record Goalscorer: David Holbauer - 159 (1984-95)
Record Appearances: Derek Walker - 601
Additional Records: Paid £2,700 to Barnet for Elwun Edwards 1981
Received £20,000 from Oxford United for Matt Murphy 1993

Senior Honours: United Counties League 1950-51, 51-52. Southern League Premier Division 2008-09.
Northants Senior Cup x6.

10 YEAR RECORD

01-02	02-03	03-04	04-05	05-06	06-07	07-08	08-09	09-10	10-11
SthE 21	SthE 19	SthE 15	SthW 12	SthE 2	SthP 20	SthP 16	SthP 1	Conf N 6	Conf N 13

CORBY TOWN

No.	Date	Comp	H/A	Opponents	Att:	Result	Goalscorers	Pos
1	Sat-14-Aug	BSN	H	Harrogate Town	360	W 2-1	Mackey 15, Hall 65	5
2	Tue-17-Aug	BSN	A	Gloucester City	386	W 2-0	Mackey 59, Diggin 85	5
3	Sat-21-Aug	BSN	A	Blyth Spartans	406	D 1-1	Mackey 24	5
4	Wed-25-Aug	BSN	H	Redditch United	307	W 3-2	Mackey 2 (40, 54), Pitham 45	4
5	Sat-28-Aug	BSN	A	Eastwood Town	432	L 1-2	Walker 12	7
6	Mon-30-Aug	BSN	H	Hinckley United	543	W 2-0	Walker 27, Hope 43	5
7	Sat-04-Sep	BSN	H	Boston United	907	D 0-0		5
8	Sat-11-Sep	BSN	A	Hyde FC	268	L 1-2	Mackey pen 44	7
9	Sat-18-Sep	BSN	H	AFC Telford	588	D 0-0		7
10	Sat-02-Oct	BSN	A	Guiseley	467	L 0-4		9
11	Sat-16-Oct	BSN	H	Gainsborough Trinity	443	W 3-1	Towers 2 (24, 50), Jarman 85	8
12	Sat-30-Oct	BSN	H	Blyth Spartans	641	L 3-4	Mackey 49, Hope 57, Og (Groves) 58	9
13	Tue-09-Nov	BSN	A	Boston United	1279	L 0-1		10
14	Sat-13-Nov	BSN	H	Workington	374	W 1-0	Jarman 70	10
15	Sat-01-Jan	BSN	H	Nuneaton Town	636	L 2-3	Webster 2, Hall 11	11
16	Mon-03-Jan	BSN	A	Hinckley United	502	D 3-3	Mackey 7, Og (Bains) 33, Diggin 88	11
17	Sat-08-Jan	BSN	H	Guiseley	370	D 2-2	Mackey 20, Webster 32	12
18	Mon-10-Jan	BSN	A	Worcester City	478	W 2-0	Watt 50, Hall 87	9
19	Tue-18-Jan	BSN	A	Vauxhall Motors	184	L 2-3	Mackey 32, Jarman 65	11
20	Sat-22-Jan	BSN	A	Stafford Rangers	432	W 5-3	Hall 3 (3, 42, pen 79), Og (Francis) 10, Diggin 64	9
21	Sat-29-Jan	BSN	H	Eastwood Town	418	L 1-6	Jarman 22	10
22	Sat-05-Feb	BSN	A	Harrogate Town	308	W 1-0	Sansara 72	9
23	Sat-12-Feb	BSN	A	Solihull Moors	366	L 2-7	Webster 30, Hall 70	11
24	Sat-19-Feb	BSN	H	Stalybridge Celtic	314	D 2-2	Hope 16, Towers 43	11
25	Tue-01-Mar	BSN	A	Nuneaton Town	681	W 3-2	Fitzpatrick 20, Jarman 2 (26, 49)	10
26	Sat-05-Mar	BSN	H	Worcester City	282	D 1-1	Jarman 90	11
27	Wed-09-Mar	BSN	H	Gloucester City	177	L 0-2		12
28	Sat-12-Mar	BSN	A	Alfreton Town	705	L 0-6		14
29	Wed-16-Mar	BSN	A	Stalybridge Celtic	315	D 1-1	Towers 53	14
30	Sat-19-Mar	BSN	H	Solihull Moors	243	L 0-2		14
31	Wed-23-Mar	BSN	H	Vauxhall Motors	168	W 3-1	Walker 2, Dolman 6, Mooney 9	11
32	Sat-26-Mar	BSN	A	Workington	314	W 2-1	Smith 82, Diggin 89	11
33	Wed-30-Mar	BSN	H	Alfreton Town	323	L 0-1		11
34	Tue-05-Apr	BSN	A	AFC Telford	1370	L 0-5		12
35	Sat-09-Apr	BSN	A	Droylsden	200	D 1-1	Fairclough 18	12
36	Sat-16-Apr	BSN	A	Gainsborough Trinity	375	L 1-3	Malone 13	14
37	Wed-20-Apr	BSN	H	Droylsden	203	W 1-0	Diggin 90	12
38	Sat-23-Apr	BSN	H	Stafford Rangers	295	L 1-3	Spruce 65	12
39	Mon-25-Apr	BSN	A	Redditch United	335	D 2-2	Malone 28, Johnson 79	13
40	Sat-30-Apr	BSN	H	Hyde FC	404	L 1-2	Og (Lees) 42	13

CUPS

No.	Date	Comp	H/A	Opponents	Att:	Result	Goalscorers
1	Sat-25-Sep	FAC 2Q	A	Bedworth United	241	W 1-0	Frew 11
2	Sat-09-Oct	FAC 3Q	H	Worcester City	520	W 2-1	Mackey 28, Hall 90
3	Sat-23-Oct	FAC 4Q	H	Salisbury City	957	W 3-0	Jarman 2 (63, 88), Mackey 75
4	Sat-06-Nov	FAC 1	H	Luton Town	1750	D 1-1	Mackey 14
5	Wed-17-Nov	FAC 1R	A	Luton Town	3050	L 2-4	Walker 84, Hope 86
6	Sat-20-Nov	FAT 3QR	A	AFC Telford	1028	L 1-2	Jarman 18

League
Starts
Substitute
Unused Sub

Cups
Starts
Substitute
Unused Sub

Goals (Lg)
Goals (Cup)

MACKENZIE	PITHAM	CHARLTON	DOLMAN	GULLIVER	LAVERY	HALL	TOWERS	JARMAN	MACKEY	WALKER	DIGGIN	FREW	WEST	HOPE	GOODING	WEBSTER	KIRK	THACKERAY	GREEN	BURGESS	WHITE	SANSARA	WATT	DRURY	JASZCZUN	RUDDICK	FARDEN	FITZPATRICK	JOHNSON	JAHRALDO-MARTIN	ADEKOTUJO	BUTCHER	MOONEY	WILCOX	MANSHIP	DIEYTE	WINDRUM	FAIRCLOUGH	SPRUCE	SMITH	TEIXEIRA	MALONE	INGRAM
X	X	X	X	X	X	X	X	X	X	X	S	S	U	U	U																												
X	X	X	X	X	X	X	X	X	X	X	S	S	U	U	U																												
X	X	X	X	X	X	X	X	X	X	X	S	U	S	U	U																												
X	X	X	X	X	X	X	X	X	X	X	S	U	U	S	U																												
X	X	X	X	X	X	X	X	X	X	X	S	U	U	S	S																												
X	X	X	U	X	X	X	X	S	X	X	X	S	U	X	U																												
X	X	X	U	X	X	S	X	X	X	X	S	S	U	X		X																											
X	X	X	U	X	X	X	X	S	X	X	U	U		X		X	U																										
X	U	X		X	X	U	X	X	S	X	S	X	X	X		X	S																										
X			X	X	X	S	X	U	X	X	U	X	X	X	X	S			S																								
X	X	X	U	X	X	X	X	S	X	X	X		U	X		S			U																								
X	X	X	U	X	X	X	X	X	X	X	S		U	X		S			S																								
X	X	X		X	X	X	X	X	X	X	S	S		X		S		U	U																								
X	X		S	X	X	X	X	X	X	X	S	U		X		S		U	X																								
X	X		U	X	S	X	X		X	X	S	S	U	X		X				X		X																					
X	S		U	X		X	X		X	X	S	S	X	X		X		U		X		X																					
X		U	S	X		X	X		X	S	S	U	X	X		X				X		X	X																				
X			S	X		S	X	X	X	S	U	U	X	X		X				X		X	X																				
X		S	X	X		X	X	X	X	S	S		X	X		X						X		U	U																		
X		S	X	X		X	X	X			X		X	X		X					S	X		U	S	U																	
X		X	U	X		X	X	X			X		X	X		X					U	X			S	S	U																
X		X		X		X	X			S	X		X	X		X					X	S		U		X	S																
		X		X		X	X	X		X	S			X		X		X				S				X		X	S	U	U												
		X		X		X	X	X		X	S		X	X		X						S				U		X	S			X											
			X	X	S	X	X	X		X	S		X			X						X				S		X	U			X	U										
			X	X	X	X	X	X		X	X											X				S		S	U			X	S	X	U								
			X	X	X		X	X		X	S					X						S				S		X	U			X	U	X		X							
			X	X			X			X	X					X						X		U	X	S		X	S			X		X									
			X	X			X			X	X											U		U	X	U		X	S			X	X	X	X								
			X	X			X			X	X											S			X	S		X	S			X	X	X	X								
			X	X			X			X	X											X				U		X	S			U	X		X		X	X	S				
				X			X			X	X											X				U		X	U				X	X	X		X	X	S	S			
				X			X			X	X											X		U		U		X	S				S	X	X		X	X	S	X			
			U	X			X			X	X											X						X	S				S	X	S		U	X		X	X	X	
			U	X			X			X	X											X							X					X	U		X	X		X		X	
			U	X			X			X	X											X			U			S					S	X	X		X	X	S	X		X	
			U	X			X			X	S											X			U			S	X				X	X	S		X		X	X		X	
			S	S			X			X	S											X						X	U				X	X	U		X	X	X	X		X	
			X	X			X			X	X											S			X			S	S				U		X		X	X	X			X	
			X	X			X			X	X											X			S			S	S					X			X	X	U	X		X	U
X	X	U	U	X	X	U	X	X		X	U	X	X	X	U	X		U																									
X	X	X	U	X	X	X	X		X	X	X	U	U	X	U	S		U	S																								
X	X	X	U	X	X	X	X	S	X	X	X	U	U	X		S		U	S																								
X	X	X	U	X	X	X	X	X	X	X	S	U	U	X		S		U	U																								
X	X	X	S	X	X	X	X	X	X	X	S	U	U	X		U		U	S																								
U	X		X	X		X	S	X	S	X	X	S		X				X	X	X	U																						
22	13	16	17	39	16	22	40	19	18	34	17	2	11	19	1	16	0	1	1	4	1	19	2	0	4	2	0	12	2	0	0	7	6	13	7	1	9	9	3	7	1	7	0
0	1	2	4	1	2	3	0	3	1	4	20	7	1	2	1	5	1	0	2	0	1	6	0	0	3	6	1	5	10	0	0	0	4	0	2	0	0	0	4	1	0	0	0
0	1	1	12	0	0	1	0	1	0	0	3	7	9	3	5	0	1	3	2	0	1	1	0	6	3	6	1	0	5	1	1	1	3	0	3	0	1	0	1	0	0	0	1
5	6	4	1	6	5	5	5	4	4	6	3	1	1	6	0	1	0	1	1	1	0	0	0	0	0	0	0	0	0	0	0	0	0	0	0	0	0	0	0	0	0	0	0
0	0	0	1	0	0	0	1	1	1	0	2	1	0	0	0	3	0	0	3	0	0	0	0	0	0	0	0	0	0	0	0	0	0	0	0	0	0	0	0	0	0	0	0
1	0	1	4	0	0	1	0	0	0	0	1	4	4	0	2	1	0	5	1	0	1	0	0	0	0	0	0	0	0	0	0	0	0	0	0	0	0	0	0	0	0	0	0
0	1	0	1	0	0	7	4	7	10	3	5	0	0	3	0	3	0	0	0	0	0	1	1	0	0	0	0	1	1	0	0	0	1	0	0	0	0	1	1	1	0	2	0
0	0	0	0	0	0	1	0	3	3	1	0	1	0	1	0	0	0	0	0	0	0	0	0	0	0	0	0	0	0	0	0	0	0	0	0	0	0	0	0	0	0	0	0

PLAYING SQUAD 2011/12

Existing Players		SN	HT	WT	DOB	AGE	POB	Career	Apps	Goals
GOALKEEPERS										
Damian	Clarke							Holbrook Sports 99, Mickleover Sports, Corby T 6/11		
Will	Jones							Stamford, FCUM 1/10, Stalybridge 8/10, Corby T 8/11		
Chris	Mackenzie		6'00"	12 09	14/05/1972	39	Northampton	Corby T, Hereford £15,000 7/94, L.Orient 10/97 Rel c/s 99, Nuneaton (L) 3/99, Nuneaton 8/99, Telford 6/03, Hereford (L) 4/04, Chester 5/04, Shrewsbury 5/06, Kidderminster (2ML) 9/07, Kidderminster Undisc 1/08 Rel 5/08, Hinckley U 6/08, Corby T 5/10, Alfreton Undisc 2/11 Rel 7/11, Corby T 7/11	22	0
DEFENDERS										
Delroy	Gordon				16/08/1984	27	Northampton	Rushden & D (Trainee), Kettering 1/03, Stamford 6/04, Rugby T c/s 05, Oxford C 3/10, Banbury U 8/10, Corby T 6/11		
Philip	Gulliver		6'02"	13 05	12/09/1982	28	Bishop Auckland	Middlesbrough Rel c/s 04, Blackpool (L) 11/02, Carlisle (L) 12/02, Bournemouth (SL) 3/03, Bury (2ML) 10/03, Scunthorpe (L) 1/04, Rushden & D 8/04, Hereford 7/06, Rushden & D 5/07 Rel 10/08, Oxford C 11/08, Corby 12/08	40	0
Tom	Land				22/11/1989	21		Derby (Yth), Sheff Wed (Scholar), Burton, Borrowash Vic, Gresley FC 1/10, Graham Street Prims (L) 2/11, Corby T 6/11, Stamford (L) 8/11		
Paul	Malone							Corby T (Yth), Desborough (L) 10/07 Perm, S & L Corby c/s 08, Stamford 7/09, Corby T (Small Fee) 3/11	7	2
Paul	Mayo		5'11"	11 09	13/10/1981	29	Lincoln	Notts Forest (Scholar), Lincoln C (Sch) 10/99 Pro 4/00, Dag & Red (L) 10/02, Watford £65,000 3/04, Lincoln C 8/05, Notts County 7/07, Darlington (L) 1/08, Mansfield 1/09 Rel 5/09, Corby T 6/09, Gainsborough 5/10 Rel 5/11, Corby T 6/11		
Aynsley	McDonald				25/01/1992	19	Earls Barton	Rushden & D, Wingate & F (L) 8/09, Banbury U (L) 1/10, Billericay (WE) 3/10, AFC Sudbury (L) 9/10, Banbury U (L) 10/10, Corby T 6/11		
Jordan	Spruce							Watford (Yth), Newport Pagnell, Corby T 3/11, S & L Corby (Dual) 8/11	7	1
MIDFIELDERS										
Andy	Burgess		6'02"	11 11	10/08/1981	29	Bedford	Luton (Jun), Rushden & D, Oxford U 1/06, Rushden & D 8/07, Luton 5/09, Mansfield (5WL) 11/09 Perm 1/10 Rel 4/10, Chester FC Rel 10/10, Fleetwood 10/10, Corby T 11/10 Rel 1/11, Droylsden 1/11, Woking 3/11, Corby T (Pl/Coach) 5/11	4	0
Andy	Hall				25/01/1986	25	Northampton	Coventry (Scholar), Kettering 7/05 Rel c/s 08, Halesowen T (SL) 3/08, Hinckley U 7/08, Corby T 5/10, Nuneaton T 3/11, Corby T 6/11	25	7
Leon	Hibbert		6'04"		06/11/1981	29	Watford	Tring T, Welwyn Garden c/s 03, Berkhamstead 8/04, Hemel Hempstead c/s 06, Barton R 11/07, Corby T 7/08, Slough (L) 10/09, Lincoln C (Trial) 5/10, Gainsborough 6/10 Rel 5/11, Corby T 6/11		
Sam	Ives				24/06/1991	20	Cambridge	Cambridge C (Yth), Cambridge U Rel 5/11, Bury T (L) 12/10, Corby T 6/11		
James	Ozmen							Holbrook Sports, Corby T 6/11		
Steve	Towers				17/08/1985	26		Oadby, Rothwell c/s 04, Corby 6/06 Rel 10/07, Stamford 10/07, Corby 5/08	40	4
FORWARDS										
Matt	Rhead		6'04"		31/05/1984	27	Stoke	Stallington, Kidsgrove Ath c/s 04, Eastwood T Undisc 10/07, Kidsgrove Ath (L) 9/08, Nantwich 6/09, Congleton (L) 12/09 Perm, Eastwood T 6/10, Corby T 7/11		
Nick	Rogan		5'10"	12 12	15/10/1983	27	Blackpool	Kendal T, Morecambe 7/02 Rel 5/05, Workington (L) 3/05, Leigh RMI (Trial) 5/05, Lancaster 7/05, Southport 10/05, Barrow 2/06 Rel 5/09, Vauxhall Motors (L) 10/08, Fleetwood 6/09 Rel 5/11, Barrow (L) 9/09, Chester FC (L) 8/10, Workington (3ML) 1/11, Altrincham (Trial) 7/11, Corby T 7/11		
Greg	Smith				24/01/1990	21		Newhall U, Daventry U, Rugby T 12/09, Sleaford T 1/10, Shepshed D 10/10, Corby T 3/11, Stamford (L) 8/11	8	1
Jordan	Smith				09/04/1988	23		Thurnby Nirvana, Corby T 6/11		

DROYLSDEN

Chairman: David Pace
Secretary: Alan Slater **(T)** 07989 024 777 **(E)** alans83@btinternet.com
Additional Committee Members:
Bryan Pace, Stella Quinn

Manager: David Pace
Programme Editor: Steven Jarvis **(E)** stevenjjarvis@googlemail.com

Club Factfile

Founded: 1892 **Nickname:** The Bloods
Previous Names: None
Previous Leagues: Manchester, Lancashire Combination 1936-39, 50-68, Cheshire County 1939-50, 68-82, North West Counties 1982-87, Northern Premier 1986-2004
Club Colours (change): All red (All royal blue)

Ground: The Butchers Arms Ground, Market Street, Droylsden, M43 7AY **(T)** 0161 370 1426
Capacity: 3,500 **Seats:** 500 **Covered:** 2,000 **Clubhouse:** Yes **Shop:** Yes

Directions
From junction 23 M60 follow signs A635 Manchester, then A662 signed Droylsden, at town centre traffic lights turn right into Market Street, through next set of lights and the main entrance to the ground is 75 yards on your left.

Previous Grounds:

Record Attendance: 4,250 v Grimsby
Record Victory: 13-2 v Lucas Sports Club
Record Defeat: Not known
Record Goalscorer: E. Gillibrand - 275 (1931-35)
Record Appearances: Paul Phillips - 326
Additional Records: Received £11,000 from Crewe Alexandra for Tony Naylor 1990

Senior Honours: Northern Premier League Division 1 1998-99. Conference North 2006-07.
Manchester Premier Cup x3. Manchester Senior Cup x3.

10 YEAR RECORD

01-02	02-03	03-04	04-05	05-06	06-07	07-08	08-09	09-10	10-11
NP P 11	NP P 9	NP P 2	Conf N 3	Conf N 4	Conf N 1	Conf 24	Conf N 7	Conf N 5	Conf N 8

DROYLSDEN

No.	Date	Comp	H/A	Opponents	Att:	Result	Goalscorers	Pos
1	Sat-14-Aug	BSN	H	Eastwood Town	372	W 4-2	Lloyd 23, Kilheeney 34, Holden 51, Brown 70	2
2	Tue-17-Aug	BSN	A	Harrogate Town	296	D 3-3	Lloyd 18, Kilheeney pen 57, McNiven 90	7
3	Sat-21-Aug	BSN	A	Nuneaton Town	902	D 1-1	Kerr 73	8
4	Wed-25-Aug	BSN	H	Hyde FC	433	W 3-1	McNiven 37, Kilheeney 55, Halford 60	7
5	Sat-28-Aug	BSN	A	Hinckley United	336	D 1-1	Holden 67	8
6	Mon-30-Aug	BSN	H	Blyth Spartans	418	L 0-3		10
7	Sat-04-Sep	BSN	H	Stafford Rangers	385	W 2-0	Kilheeney 9, Brown 77	7
8	Sat-11-Sep	BSN	A	Gainsborough Trinity	297	W 3-0	Holden 31, Kilheeney 2 (69, 77)	5
9	Sat-02-Oct	BSN	A	Gloucester City	304	D 1-1	McNiven 30	7
10	Sat-16-Oct	BSN	H	Redditch United	284	W 3-0	Banim 23, Brown 48, Kilheeney pen 62	7
11	Sat-30-Oct	BSN	H	Workington	358	W 3-0	Connors 16, Holden 48, Kerr 78	6
12	Mon-08-Nov	BSN	H	AFC Telford	391	L 2-4	Banim 60, Smith 75	6
13	Sat-13-Nov	BSN	H	Boston United	364	W 4-0	Connors 39, Byron 53, McNiven 79, Kilheeney 89	7
14	Tue-16-Nov	BSN	A	Stalybridge Celtic	626	L 0-4		7
15	Tue-23-Nov	BSN	A	Guiseley	338	L 1-2	Kilheeney 35	7
16	Sat-01-Jan	BSN	H	Vauxhall Motors	223	L 1-3	Brownhill 22	9
17	Mon-03-Jan	BSN	A	Blyth Spartans	517	W 4-2	Og (Morris) 23, McNiven 2 (24, 82), Gardner 90	7
18	Sat-08-Jan	BSN	H	Worcester City	264	W 2-1	Cryan 54, McNiven 90	6
19	Tue-18-Jan	BSN	A	Solihull Moors	209	D 2-2	Kilheeney 10, Banim 84	7
20	Mon-24-Jan	BSN	H	Stalybridge Celtic	476	D 2-2	Holden 25, Banim 87	7
21	Tue-01-Feb	BSN	A	Vauxhall Motors	187	W 1-0	McNiven 50	8
22	Sat-12-Feb	BSN	H	Nuneaton Town	320	W 1-0	Killeen 31	8
23	Mon-21-Feb	BSN	H	Hinckley United	192	W 3-2	Kilheeney 2 (48, 60), Rouse 82	8
24	Sat-26-Feb	BSN	H	Gainsborough Trinity	272	L 1-3	Banim 40	8
25	Tue-01-Mar	BSN	A	AFC Telford	1432	D 1-1	McNiven 82	8
26	Sat-05-Mar	BSN	A	Boston United	1139	L 0-2		8
27	Mon-07-Mar	BSN	H	Solihull Moors	204	L 0-5		8
28	Sat-12-Mar	BSN	A	Workington	389	L 0-2		8
29	Tue-15-Mar	BSN	A	Redditch United	70	W 3-1	Jones 48, Kilheeney 52, Miles 61	8
30	Sat-19-Mar	BSN	H	Alfreton Town	349	W 2-1	Kilheeney 3, McEvilly 45	8
31	Mon-21-Mar	BSN	A	Worcester City	500	W 1-0	McEvilly 26	6
32	Sat-02-Apr	BSN	A	Alfreton Town	707	L 0-4		9
33	Wed-06-Apr	BSN	A	Eastwood Town	340	L 0-2		9
34	Sat-09-Apr	BSN	H	Corby Town	200	D 1-1	McEvilly 49	9
35	Mon-11-Apr	BSN	H	Guiseley	244	L 0-3		9
36	Sat-16-Apr	BSN	A	Stafford Rangers	405	W 5-1	Kilheeney 4 (9, 44, 46, pen 55), Rouse 69	9
37	Wed-20-Apr	BSN	A	Corby Town	203	L 0-1		9
38	Sat-23-Apr	BSN	H	Harrogate Town	206	W 5-1	Kilheeney 32, Rouse 38, Chalmers 51, Connor 59, Miles 68	8
39	Mon-25-Apr	BSN	A	Hyde FC	472	D 1-1	Holden 16	8
40	Sat-30-Apr	BSN	H	Gloucester City	352	L 2-4	Kilheeney 5, Rose 20	8

CUPS

No.	Date	Comp	H/A	Opponents	Att:	Result	Goalscorers
1	Sat-25-Sep	FAC 2Q	A	Hyde FC	375	D 0-0	
2	Mon-27-Sep	FAC 2QR	H	Hyde FC	354	W 3-1	Kilheeney 5, Beck 40, Gardner 90
3	Sat-09-Oct	FAC 3Q	A	Ashington	543	W 4-1	Kilheeney 24, Beck 28, Banim 85, Brownhill 89
4	Sat-23-Oct	FAC 4Q	H	Barwell	411	W 3-0	Connors 24, McNiven 60, Kilheeney 88
5	Sat-06-Nov	FAC 1	A	Havant & Waterlooville	1102	W 2-0	Hardiker 57, Kilheeney 89
6	Sat-20-Nov	FAT 3Q	H	Stourbridge	246	W 3-2	Connors 12, Banim 18, Smith 49
7	Mon-29-Nov	FAC 2	H	Leyton Orient	1762	D 1-1	Kilheeney 24
8	Tue-07-Dec	FAC 2R	A	Leyton Orient	1345	L 2-8 (aet)	Kilheeney 6, Brown 54
9	Sat-11-Dec	FAT 1	H	Hinckley United	175	W 4-3	Hardiker 45, Banim 48, Holden 59, Gardner 79
10	Sat-15-Jan	FAT 2	H	Ebbsfleet United	336	W 1-0	Banim 35
11	Sat-05-Feb	FAT 3	A	Blyth Spartans	708	D 2-2	Boyd 30, Kilheeney 81
12	Mon-07-Feb	FAT 3R	H	Blyth Spartans	229	L 0-4	

League
Starts
Substitute
Unused Sub

Cups
Starts
Substitute
Unused Sub

Goals (Lg)
Goals (Cup)

PHILLIPS	VAUGHAN	BROWNHILL	KERR	HALFORD	BROWN	LLOYD	GARDNER	KILHEENEY	KILLEEN	HOLDEN	WHALLEY	CRYAN	BOOTH	ROCHE	TOWNS	BECK	MCNIVEN	ROUSE	HARDIKER	BYRON	CONNORS	SMITH	BANIM	LOWRY	TANDY	BOYD	CONNOR	BURGESS	WORSNOP	HANLEY	STOCKLEY	WALKER	HUNT	JONES	MCEVILLY	LAKE	MILES	CHALMERS	LOGAN
X	X	X	X	X	X	X	X	X	X	X	S	S	S	U	U																								
X	X	X	X	X	X	X	S	X	X	X		U	S	U		X	S																						
X	U	X	X	U	X	X	X	X	X	X		X	S	X		S	S																						
X	X	X	X	X	X		S	X	X	X			S	U		X	X	S	U																				
X	X	X	X	X	X	X	U		X	X			S	S		X	X	U	U																				
X	U	X	X	S		X	X	X	X	X			X	X	U		S		X	S																			
X		X	X		X	S	U	X	X	X				X	U	X	X	S	X	S																			
X	U	X	U		X		S	X	X	X				X	U		X	U	X	X	X																		
X		X			S			X	X	X		U		X	U	X	X		X	X	X	S	S																
X		X	X		X		S	X	X	X				X	U		S		X	U	X	S	X																
X	X	X	X		X		U	X	X	X							S	S	X	U	X	S	X																
X	U	X	X		X		S	X	X					X			X	S	X	U	X	S	X																
X	X	X	U		X		S	X	X	X		U					S	S	X	X	X		X																
X		X	S		X		U	X	X	X		U		X			X	S	X	X	X		S																
X	X	X			X		U	X	X	X		U		U			X		X	X	X	U	U																
X	X	X					X	X	X	X		X			U		S	U	X				X		S	X	S												
X	X	X					X	U	X	X		X			U		X	S	X				X		U	U	X												
X	X	X					X	S	X	X		X			U		X	S	X				X		U	X	S												
	X	X	X				S	X	X	X		U			X		X	S	X				X			X	U	S											
X	X	X					S	X	X	X		X		S			X	U	X				X			X	S		U										
X	X	X					X	X	X	X		X		S			S	U	X				X				X		U	S									
X	X	X	U				S		X	X		X		U			X	S	X				X			X	X				U								
X	X				U		S	X	X	X		X					X	S	X				X			X	X			U	S								
X	X						X	X	X	X		X					S	X	X				X			X	S			U		S	U						
X	X						S	X	X	U		X					S		X				X			X	X					S	U	X	X				
X		X					X	X	X	S		U					S		X				X			X	S					X	U	X	X				
X	U	X					X	S	X								X	S	X				X			X	U					X		X	X	U			
X	X	X	X				S	X	X	X		U											X			X	S					U		X		U	X		
X	X	X	X				X	X	X	X		U						S								X						S		X	S	U	X		
X	X	X	X					X	X	X		U						S								X						U		X	X	U	X	S	
X	X	X	X				X	X	X			U						S								X	S							X	X	U	X	S	
X	X	X	X				X	X	X			U						S								X	X							X	X	U		S	S
X	X	X	X				S	X	X	X		U						S								X								X	X	U	S	X	
X	X	X			S		X	X	X	X		U						S	X							X								X	X		S	U	
X	U	X	X		S		S	X		X		X						X								X	X								S		X	X	U
X	X	X			S			X	U	X		U						X								X	X								X	S	X	X	S
U	X	X	U		S		U	X		X								X								X	X								X	X	X	X	U
X	X	X	X		U		S	X	S	X								X								X	X								X	U	X	S	
X	X	X			X		S	X	U	X								X									X							S	X	U	X	X	S
X	X	X	U		S		S	X		X								X								X	X								X	U	X	X	S
X		X	U		X		S	X	X	X		U		X	U	S	S		X	X	X	X	U																
X		X	U		U		S	X	X	X		U		X	U	X	S		X	X	X	X	S																
X	U	X	X		S		S	X	X	X		U		X	U	X	X		X		X	U	S																
X	U	X	X		X		S	X	X	X		U		X	U		S		X	U	X	S	X																
X	U	X	X		X		S	X	X			U		X	U		X	S	X	U	X	S	X																
X	X	X			X		X	U	S	X		X		U			X			X	X	S	X		S														
X	U	X	X		X		S	X	X	X		U		X	U		S	S	X		X	U	X																
X	U	X	X		X		X	X	X			S		X	U		X	S	X	S		U	X																
X	X	X	X				S	X	X	X		U			U				X		X	S	X	X	S														
X	X	X	U				S	X	X	X		X		U	S		X	S	X				X			X													
X	X	X	S				S	X	X	X		X		U			X	S	X				X			X				U									
X	U	X	X		U		X		X	X				X	U		X	S	X				X			X				S									
38	29	37	19	4	14	5	14	35	34	34	0	11	1	8	1	5	15	7	23	5	8	0	17	0	0	22	12	0	0	0	0	2	0	10	13	1	10	6	0
0	0	0	1	1	6	1	17	2	1	1	1	1	5	3	0	1	11	18	0	2	0	4	2	0	1	0	7	1	0	1	1	3	0	1	2	1	2	4	4
1	6	0	5	1	2	0	6	1	2	1	0	15	0	5	9	0	0	5	2	3	0	1	1	0	2	1	2	0	2	2	1	2	3	0	0	10	0	1	2
12	4	12	7	0	6	0	3	10	11	10	0	3	0	8	0	2	7	0	11	3	8	2	9	1	0	3	0	0	0	0	0	0	0	0	0	0	0	0	0
0	0	0	1	0	1	0	9	0	1	0	0	1	0	0	1	1	4	6	0	1	0	4	2	0	2	0	0	0	0	1	0	0	0	0	0	0	0	0	0
0	6	0	3	0	2	0	0	1	0	0	0	7	0	3	9	0	0	0	0	2	0	3	1	0	0	0	0	0	0	1	0	0	0	0	0	0	0	0	0
0	0	1	2	1	4	2	1	20	1	6	0	1	0	0	0	0	9	3	0	1	2	1	5	0	0	0	1	0	0	0	0	0	0	1	3	0	2	1	0
0	0	1	0	0	2	0	2	7	0	1	0	0	0	0	0	2	1	0	2	0	2	1	4	0	0	1	0	0	0	0	0	0	0	0	0	0	0	0	0

PLAYING SQUAD 2011/12

Existing Players		SN	HT	WT	DOB	AGE	POB	Career	Apps	Goals
GOALKEEPERS										
Sean	Lake				19/09/1987	23		Everton (Scholar), Shrewsbury, Chester 11/05, Vauxhall Motors 3/06, Radcliffe B 11/07, Cammell Laird 1/08, Marine 6/08, Southport 12/09 Rel c/s 10, Burscough c/s 10, Droylsden 2/11	2	0
Paul	Phillips				15/11/1978	32	Manchester	Man Utd, Bury, Buxton, Curzon Ashton, Droylsden 12/99, Stalybridge 5/08, Droylsden 11/09	38	0
DEFENDERS										
Ricky	Anane		5'08"	11 02	18/02/1989	22	Manchester	Bradford C (Yth), Bury Rel c/s 09, Workington (L) 2/09, Fleetwood (SL) 3/09, Woking 7/09, Droylsden 7/11		
Chris	Brown		6'05"	12 04	21/02/1992	19	Hazel Grove	Rochdale Rel c/s 11, Bamber Bridge (WE) 2/10, Droylsden (WE) 3/10, Ashton U (L) 8/10, Bamber Bridge (L) 1/11, Hyde FC (L) 3/11, Droylsden 7/11		
John	Hardiker		5'11"	11 01	07/07/1982	29	Preston	Morecambe, Stockport £150,000 1/02 Rel c/s 05, Bury 7/05, Morecambe (3ML) 10/05 Perm 1/06, Fleetwood 7/06, Forest Green (L) 11/06 Perm 12/06 Rel 3/09, Stalybridge 3/09, Droylsden 8/10	23	0
Andrew	Langford		5'11"	12 05	03/07/1988	23	Manchester	Morecambe Rel c/s 08, Leek T (L) 11/07, Workington 12/08 Rel 5/11, Droylsden 8/11		
Craig	Robinson				29/09/1982	28		Blackpool (Scholar), Morecambe, Vauxhall Motors 7/02, Droylsden 8/04 Rel 8/07, Hyde U 8/07, Vauxhall Motors 1/08, Ashton U 7/08, Droylsden 6/11		
James	Vaughan		5'10"	12 09	06/12/1986	24	Liverpool	Tranmere, Chester 1/06, Droylsden (L) 12/06, Wollongong Community (Aust) 4/09, Sydney FC (Aust), Gold Coast (Aust), Chester 8/09, Droylsden 10/09	29	0
MIDFIELDERS										
Paul	Brown		5'11"	12 00	10/09/1984	26	Liverpool	Tranmere Rel c/s 06, Accrington (L) 8/05, Barrow 7/06, Kingston City (Aus) 2/07, Barrow 8/07 Rel 5/09, Droylsden 6/09 Rel 3/10, Witton 3/10, Vauxhall Motors 3/10, Droylsden 8/11		
Michael	Connor				10/09/1989	21		Man City (Scholar), Sunday Football, Mossley 9/08, Salford C, Woodley Sports, Northwich 7/09, Droylsden 12/10	19	1
Dan	Gardner		6'01"	12 08	30/11/1989	21	Manchester	Celtic Rel 5/09, Flixton 7/09, Crewe 2/10 Rel c/s 10, Droylsden 8/10	31	1
Stephen	Hall							New Mills, Ashton U 11/10, Altrincham (Trial), Droylsden 8/11		
Andy	Kilheeney							Abbey Hey, Droylsden 7/11		
Lewis	Killeen		5'09"	10 07	23/09/1982	28	Peterborough	Sheff Utd Rel c/s 03, Halifax (3ML), Halifax 6/03, Crawley 5/08 Rel 5/10, Droylsden 7/10	35	1
Carlos	Logan		5'07"	11 00	07/11/1985	25	Wythenshawe	Man City Rel c/s 05, Chesterfield (SL) 3/05, Darlington 8/05 Rel c/s 07, Bradford C (L) 1/07, Altrincham 8/07 Rel 2/08, Drogheda U (Trial) 2/08, Flixton 3/08, Barrow 8/07 Rel 5/10, Hyde FC 8/10 Rel 9/10, AFC Telford 12/10, Northwich 1/11, Droylsden 3/11	4	0
Warren	Peyton		5'09"	11 03	13/12/1979	31	Manchester	Bolton, Rochdale 10/99 Rel c/s 00, Bury 9/00, Nuneaton 7/01, Doncaster 12/02, Leigh RMI 7/03 Rel c/s 05, Altrincham 11/05 Rel 5/09, Stalybridge 6/09, Guiseley 6/10 Rel c/s 11, Droylsden 7/11		
David	Poole		5'08"	12 00	12/11/1984	26	Manchester	Man Utd Rel c/s 05, Yeovil 6/05, Stockport (3ML) 9/06 Stockport £10,000 1/07, Darlington 7/08 Rel c/s 09, Stockport 8/09 Rel c/s 11, Droylsden 8/11		
FORWARDS										
Jordan	Gerrard				20/11/1990	20		Everton (Yth), Accrington (Yth), Leigh Genesis 8/10, Droylsden 8/11		
Dale	Johnson		6'00"	11 08	03/05/1985	26	Ashton	Woodley Sports, Hyde U 2/04, Droylsden (6WL) 3/08, Altrincham 6/08 Rel 9/10, Hyde FC 9/10, Altrincham 3/11 Rel c/s 11, Droylsden 7/11		
Steve	Jones		5'10"	10 05	25/10/1976	34	Derry, NI	Chadderton (Yth), Blackpool Rel c/s 96, Bury 7/96 Rel c/s 97, Sligo R 8/97, Bray W (L), Chorley, Leigh RMI c/s 99, Tranmere (Trial) 7/01, Crewe £75,000 7/01, Rochdale (2ML) 2/02, Burnley 6/06, Crewe (SL) 3/08, Huddersfield (5WL) 10/08, Bradford C (SL) 11/08, Walsall 7/09 Rel c/s 11, Motherwell (SL) 1/11, Droylsden 8/11		
Ciaren	Kilheeney		5'11"	11 09	09/01/1984	27	Stockport	Man City (Trainee), Mossley 1/03, Exeter 3/03, Droylsden 5/03, Radcliffe B 11/04, Ashton U 9/05, Burscough 9/06, Southport 6/08, Droylsden 7/10	37	20
Domaine	Rouse		5'06"	10 10	04/07/1989	22	Stretford	Bury Rel 9/09, Droylsden (L) 9/08, Fleetwood (SL) 3/09, Hyde U 3/10, Droylsden 8/10	25	3
Danny	Rowe							Preston (Yth), Man Utd (Yth) Undisc, Kendal T c/s 08, Fleetwood 12/10, Droylsden (L) 8/11		

EASTWOOD TOWN

Chairman: Michael Johnson
Secretary: Mrs Rachel Thornton **(T)** 07971 655 983 **(E)** rachel@eastwoodtownfc.co.uk
Additional Committee Members:
Jamie Brough, Liz Morley, Clare Hanson.

Manager: Craig Armstrong and Jamie Brough
Programme Editor: TBC **(E)**

Back Row (L-R): Jermaine Holis, Adam Muller, Jonathan D'Laryea, Lee Stevenson, Anton Foster, Ryan Handbury, Kieran Kenlock.
Middle Row: Unknown, Matt Rhead, David Haggerty, Ian Deakin, Mat Bailey, John Danby, Adrian Hawes, Russell Cooke, Andy Todd
Front Row: Sam Ralph(Coach), Lindon Meikle, Michael Simpson, Rachel Thornton(Secretary), Paul Cox (Manager), Richard Cooper(Assistant Manager), Sam Duncum, Paul Riley, Nick Taylor (Physio).

Club Factfile

Founded: 1953 **Nickname:** The Badgers
Previous Names: None
Previous Leagues: Notts Alliance 1953-61, Central Alliance 1961-67, East Midlands 1967-71, Midland Counties 1971-82, Northern Counties East 1982-87, 2003-04, Northern Premier 1987-2003, 04-09

Club Colours (change): Black & white stripes/white/black (All sky blue hoops)

Ground: Coronation Park, Eastwood, Notts NG16 3GL **(T)** 01773 711 819
Capacity: 5,500 **Seats:** 650 **Covered:** 1,150 **Clubhouse:** Yes **Shop:** Yes

Directions
M1 TRAVELLING SOUTH At junction 27, leave the motorway (A608) Heanor. At roundabout take 3rd exit A608. Past the Sandhills Tavern to a T- junction signposted Brinsley Heanor. Going through Brinsley will take you to Eastwood. At the lights turn left onto Nottingham Road. Look for the Fire Station on your right, then turn 1st right into Chewton Street. Ground is 150 metres on your right.
M1 TRAVELLING NORTH Exit junction 26. At roundabout take exit onto A610 Ripley. Leave the A610 at the first junction signed Ilkeston. Turn right at junction onto B6010, following the signs for Eastwood. Turn 1st left after the Man In Space pub into Chewton Street. Ground is 150 metres on your right.

Previous Grounds: Not known

Record Attendance: 2,723 v Enfield - FA Amateur Cup February 1965
Record Victory: 21-0 v Rufford Colliery - 1954-55
Record Defeat: 0-8 v Hucknall Town (A) - 2000-01
Record Goalscorer: Martin Wright - 147
Record Appearances: Arthur Rowley - 800+ with no bookings (1955-76)
Additional Records: Paid £500 to Gainsborough Trinity for Jamie Kay
Recieved £72,500 from Middlesbrough for Richard Liburd

Senior Honours: Midland League 1975-76. Northern Premier League Premier Division 2008-09
Notts Senior Cup x10

10 YEAR RECORD

01-02	02-03	03-04	04-05	05-06	06-07	07-08	08-09	09-10	10-11
NP 1 8	NP 1 21	NCEP 2	NP 1 6	NP 1 7	NP 1 3	NP P 4	NP P 1	Conf N 10	Conf N 4

EASTWOOD TOWN

No.	Date	Comp	H/A	Opponents	Att:	Result	Goalscorers	Pos
1	Sat-14-Aug	BSN	A	Droylsden	372	L 2-4	Meikle 8, Nightingale pen 90	19
2	Tue-17-Aug	BSN	H	Worcester City	477	L 2-4	Duncum 65, Rhead 70	20
3	Sat-21-Aug	BSN	H	Workington	404	L 0-2		20
4	Tue-24-Aug	BSN	A	Solihull Moors	265	L 0-2		20
5	Sat-28-Aug	BSN	H	Corby Town	432	W 2-1	Muller 20, Rhead 45	19
6	Mon-30-Aug	BSN	A	Boston United	1579	L 0-1		20
7	Sat-11-Sep	BSN	H	Gloucester City	358	L 1-2	Muller 33	20
8	Sat-18-Sep	BSN	H	Hinckley United	347	W 6-2	Stevenson 3 (23, 78, 85), Meikle 29, Simpson 41, Muller 67	17
9	Sat-02-Oct	BSN	A	Gainsborough Trinity	371	W 3-1	Stevenson 49, Og (Barnes) 73, Meikle 80	14
10	Sat-16-Oct	BSN	H	Blyth Spartans	483	L 0-2		15
11	Mon-25-Oct	BSN	A	Hyde FC	261	W 2-1	Muller 62, Stevenson 90	13
12	Sat-30-Oct	BSN	H	Guiseley	495	L 0-1		15
13	Tue-02-Nov	BSN	A	Harrogate Town	191	L 1-2	Matt Bailey 83	15
14	Sat-13-Nov	BSN	A	Nuneaton Town	891	L 1-2	Rhead 14	18
15	Tue-16-Nov	BSN	H	Gainsborough Trinity	316	W 2-0	Todd 33, Stevenson 47	15
16	Sat-01-Jan	BSN	A	Alfreton Town	914	D 2-2	Stevenson 41, Todd 66	17
17	Mon-03-Jan	BSN	H	Boston United	675	D 2-2	Stevenson 2 (13, 87)	15
18	Tue-25-Jan	BSN	A	Workington	291	W 3-0	Hawes 12, Stevenson 40, Foster 51	16
19	Sat-29-Jan	BSN	A	Corby Town	418	W 6-1	Stevenson 10, Hawes 44, Rhead 53, Knox 3 (80, 82, 90)	14
20	Sat-05-Feb	BSN	H	Vauxhall Motors	293	W 3-1	Stevenson 2 (6, 47), Rhead 61	13
21	Tue-08-Feb	BSN	A	Stalybridge Celtic	327	L 1-2	Knox 23	13
22	Sat-12-Feb	BSN	A	Blyth Spartans	502	D 0-0		14
23	Sat-26-Feb	BSN	A	Gloucester City	345	W 3-1	Rhead 26, Stevenson 33, Og (Morford) 72	14
24	Tue-01-Mar	BSN	H	Harrogate Town	263	W 2-0	Stevenson 2 (4, 18)	13
25	Sat-05-Mar	BSN	H	Nuneaton Town	566	W 2-1	Meikle 4, Rhead 87	12
26	Sat-12-Mar	BSN	H	Redditch United	343	W 2-1	Todd 8, Stevenson 90	11
27	Wed-16-Mar	BSN	A	Hinckley United	271	W 3-2	Rhead 2 (23, pen 60), Knox 57	10
28	Sat-19-Mar	BSN	A	Vauxhall Motors	177	W 2-1	Meikle 2 (56, 63)	9
29	Tue-22-Mar	BSN	A	AFC Telford	1689	D 2-2	Stevenson 8, Rhead 50	9
30	Sat-26-Mar	BSN	H	Stafford Rangers	389	W 3-0	Meikle 52, Stevenson 60, Knox 89	9
31	Wed-30-Mar	BSN	H	Hyde FC	354	W 1-0	Todd 88	8
32	Sat-02-Apr	BSN	H	AFC Telford	668	W 3-0	Cooke 24, Hawes 34, Stevenson 47	8
33	Wed-06-Apr	BSN	H	Droylsden	340	W 2-0	Meikle 33, Rhead 45	6
34	Sat-09-Apr	BSN	A	Redditch United	239	W 6-0	Haggerty 2, Stevenson 2 (9, 53), Og (Warmer) 43, Rhead 45, Foster 75	6
35	Tue-12-Apr	BSN	H	Alfreton Town	1112	W 4-2	Rhead 12, Simpson 30, Haggerty 48, Todd 81	5
36	Sat-16-Apr	BSN	H	Stalybridge Celtic	437	D 1-1	Hawes 48	6
37	Tue-19-Apr	BSN	A	Stafford Rangers	339	W 2-0	Og (Johnson) 15, Knox 90	5
38	Sat-23-Apr	BSN	A	Worcester City	509	D 1-1	Hawes 35	6
39	Mon-25-Apr	BSN	H	Solihull Moors	440	W 2-1	Meikle 25, Stevenson 40	4
40	Sat-30-Apr	BSN	A	Guiseley	557	D 2-2	Todd 4, Hawes 67	4
	Ilkeston record expunged 16/09							
7	Sat-04-Sep	BSN	A	Ilkeston Town	670	D 0-0		20
CUPS								
1	Sat-25-Sep	FAC 2Q	H	Stafford Rangers	347	D 1-1	Muller 29	
2	Tue-28-Sep	FAC 2QR	A	Stafford Rangers	429	W 3-1	Stevenson 2 (11, 83), Muller 13	
3	Sat-09-Oct	FAC 3Q	A	Matlock Town	655	W 3-0	Duncum 2, Muller 38, Stevenson 65	
4	Sat-23-Oct	FAC 4Q	A	Stalybridge Celtic	659	W 2-1	Stevenson 8, Meikle 84	
5	Sat-06-Nov	FAC 1	A	Swindon Supermarine	1159	L 1-2	Stevenson 47	
6	Sat-20-Nov	FAT 3Q	H	Cambridge City	246	W 2-0	Matt Bailey 16, Stevenson 80	
7	Sat-11-Dec	FAT 1	A	Rushden & Diamonds	657	D 1-1	Stevenson 47	
8	Sat-15-Jan	FAT 2	A	AFC Telford	1159	L 0-1		

League
Starts
Substitute
Unused Sub

Cups
Starts
Substitute
Unused Sub

Goals (Lg)
Goals (Cup)

DANBY	COOKE	RILEY	SIMPSON	HAGGERTY	HAWES	D'LARYEA	FOSTER	RHEAD	TODD	MEIKLE	NIGHTINGALE	DUNCUM	STEVENSON	MULLER	HOLLIS	MATT BAILEY	HANDBURY	LEONARD	MARKEL BAILEY	HURREN	LEE	PREECE	BEARDSLEY	SHAW	WARD	KNOX	NWADIKE
X	X	X	X	X	X	X	X	X	X	X	S	S	S	U	U												
X	X	X	X		X	X	S	X	S	X	U	X	X	U		X	S										
X	X	X	U		X	X	X	X	X	X	S	X	U	S			U	X									
X	X	X	S	X	U	X	X	X	X	X	U	X	S	S				X									
X	X	X	X	X		X	X	X	S	X	S	X	U	X					U								
X	X	X	X	X	U	U	X		S	X	S	X	X	X					X	S							
X	X	X	X	X	S	U	U			X	S	X	X	X		S			X	X							
X	S	U	X	X	U	X	U			X	S	X	X	X		X			X		X						
X	X	X	X	X	U	X	U	S	S	X		X	X	X					X	U							
X	X	X	X	X	U	X	U	S	S	X	U	X	X	X					X								
X	X		X	X	U	X	U	S	S	X		X	X	X		U			X				X				
X	X	X	X	X	U	X	S	S	X	X	U		X	X		S							X				
X	X	X	X	X		X	U	S	U	X		X	X	X		X			U				U				
X	X	U	X	X		U	X	X	X	S		U	X	X		X							U	X			
X	X	S	X	X		S	X	X	X	X	U	U	X	S		X								X			
X	X		X	X	U		X	X	X	X		U	X	U		X			U					X		U	
X	X		X	X	U	U	X	X	X	X		S	X	S		X								X		S	
X	X	X	X	X	X	S	X	X	X	X		U	X	S		U										S	
X	X	X	X	X	X	S	X	X	X	X		S	X	U		U										S	
X		X	X	X	X	U	X	X	X				X	S		X			U					S	U	X	
X		X	X	X	X	U	X	X	X	S			X	U		X			U					S		X	
X		X	X	X	X	U	X	X	X	X			X	S		X			U					U		S	
X	U	X	X	X	X	X		X	X	X			X	U		X			U					U		S	
X	U	X	X	X	X	X	S	X	X	S			X	U		X								S		X	
X	U	X	X	X	X	X	S	X	X	X			X	U		X								U		S	
X	U	X	X	X	X	X	U	X	X	X		S	X	S		X								U			
X	S	X	X	X	X	X	U	X	X	S		U	X	U		X										X	
X	U	U	X	X	X	X	U	X	X	X			X	S		X			U					X			
X	S	X	X	X	X	X	S	X	X	X			X	U		X			U					U			
X	X	X	X		X	X	S	X	X	X			X	U		X								U		S	S
X	X	X	X	U	X	X	S	X	X	X			X	S		X								U		S	
X	X	X	X	S	X	X	U	X	X	X			X	U		X								U		U	
X	X		X	U	X	X	U	X	X	X			X	U		X								X		S	U
X		U	X	X	X	X	S	X	X	X			X	U		X								X		S	S
X	U	U	X	X	X	X	S	X	X	X			X	S		X								X		U	
X	S	U	X	X	X	X	S	X	X	X			X	U		X								X		U	
X	X	U	X	X	X	X	U	X	X	X			X	U										X		S	S
X	X		X	X	X	X	S	X	X	S			X	U		U								X		X	S
X	U	X	X	X	X	X	U	X	X	X			X	U		X								U		U	
X	S	U	X	X	X	X	S	X	X	X			X	U		X								X		S	
X	X	X	X	X	U	U	U	X		X	U	X	S	X					X	X							
X	U	U	X	X	U	X	U		X	X	U	X	X	X					X			X					
X	U	X	X	X	U	X	U	U	S	X		X	X	X					X			X					
X	X	X	X	X	U	X	U	S	S	X		X	X	X					X	U							
X	X	X	X	X	U	X	U	U	S	X		X	X	X		U			X								
X	X	X	X	X	U	X	U	S	S	X		X	X	X		S			X				U				
X	X	U	X	X		U	X	X	X	X		U	X	S		X							U	X			
X	X	U	X	X		S	X	X	X	X	U		X	S		X								X	U		
X	U		X	X	X	U	X	X	X	U		S	X	X		X			U					X			
40	24	26	38	34	26	29	14	32	31	34	0	11	36	10	0	26	0	2	6	1	1	0	2	12	0	5	0
0	5	1	1	1	1	3	12	5	6	5	6	4	2	11	0	2	1	0	0	1	0	0	0	3	0	12	4
0	7	8	1	2	9	7	13	0	1	0	5	5	2	19	1	4	1	0	9	1	0	0	2	9	1	5	1
8	5	4	8	8	1	5	3	3	4	7	0	5	8	6	0	3	0	0	5	0	0	2	0	3	0	0	0
0	0	0	0	0	0	1	0	2	4	0	0	1	0	2	0	1	0	0	0	0	0	0	0	0	0	0	0
0	3	3	0	0	5	2	5	2	0	1	2	1	0	0	0	1	0	0	1	1	0	0	2	0	1	0	0
0	1	0	2	2	6	0	2	13	6	9	1	1	23	4	0	1	0	0	0	0	0	0	0	0	0	7	0
0	0	0	0	0	0	0	0	0	0	1	0	1	7	3	0	1	0	0	0	0	0	0	0	0	0	0	0

PLAYING SQUAD 2011/12

Existing Players		SN	HT	WT	DOB	AGE	POB	Career	Apps	Goals
GOALKEEPERS										
Ian	Deakin		6'00"	14 03	05/02/1987	24	Birmingham	Notts Forest, Eastwood T c/s 06 Rel c/s 10, Retford U (L) 10/09, Hinckley U 1/11, Eastwood T 6/11		
James	Severn		6'04"	14 11	10/10/1991	19	Nottingham	Derby, Tamworth (L) 10/10, Eastwood T (5ML) 8/11		
Jake	Want							Dunkirk FC, Eastwood T 8/11		
DEFENDERS										
Sam	Benjamin		6'01"		21/12/1991	19		Notts Forest (Scholar) Rel c/s 11, Eastwood T 6/11		
Gavin	Caines		6'01"	12 00	20/09/1983	27	Birmingham	Walsall Rel c/s 04, Stafford R (2ML) 12/03, Cheltenham 7/04 Rel c/s 09, Kidderminster 8/09, Luton (SL) 3/10, Forest Green 8/10 Rel 6/11, Eastwood T 8/11		
James	Cullingworth				18/09/1987	23	Nottingham	Notts Forest, Shepshed D 1/07, Hucknall 7/07 Rel 9/08, Stafford R 10/08, Gainsborough 12/08 Rel 5/09, Boston U 6/09 Rel 5/11, Eastwood T 6/11		
Aaron	Mitchell		6'05"	11 02	05/02/1990	21	Nottingham	Notts Forest Rel 1/10, Ilkeston (2ML) 10/09, Burton (Trial) 2/10, Hucknall 3/10, Tamworth 3/10, Eastwood T 6/11		
Alex	Troke							Calverton, Notts County (Scholar), Eastwood T 7/11		
MIDFIELDERS										
Craig	Armstrong		5'11"	12 09	23/05/1975	36	South Shields	Notts Forest, Burnley (3ML) 12/94, Bristol R (L) 1/96, Bristol R (SL) 3/96, Gillingham (2ML) 10/96, Watford (L) 1/97, Watford (6WL) 3/97, Huddersfield £750,000 2/99, Sheff Wed £100,000 2/02, Grimsby (2ML) 2/04, Bradford C 1/05 Rel c/s 05, Cheltenham 7/05 Rel c/s 07, Gillingham 7/07 Rel 1/08, Cheltenham 2/08 Rel 1/09, Burton (6WL) 11/08, Kidderminster 1/09 Rel 5/09, Mansfield 6/09 Rel 4/10, Forest Green (SL) 2/10, Forest Green (Pl/Coach) 6/10 Rel 5/11, Eastwood T (Jt Pl/Man) 5/11		
Josh	Burge				29/06/1990	21		Grimsby (Scholar) Rel c/s 08, Aston Villa (Trial) 1/07, Appalachian State University (USA) c/s 08, Ilkeston 6/09 Rel 9/10, Boston U 11/10 Rel 11/10, Rainworth MW 12/10, Hucknall 1/11, Eastwood T 6/11		
Daniel	Elliott		5'10"	11 02	18/09/1991	19		Notts Forest (Scholar) Rel c/s 10, Tamworth 9/10 Rel c/s 11, Hucknall 6/11, Eastwood T 8/11		
Jermaine	Hollis				07/10/1986	24		Hucknall, Rainworth MW, Eastwood T 8/10	0	0
Steven	Istead		5'08"	11 04	23/04/1986	25	South Shields	Newcastle (Yth), Hartlepool Rel c/s 06. Gateshead 7/06, Consett 1/07, Peterhead c/s 07, Ilkeston 6/08, Mansfield 6/09 Rel 5/11, Alfreton (6WL) 11/09, Eastwood T 6/11		
Lee	Morris		5'10"	11 07	30/04/1980	31	Blackpool	Sheff Utd, Derby £1.8 mill 10/99, Huddersfield (L) 3/01, Leicester £120,000 2/04 Rel 4/06, Bristol C (Trial) 5/06, Yeovil 8/06 Rel 3/08, Burton 8/08 Rel c/s 09, Hereford 7/09 Rel 4/10, Mansfield (5WL) 11/09, Forest Green (SL) 3/10, Bradford C (Trial) 7/10, Kidderminster 7/10, Eastwood T (Pl/Coach) 7/11		
Danny	Poole							Rolls Royce Leisure, Eastwood T 1/09, Rolls Royce Leisure, Carlton T 0/09, Hucknall 6/10, Eastwood T 6/11		
Paul	Riley		5'09"	10 07	29/09/1982	28	Nottingham	Notts County Rel c/s 04, Hucknall (Trial) c/s 04, Alfreton 9/04, Ilkeston 0/04 Rel 11/04, Matlock 11/04, Eastwood T 9/09	27	0
Jake	Sheridan		5'09"	11 06	08/07/1986	25	Nottingham	Notts County (Yth), Dunkirk, Notts County 8/05 Rel c/s 07, Tamworth 7/07, astwood T 7/11		
Curtis	Woodhouse		5'08"	11 00	17/04/1980	31	Driffield	Sheff Utd, Birmingham £1 million 2/01, Rotherham (3ML) 2/03, Peterborough 10/03, Hull C £25,000 5/05, Grimsby 1/06 Retired c/s 06, Pro Boxer, Rushden & D 11/06 Rel 1/07, Rushden & D 3/07, Mansfield 1/09, Harrogate T 6/09 Rel 2/10, Sheffield FC 2/10, Eastwood T 6/11		
FORWARDS										
Jason	Bradley		6'03"	13 00	16/03/1989	22	Sheffield	Sheff Wed Rel c/s 08, Buxton (L) 10/07, Darlington 7/08, Buxton (L) 9/08, Blyth (L) 11/08, Gainsborough (SL) 2/09, Mansfield 7/09 Rel 4/10, Newport (L) 8/09, Kings Lynn (L) 9/09, Harrogate T (SL) 12/09, Brackley T 6/10, Tamworth 1/11, Eastwood T 6/11		
Jevais	Christie				11/06/1992	19		Notts Forest (Yth), Arnold T c/s 09, Tamworth 1/11, Eastwood T 7/11		
Ben	Fairclough		5'06"	09 10	18/04/1989	22	Nottingham	Notts Forest (Scholar), Notts County 8/08 Rel c/s 10, Ilkeston (L) 8/09, Hinckley U 8/10, Eastwood T 6/11		
Jarrod	Westcarr							Dunkirk FC, Eastwood T 8/11		

FC HALIFAX TOWN

Chairman: David Bosmworth
Secretary: Hayley Horne **(T)** 01422 341 222 **(E)** hayleyhorne@halifaxafc.co.uk
Additional Committee Members:
D Paul Anderson, Bobby Ham, Stuart Peacock

Manager: Neil Aspin
Programme Editor: Greg Stainton **(E)** marketing@sandalbmw.net

Back Row: Dan Codman, Nicky Gray, James Riley, Phil Senior, Jonathan Hedge, Steve Payne, Paul Sykes, Sam Jerome

Middle Row: Trevor Storton Assistant Manager, James Dean, Mark Whitehouse, Luke Smith, Neil Ross, Ross Clegg, Alan Russell-Cox Physio, Kevin Gillespie Fitness Coach

Front Row: Richard Marshall, Aaron Hardy, Daniel Lowe, Ryan Crossley, Neil Aspin Manager, Tom Baker, Scott Phelan, Mark Peers, Mark Hotte

Club Factfile

Founded: 1911 **Nickname:** Shaymen
Previous Names: Halifax Town 1911-2008 then reformed as F.C. Halifax Town
Previous Leagues: Yorkshire Combination 1911-12, Midland 1912-21, Football League 1921-93, 98-2002, Conference 1993-98, 2002-08
Club Colours (change): All blue (White/black & white/black & white)

Ground: The Shay Stadium, Shay Syke, Halifax HX1 2YT **(T)** 01422 341 222
Capacity: 6,561 **Seats:** 2,330 **Covered:** 4,231 **Clubhouse:** Yes **Shop:** Yes

Directions
M62, junction 24, head towards Halifax on A629 and the Town Centre.
After 3-4 miles, ground is on the right (Shaw Hill) sign posted The Shay.

Previous Grounds: Sandhall Lane 1911-15, Exley 1919-20

Record Attendance: 36,885 v Tottenham Hotspur - FA Cup 5th Round 14/02/1953
Record Victory: 12-0 v West Vale Ramblers - FA Cup 1st Qualifying Road 1913-14
Record Defeat: 0-13 v Stockport County - Division 3 North 1933-34
Record Goalscorer: Albert Valentine
Record Appearances: John Pickering
Additional Records:

Senior Honours: Conference 1997-98. Northern Premier League Division 1 North 2009-10, Premier Division 2010-11.

10 YEAR RECORD

01-02		02-03		03-04		04-05		05-06		06-07		07-08		08-09		09-10		10-11	
FL 3	24	Conf	8	Conf	19	Conf	9	Conf	4	Conf	16	Conf	20	NP1N	8	NP1N	1	NP P	1

F.C. HALIFAX TOWN

No.	Date	Comp	H/A	Opponents	Att:	Result	Goalscorers	Pos
1	Aug-02	NPL P	H	Buxton	1756	W 2 - 1	Holland 13 Vardy 75	4
2	24		A	Frickley Athletic	748	D 0 - 0		
3	28		A	Chasetown	611	L 1 - 2	Taylor 20	11
4	30		H	Colwyn Bay	1561	D 1 - 1	Marshall 55	
5	Sept 4		A	Mickleover Sports	676	W 3 - 2	Holland 10 Vardy 26 70	
6	7		H	Northwich Victoria	1166	D 1 - 1	Holland 14	9
7	**11**	**FAC 1Q**	**H**	**Whitby Town**	**976**	**W 2 - 0**	**Metcalfe 73 Dean 77**	
8	18		H	Whitby Town	1271	W 5 - 1	DEAN 3 (22 54 84) Holland 46 61	6
9	22		A	Stocksbridge Park Steels	658	W 5 - 3	Holland 7 72 Dean 12 Metcalfe 50 Garner 90	
10	**25**	**FAC 2Q**	**A**	**Ashton United**	**525**	**W 2 - 1**	**Taylor 75 82**	
11	28		H	Hucknall Town	1191	W 4 - 0	Dean 49 56 Baker 68 (pen) Garner 90	
12	Oct 2		A	Ashton United	543	W 3 - 0	Holland 44 Dean 50 Baker 61 (pen)	1
13	5		A	Burscough	494	W 2 - 0	Garner 86 Bayliss 64 (og)	
14	**9**	**FAC 3Q**	**H**	**Harrogate Town**	**1835**	**W 4 - 0**	**Baker 31 (pen) Vardy 52 Taylor 81Holland 83**	
15	**16**	**FAT 1Q**	**A**	**Durham City**	**282**	**W 2 - 0**	**Gray 9 Dean 73**	
16	19		H	Bradford P.A.	2011	W 1 - 0	Holland 16	1
17	**23**	**FAC 4Q**	**H**	**Mansfield Town**	**2986**	**L 0 - 1**		
18	26		H	Burscough	1264	W 3 - 2	Marshall 24 Baker 60 (pen) Dean 65	
19	**30**	**FAT 2Q**	**A**	**Curzon Ashton**	**392**	**L 1 - 2**	**Vardy 70**	
20	Nov 6		A	Marine	726	W 6 - 0	Holland 7 Dean 13 87 Baker 57 (pen) Vardy 78 84	1
21	13		H	Retford United	1589	W 3 - 0	Vardy 2 5 Bower 39	1
22	16		A	Matlock Town	549	W 2 - 1	Dean 14 59	
23	20		H	North Ferriby United	1605	L 0 - 2		1
24	Dec 11		A	FC United	2805	W 1 - 0	Garner 53	1
25	Jan 1		H	F.C.United	4023	W 4 - 1	Vardy 41 Gregory 55 Marshall 89 Taylor 90	
26	3		A	Colwyn Bay	827	L 1 - 2	Phelan 27	
27	8		A	Northwich Victoria	676	W 3 - 0	Dean 15 Gregory 37 Baker 66	1
28	18		H	Ossett Town	1284	W 8 - 1	Dean 27 35 Gregory 42 65 Vardy 45 79 Phelan 51 Marshall 77	
29	24		A	Bradford P.A.	1325	W 3 - 1	Vardy 2 Dean 36 Baker 59 (pen)	1
30	29		A	North Ferriby United	743	W 3 - 0	Vardy 1 56 Gregory 45	1
31	Feb 12		A	Worksop Town	775	D 1 - 1	Baker 81 (pen)	1
32	15		H	Kendal Town	1232	W 3 - 0	Baker 32 (pen) Gregory 35 71	
33	22		A	Nantwich Town		W 6 - 0	Baker 54 GREGORY 3 (57 59 79) Vardy 65 Marshall 82	
34	March 1		H	Worksop Town	1318	D 0 - 0		
35	5		H	Ashton United	1648	W 1 - 0	Vardy 89	1
36	12		A	Buxton	803	L 1 - 2	Baker 69 (pen)	1
37	15		H	Stocksbridge P.S.	1073	W 5 - 1	HOLLAND 3 (21 24 74) Baker 61(pen) Vardy 84	
38	19		A	Hucknall Town	527	W 2 - 1	Gregory 14 85	1
39	22		H	Chasetown	1343	W 3 - 2	VARDY 3 (84 89 90)	
40	26		A	Kendal Town	891	W 4 - 2	Lowe 16 VARDY 3 (51 81 86)	1
41	29		H	Nantwich Town	1346	W 3 - 1	Vardy 33 81 Hogan 73	
42	April 2		H	Matlock Town	2132	D 2 - 2	Gregory 3 31	1
43	9		A	Retford United	829	W 2 - 0	Holland 23 Hogan 43	1
44	13		A	Whitby Town	491	W 5 - 1	Gregory 27 Holland 34 Phelan 40 85 Baker 63 (Pen)	Champions
45	16		H	Marine	1844	W 1 - 0	Holland 70	1
46	19		H	Frickley Athletic	1106	W 3 - 1	Gregory 18 Holland 20 Baker 66	
47	23		H	Mickleover Sports	2404	D 1 - 1	Holland 74	1
48	25		A	Ossett Town	890	D 0 - 0		1

PLAYING SQUAD 2011/12

Existing Players		SN	HT	WT	DOB	AGE	POB	Career	Apps	Goals
GOALKEEPERS										
Simon	Eastwood		6'02"	13 13	24/07/1989	22	Luton	Huddersfield, Woking (3ML) 11/08 (08/09 12,0), Bradford C (5ML) 7/09, Oxford U 6/10 Rel c/s 11, FC Halifax 6/11		
Phil	Senior		5'11"	10 12	30/10/1982	28	Huddersfield	Huddersfield Rel 5/06, Northwich 6/06, Droylsden 6/07, Alfreton 12/07, Ilkeston 2/08, FC Halifax 7/08		
DEFENDERS										
Gregg	Anderson				01/11/1984	26		Tadcaster A, Clitheroe 3/06, Buxton 4 Fig 10/07, FC Halifax 7/11		
Simon	Garner		5'10"	11 07	15/08/1982	29		Blackburn (Yth), Accrington, Great Harwood, Clitheroe c/s 02, Kendal T, Prescot Cables 1/04, Hyde U 5/05, Clitheroe 8/05, Stalybridge 6/07, Fleetwood 6/08 Rel 9/08, FCUM 9/08, Clitheroe 2/10, FC Halifax 5/10		
David	Haggerty		6'04"	13 01	28/03/1991	20	Sheffield	Rotherham Rel c/s 10, Sheffield FC (L) 11/08, Ilkeston (WE) 1/09, Eastwood T 8/10, FC Halifax 5/11		
Aaron	Hardy		5'08"	11 04	26/05/1986	25	South Emsall	Huddersfield Rel c/s 08, Harrogate T 7/08, FC Halifax 7/09		
Liam	Hogan		6'00"	12 00	08/02/1989	22		Irlam FC, Flixton, Woodley Sports 3/08, FC Halifax 5/10		
Danny	Lowe		5'11"	12 00	12/01/1984	27	Barnsley	Northampton Rel c/s 03, Harrogate T 7/03, Harrogate RA (L) 8/03, Liversedge, Harrogate RA 12/06, Harrogate T 3/08 Rel c/s 09, FC Halifax 8/09		
Scott	McManus		6'00"	11 00	28/05/1989	22	Prestwich	Man Utd (Yth), Prestwich Heys, Ashton U (Trial) 10/07, Curzon Ashton c/s 08, Notts Forest (Trial) 7/08, Crewe Undisc 8/08 Rel 12/09, Curzon Ashton (2ML) 9/09, FCUM c/s 10, FC Halifax 5/11		
MIDFIELDERS										
Tom	Baker		5'06"	11 00	28/03/1985	26	Salford	Barnsley Rel c/s 05, Gainsborough 7/05, Scarborough 1/06 Rel 5/06, Bradford PA c/s 06, FC Halifax 10/08		
Anton	Foster				25/06/1982	29		Ilkeston, Alfreton (L) (00/01), Eastwood (L) 1/03, Gedling T c/s 03, Belper 7/04, Sheffield FC 8/05, Buxton 10/05, Eastwood T £10,000 7/08, FC Halifax 7/11		
Nicky	Gray		6'02"	12 07	17/10/1985	25	Harrogate	Leeds, Halifax 9/06, Harrogate T 6/08, FC Halifax 7/09		
Scott	Hogan				13/04/1992	19		Rochdale, Woodley Sports c/s 10, FC Halifax 11/10, Woodley Sports (L) 11/10, Mossley (Dual) 8/11		
Liam	Needham		5'11"	12 02	19/10/1985	25	Sheffield	Sheff Wed Rel c/s 05, Notts County (Trial) 8/05, Gainsborough 8/05, Notts County 11/05 Rel 12/06, Gainsborough (L) 11/06, Gainsborough 12/06 Rel 5/09, Guiseley c/s 09, FC Halifax 6/11		
Ryan	Toulson				18/11/1985	25		Halifax, Stocksbridge (L) 9/05, Altrincham (SL) 1/08, Harrogate T 6/08, Gainsborough 5/09, Guiseley 5/10 Rel c/s 11, FC Halifax 7/11		
Harry	Winter		6'01"	12 00	16/06/1989	22		Trafford, Northwich 7/09, Salford C (L) 12/09, FC Halifax (L) 1/10, FC Halifax 7/10		
FORWARDS										
James	Dean		6'03"	13 07	15/05/1986	25	Blackburn	Great Harwood, Clitheroe c/s 06, Northwich 1/07, Halifax (Trial) 7/07, Bridlington T 7/07, Bury 8/07 Rel 2/08, Altrincham (L) 10/07, Stalybridge (L) 11/07, Stalybridge (L) 1/08, Stalybridge 2/08, Hyde U 6/08, Harrogate T 9/08, FC Halifax 7/09		
Lee	Gregory				26/08/1988	23	Sheffield	Sheff Utd (Scholar), Staveley MW, Mansfield 9/09, Glapwell (3ML) 9/09, Harrogate T (3ML) 12/09, FC Halifax (L) 3/10, FC Halifax 12/10 Danny		
Holland				18/02/1983 28			Mansfield	Sheff Utd (Yth), Chesterfield (Yth), Staveley MW, Matlock 8/02, Grimsby (Trial) 7/04, Hucknall 8/04, Harrogate T (L) 11/04 Perm 12/04, Eastwood T Undisc 2/09, FC Halifax 7/10		
Jamie	Vardy		5'10"		11/01/1987	24	Sheffield	Stocksbridge PS, FC Halifax 5/10		

Caught in action....

Harrogate Town players close in on Alfreton's Chris Hall during this Blue Square North match.

Photo by Bill Wheatcroft

GAINSBOROUGH TRINITY

Chairman: Peter Swann
Secretary: Peter Wallace (T) 07841 163 110 (E) petewallace@aol.com
Additional Committee Members:
Karin Swann, Geoff Holmes

Manager: Brian Little
Programme Editor: Nicky Hodgson (E) nicky@the-sands.co.uk

Club Factfile

Founded: 1873 **Nickname:** The Blues
Previous Names: None
Previous Leagues: Midland Counties 1889-96, 1912-60, 61-68, Football League 1896-1912, Central Alliance 1960-61, Northern Premier 1968-2004
Club Colours (change): All blue (All yellow)

Ground: The Northolme, Gainsborough, Lincolnshire DN21 2QW **(T)** 01427 613 295 (office) 613 688 (Social C)
Capacity: 4,340 **Seats:** 504 **Covered:** 2,500 **Clubhouse:** Yes **Shop:** Yes

Directions
The Northolme is situated on the A159, Gainsborough to Scunthorpe road, approximately a third of a mile north of the Town Centre. Public Car Park on the right 150 yards before the Ground. Any person parked illegally in the Streets around the Ground will be issued with a ticket from the Police.

Previous Grounds: Not known

Record Attendance: 9,760 v Scunthorpe United - Midland League 1948
Record Victory: 7-0 v Fleetwood Town and v Great Harwood Town
Record Defeat: 1-7 v Stalybridge Celtic - Northern Premier 2000-01 and v Brentford - FA Cup 03-04.
Record Goalscorer: Not known
Record Appearances: Not known
Additional Records: Paid £3,000 to Buxton for Stuart Lowe
Received £30,000 from Lincoln City for Tony James

Senior Honours: Midland Counties League 1890-91, 1927-28, 48-49, 66-67
Lincolnshire Senior Cup x12

10 YEAR RECORD

01-02	02-03	03-04	04-05	05-06	06-07	07-08	08-09	09-10	10-11
NP P 19	NP P 15	NP P 10	Conf N 11	Conf N 16	Conf N 12	Conf N 11	Conf N 13	Conf N 14	Conf N 18

GAINSBOROUGH TRINITY

No.	Date	Comp	H/A	Opponents	Att:	Result	Goalscorers	Pos
1	Sat-14-Aug	BSN	A	Worcester City	750	W 2-1	Louis 2, Aiston 21	6
2	Tue-17-Aug	BSN	H	Guiseley	400	L 1-3	Mettam 14	14
3	Sat-21-Aug	BSN	H	AFC Telford	470	L 0-5		17
4	Tue-24-Aug	BSN	A	Alfreton Town	542	L 1-2	Mettam 47	18
5	Sat-28-Aug	BSN	H	Workington	362	D 1-1	Milne 88	17
6	Sat-04-Sep	BSN	A	Stalybridge Celtic	414	L 0-2		15
7	Sat-11-Sep	BSN	H	Droylsden	297	L 0-3		16
8	Sat-18-Sep	BSN	A	Stafford Rangers	402	L 1-3	Beckett 17	19
9	Sat-02-Oct	BSN	H	Eastwood Town	371	L 1-3	Peat 20	21
10	Sat-09-Oct	BSN	A	Blyth Spartans	427	W 3-1	Kendall 2 (39, 67), McMahon 55	19
11	Sat-16-Oct	BSN	A	Corby Town	443	L 1-3	Cowan 9	19
12	Sat-30-Oct	BSN	A	Gloucester City	360	W 2-0	Cowan 4, Kendall 57	17
13	Sat-06-Nov	BSN	H	Redditch United	372	W 3-0	Kendall 3 (7, 70, 84)	16
14	Sat-13-Nov	BSN	A	Hyde FC	235	D 1-1	Mettam 52	16
15	Tue-16-Nov	BSN	A	Eastwood Town	316	L 0-2		17
16	Sat-01-Jan	BSN	A	Boston United	1559	W 3-1	Aiston 20, Kendall 2 (60, 72)	15
17	Sat-08-Jan	BSN	A	Vauxhall Motors	206	L 0-1		16
18	Tue-11-Jan	BSN	H	Vauxhall Motors	222	D 1-1	Beckett pen 62	15
19	Sat-15-Jan	BSN	A	Redditch United	163	W 4-1	Beckett 2 (10, 21), Boyce 56, Kendall 81	13
20	Tue-18-Jan	BSN	H	Nuneaton Town	423	L 1-2	Mettam 59	14
21	Sat-22-Jan	BSN	H	Solihull Moors	353	D 1-1	Kendall 75	14
22	Tue-25-Jan	BSN	H	Blyth Spartans	264	L 0-2		15
23	Sat-29-Jan	BSN	A	Hinckley United	461	L 1-3	Greaves 18	17
24	Sat-05-Feb	BSN	A	Workington	273	L 2-4	Mettam 2 (14, 90)	17
25	Tue-08-Feb	BSN	H	Boston United	648	L 0-3		18
26	Sat-12-Feb	BSN	H	Harrogate Town	321	L 1-3	Kendall 6	19
27	Sat-19-Feb	BSN	H	Stafford Rangers	436	D 2-2	McMahon pen 43, Peat 52	18
28	Tue-22-Feb	BSN	H	Gloucester City	253	W 2-0	Mettam 64, Kendall 90	18
29	Sat-26-Feb	BSN	A	Droylsden	272	W 3-1	McMahon 53, Mettam 54, Mayo 84	17
30	Sat-05-Mar	BSN	H	Stalybridge Celtic	354	L 1-3	Cowan 71	18
31	Tue-08-Mar	BSN	A	AFC Telford	1408	L 1-2	Cowan 31	18
32	Sat-12-Mar	BSN	A	Harrogate Town	266	L 1-3	Kendall 49	18
33	Sat-19-Mar	BSN	H	Hinckley United	345	L 0-1		18
34	Sat-26-Mar	BSN	H	Worcester City	309	L 0-2		18
35	Sat-02-Apr	BSN	H	Hyde FC	394	W 2-1	Kendall 75, Boyce 77	18
36	Sat-09-Apr	BSN	A	Nuneaton Town	902	W 2-1	Mettam 23, Kendall 61	18
37	Sat-16-Apr	BSN	H	Corby Town	375	W 3-1	Waterfall 61, Mettam 63, Robinson 67	18
38	Sat-23-Apr	BSN	A	Guiseley	412	L 0-2		18
39	Mon-25-Apr	BSN	H	Alfreton Town	474	L 0-3		18
40	Sat-30-Apr	BSN	A	Solihull Moors	235	W 2-0	McMahon 50, R Williams 90	18
	Ilkeston Record Expunged 16/09							
6	Mon-30-Aug	BSN	A	Ilkeston Town	361	W 5-2	Mettam 2 (3, 55), Waterfall 2 (29, 41), Louis 57	13
CUPS								
1	Sat-25-Sep	FAC 2Q	A	FC United of Manchester	1037	L 1-2	McMahon pen 40	
2	Sat-20-Nov	FAT 3Q	A	Boston United	1136	L 1-2	Cowan 74	

League
Starts
Substitute
Unused Sub

Cups
Starts
Substitute
Unused Sub

Goals (Lg)
Goals (Cup)

BARNES	CLARKE	GREAVES	MAYO	BOYCE	WATERFALL	AISTON	HIBBERT	LOUIS	METTAM	PEAT	BECKETT	MCMAHON	SPAFFORD	FROST	WARD	HUME	DAVIES	MILNE	D WILLIAMS	KENDALL	ROBINSON	COWAN	R WILLIAMS
X	X	X	X	X	X	X	X	X	X	X	S	S	U	U	U								
X	X	U	X	X	X	X	X	X	X	X	S	X	U	U	U								
X	X	X	X	U	X	X	X	X	X	X		S	S	S	U	X							
X	X	X	X	X	X	X	X	X	X	U		U	U	S		X	S						
X	X	U	X	X	X		X	X	X	U		S	U	X		X	S	X					
X	X	U	X	X	X	X	X	X	X	U		X	U			S	S	X					
X	S	S	X		X	X	X	X	X	U	X	U	U			X	X	X					
X	U	X	X		X	X	U	S	X	X	X	X	U			X	S	X					
X	S	X	S	S	X	X		X		X		X				U	U		X	X	X	X	
X	X	X	U	U	X	X				S		X				S	S		X	X	X	X	X
X	X	X	U	X		X			S	S		X				S	U		X	X	X	X	X
X	U	S	S	X	X	X	X			U		X				U			X	X	X	X	X
X	U	U	U	X	X	X	X		S	S		X							X	X	X	X	X
X	S	X	U	X	X	X			X	S	U						U		X	X	X	X	X
X	U	U	S	X	X	X	X		S	S		X							X	X	X	X	X
X	U		X	X	X	X	X		S	X	U	X					S		X	X	S	X	
X	X	U	X	X	X	X			S	X	S	X					U		X	X	U	X	
X	X	X	U	X	X	X			X	X	X	S					S		U	S	X	X	
X	U	U	U	X	X	X			S	X	X	X					S		X	X	X	X	
X	U	S	U	X	X	X			S	X	X	X					U		X	X	X	X	
X	S	X	S	S	X	X			X	X	U	X					U		X	X	X	X	
X	X		X	X	X		S		S	U	X	X			S		U		X	X	X	X	
		X	U	S	X	X	X		S	X	U	X			X		S		X	X	X	X	
		S	U	X	X	X	X		X	X	S	X	U		X		U		X	X		X	
	U	U	U	X	X	S			X	X	U	X	X		X		X			X		X	X
	U	S	U	X	X	S			X	X	S	X	X		X		X			X		X	X
X		S	X	X	X	S			X	X	U	X	U		U		X			X		X	X
X	U	S	X	X	X	U			X	X	U	X	S				X			X		X	X
X	U	S	X	X		S	U		X	X	U	X	X				X			X		X	X
X	U	X		X		U	U		X	X	S	X	X		U		X			X		X	X
X	U	U	X	X	U	X			S	X	U	X	X				X			X		X	X
X	S	S	X	X	S	X			X	X			X		U		X			X		X	X
X	U	S		X	X	U			X	X			X		U		X		U	X	X	X	X
X	U	X	X	X	X	U			X	X			X				S		U	X	U	X	X
X		S	X	X	X	S			X	X		X	X				U		U	X	U	X	X
X		S	X	X	X	S			X	X		X	X				U		U	X	S	X	X
X	U	S	X		X	S			X	X		X	X				X		U	X	S	X	X
X	S	X	S		X	U			X	X		X	X				U		U	X	X	X	X
X	U	X	S		X	S			X	X		X	X		U		U		X	X	X		X
X	U	X	S		X	S			X	X		X			U		S		X	X	X	X	X
X	X	S	X	X	X	X	X	X	X	U		X	U	S			S	X					
X	X	X	U	U	X	X	S	X		X	X	X	U		U	X	S		X	S			
X	U		X	X	X	X	X		S	X	S	X					S		X	X	U	X	
36	11	16	20	29	35	24	13	8	27	29	6	30	13	1	4	5	11	4	17	31	17	31	22
0	6	13	7	3	1	9	1	1	10	5	6	4	2	2	1	3	11	0	0	1	3	0	0
0	18	9	11	2	1	5	3	0	0	6	9	2	9	2	9	2	12	0	7	0	3	0	0
2	1	1	1	1	2	2	1	1	0	2	1	2	0	0	0	1	0	0	2	1	0	1	0
0	0	0	0	0	0	0	1	0	1	0	1	0	0	0	0	0	2	0	0	1	0	0	0
0	1	0	1	1	0	0	0	0	0	0	0	0	1	0	1	0	0	0	0	0	1	0	0
0	0	1	1	2	1	2	0	1	10	2	4	4	0	0	0	0	0	1	0	15	1	4	1
0	0	0	0	0	0	0	0	0	0	0	0	1	0	0	0	0	0	0	0	0	0	1	0

PLAYING SQUAD 2011/12

Existing Players		SN	HT	WT	DOB	AGE	POB	Career	Apps	Goals
GOALKEEPERS										
Phil	Barnes		6'01"	11 01	02/03/1979	32	Sheffield	Rotherham, Blackpool £100,000 7/97 Rel c/s 04, Sheff Utd 7/04, Torquay (L) 2/05, QPR (L) 2/06, Grimsby Undisc 6/06 Rel 3/09, Gainsborough 4/09	36	0
Andrew	Pettinger		6'00"	12 02	21/04/1984	27	Scunthorpe	Scunthorpe (Yth), Everton £45,000 4/00, Grimsby 12/02 Rel c/s 04, Ossett T c/s 04, Armthorpe Wel c/s 05, Oldham (Trial), Brigg T 10/09, Gainsborough 6/11		
Gavin	Ward		6'03"	14 12	30/06/1970	41	Sutton Coldfield	Aston Villa (Trainee), Shrewsbury 9/88 Rel c/s 89, West Brom 9/89, Cardiff C 10/89, Leicester £175,000 7/93, Bradford C £175,000 7/95, Bolton £300,000 3/96, Burnley (3ML) 6/98, Stoke 2/99 Rel c/s 02, Wigan (Trial) 7/02, Walsall 8/02 Rel c/s 03, Coventry C 8/03 Rel c/s 04, Barnsley (L) 4/04, Preston 8/04 Rel c/s 06, Tranmere 7/06, Chester 7/07, Wrexham 1/08 Rel 4/09, Hednesford 7/09, Gainsborough (Pl/Ass Man) 12/09 Retired c/s 11	5	0
DEFENDERS										
Andrew	Boyce				05/11/1989	21		Doncaster Rel c/s 09, Worksop (WE) 3/08, Worksop (SL) 8/08, Mansfield (Trial) 4/09, Kings Lynn 7/09, Gainsborough 12/09	32	2
Rory	Coleman		6'00"	11 09	22/12/1990	20	Rotherham	Scunthorpe Rel c/s 11, Harrogate T (3ML) 8/09, Ilkeston (SL) 1/10, Boston U (L) 11/10, Boston U (L) 1/11, Gainsborough 6/11		
Gavin	Cowan		6'04"	14 04	24/05/1981	30	Hanover(Ger)	Exeter (Trainee), Braintree 7/99, Canvey Island 12/02, Nuneaton (L) 12/04, Nuneaton (L) 2/05, Shrewsbury £5,000 + 3/05, Kidderminster (L) 8/06, Grays 1/07 Rel 6/07, Nuneaton (L) 3/07, Nuneaton 6/07, AFC Telford 5/08 Rel 1/10, Fleetwood 1/10, Gainsborough 3/10	31	4
Mark	Gray				19/12/1991	19	Grimsby	Grimsby Rel 4/11, Spalding U (WE) 12/09, Spalding U (2ML) 10/10, Gainsborough 6/11		
Dominic	Roma		5'10"	11 11	29/11/1985	25	Sheffield	Sheff Utd Rel c/s 07, Boston U (L) 2/05, Notts County (Trial) 7/05, Tamworth (SL) 2/06, Hinckley U 7/07, Alfreton 5/09, Harrogate T 6/10, Gainsborough 5/11		
Kevin	Sandwith		5'11"	13 06	30/04/1978	33	Workington	Carlisle, Barrow 9/98, Telford 2/99, Doncaster 5/01 Rel 9/02, Halifax 11/02, Lincoln C 3/04, Macclesfield 7/05, Swansea (Trial) 11/05, Chester 6/06 Rel c/s 08, Weymouth 7/08 Rel 2/09, Oxford U 2/09, Mansfield 5/10 Rel 5/11, Gainsborough 8/11		
Luke	Waterfall		6'02"	12 11	30/07/1990	21	Sheffield	Barnsley (Scholar), Tranmere 7/08 Rel c/s 09, Altrincham (L) 10/08, Oxford U (Trial) 7/09, York C (Trial) 7/09, Ilkeston 8/09, Gainsborough 5/10	36	1
Jonathan	Williams				26/03/1992	19		Scunthorpe Rel c/s 11, Boston U (L) 11/10, Brigg T (L) 3/11, Gainsborough 5/11		
MIDFIELDERS										
Shane	Clarke		6'01"	13 03	07/11/1987	23	Lincoln	Lincoln C Rel 8/10, Stamford (WE) 1/06, Gateshead 10/10 Rel 11/10, Boston U 11/10, Chicago Fire (USA) (Trial) 2/11, Gainsborough 6/11		
Jonathan	D'Laryea		5'10"	12 02	03/09/1985	25	Manchester	Man City, Mansfield (3ML) 10/05, Mansfield 1/06, Northwich (3ML) 8/09 Perm 11/09, Eastwood T Undisc 2/10, Gainsborough 6/11		
Michael	Leary		5'11"	12 03	17/04/1983	28	Ealing	Luton Rel c/s 07, Bristol R (3ML) 8/05, Walsall (SL) 1/06, Torquay (L) 11/06, Brentford (SL) 1/07, Barnet 7/07 Rel c/s 09, Grimsby 7/09 Rel 5/11, Gainsborough 7/11		
Lewis	McMahon		5'09"	10 10	02/05/1985	26	Doncaster	Sheff Wed, Notts County 7/05 Rel c/s 06, York C 8/06 Rel 5/07, Gainsborough 7/07	34	4
Craig	Nelthorpe		5'10"	11 00	10/06/1987	24	Doncaster	Doncaster Rel 1/09, Hucknall (L) 12/05, Kidderminster (L) 10/06, Gateshead (2ML/Dual) 11/06, Halifax (L) 1/08, Darlington (SL) 3/08, Gateshead (3ML) 8/08, Oxford U 1/09, York C 5/09 Rel 5/10, Barrow (7WL) 11/09, Luton (SL) 1/10, Gateshead 6/10 Rel 5/11, Gainsborough 6/11		
Ryan	Williams		5'04"	11 02	31/08/1978	33	Chesterfield	Mansfield, Tranmere £70,000 + 8/97, Chesterfield (3ML) 11/99 £80,000 2/00, Hull C £150,000 7/01, Bristol R (2ML) 10/03 Perm 12/03, Forest Green (2ML) 12/04, Aldershot (L) 8/05, Aldershot 1/06 Rel 4/08, Weymouth 5/08 Rel 2/09, Mansfield 2/09 Rel 1/11, Gainsborough (2ML) 10/10, Gainsborough 1/11	22	1
Jamie	Yates		5'07"	10 11	24/12/1988	22	Sheffield	Rotherham Rel 5/09, Burton (3ML) 1/09, Kettering 7/09 Rel 9/09, Retford U 9/09, Alfreton 9/09, Boston U (2ML) 9/09 Perm 11/09, Gainsborough 5/11		
FORWARDS										
Daryl	Clare		5'09"	11 00	01/08/1978	33	Jersey	Grimsby Rel c/s 01, Northampton (3ML) 11/99, Northampton (L) 11/00, Cheltenham (L) 12/00, Boston U 7/01, Chester £25,000 10/02, Boston U Undisc 11/04, Crawley 8/05 £60,000, Burton 3/06, Rushden & D 5/08, Mansfield (SL) 3/09, Mansfield 5/09, Gateshead (3ML) 10/09 Perm 1/10, Cambridge U £10,000 6/10, Alfreton (SL) 2/11, Gainsborough (L) 8/11		
Ryan	Kendall		6'01"	12 08	14/09/1989	21	Hull	Hull C Rel c/s 10, Bradford C (SL) 3/10, Harrogate T 8/10, Gainsborough 9/10	32	15
Leon	Mettam		5'09"	11 01	09/12/1986	24	Lincoln	Lincoln C Rel c/s 07, Stamford 6/07, Corby T Undisc 2/08, Gainsborough 5/10	37	10
Ryan	Paczkowski				02/02/1990	21	Doncaster	Haworth Coll, Winterton R, Brigg T c/s 10, Gainsborough 6/11		
Darryn	Stamp		6'01"	11 10	21/09/1978	32	Beverley	Hessle, Scunthorpe 7/97 Rel c/s 01, Halifax (L) 2/00, Scarborough (L) 3/01, Scarborough 5/01, Northampton £30,000 5/02, Chester 8/03, Kidderminster (L) 11/04, Stevenage 1/05, York C (3ML) 10/06, Halifax 1/07, Northwich (SL) 3/08, Northwich 8/08, Gateshead (SL) 3/09, Gainsborough 6/09 Rel c/s 10, Guiseley 7/10, Gainsborough 6/11		
Owain	Warlow		6'00"	12 00	03/07/1988	23	Pontypridd	Lincoln C Rel 5/09, Kettering (L) 8/08, Llanelli 6/09 Rel 3/11, Gainsborough 8/11		

GLOUCESTER CITY

Chairman: Nigel Hughes
Secretary: Shaun Wetson **(T)** 07813 931 781 **(E)** swgcfc@gmail.com
Additional Committee Members:
John Print, Mike Dunstan, Eamonn McGurk.

Manager: David Mehew
Programme Editor: Mike Dunstan **(E)** mikedunstan@blueyonder.co.uk

Club Factfile

Founded: 1889 **Nickname:** The Tigers
Previous Names: Gloucester Y.M.C.A.
Previous Leagues: Bristol & District (now Western) 1893-96, Gloucester & Dist. 1897-1907, North Gloucestershire 1907-10, Gloucestershire North Senior 1920-34, Birmingham Combination 1935-39, Southern 1939-2000

Club Colours (change): Yellow & black/black/black (Sky blue/navy blue/sky blue)

Ground: Cheltenham Tn FC, The Abbey Business Stad., Whaddon Rd GL52 5NA **(T)** 01242 573558 (Cheltenham Town No.)
Capacity: 7,289 **Seats:** Yes **Covered:** Yes **Clubhouse:** Yes **Shop:** Yes

Directions
From the North (M5) leave at Jnctn 10, follow road A4019) towards Cheltenham, keep going straight through traffic lights until you reach a roundabout, PC World will be on your left and McDonalds on your right. Turn left here, after 500 yards you will then come to a double roundabout, go straight over, keep going for another 300 yards then turn right into Swindon Lane, follow the road over the level crossing and 2 mini roundabouts until you come to a large roundabout, go straight over, signposted Prestbury, continue past Racecourse and turn right into Albert Road, follow this to the end then turn left at roundabout into Prestbury Road, 200yards turn into Whaddon Rd.

Previous Grounds: Longlevens 1935-65, Horton Road 1965-86, Meadow Park 1986-2007, Corinium Stadium Cirencester 2007-10

Record Attendance: Longlevens: 10,500 v Tottenham - Friendly 1952. Meadow Park: 4,000 v Dagenham & Red. - FAT 3rd Q Rnd 12/04/97
Record Victory: 10-1 v Sudbury Town (H) - FA Cup 3rd Qualifying Round 17/10/98
Record Defeat: 1-12 v Gillingham - 09/11/46
Record Goalscorer: Reg Weaver - 250 (1930s)
Record Appearances: Stan Myers & Frank Tredgett - (1950s)
Additional Records: Paid £25,000 to Worcester City for Steve Ferguson 1990-91
Received £25,000 from AFC Bournemouth for Ian Hedges 1990

Senior Honours: Southern League Cup 1955-56, Midland Division 1988-89, Premier Division Play-off 2008-09.
Gloucestershire Senior Cup x19

10 YEAR RECORD

01-02	02-03	03-04	04-05	05-06	06-07	07-08	08-09	09-10	10-11
SthW 14	SthW 5	SthW 2	SthP 15	SthP 13	SthP 10	SthP 6	SthP 3	Conf N 18	Conf N 14

GLOUCESTER CITY

No.	Date	Comp	H/A	Opponents	Att:	Result	Goalscorers	Pos
1	Sat-14-Aug	BSN	A	Workington	523	L 1-2	Richards 87	12
2	Tue-17-Aug	BSN	H	Corby Town	386	L 0-2		16
3	Tue-24-Aug	BSN	A	AFC Telford	1906	L 0-2		17
4	Sat-28-Aug	BSN	A	Solihull Moors	263	L 1-2	Mullings 88	18
5	Mon-30-Aug	BSN	H	Redditch United	465	W 5-0	Tambling 10, Mullings 2 (55, 86), Symons 2 (59, pen 78)	14
6	Sat-04-Sep	BSN	H	Hyde FC	401	W 1-0	Symons 50	11
7	Sat-11-Sep	BSN	A	Eastwood Town	358	W 2-1	Mullings 29, Morford 50	8
8	Sat-18-Sep	BSN	H	Guiseley	380	L 1-2	Morford 51	13
9	Sat-02-Oct	BSN	H	Droylsden	304	D 1-1	Coupe 86	12
10	Sat-16-Oct	BSN	H	Harrogate Town	325	W 3-2	Smith pen 20, Barnes 24, Davies 26	11
11	Sat-23-Oct	BSN	A	Stafford Rangers	599	W 2-0	Symons 4, Barnes 89	9
12	Sat-30-Oct	BSN	H	Gainsborough Trinity	360	L 0-2		11
13	Sat-13-Nov	BSN	H	Blyth Spartans	305	L 1-2	Smith pen 76	12
14	Sat-01-Jan	BSN	A	Worcester City	833	L 0-2		16
15	Mon-03-Jan	BSN	H	Solihull Moors	325	L 2-4	Morford 2 (15, 75)	17
16	Sat-08-Jan	BSN	H	Boston United	385	L 0-1		17
17	Sat-22-Jan	BSN	H	Workington	315	W 2-0	Mullings 4, Edwards 81	17
18	Wed-26-Jan	BSN	H	Worcester City	425	D 1-1	Mullings pen 56	17
19	Sat-29-Jan	BSN	A	Vauxhall Motors	211	L 1-2	Edwards 59	18
20	Mon-07-Feb	BSN	A	Hinckley United	337	L 0-3		19
21	Sat-12-Feb	BSN	A	Hyde FC	295	W 3-1	Edwards 3 (6, 65, 90)	17
22	Tue-15-Feb	BSN	H	Vauxhall Motors	205	W 1-0	Edwards 32	17
23	Tue-22-Feb	BSN	A	Gainsborough Trinity	253	L 0-2		17
24	Sat-26-Feb	BSN	H	Eastwood Town	345	L 1-3	Mullings pen 82	18
25	Tue-01-Mar	BSN	A	Alfreton Town	418	L 0-4		18
26	Sat-05-Mar	BSN	A	Redditch United	309	W 1-0	Edwards pen 90	16
27	Tue-08-Mar	BSN	A	Corby Town	177	W 2-0	Edwards 2 (32, 86)	15
28	Sat-12-Mar	BSN	A	Boston United	1377	L 0-1		16
29	Tue-15-Mar	BSN	A	Nuneaton Town	592	D 0-0		15
30	Sat-19-Mar	BSN	H	Stafford Rangers	320	L 1-2	Weir 45	17
31	Tue-22-Mar	BSN	H	Hinckley United	201	W 2-1	Mullings 2 (21, 74)	16
32	Sat-26-Mar	BSN	A	Harrogate Town	262	L 0-3		17
33	Wed-30-Mar	BSN	H	Stalybridge Celtic	225	L 0-2		17
34	Sat-02-Apr	BSN	H	Nuneaton Town	470	L 0-3		17
35	Sat-09-Apr	BSN	A	Blyth Spartans	414	W 2-0	Mullings 20, Edwards pen 36	17
36	Sat-16-Apr	BSN	H	Alfreton Town	375	W 2-1	Edwards 2 (32, pen 37)	16
37	Tue-19-Apr	BSN	A	Guiseley	325	D 1-1	Edwards 59	15
38	Sat-23-Apr	BSN	A	Stalybridge Celtic	416	L 3-4	Symons pen 7, Malsom 71, Tambling 86	17
39	Mon-25-Apr	BSN	H	AFC Telford	702	D 2-2	Mann 68, Morford 75	16
40	Sat-30-Apr	BSN	A	Droylsden	352	W 4-2	Morford 2 (18, 41), Mullings 2 (33, 44)	14

Ilkeston Record Expunged 16/09

No.	Date	Comp	H/A	Opponents	Att:	Result	Goalscorers	Pos
3	Sat-21-Aug	BSN	H	Ilkeston Town	402	W 2-0	Harris 43, Symons 77	15

CUPS

No.	Date	Comp	H/A	Opponents	Att:	Result	Goalscorers
1	Sun-26-Sep	FAC 2Q	H	Weston-Super-Mare	380	L 0-2	
2	Sun-21-Nov	FAT 3Q	H	Chelmsford City	318	W 1-0	Mullings 46
3	Sat-11-Dec	FAT 1	A	Cirencester Town	406	D 1-1	Smith 59
4	Wed-15-Dec	FAT 1R	H	Cirencester Town	226	W 3-0	Symons 4, Smith 2 (pen 39, 88)
5	Sat-15-Jan	FAT 2	A	Boston United	1110	W 1-0	Mullings 67
6	Fri-04-Feb	FAT 3	A	Luton Town	2212	L 0-1	

League
Starts
Substitute
Unused Sub

Cups
Starts
Substitute
Unused Sub

Goals (Lg)
Goals (Cup)

SAWYER	MUSTOE	HARRIS	RICHARDS	HAMBLIN	ROSE	O'HARA	WEBB	MULLINGS	SYMONS	BARNES	BRYANT	PARRINELLO	TAMBLING	PREECE	LEWIS	GREEN	MORFORD	MEHEW	ARCHER	CLARKE	COUPE	JAMES	LLOYD	SMITH	DAVIES	MANN	EDWARDS	MACKIE	POUNTNEY	FAWKE	MALSOM	WEIR	EVANS	LIDIARD
X	X	X	X	X	X	X	X	X	X	X	S	S	S	U	U																			
X	U	X	X	X	S	X	X	X	X	S	X	X	S		U	X																		
X	S		X	X	X	X	X	X	X	U	X	X	S		U	X	S																	
X	X		X	X	X	S	X	X	X	S	X	X	S			U	X	U																
X	U		S	X	S		X	X	X	X	X	X	X	S		X	U		X															
X	U		X	X	X			X	X	S	X	X	X	U		X	U	S	X															
X	S		X	X	X			X	X	S		X	X	U	U	X	X	S		X														
X	X			U				X	X			X	X	S	U	X	X	U	X	X	X	S												
X	S			X	X		U	X	S			X	S	U		X	X			X	X			X	X									
X	X				X		S		X	X	X	X	S	U		X	S				X			X	X	U								
X	U				X		X		X	X	X	X	U	S		X	S				X			X	X	S								
X	X				X		X		X	X	X	X	S	S		X	S	U						X	X	U								
X	X	U		X	X		X	S	X	X	S		U			X	X							X	X	U								
X	X	X			X		X	X	X			X	U			X	U				X					S	X	S	S					
X	S			X	U		X	X	X			X	X	U		X	X				X					S		X	S					
X	U			X	X		X		X			X	S	U		X	X				X					S	S	X	X					
X	U				X		X	X	X			X	S	U		X	X				X					S	X	X	S					
X	S				X		X	X	X			X	U	U		X	X				X					U	X	X	S					
X	X						X	X	S			X	X	U		X	S	U			X					U	X	X	X					
X	S						X	X	X			X	U	S		X	X	U			X						X	X	S	X				
X	S			X			X	X	S			X	S	U		X	X				X					X	X		U		X			
X	S			X	U		X	X	S			X	U	U		X	X				X					X	X				X			
X	S				X		X	X	S			X	S			X	X	U			X					X	X				X			
X	S			X	S		X	X	S			X	U			X	X	U			X					X	X				X			
X	X				X		X	X	X			X	X				S	U			X					S	X				S	X		
X	X			X	X		X	X	X			X	S				X	U			X					S	X					S		
X	S				X		X	X	X			X	S				X	U			X						X					X	X	
X	S				X		X	X	X			X	X				S	U			X					U	X				S	X	X	
X	X				X			S	X			S	U				X				X		X			U				X	X	X	S	X
X	U				X		X	X	X			X	S			S	X				X		S				X					X	X	
X	U				S		X	X	S			X	U			X	X				X						X			U	X	X	X	
X	X				X		S	X	S			X	X			X		U								S	X				X	X	X	
X	U				X		X	X	X			X	S			X					X					S	X			X		X	S	
X	U				X		X	X	X			X	S			X					X		S			X	X					X		
X	S				S		X	X	X			X	U			X					X		U			S	X				X	X	X	
X	X				X		X	X	S			X	S								X		U			S	X				X	X	X	
X	X						X	X	X			X	S				U	U			X		S			X	X					X	X	
X	X				X		U	S	X			U	X	X			X				X		X			X	S				S	X		
X	S				X		X	X	X			X	U				X	U			X					S	X				X	X		
X	X				X		X	X	S			X	S				X	U			X					X	X				S	X		
X	U	X	X	X	X	S	X	X	X	S	X	X	U		U	X																		
X	S			X	X			X	X	U	X	X	S	U	U	X	X		U	X	X		S											
X	U	U		X	X		X	X	X	U	S	X	X			X	X							X		U								
X	S	X		X	X			X				X	S	U		X	X	U			X			X		U	X							
X	U	S		X	X		X	X	X			X	U			X	S				X			X		S	X							
X	U			X	X		X	X	X			X	U	U		X	X	U			X					U	X							
X	U			X	U		X	X	X			X	S	S		X	X				X					X	X			S				
40	16	3	6	15	28	3	32	33	30	6	8	36	10	1	0	27	22	0	3	3	30	0	2	5	5	8	23	6	2	3	10	15	8	1
0	14	0	1	0	5	1	2	3	10	4	2	2	19	5	0	1	7	2	0	0	0	1	3	0	0	12	2	1	5	0	4	1	2	0
0	10	1	0	1	2	0	2	0	0	1	0	1	11	12	5	1	4	15	0	0	0	0	2	0	0	7	0	0	1	1	0	0	0	0
6	0	1	0	6	5	0	4	6	5	0	1	6	1	0	0	6	5	0	0	1	5	0	0	3	0	1	4	0	0	0	0	0	0	0
0	2	1	0	0	0	0	0	0	0	0	1	0	3	1	0	0	1	0	0	0	0	0	1	0	0	1	0	0	0	1	0	0	0	0
0	4	1	0	0	1	0	0	0	0	2	0	0	2	3	1	0	0	2	1	0	0	0	0	0	0	3	0	0	0	0	0	0	0	0
0	0	0	1	0	0	0	0	12	5	2	0	0	2	0	0	0	7	0	0	0	1	0	0	2	1	1	13	0	0	0	1	1	0	0
0	0	0	0	0	0	0	0	2	1	0	0	0	0	0	0	0	0	0	0	0	0	0	0	3	0	0	0	0	0	0	0	0	0	0

PLAYING SQUAD 2011/12

Existing Players		SN	HT	WT	DOB	AGE	POB	Career	Apps	Goals
GOALKEEPERS										
Mike	Green		6'01"	13 01	23/07/1989	22	Bristol	Bristol R Rel c/s 11, Mangotsfield (L) 9/06, Clevedon T (L) 3/09, Gloucester (SL) 7/09, Cheltenham (Trial) 7/11, Eastleigh NC 8/11, Gloucester 8/11		
Kevin	Sawyer				14/04/1980	31	Swindon	Cirencester, Salisbury 8/02, Cirencester Undisc 8/06, Gloucester 5/07, Weston-Super-Mare (L) 3/08, Weston-Super-Mare 5/09, Gloucester 6/10	40	0
DEFENDERS										
James	Bloom		6'00"		11/08/1991	20	Cardiff	Cardiff (Yth), Falkirk 7/09 Rel c/s 11, Alloa (L) 1/10, Alloa (SL) 1/11, Gloucester 8/11		
Matt	Coupe				07/10/1978	32	St Asaph	Bristol C, Forest Green, Gloucester c/s 99, Clevedon T 9/99, Bath C c/s 01, Aberystwyth, Forest Green 1/02, Chippenham (L) 1/03, Bath C 2/03 Rel 9/10, Gloucester 9/10	30	1
Mike	Green		5'09"	11 04	18/12/1984	26	Gloucester	Southampton, Chippenham (L) 12/03 (L) 3/04, Forest Green 3/04 Rel 4/05, Cinderford c/s 05, Bath C 6/06, Clevedon (3ML) 8/07 Dual 11/07, Weston-Super-Mare 12/07, Gloucester 6/10	28	0
Tom	Hamblin		6'01"		15/09/1986	24		Mangotsfield (Yth), Bristol Manor Farm, Gloucester 5/06	15	0
Matt	Lock		5'11"	11 04	10/03/1984	27	Barnstaple	Exeter Rel c/s 03, Team Bath 8/03, Tiverton 7/04, Mangotsfield (SL) 12/04 Perm 6/05 Rel 9/06, Team Bath 10/06, Newport C (Trial) 6/09, Chelmsford 7/09 Rel 5/11, Gloucester 6/11		
Neil	Mustoe		5'09"	12 10	05/11/1976	34	Gloucester	Man Utd, Wigan Undisc 1/98 Cambridge U 7/98 Rel c/s 02, Hartlepool (Trial) 7/01, Cambridge C (L) 9/01, Gloucester 8/02, Stevenage 1/03, Yeovil 2/03 Rel c/s 03, Gloucester 8/03 Temp Man 1/06	30	0
MIDFIELDERS										
Matt	Barnes				30/10/1991	19		Swindon (Scholar) Rel 4/10, Cinderford c/s 10, Gloucester (Dual) 7/11		
Scott	Claridge							Gloucester		
Steve	Davies		5'09"	12 03	27/04/1989	22	Swansea	Afan Lido, Cirencester 7/08, Forest Green 7/09 Rel 5/11, Gloucester (3ML) 9/10, Gloucester 5/11	5	1
Jack	Harris				07/06/1989	22	Bristol	Avonmouth, Hallen, Gloucester c/s 08	2	0
Brett	James				10/09/1991	19		Gloucester	1	0
Matt	Liddiard							Gloucester	1	0
George	Lloyd				01/05/1983	18		Bristol R (Yth), Old Abbotonians, Gloucester c/s 10, Team Bath (Dual)	5	0
Adam	Mann							Shortwood, Gloucester	20	1
Darren	Mullings		6'01"	12 00	03/03/1987	24	Bristol	Bristol R, Clevedon (L) 12/06, Torquay 6/07 Rel 5/08, Tiverton (L) 11/07, Weston-Super-Mare 8/08, Gloucester 7/10	36	12
Sam	Rawlings							Cheltenham (Scholar) Rel c/s 11, Gloucester 8/11		
Matt	Rose				03/05/1976	35	Cheltenham	Cheltenham, St Marks, Moreton T, Cirencester, Gloucester 8/99, Newport C 3/00, Weston-Super-Mare 4 fig 10/03, Gloucester 6/07	33	0
Tom	Webb				02/05/1984	27		Luton (Yth), Gloucester 7/00, Viney St Swithens (L), Highworth T (L), Yate T (L) 8/09	34	0
Tyler	Weir		5'10"	11 10	21/12/1990	20	Hereford	Hereford, Gloucester (SL) 3/11, Gloucester (L) 8/11	16	1
FORWARDS										
Darren	Edwards				04/08/1980	31	Bristol	Bristol Manor Farm, Mangotsfield 98, Bristol R (Trial) 4/02,, Tiverton 1/04, Mangotsfield 9/04, Yate T 1/05, Bath C 12/06 Rel 11/10, Cinderford (L) 11/10, Gloucester 11/10	25	13
Will	Morford				28/04/1986	25		Staunton & Corse, Tuffley Rovers, Slimbridge, Gloucester 10/07	29	7

GUISELEY

Chairman: Philip Rogerson
Secretary: Adrian Towers **(T)** 07946 388 739 **(E)** admin@guiseleyafc.co.uk
Additional Committee Members:
Phil Rogerson, Stuart Allen, Steve Parkin, John Gill, Gary Douglas, Keith Hanvey, Matthew Rogerson.
Manager: Steve Kittrick
Programme Editor: Rachel O'Connor **(E)** rachel.football@hotmail.co.uk

Back Row (L-R): Adrian Towers (General Manager),Gavin Rothery, Danny Boshell, Lee Ellington, Danny Ellis, Gavin Allott, Jacob Giles (gk) Steve Drench(gk), Jamie Clarke, Mark Bower, Simon Ainge, Peter Davidson, Joe O'Neill, Joey Spivack.
Front Row: Alex Davidson, Ciaran Toner, Michael Burns, Chris Holland (Ass't Mgr), SteveKittrick (Mgr) Martin Stringfellow (Therapist), Dave Merris, James Booker, Danny Forrest.

Club Factfile

Founded: 1909 **Nickname:** The Lions
Previous Names: Not known
Previous Leagues: Wharfedale, Leeds, West Riding Counties, West Yorkshire, Yorkshire 1968-82, Northern Counties East 1982-91, Northern Premier 1991-2010

Club Colours (change): White/navy/navy (All yellow)

Ground: Nethermoor Park, Otley Road, Guiseley, Leeds LS20 8BT **(T)** 01943 873 223 (Office) 872 872 (Club)
Capacity: 3,000 **Seats:** 427 **Covered:** 1,040 **Clubhouse:** Yes **Shop:** Yes

Directions
From the West M62, M606 then follow signs to A65 through Guiseley to Ground on Right. From South and East M1 and M621 towards Leeds City Centre. Continue on M621 to Junction 2, follow Headingly Stadium signs to A65 towards Ilkley then as above. From North West From Skipton, A65 Ilkley, via Burley By-pass A65 towards Leeds, Ground quarter of a mile on left after Harry Ramsden's roundabout From North/NE A1M, leave at A59, towards Harrogate, then A658 signed Leeds Bradford Airport, at Pool turn right onto A659 Otley, continue towards Bradford/Leeds, to Harry Ramsden roundabout then A65 Leeds ground quarter of a mile on left.

Previous Grounds: Not known

Record Attendance: 2,486 v Bridlington Town - FA Vase Semi-final 1st Leg 1989-90
Record Victory: Not known
Record Defeat: Not known
Record Goalscorer: Not known
Record Appearances: Not known
Additional Records:

Senior Honours: Northern Counties East 1990-91. FA Vase 1990-91.
Northern Premier League Division 1 1993-94, Premier Division 2009-10, Challenge Cup 2008-09.

10 YEAR RECORD

01-02	02-03	03-04	04-05	05-06	06-07	07-08	08-09	09-10	10-11
NP 1 11	NP 1 14	NP 1 9	NP P 10	NP P 14	NP P 6	NP P 6	NP P 3	NP P 1	Conf N 5

GUISELEY

No.	Date	Comp	H/A	Opponents	Att:	Result	Goalscorers	Pos
1	Sat-14-Aug	BSN	H	Nuneaton Town	500	L 1-2	Walshaw 28	13
2	Tue-17-Aug	BSN	A	Gainsborough Trinity	400	W 3-1	Peyton 2 (24, 57), Needham 26	11
3	Sat-21-Aug	BSN	A	Stafford Rangers	438	D 2-2	Walshaw 2 (4, 58)	10
4	Tue-24-Aug	BSN	H	Blyth Spartans	342	D 0-0		12
5	Sat-28-Aug	BSN	A	Vauxhall Motors	178	D 2-2	Peyton 39, Stamp 89	11
6	Mon-30-Aug	BSN	H	Hyde FC	406	W 1-0	Needham 18	9
7	Sat-04-Sep	BSN	H	Redditch United	362	W 3-1	Walshaw 3 (pen 10, pen 34, 52)	6
8	Sat-11-Sep	BSN	A	Hinckley United	371	W 2-1	Walshaw 2 (14, 21)	6
9	Sat-18-Sep	BSN	A	Gloucester City	380	W 2-1	Walshaw 2 (4, 73)	5
10	Sat-02-Oct	BSN	H	Corby Town	467	W 4-0	Stamp 3 (10, 33, 73), James 90	5
11	Sat-16-Oct	BSN	A	Solihull Moors	243	W 1-0	O'Neill 36	3
12	Sat-30-Oct	BSN	A	Eastwood Town	495	W 1-0	O'Neill 90	3
13	Tue-02-Nov	BSN	H	Boston United	432	D 0-0		3
14	Tue-09-Nov	BSN	A	Workington	333	W 1-0	Walshaw 23	3
15	Sat-13-Nov	BSN	H	Stalybridge Celtic	518	W 3-1	O'Neill 10, Walshaw 46, Needham 86	3
16	Tue-23-Nov	BSN	H	Droylsden	338	W 2-1	Walshaw 2 (19, 80)	2
17	Sat-27-Nov	BSN	A	AFC Telford	2315	L 0-1		2
18	Sat-01-Jan	BSN	H	Harrogate Town	624	W 1-0	O'Neill 68	1
19	Mon-03-Jan	BSN	A	Hyde FC	342	W 1-0	Walshaw 51	1
20	Sat-08-Jan	BSN	H	Corby Town	370	D 2-2	O'Neill 75, Ellis 87	2
21	Sat-22-Jan	BSN	A	Boston United	1354	D 1-1	Ainge 67	3
22	Tue-25-Jan	BSN	H	Hinckley United	366	W 3-2	Peyton 25, Rothery 2 (59, 65)	2
23	Tue-22-Feb	BSN	A	Harrogate Town	301	D 0-0		5
24	Tue-01-Mar	BSN	H	Vauxhall Motors	203	L 1-2	Walshaw 67	5
25	Sat-05-Mar	BSN	H	AFC Telford	567	L 0-3		6
26	Sat-12-Mar	BSN	H	Worcester City	394	L 0-1		6
27	Tue-15-Mar	BSN	H	Workington	274	D 2-2	Walshaw 2 (28, 50)	6
28	Sat-19-Mar	BSN	A	Stalybridge Celtic	507	D 0-0		6
29	Tue-22-Mar	BSN	H	Alfreton Town	458	L 1-2	Walshaw 22	8
30	Sat-26-Mar	BSN	A	Nuneaton Town	761	W 1-0	Forrest 37	7
31	Tue-29-Mar	BSN	H	Stafford Rangers	258	D 1-1	Walshaw 11	7
32	Sat-02-Apr	BSN	H	Solihull Moors	374	W 1-0	Forrest 74	6
33	Tue-05-Apr	BSN	A	Alfreton Town	750	L 0-6		7
34	Sat-09-Apr	BSN	A	Worcester City	458	W 2-1	Stamp 51, Ainge 75	7
35	Mon-11-Apr	BSN	A	Droylsden	244	W 3-0	Rothery 22, Walshaw 26, O'Neill 89	5
36	Sat-16-Apr	BSN	A	Redditch United	165	W 3-2	Baldry 2 (67, 90), Walshaw pen 89	5
37	Tue-19-Apr	BSN	H	Gloucester City	325	D 1-1	Walshaw 21	6
38	Sat-23-Apr	BSN	H	Gainsborough Trinity	412	W 2-0	Rothery 8, Baldry 55	5
39	Mon-25-Apr	BSN	A	Blyth Spartans	459	D 0-0		6
40	Sat-30-Apr	BSN	H	Eastwood Town	557	D 2-2	Baldry 25, Walshaw 45	5

CUPS

No.	Date	Comp	H/A	Opponents	Att:	Result	Goalscorers
1	Sat-25-Sep	FAC 2Q	A	Colwyn Bay	457	D 1-1	O'Neill 39
2	Tue-28-Sep	FAC 2QR	H	Colwyn Bay	256	W 3-0	Walshaw 45, James 52, O'Neill 72
3	Sat-09-Oct	FAC 3Q	H	Whitley Bay	704	W 3-0	Walshaw 2 (30, 80), O'Neill 40
4	Sat-23-Oct	FAC 4Q	H	Redditch United	808	W 2-1	Needham 62, Peyton 78
5	Sat-06-Nov	FAC 1	H	Crawley Town	1609	L 0-5	
6	Sat-20-Nov	FAT 3Q	A	Chorley	890	W 1-0	O'Neill 72
7	Sat-11-Dec	FAT 1	A	Barrow	923	W 3-2	Walshaw 2 (5, 14), Boshell 19
8	Sat-15-Jan	FAT 2	H	Stalybridge Celtic	417	W 2-1	Walshaw pen 40, Needham 89
9	Sat-05-Feb	FAT 3	A	Eastbourne Borough	471	D 1-1	O'Neill 71
10	Tue-08-Feb	FAT 3R	H	Eastbourne Borough	446	W 2-1	Walshaw 47, O'Neill 86
11	Sat-26-Feb	FAT 4	H	Luton Town	1152	L 0-1	
12	Tue-03-May	PO SF 1	H	Boston United	1022	W 1-0	Peyton 75
13	Sun-08-May	PO SF 2	A	Boston United	2640	L 2-3 aet	(W 3-2 pens) Rothery 60, Stamp 108
14	Sun-15-May	PO Final	A	AFC Telford	5436	L 2-3	Walshaw pen 44, Stamp 46

League
Starts
Substitute
Unused Sub

Cups
Starts
Substitute
Unused Sub

Goals (Lg)
Goals (Cup)

DRENCH	TOULSON	MERRIS	PEYTON	AINGE	COTTERILL	ROTHERY	SHARRY	O'NEILL	WALSHAW	NEEDHAM	FITZGERALD	PENFORD	STAMP	BURTON	SCARSELLA	ELLIS	MCENEANEY	BOSHELL	JAMES	MARTENS	HOLLAND	SPIVACK	LLOYD	BALDRY	FORREST	COATES
X	X	X	X	X	X	X	X	X	X	X	S	S	S	U	U											
X	X	X	X	X		X	X	X	X	X	U	S	S	S	U	X										
X	X	X	X	X		X	X	X	X	X		S	U	U	U	X	U									
X	X	X	X	X	U	X	X	X	X	X		U	S	S	U	X										
X		X	X		X	X	X	X	X	X	U		S	S	U	X	X	U								
X	X	X	X	X	U	X	U	X	X	X			X	S	U	X		S								
X	X	X	X	X	U	X	S	X	X	X			X	S	U	X		S								
X	X	X	X	X	U	X	S	X	X	X			X		U	X		S	S							
X	X	X	X	X		X	S	X	X	X	U		X			X		S		U						
X	X	X	X	X		S	S	X	X	X	U		X			X		X	S	U						
X	X	X	X	X		X	X	X	X	X	U					X	U	S	S	U						
X	X	X	X	X	U	S	X	X	X	X					U	X	U	S	X							
X	X	X	X	X	U	S	X	X	X	X	S				U	X		S	X							
X	X	X	X	X		U	S	X	X	X	U		X		U	X		X	S							
X	X	X	X	X		S	S	X	X	X	U		S		U	X		X	X							
X	X	X	X	X		X	X	X	X		S		S			X		X	S	U		U				
X	X	X	X	X		X	X	X	X		U				U	X	U	X	S			U				
X		X	X		X	X	X	X	X	X							X		S	U	U	U		X		
X	X	X	X	X	X	X	X	X	X	X			S				U			U		U		S		
X	X	X	X	X	U	X	X	X	X	X			S			X		S		U				S		
X	X	X	X	X	U	X	U	X	X	X			U			X		X		U				S		
X	X	X	X	X		X	U	X	S	X			U			X		X		S				U	X	
X		X	X	X		X	S	X		X			X				X	X			U	U		X	S	U
X	X	X	X	X		X	S	X	X	X			U			X		X						S	U	S
X	U	X	S	X		U	X	X	X	X			S			X		X						X	X	U
X	X	X	S	X		S	X	X	X				S			X	U	X						X	X	U
	X	X	X	X		X	U	X	X				X				U	X		U				X	S	X
X	X	X	X	X		X	S	X	X				S			X	U	X						X	S	U
X	X	X	X	X		U	U	X	X				U			X	U	X						X	X	U
X	X	X	X	X		S	U	X	X				S			X	U	X						X	X	U
X	X	X	X	X		S	S	X	X				S			X	U	X						X	X	U
X	X	X	U	X		X	U	X	X				U			X	U	X						X	X	U
	X	X	X	X		X	U	X	S				X			X	S	S		U				X	X	X
	X	X	X	X		X	S	S	X				X			X	S	X		U	U			X		X
X	X	X	U	X		X	X	X	X				S			X	U	X			U			X		U
X	X	X	U	X		X	X		X		U		X			X	U	X				U		X		U
X	X	X	S	X		X	X		X		U		X			X	S	X				U		X		U
X	X	X	S	X		X	X		X		U		X			X	U	X				S		X		U
X	X	X	X	X		X	X		X		U					X	U	X			U	U		X		U
X	X	X	U	X		X	X		X		U		X			X	U	X				U		X		U
X	X	X	X	X		X	S	X	X	X	U		X			X		S	S	U	U					
X	X	X	X	X		S	S	X	X	X	S					X		X	X	U	U					
X	X	X	X	X		S	X	X	X	X	S		X			X		U	S	U	U					
X	X	X	X	X	U	X	X	X	X	X		U				X	U	U	S	U	U					
X	X	X	X	X	U	X	X	X	X	X	U		S		U	X	U	S	S							
X	X	X	X	X		X	S	X	X	X	U		S		U	X		X	S							
X	X	X	X	X		X	X	X	X		U					X		X	S	U		U	S			
X	X	X	X	X	U	S	S	X	X	X			X			X		X		U		U				
	X	X	X	X		X	S	X	X	X			S			X	U	X		U					U	X
X	X	X	X	X		X	U	X	X	X			S			X	U	X							U	U
X	X	X	X	X		X	S	X	X	X			S			X	U	X							S	U
X	X	X	X	X		X	X	X			S		X			X	U				U	S		X		U
X	X	X	X	X		X	S		X	S	U		X			X		X				U		X		U
X	X	X	X	X		X	S	S	X	U	S		X			X		X						X		U
									1				1													
37	36	40	32	38	4	30	21	34	37	23	0	0	14	0	0	35	3	24	3	0	0	0	0	18	8	3
0	0	0	4	0	0	7	11	1	2	0	3	3	14	5	0	0	3	9	7	1	0	1	0	4	3	1
0	1	0	4	0	8	3	8	0	0	0	13	1	6	2	13	0	17	1	0	11	5	9	0	1	1	14
13	14	14	14	14	0	11	5	12	13	10	0	0	6	0	0	14	0	9	1	0	0	0	0	3	0	1
0	0	0	0	0	0	3	8	1	0	1	4	0	5	0	0	0	0	2	6	0	0	1	1	0	1	0
0	0	0	0	0	3	0	1	0	0	1	5	1	0	0	2	0	6	2	0	7	5	3	0	0	2	5
0	0	0	4	2	0	4	0	6	24	3	0	0	5	0	0	1	0	0	1	0	0	0	0	4	2	0
0	0	0	2	0	0	1	0	6	8	2	0	0	2	0	0	0	0	1	1	0	0	0	0	0	0	0

PLAYING SQUAD 2011/12

Existing Players		SN	HT	WT	DOB	AGE	POB	Career	Apps	Goals
GOALKEEPERS										
Steven	Drench				11/09/1985	25		Blackburn Rel 5/06, Morecambe (SL) 11/05, Morecambe c/s 06, Southport (L) 1/08, Southport 6/08, Cambridge U (4ML) 8/08, Leigh Genesis 3/09, Guiseley 8/10	37	0
Jacob	Giles				12/10/1985	25	Huddersfield	Huddersfield (Yth), Team Bath, Taunton 9/05, Newport C 6/06 Rel 8/07, Gloucester (L) 10/06, Bradford PA 10/07, Harrogate RA 12/07, Leeds Carnegie, Guiseley 8/11		
DEFENDERS										
Simon	Ainge		6'01"	12 02	18/02/1988	23	Shipley	Bradford C Rel c/s 09, Halifax (SL) 1/08, Cambridge U (SL) 3/09, Bradford PA c/s 09, Guiseley (L) 11/09 Perm 12/09	38	2
James	Booker		5'09"		11/09/1992	18		Leeds (Scholar) Rel c/s 11, Scunthorpe (Trial) 4/11, Guiseley 5/11		
Mark	Bower		5'10"	11 00	23/01/1980	31	Bradford	Bradford C Rel c/s 09, York C (SL) 2/00, York C (SL) 11/00, Luton (3ML) 1/09, Darlington 7/09, FC Halifax 6/10, Guiseley 5/11		
Michael	Burns		5'10"	11 07	04/10/1988	22	Huyton	Liverpool (Scholar), Bolton 7/07, Gillingahm (Trial) c/s 08, Carlisle 1/09, Stafford R (2ML) 1/10, Runcorn Linnets, Newport C 1/11 Rel 2/11, Guiseley 6/11		
Danny	Ellis		6'00"	12 00	23/11/1985	25	Bradford	Bradford C Rel c/s 06, Guiseley c/s 06	35	1
Dave	Merris		5'07"	10 06	13/10/1980	30	Rotherham	Rotherham (Scholar), Guiseley 7/98, Harrogate T 9/99, York 8/03 Rel 5/06, Harrogate T 6/06, Guiseley 3/08	40	0
MIDFIELDERS										
Simon	Baldry		5'10"	11 06	12/02/1976	35	Huddersfield	Huddersfield Rel c/s 03, Bury (L) 9/98, Notts County 8/03 Rel c/s 04, Injured, Ossett T 1/08, Bradford PA 7/09 (Pl/Ass Man) c/s 10, Guiseley 12/10	22	4
Danny	Boshell		5'11"	11 10	30/05/1981	30	Bradford	Oldham, Bury (L) 3/05, Stockport 8/05 Rel c/s 06, Grimsby 8/06 Rel 2/10, Chesterfield 2/10 Rel c/s 10, Guiseley 8/10	33	0
Jamie	Clarke		6'02"	12 03	18/09/1982	28	Sunderland	Mansfield Rel c/s 04, Rochdale 7/04, Boston U 1/06 Rel c/s 07, Grimsby Rel 2/10, York C 2/10 Rel 5/10, Darlington (Trial) 7/10, Gateshead (Trial) 8/10, St Johnstone (Trial) 8/10, Gainsborough 8/10, Guiseley 7/11		
Peter	Davidson							Hull C (Yth), Hessle Sporting, North Ferriby, Guiseley 6/11		
Chris	Holland		5'09"	11 05	11/09/1975	35	Whalley	Preston, Newcastle £100,000 1/94, Birmingham (2ML) 9/96 £600,000 10/96, Huddersfield £150,000 2/00, Boston U 3/04, Southport 1/07, Leigh Genesis 7/08, Fleetwood 11/08, Burscough 3/09, Guiseley 7/09 (Pl/Coach) 8/10	0	0
Gavin	Rothery		5'09"	10 10	22/09/1987	23	Leeds	Leeds Rel 4/08, York C 10/08, Harrogate T 12/08, Carlisle 3/09 Rel c/s 10, Barrow (6WL) 11/09, Guiseley 7/10	37	4
Joe	Spivack						New Jersey, USA	Metro Stars/Red Bull Academy (USA), Royal Racing Football Club Montegnée (Bel), Eccleshill, Bradford C (Trial), IASA, Guiseley 11/10, Huddersfield (Trial) 4/11	1	0
Ciaren	Toner		5'11"	12 04	30/06/1981	30	Craigavon, NI	Tottenham Rel 3/02, Peterborough (L) 12/01, Bristol R 3/02, L.Orient 5/02 Rel c/s 04, Lincoln C 8/04 Rel c/s 05, Cambridge U (L) 3/05, Grimsby 7/05 Rel c/s 08, Rochdale 8/08, Harrogate T 8/10, Guiseley 7/11		
FORWARDS										
Gavin	Allott							Parkgate, Gainsborough (L) 11/07, Buxton (L) 1/08, Belper, Dinnington 7/08, Goole AFC 9/09, Dinnington 2/10, Parkgate 12/10, Goole AFC 1/11, Guiseley 6/11		
Alex	Davidson				24/03/1988	23		North Ferriby, Guiseley 6/11		
Lee	Ellington		5'10"	11 07	03/07/1980	31	Bradford	Eccleshill Utd, Hull C, Altrincham (Trial), Exeter 3/00, Walton & H 4/00, Gainsborough 10/00, Stalybridge 7/05, Farsley Celtic 6/09, Droylsden 3/10 Rel 3/10, Harrogate T 3/10, FC Halifax (L) 3/11, Guiseley 6/11		
Danny	Forrest		5'10"	11 07	23/10/1984	26	Keighley	Bradford C Rel 5/06, Halifax (SL) 8/05, Halifax 6/06, Hucknall (L) 1/08, Crawley 5/08 Rel 5/10, Barrow 6/10 Rel 5/11, Guiseley (3ML) 1/11, Guiseley 5/11	11	2
Joe	O'Neill		6'00"	10 05	28/10/1982	28	Blackburn	Preston, Bury (SL) 7/03, Mansfield (3ML) 8/04, Chester (3ML) 1/05, York 7/05 Rel 5/06, Altrincham 6/06 Rel 5/09, Stalybridge 6/09, Guiseley 6/10	35	6

HARROGATE TOWN

Chairman: Bill Fotherby
Secretary: Kate Sewell **(T)** 0787 928 1207 **(E)** harrogatetown@unicombox.co.uk
Additional Committee Members:
Andrew Thurkill, Bernard Fotherby, Howard Matthews, David Bolton, Peter Arnett.

Manager: Simon Weaver
Programme Editor: Peter Arnett **(E)** peterarnett@btinternet.com

Club Factfile

Founded: 1919 **Nickname:** Town
Previous Names: Not known
Previous Leagues: West Riding 1919-20, Yorkshire 1920-21, 22-31, 57-82, Midland 1921-22, Northern 1931-32, Harrogate & Dist. 1935-37, 40-46, W. Riding Co.Am. 1937-40, W. Yorks. 1946-57, N.C.E. 1982-87, N.P.L. 1987-2004

Club Colours (change): White/black/black (All grey)

Ground: The CNG Stadium, Wetherby Road, Harrogate HG2 7SA **(T)** 01423 883 671
Capacity: 3,291 **Seats:** 502 **Covered:** 1,300 **Clubhouse:** Yes **Shop:** Yes

Directions
A61 to Harrogate, turn right on to A658, and at roundabout take A661, proceed through second set of lights (Woodlands pub) ground approx. 500 mtrs on the right. From A1 Wetherby. Leave A1 at Wetherby on to A661 to Harrogate. Stay on this road and when reaching Harrogate at Woodland pub lights, ground 500mtrs on the right.

Previous Grounds: Not known

Record Attendance: 4,280 v Railway Athletic - Whitworth Cup Final 1950
Record Victory: 13-0 v Micklefield
Record Defeat: 1-10 v Methley United - 1956
Record Goalscorer: Jimmy Hague - 135 (1956-58 and 1961-76)
Record Appearances: Paul Williamson - 428 (1980-81, 1982-85, and 1986-93)
Additional Records:

Senior Honours: West Riding County Cup 1962-63, 72-73, 85-86. Northern Premier League Division 1 2001-02.
West Riding Challenge Cup x2.

10 YEAR RECORD

01-02	02-03	03-04	04-05	05-06	06-07	07-08	08-09	09-10	10-11
NP 1 1	NP P 6	NP P 5	Conf N 6	Conf N 5	Conf N 6	Conf N 6	Conf N 9	Conf N 21	Conf N 12

HARROGATE TOWN

No.	Date	Comp	H/A	Opponents	Att:	Result	Goalscorers	Pos
1	Sat-14-Aug	BSN	A	Corby Town	360	L 1-2	Armstrong 80	14
2	Tue-17-Aug	BSN	H	Droylsden	296	D 3-3	Hardy 2 (21, 25), Armstrong 54	15
3	Sat-21-Aug	BSN	H	Solihull Moors	301	W 2-0	Hardy 10, Armstrong pen 66	11
4	Tue-24-Aug	BSN	A	Workington	610	L 1-2	Armstrong 23	13
5	Sat-28-Aug	BSN	H	Boston United	447	L 3-6	Hardy 2 (26, 72), Nowakowski 40	16
6	Mon-30-Aug	BSN	A	Stalybridge Celtic	365	W 1-0	Armstrong pen 78	12
7	Sat-04-Sep	BSN	H	Hinckley United	310	D 2-2	Toner 15, Armstrong pen 41	13
8	Sat-11-Sep	BSN	A	Vauxhall Motors	176	D 1-1	Phillips 88	14
9	Sat-18-Sep	BSN	A	Nuneaton Town	839	L 0-3		14
10	Sat-02-Oct	BSN	H	Hyde FC	306	L 1-3	Armstrong pen 65	15
11	Sat-16-Oct	BSN	A	Gloucester City	325	L 2-3	Hadley 2 (4, 32)	16
12	Sat-23-Oct	BSN	A	Worcester City	713	W 3-2	Armstrong 4, James 82, Ellington 84	14
13	Sat-30-Oct	BSN	A	Redditch United	329	W 1-0	Bowey 62	13
14	Tue-02-Nov	BSN	H	Eastwood Town	191	W 2-1	Hadley 49, Armstrong 79	10
15	Sat-06-Nov	BSN	A	Hyde FC	343	L 0-1		11
16	Tue-09-Nov	BSN	A	Blyth Spartans	370	L 0-1		11
17	Sat-13-Nov	BSN	A	Alfreton Town	662	L 0-6		11
18	Sat-01-Jan	BSN	A	Guiseley	624	L 0-1		14
19	Mon-03-Jan	BSN	H	Stalybridge Celtic	378	W 2-0	Pell 25, Armstrong 56	12
20	Sat-15-Jan	BSN	H	Nuneaton Town	306	L 1-2	Armstrong pen 82	14
21	Tue-18-Jan	BSN	H	Stafford Rangers	147	W 3-2	King 2, Hutchinson 33, Ellington 41	12
22	Sat-29-Jan	BSN	A	Solihull Moors	245	D 2-2	Armstrong pen 78, Picton 88	12
23	Sat-05-Feb	BSN	H	Corby Town	308	L 0-1		14
24	Sat-12-Feb	BSN	A	Gainsborough Trinity	321	W 3-1	Armstrong pen 16, Phillips 71, King 79	13
25	Mon-14-Feb	BSN	A	Hinckley United	309	L 0-4		14
26	Tue-22-Feb	BSN	H	Guiseley	301	D 0-0		15
27	Tue-01-Mar	BSN	A	Eastwood Town	263	L 0-2		16
28	Tue-08-Mar	BSN	H	Blyth Spartans	225	D 2-2	James 67, Armstrong 78	15
29	Sat-12-Mar	BSN	H	Gainsborough Trinity	266	W 3-1	Armstrong 2 (54, pen 71), James 56	15
30	Sat-19-Mar	BSN	A	Boston United	1369	D 2-2	Nowakowski 30, Marshall 37	15
31	Tue-22-Mar	BSN	H	Redditch United	207	W 3-0	Armstrong 2 (2, pen 31), Phillips 63	15
32	Sat-26-Mar	BSN	H	Gloucester City	262	W 3-0	Chilaka 3 (3, 35, 78)	14
33	Tue-29-Mar	BSN	H	AFC Telford	305	D 0-0		13
34	Sat-02-Apr	BSN	A	Stafford Rangers	401	D 1-1	Toner 78	14
35	Sat-09-Apr	BSN	H	Vauxhall Motors	250	D 0-0		14
36	Sat-16-Apr	BSN	H	Worcester City	304	W 1-0	Armstrong 25	12
37	Tue-19-Apr	BSN	H	Alfreton Town	456	D 1-1	Armstrong 78	12
38	Sat-23-Apr	BSN	A	Droylsden	206	L 1-5	Armstrong 81	13
39	Mon-25-Apr	BSN	H	Workington	339	W 2-0	Marshall 52, Armstrong 85	12
40	Sat-30-Apr	BSN	A	AFC Telford	2176	L 0-3		12

CUPS

No.	Date	Comp	H/A	Opponents	Att:	Result	Goalscorers
1	Sat-25-Sep	FAC 2Q	A	New Mills	309	W 2-0	Og (Innes) 11, Armstrong pen 36
2	Sat-09-Oct	FAC 3Q	A	FC Halifax Town	1835	L 0-4	
3	Sat-20-Nov	FAT 3Q	H	Witton Albion	243	D 1-1	Bradley 10
4	Wed-24-Nov	FAT 3QR	A	Witton Albion	175	W 2-1	Bowey 25, Toner 74
5	Sat-11-Dec	FAT 1	H	AFC Telford	247	L 0-3	

League
Starts
Substitute
Unused Sub

Cups
Starts
Substitute
Unused Sub

Goals (Lg)
Goals (Cup)

DOOTSON	ROMA	SHEPHERD	JAMES	PELL	BLOOMER	FOSTER	BOWEY	ARMSTRONG	HARDY	PHILLIPS	NOWAKOWSKI	WILLIAMS	NAYLOR	WRIGHT	TALBOT	KENDALL	JACKLIN	MYERS	SAVORY	TONER	GONZALEZ	ELLINGTON	PICTON	HADLEY	GARDNER	BRADLEY	COOK	MCPHILLIPS	MAGUIRE	WILKINSON	KING	HUTCHINSON	DRURY	CHILAKA	LEONARD	ELLIOT	MARSHALL	FORSYTH
X	X	X	X	X	X	X	X	X	X	X	S	S	S	U	U																								
X	X	X		X	X	X		X	X	X	X	X	S	U		S	S	U																					
X	X	X		X	X	X		X	X	X	X	X	U	S	U		U		S																				
X	X	X	S	X	X			X	X	X	X	X		X			S	U	S																				
X	X	X	S	X	X			X	X	X	X	U	X	U			S		S	X																			
X	X	X	X	U	S			X	X	S	U	X	X	U			X		X	X																			
X	X	X	X	U	S			X	X	X	U	X	X	U			X		S	X																			
	X		U	X	X	X		X	X	X	X		U		X		U		S	X	X	S																	
	X	U	U	X	X	X	X	X	X	X			S		X				S	X	X	S																	
	X	X	S	X	X	X		X	X	X	X		U						U	X	X	S	S																
	X	S	X	U	X	U	X	X	S		X							U		X	X	X	X	X															
	X	U	S		U	X	X	X		S	U									X	X	X	X	X	X	X													
	X	U	X		U	X	X	X		S	U									X		X	X	X		X	X	U											
	X	S	X	U	X	X	X	X		S	U									X		X		X		X	X	U											
	X		X		U	X	X	X		S	U									X	U	X	X	X		X	X	U											
	X	S	X	U	U	X	X	X		X	S									X	U	X	X			X	X												
	X		X	U	U	X	X	X		X	U									X	U	X	X			X	X	S											
	X			X	X		U	X		S	X		U							X		S	X	S			X		X	X	X							
U	X			X	S	S	X	X			X		U							X		X	X	U			X			X	X							
	X		U	X	U	U	X	S			X							X		X		X	X	S						X	X	X						
	X			X	U	S	X	S		U	X							X		X		X	X						S	X	X	X						
	X			X	S	U	X	S		S	X											X	X				X		X	X	X	X	U					
	X		S	X	X			X		S	X							U		X		X	X				X		X	U	X	S						
	X		U	X	X	X	X	X		X								S		X		X	X				X		U		S			S				
	X		S	X	X	X		X		X	U							X		X		S	X						S		X			X	U			
	X		X		X	X		S		S	U			U						X		X	X	X							X			U	X	X		
	X		X		X	X	U	X		X	X									X		U		S					U		X			S	X	X		
	X		X		X	X	S	X		X	U									X			X		U							S			S		X	X	X
	X		X		X	X	X	X	S	X	U			U									X		U		X				U			X			X	
	X		X		X	X	U	X	U	X	X			U									X		U		X				S			X			X	
	X		X		X	X	S	X	U	X	X			U									X		S		X				S			X			X	
	X		X		X	X	U		S	X	X			U						S			X		U		X				X			X			X	
	X		X		X	X	U	X	U	X	X			U						U			X		U		X				X						X	
	X				X	X	S	X	S	X	X									X			X		U		X				X						X	
	X		U		X	X	U	X	X	X	X			S						X			X				X				U						X	
	X		U		X	X	U	X	X	X	X			S						X		U	X		U		X										X	
	X		X	U	X	X	S	X	X		X			S						X		S	X		U		X										X	
	X		X		X	X	S	X	X	S	X			U						X		S	X		U		X										X	
	X			U	S	X	U	X	S	X	X			X						X			X		X		X				U						X	
	X		X	U	U	X	S	X	X	X				X						X		S	X		X		X				S								
	X	S		X	X	X		X	X	X	X		S		X		U		S	X	X	U																		
	X	X	X	X	X	S	X	X	X		U		X		U			U	S	X	X	S	U															
	X	X	X	S	U	X	X			S										X	U	X	X	X		X	X		U									
	X		X	X	S	X	X			S	S		U							X	U	X	X	X			X		X									
	X		X	S	S	X	X	X		S	U									X		X	X	U	X		X		X									
7	40	8	20	16	27	29	15	35	15	25	24	5	3	3	2	0	2	3	1	30	5	14	28	6	3	6	22	0	3	5	12	3	0	5	2	3	12	1
0	0	3	6	0	5	2	6	4	5	10	2	1	3	4	0	1	3	1	6	1	0	8	1	3	1	0	0	1	2	0	5	1	0	3	0	0	0	0
1	0	3	6	9	8	3	8	0	3	1	11	1	5	12	2	0	2	4	1	1	3	2	0	1	9	0	0	3	2	1	3	0	1	1	1	0	0	0
0	5	2	4	3	2	4	4	3	2	1	1	0	1	0	1	0	0	0	0	5	2	3	3	2	1	1	3	0	2	0	0	0	0	0	0	0	0	0
0	0	1	0	2	2	1	0	0	0	3	1	0	1	0	0	0	0	0	2	0	0	1	0	0	0	0	0	0	0	0	0	0	0	0	0	0	0	0
0	0	0	0	0	1	0	0	0	0	0	2	0	1	0	1	0	1	1	0	0	2	1	1	1	0	0	0	0	1	0	0	0	0	0	0	0	0	0
0	0	0	3	1	0	0	1	22	5	3	2	0	0	0	0	0	0	0	0	2	0	2	1	3	0	0	0	0	0	0	2	1	0	3	0	0	2	0
0	0	0	0	0	0	0	1	1	0	0	0	0	0	0	0	0	0	0	0	1	0	0	0	0	0	1	0	0	0	0	0	0	0	0	0	0	0	0

PLAYING SQUAD 2011/12

Existing Players		SN	HT	WT	DOB	AGE	POB	Career	Apps	Goals
GOALKEEPERS										
Mark	Cook		6'00"	12 01	07/09/1988	22	North Shields	Newcastle (Scholar) Rel c/s 08, Hartlepool 7/08 Rel c/s 10, Gateshead 8/10, Harrogate T 10/10	22	0
Chris	Elliot		5'11"	12 04	17/07/1992	19	Newcastle	Bradford C Rel c/s 11, Harrogate RA (3ML) 9/10, Harrogate T (L) 2/11, Harrogate T 7/11	3	0
DEFENDERS										
Matt	Bloomer		6'00"	13 00	03/11/1978	32	Grimsby	Grimsby Rel c/s 01, Hull C (Trial) 4/01, Hull C 7/01, Lincoln C (L) 3/02, Telford (3ML) 8/02, Lincoln C 12/02 Rel 5/06, Grimsby (L) 1/06, Cambridge U (2ML) 3/06, Cambridge U 7/06 Rel 1/07, Grimsby 1/07 Rel c/s 07, Boston U 7/07, Harrogate T 6/09	32	0
Paul	Heckingbottom		6'00"	12 05	17/07/1977	34	Barnsley	Man Utd (Trainee), Sunderland 7/95, Scarborough (SL) 10/97, Hartlepool (L) 9/98, Sheff Utd (Trial), Bolton (Trial), Stockport (Trial), Darlington 3/99 Rel c/s 02, Norwich 7/02, Bradford C 7/03, Sheff Wed 7/04, Barnsley Undisc 1/06, Bradford C (6ML) 7/07, Bradford C 1/08 Rel c/s 09, Mansfield 6/09 Rel 4/10, Gateshead (SL) 2/10, Gateshead 5/10 Rel 5/11, Harrogate T 7/11		
Richard	Pell				17/11/1982	28	Boston	Notts Forest (Jun), York C (Ass Sch), Lincoln, USA, Boston T 7/99, Chesterfield (Trial), Gainsborough 8/04, Blyth 5/08 Rel 5/09, Alfreton 5/09, Byth Undisc 12/09, Harrogate T 6/10	16	1
Jake	Picton		6'01"	12 05	06/01/1991	20	Pontefract	Scunthorpe Rel c/s 10, Gainsborough (3ML) 8/09, Ilkeston 7/10 Rel 9/10, Harrogate T 9/10	29	1
Craig	Racliffe				12/04/1989	22		Athletic Bilbao (Sp) (Yth), Middlesbrough (Yth), Durham C, Cambridge C c/s 06, Mildenhall T (L) 10/08, Bury T 11/09, Biggleswade T, Harrogate T 8/11		
Danny	Stimpson		6'03"	13 07				Huddersfield (Yth), York C (Yth), Ange IF (Swe), Luton (Trial), Harrogate T 7/11		
Simon	Weaver		6'01"	10 08	20/12/1977	33	Doncaster	Sheff Wed Rel c/s 98, Doncaster (L) 2/97, Ilkeston, Grimsby (Trial) c/s 99, Nuneaton 2/00, Lincoln C 8/02, Macclesfield (2ML) 10/04, Kidderminster 12/04 Rel c/s 05, Scarborough 6/05 Rel 5/06, York C 8/06 Rel 8/06, Tamworth 8/06 Rel c/s 07, Salisbury (Trial) c/s 07, Boston U 12/07 Rel 5/08, Kings Lynn 5/08 Rel 1/09, Redditch 1/09, Ilkeston 2/09, Harrogate T (Pl/Man) 5/09 Man c/s 10		
Greg	Wright							Sheffield FC (Yth), Alfreton, Dinnington T (L), Retford 6/05, Sheffield FC 6/08, Goole AFC, Harrogate T 8/11		
MIDFIELDERS										
Peter	Bore		6'00"	12 02	04/11/1987	23	Grimsby	Grimsby Rel 5/11, York C (L) 9/08, Harrogate T 8/11		
Lee	Elam		5'08"	10 12	24/09/1976	34	Bradford	Guiseley, Southport 11/98, Morecambe 8/02, Halifax 5/03, Yeovil (L) 10/03 Perm 11/03, Chester (L) 3/04, Hornchurch 5/04, Burton 11/04, Morecambe 11/04 Rel 5/05, Crawley 7/05 Rel 9/05, Weymouth 9/05, Exeter 1/07 Rel 5/08, Altrincham 7/08 Rel 1/09, Northwich 1/09, Bradford PA 3/10, Stalybridge 8/10, Harrogate T 8/11		
Adam	Nowakowski				22/10/1986	24		Ripon C, Harrogate T	26	2
Ian	Ross		5'10"	11 00	23/01/1986	25	Sheffield	Sheff Utd, Boston U (3ML) 8/05, Bury (SL) 3/06, Notts County (SL) 7/06, Rotherham (2ML) 11/07 Perm 1/08 Rel c/s 08, Gainsborough 8/08, Alfreton 3/09, Harrogate T 5/11		
Michael	Tait				24/06/1988	23		Darlington (Yth), Gretna Rel c/s 08, Newcastle Blue Star (SL) 1/08, Blyth 8/08, Newcastle Blue Star 9/08, Workington 11/08, Newcastle Blue Star 1/09, Blyth 6/09, Harrogate T 6/11		
Stephen	Turnbull		5'10"	11 00	07/01/1987	24	South Shields	Hartlepool Rel 5/08, Gateshead (L) 12/05, Bury (2ML) 11/06, Rochdale (L) 3/07, Gateshead 7/08 Rel 5/09, Blyth 6/09, Harrogate T 5/11		
Laurie	Wilson		5'10"	11 03	05/12/1984	26	Brighton	Sheff Wed Rel c/s 04, Burton 7/04 Rel 4/05, Gresley (L) 12/04, Grantham (L) 1/05, Belper T (L) 2/05, Kidderminster 6/05, Hucknall 3/06, Alfreton 7/07, Hucknall 6/08, Ilkeston 5/10 Rel 9/10, Staveley Miners Welfare 9/10, Alfreton 10/10, Harrogate T 5/11		
FORWARDS										
Jonny	Allan		6'00"	11 03	24/05/1983	28	Penrith	Carlisle Rel c/s 02, Workington 8/02, Oxford U (Trial) 8/02 Northwich 8/02, Tranmere (Trial) 7/03, Lancaster 11/03, Halifax 12/03, Northwich 8/04, Gateshead 5/10 Rel 5/11, Harrogate T 5/11		
Paul	Brayson		5'07"	10 10	16/09/1977	33	Newcastle	Newcastle, Swansea (3ML) 1/97, Reading £100,000 3/98, Cardiff (SL) 3/00, Cardiff 7/00 Rel c/s 02, Cheltenham 8/02 Rel 5/04, York C (Trial) 7/04, Northwich 8/04, Gateshead (L) 3/05, York C 6/07, Gateshead 1/08, Newcastle Blue Star 6/08, Durham C 6/09, Blyth Spartans 8/09, Harrogate T 5/11		
Liam	Hardy				21/12/1987	23		Armthorpe Welfare, Harrogate T 6/10	20	5
Callum	Hassan		6'04"	14 03	23/01/1993	18		Hartlepool, Harrogate T 8/11		
Will	Turl							Leeds University, Royston T, Pontefract Coll, Harrogate T 8/11		
Danny	Wright		5'08"	10 07	19/10/1990	20	York	Scunthorpe (Scholar) Rel c/s 09, Sweden, Harrogate T 8/10, Knaresborough (Dual)	7	0

HINCKLEY UNITED

Chairman: Kevin Downes
Secretary: Ray Baggott **(T)** 07802 355 249 **(E)** raybaggott@yahoo.co.uk
Additional Committee Members:
Robert Mayne, Ku Akeredolu, A Dyer, P Moss, D Newman, D Radburn, M Sutton, K Thompson, Andy Gibbs.
Manager: Dean Thomas
Programme Editor: TBC **(E)** admin@hinckleyunited.com

Back Row (L-R): Jay-Lee Hodgson, Andre Gray, Tobias Dingwall, Ben Richards-Everton, Jermaine Clarke, Craig McAughtrie, Keenen Meakin-Richards.
Middle Row: Sam Palmer (Ass. Physio), Dave Radburn (Kit Manager), Joseph Hull, Paul Lister, Robert Oddy, Daniel Haystead, Denham Hinds, Jake Holt, Mark Dudley, Nicky Platnauer (Ass. Manager), Stuart Storer (Coach), Andy Keeley (Physio).
Front Row: Lloyd Kerry, Stuart Hendrie, Andrew Gooding, Dean Thomas (Manager), Tom Byrne, David Kolodynski, Daniel Newton.

Club Factfile

Founded: 1997 **Nickname:** United
Previous Names: Today's club was formed when Hinckley Athletic and Hinckley Town merged in 1997
Previous Leagues: As United: Southern 1997-2004

Club Colours (change): Red & navy/navy/red (All orange)

Ground: The Greene King Stadium, Leicester Road, Hinckley LE10 3DR **(T)** 01455 840 088
Capacity: 4,329 **Seats:** 630 **Covered:** 2,695 **Clubhouse:** Yes **Shop:** Yes

Directions
M1 J21 take M69 (Coventry) or M6 J2 take M69 (Leicester). M69 J2 take A5 North. At 3rd roundabout (Dodwells). Take 2nd exit A47 Earl Shilton & Industrial Estates, follow A47 over three roundabouts & a set of traffic lights at next roundabout take 3rd exit B4668. Stadium is 100 yards on right.

Previous Grounds: Not known

Record Attendance: 2,278 v Nuneaton Borough - 10/12/2005
Record Victory: 9-1 v Rocester (A) - 28/08/2000
Record Defeat: 1-7 v Stalybridge Celtic (A) - Conference North 03/03/2009
Record Goalscorer: Jamie Lenton - 74
Record Appearances: Jamie Lenton - 280
Additional Records:

Senior Honours: Southern League Division 1 Western 2000-01

10 YEAR RECORD

01-02		02-03		03-04		04-05		05-06		06-07		07-08		08-09		09-10		10-11	
SthP	12	SthP	13	SthP	6	Conf N	12	Conf N	10	Conf N	4	Conf N	19	Conf N	10	Conf N	7	Conf N	15

HINCKLEY UNITED

No.	Date	Comp	H/A	Opponents	Att:	Result	Goalscorers	Pos
1	Sat-14-Aug	BSN	A	Alfreton Town	516	L 0-1		17
2	Mon-16-Aug	BSN	H	Boston United	615	L 0-1		19
3	Sat-21-Aug	BSN	H	Stalybridge Celtic	436	W 5-2	Franklin 54, King 2 (56, 76), Reid 68, Strachan 78	14
4	Mon-23-Aug	BSN	A	Worcester City	746	L 2-3	Strachan 4, Roberts 45	15
5	Sat-28-Aug	BSN	H	Droylsden	336	D 1-1	Reid 21	15
6	Mon-30-Aug	BSN	A	Corby Town	543	L 0-2		19
7	Sat-04-Sep	BSN	A	Harrogate Town	310	D 2-2	Kerry 12, Gray 73	18
8	Sat-11-Sep	BSN	H	Guiseley	371	L 1-2	Gray 73	18
9	Sat-18-Sep	BSN	A	Eastwoood Town	347	L 2-6	Reid 25, Gray 36	18
10	Sat-02-Oct	BSN	H	Stafford Rangers	444	W 4-0	Reid 32, Kerry 70, King 2 (pen 81, 83)	16
11	Sat-16-Oct	BSN	A	Vauxhall Motors	201	L 0-2		17
12	Sat-23-Oct	BSN	H	Solihull Moors	376	D 2-2	Reid 49, Roberts 70	16
13	Sat-30-Oct	BSN	A	Nuneaton Town	1412	L 0-2		18
14	Sat-06-Nov	BSN	H	Alfreton Town	514	L 1-3	Gray 90	18
15	Sat-13-Nov	BSN	A	Stafford Rangers	506	W 3-1	Reid 43, Og (Harris) 48, Newton 71	17
16	Mon-03-Jan	BSN	H	Corby Town	502	D 3-3	Clarke 5, Reid 71, Ricketts 81	18
17	Sat-08-Jan	BSN	A	Redditch United	279	W 3-2	Newton 66, Fairclough 90, Strachan 90	18
18	Tue-11-Jan	BSN	A	Boston United	955	L 0-3		18
19	Mon-17-Jan	BSN	H	Hyde FC	349	W 2-0	Reid 5, Kerry 14	15
20	Sat-22-Jan	BSN	A	AFC Telford	1516	D 2-2	Hooman 31, Clarke 71	16
21	Tue-25-Jan	BSN	A	Guiseley	366	L 2-3	Kerry 11, Reid 76	17
22	Sat-29-Jan	BSN	H	Gainsborough Trinity	461	W 3-1	Belcher 25, Clarke 2 (43, 78)	15
23	Mon-07-Feb	BSN	H	Gloucester City	337	W 3-0	Reid 2 (27, 90), Kerry 43	14
24	Sat-12-Feb	BSN	H	Vauxhall Motors	449	L 2-3	Reid pen 27, Ricketts 56	15
25	Mon-14-Feb	BSN	H	Harrogate Town	309	W 4-0	Mace 19, Kerry 2 (33, pen 88), Ricketts 58	13
26	Sat-19-Feb	BSN	A	Blyth Spartans	463	L 0-4		14
27	Mon-21-Feb	BSN	A	Droylsden	192	L 2-3	Strachan 52, Ricketts 68	14
28	Sun-27-Feb	BSN	H	Nuneaton Town	1208	L 0-3		15
29	Sat-05-Mar	BSN	H	Workington	318	L 1-2	Gooding 47	15
30	Sat-12-Mar	BSN	A	Stalybridge Celtic	448	D 1-1	Belcher 24	17
31	Wed-16-Mar	BSN	H	Eastwoood Town	271	L 2-3	Belcher 2 (44, 46)	17
32	Sat-19-Mar	BSN	A	Gainsborough Trinity	345	W 1-0	Clarke 70	16
33	Tue-22-Mar	BSN	A	Gloucester City	201	L 1-2	Belcher 52	17
34	Sat-26-Mar	BSN	H	Redditch United	356	W 4-0	Newton 26, Gray 2 (29, 50), Bains 84	16
35	Sat-02-Apr	BSN	H	Blyth Spartans	424	W 5-1	Kerry 45, Clarke 45, Belcher 54, Reid 60, Gray 78	16
36	Sat-09-Apr	BSN	A	Hyde FC	295	L 0-3		16
37	Sat-16-Apr	BSN	H	AFC Telford	625	D 1-1	Gray 7	17
38	Sat-23-Apr	BSN	A	Solihull Moors	316	W 7-2	Gray 4 (7, 29, 33, 57), Gooding 16, Ricketts 2 (22, 74)	15
39	Mon-25-Apr	BSN	H	Worcester City	398	W 3-1	Kerry pen 54, Ricketts 2 (76, 79)	14
40	Sat-30-Apr	BSN	A	Workington	336	L 1-3	Gray 86	15

CUPS

No.	Date	Comp	H/A	Opponents	Att:	Result	Goalscorers
1	Sat-25-Sep	FAC 2Q	H	Coventry Sphinx	301	W 2-0	Strachan 71, Gray 75
2	Sat-09-Oct	FAC 3Q	A	Redditch United	563	L 0-1	
3	Sat-20-Nov	FAT 3Q	A	FC United of Manchester	1249	W 2-1	Clarke 7, Kerry 35
4	Sat-11-Dec	FAT 1	A	Droylsden	175	L 3-4	Reid 31, Giddings 33, Fairclough 58

League
Starts
Substitute
Unused Sub

Cups
Starts
Substitute
Unused Sub

Goals (Lg)
Goals (Cup)

HAYSTEAD	MACE	MORLEY	DILLON	MUNDAY	FRANKLIN	KERRY	STRACHAN	FAIRCLOUGH	GRAY	REID	KING	ROBERTS	NEWTON	LISTER	BLACKWELL	BURGESS	HINDS	GIDDINGS	BAINS	DOZIE	BELCHER	CLARKE	HOOMAN	RICKETTS	GOODING	THACKERAY	DEAKIN	GUDGER	CHRISTIE	HOLT	LEE
X	X	X	X	X	X	X	X	X	X	X	S	S	S	U	U																
X	X	X	X	X	X	X	X	X	X	X	S	S	S	U	U																
X	X	X		X	X	X	X	S	X	X	X	X	U	S	S																
X	X	X			X	X	X	S	X		X	X	X	X	S																
X	X	X				X	X		X	X	X	X	S	X	S	X															
X	X	X				X	X	S	X	X	X	X	U	X	S	X															
X	X	X				X	X	S	X	X	X	X	U	X	S	X															
X	X	X	S			X		S	X	X	X	X	S	X	X	X															
X	X	X	X			X	X	X	X	X	X	S	S		S	X															
	X		X			X	X	X	X	X	S	U	S	X	S		X	X	X												
X	X					X	X	S	X	X	X	X	U	X	U	U		X	X	S											
X	X					X	X	X	S	X		X	X	X	S				X	X											
X	X					X		X	S	X	X	X	X	X	U	X			X	S											
X	X					X	X	S	X	U	U		X	X	U	X		X		S	X	X									
X						X	X	S	X	X		U	S	X	X	X		X		S	X	X									
	X					X	X	U		X			S		U	X	X	X	X	U	X	X		X	S						
	X					X	X	S		X			X		U	X			X	S	X	X		X	S	X					
	X					X	X	S		X			X		U	X			X	S	S	X		X	X	X					
	X					X	X	U	U	X			S					X	X	S	S	X	X	X	X		X				
	X					X	X	U	U	X			S						X	U	U	X	X	X	X		X	X			
	X					X	X	S	S	X			U						X	U	X	U	X	X	X		X	X			
	X					X	U	U	S	X			U						X	U	X	X	X	X	X		X	X			
	X					X	U	U	S	X			U						X	U	X	X	X	X	X		X	X			
	X					X	S	S	S	X			U						X	U	X	X	X	X	X		X	X			
	X					X	U		U	X			S					U	X	S	X	X		X	X		X	X	X		
	X					X	U		S	X			S					S	X	U	X	X		X	X		X	X	X		
	X						X	X	S	X			U				X		X	U	X			X	X			X	X		
	X					X		U	S	X			U					U	X		X	X	X	X	X		X	X	S		
	X					X	X		X	X			S				X	U	U		S		X	X	X		U	X	X		
	U					X	X		U	X			U				X	X	X		X		X	X	X		U	S	X		
	U					X	X		U	X			S					X	X	U	X		X	X	X		X	S	X		
	U					X			U	X			S					X	X	U	X	X	X	X	X		X	S	X		
	X					X			S	X			X		S		U		X	S	X	X	X	X	X		X				
	X					X			X	X			X		S		U		X	S	X	X			X		X	X		S	
	X					X			X	X			S		S		U		X	S	X	X			X		X	X		U	X
	X					X			X	X			S		S		X		X	S	X			X	X			X		U	X
						X			X	X			S		U			U	X	U	X	X		X	X		X	X		U	X
						X			X	X			U		S			U	X	S	X	X		X	X		X	X		S	X
						X			X	X			X					S	X	S		X		X	X		X	X		S	X
						X			X	X			X		S			S	X			X		X	X		X	X		S	X
X	X	X	X			X	X	S	X	X	X	U	S	X	S	X															
X	X					X	X	S	X	X	X	U	S	X	X	U		X	X												
X						X	X	S	X	X		U	S	X	U	U		X	X		X	X	X								
X	U					X	X	S	X	X		X	U			X		X	X	S		X	X								
14	32	9	4	3	4	39	23	7	21	38	9	9	10	11	2	11	6	9	28	1	21	21	12	23	23	2	18	17	7	0	6
0	0	0	1	0	0	0	1	12	10	0	3	3	18	1	14	0	0	3	0	14	3	0	0	0	2	0	0	3	1	4	0
0	3	0	0	0	0	0	4	6	6	1	1	2	12	2	9	1	3	5	1	11	1	1	0	0	0	0	2	0	0	3	0
4	2	1	1	0	0	4	4	0	4	4	2	1	0	3	1	2	0	3	3	0	1	2	2	0	0	0	0	0	0	0	0
0	0	0	0	0	0	0	0	4	0	0	0	0	3	0	1	0	0	0	0	1	0	0	0	0	0	0	0	0	0	0	0
0	1	0	0	0	0	0	0	0	0	0	0	3	1	0	1	2	0	0	0	0	0	0	0	0	0	0	0	0	0	0	0
0	1	0	0	0	1	9	4	1	13	13	4	2	3	0	0	0	0	0	1	0	6	6	1	8	2	0	0	0	0	0	0
0	0	0	0	0	0	1	1	1	1	1	0	0	0	0	0	0	0	1	0	0	0	1	0	0	0	0	0	0	0	0	0

PLAYING SQUAD 2011/12

Existing Players		SN	HT	WT	DOB	AGE	POB	Career	Apps	Goals
GOALKEEPERS										
Danny	Haystead		6'01"	11 09	13/02/1986	25	Chesterfield	Sheff Utd Rel c/s 05, Scarborough (L) 11/04, Hinckley U 8/05 Rel c/s 07, Moor Green (L) 8/05, Quorn (SL) (06/07), Quorn c/s 07, Sheffield FC 2/08, Ilkeston 6/08, Hucknall 6/09, Hinckley U 6/10, Boston U 12/10 Rel 5/11, Hinckley U 5/11	14	0
Denham	Hinds				26/05/1992	19		Leicester (Yth), Hinckley U, Oadby T, Hinckley U 9/09	6	0
DEFENDERS										
Mark	Dudley		5'10"	12 02	29/01/1990	21	Doncaster	Derby Rel c/s 10, Tamworth (L) 3/09, Alfreton (L) 10/09, Hinckley U (L) 11/09, Hinckley U (L) 2/10, St Paricks (Ire) 6/10, Stafford R 8/10, Hinckley U 8/11		
Louis	Horne		6'02"	12 07	28/05/1991	20	Bradford	Bradford C Rel c/s 11, Barrow (L) 2/09, Fleetwood (L) 10/10 (10/11 1,0), FC Halifax (L) 11/10, Hinckley U 8/11		
Joseph	Hull				18/12/1991	19		Bromsgrove, Kidderminster 8/09, Redditch 8/10, Hinckley U 5/11		
Paul	Lister				03/12/1989	21	Sheffield	Chesterfield (Jun), Burton, Grantham (SL) 11/08, Hinckley U 7/09, Alfreton 12/10 Rel 5/11, Frickley (2ML) 3/11, Hinckley U 5/11	12	0
Craig	McAughtrie		6'04"	13 10	03/03/1981	30	Burton	Sheff Utd Rel c/s 00, Carlisle 8/00 Rel c/s 02, Stafford R 7/02, Tamworth Undisc 9/07 Rel 5/09, Kings Lynn 6/09, Eastwood T 9/09 Rel 4/10, Stafford R (SL) 1/10, Stafford R 5/10, Hinckley U 6/11		
Rob	Oddy				13/11/1985	25	Coventry	Coventry (Scholar) Rel c/s 04, Nuneaton (SL) 3/04, Nuneaton 8/04 Rel 5/11, Rugby T (L) 3/08, Hinckley U 6/11		
Ben	Richards-Everton					17/10/1991		19 Romulus, Carlisle (Scholar) 9/09, Romulus 1/10, Cradley T, Kettering (Trial) 4/11, Kidderminster (Trial) 4/11, Hinckley U 8/11	Birmingham	
MIDFIELDERS										
Jacob	Blackwell		6'01"	12 13	15/11/1991	19	Coventry	Coventry (Scholar), Hinckley U 8/10, Loughborough D (L) 1/11	16	0
Tom	Byrne				17/05/1988	23		Kidderminster Rel c/s 06, Quorn 7/06, Grantham 1/07, Quorn 3/08, Hinckley U 6/11		
Andy	Gooding		5'07"	10 05	30/04/1988	23	Coventry	Coventry Rel 1/08, Burton (2ML) 8/07, Rushden & D 1/08 Rel 5/08, Hinckley U 7/08, Corby T 5/10, Solihull Moors (L) 10/10, Hinckley U (SL) 12/10, Hinckley U 5/11	25	2
Lloyd	Kerry		6'02"	12 04	22/01/1988	23	Chesterfield	Sheff Utd Rel c/s 08, Torquay (2ML) 2/07, Chesterfield (SL) 2/08, Chesterfield 8/08 Rel c/s 10, Alfreton (L) 11/09, Kidderminster (L) 3/10, Hinckley U 7/10	39	9
Keenan	Meakin-Richards							Wolves (Yth), Walsall (Yth) Rel c/s 06, Hednesford c/s 06, Stafford R 2/08 Rel 3/08, Bromsgrove 3/08, Evesham, Coleshill T 3/09, Rocester, Willenhall 9/09, Chasetown 12/09, Highgate U 1/10, Bromsgrove 3/10, Stourport, Halesowen T 1/11, Hinckley U 8/11		
FORWARDS										
Jermaine	Clarke				10/12/1983	27		Aston Villa (Yth), Walsall (Scholar), Local Football, Castle Vale Kings Heath, Evesham 1/04, Redditch (2ML) 10/05, Redditch (L) 1/06 Perm, Halesowen T (L) 11/06, Bromsgrove (L) 3/07, Bromsgrove, Newport C 11/07 Rel 6/08, Bromsgrove, Rushall O (L) 11/08 Perm, Romulus 2/09, Evesham 3/09, Weston-Super-Mare 12/09 Rel c/s 10, Evesham, Hinckley U 11/10	21	6
Andre	Gray		5'11"	12 06	26/06/1991	20	Wolverhampton	Shrewsbury Rel c/s 10, AFC Telford (2ML) 11/09, Hinckley U (L) 3/10, Hinckley U 6/10	31	13
Stuart	Hendrie		5'09"	11 00	01/11/1989	21	Solihull	Walsall (Yth), Coleshill T, Stratford T, Coleshill T, Alvechurch 3/09, Atherstone c/s 09, Morecambe 8/10 Rel c/s 11, Tamworth (L) 3/11 (10/11 4,0), Hinckley U 7/11		
Jaylee	Hodgson		5'11"		17/10/1981	29	Nottingham	Heanor, Long Eaton 9/10, Rainworth MW, Loughborough D 11/10, Shepshed D 3/11, Boston U (Trial) 7/11, Hinckley U 8/11		
Jake	Holt							Hinckley U	4	0
David	Kolodynski				25/02/1989	22	Rugby	Rugby T, Cambridge C £1,500 6/10, Hinckley U 6/11		
Daniel	Newton				18/03/1991	20		Hinckley Downes, Hinckley U (Dual) 12/09, Hinckley U 6/10	28	3

HISTON

Chairman: Russell Hands
Secretary: Howard Wilkins (T) 01223 237 373 (E) secretary@histonfc.co.uk
Additional Committee Members:
Angelo Dama, Graham Muncey, Graham Eales.

Manager: David Livermore
Programme Editor: Howard Wilkins (E) secretary@histonfc.co.uk

Back Row (l-r): Daniel Sparkes, Zak Mills, Harri Hawkins, Jorg Stadelmann, David Knight, Jim Stevenson, Remy Clerima, Ollie Cleaver
Middle: Lewis Taaffe, Grant Roberts, Dan Holman, Dallas Moore, Danny Fitzsimons, Omer Riza, Matt Breeze, Jay Dowie
Front: Joe Asensi, Jack Sessions, Nick Whitehouse (Physio), Brian Page (Asst Manager), David Livermore (Manager), Howard Willmott (Academy Director), Charlie Day, Eugene Libertucci

Club Factfile

Founded: 1904 **Nickname:** The Stutes
Previous Names: Histon Institute
Previous Leagues: Cambridgeshire 1904-48, Spartan 1948-60, Delphian 1960-63, Eastern Counties 1966-2000, Southern 2000-05.
Club Colours (change): Red and black stripes/black/black (All blue)

Ground: The Glassworld Stadium, Bridge Road, Impington, Cambridge CB4 9PH (T) 01223 237 373
Capacity: 3,250 **Seats:** 450 **Covered:** 1,800 **Clubhouse:** Yes **Shop:** Yes

Directions
From the M11 (Northbound) Junc 14, take the A14 eastbound signed towards Newmarket. Take the first exit off the A14 and at the roundabout, take the first exit onto the B1049. Go straight over the traffic lights, past the Holiday Inn Hotel (on your right) and the entrance to the club is half a mile on your right.

Previous Grounds: Not known

Record Attendance: 6,400 v King's Lynn - FA Cup 1956
Record Victory: 11-0 v March Town - Cambridgeshire Invitation Cup 15/02/01
Record Defeat: 1-8 v Ely City - Eastern Counties Division One 1994
Record Goalscorer: Neil Kennedy - 292
Record Appearances: Neil Andrews and Neil Kennedy
Additional Records: Paid £6,000 to Chelmsford City for Ian Cambridge 2000. Received £30,000 from Manchester United for Guiliano Maiorana.
Senior Honours: Eastern Counties League Cup 1990-91, Eastern Counties League 1999-2000, Southern League Premier 2004-05, Conference South 2006-07.

10 YEAR RECORD

01-02	02-03	03-04	04-05	05-06	06-07	07-08	08-09	09-10	10-11
SthE 4	SthE 10	SthE 2	SthP 1	Conf S 5	Conf S 1	Conf 7	Conf 3	Conf 18	Conf 24

HISTON

No.	Date	Comp	H/A	Opponents	Att:	Result	Goalscorers	Pos
								- 5 points Jan
1	Sat-14-Aug	BSP	H	Barrow	533	W 3-1	McCrae 29, Attwood 2 (45, 70)	2
2	Tue-17-Aug	BSP	A	AFC Wimbledon	3126	L 0-2		13
3	Sat-21-Aug	BSP	A	Newport County	1927	D 2-2	McCrae 29, Okay 64	10
4	Tue-24-Aug	BSP	H	Eastbourne Borough	421	D 1-1	Oyebanjo 87	11
5	Sat-28-Aug	BSP	H	Kettering Town	681	L 0-3		21
6	Mon-30-Aug	BSP	A	Grimsby Town	2925	L 1-2	Wootton 23	22
7	Sat-04-Sep	BSP	A	Hayes & Yeading United	359	W 2-1	Murray 34, Riza pen 50	16
8	Sat-11-Sep	BSP	H	Crawley Town	497	L 0-2		20
9	Sat-18-Sep	BSP	H	Tamworth	653	L 1-2	Riza 41	20
10	Tue-21-Sep	BSP	A	Rushden & Diamonds	926	L 0-2		21
11	Sat-25-Sep	BSP	A	Wrexham	2376	L 0-4		23
12	Tue-28-Sep	BSP	H	Gateshead	285	L 1-3	Riza pen 90	23
13	Sat-02-Oct	BSP	A	Fleetwood Town	1458	D 1-1	Murray 67	23
14	Tue-05-Oct	BSP	H	Southport	368	W 2-1	Clerima 9, Murray 19	22
15	Sat-09-Oct	BSP	H	Altrincham	655	W 3-0	Oyebanjo pen 15, Murray 74, D Mills 90	21
16	Sat-16-Oct	BSP	A	Forest Green Rovers	741	W 1-0	Sparkes 46	17
17	Sat-30-Oct	BSP	H	Wrexham	914	D 1-1	Murray 90	17
18	Sat-13-Nov	BSP	H	Kidderminster Harriers	571	L 0-1		19
19	Sat-20-Nov	BSP	A	Luton Town	5963	L 1-5	Murray 43	21
20	Thu-25-Nov	BSP	H	Bath City	470	L 1-2	Sparkes 77	21
21	Sat-01-Jan	BSP	A	Cambridge United	3225	D 0-0		21
22	Mon-03-Jan	BSP	H	Grimsby Town	1122	L 1-6	Riza 83	22
23	Tue-11-Jan	BSP	A	Darlington	1725	L 1-3	Murray 60	24
24	Sat-15-Jan	BSP	H	York City	578	L 1-2	Stevenson 40	24
25	Sat-22-Jan	BSP	A	Mansfield Town	1880	L 0-1		24
26	Tue-25-Jan	BSP	A	Barrow	883	D 1-1	Clerima 2	24
27	Sat-29-Jan	BSP	H	Newport County	452	D 0-0		24
28	Tue-01-Feb	BSP	H	Fleetwood Town	255	W 1-0	Riza 13	24
29	Sat-05-Feb	BSP	A	Tamworth	885	W 1-0	Riza pen 38	23
30	Sat-12-Feb	BSP	H	Hayes & Yeading United	463	L 0-1		23
31	Tue-15-Feb	BSP	A	Altrincham	621	W 3-0	Attwood 47, Riza 72, Clerima 86	22
32	Sat-19-Feb	BSP	A	Eastbourne Borough	783	D 2-2	Riza 39, Clerima 49	23
33	Tue-22-Feb	BSP	H	Cambridge United	1903	L 0-2		23
34	Tue-01-Mar	BSP	A	Southport	652	L 1-3	Riza pen 90	23
35	Sat-05-Mar	BSP	A	Crawley Town	3031	L 0-5		24
36	Tue-15-Mar	BSP	A	Kettering Town	782	L 3-4	Riza 16, Clerima 31, Murray 38	24
37	Tue-22-Mar	BSP	H	Mansfield Town	380	L 2-3	Riza pen 41, Stevenson 45	24
38	Sat-26-Mar	BSP	A	York City	2364	L 0-1		24
39	Sat-02-Apr	BSP	H	Forest Green Rovers	426	L 0-3		24
40	Tue-05-Apr	BSP	H	Rushden & Diamonds	363	L 0-2		24
41	Sat-09-Apr	BSP	A	Gateshead	567	L 0-2		24 Relegated
42	Tue-12-Apr	BSP	H	Darlington	277	L 0-1		24
43	Sat-16-Apr	BSP	H	AFC Wimbledon	750	L 0-4		24
44	Sat-23-Apr	BSP	A	Bath City	754	L 1-2	Sparkes 62	24
45	Mon-25-Apr	BSP	H	Luton Town	1159	L 0-4		24
46	Sat-30-Apr	BSP	A	Kidderminster Harriers	1496	D 2-2	Riza 40, Murray 77	24

CUPS

No.	Date	Comp	H/A	Opponents	Att:	Result	Goalscorers
1	Sat-23-Oct	FAC 4Q	A	Havant & Waterlooville	905	L 0-2	
2	Sat-11-Dec	FAT 1	H	Bath City	263	L 2-3	Sparkes 30, Attwood 55

League
Starts
Substitute
Unused Sub

Cups
Starts
Substitute
Unused Sub

Goals (Lg)
Goals (Cup)

WELCH	OYEBANJO	OKAY	CLERIMA	ILESANMI	SPARKES	Z MILLS	MCCRAE	ATTWOOD	WOOTTON	D MILLS	ADJEI	STEWART	LAWTON	STEVENSON	SAGNA	PAVETT	DIARRA	MURRAY	TAAFFE	RIZA	SMITH	CLARKE	FITZSIMONS	LIVERMORE	AINSLEY	DOWIE	YORK	EVERDELL	OKOJIE	SESSIONS	FODERINGHAM	ASAFU-ADJAYE	COX	DAY	HAWKINS	ASENSI								
1	2	4	5	6	11	17	13	14	8	12	21	3	16	18	23	22	15	9	19	7	22	10	24	25	23	20	26	27	28	21	30	6	13	12	23	29								
X	X	X	X	X	X	X	X	X	X	X	S	U	U	U	U																													
X	X	X	X	X	X	X	X	X		X	X		U	S	S	S	U																											
X	X	X	X			X	X	X	X	X	S	X	U	U		X	S	U																										
X	X	X	X	S		X	X	X	X	X	U	X	U			X		S	S																									
X	X	X	X	X		X	X		X	X	S	U	U	S				X	S	X																								
X	X	X	X	X		S	X		X	X	S	X	U	U				X	S	X																								
X		X	X	X		X	X	S	X	X	U	X	U	U				X	S	X																								
X		X	X	X	X	X	X	X	X	X	U		U		U					X	S	S																						
X		X	X	X	X	X	X	X	X	X	U		U						U	X	S	S																						
X		X	X	X	X	X	X	X		X	S		U	S					U	X	S	X																						
X		X	X	X	X		X			X	S		U	S						X	X	X	X	U																				
X		X	X	X	X		X		X	X	S		U	U						X	X	U	X	U																				
X	X	X	X	X	X		X		X	S	U		U	U				X			X	U	X																					
X	X	X	X	X	X		X		X	S	U		U	U				X			X	U	X																					
X	X	X	X	X	X		X	S	X	S			U					X		S	X	U	X																					
X	X	X	X	X	X	U	X	U	X	U	U		U					X			X		X																					
X	X	X	X	X	X	X	U	S	X	S	X		U	U				X			X																							
X	X	X	X		X	X	U	S	X	X	S	S	U					X			X			X																				
X		X	X		X	X	S	U	X	U		X	S	X				X	S		X				X																			
X	X		X		X	U	X	U	X	S		X	U	X				X	U		X				X																			
X	X	X	X		X	X		S	X				U	U				X	S	X	X			X		U																		
X	X		X			X		X	X				U	X				X	S	X	X			X		U	S	U																
X	X	X	X		S	X		X	X				U	S				X	S	X	X			X		U																		
X	X	X	X			X		X	X			U	U	X				X	S	X	X						U		S															
X	X	X	X		S	X		X	X				U	X				X	U	X	X			U					U															
X	X	X	X		X	X			X				U	S				X	S	X	X			X			U		U															
X	X	X	X		X	X		S	X			U	U	X				X	S	X	X						U																	
X	X	X	X		X	X		S	X			U	U	X				X	S	X	X						U																	
X	X	X	X		X	X		S	X				U	X				X	U	X	X			S					U															
X	X	X	X		X	X		S	X				U	X				X	S	X	X			U					S															
X	X	S	X		U	X		X	X				U	X				X	X	X	S			X			S																	
X	X	S	X		U	X		X	X			U	U	X				X	X	X	S			X																				
X	X	X	X		S	X		X	U			U	U	X				X	X	X	S			X																				
X	X	X	X		S	X		X	S			U	U	U				X	X	X	X			X																				
X	X	X	X		S	X			X			U	S	S				X	X	X	X			X					U															
	X	X	X		X	X						X	X	S				X	X	X	X					U	U		U	U														
X	X	X	X		X	X						S	U	X				X	X	X	X			S		S				U														
			X		X	X		S				U	U	X				X	S	X	X			X		U					X	X	X											
	X		X			X		X				U	U	X					X	X	X			U		X			S		X	X		S										
	X		X		S	X						U	U	X					X	X	X					X			S	S	X	X		X										
	X	X				X			X			U	U	X				X	X	X	X					S			S		X	X		S										
	X	X				X			U			U	U	X				X	X	X	X					X			S		X		S		X									
	X	X			X	X							U	X				X		X	X			S		S			U		X	X	X		S									
	X	X	X		X	X							U	X				X		X	X					U			X		X		S		S	S								
	X	X	X		X	X							U	X				X	S	X	X					U			X		X		S		U									
	X	X	X		X	X							U	S				X	U	X	X								X		X		U		X	U								
X	X	X	X	X	X	X	X	U	X	S	S		U	U				X			X																							
X	X	X	X		X	U	S	X	X	U		X	U	U				X			X				X																			
36	38	39	43	15	28	38	17	16	31	13	2	7	1	21	0	2	0	35	11	34	33	2	6	11	2	3	0	0	3	0	9	5	2	1	2	0	0	0	0	0	0	0	0	0
0	0	2	0	1	6	1	1	10	1	5	8	2	2	9	1	1	1	1	15	1	6	2	0	3	0	3	2	0	6	1	0	0	3	2	2	1	0	0	0	0	0	0	0	0
0	0	0	0	0	2	2	2	3	2	2	7	14	43	10	2	0	1	1	6	0	0	4	0	5	0	7	5	1	6	2	0	0	1	0	1	1	0	0	0	0	0	0	0	0
2	2	2	2	1	2	1	1	1	2	0	0	1	0	0	0	0	0	2	0	0	2	0	0	0	1	0	0	0	0	0	0	0	0	0	0	0	0	0	0	0	0	0	0	0
0	0	0	0	0	0	0	1	0	0	1	1	0	0	0	0	0	0	0	0	0	0	0	0	0	0	0	0	0	0	0	0	0	0	0	0	0	0	0	0	0	0	0	0	0
0	0	0	0	0	0	1	0	1	0	1	0	0	2	2	0	0	0	0	0	0	0	0	0	0	0	0	0	0	0	0	0	0	0	0	0	0	0	0	0	0	0	0	0	0
0	2	1	5	0	3	0	2	3	1	1	0	0	0	2	0	0	0	9	0	12	0	0	0	0	0	0	0	0	0	0	0	0	0	0	0	0	0	0	0	0	0	0	0	0
0	0	0	0	0	1	0	0	1	0	0	0	0	0	0	0	0	0	0	0	0	0	0	0	0	0	0	0	0	0	0	0	0	0	0	0	0	0	0	0	0	0	0	0	0

PLAYING SQUAD 2011/12

Existing Players		SN	HT	WT	DOB	AGE	POB	Career	Apps	Goals
GOALKEEPERS										
Calum	Kitscha						Edmonton	Bishops Stortford (Yth), Histon 7/11		
David	Knight		6'00"	11 07	15/01/1987	24	Houghton-le-Spring	Middlesbrough, Darlington (2WL) 12/05, Oldham (L) 8/06, Swansea 8/07 Rel c/s 08, Mansfield 10/08 Rel 11/08, Middlesbrough 11/08, Darlington 7/09 Rel 12/09, Histon 2/10, York C (SL) 7/10		
Jorg	Stadelmann				05/03/1980	31	Austria	FC Blau-Weiß Feldkirch Jugend (Aust), SK Brederis (Aust) 7/98, FC Blau-Weiß Feldkirch 7/99, Rot-Weiß Rankweil (Aust) 7/02, FC Blau-Weiß Feldkirch (Aust0, FC Hard (Aust) 7/07, Histon 6/11		
DEFENDERS										
Remy	Clerima				20/09/1990	20		L'Orient (Fra), Histon 8/10	43	5
Danny	Fitzsimons		6'00"	11 02	05/05/1992	19		Millwall (Scholar), QPR 7/10 Rel 12/10, Histon (L) 9/10, Boreham Wood 1/11, Yeovil 2/11 Rel c/s 11, Histon 8/11	6	0
Harri	Hawkins							Histon	4	0
Sam	Hearn							Histon		
Lewis	McDonald							Histon		
Zak	Mills				28/05/1992	19		Histon	39	0
Dallas	Moore							Grimsby (Scholar) c/s 10, Halesowen T 8/10, St Neots 1/11, Histon 8/11		
MIDFIELDERS										
Joe	Asensi							Histon	1	0
Matt	Breeze				06/02/1993	18	Peterborough	Peterborough, Shepshed D (WE) 12/10, Histon (SL) 8/11		
Ollie	Cleaver		6'00"	13 00	25/01/1992	19	Enfield	Luton (Scholar), Harlow 10/09, Cheshunt 3/10, Forest Green 8/10, Histon 3/11		
Charlie	Day							Histon	3	0
Jay	Dowie				28/12/1991	19		Histon	6	0
Eugene	Libertucci							Histon		
David	Livermore		5'11"	12 02	20/05/1980	31	Edmonton	Arsenal, Millwall (5WL) 7/99 £30,000 9/99, Leeds £400,000 7/06, Hull C £400,000 8/06 Rel c/s 08, Oldham (2ML) 1/08, Brighton 7/08 Rel 2/10, Luton (2ML) 3/09, Barnet 2/10, Histon (Pl/Man) 8/10	14	0
Grant	Roberts							Leeds (Yth), Sheff Utd (Scholar), Ossett T 11/09, Guiseley (Reserves) c/s 10, Histon 8/11		
Iain	Salt							Cambridge C, Haverhill R 8/06, Wivenhoe 2/08 Rel 3/08, Ely C, Broxbourne B 11/09, Cheshunt 12/09, Histon 8/11		
James	Stevenson				17/05/1992	19		Histon	30	2
FORWARDS										
Dan	Holman							Long Buckby, Oxford C 8/10, Long Buckby 9/10, Histon 7/11		
Omer	Riza		5'08"	11 02	08/11/1979	31	Edmonton	Arsenal, Den Haag (Holl) (SL) 2/99, West Ham £20,000 12/99 Rel c/s 02, Barnet (3ML) 10/00, Cambridge U (SL) 3/01, Aberdeen (Trial) 7/02, Cambridge U 8/02 Rel c/s 03, Denizlispor (Tur) 7/03, Trabzonspor (Tur) 1/06 Rel 1/08, Shrewsbury 4/09 Rel 1/10, Aldershot T 2/10 Rel c/s 10, Stevenage (Trial) c/s 10, Histon 8/10	35	12
Jack	Sessions							Norwich U, Histon	1	0
Kaine	Sheppard							L.Orient, St Albans (WE) 1/11, Histon (WE) 8/11		
Daniel	Sparkes		6'04"	14 09	20/07/1991	20	Peterborough	Histon	34	3
Lewis	Taaffe				18/10/1991	19		Histon	26	0

HYDE FC

Chairman: Allan Kenyon
Secretary: Andrew McAnulty (T) 07866 165 957 (E) secretary@hydefc.co.uk
Additional Committee Members:
Ted Davies, Jonathan Manship, Howard Eggleston, Luke Edwards, Alan Hackey, Steve Johnson.
Manager: Gary Lowe
Programme Editor: Mark Dring (E) mark@dring16.fsnet.co.uk

Club Factfile

Founded: 1919 **Nickname:** The Tigers
Previous Names: Hyde F.C., Hyde United > 2011.
Previous Leagues: Lancashire & Cheshire 1919-21, Manchester 1921-30, Cheshire County 1930-68, 1970-82, Northern Premier 1968-70, 1983-2004

Club Colours (change): Red/navy/navy (Navy/white/red)

Ground: Ewen Fields, Walker Lane, Hyde SK14 2SB (T) 0871 200 2116
Capacity: 4,250 **Seats:** 550 **Covered:** 4,000 **Clubhouse:** Yes **Shop:** Yes

Directions
M60 (Manchester Orbital Motorway) to Junction 24, take the M67 (towards Sheffield) to junction 3 (Hyde/Dukinfield/Stalybridge). Once on exit slipway, keep to the right-hand lane heading for Hyde town centre. At the traffic lights at end of the slipway turn right, then at the second set of lights turn left (Morrisons on left) onto Mottram Road. Turn right at next lights onto Lumn Road. Left at Give Way sign onto Walker Lane. Ground entrance is on left, just after Hyde Leisure Pool, and is clearly signposted. Please note for Satnav, use SK14 5PL

Previous Grounds:

Record Attendance: 9,500 v Nelson - FA Cup 1952
Record Victory: 9-1 v South Liverpool 04/1991
Record Defeat: 0-26 v Preston North End - FA Cup 1887
Record Goalscorer: David Nolan - 117 in 404 appearances (1992-2003). Ged Kimmins - 117 in 274 appearances (1993-98)
Record Appearances: David Nolan - 404 (1992-2003)
Additional Records: Paid £8,000 to Mossley for Jim McCluskie 1989
Received £50,000 from Crewe Alexandra for Colin Little 1995

Senior Honours: Northern Premier League Division 1 2003-04, Premier Division 2004-05, League Cup x3
Cheshire Senior Cup x6. Manchester Premier cup x6.

10 YEAR RECORD

01-02	02-03	03-04	04-05	05-06	06-07	07-08	08-09	09-10	10-11
NP P 22	NP P 23	NP 1 1	NP P 1	Conf N 11	Conf N 8	Conf N 9	Conf N 20	Conf N 15	Conf N 19

HYDE UNITED

No.	Date	Comp	H/A	Opponents	Att:	Result	Goalscorers	Pos
1	Sat-14-Aug	BSN	A	AFC Telford	1501	L 0-5		22
2	Mon-16-Aug	BSN	H	Workington	372	L 2-3	Mooney 61, Pugh 89	22
3	Sat-21-Aug	BSN	H	Alfreton Town	396	L 1-5	Smart pen 30	21
4	Wed-25-Aug	BSN	A	Droylsden	433	L 1-3	Smart pen 59	21
5	Mon-30-Aug	BSN	A	Guiseley	406	L 0-1		21
6	Sat-04-Sep	BSN	A	Gloucester City	401	L 0-1		21
7	Sat-11-Sep	BSN	H	Corby Town	268	W 2-1	Whalley 8, Johnson 77	21
8	Sat-18-Sep	BSN	H	Redditch United	340	L 1-4	Johnson 84	21
9	Sat-02-Oct	BSN	A	Harrogate Town	306	W 3-1	Mooney 15, Johnson 56, Og (Picton) 69	20
10	Sat-09-Oct	BSN	H	Boston United	479	L 0-3		21
11	Sat-16-Oct	BSN	H	Worcester City	341	L 0-2		21
12	Sat-23-Oct	BSN	A	Blyth Spartans	362	L 0-3		21
13	Mon-25-Oct	BSN	H	Eastwood Town	261	L 1-2	Holsgrove 56	21
14	Sat-30-Oct	BSN	A	Vauxhall Motors	210	L 2-3	Whalley 4, Holsgrove 62	21
15	Sat-06-Nov	BSN	H	Harrogate Town	343	W 1-0	D Stott 32	20
16	Sat-13-Nov	BSN	H	Gainsborough Trinity	235	D 1-1	Johnson 85	19
17	Sat-01-Jan	BSN	A	Stalybridge Celtic	742	W 2-1	Manship 49, Whalley 75	18
18	Mon-03-Jan	BSN	H	Guiseley	342	L 0-1		19
19	Sat-08-Jan	BSN	H	Stafford Rangers	301	W 1-0	Halford 7	19
20	Sat-15-Jan	BSN	H	Solihull Moors	253	L 1-2	Turner 76	19
21	Mon-17-Jan	BSN	A	Hinckley United	349	L 0-2		19
22	Sat-22-Jan	BSN	H	Blyth Spartans	303	L 0-2		19
23	Tue-25-Jan	BSN	A	Nuneaton Town	775	W 2-1	Og (Christie) 38, Johnson 66	19
24	Sat-05-Feb	BSN	A	Redditch United	201	W 1-0	Smart pen 39	18
25	Mon-07-Feb	BSN	H	Nuneaton Town	320	D 1-1	Christopher Lynch 48	17
26	Sat-12-Feb	BSN	H	Gloucester City	295	L 1-3	Holsgrove 7	18
27	Mon-14-Feb	BSN	A	Worcester City	472	L 2-4	Holsgrove 23, Christopher Lynch 26	18
28	Mon-21-Feb	BSN	H	Stalybridge Celtic	606	L 0-2		19
29	Sat-26-Feb	BSN	H	Vauxhall Motors	311	L 1-2	Smart pen 15	19
30	Sat-05-Mar	BSN	A	Stafford Rangers	508	W 5-0	Johnson 3 (6, 9, pen 69), Smart 2 (28, pen 33)	19
31	Sat-12-Mar	BSN	A	Solihull Moors	288	L 2-3	Barlow 53, Christopher Lynch 72	19
32	Mon-14-Mar	BSN	H	AFC Telford	524	L 0-3		19
33	Sat-26-Mar	BSN	A	Alfreton Town	643	D 0-0		19
34	Wed-30-Mar	BSN	A	Eastwood Town	354	L 0-1		19
35	Sat-02-Apr	BSN	A	Gainsborough Trinity	394	L 1-2	Holsgrove 29	20
36	Sat-09-Apr	BSN	H	Hinckley United	295	W 3-0	Holsgrove 12, Barlow 57, Christopher Lynch pen 72	19
37	Sat-16-Apr	BSN	A	Boston United	1536	D 2-2	Holsgrove 18, Smart 77	19
38	Sat-23-Apr	BSN	A	Workington	326	D 1-1	Christopher Lynch 39	19
39	Mon-25-Apr	BSN	H	Droylsden	472	D 1-1	Barlow 43	19
40	Sat-30-Apr	BSN	A	Corby Town	404	W 2-1	Halford 44, D McNiven 54	19
	Ilkeston Record Expunged 16/09							
5	Sat-28-Aug	BSN	H	Ilkeston Town	319	D 1-1	Mooney 9	21
CUPS								
1	Sat-25-Sep	FAC 2Q	H	Droylsden	375	D 0-0		
2	Mon-27-Sep	FAC 2QR	A	Droylsden	354	L 1-3	Johnson 57	
3	Sat-20-Nov	FAT 3Q	A	Leamington	522	W 2-1	Smart 67, Johnson 89	
4	Tue-14-Dec	FAT 1	A	Alfreton Town	254	L 0-3		

League
Starts
Substitute
Unused Sub

Cups
Starts
Substitute
Unused Sub

Goals (Lg)
Goals (Cup)

MAWSON	D STOTT	CHRISTOPHER LYNCH	CHRIS LYNCH	TAYLOR	SORVEL	WILSON	BURKE	A STOTT	LEA	SMART	STEWART	MOONEY	MORRIS	RICK	PUGH	LOGAN	TRAYNOR	LEES	WHALLEY	POLITT	S MCNIVEN	TOLSON	CALVERT	RIMMER	SAUNDERS	MANSHIP	JOHNSON	HALFORD	HOLSGROVE	YOUNG	TURNER	BURNS	CLANCY	HUDSON	MACKRETH	BARLOW	DOUGHTY	SIMPSON	D MCNIVEN	BROWN	ROBERTS	BYRNE	CALVER
X	X	X	X	X	X	X	X	X	X	X	S	S	S	U	U																												
X	X	X	X	X		X	X	X		X	U	S	U	X	S	X	S																										
X	X	X		X			X	X		X		S	S	X	S	X	U	X	X	U																							
X	X	X		X			X	S		X		X	U	X	S	X	U	X			X	S																					
X	X	X		X			X	S		X			S	X	U	X	X	X	X				S	U																			
	X	X		X			X			X	U		U	S		X	U	X	X		X	X		S	X																		
	X	X		X			X				U		U	U		X	S	X	X		X	X			X	X	S																
	X	X		X		X	X			X	S		U	X		X	U	X			X		U		X		S																
	X	X		X			X			X		X	S	S			S	X	X			U		U	X		X	X															
	X			X			X					X	S	X			U	X	X		X	S	U	U	X		X	X															
	X			X			X				U	X	U	U			X	X	X		X	S	U		X		X	X															
				X			X			X		X	U	S			U	X	X		X		U	U	X	X	X	X															
	X			X			X					S	U	S			U	X	X		X			U	X	X	X	X	X														
	X	X					X			X		S	U	U			S	X	X					U	X	X	X	X	X														
	X	X					X			X		S	S	S				X	X				U	U	X	X	X	X	X														
	X	X					X			X		X	S	S				X					U	S	X	X	X	X	X	U													
	X	X								X		X	S	S				X	X		X		U	U	X	X	X	X			S												
	X	X								X		X	U	U				X	X		X		S	S	X	X	X	X			S												
	X	X					X			X			U	U				X	X		X	S	U		X	X	X	X			U												
	X	X					X			X		S	U	U				X	X		X				X	X	X	X		S	S												
	X	S					X			X		X	U	S				X			X				X	X		X	X	X	S	U											
		X					X			X		S	S	U				X	X		U				X	X	X	X	X	X	S												
	U	X					X			X		U	U	X				X			X			U	X	X	X		X	X	U												
	U	X								X		S	U	X				X			X			U	X	X	X	X	X	X		U											
	U	X								X		S	U	X				X			X			U	X	X	X	X	X	X		U											
	S	X								X		S		X				X			X			U		X	X	X	X	X		U	X	S									
	X	X								X		S	S	X				X			X			S		X	U		X	X		U	X	X									
	U	X					S			X		U	U	X				X			X					X	X		X	X			X	X	S								
	X	X					X			X			U	U				X			X			U			X		X	X			X	S	S	X							
	X	X					X			X				S				X			U				X		X	X	X	X			U	S	S	X							
	X	X					X			X			U	U				X			S				X		X	X	X	X				S	S	X							
	X	X					X			X			U	U				X			U				X		X	X	S	X				S	X	X							
		X					X			X			U	U				X			X				X			X	X	X		U				X	X						
		X					X			X			U					X		X	X			U	X			X	X							X	X	S	U				
	X	X					X			X								X			X				X			X	X							X	X	S	S	S	U	U	
	X	X					X			S								X			X				X			X	X							X	X	U	S	U	S	X	
	X	X					X			X								X			X				X			X	X							X	U	U	S	U		X	U
	X	X					X			X								X			X			U	X			X				U				X	U	S	X	U		X	
	X	X					X			X			U					X			X			U	X			X								X	U	S	X	U		X	
	X	X					X			X			U					X			X		U	U	X			X				U				X		X	X	U			
X	X	X		X			X	S		X		X	U	U		X	U	X	X		X	S																					
	X	X		X		U	X			X		X	U	U		S	U	X	X		X	U		U	X		X																
	X	X		X		S	X			X		X	U	U		S	U	X	X		X	S		U	X		X																
	X			X			X			X		S	U	U				X	X		X		U	U	X	X	X	X															
	X	X								X		X	S					X	X		X	S	X	S	X	X	U	X															
5	31	35	2	13	1	3	33	3	1	35	0	9	0	12	0	7	2	38	16	1	28	2	0	0	31	18	22	28	20	13	0	0	4	2	1	12	4	1	3	0	0	4	0
0	1	1	0	0	0	0	1	2	0	1	2	12	10	9	3	0	4	0	0	0	1	4	2	4	0	0	2	0	1	1	5	0	0	5	4	0	0	4	3	1	1	0	0
0	4	0	0	0	0	0	0	0	0	0	4	2	24	12	2	0	7	0	0	1	3	1	9	17	0	0	1	0	0	1	2	8	1	0	0	0	3	2	1	5	1	1	1
0	4	3	0	3	0	0	3	0	0	4	0	3	0	0	0	0	0	4	4	0	4	0	1	0	4	2	3	2	0	0	0	0	0	0	0	0	0	0	0	0	0	0	0
0	0	0	0	0	0	1	0	0	0	0	0	1	1	0	0	2	0	0	0	0	0	2	0	1	0	0	0	0	0	0	0	0	0	0	0	0	0	0	0	0	0	0	0
0	0	0	0	0	0	1	0	0	0	0	0	0	3	3	0	0	2	0	0	0	0	1	1	3	0	0	1	0	0	0	0	0	0	0	0	0	0	0	0	0	0	0	0
0	1	5	0	0	0	0	0	0	0	7	0	2	0	0	1	0	0	0	3	0	0	0	0	0	0	1	8	2	7	0	1	0	0	0	0	3	0	0	1	0	0	0	0
0	0	0	0	0	0	0	0	0	0	1	0	0	0	0	0	0	0	0	0	0	0	0	0	0	0	0	2	0	0	0	0	0	0	0	0	0	0	0	0	0	0	0	0

PLAYING SQUAD 2011/12

Existing Players		SN	HT	WT	DOB	AGE	POB	Career	Apps	Goals
GOALKEEPERS										
David	Carnell				18/04/1985	26		Man Utd (Yth), Oldham T, Hyde U c/s 06, Curzon Ashton (L) Perm, Stalybridge 11/09 Rel c/s 10, Curzon Ashton c/s 10, Hyde FC 6/11		
Andrew	Farrimond							Leigh Genesis, Hyde FC 8/11		
DEFENDERS										
Adam	Griffin		5'07"	10 04	26/08/1984	27	Salford	Oldham, Chester (L) 1/03, Oxford U (2ML) 11/05, Stockport (SL) 1/06, Stockport Undisc 8/06, Darlington 7/08 Rel c/s 09, Stockport 8/09 Rel c/s 11, Hyde FC 8/11		
Gianluca	Havern		6'01"	13 00	24/09/1988	22	Gorton	Stockport Rel 1/09, Radcliffe B (L) 2/07, Ashton U (L) 11/07, Mansfield 2/09 Rel 5/09, Stockport 8/09 Rel 8/10, Mossley 9/10, Ashton U 10/10, Hyde FC 6/11		
Nathan	Martin							Curzon Ashton, Hyde FC 6/11		
Andrew	Pearson		6'00"	13 04	21/12/1989	21	Manchester	Bolton (Yth), Wigan Rel c/s 09, Salford C 8/09, Altrincham 8/09 Rel 1/10, Rhyl 1/10, Hyde FC 8/11		
Brett	Renshaw				23/12/1980	30	Barnsley	Worsbrough Bridge, Grimethorpe Welfare, Pontefract Coll, Worsbrough Bridge, Garforth 9/03 Rel c/s 10, Bradford PA (L) 2/10, Curzon Ashton c/s 10, Bradford PA 12/10, Hyde FC 6/11		
Joel	Richardson		5'11"	11 00	22/09/1990	20	Liverpool	Tranmere (Scholar) Rel c/s 09, Aberystwyth 12/09, IK Hammerby (Swe), Hyde FC 6/11		
MIDFIELDERS										
David	Birch				14/01/1981	30		Glossop NE, Curzon Ashton 7/01, Hyde FC 8/11		
Adam	Birchall							Crewe (Trainee), Clitheroe, Runcorn 2/06, Formby, Skelmersdale c/s 06, Lancaster 1/10, Skelmersdale 3/11, Hyde FC 8/11		
Callum	Byrne		5'07"		05/02/1992	19	Liverpool	Rochdale Rel c/s 11, Trafford (L) 9/10, Mossley (2ML) 11/10, Hyde FC (L) 3/11, Hyde FC 7/11	4	0
Joseph	Evans				21/12/1990	20		Formby, Leigh Genesis 8/10, Curzon Ashton 2/11, Hyde FC 6/11		
Rory	Fallon							Loughborough University, Hyde FC 8/11		
Joe	Fox		5'10"		03/12/1991	19	York	Hull C Rel c/s 11, Grimsby (Trial), Lincoln C (Trial), Hyde FC 8/11		
Thomas	Ingram							Notts County (Scholar), Stafford R 8/07, Brackley (L) 3/08, Hinckley U 12/08, Bedworth 1/09, Quorn c/s 09, Stirling Lions (Aust) 1/10, Corby T, Hyde FC 8/11		
Luke	Mack							Maine Road, Curzon Ashton, Hyde FC 6/11		
Chris	Worsley							Curzon Ashton, Hyde FC 8/11		
FORWARDS										
Matthew	Berkeley		5'11"	10 10	03/08/1987	24	Manchester	Fletcher Moss, Burnley, Gretna 6/04, Workington (2ML) 2/06, Rel c/s 07, Altrincham 8/07 (07/08 2,0) Rel 9/07, Workington 10/07, Droylsden 6/08, Leigh Genesis 8/08, Mossley 11/08, Hyde U 11/08, The New Saints 1/09, Hyde FC 8/11		
Dan	Broadbent		5'10"	12 00	02/03/1990	21	Leeds	Huddersfield Rel 5/09, Rushden & D (L) 1/09, Gateshead (L) 2/09, Harrogate T (SL) 3/09, Harrogate T 8/09, Frickley (SL) 3/10, Frickley 7/10, Curzon Ashton 9/10, Hyde FC 8/11		
Ryan	Crowther		5'11"	11 00	17/09/1988	22	Stockport	Stockport, Liverpool Undisc 7/07 Rel 5/09, Bournemouth (Trial) 9/09, Grimsby (Trial) 10/09, Stalybridge 8/10 Rel 9/10, Jail, Ashton U 11/10, Hyde FC 6/11		
Scott	Spencer		5'11"	12 08	01/01/1989	22	Oldham	Oldham (Scholar), Everton 6/06 Rel c/s 09, Yeovil (L) 1/08, Macclesfield (L) 3/08, Rochdale 8/09 Rel 11/09, Southend 1/10, Lincoln C 1/11 Rel c/s 11, Barrow (Trial), Hyde FC 8/11		
Mike	Whitwell		6'00"	12 00	21/11/1991	19		Leeds (Scholar) Rel c/s 10, Frickley (Trial), York (Trial), Rotherham (Trial), Frickley 9/10, Harrogate RA 10/10, Hyde FC 8/11		
Ben	Williamson		5'11"	11 13	25/12/1988	22	London	Millwall (Yth), Croydon Ath (Yth), Worthing 8/09, Glen Hoddle Academy c/s 10, Bournemouth 1/11, Hyde FC 6/11, Port Vale (SL) 6/11		

NUNEATON TOWN

Chairman: Ian Neale
Secretary: Ian Brown **(T)** 07976 375292 **(E)** ian.brown@nuneatontownfc.com
Additional Committee Members:
Kirk Stephens, Neil Hodgson, Dave Allen, Mary Mills.

Manager: Kevin Wilkin
Programme Editor: Ian Brown & Deborah Carney **(E)** ian.brown@nuneatontownfc.com

Club Factfile

Founded: 2008 **Nickname:** The Boro
Previous Names: Nuneaton Borough 1937-2008
Previous Leagues: Central Amateur 1937-38, Birmingham Combination 1938-52, West Midlands 1952-58, Southern 1958-79 81-82, 88-90, 2003-04, 08-10, Conference 1979-81, 82-88, 99-03, 04-08

Club Colours (change): Blue & white stripes/blue or white/blue or white (Red & black hoops/black or red/black & red hoops)

Ground: Triton Showers Community Arena, Liberty Way, Nuneaton CV11 6RR **(T)** 02476 385 738
Capacity: **Seats:** **Covered:** **Clubhouse:** **Shop:**

Directions
From the South, West and North West, exit the M6 at Junction 3 and follow the A444 into Nuneaton. At the Coton Arches roundabout turn right into Avenue Road which is the A4254 signposted for Hinckley. Continue along the A4254 following the road into Garrett Street, then Eastboro Way, then turn left into Townsend Drive. Follow the road round before turning left into Liberty Way for the ground. From the North, exit the M1 at Junction 21 and follow the M69. Exit at Junction 1 and take the 4th exit at roundabout onto A5 (Tamworth, Nuneaton). At Longshoot Junction turn left onto A47, continue to roundabout and take the 1st exit onto A4254, Eastboro Way. Turn right at next roundabout into Townsend Drive, then right again into Liberty Way, CV11 6RR.

Previous Grounds: Manor Park

Record Attendance: 22,114 v Rotherham United - FA Cup 3rd Round 1967 (At Manor Park)
Record Victory: 11-1 - 1945-46 and 1955-56
Record Defeat: 1-8 - 1955-56 and 1968-69
Record Goalscorer: Paul Culpin - 201 (55 during season 1992-93)
Record Appearances: Alan Jones - 545 (1962-74)
Additional Records: Paid £35,000 to Forest green Rovers for Marc McGregor 2000
Received £80,000 from Kidderminster Harriers for Andy Ducros 2000

Senior Honours: Southern League Midland Division 1981-82, 92-93, Premier Division 1988-99, Premier Division Play-offs 2009-10.
Birmingham Senior Cup x7.

10 YEAR RECORD

01-02		02-03		03-04		04-05		05-06		06-07		07-08		08-09		09-10		10-11	
Conf	10	Conf	20	SthP	4	Conf N	2	Conf N	3	Conf N	10	Conf N	7	SthE	2	SthP	2	Conf N	6

NUNEATON TOWN

No.	Date	Comp	H/A	Opponents	Att:	Result	Goalscorers	Pos
1	Sat-14-Aug	BSN	A	Guiseley	500	W 2-1	Daniel 52, Dillon 68	8
2	Sat-21-Aug	BSN	H	Droylsden	902	D 1-1	L Moore 48	9
3	Tue-24-Aug	BSN	A	Boston United	1681	W 2-1	L Moore 12, Hadland 63	6
4	Sat-28-Aug	BSN	H	Stalybridge Celtic	833	W 2-1	L Moore 41, Storer 60	5
5	Mon-30-Aug	BSN	A	AFC Telford	2371	L 1-4	Marsden 87	7
6	Sat-04-Sep	BSN	A	Worcester City	1070	D 2-2	L Moore 32, Storer 57	9
7	Sat-11-Sep	BSN	H	Alfreton Town	1138	L 1-3	Dillon 90	11
8	Sat-18-Sep	BSN	H	Harrogate Town	839	W 3-0	Marsden 12, Nisevic 15, L Moore 20	9
9	Sat-02-Oct	BSN	A	Workington	522	W 1-0	Storer pen 65	6
10	Sat-16-Oct	BSN	H	Stafford Rangers	1002	W 1-0	Storer 14	6
11	Sat-30-Oct	BSN	H	Hinckley United	1412	W 2-0	L Moore 48, Nisevic 59	5
12	Tue-09-Nov	BSN	H	Solihull Moors	665	W 2-1	Storer 2 (22, pen 71)	5
13	Sat-13-Nov	BSN	H	Eastwood Town	891	W 2-1	Armson 13, Simmonds 38	5
14	Sat-11-Dec	BSN	A	Solihull Moors	417	D 1-1	Armson 46	5
15	Tue-14-Dec	BSN	A	Redditch United	163	W 5-0	Og (Ayres) 15, Forsdick 36, Spencer 41, Dillon 2 (87, 90)	5
16	Sat-01-Jan	BSN	A	Corby Town	636	W 3-2	Walker 49, Spencer 66, Hadland 75	4
17	Mon-03-Jan	BSN	H	AFC Telford	1502	D 0-0		4
18	Sat-08-Jan	BSN	H	Blyth Spartans	833	W 3-2	Spencer 51, Storer 52, L Moore 84	4
19	Tue-11-Jan	BSN	A	Stalybridge Celtic	368	W 2-0	Storer 43, Marsden 71	4
20	Sat-15-Jan	BSN	A	Harrogate Town	306	W 2-1	Noon 54, Storer pen 90	2
21	Tue-18-Jan	BSN	A	Gainsborough Trinity	423	W 2-1	Walker 21, Noon 42	1
22	Sat-22-Jan	BSN	A	Vauxhall Motors	327	D 1-1	Storer pen 49	1
23	Tue-25-Jan	BSN	H	Hyde FC	775	L 1-2	Armson 68	1
24	Sat-29-Jan	BSN	H	Redditch United	965	D 1-1	L Moore 83	1
25	Sat-05-Feb	BSN	A	Stafford Rangers	529	W 2-1	Forsdick 4, Marsden 49	1
26	Mon-07-Feb	BSN	A	Hyde FC	320	D 1-1	Walker 26	1
27	Sat-12-Feb	BSN	A	Droylsden	320	L 0-1		1
28	Sat-19-Feb	BSN	H	Worcester City	901	W 2-1	Walker 44, Spencer 79	1
29	Sun-27-Feb	BSN	A	Hinckley United	1208	W 3-0	Storer 17, Burns 18, Walker 31	1
30	Tue-01-Mar	BSN	H	Corby Town	681	L 2-3	L Moore 16, Spencer 33	1
31	Sat-05-Mar	BSN	A	Eastwood Town	566	L 1-2	Harris 89	1
32	Sat-12-Mar	BSN	H	Vauxhall Motors	726	W 3-0	Marsden 8, Hadland 2 (48, 70)	1
33	Tue-15-Mar	BSN	H	Gloucester City	592	D 0-0		1
34	Sat-19-Mar	BSN	A	Blyth Spartans	496	L 0-1		3
35	Sat-26-Mar	BSN	H	Guiseley	761	L 0-1		4
36	Sat-02-Apr	BSN	A	Gloucester City	470	W 3-0	Marsden 47, Forsdick 52, Hall 90	4
37	Sat-09-Apr	BSN	H	Gainsborough Trinity	902	L 1-2	Storer 53	4
38	Sat-16-Apr	BSN	H	Workington	801	W 2-1	Spencer 11, Oddy 71	4
39	Mon-25-Apr	BSN	H	Boston United	1525	D 1-1	Hadland 7	5
40	Sat-30-Apr	BSN	A	Alfreton Town	1123	L 2-3	Burns 18, I Christie 50	6
	Ilkeston Record Expunged 16/09							
2	Tue-17-Aug	BSN	H	Ilkeston Town	1072	D 2-2	Storer 2 (43, 65)	9

CUPS

No.	Date	Comp	H/A	Opponents	Att:	Result	Goalscorers
1	Sat-25-Sep	FAC 2Q	A	Brigg Town	276	D 3-3	L Moore 40, Pierpoint 64, Dillon 80
2	Tue-28-Sep	FAC 2QR	H	Brigg Town	545	W 2-0	Simmonds 3, Nisevic 70
3	Sat-09-Oct	FAC 3Q	H	Coleshill Town	965	W 6-0	Marsden 2 (25, 36), Simmonds 2 (38, 40), Storer 48, Burns 77
4	Sat-23-Oct	FAC 4Q	A	Workington	520	D 1-1	Nisevic 7
5	Tue-26-Oct	FAC 4QR	H	Workington	943	W 1-0	Dean 47
6	Sat-06-Nov	FAC 1	A	Lincoln City	3084	L 0-1	
7	Sat-20-Nov	FAT 3Q	H	Worcester City	582	L 1-2	Spencer 80
8	Tue-03-May	PO SF 1	H	AFC Telford	2089	D 1-1	Storer 74
9	Sun-08-May	PO SF 2	A	AFC Telford	3442	L 1-2	Spencer 56

League
Starts
Substitute
Unused Sub

Cups
Starts
Substitute
Unused Sub

Goals (Lg)
Goals (Cup)

ALCOCK	ODDY	FORSDICK	NOON	HADLAND	DANIEL	ARMSON	STORER	L MOORE	DILLON	COLLINS	NISEVIC	WALKER	MARSDEN	BATES	A MOORE	PIERPOINT	SPENCER	DEAN	BERWICK	SIMMONDS	BURNS	SHARIFF	MATTHEWS	TAYLOR	C CHRISTIE	QUIRKE	HARRIS	HALL	LAVERY	I CHRISTIE
X	X	X	X	X	X	X	X	X	X	X	S	S	S	U	U															
X	X	X	X	X	X	S	X	X	X	U	U	X	S			X	S													
X	X	X	X	X		U	X	X	S	S	S	X	X			X		X	U											
X	X	X	X		X	S	X	X		S	U	X	X			X	S	X	U											
X	X	X	X	X	U	S	X	X		S	S	X	X			X	U	X												
X	U	X	X	X		X	X	X	S	X	S	U	X	U		X		X												
X	S	X	X		U	X	X	X	S	X	X	S	X	U		X		X												
X	S	X	X		U	S		X	S	X	X	X	X	U		X		X		X										
X	U		X	X	U	X	X	X	S		X	U	X			X		X		X	U									
X	U	S	X	X		X	X	X	S		X	U	X			X	S	X		X										
X	U	U	X	X		X	X	X	X		X	S	X			X	S	X		S										
X	X	X	X	X		S	X	S	U		S	U	X			X	X	X		X										
X	X	X	X	X		X	X	X			S	S	S			X		X		X	U									
X	X	X		X		X	X	U	U		X	X	X				X	X			U	U	U							
X	X	X	X	X			X	X	S		S	U	X			X	X	X			U	S								
X	X	X	X	X		S		X	S		S	X	X			X	X	X			U	U								
X	X	X	X	X		S		X	X			X	X				X	X				S	U	U						
X	U	X	X	X		X	X	X	X			X	S				X	X			U	U	S							
X	U	X	X	X		X	X	X	S			X	X				X	X			S	S	U							
X		X	X	X		X	X	X	S			X	X				X	X			U	U	U		S					
X		X	X	X		X	X	X	S			X	X				X	X			U	U	U		S					
X		X	X	X		X	X	X	U			X	X				X	X			U	U	U		S					
X		X	X	X		S	X	X	S			X	X				X	X			U	U	S		X					
	S	X	X	X		X	X	X	X			S	S				X	X			U		U		X	X				
X	X	X	X	X		S	X	X	S		S	X	X				X	X			U				U					
X	X	X		X		U	X	X	S		X	X	X			U	X	X			U		S							
X	X	X		X		S	X	X			X	X				U	X	X			S		U				X			
X	X	X		X		S	X	X			S	X	X			U	X	X			X		U				S			
X	X	X		X		S	X	X			S	X	X			U	X	X			X		U				S			
X		X		X		X	X	X			S	X	X			U	X	X			X		U	U			S			
X	S	X		X		X	X	X			S	X	X			X	X	X			U		U				S			
X	U	X		X		X	X	X			S	X	X			X	X	X			U						S	S		
X	U	X		X		X	X	X			S	X	X			X	X	X			U						S	S		
X	X	X		X			X	X			S	X	X			X	X	X			U		U				S	S		
X	S	S		X			X	X			X	X	X			X	X	X			U						S	X		
X	U	X		X		X	X	S				S	X			X	S	X									U	X	X	X
X		X	S	X		X	X	S			S	U	X			X	U	X										X	X	X
X	X	X	X	X			X	X			U	X	U			X	X	X									S	S		U
X	X	X	X	X		S	X	X				X				X	X	X			U							U	S	S
X	U	U	X			X	S	S			X	X					S	X			X						X	X	X	X
X	X	X	X	X	X	X	X	X	X	U	U	S	U			X	S													
X		X	X	U		U	X	X	S		X	X	X	S	U	X		X		X	U									
X		X	X	U	U	S	X	X	X		X	X	S		U	X		X		X	S									
X	U	U	X	X	U	X	X	X	S		X	S	X	U		X		X		X	S									
X	U	S	X	X	U	X	X	X	S		X	S	X			X	U	X		X	U									
X	U	S	X	X	U	X	X	X	X		X	U	X			X	U	X		S	U									
X	U	S	X	X	U	X		X	X		X	X	X			X	S	X		S	U									
X	X	S	X	X		X	X	X	S		X	U				X	S	X		X	U									
X	X	X	X	X		S	X	X				U	X			U	X	X			U								X	S
X	X	X	X	X		S	X	X				U	X			S	X	X			U								X	S
39	19	35	27	36	3	21	36	35	6	4	10	28	31	0	0	23	25	38	0	5	4	0	0	0	2	1	2	4	3	3
0	5	2	1	0	0	13	1	4	14	3	17	6	5	0	0	0	6	0	0	1	2	3	3	0	3	0	9	4	1	1
0	10	2	0	0	4	2	0	1	3	1	3	6	1	4	1	5	2	0	2	0	19	7	13	2	1	0	1	1	0	1
9	3	4	9	7	0	5	8	9	3	0	7	3	7	0	0	7	2	9	0	5	0	0	0	0	0	0	0	0	2	0
0	0	4	0	0	0	3	0	0	4	0	0	2	1	1	0	1	2	0	0	2	2	0	0	0	0	0	0	0	0	2
0	4	1	0	2	5	1	0	0	0	0	0	4	0	1	2	1	2	0	0	0	7	0	0	0	0	0	0	0	0	0
0	1	3	2	5	1	3	12	9	4	0	2	5	6	0	0	0	6	0	0	1	2	0	0	0	0	0	1	1	0	1
0	0	0	0	0	0	0	2	1	1	0	2	0	2	0	0	1	2	1	0	3	1	0	0	0	0	0	0	0	0	0

PLAYING SQUAD 2011/12

Existing Players		SN	HT	WT	DOB	AGE	POB	Career	Apps	Goals
GOALKEEPERS										
Danny	Alcock		5'11"	11 03	15/02/1984	27	Salford	Stoke, Barnsley 10/03 Rel c/s 04, Accrington 8/04 Rel 5/06, Stafford R 8/06, Tamworth 12/08, Nuneaton T 8/10	39	0
Neil	Collett				02/10/1989	21	Coventry	Coventry Rel c/s 09, Nuneaton T 5/09, Mansfield 1/10, Nuneaton T (L) 7/11		
Sam	Slater							Nuneaton T		
DEFENDERS										
Mark	Albrighton		6'01"	12 07	06/03/1976	35	Nuneaton	Nuneaton, Atherstone 8/95, Telford £15,000 10/99, Doncaster 5/02, Chester (2ML) 2/06, Boston U 5/06, Darlington (L) 11/06, Rushden & D (L) 1/07, Cambridge U 6/07, Stevenage 5/08 Rel 6/10, Kidderminster 6/10, Nuneaton T 5/11		
Gareth	Dean				25/01/1990	21		Nuneaton T	38	0
Alex	Gudger							Nuneaton T		
Guy	Hadland		6'01"	12 11	23/01/1979	32	Nuneaton	Aston Villa Rel c/s 98, Injured, Hinckley U 1/00, Evesham (L) 10/01, Bedworth 10/03, Solihull B 8/04, Bedworth 12/04, Evesham 8/05, Brackley 11/05, Nuneaton 6/08	36	5
Aaron	James							Stirling Univ, Nuneaton 8/11		
Eddie	Nisevic				19/05/1991	20		Nuneaton T, Shepshed D (L) 9/09	27	2
MIDFIELDERS										
James	Armson				22/01/1990	21		Nuneaton T	34	3
Sam	Belcher		5'11"		05/01/1992	19	Nuneaton	Coventry (Yth), Wycombe Rel 5/11, Chertsey (WE) 12/09, Hinckley U (SL) 10/10, Nuneaton 6/11		
Robbie	Burns		6'00"	11 12	15/11/1990	20	Milton Keynes	Leicester Rel c/s 10, Tranmere (SL) 3/09, Ipswich (Trial) 7/10, Nuneaton T 9/10	6	2
Simon	Forsdick				27/04/1983	28	Cambridge	Coventry (Ass Sch), Stratford, Loughborough Univ, Shepshed D, Halesowen T 1/04, Hednesford T 7/07, AFC Telford 9/07, Nuneaton T (L) 8/08, Bloxwich U (L) 8/08, Rushall O (Dual) 2/09, Stratford T (Dual) 3/09, Nuneaton T (L) 3/09 Perm 6/09	37	3
Richard	Lavery				28/05/1977	34	Coventry	Bedworth, Hinckley A, Nuneaton, Stratford T, Massey Ferguson, Sutton Coldfield, Atherstone 11/99, Tamworth 2/00, Hinckley U 7/00, Nuneaton 7/01, Telford 7/03, Hinckley U 6/04, Leamington (L) 10/08, Corby T 6/10 Rel 3/11, Nuneaton T 3/11	4	0
Mark	Noon		5'10"	12 04	23/09/1983	27	Leamington Spa	Coventry, Tamworth 3/04, Nuneaton B/T 7/04	28	2
Luke	Taylor						Nuneaton	Nuneaton T	0	0
Adam	Walker		5'06"	09 00	22/01/1991	20	Coventry	Coventry Rel 4/10, Nuneaton T (3ML) 10/09, Nuneaton T 4/10	34	5
Graham	Ward		5'08"	11 09	25/02/1983	28	Dublin	Wolves, Cambridge U (Trial) 3/03, Bournemouth (Trial) 4/03, Kidderminster Free 8/03 Rel c/s 04, Cheltenham 8/04, Rel c/s 05, Burton (L) 3/05, Tamworth 5/05, Worcester (L) 10/06 Perm Rel 5/11, Nuneaton T 5/11		
FORWARDS										
Danny	Glover		6'00"	11 02	24/10/1989	21	Crewe	Port Vale Rel c/s 10, Salisbury (L) 8/09, Rochdale (L) 11/09, Stafford R (L) 3/10, Worcester 8/10, Nuneaton 6/11		
Justin	Marsden				07/03/1984	27	Coventry	Rugby U, Solihull B 7/05, AFC Telford 5/06, Bedworth U (L) 2/08, Leamington (L) 3/08, Brackley 6/08, Nuneaton T 9/08	36	6
Kurtis	Mewies							Bedworth, Nuneston T 8/11		
Lee	Moore				09/11/1985	25	Bathgate	Coventry (Jun), Bedworth 7/02, Tamworth 7/06, AFC Telford (3ML) 9/06 £5,000 12/06, Nuneaton T 6/09	39	9
Lee	Smith		5'06"	13 02	08/09/1983	27	Coney Hill	Gloucester, Cirencester 6/05, Weston-Super-Mare 6/07, Gloucester 9/07, Forest Green 6/10 Rel 5/11, Gloucester (3ML) 9/10, AFC Telford (L) 1/11, Chippenham (L) 2/11, Weymouth (SL) 3/11, Nuneaton T 7/11		

SOLIHULL MOORS

Chairman: Nigel Collins
Secretary: Robin Lamb (T) 07976 752 493 (E) robin.lamb5@btinternet.com
Additional Committee Members:
Graham Davison, Margaret Smith, Trevor Stevens, Geoff Hood, Ray Bird, Danny Thomas, Tony Harris, Ronald Crane.
Manager: Marcus Bignot
Programme Editor: John Clothier (E) solihullmoors@aol.com

Club Factfile

Founded: 2007 **Nickname:**
Previous Names: Today's club was formed after the amalgamation of Solihull Borough and Moor Green in 2007
Previous Leagues: None

Club Colours (change): White/black/white (Pink/white/white)

Ground: Damson Park, Damson Parkway, Solihull B91 2PP (T) 0121 705 6770
Capacity: 3,050 **Seats:** 280 **Covered:** 1,000 **Clubhouse:** Yes **Shop:** Yes

Directions
M42 junction 6 take the A45 towards Birmingham after approx 1.5 miles take the left filter lane at the traffic lights onto Damson Parkway. Ground approx 1 mile on the right.

Previous Grounds: None

Record Attendance: 1,076 v Rushden & Diamonds - FA Cup 4th Qualifying Round 27/10/2007
Record Victory: 4-1 v Southport - Conference South 05/04/2008
Record Defeat: 1-6 v Kettering Town - Conference South 01/01/2008
Record Goalscorer: Not known
Record Appearances: Carl Motteram - 71 (2007-09)
Additional Records:

Senior Honours: None

10 YEAR RECORD

01-02	02-03	03-04	04-05	05-06	06-07	07-08	08-09	09-10	10-11
						Conf N 17	Conf N 16	Conf N 17	Conf N 7

SOLIHULL MOORS

No.	Date	Comp	H/A	Opponents	Att:	Result	Goalscorers	Pos
1	Sat-14-Aug	BSN	H	Blyth Spartans	242	W 2-0	West 2 (1, 30)	3
2	Tue-17-Aug	BSN	A	Stafford Rangers	501	L 0-1		12
3	Sat-21-Aug	BSN	A	Harrogate Town	301	L 0-2		16
4	Tue-24-Aug	BSN	H	Eastwood Town	265	W 2-0	Og (Cooke) 45, Grandison 89	9
5	Sat-28-Aug	BSN	H	Gloucester City	263	W 2-1	Beswick pen 44, Cunnington 48	9
6	Mon-30-Aug	BSN	A	Worcester City	886	W 1-0	Beswick 32	6
7	Sat-04-Sep	BSN	A	Workington	648	L 1-2	Beswick pen 42	8
8	Sat-11-Sep	BSN	H	AFC Telford	641	L 0-1		9
9	Sat-18-Sep	BSN	H	Stalybridge Celtic	240	W 3-1	Eze 11, Cunnington 2 (41, 88)	8
10	Sat-16-Oct	BSN	H	Guiseley	243	L 0-1		9
11	Sat-23-Oct	BSN	A	Hinckley United	376	D 2-2	Johnson 11, West 15	11
12	Sat-30-Oct	BSN	H	Stafford Rangers	289	D 1-1	Cunnington 58	10
13	Sat-06-Nov	BSN	A	AFC Telford	1774	W 4-2	Johnson 21, English 54, Streete 63, Beswick 90	8
14	Tue-09-Nov	BSN	A	Nuneaton Town	665	L 1-2	Og (Pierpoint) 19	9
15	Sat-13-Nov	BSN	H	Worcester City	321	W 2-0	Beswick 25, Cunnington 64	8
16	Sat-11-Dec	BSN	H	Nuneaton Town	417	D 1-1	Johnson 36	9
17	Sat-01-Jan	BSN	H	Redditch United	318	W 3-0	Cunnington 2 (57, 85), Grandison 90	6
18	Mon-03-Jan	BSN	A	Gloucester City	325	W 4-2	Johnson 16, Beswick 37, Cunnington 42, O'Loughlin 50	6
19	Sat-15-Jan	BSN	A	Hyde FC	253	W 2-1	Cunnington 27, Beswick 66	6
20	Tue-18-Jan	BSN	H	Droylsden	209	D 2-2	Grandison 11, Beswick 30	6
21	Sat-22-Jan	BSN	A	Gainsborough Trinity	353	D 1-1	Johnson 77	6
22	Tue-25-Jan	BSN	H	Vauxhall Motors	205	W 1-0	O'Loughlin 30	6
23	Sat-29-Jan	BSN	H	Harrogate Town	245	D 2-2	English 38, Cunnington 75	6
24	Sat-05-Feb	BSN	A	Stalybridge Celtic	321	D 1-1	Smith 88	6
25	Sat-12-Feb	BSN	H	Corby Town	366	W 7-2	Beswick 33, O'Loughlin 42, Smith 2 (48, 64), Johnson 63, Omwubiko 2 (90, 90)	6
26	Tue-22-Feb	BSN	A	Boston United	1042	D 1-1	Smith 59	7
27	Sat-26-Feb	BSN	H	Workington	267	W 2-0	Langdon 59, English 69	6
28	Sat-05-Mar	BSN	A	Blyth Spartans	420	W 1-0	English 44	5
29	Mon-07-Mar	BSN	A	Droylsden	204	W 5-0	Smith 2 (25, 57), Beswick 62, English 67, Johnson 90	5
30	Sat-12-Mar	BSN	H	Hyde FC	288	W 3-2	Beswick 17, Smith 2 (38, 90)	5
31	Sat-19-Mar	BSN	A	Corby Town	243	W 2-0	Smith 2, English 36	5
32	Sat-26-Mar	BSN	H	Boston United	512	W 1-0	Smith 75	5
33	Mon-28-Mar	BSN	A	Alfreton Town	791	L 0-2		5
34	Sat-02-Apr	BSN	A	Guiseley	374	L 0-1		5
35	Tue-05-Apr	BSN	A	Redditch United	252	D 0-0		5
36	Sat-09-Apr	BSN	H	Alfreton Town	459	L 0-1		5
37	Sat-16-Apr	BSN	A	Vauxhall Motors	164	D 3-3	Beswick 2 (25, 67), Smith 89	7
38	Sat-23-Apr	BSN	H	Hinckley United	316	L 2-7	O'Loughlin 5, Smith 10	7
39	Mon-25-Apr	BSN	A	Eastwood Town	440	L 1-2	Johnson 10	7
40	Sat-30-Apr	BSN	H	Gainsborough Trinity	235	L 0-2		7

CUPS

No.	Date	Comp	H/A	Opponents	Att:	Result	Goalscorers
1	Sat-25-Sep	FAC 2Q	H	Kidsgrove Athletic	233	W 2-0	Cunnington 10, Grandison 71
2	Sat-09-Oct	FAC 3Q	H	Barwell	387	D 1-1	Cunnington 62
3	Tue-12-Oct	FAC 3QR	A	Barwell	343	L 1-3	English 21
4	Sat-20-Nov	FAT 3Q	A	Curzon Ashton	162	L 1-2	Beswick pen 89

League
Starts
Substitute
Unused Sub

Cups
Starts
Substitute
Unused Sub

Goals (Lg)
Golas (Cup)

SINGH	TIERNAN	LANGDON	PRICE	STREETE	O'LOUGHLIN	ENGLISH	GRANDISON	CUNNINGTON	WEST	BESWICK	ADKINS	LEA	GARDNER	RACHEL	DEMPSTER	EZE	MIDWORTH	SHELDON	JOHNSON	ATKINS	GOODING	AMOO	BLACKWOOD	CLARKE	OMWUBIKO	GREEN	SMITH	AYRES
X	X	X	X	X	X	X	X	X	X	X	S	S	U	U	U													
X	X	X	X	X	X	X	X	X		X	X	S	S		S													
X	X	X	X	X	X	X	X	X	X	X	U	S		U		S	U											
X	S	X	X	X	X	X	X	X	X	X	U	S		U		S	X											
X	X	X	X	X		X	X	X		X	S	X	S	U	U	S	X											
X	X	X		X		X	X	X		X	U	X	U	U	S	X	X	U										
X	X	X		X		X	X	X	X	X	S	S		U	U	X	X	S										
X	X	X		X		X	X	X	X	X	X				U	X	U	S	S	U								
X	X	X	S	X	U	X	X	X	X	X				U		X	X	S	S									
X	U	U	X	X	X	X	X	X	X	X	X	S		U		S		X										
X		U	S	X	X	X			X	X	X	S		U		X		X	X		X							
X		X	X	X			S	X	S	X		X		U		S		U	X		X	X	X					
X		X	X	X	U	X		X	S	X				U		S	S		X		X	X	X					
X		X	X	X	S	X		X	X		S			U		X	X		X		U	U	X					
X		X	X	X	S	X		X	U	X				U		U	X		X		X	S	X					
X		X	X	X	U	X		X	S	X	U			U			X		X				X	X	U			
X	U			X	X	X	S	X	S	X	X			U			X	S	X					X	X			
X	U	S		X	X	X	X	X	S	X	X						X	S	X					X	U			
X		U		X	X	X	X	X	S	X	X			U			X		X					X	U	U		
X		S	U	X	X	X	X	X	U	X	X			U			X		X					X	U			
X		U	U	X	X	X	X	X	U	X	X			U			X		X					X	S			
X		U	S	X	X	X	X	X	U	X	X			U			X		X					X	U			
X		U	U	X	X	X	S	X	X	X	X			U			X		X					X	U			
X		X	U		X	X	S		X	X	X			U			X		X					X	U	S	X	
X		X	S		X	X	S		U	X	X			U			X		X					X	S	X	X	
X		X	S		X	X	S		U	X	X			U			X		X					X	U	X	X	
X		X	S		X	X	U		S	X	X			U			X		X					X	S	X	X	
X		X	X		X	X	X		U	X	X			U			X							S	S	X	X	S
X		X	X		X	X	U		S	X	X						X		S					X	S	X	X	U
X		X			X	X	U		S	X	X			U			X		X					X	U	X	X	S
X		X	S		X	X	U			X	X				U		X		X					X	S	X	X	U
X		X	U		X	X	S			X	X			U			X		X					X	U	X	X	U
X		X	S		X	X	S			X	X			U	U		X		X					X		X	X	U
X		X	X		X	X	U			X	X			U	S		X		X					X	S		X	S
X		X	X		X	X	X		U	X	S				S		X		X					U	U		X	X
X		X	X		X	X	X			X	X			U	U		X		X					U	S		X	S
X		X	S		X	X	X			X	X			U		U	X		X					X	S		X	U
X		X	S		X		X			X	X			U	U	X	X		X					X	S		X	S
X		U	X		U	X	U			X	X			U	X	X	X		X					U	X			X
X			X		U	X	S		S	X	X			U	X	X			X					X	X			X
X	X	X	U	X	U	X	S	X	X	X	S	U				X	X	S	X									
X	X	X	U	X		X	S	X	X	X	S	U		U		X	X	U	X									
X		X	S	X	X	X	X	U	X	X	U	S		U		X	X	U	X									
X		X	S	X	U	X		X	S	X	S			U			X		X		X		X		X			
40	8	29	18	23	28	38	20	22	11	39	27	3	0	0	2	9	31	2	28	0	4	2	5	21	3	9	15	3
0	1	2	10	0	2	0	9	0	10	0	5	7	2	0	4	6	1	5	3	0	0	1	0	1	10	1	0	5
0	3	7	5	0	5	0	6	0	8	0	4	0	2	34	8	2	2	2	0	1	1	1	0	3	11	1	0	5
4	2	4	0	4	1	4	1	3	3	4	0	0	0	0	0	3	4	0	4	0	1	0	1	0	1	0	0	0
0	0	0	2	0	0	0	2	0	1	0	3	1	0	0	0	0	0	1	0	0	0	0	0	0	0	0	0	0
0	0	0	2	0	2	0	0	1	0	0	1	2	0	3	0	0	0	2	0	0	0	0	0	0	0	0	0	0
0	0	1	0	1	4	6	3	10	3	13	0	0	0	0	0	1	0	0	8	0	0	0	0	0	2	0	12	0
0	0	0	0	0	0	1	1	2	0	1	0	0	0	0	0	0	0	0	0	0	0	0	0	0	0	0	0	0

PLAYING SQUAD 2011/12

Existing Players		SN	HT	WT	DOB	AGE	POB	Career	Apps	Goals
GOALKEEPERS										
Adam	Rachel		5'11"	12 08	10/12/1976	34	Birmingham	Aston Villa, Blackpool 9/99, Northwich (L) 10/00, Moor Green/Solihull Moors 7/01	0	0
Jasbir	Singh		6'02"	13 05	12/03/1990	21		Shrewsbury Rel c/s 09, Bridgnorth (L) 8/08, Hinckley U (L) 10/08, Sutton Coldfield (L) 1/09, Kidderminster 8/09 Rel 5/10, Solihull Moors 7/10	40	0
DEFENDERS										
Karl	Broadhurst		6'00"	11 07	18/03/1980	31	Portsmouth	Bournemouth Rel c/s 07, Hereford 7/07 Rel c/s 09, Bournemouth (Trial) 7/08, Crawley 8/09 Rel 4/10, AFC Telford 8/10 Rel 8/10, Solihull Moors 8/11		
Ashley	Buswell				12/07/1990	21		Aston Villa (Yth), Cardiff (Scholar), Glen Hoddle Academy, Cardiff C (Trial) 7/11, Solihull Moors 8/11		
Andre	Francis				25/04/1985	26	Birmingham	Stafford R, Rushall O, Halesowen T 6/07, Romulus 1/08, Stafford R 7/08, Solihull Moors 5/11		
Craig	Hinton		6'00"	12 00	26/11/1977	33	Wolverhampton	Birmingham C Rel c/s 98, Kidderminster 9/98, Bristol R Bosman 6/04, Northampton 7/09, Luton (6WL) 11/10, Bristol R (Ass Man) 3/11, Solihull Moors 8/11		
Dominic	Langdon		6'02"	11 00	14/09/1988	22	Kettering	Rushden & D Rel c/s 07, Tamworth 7/07, Atherstone (L) 11/09, Brackley 1/10, Solihull Moors 8/10	31	1
Phil	Midworth				17/05/1985	26		WBA (Sch), Burton 2/05, Moor Green/Solihull Moors 3/05. Bromsgrove (L) 3/09	32	0
Stuart	Pierpoint				17/02/1982	29	Halesowen	Oldbury U, Sutton Coldfield, Halesowen T 8/05, Stafford R 7/08, Nuneaton T 6/09 Rel 5/11, Solihull Moors 6/11		
MIDFIELDERS										
Sam	Adkins		5'10"	11 07	03/12/1991	19	Birmingham	Walsall Rel c/s 10, Hednesford (L) 1/10, Solihull Moors 8/10	32	0
Ryan	Beswick				12/01/1988	23	Walton-on-Thames	Leicester, Redditch (SL) 1/09, Kettering 5/09, Kings Lynn (2ML) 8/09, Solihull Moors 10/09	39	13
Luke	Bottomer		5'08"		05/09/1992	18		Coventry (Scholar) Rel c/s 11, Worcester (L) 3/11, Solihull Moors 8/11		
Junior	English				08/10/1985	25		Moor Green/Solihull Moors	38	6
Henry	Eze				01/04/1986	25		Halesowen T, Evesham 8/10, Solihull Moors 8/10	15	1
Jordan	Fitzpatrick		6'00"	12 00	15/06/1988	23	Stourbridge	Wolves (Scholar), Hereford 9/06 Rel c/s 08, Bromsgrove (L) 3/08, Worcester 8/08 Rel 2/10, Redditch 7/10, Corby T 2/11 Rel 6/11, Solihull Moors 7/11		
Joel	Grandison		6'01"	11 11	22/05/1992	19		Coventry (Scholar) Rel c/s 10, Doncaster (Trial) 7/10, Solihull Moors 8/10	29	3
Alex	Price				15/04/1991	20		Solihull Moors, Stratford T (L) 3/09	28	0
Will	Richards				18/12/1991	19		Shrewsbury, AFC Telford 8/10, Market Drayton (L) 9/10, Redditch (L) 2/11, Solihull Moors 8/11		
FORWARDS										
Mitch	Fellows				10/06/1989	22		Wednesfield, Willenhall c/s 10, Solihull Moors 5/11		
Steve	Jackson							Solihull Moors		
Simon	Johnson		5'09"	11 09	09/03/1983	28	West Bromwich	Leeds Rel 6/05, Hull C (2ML) 12/02, Blackpool (L) 12/03, Sunderland (6WL) 9/04, Doncaster (2ML) 12/04, Barnsley (SL) 2/05, Darlington 7/05 Rel c/s 07, Bradford C (Trial) 7/07, Hereford 8/07 Rel 4/09, Bury 8/09, Halesowen T 10/09 Rel 2/10, Burton (Trial) 2/10, Solihull Moors 2/10, Guiseley 3/10, Solihull Moors (3ML) 9/10 Perm 1/11	31	8
James	McPike		5'10"	11 02	04/10/1988	22	Birmingham	Birmingham, Solihull Moors (3ML) 1/09, Kettering 5/09, Solihull Moors 9/09, Leamington 2/10, Solihull Moors 8/11		
Danny	Spencer				29/11/1981	29		St Andrews, Atherstone U, St Andrews, Rothwell 1/04, Barwell, Brackley, Redditch 11/07, Brackley 2/08, Kings Lynn 9/09, Oadby T 11/09, Nuneaton T 3/10, Solihull Moors 6/11		

STALYBRIDGE CELTIC

Chairman: Rob Gorski
Secretary: Martyn Torr **(T)** 07860 841 765 **(E)** martyn@newimage.co.uk
Additional Committee Members:
Syd White, Gerald Crossley, Dorothy Norton, John Dillon, Mark Hagan, Gordon Greenwood, Bill McCallum, Dorothy Norton, Andrew Parish, Les Taylor, Keith Trudgeon.
Manager: Jim Harvey
Programme Editor: Nick Shaw **(E)** nick@newimage.co.uk

Back row (L-R): Alan Keeling (U21 Pro manager), Connor Jennings, Phil Marsh, Adam Kay, Greg Wilkinson, Lloyd Ellams, Jan Budtz, Ashley Woodhouse, Craig Hobson, Chris Lynch, Kristian Platt, Joel Bembo - Leta, Mitchell Austin, David Pover (Sports Therapist).
Front Row: Jim Harvey (Manager), Tom Buckley, Jack Rea, Andy McWilliams, Syd White (Chief Executive), Rhys Meynell (Captain), Rob Gorski (Chairman), Callum Warburton, Dennis Sheriff, Arthur Gnahoua, Tim Ryan (Assistant Manager).

Club Factfile

Founded: 1909 **Nickname:** Celtic
Previous Names: Not known
Previous Leagues: Lancashire Combination 1911-12, Central League 1912-21, Southern 1914-15, Football League 1921-23, Cheshire Co. 1923-82, North West Co. 1982-87, N.P.L. 1987-92, 98-2001, Conference 1992-98, 01-02
Club Colours (change): Royal blue & white/white/blue (All yellow)

Ground: Bower Fold, Mottram Road, Stalybridge, Cheshire SK15 2RT **(T)** 0161 338 2828
Capacity: 6,108 **Seats:** 1,200 **Covered:** 2,400 **Clubhouse:** Yes **Shop:** Yes

Directions Leave the M6 at junction 19 (Northwich). At the roundabout at the end of the slip road turn right (exit 3 of 4) to join the A556 towards Altrincham. Stay on the A556 for 5 miles to a roundabout with the M56. Turn right at the roundabout (exit 3 of 4) onto the M56. Stay on the M56 for 6 1/2 miles to junction 3 (M60 signposted Sheffield, M67) Stay on the M60 for 7 miles to junction 24 (M67, Denton) At the roundabout turn right (exit 4 of 5) to join the M67. Stay on the M67 to the very end, Junction 4. At the roundabout turn left (exit 1 of 4) onto the A57 (Hyde Road). After 1/2 a mile you will reach a set of traffic lights (signposted Stalybridge). Turn left onto B6174 (Stalybridge Road). Almost immediately, there is a mini roundabout. Turn left (exit 1 of 5) onto Roe Cross Road (A6018). Follow this road for 1 3/4 miles passing the Roe Cross Inn on the right and through the cutting (the road is now called Mottram Road). When you pass the Dog and Partridge on the right, you will be almost there. Bower Fold is on the left opposite a sharp right turn next to the Hare and Hounds pub. If the car park is full (it usually is), parking can be found on the streets on the right of Mottram Road.

Previous Grounds: Not known

Record Attendance: 9,753 v West Bromwich Albion - FA Cup replay 1922-23
Record Victory: 16-2 v Manchester NE - 01/05/1926 and v Nantwich - 22/10/1932
Record Defeat: 1-10 v Wellington Town - 09/03/1946
Record Goalscorer: Harry Dennison - 215
Record Appearances: Kevan Keelan - 395
Additional Records: Cecil Smith scored 77 goals during the 1931-32 season
Paid £15,000 to Kettering Town for Ian Arnold 1995. Received £16,000 from Southport for Lee Trundle.

Senior Honours: Manchester Senior Cup 1922-23.
Northern Premier League Premier Division 1991-92, 2000-01.
Cheshire Senior Cup x2.

10 YEAR RECORD

01-02	02-03	03-04	04-05	05-06	06-07	07-08	08-09	09-10	10-11
Conf 21	NP P 4	NP P 11	Conf N 19	Conf N 7	Conf N 18	Conf N 2	Conf N 6	Conf N 9	Conf N 10

STALYBRIDGE CELTIC

No.	Date	Comp	H/A	Opponents	Att:	Result	Goalscorers	Pos
1	Sat-14-Aug	BSN	H	Redditch United	508	W 2-0	Marsh 9, Banim pen 11	4
2	Tue-17-Aug	BSN	A	Blyth Spartans	443	W 2-1	Hobson 2, Marsh 42	3
3	Sat-21-Aug	BSN	A	Hinckley United	436	L 2-5	Banim 3, Marsh 49	7
4	Tue-24-Aug	BSN	H	Vauxhall Motors	390	L 1-4	Banim pen 45	10
5	Sat-28-Aug	BSN	A	Nuneaton Town	833	L 1-2	Jennings 74	12
6	Mon-30-Aug	BSN	H	Harrogate Town	365	L 0-1		15
7	Sat-04-Sep	BSN	H	Gainsborough Trinity	414	W 2-0	Marsh 2 (14, pen 32)	12
8	Sat-11-Sep	BSN	A	Stafford Rangers	511	W 3-1	Jennings 40, Marsh 48, Ryan pen 74	10
9	Sat-18-Sep	BSN	A	Solihull Moors	240	L 1-3	Ryan pen 13	10
10	Sat-02-Oct	BSN	H	Alfreton Town	1336	L 1-2	Marsh 54	11
11	Sat-16-Oct	BSN	A	Boston United	1602	L 0-1		13
12	Sat-30-Oct	BSN	H	AFC Telford	607	L 0-1		16
13	Sat-06-Nov	BSN	A	Workington	398	W 5-0	Ellams 15, Marsh 4 (20, 47, 57, 66)	13
14	Sat-13-Nov	BSN	A	Guiseley	518	L 1-3	Jennings 90	14
15	Tue-16-Nov	BSN	H	Droylsden	626	W 4-0	Marsh 2 (27, 90), McWilliams 51, Elam 62	11
16	Sat-01-Jan	BSN	H	Hyde FC	742	L 1-2	Marsh 81	13
17	Mon-03-Jan	BSN	A	Harrogate Town	378	L 0-2		14
18	Sat-08-Jan	BSN	A	Alfreton Town	653	L 3-5	Warburton 16, Brogan 34, Davies 83	14
19	Tue-11-Jan	BSN	H	Nuneaton Town	368	L 0-2		14
20	Sat-22-Jan	BSN	A	Redditch United	181	W 3-1	Meynell 52, Hobson 64, Elam 89	15
21	Mon-24-Jan	BSN	A	Droylsden	476	D 2-2	Brogan pen 33, Jennings 61	14
22	Sat-05-Feb	BSN	H	Solihull Moors	321	D 1-1	Jennings 44	15
23	Tue-08-Feb	BSN	H	Eastwood Town	327	W 2-1	Hobson 2 (38, 78)	15
24	Sat-12-Feb	BSN	A	Worcester City	625	L 0-1		16
25	Tue-15-Feb	BSN	H	Boston United	331	W 3-1	Marsh 15, Og (Pearson 27), Jennings 32	14
26	Sat-19-Feb	BSN	A	Corby Town	314	D 2-2	Jennings 75, Marsh 85	13
27	Mon-21-Feb	BSN	A	Hyde FC	606	W 2-0	Marsh 26, Brogan pen 74	11
28	Tue-01-Mar	BSN	H	Worcester City	306	D 0-0		12
29	Sat-05-Mar	BSN	A	Gainsborough Trinity	354	W 3-1	Jennings 2 (26, 65), Ellams 90	10
30	Sat-12-Mar	BSN	H	Hinckley United	448	D 1-1	Elam 56	12
31	Wed-16-Mar	BSN	H	Corby Town	315	D 1-1	Jennings pen 17	12
32	Sat-19-Mar	BSN	H	Guiseley	507	D 0-0		11
33	Sat-26-Mar	BSN	A	AFC Telford	1744	L 0-1		13
34	Wed-30-Mar	BSN	A	Gloucester City	225	W 2-0	Marsh 2 (12, 30)	12
35	Sat-02-Apr	BSN	H	Workington	390	W 2-1	Marsh pen 45, McWilliams 77	10
36	Tue-05-Apr	BSN	H	Blyth Spartans	366	D 0-0		10
37	Sat-16-Apr	BSN	A	Eastwood Town	437	D 1-1	Jennings 88	11
38	Sat-23-Apr	BSN	H	Gloucester City	416	W 4-3	Jennings 2 (22, 63), Ellams 40, Kay 45	10
39	Mon-25-Apr	BSN	A	Vauxhall Motors	297	W 3-0	Meynell 51, Jennings 2 (63, 81)	10
40	Sat-30-Apr	BSN	H	Stafford Rangers	583	W 3-2	Jennings 13, Gnahoua 58, J Bembo-Leta 75	10

CUPS

No.	Date	Comp	H/A	Opponents	Att:	Result	Goalscorers
1	Sat-25-Sep	FAC 2Q	H	Alfreton Town	373	D 1-1	Elam 60
2	Tue-28-Sep	FAC 2QR	A	Alfreton Town	387	W 2-1 aet	Platt 42, Ellams 114
3	Sat-09-Oct	FAC 3Q	A	Warrington Town	429	W 3-1	Hobson 45, Marsh 2 (56, 90)
4	Sat-23-Oct	FAC 4Q	H	Eastwood Town	659	L 1-2	Marsh 34
5	Sat-20-Nov	FAT 3Q	A	Vauxhall Motors	280	W 3-1	Jennings pen 16, Ellams 48, Hobson 90
6	Sat-11-Dec	FAT 1	H	Nantwich Town	321	W 2-1	Marsh 10, Ellams 57
7	Sat-15-Jan	FAT 2	A	Guiseley	417	L 1-2	Jennings 30

League
Starts
Substitute
Unused Sub

Cups
Starts
Substitute
Unused Sub

Goals (Lg)
Goals (Cup)

BUDTZ	RULE	MCWILLIAMS	REA	ESDAILLE	PLATT	BANIM	WILKINSON	MARSH	HOBSON	JENNINGS	ELLAMS	ELAM	J BEMBO-LETA	LAW	WARBURTON	RYAN	WOODS	CROWTHER	STANFORD	KAY	WHITE	SHERRIFF	F BEMBO-LETA	AUSTIN	DAVIES	GARSIDE	MEYNELL	GNAHOUA	WOODHOUSE	BROGAN	BUCKLEY	KELLY
X	X	X	X	X	X	X	X	X	X	X	S	S	U	U	U																	
X	X	X	X	X	X	X	X	X	X	X	S	S	U	U	S																	
X	X	X	X	X	X	X	X	X	X	X	S	S	U	U	S																	
X	X		X	X	X	X	X	X	X	X	S	S	S	X	U	U																
X	X	X	S		U	X	X	X		X		X	X	U	S	X	X	S														
X	X	X	X		U		X	X		X	X	X	U	S		X	X	S	S													
X	X	X	X		U		X	X		X	X	X	S	S	S	X	X		U													
X	X	X	X	U	U		X	X	S	X	X	X	S		S	X	X															
X	X	X	X	U	X		X	X	S	X	X	X	U		S	X				S												
X	X	X	X		S		X	S	X	X	X	S	U		U	X				X	X											
X	X	X	X		U		X	X	X	X	S	X	X	U	S					S	X											
X	X	X	X	U	X		X	X	X		S	S	U		X					X	X	S										
X	X	X	X		X		X	X	S	U	X	U		S	X					X	X			S								
X	X	X	X		X		X	X	S	S	X	S	U	U	X					X	X											
X	X	X	X		X		X	X	S	X	X	S	S	U	X					U	X											
X	X	X	X	U	X		X	X	S	X	X	X	S												S		X	U				
	X	X	X	U	X			X	X	X	U	X	X									S			S		X	S	X			
	X	X	S		X		X	X	X	S	U	X	U		X										S		X		X	X		
X	X	X	X		X			X	X	S	U		U		X	X									S		X		U	X		
X	X		S		X			X	X	X	X	S	U		X	X								S	U		X			X		
X	X		X		X			S	X	X	X	X	U		S	X									S		X			X		
X			X		X			S	X	X	X	S	X		X	X				U					U		X			X		U
X	S		X		X			S	X	X	X	U	X		X	X				S							X			X		U
X	X		X		X			X	X	X			U		X	X				U				U	U		X			X		U
X	X		X		X			X	X	X		U	U		X	X				S				S	S		X			X		
X	X		X		X			X	X	X		S	U		X	X				S				S	U		X			X		
X	X		X		X			X	U	X		S	S		S	X				X				X	U		X			X		
X			X		X		U	X	S	X	U	S	X		S					X				X			X			X	X	
X			X		X		X	X	S	X	X	U	S		X					S				U			X			X	X	
X			X		X		X	X	S	X	X	S	X		X					S				U	U		X				X	
X		X	X		X		X	S	X	X	S	X	X							S				U	X		X				U	
X	X	X	X				X	X	X		X	U	X			U				X		S					X	U			S	
X		X	X		X		X	X	X		X	S	X		S	U				X							X	U			S	
X		X	X		X		X	X	X	S	X	U	S		X	U				X							X					
X		X	X		X		X	X	X	S	X	S	S		X	U				X			U				X					
X	U	X	X		X		X	X	X	S	X	S	X		S	U				X							X					
X	S	X	S		X		X	X	X	S	X	U	X		X					X		U					X					
X		X	S		X		X	S	X	X	X		X		X					X		U	S	U			X					
X	X		X		X		X		X	X	X	U	U		X					X		S	S	S			X					
X	X	X	X		X		X		X	X	X		S		X					U		S					X	S			U	
X	X	X	X	U	X		X	X	X	X	S	X	U		S	X				U												
X	X	X	X	U	X		X	X	X	X	S	X	U		S	X				S												
X	X	X	X	U			X	X	X	X			X	U	X					S	X	U										
X	X	X	X	U	U		X	X	X	X	S	X	X	S	U					S	X			U								
X	X	X	X	U	X		X	X	S	X	X	X	S	X						U				S								
X	X		X	X	X			X	X	X	X		X	X								S	U		S	U						
X	X		X		X			X	X	X	X		S		X	X				U				S	S		X				U	
38	28	27	35	4	33	5	29	32	27	29	24	11	13	1	20	15	4	0	0	14	6	0	0	2	1	0	25	0	2	12	3	0
0	2	0	5	0	1	0	0	6	9	7	7	17	10	3	12	0	0	2	1	8	0	5	2	5	6	0	0	2	0	0	2	0
0	1	0	0	5	5	0	1	0	1	1	4	8	16	7	3	6	0	0	1	4	0	2	1	5	6	0	0	3	1	0	2	3
7	7	5	7	1	5	0	5	7	6	7	3	4	3	2	2	3	0	0	0	0	2	0	0	0	0	0	1	0	0	0	0	0
0	0	0	0	0	0	0	0	0	1	0	3	0	2	1	2	0	0	0	0	3	0	1	0	2	2	0	0	0	0	0	0	0
0	0	0	0	5	1	0	0	0	0	0	0	0	2	1	1	0	0	0	0	3	0	1	1	1	0	1	0	0	0	0	1	0
0	0	2	0	0	0	3	0	20	4	16	3	3	1	0	1	2	0	0	0	1	0	0	0	0	1	0	2	1	0	3	0	0
0	0	0	0	0	1	0	0	4	2	2	3	1	0	0	0	0	0	0	0	0	0	0	0	0	0	0	0	0	0	0	0	0

PLAYING SQUAD 2011/12

Existing Players		SN	HT	WT	DOB	AGE	POB	Career	Apps	Goals
GOALKEEPERS										
Jan	Budtz		6'05"	13 05	20/04/1979	32	Hillerod, Den	B1909 (Den), FC Nordsjaelland (Den) 1/05 Rel c/s 05, Doncaster 7/05, Wolves (3ML) 1/07, Hartlepool 9/07 Rel c/s 09, Oldham (L) 2/09, Eastwood T 9/09 Rel 3/10, Stalybridge 8/10	38	0
DEFENDERS										
Tom	Buckley		5'11"	11 01	08/10/1991	19	Manchester	Rochdale (Scholar) Rel c/s 10, Woodley Sports 6/10, Stalybridge 1/11	5	0
Chris	Lynch		6'03"	15 06	31/01/1991	20	Blackburn	Burnley Rel c/s 11, Chester (5ML) 8/09, Hyde FC (L) 8/10, Stalybridge 8/11		
Andy	McWilliams		5'08"		05/11/1989	21	Stockton	York C, Stalybridge (SL) 8/10, Stalybridge 6/11	27	2
Rhys	Meynell		5'11"	12 03	17/08/1988	23	Barnsley	Barnsley Rel c/s 08, Ossett A (L) 3/07, Gretna (SL) 1/08, Barnet (Trial) c/s 08, Stalybridge 8/08, AFC Telford (Trial) 6/09, Chester 7/09 Rel 2/10, Galway U 2/10, Stalybridge 12/10	25	2
Kristian	Platt		6'02"	11 13	15/12/1991	29	Rock Ferry	Chester Rel 2/10, Stalybridge 7/10	34	0
Glenn	Rule		5'11"	11 07	30/11/1989	21	Birkenhead	Chester, Colwyn Bay 3/10, Stalybridge 7/10	30	0
Tim	Ryan		6'00"	11 07	10/12/1974	36	Stockport	Scunthorpe, Buxton 11/94, Doncaster 8/96 Rel c/s 97, Altrincham (2ML) 3/97, Southport 8/97, Doncaster 5/00 Rel 1/06, Peterborough 3/06 Rel c/s 06, Boston U 7/06, Darlington Undisc 1/07 Rel c/s 09, Harrogate T (L) 8/08, Chester 7/09 Rel 3/10, Stalybridge 3/10 (Pl/Ass Man) 6/10	15	2
Callum	Warburton				25/02/1989	22		Rochdale Rel 12/07, Northwich (L) 3/07, Kendal (4ML) 8/07, Kendal 12/07, Stalybridge 8/10	32	1
MIDFIELDERS										
Mitchell	Austin		6'02"	11 10	03/04/1991	20	Rochdale	Rotherham (Scholar) Rel c/s 10, Stalybridge 10/10	7	0
Grant	Darley				25/02/1990	21		Rotherham Rel 5/11, Ossett T (L) 1/11, Boston U (L) 2/11, Frickley (L) 3/11, Stalybridge 8/11		
Adam	Kay				05/03/1990	21		Burnley Rel c/s 10, Accrington (SL) 3/09, Chester (5ML) 8/09, Stalybridge 9/10	22	1
Jack	Rea				15/04/1992	19		Chester Rel 2/10, Stalybridge 8/10	40	0
Greg	Wilkinson				03/10/1989	21		East Manchester, Stalybridge 2/08	29	0
FORWARDS										
Joel	Bembo-Leta				15/02/1992	19		Oldham (Yth), Stalybridge	23	1
Lloyd	Ellams		6'02"	12 00	11/01/1991	20	Chester	Chester Rel 3/10, Droylsden (L) 9/08, Marine 3/10, Stalybridge 7/10	31	3
Arthur	Gnahoua							Stalybridge	2	1
Craig	Hobson				25/02/1988	23		Kendal T, Stalybridge 9/09	36	4
Conner	Jennings				29/10/1991	19		Stalybridge	36	16
Phil	Marsh		5'10"	11 13	15/11/1986	24	St Helens	Man Utd Rel c/s 07, Inverness Caledonian (Trial) 7/07, Blackpool 9/07 Rel c/s 08, Bury (Trial) 7/08, Northwich 8/08 Rel 9/08, Hyde U 10/08 Rel 11/08, Leigh Genesis 12/08, FCUM 3/09, Stalybridge 8/10	38	20
Dennis	Sherriff		6'01"	11 03	22/01/1992	19		Rochdale (Scholar) Rel c/s 10, Woodley Sports (SWE) 1/10, Woodley Sports 6/10, Stalybridge 9/10	5	0

VAUXHALL MOTORS

Chairman: Alan Bartlam
Secretary: Mike Harper (T) 07817 400 202 (E) mike.harper@sky.com
Additional Committee Members:
Stephen McInerney, A Woodley, L Jones, D Mathers, Mrs L Bartlam, A Harper, N Kelly, P Jarvis, A Marley, Mrs L Edmunds, Miss M Jones, Mrs C Mathers, C Wheelwright, Mrs T Wheelwright
Manager: Anthony Wright
Programme Editor: Ceri Richards (E) saririchards@ntlworld.com

Club Factfile

Founded: 1963 **Nickname:** The Motormen
Previous Names: Vauxhall Motors 1963-87, Vauxhall GM 1995-99
Previous Leagues: Ellesmere Port, Wirral Combination, West Cheshire 1966-87, 92-95, North West Co. 1987-92, 95-2000, Northern Premier 2000-04
Club Colours (change): White/blue/blue (Yellow/black/black)

Ground: Rivacre Park, Rivacre Road, Ellesmere Port, South Wirrall CH66 1NJ **(T)** 0151 328 1114 (Club) 327 2294 (Social)
Capacity: 3,500 **Seats:** 266 **Covered:** 1,000 **Clubhouse:** Yes **Shop:** Yes

Directions
Leave M53 at junction 5 and take A41 towards North Wales. At first set of traffic lights (Hooton Crossroads) turn left into Hooton Green. At 'T' junction turn left into Hooton Lane. At next 'T' junction turn right into Rivacre Road. Ground is 200 yards on right.

Previous Grounds: Not known

Record Attendance: 1,500 - FA XI fixture for the opening of Rivacre Park 1987
Record Victory: Not known
Record Defeat: Not known
Record Goalscorer: Terry Fearns - 111
Record Appearances: Carl Jesbitt - 509
Additional Records:

Senior Honours: North West Counties League Division 2 1988-89, 95-96, Division 1 1999-2000.
Wirral Senior Cup 1987.

10 YEAR RECORD

01-02	02-03	03-04	04-05	05-06	06-07	07-08	08-09	09-10	10-11
NP P 2	NP P 3	NP P 9	Conf N 15	Conf N 18	Conf N 15	Conf N 21	Conf N 11	Conf N 20	Conf N 17

VAUXHALL MOTORS

No.	Date	Comp	H/A	Opponents	Att:	Result	Goalscorers	Pos
1	Tue-17-Aug	BSN	H	AFC Telford	377	L 0-1		17
2	Sat-21-Aug	BSN	H	Worcester City	179	L 2-3	Wilson 7, Moogan pen 71	19
3	Tue-24-Aug	BSN	A	Stalybridge Celtic	390	W 4-1	Og (Esdaille) 48, Anoruo 62, Wilson 74, Prince 82	16
4	Sat-28-Aug	BSN	H	Guiseley	178	D 2-2	Anoruo 9, Wilson 50	14
5	Mon-30-Aug	BSN	A	Workington	707	L 1-2	Anoruo 80	18
6	Sat-04-Sep	BSN	A	Alfreton Town	603	L 0-2		19
7	Sat-11-Sep	BSN	H	Harrogate Town	176	D 1-1	Anoruo 59	19
8	Sat-18-Sep	BSN	A	Blyth Spartans	437	D 2-2	Mahon 5, Brown 55	16
9	Sat-02-Oct	BSN	H	Boston United	227	D 0-0		18
10	Sat-16-Oct	BSN	H	Hinckley United	201	W 2-0	Anoruo 2 (5, 86)	14
11	Sat-30-Oct	BSN	H	Hyde FC	210	W 3-2	Nicholas 2 (11, 90), Noone 80	14
12	Sat-13-Nov	BSN	A	Redditch United	158	D 2-2	Anoruo 10, Prince 57	15
13	Tue-23-Nov	BSN	H	Stafford Rangers	181	W 2-1	Grice 42, Mahon 65	13
14	Mon-13-Dec	BSN	A	Worcester City	408	L 1-4	Wilson 5	14
15	Sat-01-Jan	BSN	A	Droylsden	223	W 3-1	Nicholas 15, Wilson 30, Anoruo 86	12
16	Sat-08-Jan	BSN	H	Gainsborough Trinity	206	W 1-0	Anoruo 67	10
17	Tue-11-Jan	BSN	A	Gainsborough Trinity	222	D 1-1	Wilson 19	11
18	Sat-15-Jan	BSN	A	Stafford Rangers	375	L 0-1		11
19	Tue-18-Jan	BSN	H	Corby Town	184	W 3-2	Wilson 53, Grice 60, McGivern 87	10
20	Sat-22-Jan	BSN	H	Nuneaton Town	327	D 1-1	McGivern 88	11
21	Tue-25-Jan	BSN	A	Solihull Moors	205	L 0-1		11
22	Sat-29-Jan	BSN	H	Gloucester City	211	W 2-1	McGivern 15, Anoruo 62	9
23	Tue-01-Feb	BSN	H	Droylsden	187	L 0-1		9
24	Sat-05-Feb	BSN	A	Eastwood Town	293	L 1-3	Grice 74	11
25	Sat-12-Feb	BSN	A	Hinckley United	449	W 3-2	Wilson 33, Anoruo 40, Mannix 67	9
26	Tue-15-Feb	BSN	A	Gloucester City	205	L 0-1		9
27	Sat-26-Feb	BSN	A	Hyde FC	311	W 2-1	McGivern 2 (36, 50)	9
28	Tue-01-Mar	BSN	A	Guiseley	203	W 2-1	Anoruo 2 (15, 26)	9
29	Sat-05-Mar	BSN	H	Alfreton Town	263	L 0-2		9
30	Tue-08-Mar	BSN	H	Workington	167	L 1-2	McGivern 88	9
31	Sat-12-Mar	BSN	A	Nuneaton Town	726	L 0-3		10
32	Sat-19-Mar	BSN	H	Eastwood Town	177	L 1-2	McGivern 45	12
33	Wed-23-Mar	BSN	A	Corby Town	168	L 1-3	Anoruo 51	13
34	Sat-26-Mar	BSN	H	Blyth Spartans	159	L 2-6	Anoruo 24, McGivern 45	15
35	Sat-02-Apr	BSN	H	Redditch United	143	W 2-1	Og (Hickman) 66, Anoruo 79	13
36	Sat-09-Apr	BSN	A	Harrogate Town	250	D 0-0		13
37	Sat-16-Apr	BSN	H	Solihull Moors	164	D 3-3	Mahon 44, Hannigan 76, McGivern 87	13
38	Sat-23-Apr	BSN	A	AFC Telford	1617	L 1-4	McGivern 19	14
39	Mon-25-Apr	BSN	H	Stalybridge Celtic	297	L 0-3		15
40	Sat-30-Apr	BSN	A	Boston United	1610	L 0-2		17
	Ilkeston Record expunged 16/09							
1	Sat-14-Aug	BSN	A	Ilkeston Town	270	L 1-2	Anoruo 19	15
CUPS								
1	Sat-25-Sep	FAC 2Q	H	Blyth Spartans	216	W 5-1	Hannigan 20, Prince 2 (34, 86), Brown 2 (37, 57)	
2	Sat-09-Oct	FAC 3Q	A	North Ferriby United	369	D 2-2	Anoruo 24, Wilson pen 55	
3	Tue-12-Oct	FAC 3QR	H	North Ferriby United	202	D 1-1	(aet W 4-3 pens) Wilson 10	
4	Sat-23-Oct	FAC 4Q	H	Newcastle Town	323	W 1-0	Mannix 62	
5	Sat-06-Nov	FAC 1	A	Hartlepool Town	2381	D 0-0		
6	Tue-16-Nov	FAC 1R	H	Hartlepool Town	2406	L 0-1		
7	Sat-20-Nov	FAT 3Q	H	Stalybridge Celtic	280	L 1-3	Wilson pen 71	
								League
								Starts
								Substitute
								Unused Sub
								Cups
								Starts
								Substitute
								Unused Sub
								Goals (Lg)
								Goals (Cup)

TYNAN	NOONE	MARSH-EVANS	TAYLOR	HANNIGAN	MOOGAN	BROWN	SMITH	WILSON	ANORUO	GRICE	WRIGHT	EGERTON	MACAULEY	MBOA	DAMES	PRINCE	NIXON	MAHON	RITCHIE	CHAMBERS	BRIERLEY	ASGARI	NICHOLAS	MANNIX	KING	HALLIGAN	CLANCY	MCGIVERN	GROCUTT	ROBERTS	MCMURRAY
X	X	X	X		X		X	X	X	X	S	S		U	X	X															
X	X	X	X	S	X	S	X	X	X	X	S	U		U	X	X															
X	X	X	X	X	X		U	X	X	X	S	S		S	X	X	U														
X	X	X	X	X	X	S	S	X	X	S	U	X			X	X	U														
X	X	X	X	X	X		X	X	X	U	S			S	X	X	U														
X	X	X	X	X	X	X		X	X		U	X		U	X		U	S													
X	X	X	X	X		X	S	X	X		U			U	X	X		X													
X	X	X	S	X		X	X	X	X		U			U	X	X		X	U												
X	X	X	S	X		X	X	X	X		S		U	U	X	X		X	U												
X	X		X			X		X	X	S	U			U	X	X		X	U				X	X	S						
X	X		X			X	U	X	X	S				U	X	X		X	U				X	X	S						
	X		X	U		X	U	X	X	U					X	X		X	U				X	X	U		X				
	X		X				S	X	X	X	U			U		X		X	U				X	X	S	X	X				
	X		X	X		X		X	X	X				U		X		X	U				X		S		X				
	X		X			X	U	X	X	X	U			U	X	U		X	U				X	X			X				
	X		X	S		X	U	X	X	X				U	X	S		X	U				X	X			X				
	X		X	X		X	S	X		X	U		U		X	X		X	X					X							
	X		X	X		X	U	X	X	X	U			U	X	X		X	X								U				
	X		X	X		X	S	X	X	X	U			U	X	X		X	X						S			S			
U	X		X	X		X	S	X	X	X	U				X	X		X	X						S			S			
U	X		X	X		S	U	X	X	X	U				X	X		X	X						U			X			
X	X		X	X		S	S	X	X	X	U				X	X		X	U						U			X			
X	X			X		X	X	X		X	U					X		X	U					S	S			X	X		
X	X			X				X	X	X	U					X		X	U					X	S			X	X	S	
X	X		X	X			X	X	X	X	U					S		X	U					X	S				X	S	
X	X		X	X			X	X	X	U	U							X	U					X	S			S	X	X	
X	X		X	X			U	X	U	X	U					X		X	U					X				X	X	U	
X	X		X	X			S		X	X	U		U		X	X		X	U					X						X	
X	X		X	X			S		X	X	U				X	X		X	U					X				X		S	
X	X		X	X		U	S		X	X					X	X		X	U					X	U			X		S	
X	X		X	X		S	X	X	X	S	U				X			S	U					X				X		X	
X	X		X	X		S		X	X		U				X			X	U					X	U			X		X	
X	X		X	X	S	X		X	X		U		U		X			X						X				X		S	
X			X	X	S	X		X	X		U				X			X	U					X				X	X	S	
X	X		X		X	X		X	X		S				U	U		X	U					X	U				X	X	
X	X		X	X	X	X			X	X	U		U					X	U					X					X		
X	X		X	X	X	X			X	X	U				S			X	U					X				S	X	S	
X	X		X	X	X	X				X	U				X			X	U					X				X		S	
X	X		X		X	X				X	S		U		X			X	U					X		S			X	S	X
X	X		X	X	X	X				X	U		U		S			X	U		X			X		X					S
X	X	X	X	X	X	X	X	X	X	X	S	S	U	U																	
X	X	X		X		X	X	X	X	S	U		U	S	X	X		X	U												
X	X	X		X		X	X	X	X		S	U	U	S	X	X		X	U												
X	X		X			X	X	X	X	S	U	U		U	X	X		X	U	X	S	U									
X	X		X	X		X	S	X	X	S	U			U		X		X	U	U	U		X	X							
X	X		X	S		X	U	X	X	U	U				X	X		X	S		U		X	X		U					
	X		X	S		X	U	X	X	S	U			U	X	X		X	X		U		X	X		U					
	X		X	S		X	S	X	X	S				U	X	X		X	X				X	X	U						
30	39	9	36	30	12	23	9	32	34	25	0	2	0	0	29	25	0	33	5	0	1	0	7	24	0	2	5	12	10	5	1
0	0	0	2	2	2	6	10	0	0	4	7	2	0	2	2	2	0	2	0	0	0	0	0	1	10	1	0	4	0	9	1
2	0	0	0	1	0	1	8	0	1	3	28	1	7	14	1	2	4	0	27	0	0	0	0	0	6	0	1	0	0	1	0
5	7	2	5	3	0	7	3	7	7	0	0	0	0	0	6	7	0	7	2	1	0	0	4	4	0	0	0	0	0	0	0
0	0	0	0	3	0	0	2	0	0	5	1	0	0	2	0	0	0	0	1	0	1	0	0	0	0	0	0	0	0	0	0
0	0	0	0	0	0	0	2	0	0	1	5	2	2	4	0	0	0	0	4	1	3	1	0	0	1	2	0	0	0	0	0
0	1	0	0	1	1	1	0	8	16	3	0	0	0	0	0	2	0	3	0	0	0	0	3	1	0	0	0	10	0	0	0
0	0	0	0	1	0	2	0	3	1	0	0	0	0	0	0	2	0	0	0	0	0	0	0	1	0	0	0	0	0	0	0

PLAYING SQUAD 2011/12

Existing Players		SN	HT	WT	DOB	AGE	POB	Career	Apps	Goals
GOALKEEPERS										
Josh	O'Connell							Accrington (Scholar) Rel c/s 11, Vauxhall Motors 8/11		
Scott	Tynan		6'02"	13 03	27/11/1983	27	Huyton	Wigan (Sch), Notts Forest Rel c/s 04, Telford (2ML) 12/03, Barnet 9/04, Rushden & D 1/06 Rel 5/07, Hereford (2ML) 8/06, Ebbsfleet 8/07 Rel 9/07, Northwich 10/07 Rel c/s 09, Salford C 2/10, Vauxhall Motors 7/10	30	0
DEFENDERS										
Lee	Dames				21/01/1986	25	Liverpool	Tranmere (Yth), Burscough, Vauxhall Motors 6/06	31	0
Jonathan	Egerton				19/09/1988	22		Vauxhall Motors	4	0
Kevin	Grocott		5'10"	12 03	30/07/1992	19		Derby (Yth), Notts County (Yth), Burton Rel 3/11, Vauxhall Motors (L) 1/11, Vauxhall Motors 3/11	10	0
Tom	Hannigan				30/06/1988	23		Vauxhall Motors	32	1
Michael	Jackson		6'01"	12 09	14/12/1979	31	Liverpool	Southport, Rhyl 7/01, Welshpool 7/04, The New Saints 3/05, Prottur (Ice) 5/07, Caernarfon 1/09, Marine 7/09, Droylsden 8/10, Newtown 8/10, Marine 10/10, Newtown 1/11 Rel c/s 11, Vauxhall Motors 8/11		
Andy	Taylor		6'00"		28/12/1985	25	Liverpool	Austin Aztex (USA), Forest Green 6/09 Rel 11/09, Burscough 12/09, Vauxhall Motors 8/10	38	0
MIDFIELDERS										
Steven	Beck				04/06/1984	27	Liverpool	Everton Rel 6/03, Wigan (Trial) c/s 03, TNS/The New Saints 7/03, Droylsden 10/08, Australia 2/10, Droylsden 8/10, Chester FC 10/10 Rel 3/11, Vauxhall Motors 8/11		
John	Bennett				26/09/1991	19		Altrincham, Flixton c/s 10, Vauxhall Motors 7/11		
Tom	Field				02/08/1985	26	Liverpool	Everton (Trainee), Leigh RMI, TNS c/s 05, Stalybridge 8/05, Southport 10/05, Witton 11/05, Vauxhall Motors 12/05, Leigh RMI/Leigh Genesis 5/08, Vauxhall Motors 11/08, AFC Telford 6/09, Droylsden 11/09, Chester FC 8/10 Rel 5/11, Vauxhall Motors 8/11		
Tom	Grice				02/02/1990	21		Everton (Yth), Burscough, Cavecanen, Caernarfon 7/08, Marine c/s 09, Vauxhall Motors 10/09	29	3
Sean	Highdale				04/03/1991	21	Liverpool	Liverpool Rel c/s 11, Oldham (L) 8/10, Newtown (SL) 1/11, Vauxhall Motors 7/11		
David	Mannix		5'08"	11 06	24/09/1985	25	Winsford	Liverpool Rel 1/07, Accrington (L) 11/06, Ham Kam (Nor) 1/07, Accrington 1/08 Rel c/s 08, Chester 6/08 Rel 8/09, Banned, Morecambe (Trial) 7/10, Interhaching (Ger) (Trial), Vauxhall Motors 10/10	25	1
Paul	Wheeler							Cammell Laird, Vauxhall Motors 8/11		
Sean	Williams		5'07"		20/01/1992	19	Liverpool	Stockport (Scholar) Rel c/s 11, Vauxhall Motors 8/11		
Josh	Wilson				05/07/1988	23	Liverpool	Stoke (Scholar) Rel 6/06, Abroad, Northwich 7/07 Rel 5/08, Leigh RMI/ Leigh Genesis 5/08, Burscough 11/08, Vauxhall Motors 8/09	32	8
FORWARDS										
Craig	Mahon		5'07"	09 10	21/06/1989	22	Dublin	Lourdes Celtic (Yth), Wigan Rel c/s 09, Accrington (L) 11/08, Salford C c/s 09, Burscough 2/10, Vauxhall Motors 9/10	35	3
Leighton	McGivern		5'08"	11 01	02/06/1984	27	Liverpool	Waterloo Dock, Aberystwyth 1/03, Kidsgrove 7/03, Vauxhall Motors 3/04, Rochdale 7/04, Vauxhall Motors 8/05, Waterloo Dock, Chester (Trial) 10/06, Accrington 11/06 Rel c/s 08, Waterloo Dock c/s 08, Vauxhall Motors 1/11, Stockport (Trial) 7/11	16	10
Liam	Nethercote							St Johns, East Villa, Vauxhall Motors 7/11		
Anthony	Wright		5'11"	11 00	06/03/1978	33	Liverpool	Wrexham, Barrow, Droylsden 9/98, TNS, Aberystwyth, Hyde (L) 8/03, Vauxhall Motors 8/04, Colwyn Bay 1/08, Vauxhall Motors 5/08 (PL/Man) 5/11	7	0

WORCESTER CITY

Chairman: Anthony Hampson
Secretary: Joe Murphy **(T)** 07837 086 205 **(E)** joemurphy77@yahoo.co.uk
Additional Committee Members:
Jim Painter, Colin Layland, Andrew Watson, Mike Davis, Philip Williamson

Manager: Carl Heeley
Programme Editor: Rob Bazley **(E)** programme@worcestercityfc.co.uk

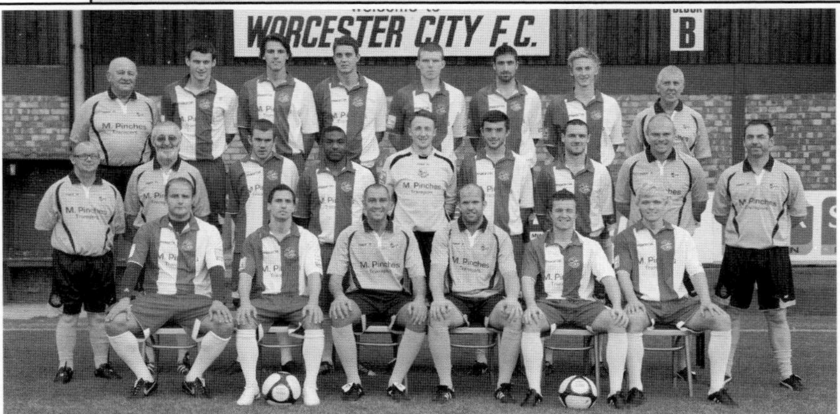

Back Row (L-R): Ernie North (Kitman), Simon Richman, Shabir Khan, RobElvins, Danny Glover, Kevin O'Connor, Jamie Price, MartinObrey (Assistant Therapist) Middle Row : Kevin Gardiner (Kit Manager), Pete O'Connell (Chiropodist), Jason Pike, Dan Polan, Mark Wright, Brad Birch, Gary Walker, Mark Owen (First Team Coach), Steve Ball (Head Therapist)
Front Row : Marc McGregor, Mark Danks, Carl Heeley (Manager), Mark Clyde (Assistant Manager), Graham Ward (Captain), Tom Thorley

Club Factfile

Founded: 1902 **Nickname:** City
Previous Names: Not known
Previous Leagues: West Midlands, Birmingham, Southern 1938-79, 85-2004, Alliance 1979-85

Club Colours (change): Blue/blue/white (Green & white hoops/green/green & white hoops)

Ground: St George's Lane, Barbourne, Worcester WR1 1QT **(T)** 01905 23003
Capacity: 4,004 **Seats:** 1,125 **Covered:** 2,000 **Clubhouse:** Yes **Shop:** Yes

Directions
Leave the M5 at Junction 6 (Worcester North) and take the A449 dual-carriageway towards Kidderminster. At the first island take the 2nd exit towards Worcester. After around 3 miles, at traffic lights/T-junction turn right towards Worcester City Centre. Take the 3rd turning on the left - St. George's Lane North. Ground on the left.

Previous Grounds: Severn Terrace, Thorneloe, Flagge Meadow

Record Attendance: 17,042 v Sheffield United - FA Cup 4th Round 24/01/1959
Record Victory: 18-1 v Bilston - Birmingham League 21/11/1931
Record Defeat: 0-10 v Wellington - Birmingham League 29/08/1920
Record Goalscorer: John Inglis - 189 (1970-77)
Record Appearances: Bobby McEwan - 596 (1959-75)
Additional Records: Paid £8,500 to Telford United for Jim Williams 1981
Received £27,000 from Everton for John Barton

Senior Honours: Birmingham League 1913-14, 24-25, 28-29, 29-30.
Southern League Cup 1939-40, 2000-01, Division 1 1967-68, 76-77, Premier 1978-79.
Birmingham Senior Cup 1975-76. Worcestershire Senior Cup x26 (last win 1996-97)

10 YEAR RECORD

01-02	02-03	03-04	04-05	05-06	06-07	07-08	08-09	09-10	10-11
SthP 8	SthP 6	SthP 5	Conf N 7	Conf N 8	Conf N 9	Conf N 12	Conf S 16	Conf S 20	Conf N 16

WORCESTER CITY

No.	Date	Comp	H/A	Opponents	Att:	Result	Goalscorers	Pos
1	Sat-14-Aug	BSN	H	Gainsborough Trinity	750	L 1-2	Cartwright 41	16
2	Tue-17-Aug	BSN	A	Eastwood Town	477	W 4-2	Clyde 2 (29, 36), Danks 34, Glover 45	10
3	Sat-21-Aug	BSN	A	Vauxhall Motors	179	W 3-2	O'Connor 11, Danks 26, Glover 34	6
4	Mon-23-Aug	BSN	H	Hinckley United	746	W 3-2	Danks 4, Birley 9, Richman 80	4
5	Sat-28-Aug	BSN	A	Stafford Rangers	557	D 1-1	Birley 17	6
6	Mon-30-Aug	BSN	H	Solihull Moors	886	L 0-1		8
7	Sat-04-Sep	BSN	H	Nuneaton Town	1070	D 2-2	Birley 48, Danks 58	10
8	Sat-11-Sep	BSN	A	Blyth Spartans	397	L 0-3		12
9	Sat-18-Sep	BSN	H	Workington	758	L 1-2	Danks 16	11
10	Sat-02-Oct	BSN	A	AFC Telford	2508	D 1-1	Danks pen 12	10
11	Sat-16-Oct	BSN	A	Hyde FC	341	W 2-0	Thorley 29, Cartwright 65	10
12	Sat-23-Oct	BSN	H	Harrogate Town	713	L 2-3	Glover 2 (13, 15)	12
13	Sat-30-Oct	BSN	A	Alfreton Town	657	L 1-2	Clarke 72	12
14	Mon-08-Nov	BSN	H	Redditch United	808	D 1-1	Danks 26	13
15	Sat-13-Nov	BSN	A	Solihull Moors	321	L 0-2		13
16	Mon-13-Dec	BSN	H	Vauxhall Motors	408	W 4-1	Thorley 43, Danks 76, Og (Hannigan) 78, Glover 90	11
17	Sat-01-Jan	BSN	H	Gloucester City	833	W 2-0	McGregor 37, Glover 45	10
18	Mon-03-Jan	BSN	A	Redditch United	505	D 0-0		10
19	Sat-08-Jan	BSN	A	Droylsden	264	L 1-2	Clyde 7	11
20	Mon-10-Jan	BSN	H	Corby Town	478	L 0-2		12
21	Wed-26-Jan	BSN	A	Gloucester City	425	D 1-1	Walker 49	12
22	Sat-05-Feb	BSN	H	Boston United	637	W 2-0	Glover pen 33, Thorley 80	12
23	Sat-12-Feb	BSN	H	Stalybridge Celtic	625	W 1-0	McGregor 90	12
24	Mon-14-Feb	BSN	H	Hyde FC	472	W 4-2	Glover 3 (8, 11, 72), Elvins 13	10
25	Sat-19-Feb	BSN	A	Nuneaton Town	901	L 1-2	Danks 14	10
26	Tue-01-Mar	BSN	A	Stalybridge Celtic	306	D 0-0		11
27	Sat-05-Mar	BSN	A	Corby Town	282	D 1-1	Charlton 12	14
28	Mon-07-Mar	BSN	H	Alfreton Town	579	L 1-2	Glover 10	14
29	Sat-12-Mar	BSN	A	Guiseley	394	W 1-0	Glover 55	13
30	Sat-19-Mar	BSN	H	AFC Telford	1068	L 0-3		13
31	Mon-21-Mar	BSN	H	Droylsden	500	L 0-1		13
32	Sat-26-Mar	BSN	A	Gainsborough Trinity	309	W 2-0	Glover 42, McGregor 81	12
33	Sat-02-Apr	BSN	A	Boston United	1352	L 0-1		15
34	Mon-04-Apr	BSN	H	Stafford Rangers	493	D 2-2	Thorley 14, McGregor 60	14
35	Sat-09-Apr	BSN	H	Guiseley	458	L 1-2	Glover 64	15
36	Tue-12-Apr	BSN	A	Workington	246	L 0-2		15
37	Sat-16-Apr	BSN	A	Harrogate Town	304	L 0-1		15
38	Sat-23-Apr	BSN	H	Eastwood Town	509	D 1-1	Charlton 75	16
39	Mon-25-Apr	BSN	A	Hinckley United	398	L 1-3	Richman 10	17
40	Sat-30-Apr	BSN	H	Blyth Spartans	509	W 1-0	K Evans 7	16

CUPS

No.	Date	Comp	H/A	Opponents	Att:	Result	Goalscorers
1	Sat-25-Sep	FAC 2Q	A	Boston United	1352	W 3-2	Danks 15, Thorley 20, Glover 89
2	Sat-09-Oct	FAC 3Q	A	Corby Town	520	L 1-2	McGregor pen 90
3	Sat-20-Nov	FAT 3Q	A	Nuneaton Town	582	W 2-1	Glover 60, McGregor 90
4	Sat-11-Dec	FAT 1	H	Northwich Victoria	577	W 1-0	Cartwright 23
5	Sat-15-Jan	FAT 2	A	Eastleigh	407	D 3-3	Glover 23, Danks 42, Richman 83
6	Mon-17-Jan	FAT 2R	H	Eastleigh	564	L 1-4	Glover 7

League
Starts
Substitute
Unused Sub

Cups
Starts
Substitute
Unused Sub

Goals (Lg)
Goals (Cup)

SANDERCOMBE	WARD	KHAN	THORLEY	ELVINS	CLYDE	CARTWRIGHT	O'CONNOR	DANKS	GLOVER	BIRLEY	RICHMAN	MCGREGOR	T EVANS	WALKER	PRICE	WRIGHT	POLAN	HEELEY	CLARKE	BIRCH	PIKE	K EVANS	MACE	PARTON	EMERY	COLEMAN	HURREN	QUAYNOR	FANKEM	CHARLTON	BOTTOMER	DUGGAN	DINSMORE
X	X	X	X	X	X	X	X	X	X	X	S	U	U	U	U																		
X	X	X	X	X	X	X	X	X	X	X	S	U	U	S	U																		
X	X	X	X	X	X	X	X	X	X	X	S	U	S	S	U																		
X		X	X	X	X	X	X	X	X	X	S	U	X	S	S	U																	
X	X		X		X	X	X	X	X	X	S	S	X	U	X	U	U																
X	X		X		X	X	X	X	X	X	U	S	X	U	X	U	U																
X	X		X		X	X	X	X	X	X	S	X		S	X	U	U	U															
X	X		X		X	X	X	X	X	X	S	X	X	S	U	U	S																
X			X			X	X	X	X	X	X	X	X	U	U	U	U		X	U													
X			X	X		X	X	X	X	X	X	S	X		U	U	U		X			U											
X	X		X	X		X	X	X	X	X	S	S	X	S		U	U		X														
	X		X	X		X	X	X	X	X	S		X	U		U	U		X			U	X										
X	X		X	X		X	X	X	X		S		X	X		U	U		X	U		U											
X			X	X		X	X	X	X	U	X	U	X	S	X	U	U		X														
X			X	X		X	X	X	X	X	X		X	S	U	U	U		X	U													
	X		X	X	U	X	X	S	S	X	X	X		X	U	X			X				U										
	X		X	X	S	X	X	X	X	S	X	X		U		U			X			U		X									
	X		X	X	S	X	X	X	X	S	X	X	U	U		U			X					X									
	X		X	X	X		X	X	X	X	X		U	U					X			U		X	U	U							
	X		X	X			X	X	X	X	X		X	S					X	U		S		X	S	U							
	X		X	X		X		X	X	S	X		X	X					X	U		S	U		S	X							
	X		X	X		X	X	X	X	X		S	S						X			U	S		U	X	X						
	X		X	X			X	X	X	X	S	S	X	S					X				U		U	X	X						
	X		X	X		S	X	X	X		U	X		U					X				U		U	X	X	X					
	X		X	X		X		X	X	S	S	X	U	X					X				U				X	U	X				
	X		X	X		X	X	S	X	U	S	X		X					X				U			X	U			X			
	X		X			X	X	X	X	U	X			X					X			U	U			X	U	S		X			
	X		X			X	X		X		X	S		X					X			U	U		S	X	X	U		X			
	X		X	S		X	X		X		X	U		X					X			U	U			X	X	S		X			
	X		X				X	X	X		X	S		X				U	X		U	S			X	X		S		X			
	X		X	X		X	X	X	X					S					X		U	U			X	X		U		X			
	X		X	X		X	X	X	X	U		S		X					X			U				X		U		X			
	X		X	X		X	X	S	X	S		X		X					X			U				X		U		X	S		
			X	X		X	X	S	X	X	X	X		U					X							X		U		X	S	U	
	X		X	X		X	X	S	X			X		X					X			U				X		U		X	S		
			X	X	U	X	X		X	X	U	X		X								S				X		X		X	S		S
					U	X	X		X	X	X			X					X			X				X	U	X		X	S		U
			X	X	S	X	X		X	X	X			X					X			U				X		U		X	S		S
			X	X	U	X	X		X	S	X								X			U				X	U	X		X	X		S
			X	X	U	X	X		S	U	X	X							X			X				X	U	U		X	X		
X			X	S	X	X	X	X	X	X	X		X	S	S	U	U		X	U	U												
X	U		X	X		X	X	X	X	X	X	S	X	U		S	S		X	U		U											
X	U		X	X	U	X	X	S	X	X	S	X	X	X		U			X														
	X		X	X	S	X	X			X	X	X		X	U	X			X	U	U		U										
	X		X	X	X	S	X	X	X	X	X		U	S		U			X			U		X									
	X		X	X		X	X	X	X	X	X		S	U		U			X			U		X	U								
14	29	4	39	30	9	35	38	28	38	22	19	14	14	15	4	1	0	0	31	0	0	2	1	4	2	19	6	4	1	15	2	0	0
0	0	0	0	1	3	1	0	5	2	6	13	9	2	11	1	0	1	0	0	0	0	4	1	0	3	0	0	3	0	0	6	0	3
0	0	0	0	0	5	0	0	0	0	5	3	6	5	10	8	14	10	2	0	5	2	15	9	0	4	2	5	9	0	0	0	1	1
3	3	0	6	5	2	5	6	4	5	6	5	2	3	2	0	1	0	0	6	0	0	0	0	2	0	0	0	0	0	0	0	0	0
0	0	0	0	1	1	1	0	1	0	0	1	1	1	2	1	1	1	0	0	0	0	0	0	0	0	0	0	0	0	0	0	0	0
0	2	0	0	0	1	0	0	0	0	0	0	0	1	2	1	4	1	0	0	3	2	3	1	0	1	0	0	0	0	0	0	0	0
0	0	0	4	1	3	2	1	9	14	3	2	4	0	1	0	0	0	0	1	0	0	1	0	0	0	0	0	0	0	2	0	0	0
0	0	0	1	0	0	1	0	2	4	0	1	2	0	0	0	0	0	0	0	0	0	0	0	0	0	0	0	0	0	0	0	0	0

PLAYING SQUAD 2011/12

Existing Players		SN	HT	WT	DOB	AGE	POB	Career	Apps	Goals
GOALKEEPERS										
James	Dormand		6'01"	14 09	13/06/1986	25	Birmingham	Birmingham Rel 5/06, Bromsgrove (L) 8/03, Stafford R (3ML) 9/04, Tamworth (3ML) 8/05, Boston U (Trial) 7/06, Tamworth 7/06 (06/07 1,0), Rel 9/06, Halesowen T 10/06, Stratford T (L) 12/07, Stratford T (2ML) 1/08, Bromsgrove 6/08, Halesowen T 1/09, Redditch 12/10 Rel 2/11, Solihull Moors 3/11, Worcester 6/11		
Matt	Sargeant							Stafford R (Yth), Chasetown 8/07, Tipton, Worcester 7/11		
DEFENDERS										
Lee	Ayres		6'02"	12 06	28/08/1982	29	Birmingham	Walsall (Yth), Evesham, Kidderminster 6/01, Stourport (L) 02, Tamworth (L) 9/03, Tamworth 11/03, Notts County (Trial) 7/04, Burton £10,000 8/04 Rel 4/06, Bristol R (Trial) c/s 06, Moor Green/Solihull Moors c/s 06, Bristol R (Trial) 10/06, Redditch 7/08, Forest Green 12/08, Halesowen T 8/10, Redditch 10/10, Solihull Moors 2/11, Worcester 7/11		
Asa	Charlton		5'11"	12 00	07/12/1977	33	Cosford	Stoke, Kidderminster, Willenhall 8/96, Telford c/s 97, Willenhall, Sandwell B, Rushall O c/s 99, Stourport S 7/01, Worcester 8/02, Halesowen T 1/03 Rel 10/04, Redditch 10/04, Mansfield 11/06 Rel 5/07, AFC Telford 5/07, Hednesford (L) 9/08, Redditch 10/08, Corby T 5/10, Worcester 2/11	15	2
Ryan	Clarke				22/01/1984	27		Notts County (Scholar), Boston U 7/03, Kings Lynn (L) 10/04, Leigh RMI (L) 12/04 Perm 3/05, Alfreton 7/05, Worcester 6/07, Boston U 5/08, Grantham 7/09, Eastwood T 8/09 Rel 11/09, Northwich 12/09, Ilkeston 5/10 Rel 9/10, Worcester 9/10	31	1
Rob	Elvins		6'02"	12 04	17/09/1986	24	Alvechurch	West Brom, Cheltenham (L) 9/06, York C (2ML) 1/07, Aldershot 6/07 Rel c/s 09, Woking (2ML) 2/09, Worcester 7/09	31	1
Carl	Heeley				17/10/1969	41		Worcester (Pl/Man)	0	0
Shabir	Khan				10/11/1985	25		Worcester	4	0
Jacob	Rowe				09/12/1990	20		Derby (Yth), Solihull Moors (Yth), Birmingham, Redditch (L) 12/09, Rochdale (Trial) 7/10, Tamworth (Trial) 8/10 AFC Telford 8/10, Redditch 10/10, Worcester 6/11		
Jared	Wilson		5'08"	10 10	24/11/1989	21	Cheltenham	Birmingham Rel c/s 10, Chesterfield (SL) 2/09, Redditch 10/10, Worcester 8/11		
MIDFIELDERS										
Matt	Birley		5'08"	11 01	26/07/1986	25	Bromsgrove	Birmingham Rel c/s 07, Lincoln C (L) 11/06, Bournemouth (Trial) 5/07, Bromsgrove c/s 07, Tamworth 10/08, Kings Lynn 6/09 Rel 9/09, Worcester 9/09	28	3
Neil	Cartwright				25/06/1982	29	Wrexham	Hinckley U, Corby T 6/10, Worcester 8/10	36	2
Danny	Edwards				27/10/1983	27	Wellington	Shrewsbury, Stafford R (SL) 3/03, Stafford R 8/03, Redditch 6/07, AFC Telford 11/08, Halesowen T (L) 11/09, Leamington 7/10, Chasetown 9/10, Stafford R 1/11, Worcester 6/11		
Josh	Emery		5'06"	10 10	30/09/1990	20	Ledbury	Cheltenham Rel 12/10, Worcester (L) 8/09, Oxford C (WE) 11/09, Worcester (L) 2/10, Cirencester (L) 8/10, Worcester 1/11	5	0
Kyonn	Evans							Worcester	6	1
Emeka	Nwadike		6'00"	12 07	09/08/1978	33	Camberwell	Wolves, Shrewsbury 12/96 Rel c/s 98, Grantham 6/98, Kings Lynn 11/99, Ilkeston 1/01, Alfreton 6/03, Worcester 6/07, AFC Telford NC 3/08, Hinckley U (2ML) 11/08, Eastwood T 6/09, Gainsborough 5/10, Eastwood T 3/11, Worcester 7/11		
Kevin	O'Connor		5'11"	12 02	19/10/1985	25	Dublin	Wolves Rel c/s 08, Stockport (L) 3/06, Port Vale (Trial) 9/08, Injured, AFC Telford NC 1/10, Worcester 6/10	38	1
Tom	Thorley		5'10"	11 08	05/04/1990	21	Stafford	Stoke Rel 6/09, Stafford R (3ML) 7/08, Burscough (L) 10/08, Stafford R (SL) 1/09, Stafford R 7/09, Worcester 6/10	39	4
FORWARDS										
Simon	Brown		5'10"	11 00	18/09/1983	27	West Bromwich	West Brom, Kidderminster (SL) 3/04, Kidderminster (3ML) 7/04, Mansfield £50,000 12/04 Rel c/s 08, Wrexham 6/08 Rel 3/10, Rushden & D (5WL) 11/08, York C (SL) 1/09, Tamworth (2ML) 11/09, Eastwood T 3/10, Corby T 6/10, Hednesford (Dual) 10/10, Redditch 1/11, Worcester 6/11		
Danny	Carey-Bertram		5'11"	13 00	14/06/1984	27	Birmingham	WBA, Hereford 9/03 Rel 6/06, Cambridge U 6/06 Rel 1/07, Forest Green Rovers 1/07 Rel 4/08, Bath C 8/08, AFC Telford 10/08 Rel 5/11, Worcester (L) 12/09, Hednesford (L) 10/10, Worcester 6/11		
Luke	Corbett		6'00"	11 02	10/08/1984	27	Worcester	Cheltenham Rel c/s 05, Cirencester (L) 12/02, Hednesford (L) 3/03, Chelmsford (L) 8/03, Weston-Super-Mare (2ML) 12/03, Weston-Super-Mare (L) 11/04, Bath C (2ML) 12/04, Cirencester (Trial) 7/05, Mangotsfield 7/05 Rel 10/05, Gloucester 10/05 Rel 9/06, Bishops Cleeve 9/06, Leamington 6/08, Worcester 5/11		
Marc	McGregor		5'09"	11 10	30/04/1978	33	Southend	Oxford U Rel c/s 97, Endsleigh c/s 97, Forest Green 8/98, Cirencester (L) 10/98, Nuneaton £35,000 6/00, Weston Super-Mare (L) 8/02, Macclesfield (Trial) 1/03, Tamworth 8/03, Chippenham (L) 9/03, Weston-Super-Mare (L) 10/03, Weston-Super-Mare (L) 12/03, Weston-Super-Mare 3/04, Hinckley U 5/05, Weston-Super-Mare 5/06, Worcester 10/09 (Pl/Coach) 8/11	23	4
Michael	Symons				22/07/1986	25	Gloucester	Ilfracombe, Barnstaple 7/04, Slimbridge (Dual) 12/04, Bideford 9/05, Cirencester 1/06, Clevedon T 3/07, Forest Green 8/08, Gloucester (L) 8/08, Gloucester (SL) 2/09, Gloucester 5/09 Rel 5/11, Worcester 6/11		
Michael	Taylor							Earlswood, Worcester 8/11		

WORKINGTON

Chairman: Humphrey Dobie

Secretary: Steve Durham **(T)** 07899 938 156 **(E)** sbj.durham@btinternet.com

Additional Committee Members:
Jos Taylor, Paul Armstrong, Colin Doorbar, Alec Graham, Thex Johnston, Jos Taylor, Dave Wilson, Les Smallwood.

Manager: Darren Edmondson

Programme Editor: Paul Armstrong **(E)** paul@workingtonafc.com

Back row (L-R): Anthony Wright, Lee Andrews, Dan Wordsworth, David Hewson, Simon Tucker, Gareth Arnison, Aaran Taylor, Andy Murray-Jones, Jonny Wright, Phil McLuckie, Adam Main, Tony Hopper, Kyle May.
Front row: Stuart Green, Mark Sloan, Jonny Blake, Dan Dillon, Darren Edmondson (manager), Viv Busby (assistant manager), Mark Boyd, Jacob Simpson, Gari Rowntree, David McNiven.

Club Factfile

Founded: 1884 **Nickname:** Reds

Previous Names: None

Previous Leagues: Cumberland Assoc. 1890-94, Cumberland Senior 1894-1901, 03-04. Lancashire 1901-03, Lancashire Comb. 1904-10, North Eastern 1910-11, 21-51, Football League 1951-77, N.P.L. 1977-2005

Club Colours (change): Red/white/red (Sky blue/navy/sky blue)

Ground: Borough Park, Workington, Cumbria CA14 2DT **(T)** 01900 602 871

Capacity: 2,500 **Seats:** 500 **Covered:** 1,000 **Clubhouse:** Yes **Shop:** Yes

Directions A66 into Workington. At traffic lights at bottom of hill (HSBC opposite), turn left towards town centre. Approach traffic lights in centre lane (Washington Central Hotel on your right) and turn right. Continue on this road, passing over a mini roundabout, a pedestrian crossing and a further set of traffic lights. You will come to the Railway Station (facing you), carry on through the junction and bear right, passing the Derwent Park Stadium (Rugby League/speedway), then left and Borough Park becomes visible ahead of you.

Previous Grounds: Various 1884-1921, Lonsdale Park 1921-37

Record Attendance: 21,000 v Manchester United - FA Cup 3rd round 04/01/1958
Record Victory: 17-1 v Cockermouth Crusaders - Cumberland Senior League 19/01/1901
Record Defeat: 0-9 v Chorley (A) - Northern Premier League 10/11/1987
Record Goalscorer: Billy Charlton - 193
Record Appearances: Bobby Brown - 419
Additional Records: Paid £6,000 to Sunderland for Ken Chisolm 1956
Received £33,000 from Liverpool for Ian McDonald 1974

Senior Honours: North West Counties League 1998-99
Cumberland County Cup x23

10 YEAR RECORD

01-02	02-03	03-04	04-05	05-06	06-07	07-08	08-09	09-10	10-11
NP 1 16	NP 1 10	NP 1 7	NP P 2	Conf N 13	Conf N 3	Conf N 14	Conf N 12	Conf N 4	Conf N 11

WORKINGTON

No.	Date	Comp	H/A	Opponents	Att:	Result	Goalscorers	Pos
1	Sat-14-Aug	BSN	H	Gloucester City	523	W 2-1	McLuckie 34, Tymon 84	9
2	Mon-16-Aug	BSN	A	Hyde FC	372	W 3-2	Hewson 19, J Wright 21, McLuckie 41	1
3	Sat-21-Aug	BSN	A	Eastwood Town	404	W 2-0	Vipond 2 (46, 75)	4
4	Tue-24-Aug	BSN	H	Harrogate Town	610	W 2-1	J Wright 18, Rowntree 38	3
5	Sat-28-Aug	BSN	A	Gainsborough Trinity	362	D 1-1	Hewson 25	3
6	Mon-30-Aug	BSN	H	Vauxhall Motors	707	W 2-1	J Wright 54, Vipond 85	3
7	Sat-04-Sep	BSN	H	Solihull Moors	648	W 2-1	Og (Midworth) 88, Arnison 90	2
8	Sat-11-Sep	BSN	A	Boston United	1556	L 0-4		4
9	Sat-18-Sep	BSN	A	Worcester City	758	W 2-1	Tymon 2 (75, 89)	3
10	Sat-02-Oct	BSN	H	Nuneaton Town	522	L 0-1		4
11	Sat-30-Oct	BSN	A	Droylsden	358	L 0-3		7
12	Sat-06-Nov	BSN	H	Stalybridge Celtic	398	L 0-5		7
13	Tue-09-Nov	BSN	H	Guiseley	333	L 0-1		8
14	Sat-13-Nov	BSN	A	Corby Town	374	L 0-1		9
15	Tue-16-Nov	BSN	A	AFC Telford	1459	L 0-1		9
16	Sat-11-Dec	BSN	A	Stafford Rangers	353	W 2-0	Arnison pen 13, A Wright 29	8
17	Sat-01-Jan	BSN	H	Blyth Spartans	385	D 1-1	A Wright 57	8
18	Tue-11-Jan	BSN	A	Alfreton Town	440	L 0-2		10
19	Tue-18-Jan	BSN	H	Redditch United	300	W 5-1	Arnison 3 (3, 10, 62), Vipond 38, May 56	9
20	Sat-22-Jan	BSN	A	Gloucester City	315	L 0-2		10
21	Tue-25-Jan	BSN	H	Eastwood Town	291	L 0-3		10
22	Tue-01-Feb	BSN	H	AFC Telford	262	L 0-1		11
23	Sat-05-Feb	BSN	H	Gainsborough Trinity	273	W 4-2	Hewson 13, May 41, McLuckie 59, Greulich 75	10
24	Sat-12-Feb	BSN	H	Alfreton Town	348	D 0-0		10
25	Sat-19-Feb	BSN	H	Boston United	379	L 3-5	Rogan 33, A Wright 37, Arnison 50	12
26	Sat-26-Feb	BSN	A	Solihull Moors	267	L 0-2		13
27	Sat-05-Mar	BSN	A	Hinckley United	318	W 2-1	Arnison 2 (46, 66)	13
28	Tue-08-Mar	BSN	A	Vauxhall Motors	167	W 2-1	Tinnion 89, Murray-Jones 90	10
29	Sat-12-Mar	BSN	H	Droylsden	389	W 2-0	J Wright 58, Rogan 76	9
30	Tue-15-Mar	BSN	A	Guiseley	274	D 2-2	Arnison 2 (45, 83)	9
31	Sat-19-Mar	BSN	A	Redditch United	208	D 1-1	J Wright 84	10
32	Tue-22-Mar	BSN	A	Blyth Spartans	408	L 1-2	Rogan 67	10
33	Sat-26-Mar	BSN	H	Corby Town	314	L 1-2	Murray-Jones 88	10
34	Sat-02-Apr	BSN	A	Stalybridge Celtic	390	L 1-2	J Wright 82	11
35	Sat-09-Apr	BSN	H	Stafford Rangers	402	W 2-0	Arnison 2 (pen 63, pen 76)	11
36	Tue-12-Apr	BSN	H	Worcester City	246	W 2-0	Arnison 2 (43, pen 56)	10
37	Sat-16-Apr	BSN	A	Nuneaton Town	801	L 1-2	Murray-Jones 79	10
38	Sat-23-Apr	BSN	H	Hyde FC	326	D 1-1	May 86	11
39	Mon-25-Apr	BSN	A	Harrogate Town	339	L 0-2		11
40	Sat-30-Apr	BSN	H	Hinckley United	336	W 3-1	Blake 9, Arnison 83, Vipond 74	11

CUPS

No.	Date	Comp	H/A	Opponents	Att:	Result	Goalscorers
1	Sat-25-Sep	FAC 2Q	H	West Auckland Town	413	W 2-1	Andrews 77, Tymon 85
2	Sat-09-Oct	FAC 3Q	H	Shildon	513	W 2-1	Arnison 9, A Wright 13
3	Sat-23-Oct	FAC 4Q	H	Nuneaton Town	520	D 1-1	Arnison 18
4	Tue-26-Oct	FAC 4QR	A	Nuneaton Town	943	L 0-1	
5	Sat-20-Nov	FAT 3Q	H	Chasetown	305	D 0-0	
6	Tue-23-Nov	FAT 3QR	A	Chasetown	334	L 0-4	

League
Starts
Substitute
Unused Sub

Cups
Starts
Substitute
Unused Sub

Goals (Lg)
Goals (Cup)

TAYLOR	LANGFORD	ROWNTREE	MAY	WHITE	MCLUCKIE	VIPOND	HEWSON	J WRIGHT	ARNISON	A WRIGHT	TINNION	TYMON	RUTTLEDGE	HINDMARCH	MAIN	ANDREWS	BLAKE	BOWMAN	SMITH	SMYTH	MURRAY-JONES	ROGAN	GREULICH	SLOAN	SWINGLEHURST	RUDD
X	X	X	X	X	X	X	X	X	X	X	S	S	S	U	U											
X	X	X	X	X	X	X	X	X	X	X	S	S	U	S	U											
X	X	X	X	X	X	X	X	X	X	X	U	S		S	U	U										
X	X	X	X	X	X	X	X	X	X	X	S	U		U		U	U									
X	X	X	X	X	X	X	X	X	X	X	S	U		U		U	U									
X	X	X	X	U	X	X		X	X	X	S	S		U	X	X	U									
X	X	X	X	X	X	X	X	X	X		S	X		S	U	S	U									
X	X	X	X	X	X	X		X	X	S	X	S		X	U	S	U									
X	X	X	X	U		X	S	X	X	X	X	S		X	U	X	S									
X	X	X	X	U		X	X	X	X	X	S	X		S	U	X	U									
X	U	X	X	X		X		X	X		U	S		X	S	X	X	X	S							
X	X		X	X		X		U	X	X	S	S		X	S	X	U	X	X							
X	X		X	U		X	X	S	X	X	S	U		X	U	X		X	X							
X	X		X	U		X	X	S	X	X	S	S		X	U	X		X	X							
X	X		X	U		X	X	X	X	X	U	S		X	S	X		X	S							
X	X		X	U	X	X	X		X	X	S			U	X	X	S			X	S					
X	X		X	U	X	X	X		X	X	S				X	X	S			X	S					
X	X		X	U	X	X	X		X	X	S				X	X	S			X	S					
X	X		X	U	X	X	X		X	X	S				X	X	S			X	U	S				
X	X		X	U	X	X	X		X		X			U	S	X	S			X	S	X				
X	X		X	U	X	X	X		X		S				S	X	U			X	S	X	X			
X	X		X		X	X	X		X	X	S				U	X	U			X	S	X	S			
X	X		X		X	X	X		X	X	U				S	X	S			X	U	X	S			
X	X		X		X	X	X	S	X	X	U				S	X	U			X	U	X				
X	X		X		X	X	X	S	X	X	U				U	X	U			X	S	X				
X	X		X		X	X	X	X		X	S			U	S	X	U			X	S	X				
X	X		X		X	X	X	X	X	X	U			S	S	X	S				U	X				
X	X		X		S	X	X	X	X	X	S			U	X	X	U				S	X				
X	X		X		S	X	X	X	X	X	U			U	X	X	S				S	X				
X	X		X		S	X	X	X	X	X	S			U	X	X	U				U	X				
X	X		X		S	X	X	X	X	X	S			U	X	X	S					X				
X	S		X		X	X	X	X	X	X	S			U	S	X	X				U	X				
X	X		X			S	X	X	X	X	X			U	S	X	X				S	X				
X	X		X			S	X	X	X	X	X			U	S	X	X				S	X		U		
X	X		X			X	X	X	X	X	X			S	U	X	U				S	X			S	
X	X		X			X	X	X	X	X	X			S	S	X	U				S	X			U	
X	X		X			X	X	X	X	X	X			S	U	X	U				S	X			S	
X	X		X			S	U	X	X		X				X	X	X				X			S	X	
X	X		X			X	X	X	X						X	X	S				S			X	X	S
X	X					X	X	X	X						X	X	X				S			X	X	S
X	X	S	S	X		U	X	X	X	X	X	X		X	U	X	S									
X	X	X	X	S		X	X	X	X	X	S	S		X	U	X	U									
X	X	X	X	U		X		S	X	X	X	U		X	U	X	U	X								
X	X	X	X	U		X		S	X	X	X	S		X	U	X	U	X								
X	X		X	X	S	X			X	X	S	U		X	X	X		X	U							
X	X		X	U	S	X			X	X	X	S		X	X	X	U		X							
40	38	11	39	9	21	37	34	27	39	32	9	2	0	7	12	33	6	5	3	11	1	18	1	2	3	0
0	1	0	0	0	4	3	1	4	0	1	21	10	1	8	13	2	11	0	2	0	17	1	2	1	2	2
0	1	0	0	12	0	0	1	1	0	0	8	3	1	14	13	3	17	0	0	0	6	0	0	1	1	0
6	6	3	5	2	0	5	2	2	6	6	4	1	0	6	2	6	0	3	1	0	0	0	0	0	0	0
0	0	1	1	1	2	0	0	2	0	0	2	3	0	0	0	0	1	0	0	0	0	0	0	0	0	0
0	0	0	0	3	0	1	0	0	0	0	0	2	0	0	4	0	4	0	1	0	0	0	0	0	0	0
0	0	1	3	0	3	5	3	6	15	3	1	3	0	0	0	0	1	0	0	0	3	3	1	0	0	0
0	0	0	0	0	0	0	0	0	2	1	0	1	0	0	0	1	0	0	0	0	0	0	0	0	0	0

PLAYING SQUAD 2011/12

Existing Players		SN	HT	WT	DOB	AGE	POB	Career	Apps	Goals
GOALKEEPERS										
Lee	Jolly							Workington		
Aaron	Taylor				20/11/1986	24		Annan Ath, Penrith, Workington c/s 07, Barrow 7/08 Rel 9/08, Penrith, Workington (Trial) 2/09, Workington 3/09	40	0
Defenders										
Lee	Andrews		6'00"	11 06	23/04/1983	28	Carlisle	Carlisle Rel 5/06, Rochdale (L) 2/03, York (2ML) 11/05, Torquay (L) 3/06, Torquay 5/06 Rel c/s 07, Newcastle Blue Star 9/07, Workington 1/08	35	0
Kyle	May				07/09/1982	28	Doncaster	Carlisle Rel c/s 02, Gretna 8/02, Workington (5ML) 8/04, Workington 1/05	39	3
Dan	McDermott							Workington		
Phil	McLuckie				13/04/1989	22		Morecambe, Workington (3ML) 12/07 Perm 3/08	25	3
Gari	Rowntree				05/10/1986	24		Carlisle (Yth), Blackburn, Workington 3/07	11	1
Dan	Wordsworth						Carlisle	Carlisle Rel 1/09, Kendal T (L) 9/08, Kendal T (L) 11/08, Kendal T 1/09, Workington (Trial) c/s 10, Harraby Catholic Club, Workington 7/11		
MIDFIELDERS										
Jonny	Blake		5'08"	11 00	04/02/1991	19	Carlisle	Carlisle, Workington 3/10	17	1
Marc	Boyd		5'10"	12 04	22/10/1981	29	Carlisle	Newcastle Rel c/s 02, Carlisle (Trial) 3/02, Port Vale 7/02, Carlisle 3/04 Rel c/s 04, Gretna 7/04 Rel 1/06, Macclesfield (SL) 1/05, Accrington 2/06, Southport 6/06, Sligo R c/s 07, Barrow 1/08, Droylsden (L) 1/11 Perm 1/11, Workington 6/11		
Dan	Dillon		5'09"	10 07	06/09/1986	24	Huntingdon	Carlisle Rel 3/06, Workington (4ML) 8/05, Workington 3/06, Team Bath 7/06, Worcester (Trial) 5/09, Hinckley U 6/09, Alfreton 10/10, Stocksbridge (Dual) 10/10, Workington 6/11		
Stuart	Green		5'10"	11 04	15/06/1981	30	Whitehaven	Newcastle, Carlisle (3ML) 12/01, Hull C (6ML) 7/02 £150,000 12/02, Carlisle (2ML) 2/03, C.Palace £75,000 8/06, Blackpool 1/08 Rel c/s 10, Crewe (L) 11/08, Wycombe 7/09 Rel c/s 11, Workington 7/11		
David	Hewson				05/05/1983	28		Gretna, Workington, Harraby CC (L)	35	3
Tony	Hopper		5'11"	12 08	31/05/1976	35	Carlisle	Carlisle Rel c/s 00, Barrow (L) 3/93, Bohemians 8/00, Workington 1/01, Carlisle 2/01 Rel c/s 02, Barrow 8/02, Workington 10/02 Rel c/s 10, Workington 8/11		
Adam	Main				16/01/1992	19		Workington	25	0
Jake	Simpson		5'11"	12 03	27/10/1990	20	Oxford	Blackburn (Scholar), Shrewsbury 7/09 Rel c/s 10, Carlisle (Trial) c/s 10, Morecambe (Trial) c/s 10, Wrexham (Trial) c/s 10, Tranmere (Trial) c/s 10, Stockport 9/10 Rel c/s 11, Hyde FC (L) 3/11, Workington 8/11		
Anthony	Wright				13/04/1986	25		Penrith, Workington 6/06	33	3
FORWARDS										
Gareth	Arnison				18/09/1986	24		Morecambe, Workington 8/05, Kendal (L) 12/06 Perm 1/07, Workington 8/08	39	15
David	McNiven		5'10"	12 00	27/05/1978	33	Leeds	Oldham Rel c/s 00, Linfield (L) 3/97, Scarborough (L) 2/00, Southport (L) 3/00, York 8/00 Rel c/s 01, Chester 7/01, Hamilton 10/01, Northwich 7/02, Kidsgrove (L) 11/02, Leigh RMI 8/03, Q.O.South 7/04, Scarborough 1/06, Morecambe 6/06, Stafford R (L) 1/07, Stafford R 8/07, Farsley Celtic (L) 2/08, Hyde U 7/09, Droylsden 8/10 Rel 3/11, Hyde FC 3/11 Rel c/s 11, Workington 7/11		
Andy	Murray-Jones							Workington	18	3
Mark	Sloan		5'09"		07/09/1992	18		Carlisle U (Scholar) Rel c/s 11, Workington (SL) 3/11, Workington 7/11	3	0
Simon	Tucker				19/10/1980	30		Carlisle, Barrow, North Bank, Loughborough University, Gresley R, Leek T 6/01, Gresley R, Sutton Coldfield 6/02, Hednesford, Hinckley U, Sutton Coldfield, Kidsgrove 10/03, Workington, Northbank Carlisle, Annan Ath, Workington 8/11		
Johnny	Wright				31/10/1985	25		Whitehaven Amateurs, Workington 8/07	31	6

BASINGSTOKE TOWN

Chairman: Rafi Razzak
Secretary: Richard Trodd (T) 07887 507 447 (E) richard.trodd@ntlworld.com
Additional Committee Members:
Ian Halloway, David Knight, Sarah Parsons, Geoff Yates, David Partridge, John Gaston

Manager: Frank Gray
Programme Editor: David Partridge (E) dave.partridge@btfc.co.uk

Club Factfile

Founded: 1896 **Nickname:** Dragons
Previous Names: None
Previous Leagues: Hampshire 1900-40, 45-71, Southern 1971-87, Isthmian 1987-2004

Club Colours (change): Blue and yellow/blue/yellow (All red)

Ground: Camrose Road, Western Way, Basingstoke RG22 6EZ (T) 01256 327 575
Capacity: 6,000 **Seats:** 651 **Covered:** 2,000 **Clubhouse:** Yes **Shop:** Yes

Directions
Leave M3 at junction 6 and turn left onto South Ringway which is the A30.
Straight over first roundabout. At second roundabout turn left into Winchester Road.
Proceed past ground on right to roundabout.
Take fifth exit into Western Way. Ground on right.

Previous Grounds: Castle Field 1896-1947

Record Attendance: 5,085 v Wycombe Wanderers - FA Cup 1st Round replay 1997-98
Record Victory: 10-1 v Chichester City (H) - FA Cup 1st Qualifying Round 1976
Record Defeat: 0-8 v Aylesbury United - Southern League April 1979
Record Goalscorer: Paul Coombs - 159 (1991-99)
Record Appearances: Billy Coomb
Additional Records: Paid £4,750 to Gosport Borough for Steve Ingham

Senior Honours: Hampshire League 1967-68, 69-70, 70-71. Southern League Southern Division 1984-85.
Hampshire Senior Cup 1970-71, 89-90, 95-96, 2007-08.

10 YEAR RECORD

01-02	02-03	03-04	04-05	05-06	06-07	07-08	08-09	09-10	10-11
Isth P 18	Isth P 5	Isth P 14	Conf S 6	Conf S 19	Conf S 19	Conf S 15	Conf S 18	Conf S 15	Conf S 13

BASINGSTOKE TOWN

No.	Date	Comp	H/A	Opponents	Att:	Result	Goalscorers	Pos
1	Sat-14-Aug	BSS	H	Chelmsford City	559	L 2-3	Rice pen 20, Pattison 90	15
2	Tue-17-Aug	BSS	A	St Albans City	311	D 0-0		15
3	Sat-21-Aug	BSS	A	Lewes	571	D 0-0		18
4	Mon-23-Aug	BSS	H	Dorchester Town	336	W 1-0	Pratt 33	10
5	Sat-28-Aug	BSS	H	Farnborough	702	W 1-0	Frewen 82	8
6	Mon-30-Aug	BSS	A	Weston-Super-Mare	260	L 0-1		10
7	Sat-04-Sep	BSS	H	Braintree Town	405	L 0-2		15
8	Sat-11-Sep	BSS	A	Woking	1112	L 0-2		17
9	Sat-18-Sep	BSS	H	Thurrock	372	D 2-2	Rice 2 (pen 63, 75)	17
10	Sat-02-Oct	BSS	A	Eastleigh	604	W 1-0	R Adams 9	15
11	Sat-16-Oct	BSS	H	Bromley	502	W 4-1	Draper 7, Warner 48, Sam-Yorke 2 (79, 88)	11
12	Sat-30-Oct	BSS	H	Welling United	429	L 1-3	Pratt 79	13
13	Sat-13-Nov	BSS	H	Bishops Stortford	358	L 0-1		17
14	Mon-15-Nov	BSS	A	Havant & Waterlooville	613	L 0-2		17
15	Tue-28-Dec	BSS	A	Farnborough	1011	D 1-1	Draper 63	17
16	Sat-01-Jan	BSS	A	Maidenhaed United	349	D 1-1	Pratt 86	17
17	Mon-03-Jan	BSS	H	Weston-Super-Mare	294	D 2-2	Smart 2, R Adams 61	17
18	Sat-08-Jan	BSS	H	Woking	604	W 1-0	Warner 53	16
19	Sat-15-Jan	BSS	A	Bromley	427	W 1-0	Lake 84	14
20	Sat-22-Jan	BSS	H	St Albans City	303	L 0-2		14
21	Tue-25-Jan	BSS	A	Dorchester Town	304	W 1-0	Warner 54	14
22	Sat-29-Jan	BSS	A	Hampton & Richmond Borough	335	D 2-2	Draper 45, Sam-Yorke 88	13
23	Tue-01-Feb	BSS	H	Staines Town	284	W 4-1	Smart 1, Draper 40, Sam-Yorke 2 (49, 68)	11
24	Sat-05-Feb	BSS	H	Dover Athletic	431	W 3-2	Draper 3 (25, 37, 40)	9
25	Mon-07-Feb	BSS	A	Chelmsford City	618	L 0-4		9
26	Sat-12-Feb	BSS	H	Eastleigh	447	L 1-2	Warner 60	11
27	Sat-19-Feb	BSS	A	Ebbsfleet United	777	L 1-3	Rice pen 59	12
28	Tue-22-Feb	BSS	A	Braintree Town	513	L 2-5	Lake 50, Sam-Yorke 71	12
29	Sat-26-Feb	BSS	A	Staines Town	378	D 1-1	Draper 7	12
30	Tue-01-Mar	BSS	A	Dartford	631	L 0-1		14
31	Sat-05-Mar	BSS	H	Lewes	326	D 1-1	Pratt 80	14
32	Tue-08-Mar	BSS	A	Thurrock	157	W 3-0	Wheeler 47, Sam-Yorke 53, Draper 60	14
33	Sat-12-Mar	BSS	H	Dartford	480	D 2-2	Sam-Yorke 2 (1, 38)	13
34	Sat-19-Mar	BSS	A	Boreham Wood	201	L 0-1		14
35	Sat-26-Mar	BSS	H	Havant & Waterlooville	325	L 0-2		14
36	Sat-02-Apr	BSS	H	Ebbsfleet United	407	L 1-2	Draper 32	14
37	Mon-04-Apr	BSS	H	Maidenhaed United	259	L 3-4	Draper 8, Sam-Yorke 33, Pratt 79	14
38	Sat-09-Apr	BSS	A	Bishops Stortford	338	W 2-0	Lake 34, Ogunbote 81	14
39	Sat-16-Apr	BSS	H	Hampton & Richmond Borough	360	W 4-0	Draper 3 (54, 75, 81), Pratt 90	13
40	Fri-22-Apr	BSS	A	Dover Athletic	1065	L 0-3		13
41	Mon-25-Apr	BSS	H	Boreham Wood	296	W 1-0	Draper 70	13
42	Sat-30-Apr	BSS	A	Welling United	705	L 0-4		13

CUPS

No.	Date	Comp	H/A	Opponents	Att:	Result	Goalscorers
1	Sat-25-Sep	FAC 2Q	A	Bristol Manor Farm	183	D 2-2	Draper 2 (42, 47)
2	Mon-27-Sep	FAC 2QR	H	Bristol Manor Farm	223	W 1-0	Draper 41
3	Sat-09-Oct	FAC 3Q	A	Didcot Town	401	W 4-0	Pratt 28, Warner 36, Pattison 44, Draper 64
4	Sat-23-Oct	FAC 4Q	H	AFC Wimbledon	1750	L 0-1	
5	Sat-20-Nov	FAT 3Q	H	Havant & Waterlooville	301	D 2-2	Reynolds 10, Rice pen 45
6	Mon-22-Nov	FAT 3QR	A	Havant & Waterlooville	353	W 2-1	Warner 53, Rice pen 72
7	Sat-11-Dec	FAT 1	H	Salisbury City	475	L 0-2	

League
Starts
Substitute
Unused Sub

Cups
Starts
Substitute
Unused Sub

Goals (Lg)
Goals (Cup)

TARDIF	FINLAY	RICE	R ADAMS	GASSON	LAKE	PATTISON	LAIDLER	PRATT	WILLIAMSON	WARNER	DRAPER	OGUNBOTE	DOWNES	HANKIN	SMART	ALLEN	FREWEN	POWELL	SAM-YORKE	CHARLICK	HOBDEN	T ADAMS	MOORE	REYNOLDS	LOCKE	OTOBO	RAYMOND	RANIERI	MILLAR	DOLAN	MORRIS	WHEELER	DUNN
X	X	X	X	X	X	X	X	X	X	X	S	S	S	U	U																		
X	X	X	X	X	U	X	X	X	X	X	X	U	S	U	U																		
X	X	X	X	X	U		X	X	X	X	X	U	S	U	X	U																	
X	X	X	X	X	X	X	X	X	U	S	U	X	S		S		X																
X		X	X	X	X	X	X	X	X	X	S	U	U	X	S		S																
X	X	X	X	X		X	X	X	X	X	S	U	S	U	X		S																
X	X	X	X		X	X	X	X	U	X	X	U	S	X	S		S																
X	S	X	X	X	X	X	X			X	S	X	X		X	U	S	U															
X	X	X	X	X	X	X	X			X	X	U	S		U		S	U	X														
X	X	U	X	X	X	X		X	U	X	X	X	S		X	U	U																
	X	S	X	X	X	X	S	X		X	X	X			X		U		S				X	U									
	X	X	X	X	X	X	S	X		X	S	X	U		U				X				X	S									
	X	U		X	U	X	X	X	U	X	X	X	S		X				S				X	X									
		X	X	X	X	S	X	X	U	X		X	S			U			X				X	X									
		X	X	X	X		X	X	S	X	X	S	S		X	U		U					X	X									
	S	X	X	X	X	S	X	X	S	X	X	U	U		X								X	X									
	U	X	X	X	U	U	X	X	X	X	X	S	S		X								X	X									
		X	X	X	X	X	U	X	U	X	U	X	U		X			U						X	X								
	U	X	X	X	X	X	S	X	U	X	U	X			X									X	X	U							
	U	X	X	X	X	X	S	X	U	X	S	X	S		X									X	X								
	X	X		X	X	X	X		S	X	X	U	S		S				X					X	X	U							
	X	X		X	X	X	X		S	X	X	U	S		S				X					X	X	U							
	U	X	X	X	X	S	U		X	X	X	U	S		X				X					X	X								
	X	X	X	X	X	U	S	S	X	X	X	U	S		X				X						X								
	X	X	X	X	X	S	X	S	U		X	S	U		X				X					X	X								
	X	X	X	X	X	U		S	U	X	X	S			X				X					X	X		U						
	X	X		X	X	X		X		X	U	S	X		X				S								X	X	S				
				X	X	S		X		X	U	X	U		X		S		X					X			X	X	U	X			
		X		X	X	S		S		X	X	X			X	U	U		X								X		S	X	X		
	S			X	X	X		X		X	X	S			X	U					U			X			X		S	X	X		
	X			X	S	U		X		S	S	X			X				X					X			X		U	X	X	X	
	X				X	X		X		X	X	U			S	U			X					X			U		S	X	X	X	
	X	S		X	X	X		X			X	U			S				X					X			U		S	X	X	X	
		X	X	X	X	X		X			X	X			X					U				X					S	U	X		
	X	X	X	X		X		X		X	X	U			X				S					X			U		U		X		S
	X	X	X	X	X	S		X		X	X	U			U				X					X							X		U
	U	X	X	X	X	X		X		X	X	U			U				X					X					U		X		U
		X	X	X	X	S		X		X	X	X			S		U		X					X					U		X		
	U	X	X	X	X	S		X		X	X	X			S				X					X	X		S				U		
	U	X	X	X	X	U		X		X	X	X			U				X					X	X		U				U		
	S	X	X	X	X	S		X		X	X	X			U				X					X	X		U				U		
		X	X	X	X			X		X	X	X			S				X	U				X	X	U					U		
X	X	X		X	X	X	X			X	X	S	X		X	U	S	S		U	U	U											
	S	X	X	X	X	S	X			S	X	X	U		X	X	X	X		U	U	U											
X	X	U	X	X	X	X	S	X	U	X	X	X	S		X	U	S																
	X	U	X	X	X	X	S	X	U	X	X	X	S		X	U	U						X	S									
	U	X	X	X	X	S	X	X	X	X			X		S	S	U						X	X									
	X	X	X		X	X	X		X	X			X		S	U	U			U	U		X	X									
X	X	X			X	X	X	S	X	X		S	X		X	U	S	U						X									
10	22	34	32	40	35	24	17	33	8	37	29	19	2	2	23	0	1	0	21	0	0	0	7	27	13	0	5	2	0	6	10	3	0
0	4	2	0	0	1	10	5	4	4	2	7	7	17	0	10	0	6	0	4	0	0	0	0	1	0	0	1	0	6	0	0	0	1
0	7	2	0	0	4	5	2	0	10	0	5	16	6	4	8	8	4	4	0	2	1	0	0	1	0	4	6	0	5	1	4	0	2
3	5	5	5	5	7	5	5	3	3	6	4	3	4	0	5	1	1	1	0	0	0	0	3	3	0	0	0	0	0	0	0	0	0
0	1	0	0	0	0	2	2	1	0	1	0	2	2	0	2	1	3	1	0	0	0	0	0	1	0	0	0	0	0	0	0	0	0
0	1	2	0	0	0	0	0	0	2	0	0	0	1	0	0	5	3	1	0	3	3	2	0	0	0	0	0	0	0	0	0	0	0
0	0	4	2	0	3	1	0	6	0	4	15	1	0	0	2	0	1	0	10	0	0	0	0	0	0	0	0	0	0	0	0	1	0
0	0	2	0	0	0	1	0	1	0	2	4	0	0	0	0	0	0	0	0	0	0	0	0	1	0	0	0	0	0	0	0	0	0

PLAYING SQUAD 2011/12

Existing Players		SN	HT	WT	DOB	AGE	POB	Career	Apps	Goals
GOALKEEPERS										
Ashley	Bayes		6'01"	13 05	19/04/1972	39	Lincoln	Brentford Rel c/s 93, Torquay 8/93 Rel c/s 96, Exeter 7/96 Rel c/s 99, L.Orient 7/99 Rel c/s 02, Bohemians (Ire) c/s 02, Woking 3/03, Hornchurch 5/04, Grays 11/04 Rel 5/07, Crawley 6/07 Rel 5/08, Stevenage 5/08, Basingstoke 6/11		
Joe	McDonnell							Basingstoke, Benfica (Trial) 12/10		
Chay	Morris							Wycombe (Scholar), Beaconsfield SYCOB 2/05, Arlesey, Burnham 8/09, Hemel Hempstead 7/10, Burnham 8/10, Beaconsfield SYCOB 2/11, Basingstoke 2/11	10	0
DEFENDERS										
Ross	Adams		5'11"	12 04	11/03/1983	28	Birmingham	Swindon (Sch), Highworth T, Chippenham 7/05, Basingstoke 5/10	32	2
Callum	Eagle							Woking (Yth), Basingstoke 8/11		
Jay	Gasson				29/12/1984	26		Fulham (Yth), Croydon A, Whyteleafe 10/03, Croydon A 2/04, Corinthian Casuals 7/04, Farnborough 6/05, Woking 6/07 Rel 5/08, Havant & W 5/08, Basingstoke 5/10	40	0
Robert	Rice		5'08"	11 11	23/02/1989	22	Hendon	Fulham (Yth), Wycombe Rel c/s 09, Wealdstone (L) 1/08, Basingstoke 6/09	36	4
Nathan	Smart				18/04/1985	26		Fleet T, Basingstoke 7/10	33	2
MIDFIELDERS										
Wes	Daly				07/03/1984	27		QPR, Gravesend (L) 10/03, Barnet (Trial) 12/03, Grays (L) 1/04, Raith (L) 8/04, Grays 2/05, AFC Wimbledon c/s 05, Maidenhead 7/07 Rel 5/08, Boreham Wood c/s 08, Carshalton c/s 09, Hendon 10/09, Bromley 12/09, Basingstoke 7/11		
Simon	Dunn							Basingstoke	1	0
Wilson	Gondwe							AFC Wimbledon, Basingstoke 7/11		
Stuart	Lake				17/11/1979	31	London	Wimbledon, Walton & Hersham, Farnborough 10/98, Northwood 3/99, Yeading, Northwood, Marlow 2/03, Uxbridge 7/04, Ashford T (Middx), Hampton & R 2/07, Basingstoke 6/10	36	3
Toby	Little				19/02/1989	22		Hayes/Hayes & Yeading, Woking NC 8/10, Staines 2/11, Basingstoke 7/11		
Shaun	McAuley				16/02/1987	24		Hayes & Yeading, Hampton & R c/s 07, Walton Casuals (Dual) 10/07, Eastleigh 7/09 Rel 5/11, Basingstoke 7/11		
Jide	Ogunbote				17/08/1988	23		Woking, Corinthian C (L) 9/07, Basingstoke 8/08	26	1
Matt	Warner				12/05/1985	26	Farnham	Wycombe, Baingstoke (2ML) 10/03, Team Bath, Farnborough 6/05, Basingstoke 7/06	39	4
FORWARDS										
Rob	Gradwell		6'02"	13 07	16/12/1990	20	Hillingdon	Birmingham (Scholar) Rel c/s 09, Luton (Trial) 4/09, Lincoln C (Trial) 7/09, Hayes & Yeading c/s 09 Rel 5/10, Lewes (L) 3/10, Lewes 5/10 Rel 1/11, Dulwich H (L) 11/10, Dulwich H 1/11, Basingstoke 7/11		
David	Pratt				01/08/1987	24		Swindon Supermarine, Chippenham 6/07, Basingstoke 5/09	37	6
Delano	Sam-Yorke		6'01"	13 04	20/01/1989	22		Woking Rel 5/10 Cray W (L) 11/09, AFC Wimbledon 7/10 Rel 5/11, Basingstoke (L) 9/10, Basingstoke (SL) 1/11, Basingstoke 6/11	25	10
Tim	Sills		6'02"	12 02	10/09/1979	31	Romsey	Millwall (Yth), Camberley 7/97, Basingstoke 7/99, Staines (L) 9/00, Kingstonian (L) 1/02, Kingstonian 3/02, Aldershot 5/03, Oxford U £50,000 1/06 Rel c/s 06, Hereford 6/06, Torquay 6/07, Stevenage Undisc 1/10, Rushden & D (3ML) 9/10, Aldershot 1/11 Rel 5/11, Basingstoke T 7/11		

BOREHAM WOOD

Chairman: Danny Hunter
Secretary: Dell Ward **(T)** 07867 661 592 **(E)** ddelldell@aol.com
Additional Committee Members:
Bill Hunter, Matthew Hunter, John Gill

Manager: Ian Allinson
Programme Editor: John Gill **(E)** johndgill2002@yahoo.co.uk

Back Row (L-R): Karl Beaumont (Asst. Groundsman), Elliott Godfrey, Michael Kamara, Gareth Risbridger, Ola Sogbanmu, Elvijs Putnins, Luke Wilkinson, Cameron Baker-Owers, Ryan Moran, Daniel Brathwaite, Greg Morgan, Jerome Maledon, Megan Reid (Physiotherapist).
Front Row: Charlie Hunter, David Bryant, Mario Noto (Team Captain), Daniel Hunter (Groundsman), Jason Goodliffe (Asst. Manager), Danny Hunter (Chairman), Ian Allinson (Team Manager), Martin Paine (Coach), Luke Garrard (Club Captain), Nicky Nicolau, Sam Hurrell. Photo by John D. Gill.

Club Factfile

Founded: 1948 **Nickname:** The Wood
Previous Names: Boreham Wood Rovers and Royal Retournez amalgamated in 1948 to form today's club
Previous Leagues: Mid Herts 1948-52, Parthenon 1952-57, Spartan 1956-66, Athenian 1966-74, Isthmian 1974-2004, Southern 2004-10

Club Colours (change): White/black/white (Sky blue/white/white)

Ground: Meadow Park, Broughinge Road, Boreham Wood WD6 5AL **(T)** 0208 953 5097
Capacity: 4,502 **Seats:** 600 **Covered:** 1,568 **Clubhouse:** Yes **Shop:** Yes

Directions
Leave A1 at A5135 and follow A5135 towards Borehamwood.
Cross two mini roundabouts then at large roundabout turn right (second exit) into Brook Road then take first right after car park for Broughinge Road.

Previous Grounds: Eldon Avenue 1948-63

Record Attendance: 4,030 v Arsenal - Friendly 13/07/2001
Record Victory: Not known
Record Defeat: Not known
Record Goalscorer: Mickey Jackson
Record Appearances: Dave Hatchett - 714
Additional Records: Received £5,000 from Dagenham & Redbridge for Steve Heffer

Senior Honours: Athenian League 1973-74. Isthmian League Division 2 1976-77, Division 1 1994-95, 2000-01.
Southern League East 2005-06, Premier Division Play-off 2009-10.
Herts Senior cup 1971-72, 98-99, 2001-02. London Challenge Cup 1997-98.

10 YEAR RECORD

01-02	02-03	03-04	04-05	05-06	06-07	07-08	08-09	09-10	10-11
Isth P 15	Isth P 22	Isth1N 9	SthE 7	SthE 1	Isth P 7	Isth P 19	Isth P 18	Isth P 4	Conf S 14

BOREHAM WOOD

No.	Date	Comp	H/A	Opponents	Att:	Result	Goalscorers	Pos
1	Sat-14-Aug	BSS	A	Weston-Super-Mare	186	L 0-2		21
2	Tue-17-Aug	BSS	H	Bromley	198	L 2-4	Noto 30, Morgan 54	20
3	Sat-21-Aug	BSS	H	Thurrock	138	D 2-2	Godfrey 2 (12, 83)	21
4	Tue-24-Aug	BSS	A	Braintree Town	438	L 2-3	Godfrey 65, Noto pen 90	21
5	Sat-28-Aug	BSS	A	Staines Town	295	D 0-0		21
6	Mon-30-Aug	BSS	H	Woking	301	D 0-0		21
7	Sat-04-Sep	BSS	A	Welling United	561	L 1-3	Hawes 44	21
8	Sat-11-Sep	BSS	H	Bishops Stortford	202	L 1-2	Allinson 52	21
9	Sat-18-Sep	BSS	A	Dorchester Town	420	L 1-3	Braithwaite 90	22
10	Sat-02-Oct	BSS	H	Dartford	351	W 3-1	Og (Bonner) 46, Noto 2 (pen 70, 84)	20
11	Sat-16-Oct	BSS	H	Ebbsfleet United	265	L 0-1		21
12	Sat-30-Oct	BSS	A	Eastleigh	616	L 0-3		22
13	Sat-06-Nov	BSS	H	Hampton & Richmond Borough	152	D 2-2	Hurrell 56, Moran 65	21
14	Sat-13-Nov	BSS	H	Dover Athletic	273	L 2-3	Hurrell 2 (26, 52)	21
15	Tue-07-Dec	BSS	H	Weston-Super-Mare	105	W 6-3	Noto 13, Chaaban 31, Morgan 2 (58, 65), Nicolau 2 (67, 81)	21
16	Tue-14-Dec	BSS	A	Maidenhead United	145	D 1-1	Chaaban 88	21
17	Sat-01-Jan	BSS	H	St Albans City	334	L 0-3		22
18	Mon-03-Jan	BSS	A	Woking	1084	L 0-3		22
19	Sat-08-Jan	BSS	A	Bishops Stortford	311	L 0-2		22
20	Sat-15-Jan	BSS	H	Chelmsford City	379	W 2-0	Sogbanmu 20, Clements 56	21
21	Sat-22-Jan	BSS	A	Havant & Waterlooville	574	L 1-2	Noto 81	21
22	Tue-25-Jan	BSS	H	Welling United	118	L 0-1		21
23	Sat-29-Jan	BSS	H	Maidenhead United	149	W 4-2	Chaaban 24, Godfrey 2 (39, 63), Moran 60	21
24	Tue-01-Feb	BSS	A	St Albans City	294	W 1-0	Morgan 41	21
25	Sat-05-Feb	BSS	A	Lewes	482	D 2-2	Sogbanmu 7, Chaaban 18	21
26	Wed-09-Feb	BSS	A	Farnborough	432	W 1-0	Godfrey 56	19
27	Sat-12-Feb	BSS	H	Dorchester Town	180	D 0-0		18
28	Mon-14-Feb	BSS	A	Chelmsford City	697	L 1-3	Sogbanmu 34	18
29	Tue-22-Feb	BSS	H	Staines Town	151	D 2-2	Nicolau 17, Bryant 54	19
30	Tue-01-Mar	BSS	A	Thurrock	183	W 3-1	Godfrey 2 (15, 62), Noto 36	17
31	Sat-05-Mar	BSS	A	Ebbsfleet United	800	D 2-2	Sogbanmu 65, Cestor 67	17
32	Sat-12-Mar	BSS	A	Bromley	399	D 1-1	Bryant 82	17
33	Sat-19-Mar	BSS	H	Basingstoke Town	201	W 1-0	Bryant 71	15
34	Sat-26-Mar	BSS	A	Dover Athletic	577	L 0-1		17
35	Tue-29-Mar	BSS	H	Farnborough	235	L 2-4	Og (Stevens) 77, Sogbanmu 89	17
36	Sat-02-Apr	BSS	A	Hampton & Richmond Borough	419	D 0-0		17
37	Tue-05-Apr	BSS	H	Braintree Town	227	L 0-2		18
38	Sat-09-Apr	BSS	H	Havant & Waterlooville	168	W 1-0	Morgan 9	17
39	Sat-16-Apr	BSS	A	Dartford	1118	W 4-1	Nicolau 43, Noto 2 (50, 67), Bryant 71	16
40	Fri-22-Apr	BSS	H	Eastleigh	220	W 2-1	Noto 2 (pen 24, 45)	15
41	Mon-25-Apr	BSS	A	Basingstoke Town	296	L 0-1		16
42	Sat-30-Apr	BSS	H	Lewes	202	W 3-0	Risbridger 45, Wilkinson 68, Garrard 71	14

CUPS

No.	Date	Comp	H/A	Opponents	Att:	Result	Goalscorers
1	Sat-25-Sep	FAC 2Q	A	Bedford Town	361	W 2-0	Kersey 42, McKenzie 45
2	Sat-09-Oct	FAC 3Q	H	Enfield Town	361	W 3-1	Garrard 63, Benjamin 79, Allinson 90
3	Sat-23-Oct	FAC 4Q	A	Ebbsfleet United	1005	L 0-3	
4	Sat-20-Nov	FAT 3Q	H	Romford	103	W 3-0	Chaaban 5, Og (Toms) 36, Hurrell 80
5	Sat-11-Dec	FAT 1	A	Eastbourne Borough	422	L 1-3	Cochrane 11

League
Starts
Substitute
Unused Sub

Cups
Starts
Substitute
Unused Sub

Goals (Lg)
Goals (Cup)

WILLIAMS	GARRARD	HAWES	NOTO	FRASER	MORAN	STANLEY	GODFREY	BLACKBURNE	ALLINSON	MORGAN	KIRBY	HUNTER	DADSON	BAKER-OWENS	LEWIS	KERSEY	KING	SEANLA	CLARKE	BRAITHWAITE	JONES	MCKENZIE	COCHRANE	BENJAMIN	HURRELL	KAMARA	CHAABAN	CHARGE	WILKINSON	RISBRIDGER	CLOSE	NICOLAU	AISIEN	GREEN	AKINOLA	HIBBERT	PUTNINS	CESTOR	SOGBANMU	ADJEI	INNS	MALEDON	FODERINGHAM	BRYANT
X	X	X	X	X	X	X	X	X	X	X	S	S	S	U																														
X	X	X	X	X	X	X	X	X	X	S	X	S	S		U																													
X	X	X	X		X	X	X	X	X	X	U	S	S		U	X	U																											
X	X	X	X		X	S	X	S	X	X	U	U	X			X		X	S																									
X	X		X		X		X	S	X	X	U	U	U			X	S	X	X	X																								
X	X	X	X		X		X	X	X	S	U		S			X	S	X	U	X																								
X	X	X			X			S	X	X	U	S	S	U		X	X	X	X	X																								
	X		X		X		X		X	X	U	U	S			X	S	S	X	X	X	X																						
	X		X	U			S			S	U		X	U		X	X	X		X	X	X	X	X																				
	X		X		X		X		S	X			S	U		X	U			X	X	X	X	X																				
	X		X		X		X			X			U	U		X	S			X	X	X	X	X																				
	X		X	U	X		X			U	U			U		X	X			X	X		X	S	X																			
	X		X		X		X			X				U			U			X	X		X	S	X	X	X	S																
	X		X		X		X								U	U	S			X	X			S	X	S	X	X	X	X														
	X		X		X		X			X		U		U						S	X		S			X	X	S	X	X		X												
	X		X	U	X		X			X		U		U							X		X				X	X	X		U	X	U											
	X		X		X					X		U			U						X		X			U	X		X	X		X	S	X	S									
	X		X									S			U						X		X			S	X		X	X	U	X	X	X	S									
	X		X		U					X											X					U	X		X	S		S	X	X	X	X								
	X		X		X					X																	X		X	X		U	S	U		S	X	X	X	S				
	X		X		X					S				U												U	X		X	X		S		X		X	X	X	X	S				
	X		X		X		S			X																U	X		X	X		X		U		S	X	X	X	S				
	X		X		X		X			X																S	X		X			X	U			X	X	X	S	U				
	X		X		X		X			X																U	X		X	X		X	U			S	X	X	S	U				
	X		X		X		X			X																U	X		X	X	U		S			S	X	X	X	U				
			X		X		X			X		U			U											X	X		X	X		X				S		X	S	U				
			X		U		X			X					U										S	X	X		X	X		X						X	S		X	S		
			X		U		X			X				U											S	X			X	S		X						X	X	S	X	X		
			X		S		X			X					U					X					S	X			X	U		X							S		X	X	X	X
			X	X	X		X			X					U					X			U		S	X				X		X							S			S	X	X
			X	S			X							U						X					S	X				X	U	X						X	X		X	S	X	X
	S		X				X			S													U		S	X			X	X		X					U	X	X			X	X	X
	X		X		U		X			X										X					S	U			X	X		X						X	S			U	X	X
	U		X		U		X			S										X					X	X			X	X		U					X	X	X			U		X
	X		X		S		X			X										X					S	U			X	X							X	X	S		U	X		X
	X		X		U		X			X										X					S	U			X	X							X	X	X		U	S		X
	X		X		U		X			X										X						U			X	X		S			S		X	X			U	X		X
	X		X		X		X			X										S						X			X	U		X					X	X	S		S	U		X
	X		X		X		X							U						S						X			U	X		X					X	X	S		X	S		X
	X		X		X		X			S				U											X	X			X	X		X					X		S			S		X
	X		X		X		X			U		S								X					S	X			X	X		X					X		S					X
	X		X		X		X			S		S		U						X					U	X			X	X		X					X		S					X
	X		X		X		X		S	S	U		U	U		X	X	U		X	X	X	X	X																				
	X		X		X		X		S	X	U	U	U			X	S			X	X	X	X	X																				
	X		X		X		X			S	U	U			U	X	X			X	X	X	X	X																				
	X		X		X					X		S		U						S	X		X		X	X	X		X	X	S													
	X		X	S	X		X					X		U							X		X				X		X	X	S	X												
7	34	6	41	3	29	3	34	4	8	28	1	0	2	0	0	10	3	5	3	20	12	4	8	3	5	15	15	2	26	23	0	20	2	4	1	3	15	18	9	0	5	5	5	14
0	1	0	0	1	2	1	2	3	1	8	1	7	7	0	0	0	5	1	1	3	0	0	1	3	10	3	0	2	0	2	0	3	3	0	3	5	0	0	13	4	1	6	0	0
0	1	0	0	3	7	0	0	0	0	2	8	7	2	15	9	1	3	0	1	0	0	0	2	0	1	10	0	0	1	2	4	2	3	2	0	0	1	0	0	4	3	3	0	0
0	5	0	5	0	5	0	4	0	0	2	0	1	0	0	0	3	2	0	0	3	5	3	5	3	1	1	2	0	2	2	0	1	0	0	0	0	0	0	0	0	0	0	0	0
0	0	0	0	1	0	0	0	0	2	2	0	1	0	0	0	0	1	0	0	1	0	0	0	0	0	0	0	0	0	0	2	0	0	0	0	0	0	0	0	0	0	0	0	0
0	0	0	0	0	0	0	0	0	0	0	3	2	2	3	1	0	0	1	0	0	0	0	0	0	0	0	0	0	0	0	0	0	0	0	0	0	0	0	0	0	0	0	0	0
0	1	1	11	0	2	0	8	0	1	5	0	0	0	0	0	0	0	0	0	1	0	0	0	0	3	0	4	0	1	1	0	4	0	0	0	0	0	1	5	0	0	0	0	4
0	1	0	0	0	0	0	0	0	1	0	0	0	0	0	0	1	0	0	0	0	0	1	1	1	1	0	1	0	0	0	0	0	0	0	0	0	0	0	0	0	0	0	0	0

ALSO PLAYED: LAWAL U(1,2). SCOTT-MORRIS U(C1,C2,C4). CRACKNELL S(10,11)X(12). ONIBUJE S(11,C2,C3). WALKER S(C5). LANCASTE U(C5). CLEMENTS X(18,20), S(19). FITZSIMONS X(18). GRAHAM U(23). READING X(26,27,28). YALA U(40,41).

PLAYING SQUAD 2011/12

Existing Players		SN	HT	WT	DOB	AGE	POB	Career	Apps	Goals
GOALKEEPERS										
Cameron	Baker-Owens				17/01/1993	18		Boreham Wood	0	0
Michael	Jordan		6'02"	13 02	07/04/1986	25	Enfield	Arsenal Rel c/s 06, Yeovil (SL) 3/06, Chesterfield 7/06 Rel 3/08, Lewes 3/08, Stevenage 8/08, Eastbourne B 1/09 Rel 2/10, Farnborough 2/10, Boreham Wood 6/11		
Daniel	Lewis				05/12/1989	21		Boreham Wood	0	0
Elvijs	Putnins				12/04/1991	20	Latvia	FK Auda (Lat) (Yth), QPR, Hemel Hempstead (L) 2/10, Boreham Wood (SL) 1/11, Boreham Wood (L) 8/11	15	0
DEFENDERS										
Daniel	Braithwaite				16/10/1981	29	London	Enfield, Chesham, Boreham Wood 8/03, Dover c/s 04, Ashford T 7/07, Harrow, Ashford T 8/08, Boreham Wood c/s 09	23	1
Lee	Close							Boreham Wood	0	0
Luke	Garrard		5'10"	10 09	22/09/1985	25	Barnet	Tottenham (Scholar), Swindon 7/02 Rel c/s 05, Bishops Stortford 7/05, Boreham Wood 10/05, Northwood 11/05, AFC Wimbledon 3/06, Boreham Wood (3ML) 10/09 Perm 1/10	35	1
Michael	Kamara				17/05/1989	22	Sierra Leone	C.Palace, Bromley (WE) 3/07, Brighton (Trial), Swindon (Trial), Chesterfield (Trial), Colchester (Trial), AFC Wimbledon, St Albans, Bishops Stortford Rel 10/07, Welling 3/08, Fisher 8/08, Woking 12/08 Rel 5/09, Staines 8/09, Boreham Wood 11/10	18	0
Charlie	O'Loughlin		6'01"	13 02	17/03/1989	22	Birmingham	Port Vale Rel 4/08, Nantwich (L) 11/07, Hinckley U (L) 1/08, Nantwich 6/08, Ilkeston 6/09, Solihull Moors 7/10, Boreham Wood 5/11		
Osei	Sankofa		6'00"	12 04	19/03/1985	26	London	Charlton Rel c/s 08, Bristol C (2ML) 9/05, Brentford (SL) 1/08, Southend 7/08 Rel c/s 10, Farnborough 9/10, Boreham Wood 7/11		
James	Smith		6'01"	13 12	30/08/1986	25	London	Cambridge U (Sch), Welling 10/04, Gravesend £3,000 + 6/05, Margate (L) 9/05, Farnborough 6/09 Rel 6/11, Boreham Wood 6/11		
Tony	Walker							Boreham Wood	0	0
Luke	Wilkinson		6'02"	11 08	02/12/1991	19	Wells	Bristol C (Scholar), Portsmouth 7/09, Northampton (L) 1/10, Eastleigh (2ML) 2/10, Dag & Red 7/10, Boreham Wood (SL) 11/10, Boreham Wood (6ML) 7/11	26	1
Ruddock	Yala				06/03/1992	19		Boreham Wood	0	0
MIDFIELDERS										
Darren	Currie		5'11"	12 07	29/11/1974	36	Hampstead	West Ham, Shrewsbury (2ML) 9/94, Shrewsbury (L) 2/95, L.Orient (2ML) 11/95, Shrewsbury £70,000 2/96, Plymouth 3/98, Barnet 7/98, Wycombe £200,000 6/01 Rel c/s 04, Colchester (Trial) 7/04, Brighton 8/04, Ipswich £250,000 12/04 Rel c/s 07, Coventry (6WL) 11/06, Los Angeles Galaxy (Trial) 3/07, Derby (SL) 3/07, Luton 7/07 Rel c/s 08, Chesterfield 7/08, Dag & Red (6WL) 11/09, Dag & Red 1/10, Boreham Wood (Pl/Coach) 8/11		
Charlie	Hunter				11/03/1993	18		Boreham Wood	7	0
Sam	Hurrell				13/07/1988	23	Hillingdon	North Greenford, Chelsea Rel c/s 07, L.Orient (Trial), Bradford C (Trial), Chelsea (Youngsters Coach) 2/08, St Albans 10/08, Welling 2/09, Woking 5/10, Boreham Wood (L) 10/10, Boreham Wood 2/11	15	3
Jordan	Lawal				01/01/1992	19		Boreham Wood	0	0
Darryl	McMahon		5'11"	12 02	10/10/1983	27	Dublin	West Ham Rel c/s 04, Torquay (L) 3/04, Port Vale 9/04, L.Orient 11/04, Notts County (2ML) 11/06, Stevenage 1/07, Cambridge U 1/09, Farnborough 7/09 Rel 6/11, Boreham Wood 6/11		
Mario	Noto				24/10/1984	26	Enfield	Tottenham (Scholar), Reading (Scholar), Wycombe (Trial) 2/04, Southend (Trial) 4/04, C.Palace (Trial) c/s 04, Darlington (Trial) 12/04, Canvey Island 1/05, Chelmsford 7/06 Rel 7/08, Boreham Wood c/s 08	41	11
Stephen	O'Leary		5'10"	11 08	02/02/1985	26	London	Luton Rel c/s 08, Tranmere (L) 11/05, Tranmere (SL) 1/06, Hereford 8/08 Rel c/s 09, Bradford C 8/09 Rel c/s 10, Kettering 8/10 Rel 8/10, Personal Trainer, Boreham Wood 8/11		
Pelly	Ruddock							Boreham Wood		
FORWARDS										
Simeon	Akinola							Boreham Wood	4	0
David	Bryant				09/06/1982	29		Dag & Red, Maldon, Aveley, Thurrock 3/07, Braintree 5/08 Rel 8/08, Thurrock 8/08, Braintree 8/10 Rel 2/11, Boreham Wood 2/11	14	4
Ali	Chaaban				16/03/1982	29	Lebanon	Dorking, Leatherhead 7/02, Farnborough 6/03 Rel 1/05, Lewes 3/04, Farnborough 8/04, Exeter 2/05 Rel 2/05, Sutton U 8/05 Rel 9/05, Break, Sutton U 12/05, Staines 1/06, Bromley 6/07 Rel, Break, Bromley 1/09 Rel c/s 09, Staines (Dual) 4/09, Gillingham (Trial) c/s 09, Bromley 8/09, Staines 9/09, Boreham Wood 11/10, Chelmsford 2/11, Boreham Wood 7/11	15	4
Inih	Effiong				02/03/1991	20		St Albans, Northwood (L) 10/08, Boreham Wood 8/09, St Albans c/s 10, Boreham Wood 7/11		
Oliver	Palmer				21/01/1992	19		Woking, St Albans (2ML) 11/10, Boreham Wood (6ML) 7/11		
Harvey	Scott-Morris							Boreham Wood	0	0

BROMLEY

Chairman: Ashley Reading
Secretary: Colin Russell **(T)** 07970 031 511 **(E)** colin@bromleyfc.co.uk
Additional Committee Members:
Paul Greenwood, Michael Coles, Jeremy Dolke, Jeff Hutton.

Manager: Mark Goldberg
Programme Editor: Jeff Hutton **(E)** info@bromleyfc.net

Club Factfile

Founded: 1892 **Nickname:** The Lillywhites
Previous Names: Not known
Previous Leagues: South London, Southern, London, West Kent, South Surburban, Kent, Spartan 1907-08, Isthmian 1908-11, 52-2007, Athenian 1919-1952

Club Colours (change): White/black/black (All red)

Ground: The Stadium, Hayes Lane, Bromley, Kent BR2 9EF **(T)** 020 8460 5291
Capacity: 5,000 **Seats:** 1,300 **Covered:** 2,500 **Clubhouse:** Yes **Shop:** Yes

Directions From M25 Motorway: Leaving the M25 at Junction 4, follow the A21 to Bromley and London, for approximately 4 miles and then fork left onto the A232 signposted Croydon/Sutton. At the 2nd set of traffic lights turn right into Baston Road (B265), following it for about 2 miles as it becomes Hayes Street and then Hayes Lane. Bromley FC is on right hand side of road just after a mini roundabout. From the Croydon/Surrey areas use the A232, turn left into Baston Road (B265), following it for about 2 miles as it becomes Hayes Street and then Hayes Lane. From West London use the South Circular Road as far as West Dulwich and then via Crystal Palace, Penge, Beckenham and Bromley South areas. From North and East London use the Blackwall Tunnel and then the A20 road as far as Sidcup. Then use the A232 to Keston Common, turn right into Baston Road (B265), following it for about 2 miles as it becomes Hayes Street and then Hayes Lane.

Previous Grounds: Not known

Record Attendance: 10,798 v Nigeria - 1950
Record Victory: 13-1 v Redhill - Athenian League 1945-46
Record Defeat: 1-11 v Barking - Athenian League 1933-34
Record Goalscorer: George Brown - 570 (1938-61)
Record Appearances: George Brown
Additional Records: Received £50,000 from Millwall for John Goodman

Senior Honours: Isthmian League 1908-10, 53-54, 60-61. Athenian League 1922-23, 48-49, 50-51.
Kent Senior Cup x5. Kent Amateur Cup x12. London Senior Cup x4

10 YEAR RECORD

01-02	02-03	03-04	04-05	05-06	06-07	07-08	08-09	09-10	10-11
Isth1 19	Isth1S 6	Isth1S 8	Isth1 4	Isth P 11	Isth P 2	Conf S 11	Conf S 13	Conf S 12	Conf S 11

BROMLEY

No.	Date	Comp	H/A	Opponents	Att:	Result	Goalscorers	Pos
1	Sat-14-Aug	BSS	H	Dorchester Town	412	W 2-1	Vines 34, McBean 72	5
2	Tue-17-Aug	BSS	A	Boreham Wood	198	W 4-2	Sobers 18, McDonnell 24, Finn 34, Dolby 40	3
3	Sat-21-Aug	BSS	A	Hampton & Richmond Borough	582	W 2-1	Vines 20, Sobers 70	2
4	Tue-24-Aug	BSS	H	Havant & Waterlooville	525	W 1-0	McBean 60	1
5	Sat-28-Aug	BSS	H	Welling United	940	W 2-1	McBean 2 (64, 72)	1
6	Mon-30-Aug	BSS	A	Bishops Stortford	464	W 1-0	Dunk pen 76	1
7	Sat-04-Sep	BSS	A	Maidenhead United	410	W 2-0	McBean 58, Scarborough 76	1
8	Sat-11-Sep	BSS	H	St Albans City	819	D 1-1	Finn 45	1
9	Sat-18-Sep	BSS	A	Dartford	1834	D 2-2	McDonnell 37, Dunk 88	1
10	Sat-02-Oct	BSS	H	Ebbsfleet United	1010	D 1-1	Vines 8	1
11	Sat-16-Oct	BSS	A	Basingstoke Town	502	L 1-4	Henriques 47	3
12	Tue-26-Oct	BSS	H	Lewes	432	D 1-1	Finn 29	3
13	Sat-30-Oct	BSS	A	Thurrock	353	W 2-1	Dolby 42, McBean 52	2
14	Sat-06-Nov	BSS	H	Farnborough	818	D 0-0		2
15	Tue-09-Nov	BSS	H	Woking	408	D 2-2	McBean 33, Scarborough 62	2
16	Sat-13-Nov	BSS	A	Braintree Town	772	W 2-0	Ibrahima 53, Finn 90	1
17	Sat-11-Dec	BSS	A	Weston-Super-Mare	173	L 0-7		2
18	Thu-30-Dec	BSS	H	Maidenhead United	535	L 0-2		2
19	Sat-01-Jan	BSS	A	Dover Athletic	1201	D 1-1	Henriques 60	2
20	Mon-03-Jan	BSS	H	Bishops Stortford	645	W 4-3	McKenzie 3 (4, 74, 82), Henriques 42	2
21	Sat-08-Jan	BSS	A	St Albans City	347	D 1-1	McKenzie 65	2
22	Tue-11-Jan	BSS	H	Chelmsford City	441	L 0-3		4
23	Sat-15-Jan	BSS	H	Basingstoke Town	427	L 0-1		5
24	Wed-19-Jan	BSS	A	Lewes	340	D 0-0		4
25	Sat-22-Jan	BSS	A	Ebbsfleet United	1095	W 2-1	Dunk 20, Harding 46	3
26	Sat-29-Jan	BSS	H	Weston-Super-Mare	424	W 3-2	McKenzie 20, Harding 32, Dunk 72	2
27	Tue-01-Feb	BSS	H	Dover Athletic	420	L 0-2		3
28	Sat-12-Feb	BSS	H	Staines Town	475	L 0-1		5
29	Sat-19-Feb	BSS	A	Dorchester Town	545	D 0-0		7
30	Wed-02-Mar	BSS	A	Welling United	525	L 1-3	Harding pen 75	9
31	Sat-05-Mar	BSS	A	Havant & Waterlooville	508	L 0-2		9
32	Tue-08-Mar	BSS	A	Eastleigh	403	L 0-1		9
33	Sat-12-Mar	BSS	H	Boreham Wood	399	D 1-1	Henriques 68	9
34	Sat-19-Mar	BSS	A	Woking	1381	L 0-1		9
35	Sat-26-Mar	BSS	H	Hampton & Richmond Borough	374	L 1-2	Nnamani 90	10
36	Tue-29-Mar	BSS	H	Thurrock	210	W 1-0	McKenzie 70	10
37	Sat-02-Apr	BSS	A	Farnborough	777	D 2-2	Harding pen 3, McKenzie 37	10
38	Sat-09-Apr	BSS	H	Braintree Town	507	L 0-3		11
39	Sat-16-Apr	BSS	A	Staines Town	263	W 2-0	Harding 1, Dunk 67	9
40	Fri-22-Apr	BSS	H	Dartford	922	W 4-1	Nnamani 19, Sobers 22, McKenzie 57, McBean 72	9
41	Mon-25-Apr	BSS	A	Chelmsford City	844	L 0-2		10
42	Sat-30-Apr	BSS	H	Eastleigh	388	L 0-2		11

CUPS

No.	Date	Comp	H/A	Opponents	Att:	Result	Goalscorers	Pos
1	Sat-25-Sep	FAC 2Q	A	Bishops Stortford	357	D 2-2	McBean 58, S Butler 75	
2	Tue-28-Sep	FAC 2QR	H	Bishops Stortford	347	W 2-1	Graves 42, Finn 90	
3	Sat-09-Oct	FAC 3Q	A	Chelmsford City	1011	D 2-2	Scarborough 23, McDonnell 56	
4	Tue-12-Oct	FAC 3QR	H	Chelmsford City	619	L 0-3		
5	Tue-23-Nov	FAT 3Q	A	Ebbsfleet United	611	L 0-4		

League
Starts
Substitute
Unused Sub

Cups
Starts
Substitute
Unused Sub

Goals (Lg)
Goals (Cup)

J BUTLER	GRAVES	DUNK	DALY	HENRIQUES	SCARBOROUGH	SOBERS	FINN	VINES	MCDONNELL	DOLBY	MCBEAN	BOYLE	JORDAN	JONES	FRAY	IBRAHIMA	FODERINGHAM	GREENE	S BUTLER	DAVISSON	AGU	PATTERSON	HOLLOWAY	HARDING	MCKENZIE	HARWOOD	AFUSI	HOCKTON	NEWTON	SHARP	LODGE	HARRIS	IDE	NNAMANI	ENGLAND	WEDGEWORTH	HALL	LOVELOCK	UDOJI	BRITNELL
X	X	X	X	X	X	X	X	X	X	X	S	S	U	U	U																										
X	X	X	X	X	X	X	X	X	X	X	S	U		U	U	S																									
	X	X	X	U	X	X	X	X	U	X	X			U	U	X	X	S																							
	X	X	X	S	X	X	X	X	U	X	X			U	U	X	X	S																							
	X	X	X	X	X		X	X	S	X	X		U	U	U	X	X	S																							
	X	X	X	X	X	X	X	X	S	X	X		U	U	U		X	S																							
	X	X	X	X	X	X	X	X	S	X	X	U			U		X	S	U																						
	X	X	X	X	X	X	X	X	S	X	X	U			U		X	S	S																						
	X	X	X	X	X	X	X	X	X	X	U				S	S	X	U		S																			
	X		X	X	X		X	X	S		X	X	U			X	X	S	S	U		X																	
		X	X	X	X	X	S	X		X	U			X	U	X	S	X	S		X																	
		X	X	X	X	X	X	X		S	X	U				U	X	X				X		S	S														
	X		X	X	X		X	X		X	X	U		U		U	X	U				X	U	X															
	X	S	X	X	X	U	X	X		X	X					U	X						X	U	X		U													
	X	S	X	X	X	U	X	X		X	X					S						X	X	X		S	U												
	X	X	S	X	X	X	X	X		X	X					X	X					U	U	S		S													
	X	X	X	X		X	X			X	X	U						U				S	X	X	X			S	S											
		X	X			X	X			U	X	S			X	X		U				X	X	S	X			S		X									
	X	X	U	X		X	X				X	U			S	U						X	X	X	X			U		X									
		X	X	X		X	S			X	S	U				X		S				U	X	X	X			X		X									
		S	X	X		X	S	S		X	X	U			X			U				X	X	X	X					X									
		X	S	X		X	X	X		X		S			X	S		U				U	X	X	X					X									
	X	X	X	X		X	X	S		X	X	U			U			U				U	X	X	X														
	X		X	X		X	X	X		X	S	U			U	U		S				X	X	X	X														
	X	X	X	X			X	S		X	X	S			X	S							U	X	X	X						U									
		X	X	X			X	S		X	X	X			X	S		U				U	X	X	X						S									
	X		X	X		X	X	S		X	X	U			U	U							X	X	X	X						S									
	X		X	X		X	X			U	S				X	S							X	X	U	X						X	X	S							
	X		S				X					U			U	X	X							X	X	X	X							X	X	X	S	S				
	X	X	X				X			X	X											U		X	X		X							S	X	X	S	U	S			
	X	X	X	X			X			X	X											U			S	X	X									X	S	U	U	X		
	X	X	S	X			X	X			S													X		X							X	X	X	U	U	X		
	X	X	S	X			X				X													X	U	X							X	X	X	U	U	X	U	
	X	X		X		S	X				X											U	X	X	X								X	X		U	X	U	
	X	X	X			U	X								U									X	X	X							X	X	X	S		X	U	S
	X	X	X	X		X	U														U		X	X	X							X	X	U	U		X	S	
	X	X	X	X		X	S				U			U									X	X	X	X							X	X	U				U	
	X	X	X	X		X	S				S			U	U								X	X	X	X							X	X					U	
	X	X	X	X			X				X			S	U							X	X		X							X	X	S				S	
	X	X	X	X		X	U				X				S									X	X	X							U	X	S			X	S	
	X	X	X	X		X	X				X			S							X			S		X							X	X				S	
	X	X	X	X			X				X			S	X						U		X	X			X							X	S	U				S	
	X		X	X	X	X	X	S	X	X	X	U	U			S	X	X	S		U																				
	X		X	X	X	X	S	X	S	X	X	U	U			X	X	X	S		U																				
	X	X	X	X	X		X	X	X	U	S	X	U			S	X	U	U			X	U																	
	X	X	X	X	X	S	X	X	X	U	S	X				U	X	U	S		U	X																		
		X		X	X	X	X	X			X	U	S			X		X			U	X	X			S	S													
2	35	32	35	36	16	26	36	18	4	24	29	2	0	0	9	8	13	1	1	0	1	12	19	25	20	14	0	1	0	5	1	2	10	13	5	0	0	7	0	0
0	0	3	5	1	0	1	4	6	5	1	7	4	0	3	3	7	0	10	2	2	0	1	0	5	1	2	0	2	1	0	2	1	1	1	5	2	1	0	5	1
0	0	0	1	1	0	3	2	0	2	2	3	13	4	10	14	7	0	8	1	1	4	6	4	1	1	1	1	1	0	0	1	0	1	0	3	5	4	0	5	0
0	4	3	4	5	5	3	4	4	3	2	3	2	0	0	0	2	4	3	0	0	0	3	1	0	0	0	0	0	0	0	0	0	0	0	0	0	0	0	0	0
0	0	0	0	0	0	1	1	1	1	0	2	0	1	0	0	2	0	0	3	0	0	0	0	0	0	1	1	0	0	0	0	0	0	0	0	0	0	0	0	0
0	0	0	0	0	0	0	0	0	0	2	0	3	3	0	0	1	0	2	1	0	4	0	1	0	0	0	0	0	0	0	0	0	0	0	0	0	0	0	0	0
0	0	5	0	4	2	3	4	3	2	2	8	0	0	0	0	1	0	0	0	0	0	0	0	5	8	0	0	0	0	0	0	0	0	2	0	0	0	0	0	0
0	1	0	0	0	1	0	1	0	1	0	1	0	0	0	0	0	0	0	1	0	0	0	0	0	0	0	0	0	0	0	0	0	0	0	0	0	0	0	0	0

PLAYING SQUAD 2011/12

Existing Players		SN	HT	WT	DOB	AGE	POB	Career	Apps	Goals
GOALKEEPERS										
Paul	Agu				31/10/1988	22		Bromley	1	0
Dean	Santaneglo				10/12/1993	17	Switzerland	Reading, Bromley (WE) 8/11		
DEFENDERS										
Ryan	Adams				28/08/1986	25		Walton Casuals, Croydon A 2/07, Westwood U, Fisher 12/08, Dulwich H, Walton & H, Worthing 3/10, Hampton & R 8/10, Walton & H 1/11, Billericay 6/11, Bromley 8/11		
Joe	Dolan		6'03"	13 05	27/05/1980	31	Harrow	Chelsea (Trainee), Millwall 4/98, Walton & H (L) 9/04, Crawley (3ML) 10/04, Stockport (2ML) 1/05, Brighton (L) 3/05, L.Orient 7/05, Stockport (L) 10/05, Fisher (2ML) 11/05, Canvey Island 1/06, Basingstoke 7/06 Rel 10/09, Carshalton, Croydon Ath 3/10, Cray W 11/10, Kingstonian 12/10, Basingstoke 2/11, Lewes 3/11, Bromley 8/11		
Rob	Gillman		6'02"	13 08	26/04/1984	27	London	Luton, Enfield (L) 3/03, Ashford T (Middx) 8/03, Bishops Stortford 7/04, Ashford T (Middx) 7/07, Bishops Stortford 12/07, Bromley 5/08, Dover 7/10 Rel c/s 11, Bromley 8/11		
Liam	Harwood				10/03/1988	23		Chipstead, Carshalton 7/06, Bristol R Undisc 9/08, Margate (2ML) 12/08, Carshalton 3/09, Margate 10/09, Tonbridge A 11/09, Bromley 11/10, Dulwich H 11/10, Thurrock 1/11, Bromley 2/11	16	0
Tutu	Henriques				06/06/1982	29	Zimbabwe	University of Luton, Carshalton c/s 02, Bromley 7/04	37	4
Marlon	Patterson		5'09"	11 10	24/06/1983	28	London	Millwall (Trainee), Chelsea (Trainee), Crawley 8/02, Fisher 1/03, Billericay, Fisher 12/03, Carshalton 3/04, Dulwich Hamlet 12/04, Carshalton 7/05, Hayes & Yeading 7/06, Dag & Red NC 8/07, Welling (3ML) 9/07, Grays (SL) 2/08, Bishops Stortford (L) 11/08, Histon 1/09, Bishops Stortford (SL) 2/09, Staines (Trial) 8/09, Bishops Stortford 8/09, Chelmsford 12/09, Bromley 9/10, Thurrock 2/11, Billericay 3/11, Bromley 8/11	13	0
Emmanuel (Udo)	Udoji		6'00"	13 05	09/01/1989	22		Rushden & D, Portsmouth, Glen Hoddle Soccer Academy, Stafford R 9/09, Bromley 3/10, Aveley 8/10, Ebbsfleet 8/10 Rel 10/10, Havant & W 11/10, Aveley, Bromley 3/11	5	0
Midfielders										
Ryan	Dolby				02/12/1989	21		Bromley, Welling 3/11, Bromley 8/11	25	2
Harry	Harding				06/12/1991	19		Bromley, Reading Rel c/s 11, Bromley (WE) 12/09, Oxford C (L) 3/10, Kettering (WE) 9/10, Croydon Ath (L) 10/10, Bromley (SL) 10/10, Bromley 7/11	30	5
Salifou	Ibrahima				14/10/1980	30	Cameroon	SG Dornheim (Ger), TG Darmstadt (Ger), FC Arheilgen (Ger), SV Erzhausen (Ger) FV Bad Vilbel (Ger), SV Buchonia Flieden (Ger) 7/05, SG Rot-Weiß Frankfurt (Ger) 7/06, TSG Worsdorf (Ger) 7/07, SV Viktoria Aschaffenburg (Ger) 8/08 Rel 1/09, Bromley 8/09	15	1
Orlando	Smith							Rel Mona (Jam), Beckenham, Chipstead, Barnet (Trial) c/s 07, Welling 8/07 Rel 5/09, Ashford T (2ML) 2/09, Farnborough, Carshalton (Dual), Bromley 3/10, Aveley, Bromley 8/11		
Danny	Waldren							Waltham Forest, Croydon A 12/06, Tooting & M 9/10, Croydon A 12/10, Bromley 8/11		
FORWARDS										
Hakeem	Araba				12/02/1990	21		Peterborough, Boston U (SL) 2/08, Dag & Red 8/08 Rel 6/10, Thurrock (3ML) 8/08, Redbridge (L) 11/08, Redbridge (L) 1/09, Bishops Stortford 8/10, Billericay 9/10, East Thurrock 10/10, Bromley 8/11		
Danny	Hockton		6'01"	12 08	07/02/1979	32	Barking	Millwall, L.Orient (L) 9/99, Stevenage 1/00, Barry T (L) 9/00, Dover £7,500 12/00, Chelmsford 8/01 Rel 5/02, Crawley 5/02, Billericay 7/03, Margate 1/06, Bromley 6/07, Braintree 4 Fig 9/08 Rel 5/09, Chelmsford 6/09 Rel 11/09, Maidstone U 11/09, Bromley (L) 12/10, Thurrock 3/11, Bromley 8/11	3	0
Mike	Jones							Bromley		
Leon	McKenzie				18/10/1984	26		L.Orient, Waltham Forest, Thurrock 6/06 Rel 12/08, Luton (Trial) 12/08, Grays 12/08 Rel 1/09, Bishops Stortford 6/09, Thurrock 9/09, Bromley 8/10, Billericay 8/10, Boreham Wood 9/10 Rel 10/10, Bromley 10/10	21	8
Gareth A	Williams		5'10"	11 13	10/09/1982	28	Germiston	C.Palace, Colchester (2ML) 1/03, Cambridge U (L) 10/03, Bournemouth (L) 2/04, Colchester (SL) 3/04, Colchester P/E 9/04 Rel 5/06, Blackpool (SL) 3/06, Yeovil (Trial) 8/06, Bromley 9/06, Weymouth 9/06, Basingstoke 10/06, Bromley 10/06, Braintree 5/08 Rel 5/09, Bromley 6/09, Croydon Ath 1/10, Ebbsfleet 9/10 Rel 6/11, Bromley 8/11		

CHELMSFORD CITY

Chairman: Mansell Wallace
Secretary: Alan Brown **(T)** 07963 626 381 **(E)** algbrown@blueyonder.co.uk
Additional Committee Members:
Trevor Smith, Trevor Wright, Martyn Gard, Martin Bissett, Mick Hooker, Chris Evans

Manager: Glenn Pennyfather
Programme Editor: Trevor Smith **(E)** trevor.2.smith@openreach.co.uk

Club Factfile

Founded: 1938 **Nickname:** City or Clarets
Previous Names: Not known
Previous Leagues: Southern League 1938-2004. Isthmian 2004-08

Club Colours (change): All claret (All white)

Ground: Melbourne Park Stadium, Salerno Way, Chelmsford CM1 2EH **(T)** 01245 290 959
Capacity: 3,000 **Seats:** 1,300 **Covered:** 1,300 **Clubhouse:** Yes **Shop:** Yes

Directions Leave A12 at J15 and head towards Chelmsford. At the roundabout turn left into Westway. Turn left onto the A1060 signposted Sawbridgeworth. At the second set of traffic lights turn right into Chignal Road. Turn right into Melbourne Avenue. Salerno Way is on your left. At the end of the football pitches and immediately before the block of flats, turn left at the mini roundabout in Salerno Way to enter the Stadium car park.

Previous Grounds: New Writtle Street 1938-97, Maldon Town 1997-98, Billericay Town 1998-2005

Record Attendance: 16,807 v Colchester United - Southern League 10/09/1949. Salerno Way: 2,998 v Billericay Town - Isthmian Jan. 2006
Record Victory: 10-1 v Bashley (H) - Southern League 26/04/2000
Record Defeat: 1-10 v Barking (A) - FA Trophy 11/11/1978
Record Goalscorer: Tony Butcher - 287 (1957-71)
Record Appearances: Derek Tiffin - 550 (1950-63)
Additional Records: Paid £10,000 to Dover Athletic for Tony Rogers 1992
Received £50,000 from Peterborough United for David Morrison

Senior Honours: Southern League 1945-46, 67-68, 71-72, Southern Division 1988-89, League Cup 1945-46, 59-60, 90-91.
Essex Professional Cup 1957-58, 69-70, 70-71, 73-74, 74-75. Non-League Champions Cup 1971-72.
Essex Senior Cup 1985-86, 88-89, 92-93, 2002-03. Isthmian League Premier Division 2007-08.

10 YEAR RECORD

01-02	02-03	03-04	04-05	05-06	06-07	07-08	08-09	09-10	10-11
SthP 18	SthP 9	SthP 18	Isth P 8	Isth P 10	Isth P 3	Isth P 1	Conf S 5	Conf S 3	Conf S 4

CHELMSFORD CITY

No.	Date	Comp	H/A	Opponents	Att:	Result	Goalscorers	Pos
1	Sat-14-Aug	BSS	A	Basingstoke Town	559	W 3-2	Lock 17, Martin 66, Bricknell 85	3
2	Mon-16-Aug	BSS	H	Woking	948	W 3-0	Nunn 9, Higgins 15, Rainford 22	1
3	Sat-21-Aug	BSS	H	Eastleigh	707	W 3-0	Rainford 2 (pen 7, pen 30), Ake 46	1
4	Tue-24-Aug	BSS	A	Welling United	652	L 2-3	Higgins 20, Rainford pen 62	3
5	Sat-28-Aug	BSS	A	Braintree Town	1265	L 0-3		4
6	Mon-30-Aug	BSS	H	Dartford	1111	W 2-0	Bricknell 28, Cook 85	4
7	Sat-04-Sep	BSS	H	Dorchester Town	821	W 2-0	Higgins 2 (81, 83)	3
8	Sat-11-Sep	BSS	A	Weston-Super-Mare	282	D 2-2	Edmans 25, Higgins 47	5
9	Sat-18-Sep	BSS	A	Lewes	1326	W 1-0	Higgins 50	5
10	Sat-02-Oct	BSS	H	Maidenhead United	827	W 2-0	Reed 39, Ake 90	3
11	Sat-16-Oct	BSS	A	Dover Athletic	1142	W 3-2	Rainford 2 (pen 45, 82), Edmans 63	2
12	Sat-30-Oct	BSS	A	Farnborough	651	L 1-3	Cook 22	3
13	Mon-01-Nov	BSS	H	St Albans City	738	D 1-1	Cook 77	3
14	Sat-13-Nov	BSS	A	Woking	1198	D 2-2	Lock 55, Modeste 71	4
15	Sat-01-Jan	BSS	H	Thurrock	876	W 6-1	Cook 2 (22, 29), Rainford 59, Reed 2 (84, 90), Edmans 89	7
16	Mon-03-Jan	BSS	A	Dartford	1321	W 2-1	Bricknell 58, Edmans 65	6
17	Sat-08-Jan	BSS	H	Weston-Super-Mare	711	W 1-0	Ake 90	4
18	Tue-11-Jan	BSS	A	Bromley	441	W 3-0	Higgins 2 (7, 37), Rainford 19	2
19	Sat-15-Jan	BSS	A	Boreham Wood	379	L 0-2		2
20	Sat-22-Jan	BSS	H	Bishops Stortford	883	W 4-1	Reed 2 (13, 37), Bricknell 43, Lock 75	2
21	Sat-29-Jan	BSS	A	Staines Town	459	L 1-2	Bricknell 52	4
22	Tue-01-Feb	BSS	A	Dorchester Town	361	D 1-1	Edmans 52	5
23	Sat-05-Feb	BSS	H	Havant & Waterlooville	770	L 1-2	Lock 76	5
24	Mon-07-Feb	BSS	H	Basingstoke Town	618	W 4-0	Edmans 10, Rainford 2 (20, pen 37), Gray 21	3
25	Sat-12-Feb	BSS	A	St Albans City	428	W 2-0	Edmans 55, Gray 79	3
26	Mon-14-Feb	BSS	H	Boreham Wood	697	W 3-1	Rainford pen 45, Lock 2 (64, 71)	2
27	Tue-22-Feb	BSS	A	Thurrock	479	D 1-1	Rainford pen 67	2
28	Sat-26-Feb	BSS	H	Ebbsfleet United	931	L 2-3	Gray 2 (5, 21)	4
29	Mon-28-Feb	BSS	H	Braintree Town	1710	D 0-0		4
30	Sat-05-Mar	BSS	A	Eastleigh	610	L 1-2	Rainford pen 58	5
31	Tue-08-Mar	BSS	A	Hampton & Richmond Borough	303	L 0-3		5
32	Sat-12-Mar	BSS	H	Lewes	782	W 4-0	Gray 2 (28, 82), Rainford 2 (32, pen 71)	4
33	Mon-14-Mar	BSS	H	Dover Athletic	751	D 2-2	Edmans 2 (42, 61)	4
34	Sat-19-Mar	BSS	A	Maidenhead United	509	W 2-1	Gray 28, Edmans 50	5
35	Tue-22-Mar	BSS	A	Bishops Stortford	648	D 2-2	Modeste 53, Chaaban 54	4
36	Sat-26-Mar	BSS	H	Welling United	784	L 0-2		5
37	Sat-02-Apr	BSS	A	Havant & Waterlooville	820	W 2-1	Gray 48, Rainford 51	5
38	Sat-09-Apr	BSS	H	Staines Town	590	W 3-1	Modeste 30, Chaaban 49, Rainford pen 70	5
39	Sat-16-Apr	BSS	H	Farnborough	941	L 0-1		7
40	Fri-22-Apr	BSS	A	Ebbsfleet United	1368	W 3-1	Edmans 28, Haines 52, Chaaban 88	6
41	Mon-25-Apr	BSS	H	Bromley	844	W 2-0	Gray pen 50, Tann 62	4
42	Sat-30-Apr	BSS	H	Hampton & Richmond Borough	1178	W 3-1	Gray 2 (29, pen 51), Martin 88	4

CUPS

No.	Date	Comp	H/A	Opponents	Att:	Result	Goalscorers
1	Sat-25-Sep	FAC 2Q	H	Chertsey Town	623	W 7-0	Higgins 4 (7, 48, 49, 63), Cook 24, Rainford 2 (pen 36, 64)
2	Sat-09-Oct	FAC 3Q	H	Bromley	1011	D 2-2	Og (Graves) 45, Rainford pen 90
3	Tue-12-Oct	FAC 3QR	A	Bromley	619	W 3-0	Bricknell 19, Higgins 50, Cook 85
4	Sat-23-Oct	FAC 4Q	A	Carshalton Athletic	1024	D 1-1	Edmans 90
5	Mon-25-Oct	FAC 4QR	H	Carshalton Athletic	1069	W 3-2	Cook 15, Higgins 2 (pen 26, 79)
6	Sat-06-Nov	FAC 1	H	Hendon	1685	W 3-2	Higgins 8, Bricknell 28, Cook 68
7	Sun-21-Nov	FAT 3Q	A	Gloucester City	318	L 0-1	
8	Sat-27-Nov	FAC 2	A	Wycombe Wanderers	3205	L 1-3	Higgins 59
9	Tue-03-May	PO SF 1	H	Ebbsfleet United	1701	L 1-4	Modeste 45
10	Sun-08-May	PO SF 2	A	Ebbsfleet United	1538	L 1-2	Gray 62

League
Starts
Substitute
Unused Sub

Cups
Starts
Substitute
Unused Sub

Goals (Lg)
Goals (Cup)

PULLEN	NUNN	PATTERSON	TANN	EL-ABD	RAINFORD	LOCK	REED	HIGGINS	COOK	AKE	BRICKNELL	MARTIN	EDMANS	HAINES	L BATCHFORD	MODESTE	BELLAMY	HARRISON	SCARLETT	LOPES	COKER	COOPER	MULLEY	EGBUNA	ROWE	CRICK	GREEN	ROBINSON	HENSHAW	GRAY	SANDERSON	CHAABAN	WILLIAMS	HUGHES-MASON	BOYLAN	PENTNEY	LADOPO	SWAINE
X	X	X	X	X	X	X	X	X	X	X	S	S	U	U	U																							
X	X	X	X	X	X	X	U	X	X	X	S	X	S	U	U																							
X	X	X	X	X	X	X	S	X	X	X	S	X	U	U		S																						
X		X	X	X	X	X	U	X	X	X	S	X	S	S		X	U																					
X		X	X	X	X	X	S	X	X	X	S	X	S	U		X	U																					
		X	X	X	X		X	U	X	X	X	X	S	X	U	S	U	X																				
		X	X	X	X		X	S	X	S	X	X	S	X		X	U	X																				
X		X	X	X	X	U	X	X	X	U		X	X	X	U	S	U																					
X		X	X	X	X	X	X	X	X		S	X	X	U	U	S			U																			
X			X	X	X	X	X	X	X	S	X	X		S	U	S			U		X																	
X	S		X		X	X	U	X		S	X	X	S	X		X					X	U	X															
X	X		X	X		X	U	X	X	S	X	X		S		X					X		U		S													
X	X		X	X		X	S	X	X	X	X	X		S		S						U	U		X													
X	X			X		X	X	X	X	S	S	X		X		X					X	U	S															
X	X		U	X	X	X	S		X	X		X	S	X	U	X										S		X										
X	X		U	X	X	X	S	U	X	X	S	X	S	X		X												X										
X	X		U	X	X	X	S	X	X	S	X	X	S	X											U			X										
X	X		U	X	X	U	X	X		X	X	X	S	X											U			X										
X	X		S	X	X	U	X	X		X	X	X	S	X											U			X										
X	X		X	X	X	X	X	X		X	X		S	S											S	U		X										
X	X		X	X	X	X	X	X		X	X		S	U		S												X	U									
X	X		X	U	X	X	U	U		S	X		X	X		X												X	S	X								
X	X		X	U	X	X	S	U		X			X	X		X												X	U	X								
X	X		X	X	X	X	U	U		X		X	X	U		S												X	U	X								
X	X		X	X	X	X				X		X	X	U		S			U							U		X		X								
X	X		X	X	X	X				X		X	X	U		S			U									X		X	S							
X	X		X	X	X	X				X		X	X	U		S												X		X	U	S	U					
X	X		X	X	X	X				U		X	S	S		X												U		X		X	X	S				
X	X		X	X	X					U	U	X	S			X												U		X	X	X	X	S				
X	X		X	X	X					X	U	X	S	U														X		X		X	X	S	S			
X	X		X	X	X	X					X	X	S	U		U												X		X			S	X	S			
	X		X		X	X				U		U	X	X		S												X		X	X	S		X	S	X		
	X		X		X	X				U		S	X	X		S												X		X	X	S		X	U	X		
	X		X	S	X	X				S			X	X		X												X		X	X	U		U	S	X		
	X		X	X	X	X				S		S	X	X		X														X	X	S	U		U	X		
	X		X	X	X					S		X		U		X			S									X		X	X	X	S			X		
	X		X	X	X					U		X		X		X			U									U		X	S	X	X			X	S	
			X	X	X					X		X	S	X		X			U									X		X	S	X	U			X	U	
	X		X	X						X		X	S	X	U	X			U											X	X	S	X			X	U	
	X		X	X						X		X	X	X	U	X												X		X	U	S				X	S	
	X		X	X						X		X	X	X	U	X												X		X	U	S	U			X	U	
	X		X	X	U					X		X	X	X		X			U									X		X		S				X	U	U
X			X	X	X	X	X	X	X	S	S	X	X	U	U	X			S	U																		
X	U		X	X	X	X	X	X	X	S	X	X		U		S		U	U	U		X																
X	U		X	X	X	X	U	X	X	S	X	X	U	X		X		U	U			U																
X	X		X	X	X			X	X	S	X	X	S	U		X		U				U	X	S	U													
X	X		X	X		X	U	X	X	S	S	X	X	U		X		U				U	U		X													
X	X			X		X	S	X	X	S	X	X		X		X		S			X	U	U		U	U												
	X			X	X	X	S	X	X		S	X		X		S		X			X		U		U		X											
X	X			X	X	X	U	X	X		S	X		X		X		U			X	U	S		U		S											
	X		X	X	S					X	S	X		X	U	X												X		X		X				X	U	S
	X		X	X						X	U	X		X		X			U						U			U		X		X				X	S	X
29	33	9	36	36	35	28	11	17	16	24	13	33	15	22	0	21	0	2	0	0	4	0	1	0	1	0	0	23	0	21	7	6	5	3	0	11	0	0
0	1	0	1	1	0	0	7	1	0	10	8	3	19	6	0	13	0	0	1	0	0	0	1	0	2	1	0	0	1	0	3	8	2	3	4	0	2	0
0	0	0	4	2	1	3	6	5	0	6	2	1	2	13	10	1	5	0	8	0	0	3	2	0	3	2	0	3	3	0	3	1	4	1	2	0	4	1
7	7	0	7	10	6	7	2	8	8	2	4	10	2	6	0	8	0	1	0	0	3	1	1	0	1	0	1	1	0	2	0	2	0	0	0	2	0	1
0	0	0	0	0	1	0	2	0	0	6	5	0	1	0	0	2	0	1	1	0	0	0	1	1	0	0	1	0	0	0	0	0	0	0	0	0	1	1
0	2	0	0	0	0	0	3	0	0	0	1	0	1	4	2	0	0	5	3	2	0	5	3	0	5	1	0	1	0	0	0	0	0	0	0	0	1	0
0	1	0	1	0	17	6	5	8	5	3	5	2	11	1	0	3	0	0	0	0	0	0	0	0	0	0	0	0	0	11	0	3	0	0	0	0	0	0
0	0	0	0	0	3	0	0	9	4	0	2	0	1	0	0	1	0	0	0	0	0	0	0	0	0	0	0	0	0	1	0	0	0	0	0	0	0	0

PLAYING SQUAD 2011/12

Existing Players		SN	HT	WT	DOB	AGE	POB	Career	Apps	Goals
GOALKEEPERS										
Lewis	Batchford				30/09/1991	19		Chelmsford	0	0
Stuart	Searle		6'03"	12 04	27/02/1979	32	Wimbleson	Tooting & Mitcham (Yth), Wimbledon Rel c/s 97, Woking c/s 97, Carshalton 8/98, Aldershot 12/99, Molesey (L) 3/00, Molesey (L) 9/00, Carshalton (L) 3/01, Carshalton £2,500 7/01, Basingstoke 11/05 (Also Chelsea Academy coach), Chelsea (Pl/Coach) 7/07, Walton & H (Dual) 7/07, Carshalton 7/08, Watford 1/09, MK Dons 7/09 Rel c/s 11, Chelmsford 8/11		
Joe	Woolley				20/09/1989	21		Charlton (Yth), Grays c/s 08 Rel 8/08, Thurrock 10/08, Harlow (Dual) 3/11, Chelmsford 8/11		
DEFENDERS										
Ryan	Batchford				05/11/1992	18		Chelmsford		
Kenny	Clark				12/08/1988	23		Dag & Red, Heybridge (L) 3/06, Thurrock 6/06, Chelmsford 6/11		
Anthony	Cook		5'07"	11 02	10/08/1989	22	London	Cardiff (Yth), Croydon Ath, Dag & Red 8/07, Carshalton (L) 10/08, Concord R (L) 12/08 Perm, Braintree (Dual) 3/09, Chelmsford 7/09	16	5
Mark	Haines		6'03"		28/09/1989	21		Northampton, Cheshunt (WE) 2/08, Grays (WE) 3/08, Grays 5/08, East Thurrock (L) 9/08, Chelmsford 7/09	28	1
Justin	Miller		6'00"	11 10	16/12/1980	30	Johannesburg, SA	Ipswich, L.Orient (3ML) 9/02, L.Orient 1/03 Rel c/s 07, Port Vale 7/07 Rel 4/08, Chelmsford 7/08 Rel 1/09, Bidvest Wits (SA) 1/09, Rushden & D 6/10, Chelmsford 5/11		
Ben	Nunn				25/10/1989	21		Boston U, Rushden & D Rel 7/08, Cambridge C 8/08 Rel 6/09, Bishops Stortford c/s 09, Chelmsford 3/10	34	1
Aiden	Palmer		5'08"	10 10	02/01/1987	24	Enfield	L.Orient Rel c/s 09, Dag & Red (L) 1/09, Prison, Bishops Stortford 12/09, Cambridge U 1/10 Rel 4/10, Bishops Stortford 7/10, Chelmsford 6/11		
Adam	Tann		6'00"	12 08	12/05/1982	29	Fakenham	Norwich (Yth), Cambridge U Rel c/s 05, Cambridge C (SL) 3/01, Reading (Trial) 7/05, Ipswich (Trial) 8/05, Rushden & D (Trial), Gravesend 10/05, Notts County 11/05, L.Orient 1/06 Rel c/s 07, Notts County 8/07 Rel c/s 09, Histon 7/09, Chelmsford 7/10	37	1
MIDFIELDERS										
Sam	Corcoran		5'11"	12 02	05/02/1991	20	Enfield	Colchester Rel c/s 11, Wealdstone (2ML) 12/09, Lowestoft (L) 3/11, Chelmsford 7/11		
Max	Cornhill							Local, Romford, East Thurrock 9/06, Chelmsford 5/11		
Mark	Crick				14/04/1989	22		Chelmsford	1	0
Daniel	Lopes				03/04/1991	20		Chelmsford	0	0
Ricky	Modeste				20/02/1988	23		Chelmsford	34	3
Greg	Morgan				30/09/1987	23		Boreham Wood Rel 5/11, Chelmsford 6/11		
Craig	Parker							Bury T, Needham Market, Chelmsford 5/11		
Dave	Rainford		6'00"	11 11	21/04/1979	32	Stepney	Colchester Rel c/s 99, Scarborough (L) 12/98, Slough 6/99, Grays c/s 01, Heybridge S 7/02, Slough 11/02, Ford U 1/03, Bishops Stortford 3/03, Dag & Red 5/06, Chelmsford 6/08	35	17
FORWARDS										
Cliff	Akurang		6'02"	12 03	27/02/1981	30	Ghana	Chelsea (Jun), Luton (Trainee), Chesham, Hitchin 8/00 Rel 12/01, Purfleet/ Thurrock 12/01, Heybridge Swifts 2/05, Dag & Red (L) 11/05, Dag & Red 1/06, Thurrock (SL) 1/07, Histon 5/07, Barnet Undisc 1/08 Rel c/s 10, Weymouth (SL) 3/09, Rushden & D (SL) 7/09, Thurrock 7/10, Maidenhead 11/10, Braintree 2/11, Chelmsford 6/11		
Joe	Benjamin		5'10"	11 04	08/10/1990	20	Woodford	West Ham (Yth), Northampton Rel c/s 10, Brackley T (WE) 1/08, Eastbourne B (L) 11/09, Eastbourne B (SL) 1/10, Ebbsfleet 8/10 Rel 9/10, Boreham Wood 9/10, AFC Hornchurch 11/10, Wealdstone 3/11, Chelmsford 7/11		
Jermaine	Brown		5'11"	11 04	12/01/1983	28	Lambeth	Arsenal Rel c/s 03, Bristol C (Trial) 8/03, Colchester 10/03, C.Palace (Trial) 1/04, Boston U 2/04 Rel c/s 04, Kings Lynn (L) 3/04, Lewes 7/05, Aldershot T 8/05, Margate 8/05 Rel 10/05, Out of Game, Chelmsford 7/11		
Kezie	Ibe		5'10"	12 00	06/12/1982	28	London	Arsenal (Jun), Bournemouth (Jun), Leatherhead 9/01, Hampton & R 12/01, Aylesbury c/s 02, Staines 6/03, Yeovil 8/04, Tiverton (L) 10/04, Exeter (L) 12/04, Weymouth (L) 2/05, St Albans (L) 3/05, Canvey Island 8/05, Chelmsford 8/06 Rel 7/08, Ebbsfleet 8/08, AFC Wimbledon (L) 3/09, Farnborough c/s 09, Chelmsford 6/11		
Tyrone	Scarlett				24/11/1991	19		Chelmsford	1	0
Warren	Whitely				11/09/1985	26		Croydon, Three Bridges, Harrow 9/08, Northwood (Dual) 11/10 Perm, Ashford T (Middx) 3/11, Chelmsford 8/11		

DARTFORD

Chairman: Bill Archer & David Skinner
Secretary: Peter Martin (T) 07976 054 202 (E) peter@martinpe.freeserve.co.uk
Additional Committee Members:
Steve Irving, David Boswell, Bob Blair,Mark Brenlund,Tony Burman, Harry Extance, Dave Francis, Norman Grimes, Jeremy Kite,Jason Outram, Nicola Collett.
Manager: Tony Burman
Programme Editor: Tony Jaglo (E) tonyjaglo@tiscali.co.uk

Top row (L-R): Adam Green, Matt Jones, Charlie Sheringham, Tom Bonner, Danny Harris, James Rogers.
Middle row: Dave Phillips (Physio), Ryan Cooper, Richard Graham, Paul Goodacre, Andrew Young, Deren Ibrahim, Elliot Bradbrook, Billy Eves, Lee Burns, John Macrae (Goalkeeping Coach)
Front row: Jack Pallen, Ryan Hayes, Steve Mosely (First Team Coach), Tony Burman (First Team Manager), Paul Sawyer (First Team Coach), Lee Noble and Jon Wallis.

Club Factfile

Founded: 1888 **Nickname:** The Darts
Previous Names: None
Previous Leagues: Kent League 1894-96, 97-98, 99-1902, 09-14, 21-26, 93-96, Southern 1996-2006

Club Colours (change): White/black/black (Royal blue & red/red/blue)

Ground: Princes Park Stadium, Grassbanks, Darenth Road, Dartford DA1 1RT (T) 01322 299 990
Capacity: 4,097 **Seats:** 640 **Covered:** Yes **Clubhouse:** Yes **Shop:** Yes

Directions From M25 clockwise leave at Junction 1 B to roundabout controlled by traffic lights. Take third exit onto Princes Road, (A225) then second exit at next roundabout. Continue down hill to traffic lights (ground on your left), turn left into Darenth Road then second turning on your left into Grassbanks leading to car park. From M25 anti-clockwise leave at Junction 2 onto slip road A225 to roundabout, then first exit, second exit at next roundabout then down hill to traffic lights turn left into Darenth Road, then second turning on your left into Grassbanks leading to car park.

Previous Grounds: The Brent/Westgate House, Potters Meadow, Engleys Meadow, Summers Meadow, Watling Street

Record Attendance: 4,097 v Horsham YMCA - Isthmian Division 1 South 11/11/2006 and v Crystal Palace - Friendly 20/07/2007
Record Victory: Not known
Record Defeat: Not known
Record Goalscorer: Not known
Record Appearances: Steve Robinson - 692
Additional Records: Paid £6,000 to Chelmsford City for John Bartley
Received £25,000 from Redbridge Forest for Andy Hessenthaler

Senior Honours: Southern League Division 2 1896-97, Eastern Section 1930-31, 31-32, Southern Championship 30-31, 31-32, 73-74, 83-84, Southern Division 1980-81, League Cup 1976-77, 87-88, 88-89, Championship Shield 1983-84, 87-88, 88-89.
Isthmian League Division 1 North 2007-08, Premier Division 2009-10. Kent Senior Cup 1929-30, 34-35, 38-39, 69-70.

10 YEAR RECORD

01-02	02-03	03-04	04-05	05-06	06-07	07-08	08-09	09-10	10-11
SthE 8	SthE 17	SthE 16	SthE 16	SthE 7	Isth1S 7	Isth1N 1	Isth P 8	Isth P 1	Conf S 10

DARTFORD

No.	Date	Comp	H/A	Opponents	Att:	Result	Goalscorers	Pos
1	Sat-14-Aug	BSS	H	Havant & Waterlooville	1302	D 2-2	Harris 26, Hayes pen 90	9
2	Tue-17-Aug	BSS	A	Hampton & Richmond Borough	680	L 0-1		16
3	Sat-21-Aug	BSS	A	Farnborough	1016	L 1-2	Noble 90	20
4	Tue-24-Aug	BSS	H	Bishops Stortford	882	W 3-0	Harris 19, Sheringham 42, Rook 80	15
5	Sat-28-Aug	BSS	H	Ebbsfleet United	2781	D 1-1	Sheringham 73	15
6	Mon-30-Aug	BSS	A	Chelmsford City	1111	L 0-2		16
7	Sat-04-Sep	BSS	H	Weston-Super-Mare	1173	W 4-1	Sheringham 2 (pen 44, 70), White 66, Og (Slocombe) 67	13
8	Sat-11-Sep	BSS	A	Thurrock	664	D 1-1	Bradbrook 78	14
9	Sat-18-Sep	BSS	H	Bromley	1834	D 2-2	Hayes pen 73, Bradbrook 89	14
10	Sat-02-Oct	BSS	A	Boreham Wood	351	L 1-3	Noble 90	17
11	Sat-16-Oct	BSS	A	Eastleigh	727	L 0-3		17
12	Sat-30-Oct	BSS	A	Lewes	953	D 1-1	Bonner 90	18
13	Tue-09-Nov	BSS	A	Dover Athletic	1199	W 2-0	Hayes 11, Berquez 82	17
14	Sat-13-Nov	BSS	H	Dorchester Town	1105	L 0-4		18
15	Sat-27-Nov	BSS	A	Woking	896	D 2-2	Hayes 7, Purcell 50	17
16	Tue-28-Dec	BSS	A	Ebbsfleet United	2435	L 1-2	Bradbrook 15	18
17	Sat-01-Jan	BSS	A	Welling United	1540	L 1-2	Rook pen 82	18
18	Mon-03-Jan	BSS	H	Chelmsford City	1321	L 1-2	Rook 52	19
19	Sat-08-Jan	BSS	H	Thurrock	1020	L 0-1		19
20	Tue-18-Jan	BSS	H	Staines Town	774	D 1-1	White 84	20
21	Sat-22-Jan	BSS	H	Farnborough	1010	W 4-1	Sheringham 2 (12, 48), Champion 63, Harris 73	20
22	Sat-29-Jan	BSS	A	Bishops Stortford	627	W 1-0	Sheringham 74	17
23	Tue-01-Feb	BSS	H	Braintree Town	841	W 1-0	Bradbrook 79	15
24	Tue-08-Feb	BSS	A	Weston-Super-Mare	234	W 1-0	Sheringham 73	15
25	Sat-12-Feb	BSS	A	Braintree Town	771	D 1-1	Main 38	15
26	Tue-15-Feb	BSS	H	Welling United	1384	D 1-1	Hayes 82	15
27	Sat-19-Feb	BSS	H	Hampton & Richmond Borough	1043	L 0-4		15
28	Tue-22-Feb	BSS	A	Dorchester Town	457	W 2-0	Harris 73, Noble 88	14
29	Tue-01-Mar	BSS	H	Basingstoke Town	631	W 1-0	Og (Reynolds) 65	13
30	Sat-05-Mar	BSS	H	Maidenhead United	976	W 3-0	Sheringham 68, Bradbrook 2 (88, 90)	12
31	Sat-12-Mar	BSS	A	Basingstoke Town	480	D 2-2	Hayes 4, Harris 24	12
32	Tue-15-Mar	BSS	H	Eastleigh	711	D 0-0		12
33	Sat-19-Mar	BSS	A	Staines Town	402	L 0-2		13
34	Tue-22-Mar	BSS	H	St Albans City	674	D 2-2	Sheringham 2 (35, 51)	13
35	Sat-26-Mar	BSS	H	Lewes	1036	W 3-0	Harris 4, Sheringham 2 (25, 90)	13
36	Sat-02-Apr	BSS	A	St Albans City	404	W 2-1	Burns 23, Pallen 85	11
37	Sat-09-Apr	BSS	H	Woking	1206	W 3-2	Bradbrook 38, Sheringham 40, Pallen 42	10
38	Sat-16-Apr	BSS	H	Boreham Wood	1118	L 1-4	Sheringham 39	11
39	Mon-18-Apr	BSS	A	Havant & Waterlooville	456	L 0-1		11
40	Fri-22-Apr	BSS	A	Bromley	922	L 1-4	Sheringham 32	11
41	Mon-25-Apr	BSS	H	Dover Athletic	1771	W 4-0	Sheringham 2 (24, 78), Champion 54, Harris 59	11
42	Sat-30-Apr	BSS	A	Maidenhead United	534	W 3-2	Sheringham 53, Pallen 68, Hayes 72	10

CUPS

No.	Date	Comp	H/A	Opponents	Att:	Result	Goalscorers
1	Sat-25-Sep	FAC 2Q	H	Lowestoft Town	1024	W 2-1	Rook 51, Harris 57
2	Sat-09-Oct	FAC 3Q	A	Canvey Island	715	D 2-2	Hayes 70, White 77
3	Tue-12-Oct	FAC 3QR	H	Canvey Island	665	D 3-3	(aet W 9-8 pens) Harris 20, Rook 40, Goodacre 65
4	Sat-23-Oct	FAC 4Q	A	Leiston	832	D 0-0	
5	Tue-26-Oct	FAC 4QR	H	Leiston	1074	W 3-2	Harris 3, Rook 25, Bonner 61
6	Sat-06-Nov	FAC 1	H	Port Vale	3679	D 1-1	Bradbrook 39
7	Tue-16-Nov	FAC 1R	A	Port Vale	3590	L 0-4	
8	Sat-20-Nov	FAT 3Q	A	Thurrock	405	W 2-0	Rook 2 (18, 82)
9	Sat-11-Dec	FAT 1	A	Crawley Town	1031	D 3-3	Sheringham 2 (3, 69), Hayes 10
10	Tue-14-Dec	FAT 1R	H	Crawley Town	605	W 1-0	Champion 90
11	Sat-15-Jan	FAT 2	A	Ashford Town (Middx)	474	W 1-0	Purcell 59
12	Sat-05-Feb	FAT 3	A	Gateshead	501	L 0-3	

League
Starts
Substitute
Unused Sub

Cups
Starts
Substitute
Unused Sub

Goals (Lg)
Goals (Cup)

YOUNG	BURGESS	BONNER	BRUCE	GOODACRE	SHINN	HAYES	WHITE	BERQUEZ	BURNS	HARRIS	NOBLE	ROOK	BURCHALL	GROSS	IBRAHIM	BRADBROOK	CHAMPION	SHERINGHAM	WHITEHOUSE	MEDLAN	BURMAN	PURCELL	EVES	BEALES	CLARK	MAIN	JONES	FOSTER	ROGERS	PALLEN	RANKIN
X	X	X	X	X	X	X	X	X	X	X	S	S	S	U	U																
X	X	X	X	X	X	X		X	X	X	S	S	S	U	U	X															
X	X	X	X	X	X	X		X	X	X	S	S	U	U	U	X															
X	X	X	X	X	X	X		U	X	X	S	S		S	U		X	X													
	X	X	X	X	X	X		U	X	X	S	S		U		S	X	X	X												
X	X	X	X	X	U	S		X	U	X	X	U		S		X	X	X													
X		X	X		X	X	X	S	S	X	S	U		X		X	X	X	U												
X		X	X	U	X	X	X	U	S	X	S	S		X		X	X	X													
X		X	X	X	X	X	U		X	S	U	S		X		X	X	X	U												
X		X	X	X	X	X	S			X	S	U	S	X		X	X	X	U												
X		X	X	X	X	S	X	U	X		X	X	S	X		X		U	U												
	X	X	U	X	X	X	S	U	X	X	X	X	S				X	S	X												
X	X	X	S	X	X	X	S	S	X	X	U					X	X	X	U												
X	X	X	U	X	X	X	S	U	X	X	S	S				X	X	X													
X	U	X	X	X	X	X	U		X	S		X	U			X	X	S				X									
X	X	X	X	X		X	S	S	X				S			X	X	X	U		U	X									
X	X	X	U	X	X	X	S		X			S	S			X	X	X	U			X									
X	U	X	X	X	S	X	X		X	S		X	S			X	X	U				X									
X	X	X	X	X		X	X				X	X	S			X		S	U		U	X		U							
X	X	X	X	X		S	S		X	U	X	S			U	X		X				X				X					
X	X	X	X	X		U	X			S	X	S			U	X	X	X								X	S				
X	X	X	X	X		U	U			X	X	S			U	X	X	X								X	S				
X		X	X	X		U	U			X	X	S			U	X	X	X			U					X	X				
X	X	X	X	X		S	X		U	X		X			U	X	X	X									U				
	X	X	X	X		S	X		S	X		S			X	X	X	X	U							X	U				
	X	X	X	X		S			S	X	X	X			X	X	X		U							X	S	U			
U	X	X	X	X		S			S	X	X	X			X	X	X				U					X	S				
X	X	X	X	X		U			X	X	X	U			U	X	X									X	U				
X	X	X	X	X		S			S	X	X	U			U	X	X	X								X	S				
X		X	X	X		S	S		X	S	X		U		U	X	X	X								X	X				
X	U	X	X	X		X	U		X	X	U		S			X	X	X									X				
X		X	X	X		X	X		X				U			X	X	X					U			S	X	U			
X	U	X	X	X		X	U		X	S	S		S			X	X	X								X	X				
X	U	X	X	X		S	X		X	X	X		U		U		X	X								S	X				
X	U	X	X	X		S			X	X	X						X	X								U	X	S	X		
X	X	X	X	X		S	X		X	X	X					S	X	X									U			S	
X	X	X		X		S			X		X					X	X	X			U		S				U		X	X	U
X	X	X	U	X		S	S		X		X					X	X	X					U				S		X	X	
X	U	X	X	X		X	S		X		S				U	X	X	X									X		X	S	
X		U	X	X		S	X		X	S	X				U	X	X	X									X		X	S	
X		U	X	X		S	S		X	X	X				U	X	X	X									X		X	S	
X		U	X	X		X	X			U					U	X	X	X			S		S				X		X	X	
X		X	X	X	X	X	S		X	S	S	X		X		X	X	U	U	U	U										
X		X	X	X	X	S	X	S	U	X	U	X	U	U		X	X	X	U												
X		X	X	X	X	X	X	U	U	X	U	X	S	S		X	X	S	U												
U	X	X	U	X	U	S	X	X	X	S	X	S	U			X	X	X	X												
U	X	X	U	X	X	X	U	U	X	X	U	X	U		X	X	X	S													
X	X	X	U	X	X	X	U	U	X	X	U	X	U			X	X	S	U												
X	U	X	X	X	X	X	S	U	X	X	S	X	U			X	X	S	U												
X	U	X	X	X	X	X	S		X	X		X	U			X	X	U	U												
X	X	X	X	X	X	X			X	X		X	S					X	U		U		U								
X	X	X	X	X	X	X			X			X	S			X	S	X	U		S		U								
X	X	X		X		S			X	U	X	X	X		U			X			U	X	U		X						
X	X	X	X	X		S	X		U	X		S			U	X	X	X								X		U			
37	24	39	36	40	15	22	14	4	28	25	20	8	0	5	3	35	36	31	2	0	0	6	0	0	0	11	11	0	7	3	0
0	0	0	1	0	1	16	11	3	6	7	11	14	11	2	0	2	0	3	0	0	1	0	2	0	0	2	6	1	0	4	0
1	7	3	4	1	1	4	6	6	2	2	3	5	5	4	17	0	0	2	10	0	5	0	2	1	0	1	5	2	0	0	1
10	7	12	8	12	9	8	4	1	9	8	2	10	1	1	1	10	9	6	1	0	0	1	0	0	1	1	0	0	0	0	0
0	0	0	0	0	0	4	3	1	0	2	2	2	3	1	0	0	1	4	0	0	1	0	0	0	0	0	0	0	0	0	0
2	2	0	3	0	1	0	2	4	3	1	4	0	6	1	2	0	0	2	8	1	3	0	3	0	0	0	0	1	0	0	0
0	0	1	0	0	0	7	2	1	1	7	3	3	0	0	0	7	2	19	0	0	0	1	0	0	0	1	0	0	0	3	0
0	0	1	0	1	0	2	1	0	0	3	0	6	0	0	0	1	1	2	0	0	0	1	0	0	0	0	0	0	0	0	0

PLAYING SQUAD 2011/12

Existing Players		SN	HT	WT	DOB	AGE	POB	Career	Apps	Goals
GOALKEEPERS										
Deren	Ibrahim				09/03/1991	20		Gillingham (Trainee), Welling Rel 5/06, Beckenham, Ashford T, Dartford, Sittingbourne (L) 2/10, St Andrews (Mal) 8/10, Dartford 11/10, Margate (Dual) 3/11	3	0
Andy	Young				28/02/1980	31		Hoddesdon, St Margaretsbury, Bishops Stortford 7/04 Rel 7/08, Thurrock 7/08, Dartford 9/08	37	0
DEFENDERS										
Tom	Bonner		6'00"	11 06	06/02/1988	23	Camden	Northampton Rel 1/07, Bedford (SL) 2/06, Nuneaton (L) 8/06, Rushden & D 1/07 Rel 8/07, Bedford (L) 2/07, Heybridge (L) 3/07, Corby T 8/07, Hinckley U 1/08, Solihull Moors 2/09, Corby T 6/09, Ilkeston 8/09, Dartford 8/10	39	1
Tom	Champion				15/05/1986	25	London	Watford (Yth), Barnet 8/04 Rel c/s 05, Wealdstone (L) 3/05, Bishops Stortford 7/05, Braintree 1/10, Dartford 5/10	36	2
Paul	Goodacre				15/07/1984	27		Burnham Ramblers, Maldon T 8/02, Bishops Stortford 6/06 Rel 10/09, Braintree 10/09, Dartford 5/10	40	0
Adam	Green		5'11"	10 11	12/01/1984	27	Hillingdon	Fulham Rel 5/06, Sheff Wed (L) 1/05, Bournemouth (L) 3/05, Bristol C (SL) 1/06, Grays 7/06 Rel 1/07, Woking 1/07 Rel c/s 08, Grimsby (Trial) 12/08, Hayes & Yeading 7/09, Dartford 6/11		
Matt	Jones				04/03/1985	26		St Albans Rel 9/04, Bishops Stortford, Dartford 1/11	17	0
MIDFIELDERS										
Elliott	Bradbrook				28/01/1985	26		Maidstone, University (USA), Maidstone c/s 08, Dartford 5/09	37	7
Jake	Burman				05/07/1992	19		Dartford	1	0
Richard	Graham		5'10"	11 10	05/08/1979	32	Newry	QPR Rel c/s 01, Barnet 7/01, Chesham 9/01, Billericay 7/02 Rel c/s 03, Kettering 8/03, Barnet 7/04 Rel c/s 07, Dag & Red 7/07 Rel c/s 09, Kettering (SL) 1/09, Grays 7/09 Rel 5/10, Eastleigh 7/10 Rel 5/11, Dartford 6/11		
Danny	Harris				07/07/1986	25	Newnham	Tilbury, East Thurrock 12/04, Bishops Stortford 12/07, Dartford (Dual) 10/09 Perm	32	7
Ryan	Hayes				15/07/1985	26		Slade Green, Dartford 3/05	38	7
Lee	Noble				01/01/1988	23		Brentwood, Dartford 6/08, Concord R (2ML) 11/10	31	3
Jack	Pallen				16/12/1991	19		Dartford, Chatham 2/10, Sittingbourne (Dual) 8/10, St Andrews FC (Mal) 8/10, Rye U, Maidstone 2/11, Dover 3/11, Dartford 3/11	7	3
James	Rogers				09/12/1984	26		Dover, Margate (L) 9/10 Perm, Dartford 3/11	7	0
Jon	Wallis		5'07"	10 08	04/04/1986	27	Gravesend	Chelsea (Jun), Gilingham Rel 5/06, Hastings U (3ML) 8/04, Hastings U (L) 9/05 Hereford 6/06 Rel 3/07, Dover (2ML) 11/06, Dag & Red (L) 2/07, Dover 3/07, Dartford 5/11		
FORWARDS										
Lee	Burns				17/07/1982	29		East Thurrock, Braintree 10/07, Dartford 6/09	34	1
Luke	Medlen							Dartford	0	0
Charlie	Sheringham		6'01"	11 06	17/04/1988	23	Chingford	Millwall (Yth), Tottenham (Yth), Bournemouth (Trial), Ipswich (Scholar) Rel c/s 05, Charlton, C.Palace Rel 1/08, Crystal Palace Blatimore (USA) (L) 4/07 Cambridge C 3/08, Welling 6/08, Bishops Stortford £6,500 5/09, Histon (SL) 2/10, Dartford 6/10	34	19
OTHERS										
Joe	Foster							Dartford	1	0
Billy	Eves							Dartford	2	0
Ryan	Cooper							Dartford		
Jack	Moore							Dartford		
Jai	Nuttall							Dartford		
Nad	Nwitua							Dartford		
Louis	Rankin							Dartford	0	0

DORCHESTER TOWN

Chairman: Shaun Hearn
Secretary: David Martin (T) 07971 172 795 (E) dorchdave@gmail.com
Additional Committee Members:
Adam Robertson, David Diaz, Paul Harris, Keith Kellaway.

Manager: Ashley Vickers
Programme Editor: TBC (E)

Club Factfile

Founded: 1880 **Nickname:** The Magpies
Previous Names: None
Previous Leagues: Dorset, Western 1947-72

Club Colours (change): Black & white/black/black & white (All yellow)

Ground: The Avenue Stadium, Weymouth Avenue, Dorchester DT1 2SP (T) 01305 262 451
Capacity: 5,009 **Seats:** 710 **Covered:** 2,846 **Clubhouse:** Yes **Shop:** Yes

Directions
The stadium is located at the junction of A35 Dorchester Bypass and the A354 to Weymouth, adjacent to Tesco. There is a coach bay for the team coach at the front of the stadium. Any supporters coach should park on the railway embankment side of the stadium.

Previous Grounds: Council Recreation Ground, Weymouth Avenue 1908-1929, 1929-90, The Avenue Ground 1929

Record Attendance: 4,159 v Weymouth - Southern Premier 1999
Record Victory: 7-0 v Canterbury (A) - Southern League Southern Division 1986-87
Record Defeat: 0-13 v Welton Rovers (A) - Western League 1966
Record Goalscorer: Not known
Record Appearances: Derek 'Dinkie' Curtis - 458 (1950-66)
Additional Records: Denis Cheney scored 61 goals in one season. Paid £12,000 to Gloucester City for Chris Townsend 1990. Received £35,000 from Portsmouth for Trevor Sinclair.

Senior Honours: Western League 19954-55. Southern League 1985-86, Division 1 East 2002-03. Dorset Senior Cup x7

10 YEAR RECORD

01-02	02-03	03-04	04-05	05-06	06-07	07-08	08-09	09-10	10-11
SthE 3	SthE 1	SthP 17	Conf S 8	Conf S 11	Conf S 17	Conf S 21	Conf S 19	Conf S 17	Conf S 17

DORCHESTER TOWN

No.	Date	Comp	H/A	Opponents	Att:	Result	Goalscorers	Pos
1	Sat-14-Aug	BSS	A	Bromley	412	L 1-2	R Hill 7	16
2	Tue-17-Aug	BSS	H	Eastleigh	502	L 0-4		22
3	Sat-21-Aug	BSS	H	Woking	547	L 1-2	R Hill 53	22
4	Mon-23-Aug	BSS	A	Basingstoke Town	336	L 0-1		22
5	Sat-28-Aug	BSS	H	Havant & Waterlooville	488	D 0-0		22
6	Mon-30-Aug	BSS	A	Hampton & Richmond Borough	485	D 2-2	Groves 73, Moss 76	22
7	Sat-04-Sep	BSS	A	Chelmsford City	821	L 0-2		22
8	Sat-11-Sep	BSS	H	Ebbsfleet United	473	L 1-2	Ings 25	22
9	Sat-18-Sep	BSS	H	Boreham Wood	420	W 3-1	Sole pen 15, R Hill 2 (25, 77)	20
10	Sat-02-Oct	BSS	A	Thurrock	208	D 1-1	Sole pen 13	21
11	Sat-16-Oct	BSS	A	Lewes	671	W 2-0	Sole pen 21, Ings 87	19
12	Sat-23-Oct	BSS	H	Braintree Town	584	W 1-0	Critchell 13	17
13	Sat-30-Oct	BSS	A	Staines Town	296	W 2-1	Ings 55, Moss 90	14
14	Sat-06-Nov	BSS	H	Bishops Stortford	563	D 0-0		11
15	Tue-09-Nov	BSS	H	Maidenhead United	376	L 1-2	Ings 53	13
16	Sat-13-Nov	BSS	A	Dartford	1105	W 4-0	Moss 2 (64, 90), Jermyn 66, Crittenden 87	11
17	Sat-01-Jan	BSS	A	Weston-Super-Mare	320	L 0-1		16
18	Mon-03-Jan	BSS	H	Hampton & Richmond Borough	451	D 2-2	Crittenden pen 60, Devlin 71	16
19	Sat-08-Jan	BSS	A	Ebbsfleet United	786	L 2-3	Stockley 2 (10, 90)	17
20	Sat-22-Jan	BSS	A	Eastleigh	558	L 0-3		18
21	Tue-25-Jan	BSS	H	Basingstoke Town	304	L 0-1		18
22	Sat-29-Jan	BSS	H	Welling United	443	D 3-3	Bowles 20, Crittenden 23, Chris Flood 37	19
23	Tue-01-Feb	BSS	H	Chelmsford City	361	D 1-1	Moss 18	18
24	Sat-05-Feb	BSS	H	Weston-Super-Mare	363	W 1-0	Chris Flood 73	17
25	Sat-12-Feb	BSS	A	Boreham Wood	180	D 0-0		16
26	Sat-19-Feb	BSS	H	Bromley	545	D 0-0		16
27	Tue-22-Feb	BSS	H	Dartford	457	L 0-2		16
28	Sat-26-Feb	BSS	A	Farnborough	809	L 0-2		16
29	Sat-05-Mar	BSS	H	Thurrock	402	W 3-1	Connolly 13, Chris Flood 2 (59, 86)	16
30	Mon-07-Mar	BSS	A	Havant & Waterlooville	458	L 1-3	Devlin 9	16
31	Sat-12-Mar	BSS	A	Welling United	549	W 2-1	Walker 2 (35, 49)	15
32	Tue-15-Mar	BSS	H	St Albans City	372	L 1-3	Martin 33	15
33	Sat-19-Mar	BSS	A	Dover Athletic	836	L 1-2	Crittenden 32	17
34	Sat-26-Mar	BSS	H	Staines Town	482	D 3-3	Connolly 2 (3, 90), Vickers 45	16
35	Tue-29-Mar	BSS	A	St Albans City	142	W 4-1	Moss 45, Jermyn 55, Connolly 90, Devlin 90	16
36	Sat-02-Apr	BSS	A	Braintree Town	561	D 1-1	Moss 88	16
37	Tue-05-Apr	BSS	A	Woking	1028	L 1-2	Coutts pen 49	16
38	Sat-09-Apr	BSS	H	Lewes	438	D 0-0		16
39	Sat-16-Apr	BSS	H	Dover Athletic	475	D 0-0		17
40	Sat-23-Apr	BSS	A	Maidenhead United	468	D 1-1	Critchell 66	17
41	Mon-25-Apr	BSS	H	Farnborough	642	W 2-1	Critchell 5, Walker 28	15
42	Sat-30-Apr	BSS	A	Bishops Stortford	372	L 1-2	Chris Flood 81	17

CUPS

No.	Date	Comp	H/A	Opponents	Att:	Result	Goalscorers
1	Sat-25-Sep	FAC 2Q	A	Mangotsfield United	265	W 4-1	Moss 50, Crittenden 63, Ings pen 64, Martin 90
2	Sat-09-Oct	FAC 3Q	A	Havant & Waterlooville	708	L 1-4	Ings 68
3	Sat-20-Nov	FAT 3Q	A	Weston-Super-Mare	184	W 3-1	Devlin 13, Ings 71, Moss 85
4	Sat-11-Dec	FAT 1	H	St Albans City	302	W 3-0	Moss 46, Wilson 2 (49, 68)
5	Sat-15-Jan	FAT 2	H	Eastbourne Borough	402	D 3-3	Crittenden 2 (45, 70), Jermyn 77
6	Tue-18-Jan	FAT 2R	A	Eastbourne Borough	487	L 0-1	

League
Starts
Substitute
Unused Sub

Cups
Starts
Substitute
Unused Sub

Goals (Lg)
Goals (Cup)

COWARD	R HILL	JERMYN	CRITCHELL	WALKER	CRITTENDEN	K HILL	GLEESON	DEVLIN	MOSS	GROVES	COUTTS	DOUGLAS	MARTIN	FRAMPTON	EVANS	ALLEN	OTOBO	GUYETT	SOLE	INGS	BOWLES	NODWELL	VICKERS	WILSON	CONNOR FLOOD	FORD	SMEETON	GILBERT	MUDGE	WHITE	FILKINS	STOCKLEY	CHRIS FLOOD	WADE	SUTTLE	THOMAS	BERGQVIST	CONNOLLY	TAYLOR	RICHARDSON	FELLOWS	SYMES
X	X	X	X	X	X	X	X	X	X	X	S	S	U	U	U																												
X	X	X	X	X	X	X	X	X	X	X	S	S	U	U		S																										
	X	X	X	X	S	U	U	X	X	S	X	X	X	U	X	X																										
	X	X	X	X	X	U	U	X	X	S	X	U	X	U	X	X																										
	X	X	X	X	X	S	U	X	X	S	X	S	X		X	X	U																									
	X	X		X	X	X		X	S	S	X	X	X	U	X	X	U																									
	X	X	S	X	X			X	X	S	X	S	X	U	X	X	U	X																								
	X	X	X	X	X			S	X			U		U	X	X	S	X	X	X																						
	X	X	X	X	X			X	X			S		U	X	U	U	X	X	X	U																					
	X	X	X	X	X		S	X	X			S	U		X	U		X	X	X	U																					
U		X	X	X	X		X	X	X		U		X		X			X	X	S	U	U																				
U		X	X	X	X		X	X	X				X		X			X		X		U	U	U	U																		
U		X	X	X	X		X	X	X		U		X		X					X	X	U		U		U																	
U		X	X	X	X		X				S		X	U	X					X	X			X		S	X	U														
U		X	X	X	X		X	X	X		U				X					X	X			U		U	X		S													
U		X	X	X	X		X	X	X		S		X		X					X	X			S			U															
X		X	X	X	X		X	X	X	S	X		X	S						X			U			U				U											
X		X		X	X		X	X	X	S	S		X	X	U						X	U					S		X													
X				X	X		X	X	X		X		X							X	U		S			X		U			X	S										
X		X	X	X	X				X		X		X	U						X			X			U					S	X		U							
X		X	X	X	X		U	X	X		X		X	U						X			S			U					X	U									
X		X	X	X	X		U	X	X		X		X	U						X			U			U					S	X									
X		X	X	X			X	X	X		X			U						X			U			X				U	U	X									
U		X	X	X			X	X	X		X		S							X			U			X				U	X			X	U					
U		X	X	X				X	X		X		X										U				X		U		S	X			X	X					
U		X	X	X	S			X	X		X		X										U				X		U			X			X	X					
U		X	X	X				X	X				X										U				X	U		U			X			X	X	X	S			
U		X	X	X				X	X				X										X				X			U			X			X		X	S	U	U	
U		X	X	X	U			X	X				U							X		X				X			U			X			X		X	U			
U		X	X	X	S			X	X				U							X		X				X			U			X			X		X	U			
X		X		X	U		U	X	X				X							X		X				X						X					X	U			U
X		X		X	S		U	X	X				X							X		X				X						X					X	U			S
X		X	X	X	X			X	X		U		U							X		X				X						X					S	U			U
X		X		X	X		U	X	X		U		X							X		X									X					X	U			S
X		X		X	X		U	X	X		X		X							X		U									S					X	S			X
U		X		X	S		U	X	X		X		X							X										X			X	S	X	U			X
U		X	X	X	S			X	X		X		X							X						U						S			X	X	X				S
U		X	X	X				X	X		X		X	U						X						S						S			X	X	X				S
X		X	X	X	X			X	S				X	U						X						S						X				X	X	U			S
X		X	S	X	X		S	X	X		S		X	U						X						X						X						U			X
X		X	X	X	X		S	X	X		S		X	U						X						X						X						U			S
X		X	X	X	U		S	S	X		X			X						S						X						X						X			X
U	X	X	X	X	X			X	X			S	U	U	X	X		X		X	U																					
U	X	X	X	X			X	X	X			S	X		X	S		X		X	S																					
U		X	X	X	X		X	X	X		S		X		X					X	X			S		U	U															
U		X	X	X	X		X	X	X		S		X		X						X	U		X		S				U											
X		X	X	X	X		X	X	X		S		X							X			S			U					X		U	U						
X		X	X	X	X		X		X		X		X							X		U	S			S					X			U						
18	10	41	32	42	27	3	13	38	39	2	19	2	30	2	14	6	0	6	4	8	25	0	7	2	0	0	17	0	1	0	0	2	19	0	0	10	6	12	1	0	0	4
0	0	0	2	0	6	1	4	2	2	7	7	6	1	1	0	1	1	0	0	1	1	0	0	3	0	1	3	0	1	0	0	3	4	0	0	0	1	1	3	0	0	6
16	0	0	0	0	3	2	10	0	0	0	5	2	6	17	2	2	4	0	0	0	3	5	5	7	1	2	6	2	1	6	2	2	1	0	1	0	1	0	10	1	1	2
2	2	6	6	6	5	0	5	5	6	0	1	0	5	0	4	1	0	2	0	3	4	0	0	1	0	0	0	0	0	0	0	2	0	0	0	0	0	0	0	0	0	0
0	0	0	0	0	0	0	0	0	0	0	3	2	0	0	0	1	0	0	0	0	1	0	0	3	0	1	1	0	0	0	0	0	0	0	0	0	0	0	0	0	0	0
4	0	0	0	0	0	0	0	0	0	0	0	0	1	1	0	0	0	0	0	0	1	1	1	0	0	1	2	0	0	1	0	0	0	1	2	0	0	0	0	0	0	0
0	4	2	3	3	4	0	0	3	7	1	1	0	1	0	0	0	0	0	3	4	1	0	1	0	0	0	0	0	0	0	0	2	5	0	0	0	0	4	0	0	0	0
0	0	1	0	0	3	0	0	1	3	0	0	0	1	0	0	0	0	0	0	3	0	0	0	2	0	0	0	0	0	0	0	0	0	0	0	0	0	0	0	0	0	0

PLAYING SQUAD 2011/12

Existing Players		SN	HT	WT	DOB	AGE	POB	Career	Apps	Goals
GOALKEEPERS										
Simon	Evans				28/01/1988	23	Reading	Andover, Dorchester 8/06 Rel 4/08, Weymouth 2/09, Bridport (L) 10/09, Dorchester 1/10 Rel 1/11, Rushden & D 1/11, Dorchester NC 8/11	14	0
Alan	Walker-Harris				06/10/1981	29	London	Southampton (Jun), Bashley, Brockenhurst, Lymington & New Milton 7/02, Bashley, Salisbury, Winchester 2/05, Eastleigh, Brockenhurst 5/06, Wimborne, Dorchester 8/11		
DEFENDERS										
Harrison	Bell						Poole	Bournemouth (Scholar) Rel c/s 11, Dorchester 8/11		
Gary	Bowles				30/12/1988	22		Cardiff (Yth), Yeovil, Dorchester 8/07, Bournemouth (Trial) 7/11	26	1
Kyle	Critchell		6'00"	12 02	18/01/1987	24	Dorchester	Southampton, Torquay (3ML) 10/06, Chesterfield 1/07, Weymouth 6/07, Wrexham 6/08 Rel 6/09, York C (2ML) 1/09, Weymouth (L) 3/09, Weymouth 6/09, Dorchester 11/09	34	3
Neil	Martin				05/04/1989	22		Exeter, Hayes & Yeading (L) 8/08 Perm 9/08 Rel 10/08, Salisbury 1/09 Rel c/s 09, Dorchester 8/09	31	1
Nathan	Peprah-Annan				12/01/1988	23	Accra, Gha	Tottenham Rel c/s 06, Sheff Wed (Trial), Portsmouth (Trial), Kettering 11/06, Dorchester 6/07 Rel 11/07, Havant & W 12/07, Dorchester 3/08 Rel 2/09, Halesowen T 2/09, Winchester 3/09, Bournemouth FC 9/09, VT FC/Sholing 2/10, Dorchester 8/11		
Jake	Smeeton		5'08"	11	09/08/1988	23	Yeovil	Yeovil Rel c/s 07, Dorchester 8/07, Gillingham T (L) 11/09, Poole T (2ML) 8/10	20	0
Ashley	Vickers		6'03"	13 10	14/06/1972	39	Sheffield	Sheff Utd, Worcester, Malvern T, 61 Club, Heybridge Swifts, Peterborough £5,000 12/97, St Albans 8/98, Dag & Red 3/00, Weymouth 5/06, Eastleigh 3/08, Newport C (L) 8/08 Perm 9/08, Dorchester (Pl/Coach) 3/09 (Pl/Man) 3/10	7	1
Nathan	Walker				03/10/1986	24		Weymouth, Portland U (L), Dorchester, Hamworthy U, Wimborne T 1/09, Dorchester 12/09	42	3
MIDFIELDERS										
Nick	Crittenden		5'08"	10 11	11/11/1978	32	Ascot	Chelsea Rel 6/00, Plymouth (L) 11/98, Yeovil 8/00 Rel c/s 03 Re-signed, Rel c/s 04, Aldershot 6/04, Weymouth 5/06 Rel 5/08, Dorchester 6/08	33	4
Steve	Devlin				03/10/1985	25		Liverpool (Yth), Chard T, Southampton (Trial) c/s 03, Frome 1/04, Chard T 7/04, Holt U, Wincanton, Dorchester (Trial) c/s 09, Holt U, Dorchester 10/09, Dag & Red (Trial) 8/10	40	3
Chris	Flood				28/11/1989	21		Andover (Yth), Winchester (Yth), Farnborough 6/07, Brentford, Thatcham (WE) 12/07, QPR 8/08 Rel 1/09, Eastleigh 3/09, Salisbury 8/09, Crawley £10,000 7/10, Forest Green (L) 9/10, Dorchester (L) 1/11 Perm 2/11	23	5
Jamie	Gleeson		6'00"	12 03	15/01/1985	26	Poole	Southampton Rel c/s 04, Kidderminster 7/04 Rel c/s 05, Eastleigh (L) 10/04, Dorchester 8/05	17	0
Mark	Jermyn		6'00"	11 05	16/04/1981	30	Germany	Torquay Rel 2/00, Dorchester 8/00	41	2
Ashley	Nicholls		5'11"	11 11	30/10/1981	29	Ipswich	Ipswich Wan, Ipswich 7/00 Rel c/s 02, Canvey Island (L) 2/02, Hereford (Trial) 7/02, Darlington 8/02, Cambridge U (SL) 2/04, Cambridge U 7/04, Rushden & D (3ML) 8/05, Rushden & D 1/06, Grays 8/06, Boston U 7/07, Maidenhead 4/08 Rel 5/09, Bishops Stortford 5/09, Newport C (2ML) 12/09, Eastleigh 3/10, Maidenhead 6/10, Dorchester 5/11		
Jamie	Symes				17/06/1993	18		Yeovil (Scholar), Bridport c/s 09, Dorchester 10/09, Bridport (Dual) 10/09, Blackpool (Trial) 2/10, Bridport c/s 10, Dorchester 3/11	10	0
Adam	Taylor				21/05/1992	19	Dorchester	Dorchester (Yth), Weymouth, Dorchester 2/11	4	0
FORWARDS										
Ben	Dickenson							Christchurch, Dorchester 5/11		
Ryan	Dovell							Dorchester Rel 5/05, Hamworthy, Poole T, Bridport 7/10, Dorchester 6/11		
Ryan	Moss		5'11"	12 04	14/11/1986	24	Dorchester	Bournemouth Rel c/s 05, Dorchester 8/05, Bashley 7/06, Dorchester Undisc 6/08 Rel 2/09, Bashley 2/09, Dorchester c/s 09	41	7
Rico	Wilson				11/02/1991	20		Bournemouth Poppies, Poole T (L) 12/07, Bournemouth (Trial) 12/08, Yeovil (Scholar) 12/08, Bournemouth Poppies, Dorchester 8/10 Rel 2/11, Sherborne (Dual) 8/10, Jail, Dorchester 6/11	5	0

DOVER ATHLETIC

Chairman: Jim Parmenter
Secretary: Franke Clarke **(T)** 07794 102 664 **(E)** frank.clarke@doverathletic.com
Additional Committee Members:
Roger Knight, Chris Oakley, Scott Rutherford, Steve Parmenter

Manager: Martin Hayes
Programme Editor: Chris Collings **(E)** chris.collings@doverathletic.com

Club Factfile

Founded: 1983 **Nickname:** The Whites
Previous Names: Dover F.C. until club folded in 1983
Previous Leagues: Southern 1983-93, 2002-04, Conference 1993-2002, Isthmian 2004-2009

Club Colours (change): White/black/black (All light blue)

Ground: Crabble Athletic Ground, Lewisham, Dover, Kent CT17 0JB **(T)** 01304 822 373
Capacity: 6,500 **Seats:** 1,000 **Covered:** 4,900 **Clubhouse:** Yes **Shop:** Yes

Directions From outside of Kent, find your way to the M25, then take the M2/A2 (following the signs to Canterbury, then from Canterbury follow signs to Dover) as far as the Whitfield roundabout (there is a McDonald's Drive-Thru on the left). Take the fourth exit at this roundabout, down Whitfield Hill. At the bottom of the hill turn left at the roundabout and follow this road until the first set of traffic lights. At the lights turn right (180 degrees down the hill) and follow the road under the railway bridge, the ground is a little further up the road on the left. There is no parking for supporters within the ground, although parking is available in the rugby ground, which is just inside the main entrance - stewards will direct you. If you have to take the M20/A20 leave the A20 in Folkestone (the exit immediately after the tunnel through the hill) and travel through the Alkham Valley (turn left at the roundabout at the end of the slip-road and then left again, following the signs for Alkham) which will eventually take you near Kearsney train station (turn right into Lower Road just before the railway bridge, before you get to the station).

Previous Grounds: None.

Record Attendance: 4,186 v Oxford United - FA Cup 1st Round November 2002
Record Victory: 7-0 v Weymouth - 03/04/1990
Record Defeat: 1-7 v Poole Town
Record Goalscorer: Lennie Lee - 160
Record Appearances: Jason Bartlett - 359
Additional Records: Paid £50,000 to Farnborough Town for David Lewworthy August 1993
Received £50,000 from Brentford for Ricky Reina 1997

Senior Honours: Southern League Southern Division 1987-88, Premier Division 1989-90, 92-93, Premier Inter League Cup 1990-91.
Kent Senior Cup 1990-91. Isthmian League Division 1 South 2007-08, Premier Division 2008-09.

10 YEAR RECORD

01-02	02-03	03-04	04-05	05-06	06-07	07-08	08-09	09-10	10-11
Conf 22	SthP 3	SthP 19	Isth P 21	Isth1 5	Isth1S 3	Isth1S 1	Isth P 1	Conf S 2	Conf S 7

DOVER ATHLETIC

No.	Date	Comp	H/A	Opponents	Att:	Result	Goalscorers	Pos
1	Sat-14-Aug	BSS	A	Woking	1458	W 1-0	Charles 55	7
2	Tue-17-Aug	BSS	H	Welling United	1097	D 2-2	I'Anson 18, Birchall 78	6
3	Sat-21-Aug	BSS	H	Staines Town	812	D 1-1	Hunt 90	8
4	Tue-24-Aug	BSS	A	Ebbsfleet United	1139	W 2-0	Birchall 43, Nicolau 81	5
5	Sat-28-Aug	BSS	A	Lewes	721	W 3-0	Og (Barness) 19, Charles 61, Crawford 69	3
6	Mon-30-Aug	BSS	H	Thurrock	923	W 1-0	Birchall pen 18	3
7	Sat-04-Sep	BSS	H	Eastleigh	1010	L 0-1		4
8	Sat-11-Sep	BSS	A	Braintree Town	561	W 2-1	Hunt 44, Birchall 82	3
9	Sat-18-Sep	BSS	H	Farnborough	973	W 6-3	Birchall 3 (pen 12, 57, pen 79), Charles 52, Wallis 72, Baker 84	3
10	Sat-02-Oct	BSS	A	Hampton & Richmond Borough	629	L 2-3	Schulz 42, Birchall 90	4
11	Sat-16-Oct	BSS	H	Chelmsford City	1142	L 2-3	Birchall 25, Baker 40	4
12	Sat-30-Oct	BSS	A	Bishops Stortford	490	W 4-1	Birchall 2 (60, 64), Tabiri 84, Baker 85	5
13	Tue-09-Nov	BSS	H	Dartford	1199	L 0-2		7
14	Sat-13-Nov	BSS	A	Boreham Wood	273	W 3-2	Baker 2 (38, 62), Norville 65	6
15	Sat-11-Dec	BSS	H	Maidenhead United	754	D 2-2	Hunt 76, Simmonds 78	5
16	Tue-28-Dec	BSS	H	Lewes	1018	W 4-0	Baker 2 (1, 40), Birchall 2 (61, 87)	4
17	Sat-01-Jan	BSS	H	Bromley	1201	D 1-1	Cutler 89	6
18	Mon-03-Jan	BSS	A	Thurrock	495	W 7-2	Birchall 5 (20, 22, 42, 49, 78), Hunt 35, Cogan 56	4
19	Tue-11-Jan	BSS	H	Woking	765	D 2-2	Simmonds 37, Long 83	6
20	Sat-15-Jan	BSS	A	Farnborough	748	L 1-4	Birchall 58	7
21	Sat-22-Jan	BSS	A	Welling United	739	W 1-0	Simmonds 78	5
22	Sat-29-Jan	BSS	H	Ebbsfleet United	1210	L 1-3	Birchall 5	8
23	Tue-01-Feb	BSS	A	Bromley	420	W 2-0	Simmonds 61, Cogan 72	7
24	Sat-05-Feb	BSS	A	Basingstoke Town	431	L 2-3	Birchall 2 (3, 46)	7
25	Tue-08-Feb	BSS	H	Braintree Town	720	L 1-2	Birchall pen 80	8
26	Sat-12-Feb	BSS	H	Weston-Super-Mare	726	L 0-1		8
27	Mon-21-Feb	BSS	A	Eastleigh	545	W 2-0	Cogan 2, Birchall 90	8
28	Sat-26-Feb	BSS	A	St Albans City	384	W 5-1	Birchall 6, Simmonds 8, Spence 40, Gillman 46, Cogan 62	6
29	Sat-05-Mar	BSS	H	Hampton & Richmond Borough	826	W 1-0	Birchall 36	6
30	Sat-12-Mar	BSS	A	Maidenhead United	352	W 1-0	Cogan 39	8
31	Mon-14-Mar	BSS	A	Chelmsford City	751	D 2-2	Birchall 13, Spence 90	8
32	Sat-19-Mar	BSS	H	Dorchester Town	836	W 2-1	Birchall 2 (33, 68)	7
33	Tue-22-Mar	BSS	A	Staines Town	356	L 0-1		7
34	Sat-26-Mar	BSS	H	Boreham Wood	577	W 1-0	Birchall 87	7
35	Tue-29-Mar	BSS	H	Havant & Waterlooville	656	L 0-1		7
36	Sat-02-Apr	BSS	H	Bishops Stortford	784	W 2-0	Harris 28, Spence 90	6
37	Mon-04-Apr	BSS	A	Havant & Waterlooville	528	D 0-0		6
38	Sat-09-Apr	BSS	A	Weston-Super-Mare	264	W 4-1	Simmonds 21, Birchall 36, Main 2 (50, 59)	6
39	Sat-16-Apr	BSS	A	Dorchester Town	475	D 0-0		6
40	Fri-22-Apr	BSS	H	Basingstoke Town	1065	W 3-0	Harris 24, Birchall pen 36, Main 71	6
41	Mon-25-Apr	BSS	A	Dartford	1771	L 0-4		7
42	Sat-30-Apr	BSS	H	St Albans City	847	W 4-1	Ashton 21, Birchall 2 (22, 64), Simmonds 40	7
CUPS								
1	Sat-25-Sep	FAC 2Q	A	Erith Town	282	W 5-1	Charles 2 (22, 30), Long 33, Birchall 2 (40, 69)	
2	Sat-09-Oct	FAC 3Q	H	Cambridge City	820	W 3-1	Birchall 2 (pen 12, 44), Wallis 51	
3	Sat-23-Oct	FAC 4Q	A	Farnborough	845	D 1-1	Birchall 63	
4	Tue-26-Oct	FAC 4QR	H	Farnborough	1044	W 5-0	Birchall 3 (1, pen 7, 19), Charles 11, Baker 55	
5	Sat-06-Nov	FAC 1	A	Gillingham	7475	W 2-0	Birchall 18, I'Anson 28	
6	Sat-20-Nov	FAT 3Q	H	Woking	818	L 1-2	Hunt pen 69	
7	Sat-27-Nov	FAC 2	H	Aldershot Town	4123	W 2-0	Birchall 2 (54, pen 90)	
8	Sat-08-Jan	FAC 3Q	A	Huddersfield Town	7894	L 0-2		

League
Starts
Substitute
Unused Sub

Cups
Starts
Substitute
Unused Sub

Goals (Lg)
Goals (Cup)

FLITNEY	WALLIS	FISH	WYNTER	SCHULZ	GILLMAN	I'ANSON	TABIRI	CHARLES	BIRCHALL	RICE	WELFORD	HILL	BAKER	CUTLER	HOOK	NICOLAU	HUNT	HUMPHREY	CRAWFORD	AISIEN	LONG	ROGERS	NORVILLE	BAH	COGAN	RAGGETT	SIMMONDS	BRIAND	SPENCE	KELLY	SHIMMIN	WHYTE	PALLEN	ASHTON	ESSAM	HARRIS	MAIN
X	X	X	X	X	X	X	X	X	X	X	S	S	U	U	U																						
X	X	X	X	X	X	X	X	X	X	S	S	U	X	U	U																						
X	X	X	X	X	X	X	X	X	X	U		S	S			X	S	U																			
X	X	X	X	X	X	X	U	S	X	X		U	X			S	X	U																			
X	X	X	X	X	X	X	S	X	X	S			X			X		U	S	U																	
X	X	X	X	X	X	S	X	S	X	X			X			S		U	X	U																	
X	X	X	X	X	X	X		X	X	S			X	U	U	X	S			U																	
X		X	X	X	X	X	X	S	X				U	X	U	X	X			U	S																
X	S	X	X		X	X	S	X	X			U	X	X			S	U		X	X																
X	X	X	X	X	X	S	X	X	X			U	X	U	U	X							S														
X	X	X	X	X	X	X	S	X	X				X		U	X	S			U			U														
X	X	X			X		X	X	X			U	X	S		X	S	U		X	X		S														
X	U	X	X	X	X	X	X		X				X		U	X	X			U	S		S														
X		X		X	X	X	X		X				X	U	U	S	S			X	X		X	U													
X	X	X	X	X	X	X	S		X				X	U	U		S				U				X		X										
	X	X	X	X	X	X			X			U	X	S	X		S	U			S				X		X										
U		X	X	X	X	X		S	X			S	X	X	X						S				X		X	U									
X		X	X	X	X	X			X			S	S	S	U		X				X				X			X									
X	S	X	X	X	X	X			S			S	X	X	U		X				X				U		X										
X	X	X	X	X		X	X		X			U	X		U		S				X				U		X	U									
X		X	X	X	X	X	U		X				S		U		U				U				X		X		X	X							
X	S	X	X	X	X	X			X				U		U		S				S				X		X		X	X							
X	X	X	X	X	X	S			X				X		U		U				S				X		X		X	S							
X	X	X	X	X	X	U			X				S		U		X				U				X		X		X	U							
X	X	X	X	X	X				X				S		U		S				S				X		X	U	X	X							
X		X	X		X	X		S	X				X		U		S								X		X	U	X	S	X						
X	X	X	X		X	X		S	X				S		U										X		X		X	U	X	U					
X	X	X	X		X	X		S	X				S	S	U										X		X		X		X	U					
X	X	X	X		U	X		S	X				X	X	U										X		X		X			U					
X	X	X	X	X	X	X	U		X				X	S	U										X	U			X				S				
X	X	X	X	X	X	X	S	S	X				X	S	U										X				X				U				
X		X	X		X	X	X	S	X				S	X	U										X		S		X				U	X			
X	X	X	X		X	X		U	X				S	S	U										X		X		X					S	X		
X		X	X		X	S	U	X	X				X	X	U										X		S		X					S	X		
X		X	X			X		S	X				S	U	U										X		X		X					X	X	X	S
X		X	X				S	S	X				U	X	U										X		X		X					S	X	X	X
X		X	X				U	U	X				X	X	U										X	U	X		X					X		X	S
X		X	X				S	S	X				X	S	U										X	U	X		X					X		X	X
X		X	X			S		S	X				X	U	U										X		X		X					X	X	X	S
X	X	X	X		X	X		S	X				X	X	U						U				X										S	X	S
X	S	X	X	X	U	X		S	X				S		U										X		X		X						X		X
X	X	X	X	U	X			U	X				X	X	U						U				X		X		S					X			
X	X	X	X	X	X	X	S	X	X			U	X	S		S		U		U	X	U															
X	X	X	X	X	X	X	U	X	X			U	X	S	U	X	S			U			S														
X	U	X	X	X	X	X	X	S	X				X	X		S	U	U		U	S		X														
X	S	X		X	X	X	X	X	X			U	X	U		S		U		X	X		S														
X	S	X	X	X	X	X	X	X	X				X	U	S		S			U	X		U														
X	X	X		X	X		X		X				X	U	U	U	X			X	X				S	U											
X	X	X	X	X	X	X	S		X				X	U	U	U	X			U	S				X	U											
X	S	X	X	X	X	X			X			U	X	X	U		X	U			S				X	U		U									
40	24	42	40	26	34	30	11	10	41	3	0	0	27	11	2	8	6	0	1	3	6	0	1	0	26	0	22	1	20	3	3	0	0	6	6	6	3
0	4	0	0	0	0	5	7	16	1	3	2	5	11	8	0	3	12	0	1	0	7	0	3	0	0	0	2	0	1	2	0	0	1	3	1	0	4
1	1	0	0	1	2	1	5	3	0	1	0	7	4	8	34	0	2	7	0	6	5	0	1	1	2	3	0	4	0	2	0	3	2	0	0	0	0
8	4	8	6	8	8	7	4	4	8	0	0	0	8	2	0	1	3	0	0	2	4	0	1	0	2	0	0	0	0	0	0	0	0	0	0	0	0
0	3	0	0	0	0	0	2	1	0	0	0	0	0	2	1	3	2	0	0	0	3	0	2	0	1	0	0	0	0	0	0	0	0	0	0	0	0
0	1	0	0	0	0	0	1	0	0	0	0	4	0	4	4	2	1	4	0	5	0	1	1	0	0	3	0	1	0	0	0	0	0	0	0	0	0
0	1	0	0	1	1	1	1	3	34	0	0	0	7	1	0	1	4	0	1	0	1	0	1	0	5	0	7	0	3	0	0	0	0	1	0	2	3
0	1	0	0	0	0	1	0	3	11	0	0	0	1	0	0	0	1	0	0	0	1	0	0	0	0	0	0	0	0	0	0	0	0	0	0	0	0

PLAYING SQUAD 2011/12

Existing Players		SN	HT	WT	DOB	AGE	POB	Career	Apps	Goals
GOALKEEPERS										
Lee	Hook		5'09"	08 11	11/03/1979	32	Margate	Wolves (Yth), Exeter, Ramsgate, Whitstable, Sittingbourne 9/02, Eastbourne B 6/03 Rel 5/09, Dover 5/09	2	0
Ben	Humphrey				28/11/1992	18		Dover, Folkestone I (L) 1/11	0	0
Mikhael	Jaimez-Ruiz		6'00"	12 02	12/07/1984	27	Merida, Ven	Graceland University, St Gregorys University, Olimpia Gherla (Rom), CFR Cluj (Rom), Arieşul Turda (Rom), Brentford (Trial) c/s 06, Barnet 10/06, Wealdstone, Northwood 2/07, Wycombe (Trial) 3/07, Aldershot 4/07 (07/08 3,0) Rel c/s 10, Yaracuyanos (Ven) 7/10, Aldershot T 2/11 Rel c/s 11, Dover 8/11		
Ross	Kitteridge		6'02"	13 11	28/12/1989	21	Reading	Arsenal (Yth), Reading (Scholar) 7/06 Rel c/s 09, Basingstoke (Trial) c/s 07, Stevenage (Trial) c/s 07, Dover (Trial) 7/07, Eastleigh (L) 11/07, Basingstoke (SL) 7/08, Basingstoke 7/09 Rel 5/10, Aldershot T 8/10, Bishops Stortford 10/10, Dover 6/11		
DEFENDERS										
Nathan	Ashton		5'08"	09 07	30/01/1987	24	Plaistow	Charlton Rel c/s 07, Millwall (SL) 3/07, Fulham 8/07, C.Palace (SL) 3/08, Wycombe 7/08 Rel c/s 09, Gillingham (Trial) 7/09, AFC Wimbledon 10/09 Rel 11/09, Aveley 9/10, Concord R 11/10, Cray W 12/10, Slovan Bratislava (Slo) (Trial) 1/11, Marlow 2/11, Dover 3/11	9	1
Ed	Harris		6'01"	13 05	03/11/1990	20	Roehampton	QPR, AFC Wimbledon 7/10 Rel 5/11, Dover (L) 3/11, Dover 6/11	6	2
Sean	Raggett							Dover, Sittingbourne (Dual), C. Palace (Trial) 11/10	0	0
Ollie	Schulz				25/05/1985	26		Ramsgate, Dover 5/08	26	1
Phil	Starkey		6'00"	12 06	10/09/1987	23	Dartford	C.Palace Rel c/s 07, Ebbsfleet 8/07, Tonbridge A (L) 1/08 Perm, Ebbsfleet (Trial) 7/09, Braintree 8/09, Dover 6/11		
Steven	Watt		6'03"	14 00	01/05/1985	26	Aberdeen	Chelsea, Barnsley (L) 10/05, Swansea 1/06 Rel c/s 08, Inverness Cal (L) 8/07, Ross County 8/08 Rel c/s 10, Grimsby 8/10 Rel 5/11, Dover (Trial) 7/11, Mansfield (Trial) 7/11, Dover 7/11		
Tom	Wynter		5'07"	11 11	20/06/1990	21	Lewisham	Gillingham, Ramsgate (3ML) 11/08, Dover (2ML) 10/09, Dover 7/10	40	0
MIDFIELDERS										
Harry	Baker		5'10"	11 13	20/09/1990	20	Bexleyheath	L.Orient Rel c/s 10, Grays (L) 1/10, Dover 8/10	38	7
Barry	Cogan		5'09"	09 00	04/11/1984	26	Sligo	Millwall, Barnet Undisc 8/06 Rel 5/07, Gillingham 7/07, Grays (SL) 3/08, Grays 7/08, Crawley 6/09 Rel 11/10, Dover 11/10	26	5
Michael	Corcoran		5'10"	11 04	28/12/1987	23	Coalisland	Cardiff, Oxford U (3ML) 1/07, Oxford U 7/07 Rel 1/08, Rushden & D 1/08, Dover 6/11		
Sam	Cutler				11/02/1990	21	Sidcup	Cambridge U, Weymouth 5/08, Grays 8/09, Torquay (Trial), Welling 11/09, Dover 7/10	19	1
Shane	Huke		5'11"	12 07	02/10/1985	25	Reading	Rochedale Rangers (Aust), Peterborough Rel c/s 07, Kings Lynn (L) 8/03, Bedford T (L) 12/03, Heybridge (L) 3/04, Cambridge C (L) 9/04, Hornchurch (L) 11/04, Dag & Red 1/07 Rel 1/09, Central Coast Mariners (Aust) 1/09, Rushden & D 3/10, Dover 5/11		
Luke	I'Anson				02/08/1988	23		AFC Wimbledon, Athletico De Coin (Sp) Rel c/s 07, Bromley 11/07, Kingstonian 3/10, Welling 3/10, Dover 8/10	35	1
Matt	Johnson				15/04/1990	21		Aveley, Rushden & D 6/10, Dover 6/11		
Glen	Southam		5'07"	11 10	27/08/1980	31	Enfield	Fulham (Jun), Tottenham (Jun), Enfield, Bishops Stortford 7/00, Boreham Wood (L), Dag & Red 5/04, Hereford 7/09, Bishops Stortford 10/09, Histon 2/10 Rel 4/10, Barnet 6/10 Rel c/s 11, Dover 8/11		
FORWARDS										
Billy	Bricknell		5'11"		24/07/1988	23	Enfield	Tottenham (Yth), Waltham Abbey, Leyton c/s 07, Billericay 1/08, Barnet (Trial) c/s 10, Chelmsford Undisc 8/10, Dover 7/11		
George	Purcell		5'11"	11 09	08/04/1988	23	Gravesend	Gillingham, Gravesend/Ebbsfleet 8/06, Heybridge (L) 9/07, Ramsgate (L) 2/09, Braintree 5/09, York C Undisc 7/10, Dartford (L) 11/10, Eastbourne B (SL) 1/11, Dover Undisc 7/11		
Donovan	Simmonds		5'10"	11 00	12/10/1988	22	Walthamstow	Charlton (Scholar), Coventry 7/07 Rel c/s 09, Gillingham (SL) 3/08, Kilmarnock (SL) 8/08, Floriana (Mal) 8/09, Morton 2/10 Rel c/s 10, Rushden & D 8/10, Nuneaton T 9/10, Dover 12/10	24	7
James	Walker		5'11"	11 13	25/11/1987	23	Hackney	Charlton, Hartlepool (L) 1/06, Luton (Trial) 2/06, Derby (Trial) 3/06, Bristol R (L) 9/06, L.Orient (3ML) 11/06, Notts County (SL) 3/07, Yeovil (3ML) 10/07, Southend (SL) 2/08, Southend £200,000 5/08 Rel 2/10, Hereford (L) 9/09, Gillingham 2/10 Rel c/s 10, L.Orient 9/10 Rel 1/11, Grimsby (Trial), Woking 3/11, Dover 7/11		

EASTBOURNE BOROUGH

Chairman: Len Smith
Secretary: Jan Field (T) 07749 572 693 (E) footballsecretary@ebfc.co.uk
Additional Committee Members:
Mick Grimer, Mike Spooner, Angus Scott, Lorna Gosling, Steve Carter, Paul Robinson, Geoffrey Smith, Paul Maynard, Tim Cobb, Tim Firth.
Manager: Garry Wilson
Programme Editor: David Bealey (E) programme@ebfc.co.uk

Back Row: Funnell (Kit), Eke (Coach), Cole, Cobbs, Masters, Banks, Elphick, Hutchinson,Rook, Karchinski (Kit).
Middle: (Physio), Hart, Smart, Pulman, Brinkhurst, Baker, Rowe, Charman, Tuppen (Physio).
Front: Johnson, Strevett, Austin, Greenwood (Head Coach), Wilson (Manager), Crabb, Medlock, Watson.

Club Factfile

Founded: 1966 **Nickname:** Borough
Previous Names: Langney Sports > 2001
Previous Leagues: Eastbourne & Hastings, Sussex County, Southern

Club Colours (change): Red/black/red (All yellow)

Ground: Langney Sports Club, Priory Lane, Eastbourne BN23 7QH (T) 01323 766 265
Capacity: 4,151 **Seats:** 542 **Covered:** 2,500 **Clubhouse:** Yes **Shop:** Yes

Directions: From M25 take M23/A23 eastbound to A27 Polegate by pass pick up and follow signs for crematorium 50yds past crematorium turn right at mini roundabout into Priory Road Stadium 100yds on left.

Previous Grounds: None

Record Attendance: 3,770 v Oxford United - FA Cup 1st Round 05/11/05
Record Victory: 10-1 v Haywards Heath Town - Sussex County Division One 1991-92
Record Defeat: 0-8 v Sheppey United (A) - FA Vase 09/10/93 and v Peachaven & Tels (A) - Sussex Co. Div.1 09/11/93
Record Goalscorer: Nigel Hole - 146
Record Appearances: Darren Baker - 689
Additional Records: Paid £1,800 to Yeovil Town for Yemi Odoubade.
Received £15,000 from Oxford United for Yemi Odoubade.
Senior Honours: Sussex County League 1999-2000, 02-03. Sussex Senior Cup 2001-02.

10 YEAR RECORD

01-02	02-03	03-04	04-05	05-06	06-07	07-08	08-09	09-10	10-11
SthE 7	SthE 2	SthP 11	Conf S 5	Conf S 17	Conf S 7	Conf S 2	Conf 13	Conf 19	Conf 23

EASTBOURNE BOROUGH

No.	Date	Comp	H/A	Opponents	Att:	Result	Goalscorers	Pos
1	Sat-14-Aug	BSP	A	Tamworth	723	L 2-4	Pacquette 49, Elphick 83	22
2	Tue-17-Aug	BSP	H	Hayes & Yeading United	902	W 5-0	Elphick 31, Pacquette 2 (45, 90), M Crabb 71, Taylor 73	8
3	Sat-21-Aug	BSP	H	Wrexham	1055	W 4-3	Pacquette 10, Elphick 44, Weatherstone 2 (pen 52, pen 90)	3
4	Tue-24-Aug	BSP	A	Histon	421	D 1-1	Treleaven 14	3
5	Sat-28-Aug	BSP	H	AFC Wimbledon	2485	L 2-3	Weatherstone 69, Atkin 78	9
6	Mon-30-Aug	BSP	A	Cambridge United	2465	L 0-2		14
7	Sat-04-Sep	BSP	H	Darlington	1464	D 1-1	Taylor 69	14
8	Sat-11-Sep	BSP	A	Barrow	1092	L 0-4		19
9	Sat-18-Sep	BSP	H	Altrincham	1117	W 5-0	Treleaven 2 (2, 13), Pacquette 38, Austin 65, Weatherstone pen 75	14
10	Tue-21-Sep	BSP	A	Forest Green Rovers	709	W 4-3	Taylor 2 (32, 45), Pacquette 45, M Crabb 90	9
11	Sat-25-Sep	BSP	A	Mansfield Town	2312	L 0-4		14
12	Wed-29-Sep	BSP	H	Rushden & Diamonds	802	L 0-2		15
13	Sat-02-Oct	BSP	H	York City	1104	W 2-1	Taylor 44, Johnson 59	14
14	Tue-05-Oct	BSP	A	Newport County	2403	D 3-3	Weatherstone pen 9, M Crabb 47, Langston 90	14
15	Sat-09-Oct	BSP	A	Bath City	1074	D 1-1	Langston 82	14
16	Sat-16-Oct	BSP	H	Luton Town	2518	L 2-4	Cook 35, Johnson 67	15
17	Sat-30-Oct	BSP	A	Grimsby Town	2894	D 2-2	Rooney 50, Taylor 67	15
18	Tue-09-Nov	BSP	H	Forest Green Rovers	722	D 0-0		15
19	Sat-13-Nov	BSP	H	Newport County	1065	D 0-0		16
20	Sat-20-Nov	BSP	A	Kidderminster Harriers	1271	L 1-2	Pacquette 71	17
21	Tue-07-Dec	BSP	A	Hayes & Yeading United	190	L 1-2	N Crabb 86	17
22	Tue-28-Dec	BSP	A	AFC Wimbledon	3364	L 0-3		18
23	Sat-01-Jan	BSP	A	Crawley Town	1894	L 1-3	Walker 85	20
24	Mon-03-Jan	BSP	H	Cambridge United	983	L 0-2		21
25	Sat-08-Jan	BSP	H	Mansfield Town	903	L 1-3	Taylor 54	22
26	Sat-22-Jan	BSP	A	Kettering Town	1146	L 0-3		22
27	Tue-25-Jan	BSP	H	Tamworth	798	L 1-4	Taylor 69	23
28	Sat-29-Jan	BSP	H	Grimsby Town	1002	L 2-3	Taylor 30, Walker 62	23
29	Tue-01-Feb	BSP	H	Gateshead	612	L 0-3		23
30	Sat-12-Feb	BSP	A	Darlington	1660	L 1-6	Smart 85	24
31	Sat-19-Feb	BSP	H	Histon	783	D 2-2	Baker 47, Elphick 57	24
32	Tue-22-Feb	BSP	A	Rushden & Diamonds	905	L 0-2		24
33	Sat-26-Feb	BSP	A	Fleetwood Town	1222	W 1-0	Smart 83	24
34	Sat-05-Mar	BSP	H	Southport	1004	W 4-1	Elphick 36, Purcell 37, M Crabb 79, Taylor 88	23
35	Tue-08-Mar	BSP	A	Wrexham	2410	L 1-2	Taylor 8	23
36	Sat-12-Mar	BSP	A	York City	2357	L 0-1		23
37	Sat-19-Mar	BSP	H	Barrow	1041	L 0-2		23
38	Tue-22-Mar	BSP	H	Crawley Town	2054	L 1-2	Purcell 71	23
39	Sat-26-Mar	BSP	H	Kettering Town	673	L 1-3	Taylor 90	23
40	Sat-02-Apr	BSP	A	Southport	923	W 3-1	Smart 17, Pacquette 27, Og (Ledsham) 43	23
41	Sat-09-Apr	BSP	H	Fleetwood Town	864	L 0-6		23
42	Tue-12-Apr	BSP	A	Gateshead	617	L 0-3		23
43	Sat-16-Apr	BSP	H	Kidderminster Harriers	688	D 1-1	Pacquette 28	23 Relegated
44	Sat-23-Apr	BSP	A	Luton Town	6171	L 0-3		23
45	Mon-25-Apr	BSP	H	Bath City	1014	W 2-0	Pacquette 46, Taylor 83	23
46	Sat-30-Apr	BSP	A	Altrincham	1649	W 4-3	Taylor 2 (17, 21), Brinkhurst 44, Purcell 90	23

CUPS

No.	Date	Comp	H/A	Opponents	Att:	Result	Goalscorers
1	Sat-23-Oct	FAC 4Q	H	Harrow Borough	681	L 2-4	Taylor 50, Atkin 88
2	Sat-11-Dec	FAT 1	H	Boreham Wood	422	W 3-1	Langston 12, Taylor 35, Pacquette 56
3	Sat-15-Jan	FAT 2	A	Dorchester Town	402	D 3-3	Pacquette 2 (24, 62), Jenkins 90
4	Tue-18-Jan	FAT 2R	H	Dorchester Town	487	W 1-0	Pacquette 77
5	Sat-05-Feb	FAT 3	H	Guiseley	471	D 1-1	Weatherstone 27
6	Tue-08-Feb	FAT 3R	A	Guiseley	446	L 1-2	Elphick 51

League
Starts
Substitute
Unused Sub

Cups
Starts
Substitute
Unused Sub

Goals (Lg)
Goals (Cup)

BANKS	JENKINS	LANGSTON	AUSTIN	ELPHICK	M CRABB	JOHNSON	WEATHERSTONE	BROWN	PACQUETTE	TRELEAVEN	TAYLOR	BRINKHURST	SMART	BAKER	STREVETT	ATKIN	WILLS	N CRABB	O'BRIEN	COOK	MAMBO	LIGHTWOOD	ROONEY	BARTON	NELSON	PARTINGTON	JENKINSON	WALKER	NORWOOD	MASTERTON	HUTCHINSON	SPENCER	DEMETRIOU	FORECAST	PURCELL	KELLY	HOLLAND							
13	3	6	5	24	11	8	14	26	10	19	7	16	4	2	12	9	18	15	22	27	28	30	20	1	21	22	17	17	18	20	28	26	21	23	22	26	17							
X	X	X	X	X	X	X	X	X	X	X	S	S	S	U	U																													
X	X	X	X	X	X	X	X	S	X	X	X	S	S	U		U																												
X	X	X	X	X	X	X	X	U	X	X	X	S	S	S		U																												
X	X	X	X	X	X		X	S	X	X	X	S	X	U		U	U																											
X	X	X	X	X	X		X	U	X	X	X	S	X	U		S	U																											
X	U	X	U	X			X	X		X	S	X	S	X	X	X	X	S																										
X	X	X	X	X	X	S	X	S		X	X	S	X	U		X		U																										
		X	X	X	X	S	X	X		X	X	S	X	S	U	X		U	X																									
X			X		X	X	X	X	X	X	X	S	S	X		U			U	X	S																							
X			U		X	X	X	X	X		X	X	U	X	S	U		S		X	X																							
X	U			U	X	X	X	X	X		X	X	S	X	S			S		X	X																							
X	X		S		X	X	X	U	X		X	U	S	X		S		X		X	X																							
X	X	X	X		X	S	X	S	X		X	X	X			S		U		X	U																							
X	X	X	X		X	X	X	X			X	X		S	S			S		X	U	U																						
X	X	X	X	S	X	X	X	U			X	X		X	S			X			S	U																						
X	X	X	X	U	X	X	X		X		X	X		U	S	S		U		X																								
X	X	X	X			X	X		S		X	X		S	S	U		U					X		X	X																		
X	X	X	X		S	X	X		X		X	U		U				U					X		X	X	S																	
X	X	X	X			X	X		X		X	S	U	U				S				U	X			X	X																	
X	X	X	X		X	X	X		S		X	S	U	X	S							U	X				X																	
X	X	X	X		X	U	X		X		X	X	S	U	S			S								X	X																	
X	X	X	X	S	X	X			X		X	U	X	S	X	U		S							X																			
X	X		X	X	X	X					X	S	X	U	S	U		S							X			X	X															
X	X			X	X	U	U					S	X	X	X	X		S						U	X			X	X															
X	X		X	X	X						X	U	X	S	U	S		S							X			X	X	X														
X	X		X	U	X	S	U				X	X	X	X	X			S							X			S		X														
X			X	X	X	X	S				X	U		X	U			S							X			X	S	X	X													
X	X		X	X			X				X	U		X	X	S		S										X		X	U	X	S											
	X		X	X	S		X				X			X	X	X		U										X		S	S		U	X	X									
U	X			X	X	X	X		S		X	X	X	X				S													X		U	X	S									
U	X		X	X	X	S	X		X		X	X	X	X				S													U			X	S									
U	X		X	U	S	X			X		S	X	X	X	X																X		U	X	X									
U	X		X	X	X		S		X		X	U	X	X				S													X			X	X									
X	X		X	X	X	U	U		X		X	S	X	X	S																X		S		X									
X	X		X		X	S	S		X		X	S	X	X								U									X		U		X	X								
X	X		X	U		S	S		X		X	X	X	X	X																X		S			X								
X	X		X	X		S	S		X		X	U	X	X	U																X		U		X	X								
X	X		X		X	X	U		U		X	S	X	X	U																X		U		X	X								
X	X		X		X	X	S		S		X	S	X	X	U																X		U		X	X								
X	X		X		X	S	U		X		X	S	X	X																	X		S		X	X	U							
X	X		X		X	U	S		X		X	S	X	X	U																X		S		X	X								
X			X		X	X	S		X		X	X	U	X	S																X		X		S	X								
X			X		X	X	U		X		X	X	U	X	S							U									X		X		S	X								
X	S		X	U	X	X			X		X	X	S	X	U																X		X		S	X								
X	S		X	X	X	X			X		X	X	S					U				U									X		X		S	X								
X	U		X	X	X	X			X		X	X	S	U	U																X		X		S	X								
X	X	X		X	X	X	X		X	U	X	S		X	S	U		U					X	U																				
X	X	X	X		X	X	X		X		X	U	X	S	S	U		S									X																	
X	X		X		X	S			X		X	X	X	X	X			S						U	X				S															
X	X		X		X	S	U		X		X	X	X	X	X			S						U	X				U															
U	X			X	X		X		S		X	S	X	X	X			S													X	X	U	X										
U	X			X	S		X		X		X	X	X	X				S													X	U	X	X										
40	35	18	40	21	37	26	25	7	29	9	42	19	22	27	8	5	1	2	1	7	3	0	4	0	8	4	3	6	3	4	17	1	5	5	10	12	0	0	0	0	0	0	0	0
0	2	0	1	2	3	9	8	4	4	0	3	18	11	6	12	6	0	16	0	0	2	0	0	0	0	0	1	1	1	1	1	0	5	0	7	0	0	0	0	0	0	0	0	0
4	3	0	2	6	0	4	6	4	1	0	0	8	5	11	10	8	2	8	1	0	2	7	0	1	0	0	0	0	0	0	2	0	7	0	0	0	1	0	0	0	0	0	0	0
4	6	2	3	3	5	2	4	0	5	0	6	3	5	5	3	0	0	0	0	0	0	0	1	0	2	0	1	0	0	0	2	1	1	2	0	0	0	0	0	0	0	0	0	0
0	0	0	0	0	1	2	0	0	1	0	0	2	0	1	2	0	0	5	0	0	0	0	0	0	0	0	0	0	1	0	0	0	0	0	0	0	0	0	0	0	0	0	0	0
2	0	0	0	0	0	0	1	0	0	1	0	1	0	0	0	2	0	1	0	0	0	0	0	3	0	0	0	0	1	0	0	1	1	0	0	0	0	0	0	0	0	0	0	0
0	0	2	1	5	4	2	5	0	10	3	15	1	3	1	0	1	0	1	0	1	0	0	1	0	0	0	0	2	0	0	0	0	0	0	3	0	0	0	0	0	0	0	0	0
0	1	1	0	1	0	0	1	0	4	0	2	0	0	0	0	1	0	0	0	0	0	0	0	0	0	0	0	0	0	0	0	0	0	0	0	0	0	0	0	0	0	0	0	0

PLAYING SQUAD 2011/12

Existing Players		SN	HT	WT	DOB	AGE	POB	Career	Apps	Goals
GOALKEEPERS										
Rikki	Banks		6'03"	13 08	13/05/1986	25	Brighton	C.Palace, Crawley (L) 2/06, Hendon (SL) 3/06, Worthing c/s 06, Lewes 6/08, Wycombe (Trial) 12/09, Eastbourne B 5/10	40	0
Clark	Masters		6'03"	13 12	31/05/1987	24	Hastings	Brighton (Yth), Gillingham (Yth), Brentford, Redbridge (2ML) 8/05, Slough (SL) 11/05, AFC Wimbledon (L) 3/07, Welling (L) 8/07, Southend 1/08 Rel c/s 09, Stevenage (SL) 1/08, Welling (L) 11/08, Grimsby (Trial) 1/09, Aldershot Undisc 7/09, Hayes & Yeading 2/10 Rel c/s 10, Hastings U 8/10 Rel 11/10, Barrow NC 11/10 Rel 5/11, Millwall (Trial) 11/10, Eastbourne B 6/11		
DEFENDERS										
Ben	Austin		5'09"	10 01	03/04/1977	34	Hastings	Brighton (Jun), Eastbourne T, Eastbourne B 6/00	41	1
Darren	Baker		5'10"	09 06	23/11/1974	36	Eastbourne	Brighton (Ass Sch), Littlehampton (Yth), Eastbourne B 6/92	33	1
Sonny	Cobbs		6'01"	13 00	01/12/1988	22		Brighton Rel 5/08, Worthing (L) 8/06, Worthing (SL) 12/06, Worthing (3ML) 8/07, Dorchester (L) 11/07, Welling (SL) 1/08, Welling 7/08, Sutton U 6/09, Lewes 6/10, Eastbourne B 6/11		
Gary	Elphick		6'01"	13 02	17/10/1985	25	Brighton	Brighton, Eastbourne B (L) 9/04, St Albans (SL) 12/04, Aldershot (2ML) 1/06, St Albans 3/06 Rel 12/07, Havant & W 12/07, Eastbourne B 5/09	23	5
Matt	Langston		6'02"	12 04	02/04/1981	30	Brighton	Watford Rel c/s 03, Aldershot (L) 12/02, Barnet (SL) 3/03, Stevenage 8/03, Cambridge C 11/03, Histon 6/06, Crawley (6WL) 3/10, Eastbourne B 6/10	18	2
Ollie	Rowe		6'01"	11 02	22/05/1991	20	Eastbourne	Brighton (Scholar) Rel c/s 09, Ringmer c/s 09, Eastbourne T, Eastbourne B 11/09, Eastbourne T (Dual) 11/09, Lewes (L) 9/10, Chelmsford 10/10, Hastings U 1/11, Eastbourne B 5/11		
MIDFIELDERS										
Steven	Brinkhurst		5'11"	11 11	28/03/1991	20	Lewes	Brighton Rel c/s 10, Bognor Regis (WE) 1/09, Lewes (L) 12/09, Lewes (L) 3/10, Eastbourne B 6/10	37	1
Gary	Charman							Chelsea (Jun), Horsham 7/96, Walton & H c/s 05, Horsham 11/05, Eastbourne B 6/11		
Sam	Cole							Hailsham, Rye U c/s 09, Eastbourne B 7/11		
Matt	Crabb		5'10"	12 01	15/12/1981	29	Eastbourne	Eastbourne U, Eastbourne B 7/00	40	4
Eddie	Hutchinson		6'01"	13 00	23/02/1982	29	Kingston	Sutton U, Brentford £75,000 8/00, Oxford U 7/06 Rel 4/09, Crawley 5/09 Rel 11/10, Eastbourne B 1/11	18	0
Simon	Johnson		5'08"	11 11	14/04/1991	20	Hailsham	Eastbourne B	35	2
Mark	Norris							Eastbourne B		
Matt	Smart		5'10"	12 04	14/04/1976	35	Crawley	Gillingham (Trainee, Crawley, Shoreham, Horsham, Wick, Horsham, Eastbourne B 7/01	33	3
James	Smith							Eastbourne B		
FORWARDS										
Gary	Hart		5'09"	12 08	21/09/1978	32	Harlow	Stansted, Brighton £1,000 6/98 Rel c/s 11, Havant & W (L) 12/07, Eastbourne B 7/11		
Billy	Medlock							Eastbourne B		
Ian	Pulman				24/09/1984	26	Kent	Chelsea (Trainee), Gillingham (Trainee), Ramsgate (Yth), Margate 4/03, Eastbourne (3ML) 1/04, Folkestone I (L) 8/04, Erith & B (L) 12/04, Erith & B 2/05, Dartford 8/05, Ramsgate 2/06, Chatham 7/06, Faversham 3/07, Whitstable 12/07, Melbourne Knights (Aust) 5/09, Whitstable 2/10, Eastbourne B 6/11		
Carl	Rook				10/02/1983	28		Sittingbourne (Yth), Folkestone I, Sittingbourne, Deal T, Whitstable, Hastings U 9/04, Dover 9/05, Horsham 1/06, Tonbridge A Undisc 12/07, Brighton (Trial) 7/09, Dartford 1/10 Rel 5/11, Tonbridge A (L) 3/11, Eastbourne B 6/11		
Ethan	Strevett				30/11/1989	21		Eastbourne B, Eastbourne T 10/08, Eastbourne B 8/10	20	0
Ross	Treleaven		5'09"	09 13	14/12/1988	22	Brighton	Crowborough, Eastbourne B (Dual) 3/08 Perm c/s 08, Worthing (Dual) 8/08, Hastings U (Dual) 2/10	9	3
Ben	Watson		5'10"	11 02	06/12/1985	25	Shoreham	Brighton, Bognor Regis (L) 3/04, Bognor Regis 7/04, Grays 7/07, Exeter (SL) 3/08, Exeter 6/08 Rel c/s 11, Forest Green (2DL) 12/09, Forest Green (L), Bath C (L) 1/11, Eastbourne B 6/11		

EASTLEIGH

Chairman: Paul Murray
Secretary: Ray Murphy **(T)** 07801 638 158 **(E)** raymurphy@ntlworld.com
Additional Committee Members:
Stuart Deas, Alan Harding, Allen Prebble, Alan Williams, David Malone, M Andrews, D Brooks, S Brookwell, M Budny, J Dunn, C Evans, M Geddes, P McIntosh, P Murray, A Prebble, J Russell, R Vaughan, P Vickery, A White, M Geddes
Manager: Ian Baird
Programme Editor: Mike Denning **(E)** mike.denning@talk21.com

Back Row (L-R): Gordon Chittenden, Billy Tsovolos, Ben Wilson, Ross Bottomley, Tom Jordan, Gareth Barfoot, Ian Harris (Goalkeeping coach), Mike Green, Jamie Slabber, Jack Vallis, Richard Gillespie, Frankie Raymond.
Front Row: Ryan O'Hara, Danny Smith, Jamie Brown, Andy Forbes, Kevin Dixon (Kit Man), Kevin Braybrook (Coach), Ian Baird (Manager), Phil Pearpoint (Coach), Andy Cook (Physio), Andrew White, Liam Hibberd, Sam Wilson, Adam Cashin-Murray.

Club Factfile

Founded: 1946 **Nickname:** The Spitfires
Previous Names: Swaythling Athletic 1946-59, Swaythling 1973-80
Previous Leagues: Southampton Junior & Senior 1946-59, Hampshire 1950-86, Wessex 1986-2003, Southern 2003-04, Isthmian 2004-05

Club Colours (change): Blue & white/white & blue/white (Red/black/red)

Ground: Silverlake Stadium 'Ten Acres', Stoneham Lane, Eastleigh SO50 9HT **(T)** 02380 613 361
Capacity: 2,300 **Seats:** 175 **Covered:** 385 **Clubhouse:** Yes **Shop:** Yes

Directions
From junction 13 of M3, turn right into Leigh Road, turn right at Holiday Inn, at mini roundabout take second exit, at the next mini roundabout take second exit, then next mini roundabout take first exit. Then take the first turning right (signposted) ground 200 metres on the left.

Previous Grounds: Not known

Record Attendance: 2,589 v Southampton - Friendly July 2005
Record Victory: 12-1 v Hythe & Dibden (H) - 11/12/1948
Record Defeat: 0-11 v Austin Sports (A) - 01.01.1947
Record Goalscorer: Johnnie Williams - 177
Record Appearances: Ian Knight - 611
Additional Records: Paid £10,000 to Newport (I.O.W.) for Colin Matthews

Senior Honours: Southampton Senior League (West) 1950.
Wessex League Cup 1992,2003, Division One 2002-03.

10 YEAR RECORD

01-02	02-03	03-04	04-05	05-06	06-07	07-08	08-09	09-10	10-11
Wex 13	Wex1 1	SthE 4	Isth P 3	Conf S 8	Conf S 15	Conf S 6	Conf S 3	Conf S 11	Conf S 8

EASTLEIGH

No.	Date	Comp	H/A	Opponents	Att:	Result	Goalscorers	Pos
1	Sat-14-Aug	BSS	H	Bishop Stortford	428	L 1-2	Williams 59	17
2	Tue-17-Aug	BSS	A	Dorchester Town	502	W 4-0	Slabber 3 (17, 31, 52), Holland 64	8
3	Sat-21-Aug	BSS	A	Chelmsford City	707	L 0-3		13
4	Mon-23-Aug	BSS	H	Maidenhead United	354	W 3-0	Williams 2 (20, 22), Gillespie 58	4
5	Sat-28-Aug	BSS	H	Weston-Super-Mare	336	D 1-1	Graham 2	9
6	Mon-30-Aug	BSS	A	Havant & Waterlooville	1020	D 2-2	Slabber pen 45, Holland 90	8
7	Sat-04-Sep	BSS	A	Dover Athletic	1010	W 1-0	Slabber 42	7
8	Sat-11-Sep	BSS	H	Lewes	366	W 2-1	Slabber 11, Holland 84	6
9	Sat-18-Sep	BSS	A	Braintree Town	499	L 0-1		7
10	Sat-02-Oct	BSS	H	Basingstoke Town	604	L 0-1		9
11	Sat-16-Oct	BSS	H	Dartford	727	W 3-0	Graham 43, Og (Goodacre) 63, Riviere 90	7
12	Sat-30-Oct	BSS	H	Boreham Wood	616	W 3-0	Taggart 1, Gillespie 16, Holland 64	7
13	Tue-09-Nov	BSS	A	Hampton & Richmond Borough	342	D 2-2	Graham 54, Holland 56	8
14	Sat-13-Nov	BSS	H	Staines Town	585	L 1-4	Jordan 29	9
15	Tue-23-Nov	BSS	A	Woking	654	D 1-1	Gillespie 55	9
16	Tue-28-Dec	BSS	A	Weston-Super-Mare	209	W 2-0	Graham 30, Bottomley 44	9
17	Sat-01-Jan	BSS	A	Farnborough	744	W 2-1	Jordan 15, Taggart 77	8
18	Mon-03-Jan	BSS	H	Havant & Waterlooville	822	W 4-2	Williams 2 (27, 90), Jordan 72, Slabber pen 93	8
19	Sat-08-Jan	BSS	A	Lewes	483	W 4-1	Smith 30, Williams 2 (40, 60), Taggart 65	8
20	Sat-22-Jan	BSS	H	Dorchester Town	558	W 3-0	Jordan 16, Graham 24, Slabber 90	8
21	Tue-25-Jan	BSS	A	St Albans City	217	W 1-0	Graham 40	6
22	Sat-29-Jan	BSS	A	Thurrock	255	L 1-2	Slabber 11	7
23	Tue-08-Feb	BSS	A	Ebbsfleet United	695	D 2-2	Slabber 11, Riviere 47	7
24	Sat-12-Feb	BSS	A	Basingstoke Town	447	W 2-1	Slabber 28, Riviere 45	7
25	Mon-14-Feb	BSS	H	St Albans City	248	W 4-2	McAuley 18, Slabber 2 (55, pen 65), Poate 54	5
26	Sat-19-Feb	BSS	H	Braintree Town	628	L 0-2		6
27	Mon-21-Feb	BSS	H	Dover Athletic	545	L 0-2		6
28	Sat-05-Mar	BSS	H	Chelmsford City	610	W 2-1	Jordan 10, Slabber 52	7
29	Tue-08-Mar	BSS	H	Bromley	403	W 1-0	Nwokeji 67	6
30	Sat-12-Mar	BSS	A	Bishop Stortford	305	W 1-0	Nwokeji 16	6
31	Tue-15-Mar	BSS	A	Dartford	711	D 0-0		7
32	Sat-19-Mar	BSS	H	Welling United	519	L 1-4	Slabber 90	8
33	Sat-26-Mar	BSS	H	Woking	877	W 4-1	Taggart 2 (1, 69), Slabber 4, Jordan 59	8
34	Tue-29-Mar	BSS	A	Welling United	479	L 2-4	Taggart pen 20, Gillespie 75	8
35	Sat-02-Apr	BSS	A	Staines Town	393	W 5-0	Slabber 4 (7, 19, pen 35, 41), McAuley 67	7
36	Tue-05-Apr	BSS	H	Farnborough	571	L 0-3		8
37	Sat-09-Apr	BSS	H	Thurrock	441	W 3-1	Holland 30, Jordan 32, Taggart 90	7
38	Tue-12-Apr	BSS	A	Maidenhead United	215	L 0-1		7
39	Sat-16-Apr	BSS	H	Ebbsfleet United	583	L 0-3		8
40	Fri-22-Apr	BSS	A	Boreham Wood	220	L 1-2	Slabber 19	8
41	Mon-25-Apr	BSS	H	Hampton & Richmond Borough	454	W 3-0	Brown 39, Smith 42, Taggart 45	8
42	Sat-30-Apr	BSS	A	Bromley	388	W 2-0	Adeniyi 39, Riviere 42	8

CUPS

No.	Date	Comp	H/A	Opponents	Att:	Result	Goalscorers
1	Sat-25-Sep	FAC 2Q	H	Bognor Regis Town	477	W 2-0	Graham 21, Riviere 81
2	Sat-09-Oct	FAC 3Q	A	Clevedon Town	313	W 5-0	Graham 20, Smith 26, Gillespie 53, Slabber 62, Williams 75
3	Sat-23-Oct	FAC 4Q	A	Woking	1048	L 2-3	Gillespie 2, Slabber 50
4	Sat-20-Nov	FAT 3Q	H	Folkestone Invicta	253	W 2-1	Gillespie 2 (11, 56)
5	Sat-11-Dec	FAT 1	H	Sutton United	388	D 1-1	Taggart 87
6	Tue-14-Dec	FAT 1R	A	Sutton United	237	W 4-0	Holland 37, Slabber 50, Og (El-Salahi) 60, Taggart 83
7	Sat-15-Jan	FAT 2	H	Worcester City	407	D 3-3	Jordan 45, McAuley 62, Riviere 69
8	Mon-17-Jan	FAT 2R	A	Worcester City	564	W 4-1	Taggart 2 (64, 89), Adeniyi 77, Gillespie 90
9	Sat-05-Feb	FAT 3	H	Chasetown	562	L 1-3	Slabber 48

League
Starts
Substitute
Unused Sub

Cups
Starts
Substitute
Unused Sub

Goals (Lg)
Goals (Cup)

MATTHEWS	BOTTOMLEY	GOODHIND	SMITH	HOLLAND	JORDAN	PALMER	HENDRY	SLABBER	GILLESPIE	GRAHAM	WILLIAMS	BROWN	ROBINSON	BARFOOT	MASON	POATE	TOOMER	WILSON	COLLINS	EASTON	BAIRD	OSMAN	BYLES	RIVIERE	TAGGART	ADENIYI	MCAULEY	CROOK	WHITE	BENNETT	SHARP	HERRING	NWOKEJI	HIBBERD
X	X	X	X	X	X	X	X	X	X	X	S	S	U	U	U																			
X	X	X	X	X	X	S	X	X	X	X	X	S	U	U	S																			
X	X	X	X	X	X		X	X	X	X	X	S	U	U	U	S																		
X	S	X	X	X	X		X	X	X	X	X	S			U	X	S	U																
	X	X	X	X	X			X	X	X	X	X	U	X	S		U		U	U														
	X	X	X	X	X			X		X	X	X	U	X	X		U		U	U	U													
	X	X	X	X	X			X	X	X	X	X	U	X	S		U		U	U														
	X	S	X	X	X		X	X	X	X	X	X		X	U		U			U		S												
U	X	U	X	X	X		X	X	X	X	S	X		X								U	X	S										
U	X	X		X	X		X	X	X	X	S	S		X								S		X	X									
X	U	X	X	X	X		S	X	X	X	S	S		U									X	X	X									
X	S	X	X	X	X			X	X	X	U	S		U									X	X	X	S								
X	X	X		X	X			X	X	X	S			U									X	X	X	U	S							
X	X	X		X	X			X	X	X	S			U									X	X	X	S	S							
U	S	X	X	X	X			S	X	X	U			X									X	X	X	X	S							
U	X	U	X	X	X					X	X			X		U							X	X	X	X	S		S					
U	X	U	X	X	X			S		X	X			X									X	X	X	X	S		U					
U	X	S	X	X	X			S		X	X			X									X	X	X	X	S		U					
U	X	X	X	X	X			S	U	X	X			X										X	X	X	S		S					
U	S	X	S	X	X			X	S	X				X		U							X	X	X	X	X							
S	S	U	X	X	X			X	S	X				X									X	X	X	X	X			U				
X	X		X	X	X			X	S	X						U	U							X	X	X	X			S	U			
X	S	X	X	X	X			X		X						U							X	X	X	S	X			S	U			
X			X	X	X			X		X				U		S						U	X	X	X	X	X			S	U			
X			X	X	X			X	S	X				U		X						U		X	X	X	X			S	U			
S	S		X	X	X			X		X				X		X						U		X	X	X	X			S	U			
U	X		X	X	X			X		X				X		X						U		X	X	X	S			S	S			
X	X			X	X			X	S	X						X	U							X	X	X	U				U	X	S	
X	X			X	X			X	S	X				U		X							S	X	X	X	U					X	S	
X	X			X	X			X	S	X				U		X							S		X	X	S				U	X	X	
X	X	U		X	X			X	S	X				U		X							S		X	X	S					X	X	
X	X	S	U	X	X			X	S	X				U									X	X		X	S					X	X	
X		X	X	X	X			X	U	X		S		U									X	S	X	S	X					X		
X	S	X	X	X	X				S	X		X		U									X	S	X	U	X					X		
X		X	X	X	X			X	S	X		U		U									X	S	X	S	X					X		
X		X	X	X	X			X	S	X		U		U									X	S	X	S	X					X		
X		X	X	X	X			X	X	X		S		U									X	X	X	U	S					U		
X	U		X	X	X			X	X	X		S		U									X	X	X	S	S					X		
X	S		X	X	X			X	X	X		S		U									X	X	X	U	S					X		
X		X	X		X			X	S	X		S		U		X							X	X	X	U	X					S		
U	X	X	X		X			S	X	X		X		X									X	X	X	S						U		S
U	X	X	U		X			X	S	X				X									X	X	X	X	S					X		S
U	X	U	X	X	X		X	X	X	X	S	X		X								U	X	S										
X	U	X	X	X	X		S	X	X	X	S	S		U						U		U	X	X	X									
X	S	X	X	X	X			X	X	X	S	U		U								U	X	X	X	S	U							
U	X	U	X	X	X				X	X	X			X		U							X	X	X	S	S							
U	X	X	X	X				S	X	X			U	X									X	X	X	X	S							
U	X		X	X	X			X		X	X		S	X				U						X	X	X	S	U						
U	X	X	X		X			X	S	X				X		U								X	X	X	X		U					
U	X	X	X		X			X	S	X				X		U							U	X	X	X	X							
X	X	X	X	X	X			X	S	X						U	U						S		X	X	X			S				
25	24	24	32	39	42	1	7	35	18	42	11	7	0	17	1	9	0	0	0	0	0	0	24	27	32	18	12	0	0	0	0	12	3	0
2	9	3	1	0	0	1	1	5	14	0	6	12	0	0	3	2	1	0	0	0	0	2	3	5	0	8	15	0	2	6	1	1	2	2
11	2	5	2	0	0	0	0	0	2	0	2	2	6	21	4	4	6	1	3	4	1	5	0	0	0	5	2	0	2	1	7	2	0	0
3	7	6	9	7	8	0	1	7	5	9	2	1	0	6	0	0	0	0	0	0	0	0	5	7	8	5	3	0	0	0	0	0	0	0
0	1	0	0	0	0	0	1	1	3	0	3	1	1	0	0	0	0	0	0	0	0	0	1	1	0	2	3	0	0	1	0	0	0	0
6	1	2	0	0	0	0	0	0	0	0	0	1	1	2	0	4	1	1	0	1	0	3	1	0	0	0	1	1	1	0	0	0	0	0
0	1	0	2	6	7	0	0	21	4	6	7	1	0	0	0	1	0	0	0	0	0	0	0	4	8	1	2	0	0	0	0	0	2	0
0	0	0	1	1	1	0	0	4	5	2	1	0	0	0	0	0	0	0	0	0	0	0	0	2	4	1	1	0	0	0	0	0	0	0

PLAYING SQUAD 2011/12

Existing Players		SN	HT	WT	DOB	AGE	POB	Career	Apps	Goals
GOALKEEPERS										
Gareth	Barfoot		6'00"		12/11/1981	29	Southampton	BAT Sports, Christchurch c/s 05, Gosport 2/06, AFC Totton, Eastleigh 7/10	17	0
Andy	Smallpiece							Bournemouth (Yth), Basingstoke Rel 8/06, Newport IoW 8/06, Winchester, Bognor Regis, Andover 7/10, Eastleigh 8/11		
Defenders										
Henrik	Breimyr		6'01"	12 02	20/07/1993	18	Stavanger, Nor	Fulham (Yth), Reading (Yth), Aldershot. Chelsea (Trial) 2/11, Eastleigh (L) 8/11		
Tom	Jordan		6'04"	12 04	24/05/1981	30	Manchester	Bristol C Rel c/s 02, Huddersfield (Trial) 3/02, Carlisle (Trial) 7/02, Exeter (Trial) 7/02, Southend 8/02 Rel c/s 03, Tamworth 8/03, Forest Green 3/04, Havant & W 8/04, Eastleigh 6/08	42	7
Ryan	O'Hara		5'08"	08 13	24/07/1989	22		Swindon (Yth), Dundee (Yth), Gretna Rel 3/08, Forest Green (Trial) 3/09, Swindon Supermarine 9/08, Salisbury 7/09, Gloucester 3/10 Rel 8/10, Cirencester 9/10, Oxford C 10/10, Chippenham 2/11, Eastleigh 8/11		
Jordan	Rose				22/11/1989	21	Southampton	Southampton (Yth), Stade Malherbe Caen (Fra) (Yth), Bournemouth Rel c/s 08, Salisbury, Bashley, Brockenhurst, Weymouth 7/09, Paulton 3/10, Bath C (Dual) 3/10, Nike Academy, Stockport 7/10 Rel c/s 11, Eastleigh 8/11		
Ryan	Tafazoli		6'05"	12 04	28/09/1991	19	Sutton	Southampton Rel c/s 11, Salisbury (L) 10/09, Salisbury (L) 1/11, Eastleigh 8/11		
Billy	Tsovolos							Eastleigh		
Jack	Vallis				21/08/1993	18	Salisbury	Eastleigh		
Ben	Wilson				17/02/1994	17	Southampton	Eastleigh	0	0
MIDFIELDERS										
Ross	Bottomley				11/05/1984	27	Ascot	Fareham, Hamble ASSC, Aldershot (Trial) 10/05, AFC Totten, Bashley (2ML) 12/09, Eastleigh 2/10	33	1
Jamie	Brown				14/07/1981	30	Bournemouth	BAT Sports, Dorchester 7/01, Eastleigh 4 fig 9/06 Rel 12/10, Winchester 12/10, Eastleigh 3/11 Rel 5/11	19	1
Adam	Cashin-Murray				11/11/1990	20	Reading	Reading T, Hungerford T 1/11, Eastleigh c/s 11		
Joe	Collins		5'09"	10 09	29/10/1990	20	Southampton	Portsmouth Rel c/s 09, Dundee U c/s 09 Rel 2/10, Eastleigh 2/10	0	0
Liam	Hibberd							Eastleigh	2	0
Jordace	Holder-Spooner				05/11/1992	18	Reading	Southampton (Scholar) Rel c/s 11, Bournemouth (Trial) 7/11, Eastleigh 8/11		
Gary	Pryde				23/10/1988	22	Redhill	Arsenal (Yth), C.Palace (Yth), Swindon (Scholar) Rel 8/07, Not Playing, Eastleigh 8/11		
Frankie	Raymond				18/11/1992	18	Reading	Reading, Horsham (L) 12/10, Basingstoke (SL) 2/11, Eastleigh (L) 8/11		
Danny	Smith		5'11"	11 04	17/08/1982	29	Southampton	Bashley (Yth), Bournemouth Rel c/s 02, Winchester 7/02, Eastleigh 7/04, Bashley (3ML) 12/07, Bashley 3/08, Bognor Regis 7/08, Eastleigh 5/09	33	2
FORWARDS										
Andy	Forbes				28/05/1979	32	Reading	Reading, Basingstoke, Andover, Winchester 8/02, Eastleigh 8/04 Rel 5/10, Woking 5/10, Sutton U (3ML) 10/10 Perm 1/11 Rel 5/11, Eastleigh 6/11		
Richard	Gillespie				21/11/1984	26		Southampton (Yth), Bashley, Salisbury (SL) 3/05, Eastleigh Undisc 6/09	32	4
Joe	Maxwell				28/11/1989	21		Eastleigh		
Jamie	Slabber		6'02"	11 10	31/12/1984	26	Enfield	Tottenham, AB Copenhagen (L) 3/04, Swindon (L) 12/04, Aldershot 3/05 Rel 5/05, Grays 7/05, Oxford U (L) 11/06, Stevenage 12/06 Rel 5/07, Rushden & D (Trial) 7/07, Havant & W 8/07 Rel 10/08, Grays NC 10/08, Woking 12/09 Rel 5/10, Eastleigh 5/10	40	21
Andy	White				01/09/1991	19	Epsom	Reading, Croydon Ath (WE) 2/09, Basingstoke (WE) 10/09, Staines (L) 3/10, Gillingham 7/10 Rel c/s 11, Margate (L) 10/10, Bishops Stortford (L) 1/11, Eastleigh 7/11		
Sam	Wilson						Southampton	Eastleigh		
Andy	Cook				10/08/1969	42		Eastleigh (Coach)		
Ian	Baird				01/04/1964	47		Eastleigh (Manager)	0	0

FARNBOROUGH

Chairman: Simon Hollis
Secretary: Brian Berger **(T)** 07717 625 791 **(E)** farnboroughfc@btinternet.com
Additional Committee Members:
Amanda Hollis, Aidan Whelan, Dave Riche.

Manager: Garry Haylock
Programme Editor: Russell Turner **(E)** russell_turner279@hotmail.co.uk

Club Factfile

Founded: 1967 **Nickname:** Boro
Previous Names: Farnborough Town 1967-2007
Previous Leagues: Surrey Senior 1968-72, Spartan 1972-76, Athenian 1976-77, Isthmian 1977-89, 99-2001, Alliance/Conference 1989-90, 91-93, 94-99, Southern 1990-91, 93-94, 2007-10

Club Colours (change): Yellow/yellow/yellow & blue hoops (All white, red & black)

Ground: Rushmoor Stadium, Cherrywood Road, Farnborough, Hants GU14 8UD **(T)** 01252 541 469
Capacity: 4,163 **Seats:** 627 **Covered:** 1,350 **Clubhouse:** Yes **Shop:** Yes

Directions Leave the M3 at Junction 4 and take the A331 signed to Farnham, after a few hundred yards exit at the second slip road- signed A325 Farnborough, turn right at the roundabout and cross over the dual carriageway and small roundabout, passing the Farnborough Gate shopping centre on your left hand side, at the next roundabout turn left (first exit) onto the A325. Go over a pelican crossing and at the next set of lights take the right filter into Prospect Avenue. At the end of this road turn rightat the roundabout into Cherrywood Road, the ground is half a mile on the right hand side.

Previous Grounds: None as Farnborough. Queens Road as Farnborough Town

Record Attendance: 2,230 v Corby Town - Southern Premier 21/03/2009
Record Victory: 7-0 v Newport (I.O.W.) (A) - Southern League Division 1 South & West 01/12/2007
Record Defeat: 0-4 v Hednesford Town (A) - Southern League Premier Division 04/03/2010
Record Goalscorer: Dean McDonald - 35 (in 53+3 Appearances 2009-10)
Record Appearances: Nic Ciardini - 147 (2007-10)
Additional Records:

Senior Honours: Southern League Division 1 South & West 2007-08, Premier Division 2009-10.
Farnborough Town: Southern League Premier Division 1990-91, 93-94. Isthmian League Division 1 1984-85, Premier Division 2000-01. Hampshire Senior Cup 1974-75, 81-82, 83-84, 85-86, 90-91, 2003-04.

10 YEAR RECORD

01-02	02-03	03-04	04-05	05-06	06-07	07-08	08-09	09-10	10-11
Conf 7	Conf 13	Conf 20	Conf 21	Conf S 3	Conf S 11	SthW 1	SthP 2	SthP 1	Conf S 2

FARNBOROUGH

No.	Date	Comp	H/A	Opponents	Att:	Result	Goalscorers	Pos
1	Sat-14-Aug	BSS	A	Braintree Town	501	L 0-3		22
2	Tue-17-Aug	BSS	H	Ebbsfleet United	663	L 1-2	McMahon 67	20
3	Sat-21-Aug	BSS	H	Dartford	1016	W 2-1	McDonald 2 (12, 67)	15
4	Tue-24-Aug	BSS	A	Weston-Super-Mare	260	W 2-0	Ibe 50, Bubb 75	8
5	Sat-28-Aug	BSS	A	Basingstoke Town	702	L 0-1		13
6	Mon-30-Aug	BSS	H	Staines Town	660	D 0-0		14
7	Sat-04-Sep	BSS	A	Bishops Stortford	465	W 4-1	Bubb 9, Binns 43, Ibe 45, Smith 49	8
8	Sat-11-Sep	BSS	H	Maidenhead United	603	D 2-2	Booth 23, Holloway 65	11
9	Sat-18-Sep	BSS	A	Dover Athletic	973	L 3-6	Booth 6, Ibe 2 (37, 60)	13
10	Sat-02-Oct	BSS	H	Lewes	886	W 1-0	Ibe 45	10
11	Sat-16-Oct	BSS	A	Hampton & Richmond Borough	611	W 4-0	Ibe 20, J King 2 (24, 86), Sankofa 60	8
12	Sat-30-Oct	BSS	H	Chelmsford City	651	W 3-1	Ibe 50, J King 68, Og (Tann) 81	8
13	Sat-06-Nov	BSS	A	Bromley	818	D 0-0		7
14	Tue-09-Nov	BSS	A	St Albans City	232	W 2-0	J King 2 (69, 88)	6
15	Sat-13-Nov	BSS	H	Hampton & Richmond Borough	761	W 2-0	Ibe 9, McMahon 57	5
16	Sat-27-Nov	BSS	H	Welling United	651	D 2-2	Binns 21, Smith 70	4
17	Sat-11-Dec	BSS	A	Havant & Waterlooville	693	W 3-0	Binns 32, Booth 35, J King 75	3
18	Tue-28-Dec	BSS	H	Basingstoke Town	1011	D 1-1	Bubb 55	3
19	Sat-01-Jan	BSS	H	Eastleigh	744	L 1-2	Bubb 6	4
20	Mon-03-Jan	BSS	A	Staines Town	511	W 2-1	McMahon 24, Bubb 58	3
21	Sat-15-Jan	BSS	H	Dover Athletic	748	W 4-1	Bubb 3 (36, 38, pen 74), Malcolm 86	3
22	Wed-19-Jan	BSS	H	Bishops Stortford	438	W 3-2	Bubb 2 (40, pen 66), Malcolm 76	2
23	Sat-22-Jan	BSS	A	Dartford	1010	L 1-4	Bubb 20	4
24	Sat-29-Jan	BSS	H	Havant & Waterlooville	704	W 2-0	Og (Pearce) 77, Bubb 89	3
25	Sat-05-Feb	BSS	A	Ebbsfleet United	990	W 3-0	Bubb pen 2, Ibe 61, Booth 67	2
26	Wed-09-Feb	BSS	H	Boreham Wood	432	L 0-1		2
27	Sat-12-Feb	BSS	A	Thurrock	238	W 4-2	McDonald 8, Ibe 2 (12, 30), Smith 48	2
28	Sat-19-Feb	BSS	H	St Albans City	601	W 1-0	Smith 76	2
29	Sat-26-Feb	BSS	H	Dorchester Town	809	W 2-0	Bubb 64, Malcolm 67	3
30	Sat-05-Mar	BSS	A	Woking	2123	D 1-1	Binns 90	4
31	Sat-12-Mar	BSS	H	Braintree Town	942	W 2-1	Ibe 21, Smith 30	3
32	Sat-19-Mar	BSS	A	Lewes	792	W 5-1	Booth 3 (3, 5, 39), J King 34, Ibe 84	2
33	Tue-22-Mar	BSS	A	Maidenhead United	368	W 3-0	Ibe 8, J King 28, McMahon 89	2
34	Sat-26-Mar	BSS	H	Weston-Super-Mare	604	W 2-0	Holloway 5, Malcolm 88	2
35	Tue-29-Mar	BSS	A	Boreham Wood	235	W 4-2	Booth 2 (pen 9, pen 18), Ibe 53, Bubb 85	2
36	Sat-02-Apr	BSS	H	Bromley	777	D 2-2	J King 2 (16, 23)	2
37	Tue-05-Apr	BSS	A	Eastleigh	571	W 3-0	Malcolm 35, Booth 2 (48, 74)	2
38	Sat-09-Apr	BSS	A	Welling United	807	L 0-1		2
39	Sat-16-Apr	BSS	A	Chelmsford City	941	W 1-0	Binns 69	2
40	Sat-23-Apr	BSS	H	Woking	1879	L 1-2	McDonald 84	2
41	Mon-25-Apr	BSS	A	Dorchester Town	642	L 1-2	J King 80	2
42	Sat-30-Apr	BSS	H	Thurrock	839	W 3-2	Bubb 2 (7, 61), Malcolm 15	2

CUPS

No.	Date	Comp	H/A	Opponents	Att:	Result	Goalscorers
1	Sat-25-Sep	FAC2Q	A	Chippenham Town	486	W 1-0	Bubb 11
2	Sat-09-Oct	FAC 3Q	H	Hamble ASSC	503	W 2-0	Bubb 2 (29, 60)
3	Sat-23-Oct	FAC 4Q	H	Dover Athletic	845	D 1-1	J King 22
4	Tue-26-Oct	FAC 4QR	A	Dover Athletic	1044	L 0-5	
5	Sat-20-Nov	FAT 3Q	A	Braintree Town	255	L 0-2	
6	Wed-04-May	PO SF 1	A	Woking	2726	W 1-0	Holloway 71
7	Sun-08-May	PO SF 2	H	Woking	2137	D 1-1 aet	McDonald 111
8	Sun-15-May	PO Final	H	Ebbsfleet United	4267	L 2-4	McMahon 88, Booth 90

League
Starts
Substitute
Unused Sub

Cups
Starts
Substitute
Unused Sub

Goals (Lg)
Goals (Cup)

JORDAN	BRAHAM-BARRETT	OPINEL	J KING	STEVE ROBINSON	SMITH	CIARDINI	WOLLEASTON	BUBB	MCDONALD	MCCOLLIN	IBE	BINNS	FERGUSON	PRICE	STEVENS	CONROY	MCMAHON	JEAN-ZEPHIRIN	HOLLOWAY	BOOTH	ASPIN	THOMAS	SANKOFA	FROSTICK	L KING	WILSON	CROWELL	MALCOLM	STUART ROBINSON	WALLACE	DAVIES
X	X	X	X	X	X	X	X	X	X	X	S	S	S	U	U																
X			X	X	X	X	X	X	X	S	X	S	U	U	U	X	X														
			X	U	X	X	U	X	X	S	X	S	S		X	X	X	X	X												
	S		X		X	X	U	X	X		X	S	S	U	X	X	X	X	X												
	U		X	X		X	U	X	X		X	S	U		X	X	X	X	X	S											
	X		S	X		U	X	X	X		X	S	S		X	X	X	X	X	U											
	X		X		X	S	U	X	U		X	X	S	S		X	X	X	X	X											
	X		X		X	U	U	X			X	X	S	U			X	X	X	X	X	U									
U	X		X	X	U	U		X			X	X		U			X	X	X	X		U	X								
X	S		X	X		X		X	S		X	X		U		X	S		X	X		U	X								
X	U		X	X		X		X	X		X	S		S	U	X	X		X	S			X								
X	X		X	X	X	U		X	S		X	U		U	X	X	X	U	X												
X	X		X	X	X	U		X	U		X	U		U	X	X	X		X	S											
X	X		X	X	X	U		X	U		X	S		U	X	X	X		X	S											
X	X		X		X	U		S	X		X	X		S	X	X	X		X	S			U								
X	X		X	X	X	U			X		X	X			X		X		X	S											
X	X		X	X	X	S		S	X		S	X			U		X		X	X			X								
X	X		X	X		U		S	X		S	X			X				X	X			X				X	S			
X	X		X	X	X	X		X			U	S			U		X		X	U							X	X			
X	X		X	X		S		X			X				X		X		X	X								X			
X	X		X	X	S	S		X	U		X	S		U		X	X		X	X								X			
X	X		X	X	X	U		X	U		X	S		X		X	X			U			U					X			
X	X		X	X	X	S		X	S		S	U		U		X	X		X	X								X			
	U			X		X		X	S		X	X		X		X	X		X	S			X					S	X	U	
X	S		X	X	S	X		X	U		X	X		U			X		X	X			X					S			
X	U		X	X	X	X		S	X		X	X		U						X			X					X	U		
X	X		X	X	X	X		X	X		X	S		X					X	S		S	U					U			
X	X		X	X	X	X		S	X		X	S		X					X	S		X	U					U			
X	X		X	X	X	U		X	X		S	S		U					X	X		S	X					X			
X	X		X	X	X	U		X	X		X	X		U					X	S		S	X					S			
X	X		X	X	X			X	U		X	X		U	S		X		X	S			X					S			
X	X		X	X	X	U			S		X	X		S	U		X		X	X			X					S			
X	X		X	X	X	U			S		X	X		U	U		X		X	X			X					S			
X	X		X	X	X	S			U		X	X		U	S		X		X	X			X					S			
X	X		X	X		S		S	U		X	X		U	X		X		X	X			X					S			
X	X		X	X		X		S	U		X	X		U	X		X		X	X								S			S
X			X		X	X		X	S			X				X	X		X	X			S					X	U		S
X	S		X	X		X			S		X	X			U	X	X		X	X			U					X			S
X	X		X	X	X	U		U	U			X			S	X	X		X	X								X			U
X	X		X	X	X	U			S			X		U	U	X	X		X	X								X			S
X	X		X		X	U			X			X		U	X	U	S		X	X			X					S			X
X	X		X		X	U		X	S		X			S		X	X		X	S			U					X			X
X	S		X	X		X		X			X	X		S		X		U	X	X		U	X	U							
X	U		X	X	X	X		X	X		X	S		S	U	X	X	U	X	S			U								
X	U		X	X	S	X		X	X		X	S		U	U	X	X	U	X	U			X								
X	U		X	X	U	X		X	X		U	X		U	U	X	X	U	X	U			X								
X	X		X	U	X	U			X		X	X		U	X	X	X		X	S			U								
X	X		X	X	X			X	U		X				S	X	X		X	S								X	U		S
X	X		X	X	X			X	S		X	X			S		X			S			X					X	U		U
X	X		X	X	X			X	S		X	X			U		X			S			X					X	U		S
34	31	1	40	34	29	16	3	27	17	1	32	23	0	4	14	21	33	7	38	22	1	1	16	0	0	0	2	12	1	0	2
0	4	0	1	0	2	7	0	7	10	2	5	14	6	5	3	0	2	0	0	12	0	3	1	0	0	0	0	11	0	0	4
1	4	0	0	1	1	18	5	1	11	0	1	3	2	22	9	1	0	1	0	3	0	3	6	0	0	0	0	2	2	1	1
8	4	0	8	7	5	4	0	7	4	0	7	5	0	0	1	6	7	0	6	1	0	0	5	0	0	0	0	3	0	0	0
0	1	0	0	0	1	0	0	0	2	0	0	2	0	2	2	0	0	0	0	5	0	0	0	0	0	0	0	0	0	0	2
0	3	0	0	1	1	1	0	0	1	0	1	0	0	3	4	0	0	4	0	2	0	1	2	1	0	0	0	0	3	0	1
0	0	0	11	0	5	0	0	17	4	0	15	5	0	0	0	0	4	0	2	11	0	0	1	0	0	0	0	6	0	0	0
0	0	0	1	0	0	0	0	3	1	0	0	0	0	0	0	0	1	0	1	1	0	0	0	0	0	0	0	0	0	0	0

PLAYING SQUAD 2011/12

Existing Players		SN	HT	WT	DOB	AGE	POB	Career	Apps	Goals
GOALKEEPERS										
Jake	Somerville							Farnborough		
Alex	Tokarczyk							Hayes & Yeading, C.Palace (Trial) 5/09, Farnborough 8/11		
Defenders										
Billy	Barnes							Farnborough		
Doug	Bergqvist		6'00"	13 07	29/03/1993	18	Stockholm, Swe	Reading (Yth), QPR (Yth), Aldershot, Thatcham (WE) 1/11, Dorchester (WE) 2/11, Dorchester (L) 3/11, Farnborough (6ML) 7/11		
Adam	Bygrave		5'09"	12 02	24/02/1989	22	Walthamstow	Reading Rel c/s 08, Gillingham (SL) 11/07, Weymouth 5/08, Histon £5,000 1/09, Hayes & Yeading 8/10, Farnborough 6/11		
Jordan	Chandler							Oxford U (Yth), Ascot U, Farnborough 8/11		
Joel	Jacobs							Farnborough		
Esmond	James				04/02/1990	21		Hayes & Yeading, Farnborough 6/11		
Ben	Myers							Farnborough		
MIDFIELDERS										
Phil	Appiah				25/10/1989	21	Toronto, Can	Fulham (Jun), Preston Rel c/s 09, Hayes & Yeading 8/10, Hemel Hempstead (Dual) 10/10, Farnborough 7/11		
Kevin	Asare-Addai							Farnborough		
Callum	Cobb							Farnborough		
Brad	Fraser							Farnborough		
Matt	Pattison				24/03/1984	27	Surrey	Camberley, Farnborough 7/03, Woking 6/07 Rel 5/09, Rushden & D 6/09 Rel 5/10, Basingstoke 5/10 Rel 5/11, Farnborough 8/11		
Josh	Pearson							Aldershot (Scholar), AFC Wimbledon, Farnborough, Fleet T (L) 2/11		
Nathan	Webb				05/06/1992	19		Hayes & Yeading Rel 8/11, Farnborough 8/11		
Ashley	Winn		5'11"	11 02	01/12/1985	25	Stockton	Middlesbrough (Yth), Oldham Rel 5/05, York C 8/05 Rel 5/06, Stalybridge (L) 3/06, Stalybridge 7/06, Barrow 7/08, Southport (L) 12/08, Southport 1/09, Gateshead (2ML) 11/10 £2,500 1/11, Farnborough 7/11		
FORWARDS										
Reece	Connolly		6'00"	11 09	22/01/1992	19	Frimley	C.Palace (Jun), Aldershot, Salisbury (SL) 1/10, Didcot T (2ML) 10/10, Dorchester (SL) 2/11, Farnborough (6ML) 7/11		
Tony	Garrod		6'02"	11 08	14/09/1991	19	Crawley	Southampton Rel c/s 11, Bishops Stortford (L) 2/11, Farnborough 7/11		
Kunjan	Gurung						Pokhara, Nepal	Farnborough		
Tom	Murphy		5'11"	10 12	19/12/1991	19	Gillingham	Gillingham (Scholar) Rel c/s 10, Ashford T (WE) 1/10, Lewes 8/10 Rel 2/11, Thurrock 2/11, Horsham (Trial) 7/11, Farnborough 8/11		

HAMPTON & RICHMOND BOROUGH

Chairman: Steve McPherson
Secretary: Nick Hornsey **(T)** 07768 861 446 **(E)** hrbfcsecretary@gmail.com
Additional Committee Members:
Quenton Hire, Nick Lyon, Chas Milner, Kevin Childs, Stefan Rance

Manager: Mark Harper
Programme Editor: Stefan Rance **(E)** stef_hrbfc@hotmail.com

Front Row (L-R): Dean Inman, Billy Jeffreys, Lewis Ferrell, Andy Smith (Assistant Manager), Mark Harper (Manager), Nigel Edgecombe (Coach), Matt Ruby, Charlie Moone, Gustavo Sousa Mota.
Middle Row: Nathan Collier, Callum Stewart, Paul Johnson, Dan Thompson, Matt Lovett, Luke Edgecombe, Rondey Chiweshe, Josh Huggins, Jonny Sutton, Trevor Adij, Ricky Machel.
Back Row: Malcolm Taylor (Kit Man), James Walters, Joe Kelly, Stuart Duff, James Simmonds, Dave Tarpey, Darrell Ellams, Tom Hickey, Roger Hoare (Physiotherapist).

Club Factfile

Founded: 1921 **Nickname:** Beavers or Borough
Previous Names: Hampton > 1999
Previous Leagues: Kingston & District, South West Middlesex, Surrey Senior 1959-64, Spartan 1964-71, Athenian 1971-73, Isthmian 1973-2007

Club Colours (change): Red & blue/red/red (Sky blue & white/black/sky blue)

Ground: Beveree Stadium, Beaver Close, Station Road, Hampton TW12 2BX **(T)** 0208 8979 2456
Capacity: 3,000 **Seats:** 300 **Covered:** 800 **Clubhouse:** Yes **Shop:** Yes

Directions
From M25; Exit M25 at Junction 10 (M3 Richmond). Exit M3 at Junction 1 and take 4th exit (Kempton Park, Kingston). After approximately 3 miles turn left in to High Street, Hampton. Immediately turn left on to Station Road. The entrance to the ground is 200 yards on the right hand side.

Previous Grounds: Not known

Record Attendance: 2,520 v AFC Wimbledon - 11/10/2005
Record Victory: 11-1 v Eastbourne United - Isthmian League Division 2 South 1991-92
Record Defeat: 0-13 v Hounslow Town - Middlesex Senior Cup 1962-63
Record Goalscorer: Peter Allen - 176 (1964-73)
Record Appearances: Tim Hollands - 750 (1977-95)
Additional Records: Paid £3,000 to Chesham United for Matt Flitter June 2000
Received £40,000 from Queens Park Rangers for Leroy Phillips

Senior Honours: Isthmian League Premier Division 2006-07.
Spartan League x4. London Senior Cup x2.

10 YEAR RECORD

01-02	02-03	03-04	04-05	05-06	06-07	07-08	08-09	09-10	10-11
Isth P 20	Isth P 24	Isth1S 5	Isth P 6	Isth P 5	Isth P 1	Conf S 3	Conf S 2	Conf S 14	Conf S 18

HAMPTON & RICHMOND BOROUGH

No.	Date	Comp	H/A	Opponents	Att:	Result	Goalscorers	Pos
1	Sat-14-Aug	BSS	A	Welling United	510	D 0-0		13
2	Tue-17-Aug	BSS	H	Dartford	680	W 1-0	Wells 68	7
3	Sat-21-Aug	BSS	H	Bromley	582	L 1-2	Tarpey 65	11
4	Tue-24-Aug	BSS	A	Thurrock	237	D 2-2	Wells 14, Moone 34	13
5	Sat-28-Aug	BSS	A	St Albans City	307	D 1-1	Simmonds 66	11
6	Mon-30-Aug	BSS	H	Dorchester Town	485	D 2-2	Tarpey 69, Yaku 77	12
7	Sat-04-Sep	BSS	A	Lewes	694	W 2-1	Og (Manning) 33, Moone 79	9
8	Sat-11-Sep	BSS	H	Havant & Waterlooville	512	L 0-1		13
9	Sat-18-Sep	BSS	A	Bishops Stortford	349	W 2-0	Yaku 7, Matthews pen 32	8
10	Sat-02-Oct	BSS	H	Dover Athletic	629	W 3-2	Hodges 2, Moone 2 (31, 36)	7
11	Sat-16-Oct	BSS	H	Farnborough	611	L 0-4		10
12	Sat-23-Oct	BSS	A	Weston-Super-Mare	238	D 0-0		9
13	Sat-30-Oct	BSS	H	Woking	796	L 1-2	Inman 17	9
14	Sat-06-Nov	BSS	A	Boreham Wood	152	D 2-2	Hodges 9, Inman 74	9
15	Tue-09-Nov	BSS	H	Eastleigh	342	D 2-2	Stevens 32, Yaku 90	9
16	Sat-13-Nov	BSS	A	Farnborough	761	L 0-2		12
17	Sat-01-Jan	BSS	H	Staines Town	694	D 0-0		15
18	Mon-03-Jan	BSS	A	Dorchester Town	451	D 2-2	Moone 2 (54, 73)	15
19	Tue-11-Jan	BSS	A	Ebbsfleet United	679	L 0-1		16
20	Sat-22-Jan	BSS	A	Braintree Town	506	L 1-3		16
21	Sat-29-Jan	BSS	H	Basingstoke Town	335	D 2-2	Hodges 2 (22, 84)	18
22	Tue-01-Feb	BSS	H	Ebbsfleet United	295	L 2-4	Simmonds pen 45, Tarpey 84	19
23	Sat-05-Feb	BSS	H	St Albans City	404	D 0-0		19
24	Sat-12-Feb	BSS	H	Welling United	429	L 0-1		20
25	Tue-15-Feb	BSS	H	Lewes	299	L 1-2	Matthews 49	20
26	Sat-19-Feb	BSS	A	Dartford	1043	W 4-0	Wells 24, Hodges 39, Yaku 2 (46, 50)	17
27	Tue-01-Mar	BSS	A	Staines Town	251	W 2-1	Tarpey 2 (39, 60)	16
28	Sat-05-Mar	BSS	A	Dover Athletic	826	L 0-1		18
29	Tue-08-Mar	BSS	H	Chelmsford City	303	W 3-0	Tarpey 56, Moone 73, Simmonds pen 83	15
30	Sat-12-Mar	BSS	H	Weston-Super-Mare	442	L 0-1		16
31	Tue-15-Mar	BSS	A	Woking	1037	L 1-2	Thompson 52	16
32	Sat-19-Mar	BSS	H	Thurrock	365	D 0-0		16
33	Sat-26-Mar	BSS	A	Bromley	374	W 2-1	Tarpey 58, Simmonds 81	15
34	Tue-29-Mar	BSS	H	Maidenhead United	315	D 1-1	Yaku 61	15
35	Sat-02-Apr	BSS	H	Boreham Wood	419	D 0-0		15
36	Tue-05-Apr	BSS	H	Bishops Stortford	261	L 0-3		15
37	Sat-09-Apr	BSS	A	Maidenhead United	341	D 0-0		15
38	Mon-11-Apr	BSS	A	Havant & Waterlooville	378	W 2-1	Yaku 2 (26, 52)	15
39	Sat-16-Apr	BSS	A	Basingstoke Town	360	L 0-4		15
40	Fri-22-Apr	BSS	H	Braintree Town	607	L 0-1		16
41	Mon-25-Apr	BSS	A	Eastleigh	454	L 0-3		17
42	Sat-30-Apr	BSS	A	Chelmsford City	1178	L 1-3	Witham 59	18

CUPS

No.	Date	Comp	H/A	Opponents	Att:	Result	Goalscorers
1	Sat-25-Sep	FAC 2Q	A	Romford	193	W 4-0	Inman 18, Hodges 33, Matthews pen 75, Tarpey 87
2	Sat-09-Oct	FAC 3Q	A	Harrow Borough	342	L 1-2	Yarney 63
3	Sat-20-Nov	FAT 3Q	A	Bognor Regis Town	376	D 2-2	Hodges 32, Inman 74
4	Tue-23-Nov	FAT 3QR	H	Bognor Regis Town	200	W 2-0	Jeffrey 70, Yaku 89
5	Sat-11-Dec	FAT 1	A	AFC Sudbury	379	W 4-1	Robinson 2, Yaku 40, Simmonds 48, Hodges 61
6	Sat-15-Jan	FAT 2	A	Gateshead	336	L 0-6	

League
Starts
Substitute
Unused Sub

Cups
Starts
Substitute
Unused Sub

Goals (Lg)
Goals (Cup)

LOVETT	ALLEN-PAGE	TANNER	INMAN	STEVENS	WELLS	SIMMONDS	COLLIER	HODGES	TARPEY	MATTHEWS	MOONE	AHMAD	ADAMS	LUCIEN	GIBBS	GOODMAN	YAKU	ROBINSON	WITHAM	JEFFREY	ROCHESTER	BOATENG	YARNIE	BEADLE	O'BRIEN	TALBOT	LETTEJALLOW	O'CONNOR	CARPENTER	ELLAMS	QUARM	HOLNESS	HARPER	DUFF	THOMPSON	THOMAS	SOUSA-MOTA	STONE	JOHNSON	MULLAN	BRAITHWAITE
X	X	X	X	X	X	X	X	X	X	X	S	S	U	U	U																										
X	X	X		X	X	X	X	X	X	X	S	S	U	U	S	X																									
X	X	X	X	X	X	X	X		X	X	X	S		S	U		S																								
X	X	X	X	X	X	X	X		X	X	X			S	U	S	S	U																							
X	X	X	X	X	X	X	X	S	X	X	X		U	U			S	U																							
X		X	X	X	X	X	X	S	X	X	X		X	S	U		S		U																						
X	X	X	X	X	X	X	X	U	X	X	X		S	U			S			S																					
X	X		X	X	X	X	X	S	X	X	X		X	S			S				U	U																			
X	X		X	X	X	X	X	X	S	X	S		U	U			X	U				X																			
X	X	X	X	X			X	X	S	X	X		S	U			U			X	U	X																			
X	X			X	X	X	X	X	X	X	U		U				X			X			S	S	S																
X	X	X	X	X	X	X		S	S	X	X		U	U			X			X				U																	
X	X	X	X	X		X		S	X	S	X		U				S			X	U	X		X																	
		X	X	X		X	X	X	U	U	X		X				S			X		X	S	U		X															
		X	X	X		X	X	X	S	U	U		X				S			X		X	X	S		X															
		X	X	X		X	X		X	X	X		U				U			X	S	X	S	S		X															
		X	X	X	X	X	X	X	U	U	S		U				X			X						X	S	X													
		X	X	X	X	X	U		X	U	X		X				S			U	U					X	X	X													
				X	X	X	X	S	X	X	X		S				S			X	U						X	X	X	U											
		X	X	X	X	X	X	X	S	U	X						S			X	U			S			X		X												
X		X	X		X	X	X	X	U	X	X						S			X	U						S		U		X										
X		X	X		X	X	X	X	S	X	X						S			X	S						U		U		X										
X		X	X		X	X	X	X	S	X	X									X	U		U				X														
X		X	X		X	X	X	X	X	U	S						S			X	U						U	X				X									
X		X	X		X		X	X	S	X	S						X			U	U						U	X			X	X									
X		X	X		X		X	X	S	X	U						X			X	U						S	X			X										
X		X	X		X	X		X	X	X	X			S					U		S							X		S		X	U								
X		X	X		X	S		X	X	X	S			U						X	U							X			X	X		U							
X			X		X	X		X	X	X	X			S					S	X	U							X			X	U	S								
X			X		X	X		X	X		X									X	S							X			X	U	X		S	U					
X			X		X	X		X	X		X						S			X	U							X			X		X		S		U				
X		X	X		X	X			X	S	X						X			X	U							X			X		U			S	U				
		X	X		X	X			X	X	X						S				U										X		X	S			U	X	X	S	
X			X		X	X			X	U	X						X		U	X											X		X	S				U	X	U	
X			X		X	X	S	S	X	S	X						X			X	U										X		X					U	X		
X		X	X			X	S	X	X	S	X						S		U	X											X		X					U	X		
X		X	X		X		X		S	S	X						X			X	U		S			U					X		X						X		
X			X		X		X		X	X	X						X			X	S		S			U				S							X	U	X		
X		S	X		X		X	S	X	X	X						X		U	X	U		S														X		X		
X		X	X				X	X	X	S	S						X		X	X	U		S								X		U						X		
X			X			X	X	X	S	X	U						X		X	X	U		S										X						X		S
		X	X	U		X	X		S								X		X	U	X		S			X					X		U						X		X
X	X		X	X	X	X	X	X	S	X	S		U				X	U		S	U	X																			
X	X	X	X	X	X	X	X		X		X		U	U			S		U		U	X	S	S																	
		X	X	X		X	S	X	X	X			U				U			X		X	U	S		X	X														
		X	X	X		X	X	X	X				X				S			X	U	U	S	S		X	X														
		X			X	X	X	X	S	S	U		X				X			X		U	S			X	X	X													
U		X	X	X	X		X	X	S	X	U		X				X			X	S						S		X												
33	12	30	39	20	33	34	29	23	27	26	29	0	5	0	0	1	15	0	3	28	1	6	1	1	0	6	4	12	2	0	16	4	8	0	0	0	2	1	10	0	1
0	0	1	0	0	0	1	2	8	12	6	8	3	3	6	1	1	18	0	1	1	5	0	9	4	1	0	3	0	0	2	0	0	1	2	2	1	0	0	0	1	1
0	0	0	0	1	0	0	1	1	3	7	4	0	9	8	4	0	2	3	5	3	21	1	1	2	0	2	3	0	2	1	0	2	4	1	0	1	3	4	0	1	0
2	2	5	5	5	4	5	5	5	3	3	1	0	3	0	0	0	3	0	0	4	0	3	0	0	0	3	3	1	1	0	0	0	0	0	0	0	0	0	0	0	0
0	0	0	0	0	0	0	1	0	3	1	1	0	0	0	0	0	2	0	0	1	1	0	3	3	0	0	1	0	0	0	0	0	0	0	0	0	0	0	0	0	0
1	0	0	0	0	0	0	0	0	0	0	2	0	3	1	0	0	1	1	1	0	3	2	1	0	0	0	0	0	0	0	0	0	0	0	0	0	0	0	0	0	0
0	0	0	2	1	3	4	0	5	7	2	7	0	0	0	0	0	8	0	1	0	0	0	0	0	0	0	0	0	0	0	0	0	0	0	1	0	0	0	0	0	0
0	0	0	2	0	0	1	0	3	1	1	0	0	0	0	0	0	2	1	0	1	0	0	0	0	0	0	0	0	0	0	0	0	0	0	0	0	0	0	0	0	0

PLAYING SQUAD 2011/12

Existing Players		SN	HT	WT	DOB	AGE	POB	Career	Apps	Goals
GOALKEEPERS										
Rodney	Chiweshe							QPR (Yth), Staines, Aldershot T, Godalming, Woking (Trial) c/s 09, Hampton & R 8/11		
Matt	Lovett				05/09/1979	31	Middlesex	Staines, Hampton & R 6/05	33	0
Defenders										
Darrell	Ellams		5'10"	10 07	03/11/1989	21		Wycombe Rel c/s 09, Hitchin (3ML) 11/08, Enfield T 8/09, Hampton & R 8/10	2	0
Lewis	Ferrell		6'00"	10 07	08/03/1991	20		Brentford, Hayes & Yeading 8/10, Hampton & R 7/11		
Dean	Inman				25/10/1990	20		Hampton & R, Chertsey (3ML) 8/09, QPR (Trial) 8/11	39	2
Billy	Jeffreys		6'03"	12 05				Millwall (Scholar) Rel c/s 08, Ashford T (Middx) c/s 08, Hampton & R 7/11		
Ricky	Machel				22/05/1987	24		QPR (Yth), Beaconsfield SYCOB, Belhaven College (USA) c/s 05, Mississippi Brilla (USA), AFC Hayes, Northwood 2/11, Hampton & R 8/11		
Matt	Ruby				18/03/1986	25	Chertsey	Woking Rel 8/08, Northwood (L) 10/05, Fleet T (L) 1/06, Basingstoke (L) 3/06, Walton & H (L) 8/06, Bognor Regis (L) 3/07, Hayes & Yeading 8/08 (09/10 41,1), Havant & W 8/10 Rel 8/10, Kingstonian 10/10, Chertsey (L) 11/10, Hampton & R 6/11		
Callum	Stewart		5'09"	12 06	01/10/1990	20	Cambridge	Ipswich (Yth), Histon Rel 5/11, Fulham (Trial) 4/10, Hampton & R 7/11		
James	Walters							Bedfont T, Uxbridge 2/11, Hampton & R 8/11		
Billy	Witham				07/07/1993	18		Hampton & R, Ashford T (Middx) (Dual) 7/11	4	1
MIDFIELDERS										
Nathan	Collier				15/08/1985	26		Hampton & R	31	0
Gary	Frewen				21/11/1990	20		Reading Rel c/s 09, Basingstoke 8/09, Walton & H (Dual) 11/10, Hayes & Yeading (Trial) 7/11, Hampton & R 8/11		
Tom	Hickey							Camberley, Hampton & R 8/11		
Paul	Johnson				10/06/1982	29	London	Wimbledon (Yth), Chelsea (Yth), QPR (Yth), Wycombe (Scholar), Hendon 8/00, Edgware 10/01, Staines 11/01, Tooting & M (L) 11/03, Ashford T (Middx) 12/03, Carshalton 5/10, Hampton & R 3/11	10	0
Joe	Kelly							Hampton & R		
Aaron	Morgan							Cambridge U (Yth), Southend, California State University (USA), Hampton & R 8/11		
Jack	Mullan							Hampton & R, Ashford T (Middx) (L) 7/11	1	0
James	Simmonds				03/12/1987	23	Hammersmith	Chelsea, Glen Hoddle Academy, Écija Balompié (Spa), Hampton & R 3/10, Carshalton 6/11, Hampton & R 7/11	35	4
Gustavo	Sousa-Mota				15/06/1993	18		Hampton & R	2	0
Ed	Thomas							Hampton & R		
FORWARDS										
Stuart	Duff							Hampton & R	2	0
Jacob	Erskine		6'01"	14 00	13/01/1989	22	Lambeth	Croydon A, Wingate & F 10/07, Dag & Red 10/07 Rel c/s 09, Tooting & M (L), 12/07, Maidstone (L) 1/08, Margate (L) 12/08, Sutton U (L) 1/09, Dorchester (6WL) 3/09, Bromley 6/09, Gillingham 8/09, Bromley (L) 10/09, Bishops Stortford (L) 2/10, Croydon Ath (SL) 3/10, Concord R 7/10, Forest Green 1/11, Swindon Supermarine (SL) 1/11, Ebbsfleet 2/11, Bromley (Trial) 7/11, Hampton & R 8/11		
Charlie	Moone				14/11/1988	22		Woking Rel 5/10, Walton & H (L) 9/09, Hampton & R 8/10	37	7
Leon	Simpson		6'10"		28/02/1985	26		Hitchin, St Neots 7/09, Aylesbury 8/09, Merstham 9/09, Farnborough 11/09, Leatherhead 12/09, St Albans 8/10 Rel 8/10, Brackley 8/10, Barton R 10/10, Rugby T 2/11, Hampton & R 8/11		
David	Tarpey				14/11/1988	22		C.Palace (Yth), Basingstoke 8/06 Rel 5/09, Hampton & R 7/09, Walton & H (Dual) 9/09	39	7
Dan	Thompson							Hampton & R	3	1

HAVANT AND WATERLOOVILLE

Chairman: Derek Pope
Secretary: Trevor Brock **(T)** 07768 271 143 **(E)** trevor.brock52@yahoo.com
Additional Committee Members:
Ray Jones, Adrian Hewett , Kevin Moore, Michael Jenkins, Adrian Aymes

Manager: Shaun Gale
Programme Editor: Adrian Aymes **(E)** aaymes2125@aol.com

Club Factfile

Founded: 1998 **Nickname:** Hawks
Previous Names: Havant Town and Waterlooville merged in 1998
Previous Leagues: Southern 1998-2004

Club Colours (change): Blue & white hoops/white/white (Yellow & blue/blue/yellow)

Ground: Westleigh Park, Martin Road, West Leigh, Havant PO9 5TH **(T)** 02392 787 822
Capacity: 4,800 **Seats:** 562 **Covered:** 3,500 **Clubhouse:** Yes **Shop:** Yes

Directions
Ground is a mile and a half from Havant Town Centre. Take A27 to Havant then turn onto B2149 (Petersfield Road). Turn right at next junction after HERON pub into Bartons Road then take first right into Martin Road.

Previous Grounds: Not known

Record Attendance: 4,400 v Swansea City - FA Cup 3rd Round 05/01/2008
Record Victory: 9-0 v Moneyfields - Hampshire Senior Cup 23/10/2001
Record Defeat: 0-5 v Worcester City - Southern Premier 20/03/2004
Record Goalscorer: James Taylor - 138
Record Appearances: James Taylor - 297
Additional Records: Paid £5,000 to Bashley for John Wilson
Received £15,000 from Peterborough United for Gary McDonald

Senior Honours: Southern League Southern Division 1998-99. Russell Cotes Cup 2003-04

10 YEAR RECORD

01-02	02-03	03-04	04-05	05-06	06-07	07-08	08-09	09-10	10-11
SthP 3	SthP 8	SthP 12	Conf S 13	Conf S 6	Conf 4	Conf S 7	Conf S 15	Conf S 6	Conf S 9

HAVANT & WATERLOOVILLE

No.	Date	Comp	H/A	Opponents	Att:	Result	Goalscorers	Pos
1	Sat-14-Aug	BSS	A	Dartford	1302	D 2-2	Hopkinson pen 45, Fogden 88	10
2	Mon-16-Aug	BSS	H	Weston-Super-Mare	732	D 0-0		9
3	Sat-21-Aug	BSS	H	Welling United	783	L 1-3	Hopkinson pen 52	19
4	Tue-24-Aug	BSS	A	Bromley	525	L 0-1		20
5	Sat-28-Aug	BSS	A	Dorchester Town	488	D 0-0		20
6	Mon-30-Aug	BSS	H	Eastleigh	1020	D 2-2	Igoe 28, Tiryaki 82	18
7	Sat-04-Sep	BSS	H	Thurrock	692	W 4-1	Fogden 2 (44, 90), Williams 48, Tiryaki 64	17
8	Sat-11-Sep	BSS	A	Hampton & Richmond Borough	512	W 1-0	Williams 43	12
9	Sat-18-Sep	BSS	H	St Albans City	755	L 0-1		15
10	Sat-02-Oct	BSS	A	Staines Town	333	W 1-0	Tiryaki 77	11
11	Sat-16-Oct	BSS	A	Bishops Stortford	571	W 5-1	Williams 2 (15, 49), Fogden 3 (42, 66, 84)	9
12	Sat-13-Nov	BSS	A	Welling United	503	W 2-0	Williams 49, Fogden 84	10
13	Mon-15-Nov	BSS	H	Basingstoke Town	613	W 2-0	Sole 2 (11, 90)	8
14	Sat-11-Dec	BSS	H	Farnborough	693	L 0-3		11
15	Sun-26-Dec	BSS	A	Woking	1182	L 1-3	Tiryaki 29	12
16	Sat-01-Jan	BSS	H	Woking	986	D 1-1	Tiryaki 51	13
17	Mon-03-Jan	BSS	A	Eastleigh	822	L 2-4	Cashman 39, Tiryaki 45	13
18	Sat-15-Jan	BSS	A	Weston-Super-Mare	205	D 1-1	Sole 85	13
19	Sat-22-Jan	BSS	H	Boreham Wood	574	W 2-1	Sole 66, Fogden 82	13
20	Sat-29-Jan	BSS	A	Farnborough	704	L 0-2		14
21	Mon-31-Jan	BSS	H	Maidenhead United	518	W 2-1	Williams pen 10, Sole 90	11
22	Sat-05-Feb	BSS	A	Chelmsford City	770	W 2-1	Keehan 28, Pearce 53	10
23	Sat-12-Feb	BSS	H	Ebbsfleet United	857	L 2-3	Keehan 40, Sole 69	13
24	Sat-19-Feb	BSS	A	Lewes	717	L 1-2	Selley 87	13
25	Tue-01-Mar	BSS	A	Maidenhead United	116	W 1-0	Fogden 84	12
26	Sat-05-Mar	BSS	H	Bromley	508	W 2-0	Williams pen 49, Tiryaki 81	11
27	Mon-07-Mar	BSS	H	Dorchester Town	458	W 3-1	Tiryaki 58, Fogden 76, Ramsey 90	10
28	Sat-12-Mar	BSS	A	Ebbsfleet United	879	L 1-2	Fogden 6	11
29	Mon-14-Mar	BSS	H	Braintree Town	582	L 1-2	McDonald 3	11
30	Sat-19-Mar	BSS	H	Bishops Stortford	752	W 4-1	Sole 16, Newton 40, Igoe 47, Fogden 62	11
31	Tue-22-Mar	BSS	A	Thurrock	152	D 1-1	Williams 71	10
32	Sat-26-Mar	BSS	A	Basingstoke Town	325	W 2-0	Fogden 35, Williams pen 40	9
33	Tue-29-Mar	BSS	A	Dover Athletic	656	W 1-0	Sole 5	9
34	Sat-02-Apr	BSS	H	Chelmsford City	820	L 1-2	Sole 9	9
35	Mon-04-Apr	BSS	H	Dover Athletic	528	D 0-0		9
36	Sat-09-Apr	BSS	A	Boreham Wood	168	L 0-1		9
37	Mon-11-Apr	BSS	H	Hampton & Richmond Borough	378	L 1-2	Scott 89	9
38	Sat-16-Apr	BSS	A	Boreham Wood	693	L 0-2		10
39	Mon-18-Apr	BSS	H	Dartford	456	W 1-0	Fogden 33	9
40	Sat-23-Apr	BSS	H	Lewes	464	L 1-2	Tiryaki 67	10
41	Mon-25-Apr	BSS	A	St Albans City	252	D 1-1	Williams 66	9
42	Sat-30-Apr	BSS	H	Staines Town	602	D 1-1	Williams 34	9

CUPS

No.	Date	Comp	H/A	Opponents	Att:	Result	Goalscorers
1	Sat-25-Sep	FAC 2Q	H	Frome Town	448	W 1-0	Williams 63
2	Sat-09-Oct	FAC 3Q	H	Dorchester Town	708	W 4-1	Tiryaki 2 (14, 72), Williams 21, Fogden 52
3	Sat-23-Oct	FAC 4Q	H	Histon	905	W 2-0	Fogden 3, Tiryaki 62
4	Wed-06-Oct	FAC 1	H	Droylsden	1102	L 0-2	
5	Sat-20-Nov	FAT 3Q	A	Basingstoke Town	301	D 2-2	Tiryaki 35, Cashman 50
6	Mon-22-Nov	FAT 3QR	H	Basingstoke Town	353	L 1-2	Fogden 32

League
Starts
Substitute
Unused Sub

Cups
Starts
Substitute
Unused Sub

Goals (Lg)
Goals (Cup)

R MARTIN	NEWTON	MCDONALD	SELLEY	PEARCE	IGOE	SIMPEMBA	HOPKINSON	RAMSEY	TIRYAKI	HINSHELWOOD	FOGDEN	WHYTE	RUBY	SEWELL	ROBSON	HOWE	MOLLOY	WILLIAMS	BALDACCHINO	WOODFORD	ASHMORE	STEFANOVIC	ADELAKUN	GAISIE	SOLE	WILKINSON	UDOJI	CASHMAN	ABNETT	EDWARDS	E MARTIN	GADD	KEEHAN	GILBERT	SCOTT	TYRELL
X	X	X	X	X	X	X	X	X	X	X	S	S	S	U	U																					
	X	X	X		X	X	X	X	X	U	X	S	X	U	U	X	S																			
	X	X	X		X	X	X	U	X	X	X	S	X	U	U	X		S																		
	X			X	X	X	X	X	X	X	X	S		U	X	X	U	S	S																	
	X		U	X	X	X	X		X	X	X	U		S	X	X	U	X	U																	
	X		X	X	X	X	X	S	X	X	X	U		X		X	U	S	U																	
	X		X	X	X	X	X	S	X	X	X	U			S	X	S	X	U																	
	X		X	X	X	X	X	U	X	X	X	U			S	X	S	X	U																	
	X		X	X	X	X	X	S	X	X	X	S		U		X	U	X		U																
	X	S	X	X	X	X		X	X	X	X	U		S	X	X				U	U															
		X		X		X		X	X	X	X			S	X	X		X	U	X	U		S	S												
	X	X	X	X	X	X	S		S	X	X					X		X			U		U		X		S									
	X		S	X	S	X	X		X	X	X			S		X		X			U		U		X		X									
	X	X	X		X			S		X	X			S		X		X		X	U				X		S	X		U						
	X			X	U	X	X	S	X	X	X			S		X		X	U	X	U							X								
	X	X		X	X	X	X	X	X	S	X			U		X		X			U				S			S								
	X	X		X		X	X		X	U	X			S		X		X	U		U				X			X		U						
	X	X	S	X		X	X	S	X	X	X			U		X		X			U				X					U						
	X	X	X	X		X	X	S	X	X	X			U		X					U				X						S	U				
	X	X	X	X		X		U	X	X	X					X		S			U				X						S	U	X			
	X	X	X	X		X		X	S	X	X					U		X			X				X						U	U	U			
	X	X	X	X		X		S	S	X	X					X		X			U				X			S			U		X			
	X	X	X	X	S	X		X		X						X		X			U				X						U	U	X	U		
	X	X	X		S	X		X	S	X	X					U		X			X							X			U		X		U	
	X	X	X	X	S	X		X	X	X	X					U		X			X												S		U	U
	X		X	X	S	X		X	S	X	X					U		X			X				X			X					S			U
	X		S	X	X	X		X	S	X	X					U		X	U		X				X										S	X
	X		X	X	X	X		X	X	X	X				U	U			U		X				S										U	X
	X	X	S	X	X	X		X	X	X	X				U	U					X				X										U	U
	X	X	S	X	X	X		X	X	X	X				U	U					X				X										S	S
	X	X	S	X	X	X		X	X	X	X					U		S			X				X										U	S
	X	X	X	U	X	X		X	S		X					X		X			U				S			X							S	X
	X		X	X	X			X		X	X			S	S	X		X	U		U				X										U	X
	X		X	X	X			X		X	X	U		S	S	X		X			U				X										U	X
	X		X	X	X	X		X	S	X	X			U	U	X		X			U				X										U	
	X		X	X	X	X		X	S	X	X			S		X		X			S				X										U	U
	X	X	X	U	S	X		X	X	X	X			U				X			X				S										S	X
	X			X	X	X			X	X	X	U		X		U		S			X				X										S	X
		X		X	X	X		X	S	X	X			S		X		X			U				S			X							X	U
	X	X		X	X	X		X	X	X	X			U		X		X			U				S										S	S
	X	U	X		U	X		X	S	X	X			X				S			X				S			X							X	X
	X	X	S		X	X		X	X		X	U		U				X			X				S			X							S	X
	X		X	X	X	X	X	U	X	X	X	U		S	S	X	U	X		S	U															
	X	S	X	X	X	X		S	X	X	X	U		S	X	X		X		U	U	U														
	X	X	X	X		X	S	X	X	X	X			S		X		X		U	U		U	U	S											
		X	X	X	X	X	X		X	X	X			S	U	X		X		S	U				S	U										
			S	X	X	X	X		X	X						U		U			X		X	S	X		X	X	S							
	X		X	X	X	X	X		X	U	X			S		X					U				X		S	X	U							
1	40	24	26	34	27	39	15	26	27	37	40	0	2	3	4	28	0	28	0	3	13	0	0	0	20	0	1	9	0	0	0	0	4	0	2	9
0	0	1	7	0	6	0	1	8	11	1	1	5	1	11	4	0	3	7	1	0	1	0	1	1	8	0	2	2	0	0	2	0	2	0	7	3
0	0	1	1	2	2	0	0	3	0	2	0	8	0	12	7	10	4	0	10	2	19	0	2	0	0	0	0	0	0	3	4	4	1	1	9	5
0	4	2	5	6	5	6	4	1	6	5	5	0	0	0	1	5	0	4	0	0	1	0	1	0	2	0	1	2	0	0	0	0	0	0	0	0
0	0	1	1	0	0	0	1	1	0	0	0	0	0	5	1	0	0	0	0	2	0	0	0	1	2	0	1	0	1	0	0	0	0	0	0	0
0	0	0	0	0	0	0	0	1	0	1	0	2	0	0	1	1	1	1	0	2	5	1	1	1	0	1	0	0	1	0	0	0	0	0	0	0
0	1	1	1	1	2	0	2	1	9	0	14	0	0	0	0	0	0	11	0	0	0	0	0	0	9	0	0	1	0	0	0	0	2	0	1	0
0	0	0	0	0	0	0	0	0	4	0	3	0	0	0	0	0	0	2	0	0	0	0	0	0	0	0	0	1	0	0	0	0	0	0	0	0

PLAYING SQUAD 2011/12

Existing Players		SN	HT	WT	DOB	AGE	POB	Career	Apps	Goals
GOALKEEPERS										
Nathan	Ashmore				22/02/1990	21		Havant & W	14	0
Lyall	Beazely							Jomo Cosmos (SA), Farnborough FC, Fleet T c/s 09, South Africa 9/10, Fleet T 10/10, Havant & W c/s 11		
DEFENDERS										
Chi	Eberendu				02/07/1992	19		Bishops Stortford, Havant & W 8/11		
Ryan	Gadd							Havant & W	0	0
Paul	Hinshelwood		6'02"	14 00	11/10/1987	23	Chatham	Brighton Rel c/s 07, Burgess Hill (L) 8/06, Torquay 6/07 Rel 5/08, Tiverton (L) 11/07, Bognor 8/08, Havant & W 1/09	38	0
Chris	Holland		6'00"	10 06	29/08/1980	31	Taunton	Bournemouth (Trainee), Bristol C Rel c/s 00, Exeter (L), Team Bath 9/00, Bath C (L) 3/05, Bath C 8/05 Rel 5/10, Weston-Super-Mare (2ML) 11/05, Gloucester (L) 2/06, Eastleigh 5/10, Havant & W 6/11		
Jon	McDonald				18/05/1985	26	Kingston	Staines, Hampton & R 3/09, Havant & W 11/09	25	1
Jake	Newton				09/06/1984	27	Hammersmith	Hampton & R (Yth), Kingston Academy, Staines c/s 03, Chalfont St Peter (L) 2/04, Bashley 2/05, Staines 7/05, Havant & W 7/09	40	1
Sam	Pearce				11/02/1987	24	Portsmouth	Havant & W, Fleet T 3/06, South Africa, Bognor Regis 8/08, Salisbury 3/09, Havant & W 6/09	34	1
Perry	Ryan				10/04/1992	19		Portsmouth Rel c/s 11, Bognor Regis (2ML) 12/10, Havant & W 8/11		
Harvey	Whyte				24/08/1991	20		Havant & W	5	0
Ryan	Woodford		5'11"	11 08	14/08/1991	20		Portsmouth (Scholar) Rel c/s 09, Havant & W 7/09	3	0
MIDFIELDERS										
Craig	Braham-Barrett				01/09/1988	22		Charlton (Yth), Sheff Wed (Yth), Aveley, Dulwich H 7/07, Potters Bar 10/07, Eastleigh, East Thurrock 2/08, Welling 5/08, Peterborough £10,000 + 10/08 Rel 7/09, Kettering (L) 1/09, Grays 8/09 Rel 1/10, Farnborough 1/10, Havant & W 6/11		
Bobby	Hopkinson		5'08"	13 07	03/07/1990	21	Plymouth	Plymouth (Scholar),Tiverton 3/08, Aldershot Undisc 8/09 Rel 3/10, Farnborough (Dual) 1/10, Havant & W 3/10	16	2
Sammy	Igoe		5'07"	10 00	30/09/1975	36	Spelthorne	Portsmouth, Reading 3/00, Luton (L) 3/03, Swindon 6/03 Rel c/s 05, Millwall 7/05 Rel c/s 06, Bristol R (4ML) 1/06, Bristol R 7/06 Rel c/s 08, Hereford (L) 3/08, Bournemouth 8/08 Rel c/s 10, Havant & W 6/10	33	2
Steven Ramsey (was Walker)					23/11/1989	21		Portsmouth (Scholar), Rel c/s 08 Havant & W 5/08	34	1
FORWARDS										
Wesley	Fogden		5'08"	10 04	12/04/1988	23	Brighton	Brighton Rel 9/08, Dorchester (L) 8/08, Dorchester 9/08, Havant & W 2/09	41	14
Scott	Jones							Brading T, Havant & W c/s 11		
Warren	McBean				13/02/1986	25	London	Watford (Jun), Broxbourne B, Barnet 7/04, Waltham Forest (L) 3/05, Farnborough 8/05 Rel 8/06, Braintree 8/06 Rel 10,06, St Albans 10/06 Rel 10/06, Sutton U 10/06, Eastleigh (2ML) 2/08, Bromley 6/08, Chelmsford (SL) 3/10, Lewes 7/11, Havant & W 8/11		
Mark	Nwokeji		5'10"	11 04	30/01/1982	29	London	Charlton (Jun), Colchester (Jun), Harlow, Leatherhead, Protec Academy, Chesham 8/02, Walton & H 9/03, St Albans 1/06, Staines (Dual) 2/06 Perm 2/06, Dag & Red 5/08 Rel c/s 10, Luton (6WL) 11/09, Luton (SL) 1/10, AFC Wimbledon 6/10 Rel 5/11, Eastleigh (L) 2/11, Havant & W 6/11		
Lee	Peacock		6'00"	12 08	09/10/1976	34	Paisley	Carlisle, Mansfield £90,000 10/97, Man City £500,000 11/99, Bristol C £600,000 8/00, Sheff Wed 7/04 Rel 1/06, Swindon 1/06, Grimsby 1/10 Rel 5/11, Havant & W 6/11		
Bobby	Scott							Southampton (Scholar), L.Orient (Scholar), Havant & W	9	1
Liam	Sewell				01/02/1991	20		Petersfield, Havant & W 12/09, Gosport B (2ML) 1/11, Gosport B (SL) 7/11	14	0

MAIDENHEAD UNITED

Chairman: Peter Griffin
Secretary: Ken Chandler **(T)** 07726 351 286 **(E)** kenneth.chandler@btinternet.com
Additional Committee Members:
Robert Hussey, Una Loughrey, Mark Stewart, Steve Jinman, Suzanne Loughrey, Graham Alfred, Mark Smith, Roy Bannister
Manager: Johnson Hippolyte
Programme Editor: Mark Roach **(E)** markroachonline@yahoo.co.uk

Club Factfile

Founded: 1870 **Nickname:** Magpies
Previous Names: Maidenhead F.C and Maidenhead Norfolkians merged to form today's club
Previous Leagues: Southern 1894-1902, 2006-07, West Berkshire 1902-04, Gr. West Suburban 1904-22, Spartan 1922-39, Gr. West Comb. 1939-45, Corinthian 1945-63, Athenian 1963-73, Isthmian 1973-2004, Conf. 2004-06

Club Colours (change): Black & white stripes/black/white (Yellow/blue/yellow)

Ground: York Road, Maidenhead, Berkshire SL6 1SF **(T)** 01628 636 314
Capacity: 4,500 **Seats:** 400 **Covered:** 2,000 **Clubhouse:** Yes **Shop:** Yes

Directions
The Ground is in the town centre.
200 yards from the station and two minutes walk from the High Street.
Access from M4 Junctions 7 or 8/9.

Previous Grounds: Not known

Record Attendance: 7,920 v Southall - FA Amateur Cup Quarter final 07/03/1936
Record Victory: 14-1 v Buckingham Town - FA Amateur Cup 06/09/1952
Record Defeat: 0-14 v Chesham United (A) - Spartan League 31/03/1923
Record Goalscorer: George Copas - 270 (1924-35)
Record Appearances: Bert Randall - 532 (1950-64)
Additional Records: Received £5,000 from Norwich City for Alan Cordice 1979

Senior Honours: Corinthian League 1957-58, 60-61, 61-62.
Berks & Bucks Senior Cup x19.

10 YEAR RECORD

01-02	02-03	03-04	04-05	05-06	06-07	07-08	08-09	09-10	10-11
Isth P 16	Isth P 10	Isth P 12	Conf S 20	Conf S 22	SthP 4	Conf S 17	Conf S 6	Conf S 16	Conf S 19

MAIDENHEAD UNITED

No.	Date	Comp	H/A	Opponents	Att:	Result	Goalscorers	Pos
1	Sat-14-Aug	BSS	A	Ebbsfleet United	790	W 2-1	Knight pen 60, Powell 78	6
2	Tue-17-Aug	BSS	H	Braintree Town	262	L 0-3		10
3	Sat-21-Aug	BSS	H	Weston-Super-Mare	227	W 1-0	Barney 90	6
4	Mon-23-Aug	BSS	A	Eastleigh	354	L 0-3		7
5	Sat-28-Aug	BSS	A	Woking	952	W 2-0	Og (Doyle) 29, St Aimie 68	6
6	Mon-30-Aug	BSS	H	St Albans City	307	W 2-1	Fagan 50, Smith 75	5
7	Sat-04-Sep	BSS	H	Bromley	410	L 0-2		6
8	Sat-11-Sep	BSS	A	Farnborough	603	D 2-2	St Aimie 2 (10, pen 77)	8
9	Sat-18-Sep	BSS	H	Staines Town	280	L 2-3	Nicholls 5, St Aimie pen 63	10
10	Sat-02-Oct	BSS	A	Chelmsford City	827	L 0-2		13
11	Sat-16-Oct	BSS	H	Welling United	275	L 0-3		16
12	Tue-09-Nov	BSS	A	Dorchester Town	376	W 2-1	Smith 2, Knight 45	15
13	Sat-13-Nov	BSS	H	Ebbsfleet United	325	D 1-1	Wilson 59	16
14	Tue-16-Nov	BSS	A	Weston-Super-Mare	172	L 1-3	Collins 20	16
15	Sat-27-Nov	BSS	A	Bishops Stortford	259	D 0-0		16
16	Sat-11-Dec	BSS	A	Dover Athletic	754	D 2-2	Akurang 86, St Aimie 89	16
17	Tue-14-Dec	BSS	H	Boreham Wood	145	D 1-1	Akurang 45	16
18	Thu-30-Dec	BSS	A	Bromley	535	W 2-0	Brown 56, Nicholls 61	11
19	Sat-01-Jan	BSS	H	Basingstoke Town	349	D 1-1	Wall 16	12
20	Mon-03-Jan	BSS	A	St Albans City	366	L 0-1		12
21	Sat-22-Jan	BSS	H	Thurrock	233	L 1-3	St Aimie pen 66	15
22	Sat-29-Jan	BSS	A	Boreham Wood	149	L 2-4	Smith 44, St Aimie pen 45	16
23	Mon-31-Jan	BSS	A	Havant & Waterlooville	518	L 1-2	Nicholls pen 80	16
24	Sat-05-Feb	BSS	H	Bishops Stortford	232	D 2-2	Akurang 29, Brown 37	18
25	Sat-12-Feb	BSS	H	Lewes	236	L 0-2		19
26	Sat-19-Feb	BSS	A	Welling United	383	L 1-2	Wall 61	20
27	Tue-22-Feb	BSS	H	Woking	402	L 0-1		20
28	Tue-01-Mar	BSS	H	Havant & Waterlooville	116	L 0-1		20
29	Sat-05-Mar	BSS	A	Dartford	976	L 0-3		20
30	Sat-12-Mar	BSS	H	Dover Athletic	352	L 0-1		20
31	Sat-19-Mar	BSS	H	Chelmsford City	509	L 1-2	Bates 87	20
32	Tue-22-Mar	BSS	H	Farnborough	368	L 0-3		20
33	Sat-26-Mar	BSS	A	Braintree Town	442	L 1-3	A Thomas pen 88	21
34	Tue-29-Mar	BSS	A	Hampton & Richmond Borough	315	D 1-1	Louis 54	21
35	Sat-02-Apr	BSS	A	Lewes	626	L 0-1		21
36	Mon-04-Apr	BSS	A	Basingstoke Town	259	W 4-3	A Thomas pen 29, Worsfold 45, Faulconbridge 49, Soloman 57	21
37	Sat-09-Apr	BSS	H	Hampton & Richmond Borough	341	D 0-0		21
38	Tue-12-Apr	BSS	H	Eastleigh	215	W 1-0	Hendry 48	20
39	Sat-16-Apr	BSS	A	Thurrock	225	W 2-1	A Thomas pen 4, Worsfold 90	18
40	Tue-19-Apr	BSS	A	Staines Town	271	W 2-1	Wall 36, Smith 87	18
41	Sat-23-Apr	BSS	H	Dorchester Town	468	D 1-1	Louis pen 48	18
42	Sat-30-Apr	BSS	H	Dartford	534	L 2-3	Faulconbridge 79, Louis 86	19

CUPS

No.	Date	Comp	H/A	Opponents	Att:	Result	Goalscorers
1	Sat-25-Sep	FAC 2Q	H	Truro City	237	W 1-0	Wall 62
2	Sat-09-Oct	FAC 3Q	A	Cinderford Town	218	W 4-0	Wall 2 (20, 48), Smith 78, Knight 89
3	Sat-23-Oct	FAC 4Q	A	Forest Green Rovers	580	L 0-1	
4	Sat-20-Nov	FAT 3Q	H	Uxbridge	211	L 2-4	Collins 2 (31, 60)

League
Starts
Substitute
Unused Sub

Cups
Starts
Substitute
Unused Sub

Goals (Lg)
Goals (Cup)

WILLIAMS	BEHZADI	FYFIELD	NICHOLLS	NISBET	FAGAN	SMITH	QUAMINA	BROWN	ST AIMIE	KNIGHT	WALL	POWELL	BRADSHAW	CARTER	LATAILLE	COLLINS	MUNDAY	BARNEY	SACKEY	ANDERSON	N THOMAS	WILSON	MARSHALL	BURT	MPI	HENDRY	AKURANG	ROSE	OCHOA	BADDELEY	MURPHY	SOLOMAN	HINDS	CLEMENT	WORSFOLD	FEDERICO	LOUIS	FAULCONBRIDGE	CLAYTON	BATES	A THOMAS	SCARBOROUGH	SAROYA	COOPER
X	X	X	X	X	X	X	X	X	X	X	S	S	S	U	U																													
X	X	X	X	X		X	X		X	X	S	S	X	U	S	X	U																											
X	X	X	X	X		S	X	S	X	X	X	X	U	U		X		S																										
X	X	X	X	X		U	X	S	X	S	X	X		U		X	X	S																										
X	X		X	X	X	X	X	S	X	X	X		X	U			U	S	S																									
X		X	X	X	X	X	X	U	X	X	X	U	X	U			U	S																										
X	S	X		X	X	X	X	X	X	X		S	X	U		S		X	U																									
X	X		X	X	X	X	X	X	X	X		S	U	U		X	U		S																									
X	X		X	X	X	X	X	X	X	X		U	U			X	U		U	S																								
X	X		X	X	X	X		X		X	X	S	U			X	U	S				X	U																					
X	X		X	X	X	X	X	X	X	S		S	S			X			U			X		U																				
X	X		X	X	X	X	X	U	S	X	X	S				X	U					X		U																				
X	X		X	X	X	S	X		S	X	X	S				X	U					X		U		X																		
	X		X	X	X	S	X	U	S	X	X	S				X	U					X		X		X																		
X	X		X	X	X	S	X	X		S	U					X						X		U		X	X	U																
X			X		X	S	X	X	S	X	U	S				X	X					X		U			X	X																
X			X	X	X	X		X	S	S	X					X	S					X		U			X	X	U															
X	X		X		X			X	X	X	S	S				X	U							U		S	X	X		X														
X	X		X		X			X	X	X	X	X				S	U	S						U			S	X		X														
X	X		X		S	X	X		S	U	X	X				S	X					X	U				X	X																
X	X		X		X	X	X		S		X	X				S	U							U		S	X	X		X														
X	X		X		X	X	X		X		X	S				S	U	S						U			X	X		X														
X	X		X		X	S	X	X			X	S			S	X	X	U					U					X		X														
X	X	X	X		X	S	X	X	U		X	S				X							U				X	S		X														
X	X	X	X	X	X	X		X	X		S	U				X		S									X	S			U													
X		X			S	X		U	X		X	X				S		S					U				X	X		X		X	X											
X		X	X	X	S	U		S	X	S	X	X											U				X			X		X	X											
		X	X	X	U			S	S	X	X	X						S					U							X		X	X	X	X									
X	S	X	X	X	S					X	X	X																U		X		X	X	U	X	S								
X	X		X		X			X			S	U																X				X	X	U	X	S	X	X	S					
	X		X		X	S																				S		X		U	U	X	X	X	X	X	X	X		S				
U	X		X		S	X						S														X		X				X	X	X	U		X	X	X	S				
X	X		X	X	X	S																				X				U		X	X	U	X		X	X		S	S			
X	X		X	X	X																					X		U		X		S	X	U	S		X	S		X	X			
X	X		X	X	X						S															X				X		U	X	U	S		X	S		X	X			
X	X		X	X	X			S			S																			S		X	X	U	X		X	X		U	X			
X	X		X								S															S						X	X	U	X		X	X		S	X	X	X	U
X	X		X		S	U		X			S															X						X		U	X		X	S			X	X		X
X	X		X		U	S		X			S	S														X						X		U	X			X			X	X	X	
X	X		X		U	S		X			X															X						X	S	U	X		S				X	X	X	
X	X		X			S		X			X															S						X	S	U	X		X				X	X	X	U
X	X		X	U		S		X																		S						X	X	U	X		X	S			X	X		X
X	X		X	X	X	X	X	X	X	X	S	U				X	U	S	U		U																							
X	X		X	X	X	X	X	X	X	S	X	S	U			X	U		S				U																					
X	X		X	X	X	X	X	X	X	S	X	S	U			X			U				U		S																			
	X		S	X	X	X	X	U	X	S	S	X				X	U					X		X		X																		
38	34	12	40	24	27	17	20	20	16	17	21	9	4	0	0	17	4	1	0	0	0	9	0	1	0	10	11	12	0	12	0	15	13	3	12	1	11	7	1	2	9	6	4	2
0	2	0	0	0	6	13	0	6	8	5	10	16	2	0	2	6	1	10	2	1	0	0	0	0	0	6	1	2	0	1	0	1	2	0	2	2	1	4	1	4	1	0	0	0
1	0	0	0	1	3	3	0	4	1	1	2	4	4	8	1	0	13	1	3	0	0	0	7	10	0	0	0	3	1	2	2	1	0	12	1	0	0	0	0	1	0	0	0	2
3	4	0	3	4	4	4	4	3	4	1	2	1	0	0	0	4	0	0	0	0	0	1	0	1	0	1	0	0	0	0	0	0	0	0	0	0	0	0	0	0	0	0	0	0
0	0	0	1	0	0	0	0	0	0	3	2	2	0	0	0	0	0	1	1	0	0	0	0	0	1	0	0	0	0	0	0	0	0	0	0	0	0	0	0	0	0	0	0	0
0	0	0	0	0	0	0	0	1	0	0	0	1	2	0	0	0	3	0	2	0	1	0	2	0	0	0	0	0	0	0	0	0	0	0	0	0	0	0	0	0	0	0	0	0
0	0	0	3	0	1	4	0	2	7	2	3	1	0	0	0	1	0	1	0	0	0	1	0	0	0	1	3	0	0	0	0	1	0	0	2	0	3	2	0	1	3	0	0	0
0	0	0	0	0	0	1	0	0	0	1	3	0	0	0	0	2	0	0	0	0	0	0	0	0	0	0	0	0	0	0	0	0	0	0	0	0	0	0	0	0	0	0	0	0

PLAYING SQUAD 2011/12

Existing Players		SN	HT	WT	DOB	AGE	POB	Career	Apps	Goals
GOALKEEPERS										
Nick	Bussey				21/09/1984	26		Dag & Red, Arlesey (L) 8/04. Kettering, Halesowen T 8/08 Rel 5/10, Kettering (Dual) 9/09, Redditch 8/10, Halesowen T 11/10, Kettering 1/11 Rel 1/11, Kettering 3/11, Maidenhead 8/11		
Jordan	Clement		6'01"	12 08	12/06/1993	28	Chertsey	Aldershot, Blackfield & Langley (WE) 10/10, Maidenhead (L) 2/11, Maidenhead (SL) 7/11	3	0
Billy	Lumley		6'05"	14 13	28/12/1989	21	Loughton	Wolves (Scholar), Glen Hoddle Academy 11/08, Brentford (Trial) 7/09, Grays 8/09 Rel 9/09, Stafford R 9/09 Rel 11/09, Northampton 12/09, Eastleigh 3/10, Billericay 7/10, Jerez Industrial CF (Spa) 8/10, Bournemouth (Trial) 4/11, Maidenhead 8/11		
Rhys	Marshall				27/05/1993	18		Maidenhead	0	0
DEFENDERS										
Bobby	Behzadi				08/02/1981	30	London	Stevenage, Wealdstone (L) 1/00, Hayes 3/00, Yeading 8/01, Maidenhead 1/07	36	0
Andrew	Fagan				23/09/1983	27		Leighton T, Windsor & E 7/08, Maidenhead 7/10	33	1
Leigh	Henry		5'10"	11 11	29/09/1986	24	Swindon	Swindon Rel 12/06, Bath C (WE) 3/05, Weston-Super-Mare (2ML) 8/06, Swindon Supermarine 2/07, Bath C 2/11 Rel 5/11, Swindon Supermarine (Dual) 3/11, Maidenhead 6/11		
Jon	Munday				13/04/1988	23		QPR, Hendon (L) 11/06, Hayes 3/07, Kidderminster 7/07 Rel 5/08, Worcester (L) 1/08, Grays 8/08 Rel 8/08, Lewes (Trial) 9/08, St Albans 11/08, Sutton U 1/09, Hitchin 2/09, Croydon Ath 7/09, Carshalton 10/09, Hemel Hempstead 12/09, Maidenhead 8/10, Walton & H (Dual) 11/10, Walton & H (Dual) 8/11	5	0
Mark	Nisbet				29/11/1986	24		Flackwell Heath, Maidenhead 7/06	24	0
Marcus	Rose				04/06/1990	21		QPR (Yth), Barnet (Scholar), Hitchin (2ML) 11/08, Leyton c/s 09, Maidenhead 11/09	14	0
Nevin	Saroya		6'03"	13 01	15/09/1980	30	Hillingdon	Brentford, Grays 10/00, Hampton & R 1/01, Yeading/Hayes & Yeading 8/01 Rel 12/08, Maidenhead 12/08, Australia 3/10, Maidenhead 3/11	4	0
John	Scarborough		6'01"		13/03/1979	31	Gravesend	Gravesend, Ashford T, Herne Bay, Eastbourne B, Tilbury, Billericay c/s 03, Tilbury 2/04, Chelmsford (Trial) c/s 04, Dover 9/04, Sutton U 9/04, Hampton & R 6/08, Bromley 8/10 Rel 12/10, Lewes 12/10, Maidenhead 3/11	6	0
Leon	Soloman				18/02/1986	25		Millwall (Junior), Gillingham (Scholar) 7/02, Hastings U (L) 8/04, Worthing (L) 12/04, Welling 9/05, Hayes & Yeading 8/08, Walton Casuals (L) 12/08, Bracknell 1/09, Hemel Hempstead c/s 09, Harrow 8/10, Windsor & E 10/10, Maidenhead 2/11	16	1
MIDFIELDERS										
Daniel	Brown				28/10/1988	22		Northwood, Maidenhead 8/09	26	2
Aaron	Harris							Maidenhead		
Will	Hendry		5'11"	12 10	10/11/1986	24	Slough	Millwall Rel 8/06, Hayes 10/06, Grays 11/06, Hayes/Hayes & Yeading 1/07 Rel c/s 09, Maidenhead 9/09, AFC Wimbledon 11/09 Rel 4/10, Eastleigh 8/10 Rel 10/10, Maidenhead 11/10	16	1
Lewis	Ochoa		5'10"	11 02	24/06/1991	20	London	Brentford (Scholar) Rel c/s 09, Wycombe (Trial) 3/09, Maidenhead 8/09, Hendon (L) 10/09	0	0
Martel	Powell				28/09/1991	19		MK Dons (Scholar) Rel c/s 10, Maidenhead 8/10	25	1
Chris	Taylor		5'08"	10 05	30/10/1985	25	Swindon	Swindon Rel c/s 06, Newport C (L) 3/05, Newport C (L) 8/05, Swindon Supermarine 8/06, Dandedong Thunder (Aust) 1/11, Maidenhead 7/11		
Max	Worsfold		5'09"	12 06	25/10/1992	18	Chertsey	Aldershot, Wealdstone (WE) 1/11, Maidenhead (L) 2/11, Maidenhead (SL) 7/11	14	2
FORWARDS										
Lee	Barney				01/04/1992	19		Maidenhead, Walton & H (Dual) 2/11, Beaconsfield SYCOB (L) 8/11	11	1
Ashan	Holgate		6'02"	12 00	09/11/1986	24	Swindon	Swindon Rel c/s 07, Salisbury (L) 3/06, Newport C (L) 10/06, Macclesfield (SL) 1/07, Weston-Super-Mare 8/07, Eastleigh 4 fig 12/07, Cirencester (L) 2/08, Weston-Super-Mare 3/08, Newport C 10/09 Rel 1/10, Swindon Supermarine 3/10, Maidenhead 6/11		
Kerran	Lataille				30/12/1992	18		QPR, Maidenhead 8/10, Walton & H (Dual) 8/11	2	0
Anthony	Thomas		5'11"	12 08	30/08/1982	29	Hammersmith	Ashford T, Edgware 7/04, Hemel Hempstead 7/05, Barnet Undisc 7/07 Rel c/s 08, Cambridge C (L) 10/07, Stevenage 5/08, Hemel Hempstead 12/08, Farnborough 6/09, Hendon (L) 2/10, Slough (L) 10/10, Brackley (L) 11/10, Maidenhead (SL) 3/11, Maidenhead 7/11	10	3
Reece	Tison-Lascaris							Boreham Wood, Maidenhead 7/11		
Alex	Wall				22/09/1990	20		Thatcham, Maidenhead 8/09	31	3
Manny	Williams				13/11/1981	29	London	Notts County (Yth), Millwall (Yth), Concord R, Bowers Utd, Leyton 7/01, Yeading 9/05, Leyton 7/06, Maidenhead 8/07, Woking 5/08 Rel 5/09, Maidenhead (2ML) 11/08, Weston-Super-Mare (3ML) 1/09, Havant & W 6/09, Maidenhead 6/11		

SALISBURY CITY

Chairman: W. Harrison-Allen
Secretary: Alec Hayter **(T)** 07884 477 168 **(E)** alechayter@googlemail.com
Additional Committee Members:
Jeff Hooper, Chris Brammall, Peter Matthiae

Manager: Darrell Clarke
Programme Editor: Paul Osborn **(E)** info@sarumgraphics.co.uk

Club Factfile

Founded: 1947 **Nickname:** The Whites
Previous Names: Salisbury F.C.
Previous Leagues: Western 1947-68, Southern 1968-2004, 2010-11, Isthmian 2004-05, Conference 2005-10.

Club Colours (change): All white (Yellow/blue/yellow)

Ground: Raymond McEnhill Stadium, Partridge Way, Old Sarum SP4 6PU **(T)** 01722 776 655
Capacity: 5,000 **Seats:** 500 **Covered:** 2,247 **Clubhouse:** Yes **Shop:** Yes

Directions
Situated A345 Salisbury/Amesbury Road.
From North/East/West: Leave A303 at Countess roundabout at Amesbury and take A345 towards Salisbury until Park and Ride roundabout from where the ground is signposted.
From South: Proceed to A345 and then follow directions to Amesbury until Park and Ride roundabout from where the ground is signposted.

Previous Grounds: Victoria Park

Record Attendance: 3,100 v Nottingham Forest - FA Cup 2nd Round 2006
Record Victory: 11-1 v RAF Colerne (H) - Western League Division 2 1948
Record Defeat: 0-7 v Minehead (A) - Southern League 1975
Record Goalscorer: Royston Watts - 180 (1959-65)
Record Appearances: Barry Fitch - 713 (1963-75)
Additional Records: Paid £15,000 to Bashley for Craig Davis
Received £20,000 from Forest Green Rovers for Adrian Randall

Senior Honours: Western League 1957-58, 60-61. Southern League Premier Division 1994-95, 2005-06.

10 YEAR RECORD

01-02	02-03	03-04	04-05	05-06	06-07	07-08	08-09	09-10	10-11
SthP 22	SthE 4	SthE 6	Isth P 12	SthP 1	Conf S 2	Conf 12	Conf 16	Conf 12	SthP 3

SALISBURY CITY

No.	Date	Comp	H/A	Opponents	Att:	Result	Goalscorers	Pos
1	Aug 14	Sth Prem	H	Stourbridge	871	W 3 - 0	Giles 33 McLaggon 48 Clarke 57	2
2	17		A	Bashley	612	W 2 - 0	Joyce 12 Clarke 13	
3	21		A	Cambridge CIty	319	D 3 - 3	McLaggon 40 (pen) Kelly 87 Purley 90	2
4	24		H	Weymouth	896	W 3 - 2	Gray 75 89 (pen) Joyce 90	
5	28		H	Hemel Hempstead Town	706	D 1 - 1	Wright 70	2
6	30		A	Chippenham Town	858	D 1 - 1	Wright 38	
7	Sept 4		H	Cirencester Town	659	W 4 - 1	Joyce 38 Wright 45 Clarke 62 Kelly 89	4
8	11	FAC 1Q	A	Highworth Town	422	D 1 - 1	Giles 76	
9	14	FAC 1Qr	H	Highworth Town	596	W 5 - 0	Giles 20 Dutton 30 McLaggon 45 Joyce 71 Knight 78	
10	18		A	Hednesford Town	324	L 0 - 3		5
11	25	FAC 2Q	A	Sholing	360	D 2 - 2	Adlesbury 10 McLaggon 74	
12	28	FAC 2Qr	H	Sholing	604	W 5 - 1	REID 3 (31 44 52) McLaggon 51 55	
13	Oct 2		H	Bedford Town	699	W 4 - 1	McLaggon 7 Hoyle 45 (og) Kelly 46 Reid 57	5
14	5		H	Oxford City	682	W 2 - 0	Laggon 11 (pen) Adlesbury 81	
15	9	FAC 3Q	H	Weston-s-Mare	871	W 1 - 0	McLaggon 28	
16	13		A	Tiverton Town	289	W 3 - 1	Ellis 3 (og) McLaggon 9 (pen) Knight 43	3
17	16	FAT Q1	A	Chesham United	297	D 1 - 1	Dutton 77	
18	19	FAT 1Qr	H	Chesham United	463	W 2 - 1	Lambert 43 (og) Reid 63	
19	23	FAC 4Q	A	Corby Town	957	L 0 - 3		
20	30	FAT 2Q	H	Almondsbury Town	577	W 2 - 1	Joyce 53 McLaggon 86 (pen)	
21	Nov 2		A	Brackley Town	204	W 3 - 0	Turley 35 Knight 45 Giles 59	
22	6		A	Banbury United	316	W 1 - 0	Silver 30	3
23	9		H	Chesham United	566	W 3 - 2	Ledger 68 (og) Turley 72 Silver 89	
24	13		H	Leamington	954	D 0 - 0		2
25	16		A	Truro City	744	D 1 - 1	Casey 65	
26	20	FAT 3Q	A	Lewes	598	W 2 - 1	Kelly 21 Clarke 29 86	
27	Dec 4	17	H	Didcot Town	608	W 4 - 2	Reid 26 71 Kelly 42 Heapy 47 (og)	2
28	11	FAT 1	A	Basingstoke Town	475	W 2 - 0	Clarke 54 McLaggon 78	
29	14		H	Halesowen Town	471	W 7 - 1	McLaggon 4 22 Giles 31 Reid 61 Clarke 67 Fitchett 81 Kelly 90	
30	Jan 3		H	Chippen ham Town	1095	W 4 - 0	Knight 10 Joyce 24 34 (pen) Dutton 40	
31	8		H	Hednesford Town	659	W 2 - 1	Kelly 58 Joyce 62 (pen)	2
32	15	FAT 2	H	Wrexham	1032	W 1 - 0	Reid 26 (pen)	
33	22		H	Bashley	774	W 2 - 1	Dutton 19 Tasazolli 58a	2
34	26		A	Swindon Supermarine	282	W 2 - 1	Reid 21 Turley 34	
35	29		A	Stourbridge	381	D 0 - 0		2
36	Feb 1		A	Hemel Hempstead	150	W 3 - 0	Boyle 8 Reid 41 (pen) 64	
37	5	FAT 3	A	Woking	1551	W 2 - 0	Reid 46 Clarke 55	
38	8		A	Evesham United	127	D 0 - 0		
39	12		A	Weymouth	837	L 0 - 2		2
40	19		A	Halesowen Town	284	W 4 - 0	REID 3 (9 31pen 64 pen) Joyce 27	1
41	22		H	Truro City	1682	L 0 - 6		
42	26	FAT 4	A	Gateshead	1864	L 1 - 2	Clarke 90	
43	March 1		H	Tiverton Town	599	W 3 - 0	Knight 14 Gardner 45 (og) Adelsbury 59	1
44	5		A	Didcot Town	347	D 1 - 1	Kelly 18	2
45	8		A	Cirencester Town	152	W 3 - 0	Kelly 14 Knight 44 45	
46	12		H	Banbury United	905	W 4 - 1	Shephard 52 57 Reid 59 Clarke 90	1
47	15		H	Cambridge City	860	L 1 - 3	Turley 39	
48	19		A	Leamington	664	L 0 - 2		1
49	22		H	Swindon Supermarine	604	W 3 - 0	Reid 33 McLaggon 78	
50	April 2		A	Oxford City	365	D 2 - 2	Clarke 54 Dutton 90	2
51	9		H	Evesham United	895	L 0 - 3		2
52	16		A	Chesham United	545	D 1 - 1	Fitchett 33	3
53	19		H	Brackley Town	565	W 3 - 1	Wright 21 McLaggon 60 88	
54	23		A	Bedford Town	373	L 0 - 1		3
55	28	P-Off SF	H	Cambridge City	1126	W 1 - 0	Knight 36	
56	May 2	P-Off Final	A	Hednesford	1903	D 2 2*	Wright 84 Adelsbury 118 Salisbury City won 3-2 on penalties	

PLAYING SQUAD 2011/12

Existing Players		SN	HT	WT	DOB	AGE	POB	Career	Apps	Goals
GOALKEEPERS										
Conor	Gough		6'05"		09/08/1993	18	Fyfield	C.Palace (Yth), Gillingham (Yth), Charlton, Lewes (WE) 3/11, St Albans (SWE) 3/11, Salisbury (L) 8/11		
Tommy	Smith				14/09/1991	19		Reading (Yth), Watford (Yth), Fulham (Yth), Portsmouth (Scholar), Salisbury 7/10		
DEFENDERS										
Ryan	Brett				11/11/1990	20		Plymouth Rel 12/09, Glen Hoddle Academy (Trial), Plymouth Parkway 2/10, Salisbury 7/10		
Brian	Dutton		5'11"	12 00	12/04/1985	26	Malton	Pickering T, Scarborough (Trial), Swindon (Trial), Cambridge U 11/03 Rel c/s 04, Pickering T 6/04, Weymouth 3/05, Eastleigh 5/06 Rel 10/06, Weymouth 1/07 Rel c/s 07, York C (Trial) c/s 07, Mangotsfield (Trial), Dorchester 9/07 Rel 10/07, Pickering T 3/08, Salisbury 8/08, Harrogate T 7/09, Northwich 12/09, Salisbury c/s 10		
Chris	Giles		6'02"	13 00	16/04/1982	29	Milborne Port	Sherborne, Yeovil 7/99, Weston-S-Mare (2ML) 3/01, Weymouth (L) 8/02, Gravesend (L) 12/02, Woking (L) 2/04, Aldershot 3/04 Rel 5/05, Crawley 7/05, Forest Green 7/06 Rel 7/06 Injured, Forest Green 11/06 Rel 4/08, Crawley 5/08 Rel 1/10, Salisbury 1/10		
Callum	Hart		6'00"	11 00	21/12/1985	25	Cardiff	Bristol C (Scholar) Rel c/s 05, Bournemouth 8/05 Rel c/s 07, Weymouth NC 11/07 Rel 1/08, Newport C 10/08, Farnborough 2/09, Weymouth 3/09 Rel c/s 09, Bath C 9/09 Rel 10/09, Weston-Super-Mare 10/09, Bath C c/s 10, Paulton R (Dual) 9/10, Salisbury 3/11		
Charlie	Knight				08/12/1987	23	Winchester	Salisbury, Andover (L) 9/06, Andover (L) 12/06, Chippenham (2ML) 2/07, Bashley 7/08, Salisbury c/s 10		
Luke	Ruddick		6'00"		03/03/1990	21	Ashford	Brentford, Ashford T (Middx), Walton Casuals 9/08, Hampton & R 10/08 Harrow 11/08, Salisbury 11/08, Bath C 6/10, Salisbury 8/11		
MIDFIELDERS										
Ben	Adelsbury				20/10/1990	20		Plymouth (Yth), Swansea, Salisbury 12/09		
Stuart	Anderson		6'0"	11 09	22/04/1986	25	Banff	Southampton, Blackpool 12/04 Rel c/s 06, Ross C (SL) 1/06, Ross C c/s 06, Livingston 3/07, Peterhead c/s 07, Salisbury 7/09		
Josh	Casey				19/10/1991	19		Reading (Yth), Southampton (Yth), Aldershot (Scholar) Rel c/s 10, Salisbury 8/10		
Darrell	Clarke		5'10"	10 11	16/12/1977	33	Mansfield	Mansfield, Hartlepool Undisc 7/01 Rel c/s 07, Stockport (L) 1/05, P ort Vale (L) 9/05, Rochdale (5ML) 7/06, Salisbury 7/07 (Pl/Man) 7/10		
Adam	Kelly				11/02/1988	23		Tiverton, Winchester, Bashley 3/09, Salisbury c/s 10		
FORWARDS										
Danny	Fitchett				28/03/1991	20		Reading (Yth), Wycombe Rel c/s 11, Badshot Lea (L) 2/10, Oxford C (L) 9/10, Salisbury (SL) 11/10, Salisbury 6/11		
Claudio	Herbert							Salisbury, Andover (SL) 8/10		
Jake	Reid				22/06/1987	24	London	Yeovil (Yth), Team Bath, Paulton (L) 1/07, Yate T (L) 3/07, Chippenham 6/07, Mangotsfield (L) 1/08, Yate (L) 3/08, Weymouth 8/09, Grays 12/09, Weymouth 1/10 Rel 3/10, Salisbury 3/10, Bath C 7/10 Rel 9/10, Salisbury 9/10		
Matt	Wright		6'04"	14 06	13/04/1991	20	Plymouth	Plymouth (Yth), Swansea (Scholar), C.Palace (Trial) 5/09, C.Palace 7/09, Maidstone (2ML) 9/09, Woking (5WL) 11/09, Salisbury c/s 10, Weymouth (3ML) 10/10, Andover (2ML) 1/11		

Caption competition....

Send in your suggestions to tw.publications@btinternet.com and you could win a copy of the 2013 edition of the Directory...

Photo by Keith Clayton

STAINES TOWN

Chairman: TBC

Secretary: Steven Parsons **(T)** 07876 672 458 **(E)** catspar57@aol.com

Additional Committee Members:
Matthew & Corinne Boon,Chris Boyce,Darren & Vanessa Cox,Hilary Denning,Graham Gould,Glenn Gulyas,John Hanson, Mike Holland,Andy Jones,Barbara Moss,Sally Payne,Jesse Richards,Kim Sherwood,Angie Payne,Chris Wainwright

Manager: Steve Cordery

Programme Editor: S. Moore & S. Parsons **(E)** catspar57@aol.com

Staines Town FC Squad, August 2010, with the Middlesex Super Cup (George Ruffell Shield) and Middlesex Senior Cup
Back Row (left to right): Craig Maskell (Asst Mgr), Michael Kamara, Danny Gordon, Marc Charles-Smith, Gareth Risbridger, Dominic Sterling, James Courtnage, Louis Wells, Richard Orlu, Marien Ifura, Dean Thomas, Darty Brown, Simon Jackson, René Steer, Trent Phillips (Coach).
Front Row: Gareth Workman (Physio'),Ryan Peters, Scott Taylor, Warren Harris, Richard Butler, Alan Boon (Chairman), Steve Cordery (Manager), James King, Leroy Griffiths, Ali Chaaban, André Scarlett, Paul Midwinter (Physio').

Club Factfile

Founded: 1892 **Nickname:** The Swans

Previous Names: Staines Albany & St Peters Institute merged in 1895. Staines 1905-18, Staines Lagonda 1918-25, Staines Vale (WWII)

Previous Leagues: Great Western Suburban, Hounslow & District 1919-20, Spartan 1924-35, 58-71, Middlesex Senior 1943-52, Parthenon 1952-53, Hellenic 1953-58, Athenian 1971-73, Isthmian 1973-2009

Club Colours (change): Old gold & blue/blue or old gold/blue or old gold (White with blue trim/white with blue trim/white)

Ground: Wheatsheaf Park, Wheatsheaf Lane, Staines TW18 2PD **(T)** 01784 225 943 / 463 100

Capacity: 3,000 **Seats:** 300 **Covered:** 850 **Clubhouse:** Yes **Shop:** Yes

Directions Leave M25 at Junction 13. If coming from the North (anticlockwise), bear left onto A30 Staines By-Pass; if coming from the South (clockwise), go round the roundabout and back under M25 to join By-Pass. Follow A30 to Billet Bridge roundabout, which you treat like a roundabout, taking last exit, A308, London Road towards Town Centre. At 3rd traffic lights, under iron bridge, turn left into South Street, passing central bus station, as far as Thames Lodge (formerly Packhorse). Turn left here, into Laleham Road, B376, under rail bridge. After 1km, Wheatsheaf Lane is on the right, by the traffic island. Ground is less than 100 yds on left. Please park on the left.

Previous Grounds: Not known

Record Attendance: 2,750 v Banco di Roma - Barassi Cup 1975 (70,000 watched the second leg)
Record Victory: 14-0 v Croydon (A) - Isthmian Division 1 19/03/1994
Record Defeat: 1-18 - Wycombe Wanderers (A) - Great Western Suburban League 27/12/1909
Record Goalscorer: Alan Gregory - 122
Record Appearances: Dickie Watmore - 840
Additional Records:

Senior Honours: Spartan League 1959-60. Athenian League Division 2 1971-72, Division 1 1974-75, 88-89.
Middlesex Senior cup 1975-76, 76-77, 77-78, 88-89, 90-91, 94-95, 97-98, 2009-10. Barassi Cup 1975-76.
Isthmian Full Members Cup 1994-95, Premier Division Play-off 2008-09.

10 YEAR RECORD

01-02	02-03	03-04	04-05	05-06	06-07	07-08	08-09	09-10	10-11
Isth1 16	Isth1S 15	Isth1S 6	Isth P 9	Isth P 6	Isth P 12	Isth P 2	Isth P 2	Conf S 8	Conf S 15

STAINES TOWN

No.	Date	Comp	H/A	Opponents	Att:	Result	Goalscorers	Pos
1	Sat-14-Aug	BSS	H	Lewes	411	W 1-0	Griffiths 41	8
2	Tue-17-Aug	BSS	A	Bishops Stortford	381	L 1-2	Scarlett 8	9
3	Sat-21-Aug	BSS	A	Dover Athletic	812	D 1-1	Butler 28	10
4	Tue-24-Aug	BSS	H	St Albans City	307	D 2-2	Charles-Smith 46, Griffiths 69	12
5	Sat-28-Aug	BSS	H	Boreham Wood	295	D 0-0		12
6	Mon-30-Aug	BSS	A	Farnborough	660	D 0-0		13
7	Sat-04-Sep	BSS	A	Ebbsfleet United	832	D 1-1	Chaaban 48	14
8	Sat-11-Sep	BSS	H	Welling United	314	L 1-2	Brown 90	16
9	Sat-18-Sep	BSS	A	Maidenhead United	280	W 3-2	Harris 70, Orlu 90, Gordon 90	12
10	Sat-02-Oct	BSS	H	Havant & Waterlooville	333	L 0-1		16
11	Sat-16-Oct	BSS	H	Woking	914	W 1-0	Scarlett 88	14
12	Sat-30-Oct	BSS	H	Dorchester Town	296	L 1-2	Scarlett 70	16
13	Sat-13-Nov	BSS	A	Eastleigh	585	W 4-1	Butler 2 (12, pen 77), Griffiths 21, Charles-Smith 67	15
14	Tue-16-Nov	BSS	A	Thurrock	204	L 1-2	Mingle 10	15
15	Tue-23-Nov	BSS	H	Weston-Super-Mare	191	W 2-1	Charles-Smith 56, Orlu 66	12
16	Sat-27-Nov	BSS	H	Braintree Town	248	D 4-4	Butler 2 (1, 31), Gordon 64, Mingle 68	12
17	Sat-01-Jan	BSS	A	Hampton & Richmond Borough	694	D 0-0		14
18	Mon-03-Jan	BSS	H	Farnborough	511	L 1-2	Brown 48	14
19	Sat-08-Jan	BSS	A	Welling United	503	L 0-4		14
20	Sat-15-Jan	BSS	H	Bishops Stortford	251	W 3-0	Taylor 2 (33, 80), Griffiths pen 40	12
21	Tue-18-Jan	BSS	A	Dartford	774	D 1-1	Gordon 63	12
22	Sat-22-Jan	BSS	A	Lewes	509	W 1-0	Newton 25	11
23	Sat-29-Jan	BSS	H	Chelmsford City	459	W 2-1	Charles-Smith 63, Griffiths pen 83	9
24	Tue-01-Feb	BSS	A	Basingstoke Town	284	L 1-4	Taylor 36	9
25	Sat-05-Feb	BSS	H	Thurrock	273	D 1-1	Butler 1	11
26	Sat-12-Feb	BSS	A	Bromley	475	W 1-0	Gordon 34	10
27	Sat-19-Feb	BSS	A	Woking	1219	L 0-2		11
28	Tue-22-Feb	BSS	A	Boreham Wood	151	D 2-2	Og (Wilkinson) 49, Thomas 77	10
29	Sat-26-Feb	BSS	H	Basingstoke Town	378	D 1-1	Lee pen 34	10
30	Tue-01-Mar	BSS	H	Hampton & Richmond Borough	251	L 1-2	D'Sane 80	10
31	Sat-05-Mar	BSS	A	Braintree Town	581	D 0-0		13
32	Sat-12-Mar	BSS	A	St Albans City	274	L 0-2		14
33	Sat-19-Mar	BSS	H	Dartford	402	W 2-0	Scarlett 5, Taylor 41	12
34	Tue-22-Mar	BSS	H	Dover Athletic	356	W 1-0	Onochie 75	12
35	Sat-26-Mar	BSS	A	Dorchester Town	482	D 3-3	Lee pen 18, Newton 51, Harris 70	11
36	Sat-02-Apr	BSS	H	Eastleigh	393	L 0-5		12
37	Tue-05-Apr	BSS	H	Ebbsfleet United	251	L 0-2		12
38	Sat-09-Apr	BSS	A	Chelmsford City	590	L 1-3	Charles-Smith 21	12
39	Sat-16-Apr	BSS	H	Bromley	263	L 0-2		14
40	Tue-19-Apr	BSS	H	Maidenhead United	271	L 1-2	Harris 60	14
41	Sat-23-Apr	BSS	A	Weston-Super-Mare	803	L 1-2	Onochie 63	12
42	Sat-30-Apr	BSS	A	Havant & Waterlooville	602	D 1-1	Quiassaca 73	15

CUPS

No.	Date	Comp	H/A	Opponents	Att:	Result	Goalscorers
1	Sat-25-Sep	FAC 2Q	A	Tooting & Mitcham United	378	W 4-1	Scarlett 20, Og (Nyang) 59, Walcott 2 (68, 90)
2	Sat-09-Oct	FAC 3Q	A	Bury Town	918	D 2-2	Griffiths 4, Charles-Smith 35
3	Tue-12-Oct	FAC 3QR	H	Bury Town	274	W 2-0	Scarlett 25, Walcott 53
4	Sat-23-Oct	FAC 4Q	A	Hythe Town	808	L 0-2	
5	Sat-20-Nov	FAT 3Q	A	St Albans City	249	L 1-3	Onochie 79

League
Starts
Substitute
Unused Sub

Cups
Starts
Substitute
Unused Sub

Goals (Lg)
Goals (Cup)

WELLS	JACKSON	STEER	GORDON	KAMARA	RISBRIDGER	TAYLOR	BROWN	GRIFFITHS	SCARLETT	BUTLER	CHAABAN	CHARLES-SMITH	KING	HARRIS	ORLU	IFURA	COURTNAGE	STERLING	WALCOTT	KALIPHA	MINGLE	ONOCHIE	PERRING	MAMBO	NEWTON	WARREN	DUFFY	QUIASSACA	LEE	THOMAS	LITTLE	D'SANE	ALLAWAY
X	X	X	X	X	X	X	X	X	X	X	S	S	U	U	U																		
X	X	X	X	X	X	X	X	X	X	X	S	S	U	S	U																		
X	X	U	X	X	X	U	X	X	X	X	S	X	S	U		X																	
X	X	X	X	U	X	U	X	X	X	X	S	X	U	S	X																		
X	X	X	X	U	U	S	X	X	X		X	X	X	S	U	X																	
X	X	U	X	X	X	U	X	X	X		X		U	X	U	X	U																
X	X	X	X	X	X	S		X	X		X	S	U	X	S	X	U																
X	X	X	X	X	X	S	X	X	S		X	S		X	U	X		U															
X	X	X	X	U		X	X		X		X	S	X	S	X		U		X	S													
X	X	X	X		S		X	X	X		X	X	U	X	S	X		U		S													
X	X	X		U	U	U	X	X	X			X		S	X	X			X	U	X												
X		X			U	U	X	X	X			U	U	X	X	X		X	X	S	X												
X	X	S	X			U	X	X	X	X		S		U	S	X		X	X		X												
X	X	U	X			S	X	X	X	X		S		S	U	X		X	X		X												
X	X	X	X			S	X		X	X		X	U	X	X	U		U			X	S											
X	X	X	X			U	X	S	X	X		X		X	X			U			X	S	U										
U	X					U		X				X	U	X	X		X	X			X	S		X	X	X	U						
	X	U	X			U	X	X				X		S	U		X	X			X	S		X	X	X							
X	X	S	X			X	X	S				X		X	U			X			X	U		X	X		S						
X	X	S	X			X	X	X	X			X		S	X		U	U					U	X	X								
X	X	X	X			X	X	X	X			X		U	X		U	S				U	U		X								
X	X	X	X				X	X	X	U				S	X		U	S					U		X								
X	X	X	X			X	X	X	X	S		X		X	X		U	S				U	U										
X	X	X	X			X	X		X	S		X		X	X		U	X					S					U					
X	X	X	X			X	X		X	X		X		S	X		U	S					U				X						
X	X	X	X						X	X		X		S	X			S					U		X		U		X	X	U		
X	X	X	X			S	U		X	X		X		S	X			U							X		S		X	X			
X	X	X	X			X				X				S	X			U					U		X		X		X	X	U		
X	X	X	X							X				X	X			X					U		X		S	U	X	X	U		
	X	X	X				X			X				S	X		X	X									S	U	X	X	U	X	U
X	X	X	X				X		X					X	X			X					U		S		X	S	X	S	U		
X	X	X	X			X	X		X	X				X	X			X							U		S	S	U	U			
X	X	X				X	X		X					X	X			X				X	U				S	U	X	S			U
X	X	X	U			X	X		X					X	X			X				X					U	U	X	S			U
X	X	X	U			X			X	X		S		X	X			X							X		U		X	U			U
X	X	X	S			X			X	X		S		X	X			X							X		U		X	U			U
X		X	X			X				X		X		S	X			X				X			X			S	X	U	S		U
X	X	X	X			X			X			X		X	X			S				S			X		S		X				U
X	X	X				X	U		X			X		X	X			X				X					S	S	X		S		U
X	X					X	X		X			X	X	X	X	U		X				S					S	U			X		U
X	X	X	U			X	X		X			S	X	X	X			X				X			S			U			X		
X		X				X			X				X	X	X	X		U							X		X	S			X		U
X	X	X		U	S	U	X	X	X		X	X	S	S	X	X	U	U	X														
X	X	X	X	S	S	U	X	X	X			X	U	U	S	X	U		X		X												
X	X	X		S	S	U	X	X	X			X	U	U	X	X	U	U	X		X												
X	X	X		U	U	S	X	X	X			X	U	S	X	X	U	U	X		X												
X	X	S	X				X	X	X	X		X		S	U	X		X	U		X	S											
39	39	33	31	6	7	21	30	19	34	18	6	21	5	23	30	11	3	19	5	0	9	5	0	4	15	2	4	0	13	5	3	1	0
0	0	3	1	0	1	6	0	2	1	2	4	10	1	15	3	0	0	6	0	3	0	6	1	0	2	0	9	5	0	3	2	0	0
1	0	4	3	4	3	9	2	0	0	1	0	1	9	4	8	2	9	8	0	1	0	3	11	0	1	0	5	7	1	4	5	0	10
5	5	4	2	0	0	0	5	5	5	1	1	5	0	0	3	5	0	1	4	0	4	0	0	0	0	0	0	0	0	0	0	0	0
0	0	1	0	2	3	1	0	0	0	0	0	0	1	3	1	0	0	0	0	0	0	1	0	0	0	0	0	0	0	0	0	0	0
0	0	0	0	2	1	3	0	0	0	0	0	0	3	2	1	0	4	3	1	0	0	0	0	0	0	0	0	0	0	0	0	0	0
0	0	0	4	0	0	4	2	5	4	6	1	5	0	3	2	0	0	0	0	0	2	2	0	0	2	0	0	1	2	1	0	1	0
0	0	0	0	0	0	0	0	1	2	0	0	1	0	0	0	0	0	0	3	0	0	1	0	0	0	0	0	0	0	0	0	0	0

PLAYING SQUAD 2011/12

Existing Players		SN	HT	WT	DOB	AGE	POB	Career	Apps	Goals
GOALKEEPERS										
Shaun	Allaway		5'10"	11 13	16/02/1983	28	Reading	Reading, Leeds £300,000 3/00 Rel c/s 04, Grimsby (L) 8/02, Walsall (3ML) 10/03, Blackpool (Trial) 5/04, Oldham (Trial) 7/04, QPR (Trial) 10/04, Slough 11/04, Staines 7/05, Injured 12/07, Reading T 10/10, Staines 2/11	0	0
Kyle	Merson							Staines		
Louis	Wells				22/02/1982	29		Hayes, Aldershot 6/06, Maidenhead 8/07, Uxbridge 3/08, Staines c/s 08	39	0
DEFENDERS										
Adam	Everitt				28/06/1982	29	Hemel Hempstead	Hemel Hempstead, Harrow c/s 00, Luton, Harrow 10/01, Hayes 6/03 Rel 5/05, Yeading (Trial) c/s 05, Yeading 9/05, Cambridge C 5/07, Eastleigh Undisc 10/07 Rel 5/08, AFC Hornchurch 8/08, Bromley 8/08, St Albans 11/08, Staines 6/11		
Danny	Gordon				20/12/1981	29	Aylesbury	Aylesbury, Staines 7/04	32	4
Marien	Ifura				07/09/1984	26		QPR (Sch) Rel c/s 04, Aylesbury (SL) 3/03, Farnborough (3ML) 9/03, Hendon (L) 1/04, Kingstonian 9/04, Staines 1/05, Studying, Windsor & E 11/06, Staines 3/08	11	0
Simon	Jackson				04/04/1985	26	Lewisham	Charlton (Sch) Rel 03/04, Woking 8/04 Rel 5/07, Fisher (L) 2/07, Fisher c/s 07, Bognor Regis 8/08, Sutton U 10/08, Staines 8/09	39	0
Richard	Orlu				12/07/1988	23		Staines, Northwood (5ML) 7/08, Walton Casuals (SL) 12/08, Walton Casuals (2ML) 8/09, Harrow (L) 10/09	33	2
Jack	Pattison				11/01/1991	20		Exeter, Hayes & Yeading (WE) 3/09 Perm (10/11), Chesham (Dual) 11/09, Burnham (Dual) 2/11, Staines 8/11		
Peter	Smith				11/09/1985	25		Lymington & New Milton, Winchester, Salisbury, Poole T, St Albans 11/09, Staines 8/11		
James	Tyrell		6'02"	13 04	26/04/1989	22	Oxford	Bristol R Rel c/s 10, Paulton R (3ML) 8/09, Clevedon T (SL) 3/10, Glen Hoddle Academy/Jerez Industrial (Spa) 8/10, Havant & W 2/11, Staines 7/11		
MIDFIELDERS										
Warren	Harris				27/02/1991	20		Tottenham (Yth), Ashford T (Middx), Staines 8/10	38	3
James	King				02/12/1990	20		Staines, Harrow (Dual) 2/10, Croydon Ath (Dual) 2/11	6	0
Howard	Newton				16/03/1982	29	Hammersmith	Sutton U, Hampton & R, Wembley, Hitchin, Staines, Epsom & E, Dag & Red, Harrow 9/04, Staines 7/06, Gillingham (Trial) 7/09, Hamilton Wanderers (NZ) c/s 10, Bromley 12/10, Staines 12/10	17	2
Gareth	Risbridger		5'10"	11 05	31/10/1981	29	High Wycombe	Marlow (Yth), Yeovil c/s 98, Southend 7/01 Rel 1/02, Dover (L) 10/01, Salisbury 2/02, Aylesbury 3/02, Staines 12/03, Boreham Wood 11/10, Staines 7/11	8	0
Andre	Scarlett		5'04"	09 06	11/01/1980	31	Wembley	Luton Rel c/s 01, Chelmsford 8/01, Boreham Wood, Hemel Hempstead, Stevenage, Wealdstone, Hitchin 3/02, Chesham 7/02, Staines 12/05	35	4
David	Wheeler				04/10/1990	20		Lewes, Staines 6/11		
FORWARDS										
Belal	Aite-Ouakrim				12/04/1985	26	London	Fulham (Yth), Berkhamstead, Windsor & E 2/05, Wycombe (Trial) c/s 05, Kingstonian (trial) c/s 05, Hendon 8/05, AFC Wimbledon 6/08 Rel 5/09, Maidenhead (L) 3/09, Hendon 2/10, Staines 6/11		
Richard	Butler				01/05/1985	26	Ashford	Ashford T (Middx), AFC Wimbledon 8/04, St Albans 11/07, Staines 2/08, Bromley 1/10 Rel 7/10, Staines 7/10	20	6
Marc	Charles-Smith				01/07/1984	27		Leatherhead, Staines c/s 07, Boreham Wood (L) 3/09	31	5
Dominic	Ogun							Staines		
Chan	Quan							Fisher FC, Staines 8/11		
Saheed	Sankoh				01/04/1988	23		Fulham, Woking 8/06 (06/07 16,0), Kingstonian (L) 1/07, Kingstonian (L) 3/07, Kingstonian 8/07, Met Police, Corinthian Casuals 3/09, Godalming T 12/09, Corinthian Casuals 3/10, Staines 8/11		
Scott	Taylor		5'10"	11 06	05/05/1976	35	Chertsey	Staines, Millwall £15,000 2/95, Bolton £150,000 3/96, Rotherham (2ML) 12/97, Blackpool (L) 3/98, Tranmere £50,000 10/98 Rel c/s 01, Stockport 8/01, Blackpool 1/02, Plymouth £100,000 12/04, MK Dons £100,000 1/06, Brentford (L) 3/07, Rochdale (L) 10/07, Grays 1/08 Rel c/s 08, Lewes 7/08, Staines 11/08	27	4

SUTTON UNITED

Chairman: Bruce Elliott
Secretary: Gerard Mills **(T)** 0793 270 2375 **(E)** honsec@suttonunited.net
Additional Committee Members:
Dave Farebrother, Graham Starns, Lee Wallis, David Mathers, Adrian Barry, Michael Bidmead, Tony Holland, Steve Moore, Brian Williams, Graham Baker.
Manager: Paul Doswell
Programme Editor: Lyall Reynolds **(E)** suttoneditor@hotmail.com

Club Factfile

Founded: 1898 **Nickname:** The U's
Previous Names: None
Previous Leagues: Sutton Junior, Southern Suburban, Athenian 1921-63, Isthmian 1963-86, 91-99, 2000-04, 2008-11, Conference 1999-2000, 04-08
Club Colours (change): All amber (All white)

Ground: Borough Sports Ground, Gander Green Lane, Sutton, Surrey SM1 2EY **(T)** 0208 644 4440
Capacity: 7,032 **Seats:** 765 **Covered:** 1,250 **Clubhouse:** Yes **Shop:** Yes

Directions
Travel along the M25 to junction 8. Then north on the A217 for about 15-20 minutes. Ignoring signs for Sutton itself, stay on the A217 to the traffic lights by the Gander Inn (on the left), turn right into Gander Green Lane. The Borough Sports Ground is about 200 yards up this road on the left hand side, if you reach West Sutton station you have gone too far.

Previous Grounds: Western Road, Manor Lane, London Road, The Find

Record Attendance: 14,000 v Leeds United - FA Cup 4th Round 24/01/1970
Record Victory: 11-1 v Clapton - 1966 and v Leatherhead - 1982-83 both Isthmian League
Record Defeat: 0-13 v Barking - Athenian League 1925-26
Record Goalscorer: Paul McKinnon - 279
Record Appearances: Larry Pritchard - 781 (1965-84)
Additional Records: Received £100,000 from AFC Bournemouth for Efan Ekoku 1990

Senior Honours: Anglo Italian Cup 1979. Isthmian League (x4) 2010-11. Athenian League x3. London Senior Cup x2. Surrey Senior Cup x2.

10 YEAR RECORD

01-02	02-03	03-04	04-05	05-06	06-07	07-08	08-09	09-10	10-11
Isth P 12	Isth P 6	Isth P 2	Conf S 15	Conf S 13	Conf S 13	Conf S 22	Isth P 5	Isth P 2	Isth P 1

SUTTON UNITED

No.	Date	Comp	H/A	Opponents	Att:	Result	Goalscorers	Pos
1	Aug 21	Isth Prem	A	Concord Rangers	242	D 0 - 0		15
2	24		H	Horsham	529	W 2 - 0	Dundas 26 Jolly 70	
3	28		H	Folkestone Invicta	503	W 1 - 0	Jolly 13	3
4	30		A	Tooting & Mitcham United	654	W 3 - 0	Jolly11 Orilonishe 60 Woods-Garness 90	
5	Sept 4		H	Billericay Town	733	W 1 - 0	Woods-Garness 10	1
6	7		A	Hastings United	541	W 3 - 2	Davis 27 Jolly 37 Woods-Garness 50	
7	**11**	**FAC 1Q**	**H**	**Alton Town**	**298**	**L 1 - 2**	**Woods-Garness 24**	
8	21		H	Harrow Borough	478	W 2 - 1	Jolly 1 Woods-Garness 11	1
9	Oct 2		H	Margate	1253	W 2 - 1	Hammond 46 Davis 78	1
10	4		A	Kingstonian	750	L 0 - 1		
11	9		A	Lowestoft Town	1265	D 0 - 0		2
12	**16**	**FAT 1Q**	**H**	**Tooting & Mitcham United**	**448**	**W 3 - 1**	**Forbes 37 Page 84 Adjei 88**	
13	23		H	Cray Wanderers	497	D 1 - 1	Murray 31	3
14	26		H	Tonbridge Angels		D 2 - 2	Jolly 35 Murray 45	
15	**30**	**FAT 2Q**	**A**	**Evesham United**	**188**	**W 1 - 0**	**Woods-Garness 70**	
16	Nov 3		A	Croydon Athletic	274	W 3 - 0	Dundas 55 Wood-Garness 67 Forbes 79	
17	6		A	Maidstone United	405	W 3 - 0	Davis 25 Forbes 43 Kavanagh 49	1
18	9		H	Kingstonian	779	W 2 - 0	Ebsworth 22 Dundas 43	
19	13		A	Margate	397	L 2 - 3	Adjei 29 Woods-Garness 49	1
20	**20**	**FAT 3Q**	**H**	**Billericay Town**	**329**	**W 4 - 2**	**FORBES 3 (4 44 76) Woods-Garness 89**	
21	23		A	Harrow Borough	163	D 0 - 0		
22	27		H	Wealdstone	527	W 4 - 3	Forbes 44 Hammond 62 (og) Downer 89 Page 90	1
23	**Dec 11**	**FAT 1**	**A**	**Eastleigh**	**388**	**D 1 - 1**	**Dundas 5**	
24	**14**	**FAT 1r**	**H**	**Eastleigh**	**237**	**L 0 - 4**		
25	27		A	Carshalton Athletic	1056	W 2 - 0	Forbes 45 Woods -Garness 55	
26	Jan 1		H	Tooting & Mitcham	746	D 2 - 2	Davis 16 Woods-Garness 33	1
27	8		A	Horsham	416	L 1 - 3	Dundas 57	
28	11		A	Canvey Island		W 3 - 1	Forbes 37 51 Woods-Garness 85	
29	15		H	Concord Rangers	568	D 1 - 1	Woods-Garness 50	1
30	22		A	Bury Town	720	L 1 - 2	El-Salahi 2	1
31	25		H	Croydon Athletic	410	W 5 - 0	Hughes 9 (og) Ebsworth 28 Forbes 45 Dundas 47 Page 55	
32	29		H	Aveley	459	W 2 - 1	Dundas 46 (pen) Page 62	1
33	Feb 5		A	Cray Wanderers	269	W 2 - 0	Dundas 70 Woods-Garness 85	1
34	8		H	AFC Hornchurch	481	W 3 - 0	Dundas 75 81 Griffiths 88	
35	12		H	Lowestoft Town	803	W 2 - 1	Forbes 26 (pen) 54	1
36	16		A	Hendon	167	L 0 - 1		
37	19		A	Tonbridge Angels	744	W 1 - 0	Dundas 56	1
38	26		H	Maidstone United	622	W 5 - 1	Ebsworth 24 Jolly 31 56 Griffiths 61 Woods-Garness 89	1
39	March 5		A	Wealdstone	556	L 1 - 2	Dundas 57	1
40	12		H	Hendon	586	W 3 - 0	Griffiths 6 Jolly 33 Dundas 64	1
41	19		A	AFC Hornchurch	337	D 1 - 1	Griffiths 86	1
42	26		H	Canvey Island	714	W 2 - 0	Dundas 65 Griffiths 86	1
43	April 2		A	Aveley	236	D 0 - 0		1
44	9		H	Bury Town	967	W 2 - 0	Forbes 36 Dundas 65	1
45	16		H	Hastings United	1552	W 2 - 1	Griffiths 33 Forbes 54 (pen)	Champions
46	23		A	Folkestone United	369	W 2 - 0	Jolly 16 Orilonishe 32	1
47	26		H	Carshalton Athletic	1367	W 2 - 0	Orilonishe 39 Woods-Garness 69	1

PLAYING SQUAD 2011/12

Existing Players		SN	HT	WT	DOB	AGE	POB	Career	Apps	Goals
GOALKEEPERS										
Kevin	Scriven				27/11/1984	26	Bournemouth	Bournemouth Rel c/s 05, Bournemouth FC (L) 8/03, Farnborough 6/05, Havant & W 6/07, Sutton U 6/09		
Wayne	Shaw				29/10/1970	40	Southampton	Southampton (Jun), Reading (Trainee), Basingstoke, Bashley, Wimborne, Gosport, AFC Lymington, Bournemouth FC, Fleet, BAT Sports, Lymington & New Milton, AFC Totten, Eastleigh (Pl/Coach) 6/03, Sutton U (Pl/Coach) c/s 09		
DEFENDERS										
Alan	Bray							Sutton U, Croydon Ath (L) 3/11		
Jay	Conroy		6'02"	12 02	02/03/1986	25	Ryegate	C.Palace, AFC Wimbledon (L) 9/04, AFC Wimbledon (3ML) 11/04, Aldershot (Trial) c/s 05, Canvey Island 8/05, Sutton U (3ML) 12/05, Chelmsford 6/06, Lewes 7/07 Rel 5/08, Havant & W 5/08 Rel 1/09, Northwich 1/09 Rel 2/09, AFC Wimbledon 3/09 Rel 4/10, Farnborough 8/10, Sutton U 5/11		
Simon	Downer		5'11"	12 08	19/10/1981	29	Romford	L.Orient Rel 5/04, Newcastle (Trial) 2/01, Aldershot (SL) 3/04, Retired, Hornchurch 11/04 Rel c/s 05, Weymouth 7/05, Grays 1/07 Rel 10/08, Wivenhoe 10/08, Sutton U 11/08, Rushden & D 1/09 Rel 6/10, Sutton U 7/10		
Karim	El-Salahi		6'02"	13 09	24/11/1986	24	London	C.Palace Rel c/s 05, Woking 7/05 Rel 1/07, Eastleigh (L) 12/06, Eastleigh 1/07, Sutton U (L) 1/08, Sutton U 3/08		
Neil	Jenkins		5'06"	10 08	06/01/1982	29	Carshalton	Wimbledon Rel c/s 02, Southend 8/02 Rel c/s 04, Crawley 6/04, Eastbourne B 7/06 Rel 5/11, Sutton U 5/11		
Sam	Page		6'04"	13 02	30/10/1987	23	Croydon	C.Palace (Yth), MK Dons Rel 1/08, Aylesbury (L) 8/06, Hendon (L) 9/06, Cambridge U (SL) 2/07 (06/07 8,0), Walton & H (L) 9/07, Hendon (3ML) 10/07, Rushden & D (Trial) 1/08, Hendon 1/08, Horsham 6/08, Sutton U 7/10		
MIDFIELDERS										
Harry	Beautyman				01/04/1992	19	Newham	L.Orient (Pro 5/10) Rel c/s 11, St Albans (L) 10/10, Hastings U (L) 1/11, Sutton U 8/11		
Tom	Kavanagh							Sutton U		
Romone	McCrae		6'01"	12 07	01/08/1990	21	Southwark	Crawley, Peterborough Undisc 7/09 Rel c/s 11, Histon (5ML) 7/10, Kettering (SL) 2/11, Sutton U 7/11		
Steve	McKimm				30/07/1975	36	London	Malden Vale, Hendon, Molesey, Dulwich H 8/96, Farnborough 4 Fig 1/99, Hayes £4,000 c/s 99, Kingstonian 6/01, Gravesend 10/01 Rel 5/06. Margate 5/06, Sutton U (Pl/Coach) 5/08		
Karl	Murray		5'11"	12 06	26/08/1982	29	London	Shrewsbury, Sheff Utd (Trial) 8/99, Northwich (L) 11/03, Woking 1/04, Grays 5/07 Rel 2/08, Eastleigh 2/08, Bromley 6/08, Sutton U (L) 9/08, Ebbsfleet (2ML) 11/08, Northwich (L) 1/09, Croydon Ath 2/09, Carshalton 10/09, Sutton U 9/10		
Fola	Orilonishe				14/07/1986	25	St Etienne, Fra	Eton Manor, Watham Forest c/s 06, Thurrock 8/07, Sutton U 5/10		
Helge	Orome							Croydon Ath, Sutton U 8/11		
Chris	Piper				20/10/1981	29	London	Charlton, St Albans, Farnborough 2/01, Dag & Red 6/03, Fisher 6/04 Rel 5/07, Eastleigh 7/07 Rel 5/08, Braintree 7/08 Rel 5/09, Croydon Ath c/s 09, Tonbridge A 10/10, Sutton U 8/11		
Anthony	Riviere				09/11/1978	32	Kent	Faversham, Welling 11/98, Fisher 6/04 Rel 5/07, Eastleigh 7/07 Rel 5/11, Sutton U 5/11		
Tony	Taggart		5'10"	11 02	07/10/1981	29	London	Brentford Rel c/s 00, Farnborough c/s 00, Barnet 6/03, Farnborough 8/04, Weymouth 6/05, Havant & W 12/05, Eastleigh 7/08, Newport C 5/10, Eastleigh (2ML) 10/10 Perm 12/10, Sutton U 5/11		
FORWARDS										
Craig	Dundas				16/02/1981	30		Local, Croydon, Dulwich H 1/04, Cyprus c/s 04, Dulwich H c/s 05, Carshalton 11/05, Sutton U 11/07 Rel c/s 09, Carshalton (Trial) 7/09, Tooting & M (Trial) 8/09, Hampton & R 8/09, Sutton U 5/10		
Leroy	Griffiths		5'11"	13 05	30/12/1976	34	London	Sutton U, Banstead, Corinthian C, Hampton & Richmond 2/00, QPR £40,000 5/01 Rel 7/03, Farnborough (L) 8/02, Margate (L) 11/02, Farnborough 8/03, Grays 9/03, Fisher 5/05 Rel 5/07, Aldershot (3ML) 1/06, Grays (SL) 2/07, Havant & W 7/07, Corinthian Casuals 10/07, Lewes 10/07, Gillingham (6WL) 11/07 Perm 1/08 Rel c/s 08, Eastleigh 8/08, Staines 8/08, Sutton U 1/11		
Bajrush	Halili							Sutton U		
Craig	Watkins				04/05/1986	25	Croydon	Epsom & E, Sutton U 7/04, Exeter 8/05 Rel 2/06, Sutton U (L) 10/05, Lewes (L) 12/05, Staines (L) 1/06, Havant & W 3/06, Sutton U 7/07, Havant & W 10/07 Rel c/s 09, Woking 8/09 Rel 10/09, Hayes & Yeading 11/09 Rel 5/10, Met Police 6/10, Sutton U 6/11		
Bradley	Woods-Garness				27/06/1986	25		Chelsea (Jun), Barnet, Welwyn Garden (Dual) 8/05, Farnborough 7/06, Billericay 8/07, Dartford (L) 3/09, Sutton U 6/09, Billericay (L) 11/09, Hendon (2ML) 12/09		

SOCCER BOOKS LIMITED

72 ST. PETERS AVENUE (Dept. NLD)
CLEETHORPES
N.E. LINCOLNSHIRE
DN35 8HU
ENGLAND

Tel. 01472 696226 Fax 01472 698546

Web site www.soccer-books.co.uk
e-mail info@soccer-books.co.uk

Established in 1982, Soccer Books Limited has one of the largest ranges of English-Language soccer books available. We continue to expand our stocks even further to include many new titles including German, French, Spanish, Italian and other foreign-language books.

With well over 100,000 satisfied customers already, we supply books to virtually every country in the world but have maintained the friendliness and accessibility associated with a small family-run business. The range of titles we sell includes:

YEARBOOKS – All major yearbooks including many editions of the Sky Sports Football Yearbook (previously Rothmans), Supporters' Guides, Playfair Annuals, European Football Yearbooks and Asian, African and North, Central and South American yearbooks.

CLUB HISTORIES – Complete Statistical Records, Official Histories, Definitive Histories plus many more.

WORLD FOOTBALL – World Cup books, International Line-up & Statistics Series, European Championships History, International and European Club Cup competition Statistical Histories and much more.

BIOGRAPHIES & WHO'S WHOS – of managers and players plus Who's Whos etc.

ENCYCLOPEDIAS & GENERAL TITLES – Books on stadia, hooligan and sociological studies, histories and hundreds of others, including the weird and wonderful!

DVDs – Season's highlights, histories, big games, World Cup matches, player profiles, a selection of over 40 F.A. Cup Finals with many more titles becoming available all the time.

For a current printed listing containing a selection of our titles, please contact us using the details at the top of this page. Alternatively, our web site offers a secure ordering system for credit and debit card holders and lists our full range of over 1,900 books and 400 DVDs.

THURROCK

Chairman: Tommy South
Secretary: Mark Southgate (T) 07979 525 117 (E) mark.southgate@purcom.com
Additional Committee Members:
Norman Posner, Gary Reed, Tony Flood, Mike Pink.

Manager: Robbie Garvey
Programme Editor: Tony Flood (E) thurrockfcpressoffice@gmail.com

THURROCK FC 2011 - 2012

Club Factfile

Founded: 1985 **Nickname:** Fleet
Previous Names: Purfleet > 2003
Previous Leagues: Essex Senior 1985-89, Isthmian 1989-2004

Club Colours (change): Yellow & green/green/green (All purple)

Ground: Thurrock Hotel, Ship Lane, Grays, Essex RM19 1YN (T) 01708 865 492
Capacity: 4,500 **Seats:** 300 **Covered:** 1,000 **Clubhouse:** Yes **Shop:** Yes

Directions Approaching the ground from the North - along the M25 in a clockwise direction. Leave the motorway at junction 30. At the roundabout take the second exit and stay in the left hand lane. This leads to a large roundabout controlled by traffic lights. The fifth exit is Ship Lane and the ground is approximately 50 yards on the right hand side. Approaching the ground from the South - anti-clockwise on the M25. When going through the Dartford Tunnel take the left hand bore. On coming out of the tunnel take the first exit - junction 31. This leads to a large roundabout controlled by traffic lights. Take the third exit which is Ship Lane. The ground is situated approximately 50 yards on the right hand side.

Previous Grounds: Not known

Record Attendance: 2,572 v West Ham United - Friendly 1998
Record Victory: 10-0 v Stansted (H) - Essex Senior Lge 1986-87 and v East Ham United (A) - Essex Senior Lge 1987-88
Record Defeat: 0-6 v St Leonards Stamco (A) - FA Trophy 1996-97 and v Sutton United (H) - Isthmian League 1997-98
Record Goalscorer: George Georgiou - 106
Record Appearances: Jimmy McFarlane - 632
Additional Records:

Senior Honours: Isthmian League Division 2 1991-92.
Essex Senior Cup 2003-04, 05-06.

10 YEAR RECORD

01-02	02-03	03-04	04-05	05-06	06-07	07-08	08-09	09-10	10-11
Isth P 5	Isth P 8	Isth P 3	Conf S 3	Conf S 10	Conf S 18	Conf S 12	Conf S 20	Conf S 10	Conf S 20

THURROCK

No.	Date	Comp	H/A	Opponents	Att:	Result	Goalscorers	Pos
1	Sat-14-Aug	BSS	H	St Albans City	306	D 2-2	Akurang 2 (64, pen 73)	12
2	Tue-17-Aug	BSS	A	Lewes	601	L 1-2	Akurang 64	16
3	Sat-21-Aug	BSS	A	Boreham Wood	138	D 2-2	Bodkin 40, Roache 45	17
4	Tue-24-Aug	BSS	H	Hampton & Richmond Borough	237	D 2-2	Gilbey 25, Roache 82	19
5	Sat-28-Aug	BSS	H	Bishops Stortford	248	L 1-3	Akurang 25	19
6	Mon-30-Aug	BSS	A	Dover Athletic	923	L 0-1		20
7	Sat-04-Sep	BSS	A	Havant & Waterlooville	692	L 1-4	Akurang 2	20
8	Sat-11-Sep	BSS	H	Dartford	664	D 1-1	Lettejallow 65	19
9	Sat-18-Sep	BSS	A	Basingstoke Town	372	D 2-2	Hart 32, Akurang pen 65	19
10	Sat-02-Oct	BSS	H	Dorchester Town	208	D 1-1	Olima 18	19
11	Sat-16-Oct	BSS	A	Braintree Town	455	L 0-1		20
12	Sat-30-Oct	BSS	H	Bromley	353	L 1-2	Akurang pen 45	20
13	Sat-06-Nov	BSS	H	Braintree Town	305	L 0-3		22
14	Sat-13-Nov	BSS	A	Weston-Super-Mare	150	L 1-2	Cracknell pen 40	22
15	Tue-16-Nov	BSS	H	Staines Town	204	W 2-1	Cracknell pen 58, Swaine 74	21
16	Sat-27-Nov	BSS	H	Lewes	274	W 3-1	Lalite 17, Cracknell pen 69, Knight 90	20
17	Sat-11-Dec	BSS	A	Bishops Stortford	251	L 0-1		20
18	Sat-01-Jan	BSS	A	Chelmsford City	876	L 1-6	Carlos 68	21
19	Mon-03-Jan	BSS	H	Dover Athletic	495	L 2-7	Knight 15, Roache 90	21
20	Sat-08-Jan	BSS	A	Dartford	1020	W 1-0	Bodkin 68	20
21	Sat-15-Jan	BSS	H	Welling United	394	W 2-1	Richards 38, Knight 48	18
22	Sat-22-Jan	BSS	A	Maidenhead United	233	W 3-1	Swaine 9, Richards 62, Olima 79	17
23	Tue-25-Jan	BSS	A	Ebbsfleet United	656	D 2-2	Knight 34, Clark 61	16
24	Sat-29-Jan	BSS	H	Eastleigh	255	W 2-1	Clark 33, Richards pen 78	15
25	Tue-01-Feb	BSS	A	Woking	707	L 0-1		16
26	Sat-05-Feb	BSS	A	Staines Town	273	D 1-1	Bodkin 39	15
27	Sat-12-Feb	BSS	H	Farnborough	238	L 2-4	Carlos 7, Swaine 43	17
28	Tue-22-Feb	BSS	H	Chelmsford City	479	D 1-1	Clark 62	17
29	Tue-01-Mar	BSS	H	Boreham Wood	183	L 1-3	Ladapo 49	19
30	Sat-05-Mar	BSS	A	Dorchester Town	402	L 1-3	Clark 6	19
31	Tue-08-Mar	BSS	H	Basingstoke Town	157	L 0-3		19
32	Sat-12-Mar	BSS	H	Woking	415	L 0-1		19
33	Sat-19-Mar	BSS	A	Hampton & Richmond Borough	365	D 0-0		19
34	Tue-22-Mar	BSS	H	Havant & Waterlooville	152	D 1-1	Clark 90	19
35	Sat-26-Mar	BSS	A	St Albans City	235	W 2-0	Richards pen 51, Lee 90	19
36	Tue-29-Mar	BSS	A	Bromley	210	L 0-1		19
37	Sat-02-Apr	BSS	H	Weston-Super-Mare	163	W 3-0	Boylan 3 (34, 50, 73)	18
38	Sat-09-Apr	BSS	A	Eastleigh	441	L 1-3	Boylan 57	19
39	Sat-16-Apr	BSS	H	Maidenhead United	225	L 1-2	Cracknell 23	20
40	Fri-22-Apr	BSS	A	Welling United	753	D 1-1	Hockton pen 90	19
41	Mon-25-Apr	BSS	H	Ebbsfleet United	647	D 0-0		20
42	Sat-30-Apr	BSS	A	Farnborough	839	L 2-3	Olima 48, Hockton 69	20

CUPS

No.	Date	Comp	H/A	Opponents	Att:	Result	Goalscorers	Pos
1	Sat-25-Sep	FAC 2Q	H	Stamford AFC	122	W 3-1	Akurang 32, Roache 2 (87, 90)	
2	Sat-09-Oct	FAC 3Q	A	Lewes	854	L 1-2	Bodkin 88	
3	Sat-20-Nov	FAT 3Q	H	Dartford	405	L 0-2		

PLAYING SQUAD 2011/12

Existing Players		SN	HT	WT	DOB	AGE	POB	Career	Apps	Goals
GOALKEEPERS										
Tommy	Forecast		6'07"	11 11	15/10/1986	24	Newham	Tottenham, Southampton Undisc 7/08, Grimsby (L) 8/09, Eastbourne B (L) 1/11, Thurrock (L) 8/11		
Craig	Holloway				10/08/1984	27	Blackheath	Arsenal Rel c/s 04, Farnborough 6/04, Southend (2ML) 1/05, Gravesend 8/05, Injured, Bromley 3/08, Braintree 5/08, Chelmsford 7/09, Braintree 12/09, Bromley 7/10, Thurrock c/s 11		
Tey	Lynn-Jones							Tilbury, Thurrock 7/11		
DEFENDERS										
Joe	Bruce		6'00"	12 00	05/07/1983	27	London	Luton Rel c/s 02, Wingate & Finchley (SL) 1/02, Molesey, Hitchin 3/03, Grays 8/03 Rel 5/06, Maidenhead (2ML) 1/06, Basingstoke 6/06, Welling 3/07, Cambridge C 6/07, Braintree 7/08, Dartford 6/10 Rel 5/11, Thurrock 8/11		
Arron	Fray		5'11"	11 02	01/05/1987	24	Bromley	C. Palace Rel c/s 08, Dag & Red 9/08 Rel c/s 09, Bromley 2/09, Thurrock 7/11		
Rickie	Hayles							Brentwood, Ilford, Eton Manor, Tilbury 12/08, AFC Hornchurch 2/10, Thurrock 6/11		
David	Partridge		6'00"	13 05	26/11/1978	32	Westminster	West Ham, Dundee U £40,000 3/99 Rel c/s 02, L.Orient (3ML) 1/02, Motherwell 7/02, Bristol C £150,000 7/05 Rel 8/07, MK Dons (SL) 1/06, L.Orient (L) 7/06, Brentford (L) 1/07, Swindon (L) 3/07, Brentford 12/07 Rel 1/08, St Patricks 1/08, Cambridge U 1/10 Rel 5/11, Thurrock 8/11		
Kurt	Robinson		5'08"	11 00	21/10/1989	21	Basildon	West Ham (Yth), Southend (Yth), Ipswich Rel 5/09, Northampton (6WL) 11/08, Rushden & D (SL) 1/09, Rushden & D 7/09, Chelmsford (L) 12/10 Perm 1/11, Thurrock 8/11		
MIDFIELDERS										
Ben	Bowditch		5'10"	12 00	19/02/1984	27	Bishops Stortford	Tottenham, AB Copenhagen (Den) (3ML) 3/04, Colchester 8/04, Barnet 8/05, Yeading (L) 3/06, Cambridge C 7/06, St Albans 8/08 Rel 10/08, Bishops Stortford 7/09, Thurrock 7/11		
Dean	Cracknell		5'10"	12 04	12/10/1983	27	Hitchin	Watford (Ass Sch), Northampton Rel 2/04, Stevenage 3/04 Rel c/s 04, Aylesbury 7/04, Barnet (Trial) 1/05, Bishops Stortford 2/05, St Albans 5/05, Staines (L) 9/06, Hemel Hempstead 5/07, St Albans 1/08, Cambridge C 3/08, Brackley 6/08, Welling 7/09 Rel 9/10, Boreham Wood 10/10, Thurrock 11/10	30	4
Reece	Harris				12/02/1991	20		Stanway R, Heybridge 10/09, Braintree 12/09, Concord R (L) 11/10, Thurrock (SL) 2/11, Thurrock 8/11	14	0
Reece	Morgan							Heybridge, Thurrock 8/11		
Idemudia (Dee)	Okojie							Wycombe, Aveley, Arlesey 11/07, Leyton, Bishops Stortford 8/08 Rel 12/08, Harlow, Billericay 3/09, Boreham Wood 6/09, Redbridge 9/09, Brentwood 10/09, Histon 1/11, Thurrock 8/11		
Glenn	Poole		5'07"	11 04	03/02/1981	30	Barking	Tottenham (Trainee), Witham T 99/00, Yeovil 11/99, Bath C (L) 9/01, Ford U/Redbridge 2/02, Thurrock 11/04, Grays 7/05, Rochdale (SL) 3/07, Brentford 5/07 Rel c/s 09, Grays 8/09, AFC Wimbledon 1/10 Rel 4/10, Barnet 6/10, Braintree 2/11, Thurrock 7/11		
Paul	Terry		5'10"	12 06	03/04/1979	32	Barking	Charlton, Bromley, Dag & Red, Yeovil 8/03, L.Orient 8/07, Grays 8/09, Rushden & D 8/09 Rel 6/10, Darlington 8/10 Rel c/s 11, Thurrock 8/11		
James	White				05/08/1988	23		Southend (Yth), Tottenham (Yth), Arsenal (Yth), Great Wakering, Dartford 8/08 Rel 5/11, Thurrock 8/11		
FORWARDS										
Rocky	Baptiste		6'02"	11 11	07/07/1972	39	Clapham	Chelsea (Jun), Willesden Hawkeye, Wealdstone, Staines, Hayes 7/00, Luton 10/00, Hayes (L) 3/01, Farnborough 6/01, Southend (Trial) 4/03, Stevenage 6/03, Margate 2/04, Havant & W 9/05, Maidenhead 10/08, AFC Wimbledon 3/09, Harrow c/s 09, Thurrock 8/11		
Lee	Boylan		5'06"	11 06	02/09/1978	32	Witham	West Ham Rel c/s 99, Kingstonian (L) 12/98, Trelleborgs (Swe) c/s 99, Exeter (2ML) 11/99, Kingstonian 2/00 Rel c/s 00, Southend (Trial), Hayes 10/00, Stevenage, Heybridge S, Canvey Island 8/01, Grays 7/06, Chelmsford (L) 2/07, Cambridge U 5/07, Stevenage Undisc 6/08 Rel 1/11, Southend (Trial) 2/11, Chelmsford 3/11, Thurrock 3/11	6	4
Kris	Newby							East Thurrock, Aveley 3/07, East Thurrock 3/07, Thurrock 6/11		
Jamie	Richards							Tottenham (Jun), Enfield, St Margartesbury, Leyton Pennant, East Thurrock, Arlesey, Braintree 8/02, Hayes 6/03, St Albans 11/03, Braintree 1/04, Enfield 7/04, Chelmsford c/s 05, Fisher 3/06 Rel 5/06, Heybridge 6/06, East Thurrock c/s 07, AFC Hornchurch 1/08, Harlow c/s 08, Thurrock 2/09, Harlow 3/09, Boreham Wood 5/09, AFC Hornchurch c/s 10, Harlow 10/10, Thurrock 1/11	19	4

Caption competition....

Send in your suggestions to tw.publications@btinternet.com and you could win a copy of the 2013 edition of the Directory...

Photo by Keith Clayton

TONBRIDGE ANGELS

Chairman: Steve Churcher

Secretary: Keith Masters (T) 07770 578 222 (E) keith.master@yahoo.co.uk

Additional Committee Members:
John Gibbons, Chris Drew, Colin Fry, Darren Apps.

Manager: Tommy Warrilow

Programme Editor: Geoff Curtis (E) curtis.g10@ntlworld.com

Front Row: Tina Jenner, Ben Judge, Lewis Taylor, Ade Olorunda, Sonny Miles, Scott Kinch, Lee Worgan, Alwayne Jones, Jon Heath, Tim Olorunda, Jake Beecroft, Sam Bewick, Melvin Slight
Back Row: Anthony Storey, Chris Henry, Jon Main, Alex O'Brien, Tommy Warrilow, Terry Sedge, Frannie Collin, Lee Browning, Danny Walder.

Club Factfile

Founded: 1948 **Nickname:** Angels

Previous Names: Tonbridge Angels, Tonbridge F.C., Tonbridge A.F.C.

Previous Leagues: Southern 1948-80, 93-2004, Kent 1989-93, Isthmian 2004-11.

Club Colours (change): All blue (All white)

Ground: Longmead Stadium, Darenth Avenue, Tonbridge, Kent TH10 3JW (T) 01732 352 417

Capacity: 2,500 **Seats:** 707 **Covered:** 1,500 **Clubhouse:** Yes **Shop:** Yes

Directions From M25. Take A21 turning at Junction 5 to junction with A225/b245 (signposted Hildenborough). After passing Langley Hotel on left thake slightly hidden left turn into Dry Hill Park Road. Left again at mini roundabout into Shipbourne Road (A227) and then left again at next roundabout into Darenth Avenue' Longmead stadium can be found at the bottom of the hill at the far end of the car park.

Previous Grounds: The Angel 1948-80

Record Attendance: 8,236 v Aldershot - FA Cup 1951
Record Victory: 11-1 v Worthing - FA Cup 1951
Record Defeat: 2-11 v Folkstone - Kent Senior Cup 1949
Record Goalscorer: Jon Main scored 44 goals in one season including seven hat-tricks
Record Appearances: Mark Giham
Additional Records:

Senior Honours: Kent Senior Cup 1964-65, 74-75

10 YEAR RECORD

01-02	02-03	03-04	04-05	05-06	06-07	07-08	08-09	09-10	10-11
SthE 19	SthE 9	SthE 3	Isth P 20	Isth1 3	Isth P 11	Isth P 8	Isth P 3	Isth P 8	Isth P 2

TONBRIDGE ANGELS

No.	Date	Comp	H/A	Opponents	Att:	Result	Goalscorers	Pos
1	Aug 21	Isth Prem	A	Billericay Town	457	L 0 - 3		22
2	24		H	Bury Town	429	L 2 - 3	Booth 44 (pen) 45	
3	28		H	Harrow Borough	349	L 1 - 2	Collin 84	22
4	30		A	Folkestone Invicta	394	D 0 - 0		
5	Sept 4		H	Horsham	435	W 2 - 0	Stanley 64 Collin 85 (pen)	17
6	7		A	Carshalton Athletic	226	L 2 - 3	Kinch 30 Stanley 56	
7	**11**	**FAC 1Q**	**H**	**Guildford City**	**385**	**L 0 - 1**		
8	18		A	Concord Rangers	184	W 2 - 1	Browning 45 Collin 64	17
9	21		H	Cray Wanderers	328	L 0 - 4		18
10	Oct 2		H	AFC Hornchurch	383	W 7 - 1	COLLIN 3 (4 42 89) Seanla 34 54 Piper 40 England 46	13
11	5		A	Margate	341	W 1 - 0	Browning 75	
12	9		H	Croydon Athletic	485	W 1 - 0	Collin 75	8
13	**16**	**FAT 1Q**	**H**	**Concord Rangers**	**384**	**W 3 - 2**	**Collin 29 32 Seanla 34**	
14	23		A	Aveley	203	W 3 - 0	SEANLA 3 (38 42 44)	5
15	26		A	Sutton United	561	D 2 - 2	England 43 Collin 82	
16	**30**	**FAT 2Q**	**H**	**Enfield Town**	**517**	**W 2 - 1**	**Miles 30 Walder 45**	
17	Nov 9		H	Margate	326	D 1 - 1	Browning 62	
18	13		A	AFC Hornchurch	301	L 1 - 3	Collin 81	11
19	**20**	**FAT 3Q**	**A**	**Welling United**	**431**	**L 0 - 1**		
20	23		A	Cray Wanderers	203	W 1 - 0	Piper 8	
21	27		H	Kingstonian	501	D 1 - 1	May 64	10
22	Jan 3		H	Folkestone Invicta	589	W 1 - 0	Judge 8	
23	8		A	Bury Town	592	W 2 - 1	May 78 Hill 90	8
24	11		H	Hendon	267	W 2 - 1	Olorundo 27 Collin 74 (pen)	
25	15		H	Billericay Town	522	W 3 - 1	Browning 22 88 Taylor 30	5
26	22		A	Tooting & Mitcham U	328	W 5 - 1	Collin 3 Olorundo 6 May 9 Walder 45 Taylor 85	4
27	29		H	Lowestoft Town	621	D 3 - 3	Beales 18 Collin 26 May 34	6
28	Feb 1		A	Maidstone United	348	W 3 - 0	COLLIN 3 (14 38 66)	
29	5		H	Aveley	436	W 1 - 0	Collin 77	3
30	8		H	Concord Rangers	388	W 3 - 2	Judge 10 Olorundo 48 Browning 78	
31	12		A	Croydon Athletic	178	L 0 - 2		3
32	19		H	Sutton United	744	L 0 - 1		3
33	22		A	Hastings United	562	W 2 - 1	Logan 8 Olorundo 45	
34	March 1		H	Canvey Island	303	D 1 - 1	Beales 79	
35	5		A	Kingstonian	405	D 1 - 1	Beecroft 78	4
36	7		A	Wealdstone	432	D 0 - 0		
37	12		H	Maidstone United	802	W 1 - 0	Rook 38	3
38	19		A	Canvey Island	477	L 0 - 1		3
39	26		H	Wealdstone	505	W 2 - 0	Olorundo 30 Rook 80	3
40	April 2		A	Lowestoft Town	767	D 0 - 0		5
41	9		H	Tooting & Mitcham	534	D 3 - 3	Collin 29 Kinch 33 Olorundo 63	8
42	12		A	Hendon	149	W 3 - 0	Collin 57 Rook 77 (pen) Olorundo 79	
43	16		H	Carshalton Athletic	472	W 4 - 0	Rook 44 Olorundo 55 Stone 78 89	2
44	23		A	Harrow Borough	362	L 0 - 2		4
45	26		H	Hastings United	817	W 2 - 0	Walder 14 Jones 75	
46	30		A	Horsham	492	W 2 - 0	Logan 45 Kinch 86	2
47	**May 3**	**P-Off SF**	**H**	**Harrow Borough**	**1124**	**W 3 - 2***	**Piper 6 Kinch 23 Olorundo 110**	
48	**7**	**P-Off Final**	**H**	**Lowestoft Town**	**2411**	**W 4 - 3**	**Olorundo 12 Piper 22 Walder 39 (pen) Taylor 78**	

PLAYING SQUAD 2011/12

Existing Players		SN	HT	WT	DOB	AGE	POB	Career	Apps	Goals
GOALKEEPERS										
Joe	Hagan				08/11/1991	19		Ebbsfleet Rel 2/11, Tonbridge A 3/11		
Lee	Worgan		6'01"	13 10	01/12/1983	27	Eastbourne	Wimbledon Rel c/s 04, Aylesbury (SL) 12/02, Wycombe (L) 4/04, Rushden & D 8/04 Rel c/s 05, Eastbourne B 8/05, Cardiff C 10/05 Rel c/s 06, Merthyr (L) 1/06, Eastbourne B 7/06, Hastings U 10/06, Tonbridge A 5/08		
DEFENDERS										
Ben	Andrews		6'01"	12 13	18/11/1980	30	Burton	Brighton, Worthing 9/00, St Albans 1/01, West Chiltington c/s 01, Horsham YMCA 3/02, Burgess Hill 8/02, Worthing 10/05, Horsham c/s 09 Rel c/s 11, Tonbridge A 6/11		
Jon	Heath							Tonbridge A		
Ben	Judge				22/05/1977	34	Redhill	C.Palace (Jun), Croydon (94), Crawley 11/01 Rel 8/07, Bromley 9/07 Rel 3/08, AFC Wimbledon 3/08 Rel 4/10, Croydon Ath 7/10, Tonbridge A 10/10		
Sonny	Miles							Tonbridge A		
Danny	Walder				03/09/1989	21	Chatham	Gillingham Rel 1/09, Ramsgate (3ML) 10/08 Perm 1/09, Dover 8/09 Rel 5/10, Tonbridge A 5/10		
MIDFIELDERS										
Jake	Beecroft				04/09/1989	21		Rushden & D Rel 5/10, Solihull Moors (6WL) 11/08, Ilkeston (3ML) 9/09, St Albans (2ML) 1/10, Tonbridge A 5/10		
Chris	Henry				27/06/1984	27	London	Harrow, Roundwood, Edgware, Chalfont St Peter, Flackwell Heath, Bedfont T, Carshalton Rel 3/11, Tonbridge A 3/11		
Scott	Kinch							Carshalton, Tooting & M 8/03, Tonbridge A 5/06, Cray W 6/08, Concord R 12/09, Tonbridge A 1/10		
Tim	Olorunda				01/09/1984	26		Hastings U, St Leonards, Rye & Iden, Hastings U 5/05, Tonbridge A 5/08, Hastings U 6/09, Tonbridge A 6/11		
Anthony	Storey				16/11/1983	27	Bishop Auckland	Middlesbrough, Sheff Wed (SL) 2/03, Dunfermline 5/03, Lewes 7/04, Eastbourne B (L) 10/04, Eastbourne B 6/05 Rel 5/06, Lewes 6/06, Tonbridge A (L) 12/06, Basingstoke (L) 3/07, Tonbridge A 5/07, Hastings U 5/10, Horsham 9/10, Tonbridge A 6/11		
Lewis	Taylor		6'00"	11 07	01/08/1986	25	Sutton	AFC Wimbledon Rel 9/04, Whyteleafe 9/04, Horsham 8/06, AFC Wimbledon 5/08 Rel 4/10, Tonbridge A 7/10		
FORWARDS										
Lee	Browning				06/05/1987	24		Gillingham (Jun), Aston Villa (Trial), Derby (Trial), Sittingbourne 7/03, Dover 9/07 Rel 3/10, Tonbridge A 5/10		
Frannie	Collin		5'11"	11 11	20/04/1987	24	Chatham	Chatham, Gillingham c/s 05 Rel c/s 07, Dover 6/07 Rel 5/10, Tonbridge A 5/10		
Alwayne	Jones							Tonbridge A		
Jon	Main		5'10"	12 01	07/03/1981	30	Greenwich	VCD Ath, Cray W, Tonbridge A 1/06, Wolves (Trial) 3/07, Norwich (Trial) 3/07, AFC Wimbledon Undisc 11/07 Rel 5/11, Dartford (3ML) 1/11, Dover (SL) 3/11, Tonbridge A 6/11		
Ade	Olorunda				10/07/1982	29		Hastings U, St Leonards, Rye & Iden, Hastings U 5/05, Tonbridge A 5/08, Hastings U 6/09, Tonbridge A 12/10		

Caption competition....

Send in your suggestions to tw.publications@btinternet.com and you could win a copy of the 2013 edition of the Directory...

Photo by Keith Clayton

TRURO CITY

Chairman: Kevin Heaney
Secretary: Ian Rennie (T) 07881 498 916 (E) ian-rennie@musikfolk.com
Additional Committee Members:
Chris Webb, Julia Sincock, John Richardson.

Manager: Lee Hodges
Programme Editor: Ian Rennie (E) ian-rennie@musikfolk.com

Club Factfile

Founded: 1889 **Nickname:** City
Previous Names: None
Previous Leagues: Cornwall County, Plymouth & District, South Western, Western 2006-08, Southern 2008-11.

Club Colours (change): All white (All royal blue)

Ground: Treyew Road, Truro, Cornwall TR1 2TH (T) 01872 225 400 / 278 853
Capacity: Nk **Seats:** 750 **Covered:** Yes **Clubhouse:** Yes **Shop:**

Directions On arriving at Exeter, leave the M5 at junction 31 and join the A30. Travel via Okehampton, Launceston, and Bodmin.. At the end of the dual carriageway (windmills on right hand side) take left hand turning signposted Truro. After approximately 7 miles turn right at traffic lights, travel downhill crossing over three roundabouts, following signs for Redruth. Approximately 500 metres after third roundabout signed 'Arch Hill', ground is situated on left hand side.

Previous Grounds: None

Record Attendance: 1,400 v Aldershot - FA Vase
Record Victory: Not known
Record Defeat: Not known
Record Goalscorer: Not known
Record Appearances: Not known
Additional Records: Most League points and goals in a season:
115 points & 185 goals, Western League Division One (42 games) 2006-07.

Senior Honours: South Western League 1960-61, 69-70, 92-93, 95-96, 97-98. Western League Division 1 2006-07, Premier Division 07-08.
FA Vase 2006-07. Southern League Division 1 South & West 2008-09, Premier Division 2010-11.
Cornwall Senior Cup x15

10 YEAR RECORD

01-02		02-03		03-04		04-05		05-06		06-07		07-08		08-09		09-10		10-11	
SWest	17	SWest	16	SWest	15	SWest	6	SWest	2	West1	1	WestP	1	Sthsw	1	SthP	11	SthP	1

TRURO CITY

No.	Date	Comp	H/A	Opponents	Att:	Result	Goalscorers	Pos
1	Aug 14	Sth Prem	H	Chesham United	435	L 0 - 3		21
2	17		A	Evesham United	118	W 4 - 3	Watkins 35 Ash 52 Taylor 69 Afful 86	
3	21		A	Bedford Town	344	D 1 - 1	Jeannin 65	9
4	24		H	Bashley	301	W 2 - 1	Smith 21 McConnell 59 (pen)	
5	28		H	Oxford City	371	W 2 - 1	Watkins 18 Adams 82	6
6	30		A	Tiverton Town	496	W 2 - 1	McConnell 45 (pen) 52 (pen)	
7	Sept 4		H	Hednesford Town	469	W 1 - 0	Yetton 80	3
8	**11**	**FAC 1Q**	**H**	**Bridgwater Town**	**420**	**W 8 - 2**	**McConnell 2 (Pen) 8 (pen) Watkins13 Smith 40 Yetton 3 (51 63 78) Taylor 87**	
9	18		A	Hemel Hempstead	257	D 1 - 1	Watts 8	4
10	**25**	**FAC 2Q**	**A**	**Maidenhead United**	**237**	**L 0 - 1**		
11	Oct 2		H	Banbury United	397	W 1 - 0	Smith 70	4
12	6		A	Swindon Supermarine	181	W 2 - 0	Watkins 18 Robinson 65 (og)	
13	9		H	Halesowen Town	407	W 6 - 0	Smith 14 61 Martin 28 64 Watkins 47 Hayles 77	2
14	12		A	Cirencester Town	113	W 3 - 0	Hayles 58 Watts 77 Martin 83	
15	**16**	**FAT 1Q**	**H**	**Bishop's Cleeve**	**330**	**W 1 - 0**	**Smith 36**	
16	23		A	Leamington	603	L 2 - 3	Watkins 33 Hayles 38	2
17	**30**	**FAT Q2**	**H**	**Horsham**	**361**	**W 2 - 0**	**Watkins 54 Pugh 87**	
18	Nov 6		H	Brackley Town	432	W 1 - 0	Hayles 90	1
19	9		H	Chippenham Town	379	W 5 - 0	Yetton 33 54 Watkins 41 59 Afful 76	
20	13		A	Didcot Town	189	W 3 - 0	Yetton 13 30 Smith 48	1
21	16		H	Salisbury City	744	D 1 - 1	Martin 90	1
22	**20**	**FAT 3Q**	**H**	**AFC Sudbury**	**349**	**L 1 - 2**	**Hayles 77**	
23	27		H	Stourbridge	355	W 3 - 1	Hayles 36 Watkins 60 Martin 87	1
24	Dec 11		A	Oxford City	235	D 1 - 1	Martin 45 (pen)	1
25	27		A	Weymouth	824	W 4 - 0	Watkins 30 Martin 31 43 Taylor 33	1
26	Jan 3		H	Tiverton Town	639	W 3 - 0	Hayles 30 Martin 42 67	
27	8		H	Hemel Hempstead	491	W 3 - 0	Smith 35 Watkins 67 Watts 80	1
28	15		A	Hednesford Town	394	L 0 - 1		1
29	22		H	Evesham United	351	D 1 - 1	Martin 52	1
30	25		A	Cambridge City	347	W 1 - 0	Yetton 16	
31	29		A	Chesham United	393	L 0 - 1		1
32	Feb 1		H	Cirencester Town	303	W 2 - 0	Watts 59 Afful 80	
33	5		H	Bedford Town	321	L 0 - 1		1
34	12		A	Bashley	285	L 1 - 2	Hayles 4	1
35	22		A	Salisbury City	1682	W 6 - 0	Taylor 23 HAYLES 3(34 76 90) Afful 88 90	
36	26		A	Stourbridge	327	D 2 - 2	Taylor 18 Ash 27	1
37	March 5		H	Cambridge City	611	W 2 - 0	Hayles 55 59	1
38	12		A	Brackley Town	253	L 2 - 3	Hayles 7 McConnell 79 (pen)	2
39	19		H	Didcot Town	381	W 2 - 1	Hayles 10 Pugh 79	2
40	26		A	Halesowen Town	207	W 3 - 0	Afful 31 Taylor 59 McConnell 73	2
41	April 2		H	Swindon Supermarine	528	W 7 - 2	Robinson 6 (og) HAYLES 3 (32 34 63pen) Smith 48 Martin 66 Taylor 89	1
42	9		A	Chippenham Town	562	W 2 - 1	Martin 81 Taylor 90	1
43	16		H	Leamington	927	W 3 - 1	Afful 49 87 Taylor77	1
44	23		A	Banbury United	499	W 3 - 0	Afful 19 Hayles 69 Watkins 85	Champions
45	25		H	Weymouth	1696	W 3 - 2	Martin 4 Walker 20 (pen) Broad 84	1

PLAYING SQUAD 2011/12

Existing Players		SN	HT	WT	DOB	AGE	POB	Career	Apps	Goals
GOALKEEPERS										
Tom	Brooks							Plymouth (Scholar), Truro C 7/09		
Timothy	Sandercombe		6'04"	13 12	15/06/1989	22	Plymouth	QPR (Yth), Plymouth (Scholar) Rel c/s 07, Tiverton (L) 11/06, Notts County 7/07 Rel c/s 08, Torquay (Trial), Stafford R 9/08, Mansfield 5/09, Weymouth 2/10, Worcester 7/10 Rel 4/11, Truro C 7/11		
DEFENDERS										
Steve	Adams		6'00"	12 04	25/09/1980	30	Plymouth	Plymouth, Sheff Wed 3/05 Rel c/s 07, Swindon 8/07, Torquay 1/08 Rel c/s 10, Forest Green (L) 8/09, Truro C (SL) 10/09, Truro C 7/10		
Jake	Ash		6'01"	13 04	26/07/1983	28		Exeter (Trainee), Falmouth, Truro C		
Kieran	Conibear-Trathen							Charlestown (Yth), Elburton Villa (Yth), Sticker AFC (Yth), St Austell, Truro C		
Barry	McConnell		5'11"	10 03	01/01/1977	34	Exeter	Exeter Rel c/s 00, Re-signed c/s 00, Weston S.M (2ML) 9/00, Bath C (L) 11/05, Tamworth 12/05 Rel 1/06, Forest Green 2/06 Rel 3/06, Tiverton 3/06 Rel 11/06, Weston-super-Mare 11/06, Dorchester 1/07, Weston-Super-Mare 6/07, Truro 6/08		
Ed	Palmer				13/11/1991	19		Torquay, Tiverton (L) 12/10, Weymouth (2ML) 2/11, Truro C (6ML) 7/11		
Arran	Pugh		6'06"					Dorchester (Yth), Dawlish T, Tiverton T 7/08, Truro C 7/09		
Martin	Watts		5'11"	10 08	20/11/1988	22	Truro	Plymouth, Truro 3/08		
MIDFIELDERS										
Les	Afful		5'06"	10 00	04/02/1984	27	Liverpool	Exeter Rel 5/06, Torquay (SL) 1/06, Forest Green 5/06, Truro C 7/09		
Joe	Broad		5'11"	12 07	24/08/1982	29	Bristol	Plymouth, Weymouth (Trial) c/s 01, Yeovil (L) 11/01, Torquay 9/03 Rel c/s 04, Walsall 8/04, Redditch (L) 9/05, Redditch (6WL) 11/05, Truro 1/06		
Daniel	Clay				15/12/1985	25	Doncaster	Exeter, Tiverton (2ML) 12/05, Crawley (2ML) 2/06, Salisbury 11/06, Dorchester (SL) 1/08, Dorchester 6/08 Rel 1/09, Dorchester 2/09, Truro C (L) 3/09, Truro C 6/09		
Cody	Cooke							Penryn Ath, Truro C 12/10		
Lee	Hodges		6'00"	12 01	04/09/1973	37	Epping	Tottenham Rel c/s 94, Plymouth (L) 2/93, Wycombe (L) 12/93, Barnet 5/94, Reading £100,000 7/97 Rel c/s 01, Plymouth 8/01 Rel 5/08, Torquay 6/08, Truro C (SL) 10/09, Truro C (Pl/Man) 5/10		
Marcus	Martin				09/02/1985	26	Torquay	Plymouth (Sch), Exeter (SL) 8/04, Truro C 1/06		
Dan	Smith		5'10"	10 07	07/06/1989	22	Plymouth	Plymouth Rel 5/09, Morecambe (L) 9/08, Eastbourne B (3ML) 11/08, Eastbourne B 5/09 Rel 2/10, Weymouth NC 2/10 Rel 2/10, Saltash 2/10, Truro C 7/10		
Andy	Taylor		5'09"	12 10	17/09/1982	28	Exeter	Man Utd Rel c/s 02, Northwich 7/02 Rel c/s 03, Kidsgrove A (L) 3/03, Cheltenham (Trial) 9/03, Exeter 10/03 Rel 5/08, Weymouth (Trial) c/s 08, Truro C 8/08		
Scott	Walker		5'08"	11 00	17/03/1980	31	Exeter	Exeter, Bath C 3/99, Newport 8/01, Chippenham 3/03, Weston-Super-Mare 6/05, Truro C Undisc 1/07		
FORWARDS										
Barry	Hayles		5'09"	13 00	17/05/1972	39	Lambeth	Willesden Hawkeye, Stevenage 7/93, Bristol R £250,000 6/97, Fulham £2 million 11/98 Rel c/s 04, Sheff Utd 6/04, Millwall Undisc 9/04, Plymouth £100,000 7/06, Leicester £150,000 1/08 Rel c/s 09, Cheltenham (2ML) 8/08, Cheltenham (2ML) 11/08, Cheltenham 7/09 Rel c/s 10, Truro C 9/10		
Andy	Watkins							Bideford, Truro C 7/06		
Stewart	Yetton		5'08"	10 03	27/07/1985	26	Plymouth	Plymouth, Weymouth (L) 1/04, Weymouth (L) 11/04, Tiverton 2/05, Truro C 10/05		

Soccer Books Limited

72 ST. PETERS AVENUE (Dept. NLD)
CLEETHORPES
N.E. LINCOLNSHIRE
DN35 8HU
ENGLAND

Tel. 01472 696226 Fax 01472 698546

Web site www.soccer-books.co.uk
e-mail info@soccer-books.co.uk

Established in 1982, Soccer Books Limited has one of the largest ranges of English-Language soccer books available. We continue to expand our stocks even further to include many new titles including German, French, Spanish, Italian and other foreign-language books.

With well over 100,000 satisfied customers already, we supply books to virtually every country in the world but have maintained the friendliness and accessibility associated with a small family-run business. The range of titles we sell includes:

Yearbooks – All major yearbooks including many editions of the Sky Sports Football Yearbook (previously Rothmans), Supporters' Guides, Playfair Annuals, European Football Yearbooks and Asian, African and North, Central and South American yearbooks.

Club Histories – Complete Statistical Records, Official Histories, Definitive Histories plus many more.

World Football – World Cup books, International Line-up & Statistics Series, European Championships History, International and European Club Cup competition Statistical Histories and much more.

Biographies & Who's Whos – of managers and players plus Who's Whos etc.

Encyclopedias & General Titles – Books on stadia, hooligan and sociological studies, histories and hundreds of others, including the weird and wonderful!

DVDs – Season's highlights, histories, big games, World Cup matches, player profiles, a selection of over 40 F.A. Cup Finals with many more titles becoming available all the time.

For a current printed listing containing a selection of our titles, please contact us using the details at the top of this page. Alternatively, our web site offers a secure ordering system for credit and debit card holders and lists our full range of over 1,900 books and 400 DVDs.

WELLING UNITED

Chairman: Paul Websdale
Secretary: Barrie Hobbins (T) 07782 347 432 (E) wellingutdfcsecretary@hotmail.co.uk
Additional Committee Members:
Steve Pain, Matthew Panting

Manager: Jamie Day
Programme Editor: Paul Carter (E) paul_carter40@yahoo.co.uk

Club Factfile

Founded: 1963 **Nickname:** The Wings
Previous Names: None
Previous Leagues: Eltham & District 1963-71, London Spartan 1971-77, Athenian 1978-81, Southern 1981-86, 2000-04, Conference 1986-2000

Club Colours (change): Red/red/white (All blue)

Ground: Park View Road Ground, Welling, Kent DA16 1SY (T) 0208 301 1196
Capacity: 4,000 **Seats:** 1,070 **Covered:** 1,500 **Clubhouse:** Yes **Shop:** Yes

Directions
M25 to Dartford then A2 towards London.
Take Bexleyheath/Blackfen/Sidcup,turn off (six miles along A2) then follow A207 signed welling.
Ground is 1 mile From A2 on main road towards Welling High Street.

Previous Grounds: Butterfly Lane, Eltham 1963-78

Record Attendance: 4,100 v Gillingham - FA Cup
Record Victory: 7-1 v Dorking - 1985-86
Record Defeat: 0-7 v Welwyn Garden City - 1972-73
Record Goalscorer: Not known
Record Appearances: Not known
Additional Records: Paid £30,000 to Enfield for Gary Abbott
Received £95,000 from Birmingham City for Steve Finnan 1995

Senior Honours: Southern League 1985-86. Kent Senior Cup 1985-86, 98-99, 2008-09.
London Senior Cup 1989-90. London Challenge Cup 1991-92.

10 YEAR RECORD

01-02	02-03	03-04	04-05	05-06	06-07	07-08	08-09	09-10	10-11
SthP 15	SthP 15	SthP 9	Conf S 16	Conf S 9	Conf S 8	Conf S 16	Conf S 7	Conf S 9	Conf S 6

WELLING UNITED

No.	Date	Comp	H/A	Opponents	Att:	Result	Goalscorers	Pos
								- 5 POINTS OCT
1	Sat-14-Aug	BSS	H	Hampton & Richmond Borough	510	D 0-0		14
2	Tue-17-Aug	BSS	A	Dover Athletic	1097	D 2-2	Healy 37, Pugh 51	13
3	Sat-21-Aug	BSS	A	Havant & Waterlooville	783	W 3-1	Fazackerley 47, Parkinson 80, Day 87	7
4	Tue-24-Aug	BSS	H	Chelmsford City	652	W 3-2	Cumbers 2 (53, 90), Pugh 65	4
5	Sat-28-Aug	BSS	A	Bromley	940	L 1-2	Billings 90	7
6	Mon-30-Aug	BSS	H	Lewes	591	W 2-1	Andrews 5, Pugh 68	6
7	Sat-04-Sep	BSS	H	Boreham Wood	561	W 3-1	Omogbehin 48, Cumbers 72, Og (Moran) 84	5
8	Sat-11-Sep	BSS	A	Staines Town	314	W 2-1	Pugh 43, Fazackerley 51	4
9	Sat-18-Sep	BSS	H	Woking	708	W 2-0	Pugh 55, Pires 78	4
10	Sat-02-Oct	BSS	A	Weston-Super-Mare	258	L 0-2		5
11	Sat-16-Oct	BSS	A	Maidenhead United	275	W 3-0	Cumbers 47, Pires 69, Healy 71	6
12	Sat-23-Oct	BSS	H	Bishops Stortford	515	W 3-1	Pires 23, Clarke 59, Cumbers 77	4
13	Sat-30-Oct	BSS	A	Basingstoke Town	429	W 3-1	Pires 39, Parkinson 80, Clarke prn 90	4
14	Sat-06-Nov	BSS	H	St Albans City	555	W 6-0	Healy 2 (6, 15), Obersteller 8, Pugh 17, Clarke 23, Cumbers 90	3
15	Tue-09-Nov	BSS	A	Ebbsfleet United	942	L 0-4		3
16	Sat-13-Nov	BSS	H	Havant & Waterlooville	503	L 0-2		3
17	Sat-27-Nov	BSS	A	Farnborough	651	D 2-2	Clarke 49, Day 90	3
18	Sat-01-Jan	BSS	H	Dartford	1540	W 2-1	Clarke 42, Cumbers 53	5
19	Mon-03-Jan	BSS	A	Lewes	766	W 3-1	Pugh 2 (33, 60), Clarke 37	5
20	Sat-08-Jan	BSS	H	Staines Town	503	W 4-0	Fazackerley 4, Pugh 9, Pires 70, Cumbers 90	3
21	Sat-15-Jan	BSS	A	Thurrock	394	L 1-2	Pugh pen 77	6
22	Sat-22-Jan	BSS	H	Dover Athletic	739	L 0-1		7
23	Tue-25-Jan	BSS	A	Boreham Wood	118	W 1-0	Cumbers 46	5
24	Sat-29-Jan	BSS	A	Dorchester Town	443	D 3-3	Clarke 5, Cumbers 30, Pires 68	6
25	Sat-05-Feb	BSS	H	Braintree Town	622	L 1-3	Day 54	6
26	Sat-12-Feb	BSS	A	Hampton & Richmond Borough	429	W 1-0	Clarke pen 24	6
27	Tue-15-Feb	BSS	A	Dartford	1384	D 1-1	Parkinson 66	6
28	Sat-19-Feb	BSS	H	Maidenhead United	383	W 2-1	Cumbers 29, Fazackerley 88	5
29	Sat-26-Feb	BSS	H	Weston-Super-Mare	470	W 1-0	Clarke 70	5
30	Wed-02-Mar	BSS	H	Bromley	525	W 3-1	Clarke 47, Fazackerley 59, Pugh 64	5
31	Sat-05-Mar	BSS	A	Bishops Stortford	401	W 4-0	Pugh 3 (12, 63, 90), Pires 87	3
32	Sat-12-Mar	BSS	H	Dorchester Town	549	L 1-2	Pires 50	5
33	Sat-19-Mar	BSS	A	Eastleigh	519	W 4-1	Pugh 2 (8, 21), Cumbers 29, Day 87	6
34	Tue-22-Mar	BSS	H	Ebbsfleet United	1010	D 1-1	Martin 32	6
35	Sat-26-Mar	BSS	A	Chelmsford City	784	W 2-0	Pires 37, Cumbers 90	3
36	Tue-29-Mar	BSS	H	Eastleigh	479	W 4-2	Clarke 4 (25, pen 45, 51, pen 86)	3
37	Sat-02-Apr	BSS	A	Woking	1475	D 0-0		3
38	Sat-09-Apr	BSS	H	Farnborough	807	W 1-0	Pugh 19	4
39	Sat-16-Apr	BSS	A	St Albans City	337	L 0-1		4
40	Fri-22-Apr	BSS	H	Thurrock	753	D 1-1	Day 71	4
41	Mon-25-Apr	BSS	A	Braintree Town	1645	L 1-3	Clarke 72	6
42	Sat-30-Apr	BSS	H	Basingstoke Town	705	W 4-0	Cumbers 14, Martin 22, Obersteller 30, Coyle 84	6

CUPS

No.	Date	Comp	H/A	Opponents	Att:	Result	Goalscorers
1	Sat-25-Sep	FAC 2Q	A	Braintree Town	433	L 0-2	
2	Sat-20-Nov	FAT 3Q	H	Tonbridge Angels	431	W 1-0	Cumbers 59
3	Sun-12-Dec	FAT 1	A	Luton Town	1639	D 0-0	
4	Tue-14-Dec	FAT 1R	H	Luton Town	404	L 1-2	Cumbers 45

League
Starts
Substitute
Unused Sub

Cups
Starts
Substitute
Unused Sub

Goals (Lg)
Goals (Cup)

MITTEN	COYLE	OBERSTELLER	DAY	ANDREWS	PARKINSON	FAZACKERLEY	CRACKNELL	CUMBERS	PUGH	HEALY	SAMBROOK	WHITNELL	BILLINGS	OMOGBEHIN	JOHNSON	CLARKE	PIRES	TAYLOR	STEWART	ACHEAMPONG	OBAMWONYI	FARRELL	WALL	WALKER	BELLAMY	LOVELOCK	WHITEHOUSE	MARTIN	HEFFERNAN	DOLBY	DENNIS
X	X	X	X	X	X	X	X	X	X	X	S	S	S	U	U																
X	X	X	X	X	X	X		X	X	X	X	U	S	U	U																
X	X	X	X	X	X	X		X	X	X	X	S	U	U	U																
X	X	X	X	X	X	X		X	X	X	X	U	U	S	S																
X	X	X	X	X	X			X	X	X	X	S	S	S	X																
X	X	X	X	X	X		S	X	X	S	X	X	X	S	U																
X		X	X	X	X	S	U	X	X	X	X	X	U	X	U																
X	X	X	X	X	X	X	S	X	X	X	X	S	S	U	U																
X	X	X	X	X		X	S	X	X	X	X		U	U	U	X	S														
	X	X	X	X		X		X	X	X	U			X	U	X	S		X	U											
	X	X	X	X	X	S		X	X	X				U	S	X	X		X	U											
	X	X	X	X	X	S		X	X	X				U	S	X	X		X	U											
	X	X	X	X	X	S		X	X	X					U	X	X		X	U	U										
	X	X	X	X	X	X		S	X	X	U				S	X	X		X	S	U										
	X	X	X	X	X	X		X	X	S	U				U	X	X		X	S	U										
	X	X	X	X	X	X		S	X	X	U				U	X	X		X	U	U										
	X	X	X	X	X	X		X	U	X	U				U	X	X		X	S	U										
	X	X	X	U	X	X		X	X	X	X				U	X			X	S	U										
	X	X	X	U	X	X		X	X	X	X				S	X	S		X	U	U										
	X	X	X	S	X	X		X	X		X				S	X	X		X	S	U										
	X	X	X	U	X	X		X	X	X	X				U	X	S				U			X							
	X	X	X	U	X	X		X	X	X	X				S	X	S			U				X	U						
	U	X	X	X	X	X		X	X	S	X				U	X	X			U				X	S						
	X	X	S	X	X			X	X	X	X				S	X	X			U				X	U						
	X		X	X	X	X		X	X	X	X					X				U				X	S						
	X		X	X	X	X		X	X		U				U	X	U			X				X	X						
	X		X	X	X	X		X	X		U				U	X	S			X		U			X	X					
	X			X	X	X		X	X		X				S	X	X			X		U			U		X				
	X	X	U	U	X	X		X	X		X				S	X	X			X		U			S		X				
	X	X	U	U	X	X		X	X		X				S	X	X			X		U			S		X				
	X	X	X	X	X	U		X	X	S	U				S	X	X			X					S		X				
	S	X	S	X	X	X		X	X		X				U	X	X			X					S		X				
		X	X		X			X	X		X				S	X	X			X					S		X	X	U		
		X	X	U	X			X			X					X	X			X					U		X	X	U	X	U
	S	X	X	S	X	S		X	U		X					X	X			X							X	X		X	U
	U	X	X	X	X	S		X	X		X					X	X			X					U		X			S	U
		X	X	X	X	X		X	X		U				U	X	X			X					U		X			U	U
	U	X	X	X	X	X		U	X		X				U	X	X			X							X	S		U	
	X	X	U	X	X	X		X	X		U				U	X	X								U		X	X	U		
	S	X	X	X	X	X		X	X		X				U	X	S			X							X	U		S	
	X	X	X	U	U	X		S	X						S	X	X			X							X	X	U	X	
	X	X	X	S	X	X		X	X	S	U				S	X				X							X	X		U	
X		X	X	X		X	X	X	X	S	X		U	U	U	X	X	U													
	X	X	X	X	X	X		X		X					S	X	X		X	U	U										
	X	X		X	X	X		X	X		X				S	X	X		X	U	U	U	U								
	X	X	X	X	X	X		X		X					U	X	X		X	U		U	U								
9	32	38	36	30	39	30	1	38	39	21	26	2	1	2	1	34	23	0	11	16	0	0	0	6	2	1	15	6	0	3	0
0	3	0	2	3	0	6	3	3	0	5	1	4	4	3	15	0	7	0	0	5	0	0	0	0	7	0	0	1	0	2	0
0	3	0	3	8	1	1	1	1	2	0	11	2	4	7	22	0	1	0	0	10	9	4	0	0	7	0	0	1	4	3	4
1	3	4	3	4	3	4	1	4	2	2	2	0	0	0	0	4	4	0	3	0	0	0	0	0	0	0	0	0	0	0	0
0	0	0	0	0	0	0	0	0	0	1	0	0	0	0	2	0	0	0	0	0	0	0	0	0	0	0	0	0	0	0	0
0	0	0	0	0	0	0	0	0	0	0	0	0	1	1	2	0	0	1	0	3	2	2	2	0	0	0	0	0	0	0	0
0	1	2	5	1	3	5	0	14	17	4	0	0	1	1	0	15	9	0	0	0	0	0	0	0	0	0	0	2	0	0	0
0	0	0	0	0	0	0	0	2	0	0	0	0	0	0	0	0	0	0	0	0	0	0	0	0	0	0	0	0	0	0	0

PLAYING SQUAD 2011/12

Existing Players		SN	HT	WT	DOB	AGE	POB	Career	Apps	Goals
GOALKEEPERS										
Deniz	Mehmet		6'03"		19/09/1992	18		West Ham (Scholar) Rel c/s 11, Bishops Stortford (WE) 2/10, Wycombe (Trial) 7/11, Welling 8/11		
Dan	Thomas		6'02"	13 01	01/09/1991	19	Poole	Brockenhurst College, Bournemouth, Dorchester (L) 2/11, Dorchester (L) 3/11, Welling (L) 8/11		
John	Whitehouse				31/05/1977	34		Charlton (Jun), Corinthian, Erith & B, Fisher, Greenwich B, Fisher, Greenwich B, Ashford T 8/01, Dartford c/s 05, Tunbridge Wells c/s 05, Chatham T 7/06, Dover 1/08 Rel 5/10, Dartford 8/10, Maldon & Tiptree (Dual), Sittingbourne (Dual) 1/11, Welling 2/11	15	0
DEFENDERS										
Anthony	Acheampong		6'03"	12 05				Cardiff (Trainee) Rel c/s 08, Aldershot (Trial) 8/08, Horsham 10/08, Welling (Trial) c/s 10, Welling 9/10, Aveley (Dual) 9/10	21	0
Ben	Martin		6'07"	13 08	25/11/1982	28	Harpenden	Harpenden, Aylesbury 3/03, Swindon 8/03 Rel c/s 04, Lincoln C (L) 10/03, Farnborough (L) 1/04, St Albans 8/04, Staines (L) 11/06, Leighton (L) 1/07, Wealdstone (L) 1/07, Chelmsford 7/09, St Albans 8/10, Welling 3/11	7	2
Jack	Obersteller		6'02"	13 00	10/10/1988	22	Newham	Millwall, Crawley (L) 3/07, Wycombe 7/07 Rel 5/08, Grays (SL) 10/07, Exeter 5/08, Grays NC 8/09, Welling 11/09, Gillingham (Trial) 7/11	38	2
Oliver	Poole							Millwall (Yth), Welling 8/11		
Andrew	Sambrook		5'10"	11 09	13/07/1979	32	Chatham	Gillingham (AS), USA Scholarship (Hartwick College) c/s 97, Gillingham 3/01 Rel 6/01, Rushden & D 8/01 Rel c/s 05, Grays 7/05, Fisher 7/08, Thurrock 11/08, AFC Wimbledon 1/09, Welling 5/09	27	0
MIDFIELDERS										
Zac	Attwood				14/12/1989	21		Eastbourne B, Bognor Regis 9/08, Hastings U (L) 10/08 Perm, USA c/s 09, Histon 8/10 Rel 6/11, Welling 7/11		
Stephen	Camacho				14/09/1992	18		Charlton (Scholar) Rel c/s 11, Welling 8/11		
Jamie	Day		5'10"	11 04	13/09/1979	31	Bexley	Arsenal, Bournemouth £20,000 3/99 Rel c/s 01, Dover 7/01, Welling 5/04, Grays 5/07, Eastbourne (L) 9/07, Havant & W (SL) 3/08, Dartford 8/08, Welling (Pl/Man) 11/09	38	5
Louis	Fazackerley				24/07/1984	27	Winchester	Fulham Rel c/s 04, Northampton (Trial) c/s 04, Farnborough (Trial) c/s 04, Sutton U 8/04, Eastbourne B 11/04, Leyton 7/06, Bishops Stortford 8/07, Bromley 5/08, Welling 10/08	36	5
Conor	Heffernan							West Ham (Yth), Gillingham (Yth), Dartford, FC Torrevieja (Spa) (Trial) 8/10, Sittingbourne 1/11, Aveley 3/11, Welling 3/11, Dag & Red (Trial) 7/11	0	0
Jordan	Johnson				09/04/1992	19		Croydon A (Yth), Bromley (Yth), Cambridge U (Scholar) 11/09, Welling 8/10	16	0
Jack	Parkinson				23/07/1989	22		Tonbridge A (Yth), VCD Ath, Welling 7/08, Margate (L) 10/08, Bournemouth (Trial) 3/10, Southend (Trial) 7/11	39	3
Loick	Pires		6'03"	13 02	20/11/1989	21	Lisbon, Port	Stoke (Yth), L.Orient Rel c/s 10, Welling 7/10, Crewe (Trial) 7/11	30	9
FORWARDS										
Lee	Clarke		5'11"	10 08	28/07/1983	28	Peterborough	Yaxley, Peterborough Undisc 10/01, Kettering (SL) 3/03, Kettering (2ML) 8/03, St Albans (SL) 1/04, St Albans 7/04 Rel 4/09, Welling 5/09, Cambridge C (L) 9/09	34	15
Quentin	Conteh							Cambridge U (Yth), Beckenham (Dual), Welling c/s 11		
Luis	Cumbers		6'00"	11 10	06/09/1988	22	Chelmsford	Gillingham Rel c/s 10, Maidstone (L) 9/07, Grays (L) 11/07, AFC Wimbledon (SL) 3/08, Ebbsfleet (L) 3/09, Ebbsfleet (L) 9/09, AFC Wimbledon (2ML) 11/09, Dover (L) 2/10, Welling 7/10	41	14
Joe	Healy		6'00"	12 04	26/12/1986	24	Sidcup	Millwall, Crawley (L) 2/05, Walton & H (L) 2/06, Fisher 8/06, Yeading (SL) 3/07, Beckenham c/s 07, Welling 7/08 Rel 10/08, Beckenham 10/08, Margate 12/08 Rel 2/10, Welling 3/10	26	4
Andy	Pugh		5'09"	12 02	28/01/1989	22	Gravesend	Gillingham Rel c/s 10, Welling (L) 10/07, Maidstone (L) 2/08, Folkestone I (L) 8/08, Grays (SL) 1/09, Dover (L) 9/09, Welling (2ML) 11/09, Histon (L) 3/10, Welling 7/10	39	17

WESTON-SUPER-MARE

Chairman: Paul Bliss
Secretary: Richard Sloane **(T)** 0771 107 8589 **(E)** wsmsecretary@hotmail.co.uk
Additional Committee Members:
Dennis Usher, Oliver Bliss, Phil Sheridan

Manager: Craig Laird
Programme Editor: Phil Sheridan **(E)**

Back Row (L-R): Ricky Bennett, Chris Young, Callum Laird, Jamie Laird, George Booth, Mike Mackey, Llloyd Irish, Ben Kirk, Jermaine Jones, Jamie Price, James Richards, Martin Slocombe, Robbie Maggs, Kane Ingram.
Middle Row: Sahr Kabba, Matt Huxley, Nabi Diallo, Steve Orchard, Brett Trowbridge, Matt Villis, Ben Hunt, Nat Pepperell, Craio Laird, Jnr Jak Martin, Jack Camm, Marcus Duharty.
Front Row: Dave Callow Physio Jon Haile Assistant Manager, Sponsor, Oli Bliss Director, Bob Flaskett Groundsman Sponsor, Craig laird Manager, Ryan Northmore Academy Director,

Club Factfile

Founded: 1899 **Nickname:** Seagulls
Previous Names: Borough or Weston-super-Mare
Previous Leagues: Somerset Senior, Western League

Club Colours (change): White/black/black (All red)

Ground: Woodspring Stadium, Winterstoke Road, Weston-super-Mare BS24 9AA **(T)** 01934 621 618
Capacity: 3,000 **Seats:** 278 **Covered:** 2,000 **Clubhouse:** Yes **Shop:** Yes

Directions
Leave the M5 at Junction 21, take the dual carriageway A370 and continue straight until the 4th roundabout with ASDA on the right. Turn left into Winterstoke Road, bypassing a mini roundabout and continue for 1/2 mile. Woodspring Stadium is on the right.

Previous Grounds: Langford Road, Winterstoke Road

Record Attendance: 2,623 v Woking - FA Cup 1st Round replay 23/11/1993 (At Winterstoke Road)
Record Victory: 11-0 v Paulton Rovers
Record Defeat: 1-12 v Yeovil Town Reserves
Record Goalscorer: Matt Lazenby - 180
Record Appearances: Harry Thomas - 740
Additional Records: Received £20,000 from Sheffield Wednesday for Stuart Jones

Senior Honours: Somerset Senior Cup 1923-24, 26-67.
Western League 1991-92.

10 YEAR RECORD

01-02	02-03	03-04	04-05	05-06	06-07	07-08	08-09	09-10	10-11
SthW 3	SthW 2	SthP 10	Conf S 11	Conf S 14	Conf S 21	Conf S 20	Conf S 17	Conf S 21	Conf S 12

WESTON-SUPER-MARE

No.	Date	Comp	H/A	Opponents	Att:	Result	Goalscorers	Pos
1	Sat-14-Aug	BSS	H	Boreham Wood	186	W 2-0	Duharty 72, Pepperell pen 85	2
2	Mon-16-Aug	BSS	A	Havant & Waterlooville	732	D 0-0		2
3	Sat-21-Aug	BSS	A	Maidenhead United	227	L 0-1		9
4	Tue-24-Aug	BSS	H	Farnborough	260	L 0-2		18
5	Sat-28-Aug	BSS	A	Eastleigh	336	D 1-1	Dayle Grubb 73	17
6	Mon-30-Aug	BSS	H	Basingstoke Town	260	W 1-0	Price 30	11
7	Sat-04-Sep	BSS	A	Dartford	1173	L 1-4	Duharty 47	16
8	Sat-11-Sep	BSS	H	Chelmsford City	282	D 2-2	Trowbridge 2 (51, 56)	15
9	Sat-18-Sep	BSS	A	Ebbsfleet United	911	L 1-3	Pepperell pen 29	18
10	Sat-02-Oct	BSS	H	Welling United	258	W 2-0	Duharty 2 (12, 19)	14
11	Sat-16-Oct	BSS	A	St Albans City	284	W 4-3	Duharty 75, Kabba 2 (75, 89), Ingram 80	12
12	Sat-23-Oct	BSS	H	Hampton & Richmond Borough	238	D 0-0		11
13	Sat-30-Oct	BSS	A	Braintree Town	471	L 0-4		12
14	Sat-06-Nov	BSS	H	Lewes	214	L 0-3		13
15	Sat-13-Nov	BSS	H	Thurrock	150	W 2-1	Dayle Grubb 18, Slocombe 33	13
16	Tue-16-Nov	BSS	H	Maidenhead United	172	W 3-1	Pepperell 37, Dayle Grubb 54, Ingram 75	9
17	Tue-23-Nov	BSS	A	Staines Town	191	L 1-2	Dean Grubb 23	10
18	Tue-07-Dec	BSS	A	Boreham Wood	105	L 3-6	Duharty 2, Pepperell 2 (7, pen 68)	11
19	Sat-11-Dec	BSS	H	Bromley	173	W 7-0	Price 2, Pepperell 11, Slocombe 15, Kirk 70, Duharty 2 (86. 90), Gilbert 90	9
20	Tue-28-Dec	BSS	H	Eastleigh	209	L 0-2		10
21	Sat-01-Jan	BSS	H	Dorchester Town	320	W 1-0	Dean Grubb 80	9
22	Mon-03-Jan	BSS	A	Basingstoke Town	294	D 2-2	Porter 66, Rand 83	9
23	Sat-08-Jan	BSS	A	Chelmsford City	711	L 0-1		9
24	Tue-11-Jan	BSS	A	Bishops Stortford	217	D 1-1	Ingram 27	9
25	Sat-15-Jan	BSS	H	Havant & Waterlooville	205	D 1-1	Kabba 87	9
26	Sat-29-Jan	BSS	A	Bromley	424	L 2-3	Kirk 16, Dayle Grubb 45	10
27	Sat-05-Feb	BSS	A	Dorchester Town	363	L 0-1		13
28	Tue-08-Feb	BSS	H	Dartford	234	L 0-1		13
29	Sat-12-Feb	BSS	A	Dover Athletic	726	W 1-0	Ingram 25	12
30	Sat-19-Feb	BSS	H	Bishops Stortford	191	W 3-1	Gilbert 2 (23, 57), Porter 88	10
31	Sat-26-Feb	BSS	A	Welling United	470	L 0-1		11
32	Sat-05-Mar	BSS	H	St Albans City	219	W 2-1	Pepperell pen 4, Ingram 86	10
33	Tue-08-Mar	BSS	H	Woking	175	L 0-1		11
34	Sat-12-Mar	BSS	A	Hampton & Richmond Borough	442	W 1-0	Ingram 22	10
35	Sat-19-Mar	BSS	H	Ebbsfleet United	366	W 3-2	Ingram 19, Kabba 50, Pepperell 83	10
36	Sat-26-Mar	BSS	A	Farnborough	604	L 0-2		12
37	Sat-02-Apr	BSS	A	Thurrock	163	L 0-3		13
38	Sat-09-Apr	BSS	H	Dover Athletic	264	L 1-4	Dayle Grubb 77	13
39	Sat-16-Apr	BSS	A	Lewes	656	D 1-1	Ingram 64	12
40	Sat-23-Apr	BSS	H	Staines Town	803	W 2-1	Kabba 83, Ingram pen 90	12
41	Mon-25-Apr	BSS	A	Woking	1975	L 3-4	Price 4, Kirk 2 (25, 73)	12
42	Sat-30-Apr	BSS	H	Braintree Town	355	W 2-1	Kabba 45, Price 78	12

CUPS

No.	Date	Comp	H/A	Opponents	Att:	Result	Goalscorers
1	Sun-26-Sep	FAC 2Q	A	Gloucester City	380	W 2-0	Ingram 2 (38, 65)
2	Sat-09-Oct	FAC 3Q	A	Salisbury City	871	L 0-1	
3	Sat-20-Nov	FAT 3Q	H	Dorchester Town	184	L 1-3	Og (Moss) 78

League
Starts
Substitute
Unused Sub

Cups
Starts
Substitute
Unused Sub

Goals (Lg)
Goals (Cup)

IRISH	PRICE	J LAIRD	RAND	VILLIS	INGRAM	TROWBRIDGE	KIRK	DUHARTY	PORTER	DEAN GRUBB	PEPPERELL	KABBA	GILBERT	WRING	MIDDLETON	ORCHARD	SLOCOMBE	DAYLE GRUBB	FARMER	MAWFORD	WOOD	TAYLOR	JONES	CURETON	KLEIN-DAVIES	LEONARD	DIALLO	C LAIRD	BENNETT	MARTIN
X	X	X	X	X	X	X	X	X	X	X	S	S	S	U	U															
X	X	X	X	X	X	S	X	U	X	X	S	X	X		S	U														
X	X	X	X	X	X	X	X	X		S	X	S	X	U	U	S														
X	X		X	X	X	X	S	S	X	U	X	X	U		U	X	X													
X	X		X	X	X	S	X	S	X	U	U	X	X			S	X	X												
X	X		X	X	S	X	X	X	S	X	X	S	U			U	X	X												
X	X	U	X	X	X	S		X	X	S	U	S	X			X	X	X												
X	X	U	X	X	X	X	U	S	S	U	X	X	X				X	X												
X	X	U	X	X	X	X	X	X	S	S	X	S	X				X	U												
X		X	X	X	X	X	X	X	X	X		S	U				U	S	X	S										
X	X	X	X	X	X			X	X	X		S	X				S	X	U	S				U						
X	X	X	X	X	X	S		X	X	X	S	S					X	X	U	U										
X	X	X	X	X		X	S	S	X	X	U	X					U	X		X				U						
X	X	S	X	X	X	X	X	X	U	U	X	S	U				X	X												
X		U	X	X	X	X	X	X	X	U	X	S	U				X	X		U										
X		X	X	X	X	S	X	S	X	U	X	X	X				U	X		U										
X	X	X	X	X		X		X		X	X	S	X				U	X		U					S					
X	X	X	X	X		X	S	X	X	X	X	S					U	X		U					S					
X	X		X	X	X	X	X	S	U	U	X	X	X				X	S								S				
X	X	U	X	X	X		X	S	X	U	X	X	X				X	S								S				
X	X	U	X	X	X	X	X	X	U	S	X	S					X	X								S				
X	X	X	X			X			X	X	U	X					X	X			U	S				X	U			
X	X	X	X	S	S	X	X	U	X		U	S					X	X								X	X			
X		X	X	X	X	U	X		X	U		X	U				X	X				U					X	U		
X	X	S	X	X	X	S	X	U	X	U		X	U				X	X									X			
X	X	S	X	X		X	X	S	X	S		X	U				X	X		U							X			
X	X	X	X			X	X	S		S		X	X				X	X		S				U			X		U	
X	X	X	X		X	X	X	X	X	S		S	X				X	S						U			U			
X	X	X	X	U	X	X	X	X	X	U		S	X				X	S									S			
X	X	X	X	U	X	X	X	X	X	S		S	X				X	S									U			
X	X	X	X	S	X	X	X		X		S	X	U				X	S		U							X			
X	X	X	U	X	X	X	X				X	X	S				X	X		U							S	S		
X		X	X	X	X	X	X	U				S	S				X	X		S							X	X	U	
X	X	X	X		X	X	X	U	S		U	U	S				X	X									X	X		
X	X	X			X	X	X		U		X	X	X				X	S		U				U			S			X
X	X	X	U		X	X	X	S	U		X	X	X				X	S									S			X
X	X	X	X		S	U	U	X	X		U		X				X	X									X	U		X
X	X	X	X		X	S	X	X	X		X		U				X	X									S	S		U
X	X	X	X		X	X	X	X	U		X	S	X				X	U									U			U
X	U	X	X		X	X	X	U	X		X	X	X				U	S									S			X
X	X	X			X	X	X	X	S		U	S	X				X	S									X	U		X
X	X	U	X		S	X	X	S	X		X	X					X	S									X	U		X
X	X	X	X	X	X	X	X	S	X	S	X	X					U	U	U	U	U									
X	X	X	X	X	X	X		S	X	X		X	U				U	X	U	S		U	U							
X	U	X	X	U		X	X	U	X	X	X	X	X				X	S		U										
42	36	28	38	26	32	31	32	20	26	10	20	19	21	0	0	2	32	24	1	1	0	0	0	0	0	2	11	2	0	6
0	0	3	0	2	4	7	3	11	5	8	4	20	4	0	1	2	1	12	0	4	0	1	0	0	2	3	6	2	0	0
0	1	7	2	2	0	2	2	6	6	11	8	1	10	2	3	2	6	2	2	9	1	1	0	5	0	0	4	4	2	2
3	2	3	3	2	2	3	2	0	3	2	2	3	1	0	0	0	1	1	0	0	0	0	0	0	0	0	0	0	0	0
0	0	0	0	0	0	0	0	2	0	1	0	0	0	0	0	0	0	1	0	1	0	0	0	0	0	0	0	0	0	0
0	1	0	0	1	0	0	0	1	0	0	0	0	1	0	0	0	2	1	2	2	1	1	1	0	0	0	0	0	0	0
0	4	0	1	0	9	2	4	8	2	2	8	6	3	0	0	0	2	5	0	0	0	0	0	0	0	0	0	0	0	0
0	0	0	0	0	1	0	0	0	0	0	0	0	0	0	0	0	0	0	0	0	0	0	0	0	0	0	0	0	0	0

PLAYING SQUAD 2011/12

Existing Players		SN	HT	WT	DOB	AGE	POB	Career	Apps	Goals
GOALKEEPERS										
Lloyd	Irish				07/09/1988	22		Yeovil Rel 10/09, Chard T (Dual) c/s 07, Taunton (Dual) c/s 08, Bridgwater, Weston-Super-Mare 7/10	42	0
Jermaine	Jones							Weston-Super-Mare	0	0
DEFENDERS										
Jory	Cureton				03/05/1993	18		Weston-Super-Mare, Wellington (L) 1/11	0	0
Craig	Laird							Plymouth (Yth), Bridgwater, Weston-Super-Mare, Exeter (Trial)	4	0
Jamie	Laird				18/06/1989	21		Plymouth (Yth) Rel c/s 07, Ange IF (Swe), Bridgwater 10/07, Teramo Calcio (Ita) (Trial) 11/07, Bath C NC 4/08 Rel c/s 08, Bridgwater 11/08, Weston-Super-Mare 7/10	31	0
Jak	Martin							Exeter, Taunton, Willand R, Tiverton, Bridgwater 11/07, Weston-Super-Mare, Tiverton (6ML) 8/10	6	0
Jamie	Price				13/05/1987	24		Yeovil (Trainee), Taunton c/s 05, Bridgwater c/s 06, Taunton 7/08, Bridgwater 12/08, Weston-Super-Mare 8/10	36	4
Craig	Rand		6'01"	11 00	24/06/1982	29	Bishop Auckland	Sheff Wed, Whitby 3/02, Stocksbridge PS 12/02, Spennymoor 5/03, Thornaby 10/03, Durham 8/04, Team Bath 10/05, Weston-Super-Mare 11/05	38	1
James	Richards							Exeter (Yth), Plymouth (Yth), Swindon (Scholar), Bournemouth (Trial) 7/11, Exeter (Trial) 7/07, Weston-Super-Mare 8/11		
Martin	Slocombe				08/11/1988	22	Weston-Super-Mare	Bristol C Rel c/s 08, Bath C 8/08, Weymouth 7/09, Chippenham 3/10, Bath C (Dual) 3/10, Weston-Super-Mare 8/10	33	2
Matt	Villis		6'03"	12 07	13/04/1984	27	Bridgwater	Bridgwater, Plymouth 9/02 Rel c/s 05, Torquay (SL) 7/04, Torquay 7/05 Rel c/s 07, Bridgwater (Trial) 7/07, Tiverton 7/07, Bridgwater 10/09, Weston-Super-Mare 7/10	28	0
MIDFIELDERS										
Ricky	Bennett							Weston-Super-Mare	0	0
George	Booth		5'08"		18/02/1992	19		Bristol R Rel c/s 11, Longwell Green Sports (L) 1/11, Weston-Super-Mare (L) 3/11, Weston-Super-Mare 8/11		
Jack	Camm							Bristol R (Scholar) Rel c/s 11, Weston-Super-Mare 8/11		
Simon	Gilbert				07/04/1985	26		Larkhall, Chippenham, Bath C, Almondsbury T, Weston-Super-Mare 7/10	25	3
Dayle	Grubb				24/07/1991	20		Weston-Super-Mare	36	5
Kane	Ingram				15/09/1987	23		Bristol C (Yth), Bath C, Taunton 9/06, Almondsbury T, Paulton 10/09, Cinderford 1/10, Weston-Super-Mare 7/10	36	9
Ben	Kirk				30/09/1984	26		Bridgwater, Chippenham 8/04, Weston-Super-Mare 6/06, Bridgwater Undisc 8/06, Weston-Super-Mare 7/10	35	4
Jake	Mawford				07/06/1993	28		Weston-Super-Mare, Wellington (L) 1/11, Street (L) 1/11	5	0
Steve	Orchard				18/02/1985	26		Weymouth, Bideford 7/04, Bridgwater, Weston-Super-Mare 7/10		4
0										
Brett	Trowbridge				19/07/1986	25		Bridgwater, Weston-Super-Mare 8/10	38	2
FORWARDS										
Nabi	Diallo				27/12/1990	20		Bristol R (Yth), Minehead, Gloucester 11/09, Weston-Super-Mare, Bridgwater (Dual) 8/10	17	0
Marcus	Duharty				22/02/1986	25		Cadbury Heath, Mangotsfield 9/08, Bridgwater T 1/09, Weston-Super-Mare 7/10	31	8
Ben	Hunt		6'01"	11 00	23/01/1990	21	Southwark	West Ham (Scholar), Bristol R c/s 08, Kingstonian (L) 10/09, Gloucester (3ML) 12/09, Newport C (L) 3/10, Dover 7/10, Lewes (SL) 2/11 Perm 3/11, Weston-Super-Mare 8/11		
Max	Huxley							Oldland Abbotonians, Weston-Super-Mare (Dual) 6/11		
Sahr	Kabba				13/04/1989	22		Bristol R (Yth), Almondsbury T, Weston-Super-Mare 7/10	39	6
Michael	Mackay						Taunton	Bristol C, Australia, Bridgwater, Weston-Super-Mare 8/11		
Robbi	Maggs		5'09"		23/10/1992	18		Bristol R (Scholar) Rel c/s 11, Lincoln C (Trial) 4/11, Weston-Super-Mare 8/11		
Nat	Pepperell				08/02/1988	23		Bridgwater, Swansea, Bath C 8/06, Tiverton 10/06, Taunton (L) 3/07, Bridgwater, Weston-Super-Mare 8/10	24	8
Chris	Young							Bridgwater T, Lunn University (USA), Bridgwater T 12/06, Tiverton 6/07, Bridgwater T (L) 2/08, Bridgwater T 7/08, Weston-Super-Mare 6/11		

WOKING

Chairman: Mike Smith
Secretary: Derek Powell (T) 01483 772 470 (E) derek.powell@wokingfc.co.uk
Additional Committee Members:
James Aughterson, Peter Jordan, James Aughterson, Geoff Chapple, Rosemary Jonhson, David Holmes. John Moore.
Manager: Garry Hill
Programme Editor: David Horncastle (E) raetec.david@btinternet.com

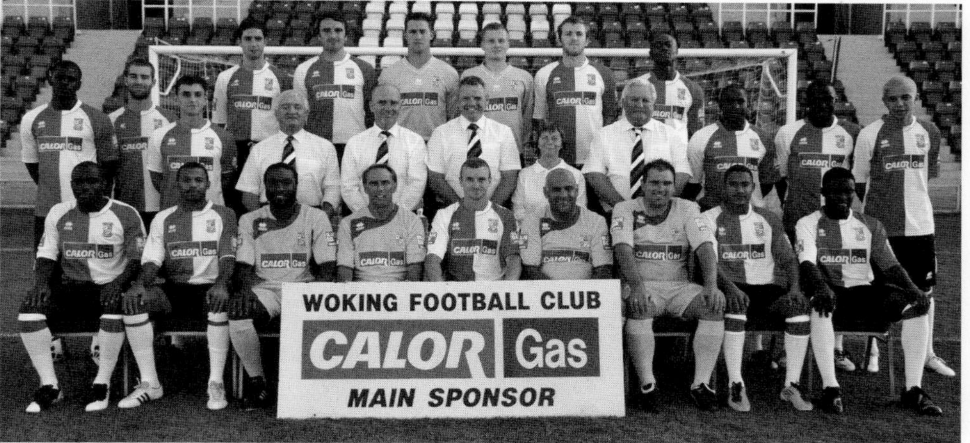

Club Factfile

Founded: 1889 **Nickname:** The Cards
Previous Names: None
Previous Leagues: Isthmian 1911-92

Club Colours (change): Red and white/black/white (All yellow)

Ground: Kingfield Stadium, Kingfield Road, Woking, Surrey GU22 9AA (T) 01483 772 470
Capacity: 6,000 **Seats:** 2,500 **Covered:** 3,900 **Clubhouse:** Yes **Shop:** Yes

Directions
Exit M25 Junction 10 and follow A3 towards Guildford. Leave at next junction onto B2215 through Ripley and join A247 to Woking. Alternatively exit M25 junction 11 and follow A320 to Woking Town Centre. The ground is on the outskirts of Woking opposite the Leisure Centre.

Previous Grounds: Wheatsheaf, Ive Lane (pre 1923)

Record Attendance: 6,000 v Swansea City - FA Cup 1978-79 and v Coventry City - FA Cup 1996-97
Record Victory: 17-4 v Farnham - 1912-13
Record Defeat: 0-16 v New Crusaders - 1905-06
Record Goalscorer: Charlie Mortimore - 331 (1953-65)
Record Appearances: Brian Finn - 564 (1962-74)
Additional Records: Paid £60,000 to Crystal Palace for Chris Sharpling
Received £150,000 from Bristol Rovers for Steve Foster

Senior Honours: Surrey Senior Cup 1912-13, 26-27, 55-56, 56-57, 71-72, 90-91, 93-94, 95-96, 99-2000, 2003-04. FA Amateur Cup 1957-58.
Isthmian League Cup 1990-91, Premier Division 1991-92. FA Trophy 1993-94, 94-95, 96-97.
Vauxhall Championship Shield 1994-95. GLS Conference Cup 2004-05.

10 YEAR RECORD

01-02		02-03		03-04		04-05		05-06		06-07		07-08		08-09		09-10		10-11	
Conf	19	Conf	19	Conf	9	Conf	8	Conf	11	Conf	15	Conf	17	Conf	21	Conf S	5	Conf S	5

WOKING

No.	Date	Comp	H/A	Opponents	Att:	Result	Goalscorers	Pos
1	Sat-14-Aug	BSS	H	Dover Athletic	1458	L 0-1		20
2	Mon-16-Aug	BSS	A	Chelmsford City	948	L 0-3		22
3	Sat-21-Aug	BSS	A	Dorchester Town	547	W 2-1	Gilroy 2 (35, 89)	16
4	Tue-24-Aug	BSS	H	Lewes	994	W 2-1	Gilroy 2 (2, 31)	9
5	Sat-28-Aug	BSS	H	Maidenhead United	952	L 0-2		14
6	Mon-30-Aug	BSS	A	Boreham Wood	301	D 0-0		15
7	Sat-04-Sep	BSS	A	St Albans City	490	W 1-0	Anane 34	10
8	Sat-11-Sep	BSS	H	Basingstoke Town	1112	W 2-0	Faulconbridge 2 (73, 90)	7
9	Sat-18-Sep	BSS	A	Welling United	708	L 0-2		9
10	Sat-02-Oct	BSS	H	Braintree Town	1056	L 0-1		12
11	Sat-16-Oct	BSS	A	Staines Town	914	L 0-1		15
12	Sat-30-Oct	BSS	A	Hampton & Richmond Borough	796	W 2-1	Hammond 2 (81, 90)	11
13	Tue-09-Nov	BSS	A	Bromley	408	D 2-2	Gilroy 2 (23, pen 90)	11
14	Sat-13-Nov	BSS	H	Chelmsford City	1198	D 2-2	Ademola 36, Faulconbridge pen 90	14
15	Tue-23-Nov	BSS	H	Eastleigh	654	D 1-1	Og (Jordan) 37	15
16	Sat-27-Nov	BSS	H	Dartford	896	D 2-2	Hammond 22, Faulconbridge 45	13
17	Sun-26-Dec	BSS	H	Havant & Waterlooville	1182	W 3-1	Anane 18, Keehan 32, Ademola 90	10
18	Sat-01-Jan	BSS	A	Havant & Waterlooville	986	D 1-1	Keehan 72	11
19	Mon-03-Jan	BSS	H	Boreham Wood	1084	W 3-0	Hurrell 1, Faulconbridge 63, Gilroy 81	10
20	Sat-08-Jan	BSS	A	Basingstoke Town	604	L 0-1		11
21	Tue-11-Jan	BSS	A	Dover Athletic	765	D 2-2	Hammond 31, Ademola 76	11
22	Sat-29-Jan	BSS	A	Braintree Town	713	L 0-2		12
23	Tue-01-Feb	BSS	H	Thurrock	707	W 1-0	Hammond 32	10
24	Tue-08-Feb	BSS	H	St Albans City	690	W 2-0	Ademola 51, Murtagh 78	9
25	Sat-12-Feb	BSS	A	Bishops Stortford	422	W 4-0	Ademola 42, Murtagh 2 (45, 74), Palmer 86	9
26	Sat-19-Feb	BSS	H	Staines Town	1219	W 2-0	Ademola 28, Hammond 68	9
27	Tue-22-Feb	BSS	A	Maidenhead United	402	W 1-0	Hammond 72	9
28	Sat-26-Feb	BSS	A	Lewes	834	W 4-0	Dobson 2 (13, 22), Murtagh 78, Thomas 80	8
29	Tue-01-Mar	BSS	H	Ebbsfleet United	1005	W 3-0	Hammond 14, McNerney 26, Dobson 31	6
30	Sat-05-Mar	BSS	H	Farnborough	2123	D 1-1	Murtagh 4	8
31	Tue-08-Mar	BSS	A	Weston-Super-Mare	175	W 1-0	Palmer 79	7
32	Sat-12-Mar	BSS	A	Thurrock	415	W 1-0	Hammond 90	7
33	Tue-15-Mar	BSS	H	Hampton & Richmond Borough	1037	W 2-1	Ademola 34, Ricketts 74	4
34	Sat-19-Mar	BSS	H	Bromley	1381	W 1-0	Dobson 67	3
35	Sat-26-Mar	BSS	A	Eastleigh	877	L 1-3	Burgess 13	6
36	Sat-02-Apr	BSS	H	Welling United	1475	D 0-0		8
37	Tue-05-Apr	BSS	H	Dorchester Town	1028	W 2-1	Doyle 41, Taylor 51	5
38	Sat-09-Apr	BSS	A	Dartford	1206	L 2-3	Burgess 30, Dobson pen 84	8
39	Sat-16-Apr	BSS	H	Bishops Stortford	1281	W 2-0	Ademola 26, Walker 47	5
40	Sat-23-Apr	BSS	A	Farnborough	1879	W 2-1	Hammond 21, Og (Jordan) 51	5
41	Mon-25-Apr	BSS	H	Weston-Super-Mare	1975	W 4-3	Dobson 29, Ademola 43, Hammond 59, Burgess 82	5
42	Sat-30-Apr	BSS	A	Ebbsfleet United	1721	D 1-1	Hammond 13	5

CUPS

No.	Date	Comp	H/A	Opponents	Att:	Result	Goalscorers
1	Sat-25-Sep	FAC 2Q	A	Bishops Cleeve	252	W 2-1	Faulconbridge 2 (82, 87)
2	Sat-09-Oct	FAC 3Q	A	Brentwood Town	748	D 1-1	McNerney 90
3	Tue-12-Oct	FAC 3QR	H	Brentwood Town	460	W 1-0	Sogbanmu 83
4	Sat-23-Oct	FAC 4Q	H	Eastleigh	1048	W 3-2	Maledon 30, Faulconbridge 41, Hammond 67
5	Sat-06-Nov	FAC 1	A	Brighton & Hove Albion	5868	D 0-0	
6	Tue-16-Nov	FAC 1R	H	Brighton & Hove Albion	4193	D 2-2	(aet L 0-3 pens) Og (Greer) 72, Sogbanmu 103
7	Sat-20-Nov	FAT 3Q	A	Dover Athletic	818	W 2-1	Federico 2 (16, 18)
8	Sat-11-Dec	FAT 1	A	Harlow Town	324	W 2-0	Hammond 2 (18, 30)
9	Sat-15-Jan	FAT 2	A	AFC Wimbledon	2265	W 3-2	Ademola 2 (3, 47), Hammond 87
10	Sat-05-Feb	FAT 3	H	Salisbury City	1551	L 0-2	
11	Wed-04-May	PO SF 1	H	Farnborough	2726	L 0-1	
12	Sun-08-May	PO SF 2	A	Farnborough	2137	D 1-1 aet	(L 1-2 agg) Hammond 45

League
Starts
Substitute
Unused Sub

Cups
Starts
Substitute
Unused Sub

Goals (Lg)
Goals (Cup)

PIDGELEY	ANANE	THOMAS	RICKETTS	INNS	MCNERNEY	ADEMOLA	QUARM	FAULCONBRIDGE	GILROY	HURRELL	T LITTLE	FORBES	SOGBANMU	TURNBULL	PEGLER	MALEDON	HENNESSY	DOYLE	DALI	BUSH	PALMER	A LITTLE	WATKINS	BLAKE	VASSELL	HAMMOND	KENNEDY	FEDERICO	SAWYER	SINTIM	COUSINS	KEEHAN	NOEL	MURTAGH	DAVIES	DOBSON	KORANTENG	BURGESS	WALKER	TAYLOR	DOUGHTY	PULLEN	BEWICK
X	X	X	X	X	X	X	X	X	X	X	S	S	S	U	U																												
X	X	X	X	X	X	X	U	X	S	X	X	S			U	X	S																										
X	X	X	X	X		X	U	S	X	X	S	X	U			S	X	X																									
X		X	X	X	X	X	U	S	X	S	X	X				X	U	X	S																								
X		X	X	X	X	X	U	S	X	S	X	X				X	S	X	U																								
X			X	U	X	X	X	U	X	X	X		U			X		X	S	X	S																						
X	X	X	X	S	X	X	X	U	X	S	X				U	X		X	S																								
X	X		X	S	X	X	X	S	X	S	X	U			U	X		X		X																							
X	X		X	U	X	X	X	S	X	S	X		S		U	X		X		X																							
		U	X	X	X	S	X	X	S	U	X	X				S		X				X		X	X																		
	X	X	X	X	X	X	X	X	U	X			X			S						X		S		S	U																
	X	X	X	U	X	X	S	X	S				S		U	X		X				X		X		X																	
	X	X	X	X	X	S	X	X	X				U	S		X						X				S	U	X															
	X	X		U	X	X		S	X				S	S	U	X		X				X				X		X	X														
	X	X	X		X	X	U	S	U				S			X		X				X				X		X	X	S													
	X	X	X		X	X		X	S					U	U	S		X				X				X		X	X	U													
	X	S	X	U	X	S		U	X	X						S		X				X				X			X			X	X										
	X	S	U	U	X	X		S	S	X						X		X				X				X			X			X	X										
	X	X		X	X	S		X	S	X					U			X				X	U			X			X		S	X											
	X	S	X	X	U	S		X	S	X								X				X				X			X		U	X	X										
	X	X	X	U	X	X		S	S	X					U	X		X				X				X			X				U										
	X	X	X	U	X	X		S	X	S					U	X		X			U	X				X							X										
	U	X	X	S	X	X		S	X	X					U	S		X				X				X							X	X									
	X	X	X	U	X	X		S		X					U	U		X			S	X				X							X	X									
	X	X	X		X	X		U						U	U			X			S	X				X					S		X	X	X								
	X	X	X		X	X		U						S	U			X			S	X				X							X	X	X	S							
	X	X	X		X	X		U						S	U			X			S	X				X							X	X	X	S							
	X	X	X		X	X		S	U					S	U			X			S	X				X								X	X	X							
	X	X	X		X	X		S	U						U			X			S	X				X							S	X	X	X							
	X	X	X		X	X		U							U			X			S	X				X							S	X	X	X	S						
	X	X	X			X		U						S	U			X			S	X				X							X	X	X	X	U						
	X	X	X			X									U			X			S	X				X							X	X	X	X	S	S	U				
	X	X	X			X									U			X			S	X				X					U		S	X	X		X	X	S				
	X		X		X	X									U			X			S	X				X							U	X	X	S	S	X	X				
	X		X		X	X			U						U			X			S	X				X							X		X	X	S	X	S				
	X	X	X		X	S												X				X				X							U			X	S	X	S	X	X	U	
	X	X	X		X	S												X			S	X				X							U			X	S	X	X	X		U	
		X	X		X	S												X			S	X				X							X			X	U	X	X	X	U	U	
	X	X	X		X	X												X			S	X				X										X	S	U	X		X	U	S
	X	X	X	X	X	X			U												S	X				X										X	S	X	U		X	U	
	X	X		X	X	X			U												S	X				X										X	S	X	X	S	X	U	
	X	X	X	S	X	X												X			S	X				X										X	S	X	U	X		U	
		X	X	X	X	X		X	X	X	S	S	S		U	X		X				X	U																				
	X	X	X	X	S	X	U	X	X	X		S	S		U	X		X				X	U	U																			
	X	X	X		X	X	X	S	X	X		X	S		U	S		X			U	X	U																				
	X	X	X	S	X	X	S	X	S	U			U		U	X		X				X	U	X		X																	
	X	X	X	U	X	X	X	U	U				S	S	U	X		X				X	S			X		X															
	X	X	X		X	X	X	S	U				S	S	U	X		X			U	X				X		X		U													
	X	X	X		X	X	S	U	S				S			X		X				X				X		X	X	U													
	X		X	X	X	X		S	S					U	U	S		X				X				X			X		X	X											
	X	X	X	S	X	X		S	S						U	X		X				X				X			X		X												
	S	X	X	X	X	X		S	X					U	U	X		X				X				X					U			X									
	X	X	X	U	X	X												X			S	X				X										X	U	X		X	S	U	
	X	X	X	S	X	X			U				S					X				X				X										X		X		S	X	U	
9	36	33	38	12	37	34	8	9	13	12	8	4	1	0	0	14	1	36	0	3	0	33	0	2	1	30	0	4	8	0	0	4	13	12	11	13	1	9	5	4	4	0	0
0	0	3	0	4	0	8	1	14	8	6	2	2	5	6	0	6	2	0	3	0	19	0	0	1	0	2	0	0	0	1	2	0	3	0	0	3	10	1	3	1	0	0	1
0	1	1	1	9	1	0	5	8	7	1	0	1	3	3	24	1	1	0	1	0	1	0	1	0	0	0	2	0	0	1	2	0	4	0	0	0	2	1	3	0	1	7	0
0	10	11	12	4	11	12	3	3	4	3	0	1	0	0	0	8	0	12	0	0	0	12	0	1	0	9	0	3	3	0	2	1	0	1	0	2	0	2	0	1	1	0	0
0	1	0	0	3	1	0	2	5	4	0	1	2	7	2	0	2	0	0	0	0	1	0	1	0	0	0	0	0	0	0	0	0	0	0	0	0	0	0	0	1	1	0	0
0	0	0	0	2	0	0	1	2	3	1	0	0	1	2	9	0	0	0	0	0	2	0	4	1	0	0	0	0	0	2	1	0	0	0	0	0	1	0	0	0	0	2	0
0	2	1	1	0	1	9	0	5	7	1	0	0	0	0	0	0	0	1	0	0	2	0	0	0	0	12	0	0	0	0	0	2	0	5	0	6	0	3	1	1	0	0	0
0	0	0	0	0	1	2	0	3	0	0	0	0	2	0	0	1	0	0	0	0	0	0	0	0	0	5	0	2	0	0	0	0	0	0	0	0	0	0	0	0	0	0	0

PLAYING SQUAD 2011/12

Existing Players		SN	HT	WT	DOB	AGE	POB	Career	Apps	Goals
GOALKEEPERS										
Jordan	Kennedy							Woking	0	0
Aaron	Howe				05/10/1987	23		Woking Rel 5/07, Carshalton (L) 2/07, Carshalton c/s 07, Hayes & Yeading 8/08, Havant & W 7/09, Woking 7/11		
Andy	Little		6'03"	13 10	03/10/1974	36	Sheffield	Sheff Wed (Jun), Croydon 9/94, Sutton U 9/99, Banstead A 10/99, Crawley 11/99, Basingstoke (L) 2/05, AFC Wimbledon 6/05, Croydon Ath 2/10 Rel 9/10, Woking 9/10	33	0
Matt	Pegler				12/08/1991	20		Fulham (Yth), QPR (Yth), Aldershot (Yth), Woking c/s 09, Fleet T (L) 3/11, Badshot Lea (L) 7/11	0	0
DEFENDERS										
Mike	Cestor				30/04/1992	19	Paris, Fra	L.Orient, Breham Wood (SL) 1/11, Woking (L) 8/11		
Adam	Doyle				23/03/1986	25		Alton T, Farnborough 10/07, Bisley (Dual) 10/07, Woking 8/10	36	1
Derek	Duncan		5'10"	10 11	23/04/1987	24	Newham	L.Orient Rel 5/07, Lewes (L) 9/06, Grays 5/07, Wycombe 7/07, Lewes (2ML) 11/07, Ebbsfleet 1/09, AFC Wimbledon 6/09 Rel 4/10, Ebbsfleet 7/10, Woking 7/11		
Alan	Inns				05/06/1982	29	Reading	Oxford C (Jun), Wokingham, Hampton & R 9/02, AFC Wimbledon 5/08 Rel 4/10, Woking 5/10, Boreham Wood (SL) 2/11	16	0
Joseph	McNerney				24/01/1990	21		Woking, Corinthian Casuals (L) 10/09, Ashford T (Middx) (L) 3/10	37	1
Josh	Watkins							Woking	0	0
MIDFIELDERS										
Dale	Binns				08/07/1981	30	London	Hendon, Cambridge C 8/04, Stevenage 6/06 Rel 5/07, Lewes 7/07, Maidenhead 5/08, Hayes & Yeading 2/09 Rel 5/10, Farnborough 6/10 Rel 6/11, Woking 6/11		
Jay	Davies		5'07"	11 02	26/12/1991	19	Dagenham	Peterborough, Woking (6WL) 2/11, Farnborough 3/11, Woking 6/11	11	0
Josh	Griffiths				27/03/1992	19		Croydon Ath (Yth), Woking		
Jack	King				20/08/1985	26		Didcot, Brackley 6/04, Didcot 11/05, Farnborough 8/09 Rel 6/11, Woking 6/11		
Nathan	Koranteng		6'02"	12 08	26/05/1992	19	London	Peterborough Rel 3/11, Tamworth (L) 9/09, Spalding U (WE) 12/09, Boston U (WE) 1/10, Rushden & D (L) 8/10, Boston U (2ML) 1/11, Woking 3/11	11	0
Adam	Newton		5'10"	11 06	04/12/1980	30	Grays	West Ham Rel c/s 02, Portsmouth (2ML) 7/99, Notts County (SL) 11/00, L.Orient (6WL) 3/02, Peterborough 7/02, Brentford 6/08 Rel c/s 09, Luton 7/09 Rel c/s 11, Woking 6/11		
Mark	Ricketts		6'00"	11 02	07/10/1984	26	Sidcup	Charlton Rel c/s 06, MK Dons (3ML) 11/05, Gravesend/Ebbsfleet 8/06, Woking 6/09	38	1
Charlie	Turnbull				08/12/1990	20		Woking, Corinthian Casuals (L) 11/08, Walton & H (L) 9/10	6	0
FORWARDS										
Moses	Ademola		5'06"	10 08	18/07/1989	22	Bermondsey	Cray W (Yth), Croydon A, Brentford Undisc 7/08, Welling (L) 11/08 Recalled 1 day, Welling (L) 12/08, Welling (2ML) 2/09, Woking (6ML) 7/09, Woking 1/10	42	9
Anson	Cousins				22/11/1991	19		Woking, Godalming (L) 11/09	2	0
Paris	Cowan-Hall		5'08"	11 08	05/10/1990	21	Hillingdon	Rushden & D (Yth), Portsmouth Rel c/s 10, Grimsby (L) 1/10, Grimsby (2ML) 1/10, Scunthorpe 10/10 Rel c/s 11, Rushden & D (SL) 2/11, Gillingham (Trial) 7/11, Newport C (Trial) 7/11, Woking 8/11		
Wayne	Gray		5'10"	11 05	07/11/1980	30	Dulwich	Wimbledon Rel c/s 04, Swindon (2ML) 3/00, Port Vale (L) 10/00, L.Orient (3ML) 11/01, Brighton (L) 3/02, Southend 7/04 Rel c/s 06, Yeovil 7/06, L.Orient Undisc 7/07 Rel c/s 09, Rotherham (Trial) c/s 09, Exeter (Trial) c/s 09, Port Vale (Trial) 9/09, AFC Hornchurch 10/09, Grays 1/10 Rel 5/10, Cambridge U 8/10 Rel 1/11, Chelmsford 1/11, Woking 7/11		
Elvis	Hammond		5'10"	10 10	06/10/1980	30	Accra, Gha	Fulham, Bristol R (2ML) 8/01, Norwich (L) 8/03, RBC Roosendaahl (Holl) (SL) 1/05, Leicester (L) 8/05 £225,000 8/05 Rel c/s 08, Cheltenham 11/08 Rel 3/10, Sutton U 10/10, Woking 10/10	32	12
Oliver	Palmer				21/01/1992	19		Woking, St Albans (2ML) 11/10, Boreham Wood (6ML) 7/11	19	2
Ola	Sogbanmu				06/03/1992	19		Woking, Kingstonian (L) 11/10, Boreham Wood (SL) 1/11	6	0
Giuseppe	Sole				08/01/1988	23	Woking	Woking, Basingstoke (L) 3/06, Ebbsfleet (SL) 1/09, Newport C 5/10, Dorchester (L) 9/10, Havant & W (3ML) 10/10 Perm 1/11 Rel c/s 11, Woking 6/11		

PREMIER DIVISION

		P	W	D	L	F	A	Pts
1	FC Halifax Town	42	30	8	4	108	36	98
2	Colwyn Bay	42	24	7	11	67	56	79
3	Bradford Park Avenue	42	23	8	11	84	55	77
4	FC United of Manchester	42	24	4	14	76	53	76
5	North Ferriby United	42	22	7	13	78	51	73
6	Buxton	42	20	10	12	71	52	70
7	Worksop Town	42	21	6	15	72	54	69
8	Kendal Town	42	21	5	16	80	77	68
9	Marine	42	20	7	15	74	64	67
10	Chasetown	42	20	6	16	76	59	66
11	Matlock Town	42	20	6	16	74	59	66
12	Northwich Victoria	42	18	9	15	66	55	63
13	Stocksbridge Park Steels	42	17	6	19	75	75	57
14	Ashton United	42	16	5	21	57	62	53
15	Mickleover Sports	42	15	7	20	70	76	52
16	Whitby Town	42	14	9	19	58	77	51
17	Nantwich Town	42	13	7	22	68	90	46
18	Frickley Athletic	42	11	11	20	43	68	44
19	Burscough	42	12	7	23	56	73	43
20	Hucknall Town	42	11	10	21	57	80	43
21	Ossett Town	42	9	5	28	45	103	32
22	Retford United	42	5	2	35	31	111	17

PLAY-OFFS

Semi-Finals

Bradford Park Avenue 0-2 FC United of Manchester

Colwyn Bay 2-0 North Ferriby United

Final (@ Colwyn Bay, 2/5/11)

Colwyn Bay 1-0 FC United of Manchester

	1	2	3	4	5	6	7	8	9	10	11	12	13	14	15	16	17	18	19	20	21	22
1 Ashton United		1-3	1-0	2-1	2-3	3-0	0-3	1-0	3-6	4-0	1-2	1-0	3-1	2-3	2-4	0-1	2-1	0-1	1-0	3-1	1-3	3-1
2 Bradford Park Avenue	2-0		3-1	4-1	2-1	1-4	1-3	4-1	2-3	6-0	5-2	2-1	3-1	1-0	1-0	1-2	2-2	0-1	2-0	3-0	1-1	4-0
3 Burscough	4-1	2-3		1-2	0-3	0-0	0-2	0-2	3-0	3-0	2-4	1-2	0-3	3-2	3-1	2-2	0-0	0-1	0-1	0-2	1-0	3-1
4 Buxton	1-1	1-1	1-0		2-0	0-0	2-1	2-2	7-1	0-4	3-0	2-1	1-3	1-2	2-1	0-0	2-2	2-0	7-0	0-0	2-0	0-1
5 Chasetown	2-1	5-0	5-0	0-1		2-2	2-1	2-0	2-0	1-0	0-1	0-1	2-1	2-3	2-2	2-2	1-0	1-0	6-0	0-2	1-1	2-6
6 Colwyn Bay	0-3	2-2	2-1	2-1	1-0		2-1	3-1	4-0	2-0	1-2	0-3	0-1	1-1	2-0	0-2	0-6	3-1	1-0	3-4	2-0	2-1
7 FC Halifax Town	1-0	1-0	3-2	2-1	3-2	1-1		4-1	3-1	4-0	3-0	1-0	2-2	1-1	3-1	0-2	1-1	8-1	3-0	5-1	5-1	0-0
8 FC United Of Manchester	2-1	2-0	3-1	1-2	4-2	0-1	0-1		4-1	4-1	1-2	2-1	1-5	0-0	1-0	2-0	1-0	4-1	5-1	1-4	4-0	2-1
9 Frickley Athletic	0-0	2-2	0-1	2-2	2-1	0-1	0-0	0-0		1-0	0-2	2-3	0-1	1-0	3-0	0-1	2-1	0-1	1-2	1-1	0-0	1-0
10 Hucknall Town	0-0	2-2	2-2	0-1	2-2	0-1	1-2	1-2	2-0		4-3	0-3	2-2	1-0	3-1	3-2	0-2	3-3	5-3	2-2	1-2	1-2
11 Kendal Town	1-0	4-1	1-2	1-1	4-0	1-4	2-4	3-2	1-0	0-0		2-1	1-0	1-2	2-1	2-5	1-1	5-4	4-1	2-3	2-1	2-1
12 Marine	4-0	1-0	2-2	1-2	2-0	1-3	0-6	0-2	1-1	1-1	2-0		2-4	1-2	4-3	2-2	3-1	4-3	2-0	5-4	1-3	2-4
13 Matlock Town	1-1	0-1	2-1	1-3	3-4	3-0	1-2	1-2	1-0	1-2	3-1	0-1		1-2	4-2	2-1	1-1	2-0	4-2	1-0	2-2	1-0
14 Mickleover Sports	0-1	1-3	2-1	2-4	1-3	4-0	2-3	2-0	3-0	1-1	1-3	0-0	1-0		6-6	3-4	2-3	2-4	4-1	2-0	2-4	0-1
15 Nantwich Town	0-2	0-1	3-2	1-1	0-4	2-1	0-6	1-4	3-2	1-2	5-3	1-1	2-3	0-0		2-1	2-1	2-1	1-0	4-3	3-1	1-2
16 North Ferriby United	3-2	1-2	2-1	2-0	0-1	1-3	0-3	1-1	4-0	3-0	4-1	0-1	3-1	4-2	1-2		1-2	4-0	0-1	2-1	6-0	3-0
17 Northwich Victoria	1-0	2-1	3-0	4-2	1-1	0-1	0-3	1-0	0-1	4-0	1-6	4-3	2-3	1-0	1-1	1-1		0-1	4-1	0-1	2-0	3-1
18 Ossett Town	0-5	0-6	1-2	0-1	2-4	2-3	0-0	0-3	1-2	1-6	0-0	0-2	0-0	1-2	0-5	0-0	0-2		2-1	3-5	0-4	2-3
19 Retford United	1-2	0-0	0-2	1-3	0-4	3-5	0-2	0-4	1-3	2-5	2-1	0-3	0-4	0-2	3-2	1-2	0-1	0-2		0-0	0-3	0-3
20 Stocksbridge Park Steels	0-0	0-1	2-4	1-4	2-0	0-1	3-5	1-2	1-1	1-0	2-1	1-3	3-1	7-3	3-1	0-1	3-0	3-0	3-2		2-1	2-3
21 Whitby Town	2-1	1-2	2-2	1-0	0-1	2-2	1-5	0-1	2-2	1-0	2-2	1-1	1-2	3-2	3-1	0-1	2-4	3-1	2-1	2-0		0-3
22 Worksop Town	3-0	3-3	1-1	3-0	2-0	0-1	1-1	1-2	1-1	2-0	1-2	1-2	2-1	2-0	0-0	4-1	2-0	1-4	1-0	2-1	5-0	

DIVISION ONE NORTH

		P	W	D	L	F	A	Pts
1	Chester	44	29	10	5	107	36	97
2	Skelmersdale United	44	30	7	7	117	48	97
3	Chorley	44	25	11	8	87	43	86
4	Curzon Ashton	44	25	10	9	85	49	85
5	AFC Fylde	44	24	9	11	91	59	81
6	Clitheroe	44	19	13	12	82	70	70
7	Bamber Bridge	44	20	10	14	70	60	70
8	Lancaster City	44	21	5	18	80	61	68
9	Warrington Town (-3)	44	18	16	10	70	52	67
10	Witton Albion	44	15	17	12	75	64	62
11	Woodley Sports	44	17	11	16	71	75	62
12	Salford City	44	17	11	16	68	73	62
13	Garforth Town	44	13	13	18	67	71	52
14	Trafford	44	15	7	22	73	92	52
15	Mossley	44	14	9	21	75	77	51
16	Wakefield	44	14	8	22	55	74	50
17	Durham City (-1)	44	13	10	21	75	92	48
18	Radcliffe Borough	44	12	12	20	60	89	48
19	Cammell Laird	44	13	8	23	66	94	47
20	Harrogate Railway Athletic	44	13	7	24	82	103	46
21	Prescot Cables	44	9	15	20	52	79	42
22	Ossett Albion (-3)	44	6	11	27	60	134	26
23	Leigh Genesis	44	5	8	31	39	112	23

PLAY-OFFS

Semi-Finals

Skelmersdale United 0-1 A F C Fylde

Chorley 2-1 Curzon Ashton

Final (@ Chorley, 6/5/11)

Chorley 2-0 A F C Fylde

	1	2	3	4	5	6	7	8	9	10	11	12	13	14	15	16	17	18	19	20	21	22	23
1 AFC Fylde		0-2	1-1	1-3	3-0	0-1	3-1	4-2	1-0	5-2	4-1	4-0	0-2	2-0	2-1	5-2	1-3	2-3	3-2	4-0	3-0	1-1	3-2
2 Bamber Bridge	3-2		1-0	0-5	1-1	1-2	2-0	1-0	1-1	2-3	2-1	3-0	2-2	5-0	0-1	2-1	2-2	0-0	1-2	4-1	1-1	3-3	2-1
3 Cammell Laird	0-3	2-4		1-2	1-1	3-0	2-5	4-2	3-2	4-8	2-1	0-0	1-2	5-1	2-2	4-0	3-3	0-2	1-0	3-2	2-3	0-1	1-2
4 Chester	2-2	2-0	2-0		1-2	5-0	2-2	3-1	2-0	3-2	3-0	1-1	3-0	6-0	1-1	2-3	3-1	4-0	6-0	3-1	2-2	0-0	3-0
5 Chorley	0-0	2-0	3-0	0-1		1-1	1-0	5-0	1-2	1-2	2-1	3-1	2-1	2-1	5-2	4-1	1-0	2-0	0-1	2-1	0-3	2-2	6-0
6 Clitheroe	2-2	1-1	3-3	0-5	0-2		0-3	4-1	3-3	3-3	2-0	6-0	5-0	2-2	2-0	2-0	4-5	2-2	2-3	2-3	2-2	3-1	0-1
7 Curzon Ashton	1-1	2-2	3-0	3-1	2-6	0-0		4-1	4-1	5-2	0-1	2-0	1-0	7-0	1-1	3-0	1-0	2-3	3-2	3-2	0-2	2-0	3-1
8 Durham City	1-3	2-1	3-3	0-3	0-3	1-1	1-1		0-0	1-1	5-0	3-1	3-2	4-2	1-1	0-2	6-2	3-3	0-2	3-1	1-3	1-1	6-2
9 Garforth Town	1-1	0-1	0-1	2-1	1-1	0-1	0-2	1-1		2-6	2-4	3-1	2-1	4-0	0-0	2-2	2-1	0-3	2-1	4-0	3-0	0-0	4-3
10 Harrogate Railway Ath.	2-3	0-1	5-1	1-4	3-2	1-4	1-2	4-1	1-4		2-3	0-1	4-3	2-3	0-0	2-1	0-1	2-4	3-2	0-1	1-3	1-1	0-2
11 Lancaster City	2-0	3-1	1-0	2-1	0-2	1-2	0-2	4-0	5-2	4-1		6-0	2-0	4-1	1-2	0-1	0-0	1-0	2-2	2-1	0-4	2-0	2-0
12 Leigh Genesis	0-1	1-3	1-3	1-1	1-2	1-2	1-2	0-4	1-0	1-2	0-0		1-3	3-3	1-1	2-1	0-3	2-3	3-2	0-1	3-3	0-8	2-3
13 Mossley	2-0	0-1	1-2	0-1	1-3	3-2	1-1	0-2	2-1	3-0	2-4	0-2		4-0	1-2	1-1	1-3	1-4	6-0	3-0	1-1	3-3	0-0
14 Ossett Albion	2-5	2-6	3-2	0-3	2-2	1-1	2-3	2-1	1-1	2-2	0-4	2-1	1-1		1-3	3-3	6-2	2-5	2-0	1-1	1-3	1-3	2-5
15 Prescot Cables	0-1	0-2	1-1	0-1	0-2	1-2	2-1	3-4	1-1	1-2	0-4	4-0	1-5	2-2		2-0	1-2	1-4	2-2	0-1	3-1	1-2	2-2
16 Radcliffe Borough	1-1	1-0	0-2	2-2	1-2	2-3	0-0	0-3	2-5	1-0	2-2	3-2	0-4	4-1	1-1		1-1	1-4	5-3	0-0	1-0	1-2	2-3
17 Salford City	3-1	1-2	1-0	0-4	0-2	2-3	0-1	4-0	1-2	1-1	2-2	2-0	2-2	1-0	0-0	1-2		0-5	2-2	2-1	1-2	1-0	1-1
18 Skelmersdale United	1-3	6-0	8-0	0-1	1-1	1-2	1-1	2-0	1-0	1-0	2-1	4-0	4-0	7-2	3-0	2-2	2-2		5-2	2-1	1-2	6-1	1-0
19 Trafford	1-4	0-2	4-1	0-2	0-4	1-1	0-2	3-1	2-2	5-2	1-0	4-1	1-4	3-1	1-2	2-0	2-1	0-3		2-0	1-2	1-1	0-1
20 Wakefield	0-1	1-0	2-1	1-2	2-2	1-0	0-1	1-4	3-2	3-2	2-0	3-0	3-2	1-1	6-0	1-2	1-2	0-2	0-3		1-1	1-1	1-0
21 Warrington Town	1-1	1-1	0-1	1-1	1-0	0-2	0-1	3-1	2-2	4-0	2-1	2-1	1-1	2-0	2-2	1-2	1-2	0-1	3-1	1-1		2-0	1-1
22 Witton Albion	3-4	2-0	3-0	2-3	0-0	2-0	1-1	1-1	1-0	2-2	0-5	5-1	2-0	5-0	3-1	3-3	0-1	0-1	2-5	3-1	1-1		2-2
23 Woodley Sports	2-0	2-1	2-0	1-1	2-2	0-2	3-1	1-0	2-1	2-4	2-1	1-1	3-4	2-1	3-1	4-0	2-3	2-4	2-2	1-1	0-0	0-1	

DIVISION ONE SOUTH

		P	W	D	L	F	A	Pts
1	Barwell	42	30	4	8	84	46	94
2	Newcastle Town	42	27	9	6	104	48	90
3	Rushall Olympic	42	26	3	13	78	45	81
4	Brigg Town	42	24	8	10	74	57	80
5	Grantham Town	42	23	10	9	69	48	79
6	Sutton Coldfield Town	42	23	6	13	89	60	75
7	Kidsgrove Athletic	42	23	6	13	88	59	75
8	Carlton Town	42	21	10	11	88	50	73
9	Glapwell	42	21	6	15	82	58	69
10	Romulus	42	20	7	15	71	65	67
11	Sheffield	42	15	10	17	73	86	55
12	Lincoln United	42	14	12	16	70	77	54
13	Goole	42	16	6	20	78	93	54
14	Belper Town	42	16	5	21	70	74	53
15	Quorn	42	11	14	17	57	61	47
16	Leek Town	42	14	5	23	64	74	47
17	Loughborough Dynamo	42	13	7	22	72	89	46
18	Market Drayton	42	13	5	24	67	91	44
19	Stamford	42	10	12	20	62	74	42
20	Rainworth Miners Welfare	42	11	7	24	53	85	40
21	Shepshed Dynamo	42	4	9	29	44	103	21
22	Spalding United	42	3	7	32	33	127	16

PLAY-OFFS

Semi-Finals

Newcastle Town 0-3 Grantham Town

Rushall Olympic 2-0 Brigg Town

Final (@ Rushall Olympic, 2/5/11)

Rushall Olympic 2-0 Grantham Town

	1	2	3	4	5	6	7	8	9	10	11	12	13	14	15	16	17	18	19	20	21	22
1 Barwell		1-0	3-2	1-2	1-0	4-1	2-1	2-1	2-0	0-4	4-0	4-0	1-1	3-2	3-0	3-1	2-0	3-0	3-3	1-0	2-1	1-0
2 Belper Town	0-1		0-1	0-0	2-1	0-1	0-2	0-1	3-5	1-1	1-0	5-1	0-5	1-5	2-2	4-1	1-2	2-3	2-1	5-0	4-5	1-4
3 Brigg Town	0-2	1-2		1-0	2-1	3-0	1-1	2-0	1-1	0-2	1-7	4-3	0-2	4-0	1-1	2-1	4-3	0-0	2-1	2-1	3-2	1-0
4 Carlton Town	4-2	0-3	1-2		0-0	4-5	2-2	3-3	1-0	3-0	4-0	5-2	0-0	0-0	2-1	0-1	0-0	2-0	7-2	4-0	3-1	2-0
5 Glapwell	0-1	0-3	0-4	1-0		3-0	7-1	3-0	2-1	4-1	1-2	3-1	1-3	3-0	2-0	5-0	3-5	4-2	1-2	2-1	1-0	0-2
6 Goole	1-4	0-1	1-3	3-6	1-0		2-1	1-1	4-2	5-1	0-1	1-3	4-4	2-1	5-1	1-2	1-0	2-5	4-1	4-1	1-0	1-2
7 Grantham Town	5-2	2-1	2-0	1-0	0-0	1-2		2-1	2-0	1-1	2-1	1-2	3-0	1-1	1-3	1-0	1-0	3-1	2-2	0-0	4-1	0-3
8 Kidsgrove Athletic	0-2	4-2	1-2	2-5	4-0	5-3	1-2		3-2	1-0	2-0	3-1	1-2	2-1	4-0	5-1	2-0	2-2	0-0	3-1	4-3	1-2
9 Leek Town	2-3	0-2	0-1	2-1	0-2	4-1	2-1	0-1		4-3	3-3	4-0	0-1	1-0	2-3	0-2	1-2	0-2	2-0	2-2	1-0	1-2
10 Lincoln United	3-2	1-2	2-2	0-2	3-2	0-0	2-5	2-2	1-1		6-1	1-1	1-1	0-0	3-0	2-0	0-1	4-2	1-1	6-1	2-0	1-3
11 Loughborough Dynamo	0-3	5-4	2-2	1-4	1-4	4-1	1-1	0-3	2-3	6-0		0-1	3-1	2-1	1-2	1-1	2-5	1-3	5-1	5-0	2-2	1-2
12 Market Drayton Town	2-2	2-4	2-2	0-2	0-1	2-1	0-3	0-1	2-1	2-2	4-0		1-8	0-2	1-2	2-4	0-2	3-1	6-0	3-0	0-3	3-4
13 Newcastle Town	4-1	2-3	1-2	2-1	3-0	3-1	1-1	3-0	1-2	3-0	3-1	2-1		1-1	4-1	3-1	5-2	1-1	5-2	3-1	4-0	1-2
14 Quorn	1-2	2-0	0-3	2-1	2-3	3-3	1-2	3-3	0-1	1-2	4-1	1-1	0-0		3-1	2-3	1-0	1-3	0-0	3-0	0-1	2-1
15 Rainworth Miners Welfare	0-2	0-2	3-2	2-2	1-1	0-1	1-2	0-1	2-1	2-3	1-2	0-2	0-2	1-2		3-5	3-1	0-0	3-2	2-0	2-2	1-2
16 Romulus	2-1	2-0	0-1	0-1	2-2	0-5	0-1	1-0	2-2	5-1	2-0	2-0	0-2	3-3	3-0		0-0	0-2	4-2	3-2	0-1	2-1
17 Rushall Olympic	0-1	3-2	2-0	2-1	2-2	3-1	1-0	2-0	2-0	2-1	0-2	2-1	2-3	0-1	2-0	0-1		5-0	2-0	6-0	1-0	3-0
18 Sheffield	0-3	1-1	5-0	1-1	1-3	2-1	1-2	2-4	4-3	1-1	1-1	2-1	1-4	2-2	1-4	1-3	2-3		3-2	2-1	3-2	2-1
19 Shepshed Dynamo	1-1	1-0	0-2	1-3	0-5	3-3	0-1	1-4	0-2	0-2	0-1	0-2	0-2	1-1	3-1	1-2	0-2	1-2		5-1	1-4	0-4
20 Spalding United	1-2	0-1	0-4	0-4	0-2	1-2	0-2	1-6	0-4	2-1	2-2	2-4	3-3	1-1	0-3	0-7	0-3	3-2	2-1		0-4	1-1
21 Stamford	0-1	2-2	2-3	2-2	2-2	1-1	1-1	0-4	2-1	1-2	1-0	1-3	2-3	1-0	0-0	1-1	0-3	2-2	1-1	6-1		1-1
22 Sutton Coldfield Town	1-0	3-1	1-1	2-3	2-5	7-2	1-2	0-2	6-1	4-1	3-2	3-2	1-2	1-1	5-1	1-1	1-2	4-2	3-1	1-1	2-1	

LEAGUE CHALLENGE CUP

PRELIMINARY ROUND

Belper Town 1-5 Glapwell
Goole 4-3 Harrogate Railway Athletic
Loughborough Dynamo 3-0 Shepshed Dynamo
Mossley 1-2 Trafford
Newcastle Town 3-3 Sutton Coldfield Town
(Newcastle Town won 3-2 on penalties)

ROUND 1

AFC Fylde 3-4 Skelmersdale United
Bamber Bridge 0-1 Chorley
Cammell Laird 1-0 Prescot Cables
Carlton Town 6-0 Brigg Town
Chester 3-1 Rushall Olympic
Curzon Ashton 3-1 Leigh Genesis
Garforth Town 3-2 Ossett Albion
Goole 3-5 Sheffield
Grantham Town 6-4 Loughborough Dynamo
Kidsgrove Athletic 2-2 Leek Town
(Kidsgrove Athletic won 4-1 on penalties)
Lancaster City 5-2 Clitheroe
Lincoln United 2-3 Stamford
Market Drayton Town 2-3 Newcastle Town
Quorn 3-0 Romulus
Radcliffe Borough 1-0 Trafford
Rainworth Miners Welfare 3-4 Barwell
Spalding United 2-1 Glapwell
Wakefield 2-2 Durham City
(Durham City won 4-3 on penalties)
Warrington Town 2-4 Witton Albion
Woodley Sports 5-1 Salford City

ROUND 2

Barwell 3-0 Spalding United
Chorley 2-1 Curzon Ashton
Kidsgrove Athletic 7-2 Cammell Laird
Newcastle Town 2-0 Chester
Quorn 0-2 Carlton Town
Sheffield 1-3 Durham City (@ Durham City)
Skelmersdale United 4-0 Witton Albion
Stamford 0-3 Grantham Town
Woodley Sports 4-3 Garforth Town

ROUND 3

Ashton United 3-1 FC United of Manchester
Barwell 4-1 Retford United
Bradford Park Avenue 0-3 FC Halifax Town
(tie awarded to Bradford Park Avenue)
Burscough 1-2 Marine
Chasetown 2-3 Newcastle Town
Chorley 1-0 Radcliffe Borough
Durham City 2-0 Frickley Athletic
Hucknall Town 2-0 Worksop Town
Kidsgrove Athletic 0-2 Colwyn Bay
Matlock Town 3-0 Grantham Town
Mickleover Sports 2-3 Carlton Town
Nantwich Town 3-7 Northwich Victoria
Ossett Town 1-4 Stocksbridge Park Steels
Skelmersdale United 6-1 Buxton
Whitby Town 1-3 North Ferriby United
Woodley Sports 3-1 Kendal Town

ROUND 3

Matlock Town 3-0 Barwell
Newcastle Town 1-2 Northwich Victoria
Stocksbridge Park Steels 3-2 North Ferriby United
Colwyn Bay 2-2 Chorley
(Colwyn Bay won 7-6 on penalties)
Durham City 1-3 Bradford Park Avenue
Carlton Town 4-5 Hucknall Town
Skelmersdale United 5-0 Woodley Sports
Ashton United 3-2 Marine

QUARTER FINALS

Ashton United 2-1 Colwyn Bay
Bradford Park Avenue 4-2 Hucknall Town
Skelmersdale United 0-2 Northwich Victoria
Stocksbridge Park Steels 0-5 Matlock Town

SEMI-FINALS

Ashton United 1-0 Matlock Town
Northwich Victoria 3-1 Bradford Park Avenue

FINAL (@ Northwich Victoria, 30/4/11)
Northwich Victoria 0-1 Ashton United

PRESIDENT'S CUP

PRELIMINARY ROUND

Cammell Laird 1-4 Woodley Sports
(@ Woodley Sports)
Lancaster City 2-1 Chorley
Leek Town 0-2 Chester
Lincoln United 4-1 Grantham Town
Ossett Albion 0-2 Durham City
Quorn 2-1 Barwell
Radcliffe Borough 1-2 Curzon Ashton
Rainworth MW 0-3 Carlton Town
Rushall Olympic 4-1 Romulus
Sheffield 3-5 Garforth Town
Skelmersdale United 1-0 Leigh Genesis
Stamford 2-0 Spalding United
Wakefield 2-1 Brigg Town

ROUND 1

Sutton Coldfield Town 2-0 Kidsgrove Athletic
AFC Fylde 7-1 Warrington Town
Belper Town 2-1 Quorn
Clitheroe 1-2 Bamber Bridge
Durham City 2-3 Harrogate Railway Athletic
Garforth Town 2-3 Goole
Lancaster City 3-0 Prescot Cables
Loughborough Dynamo 0-4 Lincoln United
Mossley 0-2 Curzon Ashton
Newcastle Town 5-0 Trafford
Rushall Olympic 3-5 Market Drayton Town
Shepshed Dynamo 0-1 Glapwell
Skelmersdale United 4-3 Salford City
Stamford 2-1 Carlton Town
Woodley Sports 1-2 Wakefield
Chester 3-1 Witton Albion

ROUND 2

Lincoln United 0-6 Belper Town
Stamford 1-2 Glapwell
Wakefield 1-3 Harrogate Railway Athletic
Chester FC 3-0 Sutton Coldfield Town
Bamber Bridge 1-3 AFC Fylde
Curzon Ashton 5-0 Goole
Market Drayton Town 2-4 Newcastle Town
Lancaster City 2-1 Skelmersdale United

QUARTER FINALS

Newcastle Town 1-0 Glapwell
Belper Town 3-2 Harrogate Railway Athletic
AFC Fylde 0-3 Chester
Lancaster City 3-0 Curzon Ashton

SEMI FINALS

Belper Town 2-0 Newcastle Town
Lancaster City 2-1 Chester

FINAL (@ Northwich Victoria, 5/4/11)
Belper Town 1-3 Lancaster City

PREMIER LEAGUE STATS 2010-11
(League, FA Cup and FA Trophy)

Top Scoring Clubs:
119 F.C.Halifax,101, F.C. United of Manchester
90 Matlock Town

Clubs with Highest Aggregate of goals in their matches
190 Nantwich Town (88-102), 176 Stocksbridge P.S.(87-89)
172 Mickleover Sports (85-87) and Kendal Town 171 (88-83)
Not surprisingly the Mickleover Sports v Nantwich Town match resulted in a 6-6 draw!

Clubs' most consecutive scoring matches:
16 Nantwich Town (Goals Tally 46-37)
15 Northwich Victoria (33-16 in first fifteen games of the season)

Top Individual Goalscorers:
44 Ross Hannah (Matlock Town)
32 Mike Norton (F.C. United of Manchester)
32 Jamie Rainford (Marine)
26 Ben Tomlinson (Worksop Town)
26 Jamie Vardy (F.C. Halifax Town)

Scored in Most Games last season:
26 Ross Hannah (Matlock Town)
23 Mike Norton (F.C. United of Manchester)

Best Consecutive Individual Scoring Runs
6 matches: Gary Bradshaw (North Ferriby United),
6 Aaron Burns (Ashton United),Mike Norton (F.C. United),
6 Jamie Rainford (Marine) & Ben Tomlinson (Worksop Town)

Most Individual Goalscorers during the season
22 Bradford P.A.

Least Individual Goalscorers during the season
10 North Ferriby United

Clubs with most players scoring 10+
5 F.C. Halifax Town: Jamie Vardy 26, Danny Holland 19, James Dean 18, Lee Gregory 16 and Tom Baker 14

Most Hat Tricks
5 F.C. Halifax Town:
Jamie Vardy 2, James Dean, Lee Gregory and Danny Holland

Most Penalties scored by clubs in the season
11 F.C. Halifax Town, 8 Ashton United

Least Penalties scored by clubs in the season
1 Colwyn Bay, Nantwich Town, Ossett Town and Retford United

Most Penalties scored by an individual player.
11 Tom Baker (F.C. Halifax Town), 9 Keiran Walmsley (Kendal Town)

Least Goals scored in the season.
33 Retford United, 48 Ossett Town

Least Goals conceded in their League Season:
40 F.C. Halifax Town

Most Goals conceded in the Season:
117 Retford United, 108 Ossett Town and 102 Nantwich Town

Failing to scorein Least Games during the Season
5 F.C. Halifax Town, 6 Kendall Town, Marine and Matlock Town

Most matches in which the club failed to score:
24 Retford United
17 Ossett Town

Most consecutive matches without scoring:
7 Retford United (the last seven games of the season)
4 Northwich Victoria

Clubs credited with most 'Own Goals' scored by opponents:
4.Bradford P.A and F.C. United of Manchester

Most Clean Sheets
18 F.C. United of Manchester
17 Colwyn Bay
Least Clean Sheets in the season
4 Retford United and Whitby Town

Most Consecutive Clean Sheets
5 Bradford P.A.
4 Ashton United
4 Colwyn Bay (also 10 in 14 games)
4 Ossett Town (4 in first 5 games of season)

Most games without a clean sheet:
25 Whitby Town (36-46 goal tally) in first 25 games of season including a run of one defeat in twelve games.
20 Nantwich Town (goal tally 50-46)
19 Burscough (goal tally 33 -40)
19 Hucknall Town (goal tally 21-37)

Most Consecutive victories:
10 F.C. Halifax Town, 8 Bradford P.A.(Also 12 in 15 games)
Most Consecutive defeats:
8 Retford United, Nantwich Town, 7 Ossett Town, 6 Burscough

Most Consecutive games without a Victory:
20 Retford United
13 Hucknall Town

Best Unbeaten Run:
19 Chasetown (13 victories and six draws)
16 F.C. United of Manchester

Best League Attendances:
4023 F.C. Halifax Town v F.C. United of Manchester
2839 F.C. United of Manchester v Kendal Town
2805 F.C. United of Manchester v F.C. Halifax Town
Best Average Home League Attendance:
1867 F.C. United of Manchester
1673 F.C. Halifax Town
Smallest Average Home League Attendance:
173 Ossett Town
212 Burscough
315 Mickleover Sports

Best League Victories:

Home:			
F.C. Halifax	8	Ossett Town	1
Buxton	7	Retford United	0
Buxton	7	Frickley Athletic	1
Away:			
Colwyn Bay	0	Northwich Victoria	6
Marine	0	F.C. Halifax Town	6
Nantwich T	0	F.C. Halifax Town	6
Ossett Town	0	Bradford P.A.	6

Club Goalscorers with 10+ for season 2010-2011 in League, F A Cup, F A Trophy and Play-Offs

Five Goalscorers with ten goals or more in 2010-2011 season.

F.C. Halifax Town	(14)	Jamie Vardy 26, Danny Holland 19 James Dean 18, Lee Gregory 16 and Tom Baker 14

Four Goalcorers

Mickleover Sports	(13)	Alex Steadman and 19 Karl Ashton 16 Kieran O'Connell 12 and Martin Smythe 10

Three Goalscorers

Buxton	(13)	Kieron Lugsden 23, Mark Reed 21 and Mchael Towey 15
Chasetown	(17)	Gary Birch 16, Ben Jevons 16 and Dean Perrow 13
F.C. United of Manchester	(15)	Mike Norton 32, Jerome Wright 16 and Matt Wolfenden 11
North Ferriby United	(10)	Gary Bradshaw 23, Alex Davidson 18 and Chris Bolder 15
Northwich Victoria	(19)	Andy Fowler, 18 Wayne Riley 15 and Ollie Ryan 12
Stocksbridge Park Steels	(18)	Jack Muldoon 16, Mark Ward 16 and Andy Ring 10

Two Goalscorers

Bradford P.A.	(22)	Tom Greaves 19 and Aiden Savoury 16
Burscough	(17)	Warren Byers 14 and Kevin Leadbetter 10
Colwyn Bay	(15)	Jon Newby 14 and Rob Hopley 12
Kendal Town	(18)	Keiran Walmsley 17 and Carl Osman 11
Marine	(18)	Jamie Rainford 32 and Neil Harvey 11
Worksop Town	(16)	Ben Tomlinson 26 and Jamie Jackson 16

One Goalscorer

Ashton United	(17)	Aaron Burns 25
Matlock Town	(18)	Ross Hannah 44
Nantwich Town	(18)	Michael Lennon 28
Ossett Town	(18)	Dave Boardman 11
Whitby Town	(12)	Jimmy Beadle 16

Clubs with no goalscorers totalling 10 or over in 2010-2011

Frickley Athletic	(19)	Top Scorers: Ashley Burbeary and Danny Walsh 7
Hucknall Town	(19)	Top Scorer: Anthony Griffiths-Junior 9
Retford United	(13)	Top Scorer: Niall O'Brien 6

The figures in brackets indicate the number of individual goalscorers for the club during the past season

NATIONAL CUP FOOTBALL 2010-2011

All twenty two clubs in the senior Evo-Stik Premier division play in the F.A. Challenge Cup early in the season and then enter the F.A. Challenge Trophy in The First Qualifying Round which was played on the 16th October. To reach the First Round Proper of the F.A. Cup and the chance to face Football League opposition, an Evo-Stik club has to survive four qualifying rounds. In The F.A. Trophy the junior clubs may play in a Preliminary Round but Evo-Stik Premier clubs will hope to compete successfully in the three Qualifying Rounds.

Only one Evo-Stik club reached the Fourth Qualifying Round of the F.A. Cup and sadly five clubs failed to register a goal in the competition. The two new names, F.C. Halifax Town and F.C. United again dominated proceedings, with the Manchester club being the only Evo Stik representative reaching the competition proper. A fine victory at League One club Rochdale was followed by an excellent draw at high flying Brighton & Hove Albion, but the League leaders made their seniority pay in the replay, although television viewers had been introduced to the fine spirit and quality existing at the F.C. United club.

THE F A CHALLENGE CUP

	Games	Round	Goals
Ashton United	3	2Q	7
Bradford P.A.	1	1Q	1
Burscough	1	1Q	0
Buxton	4	3Qr	9
Chasetown	1	1Q	0
Colwyn Bay	4	2Qr	4
F.C. Halifax Town	4	4Q	8
F.C. United	**7**	**2Rd r**	**15**
Frickley Athletic	4	3Qr	7
Hucknall Town	1	1Q	0
Kendal Town	1	1Q	2
Marine	2	1Qr	1
Matlock Town	3	3Q	4
Mickleover Sports	4	3Q	11
Nantwich Town	2	2Q	6
North Ferriby United	4	3Qr	10
Northwich Victoria	3	2Qr	4
Ossett Town	1	1Q	1
Retford United	1	1Q	0
Stocksbridge P.S.	2	2Q	6
Whitby Town	1	1Q	0
Worksop Town	1	1Q	1

r denotes lost after a replay

Leading Evo Stik League F.A. Cup Goalscorers

Mike Norton (F.C. United of Manachester)	6
Danny Walsh (Frickley Atletic)	4
Glynn Hurst (F.C. United of Manchester)	3
Keiran Lugsden (Buxton)	3
Mark Reed (Buxton)	3
Ben Smith (Ashton United)	3
Nathan Taylor (F.C. Halifax Town)	3

Evo-Stik clubs' ties in The Competition Proper.

First Round

Rochdale (League One) 2 — **F.C. United of Manchester 3**

Att: 7,048 — (Platt, Cotterill, Norton)

Second Round

Brighton & Hove Albion (League One) 1 — **F.C. United 1**

Att. 5,362 — (Platt)

F.C. United 0 Brighton & Hove Albion 4

Att: 7,000

FACHALLENGE TROPHY

This was a wonderful campaign for Chasetown who recorded one of the highlights of the club's history by reaching the quarter finals of the F.A. Challenge Trophy, only losing away to Blue Square Premier club Mansfield Town after a replay in their tenth Trophy tie. Their 24 goals were impressive but for individual goalscoring, Matlock Town's ace striker Ross Hannah grabbed all the headlines. After scoring seven against Bedworth Town at home in the First Qualifying Round he scored his clubs two goals when eventually losing after a replay to Kendal Town. And just to show he could produce the goals in the league as well, he registered a hat trick plus a double between the First and Second Qualifying Trophy ties, and was credited with 23 goals by the end of November! Worksop Town and Nantwich Town, with half their 14 goals scored by Michael Lennon who hit four against Prescot Cables, also reached the competition proper, while Northwich Victoria jogged their supporters memories of past F.A. Trophy heroics at Wembley with a First Round appearance.

	Games	Round	Goals
Ashton United	2	1Qr	3
Bradford P.A.	1	1Q	0
Burscough	1	1Q	0
Buxton	1	1Q	1
Chasetown	**10**	**Q-F**	**23**
Colwyn Bay	2	2Q	3
F.C. Halifax Town	2	2Q	3
F.C. United of Manchester	3	3Q	8
Frickley Athletic	1	1Q	1
Hucknall Town	1	1Q	1
Kendal Town	4	3Q	6
Marine	3	2Q	6
Matlock Town	3	2Qr	12
Mickleover Sports	2	2Q	4
Nantwich Town	**4**	**1st Rd**	**14**
North Ferriby United	1	1Q	0
Northwich Victoria	**5**	**1st Rd**	**9**
Ossett Town	1	1Q	1
Retford United	2	1Qr	3
Stocksbridge Park Steels	3	3Q	6
Whitby Town	3	3Q	7
Worksop Town	**5**	**1st Rd**	**8**

r denotes lost after a replay

Leading Evo-Stik club goalscorers in the F.A. Trophy:

9	Ross Hannah (Matlock Town)
7	Michael Lennon (Nantwich Town)
4	Gary Birch (Chasetown)
4	Jamie Rainford (Marine)
4	Ben Tomlinson (Worksop Town)
3	Aaron Burns (Ashton United)
3	Ben Deegan (F.C. United)
3	David Egan (Chasetown)
3	Andy Fowler (Northwich Victoria)
3	Olie Ryan (Chasetown)

First Round F.A. Trophy Results for Evo-Stik clubs.

1st Rd Chasetown 3 Kettering Town (Blue Square Premier) 3
Replay Kettering Town 1 **Chasetown 2***
2nd Rd Chasetown 2 Grimsby Town (Blue Square Premier) 1
3rd Rd Eastleigh (Blue Square South)1 **Chasetown 3**
4th Rd Chasetown 2 Mansfield Town (Blue Square Premier) 2
Replay Mansfield Town 3 **Chasetown 1**
1st Rd Stalybridge Celtic (Blue Square North) 1 **Nantwich Town 1**
1st Rd Worcester City (Blue Square North) 1 **Northwich Victoria 0**
1st Rd Worksop Town 0 Mansfield Town (Blue Square Premier) 5

ASHTON UNITED

Chairman: David Aspinall
Secretary: Bryan Marshall **(T)** 07944 032 362 **(E)** bmarshall.aufc@btinternet.com
Additional Committee Members:
Tony Collins, John Milne, Eric Stafford, Jackie Tierney, Michael Cummings, Denise Pinder, Jim Pinder, Tony Robinson, Jan Sutherland, Steve Hobson, Andrew Evans, Ronnie Thommasson
Manager: Danny Johnson
Programme Editor: Ken Lee **(E)** kenlee1947@hotmail.co.uk

The Ashton squad celebrate their League Cup Final victory.

Club Factfile

Founded: 1878 **Nickname:** Robins
Previous Names: Hurst 1878-1947
Previous Leagues: Manchester, Lancashire Combination 1912-33, 48-64, 66-68, Midland 1964-66, Cheshire County 1923-48, 68-82, North West Counties 1982-92

Club Colours (change): Red and white halves/black/red (Navy and sky stripes/navy/sky)

Ground: Hurst Cross, Surrey Street, Ashton-u-Lyne OL6 8DY **(T)** 0161 339 4158 (Club) 330 1511 (Social)
Capacity: 4,500 **Seats:** 250 **Covered:** 750 **Clubhouse:** Yes **Shop:** Yes

Directions
From the M62 (approx 7.5 miles) Exit at Junction 20, take A627M to Oldham exit (2.5 miles) Take A627 towards Oldham town centre At King Street Roundabout take Park Road Continue straight onto B6194 Abbey Hills Road Follow B6194 onto Lees Road Turn right at the stone cross memorial and 1st right into the ground. From the M60 (approx 2.5 miles); Exit at Junction 23, take A635 for Ashton town centre Follow by-pass to B6194 Mossley Road. At traffic lights turn left into Queens Road Continue onto B6194 Lees Road Turn left at the stone cross memorial and 1st right into the ground.

Previous Grounds: Rose HIll 1878-1912

Record Attendance: 11,000 v Halifax Town - FA Cup 1st Round 1952
Record Victory: 11-3 v Stalybridge Celtic - Manchester Intermediate Cup 1955
Record Defeat: 1-11 v Wellington Town - Cheshire League 1946-47
Record Goalscorer: Not known
Record Appearances: Micky Boyle - 462
Additional Records: Paid £9,000 to Netherfield for Andy Whittaker 1994
Received £15,000 from Rotherham United for Karl Marginson 1993

Senior Honours: Manchester Challenge Shield 1992-93. Northern Premier League Division 1 Cup 1994-95, League Cup 2010-11. Manchester Senior Cup x4. Manchester Premier Cup x5, Manchester Junior Cup x3.

10 YEAR RECORD

01-02	02-03	03-04	04-05	05-06	06-07	07-08	08-09	09-10	10-11
NP 1 3	NP P 16	NP P 14	Conf N 21	NP P 15	NP P 18	NP P 10	NP P 9	NP P 12	NP P 14

ASHTON UNITED

No.	Date	Comp	H/A	Opponents	Att:	Result	Goalscorers	Pos
1	Aug 21	NPL P	H	Burscough	187	W 1 - 0	Steele 31	6
2	24		A	Colwyn Bay	393	W 3 - 0	Steele 37 O'Neill 62 Dawson 77	
3	28		A	Frickley Athletic	149	D 0 - 0		3
4	30		H	F.C.United	1069	W 1 - 0	Steele 44	
5	Sept 4		A	Stocksbridge Park Steels	231	D 0 - 0		2
6	6		H	Chasetown	184	L 2 - 3	Burns 18 Owens 80	
7	**11**	**FAC 1Q**	**A**	**Prescot Cables**	**142**	**D 2 - 2**	**Steele 15 Dawson 19**	
8	**13**	**FAC 1Qr**	**H**	**Prescot Cables**	**160**	**W 4 - 0**	**SMITH 3 (16 58 82) Piana 88**	
9	18		A	Matlock Town	362	D 1 - 1	Rigoglioso 45	8
10	20		H	Marine	177	W 1 - 0	Rigoglioso 30	4
11	**25**	**FAC 2Q**	**H**	**F.C. Halifax Town**	**525**	**L 1 - 2**	**Steele 1**	
12	28		A	Kendal Town	161	L 0 - 1		
13	Oct 2		H	F.C.Halifax	543	L 0 - 3		11
14	4		H	Bradford P.A.	184	L 1 - 2	Smith 32 (pen)	16
15	9		A	Worksop Town	269	L 0 - 3		
16	12		A	Ossett Town	65	W 5 - 0	BURNS 3 (17 73 90) Bennett 35 Moyo-Modise 77	14
17	**16**	**FAT 1Q**	**A**	**Marine**	**216**	**D 2 - 2**	**Burns 29 63**	
18	**18**	**FAT 1Qr**	**H**	**Marine**	**130**	**L 1 - 3**	**Burns 22**	
19	23		H	Hucknall Town	115	W 4 - 0	Burns 17 52 Bennett 28 Frost 67	10
20	30		A	North Ferriby United	208	L 2 - 3	Burns 58 (pen) 87 (pen)	
21	Nov 6		H	Whitby Town	154	L 1 - 3	Burns 45 (pen)	13
22	13		A	Chasetown	312	L 1 - 2	Moyo-Modise 14	
23	20		H	Ossett Town	108	L 0 - 1		14
24	Jan 1		H	Colwyn Bay	154	W 3 - 0	Dawson 53 (pen) 83 O'Neill 80	14
25	3		A	F.C. of Manchester	2062	L 1 - 2	Dawson 5	
26	8		A	Burscough	133	L 1 - 4	Burns 79	14
27	15		H	Frickley Athletic	123	L 3 - 6	Crowther 18 52 Burns 78	17
28	22		A	Retford United	121	W 2 - 1	Burns 55 60	15
29	24		H	Northwich Victoria	203	W 2 - 1	Bathurst 30 Jackson 79	
30	Feb 7		H	Nantwich Town	120	L 2 - 4	Burns 48 90 (pen)	
31	12		H	Mickleover Sports	118	L 2 - 3	Bathurst 45 Burns 90 (pen)	16
32	19		A	Marine	324	L 0 - 4		16
33	26		H	Buxton	237	W 2 - 1	Burns 82 (pen) 85	15
34	March 5		A	F.C.Halifax Town	1648	L 0 - 1		15
35	7		H	Kendal Town	156	L 1 - 2	Bathurst 38	
36	12		A	Nantwich Town	316	W 2 - 0	Bathurst 51 Burns 61	
37	19		H	North Ferriby United	126	L 0 - 1		16
38	22		A	Buxton	246	D 1 - 1	Burns 40	
39	26		H	Retford United	122	W 1 - 0	Dawson 22	13
40	30		A	Mickleover Sports	170	W 1 - 0	Metcalf 49	
41	April 2		A	Hucknall Town	128	D 0 - 0		14
42	9		H	Worksop Town	164	W 3 - 1	Smith 55 (pen) Dawson 73 Bathurst 75	14
43	11		H	Matlock Town	122	W 3 - 1	Robinson 25 Dawson 72 Madeley 78	
44	16		A	Whitby Town	318	L 1 - 2	Madeley 84	15
45	18		A	Bradford P.A.	394	L 0 - 2		
46	23		H	Stocksbridge P.S.	137	W 3 - 1	Madeley 58 Burns 78 81	14
47	25		A	Northwich Victoria	322	L 0 - 1		14

BRADFORD PARK AVENUE

Chairman: Dr. John Dean
Secretary: Trevor Jowett **(T)** 07863 180 787 **(E)** tjj@21thirlmere.freeserve.co.uk
Additional Committee Members:
Robert Blackburn, Kevin Hainsworth

Manager: John Deacey
Programme Editor: Tim Parker **(E)** timparker79@yahoo.co.uk

Club Factfile

Founded: 1907 **Nickname:** Avenue
Previous Names: Reformed in 1988
Previous Leagues: Southern 1907-08, Football League 1908-70, Northern Premier 1970-74, West Riding Co.Am. 1988-89, Central Midlands 1989-90, North West Counties 1990-95

Club Colours (change): Green and white stripes/white/white (Red & blue stripes/blue/blue)

Ground: Horsfall Stadium, Cemetery Road, Bradford, West Yorkshire BD6 2NG **(T)** 01274 604 578
Capacity: 5,000 **Seats:** 1,247 **Covered:** 2,000 **Clubhouse:** Yes **Shop:** Yes

Directions
M62 to junction 26. Join M606 leave at second junction. At the roundabout take 2nd exit (A6036 signposted Halifax) and pass Odsal Stadium on the left hand side. At next roundabout take the 3rd exit (A6036 Halifax, Horsfall Stadium is signposted). After approximately one mile turn left down Cemetery Road immediately before the Kings Head Public House. Ground is 150 yards on the left.

Previous Grounds: Park Ave. 1907-73, Valley Parade 1973-74, Manningham Mills 1988-89, McLaren Field 1985-93, Batley 1993-96

Record Attendance: 2,100 v Bristol City - FA Cup 1st Round 2003
Record Victory: 11-0 v Derby Dale - FA Cup 1908
Record Defeat: 0-7 v Barnsley - 1911
Record Goalscorer: Len Shackleton - 171 (1940-46)
Record Appearances: Tommy Farr - 542 (1934-50)
Additional Records: Paid £24,500 to Derby County for Leon Leuty 1950
Received £34,000 from Derby County for Kevin Hector 1966

Senior Honours: Football League Division 3 North 1928.
North West Counties League 1994-95. Northern Premier League Division 1 2000-01, Division 1 North 2007-08.
West Riding Senior Cup x9. West Riding County Cup x2.

10 YEAR RECORD

01-02	02-03	03-04	04-05	05-06	06-07	07-08	08-09	09-10	10-11
NP P 10	NP P 7	NP P 17	Conf N 22	NP P 21	NP 1 4	NP1N 1	NP P 7	NP P 2	NP P 3

BRADFORD PARK AVENUE

No.	Date	Comp	H/A	Opponents	Att:	Result	Goalscorers	Pos
1	Aug-21	NPL P	H	Chasetown	448	W 2 - 1	Cohen 32 (og) Greaves 90	3
2	24		A	Northwich Vctoria	464	L 1 - 2	Clayton 65	
3	28		A	Colwyn Bay	440	D 2 - 2	Facey 30 Knowles 45	10
4	30		H	Ossett Town	363	L 0 - 1		
5	Sept 4		A	Worksop Town	320	D 3 - 3	Greaves 56 Sanasy 77 90 (pen)	14
6	8		H	F.C.United	990	W 4 - 1	Riordon 9 GREAVES 3 (76 87 89)	
7	**11**	**FAC 1Q**	**A**	**West Auckland Town**	**180**	**L 1 - 3**	**Greaves 6**	
8	18		H	Nantwich Town	303	W 1 - 0	Facey 18	11
9	21		A	Hucknall Town	228	D 2 - 2	Greaves 43 Heagney 62	
10	25		A	Chasetown	455	L 0 - 5		14
11	27		H	Whitby Town	277	D 1 - 1	Burton 2	
12	Oct 2		A	Stocksbrdge Park Steels	221	W 1 - 0	Burton 72 (pen)	9
13	4		A	Ashton United	184	W 3 - 1	Clayton 25 26 Burton 90	
14	9		H	Marine	365	W 2 - 1	Heagney 86 Greaves 90	4
15	**16**	**FAT 1Q**	**A**	**Colwyn Bay**	**337**	**L 0 - 2**		
16	19		A	F.C.Halifax Town	2011	L 0 - 1		
17	23		A	Kendal Town	306	L 1 - 4	Savory 5	8
18	30		H	Frickley Athletic	353	L 2 - 3	Burton 17 (pen) Clayton 85	11
19	Nov 6		A	Retford United	195	D 0 - 0		11
20	20		A	Buxton	359	D 1 - 1	Tiani 90	13
21	Dec 11		A	Burscough	167	W 3 - 2	Savory 42 86 Chiluka 90	
22	Jan 1		A	Ossett Town	265	W 6 - 0	Greaves 8 79 Gibson 27 Savory 37 Claisse 60 Tiani 76	6
23	8		A	F.C.United	1862	L 0 - 2		12
24	15		H	Colwyn Bay	281	L 1 - 4	Savory 18	12
25	22		A	Nantwich Town	369	W 1 - 0	Greaves 50	11
26	24		H	F.C.Halifax Town	1325	L 1 - 3	Savory 47	
27	Feb 2		H	Buxton	225	W 4 - 1	Savory 3 James 21 87 Boshell 45	11
28	12		A	North Ferriby United	236	W 2 - 1	Greaves 44 Savory 77	10
29	14		H	Northwich Victoria	266	D 2 - 2	Clayton 55 Evans 65 (og)	
30	28		H	North Ferriby United	241	L 1 - 2	Clayton 35	
31	March 5		H	Stocksbridge P.S.	253	W 3 - 0	Knowles 24 Hotte 38 Taylor 44	12
32	12		A	Whitby Town	323	W 2 - 1	James 31 O'Brien 69	11
33	14		H	Mickleover Sports	213	W 1 - 0	O'Brien 70	
34	19		H	Matlock Town	318	W 3 - 1	Greaves 9 O'Brien 21(pen) 59 (pen)	8
35	22		A	Frickley Athletic	248	D 2 - 2	James 45 Lister 72 (og)	
36	26		A	Marine	378	L 0 - 1		10
37	28		H	Burscough	236	W 3 - 1	Greaves 20 70 James 63	
38	April 2		H	Kendal Town	396	W 5 - 2	Savoury 18 O'Brien 27 Boshell 32 37 Drury 87 (pen)	8
39	9		A	Matlock Town	395	W 1 - 0	Savory 81 (pen)	7
40	11		H	Hucknall Town	295	W 6 - 0	GREAVES 3 (27 45 48) Savory 40 (pen) 43 Tiani 82	
41	16		H	Retford United	402	W 2 - 0	Robinson 59 (og) Clayton 73	5
42	18		H	Ashton United	394	W 2 - 0	Riley 21 Savory 37	
43	23		H	Worksop Town	528	W 4 - 0	Hotte 22 Greaves 48 Savory 64 Claisse 80	4
44	25		A	Mickleover Sports	290	W 3 - 1	Plummer 33 Savory 78 90	3
45	**28**	**Play Off SF**	**H**	**F.C.United**	**2785**	**L 0 - 2**		

BURSCOUGH

Chairman: Gary Wright
Secretary: Stan Petheridge **(T)** 0781 595 4304 **(E)** (club) sharon@heskethservices.co.uk
Additional Committee Members:
Mr D Hughes, Mr P Gilchrist, Mr M Gilchrist, Mr D McIlwain, Mr F Duffy, Mr S Heaps.
Club President: Mr R Cottam.
Manager: Christopher Stammers
Programme Editor: Ashley Fletcher **(E)**

Burscough 's squad for the 2000-2001 season with the Unibond League Division One Runners-Up Trophy. (What a smart photo!)
Back row ; left to right: Mark Wilde, Andy McMullen, Paul Blasbery, Greg Price, Billy Knowles and Ray Birch.
Middle row: Peter King (Assistant Manager), John Lawless, Lee McEvilly, Michael Clandon, Darren Saint, Brian Holmes, Neil Hanson, and John Davison (Manager). Front row: Robbie Talbot, Ryan Lowe, Ged Nolan, Bil Ashcroft, John Newman and Marvin Molyneux.

Club Factfile

Founded: 1946 **Nickname:** Linnets
Previous Names: Not known
Previous Leagues: Liverpool County Combination 1946-53, Lancashire Combination 1953-70, Cheshire County 1970-82, North West Counties 1982-98, Northern Premier League 1998-2007, Conference 2007-09
Club Colours (change): All green (All pale blue)

Ground: Victoria Park, Bobby Langton Way, Mart Lane, Burscough L40 0SD **(T)** 01704 893 237
Capacity: 2,500 **Seats:** 270 **Covered:** 1,000 **Clubhouse:** Yes **Shop:** Yes

Directions
M6 to J27. Follow signs for 'Parbold' (A5209), carry on through Newburgh into Burscough passing Briars Hall Hotel on left. Turn right at second mini-roundabout into Junction Lane (signposted 'Burscough & Martin Mere') into village, over canal. Take second left into Mart Lane to ground at end.

Previous Grounds: Not known

Record Attendance: 4,798 v Wigan Athletic - FA Cup 3rd Qualifying Round 1950-51
Record Victory: 10-0 v Cromptons Rec - 1947 and v Nelson - 1948-49 both Lancashire Combination
Record Defeat: 0-9 v Earltown - Liverpool County Combination 1948-49
Record Goalscorer: Wes Bridge - 188
Record Appearances: Not known
Additional Records: Johnny Vincent scored 60 goals during the 1953-64 season
Louis Bimpson scored 7 goals in one game.
Senior Honours: North West Counties League Division 1 1982-83. FA Trophy 2002-03. Northern Premier League Premier Division 2006-07.
Liverpool Challenge Cup x3. Liverpool Non-League Senior Cup x2.

10 YEAR RECORD

01-02	02-03	03-04	04-05	05-06	06-07	07-08	08-09	09-10	10-11
NP P 18	NP P 18	NP P 19	NP P 6	NP P 7	NP P 1	Conf N 8	Conf N 21	NP P 16	NP P 19

BURSCOUGH

No.	Date	Comp	H/A	Opponents	Att:	Result	Goalscorers	Pos
1	Aug-02	NPL P	A	Ashton United	187	L 0 - 1		18
2	24		H	Matlock Town	159	L 0 - 3		
3	28		H	North Ferriby United	143	D 2 - 2	McEvatt 31 (pen) Mahon 70	19
4	30		A	Kendal Town	276	W 2 - 1	Brookfield 67 Mahon 88	17
5	Sept 4		H	Retford United	195	L 0 - 1		
6	**11**	**FAC 1Q**	**A**	**Nantwich Town**	**247**	**L 0 - 4**		
7	14		A	Ossett Town	79	W 2 - 1	Byers 79 McEvatt 87	
8	18		A	Frickley Athletic	183	W 1 - 0	Byers 31	13
9	21		H	F.C.United	468	L 0 - 2		
10	25		H	Whitby Town	171	W 1 - 0	Byers 7	13
11	Oct 2		H	Worksop Town	174	W 3 - 0	BYERS 3 (5 50 54 pen)	10
12	5		H	F.C.Halifax Town	494	L 0 - 2		
13	9		A	Chasetown	474	L 0 - 5		14
14	12		A	Colwyn Bay	206	L 1 - 2	Byers 7	
15	**16**	**FAT 1Q**	**H**	**Clitheroe**	**201**	**L 0 - 2**		
16	23		H	Northwich Victoria	241	D 0 - 0		14
17	26		A	F.C.Halifax Town	1264	L 2 - 3	Byers 38 (pen) Fields 68	
18	30		H	Hucknall Town	151	W 3 - 0	Byers 38 47 Leadbetter 45	14
19	Nov 6		H	Mickleover Sports	167	W 3 - 2	Connolly 24 76 Leadbetter 90	12
20	9		H	Colwyn Bay	147	D 0 - 0		
21	13		A	Whitby Town	266	D 2 - 2	Bowen 73 Leadbetter 80	10
22	16		A	Nantwich Town	236	L 2 - 3	Leadbetter 44 Bowen 90	
23	20		H	Frickley Athletic	163	W 3 - 0	Leadbetter 35 Parry 67 Byers 80	
24	Dec 11		H	Bradford P.A.	167	L 2 - 3	Leadbetter 10 Byers 22	
25	Jan1		H	Burscough	236	L 2 - 4	McEvilly 27 35	11
26	3		A	Matlock Town	305	L 1 - 2	McEvatt 73 (pen)	
27	8		H	Ashton United	133	W 4 - 1	McEVATT 3 (38 58 65) Connolly 81	10
28	15		A	North Ferriby United	154	L 1 - 2	Byers 86	10
29	25		A	Marine	303	D 2 - 2	Lawless 53 McEvatt 60	
30	Feb 12		H	Buxton	247	L 1 - 2	Byers 49	14
31	19		A	F.C.United	3030	L 1 - 3	Cass 84	14
32	26		H	Nantwich Town	225	W 3 - 1	Parry 36 Farley 65 Leadbetter 68	13
33	March 1		A	Stocksbridge P.S.	76	W 4 - 2	Brookfield 12 90 Leadbetter 36 43	
34	5		A	Worksop Town	232	D 1 - 1	Leadbetter 59	13
35	12		H	Chasetown	206	L 0 - 3		13
36	19		H	Ossett Town	146	L 0 - 1		13
37	25		A	Buxton	292	L 0 - 1		16
38	28		A	Bradford P.A.	236	L 1 - 3	Higgins 30	
39	April 2		A	Northwich Victoria	327	L 0 - 3		17
40	6		H	Stocksbridge P.S.	115	L 0 - 2		
41	9		A	Hucknall Town	234	D 2 - 2	Jones 51 77	19
42	16		A	Mickleover Sports	203	L 1 - 2	McCulloch 42	20
43	22		A	Retford United	184	W 2 - 0	Gornell 8 11	
44	24		H	Marine	296	L 1 - 2	Jones 87	19

BUXTON

Chairman: Tony Tomlinson
Secretary: Don Roberts **(T)** 07967 822 448 **(E)** admin@buxtonfc.co.uk
Additional Committee Members:
Chris Brindley, Gary Taylor, Paul Jenner, David Belfield, David Hopkins, John Yates, Mike Barton
Manager: John Reed
Programme Editor: Mike Barton **(E)** mike@buxtonfc.co.uk

Club Factfile

Founded: 1877 **Nickname:** The Bucks
Previous Names: Not known
Previous Leagues: Combination 1891-99, Manchester 1899-1932, Cheshire County 1932-40, 46-73, Northern Premier 1973-98, Northern Counties East 1998-2006

Club Colours (change): All royal blue (White/black/black)

Ground: The Silverlands, Buxton, Derbyshire SK17 6QH **(T)** 01298 231 197
Capacity: 4,000 **Seats:** 490 **Covered:** 2,500 **Clubhouse:** Yes **Shop:** Yes

Directions
FROM STOCKPORT (A6): Turn left at first roundabout after dropping down the hill into the town, turn right at next roundabout, right at traffic lights (London Road pub) to Buxton Market Place. After two sets of pedestrian lights turn right at Royles shop then turn immediate left and follow road approx 500 metres to ground (opposite police station.) FROM BAKEWELL (A6): Turn left at roundabout on to Dale Road and follow road to traffic lights then as above. FROM MACCLESFIELD/CONGLETON/LEEK: Follow road to Burbage traffic lights and take right fork in the road at the Duke of York pub (Macclesfield Road.) Then at next traffic lights turn left (London Road pub) and follow as above. FROM ASHBOURNE (A515): Go straight on at first traffic lights (London Road pub) and follow directions as above.

Previous Grounds: Not known

Record Attendance: 6,000 v Barrow - FA Cup 1st Round 1961-62
Record Victory: Not known
Record Defeat: Not known
Record Goalscorer: Mark Reed - 164 (in 265 appearances 2002-07, 2009-)
Record Appearances: David Bainbridge - 642
Additional Records: Paid £5,000 to Hyde United for Gary Walker 1989
Received £16,500 from Rotherham for Ally Pickering 1989

Senior Honours: Manchester League 1931-32, Lge cup 1925-26, 26-27. Cheshire Co. League 1972-73, Lge Cup 1956-57, 57-58, 68-69. N.C.E. League 2005-06, Presidents Cup 2004-05, 05-06. N.P.L. Division 1 2006-07, President's Cup 1981-82, 2006-07. Derbyshire Senior Cup 1938-39, 45-46, 56-57, 59-60, 71-72, 80-81, 85-86, 86-87, 2008-09.

10 YEAR RECORD

01-02	02-03	03-04	04-05	05-06	06-07	07-08	08-09	09-10	10-11
NCEP 19	NCEP 4	NCEP 7	NCEP 9	NCEP 1	NP 1 1	NP P 5	NP P 14	NP P 8	NP P 6

BUXTON

No.	Date	Comp	H/A	Opponents	Att:	Result	Goalscorers	Pos
1	Aug 21	NPL P	A	F.C.Halifax Town	1756	L 1 - 2	Towey 50	15
2	25		H	Hucknall Town	225	L 0 - 4		
3	28		H	Whitby Town	279	W 2 - 0	Hunter 41 Lugsden 69	16
4	30		A	Marine	383	W 2 - 1	Ridley 58 Towey 61	
5	Sept 4		H	Nantwich Town	359	W 2 - 1	Lugsden 38 59	7
6	7		A	Retford United	187	W 3 - 1	TOWEY 3 (33 55 63)	
7	**11**	**FAC 1Q**	**A**	**Bottesford Town**	**135**	**W 3 - 0**	**Ridley 7 Lugsden 32 70**	
8	18		A	North Ferriby United	223	L 0 - 2		9
9	22		H	Kendal Town	267	W 3 - 0	Reed 39 90 Ridley 63	
10	**25**	**FAC 2Q**	**A**	**Brackley Town**	**306**	**W 3 - 1**	**Ridley 16 Reed 63 90**	
11	28		A	F.C.United	1761	W 2 - 1	Anderson 79 Reed 85 (pen)	
12	Oct 2		H	Frickley Athletic	371	W 7 - 1	Towey 6 Anderson 8 LUGSDEN 3 (8 2 79) Maxfield 45 74	2
13	6		H	Mickleover Sporta	306	L 1 - 2	Reed 45 (pen)	
14	**9**	**FAC 3Q**	**H**	**A.F.C.Telford United**	**836**	**D 1 - 1**	**Anderson 78**	
15	**12**	**FAC 3Qr**	**A**	**AFC Telford United**	**1122**	**D 2 - 2***	**Lugsden 2 Whight 120 Won 5-4 on penalties**	
16	**16**	**FAT 1Q**	**H**	**Stocksbridge Park Steels**	**321**	**L 1 - 2**	**Anderson 82**	
17	**23**	**FAC 4Q**	**A**	**Fleetwood Town**	**1181**	**L 1 - 2**	**Reed 20 (pen)**	
18	27		A	Mickleover Sports	424	W 4 - 2	Towey 8 Ridley 61 Reed 63 Lugsden 90	
19	30		H	Ossett Town	336	W 2 - 0	Lugsden 49 Agus 65	3
20	Nov 6		H	Worksop Town	421	L 0 - 1		4
21	10		H	Chasetown	230	W 2 - 0	Lugsden 32 Farmer 85 (og)	
22	13		A	Colwyn Bay	376	L 1 - 2	Reed 61	2
23	20		H	Bradford P.A.	359	D 1 - 1	Reed 13 (pen)	3
24	Jan 1		H	Marine	354	W 2 - 1	Lugsden 26 Towey 72	3
25	8		H	Retford United	303	W 7 - 0	REED 3 (18pen 22 81) Towey 30 71 Lugsden 34 Whight 80	3
26	Feb 2		A	Bradford P.A.	225	L 1 - 4	Towey 43	9
27	8		A	Chasetown	408	W 1 - 0	Lugsden 47	
28	12		A	Burscough	247	W 2 - 1	Towey 58 Reed 61	5
29	19		A	Kendal Town	219	D 1 - 1	Reed 36	5
30	23		H	Stocksbridge PS	231	D 0 - 0		
31	26		A	Ashton United	237	L 1 - 2	Ovington 65	7
32	March 1		H	Northwich Victoria	202	D 2 - 2	Reed 32 85 (pen)	
33	5		A	Frickley Athletic	314	D 2 - 2	Stevens 16 Reed 80	7
34	9		A	Hucknall Town	186	W 1 - 0	Towey 55	
35	12		H	F.C.Halifax Town	803	W 2 - 1	Lugsden 76 81	5
36	15		A	Matlock Town	654	W 3 - 1	Lugsden 29 64 Towey 68	
37	19		H	F.C.United	1726	D 2 - 2	Lugsden 3 54	4
38	22		H	Ashton United	246	D 1 - 1	Reed 22	
39	25		H	Burscough	292	W 1 - 0	Lugsden 18	4
40	30		H	North Ferriby United	289	D 0 - 0		
41	April 2		A	Ossett Town	172	W 1 - 0	Ovington 82	3
42	6		A	Whitby Town	244	L 0 - 1		
43	9		H	Colwyn Bay	408	D 0 - 0		4
44	12		A	Stocksbridge Park Steels	182	W 4 - 1	Reed 10 (pen) Towey 21 Ridley 45 Maguire 60	
45	16		A	Worksop Town	285	L 0 - 3		4
46	18		A	Northwich Victoria	303	L 2 - 4	Reed 22 Lugsden 62	
47	23		A	Nantwich Town	517	D 1 - 1	Reed 53 (pen)	6
48	25		H	Matlock Town	595	L 1 - 3	Wilde 23	6

CHASETOWN

Chairman: John Donnelly
Secretary: John Richards **(T)** 07866 902 093 **(E)** (club) chastownfc@gmail.com
Additional Committee Members:
Brian Baker, Michael Joiner, Alan Smith, Janice Brookes, John Goddard, Steve Maden, Mark Prince, Dave Goddard, Robert Brookes, Barbara Hawkes, Dave Birt, Paul Mullins, Lawrence Hawkes, John Franklin, Mike Hampton, Colin Faunch
Manager: Charlie Blakemore
Programme Editor: Russell Brown **(E)** rwbcfc@googlemail.com

Front Row (L-R): Andrews Westwood, John Branch, Richard Teesdale, Charlie Blakemore (Manager), Mick Joiner (Chief Executive), Andy Cox (Assistant Manager), Darren Stride, Dean Perrow, Mark Branch. **Middle:** Mick Andrews (Sports Therapist), Andy Turner (Scholarship Manager), Malachi Farquharson, Alex Steadman, Lee Parsons, Ben Jevons, Mark Wiggins, Ryan Price, Jake Sedgemore, Gary Birch, Matty Cohen, Jack Stone, Kevin Thompson (Coach), Ted Highfield (Sports Therapist). **Back:** Emma Archer (Sports Therapist), Theo Robinson, Jack Farmer, Karl Edwards, Ramone Stephens, Danny Smith, Andy Penny, Gary Hay, Gavin Hurran, Jimmy Turner, Chris Peel, Chris Slater, John Birt (Goalkeeping Coach)

Club Factfile

Founded: 1954 **Nickname:** The Scholars
Previous Names: Chase Terrace Old Scholars 1954-72
Previous Leagues: Cannock Youth 1954-58, Lichfield & District 1958-61, Staffordshire County 1961-72, West Midlands 1972-94, Midland Alliance 1994-2006, Southern 2006-09

Club Colours (change): Royal blue/royal blue/white (Bright red/bright red/white)

Ground: The Scholars, Church Street, Chasetown, Walsall WS7 8QL **(T)** 01543 682 222
Capacity: 2,000 **Seats:** 151 **Covered:** 220 **Clubhouse:** Yes **Shop:** Yes

Directions
From the M42 junction10 towards Tamworth or from the M6 Junction 11 or 12 towards Cannock or the A38 southbound from Derby - follow signs for A5 towards Brownhills, At the traffic lights at the Terrace Restaurant turn towards Burntwood onto the A5195. Straight over first island towards Chasetown and Hammerwich, over toll road and at second island turn left into Haney Hay Road which leads into Highfields Road signposted Chasetown, up the hill to mini island, then straight on into Church Street past the church on left and school on right. Ground is on the left at end of road. If using M6 Toll exit at junction T6 Burntwood - turn left out of Toll booths and left at second island and follow over toll road as above.

Previous Grounds: Burntwood Recreation

Record Attendance: 2,420 v Cardiff City - FA Cup 3rd Round January 2008
Record Victory: 14-1 v Hanford - Walsall Senior Cup 1991-92
Record Defeat: 1-8 v Telford United Reserves - West Midlands League
Record Goalscorer: Tony Dixon - 197
Record Appearances: Not known
Additional Records:

Senior Honours: West Midlands League 1978, League Cup x2.
Midland Alliance 2005-06.
Walsall Senior Cup x2.

10 YEAR RECORD

01-02	02-03	03-04	04-05	05-06	06-07	07-08	08-09	09-10	10-11
MidAl 18	MidAl 9	MidAl 7	MidAl 2	MidAl 1	SthM	SthM 7	SthM 4	NP1S 2	NP P 10

CHASETOWN

No.	Date	Comp	H/A	Opponents	Att:	Result	Goalscorers	Pos
1	Aug-02	NPL P	A	Bradford P.A.	448	L 1 - 2	Hay 37	16
2	24		H	Marine	418	L 0 - 1		
3	28		H	F.C.Halifax Town	611	W 2 - 1	Birch 61 Jevons 84	15
4	30		A	North Ferriby United	221	W 1 - 0	Ryan 61	
5	Sept 4		H	Kendal Town	414	L 0 - 1		13
6	6		A	Ashton United	184	W 3 - 2	Birch 62 84 Jevons 79	
7	**11**	**FAC 1Q**	**A**	**Kidsgrove Athletic**	**230**	**L 0 - 3**		
8	18		A	Worksop Town	278	L 0 - 2		15
9	22		H	Colwyn Bay	406	D 2 - 2	Perrow 48 Birch 70	
10	25		H	Bradford P.A.	455	W 5 - 0	PERROW 3 (8 pen 28 30) Jevons 47 Birch 75	10
11	28		A	Matlock Town	316	W 4 - 3	Egon 22 Jevons 25 Hay 75 78	
12	Oct 2		H	Ossett Town	410	W 1 - 0	Hay 54	4
13	9		H	Burscough	474	W 5 - 0	Edwards 37 Hay 50 59 Jevons 63 Egan 89	3
14	**16**	**FAT 1Q**	**A**	**Sheffield**	**240**	**D 1 - 1**	**Branch 42**	
15	26		H	Nantwich Town	328	D 2 - 2	Hay 23 Teesdale 88	
16	**30**	**FAT 2Q**	**A**	**Mickleover Sports**	**250**	**W 5 - 2**	**Hay 5 EGAN 3 (56 82 90) Jevons 65**	
17	Nov 13		H	Ashton United	312	W 2 - 1	Rgan 6 Jevons 20	8
18	**20**	**FAT 3Q**	**A**	**Workington**	**305**	**D 0 - 0**		
19	**23**	**FAT 3Qr**	**H**	**Workington**	**334**	**W 4 - 0**	**Hay 21 Stephens 52 McLuckie 85 (og) Ryan 90**	
20	**Dec 11**	**FAT 1**	**H**	**Kettering Town**	**444**	**D 3 - 3**	**Jack 48 (og) Birch 63 83**	
21	**14**	**FAT 1r**	**A**	**Kettering Town**	**581**	**W 2 - 1***	**Birch 87 Ryan 121**	
22	Jan 1		H	North Ferriby United	428	D 2 - 2	Jevons 8 Stephens 44	12
23	8		A	Nantwich Town	301	W 4 - 0	Peel 20 Smith 37 Perrow 88 90	11
24	**15**	**FAT 2**	**H**	**Grimsby Town**	**1012**	**W 2 - 1**	**Birch 54 Davies 57**	
25	18		H	Matlock Town	342	W 2 - 1	Birch 16 Stephens 32	
26	22		A	Whitby Town	282	W 1 - 0	Stephens 76	8
27	**Feb 5**	**FAT 3**	**A**	**Eastleigh**	**562**	**W 3 - 1**	**Davies 32 Smith 60 Jevons 74**	
28	8		H	Buxton	408	L 0 - 1		
29	12		H	Hucknall Town	416	W 1 - 0	Perrow 2	9
30	16		A	F.C.United	1445	L 2 - 4	Perrow 44 (pen) Jevons 84	
31	19		A	Colwyn Bay	485	L 0 - 1		11
32	22		A	Hucknall Town	143	D 2 - 2	Abbott 18 Perrow 74	
33	**March 1**	**FAT 4**	**H**	**Mansfield Town**	**2000**	**D 2 - 2**	**Turner 59 Grog 89 (og)**	
34	5		A	Ossett Town	124	W 4 - 2	Jevons 14 Perrow 25 Abbott 82 Birch 90	11
35	**8**	**FAT 4r**	**A**	**Mansfield Town**	**2295**	**L 1 - 3**	**Teesdale 52**	
36	10		H	Mickleover Sports	254	L 2 - 3	Abbott 14 Jevons 54	
37	12		A	Burscough	206	W 3 - 0	Teesdale 58 (pen) Stephens 85 Davies 88	10
38	15		H	Northwich Victoria	312	W 1 - 0	Birch 54	
39	19		H	Whitby Town	405	D 1 - 1	Jevons 9	9
40	22		A	F.C.Halifax Town	1343	L 2 - 3	Jevons 72 Birch 90	
41	26		H	Frickley Athletic	347	W 2 - 0	Hay 43 Branch 61	9
42	29		A	Retford UNited	152	W 4 - 0	Morris 43 Jevons 55 Parsons 69 Smith 90	
43	April 2		H	Stocksbridge P.S.	416	L 0 - 2		9
44	6		A	Mickleover Sports	238	W 3 - 1	Birch 20 53 Perrow 47	
45	9		A	Frickley Athletic	193	L 1 - 2	Davies 19	8
46	12		A	Northwich Victoria	253	D 1 - 1	Teesdale 78 (pen)	
47	16		H	F.C.United	1069	W 2 - 0	Davies 45 Branch 90	7
48	19		H	Worksop Town	419	L 2 - 6	Teesdale 65 Perrow 76 (pen)	
49	23		A	Kendal Town	240	L 0 - 4		11
50	25		H	Retford United	489	W 6 - 0	Jevons 11 Branch 18 Birch 30 Davies 57 Teesdale 73 Perrow 89	10

CHESTER

Chairman: Chris Pilsbury
Secretary: Calvin Hughes (T) 07739 351 711 (E) info@chesterfc.com
Additional Committee Members:
Steve Ashton, Chris Pilsbury, Mike Vickers, Jane Hipkiss , Jeff Banks, David Evans, Mark Howell, Jim Green, Campbell Smith.
Manager: Neil Young
Programme Editor: Rob Ashcroft (E) rob.ashcroft@chesterfc.com

Back Row: Mark Reed, Joe Ormrod, Rob Marsh-Evans, Matty McNeil, Chris Simm, Wes Baynes.
Middle Row: Chris Pilsbury (Chairman), Alex Hay (Chief Scout), Bradley Barnes, Jerome Wright, Robbie Booth, John Danby, Jamie Rainford, Michael Taylor, Michael Powell, Gary Jones (Assistant Manager), Gary Powell (First Team Coach).
Front Row: Michael Wilde, Greg Stones, Iain Howard, Neil Young (Manager), George Horan (Captain), Ashley Williams, Alex Brown, Liam Brownhill.

Club Factfile

Founded: 1885 **Nickname:** Blues
Previous Names: Chester > 1983, Chester City 1983-2010
Previous Leagues: Cheshire 1919-31, Football League 1931-2000, 2004-09, Conference 2000-04, 09-10 (Did not finish the season)

Club Colours (change): Blue and white stripes/black/blue and white hoops (All yellow)

Ground: Exacta Stadium, Bumpers Lane, Chester. CH1 4LT (T) 01244 371 376
Capacity: 6,012 **Seats:** 3,284 **Covered:** Yes **Clubhouse:** Yes **Shop:** Yes

Directions
Stay on the M56 until you reach a roundabout at the end of the motorway. Follow the signs to North Wales & Queensferry A5117. After around one and a half miles you will reach a set of traffic lights where you need to bear left on to the A550 (signposted North Wales & Queensferry). Then from the A550, take the A548 towards Chester. Head straight through the first set of traffic lights and after passing a Vauxhall and then a Renault garage on your left, turn right at the next lights into Sovereign Way. Continue to the end of Sovereign Way and then turn right into Bumpers Lane and the entrance to the Club car park is just down on the right.

Previous Grounds: Faulkner Street 1885-98, The Old Showground 98-99, Whipcord Lane 1901-06, Sealand Road 06-90, Macclesfield FC 90-92

Record Attendance: 20,378 v Chelsea - FA Cup 3rd Round replay 16/01/1952
Record Victory: 12-0 v York City - 01/02/1936
Record Defeat: Not known
Record Goalscorer: Stuart Rimmer - 135
Record Appearances: Ray Gill - 406 (1951-62)
Additional Records: Paid £100,000 to Rotherham for Gregg Blundell.
Received £300,000 from Liverpool for Ian Rush

Senior Honours: Conference 2003-04.
Cheshire Senior Cup 1894-95, 96-97, 1903-04, 07-08, 08-09, 30-31, 31-32. Herefordshire Senior Cup 1991-92 (shared).
Welsh Cup 1907-08, 32-33, 46-47. NPL Division One North 2010-11.

10 YEAR RECORD

01-02		02-03		03-04		04-05		05-06		06-07		07-08		08-09		09-10		10-11	
Conf	14	Conf	4	Conf	1	FL 2	20	FL 2	15	FL 2	18	FL 2	22	FL 2	23	Conf	dnf	NP1N	1

CHORLEY

Chairman: Ken Wright
Secretary: Harold Taylor **(T)** 07749 643 310 **(E)** harold@harold7.wanadoo.co.uk
Additional Committee Members:
Brian Pilkington, Tony Garner, Geoff Haslam, Peter Hardcastle, Brian Haslam

Manager: Gary Flitcroft
Programme Editor: Mark Locke **(E)**

Club Factfile

Founded: 1883 **Nickname:** Magpies
Previous Names: Not known
Previous Leagues: Lancashire Alliance 1890-94, Lancashire 1894-1903, Lancashire Combination 1903-68, 69-70, Northern Premier 1968-69, 70-72, 82-88, Cheshire County 1970-82, Conference 1988-90

Club Colours (change): Black and white stripes/black/black (All sky blue)

Ground: Victory Park, Duke Street, Chorley, Lancs PR7 3DU **(T)** 01257 263 406
Capacity: 4,100 **Seats:** 2,800 **Covered:** 900 **Clubhouse:** Yes **Shop:** Yes

Directions
M61 leave at junction 6, follow A6 to Chorley, going past the Yarrow Bridge Hotel on Bolton Road. Turn left at first set of traffic lights into Pilling Lane, first right into Ashley St. Ground 2nd entrance on left.

M6 junction 27, follow Chorley, turn left at lights, A49 continue for 2 ½ miles, turn right onto B5251. Drive through Coppull and into Chorley for about 2 miles. On entering Chorley turn right into Duke Street 200 yards past Plough Hotel. Turn right into Ashby Street after Duke Street school, and first right into Ground.

Previous Grounds: Dole Lane 1883-1901, Rangletts Park 1901-05, St George's Park 1905-20

Record Attendance: 9,679 v Darwen - FA Cup 1931-32
Record Victory: Not known
Record Defeat: Not known
Record Goalscorer: Peter Watson - 371 (158-66)
Record Appearances: Not known
Additional Records: Received £30,000 from Newcastle United for David Eatock 1996

Senior Honours: Lancashire Alliance 1892-93. Lancashire League 1896-97, 98-99. Lancashire Combination x11. Cheshire County League 1975-76, 76-77, 81-82. Northern Premier League 1987-88. Lancashire FA Trophy x14. Lancashire Combination League cup x3.

10 YEAR RECORD

01-02	02-03	03-04	04-05	05-06	06-07	07-08	08-09	09-10	10-11
NP 1 13	NP 1 5	NP 1 18	NP 1 16	NP 1 18	NP 1 23	NP1N 14	NP1N 14	NP1N 16	NP1N 3

F.C. UNITED OF MANCHESTER

Chairman: Andy Walsh (General Manager)
Secretary: Lindsey Howard **(T)** 0161 273 8950 **(E)** office@fc-utd.co.uk
Additional Committee Members:
Adam Brown, Scott Fletcher, Alan Hargrave, Rob Nugent, Martin Morris, Helen Lambert, Phil Sheeran, Mike Sherrard, Jules Spencer, Steve Pagnam, Alison Watt.
Manager: Karl Marginson
Programme Editor: Lindsey Howard **(E)** office@fc-utd.co.uk

FC United's No.9 gets a shot away against Stafford. Photo: Russell Hart.

Club Factfile

Founded: 2005 **Nickname:** F.C.
Previous Names: None
Previous Leagues: North West Counties 2005-07

Club Colours (change): Red/white/black (White/black/white)

Ground: Bury F.C., Gigg Lane, Bury B19 9HR **(T)** 0161 273 8950 / 764 4881
Capacity: 11,840 **Seats:** NK **Covered:** NK **Clubhouse:** Yes **Shop:** Yes

Directions Exit M60 at junction 17 (s/p A56 Whitefield, Salford). At roundabout follow signs to Whitfield A56, Radcliffe (A665), Bury A56 onto the A56. After 0.3 miles go straight over double traffic lights passing McDonalds on LHS (s/p Bury A56, Radcliffe A665). At lights after 0.8 miles (just after the Bulls Head pub) bear right (s/p Bury A56). Straight on at lights after 1.0 miles (s/p Town Centre). After 1.0 miles turn right (s/p Football Ground) into Gigg Lane. Ground is on RHS after 0.1 miles. From North and East (via M66): Exit M66 at junction 2 and follow signs to Bury A58, Football Ground onto the A58 Rochdale Road. After 0.5 miles turn left at traffic lights by the Crown Hotel (s/p Football Ground) onto Heywood Street. After 0.4 miles turn right at second mini-roundabout (s/p Football Ground, Manchester, Salford B6219) into Wellington Road. At next mini-roundabout turn left into Market Street. Straight on over mini-roundabout after 0.1 miles and right at T-junction after 0.2 miles into Gigg Lane.

Previous Grounds: None

Record Attendance: 6,023 v Great Harwood Town - 22/04/2006
Record Victory: 10-2 v Castleton Gabriels - 10/12/2005
Record Defeat: 1-5 v Bradford Park Avenue - 24/03/2010
Record Goalscorer: Rory Patterson - 99 (2005-08)
Record Appearances: Simon Carden - 199 (2005-10)
Additional Records: Simon Carden scored 5 goals against Castleton Gabriels 10/12/2005

Senior Honours: North West Counties League Division 2 2005-06, Division 1 2006-07.
Northern Premier League Division 1 North Play-off 2007-08.

10 YEAR RECORD

01-02	02-03	03-04	04-05	05-06	06-07	07-08	08-09	09-10	10-11
				NWC2 1	NWC1 1	NP1N 2	NP P 6	NP P 13	NP P 4

F.C. UNITED OF MANCHESTER

No.	Date	Comp	H/A	Opponents	Att:	Result	Goalscorers	Pos
1	Aug 21	NPL P	A	Marine	933	W 2 - 0	Norton 15 (pen) 54	
2	25		H	Nantwich Town	1866	W 1 - 0	Wright 21	
3	28		H	Retford United	1785	W 5 - 1	Parker 2 Roca 29 Cottrell 39 Little 67 85	1
4	30		A	Ashton United	1069	L 0 - 1		
5	Sept 5		H	Matlock Town	1801	L 1 - 5	Norton 61	
6	8		A	Bradford P.A.	990	L 1 - 4	Ovington 8	11
7	**11**	**FAC 1Q**	**H**	**Radcliffe Borough**	**1144**	**W 3 - 0**	**Holden 24 Norton 77 87**	
8	18		H	Stocksbridge Park Steels	1793	L 1 - 4	Hurst 63	16
9	22		A	Burscough	468	W 2 - 0	Norton 69 Connolly 72 (og)	
10	**25**	**FAC 2Q**	**H**	**Gainsborough Trinity**	**1037**	**W 2 - 1**	**Hurst 43 46**	
11	29		H	Buxton	1761	L 1 - 2	Hurst 38	
12	Oct 2		A	Mickleover Sports	1074	L 0 - 2		17
13	6		A	Ossett Town	1333	W 4 - 1	Norton 13 Wright 18 Roca 47 90	
14	**9**	**FAC3 Q**	**A**	**Norton & Stockton**	**1526**	**W 5 - 2**	**NORTON 3 (5 74 90) Hurst 64 Deegan 86**	
15	**16**	**FAT 1Q**	**H**	**Newcastle Town**	**1035**	**W 5 - 0**	**Norton 24 54 DEEGAN 3 (32 79 90)**	
16	**24**	**FAC 4Q**	**H**	**Barrow**		**W 1 - 0**	**Roca 77**	
17	26		A	Ossett Town	387	W 3 - 0	Wright 72 86 Platt 73	
18	**30**	**FAT 2Q**	**H**	**Colwyn Bay**	**1259**	**W 2 - 1**	**Ovington 5 Wright 40**	
19	**Nov 6**	**FAC 1**	**A**	**Rochdale**	**7048**	**W 3 - 2**	**Platt 42 Cotterill 49 Norton 90**	
20	13		A	Northwich Victoria	1663	L 0 - 1		18
21	16		A	Colwyn Bay	1003	L 1 - 3	Norton 10	
22	**20**	**FAT 3Q**	**H**	**Hinckley United**	**1249**	**L 1 - 2**	**Wright 87**	
23	**27**	**FAC 2**	**A**	**Brighton & Hove A**	**5362**	**D 1 - 1**	**Platt 40**	
24	**Dec 8**	**FAC 2r**	**H**	**Brighton & Hove A**	**7000**	**L 0 - 4**		
25	11		H	F.C.Halifax Town	2805	L 0 - 1		21
26	Jan 1		A	F.C.Halifax Town	4023	L 1 - 4	Wright 32 (pen)	21
27	3		H	Ashton U nited	2062	W 2 - 1	Norton 18 Wolfenden 24	
28	8		H	Bradford P.A.	1862	W 2 - 0	Roca 83 Wright 90	15
29	15		A	Retford United	544	W 4 - 0	Ashton 3 Wright 21 Wolfenden 71 Cottrell 77	
30	22		H	Hucknall Town	1883	W 4 - 1	Norton 5 Wright 37 Wolfenden 78 Cottrell 88	13
31	25		A	Kendall United	508	L 2 - 3	Carden 42 Wright 49	
32	Feb 2		H	Colwyn Bay	1560	L 0 - 1		12
33	5		A	Hucknall Town	432	W 2 - 1	Carden 75 Norton 64	
34	8		A	Frickley United		D 0 - 0		
35	12		H	Whitby Town	1662	W 4 - 0	Holden 16 Woffenden 45 Norton 56 Lyth 90 (og)	12
36	16		H	Chasetown	1445	W 4 - 2	Cottrell 45 Norton 66 77 Wolfenden 87	
37	19		H	Burscough	2030	W 3 - 0	Norton 55 Wright 77 Roca 89	7
38	26		A	Stocksbridge P.S.	837	W 2 - 1	Wolfenden 31 40	6
39	March 1		A	Nantwich Town	616	W 4 - 0	WOLFENDEN 3 (44 60 73) Roca 62	
40	5		H	Mickleover Sports	2159	D 0 - 0		6
41	12		H	Worksop Town	1886	W 2 - 1	Norton 44 Cotterill 62 (og)	6
42	15		A	North Ferriby United	472	D 1 - 1	Denton (og)	
43	19		A	Buxton	1726	D 2 - 2	Norton 65 90	7
44	23		A	Whitby Town	588	W 1 - 0	Norton 77	
45	26		H	North Ferriby United	2827	W 2 - 0	Norton 65 81	5
46	April 2		A	Worksop Town	892	W 2 - 1	Norton 71 Wright 90 (pen)	5
47	9		H	Northwich Victoria	2250	W 1 - 0	Norton 77	3
48	13		A	Frickley Atletic	1731	W 4 - 1	Wright 37 McManus 52 Norton 63 Deegan 90	
49	16		A	Chasetown	1089	L 0 - 2		3
50	20		H	Marine	1848	W 2 - 1	Norton 42 Deegan 73	
51	23		A	Matlock Town	1249	W 2 - 1	Wolfenden 38 Wright 53	2
52	25		H	Kendal Town	2839	L 1 - 2	Norton 49	4
53	**28**	**P-Off SF**	**A**	**Bradford P.A.**	**2785**	**W 2 - 0**	**Wolfenden 8 Wright 47**	
54	**May 2**	**P-Off Final**	**A**	**Colwyn Bay**	**2000**	**L 0 - 1**		

FRICKLEY ATHLETIC

Chairman: Peter Bywater
Secretary: Steve Pennock **(T)** 07985 291 074 **(E)** steve@pennocks.freeserve.co.uk
Additional Committee Members:
Gareth Dando, Steve Shorthouse, Barry Johnson, Colin Theedom.

Manager: Peter Rinkcavage
Programme Editor: Darren Haynes **(E)** Darren_haynes@live.co.uk

Club Factfile

Founded: 1910 **Nickname:** The Blues
Previous Names: Frickley Colliery
Previous Leagues: Sheffield, Yorkshire 1922-24, Midland Counties 1924-33, 34-60, 70-76, Cheshire County 1960-70, Northern Premier 1976-80, Conference 1980-87

Club Colours (change): Blue and white stripes/blue/blue (White/black/black)

Ground: Tech5 Stadium, Westfield Lane, South Elmsall, Pontefract WF9 2EQ **(T)** 01977 642 460
Capacity: 2,087 **Seats:** 490 **Covered:** 700 **Clubhouse:** Yes **Shop:** Yes

Directions

From North : Leave A1 to join A639, go over flyover to junction. Turn left and immediately right, signed South Elmsall. Continue to roundabout and take 2nd exit to traffic lights and turn left onto Mill Lane (B6474). Turn right at the T-junction and continue down hill to next T-junction. Turn right and immediately left up Westfield Lane. The ground is signposted to the left after about half a mile.

From South : Exit M18 at J2 onto A1 (North). Leave A1 for A638 towards Wakefield. Continue on A638, going straight on at the first roundabout and turn left at next roundabout to traffic lights. Continue as above from traffic lights.

Previous Grounds: Not known

Record Attendance: 6,500 v Rotherham United - FA Cup 1st Round 1971
Record Victory: Not known
Record Defeat: Not known
Record Goalscorer: K Whiteley
Record Appearances: Not known
Additional Records: Received £12,500 from Boston United for Paul Shirtliff and from Northampton Town for Russ Wilcox

Senior Honours: Hallamshire Senior Cup x10

10 YEAR RECORD

01-02	02-03	03-04	04-05	05-06	06-07	07-08	08-09	09-10	10-11
NP P 13	NP P 20	NP P 22	NP P 18	NP P 2	NP P 16	NP P 14	NP P 11	NP P 15	NP P 18

FRICKLEY ATHLETIC

No.	Date	Comp	H/A	Opponents	Att:	Result	Goalscorers	Pos
1	Aug 21	NPL P	A	Kendal Town	228	L 0 - 1		19
2	24		H	F.C.Halifax Town	748	D 0 - 0		
3	28		H	Ashton United	149	D 0 - 0		18
4	30		A	Whitby Town	331	D 2 - 2	O'Rafferty 15 Clarke 66	
5	Sept 4		H	Marine	268	L 2 - 3	Clarke 25 73 (pen)	19
6	7		A	Matlock Town	255	L 0 - 1		
7	**11**	**FAC 1Q**	**H**	**Kendal Town**	**185**	**W 3 - 0**	**Morris 17 (pen) Clarke 78 Walsh 80**	
8	18		H	Burscough	183	L 0 - 1		20
9	22		A	Retford United	160	W 3 - 1	Henry 18 Walsh 29 (pen) Chapman 71	
10	**25**	**FAC 2Q**	**H**	**Newcastle BBP**	**217**	**W 2 - 1**	**Walsh 45 48**	
11	28		H	Stocksbridge P.S.	217	D 1 - 1	Lee 76	
12	Oct 2		A	Buxton	371	L 1 - 7	Jackson 70	20
13	5		H	Hucknall Town	200	W 1 - 0	Sturdy 25	
14	**9**	**FAC 3Q**	**A**	**Sheffield**	**632**	**D 1 - 1**	**Walsh 90**	
15	**12**	**FAC 3Qr**	**H**	**Sheffield F.C.**	**322**	**L 1 - 2**	**Morris 20**	
16	**16**	**FAT 1Q**	**A**	**Kendal Town**	**182**	**L 0 - 3**		
17	23		H	Mickleover Sports	203	W 1 - 0	Kay 59	18
18	26		A	Hucknall Town	182	L 0 - 2		
19	30		A	Bradford P.A.	353	W 3 - 2	Whitehouse 23 Lee 45 Longstaff 83	11
20	Nov 6		H	Northwich Victoria	245	W 2 - 1	Whitehouse 30 Sanasy 34	15
21	13		A	Worksop Town	415	D 1 - 1	Lee 28	
22	20		A	Burscough	163	L 0 - 3		17
23	Jan 3		A	Nantwich Town	313	L 2 - 3	Burton 76 (og) Smythe 78	
24	8		H	Matlock Town	223	L 0 - 1		20
25	15		A	Ashton United	123	W 6 - 3	Smith 12 (og) SANASY 3 (37 43 90) Bennett 61 (og) Burbeary 70	
26	18		A	North Ferriby United	224	L 0 - 4		
27	Feb 8		H	F.C.United		D 0 - 0		
28	12		H	Colwyn Bay	183	L 0 - 1		20
29	15		A	Ossett Town	132	W 2 - 1	Burbeary 62 Whitehouse 77	
30	26		H	Ossett Town	201	L 0 - 1		19
31	March 1		H	Retford United	158	L 1 - 2	Burbeary 12 (pen)	
32	5		H	Buxton	214	D 2 - 2	Burbeary 65 Longstaff 69	20
33	12		A	Stocksbridge P.S.	161	D 1 - 1	Longstaff 36	20
34	15		H	Nantwich Town	150	W 3 - 0	Smith 53 Burbeary 59 Longstaff 72	
35	19		A	Colwyn Bay	288	L 0 - 4		19
36	22		H	Bradford PA	248	D 2 - 2	Walsh 15 (pen) Catton 71	
37	26		A	Chasetown	347	L 0 - 2		20
38	29		H	Worksop Town	262	W 1 - 0	Longstaff 61	
39	April 2		A	Mickleover Sports	211	L 0 - 3		20
40	5		H	Kendal Town	178	L 0 - 2		
41	9		H	Chasetown	183	W 2 - 0	Darley 44 Watts 83	20
42	13		A	F.C.United	1731	L 1 - 4	Burbeary 22 (pen)	
43	16		A	Northwich Victoria	287	W 1 - 0	Burbeary 66 (pen)	19
44	19		A	F.C.Halifax	1106	L 1 - 3	Whitehouse 12	
45	23		A	Marine	401	D 1 - 1	Walsh 13 (pen)	18
46	25		H	North Ferriby United	327	L 0 - 1		18

HEDNESFORD TOWN

Chairman: Stephen Price
Secretary: Terry McMahon **(T)** 07901 822 040 **(E)** admin@hednesfordfc.co.uk
Additional Committee Members:
Carole Price, Michael Johnson, David Smith

Manager: Robert Smith
Programme Editor: Michael Johnson **(E)** admin@hednesfordfc.co.uk

Club Factfile

Founded: 1880 **Nickname:** The Pitmen
Previous Names: Hednesford 1938-74
Previous Leagues: Walsall & District, Birmingham Combination 1906-15, 45-53, West Midlands 1919-39, 53-72, 74-84, Midland Counties 1972-74, Southern 1984-95, 2001-2005, 2009-11, Conference 1995-2001, 05-06, Northern Premier 2006-09

Club Colours (change): All white (Navy with red trim/navy/navy)

Ground: Keys Park, Park Road, Hednesford, Cannock WS12 2DZ **(T)** 01543 422 870
Capacity: 6,039 **Seats:** 1,010 **Covered:** 5,334 **Clubhouse:** Yes **Shop:** Yes

Directions: Leave M6 at J11 and follow the signs for Cannock. At the next island take the third exit towards Rugeley (A460). On reaching the A5 at Churchbridge island, rejoin the A460 signposted Rugeley and follow this road over five traffic islands. At the sixth traffic island, by a Texaco petrol station, turn right past a McDonalds restaurant and follow this road to the next island which is 'Cross Keys Island'. Go over this island to the next small island and turn right. Keys Park football ground is on left.

Previous Grounds: Not known

Record Attendance: 3,169 v York City - FA Cup 3rd Round 13/01/1997
Record Victory: 12-1 v Redditch United - Birmingham Combination 1952-53
Record Defeat: 0-15 v Burton - Birmingham Combination 1952-53
Record Goalscorer: Joe O'Connor - 230 in 430 games
Record Appearances: Kevin Foster - 463
Additional Records: Paid £12,000 to Macclesfield Town for Steve Burr
Received £50,000 from Blackpool for Kevin Russell

Senior Honours: Southern League Premier Division 1994-95. FA Trophy 2004-05.
Staffordshire Senior Cup x2. Birmingham Senior Cup 1935-36.

10 YEAR RECORD

01-02	02-03	03-04	04-05	05-06	06-07	07-08	08-09	09-10	10-11
SthP 16	SthP 11	SthP 20	SthP 4	Conf N 22	NP P 7	NP P 8	NP P 8	SthP 4	SthP 2

HEDNESFORD TOWN

No.	Date	Comp	H/A	Opponents	Att:	Result	Goalscorers	Pos
1	Aug 14	Sth Prem	H	Chippenham Town	379	L 0 - 2		19
2	17		A	Banbury United	230	W 4 - 0	Carter 13 Bridgwater 20 Gibson 58 Denny 90	
3	21		A	Hemel Hempstead Town	227	W 1 - 0	Carter 59	4
4	24		H	Cambridge City	325	L 0 - 2		
5	28		A	Didcot Town	191	W 3 - 0	Patterson 35 63 Osbourne 42	8
6	30		H	Leamington	535	D 1 - 1	Clements 7	
7	Sept 4		A	Truro City	469	L 0 - 1		7
8	**11**	**FAC 1Q**	**H**	**Newcastle Town**	**305**	**L 1 - 2**	**Durrell 10**	
9	14		H	Swindon Supermarine	210	D 1 - 1	Patterson 15	
10	18		H	Salisbury City	324	W 3 - 0	Carter 43 60 Gibson 54	7
11	Oct 2		A	Brackley Town	259	D 0 - 0		9
12	5		H	Evesham United	319	W 1 - 0	Osbourne 19	
13	9		A	Oxford City	192	D 1 - 1	Carey-Bertram 47	8
14	**16**	**FAT 1Q**	**H**	**Whitby Town**	**313**	**L 1 - 2**	**Patterson 59**	
15	23		H	Weymouth	334	W 9 - 0	Hurren10(pen) ROBINSON 4(28 47 53 66) CAREY-BERTRAM 3 (35 53 68) Brown 88	
16	30		A	Bedford Town	275	L 1 - 2	Carey Bertram 40	
17	Nov 6		A	Tiverton Town	272	W 2 - 2	Brown 45 Quinn 89	5
18	13		H	Cirencester Town	324	W 3 - 1	Brown 44 (pen) Robinson 64 Clements 73	5
19	16		H	Stourbridge	493	L 2 - 3	Quinn 11 14	
20	20		A	Chesham United	301	L 1 - 2	Quinn 83	7
21	Jan 3		A	Leamington	702	W 2 - 1	Quinn 13 Wellecomme 60	
22	8		A	Salisbury City	659	L 1 - 2	Quinn 50	9
23	15		H	Truro City	394	W 1 - 0	Quinn 69	8
24	29		A	Chippenham Town	351	W 1 - 0	Quinn 23	8
25	Feb 1		H	Bashley	240	W 1 - 0	Francis 9	
26	5		H	Hemel Hempstead Town	277	W 2 - 0	Patterson 14 (pen) Denny 51	5
27	12		A	Cambridge City	471	L 2 - 3	Compton 4 Patterson 58	6
28	19		H	Chesham United	404	W 3 - 2	Melbourne 15 Davidson 50 Wellecomme 64	6
29	23		A	Stourbridge	389	W 2 - 1	Robinson 81 Patterson 84	
30	26		A	Bashley	284	W 4 - 0	WELLECOMME 4 (2 63 79 87)	6
31	March 9		A	Swindon Supermarine	129	W 2 - 1	Clements 29 Patterson 90	
32	12		H	Tiverton Town	437	W 2 - 0	Patterson 66 Wellecomme 89	6
33	15		H	Banbury United	321	W 1 - 0	Patterson 20	
34	19		A	Cirencester Town	151	W 1 - 0	Dunkley 18	4
35	22		H	Halesowen Town	423	W 4 - 2	Francis 3 Campion 15 86 Robinson 70 (pen)	
36	26		H	Oxford City	548	W 2 - 1	Wellecomnme 14 Clements 73	3
37	29		H	Didcot Town	507	D 1 - 1	Campion 32	
38	April 2		A	Evesham United	210	L 1 - 4	Patterson 27	4
39	9		H	Bedford Town	422	W 4 - 1	PATTERSON 3 (12pen 52 62 pen) Clements 18	3
40	16		A	Weymouth	489	W 4 - 2	Patterson 39 Clements 42 Wellecomme 87 Quinn 90	
41	23		H	Brackley Town	526	W 2 - 0	Dunkley 57 Melbourne 90	2
42	25		A	Halesowen Town	286	W 6 - 0	ROBINSON 3 (18 31 73pen) Clements 61 Smith 82(og) Wellecomme 90	2
43	**29**	**P-Off SF**	**H**	**Leamington**	**1504**	**W 3 - 1**	**Patterson 9 Francis 45 Clements 70**	
44	**May 2**	**P-Off Final**	**H**	**Salisbury City**	**1903**	**D 2 - 2***	**Wellecomme 63 Quinn 106 Salisbury City won 3-2 on penalties.**	

KENDAL TOWN

Chairman: Haydon Munslow
Secretary: Craig Campbell **(T)** 07980 660 428 **(E)** info@kendaltownfootballclub.co.uk
Additional Committee Members:
Graham O'Callaghan, T Roe, Steve Dixon, Meril Tummey, D Shankley

Manager: Lee Ashcroft
Programme Editor: Steve Presnail **(E)** info@kendaltownfootballclub.co.uk

Club Factfile

Founded: 1919 **Nickname:** Town
Previous Names: Netherfield
Previous Leagues: Westmorland, North Lancashire Combination 1945-68, Northern Premier 1968-83, North West Counties 1983-87

Club Colours (change): Black and white stripes/black/red (All red)

Ground: Parkside Road, Kendal, Cumbria LA9 7BL **(T)** 01539 727 472
Capacity: 2,490 **Seats:** 450 **Covered:** 1000 **Clubhouse:** Yes **Shop:** Yes

Directions
M6 junction 36, via A590/591/A6 to Kendal (South). At first traffic lights turn right, left at roundabout, right into Parkside Road. Ground on right over brow of hill.

Previous Grounds: Not known

Record Attendance: 5,184 v Grimsby Town - FA Cup 1st Round 1955
Record Victory: 11-0 v Great Harwood - 22/03/1947
Record Defeat: 0-10 v Stalybridge Celtic - 01/09/1984
Record Goalscorer: Tom Brownlee
Record Appearances: Not known
Additional Records: Received £10,250 from Manchester City for Andy Milner 1995

Senior Honours: Westmorlands Senior Cup x12. Lancashire Senior Cup 2002-03.

10 YEAR RECORD

01-02	02-03	03-04	04-05	05-06	06-07	07-08	08-09	09-10	10-11
NP 1 21	NP 1 12	NP 1 21	NP 1 5	NP 1 3	NP P 19	NP P 11	NP P 5	NP P 5	NP P 8

KENDAL TOWN

No.	Date	Comp	H/A	Opponents	Att:	Result	Goalscorers	Pos
1	Aug 21	NPL P	H	Frickley Athletic	238	W 1 - 0	Foster 42	
2	24		A	Ossett Town	100	D 0 - 0		
3	28		A	Mickleover Town	206	W 3 - 1	Osman 76 Rowe 84 90	5
4	30		H	Burscough	276	L 1 - 2	Rowe 39	
5	Sept 4		A	Chasetown	414	W 1 - 0	Wisdom 52	
6	7		H	Colwyn Bay	167	L 1 - 4	Osman 66	8
7	**11**	**FAC 1Q**	**A**	**Frickley Athletic**	**185**	**L 2 - 3**	**Mulvaney 25 Stopforth 66**	
8	18		H	Retford United	167	W 4 - 1	Foster 19 Osman 33 72 Walmsley 63	4
9	21		A	Buxton	267	L 0 - 3		
10	25		H	Hucknall Town	168	D 0 - 0		8
11	28		H	Ashton United	161	W 1 - 0	Wisdom 39	
12	Oct 2		A	Nantwich Town	314	L 3 - 5	Rowe 38 61 Tickle 90 (og)	6
13	5		H	Northwich Victoria	241	D 1 - 1	Walmsley 60 (pen)	
14	9		A	Whitby Town	301	D 2 - 2	Walmsley 82 Osman 88	7
15	**16**	**FAT 1Q**	**H**	**Frickley Athletic**	**182**	**W 3 - 0**	**Walmsley 42 (pen) Dunn 60 Rowe 77**	
16	23		H	Bradford P.A.	306	W 4 - 1	Lloyd 8 Taylor 32 Rowe 65 Dunn 90	7
17	26		A	Northwich Victoria	480	W 6 - 1	TAYLOR 3 (12 26 50) Wisdom 56 Lloyd 63 Osman 81	
18	**30**	**FAT 2Q**	**H**	**Matlock Town**	**242**	**D 1 - 1**	**Rowe 51**	
19	**Nov 2**	**FAT 2Qr**	**A**	**Matlock Town**	**212**	**W 2 - 1**	**Osman 20 Stopforth 62**	
20	6		H	North Ferriby United	217	L 2 - 5	Rowe 49 Gardner 89	8
21	13		A	Hucknall Town	207	L 3 - 4	Walmsley 28 90 Gardner 86	9
22	**20**	**FAT 3Q**	**A**	**Alfreton Town**	**399**	**L 0 - 4**		
23	Jan 1		A	Burscough	236	W 4 - 2	JACKSON 3 (15 20 53) Taylor 45	10
24	8		A	Colwyn Bay	309	W 2 - 1	Jackson 5 Dunn 55	9
25	15		H	MIckleover Sports	159	L 1 - 2	Taylor 75	9
26	22		H	Worksop Town	245	W 2 - 1	Walmsley 50 Dunn 55	10
27	25		H	F.C.United	508	W 3 - 2	Gray 39 70 Osman 51	
28	Feb 1		H	Whitby Town	141	W 5 - 4	Dunn 11 Walmsley 51 (pen) Winters 68 75 Ashcroft 73	9
29	5		H	Stocksbridge PS	205	L 2 - 3	Walmsley 88 Winters 90	6
30	12		A	Matlock Town	327	L 1 - 3	Winters 7	7
31	15		A	F.C.Halifax Town	1231	L 0 - 1		
32	19		H	Buxton	219	W 1 - 0	Williams 57	9
33	March 5		H	Nantwich Town	231	W 2 - 1	Donnelly 64 Walmsley 90(pen)	
34	7		A	Ashton United	156	W 2 - 1	Jackson 49 71	
35	12		H	Matlock Town	222	W 1 - 0	Foster 88	9
36	15		A	Marine	306	L 0 - 2		
37	19		A	Retford United	87	L 1 - 2	Gray 76	12
38	22		H	Marine	18	W 2 - 1	McEvatt 28 Jackson 65	
39	26		H	F.C.HalifaxTown	891	L 2 - 4	Walmsley 28 (pen) Osman 79	11
40	29		A	Stocksbridge P.S.	131	L 1 - 2	Walmsley 25 (pen)	
41	April 2		A	Bradford P.A.	396	L 2 - 5	Walmsley 41 (pen) 71 (pen)	12
42	5		A	Frickley Athletic	178	W 2 - 0	Taylor 8 Jackson 85	
43	9		H	Whitby Town	160	W 2 - 1	Taylor 12 Dunn 14	11
44	11		A	Worksop Town	165	W 2 - 1	Osman 13 Walmsley74 (pen)	
45	16		A	North Ferriby United	158	L 1 - 4	Dunn 41	10
46	23		H	Chasetown	240	W 4 - 0	Walmsley 28 90 Gray 45 Osman 84	
47	25		A	F.C. United	2839	W 2 - 1	Jackson 8 Williams 90	7

MARINE

Chairman: Paul Leary
Secretary: Richard Cross **(T)** 07762 711 714 **(E)** info@marinefc.com
Additional Committee Members:
Brian Lawlor, Jean-Pierre Hall, Geoff Kewlsey, Mark Prescott, Barry Godfrey, Graham Gibson, Paul Eustace, Peter McCormick, Dave McMillan, Mark Williams, John Wildman, David Wotherspoon
Manager: Kevin Lynch
Programme Editor: Gary Langley **(E)** info@marinefc.com

Back row (l-r): Joe Fowler, Darren Byers, Paul Lundon, Callum Williams, Tom Soffe, John Shaw, Dave Roberts, Sam Barnes, Matty Brown, Neil Harvey. **Middle Row:** Gary Trowler (Kit Manager), Phil Brazier (Assistant Manager), Ian Latham, Paul Henry, Jack Booth, Kevin Lynch (Manager), Stephen Johnson, Louis Barnes, Andy Fowler, Thomas Moore, Aaron Rey, Peter Cumiskey (Coach), Nick McCarthy (Head Therapist). **Front Row:** Geoff Kewley (Joint Treasurer), Dave McMillan, Richard Cross (Club Secretary), Jean-Pierre Hall (President), Paul Leary (Chairman), Peter McCormack, Mark Williams, Paul Eustace & Barry Godfrey. Photo copyright Ray Farley.

Club Factfile

Founded: 1894 **Nickname:** Mariners
Previous Names: Not known
Previous Leagues: Liverpool Zingari, Liverpool County Combination, Lancashire Combination 1935-39, 46-69, Cheshire County 1969-79

Club Colours (change): White/black/black (Yellow/green/green)

Ground: Arriva Stadium, College Road, Crosby, Liverpool L23 3AS **(T)** 0151 924 1743
Capacity: 3,185 **Seats:** 400 **Covered:** 1,400 **Clubhouse:** Yes **Shop:** Yes

Directions
From the East & South: Leave the M62 at junction 6 and take the M57 to Switch Island at the end. At the end of the M57 take the A5036 (signposted Bootle & Docks). At the roundabout, at the end of the road (by Docks), turn right onto the A565 following signs for 'Crosby' and 'Marine AFC' and follow this road for 1 mile. After passing the Tesco Express on your right, turn left at the traffic lights (by Merchant Taylors' School) into College Road. The ground is half a mile on your left
From the North: Leave the M6 at junction 26 and join the M58. Travel along the M58 to Switch Island at the end. Take the A5036 (signposted Bootle & Docks) and follow directions above.

Previous Grounds: Waterloo Park 1894-1903

Record Attendance: 4,000 v Nigeria - Friendly 1949
Record Victory: 14-0 v Sandhurst - FA Cup 1st Qualifying Round 01/10/1938
Record Defeat: 2-11 v Shrewsbury Town - FA Cup 1st Round 1995
Record Goalscorer: Paul Meachin - 200
Record Appearances: Peter Smith 952
Additional Records: Paid £6,000 to Southport for Jon Penman October 1985
Received £20,000 from Crewe Alexandra for Richard Norris 1996

Senior Honours: Northern Premier League Premier Division 1993-94, 84-95.
Lancashire Junior Cup 1978-79, Lancashire Trophy x3. Lancashire Amateur Cup x5. Lancashire Senior Cup x6.
Liverpool Non-League Cup x3. Liverpool Challenge Cup x3.

10 YEAR RECORD

01-02	02-03	03-04	04-05	05-06	06-07	07-08	08-09	09-10	10-11
NP P 17	NP P 11	NP P 16	NP P 15	NP P 3	NP P 4	NP P 7	NP P 13	NP P 9	NP P 9

MARINE

No.	Date	Comp	H/A	Opponents	Att:	Result	Goalscorers	Pos
1	Aug 21	NPL P	H	F.C.United	933	L 0 - 2		
2	25		A	Chasetown	393	W 1 - 0	Rainford 46	
3	28		A	Worksop Town	235	W 2 - 1	Hussey 8 (pen) Rainford 40	8
4	30		H	Buxton	383	L 1 - 2	Rainford 56	
5	Sept 4		A	Frickley Athletic	288	W 3 - 2	Johnson 45 Hussey 54 (pen) Rainford 82	6
6	7		H	Stocksbridge Park Steels	258	W 5 - 4	RAINFORD 4 (8 14 35 36) Doherty 19	
7	**11**	**FAC 1Q**	**H**	**Colwyn Bay**	**312**	**D 1 - 1**	**Leadbetter 57**	
8	**14**	**FAC 1Qr**	**A**	**Colwyn Bay**		**L 0 - 2**		
9	18		H	Hucknall Town	316	D 1 - 1	Rainford 71	5
10	20		A	Ashton United	177	L 0 - 1		12
11	25		H	Worksop Town	302	L 2 - 4	Johnson 72 Moore 78	12
12	Oct 2		A	Retford United	151	W 3 - 0	Rushton 76 Hussey 81 (pen) Rainford 89	
13	5		H	Colwyn Bay	321	L 1 - 3	Rainford 45	
14	9		A	Bradford P.A.	365	L 1 - 2	Rainford 71	12
15	12		A	Northwich Victoria	425	L 3 - 4	Rainford 44 Cumiskey 63 Johnson 79	
16	**16**	**FAT 1Q**	**H**	**Ashton United**	**216**	**D 2 - 2**	**Rainford 55 85**	
17	**18**	**FAT 1Qr**	**A**	**Ashton United**	**130**	**W 3 - 1**	**Rainford 4 87 Brown 25**	
18	23		H	North Ferriby United	306	D 2 - 2	Rushton 9 Siadankey 88	13
19	26		A	Colwyn Bay	283	W 3 - 0	Harvey 17 63 Rainford 90	
20	**30**	**FAT 2Q**	**A**	**Chorley**	**834**	**L 1 - 3**	**Harvey 35**	
21	Nov 6		H	F.C.Halifax	726	L 0 - 6		14
22	13		A	Mickleover Sports	214	D 0 - 0		14
23	16		H	Northwich Victoria	344	W 3 - 1	RAINFORD 3 (18 31 45)	
24	20		A	Hucknall Town	170	W 3 - 0	Shaw 41 Rainford 57 60	9
25	Dec 11		H	Whitby Town	232	L 1 - 3	Harvey 59	
26	Jan 1		A	Buxton	354	L 1 - 2	Rainford 36	13
27	3		H	Chasetown	292	W 2 - 0	Hussey 63 Moore 69	
28	8		A	Stocksbridge P.S.	120	W 3 - 1	Rainford 55 Harvey 59 Hussey 73 (pen)	6
29	15		H	Ossett Town	308	W 4 - 3	Hussey 16 (pen) Moore 44 Rainford 55 Cumiskey 90	6
30	22		A	Matlock Town	367	W 1 - 0	Goulding 55	5
31	25		H	Burscough	303	D 2 - 2	Rainford 18 90	
32	Feb 5		A	Whitby Town	248	D 1 - 1	Henry 56	5
33	12		A	Ossett Town	122	W 2 - 0	Davies 42 Harvey 67	4
34	15		H	Nantwich Town	255	W 4 - 3	Rainford 47 56 Moore 60 Harvey 79	
35	19		H	Ashton United	324	W 4 - 0	Lundon 23 Harvey 44 55 Moore 70	3
36	26		H	Matlock Town	358	L 2 - 4	Harvey 31 Rainford 47	5
37	March 5		H	Retford United	361	W 2 - 0	Johnson 39 Austin 72 (og)	5
38	15		H	Kendal Town	306	W 2 - 0	Henry 61 Harvey 76	
39	19		A	Nantwich Town	342	D 1 - 1	Rigoglioso 83	6
40	22		A	Kendal Town	189	L 1 - 2	Johnson 51	
41	26		H	Bradford P.A.	378	W 1 - 0	Rey 56	6
42	April 2		A	North Ferriby United	219	W 1 - 0	Rey 32	6
43	9		H	Mickleover Sports	286	L 1 - 2	Rainford 61	6
44	16		A	F.C.Halifax	1844	L 0 - 1		9
45	20		A	F.C.United	1848	L 1 - 2	Shaw 19	
46	23		H	Frickley Athletic	401	D 1 - 1	Brown 90	9
47	25		A	Burscough	296	W 2 - 1	Rey 56 77	8

MATLOCK TOWN

Chairman: Tom Wright
Secretary: Keith Brown (T) 07831 311 427 (E) clubshop@matlocktownfc.com
Additional Committee Members:
S Baker, P Bates, J Beaumont, S Else, Mrs C Else, P Eyre, S Greenhough, D Reynolds, I Richardson, A Smith, G Taylor, G Tomlinson, Mrs L H West, T Weston, T Wright
Manager: Mark Atkins
Programme Editor: Mike Tomlinson (E) clubshop@matlocktownf.co.uk

Club Factfile

Founded: 1885 **Nickname:** The Gladiators
Previous Names: Not known
Previous Leagues: Midland Combination 1894-96, Matlock and District, Derbyshire Senior, Central Alliance 1924-25, 47-61, Central Combination 1934-35, Chesterfield & District 1946-47, Midland Counties 1961-69

Club Colours (change): All royal blue (Tangerine/black/tangerine)

Ground: Reynolds Stadium, Causeway Lane, Matlock, Derbyshire DE4 3AR (T) 01629 583 866
Capacity: 5,500 **Seats:** 560 **Covered:** 1,200 **Clubhouse:** Yes **Shop:** Yes

Directions
On A615, ground is 500 yards from Town Centre and Matlock BR.

Previous Grounds: Not known

Record Attendance: 5,123 v Burton Albion - FA Trophy 1975
Record Victory: 10-0 v Lancaster City (A) - 1974
Record Defeat: 0-8 v Chorley (A) - 1971
Record Goalscorer: Peter Scott
Record Appearances: Mick Fenoughty
Additional Records: Paid £2,000 for Kenny Clark 1996
Received £10,000 from York City for Ian Helliwell

Senior Honours: FA Trophy 1974-75. Anglo Italian Non-League Cup 1979.
Derbyshire Senior Cup x7.

10 YEAR RECORD

01-02		02-03		03-04		04-05		05-06		06-07		07-08		08-09		09-10		10-11	
NP 1	14	NP 1	8	NP 1	2	NP P	11	NP P	9	NP P	5	NP P	16	NP P	15	NP P	7	NP P	11

MATLOCK TOWN

No.	Date	Comp	H/A	Opponents	Att:	Result	Goalscorers	Pos
1	Aug 21	NPL P	H	Stocksbridge Park Steels	337	W 1 - 0	Featherstone 72	
2	24		A	Burscough	393	W 3 - 0	Marrison 5 Hannah 37 Haran 56	
3	28		A	Ossett Town	166	D 0 - 0		4
4	30		H	Mickleover Sports	434	L 1 - 2	Joynes 50	
5	Sept 5		A	F.C.United	1801	W 5 - 1	Hannah 3 89 Knowles 63 Cropper 81 90	
6	7		H	Frickley Athletic	255	W 1 - 0	Knowles 21	1
7	**11**	**FAC 1Q**	**H**	**Worksop Town**	**428**	**W 3 - 1**	**Hannah 6 Cropper 51 57**	
8	18		H	Ashton United	362	D 1 - 1	Hannah 62	2
9	**25**	**FAC 2Q**	**A**	**Carlton Town**	**199**	**W 1 - 0**	**Bowler 12**	
10	28		H	Chasetown	316	L 3 - 4	Marrison 34 Hannah 34 90	
11	Oct 2		A	Northwich Victoria	534	W 3 - 2	Cropper 22 Haran 53 Joynes 90	5
12	**9**	**FAC 3Q**	**H**	**Eastwood Town**	**655**	**L 0 - 3**		
13	**16**	**FAT 1Q**	**H**	**Bedworth United**	**266**	**W10- 0**	**HANNAH 7 (7 10 65 77 80 86 89) Williams 63 (og) Joynes 78 Algar 82**	
14	19		A	Nantwich Town	253	W 3 - 2	HANNAH 3 (16 75 87)	
15	23		H	Ossett Town	285	W 2 - 0	Hannah 41 58	3
16	27		A	Worksop Town	360	L 1 - 2	Cropper 90	
17	30	FAT 2Q	A	Kendal Town	242	D 1 - 1	Hannah 65	
18	Nov 2	FAT 2Qr	H	Kendal Town	212	L 1 - 2	Hannah 55	
19	6		H	Hucknall Town	420	L 1 - 2	King 20	9
20	16		H	F.C.Halifax Town	549	L 1 - 2	Morris 56	
21	20		H	Colwyn Bay	309	W 3 - 0	Hannah 18 72 (pen) Cropper 90	10
22	Dec 11		H	Retford United	253	W 4 - 2	Joynes 40 63 King 66 Davies 78	6
23	Jan 1		A	Mickleover Sports	575	L 0 - 1		7
24	3		H	Burscough	305	W 2 - 1	Wayne 39 Joynes 85	
25	8		A	Frickley Athletic	223	W 1 - 0	Hannah 74	4
26	11		H	North Ferriby United	224	W 2 - 1	Hannah 21Morris 59	
27	15		H	Worksop Town	474	W 1 - 0	Hannah 21	3
28	18		A	Chasetown	342	L 1 - 2	Hannah 19	
29	22		H	Marine	367	L 0 - 1		3
30	25		A	Stocksbridge P.S.	148	L 1 - 3	Hannah 37	
31	Feb 5		A	Retford Town	185	W 4 - 0	Lukic 16 Knowles 65 Hannah 77 Wilson 87	3
32	12		H	Kendal Town	327	W 3 - 1	Hannah 13 67 King 90	3
33	22		A	Colwyn Bay	371	W 1 - 0	Lukic 88	
34	26		A	Marine	368	W 4 - 2	Joynes 20 HANNAH 3 (37 79 83)	2
35	March 5		H	Northwich Victoria	392	D 1 - 1	Warne 75	3
36	9		A	Whitby Town	211	W 2 - 1	King 64 Hannah 86	
37	12		A	Kendal Town	222	L 0 - 1		3
38	15		H	Buxton	654	L 1 - 3	Hannah 48 (pen)	
39	19		A	Bradford P.A.	318	L 1 - 3	Hannah 3	5
40	22		A	North Ferriby United	313	L 1 - 3	Mallon 58	
41	26		H	Whitby Town	340	D 2 - 2	Joynes 7 Morris 30	
42	April 2		A	F.C.Halifax	2132	D 2 - 2	Hannah 14 (pen) Morris 88 (pen)	7
43	9		H	Bradfoord P.A.	395	L 0 - 1		9
44	11		A	Ashton United	122	L 1 - 3	Lukic 28	
45	16		A	Hucknall Town	211	D 2 - 2	Hannah 29 55	11
46	19		H	Nantwich Town	328	W 4 - 2	Sedgemore 45 (og) McAliskey 46 55 Hannah 90	10
47	23		H	F.C.United	1249	L 1 - 2	Lukic 46	
48	25		A	Buxton	595	W 3 - 1	HANNAH 3 (20 87 90)	11

MICKLEOVER SPORTS

Chairman: Stuart Clarke

Secretary: Tony Shaw **(T)** 07966 197 246 **(E)** tony@warren-shaw.co.uk

Additional Committee Members:
Ray Garlic, Roger Lee, Keith Jenkinson, Charlie Divers, James Edge, Phil Taylor, Kevin Haddon, Alan Brown, Russell Sellars, Stephen Rigg, Michael Robinson, Matthew Glazier, Ken Blackshaw, David Chambers, David McKenzie.

Manager: Richard Pratley

Programme Editor: James Edge **(E)** tony@warren-shaw.co.uk

Club Factfile

Founded: 1948 **Nickname:** Sports

Previous Names: Not known

Previous Leagues: Central Midlands 1993-99, Northern Counties East 1999-2009

Club Colours (change): Red and black stripes/black/red (Blue/white/blue)

Ground: Mickleover Sports Club, Station Road, Mickleover Derby DE3 9FB **(T)** 01332 512 826

Capacity: 1,500 **Seats:** 280 **Covered:** 500 **Clubhouse:** Yes **Shop:** Yes

Directions

M1 NORTH - J28. A38 to Derby. At Markeaton Island right A52 Ashbourne, 2nd left Radbourne Lane, 3rd Left Station Road 50 yds.

M1 SOUTH – J25. A52 to Derby. Follow signs for Ashbourne, pick up A52 at Markeaton Island (MacDonalds) then as above.

FROM STOKE A50 – Derby. A516 to A38 then as above.

Previous Grounds: Not known

Record Attendance: Not known
Record Victory: Not known
Record Defeat: Not known
Record Goalscorer: Not known
Record Appearances: Not known
Additional Records: Won 16 consecutive League matches in 2009-10 - a Northern Premier League record

Senior Honours: Central Midlands Supreme Division 1998-99. Northern Counties East Division 1 2002-03, Premier Division 2008-09.
Northern Premier League Division 1 South 2009-10.

10 YEAR RECORD

01-02	02-03	03-04	04-05	05-06	06-07	07-08	08-09	09-10	10-11
NCE1 5	NCE1 1	NCEP 13	NCEP 7	NCEP 13	NCEP 7	NCEP 14	NCEP 1	NP1S 1	NP P 15

MICKLEOVER SPORTS

No.	Date	Comp	H/A	Opponents	Att:	Result	Goalscorers	Pos
1	Aug 21	NPL P	A	Whitby Town	306	L 2 - 3	Walshe 27 Smythe 58	14
2	25		H	North Ferriby United	197	L 3 - 4	Martin 16 85 Graves 40	
3	28		H	Kendal Town	206	L 1 - 3	Steadman 26	20
4	30		A	Matlock Town	434	W 2 - 1	Smythe Steadman 28	
5	Sept 4		H	F.C.Halifax	676	L 2 - 3	Steadman 36 80	
6	8		A	Hucknall Town	227	L 0 - 1		21
7	**11**	**FAC 1Q**	**A**	**Retford United**	**144**	**W 5 - 0**	**Strzyzewski 32 50 Hoyle 46 O'Connell 80 Steadman 86**	
8	18		A	Colwyn Bay	350	D 1 - 1	O'Connell 35	
9	22		H	Ossett Town	246	L 2 - 4	Ashton 60 Steadman 90	
10	**25**	**FAC 2Q**	**A**	**Stewarts & Lloyds**	**110**	**D 2 - 2**	**Smythe 9 18**	
11	**29**	**FAC 2Qr**	**H**	**Stewarts & Lloyds**	**120**	**W 3 - 2**	**Ashton 49 115 O'Connell 53**	
12	Oct 2		H	F.C.United	1074	W 2 - 0	O'Connell 85 Ashton 77	19
13	6		A	Buxton	306	W 2 - 1	Steadman 13 77	
14	**9**	**FAC 3Q**	**H**	**Newcastle Town**	**562**	**L 1 - 2**	**Steadman 70 (pen)**	
15	13		H	Nantwich Town	185	D 6 - 6	Everett-Elliott13 Graves 23 O'Connell 41 Steadman 59 67 Ashton 61	
16	**16**	**FAT 1Q**	**H**	**Hucknall Town**	**186**	**W 2 - 1**	**O'Connell 26 Steadman 56**	
17	23		A	Frickley Athletic	203	L 0 - 1		20
18	27		H	Buxton	424	L 2 - 4	Graves 55 Walshe 83	
19	**30**	**FAT 1Q**	**H**	**Chasetown**	**250**	**L 2 - 5**	**O'Connell 29 49**	
20	Nov 6		A	Burscough	167	L 2 - 3	Graves 45 Hoyle 58 (pen)	21
21	13		H	Marine	214	D 0 - 0		21
22	20		A	Retford United	157	W 2 - 0	Ashton 70 O'Connell 76	
23	Dec 11		H	Colwyn Bay	175	W 4 - 0	Everett-Elliott 5 Steadman 28 Smythe 40 O'Connell 75	20
24	Jan 1		H	Matlock Town	575	W 1 - 0	Strzyzewski 45	17
25	3		A	North Ferriby United	233	L 2 - 4	Burton 76 (og) Smythe78	
26	8		H	Hucknell Town	276	D 1 - 1	Graves 45	19
27	15		A	Kendal Town	159	W 2 - 1	Ashton 4 Smythe 20	16
28	22		A	Northwich Victoria	357	L 0 - 1		17
29	26		A	Worksop Town	203	L 0 - 2		
30	Feb 1		A	Nantwich Town	181	D 0 - 0		18
31	12		A	Ashton Uited	118	W 3 - 2	Ashton 8 Smythe 26 Hoyle 77 (pen)	18
32	23		H	Northwich Victoria	180	L 2 - 3	Steadman 7 28	
33	March 5		A	F.C.United	2159	D 0 - 0		19
34	10		A	Chasetown	254	W 3 - 2	Graves 36 O'Connell 47 Steadman 51	
35	12		H	Retford United	245	W 4 - 0	Ashton 41 56 Smythe 49 Steadman 50	14
36	14		A	Bradford P.A.	213	L 0 - 1		
37	19		H	Worksop Town	247	L 0 - 1		14
38	23		H	Stocksbridge PS	202	W 2 - 0	Bryant 19 Steadman 38	
39	26		A	Stocksbridge PS	131	L 3 - 7	Middleditch 24 Steadman 37 Hoyle 53	15
40	30		H	Ashton United	170	L 0 - 1		
41	April 2		H	Frickley Athetic	211	W 3 - 0	Ashton 22 43 Walshe 84	15
42	6		H	Chasetown	238	L 1 - 3	Hoyle 37	
43	9		A	Marine	286	W 2 - 1	Martin 15 O'Connell 33	15
44	12		A	Ossett Town	58	W 2 - 1	Ashton 15 Hoyle 63 (pen)	
45	16		H	Burscough	203	W 2 - 1	Ashton 19 55	14
46	19		H	Whitby Town	184	L 2 - 4	Farthing 52 Smythe 55	
47	23		A	F.C.Halifax Town	2404	D 1 - 1	Hoyle 57 (pen)	15
48	25		H	Bradford P.A.	290	L 1 - 3	Ashton 88	15

NANTWICH TOWN

Chairman: Jon Gold
Secretary: Bernard Lycett **(T)** 07876 230 280 **(E)** nantwichtownfc@hotmail.co.uk
Additional Committee Members:
Edward Beeston, Michael Chatwin, Charles Grant, Clive Jackson, Jon Gold, Bob Melling (Non Executive), Steve Smithies.
Manager: Jimmy Quinn
Programme Editor: Chris Bunn **(E)** nantwichtownfc@hotmail.co.uk

Back Row (L-R): Paul Melling (Goalkeeper Coach), Triston Hendricks-Hamilton, Louis James, Niall Maguire, Matthew Worrall, Ben Mills, Chris Flynn, Jonny Brain, Mat Bailey, Ben Chapman, Liam Prince, Darren Moss, Rodney Jack, Marco Adaggio, Sam Aspinwall, Michelle Pennell (Physio).
Front Row: Zak Foster, Michael Lennon, Andy Nicholls, Jimmy Quinn (Manager), Jimmy Kelly (captain), Martin Stubbs (Assistant Manager), Ashley Carter, Carl Ruffer, Matt Lowe.
Photo Courtesy of Simon J. Newbury Photography.

Club Factfile

Founded: 1884 **Nickname:** Dabbers
Previous Names: Not known
Previous Leagues: Shropshire & Dist. 1891-92, Combination 1892-94, 191-10, Cheshire Junior 1894-95, Crewe & Dist. 1895-97, North Staffs & Dist. 1897-1900, Cheshire 1900-01, Manchester 1910-12, 65-68, Lancs. Com. 1912-14, Cheshire Co. 1919-38, 68-82, Crewe & Dist. 1938-39, 47-48, Crewe Am. Comb. 1946-47, Mid-Cheshire 1948-65, North West Co. 1982-2007
Club Colours (change): Green & white halves/green/green (Yellow & black stripes/black/black)

Ground: Weaver Stadium, Waterlode, Kingsley Fields, Nantwich, CW5 5BS **(T)** 01270 621 771
Capacity: 3,500 **Seats:** 350 **Covered:** 495 **Clubhouse:** Yes **Shop:** Yes

Directions
M6 Jun 16 A500 towards Nantwich. Over 4 roundabouts onto A51 towards Nantwich Town Centre, through traffic lights and over railway crossing. Over next r/bout then left at next r/bout past Morrisons supermarket on right. Continue over r/bout through traffic lights. Ground on right at next set of traffic lights.

Previous Grounds: Not known

Record Attendance: 5,121 v Winsford United - Cheshire Senior Cup 2nd Round 1920-21
Record Victory: 15-0 v Ashton United - Manchester League 1966-67
Record Defeat: 0-12 v Chirk - FA Cup 2nd Qualifying Round 1889-90
Record Goalscorer: Bobby Jones - 60
Record Appearances: Not known
Additional Records: Gerry Duffy scored 42 during season 1961-62
Received £4,000 from Stafford Rangers for D Dawson

Senior Honours: Cheshire Senior Cup 1975-76.
FA Vase 2005-06

10 YEAR RECORD

01-02	02-03	03-04	04-05	05-06	06-07	07-08	08-09	09-10	10-11
NWC1 15	NWC1 6	NWC1 13	NWC1 16	NWC1 4	NWC1 3	NP1S 3	NP P 3	NP P 10	NP P 17

NANTWICH TOWN

No.	Date	Comp	H/A	Opponents	Att:	Result	Goalscorers	Pos
1	Aug 21	NPL P	H	Worksop Town	455	L 1 - 2	Flynn 5	17
2	25		A	F.C.United	1866	L 0 - 1		
3	28		A	Stocksbridge Park Steels	147	L 1 - 3	Lennon 4	21
4	30		H	Northwich Victoria	863	W 2 - 1	Blake 49 Mahmood 66	
5	Sept 4		A	Buxton	359	L 1 - 2	Lennon 27	21
6	**11**	**FAC 1Q**	**H**	**Burscough**	**247**	**W 4 - 0**	**Whittaker 7 37 Lennon 50 Blake 80**	
7	18		A	Bradford P.A.	303	L 0 - 1		21
8	**25**	**FAC 2Q**	**H**	**Whitley Bay**	**344**	**L 2 - 3**	**Williams 19 (og) Jack 70**	
9	Oct 2		H	Kendal Town	314	W 5 - 3	Blackhurst 11 Jack 13 Carr 30 Lennon 32 Connerton 59	21
10	9		A	Hucknall Town	219	L 1 - 3	Carr 90	21
11	13		A	Mickleover Sports	185	D 6 - 6	Tickle 9 Southern 58 Lennon 69 90 Aspinwall 84 Sedgemore 87	
12	**16**	**FAT 1Q**	**H**	**Prescot Cables**	**274**	**W 6 - 2**	**LENNON 4 (2 29 34 45) Blake 83 Whittaker 90**	
13	19		H	Matlock Town	253	L 2 - 3	Lennon 11 Reeves 80	
14	23		H	Whitby Town	273	W 3 - 1	Blackhurst 6 Carr 46 Whittaker 61	
15	26		A	Chasetown	328	D 2 - 2	Southern 30 Carter 65	
16	**30**	**FAT 2Q**	**A**	**Mossley**	**194**	**W 3 - 2**	**Lennon 37 Blackhurst 52 Jack 75**	
17	Nov 6		H	Ossett Town	366	W 2 - 1	Reeves 27 Lennon 48	20
18	13		A	North Ferriby United	255	W 2 - 1	Blake 56 Lennon 57	
19	16		H	Burscough	236	W 3 - 2	Blake 2 Reeves 45 Carr 60	15
20	**20**	**FAT 3Q**	**A**	**Harrogate R.A.**	**142**	**W 4 - 3**	**Lennon 44 80 Flynn 52 Blackhurst 63**	
21	**Dec 11**	**FAT 1**	**A**	**Stalybridge Celtic**	**321**	**L 1 - 2**	**Jack 54**	
22	Jan 1		A	Northwich Victoria	587	D 1 - 1	Short 4	18
23	3		H	Frickley Athletic	313	W 3 - 2	Whittaker 47 Lennon 55 McAnulty 87	
24	8		H	Chasetown	301	L 0 - 4		16
25	15		H	Stocksbridge P.S.	229	W 4 - 3	Connerton 5 35 Flynn 29 Lennon 65	15
26	22		H	Bradford P.A.	369	L 0 - 1		16
27	Feb 1		H	Mickleover Sports	181	D 0 - 0		
28	7		A	Ashton United	120	W 4 - 2	Lennon 13 Flynn 24 Connerton 31 47	
29	12		H	Retford United	358	W 1 - 0	Lennon 41	13
30	15		A	Marine	255	L 3 - 4	Whittaker 28 Mahmood 80 Carr 82	
31	22		H	F.C.Halifax Town	529	L 0 - 6		
32	26		A	Burscough	225	L 1 - 3	Connerton 47	14
33	March 1		H	F.C.United	616	L 1 - 4	Connerton 4	
34	5		A	Kendal Town	231	L 1 - 2	Lennon 79	14
35	8		A	Retford United	81	L 2 - 3	Lennnon 73 Connerton 89	
36	12		H	Ashton United	316	L 0 - 2		16
37	15		A	Frickley Athletic	150	L 0 - 3		
38	19		H	Marine	342	D 1 - 1	Connerton 45	18
39	22		H	Colwyn Bay	240	W 2 - 1	Lennon 5 Sedgemoor 57 (pen)	
40	26		H	Hucknall Town	303	L 1 - 2	Reeves 44	17
41	29		A	F.C.Halifax Town	1346	L 1 - 3	Carr 51	
42	April 2		A	Whitby Town	293	L 1 - 3	Aspinwall 83	19
43	9		H	North Ferriby United	337	W 2 - 1	Oswell 45 76	
44	13		A	Worksop Town	146	D 0 - 0		
45	16		A	Ossett Town	90	W 5 - 0	LENNON 3 (7 42 52) Blackhurst 20 Aspinwall 30	17
46	19		A	Matlock Town	328	L 2 - 4	Oswell 34 Lennon 37	
47	23		H	Buxton	517	D 1 - 1	Lennon 81	17
48	25		A	Colwyn Bay	748	L 0 - 2		17

NORTH FERRIBY UNITED

Chairman: Les Hare
Secretary: Steve Tather **(T)** 07845 378 512 **(E)** info@northferribyunitedfc.co.uk
Additional Committee Members:
Colin Wicks, Alan Sage, Steve Turtle, Richard Hodgkinson, Jim White, Phil Withers, Chris Holbrough
Manager: John Anderson
Programme Editor: Richard Watts **(E)** info@northferribyunitedfc.co.uk

Club Factfile

Founded: 1934 **Nickname:** United
Previous Names: Not known
Previous Leagues: East Riding Church, East Riding Amateur, Yorkshire 1969-82, Northern Counties East 1982-2000

Club Colours (change): White with green trim/green/green (Yellow with green trim/yellow/yellow)

Ground: Rapid Solicitors Stadium, Church Road, North Ferriby HU14 3AA **(T)** 01482 634 601
Capacity: 3,000 **Seats:** 250 **Covered:** 1,000 **Clubhouse:** Yes **Shop:** Yes

Directions
Main Leeds to Hull road A63 or M62. North Ferriby is approx. 8 miles west of Hull.
Proceed through village past the Duke of Cumberland Hotel.
Turn right down Church Road. Ground mile down on left.

Previous Grounds: Not known

Record Attendance: 1,927 v Hull City - Charity game 2005
Record Victory: 9-0 v Hatfield Main - Northern Counties East 1997-98
Record Defeat: 1-7 v North Shields - Northern Counties East 1991
Record Goalscorer: Mark Tennison - 161
Record Appearances: Paul Sharp - 497 (1996-2006)
Additional Records: Andy Flounders scored 50 during season 1998-99
Received £60,000 from Hull City for Dean Windass

Senior Honours: Northern Counties East 1999-2000. Northern Premier League Division 1 2004-05.
East Riding Senior Cup x11.

10 YEAR RECORD

01-02	02-03	03-04	04-05	05-06	06-07	07-08	08-09	09-10	10-11
NP 1 12	NP 1 4	NP 1 17	NP 1 1	NP P 5	NP P 13	NP P 15	NP P 10	NP P 4	NP P 5

NORTH FERRIBY UNITED

No.	Date	Comp	H/A	Opponents	Att:	Result	Goalscorers	Pos
1	Aug 21	NPL P	H	Colwyn Bay	158	L 1 - 3	Bradshaw 78 (pen)	22
2	25		A	Mickleover Sports	197	W 4 - 3	Fry 30 Bolder 31 White 77 Brooksby 86	
3	28		A	Burscough	143	D 2 - 2	Brooksby 10 Bradshaw 18	12
4	30		H	Chasetown	221	L 0 - 1		
5	Sept 4		A	Ossett Town	127	D 0 - 0		16
6	7		H	Worksop Town	182	W 3 - 0	Fry 20 Bradshaw 68 Davidson 88	
7	**11**	**FAC 1Q**	**H**	**Ossett Town**	**112**	**W 2 - 1**	**Brooksby 29 Horsley 81 (pen)**	
8	18		H	Buxton	223	W 2 - 0	Foot 24 Bradshaw 63	12
9	22		A	Whitby Town	266	W 1 - 0	Davidson 64	
10	**25**	**FAC 2Q**	**H**	**Stocksbridge Park Steels**	**196**	**W 5 - 2**	**Denton 28 Bolder 33 76 Davidson 42 Horsley 78 (pen)**	
11	28		H	Retford United	214	L 0 - 1		
12	Oct 2		A	Hucknall Town	216	L 2 - 3	Bradshaw 62 Fry 68	
13	5		A	Stocksbridge Park Steels	126	L 0 - 1		9
14	**9**	**FAC 3Q**	**H**	**Vauxhall Motors**	**369**	**D 2 - 2**	**Brooksby 60 Fry 77**	
15	**12**	**FAC 3Qr**	**A**	**Vauxhall Motors**	**202**	**D 1 - 1**	**Bolder 75**	
16	**16**	**FAT 1Q**	**H**	**Bamber Bridge**	**179**	**L 0 - 2**		
17	23		A	Marine	306	D 2 - 2	Bradshaw 60 90	12
18	26		H	Stocksbridge Park Steels	191	W 2 - 1	Davidson 49 90	
19	30		H	Ashton United	208	W 3 - 2	Horsley 29 Bolder 63 Davidson 78	6
20	Nov 6		A	Kendal Town	217	W 5 - 2	DAVIDSON 4 (2 24 38 73) Bolder 63	5
21	13		H	Nantwich Town	255	L 1 - 2	Bolder 90	7
22	20		A	F.C.Halifax Town	1605	W 2 - 0	Fry 27 Bradshaw 76	5
23	Jan 1		A	Chasetown	428	D 2 - 2	Bradshaw 30 Bolder 47	5
24	3		H	Mickleover Sports	233	W 4 - 2	Fry 12 Bradshaw 20 57 Davidson 81	
25	11		A	Matlock Town	224	L 1 - 2	Bradshaw 6	
26	15		H	Burscough	154	W 2 - 1	Bradshaw 14 Brooksby 30	5
27	18		H	Frickley Athletic	224	W 4 - 0	Bolder 4 Davidson 31 Bradshaw 88 Fry 90	
28	29		H	F.C.Halifax Town	743	L 0 - 3		4
29	Feb 5		A	Northwich Victoria	395	D 1 - 1	Bradshaw 78	
30	12		H	Bradford P.A.	236	L 1 - 2	Bradshaw 36	6
31	15		A	Retford United	61	W 2 - 1	Bradshaw 41 Bolder 64	
32	22		H	Whitby Town	204	W 6 - 0	Bradshaw 12 77 White 36 42 Brooksby 83 Bolder 86	
33	26		A	Colwyn Bay	377	W 2 - 0	Bolder 20 Bradshaw 32	4
34	28		A	Bradford P.A.	241	W 2 - 1	Fry 27 Denton 68	
35	March 5		H	Hucknall Town	223	W 3 - 0	White 27 Burton 84 Davidson 87	2
36	12		H	Northwich Victoria	268	L 1 - 2	Davidson 45 (pen)	4
37	15		H	F.C.United	472	D 1 - 1	Bolder 58	
38	19		A	Ashton United	126	W 1 - 0	Davidson 54 (pen)	3
39	22		H	Matlock Town	313	W 3 - 1	Foot 22 Davidson 61 Bolder 69	
40	26		A	F.C.United	2827	L 0 - 2		3
41	30		A	Buxton	289	D 0 - 0		
42	April 2		H	Marine	219	L 0 - 1		4
43	6		A	Worksop Town	162	L 1 - 4	Bolder 71	
44	9		A	Nantwich Town	337	L 1 - 2	Bradshaw 79	5
45	16		H	Kendal Town	158	W 4 - 1	Brooksby 20 Harsley 59 (pen) Davidson 65 Bradshaw 70	6
46	22		H	Ossett Town	281	W 4 - 0	Horsley 24 (pen) Brooksby 42 Bradshaw 46 Davidson 67	5
47	25		A	Frickley Athletic	327	W 1 - 0	Horsley 24	5

NORTHWICH VICTORIA

Chairman: James Rushe
Secretary: Dave Thomas **(T)** 07798 564 596 **(E)** dave.thomas@northwichvics.co.uk
Additional Committee Members:
Martin Rushe, Howard Roberts

Manager: Andy Preece
Programme Editor: David Thomas **(E)** david.thomas@northwichvics.co.uk

Club Factfile

Founded: 1874 **Nickname:** Vics, Greens or Trickies
Previous Names: Not known
Previous Leagues: The Combination 1890-92, 1894-98, Football League 1892-94, Cheshire 1898-1900, Manchester 1900-12 Lancashire 1912-19, Cheshire County 1919-68, Northern Premier 1968-79, Conference 1979-2010

Club Colours (change): Green and white hoops/white/white (Yellow/blue/blue)

Ground: Victoria Stadium, Wincham Avenue, Northwich, Cheshire CW9 6GB **(T)** 01606 815 208
Capacity: 5,300 **Seats:** 1,180 **Covered:** 3,700 **Clubhouse:** Yes **Shop:** Yes

Directions
From M6, leave at Junction 19. Follow A556 towards Northwich for approx 3 miles. Turn right onto the A559 towards Lostock Gralam. (at the point where A556 becomes dual carriageway) Turn right at traffic lights before "Slow & Easy" Public House. Follow brown signs to "Victoria Stadium" (Distance 1.5 miles)

Previous Grounds: The Drill Field

Record Attendance: 11,290 v Witton Albion - Cheshire League Good Friday 1949
Record Victory: 17-0 v Marple Association 1883
Record Defeat: 3-10 v Port Vale - 1931
Record Goalscorer: Peter Burns - 160 (1955-65)
Record Appearances: Ken Jones - 970 (1969-85)
Additional Records: Paid £12,000 to Hyde United for Malcolm O'Connor August 1988. Received £50,000 from Leyton Orient for Gary Fletcher June 1921 and from Chester City for Neil Morton October 1990.

Senior Honours: FA Trophy 1983-84.
Conference North 2005-06.
Cheshire Senior Cup x15. Staffordshire Senior Cup x3.

10 YEAR RECORD

01-02	02-03	03-04	04-05	05-06	06-07	07-08	08-09	09-10	10-11
Conf 13	Conf 14	Conf 22	Conf 19	Conf N 1	Conf 13	Conf 19	Conf 22	Conf N 12	NP P 12

NORTHWICH VICTORIA

No.	Date	Comp	H/A	Opponents	Att:	Result	Goalscorers	Pos
1	Aug 21	NPL P	A	Retford United	271	W 1 - 0	Bennett 90	20
2	25		H	Bradford P.A.	464	W 2 - 1	Fowler 28 Riley 45	
3	28		H	Hucknall Town	424	W 4 - 0	Connor12 Fodor 41 Ryan 47 Riley 65	2
4	30		A	Nantwich Town	863	L 1 - 2	McAliskey 86	
5	Sept 4		H	Whitby Town	476	W 2 - 0	Fowler 75 Connor 81	1
6	7		A	F.C.Halifax	1166	D 1 - 1	Riley 65	
7	**11**	**FAC 1Q**	**A**	**Salford City**	**210**	**W 1 - 0**	**Ryan 45**	
8	18		A	Ossett Town	170	W 2 - 0	McAliskey 19 30	1
9	21		H	Worksop Town	454	W 3 - 1	Riley 27 Ryan 61 71	
10	**25**	**FAC 2Q**	**A**	**Sheffield**	**422**	**D 2 - 2**	**Fowler 38 McAliskey 55**	
11	**28**	**FAC 2Qr**	**H**	**Sheffield**	**429**	**L 1 - 2**	**Riley (pen) 90**	
12	Oct 2		H	Matlock Town	534	L 2 - 3	Fowler 30 Riley 88	3
13	5		A	Kendal Town	241	D 1 - 1	Ryan 21	
14	9		A	Colwyn Bay	556	W 6 - 0	Riley 24 51 RYAN 4 (29 75 85 89)	2
15	12		H	Marine	425	W 4 - 3	Riley 15 Ryan 52 Fowler 80 Crane 90	
16	**16**	**FAT 1Q**	**H**	**Lincoln United**	**367**	**D 0 - 0**		
17	**19**	**FAT 1Qr**	**A**	**Lincoln United**	**101**	**W 3 - 2**	**Fowler 11 Ryan 22 Riley 79**	
18	23		A	Burscough	241	D 0 - 0		1
19	26		H	Kendal Town	480	L 1 - 6	Ryan 8	
20	**30**	**FAT 2Q**	**H**	**Glapwell**	**323**	**W 4 - 0**	**Peers 37 McAliskey 58 Fowler 62 64**	
21	Nov 6		A	Frickley Athletic	245	L 1 - 2	Sumner 15	3
22	13		H	F.C.United	1663	W 1 - 0	Fowler 62	
23	16		A	Marine	344	L 1 - 3	Riley 53	
24	**20**	**FAT 3Q**	**A**	**Whitby Town**	**247**	**D 2 - 2**	**Liversedge 24 (og) McAliskey 84**	
25	**Dec 11**	**FAT 1**	**A**	**Worcester City**	**577**	**L 0 - 1**		
26	Jan 1		H	Nantwich Town	587	D 1 - 1	Wellstead 83	4
27	8		H	F.C.Halifax Town	676	L 0 - 3		8
28	15		A	Hucknall Town	170	W 2 - 0	Fowler 37 Riley 45	8
29	22		H	Mickleover Sports	357	W 1 - 0	Riley 90	7
30	24		A	Ashton Uited	203	L 1 - 2	Peers 5	
31	Feb 5		H	North Ferriby United	395	D 1 - 1	Collins 33	8
32	12		A	Stocksbridge PS	167	L 0 - 3		11
33	14		A	Bradford P.A.	266	D 2 - 2	Evans 9 Riley 39	
34	23		A	Mickleover Sports	180	W 3 - 2	Evans 16 Riley 78 Roberts 88	
35	26		H	Retford United	350	W 4 - 1	Fowler 37 Evans 41 78 Barnes 83	8
36	March 1		A	Buxton	202	D 2 - 2	Fowler 61 (pen) Fitzpatrick 69	
37	5		A	Matlock Town	392	D 1 - 1	Collins 27	8
38	8		H	Colwyn Bay	322	L 0 - 1		
39	12		A	North Ferriby United	268	W 2 - 1	Fowler4 Allen 21	8
40	15		A	Chasetown	312	L 0 - 1		
41	19		H	Stocksbridge PS	387	L 0 - 1		11
42	24		A	Worksop Town	210	L 0 - 2		
43	26		H	Ossett Town	277	L 0 - 1		12
44	April 2		H	Burscough	327	W 3 - 0	Evans 47 Allen 55 Clarke 71	
45	9		A	F.C.United	2250	L 0 - 1		12
46	12		H	Chasetown	253	D 1 - 1	Fowler 6	
47	16		H	Frickley Athletic	287	L 0 - 1		12
48	18		H	Buxton	303	W 4 - 2	FOWLER 3 (18 48 60) Clarke 42	
49	22		A	Whitby Town	337	W 4 - 2	Clarke 69 Roddy 71 Evans 74 75	
50	25		H	Ashton United	322	W 1 - 0	Fowler 73 (pen)	12

Action between Witton Albion and Sutton Coldfield Town.
Turn to page 436 to see 'what happened next'

Photo by Keith Clayton

RUSHALL OLYMPIC

Chairman: John C Allen
Secretary: Peter Athersmith (T) 07771 361 002 (E) rushallolympic@yahoo.co.uk
Additional Committee Members:
Nicholas J Allen, Brian Greenwood, Raymond Barrow, Darren Stockall, Robert Thomas, Stuart Perry, Daniel Hopley, Steve Stuart, Simon Haynes.
Manager: Neil Kitching
Programme Editor: Darren Stockall (E) rushallolympic@yahoo.co.uk

Club Factfile

Founded: 1951 **Nickname:** The Pics
Previous Names: Not known
Previous Leagues: Walsall Amateur 1952-55, Staffordshire County (South) 1956-78, West Midlands 1978-94, Midland Alliance 1994-2005, Southern 2005-08
Club Colours (change): Black and gold/black/gold (Red and white stripes/red/red)

Ground: Dales Lane off Daw End Lane, Rushall, Nr Walsall WS4 1LJ (T) 01922 641 021
Capacity: 2,500 **Seats:** 200 **Covered:** 200 **Clubhouse:** Yes **Shop:** Yes

Directions
M6 J10 follow signs for Walsall stay on this dual carriage way for about four miles until you come to the Walsall Arboretum and turn left following signs for Lichfield A461. Go under the bridge and you will come to McDonald's on your right, turn right into Daw End Lane. Go over the canal bridge and turn right opposite the Royal Oak Public House and the ground is on the right.
Alternative: From the A38 to it's junction with the A5 (Muckley Corner Hotel) take the A461 to Walsall after about five miles you will reach some traffic lights in Rushall by Mcdonald's, turn left into Daw End Lane go over the canal bridge and turn right opposite The Royal Oak Public House the ground is on the right.

Previous Grounds: Rowley Place 1951-75, Aston University 1976-79

Record Attendance: 2,000 v Leeds United Ex players
Record Victory: Not known
Record Defeat: Not known
Record Goalscorer: Graham Wiggin
Record Appearances: Alan Dawson - 400+
Additional Records:

Senior Honours: West Midlands League 1979-80. Midland Alliance 2004-05.

10 YEAR RECORD

01-02	02-03	03-04	04-05	05-06	06-07	07-08	08-09	09-10	10-11
MidAl 5	MidAl 2	MidAl 14	MidAl 1	SthW 10	SthM 15	SthM 5	NP1S 5	NP1S 12	NP1S 3

STAFFORD RANGERS

Chairman: Mike Hughes
Secretary: Robbie Mullin (T) 07977 038 534 (E) srfcmarstonroad@tiscali.co.uk
Additional Committee Members:
Cliff Went, Reg Bates, Roly Tonge, Rod Woodward.

Manager: Greg Clowes
Programme Editor: Ken Hunt (E) srfcmarstonroad@tiscali.co.uk

Back Row (L-R): John Sheldon, Neville Thompson, Liam Shotton, Luke Chapman, Dave Hall (Kit Man), Ryan Dicker, Chris Budrys, Mike Douglas. Middle Row: Andy Bates (Scout), Jordan Wood, Dan Skelton, Sean Kinsella, Danny Read, Glyn Blackhurst, Sean Jones, Peter Heler, Gareth Barker & Mick Hathaway (Coach)
Front Row: Joe Rogers, Alex Ford, Rob Stevenson, Greg Clowes (Manager), Paul Donnelly (Captain), Dorian Garner (Asst Manager), Charlie Reeves, Hayley Brennan (Physio), Alan Nagington & Kevin Street.

Club Factfile

Founded: 1876 **Nickname:** Rangers
Previous Names: Not known
Previous Leagues: Shropshire 1891-93, Birmingham 1893-96, N. Staffs. 1896-1900, Cheshire 1900-01, Birmingham Comb. 1900-12, 46-52, Cheshire County 1952-69, N.P.L. 1969-79, 83-85, Alliance 1979-83, Conf. 1985-95, 2005-11. Southern >2005.
Club Colours (change): Black & white stripes/black/black (All red)

Ground: Marston Road, Stafford ST16 3BX (T) 01785 602 430
Capacity: 6,000 **Seats:** 4,264 **Covered:** 3,500 **Clubhouse:** Yes **Shop:** Yes

Directions
M6 Junction 14. Follow signs for Uttoxeter and Stone. Straight over at 1st and 2nd (A34) islands, 3rd right sign posted Common Road and Astonfields Road Ind. Estate. The ground is straight ahead after three quarters of a mile. The route from the Motorway is highlighted by the standard football road signs.

Previous Grounds: Not known

Record Attendance: 8,536 v Rotherham United - FA Cup 3rd Round 1975
Record Victory: 14-0 v Kidsgrove Athletic - Staffordshire Senior Cup 2003
Record Defeat: 0-12 v Burton Town - Birmingham League 1930
Record Goalscorer: M. Cullerton - 176
Record Appearances: Jim Sargent
Additional Records: Paid £13,000 to VS rugby for S. Butterworth
Received £100,000 from Crystal Palace for Stan Collymore

Senior Honours: Northern Premier League 1971-72, 84-85. FA trophy 1971-72.
Staffordshire Senior Cup x7

10 YEAR RECORD

01-02	02-03	03-04	04-05	05-06	06-07	07-08	08-09	09-10	10-11
SthP 9	SthP 2	SthP 3	Conf N 8	Conf N 2	Conf 20	Conf 23	Conf N 18	Conf N 16	Conf N 20

STAFFORD RANGERS

No.	Date	Comp	H/A	Opponents	Att:	Result	Goalscorers	Pos
1	Sat-14-Aug	BSN	A	Boston United	1604	L 0-1		18
2	Tue-17-Aug	BSN	H	Solihull Moors	501	W 1-0	Sterling 53	13
3	Sat-21-Aug	BSN	H	Guiseley	438	D 2-2	Sterling 22, Clarke 50	12
4	Sat-28-Aug	BSN	H	Worcester City	557	D 1-1	Sterling 56	10
5	Mon-30-Aug	BSN	A	Alfreton Town	744	L 0-2		11
6	Sat-04-Sep	BSN	A	Droylsden	385	L 0-2		14
7	Sat-11-Sep	BSN	H	Stalybridge Celtic	511	L 1-3	Clarke 68	15
8	Sat-18-Sep	BSN	H	Gainsborough Trinity	402	W 3-1	Sterling 2 (8, 31), Mills 14	15
9	Sat-02-Oct	BSN	A	Hinckley United	444	L 0-4		17
10	Sat-16-Oct	BSN	A	Nuneaton Town	1002	L 0-1		18
11	Sat-23-Oct	BSN	H	Gloucester City	599	L 0-2		18
12	Sat-30-Oct	BSN	A	Solihull Moors	289	D 1-1	Clarke 62	19
13	Sat-13-Nov	BSN	H	Hinckley United	506	L 1-3	Mills pen 45	20
14	Tue-23-Nov	BSN	A	Vauxhall Motors	181	L 1-2	Francis 60	20
15	Sat-11-Dec	BSN	H	Workington	353	L 0-2		20
16	Sat-01-Jan	BSN	A	AFC Telford	2232	D 0-0		20
17	Mon-03-Jan	BSN	H	Alfreton Town	544	L 0-1		20
18	Sat-08-Jan	BSN	A	Hyde FC	301	L 0-1		20
19	Tue-11-Jan	BSN	H	AFC Telford	763	L 0-2		20
20	Sat-15-Jan	BSN	H	Vauxhall Motors	375	W 1-0	Francis 77	20
21	Tue-18-Jan	BSN	A	Harrogate Town	147	L 2-3	McAughtrie 59, Johnson 90	20
22	Sat-22-Jan	BSN	H	Corby Town	432	L 3-5	Benjamin 2 (8, pen 22), Mills 90	20
23	Sat-29-Jan	BSN	A	Blyth Spartans	501	L 2-3	Benjamin 9, L Reid 71	20
24	Sat-05-Feb	BSN	H	Nuneaton Town	529	L 1-2	Moss 87	20
25	Sat-12-Feb	BSN	H	Redditch United	365	W 2-1	Mills pen 61, Clarke 67	20
26	Sat-19-Feb	BSN	A	Gainsborough Trinity	436	D 2-2	Maguire 5, L Reid 58	20
27	Tue-01-Mar	BSN	A	Redditch United	131	W 1-0	Mills 3	20
28	Sat-05-Mar	BSN	H	Hyde FC	508	L 0-5		20
29	Tue-08-Mar	BSN	H	Boston United	260	L 0-4		20
30	Sat-12-Mar	BSN	H	Blyth Spartans	334	W 2-1	Adaggio 53, Mills 69	20
31	Sat-19-Mar	BSN	A	Gloucester City	320	W 2-1	Johnson 18, Maguire 90	19
32	Sat-26-Mar	BSN	A	Eastwood Town	389	L 0-3		20
33	Tue-29-Mar	BSN	A	Guiseley	258	D 1-1	Francis 86	20
34	Sat-02-Apr	BSN	H	Harrogate Town	401	D 1-1	Maguire 25	19
35	Mon-04-Apr	BSN	A	Worcester City	493	D 2-2	Maguire 53, Kinsella 69	19
36	Sat-09-Apr	BSN	A	Workington	402	L 0-2		20
37	Sat-16-Apr	BSN	H	Droylsden	405	L 1-5	Keen 71	20
38	Tue-19-Apr	BSN	H	Eastwood Town	339	L 0-2		20
39	Sat-23-Apr	BSN	A	Corby Town	295	W 3-1	Keen 2 (10, 30), Maguire 77	20
40	Sat-30-Apr	BSN	A	Stalybridge Celtic	583	L 2-3	Francis 66, Adaggio 76	20 Relegated
	Ilkeston Record Expunged 16/09							
4	Tue-24-Aug	BSN	A	Ilkeston Town	292	W 2-0	Kasiama 15, Davidson 77	7
CUPS								
1	Sat-25-Sep	FAC 2Q	A	Eastwood Town	347	D 1-1	Sterling 24	
2	Tue-28-Sep	FAC 2QR	H	Eastwood Town	429	L 1-3	Wellecomme 74	
3	Sat-20-Nov	FAT 3Q	A	Blyth Spartans	391	L 0-1		

STOCKSBRIDGE PARK STEELS

Chairman: Allen Bethel
Secretary: Michael Grimmer (T) 07801 626 725 (E) mickgrimmer@gmail.com
Additional Committee Members:
Trevor Grayson, Andrew Horsley, Wayne Cefferty, Dean Cefferty, Peter Kenney, Jack Newton, William Fieldsend, Ron Sellers, John Gosling, Philip Birkinshaw.
Manager: Gary Marrow
Programme Editor: Philip Birkenshaw (E) mickgrimmer@gmail.com

Club Factfile

Founded: 1986 **Nickname:** Steels
Previous Names: Stocksbridge Works and Oxley Park merged in 1986
Previous Leagues: Northern Counties East 1986-96

Club Colours (change): Yellow/royal blue/blue (Red/white/red)

Ground: Look Loacl Stadium, Bracken Moor Lane, Stocksbridge, Sheffield S36 2AN (T) 0114 288 8305
Capacity: 3,500 **Seats:** 400 **Covered:** 1,500 **Clubhouse:** Yes **Shop:** Yes

Directions
From West onto A616. Immediately you reach the Stocksbridge bypass turn Right signed (Stocksbridge West), then continue until you reach the shopping centre approx 1.5 miles. 300 yards past the centre you will see Gordons Autos on your left. Turn right directly opposite signed (Nanny Hill) and continue up the hill for Approx 500 yds, Ground is on the Left.
From M1- From North Junction 36 on to A61 Sheffield to McDonalds Roundabout. From South Junction 35a on to A616 Manchester to McDonalds Roundabout. From McDonalds roundabout on A616 Manchester for approx 6 miles then take Stocksbridge West exit, then continue until you reach the shopping centre approx 1.5 miles. 300yds past the centre you will see Gordons Autos on your Left. Turn right directly opposite signed (Nanny Hill) and continue up the hill for Approx 500yds, ground on Left.

Previous Grounds: Stonemoor 1949-51, 52-53

Record Attendance: 2,050 v Sheffield Wednesday - opening of floodlights October 1991
Record Victory: 17-1 v Oldham Town - FA Cup 2002-03
Record Defeat: 0-6 v Shildon
Record Goalscorer: Trevor Jones - 145
Record Appearances: Not known
Additional Records: Paul Jackson scored 10 v Oldham Town in the 2002-03 FA Cup - a FA Cup record
Received £15,000 from Wolverhampton Wanderers for Lee Mills

Senior Honours: Northern Counties East Division 1 1991-92, Premier Division 1993-94, League Cup 1994-95.
Sheffield Senior Cup 1951-52, 92-93, 95-96, 98-99

10 YEAR RECORD

01-02	02-03	03-04	04-05	05-06	06-07	07-08	08-09	09-10	10-11
NP 1 20	NP 1 17	NP 1 19	NP 1 14	NP 1 6	NP 1 6	NP1S 5	NP1S 3	NP P 11	NP P 13

STOCKSBRIDGE PARK STEELS

No.	Date	Comp	H/A	Opponents	Att:	Result	Goalscorers	Pos
1	Aug 21	NPL P	A	Matlock Town	337	L 0 - 1		21
2	25		H	Retford United	186	W 3 - 2	Callery 5 Ward 20 84	
3	28		H	Nantwich Town	147	W 3 - 1	Ward 24 Riley 58 Ring 89	7
4	30		A	Hucknall Town	272	D 2 - 2	Leonard 59 Longstaff 90	
5	Sept 4		H	Ashton United	231	D 0 - 0		8
6	7		A	Marine	258	L 4 - 5	Ward 57 Ring 59 Muldoon 60 Leonard 90	
7	**11**	**FAC 1Q**	**H**	**Trafford**	**120**	**W 4 - 2**	**Muldoon 10 Callery 45 Davies 47 Riley 85**	
8	18		A	F.C.United	1793	W 4 - 1	Muldoon 32 Davies 42 Woolley 58 Leonard 76	10
9	21		H	F.C.Halifax Town	658	L 3 - 5	Ward 6 44 (pen) Davies 37	
10	**25**	**FAC 2Q**	**A**	**North Ferriby United**	**196**	**L 2 - 5**	**Ward 11 Muldoon 32**	
11	28		A	Frickley Athletic	217	D 1 - 1	Ward 1	
12	Oct 2		H	Bradford `P A.	221	L 0 - 1		16
13	5		H	North Ferriby United	126	L 0 - 1		17
14	13		A	Worksop Town	265	L 1 - 2	Dempsey 57	
15	**16**	**FAT 1Q**	**A**	**Buxton**	**321**	**W 2 - 1**	**Ward 2 Muldoon 65**	
16	23		H	Chasetown	152	W 2 - 0	Ward 36 Dillon 39	16
17	26		A	North Ferriby United	191	L 1 - 2	Matthews (og)	
18	**30**	**FAT 2Q**	**H**	**Rugby Town**	**152**	**W 3 - 2**	**Haigh 27 Ring 50 90**	
19	Nov 6		H	Colwyn Bay	180	L 0 - 1		19
20	13		A	Ossett Town	113	W 5 - 3	Ring 19 52 Muldoon 25 Marrison 39 Leonard 44l	17
21	**21**	**FAT 3Q**	**A**	**Worksop Town**	**290**	**L 1 - 4**	**Muldoon 12**	
22	Jan 1		H	Hucknall Town	160	W 1 - 0	Marrison 34	16
23	3		A	Retford United	149	D 0 - 0		
24	8		H	Marine	120	L 1 - 3	Lovell 74	18
25	11		H	Worksop Town	163	L 2 - 3	Marrison 31 Ward 51	
26	15		A	Nantwich Town	229	L 3 - 4	Marrison 2 84 Stirrup 7	20
27	25		H	Matlock Town	148	W 3 - 1	Ward 31 Ring 46 Muldoon 82	
28	Feb 5		A	Kendal Town	205	W 3 - 2	Ward 29 (og) Ring 55 Stirrup 78	16
29	9		A	Whitby Town	224	L 0 - 2		
30	12		H	Northwich Victoria	167	W 3 - 0	Dillon 43 Ward 46 Muldoon 86	
31	23		A	Buxton	231	D 0 - 0		
32	26		H	F.C.United	837	L 1 - 2	Dillon 2	16
33	March 1		H	Burscough	76	L 2 - 4	Ward 3 Davies 73	
34	5		A	Bradford P.A.	253	L 0 - 3		16
35	12		H	Frickley Athletic	161	D 1 - 1	Muldoon 62	17
36	15		A	F.C.Halifax Town	1073	L 1 - 5	Muldoon 29	
37	19		A	Northwich Victoria	387	W 1 - 0	Muldoon 24	15
38	23		A	Mickleover Sports	202	L 0 - 2		
39	26		H	Mickleover Sports	131	W 7 - 3	Callery 11 Ring 17 Stirrup 19 Marrison 43 Hall 46 Muldoon 56 83	
40	29		H	Kendal Town	131	W 2 - 1	Lovell 75 Dillon 78	
41	April 2		A	Chasetown	416	W 2 - 0	Callery 37 Ring 41	13
42	6		A	Burscough	115	W 2 - 0	Marrison 82 Ward 90	
43	9		H	Ossett Town	127	W 3 - 0	Marrison 15 Muldoon 22 Ring 55	13
44	12		H	Buxton	182	L 1 - 4	Dillon 58 (pen)	
45	16		A	Colwyn Bay	496	W 4 - 3	Ward 25 Stirrup 84 Muldoon 75 82	13
46	23		A	Ashton United	137	L 1 - 3	Joynes 84	13
47	25		H	Whitby Town	158	W 2 - 1	Stirrup 2 Marrison 53	13

WHITBY TOWN

Chairman: Anthony Graham Manser
Secretary: Peter Tyreman (T) 01947 605 153 (E)
Additional Committee Members:
A J Spenceley, M Agar, J Nellist, C Bone, G Osbourne, M Osbourne, D Griffiths, J Smith, M Green
Manager: Tommy Cassidy
Programme Editor: Lee West (E)

Club Factfile

Founded: 1926 **Nickname:** Seasiders
Previous Names: Whitby United (pre 1950)
Previous Leagues: Northern League 1926-97

Club Colours (change): All royal blue (All white)

Ground: Turnbull Ground, Upgang Lane, Whitby, North Yorks YO21 3HZ (T) 01947 604 847
Capacity: 2,680 **Seats:** 622 **Covered:** 1,372 **Clubhouse:** Yes **Shop:** Yes

Directions
On entering Whitby from both the A169 and A171 roads, take the first fork and follow signs for the "West Cliff". Then turn left at the Spa Shop and Garage, along Love Lane to junction of the A174. Turn right and the ground is 600 yards on the left.

Previous Grounds: Not known

Record Attendance: 4,000 v Scarborough - North Riding Cup 18/04/1965
Record Victory: 11-2 v Cargo Fleet Works - 1950
Record Defeat: 3-13 v Willington - 24/03/1928
Record Goalscorer: Paul Pitman - 382
Record Appearances: Paul Pitman - 468
Additional Records: Paid £2,500 to Newcastle Blue Star for John Grady 1990
Received £5,000 from Gateshead for Graham Robinson 1997

Senior Honours: Rothmans National Cup 1975-76, 77-78. Northern League 1992-93. FA Vase 1996-97.
Northern Premier League Division 1 1997-98.
North Riding Senior Cup x5.

10 YEAR RECORD

01-02	02-03	03-04	04-05	05-06	06-07	07-08	08-09	09-10	10-11
NP P 15	NP P 10	NP P 15	NP P 4	NP P 6	NP P 11	NP P 12	NP P 19	NP P 14	NP P 16

WHITBY TOWN

No.	Date	Comp	H/A	Opponents	Att:	Result	Goalscorers	Pos
1	Aug 21	NPL P	H	Mickleover Sports	306	W 3 - 2	Campbell 12 Beadle 73 Owens 78	2
2	25		A	Worksop Town	245	L 0 - 5		
3	28		A	Buxton	270	L 0 - 2		17
4	30		H	Frickley Athletic	331	D 2 - 2	Owens 30 Craddock 71	
5	Sept 4		A	Northwich Victoria	476	L 0 - 2		18
6	8		H	Ossett Town	231	W 3 - 1	Owens 10 Beadle 73 Hackworth 83	
7	**11**	**FAC 1Q**	**A**	**F.C.Halifax Town**	**976**	**L 0 - 2**		
8	18		A	F.C.Halifax Town	1271	L 1 - 5	McTiernon 57	18
9	22		H	North Ferriby United	266	L 0 - 1		
10	25		A	Burscough	171	L 0 - 1		18
11	27		A	Bradford P.A.	277	D 1 - 1	Leeson 85	
12	Oct 2		H	Colwyn Bay	248	D 2 - 2	Beadle 16 Leeson 64	18
13	5		A	Retford United	149	W 3 - 2	Hackworth 33 (pen) Leeson 36 82	
14	9		H	Kendal Town	301	D 2 - 2	Beadle18 90	17
15	**16**	**FAT 1Q**	**A**	**Hednesford Town**	**313**	**W 2 - 1**	**Campbell 51 Southern 89**	
16	23		A	Nantwich Town	273	L 1 - 2	Beadle 73	19
17	27		H	Retford United	299	W 2 - 1	Hackworth 44 Burgess 82	
18	**30**	**FAT 2Q**	**H**	**Clitheroe**	**265**	**W 3 - 1**	**Hackworth 29 Southern 68 Batchelor 70**	
19	Nov 6		A	Ashton United	154	W 3 - 1	Leeson 42 Batchelor 85 Campbell 90	16
20	13		H	Burscough	266	D 2 - 2	Hackworth 6 Beadle 42	16
21	**20**	**FAT 3Q**	**H**	**Northwich Victoria**	**247**	**D 2 - 2**	**Batchelor 55 Campbell 83**	
22	Dec 11		A	Marine	232	W 3 - 1	Campbell 17 89 Hackworth 69	14
23	Jan 3		H	Worksop Town	276	L 0 - 3		
24	22		H	Chasetown	282	L 0 - 1		18
25	Feb 5		H	Marine	248	D 1 - 1	Batchelor 73	19
26	9		H	Stocksbridge Park Steels	227	W 2 - 0	McTiernan 40 Davies 90	
27	12		A	F.C.United	1662	L 0 - 4		19
28	22		A	North Ferriby United	204	L 0 - 6		
29	March 1		A	Ossett Town	79	W 4 - 0	BEADLE 3 (34 41 88) Southern 89	
30	5		A	Colwyn Bay	347	L 0 - 2		17
31	9		H	Matlock Town	211	L 1 - 2	Scott 38	
32	12		H	Bradford P.A.	323	L 1 - 2	Batchelor 90	18
33	16		A	Hucknall Town	118	W 2 - 1	Leeson 44 Beadle 88	
34	19		A	Chasetown	405	D 1 - 1	Burgess 66	17
35	23		H	F.C.United	588	L 0 - 1		
36	26		A	Matlock Town	340	D 2 - 2	McTiernan 40 Beadle 45	19
37	30		H	Hucknall Town	251	W 1 - 0	Hackworth 10 (pen)	
38	April 2		H	Nantwich Town	293	W 3 - 1	Campbell 18 Beadle 23 McTiernan 81	16
39	6		H	Buxton	244	W 1 - 0	Campbell 60	
40	9		A	Kendal Town	165	L 1 - 2	Burgess 65	16
41	13		H	F.C.Halifax Town	491	L 1 - 5	Beadle 60	
42	16		H	Ashton United	318	W 2 - 1	Burgess 59 Rose 62 (og)	16
43	19		A	Mickleover Sports	184	W 4 - 2	Beadle 23 Burgess 30 Campbell 49 Hackworth 66	
44	22		H	Northwich Victoria	337	L 2 - 4	Burgess 19 Davies 85	16
45	25		A	Stocksbridge P.S.	158	L 1 - 2	Beadle 45 (pen)	16

WORKSOP TOWN

Chairman: Jason Clark
Secretary: Keith Ilett (T) 07734 144 961 (E) k.ilett@sky.com
Additional Committee Members:
Chris Smith, Ian Smith, Kevin Keep.

Manager: Martin Macintosh
Programme Editor: Steve Jarvis (E) k.ilett@sky.com

Club Factfile

Founded: 1861 **Nickname:** Tigers
Previous Names: Not known
Previous Leagues: Midland Co. 1896-98, 1900-30, 49-60, 61-68, 69-74, Sheffield Amateur 1898-99, 1931-33, Central Combination 1933-35, Yorkshire 1935-39, Central Alliance1947-49, 60-61, Northern Premier 1968-69, 74-2004, Conference 2004-07

Club Colours (change): Amber and black/black/amber (Light blue and white stripes/navy/light blue)

Ground: Babbage Way, off Sandy Lane, Worksop S80 1TN (T) 07734 144 961
Capacity: NK **Seats:** NK **Covered:** NK **Clubhouse:** Yes **Shop:** NK

Directions
From M1 junc 31 take A57 Worksop after 7 miles carry on to by-pass at 3rd roundabout take 1st exit Sandy Lane industrial estate Ground 1ml on left at side of Tyre Centre.

From A1 junc34 take B6045 Blyth, then take A57 Worksop at 1st set of lights go straight on pass the Hospital on the left,next set of lights straight on, at the next set go under the bridge,the next set of lights turn right,100mts up the road 1st right then turn first left into the ground.

Previous Grounds: Central Avenue, Sandy Lane, shared with Ilkeston Town (New Manor Ground)

Record Attendance: 8,171 v Chesterfield - FA Cup 1925 (Central Avenue)
Record Victory: 20-0 v Staveley - 01/09/1984
Record Defeat: 1-11 v Hull City Reserves - 1955-56
Record Goalscorer: Kenny Clark - 287
Record Appearances: Kenny Clark - 347
Additional Records: Paid £5,000 to Grantham Town for Kirk Jackson
Received £47,000 from Sunderland for Jon Kennedy 2000

Senior Honours: Sheffield Senior Cup 1923-24, 52-53, 54-55, 65-66, 69-70,72-73, 81-82, 84-85, 94-95, 96-97, 2002-03.
Northern Premier League President's Cup 1985-86, 96-97, Chairman's Cup 2001-02.

10 YEAR RECORD

01-02	02-03	03-04	04-05	05-06	06-07	07-08	08-09	09-10	10-11
NP P 4	NP P 5	NP P 7	Conf N 17	Conf N 9	Conf N 21	NP P 9	NP P 17	NP P 18	NP P 7

WORKSOP TOWN

No.	Date	Comp	H/A	Opponents	Att:	Result	Goalscorers	Pos
1	Aug 21	NPL P	A	Nantwich Town	455	W 2 - 1	Mallon 23 Knox 63	5
2	25		H	Whitby Town	245	W 5 - 0	Mikel 49 KNOX 3 (79 84 86) Jackson 84	
3	28		H	Marine	235	L 1 - 2	Bettney 51	6
4	30		A	Retford United	501	W 3 - 0	Bettney 16 76 White 44 (og)	
5	Sept 4		H	Bradford P A.	320	D 3 - 3	Mallon 13 Knox 26 Tomlinson 80	3
6	7		A	North Ferriby United	182	L 0 - 3		
7	**11**	**FAC 1Q**	**A**	**Matlock Town**	**428**	**L 1 - 3**	**Shiels 42**	
8	18		H	Chasetown	278	W 2 - 0	Tomlinson 10 73	3
9	21		A	Northwich Victoria	454	L 1 - 3	Jackson 51	
10	25		A	Marine	302	W 4 - 2	Tomlinson 14 56 Jackson 16 40	2
11	Oct 2		A	Burscough	174	L 1 - 3	Jackson 70	7
12	9		H	Ashton Uited	269	W 3 - 0	TOMLINSON 3 (57 64 82 pen)	
13	13		H	Stocksbridge Park Steels	265	W 2 - 1	Jackson 42 Tomlinson 63	
14	**16**	**FAT 1Q**	**A**	**Market Drayton**	**147**	**D 1 - 1**	**Bacon 38**	
15	**20**	**FAT 1Qr**	**H**	**Market Drayton**	**159**	**W 1 - 0**	**Tomlinson 72**	
16	27		H	Matlock Town	360	W 2 - 1	Young 20 Tomlinson 63	4
17	**30**	**FAT 2Q**	**H**	**Lancaster City**	**262**	**W 2 - 1**	**Tomlinson 2 Bacon 21**	
18	Nov 6		A	Buxton	421	W 1 - 0	Tomlinson 78	2
19	13		H	Frickley Athletic	415	D 1 - 1	Tomlinson 40	5
20	**21**	**FAT 3Q**	**H**	**Stocksbridge P.S.**	**290**	**W 4 - 1**	**Jackson 12 Tomlinson 18 74 Bettney77**	
21	**Dec 14**	**FAT 1**	**H**	**Mansfield Town**	**682**	**L 0 - 5**		
22	Jan 3		A	Whitby Town	276	W 3 - 0	Tomlinson 18 (pen) Jackson 83 Thompson 90	
23	11		A	Stocksbridge P.S.	163	W 3 - 2	Tomlinson 7 89 Jackson 62	
24	15		A	Matlock Town	474	L 0 - 1		7
25	22		A	Kendal Town	245	L 1 - 2	Melling 43 (og)	9
26	26		H	Mickleover Sports	203	W 2 - 0	Shiels 25 Jackson 40	
27	29		H	Ossett Town	261	L 1 - 4	Bettney 49	6
28	Feb 12		H	F.C.Halifax Town	776	D 1 - 1	Suarez 21	8
29	15		A	Hucknall Town	135	W 2 - 1	Jackson 23 75	
30	March 1		A	F.C.Halifax Town	1318	D 0 - 0		
31	5		H	Burscough	232	D 1 - 1	Jackson 20	9
32	12		A	F.C.United	1886	L 1 - 2	Beckett 61	12
33	15		A	Colwyn Bay	269	L 1 - 2	Beckett 82	
34	17		H	Retford United	286	W 1 - 0	Tomlinson 78 (pen)	
35	19		A	Mickleover Sports	247	W 1 - 0	Beckett 15	10
36	22		A	Ossett Town	171	W 3 - 2	Wood 2 Tomlinson 21 75	
37	24		H	Norhwich Victoria	210	W 2 - 0	McIntosh 11 Jackson 90	
38	26		H	Colwyn Bay	275	L 0 - 1		8
39	29		A	Frickey Athletic	262	L 0 - 1		
40	April 2		H	F.C.United	892	L 1 - 2	Cotterill 8	10
41	6		H	North Ferriby United	162	W 4 - 1	Bettney 9 Beckett 18 Duncum 48 Tomlinson 77	
42	9		A	Ashton United	164	L 1 - 3	Duncum 65	10
43	11		H	Kendall Town	165	L 1 - 2	Tomlinson 82	
44	13		H	Nantwich Town	146	D 0 - 0		
45	16		H	Buxton	285	W 3 - 0	Shiels 2 Suarez 10 34	8
46	19		A	Chasetown	419	W 6 - 2	Thompson 45 Young 48 McIntosh 75 89 Tomlinson 79 Jackson 90	
47	23		A	Bradford P.A.	528	L 0 - 4		7
48	25		H	Hucknall Town	265	W 2 - 0	Jackson 54 Tomlinson 90	9

A.F.C. FYLDE

Chairman: David Haythornthwaite
Secretary: Martin Benson **(T)** 07545 735 154 **(E)** info@afcfylde.co.uk
Additional Committee Members:
Dai Davis, Stuart King, Martin Booker, Eric Picton

Manager: Kelham O'Hanlon
Programme Editor: Martin Booker **(E)** info@afcfylde.co.uk

Back Row (L-R): Baldwin (Kit man), Stopforth, Allen, Thorpe, Betts, Whiteside, Steel, MacDonald, Doughty, Stringfellow, Waddington, Wilson, Fraser (Physio).
Front Row: Clarkson (Reserve Team Coach), Penswick, Barnes, Heywood, Kay, Steel, Fuller (Assistant Manager), Mercer (Capt), O'Hanlon, Mercer, Booth, Swarbrick, Jarvis, McNiven (1st Team Coach), Mitchell (Goalkeeping Coach).

Club Factfile

Founded: 1988 **Nickname:**
Previous Names: Wesham FC and Kirkham Town amalgamated in 1988 to form Kirkham & Wesham > 2008
Previous Leagues: West Lancashire, North West Counties 2007-09

Club Colours (change): All white (red and blue stripes/blue/blue)

Ground: Kellamergh Park, Bryning Lane, Warton, Preston PR4 1TN **(T)** 01772 682 593
Capacity: 1,426 **Seats:** 282 **Covered:** 282 **Clubhouse:** Yes **Shop:** Yes

Directions
EXIT via Junction 3 M55 (signposted A585 Fleetwood/Kirkham). Up approach and turn left towards signs for Kirkham.In around 3/4 mile you will approach a roundabout. Then follow the signs for Wrea Green and Lytham St. Annes (2nd exit) B5259.After another 500 yards you will approach a new roundabout (go straight on) and 1/4 mile you will go over main Preston/Blackpool railway bridge and drop down almost immediately to a small mini roundabout (pub on left called Kingfisher). Carry on straight over this and up to main roundabout (another 200 yards) at junction of main Preston/Blackpool A583. Go straight over roundabout and drive on into Wrea Green Village.At 2nd mini roundabout in the centre of the village (Church on right l) take left turn into Bryning Lane, signposted on The Green (small white signpost) to Warton (2 miles).The Green will now be on your right as you exit out of the village and in around 1.8 miles you will come to the Birley Arms Pub on your left. Turn immediately left into The Birley Arms Pub Car park and continue to drive through the car park TO BOTTOM LEFT CORNER until you reach access road and park in the Main Club Car Park located behind the Main Stand. Approximate mileage from motorway to the ground is 5 miles and will take around 10 minutes to travel in a car.

Previous Grounds: Coronation Road > 2006

Record Attendance: 1,217 v New Mills - North West Counties 09/05/2009
Record Victory: Not known
Record Defeat: Not known
Record Goalscorer: Not known
Record Appearances: Not known
Additional Records:

Senior Honours: West Lancashire League 1999-2000, 00-01, 01-02, 03-04, 04-05, 05-06, 06-07.
FA Vase 2007-08.
North West Counties League 2008-09

10 YEAR RECORD

01-02		02-03		03-04		04-05		05-06		06-07		07-08		08-09		09-10		10-11	
WYkP	1	WYkP	2	WYkP	1	WYkP	1	WYkP	1	WYkP	1	NWC2	2	NWCP	1	NP1N	13	NP1N	5

BAMBER BRIDGE

Chairman: David Spencer
Secretary: George Halliwell **(T)** 07970 042 954 **(E)**
Additional Committee Members:
Dennis Allen, Terry Gammans, George Halliwell, Geoff Wright, Gerry Lawson, Dave Rowland.
Manager: Neil Crowe
Programme Editor: Dave Rowland **(E)**

Club Factfile

Founded: 1952 **Nickname:** Brig
Previous Names: Not known
Previous Leagues: Preston & District 1952-90, North West Counties 1990-93

Club Colours (change): White/black/black (All yellow)

Ground: Irongate Ground, Brownedge Road, Bamber Bridge PR5 6UX **(T)** 01772 909 690
Capacity: 3,000 **Seats:** 554 **Covered:** 800 **Clubhouse:** Yes **Shop:** Yes

Directions
Junction 29, A6 (Bamber Bridge by-pass)onto London Way. First roundabout take 3rd exit Brownedge Road (East) then take first right. Ground on left at the bottom of the road.

Previous Grounds: King George V, Higher Wallton 1952-86

Record Attendance: 2,300 v Czech Republic - Pre Euro '96 friendly
Record Victory: 8-0 v Curzon Ashton - North West Counties 1994-95
Record Defeat: Not known
Record Goalscorer: Not known
Record Appearances: Not known
Additional Records: Paid £10,000 to Horwich RMI for Mark Edwards
Received £15,000 from Wigan Athletic for Tony Black 1995

Senior Honours: ATDC Lancashire Trophy 1994-95.
Northern Premier League Premier Division 1995-96, Challenge Cup 1995-96.

10 YEAR RECORD

01-02	02-03	03-04	04-05	05-06	06-07	07-08	08-09	09-10	10-11
NP P 23	NP 1 13	NP 1 10	NP P 21	NP 1 13	NP 1 13	NP1N 5	NP1N 11	NP1N 14	NP1N 7

CAMMELL LAIRD

Chairman: George Higham
Secretary: Anthony R Wood **(T)** 07931 761 429 **(E)** Nk
Additional Committee Members:
George Higham, Chris Wood, Janet Griffiths, Steve Major, John Lynch.

Manager: Tony Sullivan
Programme Editor: Debbie Smaje **(E)** Nk

Club Factfile

Founded: 1907 **Nickname:** Lairds
Previous Names: Not known
Previous Leagues: West Cheshire, North West Counties

Club Colours (change): All royal blue (All yellow)

Ground: St Peter's Road, Rock Ferry, Birkenhead CH42 1PY **(T)** 0151 645 3132
Capacity: 2,000 **Seats:** 150 **Covered:** Yes **Clubhouse:** Yes **Shop:** Yes

Directions
FROM CHESTER: M53, leave at Junction 5, take third exit on to A41 and travel towards Birkenhead. At New Ferry signpost take B5136 towards New Ferry. After approx 1 mile at sign for Lairds Sports Club, turn right down Proctor Road, ground on the left.
FROM LIVERPOOL: Take the Birkenhead Tunnel then A41 signposted North Wales for approx 1 mile. At large roundabout take B5136 signposted New Ferry, Rock Ferry. Follow until 2nd set of traffic lights at Abbotsford pub. Turn left then first right into St Peters Road. Ground at bottom of road on right.

Previous Grounds: Not known

Record Attendance: 1,700 v Harwich & Parkeston - FA Vase 5th Round 1990-91
Record Victory: Not known
Record Defeat: Not known
Record Goalscorer: Not known
Record Appearances: Not known
Additional Records:

Senior Honours: North West Counties League Division 2, League Cup and Trophy 2004-05, Division 1 2005-06.
West Cheshire League x19 (Most recently 2000-01). Cheshire Amateur Cup x11.
Wirral Senior Cup.

10 YEAR RECORD

01-02		02-03		03-04		04-05		05-06		06-07		07-08		08-09		09-10		10-11	
WCh1	2	WCh1	3	WCh1	2	NWC2	1	NWC1	1	NP 1	2	NP1S	2	NP P	18	NP1S	16	NP1N	19

CLITHEROE

Chairman: Anne Barker
Secretary: Colin Wilson **(T)** 07949 031 039 **(E)** wilsoncfc424370@aol.com
Additional Committee Members:
Andrew Jackson

Manager: Carl Garner
Programme Editor: Chris Musson **(E)** wilsoncfc424370@aol.com

Club Factfile

Founded: 1877 **Nickname:** The Blues
Previous Names: Not known
Previous Leagues: Blackburn & District, Lancashire Combination 1903-04, 05-10, 25-82, North West Counties 1982-85

Club Colours (change): Blue/blue/red (All red)

Ground: Shawbridge, off Pendle Road, Clitheroe, Lancashire BB7 1DZ **(T)** 01200 444 487
Capacity: 2,400 **Seats:** 250 **Covered:** 1,400 **Clubhouse:** Yes **Shop:**

Directions
M6 junction 31, A59 to Clitheroe (17 miles) at 5th roundabout turn left after half a mile at Pendle Road. Ground is one mile behind Bridge Inn on the right.

Previous Grounds: Not known

Record Attendance: 2,050 v Mangotsfield - FA Vase Semi-final 1995-96
Record Victory: Not known
Record Defeat: Not known
Record Goalscorer: Don Francis
Record Appearances: Lindsey Wallace - 670
Additional Records: Received £45,000 from Crystal Palace for Carlo Nash

Senior Honours: North West Counties League 1984-85, 2003-04.
Lancashire Challenge Trophy 1984-85. East Lancashire Floodlit Trophy 1994-95.

10 YEAR RECORD

01-02	02-03	03-04	04-05	05-06	06-07	07-08	08-09	09-10	10-11
NWC1 6	NWC1 2	NWC1 1	NP 1 19	NP 1 16	NP 1 16	NP1N 13	NP1N 12	NP1N 8	NP1N 6

CURZON ASHTON

Chairman: Harry Galloway
Secretary: Robert Hurst **(T)** 07713 252 310 **(E)** office@curzon-ashton.co.uk
Additional Committee Members:
Harry Twamley, Ronnie Capstick, Simon Shuttleworth, Paul Price, James Newall, David Jones, Steve Ball, Ian Seymour, Nigel Seymour, Ron Walber, Wayne Salkeld.
Manager: John Flanagan
Programme Editor: Ian Seymour **(E)** office@curzon-ashton.co.uk

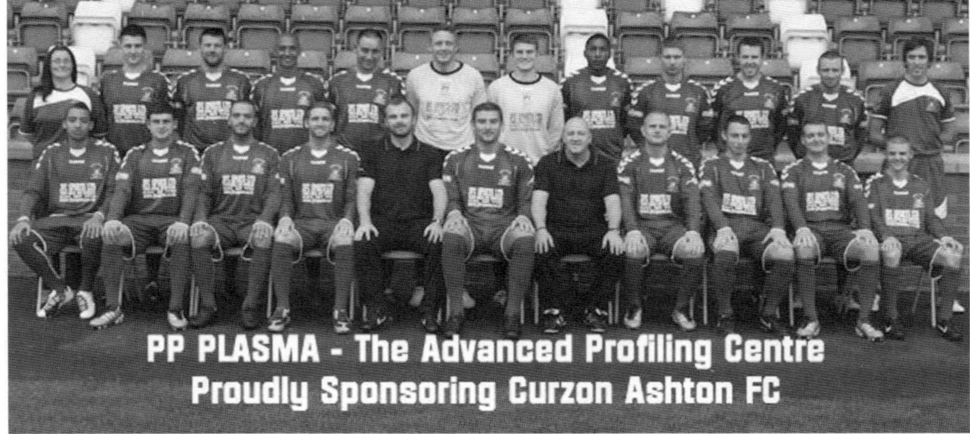

Club Factfile

Founded: 1963 **Nickname:** Not known
Previous Names: None
Previous Leagues: Manchester Amateur, Manchester > 1978, Cheshire County 1978-82,
North West Counties 1982-87, 98-2007, Northern Premier 1987-97, Northern Counties East 1997-98,

Club Colours (change): All royal blue (All red)

Ground: Tameside Stadium, Richmond Street, Ashton-u-Lyme OL7 9HG **(T)** 0161 330 6033
Capacity: 5,000 **Seats:** 504 **Covered:** Yes **Clubhouse:** Yes **Shop:** Yes

Directions
From Stockport (south) direction Leave the M60 at junc 23 (Ashton-U-Lyne). Turn left at the top of the slip road, go straight through the next set of lights, and bear right (onto Lord Sheldon Way) at the next set. Continue on this road until you come to a set of traffic lights with the Cineworld Cinema on your right. Turn left here onto Richmond St. Over the bridge, across the mini-roundabout and then first left down to the ground. From Oldham (north) direction Leave the M60 at junc 23 (Ashton-U-Lyne) and turn right at the top of the slip road signposted A635 Manchester. Turn right at the second set of traffic lights, sign posted Ashton Moss, and then follow directions as from the south.

Previous Grounds: Katherine Street > 204, Stalybridge Celtic FC 2004-06

Record Attendance: 1,826 v Stamford - FA Vase Semi-final
Record Victory: 7-0 v Ashton United
Record Defeat: 0-8 v Bamber Bridge
Record Goalscorer: Alan Sykes
Record Appearances: Alan Sykes
Additional Records:

Senior Honours: Manchester Premier Cup x5

10 YEAR RECORD

01-02	02-03	03-04	04-05	05-06	06-07	07-08	08-09	09-10	10-11
NWC1 13	NWC1 18	NWC1 7	NWC1 4	NWC1 7	NWC1 2	NP1N 4	NP1N 4	NP1N 3	NP1N 4

DURHAM CITY

Chairman: Austin Carney
Secretary: Kevin Walters (T) 0191 385 4313 (E) kevin@jeck.co.uk
Additional Committee Members:
Ian Walker, Stewart Dawson, Terry Brown, Brian Johnson, James Cairns, Simon Carey.

Manager: Lee Collings
Programme Editor: Kevin Hewitt (E) kevin@jeck.co.uk

Club Factfile

Founded: 1949 **Nickname:** City
Previous Names: Original club founded in 1918 disbanded in 1938 and reformed in 1949
Previous Leagues: Victory 1918-19, North Eastern 1919-21, 28-38, Football League 1921-28, Wearside 1938-39, 50-51, Northern 1951-2008

Club Colours (change): Yellow & blue halves/blue/blue & yellow (White/white/red & white)

Ground: The Durham UTS Arena, New Ferens Park, Belmont Ind.Est. DH1 1GG (T) 0191 386 9616
Capacity: 2,700 **Seats:** 270 **Covered:** 750 **Clubhouse:** Yes **Shop:** No

Directions
Leave the A1M at J62 (signed Durham City) At the top of the slip road turn left.
After about 1/2 mile bear left (signed Belmont + Dragonville).
At the top of the slip road turn left.
At traffic lights turn left then take the 2nd left, the stadium is on your right.

Previous Grounds: Holiday Park 1921-38, Ferens Park 1949-94

Record Attendance: 2,750 v Whitley Bay - FA Vase Semi-final 2001-02
Record Victory: Not known
Record Defeat: Not known
Record Goalscorer: Not known
Record Appearances: Joe Raine - 552
Additional Records: Lee Ludlow scored 45 goals in one season

Senior Honours: Northern League 1994-95, 2007-08. Northern Premier League Division 1 North 2008-09, Chairman's Cup 2008-09.

10 YEAR RECORD

01-02	02-03	03-04	04-05	05-06	06-07	07-08	08-09	09-10	10-11
NL 1 6	NL 1 5	NL 1 2	NL 1 6	NL 1 11	NL 1 8	NL 1 1	NP1N 1	NP P 20	NP1N 17

FARSLEY A.F.C.

Chairman: John Palmer
Secretary: Joshua Greaves **(T)** 07725 999 758 **(E)** fcfcsecretary@live.com
Additional Committee Members:
J Farrell, Mrs D Farrell, Mrs M Palmer, P Palmer, S Palmer.

Manager: Neil Parsley
Programme Editor: Phil Morris **(E)** fcfcsecretary@live.com

Club Factfile

Founded: 2010 **Nickname:** The Villagers
Previous Names: Farsley Celtic > 2010
Previous Leagues: Northern Counties East 2010-11.

Club Colours (change): All blue (All green)

Ground: Throstle Nest, Newlands, Pudsey, Leeds, LS28 5BE **(T)** 0113 255 7292
Capacity: 4,000 **Seats:** 300 **Covered:** 1,500 **Clubhouse:** Yes **Shop:** Yes

Directions
Farsley is sandwiched between Leeds and Bradford approximately 1 mile from the junction of the Leeds Outer Ring Road (A6110) and the A647 towards Bradford. At the junction, take the B6157 towards Leeds, passing the police station on the left hand side. At New Street (the junction cornered by Go Outdoors) turn left. Newlands is approximately 300 yards on the right. Throstle Nest is situated at the end of Newlands with parking available outside the ground.

Previous Grounds: Not known

Record Attendance: None
Record Victory: 8-0 v Arnold Town (H) Northern Counties East Premier 2010-11.
Record Defeat: 5-1 v Tadcaster Albion, President's Cup Final 27/04/11.
Record Goalscorer: Not known
Record Appearances: Not known
Additional Records: None

Senior Honours: Northern Counties East Premier Division 2010-11.

10 YEAR RECORD

01-02	02-03	03-04	04-05	05-06	06-07	07-08	08-09	09-10	10-11
									NCEP 1

GARFORTH TOWN

Chairman: Tom Murray
Secretary: Paul Bracewell **(T)** 07870 993 628 **(E)** info@garforthtown.com
Additional Committee Members:
Norman Hebbron, Simon Clifford, Gillian Clifford, Brian Close, Jane Close, Steve Nichol.

Manager: Steve Nichol
Programme Editor: Jason Broadbelt **(E)** info@garforthtown.com

Club Factfile

Founded: 1964 **Nickname:** The Miners
Previous Names: Garforth Miners 1964-85
Previous Leagues: Leeds Sunday Combination 1964-72, West Yorkshire 1972-78, Yorkshire 1978-83, Northern Counties East 1983-2007
Club Colours (change): Yellow/blue/white (Blue and white stripe/white/blue)

Ground: Genix Healthcare Stadium, Cedar Ridge, Garforth, Leeds LS25 2PF **(T)** 0113 287 7145
Capacity: 3,000 **Seats:** **Covered:** 200 **Clubhouse:** Yes **Shop:** Yes

Directions
From North: travel south on A1 and join M1. Turn off at 1st junc (47). From South: M1 to junc 47. From Leeds area: join M1 at junc 44 or 46 and turn off at junc 47. From West: M62 to junc 29, join M1 and off at junc 47. From junc 47: take turning signe 'Garforth' (A642). Approx. 200 yds turn left into housing estate opposite White House. (Cedar Ridge). Stadium at end of lane. From the South (alternative): A1, turn off on to A63 signposted 'Leeds' immediately after 'Boot & Shoe' Public House. At 1st roundabout turn right on to A656 and follow to next roundabout. Take 1st left on to A642 (Garforth) and follow from M1 junc 47.

Previous Grounds: Not known

Record Attendance: 1,385 v Tadcaster Albion - Socrates debut - Northern Counties East League record
Record Victory: Not known
Record Defeat: Not known
Record Goalscorer: Simeon Bambrook - 67
Record Appearances: Philip Matthews - 1982-93
Additional Records:

Senior Honours: Northern Counties East Division 1 1997-98

10 YEAR RECORD

01-02	02-03	03-04	04-05	05-06	06-07	07-08	08-09	09-10	10-11
NCEP 20	NCEP 20	NCE1 6	NCE1 2	NCEP 10	NP1N 4	NP1N 10	NP1N 16	NP1N 20	NP1N 13

HARROGATE RAILWAY ATHLETIC

Chairman: Mick Gray
Secretary: David Shepherd **(T)** 07816 986 799 **(E)** mail4rail@ntlworld.com
Additional Committee Members:
Paddy Hall, David Greenwood

Manager: Nigel Danby
Programme Editor: David Shepherd **(E)** mail4rail@ntlworld.com

Club Factfile

Founded: 1935 **Nickname:** The Rail
Previous Names: Not known
Previous Leagues: West Yorkshire, Harrogate & District, Yorkshire 1955-73, 80-82, Northern Counties East 1982-2006

Club Colours (change): Red/green/red (White/black/white)

Ground: Station View, Starbeck, Harrogate, North Yorkshire HG2 7JA **(T)** 01423 883 104
Capacity: 3,500 **Seats:** 800 **Covered:** 600 **Clubhouse:** Yes **Shop:** No

Directions
From All Areas I would suggest using the M1 A1 Link Road heading North. Once on the A1 North stay on it until Junction 47. Exit at Junction 47 and take the 1st Exit at the Roundabout A59 heading towards Knaresborough and Harrogate. At the next Roundabout take the 3rd exit A59 Knaresborough. Stay on the A59 through Knaresborough and on towards Harrogate, after approx 1 mile from Knaresborough you will enter Starbeck. Proceed through Starbeck over the Railway Crossing. Station View is the 1st Right after the Railway Crossing. The Ground is at the far end of Station View. If you are coming from Harrogate towards Knaresborough on the A59 turn left immediately prior to pelican crossing just before the Railway Crossing. The Ground is at the far end of Station View.

Previous Grounds: Not known

Record Attendance: 3,500 v Bristol City - FA Cup 2nd Round 2002-03
Record Victory: Not known
Record Defeat: Not known
Record Goalscorer: Not known
Record Appearances: Not known
Additional Records: Received £1,000 from Guiseley for Colin Hunter

Senior Honours: Northern Counties East Division 2 North & League cup 1983-84, Division 1 1989-99.

10 YEAR RECORD

01-02	02-03	03-04	04-05	05-06	06-07	07-08	08-09	09-10	10-11
NCEP 5	NCEP 10	NCEP 12	NCEP 3	NCEP 3	NP 1 12	NP1N 12	NP1N 18	NP1N 17	NP1N 20

LANCASTER CITY

Chairman: Mick Hoyle
Secretary: Barry Newsham **(T)** 07539 615 866 **(E)** lancastercityfc@btinternet.com
Additional Committee Members:
Stuart Houghton, John Bagguley, David Needham, Ian Sharp, Norman Wilson, Steve Ball, Eric Williams.
Manager: Tony Hesketh
Programme Editor: Barry Newsham **(E)** lancastercityfc@btinternet.com

Club Factfile

Founded: 1905 **Nickname:** Dolly Blues
Previous Names: Not known
Previous Leagues: Lancashire Combination 1905-70, Northern Premier League 1970-82, 87-2004, North West Counties 1982-87, Conference 2004-07
Club Colours (change): Blue/white/blue (Yellow/blue/yellow)

Ground: Giant Axe, West Road, Lancaster LA1 5PE **(T)** 01524 382 238
Capacity: 3,064 **Seats:** 513 **Covered:** 900 **Clubhouse:** Yes **Shop:** Yes

Directions
From the South: Exit M6 at Junction 33. At roundabout take the second exit onto the A6, pass through Galgate and then Lancaster University on the right until the next roundabout. Take the second main exit into Lancaster and follow signs for the railway station. At the traffic lights by Waterstones Bookshop turn immediately left. Take the second right onto Station Road and follow downhill on West Road and take the first right into the ground. From the North: Exit M6 at Junction 34 and turn left onto the A683. Follow signs for railway station into City around the one way system. Move over to the right hand side lane at the police station and through traffic lights. Manoeuvre into the left-hand lane until traffic lights at Waterstones Bookshop. Follow directions as from the south.

Previous Grounds: Not known

Record Attendance: 7,500 v Carlisle United - FA Cup 1936
Record Victory: 8-0 v Leyland Motors (A) - 1983-84
Record Defeat: 0-10 v Matlock Town - Northern Premier League Division 1 1973-74
Record Goalscorer: David Barnes - 130
Record Appearances: Edgar J Parkinson - 591
Additional Records: Paid £6,000 to Droylsden for Jamie Tandy
Received £25,000 from Birmingham City for Chris Ward
Senior Honours: Lancashire Junior Cup (ATS Challenge Trophy) 1927-28, 28-29, 30-31, 33-34, 51-52, 74-75.
Northern Premier League Division 1 1995-96.

10 YEAR RECORD

01-02	02-03	03-04	04-05	05-06	06-07	07-08	08-09	09-10	10-11
NP P 3	NP P 17	NP P 8	Conf N 13	Conf N 15	Conf N 24	NP1N 11	NP1N 7	NP1N 2	NP1N 8

MOSSLEY

Chairman: Vacant
Secretary: Harry Hulmes **(T)** 07944 856 343 **(E)** harry.hulmes@btinternet.com
Additional Committee Members:
Steve Burgess, Colin Fielding, Mark Griffin, John Lamer, Bob Murphy, Joanne Blackshaw, John Cawthorne, Elaine Field, Colin Fielding, Linda Hughes, Steve Porter, Steve Tague.
Manager: Gareth McClelland
Programme Editor: John Cawthorne **(E)** harry.hulmes@btinternet.com

Club Factfile

Founded: 1903 **Nickname:** Lilywhites
Previous Names: Park Villa 1903-04, Mossley Juniors
Previous Leagues: Ashton, South East Lancashire, Lancashire Combination 1918-19, Cheshire County 1919-72, Northern Premier 1972-95, North West Counties 1995-2004

Club Colours (change): All white (Orange/black/black)

Ground: Seel Park, Market Street, Mossley, Lancashire OL5 0ES **(T)** 01457 832 369
Capacity: 4,500 **Seats:** 200 **Covered:** 1,500 **Clubhouse:** Yes **Shop:** Yes

Directions
Exit M60 Junction 23 following A635 Ashton-under-Lyne. Take 3rd exit off roundabout then 3rd exit off next roundabout (Asda) and then 3rd exit off next roundabout signed Mossley A670. At junction turn right on to Mossley Rd through traffic lights. After approx 2.5 miles drop down hill entering Mossley town centre. Passing supermarket on left turn right before next traffic lights. Continue up the hill and left into Market Street. Ground is approx 200 yards on the left.

Previous Grounds: Not known

Record Attendance: 7,000 v Stalybridge Celtic 1950
Record Victory: Not known
Record Defeat: Not known
Record Goalscorer: David Moore - 235 (1974-84)
Record Appearances: Jimmy O'Connor - 613 (1972-87)
Additional Records: Paid £2,300 to Altrincham for Phil Wilson
Received £25,000 from Everton for Eamonn O'Keefe

Senior Honours: Northern Premier League 1978-79, 79-80, Challenge Cup 78-79, Division 1 2005-06

10 YEAR RECORD

01-02	02-03	03-04	04-05	05-06	06-07	07-08	08-09	09-10	10-11
NWC1 8	NWC1 3	NWC1 2	NP 1 7	NP 1 1	NP P 20	NP1N 15	NP1N 10	NP1N 7	NP1N 15

OSSETT ALBION

Chairman: Steven Hanks
Secretary: Alan Nash **(T)** 07585 952 295 **(E)** ossettalbion@sky.com
Additional Committee Members:
N Wigglesworth,P Hanks,S Chambers,L Burns,J Bowker,A Lightfoot,J Hirst,K Fletcher,J Ferguson,M Baker, N Yarrow,P Riordan,J Butterworth,J Shaw,P Eaton,J Murgatroyd,J McGinty,A Weatherill,S Garside.
Manager: Lloyd Fellow & Paul Watson
Programme Editor: Stephen Hanks **(E)** ossettalbion@sky.com

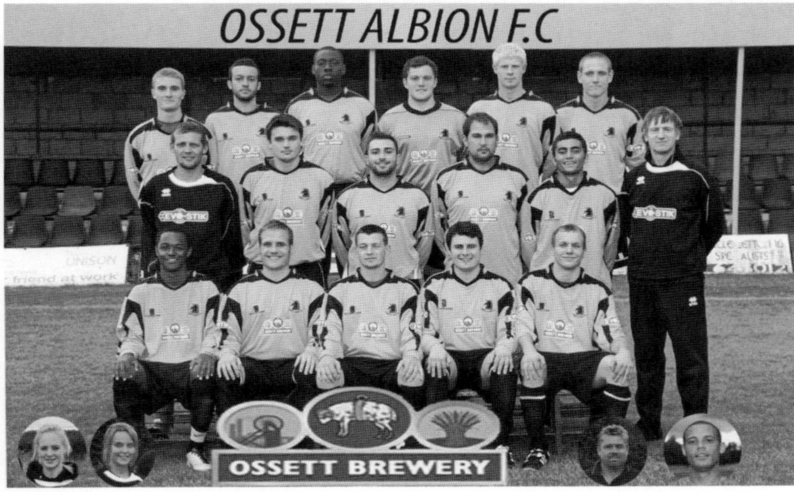

Club Factfile

Founded: 1944 **Nickname:** Albion
Previous Names: Not known
Previous Leagues: Heavy Woollen Area 1944-49, West Riding County Amateur 1949-50, West Yorkshire 1950-57, Yorkshire 1957-82, Northern Counties East 1982-2004
Club Colours (change): Old gold/black/black (All white)

Ground: The Warehouse Systems Stadium, Dimple Wells, Ossett, Yorkshire **(T)** 01924 273 746
Capacity: 3,000 **Seats:** Yes **Covered:** 750 **Clubhouse:** Yes **Shop:** Yes

Directions
From M1 Junction 40: Follow Wakefield signs for 200 yards. Turn right at traffic lights (Holiday Inn on the corner). At the end of Queens Drive turn right and then 2nd left onto Southdale Road. At the end of Southdale Road turn right then immediately left onto Dimple Wells Road, the ground is facing. NOTE: There is a weight limit on Southdale Road. Coaches will need to continue on Station Road to the end, turn left, then at the end left again. Take 1st right onto Priory Road following for 200 yards turning left twice.

Previous Grounds: Fearn House

Record Attendance: 1,200 v Leeds United - Opening of floodlights 1986
Record Victory: 12-0 v British Ropes (H) - Yorkshire League Division 2 06/05/1959
Record Defeat: 2-11 v Swillington (A) - West Yorkshire League Division 1 25/04/1956
Record Goalscorer: John Balmer
Record Appearances: Peter Eaton - 800+ (22 years)
Additional Records:

Senior Honours: Northern Counties East League Division 1 1986-87, Premier Division 1998-99, 2003-04, League Cup 1983-84, 2002-03. West Riding County Cup x4.

10 YEAR RECORD

01-02	02-03	03-04	04-05	05-06	06-07	07-08	08-09	09-10	10-11
NP 1 22	NCEP 5	NCEP 1	NP 1 12	NP 1 14	NP 1 11	NP1N 6	NP1N 6	NP1N 21	NP1N 22

OSSETT TOWN

Chairman: Graham Firth
Secretary: Simon Turfrey (T) 07773 649 251 (E) simonturfrey@aol.com
Additional Committee Members:
Martin Voakes, Tristan Jackson, Bruce Saul.

Manager: Philip Sharp
Programme Editor: Bruce Saul (E) simonturfrey@aol.com

Club Factfile

Founded: 1936 **Nickname:** Town
Previous Names: Not known
Previous Leagues: Leeds 1936-39, Yorkshire 1945-82, Northern Counties East 1983-99

Club Colours (change): All red (All blue)

Ground: Ingfield, Prospect Road, Ossett, Wakefield WF5 9HA (T) 01924 280 028
Capacity: 4,000 **Seats:** 360 **Covered:** 1,000 **Clubhouse:** Yes **Shop:** Yes

Directions
From M1 Junction 40: Take A638 signposted Ossett Town Centre. Take first left off A638 onto Wakefield Road, sixth left turn into Dale Street (B6120) to traffic lights. Turn left at lights. The Ground is in front of you opposite the bus station. The entrance to the Ground is just before the Esso petrol station.

Previous Grounds: Not known

Record Attendance: 2,600 v Manchester United - Friendly 1989
Record Victory: 10-1 v Harrogate RA (H) - Northern Counties East 27/04/1993
Record Defeat: 0-7 v Easington Colliery - FA Vase 08/10/1983
Record Goalscorer: Dave Leadbitter
Record Appearances: Steve Worsfold
Additional Records: Received £1,350 from Swansea Town for Dereck Blackburn

Senior Honours: West Riding County Cup 1958-59, 81-82

10 YEAR RECORD

01-02	02-03	03-04	04-05	05-06	06-07	07-08	08-09	09-10	10-11
NP 1 2	NP 1 20	NP 1 14	NP P 16	NP P 11	NP P 10	NP P 18	NP P 12	NP P 19	NP P 21

PRESCOT CABLES

Chairman: Tony Zeverona
Secretary: Doug Lace (T) 07753 143 273 (E) prescotcables@hotmail.com
Additional Committee Members:
D Bellairs, G Conway, M Flaherty, P Kneale, D Lace, N Parr.

Manager: David Ridler
Programme Editor: Paul Watkinson (E) prescotcables@hotmail.com

Club Factfile

Founded: 1884 **Nickname:** Tigers
Previous Names: Prescot > 1995
Previous Leagues: Liverpool County Combination, Lancashire Combination 1897-98, 1918-20, 27-33, 36-76, Mid Cheshire 1976-78, Cheshire County 1978-82, North West Counties 1982-2003
Club Colours (change): Amber/black/black (All sky blue)

Ground: Valerie Park, Eaton Street, Prescot L34 6HD (T) 0151 430 0507
Capacity: 3,000 **Seats:** 500 **Covered:** 600 **Clubhouse:** Yes **Shop:** Yes

Directions
From North: M6 to Junction 26, onto M58 to Junction 3. Follow A570 to junction with A580 (East Lancs Road). (Approach junction in right hand lane of the two lanes going straight on). Cross A580 and take first road on right (Bleak Hill Road). Follow this road through to Prescot (2 miles). At traffic lights turn right, straight on at large roundabout (do not follow route onto Prescot by-pass) and right at next lights. 100 yards turn right at Hope and Anchor pub into Hope Street. Club will be in sight at bottom of road. **From South:** M6 to Junction 21a (M62 junction 10). Follow M62 towards Liverpool, to junction 7. Follow A57 to Rainhill and Prescot. Through traffic lights at Fusilier pub, 100 yards turn right at Hope and Anchor pub (as above). **From East:** Follow M62 as described in 'From South' or A580 East Lancs Road to Junction with A570 (Rainford by-pass), turn left and take first right. Follow route as 'From North'.

Previous Grounds: Not known

Record Attendance: 8,122 v Ashton National - 1932
Record Victory: 18-3 v Great Harwood - 1954-55
Record Defeat: 1-12 v Morecambe - 1936-37
Record Goalscorer: Freddie Crampton
Record Appearances: Harry Grisedale
Additional Records:

Senior Honours: Lancashire Combination 1956-57. North West Counties League 2002-03.
Liverpool Non-League Cup x4. Liverpool Challenge Cup x6.

10 YEAR RECORD

01-02	02-03	03-04	04-05	05-06	06-07	07-08	08-09	09-10	10-11
NWC1 2	NWC1 1	NP 1 12	NP P 5	NP P 13	NP P 14	NP P 13	NP P 22	NP1N 15	NP1N 21

RADCLIFFE BOROUGH

Chairman: Vacant
Secretary: John Walker **(T)** 0782 464 7289 **(E)** rbfc@hotmail.co.uk
Additional Committee Members:
Graham Fielding, David Chalmers

Manager: Benny Phillips
Programme Editor: John Walker **(E)** rbfc@hotmail.co.uk

Back Row (L-R): Reece Kelly, Steve Howson, Griff Jones, Ben Wharton, Nick Culkin, Mark Jones, Simon Kelly, James Mullineux, Daniel Thomas, Craig Flowers.
Front Row: Shaun Connor, Alastair Brown, Jordan Hadfield, Dave Sherlock, Tom Brooks, Steve Burke and Ryan Broadhead.

Club Factfile

Founded: 1949 **Nickname:** Boro
Previous Names: Not known
Previous Leagues: South East Lancashire, Manchester 1953-63, Lancashire Combination 1963-71, Cheshire County 1971-82, North West Counties 1982-97

Club Colours (change): Blue & black stripes/black/blue (Red and black stripes/black/white)

Ground: Stainton Park, Pilkington Road, Radcliffe, Lancashire M26 3PE **(T)** 0161 724 8346
Capacity: 3,000 **Seats:** 350 **Covered:** 1,000 **Clubhouse:** Yes **Shop:** Yes

Directions
M62 junction 17 – follow signs for 'Whitefield' and 'Bury'.
Take A665 to Radcliffe via by-pass to Bolton Road. Signposted to turn right into Unsworth Street opposite Turf Hotel.
The Stadium is on the left approximately half a mile turning Colshaw Close East.

Previous Grounds: Not known

Record Attendance: 2,495 v York City - FA Cup 1st Round 2000-01
Record Victory: Not known
Record Defeat: Not known
Record Goalscorer: Ian Lunt - 147
Record Appearances: David Bean - 401
Additional Records: Paid £5,000 to Buxton for Gary Walker 1991
Received £20,000 from Shrewsbury Town for Jody Banim 2003

Senior Honours: North West Counties 19984-85. Northern Premier League Division 1 1996-97.

10 YEAR RECORD

01-02		02-03		03-04		04-05		05-06		06-07		07-08		08-09		09-10		10-11	
NP 1	5	NP 1	3	NP P	20	NP P	9	NP P	18	NP P	21	NP1N	16	NP1N	16	NP1N	10	NP1N	18

SALFORD CITY

Chairman: Darren Quick
Secretary: Andrew Giblin (T) 07867 823 713 (E) andrewgiblin@aol.com
Additional Committee Members:
H Blears, D Russell, D Dore, J Barton, D Brent, P Byram, G Carter, L Flint, B Gaskill, T Gaskill, I Jolly, I Malone, F McCauley, P Raven, G Russell, J Simpson, P Smith, B Taylor, D Taylor, D Wilson.
Manager: Rhodri Giggs
Programme Editor: Billy Lines-Rowlands (E) andrewgiblin@aol.com

Back row (L-R): Jamie Tandy, Dean Cooper, Billy McCartney, Andy Robertson, Rhodri Giggs, Steve Foster
Front row: Darren Hockenhull, Alex Mortimer (c), Matt Cross, Gareth Thomas, Ashley Kelly

Club Factfile

Founded: 1940 **Nickname:** Ammies
Previous Names: Salford Central 1940-63, Salford Amateurs 1963 until merger with Anson Villa, Salford F.C. > 1990
Previous Leagues: Manchester 1963-80, Cheshire County 1980-82, North West Counties 1982-2008

Club Colours (change): Tangerine/black/tangerine (Lime green and white stripes/lime green/lime green)

Ground: Moor Lane, Kersal, Salford, Manchester M7 3PZ (T) 0161 792 6287
Capacity: 8,000 **Seats:** 260 **Covered:** 600 **Clubhouse:** Yes **Shop:** No

Directions
M62 to Junction 17 (Prestwich, Whitefield). Take A56 Bury New Road towards Manchester. Continue through four sets of traffic lights. Turn right into Moor Lane. Ground 500 yards on left. Take first left after ground (Oaklands Road), first left again into Nevile Road and follow along to main entrance.

Previous Grounds: Not known

Record Attendance: 3,000 v Whickham - FA Vase 1980
Record Victory: Not known
Record Defeat: Not known
Record Goalscorer: Not known
Record Appearances: Not known
Additional Records:

Senior Honours: Manchester League Premier Division 1975, 76, 77, 79. North West Counties League Cup 2006.

10 YEAR RECORD

01-02	02-03	03-04	04-05	05-06	06-07	07-08	08-09	09-10	10-11
NWC1 3	NWC1 9	NWC1 15	NWC1 18	NWC1 5	NWC1 4	NWC1 2	NP1N 20	NP1N 11	NP1N 12

SKELMERSDALE UNITED

Chairman: Paul Griffiths
Secretary: Bryn Jones **(T)** 07904 911 234 **(E)** skelmersdaleunited@hotmail.com
Additional Committee Members:
Mrs L Boardman, Mr M Boardman, Mr D Bolderston, Mr A Gore, Mr T Garner, Mr N Leatherbarrow, Mr B Jones, Mr P McGee, Mr J Sewell, Mr M Sewell.
Manager: Tommy Lawson
Programme Editor: Neil Leatherbarrow **(E)** skelmersdaleunited@hotmail.com

Club Factfile

Founded: 1882 **Nickname:** Skem
Previous Names: Not known
Previous Leagues: Liverpool County Combination, Lancashire Combination 1891-93, 1903-07, 21-24, 55-56, 76-78, Cheshire County 1968-71, 78-82, Northern Premier 1971-76, North West Counties 1983-2006

Club Colours (change): All royal blue (All red)

Ground: West Lancashire College Stadium, Selby Place, Statham Road WN8 8EF **(T)** 01695 722 123
Capacity: 2,300 **Seats:** 240 **Covered:** 500 **Clubhouse:** Yes **Shop:** Yes

Directions
Exit M58 J4 (signposted Skelmersdale), carry straight on at next roundabout (Hope Island) into Glenburn Road, left at next roundabout (Half Mile Island) into Neverstitch Road (signposted Stanley Industrial Estate). Immediately right at next roundabout into Staveley Road and then left into Statham Road. Ground is 500 yards on left in Selby Place.

Previous Grounds: Not known

Record Attendance: 7,000 v Slough Town - FA Amateur Cup Semi-final 1967
Record Victory: Not known
Record Defeat: Not known
Record Goalscorer: Stuart Rudd - 230
Record Appearances: Robbie Holcroft - 422 including 398 consecutively
Additional Records: Paid £2,000 for Stuart Rudd
Received £4,000 for Stuart Rudd

Senior Honours: FA Amateur Cup 1970-71. Barassi Anglo-Italian Cup 1970-71.
Lancashire Junior Cup x2. Lancashire Non-League Cup x2.

10 YEAR RECORD

01-02	02-03	03-04	04-05	05-06	06-07	07-08	08-09	09-10	10-11
NWC1 9	NWC1 5	NWC1 8	NWC1 6	NWC1 2	NP 1 15	NP1N 3	NP1N 2	NP1N 5	NP1N 2

TRAFFORD

Chairman: Howard Nelson
Secretary: Graham Foxall **(T)** 07796 864 151 **(E)** davem@traffordfc.co.uk
Additional Committee Members:
D Brown, D Law, D Murray, T Walmsley, B Whitten, M.Brown, N.Brown, B Griffin, A Heathcote, L.Knights, H Nelson, P Thomas, J Williams.
Manager: Garry Vaughan
Programme Editor: Dave Murray **(E)** davem@traffordfc.co.uk

Back Row L-R): G. Vaughan (Manager), K. Coppin, K. Harrop, T. Bailey, C. Lawton, N. Bayunu, T. Read, A. Lundy, L. Hargreaves, T. Smith, S. Woodford, T. Turner, R. Marley, J. McComb (Ass. Manager), J. McDermott (Coach)
Front Row: S. Gallanders, P. Ashton, D. White, M. Keddie, J. Shaw, W. Collier, N. Papargiris, S. Barlow.

Club Factfile

Founded: 1990 **Nickname:** The North
Previous Names: North Trafford 1990-94
Previous Leagues: Mid Cheshire 1990-92, North West Counties 1992-97, 2003-08, Northern Premier 1997-2003

Club Colours (change): All white (All yellow)

Ground: Shawe View, Pennybridge Lane, Flixton Urmston M41 5DL **(T)** 0161 747 1727
Capacity: 2,500 **Seats:** 292 **Covered:** 740 **Clubhouse:** Yes **Shop:** Yes

Directions
Anti-Clockwise exit at J10 (Trafford Centre) and turn right towards Urmston B5214. Straight across two roundabouts. First lights turn right into Moorside Road, at next roundabout take second exit in to Bowfell Road. At next lights turn sharp left then immediately right in to Pennybridge Lane next to Bird In Hand Pub, parking on left 100 yards.
Or Leave M60 at J8, taking A6144 towards Lymm, Partington, Carrington. At second set of traffic lights turn right on B5158 towards Flixton. Remain on B5158 crossing railway bridge at Flixton Station and turn right at next set of traffic lights. Passing Bird in Hand Pub take immediate right in to Pennybridge Lane. Parking on left 100 yards.

Previous Grounds: Not known

Record Attendance: 803 v Flixton - Northern Premier League Division 1 1997-98
Record Victory: Not known
Record Defeat: Not known
Record Goalscorer: Garry Vaughan - 88
Record Appearances: Garry Vaughan - 293
Additional Records:

Senior Honours: North West Counties Division 1 1996-97, 2007-08.
Manchester Challenge Trophy 2004-05. Northern Premier President's Cup 2008-09.

10 YEAR RECORD

01-02		02-03		03-04		04-05		05-06		06-07		07-08		08-09		09-10		10-11	
NP 1	15	NP 1	22	NWC1	16	NWC1	12	NWC1	15	NWC1	5	NWC1	1	NP1N	15	NP1N	12	NP1N	14

WAKEFIELD

Chairman: Vacant
Secretary: Peter Matthews (T) 0794 382 9818 (E) peter.matthews@wakefieldfc.com
Additional Committee Members:
Alan Blackman, Pete Belvis, Daniel Brownhill.

Manager: Steve Nicholson
Programme Editor: Dan Brownhill (E) daniel.brownhill@wakefieldfc.com

Club Factfile

Founded: 1903 **Nickname:** The Bears
Previous Names: Emley AFC 1903-2002, Wakefield & Emley AFC 2002-04, 2004-06 Wakefield - Emley AFC
Previous Leagues: Huddersfield > 1969, Yorkshire 1969-82, Northern Counties East 1982-89

Club Colours (change): All nike royal blue (Nike hooped volt (Fluo Yellow) and black/black/black)

Ground: Ingfield, Prospect Road, Ossett, West Yorkshire WF5 9HA (T) 01924 280 028 (office) / 272 960 (club)
Capacity: Nk **Seats:** Nk **Covered:** Nk **Clubhouse:** Yes **Shop:** Nk

Directions From M1 Junction 40: Take A638 signposted Ossett Town Centre. Take first left off A638 onto Wakefield Road, sixth left turn into Dale Street (B6120) to traffic lights. Turn left at lights. The Ground is in front of you opposite the bus station. The entrance to the Ground is just before the Esso petrol station.

Previous Grounds: Welfare Ground 1903-2000, Belle Vue 2000-06

Record Attendance: 5,134 v Barking - FA Amateur Cup 3rd Round 01/02/1969 at Welfare Ground
Record Victory: 12-0 v Ecclesfield Red Rose - Sheffield & Hallamshire Senior Challenge Cup 2nd Round 10/12/1996
Record Defeat: 1-7 v Altrincham - Northern Premier League Premier Division 25/04/1998
Record Goalscorer: Mick Pamment - 305
Record Appearances: Ray Dennis - 762
Additional Records: Received £60,000 from Ayr United for Michael Reynolds 1998

Senior Honours: Yorkshire League 1975-76, 77-78, 79-80, 81-82, League Cup 1969-70, 78-79, 81-82.
Northern Counties East 1987-88, 88-89.
Sheffield & Hallamshire Senior Cup 1975-76, 79-80, 80-81, 83-84, 88-89, 90-91, 91-92, 97-98.

10 YEAR RECORD

01-02	02-03	03-04	04-05	05-06	06-07	07-08	08-09	09-10	10-11
NP P 5	NP P 12	NP P 23	NP P 13	NP P 20	NP 1 21	NP1N 7	NP1N 9	NP1N 18	NP1N 16

WARRINGTON TOWN

Chairman: Gary Skeltenbury
Secretary: Keith Maguire **(T)** 07969 123 786 **(E)** info@warringtontown.co.uk
Additional Committee Members:
Richard Sutton, Toby McCormac, Kevin Read, Bill Carr, David Hughes, Jeff Greenwood, Martin Simcock, Ken Lacey.
Manager: Joey Dunn
Programme Editor: Paul Roach **(E)** info@warringtontown.co.uk

Club Factfile

Founded: 1948 **Nickname:** The Town
Previous Names: Stockton Heath 1949-62
Previous Leagues: Warrington & District 1949-52, Mid Cheshire 1952-78, Cheshire County 1978-82, North West Counties 1982-90 Northern Premier 1990-97

Club Colours (change): Yellow and blue/blue/blue (All red)

Ground: Cantilever Park, Common Lane, Latchford, Warrington WA4 2RS **(T)** 01925 653 044
Capacity: 2,000 **Seats:** 350 **Covered:** 650 **Clubhouse:** Yes **Shop:** Yes

Directions
From M62 Junction 9 Warrington Town Centre: Travel 1 mile south on A49, turn left at traffic lights into Loushers Lane, ground ½ mile on right hand side. From M6 North or South Junction 20: Follow A50 (Warrington signs) for 2 miles, cross Latchford Swingbridge, turn immediate left into Station Road, ground on left.

Previous Grounds: Not known

Record Attendance: 2,600 v Halesowen Town - FA Vase Semi-final 1st leg 1985-86
Record Victory: Not known
Record Defeat: Not known
Record Goalscorer: Steve Hughes - 167
Record Appearances: Neil Whalley
Additional Records: Paid £50,000 to Preston North End for Liam Watson
Received £60,000 from Preston North End for Liam Watson

Senior Honours: North West Counties 1989-90, Division 2 2000-01, League Cup 1985-86, 87-88, 88-89

10 YEAR RECORD

01-02	02-03	03-04	04-05	05-06	06-07	07-08	08-09	09-10	10-11
NWC1 11	NWC1 16	NWC1 5	NP 1 20	NP 1 19	NP 1 22	NP1S 13	NP1N 19	NP1N 9	NP1N 9

WITTON ALBION

Chairman: Mark Harris
Secretary: Graham Shuttleworth **(T)** 07966 289 434 **(E)** wafc43008@o2.co.uk
Additional Committee Members:
Reg Hardingham, Alison Atkins, Vijay Anthwal, Ernest Fryer, Graham Pickering, Paul Worthington.
Manager: Brian Pritchard
Programme Editor: Jamie Thompson **(E)** jamie.thompson4@talktalk.net

Club Factfile

Founded: 1887 **Nickname:** The Albion
Previous Names: Not known
Previous Leagues: Lancashire Combination, Cheshire County > 1979, Northern Premier 1979-91, Conference 1991-94

Club Colours (change): Red & white stripes/black/red (Blue & yellow/yellow/blue)

Ground: Help for Heros Stadium, Wincham Park, Chapel Street, Wincham, CW9 6DA **(T)** 01606 430 08
Capacity: 4,500 **Seats:** 650 **Covered:** 2,300 **Clubhouse:** Yes **Shop:** Yes

Directions
M6 Junction 19: Follow A556 for Northwich for three miles, through two sets of traffic lights. Turn right at the beginning of the dual carriageway onto A559. After ¾ mile turn right at traffic lights by Slow & Easy Public House, still following A559. After a further ¾ mile turn left a Black Greyhound Public House (signposted). Follow the road through the industrial estate for about ½ mile. Turn left immediately after crossing the canal bridge (signposted) **From M56 Junction 10:** Follow the A558 (Northwich Road) towards Northwich for approximately 6 miles. Turn right at the crossroads by the Black Greyhound Public House (signposted). Follow the road through the industrial estate for about ½ mile. Turn left immediately after crossing the canal bridge (signposted)

Previous Grounds: Central Ground (1910-1989)

Record Attendance: 3,940 v Kidderminster Harries - FA Trophy Semi-final 13/04/1991
Record Victory: 13-0 v Middlewich (H)
Record Defeat: 0-9 v Macclesfield Town (A) - 18/09/1965
Record Goalscorer: Frank Fidler - 175 (1947-50)
Record Appearances: Brian Pritchard - 729
Additional Records: Paid £12,500 to Hyde United for Jim McCluskie 1991
Received £11,500 from Chester City for Peter Henderson

Senior Honours: Northern Premier League 1990-91. Cheshire Senior Cup x7.

10 YEAR RECORD

01-02	02-03	03-04	04-05	05-06	06-07	07-08	08-09	09-10	10-11
NP P 10	NP P 7	NP P 5	NP 1 8	NP 1 8	NP P 2	NP P 2	NP P 20	NP1S 7	NP1N 10

WOODLEY SPORTS

Chairman: Vacant
Secretary: Wayne Ashworth **(T)** 07786 028 219 **(E)** washworth@woodleysportsfc.com
Additional Committee Members:
Dave Parsonage, John Rourke, Darrin Whittaker, Peter Ross.

Manager: Chris Wilcock
Programme Editor: Wayne Ashworth **(E)** washworth@woodleysportsfc.com

Club Factfile

Founded: 1970 **Nickname:** The Steelmen
Previous Names: Woodley Athletic
Previous Leagues: Lancashire and Cheshire, Manchester, North West Counties

Club Colours (change): Blue/blue/white (Red/red/white)

Ground: The Neil Rourke Stadium, Lambeth Grove, Woodley SK6 1QX **(T)** 0161 406 6896 (office) / 494 6429 (club)
Capacity: 2,300 **Seats:** 300 **Covered:** Yes **Clubhouse:** Yes **Shop:** Nk

Directions
Woodley Sports Football Club is located in Woodley, a suburb of Stockport in the North West of England. The ground lies a short distance from the new Manchester Ring Road, the M60. To reach us from the motorway, you should leave at Junction 25, which is signposted for Bredbury. Follow signs from here for the A560 towards Bredbury and Sheffield. Just after passing the McDonalds Drive-Thru, take a left at the traffic lights and proceed down Stockport Road towards Woodley, passing under the railway bridge at Bredbury Railway Station. Having passed St Mark's Church on the right, you reach a set of traffic lights. Immediately after the lights, at The Lowes Arms and before the Waggon & Horses Pub, turn left onto Mill Street. Proceed over the bridge on Mill Lane and then follow the signs to the ground.

Previous Grounds: None

Record Attendance: 1,500 v Stockport County
Record Victory: Not known
Record Defeat: Not known
Record Goalscorer: Not known
Record Appearances: Not known
Additional Records:

Senior Honours: North West Counties League Division 2 1999-2000.
Cheshire Senior Cup 2003-04.

10 YEAR RECORD

01-02	02-03	03-04	04-05	05-06	06-07	07-08	08-09	09-10	10-11
NWC1 10	NWC1 17	NWC1 4	NP 1 11	NP 1 4	NP 1 10	NP1N 17	NP1N 13	NP1N 19	NP1N 11

BELPER TOWN

Chairman: Vaughan Williams
Secretary: David Laughlin **(T)** 07768 010 604 **(E)** info@belpertownfc.co.uk
Additional Committee Members:
Phil Varney, Christopher Balls, Rex Barker, Alan Benfield, Graham Boot, Steve Boxall, Andrew Carter, Graham Hulland, David Winterbotham.
Manager: Tommy Taylor
Programme Editor: David Laughlin **(E)** info@belpertownfc.co.uk

Back Row (L-R): Ollie Graham, Deon Meikle, Rob Ludlam, Ben Spargo, Matt Plant, Andy Richmond, Tommy Hannigan, Matty Thorpe, Richard Adams, Ruben Wiggins-Thomas, Liam Davis, Paris Simmons, Jinesh Lal (Physio).

Front Row: Paul Bennett (Kitman), Aaron Pride, Joaquin Ortuno, Luke Fedorenko, Lee Morris, Jon Froggatt, Tommy Taylor (Manager), Damien Magee, Andy Rushbury, Mark Camm, Jamie Smith, David Bennett (Kitman).

Club Factfile

Founded: 1883 **Nickname:** Nailers
Previous Names: Not known
Previous Leagues: Central Alliance 1957-61, Midland Counties 1961-82, Northern Counties East 1982-97

Club Colours (change): Yellow/black/black (All white)

Ground: Christchurch Meadow, Bridge Street, Belper DE56 1BA **(T)** 01773 825 549
Capacity: 2,650 **Seats:** 500 **Covered:** 850 **Clubhouse:** Yes **Shop:** Yes

Directions
From North: Exit M1: Exit junction 28 onto A38 towards Derby. Turn off at A610 (signposted 'Ripley/Nottingham') 4th exit at roundabout towards Ambergate. At junction with A6 (Hurt Arms Hotel) turn left to Belper. Ground on right just past first set of traffic lights. Access to the ground is by the lane next to the church.
From South: Follow A6 north from Derby towards Matlock. Follow A6 through Belper until junction with A517. Ground on left just before traffic lights at this junction. Access to the ground is by the lane next to the church.
NB. Please do not attempt to bring coaches into the ground – these can be parked outside

Previous Grounds: Acorn Ground > 1951

Record Attendance: 3,200 v Ilkeston Town - 1955
Record Victory: 15-2 v Nottingham Forest 'A' - 1956
Record Defeat: 0-12 v Goole Town - 1965
Record Goalscorer: Mick Lakin - 231
Record Appearances: Craig Smithurst - 678
Additional Records: Paid £2,000 to Ilkeston Town for Jamie Eaton 2001
Received £2,000 from Hinckley United for Craig Smith

Senior Honours: Central Alliance League 1958-59, Derbyshire Senior Cup 1958-59, 60-61, 62-63, 79-80.
Midland Counties 1979-80. Northern Counties East 1984-85.

10 YEAR RECORD

01-02	02-03	03-04	04-05	05-06	06-07	07-08	08-09	09-10	10-11
NP 1 18	NP 1 6	NP 1 20	NP 1 17	NP 1 9	NP 1 19	NP 1 8	NP1S 2	NP1S 6	NP1S 14

BRIGG TOWN

Chairman: Kiron Brown
Secretary: Martin North (T) 07891 122 242 (E) briggtownfc@chessmail.co.uk
Additional Committee Members:
John Martin, Carolyn Smith, Bob Taylor, Jack Dunderdale, Kenny Bowers, Mark Cawkwell, Carl Atkinson, Mike Smith, Simon Harris, Tim Harris, Kenny Bowers, Carolyn Smith
Manager: Peter Daniel
Programme Editor: Michael Harker (E) briggtownfc@chessmail.co.uk

Club Factfile

Founded: 1864 **Nickname:** Zebras
Previous Names: Not known
Previous Leagues: Lincolnshire 1948-76, Midland Counties 1976-82, Northern Counties East 1982-2004

Club Colours (change): Black and white stripes/black/red (All green)

Ground: The Hawthorns, Hawthorn Avenue, Brigg DN20 8PG* (T) 01652 651 605
Capacity: 2,500 **Seats:** 370 **Covered:** Yes **Clubhouse:** Yes **Shop:** Yes

Directions
From M180 (Exit 4 - Scunthorpe East) A18 to Brigg. Leave Town via Wrawby Road, following signs for Airport and Grimsby. 100 metres after Sir John Nelthorpe Lower School, and immediately after bus stop/shelter, turn left into Recreation ground (signposted "Football Ground") and follow road into club car park.

*SAT NAV postcode DN20 8DT

Previous Grounds: Old Manor House Convent, Station Road > 1939, Brocklesby 1939-59

Record Attendance: 2,000 v Boston United - 1953
Record Victory: Not known
Record Defeat: Not known
Record Goalscorer: Not known
Record Appearances: Not known
Additional Records:

Senior Honours: Midland Counties League 1977-78. FA Vase 1995-96, 2002-03. Northern Counties East Premier Division 2000-01. Lincolnshire League x8, League Cup x5. Lincolnshire 'A' Senior Cup x4. Lincolnshire 'B' Senior Cup x5.

10 YEAR RECORD

01-02		02-03		03-04		04-05		05-06		06-07		07-08		08-09		09-10		10-11	
NCEP	2	NCEP	2	NCEP	3	NP 1	8	NP 1	8	NP 1	17	NP 1	16	NP1S	20	NP1S	15	NP1S	4

CARLTON TOWN

Chairman: Michael Garton
Secretary: Paul Shelton **(T)** 07854 586 875 **(E)** info@carltontownfc.co.uk
Additional Committee Members:
Terry Fowler, Roger Smith, Jennie Shaw, Ian White, Mark Steggles, Tim Bee, Bob Sharp, Brian Dennett, Alan Murphy.
Manager: Les McJannet
Programme Editor: John Hickling **(E)** info@carltontownfc.co.uk

Photo: Keith Clayton.

Club Factfile

Founded: 1904 **Nickname:** Town
Previous Names: Sneinton
Previous Leagues: Notts Alliance, Central Midlands, Northern Counties East

Club Colours (change): Navy & yellow stripes/navy & yellow/navy & yellow (White & red/red & white/red)

Ground: Bill Stokeld Stadium, Stoek Lane, Gedling, Nottingham NG4 2QP* **(T)** 0115 940 3192 / 940 2531
Capacity: 1,500 **Seats:** 164 **Covered:** 100 **Clubhouse:** Yes **Shop:** No

Directions
From M1 J26 take A610 to Nottingham Ring Road. Follow signs for Mansfield (A60) for approx 4 miles via 2 roundabouts until reaching junction with A60 at Arnold. Take right turn at Vale Hotel on to Thackerays Lane. Proceed to roundabout and take 3rd exit on to Arno Vale Road. Proceed through traffic lights to top of hill and continue straight on at next lights on to Arnold Lane. Continue past golf course, the old Gedling Colliery and church to mini roundabout. Continue straight on to the old junction with A612. (Southwell) must turn right here and at next set of lights turn left and follow the loop road to the next junction. Take left turn on to the new A612 Gedling By Pass and follow to the next set of traffic lights at Severn Trent Works. Turn left on to Stoke Lane. Entrance to Carlton Town is immediate right. **[Ground must be accessed via the new A612 between Netherfield and Burton Joyce. Football club is signposted in both directions on the approach to the ground).** *Sat Nav postcode NG4 2QW

Previous Grounds: Not known

Record Attendance: 1,000 - Radio Trent Charity Match
Record Victory: Not known
Record Defeat: Not known
Record Goalscorer: Not known
Record Appearances: Not known
Additional Records:

Senior Honours: Notts Alliance League Division 2 1984-85, Division 1 1992-93. Central Midlands Supreme Division 2002-03.
Northern Counties East Division 1 2005-06

10 YEAR RECORD

01-02	02-03	03-04	04-05	05-06	06-07	07-08	08-09	09-10	10-11
	CM Su 1	NCE1 9	NCE1 3	NCE1 1	NCEP 3	NP 1 10	NP1S 4	NP1S 9	NP1S 8

COALVILLE TOWN

Chairman: Glyn Rennocks
Secretary: James Jarvis **(T)** 07791 231 860 **(E)** web@coalvilletownfc.co.uk
Additional Committee Members:
Mick Jordan, Robert Brooks, Jack Sarson, Dan Gallacher, Jon Bailiss.

Manager: Adam Stevens
Programme Editor: Jon Bailiss **(E)** web@coalvilletownfc.co.uk

Club Factfile

Founded: 1994 **Nickname:** The Ravens
Previous Names: Ravenstoke Miners Ath. 1925-58. Ravenstoke FC 58-95. Coalville 95-98.
Previous Leagues: Coalville & Dist. Amateur. North Leicester. Leicestershire Senior. Midland Alliance > 2011.

Club Colours (change): Black & white stripes/white/white (Red & yellow stripes/red/red)

Ground: Owen Street Sports Ground, Owen St, Coalville LE67 3DA **(T)** 01530 833 365
Capacity: 2,000 **Seats:** 240 **Covered:** 240 **Clubhouse:** Yes **Shop:** Yes

Directions From the M42/A42 take the exit signposted Ashby and follow A511 to Coalville and Leicester. After approx. 3 miles and at the first roundabout take the second exit (A511). At the next roundabout take the 3rd exit into Coalville Town Centre. At the traffic lights go straight over to mini-roundabout then straight on for 50 meters before turning right into Owen Street. Ground is at the top of Owen Street on the left.

Previous Grounds: Not known

Record Attendance: 1,500.
Record Victory: Not known
Record Defeat: Not known
Record Goalscorer: Not known
Record Appearances: Nigel Simms.
Additional Records:

Senior Honours: Leicestershire Senior Cup 1999-00. Leicestershire Senior 2001-02, 02-03. Midland Football Alliance 2010-11.

10 YEAR RECORD

01-02	02-03	03-04	04-05	05-06	06-07	07-08	08-09	09-10	10-11
LeicS 1	LeicS 1	MidAl 8	MidAl 3	MidAl 8	MidAl 18	MidAl 8	MidAl 3	MidAl 2	MidAl 1

GOOLE

Chairman: Chris Hoff
Secretary: Mrs Ann Smith **(T)** 07837 607 233 **(E)** asmith1940@hotmail.co.uk
Additional Committee Members:
Phil Jones

Manager: Karl Rose
Programme Editor: Chris Hoff **(E)** asmith1940@hotmail.co.uk

Club Factfile

Founded: 1997 **Nickname:** The Badgers
Previous Names: Not known
Previous Leagues: Central Midlands 1997-98, Northern Counties East 2000-04

Club Colours (change): All red (All yellow)

Ground: Victoria Pleasure Gardens, Marcus Road, Goole DN14 6DW **(T)** 01405 762 794 (MD) / 07970 626954
Capacity: 3,000 **Seats:** 200 **Covered:** 800 **Clubhouse:** Yes **Shop:** Yes

Directions
Leave the M62 at Junction 36 and follow signs to Goole Town Centre. Turn right at the 2nd set of traffic lights into Boothferry Road. Turn right again after 300 yards into Carter Street. The Victoria Pleasure Grounds is at the end of the road. 366 Metres from Goole Railway Station.

Previous Grounds: Not known

Record Attendance: 976 v Leeds United - 1999
Record Victory: Not known
Record Defeat: Not known
Record Goalscorer: Kevin Severn (1997-2001)
Record Appearances: Phil Dobson - 187 (1999-2001)
Additional Records:

Senior Honours: Central Midlands 1997-98. Northern Counties East Division 1 1999-2000, Premier Division 2003-04.

10 YEAR RECORD

01-02	02-03	03-04	04-05	05-06	06-07	07-08	08-09	09-10	10-11
NCEP 12	NCEP 3	NCEP 6	NCEP 1	NP 1 21	NP 1 7	NP 1 9	NP1S 18	NP1S 18	NP1S 13

GRANTHAM TOWN

Chairman: Steve Boam
Secretary: Patrick Nixon **(T)** 07747 136 033 **(E)** psnixon@hotmail.com
Additional Committee Members:
Roger Booth, Barry Palmer, Peter Railton, Darren Quinn

Manager: Wayne Hallcro and Jimmy Albans
Programme Editor: Mike Koranski **(E)** psnixon@hotmail.com

Back row (l-r): Phil Watt, Sam Saunders, Niall O'Rafferty, Alistair Asher, Rob Murray, Grant Brindley, Rhys Lewis, Lee Potts.
Middle Row: Tris Whitman, Tom Maddison, Jamie McGhee, Sam Purcicoe, Gio Carchedi, Matt Glass, Rob Norris, Steve Melton, Paul Grimes, Martin Ball, Joe Briers.
Front row: Nige Marshall (Physio), Dennis Rhule (Coach), Pat Nixon (Secretary), Pete Railton (Director), Steve Boam (Chairman), Darron Quinn (Director), Wayne Hallcro (Joint Manager), Becky Cope (Commercial Assistant).

Club Factfile

Founded: 1874 **Nickname:** Gingerbreads
Previous Names: Not known
Previous Leagues: Midland Amateur Alliance, Central Alliance 1911-25, 59-61, Midland Counties 1925-59, 61-72, Southern 1972-79, 85-2006, Northern Premier 1979-85

Club Colours (change): White/black/black (Red and black stripes/red/red)

Ground: South Kesteven Sports Stadium, Trent Road, Gratham NG31 7XQ **(T)** 01476 402 224
Capacity: 7,500 **Seats:** 750 **Covered:** 1,950 **Clubhouse:** Yes **Shop:** Yes

Directions
FROM A1 NORTH Leave A1 At A607 Melton Mowbray exit. Turn left at island on slip road into Swingbridge Lane. At T junction turn left into Trent Road ground is 100yds on right.
FROM A52 NOTTINGHAM. Pass over A1 and at first island turn right into housing estate & Barrowby Gate. Through housing estate to T junction. Turn right and then immediately left into Trent road ground is 100 yards on the left.
FROM A607 MELTON MOWBRAY. Pass under A1 and take next left A1 South slip road. At island turn right into Swingbridge Road then as for A1 North above. From all directions follow brown signs for Sports Complex, which is immediately behind the stadium.

Previous Grounds: London Road

Record Attendance: 3,695 v Southport - FA Trophy 1997-98
Record Victory: 13-0 v Rufford Colliery (H) - FA Cup 15/09/1934
Record Defeat: 0-16 v Notts County Rovers (A) - Midland Amateur Alliance 22/10/1892
Record Goalscorer: Jack McCartney - 416
Record Appearances: Chris Gardner - 664
Additional Records: Received £20,000 from Nottingham Forest for Gary Crosby

Senior Honours: Southern League Midland Division 1997-98. Lincolnshire Senior Cup x20. Lincolnshire County Senior Cup x2.

10 YEAR RECORD

01-02	02-03	03-04	04-05	05-06	06-07	07-08	08-09	09-10	10-11
SthE 2	SthP 16	SthP 22	SthP 13	SthP 11	NP P 22	NP 1 6	NP1S 13	NP1S 11	NP1S 5

HUCKNALL TOWN

Chairman: David Gamble
Secretary: Tony Knowles **(T)** 07775 001 266 **(E)** commercialmanager@hucknalltownfc.com
Additional Committee Members:
Brian Holmes, John Coleman, Geoff Gospel, Andy Johnson, Lynne Taylor, Andy Graves.

Manager: Tommy Brooklands
Programme Editor: Gary Stones **(E)** commercialmanager@hucknalltownfc.com

Club Factfile

Founded: 1987 **Nickname:** The Town
Previous Names: Not known
Previous Leagues: Bulwell & District 1946-59, 60-65, Central Alliance 1959-60 Notts Spartan 1965-70, Central Midlands 1989-92

Club Colours (change): Yellow/black/yellow (All white)

Ground: Watnall Road, Hucknall, Notts NG15 6EY **(T)** 01159 30206
Capacity: 3,013 **Seats:** 500 **Covered:** 900 **Clubhouse:** Yes **Shop:** Yes

Directions
Exit the M1 at Junction 27 and take the A608 towards Hucknall. Turn right onto the A611 to Hucknall then take the Hucknall bypass. At the second roundabout join Watnall Road (B6009) and the ground is 100 yards on the right.

Previous Grounds: Not known

Record Attendance: 1,841 v Bishop's Stortford - FA Trophy Semi-final 2004-05
Record Victory: 12-1 v Teversal - Notts Senior Cup 1989-90
Record Defeat: Not known
Record Goalscorer: Maurice Palethorpe - 400 approx. (1980-90)
Record Appearances: Dave McCarthy - 282
Additional Records: Received £10,000 from Brentford for Stuart Nelson 2003-04

Senior Honours: Central Midlands League 1989-90, 90-91, League Cup x3. Northern Counties East 1997-98, League Cup x3.
Northern Premier League Premier Division 2003-04.
Notts Senior Cup x5.

10 YEAR RECORD

01-02	02-03	03-04	04-05	05-06	06-07	07-08	08-09	09-10	10-11
NP P 16	NP P 8	NP P 1	Conf N 10	Conf N 12	Conf N 13	Conf N 20	Conf N 22	NP P 17	NP P 20

ILKESTON

Chairman: David Mantle
Secretary: Andrew Raisin **(T)** 07813 357 393 **(E)** a.raisin@ilkestonfc.co.uk
Additional Committee Members:
David Mantle, Paul Riley.

Manager: Kevin Wilson
Programme Editor: Terry Bowles **(E)** a.raisin@ilkestonfc.co.uk

Back row (left to right): Joe Maguire, Dan Partridge, Josh Hill, Liam Green, Ryan Swift, Aaron Butcher, Josh Wisdom, Ryan Wlson, Tyrell Waite, Jerome Palmer.
Front row: Joe Wilcox, Will McCall, Daryll Thomas, Jimmy Davison (physio), Kevin Wilson (manager), Darren Caskey (player-coach), Adam Colton, Russell Peel, Andrew Osei-Siribour.

Club Factfile

Founded: 1945 **Nickname:** The Robins
Previous Names: Ikeston Town > 2011.
Previous Leagues: Notts & Derbyshire 1945-47, Central Alliance 1947-61, Midlands counties 1961-71, 73-82, Southern 1971-73, 95-2004, N.C.E. 1982-86, Central Midlands 1986-90, West Midlands Reg. 1990-94, N.P.L. 2004-09

Club Colours (change): All red & white (Blue & black stripes/black/black)

Ground: New Manor Ground, Awsworth Road, Ilkeston, Derbyshire DE7 8JF **(T)** 0115 944 428
Capacity: 3,029 **Seats:** 550 **Covered:** 2,000 **Clubhouse:** Yes **Shop:** Yes

Directions M1 Junction 26, take the A610 signed Ripley, leave at the first exit on to the A6096 signed Awsworth / Ilkeston, at the next island take the A6096 signed Ilkeston, keep on this road for about half a mile, then turn right into Awsworth Road, Signed Cotmanhay (Coaches can get down this road) the ground is about half a mile on the left hand side down this road. Car Parking available at the ground £1 per car.

Previous Grounds: Manor Ground 1945-1992

Record Attendance: Manor Ground: 9,592 v Peterborough - FAC 4thQ 1955-56. New Manor: 2,538 v Rushden & D. - FAC 1st Rnd 1999/00
Record Victory: 14-2 v Codnor M.W. - 1946-47
Record Defeat: 1-11 v Grantham Town - 1947-48. 0-10 v VS Rugby - 1985-86
Record Goalscorer: Jackie Ward - 141
Record Appearances: Terry Swincoe - 377
Additional Records: Paid £7,500 to Southport for Justin O'Reilly 1998
Received £25,000 from Peterborough United for Francis Green

Senior Honours: Derbyshire Senior Cup 1948-49, 52-53, 55-56, 57-58, 62-63, 82-83, 92-93, 98-99, 99-00, 05-06, 06-07.
Central Alliance 1951-52, 52-53, 53-54, 54-55, League Cup 1957-58. Midland Counties League 1967-68. Central Midlands League Cup 1986-87. West Midlands Div.1 1991-92, Premier 93-94, Div.1 League Cup 91-92, Premier League Cup 93-94.

10 YEAR RECORD

01-02	02-03	03-04	04-05	05-06	06-07	07-08	08-09	09-10	10-11
SthP 10	SthP 21	SthW 10	NP 1 2	NP P 16	NP P 12	NP P 17	NP P 2	Conf N 8	Conf N Exp

KIDSGROVE ATHLETIC

Chairman: Michael Fitzjohn
Secretary: Lisa Fitzjohn (T) 07960 560 391 (E)
Additional Committee Members:
David James, John Rowley, Ray Green.

Manager: Peter Ward
Programme Editor: TBC (E)

Back row L-R: Craig Dove, Lisa Fitzjohn(Secretary), Dave Beswick (Coach), Adam Beasley, Matt Haddrell, Dan Schwarz, Peter Ward (Manager), Paul Lawton, Aiden Matranga, Liam Shotton, Nick Ward, Karl Charlton, Sam Hall,Wayne Johnson, Steve Hodgson, Graham Plant(Medical Attendant)
Front Row: Tom Urwin, Danny Smith, Ricky Bridge, Tim Sanders, Dave Walker

Club Factfile

Founded: 1952 **Nickname:** The Grove
Previous Names: Not Known
Previous Leagues: Buslem and Tunstall 1953-63, Staffordshire County 1963-66, Mid Cheshire 1966-90, North West Counties 1990-2002
Club Colours (change): All blue (All green)

Ground: The Seddon Stadium, Hollinwood Road, Kidsgrove, Staffs ST7 1DQ (T) 01782 782 412
Capacity: 4,500 **Seats:** 1,000 **Covered:** 800 **Clubhouse:** Yes **Shop:** Yes

Directions Leave the M6 at Junction 16, join the A500 towards Stoke-on-Trent. Take the 2nd exit signposted Newcastle & Kidsgrove. Top of the slip road, turn left onto A34 Kidsgrove/Congleton. Straight over at roundabout. At 1st set of traffic lights (by Caudwell Arms pub) turn right onto A34. Continue to next set of lights, turn right into Cedar Avenue. Continue then take 2nd right into Lower Ash Road. Take 3rd left into Hollinwood Road, Ground on left at top.

Previous Grounds: Vickers and Goodwin 1953-60

Record Attendance: 1,903 v Tiverton Town - FA Vase Semi-final 1998
Record Victory: 23-0 v Cross Heath W.M.C. - Staffordshire Cup 1965
Record Defeat: 0-15 v Stafford Rangers - Staffordshire Senior Cup 20/11/2001
Record Goalscorer: Scott Dundas - 53 (1997-98)
Record Appearances: Not known
Additional Records: Paid £10,000 to Stevenage Borough for Steve Walters
Received £3,000 for Ryan Baker 2003-04

Senior Honours: Mid Cheshire League x4, League Cup x3.
North West Counties Division 1 1997-98, 2001-02, Challenge Cup 1997-98.
Staffordshire Senior Cup 2010-11.

10 YEAR RECORD

01-02		02-03		03-04		04-05		05-06		06-07		07-08		08-09		09-10		10-11	
NWC1	1	NP 1	19	NP 1	22	NP 1	10	NP 1	17	NP 1	8	NP 1	17	NP1S	15	NP1S	4	NP1S	7

LEEK TOWN

Chairman: Andrew Wain
Secretary: Brain Wain (T) 07967 204 470 (E)
Additional Committee Members:
C Hermiston, A Reeves, Mrs T Reynolds, N Baker, P Bateman, Dr D Bates.

Manager: Lee Casswell
Programme Editor: Steve & Tracy Reynolds (E)

Back Row (L-R): Ken Ashford (Kit Man/Physio), Ashley Miller, Wayne Corden, Leon Ashman, Matt Bradbury, John Ritchie, Paul Heeps, Pete Johnson, Rob Hawthorne, Paul Rutter, Dean Crowe, Chris Hermiston (Groundsman/Director)
Front Row: Joe Wolliscroft, Dan Cope, Mitch Shenton, Bobby Gee, Wayne Johnson (Manager), Andy Wain (Chairman), Paul Macari (Asst Manager), Matt Johnson, Luke Robinson, Andy Taylor, Tom France

Club Factfile

Founded: 1946 **Nickname:** The Blues
Previous Names: Not known
Previous Leagues: Staffordshire Co., Manchester 1951-54, 57-73, West Midlands (B'ham) 1954-56,Cheshire Co. 1973-82, North West Counties 1982-87, N.P.L. 1987-94, 95-97, Southern 1994-95, Conference 1997-99

Club Colours (change): All blue (Red and black stripes/black/black)

Ground: Harrison Park, Macclesfield Road, Leek, Cheshire ST13 8LD (T) 01538 399 278
Capacity: 3,600 **Seats:** 625 **Covered:** 2,675 **Clubhouse:** Yes **Shop:** Yes

Directions
From the South: Leave M6 at J15, over roundabout on to the A500, go over the flyover, up the slip road, onto the A50 and follow the signs to Leek. Go straight over the roundabout (Britannia Building on the left) to large set of lights. Go straight across St. Georges Street to top of road to junction, turn left, go down the hill for about a half a mile. The Ground is on the left. **From the North:** Leave M6 at J19. Take Macclesfield signs. Follow into Macclesfield then take A523 Leek/Buxton signs. Follow these to Leek. Ground is situated on the right as you come into Leek. From West Midlands: M6 J15. A500 towards Stoke, over flyover, take A50 past Brittania Stadium. After approx 3 miles join A53 signposted Leek. On entering the town, straight ahead up St Edwards St. (Remainder as above)

Previous Grounds: Not known

Record Attendance: 5,312 v Macclesfield Town - FA Cup 1973-74
Record Victory: Not known
Record Defeat: Not known
Record Goalscorer: Dave Sutton - 144
Record Appearances: Gary Pearce - 447
Additional Records: Paid £2,000 to Sutton Town for Simon Snow
Received £30,000 from Barnsley for Tony Bullock

Senior Honours: Northern Premier League 1996-97. Staffordshire Senior Cup 1995-96.

10 YEAR RECORD

01-02	02-03	03-04	04-05	05-06	06-07	07-08	08-09	09-10	10-11
NP 1 6	NP 1 9	NP 1 8	NP P 7	NP P 12	NP P 17	NP P 19	NP1S 9	NP1S 8	NP1S 16

LINCOLN UNITED

Chairman: John Joe Dolan
Secretary: John Wilkinson **(T)** 07773 284 017 **(E)** johnwilk@live.co.uk
Additional Committee Members:
Vic Sahunta, Maurise Bull, Chris Bestford, Allen Crombie, Malcolm Cowling.

Manager: Terry Fleming
Programme Editor: John Wilkinson **(E)** johnwilk@live.co.uk

Back Row (l-R): Scott Coupland, Josh Raby, Craig Leverett, Alex Troughton, Peter McDaid, Sean Wright, Stuart Reddington, Nigel Wallace, James Stokes, Jordan Hempenstall, Lee Pickering, David Coyde
Front Row: Steve Churcher(Kit Manager), George Zuerner, Liam Bull, Chris Funnell, Terry Fleming, Darren Dye, Brendan McDaid, Kallum Smith, Jack McGovern, Phil McGann

Club Factfile

Founded: 1938 **Nickname:** United
Previous Names: Lincoln Amateurs > 1954
Previous Leagues: Lincolnshire 1945-46, 60-67, Lincoln 1946-60, Yorkshire 1967-82, Northern Counties East 1982-86, 92-95, Central Midlands 1982-92

Club Colours (change): White/red/red (Red/black/black)

Ground: Ashby Avenue, Hartsholme, Lincoln LN6 0DY **(T)** 01522 696 400
Capacity: 2,714 **Seats:** 400 **Covered:** 1,084 **Clubhouse:** Yes **Shop:** Yes

Directions
Along Lincoln Relief Road (A46) until reaching roundabout with exit for Birchwood. Take this exit which is Skellingthorpe Road for approximately 1 mile, at 30 mph sign turn right into Ashby Avenue. Entrance to ground is 200 yards on right.

Previous Grounds: Skew Bridge 1940s, Co-op Sports Ground > 1960s, Hartsholme Cricket Club > 1982

Record Attendance: 2,000 v Crook Town - FA Amateur Cup 1st Round 1968
Record Victory: 12-0 v Pontefract Colliery - 1995
Record Defeat: 0-7 v Huddersfield Town - FA Cup 1st Round 16/11/1991
Record Goalscorer: Tony Simmons - 215
Record Appearances: Steve Carter - 447
Additional Records: Paid £1,000 to Hucknall Town for Paul Tomlinson December 2000
Received £3,000 from Charlton Athletic for Dean Dye July 1991

Senior Honours: Northern Counties East Division 1 1985-86, 92-93, Premier Division 1994-95.

10 YEAR RECORD

01-02	02-03	03-04	04-05	05-06	06-07	07-08	08-09	09-10	10-11
NP 1 19	NP 1 16	NP 1 4	NP P 14	NP P 19	NP P 15	NP P 20	NP1S 10	NP1S 19	NP1S 12

LOUGHBOROUGH DYNAMO

Chairman: Frank Fall
Secretary: Brian Pugh (T) 07775 825 321 (E) contact@loughboroughdynamofc.co.uk
Additional Committee Members:
Ian Beach, Greg Blood, John Cherry, Keith Hawes, Colin Westley.

Manager: Scott Clamp
Programme Editor: Rob Smith (E) contact@loughboroughdynamofc.co.uk

Club Factfile

Founded: 1955 **Nickname:** Dynamo
Previous Names: Not known
Previous Leagues: Loughborough Alliance 1957-66, Leicestershire & District 1966-71, East Midlands 1971-72, Central Alliance 1972-89, Leicestershire Senior 1989-2004, Midland Alliance 2004-08
Club Colours (change): Gold/black/gold (Green and white hoops/white/green and white hoops)

Ground: Nanpantan Sports Ground, Nanpantan Road, Loughborough LE11 3YE (T) 01509 237 148
Capacity: 1,500 **Seats:** 250 **Covered:** Yes **Clubhouse:** Yes **Shop:** No

Directions
From M1: At Junction 23 turn towards Loughborough (A512). At 1st set of traffic lights turn right on to Snells Nook Lane.. At 1st crossroads ("Priory" pub on left) turn left on to Nanpantan Rd. Turn (1st) right after 0.75 miles on to Watermead Lane. The ground is at the end of the lane. **From Leicester (A6):** Turn left at 3rd roundabout on Epinal Way (Ring Road) on to Forest Road. After 2 miles turn (5th) left on to Watermead Lane. **From Nottingham (A60):** Turn right at 1st set of traffic lights in Loughborough. Go through next 4 sets of traffic lights. Turn left at the first roundabout on to Epinal Way straight on at next roundabout and then take the third exit at following roundabout on to Forest Road. After 2 miles turn (5th) left on to Watermead Lane.

Previous Grounds: Not known

Record Attendance: Not known
Record Victory: Not known
Record Defeat: Not known
Record Goalscorer: Not known
Record Appearances: Not known
Additional Records:

Senior Honours: Leicestershire Senior League Division 1 2001-02, Premier Division 2003-04.
Leicestershire Senior Cup 2002-03, 03-04.

10 YEAR RECORD

01-02		02-03		03-04		04-05		05-06		06-07		07-08		08-09		09-10		10-11	
LeicS1	1	LeicS	4	LeicS	1	MidAl	14	MidAl	13	MidAl	9	MidAl	2	NP1S	14	NP1S	14	NP1S	17

MARKET DRAYTON TOWN

Chairman: Julian Parton
Secretary: Brian Garratt (T) 07854 725 957 (E)
Additional Committee Members:
Nick Alsop, Clive Jones, Frank Hodgkiss, Pauline Mellor, Alex Mutch, Mark Paton, Gary Burns, Paul Littlehales, Stuart Holloway, Mick Murphy, Tom Mellor, Ian Macintosh, Ron Ebrey.
Manager: Neil Wooliscroft
Programme Editor: Stuart Holloway (E)

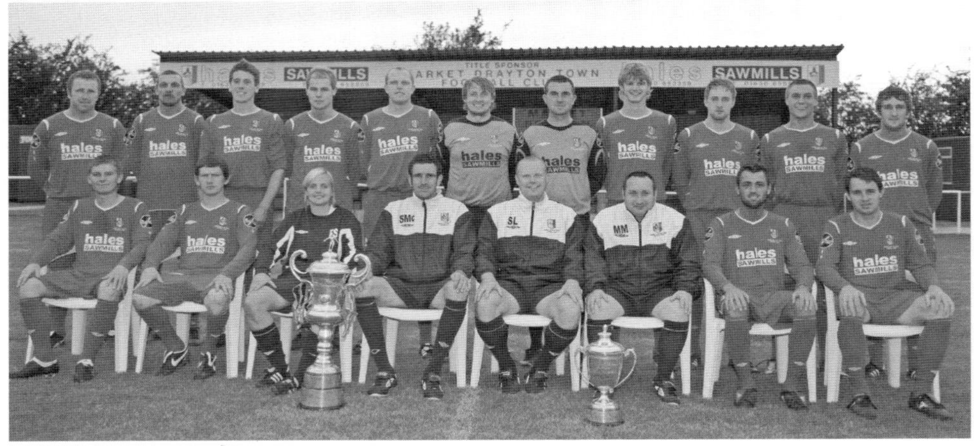

Club Factfile

Founded: 1969 **Nickname:**
Previous Names: Little Drayton Rangers > 2003
Previous Leagues: West Midlands (Regional) 1969-2006, Midland Alliance 2006-09

Club Colours (change): All red (All navy blue)

Ground: Greenfields Sports Ground, Greenfields Lane, Market Drayton TF9 3SI (T) 01630 655 088
Capacity: Nk **Seats:** Nk **Covered:** Nk **Clubhouse:** Yes **Shop:** Nk

Directions
Take the A41 to Ternhill Island, turn right on A53 for Newcastle-under-Lyne. Straight on at first island (by Muller factory). At next island turn right to town centre (by Gingerbread Inn). Approx 200yds take 2nd right into Greenfields Lane. Ground 150 yards on right, car park opposite.

From Stoke-on-Trent take A53 for Shrewsbury, at Gingerbread Inn turn left for town centre then as above.

Previous Grounds: Not known

Record Attendance: Not known
Record Victory: Not known
Record Defeat: Not known
Record Goalscorer: Not known
Record Appearances: Not known
Additional Records:

Senior Honours: West Midlands (Regional) League 2005-06. Midland Alliance 2008-09.

10 YEAR RECORD

01-02		02-03		03-04		04-05		05-06		06-07		07-08		08-09		09-10		10-11	
WMP	4	WMP	4	WMP	7	WMP	2	WMP	1	MidAl	13	MidAl	3	MidAl	1	NP1S	13	NP1S	18

NEW MILLS

Chairman: Ray Coverley
Secretary: Duncan Hibbert **(T)** 07957 482 343 **(E)** duncanhibbert@newmillsafc.co.uk
Additional Committee Members:
Andrew Bowers, Sue Hyde, Patrick Kenyon, Andrew Thomas, John Bradbury, Glyn Jones, Allan Jones, Michael Bradbury.
Manager: Ally Pickering
Programme Editor: Glyn Jones **(E)** glynjones@newmillsafc.co.uk

Club Factfile

Founded: pre1890 **Nickname:** The Millers
Previous Names: New Mills St Georges until 1919
Previous Leagues: Manchester, North West Counties, Cheshire

Club Colours (change): Amber & black/amber & black/black (White/white/black).

Ground: Church Lane, New Mills, SK22 4NP **(T)** 01663 747 435
Capacity: 1,650 **Seats:** 120 **Covered:** 400 **Clubhouse:** Yes **Shop:**

Directions
Via Buxton: Follow the A6 By-Pass, go straight through the roundabout, under railway bridge and about 1 mile further on turn right onto Marsh Lane (Past Furness Vale primary school), this road takes you straight to the ground. Coach drivers should proceed on the A6 a couple of miles turning right opposite the Swan.

From Chesterfield, take the A619 then the A623 and after the hair pin bend at Sparrow pit, proceed down the A623 turning right onto the A6 By-Pass, Follow directions as above.

Previous Grounds: Not known

Record Attendance: **Att:** 4,500 v Hyde United, Manchester Junior Cup 09/09/1922
Record Victory: 20-3 v Winton United, Manchester Junior Cup 10/11/1962
Record Defeat: Not known
Record Goalscorer: In a season - Neville Holdgate - 62 1937-38
Record Appearances: Not known
Additional Records:

Senior Honours: Manchester League Premier Division 1924, 26, 56, 63, 65, 66, 67, 68, 70, 71.
North West Counties Division Two 2007-08, Challenge Cup 2008-09, Premier Division 2010-11.

10 YEAR RECORD

01-02	02-03	03-04	04-05	05-06	06-07	07-08	08-09	09-10	10-11
MancP 5	MancP 10	MancP 14	NWC2 9	NWC2 12	NWC2	NWC2 1	NWCP 2	NWCP 2	NWCP 1

NEWCASTLE TOWN

Chairman: Paul Ratcliffe
Secretary: Ray Tatton **(T)** 07792 292 849 **(E)** rftatton@tiscali.co.uk
Additional Committee Members:
Michael Pagett, Alan Salt, Terry Donlan, Geoff Eccleston, Ken Walshaw, Les Morris, Colin Spencer, Tony Caveney.
Manager: John Diskin
Programme Editor: Ray Tatton **(E)** rftatton@tiscali.co.uk

Club Factfile

Founded: 1964 **Nickname:** Castle
Previous Names: Parkway Hanley, Clayton Park & Parkway Clayton. Merged as NTFC 86
Previous Leagues: Newcatle & District, Staffs Co & Mid Cheshire, North West Counties

Club Colours (change): Royal blue/royal blue/white (All white)

Ground: Lyme Valley Parkway Stadium, Buckmaster Avenue, Clayton, ST5 3BX **(T)** 01782 662 351
Capacity: 4,000 **Seats:** 300 **Covered:** 1,000 **Clubhouse:** Yes **Shop:** Yes

Directions
FROM M6: Leave the M6 at Junction 15 and immediately turn left up the bank (signposted A519 Newcastle.) Go to the second roundabout and turn right into Stafford Avenue. Take the first left into Tittensor Road (signposted Newcastle Town FC.) Go to the end and the ground is below in the parkway. (Entrance through the gateway signposted Newcastle Town FC.) **FROM A50 DERBY:** Follow the A50 to the end and join the A500 (signposted M6 South) just past Stoke City Football Ground. Follow the A500 to the Motorway and at the roundabout turn right up the bank (A519 Newcastle.) Go to the second roundabout and turn right into Stafford Avenue. Take the first left into Tittensor Road (signposted Newcastle Town FC.) Go to the end and the ground is below in the parkway. (Entrance through the gateway signposted Newcastle Town FC.)

Previous Grounds: Not known

Record Attendance: 3,948 v Notts County - FA Cup 1996
Record Victory: Not known
Record Defeat: Not known
Record Goalscorer: Andy Bott - 149
Record Appearances: Dean Gillick - 632
Additional Records:

Senior Honours: Mid Cheshire League 1985-86. Walsall Senior Cup 1993-94, 94-95.

10 YEAR RECORD

01-02	02-03	03-04	04-05	05-06	06-07	07-08	08-09	09-10	10-11
NWC1 5	NWC1 4	NWC1 6	NWC1 2	NWC1 6	NWC1 12	NWC1 3	NWCP 3	NWCP 1	NP1S 2

QUORN

Chairman: Stuart Turner
Secretary: Reg Molloy (T) 07729 173 333 (E) quornfc@btconnect.com
Additional Committee Members:
J Nooney, S Warrington, M Berry, A Webb, L Caunt, J Penny, H Simpson, J Simpson, M Unwin, M Hall.
Manager: Dougie Keast
Programme Editor: Stewart Warrington (E) quornfc@btconnect.com

Club Factfile

Founded: 1924 **Nickname:** Reds
Previous Names: Quorn Methodists
Previous Leagues: Leicestershire Senior, Midland Alliance

Club Colours (change): All red (Yellow/blue/blue)

Ground: Farley Way Stadium, Farley Way, Quorn, Leicestershire LE12 8RB **(T)** 01509 620 232
Capacity: 1,550 **Seats:** 350 **Covered:** 250 **Clubhouse:** Yes **Shop:** Nk

Directions
Exit Junction 24 M1 Southbound on A6 through Kegworth, continue on A6 signposted Leicester/Loughborough bypass. Through Loughborough and at first roundabout take 2nd exit signposted Quorn. Turn left at traffic lights 200 yards from island and the ground is situated just inside on the left.

Previous Grounds: Not known

Record Attendance: Not known
Record Victory: Not known
Record Defeat: Not known
Record Goalscorer: Not known
Record Appearances: Not known
Additional Records:

Senior Honours: Leicestershire Senior Cup 1940, 1952, 1954.
Leicestershire Senior League 2000-01

10 YEAR RECORD

01-02		02-03		03-04		04-05		05-06		06-07		07-08		08-09		09-10		10-11	
MidAl	7	MidAl	5	MidAl	4	MidAl	4	MidAl	7	MidAl	3	NP 1	12	NP1S	12	NP1S	20	NP1S	15

RAINWORTH MINERS WELFARE

Chairman: Derek Blow
Secretary: Leslie Lee (T) 07740 576 958 (E) leslie.lee7@ntlworld.com
Additional Committee Members:
Derek Bentley, Eileen Wright, Robbie Blamford, Gordon Foster, Brian Martin, Frank Bramwell, John Lock.
Manager: Billy Millar & Lee Wilkinson
Programme Editor: Gordon Foster (E) leslie.lee7@ntlworld.com

Club Factfile

Founded: 1922 **Nickname:** The Wrens
Previous Names: Rufford Colliery
Previous Leagues: Notts Alliance 1922-03, Central Midlands League 2003-07, Northern Counties East 2007-10

Club Colours (change): All White (Red/black/black).

Ground: Welfare Ground, Kirklington Road, Rainworth, Mansfield NG21 0JY (T) 01623 792 495
Capacity: 2,000 **Seats:** 221 **Covered:** 350 **Clubhouse:** Yes **Shop:** No

Directions
From M1 (Junction 29) – take A617. At Pleasley turn right onto the new Mansfield Bypass road which is still the A617 and follow to Rainworth. At roundabout with B6020 Rainworth is off to the right, but it is better to go straight over onto the new Rainworth Bypass and then right at the next roundabout (the ground can be seen on the way along the Bypass) At mini roundabout, turn right onto Kirklington Road and go down the hill for ¼ mile – ground and car park on the right
Alternatively you can reach the new A617 Bypass from the A38 via Junction 28 on the M1. From A614 at roundabout, take the A617 to Rainworth for 1 mile. Left at 1st roundabout into village. At mini roundabout right into Kirklington road – ¼ mile down hill as above.

Previous Grounds: Not known

Record Attendance: 5,071 v Barton Rovers FA Vase SF 2nd Leg, 1982.
Record Victory: Not known
Record Defeat: Not known
Record Goalscorer: Not known
Record Appearances: Not known
Additional Records:

Senior Honours: Notts Senior Cup Winners 1981-82

10 YEAR RECORD

01-02	02-03	03-04	04-05	05-06	06-07	07-08	08-09	09-10	10-11
NottS 8	NottS 5	CM P 3	CM Su 20	CM Su 9	CM Su 3	NCE1 4	NCE1 2	NCEP 2	NP1S 20

ROMULUS

Chairman: Richard Evans
Secretary: Peter Lowe (T) 07738 604 391 (E) peterwloweuk@yahoo.co.uk
Additional Committee Members:
Roger Evans, Andy Fitchett, Peter Morgan, Paul Dockerill, Tom Clarke, Philip Hobson, Keith Brown, Keith Higham, Andy Mitchell, Mark Taylor.
Manager: Richard Evans
Programme Editor: Paul Dockerill (E) peterwloweuk@yahoo.co.uk

Back row (L-R): Michael Easthope (Kit man), Ruth Willey (Physiotherapist), Marvin Johnson, Gavin Day, Dean Baker, Nathan Blissett, Lewis Exall, Luke Paskin, Wayne Dyer, Luke Edwards, Jon Powis, Derek Dudley, Dan Simpson (Chief Scout).
Front Row (L-R): Jamal Pinnock, Nathan Walker, Ross Dempster, Richard Evans Jnr, Dave Barnett (First Team Coach), Paul Dockerill (Vice-Chairman), Richard Evans (Manager), Ashley Jackson, Robert Evans, Peter Faulds, Marcus Brown.

Club Factfile

Founded: 1979 **Nickname:** The Roms
Previous Names: Not known
Previous Leagues: Midland Combination 1999-2004, Midland Alliance 2004-07, Southern 2007-2010

Club Colours (change): Red and white stripes/red/red (Black and green stripes/black/green)

Ground: Sutton Coldfield FC, Central Ground,Coles Lane B72 1NL (T) 0121 354 2997
Capacity: 4,500 **Seats:** 200 **Covered:** 500 **Clubhouse:** Yes **Shop:** Yes

Directions
From M42 Junc 9, take A4097 (Minworth sign). At island, follow signs to Walmley Village. At traffic lights turn right (B4148). After shops turn left at traffic lights into Wylde Green Road. Over railway bridge turn right into East View Road, which becomes Coles Lane.

Previous Grounds: Not known

Record Attendance: Not known
Record Victory: Not known
Record Defeat: Not known
Record Goalscorer: Not known
Record Appearances: Not known
Additional Records:

Senior Honours: Midland Combination Division One 1999-00, Premier Division 2003-04, Challenge Cup 03-04.

10 YEAR RECORD

01-02		02-03		03-04		04-05		05-06		06-07		07-08		08-09		09-10		10-11	
MCmP	4	MCmP	5	MCmP	1	MidAl	12	MidAl	4	MidAl	2	SthM	10	SthM	11	SthM	8	NP1S	10

SHEFFIELD

Chairman: Richard Tims
Secretary: Stephen Hall (T) 07761 207 447 (E)
Additional Committee Members:
I Cameron, R Dyson, P. Hancock, J. Harrison, A. Methley, J Ball, P. Bowden, N. Hughes,D. Risely, M. Turnidge, L Walshaw, C. Williamson, Mrs. D. Risely, Mrs. J. Towning.
Manager: Mark Shaw
Programme Editor: Craig Williamson (E)

Club Factfile

Founded: 1857 **Nickname:** Not known
Previous Names: None
Previous Leagues: Yorkshire 1949-82

Club Colours (change): Red/black/red (All blue)

Ground: The BT Local Business Stadium, Sheffield Road, Dronfield S18 2GD (T) 01246 292 622
Capacity: 1,456 **Seats:** 250 **Covered:** 500 **Clubhouse:** Yes **Shop:** Yes

Directions
From the South – M1 to Junc 29, A617 into Chesterfield. At Roundabout follow A61 Sheffield. This is a dual carriageway passing over 2 roundabouts. At the 3rd roundabout take the 3rd exit signposted Dronfield. The Coach and Horses Public House is at the bottom of the hill on the right and the BT Local Business Stadium directly behind it. Entrance to the ground is by turning right at the traffic lights and immediate right into the Club Car Park. **From the East** - M18 to M1 north to Junc 33 (Sheffield). Turn towards Sheffield and take the 3rd exit from dual carriageway signposted' Ring Road / Chesterfield'. Go straight on at traffic island so that you are travelling alongside dual carriageway for a short period. At the junction turn left onto A61 Chesterfield. This is a dual carriageway passing through numerous traffic lights and two traffic islands. Follow Chesterfield sign at all times. After passing Graves Tennis centre on your left, turn left at next traffic island (still signposted Chesterfield). At next traffic island take 2nd exit signposted Dronfield The Coach and Horses Public House is at the bottom of the hill on the right and the BT Local Business Stadium directly behind it. Entrance to the ground is by turning right at the traffic lights and immediate right into the Club Car Park.

Previous Grounds: Abbeydale Park, Dore 1956-89, Sheffield Amateur Sports Stadium, Hillsborough Park 1989-91, Don Valley Stadium 1991-97

Record Attendance: 2,000 v Barton Rovers - FA Vase Semi-final 1976-77
Record Victory: Not known
Record Defeat: Not known
Record Goalscorer: Not known
Record Appearances: Not known
Additional Records: Paid £1,000 to Arnold Town for David Wilkins. Received £1,000 from Alfreton for Mick Godber 2002. World's first ever Football Club.
Senior Honours: FA Amateur Cup 1902-03. Northern Counties East Division 1 1988-89, 90-91, League Cup 2000-01, 04-05. Sheffield and Hallamshire Senior Cup 1993-94, 2004-05, 05-06.

10 YEAR RECORD

01-02		02-03		03-04		04-05		05-06		06-07		07-08		08-09		09-10		10-11	
NCEP	9	NCEP	7	NCEP	4	NCEP	4	NCEP	4	NCEP	2	NP 1	4	NP1S	11	NP1S	5	NP1S	11

SHEPSHED DYNAMO

Chairman: Peter Bull
Secretary: Danny Pole **(T)** 07866 500 187 **(E)**
Additional Committee Members:
Elaine Hunt, Alan Spendlove, Mick Voce, N.Attwal, M.Widdowson, P.Robinson, P.Bailey, M.Bailey, S.Bailey, S.Straw, A.Gibson, J.Crowson, S.Baker, S.Gardener.
Manager: John Ramshaw
Programme Editor: Ben Reed **(E)** ben@shepsheddynamo.co.uk

Club Factfile

Founded: 1994 **Nickname:** Dynamo
Previous Names: Shepshed Albion/Charterhouse > 1994
Previous Leagues: Leicestershire Senior 1907-16, 19-27, 46-50, 51-81, Midland Counties 1981-82, N.C.E. 1982-83, Southern 1983-88, 96-2004, N.P.L. 1988-93, Midland Combination 1993-94, Midland Alliance 1994-95

Club Colours (change): Black and white stripes/black/black (All yellow)

Ground: The Dovecote, Butt Hole Lane, Shepshed, Leicestershire LE12 9BN **(T)** 01509 650 992
Capacity: 2,050 **Seats:** 570 **Covered:** 400 **Clubhouse:** Yes **Shop:** Yes

Directions
From M1: Leave at Junction 23 and take A512 (Ashby). At first traffic lights turn right into Leicester Road and continue to garage on right. Turn right at mini roundabout into Forest Street and continue to Black Swan pub on left. Turn right into Butt Hole Lane, ground 100 yards. **From M6:** Leave at Junction 15 (Stoke-on-Trent) and take A50 to join M1 at Junction 24 South. At Junction 23 leave M1 and continue as above.

Previous Grounds: Not known

Record Attendance: 2,500 v Leicester City - Friendly 1996-97
Record Victory: Not known
Record Defeat: Not known
Record Goalscorer: Lee McGlinchey - 107
Record Appearances: Lee McGlinchey - 255
Additional Records:

Senior Honours: Midland Counties League 1981-82, League Cup 81-82. Northern Counties East 1982-83, League Cup 82-83. Midland Alliance 1995-96. Leicestershire Senior Cup x7

10 YEAR RECORD

01-02	02-03	03-04	04-05	05-06	06-07	07-08	08-09	09-10	10-11
SthW 16	SthW 17	SthW 21	NP 1 15	NP 1 10	NP 1 20	NP 1 15	NP1S 8	NP1S 17	NP1S 21

STAMFORD

Chairman: John Drewnicki
Secretary: Phil Bee (T) 07772 646 776 (E) phil.bee@queen-eleanor.lincs.sch.uk
Additional Committee Members:
Guy Walton, John Burrows, John Drewnicki, Dave Salisbury, Roger Twiddy, David Whitby, Keith Scarber.
Manager: Simon Clark
Programme Editor: John Burrows (E) phil.bee@queen-eleanor.lincs.sch.uk

Back row (L-R): Luke Weston (coach), Becky Moss (physio), Ross Watson, Tony Battersby, Lee Beeson, Chris Wright, Miles Chamberlain (Captain), Richard Stainsby, Ben Sedgemore (assistant manager), Andy Toyne, Paul Malone, Stuart King, Simon Clark (manager).
Front row (L-R): Ricky Miller, David Sheridan, Craig Rook, Liam Hook, Dan Cotton, Adam Weston, Nick Jackson, Callum Reed, Simon Mowbray.

Club Factfile

Founded: 1894 **Nickname:** The Daniels
Previous Names: Stamford Town and Rutland Ironworks amalgamated in 1894 to form Rutland Ironworks > 1896
Previous Leagues: Peterborough, Northants (UCL) 1908-55, Central Alliance 1955-61, Midland counties 1961-72, United Counties 1972-98, Southern 1998-2007

Club Colours (change): Red/red/red (All navy blue)

Ground: Kettering Road, Stamford, Lincs PE9 2JS (T) 01780 763 079
Capacity: 2,000 **Seats:** 250 **Covered:** 1,250 **Clubhouse:** Yes **Shop:** Yes

Directions
Travel on A1 Southbound. Leave A1 by A43 slip road.
At junction turn left. Ground is one mile on the left.

Previous Grounds: None

Record Attendance: 4,200 v Kettering Town - FA Cup 3rd Qualifying Round 1953
Record Victory: 13-0 v Peterborough Reserves - Northants League 1929-30
Record Defeat: 0-17 v Rothwell - FA Cup 1927-28
Record Goalscorer: Bert Knighton - 248
Record Appearances: Dick Kwiatkowski - 462
Additional Records:

Senior Honours: FA Vase 1979-80. United Counties League x7. Lincolnshire Senior Cup, Senior Shield. Lincolnshire Senior 'A' Cup x3.

10 YEAR RECORD

01-02	02-03	03-04	04-05	05-06	06-07	07-08	08-09	09-10	10-11
SthE 5	SthE 3	SthE 7	SthE 21	SthE 4	SthP 8	NP P 20	NP1S 7	NP1S 10	NP1S 19

SUTTON COLDFIELD TOWN

Chairman: Tom Keogh
Secretary: Bill Worship (T) 07837 375 369 (E) billandpatworship@tiscali.co.uk
Additional Committee Members:
Bernard Bent, Bernard Cheek, Ken Hawkins, Mrs Chris Rogers, Andy Taylor, Neil Murrall, Nick Thurston.
Manager: Chris Keogh
Programme Editor: Lyn Coley (E) billandpatworship@tiscali.co.uk

Club Factfile

Founded: 1897 **Nickname:** Royals
Previous Names: Sutton Coldfield F.C. 1879-1921
Previous Leagues: Central Birmingham, Walsall Senior, Staffordshire County, Birmingham Combination 1950-54, West Midlands (Regional) 1954-65, 79-82, Midlands Combination 1965-79

Club Colours (change): All blue (All yellow)

Ground: Central Ground, Coles Lane, Sutton Coldfield B72 1NL (T) 0121 354 2997
Capacity: 4,500 **Seats:** 200 **Covered:** 500 **Clubhouse:** Yes **Shop:** Yes

Directions
From M42 Junc 9, take A4097 [Minworth sign]. At island, follow signs to Walmley Village. At traffic lights turn right [B4148]. After shops turn left at traffic lights into Wylde Green Road. Over railway bridge turn right into East View Road, which becomes Coles Lane.

Previous Grounds: Meadow Plat 1879-89, Coles Lane 1890-1919

Record Attendance: 2,029 v Doncaster Rovers - FA Cup 1980-81
Record Victory: Not known
Record Defeat: Not known
Record Goalscorer: Eddie Hewitt - 288
Record Appearances: Andy Ling - 550
Additional Records: Paid £1,500 to Gloucester for Lance Morrison, to Burton Albion for Micky Clarke and to Atherstone United for Steve Farmer 1991. Received £25,000 from West Bromwich Albion for Barry Cowdrill 1979

Senior Honours: West Midlands League 1979-80. Midland Combination x2.

10 YEAR RECORD

01-02	02-03	03-04	04-05	05-06	06-07	07-08	08-09	09-10	10-11
SthW 6	SthW 11	SthW 8	SthW 18	SthW 7	SthM 12	SthM 4	SthM 6	SthM 6	NP1S 6

This is what happened next....

Further action between Witton Albion and Sutton Coldfield Town.

Photo by Keith Clayton

PREMIER DIVISION

		P	W	D	L	F	A	Pts
1	Truro City	40	27	6	7	91	35	87
2	Hednesford Town	40	26	5	9	82	38	83
3	Salisbury City	40	23	10	7	82	45	79
4	Cambridge City	40	24	7	9	74	40	79
5	Leamington	40	24	6	10	68	39	78
6	Chesham United	40	20	11	9	64	35	71
7	Chippenham Town	40	18	14	8	54	41	68
8	Stourbridge	40	18	8	14	72	61	62
9	Brackley Town	40	16	10	14	67	47	58
10	Swindon Supermarine	40	17	7	16	56	58	58
11	Bashley	40	14	10	16	55	63	52
12	Evesham United	40	14	9	17	54	49	51
13	Cirencester Town	40	13	8	19	59	67	47
14	Oxford City	40	11	12	17	48	54	45
15	Hemel Hempstead Town	40	13	6	21	50	59	45
16	Banbury United (-1)	40	11	8	21	44	67	40
17	Bedford Town	40	10	7	23	41	76	37
18	Weymouth (-10)	40	12	8	20	55	85	34
19	Didcot Town	40	7	11	22	39	69	32
20	Tiverton Town	40	7	8	25	33	77	29
21	Halesowen Town	40	5	9	26	24	107	24
	Windsor & Eton - record expunged							

PLAY-OFFS

Semi-Finals

Hednesford Town 3-1 Leamington

Salisbury City 1-0 Cambridge City

Final (@ Hednesford Town, 2/5/11)

Hednesford Town 2-2 Salisbury City (Salisbury City won 3-2 on penalties)

	1	2	3	4	5	6	7	8	9	10	11	12	13	14	15	16	17	18	19	20	21
1 Banbury United		1-4	2-0	0-0	2-0	2-1	1-2	0-2	2-1	1-1	0-2	0-4	0-4	1-1	0-2	0-1	4-0	0-0	2-2	0-3	3-0
2 Bashley	2-1		2-5	0-3	1-1	1-1	1-4	1-2	1-1	1-0	0-0	0-4	1-0	0-4	3-1	0-2	0-0	2-0	1-0	2-1	5-1
3 Bedford Town	0-1	1-0		2-1	1-2	1-2	1-1	1-6	1-1	1-2	0-0	2-1	0-1	0-2	0-1	1-0	2-1	0-6	1-3	1-1	4-1
4 Brackley Town	2-0	3-4	4-0		0-0	1-1	1-1	4-1	2-1	5-0	6-0	0-0	3-1	0-0	1-0	0-3	0-0	1-4	1-0	3-2	1-1
5 Cambridge City	1-1	1-1	2-0	2-3		0-0	0-1	1-2	4-2	2-0	7-1	3-2	3-2	3-2	3-0	3-3	3-0	2-0	5-0	0-1	1-0
6 Chesham United	0-2	0-0	0-0	1-0	1-0		2-0	6-1	1-1	1-0	3-0	2-1	3-3	1-0	2-0	1-1	2-0	4-0	5-0	1-0	2-1
7 Chippenham Town	4-0	1-0	3-1	3-2	1-0	1-0		0-0	1-1	1-0	3-1	0-1	2-0	0-0	1-2	1-1	0-0	3-1	4-1	1-2	1-0
8 Cirencester Town	1-1	2-1	4-2	0-3	1-2	3-2	1-1		0-0	1-2	5-0	0-1	3-2	0-1	4-1	0-3	1-2	1-2	1-0	0-3	3-0
9 Didcot Town	0-2	0-2	1-0	1-1	1-2	1-0	1-1	1-2		1-2	1-1	0-3	0-1	1-2	0-3	1-1	1-4	1-4	2-0	0-3	2-2
10 Evesham United	4-3	2-2	0-0	1-0	1-2	0-0	2-2	2-1	3-0		0-0	4-1	1-0	0-1	3-0	0-0	2-3	0-1	3-1	3-4	1-3
11 Halesowen Town	3-1	0-2	0-3	5-3	0-1	1-4	1-2	1-1	1-0	0-8		0-6	1-6	0-3	0-3	0-4	0-3	1-1	0-1	0-3	0-0
12 Hednesford Town	1-0	1-0	4-1	2-0	0-2	3-2	0-2	3-1	1-1	1-0	4-2		2-0	1-1	2-1	3-0	2-3	1-1	2-0	1-0	9-0
13 Hemel Hempstead Town	1-2	0-2	1-0	1-0	0-2	0-1	1-2	2-2	0-1	1-0	1-0	0-1		1-0	0-2	0-3	2-2	1-2	2-1	1-1	1-2
14 Leamington	3-1	2-1	5-0	2-1	2-3	3-2	0-0	1-0	2-1	1-0	3-0	1-2	2-3		2-0	2-0	3-2	2-1	2-1	3-2	1-0
15 Oxford City	2-2	1-1	1-1	0-2	0-1	0-2	0-0	3-3	0-3	0-1	0-0	1-1	3-0	2-3		2-2	0-2	2-1	3-1	1-1	5-0
16 Salisbury City	4-1	2-1	4-1	3-1	1-3	3-2	4-0	4-1	4-2	0-3	7-1	2-1	1-1	0-0	2-0		3-0	2-0	3-0	0-6	3-2
17 Stourbridge	2-1	6-1	3-0	2-1	3-0	1-1	1-0	2-1	3-1	3-1	0-2	1-2	1-5	4-3	0-3	0-0		5-1	0-0	2-2	7-2
18 Swindon Supermarine	3-0	4-2	1-0	1-5	0-2	0-0	3-1	1-0	2-0	1-1	3-0	1-2	1-3	1-0	1-1	1-2	2-1		3-0	0-2	0-1
19 Tiverton Town	1-0	2-2	3-5	1-3	2-2	1-2	0-0	2-2	2-3	1-0	0-0	1-2	1-0	1-0	0-0	1-3	1-0	0-1		1-2	0-4
20 Truro City	1-0	2-1	0-1	1-0	2-0	0-3	5-0	2-0	2-1	1-1	6-0	1-0	3-0	3-1	2-1	1-1	3-1	7-2	3-0		3-2
21 Weymouth	2-4	1-4	3-1	0-0	0-3	3-0	3-3	1-0	1-2	2-0	3-0	2-4	2-2	1-2	1-1	2-0	3-2	0-0	3-1	0-4	

DIVISION ONE CENTRAL

		P	W	D	L	F	A	Pts
1	Arlesey Town (-9)	42	30	7	5	108	34	88
2	Hitchin Town	42	26	9	7	107	44	87
3	Daventry Town (-6)	42	26	9	7	95	47	81
4	Biggleswade Town	42	24	9	9	89	51	81
5	Slough Town	42	24	4	14	91	66	76
6	Rugby Town	42	20	11	11	74	56	71
7	Leighton Town	42	19	12	11	72	50	69
8	Aylesbury	42	19	11	12	73	62	68
9	Woodford United	42	18	9	15	61	59	63
10	Bedfont Town	42	17	12	13	66	66	63
11	Marlow	42	15	9	18	68	65	54
12	Barton Rovers	42	14	9	19	59	64	51
13	Uxbridge	42	14	8	20	76	87	50
14	Burnham	42	14	7	21	61	87	49
15	Bedworth United	42	12	12	18	49	62	48
16	Ashford Town (Middx)	42	13	8	21	69	85	47
17	Soham Town Rangers	42	10	10	22	55	81	40
18	North Greenford United	42	10	10	22	51	86	40
19	AFC Hayes	42	11	6	25	54	96	39
20	Northwood	42	11	6	25	59	106	39
21	Atherstone Town	42	10	6	26	61	118	36
22	Beaconsfield SYCOB	42	7	12	23	49	75	33

PLAY-OFFS

Semi-Finals

Daventry Town 2-0 Biggleswade Town

Hitchin Town 4-1 Slough Town

Final (@ Hitchin Town, 2/5/11)

Hitchin Town 2-0 Daventry Town

	1	2	3	4	5	6	7	8	9	10	11	12	13	14	15	16	17	18	19	20	21	22
1 AFC Hayes		1-2	0-2	6-2	0-1	1-1	1-1	1-2	2-0	2-1	2-0	2-2	0-5	0-4	2-2	2-3	4-2	0-4	2-4	2-0	2-1	1-2
2 Arlesey Town	3-0		2-0	12-0	4-0	2-1	1-0	3-0	3-0	0-0	8-0	0-1	1-2	1-1	3-1	5-0	2-1	4-1	2-1	6-1	3-1	3-2
3 Ashford Town (Middx)	4-2	0-3		1-1	1-2	1-0	3-1	1-1	2-2	2-3	2-2	1-4	3-0	0-3	0-3	3-2	0-0	3-4	1-2	4-2	3-0	2-3
4 Atherstone Town	2-1	0-3	1-3		3-1	3-1	1-3	0-3	0-1	0-3	2-3	1-2	1-3	1-2	0-7	2-0	4-0	1-1	1-2	3-4	3-3	0-4
5 Aylesbury	4-1	2-2	1-3	4-2		2-0	2-2	0-1	0-1	2-2	3-0	1-0	1-3	1-1	1-0	0-0	3-2	1-3	1-2	1-5	4-3	1-1
6 Barton Rovers	1-2	1-2	6-2	0-1	0-1		2-2	4-1	3-1	4-2	0-0	2-3	2-5	0-1	1-0	1-3	1-1	1-1	2-0	1-0	2-1	0-1
7 Beaconsfield S Y C O B	4-3	2-3	2-3	1-2	1-1	0-1		1-1	3-1	0-1	0-2	3-5	1-4	1-0	1-1	2-3	0-1	1-2	1-0	1-3	0-0	4-2
8 Bedfont Town	3-1	0-0	2-5	1-1	1-1	1-0	4-2		3-2	2-1	2-1	0-0	1-1	1-0	1-1	7-0	3-1	2-3	1-2	2-1	1-1	0-3
9 Bedworth United	1-1	1-2	2-1	1-2	1-3	0-1	0-0	0-1		0-0	2-0	1-2	0-1	0-0	2-1	1-1	2-1	1-0	1-1	1-1	1-0	2-1
10 Biggleswade Town	4-0	2-2	4-0	5-1	2-4	3-1	2-1	1-0	3-4		5-2	1-0	1-2	2-1	3-1	2-0	6-2	1-1	1-5	1-1	2-1	1-0
11 Burnham	0-2	1-2	1-0	6-1	0-3	3-3	0-2	1-1	2-1	2-1		2-2	1-2	3-1	1-3	5-3	2-3	2-1	0-2	0-4	1-1	2-1
12 Daventry Town	3-1	1-1	4-2	3-1	1-0	5-0	1-0	5-1	2-2	1-2	2-0		1-1	2-0	0-1	3-2	4-1	4-2	1-2	0-0	4-1	3-2
13 Hitchin Town	2-0	0-1	3-3	5-2	4-2	1-2	4-0	5-1	2-1	1-2	3-0	2-0		5-0	3-0	2-0	1-0	1-2	3-2	9-1	2-2	0-0
14 Leighton Town	2-1	1-2	3-0	2-2	0-0	4-1	0-0	3-1	1-0	0-3	1-1	5-0	3-2		1-1	1-1	5-0	4-1	3-1	4-1	2-1	2-1
15 Marlow	4-1	1-1	2-1	2-0	1-3	0-5	0-0	1-2	4-1	0-0	2-3	1-2	1-1	1-1		3-0	1-2	0-3	1-4	1-0	4-7	0-1
16 North Greenford United	1-2	2-0	2-0	3-3	1-1	2-2	2-0	1-1	2-2	1-1	1-0	0-3	1-5	1-0	1-3		0-2	0-2	1-3	2-1	2-2	2-3
17 Northwood	3-1	1-5	2-2	2-5	1-1	1-2	2-1	5-2	3-4	0-3	3-1	0-6	0-7	1-3	1-6	0-1		0-0	1-5	2-1	0-2	5-0
18 Rugby Town	4-0	1-3	0-1	3-1	0-2	2-2	1-1	4-2	1-0	0-0	1-4	1-4	1-1	2-2	2-0	2-1	1-0		1-0	5-1	4-0	0-0
19 Slough Town	5-0	0-3	2-0	3-0	3-2	2-1	6-4	1-1	2-1	3-2	2-3	1-3	1-1	0-1	1-3	2-1	4-3	1-3		2-1	5-2	3-3
20 Soham Town Rangers	0-0	0-1	1-1	3-1	1-2	0-1	0-0	1-0	2-2	0-3	0-2	0-0	2-3	3-3	1-2	2-0	3-1	1-4	1-0		2-2	3-0
21 Uxbridge	0-2	2-1	3-2	1-2	1-3	1-0	3-0	1-3	2-3	1-4	4-2	1-6	1-0	3-1	0-1	3-1	2-2	3-0	2-1	5-1		5-1
22 Woodford United	5-0	2-1	2-1	4-2	2-5	0-0	1-0	0-3	0-0	1-3	3-0	0-0	0-0	2-0	1-0	2-1	0-1	0-0	1-3	1-0	3-0	

DIVISION ONE SOUTH & WEST

		P	W	D	L	F	A	Pts
1	AFC Totton	40	31	4	5	121	35	97
2	Sholing	40	30	5	5	90	28	95
3	Mangotsfield United	40	26	7	7	79	48	85
4	Frome Town	40	24	7	9	77	31	79
5	Thatcham Town	40	20	7	13	70	43	67
6	North Leigh	40	19	8	13	81	81	65
7	Hungerford Town	40	17	12	11	58	43	63
8	Almondsbury Town	40	17	12	11	63	54	63
9	Taunton Town	40	16	10	14	49	49	58
10	Bideford	40	17	7	16	68	73	58
11	Paulton Rovers	40	15	12	13	64	63	57
12	Cinderford Town	40	16	8	16	63	61	56
13	Gosport Borough	40	16	7	17	58	65	55
14	Yate Town	40	12	8	20	43	48	44
15	Bishops Cleeve	40	10	12	18	47	59	42
16	Abingdon United	40	11	7	22	56	85	40
17	Stourport Swifts	40	10	10	20	52	81	40
18	Bridgwater Town	40	9	11	20	47	86	38
19	Wimborne Town	40	10	5	25	45	81	35
20	Clevedon Town	40	6	8	26	46	86	26
21	Andover	40	2	5	33	32	109	11

Bromsgrove Rovers resigned just before the start of the 2010/11 season.

PLAY-OFFS

Semi-Finals

Mangotsfield United 1-3 Frome Town

Sholing 2-0 Thatcham Town

Final @ Sholing, 2/5/11)

Sholing 0-1 Frome Town

	1	2	3	4	5	6	7	8	9	10	11	12	13	14	15	16	17	18	19	20	21
1 Abingdon United		1-0	1-2	1-2	0-2	2-1	1-2	5-4	2-0	1-4	1-3	2-2	1-3	2-0	1-1	0-1	1-1	1-3	0-3	0-0	3-1
2 AFC Totton	7-0		3-0	9-0	5-1	0-0	4-2	3-1	0-1	3-2	5-2	7-0	1-2	3-1	5-1	2-1	3-2	3-1	3-0	5-2	4-1
3 Almondsbury Town	3-1	1-0		3-2	1-5	0-0	4-0	2-0	1-0	0-1	4-0	0-0	3-3	1-0	2-0	0-0	2-2	0-2	3-2	3-2	3-1
4 Andover	1-5	0-2	0-2		3-4	0-5	0-4	1-2	1-2	0-3	0-1	0-3	0-2	1-4	0-3	0-0	1-2	2-2	0-2	1-3	0-1
5 Bideford	4-2	1-1	0-0	2-1		2-0	0-2	0-3	3-1	1-4	2-0	0-0	3-4	0-2	3-0	2-5	1-1	1-2	1-1	1-2	2-1
6 Bishops Cleeve	2-2	0-2	2-2	2-0	1-2		1-1	0-1	1-1	0-1	3-0	1-0	1-2	3-3	1-5	0-0	0-0	0-0	3-0	0-1	2-1
7 Bridgwater Town	0-3	0-3	2-2	1-0	3-1	1-1		2-3	1-4	2-5	4-2	1-2	0-2	4-0	0-2	0-4	0-0	0-0	0-4	0-1	0-5
8 Cinderford Town	3-2	1-2	1-0	2-2	0-3	4-0	1-0		4-1	1-0	1-1	2-2	1-3	1-2	3-3	2-0	3-2	1-2	0-4	5-1	0-0
9 Clevedon Town	2-2	2-2	2-3	5-0	2-2	1-4	1-1	0-2		1-3	1-1	1-3	1-2	2-3	0-2	2-3	1-3	0-3	2-1	1-0	0-1
10 Frome Town	5-0	0-3	1-4	3-0	0-2	1-1	6-0	4-0	2-1		2-1	0-1	2-0	8-0	1-0	1-0	1-1	0-0	2-0	3-1	0-0
11 Gosport Borough	3-2	0-1	1-1	1-2	4-1	1-0	1-1	1-0	3-1	1-0		1-1	1-3	2-1	3-3	1-1	3-0	2-0	2-1	3-2	2-1
12 Hungerford Town	3-2	0-3	4-1	6-1	3-0	1-2	2-0	0-0	2-0	0-1	3-0		0-1	1-2	0-0	0-1	4-1	1-0	0-0	1-1	1-0
13 Mangotsfield United	4-0	1-2	1-1	1-1	4-0	3-1	2-2	3-2	2-1	0-2	3-2	2-0		3-3	1-1	1-2	1-0	1-0	4-2	3-2	0-1
14 North Leigh	1-1	0-3	5-4	2-1	5-4	6-2	6-3	1-1	5-2	1-2	1-2	1-1	1-2		1-1	0-4	4-2	0-2	0-3	2-1	2-2
15 Paulton Rovers	0-2	1-3	4-1	2-1	0-0	2-1	3-0	1-0	2-2	1-1	2-0	1-4	0-1	3-4		1-6	3-0	1-0	2-2	2-1	2-1
16 Sholing	4-1	2-0	2-1	3-0	2-0	6-1	6-0	1-0	2-1	2-1	3-2	1-0	1-0	1-2	2-1		4-1	5-0	2-1	3-0	2-0
17 Stourport Swifts	0-1	0-5	1-1	4-2	1-4	2-0	1-1	2-1	1-0	1-2	0-2	4-4	0-2	0-4	3-3	1-3		1-3	0-1	3-1	0-3
18 Taunton Town	3-1	1-4	1-0	2-1	2-3	2-0	1-1	1-3	1-1	1-0	3-1	1-1	3-1	0-0	3-2	1-1	1-3		0-2	0-0	0-2
19 Thatcham Town	4-0	1-4	1-0	2-0	3-0	1-0	1-1	1-1	5-0	0-0	1-0	2-0	3-4	1-2	3-0	1-0	3-4	1-0		0-1	1-1
20 Wimborne Town	0-3	1-4	0-1	4-3	1-3	0-4	1-2	2-1	5-0	0-3	3-2	0-1	1-1	1-2	1-1	1-3	1-0	0-2	1-4		0-3
21 Yate Town	1-0	2-2	1-1	2-2	1-2	0-1	0-3	1-2	2-0	0-0	1-0	0-1	0-1	1-2	0-2	0-1	1-2	2-0	0-2	2-0	

LEAGUE CUP

PRELIMINARY ROUND

Daventry Town 3-2 Brackley Town
Truro City 0-1 Bideford

ROUND 1

Abingdon United 2-3 Banbury United
AFC Hayes 3-2 Bedfont Town
AFC Totton 1-2 Sholing
Ashford Town (Middlesex) 2-2 Northwood
(Ashford Town (Middlesex) won 4-3 on penalties)
Atherstone Town 0-1 Cinderford Town
Barton Rovers 0-2 Cambridge City
Bashley 5-2 Weymouth
Beaconsfield SYCOB 3-2 Marlow
Bedworth United 3-1 Stourport Swifts
Bideford 1-2 Tiverton Town
Biggleswade Town 0-2 Arlesey Town
Bishops Cleeve 0-2 Stourbridge
Burnham 1-1 North Greenford United
(North Greenford United won 4-1 on penalties)
Cirencester Town 6-4 North Leigh
Clevedon Town 4-0 Almondsbury Town
Daventry United 4-1 Woodford United
Didcot Town 1-2 Chippenham Town
Evesham United 0-0 Leamington
(Leamington won 3-1 on penalties)
Frome Town 1-1 Paulton Rovers
(Paulton Rovers won 5-4 on penalties)
Gosport Borough 2-0 Andover
Halesowen Town 1-3 Rugby Town
Hemel Hempstead Town 2-1 Soham Town Rgers
Hitchin Town 2-1 Bedford Town
Leighton Town 1-3 Slough Town
Mangotsfield United 3-0 Yate Town
Oxford City 2-1 Thatcham Town
Swindon Supermarine 3-4 Hungerford Town
Taunton Town 3-0 Bridgwater Town
Uxbridge 2-4 Aylesbury
Wimborne Town 1-2 Salisbury City
Windsor & Eton 3-2 Chesham United

ROUND 2

Cinderford Town 0-3 Stourbridge
Cirencester Town 3-1 Hungerford Town
AFC Hayes 1-5 Windsor & Eton
Ashford Town (Middx) 2-1 Aylesbury
Bedworth United 0-1 Daventry Town
Oxford City 0-2 Slough Town
Arlesey Town 1-3 Cambridge City
Bashley 0-3 Salisbury City
Chippenham Town 1-0 Paulton Rovers
Clevedon Town 3-0 Tiverton Town
Hednesford Town 2-0 Banbury United
Hitchin Town 1-2 Hemel Hempstead Town
Leamington 3-0 Rugby Town
North Greenford United 5-1 Beaconsfield SYCOB
Sholing 5-2 Gosport Borough
Taunton Town 2-2 Mangotsfield United
(Taunton Town won 5-4 on penalties)
Hednesford Town - Bye

ROUND 3

Cambridge City 1-0 North Greenford United
Cirencester Town 1-4 Sholing
Stourbridge 2-1 Daventry Town
Ashford Town (Middx) 1-2 Slough Town
Clevedon Town 1-3 Taunton Town
Leamington 0-1 Hednesford Town
Salisbury City 2-3 Chippenham Town
Windsor & Eton 2-0 Hemel Hempstead Town
(Windsor & Eton folded, Hemel Hempstead Town re-instated)

QUARTER FINALS

Cambridge City 3-2 Slough Town
Hednesford Town 4-2 Stourbridge
Hemel Hempstead Town 2-2 Sholing (Hemel Hempstead Town won 4-3 on penalties)
Taunton Town 0-2 Chippenham Town

SEMI-FINALS

Chippenham Town 0-1 Hednesford Town
Hemel Hempstead Town 2-1 Cambridge City

FINAL (2 Legs, 5/4/11 & 12/4/11)

Hemel Hempstead Town 1-2 Hednesford Town
Hednesford Town 3-0 Hemel Hempstead Town

PREMIER LEAGUE STATS 2010-11
(League, FA Cup and FA Trophy)

Top Scoring Club
113 Salisbury City
103 Truro City

Clubs with highest aggregate of goals in their matches

173	Salisbury City	113-60
153	Chippenham Town	75-78
153	Cirencester Town	76-77
153	Swindon Supermarine	83-70
153	Weymouth	60-93

Clubs' most consecutive scoring matches

33 Hednesford Town (5th October until the end of season)
17 Truro City

Top Individual Goalscorers

33	Craig Hammond	(Cambridge City)
22	Warren Byerley	(Weymouth)
22	Denis Fenemore	(Hemel Hempstead T)
22	Ryan Rowe	(Stourbridge)

Scored in Most Games last season
29 games Craig Hammond (Cambridge City)
21 games Ryan Rowe (Stourport)

Best Consecutive Individual Scoring Runs

6 matches	Ryan Rowe	(Stourport)
5 matches	Craig Hammond	(Cambridge City)
5 matches	David Kolodynski	(Cambridge City)

Clubs with most individual Goalscorers in the season:
22 Hednesford Town
20 Leamington
20 Swinson Supermarine

Clubs with least individual goalscorers in the season:
11 Bedford Town
13 Stourbridge

Clubs with most players scoring 10+ in the season
4 Hednesford Town (Kyle Patterson 16 Neil Wellecomme 11,
Marvin Robinson and Danny Quinn 10)

Clubs with most hat trick scorers
5 Hednesford Town: Marvin Robinson 2, Kyle Patterson Neil Wellecomme and Danny Carey-Bertram

Most Penalties scored by clubs
11 Salisbury City, 10 Truro City and 8 Swindon Supermarine

Most Penalties by Individual Players
7 Nick Stanley (Swindon Supermarine)
6 Barry McConnell (Truro City)

Least Goals scored in the League Season
24 Halesowen Town 33 Tiverton Town

Least League Goals conceded in the Season
35 Chesham United and Truro City

Most League Goals conceded in the Season
107 Halesowen Town 85 Weymouth

Most matches in which the clubs failed to score
Halesowen Town 23, Bedford Town and Tiverton Town 17

Most Consecutive Matches without scoring
6 & 5 matches Halesowen Town and 12 in16 matches
4 matches Evesham United and 6 in 7 matches
3 matches Bedford Town and 5 in 6 matches

Clubs benefitting from 'own goals' from opponents
6 Salisbury City
4 Leamington

Most 'Clean Sheets' (your opponents failing to score)
20 Chesham United and Salisbury City

Least Clean Sheets
8 Didcot Town
9 Banbury United and Bedford Town

Most Consecutive Clean Sheets

7 Cambridge City (also 8 in first 10 matches of the season)
5 & 4 Truro City (and 9 in 10 matches)
4 Chesham United (first four games of the season)
4 Hednesford Town

Most Games without keeping a Clean Sheet
15 Didcot Town (goal tally 12-29)
13& 12 Bedford Town also had 4 consecutive clean sheets! (goal tallies 17-32 & near the end of season 10-33)
13 Oxford City (goal tally 6-21) start of seson

Most Consecutive Victories
9 Hednesford Town, Leamington and Salisbury City
7 Cambridge City and Truro City
In 2011 Hednesford Town won 19 of 24 games but failed to gain promotion.

Most Consecutive Defeats
7&6 matches Halesowen Town
7 Tiverton Town
6 Bedford Town & Hemel Hempstead

Most Consecutive Games without a Victory
15 Didcot Town and Tiverton Town
14 Halesowen Town
Oxford City (First games of the season)

Best Unbeaten Run
19 Salisbury City
12 Cambridge City (first 12 of season)
10 Hednesford Town & Leamington

Best League Attendances
1696 Truro City v Weymouth
1095 Salisbury City v Chippenham Town

Best Average League Attendances
778 Salisbury City, 518Truro City and 500 Leamington

Smallest Average League Attendance
134 Evesham United, 144 Cirencester Town
154 Swindon Supermarine

Best League Victories

Home:			
Hednesford Town	9	Weymouth	0
Cambridge City	7	Halesowen T	1
Salisbury City	7	Halesowen T	1
Away:			
Halesowen Town	0	Evesham Utd	8
Salisbury City	0	Truro City	6

Club Goalscorers with 10+ for season 2010-2011 in League, F.A.Cup. F.A.Trophy and Play-Off matches

Four Goalscorers

Hednesford Town	(22)	Kyle Patterson 16, Nick Wellecomme 11, Danny Quinn 10 and Marvin Robinson 10

Three Goalscorers

Brackley Town	(17)	Tom Winters 13 Owen Story 12 Francis Green 10
Salisbury City	(19)	Jake Reid 18, Kayne McLaggon 15 and Darrell Clarke 12
Stourbridge	(13)	Ryan Rowe 22, Linden Dovey 12 and Ben Billingham 10
Truro City	(15)	Barry Hayles 19, Marcus Martin 14 and Andy Watkins 13

Two Goalscorers

Bashley	(13)	Mark Gamble 16 and Chris Knowles 11
Cambridge City	(15)	Craig Hammond 33 David Kolodynski 18
Chesham United	(19)	Steve Wales 15 and Leon Archer 13
Chippenham Town	(16)	Alan Griffin 16 and Lewis Powell 15
Evesham United	(13)	Isaac Shaze 16 and David Accam 10
Leamington	(20)	Luke Corbett 18 and James Rowe 15
Swindon Supermarine	(20)	Nick Stanley 14 and Jamie Gosling 10

One Goalscorer

Bedford Town	(11)	Ian Draycott 17
Cirencester Town	(16)	Jody Bevan 20
Hemel Hempstead Town	(14)	Denis Fenemore 22
Oxford City	(17)	Lee Steele 13
Weymouth	(19)	Warren Byerley 22

Clubs with no goalscorer totalling 10 or more in 2010-2011

Banbury United	(17)	Top Goalscorer: Nabil Shariff 9
Didcot Town	(15)	Top Goalscorer: Dave Laurence 9
Halesowen Town	(14)	Top Goalscorer: Stefan Moore and Justin Nisbett 4 each
Tiverton Town	(14)	Top Goalscorer: Joe Bushin and Ian Sampson 6 each

National Cup Football 2010-2011

Only one Southern League club emerged from the Qualifying Rounds to compete in the competition proper, but **Swindon Supermarine** certainly enjoyed their seven game F.A. Cup run with an excellent tally of seventeen goals shared between ten individual scorers. A thrilling 4-3 replay victory at Blue Square Premier club Bath City in the Fourth Qualifying Round was one of the highlights of the season, before 'Marine' beat Eastwood Town to qualify for a trip to Colchester United where a single goal decided the game .

Salisbury City, scoring fourteen F.A. Cup goals, were the only other Southern League club to reach the Fourth Qualifying Round where they lost at Corby. **Truro City**, helped by a hat trick from Stewart Yetton, enjoyed a spectacular 8-1 victory over Bridgwater Town but lost their next tie at Maidenhead United. The next highest scores were **Cambridge City** with seven, all scored by different marksmen, but in general it was a disappointing F.A. Cup campaign for the Premier Division.

F.A. CHALLENGE CUP

	Games	Round	Goals
Banbury United	1	1Q	1
Bashley	4	3Q	8
Bedford Town	3	2Q	3
Brackley Town	3	2Q	5
Cambridge City	3	2Qr	7
Chesham United	3	2Qr	6
Chippenham Town	2	2Q	2
Cirencester Town	2	1Qr	2
Didcot Town	4	3Q	4
Evesham United	1	1Q	1
Hednesford Town	1	1Q	1
Hemel Hempstead T	1	1Q	1
Leamington	2	1Qr	2
Oxford City	1	1Q	0
Salisbury City	6	4Q	14
Stourbridge	2	2Q	4
Swindon Supermarine	**7**	**2nd Rd**	**17**
Tiverton Town	2	1Qr	1
Truro City	2	2Q	8
Weymouth	1	1Q	2

Halesowen Town didn't compete in last season's F.A. Cup

Leading F.A. Cup Goalscorers

5	Kayne McLaggon (Salisbury City)
4	Jamie Gosling (Swindon Supermarine)
4	Nick Stanley (Swindon Supermarine)
3	Mark Gamble (Bashley)
3	Chris Knowles (Bashley)
3	Jake Reid (Salisbury City)
3	Stewart Yetton (Truro City)

Zamaretto Clubs' First Round F.A. Cup Tie 2010-2011

First Round

Swindon Supermarine 2 Eastwood Town 1
Holgate, Wells — Stevenson — Att: 1159

Second Round

Colchester United 1 Swindon Supermarine 0
Mooney
Att: 3047

F.A. CHALLENGE TROPHY

It certainly wasn't a special season for the majority of Southern League clubs in the national cup competitions, as only Salisbury City, a club with recent senior league experience, and Cirencester Town really did themselves justice in The F.A. Challenge Trophy. Swindon Supermarine bursting with F.A. Cup pride did manage ten Trophy goals, but possibly the pressure of playing ten exciting cup ties before the end of November, proved just too much and they lost after a long journey to a very consistent Lowestoft Town side. Perhaps Cirencester Town had a little luck when drawn to play two clubs under severe administrative pressure, in Halesowen Town and Weymouth, and a third success, in a replay against Grays Athletic brought a 'local derby' with Gloucester City and defeat after another replay. Salisbury City however, made up for the rest of the Premier League's disappointing cup season with an astonishing fourteen F.A. Cup and F.A. Trophy ties to warm them up for their successful play off matches at the end of the season. After Chesham United, Almondsbury Town, Lewes and Basingstoke Town had been seen off, the victories over Wrexham at home and Woking away, really lifted the club, and although a difficult pairing away to Gateshead brought an honourable end to the Trophy run, the club's confidence and spirit was obviously boosted for their end of season heroics.

	Games	Round	Goals
Banbury United	3	2Q	5
Bashley	1	1Q	0
Bedford Town	1	1Q	2
Brackley Town	3	3Q	4
Cambridge City	3	3Q	3
Chesham United	2	1Qr	2
Chippenham Town	4	2Qr	7
Cirencester Town	**6**	**1st Rd**	**9**
Didcot Town	1	1Q	0
Evesham United	2	2Q	1
Halesowen Town	1	1Q	0
Hednesford Town	1	1Q	1
Hemel Hempstead T	1	1Q	2
Leamington	3	3Q	7
Oxford City	1	1Q	1
Salisbury City	**8**	**4th Rd**	**13**
Stourbridge	3	3Q	6
Swindon Supermarine	3	3Q	10
Tiverton Town	1	1Q	1
Truro City	3	3Q	4
Weymouth	2	2Q	3

Leading F.A. Challenge Trophy Goalscorers

4	Ian Brown (Cirencester Town)
4	Darell Clarke (Salisbury Cty)
3	Steve Cook (Swindon Supermarine)
3	Nabil Shariff (Banbury United)

F.A.Trophy ties in the Competition Proper

First Round

Cirencester Town 1	Gloucester City	1
Brown	Smith	Att: 406
Gloucester City 3	Cirencester Town	0
Symons Smith 2 (1pen)		Att: 226
Basingstoke Town 0	Salisbury City	2
	Clarke McLaggon	Att: 475

Second Round

Salisbury City 1	Wrexham	0
Reid (pen)		Att: 1032

Third Round

Woking 0	Salisbury City	2
	Reid , Clarke	Att: 1551

Fourth Round

Gateshead 2	Salisbury City	1
Smith, Hatch	Clarke	Att: 1884

AFC TOTTON

Chairman: Phil Shephard
Secretary: Norman Cook (T) 07580 547 905 (E) secretary@afctotton.com
Additional Committee Members:
John Heskins, Sean McGlead

Manager: Stuart Ritchie
Programme Editor: Steve Chadwick (E) programme@afctotton.com

Club Factfile

Founded: 1886 **Nickname:** Stags
Previous Names: Totton FC until merger with Totton Athletic in 1979
Previous Leagues: Hampshire 1982-86, Wessex 1986-2008

Club Colours (change): White/navy/white (All yellow)

Ground: Testwood Stadium, Salisbury Road, Calmore, Totton SO40 2RW (T) 02380 868 981
Capacity: 2,000 **Seats:** 500 **Covered:** 500 **Clubhouse:** Yes **Shop:** Yes

Directions
From the M27 Junction 2. From the east take the first exit at the roundabout or from the west take the third exit at the roundabout.
Take the first left within 100 yards, signposted Totton Central.
At the T junction turn left and you will find the entrance to the ground approximately 1 mile on the left hand side, just before the Calmore Roundabout.

Previous Grounds: Not known

Record Attendance: 600 v Windsor & Eton - FA Cup 4th Qualifying Round 1982-83
Record Victory: Not known
Record Defeat: Not known
Record Goalscorer: Not known
Record Appearances: James Sherlington
Additional Records:

Senior Honours: Hampshire League 1981-82, 84-85. Wessex League Premier Division 2007-08.
Southern League Division South & West 2010-11.
Hampshire Senior Cup 2010-11.

10 YEAR RECORD

01-02	02-03	03-04	04-05	05-06	06-07	07-08	08-09	09-10	10-11
Wex 3	Wex 3	Wex 8	Wex1 8	Wex1 4	WexP 2	WexP 1	Sthsw 3	Sthsw 2	Sthsw 1

ARLESEY TOWN

Chairman: Manny Cohen
Secretary: Chris Sterry **(T)** 07540 201 473 **(E)** chris.sterry@ntlworld.com
Additional Committee Members:
Paul Ison, Trevor Flint, Ken Gear

Manager: Zema Abbey
Programme Editor: Tony Smith **(E)** cricketfants@sky.com

Club Factfile

Founded: 1891 **Nickname:** The Blues
Previous Names: Not known
Previous Leagues: Biggleswade & Dist., Bedfordshire Co. (South Midlands) 1922-26, 27-28, Parthenon, London 1958-60, United Co. 1933-36, 82-92, Spartan South Mid. 1992-2000, Isthmian 2000-04, 06-08, Southern 2004-07

Club Colours (change): Light blue/dark blue/dark blue (All yellow)

Ground: Armadillo Stadium, Hitchin Road, Arlesey SG15 6RS **(T)** 01462 734 504
Capacity: 2,920 **Seats:** 150 **Covered:** 600 **Clubhouse:** Yes **Shop:** Yes

Directions
From the A1 exit at Baldock(J10) and follow the signs for Stotfold then Arlesey. You will enter Arlesey from the area known as Church End, this is the opposite end of Arlesey, but as there is only one main street just follow keep driving until you pass the Biggs Wall building and the ground is on your left.

Coming of the M1 at Luton and follow the signs for Hitchin, pass Hitchin Town FC on the Shefford Road and turn right into Turnpike Lane, this is Ickleford. Follow the road out of Ickleford and bear left away from the Letchworth turning, the ground is a little further on, on the right.

Previous Grounds: Not known

Record Attendance: 2,000 v Luton Town Reserves - Bedfordshire Senior Cup 1906
Record Victory: Not known
Record Defeat: Not known
Record Goalscorer: Not known
Record Appearances: Gary Marshall
Additional Records:

Senior Honours: South Midlands Premier Division x5. United Counties Premier Division 1984-85. FA Vase 1994-95.
Isthmian League Division 3 2000-01. Southern League Division 1 Central 2010-11.
Bedfordshire Senior Cup 1965-66, 78-79, 96-97, 2010-11.

10 YEAR RECORD

01-02		02-03		03-04		04-05		05-06		06-07		07-08		08-09		09-10		10-11	
Isth2	4	Isth1N	16	Isth1N	8	SthE	14	SthE	10	Isth1N	18	Isth1N	15	SthC	18	SthC	9	SthC	1

BANBURY UNITED

Chairman: Paul Jones
Secretary: Barry Worlsey **(T)** 07941 267 567 **(E)** bworsley@btinternet.com
Additional Committee Members:
Nigel Porter, David Bennett, Richard Cox, Peter Meadows, Sandra Mold.

Manager: Ady Fuller
Programme Editor: David Shadbolt **(E)** djshadbolt@tiscali.o.uk

Club Factfile

Founded: 1933 **Nickname:** Puritans
Previous Names: Banbury Spencer. Club reformed in 1965 as Banbury United
Previous Leagues: Banbury Junior 1933-34, Oxon Senior 1934-35, Birmingham Combination 1935-54, West Midlands 1954-66, Southern 1966-90, Hellenic 1991-2000

Club Colours (change): Red with gold trim/red/red/ (White/blue/blue)

Ground: Spencer Stadium, off Station Road, Banbury OX16 5TA **(T)** 01295 263 354
Capacity: 6,500 **Seats:** 250 **Covered:** 50 **Clubhouse:** Yes **Shop:** Yes

Directions
From M40, Junction 11, head towards Banbury, over first roundabout, left at next roundabout into Concorde Avenue. Straight on at next roundabout, taking left hand lane, and turn left at traffic lights, turn first right into Station Approach. At station forecourt and car park, take narrow single track road on extreme right and follow to Stadium.(Direct SatNav to OX16 5AB).

Previous Grounds: Not known

Record Attendance: 7,160 v Oxford City - FA Cup 3rd Qualifying Round 30/10/1948
Record Victory: 12-0 v RNAS Culham - Oxon Senior Cup 1945-46
Record Defeat: 2-11 v West Bromwich Albion 'A' - Birmingham Combination 1938-39
Record Goalscorer: Dick Pike and Tony Jacques - 222 (1935-48 and 1965-76 respectively)
Record Appearances: Jody McKay - 576
Additional Records: Paid £2,000 to Oxford United for Phil Emsden
Received £20,000 from Derby County for Kevin Wilson 1979

Senior Honours: Hellenic Premier 1999-2000. Oxford Senior Cup 1978-79, 87-88, 2003-04.

10 YEAR RECORD

01-02	02-03	03-04	04-05	05-06	06-07	07-08	08-09	09-10	10-11
SthE 15	SthE 8	SthE 8	SthP 17	SthP 7	SthP 13	SthP 9	SthP 19	SthP 12	SthP 16

BANBURY UNITED

No.	Date	Comp	H/A	Opponents	Att:	Result	Goalscorers	Pos
1	Aug 14	Sth Prem	A	Cirencester Town	211	D 1 - 1	Foster 90	7
2	17		H	Hednesford Town	230	L 0 - 4		
3	21		H	Tiverton Town	200	D 2 - 2	Gordon 11 Shariff 36	17
4	24		A	Halesowen Town	285	L 1 - 3	Taylor 66	
5	28		A	Chesham United	304	W 2 - 0	Banjamin 32 Shariff 88	12
6	30		H	Evesham United	297	D 1 - 1	Shariff 85	
7	Sept 4		A	Didcot Town	225	W 2 - 0	Shariff 27 Taylor 79 (Pen)	10
8	**11**	**FAC 1Q**	**H**	**Chippenham Town**	**277**	**L 1 - 2**	**Taylor 36**	
9	14		H	Bashley	171	L 1 - 4	Benjamin 35	
10	18		H	Swindon Supermarine	213	D 0 - 0		12
11	25		H	Hemel Hempstead	209	L 0 - 4		13
12	Oct 2		A	Truro City	397	L 0 - 1		16
13	9		A	Bedford Town	285	W 1 - 0	Shariff 27	12
14	**16**	**FAT 1Q**	**H**	**Wimborne Town**	**239**	**D 1 - 1**	**Leroyd 41**	
15		**FAT 1Qr**	**A**	**Wimborne Town**	**100**	**W 3 - 1***	**Shariff 55 108 Lockyer 91 (og)**	
16	23		H	Oxford City	258	L 0 - 2		17
17	**30**	**FAT 2Q**	**A**	**Billericay Town**	**285**	**L 1 - 2**	**Shariff 90 (pen)**	
18	Nov 2		A	Stourbridge	245	L 1 - 2	Shariff 57	
19	6		H	Salisbury City	316	L 0 - 1		18
20	16		H	Cambridge City	165	W 2 - 0	Benjamin 18 Taylor 43	
21	20		A	Chippenham Town	373	L 0 - 4		15
22	27		H	Leamington	476	D 1 - 1	Learoyd 9	
23	Dec 4		A	Weymouth	530	W 4 - 2	Coleman 4 (pen) 34 Staff 12 Martin 56	14
24	11		H	Chesham United	275	W 2 - 1	Martin 29 Maddox 78	12
25	Jan 3		A	Evesham United	110	L 3 - 4	Martin 50 Benjamin 65 Owen 84	
26	8		A	Swindon Supermarine	167	L 0 - 3		13
27	15		H	Didcot Town	250	W 2 - 1	Martin 31 Stone 45	12
28	29		H	Cirencester Town	223	L 0 - 2		15
29	Feb 5		A	Tiverton Town	255	L 0 - 1		15
30	8		H	Brackley Town	397	D 0 - 0		
31	12		H	Halesowen Town	219	L 0 - 2		15
32	15		A	Bashley	148	L 1 - 2	Maddox 31	
33	19		H	Chippenham Town	239	L 1 - 2	Benjamin 6	16
34	22		A	Cambridge City	276	D 1 - 1	Staff 32	
35	26		A	Leamington	626	L 1 - 3	Stone 87	16
36	March 5		H	Weymouth	300	W 3 - 0	Maddox 11 (pen) Ashton 45 Rose 58	16
37	12		A	Salisbury City	905	L 1 - 4	Farquarson 28	16
38	15		A	Hednesford Town	321	L 0 - 1		
39	26		H	Bedford Town	243	W 2 - 0	Stone 2 53	16
40	April 2		A	Hemel Hempstead	208	W 2 - 1	Learoyd 26 Maddox 64	16
41	9		H	Stourbridge	298	W 4 - 0	Haisley 40 STONE 3 (49 80 82 (pen)	16
42	16		A	Oxford City	261	D 2 - 2	Ashton 37 Green 54	16
43	23		H	Truro City	499	L 0 - 3		16
44	25		A	Brackley Town	528	L 0 - 2		

Caught in action....

Adam Confue (Daventry) crosses under pressure from Bedfont's Carl McCluskey.

Photo by Keith Clayton

BARWELL

Chairman: David Laing
Secretary: Mrs Shirley Brown **(T)** 07961 905 141 **(E)** shirley.brown16@ntlworld.com
Additional Committee Members:
Mandy French, Colin Burton, Vic Coleman, Mervyn Nash

Manager: Jimmy Ginnelly
Programme Editor: Dave Richardson **(E)** daverichardson@cleartherm.com

Back row (L-R): JIMMY GINNELLY (MANAGER) GUY SANDERS, CHRIS HOLLIST, ADAM WYKES, JAI STANLEY, JAMIE TOWERS, LUKE BARLONE, RICHARD LETTS, SCOTT HADLAND (CAPT) SCOTT RICKARDS, CRAIG DUTTON (now retired), MARTIN HIER (ASST MANAGER) PAUL O'BRIEN (now at Tamworth).
Front row: FRANCINO FRANCIS (now at Tamworth) KEV CHARLEY, SCOTT LOWER, mascot, mascot, LIAM CASTLE, JAMES GINNELLY LEWIS DODD.

Club Factfile

Founded: 1992 **Nickname:** Canaries
Previous Names: Barwell Athletic FC and Hinckley FC amalgamated in 1992.
Previous Leagues: Midland Alliance 1992-2010, Northern Premier League 2010-11.

Club Colours (change): Yellow with green trim/green/yellow (Blue with white trim/blue/blue)

Ground: Kirkby Road Sports Ground, Kirkby Road, Barwell LE9 8FQ **(T)** 01455 843 067
Capacity: 2,500 **Seats:** 256 **Covered:** 750 **Clubhouse:** Yes **Shop:** No

Directions
FROM M6 NORTH/M42/A5 NORTH: From M6 North join M42 heading towards Tamworth/Lichfield, leave M42 at Junction 10(Tamworth Services) and turn right onto A5 signposted Nuneaton. Remain on A5 for approx 11 miles, straight on at traffic lights at Longshoot Motel then at next roundabout take first exit signposted A47 Earl Shilton. In about 3 miles at traffic lights go straight on and in 1 mile at roundabout take first exit signposted Barwell. In about 1.5 miles, centre of village, go straight over mini roundabout and then in 20 metres turn right into Kirkby Road. Entrance to complex is 400 metres on right opposite park. **FROM M1 SOUTH:** From M1 South Take M69)Signposted Coventry) Take Junction 2 Off M69 (Signposted Hinckley) Follow signs to Hinckley . Go straight on at traffic lights with Holywell Pub on the right. The road bears to the right at next traffic lights turn right signposted Earl Shilton/Leicester. Keep on this road past golf club on right at Hinckley United Ground on left and at large roundabout take second exit signposted Barwell. In about 1.5 miles, centre of village, go straight over mini roundabout and then in 20 metres turn right into Kirkby Road. Entrance to complex is 400 metres on right opposite park.

Previous Grounds: Not known

Record Attendance: Not known
Record Victory: Not known
Record Defeat: Not known
Record Goalscorer: Andy Lucas
Record Appearances: Adrian Baker
Additional Records:

Senior Honours: Midland Alliance League Cup 2005-06, Champions 2009-10.
Northern Premier Division One South 2010-11.

10 YEAR RECORD

01-02		02-03		03-04		04-05		05-06		06-07		07-08		08-09		09-10		10-11	
MidAl	8	MidAl	12	MidAl	18	MidAl	13	MidAl	9	MidAl	6	MidAl	10	MidAl	2	MidAl	1	NP1S	1

BASHLEY

Chairman: Richard Millbery
Secretary: Dave Grant **(T)** 07800 800 308 **(E)** bashdave@hotmail.co.uk
Additional Committee Members:
Chris Brown, Pat Bowring.

Manager: Steve Riley
Programme Editor: Richard Millbery **(E)** rw_millbery@lineone.net

Club Factfile

Founded: 1947 **Nickname:** The Bash
Previous Names: Not known
Previous Leagues: Bournemouth 1953-83, Hampshire 1983-86, Wessex 1986-89, Southern 1989-2004, Isthmian 2004-06

Club Colours (change): Gold/black/black (White/blue/blue)

Ground: Bashley Road Ground, Bashley Road, New Milton, Hampshire BH25 5RY **(T)** 01425 620 280
Capacity: 4,250 **Seats:** 250 **Covered:** 1,200 **Clubhouse:** Yes **Shop:** Yes

Directions
Take the A35 from Lyndhurst towards Christchurch, turn left onto B3058 towards New Milton.
The ground is on the left hand side in Bashley village.

Previous Grounds: Not known

Record Attendance: 3,500 v Emley - FA Vase Semi-final 1st Leg 1987-88
Record Victory: 21-1 v Co-Operative (A) - Bournemouth League 1964
Record Defeat: 2-20 v Air Speed (A) - Bournemouth League 1957
Record Goalscorer: Richard Gillespie - 134
Record Appearances: John Bone - 829
Additional Records: Paid £7,500 to Newport (IOW) for Danny Gibbons and from Dorchester Tn for David Elm. Received £15,000 from Salisbury for Craig Davis, from Eastleigh for Paul Sales and from AFC Bournemouth for Wade Elliott.

Senior Honours: Wessex League 1986-87, 87-88, 88-89. Southern League Southern Division 1989-90, Division 1 South & West 2006-07.

10 YEAR RECORD

01-02		02-03		03-04		04-05		05-06		06-07		07-08		08-09		09-10		10-11	
SthE	10	SthE	5	SthE	11	Isth1	14	Isth1	9	Sthsw	1	SthP	5	SthP	14	SthP	7	SthP	11

BASHLEY

No.	Date	Comp	H/A	Opponents	Att:	Result	Goalscorers	Pos
1	Aug 14	Sth Prem	A	Leamington	513	L 1 - 2	Knowles 16 (pen)	16
2	17		H	Salisbury City	613	L 0 - 2		
3	21		H	Didcot Town	277	D 1 - 1	Gamble 11	21
4	24		A	Truro City	301	L 1 - 2	Roberts (Adam) 90	
5	30		A	Weymouth	673	W 4 - 1	Maxwell 5 White 24 (og) Oliver 38 T.Hill 82	
6	Sept 4		H	Chippenham Town	269	L 1 - 4	T.Hill 64	18
7	**11**	**FAC 1Q**	**A**	**Walton & Hersham**	**160**	**W 4 - 1**	**T.Hill 8 Knowles 30 Gamble 65 73**	
8	14		A	Banbury United	171	W 4 - 1	Gamble 4 T.Hill 43 79 Roberts 90	
9	18		A	Bedford Town	285	L 0 - 1		15
10	**25**	**FAC 2Q**	**H**	**Fleet Town**	**195**	**D 2 - 2**	**Gamble 39 Knowles 69 (pen)**	
11	**28**	**FAC 2Qr**	**A**	**Fleet Town**	**146**	**W 2 - 0**	**Allen 15 Knowles 87 (pen)**	
12	Oct 2		H	Stourbridge	240	D 0 - 0		17
13	5		H	Chesham United	222	D 1 - 1	Middleton 35	
14	**9**	**FAC 3Q**	**A**	**Poole Town**	**838**	**L 0 - 1**		
15	**16**	**FAT 1Q**	**A**	**Weymouth**	**363**	**L 0 - 2**		
16	23		H	Evesham United	245	W 1 - 0	Middleton 11	14
17	30		A	Hemel Hempstead	183	W 2 - 0	R.Hill 43 Allen 46	11
18	Nov 6		H	Cambridge City	287	D 1 - 1	T.Hill 56	11
19	13		A	Halesowen Town	185	W 2 - 0	Whitley 54 Knowles 89	
20	16		A	Oxford City	164	D 1 - 1	T.Hill 35	
21	Dec 4		H	Cirencester Town	207	L 1 - 2	T.Hill 29	12
22	14		A	Brackley Town	118	W 4 - 3	Gamble 15 90 Thackery 32 (og) Middleton 54	
23	Jan 3		H	Weymouth	346	W 5 - 1	Spinney 53 GAMBLE 3 (54 62 67) Middleton 64	
24	8		H	Bedford Town	228	L 2 - 5	R. Hill 58 Meade 90	11
25	15		A	Chippenham Town	352	L 0 - 1		11
26	18		H	Swindon Supermarine	175	W 2 - 0	Gamble 39 R.Hill 63	
27	22		A	Salisbury City	774	L 1 - 2	Oliver 8	11
28	29		H	Leamington	272	L 0 - 4		13
29	Feb 1		A	Hednesford Town	240	L 0 - 1		
30	5		A	DidcotTown	138	W 2 - 0	Knowles 23 75	13
31	8		A	Tivertn Town	190	D 2 - 2	T.Hill 3 Knowles 88	
32	12		H	Truro City	285	W 2 - 1	Gamble 21 Allen 65	10
33	15		H	Banbury United	148	W 2 - 1	Gamble 10 Knowles 44	
34	19		A	Swindon Supermarine	137	L 2 - 4	Knowles 1 (pen) 90	10
35	22		H	Oxford City	188	W 3 - 1	Whitley 11 28 Gamble 47	
36	26		H	Hednesford Town	264	L 0 - 4		10
37	March 5		A	Cirencester Town	87	L 1 - 2	Mason 18	10
38	12		A	Cambridge City	329	D 1 - 1	Allen 17	10
39	19		H	Halesowen Town	205	D 0 - 0		11
40	26		H	Hemel Hempstead	180	W 1 - 0	Gamble 89	10
41	April 2		A	Chesham United	361	D 0 - 0		11
42	9		H	Brackley Town	238	L 0 - 3		11
43	12		A	Evesham United	109	D 2 - 2	Gamble 55 Allen 67	
44	23		A	Stourbridge	291	L 1 - 6	Mason 86	11
45	25		H	Tiverton Town	231	W 1 - 0	Allen 58	

Bedford Town F.C.

BEDFORD TOWN

Chairman: David Howell
Secretary: Dave Swallow **(T)** 07939 812 965 **(E)** david.swallow@bedfordeagles.net
Additional Committee Members:
Paul Searing, Gerry Edmunds, Mick Hooker, Tony Luff, Dave Redman,

Manager: Ady Hall
Programme Editor: Dave Swallow **(E)** david.swallow@bedfordeagles.net

Back Row L to R: Chris Gibbons(Physio), Mark Ducket, Josh Beech, Graham Clark, Wes Lewis, Ian Brown, Michael Kavanagh, James Faulkner, Gavin Hoyte, Gareth Price, Jermaine Ivy, Jermaine Hall, Seb Simpson.
Front Row: Paul Cooper, Callum lewis, Drew Roberts, Steve Jackman (Coach), David Howell (Chairman), Ady Hall (Manager), Tom Damon, Manny Richardson, Jamie Cole.

Club Factfile

Founded: 1989 **Nickname:** The Eagles
Previous Names: Original Bedford Town founded in 1908 folded in 1982
Previous Leagues: South Midlands 1989-94, Isthmian 1994-2004, Southern 2004-06, Conference 2006-07

Club Colours (change): Blue with white trim/blue/blue (White/navy/white)

Ground: The Eyrie, Meadow Lane, Cardington, Bedford MK44 3SB **(T)** 01234 831 558
Capacity: 3,000 **Seats:** 300 **Covered:** 1,000 **Clubhouse:** Yes **Shop:** Yes

Directions
From A1: Take A603 from Sandy to Bedford, go through Willington and ground is a mile and a half on right, signposted Meadow Lane. From M1: Off at Junction 13, take A421, carry on A421 onto Bedford Bypass and take A603 Sandy turn off. Ground is on left.

Previous Grounds: Allen Park, Queens Park, Bedford Park Pitch 1991-93

Record Attendance: 3,000 v Peterborough United - Ground opening 06/08/1993
Record Victory: 9-0 v Ickleford and v Cardington
Record Defeat: 0-5 v Hendon
Record Goalscorer: Jason Reed
Record Appearances: Eddie Lawley
Additional Records:

Senior Honours: Isthmian League Division 2 1998-99. Bedfordshire Senior Cup 1994-95. Southern League Play-offs 2005-06.

10 YEAR RECORD

01-02	02-03	03-04	04-05	05-06	06-07	07-08	08-09	09-10	10-11
Isth P 17	Isth P 9	Isth P 15	SthP 5	SthP 5	Conf S 22	SthP 19	SthP 15	SthP 18	SthP 17

BEDFORD TOWN

No.	Date	Comp	H/A	Opponents	Att:	Result	Goalscorers	Pos
1	Aug 14	Sth Premier	A	Oxford City	151	D 1 - 1	Sozzo 23	8
2	18		H	Halesowen Town	230	D 0 - 0		
3	21		H	Truro City	344	D 1 - 1	Daniel 10	11
4	24		A	Didcot Town	145	L 0 - 1		
5	28		A	Swindon Supermarine	141	L 0 - 1		18
6	30		H	Chesham United	369	L 1 - 2	Clark 39	
7	Sept 5		A	Evesham United	146	D 0 - 0		20
8	**11**	**FAC 1Q**	**A**	**Stanway Rovers**	**128**	**D 1 - 0**	**Lewis 70**	
9	**14**	**FAC 1Qr**	**H**	**Stanway Rovers**	**221**	**W 2 - 0**	**Draycott 33 80 (pen)**	
10	18		H	Bashley	285	W 1 - 0	Daniel 81	19
11	**25**	**FAC 2Q**	**H**	**Boreham Wood**	**361**	**L 0 - 2**		
12	28		H	Leamington	238	L 0 - 2		
13	Oct 2		A	Salisbury City	699	L 1 - 4	Sozzo 15	20
14	5		A	Cirencester Town	80	L 2 - 4	Daniel 10 Sozzo 86	
15	9		H	Banbury United	285	L 0 - 1		20
16	**16**	**FAT 1Q**	**A**	**Harlow Town**	**248**	**L 2 - 3**	**Sozzo 47 Wall 78**	
17	23		A	Tiverton Town	219	W 5 - 3	DRAYCOTT 3 (14 16pen 69) Sozzo 17 90	20
18	30		H	Hednesford Town	275	W 2 - 1	Stupple 68 Cole 90	17
19	Nov 6		A	Hemel Hempstead	210	L 0 - 1		17
20	13		H	Stourbridge	287	W 2 - 1	Draycott 10 Lewis 79	14
21	16		H	Brackley Town	178	W 2 - 1	Sozzo 36 Clark 84	
22	20		A	Weymouth	431	L 1 - 3	Lewis 53	14
23	Dec 11		H	Swindon Supermarine	242	L 0 - 6		15
24	Jan 3		A	Chesham United	367	D 0 - 0		
25	8		A	Bashley	228	W 5 - 2	Daniel 45 Ian Draycott 63 Duckett 67 Ivy 82 Whitley 86 (og)	
26	15		H	Evesham United	279	L 1 - 2	Ian Draycott 38	17
27	18		A	Chippenham Town	277	L 1 - 3	Ian Draycott 18	
28	22		A	Halesowen Town	164	W 3 - 0	Ian Draycott 38 77 Richardson 50	16
29	29		H	Oxford City	220	L 0 - 1		16
30	Feb 5		A	Truro City	321	W 1 - 0	Ivy 40	15
31	12		H	Didcot Town	285	D 1 - 1	Draycott 64	13
32	March 5		H	Chippenham Town	241	D 1 - 1	Ivy 47	15
33	8		A	Leamington	345	L 0 - 5		
34	12		H	Hemel Hempstead	276	L 0 - 1		15
35	19		A	Stourbridge	619	L 0 - 3		16
36	22		H	Cambridge City	297	L 1 - 2	Draycott 60	
37	26		A	Banbury United	243	L 0 - 2		17
38	29		A	Brackley Town	171	L 0 - 4		
39	April 2		H	Cirencester Town	234	L 1 - 6	Draycott 15	17
40	5		H	Weymouth	192	W 4 - 1	Draycott 48 Sozzo 53 Daniel 76 Wall 85	
41	9		A	Hednesford Town	422	L 1 - 4	Draycott 53	17
42	16		H	Tiverton Town	251	L 1 - 3	Draycott 19	
43	23		H	Salisbury City	373	W 1 - 0	Ivy 51	17
44	25		A	Cambridge City	541	L 0 - 2		

BRACKLEY TOWN

Chairman: Sara Crannage
Secretary: Pat Ashby **(T)** 07969 825 636 **(E)** pat.ashby55@btinternet.com
Additional Committee Members:
Dave Boynton, Phil Hedges, Francis Oliver, Tim Carroll.

Manager: Jon Brady
Programme Editor: Brian Martin **(E)** brianmartin2905@aol.com

Back Row (L-R): Barry Quinn, Brett Solkhon, Jefferson Louis, Jamie Gould, Tom Winters, Francis Green, Elliot Sandy, Tom Kemp, Billy Turley.
Front Row: Tommy Jaszczun, Owen Story, James Clifton, Paul Dempsey, Ellis Myles, Chris WIllmott.
Photo by Brian Martin, taken after Brackley's 1-0 victory over Northampton Town in the Maunsell Cup during the 2011-12 pre-season.

Club Factfile

Founded: 1890 **Nickname:** Saints
Previous Names: Not known
Previous Leagues: Banbury & District, North Buckinghamshire, Hellenic 1977-83, 94-97, 99-2004, United Counties 1983-84, Southern 1997-99
Club Colours (change): Red and white stripes/red/white (All yellow)

Ground: St James Park, Churchill Way, Brackley NN13 7EJ **(T)** 01280 704 077
Capacity: 3,500 **Seats:** 300 **Covered:** 1,500 **Clubhouse:** Yes **Shop:** Yes

Directions
Take A43 from Northampton or Oxford, or A422 from Banbury to large roundabout south of town. Take exit marked Brackley and follow towards the town (Tesco store on left). Pass the Locomotive public house and take first turning right, signposted Football Club, into Churchill Way - road leads into Club car park.

Previous Grounds: Banbury Road, Manor Road, Buckingham Road > 1974

Record Attendance: 960 v Banbury United - 2005-06
Record Victory: Not known
Record Defeat: Not known
Record Goalscorer: Paul Warrington - 320
Record Appearances: Terry Muckelberg - 350
Additional Records: Received £2,000 from Oxford City for Phil Mason 1998

Senior Honours: Hellenic League Premier Division 1996-97, 2003-04, Division 1 Cup 1982-83. Southern League Division 1 Midlands 2006-07

10 YEAR RECORD

01-02		02-03		03-04		04-05		05-06		06-07		07-08		08-09		09-10		10-11	
Hel P	7	Hel P	7	Hel P	1	SthW	7	SthW	3	SthM	1	SthP	8	SthP	11	SthP	5	SthP	9

BRACKLEY TOWN

No.	Date	Comp	H/A	Opponents	Att:	Result	Goalscorers	Pos
1	Aug 14	Sth Prem	H	Cambridge City	235	D 0 - 0		13
2	17		A	Heme Hempstead Town	221	L 0 - 1		
3	21		A	Chesham United	281	L 0 - 1		19
4	24		H	Chippenham Town	202	D 1 - 1	Winters 9	
5	28		H	Stourbridge	217	D 0 - 0		19
6	30		A	Oxford City	348	W 2 - 0	Appiah 15 Story 39	
7	**11**	**FAC 1Q**	**A**	**Leamington**	**532**	**D 2 - 2**	**Basham 14 Francis Green 20**	
8	**14**	**FAC 1Qr**	**H**	**Leamington**	**306**	**W 2 - 0**	**Basham 35 (pen) Willmott 68**	
9	18		A	Cirencester Town	117	W 3 - 0	Appiah 2 Basham 41 48	13
10	**25**	**FAC 2Q**	**H**	**Buxton**	**306**	**L 1 - 3**	**Palmer 33**	
11	Oct 2		H	Hednesford Town	259	D 0 - 0		14
12	5		A	Leamington	503	L 1 - 2	Appiah 90	
13	**16**	**FAT 1Q**	**A**	**Burnham**	**102**	**D 0 - 0**		
14	**30**	**FAT 2Q**	**H**	**Windsor & Eton**	**187**	**W 4 - 0**	**Winters 25 Basham 36 Story 56 Taylor 69**	**20**
15	Nov 2		H	Salisbury City	204	L 0 - 3		
16	6		A	Truro City	432	L 0 - 1		20
17	11		A	Weymouth	271	D 0 - 0		
18	13		H	Tiverton Town	152	W 1 - 0	Bradley 24	16
19	16		A	Bedford Town	178	L 1 - 2	Bradley 74 (pen)	
20	**20**	**FAT 3Q**	**H**	**Wealdstone**	**302**	**L 0 - 1**		
21	23		H	Didcot Town	151	W 2 - 1	Thomas 62 Francis Green 65	
22	27		A	Halesowen Town	122	L 3 - 5	Thomas 16 Anderson 57 Moore 65 (og)	16
23	Dec 11		A	Stourbridge	208	L 1 - 2	Gould 4	16
24	14		H	Bashley	118	L 3 - 4	Palmer 53 Winters 59 Francis Green 65	
25	Jan 3		H	Oxford City	268	W 1 - 0	Francis Green 55	
26	8		H	Cirencester Town	177	W 4 - 1	WINTERS 3 (6 48 78 pen) Francis Green 42	14
27	22		H	Hemel Hempstead	181	W 3 - 1	Thomas 14 Story 43 Winters 90	12
28	25		H	Evesham United	105	W 5 - 0	Francis Green 35 81 Winters 50 Palmer 78 Sandy 80	
29	29		A	Cambridge City	313	W 3 - 2	Thomas 30 Story 61 87	11
30	Feb 5		H	Chesham United	202	D 1 - 1	Thomas 55	10
31	8		A	Babury United	397	D 0 - 0		
32	12		A	Chippenham Town	391	L 2 - 3	Sandy 48 Story 59	11
33	19		A	Didcot Town	190	D 1 - 1	Sandy 19	12
34	March 2		A	Swindon Supermarine	203	W 5 - 1	Kemp 36 Winters 45 (pen) Palmer 68 88 Francis Green 77	
35	5		A	Evesham United	124	L 0 - 1		12
36	12		H	Truro City	253	W 3 - 2	Kemp 14 Francis Green 53 Chennels 86	11
37	15		H	Weymouth	171	D 1 - 1	Story 82	
38	19		A	Tiverton Town	208	W 3 - 1	Winters 2 (pen) Chennels 58 Story 90	10
39	29		H	Bedford Town	171	W 4 - 0	Basham 26 86 Kemp 73 Sandy 77	
40	April 2		H	Leamington	376	D 0 - 0		9
41	5		H	Halesowen Town	135	W 6 - 0	Francis Green 6 Winters 8 80 Basham 13 Story 47 49	
42	9		A	Bashley	238	W 3 - 0	Sandy 1 80 Quinn 82	9
43	16		H	Swindon Supermarine	225	L 1 - 4	Basham 52 (pen)	9
44	19		A	Salisbury City	565	L 1 - 3	Story 41	
45	23		A	Hednesford Town	526	L 0 - 2		9
46	25		H	Banbury United	528	W 2 - 0	Sandy 65 Story 90	

CAMBRIDGE CITY

Chairman: Kevin Satchell
Secretary: Andy Dewey **(T)** 07720 678 585 **(E)** andy.dewey@btinternet.com
Additional Committee Members:
Sharon Pettengell, Terry Dunn, Ken Ledran, Gill Wordingham, Roger de Ste Croix.

Manager: Gary Roberts
Programme Editor: Chris Farrington **(E)** ccfc.editor@googlemail.com

Back row (L-R): Robbie Nightingale, Scott Paterson, Luke Robins, Dubi Ogbonna.
Middle row: Lee chaffey, Joey Abbs, Craig Hammond, Zac Barrett, Dave Theobald, James Krause, Miles Smith.
Front row: Neil Midgley, Joe Miller (sports therapist), Gary Roberts (manager), Adrian Cambridge, Lee Clift.

Club Factfile

Founded: 1908 **Nickname:** Lilywhites
Previous Names: Cambridge Town 1908-51
Previous Leagues: Bury & District 1908-13, 19-20, Anglian 1908-10, Southern Olympian 1911-14, Southern Amateur 1913-35, Spartan 1935-50, Athenian 1950-58, Southern 1958-2004

Club Colours (change): White/black/black (All light blue)

Ground: City Ground, Milton Road, Cambridge CB4 1UY **(T)** 01223 357 973
Capacity: 2,000 **Seats:** 533 **Covered:** 1,400 **Clubhouse:** Yes **Shop:** Yes

Directions
Take Junction 13 on M11 and head for City Centre. At mini roundabout turn left then straight on at traffic lights. The road then runs parallel with the river. On reaching traffic lights controlling entry to one way system, get into middle lane up beside Staples Office Furniture and follow lane behind Staples where it becomes nearside lane. Stay in this lane until road straightens then take first left. Ground is behind Westbrook Centre.

Previous Grounds: Not known

Record Attendance: 12,058 v Leytonstone - FA Amateur Cup 1st Round 1949-50
Record Victory: Not known
Record Defeat: Not known
Record Goalscorer: Gary Grogan
Record Appearances: Mal Keenan
Additional Records: Paid £8,000 to Rushden & Diamonds for Paul Coe
Received £100,000 from Millwall for Neil Harris 1998

Senior Honours: Southern League 1962-63, Southern Division 1985-86.
Suffolk Senior Cup 1909-10. East Anglian x9.

10 YEAR RECORD

01-02	02-03	03-04	04-05	05-06	06-07	07-08	08-09	09-10	10-11
SthP 14	SthP 18	SthP 8	Conf S 2	Conf S 7	Conf S 13	Conf S 14	SthP 4	SthP 6	SthP 4

CAMBRIDGE CITY

No.	Date	Comp	H/A	Opponents	Att:	Result	Goalscorers	Pos
1	Aug 14	Sth Prem	A	Brackley Town	235	D 0 - 0		14
2	17		H	Leamington	312	W 3 - 2	Burke 41 Hammond 57 Cambridge 60	
3	21		H	Salisbury City	319	D 3 - 3	Hammond 45 85 Fuller 75	7
4	24		A	Hednesford Town	325	W 2 - 0	Hammond 59 Kolodynski 71	
5	28		H	Tiverton Town	267	W 5 - 0	Kolodynski 8 Hammond 9 Burke 11 Nicel 36 Abbs 86	7
6	30		A	Hemel Hempstead Town	390	W 2 - 0	Kolodynski 48 58	
7	Sept 4		H	Stourbridge	365	W 3 - 0	Cambridge 49 Theobald 65 Kolodynski 85	1
8	**11**	**FAC 1Q**	**H**	**Long Buckby**	**270**	**W 3 - 0**	**Kolodynski 31 (pen) Chaffy 48 Wade 83**	
9	14		A	Oxford City	147	W 1 - 0	Hammond 8	
10	18		A	Weymouth	506	W 3 - 0	Hammond 29 89 Chaffey 37	1
11	**25**	**FAC 2Q**	**H**	**HItchin Town**	**388**	**D 2 - 2**	**Hammond 5 Cambridge 90**	
12	**28**	**FAC 2Qr**	**A**	**Hitchin Town**	**324**	**W 2 - 0**	**Burke 57 Theobald 81**	
13	Oct 2		H	Chippenham Town	322	L 0 - 1		1
14	5		A	Halesowen Town	176	W 1 - 0	Theobald 38	
15	**16**	**FAT 1Q**	**H**	**Aveley**	**243**	**W 1 - 0**	**Hammond 1**	
16	23		A	Cirencester Town	147	W 2 - 1	Hammond 19 86	1
17	**30**	**FAT 2Q**	**A**	**Daventry Town**	**311**	**W 2 - 1**	**Hammond 17 54**	
18	Nov 6		A	Bashley	287	D 1 - 1	Theobald 11	2
19	13		H	Chesham United	356	D 0 - 0		3
20	16		A	Banbury United	165	L 0 - 2		
21	**20**	**FAT 3Q**	**A**	**Eastwood Town**	**246**	**L 0 - 2**		
22	27		A	Didcot Town	100	W 2 - 1	Hammond 25 Hughes 45	3
23	Dec 12		A	Tiverton Town	192	D 2 - 2	Hammond 20 Robbins 59	3
24	14		H	Swindon Supermarine	211	W 2 - 2	Hammond 55 Kolodynski 80	
25	Jan 3		H	Hemel Hempstead U	357	W 3 - 2	Theobald 35 Robins 78 Hammond 82	3
26	8		H	Weymouth	352	W 1 - 0	Hammond 4	3
27	15		A	Stourbridge	305	L 0 - 3		3
28	22		A	Leamington	543	W 3 - 2	Abbs 3 Kolodynski 13 38	3
29	25		H	Truro City	347	L 0 - 1		
30	29		H	Brackley Town	313	L 2 - 3	Hammond 44 Midgeley 83	3
31	Feb 1		H	Oxford City	194	W 3 - 0	Kolodynski 20 85 Hammond 38	
32	12		H	Hednesford Town	471	W 3 - 2	Kolodynski 50 (pen) 89 Hammond 77	3
33	15		H	Evesham United	197	W 2 - 0	Abbs 8 Kolodynski 13	
34	19		A	Evesham United	140	W 2 - 1	Theobald 14 Hammond 52	3
35	22		H	Banbury United	276	D 1 - 1	Kolodynski 38 (pen)	
36	March 5		A	Truro City	611	L 0 - 2		3
37	12		H	Bashley	329	D 1 - 1	Hammond 67	4
38	15		A	Salisbury City	860	W 3 - 1	Hammond 29 Kolodynski 49 Abbs 63	
39	19		A	Chesham United	473	L 0 - 1		6
40	22		A	Bedford Town	297	W 2 - 1	Krause 4 Abbs 7	
41	26		A	Swindon Supermarine	137	W 2 - 0	Hammond 16 45	4
42	April 2		H	Halesowen Town	345	W 7 - 1	HAMMOND 4 (17 24pen 44 48) Abbs 56 87 Kolodynski 65	3
43	12		H	Didcot Town	219	W 4 - 2	Nightingale 7 10 Abbs 27 63	
44	16		H	Cirencester Town	446	L 1 - 2	Hammond 35	4
45	23		A	Chippenham Town	353	L 0 - 1		7
46	25		H	Bedford Town	541	W 2 - 0	Hammond 18 Kolodynski 48	4
47	**28**	**P-Off SF**	**A**	**Salisbury City**	**1126**	**L 0 - 1**		

CHESHAM UNITED

Chairman: Alan Calder
Secretary: Brian McCarthy **(T)** 07900 376 491 **(E)** brian_mccarthy@ntlworld.com
Additional Committee Members:
Mike Dragisic, D. Jeffrey, G. Stevenson, M. Warrick, C Beton.

Manager: Andy Leese
Programme Editor: Steve Doman **(E)** cufcprogramme@talktalk.net

Club Factfile

Founded: 1919 **Nickname:** The Generals
Previous Names: Not known
Previous Leagues: Spartan 1917-47, Corinthian 1947-63, Athenian 1963-73, Isthmian 1973-2004

Club Colours (change): All claret (Yellow/black/yellow)

Ground: The Meadow, Amy Lane, Amersham Road, Chesham HP5 1NE **(T)** 01494 783 964
Capacity: 5,000 **Seats:** 284 **Covered:** 2,500 **Clubhouse:** Yes **Shop:** Yes

Directions
From M25 Junction 20 take A41 (Aylesbury), leave A41 at turn-off for Chesham (A416), pass through Ashley Green into Chesham. Follow signs to Amersham, still on A416 pass two petrol stations opposite each other and at next roundabout take third exit into ground.
From M1 Junction 8 follow signs for Hemel Hempstead then joining the A41 for Aylesbury, then as above.

Previous Grounds: Not known

Record Attendance: 5,000 v Cambridge United - FA Cup 3rd Round 05/12/1979
Record Victory: Not known
Record Defeat: Not known
Record Goalscorer: John Willis
Record Appearances: Martin Baguley - 600+
Additional Records: Received £22,000 from Oldham Athletic for Fitz Hall

Senior Honours: Isthmian League 1992-93, Division 1 1986-87, 97-97. Berks & Bucks Senior Cup x12.

10 YEAR RECORD

01-02	02-03	03-04	04-05	05-06	06-07	07-08	08-09	09-10	10-11
Isth P 7	Isth P 21	Isth1N 4	SthP 12	SthP 22	Sthsw 15	SthM 6	SthM 5	SthM 4	SthP 6

CHESHAM UNITED

No.	Date	Comp	H/A	Opponents	Att:	Result	Goalscorers	Pos
1	Aug 14	Sth Prem	A	Truro City	435	W 3 - 0	Wales 49 87 Fanibuyan 58	1
2	17		H	Oxford City	275	W 2 - 0	Wales 5 Marsala 84	
3	21		H	Brackley Town	281	W 1 - 0	Bangura 54	1
4	25		A	Swindon Supermarine	101	D 0 - 0		
5	28		H	Banbury United	304	L 0 - 2		4
6	30		A	Bedford Town	369	W 2 - 1	Crace 14 Talbot 13 (pen)	
7	Sept 4		H	Tiverton Town	340	W 5 - 0	Talbot 29 (pen) Fanbuyan 36 Bangura 43 Fotherington 87 Wales 90	2
8	**11**	**FAC 1Q**	**A**	**Burnham Ramblers**	**115**	**W 3 - 0**	**Archer 45 Bartley 46 Bangura 60**	
9	18		A	Stourbridge	231	D 1 - 1	Moone 72 (og)	3
10	**25**	**FAC 2Q**	**H**	**Wealdstone**	**504**	**D 2 - 2**	**Crace 18 Wales 90**	
11	**27**	**FAC 2Qr**	**A**	**Wealdstone**	**366**	**L 1 - 4**	**Bartley 50**	
12	Oct 2		H	Weymouth	311	W 2 - 1	Ledger 20 Obeng 49	3
13	5		A	Bashley	222	D 1 - 1	Fanibuyan 10	
14	9		H	Chippenham Town	405	W 2 - 0	Bartley 13 Wales 90	3
15	**16**	**FAT 1Q**	**H**	**Salisbury City**	**297**	**D 1 - 1**	**Fanibuyan 30**	
16	**19**	**FAT 1Qr**	**A**	**Salisbury City**	**463**	**L 1 - 2**	**Elsegood 15**	
17	Nov 6		H	Didcot Town	314	D 1 - 1	Potton 41	6
18	9		A	Salisbury City	566	L 2 - 3	Archer 6 Wales 42	
19	13		A	Cambridge United	356	D 0 - 0		6
20	16		A	Cirencester Town	53	L 2 - 3	Archer 73 Elsegood 90	
21	20		H	Hednesford Town	301	W 2 - 1	Wales 2 45	6
22	Dec 11		A	Banbury United	275	L 1 - 2	Wales 5	8
23	Jan 3		H	Bedford Town	367	D 0 - 0		
24	8		H	Stourbridge	268	W 2 - 0	Archer 20 Wales 74	5
25	15		A	Tiverton Town	235	W 2 - 1	Wales 15 Talbot 23 (pen)	5
26	18		A	Evesham United	95	D 0 - 0		
27	22		A	Oxford Cty	176	W 2 - 0	Archer 12 Fotheringham 21	4
28	29		H	Truro City	393	W 1 - 0	Archer 57	4
29	Feb 5		A	Brackley Town	202	D 1 - 1	Archer 78	4
30	12		H	Swindon Supermarine	359	W 4 - 0	Bartley 2 Talbot 37 (pen) Potton 65 Robinson 85	4
31	15		H	Leamington	278	W 1 - 0	Bangura 50	
32	19		A	Hednesford Town	404	L 2 - 3	Ledger 81 Archer 89	4
33	22		H	Cirencester Town	253	W 6 - 1	ROBINSON 3 (3 45 62) Obeng 44 Talbot 54 Archer 72	
34	March 5		A	Halesowen Town	187	W 4 - 1	ARCHER 3 (1 31 71) Wales 75	4
35	8		A	Hemel Hempstead	263	W 1 - 0	Robinson 1	
36	12		A	Didcot Town	205	L 0 - 1		5
37	15		H	Halesowen Town	260	W 3 - 0	Banjura 17 Bartley 37 Wales 89	
38	19		H	Cambridge City	473	W 1 - 0	Theobald 28 (og)	3
39	22		H	Evesham United	243	W 1 - 0	Wales 59	
40	26		A	Chippenham Town	457	L 0 - 1		5
41	April 2		H	Bashley	361	D 0 - 0		5
42	9		A	Leamington	667	L 2 - 3	Archer 49 Lambert 61	6
43	16		H	Salisbury City	545	D 1 - 1	Kyriacou 62	6
44	23		A	Weymouth	643	L 0 - 3		6
45	26		H	Hemel Hempstead	451	D 3 - 3	Couch 10 Bangura 44 Watters 54	

CHIPPENHAM TOWN

Chairman: John Applegate
Secretary: Angela Townsley **(T)** 07909 634 875 **(E)** angelatownsley_chiptownfc@talktalk.net
Additional Committee Members:
Leila Garraway, Barry Stephens, Doug Webb, Richard Chappell, Barry Lane, Avril Mays, Hazel Ralph, Robin Townsley.
Manager: Adie Mings
Programme Editor: Angela Townsley **(E)** angelatownsley_chiptownfc@talktalk.net

Club Factfile

Founded: 1873 **Nickname:** The Bluebirds
Previous Names: Not known
Previous Leagues: Hellenic, Wiltshire Senior, Wiltshire Premier, Western

Club Colours (change): Royal blue/royal blue/blue (All white)

Ground: Hardenhuish Park, Bristol Road, Chippenham SN14 6LR **(T)** 01249 650 400
Capacity: 3,000 **Seats:** 300 **Covered:** 1,000 **Clubhouse:** Yes **Shop:** Yes

Directions
Exit 17 from M4. Follow A350 towards Chippenham for three miles to first roundabout, take second exit (A350); follow road to third roundabout (junction with A420). Turn left and follow signs to town centre. Ground is 1km on left hand side adjacent to pedestrian controlled traffic lights. Car/Coach park next to traffic lights.

Previous Grounds: Not known

Record Attendance: 4,800 v Chippenham United - Western League 1951
Record Victory: 9-0 v Dawlish Town (H) - Western League
Record Defeat: 0-10 v Tiverton Town (A) - Western League
Record Goalscorer: Dave Ferris
Record Appearances: Ian Monnery
Additional Records:

Senior Honours: Western League 1951-52. Les Phillips Cup 1999-2000. Wiltshire Senior Cup. Wiltshire Senior Shield x4.

10 YEAR RECORD

01-02	02-03	03-04	04-05	05-06	06-07	07-08	08-09	09-10	10-11
SthW 2	SthP 5	SthP 21	SthP 2	SthP 4	SthP 7	SthP 4	SthP 8	SthP 3	SthP 7

CHIPPENHAM TOWN

No.	Date	Comp	H/A	Opponents	Att:	Result	Goalscorers	Pos
1	Aug 14	Sth Prem	A	Hednesford Town	379	W 2 - 0	Powell 48 Benison 90	3
2	17		H	Tiverton Town	446	W 4 - 1	POWELL 3 (4 39 66) Lamb 76 (pen)	
3	21		H	Cirencester Town	402	D 0 - 0		3
4	24		A	Brackley Town	202	D 1 - 1	Allison 53	
5	28		A	Leamington	463	D 0 - 0		7
6	30		H	Salisbury City	858	D 1 - 1	Allison 56	
7	Sept 4		A	Bashley	269	W 4 - 1	Gullick 6 72 Powell 62 Griffin 65	5
8	**11**	**FAC 1Q**	**A**	**Banbury United**	**277**	**W 2 - 1**	**Harvey 58 Griffin 88**	
9	14		H	Halesowen Town	321	W 3 - 1	Powell 66 Griffin 68 Martin 81	
10	18		H	Didcot Town	409	D 1 - 1	Tindle 87	2
11	**25**	**FAC 2Q**	**H**	**Farnborough**	**486**	**L 0 - 1**		
12	Oct 2		A	Cambridge City	322	W 1 - 0	Edenborough 90	2
13	5		H	Stourbridge	401	D 0 - 0		
14	9		A	Chesham United	405	L 0 - 2		5
15	**16**	**FAT 1Q**	**A**	**Slough Town**	**251**	**D 1 - 1**	**Powell 54**	
16	**19**	**FAT 1Qr**	**H**	**Slough Town**	**244**	**W 4 - 1**	**Allison 3 Harvey 43 Gullick 66 Edenborough 80**	
17	23		H	Hemel Hempstead	408	W 2 - 0	Tindle 37 Benison 90	5
18	**30**	**FAT 2Q**	**H**	**Lowestoft Town**	**383**	**D 1 - 1**	**Griffin 72**	
19	**Nov 2**	**FAT 2Qr**	**A**	**Lowestoft Town**	**577**	**L 1 - 3**	**Griffin 63**	
20	9		A	Truro City	379	L 0 - 5		
21	13		A	Weymouth	485	D 3 - 3	Powell 25 Griffin 46 Williams 71	7
22	16		A	Evesham United	94	D 2 - 2	Griffin 70 Tindle 81	
23	20		H	Banbury United	373	W 4 - 0	Powell 13 Lye 38 Gullick 45 Griffin 61	4
24	27		A	Oxford City	136	D 0 - 0		4
25	Jan 3		A	Salisbury City	1095	L 0 - 4		
26	8		A	Didcot Town	234	D 1 - 1	Lamb 45	7
27	15		H	Bashley	352	W 1 - 0	Kite 82	7
28	18		H	Bedford Town	277	W 3 - 1	Edenborough 52 77 Powell 63	
29	29		H	Hednsford Town	351	L 0 - 1		7
30	Feb 5		A	Cirencester Town	167	D 1 - 1	Powell 43	9
31	12		H	Brackley Town	391	W 3 - 2	Griffin 17 Green 43 (og) Alison 61	8
32	19		A	Banbury United	239	W 2 - 1	Griffin 15 89	7
33	22		H	Evesham United	330	W 1 - 0	Smith 6	
34	26		H	Oxford City	367	L 1 - 2	Powell 78	7
35	March 5		A	Bedford Town	241	D 1 - 1	Tindall 88	8
36	8		A	Halesowen Town	102	W 2 - 1	Powell 69 Gullick 79	
37	15		H	Swindon Supermarine	343	W 3 - 1	Griffin 12 76 (pen) Powell 67	
38	19		H	Weymouth	432	W 1 - 0	Griffin 90	7
39	22		H	Leamington	387	D 0 - 0		
40	26		H	Chesham United	457	W 1 - 0	Powell 63	7
41	29		A	Tiverton Town	210	D 0 - 0		
42	April 2		A	Stourbridge	268	L 0 - 1		7
43	9		H	Truro City	422	L 1 - 2	Guthrie 73	7
44	16		A	Hemel Hempstead	170	W 2 - 1	Osman 11 39	7
45	23		H	Cambridge City	353	W 1 - 0	Griffin 87	7
46	25		A	Swindon Supermarine	258	L 1 - 3	Griffin 61 (pen)	

CIRENCESTER TOWN

Chairman: Stephen Abbley
Secretary: Steve Hale (T) 01285 654 543 (E) steve.hale@cirentownfc.com
Additional Committee Members:
Alan Sykes, Peter Mills, Robert Saunders, Alan Lloyd, David Bougen.

Manager: Brian Hughes
Programme Editor: Mark O'Brien (E) obrienm2uk@aol.com

Club Factfile

Founded: 1889 **Nickname:** Centurions
Previous Names: Not known
Previous Leagues: Hellenic

Club Colours (change): Red and black stripes/black/red (All orange)

Ground: The Corinium Stadium, Kingshill Lane, Cirencester GL7 1HS (T) 01285 654 543
Capacity: 4,500 **Seats:** 550 **Covered:** 1,250 **Clubhouse:** Yes **Shop:** Yes

Directions
Leave bypass at Burford Road roundabout.
Aim for Stow, turn right at traffic lights, then right again at next junction, first left into Kingshill Lane.
Ground 500 yards on right.

Previous Grounds: Smithfield Stadium

Record Attendance: 2,600 v Fareham Town - 1969
Record Victory: Not known
Record Defeat: Not known
Record Goalscorer: Not known
Record Appearances: Not known
Additional Records: Paid £4,000 to Gloucester City for Lee Smith

Senior Honours: Hellenic League Premier Division 1995-96.
Gloucestershire Senior Amateur Cup 1989-90. Gloucestershire County Cup 1995-96.

10 YEAR RECORD

01-02		02-03		03-04		04-05		05-06		06-07		07-08		08-09		09-10		10-11	
SthW	13	SthW	14	SthW	3	SthP	7	SthP	18	SthP	21	SthP	21	Sthsw	14	Sthsw	5	SthP	13

CIRENCESTER TOWN

No.	Date	Comp	H/A	Opponents	Att:	Result	Goalscorers	Pos
1	Aug 14	Sth Prem	H	Banbury United	211	D 1 - 1	Hoskin 17	9
2	21		A	Chippenham Town	402	D 0 - 0		6
3	24		H	Stourbridge	134	L 1 - 2	Palmer 65	
4	28		A	Halesowen Town	302	D 1 - 1	Sysum 49	10
5	30		H	Swindon Supermarine	227	L 1 - 2	Bevan 72	
6	Sept 4		A	Salisbury City	659	L 1 - 4	Bevan 33	15
7	**11**	**FAC 1Q**	**H**	**Didcot Town**	**79**	**D 0 - 0**		
8	**14**	**FAC 1Qr**	**A**	**Didcot Town**	**136**	**L 2 - 3**	**Emery 8 Bevan 79**	
9	18		H	Brackley Town	117	L 0 - 3		20
10	Oct 2		A	Didcot Town	156	W 2 - 1	Mortimer-Jones 62 Tomkins 84	18
11	5		H	Bedford Town	80	W 4 - 2	BEVAN 3 (25 29pen 81) Griffin 90	
12	9		A	Weymouth	449	L 0 - 1		13
13	12		H	Truro City	113	L 0 - 3		
14	**16**	**FAT 1Q**	**H**	**Halesowen Town**	**112**	**W 3 - 0**	**Bevan 59 Palmer 77 Sysum 80**	
15	19		A	Hemel Hempstead	116	D 2 - 2	Reid 8 Tomkins 15	
16	23		H	Cambridge City	147	L 1 - 2	Reid 40	16
17	**30**	**FAT 2Q**	**H**	**Weymouth**	**95**	**W 2 - 1**	**Brown 25 77**	
18	Nov 6		H	Oxford City	196	W 4 - 1	Palmer 43 Sysum 45 74 Bevan 76	12
19	13		A	Hednesford Town	324	L 1 - 3	Wood 40 (pen)	13
20	16		H	Chesham United	53	W 3 - 2	Bevan 34 Tomkins 67 86	
21	**20**	**FAT 3Q**	**H**	**Grays Athletic**	**157**	**D 2 - 2**	**Sysum 43 Brown 58**	
22	**23**	**FAT 3Qr**	**A**	**Grays Athletic**	**153**	**W 1 - 0**	**Bevan 31**	
23	27		H	Tiverton Town	89	W 1 - 0	Mark Draycott 62	11
24	Dec 4		A	Bashley	207	W 2 - 1	Tomkins 45 Palmer 90	10
25	**11**	**FAT 1Q**	**H**	**Gloucester City**	**406**	**D 1 - 1**	**Brown 63**	
26	**15**	**FAT 1Qr**	**A**	**Gloucester City**	**226**	**L 0 - 3**		
27	Jan 3		A	Swindon Supermarine	232	L 0 - 1		
28	8		A	Brackey Town	177	L 1 - 4	Etheridge 56	12
29	11		H	Evesham United	67	L 1 - 2	Mark Draycott 33	
30	25		A	Leamington	275	L 0 - 1		
31	29		A	Banbury Uited	223	W 2 - 0	Mark Draycott 31 Bevan 90	14
32	Feb 1		A	Truro City	303	L 0 - 2		
33	5		H	Chippenham Town	187	D 1 - 1	Hoskin 82	14
34	12		A	Stourbridge	211	L 1 - 2	Sysum 49	16
35	15		H	Halesowen Town	47	W 5 - 0	BEVAN 3 (9 43 70) Draycott 77 86	
36	19		H	Leamington	241	L 0 - 1		14
37	22		A	Chesham United	53	L 1 - 6	Edenborough 42 (pen)	
38	26		A	Tiverton Town	231	D 2 - 2	Hoskin 49 Bevan 81	
39	March 5		H	Bashley	87	W 2 - 1	Hoskin 3 Bevan 25	13
40	8		H	Salisbury City	152	L 0 - 3		
41	12		A	Oxford City	175	D 3 - 3	Tomkins 44 59 Hoskin 45	14
42	19		H	Hednesford Town	151	L 0 - 1		15
43	26		H	Weymouth	217	W 3 - 0	Mortimer-Jones 23 Bevan 47 Sysum 53	15
44	April 2		A	Bedford Town	234	W 6 - 1	Bevan 21 36 Dunton 32 Draycott 39 45 Brown 84	14
45	9		H	Hemel Hempstead	95	W 3 - 2	Edenborough 46 Bevan 48 Tomkins 75	13
46	11		A	Cambridge City	446	W 2 - 1	Mortimer-Jones 25 Brown 86	13
47	23		H	Didcot Town	291	D 0 - 0		13
48	25		A	Evesham United	156	L 1 - 2	Westlake 85	

EVESHAM UNITED

Chairman: Jim Cockerton
Secretary: Mike Peplow **(T)** 07889 011 539 **(E)** rwestmacot@aol.com
Additional Committee Members:
Andy Beasley, Steve Lane, Roger Westmacott.

Manager: Paul West
Programme Editor: Mike Peplow **(E)** rwestmacot@aol.com

Club Factfile

Founded: 1945 **Nickname:** The Robins
Previous Names: Not known
Previous Leagues: Worcester, Birmingham Combination, Midland Combination 1951-55, 65-92, West Midlands (Regional) 1955-62
Club Colours (change): Red and white stripes/white/red (Blue and white stripes/blue/blue)

Ground: Worcester City FC, St George's Lane, Worcester WR1 1QT **(T)** 01905 23003
Capacity: 2,000 **Seats:** 350 **Covered:** 600 **Clubhouse:** Yes **Shop:** Yes

Directions Leave M5 at Junction 6 (Worcester North), follow signs for Worcester along the A449. Follow the dual carrigeway until you come to roundabout, take second turning towards Worcester. Stay on this road for about one mile (Ombersley Road) until you reach T-junction and traffic lights. Turn right at lights. St George's Lane is third turning on left between tool hire shop and 'In Toto Kitchen' showrooms. Ground is 500 yards on left.

Previous Grounds: The Crown Meadow > 1968, Common Reed 1968-2006

Record Attendance: 2,338 v West Bromwich Albion - Friendly 18/07/1992
Record Victory: 11-3 v West Heath United
Record Defeat: 1-8 v Ilkeston Town
Record Goalscorer: Sid Brain
Record Appearances: Rob Candy
Additional Records: Paid £1,500 to Hayes for Colin Day 1992
Received £5,000 from Cheltenham Town for Simon Brain

Senior Honours: Midland Combination Premier Division 1991-92, Division 1 1965-66, 67-68, 68-69.
Southern League Division 1 Midlands 2007-08.
Worcestershire Senior Urn x2

10 YEAR RECORD

01-02	02-03	03-04	04-05	05-06	06-07	07-08	08-09	09-10	10-11
SthW 12	SthW 12	SthW 14	SthW 3	SthP 20	SthM 5	SthM 1	SthP 9	SthP 16	SthP 12

EVESHAM UNITED

No.	Date	Comp	H/A	Opponents	Att:	Result	Goalscorers	Pos
1	Aug 14	Sth Prem	A	Didcot Town	152	W 2 - 1	Nisbett 55 Agbor 70	4
2	17		H	Truro City	118	L 3 - 4	Agbor 48 50 Nisbett 78	
3	21		H	Halesowen Town	191	D 0 - 0		8
4	24		A	Tiverton Town	273	L 0 - 1		
5	28		H	Weymouth	160	L 1 - 3	Lennon 82	16
6	30		A	Banbury United	297	D 1 - 1	Agbor 89	
7	Sept 5		H	Bedford Town	146	D 0 - 0		17
8	**11**	**FAC 1Q**	**H**	**Coleshill Town**	**89**	**L 1 - 3**	**Agbor 84**	
9	14		A	Stourbridge	289	L 1 - 3	Agbor 62	
10	18		A	Oxford City	176	W 1 - 0	Shaze 68	14
11	Oct 2		H	Hemel Hempstead	104	W 1 - 0	Shaze 48	11
12	5		A	Hednesford Town	319	L 0 - 1		
13	9		H	Windsor & Eton	111	D 0 - 0		11
14	**16**	**FAT 1Q**	**H**	**Frome Town**	**107**	**W 1 - 0**	**Shaze 45**	
15	23		A	Bashley	243	L 0 - 1		15
16	**30**	**FAT 2Q**	**H**	**Sutton United**	**188**	**L 0 - 1**		
17	Nov 6		A	Leamington	565	L 0 - 1		16
18	13		H	Swindon Supermarine	94	L 0 - 1		19
19	16		H	Chippenham Town	94	D 2 - 2	Scheppel 25 (pen) Brown 62	
20	Dec 11		A	Weymouth	486	L 0 - 2		20
21	Jan 3		H	Banbury United	110	W 4 - 3	Accam 10 Palmer 41 Scheppel 62 Shaze 82	
22	8		H	Oxford City	106	W 3 - 0	Shaze 10 Brown 30 Scheppel 63 (pen)	
23	11		A	Cirencester Town	67	W 2 - 1	Palmer 39 Brown 76	
24	15		A	Bedford Town	279	W 2 - 1	Palmer 14 Clark 41 (og)	
25	18		H	Chesham United	95	D 0 - 0		
26	22		A	Truro City	351	D 1 - 1	Blake 90	13
27	25		A	Brackley Town	105	L 0 - 5		
28	29		H	Didcot Town	104	W 3 - 0	Palmer 40 (pen) Accam 49 Shaze 54	12
29	Feb 5		A	Halesowen Town	175	W 8 - 0	Palmer 18 Ibhadon 39 (og) Shaze 34 45 ACCAM 3 (39 46 57) Mensah 81	12
30	8		H	Salisbury City	127	D 0 - 0		
31	13		H	Tiverton Town	116	W 3 - 1	Shaze 24 67 Palmer 31	
32	15		A	Cambridge City	197	L 0 - 2		12
33	19		H	Cambridge City	140	L 1 - 2	Palmer 90	11
34	22		A	Chippenham Town	330	L 0 - 1		
35	March 1		H	Stourbridge	138	L 2 - 3	Shaze 47 Accam 86	
36	5		H	Brackley Town	124	W 1 - 0	Accam 35 (pen)	11
37	12		H	Leamington	268	L 0 - 1		12
38	19		A	Swindon Supermarine	131	D 1 - 1	Accam 51	12
39	22		A	Chesham United	243	L 0 - 1		
40	April 2		H	Hednesford Town	210	W 4 - 1	Jones 10 Shaze 20 Accam 76 Palmer 79	12
41	9		A	Salisbury City	895	W 3 - 0	Accam 34 (pen) Shaze 43 63	12
42	16		H	Bashley	109	D 2 - 2	Shaze 77 82	12
43	23		A	Hemel Hempdstead	161	L 0 - 1		12
44	25		H	Cirencester Town	156	W 2 - 1	Palmer 5 Wilding 73	

Caught in action....

Frome Town in action against Evesham in last year's FA Trophy.

Photo by Jonathan Holloway

FROME TOWN

Chairman: Jeremy Alderman
Secretary: Ian Pearce (T) 07811 511 222 (E) ian@frometownfc.co.uk
Additional Committee Members:
Terry Wolff, Ian Pearce, Richard Hudson, Ivan Carver, Neil Clark, Gary Collison, Jon Curle, Brian Stevens.
Manager: Darren Perrin
Programme Editor: Andrew Meaden (E) programmes@amprintcopy.co.uk

Back row: LR - Derek Graham (Assistant Manager), Shaun Baker (Kit Manager), Darren White, Twaine Plummer, Alex Lapham, Kyle Tooze, Ed Quelch, Tom Drewitt, Darren Chitty, Ryan Bennett, Ben Thomson, Mike Perrott, Dean Flockton, Mike Reaney, Sam Babatunde, Matt Peters, Reynold Turnock, Lloyd Chamberlain (GK Coach), Mike Kilgour (Coach).
Front Row: Ricky Hulbert, Josh Brigham, Luke Ballinger, Richard Hudson (Treasurer), Gary Collinson (Community Development), Jeremy Alderman (Chairman), Terry Wolff (Vice-Chairman), Ian Pearce (Club Secretary), Jamie Cheeseman, Dean Evans, Simeon Allison, Kris Miller.

Club Factfile

Founded: 1904 **Nickname:** The Robins
Previous Names: None
Previous Leagues: Wiltshire Premier 1904, Somerset Senior 1906-19, Western 1919, 63-2009

Club Colours (change): All red (All white)

Ground: Aldersmith Stadium, Badgers Hill, Berkley Road, Frome BA11 2EH (T) 01373 464 087
Capacity: 2,000 **Seats:** 150 **Covered:** 200 **Clubhouse:** Yes **Shop:** Yes

Directions
From Bath, take A36 and then A361. At third roundabout, follow A361 and at fourth roundabout take A3098. Take first right and ground is one mile on left hand side. From south follow A36 (Warminster) and take A3098 to Frome. At T Junction turn right and take second exit at roundabout. Ground is first right and follow road for one mile on left hand side.

Previous Grounds: Not known

Record Attendance: 8,000 v Leyton Orient - FA Cup 1st Round 1958
Record Victory: Not Known
Record Defeat: Not Known
Record Goalscorer: Not Known
Record Appearances: Not Known
Additional Records:

Senior Honours: Somerset County League 1906-07, 08-09, 10-11.
Western League Division 1 1919-20, 2001-02, Premier Division 1962-63, 78-79.
Somerset Senior Cup 1932-33, 33-34, 50-51 Somerset Premier Cup 1966-67, 68-69 (shared), 82-83, 2008-09.

10 YEAR RECORD

01-02	02-03	03-04	04-05	05-06	06-07	07-08	08-09	09-10	10-11
West1 1	WestP 11	WestP 3	WestP 3	WestP 7	WestP 3	WestP 4	WestP 2	Sthsw 6	Sthsw 4

HEMEL HEMPSTEAD TOWN

Chairman: David Boggins
Secretary: Dean Chance **(T)** 07858 990 550 **(E)** dean.chance@ntlworld.com
Additional Committee Members:
Mick Dorer, Phil Smith, Chris Brooks, John Adams, Darren Kelly.

Manager: Colin Payne
Programme Editor: Tony Conway **(E)** tonyconway@yahoo.com

Club Factfile

Founded: 1885 **Nickname:** The Tudors
Previous Names: Hemel Hempstead FC
Previous Leagues: Spartan 1922-52, Delphian 1952-63, Athenian 1963-77, Isthmian 1977-2004

Club Colours (change): All red (All green)

Ground: Vauxhall Road, Adeyfield Road, Hemel Hempstead HP2 4HW **(T)** 01442 259 777
Capacity: 3,152 **Seats:** 300 **Covered:** 900 **Clubhouse:** Yes **Shop:** Yes

Directions
Leave M1 at Junction 8 - follow dual carriageway over two roundabouts.
Get into outside lane and after 100 yards turn right.
Follow road to mini-roundabout turn left, next large roundabout take third exit into ground car park.

Previous Grounds: Crabtree Lane

Record Attendance: 3,500 v Tooting & Mitcham - Amateur Cup 1962 (Crabtree Lane)
Record Victory: Not known
Record Defeat: Not known
Record Goalscorer: Dai Price
Record Appearances: John Wallace - 1012
Additional Records:

Senior Honours: Isthmian League Division 3 1998-99. Herts Senior Cup x7. Herts Charity Cup x6.

10 YEAR RECORD

01-02	02-03	03-04	04-05	05-06	06-07	07-08	08-09	09-10	10-11
Isth2 10	Isth1N 3	Isth1N 6	SthP 19	SthW 4	SthP 5	SthP 7	SthP 5	SthP 20	SthP 15

HEMEL HEMPSTEAD TOWN

No.	Date	Comp	H/A	Opponents	Att:	Result	Goalscorers	Pos
1	Aug 14	Sth Prem	A	Swindon Supermarine	133	W 3 - 1	Wilson 25 Lafayetti 36 Blake 85	5
2	17		H	Brackley Town	221	W 1 - 0	Fenemore 33	
3	21		H	Hednesford Town	227	L 0 - 1		5
4	24		A	Leamington	388	W 3 - 2	Fenemore 18 Lafayette 50 61	
5	28		A	Salisbury City	706	D 1 - 1	Fenemore 78	5
6	30		H	Cambridge City	390	L 0 - 2		
7	Sept 4		A	Halesowen Town	324	W 6 - 1	May 9 Fenemore 15 (pen) 26 LAFAYETTE 3 (20 69 90)	
8	**11**	**FAC 1Q**	**H**	**Concord Rangers**	**184**	**L 1 - 2**	**Goss 56**	
9	18		H	Truro City	257	D 1 - 1	Fennemore 18	8
10	25		A	Banbury United	209	W 4 - 0	FENEMORE 3 (10 76 82) Stone 85	2
11	Oct 2		A	Evesham United	104	L 0 - 1		6
12	10		H	Didcot Town	129	L 0 - 1		
13	**16**	**FAT 1Q**	**H**	**Rugby Town**	**167**	**L 2 - 3**	**Fenemore 6 (pen) 16**	
14	19		H	Cirencester Town	116	D 2 - 2	Vincente 10 Fenemore 83 (pen)	
15	23		A	Chippenham Town	408	L 0 - 2		9
16	30		H	Bashley	183	L 0 - 2		10
17	Nov 6		H	Bedford Town	210	W 1 - 0	Fenemore 40	10
18	13		A	Oxford City	157	L 0 - 3		10
19	Jan 3		A	Cambridge City	357	L 2 - 3	Ash 32 Fenemore 48	
20	8		A	Truro City	491	L 0 - 3		16
21	15		H	Halesowen Town	169	W 1 - 0	Hammond 16	
22	18		H	Weymouth	164	L 1 - 2	May 16	
23	22		A	Brackley Town	181	L 1 - 3	Hammond 87	17
24	25		A	Tiverton Town	124	L 0 - 1		
25	29		H	Swindon Supermarine	156	L 1 - 2	Fenemore 84	17
26	Feb 1		H	Salisbury City	150	L 0 - 3		
27	5		A	Hednesford Town	277	L 0 - 2		17
28	12		H	Leamington	233	W 1 - 0	Fenemore 73	14
29	26		A	Weymouth	538	D 2 - 2	Fenemore 44 (pen) 77	15
30	March 5		H	Tiverton Town	175	W 2 - 1	Butler 74 McEntegart 89	14
31	8		H	Chesham United	265	L 0 - 1		
32	12		A	Bedford Town	276	W 1 - 0	Pearce 50	13
33	19		H	Oxford City	201	L 0 - 2		13
34	22		A	Didcot Town	148	W 1 - 0	Pearce 57	
35	26		A	Bashley	180	L 0 - 1		14
36	29		A	Stourbridge	255	W 5 - 1	Williams 44 66 FENEMORE 3 (62 89 (0)	
37	April 2		H	Banbury United	208	L 1 - 2	Pearce 60	13
38	9		A	Cirencester Town	95	L 2 - 3	Blake 56 Williams 58	15
39	16		H	Chippenham Town	170	L 1 - 2	Blake 17	15
40	19		H	Stourbridge	144	D 2 - 2	Fennemore 9 Wilson 74	
41	23		H	Evesham United	161	W 1 - 0	Williams 55	14
42	25		A	Chesham United	451	D 3 - 3	Wilson 32 Blake 39 Pearce 71	

Caught in action....

O'Brian, Brentwood, and Berwick (No.9) of Daventry tussle for the ball.

Photo by Keith Clayton

HITCHIN TOWN

Chairman: Terry Barratt

Secretary: Roy Izzard **(T)** 07803 202 498 **(E)** roy.izzard@bjca.co.uk

Additional Committee Members:
Eileen Bone, John Morrell, Andy Melvin, Mark Burke, Fred Andrews, Tony Gill, Neil Jensen, Mrs Chris Morrell, Chris Newbold, Stewart Virgo.

Manager: Carl Williams

Programme Editor: Neil Jensen **(E)** neil.jensen@db.com

Club Factfile

Founded: 1865 **Nickname:** Canaries

Previous Names: Re-formed in 1928

Previous Leagues: Spartan 1928-39, Herts & Middlesex 1939-45, Athenian 1945-63, Isthmian 1964-2004

Club Colours (change): Yellow/green/green (Green/yellow/yellow)

Ground: Top Field, Fishponds Road, Hitchin SG5 1NU **(T)** 01462 459 028 (match days only)

Capacity: 5,000 **Seats:** 500 **Covered:** 1,250 **Clubhouse:** Yes **Shop:** Yes

Directions
From East A1 to J8 onto A602 to Hitchin.
At Three Moorhens Pub roundabout, take third exit (A600) towards Bedford, over next roundabout and lights, turn right at next roundabout, turnstiles on left, parking 50 yards on.

Previous Grounds: Not known

Record Attendance: 7,878 v Wycombe Wanderers - FA Amateur Cup 3rd Round 08/02/1956

Record Victory: 13-0 v Cowley and v RAF Uxbridge - both Spartan League 1929-30

Record Defeat: 0-10 v Kingstonian (A) and v Slough Town (A) - 1965-66 and 1979-80 respectively

Record Goalscorer: Paul Giggle - 214 (1968-86)

Record Appearances: Paul Giggle - 769 (1968-86)

Additional Records: Paid £2,000 to Potton United for Ray Seeking
Received £30,000 from Cambridge United for Zema Abbey, January 2000

Senior Honours: AFA Senior Cup 1931-32. London Senior Cup 1969-70. Isthmian League Division 1 1992-93.
Herts Senior Cup x19 (a record)

10 YEAR RECORD

01-02	02-03	03-04	04-05	05-06	06-07	07-08	08-09	09-10	10-11
Isth P 11	Isth P 14	Isth P 20	SthP 18	SthP 14	SthP 11	SthP 18	SthP 20	SthC 2	SthC 2

LEAMINGTON

Chairman: Jim Scott
Secretary: Richard Edy **(T)** 07508 207 053 **(E)** matchsecretary@leamingtonfc.co.
Additional Committee Members:
Jim Scott, Shaun Brady, Nic Sproul, Russell Davis, Graham Moody, Kevin Watson.

Manager: Paul Holleran
Programme Editor: Sally Ellis **(E)** programme@leamingtonfc.co.uk

Back Row (L-R): Ron Ainsworth (Kitman), Alex Taylor, Kyle Cartwright, Richard Batchelor, Jacob Blyth, Liam Daly, Tony Breeden (GK), Craig Owen, James Mace, Tom Berwick, Dave Ward (Sports Therapist).
Front Row: Ben Mackey, James Husband, Dior Angus, Jamie Hood, Lee Williams (Assistant Manager), Paul Holleran (Manager), Liam O'Neill (Coach), Lee Downes (Captain), Stephan Morley, Jamie Sheldon, Michael Tuohy.

Club Factfile

Founded: 1892 **Nickname:** The Brakes
Previous Names: Leamington Town 1892-1937, Lockheed Borg & Beck 1944-46 , Lockheed Leamington 1946-73, AP Leamington 1973-88
Previous Leagues: Birmingham Combination, Birmingham & District, West Midlands Regional, Midland Counties, Southern, Midland Combination, Midland Alliance

Club Colours (change): Gold and black/black with gold trim/black (Blue with yellow trim/blue/blue)

Ground: New Windmill Ground, Harbury Lane, Whitmarsh, Leamington CV33 9QB **(T)** 01926 430 406
Capacity: 5,000 **Seats:** 120 **Covered:** 720 **Clubhouse:** Yes **Shop:** Yes

Directions
From West and North – M40 Southbound – Exit J14 and take A452 towards Leamington. Ahead at 1st island. Next island take 2nd exit A452 (Europa Way). Next island take 4th exit (Harbury Lane) signposted Harbury and Bishops Tachbrook. Next island take 3rd exit (Harbury Lane). At traffic lights continue straight ahead Harbury Lane. Ground is 1.5 miles on left.
From South – M40 northbound – Exit J13. Turn right onto A452 towards Leamington. At 1st island take 3rd exit A452 (Europa Way) and follow as above (Europa Way onwards).

Previous Grounds: Old Windmill Ground

Record Attendance: 1,380 v Retford United - 17/02/2007
Record Victory: Not known
Record Defeat: Not known
Record Goalscorer: Josh Blake - 166
Record Appearances: Josh Blake - 314
Additional Records:

Senior Honours: Birmingham & District 1961-62. West Midlands Regional 1962-63. Midland Counties 1964-65.
Southern League 1982-83, Division 1 Midlands 2008-09.
Midland Combination Division 2 2000-01, Premier Division 2004-05. Midland Alliance 2006-07, League cup 2005-06.

10 YEAR RECORD

01-02		02-03		03-04		04-05		05-06		06-07		07-08		08-09		09-10		10-11	
MCm1	2	MCmP	3	MCmP	2	MCmP	1	MidAl	5	MidAl	1	SthM	2	SthM	1	SthP	10	SthP	5

LEAMINGTON

No.	Date	Comp	H/A	Opponents	Att:	Result	Goalscorers	Pos
1	Aug 14	Sth Prem	H	Bashley	513	W 2 - 1	Corbett 26 73	6
2	17		A	Cambridge City	312	L 2 - 3	Daley 52 Corbett 63	
3	24		H	Hemel Hempstead Town	388	L 2 - 3	Jackson 3 Corbett 32	15
4	28		H	Chippenham Town	463	D 0 - 0		
5	30		A	Hednesford Town	535	D 1 - 1	Corbett 15	
6	Sept 4		H	Weymouth	603	W 1 - 0	Batchelor 20	13
7	**11**	**FAC 1Q**	**H**	**Brackley Town**	**532**	**D 2 - 2**	**Murphy 25 Wilding 81**	
8	**14**	**FAC 1Qr**	**A**	**Brackley Town**	**306**	**L 0 - 2**		
9	18		A	Tiverton Town	309	L 0 - 1		16
10	25		A	Halesowen Town	376	W 3 - 0	LEWIS 3 (40 45 71pen)	
11	28		A	Bedford Town	238	W 2 - 0	Husband 25 Lewis 28 (pen)	
12	Oct 2		H	Oxford City	570	W 2 - 0	Hood 56 Lewis 65	7
13	5		H	Brackley Town	503	W 2 - 1	Corbett 65 Batchelor 83	
14	**16**	**FAT 1Q**	**A**	**Woodford United**	**298**	**W 3 - 1**	**Husband 25 Wilding 40 Daley 82**	
15	23		H	Truro City	603	W 3 - 2	Batchelor 12 Brooks 25 (og) Lewis 44 (pen)	6
16	**30**	**FAT 2Q**	**H**	**Bamber Bridge**	**510**	**W 3 - 0**	**Lewis 26 Bachelor 35 Rowe 37**	
17	Nov 6		H	Evesham United	565	W 1 - 0	Corbett 77	4
18	9		A	Didcot Town	210	W 2 - 1	Gunn 8 (og) Jackson 35	
19	13		A	Salisbury City	954	D 0 - 0		4
20	**20**	**FAT 3Q**	**H**	**Hyde United**	**522**	**L 1 - 2**	**Rowe 10**	
21	27		A	Banbury United	476	D 1 - 1	Rowe 13	5
22	Jan 3		H	Hednesford Town	702	L 1 - 2	Corbett 3	
23	8		H	Tiverton Town	444	W 2 - 1	Corbett 59 (pen) 81	4
24	15		A	Weymouth	508	W 2 - 1	Rowe 4 44	4
25	22		H	Cambridge City	543	L 2 - 3	Husband 78 Corbett 90	7
26	25		H	Cirencester Town	275	W 1 - 0	Rowe 63	
27	29		A	Bashley	272	W 4 - 0	Corbett 5 (pen) 57 Rowe 12 13	4
28	Feb 8		H	Swindon Supermarine	362	W 2 - 0	Rowe 46 Corbett 77	
29	12		A	Hemel Hempstead	233	L 0 - 1		5
30	15		A	Chesham United	278	L 0 - 1		
31	19		A	Cirencester Town	241	W 1 - 0	Daley 26	5
32	22		H	Halesowen Town	375	W 3 - 0	Rowe 61 68 Corbett 90	
33	26		H	Banbury United	626	W 3 - 1	Taylor 45 Tuohy 70 Bythe 74	4
34	March 5		A	Swindon Supermarine	208	L 0 - 1		5
35	8		H	Bedford Town	345	W 5 - 0	Blyth 8 Wall 3(og) Husband 66 Corbett 75 Downes 90	
36	12		A	Evesham United	268	W 1 - 0	Corbett 90	3
37	16		A	Stourbridge	443	L 3 - 4	Blyth 56 Barnfield 66 Rowe 74	
38	19		H	Salisbury City	664	W 2 - 0	Blyth 21 Rowe 86	5
39	22		A	Chippenham Town	387	D 0 - 0		
40	26		H	Didcot Town	503	W 2 - 1	A.Williams 5 (og) Sheldon 33	6
41	April 2		A	Brackley Town	376	D 0 - 0		6
42	9		H	Chesham United	667	W 3 - 2	Breeden 16 Bartley 76(pen) Blyth 84	
43	16		A	Truro City	927	L 1 - 3	Stanley 25	5
44	23		A	Oxford City	373	W 3 - 2	Rowe 16 78 Lysett 51	5
45	25		H	Stourbridge	793	W 3 - 2	Sheldon 60 Batchelor 75 Corbett 85 (pen)	5
46	**28**	**P-Off SF**	**A**	**Hednesford Town**	**1504**	**L 1 - 3**	**Batchelor 42**	

OXFORD CITY

Chairman: Brian Cox
Secretary: John Shepperd (T) 07748 628 911 (E) shepoxf@tiscali.co.uk
Additional Committee Members:
Peter Knapton, Paul Cotterell, Colin Taylor, Peter Burden, Paul Townsend.

Manager: Mike Ford
Programme Editor: Colin Taylor (E) ctoxford@btinternet.com

Club Factfile

Founded: 1882 **Nickname:** City
Previous Names: Not known
Previous Leagues: Isthmian 1907-88, 94-2005, South Midlands 1990-93, Spartan South Midlands 2005-06

Club Colours (change): Blue and white hoops/blue/blue (All yellow)

Ground: Court Place Farm, Marsh Lane, Marston, Oxford OX3 0NQ (T) 01865 744 493
Capacity: 3,000 **Seats:** 300 **Covered:** 400 **Clubhouse:** Yes **Shop:** Yes

Directions
Ground lies off A40 ring road, northern by-pass.
Follow signs for J.R. Hospital in yellow and small green signs to Court Place Farm Stadium.

Previous Grounds: The White House 1882-1988, Cuttleslowe Park 1990-91, Pressed Steel 1991-93

Record Attendance: 9,500 v Leytonstone - FA Amateur Cup - 1950
Record Victory: Not known
Record Defeat: Not known
Record Goalscorer: John Woodley
Record Appearances: John Woodley
Additional Records: Paid £3,000 to Woking for S Adams
Received £15,000 from Yeovil Town for Howard Forinton

Senior Honours: FA Amateur Cup 1905-06. Oxford Senior Cup x3
Spartan South Midlands League Premier Division 2005-06.

10 YEAR RECORD

01-02	02-03	03-04	04-05	05-06	06-07	07-08	08-09	09-10	10-11
Isth1 10	Isth1N 15	Isth1N 19	SthW 21	SSM P 1	SthW 12	SthW 4	SthP 6	SthP 13	SthP 14

OXFORD CITY

No.	Date	Comp	H/A	Opponents	Att:	Result	Goalscorers	Pos
1	Aug 14	Sth Prem	H	Bedford Town	151	D 1 - 1	Ballard 64	10
2	17		A	Chesham United	275	L 0 - 2		
3	21		A	Weymouth	534	D 1 - 1	Harding 52	15
4	28		A	Truro City	371	L 1 - 2	Sandy 68	20
5	30		H	Brackley Town	348	L 0 - 2		
6	Sept 4		H	Swindon Supermarine	212	D 1 - 1	Holman 90	20
7	**11**	**FAC 1Q**	**H**	**Mangotsfield United**	**155**	**L 0 - 1**		
8	14		H	Cambridge City	147	L 0 - 1		
9	18		H	Evesham United	176	L 0 - 1		21
10	Oct 2		A	Leamington	570	L 0 - 2		21
11	5		A	Salisbury City	692	L 0 - 2		
12	9		H	Hednesford Town	192	D 1 - 1	Savage 53 (pen)	21
13	**16**	**FAT 1Q**	**H**	**Daventry Town**	**152**	**L 1 - 4**	**Pritchard 34**	
14	19		H	Halesowen Town	156	D 0 - 0		
15	23		A	Banbury United	258	W 2 - 0	Lyon 43 McIlwain 78	21
16	Nov 6		A	Cirencester Town	196	L 1 - 4	Blossom 20	21
17	13		H	Hemel Hempstead	157	W 3 - 0	McIlwain 13 Steele 53 Kington 90	20
18	16		H	Bashley	164	D 1 - 1	Steele 90	
19	20		A	Tiverton Town	195	D 0 - 0		19
20	27		H	Chippenham Town	136	D 0 - 0		19
21	Dec 11		H	Truro City	235	D 1 - 1	Steele 44	18
22	Jan 3		A	Brackley Town	268	L 0 - 1		
23	8		A	Evesham United	106	L 0 - 3		20
24	15		H	Swindon Supermarine	206	W 2 - 1	McIlwain 2 Mekki 70	19
25	22		H	Chesham United	176	L 0 - 2		19
26	29		A	Bedford Town	220	W 1 - 0	Malone 57	18
27	Feb 1		A	Cambridge City	194	L 0 - 3		
28	5		H	Weymouth	244	W 5 - 0	FAULKNER 3 (35 68 80pen) Steele 43 Mekki 57	18
29	8		H	Didcot Town	315	L 0 - 3		
30	22		A	Bashley	188	L 1 - 3	Ballard 88	
31	26		A	Chippenham Town	367	W 2 - 1	Barcelos 48 Lyons 52	17
32	March 5		H	Stourbridge	161	L 0 - 2		17
33	12		H	Cirencester Town	175	D 3 - 3	Steele 1 55 Savage 73	17
34	15		H	Tiverton Town	101	W 3 - 1	Steele 45 88 Pearson 60	
35	19		A	Hemel Hempstead	201	W 2 - 0	Steele 29 Barcelos 74	14
36	22		A	Stourbridge	319	W 3 - 0	BARCELLOS 3 (29 76 83)	
37	26		A	Hednesford Town	546	L 1 - 2	Lyon 85	13
38	April 2		H	Salisbury City	365	D 2 - 2	Blossom 17 Savage 90 (pen)	15
39	9		A	Halesowen Town	167	W 3 - 0	Barcellos 46 65 Anderson 63	14
40	16		H	Banbury United	261	D 2 - 2	Ballard 18 90	14
41	23		H	Leamington	373	L 2 - 3	Steele 12 Anderson 37	15
42	25		A	Didcot Town	411	W 3 - 0	STEELE (3 9 49 86pen)	

REDDITCH UNITED

Chairman: Chris Swan
Secretary: Tim Delaney **(T)** 07827 963 212 **(E)** sec.rufc@yahoo.co.uk
Additional Committee Members:
Jeff Sharp, Sallie Swan, Mark Fenemore.

Manager: Martin Sockett
Programme Editor: Sallie Swan & Craig Swan **(E)** programmeeditor.reds@yahoo.com

Club Factfile

Founded: 1891 **Nickname:** The Reds
Previous Names: Redditch Town
Previous Leagues: Birmingham combination 1905-21, 29-39, 46-53, West Midlands 1921-29, 53-72, Southern 1972-79, 81-2004, Alliance 1979-80. Conference 2004-11.

Club Colours (change): Red/black/black (White/blue/blue)

Ground: Valley Stadium, Bromsgrove Road, Redditch B97 4RN **(T)** 01527 67450
Capacity: 5,000 **Seats:** 400 **Covered:** 2,000 **Clubhouse:** Yes **Shop:** Yes

Directions
M42 J2, at island first exit onto the A441 for 2 miles, next island first exit onto Birmingham Road A441 for 1.2 miles then at island third exit onto Middlehouse Lane B4184 for 0.3 miles. At traffic lights (next to the fire station) turn left onto Birmingham Road for 0.2 miles then turn right into Clive Road for 0.3 miles. At island take first exit onto Hewell Road for 0.2 miles then at 'T' junction right onto Windsor Street for 0.1 miles. At traffic lights (next to bus station) continue straight ahead onto Bromsgrove Road for 0.3 miles and at the brow of the hill, turn right into the ground's entrance.

Previous Grounds: HDA Sports Ground, Millsborough Road

Record Attendance: 5,500 v Bromsgrove Rovers - Wets Midlands League 1954-55
Record Victory: Not known
Record Defeat: Not known
Record Goalscorer: Not known
Record Appearances: Not known
Additional Records: Paid £3,000 to Halesowen Town for Paul Joinson
Received £40,000 from Aston Villa for David Farrell

Senior Honours: Worcestershire Senior Cup 1893-94, 29-30, 74-75, 76-76, 2007-08.
Birmingham Senior Cup 1924-25, 31-32, 38-39, 76-77, 2004-05.
Southern League Division 1 North 1975-76, Western Division 2003-04. Staffordshire Senior Cup 1990-91.

10 YEAR RECORD

01-02	02-03	03-04	04-05	05-06	06-07	07-08	08-09	09-10	10-11
SthW 18	SthW 7	SthW 1	Conf N 9	Conf N 20	Conf N 19	Conf N 13	Conf N 14	Conf N 19	Conf N 21

REDDITCH UNITED

No.	Date	Comp	H/A	Opponents	Att:	Result	Goalscorers	Pos
								- 5 points Mar
1	Sat-14-Aug	BSN	A	Stalybridge Celtic	508	L 0-2		21
2	Tue-17-Aug	BSN	H	Alfreton Town	287	L 1-5	Jones 40	22
3	Sat-21-Aug	BSN	H	Boston United	456	L 0-9		22
4	Wed-25-Aug	BSN	A	Corby Town	307	L 2-3	M Smith 42, Ravenhill 83	22
5	Sat-28-Aug	BSN	H	AFC Telford	606	D 1-1	M Smith 16	22
6	Mon-30-Aug	BSN	A	Gloucester City	465	L 0-5		22
7	Sat-04-Sep	BSN	A	Guiseley	362	L 1-3	Adaggio 19	22
8	Sat-18-Sep	BSN	A	Hyde FC	340	W 4-1	M Smith 3 (5, 76, 81), Adaggio 78	20
9	Sat-02-Oct	BSN	H	Blyth Spartans	254	W 2-1	P Green 90, N Smith pen 90	19
10	Sat-16-Oct	BSN	A	Droylsden	284	L 0-3		20
11	Sat-30-Oct	BSN	H	Harrogate Town	329	L 0-1		20
12	Sat-06-Nov	BSN	A	Gainsborough Trinity	372	L 0-3		21
13	Mon-08-Nov	BSN	A	Worcester City	808	D 1-1	Fitzpatrick 90	21
14	Sat-13-Nov	BSN	H	Vauxhall Motors	158	D 2-2	J Richards 64, P Green 78	21
15	Tue-14-Dec	BSN	H	Nuneaton Town	163	L 0-5		21
16	Tue-28-Dec	BSN	A	AFC Telford	1690	L 1-3	Quaynor 19	21
17	Sat-01-Jan	BSN	A	Solihull Moors	318	L 0-3		21
18	Mon-03-Jan	BSN	H	Worcester City	505	D 0-0		21
19	Sat-08-Jan	BSN	H	Hinckley United	279	L 2-3	M Smith 2 (53, 62)	21
20	Sat-15-Jan	BSN	H	Gainsborough Trinity	163	L 1-4	M Smith 84	21
21	Tue-18-Jan	BSN	A	Workington	300	L 1-5	P Green 12	21
22	Sat-22-Jan	BSN	H	Stalybridge Celtic	181	L 1-3	Og (Ryan) 43	21
23	Tue-25-Jan	BSN	A	Boston United	994	L 0-1		21
24	Sat-29-Jan	BSN	A	Nuneaton Town	965	D 1-1	P Green 79	21
25	Sat-05-Feb	BSN	H	Hyde FC	201	L 0-1		21
26	Sat-12-Feb	BSN	A	Stafford Rangers	365	L 1-2	McKenzie 13	21
27	Tue-22-Feb	BSN	A	Blyth Spartans	528	L 0-2		21
28	Tue-01-Mar	BSN	H	Stafford Rangers	131	L 0-1		21
29	Sat-05-Mar	BSN	H	Gloucester City	309	L 0-1		21
30	Sat-12-Mar	BSN	A	Eastwood Town	343	L 1-2	S Brown 78	21
31	Tue-15-Mar	BSN	H	Droylsden	70	L 1-3	McKenzie 38	21
32	Sat-19-Mar	BSN	H	Workington	208	D 1-1	S Brown pen 14	21
33	Tue-22-Mar	BSN	A	Harrogate Town	207	L 0-3		21
34	Sat-26-Mar	BSN	A	Hinckley United	356	L 0-4		21 Relegated
35	Sat-02-Apr	BSN	A	Vauxhall Motors	143	L 1-2	Og (Grocutt) 73	21
36	Tue-05-Apr	BSN	H	Solihull Moors	252	D 0-0		21
37	Sat-09-Apr	BSN	H	Eastwood Town	239	L 0-6		21
38	Sat-16-Apr	BSN	H	Guiseley	165	L 2-3	Geathers 31, Harris 55	21
39	Sat-23-Apr	BSN	A	Alfreton Town	1364	L 0-4		21
40	Mon-25-Apr	BSN	H	Corby Town	335	D 2-2	McKenzie 2 (22, 65)	21

CUPS

No.	Date	Comp	H/A	Opponents	Att:	Result	Goalscorers
1	Sat-25-Sep	FAC 2Q	A	Loughborough Dynamo	185	W 2-0	P Green 67, J Richards 75
2	Sat-09-Oct	FAC 3Q	H	Hinckley United	563	W 1-0	Adaggio pen 34
3	Sat-23-Oct	FAC 4Q	A	Guiseley	808	L 1-2	N Smith 63
4	Sat-11-Dec	FAT 1	A	Grimsby Town	1116	L 0-3	

ST ALBANS CITY

Chairman: Ian Ridley
Secretary: Steve Eames (T) 07805 769 083 (E) steveeames@sacfc.co.uk
Additional Committee Members:
Nick Crowther, Nick Archer, Lawrence Levy, John McGowan.

Manager: David Howell
Programme Editor: Steve Eames (E) steveeames@sacfc.co.uk

St Abans City in 1997. Back row, left to right: Gary Cobb, Richard Evans, Andy Polston, Kevin Mudd, Rob Haworth, Jon Daly, and Steve Clark. Front row: Gareth Howells, Erskine Smart, Greg Howell, Peter Risley, Naseem Bashir, Tony Kelly and Jay Thomas.

Club Factfile

Founded: 1908 **Nickname:** The Saints
Previous Names:
Previous Leagues: Herts County 1908-10, Spartan 1908-20, Athenian 1920-23, Isthmian 1923-2004, Conference 2004-11.

Club Colours (change): Yellow/blue/yellow (Red/black/red)

Ground: Clarence Park, York Road, St. Albans, Herts AL1 4PL (T) 01727 848 914
Capacity: 5,007 **Seats:** 667 **Covered:** 1,900 **Clubhouse:** Yes **Shop:** Yes

Directions From the M25 (Clockwise) Exit M25 at junction 21A(A405). Follow signs to St. Albans from slip road. At Noke Hotel roundabout (Shell garage will be straight ahead), bear right on A405 and stay on A405 until London Colney roundabout (traffic light controlled). Turn left onto A1081. Follow road for approx 1 mile until mini roundabout (Great Northern pub on left). Turn right into Alma Road. At traffic lights turn right into Victoria Street and continue to junction with Crown pub. Go straight across into Clarence Road, ground is first on left about 50 yards past junction or take the next turning on the left into York Road, ground entrance is at the end of the road on the left. From the M25 (Counter-clockwise) Exit M25 at junction 22 (A1081). Follow signs to St. Albans from slip road. At London Colney roundabout (traffic light controlled) exit onto A1081. Follow road for approx 1 mile until mini roundabout (Great Northern pub on left). Turn right into Alma Road. At traffic lights turn right into Victoria Street and continue to junction with Crown pub. Go straight across into Clarence Road, ground is first on left about 50 yards past junction or take the next turning on the left into York Road, ground entrance is at the end of the road on the left.

Previous Grounds: None

Record Attendance: 9,757 v Ferryhill Athletic - FA Amateur Cup 1926
Record Victory: 14-0 v Aylesbury United (H) - Spartan League 19/10/1912
Record Defeat: 0-11 v Wimbledon (H) - Isthmian League 1946
Record Goalscorer: Billy Minter - 356 (Top scorer for 12 consecutive season from 1920-32)
Record Appearances: Phil Wood - 900 (1962-85)
Additional Records: Paid £6,000 to Yeovil Town for Paul Turner August 1957
Received £92,759 from Southend United for Dean Austin 1990

Senior Honours: Athenian League 1920-21, 21-22. Isthmian League 1923-24, 26-27, 27-28.
London Senior Cup 1970-71.

10 YEAR RECORD

01-02	02-03	03-04	04-05	05-06	06-07	07-08	08-09	09-10	10-11
Isth P 10	Isth P 4	Isth P 19	Conf S 14	Conf S 2	Conf 24	Conf S 19	Conf S 12	Conf S 13	Conf S 22

ST ALBANS CITY

No.	Date	Comp	H/A	Opponents	Att:	Result	Goalscorers	Pos
								- 10 points Feb
1	Sat-14-Aug	BSS	A	Thurrock	306	D 2-2	Roberts 49, Effiong 52	11
2	Tue-17-Aug	BSS	H	Basingstoke Town	311	D 0-0		12
3	Sat-21-Aug	BSS	H	Braintree Town	330	D 0-0		14
4	Tue-24-Aug	BSS	A	Staines Town	307	D 2-2	Fisher 16, Effiong 28	16
5	Sat-28-Aug	BSS	H	Hampton & Richmond Borough	307	D 1-1	A Martin 50	16
6	Mon-30-Aug	BSS	A	Maidenhead United	307	L 1-2	Frater 89	17
7	Sat-04-Sep	BSS	H	Woking	490	L 0-1		18
8	Sat-11-Sep	BSS	A	Bromley	819	D 1-1	Peters 51	18
9	Sat-18-Sep	BSS	A	Havant & Waterlooville	755	W 1-0	Sigere 61	16
10	Sat-02-Oct	BSS	H	Bishops Stortford	354	L 1-4	Deeney 18	18
11	Sat-16-Oct	BSS	H	Weston-Super-Mare	284	L 3-4	Peters 31, Sigere 74, Effiong 78	18
12	Sat-30-Oct	BSS	H	Ebbsfleet United	472	L 1-2	Effiong 34	19
13	Mon-01-Nov	BSS	A	Chelmsford City	738	D 1-1	Beautyman 58	19
14	Sat-06-Nov	BSS	A	Welling United	555	L 0-6		19
15	Tue-09-Nov	BSS	H	Farnborough	232	L 0-2		19
16	Sat-13-Nov	BSS	A	Lewes	727	L 1-3	Everitt 76	20
17	Sat-01-Jan	BSS	A	Boreham Wood	334	W 3-0	Effiong 2 (17, 44), Smith 27	19
18	Mon-03-Jan	BSS	H	Maidenhead United	366	W 1-0	Effiong 55	18
19	Sat-08-Jan	BSS	H	Bromley	347	D 1-1	Hutton 8	18
20	Sat-22-Jan	BSS	A	Basingstoke Town	303	W 2-0	Effiong 41, Smith 73	19
21	Tue-25-Jan	BSS	H	Eastleigh	217	L 0-1		19
22	Sat-29-Jan	BSS	H	Lewes	338	D 0-0		20
23	Tue-01-Feb	BSS	H	Boreham Wood	294	L 0-1		20
24	Sat-05-Feb	BSS	A	Hampton & Richmond Borough	404	D 0-0		20
25	Tue-08-Feb	BSS	A	Woking	690	L 0-2		20
26	Sat-12-Feb	BSS	H	Chelmsford City	428	L 0-2		22
27	Mon-14-Feb	BSS	A	Eastleigh	248	L 2-4	Effiong 13, Deeney 72	22
28	Sat-19-Feb	BSS	A	Farnborough	601	L 0-1		22
29	Sat-26-Feb	BSS	H	Dover Athletic	384	L 1-5	Chaves 89	22
30	Sat-05-Mar	BSS	A	Weston-Super-Mare	219	L 1-2	Battersby 75	22
31	Sat-12-Mar	BSS	H	Staines Town	274	W 2-0	Battersby 21, O'Donnell 58	22
32	Tue-15-Mar	BSS	A	Dorchester Town	372	W 3-1	Effiong 3 (8, pen 73, 83)	22
33	Sat-19-Mar	BSS	A	Braintree Town	576	D 1-1	Petrucci 83	22
34	Tue-22-Mar	BSS	A	Dartford	674	D 2-2	Effiong 33, O Kelly 53	22
35	Sat-26-Mar	BSS	H	Thurrock	235	L 0-2		22
36	Tue-29-Mar	BSS	H	Dorchester Town	142	L 1-4	Everitt 87	22
37	Sat-02-Apr	BSS	H	Dartford	404	L 1-2	Battersby 55	22
38	Sat-09-Apr	BSS	A	Ebbsfleet United	840	L 0-4		22 Relegated
39	Sat-16-Apr	BSS	H	Welling United	337	W 1-0	Effiong 79	22
40	Sat-23-Apr	BSS	A	Bishops Stortford	401	L 0-4		22
41	Mon-25-Apr	BSS	H	Havant & Waterlooville	252	D 1-1	Everitt 35	22
42	Sat-30-Apr	BSS	A	Dover Athletic	847	L 1-4	Smith 52	22

CUPS

No.	Date	Comp	H/A	Opponents	Att:	Result	Goalscorers
1	Sat-25-Sep	FAC 2Q	H	Beckenham Town	303	W 3-1	Sigere 6, Roberts pen 53, Og (Hill) 83
2	Sat-09-Oct	FAC 3Q	H	Kingstonian	484	D 0-0	
3	Mon-11-Oct	FAC 3QR	A	Kingstonian	367	W 2-1	Gomez 2 (17, 72)
4	Sat-23-Oct	FAC 4Q	A	Luton Town	4144	L 0-4	
5	Sat-20-Nov	FAT 3Q	H	Staines Town	249	W 3-1	Palmer 11, Everitt 35, Peters 75
6	Sat-11-Dec	FAT 1	A	Dorchester Town	302	L 0-3	

STOURBRIDGE

Chairman: Ian Pilkington
Secretary: Clive Eades **(T)** 07958 275 986 **(E)** clive.eades2@capita.co.uk
Additional Committee Members:
Gordon Thomas, Andy Pountney, Neil Smith, Andy Bullingham, Hugh Grant, Nigel Gregg, Sharon Hyde, Stephen Hyde, Jonathan Martin, Gordon Thomas.
Manager: Gary Hackett
Programme Editor: Nigel Gregg **(E)** ng004f7624@blueyonder.co.uk

Back Row (L to R): Sean Geddes, Aaron Griffiths, James Dyson, Aaron Drake, Leon Broadhurst, Craig Slater, Nathan Bennett, Lewis Solly, Sam Smith, Linden Dovey, Jamie Oliver, Josh Craddock, Paul McCone, Ashley Edwards, Will Worthington.
Front Row: Paul Lloyd, David Plinston, Sam Rock, Steve Johnson (GK coach), Richard Drewett (physio), Jon Ford (Asst Manager), Ian Pilkington (Chairman), Gary Hackett (Manager), Mark Clifton (Coach), Ben Billingham, Ryan Rowe, Ryan Mahon, Drew Canavan.
Photo courtesy of Andrew Roper.

Club Factfile

Founded: 1876 **Nickname:** The Glassboys
Previous Names: Not known
Previous Leagues: West Midlands (Birmingham League) 1892-1939, 54-71, Birmingham Combination 1945-53, Southern 1971-2000

Club Colours (change): Red and white stripes/red/red (Yellow/green/yellow)

Ground: War Memorial Athletic Ground, High Street, Amblecote DY8 4HN **(T)** 01384 394 040 / 444 075
Capacity: 2,000 **Seats:** 250 **Covered:** 750 **Clubhouse:** Yes **Shop:** Yes

Directions
From Stourbridge Ring-Road follow signs A491 to Wolverhampton.
The ground is on the left within 300 yards immediately beyond the third traffic lights and opposite the Royal Oak public house.

Previous Grounds: Not known

Record Attendance: 5,726 v Cardiff City - Welsh Cup Final 1st Leg 1974
Record Victory: Not known
Record Defeat: Not known
Record Goalscorer: Ron Page - 269
Record Appearances: Ron Page - 427
Additional Records: Received £20,000 from Lincoln City for Tony Cunningham 1979

Senior Honours: Southern League Division 1 North 1973-74, Midland Division 90-91, League Cup 92-93. Midland Alliance 2001-02, 02-03. Worcestershire Junior Cup 1927-28. Hereford Senior Cup 1954-55. Birmingham Senior Cup x3. Worcestershire Senior Cup x9

10 YEAR RECORD

01-02		02-03		03-04		04-05		05-06		06-07		07-08		08-09		09-10		10-11	
MidAl	1	MidAl	1	MidAl	9	MidAl	8	MidAl	2	SthM	7	SthM	3	SthP	16	SthP	9	SthP	8

STOURBRIDGE

No.	Date	Comp	H/A	Opponents	Att:	Result	Goalscorers	Pos
1	Aug 14	Sth Prem	A	Salisbury City	871	L 0 - 3		20
2	17		H	Didcot Town	252	W 3 - 1	Brady 29 47 Dovey 79	
3	22		H	Swindon Supermarine	167	W 5 - 1	BRADY 3 (31 37 76) McCone 59 Plinston 88	10
4	24		A	Cirencester Town	134	W 2 - 1	Bennett 63 Rowe 84	
5	28		A	Brackley Town	217	D 0 - 0		3
6	31		H	Halesowen Town	769	L 0 - 2		
7	Sept 4		A	Cambridge City	365	L 0 - 3		8
8	**11**	**FAC 1Q**	**H**	**Romulus**	**224**	**W 2 - 0**	**Brady 45 Rowe 57**	
9	14		H	Evesham United	289	W 3 - 1	Rowe 47 Plinston 59 Drake 87	
10	18		H	Chesham United	231	D 1 - 1	Rowe 25	9
11	**25**	**FAC 2Q**	**A**	**AFC Telford United**	**1447**	**L 2 - 5**	**Canavan 3 Rowe 23**	
12	Oct 2		A	Bashley	240	D 0 - 0		10
13	5		A	Chippenham Town	401	D 0 - 0		
14	9		H	Tiverton Town	424	D 0 - 0		10
15	**16**	**FAT 1Q**	**A**	**Bridgwater Town**	**201**	**W 3 - 1**	**Dovey 19 29 Rowe 84**	
16	**30**	**FAT 2Q**	**A**	**Rushall Olympic**	**241**	**W 1 - 0**	**Dovey 63**	
17	Nov 2		H	Banbury United	245	W 2 - 1	Dovey 49 65	
18	6		H	Weymouth	388	W 7 - 2	Drake 6 59 Rowe 41 Dovey 45 Billingham 53 85 Rock 83	8
19	13		A	Bedford Town	287	L 1 - 2	Rowe 9	8
20	16		A	Hednesford Town	493	W 3 - 2	Billingham 9 Bennett 49 Rowe 82	
21	**20**	**FAT 3Q**	**A**	**Droylsden**	**246**	**L 2 - 3**	**Rowe 34 Drake 85**	
22	27		A	Truro City	355	L 1 - 3	Rowe 31	9
23	Dec 11		H	Brackley Town	208	W 2 - 1	Billingham 65 Rock 69	
24	Jan 3		A	Halesowen Town	835	W 3 - 0	Billingham 36 (pen) 45 Plinston 75	
25	8		A	Chesham United	268	L 0 - 2		6
26	15		H	Cambridge City	305	W 3 - 0	Billingham 7 Rowe 73 Dovey 87	
27	22		A	Didcot Town	152	W 4 - 1	Rowe 14 Broadhurst 26 Canavan 85 Dovey 90	
28	29		H	Salisbury City	381	D 0 - 0		6
29	Feb 5		A	Swindon Supermarine	123	L 1 - 2	Rowe 53	7
30	12		H	Cirencester Town	211	W 2 - 1	Broadhurst 35 Canavan 45	7
31	23		H	Hednesford Town	389	L 1 - 2	Rowe 49	
32	26		H	Truro City	327	D 2 - 2	Broadhurst 39 Rowe 65	9
33	March 1		A	Evesham United	138	W 3 - 2	Dovey 11 (pen) Rowe 34 Bennett 63	
34	5		A	Oxford City	161	W 2 - 0	Broadhurst 25 Rowe 41	7
35	12		A	Weymouth	497	L 2 - 3	Bennett 17 Rowe 90	8
36	15		H	Leamington	860	W 4 - 3	Rowe 4 Drake 28 Dovey 83 Billingham 90	
37	19		H	Bedford Town	619	W 3 - 0	Dovey 6 (pen) Billingham 62 Rock 77	8
38	22		H	Oxford City	319	L 0 - 3		
39	26		A	Tiverton Town	190	L 0 - 1		8
40	29		H	Hemel Hempstead	255	L 1 - 5	Drake	
41	April 2		H	Chippenham Town	268	W 1 - 0	Rowe 89	8
42	19		A	Hemel Hempstead	144	D 2 - 2		
43	23		H	Bashley	291	W 6 - 1	McCone 4 Craddock 11 44 Dyson 31 Bennett 41 Billingham 50	8
44	25		A	Leamington	793	L 2 - 3	Bennett 8 McCone 71	

SWINDON SUPERMARINE

Chairman: Keith Yeomans
Secretary: Judi Moore **(T)** 07785 970 954 **(E)** judimoore6@aol.com
Additional Committee Members:
Steve Gunnett, Steve Wheeler.

Manager: Matt Robinson & Gary Horgan
Programme Editor: Keith Yeomans **(E)** supermarinefc@aol.com

Club Factfile

Founded: 1992 **Nickname:** Marine
Previous Names: Club formed after the amalgamation of Swindon Athletic and Supermarine
Previous Leagues: Wiltshire, Hellenic1992-2001.

Club Colours (change): Blue and white/blue/blue (All red)

Ground: The Webbs Stadium, South Marston, Swindon SN3 4BZ **(T)** 01793 828 778
Capacity: 3,000 **Seats:** 300 **Covered:** 300 **Clubhouse:** Yes **Shop:** Yes

Directions
From M5 Junction 11a, take the A417 to Cirencester, then A419 Swindon. At the A361 junction by Honda Factory take road to Highworth. After one mile Club is on 4th roundabout.

From M4 Junction 15, take A419 towards Swindon Cirencester, take A361, then as above .

From A420 Swindon take A419 to Cirencester, near Honda factory take A361, then as above.

Previous Grounds: Supermarine: Vickers Airfield > Mid 1960s

Record Attendance: 1,550 v Aston Villa
Record Victory: Not known
Record Defeat: Not known
Record Goalscorer: Damon York - 136 (1990-98)
Record Appearances: Damon York - 314 (1990-98)
Additional Records: Paid £1,000 to Hungerford Town for Lee Hartson

Senior Honours: Hellenic League Premier Division 1997-98, 2000-01, Challenge Cup 97-97, 99-2000.

10 YEAR RECORD

01-02	02-03	03-04	04-05	05-06	06-07	07-08	08-09	09-10	10-11
SthW 19	SthW 19	SthW 17	SthW 19	SthW 5	Sthsw 4	SthP 12	SthP 13	SthP 14	SthP 10

SWINDON SUPERMARINE

No.	Date	Comp	H/A	Opponents	Att:	Result	Goalscorers	Pos
1	Aug 14	Sth Prem	H	Hemel Hempstead Town	133	L 1 - 3	Allen 80	18
2	19		A	Weymouth	743	D 0 - 0		
3	22		A	Stourbridge	167	L 1 - 5	Cook 90	20
4	25		H	Chesham United	101	D 0 - 0		
5	28		H	Bedford Town	141	W 1 - 0	Stanley 34 (pen)	13
6	30		A	Cirencester Town	227	W 2 - 1	Cook 13 Gosling 35	
7	Sept 4		H	Oxford City	212	D 1 - 1	Tooze 33	12
8	**11**	**FAC 1Q**	**H**	**Brading Town**	**110**	**W 4 - 0**	**Tooze 17 Gosling 46 C.Allen 53 Hopper 82**	
9	14		A	Hednesford Town	210	D 1 - 1	Stanley 42 (pen)	
10	18		A	Banbury United	213	D 0 - 0		10
11	**25**	**FAC 2Q**	**H**	**Weymouth**	**185**	**W 3 - 0**	**Gosling 37 81 Holgate 66**	
12	Oct 6		H	Truro City	181	L 0 - 2		
13	**9**	**FAC 3Q**	**H**	**Hungerford Town**	**365**	**W 4 - 0**	**STANLEY 3 (8 21pen 64) Gosling 66**	
14	**16**	**FAT 1Q**	**H**	**Beaconsfield SYCOB**	**111**	**W 4 - 2**	**Gosling 15 Cook 54 Hopper 65 Henry 75**	
15	19		A	Didcot Town	169	W 4 - 1	GOSLING 3 (34 64 70) Holgate 73	12
16	**23**	**FAC 4Q**	**H**	**Bath City**	**551**	**D 0 - 0**		
17	**26**	**FAC 4Qr**	**A**	**Bath City**	**665**	**W 4 - 3**	**Stanley 3 Robinson 41 Henry 45 Lapham 90**	
18	**30**	**FAT 2Q**	**A**	**Paulton Rovers**	**159**	**W 5 - 4**	**Stanley 26 Cook 46 48 Hopper 55 Morris 87**	
19	**Nov 6**	**FAC 1**	**H**	**Eastwood Town**	**1159**	**W 2 - 1**	**Holgate 16 Wells 27**	
20	13		A	Evesham United	94	W 1 - 0	Hopper 90	12
21	17		H	Tiverton Town	108	W 3 - 0	Hopper 31 Stanley 58 (pen) Cook 80	
22	**20**	**FAT 3Q**	**A**	**Lowestoft Town**	**622**	**L 1 - 2**	**Wells 20**	
23	**27**	**FAC 2**	**A**	**Colchester Town**	**3047**	**L 0 - 1**		
24	Dec 11		A	Bedford Town	242	W 6 - 0	Taylor 14 Gosling 16 Morris 22 HOLGATE 3 (54 73 78)	11
25	14		A	Cambridge City	211	L 0 - 2		
26	Jan 3		H	Cirencester Town	232	W 1 - 0	Wells 11	
27	8		H	Banbury United	167	W 3 - 0	Cook 44 Horgan 50 Wells 76	10
28	12		H	Halesowen Town	101	W 3 - 0	Morris 4 60 Stanley 41	
29	15		A	Oxford City	206	L 1 - 2	Morris 54	9
30	18		A	Bashley	175	L 0 - 2		
31	26		H	Salisbury City	282	L 1 - 2	Erskine 9	
32	29		A	Hemel Hempstead	156	W 2 - 1	Wells 43 Erskine 79	9
33	Feb 5		H	Stourbridge	123	W 2 - 0	Bampton 59 Bryant 63	8
34	8		A	Leamington	362	L 0 - 2		
35	12		A	Chesham United	359	L 0 - 4		9
36	19		H	Bashley	137	W 4 - 2	STANLEY 3 14 44 53) Robinson 16	9
37	22		A	Tiverton Town	229	W 1 - 0	Bryant 25	
38	March 2		H	Brackley Town	103	L 1 - 5	Bryant 43	
39	5		H	Leamington	208	W 1 - 0	Stanley 69 (pen)	9
40	9		H	Hednesford Town	129	L 1 - 2	Beeden 54	
41	12		A	Halesowen Town		D 1 - 1	Stanley 61	
42	15		A	Chippenham Town	343	L 1 - 3	Stanley 57 (pen)	
43	19		H	Evesham United	131	D 1 - 1	McHugh 88	9
44	22		A	Salisbury City	604	L 0 - 2		
45	26		H	Cambridge City	137	L 0 - 2		9
46	30		H	Weymouth	147	L 0 - 1		
47	April 2		A	Truro City	528	L 2 - 7	Murphy 8 72	10
48	9		H	Didcot Town	163	W 2 - 0	McHugh 17 Bampton 50	10
49	16		A	Brackley Town	225	W 4 - 1	Wells 12 Robinson 56 Hopper 64 Bryant 90	10
50	25		H	Chippenham Town	258	W 3 - 1	Bryant 15 Bampton 31 Hopper 48 (pen)	

WEYMOUTH

Chairman: Amanda Rolls

Secretary: Nigel Biddlecombe **(T)** 07880 508 240 **(E)** biddie@weymoff.com

Additional Committee Members:
David Samuel, Mark Coleman, Audrius Preidzius, Bronius Preidzius, Pranas Preidzius, Inga Preidziuviene, Lijana Preidziuviene, Eugenius Tiskus.

Manager: Brendan King

Programme Editor: Hilary Billimore **(E)** hbillimore@tiscali.co.uk

Back row (L-R): Carl Mutch (reserve team coach), Alex Halloran (now Portland), Joe Toghill, Mitch Conning, Scott Dixon, Lewis Tasker, Tom Manley, Nick Jordan, Jamie Beasley, Sam Poole, T-J Lang, Rob Wolleaston, Rex Buttle (reserve team physio).
Front Row: Stephen Reed, Ollie Tribe, Emma Tonkin, Ben Gerring, Brendon King (manager), Mattie Groves (asst. manager), Warren Byerley, Ritchy Marshallsay, Ryan McKechnie, Kyle Bassett.

Club Factfile

Founded: 1890 **Nickname:** The Terras

Previous Names: None

Previous Leagues: Dorset, Western 1907-23, 28-49, Southern 1923-28, 49-79, 89-2005, Alliance/Conference 1979-89, 2005-10

Club Colours (change): Claret with sky blue sleeves/claret/claret (All yellow)

Ground: Bob Lucas Stadium, Radipole Lane, Weymouth DT4 9XJ **(T)** 01305 785 558

Capacity: 6,600 **Seats:** 800 **Covered:** Yes **Clubhouse:** Yes **Shop:** Yes

Directions
Approach Weymouth from Dorchester on the A354.
Turn right at first roundabout onto Weymouth Way, continue to the next roundabout then turn right (signposted Football Ground).
At the next roundabout take third exit into the ground.

Previous Grounds: Not known

Record Attendance: 4,995 v Manchester United - Ground opening 21/10/97

Record Victory: Not known

Record Defeat: Not known

Record Goalscorer: W 'Farmer' Haynes - 275

Record Appearances: Tony Hobsons - 1,076

Additional Records: Paid £15,000 to Northwich Victoria for Shaun Teale
Received £100,000 from Tottenham Hotspur for Peter Guthrie 1988

Senior Honours: Southern League 1964-65, 65-66. Conference South 2005-06.
Dorset Senior Cup x27

10 YEAR RECORD

01-02	02-03	03-04	04-05	05-06	06-07	07-08	08-09	09-10	10-11
SthP 11	SthP 17	SthP 2	Conf S 7	Conf S 1	Conf 11	Conf 18	Conf 23	Conf S 22	SthP 18

WEYMOUTH

No.	Date	Comp	H/A	Opponents	Att:	Result	Goalscorers	Pos
1	Aug 14	Sth Prem	A	Halesowen Town	373	D 0 - 0	deducted 10 points for going into administration	22
2	19		H	Swindon Supermarine	743	D 0 - 0		
3	21		H	Oxford City	534	D 1 - 1	Groves 14	22
4	24		A	Salisbury City	896	L 2 - 3	Dubois 29 Gerring 35	
5	28		A	Evesham United	163	W 3 - 1	Byerley 13 (pen) Mower 23 Emati-Emati 84	22
6	30		H	Bashley	673	L 1 - 4	Dubois 15	
7	Sept 4		A	Leamington	603	L 0 - 1		22
8	**11**	**FAC 1Q**	**A**	**Taunton Town**	**288**	**W 2 - 1**	**Byerley 11 46**	
9	18		H	Cambridge City	506	L 0 - 3		22
10	**25**	**FAC 2Q**	**A**	**Swindon Supermarine**	**185**	**L 0 - 3**		
11	Oct 2		A	Chesham United	311	L 1 - 2	Byerley 41	22
12	9		H	Cirencester Town	449	W 1 - 0	Byerley 75 (pen)	22
13	**16**	**FAT 1Q**	**H**	**Bashley**	**201**	**D 2 - 2**	**P.Dean 57 S.Fitzgerald 90**	
14	21		H	Tiverton Town	461	W 3 - 1	Gerring 6 Wright 53 Byerley 61 (pen)	
15	23		A	Hednesford Town	334	L 0 - 9		22
16	**30**	**FAT 2Q**	**A**	**Cirencester Town**	**95**	**L 1 - 2**	**Groves 75**	
17	Nov 6		A	Stourbridge	388	L 2 - 7	Byerley 47 82 (pen)	22
18	13		H	Chippenham Town	485	D 3 - 3	Byerley 28 Charles 89 Gerring 90	22
19	16		A	Didcot Town	163	D 2 - 2	Wolleaston 48 Groves 70	
20	20		H	Bedford Town	431	W 3 - 1	Byerley 24 Wright 41 Groves 86	22
21	Dec 4		H	Banbury United	530	L 2 - 4	Holloran 52 84	22
22	11		H	Evesham United	486	W 2 - 0	Byerley 51 (pen) Wolleaston 77	22
23	27		H	Truro City	824	L 0 - 4		22
24	Jan 3		A	Bashley	346	L 1 - 5	Byerley 26	
25	8		A	Cambridge City	352	L 0 - 1		22
26	15		H	Leamington	58	L 1 - 2	Byerley 86	22
27	18		A	Hemel Hempstead	164	W 2 - 1	Groves 44 Byerley 81	
28	29		H	Halesowen Town	535	W 3 - 0	Clough 39 Byerley 49 71 (pen)	22
29	Feb 5		A	Oxford City	244	L 0 - 5		22
30	12		H	Salisbury City	837	W 2 - 0	Byerley 20 Beasley 56	18
31	24		H	Didcot Town	651	L 1 - 2	Wooleaston 84	
32	26		H	Hemel Hempstead	538	D 2 - 2	Reed 63 Beasley 65	19
33	March 5		A	Banbury United	300	L 0 - 3		19
34	12		H	Stourbridge	497	W 3 - 2	Mudge 5 Byerley 69 M.Groves 90	19
35	15		A	Brackley Town	171	D 1 - 1	Gerring 38	
36	19		A	Chippenham Town	432	L 0 - 1		19
37	26		A	Cirencester Town	217	L 0 - 3		19
38	30		A	Swindon Supermarine	147	W 1 - 0	Byerley 90	
39	April 5		A	Bedford Town	192	L 1 - 4	Byerley 2	
40	9		A	Tiverton Town	472	W 4 - 0	Wolleaston 36 Fowler 45 74 Gerring 88	18
41	16		H	Hednesford Town	489	L 2 - 4	Byerley 46 Beasley 70	
42	23		H	Chesham United	643	W 3 - 0	Beasley 43 Byerley 46 Groves 89	18
43	25		A	Truro City	1696	L 2 - 3	Smith 18 McConnell 48 (og)	

AFC HAYES

Chairman: B Stone
Secretary: Barry Crump **(T)** 07966 468 029 **(E)** afchayesfootballsec@hotmail.co.uk
Additional Committee Members:
Peter Betts, Roger Galloway, Dave Ball, John Handell, Keith Gavin, Perry Squires, Dave Swan.
Manager: Danny Vincent
Programme Editor: Dave Swan **(E)** daveswan03@hotmail.com

Club Factfile

Founded: 1974 **Nickname:** The Brook
Previous Names: Brook House > 2008.
Previous Leagues: Spartan South Midlands, Isthmian

Club Colours (change): Blue and white stripes/blue/blue (Red/white/red)

Ground: Farm Park, Kingshill Avenue, Hayes UB4 8DD **(T)** 020 8845 0110
Capacity: 2,000 **Seats:** 150 **Covered:** 200 **Clubhouse:** Yes **Shop:** No

Directions
From the A40 McDonalds Target roundabout take A312 south towards Hayes.
At White Hart roundabout take third exit into Yeading Lane.
Turn right at first traffic lights into Kingshill Avenue.
Ground approx one miles on the right-hand side.

Previous Grounds:

Record Attendance: Not known
Record Victory: Not known
Record Defeat: Not known
Record Goalscorer: Not known
Record Appearances: Not known
Additional Records:

Senior Honours: Spartan South Midlands Premier South 1997-98, Premier Cup 1999-2000, Challenge Trophy 2003-04.
Isthmian Associate Members Trophy 2005-06.
Middlesex Senior Cup 2008-09.

10 YEAR RECORD

01-02	02-03	03-04	04-05	05-06	06-07	07-08	08-09	09-10	10-11
Conf 20	Isth P 7	Isth P 8	Conf S 12	Conf S 20	Conf S 20	Sthsw 14	Sthsw 9	Sthsw 21	SthC 19

ASHFORD TOWN (MIDDLESEX)

Chairman: Dave Baker
Secretary: Geoff Knock **(T)** 07928 101 876 **(E)** football.secretary@atmfc.co.uk
Additional Committee Members:
Alan Constable, Bob Parker, Gareth Coates, Dan Butler, Mark Davis, Ben Murray, Terry Ryan, Mick Tilt.
Manager: Paul Burgess
Programme Editor: Phil Marshall **(E)** club.manager@atmfc.co.uk

Club Factfile

Founded: 1964 **Nickname:** Ash Trees
Previous Names: Not known
Previous Leagues: Hounslow & District 1964-68, Surrey Intermediate 1968-82, Surrey Premier 1982-90, Combined Counties 1990-2000, Isthmian 2000-04, 06-10, Southern 2004-06

Club Colours (change): Tangerine and white stripes/black/tangerine (Blue/white/blue)

Ground: Robert Parker Stadium, Stanwell, Staines TW19 7BH **(T)** 01784 245 908
Capacity: 2,550 **Seats:** 250 **Covered:** 250 **Clubhouse:** Yes **Shop:** No

Directions
M25 junction 13, A30 towards London,
third left at footbridge after Ashford Hospital crossroads,
ground sign posted after 1/4 mile on the right down Short Lane,
two miles from Ashford (BR) and Hatton Cross tube station.

Previous Grounds: Clockhouse Lane Rec

Record Attendance: 992 v AFC Wimbledon - Isthmian League Premier Division 26/09/2006
Record Victory: Not known
Record Defeat: Not known
Record Goalscorer: Andy Smith
Record Appearances: Alan Constable - 650
Additional Records: Received £10,000 from Wycombe Wanderers for Dannie Bulman 1997

Senior Honours: Surrey Premier League 1982-90. Combined Counties League 1994-95, 95-96, 96-97, 97-98.
Middlesex Charity Cup 2000-01. Middlesex Premier Cup 2006-07. Isthmian League Cup 2006-07.

10 YEAR RECORD

01-02		02-03		03-04		04-05		05-06		06-07		07-08		08-09		09-10		10-11	
Isth2	12	Isth1S	17	Isth1S	12	SthW	6	SthW	2	Isth P	17	Isth P	6	Isth P	10	Isth P	20	SthC	16

AYLESBURY

Chairman: Danny Martone
Secretary: Ian Brown **(T)** 07947 338 462 **(E)** brownzola@aol.com
Additional Committee Members:
Steve Macdonald, Bill Harrison, Maria Butler, John Franklin, Warren Sheward.

Manager: Mark Eaton
Programme Editor: Russell Williams **(E)** cmartone040@btinternet.com

Club Factfile

Founded: 1897 **Nickname:** The Moles
Previous Names: Haywood United > 2004, Haywood FC 2004-05, Aylesbury Vale 2005-09
Previous Leagues: Spartan South Midlands

Club Colours (change): Red with black trim/black/black (Yellow with blue trim/yellow/yellow)

Ground: Haywood Way, Aylesbury, Bucks. HP19 9WZ **(T)** 01296 421 101
Capacity: **Seats:** Yes **Covered:** Yes **Clubhouse:** Yes **Shop:** No

Directions
When entering Aylesbury from all major routes, join the ring road and follow signposts for A41 Bicester and Waddesdon. leave the ring road at the roundabout by the Texaco Garage and Perry dealership. From the Texaco Garage cross straight over four roundabouts. At the fifth roundabout with the Cotton Wheel Pub on the right hand side, turn right into Jackson Road. Take the second left into Haywood Way, club is at the bottom of the road. If entering Aylesbury from Bicester (A41), turn left into Jackson Road by the Cotton Wheel Pub, and then second left into Haywood Way.

Previous Grounds:

Record Attendance: Not known
Record Victory: Not known
Record Defeat: Not known
Record Goalscorer: Not known
Record Appearances: Not known
Additional Records: Not known

Senior Honours: Spartan South Midlands League Division 1 2003-04, Premier Division 2009-10.

10 YEAR RECORD

01-02	02-03	03-04	04-05	05-06	06-07	07-08	08-09	09-10	10-11
SSM2 2	SSM1 9	SSM1 1	SSM P 3	SSM P 5	SSM P 5	SSM P 9	SSM P 15	SSM P 1	SthC 8

BARTON ROVERS

Chairman: Malcolm Bright
Secretary: Darren Whiley **(T)** 07860 632 152 **(E)** brfc@ultracs.co.uk
Additional Committee Members:
Chris Larkin, Sheila Gardner. Ced Gardner.

Manager: Dan Kennoy
Programme Editor: Chris Larkin **(E)** camford@talktalk.net

Club Factfile

Founded: 1898 **Nickname:** Rovers
Previous Names: Not known
Previous Leagues: Luton & district 1947-54, South Midlands 1954-79, Isthmian 1979-2004

Club Colours (change): Royal blue with white trim/royal blue/royal blue with white bands (Yellow with black trim/black/yellow with white band)

Ground: Sharpenhoe Road, Barton-le-Clay, Bedford MK45 4SD **(T)** 01582 707 772
Capacity: 4,000 **Seats:** 160 **Covered:** 1,120 **Clubhouse:** Yes **Shop:** Yes

Directions
Leave M1 at J12 head towards Harlington.
Follow signs through Sharpenhoe Village to Barton.
At T-junction in village turn right, continue 500 yards and turn right into ground on concrete roadway adjacent to playing fields.

Previous Grounds: Not known

Record Attendance: 1,900 v Nuneaton Borough - FA Cup 4th Qualifying Round 1976
Record Victory: Not known
Record Defeat: Not known
Record Goalscorer: Richard Camp - 152 (1989-98)
Record Appearances: Tony McNally - 598 (1988-2005)
Additional Records: Paid £1,000 to Hitchin Town for B. Baldry 1980
Received £1,000 from Bishop's Stortford for B. Baldry 1981

Senior Honours: South Midlands League x8. Bedfordshire Senior Cup x7. Bedfordshire Premier Cup 1995-96.

10 YEAR RECORD

01-02	02-03	03-04	04-05	05-06	06-07	07-08	08-09	09-10	10-11
Isth2 14	Isth1N 19	Isth1N 18	SthE 8	SthE 19	SthM 20	SthM 11	SthM 17	SthM 21	SthC 12

BEACONSFIELD SYCOB

Chairman: Fred Deanus
Secretary: Robin Woolman **(T)** 07778 832 019 **(E)** robin.woolman@btinternet.com
Additional Committee Members:
Paul Witney, Jim McGirr, Paul Hughes.

Manager: Colin Davis
Programme Editor: Karl McKenzie **(E)** karlmckenzie1@hotmail.com

Club Factfile

Founded: 1994 **Nickname:** The Rams
Previous Names: Slough YCOB and Beaconsfield United merged in 1994
Previous Leagues: Spartan South Midlands 1004-2004, 07-08, Southern 2004-07

Club Colours (change): Red and white quarters/black/red and white (Yellow with blue trim/blue with yellow trim/blue)

Ground: Holloways Park, Windsor Road, Beaconsfield, Bucks HP9 2SE **(T)** 01494 676 868
Capacity: **Seats:** **Covered:** **Clubhouse:** Yes **Shop:**

Directions Leave Junction 2 of M40, take A355 towards Slough, 50 yards off roundabout turn left and at next roundabout turn complete right, coming back towards A355 to continue across A355, then turn right and 150 yards on left is sign to club. Go through gate and clubhouse is 200 yards on right.

Previous Grounds: Not known

Record Attendance: Not known
Record Victory: Not known
Record Defeat: Not known
Record Goalscorer: Allan Arthur
Record Appearances: Allan Arthur
Additional Records:

Senior Honours: Spartan South Midlands 2000-01, 03-04, 07-08. Berks and Bucks Senior Trophy 2003-04

10 YEAR RECORD

01-02	02-03	03-04	04-05	05-06	06-07	07-08	08-09	09-10	10-11
SSM P 10	SSM P 2	SSM P 1	SthE 14	SthW 13	Sthsw 22	SSM P 1	Sthsw 4	SthM 19	SthC 22

BEDFONT TOWN

Chairman: Doug White
Secretary: Stewart Cook **(T)** 07946 170 277 **(E)** stewart.cook@btinternet.com
Additional Committee Members:
Lawrence Brimicombe, Paul Spencer, Don Townsend.

Manager: Kevin Cooper
Programme Editor: Stewart Cook **(E)** stewart.cook@btinternet.com

Club Factfile

Founded: 1965 **Nickname:** The Peacocks
Previous Names: Amalgamated with Bedfont United in 1972 to create today's club
Previous Leagues: West Middlesex Sunday, Hounslow & District, Woking & District 1986-99, Guildford & Woking Alliance 1999-2001, Surrey Intermediate 2001-04, Combined Counties 2004-09

Club Colours (change): Navy/white/navy (Yellow/navy/white)

Ground: The Orchard, Hatton Road, Bedfont TW14 9QT **(T)** 0208 8907 264
Capacity: **Seats:** Yes **Covered:** Yes **Clubhouse:** Yes **Shop:**

Directions
From M4: Leave the M4 at junction 3, then at roundabout take the exit onto the A312 (Heathrow/Staines). Continue to traffic signals connecting to A30 and turn right. At traffic signals turn left into Dick Turpin Way. At traffic signals turn right onto Fagg's Road, turn left onto Hatton Road (signposted Bedfont FC). The ground is on the left opposite the Duke of Wellington Public House.
From M3: Leave the M3 at junction 2, then join the M25 motorway. Leave the M25 at junction 13, at roundabout take the 3rd exit onto the A30. At Crooked Billet continue forward. At Clockhouse Roundabout take the 1st exit onto the A30. At Hatton Cross traffic signals continue to next traffic signals and turn right into Dick Turpin Way. At traffic signals turn right onto Fagg's Road, turn left onto Hatton Road (signposted Bedfont FC). The ground is on the left opposite the Duke of Wellington Public House.

Previous Grounds: Not known

Record Attendance: Not known
Record Victory: Not known
Record Defeat: Not known
Record Goalscorer: Not known
Record Appearances: John Skeen
Additional Records:

Senior Honours: Surrey Intermediate Premier 2003-04. Combined Counties Premier 2008-09.

10 YEAR RECORD

01-02	02-03	03-04	04-05	05-06	06-07	07-08	08-09	09-10	10-11
SuI3 2	SuI2	SuIP 1	CC1 2	CCP 6	CCP 22	CCP 9	CCP 1	Sthsw 17	SthC 10

BEDWORTH UNITED

Chairman: Peter Randle
Secretary: Graham Bloxham (T) 07748 640 613 (E) graham@greenbacks1.free-online.co.uk
Additional Committee Members:
Eric Whitehead, Dave Brannan, Bill Haywood, Blake Timms.

Manager: Steve Farmer
Programme Editor: Alan Robinson (E) alanrobinson8@btinternet.com

Club Factfile

Founded: 1896 **Nickname:** Greenbacks
Previous Names: Bedworth Town 1947-68
Previous Leagues: Birmingham Combination 1947-54, Birmingham/West Midlands 1954-72

Club Colours (change): Green/green/green with white trim (All gold)

Ground: The Oval, Coventry Road, Bedworth CV12 8NN (T) 02476 314 752
Capacity: 7,000 **Seats:** 300 **Covered:** 300 **Clubhouse:** Yes **Shop:** Yes

Directions
11/2 miles from M6 J3, take B4113 Coventry–Bedworth Road and after third set of traffic lights (Bedworth Leisure Centre).
Ground 200 yards on right opposite cemetery.
Coaches to park in Leisure Centre.

Previous Grounds: British Queen Ground 1911-39

Record Attendance: 5,127 v Nuneaton Borough - Southern League Midland Division 23/02/1982
Record Victory: Not known
Record Defeat: Not known
Record Goalscorer: Peter Spacey - 1949-69
Record Appearances: Peter Spacey - 1949-69
Additional Records: Paid £1,750 to Hinckley Town for Colin Taylor 1991-92
Received £30,000 from Plymouth Argyle for Richard Landon

Senior Honours: Birmingham Combination x2. Birmingham Senior Cup x3. Midland Floodlit Cup 1981-82, 92-93.

10 YEAR RECORD

01-02	02-03	03-04	04-05	05-06	06-07	07-08	08-09	09-10	10-11
SthW 11	SthW 18	SthW 19	SthW 15	SthW 16	SthM 16	SthM 15	SthM 14	SthM 16	SthC 15

BIGGLESWADE TOWN

Chairman: Maurice Dorrington
Secretary: Andy McDonnell **(T)** 07879 802 105 **(E)** andy.mcdonnell@ntlworld.com
Additional Committee Members:
Brian Doggett, Annette Dorrington, M. Draxler.

Manager: Chris Nunn
Programme Editor: David Simpson **(E)** simpson_david@hotmail.co.uk

Club Factfile

Founded: 1874 **Nickname:** The Waders
Previous Names: Not known
Previous Leagues: Biggleswade & District, Bedford & District, Spartan South Midlands 1951-55, 80-2009, Eastern Counties 1955-63, United Counties 1963-80
Club Colours (change): Green and white stripes/green/green (Sky blue and white stripes/black/sky blue)

Ground: The Carlsberg Stadium, Langford Road, Biggleswade SG18 9JJ **(T)**
Capacity: **Seats:** **Covered:** **Clubhouse:** Yes **Shop:**

Directions From the south – up the A1, past the first roundabout (Homebase) signposted Biggleswade. At next roundabout (Sainsburys) turn right onto A6001. As you approach the Town Centre, go straight over the mini roundabout following signs for Langford (Teal Road). At traffic lights, turn right (still heading towards Langford). Continue along Hitchin Street over two mini roundabouts and as you pass under the A1, the ground entrance is 200 yards on the right. From the north – exit A1 at the Sainsburys roundabout and follow instructions as above.

Previous Grounds: Fairfield

Record Attendance: 2,000
Record Victory: Not known
Record Defeat: Not known
Record Goalscorer: Not known
Record Appearances: Not known
Additional Records:

Senior Honours: Spartan South Midlands Premier Division 2008-09. Bedfordshire Premier Cup 2009.

10 YEAR RECORD

01-02	02-03	03-04	04-05	05-06	06-07	07-08	08-09	09-10	10-11
SSM P 9	SSM P 11	SSM P 15	SSM P 10	SSM P 15	SSM P 18	SSM P 3	SSM P 1	SthM 12	SthC 4

BURNHAM

Chairman: Bob Breen
Secretary: Alan King (T) 07899 941 414 (E) alanking50@aol.com
Additional Committee Members:
Malcolm Higton, R. H. Saunders.

Manager: Martin Stone
Programme Editor: TBA (E)

Burnham (Southern League Eastern Division) celebrate after a 1-1 draw with Scarborough (Conference) in the 1999-2000 F.A.Trophy competition.

Club Factfile

Founded: 1878 **Nickname:** The Blues
Previous Names: Burnham & Hillingdon 1985-87
Previous Leagues: Hellenic 1971-77, 95-99, Athenian 1977-84, London Spartan 1984-85, Southern 1985-95

Club Colours (change): Blue and white quarters/blue/blue (Red and black quarters/black/red)

Ground: The Gore, Wymers Wood Road, Burnham, Slough SL1 8JG (T) 01628 668 654
Capacity: 2,500 **Seats:** **Covered:** **Clubhouse:** Yes **Shop:** Yes

Directions: Approx. 2 miles from M4 junction 7 and 5 miles from M40 junction 2. From M40 take A355 to A4 signposted Maidenhead. From M4 take A4 towards Maidenhead until you reach roundabout with Sainsbury Superstore on left. Turn right into Lent Rise Road and travel approx 11/2 miles over 2 double roundabouts. 100 yards after second double roundabout fork right into Wymers Wood Road. Ground entrance on right.

Previous Grounds: Baldwin Meadow until 1920s

Record Attendance: 2,380 v Halesowen Town - FA Vase 02/04/1983
Record Victory: 18-0 v High Duty Alloys - 1970-71
Record Defeat: 1-10 v Ernest Turner Sports - 1963-64
Record Goalscorer: Fraser Hughes - 65 (1969-70)
Record Appearances: Not known
Additional Records:

Senior Honours: Hellenic League 1975-76, 98-99, League Cup 1975-76, 98-99, Division 1 Cup 1971-72.

10 YEAR RECORD

01-02	02-03	03-04	04-05	05-06	06-07	07-08	08-09	09-10	10-11
SthE 11	SthE 13	SthE 17	SthW 9	SthW 4	Sthsw 3	Sthsw 10	Sthsw 17	SthM 3	SthC 14

CHALFONT ST PETER

Chairman: Dennis Mair
Secretary: John Carroll (T) 07950 981 008 (E) jc.chalfontfc@fsmail.net
Additional Committee Members:
Graham Hamilton.

Manager: Danny Edwards
Programme Editor: Ian Doorbar (E) doors8jz@hotmail.com

Club Factfile

Founded: 1926 **Nickname:** Saints
Previous Names: Not known
Previous Leagues: G W Comb. Parthernon. London. Spartan. L Spartan. Athenian. Isthmian, Spartan South Midlands 2006-11.

Club Colours (change): Red/green/red. (Yellow/blue/blue).

Ground: Mill Meadow, Gravel Hill, Amersham Road, Chalfont St Peter SL9 9QX (T) 01753 885 797
Capacity: 4,500 **Seats:** 220 **Covered:** 120 **Clubhouse:** Yes **Shop:** Yes

Directions
Follow A413 (Amersham Road).
The ground is adjacent to the Chalfont Community Centre off Gravel Hill which is part of the A413.
Players and officials can park inside the ground.
The A413 is the Denham to Aylesbury road.

Previous Grounds: Not known

Record Attendance: **Att:** 2,550 v Watford benefit match 1985 **App:** Colin Davies
Record Victory: Not known
Record Defeat: Not known
Record Goalscorer: Not known
Record Appearances: Not known
Additional Records:

Senior Honours: Isthmian Lge Div 2 87-88, Berks & Bucks Intermediate Cup 52-53.
Spartan South Midlands Premier Division 2010-11.

10 YEAR RECORD

01-02	02-03	03-04	04-05	05-06	06-07	07-08	08-09	09-10	10-11
Isth3 14	Isth2 15	Isth2 14	Isth2 11	Isth2 8	SSM P 6	SSM P 2	SSM P 3	SSM P 2	SSM P 1

CHERTSEY TOWN

Chairman: Steve Powers
Secretary: Chris Gay (T) 07713 473 313 (E) chrisegay@googlemail.com
Additional Committee Members:
Sue Powers, Wendy Blaby.

Manager: Spencer Day
Programme Editor: Chris Gay (E) chrisegay@googlemail.com

Unfortunately an up-to-date photograph was not available at the time of going to press.

Club Factfile

Founded: 1890 **Nickname:** Curfews
Previous Names: None
Previous Leagues: Metropolitan. Spartan. Athenian. Isthmian, Combined Counties 2006-11.

Club Colours (change): White with blue trim/white/white (All navy)

Ground: Alwyns Lane, Chertsey, Surrey KT16 9DW (T) 01932 561 774
Capacity: 3,000 **Seats:** 240 **Covered:** 760 **Clubhouse:** Yes **Shop:** Yes

Directions Leave M25 at junction 11, East on St. Peters Way (A317). Left at roundabout in Chertsey Road (A317). Left into Eastworth Road (A317). Straight on into Chilsey Green Road (A320), 3rd exit on roundabout (towards Staines) (A320). 1st right after car showrooms into St. Ann's Road (B375). Right at Coach & Horses in Grove Road (residential). Alwyns Lane is very narrow and not suitable for large motor coaches.

Previous Grounds: Not known

Record Attendance: Att: 2150 v Aldershot Town, Isthmian Div.2 04/12/93. **Goals:** Alan Brown (54) 1962-63.
Record Victory: Not known
Record Defeat: Not known
Record Goalscorer: Not known
Record Appearances: Not known
Additional Records:

Senior Honours: Surrey Senior Champions 1959, 61, 62. Isthmian League Cup 1994.

10 YEAR RECORD

01-02	02-03	03-04	04-05	05-06	06-07	07-08	08-09	09-10	10-11
Isth2 17	Isth1S 24	Isth2 4	Isth2 6	Isth2 6	CCP 8	CCP 8	CCP 3	CCP 2	CCP 2

DAVENTRY TOWN

Chairman: Iain Humphrey
Secretary: Matt Hogsden **(T)** 07854 468 925 **(E)** dtfcsec@hotmail.co.uk
Additional Committee Members:
Trevor Osborne, Jason Lee, Mike Tebbit, Frank Hobbs, Malcolm Hobbs, Dennis Job, Kurt Shingler, Allan Staples.
Manager: Mark Kinsella
Programme Editor: Harvey Potter **(E)** h.potter@shebanguk.net

Photo: Keith Clayton.

Club Factfile

Founded: 1886 **Nickname:** The Town
Previous Names: Not known
Previous Leagues: Northampton Town (pre-1987), Central Northways Comb 1987-89, United Counties 1989-2010.

Club Colours (change): Purple/white/white (Yellow/white/white)

Ground: Communications Park, Browns Road, Daventry, Northants NN11 4NS **(T)** 01327 311 239
Capacity: 2,000 **Seats:** 250 **Covered:** 250 **Clubhouse:** Yes **Shop:**

Directions
From Northampton or J.16 of the M1, follow A45 westbound into Daventry, crossing the A5 on the way.
At first roundabout bear left along A45 Daventry Bypass.
At next roundabout go straight over onto Browns Road.
The Club is at the top of this road on the left.

Previous Grounds:

Record Attendance: 850 v Utrecht (Holland) - 1989
Record Victory: Not known
Record Defeat: Not known
Record Goalscorer: Not known
Record Appearances: Not known
Additional Records:

Senior Honours: United Counties League Division 1 1989-90, 90-91, 2000-01, 2007-08, Premier Division 2009-10.

10 YEAR RECORD

01-02	02-03	03-04	04-05	05-06	06-07	07-08	08-09	09-10	10-11
UCL P	UCL P	UCL P	UCL P	UCL P	UCL P	UCL 1 1	UCL P 7	UCL P 1	SthC 2

FLEET TOWN

Chairman: Jamie Williamson
Secretary: John Goodyear **(T)** 07768 701 797 **(E)** goodyear.john@btinternet.com
Additional Committee Members:
Lyn Bevan, Andy Allen, Steve Cantle, Michael Gardner, Matthew Thorne.

Manager: Steve Mellor
Programme Editor: Matt Thorne **(E)** thornematthew@hotmail.com

Club Factfile

Founded: 1890 **Nickname:** The Blues
Previous Names: Fleet FC 1890-1963
Previous Leagues: Hampshire 1961-77, Athenian, Combined Counties, Chiltonian, Wessex 1989-95, 2000-02, Southern 1995-2000, 02-04, 07-08, Isthmian 2004-07, 2008-11.

Club Colours (change): All blue (Yellow & black/black/yellow & black)

Ground: Calthorpe Park, Crookham Road, Fleet, Hants GU51 5FA **(T)** 01252 623 804
Capacity: 2,000 **Seats:** 250 **Covered:** 250 **Clubhouse:** Yes **Shop:** Yes

Directions
Leave the M3 at junction 4A. Follow signs to Fleet via A3013.
At 5th roundabout (a T-junction) turn left over railway bridge.
Carry on past Oatsheaf Pub on the right, ground is a further 1/4 mile on the right.

Previous Grounds: Watsons Meadow > 1923.

Record Attendance: 1,336 v AFC Wimbledon, Isthmian League 08/01/2005
Record Victory: 15-0 v Petersfield , Wessex League 26/12/1994
Record Defeat: 0-7 v Bashley, Southern League 12/04/2004
Record Goalscorer: Mark Frampton - 428
Record Appearances: Mark Frampton - 250
Additional Records: Paid £3,000 to Aldershot for Mark Russell

Senior Honours: Wessex League 1994-95.

10 YEAR RECORD

01-02	02-03	03-04	04-05	05-06	06-07	07-08	08-09	09-10	10-11
Wex 2	SthE 20	SthE 22	Isth1 19	Isth1 14	Isth1S 5	Sthsw 2	Isth1S 3	Isth1S 6	Isth1S 13

LEIGHTON TOWN

Chairman: Richard Graham
Secretary: Ken Slater **(T)** 07816 786 621 **(E)** slatter@wrenwalk.fsnet.co.uk
Additional Committee Members:
Roy Parker, Alex Irvine, Jim Morrisroe.

Manager: Sean Downey
Programme Editor: Andrew Parker **(E)** andrewparker-leightontownfc@virginmedia.com

Club Factfile

Founded: 1885 **Nickname:** Reds
Previous Names: Leighton United 1922-63
Previous Leagues: Leighton & District, South Midlands 1922-24, 26-29, 46-54, 55-56, 76-92, Spartan 1922-53, 67-74, United Counties 1974-76, Isthmian

Club Colours (change): Red and white stripes/red/red (Yellow/black/yellow)

Ground: Lake Street, Leighton Buzzard, Beds LU7 1RX **(T)** 01525 373 311
Capacity: 2,800 **Seats:** 155 **Covered:** 300 **Clubhouse:** Yes **Shop:** No

Directions
Ground is situated just south of Town Centre on the A4146 Leighton Buzzard to Hemel Hemstead Road.
Entrance to car park and ground is opposite Morrisons Supermarket Petrol Station.
1/2 mile south of town centre.

Previous Grounds: Wayside

Record Attendance: 1,522 v Aldershot Town - Isthmian League Division 3 30/01/1993
Record Victory: v Met Railway (H) - Spartan League 1925-26
Record Defeat: 0-12 v Headington United (A) - Spartan League 18/10/1947
Record Goalscorer: Not known
Record Appearances: Not known
Additional Records:

Senior Honours: South Midlands League 1966-67, 91-92. Isthmian League Division 2 2003-04.
Bedfordshire Senior Cup 1926-27, 67-68, 69-70, 92-93.

10 YEAR RECORD

01-02		02-03		03-04		04-05		05-06		06-07		07-08		08-09		09-10		10-11	
Isth3	17	Isth2	6	Isth2	1	SthE	10	SthW	8	SthM	18	SthM	9	SthM	8	SthM	10	SthC	7

MARLOW

Chairman: Terry Staines
Secretary: Paul Burdell **(T)** 07961 145 949 **(E)** marlow.fc@virgin.net
Additional Committee Members:
Graeme Cooper, Ray Frith.

Manager: Kevin Stone
Programme Editor: Terry Staines **(E)** terry.staines@ntlworld.com

Back Row (L-R): Mark Skoyles (Physio), Stuart MacLellan, Mark Avery, Daniel Stone, Marcus Mealing, Michael Watkins, Tom Willment, Gavin Lane, James Burrell.
Front Row: Craig Roberts, Jermaine Roche, Mitchel Woodward, Aaron Couch, Leigh Mason, Johnny Gray, Jon Case, Jordan Trumpet.

Club Factfile

Founded: 1870 **Nickname:** The Blues
Previous Names: Great Marlow
Previous Leagues: Reading & District, Spartan 1908-10, 28-65, Great Western Suburban, Athenian 1965-84, Isthmian 1984-2004

Club Colours (change): Royal blue with white trim/royal/royal (All red)

Ground: Alfred Davies Memorial Ground, Oak tree Road, Marlow SL7 3ED **(T)** 01628 483 970
Capacity: 3,000 **Seats:** 250 **Covered:** 600 **Clubhouse:** Yes **Shop:**

Directions
From M40 (Junction 4 High Wycombe) or M4 (Junction 8/9 Maidenhead) take A404, leave at the A4155 junction signposted Marlow.
Follow A4155 towards Marlow then turn right at Esso service station into Maple Rise.
At crossroads follow straight ahead into Oak Tree Road.
Ground 100 yards on left.

Previous Grounds: Crown ground 1870-1919, Star Meadow 1919-24

Record Attendance: 3,000 v Oxford United - FA Cup 1st Round 1994
Record Victory: Not known
Record Defeat: Not known
Record Goalscorer: Kevin Stone
Record Appearances: Mick McKeown - 500+
Additional Records: Paid £5,000 to Sutton United for Richard Evans
Received £8,000 from Slough Town for David Lay

Senior Honours: Isthmian League Division 1 1987-88, League Cup 92-93.
Berks & Bucks Senior Cup x11

10 YEAR RECORD

01-02	02-03	03-04	04-05	05-06	06-07	07-08	08-09	09-10	10-11
Isth2 9	Isth1N 11	Isth1S 16	SthW 13	SthW 6	Sthsw 7	Sthsw 9	SthM 9	SthM 15	SthC 11

NORTH GREENFORD UNITED

Chairman: John Bivens
Secretary: Mrs Barbara Bivens **(T)** 07915 661 580 **(E)** barbarabivens@talktalk.net
Additional Committee Members:
John Chorley, Tony Tuohy, Lorraine Chorley, Pat Hillier.

Manager: Steve Ringrose
Programme Editor: Pat Hillier **(E)** agneshillier@aol.com

Unfortunately an up-to-date photograph was not available at the time of going to press.

Club Factfile

Founded: 1944 **Nickname:** Blues
Previous Names: None
Previous Leagues: London Spartan, Combined Counties 2002-10

Club Colours (change): Royal blue & white/royal blue & white/royal blue (Yellow with red trim/yellow & red/yellow)

Ground: Berkeley Fields, Berkley Avenue, Greenford UB6 0NX **(T)** 0208 422 8923
Capacity: 2,000 **Seats:** 150 **Covered:** 100 **Clubhouse:** Yes **Shop:** No

Directions
A40 going towards London. At the Greenford Flyover come down the slip road, keep in the left hand lane, turn left onto the Greenford Road (A4127). At the third set of traffic lights, turn right into Berkeley Av. Go to the bottom of the road. There is a large car park. We are on the right hand side.

Previous Grounds: Not known

Record Attendance: 985 v AFC Wimbledon
Record Victory: Not known
Record Defeat: Not known
Record Goalscorer: John Hill - 98
Record Appearances: Not known
Additional Records:

Senior Honours: Combined Counties League Premier Division 2009-10

10 YEAR RECORD

01-02	02-03	03-04	04-05	05-06	06-07	07-08	08-09	09-10	10-11
	CC 10	CCP 14	CCP 2	CCP 13	CCP 5	CCP 6	CCP 2	CCP 1	SthC 20

NORTHWOOD

Chairman: Ian Barry
Secretary: Alan Evans **(T)** 07960 744 349 **(E)** alan.evansnfc@btopenworld.com
Additional Committee Members:
Ken Green, Tino Nannavecchia, Pat Byrne, Peter Barry, Betty Walley.

Manager: Gary Meakin
Programme Editor: Ken Green **(E)** ken.green01@ntlworld.com

Back row: Mark Barnham (Manager), Sam Sharples, Rodney Hicks, Scott Raper, John Sonuga, Troy Roach, Leon Osei, Andrew Iwediuno, Dean Wallace, Jamie Lindsay, Marie Scott (Physio).
Front row: Kyle Matthews, John Christian, Mark Burgess, Mitch Swain, Ryan Tackley, Wayne Jackson, Scott Orphanou.
Photo: James Brown

Club Factfile

Founded: 1899 **Nickname:** Woods
Previous Names: Northwood Town
Previous Leagues: Harrow & Wembley 1932-69, Middlesex 1969-78, Hellenic 1979-84, London Spartan 1984-93, Isthmian 1993-2005, 2007-10, Southern 2005-07

Club Colours (change): All red (All yellow)

Ground: Northwood Park, Chestnut Avenue, Northwood, Middlesex HA6 1HR **(T)** 01923 827 148
Capacity: 3,075 **Seats:** 308 **Covered:** 932 **Clubhouse:** Yes **Shop:** No

Directions
M25 Junction 18, take A404 through Rickmansworth to Northwood. After passing under grey railway bridge, take first right into Chestnut Avenue. Ground is in grounds of Northwood Park, entrance is 400 metres on left. (Ground is 20 minutes from J.18).

Previous Grounds:

Record Attendance: 1,642 v Chlesea - Friendly July 1997
Record Victory: 15-0 v Dateline (H) - Middlesex Intermediate Cup 1973
Record Defeat: 0-8 v Bedfont - Middlesex League 1975
Record Goalscorer: Not known
Record Appearances: Chris Gell - 493+
Additional Records: Lawrence Yaku scored 61 goals during season 1999-2000

Senior Honours: Isthmian League Division 1 North 2002-03, Charity Shield 2002.
Middlesex Premier Cup 1994-95.

10 YEAR RECORD

01-02	02-03	03-04	04-05	05-06	06-07	07-08	08-09	09-10	10-11
Isth1 5	Isth1N 1	Isth P 21	Isth P 17	SthP 19	SthP 22	Isth1N 10	Isth1N 6	Isth1N 10	SthC 20

RUGBY TOWN

Chairman: Brian Melvin
Secretary: Doug Wilkins **(T)** 07976 284 614 **(E)** dougwilkins44@hotmail.com
Additional Committee Members:
Mike Yeats, Les Leeson, Danny Lorden, Lisa Melvin, Darren Knapp, Jim Melvin.

Manager: Dave Stringer
Programme Editor: Neil Melvin **(E)** neilmelvin@melbros.com

Club Factfile

Founded: 1956 **Nickname:** The Valley
Previous Names: Valley Sports 1956-71, Valley Sport Rugby 1971-73, VS Rugby 1973-2000, Rugby United 2000-05
Previous Leagues: Rugby & District 1956-62, Coventry & Partnership, North Warwickshire 1963-69, United Counties 1969-75 West Midlands 1975-83

Club Colours (change): Sky blue/white/sky blue (Maroon/maroon/sky blue)

Ground: Butlin Road, Rugby, Warwicks CV21 3SD **(T)** 01788 844 806
Capacity: 6,000 **Seats:** 750 **Covered:** 1,000 **Clubhouse:** Yes **Shop:** Yes

Directions
From M6 J.1 North and South, take A426 signed Rugby at third island turn left into Boughton Road.
Continue along Boughton Road after passing under viaduct turn right at traffic lights, B5414 up the hill take second left at mini island into Butlin Road.

Previous Grounds:

Record Attendance: 3,961 v Northampton Town - FA Cup 1984
Record Victory: 10-0 v Ilkeston Town - FA Trophy 04/09/1985
Record Defeat: 1-11 v Ilkeston Town (A) - 18/04/1998
Record Goalscorer: Danny Conway - 124
Record Appearances: Danny Conway - 374
Additional Records: Paid £3,500 for R Smith, I Crawley and G Bradder
Received £15,000 from Northampton Town for Terry Angus

Senior Honours: FA Vase 1982-83. Southern League Midland Division 1986-87. Midland Combination Division 1 2001-02.
Birmingham Senior Cup 1988-89, 91-92

10 YEAR RECORD

01-02	02-03	03-04	04-05	05-06	06-07	07-08	08-09	09-10	10-11
MCm1 1	MCmP 6	MCmP 3		SthP 15	SthP 17	SthP 15	SthP 17	SthP 22	SthC 6

SLOUGH TOWN

Chairman: Steve Easterbrook
Secretary: Kath Lathey **(T)** 07792 126 124 **(E)** gensec@sloughtownfc.net
Additional Committee Members:
Roy Merryweather, Glen Riley, Alan Harding,
Mike Lightfoot, Gary Thomas, Chris Sliski, Kevin Merryweather
Manager: Steve Bateman
Programme Editor: Glen Riley **(E)** programme@sloughtownfc.net

Slough Town were one of the most powerful non-league clubs in 'The Sixties.' Back row, left to right: Gerry Ford (Traynor), Stevens, Hatt, Hartridge, Reynolds, Bell, Sleap and Bob Gibbs (Manager). Front row: Connell, Gamblin, Delaney, Clarke, Gaynor and Kent.

Club Factfile

Founded: 1890 **Nickname:** The Rebels
Previous Names: Not known
Previous Leagues: Southern Alliance 1892-93, Berks & Bucks 1901-05, Gt Western Suburban 1909-19, Spartan 1920-39, Herts & Middx 1940-45, Corinthian 1946-63, Athenian 1963-73, Isthmian 1973-90, 94-95, Conf. 1990-94
Club Colours (change): Amber/navy blue/amber (Red and navy shirts/black/red)

Ground: Sharing with Beaconsfield SYCOB, Holloways Park, Slough Rd HP9 2SG **(T)** 01494 676 868
Capacity: 3,500 **Seats:** 200 **Covered:** Yes **Clubhouse:** Yes **Shop:** Yes
Directions Leave M40 at Junction 2, take A355 towards Slough, only 50 yards off the roundabout on the A355 is slip road on right with sign giving Club name. Turn right through gate and clubhouse is 200 metres on the right. The ground is 'signposted' from both sides of the carriageway (A355).

Previous Grounds: Not known

Record Attendance: 8,000 v Liverpool - Schoolboys 1976
Record Victory: 17-0 v Railway Clearing House - 1921-22
Record Defeat: 1-11 v Chesham Town - 1909-10
Record Goalscorer: Tony Norris - 84 (1925-26)
Record Appearances: Terry Reardon - 458 (1964-81)
Additional Records: Paid £18,000 to Farnborough Town for Colin Fielder
Received £22,000 from Wycombe Wanderers for Steve Thompson
Senior Honours: Isthmian League 1980-81, 89-90. Athenian League x3. Berks & Bucks Senior Cup x10.

10 YEAR RECORD

01-02	02-03	03-04	04-05	05-06	06-07	07-08	08-09	09-10	10-11
Isth1 8	Isth1S 4	Isth1S 4	Isth P 13	Isth P 17	Isth P 22	Sthsw 21	Sthsw 16	SthM 5	SthC 5

ST. NEOTS TOWN

Chairman: Mike Kearns
Secretary: Peter Naylor (T) 07702 400 205 (E) secretary@stneotsfc.com
Additional Committee Members:
Lee Kearns, Marian Izzard.

Manager: Dennis Greene
Programme Editor: Mike Davies (E) mark@blueprwandesign.co.uk

Back Row (L-R): Richard King (coach), Adrian Sears, Chris Hope, Dan Jacob, Kieron Davies, Max Harradine, Aaron Greene, Danny Nicholls (coach).
Middle Row: Neil MacKenzie, Peter Grant, Jordan Gent, Tim Trebes, Michael Duggan, Craig Grieve, Junior Konadu, Will Fordham, Pete Naylor (secretary).
Front row: Tony Scully (player/coach), Lewis Hilliard, Dennis Greene (manager), Stefan Moore, Mike Kearns (chairman/owner), Shane Tolley, John Walker (club president).

Club Factfile

Founded: 1879 **Nickname:** Saints
Previous Names: St. Neots & District > 1951.
Previous Leagues: S Midlands, Cent. Alliance, UCL, Eastern Co., Hunts, United Counties > 2011.

Club Colours (change): Light blue/dark blue/dark blue (All red)

Ground: Hunts Post Community Stadium, Cambridge Road, St Neots, PE19 6SN (T) 01480 470 012
Capacity: 3,000 **Seats:** 250 **Covered:** 850 **Clubhouse:** Yes **Shop:** No

Directions From St Neots town centre, take the B1428 Cambridge Road, after going under the railway bridge, turn left at the first roundabout into Dramsell Rise. Follow the road up the hill to Kester Way and the ground. If approaching from Cambridge on the A428, turn right at the first roundabout as you approach St Neots onto the Cambridge Road. At the second roundabout, turn right into Dramsell Rise and follow as above. If travelling via the A1, follow signs for the A428 Cambridge. Go straight over roundabout with Tescos on left hand side, then turn left at next roundabout. Follow final instructions above as if approaching from Cambridge.

Previous Grounds: Not known

Record Attendance: Att: 2,000 v Wisbech 1966
Record Victory: Not known
Record Defeat: Not known
Record Goalscorer: Not known
Record Appearances: Not known
Additional Records:

Senior Honours: United Counties League 1967-68, 2010-11. Division One 1994-95.
Huntingdonshire Senior Cup x35 2009-10 the most recent. Huntingdonshire Premier Cup 2001-02.

10 YEAR RECORD

01-02	02-03	03-04	04-05	05-06	06-07	07-08	08-09	09-10	10-11
UCL P 6	UCL P 13	UCL P 4	UCL P 14	UCL P 4	UCL P 17	UCL P 8	UCL P 17	UCL P 2	UCL P 1

UXBRIDGE

Chairman: Alan Holloway
Secretary: Roger Stevens **(T)** 07773 513 405 **(E)** sec@uxbridgefc.co.uk
Additional Committee Members:
Mick Burrell, Averill Hinde, D Gill, D Marshall, C Rycraft, D Tucker, R Turton.

Manager: Tony Choules
Programme Editor: Zoe Nealon **(E)** program.editor@uxbridgefc.co.uk

Back Row: Stuart Everley, Adam Tonne, Michael Murray, Craige Tomkins, Tom Bentley, Howard Hall, Matt Elston-Bull, Michael Parkin, Matt Burton, Rob Fitzgerald, Danny Julienne, Stuart Farrell, Mark Smith, Jake Girt, Scott Everley

Front Row: Andrew Perring, Jake Lovell, Ryan Fenton, Gavin Brown (Vice Captain), Paul Mills (Ass't Manager), Tony Choules (Manager), Wayne Carter (Captain), Dave Thomas, Mohamed Hashi, Chris Moore

Club Factfile

Founded: 1871 **Nickname:** The Reds
Previous Names: Uxbridge Town 1923-45
Previous Leagues: Southern 1894-99, Gt Western Suburban 1906-19, 20-23, Athenian 1919-20, 24-37, 63-82, Spartan 1937-38, London 1938-46, Gt Western Comb. 1939-45, Corinthian 1946-63, Isthmian

Club Colours (change): Red/white/red (Sky blue/navy/navy)

Ground: Honeycroft Road, West Drayton, Middlesex UB7 8HX **(T)** 01895 443 557
Capacity: 3,770 **Seats:** 339 **Covered:** 760 **Clubhouse:** Yes **Shop:**

Directions
M4 to Junction 4 (Heathrow),
take A408 towards Uxbridge for 1 mile,
turn left into Horton Road.
Ground 1/2 mile on right.

Previous Grounds: RAF Stadium 1923-48, Cleveland Road 1948-78

Record Attendance: 1,000 v Arsenal - Opening of the floodlights 1981
Record Victory: Not known
Record Defeat: Not known
Record Goalscorer: Phil Duff - 153
Record Appearances: Roger Nicholls - 1,054
Additional Records:

Senior Honours: Middlesex Senior Cup 1893-94, 95-96, 1950-51, 2000-01. London Challenge Cup 1993-94, 96-97, 98-99.

10 YEAR RECORD

01-02		02-03		03-04		04-05		05-06		06-07		07-08		08-09		09-10		10-11	
Isth1	9	Isth1N	5	Isth1N	13	SthE	4	SthE	14	Sthsw	8	Sthsw	5	Sthsw	13	Sthsw	15	SthC	13

WOODFORD UNITED

Chairman: Andrew Worrall
Secretary: David Allen (T) 07889 847 428 (E) allend@wufc.biz
Additional Committee Members:
Yvonne Worrall, R Adams, D Grogan.

Manager: Phil Mason
Programme Editor: Richard Usher (E) richard-usher@sky.com

Club Factfile

Founded: 1946 **Nickname:** Reds
Previous Names: Not known
Previous Leagues: Central Northants Combination 1946-70, United Counties 1971-2006

Club Colours (change): All red (Yellow/black/yellow)

Ground: Byfield Road, Woodford Halse, Daventry, Northants NN11 3QR (T) 01327 263 734
Capacity: 3,000 **Seats:** 252 **Covered:** 252 **Clubhouse:** Yes **Shop:** No

Directions
From M1 J18, M40 J11,
take A361 Banbury to Daventry road.
Exit A361 in Byfield, follow signs for Woodford Halse.
Ground on left 200 yards past industrial estate.

Previous Grounds: Not known

Record Attendance: 1,500 v Stockport County
Record Victory: Not known
Record Defeat: Not known
Record Goalscorer: Not known
Record Appearances: Not known
Additional Records:

Senior Honours: United Counties League Division 2 1973-74, Premier Division 2005-06.

10 YEAR RECORD

01-02		02-03		03-04		04-05		05-06		06-07		07-08		08-09		09-10		10-11	
UCL 1	3	UCL P	14	UCL P	12	UCL P	7	UCL P	1	SthM	8	SthM	19	SthM	20	SthM	7	SthC	9

ABINGDON UNITED

Chairman: Mrs Deborah Blackmore
Secretary: John Blackmore **(T)** 07747 615 691 **(E)** john.blackmore2@ntlworld.com
Additional Committee Members:
Alf White, Pat Evans, Shirley Evans, Bill Fletcher, Doreen White, Chris Jane, Derek Turner, Robin Yuill.

Manager: Richie Bourne
Programme Editor: Bill Fletcher **(E)** billfletcher@ntlworld.com

Back Row (L-R): Shane Sherbourne (Goalkeeper Coach), Chris Harper, John McMahon, Luke Carnell, Tom Franklin, Gareth Tucker, Jon Beames, Richard Peirson (Player Coach), Steve Davis, John Mills, Sam Elkins, Andy Lawson (Club Physio)
Front Row: Andy Younie, Anaclet Odhiambo, Tom Melledew, Richie Bourne (Manager), Jim Smith , James Organ, Pablo Haysham

Club Factfile

Founded: 1946 **Nickname:** The U's
Previous Names: Not known
Previous Leagues: North Berkshire 1949-58, Hellenic 1958-2006

Club Colours (change): All yellow (White/red/white)

Ground: The North Court, Northcourt Road, Abingdon OX14 1PL **(T)** 01235 203 203
Capacity: 2,000 **Seats:** 158 **Covered:** 258 **Clubhouse:** Yes **Shop:**

Directions
From the north – Leave A34 at Abingdon north turning. Ground on right at first set of traffic lights.
From the south – Enter Town Centre, leave north on A4183 (Oxford Road).
Ground on left after one mile.

Previous Grounds: Not known

Record Attendance: 1,500 v Oxford United - Friendly 1994
Record Victory: Not known
Record Defeat: Not known
Record Goalscorer: Not known
Record Appearances: Not known
Additional Records:

Senior Honours: Hellenic League Division 1 1981-82, League Cup 1965-66. Berks & Bucks Senior Trophy x2.

10 YEAR RECORD

01-02	02-03	03-04	04-05	05-06	06-07	07-08	08-09	09-10	10-11
Hel P 4	Hel P 8	Hel P 11	Hel P 5	Hel P 3	Hel P 18	Sthsw 16	Sthsw 15	Sthsw 14	Sthsw 16

BIDEFORD

Chairman: Roy Portch
Secretary: Kevin Tyrrell **(T)** 07929 078 613 **(E)** k.tyrrell@talktalk.net
Additional Committee Members:
Ian Knight

Manager: Sean Joyce
Programme Editor: Ian Knight **(E)** ianknight160@btinternet.com

Club Factfile

Founded: 1949 **Nickname:** The Robins
Previous Names: Bideford Town
Previous Leagues: Devon & Exeter 1947-49, Western 1949-72, 75-2010, Southern 1972-75

Club Colours (change): All red (All blue)

Ground: The Sports Ground, Kingsley Road, Bideford EX39 2LH **(T)** 01237 474 974
Capacity: 6,000 **Seats:** 375 **Covered:** 1,000 **Clubhouse:** Yes **Shop:**

Directions
Exit M5 at J.27. A361 to Barnstaple. Turn left onto A39 to Bideford.
9 miles turn left into town.
Ground on right hand side as entering town centre.

Previous Grounds:

Record Attendance: 6,000 v Gloucester City - FA Cup 4th Qualifying Round
Record Victory: Not known
Record Defeat: Not known
Record Goalscorer: Tommy Robinson - 259
Record Appearances: Derek May - 527
Additional Records:

Senior Honours: Western LEague 1963-64, 70-71, 71-72, 81-82, 82-83, 2001-02, 03-04, 04-05, 05-06, 09-10, Division 1 1951-52,
Division 3 1949-50.
Devon Senior Cup 1979-80

10 YEAR RECORD

01-02	02-03	03-04	04-05	05-06	06-07	07-08	08-09	09-10	10-11
WestP 1	WestP 3	WestP 1	WestP 1	WestP 1	WestP 4	WestP 6	WestP 6	WestP 1	Sthsw 10

BISHOP'S CLEEVE

Chairman: David Walker
Secretary: Nigel Green **(T)** 07919 518 880 **(E)** negreen@tiscali.co.uk
Additional Committee Members:
Dave Lewis, Hanif Tai, Bob Weaver, Lyn Weaver, Malcolm Eustace, Paul Price, Hilary Green. John Pickup.
Manager: Alex Sykes
Programme Editor: TBA **(E)**

Unfortunately an up-to-date photograph was not available at the time of going to press.

Club Factfile

Founded: 1892 **Nickname:** Villagers
Previous Names:
Previous Leagues: Cheltenham, North Gloucestershire, Hellenic 1983-2006

Club Colours (change): Blue & white/blue/blue (Yellow & white/yellow/yellow)

Ground: Kayte Lane, Bishop's Cleeve, Cheltenham GL52 3PD **(T)** 01242 676 166
Capacity: 1,500 **Seats:** 50 **Covered:** 50 **Clubhouse:** Yes **Shop:** Yes

Directions
From Cheltenham take A435 towards Evesham.
Pass racecourse, take right at traffic lights then first left into Kayte Lane.
Ground 1/2 mile on left.

Previous Grounds: Stoke Road and ground shared with Moreton Town, Wollen Sports, Highworth Town and Forest Green Rovers

Record Attendance: 1,300 v Cheltenham Town - July 2006
Record Victory: Not known
Record Defeat: Not known
Record Goalscorer: Kevin Slack
Record Appearances: John Skeen
Additional Records:

Senior Honours: Hellenic League Division 1 1986-87, Premier League Cup 1988.
Gloucestershire Junior Cup North. Gloucestershire Senior Amateur Cup North x3.

10 YEAR RECORD

01-02	02-03	03-04	04-05	05-06	06-07	07-08	08-09	09-10	10-11
Hel P 10	Hel P 9	Hel P 3	Hel P 3	Hel P 2	SthM 13	SthM 12	Sthsw 18	Sthsw 11	Sthsw 15

BRIDGWATER TOWN 1984

Chairman: Alan Hurford
Secretary: Roger Palmer **(T)** 07587 775 227 **(E)** palmer449@btinternet.com
Additional Committee Members:
Keith Setter, Jennie Parker.

Manager: Rob Dray
Programme Editor: Roger Palmer **(E)** palmer449@btinternet.com

Back Row (L-R): Winston Davey (Vice Chairman), Kevin Milsom (Assistant Manager), Carl Tucker, Neil Peek, Josh Turner, Luke Buckingham, Mat Pitcher, Rob Snook, Simon Lyons, Andrew Forward, Leigh Bailey, Josh Ford, Ian Bellinger, Adam Sparks, Becky Bidgood (Physio)
Front Row: Rob Dray (Manager), Eddie Pike (Committee Member), Shane Kingston, Sean Kenny, Andy Robertson, Lee Singleton (from Sponsors TMB), Chris Young (Captain), Mike Mackay, Tom Parsons, Sam Peppin, Keith Setter (President), Steve Perkins (Player/Coach)

Club Factfile

Founded: 1984 **Nickname:** The Robins
Previous Names: Bridgwater Town
Previous Leagues: Somerset Senior, Western

Club Colours (change): Red/white/white (White/yellow/yellow)

Ground: Fairfax Park, College Way, Bath Road, Bridgwater, Somerset TA6 4TZ **(T)** 01278 446 899
Capacity: 2,500 **Seats:** 128 **Covered:** 500 **Clubhouse:** Yes **Shop:** Yes

Directions
Southbound from Bristol M5 J.23- enter town on A39 from Glastonbury. Ground is between Bridgwater College and Rugby Ground by railway bridge.
Northbound from Taunton – M5 J.24- enter town on A38, follow signs for Glastonbury (A39). Ground is between Bridgwater College and Rugby Ground as you pass over railway bridge.

Previous Grounds: Not known

Record Attendance: 1,112 v Taunton Town - 26/02/1997
Record Victory: Not Known
Record Defeat: Not Known
Record Goalscorer: Not Known
Record Appearances: Not Known
Additional Records:

Senior Honours: Somerset Senior League x3. Somerset Senior Cup 1993-94, 95-96. Western League Division 1 1995-96.

10 YEAR RECORD

01-02	02-03	03-04	04-05	05-06	06-07	07-08	08-09	09-10	10-11
WestP 8	WestP 6	WestP 6	WestP 6	WestP 11	WestP 2	Sthsw 6	Sthsw 7	Sthsw 3	Sthsw 18

CINDERFORD TOWN

Chairman: Ashley Saunders
Secretary: Robert Maskell (T) 07835 511 774 (E) maskellbilly@yahoo.co.uk
Additional Committee Members:
Stuart Tait, Ray Reed, Mike James, Alan Jones, Robert Knight, Ken McNally, Beryl Reed, Barry Turner, Chris Warren.
Manager: Steve Peters
Programme Editor: Liam Maskell (E) liammaskell@googlemail.com

Action from Cinderford's FA Trophy Preliminary Round tie against Mangotsfield United. Photo: Peter Barnes.

Club Factfile

Founded: 1922 **Nickname:** The Foresters
Previous Names: Not known
Previous Leagues: Gloucestershire Northern Senior 1922-39, 60-62, Western 1946-59, Warwickshire Combination 1963-64, West Midlands 1965-69, Gloucestershire Co. 1970-73, 85-89, Midland Comb. 1974-84, Hellenic 1990-95

Club Colours (change): All white (All yellow)

Ground: The Causeway, Hildene, Cinderford, Gloucestershire GL14 2QH (T) 01594 827 147 / 822 039
Capacity: 3,500 **Seats:** 250 **Covered:** 1,000 **Clubhouse:** Yes **Shop:** Yes

Directions Take A40 west out of Gloucester, then A48 for 8 miles. Turn right at Elton Garage onto A4151 (Forest of Dean). Continue through Littledean, climb steep hill, turn right at crossroads (football ground), then second left into Latimer Road. Or if coming from Severn Bridge take A48 Chepstow through Lydney, Newnham then left at Elton Garage – then as above.

Previous Grounds: Mousel Lane, Royal Oak

Record Attendance: 4,850 v Minehead - Western League 1955-56
Record Victory: 13-0 v Cam Mills - 1938-39
Record Defeat: 0-10 v Sutton Coldfield - 1978-79
Record Goalscorer: Not known
Record Appearances: Russel Bowles - 528
Additional Records:

Senior Honours: Western League Division 2 1956-57. Midland Combination 1981-82. Hellenic Premier Division 1994-95, League Cup 94-95. Gloucestershire Senior Amateur Cup North x6. Gloucestershire Junior Cup North 1980-81. Gloucestershire Senior Cup 2000-01.

10 YEAR RECORD

01-02	02-03	03-04	04-05	05-06	06-07	07-08	08-09	09-10	10-11
SthW 15	SthW 15	SthW 20	SthW 16	SthW 15	SthM 9	SthM 16	SthM 11	Sthsw 16	Sthsw 12

CLEVEDON TOWN

Chairman: John Croft
Secretary: Brian Rose (T) 07768 100 632 (E) brian.rose@blueyonder.co.uk
Additional Committee Members:

Manager: Micky Bell
Programme Editor: Dave Wright (E) smallwavedave@hotmail.com

Club Factfile

Founded: 1880 **Nickname:** Seasiders
Previous Names: Clevedon FC and Ashtonians merged in 1974
Previous Leagues: Weston & District, Somerset Senior, Bristol Charity, Bristol & District, Bristol Suburban, Western 1974-93

Club Colours (change): Royal blue & white stripes/royal/royal (All green)

Ground: Hand Stadium, Davis Lane, Clevedon BS21 6TG (T) 01275 871 600
Capacity: 3,500 **Seats:** 300 **Covered:** 1,600 **Clubhouse:** Yes **Shop:** Yes

Directions
Exit J20 from M5, at bottom of slip road, turn left at roundabout into Central Way.
At next roundabout turn left to Kenn Road.
Stay on Kenn Road out of town, cross river, take 1st left into Davis Lane, over motorway.
Ground 200m on right.

Previous Grounds: Dial Hill until early 1890s, Teignmouth Road > 1991

Record Attendance: 2,300 v Billingham Synthonia - FA Amateur Cup 1952-53
Record Victory: 18-0 v Dawlish Town (H) - Western League Premier Division 24/04/1993
Record Defeat: 3-13 v Yate YMCA (A) - Bristol Combination 1967-68
Record Goalscorer: Not known
Record Appearances: Not known
Additional Records:

Senior Honours: Somerset Senior Cup 1901-02, 04-05, 28-29, 2000-01, 01-02. Somerset Premier Cup x4.
Southern League Western Division 1992-93, 2005-06, Midland Division 1998-99.

10 YEAR RECORD

01-02	02-03	03-04	04-05	05-06	06-07	07-08	08-09	09-10	10-11
SthW 10	SthW 13	SthW 11	SthW 4	SthW 1	SthP 18	SthP 11	SthP 18	SthP 21	Sthsw 20

DIDCOT TOWN

Chairman: John Bailey
Secretary: Pat Horsman **(T)** 07882 154 612 **(E)** didcot@fernring.co.uk
Additional Committee Members:
Justin Lambourne.

Manager: Francis Vines
Programme Editor: Steve Clare **(E)** stclare@tiscali.co.uk

Didcot players celebrate scoring against Tiverton Town. Photo: Jonathan Holloway.

Club Factfile

Founded: 1907 **Nickname:** Railwaymen
Previous Names: Not known
Previous Leagues: Metropolitan 1957-63, Hellenic 1963-2006

Club Colours (change): Red with white sleeves/white/red & white (Gold/black/black)

Ground: NPower Loop Meadow Stadium, Bowmont Water, Didcot OX11 7GA **(T)** 01235 813 138
Capacity: 5,000 **Seats:** 250 **Covered:** 200 **Clubhouse:** Yes **Shop:** Yes

Directions
From A34 take A4130 towards Didcot. At first roundabout take first exit, at next roundabout take third exit, then straight across next two roundabouts. At fifth roundabout turn right into Avon Way. Follow Avon Way for 1/2 mile till you get to a mini roundabout. Straight across it, ground is on the left after 100 yards, in Bowmont Water.

Previous Grounds: Not known

Record Attendance: 1,512 v Jarrow roofing - FA Vase Semi-final 2005
Record Victory: Not known
Record Defeat: Not known
Record Goalscorer: Ian Concanon
Record Appearances: Not known
Additional Records:

Senior Honours: Hellenic League Premier Division 1953-54, 2005-06, Division 1 1976-77, 87-88, League Cup x6.
FA Vase 2004-05. Berks & Bucks Senior Trophy 2001-02, 02-03, 05-06.

10 YEAR RECORD

01-02	02-03	03-04	04-05	05-06	06-07	07-08	08-09	09-10	10-11
Hel P 5	Hel P 5	Hel P 5	Hel P 2	Hel P 1	Sthsw 10	Sthsw 3	Sthsw 5	SthP 15	SthP 19

GOSPORT BOROUGH

Chairman: Mark Hook
Secretary: Brian Cosgrave (T) 07984 960 537 (E) brian.cosgrave@hotmail.co.uk
Additional Committee Members:
Mick Marsh, John Simpson, Paul Hook.

Manager: Alex Pike
Programme Editor: Jeremy Fox (E) programme@gosportboroughfc.co.uk

Gosport Borough 1992-1993 in the Jewson Wessex League . Back row , left to right: R.Sherwood (Manager), B.Williamson (Physio), J.Diaper, D.Wood, G.Payne, A.Gage, D.Fear (Captain), S.Preston, K.White, I. Rew, P.Smith (Assistant Manager) and G.Bramble (Physio). Front Row: S.Hare, N.Goater, A.Williams, K.Maddock and N.Long.

Club Factfile

Founded: 1944 **Nickname:** The 'Boro'
Previous Names: Gosport Borough Athletic
Previous Leagues: Portsmouth 1944-45, Hampshire 1945-78, Southern 1978-92, Wessex 1992-2007

Club Colours (change): Yellow/navy/navy (White/red/red)

Ground: Privett Park, Privett Road, Gosport, Hampshire PO12 0SX (T) 023 9250 1042 (Match days only)
Capacity: 4,500 **Seats:** 450 **Covered:** 600 **Clubhouse:** Yes **Shop:** Yes

Directions
Exit M27 at J11. TakeA32 Fareham to Gosport road.
After 3 miles take the 3rd exit at Brockhurst r/a, into Military Road.
At next r/a take 1st exit into Privett Road. Ground is approx. 400 yards on left.

Previous Grounds: Not known

Record Attendance: 4,770 v Pegasus - FA Amateur Cup 1951
Record Victory: 14-0 v Cunliffe Owen - Hampshire League 1945-46
Record Defeat: 0-9 v Gloucester City - Southern Premier Division 1989-90 and v Lymington & N.M. - Wessex Lge 99-2000
Record Goalscorer: Ritchie Coulbert - 192
Record Appearances: Tony Mahoney - 765
Additional Records:

Senior Honours: Hampshire League 1945-46, 76-77, 77-78. Hampshire Senior Cup 1987-88. Wessex League Cup 1992-93. Wessex League 2006-07.

10 YEAR RECORD

01-02		02-03		03-04		04-05		05-06		06-07		07-08		08-09		09-10		10-11	
Wex	4	Wex	2	Wex	3	Wex1	4	Wex1	5	WexP	1	Sthsw	11	Sthsw	12	Sthsw	8	Sthsw	13

HALESOWEN TOWN

Chairman: Steven Lynch
Secretary: Andrew While **(T)** 07976 769 972 **(E)** andrew.while@blueyonder.co.uk
Additional Committee Members:
Michael Serdetschniy.

Manager: Shaun Cunnington
Programme Editor: Andrew While **(E)** andrew.while@blueyonder.co.uk

Club Factfile

Founded: 1873 **Nickname:** Yeltz
Previous Names: Not known
Previous Leagues: West Midlands 1892-1905, 06-11, 46-86, Birmingham Combination 1911-39

Club Colours (change): Blue/blue/blue (All green)

Ground: The Grove, Old Hawne Lane, Halesowen B63 3TB **(T)** 0121 550 9433
Capacity: 3,150 **Seats:** 525 **Covered:** 930 **Clubhouse:** Yes **Shop:** Yes

Directions
Leave M5 at Junction 3, follow A456 Kidderminster to first island and turn right (signposted A459 Dudley).
Turn left at next island (signposted A458 Stourbridge).
At next island take third exit into Old Hawne Lane.
Ground about 400 yards on left.

Previous Grounds: Not known

Record Attendance: 5,000 v Hendon - FA Cup 1st Round Proper 1954
Record Victory: 13-1 v Coventry Amateurs - Birmingham Senior cup 1956
Record Defeat: 0-8 v Bilston - West Midlands League 07/04/1962
Record Goalscorer: Paul Joinson - 369
Record Appearances: Paul Joinson - 608
Additional Records: Paid £7,250 to Gresley Rovers for Stuart Evans
Received £40,000 from Rushden & Diamonds for Jim Rodwell

Senior Honours: FA Vase 1984-85, 85-86 (R-up 1982-83). Southern League Midland Division 1989-90, Western Division 2001-02.
Birmingham Senior Cup 1983-84, 97-98. Staffordshire Senior Cup 1988-89.
Worcestershire Senior Cup 1951-52, 61-62, 2002-03, 04-05.

10 YEAR RECORD

01-02	02-03	03-04	04-05	05-06	06-07	07-08	08-09	09-10	10-11
SthW 1	SthP 19	SthW 4	SthP 9	SthP 8	SthP 6	SthP 3	SthP 10	SthP 8	SthP 21

HUNGERFORD TOWN

Chairman: Steve Skipworth
Secretary: Ken Holmes **(T)** 07932 890 336 **(E)** kensven@tiscali.co.uk
Additional Committee Members:
Ron Tarry, Duncan Groves, Mick Butler, Norman Matthews, Steve Puffett, John Smyth, John Sopp, Nigel Warrick, Terry Wild.
Manager: Bobby Wilkinson
Programme Editor: John Smyth **(E)** john.smyth@saxon-brands.com

Club Factfile

Founded: 1886 **Nickname:** The Crusaders
Previous Names: None
Previous Leagues: Newbury & District, Swindon & District, Hellenic 1958-78, 2003-09, Isthmian 1978-2003

Club Colours (change): All white (All red)

Ground: Bulpitt Lane, Hungerford RG17 0AY **(T)** 01488 682 939
Capacity: 2,500 **Seats:** 170 **Covered:** 400 **Clubhouse:** Yes **Shop:** Yes

Directions
From M4 Junction, take A338 to Hungerford. First Roundabout turn right on to A4, next roundabout first left, 100 yards roundabout 1st left up High Street, go over three roundabouts, at fourth roundabout turn first left signposted 'Football Club'. Take second left into Bulpitt Lane, go over crossroads, ground on left.

Previous Grounds: None

Record Attendance: 1,684 v Sudbury Town - FA Vase Semi-final 1988-89
Record Victory: Not known
Record Defeat: Not known
Record Goalscorer: Ian Farr - 268
Record Appearances: Dean Bailey and Tim North - 400+
Additional Records: Paid £4,000 to Yeovil Town for Joe Scott
Received £3,800 from Barnstaple Town for Joe Scott

Senior Honours: Hellenic Division 1 1970-71, Premier Division 2008-09, League Cup 2006-07, 07-08.
Berks & Bucks Senior Cup 1981-82.
Isthmian representatives in Anglo Italian Cup 1981.

10 YEAR RECORD

01-02	02-03	03-04	04-05	05-06	06-07	07-08	08-09	09-10	10-11
Isth2 15	Isth2 5	Hel P 6	Hel P 17	Hel P 16	Hel P 3	Hel P 3	Hel P 1	Sthsw 17	Sthsw 7

MANGOTSFIELD UNITED

Chairman: Mike Richardson

Secretary: Sophie Dyer **(T)** 07977 585 880 **(E)** sophie.dyer@filton.ac.uk

Additional Committee Members:
Mike Hamilton, Roger Gray.

Manager: Phil Bater

Programme Editor: Bob Smale **(E)** bob_smale@yahoo.co.uk

Back Row (L-R): Dean Griffiths, Lee Marshall, Gary Colborne, Sam Alexander, Tom Billing, Sam O'Sullivan
Front Row: Daine O'Connor, Alex Hoyle, Tom Knighton, Ryan Newman, Geraint Bater, Harley Purnell, Tom Parrinello, Mitchell Page, Mike Baker. **Inset:** Matt Groves

Club Factfile

Founded: 1950 **Nickname:** The Field

Previous Names: None

Previous Leagues: Bristol & District 1950-67. Avon Premier Combination 1967-72. Western 1972-2000.

Club Colours (change): Sky blue/maroon/sky blue (Yellow/black/yellow)

Ground: Cossham Street, Mangotsfield, Bristol BS16 9EN **(T)** 0117 956 0119

Capacity: 2,500 **Seats:** 300 **Covered:** 800 **Clubhouse:** Yes **Shop:** Yes

Directions
Exit the M32 at Junction 1 and follow the A4174 towards Downend following signs to Mangotsfield. Turn left into Cossham Street, the ground is approx 300 yards on the right.

Previous Grounds: None

Record Attendance: 1,253 v Bath City - F.A. Cup 1974

Record Victory: 17-0 v Hanham Sports (H) - 1953 Bristol & District League

Record Defeat: 3-13 v Bristol City United - Bristol & District League Division 1

Record Goalscorer: John Hill

Record Appearances: John Hill - 600+

Additional Records: In the last 10 matches of the 2003/04 season, the club went 738 minutes (just over 8 games) without scoring and then finished the campaign with 13 goals in the last two, which included a 9-0 away win.

Senior Honours: Gloucestershire Senior Cup 1968-69, 75-76, 2002-03. Somerset Premier Cup 1987-88. Western League 1990-91. Southern League Division One West 2004-05. Gloucestershire F.A. Trophy x6.

10 YEAR RECORD

01-02	02-03	03-04	04-05	05-06	06-07	07-08	08-09	09-10	10-11
SthW 7	SthW 6	SthW 13	SthW 1	SthP 10	SthP 9	SthP 14	SthP 22	Sthsw 9	Sthsw 3

NORTH LEIGH

Chairman: Peter King
Secretary: Keith Huxley (T) 07775 818 066 (E) keith.huxley08@tiscali.co.uk
Additional Committee Members:
Mike Burnell, Stacey McDonough, Pete Dix, Phil Horne, Barry Norton, Wayne Reynolds, Maureen Webb.
Manager: Mark Gee
Programme Editor: Mike Burnell (E) michael.burnell1@ntlworld.com

Club Factfile

Founded: 1908 **Nickname:** The Millers
Previous Names: Not known
Previous Leagues: Witney & District, Hellenic 1990-2008

Club Colours (change): Yellow/black/yellow (All sky blue)

Ground: Eynsham Hall Park, North Leigh, Witney, Oxon OX29 6SL (T) 07583 399 577
Capacity: 2,000 **Seats:** 100 **Covered:** 200 **Clubhouse:** Yes **Shop:** No

Directions
Ground is situated off A4095 Witney to Woodstock road, three miles east of Witney.
Entrance 300 yards east of main park entrance.

Previous Grounds: Not known

Record Attendance: 426 v Newport County - FA Cup 3rd Qualifying Round 16/10/2004
Record Victory: Not known
Record Defeat: Not known
Record Goalscorer: P Coles
Record Appearances: P King
Additional Records:

Senior Honours: Hellenic Premier Division 2001-02, 02-03, 07-08. Oxon Charity Cup x2.

10 YEAR RECORD

01-02	02-03	03-04	04-05	05-06	06-07	07-08	08-09	09-10	10-11
Hel P 1	Hel P 1	Hel P 8	Hel P 7	Hel P 4	Hel P 2	Hel P 1	Sthsw 8	Sthsw 10	Sthsw 6

PAULTON ROVERS

Chairman: David Bissex
Secretary: Andrew Harris **(T)** 07760 377 302 **(E)** ahbr23112@blueyonder.co.uk
Additional Committee Members:
David Bissex, Lar Rogers, Paul Rowlands, Les Rogers, Rob Filer, Tim Pow, Andrew Harris.

Manager: Mark Harrington
Programme Editor: Peter Lord **(E)** lord_p7@sky.com

Front Row (L-R): Stuart Tovey, Mark Harrington (coach), Callum Hart, Dan Cleverley, Matt Cooper, Chris Lane, Ben Cleverley, Jack Allward, Daine O'Connor, Lee Marshall, Charlie Rich.
Back Row (L-R): Andrew Jones (Manager), Paul Milsom (Asst Manager), Joe Bradley, Ollie Price, Rob Claridge, Josh Jeffries, Ben Lacey, Kyle Phillips, Phil Waters, Craig Loxton, Craig Burchill, Lee Williams (physio), Colin Parsons (kit manager).

Club Factfile

Founded: 1881 **Nickname:** The Robins or Rovers
Previous Names: Not known
Previous Leagues: Wiltshire Premier, Somserset Senior, Western

Club Colours (change): All maroon (All white)

Ground: Athletic Ground, Winterfield Road, Paulton, Bristol BS39 7RF **(T)** 01761 412 907
Capacity: 5,000 **Seats:** 253 **Covered:** 2,500 **Clubhouse:** Yes **Shop:** Yes

Directions
From A39 at Farrington Gurney, follow A362 marked Radstock for two miles.
Turn left at roundabout, take B3355 to Paulton and ground is on the right.

Previous Grounds: Chapel Field, Cricket Ground, Recreation Ground

Record Attendance: 2,000 v Crewe Alexandra - FA Cup 1906-07
Record Victory: Not known
Record Defeat: Not known
Record Goalscorer: Graham Colbourne
Record Appearances: Steve Tovey
Additional Records:

Senior Honours: Somerset Senior Cup x12

10 YEAR RECORD

01-02	02-03	03-04	04-05	05-06	06-07	07-08	08-09	09-10	10-11
WestP 7	WestP 5	WestP 2	SthW 8	SthW 17	Sthsw 2	Sthsw 7	Sthsw 10	Sthsw 7	Sthsw 11

POOLE TOWN

Chairman: Clive Robbins
Secretary: Bill Reid (T) 01794 517 991 (E) secretary@pooletownfc.co.uk
Additional Committee Members:
Andrew James, Chris Reeves, Doug Huggins, Stella Ayling, Rob Ballston, Mark Bumford, Peter Hough.
Manager: Tommy Killick
Programme Editor: Ian Claxton (E) ian.claxton@btinternet.com

Poole's Michael Walker puts in a strong challenge on Spennymoor's Lewis Dodds during this FA Vase tie from last season. Photo: Graham Brown.

Club Factfile

Founded: 1890 **Nickname:** The Dolphins
Previous Names: Poole Rovers 1884, Poole Hornets 1886 - amalgamated on 20.09.1890 to form Town.
Previous Leagues: Western 1922-26, Southern 1926-30, Western 1930-57, Southern 5197-96, Hampshire 1996-2004, Wessex 2004-11.

Club Colours (change): Red & white halves/red/red & white (Sky blue/white/sky blue).

Ground: Tatnam Ground, Oakdale School, School Lane, Poole BH15 3JR (T) 07771 604 289 (Match days)
Capacity: 2,000 **Seats:** 154 **Covered:** 120 **Clubhouse:** Yes **Shop:**

Directions
Follow the A35 into Poole and at the roundabout by the fire station take the second exit into Holes Bay Road (A350). At next roundabout take 1st exit onto Broadstone Way (A349) and turn right at Wessex Gate East traffic lights into Willis Way. Turn right into Fleets Way and continue until you see Poole Motor Cycles. Turn left into Palmer Road opposite Poole
Motor Cycles and take first right into School Lane which will take you into the Club/School car park. The ground is on the right hand side. Nearest Railway Station: Poole (3/4 mile)

Previous Grounds:

Record Attendance: **Att:** 10,224 v Queens Park Rangers, FA Cup 1st Rnd Replay, 1946 (at Poole Stadium).
Record Victory: 11-0 v Horndean (A) Hampshire League 11/02/1998
Record Defeat: 1-8 v East Cowes VA (A) Hampshire League 01/05/2001.
Record Goalscorer: Not known
Record Appearances: Not known
Additional Records: Got to 3rd Round of FA Cup in 1926 v Everton.

Senior Honours: Western League 1956-57. Dorset Senior Cup (12).
Wessex League Champions 2008-09, 09-10, 10-11.

10 YEAR RECORD

01-02		02-03		03-04		04-05		05-06		06-07		07-08		08-09		09-10		10-11	
HantP	5	HantP	4	HantP	3	Wex2	2	Wex1	8	WexP	4	WexP	4	WexP	1	WexP	1	WexP	1

SHOLING

Chairman: Trevor Lewis
Secretary: Colin Chamberlain **(T)** 07770 452 660 **(E)** secretary.sholingfc@gmail.com
Additional Committee Members:
David Fear, Arthur Fox, Bill Boyle, Kevin Harnett, Malcolm Stokes.

Manager: David Diaper
Programme Editor: Mrs Chris Lewis **(E)** chrislewis@tiscali.co.uk

Back Row (L-R): Marvin McLean,Jack McCarthy,Iain Seabrook,Jamie Austen,Lee Webber,Mike Hookway,Dave Marden,Lee Bright, Lee Wort,Mike Carter.
Front Row: Byron Mason,Barry Mason,Kevin Gibbens,Kevin Harnett(Director of Football),Dave Diaper (Manager),Mick Marsh(Coach), Adam Camfield, Tyronne Bowers,Nick Watts.

Club Factfile

Founded: 1916 **Nickname:** The Boatmen
Previous Names: Woolston Works, Thornycrofts (Woolston) 1918-52, Vospers 1960-2003, VT FC 2003-10
Previous Leagues: Hampshire 1991-2004, Wessex 2004-09

Club Colours (change): Red & white stripes/black/red (Yellow and blue stripes/yellow/yellow)

Ground: VT Group Sportsground, Portsmouth Road, Sholing, SO19 9PW **(T)** 02380 403 829
Capacity: **Seats:** Yes **Covered:** Yes **Clubhouse:** Yes **Shop:**

Directions
Leave the M27 at J8 and follow the signs towards Hamble. As you drive up dual carriageway (remain in the L/H lane), you come to Windover roundabout. Take the second exit towards Hamble. Take the R/H lane and carry on straight across the small roundabout. After 200 yards bear right across a second small roundabout (2nd exit). After about 100 yards turn right into Portsmouth Road. Follow straight on for about half mile. VT ground is on right opposite a lorry entrance.

Previous Grounds: Not known

Record Attendance: 150
Record Victory: Not known
Record Defeat: Not known
Record Goalscorer: George Diaper - 100+
Record Appearances: Not known
Additional Records:

Senior Honours: Hampshire Premier Division 2000-01, 03-04

10 YEAR RECORD

01-02	02-03	03-04	04-05	05-06	06-07	07-08	08-09	09-10	10-11
		HantP 1	Wex1 12	Wex1 13	WexP 3	WexP 2	WexP 2	Sthsw 4	Sthsw 2

STOURPORT SWIFTS

Chairman: Chris Reynolds
Secretary: Laura McDonald **(T)** 07793 768 793 **(E)** Lmacca65@hotmail.com
Additional Committee Members:
Chris Knight, Roy Crowe, John McDonald, Val Lavery, Paul Morris.

Manager: Rod Brown
Programme Editor: Mike Cooper **(E)** mike.cooper@allmediapm.co.uk

Back Row (L-R): Lee Phillips (GK Coach) Tom Reynolds, Lee Mussell, Jamie Willets, Aaron Lloyd, Haydn Whitcombe, Chris Knight, Mark Benbow, Nathan Hayward, Kyonn Evans and Dave Connell (Assistant Manager)
Front Row (L-R): Daniel Pitt, Adam Granger, Chris Duggan, John Griffin, Dene Whittal Williams, Rod Brown (Manager) Dennis Pearce, Nathan Demonte, Julian Triana and Matt Clarke

Club Factfile

Founded: 1882 **Nickname:** Swifts
Previous Names: Not known
Previous Leagues: Kidderminster/Worcestershire/West Midlands (Regional) > 1998, Midland Alliance 1998-2001

Club Colours (change): Gold/black/black (All blue)

Ground: Walshes Meadow, Harold Davis Drive, Stourport on Severn DY13 0AA **(T)** 01299 825 188
Capacity: 2,000 **Seats:** 250 **Covered:** 150 **Clubhouse:** Yes **Shop:** Yes

Directions
Follow the one way system through Stourport Town Centre signposted 'Sports Centre'.
Go over river bridge and turn left into Harold Davies Drive.
Ground is at rear of Sports Centre.

Previous Grounds: Bewdley Road, Moor Hall Park, Feathers Farm, Olive Grove, Hawthorns

Record Attendance: 2,000
Record Victory: 10-0
Record Defeat: 1-7
Record Goalscorer: Gary Crowther
Record Appearances: Ian Johnson
Additional Records:

Senior Honours: Midland Alliance 2000-01

10 YEAR RECORD

01-02	02-03	03-04	04-05	05-06	06-07	07-08	08-09	09-10	10-11
SthW 8	SthW 16	SthW 18	SthW 14	SthW 20	SthM 22	SthM 17	SthM 16	SthM 17	Sthsw 17

TAUNTON TOWN

Chairman: Kevin Sturmey
Secretary: Martin Dongworth **(T)** 07791 948 686 **(E)** admin@tauntontown.com
Additional Committee Members:
Christopher Mayhew, Harold Needs, Gordon Nelson, Brian Pollard, Andrew Power.

Manager: Paul West
Programme Editor: James Wright **(E)** james.m.wright@talk21.com

Club Factfile

Founded: 1947 **Nickname:** The Peacocks
Previous Names: None
Previous Leagues: Western 1954-77, 83-2002, Southern 1977-83

Club Colours (change): Sky blue/claret/sky blue (All yellow)

Ground: Wordsworth Drive, Taunton, Somerset TA1 2HG **(T)** 01823 278 191
Capacity: 2,500 **Seats:** 300 **Covered:** 1,000 **Clubhouse:** TBA* **Shop:** Yes

Directions
From M5 Junction 25 follow signs to Town Centre.
Proceed along Toneway then bear left at roundabout into Chritchard Way.
At traffic lights proceed into Wordsworth Drive and the ground is on the left.

*Clubhouse burnt down during the 2011 close season.

Previous Grounds: Not known.

Record Attendance: 3,284 v Tiverton Town - FA Vase Semi-final 1999
Record Victory: 12-0 v Dawlish Town (A) - FA Cup Preliminary Round 28/08/1993
Record Defeat: 0-8 v Cheltenham Town (A) - FA Cup 2nd Qualifying Round 28/09/1991
Record Goalscorer: Tony Payne
Record Appearances: Tony Payne
Additional Records: Reg Oram scored 67 in one season

Senior Honours: Western League 1968-69, 89-90, 95-96, 98-99, 99-2000, 2000-01. FA Vase 2000-01.
Somerset Premier Cup 2002-03, 05-06.

10 YEAR RECORD

01-02	02-03	03-04	04-05	05-06	06-07	07-08	08-09	09-10	10-11
WestP 2	SthW 10	SthW 15	SthW 17	SthW 18	Sthsw 5	Sthsw 18	Sthsw 20	Sthsw 19	Sthsw 9

THATCHAM TOWN

Chairman: Eric Bailey
Secretary: Alan Lovegrove (T) 07817 723 846 (E) mail@alanlovegrove.wanadoo.co.uk
Additional Committee Members:
David Tait, Sylvia Bailey, Peter Woodage.

Manager: Gary Ackling
Programme Editor: Andy Morris (E) acmorris@madasafish.com

Back Row (L-R): Richard Fox (Physio), Callum Willmoth, Sean Cook, Mark James, Paul Strudley, Gareth Thomas (Captain), Steve Howe, Sam Flegg, Marc Green, Tom Melledew.
Front Row: Sam Hamilton, Paul Taplin, Scott Rees, James Clark, Gary Ackling (Manager), Eric Bailey (Chairman), Will Bratt (Player/Coach), Mark Hughes, Matt Pedder, Robbie Sadler.

Club Factfile

Founded: 1895 **Nickname:** The Kingfishers
Previous Names: Not known
Previous Leagues: Hellenic 1974-82, Athenian 1982-84, London Spartan 1984-86, Wessex 1986-2006

Club Colours (change): Blue and white stripes/blue/blue (Red/black/black)

Ground: Waterside Park, Crookham Hill, Thatcham, Berks RG19 4PA (T) 01635 862 016
Capacity: 3,000 **Seats:** 300 **Covered:** 300 **Clubhouse:** Yes **Shop:** Yes

Directions
A4 Thatcham at Sony roundabout turn into Pipers Way.
At next roundabout turn left, crossing over the railway line.
Entrance to Waterside Park 300 metres on left-hand side.

Previous Grounds: Station Road 1946-52, Lancaster Close 1952-92

Record Attendance: 1,400 v Aldershot - FA Vase
Record Victory: Not known
Record Defeat: Not known
Record Goalscorer: Not known
Record Appearances: Not known
Additional Records:

Senior Honours: Hellenic League 1974-75. Wessex League 1995-96.

10 YEAR RECORD

01-02	02-03	03-04	04-05	05-06	06-07	07-08	08-09	09-10	10-11
Wex 12	Wex 9	Wex 10	Wex1 3	Wex1 2	Sthsw 6	Sthsw 15	Sthsw 6	Sthsw 12	Sthsw 5

TIVERTON TOWN

Chairman: David Graham
Secretary: Ramsey Findlay **(T)** 07761 261 990 **(E)** ramsayfindlay@hotmail.co.uk
Additional Committee Members:
Ian Humphries, Matthew Conridge, Kimm Smith, John Smith.

Manager: Mark Saunders
Programme Editor: Alan Reidy **(E)** alanreidy@hotmail.com

Action from Tiverton's fixture away to Didcot Town. Photo: Jonathan Holloway.

Club Factfile

Founded: 1913 **Nickname:** Tivvy
Previous Names: None
Previous Leagues: Devon and Exeter, Western

Club Colours (change): All yellow (All white)

Ground: Ladysmead, Bolham Road, Tiverton, Devon EX16 6SG **(T)** 01884 252 397
Capacity: 3,500 **Seats:** 520 **Covered:** 2,300 **Clubhouse:** Yes **Shop:** Yes

Directions
M5 Junction 27, follow A361 to Tiverton's second exit at roundabout, turning left.
Continue for about 400 yards, crossing roundabout until reaching mini-roundabout.
Carry on straight across. Ground is 200 yards on right.

Previous Grounds: None

Record Attendance: 3,000 v Leyton Orient - FA Cup 1st Round Proper 1994-95
Record Victory: 10-0 v Exmouth Town, Devon St Lukes Cup 16/02/1994
Record Defeat: 2-6 v Stafford Rangers (A) - Southern League 2001-02 & Heavitree United, Les Philips Cup 29/11/1997
Record Goalscorer: Phil Everett
Record Appearances: Not known
Additional Records:

Senior Honours: FA Vase 1997-98, 98-99. Western League x5. Southern League Cup 2006-07.
Devon Senior Cup 1955-56, 65-66. East Devon Senior Cup x7.

10 YEAR RECORD

01-02	02-03	03-04	04-05	05-06	06-07	07-08	08-09	09-10	10-11
SthP 6	SthP 4	SthP 15	SthP 8	SthP 12	SthP 15	SthP 17	SthP 12	SthP 19	SthP 20

WIMBORNE TOWN

Chairman: Ken Stewart
Secretary: Peter Barham **(T)** 07956 833 316 **(E)** barhamp@tiscali.co.uk
Additional Committee Members:
Jeff Robbins, Juliet Piddington, Richard Button, Geoff Maxted.

Manager: Steve Cuss
Programme Editor: Ken Fergus **(E)** kenfergus@sky.com

Back row (l to r): George Webb, Gary Funnell, Max Cream, Matt Kemble, Tom Hunt, Jordan Cole, Brad Magookin, Matt Dear, Ryan Murray
Middle Row (l to r): Jim Cousins (reserve team asst mgr), Tim Collins (reserve team mgr), Ken Fergus (director), Tony Grant (director), Dan Ackerman, Jason Collins, Chris Batten (main sponsor), Andrew Battison (first team coach), James Harrold (physio)
Front Row (l to r): Jeff Robbins (kit), Peter Barham (secretary), Mark Jamison, Scott Arnold (captain), Steve Cuss (manager), Paul Roast (asst mgr), Ross Lloyd, Ken Stewart (chairman), Jamie Davidson

Club Factfile

Founded: 1878 **Nickname:** Magpies
Previous Names: Not known
Previous Leagues: Dorset, Dorset Combination, Western 1981-86, Wessex 1986-2010

Club Colours (change): Black and white stripes/black/black (Sky blue/white/sky blue)

Ground: The Cuthbury, Cowgrove Road, Wimborne, Dorset, BH21 4EL **(T)** 01202 884 821
Capacity: 3,250 **Seats:** 275 **Covered:** 425 **Clubhouse:** Yes **Shop:** Yes

Directions
On the Wimborne To Blandford Road (B3082), turn left into Cowgrove Road just past Victoria Hospital.
Postcode for Sat nav is BH21 4EL.

Previous Grounds: Not known

Record Attendance: 3,250 v Bamber Bridge
Record Victory: Not known
Record Defeat: Not known
Record Goalscorer: Jason Lovell
Record Appearances: James Sturgess
Additional Records:

Senior Honours: FA Vase 1991-92. Wessex League 1991-92, 93-94, 99-2000.
Dorset Senior Amateur Cup 1936-37, 63-64.

10 YEAR RECORD

01-02	02-03	03-04	04-05	05-06	06-07	07-08	08-09	09-10	10-11
Wex 8	Wex 4	Wex 2	Wex1 7	Wex1 12	WexP 6	WexP 3	WexP 4	WexP 2	Sthsw 19

YATE TOWN

Chairman: Peter Jackson
Secretary: Terry Tansley **(T)** 07875 272 126 **(E)** admin@yatetownfc.com
Additional Committee Members:
John Powell, Roger Hawkins, Robert Lomas.

Manager: Rovert Cousins
Programme Editor: Terry Tansley **(E)** admin@yatetownfc.com

Action from Yate's (White/black strip) fixture against Sholing. Photo: Jonathan Holloway.

Club Factfile

Founded: 1946 **Nickname:** The Bluebells
Previous Names: Yate YMCA 1946-70
Previous Leagues: Bristol Premier Combination > 1968, Gloucestershire County 1968-83, Hellenic 1983-89, 2000-03, Southern 1989-2000

Club Colours (change): White/blue navy/white (All yellow)

Ground: Lodge Road, Yate, Bristol BS37 7LE **(T)** 01454 228 103
Capacity: 2,000 **Seats:** 236 **Covered:** 400 **Clubhouse:** Yes **Shop:** Yes

Directions
From East: leave M4 J18, enter Yate on A432 via Chipping Sodbury bypass. Turn right at first small roundabout (Link Road), straight over next roundabout into Goose Green Way, over more roundabouts and 2 major sets of traffic lights. Turn right at third set of lights (by The Fox), then immediately left into Lodge Road. Ground 200m on right. From North: M5 (South) exit J14, B4509/B4060 into Chipping Sodbury. Turn right into Chipping Sodbury High Street, down Bowling Hill and right at first roundabout into Goose Green Way – then as above. From South: Leave M5 at J15, then join M5. Leave M4 at J19, take second exit onto M32. Leave M32 at J1, at roundabout take first exit onto A4174. Continue on A4174 over traffic lights, then at roundabout take first exit onto A432. Enter Yate on A432, at traffic lights turn left into Stover Road (B4059), then at roundabout take second exit – still on B4059. Left at traffic lights (Fox PH) and immediately left into Lodge Road.

Previous Grounds: Not known

Record Attendance: 2,000 v Bristol Rovers v Bristol Rovers Past XI - Vaughan Jones testimonial 1990
Record Victory: 13-3 v Clevedon - Bristol Premier Combination 1967-68
Record Defeat: Not known
Record Goalscorer: Kevin Thaws
Record Appearances: Gary Hewlett
Additional Records: Paid £2,000 to Chippenham Town for Matt Rawlings 2003
Received £15,000 from Bristol Rovers for Mike Davis

Senior Honours: Hellenic League 1987-88, 88-89. Gloucestershire Senior Cup 2004-05, 05-06.

10 YEAR RECORD

01-02	02-03	03-04	04-05	05-06	06-07	07-08	08-09	09-10	10-11
Hel P 3	Hel P 2	SthW 16	SthW 2	SthP 6	SthP 14	SthP 10	SthP 21	Sthsw 13	Sthsw 14

Ryman football league

PREMIER DIVISION

		P	W	D	L	F	A	Pts
1	Sutton United	42	26	9	7	76	33	87
2	Tonbridge Angels	42	22	10	10	71	45	76
3	Bury Town	42	22	10	10	67	49	76
4	Lowestoft Town	42	20	15	7	68	30	75
5	Harrow Borough	42	22	7	13	77	51	73
6	Canvey Island	42	21	10	11	69	51	73
7	Kingstonian	42	21	9	12	66	50	72
8	Concord Rangers	42	21	8	13	72	55	71
9	Cray Wanderers	42	20	9	13	72	46	69
10	AFC Hornchurch	42	19	12	11	58	46	69
11	Billericay Town	42	20	9	13	56	45	69
12	Wealdstone	42	16	10	16	58	54	58
13	Carshalton Athletic	42	14	10	18	49	57	52
14	Tooting & Mitcham United	42	13	10	19	63	85	49
15	Hendon	42	12	10	20	61	81	46
16	Margate	42	11	12	19	52	64	45
17	Horsham	42	11	11	20	43	77	44
18	Hastings United	42	9	11	22	50	65	38
19	Aveley	42	10	8	24	35	62	38
20	Maidstone United	42	9	10	23	43	75	37
21	Croydon Athletic (-3)	42	10	4	28	44	95	31
22	Folkestone Invicta	42	5	12	25	34	68	27

PLAY-OFFS

Semi-Finals

Bury Town 1-2 Lowestoft Town

Tonbridge Angels 3-2 Harrow Borough

Final (@: Tonbridge Angels, 7/5/11)

Tonbridge Angels 4-3 Lowestoft Town

	1	2	3	4	5	6	7	8	9	10	11	12	13	14	15	16	17	18	19	20	21	22
1 AFC Hornchurch		1-0	1-1	1-1	0-3	4-0	2-0	1-0	1-0	4-0	2-0	1-0	0-0	0-2	1-1	1-2	2-0	2-1	1-1	3-1	2-2	2-1
2 Aveley	1-4		0-1	0-2	1-3	2-0	1-1	0-3	3-0	1-1	0-2	1-3	0-2	1-0	1-1	0-3	1-2	1-1	0-0	0-3	3-1	0-1
3 Billericay Town	2-0	1-0		1-2	1-0	0-0	2-1	3-2	1-2	4-2	1-3	3-0	2-0	2-1	0-1	1-3	1-0	0-0	1-0	3-0	1-0	1-0
4 Bury Town	1-3	2-1	3-0		2-1	3-0	1-2	2-2	1-0	1-1	2-5	2-1	2-2	2-0	0-0	0-0	1-2	2-1	2-1	1-2	2-1	1-0
5 Canvey Island	3-0	2-1	3-2	3-0		1-1	0-4	4-2	3-2	1-0	2-0	2-2	4-1	3-1	0-2	0-0	3-0	2-0	1-3	1-0	0-2	1-1
6 Carshalton Athletic	0-0	2-2	1-3	1-0	1-0		2-4	1-1	1-2	1-0	0-1	1-1	2-1	0-0	1-3	2-0	0-0	1-3	0-2	3-2	2-0	2-3
7 Concord Rangers	1-3	0-1	1-1	2-2	1-0	1-1		2-0	3-0	2-1	3-0	2-1	3-2	2-0	2-1	0-2	3-2	0-0	0-0	1-2	3-0	1-6
8 Cray Wanderers	1-2	3-0	1-3	2-1	0-0	2-1	2-1		4-0	0-1	5-1	2-0	3-1	1-1	2-0	0-1	2-1	2-0	0-2	0-1	2-3	1-0
9 Croydon Athletic	0-3	0-2	0-0	1-3	0-4	1-4	1-3	3-1		2-1	1-3	2-0	1-4	2-4	0-4	0-2	1-2	5-3	0-3	2-0	0-1	2-2
10 Folkestone Invicta	1-1	1-2	1-1	0-2	1-2	1-2	1-1	1-1	0-2		1-0	1-3	1-2	0-0	1-0	1-4	4-0	1-2	0-2	0-0	1-3	1-1
11 Harrow Borough	1-0	1-2	1-1	2-0	6-1	2-1	0-2	1-1	3-1	2-0		2-2	2-3	6-0	1-0	2-0	2-0	0-0	0-0	2-0	2-0	2-4
12 Hastings United	0-1	2-3	1-0	0-2	0-1	0-1	0-3	1-1	3-1	2-2	2-0		1-1	2-3	1-2	0-0	1-2	3-0	2-3	1-2	3-2	2-0
13 Hendon	2-1	1-2	1-1	3-3	0-3	1-0	4-1	2-2	4-0	2-1	0-3	0-0		0-3	2-3	1-1	2-3	2-3	1-0	0-3	4-1	0-1
14 Horsham	0-0	0-0	1-2	1-4	1-1	2-1	1-3	0-4	1-1	0-0	1-7	1-1	1-2		2-3	1-2	1-1	1-1	3-1	0-2	1-0	2-1
15 Kingstonian	2-1	2-0	4-2	1-1	3-1	0-1	0-3	2-1	2-1	2-0	1-3	3-1	3-0	1-3		2-0	0-1	1-0	1-0	1-1	4-2	1-3
16 Lowestoft Town	2-0	1-0	1-1	0-1	1-1	0-0	2-0	0-1	4-0	4-1	3-0	1-1	8-1	4-0	1-1		3-3	2-1	0-0	0-0	0-0	0-0
17 Maidstone United	0-0	1-1	0-2	1-2	0-1	1-3	2-0	2-4	0-1	2-0	0-0	2-4	2-2	0-1	1-2	0-1		0-2	0-3	0-3	1-1	2-4
18 Margate	2-2	2-0	0-1	0-1	2-2	2-1	1-2	0-2	0-2	0-2	2-3	2-0	1-1	6-1	3-3	0-3	1-1		3-2	0-1	3-3	1-0
19 Sutton United	3-0	2-1	1-0	2-1	2-0	2-0	1-1	1-1	5-0	1-0	2-1	2-1	3-0	2-0	2-0	2-1	5-1	2-1		2-2	2-2	4-3
20 Tonbridge Angels	7-1	1-0	3-1	2-3	1-1	4-0	3-2	0-4	1-0	1-0	1-2	2-0	2-1	2-0	1-1	3-3	1-0	1-1	0-1		3-3	2-0
21 Tooting & Mitcham United	1-1	1-0	3-2	1-3	1-2	0-5	3-2	0-3	2-2	4-1	3-2	1-1	4-3	1-2	1-1	2-1	3-4	3-0	0-3	1-5		1-0
22 Wealdstone	0-3	2-0	1-0	0-0	3-3	0-3	1-3	0-1	4-3	1-1	1-1	2-1	1-0	3-0	2-1	0-2	1-1	0-1	2-1	0-0	3-0	

DIVISION ONE NORTH

		P	W	D	L	F	A	Pts
1	East Thurrock United	40	30	5	5	92	38	95
2	Needham Market	40	26	9	5	95	49	87
3	Wingate & Finchley	40	21	9	10	72	54	72
4	Harlow Town	40	21	8	11	61	51	71
5	Brentwood Town	40	20	9	11	75	55	69
6	Enfield Town	40	21	5	14	76	44	68
7	AFC Sudbury	40	18	12	10	82	64	66
8	Maldon & Tiptree	40	18	9	13	70	67	63
9	Heybridge Swifts	40	17	10	13	81	59	61
10	Grays Athletic	40	17	10	13	69	51	61
11	Waltham Abbey	40	16	10	14	75	63	58
12	Romford	40	16	7	17	63	66	55
13	Potters Bar Town	40	14	9	17	60	68	51
14	Ware	40	13	6	21	57	77	45
15	Great Wakering Rovers	40	13	5	22	60	82	44
16	Redbridge	40	10	9	21	51	79	39
17	Thamesmead Town	40	11	6	23	42	71	39
18	Cheshunt	40	10	8	22	49	81	38
19	Tilbury	40	11	4	25	41	66	37
20	Ilford	40	8	8	24	42	81	32
21	Waltham Forest	40	6	8	26	43	90	26
	Leyton - record expunged							

PLAY-OFFS

Semi-Finals

Needham Market 1-3 Brentwood Town

Wingate & Finchley 3-2 Harlow Town

Final (@ Wingate & Finchley, 7/5/11)

Wingate & Finchley 3-2 Brentwood Town

	1	2	3	4	5	6	7	8	9	10	11	12	13	14	15	16	17	18	19	20	21
1 AFC Sudbury		2-1	2-2	0-2	1-5	3-3	4-0	1-0	2-1	1-1	6-3	2-2	6-0	3-0	0-4	2-1	0-0	2-4	3-3	5-1	1-1
2 Brentwood Town	2-3		1-1	1-3	0-6	2-1	4-0	1-1	3-3	2-1	1-2	2-4	1-0	2-0	2-0	3-0	2-0	2-2	3-1	2-1	2-3
3 Cheshunt	0-2	1-3		0-1	0-3	0-3	2-0	0-3	1-1	5-2	1-2	2-0	1-0	1-3	2-3	2-0	1-2	2-1	1-0	3-1	0-4
4 East Thurrock United	4-2	2-2	3-3		2-0	4-0	3-2	3-0	1-2	2-1	1-0	2-1	3-1	4-1	3-0	0-2	3-2	2-1	4-1	3-0	2-1
5 Enfield Town	2-0	0-1	1-2	0-4		2-0	0-3	5-0	3-0	1-0	0-1	0-0	2-3	2-1	1-1	0-1	2-0	2-1	3-0	4-0	1-2
6 Grays Athletic	1-1	0-0	9-0	1-3	2-0		1-2	0-1	1-1	3-0	1-1	2-3	1-2	2-2	3-0	4-1	3-1	1-0	4-0	1-1	2-1
7 Great Wakering Rovers	0-4	2-7	4-1	1-1	1-3	0-1		1-1	2-1	4-2	1-2	0-1	5-6	1-3	0-1	2-0	2-0	1-3	2-2	3-2	3-2
8 Harlow Town	1-0	0-4	3-4	1-1	2-2	1-2	1-0		2-1	2-0	3-0	1-2	3-0	1-1	4-1	2-1	1-0	1-2	3-1	1-1	1-0
9 Heybridge Swifts	5-1	0-3	5-2	1-3	2-2	3-1	1-2	1-2		7-2	4-0	0-1	2-0	2-3	2-3	4-0	1-0	1-1	1-1	2-1	2-2
10 Ilford	0-1	2-0	1-0	0-4	0-1	0-2	1-3	0-2	1-4		0-1	1-2	1-0	2-0	3-2	1-0	1-2	1-1	0-1	0-3	1-3
11 Maldon & Tiptree	1-1	1-1	3-1	0-1	2-4	1-2	3-1	4-1	2-4	1-1		2-2	2-2	3-2	2-0	1-1	2-1	2-1	4-1	3-2	0-0
12 Needham Market	3-2	0-0	3-2	3-0	3-2	1-1	3-2	1-1	0-0	3-3	4-0		1-0	7-1	2-1	3-1	2-1	4-2	4-0	3-2	4-1
13 Potters Bar Town	2-2	0-0	1-0	0-2	1-0	2-3	2-2	0-1	2-1	0-1	0-2	2-2		2-2	1-2	4-1	1-0	0-4	0-0	4-0	4-4
14 Redbridge	0-1	4-0	0-0	0-3	0-2	1-1	2-1	1-2	1-4	1-1	0-5	0-5	2-1		1-3	1-2	1-1	2-2	4-1	1-1	1-2
15 Romford	1-3	0-2	2-1	0-2	2-0	2-0	3-0	2-4	0-0	3-3	3-1	1-3	1-3	3-1		0-3	0-3	2-3	5-1	3-0	1-1
16 Thamesmead Town	2-2	1-2	1-1	1-2	0-3	0-2	0-1	1-2	2-1	2-2	3-3	0-2	0-3	0-2	1-1		3-1	3-0	1-0	3-1	0-3
17 Tilbury	1-2	0-2	0-0	0-2	0-4	3-2	3-1	2-0	3-4	2-0	0-2	3-2	1-2	0-2	3-3	0-1		2-1	1-0	0-2	1-2
18 Waltham Abbey	0-2	5-2	1-1	2-2	0-2	2-0	2-1	0-1	1-1	6-2	3-2	0-2	2-2	1-0	0-1	2-0	4-0		5-4	3-0	2-4
19 Waltham Forest	3-2	0-3	2-1	0-2	2-3	0-2	0-0	1-2	1-2	2-2	4-0	1-3	1-3	2-1	1-1	1-2	0-2	1-1		4-1	0-2
20 Ware	2-2	1-3	3-1	3-2	2-1	3-0	4-2	2-2	0-1	1-2	0-4	4-3	2-0	1-2	0-2	4-1	1-0	0-1	2-0		0-0
21 Wingate & Finchley	0-3	2-1	2-1	2-1	2-2	1-1	0-2	2-1	1-3	1-0	3-0	2-1	2-4	2-1	1-0	1-0	2-0	3-3	5-0	0-2	

DIVISION ONE SOUTH

		P	W	D	L	F	A	Pts
1	Metropolitan Police	42	30	6	6	102	41	96
2	Bognor Regis Town	42	29	9	4	103	43	96
3	Whitehawk	42	26	10	6	109	44	88
4	Leatherhead	42	27	7	8	100	41	88
5	Dulwich Hamlet	42	19	8	15	79	59	65
6	Walton & Hersham	42	18	8	16	69	58	62
7	Burgess Hill Town	42	16	14	12	69	60	62
8	Faversham Town	42	15	16	11	56	48	61
9	Ramsgate	42	16	12	14	65	63	60
10	Chipstead	42	15	12	15	63	67	57
11	Sittingbourne	42	16	8	18	52	66	56
12	Walton Casuals	42	15	8	19	65	71	53
13	Fleet Town	42	14	10	18	68	90	52
14	Worthing	42	12	13	17	76	73	49
15	Whitstable Town	42	12	13	17	58	75	49
16	Whyteleafe	42	14	3	25	65	94	45
17	Godalming Town	42	13	6	23	52	82	45
18	Eastbourne Town	42	11	11	20	60	78	44
19	Merstham (-1)	42	10	15	17	60	85	44
20	Corinthian Casuals	42	11	9	22	53	80	42
21	Chatham Town	42	10	10	22	52	80	40
22	Horsham YMCA	42	5	8	29	41	119	23

PLAY-OFFS

Semi-Finals

Bognor Regis Town 1-3 Dulwich Hamlet

Whitehawk 1-1 Leatherhead (Leatherhead won 4-3 on penalties)

Final (@ Leatherhead, 7/5/11)

Leatherhead 4-3 Dulwich Hamlet

	1	2	3	4	5	6	7	8	9	10	11	12	13	14	15	16	17	18	19	20	21	22
1 Bognor Regis Town		4-1	3-1	3-0	2-2	2-0	1-3	2-0	5-0	2-0	4-1	3-2	3-3	1-0	1-1	4-1	4-0	2-0	2-1	1-1	1-0	3-1
2 Burgess Hill Town	2-1		1-1	3-0	1-1	1-1	1-1	1-1	6-0	3-1	4-0	0-2	1-2	2-2	1-1	3-1	2-3	2-2	2-2	1-1	4-0	2-0
3 Chatham Town	1-1	1-0		0-3	1-0	3-2	3-1	0-2	4-1	0-2	0-1	1-1	4-4	2-3	0-2	1-2	3-2	3-2	1-6	0-0	1-2	1-1
4 Chipstead	1-3	2-1	2-2		3-1	1-4	1-1	2-1	2-4	2-1	2-1	1-3	2-2	2-2	1-1	0-1	0-0	2-1	1-1	2-2	1-2	2-0
5 Corinthian-Casuals	1-2	4-0	2-1	2-0		3-1	0-3	1-1	1-2	1-3	3-1	1-2	2-1	0-4	2-0	3-2	1-3	1-1	3-4	2-2	3-2	1-1
6 Dulwich Hamlet	1-2	1-2	5-2	3-2	3-1		2-2	2-2	6-0	4-0	1-1	1-0	0-1	0-1	2-4	3-0	2-0	1-2	0-1	2-0	1-0	1-2
7 Eastbourne Town	1-2	2-4	2-3	2-0	0-0	0-3		4-1	1-1	1-0	4-4	1-2	0-1	1-2	0-1	4-4	2-1	0-0	3-5	1-2	2-2	1-3
8 Faversham Town	4-0	1-1	2-1	2-2	3-0	1-2	3-0		2-2	3-1	2-0	0-0	0-0	0-2	0-2	3-1	2-0	0-1	2-1	1-1	1-0	2-2
9 Fleet Town	0-2	0-2	3-1	1-1	1-0	2-2	3-1	1-1		2-0	4-2	1-3	1-1	0-2	2-1	1-0	0-3	3-1	3-3	3-2	1-2	1-1
10 Godalming Town	0-6	1-1	2-0	0-0	2-1	3-5	0-1	0-0	0-5		3-0	1-2	1-2	2-0	1-2	0-2	1-3	4-3	0-3	1-2	4-1	2-2
11 Horsham Y M C A	0-3	1-4	1-1	2-2	0-3	0-2	3-2	0-1	2-0	0-2		0-11	3-5	3-0	2-3	0-5	0-2	0-3	2-2	2-3	2-1	1-1
12 Leatherhead	3-2	1-0	2-0	1-2	0-1	2-0	7-3	3-0	2-1	0-2	6-0		4-0	0-2	3-3	2-0	2-1	2-2	2-1	3-0	1-1	1-1
13 Merstham	2-4	0-1	0-2	0-4	3-1	2-3	1-1	1-1	5-2	1-0	2-2	0-3		0-3	1-2	1-1	2-2	1-5	1-4	4-3	0-3	3-3
14 Metropolitan Police	1-1	3-0	2-2	3-1	5-0	4-0	1-1	2-0	4-1	8-1	3-1	1-0	1-0		3-0	1-0	4-2	2-0	0-3	5-2	4-5	0-3
15 Ramsgate	1-3	1-3	2-1	0-1	3-1	0-0	3-1	2-2	2-2	1-0	2-2	0-2	0-1	1-1		0-2	1-1	5-1	2-2	0-1	5-0	3-3
16 Sittingbourne	0-5	0-1	2-0	0-3	1-0	2-2	0-1	1-1	2-1	2-2	1-0	1-2	1-1	0-2	3-0		0-3	1-0	2-2	2-0	2-1	0-4
17 Walton & Hersham	1-1	1-1	0-0	1-2	1-1	0-2	0-1	3-2	3-2	0-2	3-0	0-2	3-1	0-2	3-0	0-1		1-0	0-2	3-1	1-3	3-1
18 Walton Casuals	1-2	3-0	2-0	2-1	2-1	2-2	1-0	1-2	2-1	1-1	2-0	0-5	3-0	1-4	2-3	2-2	1-3		0-1	1-2	4-1	3-1
19 Whitehawk	1-2	6-0	4-1	3-1	6-0	3-1	3-0	2-2	2-0	5-0	6-1	2-1	1-1	0-2	4-2	4-0	0-1	1-0		1-1	5-0	1-0
20 Whitstable Town	1-1	1-1	2-1	0-3	0-0	0-1	1-2	0-1	2-3	1-2	4-0	2-2	1-0	0-6	1-0	2-1	1-1	2-2	1-3		3-4	3-2
21 Whyteleafe	1-5	2-3	0-1	1-2	4-2	2-1	2-3	1-0	3-4	2-1	2-0	2-6	1-1	1-2	0-1	0-1	2-5	4-0	1-2	3-2		1-2
22 Worthing	2-2	2-0	3-1	4-1	3-0	1-4	1-0	0-1	3-3	2-3	5-0	1-2	3-3	2-3	1-2	1-2	1-6	2-3	0-0	1-2	4-0	

LEAGUE CUP

ROUND 1

Waltham Forest 1-0 Grays Athletic
Fleet Town 4-3 Horsham YMCA

ROUND 2

Hendon 1-2 Harrow Borough
Lowestoft Town 2-0 AFC Sudbury
Cheshunt 2-1 Harlow Town
Wingate & Finchley 3-01 Bury Town
Ware 0-3 Wealdstone
Potters Bar Town 2-1 Enfield Town
Waltham Abbey 2-1 Needham Market
Leyton 3-2 Redbridge
Concord Rangers 3-1 Chatham Town
East Thurrock United 1-1 AFC Hornchurch
(East Thurrock United won 5-3 on penalties)
Billericay Town 2-3 Canvey Island
Waltham Forest 0-1 Aveley
Romford 1-2 Tilbury (tie awarded to Romford)
Heybridge Swifts 3-2 Brentwood Town
Maldon & Tiptree 3-1 Great Wakering Rovers
Dulwich Hamlet 1-0 Ilford
Maidstone United 1-2 Leatherhead
Merstham 0-1 Chipstead
Croydon Athletic2-2 Folkestone Invicta
(Folkestone Invicta won 4-2 on penalties)
Whyteleafe 0-2 Cray Wanderers
Tooting & Mitcham United 2-1 Whitstable Town
Sittingbourne 2-0 Faversham Town
Tonbridge Angels 2-0 Ramsgate
Margate 2-5 Thamesmead Town
Godalming Town 1-4 Fleet Town
Horsham 5-1 Bognor Regis Town
Carshalton Athletic 0-1 Eastbourne Town
Worthing 1-6 Burgess Hill Town
Walton Casuals 1-0 Sutton United
Metropolitan Police 3-0 Corinthian-Casuals
Walton & Hersham 0-3 Kingstonian
Hastings United 3-3 Whitehawk
(Hastings United won 5-4 on penalties)

ROUND 3

Cheshunt 1-2 Lowestoft Town
Harrow Borough 3-0 Leyton
Waltham Abbey 2-3 Potters Bar Town
Wealdstone 2-2 Wingate & Finchley
(Wingate & Finchley won 5-3 on penalties)
Canvey Island 0-1 Heybridge Swifts
Concord Rangers 0-1 Dulwich Hamlet
Maldon & Tiptree 3-2 East Thurrock United
Romford 3-2 Aveley
Cray Wanderers 2-1 Folkestone Invicta
Leatherhead 1-0 Chipstead
Sittingbourne 0-2 Tooting & Mitcham United
Thamesmead Town 1-1 Tonbridge Angels
(Thamesmead Town won 5-4 on penalties)
Horsham 1-2 Hastings United
Metropolitan Police 5-1 Eastbourne Town
Kingstonian 0-1 Fleet Town
Walton Casuals 2-0 Burgess Hill Town

ROUND 4

Maldon & Tiptree 1-0 Potters Bar Town
Lowestoft Town 4-4 Heybridge Swifts
(Heybridge Swifts won 6-5 on penalties)
Harrow Borough 1-1 Wingate & Finchley
(Wingate & Finchley won 13-12 on penalties)
Dulwich Hamlet 2-1 Romford
Walton Casuals 0-3 Leatherhead
Tooting & Mitcham United 1-4 Metropolitan Police
Thamesmead Town 1-1 Cray Wanderers
(Cray Wanderers won 5-4 on penalties)
Hastings United 1-2 Fleet Town

QUARTER FINALS

Wingate & Finchley 5-2 Metropolitan Police
Heybridge Swifts 0-2 Dulwich Hamlet
Cray Wanderers 0-2 Leatherhead
Fleet Town 0-2 Maldon & Tiptree

SEMI-FINALS

Leatherhead 1-5 Dulwich Hamlet
Wingate & Finchley 2-1 Maldon & Tiptree

FINAL (@ Metropolitan Police, 30/3/11)
Dulwich Hamlet 0-2 Wingate & Finchley

PREMIER LEAGUE STATS 2010-11
(League, FA Cup and FA Trophy)

Top Scoring Clubs:
97 Lowestoft Town, 86 Sutton United and 82 Bury Town

Club with highest aggregate of goals in their matches
190 Tooting & Mitcham U (69-91),148 Wealdstone (83-65),
144 Lowestoft Town (97-47)

Clubs' most consecutive scoring matches:
19 Concord Rangers (Goal tally 37-28)

Top individual goalscorers:
27 Rocky Baptiste (Harrow Borough)
27 Bobby Traynor (Kingstonian)

Scored in most games last season:
21games Bobby Traynor (Kingstonian),
19 Rocky Baptiste (Harrow Borough)

Best consecutive individual Scoring Run
5 games. Tony Stokes (Concord Rangers) plus 11 in 14 games
5 games. Paul Vines (Kingstonian
5 games. Laurent Hamici (Cray Wanderers) (scored 11 in first 8 games of season)
5 games. Bradley Woods-Garness (Sutton United)

Most Individual goalscorers
23 Billericay Town

Least individual goalscorers
11 Folkestone Invicta

Club with most players scoring 10+ in the season
4 Canvey Island (Robbie King 19, Danny Heale15,
Alex Rhodes 13 & Jason Hallett 10)
4 Sutton United (Bradley Woods-Garness 16, Craig.Dundas 15,
Andy Forbes 15 & Richard Jolly 10)

Most hat tricks
3 Canvey Island: Robbie King, Alex Rhodes and Jason Hallett
3 Carshalton Athletic: Byron Harrison (2) and Joel Ledgister

Most Penalties scored by club in the season
9 Kingstonian, 8 Aveley and Bury Town

Least Penalties scored by a club in the season
1 Croydon Athletic, 2 Horsham and Maidstone United

Most Penalties scored by individual players
8 Bobby Traynor (Kingstonian),
6 Chris Henderson (Bury Town)

Least Goals scored by a club in the season
36 Aveley and 44 Croydon Athletic

Least Goals conceded in the season
41 Sutton United

Most Goals conceded in the season
92 Croydon Athletic & Hendon,
91 Tooting & Mitcham U

Failing to Score in Least Games during the Season:
7 Bury Town, Cray Wanderers and Sutton United

Most matches in which the club failed to score
17 Croydon Athletic

Most Consecutive matches without scoring
5 Maidstone United and Wealdstone

Clubs credited with most 'o.g.s' scored by opponents
3 for Harrow Borough & Lowestoft Town

Most Clean Sheets
22 Sutton United, 21 Lowestoft Town

Least Clean Sheets
6 Hastings United,
7 Maidstone United and Tooting & Mitcham U

Most Consecutive Clean Sheets
6 Lowestoft Town, 5 Sutton United
5 Billericay Town within a run of 8 in 9 games

Most games without a clean sheet
18 Wealdstone (Goals Tally 35-29)
16 Margate (Goals Tally 20-32)

Most consecutive victories
5 AFC Hornchurch,
5 Billericay Town in a run of 8 in 9 games
5 Canvey Island, Harrow Borough,
Sutton United x 2,Tonbridge Angels x 2

Most consecutive defeats
9 Hastings United,
6 Maidstone United in a run of 11 in12 games

Most consecutive games without a victory
20 Hastings United

Best Unbeaten Run
12 AFC Hornchurch,
11 Tonbridge Angels, Wealdstone

Best League attendances
Sutton United 1552 v Hastings United,
Lowestoft T 1246 v Bury Town,
Canvey Island 1163 v Concord Rangers
Carshalton Ath1056 v Sutton United

Best average Home league attendance
694 Sutton United, 679 Lowestoft Town

Smallest Home League average attendance

132 Croydon Athletic, 176 Aveley,
194 Cray Wanderers and Harrow Borough

Best league victories

Home:			
Lowestoft Town	8	Hendon	1
Harrow Borough	6	Horsham	1
Tonbridge Angels	7	AFC Hornchurch	1
Away:			
Horsham	1	Harrow Borough	7
Concord Rangers	1	Wealdstone	6

Did you know ?
That **Harrow Borough** achieved their two impressive victories against Horsham in a sixteen day spell in mid winter and **Rocky Baptiste** scored seven of the thirteeen goals.

Bury Town scored just one goal in each of their last seven games, winning three and losing four but still qualified for the Play-Offs

Club Goalscorers with 10+ for season 2010-2011 in League, F.A.Cup. F.A.Trophy and Play-Off matches

Four Goalscorers

Canvey Island	(16)	Robbie King 19, Danny Heale 15, Alex Rhodes 13 and Jason Hallett 10
Sutton United	(15)	Bradley Woods-Garness 16, Craig Dundas 15 Andy Forbes 15 and Richard Jolly 10

Three Goalscorers

Bury Town	(15)	Sam Reed 17, Craig Henderson 12 and Lee Reed 11
Harrow Borough	(14)	Rocky Baptiste 27, Troy Hewitt 17 and Kenta Nakashma 11
Hendon	(17)	Belal Aite-Quakrim 18, Jamie Busby 14 and Aaron Morgan 10

Two Goalscorers

Carshalton Athletic	(17)	Byron Harrison 13 and Joel Ledgister 13
Cray Wanderers	(19)	Laurent Hamici 22 and Leigh Bremner 13
Concord Rangers	(18)	Tony Stokes 21 and Harry Elmes 15
Folkeston Invicta	(11)	Darren Smith 13 and James Everitt 10
Margate	(15)	Shaun Welford 12 and James Pinnock 10
Tonbridge Angels	(21)	Collin 20 and Ade Olorundo 10
Wealdstone	(18)	Peter Dean 20 and Greg Ngoyi 12

One Goalscorer

AFC Hornchurch	(16)	MartinTuohy 19
Hastings United	(18)	Sam Adams 12
Kingstonian	(18)	Bobby Traynor 27
Lowestoft Town	(21)	Matt Nolan 10
Maidstone United	(18)	Danny Hockton 14

Clubs with no goalscorers totalling 10 or over in 2010-2011

Aveley	(18)	Top Scorer Orlando Smith 9
Billericay Town	(23)	Top Scorers: Tony Boot, James Lawson and Cedric Ngakam 6 each.
Croydon Athletic	(15)	Top Scorer: Danny Elgar 6
Horsham	(19)	Top Scorer: Jamie Cade 9
Tooting & Mitcham	(20)	Top Scorer: Jamie Byatt and Rob Haworth

Totals in brackets denote the number of individual goalscorers for the club in their League, F.A.Cup . F.A.Trophy and Play Off games.

NATIONAL CUP FOOTBALL 2010-2011

All twenty two clubs in the senior Ryman division play in the F.A.Challenge Cup early in the season and then enter the F.A.Challenge Trophy in The First Qualifying Round which was played on the 16th October. To reach the First Round Proper of the F.A. Cup and the chance to face Football League opposition, a Ryman club has to survive four qualifying rounds. In The F.A. Trophy the junior clubs may play in a Preliminary Round but Ryman Premier clubs will hope to compete successfully in the three Qualifying Rounds.

F.A.CHALLENGE CUP

	Games	Round	Goals
AFC Hornchurch	3	2Qr	8*
Aveley	1	1Q	1
Billericay Town	2	2Qr	2
Bury Town	5	3Qr	11
Canvey Island	4	3Qr**	10
Carshalton Athletic	6	4Q	13
Concord Rangers	4	3Q	4
Cray Wanderers	3	2Qr	5
Folkestone Invicta	3	2Q	6
Harrow Borough	**5**	**1st Rd 12**	
Hastings United	1	1Q	2
Hendon	**6**	**1st Rd 12**	
Horsham	1	1Q	2
Kingstonian	4	3Qr	4
Lowestoft Town	2	2Q	8
Maidstone United	1	1Q	1
Margate	2	2Qr	5
Sutton United	1	1Q	1
Tonbridge Angels	1	1Q	0
Tooting & Mitcham Utd	2	2Q	5
Wealdstone	5	3Qr	15

* All scored in their first tie v Oxhey Jets.

** Lost after a penalty shoot out 8-9 to Dartford.

r denotes lost after a replay

Croydon Athletic didn't compete in the F.A.Cup last season

Leading Ryman League F.A.Cup goalscorers:

Byron Harrison (Carshalton Athletic)	7
Rocky Baptiste (Harrow Borough)	5
Alex Rhodes (Canvey Island)	5
Danny Burnell (Wealdstone)	4
Jamie Busby (Hendon)	4
Scott Fitzgerald (Wealdstone)	4
Chris Henderson (Bury Town)	4
Troy Hewitt (Harrow Borough)	4
Aarron Morgan (Hendon)	4

Ryman clubs' First Round ties in 2010-2011

Harrow Borough 0 Chesterfield	2
Chelmsford Cty 3 **Hendon**	2

F.A.CHALLENGE TROPHY

Not one of the more succesful seasons for the Ryman clubs in the F.A.Trophy but four clubs featured in the First Round Proper. Lowestoft's tally of 16 in six games was impressive, with their fine overrall tally of 97 shared between 24 different goalscores with only Matt Nolan (10) reaching double figures.

	Games	Round	Goals
AFC Hornchurch	**4**	**1st Rd**	**7**
Aveley	1	1Q	0
Billericay Town	3	3Q	5
Bury Town	2	2Q	3
Canvey Island	1	1Q	1
Carshalton Athletic	2	2Q	2
Concord Rangers	1	1Q	1
Cray Wanderers	2	2Q	3
Croydon Athletic	1	1Q	0
Folkestone Invicta	4	3Q	8
Harrrow Borough	1	1Q	0
Hastings United	2	1Qr	3
Hendon	2	2Q	2
Horsham	2	2Q	3
Kingstonian	2	2Q	5
Lowestoft Town	**6**	**1st Rd**	**16**
Maidstone United	3	3Q	4
Margate	2	2Q	6
Sutton United	**5**	**1st Rdr**	**9**
Tonbridge Angels	3	3Q	5
Tooting & Mitcham U	1	1Q	1
Wealdstone	**6**	**1st Rdr**	**11**

Leading Ryman club goalscorers in the F.A.Trophy were:

3	Tommy Black	(AFC Hornchurch)
3	Andy Forbes	(Sutton United)
3	Greg Ngoyi	(Wealdstone)
3	Darren Smith	(Folkestone Invicta)
3	Shaun Welford	(Margate)

First Round F.A.Trophy Results for Ryman Premier clubs

Newport County	0	Wealdstone	0
Wealdstone	0	Newport County	1
Eastleigh	1	Sutton United	1
Sutton United	0	Eastleigh	4
Lowestoft Town	2	Uxbridge	3

AFC HORNCHURCH

Chairman: Colin McBride
Secretary: Kerry Street **(T)** 0775 834 8244 **(E)** kelafch@googlemail.com
Additional Committee Members:
Peter Butcher, Terry Fisher

Manager: Jim McFarlane
Programme Editor: Peter Butcher **(E)** peter.butcher5@btinternet.com

The Eastside Stand.

Club Factfile

Founded: 2005 **Nickname:** The Urchins
Previous Names: Formed in 2005 after Hornchurch F.C. folded
Previous Leagues: Hornchurch F.C. Athenian, Isthmian, Conference. Since 2005: Essex Senior

Club Colours (change): Red and white stripes/black/black

Ground: The Stadium, Bridge Avenue, Upminster, Essex RM14 2LX **(T)** 01708 220 080
Capacity: 3,500 **Seats:** 800 **Covered:** 1,400 **Clubhouse:** Yes **Shop:** Yes

Directions
Bridge Avenue is off A124 between Hornchurch and Upminster.

Previous Grounds:

Record Attendance: 3,500 v Tranmere Rovers - FA Cup 2nd Round 2003-04
Record Victory: Not known
Record Defeat: Not known
Record Goalscorer: Not known
Record Appearances: Not known
Additional Records: Won the Essex League with a record 64 points in 2005-06

Senior Honours: Since reformation in 2005: Essex Senior League, League Cup and Memorial Trophy 2005-06.
Isthmian League Division 1 North 2006-07

10 YEAR RECORD

01-02	02-03	03-04	04-05	05-06	06-07	07-08	08-09	09-10	10-11
Isth3 2	Isth1N 2	Isth P 5	Conf S 17	ESen 1	Isth1N 1	Isth P 4	Isth P 6	Isth P 9	Isth P 10

A.F.C. HORNCHURCH

No.	Date	Comp	H/A	Opponents	Att:	Result	Goalscorers	Pos
1	Aug 21	Isth Prem	H	Cray Wanderers	226	W 1 - 0	Tuohy 11	7
2	25		A	Lowestoft Town	709	L 0 - 2		
3	28		A	Kingstonian	336	L 1 - 2	Black 15 (pen)	15
4	30		H	Wealdstone	351	W 2 - 1	Black 71 Hunter 73	
5	Sept 4		A	Maidstone United	265	D 0 - 0		11
6	7		H	Canvey Island	227	L 0 - 3		
7	**11**	**FAC 1Q**	**H**	**Oxhey Jets**	**171**	**W 8 - 2**	**Hayles 43 87 FLACK 3 (51 54 67) Smith 71 Hunt 73 (pen) Wall 77**	
8	18		H	Hendon	260	D 0 - 0		14
9	21		A	Tooting & Mitcham	138	D 1 - 1	Hunt 31 (pen)	15
10	**25**	**FAC 2Q**	**H**	**Brentwood Town**	**279**	**D 0 - 0**		
11	**28**	**FAC 2Qr**	**A**	**Brentwood Town**	**213**	**L 0 - 1**		
12	Oct 2		A	Tonbridge Angels	383	L 1 - 7	Wall 39	16
13	5		H	Folkestone Invicta	212	W 4 - 0	Spencer 32 Tuohy 52 Hayles 70 Hunt 77	
14	9		H	BIllericay Town	422	D 1 - 1	Black 78	14
15	**16**	**FAT 1Q**	**H**	**Brentwood Town**	**214**	**W 2 - 1**	**Black 37 81**	
16	23		A	Bury Town	506	W 3 - 1	Tuohy 25 56 Hayles 58	12
17	26		A	Hastings United	301	W 1 - 0	L.Smith 62	
18	**30**	**FAT 2Q**	**A**	**Margate**	**325**	**W 2 - 1**	**Tuohy 5 Styles 90**	**10**
19	Nov 6		H	Concord Rangers	262	W 2 - 0	Curley 50 63	6
20	9		A	Folkestone Invicta	148	D 1 - 1	Tuohy 49	
21	13		H	Tonbridge Angels	301	W 3 - 1	Tuohy 39 Collis 56 Spencer 76	7
22	**20**	**FAT 3Q**	**A**	**Bideford**	**265**	**W 3 - 0**	**Hayles 66 Styles 80 Black 88**	
23	23		H	Tooting & Mitcham	214	D 2 - 2	Hunt 61 Smith 63	
24	27		A	Croydon Athletic	82	W 3 - 0	TUOHY 3 (2 17 18)	4
25	**Dec 11**	**FAT 1**	**A**	**Ashford Town (Middx)**	**131**	**L 0 - 1**		
26	Jan 1		A	Wealdstone	506	W 3 - 0	Smith 32 Coyne 36 Rankine 90	5
27	8		H	Lowestoft Town	316	L 1 - 2	Hayles 55	6
28	16		A	Cray Wanderers	227	W 2 - 1	Hunt 10 (pen) 57	
29	22		A	Carshalton Athletic	216	D 0 - 0		8
30	29		H	Horsham	235	L 0 - 3		9
31	Feb 1		H	Margate	181	W 2 - 1	Black 77 Smith 88	
32	5		H	Bury Town	293	D 1 - 1	Jackman 80	8
33	8		A	Sutton United	481	L 0 - 3		
34	12		A	Billericay Town	582	L 0 - 2		11
35	22		H	Harrow Borough	148	W 2 - 0	Smith 45 69	
36	26		A	Concord Rangers	234	W 3 - 1	Hunt 15 Hayles 67 Tuohy 82	
37	March 5		H	Croydon Athletic	214	W 1 - 0	Tuohy 4	7
38	8		H	Aveley	157	W 1 - 0	Tuohy 36	
39	12		A	Harrow Borough	171	L 0 - 1		6
40	15		H	Hastings United	168	W 1 - 0	St Aimie 88	
41	19		H	Sutton United	337	D 1 - 1	St Aimie 90	7
42	22		A	Hendon	141	L 1 - 2	Tuohy 74	
43	26		A	Margate	330	D 2 - 2	St Aimie 34 Tuohy 36	9
44	April 2		A	Horsham	190	D 0 - 0		10
45	9		H	Carshalton Athletic	204	W 4 - 0	Hunt 45 Tuohy 63 79 Curley 77	10
46	16		A	Canvey Island	469	L 0 - 3		10
47	22		H	Kingstonian	344	D 1 - 1	Styles 1	11
48	26		A	Aveley	216	W 4 - 1	Smith 43 62 Hunt 47 Tuohy 53	
49	30		H	Maidstone United	557	W 2 - 0	Curley 45 Tuohy 52	10

AVELEY

Chairman: Graham Gennings
Secretary: Craig Johnston **(T)** 0794 643 8540 **(E)** craigjohnston@aveleyfc.freeserve.co.uk
Additional Committee Members:
Terry King, Alan Suttling

Manager: Carl Griffiths
Programme Editor: Craig Johnston **(E)** craigjohnston@aveleyfc.freeserve.co.uk

2010-11 Essex Senior Cup Final team.

Club Factfile

Founded: 1927 **Nickname:** The Millers
Previous Names: Not known
Previous Leagues: Thurrock Combination 1946-49, London 1949-57, Delphian 1957-63, Athenian 1963-73, Isthmian 1973-2004, Southern 2004-06
Club Colours (change): All royal blue

Ground: Mill Field, Mill Road, Aveley, Essex RM15 4SJ **(T)** 01708 865 940
Capacity: 4,000 **Seats:** 400 **Covered:** 400 **Clubhouse:** Yes **Shop:** No

Directions
London - Southend A1306, turn into Sandy Lane at Aveley.

Previous Grounds: Not known

Record Attendance: 3,741 v Slough Town - FA Amateur Cup 27/02/1971
Record Victory: 11-1 v Histon - 24/08/1963
Record Defeat: 0-8 v Orient, Essex Thameside Trophy
Record Goalscorer: Jotty Wilks - 214
Record Appearances: Ken Riley - 422
Additional Records:

Senior Honours: Athenian League 1970-71. Isthmian League Division 1 North 2008-09.
Thameside Trophy 1980, 2005, 2007.

10 YEAR RECORD

01-02	02-03	03-04	04-05	05-06	06-07	07-08	08-09	09-10	10-11
Isth3 3	Isth1N 6	Isth1N 14	SthE 17	SthE 20	Isth1N 15	Isth1N 11	Isth1N 1	Isth P 3	Isth P 19

AVELEY

No.	Date	Comp	H/A	Opponents	Att:	Result	Goalscorers	Pos
1	Aug 2	Isth. Prem	A	Horsham	290	D 0 - 0		10
2	23		H	Folkestone Invicta	192	D 1 - 1	Edgar 47	
3	28		H	Concord Rangers	145	D 1 - 1	Knight 88	14
4	30		A	Bury Town	556	L 1 - 2	Pethers 77	
5	Sept 4		H	Hastings United	214	L 1 - 3	Knight 57	18
6	7		A	Margate	268	L 0 - 2		
7	**11**	**FAC 1Q**	**A**	**Hitchin Town**	**224**	**L 1 - 2**	**K.Smith 1**	
8	18		A	Lowestoft Town	634	L 0 - 1		21
9	24		H	Croydon Athletic	145	W 3 - 0	O.Smith 81 83 (pen) Gobel 83	19
10	Oct 2		H	Cray Wanderers	137	L 0 - 3		20
11	5		A	Harrow Borough	101	W 2 - 1	O.Smith 10 K. Smith 65	
12	9		A	Maidstone United	230	D 1 - 1	O.Smith 9 (pen)	16
13	**16**	**FAT 1Q**	**A**	**Cambridge City**	**243**	**L 0 - 1**		
14	23		H	Tonbridge Angels	203	L 0 - 3		17
15	30		H	Canvey Island	209	W 1 - 3	Llewellyn 52	19
16	Nov 6		A	Tooting & Mitcham	246	L 0 - 1		19
17	8		H	Harrow Borough	141	L 0 - 2		
18	13		A	Cray Wanderers	167	L 0 - 3		21
19	24		A	Croydon Athletic	89	W 2 - 0	Quinton 47 Thompson 62	
20	Dec 4		A	Wealdstone	410	L 0 - 2		20
21	Jan 3		H	Bury Town	166	L 0 - 2		
22	8		A	Folkestone Invicta	252	W 2 - 1	Howell 30 70	20
23	10		A	Kingstonian	272	L 0 - 2		
24	16		H	Horsham	150	W 1 - 0	O.Smith 57	18
25	22		H	Billericay Town	210	L 0 - 1		18
26	29		A	Sutton United	459	L 1 - 2	Tuna 40 (pen)	18
27	31		H	Hendon	150	L 0 - 2		
28	Feb 5		A	Tonbridge Angels	436	L 0 - 1		20
29	12		H	Kingstonian	208	D 1 - 1	Slatter 43	22
30	21		H	Carshalton Athletic	127	W 2 - 0	Stanley 40 Smith 70	
31	March 5		A	Hendon	123	W 2 - 1	Russell 9 Slatter 24	19
32	8		A	AFC Hornchurch	157	L 0 - 1		
33	12		H	Wealdstone	252	L 0 - 1		19
34	15		A	Canvey Island	241	L 1 - 2	Stanley 43	
35	19		A	Carshalton Avenue	210	D 2 - 2	Salmon 10 Beaney 45	19
36	26		H	Maidstonre United	162	L 1 - 2	Dodson 76	20
37	28		H	Lowestoft Town	153	L 0 - 3		
38	April 2		H	Sutton United	236	D 0 - 0		19
39	4		H	Tooting & Mitcham United	133	W 3 - 1	Harrison 29 Smith 53 Beaney 86 (pen)	
40	9		A	Billericay Town	392	L 0 - 1		19
41	16		H	Margate	150	D 1 - 1	Beaney 62 (pen)	19
42	22		A	Concord Rangers	192	W 1 - 0	Smith 2	19
43	26		H	AFC Hornchurch	216	L 1 - 4	Stanley 89	
44	30		A	Hastings United	737	W 3 - 2	Stanley 52 57 Beaney 83	19

BILLERICAY TOWN

Chairman: Steve Kent
Secretary: Ian Ansell **(T)** 0795 897 8154 **(E)** secretary@billericaytownfc.co.uk
Additional Committee Members:
Jim Green, Simon Williams

Manager: Craig Edwards
Programme Editor: Gary Clark **(E)** programme.editor@billericaytownfc.co.uk

Club Factfile

Founded: 1880 **Nickname:** Town or Blues
Previous Names:
Previous Leagues: Romford & District 1890-1914, Mid Essex 1918-47, South Essex Combination 1947-66, Essex Olympian 1966-71, Essex Senior 1971-77, Athenian 1977-79

Club Colours (change): Royal blue/white/royal blue

Ground: New Lodge, Blunts Wall Road, Billericay CM12 9SA **(T)** 01277 652 188
Capacity: 3,500 **Seats:** 424 **Covered:** 2,000 **Clubhouse:** Yes **Shop:** Yes

Directions
From the M25 (J29) take the A127 to the Basildon/Billericay (A176) turn-off, (junction after the Old Fortune of War r'about). Take second exit at r'about (Billericay is signposted). Then straight over (2nd exit) at the next roundabout. Continue along that road until you enter Billericay. At the first r'about take the first available exit. At the next r'about (with Billericay School on your left) go straight over (1st exit). At yet another r'about!, turn left into the one-way system. Keep in the left-hand lane and go straight over r'about. At first set of lights, turn left. Blunts Wall Road is the second turning on your right.

Previous Grounds:

Record Attendance: 3,841 v West Ham United - Opening of Floodlights 1977
Record Victory: 11-0 v Stansted (A) - Essex Senior League 05/05/1976
Record Defeat: 3-10 v Chelmsford City (A) - Essex Senior Cup 04/01/1993
Record Goalscorer: Freddie Claydon - 273
Record Appearances: J Pullen - 418
Additional Records: Leon Gutzmore scored 51 goals during the 1997-98 season.
Received £22,500+ from West Ham United for Steve Jones November 1992

Senior Honours: FA Vase 1975-76, 76-77, 78-79. Essex Senior Cup 1975-76. Athenian League 1978-79.
Essex Senior Trophy x2.

10 YEAR RECORD

01-02	02-03	03-04	04-05	05-06	06-07	07-08	08-09	09-10	10-11
Isth P 9	Isth P 12	Isth P 22	Isth P 2	Isth P 7	Isth P 4	Isth P 10	Isth P 11	Isth P 13	Isth P 11

BILLERICAY TOWN

No.	Date	Comp	H/A	Opponents	Att:	Result	Goalscorers	Pos
1	Aug 21	Isth Prem	H	Tonbridge Angels	457	W 3 - 0	Wild 61 Charge 65 Kouassi 73	1
2	23		A	Kingstonian	385	L 2 - 4	Collis 34 McKenzie 47	
3	28		A	Croydon Athletic	171	D 0 - 0		13
4	30		H	Canvey Island	628	W 1 - 0	Charge 77	
5	Sept 4		A	Sutton United	504	L 0 - 1		9
6	7		H	Wealdstone	268	W 1 - 0	Wild 49	
7	**11**	**FAC 1Q**	**H**	**Tilbury**	**329**	**W 1 - 0**	**Hyde 67**	
8	18		A	Harrow Borough	285	D 1 - 1	Araba 90 (pen)	7
9	21		H	Lowestoft Town	334	L 1 - 3	Ngakam 38	11
10	**25**	**FAC 2Q**	**H**	**Concord Rangers**	**301**	**D 1 - 1**	**Collis 81 (pen)**	
11	**28**	**FAC 2Qr**	**A**	**Concord Rangers**	**283**	**L 0 - 1***		
12	Oct 2		H	Horsham	317	W 2 - 1	Collis 30 (pen) Charge 76	8
13	5		A	Concord Rangers	228	D 1 - 1	Edgar 41	
14	9		A	AFC Hornchurch	422	D 1 - 1	Matafa	9
15	**16**	**FAT 1Q**	**A**	**Biggleswade Town**	**196**	**W 1 - 0**	**Bonnett-Johnson 45**	
16	23		H	Margate	384	D 0 - 0		9
17	26		H	Cray Wanderers	221	W 3 - 2	Brayley 2 Dodson 25 Ngakam 53	
18	**30**	**FAT 2Q**	**H**	**Banbury United**	**285**	**W 2 - 1**	**Brayley 49 (pen) Robinson 85**	
19	Nov 6		A	Carshalton Athletic	300	W 3 - 1	Bonnet-Johnson 39 Robinson 59 Brayley 89	4
20	9		H	Concord Rangers	249	W 2 - 1	Lawson 25 41	
21	13		A	Horsham	281	W 2 - 1	Lawson 33 Robinson 64	3
22	**20**	**FAT 3Q**	**A**	**Sutton United**	**329**	**L 2 - 4**	**Robinson 51 Schoburg 85**	
23	Dec 11		A	Bury Town	486	L 0 - 3		7
24	14		H	Harrow Borough	165	L 1 - 3	Robinson 23	8
25	Jan 3		A	Canvey Island	621	L 2 - 3	Chatting 5 Schoberg 70	
26	8		H	Kingstonian	349	L 0 - 1		11
27	15		A	Tonbridge Angels	522	L 1 - 3	Chatting 65	13
28	18		A	Tooting & Mitcham United	234	L 2 - 3	Hyde 12 Lawson 51	
29	22		A	Aveley	210	W 1 - 0	Paka 65	12
30	29		H	Folkestone Invicta	377	W 4 - 2	Ngakam 22 Lawson 31 89 Chatting 49	12
31	Feb 1		A	Lowestoft Town	513	D 1 - 1	Robinson 90	
32	5		A	Margate	341	W 1 - 0	Anderson 76	11
33	8		H	Maidstone United	243	W 1 - 0	Ngakam 90	
34	12		H	AFC Hornchurch	582	W 2 - 0	Ngakam 50 Kpaka 61	7
35	15		H	Hastings United	203	W 3 - 0	Hyde 15 Bevemmey 77 O'Rawe 84	
36	22		H	Hendon	219	W 2 - 0	Ngakam 43 Kpaka 61	
37	March 5		A	Hastings United	363	L 0 - 1		6
38	12		H	Tooting & Mitcham	422	W 1 - 0	Flanagan 47	
39	15		H	Carshalton Athletic	237	D 0 - 0		
40	19		A	Maidstone United	312	W 2 - 0	Boot 84 Allen 90	4
41	22		A	Cray Wanderers	191	W 3 - 1	Allen 27 Boot 47 82	
42	26		H	Bury Town	538	L 1 - 2	Chatting 87	4
43	April 2		A	Folkestone Invicta	274	D 1 - 1	Boot 43	7
44	9		H	Aveley	392	W 1 - 0	Boot 47	7
45	16		A	Wealdstone	423	L 0 - 1		9
46	22		H	Croydon Athletic	366	L 1 - 2	Chatting 3	10
47	26		A	Hendon	156	D 1 - 1	Flanagan 11 (pen)	
48	30		H	Sutton United	377	W 1 - 0	Boot 73	11

BURY TOWN

Chairman: Russell Ward
Secretary: Mrs Wendy Turner **(T)** 07795 661 959 **(E)** wturner@burytownfc.freeserve.co.uk
Additional Committee Members:
Chris Ward

Manager: Richard Wilkins
Programme Editor: Christopher Ward **(E)** cpward@burytownfc.co.uk

Club Factfile

Founded: 1872 **Nickname:** The Blues
Previous Names: Bury St Edmunds 1895-1902, Bury United 1902-06
Previous Leagues: Norfolk & Suffolk Border, Essex & Suffolk Border, Eastern Counties 1935-64, 76-87, 97-2006, Metropolitan 1964-71, Southern 1971-76, 87-97
Club Colours (change): All blue

Ground: Ram Meadow, Cotton Lane, Bury St Edmunds IP33 1XP **(T)** 01284 754 721
Capacity: 3,500 **Seats:** 300 **Covered:** 1,500 **Clubhouse:** Yes **Shop:** Yes

Directions
Follow signs to Town Centre from A14. At second roundabout take first left into Northgate Street then left into Mustow Street at T junction at lights and left again into Cotton Lane. Ground is 350 yards on the right.

Previous Grounds:

Record Attendance: 2,500 v Enfield - FA Cup 1986
Record Victory: Not known
Record Defeat: Not known
Record Goalscorer: Doug Tooley
Record Appearances: Doug Tooley
Additional Records: Paid £1,500 to Chelmsford City for Mel Springett
Received £5,500 from Ipswich Town for Simon Milton

Senior Honours: Eastern Counties League 1963-64.
Suffolk Premier Cup x9.
Southern League Division One Central 2010/11

10 YEAR RECORD

01-02	02-03	03-04	04-05	05-06	06-07	07-08	08-09	09-10	10-11
ECP 7	ECP 9	ECP 9	ECP 2	ECP 2	Isth1N 17	Isth1N 7	SthC 7	SthC 1	Isth P 3

BURY TOWN

No.	Date	Comp	H/A	Opponents	Att:	Result	Goalscorers	Pos
1	Aug 21	Isth Prem	H	Kingstonian	581	D 0 - 0		11
2	24		A	Tonbridge Angels	429	W 3 - 2	S.Reed 49 80 L.Reed 67	
3	28		A	Maidstone United	236	W 2 - 1	Bullard 39 Chaplin 41	4
4	30		H	Aveley	556	W 2 - 1	Nurse 33 Henderson 78	
5	Sept 4		A	Wealdstone	504	D 0 - 0		5
6	7		H	Cray Wanderers	439	D 2 - 2	L.Reed 27 S.Reed 86	
7	**11**	**FAC 1Q**	**A**	**Woodford United**	**89**	**W 3 - 1**	**HENDERSON 3 (30 pen 47 pen 68)**	
8	18		H	Hastings United	530	W 2 - 1	Henderson 3 Scowcroft 76	3
9	21		A	Canvey Island	303	L 0 - 3		4
10	**25**	**FAC 2Q**	**H**	**Grays Athletic**	**582**	**D 2 - 2**	**S.Reed 47 Henderson 57 (pen)**	
11	**29**	**FAC 2Qr**	**A**	**Grays Athletic**	**268**	**W 4 - 1**	**Kearns 10 Bullard 16 Leabon 70 77**	
12	Oct 2		A	Tooting & Mitcham	298	W 3 - 1	Leabon 8 Andrews 72 L.Reed 81	4
13	5		H	Hendon	487	D 2 - 2	L.Reed 7 Henderson 35	
14	**9**	**FAC 3Q**	**H**	**Staines Town**	**918**	**D 2 - 2**	**Leabon 23 Coulson 90**	
15	**12**	**FAC 3Qr**	**A**	**Staines Town**	**274**	**L 0 - 2**		
16	**16**	**FAT 1Q**	**H**	**Barton Rovers**	**353**	**W 2 - 0**	**Nurse 37 Nunn 60**	
17	23		H	AFC Hornchurch	506	L 1 - 3	Nurse 87	6
18	**30**	**FAT 2Q**	**A**	**Ashford Town (Middx)**	**120**	**L 1 - 2**	**Henderson 32**	
19	Nov 6		A	Margate	305	W 1 - 0	Scowcroft 55	5
20	9		A	Hendon	139	D 3 - 3	Henderson 10 (pen) L.Reed 30 Bullard 35	
21	13		H	Tooting & Mitcham	515	W 2 - 1	L.Reed 18 35	6
22	16		A	Carshalton Athletic	192	L 0 - 1		
23	20		A	Hastings United	314	W 2 - 0	Scowcroft 29 Hipperson 42	4
24	23		H	Canvey Island	440	W 2 - 1	S.Reed 22 Hipperson 35	3
25	Dec 11		H	Billericay Town	486	W 3 - 0	Scowcroft 35 Bullard 37 S.Reed 82	2
26	Jan 3		A	Aveley	252	W 2 - 0	Andrews 49 (og) L.Reed 52	
27	8		H	Tonbridge Angels	592	L 1 - 2	Ives 55	2
28	16		A	Kingstonian	372	D 1 - 1	S.Reed 62	
29	18		A	Concord Rangers	221	D 2 - 2	Scowcroft 22 S.Reed 47	2
30	22		H	Sutton United	720	W 2 - 1	L.Reed 14 Scowcroft 43	2
31	25		A	Folkestone Invicta	182	W 2 - 0	L.Reed 11 Nurse 83	
32	29		A	Croydon Athletic	79	W 3 - 1	S.Reed 30 Nurse 38 Scowcroft 82 (pen)	2
33	Feb 1		H	Harrow Borough	502	L 2 - 5	Nunn 9 S.Reed 17	
34	5		A	AFC Hornchurch	293	D 1 - 1	S.Reed 63	2
35	12		H	Carshalton Athletic	484	W 3 - 0	Andrews 4 Nunn 14 S.Reed 64	
36	15		H	Horsham	339	W 2 - 0	Scowcroft 25 Groves 78 (og)	
37	22		H	Lowestoft Town	931	D 0 - 0		
38	March 5		H	Folkestone Invicta	487	D 1 - 1	Chaplin 63	2
39	12		A	Horsham	217	W 4 - 1	NURSE 3 (15 48 67) L.Reed 87	2
40	15		H	Margate	408	W 2 - 1	Henderson 40 (pen) S Reed 90	
41	19		H	Concord Rangers	462	L 1 - 2	Nunn 73	2
42	22		A	Harrow Borough	145	L 0 - 2		
43	26		A	Billericay Town	536	W 2 - 1	S.Reed 29 40	2
44	April 2		H	Croydon Athletic	510	W 1 - 0	Henderson 43 (pen)	2
45	9		A	Sutton United	967	L 1 - 2	S.Reed 85	2
46	17		A	Cray Wanderers	302	L 1 - 2	Leabon 90	6
47	23		H	Maidstone United	502	L 1 - 2	Leabon 31	6
48	26		A	Lowestoft Town	1248	W 1 - 0	Flanagan 11 (pen)	
49	30		H	Wealdstone	692	W 1 - 0	S.Reed 46	3
50	**May 3**	**P-Off SF**	**H**	**Lowestoft Town**	**1427**	**L 1 - 2**	**Henderson 49**	

CANVEY ISLAND

Chairman: George Frost
Secretary: Gary Sutton (T) 0779 002 5828 (E) gary.sutton@sky.com
Additional Committee Members:
Chris Sutton, Steve Chaplin

Manager: John Batch
Programme Editor: Glen Eckett (E) gleneckett@another.com

Club Factfile

Founded: 1926 **Nickname:** The Gulls
Previous Names:
Previous Leagues: Southend & District, Thurrock & Thames Combination, Parthenon, Metropolitan, Greater London 1964-71, Essex Senior 1971-95, Isthmian 1995-2004, Conference 2004-06

Club Colours (change): Yellow and sky blue/sky blue/yellow and sky blue

Ground: The Brockwell Stadium, Park Lane, Canvey Island, Essex SS8 7PX (T) 01268 682 991
Capacity: 4,100 **Seats:** 500 **Covered:** 827 **Clubhouse:** Yes **Shop:** Yes

Directions
A130 from A13 or A127 at Sadlers Farm roundabout.
One mile through Town Centre, first right past old bus garage.

Previous Grounds:

Record Attendance: 3,553 v Aldershot Town - Isthmian League 2002-03
Record Victory: Not Known
Record Defeat: Not Known
Record Goalscorer: Andy Jones
Record Appearances: Steve Ward
Additional Records: Paid £5,000 to Northwich Victoria for Chris Duffy
Received £4,500 from Farnborough Town for Brian Horne

Senior Honours: Isthmian Division 1 1993-94, Premier Division 2003-04.
FA Trophy 2000-01. Essex Senior Cup 1998-99, 2000-01, 2001-02.

10 YEAR RECORD

01-02	02-03	03-04	04-05	05-06	06-07	07-08	08-09	09-10	10-11
Isth P 2	Isth P 2	Isth P 1	Conf N 18	Conf N 4	Isth1N 6	Isth1N 5	Isth P 12	Isth P 16	Isth P 6

CANVEY ISLAND

No.	Date	Comp	H/A	Opponents	Att:	Result	Goalscorers	Pos
1	Aug 21	Isth Prem	A	Margate	474	D 2 - 2	Heale 7 Rowe 28	
2	24		H	Harrow Borough	220	W 2 - 0	Rowe 44 51	
3	28		H	Carshalton Athletic	308	D 1 - 1	Heale 28	9
4	30		A	Billericay Town	628	L 0 - 1		
5	Sept 4		H	Tooting & Mitcham	228	L 0 - 2		13
6	7		A	AFC Hornchurch	277	W 3 - 0	KING 3 (12 53 88)	
7	**11**	**FAC 1Q**	**H**	**Newport Pagnell**	**266**	**W 4 - 1**	**Rhodes 50 76 Heale 64 Rowe 75**	
8	18		A	Cray Wanderers	189	D 0 - 0		10
9	21		H	Bury Town	303	W 3 - 0	Hallett 24 King 59 Rhodes 88	7
10	**25**	**FAC 2Q**	**H**	**Whitstable Town**	**271**	**W 1 - 0**	**Rhodes 85**	
11	Oct 2		H	Kingstonian	356	L 0 - 2		10
12	5		A	Lowestoft Town	677	D 1 - 1	Curran 60	
13	**9**	**FAC 3Q**	**H**	**Dartford**	**715**	**D 2 - 2**	**Heale 9 King 90**	
14	**12**	**FAC 3Qr**	**A**	**Dartford**	**665**	**D 3 - 3***	**Everett 17 Rhodes 67 77 Dartford won 9-8 on penalties**	
15	**16**	**FAT 1Q**	**H**	**AFC Sudbury**	**293**	**L 1 - 2**	**Moore 6**	
16	30		A	Aveley	209	W 3 - 1	Heale 4 Easterford 11 King 90 (pen)	14
17	Nov 2		H	Wealdstone	225	D 1 - 1	Rhodes 90	
18	6		H	Folkestone Invicta	322	W 1 - 0	Isa 64	7
19	13		A	Kingstonian	380	L 1 - 3	Heale 88	13
20	20		H	Cray Wanderers	314	W 4 - 2	Heale 40 King 58 Curran 70 Rhodes 90	
21	23		A	Bury Town	440	L 1 - 2	Moore 89	11
22	27		A	Horsham	226	D 1 - 1	Hallett 77	11
23	Dec 14		H	Lowestoft Town	247	D 0 - 0		
24	Jan 3		H	Billericay Town	621	W 3 - 2	Curran 7 20 Rhodes 36	
25	8		A	Harrow Borough	151	L 1 - 6	Dobinson 9	12
26	11		H	Sutton United	556	L 1 - 3	Hallett 4	
27	15		H	Margate	317	W 2 - 0	King 20 27	11
28	Jan 22		H	Maidstone United	351	W 3 - 0	King 2 89 Heale 47	10
29	29		A	Hastings United	325	W 1 - 0	Davidson 20 (pen)	8
30	Feb 5		H	Hendon	309	W 4 - 1	King 33 Curran 56 Heale 75 Gordon 90	
31	8		H	Concord Rangers	231	W 3 - 2	Heale 9 King 22 34	
32	12		A	Wealdstone	444	D 3 - 3	King 54 Gordon 78 Hallett 85	9
33	22		A	Concord Rangers	720	L 0 - 1		
34	March 1		A	Tonbridge Angels	303	D 1 - 1	Hallett 49	
5	5		H	Horsham	327	W 3 - 1	King 6 Hallett 23 Rhodes 64	10
36	12		A	Croydon Athletic	109	W 4 - 0	RHODES 3 (11 35 39) Easterford 75	10
37	15		H	Aveley	241	W 2 - 1	Heale 32 King 57	
38	19		H	Tonbridge Angels	477	W 1 - 0	Heale 20	6
39	26		A	Sutton United	714	L 0 - 2		10
40	28		A	Hendon		W 3 - 0	HALLETT 3 (44 52 59)	
41	April 2		H	Hastings United	501	D 2 - 2	Game 61 Heale 86	8
42	5		A	Folkestone Invicta	188	W 2 - 1	Hallett 35 Heale 49	
43	9		A	Maidstone United	340	W 1 - 0	King 47	4
44	16		H	AFC Hornchurch	469	W 3 - 0	Gordon 27 King 70 Heale 82	3
45	23		A	Carshalton Athletic	240	L 0 - 1		5
46	26		H	Concord Rangers	1163	L 0 - 4		
47	30		A	Tooting & Mitcham	473	W 2 - 1	Gordon 74 90	5

CARSHALTON ATHLETIC

Chairman: Alan Walker
Secretary: Frank Thompson (T) 0774 776 4349 (E) frankthompson@carshaltonathletic.co.uk
Additional Committee Members:
John Kistner, Rory Walsh, Paul williams

Manager: Paul Dipre
Programme Editor: Rory Wals (E) press@carshaltonathletic.co.uk

Club Factfile

Founded: 1905 **Nickname:** Robins
Previous Names: Not known
Previous Leagues: Southern Suburban > 1911, Surrey Senior 1922-23, London 1923-46, Corinthian 1946-56, Athenian 1956-73, Isthmian 1973-2004, Conference 2004-06

Club Colours (change): All red

Ground: War Memorial Sports Ground, Colston Avenue, Carshalton SM5 2PN (T) 0208 642 2551
Capacity: 8,000 **Seats:** 240 **Covered:** 4,500 **Clubhouse:** Yes **Shop:** Yes

Directions
Turn right out of Carshalton Station exit,
turn right again,
and then left into Colston Avenue.

Previous Grounds: Not known

Record Attendance: 7,800 v Wimbledon - London Senior Cup
Record Victory: 13-0 v Worthing - Isthmian League Cup 28/01/1991
Record Defeat: 0-11 v Southall - Athenian League March 1963
Record Goalscorer: Jimmy Bolton - 242
Record Appearances: Jon Warden - 504
Additional Records: Paid £15,000 to Enfield for Curtis Warmington
Received £30,000 from Crystal Palace for Ian Cox

Senior Honours: Isthmian League Division 1 South 2002-03.
Surrey Senior Shield 1975-76. London Challenge Cup 1991-92. Surrey Senior Cup x3.

10 YEAR RECORD

01-02	02-03	03-04	04-05	05-06	06-07	07-08	08-09	09-10	10-11
Isth1 6	Isth1S 1	Isth P 7	Conf S 19	Conf S 21	Isth P 13	Isth P 18	Isth P 4	Isth P 17	Isth P 13

CARSHALTON ATHLETIC

No.	Date	Comp	H/A	Opponents	Att:	Result	Goalscorers	Pos
1	Aug 21	Isth Prem	H	Lowestoft Town	350	W 2 - 0	Johnson 40 Harrison 64	2
2	28		A	Canvey Island	308	D 1 - 1	Johnson 13	11
3	30		H	Croydon Athletic	378	L 1 - 2	Harrison 65	
4	Sept 4		A	Hendon	201	L 0 - 1		16
5	7		H	Tonbridge Angels	228	W 3 - 2	Henry 45 Johnson 84 Harrison 89	
6	**11**	**FAC 1Q**	**H**	**Tunbridge Wells**	**250**	**W 2 - 1**	**Ledgister 48 Harrison 89**	
7	18		H	Tooting & Mitcham U	484	W 2 - 0	Johnson 26 Harrison 68	8
8	20		A	Wealdstone	406	W 3 - 0	Duncan 39 Dean 74 (og) Ledgister 76	
9	**25**	**FAC 2Q**	**A**	**East Thurrock**	**163**	**D 1 - 1**	**Joseph 37**	
10	**28**	**FAC 2Qr**	**H**	**East Thurrock**	**188**	**W 3 - 2**	**HARRISON 3 (39 42 58)**	
11	Oct 2		A	Maidstone United	263	W 3 - 1	Ledgister 28 Harrison 65 A.Lokando 90	6
12	5		H	Hastings United	219	D 1 - 1	Ray 80	
13	**9**	**FAC 3Q**	**H**	**Braintree Town**	**490**	**W 4 - 1**	**Henry 20 HARRISON 3 (38 71 80)**	
14	**16**	**FAT 1Q**	**H**	**Ilford**	**216**	**W 2 - 0**	**Henry 43 Noel 80**	
15	**23**	**FAC 4Q**	**H**	**Chelmsford City**	**1024**	**D 1 - 1**	**Joseph 89**	
16	**25**	**FAC 4Qr**	**A**	**Chelmsford City**	**1069**	**L 2 - 3**	**Roberts 40 Ledgister 45**	
17	**30**	**FAT 2Q**	**A**	**Harlow Town**	**296**	**L 0 - 2**		
18	Nov 2		A	Cray Wanderers	182	L 1 - 2	Pigden 27	
19	6		H	Billericay Town	300	L 1 - 3	Harrison 49 (pen)	13
20	9		A	Hastings United	267	W 1 - 0	Joseph 85	
21	13		H	Maidstone United	321	D 0 - 0		10
22	16		H	Bury Town	192	W 1 - 0	Boateng 69	
23	20		A	Tooting & Mitcham U	469	W 5 - 0	LEDGISTER 3 (53 57 61) Pigden 80 (pen) Noel 89	
24	23		H	Wealdstone	187	W 3 - 2	Roberts 85 Spendlove 22 Obaze 90	8
25	Dec 11		H	Concord Rangers	218	L 2 - 4	Harrison 9 (pen) Ledgister 13	
26	14		A	Horsham	182	L 1 - 2	Ray 76	
27	27		H	Sutton United	1056	L 0 - 2		
28	Jan 1		A	Croydon Athletic	217	W 3 - 1	Johnson 47 Ledgister 54 74 Noel 61	6
29	15		A	Lowestoft Town	733	D 0 - 0		9
30	22		H	AFC Hornchurch	216	D 0 - 0		11
31	25		A	Harrow Borough	125	L 1 - 2	Henry 8	
32	29		A	Kingstonian	415	W 1 - 0	Noel 72	11
33	Feb 5		H	Folkestone Invicta	235	W 1 - 0	Johnson 89	12
34	8		H	Margate	157	L 1 - 3	Ledgister 35	
35	12		A	Bury Town	484	L 0 - 3		12
36	19		H	Horsham	206	D 0 - 0		13
37	21		A	Aveley	127	L 0 - 2		
38	March 1		H	Cray Wanderers	100	D 1 - 1	Wilson-Dennis 72	
39	5		H	Harrow Borough	200	L 0 - 1		13
40	8		A	Folkestone Invictor	19	W 2 - 1	Pigden 3 Ledgister 38	
41	12		A	Margate	337	L 1 - 2	Pigden 34	13
42	15		A	Billericay Town	237	D 0 - 0		
43	19		H	Aveley	210	D 2 - 2	Reece 49 Ledgister 66	13
44	26		A	Concord Rangers	164	D 1 - 1	Henry 22	13
45	April 2		H	Kingstonian	397	L 1 - 3	Ray 80	13
46	9		A	AFC Hornchurch	204	L 0 - 4		13
47	16		A	Tonbridge Angels	472	L 0 - 4		14
48	23		H	Canvey Island	240	W 1 - 0	Ayres 80	13
49	26		A	Sutton United	1367	L 0 - 2		
50	30		H	Hendon	211	W 2 - 1	Ayres 6 70	13

CONCORD RANGERS

Chairman: Antony Smith
Secretary: Chris Crerie **(T)** 0790 952 8818 **(E)** concordrangers@btinternet.com
Additional Committee Members:
Jack Smith junior, Ron Heyfron

Manager: Danny Scopes and Danny Cowley
Programme Editor: Phil Crowe **(E)** hopesunltd@yahoo.co.uk

Back Row: Harry Elmes Nicky Cowley Lee White Dan Scopes James Dudley Danny Cowley Nick Skelton Richard Halle James Elmes

Front Row: Adam Wickenden Michael Begg Seb Dunbar Michael Noone Tom Bruno Billy Coyne Tyler Campbell David Adepide Tony Stokes Connor French Gary Ewers

Club Factfile

Founded: 1967 **Nickname:** Rangers
Previous Names: Not known
Previous Leagues: Southend & District, Southend Alliance, Essex Intermediate 1988-91, Essex Senior 1991-2008

Club Colours (change): Yellow/blue/blue

Ground: Aspect Arena, Thames Road, Canvey Island, Essex SS8 0HH **(T)** 01268 515 750
Capacity: 1,500 **Seats:** Yes **Covered:** Yes **Clubhouse:** Yes **Shop:**

Directions
A130 onto Canvey Island.
Turn right into Thorney Bay Road.
Then right again into Thames Road.

Previous Grounds: Waterside

Record Attendance: 1,500 v Lee Chapel North - FA Sunday Cup 1989-90
Record Victory: Not Known
Record Defeat: Not Known
Record Goalscorer: Not Known
Record Appearances: Not Known
Additional Records:

Senior Honours: Essex Intermediate League Division 2 1990-91. Essex Senior League 1997-98, 2003-04, 07-08

10 YEAR RECORD

01-02	02-03	03-04	04-05	05-06	06-07	07-08	08-09	09-10	10-11
ESen 4	ESen 2	ESen 1	ESen 9	ESen 7	ESen 7	ESen 1	Isth1N 5	Isth1N 2	Isth P 8

CONCORD RANGERS

No.	Date	Comp	H/A	Opponents	Att:	Result	Goalscorers	Pos
1	Aug 21	Isth Prem	H	Sutton United	242	D 0 - 0		15
2	24		A	Hendon	165	L 1 - 4	H.Elmes 45	
3	28		A	Aveley	145	D 1 - 1	Thomas 54	16
4	30		H	Lowestoft Town	236	L 0 - 2		
5	Sept 4		A	Croydon Athletic	177	W 3 - 1	Brayley 29 Lawson 52 Stokes 66	14
6	7		H	Maidstone United	172	W 3 - 2	Brayley 40 Lawson 62 King 90	
7	**11**	**FAC 1Q**	**A**	**Hemel Hempstead**	**184**	**W 2 - 1**	**Glazier 74 (pen) Stokes 85**	
8	18		H	Tonbridge Angels	184	L 1 - 2	H.Elmes 79	13
9	21		A	Hastings United	437	W 3 - 0	H.Elmes 64 King 71 Brayley 80 (pen)	
10	**25**	**FAC 2Q**	**A**	**Billericay Town**	**301**	**D 1 - 1**	**Lawson 7**	
11	**28**	**FAC 2Qr**	**H**	**Billericay Town**	**283**	**W 1 - 0***	**Stokes 101**	
12	Oct 2		A	Folkestone Invicta	259	D 1 - 1	Hawes 70	11
13	5		H	Billericay Town	228	D 1 - 1	King 64	
14	**9**	**FAC 3Q**	**H**	**Hythe Town**	**163**	**L 0 - 1**		
15	**16**	**FAT 1Q**	**A**	**Tonbridge Angels**	**394**	**L 2 - 3**	**England 40 (og) Erskine 86**	
16	23		H	Tooting & Mitcham	202	W 3 - 0	Cowley 37 Stokes 64 Erskine 80	11
17	26		H	Margate		D 0 - 0		
18	30		A	Harrow Borough	110	W 2 - 0	Cowley 12 White 65	9
19	Nov 6		A	AFC Hornchurch	262	L 0 - 2		9
20	9		A	Billericay Town	249	L 1 - 2	Stokes 17	
21	13		H	Folkestone Invicta	183	W 2 - 1	H.Elmes 34 Erskine 65	9
22	23		H	Hastings United	112	W 2 - 1	H.Elmes 4 Harris 86	9
23	Dec 11		A	Carshalton Athletic	218	W 4 - 2	H.Elmes 21 45 Stokes 73 J.Elmes 87	
24	Jan 3		A	Lowestoft Town		L 0 - 2		
25	8		H	Hendon	181	W 3 - 2	Stokes 29 (pen) Ogilvie 31 King 64	7
26	15		A	Sutton United	568	D 1 - 1	H.Elmes 18	8
27	18		H	Bury Town	221	D 2 - 2	Santag 58 H.Elmes 90	
28	22		A	Horsham	219	W 3 - 1	King 56 89 Cowley 84	7
29	29		H	Wealdstone	162	L 1 - 6	H.Elmes 65	10
30	31		A	Kingstonian	257	W 3 - 0	Ogilvie 6 White 50 Stokes 73	
31	Feb 5		A	Tooting & Mitcham	230	L 2 - 3	Stokes 16 Miller 90	10
32	8		A	Tonbridge Angles	388	L 2 - 3	H.Elmes 11 46	
33	12		H	Harrow Borough	183	W 3 - 0	Stokes 17 J.Elmes 22 59	10
34	15		H	Cray Wanderers	191	W 2 - 0	Stokes 5 J.Elmes 44	
35	22		H	Canvey Island	720	W 1 - 0	Sienna 90	
36	26		H	AFC Hornchurch	234	L 1 - 3	Stokes 40	6
37	March 5		A	Cray Wanderers	127	L 1 - 2	Stokes 82	9
38	12		H	Kingstonian	223	W 2 - 1	Stokes 49 Miller 68	8
39	19		A	Bury Town	462	W 2 - 1	H.Elmes 21 Stokes 43	9
40	22		A	Margate	236	W 2 - 1	Stokes 20 King 50	
41	26		H	Carshalton Athletic	164	D 1 - 1	H.Elmes 47	7
42	April 2		A	Wealdstone	425	W 3 - 1	J.Elmes 11 King 34 Stokes 59	6
43	9		H	Horsham	162	W 2 - 0	Stokes 40 Ogilvie 70	6
44	16		A	Maidstone UNited	407	L 0 - 2		8
45	22		H	Aveley	194	L 0 - 1		9
46	26		A	Canvey Island	1163	W 4 - 0	Stokes 13 75 King 31 Begg 90	
47	30		H	Croydon Athletic	184	W 3 - 0	H.Elmes 1 Stokes 37 Ogilvie 77	8

CRAY WANDERERS

Chairman: Gary Hillman
Secretary: Kerry Phillips **(T)** 07718 353 583 **(E)** kerryphillips@hotmail.com
Additional Committee Members:
Martin Hodson, Jerry Dowlen

Manager: Ian Jenkins
Programme Editor: Jerry Dowlen **(E)** jerry.dowlen@btopenworld.net

Back Row (L-R): John Woolf, Joe Francis (Coach), Jerome Maledon, Delano Sam-Yorke, Mark Willy, George Porter, John Guest, Jack Smelt, Arron Day, Tommy Tyne, Rob Quinn, Tyrone Sterling, Steve Aris, Mike Reeves (Sports Therapist).
Front Row (L-R) Zak Goldsmith, Shane Graham, Leigh Bremner, Jamie Wood, Lewis Wood, Colin Luckett, Ian Jenkins, Paul Blade (Director of Football)

Club Factfile

Founded: 1860 **Nickname:** Wanderers or Wands
Previous Names: Cray Old Boys (immediately after WW1); Sidcup & Footscray (start of WW2).
Previous Leagues: Kent 1894-1903, 1906-07, 1909-1914, 1934-38, 1978-2004; West Kent & South Suburban Leagues (before WW1); London 1920-1934, 1951-1959; Kent Amateur 1938-1939, 1946-1951; South London Alliance 1943-1946; Aetolian 1959-1964; Greater London 1964-1966; Metropolitan 1966-1971; Met. London 1971-1975; London Spartan 1975-1978.
Club Colours (change): Amber/black/black.

Ground: Bromley FC, Hayes Lane, Bromley, Kent BR2 9EF **(T)** 020 8460 5291
Capacity: 5,000 **Seats:** 1,300 **Covered:** 2,500 **Clubhouse:** Yes **Shop:** Yes

Directions
From M25: Leaving the motorway at junction 4, follow the A21 to Bromley and London, for approximately 4 miles and then fork left onto the A232 signposted Croydon/Sutton. At the second set of traffic lights, turn right into Baston Road (B265), following it for about two miles as it becomes Hayes Street and then Hayes Lane. Cray Wanderers FC is on the right hand side of the road just after the mini roundabout. There is ample room for coaches to drive down the driveway, turn round and park.

Previous Grounds: Star Lane (1860s), Derry Downs (until 1898), Fordcroft (1898-1936), Twysdens (1936-1939), St Mary Cray Rec (1940s),
Previous Grounds: Cont. Northfield Farm (1950-51), Tothills (aka Fordcroft, 1951-1955), Grassmeade (1955-1973), Oxford Road (1973-1998).

Record Attendance: (Grassmeade) 2,160vLeytonstone – FA Am.C 3rd Rd, 1968-69; (Oxford R) 1,523vStamford – FAV QF 79-80; (Hayes L) 1,082vAFC Wim. – 04-05
Record Victory: 15-0 v Sevenoaks - 1894-95.
Record Defeat: 2-15 (H) and 0-14 (A) v Callenders Athletic - Kent Amateur League, 1947-48.
Record Goalscorer: Ken Collishaw 274 (1954-1965)
Record Appearances: John Dorey - 500 (1961-72).
Additional Records: Unbeaten for 28 Ryman League games in 2007-2008.

Senior Honours: Kent League 1901-02, 80-81, 2002-03, 03-04 (League Cup 83-84, 2002-03); London League 1956-57, 57-58 (League Cup 54-55); Aetolian League 1962-63 (League Cup 63-64); Greater London League 1965-66 (League Cup 64-65, 65-66); Met. Lge Cup 1970-71; Met. London League & League Cup 1974-75; London Spartan League 1976-77, 77-78. Kent Amateur Cup 1930-31, 62-63, 63-64, 64-65. Kent Senior Trophy 1992-93, 2003-04.

10 YEAR RECORD

01-02		02-03		03-04		04-05		05-06		06-07		07-08		08-09		09-10		10-11	
Kent P	5	Kent P	1	Kent P	1	Isth1	6	Isth1	11	Isth1S	12	Isth1S	3	Isth1S	2	Isth P	15	Isth P	9

CRAY WANDERERS

No.	Date	Comp	H/A	Opponents	Att:	Result	Goalscorers	Pos
1	Aug 21	Isth Prem	A	AFC Hornchurch	226	L 0 - 1		17
2	28		H	Tooting & Mitcham United	254	L 2 - 3	Hamici 48 Cottrell 79	20
3	30		A	Hastings United	574	D 1 - 1	Hamici 76	
4	Sept 4		H	Harrow Borough	178	W 5 - 1	HAMICI 3 (5 65 90) Perkins 24 Saunders 83	15
5	7		A	Bury Town	439	D 2 - 2	Hamici 54 Perkins 79	
6	**12**	**FAC 1Q**	**H**	**South Park**	**150**	**W 1 - 0**	**Hamici 90**	
7	18		H	Canvey Island	189	D 0 - 0		18
8	21		A	Tonbridge Angels	328	W 4 - 0	HAMICI 3 (58 82 85) Gibbs 64	
9	**25**	**FAC 2Q**	**H**	**Ebbsfleet United**	**408**	**D 2 - 2**	**Phillips 30 Hamici 75**	
10	**28**	**FAC 2Qr**	**A**	**Ebbsfleet United**	**535**	**L 2 - 4**	**Lozano 48 Bremner 78**	
11	Oct 2		A	Aveley	137	W 3 - 0	Lover 16 Guyut 30 Willy 81	9
12	5		H	Maidstone United	234	W 2 - 1	Bremner 35 Lover 70	
13	9		H	Folkestone Invicta	223	L 0 - 1		10
14	**16**	**FAT 1Q**	**H**	**Wingate & Finchley**	**98**	**W 2 - 1**	**Day 85 Lover 90**	
15	23		A	Sutton United	497	D 1 - 1	Lover 5	
16	26		A	Billericay Town	221	L 2 - 3	Saunders 43 Lover 70	12
17	**30**	**FAT 2Q**	**H**	**Maidstone United**	**224**	**L 1 - 2**	**Willy 53**	
18	Nov 2		H	Carshalton Athletic		W 2 - 1	Lover 71 (pen) Hamici 83	
19	7		H	Wealdstone	198	W 1 - 2	Hamici 54	
20	9		A	Maidstone United		W 4 - 0	Lozano 23 Saunders 63 Phillips 79 Hamici 84	
21	14		H	Aveley	167	W 3 - 4	Lozano 3 Lover 18 38	4
22	20		A	Canvey Island	314	L 2 - 1	Willy 74 McLeod 90	5
23	23		H	Tonbridge Angels	203	L 0 - 1		7
24	Dec 11		H	Croydon Athletic	169	W 4 - 0	BREMNER 3 (5 9 87) Ashton 90	4
25	27		A	Margate	371	W 2 - 0	Willy 62 Laurent 64	
26	Jan 1		H	Hastings United	276	W 2 - 0	Bremner 6 Hamici 9	2
27	16		H	AFC Hornchurch	227	L 1 - 2	Sterling 77	
28	23		H	Kingstonian	253	W 2 - 0	Saunders 7 Guest 62	3
29	25		H	Lowestoft Town	143	L 0 - 1		
30	29		A	Hendon	151	D 2 - 2	Munnelly 8 (og) Saunders 61	5
31	Feb 5		H	Sutton United	269	L 0 - 2		7
32	8		A	Horsham	144	W 4 - 0	Gibbs 10 Dolby 45 (pen) 86 Philips 63	
33	12		A	Folkestone Invicta	243	D 1 - 1	Hamici 75	5
34	15		A	Concord Rangers	191	L 0 - 2		
35	March 1		A	Carshalton Athletic	100	D 1 - 1	Hamici 43 (pen)	
36	5		H	Concord Rangers	127	W 2 - 1	Dolby 66 Bremner 77	8
37	12		A	Lowestoft Town	824	W 1 - 0	Willy 76	7
38	19		H	Horsham	116	D 1 - 1	Vines 5	10
39	22		H	Billericay Town	191	L 1 - 3	Bremner 45	
40	26		A	Croydon Athletic	86	L 1 - 3	Hamici 78	11
41	April 2		H	Hendon	162	W 3 - 1	Bremner 14 Hamici 26 86	11
42	4		A	Wealdstone	351	W 1 - 0	Hamici 45	
9	9		A	Kingstonian	304	L 1 - 2	Phllips 32	11
44	17		H	Bury Town	302	W 2 - 1	Guest 21 Bremner 45	
45	22		A	Tooting & Mitcham	323	W 3 - 0	Bremner 30 Hamici 62 Dolby 85	8
46	26		H	Margate	199	W 2 - 0	Bremner 60 90	
47	30		A	Harrow Borough	290	D 1 - 1	Day 86	9

Come On Wombles....

....but can you spot a 'genuine' Womble!!!

Photo by Peter Barnes

EAST THURROCK UNITED

Chairman: Brian Mansbridge
Secretary: Neil Speight **(T)** 0788 531 3435 **(E)** speight.n@sky.com
Additional Committee Members:
Mick Stephens, Ian Simes

Manager: John Coventry
Programme Editor: Neil Speight **(E)** speight.n@sky.com

Club Factfile

Founded: 1969 **Nickname:** Rocks
Previous Names: Corringham Social > 1969 (Sunday side)
Previous Leagues: South Essex Combination, Greater London, Metropolitan 1972-75, London Spartan 1975-79, Essex Senior 1979-92, Isthmian 1992-2004, Southern 2004-05

Club Colours (change): Amber with black trim/black/black

Ground: Rookery Hill, Corringham, Essex SS17 9LB **(T)** 01375 644 166
Capacity: 4,000 **Seats:** 160 **Covered:** 1,000 **Clubhouse:** Yes **Shop:** No

Directions
From A13 London-Southend road,
take A1014 at Stanford-le-Hope for two and half miles,
Ground is on the left.

Previous Grounds: Billet, Stanford-le-Hope 1970-73, 74-76, Grays Athletic 1973-74, Tilbury FC 1977-82, New Thames Club 1982-84

Record Attendance: 1,215 v Woking FA Cup 2003
Record Victory: 7-0 v Coggeshall (H) - Essex Senior League 1984
Record Defeat: 0-9 v Eton Manor (A) - Essex Senior League 1982
Record Goalscorer: Graham Stewart - 102
Record Appearances: Glen Case - 600+
Additional Records: £22,000 from Leyton Orient for Greg Berry 1990

Senior Honours: Isthmian League Division Three 1999-2000, Division One North 2010-11. East Anglian Cup 2002-03.

10 YEAR RECORD

01-02	02-03	03-04	04-05	05-06	06-07	07-08	08-09	09-10	10-11
Isth2 8	Isth1N 17	Isth1N 12	SthE 2	Isth P 12	Isth P 16	Isth P 20	Isth1N 2	Isth1N 5	Isth1N 1

HARROW BOROUGH

Chairman: Peter Rogers
Secretary: Peter Rogers **(T)** 0795 618 5685 **(E)** peter@harrowboro.co.uk
Additional Committee Members:
Stuart Hobbs

Manager: Dave Anderson
Programme Editor: Peter Rogers **(E)** peter@harroboro.co.uk

Club Factfile

Founded: 1933 **Nickname:** Boro
Previous Names: Roxonian 1933-38, Harrow Town 1938-66
Previous Leagues: Harrow & District 1933-34, Spartan 1934-40, 45-58, West Middlesex Combination 1940-41, Middlesex Senior 1941-45, Delphian 1956-63, Athenian 1963-75

Club Colours (change): Red with white/red/red

Ground: Earlsmead, Carlyon Avenue, South Harrow HA2 8SS **(T)** 0844 561 1347
Capacity: 3,070 **Seats:** 350 **Covered:** 1,000 **Clubhouse:** Yes **Shop:** Yes

Directions
From the M25 junction 16, take the M40 East towards Uxbridge and London. Continue onto A40, passing Northolt Aerodrome on the left hand side. At the Target Roundabout junction (A312) turn left towards Northolt.
Just after passing Northolt Underground Station on the left hand side, turn left at the next set of traffic lights, onto Eastcote Lane, becoming Field End Road.
At next roundabout, turn right onto Eastcote Lane. At a small parade of shops, take the turning on the right into Carlyon Avenue. Earlsmead is the second turning on the right.

Previous Grounds:

Record Attendance: 3,000 v Wealdstone - FA Cup 1st Qualifying Road 1946
Record Victory: 13-0 v Handley Page (A) - 18/10/1941
Record Defeat: 0-8 on five occasions
Record Goalscorer: Dave Pearce - 153
Record Appearances: Les Currell - 582, Colin Payne - 557, Steve Emmanuel - 522
Additional Records:

Senior Honours: Isthmian League 1983-84.
Middlesex Senior Cup 1982-83, 92-93. Middlesex Premier Cup 1981-82.
Middlesex Senior Charity Cup 1979-80, 92-93, 2005-06, 06-07

10 YEAR RECORD

01-02	02-03	03-04	04-05	05-06	06-07	07-08	08-09	09-10	10-11
Isth P 21	Isth P 18	Isth P 17	Isth P 16	Isth P 16	Isth P 19	Isth P 16	Isth P 14	Isth P 14	Isth P 5

HARROW BOROUGH

No.	Date	Comp	H/A	Opponents	Att:	Result	Goalscorers	Pos
1	Aug 21	Isth Prem	H	Maidstone United	222	W 2 - 0	R.Baptiste 14 Nakashima 66	4
2	24		A	Canvey Island	220	L 0 - 2		
3	28		A	Tonbridge Angels	349	W 2 - 1	McGonigle 27 R.Baptiste 69	6
4	30		H	Hendon	235	L 2 - 3	Hewitt 45 Marney 72	
5	Sept 4		A	Cray Wanderers	178	L 1 - 5	Coleman 10 (og)	12
6	7		H	Lowestoft Town	165	W 2 - 0	Hewitt 64 Morlese 86	
7	**11**	**FAC 1Q**	**A**	**Great Wakering**		**W 4 - 2**	**R.Baptiste 25 Judd 35 (og) Hewitt 55 Dixon 69**	
8	18		H	Billericay Town	285	D 1 - 1	R.Baptiste 85	9
9	21		A	Sutton United	478	L 1 - 2	Clarke 40	12
10	**25**	**FAC 2Q**	**A**	**Redbridge**	**82**	**W 2 - 1**	**R.Baptiste 34 Morlese 76**	
11	Oct 2		A	Hastings United	374	L 0 - 2		14
12	5		H	Aveley	101	L 1 - 2	Watts 63	
13	**9**	**FAC 3Q**	**H**	**Hampton & Richmond B**	**342**	**W 2 - 1**	**R.Baptiste 2**	
14	**16**	**FAT 1Q**	**H**	**Hendon**	**174**	**L 0 - 1**		
15	**23**	**FAC 4Q**	**A**	**Eastbourne Borough**	**681**	**W 4 - 2**	**R.Baptiste 5 HEWITT 3 (21 30 49)**	
16	30		H	Concord Rangers	110	L 0 - 2		18
17	**Nov 6**	**FAC 1**	**H**	**Chesterfield**	**1050**	**L 0 - 2**		
18	8		A	Aveley	141	W 2 - 0	Hewitt 69 Clarke 84	
19	13		H	Hastings United	132	D 2 - 2	Hewitt 45 McConigle 77	
20	20		H	Croydon Athletic	112	W 3 - 0	Hewitt 21 Walters 61 R.Baptiste 90	17
21	23		H	Sutton United	163	D 0 - 0		
22	Dec 12		A	Kingstonian	319	W 3 - 1	Marney 9 Watts 34 Nakashima 34	
23	14		A	Billericay Town	165	W 3 - 1	R.Baptiste 2 29 King 56	13
24	Jan 1		A	Hendon	206	W 3 - 0	J.Reading 52 (og) Hewitt 67 Clarke 90	10
25	8		H	Canvey Island	151	W 6 - 1	R.Baptiste 5 (pen) Hewitt 7 78 Nakashima 19 McGonigle 49 51	
26	15		A	Maidstone United	320	D 0 - 0		10
27	18		A	Horsham	188	W 7 - 1	R.BAPTISTE 3 (10 42 87) Ijaha 19 McGonigle 27 Nakashima 45 Hewitt 89	
28	22		A	Folkestone Invicta	209	L 0 - 1		9
29	25		H	Carshalton Athletic	125	W 2 - 1	R.Baptiste 50 Watts 90	
30	29		H	Margate	144	D 0 - 0		7
31	Feb 1		A	Bury Town	502	W 5 - 2	Hewitt 18 77 Watts 67 Ilaha 69 McGonigle75	
32	5		H	Horsham	155	W 6 - 0	R.BAPTISTE 4 (36 50 58 pen 89) Hewitt 13 83	
33	12		A	Concord Rangers	183	L 0 - 3		8
34	22		A	AFC Hornchurch	148	L 0 - 2		
35	March 1		H	Wealdstone	337	L 2 - 4	Clarke 37 Nakashima 74	
36	5		A	Carshalton Athletic	200	W 1 - 0	R.Baptiste 28	11
37	12		H	AFC Hornchurch	171	W 1 - 0	Walters 45	11
38	15		H	Tooting & Mitcham U	148	W 2 - 0	R.Baptiste 9 Morlese18	
39	19		A	Tooting & Mitcham U	235	L 2 - 3	Morlese 4 R.Baptiste 90 (pen)	11
40	22		H	Bury Town	145	W 2 - 0	Walters 6 Hart 63	
41	26		H	Kingstonian	340	W 1 - 0	Nakashima 10	6
42	30		A	Croydon Athletic	98	W 3 - 1	Walters 15 Nakashima 41 Delgado 58	
43	April 2		A	Margate	308	W 3 - 2	Nakashima 46 84 Clarke 55	3
44	9		H	Folkestone Invicta	171	W 2 - 0	Nakashima 40 53	3
45	16		A	Lowestoft Town	724	L 0 - 3		5
46	23		H	Tonbridge Angels	362	W 2 - 0	R.Baptiste 32 Hart 44	3
47	26		A	Wealdstone	765	D 1 - 1	R.Baptiste 48 (pen)	
48	30		H	Cray Wanderers	290	D 1 - 1	Jinadu 46	5
49	**May 3**	**P-Off SF**	**A**	**Tonbridge Angels**	**1124**	**L 2 - 3**	**R.Baptiste 26 69**	

HASTINGS UNITED

Chairman: David Walters
Secretary: Tony Cosens **(T)** 0771 265 4288 **(E)** richardcosens@btinternet.com
Additional Committee Members:
Sean Adams, Louise Freeman

Manager: Jason Hopkinsin
Programme Editor: Marie O'Mara **(E)** flio10@yahoo.co.uk

Club Factfile

Founded: 1894 **Nickname:** The Us
Previous Names: Hastings and St Leonards Amateurs, Hastings Town > 2002
Previous Leagues: South Eastern 1904-05, Southern 1905-10, Sussex County 1921-27, 52-85, Southern Amateur 1927-46, Corinthian 1946-48

Club Colours (change): Claret with blue sleeves/white/white

Ground: The Pilot Field, Elphinstone Road, Hastings TN34 2AX **(T)** 01424 444 635
Capacity: 4,050 **Seats:** 800 **Covered:** 1,750 **Clubhouse:** Yes **Shop:** Yes

Directions
From A1 turn left at third roundabout into St Helens Road. Then left after one mile into St Helens Park Road leading into Downs Road. Turn left at T-junction at the end of the road. Ground is 200 yards on the right.

Previous Grounds: Bulverhythe Recreation > 1976

Record Attendance: 4,888 v Nottingham Forest - Friendly 23/06/1996
Record Victory: Not Known
Record Defeat: Not Known
Record Goalscorer: Terry White scored 33 during 1999-2000
Record Appearances: Not Known
Additional Records: Paid £8,000 to Ashford Town for Nicky Dent
Received £30,000 from Nottingham Forest for Paul Smith

Senior Honours: Southern League Division 1 1991-92, 2001-01, League Cup 1994-95.

10 YEAR RECORD

01-02	02-03	03-04	04-05	05-06	06-07	07-08	08-09	09-10	10-11
SthE 1	SthP 20	SthE 18	Isth1 11	Isth1 12	Isth1S 4	Isth P 14	Isth P 17	Isth P 7	Isth P 18

HASTINGS TOWN

No.	Date	Comp	H/A	Opponents	Att:	Result	Goalscorers	Pos
1	Aug 21	Isth Prem	H	Wealdstone	563	W 2 - 0	Ray 60 Pogue 65	5
2	25		A	Maidstone United	372	W 4 - 2	A.Olorundo 45 65 Adams 45 Pogue 76	
3	28		A	Hendon	173	D 0 - 0		1
4	30		H	Cray Wanderers	574	D 1 - 1	Adams 84 (pen)	
5	Sept 4		A	Aveley	214	W 3 - 1	Pogue 73 Olorundo 74 Logan 84	4
6	7		H	Sutton United	541	L 2 - 3	Ray 70 A.Olorundo 78	
7	**11**	**FAC 1Q**	**A**	**Bognor Regis Town**	**374**	**L 2 - 3**	**Eldridge 24 Richardson 28**	
8	18		A	Bury Town	530	L 1 - 2	Ray 89	6
9	21		H	Concord Rangers	437	L 0 - 3		10
10	Oct 2		H	Harrow Borough	374	W 2 - 0	A.Olorundo 68 Phillips 73	7
11	5		A	Carshalton Athletic	219	D 1 - 1	Beales 18	
12	9		A	Tooting & Mitcham	282	D 1 - 1	Phillips 70 (pen)	7
13	**16**	**FAT 1Q**	**A**	**Dulwich Hamlet**	**216**	**D 2 - 2**	**Beales 8 Logan 81**	
14	**19**	**FAT 1Qr**	**H**	**Dulwich Hamlet**	**243**	**L 1 - 2**	**Pogue 71**	
15	23		H	Lowestoft Town	418	D 0 - 0		8
16	26		H	AFC Hornchurch		L 0 - 1		
17	Nov 7		A	Kingstonian	329	L 1 - 3	Beales 69	
18	9		H	Carshalton Athletic	267	L 0 - 1		
19	13		A	Harrow Borough	329	D 2 - 2	Adams 39 Phillips 68	
20	20		H	Bury Town	314	L 0 - 2		14
21	23		A	Concord Rangers	112	L 1 - 2	Code 74	16
22	Dec 11		H	Horsham	251	L 2 - 3	Eldridge 66 Pogue 69	17
23	Jan 1		A	Cray Wanderers	276	L 0 - 2		18
24	8		H	Maidstone United	208	L 1 - 2	Eldridge 25	
25	19		A	Croydon Athletic	102	L 0 - 2		
26	22		A	Margate	298	L 0 - 2		19
27	24		A	Wealdstone	340	L 1 - 2	Millwood 84	
28	29		H	Canvey Island	325	L 0 - 1		19
29	Feb 1		H	Folkestone Invicta	287	D 2 - 2	Eldridge 35 Adams 73 (pen)	
30	5		A	Lowestoft Town	695	D 1 - 1	Adams 53	
31	8		H	Tooting & Mitcham	403	W 3 - 2	Adams 19 (pen) 27 (pen) Porter 53	18
32	15		A	Billericay Town	203	L 0 - 3		
33	22		H	Tonbridge Angels	562	L 1 - 2	Perkins 63	
34	March 5		H	Billericay Town	363	W 1 - 0	Rowe 43	18
35	12		A	Folkestone Invicta	328	W 3 - 1	Eldridge 15 Rowe 76 Poque 86	
36	15		A	AFC Hornchurch	168	L 0 - 1		
37	19		H	Croydon Athletic	352	W 3 - 1	Adams 42 58 (pen) Ray 69	18
38	22		H	Kingstonian	360	L 1 - 2	Porter 61	
39	26		A	Horsham	251	D 1 - 1	Rowe 65	18
40	April 2		A	Canvey Island	501	D 2 - 2	Adams 11 Beautyman 35	18
41	9		H	Margate	434	W 3 - 0	Pogue 32 Jirbandy45 Billings 90	17
42	16		A	Sutton United	1552	L 1 - 2	Beautyman 62	18
43	23		H	Hendon	431	D 1 - 1	Adams 42 (pen)	18
44	26		A	Tonbridge Angels	817	L 0 - 2		
45	30		H	Aveley	737	L 2 - 3	Hopkinson 74 Jerbandy 83	18

HENDON

Chairman: Simon Lawrence
Secretary: Graham Etchell (T) 0797 369 8552 (E) hendonfc@freenetname.co.uk
Additional Committee Members:
Steve Rogers, David Balheimer

Manager: Gary McCann
Programme Editor: Steve Rogers (E) steve_rogers2506@btinternet.com

Back Row: Parker, Hudson, Reading, Vargas, Cousins, C.Maclaren.
Front Row: Aite-Ouakrim, Burgess, Busby, Munnelley, Morgan. Photo: Andrew Aleksiejczuk.

Club Factfile

Founded: 1908 **Nickname:** Dons or Greens
Previous Names: Christ Church Hampstead > 1908, Hampstead Town > 1933, Golders Green > 1946
Previous Leagues: Finchley & District 1908-11, Middlesex 1910-11, London 1911-14, Athenian 1914-63

Club Colours (change): All green & white

Ground: Wembley FC, Vale Farm, Watford Road, Wembley HA0 3HG (T) 020 8908 3553
Capacity: 2,450 **Seats:** 350 **Covered:** 950 **Clubhouse:** Yes **Shop:**

Directions
400 yards from Sudbury Town underground station.
Or 10 minutes walk from North Wembley BR.

Previous Grounds: Claremont Road

Record Attendance: 9,000 v Northampton Town - FA Cup 1st Round 1952
Record Victory: 13-1 v Wingate - Middlesex County Cup 02/02/1957
Record Defeat: 2-11 v Walthamstowe Avenue, Athenian League 09/11/1935
Record Goalscorer: Freddie Evans - 176 (1929-35)
Record Appearances: Bill Fisher - 787 - (1940-64)
Additional Records: Received £30,000 from Luton Town for Iain Dowie

Senior Honours: FA Amateur Cup 1959-60, 64-65, 71-72. Isthmian League 1964-65, 72-73. European Amateur Champions 1972-73. Athenian League x3. London Senior Cup 1963-64, 68-69. Middlesex Senior Cup x14

10 YEAR RECORD

01-02	02-03	03-04	04-05	05-06	06-07	07-08	08-09	09-10	10-11
Isth P 8	Isth P 3	Isth P 4	Isth P 11	Isth P 19	Isth P 14	Isth P 7	Isth P 16	Isth P 10	Isth P 15

HENDON

No.	Date	Comp	H/A	Opponents	Att:	Result	Goalscorers	Pos
1	Aug 21	Isth Prem	A	Tooting & Mitcham United	331	L 3 - 4	O'Leary 32 Morgan 54 82	16
2	24		H	Concord Rangers	165	W 4 - 1	AITE-OUAKRIM 4 (37 65 72 82)	
3	28		H	Hastings United	173	D 0 - 0		10
4	30		A	Harrow Borough	235	W 3 - 2	Morgan 4 Guentchev 78 (pen) 88 (pen)	
5	Sept 4		H	Carshalton Athletic	201	W 1 - 0	Serwin 82	6
6	7		A	Horsham	151	W 2 - 1	Guentchev 27 Busby 81 (pen)	
7	**12**	**FAC 1Q**	**H**	**Cheshunt**	**182**	**W 4 - 1**	**Aite-Quakrim 55 Morgan 57 89 Busby 59**	
8	18		A	AFC Hornchurch	260	D 0 - 0		
9	20		H	Kingstonian	215	L 2 - 3	O'Leary 31 Busby 74	6
10	**26**	**FAC 2Q**	**H**	**Maldon &Tiptree**	**166**	**W 2 - 1**	**Busby 12 Morgan 51**	
11	Oct 2		H	Croydon Athletic	130	W 4 - 0	Wishart 25 45 Busby 45 Aite-Quakrim 84	5
12	5		A	Bury Town	487	D 2 - 2	Aite-Quakrim14 60	
13	**9**	**FAC 3Q**	**A**	**Whitehawk**	**178**	**W 2 - 1**	**Aite-Quakrim 14 Morgan 14**	
14	**16**	**FAT 1Q**	**A**	**Harrow Borough**	**174**	**W 1 - 0**	**O'Leary 63**	
15	19		A	Maidstone United	171	D 2 - 2	McLaren C 55 Busby 69 (pen)	8
16	**23**	**FAC 4Q**	**H**	**Metropolitan Police**	**269**	**D 0 - 0**		
17	**27**	**FAC 4Qr**	**A**	**Metropolitan Police**	**302**	**W 2 - 0**	**Aite-Quakrim 27 MacLaren 32**	
18	**30**	**FAT 2Q**	**A**	**AFC Sudbury**	**289**	**L 1 - 5**	**Guentchev 16**	
19	**Nov 6**	**FAC 1**	**A**	**Chelmsford City**	**1685**	**L 2 - 3**	**Busby 43 (pen) 80**	
20	9		H	Bury Town	139	D 3 - 3	Coulson 35 (og) Parker 82 Busby 89	12
21	13		A	Croydon Athletic	91	W 4 - 1	Coke 15 C.McLaren 45 Busby 49 Wishart 58	
22	Dec 11		H	Folkestone Invicta	157	W 2 - 1	Guentchev 21 Haule 71	10
23	Jan 1		H	Harrow Borough	206	L 0 - 3		11
24	8		A	Concord Rangers	181	L 2 - 3	Aite-Quakrim 39 52	13
25	11		A	Tonbridge Angels	267	L 1 - 2	Aite-Quakrim 10	
26	15		H	Tooting & Mitcham	172	W 4 - 1	Guentchev 28 40 Munnelly 84 O'Leary 88	12
27	22		A	Wealdstone	428	L 0 - 1		14
28	25		A	Margate	162	D 1 - 1	Busby 88	
29	29		H	Cray Wanderers	151	D 2 - 2	Ngoyi 51 Dyer 75	15
30	31		A	Aveley	150	W 2 - 0	Peacock 4 Ngoyi 60	
31	Feb 5		A	Canvey Island	309	L 1 - 4	Busby 12	
32	12		H	Maidstone United	177	L 2 - 3	Morgan 20 C.McLaren 76	16
33	16		H	Sutton United	167	W 1 - 0	Morgan 45	
34	19		A	Lowestoft Town	629	L 1 - 8	Aite-Quakrim 53	14
35	22		A	Billericay Town	219	L 0 - 2		
36	28		A	KIngstonian	271	L 0 - 3		
37	March 5		H	Aveley	123	L 1 - 2	Haule 33	
38	12		A	Sutton United	586	L 0 - 3		16
39	15		H	Lowestoft Town	125	D 1 - 1	Aite-Quakrim17	
40	19		H	Margate	164	L 2 - 3	Aite-Quakrim 52 Busby 58 (pen)	16
41	22		H	AFC Hornchurch	141	W 2 - 1	Ngoyi 45 81	
42	26		A	Folkestone	202	W 2 - 1	Aite-Quakrim 75 87	14
43	28		H	Canvey Island	170	L 0 - 3		
44	April 2		A	Cray Wanderers	162	L 1 - 3	K.MacLaren 57	15
45	9		H	Wealdstone	251	L 0 - 1		15
46	12		H	Tonbridge Angels	149	L 0 - 3		
47	16		H	Horsham	252	L 0 - 3		16
48	23		A	Hastings United	431	D 1 - 1	Diedhiou 65	15
49	26		H	Billericay Town	156	D 1 - 1	Busby 23	
50	30		A	Carshalton Athletic	211	L 1 - 2	Morgan 16	15

HORSHAM

Chairman: Kevin Borrett
Secretary: John Lines **(T)** 0772 141 8889 **(E)** linesj@tesco.net
Additional Committee Members:
Annie Raby, Adam Hammond, Tim Hewlett

Manager: Justin Luchford
Programme Editor: Adam Hammond **(E)** adam@horshampress.co.uk

HORSHAM FC 2010 - 2011
Back Row L to R. George Magnus, Steve Davies, Tom Graves, Jamal King, Jay Lovett, Alan Tait, Paul Kennett
Middle Row L to R. Darren Etheridge, Steve Elliott, Jack Page, Rob Frankland, Ben Andrews (Capt) Mark Zawadski, Steve Sargent, John Westcott, Chris Copestack, Mark Hawthorne, (Coach)
Front Row L to R. Adam Hutchings, Pat Harding, Dean Wright, John Maggs (Manager) Sam Tucknott, Mark Knee, Gary Charman

Club Factfile

Founded: 1881 **Nickname:** Hornets
Previous Names:
Previous Leagues: West Susses Senior, Sussex County 1926-51, Metropolitan 1951-57, Corinthian 1957-63, Athenian 1963-73

Club Colours (change): Amber and green halves/green/amber

Ground: Horsham YMCA, Gorings Mead, Horsham RH13 5BP **(T)** 01403 266 888
Capacity: 1,575 **Seats:** 150 **Covered:** 200 **Clubhouse:** Yes **Shop:**

Directions
From the east, take A281 (Brighton Road, and the ground is on the left and sign posted opposite Gorings Mead.

Previous Grounds: Horsham Park, Hurst Park, Springfield Park

Record Attendance: 8,000 v Swindon - FA Cup 1st Round Novmber 1966
Record Victory: 16-1 v Southwick - Sussex County League 1945-46
Record Defeat: 1-11 v Worthing - Sussex Senior Cup 1913-14
Record Goalscorer: Mick Browning
Record Appearances: Mark Stepney
Additional Records:

Senior Honours: Athenian League Division 1 1972-73. Sussex Senior Cup x7

10 YEAR RECORD

01-02	02-03	03-04	04-05	05-06	06-07	07-08	08-09	09-10	10-11
Isth2 2	Isth1S 8	Isth1S 15	Isth1 3	Isth1 2	Isth1S 9	Isth P 11	Isth P 13	Isth P 11	Isth P 17

HORSHAM

No.	Date	Comp	H/A	Opponents	Att:	Result	Goalscorers	Pos
1	Aug 21	Isth Prem	H	Aveley	290	D 0 - 0		13
2	24		A	Sutton United	529	L 0 - 2		
3	28		A	Wealdstone	383	L 0 - 3		19
4	30		H	Kingstonian	372	L 2 - 3	Lovett 17 Andrews 73	
5	Sept 4		A	Tonbridge Angels	435	L 0 - 2		22
6	7		H	Hendon	151	L 1 - 2	Tait 37	
7	**11**	**FAC 1Q**	**A**	**Folkestone Invicta**	**327**	**L 2 - 4**	**Davies 78 Harding 90**	
8	18		H	Folkestone Invicta	650	D 0 - 0		22
9	25		A	Maidstone United	249	W 1 - 0	Knee 18	22
10	Oct 2		A	Billericay Town	317	L 1 - 2	Page 21	22
11	5		H	Tooting & Mitcham	226	W 1 - 0	Harding 74	
12	9		A	Margate	347	L 1 - 6	Andrews 36	21
13	**16**	**FAT 1Q**	**H**	**Redbridge**	**188**	**W 3 - 0**	**Davies 13 75 Tait 90**	
14	**30**	**FAT 2Q**	**A**	**Truro City**	**381**	**L 0 - 2**		
15	Nov 6		A	Lowestoft Town	683	L 0 - 4		22
16	9		A	Tooting & Mitcham U		W 2 - 1	Charman 90 Butler 90 (pen)	
17	13		H	Billericay Town	281	L 1 - 2	Hector 52	20
18	23		H	Maidstone United	213	D 1 - 1	Dunn 64	
19	27		H	Canvey Island	228	D 1 - 1	Storey 68	
20	Dec 7		A	Folkestone invcta	142	D 0 - 0		
21	11		A	Hastings United	251	W 3 - 2	CHARMAN 3 (12 42 55)	18
22	14		H	Carshalton Athletic	182	W 2 - 1	Cade 65 83	
23	Jan 3		A	Kingstonian	410	W 3 - 1	Graham 30 Harding 38 Storey 40	
24	8		H	Sutton United	416	W 3 - 1	Dunn 8 Cade 11 Harding 59	14
25	15		A	Aveley	150	L 0 - 1		
26	18		H	Harrow Borough	188	L 1 - 7	Charman 8	
27	22		H	Concord Rangers	219	L 1 - 3	Andrews 6	17
28	29		A	AFC Hornchurch	235	W 2 - 0	Kennett 4 Dunn 88	
29	Feb 5		A	Harrow Borough	155	L 0 - 6		17
30	8		H	Cray Wanderers	144	L 0 - 4		
31	12		H	Margate	222	D 1 - 1	Charman 48	17
32	15		A	Bury Town	339	L 0 - 2		
33	19		A	Carshalton Athletic	206	D 0 - 0		17
34	26		H	Lowestoft Town	236	L 1 - 2	Pearoux 43	17
35	March 5		A	Canvey Island	327	L 1 - 3	Cade 89	
36	8		H	Croydon Athletic	151	D 1 - 1	Cade 20	
37	12		H	Bury Town	217	L 1 - 4	Harding 44	17
38	19		A	Cray Wanderers	116	D 1 - 1	Storey 84	17
39	26		H	Hastings United	251	D 1 - 1	Robinson 11	17
40	April 2		H	AFC Hornchurch	190	D 0 - 0		17
41	9		A	Concord Rangers	162	L 0 - 2		18
42	16		A	Hendon	252	W 3 - 0	Brotherton 20 Cade 80 Kennett 86	17
43	23		H	Wealdstone	286	W 2 - 1	Cade 37 Brotherton 68 (pen)	17
44	26		A	Croydon Athletic	108	W 4 - 2	Cade 36 74 Sefoah 55 (og) Graves 59	
45	30		H	Tonbridge Angels	492	L 0 - 2		17

KINGSTONIAN

Chairman: John Fenwick
Secretary: Gerry Petit (T) 0785 937 7778 (E) gandjpetit149@tiscali.co.uk
Additional Committee Members:
Ali Kazemi, Clinton Arthur

Manager: Alan Dowson
Programme Editor: Robert Wooldridge (E) floiing@aol.com

Club Factfile

Founded: 1885 **Nickname:** The K's
Previous Names: Kingston & Suburban YMCA 1885-87, Saxons 1887-90, Kingston Wanderers 1893-1904, Old Kingstonians 1908-19
Previous Leagues: Kingston & District, West Surrey, Southern Suburban, Athenian 1919-29, Isthmian 1929-98, Conference 1998-2001

Club Colours (change): Red and white hoops/black/red & white

Ground: Kingsmead Stadium, Kingston Road, Kingston KT1 3PB (T) 0208 8547 3528
Capacity: 4,262 **Seats:** 1,080 **Covered:** 2,538 **Clubhouse:** Yes **Shop:** Yes

Directions
Take Cambridge Road from Town Centre (A2043) to Malden Road.
From A3 turn off at New Malden and turn left onto A2043.
Ground is 1 mile on the left which is half a mile from Norbiton BR.

Previous Grounds: Several > 1921, Richmond Road 1921-89

Record Attendance: 4,582 v Chelsea - Freindly
Record Victory: 15-1 v Delft - 1951
Record Defeat: 0-11 v Ilford - Isthmian League 13/02/1937
Record Goalscorer: Johnnie Wing - 295 (1948-62)
Record Appearances: Micky Preston - 555 (1967-85)
Additional Records: Paid £18,000 to Rushden & Diamonds for David Leworthy 1997
Received £150,000 from West Ham United for Gavin Holligan 1999

Senior Honours: FA Amateur Cup 1932-33. Isthmian League 1933-34, 36-37, 97-98, Division 1 South 2008-09.
FAT Trophy 1998-99, 99-2000. Athenian League x2. London Senior Cup x3. Surrey Senior Cup x3.

10 YEAR RECORD

01-02		02-03		03-04		04-05		05-06		06-07		07-08		08-09		09-10		10-11	
Isth P	14	Isth P	11	Isth P	18	Isth P	22	Isth1	7	Isth1S	13	Isth1S	7	Isth1S	1	Isth P	5	Isth P	7

KINGSTONIAN

No.	Date	Comp	H/A	Opponents	Att:	Result	Goalscorers	Pos
1	Aug 21	Isth Prem	A	Bury Town	581	D 0 - 0		14
2	23		H	Billericay Town	385	W 4 - 2	TRAYNOR 3 (20 81pen 90pen) Thompson 27	
3	28		H	AFC Hornchurch	336	W 2 - 1	Lodge 21 Wilson-Dennis 89	2
4	30		A	Horsham	372	W 3 - 2	Traynor 53 (pen) 73 (pen) McDonald 90	
5	Sept 4		H	Margate	419	W 1 - 0	Lodge 84	2
6	7		A	Folkestone Invicta	229	L 0 - 1		
7	18		H	Maidstone United	384	L 0 - 1		5
8	20		A	Hendon	215	W 3 - 2	Bird 2 Hamlin 24 Lodge 75	3
9	**25**	**FAC 2Q**	**A**	**Margate**	**438**	**D 1 - 1**	**Traynor 23**	
10	**27**	**FAC 2Qr**	**H**	**Margate**	**350**	**D 1 - 1***	**Hall 66 Won 3-2 on penalties**	
11	Oct 2		A	Canvey Island	356	W 2 - 0	Hustwick 11 Traynor 52	3
12	4		H	Sutton United	750	W 1 - 0	Alimi 87	
13	**9**	**FAC 3Q**	**A**	**St Albans City**	**484**	**D 0 - 0**		
14	**11**	**FAC 3Qr**	**H**	**St Albans City**	**367**	**L 1 - 2**	**Traynor 45 (pen)**	
15	**16**	**FAT 1Q**	**A**	**Faversham Town**	**230**	**W 2 - 1**	**Gray 58 Lodge 80 (pen)**	
16	23		A	Croydon Athletic	199	W 4 - 0	Lodge 17 66 Traynor 64 Wilson-Dennis 78	1
17	25		A	Wealdstone	405	L 1 - 2	Traynor 4	
18	**31**	**FAT 2Q**	**A**	**Wealdstone**	**428**	**L 3 - 5**	**Gray 4 Traynor 21 (pen) 37**	
19	Nov 7		H	Hastings United	329	W 3 - 1	Lodge 25 Huckle 30 Traynor 39	
20	9		A	Sutton United	779	L 0 - 2		
21	13		H	Canvey Island	380	W 3 - 1	Jinadu 11 Traynor 49 66	2
22	27		A	Tonbridge Angels	501	D 1 - 1	Gray 38	2
23	Dec 12		H	Harrow Borough	319	L 1 - 3	King 53 (og)	
24	28		A	Tooting & Mitcham	324	D 1 - 1	Traynor 39	
25	Jan 3		H	Horsham	410	L 1 - 3	Traynor 9	
26	8		A	Billericay Town	349	W 1 - 0	Tait 22	4
27	10		H	Aveley	272	W 2 - 0	Traynor 80 Gray 86	
28	16		H	Bury Town	372	D 1 - 1	Traynor 43	5
29	22		A	Cray Wanderers	253	L 0 - 2		5
30	25		A	Maidstone United	262	W 2 - 1	Clayton 34 McDonald 90	
31	29		H	Carshalton Athletic	415	L 0 - 1		4
32	31		H	Concord Rangers	257	L 0 - 3		
33	Feb 6		H	Croydon Athletic	316	W 2 - 1	Dolan 45 Traynor 79	
34	12		A	Aveley	208	D 1 - 1	Traynor 20	4
35	15		A	Lowestoft Town	567	D 1 - 1	Alimi 27	
36	19		H	Wealdstone	386	L 1 - 3	Vines 51	6
37	28		H	Hendon	271	W 3 - 0	Vines 2 Traynor 44 Alimi 86	
38	March 5		H	Tonbridge Angels	405	D 1 - 1	Vines 37	5
39	12		A	Concord Rangers	223	L 1 - 2	Vines 89	9
40	19		H	Lowestoft Town	366	W 2 - 0	Vines 44 Clayton 45	8
41	22		A	Hastings Town	360	W 2 - 1	Harkin 88 Traynor 90	
42	26		A	Harrow Borough	340	L 0 - 1		8
43	April 2		A	Carshalton Athletic	397	W 3 - 1	P.Vines 45 Clayton 46 Hutchinson 70	9
44	9		H	Cray Wanderers	304	W 2 - 1	Hutchinson 15 Huckle 54	9
45	16		H	Folkestone Invicta	352	W 2 - 0	Bird 65 Lodge 90	7
46	22		A	AFC Hornchurch	344	D 1 - 1	Traynor 14	7
47	26		H	Tooting & Mitcham	465	W 4 - 2	Vines 3 77 Traynor 29 (pen) Hutchinson 55	
48	30		A	Margate	489	D 3 - 3	Traynor 16 (pen) 29 Vines 22	7

Caption competition....

Send in your suggestions to tw.publications@btinternet.com and you could win a copy of the 2013 edition of the Directory...

Photo by Keith Clayton

LEATHERHEAD

Chairman: Peter Ashdown
Secretary: Jean Grant **(T)** 07966 710 089 **(E)** jeanlisagrant@blackberry.orange.co.uk
Additional Committee Members:
Richard Wilkinson, John Loveridge

Manager: Mick Sullivan
Programme Editor: Rod Ellis **(E)** rodellis83@hotmail.com

Back row (L-R): Adam Goodwell, Jon Boswell, Dan Dean, Kwabena Agyei, Elliott Thompson, Adrian Jones, Chico Ramos, Antony Russell, Bentley Graham, Gabriel Odunaike, Greg Andrews, Jack Macleod.
Front row: Tom Williams, Kevin Terry, Liam Pestle, Darryl Cooper-Smith, Tommy Hutchings, Mark Simmons, Chris Boulter, Marc Elston, Jon Coke, Steve Barilli, Rob Stevenson, Arnold Okirur.

Club Factfile

Founded: 1946 **Nickname:** The Tanners
Previous Names:
Previous Leagues: Surrey Senior 1946-50, Metropolitan 1950-51, Delphian 1951-58, Corinthian 1958-63, Athenian 1963-72

Club Colours (change): Green/white/green

Ground: Fetcham Grove, Guildford Road, Leatherhead, Surrey KT22 9AS **(T)** 01372 360 151
Capacity: 3,400 **Seats:** 200 **Covered:** 45 **Clubhouse:** Yes **Shop:** Yes

Directions
M25 junction 9 to Leatherhead,
follow signs to Leisure Centre,
ground adjacent.
Half a mile from Leatherhead BR.

Previous Grounds:

Record Attendance: 5,500 v Wimbledon - 1976
Record Victory: 13-1 v Leyland Motors - Surrey Senior League 1946-47
Record Defeat: 1-11 v Sutton United
Record Goalscorer: Steve Lunn scored 46 goals during 1996-97
Record Appearances: P Caswell - 200
Additional Records: Paid £1,500 to Croydon for B Salkeld
Received £1,500 from Croydon for B Salkeld

Senior Honours: Athenian League 1963-64.
Surrey Senior Cup 1968-69. Isthmian League cup 1977-78.

10 YEAR RECORD

01-02	02-03	03-04	04-05	05-06	06-07	07-08	08-09	09-10	10-11
Isth2 11	Isth1S 14	Isth1S 13	Isth1 7	Isth1 10	Isth1S 11	Isth1S 17	Isth1S 15	Isth1S 5	Isth1S 4

LEWES

Chairman: Steve Ibbitson
Secretary: Kevin Brook (T) 07785 074 081 (E) lewes_fc@hotmail.co.uk
Additional Committee Members:
James Boyes, Lee Cobb

Manager: Steve King
Programme Editor: James Boyes (E) james-boyes@lineone.net

Unfortunately an up-to-date photograph was not available at the time of going to press.

Club Factfile

Founded: 1885 **Nickname:** Rooks
Previous Names:
Previous Leagues: Mid Sussex 1886-1920, Sussex County 1920-65, Athenian 1965-77, Isthmian 1977-2004, Conference 2004-11.

Club Colours (change): Red and black stripes/white/white

Ground: The Dripping Pan, Mountfield Road, Lewes, East Sussex BN7 2XD (T) 01273 472 100
Capacity: 3,000 **Seats:** 400 **Covered:** 1,400 **Clubhouse:** Yes **Shop:** Yes

Directions After leaving the M23, follow the A23 to Brighton. On the outskirts of Brighton join the A27 eastbound. Stay on the A27 for about 5 miles. At the roundabout take first exit into Lewes. Follow this road until you reach traffic lights outside Lewes Prison. Turn right at the lights and follow the road down the hill until you reach a mini roundabout outside the Swan public house. Turn left at roundabout into Southover High Street and continue over next mini roundabout outside the Kings Head public house. At the next roundabout go straight over into Mountfield Road. The Dripping Pan is on your right.

Previous Grounds:

Record Attendance: 2,500 v Newhaven - Sussex County League 26/12/1947
Record Victory: Not known
Record Defeat: Not known
Record Goalscorer: 'Pip' Parris - 350
Record Appearances: Terry Parris - 662
Additional Records: Paid £2,000 for Matt Allen
Received £2,500 from Brighton & Hove Albion for Grant Horscroft

Senior Honours: Mid Sussex League 1910-11, 13-14. Sussex County League 1964-65.
Sussex Senior Cup 1964-65, 70-71, 84-85, 2000-01, 05-06. Athenian League Division 2 1967-68, Division 1 1969-70.
Isthmian League Division 2 2001-02, Division 1 South 2003-04. Conference South 2007-08

10 YEAR RECORD

01-02		02-03		03-04		04-05		05-06		06-07		07-08		08-09		09-10		10-11	
Isth2	1	Isth1S	3	Isth1S	1	Conf S	4	Conf S	4	Conf	9	Conf S	1	Conf	24	Conf S	19	Conf S	21

LEWES

No.	Date	Comp	H/A	Opponents	Att:	Result	Goalscorers	Pos
1	Sat-14-Aug	BSS	A	Staines Town	411	L 0-1		19
2	Tue-17-Aug	BSS	H	Thurrock	601	W 2-1	Ide 25, Wormull 63	10
3	Sat-21-Aug	BSS	H	Basingstoke Town	571	D 0-0		12
4	Tue-24-Aug	BSS	A	Woking	994	L 1-2	Lang 57	17
5	Sat-28-Aug	BSS	H	Dover Athletic	721	L 0-3		18
6	Mon-30-Aug	BSS	A	Welling United	591	L 1-2	Wormull pen 90	19
7	Sat-04-Sep	BSS	H	Hampton & Richmond Borough	694	L 1-2	Wormull 55	19
8	Sat-11-Sep	BSS	A	Eastleigh	366	L 1-2	Wheeler 12	20
9	Sat-18-Sep	BSS	H	Chelmsford City	1326	L 0-1		21
10	Sat-02-Oct	BSS	A	Farnborough	886	L 0-1		22
11	Sat-16-Oct	BSS	H	Dorchester Town	671	L 0-1		22
12	Tue-26-Oct	BSS	A	Bromley	432	D 1-1	Og (Foderingham) 74	22
13	Sat-30-Oct	BSS	H	Dartford	953	D 1-1	Olima 35	21
14	Sat-06-Nov	BSS	A	Weston-Super-Mare	214	W 3-0	Murphy 2 (59, 87), Porter 85	20
15	Tue-09-Nov	BSS	A	Bishops Stortford	264	L 0-1		20
16	Sat-13-Nov	BSS	H	St Albans City	727	W 3-1	Olima 2 (41, 55), Godfrey 45	19
17	Sat-27-Nov	BSS	A	Thurrock	274	L 1-3	Olima 54	19
18	Tue-28-Dec	BSS	A	Dover Athletic	1018	L 0-4		19
19	Sat-01-Jan	BSS	A	Ebbsfleet United	1167	L 0-1		20
20	Mon-03-Jan	BSS	H	Welling United	766	L 1-3	Godfrey 45	20
21	Sat-08-Jan	BSS	H	Eastleigh	483	L 1-4	Murphy 72	21
22	Sat-15-Jan	BSS	A	Braintree Town	535	L 0-1		22
23	Wed-19-Jan	BSS	H	Bromley	340	D 0-0		22
24	Sat-22-Jan	BSS	H	Staines Town	509	L 0-1		22
25	Sat-29-Jan	BSS	A	St Albans City	338	D 0-0		22
26	Sat-05-Feb	BSS	H	Boreham Wood	482	D 2-2	Taylor 31, Noel 68	22
27	Sat-12-Feb	BSS	A	Maidenhead United	236	W 2-0	Tabiri 78, Barker 83	21
28	Tue-15-Feb	BSS	A	Hampton & Richmond Borough	299	W 2-1	Taylor 4, Hall 83	21
29	Sat-19-Feb	BSS	H	Havant & Waterlooville	717	W 2-1	Breach 67, Wheeler 73	21
30	Wed-23-Feb	BSS	H	Ebbsfleet United	593	L 0-3		21
31	Sat-26-Feb	BSS	H	Woking	834	L 0-4		21
32	Sat-05-Mar	BSS	A	Basingstoke Town	326	D 1-1	Wheeler 90	21
33	Sat-12-Mar	BSS	A	Chelmsford City	782	L 0-4		21
34	Sat-19-Mar	BSS	H	Farnborough	792	L 1-5	Noel 26	21
35	Wed-23-Mar	BSS	H	Braintree Town	359	W 2-1	Dolan 25, Wheeler 80	20
36	Sat-26-Mar	BSS	A	Dartford	1036	L 0-3		20
37	Sat-02-Apr	BSS	H	Maidenhead United	626	W 1-0	Noel 45	20
38	Sat-09-Apr	BSS	A	Dorchester Town	438	D 0-0		20
39	Sat-16-Apr	BSS	H	Weston-Super-Mare	656	D 1-1	Hill 56	21
40	Sat-23-Apr	BSS	A	Havant & Waterlooville	464	W 2-1	A Hutchinson 42, Hunt 89	21
41	Mon-25-Apr	BSS	H	Bishops Stortford	835	L 1-2	Hill 86	21 Relegated
42	Sat-30-Apr	BSS	A	Boreham Wood	202	L 0-3		21

CUPS

No.	Date	Comp	H/A	Opponents	Att:	Result	Goalscorers	Pos
1	Sat-25-Sep	FAC 2Q	H	Harlow Town	785	W 2-0	Breach 2 (32, 38)	
2	Sat-09-Oct	FAC 3Q	H	Thurrock	854	W 2-1	Murphy 2 (17, 73)	
3	Sat-23-Oct	FAC 4Q	A	Cambridge United	1626	L 0-3		
4	Sat-20-Nov	FAT 3Q	H	Salisbury City	598	L 1-3	Hamilton 72	

LOWESTOFT TOWN

Chairman: Gary Keyzor
Secretary: Terry Lynes **(T)** 0793 087 2947 **(E)** terrylynes@fsmail.net
Additional Committee Members:
Steven End, Simon Reeve

Manager: Micky Chapman and Ady Gallagher
Programme Editor: Terry Lynes **(E)** terrylynes@fsmail.net

Lowestoft Town of the Jewson Eastern Counties in 1992-1993. Back row, left to right: R.Butcher (Vice Chaiman), C.Rowe (Manager), J.Sturman, G.Mills, J.Mackenzie, M.Ling, A.Ames, M.Barbrook, G.Maguire, A.Moore, R.Harper (Chairman) and S,Youngman. Front Row: B.Lyons (Ball Boy), J.Clarke, P.Holland, P.Mobbs, M.Chapman, G.Atkins (Mascot) and I. Moran.

Club Factfile

Founded: 1880 **Nickname:** The Trawler Boys or Blues
Previous Names: Original club merged with Kirkley in 1887 to form Lowestoft and became Lowestoft Town in 1890
Previous Leagues: North Suffolk 1897-35, Eastern Counties 1935-2009

Club Colours (change): All blue

Ground: Crown Meadow, Love Road, Lowestoft NR32 2PA **(T)** 01502 573 818
Capacity: 3,000 **Seats:** 466 **Covered:** 500 **Clubhouse:** Yes **Shop:** Yes

Directions
Just off A12.
Ten minutes from Lowestoft BR.

Previous Grounds:

Record Attendance: 5,000 v Watford - FA Cup 1st Round 1967
Record Victory: Not Known
Record Defeat: Not Known
Record Goalscorer: Not Known
Record Appearances: Not Known
Additional Records:

Senior Honours: Eastern Counties League 1935-36 (shared), 37-38, 62-63, 64-65, 65-66, 66-67, 67-68, 69-70, 70-71, 77-78, 2005-06, 08-09.
Isthmian League Division 1 North 2009-10.
Suffolk Senior Cup 1902-03, 22-23, 25-26, 31-32, 35-36, 46-47, 47-48, 48-49, 55-56.

10 YEAR RECORD

01-02	02-03	03-04	04-05	05-06	06-07	07-08	08-09	09-10	10-11
ECP 3	ECP 4	ECP 8	ECP 4	ECP 1	ECP 3	ECP 11	ECP 1	Isth1N 1	Isth P 4

LOWESTOFT TOWN

No.	Date	Comp	H/A	Opponents	Att:	Result	Goalscorers	Pos
1	Aug 21	Isth Prem	A	Carshalton Athletic	350	L 0 - 2		19
2	24		H	AFC Hornchurch	709	W 2 - 0	Godbold 45 Halliday 77	
3	28		H	Margate	723	W 2 - 1	McGlone 27 Bloomfield 51	7
4	30		A	Concord Rangers	236	W 2 - 0	McGlone 2 Bloomfield 62	
5	Sept 4		H	Folkestone	831	W 4 - 1	Bloomfield 11 14 McGlone 72 Friend 84 (o.g.)	
6	7		A	Harrow Borough	165	L 0 - 2		2
7	**11**	**FAC 1Q**	**H**	**Desborough Town**	**566**	**W 7 - 1**	**Smith 1 Bloomfield 12 17 Ainsley 24 Forshaw 39 52 Godbold 41**	
8	18		H	Aveley	634	W 1 - 0	Forshaw 31	2
9	21		A	Billericay Town	334	W 3 - 1	Forshaw 7 Goughran 23 Godbold 44	2
10	**25**	**FAC 2Q**	**A**	**Dartford**	**1024**	**L 1 - 2**	**Cockrill 84**	
11	Oct 2		A	Wealdstone	480	W 2 - 0	Mitchell 45 Forbes 83	2
12	5		H	Canvey Island	677	D 1 - 1	McGlone 67	
13	9		H	Sutton United	1265	D 0 - 0		1
14	**16**	**FAT 1Q**	**A**	**Needham Market**	**381**	**D 2 - 2**	**Forbes 32 72 (pen)**	
15	**19**	**FAT 1Qr**	**H**	**Needham Market**	**546**	**W 6 - 2**	**Nolan 11 (pen) 26 Francis 39 Haynes-Brown 69 Fisk 80 McGlone 88**	
16	23		A	Hastings United	418	D 0 - 0		2
17	**30**	**FAT 2Q**	**A**	**Chippenham Town**	**383**	**D 1 - 1**	**Tindle 53 (og)**	
18	**Nov 2**	**FAT 2Qr**	**H**	**Chippenham Town**	**577**	**W 3 - 1***	**McGlone 20 Ainsley 109 Bloomfield 112**	
19	6		H	Horsham	683	W 4 - 0	Forbes 20 Bloomfield 30 Francis 35 Ainsley 46	2
20	13		H	Wealdstone	737	D 0 - 0		
21	**20**	**FAT 3Q**	**H**	**Swindon Supermarine**	**622**	**W 2 - 1**	**Francis 18 Forshaw 89**	**3**
22	**Dec 11**	**FAT 1**	**H**	**Uxbridge**	**609**	**L 2 - 3**	**Forbes 87 Crane 89**	
23	14		A	Canvey Island	247	D 0 - 0		5
24	Jan 3		H	Concord Rangers	786	W 2 - 0	Smith 51 Francis 57	
25	8		A	AFC Hornchurch	316	W 2 - 1	Cockrill 2 7	5
26	15		H	Carshalton Athletic	733	D 0 - 0		6
27	22		H	Croydon Athletic	657	W 4 - 0	Nolan 50 Smith 61 80 (pen) Stock 76	6
28	25		A	Cray Wanderers	143	W 1 - 0	Forshaw 48	
29	29		A	Tonbridge Angels	621	D 3 - 3	Haynes-Brown 40 Cockrill 81 Frew 86	3
30	Feb 1		H	Billericay Town	513	D 1 - 1	Cockrill 51	
31	5		H	Hastings United	695	D 1 - 1	Frew 67	4
32	8		A	Tooting & Mitcham	178	L 1 - 2	Nolan 85 (pen)	
33	12		A	Sutton United	803	L 1 - 2	Mitchell 65	6
34	15		H	Kingstonian	567	D 1 - 1	Francis 5	
35	19		H	Hendon	629	W 8 - 1	Frew 5 Nolan 16 44 Francis 43 Mitchell 46 Stock 65 Burgess 80 (og) Godbold 81	4
36	22		A	Bury Town	931	D 0 - 0		
37	26		A	Horsham	236	W 2 - 1	Frew 10 56	3
38	March 5		A	Maidstone United	311	W 1 - 0	Forshaw 52	3
39	12		H	Cray Wanderers	824	L 0 - 1		4
40	15		A	Hendon	125	D 1 - 1	Corcoran 69	
41	19		A	Kingstonian	366	L 0 - 2		5
42	22		H	Maidstone United	511	D 3 - 3	Nolan 49 52 Paul 66 (og)	
43	26		H	Tootiing & Mitcham	603	D 0 - 0		5
44	28		A	Aveley	153	W 3 - 0	Frew 8 14 Mitchell 11	
45	April 2		H	Tonbridge Angels	767	D 0 - 0		4
46	9		A	Croydon Athletic	104	W 2 - 0	Forbes 28 Guentchev 78	5
47	16		H	Harrow Borough	724	W 3 - 0	Cave-Brown 25 Francis 33 Guentchev 82	5
48	23		A	Margate	403	W 3 - 0	Forshaw 12 31 Nolan 45	2
49	26		H	Bury Town	1246	L 0 - 1		
50	30		A	Folkestone Invicta	244	W 4 - 1	Nolan 71 Forbes 78 Cave-Brown 88 Stock 90	4
51	**May 3**	**P-Off SF**	**A**	**Bury Town**	**1427**	**W 2 - 1**	**Nunn (og) 43 Guentchev 67**	
52	**7**	**P-Off Final**	**A**	**Tonbridge Angels**	**2411**	**L 3 - 4**	**Cockerill 30 Cave-Brown 48 Guentchev 75**	

MARGATE

Chairman: (Chief Exec.) Cliff Egan
Secretary: Ken Tomlinson **(T)** 0771 003 3566 **(E)** ken.tomlinson@margate-fc.com
Additional Committee Members:
Steve Wells, Peter Cove

Manager: Chris Kinnear
Programme Editor: Don Walker **(E)** don.walker@margate-fc.com

Back Row (l-r): Kevin Rayne, Kwesi Appiah, Dean Hill, Tom Bradbrook, Curtis Robinson, Richard Avery, Jack Smelt, Wayne Wilson, Craig Cloke, Dean Pooley, Laurence Ball, Mark Corneille, Jake Leberl (Coach), Paul Wilson (Physio)
Front Row (l-r): Liam Coleman, Dan Stubbs, Adam Burchell, Cliff Egan (CEO), Richard Piper (Director), Chris Kinnear (Manager), Keith Piper (Director), Colin Page (Director), Dean Grant, Matt Bodkin, Ashley Groombridge

Club Factfile

Founded: 1896 **Nickname:** The Gate
Previous Names: None
Previous Leagues: Kent 1911-23, 24-28, 29-33, 37-38, 46-59. Southern 1933-37, 59-2001, Conference 2001-04

Club Colours (change): Royal blue & white hoops/royal blue/white

Ground: Hartsdown Park, Hartsdown Road, Margate, Kent CT9 5QZ **(T)** 01843 221 769
Capacity: 3,000 **Seats:** 350 **Covered:** 1,750 **Clubhouse:** Yes **Shop:** Yes

Directions From M25 continue onto M26 merge onto M20, at junction 7, exit onto Sittingbourne Rd/A249 toward Sheerness/Canterbury/Ramsgate, continue to follow A249, take the ramp onto M2, continue onto A299 (signs for Margate/Ramsgate) keep right at the fork, at the roundabout, take the 2nd exit onto Canterbury Rd (Birchington)/A28 continue to follow A28, turn right onto The Square/A28 continue to follow A28, turn right onto George V Ave/B2052, turn right onto Hartsdown Rd/B2052, ground will be on the left.

Previous Grounds: Not known

Record Attendance: 14,500 v Tottenham Hotspur - FA Cup 3rd Round 1973
Record Victory: 8-0 v Tunbridge Wells (H) - 1966-67, v Chatham Town (H) - 1987-88 and v Stalybridge Celtic (H) - 2001-02
Record Defeat: 0-11 v AFC Bournemouth (A) - FA Cup 20/11/1971
Record Goalscorer: Jack Palethorpe scored 66 during 1929-30
Record Appearances: Bob Harrop
Additional Records: Paid £5,000 to Dover Athletic for Steve Cuggy

Senior Honours: Southern League Premier Division 1935-36, 2000-01, Division 1 1962-63, Division 1 South 1977-78.

10 YEAR RECORD

01-02	02-03	03-04	04-05	05-06	06-07	07-08	08-09	09-10	10-11
Conf 8	Conf 10	Conf 16	Conf S 21	Isth P 14	Isth P 6	Isth P 9	Isth P 19	Isth P 19	Isth P 16

MARGATE

No.	Date	Comp	H/A	Opponents	Att:	Result	Goalscorers	Pos
1	Aug 21	Isth Prem	H	Canvey Island	474	D 2 - 2	Cloke 45 Grant 79	9
2	28		A	Lowestoft Town	723	L 1 - 2	Marsden 25	17
3	30		H	Maidstone United	641	D 1 - 1	Wilson 84	
4	Sept 4		A	Kingstonian	419	L 0 - 1		19
5	7		H	Aveley	268	W 2 - 0	Welford 78 90	
6	**11**	**FAC 1Q**	**A**	**Binfield**	**394**	**W 3 - 0**	**Welford 51 Kamara 60 Osbourne 65**	
7	18		H	Wealdstone	380	W 1 - 0	Pinnock 69	12
8	21		A	Folkestone Invicta	408	W 2 - 1	Welford 6 Robinson 45	8
9	**25**	**FAC 2Q**	**H**	**Kingstonian**	**438**	**D 1 - 1**	**Pinnock 22**	
10	**27**	**FAC 2Qr**	**A**	**Kingstonian**	**350**	**D 1 - 1**	**Wilson 24 lost 2-3 on penalties**	
11	Oct 2		A	Sutton United	1253	L 1 - 2	Grant 69	12
12	5		H	Tonbridge Angels	341	L 0 - 1		
13	9		H	Horsham	347	W 6 - 1	Marsden 8 WELFORD 3 (21 77 pen 79) Saunders 51 Grant 86	11
14	**16**	**FAT 1Q**	**H**	**Whitehawk**	**227**	**W 5 - 1**	**Grant 34 Saunders 43 WELFORD 3 (57 73 82)**	
15	23		A	Billericay Town	384	D 0 - 0		13
16	26		A	Concord Rangers	136	D 0 - 0		
17	**30**	**FAT 2Q**	**H**	**AFC Hornchurch**	**325**	**L 1 - 2**	**Robinson 65**	
18	Nov 6		H	Bury Town	305	L 0 - 1		15
19	9		A	Tonbridge Angels	326	D 1 - 1	Stubbs 8	
20	13		H	Sutton United	397	W 3 - 2	Downer 20 (og) Wilson 57 73	12
21	17		A	Croydon Athletic	103	L 3 - 5	Pinnock 26 80 Seefah 28 (og)	
22	23		H	Folkestone Invicta	200	L 0 - 2		
23	27		H	Tooting & Mitcham	336	D 3 - 3	Welford 39 Pinnock 45 90	13
24	Dec 27		H	Cray Wanderers	371	L 0 - 2		
25	Jan 3		A	Maidstone United	476	W 2 - 0	Welford 18 (pen) Pinnock 90	
26	8		H	Croydon Athletic	266	L 0 - 2		16
27	10		A	Wealdstone	348	W 1 - 0	Stubbs 45	
28	15		A	Canvey Island	317	L 0 - 2		14
29	22		H	Hastings United	298	W 2 - 0	Pinnock 27 88	13
30	25		H	Hendon	162	D 1 - 1	Cloke 36	
31	29		A	Harrow Borough	144	D 0 - 0		14
32	Feb 1		A	AFC Hornchurch	173	L 1 - 2	Ball 37	
33	5		H	Billericay Town	341	L 0 - 1		15
34	8		A	Carshalton Athletic	157	W 3 - 1	Bradbrook 4 Ball 40 Cloke 42	
35	12		A	Horsham	222	D 1 - 1	Bradbrook 58	14
36	March 5		A	Tooting & Mitcham U	375	L 0 - 3		16
37	12		H	Carshalton Athletic	337	W 2 - 1	Bradbrook 12 49	14
38	15		A	Bury Town	408	L 1 - 2	Pinnock 78	
39	19		A	Hendon	164	W 3 - 2	Cloke 7 Bradbrook 15 Wilson 65	14
40	22		H	Concord Rangers	236	L 1 - 2	Wilson 87 (pen)	
41	26		H	AFC Hornchurch	330	D 2 - 2	Hill 9 Wilson 56	15
42	April 2		H	Harrow Borough	308	L 2 - 3	Langiano 2 Bradbrook 16	16
43	9		A	Hastings United	434	L 0 - 3		16
44	16		A	Aveley	150	D 1 - 1	Bradbrook 67	15
45	23		H	Lowestoft Town	403	L 0 - 3		16
46	26		A	Cray Wanderers	199	L 0 - 2		
47	30		H	Kingstonian	489	D 3 - 3	Wilson 38 47 Hill 79	16

METROPOLITAN POLICE

Chairman: Des Flanders
Secretary: Tony Brooking (T) 0796 133 4523 (E) tony.brooking@met.police.uk
Additional Committee Members:
Cliff Travis, Graham Fulcher

Manager: Jim Cooper
Programme Editor: Cliff Travis (E) cliffordtravis@hotmail.com

The Isthmian League Division One South Winning Squad
Back row, left to right: Jamal Carr, Eddie Smith, Craig Watkins, Vernon Francis, Neil Lampton, Rob Smith, Elliot Taylor.
Middle row: Paul Barrowcliff, Steve Noakes, Dominic O'Shea, Adam Broomhead, Mo Maan, Dave Smalley, Daniel Gwyther, James Field, Chris Bourne, Chris MacPherson.
Front row: Craig Brown, Steve Sutherland, Stuart Mackenzie, Gavin MacPherson(assistant manager), Jim Cooper(manager),John Nicholson, Nicky Humphrey, Tyron Smith.

Club Factfile

Founded: 1919 **Nickname:** The Blues
Previous Names: Not known
Previous Leagues: Spartan 1928-60, Metropolitan 1960-71, Southern 1971-78

Club Colours (change): All blue

Ground: Imber Court, Ember Lane, East Molesey, Surrey KT8 0BT (T) 0208 398 7358
Capacity: 3,000 **Seats:** 297 **Covered:** 1,800 **Clubhouse:** Yes **Shop:** No

Directions
From London A3 take A309 towards Scilly Isles roundabout then right into Hampton Court Way.
Left at first roundabout into Imber Court Road. Ground is in 300 yards.

Previous Grounds: Not known

Record Attendance: 4,500 v Kingstonian - FA Cup 1934
Record Victory: 10-1 v Tilbury - 1995
Record Defeat: 1-11 v Wimbledon - 1956
Record Goalscorer: Mario Russo
Record Appearances: Pat Robert
Additional Records:

Senior Honours: Spartan League x7.
Middlesex Senior Cup 1927-28, Surrey Senior Cup 1932-33. London Senior Cup 2009-10.
Isthmian League Division One South 2010-11.

10 YEAR RECORD

01-02		02-03		03-04		04-05		05-06		06-07		07-08		08-09		09-10		10-11	
Isth2	13	Isth1S	23	Isth1S	20	Isth1	5	Isth1	4	Isth1S	6	Isth1S	4	Isth1S	4	Isth1S	10	Isth1S	1

Met Police's Imber Court.

TOOTING & MITCHAM UNITED

Chairman: Chrissie Stevenson
Secretary: Gary Harding **(T)** 0770 271 0400 **(E)** gary@urspace4u.com
Additional Committee Members:
Nigel Sarsons, Dave Watters, Lyn Catchpole

Manager: Mark Beard
Programme Editor: Dave Watters **(E)** gary.harding@thehubattmufc.co.uk

Back row (L-R): Mark Gradosielski, Phil Williams, Craig Vernon, Barry Stevens, Paul Honey, Luke Garrard, Tony Nwanchu, Jason Henry, James Nicholls, Danny Bracken, Aaron Goode, Jon Dollery, Mark Waters, Adam Fletcher, Hasim Deen.
Front row: Nicola Upward, Karl Beckford, Jamie Byatt, Hsang Nyang, Kevin Cooper, Mark Beard, James Evans, Nigel Brake, Lino Gonalves, Nick Tester.

Club Factfile

Founded: 1932 **Nickname:** The Terrors
Previous Names: Not known
Previous Leagues: London 1932-37, Athenian 1937-56

Club Colours (change): Black and white stripes/black/black

Ground: Imperial Fields, Bishopsford Road, Morden, Surrey SM4 6BF **(T)** 020 8648 3248 / 020 8685 6193
Capacity: 3,50 **Seats:** 600 **Covered:** 1,200 **Clubhouse:** Yes **Shop:** Yes

Directions
M25 junction 8, take the A217 northbound, this goes through Tadworth and Cheam. It's dual carriageway most of the way, although long stretches have a 40mph speed limit. This leads to a major roundabout with lights (Rose Hill). Take the third exit (Mitcham A217), this is Bishopsford Road and the ground is a mile further on. Go through two sets of lights, the road dips, and the entrance is on the right opposite a petrol station.
From the South: M25 junction 7, M23 then A23 northbound. Turn left onto the A237 after passing under a railway bridge at Coulsdon South station. Through Hackbridge and Beddington, then turn left onto the A239. Turn left again at lights by Mitcham Cricket Green into the A217, the ground is 800 yards on the left.

Previous Grounds: Sandy Lane, Mitcham

Record Attendance: 17,500 v Queens Park Rangers - FA Cup 2nd Round 1956-57 (At Sandy Lane)
Record Victory: 11-0 v Welton Rovers - FA Amateur Cup 1962-63
Record Defeat: 1-8 v Kingstonian - Surrey Senior Cup 1966-67
Record Goalscorer: Alan Ives - 92
Record Appearances: Danny Godwin - 470
Additional Records: Paid £9,000 to Enfield for David Flint
Received £10,000 from Luton Town for Herbie Smith

Senior Honours: Athenian League 1949-50, 54-55. Isthmian League 1975-76, 59-60, Division 2 2000-01. Full Members Cup 1992-93. London Senior Cup 1942-43, 48-49, 58-59, 59-60, 2006-07, 07-08. Surrey Senior cup 1937-38, 43-44, 44-45, 52-53, 59-60, 75-76, 76 -77, 77-78, 2007-07. Surrey Senior Shield 1951-52, 60-61, 61-62, 65-66. South Thames Cup 1969-70.

10 YEAR RECORD

01-02	02-03	03-04	04-05	05-06	06-07	07-08	08-09	09-10	10-11
Isth1 12	Isth1S 11	Isth1S 11	Isth1 8	Isth1 6	Isth1S 2	Isth1S 2	Isth P 9	Isth P 12	Isth P 14

TOOTING & MITCHAM UNITED

No.	Date	Comp	H/A	Opponents	Att:	Result	Goalscorers	Pos
1	Aug 21	Isth Prem	H	Hendon	331	W 4 - 3	MASON-HUGHES 3 (26 44 48) Williams 31	6
2	23		A	Wealdstone	419	L 0 - 3		
3	28		A	Cray Wanderers	254	W 3 - 2	Haworth 38 Nicholls 66 Stevens 84	8
4	30		H	Sutton United	654	L 0 - 3		
5	Sept 4		A	Canvey Island	238	W 2 - 0	Williams 30 Hawarth 66	7
6	**11**	**FAC 1Q**	**H**	**Walton Casuals**	**450**	**W 4 - 1**	**Haworth 29 Beckford 37 50 Hall 90**	
7	18		A	Carshalton Athletic	484	L 0 - 2		11
8	21		H	AFC Hornchurch	138	D 1 - 1	Williams 11	13
9	**25**	**FAC 2Q**	**H**	**Staines Town**	**378**	**L 1 - 2**	**Williams 86**	
10	Oct 2		H	Bury Town	298	L 1 - 3	Beckford 75 (pen)	15
11	5		A	Horsham	226	L 0 - 1		
12	9		H	Hastings United	282	D 1 - 1	Stevens 58	15
13	**16**	**FAT 1Q**	**A**	**Sutton United**	**448**	**L 1 - 3**	**Haworth 62**	
14	19		H	Croydon Athletic	167	D 2 - 2	Sealey 18 George 83 (og)	
15	23		A	Concord Rangers	202	L 0 - 3		15
16	26		A	Folkestone Invicta	180	W 3 - 1	Dalhouse 15 Pitcher 16 Stevens 39	
17	Nov 6		H	Aveley	246	W 1 - 0	Pitcher 32 (pen)	
18	9		H	Horsham	173	L 1 - 2	Sealey 63	
19	13		A	Bury Town	515	L 1 - 2	Sealey 54	15
20	20		H	Carshalton Atletic	469	L 0 - 5		15
21	23		A	AFC Hornchurch	214	D 2 - 2	Crook 37 Haworth 69	
22	27		A	Margate	336	D 3 - 3	Crook 49 Mason-Hughes 74 Haworth 79	15
23	Dec 11		A	Maidstone United	302	D 1 - 1	Haworth 38	15
24	28		H	Kingstonian	324	D 1 - 1	S.Butler 35	
25	Jan 1		A	Sutton United	746	D 2 - 2	Henry 44 Mason-Hughes 90	15
26	8		H	Wealdstomne	384	W 1 - 0	Crook 63	15
27	15		A	Hendon	172	L 1 - 4	Hall 74	
28	18		H	Billericay Town	234	W 3 - 2	Byatt 31 Haworth 45 Dellow 85	
29	22		H	Tonbridge Angels	328	L 1 - 5	Hall 52	15
30	Feb 5		H	Concord Rangers	230	W 3 - 2	Byatt 20 Pinnock 32 Beckford 44 (pen)	16
31	8		H	Lowestoft Town	176	W 2 - 1	Pinnock 57 Beckford 90	
32	12		A	Hastings United	403	L 2 - 3	Byatt 50 Beckford 89	15
33	March 5		H	Margate	375	W 3 - 0	Byatt 69 Heverin 74 Sealey 90	14
34	2		A	Billericay Town	422	L 0 - 1		15
35	15		A	Harrow Borough	149	L 0 - 2		
36	19		H	Harrow Borough	235	W 3 - 2	Hall 36 Henry 40 72	15
37	26		A	Lowestoft Town	603	D 0 - 0		16
38	29		H	Folkestone Invicta	177	W 4 - 1	Dean 37 Drage 66 Byatt 69 (Pen) 82	
39	April 2		H	Maidstone United	314	L 3 - 4	Byatt 27 Henry 45 59	14
40	4		A	Aveley	133	L 1 - 3	Beckford 68	
41	9		A	Tonbridge Amgels	534	D 3 - 3	Walder 5 (og) Pinnock 25 Dixon 66	14
42	16		A	Croydon Athletic	179	W 1 - 0	Byatt 66	13
43	22		H	Cray Wanderers	323	L 0 - 3		14
44	26		A	Kingstonian	465	L 2 - 4	Crook 36 Pitcher 70 (pen)	
45	30		H	Canvey Island	473	L 1 - 2	Hall 12	14

WEALDSTONE

Chairman: Howard Krais
Secretary: Paul Fruin (T) 0779 003 8095 (E) paul@pfruin.orangehome.co.uk
Additional Committee Members:
Alan Couch, Nick Dugard, Peter Worby

Manager: Gordon Bartlett
Programme Editor: Adam Gloor (E) adamgloor@aol.com

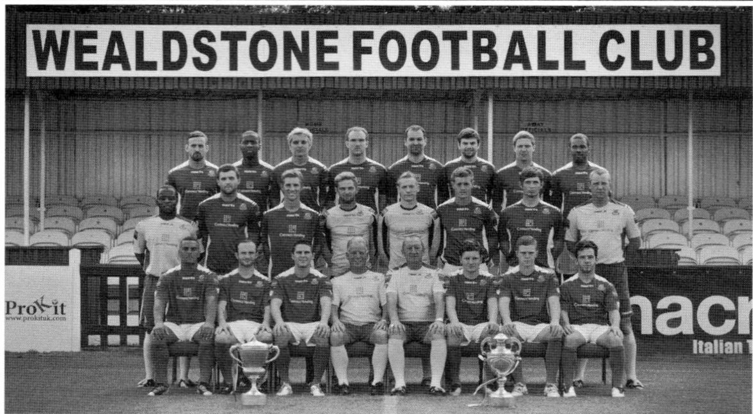

Back Row (L-R): Peter Dean, James Hammond, Danny Spendlove, Kieron Knight, Scott Fitzgerald, Wes Parker, David Hicks, Alex Dyer. **Middle Row:** Micky Johnson (Coach), Darren Locke, Jake Parsons, Jonathan North, Sam Beagle, Alan Massey, Sean Cronin, Mark Gill (Coach). **Front Row:** Kurtney Brooks, Richard Jolly, Lee Chappell, Gordon Bartlett (Manager), Leo Morris (Assistant Manager), Dean Wallace, Jordan Lumsden, Tom O'Regan. **Not Pictured:** Nikki Ahamed, Denzil Conteh, Eddie Adjei & Scott McCubbin

Club Factfile

Founded: 1899 **Nickname:** The Stones
Previous Names:
Previous Leagues: Willesden & District 1899-1906, 08-13, London 1911-22, Middlesex 1913-22, Spartan 1922-28, Athenian 1928-64, Isthmian 1964-71, 95-2006, Southern 1971-79, 81-82, 88-95, Conference 1979-81, 82-88

Club Colours (change): All blue with white trim

Ground: St. Georges Stadium, Grosvenor Vale, Ruislip, Middlesex HA4 6JQ (T) 01895 637 487
Capacity: 2,300 **Seats:** 300 **Covered:** 450 **Clubhouse:** Yes **Shop:**

Directions
From the M1: Follow Signs for Heathrow Airport on the M25. Come off at Junction 16 onto the A40, come off at The Polish War Memorial junction A4180 sign posted to Ruislip, continue on West End Road, right into Grosvenor Vale after approx 1.5 miles, the ground is at the end of the road.
From the M25: Follow Take Junction 16 Off M25 onto A40. Then come off at The Polish War Memorial junction A4180 sign posted to Ruislip, continue on West End Road, right into Grosvenor Vale after approx 1.5 miles, the ground is at the end of the road.
From the M4: Junction 4B, take the M25 towards Watford, come off Junction 16 and join A40, come off at The Polish War Memorial junction A4180 sign posted to Ruislip, continue on West End Road, right into Grosvenor Vale after approx 1.5 miles, the ground is at the end of the road.

Previous Grounds: Lower Mead Stadium, Watford FC, YEading FC, Northwood FC

Record Attendance: 13,504 v Leytonstone - FA Amateur Cup 4th Round replay 05/03/1949 (at Lower Mead Stadium)
Record Victory: 22-0 v The 12th London Regiment (The Rangers) - FA Amateur Cup 13/10/1923
Record Defeat: 0-14 v Edgware Town (A) - London Senior Cup 09/12/1944
Record Goalscorer: George Duck - 251
Record Appearances: Charlie Townsend - 514
Additional Records: Paid £15,000 to Barnet for David Gipp
Received £70,000 from Leeds United for Jermaine Beckford

Senior Honours: Athenian League 1951-52. Southern League Division 1 South 1973-74, Southern Division 1981-82. Conference 1984-85. Isthmian League Division 3 1996-97. FA Amateur Cup 1965-66. London Senior Cup 1961-62. FA Trophy 1984-85. Middlesex Senior Cup x11

10 YEAR RECORD

01-02		02-03		03-04		04-05		05-06		06-07		07-08		08-09		09-10		10-11	
Isth1	8	Isth1N	9	Isth1N	7	Isth P	18	Isth P	18	SthP	19	Isth P	13	Isth P	7	Isth P	6	Isth P	12

WEALDSTONE

No.	Date	Comp	H/A	Opponents	Att:	Result	Goalscorers	Pos
1	Aug 21	Isth Prem	A	Hastings United	563	L 0 - 2		21
2	23		H	Tooting & Mitcham United	419	W 3 - 0	Fitzgerald 14 Ngoyi 23 44	
3	28		H	Horsham	383	W 3 - 0	Ngoyi 38 Dean 43 52	5
4	30		A	AFC Hornchurch	351	L 1 - 2	Fitzgerald 53	
5	Sept 4		H	Bury Town	504	D 0 - 0		8
6	7		A	Billericay Town	268	L 0 - 1		
7	**11**	**FAC 1Q**	**H**	**Tring Athletic**	**196**	**W 7 - 1**	**Ngoyi 2 BURNELL 4 (34 48 64 80) Fitzgerald 77 (pen) 84**	
8	18		A	Margate	380	L 0 - 1		15
9	20		H	Carshalton Athletic	406	L 0 - 3		16
10	**25**	**FAC 2Q**	**A**	**Chesham United**	**504**	**D 2 - 2**	**Ngoyi 35 Fitzgerald 77**	
11	**27**	**FAC 2Qr**	**H**	**Chesham United**	**366**	**W 4 - 1**	**Fitzgerald 20 Dean 42 75 Chappell 64**	
12	Oct 2		H	Lowestoft Town	480	L 0 - 2		17
13	6		A	Croydon Athletic	134	D 2 - 2	Ngoyi 28 Dean 33	
14	**9**	**FAC 3Q**	**A**	**Metropolitan Police**	**390**	**D 1 - 1**	**Cronin 19**	
15	**13**	**FAC 3Qr**	**H**	**Metropolitan Police**	**403**	**L 1 - 2***	**O'Leary 40**	
16	**16**	**FAT 1Q**	**H**	**Potters Bar**	**201**	**D 2 - 2**	**Balic 26 Pett 90**	
17	**19**	**FAT 1Qr**	**A**	**Potters Bar**	**137**	**W 3 - 1**	**Daly 16 Spendlove 25 O'Leary 73**	
18	23		H	Maidstone United	385	D 1 - 1	Ngoyi 73	
19	25		H	Kingstonian	405	W 2 - 1	Ngoyi 45 Dean 62	16
20	**31**	**FAT 2Q**	**A**	**Kingstonian**	**428**	**W 5 - 3**	**NGOYI 3 (6 26 54) Dean 1 Spendlove 70**	
21	Nov 2		A	Canvey Island	225	D 1 - 1	Fitzgerald 76	16
22	7		A	Cray Wanderers	198	L 0 - 1		
23	9		H	Croydon Athletic	310	W 4 - 3	Dyer 7 Fitzgerald 47 78 Dean 82	
24	13		A	Lowestoft Town	737	D 0 - 0		16
25	**20**	**FAT 3Q**	**A**	**Brackley Town**	**302**	**W 1 - 0**	**Dean 89**	
26	23		A	Carshalton Athletic	187	L 2 - 3	Dyer 19 61	
27	27		A	Sutton United	527	L 3 - 4	Dyer 21 27 Spendlove 48	14
28	Dec 4		H	Aveley	410	W 2 - 0	Forbes 55 Ngoyi 78	13
29	**11**	**FAT 1**	**A**	**Newport County**	**1070**	**D 0 - 0**		
30	**14**	**FAT 1r**	**H**	**Newport County**	**324**	**L 0 - 1**		
31	Jan 1		H	AFC Hornchurch	506	L 0 - 3		14
32	8		A	Tooting & Mitcham U	394	L 0 - 1		17
33	10		H	Margate		L 0 - 1		
34	22		H	Hendon	428	W 1 - 0	Sintim 33 (og)	16
35	24		H	Hastings United	340	W 2 - 1	Jolly 4 Dean 38	
36	29		A	Concord Rangers	162	W 6 - 1	Wild 40 JOLLY 3 (45 48 53) Dean 70 (pen) 89	13
37	Feb 5		A	Maidstone United	352	W 4 - 2	Knight 11 Walker 38 (og) Jolly 65 66	13
38	12		H	Canvey Island	444	D 3 - 3	Jolly 37 90 Massey 40	13
39	15		A	Folkestone Invicta	146	D 1 - 1	Brooks 61	
40	19		A	Kingstonian	386	W 3 - 1	Brooks 11 Dean 36 90 (pen)	12
41	March 1		A	Harrow Borough	337	W 4 - 0	Dean 23 (pen) 90 Chappell 40 Dyer 50	
42	5		H	Sutton United	556	W 2 - 1	Dean 9 Chappell 90	12
43	7		H	Tonbridge Angels	432	D 0 - 0		
44	12		A	Aveley	252	W 1 - 0	Dyer 27	12
45	19		H	Folkestone Invicta	445	D 1 - 1	Dean 30	12
46	26		A	Tonbridge Angels	505	L 0 - 2		12
47	April 2		H	Concord Rangers	425	L 1 - 3	Massey 56	12
48	4		H	Cray Wanderers	351	L 0 - 1		
49	9		A	Hendon	251	W 1 - 0	Parker 51	12
50	16		H	Billericay Town	423	W 1 - 0	Dean 23	12
51	23		A	Horsham	286	L 1 - 2	Dean 89	12
52	26		H	Harrow Borough	765	D 1 - 1	Chappell 8	
53	30		A	Bury Town	692	L 0 - 1		12

Caption competition....
KEDWELL
9
easyJet
Send in your suggestions to
tw.publications@btinternet.com and you could
win a copy of the 2013 edition of the Directory...
Photo by Keith Clayton

WINGATE & FINCHLEY

Chairman: Aron Sharpe
Secretary: David Thrilling **(T)** 0797 700 7746 **(E)** secretary@wingatefinchley.com
Additional Committee Members:
Harvey Ackerman, Ricky Deller, Paul Lerman

Manager: David Norman
Programme Editor: Paul Lerman **(E)** paullerman@hotmail.com

Back Row (L-R): Ewa Trochym, David Norman, Lewis Jones, Gary Burrell, Ahmet Rifat, Bobby Smith, Gavin King, David Laird, Ajet Shehu, Ola Williams, Joe O'Brien, Dean Smith, Andrew Zeller.
Front Row: Marc Weatherstone, Murat Karagul, Josh Cooper, Jordan Fowler, Daniel Nielsen, Leon Smith, Paul Wright, Angus McLachlan, Marc Henry.

Club Factfile

Founded: 1991 **Nickname:** Blues
Previous Names: Wingate (founded 1946) and Finchley (founded late 1800s) merged in 1991
Previous Leagues: South Midlands 1991-95, Isthmian 1995-2004, Southern 2004-2006

Club Colours (change): Blue/white/white (All yellow)

Ground: Harry Abraham Stadium, Summers Lane, Finchley N12 0PD **(T)** 020 8446 2217
Capacity: 8,500 **Seats:** 500 **Covered:** 500 **Clubhouse:** Yes **Shop:** No

Directions
The simplest way to get to The Harry Abrahams Stadium is to get on to the A406 North Circular Road.
If coming from the West (eg via M1), go past Henlys Corner (taking the left fork after the traffic lights) and then drive for about 1 mile. The exit to take is the one immediately after a BP garage. Take the slip road and then turn right at the lights onto the A1000.
If coming from the East (eg via A10, M11) take the A1000 turn off. At the end of the slip road turn left at the lights. Go straight over the next set of lights. Then after 100m pass through another set of lights, then at the next set of lights turn right into Summers Lane. The Abrahams Stadium is a few hundred metres down on the right hand side.

Previous Grounds:

Record Attendance: 528 v Brentwood Town (Division One North Play-Off) 2010/11
Record Victory: 9-1 v Winslow (South Midlands League) 23/11/1991
Record Defeat: 0-9 v Edgware - Isthmian Division 2 15/01/2000
Record Goalscorer: Marc Morris 650 (including with Wingate FC) FA Record for one Club
Record Appearances: Marc Morris 720 (including with Wingate FC)FA Record for one Club
Additional Records:

Senior Honours: Isthmian League Cup 2010-11.
London Senior Cup 2010-11.

10 YEAR RECORD

01-02	02-03	03-04	04-05	05-06	06-07	07-08	08-09	09-10	10-11
Isth3 7	Isth1N 18	Isth1N 11	SthE 12	SthE 12	Isth1N 9	Isth1N 18	Isth1N 7	Isth1N 3	Isth1N 3

AFC SUDBURY

Chairman: Philip Turner
Secretary: Davis Webb **(T)** 07885 327 510 **(E)** dave-afc@supanet.com
Additional Committee Members:
Mark Peaman, Danny Crosbie

Manager: Nicky Smith
Programme Editor: Darren Theobald **(E)** theobaldd@hotmail.co.uk

Club Factfile

Founded: 1999 **Nickname:** Yellows
Previous Names: Sudbury Town (1874) and Sudbury Wanderers (1958) merged in 1999
Previous Leagues: Eastern Counties 1999-2006, Isthmian 2006-08, Southern 2008-10

Club Colours (change): Yellow/blue/yellow

Ground: Kingsmarsh Stadium, Brundon Lane, Sudbury, Suffolk CO10 7HN **(T)** 01787 376 213
Capacity: 2,500 **Seats:** 200 **Covered:** 1,500 **Clubhouse:** Yes **Shop:** Yes

Directions
Follow Halstead/Chelmsford road from Sudbury centre for a mile.
First right after bridge at foot of steep hill and first right again after left hand bend.

Previous Grounds: Not known

Record Attendance: 1,800
Record Victory: Not known
Record Defeat: Not known
Record Goalscorer: Gary Bennett - 172
Record Appearances: Paul Betson - 376
Additional Records:

Senior Honours: Eastern Counties League 2000-01, 01-02, 02-03, 03-04, 04-05.
Suffolk Premier Cup 2002, 2003, 2004.

10 YEAR RECORD

01-02	02-03	03-04	04-05	05-06	06-07	07-08	08-09	09-10	10-11
ECP 1	ECP 1	ECP 1	ECP 1	ECP 3	Isth1N 5	Isth1N 2	SthM	SthM 14	Isth1N 7

BRENTWOOD TOWN

Chairman: Brian Hallett
Secretary: Ray Stevens **(T)** 0776 800 6370 **(E)** r.w.stevens@btinternet.com
Additional Committee Members:
Ken Hobbs

Manager: Steve Witherspoon
Programme Editor: Ken Hobbs **(E)** khobbs1057@aol.com

Brentwood of the Essex Senior League in 1994. Back row, left to right: J.Holmes, L.Cook, J.Elwood, M.Hardingham, B.Douglas, B.Maltese and D.Pether. Front Row: N.Slack, G.Devlin, D.Stille, J.Taylor and R.Pike.

Club Factfile

Founded: 1955 **Nickname:** Blues
Previous Names: Manor Athletic, Brentwood Athletic, Brentwood F.C.
Previous Leagues: Romford & District, South Essex Combination, London & Essex Border, Olympian, Essex Senior

Club Colours (change): Sky blue/white/sky blue

Ground: The Arena, Brentwood Centre, Doddinghurst Road, Brentwood CM15 9NN **(T)** 01708 800 6370
Capacity: 1,000 **Seats:** 50 **Covered:** 250 **Clubhouse:** Yes **Shop:** No

Directions
From High Street (Wilson's Corner) turn north into Ongar Road.
Then at third mini roundabout turn right into Doddinghurst Road.

Previous Grounds: King George's Playing Fields (Hartswood), Larkins Playing Fields 1957-93

Record Attendance: 472 v West Ham United - 27/07/2004
Record Victory: Not known
Record Defeat: Not known
Record Goalscorer: Not known
Record Appearances: Not known
Additional Records:

Senior Honours: Essex Senior League 2000-01, 2006-07, League Cup 1975-76, 78-79, 90-91, 2006-07.
Essex Olympian League Cup 1967-68.

10 YEAR RECORD

01-02	02-03	03-04	04-05	05-06	06-07	07-08	08-09	09-10	10-11
ESen 14	ESen 11	ESen 14	ESen 14	ESen 8	ESen 1	Isth1N 6	Isth1N 3	Isth1N 12	Isth1N 5

CHATHAM TOWN

Chairman: Jeff Talbot
Secretary: Henry Longhurst **(T)** 0796 746 5554 **(E)** h.longhurst@sky.com
Additional Committee Members:
Mike Green

Manager: Kevin Watson
Programme Editor: Rachel Willett **(E)** rachel.willett@yahoo.co.uk

Terry Groom, David Hunt, Brad Potter, Jason Barton, Matt Solly, Nick Hegley, Barry Bell
Jon Hogg, Joe Fuller, Gary Cook, James Tedder GK, Adam Molloy GK, George Mitchell, Uche Ibemere, Lee Maskell, Anthony Hogg
Ryan Laker, Callum O'Shea, Danny Penny (Capt), Paul Foley (Manager), Kevin Watson (Player Coach), Gary Ward (Vice Capt), Kevin Winchcombe, Ryan Restell

Club Factfile

Founded: 1882 **Nickname:** Chats
Previous Names: Chatham FC 1882-1974, Medway FC 1974-79
Previous Leagues: Southern 1894-1900, 1920-21, 27-29, 83-88, 2001-, Kent 1894-96, 1901-1905, 29-59, 68-83, 88-2001, Aetolian 1959-64, Metropolitan 1964-68
Club Colours (change): Red & black stripes/black/black

Ground: Maidstone Road Sports Ground, Maidstone Road, Chatham ME4 6LR **(T)** 01634 812 194
Capacity: 2,000 **Seats:** 600 **Covered:** 600 **Clubhouse:** Yes **Shop:** Yes

Directions
M2, A229 Chatham turn-off,
follow signs to Chatham,
ground is one and half miles on the right opposite garage.
One mile from Chatham BR.

Previous Grounds: Great Lines, Chatham 1882-90

Record Attendance: 5,000 v Gillingham - 1980
Record Victory: Not known
Record Defeat: Not known
Record Goalscorer: Not known
Record Appearances: Not known
Additional Records: Received Transfer fee of £500

Senior Honours: Kent League 1894-95, 1903-04, 04-05, 71-72, 73-74, 75-76, 76-77, 79-80, 2000-01.
Kent Senior Cup 1888-89, 1904-05, 10-11, 18-19. Kent Senior Shield 1919-20.

10 YEAR RECORD

01-02	02-03	03-04	04-05	05-06	06-07	07-08	08-09	09-10	10-11
SthE 16	SthE 15	SthE 13	SthE 11	SthE 17	Isth1S 16	Isth1S 18	Isth1N 10	Isth1S 17	Isth1S 21

CHESHUNT

Chairman: Vince Sartori
Secretary: Alex Kalinic **(T)** 0775 483 1800 **(E)** alex@cheshuntfc.com
Additional Committee Members:
Paul Fletcher

Manager: Bob Dearie
Programme Editor: Alex Kalinic **(E)** alex@cheshuntfc.com

Back Row L to R – Iain Salt, Billy Haspineall, Nick Mountford, Joe Wright, Tom Dos Anjos, Christiaan Beaupierre, Syrus Gordon, Charie Douse, Darrell Cox. Middle Row L to R - Chris Meikle, Tom Tresadern, Michael Sharman, Graeme Butler, David Hicks, Glen Parry, Matt Thomson, Gary Schillaci, Jimmy Martin, Richard Ashie.
Front Row L to R – Howard Bailey, Adam Norman, Alex Kalinic, Paul Fletcher, Paul Halsey (Assist Manager) Bob Dearie (Manager) Alfie Noarman (Coach) Rebecca Cornish (Physio) Neil Harrison, George Norman, Vince Bates .

Club Factfile

Founded: 1946 **Nickname:** Ambers
Previous Names:
Previous Leagues: London 1947-51, 56-59, Delphian 1952-55, Aetolian 1960-62, Spartan 1963-64, 88-93, Athenian 1965-76, Isthmian 1977-87, 94-2005, Southern 2006-08

Club Colours (change): Amber/black/amber or black

Ground: Cheshunt Stadium, Theobalds Lane, Cheshunt, Herts EN8 8RU **(T)** 01992 633 500
Capacity: 3,500 **Seats:** 424 **Covered:** 600 **Clubhouse:** Yes **Shop:** No

Directions
M25, junction 25 take A10 north towards Hertford.
Third exit at roundabout towards Waltham Cross A121.
First exit at roundabout towards Cheshunt B176.
Under railway bridge then left onto Theobalds Lane.
Ground is 800 yard on the right.

Previous Grounds: Not known

Record Attendance: 5,000
Record Victory: v Bromley - FA Amateur Cup 2nd Round 28/01/1950
Record Defeat: 0-10 v Etonn Manor - London League 17/04/1956
Record Goalscorer: Eddie Sedgwick - 148 (1967-72, 1980)
Record Appearances: John Poole - 526 (1970-76, 79-83)
Additional Records: Received £10,000 from Peterborough United for Lloyd Opara

Senior Honours: London League Premier Division 1950, Division 1 1948, 49. Athenian League Premier Division 1976, Division 1 1968.
Spartan League 1963. Isthmian League Division 2 2003.
London Charity Cup 1974. East Anglian Cup 1975. Herts Charity Cup 2006, 2008.

10 YEAR RECORD

01-02	02-03	03-04	04-05	05-06	06-07	07-08	08-09	09-10	10-11
Isth2 20	Isth2 1	Isth1N 3	Isth P 19	SthP 16	SthP 16	SthP 22	Isth1N 14	Isth1N 15	Isth1N 18

ENFIELD TOWN

Chairman: Paul Millington
Secretary: Peter Coath (T) 0794 937 8931 (E) peter.coath@virginmedia.com
Additional Committee Members:
Keith Wortley, Ciaron Glennon, Dave Farenden

Manager: Steve Newing
Programme Editor: Ciaron Glennon (E) ciaron.glennon@btopenworld.com

Photo: Alison Glennon

Club Factfile

Founded: 2001 **Nickname:** ET's or Towners
Previous Names: Broke away from Enfield F.C. in 2001
Previous Leagues: Essex Senior League

Club Colours (change): White/blue/blue

Ground: Quenn Elizabeth Stadium, Donkey Lane, Enfield EN1 4BT (T) 020 8363 7398
Capacity: **Seats:** **Covered:** **Clubhouse:** **Shop:**

Directions
Turn off A10 at Carterhanger Lane,
then turn immediately into Donkey Lane.

Previous Grounds: Brimsdown Rovers FC 2001-2010

Record Attendance: 562 v Enfield - Middlesex Charity Cup 2002-03
Record Victory: 7-0 v Ilford (A) - 29/04/2003
Record Defeat: Not known
Record Goalscorer: Dan Clarke - 68
Record Appearances: Stuart Snowden - 147
Additional Records:

Senior Honours: Essex Senior League 2002-03, 04-05.

10 YEAR RECORD

01-02	02-03	03-04	04-05	05-06	06-07	07-08	08-09	09-10	10-11
ESen 2	ESen 1	ESen 4	ESen 1	SthE 3	Isth1N 3	Isth1N 12	Isth1N 12	Isth1N 4	Isth1N 6

GRAYS ATHLETIC

Chairman: Keith Burns
Secretary: Val Pepperell **(T)** 0793 173 1358 **(E)** graysathleticfc@hotmail.co.uk
Additional Committee Members:
Steve Allen, Steve Pepperell

Manager: Hakan Hayrettin
Programme Editor: Chris Jones **(E)** cmjones007@hotmail.com

Action from Grays' FA Trophy 3rd Qualifying Round tie with Cirencester Town.
Photo: Peter Barnes.

Club Factfile

Founded: 1890 **Nickname:** The Blues
Previous Names: Not known
Previous Leagues: Athenian 1912-14, 58-83, London 1914-24, 26-39, Kent 1924-26, Corinthian 1945-58, Isthmian 1958-2004, Conference 2004-10
Club Colours (change): All royal blue

Ground: East Thurrock United, Rookery Hill, Corringham, Essex SS17 9LB **(T)** 01375 644 166
Capacity: 4,000 **Seats:** 160 **Covered:** 1,000 **Clubhouse:** Yes **Shop:** No

Directions
From A13 London-Southend road,
take A1014 at Stanford-le-Hope for two and half miles.
Ground on left.

Previous Grounds: Recreation Ground Bridge Road

Record Attendance: 9,500 v Chelmsford City - FA Cup 4th Qualifying Round 1959
Record Victory: 12-0 v Tooting & Mitcham United - London League 24/02/1923
Record Defeat: 0-12 v Enfield (A) - Athenian League 20/04/1963
Record Goalscorer: Harry Brand - 269 (1944-52)
Record Appearances: Phil Sammons - 673 (1982-97)
Additional Records:

Senior Honours: Conference South 2004-05. FA Trophy 2004-05, 05-06.
Essex Senior Cup x8

10 YEAR RECORD

01-02		02-03		03-04		04-05		05-06		06-07		07-08		08-09		09-10		10-11	
Isth P	6	Isth P	19	Isth P	6	Conf S	1	Conf	3	Conf	19	Conf	10	Conf	19	Conf	23	Isth1N	10

GREAT WAKERING ROVERS

Chairman: Roy Ketteridge
Secretary: Daniel Ellis (T) 07828 048 671 (E) secretary@gwrovers.co.uk
Additional Committee Members:
Robert Lilley

Manager: Ryan Wilkinson
Programme Editor: Dan Ellis (E) danielellis@hotmail.co.uk

Great Wakering in 2005-2006, back row, left to right: Clive Taylor (Physio), Joel Ettienne-Clark, Nathan Evans, Matt Stubbs, Gianni Frankis, Nikki Beale, James Marrable, Dave Hudson Paul Pilkington, Michael Perrineau-Daley, Ryan Wilkinson (Coach) and David Patient (Assistant Manager). Front row: Fajion, Matt Reade, Glen Robson, Martin Buglione, Gary Eweters, John Heffer, Iain O'Connell (Manager0, Danny Pitts, Jason Barton, Jason Bourne and Ross Parmenter.

Club Factfile

Founded: 1919 **Nickname:** Rovers
Previous Names: Not known
Previous Leagues: Southend & District 1919-81, Southend Alliance 1981-89, Essex Intermediate 1989-92, Essex Senior 1992-99, Isthmian 1999-2004, Southern 2004-05
Club Colours (change): Green and white stripes/white/green

Ground: Burroughs Park, Little Wakering Hall Lane, Gt Wakering SS3 0HH (T) 01702 217 812
Capacity: 2,500 **Seats:** 150 **Covered:** 300 **Clubhouse:** Yes **Shop:** No

Directions
A127 towards Southend and follow signs for Shoeburyness for about four miles.
Turn left to Great Wakering on B1017 at Bournes Green.
Go down High Street for half a mile and ground is on the left.

Previous Grounds: Great Wakering Rec

Record Attendance: 1,150 v Southend United - Friendly 19/07/2006
Record Victory: 9-0 v Eton Manor - 27/12/1931
Record Defeat: 1-7 v Bowers United - Essex Senior League 01/04/1998
Record Goalscorer: Not known
Record Appearances: Not known
Additional Records:

Senior Honours: Essex Senior League 1994-95. Isthmian League Division 3.

10 YEAR RECORD

01-02	02-03	03-04	04-05	05-06	06-07	07-08	08-09	09-10	10-11
Isth2 7	Isth1N 14	Isth1N 21	SthE 20	SthE 13	Isth1N 12	Isth1N 13	Isth1N 13	Isth1N 9	Isth1N 15

HARLOW TOWN

Chairman: John Barnett
Secretary: John McClelland **(T)** 0781 639 1892 **(E)** maccahtfc@hotmail.com
Additional Committee Members:
Ray Dyer, Steve Clark

Manager: Kevin Warren
Programme Editor: John McClelland **(E)** maccahtfc@hotmail.com

Club Factfile

Founded: 1879 **Nickname:** Hawks
Previous Names: Not known
Previous Leagues: East Hertfordshire > 1932, Spartan 1932-39, 46-54, London 1954-61, Delphian 1961-63, Athenian 1963-73, Isthmian 1973-92, Inactive 1992-93, Southern 2004-06

Club Colours (change): All red

Ground: Barrows Farm Std, off Elizabeth Way, The Pinnacles, Harlow CM19 5BE **(T)** 01279 443 196
Capacity: 3,500 **Seats:** 500 **Covered:** 500 **Clubhouse:** Yes **Shop:** Yes

Directions
Barrows Farm is situated on the western side of town just off of the Roydon Road (A1169) on the Pinnacles Industrial Estate.
If coming into Harlow from the M11 (North or South) exit at Junction 7 and follow the A414 until the first roundabout where you turn left onto the A1169. Follow the A1169 signed for Roydon until you see the ground ahead of you at the Roydon Road roundabout. Go straight over the roundabout and the entrance to the ground is on the left.
If coming into town from the west on the A414 turn right at the first roundabout (the old ground was straight ahead) signed Roydon A1169. Follow the A1169 for approx 1 mile and the entrance to the ground is on the right.

Previous Grounds: Marigolds 1919-22, Green Man Field 1922-60

Record Attendance: 9,723 v Leicester City - FA Cup 3rd Round replay 08/01/1980
Record Victory: 14-0 v Bishop's Stortford - 11/04/1925
Record Defeat: 0-11 v Ware (A) - Spartan Division 1 East 06/03/1948
Record Goalscorer: Dick Marshall scored 64 during 1928-29
Record Appearances: Norman Gladwin - 639 (1949-70)
Additional Records:

Senior Honours: Athenian League Division 1 1971-72. Isthmian League Division 1 1978-79, Division 2 North 1988-89.
Essex Senior cup 1978-79

10 YEAR RECORD

01-02		02-03		03-04		04-05		05-06		06-07		07-08		08-09		09-10		10-11	
Isth1	7	Isth1N	10	Isth1N	10	SthE	15	SthE	9	Isth1N	2	Isth P	15	Isth P	20	Isth1N	22	Isth1N	4

HEYBRIDGE SWIFTS

Chairman: Nick Bowyer
Secretary: Peter Pask (T) 0777 093 0556 (E) admin@heybridgeswifts.com
Additional Committee Members:
Jill Hedgecock, Dave Buckingham, Michael Gibson

Manager: Mark Hawkes
Programme Editor: Noel Tilbrook (E) noel@steponsafety.co.uk

Club Factfile

Founded: 1880 **Nickname:** Swifts
Previous Names: No known
Previous Leagues: Essex & Suffolk Border, North Essex, South Essex, Essex Senior 1971-84

Club Colours (change): Black and white stripes/black/black

Ground: Scraley Road, Heybridge, Maldon, Essex CM9 8JA (T) 01621 852 978
Capacity: 3,000 **Seats:** 550 **Covered:** 1,200 **Clubhouse:** Yes **Shop:** Yes

Directions
Leave Maldon on the main road to Colchester,
pass through Heybridge then turn right at sign to Tolleshunt Major (Scraley Road).
The ground is on the right.

Previous Grounds: Not known

Record Attendance: 2,477 v Woking - FA Trophy 1997
Record Victory: Not known
Record Defeat: Not known
Record Goalscorer: Julian Lamb - 115 (post War)
Record Appearances: Hec Askew - 500+. John Pollard - 496
Additional Records: Paid £1,000 for Dave Rainford and for Lee Kersey
Received £35,000 from Southend United for Simon Royce

Senior Honours: Isthmian League Division 2 North 1989-90, Essex Senior League x3.
Essex Junior Cup 1931-32. East Anglian Cup 1993-94, 94-95.

10 YEAR RECORD

01-02	02-03	03-04	04-05	05-06	06-07	07-08	08-09	09-10	10-11
Isth P 13	Isth P 20	Isth P 16	Isth P 7	Isth P 2	Isth P 12	Isth P 12	Isth P 21	Isth1N 6	Isth1N 9

ILFORD

Chairman: Roger Chilvers
Secretary: Marion Chilvers **(T)** 020 8591 5313 **(E)** rogerchilvers@aol.com
Additional Committee Members:
Len Llewellyn

Manager: Colin Walton
Programme Editor: Len Llewellyn **(E)** exseniorlenl@aol.com

Ilford F.C., The Finalists in the 1958 F A Amateur Cup Final. Back row, left to right: J.Sharod, A.Whittall, G.Simmons, P.Gibbins, H.Dodkins, and E.Cross. Front Row: C.Elsworthy, D.Durston, T.Taylor, H.Butler, S.Castle and A.Sewell

Club Factfile

Founded: 1987 **Nickname:** The Foxes
Previous Names: Reformed as Ilford in 1987 after the original club merged with Leytonstone in 1980.
Previous Leagues: Spartan 1987-94, Essex Senior 1996-2004, Isthmian 2004-05, Southern 2005-06

Club Colours (change): Blue and white hoops/blue/blue

Ground: Cricklefield Stadium, 486 High Road, Ilford, Essex IG1 1UE **(T)** 020 8514 8352
Capacity: 3,500 **Seats:** 216 **Covered:** Yes **Clubhouse:** Yes **Shop:** No

Directions Taking the A127, from the east travel towards London before coming to the traffic light controlled junction at Barley Lane, Goodmayes (B177) . Turn Left by taking the slip road and follow Barley Lane to its junction with the traffic light controlled High Road, Goodmayes (A118) (it is the first set of traffic control lights for traffic rather than pedestrians on that road). Turn Right and follow the road past Seven Kings station (which should be on your right) and on towards Ilford. The entrance to the ground is some 400 yards past the station with the Ilford Swimming Baths on the left being the point at which both coaches and those in cars or on foot should turn left into the car parks. Both on Saturday and after 6pm. during the week, the public car park is free of charge.

Previous Grounds: Not known

Record Attendance: Not known
Record Victory: Not known
Record Defeat: Not known
Record Goalscorer: Not known
Record Appearances: Not known
Additional Records:

Senior Honours: Isthmian League Division Two 2004-05.

10 YEAR RECORD

01-02		02-03		03-04		04-05		05-06		06-07		07-08		08-09		09-10		10-11	
ESen	9	ESen	3	ESen	2	Isth2	1	SthE	21	Isth1N	21	Isth1N	21	Isth1N	17	Isth1N	20	Isth1N	20

LEISTON

Chairman: Andrew Crisp
Secretary: David Rees (T) 07734 600 414 (E) gagrees@aol.com
Additional Committee Members:

Manager: Mark Morsley
Programme Editor: David Rees (E) gagrees@aol.com

Leiston Town 1997-1998.

Club Factfile

Founded: 1880 **Nickname:** The Blues
Previous Names: None
Previous Leagues: Suffolk & Ipswich, Eastern Counties > 2011.

Club Colours (change): All royal blue

Ground: LTAA, Victory Road, Leiston IP16 4DQ (T) 01728 830 308
Capacity: 2,500 **Seats:** 124 **Covered:** 500 **Clubhouse:** **Shop:**

Directions Take junction 28 off the M25, take the A12/A1023 exit to Chelmsford/Romford/Brentwood, keep left at the fork, follow signs for Chelmsford/A12 (E) and merge onto A12, at the roundabout, take the 3rd exit onto the A14 ramp, merge onto A14, at junction 58, exit toward A12, keep left at the fork, follow signs for Lowestoft/Woodbridge/A12 (N) and merge onto A12, go through 7 roundabouts, turn right onto A1094, turn left onto Snape Rd/B1069, continue to follow B1069, turn left onto Victory Rd, ground will be on the left.

Previous Grounds: Not known

Record Attendance: **Att:** 271 v AFC Sudbury, 13.11.04.
Record Victory: Not known
Record Defeat: Not known
Record Goalscorer: Lee McGlone - 60 (League).
Record Appearances: Tim Sparkes - 154 (League).
Additional Records:

Senior Honours: Eastern Counties League Premier Division 2010-11.

10 YEAR RECORD

01-02		02-03		03-04		04-05		05-06		06-07		07-08		08-09		09-10		10-11	
EC1	4	EC1	7	EC1	3	ECP	10	ECP	9	ECP	5	ECP	9	ECP	7	ECP	3	ECP	1

MALDON & TIPTREE

Chairman: Ed Garty
Secretary: Phil Robinson **(T)** 0775 906 6636 **(E)** robbophil@hotmail.com
Additional Committee Members:
Peter Bond

Manager: Brad King & Glen Knight
Programme Editor: Phil Robinson **(E)** robbophil@hotmail.com

Unfortunately an up-to-date photograph was not available at the time of going to press.

Club Factfile

Founded: 2010 **Nickname:** The Hoops
Previous Names: Maldon Town (1975) and Tiptree United (1933) merged in 2010 to form today's club
Previous Leagues: None

Club Colours (change): Blue and red stripes/blue/blue

Ground: Wallace Binder Ground, Park Drive, Maldon CM9 6XX **(T)** 01621 853 762
Capacity: 2,800 **Seats:** 155 **Covered:** 300 **Clubhouse:** Yes **Shop:**

Directions
From M25 junction 28 travel north on A12 until A414 to Maldon.
Turn right at Safeways roundabout, then over next two roundabouts.
Ground is on the right.

Previous Grounds:

Record Attendance: First season as new club
Record Victory: First season as new club
Record Defeat: First season as new club
Record Goalscorer: First season as new club
Record Appearances: First season as new club
Additional Records:

Senior Honours: None

10 YEAR RECORD

01-02	02-03	03-04	04-05	05-06	06-07	07-08	08-09	09-10	10-11
									Isth1N 8

NEEDHAM MARKET

Chairman: David Bugg
Secretary: Mark Easlea **(T)** 0779 545 6502 **(E)** m.easlea@sky.com
Additional Committee Members:
Paul Collier, Wendy Hall

Manager: Danny Laws
Programme Editor: Mark Easlea **(E)** m.easlea@sky.com

Club Factfile

Founded: 1919 **Nickname:**
Previous Names: None
Previous Leagues: Suffolk & Ipswich Senior, Eastern Counties

Club Colours (change): All red

Ground: Bloomfields, Quinton Road, Needham Market IP6 8DA **(T)** 01449 721 000
Capacity: 1,000 **Seats:** 250 **Covered:** 250 **Clubhouse:** Yes **Shop:** Yes

Directions
Quinton Road is off Barretts Lane which in turn is off Needham Market High Street.

Previous Grounds: Not known

Record Attendance: 750 v Ipswich Town - Suffolk Premier Cup 2007
Record Victory: Not known
Record Defeat: Not known
Record Goalscorer: Alvin King
Record Appearances: Not known
Additional Records:

Senior Honours: Suffolk Senior Cup 1989-90, 2004-05. Suffolk & Ipswich Senior League 1995-96. East Anglian Cup 2006-07.
Eastern Counties Premier Division 2009-10.

10 YEAR RECORD

01-02		02-03		03-04		04-05		05-06		06-07		07-08		08-09		09-10		10-11	
EC1	5	EC1	11	EC1	14	EC1	2	ECP	6	ECP	4	ECP	2	ECP	3	ECP	1	Isth1N	2

POTTERS BAR TOWN

Chairman: Peter Waller
Secretary: Alan Evans **(T)** 0783 363 2965 **(E)** potters_bar_sec@hotmail.co.uk
Additional Committee Members:
Dave Quinlan

Manager: Adam Lee
Programme Editor: Jeff Barnes **(E)** jeff@jeffbarnes.co.uk

Photo: Alan Coomes.

Club Factfile

Founded: 1960 **Nickname:** Grace or Scholars
Previous Names: None
Previous Leagues: Barnet & District 1960-65, North London Combination 1965-68, Herts Senior County 1968-91, Spartan South Midlands 1991-2005, Southern 2005-06

Club Colours (change): Maroon/white/white

Ground: The South Mimms Travel Stad., Parkfield, Watkins Rise, Pot.Bar EN6 1QN **(T)** 01707 654 833
Capacity: 2,000 **Seats:** 150 **Covered:** 250 **Clubhouse:** Yes **Shop:** Yes

Directions
M25 junction 24 enter Potters Bar along Southgate Road (A111) turn right into High Street at first lights (A1000) then left into The Walk after half a mile. Ground is 200 yards on the right - opposite Potters Bar Cricket Club.

Previous Grounds:

Record Attendance: 268 v Wealdstone - FA Cup 1998 (4,000 watched a charity match in 1997)
Record Victory: Not known
Record Defeat: Not known
Record Goalscorer: Not known
Record Appearances: Not known
Additional Records:

Senior Honours: Spartan South Midlands League Premier 1996-97, 2004-05.

10 YEAR RECORD

01-02	02-03	03-04	04-05	05-06	06-07	07-08	08-09	09-10	10-11
SSM P 13	SSM P 3	SSM P 4	SSM P 1	SthE 15	Isth1N 14	Isth1N 17	Isth1N 19	Isth1N 14	Isth1N 13

REDBRIDGE

Chairman: Dan Holloway
Secretary: Bob Holloway (T) 0789 069 9907 (E) bobholloway@redbridgefc.com
Additional Committee Members:
John Taylor, Len Cordell, Adam Silver, Tim Ley

Manager: Terry Spillance
Programme Editor: Adam Silver (E) adammichaelsilver@hotmail.com

Club Factfile

Founded: 1958 **Nickname:** Motormen
Previous Names: Ford United 1958-2004
Previous Leagues: Aetolian 1959-64, Greater London 1964-71, Metropolitan 1971-74, Essex Senior 1974-97, Isthmian 1997-2004, Conference 2004-05

Club Colours (change): Red with black trim/black/black

Ground: Oakside Stadium, Station Road, Barkingside, Ilford IG6 1NB (T) 020 8550 3611
Capacity: 3,000 **Seats:** 316 **Covered:** 1,000 **Clubhouse:** Yes **Shop:** Yes

Directions
A12 from London, turn left off Eastern Avenue into Horns Road, Barkingside (Greengate). Right into Craven Gardens, right again into Carlton Drive and left into Station Road. Go over bridge and ground is on the right.
Adjacent to Barkingside Underground Station (Central Line).

Previous Grounds: Ford Sports & Social Club > 2000

Record Attendance: 58,000 v Bishop Auckland
Record Victory: Not known
Record Defeat: Not known
Record Goalscorer: Jeff Wood - 196
Record Appearances: Roger Bird
Additional Records:

Senior Honours: Aetolian League 1959-60, 61-62. Greater London League 1970-71. Essex Senior League 1991-92, 96-97.
Isthmian League Division 3 1998-99, Division 1 2001-02,

10 YEAR RECORD

01-02		02-03		03-04		04-05		05-06		06-07		07-08		08-09		09-10		10-11	
Isth1	1	Isth P	15	Isth P	13	Conf S	22	Isth P	22	Isth1N	16	Isth1N	3	Isth1N	8	Isth1N	18	Isth1N	16

ROMFORD

Chairman: Steve Gardener
Secretary: Colin Ewenson **(T)** 0797 371 7074 **(E)** ewenson@aol.com
Additional Committee Members:

Manager: Paul Martin
Programme Editor: Keith Preston **(E)** prestonruf@aol.com

Club Factfile

Founded: 1876 **Nickname:** Boro
Previous Names: Original club founded in 1876 folded during WW1, Reformed in 1929 folded again in 1978 and reformed in 1992
Previous Leagues: Athenian 1931-39, Isthmian 1945-59, 97-2002, Southern 1959-78, Essex Senior 1992-96, 2002-09

Club Colours (change): Blue and yellow stripes/blue/blue

Ground: Aveley FC, The Mill Field, Mill Road, Aveley RM15 4SJ **(T)** 01708 365 940
Capacity: 4,000 **Seats:** 400 **Covered:** 400 **Clubhouse:** Yes **Shop:**

Directions
London - Southend A1306, turn into Sandy Lane at Aveley.

Previous Grounds:

Record Attendance: 820 v Leatherhead - Isthmian Division 2
Record Victory: Not known
Record Defeat: Not known
Record Goalscorer: Danny Benstock
Record Appearances: S Horne - 234
Additional Records: Essex Senior League 1995-96, 2008-09. Isthmian League Division 2 1996-97.

Senior Honours:

10 YEAR RECORD

01-02	02-03	03-04	04-05	05-06	06-07	07-08	08-09	09-10	10-11
Isth2 22	ESen 5	ESen 5	ESen 5	ESen 12	ESen 2	ESen 5	ESen 1	Isth1N 13	Isth1N 12

SOHAM TOWN RANGERS

Chairman: Colin Murfit
Secretary: Karen Prewett **(T)** 07917 417 516 **(E)** ladykarenp@btinternet.com
Additional Committee Members:
Simon Cullum, Desmond Camp

Manager: Andrew Furnell
Programme Editor: Fred Parker **(E)** fred@fredparker.plus.com

Unfortunately an up-to-date photograph was not available at the time of going to press.

Club Factfile

Founded: 1947 **Nickname:** Town or Rangers
Previous Names: Soham Town and Soham Rangers merged in 1947
Previous Leagues: Peterborough & District, Eastern Counties 1963-2008, Southern 2008-11.

Club Colours (change): All green with white trim

Ground: Julius Martin Lane, Soham, Ely, Cambridgeshire CB7 5EQ **(T)** 01353 720 732
Capacity: 2,000 **Seats:** 250 **Covered:** 1,000 **Clubhouse:** Yes **Shop:** Yes

Directions: Take the turning off the A14 for Soham/Ely. Join the A142 following signs for Ely/Soham. On approaching Soham at the Q8 Petrol Station, continue down the Soham by-pass for approx. 1.5 miles. Turn left after the Bypass Motel, continue bearing left across the Common into Bushel Lane, at end of road, turn right into Hall Street. Julius Martin Lane is 2nd left.

Previous Grounds:

Record Attendance: 3,000 v Pegasus - FA Amateur Cup 1963
Record Victory: Not known
Record Defeat: Not known
Record Goalscorer: Not known
Record Appearances: Not known
Additional Records:

Senior Honours: Eastern Counties League Premier Division 2007-08

10 YEAR RECORD

01-02	02-03	03-04	04-05	05-06	06-07	07-08	08-09	09-10	10-11
ECP 12	ECP 3	ECP 5	ECP 7	ECP 10	ECP	ECP 1	SthC 15	SthC 11	SthC 17

THAMESMEAD TOWN

Chairman: Terry Hill
Secretary: David Joy **(T)** 0799 061 2495 **(E)** davejoyo@yahoo.co.uk
Additional Committee Members:
Colin Mare

Manager: Keith McMahon
Programme Editor: Colin Mare **(E)** marecolin@hotmail.com

Archive Team Photo - 2009-10 - Back row (L-R): Steve Waite (Assistant Manager), Alan Martin (Physio), Gabriel Momodu, Andy Constable, Pater Deadman, James Brown, Lew Tozer, Junior Baker, Tony Russell (Player/Coach), Steve Cant, Keith McMahon (Manager), Alan Woodward (Physio)
Front row (L-R): George Martin (Mascot), Scott Mulholland, Jack Hopkins, Lea Dawson, Steve Northwood, Rafael Momodu, Danny Moore, Marcus Perona, Peter Smith.

Club Factfile

Founded: 1970 **Nickname:** The Mead
Previous Names: None
Previous Leagues: Spartan 1987-91, Kent 1991-2008

Club Colours (change): Green and white/green/green

Ground: Bayliss Avenue, Thamesmead, London SE28 8NJ **(T)** 020 8311 4211
Capacity: 400 **Seats:** 161 **Covered:** 125 **Clubhouse:** Yes **Shop:**

Directions From the A2 take the A2018 exit toward Dartford/Wilmington, at the roundabout, take the 1st exit onto Shepherd's Ln/A2018. At the roundabout, take the 1st exit onto Rochester Way. Slight right at Swan Ln, continue onto Station Rd. At the roundabout, take the 1st exit onto Crayford Rd/A207, continue to follow A207, slight right to stay on A207, turn left at London Rd/A2000 continue to follow A2000, turn right at Perry St/A2000. At the roundabout, take the 2nd exit onto Northend Rd/A206, continue to follow A206. Go through 1 roundabout. At the roundabout, take the 2nd exit onto Bronze Age Way/A2016, continue to follow A2016. Go through 1 roundabout. At the roundabout, take the 2nd exit onto Eastern Way/A2016. Take the ramp. At the roundabout, take the 3rd exit onto Carlyle Rd/A2041. At the roundabout, take the 3rd exit onto Crossway. Turn right at Bayliss Ave, take the 1st left onto Chadwick Way. Ground will be on the left

Previous Grounds:

Record Attendance: 400 v Wimbledon - Ground opening 1988
Record Victory: 9-0 v Kent Police - Kent League 19/04/1994
Record Defeat: Not known
Record Goalscorer: Delroy D'Oyley
Record Appearances: Not known
Additional Records:

Senior Honours: Kent Senior Trophy 2004-05. Kent Premier 2007-08

10 YEAR RECORD

01-02	02-03	03-04	04-05	05-06	06-07	07-08	08-09	09-10	10-11
Kent P 4	Kent P 3	Kent P 2	Kent P 8	Kent P 3	Kent P 4	Kent P 1	Isth1N 18	Isth1N 7	Isth1N 17

TILBURY

Chairman: Robin Nash
Secretary: Anthony Mercer **(T)** 07718 881 593 **(E)** amercer67@googlemail.com
Additional Committee Members:
Linda Vaughan, Karl Sharman, George Hammond

Manager: Paul Vaughan
Programme Editor: Mark Kettlety **(E)** sundayonly1@aol.com

Club Factfile

Founded: 1900 **Nickname:** The Dockers
Previous Names:
Previous Leagues: Grays & District/South Essex, Kent 1927-31, London, South Essex Combination (Wartime), Corinthian 1950-57, Delphian 1962-63, Athenian 1963-73, Isthmian 1973-2004, Essex Senior 2004-05

Club Colours (change): Black & white stripes/black/red

Ground: Chadfields, St Chads Road, Tilbury, Essex RM18 8NL **(T)** 01375 843 093
Capacity: 4,000 **Seats:** 350 **Covered:** 1,000 **Clubhouse:** Yes **Shop:** No

Directions
A13 Southend bound go left at Chadwell St Mary's turning, then right after 400 metres and right again at roundabout (signed Tilbury). Right into St Chads Road after five miles, first right into Chadfields for ground.

Previous Grounds: Not known

Record Attendance: 5,500 v Gorleston - FA Cup 1949
Record Victory: Not known
Record Defeat: Not known
Record Goalscorer: Ross Livermore - 282 in 305 games
Record Appearances: Nicky Smith - 424 (1975-85)
Additional Records: Received £2,000 from Grays Athletic for Tony Macklin 1990 and from Dartford for Steve Connor 1985

Senior Honours: Athenian League 1968-69. Isthmian League Division 1 1975-76.
Essex Senior Cup x4.

10 YEAR RECORD

01-02		02-03		03-04		04-05		05-06		06-07		07-08		08-09		09-10		10-11	
Isth2	16	Isth1N	20	Isth1N	22	SthE	22	ESen	3	Isth1N	19	Isth1N	20	Isth1N	11	Isth1N	11	Isth1N	19

WALTHAM ABBEY

Chairman: Joe Collins
Secretary: Derek Bird (T) 0776 583 7246 (E) secretary@wafc.net
Additional Committee Members:
Dave Marrion

Manager: Paul Wickenden
Programme Editor: Derek Bird (E) secretary@wafc.net

Club Factfile

Founded: 1944 **Nickname:** Abbotts
Previous Names: Abbey Sports amalgamated with Beechfield Sports in 1974 to form Beechfields. Club then renamed to Waltham Abbey in 1976
Previous Leagues: Spartan, Essex & Herts Border, Essex Senior

Club Colours (change): Green and white hoops/white/green

Ground: Capershotts, Sewardstone Road, Waltham Abbey, Essex EN9 1LU (T) 01992 711 287
Capacity: 2,000 **Seats:** 300 **Covered:** 500 **Clubhouse:** Yes **Shop:** No

Directions
Exit M25 at junction 26 and take 2nd left at roundabout into Honey Lane (A121).
At the Sewardstone roundabout, take third right into Sewarstone Road which takes you over the M25.
Ground is first right before cemetery.

Previous Grounds: Capershotts

Record Attendance: Not known
Record Victory: Not known
Record Defeat: Not known
Record Goalscorer: Not known
Record Appearances: Not known
Additional Records:

Senior Honours: London Spartan League Division 1 1977-78, Senior Division 1978-79.
London Senior Cup 1999. Essex Senior Cup 2004-05.

10 YEAR RECORD

01-02	02-03	03-04	04-05	05-06	06-07	07-08	08-09	09-10	10-11
LonInt 1	ESen 10	ESen 6	ESen 3	ESen 2	Isth1N 10	Isth1N 14	Isth1N 4	Isth1N 21	Isth1N 11

WALTHAM FOREST

Chairman: Isaac Johnson
Secretary: Tony Brazier (T) 0771 564 0171 (E) bjmapbr@ntlworld.com
Additional Committee Members:
Andrzej Perkins

Manager: Olawale Ojelabi
Programme Editor: Andrzej Perkins (E) forestgimp@hotmail.co.uk

Club Factfile

Founded: 1995 **Nickname:** The Stags
Previous Names: Leyton Pennant formed when Leyton and Walthamstow Pennant merged in 1995. Changed to Waltham Forest in 2003.
Previous Leagues: Isthmian 2003-04, Southern 2004-06

Club Colours (change): White with blue trim/navy blue/navy blue

Ground: Ilford FC, Cricklefield Stadium, 486 High Road, Ilford, Essex IG1 1UE (T) 0208 514 8352
Capacity: 3,500 **Seats:** 216 **Covered:** Yes **Clubhouse:** Yes **Shop:**

Directions: Taking the A127, from the east travel towards London before coming to the traffic light controlled junction at Barley Lane, Goodmayes (B177) . Turn Left by taking the slip road and follow Barley Lane to its junction with the traffic light controlled High Road, Goodmayes (A118) (it is the first set of traffic control lights for traffic rather than pedestrians on that road). Turn Right and follow the road past Seven Kings station (which should be on your right) and on towards Ilford. The entrance to the ground is some 400 yards past the station with the Ilford Swimming Baths on the left being the point at which both coaches and those in cars or on foot should turn left into the car parks. Both on Saturday and after 6pm. during the week, the public car park is free of charge.

Previous Grounds: Wadham Lodge

Record Attendance: Not known
Record Victory: Not known
Record Defeat: Not known
Record Goalscorer: Not known
Record Appearances: Not known
Additional Records:

Senior Honours: None

10 YEAR RECORD

01-02	02-03	03-04	04-05	05-06	06-07	07-08	08-09	09-10	10-11
Isth2 6	Isth1N 22	Isth1N 16	SthE 9	SthE 8	Isth1N 8	Isth1N 19	Isth1N 20	Isth1N 16	Isth1N 21

WARE

Chairman: Mick Clarke
Secretary: Fred Plume (T) 0796 702 2714 (E) fredplume@hotmail.co.uk
Additional Committee Members:
Billy Shaw

Manager: Stuart Nethercott
Programme Editor: Mark Kettlety (E) sundayonly1@aol.com

Club Factfile

Founded: 1892 **Nickname:** Blues
Previous Names:
Previous Leagues: East Herts, North Middlesex 1907-08, Herts County 1908-25, Spartan 1925-55, Delphian 1955-63, Athenian 1963-75

Club Colours (change): Blue and white/blue/blue

Ground: Wodson Park, Wadesmill Road, Ware, Herts SG12 0UQ (T) 01920 462 064
Capacity: 3,300 **Seats:** 500 **Covered:** 312 **Clubhouse:** Yes **Shop:** Yes

Directions
A10 off junction A602 and B1001 turn right at roundabout after 300 yards and follow Ware sign, past Rank factory. Turn left at main road onto A1170 (Wadesmill Road) Stadium is on the right after 3/4 mile.

Previous Grounds: Highfields, Canons Park, London Road, Presdales Lower Park 1921-26

Record Attendance: 3,800 v Hendon - FA Amateur Cup 1956-57
Record Victory: 10-1 v Wood Green Town
Record Defeat: 0-11 v Barnet
Record Goalscorer: George Dearman scored 98 goals during 1926-27
Record Appearances: Gary Riddle - 654
Additional Records:

Senior Honours: Isthmian League Division 2 2005-06.
East Anglian Cup 1973-74. Herts Senior Cup x5.

10 YEAR RECORD

01-02	02-03	03-04	04-05	05-06	06-07	07-08	08-09	09-10	10-11
Isth3 13	Isth2 8	Isth2 8	Isth2 10	Isth2 1	Isth1N 7	Isth1N 4	Isth1N 9	Isth1N 19	Isth1N 14

BOGNOR REGIS TOWN

Chairman: Dominic Reynolds
Secretary: Simon Cook **(T)** 07527 455 167 **(E)** sajcook2@aol.com
Additional Committee Members:
Roger Nash, Jack Pearce

Manager: Jamie Howell & Darin Kilpatrick
Programme Editor: Rob Garforth **(E)** rjgarforth@hotmail.com

Club Factfile

Founded: 1883 **Nickname:** The Rocks
Previous Names:
Previous Leagues: West Sussex 1896-1926, Brighton & Hove District 1926-27, Sussex County 1927-72, Southern League 1972-81, Isthmian 1982-2004, Conference 2004-09

Club Colours (change): White with green trim/green/white

Ground: Nyewood Lane, Bognor Regis PO21 2TY **(T)** 01243 822 325
Capacity: 4,100 **Seats:** 350 **Covered:** 2,600 **Clubhouse:** Yes **Shop:** Yes

Directions
West along sea front from pier past Aldwick shopping centre then turn right into Nyewood Lane.

Previous Grounds:

Record Attendance: 3,642 v Swnsea City - FA Cup 1st Round replay 1984
Record Victory: 24-0 v Littlehampton - West Sussex League 1913-14
Record Defeat: 0-19 v Shoreham - West Sussex League 1906-07
Record Goalscorer: Kevin Clements - 206
Record Appearances: Mick Pullen - 967 (20 seasons)
Additional Records: Paid £2,000 for Guy Rutherford 1995-96. Received £10,500 from Brighton & Hove for John Crumplin and Geoff Cooper, and from Crystal Palace for Simon Rodger.

Senior Honours: Sussex Professional Cup 1973-74. Sussex Senior Cup x9.

10 YEAR RECORD

01-02	02-03	03-04	04-05	05-06	06-07	07-08	08-09	09-10	10-11
Isth1 4	Isth1S 2	Isth P 10	Conf S 9	Conf S 12	Conf S 12	Conf S 18	Conf S 21	Isth P 22	Isth1S 2

BURGESS HILL TOWN

Chairman: Kevin Newell
Secretary: Tim Spencer **(T)** 0781 264 2498 **(E)** timspencer57@hotmail.com
Additional Committee Members:
Allan Turpin

Manager: Gary Croydon
Programme Editor: Emily Hodgkinson **(E)** timspencer57@hotmail.com

Club Factfile

Founded: 1882 **Nickname:** Hillians
Previous Names: None
Previous Leagues: Mid Sussex, Sussex County > 2003, Southern 2003-04

Club Colours (change): Yellow/black/black

Ground: Leylands Park, Maple Drive, Burgess Hill, West Sussex RH15 8DL **(T)** 01444 254 832
Capacity: 2,250 **Seats:** 307 **Covered:** Yes **Clubhouse:** Yes **Shop:** Yes

Directions
Turn east from A273 London Road into Leylands Road,
take 4th left sign posted Leyland Park.
Nearest station is Wivelsfield.

Previous Grounds: None

Record Attendance: 2,005 v AFC Wimbledon - Isthmian League Division 1 2004-05
Record Victory: Not known
Record Defeat: Not known
Record Goalscorer: Ashley Carr - 208
Record Appearances: Paul Williams - 499
Additional Records:

Senior Honours: Sussex County League x6 (Most recently 2001-02, 02-03).
Sussex Senior Cup 1883-84, 84-85, 85-86.

10 YEAR RECORD

01-02		02-03		03-04		04-05		05-06		06-07		07-08		08-09		09-10		10-11	
SxC1	1	SxC1	1	SthE	9	Isth1	10	Isth1	19	Isth1S	14	Isth1S	12	Isth1S	19	Isth1S	7	Isth1S	7

CHIPSTEAD

Chairman: Nigel Scarborough
Secretary: Heather Armstrong **(T)** 07525 443 802 **(E)** heather.chipsteadfc@virginmedia.com
Additional Committee Members:
Terry Tiernan, Keith Harvey

Manager: Mark Tompkins
Programme Editor: Janet Beckett **(E)** tandj47@talktalk.net

Club Factfile

Founded: 1906 **Nickname:** Chips
Previous Names:
Previous Leagues: Surrey Intermediate 1962-82, Surrey Premier 1982-86, Combined Counties 1986-2007

Club Colours (change): Green and white hoops/black/black

Ground: High Road, Chipstead, Surrey CR5 3SF **(T)** 01737 553 250
Capacity: 2,000 **Seats:** 150 **Covered:** 200 **Clubhouse:** Yes **Shop:** No

Directions
From the Brighton Road north bound,
go left into Church Lane and left into Hogcross Lane.
High Road is on the right.

Previous Grounds: Not known

Record Attendance: 1,170
Record Victory: Not known
Record Defeat: Not known
Record Goalscorer: Mick Nolan - 124
Record Appearances: Not known
Additional Records:

Senior Honours: Combined Counties Premier 1989-90, 2006-07.

10 YEAR RECORD

01-02	02-03	03-04	04-05	05-06	06-07	07-08	08-09	09-10	10-11
CC 3	CC 16	CCP 8	CCP 8	CCP 14	CCP 1	Isth1S 15	Isth1S 21	Isth1S 19	Isth1S 10

CORINTHIAN CASUALS

Chairman: Brian Vandervilt
Secretary: Brian Vandervilt **(T)** 0773 637 7498 **(E)** chairman@corinthian-casuals.com
Additional Committee Members:
John Kelvie, Rob Cavallini, Vincent Huggett

Manager: Kim Harris
Programme Editor: Rob Cavallini **(E)** rob_cavallini@hotmail.com

Club Factfile

Founded: 1939 **Nickname:** Casuals
Previous Names: Casuals and Corinthians merged in 1939
Previous Leagues: Isthmian 1939-84, Spartan 1984-96, Combined Counties 1996-97

Club Colours (change): Chocolate and pink halves/chocolate/chocolate

Ground: King George's Field, Queen Mary Close, Hook Rise South, KT6 7NA **(T)** 0208 397 3368
Capacity: 2,000 **Seats:** 161 **Covered:** 700 **Clubhouse:** Yes **Shop:** Yes

Directions
A3 to Tolworth (Charrington Bowl) roundabout.
Hook Rise is the slip road immediately past the Toby Jug Pub.
Left under railway bridge after 1/4 mile and ground is on the right.
1/2 mile from Tolworth BR.

Previous Grounds: Kennington Oval, shared with Kingstonian and Dulwich Hamlet

Record Attendance: Not known
Record Victory: Not known
Record Defeat: Not known
Record Goalscorer: Cliff West - 219
Record Appearances: Simon Shergold - 526
Additional Records:

Senior Honours: London Spartan League Senior Division 1985-86.
Surrey Senior Cup 2010-11.

10 YEAR RECORD

01-02	02-03	03-04	04-05	05-06	06-07	07-08	08-09	09-10	10-11
Isth3 10	Isth1S 21	Isth1S 23	Isth1 13	Isth1 23	Isth1S 22	Isth1S 20	Isth1S 20	Isth1S 13	Isth1S 20

CRAWLEY DOWN

Chairman: Brian Suckling
Secretary: Jane Suckling (T) 07712 814 113 (E) b.suckling@btinternet.com
Additional Committee Members:
Richard Munn, Howard Griggs

Manager: Darren Guirey
Programme Editor: Michael Martin (E) martinmd@btinternet.com

Club Factfile

Founded: 1993 **Nickname:**
Previous Names: Crawley Down United > 1993. Crawley Down Village > 1999.
Previous Leagues: Mid Sussex, Sussex County > 2011.

Club Colours (change): All Red

Ground: The Haven Sportsfield, Hophurst Lane, Crawley Down RH10 4LJ (T) 01342 717 140
Capacity: 1,000 **Seats:** **Covered:** 50 **Clubhouse:** **Shop:**

Directions
From the North: Turn off the M23 at Junction 10 signposted East Grinstead At the roundabout at the Copthorne Hotel, take the 2nd exit, signed A264 East Grinstead. At the next roundabout (Duke's Head) take the 3rd exit, B2028 south, toward Turners Hill After approx. 1 mile turn left into Sandy Lane. (just after entering the 30mph zone and a telephone box in the layby on the right). At the end of Sandy Lane (war memorial on the right), turn left signed Felbridge.After a couple of bends the Haven Centre is on your left. **From the East:** Travel through East Grinstead on the A22 until the Junction with the A264 at the Felbridge Traffic lights. Turn left (Sign posted Crawley) and after 100 Meters take the Left Fork towards Crawley Down. Approx 1.5 Miles Haven Centre on Right. **From the South:** Travel North through Turners Hill on the B2028 after approx 2 Miles take the 2nd turning on your right (Vicarage Road). This is a Right fork and is sited just after passing over a small bridge. Follow Vicarage Road for approx 1/2 Mile past Junction with Sandy Lane and The Haven Centre is 200 Meters on your left.
Previous Grounds:

Record Attendance: **Att:** 404 v East Grinstead Town 96
Record Victory: Not known
Record Defeat: Not known
Record Goalscorer: Not known
Record Appearances: Not known
Additional Records:

Senior Honours: Sussex County Division One 2010-11.

10 YEAR RECORD

01-02	02-03	03-04	04-05	05-06	06-07	07-08	08-09	09-10	10-11
SxC2 11	SxC2 15	SxC2 11	SxC2 10	SxC2 5	SxC2 16	SxC2 6	SxC2 3	SxC1 8	SxC1 1

CROYDON ATHLETIC

Chairman: Chris Roots
Secretary: Karen Muir (T) 0775 292 6809 (E) karen@muir54.fsnet.co.uk
Additional Committee Members:
Ken Fisher

Manager: Dave Garland & Bob Langford
Programme Editor: Peter Smith (E) peter.smith59@live.co.uk

Club Factfile

Founded: 1947 **Nickname:** The Rams
Previous Names: Norwood FC and Wandsworth FC amalgamated in 1986 to form Wandsworth & Norwood > 1990
Previous Leagues: Wandsworth Parthenon 1960-64, Surrey Senior 1964-77, London Spartan 1977-79

Club Colours (change): All maroon

Ground: The Keith Tucket Stadium, off Maryfield Road, Thornton Heath CR7 6DN **(T)** 020 8664 8343
Capacity: 3,000 **Seats:** 163 **Covered:** 660 **Clubhouse:** Yes **Shop:** Yes

Directions
From M25: Exit at either Junction 6 and then take the A22 to Purley Cross and then join the A23 London Road and then directions below from Purley, or exit at Junction 7 and take the A23 London Road all the way. **From Streatham and Norbury:** Take the A23 London Road to the roundabout at Thornton Heath, continue down the A23 Thornton Road. Then take the 1st on the Right past the No Entry road (Fairlands Avenue), Silverleigh Road, 50 yards, at the fork, keep left (signposted Croydon Athletic FC) into Trafford Road, then Mayfield Road (which is a continuation of Trafford Road) Go to the end of Mayfield Road, then left at the last house. Follow the lane, passed allotments, past an open car park space and continue along the lane to our club car park.

Previous Grounds: Not known

Record Attendance: 1,372 v AFC Wimbledon 2004-05
Record Victory: Not Known
Record Defeat: Not Known
Record Goalscorer: Marc Flemington
Record Appearances: James Gibson - 300
Additional Records:

Senior Honours: London Spartan League 1994-95. Isthmian League Division 3 2001-02, Division 1 South 2009-10.

10 YEAR RECORD

01-02	02-03	03-04	04-05	05-06	06-07	07-08	08-09	09-10	10-11
Isth3 1	Isth1S 19	Isth1S 10	Isth1 12	Isth1 8	Isth1S 19	Isth1S 13	Isth1S 10	Isth1S 1	Isth P 21

DULWICH HAMLET

Chairman: Jack Payne
Secretary: Martin Eede **(T)** 0795 739 5948 **(E)** eede.martin@gmail.com
Additional Committee Members:
John Lawrence

Manager: Gavin Rose
Programme Editor: John Lawrence **(E)** john_lawrence@hotmail.co.uk

Club Factfile

Founded: 1889 **Nickname:** Hamlet
Previous Names: None
Previous Leagues: Camberwell 1894-97, Southern Suburban 1897-1900, 01-07, Dulwich 1900-01, Spartan 1907-08

Club Colours (change): Navy blue and pink/navy blue/navy blue

Ground: Champion Hill Stadium, Dog Kennell Hill, Edgar Kail Way SE22 8BD **(T)** 0207 274 8707
Capacity: 3,000 **Seats:** 500 **Covered:** 1,000 **Clubhouse:** Yes **Shop:** Yes

Directions
East Dulwich station, 200 yards.
Denmark Hill station, 10 minutes walk.
Herne Hill station then bus 37 stops near ground.
Buses 40 & 176 from Elephant & Castle, 185 from Victoria.

Previous Grounds: Woodwarde Rd 1893-95,College Farm 95-96,Sunray Ave 1896-02,Freeman's Gd,Champ Hill 02-12,Champ Hill (old grd)12-92

Record Attendance: 1,835 v Southport - FA Cup 1998-99
Record Victory: Not known
Record Defeat: Not known
Record Goalscorer: Edgar Kail - 427 (1919-33)
Record Appearances: Reg Merritt - 576 (1950-66)
Additional Records: Received £35,000 from Charlton Athletic for Chris Dickson 2007

Senior Honours: FA Amateur Cup 1919-20, 31-32, 33-34, 36-37.
Isthmian League Premier Division x4, Division 1 1977-78. London Senior Cup x5. Surrey Senior Cup x16.
London Challenge Cup 1998-99.

10 YEAR RECORD

01-02	02-03	03-04	04-05	05-06	06-07	07-08	08-09	09-10	10-11
Isth1 17	Isth1S 4	Isth1S 7	Isth1 15	Isth1 13	Isth1S 8	Isth1S 6	Isth1S 12	Isth1S 12	Isth1S 5

EASTBOURNE TOWN

Chairman: David Jenkins
Secretary: Mark Potter **(T)** 0772 084 6857 **(E)** markpotter@eastbournera.fsnet.co.uk
Additional Committee Members:
Robert Hylands

Manager: Danny Bloor
Programme Editor: Mark Potter **(E)** markpotter@eastbournera.fsnet.co.uk

Club Factfile

Founded: 1881 **Nickname:** Town
Previous Names: None
Previous Leagues: Southern Amateur 1907-46, Corinthian 1960-63, Athenian 1963-76, Sussex County 1976-2007

Club Colours (change): Yellow & dark blue halves/dark blue/dark blue

Ground: The Saffrons, Compton Place Road, Eastbourne BN21 1EA **(T)** 01323 723 734
Capacity: 3,000 **Seats:** 200 **Covered:** Yes **Clubhouse:** Yes **Shop:** No

Directions
Turn South West off the A22 into Grove Road.

Previous Grounds:

Record Attendance: 7,378 v Hastings United - 1953
Record Victory: Not known
Record Defeat: Not known
Record Goalscorer: Not known
Record Appearances: Not known
Additional Records:

Senior Honours: Sussex County League 1976-77, Sussex Senior Cup x12.
Sussex RUR Charity Cup x3. AFA Senior Cup x2.

10 YEAR RECORD

01-02	02-03	03-04	04-05	05-06	06-07	07-08	08-09	09-10	10-11
SxC2 4	SxC2 2	SxC1 5	SxC1 10	SxC1 5	SxC1 1	Isth1S 19	Isth1S 13	Isth1S 22	Isth1S 18

FAVERSHAM TOWN

Chairman: Ray Leader
Secretary: Mrs Wendy Walker **(T)** 0778 963 8367 **(E)** wendy-walker@hotmail.co.uk
Additional Committee Members:
Tony Gray

Manager: Ray Turner
Programme Editor: Mark Downs **(E)** lilywhite.editor@googlemail. com

Club Factfile

Founded: 1884 **Nickname:** Lillywhites
Previous Names: None
Previous Leagues: Metropolitan, Athenian, Kent

Club Colours (change): White/black/black

Ground: Salters Lane, Faversham Kent ME13 8ND **(T)** 01795 591 900
Capacity: 2,000 **Seats:** 200 **Covered:** 1,800 **Clubhouse:** Yes **Shop:**

Directions
From the M25 continue onto M26 9.9 miles. Continue onto M20 8.1 miles. Exit onto Slip Road (M20 J7) 0.2 miles. Bear left 0.1 miles. Continue onto Sittingbourne Road A249 0.9 miles. Bear right onto Detling Hill A249 4.6 miles. Bear left 0.1 miles. Continue onto Slip Road (M2 J5) 0.4 miles. Continue onto M2 10.5 miles. Exit onto Slip Road (M2 J6) 0.1 miles. Turn left onto Ashford Road A251 0.5 miles. Turn right onto Canterbury Road A2 0.2 miles. Turn right onto Westwood Place 0.1 miles.

Previous Grounds:

Record Attendance: Not Known
Record Victory: Not Known
Record Defeat: Not Known
Record Goalscorer: Not Known
Record Appearances: Not Known
Additional Records:

Senior Honours: Kent League 1969-70, 70-71, 89-90, 2009-10.

10 YEAR RECORD

01-02	02-03	03-04	04-05	05-06	06-07	07-08	08-09	09-10	10-11
Kent P 16	Kent P 16				Kent P 12	Kent P 13	Kent P 4	Kent P 1	Isth1S 8

FOLKESTONE INVICTA

Chairman: Lynn Woods
Secretary: Neil Pilcher (T) 07880 745 772 (E) neil.pilcher@xchanging.com
Additional Committee Members:
Elaine Orsbourne, Andy Bowden, Phil Orris

Manager: Neil Cugley
Programme Editor: Richard Murrill (E) richardmurrill@gmail.com

Back Row (L-R): Mick Dix (Asst. Manager), Luke Webb, Adam Slegg, Neil Cugley (Manager)
Middle Row: Neil Pilcher (Football Secretary), Brian Merryman (Director), Willy Webb (Kit Manager), Liam Dickson, Frankie Chappell, Liam Friend, Tyson Dennigan, Jack Delo, Josh Vincent, Pete Williams, Niall Jackson, Jo Denby (Physio), Alex Bartlett (Physio), Dave Williams (Physio)
Front Row: Paul Jones, James Everitt, Olly Bartrum, Micheal Everitt, Roland Edge, Simon Austin, Darren Smith

Club Factfile

Founded: 1936 **Nickname:** The Seasiders
Previous Names: Not known
Previous Leagues: Kent 1990-98, Southern 1998-2004

Club Colours (change): Black & amber stripes/black with amber trim/black

Ground: The Buzzlines Stadium, The New Pavilion, Cheriton Road CT19 5JU (T) 01303 257 461
Capacity: 6,500 **Seats:** 900 **Covered:** 3,500 **Clubhouse:** Yes **Shop:** Yes

Directions
On the A20 behind Morrisons Supermarket,
midway between Folkstone Central and West BR stations

Previous Grounds: South Road Hythe > 1991, County League matches on council pitches

Record Attendance: 7,881 v Margate - Kent Senior Cup 1958
Record Victory: 13-0 v Faversham Town - Kent League Division 1
Record Defeat: 1-7 v Crockenhill - Kent League Division 1
Record Goalscorer: Not Known
Record Appearances: Not Known
Additional Records:

Senior Honours: None

10 YEAR RECORD

01-02	02-03	03-04	04-05	05-06	06-07	07-08	08-09	09-10	10-11
SthP 13	SthP 22	SthE 5	Isth P 13	Isth P 13	Isth P 18	Isth P 21	Isth1S 11	Isth1S 2	Isth P 22

GODALMING TOWN

Chairman: Kevin Young
Secretary: Mrs Jane Phillips **(T)** 0788 993 3512 **(E)** secretary@godalmingtownfc.co.uk
Additional Committee Members:
Glenn Moulton, Ian Curtis

Manager: Neil Baker & Jon Underwood
Programme Editor: Glenn Moulton **(E)** info@godalmingtownfc.co.uk

In the days of Godalming & Guildford in 1997-98. Back row, left to right: Mick Wollen (Manager), Darren Burge, Nigel Kay, Liam Keane, Sean Gorman, Jez Jukes, Neil Munro, Dave Thompson, Adam Gregory and Tim Daly (Coach). Front Row: Justin Horner, Terry Vick, Dale Homersham, John Ferucci, Jamie Collin, Terry Worsfold and Len Brown (Trainer).

Club Factfile

Founded: 1950 **Nickname:** The G's
Previous Names: Godalming & Farncombe United, Godalming & Guildford
Previous Leagues: Combined Counties, Southern 2006-08

Club Colours (change): Yellow/green/yellow

Ground: Wey Court, Mead Row, Guildford, Surrey GU7 3JE **(T)** 01483 417 520
Capacity: 3,000 **Seats:** 200 **Covered:** 400 **Clubhouse:** Yes **Shop:** Yes

Directions
A3100 from Guildford, pass the Manor Inn on the left and then the petrol station on the right. Wey Court is 50 yards further along the road on the right hand side.
A3100 from Godalming, pass the Three Lions pub on the left and then turn left into Wey Court immediately after the Leathern Bottle pub.
Parking: Please note that the club car park is for players and officials only. Spectators are asked to use the public car park next door to the ground.

Previous Grounds: Not known

Record Attendance: 1,305 v AFC Wimbledon - 2002
Record Victory: Not Known
Record Defeat: Not Known
Record Goalscorer: Not Known
Record Appearances: Not Known
Additional Records:

Senior Honours: Combined Counties League Premier Division 1983-84, 2005-06.

10 YEAR RECORD

01-02		02-03		03-04		04-05		05-06		06-07		07-08		08-09		09-10		10-11	
CC	17	CC	7	CCP	11	CCP	4	CCP	1	Isth1S	22	Sthsw	12	Isth1S	9	Isth1S	4	Isth1S	17

HYTHE TOWN

Chairman: Paul Markland
Secretary: Martin Giles **(T)** 07908 763 101 **(E)** martinrgiles@sky.com
Additional Committee Members:
Richard Giles, David Skeel

Manager: Scott Porter
Programme Editor: Martin Whybrow **(E)** martinw@ibspublishing.com

Club Factfile

Founded: 1910 **Nickname:** Town
Previous Names: Hythe Town > 1988. Hythe Town 1988 Ltd > 92. Hythe United 95- 01.
Previous Leagues: Southern, Kent League > 2011.

Club Colours (change): All red

Ground: Reachfields Stadium, Fort Road, Hythe CT21 6JS **(T)** 01303 264 932
Capacity: 3,000 **Seats:** **Covered:** **Clubhouse:** Yes **Shop:** No

Directions
The Reachfields Stadium is easily accessible from the M20 motorway. Leave the M20 at junction 11, then at the roundabout take the 3rd exit onto the B2068, signposted Hastings, Hythe. At the next roundabout take the 2nd exit onto Ashford Road, A20. Continue forward onto Ashford Road, A20. Entering Newingreen, at the T-junction turn left onto Hythe Road, A261, signposted Hythe. Continue forward down London Road, A261. Entering Hythe, continue forward at the traffic lights onto Scanlons Bridge Road, A2008.
Turn right at the next set of lights onto Dymchurch Road, A259. Either take the 1st left down Fort Road and turn right at the end of Fort Road for the car-park, or after a few hundred yards turn left onto the Reachfields estate. Follow the road round and the stadium will be on your right.

Previous Grounds: Not known

Record Attendance: **Att:** 2,147 v Yeading, FA Vase Semi-Final, 1990.
Record Victory: Not known
Record Defeat: Not known
Record Goalscorer: Not known
Record Appearances: Not known
Additional Records:

Senior Honours: Kent League 1988-89, Premier Division 2010-11.
Kent Senior Trophy 1990-91.

10 YEAR RECORD

01-02		02-03		03-04		04-05		05-06		06-07		07-08		08-09		09-10		10-11	
Kent P	14	Kent P	8	Kent P	6	Kent P	6	Kent P	12	Kent P	6	Kent P	4	Kent P	2	Kent P	3	Kent P	1

MAIDENHEAD UNITED

Chairman: Peter Griffin
Secretary: Ken Chandler **(T)** 07726 351 286 **(E)** kenneth.chandler@btinternet.com
Additional Committee Members:
Robert Hussey, Una Loughrey, Mark Stewart, Steve Jinman, Suzanne Loughrey, Graham Alfred, Mark Smith, Roy Bannister
Manager: Johnson Hippolyte
Programme Editor: Mark Roach **(E)** markroachonline@yahoo.co.uk

Club Factfile

Founded: 1870 **Nickname:** Magpies
Previous Names: Maidenhead F.C and Maidenhead Norfolkians merged to form today's club
Previous Leagues: Southern 1894-1902, 2006-07, West Berkshire 1902-04, Gr. West Suburban 1904-22, Spartan 1922-39, Gr. West Comb. 1939-45, Corinthian 1945-63, Athenian 1963-73, Isthmian 1973-2004, Conf. 2004-06
Club Colours (change): Black & white stripes/black/white (Yellow/blue/yellow)

Ground: York Road, Maidenhead, Berkshire SL6 1SF **(T)** 01628 636 314
Capacity: 4,500 **Seats:** 400 **Covered:** 2,000 **Clubhouse:** Yes **Shop:** Yes

Directions
The Ground is in the town centre.
200 yards from the station and two minutes walk from the High Street.
Access from M4 Junctions 7 or 8/9.

Previous Grounds: Not known

Record Attendance: 7,920 v Southall - FA Amateur Cup Quarter final 07/03/1936
Record Victory: 14-1 v Buckingham Town - FA Amateur Cup 06/09/1952
Record Defeat: 0-14 v Chesham United (A) - Spartan League 31/03/1923
Record Goalscorer: George Copas - 270 (1924-35)
Record Appearances: Bert Randall - 532 (1950-64)
Additional Records: Received £5,000 from Norwich City for Alan Cordice 1979

Senior Honours: Corinthian League 1957-58, 60-61, 61-62.
Berks & Bucks Senior Cup x19.

10 YEAR RECORD

01-02	02-03	03-04	04-05	05-06	06-07	07-08	08-09	09-10	10-11
Isth P 16	Isth P 10	Isth P 12	Conf S 20	Conf S 22	SthP 4	Conf S 17	Conf S 6	Conf S 16	Conf S 19

MERSTHAM

Chairman: Ted Hickman
Secretary: Richard Baxter **(T)** 0772 029 0027 **(E)** richardbaxter01@hotmail.com
Additional Committee Members:
Kevin Austen, Mr M Richardson

Manager: Andrew Martin
Programme Editor: Kevin Austen **(E)** email@merst hamfc.co.uk

Club Factfile

Founded: 1905 **Nickname:** Moatsiders
Previous Names: Not known
Previous Leagues: Redhill & District, Surrey Senior 1964-78, London Spartan 1978-84, Combined Counties 1984-2008

Club Colours (change): Amber & black/black/amber

Ground: Moatside Stadium, Weldon Way, Merstham, Surrey RH1 3QB **(T)** 01737 644 046
Capacity: 2,500 **Seats:** 174 **Covered:** 100 **Clubhouse:** Yes **Shop:** No

Directions
Leave Merstham village (A23) by School Hill,
take 5th right (Weldon Way).
Clubhouse and car park on the right.
Ten minutes walk from Merstham BR.

Previous Grounds: Not known

Record Attendance: 1,587 v AFC Wimbledon - Combined Counties League 09/11/2002
Record Victory: Not Known
Record Defeat: Not Known
Record Goalscorer: Not Known
Record Appearances: Not Known
Additional Records:

Senior Honours: Combined Counties League Premier Division 2007-08.

10 YEAR RECORD

01-02	02-03	03-04	04-05	05-06	06-07	07-08	08-09	09-10	10-11
CC 20	CC 17	CCP 12	CCP 16	CCP 2	CCP 2	CCP 1	Isth1S 8	Isth1S 16	Isth1S 19

RAMSGATE

Chairman: Richard Lawson
Secretary: Martin Able **(T)** 0795 899 3959 **(E)** secretary@ramsgate-fc.co.uk
Additional Committee Members:
Edward Lucas, John Vahid

Manager: Jim Ward
Programme Editor: TBC **(E)**

Back Row L-R): Ada Hubbard, Tom Tsangarides, Warren Schulz, Luke Wheatley, Brett Mills, Conor Quinn, Liam Quinn, Gary Lockyer, Richard Langley. (Middle Row: Paul Axon, Ryan Harker, Curtis Winnett, Joe Taylor, Ashley Groombridge, Andy Hadden, Dan Dolton. Front Row: Mark Lovell, Mitchell Sherwood, Ben Laslett, Foy Manoharan-Turner, Richard Lawson, Jim Ward, Ollie Gray, James Gregory, Aaron Beech.

Club Factfile

Founded: 1945 **Nickname:** Rams
Previous Names: Ramsgate Athletic > 1972
Previous Leagues: Kent 1949-59, 1976-2005, Southern 1959-76

Club Colours (change): All red

Ground: Southwood Stadium, Prices Avenue, Ramsgate, Kent CT11 0AN **(T)** 01843 591 662
Capacity: 5,000 **Seats:** 400 **Covered:** 600 **Clubhouse:** Yes **Shop:** Yes

Directions
Approach Ramsgate via A299 (Canterbury/London) or A256 (Dover/Folkestone) to Lord of Manor roundabout.
Follow the signpost to Ramsgate along Canterbury Road East, counting via 2nd exit of the 1st roundabout.
At the 2nd roundabout, continue towards Ramsgate on London Road (2nd exit).
Take the 3rd turning on the left, into St Mildred's Avenue, then 1st left into Queen Bertha Road.
After the right hand bend, take left into Southwood Road, and 1st left into Prices Ave. The stadium is at the end of Prices Avenue.

Previous Grounds:

Record Attendance: 5,200 v Margate - 1956-57
Record Victory: 11-0 & 12-1 v Canterbury City - Kent League 2000-01
Record Defeat: Not Known
Record Goalscorer: Mick Willimson
Record Appearances: Not Known
Additional Records:

Senior Honours: Kent League Division 1 1949-50, 55-56, 56-57, Premier League 1998-99, 2004-05, Kent League Cup x6.
Isthmian League Division 1 2005-06, League Cup 2007-08.
Kent Senior Cup 1963-64, Kent Senior Trophy x3.

10 YEAR RECORD

01-02	02-03	03-04	04-05	05-06	06-07	07-08	08-09	09-10	10-11
Kent P 6	Kent P 5	Kent P 9	Kent P 1	Isth1 1	Isth P 8	Isth P 5	Isth P 22	Isth1S 14	Isth1S 9

SITTINGBOURNE

Chairman: Andy Spice
Secretary: John PItts (T) 0750 513 4135 (E) johncp49@hotmail.com
Additional Committee Members:
Peter Pitts

Manager: Richard Brady
Programme Editor: John Pitts (E) johncp49@hotmail.com

Club Factfile

Founded: 1886 **Nickname:** Brickies
Previous Names: Sittingbourne United 1881-86
Previous Leagues: Kent 1894-1905, 1909-27, 30-39, 45-59, 68-91, South Eastern 1905-09, Southern 1927-30, 59-67

Club Colours (change): Red with black stripes/black/black

Ground: Bourne Park, Central Park Stadium, Eurolink, Sittingbourne ME10 3SB (T) 01795 435 077
Capacity: 3,000 **Seats:** 300 **Covered:** 600 **Clubhouse:** Yes **Shop:** Yes

Directions
Through Sittingbourne on the main A2,
club sign posted clearly and regularly from both east and west.
One mile from Sittingbourne BR station.

Previous Grounds: Sittingbourne Rec. Ground 1881-90, Gore Court Cricket Grd 1890-92, The Bull Ground 1892-1990

Record Attendance: 5,951 v Tottenham Hotspur - Friendly 26/01/1993
Record Victory: 15-0 v Orpington, Kent League 1922-23)
Record Defeat: 0-10 v Wimbledon, SL Cup 1965-66)
Record Goalscorer: Not Known
Record Appearances: Not Known
Additional Records: Paid £20,000 to Ashford Town for Lee McRobert 1993
Received £210,000 from Millwall for Neil Emblem and Michael Harle 1993
Senior Honours: Southern League Southern Division 1992-93, 95-96. Kent League x7, League cup x4.
Kent Senior Cup 1901-02, 28-29, 29-30, 57-58.

10 YEAR RECORD

01-02	02-03	03-04	04-05	05-06	06-07	07-08	08-09	09-10	10-11
SthE 17	SthE 12	SthE 10	SthE 19	SthE 18	Isth1S 10	Isth1S 9	Isth1S 6	Isth1S 9	Isth1S 11

WALTON & HERSHAM

Chairman: Alan Smith
Secretary: Michael Groom **(T)** 0771 023 0694 **(E)** mhgroom@aol.com
Additional Committee Members:
Mervyn Rees, John Crawford, Mark Massingham

Manager: Chuck Martini
Programme Editor: Mark Massingham **(E)** mark@waltonfc.freeserve.co.uk

Williams (Walton and Hersham) makes a fine save from a long range shot against St.Neots, during a pre-season friendly. Photo: Keith Clayton.

Club Factfile

Founded: 1896 **Nickname:** Swans
Previous Names: Not known
Previous Leagues: Surrey Senior, Corinthian 1945-50, Athenian 1950-71

Club Colours (change): All red

Ground: Sports Ground, Stompond Lane, Walton-on-Thames KT12 1HF **(T)** 01932 245 263
Capacity: 5,000 **Seats:** 400 **Covered:** 2,500 **Clubhouse:** Yes **Shop:** Yes

Directions
From Walton Bridge go over and along New Zealand Avenue, down one way street and up A244 Hersham Road. Ground is second on the right.

Previous Grounds: Not known

Record Attendance: 10,000 v Crook Town - FA Amateur Cup 6th Round 1951-52
Record Victory: 10-0 v Clevedon - FA Amateur Cup 1960
Record Defeat: 3-11 v Kingstonian - Surrey Shield 1958
Record Goalscorer: Reg Sentance - 220 (During 11 seasons)
Record Appearances: Terry Keen - 449 (During 11 seasons)
Additional Records: Paid £6,000. Received £150,000 from Bristol Rovers for Nathan Ellington 1999.

Senior Honours: Athenian League 1968-69.
FA Amateur Cup 1972-73. Barassi Cup 1973-74.
Surrey Senior Cup x6. London Senior Cup.

10 YEAR RECORD

01-02	02-03	03-04	04-05	05-06	06-07	07-08	08-09	09-10	10-11
Isth1 13	Isth1S 7	Isth1S 9	Isth1 2	Isth P 9	Isth P 19	Isth1S 10	Isth1S 14	Isth1S 8	Isth1S 6

WALTON CASUALS

Chairman: Graham James
Secretary: Gus Schofield **(T)** 0782 469 6705 **(E)** g.schofield1@ntlworld.com
Additional Committee Members:
David Symonds

Manager: Neil Shipperley
Programme Editor: Duncan Saunders **(E)** duncan@brsaunders.co.uk

Back Row (L-R): Chris Drake, Jake Jenkins, Kristian Webb, Alex Brown, Luke Evans, Michael Barima, Mark Nicholls
Middle: Dick Errington (Physio), Max Howell, Alfie Arthur, Dale Burnham, Mark Philpot, Anthony Gale, Laurie Walters, Danny Buckle, Kwaku Agyemang (Fitness Coach)
Front: Liam Hind, Jess Smith (Coach), Daniel Lawson, Neil Shipperley (Manager), Craig Lewington, Gary Farrell (Asst Manager), Joe Kelly Missing- Craig Totton, Charlie Ide

Club Factfile

Founded: 1948 **Nickname:** The Stags
Previous Names: Not known
Previous Leagues: Surrey Intermediate, Surrey Senior, Suburban, Surrey Premier, Combined Counties

Club Colours (change): Tangerine/black/black

Ground: The Waterside Stadium, Waterside Drive, Walton KT12 2JP **(T)** 01932 787 749
Capacity: 2,000 **Seats:** 153 **Covered:** 403 **Clubhouse:** Yes **Shop:** Yes

Directions
Left off Terrace Road at first major roundabout out of Walton centre.
Ground is next to The Xcel Leisure Centre.

Previous Grounds: Not known

Record Attendance: 1,748 v AFC Wimbledon - Combined Counties League 12/04/2004
Record Victory: Not Known
Record Defeat: Not Known
Record Goalscorer: Greg Ball - 77
Record Appearances: Craig Carley - 234
Additional Records:

Senior Honours: Combined Counties League Premier Division 2004-05, League Cup 1999-2000.

10 YEAR RECORD

01-02	02-03	03-04	04-05	05-06	06-07	07-08	08-09	09-10	10-11
CC 9	CC 18	CCP 7	CCP 1	Isth1 15	Isth1S 17	Isth1S 16	Isth1S 17	Isth1S 21	Isth1S 12

WHITEHAWK

Chairman: Peter McDonnell
Secretary: John Rosenblatt **(T)** 07724 519 370 **(E)** johnrosenblatt@whitehawkfc.com
Additional Committee Members:
Fed Moore, Lee Brace, Keith Fowler

Manager: Darren Freeman
Programme Editor: Kevin Keehan **(E)** k.keehan@gmail.co.uk

Whitehawk's Sussex County League side in 1993-1994. Back row, left to right: A.Carr, A.Packham, S.Watts, M.Judge, P.Hubbard Coach), R.Gunn, S.Edwards, T.Flower and D.Brown.
Front row: M.Thomas, N.oad, T.Louis, S.Pierce and P.Summers. Mascots: J.Kelly and R.Powell.

Club Factfile

Founded: 1945 **Nickname:** Hawks
Previous Names: Whitehawk & Manor Farm Old Boys untill 1958
Previous Leagues: Brighton & Hove District, Sussex County > 2010

Club Colours (change): All red

Ground: Enclosed Ground, East Brighton Park, Wilson Avenue, Brighton BN2 5TS **(T)** 01273 609 736
Capacity: 3,000 **Seats:** **Covered:** 500 **Clubhouse:** Yes **Shop:** No

Directions From N (London) on M23/A23 – after passing Brighton boundary sign & twin pillars join A27 (sp Lewes); immediately after passing Sussex University (on L) leave A27 via slip rd at sp B2123, Falmer, Rottingdean; at roundabout at top of slip rd turn R onto B2123 (sp Falmer, Rottingdean); in 2m at traffic lights in Woodingdean turn R by Downs Hotel into Warren Road; in about 1m at traffic lights turn L into Wilson Ave, crossing racecourse; in 1¼m turn L at foot of hill (last turning before traffic lights) into East Brighton Park; follow lane for the ground.

Previous Grounds:

Record Attendance: 2,100 v Bognor Regis Town - FA Cup 1988-89
Record Victory: Not known
Record Defeat: Not known
Record Goalscorer: Billy Ford
Record Appearances: Ken Powell - 1,103
Additional Records:

Senior Honours: Sussex County League Division 1 1961-62, 63-64, 83-84, 2009-10. Division 2 1967-68, 80-81.
Sussex Senior Cup 1950-51, 61-62 Sussex RUR Charity Cup x3.

10 YEAR RECORD

01-02	02-03	03-04	04-05	05-06	06-07	07-08	08-09	09-10	10-11
SxC1 13	SxC1 2	SxC1 8	SxC1 3	SxC1 3	SxC1 2	SxC1 2	SxC1 13	SxC1 1	Isth1S 3

WHITSTABLE TOWN

Chairman: Joseph Brownett
Secretary: Gary Johnson **(T)** 07957 424 810 **(E)** secretary@whitstabletownfc.co.uk
Additional Committee Members:
Philip Gurr, Anthony Rouse

Manager: Peter Nott
Programme Editor: Andy Short **(E)** programme@whitstablefc.co.uk

Photo courtesy Per LaLeng

Club Factfile

Founded: 1886 **Nickname:** Oystermen or Natives
Previous Names: Not known
Previous Leagues: East Kent 1897-1909, Kent 1909-59, Aetolian 1959-60, Kent Amateur 1960-62, 63-64, South East Anglian 1962-63, Greater London 1964-67, Kent 1967-2007

Club Colours (change): Red/white/red

Ground: The D & J Tyres Belmont Grd, Belmont Rd, Belmont, Whitstable CT5 1QP **(T)** 01227 266 012
Capacity: 2,000 **Seats:** 500 **Covered:** 1,000 **Clubhouse:** Yes **Shop:** Yes

Directions
From Thanet Way (A299) turn left at Tesco roundabout and Millstrood Road.
Ground at bottom of road,
400 yards from Whitstable BR station.

Previous Grounds: Not known

Record Attendance: 2,500 v Gravesend & Northfleet - FA Cup 19/10/1987
Record Victory: Not known
Record Defeat: Not known
Record Goalscorer: Barry Godfrey
Record Appearances: Frank Cox - 429 (1950-60)
Additional Records:

Senior Honours: Kent Amateur Cup 1928-29.
Kent League 2006-07, League Trophy 2006-07.

10 YEAR RECORD

01-02	02-03	03-04	04-05	05-06	06-07	07-08	08-09	09-10	10-11
Kent P 10	Kent P 6	Kent P 5	Kent P 3	Kent P 5	Kent P 10	Isth1S 14	Isth1S 16	Isth1S 18	Isth1S 15

WHYTELEAFE

Chairman: Mark Coote
Secretary: Chris Layton (T) 0771 845 7875 (E) secretary@theleafe.co.uk
Additional Committee Members:
Brian Davis, Paul Owens

Manager: Nicky English
Programme Editor: Graham Douce (E) graham@theleafe.co.uk

Club Factfile

Founded: 1946 **Nickname:** Leafe
Previous Names: Not known
Previous Leagues: Caterham & Edenbridge, Croydon, Thornton Heath & District, Surrey Intermediate (East) 1954-58, Surrey Senior 1958-75, Spartan 1975-81, Athenian 1981-84

Club Colours (change): Green/white/white

Ground: 15 Church Road, Whyteleafe, Surrey CR3 0AR (T) 0208 660 5491
Capacity: 5,000 **Seats:** 400 **Covered:** 600 **Clubhouse:** Yes **Shop:** Yes

Directions FROM THE M25 AND THE SOUTH: From Junction 6 of the M26 head north along the A22 (signposted to London, Croydon and Caterham). At Wapses Lodge Roundabout, the Ann Summers building is clearly visible opposite, take the third exit. Take the first left adjacent to Whyteleafe South railway station and cross the level crossing. Fork right after 200 yards into Church Road. The ground is a quarter of a mile down the road on the right. FROM THE NORTH: From Purley Cross (where the A23 crosses the A22), head south signposted to Eastbourne and the M25. Pass 'My Old China' (Chinese restaurant) on your right and continue under a railway bridge. Follow the A22 through Kenley and into Whyteleafe. At the first roundabout (with Whyteleafe Tavern opposite), turn right and cross a level crossing adjacent to Whyteleafe Station. Take first left into Church Road keeping St Luke Church to your right. The ground is a quarter of a mile up the road on the left.

Previous Grounds: Not known

Record Attendance: 2,210 v Chester City - FA Cup 1999-2000
Record Victory: Not known
Record Defeat: Not known
Record Goalscorer: Not known
Record Appearances: Not known
Additional Records: Paid £1,000 to Carshalton Athletic for Gary Bowyer
Received £25,000 for Steve Milton

Senior Honours: Surrey Senior Cup 1968-69.

10 YEAR RECORD

01-02	02-03	03-04	04-05	05-06	06-07	07-08	08-09	09-10	10-11
Isth1 20	Isth1S 5	Isth1S 17	Isth1 9	Isth1 18	Isth1S 20	Isth1S 11	Isth1S 18	Isth1S 15	Isth1S 16

WORTHING

Chairman: Dave Agnew & Mrs Deborah McKail
Secretary: Gareth Nicholas **(T)** 01903 239 575 **(E)** garethbnicholas@hotmail.co.uk
Additional Committee Members:
Paul Long, Monty Hollis, John Justice

Manager: Chris White
Programme Editor: Sam Skilton **(E)** sam.skilton@tiscali.co.uk

Worthing were Isthmian League Diovison Two champions in 1993. Back row, left to right: B.Reynolds, A. Robinson, G.Penhaligan, D.Stevens, R.Tiltman, M.Ball, G.Walller, R.Knight, M.Nye, I. Cocker (Assistant Manager) and G.Armstrong (Manager). Front Row: J.Robson (Coach), C.Johnson, S.Brown, J.Kanczier, D.Freeman , D.Robson, M.Montague and S.Beckford (Mascot).

Club Factfile

Founded: 1886 **Nickname:** Rebels
Previous Names: Not known
Previous Leagues: West Sussex 1896-1904, 1905-14, 19-20, Brighton Hove & District 1919-20, Sussex County 1920-40, Corinthian 1948-63, Athenian 1963-77
Club Colours (change): All red

Ground: Woodside Road, Worthing, West Sussex BN14 7HQ **(T)** 01903 239 575
Capacity: 3,650 **Seats:** 500 **Covered:** 1,500 **Clubhouse:** Yes **Shop:**

Directions
A24 or A27 to Grove Lodge roundabout.
A24 (Town Centre exit) and right into South Farm Road.
Over five roundabouts take last on right (Pavilion Road) before level crossing.
Woodside Road on right, ground on left. 1/2 mile from BR.

Previous Grounds:

Record Attendance: 3,600 v Wimbledon - FA Cup 14/11/1936
Record Victory: 25-0 v Littlehampton (H) - Sussex League 1911-12
Record Defeat: 0-14 v Southwick (A) - Sussex County League 1946-47
Record Goalscorer: Mick Edmonds - 276
Record Appearances: Mark Knee - 414
Additional Records: Received £7,500 from Woking for Tim Read 1990

Senior Honours: Sussex League 1920-21, 21-22, 26-27, 28-29, 30-31, 33-34, 38-39. Sussex League West 1945-46.
Isthmian League Division 2 1981-82, 92-93, Division 1 1982-83.
Sussex Senior Cup x21.

10 YEAR RECORD

01-02	02-03	03-04	04-05	05-06	06-07	07-08	08-09	09-10	10-11
Isth1 15	Isth1S 12	Isth1S 2	Isth P 10	Isth P 8	Isth P 20	Isth1S 5	Isth1S 5	Isth1S 3	Isth1S 14

NO
Respect
Referee
Game
One match in three is played without a referee because of abuse from players.
Isn't it time to show some Respect?
TheFA.com/Respect
TheFA
Respect

COMBINED COUNTIES LEAGUE

Sponsored by: Cherry Red Records
Founded: 1978
Recent Champions:
2006: Godalming Town
2007: Chipstead
2008: Merstham
2009: Bedfont Green
2010: North Greenford United
combinedcountiesleague.co.uk

PREMIER DIVISION	P	W	D	L	F	A	Pts
1 Guildford City	40	28	9	3	97	38	93
2 Chertsey Town	40	29	3	8	87	40	90
3 Molesey	40	25	7	8	102	50	82
4 Camberley Town	40	25	5	10	101	47	80
5 Hanworth Villa	40	22	6	12	85	53	72
6 Badshot Lea	40	19	12	9	83	60	69
7 Sandhurst Town	40	20	8	12	77	58	68
8 Mole Valley SCR	40	17	10	13	78	71	61
9 Cove	40	16	10	14	63	56	58
10 Epsom & Ewell	40	15	7	18	60	72	52
11 Colliers Wood United	40	14	9	17	65	65	51
12 Chessington & Hook United (-3)	40	16	5	19	57	66	50
13 Egham Town (-3)	40	15	6	19	80	67	48
14 Wembley	40	13	8	19	51	74	47
15 Raynes Park Vale	40	11	13	16	52	76	46
16 Horley Town	40	10	11	19	51	73	41
17 Banstead Athletic	40	11	7	22	59	86	40
18 Ash United	40	10	8	22	47	77	38
19 Dorking	40	8	8	24	53	106	32
20 Croydon (-4)	40	8	6	26	48	92	26
21 Bookham	40	4	10	26	37	106	22

EL RECORDS PREMIER CHALLENGE CUP

ROUND 1
Badshot Lea 5-1 Chobham
Banstead Athletic 2-1 Hayes Gate
Chessington & Hook United 0-2 Hanworth Villa
Colliers Wood United 2-4 Egham Town
Cove 1-2 Epsom & Ewell
Horley Town 3-2 Eversley
Knaphill 1-3 Molesey
Mole Valley SCR 6-1 Sheerwater
Sandhurst Town 2-0 Chertsey Town
ROUND 2
Badshot Lea 0-1 Croydon
Banstead Athletic 3-4 Bedfont Sports
Bookham 2-0 Hartley Wintney
Camberley Town 2-0 CB Hounslow United
Egham Town 3-1 Hanworth Villa
Epsom & Ewell 2-2 Worcester Park
(Epsom & Ewell won 5-3 on penalties)
Croydon Municipal scr-w/o Guildford City
Farleigh Rovers 3-3 Cobham
(Farleigh Rovers won 5-4 on penalties)
Farnham Town 3-0 Feltham
Frimley Green 2-3 Staines Lammas
Horley Town 1-3 Wembley
Mole Valley SCR 3-2 Westfield
Raynes Park Vale 7-0 Farnborough North End
Sandhurst Town 7-0 Dorking
South Park 3-1 Ash United
Warlingham 0-2 Molesey
ROUND 3
Bedfont Sports 1-2 Farnham Town
Egham Town 2-2 Staines Lammas
(Egham Town won 4-2 on penalties)
Epsom & Ewell 1-3 Camberley Town
South Park 0-1 Sandhurst Town
Croydon 1-2 Wembley
Raynes Park Vale 3-3 Farleigh Rovers
(abandoned during extra time)
Mole Valley SCR 5-3 Bookham
Molesey 3-2 Guildford City
Round 3 Replay
Farleigh Rovers 2-1 Raynes Park Vale (@ Raynes Park Vale)
QUARTER FINALS
Wembley 1-0 Egham Town
Farnham Town 0-1 Sandhurst Town
Mole Valley SCR 2-1 Camberley Town
Farleigh Rovers 2-1 Molesey
SEMI-FINALS
Sandhurst Town 2-0Farleigh Rovers
Wembley 2-1 Valley SCR
FINAL (@ Farnborough, 6/5/11)
Sandhurst Town 1-0 Wembley

PREMIER DIVISION	1	2	3	4	5	6	7	8	9	10	11	12	13	14	15	16	17	18	19	20	21
1 Ash United		3-3	2-0	6-0	1-3	1-2	1-2	0-5	1-2	0-1	4-3	2-1	0-3	2-3	1-0	1-1	2-0	3-1	1-2	1-4	0-0
2 Badshot Lea	2-1		2-1	3-0	3-3	1-2	1-1	0-2	3-2	4-1	3-0	3-0	4-0	1-3	1-4	1-1	2-2	1-2	1-1	3-0	3-3
3 Banstead Athletic	3-0	0-1		3-1	0-4	0-5	0-1	3-1	2-5	4-3	4-1	2-3	0-1	1-1	3-5	1-1	3-2	1-4	1-1	1-3	1-0
4 Bookham	1-2	2-5	1-1		0-4	1-2	0-3	1-2	0-1	0-2	0-1	0-5	1-1	0-2	2-5	1-2	1-0	1-1	2-2	1-5	0-0
5 Camberley Town	2-1	1-2	1-1	2-3		2-0	1-0	0-1	4-1	4-0	4-0	2-2	2-0	0-2	2-1	1-1	5-1	1-2	7-0	3-0	4-1
6 Chertsey Town	1-0	3-1	5-1	3-1	1-0		1-2	3-0	4-0	4-1	1-0	3-1	1-2	3-0	1-0	5-2	1-3	1-2	2-0	2-1	5-2
7 Chessington & Hook Utd	1-0	1-4	0-4	1-2	1-3	0-1		2-2	0-1	3-0	6-4	6-5	3-1	0-1	1-1	2-1	1-2	1-3	2-1	1-2	0-1
8 Colliers Wood United	3-1	1-2	2-3	4-1	1-2	2-2	2-1		0-1	2-0	2-3	3-0	0-2	2-4	1-2	0-0	1-3	2-0	2-2	0-0	0-1
9 Cove	0-0	2-3	2-3	1-1	2-2	0-0	1-0	2-2		0-1	3-1	1-4	0-1	1-1	1-1	1-1	3-0	3-1	1-2	1-2	2-0
10 Croydon	1-3	1-2	3-3	1-1	0-2	2-3	1-1	4-1	2-3		1-4	1-0	0-3	1-4	0-3	0-2	2-4	1-1	3-4	1-2	1-1
11 Dorking	0-2	3-1	1-0	3-0	1-7	1-3	0-3	0-0	1-3	3-3		0-3	3-1	2-4	2-2	0-3	0-0	1-7	2-2	3-0	1-2
12 Egham Town	6-0	0-0	2-0	4-0	1-2	1-2	0-0	2-3	2-0	2-3	4-1		3-1	1-2	0-1	2-0	1-4	1-4	4-3	1-1	7-1
13 Epsom & Ewell	1-1	2-2	3-1	1-1	1-2	1-4	2-3	2-1	0-2	3-2	5-0	2-2		1-5	1-3	2-1	1-1	2-2	1-2	1-2	2-3
14 Guildford City	6-0	2-1	2-0	1-0	3-1	2-0	3-4	2-2	4-0	2-0	2-2	4-0	3-1		2-1	3-1	4-0	1-1	1-1	2-0	2-0
15 Hanworth Villa	1-0	1-2	2-0	6-1	1-3	2-0	3-0	2-1	0-0	0-2	2-0	3-1	0-1	2-1		5-0	3-3	2-0	5-2	1-1	4-2
16 Horley Town	3-0	2-2	0-1	2-3	3-6	0-4	3-1	0-2	0-3	2-0	4-0	1-0	0-2	1-1	1-3		3-0	0-4	0-0	2-2	3-1
17 Molesey	4-1	2-2	4-3	6-1	0-3	0-2	0-1	2-2	0-0	2-0	6-3	1-0	4-1	3-3	4-3	2-2		1-4	0-1	3-0	1-0
18 Mole Valley S C R	4-1	1-1	5-0	5-1	3-0	5-3	2-0	3-5	3-1	5-1	1-1	3-2	3-0	1-2	2-3	4-0	3-1		3-2	3-0	2-1
19 Raynes Park Vale	0-0	0-2	1-1	1-1	4-3	0-0	4-0	0-2	0-7	0-2	1-1	1-2	1-2	0-2	3-1	2-1	1-3	1-0		2-1	0-0
20 Sandhurst Town	1-1	2-4	3-2	6-3	1-0	0-1	2-1	4-1	1-2	2-0	2-0	1-1	3-1	1-1	3-1	4-1	1-1	1-2	4-0		7-2
21 Wembley	1-1	2-1	2-1	1-1	1-3	0-1	0-1	3-0	3-2	3-0	5-1	0-4	1-2	0-4	2-0	1-0	1-3	0-0	3-2	1-2	

DIVISION ONE		P	W	D	L	F	A	Pts
1	Worcester Park	36	24	7	5	117	45	79
2	Farnham Town	36	23	8	5	83	43	77
3	South Park	36	22	7	7	108	44	73
4	Bedfont Sports	36	21	8	7	80	47	71
5	Warlingham	36	18	10	8	83	43	64
6	Farleigh Rovers	36	19	5	12	74	61	62
7	Hartley Wintney	36	18	7	11	64	50	61
8	Cobham	36	18	3	15	74	80	57
9	Knaphill	36	16	7	13	72	66	55
10	Staines Lammas	36	15	6	15	68	54	51
11	Eversley	36	14	6	16	74	61	48
12	Hayes Gate	36	14	5	17	79	83	47
13	Westfield	36	12	8	16	53	62	44
14	CB Hounslow United	36	11	9	16	61	71	42
15	Frimley Green	36	10	6	20	45	82	36
16	Feltham	36	8	8	20	43	80	32
17	Sheerwater	36	5	7	24	29	99	22
18	Chobham	36	4	8	24	52	119	20
19	Farnborough North End	36	5	5	26	33	102	20

(Croydon Municipal resigned before the start of the season)

LEMON RECORDS DIV. ONE CHALLENGE CUP

ROUND 1
Bedfont Sports 3-0 Westfield
Chobham 3-0 Knaphill
Hartley Wintney 1-0 Frimley Green
Warlingham 1-0 Feltham

ROUND 2
CB Hounslow United 1-6 Worcester Park
Chobham 1-4 Bedfont Sports
Croydon Municipal scr-w/o Staines Lammas
Eversley 2-1 Farnborough North End
Farleigh Rovers 3-0 Hartley Wintney
Hayes Gate 3-1 Farnham Town
Sheerwater 2-3 Warlingham
South Park 3-1 Cobham

QUARTER FINALS
South Park 6-1 Hayes Gate
Eversley 0-1 Bedfont Sports
Staines Lammas 1-5 Farleigh Rovers
Worcester Park 3-0 Warlingham

SEMI-FINALS
Farleigh Rovers 0-3 Bedfont Sports
South Park 3-1 Worcester Park

FINAL (@ Molesey, 2/5/11)
Bedfont Sports 0-1South Park

RESERVE DIVISION		P	W	D	L	F	A	Pts
1	Mole Valley SCR reserves	26	17	4	5	70	30	55
2	Farnham Town reserves	26	15	5	6	56	35	50
3	Frimley Green reserves	26	14	4	8	68	44	46
4	Westfield reserves	26	12	6	8	57	39	42
5	Bedfont Sports reserves	26	13	2	11	56	48	41
6	Bookham reserves (-1)	26	11	6	9	57	50	38
7	Warlingham reserves	26	10	8	8	50	45	38
8	Worcester Park reserves	26	11	3	12	52	58	36
9	Eversley reserves	26	9	7	10	42	45	34
10	Knaphill reserves	26	9	7	10	40	44	34
11	Farleigh Rovers reserves	26	9	5	12	40	49	32
12	CB Hounslow United reserves	26	6	9	11	44	56	27
13	Sheerwater reserves	26	5	3	18	29	88	18
14	Staines Lammas reserves	26	4	5	17	30	60	17

RESERVE CHALLENGE CUP

ROUND 1
Knaphill reserves 1-4 Frimley Green reserves
Mole Valley SCR reserves 2-2 CB Hounslow reserves (Mole Valley SCR reserves won 4-2 on penalties)
Farleigh Rovers reserves 2-1 Bedfont Sports reserves
Bookham reserves 6-2 Staines Lammas reserves
Warlingham reserves 0-2 Westfield reserves
Sheerwater reserves 1-0 Farnham Town reserves

ROUND 2
Farleigh Rovers reserves 2-3 Westfield reserves
Worcester Park reserves 1-6 Bookham reserves
Eversley reserves 6-0 Sheerwater reserves
Mole Valley SCR reserves 2-0 Frimley Green reserves

SEMI-FINALS
Westfield reserves 2-1 Eversley reserves
Mole Valley SCR reserves 5-0 Bookham reserves

FINAL (@ Molesey, 20/4/11)
Mole Valley SCR reserves 4-0 Westfield reserves

DIVISION ONE		1	2	3	4	5	6	7	8	9	10	11	12	13	14	15	16	17	18	19
1	Bedfont Sports		3-3	4-0	6-0	1-1	1-1	2-1	3-0	1-1	2-0	1-0	3-2	3-2	2-1	3-1	1-1	1-1	5-2	1-1
2	C B Hounslow United	1-6		2-2	2-3	2-2	0-4	2-1	3-3	5-0	3-1	1-4	2-2	0-3	0-0	1-4	4-1	1-4	0-2	1-3
3	Chobham	2-0	0-2		2-5	0-5	3-4	0-4	0-7	1-3	4-1	3-4	2-2	2-4	5-1	1-4	2-2	1-3	0-1	2-2
4	Cobham	0-2	4-1	3-3		3-1	0-2	3-0	2-3	2-1	3-2	2-5	2-0	1-0	0-2	3-1	4-3	2-1	1-4	1-4
5	Eversley	1-2	2-1	4-0	2-3		3-0	2-1	0-1	3-2	3-1	0-1	2-3	2-3	1-1	0-2	1-1	1-1	8-2	1-1
6	Farleigh Rovers	2-1	0-3	4-2	1-0	0-4		3-0	2-0	0-0	2-3	5-2	1-2	2-3	4-1	4-4	1-0	2-1	3-1	1-4
7	Farnborough North End	0-3	3-5	1-1	1-2	0-1	0-4		1-3	2-0	0-2	0-4	2-1	0-0	1-2	3-2	3-4	0-6	1-4	0-2
8	Farnham Town	1-2	2-0	2-0	1-1	4-3	2-1	3-1		2-0	3-2	1-1	1-0	4-1	3-0	1-1	2-0	2-2	3-0	3-1
9	Feltham	1-5	2-1	2-1	1-5	1-3	1-1	1-1	1-0		1-2	0-5	6-2	2-2	1-0	1-2	2-4	0-0	1-1	1-2
10	Frimley Green	0-3	1-0	2-1	3-3	1-2	3-2	1-1	1-3	2-0		1-2	0-2	0-4	0-1	0-5	2-1	0-4	0-0	0-2
11	Hartley Wintney	1-2	2-1	3-3	3-1	1-2	3-0	1-0	0-2	1-3	2-2		0-3	2-1	0-0	1-1	2-1	0-1	2-1	2-1
12	Hayes Gate	1-3	2-3	9-2	2-3	5-4	3-2	7-1	1-3	3-4	3-0	1-3		2-0	6-2	0-3	1-1	0-3	4-1	1-9
13	Knaphill	2-0	2-2	3-1	3-1	1-0	1-2	1-1	2-6	3-1	6-4	0-2	1-3		2-2	1-1	2-0	0-2	1-0	4-1
14	Sheerwater	2-2	0-5	0-1	1-5	2-1	1-3	0-1	1-1	2-1	0-3	1-2	2-4	1-3		1-7	0-5	0-2	0-1	1-5
15	South Park	3-1	0-1	7-1	5-2	5-2	1-1	7-0	3-2	10-0	3-1	2-0	1-1	6-2	6-0		1-2	2-0	1-0	3-5
16	Staines Lammas	2-0	0-1	7-1	2-0	1-3	0-1	6-0	1-2	1-1	1-1	3-1	1-0	2-1	3-0	1-2		4-2	4-1	1-2
17	Warlingham	3-0	0-0	5-2	3-1	2-1	2-3	5-0	4-4	2-0	8-0	2-2	2-0	2-2	1-1	0-1	4-0		2-0	1-1
18	Westfield	1-2	1-1	0-0	6-1	3-2	1-3	6-2	1-2	1-0	1-1	2-0	1-1	3-4	1-0	0-0	0-2	2-1		1-1
19	Worcester Park	6-3	2-1	7-1	1-2	3-1	5-3	6-0	1-1	2-1	1-2	0-0	7-0	3-2	11-0	2-1	3-0	7-1		3-1

COMBINED COUNTIES INS & OUTS

PREM - IN: Farnham Town (P), South Park (P), Windsor (formerly Windsor & Eton) (WS - Southern League Premier Division).

OUT: Bookham (R), Chertsey Town (P - Southern League Division One Central).

DIV ONE - IN: Bookham (R), Guernsey (N), South Kilburn (S - Hellenic League Division One East), Spelthorne Sports Club (P - Surrey Elite Intermediate League).

OUT: Chobham (R - Guildford & Woking Alliance), Farnborough North End (S - Surrey Elite Intermediate League), Farnham Town (P), South Park (P), Hayes Gate (F).

ASH UNITED

Founded: 1911 Nickname: United

Secretary: Gareth Watmore **(T)** 07739 188 069 **(E)** garethwatmore@hotmail.com
Chairman: Kevin Josey **Manager:** Paul Bonner **Prog Ed:** Gareth Watmore
Ground: Youngs Drive off Shawfield Road, Ash, GU12 6RE. **(T)** 01252 320 385 / 345 757
Capacity: 2500 **Seats:** 152 **Covered:** 160 **Midweek Matchday:** Tuesday **Clubhouse:** Yes **Shop:** No

Colours(change): All green.
Previous Names: None
Previous Leagues: Surrey Intermediate
Records: **Att:** 914 v AFC Wimbledon Combined Co 2002-03. **Goals:** Shaun Mitchell (216). **Apps:** Paul Bonner (582).
Senior Honours: Aldershot Senior Cup 1998-99, 01-02.

10 YEAR RECORD

01-02	02-03	03-04	04-05	05-06	06-07	07-08	08-09	09-10	10-11
CC 2	CC 9	CCP 9	CCP 13	CCP 3	CCP 4	CCP 15	CCP 9	CCP 11	CCP 18

BADSHOT LEA

Founded: 1907 Nickname: Baggies

Secretary: Mrs Nicky Staszkiewicz **(T)** 07921 466 858 **(E)** nstaszkiewicz@ashgatepublishing.com
Chairman: Mark Board **Manager:** David Ford **Prog Ed:** Peter Collison
Ground: Godalming Town FC, Weycourt, Meadow, Farncombe, GU7 3JE **(T)** 01483 417 520
Capacity: 2,500 **Seats:** 230 **Covered:** 100 **Midweek Matchday:** Tuesday **Clubhouse:** Yes **Shop:** Yes

Colours(change): Claret & blue/claret & blue/claret & blue
Previous Names:
Previous Leagues: Surrey Intermediate. Hellenic > 2008.
Records: **Att:** 276 v Bisley, 16.04.07.
Senior Honours:

10 YEAR RECORD

01-02	02-03	03-04	04-05	05-06	06-07	07-08	08-09	09-10	10-11
		Hel1E 14	Hel1E 7	Hel1E 12	Hel1E 3	Hel P 11	CCP 7	CCP 10	CCP 6

BANSTEAD ATHLETIC

Founded: 1944 Nickname: A's

Secretary: Terry Parmenter **(T)** 07940 387 041 **(E)** terryparmenter@blueyonder.co.uk
Chairman: Terry Molloy **Manager:** Graeme Banyard **Prog Ed:** Bob Lockyar
Ground: Merland Rise, Tadworth, Surrey KT20 5JG **(T)** 01737 350 982
Capacity: 3500 **Seats:** 250 **Covered:** 800 **Midweek Matchday:** Tuesday **Clubhouse:** Yes **Shop:** Yes

Colours(change): Amber & black/black/black
Previous Names: None
Previous Leagues: London Spartan League. Athenian League. Isthmian.
Records: **Att:** 1400 v Leytonstone, FA Amateur Cup 1953. **Goals:** Harry Clark. **Apps:** Dennis Wall.
Senior Honours: London Spartan LC 65-67. Athenian LC 80-82.

10 YEAR RECORD

01-02	02-03	03-04	04-05	05-06	06-07	07-08	08-09	09-10	10-11
Isth2 5	Isth1S 16	Isth1S 18	Isth1S 17	Isth1S 20	CCP 6	CCP 17	CCP 10	CCP 20	CCP 17

CAMBERLEY TOWN

Founded: 1895 Nickname: Reds or Town

Secretary: Ben Clifford **(T)** 07876 552 210 **(E)** benjamincclifford@sky.com
Chairman: Ronnie Wilson **Manager:** Darren Barnard & Paul Miles **Prog Ed:** Andy Vaughan
Ground: Krooner Park, Krooner Road, Camberley, Surrey GU15 2QW **(T)** 01276 65392
Capacity: 1,976 **Seats:** 196 **Covered:** 300 **Midweek Matchday:** Tuesday **Clubhouse:** Yes **Shop:** Yes

Colours(change): Red and white stripes/rblue/red
Previous Names: None
Previous Leagues: Surrey Senior Lge. Spartan Lge. Athenian Lge. Isthmian Lge.
Records: **Att:** 2066 v Aldershot Town, Isthmian Div.2 25/08/90. **Apps:** Brian Ives.
Senior Honours:

10 YEAR RECORD

01-02	02-03	03-04	04-05	05-06	06-07	07-08	08-09	09-10	10-11
Isth3 22	Isth2 16	Isth2 10	Isth2 12	Isth2 14	CCP 7	CCP 3	CCP 5	CCP 3	CCP 4

CHESSINGTON & HOOK UNITED

Founded: 1921 Nickname: Chessey

Secretary: Chris Blackie **(T)** 07748 877 704 **(E)** kandcblackie@googlemail.com
Chairman: Graham Ellis **Manager:** Glyn Stevens **Prog Ed:** Eric Wicks
Ground: Chalky Lane, Chessington, Surrey KT9 2NF **(T)** 01372 745 777
Capacity: 3000 **Seats:** 167 **Covered:** 600 **Midweek Matchday:** Tuesday **Clubhouse:** Yes **Shop:** No

Colours(change): All blue
Previous Names: Chessington United.
Previous Leagues: Surrey Senior Lge. Surrey County Premier Lge.
Records:
Senior Honours:

10 YEAR RECORD

01-02	02-03	03-04	04-05	05-06	06-07	07-08	08-09	09-10	10-11
CC 11	CC 14	CCP 10	CCP 3	CCP 8	CCP 11	CCP 11	CCP 19	CCP 6	CCP 12

COLLIERS WOOD UNITED

Founded: 1874 Nickname: The Woods

Secretary: Tony Hurrell **(T)** 07956 983 947 **(E)** collierswoodutd@btconnect.com
Chairman: Tony Eldridge **Manager:** Mark Douglas **Prog Ed:** Chris Clapham
Ground: Wibandune Sports Gd, Lincoln Green, Wimbledon SW20 0AA **(T)** 0208 942 8062
Capacity: 2000 **Seats:** 102 **Covered:** 100 **Midweek Matchday:** Wednesday **Clubhouse:** Yes **Shop:** Yes

Colours(change): Blue & black/black/black
Previous Names: Vandyke Colliers United
Previous Leagues: Surrey County Senior Lge.
Records: **Att:** 151 v Guildford City 06/08/2010. **Win:** 9-1 v Bedfont 05/03/2008.
Senior Honours:

10 YEAR RECORD

01-02	02-03	03-04	04-05	05-06	06-07	07-08	08-09	09-10	10-11
SuCS 5	SuCS 2	CC1 2	CCP 14	CCP 4	CCP 13	CCP 7	CCP 14	CCP 19	CCP 11

COVE

Founded: 1897 Nickname:

Secretary: Graham Brown **(T)** 07713 250 093 **(E)** covefc1897@aol.com
Chairman: P Wentworth **Manager:** Koo Dumbaya **Prog Ed:** Graham Brown
Ground: Oak Farm Fields, 7 Squirrels Lane, Farnborough GU14 8PB **(T)** 01252 543 615
Capacity: 2500 **Seats:** 110 **Covered:** 100 **Midweek Matchday:** Tuesday **Clubhouse:** Yes **Shop:** No

Colours(change): Yellow/black/yellow
Previous Names: None
Previous Leagues: Isthmian League. Hampshire.
Records: **Att:** 1798 v Aldershot Town, Isthmian Div.3 01/05/93.
Senior Honours: Aldershot Senior Cup (x5)

10 YEAR RECORD

01-02	02-03	03-04	04-05	05-06	06-07	07-08	08-09	09-10	10-11
CC 15	CC 23	CCP 24	CCP 20	CCP 16	CCP 18	CCP 4	CCP 6	CCP 12	CCP 9

CROYDON

Founded: 1953 Nickname: The Trams

Secretary: Antonio Di Natale **(T)** 07941 576 311 **(E)** croydonfc@footballfans.co.uk
Chairman: TBC **Manager:** John Fowler **Prog Ed:** Simon Hawkins
Ground: Croydon Sports Arena, Albert Road, South Norwood SE25 4QL **(T)** 0208 654 8555
Capacity: 8,000 **Seats:** 500 **Covered:** 1,000 **Midweek Matchday:** Tuesday **Clubhouse:** Yes **Shop:** Yes

Colours(change): All sky blue
Previous Names: Croydon Amateurs > 1974.
Previous Leagues: Surrey Senior. Spartan. Athenian. Isthmian > 2006. Kent 2006-09.
Records: **Att:** 1,450 v Wycombe Wders, FA Cup 4th Qual. 1975. **Goalscorer:** Alec Jackson - 111. **Apps:** Alec Jackson - 452 (1977-88).
Senior Honours:

10 YEAR RECORD

01-02	02-03	03-04	04-05	05-06	06-07	07-08	08-09	09-10	10-11
Isth P 22	Isth1S 18	Isth1S 21	Isth1 22	Isth2 10	Kent P 3	Kent P 12	Kent P 9	CCP 16	CCP 20

DORKING
Founded: 1880 Nickname: The Chicks

Secretary: Ray Collins **(T)** 07710 010 241 **(E)** dorkingfc@aol.com
Chairman: Jack Collins **Manager:** Peter Buckland **Prog Ed:** Bryan Bletso
Ground: Meadowbank, Mill Lane, Dorking Surrey RH4 1DB **(T)** 01306 884 112
Capacity: 3500 **Seats:** 200 **Covered:** 800 **Midweek Matchday:** Tuesday **Clubhouse:** Yes **Shop:** Yes

Colours(change): Green & white hoops/green & white/green
Previous Names: Guildford & Dorking (when club merged 1974). Dorking Town 77-82
Previous Leagues: Corinthian, Athenian, Isthmian > 2006.
Records: **Att:** 4500 v Folkstone Town FAC 1955 & v Plymouth Argyle FAC 1993. **Goals:** Andy Bushell. **Apps:** Steve Lunn.
Senior Honours:

10 YEAR RECORD

01-02	02-03	03-04	04-05	05-06	06-07	07-08	08-09	09-10	10-11
Isth3 8	Isth2 14	Isth2 2	Isth1 21	Isth2 9	CCP 16	CCP 22	CC1 3	CCP 22	CCP 19

EGHAM TOWN
Founded: 1877 Nickname: Sarnies

Secretary: Daniel Bennett **(T)** 07932 612 424 **(E)** sales@beautiful-bathrooms.co.uk
Chairman: Brian Askew **Manager:** J Hamsher, W Noade & C Bartholomew **Prog Ed:** Paul Bennett
Ground: Runnymead Stadium, Tempest Road, Egham TW20 8HX **(T)** 01784 435 226
Capacity: 5500 **Seats:** 262 **Covered:** 3300 **Midweek Matchday:** Tuesday **Clubhouse:** Yes **Shop:** No

Colours(change): All red
Previous Names: Runnymead Rovers 1877-1905. Egham F.C. 05-63.
Previous Leagues: Spartan Lge. Athenian Lge. Isthmian Lge. Southern Lge.
Records: **Att:** 1400 v Wycombe Wanderers, FAC 2nd Qual. 1972-73. **Goals:** Mark Butler (153). **Apps:** Dave Jones (850+).
Senior Honours:

10 YEAR RECORD

01-02	02-03	03-04	04-05	05-06	06-07	07-08	08-09	09-10	10-11
Isth3 6	Isth1S 10	Isth1S 22	SthW 22	Isth2 5	CCP 10	CCP 12	CCP 13	CCP 4	CCP 13

EPSOM & EWELL
Founded: 1918 Nickname: E's

Secretary: Tina Nadesan **(T)** 07582 220 295 **(E)** tinanadesan@hotmail.co.uk
Chairman: Tony Jeffcoate **Manager:** Lyndon Buckwell **Prog Ed:** Richard Lambert
Ground: Merstham FC, Moatside Ground, Weldon Way, Merstham RH1 3QB **(T)** 01737 644 046
Capacity: 2,000 **Seats:** 172 **Covered:** Yes **Midweek Matchday:** Tuesday **Clubhouse:** Yes **Shop:** No

Colours(change): Royal blue & white hoops/royal blue/royal blue & white hoops
Previous Names: Epsom T (previously Epsom FC) merged with Ewell & Stoneleigh in 1960
Previous Leagues: Corinthian Lge. Athenian Lge. Surrey Senior Lge. Isthmian Lge.
Records: **Att:** 5000 v Kingstonian, FAC 2Q 15/10/49. **Goals:** Tommy Tuite - 391. **Apps:** Graham Morris - 658.
Senior Honours:

10 YEAR RECORD

01-02	02-03	03-04	04-05	05-06	06-07	07-08	08-09	09-10	10-11
Isth3 5	Isth1S 9	Isth1S 24	Isth2 14	Isth2 15	CCP 17	CCP 10	CCP 4	CCP 5	CCP 10

FARNHAM TOWN
Founded: 1906 Nickname: The Town

Secretary: Ross Moore **(T)** 07810 698 272 **(E)** rossjm@btinternet.com
Chairman: Ray Bridger **Manager:** Paul Tanner **Prog Ed:** Ross Moore
Ground: Memorial Ground, West Street, Farnham GU9 7DY **(T)** 01252 715 305
Capacity: 1,500 **Seats:** 50 **Covered:** **Midweek Matchday:** Tuesday **Clubhouse:** **Shop:**

Colours(change): Claret & sky blue/white, claret & blue/claret
Previous Names:
Previous Leagues: Spartan 1973-75, Lon. Spartan 1975-80, Combined Co. 1980-92, 93-2006, Isthmian 1992-93 (resigned pre-season).
Records:
Senior Honours: Combined Counties League 1990-91, 91-92, Division 1 2006-07.

10 YEAR RECORD

01-02	02-03	03-04	04-05	05-06	06-07	07-08	08-09	09-10	10-11
CC 14	CC 22	CCP 22	CCP 21	CCP 21	CC1 1	CC1 5	CC1 8	CC1 11	CC1 2

GUILDFORD CITY

Founded: 1996 | Nickname: The City

Secretary: Matt Howell **(T)** 07912 689 953 **(E)** secretary@guildfordcitfc.co.uk
Chairman: Chris Pegman **Manager:** Kevin Rayner **Prog Ed:** Chris Pegman
Ground: Spectrum Leisure Centre, Parkway, Guildford GU1 1UP **(T)** 01483 443 322
Capacity: 1100 **Seats:** 269 **Covered:** Yes **Midweek Matchday:** Wednesday **Clubhouse:** Yes **Shop:** Yes

Colours(change): Red & white stripes/black/black
Previous Names: AFC Guildford 1996-2005. Guildford United 05-06.
Previous Leagues: Surrey Senior.
Records: **Att:** 211 v Godalming & Guildford, 2004
Senior Honours: Combined Counties Premier Division 2010-11.

10 YEAR RECORD

01-02	02-03	03-04	04-05	05-06	06-07	07-08	08-09	09-10	10-11
SuCS 11	SuCS 9	CC1 1	CCP 12	CCP 17	CCP 21	CCP 2	CCP 20	CCP 7	CCP 1

HANWORTH VILLA

Founded: 1976 | Nickname: The Vilans

Secretary: Dave Brown **(T)** 07971 650 297 **(E)** brown@park-road.fsnet.co.uk
Chairman: Gary Brunning **Manager:** Bobby Dawson **Prog Ed:** Gary Brunning
Ground: Rectory Meadows, Park Road, Hanworth TW13 6PN **(T)** 020 8831 9391
Capacity: 600 **Seats:** 100 **Covered:** Yes **Midweek Matchday:** Tuesday **Clubhouse:** **Shop:**

Colours(change): Red & white/black/black
Previous Names:
Previous Leagues: Hounslow & District Lge. West Middlesex Lge. Middlesex County League.
Records:
Senior Honours: West Middlesex Div. 1 & Div. 2 Champions. Middlesex County Champions 2002-03, 04-05.

10 YEAR RECORD

01-02	02-03	03-04	04-05	05-06	06-07	07-08	08-09	09-10	10-11
MidCo 4	MidCo 1	MidCo 4	MidCo 1	CC1 7	CC1 6	CC1 2	CC1 2	CCP 17	CCP 5

HORLEY TOWN

Founded: 1896 | Nickname: The Clarets

Secretary: Jim Betchley **(T)** 07714 837 568 **(E)** valduxbury@gamestec.co.uk
Chairman: Mark Sale **Manager:** Ali Rennie **Prog Ed:** Abbey Cortazzi
Ground: The New Defence, Court Lodge Road, Horley RH6 8RS **(T)** 01293 822 000 / 07545 697 234
Capacity: 1800 **Seats:** 101 **Covered:** Yes **Midweek Matchday:** Tuesday **Clubhouse:** Yes **Shop:** Yes

Colours(change): Claret & sky blue/claret/claret
Previous Names: Horley >1975
Previous Leagues: Surrey Senior, London Spartan, Athenian, Surrey County Senior, Crawley & District
Records: **Att:** 1,500 v AFC Wimbledon, 2003-04. **Goalscorer:** Alan Gates. **Win:** 12-1 v Egham. **Defeat:** 2-8 v Redhill 1956/57.
Senior Honours:

10 YEAR RECORD

01-02	02-03	03-04	04-05	05-06	06-07	07-08	08-09	09-10	10-11
	SuCS 3	CCP 17	CCP 7	CCP 5	CC1 2	CCP 5	CCP 12	CCP 14	CCP 16

MOLE VALLEY SCR

Founded: 1978 | Nickname: Commoners

Secretary: Darren Salmon **(T)** 07891 308 771 **(E)** darren_ks@hotmail.com
Chairman: Alan Salmon **Manager:** Darren Salmon **Prog Ed:** Michael Bolton
Ground: River Lane Sports Ground, River Lane (off Randalls Rd) Leatherhead, KT22 0AU **(T)** 07757 980497
Capacity: 500 **Seats:** No **Covered:** Yes **Midweek Matchday:** Tuesday **Clubhouse:** Yes **Shop:** Yes

Colours(change): All red
Previous Names: Inrad FC. Centre 21 FC . SCR Plough, SCR Grapes, SRC Litten Tree, SCR Kingfisher
Previous Leagues: South Eastern Combination.
Records:
Senior Honours:

10 YEAR RECORD

01-02	02-03	03-04	04-05	05-06	06-07	07-08	08-09	09-10	10-11
							CC1 4	CC1 1	CCP 8

MOLESEY

Founded: 1953 Nickname: The Moles

Secretary: Tracey Teague **(T)** 07939 387 277 **(E)** teaguetracy90@yahoo.co.uk
Chairman: Gary Mayne **Manager:** Steve Webb **Prog Ed:**
Ground: 412 Walton Road, West Molesey KT8 2JG. **(T)** 020 8979 4283 (Clubhouse)
Capacity: 4,000 **Seats:** 160 **Covered:** Yes **Midweek Matchday:** Tuesday **Clubhouse:** Yes **Shop:** Yes

Colours(change): White/black/black.
Previous Names: None.
Previous Leagues: Surrey Senior. Spartan. Athethian. Isthmian.
Records: **Att:** 1,255 v Sutton United, Surrey Senior Cup sem-final 1966. **Goalscorer:** Michael Rose (139). **Apps:** Frank Hanley (453).
Senior Honours:

10 YEAR RECORD

01-02	02-03	03-04	04-05	05-06	06-07	07-08	08-09	09-10	10-11
Isth2 19	Isth1S 22	Isth1S 19	Isth1 16	Isth1 17	Isth1S 15	Isth1S 22	CCP 11	CCP 8	CCP 3

RAYNES PARK VALE

Founded: 1995 Nickname: The Vale

Secretary: David Brenen **(T)** 07956 304 566 **(E)** davidbrenen@blueyonder.co.uk
Chairman: Richard Cook **Manager:** Mark Williams **Prog Ed:** Syd Toulson
Ground: Prince George's Playing Field, Raynes Park SW20 9NB **(T)** 0208 540 8843
Capacity: 1500 **Seats:** 120 **Covered:** 100 **Midweek Matchday:** Wednesday **Clubhouse:** Yes **Shop:** No

Colours(change): Blue/blue/red
Previous Names: Raynes Park > 1995 until merger with Malden Vale.
Previous Leagues: Surrey County Premier Lge. Isthmian.
Records: **Att:** 1871 v AFC Wimbledon (At Carshalton Athletic).
Senior Honours:

10 YEAR RECORD

01-02	02-03	03-04	04-05	05-06	06-07	07-08	08-09	09-10	10-11
CC 7	CC 8	CCP 16	CCP 9	CCP 9	CCP 15	CCP 19	CCP 8	CCP 18	CCP 15

SANDHURST TOWN

Founded: 1910 Nickname: Fizzers

Secretary: Mike Ellsmore **(T)** 07986 484 025 **(E)** mike.ellsmore@sky.com
Chairman: CEO - Michael Morgan **Manager:** Peter Browning **Prog Ed:** Tony Dean
Ground: Bottom Meadow, Memorial Ground, Yorktown Rd, GU47 9BJ **(T)** 01252 878 768
Capacity: 1000 **Seats:** 102 **Covered:** 100 **Midweek Matchday:** Tuesday **Clubhouse:** Yes **Shop:** No

Colours(change): Red/black/black.
Previous Names: None
Previous Leagues: Reading & Dist. East Berks. Aldershot Senior. Chiltonian Lge.
Records: **Att:** 2,449 v AFC Wimbledon, Combined Counties 17.08.2002.
Senior Honours: Aldershot FA Senior Invitation Challenge Cup 2000-01, 05-06. Combined Counties Premier Challenge Cup 2010-11.

10 YEAR RECORD

01-02	02-03	03-04	04-05	05-06	06-07	07-08	08-09	09-10	10-11
CC 13	CC 6	CCP 5	CCP 5	CCP 7	CCP 12	CCP 16	CCP 16	CCP 9	CCP 7

SOUTH PARK

Founded: 1897 Nickname:

Secretary: Nick Thatcher **(T)** 07817 613 674 **(E)** spfcsecretary@hotmail.co.uk
Chairman: Colin Puplett **Manager:** Ricky Kidd **Prog Ed:** Nick Thatcher
Ground: King George's Field, Whitehall Lane, South Park RH2 8LG **(T)** 01737 245 963
Capacity: 700 **Seats:** 100 **Covered:** Yes **Midweek Matchday:** Wednesday **Clubhouse:** **Shop:**

Colours(change): All red
Previous Names: South Park & Reigate Town 2001-03.
Previous Leagues: Crawley & District > 2006.
Records: **Att:** 230 v Warlingham 10/08/2007.
Senior Honours:

10 YEAR RECORD

01-02	02-03	03-04	04-05	05-06	06-07	07-08	08-09	09-10	10-11
					CC1 7	CC1 12	CC1 14	CC1 6	CC1 3

WEMBLEY

Founded: 1946 Nickname: The Lions

Secretary: Mrs Jean Gumm **(T)** 07876 125 784 **(E)** wembleyfc@aol.com
Chairman: Brian Gunn **Manager:** Ian Bates **Prog Ed:** Richard Markiewicz
Ground: Vale Farm, Watford Road, Sudbury, Wembley HA0 3AG. **(T)** 0208 904 8169
Capacity: 2450 **Seats:** 350 **Covered:** 950 **Midweek Matchday:** Tuesday **Clubhouse:** Yes **Shop:** No

Colours(change): Red & white/red/red
Previous Names: None
Previous Leagues: Middlesex Lge. Spartan. Delphian. Corinthian. Athenian. Isthmian.
Records: **Att:** 2654 v Wealdstone, FA Amateur Cup 1952-53. **Goals:** Bill Handraham (105). **Apps:** Spud Murphy (505).
Senior Honours:

10 YEAR RECORD

01-02	02-03	03-04	04-05	05-06	06-07	07-08	08-09	09-10	10-11
Isth2 18	Isth1N 23	Isth2 11	Isth2 13	Isth2 11	CCP 3	CCP 14	CCP 17	CCP 15	CCP 14

WINDSOR

Founded: 1892 Nickname: The Royalists

Secretary: Steve Rowland **(T)** 07887 770 630 **(E)** secretary@windsorfc.net
Chairman: Kevin Stott **Manager:** Keith Scott **Prog Ed:** Hayden Wheeler
Ground: Stag Meadow, St Leonards Road, Windsor, Berks SL4 3DR **(T)** 01753 860 656
Capacity: 3,085 **Seats:** 302 **Covered:** 650 **Midweek Matchday:** Tuesday **Clubhouse:** Yes **Shop:** Yes

Colours(change): Red & green/red & green/red
Previous Names: Windsor & Eton 1892-2011.
Previous Leagues: W.Berks, Gt Western, Suburban, Athenian 22-29,63-81, Spartan 29-32, Gt W.Comb. Corinthian 45-50, Met 50-60, Delphian 60-63, Isth 63-06, Sth06-11
Records: 8,500 - Charity Match
Senior Honours: Athenian League 1979-80, 80-81. Isthmian League Division 1 1983-84. Southern League Division 1 South & West 2009-10. Berks & Bucks Senior Cup x11.

10 YEAR RECORD

01-02	02-03	03-04	04-05	05-06	06-07	07-08	08-09	09-10	10-11
Isth1 22	Isth1S 13	Isth1S 3	Isth P 15	Isth P 21	Sthsw 14	Sthsw 8	Sthsw 2	Sthsw 1	SthP Exp

Guildford City celebrate winning the Premier Division title. Photo: Eric Marsh.

BEDFONT SPORTS
Founded: 2002 Nickname: The Eagles

Secretary: David Sturt **(T)** 07712 824 112 **(E)** dave.sturt2@blueyonder.co.uk
Chairman: David Reader **Manager:** Gavin Bamford **Prog Ed:** David Sturt
Ground: Bedfont Sports Club, Hatton Road, Bedfont TW14 9QT **(T)** 0208 831 9067 **Capacity:** 3,000
Colours(change): Red/black/black

ADDITIONAL INFORMATION:
Previous League: Middlesex County.

BOOKHAM
Founded: 1905 Nickname:

Secretary: Daniel Carnota **(T)** 07792 546 041 **(E)** daniel.carnota@sonyericsson.com
Chairman: Simon Butler **Manager:** Simon Butler **Prog Ed:** Daniel Carnota
Ground: Dorking FC, Mill Lane, Dorking, Surrey RH4 1DX **(T)** 01306 884 112 **Capacity:** 3000
Colours(change): All yellow.

ADDITIONAL INFORMATION: Att: 81 v AFC Wallingford - 22.10.05.

CB HOUNSLOW UNITED
Founded: 1989 Nickname:

Secretary: Stephen Hosmer **(T)** 07900 604 936 **(E)** stephen.hosmer@btinternet.com
Chairman: Frank James **Manager:** Roy Wright **Prog Ed:** Stephen Hosmer
Ground: Osterley S.C., Tentelow Lane, Norwood Green UB2 4LW **(T)** 0208 574 7055 **Capacity:** 1000+
Colours(change): All dark blue

ADDITIONAL INFORMATION:
Previous League: Middlesex County.

COBHAM
Founded: 1892 Nickname: Hammers

Secretary: Ken Reed **(T)** 07850 211 165 **(E)** coham@hotmail.com
Chairman: Leigh Dynan **Manager:** Leigh Dynan **Prog Ed:** Ken Reed
Ground: Leg O'Mutton Field, Anvil Lane, Cobham KT11 1AA **(T)** 07787 383 407 **Capacity:** 2000
Colours(change): Red & black/black/black

ADDITIONAL INFORMATION: Att: 2000 - Charity game 1975.
Honours: Combined Counties League Cup 2001-02.

EVERSLEY
Founded: 1910 Nickname: Wild Boars

Secretary: Paul Latham **(T)** 07850 080 493 **(E)** paul.latham10@gmail.com
Chairman: Daniel Nevitt **Manager:** Ian Savage **Prog Ed:** Gavin Banks
Ground: ESA Sports Complex, Fox Lane, Eversley RG27 0NS **(T)** 0118 973 2400 **Capacity:** 300+
Colours(change): Yellow & royal blue stripes/royal blue/royal blue

ADDITIONAL INFORMATION:
Previous League: Surrey Elite Intermediate.
Honours: Surrey Elite Intermediate 2008-09.

FARLEIGH ROVERS
Founded: 1922 Nickname: The Foxes

Secretary: Mark Bassett **(T)** 07921 764 409 **(E)** m.bassett69@btinternet.com
Chairman: Mark Whittaker **Manager:** **Prog Ed:** Eddie Wilcocks
Ground: Parsonage Field, Harrow Road, Warlingham CR6 9EX **(T)** 01883 626 483 **Capacity:** 500
Colours(change): Black & red stripes/black/black

ADDITIONAL INFORMATION:
Previous League: Surrey County Premier.
Honours: Surrey County Premier 1982-83.

FELTHAM
Founded: 1946 Nickname: The Blues

Secretary: Brian Barry **(T)** 07818 465 501 **(E)** brianbarry88@hotmail.com
Chairman: Brian Barry **Manager:** Wayne Tisson **Prog Ed:** Martin Mukasa
Ground: Bedfont FC, The Orchard, Hatton Road, Bedfont TW14 9QT **(T)** 020 8890 7264 **Capacity:** 1200
Colours(change): Blue & white/blue/blue

ADDITIONAL INFORMATION:
Record Att: 1,938 v Hampton - Middx Senior Cup 1972-73. **Goalscorer:** Paul Clarke - 135. **Apps:** Colin Ryder - 363.
Honours: Isthmian Division 2 1980-81.

FRIMLEY GREEN

Founded: 1919 Nickname: The Green

Secretary: Mark O'Grady (T) 07812 026 390 (E) mogradyuk@yahoo.co.uk
Chairman: Mark O'Grady **Manager:** Anthony Yearsley **Prog Ed:** Mark O'Grady
Ground: Frimley Green Rec. Ground, Frimley Green, Camberley GU16 6SY (T) 01252 835 089 **Capacity:** 2000
Colours(change): Blue & white/blue/blue

ADDITIONAL INFORMATION:
Previous League: Surrey County Premier.
Record Att: 1,152 v AFC Wimbledon 2002-03. **Win:** 6-1 v Farnham Town 21/12/02. **Defeat:** 1-7 v Walton Casuals 2002/03.

GUERNSEY

Founded: 2011 Nickname: Green Lions

Secretary: Mark Le Tissier (T) 07781 119 169 (E) mark.letissier@guernseyfc.com
Chairman: Steve Dewsnip **Manager:** Tony Vance **Prog Ed:** Tania Mendes
Ground: Footes Lane Stadium, St Peter Port, Guernsey GY1 2UL (T) 01481 747 279 **Capacity:** 5,000
Colours(change): Green & white/white/green

ADDITIONAL INFORMATION:

HARTLEY WINTNEY

Founded: 1897 Nickname: The Row

Secretary: Luke Mullen (T) 07860 729 608 (E) mulley@ntlworld.com
Chairman: Luke Mullen **Manager:** Neville Roach **Prog Ed:** Luke Mullen
Ground: Memorial Playing Fields,Green Lane, Hartley Wintney RG27 8DL (T) 01252 843 586 **Capacity:** 2,000
Colours(change): Orange & black/black/orange

ADDITIONAL INFORMATION:
Record Att: 1,392 v AFC Wimbledon , 25/01/02.
Honours: Combined Counties League 1982-83.

KNAPHILL

Founded: 1924 Nickname: The Knappers

Secretary: Bryan Freeman (T) 07876 162 904 (E) b.freeman@btinternet.com
Chairman: Terry Chapman **Manager:** Bob Pritchard **Prog Ed:** Nick Croshaw
Ground: Brookwood Country Park, Redding Way, Knaphill GU21 2AY (T) 01483 475 150 **Capacity:** 750
Colours(change): Red/black/red

ADDITIONAL INFORMATION: **Att:** 134 v Westfield 26/12/2007. **Goalscorer:** Matt Baker - 24.
Honours: Woking & District League 1978-79. Surrey Intermediate League Division One 2005-06, Premier 06-07.

SHEERWATER

Founded: 1958 Nickname: Sheers

Secretary: Trevor Wenden (T) 07791 612 008 (E) trevor.wenden2@ntlworld.com
Chairman: Douglas Mulcahy **Manager:** **Prog Ed:** Trevor Wenden
Ground: Sheerwater Recreation Ground, Blackmore Crescent, Woking GU21 5QJ (T) 01932 348 192 **Capacity:** 1,000
Colours(change): All royal blue

ADDITIONAL INFORMATION:
Previous League: Surrey County Premier.

SOUTH KILBURN

Founded: 2005 Nickname: SK

Secretary: Amanda Jennings (T) 07595 256 309 (E) jenningsmandy@ymail.com
Chairman: Dennis Woolcock **Manager:** Mick Jennings **Prog Ed:** Amanda Jennings
Ground: Vale Farm, Watford Road, North Wembley HA0 3HE (T) 0208 908 6545 **Capacity:**
Colours(change): White & black/black/black

ADDITIONAL INFORMATION: **Att:** 65 v Rayners Lane 25/08/2008.

SPELTHORNE SPORTS

Founded: 1922 Nickname: Spelly

Secretary: Chris Devlin (T) 07956 321 558 (E) secretary.spelthornesportsfc@hotmail.co.uk
Chairman: Ian Croxford **Manager:** Steve Flatman **Prog Ed:** Chris Devlin
Ground: Spelthorne Sports Club, 296 Staines Rd West, Ashford Common, TW15 1RY (T) 01932 783 625 **Capacity:**
Colours(change):

ADDITIONAL INFORMATION: **Previous League:** Surrey Elite Intermediate.
Honours: Surrey Elite Intermediate League 2010-11.

STAINES LAMMAS

Founded: 1926 Nickname:

Secretary: Bob Parry **(T)** 07771 947 757 **(E)** bobandtracey1@btopenworld.com
Chairman: Ciaron Taylor **Manager:** Nathan Wharf **Prog Ed:** Clive Robertson
Ground: Laleham Recreation Ground, The Broadway, Laleham, Staines TW18 1RZ **(T)** 01784 465 204 **Capacity:** 255
Colours(change): All blue

ADDITIONAL INFORMATION:
Record Att: 107 v Hanworth Villa, January 2006. **Goalscorer:** Jay Coombs - 270+ **Win:** 19-1 v Cranleigh (Surrey Senior Lge) 19/03/03.
Honours: Combined Counties Division 1 2007-08, 08-09.

WARLINGHAM

Founded: 1896 Nickname: The Hammers

Secretary: Les Badcock **(T)** 07890 589 030 **(E)** lesbadcock@hotmail.com
Chairman: Steve Rolfe **Manager:** **Prog Ed:** Steve Rolfe
Ground: Verdayne Playing Fields, Verdayne Gardens, Warlingham, Surrey CR6 9RP **(T)** 01883 625 718 **Capacity:**
Colours(change): Black & white stripes/black/black

ADDITIONAL INFORMATION:
Previous League: Surrey South Eastern Combination.
Honours: Combined Counties League Division 1 2005-06.

WESTFIELD

Founded: 1953 Nickname: The Field

Secretary: Michael Lawrence **(T)** 07780 684 416 **(E)** michaelgeorgelawrence@hotmail.com
Chairman: Stephen Perkins **Manager:** Craig Moore & John Comer **Prog Ed:** Pat Kelly
Ground: Woking Park, off Elmbridge Lane, Kingfield, Woking GU22 9AE **(T)** 01483 771 106 **Capacity:** 1000
Colours(change): Yellow/black/black

ADDITIONAL INFORMATION:
Previous League: Surrey Senior.
Honours: Surrey Senior 1972-73, 73-74.

WORCESTER PARK

Founded: 1921 Nickname: The Skinners

Secretary: Tony McCarthy **(T)** 07961 829 070 **(E)**
Chairman: Sam Glass **Manager:** Mark Chapman **Prog Ed:** Alan Pearce
Ground: Skinners Field, Green Lane, Worcester Park, Surrey KT4 8AJ **(T)** 0208 337 4995 **Capacity:**
Colours(change): All blue

ADDITIONAL INFORMATION:
Previous League: Surrey County Premier.
Honours: Surrey County Premier/Senior League 1999-2000, 2000-01. Combined Counties Division One 2010-11.

Warlingham FC. Photo: Roger Turner.

GROUND DIRECTIONS

ASH UNITED - Youngs Drive GU12 6RE - 01252 320 385
FROM M3: Get off the M3 at J4, onto the A331: Take 3rd Exit off to Woking. Up to the roundabout turn left into Shawfields Road, follow road for about 500 yards, Football Ground is on the left, take next turning on your left into Youngs Drive where club is 50yards on. FROM M25: Get onto the A3 heading to Guildford/Portsmouth. Keep on this until you reach the A31(Hog's Back). Then go onto the A31 until you reach the exit for the A331 to Aldershot. Follow the signs for Aldershot, which will be the 1st exit off the A331.When you reach the roundabout take the exit for Woking, which will be the 3rd exit off. Up to the roundabout turn left into Shawfields Road, then as above.

BADSHOT LEA - Farnborough FC GU14 8UG - 01252 541 469
Leave M3 at junction 4, take A331 to Farnham, After a few hundred yards exit at 2nd slip road (A325 to Farnborough). Cross over the dual carriageway and a small roundabout, Pass the Farnborough Gate shopping centre on the left. At the next roundabout turn left onto the A325, Go over pelican crossing and at next set of lights Turn right into Prospect Avenue. At the next roundabout turn right into Cherrywood Road, Ground is half a mile down on the right.

BANSTEAD ATHLETIC - Merland Rise KT20 5JG - 01737 350 982
From M25 junction 8 follow signs to Banstead Sports Centre.

CAMBERLEY TOWN - Krooner Park GU15 2QW - 01276 65392
Exit M3 Motorway at Junction 4. At the end of the slip road take the right hand land signposted A331, immediately take the left hand lane signposted Frimley and Hospital (Red H Symbol) and this will lead you up onto the A325. Continue to the roundabout and turn left onto the B3411 (Frimley Road) Continue past Focus DIY store on Left and stay on B3411 for approx 1.5 miles. At the next Mini roundabout turn left into Wilton Road, proceed through industrial estate (past the Peugeot garage) and the entrance to the ground is right at the end.

CHESSINGTON & HOOK UNITED - Chalky Lane KT9 2NF - 01372 745 777
Chalky Lane is off A243 (Opposite Chessington World of Adventures) which leads to Junction 9 on M25 or Hook Junction on the A3.

COLLIERS WOOD UTD - Wibbandune Sports Ground SW20 0AA - 0208 942 8062
On A3 Southbound 1 mile from Robin Hood Gate.

COVE - Squirrel Lane GU14 8PB - 01252 543 615
From M3 junction 4, follow signs for A325, then follow signs for Cove FC.

DORKING - Meadowbank Stadium RH4 1DX - 01306 884 112

EGHAM TOWN - Runnymede Stadium TW20 8HX - 01784 435 226
From M25 - J13 - Take the A30, heading south. The road runs parallel with the M25 briefly, and sweeps round a sharp left hand bend, under the M25. Stay right, down to the r'about in front of you just the other side of the M25. Go round the r'about and back under the M25.This road is called The Causeway. Carry on down this road, over the small r'about at Sainsbury's and at the bigger r'about turn right (signposted B3376 - Thorpe, Chertsey, Woking). Proceed down Thorpe Rd, over a level crossing, to a mini r'about, go over, and on the left, after the green turn into Pond Road. Left into Wards Place then first right and you will see the entrance to the football ground.

EPSOM & EWELL - Merstham FC, Moatside Ground, Weldon Way, Merstham RH1 3QB - 01737 644 046
From A23 to School Hill, under two bridges, Weldon Way is 4th turning on the right.

FARNHAM TOWN - Memorial Ground, West St. GU9 7DY - 01252 715 305
Follow A31 to Coxbridge roundabout (passing traffic lights at Hickleys corner. Farnham station to left.) At next roundabout take 3rd exit to Farnham town centre. At the mini roundabout take 2nd exit. The ground is to the left.

GUILDFORD CITY - Spectrum Arena, Parkway GU1 1UP - 01483 443 322
From Guildford main line station, take no.100 shuttle bus to Spectrum. From London Road Station walk via Stoke Park. From A3, exit at Guildford – follow signs to leisure centre.

HANWORTH VILLA - Rectory Meadows, Park Road TW13 6PN - 0208 831 9391
From M25 and M3 once on the M3 towards London. This becomes the A316, take the A314 (Hounslow Rd) exit signposted Feltham & Hounslow. Turn left onto Hounslow Rd, at the second mini round about (Esso garage on the corner) turn left into Park Rd. Continue down Park Road past the Hanworth Naval Club on the right and Procter's Builders Merchants on the left. Follow the road around the 90 degree bend and continue to the end of the road past the Hanworth Village Hall. Once past the two houses next to the village hall turn left into Rectory Meadows.

HORLEY TOWN - The New Defence RH6 8RS - 07545 697 234
From centre of town go North up Victoria where it meets the A23, straight across to Vicarage Lane, 2nd left into Court Lodge Road follow it through estate and we are behind adult education centre.

MOLE VALLEY SCR - River Lane Sports Ground KT22 0AU - 07757 980 497
Exit M25 (Junction 9); Take first left onto the A224 Oxshott Road stay on it till you come to a Round About take first left into Oaklawn Road follow Road till you reach the "T" junction do a left go straight on you will see a sign post for a sewage works on the right, entrance to the ground is 300 yards on the right by mini roundabout. Ground has its own slip road to do a right hand turn into River Lane.

MOLESEY - 412 Walton Road West KT8 0JG - 0208 979 4283
Take A3 towards Cobham/London & exit at Esher-Sandown turn. 1st exit at roundabout to A244 through Esher to Marquis of Granby Pub. 1st exit A309 at next roundabout. 1st exit at end of road turn right, follow until mini roundabout left into Walton Road after 1 mile ground on left.

RAYNES PARK VALE - Prince Georges Fields SW20 9NB - 0208 540 8843
Exit Raynes Park station into Grand Drive cross Bushey Road at the traffic lights continue up Grand Drive for 400 yards entrance on the left follow drive to clubhouse. From the A3. Onto Bushey Road towards South Wimbledon. Grand Drive on the right, ground in Grand Drive on the left hand side.

SANDHURST TOWN - Bottom Meadow GU47 9BJ - 01252 878 768
Situated on A321 approx 5 miles from Junction 4 on M3, or approx 8 miles from junction 10 on the M4 Park in Council Offices car park and walk down tarmac footpath beside the stream to ground.

SOUTH PARK - King George's Field RH2 8LG - 01737 245 963
From junction 8 of the M25, take A217 and follow signs to Gatwick. Follow through the one way system via Reigate town centre and continue on until traffic lights and crossroads by The Angel public house, turn right at these lights, into Prices Lane, and continue on road. After a sharp right bend into Sandcross Lane past Reigate Garden Centre. Take next left after school into Whitehall Lane.

WEMBLEY - Vale Farm, Watford Road HA0 3AG - 0208 904 8169
From Sudbury Town Station 400 yards along Watford Road.

WINDSOR - Stag Meadow, St Leonards Road, Windsor, Berks SL4 3DR - 01753 860 656
Exit M4 at Junction 6, follow dual carriageway (signposted Windsor) to large roundabout at end, take third exit into Imperial Road, turn left at T-junction into St Leonards Road. Ground approx ½ mile on right opposite Stag & Hounds public house.

Badshot Lea FC. Photo: Alan Coomes.

South Park FC. Photo: Alan Coomes.

DIVISION ONE

BEDFONT SPORTS - Bedfont Sports Club TW14 9QT
From Junction 13, M25 – Staines. At Crooked Billet roundabout turn right onto the A30 Signposted C. London, Hounslow. At Clockhouse Roundabout take the 2nd exit onto the A315 Signposted Bedfont. Turn left onto Hatton Road. Arrive on Hatton Road, Bedfont Sports Club.

BOOKHAM - Dorking FC, Meadowbank Stadium RH4 1DX- 01306 884 112

CB HOUNSLOW UNITED - Osterley Sports Club UB2 4LW - 0208 574 7055
From the A4 (Great West Road). Turn left at Master Robert, Church Rd. Turn left at Heston Road. Follow for 1 mile. Turn right at Norwood Green (Tentelow Lane). Club is 1 mile on the Right.

COBHAM - Leg of Mutton Field - 07787 383 407
From Cobham High Street, turn right into Downside Bridge Road and turn right into Leg of Mutton Field.

EVERSLEY - ESA Sports Complex, Fox Lane, Eversley RG27 0NS - 0118 973 2400
Leave the M3 at junction 4a signposted Fleet/Farnborough. At the roundabout take the 2nd exit towards Yateley.
At the roundabout take the 2nd exit towards Yateley. At the roundabout take the 2nd exit towards Yateley.
At the roundabout take the 1st exit and proceed through Yateley on the Reading Road. At the roundabout take the 2nd exit and follow the road for about 1 mile. Turn right down the first turning for Fox Lane and then follow the road round to the right where the ground will be signposted.

FARLEIGH ROVERS - Parsonage Field, Harrow Road CR6 9EX - 01883 626 483
From M25 junction 6 left at lights up Godstone Hill (Caterham bypass) to roundabout. Take fourth turning off of roundabout. Up Succombs Hill then right into Westhall Rd. Right at the green then second left into Farleigh Rd. Left at mini round about continue still on Farleigh Road. Right at the Harrow Pub. This is Harrow Road. Right at the end of the houses and the ground is behind the houses.

FELTHAM - Bedfont FC, Beveree TW14 9QT - 0208 890 7264
Hatton Road runs alongside the A30 at Heathrow. Ground is opposite the Duke of Wellington Public House.

FRIMLEY GREEN - Frimley Green Recreation Groand GU16 6SY - 01252 835 089
Exit M3 at junction 4 and follow the signs to Frimley High Street. At the mini roundabout in front of the White Hart public house turn into Church Road. At the top of the hill by the Church the road bends right and becomes Frimley Green Road. Follow the road for approx of a mile, go over the mini roundabout which is the entrance to Johnson's Wax factory, and the Recreation Ground is the second turning on the left, just past Henley Drive, which is on your right.

GUERNSEY - Footes Lane Stadium, St Peter Port, Guernsey GY1 2UL - 01481 747 279
The ground is located centrally in the island, is easily accessible with parking for several hundred cars in the immediate vicinity and on a regular bus route stopping immediately outside the stadium. It is approximately three miles north easterly from Guernsey Airport and one mile west from St Peter Port, the island's capital.

HARTLEY WINTNEY - Memorial Playing Fields RG27 8DL - 01252 843 586
On entering Hartley Wintney via the A30 take the turn at the mini roundabout signposted A323 Fleet. Take the 1st right turn, Green Lane, which has St John's Church on the corner. Continue down Green Lane for about 800 metres and turn right into car park, which has a shared access with Greenfields School. Turn left at St John's Church if coming down the A323 from Fleet.

KNAPHILL - Wood Country Park GU21 2AY - 01483 475 150
From A3: A322 from Guildford through towards Worplesdon. At Fox Corner rounabaout, take 2bd exit onto Bagshot Road, A322 signposted Bagshot. Pat West Hill Golf Club, at traffice lights turn right onto Brookwood Lye Road, A324 signposted Woking. Turn left into Hermitage Road on A324, up to roundabout, take 1st exit onto Redding Way, then 1st left entering driveway towards car park and ground.
From M3: Take A322 towards Bisley on Guildford Road, continue forwards onto Bagshot Road A322. At traffic lights, left into Brookwood Lye Road at traffic lights - A324 Woking. At Hermitage Road roundabout, 1st exit onto Redding ay, then 1st turning on left entering driveway towards car park and ground.
From M25: Towards Woking Town Centre on A320 Chertsey Road, signposted town centre. At roundabout take 2nd exit onto Victoria Way signposted Guildford. Keep to the right and at Traffic lights turn right into Lockfield Drive A324 signpost Aldershot. At next roundabout take 2nd exit signposted Knaphill. At Robin Hood roundabout 1st exit Amstell Way marked A324 Aldershot. Up to roundabout, 2nd exit into Hermitage Road, past Woking Crematorium. Then Min-roundabout and continue forward and enter Hermitage Roundabout 2nd exit into Redding Way. Take 1st left entering driveway towards car park and ground.

SHEERWATER - Sheerwater Recreation Ground GU21 5QJ - 01932 348 192
From M25(J11) take the A320 towards Woking, At Six Cross roundabout take the exit to Monument Road. At the lights turn left into Eve Road for Sheerwater Estate. First left is Blackmore Crescent, Entrance is Quarter of a mile on left.

SOUTH KILBURN - Vale Farm, Watford Road HA0 3HE - 0208 908 6545
Leave A40 onto A404, Watford Road, continue along Watford Road, you will see the sign for Vale Farm Sports Ground on right.

SPELTHORNE SPORTS - 296 Staines Rd West, Ashford Common, TW15 1RY - 01932 783 625
From M25 (J13) take the A30 exit to London (W)/Hounslow/Staines. At the roundabout, take the 1st exit onto Staines Bypass/A30 heading to London(W)/Hounslow/Staines/Kingston/A308. Turn left onto Staines Bypass/A308 Continue to follow A308. Go through 1 roundabout. Make a U-turn at Chertsey Rd. Ground will be on the left.

STAINES LAMMAS - Laleham Recreation Ground TW18 1RZ - 01784 465 204
From M25 Junction 13 to Staines. A30 through to A308; right at Fordbridge roundabout; left at mini roundabout to B377 into Laleham; entrance opposite Turks Head Pub.

WARLINGHAM - Verdayne Playing Fields CR6 9RP - 01883 625 718
From Sanderstead take B269 towards Warlingham. Verdayne Gardens is off LImpsfield Road (B269) between Sanderstead and Warlingham.

WESTFIELD - Woking Park, off Elmbridge Lane GU22 7AA - 01483 771 106
Follow signs to Woking Leisure Centre on the A247.

WORCESTER PARK- Skinners Field, Green Lane KT4 8AJ - 0208 337 4995
From M25, come off at A3 turn off and head towards London, then come off at Worcester Park turn off, stay on this road until you pass station on your left and go under bridge, then take first left which is Green Lane, ground is 500 yards on the left.

EAST MIDLAND COUNTIES LEAGUE

Sponsored by: No sponsor

Founded: 2008

Recent Champions:
2009: Kirby Muxloe SC
2010: Dunkirk

emc-fl.com

		P	W	D	L	F	A	Pts
1	Gresley	38	28	6	4	109	36	90
2	Borrowash Victoria	38	27	7	4	79	23	88
3	Heanor Town	38	26	6	6	118	41	84
4	Gedling Miners Welfare	38	26	5	7	76	36	83
5	Barrow Town	38	23	4	11	70	44	73
6	Holbrook Sports	38	21	4	13	93	56	67
7	Radcliffe Olympic	38	19	4	15	73	53	61
8	Bardon Hill	38	18	5	15	83	65	59
9	Thurnby Nirvana	38	18	4	16	85	67	58
10	Greenwood Meadows	38	15	10	13	68	62	55
11	Hinckley (-9)	38	18	8	12	71	75	53
12	Anstey Nomads	38	15	4	19	56	102	49
13	Holwell Sports	38	11	7	20	55	73	40
14	Graham St Prims	38	10	9	19	46	80	39
15	Ellistown	38	11	5	22	52	83	38
16	Ibstock United	38	10	4	24	46	78	34
17	St Andrews (-3)	38	9	9	20	60	86	33
18	Gedling Town (-3)	38	9	4	25	53	91	28
19	Radford	38	6	4	28	50	107	22
20	Blackwell Miners Welfare	38	5	1	32	35	120	16

LEAGUE CUP

ROUND 1

Anstey Nomads 3-4 Barrow Town
Graham Street Prims 0-3 Radford
Heanor Town 4-1 Bardon Hill
Holwell Sports 4-3 Gresley

ROUND 2

Barrow Town 1-0 Radford
Gedling Miners Welfare 2-5 Thurnby Nirvana
Gedling Town v Heanor Town (tie awarded to Heanor Town)
Greenwood Meadows 4-2 Blackwell Miners Welfare
Hinckley 0-3 Ellistown
Holbrook Sports 5-2 Holwell Sports
St Andrews 1-5 Radcliffe Olympic

QUARTER FINALS

Borrowash Victorua 4-0 Ellistown
Greenwood Meadows 1-2 Thurnby Nirvana
Holbrook Sports 2-1 Heanor Town
Radcliffe Olympic 1-0 Barrow Town

SEMI-FINALS

Thurnby Nirvana 2-0 Borrowash Victoria
Holbrook Sport 2-0 Radcliffe Olympic

FINAL (@ Gresley, 10/5/11)

Thurnby Nirvana 4-2 Holbrook Sports

	1	2	3	4	5	6	7	8	9	10	11	12	13	14	15	16	17	18	19	20
1 Anstey Nomads		2-1	1-2	5-0	1-5	3-2	0-3	3-1	1-0	1-3	0-9	0-7	1-4	3-5	1-0	1-0	0-4	2-1	1-1	1-6
2 Bardon Hill	3-0		0-4	4-2	1-3	2-0	1-2	0-4	1-1	2-2	4-2	1-4	6-1	1-2	1-0	2-0	2-1	2-1	4-0	2-4
3 Barrow Town	1-1	3-3		4-0	0-2	5-2	0-1	2-1	0-0	2-0	3-2	1-0	0-1	1-4	0-0	2-1	0-2	1-0	4-1	0-1
4 Blackwell Miners Welfare	1-4	0-3	0-5		1-2	1-2	0-2	2-3	3-1	1-1	1-5	0-5	1-2	1-7	1-5	2-1	0-2	1-3	2-3	4-3
5 Borrowash Victoria	3-0	2-1	2-0	5-1		1-0	2-0	6-1	1-0	3-1	0-0	0-0	0-1	2-0	0-0	2-0	2-0	3-1	1-1	4-0
6 Ellistown	0-4	2-3	0-2	4-0	3-1		1-2	1-0	1-3	0-2	0-2	2-3	1-0	2-1	2-1	0-0	1-3	1-0	1-5	0-5
7 Gedling Miners Welfare	2-1	1-0	3-2	3-1	2-1	3-2		2-0	1-0	0-2	1-1	2-2	4-1	2-1	2-0	1-0	4-3	4-0	7-1	1-2
8 Gedling Town	1-1	0-2	1-0	0-1	1-2	1-3	1-1		1-2	2-6	1-3	0-4	1-2	0-5	1-4	4-2	4-0	5-2	1-1	3-0
9 Graham Street Prims	0-0	1-4	2-1	1-2	0-0	6-4	2-5	0-1		0-0	1-5	2-1	5-1	1-0	2-5	0-0	0-3	3-2	1-3	2-1
10 Greenwood Meadows	0-2	1-1	1-3	2-1	1-1	2-2	0-2	4-1	1-2		2-0	3-1	0-4	2-2	3-1	2-0	0-0	0-1	4-2	3-0
11 Gresley	4-0	2-1	5-0	4-1	4-0	5-1	1-0	1-1	5-1	3-5		4-1	1-0	4-0	4-1	3-2	4-1	4-2	2-1	2-0
12 Heanor Town	9-0	3-2	1-3	7-0	2-2	2-0	3-2	2-0	5-1	2-0	0-0		4-1	2-1	8-1	3-0	2-1	4-3	7-3	2-0
13 Hinckley	2-1	3-2	0-2	4-2	0-4	2-3	1-0	6-1	1-1	4-3	1-1	3-2		3-3	2-0	2-0	1-3	2-2	0-6	1-5
14 Holbrook Sports	4-1	3-2	0-1	1-0	0-1	1-1	0-0	7-1	5-2	4-0	1-3	0-3	2-3		0-2	6-2	2-1	2-1	2-1	3-0
15 Holwell Sports	1-2	3-3	0-1	3-2	0-2	3-1	1-3	4-1	0-0	2-2	0-4	1-1	1-3	0-1		1-2	0-6	2-3	0-0	0-2
16 Ibstock United	3-4	1-2	1-4	2-0	0-4	3-1	2-1	3-2	1-0	1-2	1-1	0-3	1-1	1-0	0-2		1-2	5-1	1-3	2-5
17 Radcliffe Olympic	6-1	4-0	1-2	1-0	0-1	1-0	0-2	1-0	4-0	3-1	0-2	2-2	2-2	4-6	2-1	0-1		3-0	2-1	2-1
18 Radford	0-3	1-6	1-4	1-0	0-1	1-1	0-3	1-6	5-2	3-5	1-4	0-3	2-4	1-5	1-2	3-4	2-0		1-1	2-4
19 St Andrews	1-2	0-6	0-1	8-0	0-5	3-4	0-1	2-1	1-1	1-1	0-1	0-7	1-1	0-4	0-2	2-1	3-1	1-1		1-2
20 Thurnby Nirvana	7-2	0-2	3-4	2-0	0-3	1-1	1-1	3-0	5-0	2-1	1-2	0-1	1-1	1-3	4-6	4-1	2-2	4-0	3-2	

ANSTEY NOMADS
Founded: Nickname:

Secretary: Chris Hillebrandt **(T)** 0794 685 6430 **(E)** chille1055@hotmail.com
Chairman: Tony Ford **Manager:** Andy Miller **Prog Ed:** Russ&Helen Preston-Hayes
Ground: Cropston Road, Anstey, Leicester LE7 7BP **(T)** 0116 236 4868 **Capacity:**
Colours(change): Red & white stripes/black/red

ADDITIONAL INFORMATION:
Previous League: Leicestershire Senior

BARDON HILL
Founded: Nickname:

Secretary: Adrian Bishop **(T)** 07999 879 841 **(E)** adebishop1@sky.com
Chairman: **Manager:** **Prog Ed:** Terry Gee
Ground: Bardon Close, Coalville, Leicester LE67 4BS **(T)** 01530 815 569 **Capacity:**
Colours(change): All royal blue

ADDITIONAL INFORMATION:
Previous League: Leics Senior. **Previous Name:** Bardon Hill Sports

BARROW TOWN
Founded: Nickname:

Secretary: Andy Dermott **(T)** 07875 291 365 **(E)** a.dermott514@btinternet.com
Chairman: Michael Bland **Manager:** John Folwell & Adam Beazeley **Prog Ed:** Andy Dermott
Ground: Riverside Park, Bridge Street, Quorn, Leicestershire LE12 8EN **(T)** 01509 620 650 **Capacity:**
Colours(change): Red & black stripes/black/black

ADDITIONAL INFORMATION:
Previous League: Leicestershire Senior

BLABY & WHETSTONE ATHLETIC
Founded: Nickname:

Secretary: Sue Warner **(T)** **(E)** suewarner2@aol.com
Chairman: Mark Jenkins **Manager:** Steve Orme **Prog Ed:**
Ground: Warwick Road, Whetstome, Leicester LE8 6LW **(T)** 0116 275 1182 **Capacity:**
Colours(change): Blue

ADDITIONAL INFORMATION:
Previous Lge: Leicestershire Senior > 2011.

BLACKWELL MINERS WELFARE
Founded: Nickname:

Secretary: Steve Harris **(T)** 07505 366 136 **(E)** manor2@ntlworld.com
Chairman: Steve Harris **Manager:** Gary Hayward **Prog Ed:** Chris Ryde
Ground: Primrose Hill Sports Ground, Primrose Hill, Blackwell, Alfreton DE55 5JF **(T)** 07505 366 136 **Capacity:**
Colours(change): Red & white/red/white

ADDITIONAL INFORMATION:
Previous League: Central Midlands

BORROWASH VICTORIA
Founded: Nickname:

Secretary: Ian Collins **(T)** 07733 055 212 **(E)** chunkyvics@ntlworld.com
Chairman: Ian Anderson **Manager:** Mark Wilson **Prog Ed:** Frazer Watson
Ground: Watkinsons Construction Bowl, Borrowash Rd, Spondon, Derby DE21 7PH **(T)** 01332 669 688 **Capacity:**
Colours(change): Red & white stripes/black/black

ADDITIONAL INFORMATION:
Previous League: Central Midlands

ELLISTOWN
Founded: Nickname:

Secretary: Sue Matthews **(T)** 07881 723 033 **(E)** suematthews7@hotmail.com
Chairman: Andy Roach **Manager:** **Prog Ed:** Craig Waistell
Ground: Terrace Road, Terrace Road, Ellistown, Leicestershire LE67 1GD **(T)** 01530 230 159 **Capacity:**
Colours(change): Yellow & blue/blue/yellow

ADDITIONAL INFORMATION:
Previous League: Leicestershire Senior

GEDLING MINERS WELFARE

Founded: Nickname:

Secretary: Norman Hay **(T)** 07748 138 732 **(E)** norman.hay@virginmedia.com
Chairman: Vic Hulme **Manager:** Lee Boulton **Prog Ed:** Anthony Hay
Ground: Plains Social Club, Plains Road, Mapperley, Nottingham NG3 5RH **(T)** 0115 926 6300 **Capacity:**
Colours(change): Yellow/blue/yellow

ADDITIONAL INFORMATION:
Previous League: Central Midlands

GRAHAM ST. PRIMS

Founded: 1904 Nickname:

Secretary: Peter Davis **(T)** 07969 160 574 **(E)** j.davis16@sky.com
Chairman: Wayne Harvey-Toon **Manager:** Mark Webster **Prog Ed:** Edward Davis
Ground: Asterdale Sports Centre, Borrowash Road, Spondon, Derbyshire DE21 7PH **(T)** 01332 704 064 **Capacity:**
Colours(change): Red & white/black/black

ADDITIONAL INFORMATION:
Previous League: Central Midlands

GREENWOOD MEADOWS

Founded: 1987 Nickname:

Secretary: Mark Connors **(T)** 07960 399 812 **(E)** mark@ntextiles.co.uk
Chairman: Mark Burton **Manager:** Kaz Fawzi **Prog Ed:** Martin Asher
Ground: Lenton Lane Ground, Lenton Lane, Nr Clifton Bridge, Nottingham NG7 2SA **(T)** 07712 530 706 **Capacity:**
Colours(change): Green/black/black

ADDITIONAL INFORMATION:
Previous League: Central Midlands

HEANOR TOWN

Founded: Nickname:

Secretary: Keith Costello **(T)** 07792 691 843 **(E)** ukinfo@jmcengineering.com
Chairman: **Manager:** Craig Hopkins/Glenn Kirkwood **Prog Ed:** Stan Wilton
Ground: The Town Ground, Mayfield Avenue, Heanor DE75 7EN **(T)** 01773 713 742 **Capacity:**
Colours(change): White/black/black (Red/white/white)

ADDITIONAL INFORMATION:
Previous League: Central Midlands

HOLBROOK SPORTS

Founded: 1931 Nickname:

Secretary: Chris Sadler **(T)** 07813 680 458 **(E)** chris.sadler@derby-college.ac.uk
Chairman: Howard Williams **Manager:** Leigh Grant **Prog Ed:** Chris Sadler
Ground: O'kra Ground, Shaw Lane, Holbrook, Derbyshire DE56 0TG **(T)** 07966 792 011 **Capacity:**
Colours(change): All royal blue

ADDITIONAL INFORMATION:
Previous Names: Holbrook, Holbrook Miners Welfare
Previous League: Central Midlands

HOLWELL SPORTS

Founded: Nickname:

Secretary: Chris Parkin **(T)** 07507 322 489 **(E)** chris@parkin007.co.uk
Chairman: Phil Saddington **Manager:** **Prog Ed:** Linda Parker
Ground: Welby Road, Asfordby Hill, Melton Mowbray, Leicestershire LE14 3RD **(T)** 07523 427 450 **Capacity:**
Colours(change): Yellow & green/green/green

ADDITIONAL INFORMATION:
Previous League: Leicestershire Senior

IBSTOCK UNITED

Founded: Nickname:

Secretary: Chris Pallett **(T)** 07817 772 119 **(E)** chris_iufc@hotmail.co.uk
Chairman: **Manager:** Neil Scott **Prog Ed:** Chris Pallett
Ground: The Welfare Ground, Leicester Road, Ibstock, Leicestershire LE67 6HN **(T)** 01974 657 701 **Capacity:**
Colours(change): Red & white/red/red

ADDITIONAL INFORMATION:
Previous Name: Ibstock Welfare
Previous League: Leicestershire Senior

OADBY TOWN

Founded: 1937 | Nickname: The Poachers

Secretary: Ken Farrant **(T)** 07986 359 646 **(E)** oadbytownfc@btconnect.com
Chairman: Brian Fletcher-Warington **Manager:** Lee Harriman **Prog Ed:** Kelly Marie
Ground: Green King Park, Wigston Road, Oadby LE2 5QG **(T)** 07794 088 210 **Capacity:** 5,000
Colours(change): White/red/red

ADDITIONAL INFORMATION:
Honours: Leicestershire Senior Div.2 1951-52. Prem 63-64, 67-68, 68-69, 72-73, 94-95, 96-97, 97-98, 98-99. Midland Alliance 99-00.
Previous Lge: Midland Alliance > 2011.

RADCLIFFE OLYMPIC

Founded: 1876 | Nickname:

Secretary: Michael Bradley **(T)** **(E)** knacks@hotmail.com
Chairman: Nigel Carter **Manager:** Kevin Waddley **Prog Ed:** Brendan Richardson
Ground: The Rec. Grd, Wharfe Lane, Radcliffe on Trent, Nottingham NG12 2AN **(T)** 07825 285 024 **Capacity:**
Colours(change): All navy blue (All red)

ADDITIONAL INFORMATION:
Previous Leagues: Notts Alliance, Central Midlands

RADFORD

Founded: 1964 | Nickname:

Secretary: Danny Staley **(T)** 07972 878 887 **(E)** d.staley@hotmail.co.uk
Chairman: Bob Thomas **Manager:** Simon Snow **Prog Ed:** Howard Bacon
Ground: Selhurst Street, Off Radford Road, Nottingham NG7 5EH **(T)** 0115 942 3250 **Capacity:**
Colours(change): All claret (All light blue)

ADDITIONAL INFORMATION:
Previous League: Central Midlands

ST. ANDREWS

Founded: | Nickname:

Secretary: Les Botting **(T)** 07793 500 937 **(E)** standrewsfc@btconnect.com
Chairman: Bill Wells **Manager:** Clem Dublin **Prog Ed:** Darren Creed
Ground: Canal Street, Aylestone, Leicester LE2 8LA **(T)** 0116 283 9298 **Capacity:**
Colours(change): Black & white stripes/black/red (All blue)

ADDITIONAL INFORMATION:
Previous League: Leicestershire Senior

THURNBY NIRVANA

Founded: | Nickname:

Secretary: Zak Hajat **(T)** 07811 843 136 **(E)** nirvanafc@hotmail.com
Chairman: **Manager:** Damion Qualiey **Prog Ed:** Chris Tonge
Ground: Dakyn Road, Thurnby Lodge, Leicester LE5 2ED **(T)** 0116 243 3308 **Capacity:**
Colours(change): All green

ADDITIONAL INFORMATION:
Previous Name: Thurnby Rangers
Previous League: Leicestershire Senior

EASTERN COUNTIES LEAGUE

Sponsored by: Ridgeons
Founded: 1935
Recent Champions:
2006: Lowestoft Town
2007: Wroxham
2008: Soham Town Rangers
2009: Lowestoft Town
2010: Needham Market
ridgeonsleague.co.uk

PREMIER DIVISION	P	W	D	L	F	A	Pts
1 Leiston	42	29	8	5	97	39	95
2 Dereham Town	42	25	9	8	88	42	84
3 Wroxham	42	24	8	10	85	52	80
4 Wisbech Town	42	21	13	8	77	49	76
5 Mildenhall Town	42	22	7	13	66	50	73
6 Norwich United	42	20	10	12	85	49	70
7 Stanway Rovers	42	18	13	11	83	52	67
8 Haverhill Rovers	42	18	11	13	58	55	65
9 Hadleigh United	42	18	9	15	83	72	63
10 Woodbridge Town	42	18	8	16	70	84	62
11 CRC	42	15	12	15	73	59	57
12 Kirkley & Pakefield	42	16	9	17	59	62	57
13 Brantham Athletic	42	15	6	21	86	79	51
14 Great Yarmouth Town	42	13	12	17	73	80	51
15 Ely City	42	13	10	19	58	62	49
16 FC Clacton	42	13	10	19	57	71	49
17 Walsham-le-Willows	42	9	19	14	65	72	46
18 Felixstowe & Walton United	42	11	11	20	55	84	44
19 Newmarket Town	42	10	11	21	45	89	41
20 Wivenhoe Town	42	6	14	22	48	76	32
21 Histon reserves (-1)	42	7	10	25	50	132	30
22 Debenham LC	42	7	8	27	56	107	29

LEAGUE CUP

PRELIMINARY ROUND
Felixstowe & Walton United 2-0 Wivenhoe Town
Hadleigh United 1-2 Stowmarket Town
March Town United 3-2 Fakenham Town
Newmarket Town 1-0 Haverhill Rovers
Norwich United 3-1 Debenham LC
Saffron Walden Town 7-0 Long Melford
Walsham-le-Willows 4-2 Thetford Town

ROUND 1
Brantham Athletic 3-2 Ipswich Wanderers
Dereham Town 0-1 Wisbech Town
Diss Town 2-0 Gorleston
Ely City 3-0 March Town United
F C Clacton 6-2 Whitton United
Felixstowe & Walton United 2-3 Stowmarket Town
Great Yarmouth Town 5-3 Norwich United
Halstead Town 0-1 Stanway Rovers
Histon reserves 4-0 Cornard United
Kirkley & Pakefield 16-1 Leiston
Mildenhall Town 1-2 Godmanchester Rovers
Newmrket Town 0-3 CRC
Saffron Walden Town 0-1 Cambridge University Press
Team Bury 3-0 Swaffham Town
Walsham-le-Willows 5-2 Downham Town
Wroxham 5-2 Woodbridge Town

ROUND 2
Stowmarket Town 3-1 Histon reserves
Great Yarmouth Town 1-2 Kirkley & Pakefield
Stanway Rovers 3-1 Cambridge University Press
CRC 3-1 Brantham Athletic
Team Bury 3-0 F C Clacton
Walsham-le-Willows 3-0 Ely City
Wisbech Town 4-1 Diss Town
Wroxham w/o-scr Godmanchester Rovers

QUARTER FINALS
Stanway Rovers 1-1 CRC (CRC won 4-1 on penalties)
Stowmarket Town 5-0 Team Bury
Walsham-le-Willows 0-6 Wroxham
Wisbech Town 3-1 Kirkley & Pakefield

SEMI-FINALS
Stowmarket Town 2-6 Wisbech Town
Wroxham 2-0 CRC

FINAL (@ Dereham Town, 2/5/11)
Wisbech Town 1-0 Wroxham

PREMIER DIVISION	1	2	3	4	5	6	7	8	9	10	11	12	13	14	15	16	17	18	19	20	21	22
1 Brantham Athletic		0-1	2-2	1-2	1-0	0-1	0-1	1-2	1-3	3-0	6-4	2-1	3-3	2-3	0-0	3-4	0-0	1-4	1-2	1-2	4-0	5-2
2 Cambridge Regional College	3-1		2-0	1-1	0-1	4-4	0-4	1-1	3-1	1-2	1-1	2-3	2-3	4-1	3-0	0-0	2-2	3-0	0-1	2-0	9-3	1-2
3 Debenham L C	4-0	1-3		0-2	1-0	0-2	3-0	2-5	1-4	0-1	7-0	2-3	0-2	2-2	1-2	1-3	2-5	4-0	0-2	1-1	1-1	0-3
4 Dereham Town	1-5	0-0	3-0		2-1	4-1	3-0	1-2	4-0	3-1	6-1	3-0	2-0	3-0	0-0	2-1	0-5	2-2	3-3	4-0	2-3	2-1
5 Ely City	4-1	3-1	3-3	1-2		1-0	1-2	3-1	2-4	0-1	4-2	0-0	0-1	0-0	2-1	0-0	2-1	1-1	2-3	3-3	1-4	0-0
6 F C Clacton	0-3	0-5	0-0	0-3	0-1		1-2	0-2	1-4	2-0	8-0	3-0	1-3	1-2	2-1	0-3	2-2	0-0	0-2	3-1	3-2	1-3
7 Felixstowe & Walton United	0-2	1-1	6-2	0-5	0-2	1-2		5-2	0-0	0-0	4-2	1-1	2-2	0-1	1-5	1-5	1-1	2-2	1-1	1-3	1-2	3-5
8 Great Yarmouth Town	3-2	1-1	4-0	0-4	1-1	3-1	1-2		0-2	2-2	1-2	1-1	1-4	2-4	1-1	2-3	0-2	3-2	2-1	1-1	0-1	0-2
9 Hadleigh United	1-0	3-2	2-1	2-0	1-2	1-1	4-1	1-4		3-4	2-2	0-1	1-1	1-2	5-0	0-3	3-1	1-3	0-3	3-0	2-2	0-2
10 Haverhill Rovers	3-1	4-0	1-2	2-3	1-1	1-1	1-1	1-1	3-2		1-1	0-0	0-1	2-1	3-0	0-2	0-2	1-1	2-1	1-0	3-1	0-0
11 Histon reserves	0-5	0-4	1-1	0-5	2-6	2-6	0-0	2-2	1-3	2-2		3-2	0-4	1-0	0-0	1-2	4-3	2-2	2-2	0-3	2-1	2-1
12 Kirkley & Pakefield	0-7	0-1	7-0	0-0	2-1	0-2	3-1	2-0	2-2	2-1	8-0		2-0	0-1	2-1	2-0	1-5	0-0	2-1	1-0	1-4	0-2
13 Leiston	4-0	0-3	4-1	0-1	3-0	3-0	2-0	2-1	6-3	4-0	4-0	1-0		1-0	4-0	2-0	2-2	2-1	1-3	2-2	6-3	1-0
14 Mildenhall Town	2-0	1-0	6-2	2-1	2-1	3-1	2-0	1-1	1-2	6-0	2-0	1-1	0-1		2-1	1-0	2-1	2-2	1-1	1-0	1-0	1-2
15 Newmarket Town	2-6	2-1	2-2	0-2	2-1	3-0	0-2	2-3	0-4	1-3	2-1	0-0	0-6	1-0		2-1	2-1	1-1	0-3	2-1	0-1	1-1
16 Norwich United	5-1	1-0	6-1	1-3	2-0	0-1	4-0	4-3	1-1	2-2	5-0	1-0	1-2	0-0	6-0		2-0	3-0	0-0	3-3	0-0	2-3
17 Stanway Rovers	4-1	3-0	1-0	0-0	4-0	1-2	0-2	2-2	1-2	1-0	2-0	3-0	0-0	1-3	2-2	1-4		1-1	2-0	1-1	4-1	2-1
18 Walsham-le-Willows	1-3	3-0	0-2	1-1	1-1	2-2	6-2	2-2	3-3	0-1	3-2	3-1	1-2	3-2	4-4	1-1	0-3		1-2	3-0	2-2	0-1
19 Wisbech Town	1-1	3-3	3-1	3-0	2-1	0-0	1-1	3-2	0-3	0-2	5-0	2-1	0-1	3-0	5-1	2-0	1-1	2-2		2-1	2-1	1-1
20 Wivenhoe Town	2-5	1-1	2-1	0-0	2-5	1-1	0-2	1-4	2-2	0-1	2-1	1-3	1-1	0-1	0-0	4-1	1-1	0-1	3-4		0-1	1-1
21 Woodbridge Town	0-3	1-1	2-1	0-2	1-0	2-1	3-0	3-1	3-1	0-5	1-3	1-3	2-2	3-1	4-0	3-2	1-6	1-1	0-0	2-1		3-2
22 Wroxham	2-2	0-1	9-1	2-1	1-0	0-0	3-1	2-3	2-1	2-0	4-1	3-1	0-4	3-2	2-1	1-1	2-3	3-0	3-1	2-1	4-1	

EASTERN COUNTIES - STEP 5/6

DIVISION ONE	P	W	D	L	F	A	Pts
1 Gorleston	32	22	4	6	85	32	70
2 Whitton United	32	20	9	3	79	33	69
3 Diss Town	32	20	5	7	75	27	65
4 Cambridge University Press	32	18	8	6	82	44	62
5 Thetford Town	32	16	7	9	70	47	55
6 Saffron Walden Town	32	15	8	9	68	41	53
7 Stowmarket Town	32	16	5	11	67	44	53
8 March Town United	32	15	4	13	53	53	49
9 Godmanchester Rovers	32	12	9	11	61	41	45
10 Ipswich Wanderers	32	12	6	14	60	67	42
11 Halstead Town	32	12	5	15	44	59	41
12 Long Melford	32	11	4	17	44	64	37
13 Team Bury	32	9	8	15	48	65	35
14 Fakenham Town	32	8	9	15	37	53	33
15 Swaffham Town	32	9	5	18	53	78	32
16 Downham Town	32	4	5	23	37	91	17
17 Cornard United	32	2	1	29	17	141	7

DIVISION ONE LEAGUE CUP

PRELIMINARY ROUND
Long Melford 3-1 Ipswich Wanderers

ROUND 1
Cornard United 1-2 Whitton United
Diss Town 1-2 Thetford Town
Downham Town 0-2 Swaffham Town
Fakenham Town 0-2 Gorleston
Godmanchester Rovers 4-2 Cambridge University Press
Long Melford 1-0 Halstead Town
March Town United 0-2 Saffron Walden Town
Team Bury 0-3 Stowmarket Town

QUARTER FINALS
Long Melford 1-0 Godmanchester Rovers
Saffron Walden Town 1-5 Whitton United
Swaffham Town 0-1 Gorleston
Thetford Town 2-1 Stowmarket Town

SEMI-FINALS
Gorleston 1-0 Whitton United
Thetford Town 1-0 Long Melford

FINAL (@ Diss Town, 8/4/11)
Gorleston 3-1 Thetford Town

RESERVE CHAMPIONSHIP PLAY-OFF

(Chell Trophy) (@ Bury Town, 12/5/11)
Lowestoft Town reserves 0-3 Braintree Town reserves

DIVISION ONE	1	2	3	4	5	6	7	8	9	10	11	12	13	14	15	16	17
1 Cambridge University Press		6-1	1-0	8-2	2-6	3-2	0-1	4-0	6-2	1-3	1-5	1-1	0-1	4-1	3-0	4-3	1-1
2 Cornard United	1-4		0-6	0-3	0-6	0-6	0-2	2-3	0-6	3-2	0-1	0-2	0-13	0-7	0-5	0-4	0-3
3 Diss Town	1-2	6-0		4-0	1-0	0-0	1-1	3-0	2-1	2-0	3-0	2-4	3-0	3-0	3-3	2-0	0-2
4 Downham Town	0-7	0-1	0-3		1-1	3-1	1-6	3-0	1-2	3-0	1-2	3-3	1-1	2-4	2-2	0-3	0-5
5 Fakenham Town	2-4	5-1	1-0	2-1		1-1	1-1	1-1	0-2	2-1	0-0	2-2	0-1	2-2	3-3	2-3	0-1
6 Godmanchester Rovers	2-1	1-1	0-2	1-1	3-0		1-4	6-1	1-2	5-1	2-2	2-0	1-3	4-1	3-3	0-0	0-1
7 Gorleston	3-4	6-0	4-0	5-1	0-1	1-0		2-1	1-3	3-1	2-3	1-1	4-3	7-2	4-0	3-0	0-3
8 Halstead Town	1-1	3-0	0-1	3-0	3-0	1-2	0-1		5-0	1-2	2-1	3-1	0-4	1-0	1-0	3-2	1-1
9 Ipswich Wanderers	1-1	6-2	1-1	5-2	3-0	1-3	0-3	2-1		1-3	0-4	0-3	1-1	3-1	1-1	2-5	2-3
10 Long Melford	0-0	4-0	0-3	4-0	0-1	0-5	1-3	1-1	1-3		0-1	2-1	4-3	2-1	4-2	1-0	2-6
11 March Town United	1-2	2-0	1-6	2-1	2-0	3-2	0-1	1-2	3-1	1-2		1-3	1-3	1-1	3-2	0-3	0-4
12 Saffron Walden Town	3-0	6-0	0-3	4-1	2-1	0-1	1-2	5-1	2-2	1-0	2-3		2-0	4-1	4-1	1-2	1-1
13 Stowmarket Town	1-1	3-0	4-1	4-2	0-1	2-0	0-4	0-1	3-1	1-1	3-2	1-0		4-0	0-1	0-3	0-1
14 Swaffham Town	0-3	7-0	1-4	1-0	4-1	2-2	0-4	2-0	2-4	0-0	0-4	2-2	4-3		3-2	1-3	0-5
15 Team Bury	1-3	4-3	1-1	1-0	2-0	0-4	0-2	2-1	3-0	2-1	1-1	0-1	1-2	0-2		3-1	1-1
16 Thetford Town	2-2	5-0	0-3	2-1	5-0	0-0	3-1	3-3	2-2	1-0	3-1	0-4	2-2	2-1	6-0		1-1
17 Whitton United	2-2	4-2	0-5	4-1	1-1	1-0	3-3	6-0	1-0	7-1	0-1	2-2	1-4	2-0	2-1	4-1	

EASTERN COUNTIES INS & OUTS

PREM - IN: Diss Town (P), Gorleston (P).

OUT: Debenham Leisure Centre (R), Histon Reserves (W - Cambs County League Premier Division),

Leiston (P - Isthmian League Division One North).

DIV ONE - IN: Brightlingsea Regent (P - Essex & Suffolk Border League Premier Division), Debenham Leisure Centre (R).

OUT: Diss Town (P), Gorleston (P), Saffron Walden Town (F).

BRANTHAM ATHLETIC

Founded: 1887 Nickname:

Secretary: Andy Powell **(T)** 07919 616 310 **(E)** branthamathfc@hotmail.co.uk
Chairman: Peter Crowhurst **Manager:** Tony Hall and Alan Merchant **Prog Ed:** Andy Powell
Ground: Brantham Leisure Centre, New Village, Brantham CO11 1RZ. **(T)** 01206 392 506
Capacity: 1,200 **Seats:** 200 **Covered:** 200 **Midweek Matchday:** Tuesday **Clubhouse:** Yes **Shop:**

Colours(change): All blue. (Red and black/black/black)
Previous Names: Brantham & Stutton United 1996-98.
Previous Leagues: Eastern Counties. Suffolk & Ipswich.
Records: **Att:** 1,700 v VS Rugby, FA Vase 5R 1982-83.
Senior Honours: Suffolk & Ipswich Senior League Champions 2007-08.

10 YEAR RECORD

01-02	02-03	03-04	04-05	05-06	06-07	07-08	08-09	09-10	10-11
			S&I 1 2	S&I S 14	S&I S 4	S&I S 1	EC1 8	EC1 3	ECP 13

CRC

Founded: Nickname:

Secretary: Julie Ankers **(T)** 07782 120 354 **(E)** julieankers@cambridge-united.co.uk
Chairman: Robert Smith **Manager:** Mark Bonner **Prog Ed:**
Ground: Cambridge Utd FC, R Costings Abbey Stad, Newmarket Road CB5 8LN **(T)** 01223 566 500
Capacity: 9,217 **Seats:** 200 **Covered:** Yes **Midweek Matchday:** Wednesday **Clubhouse:** **Shop:** Yes

Colours(change): Amber/black/black (All sky blue)
Previous Names: None.
Previous Leagues: None
Records:
Senior Honours:

10 YEAR RECORD

01-02	02-03	03-04	04-05	05-06	06-07	07-08	08-09	09-10	10-11
					ECP 17	ECP 13	ECP 2	ECP 2	ECP 11

DEREHAM TOWN

Founded: 1884 Nickname: Magpies

Secretary: Nigel Link **(T)** 07885 144039 **(E)** patnige1954@fsmail.net
Chairman: Mike Baldry **Manager:** Matt Henman **Prog Ed:** Barnes Print
Ground: Aldiss Park, Norwich Road, Dereham, Norfolk NR20 3PX **(T)** 01362 690 460
Capacity: 3,000 **Seats:** 50 **Covered:** 500 **Midweek Matchday:** Tuesday **Clubhouse:** Yes **Shop:** Yes

Colours(change): White & black/black/black. (Green & white/green/green)
Previous Names: Dereham and Dereham Hobbies.
Previous Leagues: Norwich District. Dereham & District. Norfolk & Suffolk. Anglian Comb.
Records: **Att:** 3000 v Norwich City, Friendly, 07/2001.
Senior Honours: Anglian Combination Division 1 Champions 1989-90, Premier Division 97-98. Norfolk Senior Cup 2005-06, 06-07.

10 YEAR RECORD

01-02	02-03	03-04	04-05	05-06	06-07	07-08	08-09	09-10	10-11
ECP 13	ECP 19	ECP 18	ECP 15	ECP 12	ECP 6	ECP 4	ECP 4	ECP 10	ECP 2

DISS TOWN

Founded: 1888 Nickname: Tangerines

Secretary: Steve Flatman **(T)** 07855 531 341 **(E)** pam@dissfc.wanadoo.co.uk
Chairman: Richard Upson **Manager:** Robert Taylor **Prog Ed:** Gary Enderby
Ground: Brewers Green Lane, Diss, Norfolk IP22 4QP **(T)** 01379 651 223
Capacity: **Seats:** **Covered:** **Midweek Matchday:** **Clubhouse:** **Shop:**

Colours(change): Tangerine/navy blue/tangerine (Sky blue/navy/navy)
Previous Names:
Previous Leagues: Anglian Combination
Records: 1,731 v Atherton LR, FA Vase Semi Final, 19.03.94.
Senior Honours: Eastern Counties Division One 1991-92. FA Vase winners 1993-94.

10 YEAR RECORD

01-02	02-03	03-04	04-05	05-06	06-07	07-08	08-09	09-10	10-11
ECP 16	ECP 5	ECP 4	ECP 12	ECP 11	ECP 20	EC1 4	EC1 9	EC1 5	EC1 3

ELY CITY

Founded: 1885 Nickname: Robins

Secretary: Derek Oakey **(T)** 07720 542 882 **(E)** derek.oakey@tesco.net
Chairman: Robert Button **Manager:** Alan Alsop **Prog Ed:** Barnes Print
Ground: Unwin Sports Ground, Downham Road, Ely CB6 2SH **(T)** 01353 662 035
Capacity: 1,500 **Seats:** 150 **Covered:** 350 **Midweek Matchday:** Tuesday **Clubhouse:** Yes **Shop:** Yes

Colours(change): All red. (All blue).
Previous Names: None.
Previous Leagues: Peterborough. Central Alliance.
Records: **Att:** 260 v Soham, Eastern Counties Div.1, 12.04.93.
Senior Honours: Cambridgeshire Senior Cup 1947-48. Eastern Counties Division 1 1996-97.

10 YEAR RECORD

01-02	02-03	03-04	04-05	05-06	06-07	07-08	08-09	09-10	10-11
ECP 9	ECP 23	EC1 10	EC1 9	EC1 7	EC1 4	EC1 2	ECP 14	ECP 9	ECP 15

FC CLACTON

Founded: 1892 Nickname: The Seasiders

Secretary: Barry Leatherdale **(T)** 07545 998 242 **(E)** secretary@fcclacton.com
Chairman: David Ballard **Manager:** Steve Pitt **Prog Ed:** Martin Oswick
Ground: Rush Green Bowl, Rush Green Rd, Clacton-on-Sea CO16 7BQ **(T)** 07545 998 242
Capacity: 3,000 **Seats:** 200 **Covered:** Yes **Midweek Matchday:** Tuesday **Clubhouse:** Yes **Shop:** Yes

Colours(change): White/royal blue/royal blue. (Yellow/black/black).
Previous Names: Clacton Town > 2007
Previous Leagues: Eastern Counties. Essex County. Southern League.
Records: **Att:** 3,505 v Romford, FA Cup 1952 at Old Road.
Senior Honours: Eastern Counties Division 1 1994-95, 98-99.

10 YEAR RECORD

01-02	02-03	03-04	04-05	05-06	06-07	07-08	08-09	09-10	10-11
ECP 4	ECP 11	ECP 6	ECP 8	ECP 22	ECP 21	EC1 10	EC1 7	EC1 2	ECP 16

FELIXSTOWE & WALTON UNITED

Founded: 2000 Nickname: Seasiders

Secretary: Adrian Hakes **(T)** 07584 644 069 **(E)** Adrian.hakes@btinternet.com
Chairman: Tony Barnes **Manager:** Kevin Witchalls **Prog Ed:** Phil Griffiths
Ground: Town Ground, Dellwood Avenue, Felixstowe IP11 9HT **(T)** 01394 282 917
Capacity: 2,000 **Seats:** 200 **Covered:** 200 **Midweek Matchday:** Tuesday **Clubhouse:** Yes **Shop:** Yes

Colours(change): Red & white stripes/white/red. (Yellow & blue/yellow/yellow).
Previous Names: Felixstowe Port & Town and Walton United merged in July 2000.
Previous Leagues: None
Records:
Senior Honours:

10 YEAR RECORD

01-02	02-03	03-04	04-05	05-06	06-07	07-08	08-09	09-10	10-11
ECP 21	EC1 16	EC1 15	EC1 17	EC1 2	ECP 13	ECP 8	ECP 12	ECP 7	ECP 18

GORLESTON

Founded: 1887 Nickname:

Secretary: Ann Santon **(T)** 07597 926 329 **(E)** santonmicks@aol.com
Chairman: Reg Cadmore **Manager:** Richard Daniels **Prog Ed:** TBA
Ground: Emerald Park, Woodfarm Lane, Gorleston, Norfolk NR31 9AQ **(T)** 01493 602 802
Capacity: **Seats:** **Covered:** **Midweek Matchday:** **Clubhouse:** **Shop:**

Colours(change): All green (All blue)
Previous Names:
Previous Leagues: Anglian Combination
Records: **Record Att:** 4,473 v Orient, FA Cup 1st Round, 29.11.51.
Senior Honours: Norfolk & Suff. Lge (x 7). Norfolk Senior Cup (x 14). Anglian Comb 1968-69. Eastern Counties 1952-53, 72-73, 79-80, 80-81. Division One 1995-96, 2010-11.

10 YEAR RECORD

01-02	02-03	03-04	04-05	05-06	06-07	07-08	08-09	09-10	10-11
ECP 5	ECP 15	ECP 20	ECP 21	EC1 18	EC1 14	EC1 8	EC1 6	EC1 4	EC1 1

GREAT YARMOUTH TOWN
Founded: 1897 Nickname:

Secretary: Colin Jones **(T)** 07872 121942 **(E)** colscanaries@hotmail.com
Chairman: Colin Jones **Manager:** Paul Tong **Prog Ed:** TBA
Ground: The Wellesley, Sandown Road, Great Yarmouth NR30 1EY **(T)** 01493 656 099
Capacity: 3,600 **Seats:** 500 **Covered:** 2,100 **Midweek Matchday:** Tuesday **Clubhouse:** Yes **Shop:** Yes

Colours(change): Amber & black stripes/black/black. (All pink).
Previous Names: None
Previous Leagues: Norfolk & Suffolk.
Records: **Att:** 8,944 v Crystal Palace FA Cup R1 52-53. **Goalscorer:** Gordon South - 298 (1927-47). **Apps:** Mark Vincent - 700 (84-05).
Senior Honours: Eastern Counties League Champions 1968-69, Division 1 2009-10. Norfolk Senior Cup (x 12)

10 YEAR RECORD

01-02	02-03	03-04	04-05	05-06	06-07	07-08	08-09	09-10	10-11
ECP 17	ECP 8	ECP 16	ECP 22	EC1 13	EC1 13	EC1 11	EC1 5	EC1 1	ECP 14

HADLEIGH UNITED
Founded: 1892 Nickname: Brettsiders

Secretary: Chris Rose **(T)** 07864 828 213 **(E)** chris1rose@btinternet.com
Chairman: Rolf Beggerow **Manager:** Stuart Crawford **Prog Ed:** Chris Towell
Ground: Millfield, Tinkers Lane, Duke St, Hadleigh IP7 5NG **(T)** 01473 822 165
Capacity: 3,000 **Seats:** 250 **Covered:** 500 **Midweek Matchday:** Tuesday **Clubhouse:** Yes **Shop:**

Colours(change): White/blue/blue (All red)
Previous Names: None
Previous Leagues: Suffolk & Ipswich.
Records: **Att:** 518 v Halstead Town, FA Vase replay, 17.01.95.
Senior Honours: Suffolk & Ipswich League Champions 1953-54, 56-57, 73-74, 76-77, 78-79.
Suffolk Senior Cup 1968-69, 71-72, 82-83, 2003-04. Eastern Counties League Champions 1993-94.

10 YEAR RECORD

01-02	02-03	03-04	04-05	05-06	06-07	07-08	08-09	09-10	10-11
EC1 14	EC1 4	EC1 18	EC1 16	EC1 21	EC1 9	EC1 5	EC1 2	ECP 18	ECP 9

HAVERHILL ROVERS
Founded: 1886 Nickname: Rovers

Secretary: Gary Brown **(T)** 07894 553 267 **(E)** gabrown306@hotmail.com
Chairman: Steve Brown **Manager:** Peter Betts **Prog Ed:** Gary Brown
Ground: The New Croft, Chalkstone Way, Haverhill, Suffolk CB9 0BW **(T)** 01440 702 137
Capacity: 3,000 **Seats:** 200 **Covered:** 200 **Midweek Matchday:** Tuesday **Clubhouse:** Yes **Shop:**

Colours(change): All red. (White/navy/navy).
Previous Names: None.
Previous Leagues: East Anglian. Essex & Suffolk Border.
Records:
Senior Honours: Essex & Suffolk Border League Champions 1947-48, 62-63, 63-64.
Eastern Counties League Cup 1964-65, League Champions 78-79. Suffolk Senior Cup 1995-96.

10 YEAR RECORD

01-02	02-03	03-04	04-05	05-06	06-07	07-08	08-09	09-10	10-11
EC1 3	EC1 10	EC1 11	EC1 5	EC1 8	EC1 2	ECP 10	ECP 21	ECP 12	ECP 8

KIRKLEY & PAKEFIELD
Founded: 1886 Nickname: The Kirks

Secretary: Barrie Atkins **(T)** 07970 659 001 **(E)** 2006@tiscali.co.uk
Chairman: Robert Jenkerson **Manager:** Jon Reynolds **Prog Ed:** Barnes Print
Ground: K. & P. Community Sports & S. Club, Walmer Rd, Lowestoft NR33 7LE **(T)** 01502 513 549
Capacity: 2,000 **Seats:** 150 **Covered:** 150 **Midweek Matchday:** Tuesday **Clubhouse:** Yes **Shop:** Yes

Colours(change): Royal blue & maroon/royal/royal. (Orange/orange/black).
Previous Names: Kirkley. Kirkley & Waveney 1929-33. Merged with Pakefield in 2007.
Previous Leagues: Norfolk & Suffolk. Anglian Combination.
Records: **Att:** 1,125 v Lowestoft Town. **Goalscorer:** Barry Dale - 241. **Apps:** Barry Dale - 495.
Senior Honours: Suffolk Senior Cup 1900-01, 01-02, 24-25, 00-01, 01-02. Anglian Combination League 2001-02, 02-03.

10 YEAR RECORD

01-02	02-03	03-04	04-05	05-06	06-07	07-08	08-09	09-10	10-11
AngP 1	AngP 1	EC1 5	EC1 3	ECP 14	ECP 7	ECP 6	ECP 6	ECP 4	ECP 12

MILDENHALL TOWN

Founded: 1898 | Nickname: The Hall

Secretary: Brian Hensby **(T)** 07932 043 261 **(E)** bhensby@talktalk.net
Chairman: Martin Tuck **Manager:** Christian Appleford **Prog Ed:** Frank Marshall
Ground: Recreation Way, Mildenhall, Suffolk IP28 7HG **(T)** 01638 713 449
Capacity: 2,00 **Seats:** 50 **Covered:** 200 **Midweek Matchday:** Tuesday **Clubhouse:** Yes **Shop:** Yes

Colours(change): Amber/black/black. (Red/white/red).
Previous Names: None
Previous Leagues: Bury & District. Cambridgeshire. Cambridgeshire Premier.
Records: **Att:** 450 v Derby County, Friendly, July 2001.
Senior Honours:

10 YEAR RECORD

01-02	02-03	03-04	04-05	05-06	06-07	07-08	08-09	09-10	10-11
ECP 11	ECP 10	ECP 12	ECP 6	ECP 5	ECP 2	ECP 5	ECP 11	ECP 6	ECP 5

NEWMARKET TOWN

Founded: 1877 | Nickname: The Jockeys

Secretary: Elaine Jeakins **(T)** 07801 815 682 **(E)** elaine.jeakins@ntlworld.com
Chairman: John Olive **Manager:** Kevin Grainger **Prog Ed:** Elaine Jeakins
Ground: Town Ground, Cricket Field Road, Off Cheveley Rd, Newmarket CB8 8BG **(T)** 01638 663 637
Capacity: 2,750 **Seats:** 144 **Covered:** 250 **Midweek Matchday:** Wednesday **Clubhouse:** Yes **Shop:** Yes

Colours(change): Yellow/blue/yellow (Blue/blue/yellow)
Previous Names: None
Previous Leagues: Bury Senior. Ipswich Senior. Essex & Suffolk B. United Counties.
Records: **Att:** 2,701 v Abbey United (now Cambridge Utd) FA Cup, 01.10.49.
Senior Honours: Suffolk Senior Cup 1934-35, 93-94. Suffolk Premier Cup 1993-94, 94-95, 96-97.
Eastern Counties League Division 1 2008-09.

10 YEAR RECORD

01-02	02-03	03-04	04-05	05-06	06-07	07-08	08-09	09-10	10-11
ECP 19	ECP 18	ECP 10	ECP 13	ECP 17	ECP 12	ECP 21	EC1 1	ECP 16	ECP 19

NORWICH UNITED

Founded: 1903 | Nickname: Planters

Secretary: Keith Cutmore **(T)** 07788 437 515 **(E)** secretary.nufc@hotmail.co.uk
Chairman: John Hilditch **Manager:** Paul Chick **Prog Ed:** Barnes Print
Ground: Plantation Park, Blofield, Norwich NR13 4PL **(T)** 01603 716 963
Capacity: 3,000 **Seats:** 100 **Covered:** 1,000 **Midweek Matchday:** Tuesday **Clubhouse:** Yes **Shop:** Yes

Colours(change): Yellow & blue/blue/blue. (All red)
Previous Names: Poringland & District > 1987
Previous Leagues: Norwich & District. Anglian Combination
Records: **Att:** 401 v Wroxham, Eastern Co. Lge, 1991-92. **Goalscorer:** M. Money. **Apps:** Tim Sayer.
Senior Honours: Anglian Combination Senior Cup 1983-84. Eastern Counties League Division One 1990-91, 01-02.

10 YEAR RECORD

01-02	02-03	03-04	04-05	05-06	06-07	07-08	08-09	09-10	10-11
EC1 1	ECP 16	ECP 11	ECP 14	ECP 20	ECP 16	ECP 15	ECP 19	ECP 15	ECP 6

STANWAY ROVERS

Founded: 1956 | Nickname: Rovers

Secretary: Paul Rogers **(T)** 07986 615 481 **(E)** paul.rogers2@ntlworld.com
Chairman: Roy Brett **Manager:** Wayne Bond **Prog Ed:** Mike Norfolk
Ground: Hawthorns, New Farm Road, Stanway, Colchester CO3 0PG **(T)** 01206 578 187
Capacity: 1,500 **Seats:** 100 **Covered:** 250 **Midweek Matchday:** Wednesday **Clubhouse:** Yes **Shop:** Yes

Colours(change): Amber & black/black/black. (Sky & navy blue/navy/navy).
Previous Names: None.
Previous Leagues: Colchester & East Essex. Essex & Suffolk Border.
Records: **Att:** 210 v Harwich & P, Eastern Co. Lge Div.1, 2004.
Senior Honours: Eastern Counties League Division 1 Champions 2005-06, League Cup 2008-09.

10 YEAR RECORD

01-02	02-03	03-04	04-05	05-06	06-07	07-08	08-09	09-10	10-11
EC1 7	EC1 5	EC1 4	EC1 6	EC1 1	ECP 14	ECP 7	ECP 9	ECP 5	ECP 7

WALSHAM-LE-WILLOWS

Founded: 1888 Nickname:

Secretary: Gordon Ross **(T)** 07742 111 892 **(E)** gordonaross@aol.com
Chairman: Mike Powles **Manager:** Christopher Soanes **Prog Ed:** Barnes Print
Ground: Walsham Sports Club, Summer Rd, Walsham-le-Willows IP31 3AH **(T)** 01359 259 298
Capacity: **Seats:** 100 **Covered:** 100 **Midweek Matchday:** Wednesday **Clubhouse:** Yes **Shop:**

Colours(change): Red with yellow trim/red and yellow/red with yellow trim (Royal blue with yellow trim/royal blue/royal blue)
Previous Names: None
Previous Leagues: Bury & District. Suffolk & Ipswich.
Records:
Senior Honours: Suffolk & Ipswich Senior League Champions 2001-02, 02-03. Suffolk Senior Cup 2005-06.
Eastern Counties League Division 1 Champions 2006-07.

10 YEAR RECORD

01-02	02-03	03-04	04-05	05-06	06-07	07-08	08-09	09-10	10-11
S&I S 1	S&I S 1	S&I S 2	EC1 4	EC1 5	EC1 1	ECP 16	ECP 10	ECP 13	ECP 17

WISBECH TOWN

Founded: 1920 Nickname: Fenmen

Secretary: Colin Gant **(T)** 07803 021 699 **(E)** colin@gant5366.freeserve.co.uk
Chairman: Barry Carter **Manager:** Steve Appleby **Prog Ed:** Spencer Larham
Ground: The Fenland Stadium, Lynn Road, Wisbech PE14 7AN **(T)**
Capacity: **Seats:** **Covered:** **Midweek Matchday:** Tuesday **Clubhouse:** **Shop:**

Colours(change): All red. (Yellow/green/yellow).
Previous Names: None
Previous Leagues: East Midlands. Peterborough. United Co. Eastern Co. Midland. Southern.
Records: **Att:** 8,044 v Peterborough Utd, Midland Lge 25/08/1957 **Goalscorer:** Bert Titmarsh - 246 (1931-37) **Apps:** Jamie Brighty - 731
Senior Honours: United Counties League Champions 1946-47, 47-48. Southern League Division 1 1961-62.
Eastern Counties League 1971-72, 76-77, 90-91, League Cup 2010-11. East Anglian Cup 1987-88.

10 YEAR RECORD

01-02	02-03	03-04	04-05	05-06	06-07	07-08	08-09	09-10	10-11
SthM 22	ECP 6	ECP 14	ECP 16	ECP 4	ECP 11	ECP 12	ECP 16	ECP 11	ECP 4

WIVENHOE TOWN

Founded: 1925 Nickname: The Dragons

Secretary: Carl Callan **(T)** 07818 596 376 **(E)** carl@nallac.com
Chairman: Carl Callan **Manager:** Mo Osman **Prog Ed:** Richard Charnock
Ground: Broad Lane, Elmstead Road, Wivenhoe CO7 7HA **(T)** 01206 827 144
Capacity: 2876 **Seats:** 161 **Covered:** 1300 **Midweek Matchday:** Tuesday **Clubhouse:** Yes **Shop:** Yes

Colours(change): All blue (All yellow)
Previous Names: Wivenhoe Rangers.
Previous Leagues: Brightlingsea & District, Colchester & East Essex. Essex & Suffolk Border, Essex Senior, Isthmian
Records: **Att:** 1,912 v Runcorn, FA Trophy, 1st Round, Feb. 1990. **Goalscorer:** (258 in 350 games). **Apps:** Keith Bain (538).
Senior Honours: Isthmian Division 2 North 1987-88. Division 1 1989-90. Essex Senior Trophy 1987-88.

10 YEAR RECORD

01-02	02-03	03-04	04-05	05-06	06-07	07-08	08-09	09-10	10-11
Isth2 21	Isth1N 21	Isth1N 17	SthE 5	SthE 6	Isth1N 11	Isth1N 22	ECP 17	ECP 20	ECP 20

WOODBRIDGE TOWN

Founded: 1885 Nickname: The Woodpeckers

Secretary: Allan Kitchen **(T)** 07951 217 060 **(E)** allan.kitchen@btinternet.com
Chairman: John Beecroft **Manager:** Mark Scopes **Prog Ed:** Richard Scott
Ground: Notcutts Park, Fynn Road, Woodbridge IP12 4DA **(T)** 01394 385 308
Capacity: 3,000 **Seats:** 50 **Covered:** 200 **Midweek Matchday:** Wednesday **Clubhouse:** Yes **Shop:** No

Colours(change): Black & white stripes/black/black. (All red).
Previous Names: None.
Previous Leagues: Ipswich & District. Suffolk & Ipswich.
Records: **Att:** 3,000 v Arsenal, for the opening of the floodlights, 02.10.90.
Senior Honours: Suffolk Senior Cup 1885, 77-78, 92-93, 93-94.
Ipswich & District Senior Champions 1912-13. Suffolk & Ipswich Senior 1988-89.

10 YEAR RECORD

01-02	02-03	03-04	04-05	05-06	06-07	07-08	08-09	09-10	10-11
ECP 8	ECP 20	ECP 17	ECP 17	ECP 16	ECP 9	ECP 17	ECP 18	ECP 19	ECP 10

WROXHAM

Founded: 1892 Nickname: Yachtsmen

Secretary: Chris Green **(T)** 07769 509 164 **(E)** secretary@wroxhamfc.com

Chairman: TBA **Manager:** David Batch **Prog Ed:** Barnes Print

Ground: Trafford Park, Skinners Lane, Wroxham NR12 8SJ **(T)** 01603 783 538

Capacity: 2,500 **Seats:** 50 **Covered:** 250 **Midweek Matchday:** Tuesday **Clubhouse:** Yes **Shop:** No

Colours(change): Blue & white stripes/blue/white (All red)

Previous Names: None

Previous Leagues: East Norfolk. Norwich City. East Anglian. Norwich & Dist. Anglian Comb.

Records: **Att:** 1,011 v Wisbech Town, Eastern Co. Lge, 16.03.93. **Goalscorer:** Matthew Metcalf. **Apps:** Stu Larter.

Senior Honours: Anglian County League 1981-82, 82-83, 83-84, 84-85, 86-87. Eastern Co. Div.1 1988-89, Prem 91-92, 92-93, 93-94, 96-97, 97-98, 98-99, 06-07. N'folk Sen'Cup 1992-93, 95-96, 97-98, 99-00, 03-04.

10 YEAR RECORD

01-02	02-03	03-04	04-05	05-06	06-07	07-08	08-09	09-10	10-11
ECP 2	ECP 2	ECP 3	ECP 5	ECP 8	ECP 1	ECP 3	ECP 5	ECP 8	ECP 3

Team Bury FC. Photo: Alan Coomes.

DIVISION ONE

BRIGHTLINGSEA REGENT

Founded: Pre 1908 Nickname: The Tics

Secretary: Ian Dixon (T) 07809 434 122 (E) janinedixon@gmail.com
Chairman: Terry Doherty **Manager:** James Webster **Prog Ed:** Mark Gridley
Ground: North Road, Brightlingsea, Essex CO7 0PL (T) 01206 304 199 **Capacity:**
Colours(change): Red & black stripes/black/black (All blue)

ADDITIONAL INFORMATION:
Previous Lge: Essex & Suffolk Border > 2011.
Honours: Essex & Suffolk Border League 2010-11.

CAMBRIDGE UNIVERSITY PRESS

Founded: 1893 Nickname:

Secretary: Gary Crick (T) 07728 344 088 (E) gary@cupfc.net
Chairman: Nigel Atkinson **Manager:** Nigel Dixon **Prog Ed:**
Ground: The Glassworld Stadium, Bridge Road, Impington, Cambridge CB24 9PH (T) 01223 237 373 **Capacity:**
Colours(change): All sky blue (All yellow)

ADDITIONAL INFORMATION:
Honours: Cambridgeshire Senior Cup 1913-14. Cambridgeshire Premier League 1934-35.

CORNARD UNITED

Founded: 1964 Nickname: Ards

Secretary: Chris Symes (T) 07811 096 832 (E) chrissymes@hotmail.com
Chairman: Neil Cottrell **Manager:** Chris Symes **Prog Ed:** Chris Symes
Ground: Blackhouse Lane, Great Cornard, Sudbury, Suffolk CO10 0NL (T) 07811 096 382 **Capacity:**
Colours(change): Royal blue & white/black/black (Lime green/black/black)

ADDITIONAL INFORMATION:
Record Att: 400 v Colchester United 1997. **Goalscorer:** Andy Smiles. **Apps:** Keith Featherstone.
Honours: Essex & Suffolk Border League Champions 1988-89. Eastern Counties Div. 1 1989-90. Suffolk Senior Cup 89-90.

DEBENHAM LC

Founded: Nickname: The Hornets

Secretary: Dan Snell (T) 07840 246 837 (E) snelly1992@hotmail.co.uk
Chairman: Stephen Anderson **Manager:** Rob Allum **Prog Ed:** Martyn Clarke
Ground: Debenham Leisure Centre, Gracechurch Street, Debenham IP14 6BL (T) 01728 861 101 **Capacity:** 1,000
Colours(change): Yellow/black/yellow. (All blue).

ADDITIONAL INFORMATION: **Att:** 400. **Goalscorer:** Lee Briggs. **Apps:** Steve Nelson.

DOWNHAM TOWN

Founded: 1881 Nickname: Town

Secretary: George Dickson (T) 07834 329 781 (E) george.dickson@britishsugar.com
Chairman: David Green **Manager:** Garth Good **Prog Ed:** Barnes Print
Ground: Memorial Field, Lynn Road, Downham Market PE38 9QE (T) 01366 388 424 **Capacity:**
Colours(change): Red/red/red & white (All blue)

ADDITIONAL INFORMATION:
Record Att: 325 v Wells Town, Norfolk Senior Cup, 1998-99. **Honours:** Peterborough Senior Cup 1962, 63, 67, 72, 87. Peterborough League 1963, 74, 79, 87, 88. Norfolk Senior Cup 1964, 66.

FAKENHAM TOWN

Founded: 1884 Nickname: Ghosts

Secretary: Andrew Mitchell (T) 07540 778 379 (E) andrewmitchell@fakenhamtownfc.co.uk
Chairman: William Clayton **Manager:** Wayne Anderson **Prog Ed:** Barnes Print
Ground: Clipbush Park, Clipbush Lane, Fakenham, Norfolk NR21 8SW (T) 01328 855 859 **Capacity:**
Colours(change): Amber & black stripes/black/amber (Blue & white/blue/blue)

ADDITIONAL INFORMATION:
Record Att: 1,100 v Watford, official opening of new ground.
Honours: Norfolk Senior Cup 1970-71, 72-73, 73-74, 91-92, 93-94, 94-95.

GODMANCHESTER ROVERS

Founded: 1911 Nickname: Goody/Rovers

Secretary: Finbarr Sheehan (T) 07887 880 717 (E) fin.catworth@virgin.net
Chairman: Keith Gabb **Manager:** David Hurst **Prog Ed:** Sue Hurst
Ground: Bearscroft Lane, Godmanchester, Huntingdon, Cambs PE29 2LQ (T) 07774 830507 **Capacity:**
Colours(change): All blue (All red)

ADDITIONAL INFORMATION:
Record Att: 138 v Cambridge City Reserves, Dec. 2003.

HALSTEAD TOWN

Founded: 1879 Nickname: The Town

Secretary: Steve Webber **(T)** 07763 078 563 **(E)** halsteadtownfc@aol.com
Chairman: Jimmy Holder **Manager:** Jimmy Holder **Prog Ed:** Barnes Print
Ground: Rosemary Lane, Broton Industrial Estate, Halstead, Essex CO9 1HR **(T)** 01787 472 082 **Capacity:**
Colours(change): Black & white halves/black/black (All blue)

ADDITIONAL INFORMATION:
Record Att: 4,000 v Walthamstowe Avenue, Essex Senior Cup 1949.
Honours: Eastern Counties Champions 1994-95, 95-96. Div.1 2002-03. Essex Senior Trophy 1994-95, 96-97.

IPSWICH WANDERERS

Founded: 1983 Nickname: Wanderers

Secretary: Mark Bright **(T)** 07775 580 134 **(E)** mark.bright@uk.henkel.com
Chairman: Terry Fenwick **Manager:** Steve Buckle **Prog Ed:** Roger Wosahlo
Ground: SEH Sports Centre, Humber Doucy Lane, Ipswich IP4 3NR **(T)** 01473 728581 **Capacity:**
Colours(change): Blue & white/blue/blue (All orange)

ADDITIONAL INFORMATION:
Record Att: 335 v Woodbridge, Eastern Counties League 1993-94.
Honours: Eastern Counties Div.1 Champions 1997-98, 04-05.

LONG MELFORD

Founded: 1868 Nickname: The Villagers

Secretary: Richard Powell **(T)** 07897 751 298 **(E)** richard.j.powell@hotmail.co.uk
Chairman: Colin Woodhouse **Manager:** Jason Maher **Prog Ed:** Andy Cussans
Ground: Stoneylands Stadium, New Road, Long Melford, Suffolk CO10 9JY **(T)** 01787 312 187 **Capacity:**
Colours(change): Black & white stripes/black/black (All red)

ADDITIONAL INFORMATION:
Honours: Essex & Suffolk Border Champions x5. Suffolk Senior Cup x8.

MARCH TOWN UNITED

Founded: 1885 Nickname: Hares

Secretary: Raymond Bennett **(T)** 07944 721 312 **(E)** r.bennett639@btinternet.com
Chairman: Philip White **Manager:** Bret Whalley **Prog Ed:** Gary Wesley
Ground: GER Sports Ground, Robin Goodfellow Lane, March, Cambs PE15 8HS **(T)** 01354 653 073 **Capacity:**
Colours(change): Tangerine/black/black (All blue)

ADDITIONAL INFORMATION:
Record Att: 7,500 v King's Lynn, FA Cup 1956.
Honours: United Counties League 1953-54. Eastern Counties 1987-88.

STOWMARKET TOWN

Founded: 1883 Nickname:

Secretary: David Marshall **(T)** 07952 288 298 **(E)** footballsecretary@stowmarkettownfc.co.uk
Chairman: Neil Sharp **Manager:** Steve Jay **Prog Ed:** Alex Moss
Ground: Greens Meadow, Bury Road, Stowmarket, Suffolk IP14 1JQ **(T)** 01449 612 533 **Capacity:**
Colours(change): Gold & black/black/black (All red)

ADDITIONAL INFORMATION:
Previous League: Essex & Suffolk Border. **Record Att:** 1,200 v Ipswich Town, friendly, July 1994.
Honours: Suffolk Senior Cup x10

SWAFFHAM TOWN

Founded: 1892 Nickname: Pedlars

Secretary: Ray Ewart **(T)** 07990 526 744 **(E)** rayewart@aol.com
Chairman: Wayne Hardy **Manager:** Paul Hunt **Prog Ed:** Barnes Print
Ground: Shoemakers Lane, Swaffham, Norfolk PE37 7NT **(T)** 01760 722 700 **Capacity:**
Colours(change): Black & white stripes/black/black (Tangerine/white/white)

ADDITIONAL INFORMATION:
Record Att: 250 v Downham Town, Eastern Counties League Cup, 03.09.91.
Honours: Eastern Counties Division 1 2000-01.

TEAM BURY

Founded: 2005 Nickname:

Secretary: Ross Wilding **(T)** 07971 199 810 **(E)** ross.wilding@wsc.ac.uk
Chairman: Alan Collen **Manager:** Ross Wilding **Prog Ed:** Ross Wilding
Ground: Bury Town FC, Ram Meadow, Cotton Lane, Bury St Edmunds IP33 1XP **(T)** 01284 754 721 **Capacity:**
Colours(change): All blue (All red)

ADDITIONAL INFORMATION:

THETFORD TOWN

Founded: 1883 Nickname:

Secretary: Bob Richards **(T)** 07795 255 160 **(E)** bobrich60@talktalk.net
Chairman: Michael Bailey **Manager:** Mark Scott **Prog Ed:** Barnes Print
Ground: Recreation Ground, Mundford Road, Thetford, Norfolk IP24 1NB **(T)** 01842 766 120 **Capacity:**
Colours(change): Claret & blue/claret/claret (Sky blue & claret/claret/claret)

ADDITIONAL INFORMATION:
Records Att: 394 v Diss Town, Norfolk Senior Cup, 1991.
Honours: Norfolk Senior Cup 1947-48, 90-91. Norfolk & Suffolk League 1954-55.

WHITTON UNITED

Founded: 1926 Nickname:

Secretary: Phil Pemberton **(T)** 07429 116 538 **(E)** pemby64@hotmail.com
Chairman: Ruel Fox **Manager:** Ian Brown **Prog Ed:** Phil Pemberton
Ground: King George V Playing Fields, Old Norwich Road, Ipswich IP1 6LE **(T)** 01473 464 030 **Capacity:**
Colours(change): All green (Yellow/black/black)

ADDITIONAL INFORMATION:
Record Att: 528 v Ipswich Town, 29.11.95.
Honours: Suffolk & Ipswich League 1946-47, 47-48, 65-66, 67-68, 91-92, 92-93. Suffolk Senior Cup 1958-59, 62-63, 92-93.

GROUND DIRECTIONS

BRANTHAM ATHLETIC - Brantham Leisure Centre CO11 1RZ - 01206 392 506

Turn off the A12 heading towards East Bergholt, stay on the B1070 through East Bergholt and go straight across the roundabout with the A137. Turn left immediately at the T-junction and follow this road around the sharp curve to the right and turn right immediately before the Village Hall. Follow this road around the sharp left hand turn and the Social Club and the car park are on the right.

CRC - The Trade Recruitment Stadium CB5 8LN - 01223 566 500

Exit the A14 at the fourth junction (situated east of Cambridge), up the slip road to the roundabout (sign posted Stow-Cum-Quy). Turn right onto the A1303, and return westwards towards Cambridge. Go straight over the first roundabout, passing Marshall Airport to the left. Go straight over two sets of traffic lights to a roundabout. The Ground's floodlights can be seen from here and McDonald's is on the right.

DEREHAM TOWN - Aldiss Park, Norwich Road NR20 3PX - 01362 690 460

Take the A47 towards Swaffham & Dereham. Do not take first slip road into Dereham. Carry on along the by-pass and take the second slip road, onto the B1110, sign posted B1147 to Bawdeswell, Swanton Morley and the Dereham Windmill. Follow the slip road round and Aldiss Park is 500 yards on your right.

DISS TOWN - Brewers Green Lane IP22 4QP - 01379 651 223

Off B1066 Diss -Thetford road near Roydon school. One and a half miles from Diss (BR).

ELY CITY - Unwin Sports Ground CB6 2SH - 01353 662 035

Follow signs for Kings Lynn/Downham Market as you approach Ely. Don't go into the city centre. After the Little Chef roundabout (junction of A10/A142) continue for approx half a mile until the next roundabout. Turn left for Little Downham (the B1411). There is also a sign for a Golf Course. The Golf Course is part of a Sports Complex which includes the football club. After turning left at the roundabout take another left after only about 50 metres into the Sports Complex entrance. The football club is at the end of the drive past the rugby club and tennis courts.

FC CLACTON - Rush Green Bowl CO16 7BQ - 01255 432 590

Leave the A12 at junction 29, then at roundabout take the 1st exit, then merge onto the A120 (sign posted Clacton, Harwich). Branch left, then merge onto the A133 (sign posted Clacton). Continue along the A133 following signs to Clacton until St Johns Roundabout (tiled Welcome to Clacton sign) take the 4th exit onto St Johns Rd - B1027 (sign posted St Osyth) Entering Clacton On Sea B1027 (fire station on left). B1027 At second mini-roundabout turn left onto Cloes Lane (Budgens on right). Continue down Cloes Lane for about 1/2 mile, passing St.Clares School on your right, at traffic lights, turn right onto Rush Green Rd. Rush Green Bowl will then appear on the right after 1/4 mile.

FELIXSTOWE & WALTON - Town Ground, Dellwood Ave IP11 9HT - 01394 282 917
The A12 meets the A14 (Felixstowe to M1/M6 trunk road) at Copdock interchange, just to the South of Ipswich. For Felixstowe take the A14 heading east over the Orwell Bridge. Follow the A14, for approx. 14 miles until you come to a large roundabout with a large water tower on your right, take the 1st exit off the roundabout, which is straight on. Take the first exit at the next roundabout, straight ahead again. At the next roundabout take the fourth exit onto Beatrice Avenue, take the first left into Dellwood Avenue. The ground is 100 yards down on the left behind tall wooden fencing.

GORLESTON - Emerald Park, Woodfarm Lane NR31 9AQ - 01493 602 802
On Magdalen Estate follow signs to Crematorium, turn left and follow road to ground.

GREAT YARMOUTH TOWN - The Wellesley, Sandown Road NR30 1EY - 01493 656 099
Just off Marine Parade 200 yards north of the Britannia Pier. Half a mile from the BR station.

HADLEIGH UNITED - Millfield, Tinkers Lane IP7 5NG - 01473 822 165
On reaching Hadleigh High Street turn into Duke Street (right next to Library), continue on for approximately 150 metres and take left turn into narrow lane immediately after going over small bridge, continue to end of the lane where you will find the entrance to club car park.

HAVERHILL ROVERS - The New Croft, Chalkstone Way CB9 0LD - 01440 702 137
Take the A143 in to Haverhill and, at the roundabout by Tesco, turn left and then right in the one in front of the store. Carry on over the next roundabout past Aldi on the left and past the Sports Centre, Cricket Club and garage on the left. Just after the Workspace Office Solutions building take a right towards the town centre (towards Parking (South). The drive way into Hamlet Croft is a small turning on the left just after Croft Lane (look for the sign for Tudor Close).

KIRKLEY & PAKEFIELD - K & P Community & Sports Club, Walmer Road, NR33 7LE - 01502 513 549.
From A12 to Lowestoft town centre and go over roundabout at Teamways Garage and past Teamways Pub. Take next left into Walmer Road.

MILDENHALL TOWN - Recreation Way, Mildenhall, Suffolk IP28 7HG - 01638 713449 (club)
Next to swimming pool and car park a quarter of a mile from town centre.

NEWMARKET TOWN - Town Ground, Cricket Field Road CB8 8BG - 01638 663 637 (club).
Four hundred yards from Newmarket BR.Turn right into Green Road and right at cross roads into new Cheveley Rd. Ground is at top on left.

NORWICH UNITED - Plantation Park, Blofield, Norwich, Norfolk NR13 4PL - 01603 716963
Off the A47.

STANWAY ROVERS - `Hawthorns', New Farm Road CO3 0PG - 01206 578 187
Leave A12 at Jct 26 to A1124. Turn right(from London)or left from Ipswich onto Essex Yeomanry Way. A1124 towards Colchester 1st right into Villa Rd,then left into Chaple Rd, and left into New Farm Rd. Ground 400 yds on left.Nearest BR station is Colchester North.

WALSHAM LE WILLOWS - Walsham Sports Club, Summer Road IP31 3AH 01359 259 298
From Bury - Diss road (A143) turn off down Summer Lane in Walsham-le-Willows and ground is on the right.

WISBECH TOWN - The Tom Wood's Fenland Stadium, Lynn Road, Wisbech PE14 7AN
The Tom Wood's Bear Fenland Stadium is on the B198 Lynn Road, just on the northern outskirts of Wisbech.

WIVENHOE TOWN - Broad Lane, Elmstead Road CO7 7HA - 01206 825 380
The ground is situated off the B1027 to the north of Wivenhoe.

WOODBRIDGE TOWN - Notcutts Park, Seckford Hall Road IP12 4DA - 01394 385 308
From Lowestoft turn left into Woodbridge at last roundabout (or first roundabout from Ipswich). Take first turning left and first left again. Drive to ground at end of road on left.

WROXHAM - Trafford Park, Skinners Lane NR12 8SJ - 01603 783 538
From Norwich, turn left at former Castle Pub and keep left to ground. Under two miles from Wroxham & Hoveton BR. Buses 722,724 and 717.

DIVISION ONE

BRIGHTLINGSEA REGENT - North Road, Brightlingsea, Essex CO7 0PL - 01206 304 199
Take exit 28 off M25, take slip road left for A12 toward Brentwood / Chelmsford / Romford, turn left onto slip road, merge onto A12, take slip road left for A120, take slip road left for A133, at roundabout, take 2nd exit, turn left onto B1029 / Great Bentley Road, turn right onto B1027 / Tenpenny Hill, and then immediately turn left onto B1029 / Brightlingsea Road, turn left to stay on B1029 / Ladysmith Avenue, bear left onto Spring Road, turn left onto North Road.

CAMBRIDGE UNI. PRESS - The Glassworld Stadium, Bridge Road, Impington, Cambridge CB24 9PH - 01223 237 373 - Take exit 14 M11, take slip road left for A14 (E) toward Ely / Newmarket, take slip road left, at roundabout, take 1st exit onto B1049 / Cambridge Road, ground 1/2 mile.

CORNARD UNITED - Blackhouse Lane CO10 0NL - 07811 096 382
Left off roundabout on A134 coming from Ipswich/Colchester into Sudbury, follow signs for Country Park - ground is immediately opposite along Blackhouse Lane.

DEBENHAM LC - Debenham Leisure Centre IP14 6BL - 01728 861 101
Approach Ipswich along the A14. Turn left at junction 51 onto the A140 signposted towards Norwich. After approx 4 miles turn right towards Mickfield and follow the road into Debenham turning left into Gracechurch Street. Debenham Leisure Centre is approx 1 mile on the right hand side.

DOWNHAM TOWN - Memorial Field, Lynn Road PE38 9QE - 01366 388 424
One and a quarter miles from Downham Market (BR) - continue to town clock, turn left and ground is three quarters of a mile down Lynn Road.

FAKENHAM TOWN - Clipbush Pk, Clipbush Lane NR21 8SW - 01328 855 859
Corner of A148 & Clipbush Lane.

GODMANCHESTER ROVERS - Bearscroft Lane PE29 2LQ - 07774 830 507
From A14 turn off for Godmanchester. Take A1198 towards Wood Green Animal Shelter, Bearscroft Lane is half mile from A14 on the left.

HALSTEAD TOWN - Rosemary Lane CO9 1HR - 01787 472 082
From A1311 Chelmsford to Braintree road follow signs to Halstead.

IPSWICH WANDERERS - SEH Sports Centre IP4 3NR 01473 728 581

LONG MELFORD - Stoneylands Stadium CO10 9JY - 01787 312 187
Turn down St Catherine Road off Hall St (Bury-Sudbury road) and then turn left into New Road.

MARCH TOWN UNITED - GER Sports Ground PE15 8HS - 01354 653 073
5 mins from town centre, 10 mins from BR station.

SAFFRON WALDEN TOWN - Catons Lane CB10 2DU - 01799 522 789
Into Castle St off Saffron-W High St. Then left at T jct and 1st left by Victory Pub.

STOWMARKET TOWN - Greens Meadow, Bury Road IP14 1JQ - 01449 612 533
About 800 yards from Stowmarket station (BR).Turn right at lights and head out of town over roundabout into Bury Road, Ground is on the right.

SWAFFHAM TOWN - Shoemakers Lane PE37 7NT - 01760 722 700

TEAM BURY - Ram Meadow, Cotton Lane IP33 1XP - 01284 754 721

THETFORD TOWN - Recreation Ground, Munford Road IP24 1NB - 01842 766 120
Off bypass (A11) at A143 junction - ground 800 yards next to sports ground.

WHITTON UNITED - King George V Playing Fields IP1 6LE - 01473 464 030
Turn off A14, junction A1156 approx 3 miles west of A12/A14 junction.

ESSEX SENIOR LEAGUE

Sponsored by: No sponsor
Founded: 1971
Recent Champions:
2006: AFC Hornchurch
2007: Brentwood Town
2008: Concord Rangers
2009: Romford
2010: Witham Town
essexseniorfootballleague.moonfruit.com

		P	W	D	L	F	A	Pts
1	Enfield 1893	32	23	4	5	83	27	73
2	Stansted (-3)	32	22	9	1	81	25	72
3	Witham Town (-1)	32	20	8	4	82	40	67
4	Bethnal Green United	32	17	6	9	59	35	57
5	Southend Manor	32	16	5	11	58	47	53
6	Barking	32	15	4	13	52	44	49
7	Burnham Ramblers	32	14	6	12	67	50	48
8	Eton Manor	32	11	10	11	59	56	43
9	Hullbridge Sports	32	10	10	12	48	53	40
10	London APSA	32	12	4	16	27	42	40
11	Mauritius Sports Association	32	11	5	16	53	62	38
12	Basildon United	32	10	4	18	45	66	34
13	Takeley	32	9	7	16	48	73	34
14	Bowers & Pitsea	32	8	8	16	41	72	32
15	Barkingside	32	9	4	19	51	78	31
16	Sawbridgeworth Town	32	10	1	21	38	75	31
17	Clapton	32	3	9	20	37	84	18

GORDON BRASTED TROPHY

ROUND 1
Bowers & Pitsea 4-4 Sawbridgeworth Town (Sawbridgeworth Town won 4-3 on penalties)

ROUND 2
Basildon United 0-4 Eton Manor
Bethnal Green United 4-0 Sawbridgeworth Town
Burnham Ramblers 2-1 Enfield 1893
Hullbridge Sports 3-2 Stansted
Mauritius Sports Association 1-3 Barkingside
Southend Manor 2-0 London APSA
(tie awarded to London APSA)
Takeley 0-3 Clapton
Witham Town 3-2 Barking

QUARTER FINALS
Barkingside 2-1 Bethnal Green United
Burnham Ramblers 6-1 Clapton
Eton Manor 2-1 London APSA
Witham Town 3-1 Hullbridge Sports

SEMI-FINALS
Eton Manor 1-0 Witham Town
Burnham Ramblers 4-2 Barkingside

FINAL (@ Burnham Ramblers, 25/4/11)
Burnham Ramblers 4-2 Eton Manor

	1	2	3	4	5	6	7	8	9	10	11	12	13	14	15	16	17
1 Barking		1-0	4-0	0-1	1-2	1-2	3-2	0-1	0-3	1-1	2-1	0-1	3-0	7-1	2-2	1-1	1-5
2 Barkingside	0-3		2-6	2-1	3-5	2-1	1-3	2-5	3-2	1-4	0-1	0-4	0-2	2-1	1-1	6-2	0-1
3 Basildon United	1-0	2-2		1-2	1-0	3-3	3-2	0-2	3-2	3-2	0-4	2-3	1-2	1-1	0-2	0-1	0-1
4 Bethnal Green United	3-1	4-3	1-2		1-0	2-0	2-1	1-0	2-2	1-0	0-0	0-2	3-0	0-1	1-1	4-0	1-1
5 Bowers & Pitsea	0-1	3-1	2-0	1-1		0-4	2-2	0-5	1-1	2-4	1-1	0-3	3-2	3-1	2-7	2-3	1-7
6 Burnham Ramblers	1-2	1-2	2-2	2-1	1-2		4-2	2-0	1-1	3-0	2-0	5-1	7-0	1-4	1-4	5-1	2-4
7 Clapton	1-0	2-3	0-4	1-3	2-2	0-2		2-6	2-2	1-1	0-1	1-1	0-4	1-4	1-8	0-0	2-2
8 Enfield	0-1	1-0	3-0	3-0	3-0	1-1	3-0		5-1	2-0	1-2	3-1	2-0	1-1	1-1	4-3	2-2
9 Eton Manor	4-1	2-2	1-2	2-5	1-1	3-1	2-2	2-4		1-3	1-0	3-2	4-0	2-2	0-0	3-0	1-3
10 Hullbridge Sports	2-3	3-3	3-2	1-0	0-2	1-3	3-2	1-4	4-0		0-1	2-2	1-1	1-0	1-4	1-1	1-1
11 London A P S A	2-1	0-3	0-3	0-3	0-0	2-0	2-0	0-3	1-2	1-0		1-0	2-0	0-3	0-3	2-2	1-2
12 Mauritius Sports Assoc. UK	2-6	1-3	6-0	2-1	3-1	0-1	0-1	1-4	0-3	2-2	1-0		0-1	2-2	0-2	3-2	2-4
13 Sawbridgeworth Town	1-2	4-0	3-2	1-6	3-1	2-0	2-1	0-5	0-4	1-2	0-1	1-2		1-0	1-5	1-4	2-3
14 Southend Manor	0-1	2-1	4-0	2-1	3-1	2-0	4-1	0-2	3-1	1-1	2-0	3-2	2-1		0-3	4-1	0-1
15 Stansted	2-0	4-1	3-1	1-1	3-0	2-2	3-0	2-1	0-0	1-2	1-0	4-1	2-1	2-0		2-0	3-2
16 Takeley	1-2	4-1	1-0	0-3	4-1	2-6	2-2	0-4	0-2	1-1	2-1	1-1	3-1	2-0	1-2		2-3
17 Witham Town	1-1	2-1	2-0	2-4	0-0	1-1	5-0	1-2	3-1	2-0	4-0	3-2	4-0	4-5	1-1	5-1	

LEAGUE CUP

Group A	P	W	D	L	F	A	Pts
1 Witham Town	4	2	1	1	11	5	7
2 Bethnal Green United	4	2	1	1	9	5	7
3 Eton Manor	4	1	0	3	5	15	3

	BGU	EM	WT
Bethnal Green United		5-1	2-2
Eton Manor	2-1		1-3
Witham Town	0-1	6-1	

Group B	P	W	D	L	F	A	Pts
1 Mauritius Sports Assoc	2	1	0	1	7	5	3
2 Barking	2	1	0	1	5	7	3

	Bk	MSA
Barking		3-2
Mauritius Sports Assoc	5-2	

Group C	P	W	D	L	F	A	Pts
1 Enfield 1893	4	3	0	1	9	4	9
2 Bowers & Pitsea	4	2	0	2	8	7	6
3 Burnham Ramblers	4	1	0	3	4	10	3

	B&P	BR	Enf
Bowers & Pitsea		2-3	0-3
Burnham Ramblers	0-3		1-2
Enfield 1893	1-3	3-0	

Group D	P	W	D	L	F	A	Pts
1 Takeley	4	3	1	0	10	4	10
2 Basildon United	4	2	1	1	7	2	7
3 Sawbridgeworth United	4	0	0	4	3	14	0

	BU	ST	Tak
Basildon United		4-0	0-0
Sawbridgeworth Town	0-2		1-3
Takeley	2-1	5-2	

Group E	P	W	D	L	F	A	Pts
1 Stansted	4	3	0	1	15	7	9
2 Barkingside	4	2	1	1	13	10	7
3 Clapton	4	0	1	3	7	18	1

	Bar	Cla	Sta
Barkingside		3-3	2-3
Clapton	2-5		1-3
Stansted	2-3	7-1	

Group F	P	W	D	L	F	A	Pts
1 Southend Manor	4	3	0	1	12	6	9
2 Hullbridge Sports	4	2	1	1	7	4	7
3 London APSA	4	0	1	3	4	13	1

	HS	LA	SM
Hullbridge Sports		3-0	2-1
London APSA	1-1		2-4
Southend Manor	2-1	5-1	

QUARTER FINALS (2 LEGS)

Bethnal Green United 4-1 Takeley
Takeley 3-4 Bethnal Green United
Bethnal Green United won 8-4 on aggregate
Mauritius Sports Association 0-2 Stansted
Stansted 6-2 Mauritius Sports association
Stansted won 8-2 on aggregate
Southend Manor 3-1 Witham Town
Witham Town 2-1 Southend Manor
Southend Manor won 4-3 on aggregate
Basildon United 0-1 Enfield 1893
Enfield 1893 2-0 Basildon United
Enfield 1893 won 3-0 on aggregate

SEMI-FINALS (2 LEGS)

Stansted 1-0 Bethnal Green United
Bethnal Green United 0-3 Stansted
Stansted won 4-0 on aggregate
Enfield 1893 3-2 Southend Manor
Southend Manor 2-2 Enfield 1893
Enfield 1893 won 5-4 on aggregate

FINAL (@ Barkingside, 2/5/11)
Stansted 3-0 Enfield 1893

Essex Senior League Champions - Enfield 1893. Photo: Gordon Whittington.

BARKING

Founded: 1880 Nickname: The Blues

Secretary: Peter Ball **(T)** 07790 594 530 **(E)** secretary@barking-fc.co.uk
Chairman: Rob O'Brien **Manager:** Steve Munday **Prog Ed:** Ashley Hanson
Ground: Mayesbrook Park, Lodge Avenue, Dagenham RM8 2JR **(T)** 0776 458 7112
Capacity: 2,500 **Seats:** 200 **Covered:** 600 **Midweek Matchday:** Tuesday **Clubhouse:** Yes **Shop:** Yes

Colours(change): Royal blue/blue/blue. (All yellow).
Previous Names: Barking Rov. Barking Woodville. Barking Working Lads Institute, Barking Institute. Barking T. Barking & East Ham U.
Previous Leagues: South Essex, London, Athenian. Isthmian. Southern.
Records: **Att:** 1,972 v Aldershot, FA Cup 2nd Rnd, 1978. **Goalscorer:** Neville Fox - 241 (65-73). **Apps:** Bob Makin - 566.
Senior Honours: Essex Senior Cup 1893-94, 95-96, 1919-20, 45-46, 62-63, 69-70, 89-90. London Senior Cup 1911-12, 20-21, 26-27, 78-79.

10 YEAR RECORD

01-02	02-03	03-04	04-05	05-06	06-07	07-08	08-09	09-10	10-11
Isth1 21	Isth1N 12	Isth1N 23	SthE 6	SthE 5	ESen 6	ESen 9	ESen 12	ESen 8	ESen 6

BARKINGSIDE

Founded: 1898 Nickname:

Secretary: Jimmy Flanagan **(T)** 07956 894 194 **(E)** confclothing@aol.com
Chairman: Jimmy Flanagan **Manager:** Tony Fenn **Prog Ed:** Jimmy Flanagan
Ground: Oakside Stadium, Station Road, Barkingside IG6 1NB **(T)** 0208 550 3611
Capacity: 3,000 **Seats:** 350 **Covered:** 850 **Midweek Matchday:** Monday **Clubhouse:** Yes **Shop:** No

Colours(change): Sky blue & navy/navy blue/navy blue. (All orange)
Previous Names: None
Previous Leagues: London. Greater London. Met London. Spartan, South Midlands.
Records: **Att:** 957 v Arsenal Reserves, London League, 1957.
Senior Honours: London Senior Cup 1996-97. Spartan South Midlands League Premier Division 1998-99. Essex Senior Cup 2008-09.

10 YEAR RECORD

01-02	02-03	03-04	04-05	05-06	06-07	07-08	08-09	09-10	10-11
ESen 13	ESen 9	ESen 11	ESen 4	ESen 4	ESen 3	ESen 3	ESen 5	ESen 9	ESen 15

BASILDON UNITED

Founded: 1963 Nickname:

Secretary: Richard Mann **(T)** 0796 435 6642 **(E)** richard@basildon-united.co.uk
Chairman: John Moran **Manager:** Paul Larke **Prog Ed:** Richard Mann
Ground: The Stadium, Gardiners Close, Basildon SS14 3AW **(T)** 01268 520 268
Capacity: 2,000 **Seats:** 400 **Covered:** 1,000 **Midweek Matchday:** Wednesday **Clubhouse:** Yes **Shop:** No

Colours(change): Gold/black/black. (All red).
Previous Names: Armada Sports.
Previous Leagues: Grays & Thurrock. Greater London. Essex Senior. Athenian. Isthmian.
Records: **Att:** 4,000 v West Ham, ground opening 11.08.70.
Senior Honours: Isthmian League Division 2 Champions 1983-84.

10 YEAR RECORD

01-02	02-03	03-04	04-05	05-06	06-07	07-08	08-09	09-10	10-11
ESen 10	ESen 13	ESen 7	ESen 7	ESen 11	ESen 10	ESen 16	ESen 8	ESen 12	ESen 12

BETHNAL GREEN UNITED

Founded: 2000 Nickname:

Secretary: Akhtar Imran Ahmed **(T)** 07590 568 422 **(E)** akhtarx@hotmail.com
Chairman: Mohammed Nural Hoque **Manager:** Justin Gardner **Prog Ed:** Akhtar Imran Ahmed
Ground: Mile End Stadium, Rhodeswell Rd, Poplar E14 7TW **(T)** 020 8980 1885
Capacity: **Seats:** Yes **Covered:** Yes **Midweek Matchday:** Wednesday **Clubhouse:** **Shop:**

Colours(change): Green & white/green & white/green. (All red)
Previous Names: None.
Previous Leagues: Middlesex 2000-09.
Records:
Senior Honours:

10 YEAR RECORD

01-02	02-03	03-04	04-05	05-06	06-07	07-08	08-09	09-10	10-11
		Midx1 2	MidxP 7			MidxP 8	MidxP 1	ESen 5	ESen 4

BOWERS & PITSEA

Founded: 1946 Nickname:

Secretary: Lee Stevens (T) 07910 626 727 (E) lee-stevens@sky.com
Chairman: Barry Hubbard **Manager:** Colin Cook **Prog Ed:** Lee Stevens
Ground: Len Salmon Stadium, Crown Avenue, Pitsea, Basildon SS13 2BE (T) 01268 581 977
Capacity: 2,000 **Seats:** 200 **Covered:** 1,000 **Midweek Matchday:** Wednesday **Clubhouse:** Yes **Shop:** Yes

Colours(change): All claret. (All sky blue).
Previous Names: Bowers United > 2004.
Previous Leagues: Thurrock & Thameside Combination. Olympian.
Records: Att: 1,800 v Billericay Town, FA Vase.
Senior Honours:

10 YEAR RECORD

01-02	02-03	03-04	04-05	05-06	06-07	07-08	08-09	09-10	10-11
ESen 6	ESen 7	ESen 8	ESen 10	ESen 15	ESen 4	ESen 7	ESen 11	ESen 17	ESen 14

BURNHAM RAMBLERS

Founded: 1900 Nickname: Ramblers

Secretary: Shaun Pugh (T) 0752 509 9914 (E) secretarybrfc@sapugh.gotadsl.co.uk
Chairman: William Hannan **Manager:** Keith Wilson **Prog Ed:** Martin Leno
Ground: Leslie Fields Stadium, Springfield Road CM0 8TE (T) 01621 783 484
Capacity: 2,000 **Seats:** 156 **Covered:** 300 **Midweek Matchday:** Tuesday **Clubhouse:** Yes **Shop:** No

Colours(change): Navy & sky blue stripes/navy/sky blue (All red).
Previous Names: None
Previous Leagues: North Essex. Mid-Essex. Olympian. South East Essex.
Records: Att: 1,500 v Arsenal, opening of stand.
Senior Honours:

10 YEAR RECORD

01-02	02-03	03-04	04-05	05-06	06-07	07-08	08-09	09-10	10-11
ESen 3	ESen 8	ESen 12	ESen 2	ESen 5	ESen 5	ESen 8	ESen 7	ESen 3	ESen 7

CLAPTON

Founded: 1878 Nickname: Tons

Secretary: Shirley Doyle (T) 0798 358 8883 (E) shirley.10@hotmail.co.uk
Chairman: Dennis Wright **Manager:** Wilfred Thomas **Prog Ed:** Dennis Wright
Ground: The Old Spotted Dog, Upton Lane, Forest Gate E7 9NU (T) 0794 400 9386
Capacity: 2,000 **Seats:** 100 **Covered:** 180 **Midweek Matchday:** Tuesday **Clubhouse:** Yes **Shop:** No

Colours(change): Red & white stripes/black/red (Black & red stripes/red/red)
Previous Names: None
Previous Leagues: Southern (founder member). London. Isthmian (founder member).
Records: Att: 12,000 v Tottenham Hotspur, FA Cup, 1898-99. First English club to play on the continent, beating a Belgian XI in 1890.
Senior Honours: Isthmian League Champions 1910-11, 22-23, Division 2 1982-83. Essex Senior Cup (x 4).

10 YEAR RECORD

01-02	02-03	03-04	04-05	05-06	06-07	07-08	08-09	09-10	10-11
Isth3 21	Isth2 9	Isth2 15	Isth2 16	Isth2 16	ESen 14	ESen 11	ESen 16	ESen 16	ESen 17

ENFIELD 1893 FC

Founded: 1893 Nickname:

Secretary: Mark Wiggs (T) 0795 764 7820 (E) enfieldfc@ntlworld.com
Chairman: Steve Whittington **Manager:** Kevin Lucas **Prog Ed:** Mark Kettlety
Ground: Goldsdown Road, Enfield, Middlesex EN3 7RP (T) 01438 210 073
Capacity: 500 **Seats:** 300 **Covered:** Yes **Midweek Matchday:** Wednesday **Clubhouse:** Yes **Shop:**

Colours(change): White/blue/white. (Yellow/blue/yellow).
Previous Names: Enfield Spartans > 1900. Enfield > 2007.
Previous Leagues: Tottenham & District, North Middlesex, London, Athenian, Isthmian, Alliance, Southern
Records: Att: 10,000 v Spurs, floodlight opening at Southbury Rd., 10.10.62. **Goals:** Tommy Lawrence - 191 (1959-64). **Apps:** Andy Pape - 643 (85-92 93-99)
Senior Honours: FA Trophy 1981-82, 87-88. Alliance League 1982-83, 85-86. FA Amateur Cup 1966-67, 69-70. Essex Senior League 2010-11.

10 YEAR RECORD

01-02	02-03	03-04	04-05	05-06	06-07	07-08	08-09	09-10	10-11
Isth P 19	Isth P 23	Isth1N 24	Isth2 2	SthE 16	Isth1N 13	ESen 2	ESen 2	ESen 4	ESen 1

ETON MANOR

Founded: 1901 | Nickname: The Manor

Secretary: Enrique Nespereira **(T)** 07740 457 686 **(E)**

Chairman: Reg Curtis **Manager:** Kevin Durrant **Prog Ed:** Reg Curtis

Ground: Waltham Abbey FC, Capershotts, Sewardstone Road, Waltham Abbey EN9 1LU **(T)** 01992 711 287

Capacity: 2,500 **Seats:** 200 **Covered:** 600 **Midweek Matchday:** Monday **Clubhouse:** Yes **Shop:**

Colours(change): Sky blue & navy. (Black & white/black/black).
Previous Names: Wildernes Leyton.
Previous Leagues: London. Greater London. Metropolitan.
Records: **Att:** 600 v Leyton Orient, opening of floodlights. **Goalscorer:** Dave Sams.
Senior Honours:

10 YEAR RECORD

01-02	02-03	03-04	04-05	05-06	06-07	07-08	08-09	09-10	10-11
ESen 15	ESen 16	ESen 9	ESen 12	ESen 13	ESen 11	ESen 4	ESen 6	ESen 15	ESen 8

HARINGEY & WALTHAM DEVELOPMENT

Founded: | Nickname:

Secretary: Lindsay Boyaram **(T)** 0743 212 1547 **(E)**

Chairman: Burk Gravis **Manager:** Tony Ievoli **Prog Ed:** TBC

Ground: Haringey Boro' FC, Coles Park, White Hart Lane N17 7JP **(T)** TBA

Capacity: **Seats:** **Covered:** **Midweek Matchday:** Wednesday **Clubhouse:** Yes **Shop:** No

Colours(change): Black & white stripes/black & white/black (All white)
Previous Names: Mauritius Sports merged with Walthamstow Avenue & Pennant 2007. Mauritius Sports Association 2007-11.
Previous Leagues: London Intermediate.
Records:
Senior Honours:

10 YEAR RECORD

01-02	02-03	03-04	04-05	05-06	06-07	07-08	08-09	09-10	10-11
LonInt 9	LonInt 8					ESen 13	ESen 15	ESen 18	ESen 11

HULLBRIDGE SPORTS

Founded: 1945 | Nickname:

Secretary: Mrs Beryl Petre **(T)** 0776 836 3791 **(E)** beryl@petre1942.fsnet.co.uk

Chairman: Andrew Burgess **Manager:** Enrico Tritera **Prog Ed:** Beryl Petre

Ground: Lower Road, Hullbridge, Hockley Essex SS5 6BJ **(T)** 01702 230 420

Capacity: 1,500 **Seats:** 60 **Covered:** 60 **Midweek Matchday:** Tuesday **Clubhouse:** Yes **Shop:** No

Colours(change): Royal blue & white stripes/royal/royal. (All pink black).
Previous Names: None
Previous Leagues: Southend & District. Southend Alliance.
Records: **Att:** 800 v Blackburn Rovers, FA Youth Cup 1999-00.
Senior Honours:

10 YEAR RECORD

01-02	02-03	03-04	04-05	05-06	06-07	07-08	08-09	09-10	10-11
ESen 12	ESen 15	ESen 16	ESen 15	ESen 14	ESen 12	ESen 14	ESen 9	ESen 11	ESen 9

LONDON APSA

Founded: 1993 | Nickname:

Secretary: Zabir Bashir **(T)** 07956 660 699 **(E)** zabirbashir23@hotmail.com

Chairman: Zulfi Ali **Manager:** Zakir Hussain **Prog Ed:** TBC

Ground: Clapton FC until Christmas then Terence McMillian Stadium, Plaistow E13 8SD **(T)** 0207 511 4477

Capacity: 4,000 **Seats:** 400 **Covered:** 400 **Midweek Matchday:** Thursday **Clubhouse:** **Shop:**

Colours(change): All blue (Green & white/green & white/green)
Previous Names: Ahle Sunnah
Previous Leagues: Asian League.
Records:
Senior Honours:

10 YEAR RECORD

01-02	02-03	03-04	04-05	05-06	06-07	07-08	08-09	09-10	10-11
		ESen 15	ESen 13	ESen 9	ESen 13	ESen 17	ESen 14	ESen 13	ESen 10

SAWBRIDGEWORTH TOWN

Founded: 1890 Nickname: Robins

Secretary: Mrs Leslie Atkins **(T)** 07762 553 924 **(E)** sawbosec@hotmail.com
Chairman: Steve Day **Manager:** Pete Wickham **Prog Ed:** Steve Tozer
Ground: Crofters End, West Road, Sawbridgeworth CM21 0DE **(T)** 01279 722 039
Capacity: 2,500 **Seats:** 175 **Covered:** 300 **Midweek Matchday:** Tuesday **Clubhouse:** Yes **Shop:** No

Colours(change): Red & black/black/black. (Green/green/white).
Previous Names: Sawbridgeworth > 1976.
Previous Leagues: Stortford. Spartan. Herts County. Essex Olympian.
Records: **Att:** 610 v Bishops Stortford.
Senior Honours:

10 YEAR RECORD

01-02	02-03	03-04	04-05	05-06	06-07	07-08	08-09	09-10	10-11
ESen 7	ESen 6	ESen 3	ESen 8	ESen 6	ESen 8	ESen 12	ESen 13	ESen 10	ESen 16

SOUTHEND MANOR

Founded: 1955 Nickname: The Manor

Secretary: John Bastin **(T)** 0778 097 7728 **(E)** john.bastin1@gmail.com
Chairman: Robert Westley **Manager:** Russell Faulker **Prog Ed:** Bob Westley
Ground: The Arena, Southchurch Pk, Lifstan Way, Southend SS1 2TH **(T)** 01702 615 577
Capacity: 2,000 **Seats:** 500 **Covered:** 700 **Midweek Matchday:** Tuesday **Clubhouse:** Yes **Shop:** No

Colours(change): Yellow/black/yellow. (White/red/red).
Previous Names: None
Previous Leagues: Southend Borough Combination. Southend & District Alliance.
Records: **Att:** 1,521 v Southend United, opening floodlights, 22.07.91.
Senior Honours: Essex Senior League Champions 1990-91. Essex Senior Trophy 92-93.

10 YEAR RECORD

01-02	02-03	03-04	04-05	05-06	06-07	07-08	08-09	09-10	10-11
ESen 5	ESen 4	ESen 10	ESen 6	ESen 10	ESen 9	ESen 6	ESen 4	ESen 7	ESen 5

SPORTING BENGAL UNITED

Founded: 1996 Nickname: Bengal Tigers

Secretary: Khayrul Alam **(T)** 0207 392 2126 **(E)** bfauk@btconnect.com
Chairman: Aroz Miah **Manager:** Mamun Chowdhury **Prog Ed:** Nasyar Miah
Ground: Mile End Stadium, Rhodeswell Rd, Off Burdett Rd E14 4TW **(T)** 020 8980 1885
Capacity: **Seats:** Yes **Covered:** **Midweek Matchday:** Wednesday **Clubhouse:** **Shop:**

Colours(change): All royal blue (All yellow).
Previous Names: None.
Previous Leagues: Asian League. London Intermediate, Kent 2003-11.
Records: **Att:** 4,235 v Touring Phalco Mohammedan S.C.
Senior Honours:

10 YEAR RECORD

01-02	02-03	03-04	04-05	05-06	06-07	07-08	08-09	09-10	10-11
LonInt 7		Kent P 17	Kent P 14	Kent P 15	Kent P 17	Kent P 17	Kent P 17	Kent P 15	Kent P 15

STANSTED

Founded: 1902 Nickname: Blues

Secretary: Terry Shoebridge **(T)** 0774 304 4824 **(E)** terry.sue.shoebridge@btinternet.com
Chairman: Terry Shoebridge **Manager:** Tony Mercer **Prog Ed:** Andy Taylor
Ground: Hargrave Park, Cambridge Road, Stansted CM24 8DL **(T)** 01279 812 897
Capacity: 2,000 **Seats:** 200 **Covered:** 400 **Midweek Matchday:** Tuesday **Clubhouse:** Yes **Shop:** No

Colours(change): All royal blue (All red).
Previous Names: None.
Previous Leagues: Spartan. London. Herts County.
Records: **Att:** 828 v Whickham, FA Vase, 1983-84.
Senior Honours:

10 YEAR RECORD

01-02	02-03	03-04	04-05	05-06	06-07	07-08	08-09	09-10	10-11
ESen 8	ESen 14	ESen 13	ESen 11	ESen 16	ESen 16	ESen 10	ESen 10	ESen 1	ESen 2

TAKELEY

Founded: 1903 Nickname:

Secretary: Michael Rabey **(T)** 0783 184 5466 **(E)** mcrab@btinternet.com
Chairman: Pat Curran **Manager:** Don Watters **Prog Ed:** David Edwards
Ground: Station Road, Takeley, Bishop's Stortford CM22 6SQ **(T)** 01279 870 404
Capacity: **Seats:** **Covered:** **Midweek Matchday:** Tuesday **Clubhouse:** **Shop:**

Colours(change): All royal blue. (All white).
Previous Names: None.
Previous Leagues: Essex Intermediate/Olympian.
Records:
Senior Honours: Essex Olympian League 2001-02.

10 YEAR RECORD

01-02	02-03	03-04	04-05	05-06	06-07	07-08	08-09	09-10	10-11
EssxO 1	EssxO 2	EssxO 6	EssxO 8	EssxO 9	EssxO 3	EssxO 2	ESen 3	ESen 6	ESen 13

WITHAM TOWN

Founded: 1947 Nickname: Town

Secretary: Mrs Alison Barker **(T)** 01376 324 324 **(E)**
Chairman: Tony Last **Manager:** Gary Kimble **Prog Ed:** David Cobb
Ground: Spicer McColl Stadium, Spa Road, Witham CM8 1UN **(T)** 01376 511 198
Capacity: 2,500 **Seats:** 157 **Covered:** 780 **Midweek Matchday:** Tuesday **Clubhouse:** Yes **Shop:** No

Colours(change): White/dark blue/dark blue (All yellow).
Previous Names: None.
Previous Leagues: Mid. Essex. Essex & Suff. B. Essex Senior 1971-87. Isthmian 1987-2009
Records: **Att:** 800 v Billericay Town, Essex Senior Lge, May 1976. **Goalscorer:** Colin Mitchell. **Appearances:** Keith Dent.
Senior Honours:

10 YEAR RECORD

01-02	02-03	03-04	04-05	05-06	06-07	07-08	08-09	09-10	10-11
Isth3 12	Isth2 7	Isth2 6	Isth2 5	Isth2 2	Isth1N 20	Isth1N 20	Isth1N 21	ESen 2	ESen 3

ESSEX SENIOR INS & OUTS

IN: Sporting Bengal United (S - Kent League Premier Division).

Mauritius Sports Association become Haringey & Waltham Development.

HELLENIC LEAGUE

Sponsored by: Uhlsport
Founded: 1953
Recent Champions:
2006: Didcot Town
2007: Slimbridge
2008: North Leigh
2009: Hungerford Town
2010: Almondsbury Town
hellenicleague.co.uk

PREMIER DIVISION	P	W	D	L	F	A	Pts
1 Wantage Town	42	29	5	8	109	51	92
2 Binfield	42	27	8	7	108	43	89
3 Ardley United	42	27	7	8	108	44	88
4 Highworth Town	42	28	4	10	108	52	88
5 Slimbridge	42	27	7	8	80	52	88
6 Shortwood United	42	25	7	10	111	53	82
7 Kidlington	42	26	4	12	93	57	82
8 Flackwell Heath (-3)	42	19	10	13	82	52	64
9 Old Woodstock Town (-3)	42	20	7	15	86	78	64
10 Thame United	42	17	10	15	66	61	61
11 Wokingham & Emmbrook	42	17	9	16	76	71	60
12 Ascot United	42	17	7	18	98	83	58
13 Reading Town (-1)	42	15	8	19	75	86	52
14 Abingdon Town	42	15	6	21	76	85	51
15 Wootton Bassett Town	42	13	7	22	55	87	46
16 Bracknell Town	42	12	10	20	65	99	46
17 Oxford City Nomads	42	14	4	24	84	120	46
18 Witney United	42	11	9	22	67	93	42
19 Carterton (-3)	42	11	7	24	60	101	37
20 Shrivenham	42	7	8	27	56	99	29
21 Fairford Town	42	4	8	30	46	125	20
22 Pegasus Juniors	42	3	4	35	39	156	13

LEAGUE CHALLENGE CUP

ROUND 1
Bracknell Town 3-3 Woodley Town
(Woodley Town won 4-2 on penalties)
Carterton 6-2 Binfield
Cheltenham Saracens 2-3 Milton United
Chinnor 2-0 Lydney Town
Clanfield 2-1 Newbury
Cricklade Town 2-5 Henley Town
Didcot Town reserves 0-1 South Kilburn
Easington Sports 3-0 Hook Norton
Farnborough reserves 2-5 Holyport
Flackwell Heath 0-0 Thame United
(Flackwell Heath won 7-6 on penalties)
Headington Amateurs 1-0 Penn & Tylers Green
Hungerford Town reserves 4-2 Winterbourne United
Malmesbury Victoria 0-2 Bicester Town
Purton 1-2 Letcombe
Rayners Lane 2-2 Launton Sports
(Rayners Lane won 5-4 on penalties)
Reading Town 8-0 Fairford Town
Trowbridge Town 0-4 Slimbridge
Tytherington Rocks 2-2 Chalfont Wasps
(Chalfont Wasps 4-1won on penalties)
Wantage Town 7-1 Finchampstead

ROUND 2
Kidlington 1-3 Highworth Town
Old Woodstock Town 3-5 Abingdon Town
Rayners Lane 1-2 Wootton Bassett Town
Oxford City Nomads 0-2 Hungerford Town reserves
Shrivenham 2-6 Chalfont Wasps
Slimbridge 2-1 Wokingham & Emmbrook
Flackwell Heath 6-5 Headington Amateurs
Milton United 1-2 Holyport
Woodley Town 3-6 Reading Town
Ardley United 6-1 Letcombe
Carterton 2-0 Easington Sports
Clanfield 1-3 Shortwood United
Chinnor 1-3 Bicester Town
Henley Town 4-0 Pegasus Juniors
South Kilburn 1-0 Ascot United
Wantage Town 5-0 WitneyUnited

ROUND 3
Slimbridge 3-1 Reading Town
Carterton 1-3 Abingdon Town
Shortwood United 0-1 Highworth Town
Chalfont Wasps 2-5 Ardley United
Holyport 1-0 Hungerford Town reserves
South Kilburn 0-3 Wantage town
Flackwell Heath 2-0 Henley Town
Wootton Bassett Town 2-2 Bicester Town (Wootton Bassett

PREMIER DIVISION	1	2	3	4	5	6	7	8	9	10	11	12	13	14	15	16	17	18	19	20	21	22
1 Abingdon Town		0-3	2-2	0-0	4-0	4-1	1-0	1-1	2-1	2-4	0-2	3-1	9-1	2-1	1-0	1-3	2-3	1-2	0-3	1-2	2-2	2-0
2 Ardley United	1-0		6-2	1-1	4-1	5-0	4-2	1-1	1-1	0-0	1-3	4-1	3-0	5-1	2-1	5-0	4-2	0-2	3-3	3-1	3-0	4-0
3 Ascot United	3-3	2-3		2-2	1-1	0-2	6-2	0-1	0-2	0-2	2-2	3-0	3-3	4-1	1-3	4-3	3-2	2-0	1-2	5-1	2-3	3-0
4 Binfield	2-1	2-1	5-3		8-0	2-0	6-1	2-1	0-2	3-0	5-0	4-3	4-2	2-0	1-0	2-0	2-2	2-0	2-0	3-1	3-1	7-1
5 Bracknell Town	3-4	4-1	0-3	1-0		3-3	1-0	0-3	0-2	3-2	2-2	2-0	3-1	2-2	2-3	1-0	2-3	2-3	0-5	2-2	0-2	3-0
6 Carterton	1-3	2-4	1-2	0-5	3-5		3-0	1-4	0-6	0-2	0-5	2-2	6-2	1-3	0-4	2-2	2-0	1-1	1-3	2-1	1-2	2-1
7 Fairford Town	1-1	2-2	0-4	0-6	0-1	1-3		1-3	1-4	0-4	2-3	0-3	2-1	1-2	2-4	2-2	1-5	2-5	1-7	1-4	1-3	1-1
8 Flackwell Heath	0-3	1-0	3-0	2-0	2-0	1-2	2-2		0-2	3-1	2-1	12-0	3-0	4-0	1-1	2-0	0-0	1-1	2-3	1-2	3-0	4-0
9 Highworth Town	4-0	0-3	3-0	0-3	4-0	3-1	2-0	7-1		1-2	3-2	6-1	4-0	3-0	3-2	3-2	2-0	1-1	5-1	1-0	1-6	5-1
10 Kidlington	3-1	2-1	5-0	1-3	2-3	1-0	7-0	1-0	2-1		1-2	5-1	4-1	4-1	2-1	1-2	2-1	2-0	1-2	1-2	2-1	1-1
11 Old Woodstock Town	2-3	0-0	3-1	1-0	4-2	2-0	1-2	2-2	1-2	0-5		2-1	3-1	3-5	4-3	1-1	2-3	3-2	0-2	3-1	5-2	2-0
12 Oxford City Nomads	4-3	0-3	2-7	2-2	5-4	1-5	1-3	2-3	2-4	2-0	6-0		6-0	3-2	5-2	5-0	1-2	2-4	0-0	2-1	1-2	0-8
13 Pegasus Juniors	2-4	0-4	0-7	0-2	3-1	1-1	0-2	0-3	0-5	2-5	2-4	0-1		0-4	0-6	2-1	1-3	2-2	1-6	0-3	3-2	0-2
14 Reading Town	3-2	0-4	3-2	1-1	2-2	5-2	3-1	0-2	2-4	2-4	1-1	2-2	5-1		2-4	2-1	1-2	1-0	4-5	0-0	1-0	2-1
15 Shortwood United	3-0	1-0	2-1	3-3	5-0	0-0	2-0	1-1	1-1	0-1	3-1	3-0	6-1	2-2		3-1	3-0	0-1	3-0	8-2	5-2	4-1
16 Shrivenham	4-3	1-6	0-2	1-4	1-2	2-3	2-2	2-2	0-2	2-2	1-0	5-4	6-1	1-2	1-3		1-2	1-1	1-2	0-2	1-2	1-2
17 Slimbridge	3-2	1-2	2-2	2-1	2-1	2-0	2-0	2-2	2-1	6-0	1-0	1-0	2-0	1-0	1-5	2-0		3-0	2-0	1-1	2-0	1-0
18 Thame United	7-0	1-3	1-2	0-2	2-2	3-1	3-0	1-0	1-1	3-1	0-2	0-1	2-1	1-0	1-1	3-1	1-2		0-0	2-1	2-5	2-2
19 Wantage Town	2-0	2-1	2-1	3-1	3-1	5-0	5-3	4-0	1-2	1-1	3-2	3-1	5-0	2-1	3-1	5-0	0-1	1-0		4-3	0-0	1-2
20 Witney United	0-2	1-3	0-4	1-1	1-1	1-4	0-0	3-2	4-3	1-2	3-4	1-3	3-3	3-2	1-2	0-1	3-3	5-2	1-5		1-1	2-1
21 Wokingham & Emmbrook	1-0	0-2	2-4	2-1	1-1	1-1	3-3	2-1	4-1	1-2	0-4	5-2	7-0	1-1	1-2	3-1	1-1	1-2	2-1	1-0		0-0
22 Wootton Bassett Town	4-1	0-2	3-2	1-3	1-1	1-0	3-1	1-0	2-0	1-3	2-2	2-5	2-1	0-3	1-5	1-1	1-2	0-1	0-4	3-2	2-1	

HELLENIC LEAGUE - STEP 5/6

DIVISION ONE WEST	P	W	D	L	F	A	Pts
1 Headington Amateurs	28	20	3	5	81	42	63
2 Bicester Town	28	18	4	6	61	30	58
3 Cheltenham Saracens	28	17	6	5	80	41	57
4 Clanfield	28	17	4	7	64	35	55
5 Lydney Town	28	14	6	8	64	42	48
6 Purton	28	14	5	9	62	51	47
7 Cricklade Town	28	13	7	8	74	46	46
8 Tytherington Rocks	28	9	8	11	48	47	35
9 Letcombe	28	9	7	12	43	59	34
10 Winterbourne United	28	9	6	13	58	54	33
11 Easington Sports	28	9	5	14	33	46	32
12 Trowbridge Town	28	9	2	17	36	65	29
13 Malmesbury Victoria	28	8	3	17	40	79	27
14 Hook Norton	28	6	5	17	38	59	23
15 Launton Sports	28	1	3	24	15	101	6

DIVISION ONE EAST	P	W	D	L	F	A	Pts
1 Holyport	26	18	4	4	62	29	58
2 Henley Town	26	16	5	5	48	23	53
3 Newbury	26	16	2	8	63	37	50
4 Milton United	26	14	5	7	57	50	47
5 Woodley Town (-3)	26	14	7	5	54	36	46
6 Chalfont Wasps	26	14	4	8	51	40	46
7 Rayners Lane	26	14	1	11	38	29	43
8 Hungerford Town reserves	26	12	3	11	48	44	39
9 Farnborough reserves	26	9	5	12	43	46	32
10 Penn & Tylers Green	26	7	6	13	37	47	27
11 Finchampstead	26	7	4	15	39	59	25
12 South Kilburn	26	5	4	17	34	58	19
13 Chinnor	26	3	8	15	29	60	17
14 Didcot Town reserves	26	2	4	20	29	74	10

LEAGUE CHALLENGE CUP continued...

QUARTER FINALS
Slimbridge 0-1 Ardley United
Holyport 5-2 Abingdon Town
Flackwell Heath 5-1 Wootton Bassett Town
Highworth Town 1-2 Wantage Town
SEMI-FINALS
Ardley United 1-0 Wantage Town
Holyport 1-1 Flackwell Heath (Holyport won 5-4 on penalties)
FINAL (@ Meadow View Park, Thame, 2/5/11)
Holyport 3-1 Ardley United

FLOODLITE CUP

ROUND 1
Abingdon United 1-3 Hungerford Town
Ardley United 1-2 Holyport
Bracknell Town 1-2 Kidlington
Carterton 2-1 Highworth Town
Cheltenham Saracens 1-2 Slimbridge
Reading Town 3-2 Didcot Town
Wantage Town 5-0 Bicester Town
ROUND 2
Ascot United 5-3 Reading Town
Binfield 8-1 Milton United
Fairford Town 2-3 Cirencester Town
Flackwell Heath 3-5 Carterton
Gloucester City 2-1 Hungerford Town
Hook Norton 1-2 Newbury
Maidenhead United 2-0 Henley Town
Malmesbury Victoria 2-5 Abingdon Town
Shortwood United 0-1 Clanfield
Shrivenham 2-1 Kidlington
Thatcham Town 2-0 Old Woodstock Town
Holyport 4-1 Lydney Town
Slimbridge 3-0 Oxford City Nomads
Wantage Town 2-0 Pegasus Juniors
Wokingham & Emmbrook 1-0 Thame United
Wootton Bassett Town 0-1 Witney Town
ROUND 3
Abingdon Town 7-0 Carterton
Binfield 3-1 Wantage Town
Clanfield 0-3 Witney United
Holyport 3-0 Cirencester Town
Maidenhead United 3-4 Slimbridge
Shrivenham 1-1 Newbury (Newbury won 3-2 on penalties)
Thatcham Town 1-0 Gloucester City
Wokingham & Emmbrook 0-3 Ascot United
QUARTER FINALS
Abingdon Town 2-1 Thatcham Town
Slimbridge 0-1 Holyport
Witney United 1-3 Ascot United
Newbury 0-1 Binfield
SEMI-FINALS
Holyport 3-2 Binfield
Abingdon Town 4-2 Ascot United
FINAL (@ Henley Town, 28/4/11)
Holyport 3-0 Abingdon Town

SUPPLEMENTARY CUP

PRELIMINARY ROUND
Bracknell Town 0-5 Oxford City Nomads
Lydney Town 1-2 Trowbridge Town
Milton United 0-1 Witney United

ROUND 2
Binfield 4-3 Wokingham & Emmbrook
Farnborough reserves 2-3 Purton
Hook Norton 3-2 Tytherington Rocks
Malmesbury Victoria 1-3 Newbury
Shrivenham 1-4 Headington Amateurs
Rayners Lane 3-3 Thame United
(Thame United won 5-4 on penalties)
Cricklade Town 1-2 Woodley Town
Letcombe 3-3 Cheltenham Saracens
(Cheltenham Saracens won 5-4 on penalties)
Oxford City Nomads 0-5 Kidlington
Easington Sports 1-1 Trowbridge Town
(Easington Sports won 3-0 on penalties)
Penn &Tylers Green 5-0 Fairford Town
Old Woodstock Town 6-4 Clanfield
Didcot Town reserves 1-3 Ascot United
Pegasus Juniors 2-0 Finchampstead
Winterbourne United 0-3 Chinnor
Lauynton Sports 0-4 Witney United

ROUND 3
Ascot United 4-1 Chinnor
Binfield w/o-scr Easington Sports
Headingon Amateurs 0-2 Cheltenham Saracens
Newbury 2-3 Purton
Witney United 1-0 Hook Norton
Penn & Tylers Green 0-1 Thame United
Woodley Sports 3-2 Pegasus Juniors
Old Woodstock Town 1-2 Kidlington

QUARTER FINALS
Binfeld 2-4 Kidlington
Cheltenham Saracens 1-5 Witney United
Thame United 1-5 Ascot United
Woodley Town 1-2 Purton

SEMI-FINALS
Kidlington 3-2 Witney United
Ascot United 3-4 Purton

FINAL (@ Abingdon Town, 7/5/11)
Kidlington 3-0 Purton

CHAIRMAN'S CUP

FINAL (@ Shrivenham, 3/5/11)

Cirencester Town reserves 1-2 Gloucester City reserves

PRESIDENT'S CUP

FINAL (@ Ardley United, 30/4/11)

Chalfont Wasps reserves 1-3 Gloucester City reserves

DIVISION ONE WEST	1	2	3	4	5	6	7	8	9	10	11	12	13	14	15
1 Bicester Town		2-0	3-0	1-1	3-0	0-2	2-1	8-1	3-3	3-1	1-0	0-1	5-0	2-0	1-3
2 Cheltenham Saracens	3-0		1-4	6-4	2-2	4-1	3-1	8-2	4-0	2-2	8-2	3-0	3-2	0-0	3-0
3 Clanfield	0-1	1-4		1-1	1-1	3-1	2-0	1-0	2-0	2-2	7-0	5-2	4-1	4-0	1-0
4 Cricklade Town	2-1	3-1	3-2		4-0	0-2	4-4	6-0	4-1	0-1	3-0	3-3	6-4	7-4	4-1
5 Easington Sports	1-2	1-2	1-2	1-4		2-3	1-0	1-0	2-0	3-1	3-0	1-2	2-1	2-1	2-2
6 Headington Amateurs	3-1	2-1	4-0	2-1	1-0		2-2	4-1	3-4	2-0	8-0	2-0	3-1	3-3	4-2
7 Hook Norton	0-3	2-5	1-6	0-4	3-0	2-2		0-1	0-2	1-0	1-1	4-0	3-0	0-2	2-3
8 Launton Sports	0-3	1-2	0-6	0-4	0-0	0-4	0-4		1-4	1-6	1-1	1-4	1-5	1-2	1-4
9 Letcombe	1-1	0-2	0-0	2-0	2-0	1-6	4-0	0-0		1-5	4-2	2-2	0-1	0-2	2-1
10 Lydney Town	0-2	1-1	1-2	2-1	6-3	6-2	2-0	4-0	2-2		2-0	5-0	1-0	1-1	2-2
11 Malmesbury Victoria	1-1	1-3	1-3	2-1	1-2	1-6	0-4	4-0	4-2	5-1		4-3	0-2	0-5	4-1
12 Purton	1-2	3-1	1-0	1-1	2-1	4-1	2-1	5-1	7-2	1-3	3-1		3-0	1-1	1-3
13 Trowbridge Town	1-4	0-4	2-3	2-1	1-0	1-3	1-1	2-0	0-1	0-4	2-0	1-3		1-1	3-2
14 Tytherington Rocks	2-3	2-2	0-1	1-1	0-1	1-2	2-1	6-1	3-3	3-0	1-2	0-5	0-1		3-1
15 Winterbourne United	2-3	2-2	4-1	1-1	0-0	1-3	5-0	3-0	2-0	2-3	1-3	2-2	7-1	1-2	

DIVISION ONE EAST	1	2	3	4	5	6	7	8	9	10	11	12	13	14
1 Chalfont Wasps		4-1	1-1	3-1	1-1	0-1	3-1	3-2	4-1	2-4	1-0	1-0	1-3	1-2
2 Chinnor	1-1		1-6	1-2	3-2	0-4	1-5	1-3	0-2	4-4	1-2	0-0	3-2	0-2
3 Didcot Town reserves	0-3	1-1		2-2	3-3	0-2	0-1	2-4	2-5	1-5	0-4	1-3	4-2	0-1
4 Farnborough reserves	1-3	0-1	5-1		2-1	1-3	2-2	1-1	2-2	2-4	1-2	2-1	4-1	2-2
5 Finchampstead	5-1	4-1	1-0	1-3		1-2	0-5	0-4	0-5	0-2	0-2	2-4	0-2	2-1
6 Henley Town	2-1	3-0	3-0	0-2	0-3		0-1	8-0	1-1	3-0	2-1	2-1	1-0	1-1
7 Holyport	1-2	1-0	4-2	2-1	1-1	2-2		2-0	3-0	2-3	5-1	2-1	5-2	1-2
8 Hungerford Town reserves	2-3	3-3	3-0	1-0	2-0	0-1	0-3		5-0	1-1	0-2	1-2	2-0	3-2
9 Milton United	2-1	2-1	3-2	3-2	5-2	1-0	1-1	6-3		2-1	4-0	0-2	4-2	0-3
10 Newbury	4-1	1-0	4-0	2-0	3-2	2-3	1-2	0-3	5-1		2-0	0-1	3-2	1-3
11 Penn & Tylers Green	2-2	1-1	3-0	3-4	5-2	1-1	1-2	0-2	0-0	0-2		1-2	2-2	3-4
12 Rayners Lane	0-2	2-1	2-0	0-1	1-2	2-0	1-3	1-0	5-0	0-4	3-1		1-0	0-1
13 South Kilburn	1-2	2-2	5-0	2-0	0-3	0-1	1-2	1-0	1-5	0-4	0-0	0-2		3-3
14 Woodley Town	1-4	1-1	3-1	2-0	1-1	2-2	1-3	2-3	2-2	2-1	4-0	2-1	4-0	

RESERVE DIVISION ONE	P	W	D	L	F	A	Pts
1 Highworth Town reserves	24	17	4	3	65	16	55
2 Abingdon United reserves	24	13	8	3	66	39	47
3 Maidenhead United reserves	24	14	4	6	58	37	46
4 Thatcham Town reserves	24	14	2	8	56	43	44
5 Ardley United reserves	24	12	5	7	43	37	41
6 Binfield reserves	24	11	4	9	56	41	37
7 Cirencester Town reserves	24	11	4	9	46	35	37
8 Fairford Town reserves	24	11	4	9	48	46	37
9 Wootton Bassett Town reserves	24	8	2	14	43	61	26
10 Kidlington reserves	24	7	4	13	43	47	25
11 Finchampstead reserves	24	6	0	18	30	77	18
12 Cheltenham Saracens reserves	24	4	5	15	41	70	17
13 Wantage Town reserves	24	4	2	18	35	81	14

Abingdon Town reserves - record expunged

Carterton reserves - record expunged

RESERVE TWO WEST	P	W	D	L	F	A	Pts
1 Gloucester City reserves	18	17	0	1	77	9	51
2 Old Woodstock Tn res	18	10	4	4	42	26	34
3 Easington Sports res	18	8	4	6	35	24	28
4 Bicester Town reserves	18	7	2	9	43	40	23
5 Letcombe reserves	18	6	5	7	36	44	23
6 Hook Norton reserves	18	6	3	9	30	45	21
7 Clanfield reserves	18	6	3	9	36	59	21
8 Milton United reserves	18	6	2	10	24	29	20
9 Shrivenham reserves	18	5	5	8	35	43	20
10 Launton Sports reserves	18	4	2	12	20	59	14

Cricklade Town reserves - record expunged

RESERVE TWO EAST	P	W	D	L	F	A	Pts
1 Thame United reserves	20	14	2	4	61	24	44
2 Rayners Lane reserves	20	13	3	4	42	20	42
3 Newbury reserves	20	10	5	5	48	31	35
4 Flackwell Heath reserves	20	9	4	7	43	29	31
5 Chalfont Wasps reserves	20	8	5	7	36	29	29
6 Penn & Tylers Green res	20	9	2	9	33	42	29
7 Holyport reserves	20	7	4	9	33	38	25
8 Henley Town reserves	20	8	1	11	27	41	25
9 Hungerford Town 'Dev'	20	5	3	12	29	55	18
10 Ascot United reserves	20	5	2	13	22	40	17
11 Chinnor reserves	20	4	5	11	27	52	17

ABINGDON TOWN

Founded: 1870 Nickname: The Abbots

Secretary: Wendy Larman **(T)** 01235 763 985 **(E)** thomas.larman@btinternet.com
Chairman: Tom Larman **Manager:** Chris Fontaine **Prog Ed:** Kenny More
Ground: Culham Road, Abingdon OX14 3HP **(T)** 01235 521 684
Capacity: 3,000 **Seats:** 271 **Covered:** 1,771 **Midweek Matchday:** Tuesday **Clubhouse:** Yes **Shop:** Yes

Colours(change): All yellow and green
Previous Names: Abingdon FC (merged with St Michaels in 1899) > 1928.
Previous Leagues: Reading Senior, Reading & District, Oxfordshire Senior, North Berkshire, Spartan, Isthmian
Records: **Att:** 4,000 v Swindon Town, Maurice Owen Benefit, 1950.
Senior Honours: Berks & Bucks Senior Cup 58-59. Spartan Lge 88-89. Isthmian Lge Div.2 South 90-91.

10 YEAR RECORD

01-02	02-03	03-04	04-05	05-06	06-07	07-08	08-09	09-10	10-11
Isth3 16	Isth2 4	Isth2 9	Isth2 7	Hel P 18	Hel P 18	Hel P 19	Hel P 19	Hel P 12	Hel P 14

ARDLEY UNITED

Founded: 1945 Nickname:

Secretary: Norman Stacey **(T)** 07711 009198 **(E)** ardley.house@virgin.net
Chairman: Norman Stacey **Manager:** Kevin Brock **Prog Ed:** Peter Sawyer
Ground: The Playing Fields, Oxford Road, Ardley OX27 7NZ **(T)** 07711 009 198
Capacity: 1,000 **Seats:** 100 **Covered:** 200 **Midweek Matchday:** Tuesday **Clubhouse:** Yes **Shop:** No

Colours(change): All sky blue.
Previous Names: None
Previous Leagues: Oxford Senior.
Records: **Att:** 278 v Kidlington, 29.08.05.
Senior Honours: Hellenic League Div.1 Champions 1996-97, 97-98.

10 YEAR RECORD

01-02	02-03	03-04	04-05	05-06	06-07	07-08	08-09	09-10	10-11
Hel1W 3	Hel1W 5	Hel1W 5	Hel P 18	Hel P 10	Hel P 4	Hel P 13	Hel P 5	Hel P 7	Hel P 3

ASCOT UNITED

Founded: 1965 Nickname: Yellaman

Secretary: Mark Gittoes **(T)** 07798 701995 **(E)** mark.gittoes@ascotunited.net
Chairman: Mike Harrison **Manager:** Jeff Lamb **Prog Ed:** Mark Gittoes
Ground: Ascot Racecourse, Car Park 10, Winkfield Rd, Ascot SL5 7RA **(T)** 07798 701995
Capacity: **Seats:** **Covered:** **Midweek Matchday:** Tuesday **Clubhouse:** Yes **Shop:**

Colours(change): Yellow/blue/yellow
Previous Names: None.
Previous Leagues: Reading Senior.
Records: **Att:** 298 30/08/2009.
Senior Honours:

10 YEAR RECORD

01-02	02-03	03-04	04-05	05-06	06-07	07-08	08-09	09-10	10-11
ReadS 12	ReadS 6	ReadS 6	ReadS 3	ReadS 4	ReadS 1	Hel1E 4	Hel1E 2	Hel P 15	Hel P 12

BINFIELD

Founded: 1892 Nickname: Moles

Secretary: Rob Challis **(T)** 07515 336989 **(E)** robchallis@binfieldfc.com
Chairman: Bob Bacon **Manager:** Mark Tallentire **Prog Ed:** Colin Byers
Ground: Hill Farm Lane, Binfield RG42 5NR **(T)** 01344 860 822
Capacity: **Seats:** **Covered:** **Midweek Matchday:** Monday **Clubhouse:** Yes **Shop:**

Colours(change): All red.
Previous Names: None.
Previous Leagues: Ascot & District. Great Western Combination. Reading & Dist. Chiltonian.
Records: **Att:** 1000+ Great Western Combination.
Senior Honours: Hellenic League Division 1 East 2008-09.

10 YEAR RECORD

01-02	02-03	03-04	04-05	05-06	06-07	07-08	08-09	09-10	10-11
Hel1E 14	Hel1E 8	Hel1E 5	Hel1E 5	Hel1E 8	Hel1E 11	Hel1E 9	Hel1E 1	Hel P 8	Hel P 2

BRACKNELL TOWN

Founded: 1896 Nickname: The Robins

Secretary: Tony Hardy **(T)** 07920 726 501 **(E)** tony.hardy@bsigroup.com
Chairman: Ian Nugent **Manager:** Steve McLurg **Prog Ed:** Rob Scully
Ground: Larges Lane Bracknell RG12 9AN **(T)** 01344 412 305
Capacity: 2,500 **Seats:** 190 **Covered:** 400 **Midweek Matchday:** Tuesday **Clubhouse:** Yes **Shop:** Yes

Colours(change): Red and white/red/red
Previous Names: None
Previous Leagues: Great Western Comb., Surrey Senior 1963-70, London Spartan 1970-75, Isthmian 1984-2004, Southern 2004-10
Records: **Att:** 2,500 v Newquay - FA Amateur Cup 1971. **Goalscorer:** Justin Day. **Apps:** James Woodcock.
Senior Honours:

10 YEAR RECORD

01-02	02-03	03-04	04-05	05-06	06-07	07-08	08-09	09-10	10-11
Isth3 4	Isth1S 20	Isth1S 14	SthW 20	SthW 19	Sthsw 19	Sthsw 20	Sthsw	Sthsw 22	Hel P 16

CHELTENHAM SARACENS

Founded: 1964 Nickname: Saras

Secretary: Bob Attwood **(T)** 07778 502 539 **(E)** bobattwood@tiscali.co.uk
Chairman: Chris Hawkins **Manager:** Gerry Oldham **Prog Ed:** Bob Attwood
Ground: Petersfield Park, Tewkesbury Road GL51 9DY **(T)** 01242 584 134
Capacity: **Seats:** **Covered:** **Midweek Matchday:** **Clubhouse:** **Shop:**

Colours(change): All navy blue
Previous Names:
Previous Leagues:
Records: **Att:** 327 v Harrow Hill 31/08/2003.
Senior Honours: Glouscestershire Senior Cup 1991-92. Hellenic League Division 1 1999-2000.

10 YEAR RECORD

01-02	02-03	03-04	04-05	05-06	06-07	07-08	08-09	09-10	10-11
Hel P 22	Hel1W 9	Hel1W 13	Hel1W 6	Hel1E 8	Hel1W 6	Hel1W 5	Hel1W 12	Hel1W 4	Hel1W 3

FAIRFORD TOWN

Founded: 1891 Nickname: Town

Secretary: William Beach **(T)** 07919 940 909 **(E)** wbeach007@btinternet.com
Chairman: TBC **Manager:** Tom Dryden **Prog Ed:** Andrew Meadon
Ground: Cinder Lane, London Road, Fairford GL7 4AX **(T)** 01285 712 071
Capacity: 2,000 **Seats:** 100 **Covered:** 250 **Midweek Matchday:** Tuesday **Clubhouse:** Yes **Shop:** Yes

Colours(change): All red.
Previous Names: None.
Previous Leagues: Cirencester & District. Swindon & District.
Records: **Att:** 1,525 v Coventry City, friendly, July 2000. **Goalscorer:** Pat Toomey.
Senior Honours:

10 YEAR RECORD

01-02	02-03	03-04	04-05	05-06	06-07	07-08	08-09	09-10	10-11
Hel P 6	Hel P 6	Hel P 10	Hel P 8	Hel P 17	Hel P 13	Hel P 20	Hel P 14	Hel P 20	Hel P 21

FLACKWELL HEATH

Founded: 1907 Nickname: Heath

Secretary: Brian Kirby **(T)** 01628 528 549 **(E)** flackwellheathfc@hotmail.co.uk
Chairman: Geoff Turner **Manager:** TBC **Prog Ed:** Geoff Turner
Ground: Wilks Park, Magpie Lane, Heath End Rd, Flackwell Hth HP10 9EA. **(T)** 01628 523 892
Capacity: 2,000 **Seats:** 150 **Covered:** Yes **Midweek Matchday:** Tuesday **Clubhouse:** Yes **Shop:** No

Colours(change): All red.
Previous Names: None.
Previous Leagues: Great Western Combination. Hellenic. Isthmian.
Records: **Att:** 1,500 v Oxford United, charity match, 1966. **Goalscorer:** Tony Wood. **Apps:** Lee Elliott.
Senior Honours:

10 YEAR RECORD

01-02	02-03	03-04	04-05	05-06	06-07	07-08	08-09	09-10	10-11
Isth3 20	Isth2 3	Isth2 5	Isth2 9	Isth2 4	Isth1N 22	Hel P 9	Hel P 16	Hel P 4	Hel P 8

HENLEY TOWN

Founded: Nickname: Lillywhites

Secretary: Geoff Biggs **(T)** 07710 795 190 **(E)** cavaman@gmail.com
Chairman: Barrie Baxter **Manager:** Dave Tuttle **Prog Ed:** Geoff Biggs
Ground: The Triangle Ground, Mill Lane, Henley RG9 4HB **(T)** 01491 411 083
Capacity: **Seats:** **Covered:** **Midweek Matchday:** Tuesday **Clubhouse:** **Shop:**

Colours(change): White/black/black
Previous Names:
Previous Leagues:
Records: **Att:** 2000+ v Reading, 1922. **Goalscorer:** M. Turner.
Senior Honours: Hellenic League Div.1 1963-64, 67-68, Div.1 East 2000-01. Chiltonian League Division 1 1987-88. Premier 1999-00.

10 YEAR RECORD

01-02	02-03	03-04	04-05	05-06	06-07	07-08	08-09	09-10	10-11
Hel P 16	Hel P 10	Hel P 15	Hel P 14	Hel P 21	Hel1E 16	Hel1E 6	Hel1E 7	Hel1E 5	Hel1E 2

HIGHWORTH TOWN

Founded: 1893 Nickname: Worthians

Secretary: Fraser Haines **(T)** 07939 032 451 **(E)** fraserhaines@btinternet.com
Chairman: Rohan Haines **Manager:** Dave Webb **Prog Ed:** Mike Markham
Ground: Elm Recreation Ground, Highworth SN6 7DD **(T)** 01793 766 263
Capacity: 2,000 **Seats:** 150 **Covered:** 250 **Midweek Matchday:** Tuesday **Clubhouse:** Yes **Shop:** No

Colours(change): Red/black/red.
Previous Names: None.
Previous Leagues: Swindon & District. Wiltshire.
Records: **Att:** 2,000 v QPR, opening of floodlights. **Goalscorer:** Kevin Higgs. **Apps:** Rod Haines.
Senior Honours: Hellenic League Champions 2004-05.

10 YEAR RECORD

01-02	02-03	03-04	04-05	05-06	06-07	07-08	08-09	09-10	10-11
Hel P 15	Hel P 4	Hel P 9	Hel P 1	Hel P 12	Hel P 15	Hel P 6	Hel P 6	Hel P 9	Hel P 4

HOLYPORT

Founded: 1934 Nickname: The Villagers

Secretary: Graham Broom **(T)** 07702 369 708 **(E)** grahambroom@btinternet.com
Chairman: Tony Andrews **Manager:** Derek Sweetman **Prog Ed:** Richard Tyrell
Ground: Summerleaze Village SL6 8SP **(T)** 07702 369 708 / 07786 167 949
Capacity: **Seats:** **Covered:** **Midweek Matchday:** Tuesday **Clubhouse:** **Shop:**

Colours(change): Claret/green/claret
Previous Names:
Previous Leagues:
Records: **Att:** 218 v Eton Wick, 2006.
Senior Honours: Norfolkian Senior Cup 1999-2000. Hellenic League Division One East 2010-11.

10 YEAR RECORD

01-02	02-03	03-04	04-05	05-06	06-07	07-08	08-09	09-10	10-11
	Hel1E 15	Hel1E 17	Hel1E 15	Hel1E 14	Hel1E 9	Hel1E 7	Hel1E 5	Hel1E 3	Hel1E 1

KIDLINGTON

Founded: 1909 Nickname:

Secretary: David Platt **(T)** 07956 531 185 **(E)** david.platt45@googlemail.com
Chairman: TBC **Manager:** Gordon Geary **Prog Ed:** Les Deabill
Ground: Yarnton Road, Kidlington, Oxford OX5 1AT **(T)** 01865 841 526
Capacity: **Seats:** Yes **Covered:** Yes **Midweek Matchday:** Tuesday **Clubhouse:** Yes **Shop:** No

Colours(change): Green/green/white
Previous Names: None.
Previous Leagues: Oxford Senior.
Records: **Att:** 2,500 v Showbiz XI, 1973.
Senior Honours:

10 YEAR RECORD

01-02	02-03	03-04	04-05	05-06	06-07	07-08	08-09	09-10	10-11
Hel1W 10	Hel1W 7	Hel1W 12	Hel1W 3	Hel P 20	Hel P 9	Hel P 15	Hel P 9	Hel P 11	Hel P 7

OXFORD CITY NOMADS

Founded: 1936 Nickname: The Nomads

Secretary: Colin Taylor **(T)** 07817 885 396 **(E)** ctoxford@btinternet.com
Chairman: Richard Lawrence **Manager:** Justin Merritt & Justin Lee **Prog Ed:** Colin Taylor
Ground: Court Place Farm Stadium, Marsh Lane, Marston OX3 0NQ **(T)** 01865 744 493
Capacity: 3,000 **Seats:** 300 **Covered:** 400 **Midweek Matchday:** Wednesday **Clubhouse:** Yes **Shop:** Yes

Colours(change): Blue & white hoops/blue/blue.
Previous Names: Quarry Nomads > 2005.
Previous Leagues: Chiltonian.
Records: **Att:** 334 v Headington Amateurs, 25.08.03.
Senior Honours:

10 YEAR RECORD

01-02	02-03	03-04	04-05	05-06	06-07	07-08	08-09	09-10	10-11
Hel1E 11	Hel1E 1	Hel1W 7	Hel1W 15	Hel1E 11	Hel1E 12	Hel1W 9	Hel1W 3	Hel P 10	Hel P 17

READING TOWN

Founded: 1966 Nickname: Town

Secretary: Richard Grey **(T)** 07762 494 324 **(E)** richardigrey@aol.com
Chairman: Roland Ford **Manager:** Mark Bartley **Prog Ed:** Richard Wickson
Ground: Reading Town Sports Ground, Scours Lane, Reading RG30 6AY **(T)** 0118 945 3555
Capacity: 2000 **Seats:** 120 **Covered:** 200 **Midweek Matchday:** Tuesday **Clubhouse:** Yes **Shop:** No

Colours(change): Red/black/black
Previous Names: Lower Burghfield, XI Utd, Vincents Utd, Reading Garage, ITS Reading T.
Previous Leagues: Chiltonian Lge. Combined Counties.
Records: **Att:** 1067 v AFC Wimbledon, Combined Counties 03.05.03.
Senior Honours:

10 YEAR RECORD

01-02	02-03	03-04	04-05	05-06	06-07	07-08	08-09	09-10	10-11
CC 21	CC 15	CCP 3	CCP 19	CCP 10	CCP 9	CCP 13	Hel P 8	Hel P 3	Hel P 13

SHORTWOOD UNITED

Founded: 1900 Nickname: The Wood

Secretary: Mark Webb **(T)** 07792 323784 **(E)** squish.shortwoodfc@live.co.uk
Chairman: Peter Webb **Manager:** John Evans **Prog Ed:** Paul Webb
Ground: Meadowbank, Shortwood, Nailsworth GL6 0SJ **(T)** 01453 833 936
Capacity: 2,000 **Seats:** 50 **Covered:** 150 **Midweek Matchday:** Tuesday **Clubhouse:** Yes **Shop:** No

Colours(change): Red & white/white/black.
Previous Names: None.
Previous Leagues: Gloucestershire County.
Records: **Att:** 1,000 v Forest Green Rovers, FA Vase 5th Rnd 1982. **Goalscorer:** Peter Grant. **Apps:** Peter Grant.
Senior Honours: Hellenic Lge Champions 84-85, 91-92. Gloucestershire Senior Cup (x 2).

10 YEAR RECORD

01-02	02-03	03-04	04-05	05-06	06-07	07-08	08-09	09-10	10-11
Hel P 9	Hel P 13	Hel P 19	Hel P 15	Hel P 15	Hel P 8	Hel P 5	Hel P 2	Hel P 2	Hel P 6

SHRIVENHAM

Founded: 1900 Nickname: Shrivy

Secretary: Emma Skilton **(T)** 07845 693 274 **(E)** emma.skilton@nationwide.co.uk
Chairman: Robb Forty **Manager:** John Fisher **Prog Ed:** Matt Hirst
Ground: The Recreation Ground, Shrivenham SN6 8BJ **(T)** 07767 371 414
Capacity: **Seats:** **Covered:** **Midweek Matchday:** Tuesday **Clubhouse:** Yes **Shop:**

Colours(change): Blue & white hoops/blue/blue.
Previous Names: None.
Previous Leagues: North Berkshire.
Records: **Att:** 800 v Aston Villa, 21.05.2000.
Senior Honours: Hellenic Division One West 2004-05.

10 YEAR RECORD

01-02	02-03	03-04	04-05	05-06	06-07	07-08	08-09	09-10	10-11
Hel1W 9	Hel1W 12	Hel1W 3	Hel1W 1	Hel P 8	Hel P 10	Hel P 8	Hel P 18	Hel P 16	Hel P 20

SLIMBRIDGE

Founded: 1899 Nickname: The Swans

Secretary: Colin Gay **(T)** 07702 070 229 **(E)** colin1956bcfc@o2.co.uk
Chairman: John Mack **Manager:** Leon Sterling **Prog Ed:** Tim Blake
Ground: Wisloe Road, Cambridge, Glos GL2 7AF **(T)** 07835 927 226
Capacity: **Seats:** Yes **Covered:** Yes **Midweek Matchday:** Tuesday **Clubhouse:** Yes **Shop:** Yes

Colours(change): Blue/blue/white.
Previous Names: None
Previous Leagues: Stroud & District. Gloucester Northern. Gloucestershire County.
Records: Since 2002-03. **Att:** 525 v Shortwood United, Hellenic Prem. 24.08.03. **Goals:** Julian Freeman - 79 (from 122 apps.).
Senior Honours: Gloucester Northern League 2007-08. Gloucestershire County League 2008-09.

10 YEAR RECORD

01-02	02-03	03-04	04-05	05-06	06-07	07-08	08-09	09-10	10-11
GlCo 2	Hel1W 1	Hel P 4	Hel P 4	Hel P 5	Hel P 1	GlN1 1	GlCo 1	Hel1W 1	Hel P 5

THAME UNITED

Founded: 1883 Nickname: United

Secretary: Tony Collingwood **(T)** 07824 883 456 **(E)** a.collingwood540@btinternet.com
Chairman: Jake Collinge **Manager:** Mark West **Prog Ed:** Jake Collinge
Ground: The ASM Stadium, Meadow View Park, Tythrop Wa, Thame, Oxon, OX9 3RN **(T)** 01844 214 401
Capacity: 2,500 **Seats:** Yes **Covered:** Yes **Midweek Matchday:** Tuesday **Clubhouse:** Yes **Shop:**

Colours(change): Red & black/black/black.
Previous Names: Thame F.C.
Previous Leagues: Oxon Senior. Hellenic. South Midlands. Isthmian. Southern.
Records: **Att:** 1,035 v Aldershot, Isthmian Div.2, 04.04.94. **Goalscorer:** Not known. **Apps:** Steve Mayhew.
Senior Honours: Isthmian Division 2 1994-95.

10 YEAR RECORD

01-02	02-03	03-04	04-05	05-06	06-07	07-08	08-09	09-10	10-11
Isth1 11	Isth1N 8	Isth1N 15	SthW 11	SthW 22	Hel P 20	Hel1E 10	Hel1E 9	Hel1E 1	Hel P 10

WANTAGE TOWN

Founded: 1892 Nickname: Alfredians

Secretary: John Culley **(T)** 07921 243 263 **(E)** john_clly@yahoo.co.uk
Chairman: Tony Woodward **Manager:** Andy Wallbridge **Prog Ed:** Tony Woodward
Ground: Alfredian Park, Manor Road, Wantage OX12 8DW **(T)** 01235 764 781
Capacity: 1,500 **Seats:** 50 **Covered:** 300 **Midweek Matchday:** Tuesday **Clubhouse:** Yes **Shop:** No

Colours(change): Green & white hoops/white/white.
Previous Names: None.
Previous Leagues: Swindon & District. North Berkshire. Reading & District.
Records: **Att:** 550 v Oxford United, July 2003.
Senior Honours:

10 YEAR RECORD

01-02	02-03	03-04	04-05	05-06	06-07	07-08	08-09	09-10	10-11
Hel P 12	Hel P 21	Hel1E 1	Hel P 10	Hel P 9	Hel P 11	Hel P 12	Hel P 11	Hel P 5	Hel P 1

WITNEY TOWN

Founded: 2001 Nickname: The Blanketmen

Secretary: Adrian Bircher **(T)** 07824 999 119 **(E)** adrian1.bircher@ntlworld.com
Chairman: Tom Amer **Manager:** Duncan Colwell **Prog Ed:** Rich Wickson
Ground: Marriot Stadium, Downs Road, Witney OX29 7WT **(T)** 01993 848 558 (Office) or 702 549 (Bar)
Capacity: 3,500 **Seats:** 280 **Covered:** 2,000 **Midweek Matchday:** Tuesday **Clubhouse:** Yes **Shop:** Yes

Colours(change): Yellow/black/yellow.
Previous Names: Witney United > 2001-11.
Previous Leagues: None.
Records: **Att:** 628 v Oxford United, 26.02.08
Senior Honours:

10 YEAR RECORD

01-02	02-03	03-04	04-05	05-06	06-07	07-08	08-09	09-10	10-11
	Hel1W 15	Hel1W 4	Hel P 11	Hel P 6	Hel P 6	Hel P 4	Hel P 3	Hel P 6	Hel P 18

WOKINGHAM & EMMBROOK

Founded: 2004 Nickname: Satsumas

Secretary: Sally Blee **(T)** 07714 732 790 **(E)** sally.blee@tesco.net
Chairman: Paul Rance **Manager:** Roger Herridge **Prog Ed:** Paul Rance
Ground: Bracknell Town FC, Larges Lane, Bracknell RG12 9AN **(T)** 01344 412 305
Capacity: 2,500 **Seats:** 190 **Covered:** 400 **Midweek Matchday:** Tuesday **Clubhouse:** Yes **Shop:**

Colours(change): Orange/black/black.
Previous Names: Club formed when Wokingham Town and Emmbrook Sports merged.
Previous Leagues: Isthmian (Wokingham). Reading (Emmbrook Sports).
Records: **Att:** 305 v Binfield, 25.03.2005.
Senior Honours:

10 YEAR RECORD

01-02	02-03	03-04	04-05	05-06	06-07	07-08	08-09	09-10	10-11
			Hel1E 11	Hel1E 3	Hel1E 8	Hel1E 12	Hel1E 4	Hel1E 2	Hel P 11

HELLENIC INS & OUTS

PREM - IN: Cheltenham Saracens (P - Division One West), Henley Town (P - Division One East), Holyport (P - Division One East).
OUT: Carterton (R - Division One West), Old Woodstock Town (R - Division One West), Pegasus Juniors (S - West Midlands League Premier Division), Wootton Bassett Town (R - Division One West).
Witney United become Witney Town.
DIV ONE EAST - IN: Highmoor-IBIS (P - Reading League Senior Division), Lambourn Sports (P - North Berks League Division One), Letcombe (S - Division One West), Maidenhead United Reserves (P - Reserve Division), Thatcham Town (P - Reserve Division).
OUT: Farnborough Reserves (S - Suburban League), Henley Town (P), Holyport (P), South Kilburn (S - Combined Counties League Divsion One).
DIV ONE WEST - IN: Brimscombe & Thrupp (P - Glos County League), Carterton (R), Cirencester Town Reserves (N), New College Swindon (P - Wiltshire League Premier Division), Old Woodstock Town (R), Wootton Bassett Town (R).
OUT: Bicester Town (F), Cheltenham Saracens (P), Launton Sports (P - Oxfordshire Senior League Premier Division), Letcombe (S - Division One East).

Headington Amateurs celebrate after winning the Hellenic Division One West title. Photo: Gordon Whittington.

ABINGDON UNITED RESERVES
Founded: Nickname: U's

Secretary: John Blackmore **(T)** 07747 615 691 **(E)** john.blackmore2@ntlworld.com
Chairman: Deborah Blackmore **Manager:** TBC **Prog Ed:** Bill Fletcher
Ground: Northcourt Road, Abingdon OX14 1PL **(T)** 01235 203 203 **Capacity:**
Colours(change): All yellow.

ADDITIONAL INFORMATION:

CHALFONT WASPS
Founded: 1922 Nickname: The Stingers

Secretary: Bob Cakeboard **(T)** 07895 094 579 **(E)** robert.cakeboard@btinternet.com
Chairman: Steve Waddington **Manager:** Martin Kenealy **Prog Ed:** Al Yeomans
Ground: Crossleys Bowstridge, Lane Chalfont, St Giles HP8 4QN **(T)** 01494 875 050 **Capacity:**
Colours(change): Yellow and black stripes/black/black

ADDITIONAL INFORMATION:
Record Att: 82 v Didcot Town 17/12/2005.
Honours: Hellenic League Division 1 East 2007-08.

CHINNOR
Founded: 1884 Nickname:

Secretary: Richard Carr **(T)** 07786 115 089 **(E)** richard.carr@eu.sony.com
Chairman: Jim Marshall **Manager:** David Ridgley **Prog Ed:** Richard Carr
Ground: Station Road, Chinnor, Oxon OX39 4PV **(T)** 01844 352 579 **Capacity:**
Colours(change): All royal blue

ADDITIONAL INFORMATION:
Previous League: Oxfordshire Senior.
Record Att: 306 v Oxford Quarry Nomads, 29.08.2005.

DIDCOT TOWN RESERVES
Founded: 1907 Nickname: Railwaymen

Secretary: Pat Horsman **(T)** 07882 154 612 **(E)** didcot@fernring.co.uk
Chairman: John Bailey **Manager:** Paul Noble **Prog Ed:** Steve Clare
Ground: NPower Loop Meadow Stadium, Bowmont Water, Didcot OX11 7GA **(T)** 01235 813 138 **Capacity:**
Colours(change): Red & white/white/red & white

ADDITIONAL INFORMATION:
Previous League: Hellenic Reserves.

FINCHAMPSTEAD
Founded: 1952 Nickname: Finches

Secretary: Nick Markman **(T)** 07793 866 324 **(E)** njm826@btinternet.com
Chairman: Richard Laugharne **Manager:** John Laugharne **Prog Ed:** Nick Markman
Ground: Memorial Park The Village, Finchampstead RG40 4JR **(T)** 0118 9732890 **Capacity:**
Colours(change): Sky blue & white/sky/sky

ADDITIONAL INFORMATION:
Record Att: 425 v Sandhurst, 1958-59.
Honours: Chiltonian League 1987-88. Reading Senior Challenge Cup 1986-87. Hellenic League Division 1 East 2001-02.

HIGHMOOR-IBIS
Founded: Nickname: Mighty Moor

Secretary: Chris Gallimore **(T)** 01189 588 518 **(E)** chris.gallimore@sjpp.co.uk
Chairman: Phllip Mullin **Manager:** Paul Hamilton **Prog Ed:** Martin Law
Ground: Palmer Park Stadium, Wokingham Road, Reading RG6 1LF **(T)** 01189 375 080 **Capacity:**
Colours(change): All blue

ADDITIONAL INFORMATION: Previous Lge: Reading Senior.
Honours: Reading League Senior Division 2010-11.

HUNGERFORD TOWN RESERVES
Founded: 1886 Nickname: The Crusaders

Secretary: John Smyth **(T)** 07824 513 390 **(E)** johnsmyth@homecall.co.uk
Chairman: Nigel Warrick **Manager:** Andy Allum **Prog Ed:** John Smyth
Ground: Bulpit Lane, Hungerford RG17 0AY **(T)** 01488 682 939 **Capacity:**
Colours(change): White/blue/white

ADDITIONAL INFORMATION:
Previous League: Hellenic Reserves.

LAMBOURN SPORTS

Founded: | Nickname:

Secretary: Micky Towell | **(T)** 07816 822 635 | **(E)** micky7owell@aol.com
Chairman: Jason Williams | **Manager:** Robin Clark | **Prog Ed:** TBC
Ground: Bockhampton Road Lambourn, Hungerford, Berkshire RG17 8PS | **(T)** 01488 72212 | **Capacity:**
Colours(change): Red/white/black

ADDITIONAL INFORMATION: Previous Lge: North Berkshire > 2011.
Honours: North Berkshire League Division One 2010-11.

LETCOMBE

Founded: 1910 | Nickname: Brooksiders

Secretary: Des Williams | **(T)** 07765 144 985 | **(E)** deswilliams45@btinternet.com
Chairman: Dennis Stock | **Manager:** Alan Gifford | **Prog Ed:** Russell Stock
Ground: Bassett Road, Letcombe Regis OX12 9JU | **(T)** 07765 144 985 | **Capacity:**
Colours(change): All purple

ADDITIONAL INFORMATION:
Record Att: 203 v Old Woodstock Town, 29/08/04.
Honours: North Berkshire League Division One 1989-90. Chiltonian League Division One 1990-91.

MAIDENHEAD UNITED RESERVES

Founded: | Nickname: Magpies

Secretary: Ken Chandler | **(T)** 07726 351 286 | **(E)** kenneth.chandler@btinternet.com
Chairman: Peter Griffin | **Manager:** Dom Lock | **Prog Ed:** Steve Jinman
Ground: York Road, Maidenhead, Berkshire SL6 1SF | **(T)** 01628 636 314 | **Capacity:**
Colours(change): Black & white stripe/black/red

ADDITIONAL INFORMATION: Previous Lge: Hellenic Reserves.

MILTON UNITED

Founded: 1909 | Nickname: Miltonians

Secretary: Sarah Banks | **(T)** 07809 777 900 | **(E)** connollysarah2002@hotmail.com
Chairman: Ron Renton | **Manager:** Shaun Smith | **Prog Ed:** Ron Renton
Ground: Potash Lane, Milton Heights, OX13 6AG | **(T)** 01235 832 999 | **Capacity:**
Colours(change): Claret & sky/claret & sky/claret

ADDITIONAL INFORMATION:
Record Att: 608 Carterton v Didcot Town, League Cup Final, 07.05.05. **Goalscorer:** Nigel Mott.
Honours: Hellenic League 1990-91.

NEWBURY

Founded: 1887 | Nickname:

Secretary: Knut Riemann | **(T)** 07855 031 000 | **(E)** kriemann@yahoo.com
Chairman: Keith Moss | **Manager:** Steve Melledew | **Prog Ed:** Martin Strafford
Ground: Faraday Road, Newbury RG14 2AD | **(T)** 01635 41031 or 07790 592 154 | **Capacity:**
Colours(change): Amber & black/black/amber & black

ADDITIONAL INFORMATION:
Record Att: 246 v Kintbury Rangers 27/12/2008.
Honours: Hellenic League 1978-79, 80-81. Athenian League 1982-83.

PENN & TYLERS GREEN

Founded: 1905 | Nickname:

Secretary: Andrea Latta | **(T)** 07904 538 868 | **(E)** hsvlatta1955@yahoo.co.uk
Chairman: Tony Hurst | **Manager:** John Sepede | **Prog Ed:** Fergus Sturrock
Ground: French School Meadows, Elm Road, Penn, Bucks HP10 8LF | **(T)** 01494 815 346 | **Capacity:**
Colours(change): Blue & white stripes/blue/blue

ADDITIONAL INFORMATION:
Previous League: Chiltonian (Founder member).
Record Att: 125 v Chalfont Wasps, August 2000.

RAYNERS LANE

Founded: | Nickname: The Lane

Secretary: Tony Pratt | **(T)** 01895 233 853 | **(E)** richard.mitchell@tesco.net
Chairman: Martin Noblett | **Manager:** Dean Gardner | **Prog Ed:** Richard Mitchell
Ground: Tithe Farm Social Club, Rayners Lane, South Harrow HA2 0XH | **(T)** 0208 868 8724 | **Capacity:**
Colours(change): Yellow/green/yellow

ADDITIONAL INFORMATION:
Record Att: 550 v Wealdstone 1983.
Honours: Hellenic League Division 1 1982-83.

THATCHAM TOWN RESERVES

Founded: Nickname: Kingfishers

Secretary: Alan Lovegrove (T) 07817 723 846 (E) mail@alanlovegrove.wanadoo.co.uk
Chairman: Eric Bailey **Manager:** Gary Cook **Prog Ed:** TBC
Ground: Waterside Park, Crookham Hill, Thatcham RG19 4PA (T) 01635 862 016 **Capacity:**
Colours(change): Blue & white/blue/blue

ADDITIONAL INFORMATION: Previous Lge: Hellenic Reserves.

WOODLEY TOWN

Founded: 1904 Nickname: Town

Secretary: John Mailer (T) 07883 341 628 (E) john_mailer@hotmail.co.uk
Chairman: Mark Rozzier **Manager:** Cyril Fairchild **Prog Ed:** Mark Beaven
Ground: East Park Farm, Park Lane, Charvil, Berks RG10 9TR (T) 07703 474 555 **Capacity:**
Colours(change): All navy blue

ADDITIONAL INFORMATION:
Previous League: Reading.
Honours: Reading Football League Senior Division 2008-09. Berkshire Trophy Centre Senior Cup 2008-09.

BRIMSCOMBE & THRUPP

Founded: Nickname: Lilywhites

Secretary: John Mutton (T) 01453 757 880 (E) johncolin123@gmail.com
Chairman: Clive Baker **Manager:** Phil Baker **Prog Ed:** Clive Baker
Ground: 'The Meadow', London Road, Brimscombe Stroud, Gloucestershire GL5 2SH (T) 07833 231 464 **Capacity:**
Colours(change): White/blue/blue.

ADDITIONAL INFORMATION: Previous Lge: Gloucestershire County > 2011.
Honours: Gloucestershire County League 2010-11.

CARTERTON

Founded: 1918 Nickname:

Secretary: Rob King (T) 07766 201 418 (E) robert.king80@virgin.net
Chairman: Rob King **Manager:** Mark Jacobsen **Prog Ed:** Andy Meaden
Ground: Kilkenny Lane, Carterton, Oxfordshire OX18 1DY. (T) 01993 842 410 **Capacity:** 1,500
Colours(change): Red with green trim/green/red.

ADDITIONAL INFORMATION: Record Att: 650 v Swindon Town, July 2001. **Goalscorer:** Phil Rodney.

CIRENCESTER TOWN RESERVES

Founded: 2011 Nickname: Centurions

Secretary: Steve Hale (T) 01285 654 543 (E) steve.hale@cirentownfc.plus.com
Chairman: Steve Abbley **Manager:** Andy Minturn **Prog Ed:** Andy James
Ground: Corinium Stadium, Kingshill Lane, Cirencester Glos GL7 (T) 01285 654 543 **Capacity:**
Colours(change): Red & black stripes/black/red.

ADDITIONAL INFORMATION:

CLANFIELD

Founded: 1890 Nickname: Robins

Secretary: John Osborne (T) 01993 771 631 (E) trevor@cuss.gotadsl.co.uk
Chairman: John Osborne **Manager:** Peter Osborne **Prog Ed:** Trevor Cuss
Ground: Radcot Road, Clanfield OX18 2ST (T) 01367 810 314 **Capacity:**
Colours(change): All red

ADDITIONAL INFORMATION:
Record Att: 197 v Kidlington August 2002.
Honours: Hellenic League Division 1 1969-70.

CRICKLADE TOWN

Founded: 1897 Nickname: Crick

Secretary: Rebecca Ross (T) 07970 066 581 (E) alisdair.ross@venuesevent.com
Chairman: Alisdair Ross **Manager:** Graham Jackson **Prog Ed:** Alisdair Ross
Ground: Cricklade Leisure Centre, Stones Lane, Cricklade SN6 6JW (T) 01793 750 011 **Capacity:**
Colours(change): Green/black/green

ADDITIONAL INFORMATION:
Record Att: 170 v Trowbridge Town 2003-04.
Honours: Wiltshire League 2000-01.

EASINGTON SPORTS
Founded: 1946 Nickname: The Clan

Secretary: Angela Clives **(T)** 07815 325 905 **(E)** aclives@btinternet.com
Chairman: Phil Lines **Manager:** Phil Lines **Prog Ed:** James Collier
Ground: Addison Road, Banbury OX16 9DH **(T)** 01295 257 006 **Capacity:**
Colours(change): Red & white/red & white/red

ADDITIONAL INFORMATION:
Record Att: 258 v Hook Norton.
Hnours: Oxfordshire Senior League 1957-58, 58-59. Division 1 1965-66. Oxfordshire Senior Ben Turner Trophy 1970-71.

HEADINGTON AMATEURS
Founded: 1949 Nickname: A's

Secretary: Donald Light **(T)** 07764 943 778 **(E)** donald.light@ntlworld.com
Chairman: Donald Light **Manager:** Shaun Pearce **Prog Ed:** Donald Light
Ground: The Pavillion, Barton Recreation Ground, Oxford OX3 9LA **(T)** 01865 760 489 **Capacity:**
Colours(change): All red

ADDITIONAL INFORMATION:
Record Att: 250 v Newport AFC, 1991. **Goalscorer:** Tony Penge. **Apps:** Kent Drackett.
Honours: Oxfordshire Senior League 1972-73, 73-74, 75-76, 76-77, Division 1 1968-69. Hellenic League Division One West 2010-11.

HOOK NORTON
Founded: 1898 Nickname: Hooky

Secretary: Garnet Thomas **(T)** 07866 035 642 **(E)** thomasz@tiscali.co.uk
Chairman: Garnet Thomas **Manager:** Mark Boyland **Prog Ed:** Mark Willis
Ground: The Bourne, Hook Norton OX15 5PB **(T)** 01608 737 132 **Capacity:**
Colours(change): Royal blue/royal blue/white

ADDITIONAL INFORMATION:
Record Att: 244 v Banbury United, 12/12/98.
Honours: Oxfordshire Senior League 1999-00, 00-01. Hellenic League Division 1 West 2001-02.

LYDNEY TOWN
Founded: 1911 Nickname: The Town

Secretary: Roger Sansom **(T)** 07887 842 125 **(E)** rsansom@glatfelter.com
Chairman: Peter Elliott **Manager:** Mark Lee **Prog Ed:** Roger Sansom
Ground: Lydney Recreation Ground, Swan Road, Lydney GL15 5RU **(T)** 01594 844 523 **Capacity:**
Colours(change): Black & white stripes/black/black & white

ADDITIONAL INFORMATION:
Record Att: 375 v Ellwood, 05.11.05.
Honours: Gloucestershire County League 2005-06. Hellenic League Division 1 West 2006-07.

MALMESBURY VICTORIA
Founded: Nickname: The Vics

Secretary: Sue Neale **(T)** 07885 092 661 **(E)** paul.neale@btconnect.com
Chairman: Paul Neale **Manager:** Simon Winstone **Prog Ed:** Andrew Meadon
Ground: Flying Monk Ground, Gloucester Road, SN16 0AJ **(T)** TBA **Capacity:**
Colours(change): Black & white/black/red

ADDITIONAL INFORMATION:
Record Att: 261 v Cirencester United, 25.08.02.
Honours: Wiltshire League 1999-00. Wiltshire Senior Cup 01-02.

NEW COLLEGE ACADEMY
Founded: Nickname: College

Secretary: Rob Hopkins **(T)** 07739 914 888 **(E)** rob.hopkins@newcollege.ac.uk
Chairman: Paul Bodin **Manager:** Mark Teasdale **Prog Ed:** Paul Smith
Ground: Sumpermarine RFC Sports & Social, Supermarine Rd, South Marston SN3 4BZ **(T)** 01793 824 828 **Capacity:**
Colours(change): All royal blue

ADDITIONAL INFORMATION: **Previous Lge:** Wiltshire > 2011.

OLD WOODSTOCK TOWN
Founded: Nickname:

Secretary: Louise Jordon **(T)** 07944 418 114 **(E)** louise.jordon@talktalk.net
Chairman: Ted Saxton **Manager:** Eddie Nix **Prog Ed:** Mark Cain
Ground: New Road, Woodstock OX20 1PD **(T)** 07748 152 243 **Capacity:**
Colours(change): Royal blue & red/royal/royal.

ADDITIONAL INFORMATION: **Att:** 258 v Kidlington, 27.08.01.

PURTON
Founded: 1923 Nickname: The Reds

Secretary: Alan Eastwood (T) 07950 889 177 (E) alan.eastwood830@ntlworld.com
Chairman: Alan Eastwood **Manager:** Chris Pethick **Prog Ed:** Alan Eastwood
Ground: The Red House, Purton SN5 4DY (T) 01793 770 262 (MD) **Capacity:**
Colours(change): All red

ADDITIONAL INFORMATION:
Honours: Wiltshire League 1945-46, 46-47, 47-48. Wiltshire County League 1985-86. Hellenic League Division 1 1995-96, Division 1 West 2003-04. Wiltshire Senior Cup 1938-39, 48-49, 50-51, 54-55, 87-88, 88-89, 94-95.

TROWBRIDGE TOWN
Founded: 1880 Nickname: Bees

Secretary: Jodie Arberry (T) 07941 776 683 (E) bobarberry@blueyonder.co.uk
Chairman: Ralph McCaldon **Manager:** Ralph McCaldon **Prog Ed:** Andy Meaden
Ground: Wood Marsh, Bradley Road, Trowbridge BA14 0SB (T) 07545 172 043 **Capacity:**
Colours(change): Yellow & black/black/yellow

ADDITIONAL INFORMATION:
Record Att: 369 v Tytherington Rocs 28/08/2005.
Honours: Wiltshire League 2003-04. Wiltshire Senior Cup 2003-04.

TYTHERINGTON ROCKS
Founded: 1896 Nickname: The Rocks

Secretary: Graham Shipp (T) 07811 318 424 (E) tramar1618@btinternet.com
Chairman: Ted Travell **Manager:** Gary Powell **Prog Ed:** Mark Brown
Ground: Hardwicke Playing Field, Tytherington Glos GL12 8UJ (T) 07837 555 776 **Capacity:**
Colours(change): Amber & black/black/black

ADDITIONAL INFORMATION:
Previous Lge: Gloucestershire County.
Record Att: 424 v Winterbourne United, 26/08/2007.

WINTERBOURNE UNITED
Founded: 1911 Nickname: The Bourne

Secretary: Robyn Maggs (T) 07976 255 666 (E) robynmaggs@hotmail.com
Chairman: Robyn Maggs **Manager:** Nick Tanner **Prog Ed:** Robyn Maggs
Ground: Oakland Park, Alomondsbury, Bristol BS32 4AG (T) 07976 255 666 **Capacity:**
Colours(change): Red & black/red/red.

ADDITIONAL INFORMATION:
Record Att: 229 v Malmesbury Victoria, 29/08/2004.
Honours: Gloucestershire County League 2000-01. Hellenic League Division 1 West 2005-06, 07-08.

WOOTTON BASSETT TOWN
Founded: 1882 Nickname:

Secretary: Ian Thomas (T) 07714 718 122 (E) nutwood43@sky.com
Chairman: Paul Harrison **Manager:** Dave Turner **Prog Ed:** Mark Smedley
Ground: Gerard Buxton Sport Ground, Rylands Way SN4 8AW (T) 01793 853 880 **Capacity:** 2,000
Colours(change): Blue & yellow/blue/yellow.

ADDITIONAL INFORMATION: **Record Att:** 2,103 v Swindon Town, July 1991. **Goalscorer:** Brian 'Tony' Ewing. **Apps:** Steve Thomas.

GROUND DIRECTIONS

ABINGDON TOWN - Culham Road OX14 3HP - 01235 521 684
From Town Centre follow signs for Culham, go over bridge, ground is 300 yards on right.

ARDLEY UNITED - The Playing Fields OX27 7NZ - 07711 009 198
From M40 Junction 10 take B430 towards Middleton Stoney the ground is on the right hand side after mile. From Oxford take B430 through Weston-on-the-Green & Middleton Stoney then on the left hand side after passing Church in village.

ASCOT UNITED - Ascot Racecourse SL5 7RA - 07798 701 995
From Ascot High Street, with Ascot Racecourse on the left, follow the A329 to the mini-roundabout, at the end of the High Street, turn left on Winkfield Rd, go through road underpass and take the first right (signposted Car Park 7&8). Follow the track past the Ascot United welcome sign, through gates into the large car park and the ground is approx. 600m further on.

BINFIELD - Hill Farm Lane RG42 5NR - 01344 860 822

From M4 Junction 10 take A329 signposted Wokingham & Binfield, at roundabout take 1st exit. Go through 1st set of traffic lights, turn left at 2nd set opposite Travel Lodge. Follow road through village over two mini-roundabouts, at 'T' junction with church in front of you turn right. Take left filter road after 150 yards into Stubbs Lane. Ground is on left at end of short lane.

BRACKNELL TOWN - Larges Lane RG12 9AN - 01344 412 305

Leave M4 at J10, take A329M signposted Wokingham & Bracknell. Follow road for 5 miles, over roundabout, pass Southern industrial estate (Waitrose etc.) on right to a 2nd r'about with traffic lights; take 2nd exit and follow signposts for M3. At next r'about take 1st exit. At next r'about take 3rd exit, Church Road dual carriageway. This brings you to another r'about with Bracknell & Wokingham college on right and Old Manor PH on left, take 5th exit for Ascot - A329. Go down hill on dual carriageway, London Road to next r'about take 4th exit back up the dual carriageway, London Road, Larges Lane last left turn before reaching r'about again. Ground 200 yards on right.

CHELTENHAM SARACENS - PETERSFIELD PARK GL51 9DY - 01242 584 134

Follow directions into Cheltenham following signs for railway station. At Station roundabout take Gloucester Road, in a Northerly direction for approx 2 miles. Turn left at lights past Tesco entrance onto Tewkesbury Rd, follow road past 'The Range' store over railway bridge. Take 1st left and then 1st left again, then left into service road into car park.

FAIRFORD TOWN - Cinder Lane London Road GL7 4AX - 01285 712 071

Take A417 from Lechlade, turn left down Cinder Lane 150 yards after 40 mph sign. From Cirencester take Lechlade Road, turn right down Cinder Lane 400 yards after passing the Railway Inn.

FLACKWELL HEATH - Wilks Park, Magpie Lane HP10 9EA - 01628 523 892

Junction 4 of M40 Follow signs A404 (High Wycombe) Turn right at traffic lights halfway down Marlow Hill, signposted Flackwell Heath. Ground three (3) miles on left.

HENLEY TOWN - The Triangle Ground RG9 4HB - 01491 411 083

From Henley Town Centre take the A4155 towards Reading. Mill Lane is approximately one mile from the Town Centre on the left immediately before the Jet Garage. From M4 Junction 11 head towards Reading on the A33 inner distribution road then follow A4155 signed to Henley, turn right into Mill Lane after the Jet Garage. Ground & Car Park on the left over the Railway Bridge.

HIGHWORTH TOWN - Elm Recreation Ground SN6 7DD - 01793 766 263

Enter Town on A361, turn into The Green by Veterinary Surgery, Ground and Car Park 100 yards on left.

HOLYPORT - Summerleaze Village SL6 8SP - 07702 369 708

From the A4 Maidenhead take the B4447 towards Cookham after mile turn right into Ray Mill Road West, at the T-junction turn left into Blackamoor Lane. As road bends sharply you will see the entrance to the ground on left, signposted Holyport FC. Please observe speed limit down track to the ground.

KIDLINGTON - Yarnton Road OX5 1AT - 01865 841 526

From Kidlington Roundabout take A4260 into Kidlington. After 3rd set of traffic lights take 2nd left into Yarnton Road. Ground 300 yards on left, just past Morton Avenue.

OXFORD CITY NOMADS - Court Place Farm Stadium OX3 0NQ - 01865 744 493

From South: From Newbury travel along the A34 towards Oxford turn onto Ring Road heading towards London (East). Follow Ring Road over 5 roundabouts to the Green Road roundabout signposted London, M40 East. Go straight over towards Banbury. A fly-over is visible, turn left onto the slip road and follow road to Court Place Farm Stadium on left. From North: At the North Oxford roundabout, travel towards London M40 on the Eastern by-pass, turn off at the flyover, the ground is visible to the left as you go over bridge.

READING TOWN - Scours Lane RG30 6AY - 0118 945 3555

Leave M4 at junction 12 and take A4 towards Reading. Turn left at 1st lights go through Tilehurst Centre turn right into Norcot Road then left into Oxford Road and 1st right into Scours Lane.

SHORTWOOD UNITED - Meadowbank GL6 0SJ - 01453 833 936

12 miles west of Cirencester head for Cirencester, proceed up Spring Hill for 30 yards turn left through the Car Park, then left at Britannia Inn. Proceed up hill for approx mile to Shortwood. Ground is on the left hand side opposite the Church.

HELLENIC LEAGUE - STEP 5/6

SHRIVENHAM - The Recreation Ground SN6 8BJ - 07767 371 414

Shrivenham village is signposted off A420 Oxford to Swindon road, six miles east of Swindon, four miles west of Faringdon. Drive through village turn into Highworth Road, ground is on right, car park on left.

SLIMBRIDGE - Wisloe Road GL2 7AF - 07835 927 226

From the A38 take the A4135 to Dursley. Ground is 100 yards on the left.

THAME UNITED - The ASM Stadium, Meadow View Park, Tythrop Wa, Thame, Oxon, OX9 3RN

01844 214 401. From the west: At the Oxford Road roundabout on the edge of Thame take the first left (sign posted Aylesbury) and follow the by-pass. At the next roundabout take the third exit on to Tythrop Way. The ground is 200 yards on the left.

From the east: Leave the M40 at Junction 6 and follow the signposts to Thame. On arriving in Thame, take the first right on to Wenman Road (B4012). Stay on the B4012 as it by-passes Thame, going straight over two roundabouts. The ground is on the right, directly off the by-pass, approximately half a mile after you pass Chinnor Rugby Club.

WANTAGE TOWN - Alfredian Park, Manor Road OX12 8DW - 01235 764 781

Proceed to Market Square. Take road at southeast corner (Newbury Street signposted to Hungerford). Continue for approximately a quarter of a mile take right turning into the ground. Clearly marked 'Wantage Town FC'.

WOKINGHAM & EMMB' - Bracknell Town FC RG12 9AN - 01344 412 305

Leave M4 at J10, take A329M signposted Wokingham & Bracknell. Follow road for 5 miles, over roundabout, pass Southern industrial estate (Waitrose etc.) on right to a 2nd r'about with traffic lights; take 2nd exit and follow signposts for M3. At next r'about take 1st exit. At next r'about take 3rd exit, Church Road dual carriageway. This brings you to another r'about with Bracknell & Wokingham college on right and Old Manor PH on left, take 5th exit for Ascot - A329. Go down hill on dual carriageway, London Road to next r'about take 4th exit back up the dual carriageway, London Road, Larges Lane last left turn before reaching r'about again. Ground 200 yards on right.

WITNEY UNITED - Polythene UK Stadium OX29 7WT - 01993 848 558

From West: A40 towards Oxford. At Minster Lovell roundabout, take the 1st exit to Minster Lovell. Two miles turn right into Downs Road (signposted for Witney Lakes Golf Club), ground half a mile on right. From Witney town centre: go west on Welch Way, at roundabout take 3rd exit into Curbridge Road. Take 3rd exit at roundabout into Deer Park Road, Left at traffic lights into Range Road, then left ground 400 yards on right.

DIVISION 1 EAST

CHALFONT WASPS - Crossleys Bowstridge Lane HP8 4QN - 01494 875 050

A413 to Chalfont St Giles, follow signposts for village centre. Bowstridge Lane is 400 yards on left immediately after the shops. Crossleys is 400 yards along Bowstridge Lane on the right. Ground is directly ahead.

CHINNOR - Station Road OX39 4PV - 01844 352 579

Leave M40 at junction 6 and follow B4009 sign posted Princes Risborough. After 3 miles enter Chinnor and turn left at Crown PH roundabout. Ground is 400 yards on right.

DIDCOT TOWN RESERVES - Npower Loop Meadow Stad' OX11 7GA - 01235 813 138

From A34 take A4130 towards Didcot, at first roundabout take first exit, at next roundabout take third exit, then straight across next two roundabouts, at 5th roundabout turn right into Avon Way, ground is on the left. Also footpath direct from Didcot Railway Station.

FINCHAMPSTEAD - Memorial Park, The Village RG40 4JR - 0118 973 2890

A321 from Wokingham, then fork right onto B3016. At the Greyhound Public House turn right onto the B3348. The ground is 200 yards on the right.

HIGHMOOR - IBIS - Palmer Park Stadium, Wokingham Road, Reading RG6 1LF - 01189 375 080

From A4 (Also indicated as London Road Reading) At the KIngs Road/A 329 Junction turn into the A329 the Palmer Park ground is approx. 300 metres on the left.

HUNGERFORD TOWN RESERVES - Bulpit Lane RG17 0AY - 01488 682 939

Leave M4 at junction 14 to A4, right then left at Bear Hotel through town centre, left into Priory Road, 2nd left into Bulpit Lane, over crossroads ground on left.

LAMBOURN SPORTS - Bockhampton Road Lambourn, Hungerford, Berkshire RG17 8PS - 01488 72212
Follow signs to Lambourn Village Church, head to village centre and into Station Road, turn left into Bockhampton Road, ground is on left.

LETCOMBE - Bassett Road OX12 9JU - 07765 144 985
Take the B4507 from Wantage (Sign posted White Horse). Turn left after half a mile to Letcombe Regis. Ground on Far side of Village, on the right hand side of road.

MAIDENHEAD UNITED RESERVES - York Road, Maidenhead, Berkshire SL6 1SF - 01628 636 314
The Ground is in the town centre. 200 yards from the station and two minutes walk from the High Street.
Access from M4 Junctions 7 or 8/9.

MILTON UNITED - Potash Lane OX13 6AG - 01235 832 999
Exit A34 at Milton, 10 miles south of Oxford & 12 miles north of junction 13 of M4. Take A4130 towards Wantage approximately 200 metres turn 1st left then right into Milton Hill. Ground 400 metres on the left.

NEWBURY - Faraday Road RG14 2AD - 01635 41031
Leave M4 at junction 13 taking Newbury road. Take A4 towards Thatcham, then take 1st right by 'Topp Tiles' into Faraday Road, ground is at end of road.

PENN & TYLERS GREEN - French School Meadows HP10 8LF - 01494 815 346
From West - 'M40 to High Wycombe leave at J4. Follow A404 to Amersham, via Wycombe. Stay on A404 up the hill past railway station approx. 3 miles at Hazlemere Crossroads turn right onto the B474 signposted to Penn and Beaconsfield. Continue for approx. one mile go past three new houses on left, turn into Elm Road, the ground is on the left. From East -Leave M40 at Junction 2 and take the road signed Beaconsfield. From Beaconsfield follow the road through Penn towards Hazlemere, pass the pond on green and entrance to ground is on the right had side of road before the hill.

RAYNERS LANE - Tithe Farm Social Club HA2 0XH - 0208 868 8724
From A40 Polish War Memorial turn left into A4180 (West End Road), approx. 500 metres turn right into Station Approach, at traffic lights turn right into Victoria Road. At next roundabout continue straight on to traffic lights at junction with Alexandra Avenue (Matrix Bar & Restaurant on left). Continue straight on over traffic lights and take second turning on left into Rayners Lane. Ground is approximately half a mile on the left.

THATCHAM TOWN RESERVES - Waterside Park, Crookham Hill, Thatcham RG19 4PA - 01635 862 016
A4 Thatcham at Sony roundabout turn into Pipers Way. At next roundabout turn left, crossing over the railway line. Entrance to Waterside Park 300 metres on left-hand side.

WOODLEY TOWN - East Park Farm, Park Lane RG10 9TR - 07703 474 555
Take A4, Bath Road & exit onto A3032 at @Wee Waif' roundabout to Twyford & Charvil. Take right exit at mini-roundabout into Park Lane then 2nd exit at mini-roundabout on Park Lane then left turn into East Park Farm. After-match Hospitality is at the Earley Home Guard Club.

DIVISION 1 WEST

BRIMSCOMBE & THRUPP - 'The Meadow', London Road, Brimscombe Stroud, Gloucestershire GL5 2SH 07833 231 464 - 9 miles north of Cirencester on A419. 2 miles south of Stroud on A419.

CARTERTON - Kilkenny Lane OX18 1DY - 01993 842 410
Leave A40 follow B4477 for Carterton continue along Monahan Way turning right at roundabout, at traffic lights turn right onto Upavon Way. At next set of lights turn right onto B4020 to Burford. Take 2nd right into Swinbrook Road carry onto Kilkenny Lane, a single-track road). Ground & car park 200 metres on left hand side.

CLANFIELD - Radcot Road OX18 2ST - 01367 810 314
Situated on A4095 at southern end of village, 8 miles west of Witney and 4 miles east of Faringdon.

CIRENCESTER TOWN RESERVES - Corinium Stadium, Kingshill Lane, Cirencester Glos GL7 - 01285 654 543
Leave bypass at Burford Road roundabout. Aim for Stow, turn right at traffic lights, then right again at next junction, first left into Kingshill Lane. Ground 500 yards on right.

HELLENIC LEAGUE - STEP 5/6

CRICKLADE TOWN - Cricklade Leisure Centre SN6 6JW - 01793 750 011
Cricklade is eight miles North of Swindon signposted off the A419. Leisure Centre is signposted off the B4040 Malmesbury Road.

EASINGTON SPORTS - Addison Road OX16 9DH - 01295 257 006
From North/South M40- Leave M40 at J11, follow A422 to Banbury, 2nd r'about take A4260 to Adderbury. Go through three sets of traffic lights, at top of hill at T-junc' turn left. Take 3rd right into Addison Rd. From South West A361 – Entering Banbury take 1st right turning into Springfield Av after 'The Easington' PH. Follow road, take T-junc' right into Grange Rd, 1st right into Addison Rd. Ground on left at end of road.

HEADINGTON AM' - Barton Recreation Ground OX3 9LA - 01865 760 489
A40 from London take last exit at Headington Roundabout. A40 from Witney take first exit. Take first left after leaving roundabout into North Way. Follow North Way to end where road merges to become Barton Village Road. Ground at bottom of hill on left.

HOOK NORTON - The Bourne OX15 5PB - 01608 737 132
From Oxford – A44 to junction with A361 turn right, take 1st left to a 'T' junction, turn right & enter village, after 30 MPH turn left then 1st right into 'The Bourne', take 1st left into ground.

LYDNEY TOWN - Lydney Recreation Ground GL15 5RU - 01594 844 523
From Gloucester – take Lydney road off A48 down Highfield Hill and into the town centre. Take 1st left into Swan Road after 2nd set of pelican lights. From Chepstow – at by-pass roundabout take Lydney road. Go over railway crossing then take 2nd right into Swan Road.

MALMESBURY VICTORIA - Flying Monk Ground SN16 0AJ
Off A429 signpost Cirencester take B4014 to Tetbury. First left signpost Town Centre Ground on right directly after Somerfield supermarket, narrow right turning into ground behind supermarket.

OLD WOODSTOCK TOWN - New Road, Woodstock OX20 1PD - 07748 152 243
A44 from Oxford, turn right opposite The Crown into Hensington Road. After half a mile road bends to right, take 1st turning right into New Road. Ground on left.

OLD WOODSTOCK TOWN - Eynsham Hall Park OX29 6PN - 07748 152 243
Ground situated on the A4095 Witney to Woodstock road, some 3 miles East of Witney. The entrance is 300 yards east of the main Eynsham Hall Park entrance. (North Leigh FC)

PURTON - THE RED HOUSE SN5 4DY - 01793 770 262 MD
Red House is near Village Hall Square; Purton is well signposted from all directions, situated on the B4041 Wootton Bassett to Cricklade Road, NW of Swindon.

TROWBRIDGE TOWN - Wood Marsh, Bradley Road BA14 0SB - 07545 172 043
Take the A350 Trowbridge by-pass towards Westbury continue through a set of traffic lights until you reach the Yarnbrook Roundabout, Texaco garage on corner. Take the 3rd exit to Trowbridge Go under a railway bridge, next roundabout take the North Bradley exit. Carry on along this road over a small roundabout and past the 'Mash Tun' PH. Ground is on the left.

TYTHERINGTON ROCKS - Hardwicke Playing Field GL12 8UJ - 07837 555 776
From M5 Junction 14 take A38 for Bristol. Tytherington turn-off is approximately three (3) miles. Enter village, ground is signposted.

WINTERBOURNE UNITED - Oakland Park, Alomondsbury, Bristol BS32 4AG - 07976 255 666
From M4 (West) leave at junction 20 to M5 (Sth West). Leave immediately at junction 16 (A38 Thornbury), turn right onto A38, then first left 100 yards from junction, in front of Motorway Police HQ, Ground next door. Signposted from A38 'Gloucestershire FA HQ'.

WOOTTON BASSETT - Gerard Buxton Sports Ground SN4 8AW - 01793 853 880
Leave M4 at junction 16 and proceed towards Wootton Bassett Town Centre. Take 1st left after BP Petrol Station in Longleaze. Take 3rd turning on right into Rylands Way. Ground 150 metres on right hand side. Approaching from Calne or Devizes Area - proceed through Wootton Bassett Town Centre, take first right after Shell Garage into Longleaze then follow previous instructions.

KENT INVICTA LEAGUE - FORMED 2011

ASHFORD UNITED

Founded: 1930 Nickname:

Secretary: Elaine Orsbourne **(T)** 01233 646 713 **(E)** orsbournes@ntlworld.com
Chairman: **Manager:** **Prog Ed:**
Ground: The Homelands, Ashford Road **(T)** **Capacity:**
Colours(change): Green & white/green/green & white (Yellow & green/yellow/yellow & green)

ADDITIONAL INFORMATION:

BEARSTED

Founded: 1895 Nickname:

Secretary: Roy Benton **(T)** 01634 240 008 **(E)** benton951@aol.com
Chairman: **Manager:** **Prog Ed:**
Ground: Otham Sports Club, Honey Lane, Otham, Maidstone ME15 8RG **(T)** 07860 360 280 **Capacity:**
Colours(change): White/blue/blue (Yellow/blue or yellow/blue or yellow)

ADDITIONAL INFORMATION:
Previous Lge: Kent County > 2011.

BLY SPARTANS

Founded: 1982 Nickname:

Secretary: Tony Wheeler **(T)** 07775 735 543 **(E)** blyspatans@yahoo.co.uk
Chairman: **Manager:** **Prog Ed:**
Ground: Bly Spartans Sports Ground, Rede Court Road, Strood, Kent ME2 3TU **(T)** 01634 710577 **Capacity:**
Colours(change): All maroon (All white)

ADDITIONAL INFORMATION:
Previous Lge: Kent County > 2011.

BRIDON ROPES

Founded: 1935 Nickname:

Secretary: Richard Clements **(T)** 0208 244 1167 **(E)** rich.clements@live.co.uk
Chairman: **Manager:** **Prog Ed:**
Ground: Meridian Sports & Social Club, Charlton Park Lane, Charlton, London SE7 8QS **(T)** 0208 8561923 **Capacity:**
Colours(change): Blue & white/blue/blue (All red)

ADDITIONAL INFORMATION:
Previous Lge: Kent County > 2011.

CROCKENHILL

Founded: 1946 Nickname:

Secretary: Jayne Martin **(T)** 01322 665 517 **(E)** jayne.martin12@live.co.uk
Chairman: **Manager:** **Prog Ed:**
Ground: Wested Meadow Ground, Eynesford Road, Crockenhill, Kent BR8 8EJ **(T)** 01322 666067 **Capacity:**
Colours(change):

ADDITIONAL INFORMATION:
Previous Lge: Kent County > 2011.

ERITH & DARTFORD TOWN

Founded: Nickname:

Secretary: Simon Kidby **(T)** **(E)** sikakima@supanet.com
Chairman: **Manager:** **Prog Ed:**
Ground: Oakwood (VCD Ath FC), Old Road, Crayford, Kent, DA1 4DN **(T)** 07501 684838 **Capacity:**
Colours(change):

ADDITIONAL INFORMATION:

HOLLANDS & BLAIR

Founded: 1970 Nickname:

Secretary: Laurence Plummer **(T)** 07540 841 799 **(E)** laurence.plummer@btinternet.com
Chairman: **Manager:** **Prog Ed:**
Ground: Star Meadow Sports Club, Darland Avenue, Gillingham, Kent ME7 3AN **(T)** 01634 573839 **Capacity:**
Colours(change): All red (Yellow & blue)

ADDITIONAL INFORMATION:
Previous Lge: Kent County > 2011.
Honours: Kent County 2010-11.

LEWISHAM BOROUGH
Founded: 2003 Nickname:

Secretary: Ray Simpson **(T)** 07958 946 236 **(E)** grancan_jamaica@yahoo.co.uk
Chairman: **Manager:** **Prog Ed:**
Ground: Ladywell Arena, Silvermere Road, Catford, London SE6 4QX **(T)** **Capacity:**
Colours(change): Yellow & blue/blue/yellow & blue (All red)

ADDITIONAL INFORMATION:
Previous Lge: Kent county > 2011.

LYDD TOWN
Founded: 1885 Nickname:

Secretary: Bruce Marchant **(T)** 01303 275 403 **(E)** brucemarchant@hotmail.com
Chairman: **Manager:** **Prog Ed:**
Ground: The Lindsey Field, Dengemarsh Road, Lydd, Kent TN29 9JH **(T)** 01797 321904 **Capacity:**
Colours(change): Green & red/green/red (Blue & white stripes/blue/blue)

ADDITIONAL INFORMATION:
Previous Lge: Kent County > 2011.

MERIDIAN
Founded: 1995 Nickname:

Secretary: Dwinder Tamma **(T)** 07977 274 179 **(E)** dtamna@meridianfc.co.uk
Chairman: **Manager:** **Prog Ed:**
Ground: Meridian Sports & Social Club, 110 Charlton Park Lane, London SE7 8QS **(T)** 0208 856 1923 **Capacity:**
Colours(change): All sky blue (All red)

ADDITIONAL INFORMATION:
Previous Lge: Kent County > 2011.

ORPINGTON
Founded: 1939 Nickname:

Secretary: Paul Wade **(T)** 01689 889 619 **(E)** paul.wade@virgin.net
Chairman: **Manager:** **Prog Ed:**
Ground: Green Court Road, Crockenhill, Kent BR8 8HJ **(T)** 01322 666442 **Capacity:**
Colours(change): Yellow/black/black

ADDITIONAL INFORMATION:
Previous Lge: Kent County > 2011.

PHOENIX SPORTS
Founded: 1935 Nickname:

Secretary: Alf Levy **(T)** 01322 526 159 **(E)** alf_levy@sky.com
Chairman: **Manager:** **Prog Ed:**
Ground: Phoenix Sports Ground, Mayplace Road East, Barnehurst, Kent DA7 6JT **(T)** 01322 526159 **Capacity:**
Colours(change): Green/black/black (All red)

ADDITIONAL INFORMATION:
Previous Lge: Kent County > 2011.

RUSTHALL
Founded: 1890 Nickname:

Secretary: Alan Hawkins **(T)** 01892 532 212 **(E)** hawkins48@btinternet.com
Chairman: **Manager:** **Prog Ed:**
Ground: Jockey Farm, Nellington Road, Rusthall, Tunbridge Wells, Kent TN4 8SH **(T)** 07865 396 299 **Capacity:**
Colours(change): Green & white stripes/green/green (Blue & black/black/black)

ADDITIONAL INFORMATION:
Previous Lge: Kent County > 2011.

SEVEN ACRE & SIDCUP
Founded: 1900 Nickname:

Secretary: Lee Hill **(T)** 07834 583 395 **(E)** ch1964@tiscali.co.uk
Chairman: **Manager:** **Prog Ed:**
Ground: Sidcup & District Conservative Club, Oxford Road, Sidcup, Kent, DA14 6LW. **(T)** 020 8300 2987 **Capacity:**
Colours(change): Red & black/black/black (Green/black/black)

ADDITIONAL INFORMATION:
Previous Lge: Kent County > 2011.

SUTTON UNITED (KENT)

Founded: 1898 Nickname:

Secretary: Peter Johnson **(T)** 07803 984 838 **(E)** pwjohnson.ltd@btinternet.com
Chairman: **Manager:** **Prog Ed:**
Ground: The Roaches Rec. Ground, Parsonage Lane, Sutton-at-Hone, Dartford, DA4 9HD **(T)** 07788 446495 **Capacity:**
Colours(change): All green & white (All black & white)

ADDITIONAL INFORMATION:
Previous Lge: Kent County > 2011.

WOODSTOCK PARK

Founded: 1970 Nickname:

Secretary: David Brown **(T)** 07795 465 384 **(E)** secretary@woodstockparkfc.co.uk
Chairman: **Manager:** **Prog Ed:**
Ground: W.E.Manin Ltd. Stadium, Woodstock Park, Broadoak Road, Sittingbourne ME9 8HL **(T)** 01795 410777 **Capacity:**
Colours(change): All navy blue (All red)

ADDITIONAL INFORMATION:
Previous Lge: Kent County > 2011.

Soccer Books Limited

72 ST. PETERS AVENUE (Dept. NLD)
CLEETHORPES
N.E. LINCOLNSHIRE
DN35 8HU
ENGLAND

Tel. 01472 696226 Fax 01472 698546

Web site www.soccer-books.co.uk
e-mail info@soccer-books.co.uk

Established in 1982, Soccer Books Limited has one of the largest ranges of English-Language soccer books available. We continue to expand our stocks even further to include many new titles including German, French, Spanish, Italian and other foreign-language books.

With well over 100,000 satisfied customers already, we supply books to virtually every country in the world but have maintained the friendliness and accessibility associated with a small family-run business. The range of titles we sell includes:

YEARBOOKS – All major yearbooks including many editions of the Sky Sports Football Yearbook (previously Rothmans), Supporters' Guides, Playfair Annuals, European Football Yearbooks and Asian, African and North, Central and South American yearbooks.

CLUB HISTORIES – Complete Statistical Records, Official Histories, Definitive Histories plus many more.

WORLD FOOTBALL – World Cup books, International Line-up & Statistics Series, European Championships History, International and European Club Cup competition Statistical Histories and much more.

BIOGRAPHIES & WHO'S WHOS – of managers and players plus Who's Whos etc.

ENCYCLOPEDIAS & GENERAL TITLES – Books on stadia, hooligan and sociological studies, histories and hundreds of others, including the weird and wonderful!

DVDs – Season's highlights, histories, big games, World Cup matches, player profiles, a selection of over 40 F.A. Cup Finals with many more titles becoming available all the time.

For a current printed listing containing a selection of our titles, please contact us using the details at the top of this page. Alternatively, our web site offers a secure ordering system for credit and debit card holders and lists our full range of over 1,900 books and 400 DVDs.

KENT LEAGUE

Sponsored by: Hurlimann
Founded: 1966
Recent Champions:
2006: Maidstone United
2007: Whitstable Town
2008: Thamesmead Town
2009: VCD Athletic
2010: Faversham Town
kentleague.com

PREMIER DIVISION	P	W	D	L	F	A	Pts
1 Hythe Town	30	21	5	4	82	33	68
2 Herne Bay	30	20	8	2	64	30	68
3 VCD Athletic	30	13	13	4	51	33	52
4 Greenwich Borough	30	16	2	12	65	42	50
5 Erith & Belvedere	30	14	7	9	60	40	49
6 Tunbridge Wells	30	13	6	11	64	48	45
7 Sevenoaks Town	30	14	3	13	45	50	45
8 Erith Town	30	11	9	10	54	44	42
9 Norton Sports	30	10	10	10	52	64	40
10 Beckenham Town	30	12	3	15	56	55	39
11 Deal Town	30	10	5	15	39	52	35
12 Corinthian	30	10	5	15	38	59	35
13 Lordswood	30	9	7	14	41	50	34
14 Holmesdale	30	5	8	17	33	54	23
15 Sporting Bengal United	30	6	5	19	39	92	23
16 Fisher	30	6	4	20	30	67	22

PREMIER DIVISION CUP

ROUND 1 (2 LEGS)
Corinthian 0-0 Deal Town
Deal Town 1-3 Corinthian
Corinthian win 3-1 on aggregate
Herne Bay 4-0 Sporting Bengal United
Sporting Bengal United 1-1 Herne Bay
Herne Bay won 5-1 on aggregate
Erith & Belvedere 1-1 Holmesdale
Holmesdale removed - second leg not played
Erith Town 2-3 Norton Sports
Norton Sports 3-1 Erith Town
Norton Sports won 6-3 on aggregate
Beckenham Town 4-0 Fisher
Fisher 1-5 Beckenham Town
Beckenham Town won 9-1 on aggregate
Lordswood 2-0 Hythe Town
Lordswood removed - second leg not played
Greenwich Borough 1-2 VCD Athletic
VCD Athletic 2-1 Greenwich Borough
VCD Athletic won 4-3 on aggregate
Sevenoaks Town 0-1 Tunbridge Wells
Tunbridge Wells 1-5 Sevenoaks Town
Sevenoaks Town won 5-2 on aggregate

QUARTER FINALS (2 LEGS)
Corinthian 1-2 (Beckenham Town
Bechenham Town 0-2 Corinthian
Corinthian won 3-2 on aggregate
Herne Bay 2-0 Norton Sports
Norton Sports 2-3 Herne Bay
Herne Bay won 5-2 on aggregate
Sevenoaks Town 2-2 Hythe Town
Hythe Town 2-1 Sevenoak Town
Hythe Town won 4-3 on aggregate
VCD Athletic 1-1 Erith & Belvedere
Erith & Belvedere 0-2 VCD Athletic
VCD Athletic won 3-1 on aggregate

SEMI-FINALS (2 LEGS)
Herne Bay 1-0 Corinthian
Corinthian 0-2 Herne bay
Herne Bay won 3-0 on aggregate
Hythe Town 2-1 VCD Athletic
VCD Athletic 1-5 Hythe Town
Hythe Town won 7-2 on aggregate

FINAL (@ Folkestone Invicta, 7/5/11)
Herne Bay 3-2 Hythe Town

PREMIER DIVISION	1	2	3	4	5	6	7	8	9	10	11	12	13	14	15	16
1 Beckenham Town		6-0	1-2	3-2	2-0	1-2	1-0	1-2	4-0	0-2	0-2	6-4	2-3	2-5	2-4	0-0
2 Corinthian	4-2		1-0	2-1	1-1	0-2	2-5	0-2	2-1	1-7	4-1	2-2	0-1	2-0	2-0	1-1
3 Deal Town	1-0	1-2		1-1	2-0	0-1	0-3	0-2	1-1	0-3	1-0	0-2	4-2	1-0	3-4	1-1
4 Erith & Belvedere	2-0	3-0	4-2		0-3	3-1	2-1	2-2	0-2	1-4	7-2	4-0	1-2	1-1	1-1	1-1
5 Erith Town	0-1	3-3	4-0	0-2		2-0	2-1	4-1	2-0	0-2	2-2	1-1	2-0	9-0	0-0	2-2
6 Fisher	2-4	0-2	3-3	1-0	2-4		1-3	0-3	1-2	0-2	1-0	1-1	0-1	1-3	0-5	2-1
7 Greenwich Borough	2-1	2-0	0-1	2-3	2-1	5-1		1-1	1-0	1-2	2-1	4-0	1-2	8-0	3-2	3-2
8 Herne Bay	2-0	1-0	3-1	1-2	4-0	2-1	3-1		2-1	0-0	3-1	1-1	2-1	2-0	5-0	2-2
9 Holmesdale	2-2	1-1	0-1	1-2	2-0	1-1	1-2	1-1		2-2	3-1	3-0	2-3	1-1	0-3	1-4
10 Hythe Town	6-2	1-0	1-2	2-1	3-0	1-0	2-0	2-2	3-2		3-4	4-2	2-1	8-0	3-1	1-1
11 Lordswood	0-2	2-0	1-1	0-1	1-1	2-0	2-2	2-2	2-0	0-3		1-1	2-1	0-1	3-0	1-3
12 Norton Sports	0-1	1-0	4-3	0-7	3-3	2-2	3-2	1-2	2-1	3-1	1-3		3-0	6-2	0-4	2-2
13 Sevenoaks Town	2-4	2-0	2-1	1-4	2-1	2-0	3-1	2-4	2-0	0-4	0-2	2-2		2-2	4-1	0-1
14 Sporting Bengal United	3-6	2-3	0-4	1-1	2-3	4-3	0-5	1-3	4-1	2-4	2-1	0-2	0-1		1-1	0-1
15 Tunbridge Wells	0-0	4-0	3-2	2-0	3-4	7-1	0-2	0-1	3-0	2-2	2-2	0-1	2-1	7-1		0-3
16 V C D Athletic	1-0	4-3	3-0	1-1	0-0	1-0	3-0	2-3	1-1	3-2	1-0	2-2	0-0	3-1	1-3	

KENT LEAGUE - STEP 5

DIVISION ONE		P	W	D	L	F	A	Pts
1	Cray Wanderers reserves	16	10	3	3	59	19	33
2	Whitstable Town res	16	7	3	6	36	37	24
3	Maidstone United res	16	6	5	5	34	40	23
4	Erith Town reserves	16	6	4	6	29	25	22
5	Herne Bay reserves	16	6	4	6	34	34	22
6	Thamesmead Town res	16	6	4	6	25	31	22
7	Chatham Town reserves	16	5	4	7	26	29	19
8	Margate reserves	16	4	6	6	30	41	18
9	Erith & Belvedere res	16	4	3	9	19	36	15
	Beckenham Town reserves - record expunged							

DIVISION TWO		P	W	D	L	F	A	Pts
1	Faversham Town res	18	15	3	0	58	16	48
2	Deal Town reserves	18	15	2	1	50	11	47
3	Holmesdale reserves	18	6	6	6	24	38	24
4	Lordswood reserves	18	6	4	8	31	40	22
5	Sevenoaks Town res	18	6	3	9	33	36	21
6	Ramsgate reserves	18	6	3	9	39	45	21
7	Greenwich Borough res	18	6	2	10	25	40	20
8	VCD Athletic reserves	18	5	4	9	31	35	19
9	Hythe Town reserves	18	4	4	10	28	39	16
10	Folkestone Invicta res	18	4	3	11	30	49	15

DIVISION ONE/TWO CUP

FINAL (@ Corinthian, 2/5/11)
Cray Wanderers reserves 3-1 Erith & Belvedere reserves

FLOODLIGHT TROPHY		P	W	D	L	F	A	Pts
1	Whitstable Town	14	10	2	2	31	19	32
2	Faversham Town	14	8	1	5	35	21	25
3	Herne Bay	14	6	4	4	31	18	22
4	Deal Town	14	6	4	4	25	27	22
5	Ramsgate	14	5	4	5	27	31	19
6	Chatham Town	14	5	1	8	24	30	16
7	VCD Athletic	14	4	2	8	19	31	14
8	Lordswood	14	0	6	8	17	32	6

Corinthian FC. Photo: Alan Coomes.

KENT LEAGUE INS & OUTS

PREM - IN: Canterbury City (P - Kent County League Premier Division),

Cray Valley Paper Mills (P - Kent County League Premier Division)

OUT: Hythe Town (P - Isthmian League Division One South), Sporting Bengal United (S - Essex Senior League)

Norton Sports become Woodstock Sports

BECKENHAM TOWN

Founded: 1887 Nickname: Reds

Secretary: Peter Palmer **(T)** 07774 728 758 **(E)** peterpalmer3@sky.com
Chairman: TBC **Manager:** Jason Huntley **Prog Ed:** Sam Percival
Ground: Eden Park Avenue, Beckenham Kent BR3 1JT **(T)** 07774 728 758
Capacity: 4,000 **Seats:** 120 **Covered:** 120 **Midweek Matchday:** Tuesday **Clubhouse:** Yes **Shop:** Yes

Colours(change): Red/red. (White/blue).
Previous Names: Stanhope Rovers.
Previous Leagues: South East London Amateur. Metropolitan. London Spartan.
Records: **Att:** 720 v Berkhamsted, FA Cup 1994-95. **Goalscorer:** Ricky Bennett. **Apps:** Lee Fabian - 985.
Senior Honours:

10 YEAR RECORD

01-02	02-03	03-04	04-05	05-06	06-07	07-08	08-09	09-10	10-11
Kent P 9	Kent P 10	Kent P 12	Kent P 10	Kent P 2	Kent P 11	Kent P 3	Kent P 15	Kent P 4	Kent P 10

CANTERBURY CITY

Founded: 1904 Nickname:

Secretary: Keith Vaughan **(T)** 07784 671 502 **(E)** keith.vaughan3@btinternet.com
Chairman: Tim Clarke **Manager:** Paul Murray **Prog Ed:** John Fabre
Ground: Herne Bay FC, Winch's Field, Standley Gardens, Heren Bay CT6 5SG **(T)**
Capacity: 3,000 **Seats:** 200 **Covered:** 1,500 **Midweek Matchday:** Tuesday **Clubhouse:** Yes **Shop:** Yes

Colours(change): Burgundy/white/burgundy (Green/white/green)
Previous Names:
Previous Leagues: Kent 1947-59, 94-01, Metropolitan 1959-60, Southern 1960-61, 94, Kent County 2007-11.
Records:
Senior Honours: Kent County League Division One East 2007-08, 08-09.

10 YEAR RECORD

01-02	02-03	03-04	04-05	05-06	06-07	07-08	08-09	09-10	10-11
						KC1E 1	KC1E 1	KC P 5	KC P 2

CORINTHIAN

Founded: 1972 Nickname:

Secretary: Sue Billings **(T)** 07734 855 554 **(E)** corinthians@billingsgroup.com
Chairman: R J Billings **Manager:** Tony Stitford **Prog Ed:**
Ground: Gay Dawn Farm, Valley Road, Longfield DA3 8LY **(T)** 01474 573 118
Capacity: **Seats:** **Covered:** **Midweek Matchday:** Tuesday **Clubhouse:** Yes **Shop:**

Colours(change): Green & white hoops/white (Yellow/green)
Previous Names: Welling United Reserves > 2009.
Previous Leagues: Southern 1985-91.
Records:
Senior Honours:

10 YEAR RECORD

01-02	02-03	03-04	04-05	05-06	06-07	07-08	08-09	09-10	10-11
							Kent 2 6	Kent P 14	Kent P 12

CRAY VALLEY PAPER MILLS

Founded: Nickname:

Secretary: Dave Wilson **(T)** 07715 961 886 **(E)** wilson433@ntlworld.com
Chairman: Doug Francis **Manager:** Steve Chapman **Prog Ed:** Doug Francis
Ground: Badgers Sports, Middle Park Avenue, Eltham SE9 5HT **(T)**
Capacity: **Seats:** **Covered:** **Midweek Matchday:** **Clubhouse:** **Shop:**

Colours(change): Green/black/black (Sky blue/white/white).
Previous Names:
Previous Leagues: Spartan 1991-97, Spartan South Midlands 1997-98, London Intermediate 1998-01, Kent County 2001-11.
Records:
Senior Honours: Kent County League Premier Division 2004-05.

10 YEAR RECORD

01-02	02-03	03-04	04-05	05-06	06-07	07-08	08-09	09-10	10-11
			KC P 1		KC P 7	KC P 9	KC P 5	KC P 6	KC P 3

DEAL TOWN

Founded: 1908 Nickname: Town

Secretary: Michelle Finn **(T)** 01304 375 574 **(E)**

Chairman: David Reid **Manager:** Derek Hares **Prog Ed:** Colin Adams

Ground: Charles Sports Ground, St Leonards Road, Deal. CT14 9BB **(T)** 01304 375 623

Capacity: 2,500 **Seats:** 180 **Covered:** 180 **Midweek Matchday:** Tuesday **Clubhouse:** Yes **Shop:** Yes

Colours(change): Black & white/black. (Blue/blue).
Previous Names: Deal Cinque Ports FC > 1920
Previous Leagues: Thanet. East Kent. Kent. Aetolian. Southern. Greater London.
Records: **Att:** 2,495 v Newcastle Town, FA Vase S-F, 26.03.2000.
Senior Honours:

10 YEAR RECORD

01-02	02-03	03-04	04-05	05-06	06-07	07-08	08-09	09-10	10-11
Kent P 3	Kent P 4	Kent P 16	Kent P 13	Kent P 9	Kent P 8	Kent P 9	Kent P 12	Kent P 9	Kent P 11

ERITH & BELVEDERE

Founded: 1922 Nickname: Deres

Secretary: Frank May **(T)** 07778 987 579 **(E)** frank.may@erithandbelvederefc.co.uk

Chairman: John McFadden **Manager:** Micky Collins **Prog Ed:** Martin Tarrant/Brian Spurrel

Ground: Welling FC, Park View Rd, Welling, DA16 1SY **(T)** 020 8304 0333

Capacity: 4,000 **Seats:** 1,070 **Covered:** 1,000 **Midweek Matchday:** Tuesday **Clubhouse:** Yes **Shop:** Yes

Colours(change): Blue & white quarters/blue. (Red & white quarters/red.
Previous Names: Belvedere & District FC (Formed 1918 restructured 1922)
Previous Leagues: Kent. London. Corinthian. Athenian. Southern.
Records: **Att:** 5,573 v Crook C.W., FA Am. Cup 1949. **Goalscorer:** Colin Johnson - 284 (61-71). **Apps:** Dennis Crawford - 504 (56-71).
Senior Honours:

10 YEAR RECORD

01-02	02-03	03-04	04-05	05-06	06-07	07-08	08-09	09-10	10-11
SthE 9	SthE 18	SthE 21	SthE 21	Kent P 4	Kent P 7	Kent P 7	Kent P 8	Kent P 12	Kent P 5

ERITH TOWN

Founded: 1959 Nickname: The Dockers

Secretary: Jim Davie **(T)** 07780 712 149 **(E)**

Chairman: Albert Putman **Manager:** Tony Russell **Prog Ed:** Ian Birrell

Ground: Erith Sports Stadium, Avenue Road, Erith DA8 3AT **(T)** 01322 350 271

Capacity: 1,450 **Seats:** 1,006 **Covered:** 1,066 **Midweek Matchday:** Monday **Clubhouse:** Yes **Shop:** No

Colours(change): Red & black/black. (Yellow/white).
Previous Names: Woolwich Town 1959-89 and 1990-97.
Previous Leagues: London Metropolitan Sunday. London Spartan.
Records: **Att:** 325 v Charlton Athletic, friendly. **Goalscorer:** Dean Bowey.
Senior Honours:

10 YEAR RECORD

01-02	02-03	03-04	04-05	05-06	06-07	07-08	08-09	09-10	10-11
Kent P 13	Kent P 15	Kent P 7	Kent P 15	Kent P 14	Kent P 14	Kent P 5	Kent P 7	Kent P 12	Kent P 8

FISHER

Founded: 1908 Nickname: The Fish

Secretary: Dan York **(T)** 07719 632 635 **(E)** dan@fisherfc.co.uk

Chairman: Ben Westmancott **Manager:** Steve Firkins **Prog Ed:** Jevon Hall

Ground: Dulwich Hamlet FC, Edgar Kail Way, East Dulwich SE22 8BD **(T)**

Capacity: 3,000 **Seats:** 500 **Covered:** 1,000 **Midweek Matchday:** Monday **Clubhouse:** Yes **Shop:** Yes

Colours(change): Black & white/white/white. (Blue/black/red).
Previous Names: Fisher Athletic. Reformed as Fisher F.C. in 2009.
Previous Leagues: Parthenon, Kent Amateur, London Spartan, Southern, Isthmian, Conference.
Records: **Att:** 4,283 v Barnet Conference 04/05/1991. **Goalscorer:** Paul Shinners - 205. **Apps:** Dennis Sharp - 720.
Senior Honours: Southern League Southern Division 1982-83, Premier 86-87, Eastern 2004-05. Kent Senior Cup 1983-84. Isthmian League Cup 2005-06.

10 YEAR RECORD

01-02	02-03	03-04	04-05	05-06	06-07	07-08	08-09	09-10	10-11
SthE 6	SthE 14	SthE 14	SthE 1	Isth P 3	Conf S 10	Conf S 4	Conf S 22	Kent P 13	Kent P 16

GREENWICH BOROUGH

Founded: 1928 Nickname: Boro

Secretary: TBC **(T)** **(E)**

Chairman: Devon Hanson **Manager:** TBC **Prog Ed:** TBC

Ground: Holmesdale FC, 68 Oakley Road, Bromley, Kent BR2 8HQ **(T)**

Capacity: **Seats:** **Covered:** **Midweek Matchday:** Tuesday **Clubhouse:** Yes **Shop:** No

Colours(change): All red. (All blue).
Previous Names: Woolwich Borough Council Athletic FC.
Previous Leagues: South London Alliance. Kent Amateur. London Spartan.
Records: **Att:** 2,000 v Charlton Athletic, turning on of floodlights, 1978.
Senior Honours: Kent League 86-87, 87-88.

10 YEAR RECORD

01-02	02-03	03-04	04-05	05-06	06-07	07-08	08-09	09-10	10-11
Kent P 15	Kent P 14	Kent P 8	Kent P 9	Kent P 13	Kent P 5	Kent P 8	Kent P 3	Kent P 5	Kent P 4

HERNE BAY

Founded: 1886 Nickname: The Bay

Secretary: John Bathurst **(T)** 07788 718 745 **(E)** johnbhbfc@aol.com

Chairman: Trevor Kennett **Manager:** Simon Halsey **Prog Ed:** John Bathurst

Ground: Safety Net Stadium, Winch's Field, Stanley Gardens, Herne Bay CT6 5SG **(T)** 01227 374 156

Capacity: 3,000 **Seats:** 200 **Covered:** 1,500 **Midweek Matchday:** Wednesday **Clubhouse:** Yes **Shop:** Yes

Colours(change): Blue & white strips/blue (Yellow/black/black)
Previous Names: None.
Previous Leagues: East Kent. Faversham & Dist. Cantebury & Dist. Kent Am. Athenian.
Records: **Att:** 2,303 v Margate, FA Cup 4th Qual. 1970-71.
Senior Honours:

10 YEAR RECORD

01-02	02-03	03-04	04-05	05-06	06-07	07-08	08-09	09-10	10-11
Kent P 7	Kent P 11	Kent P 10	Kent P 2	Kent P 7	Kent P 9	Kent P 6	Kent P 6	Kent P 2	Kent P 2

HOLMESDALE

Founded: 1956 Nickname:

Secretary: Ross Mitchell **(T)** **(E)** secretary@holmesdalefc.co.uk

Chairman: Mark Harris **Manager:** Gary Davies **Prog Ed:** TBC

Ground: Holmesdale Sp.& Soc.Club, 68 Oakley Rd, Bromley BR2 8HQ **(T)** 020 8462 4440

Capacity: **Seats:** **Covered:** **Midweek Matchday:** Tuesday **Clubhouse:** Yes **Shop:** Yes

Colours(change): Green & yellow/green. (All blue).
Previous Names: None.
Previous Leagues: Thornton Heath & Dist. Surrey Inter. Surrey South Eastern. Kent County.
Records: **Goals:** M Barnett - 410 (in 429 apps).
Senior Honours:

10 YEAR RECORD

01-02	02-03	03-04	04-05	05-06	06-07	07-08	08-09	09-10	10-11
	KC1W 4	KC1W 4	KC1W 8	KC1W 1	KC P 1	Kent P 15	Kent P 5	Kent P 10	Kent P 14

LORDSWOOD

Founded: 1968 Nickname: Lords

Secretary: Steve Lewis **(T)** 07902 107 769 **(E)** slew1953@hotmail.co.uk

Chairman: Ron Constantine **Manager:** Jason Lillis **Prog Ed:** Darell Harman

Ground: Martyn Grove, Northdane Way, Walderslade, ME5 8YE **(T)** 01634 669 138

Capacity: 600 **Seats:** 123 **Covered:** 123 **Midweek Matchday:** Tuesday **Clubhouse:** Yes **Shop:** No

Colours(change): Orange & black/black. (Blue & white/blue).
Previous Names: None.
Previous Leagues: Rochester & Dist. Kent County.
Records:
Senior Honours:

10 YEAR RECORD

01-02	02-03	03-04	04-05	05-06	06-07	07-08	08-09	09-10	10-11
Kent P 11	Kent P 13	Kent P 13	Kent P 16	Kent P 8	Kent P 13	Kent P 16	Kent P 16	Kent P 16	Kent P 13

SEVENOAKS TOWN

Founded: 1883 Nickname: Town

Secretary: Eddie Diplock **(T)** 01732 454 280 **(E)** suesmart53@hotmail.co.uk
Chairman: Tony Smart **Manager:** Darren Anslow **Prog Ed:** Vacant
Ground: Greatness Park, Seal Road, Sevenoaks TN14 5BL **(T)** 01732 741 987
Capacity: 2,000 **Seats:** 110 **Covered:** 200 **Midweek Matchday:** Tuesday **Clubhouse:** **Shop:**

Colours(change): Blue stripes/navy. (Green & white/white).
Previous Names: None.
Previous Leagues: Sevenoaks League. Kent Amateur/County.
Records:
Senior Honours:

10 YEAR RECORD

01-02	02-03	03-04	04-05	05-06	06-07	07-08	08-09	09-10	10-11
KC P 2	KC P 1	Kent P 11	Kent P 11	Kent P 16	Kent P 10	Kent P 11	Kent P 14	Kent P 6	Kent P 7

TUNBRIDGE WELLS

Founded: 1886 Nickname: The Wells

Secretary: Phill Allcorn **(T)** 07900 243 508 **(E)** secretary@twfcexec.com
Chairman: Joe Croker **Manager:** Martin Larkin **Prog Ed:** TBC
Ground: Culverden Stadium, Culverden Down, Tunbridge Wells TN4 9SG **(T)** 01892 520 517
Capacity: 3,750 **Seats:** 250 **Covered:** 1,000 **Midweek Matchday:** Tuesday **Clubhouse:** Yes **Shop:** No

Colours(change): Red/red (Blue/blue)
Previous Names: None.
Previous Leagues: Isthminan. London Spartan.
Records: **Att:** 967 v Maidstone United, FA Cup 1969. **Goalscorer:** John Wingate - 151. **Apps:** Tony Atkins - 410.
Senior Honours:

10 YEAR RECORD

01-02	02-03	03-04	04-05	05-06	06-07	07-08	08-09	09-10	10-11
Kent P 8	Kent P 12	Kent P 14	Kent P 7	Kent P 10	Kent P 15	Kent P 10	Kent P 10	Kent P 7	Kent P 6

VICKERS CRAYFORD DARTFORD ATHLETIC

Founded: 1916 Nickname: The Vickers

Secretary: Debbie Rump **(T)** **(E)** debbierump@talktalk.net
Chairman: Gary Rump **Manager:** Ricky Bennett **Prog Ed:**
Ground: VCD Athletic Club, Old Road, Crayford DA1 4DN **(T)** 01322 524 262
Capacity: **Seats:** Yes **Covered:** Yes **Midweek Matchday:** Tuesday **Clubhouse:** Yes **Shop:** No

Colours(change): Green & white/white (Blue/black)
Previous Names: Vickers (Erith). Vickers (Crayford)
Previous Leagues: Dartford & District. Kent County. Isthmian
Records:
Senior Honours:

10 YEAR RECORD

01-02	02-03	03-04	04-05	05-06	06-07	07-08	08-09	09-10	10-11
Kent P 2	Kent P 7	Kent P 3	Kent P 5	Kent P 6	Kent P 2	Kent P 2	Kent P 1	Isth1N 8	Kent P 3

WOODSTOCK SPORTS

Founded: 1927 Nickname:

Secretary: Colin Page **(T)** 07970 549 355 **(E)** c_page@blueyonder.co.uk
Chairman: R Welling **Manager:** Ben Taylor **Prog Ed:** TBC
Ground: Herne Bay FC, Winch's Field, Herne Bay CT6 5SG **(T)** 01227 374 156
Capacity: 3,000 **Seats:** 200 **Covered:** 1,500 **Midweek Matchday:** Tuesday **Clubhouse:** Yes **Shop:** Yes

Colours(change): Blue & white/black. (All red).
Previous Names: Amalgamated with Teynham & Lynsted in 1998, Norton Sports 1998-2011.
Previous Leagues: Kent County.
Records:
Senior Honours:

10 YEAR RECORD

01-02	02-03	03-04	04-05	05-06	06-07	07-08	08-09	09-10	10-11
			KC1E 1		KC P 3	KC P 1	Kent P 11	Kent P 11	Kent P 9

MIDLAND COMBINATION

Sponsored by: Athium Limited
Founded: 1927
Recent Champions:
2006: Atherstone Town
2007: Coventry Sphinx
2008: Coleshill Town
2009: Loughborough University
2010: Heath Hayes
midcomb.com

PREMIER DIVISION	P	W	D	L	F	A	Pts
1 Heather St. John's	36	25	6	5	112	34	81
2 Nuneaton Griff (-3)	36	22	7	7	93	50	70
3 Castle Vale	36	19	10	7	67	38	67
4 Coventry Copsewood	36	21	4	11	75	49	67
5 Dosthill Colts	36	19	6	11	63	52	63
6 Cadbury Athletic	36	17	9	10	61	40	60
7 Bolehall Swifts	36	18	5	13	56	43	59
8 Brocton	36	18	4	14	80	53	58
9 Walsall Wood	36	16	10	10	42	33	58
10 Southam United	36	14	10	12	43	33	52
11 Continental Star	36	14	8	14	58	52	50
12 Bartley Green	36	12	10	14	66	76	46
13 Pershore Town	36	10	9	17	47	64	39
14 Castle Vale JKS	36	11	5	20	62	86	38
15 Pilkington XXX	36	7	12	17	53	80	33
16 Massey Ferguson	36	8	9	19	51	93	33
17 Pelsall Villa	36	10	1	25	34	80	31
18 Alveston	36	8	3	25	41	110	27
19 Racing Club Warwick (-1)	36	4	10	22	45	83	21

TONY ALLDEN MEMORIAL CUP

(@ Heath Hayes, 30/7/11)
Heath Hayes 0-5 Heather St Johns

LES JAMES MEMORIAL CHALLENGE CUP

PRELIMINARY ROUND
Leamington Hibernian 0-4 Feckenham
JDG Alliance 0-9 Polesworth
Greenhill 0-1 Chelmsley Town
Blackwood 9-1 Future Legends
Young Warriors 1-3 Hampton
Burntwood Town 4-1 Lichfield City
Bromsgrove Sporting 2-0 Stretton Eagles
Aston 3-2 Perrywood
Inkberrow 1-3 Enville Athletic
Coventry Amateurs 1-2 Clements 83
Kenilworth Town KH 1-3 Henley Forest

ROUND 1
Droitwich Spa w/o-scr Brereton Social
Archdale 73 3-2 Northfield Town
Enville Athletic 1-2 Coton Green
Littleton 4-2 West Midlands Police
Bromsgrove Sporting 1-2 Chelmsley Town
Phoenix United 0-1 Aston
Feckenham 2-0 Burntwood Town
Fairfield Villa 3-1 Henley Forest
Blackwood 3-4 Polesworth
Hampton 3-1 FC Glades Sporting
Clements 83 0-1 Shirley Town

ROUND 2
Knowle 1-3 Dosthill Colts
Castle Vale JKS 1-3 Heather St Johns
Southam United 2-1 Bolehall Swifts
Pelsall Villa 4-0 Alveston
Chelmsley Town 0-2 Poleworth
Pershore Town 0-1 Littleton
Castle Vale 1-0 Brocton
Aston 5-0 Shirley Town
Fairfield Villa 1-1 Walsall Wood
(Fairfield Villa won 3-1 on aggregate)
Racing Club Warwick 2-5 Massey Ferguson
Cadbury Athletic 2-1 Nuneaton Griff
Earlswood Town 2-1 Droitwich Spa
Pilkington XXX 1-6 Coventry Copsewood
Archdale 73 1-4 Coton Green
Continental Star 2-1 Hampton
Feckenham 1-4 Bartley Green

PREMIER DIVISION	1	2	3	4	5	6	7	8	9	10	11	12	13	14	15	16	17	18	19
1 Alveston		1-2	2-1	0-3	0-6	0-2	1-2	1-4	0-1	1-3	1-4	0-5	0-7	1-0	0-1	3-2	4-3	0-3	1-3
2 Bartley Green	6-1		0-4	5-0	1-3	1-2	2-2	2-1	1-2	4-3	0-4	0-0	4-1	1-3	1-2	2-2	2-2	3-1	0-0
3 Bolehall Swifts	2-1	2-2		2-0	3-1	0-2	3-2	2-1	2-2	0-1	2-0	0-1	0-4	6-1	1-0	3-1	0-3	0-0	2-1
4 Brocton	5-0	2-3	0-1		0-1	4-1	10-2	3-3	4-3	2-4	3-3	6-1	1-2	1-2	1-0	1-2	7-0	1-0	0-0
5 Cadbury Athletic	4-0	1-1	2-0	1-1		3-0	3-0	0-4	1-3	2-2	0-2	2-2	1-2	2-0	2-0	1-0	6-2	0-0	0-2
6 Castle Vale	2-2	2-2	1-0	1-0	2-2		2-0	0-1	2-2	4-1	2-0	2-0	3-3	1-2	0-0	4-1	0-0	0-1	3-2
7 Castle Vale J K S	2-4	3-4	1-3	2-0	0-2	0-3		2-2	2-1	2-3	1-6	1-2	1-3	3-1	2-1	2-0	3-0	0-2	1-2
8 Continental Star	2-1	4-2	1-0	0-1	2-3	1-4	2-0		2-2	3-2	1-2	4-0	2-3	0-1	1-0	2-3	2-1	1-0	0-0
9 Coventry Copsewood	0-2	4-1	0-1	2-3	2-0	1-3	3-1	4-1		2-0	3-1	3-2	0-2	1-1	5-3	4-0	3-2	2-0	2-0
10 Dosthill Colts	3-1	6-1	0-3	0-2	3-2	1-1	2-4	0-1	3-2		1-0	2-1	1-1	0-1	4-2	0-2	1-0	3-1	1-1
11 Heather St Johns	8-0	3-2	3-1	5-0	1-0	1-1	5-1	1-1	5-2	2-0		6-0	3-0	6-1	0-0	2-2	4-0	2-0	2-0
12 Massey-Ferguson	1-3	1-1	3-2	0-3	2-2	1-5	0-7	4-2	0-1	2-3	0-3		0-6	1-3	5-2	2-2	1-1	0-1	6-1
13 Nuneaton Griff	7-1	7-1	1-3	2-1	2-0	1-1	3-2	2-1	2-1	0-1	1-9	7-1		1-2	1-1	1-1	2-1	1-1	0-0
14 Pelsall Villa	3-4	0-2	0-1	0-3	0-1	0-3	0-2	0-3	0-1	0-2	1-3	4-0	0-6		0-6	1-2	2-1	1-0	0-1
15 Pershore Town	2-0	1-3	1-1	0-5	1-1	0-2	1-4	2-0	1-2	1-3	0-5	4-1	1-2	2-1		1-1	2-2	1-0	1-1
16 Pilkington X X X	2-2	2-1	1-1	2-3	0-2	0-5	3-3	1-1	0-2	0-1	2-6	2-4	3-2	4-2	3-3		4-4	1-1	1-2
17 Racing Club Warwick	4-0	2-3	0-3	1-2	0-3	0-1	2-2	1-1	0-6	0-0	2-4	1-1	1-3	5-1	1-3	2-1		0-2	0-0
18 Southam United	3-3	0-0	2-0	2-1	0-0	2-0	5-0	0-0	0-1	1-1	2-0	1-1	0-3	3-0	0-1	3-0	2-1		2-4
19 Walsall Wood	2-0	2-0	2-1	0-1	0-1	3-0	0-0	2-1	1-0	0-2	1-1	0-0	1-2	1-0	3-0	1-0	2-0	1-2	

MIDLAND COMBINATION - STEP 6/7

DIVISION ONE		P	W	D	L	F	A	Pts
1	Earlswood Town	30	23	5	2	112	25	74
2	Knowle	30	21	4	5	82	30	67
3	Stretton Eagles	30	19	3	8	82	40	60
4	Fairfield Villa	30	19	1	10	59	42	58
5	Littleton	30	16	5	9	74	44	53
6	Shirley Town	30	14	6	10	71	58	48
7	FC Glades Sporting	30	15	3	12	64	66	48
8	Droitwich Spa	30	12	7	11	59	53	43
9	Kenilworth Town KH	30	13	4	13	67	62	43
10	Hampton	30	11	5	14	54	52	38
11	Northfield Town	30	10	7	13	52	60	37
12	West Midlands Police	30	8	8	14	56	80	32
13	Archdale '73	30	8	6	16	52	77	30
14	Coton Green	30	4	12	14	46	58	24
15	Phoenix United	30	5	5	20	40	78	20
16	Burntwood Town	30	0	3	27	19	164	3

Brereton Social - record expunged

PRESIDENT'S CUP

ROUND 1
Burntwood 0-2 Hampton
ROUND 2
Shirley Town 3-4 West Midlands Police
Archdale 73 0-2 Knowle
Northfield Town 0-2 Kenilworth Town KH
Brereton Social scr-w/o Fairfield Villa
Earlswood Town 2-2 Littleton (Littleton won 4-3 on penalties)
Droitwich Spa 2-3 Hampton
Phoenix United 0-1 FC Glades Sporting
Coton Green 1-2 Stretton Eagles
QUARTER FINALS
Hampton 1-2 Littleton
Kenilworth Town KH 0-3 Knowle
Fairfield Villa 2-0 Stretton Eagles
FC Glades Sporting 5-1 West Midlands Police
SEMI-FINALS (2 LEGS)
Fairfield Villa 1-2 Littleton
Littleton 4-2 Fairfield Villa (Littleton won 6-3 on aggregate)
FC Glades Sporting 0-2 Knowle
Knowle 4-4 FC Glades Sporting
(Knowle won 6-4 on aggregate)
FINAL (@ Redditch United, 12/5/11)
Knowle 0-1 Littleton

LES JAMES MEMORIAL CHALLENGE CUP

CONTINUED
ROUND 3
Bartley Green 5-2 Polesworth
Continental Star 2-0 Coton Green
Castle Vale 4-0 Dosthill Colts
Earlswood Town 1-0 Pelsall Villa
Littleton 1-2 Coventry Copsewood
Fairfield Villa 1-0 Southam United
Massey Ferguson 4-6 Aston
Heather St Johns 2-1 Cadbury Athletic
QUARTER FINALS
Earlswood Town 2-0 Bartley Green
Continental Star 2-0 Aston
Coventry Copsewood 5-0 Fairfield Villa
Heather St Johns 1-2 Castle Vale
SEMI-FINALS (2 LEGS)
Earlswood Town 6-2 Continental Star
Continental Star 1-3 Earlswood Town (Earlswood Town won 9-3 on aggregate)
Castle Vale received a walkover against Coventry Copsewood
FINAL (@ Walsall, 9/5/11)
Castle Vale 4-1 Earlswood Town

CHALLENGE VASE

ROUND 1
Henley Forest 2-1 Bromsgrove Sporting
Young Warriors 2-1 Droitwich Spa reserves
Blackwood 5-1 Cadbury Athletic reserves
Clements 83 1-2 Lichfield City
Continental Star reserves 3-1 Leamington Hibernian
Enville Athletic 3-0 Greenhill
Chelmsley Town 2-3 Feckenham
Knowle reserves 1-5 Perrywood
QUARTER FINALS
Enville Athletic 1-2 Lichfield City
Feckenham 3-1 Henley Forest
Young Warriors 2-4 Continental Star reserves
Blackwood 4-4 Perrywood (Blackwood won on penalties)
SEMI-FINALS (2 LEGS)
Lichfield City 1-1 Blackwood
Blackwood 0-4 Lichfield City
(Lichfield City won 6-1 on aggregate)
Feckenham 2-3 Continental Star reserves
Continental Star reserves 1-1 Feckenham (Continental Star reserves won 4-3 on aggregate)
FINAL (@ Coleshill Town, 10/5/11)
Continental Star reserves 1-2 Lichfield City

DIVISION ONE	1	2	3	4	5	6	7	8	9	10	11	12	13	14	15	16
1 Archdale		3-1	2-2	0-0	0-3	1-3	0-1	1-2	1-4	2-8	1-2	3-0	3-2	2-3	1-3	3-1
2 Burntwood Town	2-2		1-2	0-9	0-22	0-1	2-8	0-7	2-3	0-6	0-6	1-9	1-1	1-2	0-4	1-1
3 Coton Green	1-1	7-0		2-2	0-2	0-1	3-0	1-2	3-3	0-2	2-4	1-1	3-3	2-2	1-1	1-3
4 Droitwich Spa	0-4	3-1	0-0		2-1	0-5	1-2	2-2	1-3	1-4	3-0	5-0	4-2	2-3	3-2	0-0
5 Earlswood Town	8-0	7-0	5-1	5-0		2-1	4-2	2-2	2-2	0-0	0-0	1-1	2-1	4-1	4-1	5-1
6 Fairfield Villa	3-1	5-1	2-1	1-0	2-4		2-0	1-0	3-5	1-0	3-4	1-1	4-2	0-2	3-2	3-1
7 FC Glades Sporting	5-2	2-1	0-3	1-3	0-4	1-0		4-1	1-0	0-2	3-2	0-0	5-2	5-3	1-3	3-3
8 Hampton	3-1	4-0	2-2	0-1	2-3	2-1	3-3		4-1	0-2	1-3	0-1	4-0	1-4	0-2	0-0
9 Kenilworth Town K H	0-1	6-2	2-1	5-0	2-1	1-3	2-3	2-3		2-1	1-2	3-2	1-1	2-3	0-1	1-7
10 Knowle	2-2	6-1	2-1	1-0	0-3	3-0	4-2	3-1	3-2		1-1	6-1	3-0	2-1	3-1	0-2
11 Littleton	4-0	6-0	2-0	1-1	1-2	3-1	1-2	1-2	1-3	2-4		2-0	2-1	1-1	1-2	9-1
12 Northfield Town	1-3	6-1	3-1	1-3	0-4	1-2	4-0	1-0	3-3	1-1	1-4		3-1	3-0	1-5	2-1
13 Phoenix United	2-1	8-0	1-1	1-7	1-2	0-2	2-5	3-0	0-4	0-2	0-2	2-1		0-3	0-5	0-0
14 Shirley Town	3-5	7-0	4-1	1-1	0-3	2-3	3-4	0-3	2-1	2-1	2-2	1-3	4-1		2-2	1-0
15 Stretton Eagles	4-2	7-0	2-0	1-2	1-4	0-2	3-0	3-2	4-0	0-2	3-1	4-0	4-0	2-2		4-0
16 West Midlands Police	4-4	4-0	3-3	4-3	1-3	2-0	3-1	4-1	1-3	1-8	3-4	1-1	0-3	1-7	3-6	

DIVISION TWO	P	W	D	L	F	A	Pts
1 Blackwood	30	23	4	3	81	21	73
2 Feckenham	30	21	2	7	73	36	65
3 Bromsgrove Sporting	30	20	4	6	82	27	64
4 Lichfield City	30	19	6	5	85	33	63
5 Henley Forest (-1)	30	17	5	8	75	44	55
6 Continental Star reserves	30	13	8	9	59	47	47
7 Young Warriors (-9)	30	15	5	10	81	62	41
8 Perrywood	30	11	6	13	39	58	39
9 Cadbury Athletic reserves	30	10	4	16	37	66	34
10 Leamington Hibernian	30	9	6	15	53	82	33
11 Chelmsley Town	30	9	4	17	42	61	31
12 Droitwich Spa reserves	30	6	9	15	46	68	27
13 Greenhill	30	7	6	17	29	72	27
14 Clements '83	30	8	2	20	36	60	26
15 Enville Athletic	30	7	5	18	51	80	26
16 Knowle reserves	30	4	6	20	24	76	18

DIVISION THREE	P	W	D	L	F	A	Pts
1 Polesworth	26	21	4	1	87	27	67
2 Aston	26	19	3	4	77	22	60
3 Littleton reserves	26	18	4	4	69	34	58
4 Inkberrow	26	13	5	8	56	41	44
5 Walsall Wood reserves	26	13	4	9	53	40	43
6 Northfield Town reserves	26	13	3	10	43	42	42
7 Lichfield City reserves	26	13	3	10	43	51	42
8 Dosthill Colts reserves	26	10	3	13	35	38	33
9 Future Legends	26	10	3	13	52	57	33
10 Stratford Town "A"	26	10	2	14	50	65	32
11 Coton Green reserves	26	7	4	15	37	46	25
12 JDG Alliance	26	7	0	19	53	96	21
13 Coventry Amateurs	26	5	1	20	34	74	16
14 Alveston reserves	26	3	1	22	22	78	10

CHALLENGE URN

ROUND 1

Littleton reserves 1-2 Coton Green reserves
Aston 5-1 Northfield Town
Lichfield City reserves 4-4 Coventry Amateurs (Coventry Amateurs won 3-1 on penalties)
Stratford Town "A" 2-0 Dosthill Colts reserves
Polesworth 10-0 JDG Alliance
Alveston reserves w/o-scr Archdale reserves
Future Legends 1-2 Walsall Wood reserves

QUARTER FINALS

Stratford Town "A" 5-2 Coventry Amateurs
Alveston reserves 1-0 Coton Green reserves
Inkberrow 2-0 Walsall Wood reserves
Polesworth 1-2 Aston

SEM-FINALS (2 LEGS)

Inkberrow 1-4 Aston
Aston 5-0 Inkberrow (Aston won 9-1 on aggregate)
Stratford Town "A" 3-0 Alveston reserves
Alveston reserves 0-2 Stratford Town "A"
(Stratford Town "A" won 5-0 on aggregate)

FINAL (@ Pilkington XXX, 11/5/11)

Aston 2-2 Stratford Town "A"
(Stratford Town "A" won 4-1 on penalties)

CHALLENGE TROPHY

ROUND 1

Highgate United reserves 2-3 Tipton Town reserves
Heather St Johns reserves 3-0 Brocton reserves
Boldmere St Michaels reserves 3-2 Banbury United reserves

QUARTER FINALS

Barwell reserves 2-1 Quorn reserves
Heather St Johns reserves 0-4 Chasetown reserves
Gresley reserves 1-3 Oadby Town reserves
Tipton Town reserves 3-1 Boldmere St Michaels reserves

SEMI-FINALS (2 LEGS)

Oadby Town reserves 1-1 Tipton Town reserves
Tipton Town reserves 2-1 Oadby Town reserves
(Tipton Town reserves won 3-2 on aggregate)
Chasetown reserves 4-0 Barwell reserves
Barwell reserves 1-1 Chasetown reserves
(Chasetown reserves won 5-1 on aggregate)

FINAL (@ Chasetown, 30/4/11)

Tipton Town reserves 1-5 Chasetown reserves

DIVISION TWO	1	2	3	4	5	6	7	8	9	10	11	12	13	14	15	16
1 Blackwood		1-0	1-0	6-0	2-1	1-2	7-0	3-0	0-0	4-1	3-1	2-0	5-2	2-1	1-0	3-1
2 Bromsgrove Sporting	1-0		4-0	2-1	6-0	3-0	2-1	3-1	4-0	7-0	0-1	6-1	6-0	2-2	3-0	3-3
3 Cadbury Athletic reserves	0-6	2-3		3-1	0-0	2-1	3-1	1-2	0-3	4-2	0-3	4-2	0-1	2-1	0-3	1-4
4 Chelmsley Town	0-4	2-2	4-0		0-2	1-2	2-2	5-2	3-5	2-0	0-1	3-0	2-1	1-3	3-1	3-4
5 Clements 83	1-1	0-2	0-1	1-0		2-3	2-4	0-2	1-2	2-0	2-0	3-0	1-3	1-2	1-2	4-2
6 Continental Star reserves	1-2	0-0	0-2	1-2	4-0		4-4	3-1	3-0	3-1	3-0	1-1	4-2	2-2	1-1	1-2
7 Droitwich Spa reserves	2-1	0-4	4-0	2-2	1-3	0-1		3-1	1-1	4-1	1-2	1-1	2-2	0-3	0-1	2-6
8 Enville Athletic	0-1	0-1	3-1	3-0	3-0	3-4	3-3		1-3	1-0	3-2	1-1	1-2	1-10	1-2	1-3
9 Feckenham	1-2	1-0	3-0	3-0	3-2	2-0	3-1	2-0		2-3	1-0	7-0	3-1	0-4	4-3	1-0
10 Greenhill	2-5	1-2	0-1	0-1	2-1	1-1	1-0	2-2	0-6		0-6	1-0	2-1	2-2	0-0	0-3
11 Henley Forest	2-2	1-3	2-2	3-1	4-2	1-1	3-0	7-3	3-0	3-0		1-2	4-2	3-0	5-1	4-4
12 Knowle reserves	0-1	2-1	2-3	0-0	1-0	1-3	1-1	3-2	1-5	0-1	0-6		1-2	1-4	0-1	0-7
13 Leamington Hibs	0-6	0-6	1-1	1-0	4-0	5-3	1-3	4-4	1-3	1-1	5-1	1-1		1-9	3-0	1-1
14 Lichfield City	1-1	2-1	4-1	5-0	3-0	0-0	3-1	4-2	2-1	5-0	1-3	3-0	3-1		1-0	0-2
15 Perrywood	0-2	0-3	1-1	2-1	2-1	1-5	3-1	2-2	0-7	0-2	1-1	3-2	3-1	1-1		1-3
16 Young Warriors	1-6	5-2	4-2	0-2	1-3	4-2	1-1	5-2	0-1	3-3	1-2	2-0	6-3	1-4	2-4	

MIDLAND COMBINATION DIVISION ONE CONSTITUTION 2011-12

ALVIS	ALVIS SPORTS & SOCIAL CLUB, GREEN LANE, COVENTRY CV3 6EG	NONE
ARCHDALE	County Sports Ground, Claines Lane, Worcester WR3 7SS	07736 309670
BLACKWOOD	Hampton Sports Ground, Field Lane, Solihull B91 2RT	None
BROMSGROVE SPORTING	The Victoria Ground, Birmingham Road, Bromsgrove B61 0DR	None
COTON GREEN	Red Lion Ground, Armitage Lane, Brereton, Rugeley WS15 1ED	01889 585526
DROITWICH SPA	Droitwich Spa Leisure Centre, Briar Mill, Droitwich WR9 0RZ	01905 771212
FC GLADES SPORTING	The Glades, Lugtrout Lane, Solihull B91 2RX	None
FAIRFIELD VILLA	Recreation Ground, Stourbridge Road, Fairfield, Bromsgrove B61 9LZ	01527 877049
FECKENHAM	Studley Sports & Social Club, Eldorado Close, Studley B80 7HP	01527 852671
HAMPTON	Field Lane Sports Ground, Lugtrout Lane, Solihull B91 2RT	None
KNOWLE	Hampton Road, Knowle, Solihull B93 0NX	01564 779807
LICHFIELD CITY	Brownsfield Park, Brownsfield Road, off Eastern Avenue, Lichfield WS13 6AY	None
LITTLETON	Five Acres, Pebworth Road, North Littleton, Evesham WR11 8QL	07966 297971
NORTHFIELD TOWN	Shenley Lane Community Centre, Shenley Lane, Selly Oak, Birmingham B29 4HZ	0121 475 3870
PHOENIX UNITED	Pavilion Sports Ground, Thimblemill Road, Smethwick, Warley B66 6NR	0121 429 2459
SHIRLEY TOWN	Tilehouse Lane, Whitlocks End, Solihull B90 1PN	None
STRETTON	Shobnall Sports & Social Club, Shobnall Road, Burton-on-Trent DE14 2BB	01283 567991
WEST MIDLANDS POLICE	Tally Ho! Traing Centre, Pershore Road, Edgbaston, Birmingham B5 7RD	0121 626 8228

DIVISION THREE	1	2	3	4	5	6	7	8	9	10	11	12	13	14
1 Alveston reserves		0-3	1-3	1-4	1-0	3-2	1-1	0-3	0-3	1-2	0-1	1-3	0-3	0-4
2 Aston	5-1		3-2	5-1	0-1	1-1	4-1	5-2	9-0	2-3	2-0	5-1	7-0	1-0
3 Coton Green reserves	5-0	1-2		2-0	1-0	0-1	0-2	3-5	3-0	0-5	0-1	0-0	1-2	1-4
4 Coventry Amateurs	4-2	0-4	0-3		2-4	2-5	2-3	2-1	1-2	0-1	1-3	1-2	4-1	1-2
5 Dosthill Colts reserves	3-1	1-2	4-1	3-0		1-1	2-4	2-1	0-1	0-2	1-1	0-4	0-1	1-0
6 Future Legends	4-0	0-2	1-0	2-2	1-0		0-2	13-3	1-2	5-2	1-2	0-6	1-2	2-1
7 Inkberrow	4-2	0-0	1-1	7-1	4-1	6-0		2-1	3-1	0-1	2-0	1-5	1-0	2-2
8 J D G Alliance	3-1	0-4	3-1	1-2	0-4	2-0	4-2		6-2	2-5	1-2	0-6	2-3	2-4
9 Lichfield City reserves	5-2	0-0	4-2	3-0	0-1	1-0	1-0	4-1		0-5	1-3	2-3	3-0	2-1
10 Littleton reserves	5-0	3-1	3-2	2-0	4-2	3-0	3-3	3-1	1-1		2-2	0-4	4-1	2-2
11 Northfield Town reserves	2-1	1-3	0-3	2-0	0-1	1-4	3-2	4-2	1-1	0-1		4-5	2-1	2-0
12 Polesworth	3-0	2-1	1-1	4-1	1-1	7-1	5-1	5-2	3-1	2-1	2-0		5-0	2-0
13 Stratford Town "A"	1-0	1-3	1-1	6-1	3-2	1-5	0-2	12-2	5-1	1-5	1-4	1-4		2-2
14 Walsall Wood reserves	2-3	0-3	2-0	3-2	2-0	5-1	1-0	5-3	0-2	2-1	4-2	2-2	3-1	

MIDLAND COMBINATION DIVISION TWO CONSTITUTION 2011-12

ASTON	Moor Lane Pavilion, Moor Lane, Perry Barr, Birmingham B6 7AA	0121 331 6515
BARTON UNITED	Holland SC, Efflinch Lane, Barton-under-Needwood, Burton-upon-Trent DE13 8ET	01283 713972
BURNTWOOD TOWN	Memorial Ground, Rugeley Road, Burntwood WS7 9BE	07946 269153
CHELMSLEY TOWN	The Pavilion, Coleshill Road, Marston Green, Birmingham B37 7HW	0121 779 5400
CLEMENTS	Sedgemere Sports & Social, Sedgemere Road, Yardley, Birmingham B26 2AX	0121 783 0888
COVENTRY SPARTANS	Westwood Heath Sports Ground, Westwood Heath Road, Westwood Heath, Coventry CV4 8GP	None
ENVILLE ATHLETIC	Enville Athletic Club, Hall Drive, Enville, Stourbridge DY7 5HB	01384 872368
FC STRATFORD	Knights Lane, Tiddington, Stratford-upon-Avon CV37 7BZ	None
GREENHILL	Dudley Sports FC, Dudley S&S, Hillcrest Avenue, Brierley Hill DY5 3QH	01384 826420
HENLEY FOREST	Henley-in-Arden Sports/S Grnd, Stratford Road, Henley-in-Arden B95 6AD	01564 792022
INKBERROW	Sands Road, Inkberrow, Worcester WR7 4HJ	None
LEAMINGTON HIBERNIAN	Ajax Park, Hampton Road, Warwick CV35 8HA	01926 495786
PERRYWOOD	Neel Park, Droitwich Road, Perdiswell, Worcester WR3 7SN	07808 768222
POLESWORTH	North Warks Sports & Social, Hermitage Hill, Polesworth, Tamworth B78 1HS	01827 892482
YOUNG WARRIORS	Coventry Sphinx FC, Sphinx Drive, Siddeley Avenue, Coventry CV3 1WA	024 7645 1361

RESERVE DIVISION	P	W	D	L	F	A	Pts
1 Chasetown reserves	20	15	3	2	62	11	48
2 Quorn reserves	20	14	2	4	56	26	44
3 Barwell reserves	20	12	5	3	48	26	41
4 Tipton Town reserves	20	13	1	6	44	22	40
5 Banbury United reserves	20	13	0	7	36	21	39
6 Boldmere St. Michael's res.	20	11	1	8	38	22	34
7 Highgate United reserves	20	8	1	11	33	50	25
8 Oadby Town reserves	20	4	3	13	28	44	15
9 Gresley reserves	20	4	2	14	26	48	14
10 Brocton reserves	20	4	1	15	21	75	13
11 Heather St. John's reserves	20	2	1	17	15	62	7

CHALLENGE BOWL

FINAL (@ Boldmere St Michaels, 7/5/11)

Boldmere Michaels reserves 5-2 Tipton Town reserves

BARTLEY GREEN
Founded: 1957 Nickname:

Secretary: Phillip Wincott **(T)** 07791 687 004 **(E)** wincottnelly@aol.com
Chairman: David Shepherd **Manager:** **Prog Ed:**
Ground: Illey Lane, Halesowen, Birmingham, West Midlands B62 0HE **(T)** **Capacity:**
Colours(change): Amber/black/black

ADDITIONAL INFORMATION:
Honours: Midland Combination Division 2 2005-06, Division 1 2006-07.

BLOXWICH UNITED
Founded: 2006 Nickname:

Secretary: Ian Mason **(T)** 07771 717 349 **(E)** i.mason@blueyonder.co.uk
Chairman: Dennis Holford **Manager:** **Prog Ed:**
Ground: Red Lion Ground, Somerfield Road, Bloxwich, Walsall WS3 2EJ **(T)** 01922 405 835 **Capacity:**
Colours(change): All red

ADDITIONAL INFORMATION: **Previous Lge:** West Midlands > 2011.

BOLEHILL SWIFTS
Founded: 1953 Nickname:

Secretary: Philip Crowley **(T)** 07702 786 722 **(E)** bolehallswifts.philcrowley@hotmail.co.uk
Chairman: Geoffrey Mulvey **Manager:** **Prog Ed:**
Ground: Rene Road, Bolehall, Tamworth, Staffordshire B77 3NN **(T)** **Capacity:**
Colours(change): All yellow.

ADDITIONAL INFORMATION:
Honours: Midland Combination Division 2 1984-85.

BROCTON
Founded: 1937 Nickname:

Secretary: Terry Homer **(T)** 07791 841 774 **(E)** terryhomer@yahoo.co.uk
Chairman: Brian Townsend **Manager:** John Berks **Prog Ed:**
Ground: Silkmore Lane Sports Grd, Silkmore Lane, Stafford, Staffordshire ST17 4JH **(T)** **Capacity:**
Colours(change): Green & white/white/green

ADDITIONAL INFORMATION:

CADBURY ATHLETIC
Founded: 1994 Nickname:

Secretary: Ron Thorn **(T)** 07905 358 477 **(E)** ronald_thorn@wragge.com
Chairman: John Peckham **Manager:** Jimmy Rowe **Prog Ed:**
Ground: Alvechurch FC, Lye Meadow, Redditch Road, Alvechurch, Worcs B48 7RS **(T)** **Capacity:**
Colours(change): Purple with black & white trim/black/purple with white & black hoops

ADDITIONAL INFORMATION:

CASTLE VALE
Founded: 1964 Nickname:

Secretary: Shane Godwood **(T)** 07787 804 153 **(E)** shanegodwood@msn.com
Chairman: Gary Higgins **Manager:** G Palmer **Prog Ed:** Miss L Olley
Ground: Vale Stadium, Farnborough Road, Castle Vale, Birmingham B35 7DA **(T)** **Capacity:**
Colours(change): All red

ADDITIONAL INFORMATION:
Previous Names: Kings Heath > 2002, Castle Vale K.H. > 2005.

CASTLE VALE JKS
Founded: 1998 Nickname:

Secretary: Barry Lee **(T)** 07957 422 145 **(E)** pneumaticsys@aol.com
Chairman: Duval Palgrave **Manager:** **Prog Ed:**
Ground: Vale Stadium, Farnborough Road, Castle Vale, Birmingham B35 7DA **(T)** **Capacity:**
Colours(change): All yellow & blue

ADDITIONAL INFORMATION:
Honours: Midland Combination Division 1 2008-09.

CONTINENTAL STAR
Founded: 1975 Nickname:

Secretary: Keith John **(T)** 07956 429 046 **(E)** keith.john6@hotmail.co.uk
Chairman: Keith John **Manager:** Lincoln Moses **Prog Ed:**
Ground: Rushall Olympic FC, Dales Lane, Rushall, Walsall, West Midlands WS4 1LJ **(T)** **Capacity:**
Colours(change): Yellow & blue/blue/blue

ADDITIONAL INFORMATION:
Previous Name: Handsworth Continental Star 2001-02.
Honours: Midland Combination Division 2 1995-96.

COVENTRY COPSEWOOD
Founded: 1923 Nickname:

Secretary: David Wilson **(T)** 07807 969 327 **(E)** copsewoodfc@btopenworld.com
Chairman: Robert Abercrombie **Manager:** **Prog Ed:**
Ground: Copsewood Sports & Social Club, Allard Way, Binley, Coventry CV3 1HQ **(T)** **Capacity:**
Colours(change): All blue

ADDITIONAL INFORMATION:
Previous Names: G.P.T. Coventry > 2000, Coventry Marconi > 2005.
Honours: Midland Combination Challenge Cup 2006-07.

EARLSWOOD TOWN
Founded: 1968 Nickname:

Secretary: Clive Faulkner **(T)** 07866 122 254 **(E)** faulkner-c1@sky.com
Chairman: Graham Ashford **Manager:** **Prog Ed:**
Ground: TSA Sports Ground, Eckersall Road, Kings Norton, Birmingham B38 8SR **(T)** **Capacity:**
Colours(change): All red.

ADDITIONAL INFORMATION:
Honours: Midland Combination League Division One 2010-11.

NUNEATON GRIFF
Founded: 1972 Nickname:

Secretary: Peter Kemp **(T)** 07931 297 935 **(E)** nuneatongriff@talktalk.net
Chairman: John Gore **Manager:** **Prog Ed:**
Ground: The Pingles Stadium, Avenue Road, Nuneaton, Warwickshire CV11 4LX **(T)** **Capacity:**
Colours(change): Blue & white/blue/blue

ADDITIONAL INFORMATION:
Honours: Midland Combination Premier Division 1999-2000, 00-01.

PELSALL VILLA
Founded: 1898 Nickname:

Secretary: Shaun Mason **(T)** 07779 111 023 **(E)** shaunmason1967@yahoo.co.uk
Chairman: Shaun Mason **Manager:** Mark Bentley **Prog Ed:**
Ground: The Bush Ground, Walsall Road, Walsall, West Midlands WS3 4BP **(T)** **Capacity:**
Colours(change): Red & black stripes/black/black

ADDITIONAL INFORMATION:

PERSHORE TOWN
Founded: 1988 Nickname:

Secretary: Jane Conway **(T)** 07841 377 788 **(E)** jane.chamberlain@homecall.co.uk
Chairman: Damien Rourke **Manager:** **Prog Ed:**
Ground: King George V Playing Field, King George's Way, Pershore WR10 1AA **(T)** **Capacity:**
Colours(change): Blue & white stripes/blue/blue

ADDITIONAL INFORMATION:
Previous League: Midland Alliance (Founder members).
Honours: Midland Combination Division 2 1989-90, Premier 1993-94.

PILKINGTON XXX
Founded: 2002 Nickname:

Secretary: Kim Holland **(T)** 07508 343 981 **(E)** kimholland-pilkingtonfc@hotmail.com
Chairman: Saul Gray **Manager:** **Prog Ed:**
Ground: Triplex Sports, Eckersall Road, Kings Norton, Birmingham B38 8SR **(T)** **Capacity:**
Colours(change): Green/black/green

ADDITIONAL INFORMATION:
Previous Name: Burman Hi-Ton > 2002.
Honours: Midland Combination Division 2 2001-02.

RACING CLUB WARWICK
Founded: 1919 Nickname: Racers

Secretary: Pat Murphy **(T)** 07926 188 553 **(E)** pja.murphy@hotmail.co.uk
Chairman: Bob Dhillon **Manager:** Lee Knight **Prog Ed:**
Ground: Hampton Road, Warwick, Warwickshire CV34 6JP **(T)** 01926 495 786 **Capacity:**
Colours(change): Old gold/black/old gold.

ADDITIONAL INFORMATION:
Record Att: 1,280 v Leamington FC, Midland All.26/12/2005. **Goalscorer:** Steve Edgington - 200. **Apps:** Steve Cooper - 600+
Honours: Midland Combination Premier Division 1987-88.

SOUTHAM UNITED
Founded: 1905 Nickname:

Secretary: Charles Hill **(T)** 07802 949 781 **(E)** charles@southamunitedfc.com
Chairman: Charles Hill **Manager:** Luke Fogarty **Prog Ed:**
Ground: Banbury Road, Southam, Warwickshire CV47 2BJ **(T)** **Capacity:**
Colours(change): Yellow/royal blue/royal blue

ADDITIONAL INFORMATION:
Honours: Midland Combination Division 3 1980-81.

WALSALL WOOD
Founded: 1907 Nickname:

Secretary: John Rogers **(T)** 07504 981 141 **(E)** erogers@blueyonder.co.uk
Chairman: Ivor Osborne **Manager:** Nigel Birch **Prog Ed:**
Ground: Oak Park, Lichfield Road, Walsall Wood, Walsall WS9 9NP **(T)** **Capacity:**
Colours(change): All red

ADDITIONAL INFORMATION:
Previous League: West Midlands (Regional).
Honours: Worcestershire/Midland Combination 1951-52.

MIDLAND COMBINATION INS & OUTS

PREM - IN: Bloxwich United (P - West Midland League Premier Division), Earlswood Town (P)
OUT: Alveston (W - Stratford Alliance Division One), Dosthill Colts (merged with Midland Alliance club Coleshill Town), Heather St John (P - Midland Alliance), Massey-Ferguson (now Massey-Ferguson Ath.) (R - Coventry Alliance Division Three).
DIV ONE - IN: Alvis (P - Coventry Alliance Premier Division), Blackwood (P), Bromsgrove Sporting (P), Feckenham (P), Lichfield City (P).
OUT: Burntwood Town (R), Earlswood Town (P), Kenilworth Town KH (WS - Stratford Alliance Division One)
DIV TWO - IN: Aston (P), Barton United (S - Staffs County Senior League Division One), Burntwood Town (R), Coventry Peugeot (formerly Peugeot Sports) (P - Coventry Alliance Premier Division), Coventry Spartans (formerly Coventry Amateurs) (P), FC Stratford (formerly Stratford Tn A) (P), Inkberrow (P), Polesworth (P).
OUT: Blackwood (P), Bromsgrove Sporting (P), Cadbury Athletic Reserves (S - Reserve Division Two), Continental Star Reserves (S - Reserve Division Two), Droitwich Spa Reserves (S - Reserve Division Two), Feckenham (P), Knowle Reserves (S - Reserve Division Two), Lichfield City (P).
DIVISION THREE: Disbanded

GROUND DIRECTIONS

BLOXWICH UNITED - Ground: Red Lion Ground, Somerfield Road, Bloxwich, Walsall, West Midlands, WS3 2EJ
From junction 10 of M6 take A454 (Wolverhampton Road) towards Walsall, on to Blue Lane West. At traffic lights turn left onto Green Lane (A34). Keep straight on for approximately 1½ miles. At roundabout, go straight over onto A34. Ground is approximately ½ mile up on right hand side.

BARTLEY GREEN - Ground: Illey Lane, Halesowen , Birmingham , West Midlands , B62 0HE
From M5 junctions 3, follow the A456 for Halesowen/Kidderminster for approx 1.5 miles to Grange Island. Turn left along the B4551 Bromsgrove Road for approx 400 yards, take the 1st left into Illey Lane and the ground is approximately 1 mile on the left hand side.
Exit M42 at Junction 10, take A5 towards Tamworth, exit A5 at 2nd exit (Glascote & Amington Industrial Estate). Turn right onto Marlborough Way, at next island turn left (B5000), turn right into Argyle Street (opposite chip shop). At T-junction, turn left into Amington Road, drive over the canal bridge, and turn 2nd right into Leedham Avenue. Take right fork into Rene Rd. Club is situated 150 yards on right immediately after school.

BROCTON - Ground: Silkmore Lane Sports Ground, Silkmore Lane , Stafford , Staffordshire , ST17 4JH
From M6 J13 take A449 towards Stafford for 1.5 miles until reaching traffic lights by Esso petrol station. Turn right at lights into Rickescote Road, follow road round over railway bridge to mini island, at island bear left into Silkmore Lane. At next mini island take 4th exit for entrance to ground. From Lichfield/Rugeley. After passing Staffs Police HQ at Baswick go downhill past BMW garage and pub to large island, take 1st exit into Silkmore Lane, at next mini island take 2nd exit into ground entrance. Do not turn into Lancaster Road or Silkmore Crescent as directed by Sat Navs.

MIDLAND COMBINATION - STEP 6/7

CADBURY ATHLETIC - Ground: Lye Meadow, Redditch Road , Alvechurch , Worcestershire , B48 7RS

M42 Junction 2, Follow signs for Redditch, taking dual carriageway. At 1st island turn right (Signposted Alvechurch), ground approximately 1km on right. Car Park entrance before ground.

CASTLE VALE - Ground: Vale Stadium, Farnborough Road, Castle Vale , Birmingham , West Midlands , B35 7DA

From M6 Junction 5 turn right at the island onto the A452 to island with Spitfire sculpture, turn right into Tangmere Drive, then right into Farnborough Road. Ground is on the right hand side after approximately 1/2 mile.

CASTLE VALE JKS - Ground: Vale Stadium, Farnborough Road, Castle Vale , Birmingham , West Midlands , B35 7DA

See Castle Vale above.

CONTINENTAL STAR - Ground: Dales Lane, Rushall , Walsall , West Midlands , WS4 1LJ

From M6: Leave at Junction 10 and follow signs for Walsall on A454 (Wolverhampton Road). Keep in the left hand lane and at the 1st set of traffic lights turn left into Bloxwich Lane. Progress through a set of traffic lights, keeping in the right hand lane and at the island bear left continuing along Bloxwich Lane. At the 3rd set of lights turn into Leamore Lane (at T-junction). Continue along Leamore Lane over the 1st island (A34 Somerfield Road-Green Lane) and pass through traffic lights on B4210 Bloxwich Road into Harden Road, continue along Harden Road and go straight over a mini island, at the next island take the 2nd exit continuing along Harden Road progressing into Station Road. At the set of traffic lights at the staggered junction with the A461 Lichfield Road, turn right and then left ono the B4154 (Daw End Lane) towards Aldridge, with McDonalds on your right. Continue up Daw End Lane and over the canal bridge, Dales Lane is the next on the right opposite the Royal Oak Public House. The ground entrance is sign posted.

COVENTRY COPSEWOOD - Ground: Copsewood Sports & Social Club, Allard Way, Binley , Coventry , West Midlands , CV3 1HQ

M6 South: Leave at junction 2 and follow A4600 signs for City Centre. Go over 3 roundabouts and past 1 set of traffic lights, on reaching the 2nd set of traffic lights with Coventry Oak pub on left, turn left down Hipswell Highway. Follow road for 1 mile and reach another set of lights (Fire Station is on left and Mill Pool pub is on right). Go over lights and the ground is 300 yards on the left. From M40: Follow A46 signs to Coventry and Leicester, stay on this road until very end, you then reach a roundabout with a flyover, go round the roundabout following M69 signs. This road takes you past Asda and you reach a set of traffic lights with a roundabout. Take 2nd left turn off the roundabout, again following M69 signs, This is Allard Way and takes you past Matalan on left, Go under railway bridge and ground is 400 yards on the right. A45 from Birmingham Direction: Follow A45 until reaching a slip road signposted A46, this slip road has the Festival Pub on left side of it. It is after a roundabout with big Peugeot car showroom on left. Go down slip road and take 2nd exit. , this is another slip road leading to A46, signposted B4114 Coventry. Follow road until reaching roundabout with a flyover, and then follow as M40 directions above.

EARLSWOOD TOWN - Ground: The Pavilions, Malthouse Lane, Earlswood , Solihull , West Midlands , B94 5DX

From M42 (Junction 3) A435 Evesham to Birmingham Road, at Motorway Island take minor exit to Foreshaw Heath. Follow for 3/4 mile. Turn right into Poolhead Lane. After passing Earlswood Trading Estate (on right) turn first left into Small Lane (no road sign) just before the road crosses the motorway. The ground 1/2 mile on right hand side. From A34 Heading away from Birmingham, leave Shirley. Turn right into Blackford Road (B4102) signposted Earlswood/Redditch. Follow this road for 4 miles. After passing the crossroads at Earlswood (Reservoir Public House) turn next right into Springbrook Lane. Go to the end of Springbrook Lane, Turn left into Malthouse Lane. Ground approximately 1/4 mile on left.

NUNEATON GRIFF - Ground: The Pingles Stadium, Avenue Road , Nuneaton , Warwickshire , CV11 4LX

From M5, M42 & M6: Take M6 south to junction 3 and leave by turning left onto A444 (Nuneaton). Stay on A444 through Bermuda Park, McDonalds and George Eliot Hospital roundabouts until reaching large roundabout with footbridge over road. Carry straight on (2nd exit) and downhill, taking right hand lane. At bottom of hill you reach Coton Arches Island, take 2nd exit (A4252 Avenue Road) and travel 1/2 mile to Cedar Tree Pub traffic lights, turn left into Stadium car park service road. It is unsuitable for coaches to turn around in. From A5: Travel south following signs for Nuneaton. After passing through Atherstone travel for 2 1/2 miles until junction with A444. At this junction (Royal Red Gate Pub) turn right at staggered junction and continue on A444 through Caldecote and Weddington into Nuneaton. Join one-way system at Graziers Arms by turning left and immediately take right hand lane for 300 yards and follow A444 for Coventry. At Third Island turn left on to dual carriageway (Coton Road) for 1/2 mile and turn left at Coton Arches island on to A4252 (Avenue Road) then as above.

PELSALL VILLA - Ground: The Bush Ground, Walsall Road , Walsall , West Midlands , WS3 4BP

Leave M6 at junction 7 sign-posted A34 Birmingham. Take A34 towards Walsall to 1st Island, turn right (marked Ring Road) across 3 islands. At large island at the bottom of the hill, take last exit marked Lichfield. Up hill and across next island to traffic lights, continue to next set of lights and turn left (B4154 Pelsall). Go over Railway Bridge to Old Bush Public House, the ground is next to the public house signposted Pelsall Cricket Club. From Birmingham East: Follow A452 from Spitfire Island then follow signs towards Brownhills. At the traffic lights at the Shire Oak P.H, turn left onto A461 (Walsall) and pass the entrance to Walsall Wood FC. At the traffic lights in Shelfield (The Spring Cottage PH) turn right (signposted Pelsall). At the next set of traffic lights turn left, the Bush is approx 400 yards on left. From: Coventry: Take A45 to Stonebridge Island, turn right onto A452 but then keep to the right following A446 (signposted Lichfield). Follow the A446 to Bassett's Pole Island. Take the 3rd exit onto A38 (Lichfield). Leave the A38 at sliproad for the A5 and take the 2nd exit at the island. Follow the A5 over next 2 islands and at Muckley Corner turn left (inside lane) to join A461. Go straight on at the traffic lights and follow directions as above.

PERSHORE TOWN - Ground: King George V Playing Field, King George's Way , Pershore , Worcestershire , WR10 1AA

M5 Junction 7, take B4080 (formerly A44) to Pershore. On entering the town turn left at 2nd set of traffic lights (signposted Leisure Centre). The ground is 300 yards on the left hand side.

PILKINGTON XXX - Ground: Triplex Sports, Eckersall Road, Kings Norton , Birmingham , West Midlands , B38 8SR

From Cotteridge A441 through and past Kings Norton Station, 150 yards turn right across dual carriageway at petrol station, approximately 300 yards there is a sharp bend, turn right. Ground is on right.

RACING CLUB WARWICK - Ground: Hampton Road , Warwick , Warwickshire , CV34 6JP

M40 Junction 15, signposted Warwick. At roundabout with traffic lights take A429 to Warwick. Follow this road for 1/2 mile and you will come to houses on your left. Take the 2nd turn on the left into Shakespeare Avenue. Follow to T-junction. Turn right into Hampton Road. Entrance to ground is 50 yards on left.

SOUTHAM UNITED - Ground: Banbury Road , Southam , Warwickshire , CV47 2BJ

From Birmingham: M40 Junction 12, exit to A4451 to Southam. Approximately 6 1/2 miles to an island in Southam, turn right, at 2nd island turn right again, ground is 100 yards on right. From Coventry: take A423 Banbury Road; the ground is approximately 12 1/2 miles from Coventry.

WALSALL WOOD - Ground: Oak Park, Lichfield Road, Walsall Wood , Walsall , West Midlands , WS9 9NP

From North using M6 motorway: M6 south to junction 12. Take A5 until big island just outside Brownhills (next island after the Turn pub on left). Take A452 Chester Road North through Brownhills High Street to traffic lights at Shire Oak (pub at junction on right hand side). Turn right on to A461 for Walsall, go to next set of traffic lights, cross over and turn right immediately on to Oak Park Leisure Centre car park (rear of Kentucky Fried Chicken). Proceed diagonally over car park and follow road round to ground entrance. From South using M5/M6 motorways: M5 North past junction 1 on to M6 north. Leave at junction 9 (Wednesbury turn off). Take A4148 to Walsall. Proceed for about 2 miles over several islands until going down a hill alongside the Arboretum. At big island at bottom, turn right onto A461 for Lichfield. Take A461 for about 4 miles and go through Walsall Wood village (after Barons Court Hotel on right), up the hill after village, Oak Park is on the left opposite Fitness First, turn left and go diagonally across Oak Park Leisure Centre car park, Follow road round to the ground entrance. M5/M6 alternative M5 North and bear left after junction 1 (West Bromwich) onto M6 south. Go to next junction (Junction 7 Great Barr) and follow signs for A34 Birmingham Road to junction with Queslett Road (A4041). Turn left at the junction (traffic lights) and take A4041 past Asda and over several islands to A452 Chester Road. Turn left at this island and travel for about 4 miles to Shire Oak crossroads (traffic lights with Shire Oak pub opposite). Turn left at the lights onto A461 for Walsall. Go to next lights and cross over, Oak Park is immediately on the right opposite Fitness First. Turn right onto car park and go diagonally across, following road round to the ground entrance.

DIVISION ONE

ALVIS - Ground: Alvis Sports & Social Club, Green Lane, Coventry, West Midlands, CV3 6EA

From roundabout on A45, Kenpas Highway/Stonebridge Highway, take B4113 into St Martins Road. After turn right into Green Lane South after the school. The ground is on the left hand side.

ARCHDALE '73 - Ground: County Sports Ground, Claines Lane , Worcester , Worcestershire , WR3 7SS

M5 to Junction 6, take A449 (link road) signposted Kidderminster, down to the bottom, at island turn sharp left into Claines Lane, continue past church on right, ground is on the left (about 1/2 mile).

BLACKWOOD - Ground: Hampton Sports Club, Field Lane , Solihull , West Midlands , B91 2RT

From M42 North or South: Exit motorway at junction 5 (signposted Solihull). Take 1st Exit left (A41). Continue on A41 until you reach 1st set of traffic lights and turn right into Hampton Lane, after approx 1/2 mile turn left into Field Lane, ground is approx 3/4 mile on the right hand side.

BRERETON SOCIAL - Ground: Red Lion Ground, Armitage Lane, Brereton , Rugeley , Staffordshire , WS15 1ED

From M6 Junction 11 follow A460 to Rugeley, on reaching large roundabout at Rugeley take A51 (signposted Lichfield). At end of dual carriageway in Brereton turn left at traffic lights into Armitage Lane. Entrance is 100 yards on right.

BROMSGROVE SPORTING - Ground: The Beehive, Abbeyfields Drive , Studley , Warwickshire , B80 7BF

Leave M42 at junction 3. Take A435 towards Redditch, head south for 5 miles. Abbeyfields Drive is on the left hand side 1/2 mile past 'The Boot' public house, adjacent to a sharp left hand bend.

COTON GREEN - Ground: New Mill Lane, Fazeley , Tamworth , Staffordshire , B78 3RX

From M42 junction 9, take A446 exit towards The Belfry, at the next island turn right towards Tamworth and Drayton Manor Park (A4091), continue for approximately 4 miles, past entrance to Drayton Mark Park on your left, continue over the canal with 'Debbies Boat Hire' on your right and 'Fazeley Marina' on your left. As you enter Fazeley you need to turn right immediately after the start of the 30mph speed limit, into New Mill Lane (there is a right filter lane). Once in New Mill Lane, follow lane past houses, turn right at the bottom and follow into car park.

DROITWICH SPA - Ground: Droitwich Spa Leisure Centre, Briar Mill , Droitwich , Worcestershire , WR9 0RZ

M5 junction 5, take A38 to Droitwich, At traffic lights by Chateau Impney, go onto dual carriageway, at roundabout take 1st exit (Kidderminster Road), pass Homebase and take next right into Salwarpe Road. Go straight over at next roundabout, next right into Briarmill Road and ground is behind the all weather complex.

FAIRFIELD VILLA - Ground: Recreation Ground, Stourbridge Road, Fairfield , Bromsgrove , Worcestershire , B61 9LZ

From M42 Junction 1: Take A38 North to junction 4 M5 and then take A491 towards Stourbridge, travel 2 miles to next roundabout, then left onto B4091 up into Fairfield Village. Go past Swan Public House and approximately 200 yards on your left you will see a school warning sign and telephone booth. Turn left here, up drive to ground. From M5 Junction 4: See above From A38 South to M5 junction 4: see above.

FC GLADES SPORTING - Ground: The Glades, Lugtrout Lane , Solihull , West Midlands , B91 2RX

From M42 North or South: Exit motorway at junction 5 (signposted Solihull). Take 1st Exit left (A41). Continue on A41 until you reach 1st set of traffic lights and turn right into Hampton Lane, take the 2nd left (after approx 2 miles) into Lugtrout Lane. Continue on Lugtrout Lane past houses on either side. Entrance to the ground will be on your left (opposite cricket ground).

MIDLAND COMBINATION - STEP 6/7

FECKENHAM - Ground: Studley Sports & Social Club, Eldorado Close , Studley , Warwickshire , B80 7HP

Leave M42 at junction 3 then, at roundabout, take the 3rd exit onto the A435, signposted Redditch / Evesham. At the next roundabout take the 2nd exit staying on the A435, at the next roundabout, take the 2nd exit onto the B4092, signposted Astwood Bank, then take the 3rd turning on the right into Eldorado Close. Leave the M5 south at junction 4. At the roundabout take the 2nd exit onto the A38, signposted Bromsgrove. Travel for approximately 3 miles then turn onto the A448, signposted Redditch, the A448 will then merge with the A4189. At the next roundabout take the 3rd turning staying on the A4189. At the next roundabout take the 2nd turning still on the A4189, at the next roundabout take the 3rd turning onto the A435 signposted Evesham. At the next roundabout take the 2nd exit, staying on the A435. At the next roundabout take the 2nd exit onto the B4092, signposted Astwood Bank, then take the 3rd turning on the right into Eldorado Close.

HAMPTON - Ground: Hampton Sports Club, Field Lane , Solihull , West Midlands , B91 2RT

From M42 North or South: Exit motorway at junction 5 (signposted Solihull). Take 1st Exit left (A41). Continue on A41 until you reach 1st set of traffic lights and turn right into Hampton Lane, after approx 1/2 mile turn left into Field Lane, ground is approx 3/4 mile on the right hand side.

KNOWLE - Ground: Hampton Road, Knowle , Solihull , West Midlands , B93 0NX

Directions: M42 Junction 5, A4140 to Knowle, turn left at Toby Carvery into Hampton Road. Ground is 200 yards on right.

LICHFIELD CITY - Ground: Brownsfield Park, Brownsfield Road , Lichfield , Staffordshire , WS13 6AY

From M42 J10, follow A5 towards Brownhills, or J9 and follow A446 to Lichfield, then follow signs for A38 Lichfield/Derby. From Swinfen Roundabout take 3rd exit for A38 north and then take next off A38 onto A5192 (Cappers Lane). Follow A5192 through 2 islands onto Eastern Avenue. The Ground is on the right at the top of the hill next to Norgreen factory. From M6 J12, follow A5 towards Lichfield then A38 to Lichfield Derby, then follow instructions as above.

LITTLETON - Ground: Five Acres, Pebworth Road, North Littleton , Evesham , Worcestershire , WR11 8QL

Get on A46 and aim for Bidford-on-Avon, leave A46 at Bidford roundabout and follow signs for B439 (Bidford 0.5 miles). Come to roundabout in Bidford and take exit B4085 (Cleeve Prior), over a very narrow bridge controlled by traffic lights, straight over crossroads following sign to Honeybourne Broadway. Straight on for approx. 3 miles signpost right turn for the Littletons at crossroads, the ground is 1.25 miles on the right.

NORTHFIELD TOWN - Ground: Shenley Lane Community Association, Shenley Lane, Selly Oak , Birmingham , West Mids , B29 4HZ

From Birmingham City Centre: Take the A38 (Bristol Road) towards Bromsgrove, travel through the districts of Bournbrook and Selly Oak. Once through Selly Oak, the road changes to a dual carriageway, following this until just before the end, where the Royal Orthopaedic Hospital is situated on the left. Turn right across the carriageway at the hospital and proceed down Whitehill Lane. At the bottom turn right across the dual carriageway and 1st right again into the ground. A-Z ref 2A 104. From the M42: From the M6 North join the M42 and head towards Worcester, follow the M42 until the junction A441Redditch/Birmingham is reached. Leave the motorway and head towards Birmingham. As you head towards Birmingham you will go up a hill, at the top of the hill you will come to a mini roundabout. At this island turn left into Longbridge Lane. Follow this all the way to the end, at the end you will come to a dual carriageway, turn right on to this. The dual carriageway is the main A38 heading towards Birmingham. Follow this road until the end when you will come into Northfield centre. As you go through Northfield you will come to a junction controlled by traffic lights, turn left into Bell Lane. As you go down the hill you will join a dual carriageway, at the bottom of the hill, turn across the carriageway and the ground is facing you. From the M5: Leave the motorway at junction 4 (A38). Follow signs for Birmingham, this is a dual carriageway. After 3 miles you will come to an island, the Rover car plant at Longbridge is directly in front of you. Turn left, still on the A38. Follow this road until the end when you will come into Northfield centre. As you go through Northfield you will come to a junction controlled by traffic lights, turn left into Bell Lane. As you go down the hill you will join a dual carriageway, at the bottom of the hill, turn across the carriageway and the ground is facing you.

PHOENIX UNITED - Ground: The Pavilions, Malthouse Lane, Earlswood , Solihull , West Midlands , B94 5DX

From M42 (Junction 3) A435 Evesham to Birmingham Road, at Motorway Island take minor exit to Foreshaw Heath. Follow for 3/4 mile. Turn right into Poolhead Lane. After passing Earlswood Trading Estate (on right) turn first left into Small Lane (no road sign) just before the road crosses the motorway. The ground 1/2 mile on right hand side. From A34 Heading away from Birmingham, leave Shirley. Turn right into Blackford Road (B4102) signposted Earlswood/Redditch. Follow this road for 4 miles. After passing the crossroads at Earlswood (Reservoir Public House) turn next right into Springbrook Lane. Go to the end of Springbrook Lane, Turn left into Malthouse Lane. Ground approximately 1/4 mile on left.

SHIRLEY TOWN - Ground: Tilehouse Lane, Shirley , Solihull , West Midlands , B90 1PH

Directions: Tanworth Lane after 150yds, turn right into Dickens Heath Road (Chiswick Green Inn on Left). Follow road to island, take 3rd exit and then after 100 yards go right into Tythe Barn Lane. Follow road then approx 3/4 miles at T junction turn right into Tilehouse Lane. Ground 200 yds on Right (opposite Whitlock's End Station car park). From West & M42: Leave @ J3 onto A435 to Birmingham. After 1 1/2 miles (Beckets Island) take 4th Exit (signposted Earlswood) entering Station Road. After 3/4 miles bear right over railway bridge entering Norton Lane. After 1/4 miles turn left into Lowbrook Road. After 1/4 mile at crossroads turn left into Tilehouse lane. After 1 mile approx ground is on right hand side (opposite Whitlock's End Station Car Park).

STRETTON EAGLES - Ground: Shobnall Sports Gound, Shobnall Road , Burton-upon-Trent , Staffordshire , DE14 2BB

Take A38 to Burton on Trent, leave at A5121 and take the 3rd exit towards Burton. At the lights take left hand lane for Burton, go straight through in 200 metres (You will see Bannatynes Leisure on your right). At the roundabout go straight on (A5234 Abbots Bromley). Stay on this road across 3 mini islands, you will then pass the recycling centre before reaching another island. Turn left into Shobnall Road and follow for 400 metres before turning right into Shobnall Leisure Centre. The ground is 200 yards on the right of the driveway.

WEST MIDLANDS POLICE - Ground: Tally Ho Training Centre, Pershore Road, Edgbaston , Birmingham , West Midlands , B5 7RD

Directions: From M5: Exit at junction 3, take A456 Hagley Road to 'Five Ways', turn right on to Islington Row, turn right at traffic lights at Bristol Road. Turn left at next set of traffic lights into Priory Road, then right into Pershore Road. Tally Ho! is on your left. From M6: Exit at junction 6; take Aston Expressway (A38) through Queensway underpasses emerging in Bristol Street/Bristol Road. Turn left at traffic lights at junction with Priory Road. Turn right at next set of traffic lights. Pershore Road and Tally Ho! is on your left (A-Z Reference 3G Page 89).

MIDLAND FOOTBALL ALLIANCE

Sponsored by: Aspire
Founded: 1994
Recent Champions:
2006: Chasetown
2007: Leamington
2008: Atherstone Town
2009: Market Drayton Town
2110: Barwell
midland footballalliance.co.uk

		P	W	D	L	F	A	Pts
1	Coalville Town	44	32	4	8	153	53	100
2	Tipton Town	44	31	7	6	101	32	100
3	Boldmere St Michaels	44	26	10	8	86	33	88
4	Loughborough University	44	27	7	10	77	36	88
5	Stratford Town	44	26	8	10	92	48	86
6	Westfields	44	24	13	7	102	54	85
7	Studley	44	25	10	9	81	49	85
8	Dunkirk	44	25	9	10	104	67	84
9	Kirby Muxloe	44	25	7	12	89	58	82
10	Causeway United	44	26	2	16	85	59	80
11	Heath Hayes	44	20	11	13	84	83	71
12	Coleshill Town	44	18	11	15	67	55	65
13	Ellesmere Rangers	44	16	9	19	79	73	57
14	Rocester	44	16	5	23	57	73	53
15	Bridgnorth Town	44	14	6	24	61	84	48
16	Coventry Sphinx	44	12	9	23	66	75	45
17	Biddulph Victoria	44	12	6	26	63	81	42
18	Highgate United	44	10	9	25	59	104	39
19	Friar Lane & Epworth	44	10	3	31	69	117	33
20	Alvechurch	44	8	7	29	47	119	31
21	Willenhall Town (-1)	44	8	6	30	63	149	29
22	Oadby Town	44	5	7	32	55	129	22
23	Malvern Town	44	4	6	34	38	147	18

LEAGUE CUP

ROUND 1
Dunkirk 0-4 Loughborough University
Highgate United 2-2 Studley
(Highgate United won 5-4 on penalties)
Biddulph Victoria 2-0 Ellesmere Rangers
Bridgnorth Town 0-2 Causeway United
Friar Lane & Epworth 0-2 Oadby Town
Heath Hayes 7-3 Willenhall Town
Stratford Town 2-1 Coleshill Town

ROUND 2
Biddulph Victoria 6-1 Rocester
Causeway United 0-2 Tipton Town
Malvern Town 0-8 Westfields
Boldmere St Michaels 3-1 Heath Hayes
Highgate United 1-3 Alvechurch
Oadby Town 2-3 Kirby Muxloe
Coalville Town 1-5 Loughborough University
Coventry Sphinx 2-3 Stratford Town

QUARTER FINALS
Alvechurch 2-6 Stratford Town
Tipton Town 0-0 Westfields (Westfields won 4-2 on penalties)
Biddulph Victoria 0-2 Boldmere St Michaels
Kirby Muxloe 0-2 Loughborough University

SEMI-FINALS (2 LEGS)
Westfields 1-1 Stratford Town
Stratford Town 3-2 Westfields
Stratford Town won 4-3 on aggregate
Loughborough University 0-2 Boldmere St Michaels
Boldmere St Michaels 1-0 Loughborough University
Boldmere St Michaels won 3-0 on aggregate

FINAL (@ Walsall, 10/5/11)
Stratford Town 4-2 Boldmere St Michaels

JOE McGORRIAN CUP
(League champions v League Cup holders)

(@ Barwell, 30/7/10)
Barwell 4-1 Coventry Sphinx

	1	2	3	4	5	6	7	8	9	10	11	12	13	14	15	16	17	18	19	20	21	22	23
1 Alvechurch		0-4	1-3	2-1	1-2	0-9	0-4	1-2	5-3	3-1	2-6	1-3	1-1	0-3	0-1	0-0	5-2	1-2	1-6	0-2	1-0	1-3	2-2
2 Biddulph Victoria	4-1		1-1	4-2	1-0	0-2	1-2	0-1	2-3	0-0	4-1	1-3	0-0	1-2	3-0	2-0	6-1	1-3	0-3	0-1	2-4	0-3	2-2
3 Boldmere St Michaels	1-0	1-0		1-0	0-1	4-2	0-1	3-2	7-0	5-1	3-0	5-1	1-1	3-0	0-0	5-0	5-0	2-0	1-0	0-0	1-0	0-0	5-2
4 Bridgnorth Town	4-1	3-2	0-3		2-1	0-4	1-1	2-1	0-0	0-1	4-2	2-4	2-2	0-6	1-2	2-2	3-1	2-1	1-2	2-2	0-1	1-2	4-1
5 Causeway United	3-0	3-0	1-3	3-0		3-1	2-0	3-0	0-4	1-0	2-0	4-0	3-0	4-0	2-0	5-0	4-1	1-2	3-1	2-0	1-3	0-0	3-1
6 Coalville Town	5-1	2-1	3-0	7-0	5-1		0-2	0-0	4-4	3-0	5-0	7-0	2-1	6-0	3-2	7-0	3-0	4-0	6-1	3-5	2-0	1-2	5-1
7 Coleshill Town	2-2	3-2	2-0	1-0	6-1	2-1		1-1	0-1	1-1	3-1	1-1	1-3	0-1	2-0	5-0	3-1	1-2	0-4	0-0	0-2	2-3	1-2
8 Coventry Sphinx	0-2	3-1	0-0	0-1	4-2	1-3	1-2		1-3	1-4	3-4	1-2	1-1	3-4	0-2	1-1	3-1	0-1	5-2	2-1	1-2	1-2	4-1
9 Dunkirk	7-0	2-1	0-1	1-0	3-0	3-4	1-0	1-0		1-0	6-2	7-1	3-3	3-0	1-3	3-2	3-3	2-1	0-2	2-2	1-1	2-2	2-1
10 Ellesmere Rangers	2-1	2-0	1-2	2-1	3-1	2-2	3-4	4-1	1-1		3-2	2-3	5-0	1-2	1-2	2-1	2-2	2-2	3-4	1-0	2-3	2-2	3-0
11 Friar Lane & Epworth	1-2	1-3	1-4	1-3	0-3	2-6	0-3	1-2	1-2	4-2		1-3	3-1	0-0	0-5	0-0	3-2	2-1	1-2	0-1	0-2	3-0	5-0
12 Heath Hayes	1-1	2-2	1-0	3-0	2-3	1-4	0-0	4-1	2-4	1-0	6-1		2-4	1-1	4-2	6-1	2-1	0-3	0-1	4-1	0-0	2-3	1-0
13 Highgate United	3-0	0-2	0-1	0-3	3-3	2-3	0-1	1-4	1-5	1-2	4-4	1-1		1-2	0-1	5-4	3-1	1-0	1-3	1-4	0-3	0-1	2-3
14 Kirby Muxloe	4-1	2-0	2-2	2-0	3-1	2-1	1-1	2-1	2-1	2-4	5-0	1-2	1-0		0-1	3-1	2-1	0-2	3-1	2-0	0-2	2-2	5-1
15 Loughborough University	2-0	1-0	0-0	1-0	2-0	1-2	2-0	0-0	4-1	1-0	2-0	1-0	2-3	2-0		4-0	3-0	3-0	0-0	3-0	1-1	5-4	3-0
16 Malvern Town	0-1	5-0	1-6	0-2	0-2	0-2	3-0	0-5	1-5	1-4	2-4	1-1	0-3	0-2	0-3		4-2	0-6	1-2	1-6	0-7	0-10	3-5
17 Oadby Town	2-2	0-5	2-1	2-3	0-2	2-3	1-1	2-1	1-4	1-5	4-3	0-2	1-2	1-5	1-1	0-1		2-1	0-3	0-3	2-2	2-2	2-4
18 Rocester	1-0	1-0	0-1	0-0	1-3	1-7	0-3	0-3	1-2	2-1	3-0	1-1	2-3	1-1	0-3	2-1	4-0		1-4	1-1	0-3	0-2	5-0
19 Stratford Town	2-2	2-2	1-0	3-0	2-1	0-3	2-0	1-1	1-2	4-1	1-0	1-1	2-0	1-1	2-0	0-0	2-1	2-0		0-1	2-0	0-1	7-0
20 Studley	3-0	5-0	2-1	2-1	3-0	1-3	3-1	0-0	1-0	2-1	3-2	2-3	2-1	3-1	1-0	2-0	3-1	2-1	2-2		1-0	0-0	2-3
21 Tipton Town	4-0	1-0	0-0	4-1	2-0	2-1	1-0	3-1	1-1	1-0	4-0	5-1	6-0	2-1	1-0	5-0	6-1	2-0	0-4	1-1		3-0	6-2
22 Westfields	5-0	6-0	1-2	2-1	0-2	1-1	2-2	2-1	2-1	0-0	1-0	2-2	10-0	0-2	2-2	5-0	3-2	4-1	2-1	1-1	1-4		4-1
23 Willenhall Town	3-2	1-3	2-2	1-6	0-3	2-6	2-2	2-2	0-3	2-2	0-7	3-4	3-0	0-9	1-4	5-1	1-3	0-1	0-6	2-4	0-1	1-2	

ALVECHURCH

Founded: 1929 Nickname: The Church

Secretary: Stephen Denny **(T)** 07710 012 733 **(E)** alvechurch@btinternet.com
Chairman: Peter Eacock **Manager:** Graham Scott **Prog Ed:** Alan Deakin
Ground: Lye Meadow, Redditch Road, Alvechurch B48 7RS **(T)** 0121 445 2929
Capacity: 3,000 **Seats:** 100 **Covered:** 300 **Midweek Matchday:** Tuesday **Clubhouse:** Yes **Shop:** No

Colours(change): Gold/black/black. (All blue).
Previous Names: Alvechurch FC >1992. Re-formed in 1994.
Previous Leagues: Midland Combination
Records:
Senior Honours: Since 1994: Midland Combination Premier 2002-03. Worcestershire Senior Urn 03-04, 04-05.

10 YEAR RECORD

01-02	02-03	03-04	04-05	05-06	06-07	07-08	08-09	09-10	10-11
MCmP 20	MCmP 1	MidAl 19	MidAl 15	MidAl 14	MidAl 10	MidAl 14	MidAl 10	MidAl 7	MidAl 20

ATHERSTONE TOWN

Founded: 2004 Nickname: The Adders

Secretary: Louise Roden **(T)** 07837 509 752 **(E)** louiseroden@btinternet.com
Chairman: Robert Weale **Manager:** **Prog Ed:** Graham Reed
Ground: Sheepy Road, Atherston, Warwickshire CV9 3AD **(T)** 01827 717 829
Capacity: **Seats:** Yes **Covered:** Yes **Midweek Matchday:** **Clubhouse:** Yes **Shop:**

Colours(change): Red and white stripes/black/red (All green)
Previous Names: None
Previous Leagues: Midland Combination 2004-06, Midland Alliance 2006-08
Records: Not known
Senior Honours: Midland Combination Division 1 2004-05, Premier Division 2005-06. Midland Alliance 2007-08.

10 YEAR RECORD

01-02	02-03	03-04	04-05	05-06	06-07	07-08	08-09	09-10	10-11
			MCm1 1	MCmP 1	MidAl 8	MidAl 1	SthM 3	SthM 13	SthC 21

BOLDMERE ST. MICHAELS

Founded: 1883 Nickname: The Mikes

Secretary: Rob Paterson **(T)** 07528 177 046 **(E)** robb4paterson@btinternet.com
Chairman: Keith Fielding **Manager:** Rob Mallaband **Prog Ed:** Alan Parsons
Ground: Trevor Brown Memorial Gd, Church Rd, Boldmere B73 5RY **(T)** 0121 373 4435
Capacity: 2,500 **Seats:** 230 **Covered:** 400 **Midweek Matchday:** Tuesday **Clubhouse:** Yes **Shop:** No

Colours(change): White/black/black. (Amber/white/amber)
Previous Names: None.
Previous Leagues: West Midlands (Regional). Midland Combination.
Records:
Senior Honours: AFA Senior Cup 1947-48. Midland Combination Premier 1985-86, 88-89, 89-90.

10 YEAR RECORD

01-02	02-03	03-04	04-05	05-06	06-07	07-08	08-09	09-10	10-11
MidAl 13	MidAl 14	MidAl 15	MidAl 10	MidAl 10	MidAl 7	MidAl 4	MidAl 4	MidAl 6	MidAl 3

BRIDGNORTH TOWN

Founded: 1946 Nickname:

Secretary: Zoe Griffiths **(T)** 01746 763 001 (Club) **(E)** zoebtfc@aol.com
Chairman: John Evans **Manager:** Mark Clyde **Prog Ed:**
Ground: Crown Meadow, Innage Lane, Bridgnorth WV16 4HS **(T)** 01746 763 001
Capacity: **Seats:** **Covered:** **Midweek Matchday:** Tuesday **Clubhouse:** **Shop:** Yes

Colours(change): All blue. (All red).
Previous Names: None.
Previous Leagues: Worcestershire Combination/Midland Combination. Southern. West Mids.
Records:
Senior Honours: Midland Combination 1979-80, 82-83. West Midlands (Regional) 07-08.

10 YEAR RECORD

01-02	02-03	03-04	04-05	05-06	06-07	07-08	08-09	09-10	10-11
MidAl 11	MidAl 16	MidAl 10	MidAl 22	MCmP 5	WMP 7	WMP 1	MidAl 12	MidAl 20	MidAl 15

CAUSEWAY UNITED

Founded: 1957 Nickname:

Secretary: Frank Webb **(T)** 07977 599 847 **(E)**
Chairman: Edward Russell **Manager:** Carl Burley **Prog Ed:**
Ground: Stourbridge FC, Amblecote, Stourbridge DY8 4HN **(T)** 01384 394 040
Capacity: **Seats:** **Covered:** **Midweek Matchday:** Tuesday **Clubhouse:** Yes **Shop:**

Colours(change): All blue. (All white).
Previous Names: None.
Previous Leagues: West Midlands (Regional).
Records: **Att:** 150. **Apps:** Malcolm Power - 300+
Senior Honours:

10 YEAR RECORD

01-02	02-03	03-04	04-05	05-06	06-07	07-08	08-09	09-10	10-11
WMP 1	MidAl 11	Isth P 17	MidAl 16	MidAl 19	MidAl 17	MidAl 6	MidAl 9	MidAl 12	MidAl 10

COLESHILL TOWN

Founded: 1894 Nickname:

Secretary: Vicky Robinson **(T)** 07968 410 467 **(E)** vrobinson24@aol.com
Chairman: Paul Woodford **Manager:** **Prog Ed:** As secretary
Ground: Pack Meadow, Packington Lane, Coleshill B46 3JQ **(T)** 01675 463 259
Capacity: **Seats:** **Covered:** **Midweek Matchday:** Tuesday **Clubhouse:** Yes **Shop:**

Colours(change): White/blue/red (All green)
Previous Names: None.
Previous Leagues: Midland Combination.
Records:
Senior Honours: Midland Combination Division Two 1969-70. Premier 07-08.

10 YEAR RECORD

01-02	02-03	03-04	04-05	05-06	06-07	07-08	08-09	09-10	10-11
MCmP 10	MCmP 14	MCmP 18	MCmP 9	MCmP 11	MCmP 4	MCmP 1	MidAl 11	MidAl 8	MidAl 12

COVENTRY SPHINX

Founded: 1946 Nickname: Sphinx

Secretary: Jackie McGowan **(T)** 07843 477 799 **(E)** jackie.mcgowan@coventrysphinx.co.uk
Chairman: Joe Fletcher **Manager:** Danny McSheffrey **Prog Ed:** Neil Long
Ground: Sphinx Spts & Social Club, Sphinx Drive, Coventry CV3 1WA **(T)** 02476 451 361
Capacity: **Seats:** **Covered:** Yes **Midweek Matchday:** Tuesday **Clubhouse:** Yes **Shop:**

Colours(change): Sky blue & white stripes/navy/navy (Yellow & black/black & yellow/yellow).
Previous Names: Sphinx > 1995.
Previous Leagues: Midland Combination.
Records:
Senior Honours: Midland Combination Premier 2006-07.

10 YEAR RECORD

01-02	02-03	03-04	04-05	05-06	06-07	07-08	08-09	09-10	10-11
MCmP 2	MCmP 7	MCmP 4	MCmP 2	MCmP 2	MCmP 1	MidAl 19	MidAl 7	MidAl 9	MidAl 16

DUNKIRK

Founded: 1946 Nickname: The Boatmen

Secretary: Steve Throssell **(T)** 07903 322 446 **(E)** philallen7@supanet.com
Chairman: David Johnson **Manager:** Dave Harbottle & Ian Upton **Prog Ed:** Phil Allen & Darren Miller
Ground: Ron Steel Spts Grd, Lenton Lane, Clifton Bridge, Nottingham NG7 2SA **(T)** 0115 985 0803
Capacity: 1,500 **Seats:** 150 **Covered:** 150 **Midweek Matchday:** Tuesday **Clubhouse:** Yes **Shop:**

Colours(change): Red/black/black (White/blue/white)
Previous Names: None
Previous Leagues: Notts Amateur 1946-75, Notts Alliance 1975-95, Central Midlands 1995-2008, East Midlands Counties > 2010
Records:
Senior Honours: Notts Amateur League 1973-75. Central Midlands League Supreme Division 2004-05. East Midlands Counties 2009-10

10 YEAR RECORD

01-02	02-03	03-04	04-05	05-06	06-07	07-08	08-09	09-10	10-11
CM Su 9	CM Su 12	CM Su 6	CM Su 1	CM Su 8	CM Su 6	CM Su 4	EMC 5	EMC 1	MidAl 8

ELLESMERE RANGERS

Founded: 1969 Nickname:

Secretary: John Edge **(T)** 07947 864 357 **(E)** john.edge2@homecall.co.uk
Chairman: David Coles **Manager:** **Prog Ed:**
Ground: Beech Grove, Ellesmere, Shropshire SY12 0BT **(T)** 07947 864 357
Capacity: **Seats:** **Covered:** **Midweek Matchday:** Tuesday **Clubhouse:** **Shop:**

Colours(change): Sky blue/navy/sky blue (Yellow/black/yellow)
Previous Names:
Previous Leagues: West Midlands
Records:
Senior Honours: West Midlands League Premier Division 2009-10.

10 YEAR RECORD

01-02	02-03	03-04	04-05	05-06	06-07	07-08	08-09	09-10	10-11
			WM2 4	WM1	WMP 12	WMP 7	WMP 4	WMP 1	MidAl 13

GRESLEY

Founded: 2009 Nickname:

Secretary: Reg Shorthouse **(T)** 07779 049 847 **(E)** reg.shorthouse@gresleyfc.com
Chairman: Mark Harrison **Manager:** Gary Norton **Prog Ed:** Robert Mansfield
Ground: The Moat Ground, Moat Street, Church Gresley, Derbyshire DE11 9RE **(T)** 01283 216 315
Capacity: **Seats:** **Covered:** **Midweek Matchday:** **Clubhouse:** **Shop:**

Colours(change): Red/white/red (White/red/white)
Previous Names: Gresley Rovers
Previous Leagues: East Midlands 2009-11.
Records:
Senior Honours: East Midlands Counties League 2010-11.

10 YEAR RECORD

01-02	02-03	03-04	04-05	05-06	06-07	07-08	08-09	09-10	10-11
								EMC 2	EMC 1

HEATH HAYES

Founded: 1964 Nickname:

Secretary: Kathlyn Davies **(T)** 07969 203 063 **(E)** kathlyndavies@aol.com
Chairman: Craig Brotherton **Manager:** **Prog Ed:**
Ground: Coppice Colliery Grd, Newlands Lane, Heath Hayes, Cannock, WS12 3HH **(T)** 07969 203 063
Capacity: **Seats:** **Covered:** **Midweek Matchday:** Tuesday **Clubhouse:** **Shop:**

Colours(change): Blue & white stripes/blue/white (Yellow/black/yellow)
Previous Names:
Previous Leagues: Staffordshire County, West Midlands, Midland Combination 2006-10.
Records:
Senior Honours: Staffordshire County League Division 1 1977-78. West Midlands League Division 1 North 1998-99. Midland Combination Premier Division 2009-10.

10 YEAR RECORD

01-02	02-03	03-04	04-05	05-06	06-07	07-08	08-09	09-10	10-11
WMP 10	WMP 12	WMP 6	WMP 6	WMP 13	MCmP 8	MCmP 10	MCmP 10	MCmP 1	MidAl 11

HEATHER ST. JOHN'S

Founded: 1949 Nickname:

Secretary: Adrian Rock **(T)** 07952 633 331 **(E)** adrianrock@hotmail.co.uk
Chairman: Paul Harrison **Manager:** **Prog Ed:**
Ground: St John's Park, Ravenstone Rd, Heather LE67 2QJ. Tel: 01530 263 986. **(T)**
Capacity: **Seats:** **Covered:** **Midweek Matchday:** **Clubhouse:** **Shop:**

Colours(change): All royal blue (All white)
Previous Names: Heather Athletic 1949-2007.
Previous Leagues: Midland Combination > 2011.
Records:
Senior Honours: Midland Combination 2010-11.

10 YEAR RECORD

01-02	02-03	03-04	04-05	05-06	06-07	07-08	08-09	09-10	10-11
		MCm2 5	MCm1 13	MCm1 12	MCm1 6	MCmP 7	MCmP 5	MCmP 2	MCmP 1

HIGHGATE UNITED

Founded: 1948 Nickname: Red or Gate

Secretary: Paul Davis **(T)** 07527 941 993 **(E)** merryeric@tiscali.co.uk
Chairman: Anthony Clancy **Manager:** Mark Burge **Prog Ed:**
Ground: The Coppice, Tythe Barn Lane, Shirley Solihull B90 1PH **(T)** 0121 744 4194
Capacity: **Seats:** **Covered:** **Midweek Matchday:** Tuesday **Clubhouse:** **Shop:**

Colours(change): All red (White/black/black)
Previous Names: None.
Previous Leagues: Worcestershire/Midland Combination.
Records: Not known
Senior Honours: Midland Combination Premier 1972-73, 73-74, 74-75.

10 YEAR RECORD

01-02	02-03	03-04	04-05	05-06	06-07	07-08	08-09	09-10	10-11
MCmP 13	MCmP 9	MCmP 12	MCmP 18	MCmP 14	MCmP 3	MCmP 2	MidAl 13	MidAl 18	MidAl 18

KIRKBY MUXLOE

Founded: 1910 Nickname:

Secretary: Philip Moloney **(T)** 07775 992 778 **(E)** pmoloney1@hotmail.com
Chairman: Simon Bailey **Manager:** Gaz Keenan **Prog Ed:**
Ground: Kirby Muxloe Sports Club, Ratby Lane LE9 2AQ **(T)** 0116 239 3201
Capacity: **Seats:** **Covered:** **Midweek Matchday:** Tuesday **Clubhouse:** Yes **Shop:**

Colours(change): Sky blue & yellow stripes/blue/blue (Black & white stripes/navy/red)
Previous Names:
Previous Leagues: Leicester Mutual. Leicester City. Leicestershire Senior. East Midlands Co.
Records:
Senior Honours: Leicestershire Co. Cup 2006-07. Leicestershire Senior Champions 07-08. East Midlands Counties Champions 2008-09.

10 YEAR RECORD

01-02	02-03	03-04	04-05	05-06	06-07	07-08	08-09	09-10	10-11
LeicS 5	LeicS 7	LeicS 2	LeicS 4	LeicS 8	LeicS 2	LeicS 1	EMC 1	MidAl 10	MidAl 9

LOUGHBOROUGH UNIVERSITY

Founded: 1920 Nickname:

Secretary: Margaret Folwell **(T)** 01509226127(Office Hrs) **(E)** secretary@loughboroughfootball.co.uk
Chairman: Stuart McLaren **Manager:** Stuart McLaren **Prog Ed:**
Ground: Nanpantan Sports Ground, Nanpantan Road LE11 3YE **(T)** 01509 237 148
Capacity: **Seats:** **Covered:** **Midweek Matchday:** **Clubhouse:** **Shop:**

Colours(change): All maroon. (All sky blue).
Previous Names: None
Previous Leagues: Leicestershire Senior. Midland Combination.
Records:
Senior Honours: Midland Combination 2008-09.

10 YEAR RECORD

01-02	02-03	03-04	04-05	05-06	06-07	07-08	08-09	09-10	10-11
						MCmP 4	MCmP 1	MidAl 13	MidAl 4

ROCESTER

Founded: 1876 Nickname: Romans

Secretary: Barry Smith **(T)** 07770 762 825 **(E)** rocesterfc@btinternet.com
Chairman: Mark Deaville **Manager:** David Langston **Prog Ed:** Barry Smith
Ground: Hillsfield, Mill Street, Rocester, Uttoxeter ST14 5JX **(T)** 01889 591 301
Capacity: 4,000 **Seats:** 230 **Covered:** 500 **Midweek Matchday:** Tuesday **Clubhouse:** Yes **Shop:** Yes

Colours(change): Amber & black stripes/black/black. (All royal blue).
Previous Names: None.
Previous Leagues: Staffs Sen. (Founder Member). W.Mids (Reg). Mid.All (FM) Southern. NPL
Records: **Apps:** Peter Swanwick 1962-82.
Senior Honours: Staffordshire Senior 1985-86, 86-87. West Mids (Regional) Div.1 87-88. Midland Alliance 1998-99, 2003-04.

10 YEAR RECORD

01-02	02-03	03-04	04-05	05-06	06-07	07-08	08-09	09-10	10-11
SthW 21	SthW 21	MidAl 1	NPL 1 22	MidAl 22	MidAl 12	MidAl 5	MidAl 20	MidAl 16	MidAl 14

STRATFORD TOWN

Founded: 1944 Nickname: The Town

Secretary: Brian Rose **(T)** 07833 776 834 **(E)** brian_rose@nfumutual.co.uk
Chairman: Craig Hughes **Manager:** Morton Titterton **Prog Ed:** Mark Bickley
Ground: Knights Lane, Tiddington, Stratford Upon Avon CV37 7BZ **(T)** 01789 269 336
Capacity: **Seats:** Yes **Covered:** Yes **Midweek Matchday:** Tuesday **Clubhouse:** Yes **Shop:** Yes

Colours(change): All royal blue. (Tangerine/black/tangerine)
Previous Names: Stratford Town Amateurs 1964-70.
Previous Leagues: Worcestershire/Midland Comb. Birmingham & Dist. W.Mid (Reg). Hellenic.
Records: **Att:** 1,078 v Aston Villa, Birmingham Senior Cup, Oct. 1996.
Senior Honours: Worcestershire/Midland Combination 1956-57, 86-87.
Birmingham Senior Cup 1962-63. Midland Alliance League Cup 2002-03, 03-04, 10-11.

10 YEAR RECORD

01-02	02-03	03-04	04-05	05-06	06-07	07-08	08-09	09-10	10-11
MidAl 4	MidAl 3	MidAl 3	MidAl 11	MidAl 15	MidAl 4	MidAl 7	MidAl 6	MidAl 3	MidAl 5

STUDLEY

Founded: 1971 Nickname: Bees

Secretary: Ian Milne **(T)** 07903 319 680 **(E)** milne.ian94@googlemail.com
Chairman: Barry Cromwell **Manager:** Lee Adams **Prog Ed:** Alec James
Ground: The Beehive, Abbeyfields Drive, Studley B80 7BE **(T)** 01527 853 817
Capacity: 1,500 **Seats:** 200 **Covered:** Yes **Midweek Matchday:** Tuesday **Clubhouse:** Yes **Shop:** Yes

Colours(change): Sky blue/navy/sky blue. (All white)
Previous Names: Studley BKL > 2002.
Previous Leagues: Redditch & Sth Warwicks Sunday Combination. Midland Combination.
Records: **Att:** 810 v Leamington 2003-04. **Goalscorer:** Brian Powell. **Apps:** Lee Adams - 523.
Senior Honours: Midland Combination Div.1 1991-92. Worcestershire FA Senior Urn 00-01,01-02, 02-03.

10 YEAR RECORD

01-02	02-03	03-04	04-05	05-06	06-07	07-08	08-09	09-10	10-11
MidAl 9	MidAl 7	MidAl 5	MidAl 18	MidAl 16	MidAl 20	MidAl 13	MidAl 14	MidAl 11	MidAl 7

TIPTON TOWN

Founded: 1948 Nickname:

Secretary: Keith Birch **(T)** 07765 141 410 **(E)** birchkeith@yahoo.co.uk
Chairman: John Cross **Manager:** **Prog Ed:**
Ground: Tipton Sports Academy, Wednesbury Oak Road, Tipton DY4 0BS **(T)** 0121 502 5534
Capacity: 1,000 **Seats:** 200 **Covered:** 400 **Midweek Matchday:** Wednesday **Clubhouse:** Yes **Shop:** No

Colours(change): Black & white stripes/black/red. (All blue).
Previous Names: None.
Previous Leagues: West Midlands (Regional).
Records: **Att:** 1,100 v Wolves, 01.08.88.
Senior Honours: Wednesbury Senior Cup 1975-76, 76-77, 80-81, 95-96. West Midlands (Regional) Div.1 83-84. Prem 04-05.

10 YEAR RECORD

01-02	02-03	03-04	04-05	05-06	06-07	07-08	08-09	09-10	10-11
WestP 11	WestP 3	WestP 2	WestP 1	MidAl 11	MidAl 5	MidAl 9	MidAl 5	MidAl 4	MidAl 2

TIVIDALE

Founded: 1954 Nickname:

Secretary: Leon Murray **(T)** 07939 234 813 **(E)** loentivi@hotmail.com
Chairman: Chris Dudley **Manager:** Leon Murray **Prog Ed:**
Ground: The Beeches, Packwood Road, Tividale, West Mids B69 1UL **(T)** 01384 211 743
Capacity: **Seats:** **Covered:** **Midweek Matchday:** **Clubhouse:** **Shop:**

Colours(change): All yellow (All blue)
Previous Names: None
Previous Leagues: West Midlands (Regional) 1966- 2011.
Records: Not known
Senior Honours: West Midlands (Regional) League Division One 1972-73, Premier Division 2010-11.

10 YEAR RECORD

01-02	02-03	03-04	04-05	05-06	06-07	07-08	08-09	09-10	10-11
WMP 2	WMP 5	WMP 8	WMP 16	WMP 8	WMP 2	WMP 11	WMP 13	WMP 7	WMP 1

WESTFIELDS

Founded: 1966 Nickname: The Fields

Secretary: Andrew Morris **(T)** 07860 410 548 **(E)** andrew@andrew-morris.co.uk

Chairman: John Morgan **Manager:** Sean Edwards **Prog Ed:**

Ground: Allpay Park, Widemarsh Common, Hereford HR4 9NA **(T)** 07860 410 548

Capacity: 2,000 **Seats:** 150 **Covered:** 150 **Midweek Matchday:** Tuesday **Clubhouse:** Yes **Shop:** Yes

Colours(change): All Maroon & sky blue/sky blue/sky blue (All white)
Previous Names: None.
Previous Leagues: Herefordshire Sunday. Worcester & Dist. West Midlands (Regional).
Records: **Att:** 518 v Rushden & Daimonds, FA Cup, 1996. **Goalscorer:** Paul Burton. **Apps:** Jon Pugh.
Senior Honours: Hereford Senior Cup 1985-86, 88-89, 91-92, 95-96, 01-02, 02-03, 04-05, 05-06, 07-08.
West Midlands (Regional) Premier 2002-03.

10 YEAR RECORD

01-02	02-03	03-04	04-05	05-06	06-07	07-08	08-09	09-10	10-11
WestP 5	WestP 1	MidAl 13	MidAl 6	MidAl 20	MidAl 16	MidAl 11	MidAl 17	MidAl 5	MidAl 6

WILLENHALL TOWN

Founded: 1953 Nickname: The Lockmen

Secretary: Garry Nicholls **(T)** 07776 294 558 **(E)** wtfcclubsec@aol.co.uk

Chairman: Sean Coughlan **Manager:** **Prog Ed:**

Ground: Noose Lane, Willenhall, West Midlands WV13 3BB **(T)** 01902 636 586

Capacity: 5,000 **Seats:** 324 **Covered:** 500 **Midweek Matchday:** Tuesday **Clubhouse:** Yes **Shop:** Yes

Colours(change): All red (Blue/blue/yellow)
Previous Names: None
Previous Leagues: Staffs Co, West Mids 1975-78, 91-94, Southern 1982-91, 2005-08, Midland All. 94-2004, N.P.L 2004-05, 08-10
Records: **Att:** 3,454 v Crewe FA Cup 1st Rnd 1981. **Goalscorer & Apps:** Gary Matthews. **Win:** 11-1 v Bridgnorth Town 2001-02.
Senior Honours: Staffs County Premier 1974-75. West Mids Division 1 1975-76, Premier 77-78. Southern League Midland Division 1983-84.

10 YEAR RECORD

01-02	02-03	03-04	04-05	05-06	06-07	07-08	08-09	09-10	10-11
MidAl 12	MidAl 6	MidAl 2	NP 1 4	SthW 9	SthM 4	SthM 14	NP1S 16	NP1S 22	MidAl 21

MIDLAND FOOTBALL ALLIANCE INS & OUTS

IN: Atherstone Town (W - Southern League Division One Central), Gresley (P - East Midlands League),

Heather St John (P - Midland Alliance Premier Division), Tividale (P - West Midlands League Premier Division).

OUT: Biddulph Victoria (now Biddulph Town) (W-Staffs County League Premier Division),

Coalville Town (P-Northern Premier League Division One South), Friar Lane & Epworth (W-Leics Senior League Division One),

Malvern Town (P-West Midlands League Premier Division), Oadby Town (R-East Midlands League).

NORTH WEST COUNTIES LEAGUE

Sponsored by: Vodkat
Founded: 1982
Recent Champions:
2006: Cammell Laird
2007: FC United of Manchester
2008: Trafford
2009: AFC Fylde
2010: Newcastle Town
nwcfl.co.uk

PREMIER DIVISION	P	W	D	L	F	A	Pts
1 New Mills	42	32	6	4	102	38	102
2 Ramsbottom United	42	29	4	9	101	45	91
3 Winsford United	42	26	5	11	99	50	83
4 Padiham	42	21	10	11	84	62	73
5 Colne	42	21	10	11	90	73	73
6 Bootle	42	21	9	12	78	56	72
7 Barnoldswick Town	42	19	12	11	81	58	69
8 Congleton Town	42	18	10	14	70	60	64
9 Squires Gate	42	18	10	14	74	70	64
10 Atherton LR	42	19	6	17	75	72	63
11 Bacup Borough	42	17	10	15	68	55	61
12 Runcorn Linnets	42	16	8	18	68	77	56
13 Maine Road	42	15	9	18	69	64	54
14 Glossop North End	42	14	11	17	68	55	53
15 Flixton	42	13	9	20	78	91	48
16 Silsden	42	13	9	20	47	74	48
17 St Helens Town	42	14	5	23	79	116	47
18 Formby	42	11	10	21	67	95	43
19 Stone Dominoes	42	12	6	24	60	90	42
20 Alsager Town	42	10	8	24	57	94	38
21 Rossendale United (-1)	42	6	11	25	63	106	28
22 Ashton Athletic	42	5	6	31	45	122	21

LEAGUE CHALLENGE CUP

ROUND 1
Abbey Hey 2-3 Irlam
AFC Blackpool 2-0 Rochdale Town
AFC Darwen 1-0 Ashton Town
AFC Liverpool 1-2 Runcorn Town
Atherton Collieries 5-0 Ashton Athletic
Cheadle Town 0-1 Chadderton
Daisy Hill 3-0 Oldham Boro
Norton United 3-0 Holker Old Boys
Wigan Robin Park 2-1 Eccleshall
ROUND 2
Alsager Town 1-2 St Helens Town
Atherton Collieries 0-2 AFC Blackpool
Atherton Laburnum Rovers 4-2 Silsden
Bacup Borough 3-2 Chadderton
Barnoldswick Town 3-4 Irlam
Bootle 6-0 Runcorn Linnets
Glossop North End 2-2 Colne
Maine Road 1-2 Winsford United
New Mills 4-1 Flixton
Norton United 1-2 Wigan Robin Park
Padiham 1-2 Formby
Ramsbottom United 4-1 Daisy Hill
Runcorn Town 2-1 Congleton Town
Squires Gate 6-1 Rossendale United
Stone Dominoes 3-2 Leek CSOB
AFC Darwen - Bye
ROUND 2 REPLAY
Colne 1-2 Glossop North End
ROUND 3
AFC Blackpool 5-1 St Helens Town
AFC Darwen 0-1 Glossop North End (@ Glossop North End)
Atherton Laburnum Rovers 2-2 Runcorn Town
Bacup Borough 1-3 Winsford United
Formby 3-1 Bootle
Irlam 2-0 Squires Gate
Ramsbottom United 1-2 New Mills
Wigan Robin Park 4-3 Stone Dominoes
ROUND 3 REPLAY
Runcorn Town 4-0 Atherton Laburnum Rovers
QUARTER FINALS
AFC Blackpool 2-1 Irlam
Formby 1-2 Winsford United
Glossop North End 0-2 New Mills
Wigan Robin Park 1-6 Runcorn Town
SEMI-FINALS
New Mills 3-2 Runcorn Town
Winsford United 2-1 AFC Blackpool
FINAL (@ Curzon Ashton, 11/5./11)
New Mills 0-1 Winsford United

PREMIER DIVISION	1	2	3	4	5	6	7	8	9	10	11	12	13	14	15	16	17	18	19	20	21	22
1 Alsager Town		5-1	2-4	2-4	1-1	1-2	1-1	0-4	2-2	1-1	0-2	0-1	0-3	1-0	2-3	2-0	3-0	1-1	0-4	2-1	0-1	0-5
2 Ashton Athletic	2-4		1-4	0-3	0-5	1-2	1-3	1-2	2-3	2-2	0-2	2-4	0-2	0-1	1-3	2-2	1-3	1-3	3-0	1-3	4-1	0-4
3 Atherton Laburnum Rovers	2-2	2-1		3-2	1-0	3-0	2-0	2-0	2-1	10-4	0-0	1-0	1-2	2-1	0-4	1-3	0-2	1-0	1-3	1-0	1-4	0-2
4 Bacup Borough	3-0	1-1	2-1		1-0	2-2	0-1	1-1	1-3	3-1	0-1	0-0	0-1	1-1	3-0	2-1	0-3	0-1	3-0	7-1	1-1	1-1
5 Barnoldswick Town	5-1	1-0	0-4	2-2		1-2	4-2	1-2	2-4	4-0	2-1	2-0	1-4	3-2	2-1	1-1	3-0	1-1	4-1	3-0	3-1	2-2
6 Bootle	3-1	3-1	2-2	3-0	3-3		0-2	4-0	1-1	1-2	1-0	2-1	2-3	2-2	1-3	1-1	1-1	2-0	2-1	2-1	3-0	0-1
7 Colne	3-2	2-2	4-1	2-1	1-1	2-2		1-0	4-2	4-3	3-2	2-1	1-2	0-3	0-2	4-0	3-2	0-0	3-3	6-1	0-2	0-3
8 Congleton Town	2-2	6-1	2-1	0-1	3-3	0-4	1-2		1-0	3-0	1-1	1-1	1-2	1-1	1-1	3-0	3-2	1-0	2-2	4-1	2-0	4-0
9 Flixton	1-4	3-1	1-2	1-3	2-2	0-1	2-2	4-1		0-0	3-2	3-0	1-4	3-3	0-3	2-2	1-3	5-1	2-3	3-2	3-1	0-2
10 Formby	2-1	1-1	1-1	5-1	1-2	2-1	2-1	2-2	2-2		0-1	0-3	0-2	1-3	1-1	4-1	2-2	0-1	1-4	2-1	4-1	1-2
11 Glossop North End	0-1	8-0	3-3	2-1	0-1	1-1	1-2	0-1	5-1	3-0		1-2	2-1	1-3	0-1	1-1	2-1	7-1	1-1	2-4	2-2	2-1
12 Maine Road	4-0	0-0	4-2	1-2	2-1	1-2	4-1	1-1	0-3	2-4	2-1		3-0	1-2	0-3	4-0	2-2	0-1	1-2	0-3	2-2	0-2
13 New Mills	2-0	6-0	3-2	3-1	1-1	1-0	1-1	2-1	1-0	2-0	1-1	4-4		4-0	1-0	1-1	2-1	3-0	4-0	9-0	1-1	2-0
14 Padiham	2-0	2-3	1-3	2-3	3-0	2-0	1-1	2-0	5-3	1-1	3-0	1-1	3-1		2-1	2-0	3-2	2-0	1-2	1-3	2-1	2-2
15 Ramsbottom United	2-0	4-1	1-0	0-0	1-0	3-1	5-2	1-0	2-1	3-1	1-2	2-1	1-2	1-2		5-1	5-0	2-3	2-0	3-3	3-0	3-1
16 Rossendale United	2-4	1-2	0-2	0-3	2-4	3-4	1-4	5-1	2-4	2-3	2-0	1-0	1-2	2-5	5-7		L-W	1-1	1-1	2-4	2-4	4-4
17 Runcorn Linnets	2-2	0-2	1-0	2-0	1-3	1-3	2-2	0-1	3-0	3-2	1-1	2-1	1-4	1-1	0-5	4-2		2-1	0-0	3-5	3-0	0-3
18 Silsden	2-1	7-0	2-2	0-3	1-2	1-2	0-4	2-1	0-0	3-2	0-0	1-3	0-2	2-3	1-0	2-2	1-2		0-0	0-3	2-1	1-3
19 Squires Gate	3-0	2-1	2-3	1-4	1-1	2-1	1-3	3-2	6-2	1-0	2-2	1-4	0-5	2-4	0-1	2-0	4-2	5-0		4-0	1-1	0-2
20 St Helens Town	5-1	2-1	3-0	1-1	0-3	1-0	4-8	2-3	3-2	4-5	1-0	3-3	2-4	2-2	1-5	3-3	0-4	0-3	1-3		0-2	0-3
21 Stone Dominoes	3-6	5-0	4-1	3-2	2-0	0-5	1-2	1-3	2-3	2-1	0-5	1-3	1-2	2-1	0-2	1-2	1-3	0-1	0-0	3-2		1-4
22 Winsford United	3-0	5-1	2-1	2-0	1-1	2-4	4-1	0-2	3-1	7-1	3-0	0-2	3-0	3-1	3-5	0-1	2-1	4-0	0-1	2-3	3-1	

DIVISION ONE	P	W	D	L	F	A	Pts
1 AFC Blackpool	34	28	3	3	94	30	87
2 Runcorn Town (-3)	34	26	6	2	114	39	81
3 Holker Old Boys	34	19	6	9	77	42	63
4 AFC Liverpool	34	19	6	9	65	34	63
5 Atherton Collieries	34	18	6	10	70	44	60
6 Chadderton	34	18	6	10	64	48	60
7 Norton United	34	17	7	10	64	54	58
8 Wigan Robin Park (-3)	34	17	5	12	68	51	53
9 Irlam	34	14	5	15	63	69	47
10 Cheadle Town	34	13	7	14	54	62	46
11 Eccleshall (-3)	34	15	3	16	64	70	45
12 Leek CSOB	34	11	9	14	54	58	42
13 AFC Darwen	34	9	10	15	38	69	37
14 Daisy Hill	34	6	8	20	47	90	26
15 Abbey Hey	34	6	6	22	48	72	24
16 Ashton Town	34	5	8	21	37	86	23
17 Oldham Boro	34	5	6	23	37	77	21
18 Rochdale Town	34	2	9	23	44	107	15

RESERVE DIVISION	P	W	D	L	F	A	Pts
1 Padiham reserves	24	19	3	2	73	29	60
2 Glossop North End rese (+2)	24	16	3	5	60	29	53
3 Barnoldswick Town res (-1)	24	15	2	7	62	29	46
4 Bootle reserves (-1)	24	11	9	4	47	30	41
5 Irlam reserves	24	11	5	8	47	38	38
6 Wigan Robin Park reserves	24	11	3	10	48	45	36
7 AFC Liverpool reserves	24	10	5	9	57	44	35
8 Ashton Athletic reserves	24	10	3	11	50	42	33
9 New Mills reserves	24	10	3	11	50	50	33
10 Ashton Town reserves (-1)	24	6	4	14	47	64	21
11 Daisy Hill reserves	24	6	2	16	36	66	20
12 Cheadle Town reserves	24	4	1	19	33	87	13
13 AFC Darwen reserves (-3)	24	5	1	18	28	85	13

FIRST DIVISION CHALLENGE CUP

ROUND 1

AFC BlRound 1

Chadderton 1-2 Wigan Robin Park

Abbey Hey 2-3 Cheadle Town

Atherton Collieries 1-0 Oldham Boro

AFC Darwen 1-2 Norton United

ROUND 2

Eccleshall 0-0 Irlam (Irlam won on penalties)

Ashton Town 0-3 Leek CSOB

AFC Blackpool 4-0 Holker Old Boys

Norton United 3-2 Rochdale Town (@ Rochdale Town)

Cheadle Town 1-5 Runcorn Town

Atherton Collieries 4-1 Daisy Hill

QUARTER FINALS

AFC Blackpool 3-1 Runcorn Town

AFC Liverpool 2-2 Norton United (AFC Liverpool won on penalties)

Atherton Collieries 1-1 Leek CSOB (Atherton Collieries won on penalties)

Wigan Robin Park 0-1 Irlam

SEMI-FINALS

AFC Blackpool 1-2 AFC Liverpool

Irlam 1-3 Atherton Collieries

FINAL (@ Flixton, 9/5/11)

AFC Liverpool 2-3 Atherton Collieries (aet)

RESERVE DIVISION CHALLENGE CUP

FINAL (@ Glossop North End, 26/4/11)

Glossop North End reserves 2-2 Ashton Athletic reserves

(Glossop North End reserves won on penalties)

DIVISION ONE	1	2	3	4	5	6	7	8	9	10	11	12	13	14	15	16	17	18
1 AFC Blackpool		1-4	1-2	2-3	1-2	1-2	1-2	1-2	3-3	0-2	0-4	1-2	0-1	1-2	4-5	2-1	0-3	3-0
2 AFC Darwen	1-0		2-1	1-2	3-1	1-0	1-0	2-0	4-0	3-1	1-1	5-0	2-1	4-2	3-2	10-2	4-0	2-1
3 AFC Liverpool	1-1	1-6		1-0	3-1	1-2	2-2	0-2	1-0	1-1	0-3	2-1	1-1	0-2	0-0	3-1	1-1	2-1
4 Abbey Hey	1-0	0-1	4-0		1-0	1-1	0-2	1-1	5-0	2-0	0-1	3-1	1-1	2-1	4-1	3-0	1-2	2-1
5 Ashton Town	1-1	0-3	2-2	0-0		3-1	0-3	1-2	5-2	1-3	1-2	2-2	1-2	1-5	1-0	2-0	0-8	0-3
6 Atherton Collieries	0-2	0-0	7-0	1-1	5-1		3-1	1-1	1-0	1-1	2-3	1-2	2-1	4-1	2-0	2-1	0-1	1-2
7 Chadderton	3-1	3-2	2-4	1-0	4-0	4-3		1-1	0-1	4-1	1-0	2-1	1-1	2-3	1-1	3-2	1-2	1-1
8 Cheadle Town	1-3	0-4	1-1	2-5	5-1	0-2	3-4		3-0	1-2	1-0	1-2	1-0	2-3	1-1	1-0	2-2	0-4
9 Daisy Hill	1-4	0-1	1-1	3-4	2-2	0-4	1-0	4-5		1-0	2-3	3-3	5-1	0-0	3-1	1-1	1-3	0-0
10 Eccleshall	1-0	2-3	3-0	0-7	5-1	2-3	0-1	3-2	4-3		4-2	6-1	1-5	1-3	2-0	2-0	1-3	0-1
11 Holker Old Boys	2-2	1-2	4-0	1-2	3-2	1-3	1-2	2-1	6-1	3-0		2-1	3-0	2-2	1-1	8-0	2-2	2-1
12 Irlam	4-1	2-2	1-0	2-3	2-1	3-2	1-2	1-2	4-3	0-6	3-2		0-0	1-2	2-1	6-0	1-1	2-1
13 Leek CSOB	2-2	1-2	3-3	0-1	4-1	0-0	1-4	1-1	4-0	1-1	1-3	2-1		1-2	3-1	3-2	0-3	3-1
14 Norton United	3-0	0-2	2-1	1-1	0-0	1-6	2-1	0-1	4-0	1-2	0-0	3-0	2-1		2-1	3-0	3-3	2-4
15 Oldham Boro	4-3	0-4	0-2	0-3	2-1	1-2	0-1	1-2	0-2	4-0	0-3	0-3	3-1	1-2		2-2	1-3	0-2
16 Rochdale Town	2-2	2-4	2-1	3-2	2-2	0-4	2-2	1-3	3-3	1-2	0-3	3-6	1-3	2-2	2-2		0-3	3-3
17 Runcorn Town	5-1	2-1	4-0	1-0	5-0	6-0	2-0	5-1	9-1	5-4	2-3	3-2	4-2	2-1	6-0	6-3		5-0
18 Wigan Robin Park	0-3	1-4	5-0	2-0	0-0	1-2	4-3	3-2	1-0	6-1	2-0	1-0	2-3	5-2	4-1	3-0	2-2	

AFC BLACKPOOL

Founded: 1947 Nickname: Mechs

Secretary: William Singleton **(T)** 01253 761 721 **(E)**
Chairman: Henry Baldwin **Manager:** Stuart Parker **Prog Ed:** David Tebbett
Ground: Mechanics Ground, Jepson Way, Common Edge Road, Blackpool, FY4 5DY **(T)** 01253 761 721
Capacity: 2,000 **Seats:** 250 **Covered:** 1,700 **Midweek Matchday:** Tuesday **Clubhouse:** Yes **Shop:** Yes

Colours(change): Tangerine/white/tangerine (White/tangerine/tangerine)
Previous Names: Blackpool Mechanics. **Previous Ground:** Stanley Park 1947-49.
Previous Leagues: Fylde, Blackpool & Fylde Combination, West Lancashire, Lancashire Combination 1962-68.
Records: **Att:** 4,300 v FC United of Manchester, 18/02/2006 at Blackpool FC.
Senior Honours: Lancashire County FA Shield 1957/58, 1960/61. West Lancashire League 1960/61, 61/62. North West Counties League Division Three 1985/86, Division One 2010-11.

10 YEAR RECORD

01-02	02-03	03-04	04-05	05-06	06-07	07-08	08-09	09-10	10-11
NWC2 8	NWC2 14	NWC2 14	NWC2 10	NWC2 9	NWC1 13	NWC1 9	NWC1 15	NWC1 15	NWC1 1

AFC LIVERPOOL

Founded: 2008 Nickname:

Secretary: Pat Cushion **(T)** 0151 430 0507 **(E)** clubsec@afcliverpool.org.uk
Chairman: Chris Stirrup **Manager:** Paul Moore **Prog Ed:** Steven Horton
Ground: Prescot Cables FC, Valerie Pk, Eaton Street, Prescot, Merseyside, L34 6ND **(T)** 0151 430 0507
Capacity: 3,000 **Seats:** 500 **Covered:** 600 **Midweek Matchday:** Wednesday **Clubhouse:** Yes **Shop:** Yes

Colours(change): All red (Yellow/black/yellow)
Previous Names: None
Previous Leagues: None
Records: **Att:** 604 v Wigan Robin Park 06/09/2008.
Senior Honours: North West Counties Trophy 2008-09, 09-10.

10 YEAR RECORD

01-02	02-03	03-04	04-05	05-06	06-07	07-08	08-09	09-10	10-11
							NWC1 4	NWC1 5	NWC1 4

ALSAGER TOWN

Founded: 1968 Nickname: The Bullets

Secretary: Chris Robinson **(T)** 01270 882 336 **(E)**
Chairman: Terry Greer **Manager:** John Brown **Prog Ed:** John Shenton
Ground: Town Ground, Woodland Court, Alsager ST7 2DP **(T)** 01270 882 336
Capacity: 3,000 **Seats:** 250 **Covered:** 1,000 **Midweek Matchday:** Tuesday **Clubhouse:** Yes **Shop:** Yes

Colours(change): Black & white/black/black. (Maroon & sky blue/maroon/maroon).
Previous Names: Alsager FC (Merger of Alsager Institute & Alsager Utd) in 1965.
Previous Leagues: Crewe. Mid Cheshire. Northern Premier.
Records: **Att:** 450 v Crewe Alexandra, friendly, 2004. **Goalscorer:** Gareth Rowe. **Apps:** Wayne Brotherton.
Senior Honours: Leek Cup 2002

10 YEAR RECORD

01-02	02-03	03-04	04-05	05-06	06-07	07-08	08-09	09-10	10-11
NWC2 2	NWC1 11	NWC1 9	NWC1 7	NWC1 3	NP1S 16	NP1S 14	NWCP 7	NWCP 18	NWCP 20

ASHTON ATHLETIC

Founded: 1968 Nickname:

Secretary: Alan Greenhalgh **(T)** 01942 716 360 **(E)**
Chairman: Jimmy Whyte **Manager:** Steve Wilkes **Prog Ed:** Alan Greenhalgh
Ground: Brockstedes Park, Downall Green, Ashton in Markerfield WN4 0NR **(T)** 01942 716 360
Capacity: 600 **Seats:** 100 **Covered:** 300 **Midweek Matchday:** Tuesday **Clubhouse:** Yes **Shop:** No

Colours(change): All yellow. (All blue).
Previous Names: None.
Previous Leagues: Lancashire Combination, Manchester Amateur League
Records: **Att:** 165 v Runcorn Linnets 2006-07. **Apps:** Steve Rothwell - 50+
Senior Honours: Atherton Charity Cup 2006-07, 07-08, 08-09.

10 YEAR RECORD

01-02	02-03	03-04	04-05	05-06	06-07	07-08	08-09	09-10	10-11
Manc 5	Manc 5	Manc 10	Manc 10	Manc 4	NWC2 16	NWC2 3	NWCP 6	NWCP 21	NWCP 22

ATHERTON L.R.

Founded: 1956 Nickname: The Panthers

Secretary: Natalie Waldie **(T)** 01942 883 950 **(E)**
Chairman: (Acting) Jane Wilcock **Manager:** Phil Priestley **Prog Ed:** Jeff Gorse
Ground: Crilly Park, Spa Road, Atherton, Manchester M46 9XG **(T)** 01942 883 950
Capacity: 3,000 **Seats:** 250 **Covered:** Yes **Midweek Matchday:** Tuesday **Clubhouse:** Yes **Shop:** No

Colours(change): Yellow & blue/royal blue/yellow. (All white).
Previous Names: Laburnum Rovers
Previous Leagues: Bolton Comb, Cheshire County 80-82, NWCL 82-94 and NPL 94-97
Records: **Att:** 2,300 v Aldershot Town F.A. Vase Q-Final replay 93-94. **Goalscorer:** Shaun Parker **App:** Jim Evans
Senior Honours: North West Counties League 1992-93, 93-94. Champions Trophy 1992-93, 93-94.

10 YEAR RECORD

01-02	02-03	03-04	04-05	05-06	06-07	07-08	08-09	09-10	10-11
NWC1 20	NWC1 14	NWC1 12	NWC1 15	NWC1 20	NWC1 16	NWC1 19	NWCP 12	NWCP 20	NWCP 10

BACUP BOROUGH

Founded: 1878 Nickname: The Boro

Secretary: Wendy Ennis **(T)** 01706 878 655 **(E)**
Chairman: Frank Manning **Manager:** Brent Peters **Prog Ed:** Michael Carr
Ground: Brian Boys Stadium, Cowtoot Lane, Blackthorn, Bacup, OL13 8EE **(T)** 01706 878 655
Capacity: 3,000 **Seats:** 500 **Covered:** 1,000 **Midweek Matchday:** Wednesday **Clubhouse:** Yes **Shop:** No

Colours(change): White/black/black. (Tangerine/claret/tangerine).
Previous Names: Bacup FC
Previous Leagues: Lancashire Combination 1903-82
Records: **Att:** 4,980 v Nelson 1947 **Goalscorer:** Jimmy Clarke
Senior Honours: North West Counties League Division Two 2002-03, Challenge Cup 2003-04.

10 YEAR RECORD

01-02	02-03	03-04	04-05	05-06	06-07	07-08	08-09	09-10	10-11
NWC2 12	NWC2 1	NWC1 14	NWC1 9	NWC1 17	NWC1 15	NWC1 18	NWCP 8	NWCP 12	NWCP 11

BARNOLDSWICK TOWN

Founded: 1972 Nickname:

Secretary: Lynn James **(T)** **(E)**
Chairman: Ian James **Manager:** B. Hall, S. Airdrie & K. Richardson **Prog Ed:** Peter Naylor
Ground: Silentnight Stadium, West Close Road, Barnoldswick, Colne, BB18 5LJ **(T)** 01282 815 817
Capacity: **Seats:** **Covered:** **Midweek Matchday:** Tuesday **Clubhouse:** Yes **Shop:**

Colours(change): Yellow & Royal Blue/royal blue/royal blue socks (All red)
Previous Names: Today's club formed after the merger of Barnoldswick United and Barnoldswick Park Rovers in 2003
Previous Leagues: Craven, East Lancashire, West Lancashire.
Records:
Senior Honours: West Lancashire Division 1 1998-99

10 YEAR RECORD

01-02	02-03	03-04	04-05	05-06	06-07	07-08	08-09	09-10	10-11
WLaP 6	WLaP 9	WLaP 12	WLaP 15	WLaP 15	WLaP 13	WLaP 10	WLaP 6	NWC1 2	NWCP 7

BOOTLE

Founded: 1954 Nickname:

Secretary: Joe Doran **(T)** 0151 531 0665 **(E)**
Chairman: Frank Doran **Manager:** Chris O'Bien **Prog Ed:** Dave Miley Junior
Ground: Delta Taxi Stadium, Vestey Rd, Off Bridle Road, Bootle L30 4UN **(T)** 0151 525 4796 or 07852 742790
Capacity: **Seats:** **Covered:** **Midweek Matchday:** Tuesday **Clubhouse:** Yes **Shop:**

Colours(change): All Royal blue. (Yellow/black/black).
Previous Names: Langton Dock 1953 - 1973.
Previous Leagues: Liverpool Shipping. Lancs Comb. Cheshire. Liverpool County Comb.
Records: **Att:** 1,078 v Everton Reserves, Liverpool Senior Cup Feb 2010.
Senior Honours: Liverpool County Champions 1964-65, 65-66, 67-68, 68-69, 69-70, 70-71, 71-72, 72-73, 73-74.
North West Counties Div.1 Champions 2008-09

10 YEAR RECORD

01-02	02-03	03-04	04-05	05-06	06-07	07-08	08-09	09-10	10-11
NWC2 6	Liv 5	Liv 17	Liv 12	Liv 3	NWC2 10	NWC2 6	NWC1 1	NWCP 3	NWCP 6

COLNE

Founded: 1996 Nickname:

Secretary: Edward Lambert (T) 01282 862 545 (E)
Chairman: David Blacklock **Manager:** Nigel Coates **Prog Ed:** Ray Davies
Ground: The XLCR Stadium, Harrison Drive, Colne, Lancashire. BB8 9SL (T) 01282 862 545
Capacity: 1,800 **Seats:** 160 **Covered:** 1,000 **Midweek Matchday:** Tuesday **Clubhouse:** Yes **Shop:** Yes

Colours(change): All Red. (All sky blue).
Previous Names: None
Previous Leagues: None
Records: **Att:** 1,742 v AFC Sudbury F.A. Vase SF 2004 **Goalscorer:** Geoff Payton **App:** Richard Walton
Senior Honours: BEP Cup Winners 1996-97 North West Counties League Division Two 2003-04.

10 YEAR RECORD

01-02	02-03	03-04	04-05	05-06	06-07	07-08	08-09	09-10	10-11
NWC2 14	NWC2 10	NWC2 1	NWC1 10	NWC1 9	NWC1 11	NWC1 5	NWCP 18	NWCP 8	NWCP 5

CONGLETON TOWN

Founded: 1901 Nickname: Bears

Secretary: Ken Mead (T) 01260 278 152 (E)
Chairman: Peter Evans **Manager:** Joe Paladino **Prog Ed:** Ken Mead
Ground: Booth Street, Crescent Road, Congleton, Cheshire CW12 4DG (T) 01260 274 460
Capacity: 5,000 **Seats:** 250 **Covered:** 1,200 **Midweek Matchday:** Tuesday **Clubhouse:** Yes **Shop:** Yes

Colours(change): Black & white stripes/black/black. (All yellow).
Previous Names: Congleton Hornets
Previous Leagues: Crew & District, North Staffs, Macclesfield, Cheshire , Mid Cheshire, NW Co, NPL
Records: **Att:** 6,800 v Macclesfield, Cheshire Lge1953-54 **Goalscorer:** Mick Bidde 150+ **App:** Ray Clack 600+ Graham Harrison 600+
Senior Honours: Cheshire Senior Cup 1920-21, 37-38.

10 YEAR RECORD

01-02	02-03	03-04	04-05	05-06	06-07	07-08	08-09	09-10	10-11
NWC1 16	NWC1 8	NWC1 11	NWC1 19	NWC1 12	NWC1 10	NWC1 9	NWCP 4	NWCP 5	NWCP 8

FLIXTON

Founded: 1960 Nickname: Valiants

Secretary: Fintan Doran (T) 0161 748 2903 (E)
Chairman: Lenny Wood **Manager:** Lloyd Morrison **Prog Ed:** TBC
Ground: Valley Road, Flixton, Manchester M41 8RQ (T) 0161 748 2903
Capacity: 2,000 **Seats:** 250 **Covered:** 650 **Midweek Matchday:** Wednesday **Clubhouse:** Yes **Shop:** No

Colours(change): Blue & white Stripes, blue/blue. (All Red).
Previous Names:
Previous Leagues: S. Manc & Wythenshawe 60-63, Lancs & Che 63-73, Manc73-86, NWC 86-96, NPL 97-00
Records: **Att:** 2,050 v FC Utd of Manchester NWC Div.2, 26.12.05.
Senior Honours: North West Counties League Division Two 1994-95, Division One 1995-96.

10 YEAR RECORD

01-02	02-03	03-04	04-05	05-06	06-07	07-08	08-09	09-10	10-11
NWC1 21	NWC1 21	NWC2 5	NWC2 18	NWC2 2	NWC1 13	NWC1 8	NWCP 20	NWCP 16	NWCP 15

GLOSSOP NORTH END

Founded: 1886 Nickname: Hillmen

Secretary: Stuart Taylor (T) (E)
Chairman: David Atkinson **Manager:** Paul Colgan **Prog Ed:** Stuart Taylor
Ground: Surrey Street, Glossop, Derbys SK13 7AJ (T) 01457 855 469
Capacity: 2,374 **Seats:** 209 **Covered:** 509 **Midweek Matchday:** Wednesday **Clubhouse:** Yes **Shop:** Yes

Colours(change): Black & white/black/black (All blue).
Previous Names: Glossop North End1886-1896 and Glossop FC 1898-1992
Previous Leagues: The Football League. Cheshire County. Manchester. Lancashire Comb.
Records: **Att:** 10,736 v Preston North End F.A. Cup 1913-1914
Senior Honours: Manchester League 1927-28. Derbyshire Senior Cup 2000-01.

10 YEAR RECORD

01-02	02-03	03-04	04-05	05-06	06-07	07-08	08-09	09-10	10-11
NWC1 19	NWC1 20	NWC1 18	NWC1 13	NWC1 16	NWC1 9	NWC1 7	NWCP 5	NWCP 7	NWCP 14

MAINE ROAD
Founded: 1955 Nickname: Blues

Secretary: Derek Barber **(T)** 0161 431 8243 **(E)**
Chairman: Ron Meredith **Manager:** Ian Walker **Prog Ed:** Derek Barber
Ground: Brantingham Road, Chorlton-cum-Hardy M21 0TT **(T)** 0161 861 0344
Capacity: 2,000 **Seats:** 200 **Covered:** 700 **Midweek Matchday:** Tuesday **Clubhouse:** Yes **Shop:** No

Colours(change): All sky blue. (Red & black stripes/black/black).
Previous Names:
Previous Leagues: Rusholme Sunday 55-66, Manchester Amateur Sunday 66-72 & Manchester 72-87
Records: **Att:** 3,125 v FC United Manchester, NWC Div.1, 04.11.06, at Stalybridge Celtic.
Senior Honours: Manchester Premier League 1982-83, 83-84, 84-85, 85-86. North West Counties Division Two 1989-90, Challenge Cup 07-08.

10 YEAR RECORD

01-02	02-03	03-04	04-05	05-06	06-07	07-08	08-09	09-10	10-11
NWC1 22	NWC2 3	NWC2 2	NWC1 8	NWC1 10	NWC1 6	NWC1 4	NWCP 13	NWCP 6	NWCP 13

PADIHAM
Founded: 1878 Nickname: Caldersiders

Secretary: Alan Smith **(T)** 0777 571 7698 **(E)**
Chairman: Frank Heys **Manager:** Craig Chadwick **Prog Ed:** Alan Smith
Ground: Arbories Memories Sports Ground, Well Street, Padiham BB12 8LE **(T)** 01282 773 742
Capacity: 1,688 **Seats:** 159 **Covered:** Yes **Midweek Matchday:** Wednesday **Clubhouse:** Yes **Shop:**

Colours(change): Royal bluelue/white/royal blue. (Yellow/blue/yellow & blue).
Previous Names: None
Previous Leagues: Lancs Comb. NWC. W.Lancs,.NE Lancs. NE Lancs Comb. E.Lancs Am.
Records: **Att:** 9,000 v Burnley, Dec.1884 (at Calderside Ground).
Senior Honours:

10 YEAR RECORD

01-02	02-03	03-04	04-05	05-06	06-07	07-08	08-09	09-10	10-11
NWC2 13	NWC2 4	NWC2 12	NWC2 4	NWC2 5	NWC2 3	NWC2 12	NWC1 2	NWCP 10	NWCP 4

RAMSBOTTOM UNITED
Founded: 1966 Nickname: The Rams

Secretary: Malcolm Holt **(T)** 01204 883085 **(E)**
Chairman: Harry Williams **Manager:** A. Johnson & B. Morley **Prog Ed:** Richard Isaacs
Ground: Riverside Ground, Acre Bottom, Ramsbottom BL0 0BS. **(T)**
Capacity: **Seats:** Yes **Covered:** Yes **Midweek Matchday:** Tuesday **Clubhouse:** Yes **Shop:** No

Colours(change): Blue/blue/white (Red/black/red).
Previous Names:
Previous Leagues: Bury Amateur, Bolton Combination & Manchester League
Records: **Att:** 1,653 v FC United of Manchester 07.04.2007. **Goalscorer:** Russell Brierley - 176 (1996-2003).
Senior Honours: North West Counties Division Two 1996-97.

10 YEAR RECORD

01-02	02-03	03-04	04-05	05-06	06-07	07-08	08-09	09-10	10-11
NWC1 12	NWC1 15	NWC1 17	NWC1 5	NWC1 18	NWC1 8	NWC1 16	NWCP 14	NWCP 4	NWCP 2

RUNCORN LINNETS
Founded: 2006 Nickname: Linnets

Secretary: Lynn Johnston **(T)** 01606 43008 **(E)**
Chairman: Derek Greenwood **Manager:** Paul McNally **Prog Ed:** Mark Buckley
Ground: Millbank Linnets Stadium, Murdishaw Ave, Runcorn, Cheshire WA7 6HP **(T)** 07050 801733 (Clubline)
Capacity: **Seats:** **Covered:** **Midweek Matchday:** Tuesday **Clubhouse:** Yes **Shop:**

Colours(change): Yellow & green hoops/green/yellow & green. (Blue & white/white/blue)
Previous Names: None
Previous Leagues: None.
Records: 1,037 v Witton Albion, pre season friendly July 2010
Senior Honours:

10 YEAR RECORD

01-02	02-03	03-04	04-05	05-06	06-07	07-08	08-09	09-10	10-11
					NWC2 2	NWC1 12	NWCP 11	NWCP 11	NWCP 12

RUNCORN TOWN

Founded: 1967 | Nickname:

Secretary: Martin Fallon | **(T)** 01928 590 508 | **(E)**

Chairman: Tony Riley | **Manager:** Simon Burton | **Prog Ed:** Alan Bennett

Ground: Pavilions Sports Complex, Sandy Lane, Weston Point, Runcorn WA7 4EX | **(T)** 01928 590 508

Capacity: | **Seats:** Yes | **Covered:** Yes | **Midweek Matchday:** Monday | **Clubhouse:** | **Shop:**

Colours(change): Sky & navy/navy/navy (Yellow & black/black/yellow)
Previous Names: Mond Rangers 1967-2005 (Amalgamated with ICI Weston 1974-75).
Previous Leagues: Runcorn Sunday 1967-73, Warrington & District 1973-84, West Cheshire 1984-10.
Records: **Att:** 185 v Dunston UTS, FA Vase 4th Round 2011.
Senior Honours: West Cheshire League Division Two 2006-07. Runcorn Senior Cup 2004-05, 05-06, 07-08.

10 YEAR RECORD

01-02	02-03	03-04	04-05	05-06	06-07	07-08	08-09	09-10	10-11
WCh1	WCh2	WCh2	WCh2 2	WCh1 15	WCh2 1	WCh1 3	WCh1 4	WCh1 3	NWC1 2

SILSDEN

Founded: 1904 | Nickname:

Secretary: John Barclay | **(T)** 01535 656213 | **(E)**

Chairman: Sean McNulty | **Manager:** Chris Reape | **Prog Ed:** Peter Hanson

Ground: Keighley Road, Keighley Road, Silsden, BD20 0EH | **(T)** TBC

Capacity: | **Seats:** Yes | **Covered:** Yes | **Midweek Matchday:** Wednesday | **Clubhouse:** Yes | **Shop:**

Colours(change): Red/black/red (All yellow).
Previous Names: Reformed in 1980.
Previous Leagues: Craven & District. West Riding County Amateur.
Records: **Att:**1,564 v FC United of Manchester- March 2007
Senior Honours:

10 YEAR RECORD

01-02	02-03	03-04	04-05	05-06	06-07	07-08	08-09	09-10	10-11
			NWC2 2	NWC1 14	NWC1 14	NWC1 11	NWCP 9	NWCP 14	NWCP 16

SQUIRES GATE

Founded: 1948 | Nickname:

Secretary: John Maguire | **(T)** 01253 348 512 | **(E)**

Chairman: Stuart Hopwood | **Manager:** Russ McKenna | **Prog Ed:** Dave Gore

Ground: School Road, Marton, Blackpool, Lancs FY4 5DS | **(T)** 01253 798 583

Capacity: 1,000 | **Seats:** 100 | **Covered:** Yes | **Midweek Matchday:** Tuesday | **Clubhouse:** Yes | **Shop:** No

Colours(change): All blue. (All Red)
Previous Names: Squires Gate British Legion FC >1953.
Previous Leagues: Blackpool & District Amateur 1958-61. West Lancashire 1961-91.
Records: **Att:** 600 v Everton, friendly 1995.
Senior Honours:

10 YEAR RECORD

01-02	02-03	03-04	04-05	05-06	06-07	07-08	08-09	09-10	10-11
NWC2 3	NWC1 12	NWC1 20	NWC1 17	NWC1 13	NWC1 18	NWC1 6	NWCP 10	NWCP 13	NWCP 9

ST HELENS TOWN

Founded: 1946 | Nickname: Town

Secretary: Jeff Voller | **(T)** 0151 222 2963 | **(E)**

Chairman: John McKiernan | **Manager:** Jim McBride | **Prog Ed:** Jeff Voller

Ground: Ashton Town FC, Edge Green St, Ashton-in-Makerfield WN4 8SL | **(T)** 01942 701 483

Capacity: | **Seats:** | **Covered:** | **Midweek Matchday:** Tuesday | **Clubhouse:** | **Shop:**

Colours(change): Red & white/red/red & white. (Sky blue/navy/navy).
Previous Names: St Helen's Town formed in 1903 folded in 1923.
Previous Leagues: Liverpool Co Comb 1946-49 Lancs Comb 49-75, Chesh Co. 75-82
Records: **Att:** 4,000 v Manchester City 1950. **Goalscorer:** S. Pennington. **App:** Alan Wellens
Senior Honours: Lancashire Combination 1971-72 . FA Vase 1986-87.

10 YEAR RECORD

01-02	02-03	03-04	04-05	05-06	06-07	07-08	08-09	09-10	10-11
NWC1 4	NWC1 7	NWC1 19	NWC1 3	NWC1 8	NWC1 19	NWC1 14	NWCP 16	NWCP 9	NWCP 17

STONE DOMINOES

Founded: 1987 Nickname: The Doms

Secretary: Pauline Matthews **(T)** 01785 761 891 **(E)**

Chairman: Chris Haines **Manager:** Shaun Hollinshead **Prog Ed:** Colin Heath

Ground: Motiva Park, Yarnfield Lane, Yarnfield, Stone, Staffs ST15 0NF **(T)** 01785 761 891

Capacity: 1,000 **Seats:** 250 **Covered:** yes **Midweek Matchday:** Wednesday **Clubhouse:** Yes **Shop:**

Colours(change): Red/black/Black (All white).
Previous Names:
Previous Leagues: Midland League
Records: **Att:** 887 v FC United of Manchester 24/03/07 (at Newcastle Town).
Senior Honours: Midland League 1999-00. North West Counties League Division One 2009-10.

10 YEAR RECORD

01-02	02-03	03-04	04-05	05-06	06-07	07-08	08-09	09-10	10-11
NWC2 4	NWC2 2	NWC1 10	NWC1 11	NWC1 21	NWC1 22	NWC2 10	NWC1 3	NWC1 1	NWCP 19

WINSFORD UNITED

Founded: 1883 Nickname: Blues

Secretary: Robert Astles **(T)** 01606 558 447 **(E)**

Chairman: Mark Loveless **Manager:** Ian Street **Prog Ed:** Robert Astles

Ground: Barton Stadium, Kingsway, Winsford, Cheshire CW7 3AE **(T)** 01606 558 447

Capacity: 6,000 **Seats:** 250 **Covered:** 5,000 **Midweek Matchday:** Tuesday **Clubhouse:** Yes **Shop:** Yes

Colours(change): All royal blue. (All white).
Previous Names:
Previous Leagues: The Combination 1902-04. Cheshire County 1919-40, 47-82. N.P.L. 1987-01
Records: **Att:** 8,000 v Witton Albion, 1947. **Goalscorer:** Graham Smith 66 **Apps:** Edward Harrop 400
Senior Honours: Cheshire League 1920-21, 76-77. Cheshire Senior Cup 1958-59, 79-80, 92-93.
North West Counties League Division Two 2006-07.

10 YEAR RECORD

01-02	02-03	03-04	04-05	05-06	06-07	07-08	08-09	09-10	10-11
NWC1 7	NWC1 22	NWC2 8	NWC2 3	NWC2 4	NWC2 1	NWC1 10	NWCP 19	NWCP 19	NWCP 3

NORTH WEST COUNTIES INS & OUTS

PREM

IN: IN: AFC Blackpool (P), AFC Liverpool (P), Runcorn Town (P)

OUT: Formby (R), New Mills (P - Northern Premier League Division One South), Rossendale United (W)

DIV ONE

IN: Formby (R), Nelson (N), Northwich Villa (P - Cheshire League Division One)

OUT: AFC Blackpool (P), AFC Liverpool (P), Runcorn Town (P)

ABBEY HEY
Founded: 1902 Nickname:

Secretary: Tony McAllister **(T)** 0161 231 7147 **(E)**
Chairman: James Whittaker **Manager:** Barry Walker **Prog Ed:** Gordon Lester
Ground: The Abbey Stadium, Goredale Avenue, Gorton, Manchester M18 7HD **(T)** 0161 231 7147 **Capacity:**
Colours(change): Red/black/red (All blue)

ADDITIONAL INFORMATION: Previous Lge: Manchester Amateur, South East Lancashire, Manchester.
Record Att: 400 v Manchester City XI, October 1999.
Honours: Manchester League 1981-82, 88-89, 88-89, 91-92, 93-94, 94-95.

AFC DARWEN
Founded: 2009 (reformed) Nickname:

Secretary: Derek Slater **(T)** 07989 744 584 **(E)**
Chairman: Derek Slater **Manager:** Kenny Langford **Prog Ed:** Steve Hart
Ground: Anchor Ground, Anchor Road, Darwen, Lancs, BB3 0BB. **(T)** 07989 744 584 **Capacity:**
Colours(change): All red (All navy)

ADDITIONAL INFORMATION:
Record Att: 14,000 v Blackburn Rovers 1882.
Honours: Lancashire League 1902. North West Counties League Cup 1983. North West Alliance Cup 1996.

ASHTON TOWN
Founded: 1962 Nickname:

Secretary: Steve Barrett **(T)** 01942 701 483 **(E)**
Chairman: Mark Hayes **Manager:** John Carroll **Prog Ed:** Ian Promfrett
Ground: Edge Green Street, Ashton-in-Makerfield, Wigan, WN4 8SL **(T)** 01942 701483 **Capacity:**
Colours(change): Red/black/black (White/red/red)

ADDITIONAL INFORMATION:
Record Att: 1,865 v FC United of Manchester 2007.
Honours: Warrington League Guardian Cup.

ATHERTON COLLIERIES
Founded: 1916 Nickname: The Colts

Secretary: Emil Anderson **(T)** **(E)**
Chairman: Paul Gregory **Manager:** Steve Pilling **Prog Ed:** Emil Anderson
Ground: Alder Street, Atherton, Greater Manchester. M46 9EY. **(T)** 07968 548056 **Capacity:**
Colours(change): Black & white stripes/black/black (All orange)

ADDITIONAL INFORMATION:
Record Att: 3,300 in Lancashire Combination 1920's.
Honours: North West Counties League Division 3 1986-87.

CHADDERTON
Founded: 1947 Nickname: Chaddy

Secretary: David Shepherd **(T)** 0161 624 9733 **(E)**
Chairman: Bob Sopel **Manager:** Paul Buckley **Prog Ed:** Bob Sopel
Ground: Andrew Street, Chadderton, Oldham, Greater Manchester. OL9 0JT **(T)** 0161 624 9733 **Capacity:**
Colours(change): Red/black/red (Orange/black/black)

ADDITIONAL INFORMATION:
Record Att: 2,352 v FC United of Manchester 2006.
Honours: Gilgryst Cup 1969-70. Umbro International Cup 1999-00.

CHEADLE TOWN
Founded: 1961 Nickname:

Secretary: Brian Lindon **(T)** 0161 428 2510 **(E)**
Chairman: Chris Davies **Manager:** Steve Brokenbrow **Prog Ed:** Stuart Crawford
Ground: Park Road Stadium, Cheadle, Cheshire, SK8 2AN **(T)** 0161 428 2510 **Capacity:**
Colours(change): Green/green/white (White/black/black).

ADDITIONAL INFORMATION:
Record Att: 3,377 v FC United of Manchester (At Stockport County). **Goalscorer:** Peter Tilley. **Apps:** John McArdle.
Honours: Manchester Division One 1979-80.

DAISY HILL
Founded: 1894 Nickname:

Secretary: Robert Naylor **(T)** 01942 818 544 **(E)**
Chairman: Graham Follows **Manager:** Craig Thomas **Prog Ed:** Robert Naylor
Ground: New Sirs, St James Street, Westhoughton, Bolton, BL5 2EB **(T)** 01942 818 544 **Capacity:**
Colours(change): All royal blue (All red)

ADDITIONAL INFORMATION:
Record Att: 2,000 v Horwich RMI, Westhoughton Charity Cup Final 1979-80. **Goalscorer & Apps:** Alan Roscoe 300gls, 450app
Honours: Bolton Combination Premier Division 1962-63, 72-73, 75-76, 77-78.

ECCLESHALL
Founded: 1971 Nickname:

Secretary: Stephen Wright **(T)** 01785 851 351 (MD) **(E)**
Chairman: Andy Mapperson **Manager:** Dave Dale **Prog Ed:** Richard Marsh
Ground: Pershall Park, Chester Road, Eccleshall, ST21 6NE **(T)** 01785-851351 (MD) **Capacity:**
Colours(change): Blue & black stripes/black/black (All red)

ADDITIONAL INFORMATION:
Record Att: 2,011 v FC United of Manchester November 2005.
Honours: Midland League 1990, 2002-03.

FORMBY
Founded: 1919 Nickname: Squirrels

Secretary: Anita Shaw **(T)** 01704 833 615 **(E)**
Chairman: Hugh McAuley **Manager:** Kevin Daily **Prog Ed:** Adrian Cork
Ground: Altcar Road, Formby, Merseyside L37 4EL **(T)** 01704 833 615 **Capacity:** 2,000
Colours(change): Yellow/blue/blue (All navy)

ADDITIONAL INFORMATION: Record Att: 603 v Southport Liverpool Senior Cup 2003-04
Previous Lge: Liverpool Co. Comb, 1919-68, Lancs Comb. 68-71, Cheshire Co. 71-82

HOLKER OLD BOYS
Founded: 1936 Nickname: Cobs

Secretary: John Adams **(T)** 01229 828 176 **(E)**
Chairman: Dick John **Manager:** Dave Smith **Prog Ed:** Dick John
Ground: Rakesmoor, Rakesmoor Lane, Hawcoat, Barrow-in-Furness, LA14 4QB **(T)** 01229 828 176 **Capacity:**
Colours(change): Green & white/green/green & white (All red)

ADDITIONAL INFORMATION:
Record Att: 2,303 v FC United of Manchester FA Cup at Craven Park 2005-06. **Goalscorer:** Dave Conlin.
Honours: West Lancashire League 1986-87.

IRLAM
Founded: 1969 Nickname:

Secretary: Warren Dodd **(T)** 07718 756402/07969 946277 **(E)**
Chairman: Ron Parker **Manager:** Ryan Gilligan **Prog Ed:** Warren Dodd
Ground: Silver Street, Irlam, Manchester M44 6HR **(T)** 07718 756402 **Capacity:**
Colours(change): Blue & white/blue/blue (All red)

ADDITIONAL INFORMATION:
Previous Name: Mitchell Shackleton. **Previous League:** Manchester.
Record Att: 1,600 v Hallam FA Vase.

LEEK C.S.O.B.
Founded: 1945 Nickname:

Secretary: Stan Lockett **(T)** 01538 383734 **(E)**
Chairman: Chris McMullen **Manager:** Brett Barlow **Prog Ed:** Stan Lockett
Ground: Leek Town FC, Harrison Park, Macclesfield Road, Leek, Staffs. ST13 8LD **(T)** 01538 383734 **Capacity:**
Colours(change): Red & white stripes/red/red & white hoops (Blue/blue/blue & white hoops)

ADDITIONAL INFORMATION:
Record Att: 2,590 v FC United of Manchester August 2005.
Honours: Midland League 1995-96.

NELSON
Founded: 1883 Nickname: Blues

Secretary: Diane Whittaker **(T)** 01282 613 820 **(E)**
Chairman: Fayyaz Ahmed **Manager:** Paul Paynter **Prog Ed:** Alan Maidment
Ground: Victoria Park, Lomeshaye Way, Nelson, Lancs BB9 7BN. **(T)** 01282 613 820 **Capacity:** 1500
Colours(change): All royal blue. (Sky blue & white stripes/white/white).

ADDITIONAL INFORMATION: Att: 14,143 v Bradford Park Avenue, Div.3 North, 10.04.26.
Honours: Football League Division Three North 1922-23. **Previous Lge:** Lancashire 1889-98,1900-01. Football Lge 1898-1900. Lancashire Combination 1901-16,46-82. NWC 1982-88. West Lancashire 1988-92.

NORTHWICH VILLA
Founded: 2005 Nickname:

Secretary: Vic England **(T)** **(E)**
Chairman: Robert Millington **Manager:** Kevin Langley **Prog Ed:** Noel McCourt
Ground: Victoria Stadium, Wincham, Northwich, Cheshire CW9 6GB **(T)** 01606 815 200 **Capacity:**
Colours(change): Green & white hoops/white/white (Yellow/blue/blue).

ADDITIONAL INFORMATION: Record Att: 146 v Northwich Victoria.
Previous Lge: Cheshire 2005-11.
Honours: Cheshire League Division One 2008-09, Division One Cup 2009-10.

NORTON UNITED

Founded: 1989 Nickname:

Secretary: Dennis Vickers (T) 01782 838 290 (E)
Chairman: Stephen Beaumont **Manager:** Dave Johnson **Prog Ed:** Dennis Vickers
Ground: Norton CC & MWI Community Drive, Smallthorne, Stoke-on-Trent ST6 1QF (T) 01782 838 290 **Capacity:**
Colours(change): Red & black/black/black (All yellow)

ADDITIONAL INFORMATION:
Record Att: 1,382 v FC United of Manchester 09/04/2006.
Honours: Midland League 1996-97, 98-99, 2000-01. Staffordshire Senior Vase 1998-99, 2003-04.

OLDHAM BORO

Founded: 1964 Nickname:

Secretary: John Egan (T) 0161 624 2689 (E)
Chairman: Mark Kilgannon **Manager:** Tony Mills **Prog Ed:**
Ground: Whitebank Road, Oldham, Greater Manchester OL8 3JH (T) 0161 624 2689 **Capacity:**
Colours(change): Blue/black/white (Cream/royal blue/royal blue)

ADDITIONAL INFORMATION:
Record Att: 1,767 v FC United of Manchester 2006.
Honours: North West Counties Division Two 1997-98.

ROCHDALE TOWN

Founded: 1924 Nickname:

Secretary: Deborah Hibbert (T) 01706 527103 (E)
Chairman: Mark Canning **Manager:** Dave Brown **Prog Ed:** Deborah Hibbert
Ground: Mayfield Sports Centre, Keswick Street, Castleton, Rochdale. OL11 3AG (T) 01706 527103 **Capacity:**
Colours(change): Black & white stripes/black/black (Blue/white/blue).

ADDITIONAL INFORMATION:
Record Att: 2,473 v FC United of Manchester (at Radcliffe Borough).
Honours: Manchester Division One 1986-87.

WIGAN ROBIN PARK

Founded: 2005 Nickname:

Secretary: Taffy Roberts (T) 01942 404 950 (E)
Chairman: Steve Halliwell **Manager:** John Neafcy **Prog Ed:** Andrew Vaughan
Ground: Robin Park Arena, Loire Drive, Robin Park, Wigan, WN5 0UH (T) 01942 404 950 **Capacity:**
Colours(change): Red & white/black & red/black & red (Yellow/green/yellow)

ADDITIONAL INFORMATION: Att: 298 v AFC Liverpool 31/03/09.
Previous League: Manchester 2005-08.
Honours: Manchester Premier 2007-08, Gilgryst Cup 07-08.

GROUND DIRECTIONS

AFC BLACKPOOL - Mechanics Ground, Jepson Way, Common Edge Road, Blackpool, Lancashire FY4 5DY. 01253 761721
M6 to M55, exit at junction 4. At roundabout turn left along A583 to traffic lights, turn right into Whitehill Road, to traffic lights (2 miles). Go straight across the main road into Jepson Way, ground at top.

AFC LIVERPOOL - Valerie Park, Eaton Street, Prescot, Merseyside, L34 6ND. 0151 430 0507
From North: M6 to Junction 26, onto M58 to Junction 3. Follow A570 to junction with A580 (East Lancs Road). (Approach junction in right hand lane of the two lanes going straight on). Cross A580 and take first road on right (Bleak Hill Road). Follow this road through to Prescot (2 miles). At traffic lights turn right, straight on at large roundabout (do not follow route onto Prescot by-pass) and right at next lights. 100 yards turn right at Hope and Anchor pub into Hope Street. Club will be in sight at bottom of road. From South: M6 to Junction 21a (M62 junction 10). Follow M62 towards Liverpool, to junction 7. Follow A57 to Rainhill and Prescot. Through traffic lights at Fusilier pub, 100 yards turn right at Hope and Anchor pub (as above). From East: Follow M62 as described in 'From South' or A580 East Lancs Road to Junction with A570 (Rainford by-pass), turn left and take first right. Follow route as 'From North'

ALSAGER TOWN - The Town Ground, Woodland Court, Alsager, Staffs, ST7 2DP 01270 882336
M6 to Junction16, A500 towards Stoke, leave A500 at 2nd exit (A34 to Congleton) at 2nd set of traffic lights on A34 turn left for Alsager, turn right opposite Caradon/Twyfords Factory (500 Yards), into Moorhouse Ave, West Grove mile on right. No available parking within the ground.

ASHTON ATHLETIC - Brocstedes Park, Downall Green, Ashton in Makerfield. WN4 0NR. 01942 716360
M6 northbound to junction 25, follow the slip road to the island and turn right A49, proceed for approx 0.50 mile turning right into Soughers Lane. At the T junction turn right into Downall Green Road and go over the motorway bridge passing a church on your right. Turn 2nd right into Booths Brow Road and turn 2nd right again into Brocstedes Road which is a narrow street. After 200 yards turn right down a shale road into the car park and ground.

From The North: M6 southbound to junction 24, proceed on to the slip road keeping in the right hand lane, turn right go over the motorway bridge and immediately re-enter the M6 Northbound for approximately 100 yards. Leave at junction 25,Follow the slip road to the island and turn right A49, proceed for approx 0.50 mile turning right into Soughers Lane. At the T junction turn right into Downall Green Road and go over the motorway bridge passing a church on your right. Turn 2nd right into Booths Brow Road and turn 2nd right again into Brocstedes Road which is a narrow street. After 200 yards turn right down a shale road into the car park and ground.

ATHERTON L.R. - Crilly Park, Spa Road, Atherton, Greater Manchester. M46 9XG. 01942 883950
M61 to Junction 5, follow signs for Westhoughton, turn left onto A6, turn right at first lights into Newbrook Road, then turn right into Upton Road, passing Atherton Central Station. Turn left into Springfield Road and left again into Hillside Road into Spa Road and ground.

BACUP BOROUGH - Brian Boys Stadium, Cowtoot Lane, Blackthorn, Bacup, Lancashire. OL13 8EE. 01706 878655
From M62, take M66 onto A681, through Rawtenstall to Bacup Town Centre, turn left onto the A671 towards Burnley, after approx. 300 yards turn right immediately before the Irwell Inn climbing Cooper Street, turn right into Blackthorn Lane, then first left into Cowtoot Lane to ground.

BARNOLDSWICK TOWN - Silentnight Stadium, West Close Road, Barnoldswick, Colne, BB18 5EW. 01282 815817
ravelling from Blackburn to Colne on M65 to end, straight on at roundabout onto Vivary Way onto North Valley Road. Through two sets of traffic lights to roundabout, turn left to Barnoldswick. Straight on till you come to roundabout in Kelbrook turn left to Barnoldswick.On entering Barnoldswick straight ahead at traffic lights, straight ahead at mini roundabout. Travel through built up area past Fosters Arms pub on left set back. Take first right onto Greenberfield Lane, travel 50 yards take middle single track (signposted) travel to bottom of track and bare right to car park at rear of ground.
Travelling from Barrow on A59 from Gisburn towards Skipton turn right at Barnoldswick signpost. Travel approx 2 miles taking 1st left onto Greenberfield Lane, travel 50 yards take middle single track (signposted) travel to bottom of track bare right to car park at rear of ground.
If using a SatNav use postcode BB18 5LJ.

BOOTLE - Delta Taxi Stadium, Vestey Road, off Bridle Road, Bootle, L30 4UN. 0151 525 4796 or 07852 742790
At Liverpool end of M57and M58 follow signs for Liverpool (A59 (S)), for 1 1/2 miles. At Aintree racecourse on left and Aintree Train Station on right ,turn right at lights into Park Lane. Turn left at second set of lights into Bridle Road. After 200 yards turn left at lights into Vestey Estate , ground 200 yards.

COLNE - The XLCR Stadium, Harrison Drive, Colne, Lancashire. BB8 9SL. 01282 862545
Follow M65 to end of motorway. Turn left and follow signs for Skipton and Keighley, continue to roundabout, take 1st left up Harrison Drive, across small roundabout, follow road to ground.

CONGLETON TOWN - Booth Street, off Crescent Road, Congleton, Cheshire, CW12 4DG. 01260 274460
On approach to Congleton from M6, past Waggon & Horses Pub, at 1st roundabout 2nd exit, past fire station, 2nd right into Booth Street. Ground at top of road.

FLIXTON - Valley Road, Flixton, Manchester. M41. 0161 748 2903
Leave M60 junction 10, take the B5214, signposted Urmston, at the second roundabout take third exit, take right only lane on the exit in Davyhulme Road, follow this road to Valley Road, just after the left hand bend after 1 1/2 miles. The ground is at the other end of the road.

GLOSSOP NORTH END - Surrey Street, Glossop, Derbyshire. SK13 7AJ. 01457 855469
A57 to Glossop, turn left at traffic lights (near Tesco sign), Glossopbrook Road. Follow road to top of hill. Ground on right.

MAINE ROAD - Brantingham Road, Chorlton-cum-Hardy, Manchester. M21 0TT. 0161 861 0344
M60 to junction 7, A56 towards Manchester. At traffic island follow signs for Manchester United, Lancs CC, turn right at next set of traffic lights signposted A5145 (Chorlton-cum-Hardy/Stockport), through next set of traffic lights. Take left fork at Y junction (traffic lights) onto A6010 (Wilbraham Road) to Chorlton. Through traffic lights (ignore pedestrian lights) for approx 1 mile. Left at next traffic lights into Withington Road, first left into Brantingham Road. Ground 300 yards on left. From North: M60 clockwise to junction 5 onto A5103 towards Manchester Centre for approx 2 miles, turn left at traffic lights (Wilbraham Road) A6010, then right at 2nd set of lights (Withington Road), first left into Brantingham Road. Ground 300 yards on left.

PADIHAM - Arbories Memorial Sports Ground, Well Street, Padiham, Lancashire, BB12 8LE. 01282 773742
M65 to Junction 8, then follow A6068 signposted Clitheroe and Padiham. At traffic lights at bottom of hill turn right into Dean Range/Blackburn Road towards Padiham. At next junction turn into Holland Street opposite church, then into Well St at the side of Hare & Hounds Pub to ground.

RAMSBOTTOM UNITED - Riverside Ground, Acrebottom, Ramsbottom, Bury. BL0 0BS
M66(North) to junction 1, take A56 towards Ramsbottom. After 1 mile turn left at traffic lights down Bury New Road. Turn left after old Mondi Paper Mill (and before the railway crossing) along the road running parallel with East Lancashire Railway. Ground at bottom on the right. From North : Leave M65 at junction 8. Follow A56 to Ramsbottom exit then follow A676 (signposted Bolton) into the centre of Ramsbottom. At the traffic lights in centre of town, turn left into Bridge Street and turn right after the railway crossing.

RUNCORN LINNETS - Millbank Linnets Stadium, Murdishaw Ave, Runcorn, Cheshire. WA7 6HP. 07050 801733 (Clubline)
orth East - M56 junction 12 take A557 Widnes/Northwich. At Roundabout take 1st Exit onto A557 heading Frodsham A56, go through 1 roundabout. Turn left at Chester Rd/A56, turn left at Chester Rd/A533. At the r'about, take the 2nd exit onto Murdishaw Ave. Destination on the Right.
Head West on M56 towards Exit 11. At junction 11, take the A56 exit to Preston Brook/Daresbury. At the roundabout take the 1st exit onto Chester Rd/A56 heading to Preston Brook/Daresbury. Continue to follow Chester Rd, go through 2 roundabouts.At the roundabout take the 2nd exit onto Murdishaw Ave. Destination on the right.

RUNCORN TOWN - Pavilions Sports Complex, Sandy Lane, Weston Point, Runcorn, Cheshire WA7 4EX. 01928 590 508
M56 J12. Head towards Liverpool. Come off at 4th exit (Runcorn Docks), turn left at the top of slip road, left at T-Junction, then left into Pavilions.
M62 J7. Head towards Runcorn. When crossing Runcorn Bridge, stay in the right hand lane. Follow road around and come off at second exit (Runcorn Docks). Turn right at the top of slip road, left at T-Junction, then left into Pavilions.

SILSDEN - Keighley Road, Silsden, BD20 0EH
A629 Skipton to Keighley road, take A6034, ground in on the left after the golf driving range.

SQUIRES GATE - School Road, Marton, Blackpool, FY4 5DS. 01253 798583
From M55: At the end of the M55 (J4), continue along dual carriageway (A5230), and bear left at major roundabout, staying on A5230. At second traffic lights, turn left onto B5261. After passing Shovels pub on left, turn left at lights, and first car park is on left after approx 50 yards. Parking is also available down the lane leading to the Club, on your left, after another 40 yards. If both these are full, parking is also available on the Shovels car park, or on the car park adjacent to the playing fields (turn right at the lights after passing the pub).

ST HELENS TOWN - Ashton Town FC, Edge Green Street, Ashton-in-Makerfield, Wigan, Greater Manchester. 01942 701483
M6 to Junction 23, A49 to Ashton-in-Makerfield. Turn right at the traffic lights onto the A58 towards Bolton. After approx. three quarters of a mile, turn right into Golbourne Road. After 200 yards turn right into Edge Green Street. Ground at bottom of street.(Ashton Town FC)

STONE DOMINOES - Motiva Park, Yarnfield Lane, Yarnfield, Stone, Staffs, ST15 0NF. 01785 761891
From M6 junction 15, straight on at first roundabout following A500 to Stoke, come to first slip road)before flyover) and turn right at roundabout heading to Stone A34 (5 miles), straight on at next roundabout (Trentham Gardens on your right), through village of Tittensor (take care: cameras - 40mph), at next roundabout straight on (pub in the middle, Darlaston Inn) still on A34, 2 more roundabouts *BP garage on left) get in right hand lane and turn right into Yarnfield Lane (pub on corner called the Wayfarer) football ground is about 1 mile on left before village of Yarnfield.

WINSFORD UNITED - The Barton Stadium, Kingsway, Winsford, Cheshire. CW7 3AE. 01606 558447
From M6 junction 18, follow A54 through Middlewich for approx 3 miles, bear right at roundabout at Winsford Railway Station, follow road for approx 1 mile, turn right into Kingsway, ground is on the right.

DIVISION ONE

ABBEY HEY - The Abbey Stadium, Goredale Avenue, Gorton, Manchester M18 7HD. 0161 231 7147

M60 to junction 24, take A57 to Manchester City Centre for approx 1 mile, at first set of major traffic lights (MacDonalds on right) pass through for approx 300yards, turn left immediatley before overhead railway bridge (A.H.F.C. sign) into Woodland Avenue. Take first right, pass under railway bridge, turn first left into Goredale Avenue.

AFC DARWEN - Anchor Ground, Anchor Road, Darwen, Lancs, BB3 0BB. 07989-744584

Leave M65 at Junction 4. At traffic lights turn left onto A666 (signposted Darwen). After approx ? mile turn left between Anchor Car Sales and the Anchor Pub. Bare right and ground 200 yards on left.

ASHTON TOWN - Edge Green Street, Ashton-in-Makerfield, Wigan, Greater Manchester. WN4 8SL. 01942 701483

M6 to Junction 23, A49 to Ashton-in-Makerfield. Turn right at the traffic lights onto the A58 towards Bolton. After approx. three quarters of a mile, turn right into Golbourne Road. After 200 yards turn right into Edge Green Street. Ground at bottom of street.

ATHERTON COLLIERIES - Alder Street, Atherton, Greater Manchester. M46 9EY. 07968 548056

M61 to junction 5, follow sign for Westhoughton, turn left onto A6, turn right onto A579 (Newbrook Road/Bolton Road) into Atherton. At first set of traffic lights turn left into High Street, then second left into Alder Street to ground.

CHADDERTON - Andrew Street, Chadderton, Oldham, Greater Manchester OL9 0JT. 0161 624 9733

M62 to junction 20, following A627(M) towards Manchester. Motorway becomes a dual carriageway, turn left at first major traffic lights (A699) Middleton Road, then second left into Burnley Street, Andrew Street at the end.

CHEADLE TOWN - Park Road Stadium, Cheadle, Cheshire, SK8 2AN. 0161 428 2510

M60 to junction 2 (formerly M63 junction 11), follow A560 to Cheadle. Go through first main set of traffic lights and then first left after shops into Park Road. Ground at end of road.

DAISY HILL - New Sirs, St James Street, Westhoughton, Bolton, BL5 2EB. 01942 818 544.

M61 to junction 5, A58 (Snydale Way/Park Road) for one and a half mile, left into Leigh Road (B5235) for 1 mile to Daisy Hill. Turn right into village 200 yards after mini roundabout, then left between church and school into St James Street. Ground 250 yards on left.

ECCLESHALL - Pershall Park, Chester Road, Eccleshall, ST21 6NE. 01785-851351 (Match Days Only)

M6 to junction 14 then A5013 to Eccleshall, right at mini-roundabout and then left at next mini-roundabout into High Street B5026, ground 1 mile on right.

M6 to junction 15, then A519 to Eccleshall right at mini-roundabout to High Street B5026, ground 1 mile on right.

FORMBY - Altcar Road, Formby, Merseyside, L37 8DL. 01704 833615

A565 Liverpool to Southport Road. At traffic lights opposite Tesco's superstore, turn right into Altcar Road. The ground is located 350 yards on the right, past Tesco.

HOLKER OLD BOYS - Rakesmoor, Rakesmoor Lane, Hawcoat, Barrow-in-Furness, Cumbria. LA14 4QB. 01229 828176

M6 to junction 36. Take the A590 all the way to Barrow-in-Furness. At the borough boundary continue along the A590. After 1? miles you will pass the Kimberley Clark paper mill on your right. Immediately after passing the paper mill turn left into Bank Lane, signposted "Barrow Golf Club" on the left hand side of the A590 and "Hawcoat yard on the right hand side of the A590. Follow this road to the T- junction at the top of the hill outside the Golf Club. Turn left here into Rakesmoor Lane the ground is 200 yds. down the road on the right. *Please be advised that Rakesmoor Lane beyond the ground is a single-track road and as such is unsuitable for coaches. It is not possible to turn a coach into the ground when approaching from that direction.*

IRLAM - Irlam Football Club, Silver Street, Irlam, Manchester M44 6HR. 07718 756402/07969 946277

From Peel Green Roundabout (M60 Junction 11), take A57 to Irlam, and then B5320 into Lower Irlam. After passing Morsons Project, turn right into Silver Street, at Nags Head Pub. The ground is situated at the bottom of Silver Street on the right hand side.

LEEK C.S.O.B. - Harrison Park, Macclesfield Road, Leek, Staffs. ST13 8LD (Leek Town FC). 01538 383 734.

M6 to junction 17 - A534 to Congleton - follow signs for Leek (A54) - carry on A54 until junction with A523 - turn right onto A523 - this is road direct to Leek and ground (8 miles) - ground on right just into Leek (Macclesfield Road).

NELSON - Victoria Park, Lomeshaye Way, Nelson, Lancs BB9 7BN. 01282 613 820

M65 to Junction 13. Take first left (A6068 Fence), 2nd left (B6249 Nelson), the 2nd right, signposted Lomeshaye Village, to ground.

NORTHWICH VILLA - Victoria Stadium, Wincham, Northwich, Cheshire. 01606 815200

From M6, leave at junction 19, follow A556 towards Northwich for approx 3 miles, turn right onto the A559 towards Lostock Gralam, turn right at traffic lights before the Slow & Easy Public House, follow signs to Victoria Stadium.

NORTON UNITED - Norton CC & MWI - Community Drive, Smallthorne, Stoke-on-Trent ST6 1QF. 01782 838290

M6 to junction 16, A500 to Burslem/Tunstall, turn off bear right at traffic island to Burslem, through lights to Smallthorne, take 3rd exit on mini-roundabout, turn right by pedestrian crossing into Community Drive, ground 200 metres on left.

OLDHAM BORO - Whitebank Road, Oldham, Greater Manchester OL8 3JH. 0161 624 2689

M60 to Junction 18, join the new M60 motorway to junction 22, Hollinwood, turn left at next set of lights onto Hollins Road (A6104), follow road until you see fire station on right, turn right at fire station, follow road down to next left Whitebank Road. Ground is on your left.

ROCHDALE TOWN - Mayfield Sports Centre, Keswick Street, Castleton, Rochdale. OL11 3AG. 01706 527 103

M62 to junction 20, follow A627M towards Rochdale. Keep right on A627M and turn right at traffic lights at BMW Garage go to next roundabout, take 2nd exit into Queensway towards Castleton and through the Industrial Estate. Turn Right at traffic lights into Manchester Road, A664. Go past Castleton Rail station and turn left at Fairwell Inn, into Keswick St, go through new housing estate to ground --- Rochdale Town FC ground is next to Castlehawk Golf Club.

WIGAN ROBIN PARK - Robin Park Arena, Loire Drive, Robin Park, Wigan, WN5 0UH. 01942 404 950

M6 J25 take road into Wigan and follow signs for the DW Stadium (Wigan Athletic) Ground is next to stadium, behind Wickes DIY store on the retail park.

NORTHERN COUNTIES EAST LEAGUE

Sponsored by: Koolsport
Founded: 1982
Recent Champions:
2006: Buxton
2007: Retford United
2008: Winterton Rangers
2009: Mickleover Sports
2010: Bridlington Town
ncel.org.uk

PREMIER DIVISION	P	W	D	L	F	A	Pts
1 Farsley	38	27	4	7	108	41	85
2 Parkgate	38	23	9	6	94	55	78
3 Bridlington Town	38	20	11	7	94	55	71
4 Tadcaster Albion	38	20	8	10	90	62	68
5 Winterton Rangers	38	18	11	9	73	52	65
6 Lincoln Moorlands Railway	38	17	10	11	90	58	61
7 Pickering Town	38	18	7	13	81	71	61
8 Thackley	38	17	9	12	66	50	60
9 Nostell Miners Welfare	38	16	8	14	60	66	56
10 Scarborough Athletic	38	15	9	14	69	61	54
11 Maltby Main	38	15	9	14	59	61	54
12 Long Eaton United	38	14	12	12	47	59	54
13 Armthorpe Welfare	38	13	9	16	68	76	48
14 Hall Road Rangers	38	14	6	18	58	70	48
15 Selby Town	38	15	3	20	54	75	48
16 Brighouse Town	38	11	8	19	58	77	41
17 Liversedge (-1)	38	7	12	19	52	76	32
18 Arnold Town	38	6	12	20	61	95	30
19 Hallam	38	7	6	25	48	96	27
20 Dinnington Town	38	3	5	30	35	109	14

LEAGUE CUP

ROUND 1
AFC Emley 4-5 Barton Town Old Boys
Bottesford Town 5-0 Rossington Main
Glasshoughton Welfare 3-4 Eccleshill United
Hemsworth Miners Welfare 3-2 Brodsworth Welfare
Louth Town 8-0 Shirebrook Town
Staveley Miners Welfare 2-0 Pontefract Collieries
Teversal 0-2 Leeds Carnegie
Yorkshire Amateur 2-1 Worsbrough Bridge Athletic

ROUND 2
Appleby Frodinghm 2-1 Hemsworth Miners Welfare
Armthorpe Welfare 1-5 Parkgate
Arnold Town 4-2 Eccleshill United
Askern Villa 0-2 Hall Road Rangers
Barton Town Old Boys 4-2 Hallam
Brighouse Town 0-0 Liversedge
(Liversedge won 4-2 on penalties)
Dinnington Town 1-3 Staveley Miners Welfare
Grimsby Borough 3-4 Scarborough Athletic
Handsworth 3-1 Yorkshire Amateur
Lincoln Moorlands Railway 1-2 Bridlington Town
Long Eaton United 2-1 Nostell Miners Welfare
Louth Town 0-3 Farsley
Selby Town 0-1 Bottesford Town
Tadcaster Albion 2-3 Maltby Main
Thackley 0-2 Pickering Town
Winterton Rangers 1-0 Leeds Carnegie

ROUND 3
Appleby Frodingham 1-3 Winterton Rangers
Barton Town Old Boys 0-2 Staveley Miners Welfare
Farsley 5-0 Arnold Town
Hall Road Rangers 1-0 Long Eaton United
Liversedge 2-0 Bridlington Town
Maltby Main 0-2 Handsworth
Pickering Town 4-0 Parkgate
Scarborough Athletic 3-0 Bottesford Town

QUARTER FINALS
Handsworth 0-0 Staveley Miners Welfare
(Handsworth won 5-3 on penalties)
Liversedge 0-1 Farsley
Scarborough Athletic 1-0 Hall Road Rangers
Winterton Rangers 3-1 Pickering Town

SEMI-FINALS
Farsley 4-2 Handsworth
Winterton Rangers 3-2 Scarborough Athletic

FINAL (@ Staveley Miners Welfare, 2/5/11)
Farsley 1-0 Winterton Rangers

PREMIER DIVISION	1	2	3	4	5	6	7	8	9	10	11	12	13	14	15	16	17	18	19	20
1 Armthorpe Welfare		4-4	2-2	3-2	3-2	2-2	3-2	3-1	2-8	5-0	3-4	0-0	1-1	2-2	0-3	0-3	0-1	3-3	2-1	3-1
2 Arnold Town	2-1		1-2	2-1	2-0	2-8	2-4	2-1	3-3	0-0	0-3	3-3	1-2	0-2	5-5	3-4	5-0	1-3	1-1	2-2
3 Bridlington Town	2-0	0-0		1-1	3-0	1-2	1-1	2-0	3-2	2-0	5-0	4-2	4-3	2-2	4-2	5-0	5-1	3-1	2-4	2-1
4 Brighouse Town	2-1	1-1	1-2		4-3	1-6	0-4	3-0	4-7	1-2	0-1	0-5	1-2	1-1	3-0	1-2	0-1	1-5	0-1	4-3
5 Dinnington Town	4-2	0-1	1-3	2-2		1-4	0-4	2-1	0-2	1-1	1-1	0-3	0-0	0-3	1-4	1-7	0-2	1-3	1-5	0-3
6 Farsley	4-1	8-0	1-1	1-2	5-0		4-0	5-0	3-1	3-0	7-0	2-4	1-1	1-0	2-1	1-0	2-1	0-1	0-2	2-1
7 Hall Road Rangers	2-1	3-2	1-4	1-5	2-0	1-1		0-1	2-2	2-0	1-3	2-2	0-2	2-4	1-0	1-0	3-0	3-0	1-0	1-3
8 Hallam	2-0	1-0	1-5	3-2	1-1	1-3	1-2		1-4	2-4	0-2	2-1	1-4	2-3	1-2	2-4	1-2	1-2	2-2	0-5
9 Lincoln Moorlands Railway	1-1	3-1	1-1	0-0	2-1	2-1	4-0	1-2		1-1	5-0	4-0	4-1	1-2	1-0	3-4	1-1	0-0	2-0	5-1
10 Liversedge	2-2	2-2	5-3	2-2	1-2	1-2	3-2	1-2	3-2		0-1	1-0	1-2	1-3	2-3	2-2	1-1	1-2	1-2	2-2
11 Long Eaton United	0-3	1-1	0-0	0-0	1-0	0-1	1-0	2-2	2-2	2-0		1-1	1-1	2-1	3-3	2-1	2-0	0-2	0-2	2-2
12 Maltby Main	0-2	3-2	1-5	1-2	4-1	0-3	4-3	2-0	1-0	2-1	1-1		0-1	1-1	1-4	1-1	1-0	1-4	3-1	1-1
13 Nostell Miners Welfare	3-1	3-2	0-0	1-2	4-3	4-2	2-1	1-0	1-4	1-1	0-2	0-1		0-6	4-0	3-1	3-1	3-3	0-3	2-4
14 Parkgate	3-1	3-0	3-2	3-1	2-1	3-2	1-0	4-1	3-1	4-4	4-3	1-1	3-0		2-0	2-2	3-2	3-3	4-2	3-4
15 Pickering Town	2-1	4-2	5-4	0-0	5-1	1-5	0-0	4-2	0-3	3-2	2-1	1-3	2-1	1-5		5-0	3-1	2-3	4-2	1-1
16 Scarborough Athletic	0-1	1-0	3-3	2-3	4-0	1-2	4-1	4-4	2-2	5-1	0-1	1-2	0-0	1-1	1-0		2-1	1-0	0-1	3-1
17 Selby Town	0-3	3-3	1-4	1-0	7-2	1-4	0-1	1-0	2-1	0-2	4-2	2-1	4-1	2-3	0-5	2-0		2-0	1-3	1-5
18 Tadcaster Albion	3-4	5-1	3-1	4-2	3-0	3-4	4-1	5-0	3-4	2-0	3-0	2-1	3-2	2-1	2-2	2-3	1-2		2-2	1-1
19 Thackley	1-2	3-1	1-1	0-2	3-1	0-2	2-2	1-1	4-1	1-1	0-0	2-0	2-0	3-0	1-2	1-0	0-3	4-1		2-2
20 Winterton Rangers	1-0	2-1	2-0	3-1	2-1	0-2	4-1	5-5	2-0	2-0	1-0	0-1	0-1	1-0	0-0	0-0	2-0	1-1	2-1	

NORTHERN COUNTIES EAST LEAGUE - STEP 5/6

DIVISION ONE	P	W	D	L	F	A	Pts
1 Staveley Miners Welfare	38	26	6	6	95	46	84
2 Barton Town Old Boys	38	23	8	7	97	45	77
3 Yorkshire Amateur	38	23	6	9	81	36	75
4 Handsworth	38	24	3	11	98	66	75
5 Pontefract Collieries	38	19	11	8	85	51	68
6 Louth Town	38	18	8	12	76	59	62
7 Glasshoughton Welfare	38	19	5	14	65	48	62
8 AFC Emley	38	18	8	12	63	47	62
9 Askern Villa	38	17	6	15	66	68	57
10 Eccleshill United	38	17	5	16	76	62	56
11 Leeds Carnegie	38	16	7	15	55	56	55
12 Worsbrough Bridge Athletic	38	16	7	15	58	62	55
13 Shirebrook Town	38	16	4	18	67	72	52
14 Rossington Main	38	15	4	19	74	82	49
15 Grimsby Borough	38	13	8	17	69	69	47
16 Hemsworth Miners Welfare	38	12	6	20	64	82	42
17 Bottesford Town	38	10	10	18	56	69	40
18 Teversal	38	11	5	22	58	78	38
19 Appleby Frodingham	38	6	3	29	38	116	21
20 Brodsworth Welfare	38	0	2	36	17	144	2

PRESIDENT'S CUP

ROUND 1

AFC Emley 2-1 Winterton Rangers
Armthorpe Welfare 1-3 Leeds Carnegie
Arnold Town 1-2 Scarborough Athletic
Farsley 3-2 Brighouse Town
Hemsworth Miners Welfare 1-0 Pickering Town
Pontefract Collieries 1-3 Bridlington Town
Tadcaster Albion 0-0 Barton Town Old Boys (Tadcaster Albion won 4-2 on penalties)
Thackley 2-1 Staveley Miners Welfare

QUARTER FINALS

Bridlington Town 5-1 Leeds Carnegie
Farsley 5-2 AFC Emley
Tadcaster Albion 5-2 Hemsworth Miners Welfare
Thackley 1-3 Scarborough Athletic

SEMI-FINALS

Farsley 5-0 Scarborough Athletic
Tadcaster Albion 1-0 Bridlington Town

FINAL (@ Tadcaster Albion, 27/4/11)
Tadcaster Albion 5-1 Farsley

WILKINSON SWORD SHIELD

ROUND 1

Appleby Frodingham 0-3 Shirebrook Town
Eccleshill United 3-2 Leeds Carnegie
Grimsby Borough 0-2 Staveley Miners Welfare
Teversal 1-2 Askern Villa

ROUND 2

AFC Emley 2-1 Shirebrook Town (tie awarded to Shirebrook Town)
Askern Villa 1-2 Glasshoughton Welfare
Louth Town 7-0 Eccleshill United
Pontefract Collieries 5-3 Hemsworth Miners Welfare
Rossington Main 6-1 Brodsworth Welfare
Staveley Miners Welfare 4-3 Handsworth
Worsbrough Bridge Athletic 2-3 Barton Town Old Boys
Yorkshire Amateur 0-1 Bottesford Town (tie awarded to Yorkshire Amateur)

QUARTER FINALS

Glasshoughton Welfare 2-0 Yorkshire Amateur
Rossington Main 1-0 Barton Town Old Boys
Shirebrook Town 2-3 Louth Town
Staveley Miners Welfare 2-2 Pontefract Collieries (Pontefract Collieries won 3-2 on penalties)

SEMI-FINALS

Louth Town 3-5 Rossington Main
Pontefract Collieries 2-3 Glasshoughton Welfare

FINAL (@ Barton Town Old Boys, 26/4/11)
Glasshoughton Welfare 2-0 Rossington Main

DIVISION ONE	1	2	3	4	5	6	7	8	9	10	11	12	13	14	15	16	17	18	19	20
1 AFC Emley		3-3	0-2	3-1	2-1	7-0	1-0	1-3	1-1	6-1	2-1	1-2	5-2	3-2	1-1	3-2	0-1	1-0	1-3	1-1
2 Appleby Frodingham	0-2		0-2	0-9	2-1	2-0	1-4	0-3	1-3	1-3	1-8	1-1	1-2	0-5	0-5	2-3	1-5	1-2	1-2	0-2
3 Askern Villa	1-2	4-1		0-2	0-0	4-0	2-3	2-5	1-1	2-2	2-1	3-1	3-2	2-1	2-3	2-2	0-3	2-1	3-0	1-1
4 Barton Town Old Boys	1-3	3-0	4-1		2-3	7-0	4-1	2-1	2-1	3-1	1-1	4-0	5-0	0-0	0-1	3-2	2-2	4-1	2-2	3-1
5 Bottesford Town	0-2	0-3	5-0	2-5		7-1	3-1	0-4	0-0	5-3	0-2	0-0	1-2	1-1	1-3	3-1	0-8	2-2	0-0	1-2
6 Brodsworth Welfare	0-4	0-1	1-7	1-3	1-1		0-3	1-1	0-4	0-4	0-5	0-4	0-2	1-7	2-4	1-2	0-1	3-4	0-4	0-4
7 Eccleshill United	0-0	4-0	1-2	1-2	3-1	4-0		2-3	2-1	2-0	6-1	0-1	1-1	2-4	3-1	1-2	5-1	3-0	2-1	2-1
8 Glasshoughton Welfare	0-0	6-0	1-4	1-1	2-0	1-0	1-0		3-4	1-0	1-2	0-1	2-0	1-3	2-3	0-1	2-0	3-1	0-1	0-3
9 Grimsby Borough	0-0	1-0	4-0	3-3	1-2	7-0	5-1	0-5		3-4	3-0	1-3	0-3	1-1	0-6	1-2	1-2	1-2	2-0	0-1
10 Handsworth	4-0	6-2	4-1	2-0	4-3	4-0	2-1	4-0	3-1		1-2	3-1	2-2	3-1	4-2	2-1	3-1	1-2	3-0	2-3
11 Hemsworth Miners Welfare	3-2	3-0	0-1	1-4	1-1	3-1	1-3	0-0	1-1	0-2		3-3	1-0	3-3	3-4	0-2	0-4	1-2	1-3	2-0
12 Leeds Carnegie	1-0	0-1	1-0	1-2	3-1	2-1	3-2	0-1	0-1	0-2	0-1		1-1	2-2	1-2	3-2	2-4	4-2	3-0	0-0
13 Louth Town	1-0	3-1	1-1	1-1	0-1	2-1	2-3	4-2	3-4	1-1	7-3	3-1		0-1	5-0	4-1	0-2	2-0	3-1	1-0
14 Pontefract Collieries	0-0	1-1	5-0	0-1	1-0	4-0	4-2	1-2	1-3	3-2	4-3	4-0	2-2		4-2	3-3	2-0	1-1	1-2	1-0
15 Rossington Main	4-0	1-3	1-2	0-5	1-4	2-0	2-2	0-1	2-2	2-3	3-1	1-2	2-3	1-2		1-2	1-3	5-2	0-3	0-3
16 Shirebrook Town	2-1	5-3	2-1	0-1	2-1	3-0	1-1	1-3	2-1	1-3	3-1	1-3	1-3	1-2	1-2		1-3	3-0	5-2	1-3
17 Staveley Miners Welfare	2-0	5-1	0-3	3-3	1-0	6-1	3-0	4-0	3-2	3-2	2-1	2-1	2-2	3-3	2-0	3-1		4-1	2-1	3-1
18 Teversal	0-1	3-0	3-1	1-0	2-4	7-1	2-3	0-3	2-3	2-3	4-0	0-0	1-3	0-3	2-3	1-1	1-0		1-1	1-2
19 Worsbrough Bridge Athletic	1-2	2-1	4-1	1-2	1-1	3-0	2-2	1-0	5-2	1-3	0-4	2-4	2-1	2-0	2-2	1-0	0-0	2-1		0-2
20 Yorkshire Amateur	0-2	4-2	0-1	3-0	0-0	4-0	1-0	1-1	2-0	7-2	6-0	2-0	3-2	1-2	4-1	4-1	2-2	3-1	4-0	

NORTHERN COUNTIES EAST INS & OUTS

PREM - IN: Barton Town Old Boys (P), Retford (formerly Retford United) (R - Northern Premier League Premier Division), Staveley Miners Welfare (P).

OUT: Dinnington Town (R), Farsley (P - Northern Premier League Division One North), Hallam (R).

DIV ONE - IN: Albion Sports (P - West Riding County Amateur League Premier Division), Dinnington Town (R), Hallam (R), Worksop Parramore (formerly Sheffield Parramore) (P - Central Midlands League Supreme Division).

OUT: Barton Town Old Boys (P), Leeds Carnegie (F), Staveley Miners Welfare (P).

ARMTHORPE WELFARE
Founded: 1926 Nickname: Wellie

Secretary: Craig Trewick **(T)** **(E)** armthorpe.welfare@hotmail.co.uk
Chairman: Stephen Taylor **Manager:** Des Bennett **Prog Ed:** Martin Turner
Ground: Welfare Ground, Church Street, Armthorpe, Doncaster DN3 3AG **(T)** 07775 797 013 (Match days only)
Capacity: 2,500 **Seats:** 250 **Covered:** 400 **Midweek Matchday:** Tuesday **Clubhouse:** No **Shop:** No

Colours(change): All royal blue (All red)
Previous Names:
Previous Leagues: Doncaster Senior
Records: **Att:** 2,000 v Doncaster R Charity Match 1985-86. **Goalscorer:** Martin Johnson. **App:** Gary Leighton. **Win:** 10-0. **Defeat:** 1-7
Senior Honours: West Riding Challenge Cup 1981-82, 82-83. Northern Counties East Division 1 Central 1984-85.

10 YEAR RECORD

01-02	02-03	03-04	04-05	05-06	06-07	07-08	08-09	09-10	10-11
NCEP 6	NCEP 18	NCEP 14	NCEP 18	NCEP 10	NCEP 13	NCEP 9	NCEP 15	NCEP 3	NCEP 13

ARNOLD TOWN
Founded: 1989 Nickname: Eagles

Secretary: Roy Francis **(T)** 0115 952 2634 **(E)** mail@arnoldfc.com
Chairman: Roy Francis **Manager:** Chris Freestone/Martin Carruthers **Prog Ed:** Mick Gretton
Ground: Eagle Valley, Oxton Road, Arnold, Nottingham NG5 8PS **(T)** 0115 965 6000
Capacity: **Seats:** **Covered:** **Midweek Matchday:** Tuesday **Clubhouse:** **Shop:**

Colours(change): All maroon. (Yellow/blue/yellow)
Previous Names: Arnold F.C. (founded 1928 as Arnold St. Marys) merged with Arnold Kingswell (1962) in '1989.
Previous Leagues: Central Midland 89-93
Records: **Att:** 3,390 v Bristol Rovers FAC 1-Dec 1967 **Goalscorer:** Peter Fletcher - 100. **App:** Pete Davey - 346. **Win:** 10-1 **Defeat:** 0-7
Senior Honours: Northern Counties East 1985-86. Central Midlands 92-93. Northern Counties Div.1 93-94.

10 YEAR RECORD

01-02	02-03	03-04	04-05	05-06	06-07	07-08	08-09	09-10	10-11
NCEP 10	NCEP 15	NCEP 18	NCEP 16	NCEP 5	NCEP 15	NCEP 10	NCEP 6	NCEP 8	NCEP 18

BARTON TOWN OLD BOYS
Founded: 1995 Nickname: Swans

Secretary: Peter Mitchell **(T)** 01652 635 838 **(E)** bartontown@gmail.com
Chairman: Paul Friskney **Manager:** Dave Anderson **Prog Ed:** Phil Hastings
Ground: The Euronics Ground, Marsh Lane, Barton-on-Humber **(T)** 01652 635 838
Capacity: 3,000 **Seats:** 240 **Covered:** 540 **Midweek Matchday:** Tuesday **Clubhouse:** Yes **Shop:** No

Colours(change): Sky blue & white stripes/white/sky blue (Red & black stripes/black/black)
Previous Names:
Previous Leagues: Lincolnshire 1995-00, Humber (Founder member) 2000-01, Central Midlands 2001-07.
Records:
Senior Honours: Lincolnshire League 1996-97. Central Midlands League Supreme Division 2005-06.

10 YEAR RECORD

01-02	02-03	03-04	04-05	05-06	06-07	07-08	08-09	09-10	10-11
CM P 2	CM Su 13	CM Su 7	CM Su 4	CM Su 1	CM Su 2	NCE1 9	NCE1 5	NCE1 6	NCE1 2

BRIDLINGTON TOWN
Founded: 1918 Nickname: Seasiders

Secretary: Gavin Branton **(T)** **(E)** gavinbranton@yahoo.co.uk
Chairman: Peter Smurthwaite **Manager:** Mitch Cook **Prog Ed:** Dom Taylor
Ground: Queensgate Lane Rental Stadium, Queensgate, Bridlington YO16 7LN **(T)** 01262 606 879
Capacity: 3,000 **Seats:** 500 **Covered:** 500 **Midweek Matchday:** Tuesday **Clubhouse:** Yes **Shop:** Yes

Colours(change): All red (All white).
Previous Names: Original Bridlington Town folded in 1994. Greyhound FC changed to Bridlington Town.
Previous Leagues: Yorkshire 1924-39, 59-82, NCEL 1982-90, 99-2003, Northern Premier 1990-94, 2003-08
Records: **Att:** 1,006 v FC Utd of Manchester, NPLD1N, 03.11.07. **Goalscorer:** Neil Grimson. **Apps:** Neil Grimson - 200+ (1987-97).
Senior Honours: FA Vase 1992-93. Northern Counties East 2002-03, 2009-10, Division 1 1992-93.
ERCFA Senior Cup 1921,22,23,31,53,57,61,65,67,70,72,89,93,05

10 YEAR RECORD

01-02	02-03	03-04	04-05	05-06	06-07	07-08	08-09	09-10	10-11
NCE1 2	NCEP 1	NP 1 11	NP P 20	NP 1 11	NP 1 24	NP1N 18	NCEP 4	NCEP 1	NCEP 3

BRIGHOUSE TOWN

Founded: 1963 Nickname: Town

Secretary: Malcolm Taylor **(T)** **(E)** malctay@blueyonder.co.uk
Chairman: Chris Lister **Manager:** Mick Couzens **Prog Ed:** Malcolm Taylor
Ground: Dual Seal Stadium, St Giles Rd, Hove Edge, Brighouse, HD6 2PL. **(T)**
Capacity: 1,000 **Seats:** 100 **Covered:** 200 **Midweek Matchday:** Tuesday **Clubhouse:** Yes **Shop:** No

Colours(change): Orange/black/orange. (Yellow/green/yellow).
Previous Names:
Previous Leagues: Huddersfield Works. 1963-75. West Riding County Amateur 1975-08.
Records:
Senior Honours: West Riding County Amateur League: Prem Div - 1990/91 1994/95 1995/96 2000/01 2001/02, Prem Cup - 1993/94, 95/96 98/99, 00/01; Div 1 - 1988/89

10 YEAR RECORD

01-02	02-03	03-04	04-05	05-06	06-07	07-08	08-09	09-10	10-11
WRCP 1	WRCP 2	WRCP 3	WRCP 4	WRCP 3	WRCP 3	WRCP 8	NCE1 15	NCE1 2	NCEP 16

HALL ROAD RANGERS

Founded: 1959 Nickname: Rangers

Secretary: Sophia Graham **(T)** **(E)** hallroadrangers@yahoo.co.uk
Chairman: Darren Wilson **Manager:** Billy Heath **Prog Ed:** Alex Blackburne
Ground: Dene Park, Dene Close, Beverley Road, Dunswell HU6 0AA **(T)** 01482 850 101
Capacity: 1,200 **Seats:** 250 **Covered:** 750 **Midweek Matchday:** Tuesday **Clubhouse:** Yes **Shop:** Yes

Colours(change): Blue & white/blue/blue. (Red & black/black/black)
Previous Names:
Previous Leagues: East Riding County, Yorkshire 1968-82.
Records: **App:**1,200 v Manchester City Aug 93 **Goalscorer:** G James **App:** G James
Senior Honours: East Riding Senior Cup 1972-73, 93-94. N.C.E. Division Two 1990-91.

10 YEAR RECORD

01-02	02-03	03-04	04-05	05-06	06-07	07-08	08-09	09-10	10-11
NCE1 9	NCE1 9	NCE1 14	NCE1 11	NCE1 14	NCE1 10	NCE1 2	NCEP 16	NCEP 11	NCEP 14

LINCOLN MOORLANDS RAILWAY

Founded: 1989 Nickname: The Moors

Secretary: Ken Rooney **(T)** 07908809366 **(E)** kenneth.rooney@ntlworld.com
Chairman: Alan Hobbs **Manager:** Danny George **Prog Ed:** Graham Peck
Ground: Moorland Sports Ground, Newark Road, Lincoln LN6 0XJ **(T)** 01522 874 111
Capacity: 200 **Seats:** 200 **Covered:** 100 **Midweek Matchday:** Wednesday **Clubhouse:** Yes **Shop:** No

Colours(change): Claret & blue/claret/claret & blue. (Yellow/royal blue/yellow).
Previous Names:
Previous Leagues: Central Midlands.
Records:
Senior Honours: Central Midlands Supreme 1999-00. Lincolnshire Senior Cup 2006-07.

10 YEAR RECORD

01-02	02-03	03-04	04-05	05-06	06-07	07-08	08-09	09-10	10-11
NCE1 4	NCE1 7	NCE1 8	NCE1 4	NCE1 7	NCE1 5	NCEP 19	NCEP 18	NCEP 17	NCEP 6

LIVERSEDGE

Founded: 1910 Nickname: Sedge

Secretary: Bryan Oakes **(T)** 01274 683 327 **(E)** bryan@bryanoakes.orangehome.co.uk
Chairman: Steve Newton **Manager:** Billy Miller **Prog Ed:** Andrew Taylor
Ground: Clayborn Ground, Quaker Lane, Hightown Road, Cleckheaton WF15 8DF **(T)** 01274 682 108
Capacity: 2,000 **Seats:** 250 **Covered:** 750 **Midweek Matchday:** Tuesday **Clubhouse:** Yes **Shop:** Yes

Colours(change): Sky blue/navy/sky blue. (All red).
Previous Names:
Previous Leagues: Spen Valley, West Riding Co. Amateur 1922-72, Yorkshire 1972-82
Records: **Att:** 986 v Thackley **Goalscorer:** Denis Charlesworth **App:** Barry Palmer
Senior Honours: Northern Counties East League Cup 2005-06.

10 YEAR RECORD

01-02	02-03	03-04	04-05	05-06	06-07	07-08	08-09	09-10	10-11
NCEP 11	NCEP 9	NCEP 9	NCEP 6	NCEP 2	NCEP 12	NCEP 4	NCEP 14	NCEP 9	NCEP 17

LONG EATON UNITED

Founded: 1956 Nickname: Blues

Secretary: Jim Fairley **(T)** **(E)** jim@longeatonutd.co.uk
Chairman: Jim Fairley **Manager:** Craig Weston (Care taker) **Prog Ed:** Jim Fairley
Ground: Grange Park, Station Rd, Long Eaton, Derbys NG10 2EF **(T)** 0115 973 5700
Capacity: 1,500 **Seats:** 150 **Covered:** 500 **Midweek Matchday:** Tuesday **Clubhouse:** Yes **Shop:** No

Colours(change): All blue. (All yellow).
Previous Names:
Previous Leagues: Central Alliance 1956-61, Mid Co Football Lge 1961-82, NCE 1982-89, Central Midlands 1989-2002
Records: **Att:** 2,019 v Burton Albion FA Cup 1973
Senior Honours: Derbyshire Senior Cup 1964-65, 75-76. Northern Counties East Div1S 1984-85. League Cup 2008-09.

10 YEAR RECORD

01-02	02-03	03-04	04-05	05-06	06-07	07-08	08-09	09-10	10-11
CM Su 3	NCE1 3	NCE1 2	NCEP 12	NCEP 19	NCEP 11	NCEP 12	NCEP 2	NCEP 10	NCEP 12

MALTBY MAIN

Founded: 1916 Nickname: Miners

Secretary: John Mills **(T)** 01709 813 609 **(E)** john_mills_@hotmail.co.uk
Chairman: Graham McCormick **Manager:** Steve Adams **Prog Ed:** Nick Dunhill
Ground: Muglet Lane, Maltby, Rotherham S66 7JQ. **(T)** 07795 693 683
Capacity: 2,000 **Seats:** 150 **Covered:** 300 **Midweek Matchday:** Wednesday **Clubhouse:** No **Shop:** No

Colours(change): Red/black/red (Yellow/black/grey)
Previous Names: Maltby Miners Welfare 1970-96
Previous Leagues: Sheffield Co Senior. Yorkshire League 1973-84
Records: **Att:** 1,500 v Sheffield Weds (friendly) 1991-2
Senior Honours: Sheffield & Hallamshire Senior Cup1977-78

10 YEAR RECORD

01-02	02-03	03-04	04-05	05-06	06-07	07-08	08-09	09-10	10-11
NCE1 6	NCE1 15	NCE1 3	NCEP 19	NCEP 18	NCEP 10	NCEP 18	NCEP 12	NCEP 16	NCEP 11

NOSTELL MINERS WELFARE

Founded: 1928 Nickname: The Welfare

Secretary: Granville Marshall **(T)** 01924 864 462 **(E)** nostwellmwfc@hotmail.com
Chairman: Granville Marshall **Manager:** Alan Colquhoun **Prog Ed:** Malcolm Lamb
Ground: The Welfare Grd, Crofton Co. Centre, Middle Lane, New Crofton WF4 1LB **(T)** 01924 866 010
Capacity: 1500 **Seats:** 100 **Covered:** 200 **Midweek Matchday:** Tuesday **Clubhouse:** Yes **Shop:** No

Colours(change): Yellow/black/black. (All blue).
Previous Names:
Previous Leagues: Wakefield 1950-66, 69-82, West Yorkshire 1966-68, 82-2006
Records:
Senior Honours: West Yorkshire Premier Division 2004-05

10 YEAR RECORD

01-02	02-03	03-04	04-05	05-06	06-07	07-08	08-09	09-10	10-11
WYkP 8	WYkP 3	WYkP 5	WYkP 1	WYkP 3	NCE1 4	NCE1 5	NCEP 13	NCEP 18	NCEP 9

PARKGATE

Founded: 1969 Nickname: The Steelmen

Secretary: Bruce Bickerdike **(T)** **(E)** brucebickerdike@hotmail.co.uk
Chairman: Albert Dudill **Manager:** Doug Shelley **Prog Ed:** Dave PLatts
Ground: Roundwood Sports Complex, Green Lane, Rawmarsh, S62 6LA **(T)** 01709 826 600
Capacity: 1,000 **Seats:** 300 **Covered:** 300 **Midweek Matchday:** Tuesday **Clubhouse:** Yes **Shop:** No

Colours(change): All Red & White. (All green & white).
Previous Names: BSC Parkgate (1982-86) RES Parkgate (pre 1994)
Previous Leagues: BIR County Senior. Yorkshire 1974-82.
Records: **Att:** v Worksop 1982
Senior Honours: N.C.E. Division One 2006-07. Wilkinson Sword Trophy 2006-07.

10 YEAR RECORD

01-02	02-03	03-04	04-05	05-06	06-07	07-08	08-09	09-10	10-11
NCE1 14	NCE1 8	NCE1 10	NCE1 12	NCE1 6	NCE1 1	NCEP 8	NCEP 11	NCEP 14	NCEP 2

PICKERING TOWN

Founded: 1888 Nickname: Pikes

Secretary: Keith Usher **(T)** 01751 473 317 **(E)**
Chairman: Keith Usher **Manager:** Paul Vasey **Prog Ed:** Alasdair Dinnewell
Ground: Recreation Club, off Mill Lane, Malton Road, Pickering YO18 7DB **(T)** 01751 473 317
Capacity: 2,000 **Seats:** 200 **Covered:** 500 **Midweek Matchday:** Tuesday **Clubhouse:** Yes **Shop:** No

Colours(change): All blue. (All yellow).
Previous Names:
Previous Leagues: Beckett, York & District, Scarborough & District, Yorkshire 1972-1982
Records: **Att:** 1,412 v Notts County (friendly) in August 1991
Senior Honours: N.C.E. Div 2 1987-88. North Riding Cup 1990-91. Wilkinson Sword Trophy 2000-01

10 YEAR RECORD

01-02	02-03	03-04	04-05	05-06	06-07	07-08	08-09	09-10	10-11
NCEP 4	NCEP 13	NCEP 5	NCEP 5	NCEP 6	NCEP 9	NCEP 3	NCEP 9	NCEP 7	NCEP 7

RETFORD

Founded: 1987 Nickname: Badgers

Secretary: Annie Knight **(T)** **(E)** annierufc@sky.com
Chairman: Bill Wyles **Manager:** Brett Marshall **Prog Ed:** Jon Knight
Ground: Cannon Park, Leverton Road, Retford, Notts DN22 6QF **(T)** 01777 869 468 / 710 300
Capacity: 2,000 **Seats:** 150 **Covered:** 200 **Midweek Matchday:** Tuesday **Clubhouse:** Yes **Shop:** Yes

Colours(change): Black and white stripes/black/black (All yellow)
Previous Names: Retford United > 2011.
Previous Leagues: Gainsborough & Dist, Nottinghamshire Alliance > 2001, Central Midlands 2001-04, Northern Counties East 2004-07
Records: 1,527 v Doncaster Rovers - Friendly July 2006
Senior Honours: Notts All. Div.1 2000-01. Central Mids Div.1 01-02, Supreme Division 03-04, Lge Cup 01-02, 03-04, Floodlit Cup 03-04. N.C.E. Prem. Division 06-07, Presidents Cup 06-07. N.P.L. Div.1S 07-08, 08-09, Chairmans Cup 07-08. Notts Sen. Cup 08-09.

10 YEAR RECORD

01-02	02-03	03-04	04-05	05-06	06-07	07-08	08-09	09-10	10-11
CM P 1	CM Su 4	CM Su 1	NCE1 8	NCE1 2	NCEP 1	NP1S 1	NP1S 1	NP P 6	NP P 22

SCARBOROUGH ATHLETIC

Founded: 2007 Nickname: The Seadogs

Secretary: John Clarke **(T)** **(E)** john@scarboroughathletic.com
Chairman: David Holland **Manager:** Rudy Funk **Prog Ed:** James Hunter
Ground: Bridlington FC, Queensgate Stadium, Bridlington, East Yorks YO11 3EP **(T)** 01262 606 879
Capacity: 3000 **Seats:** 500 **Covered:** 1,200 **Midweek Matchday:** Tuesday **Clubhouse:** Yes **Shop:** No

Colours(change): All Red (White/red/red).
Previous Names: Formed after Scarborough F.C. folded in 2007.
Previous Leagues: N/A
Records: **Att:** 791 v Leeds Carnegie N.C.E. Div.1 - 25.04.09.
Senior Honours: N.C.E. Division One 2008-09.

10 YEAR RECORD

01-02	02-03	03-04	04-05	05-06	06-07	07-08	08-09	09-10	10-11
						NCE1 5	NCE1 1	NCEP 5	NCEP 10

SELBY TOWN

Founded: 1919 Nickname: The Robins

Secretary: Thomas Arkley **(T)** 07830 218 657 **(E)** toonarkley@yahoo.co.uk
Chairman: Ralph Pearse **Manager:** Leon Sewell **Prog Ed:** Thomas Arkley
Ground: Selby Times Stadium, Richard Street, Scott Road, Selby YO8 0DB **(T)** 01757 210 900
Capacity: 5,000 **Seats:** 220 **Covered:** 350 **Midweek Matchday:** Tuesday **Clubhouse:** Yes **Shop:** Yes

Colours(change): All red (Black & white/white/black).
Previous Names:
Previous Leagues: Yorkshire 1920-82
Records: **Att:** 7,000 v Bradford PA FA Cup1st Round 1953-54
Senior Honours: Yorkshire League 1934-35, 35-36, 52-53, 53-54. NCE Div.1 95-96.

10 YEAR RECORD

01-02	02-03	03-04	04-05	05-06	06-07	07-08	08-09	09-10	10-11
NCEP 7	NCEP 16	NCEP 8	NCEP 2	NCEP 8	NCEP 5	NCEP 7	NCEP 3	NCEP 13	NCEP 15

STAVELEY MINERS WELFARE

Founded: 1989 Nickname: The Welfare

Secretary: Ele Reaney **(T)** 01246 471 441 **(E)** staveleyed@hotmail.co.uk
Chairman: Terry Damms **Manager:** Billy Fox **Prog Ed:** Ele Reaney
Ground: Inkersall Road, Staveley, Chesterfield, S43 3JL **(T)** 01246 471 441
Capacity: 5,000 **Seats:** 220 **Covered:** 400 **Midweek Matchday:** Wednesday **Clubhouse:** Yes **Shop:** Yes

Colours(change): Blue & white/blue/blue (All orange)
Previous Names:
Previous Leagues:
Records: 292 v Scarborough Athletic, NCE Division 1 01/12/2007. **Goalscorer:** Mick Godber. **Apps:** Shane Turner.
Senior Honours: County Senior League Division 3 1991-92, Division 2 1992-93. N.C.E. Division One 2010-11.

10 YEAR RECORD

01-02	02-03	03-04	04-05	05-06	06-07	07-08	08-09	09-10	10-11
NCE1 15	NCE1 17	NCE1 16	NCE1 9	NCE1 10	NCE1 6	NCE1 8	NCE1 4	NCE1 4	NCE1 1

TADCASTER ALBION

Founded: 1892 Nickname: The Brewers

Secretary: Howard Clarke **(T)** **(E)** sandra.clarke1@tiscali.co.uk
Chairman: Rob Northfield **Manager:** Paul Marshall **Prog Ed:** Kevin Axtell
Ground: The Park, Ings Lane, Tadcaster LS24 9AY **(T)** 01937 834 119
Capacity: 1,500 **Seats:** 150 **Covered:** 400 **Midweek Matchday:** Tuesday **Clubhouse:** Yes **Shop:** No

Colours(change): Yellow/navy/navy (Red/navy)
Previous Names: None
Previous Leagues: York, Harrogate, Yorkshire (73-82)
Records: **Att:** 1,200 v Winterton FA Vase 4th Round 1996-7
Senior Honours: Northern Counties East Division 1 2009-10.

10 YEAR RECORD

01-02	02-03	03-04	04-05	05-06	06-07	07-08	08-09	09-10	10-11
NCE1 13	NCE1 16	NCE1 18	NCE1 6	NCE1 3	NCE1 7	NCE1 12	NCE1 17	NCE1 1	NCEP 4

THACKLEY

Founded: 1930 Nickname: Dennyboys

Secretary: Mick Lodge **(T)** **(E)** mick.lodge@btinternet.com
Chairman: Mike Smith **Manager:** Vince Brockie & Sean Regan **Prog Ed:** John McCreery
Ground: Dennyfield, Ainsbury Avenue, Thackley, Bradford BD10 0TL **(T)** 01274 615 571
Capacity: 3000 **Seats:** 300 **Covered:** 600 **Midweek Matchday:** Tuesday **Clubhouse:** Yes **Shop:** Yes

Colours(change): Red/white/red. (White/black/white).
Previous Names: Thackley Wesleyians 1930-39
Previous Leagues: Bradford Am, W. Riding Co. Am., West Yorks, Yorks 1967-82
Records: **Att:** 1,500 v Leeds United 1983
Senior Honours: W. Riding County Cup 1963-64, 66-67, 73-74, 74-75. Bradford & District Senior Cup (x13).

10 YEAR RECORD

01-02	02-03	03-04	04-05	05-06	06-07	07-08	08-09	09-10	10-11
NCEP 8	NCEP 6	NCEP 11	NCEP 8	NCEP 9	NCEP 18	NCEP 16	NCEP 7	NCEP 4	NCEP 8

WINTERTON RANGERS

Founded: 1930 Nickname: Rangers

Secretary: Mark Fowler **(T)** 07775 907 606 **(E)** mark-fowler-68@hotmail.co.uk
Chairman: David Crowder **Manager:** Richard Sennett & Mark Turner **Prog Ed:** Brian Crowder
Ground: West Street, Winterton, Scunthorpe DN15 9QF. **(T)** 07956 088 472 / 01724 732 628
Capacity: 3,000 **Seats:** 245 **Covered:** 200 **Midweek Matchday:** Wednesday **Clubhouse:** Yes **Shop:** No

Colours(change): All royal blue. (All red).
Previous Names:
Previous Leagues: Scunthorpe & Dist. 1945-65. Lincs 1965-70. Yorkshire 1970-82.
Records: **Att:** 1,200 v Sheffield United, flood lights switch on, October 1978.
Senior Honours: NCE Premier 07-08.

10 YEAR RECORD

01-02	02-03	03-04	04-05	05-06	06-07	07-08	08-09	09-10	10-11
NCE1 7	NCE1 10	NCE1 11	NCE1 10	NCE1 5	NCE1 2	NCEP 1	NCEP 5	NCEP 6	NCEP 5

A.F.C. EMLEY

Founded: 2005 Nickname: Pewits

Secretary: John Whitehead **(T)** **(E)** afcemley@tiscali.co.uk
Chairman: Graham Roys **Manager:** Darren Hepworth **Prog Ed:** Rob Dixon
Ground: The Welfare Ground, Off Upper Lane, Emley, nr Huddersfield, HD8 9RE. **(T)** 07702 712 287 **Capacity:** 2,000
Colours(change): Sky blue & maroon/sky blue/maroon (Green/white/green)

ADDITIONAL INFORMATION:
Previous League: West Yorkshire 2005-06.

ALBION SPORTS

Founded: 1974 Nickname: Lions

Secretary: Jaj Singh **(T)** **(E)**
Chairman: Kultar Singh **Manager:** Kulwinder Singh Sandhu **Prog Ed:** Chris Kaye/Balbinder Singh
Ground: Cemetery Road, off Halifax Road, Bradford BD6 2NG **(T)** 01274 604 568 **Capacity:** 3,500
Colours(change): Yellow & royal blue/royal blue/royal blue (All red)

ADDITIONAL INFORMATION:
Previous Lge: West Riding County Amateur > 2011.

APPLEBY FRODINGHAM

Founded: 1990 Nickname: The Steelmen

Secretary: Steve Lumley-Holmes **(T)** **(E)** lumleyholmes@btinternet.com
Chairman: Steve Lumley-Holmes **Manager:** Simon Shorthose/John Simpson **Prog Ed:** Dick Drury
Ground: Brumby Hall Sports Ground, Ashby Road, Scunthorpe, DN16 1AA **(T)** 01724 402134 / 843024 **Capacity:**
Colours(change): Black & red halves/black/black (Royal blue & white halves/royal/royal)

ADDITIONAL INFORMATION:
Previous League: Central Midlands.
Honours: Lincolnshire League: 1962-63, 76-77, 77-98, 93-94; Lincolnshire Challenge Cup: 1962-63, 75-76, 76-77, 77-78, 92-93

ASKERN VILLA

Founded: 1924 Nickname: Welly or Villa

Secretary: Dave Hall **(T)** 07799 752 890 **(E)** davidhallgfx@btinternet.com
Chairman: Ted Ellis **Manager:** Brian Johnston **Prog Ed:** Dave Hall
Ground: Askern Villa Sports Ground, Manor Way, Doncaster Road, Askern, DN6 0AJ **(T)** 01302 700597 **Capacity:** 2,000
Colours(change): Black & white/black/black & white (All red)

ADDITIONAL INFORMATION:
Previous League: Central Midlands.
Honours: Central Midlands League 2007-08.

BOTTESFORD TOWN

Founded: 1974 Nickname: The Poachers

Secretary: Tony Reeve **(T)** 07711 152 965 **(E)** anthony.reeve3@ntlworld.com
Chairman: Tony Reeve **Manager:** Dave Andrews **Prog Ed:** Liz Gray
Ground: Birch Park, Ontario Road, Bottesford, Scunthorpe, DN17 2TQ **(T)** 01724 871 883 **Capacity:** 1,000
Colours(change): All blue & yellow (Red & black/black & red/black & red)

ADDITIONAL INFORMATION:
Previous League: Central Midlands 2000-07.
Honours: Lincolnshire League 1989-90, 90-91, 91-92. Central Midlands League Supreme Division 2006-07.

DINNINGTON TOWN

Founded: 2000 Nickname: Dinno

Secretary: Chris Dearns **(T)** 07802 542 335 **(E)** chris.dearns@gmail.com
Chairman: Mick Kent **Manager:** Steve Toyne **Prog Ed:** Wayne Rutledge
Ground: 131 Laughton Road, Dinnington, Nr Sheffield S25 2PP **(T)** 07802 542 335 **Capacity:** 2000
Colours(change): Yellow & black/black/black. (All white).

ADDITIONAL INFORMATION:
Northern Counties East Division One 2007-08, League Cup 2009-10.

ECCLESHILL UNITED

Founded: 1948 Nickname: The Eagles

Secretary: David Heaney **(T)** 07501 096945 **(E)** dp.heaney@hotmail.co.uk
Chairman: Adrian Benson **Manager:** Ian Banks **Prog Ed:** Paul Everett
Ground: The Smith Butler Stadium, Kingsway, Wrose, Bradford, BD2 1PN **(T)** 01274 615 739 **Capacity:** 2,225
Colours(change): Blue & white/blue/blue (All red).

ADDITIONAL INFORMATION:
Record Att: 715 v Bradford City 1996-97. **Win:** 10-1. **Defeat:** 0-6.
Honours: Bradford Senior Cup 1985-86. Northern Counties East Division 1 1996-97.

GLASSHOUGHTON WELFARE

Founded: 1964 Nickname: Welfare or Blues

Secretary: Frank MacLachlan **(T)** 07710 586 447 **(E)** frank.maclachlan@btinternet.com
Chairman: Phil Riding **Manager:** Craig Elliott **Prog Ed:** Nigel Lea
Ground: Glasshoughton Centre, Leeds Road, Glasshoughton, Castleford WF10 4PF **(T)** 01977 511 234 **Capacity:** 2,000
Colours(change): Royal blue & white/royal blue/royal blue (All yellow)

ADDITIONAL INFORMATION:
Record Att: 300 v Bradford City 1990. **Win:** 8-1. **Defeat:** 0-8.
Honours: West Riding County Cup 1993-94.

GRIMSBY BOROUGH

Founded: 2003 Nickname: The Wilderness Boys

Secretary: Nigel Fanthorpe **(T)** 01472 605 177 **(E)** nigelfanthorpe@hotmail.co.uk
Chairman: Kenneth Vincent **Manager:** Steve Newby & Nigel Fanthorpe **Prog Ed:** Brian Sylvester
Ground: Grimsby Community Stadium, Bradley Road, Grimsby, DN37 0AG **(T)** **Capacity:** 1,500
Colours(change): Royal blue/royal blue/white (Yellow/white/royal blue)

ADDITIONAL INFORMATION:
Previous League: Central Midlands 2004-08.

HALLAM (SECOND OLDEST CLUB IN THE WORLD)

Founded: 1860 Nickname: Countrymen

Secretary: Mark Radford **(T)** 0114 249 7287 **(E)** markradford34@yahoo.com
Chairman: David Slater **Manager:** Julian Watts **Prog Ed:** Mark Radford
Ground: Sandygate Road, Crosspool, Sheffield S10 5SE **(T)** 0114 230 9484 **Capacity:** 1,000
Colours(change): All blue (All yellow).

ADDITIONAL INFORMATION: Att: 2,000 v Hendon F.A. Amateur Cup. **Goalscorer:** A Stainrod 46. **App:** P. Ellis 500+. **Win:** 7-0 x2. **Defeat:** 0-7.
Honours: Northern Counties East League Cup 2003-04.
Previous Lge: Yorkshire 1952-82.

HANDSWORTH

Founded: 2003 Nickname: Amber & Blacks

Secretary: Dave Wragg **(T)** 07885 240 308 **(E)** davewragg1@btinternet.com
Chairman: John Ward **Manager:** Russ Eagle **Prog Ed:** Dave Wragg
Ground: Handsworth Junior Sporting Club, Olivers Mount, Handsworth, S9 4PA **(T)** **Capacity:**
Colours(change): Amber & black/black/black (Red/white/red).

ADDITIONAL INFORMATION:
Previous League: Sheffield & Hallamshire County Senior 2003-10.
Honours: Sheffield & Hallamshire County Senior League Division 1 2007-08.

HEMSWORTH MINERS WELFARE

Founded: 1981 Nickname: Wells

Secretary: Mark Crapper **(T)** 01977 614 723 **(E)** crapperbruce@aol.com
Chairman: Tony Benson **Manager:** Andrew Cracknell **Prog Ed:** Mark Crapper
Ground: Fitzwilliam Stadium, Wakefield Road, Fitzwilliam, Pontefract, WF9 5AJ **(T)** 01977 614 997 **Capacity:** 2,000
Colours(change): Royal blue/royal blue/white (White/white/royal blue)

ADDITIONAL INFORMATION:
Previous League: West Riding County Amateur 1995-2008.

LOUTH TOWN

Founded: 2007 Nickname: The White Wolves

Secretary: Matt Jones **(T)** **(E)** m.jones255@btinternet.com
Chairman: Eddie Clark **Manager:** Paul Walden **Prog Ed:** Dave Wilson
Ground: The Park Avenue Stadium, Park Avenue, Louth, LN11 8BY **(T)** 07891 965531 **Capacity:** 1,500
Colours(change): White/black/black (All blue)

ADDITIONAL INFORMATION:
Previous League: Central Midlands 2007-10.
Honours: Central Midlands League Premier Division 2008-09, Supreme Division 2009-10.

PONTEFRACT COLLIERIES

Founded: 1958 Nickname: Colls

Secretary: Darren Angell **(T)** 07796 136 415 **(E)** darren@pontecolls.co.uk
Chairman: Guy Nottingham **Manager:** Brendan Ormsby **Prog Ed:** Eddie Fogden
Ground: Skinner Lane, Pontefract, WF8 4QE **(T)** 01977 600 818 **Capacity:** 1,200
Colours(change): All royal blue (All claret)

ADDITIONAL INFORMATION:
Previous League: Yorkshire 1979-82.
Honours: Northern Counties East League Division 1 1983-84, 95-96.

ROSSINGTON MAIN
Founded: 1919 Nickname: The Colliery

Secretary: Gerald Parsons **(T)** **(E)** g-parsons2@sky.com
Chairman: Carl Stokes **Manager:** Steve Lodge **Prog Ed:** Peter Murden
Ground: Welfare Ground, Oxford Street, Rossington, Doncaster, DN11 0TE **(T)** 01302 865 524 **Capacity:** 2,000
Colours(change): All blue (All red)

ADDITIONAL INFORMATION:
Record Att: 1,200 v Leeds United 06/08/1991. **Goalscorer:** Mark Illam. **Apps:** Darren Phipps.
Honours: Central Midlands League Premier Division 1984-85, League Cup 1983-84, 84-85.

SHIREBROOK TOWN
Founded: 1985 Nickname: None

Secretary: Aimee Radford **(T)** 01623 742 535 **(E)** aimeeradford@yahoo.co.uk
Chairman: Gary Meredith **Manager:** Mickey Taylor **Prog Ed:** Peter Craggs
Ground: Shirebrook Spts and So C, Langwith Rd, Shirebrook, Mansfield, NG20 8TF **(T)** 01623 742 535 **Capacity:** 2,000
Colours(change): Red & black/black/red (All white)

ADDITIONAL INFORMATION:
Record Goalscorer: Craig Charlesworth - 345.
Honours: Central Midlands League Supreme Division 2000-01, 01-02, Northern Counties East Division 1 2003-04.

TEVERSAL
Founded: 1918 Nickname: Tevie Boys

Secretary: Kevin Newton **(T)** 07711 358 060 **(E)** kevin.newton@teversalfc.co.uk
Chairman: Peter Cockerill **Manager:** Jamie Hudson **Prog Ed:** Kevin Newton
Ground: Teversal Grange Spts and So.Centre, Carnarvon St, Teversal, NG17 3HJ **(T)** 07773 922 539 **Capacity:**
Colours(change): Red/black/black (White/red/red)

ADDITIONAL INFORMATION:
Previous Name: Teversal Grange. **Previous League:** Central Midlands.
Honours: Central Midlands League 2004-05.

WORKSOP PARRAMORE
Founded: 1936 Nickname: None

Secretary: Max Ross **(T)** **(E)**
Chairman: Pete Whitehead **Manager:** TBC **Prog Ed:** Max Ross
Ground: The Windsor Foodservice Stadium, Sandy Land, Worksop S80 1TJ **(T)** 01909 479 955 **Capacity:** 2,500
Colours(change): Sky blue/black/sky blue (Orange/black/black).

ADDITIONAL INFORMATION:
Previous Name: Sheffield Parramore 1936-2011.
Previous Lge: Central Midlands > 2011.

WORSBROUGH BRIDGE ATHLETIC
Founded: 1923 Nickname: Briggers

Secretary: Charlie Wyatt **(T)** 01226 284 452 **(E)** charlie@worsbroughbridgefc.com
Chairman: John Cooper **Manager:** Ian Shirt & Chris Hilton **Prog Ed:** Charlie Wyatt
Ground: Park Road, Worsbrough Bridge, Barnsley, S70 5LJ **(T)** 01226 284 452 **Capacity:** 2,000
Colours(change): Red & white/black/black (All blue)

ADDITIONAL INFORMATION:
Record Att: 1,603 v Blyth Spatans, FA Amateur Cup 1971.
Honours: County Senior League Division 1 1965-66, 69-70.

YORKSHIRE AMATEUR
Founded: 1918 Nickname: Ammers

Secretary: Keith Huggins **(T)** 0113 262 4093 **(E)** keith.huggins@tiscali.co.uk
Chairman: Jeni French **Manager:** Paul Lines **Prog Ed:** Jeni French
Ground: Bracken Edge, Roxholme Road, Leeds, LS8 4DZ (Sat. Nav. LS7 4JG) **(T)** 0113 262 4093 **Capacity:** 1,550
Colours(change): White/blue/red (All red)

ADDITIONAL INFORMATION:
Record Att: 4,000 v Wimbledon, FA Amateur Cup Quarter Final 1932.
Honours: Yorkshire League: 1931-32, Div 2 - 1958-59, Div 3 - 1977-78. Leeds & District Senior Cup.

GROUND DIRECTIONS

ARMTHORPE WELFARE - Welfare Ground, Church Street, Armthorpe, Doncaster, DN3 3AG. Tel: (01302) 842795 - Match days only
From the north, turn left at main roundabout in the centre of Doncaster and straight across at next roundabout on to Wheatley Hall Road. Turn right on to Wentworth Road, go to top of hill towards the Hospital on to Armthorpe Road. From the south, take the M18 to J4 on to the A630. At 2nd roundabout, turn left and proceed to next roundabout, then turn right. Ground 400 yards on left behind Netto.

ARNOLD TOWN - Eagle Valley, Oxton Road, Arnold, Nottingham, NG5 8PS. Tel: 0115 965 6000.
From South: From Nottingham, take the A60 Mansfield road. At the first traffic island half a mile north of Arnold, join the A614 towards Doncaster. After 200 yards, go through traffic lights and, after 300 yards, take the next turn right. The ground entrance is 200 yards on the right.
From North: A614 towards Nottingham. As you approach the first set of traffic lights, turn left 300 yards before the lights. The ground entrance is 200 yards on the right.
From M1: Leave at Junction 27. Head towards Hucknall/Nottingham. After one mile, turn right at the first set of traffic lights. One mile, turn first left at island and stay on this road for two miles until junction with A60. Turn right and, at the next island, turn left onto the A614 towards Doncaster. After 200 yards, go through traffic lights and, after 300 yards, take the next right turn. The ground entrance is 200 yards on the right.

BARTON TOWN OLD BOYS - The Euronics Ground, Marsh Lane, Barton-on-Humber. Tel: (01652) 635838

Approaching from the South on A15, Barton is the last exit before the Humber Bridge. Follow the A1077 into the town. Turn right at the mini roundabout at the bottom of the hill into Holydyke. Take second left onto George Street and then into King Street. Marsh Lane is opposite the junction of King Street and High Street. The ground is at the end of Marsh Lane, on the right, immediately after the cricket ground.

BRIDLINGTON TOWN - Queensgate Stadium, Queensgate, Bridlington, East Yorkshire, YO16 7LN. Tel: (01262) 606879

From South (Hull, Beeford, Barmston): Approach Bridlington on the A165, passing golf course on right and Broadacres Pub, Kingsmead Estate on left. Straight through traffic lights to roundabout by B&Q. Turn right. At traffic lights turn left and over the railway bridge. At roundabout bear left and carry on heading north up Quay Road. After traffic lights turn right into Queensgate. Ground is 800 yards up the road on the right.

From South and West (Driffield, Hull, York): Approach Bridlington on A614. (This was formally the A166). Straight on at traffic lights (Hospital on right) and follow the road round the bend. At roundabout straight across to mini roundabout and bear right (second exit). Follow road around to right and to traffic lights. Straight on. At next traffic lights (just after Kwikfit) turn left into Queensgate. Ground is 800 yards up the road on the right.

From North (Scarborough): Approach Bridlington (Esso garage on right) at roundabout turn left then at mini roundabout second exit. Follow road around to right and to traffic lights. Straight on. At next traffic lights (just after Kwikfit) turn left into Queensgate. Ground is 800 yards up the road on the right.

BRIGHOUSE TOWN - Dual Seal Stadium, St Giles Road, Hove Edge, Brighouse, West Yorkshire, HD6 2PL.

M1 to M62 travel westwards to J26 then come off motorway and go on to A58 Halifax to third set of traffic lights at Hipperholme. At lights, turn left onto A644 to Brighouse. Travel approx. one mile passing the Dusty Miller pub, take next left and, within 30-40 metres, turn left on to Spouthouse Lane. Follow this road for approximately 1/4 of a mile until road swings left at this point. Turn right in to car park. Be careful of oncoming traffic on bend.

HALL ROAD RANGERS - Dene Park, Dene Close, Beverley Road, Dunswell, nr Hull, HU6 0AA. Tel: (01482) 850101

M62 to A63, turn left before Humber Bridge onto A164 to Beverley, after approx. 5 miles turn right onto A1079. In 2 miles, turn left at large roundabout to ground 20 yards on right.

LINCOLN MOORLANDS RAILWAY - Lincoln Moorlands Railway Sports Ground, Newark Road, Lincoln, LN6 8RT. Tel: (01522) 874111

From North: A1 to Markham Moor. Take A57 until Lincoln by-pass. At Carholme Roundabout take 3rd. exit towards Lincoln South. Travel 1.7 miles to Skellingthorpe Roundabout and take 2nd. Exit towards Lincoln South. Travel 1.6 miles to Doddington Roundabout and take 1st. exit B1190 towards Lincoln South. Travel 2.1 miles until T-Junction. Turn left onto A1434 and travel 0.4 mile. Entrance to ground is on left immediately after Chancery Close.

From Newark: A46 to Lincoln by-pass. At roundabout take last exit onto A1434 towards Lincoln. Travel for 3.1 miles, entrance to ground on left immediately after Chancery Close signposted 'Moorlands Railway Club'.

LIVERSEDGE - Clayborn Ground, Quaker Lane, Hightown Road, Cleckheaton, WF15 8DF. Tel: (01274) 682108

M62 J26, A638 into Cleckheaton, right at lights on corner of Memorial Park, through next lights and under railway bridge, first left (Hightown Rd) and Quaker Lane is approx 1/4 mile on left and leads to ground. From M1 J40, A638 thru Dewsbury and Heckmondwike to Cleckheaton, left at Memorial Park lights then as above. Buses 218 & 220 (Leeds - Huddersfield) pass top of Quaker Lane.

LONG EATON UNITED - Grange Park, Station Road, Long Eaton, NG10 2EG. Tel: (0115) 973 5700

M1 Junc 25, take A52 towards Nottingham, to island by Bardills Garden Centre, right onto B6003. Approx 2 miles to end of road to T-junction. At traffic lights, turn right A453 and take 2nd left into Station Road. Entrance on left down un-named road opposite disused car park next to Grange School.

MALTBY MAIN - Muglet Lane, Maltby, Rotherham, S66 7JQ. Tel: (07795) 693683

Exit M18 at Junc 1 with A631. Two miles into Maltby, right at traffic lights at Queens Hotel corner on to B6427 Muglet Lane. Ground 3/4 mile on left.

NOSTELL MINERS WELFARE - The Welfare Ground, Crofton Community Centre, Middle Lane, New Crofton, Wakefield, WF4 1LB. Tel: (01924) 866010

M1 J39, head towards Wakefield (A638), Denby Dale road. Leave Wakefield on the A638 (Doncaster Rd), towards Wakefield Trinity Ground. Continue on this road for another 2 miles, you will pass the Red Beck Motel on your right. Go under the bridge and turn right opposite the Public house 'Crofton Arms'. Follow road through Crofton village (1 1/4 miles). Turn left at 'Slipper' public house, then right onto Middle Lane, follow road round to reach Crofton Community Centre.

PARKGATE - Roundwood Sports Complex, Green Lane, Rawmarsh, Rotherham, S62 6LA. Tel: (01709) 826600

From Rotherham A633 to Rawmarsh. From Doncaster A630 to Conisbrough, then A6023 through Swinton to Rawmarsh. Grd at Green Lane - right from Rotherham, left from Conisbrough at the Crown Inn. Ground 800yds on right.

PICKERING TOWN - Recreation Club, off Mill Lane, Malton Rd, Pickering, YO18 7DB. Tel: (01751) 473317

A169 from Malton. On entering Pickering, take 1st left past Police Station and BP garage into Mill Lane, ground 200 yds on right.

RETFORD - Cannon Park, Leverton Road, Retford, Notts DN22 6QF. Tel: (01777) 869 468 / 710 300

Leave the A1 at Ranby and follow the A620 towards Retford. Go past Ranby prison and go straight on at the next 2 mini roundabouts. At the 3rd roundabout take the 3rd exit signposted Gainsborough. Passing Morrisons on the left, go through the traffic lights and move into the right hand lane. Turn right at the traffic lights. Turn left at the traffic lights by the Broken Wheel Public House into Leverton Road. Go past the Masons Arms Public House and go over 2 hump backed bridges. The ground is signposted and is on the right.

SCARBOROUGH ATHLETIC - Queensgate Stadium, Bridlington, East Yorkshire, YO16 7LN. Tel: (01262) 606879

From South (Hull, Beeford, Barmston): Approach Bridlington on the A165, passing golf course on right and Broadacres Pub, Kingsmead Estate on left. Straight through traffic lights to roundabout by B&Q. Turn right. At traffic lights turn left and over the railway bridge. At roundabout bear left and carry on heading north up Quay Road. After traffic lights turn right into Queensgate. Ground is 800 yards up the road on the right.

From South and West (Driffield, Hull, York): Approach Bridlington on A614. (This was formally the A166). Straight on at traffic lights (Hospital on right) and follow the road round the bend. At roundabout straight across to mini roundabout and bear right (second exit). Follow road around to right and to traffic lights. Straight on. At next traffic lights (just after Kwikfit) turn left into Queensgate. Ground is 800 yards up the road on the right.

From North (Scarborough): Approach Bridlington (Esso garage on right) at roundabout turn left then at mini roundabout second exit. Follow road around to right and to traffic lights. Straight on. At next traffic lights (just after Kwikfit) turn left into Queensgate. Ground is 800 yards up the road on the right.

SELBY TOWN - The Selby Times Stadium, Richard St, Scott Rd, Selby, YO8 4BN. Tel: (01757) 210900

From Leeds, left at main traffic lights in Selby down Scott Rd, then 1st left into Richard St. From Doncaster, go straight across main traffic lights into Scott Rd then 1st left. From York, right at main traffic lights into Scott Rd and 1st left.

STAVELEY MINERS WELFARE - Inkersall Road, Staveley, Chesterfield, S43 3JL. Tel: (01246) 471441

M1 J30 follow A619 Chesterfield. Staveley is 3 miles from J30. Turn left at GK Garage in Staveley town centre into Inkersall Road. Ground is 200 yards on right at side of Speedwell Rooms.

TADCASTER ALBION - 2inspire Park, Ings Lane, Tadcaster, LS24 9AY

From West Riding and South Yorks - Turn right off A659 at John Smith's Brewery Clock. From East Riding - Turn left off A659 after passing over river bridge and pelican crossing (New Street).

THACKLEY - Dennyfield, Ainsbury Avenue, Thackley, Bradford, BD10 0TL. Tel: (01274) 615571

On main Leeds/Keighley A657 road, turn off at Thackley corner which is 2 miles from Shipley traffic lights and 1 mile from Greengates lights. Ainsbury Avenue bears to the right 200yds down the hill. Ground is 200yds along Ainsbury Avenue on the right.

WINTERTON RANGERS - West Street, Winterton, Scunthorpe, DN15 9QF. Tel: (01724) 732628

From Scunthorpe - Take A1077 Barton-on-Humber for 5 miles. On entering Winterton take 3rd right (Eastgate), 3rd left (Northlands Rd) and 1st Right (West St). Ground 200 yards on left.

DIVISION ONE

A.F.C. EMLEY - The Welfare Ground, Off Upper Lane, Emley, nr Huddersfield, HD8 9RE. Tel: 01924 849392 or 07702 712287

From M1 J38: Travel on road signposted to Huddersfield through the village of Bretton to the first roundabout. Take first exit off this roundabout signposted Denby Dale. After approximately one mile turn right at road signposted Emley. After 2 miles enter the village of Emley. Entrance to ground is opposite a white bollard in centre of road. (Narrow entrance).

From M1 J39: Travel on road signposted toward Denby Dale. Travel for approximately 3 miles up hill to first roundabout. Take 2nd exit and follow directions as above.

ALBION SPORTS - Cemetery Road, off Halifax Road, Bradford BD6 2NG. Tel: 01274 604 568

M62 to J26. Join M606. Leave at second junction. At roundabout take second exit (A6036 signposted Halifax) and pass Odsal Stadium on left hand side. At next roundabout, take third exit (A6036 Halifax, Horsfall Stadium is signposted). After approximately 1 mile, turn left down Cemetery Road immediately before Kings Head Public House. Ground is 150 yards on the left.

APPLEBY FRODINGHAM - Brumby Hall Sports Ground, Ashby Road, Scunthorpe, DN16 1AA. Tel: 01724 402134 or 01724 843024

From M18, take J5 on to the M180. From M180, take J3 onto the M181 (Scunthorpe West). At the roundabout, turn right onto A18. Straight on at the mini roundabout (McDonalds). At the next large roundabout, take the third exit (A18) up the hill to the next roundabout, turn left and the entrance to the ground is 100 metres on the left.

ASKERN VILLA - Askern Villa Sports Ground, Manor Way, Doncaster Road, Askern, DN6 0AJ. Tel: (01302) 700597

Via A1 - Leave the A1 at Junction A639. Follow Signs Askern/Campsall. At T-Junction turn right towards Sutton. Take left turn at Anne Arms Public House. Take second right on to Manor Way. Car park in grounds of Askern Miners Welfare; Via M62 - Exit Junction 34 follow signs for Doncaster (A19) for about 6 miles take 1st right after "The Askern" Public House. Clubhouse on the left.

BOTTESFORD TOWN - Birch Park, Ontario Road, Bottesford, Scunthorpe, DN17 2TQ. Tel: (01724) 871883

Exit M180 via M181-Scunthorpe. At circle (Berkeley Hotel), turn right into Scotter Road. At circle (Asda) straight ahead, 2nd left into South Park road then on to Sunningdale Road, turn right into Goodwood Road, Birch Park at end (right turn). Please note that Goodwood Road is not suitable for large vehicles. Instead, take 2nd right off Sunningdale Road which is Quebec Road, then 2nd right which is Ontario Road down to the bottom and ground is on the left.

BRODSWORTH WELFARE - Welfare Ground, Woodlands, Nr. Doncaster, DN6 7PP. Tel: (01302) 728380

From A1 take A638 to Doncaster, take left after Woodlands Pub into Welfare Road, ground 50 yards on left.

DINNINGTON TOWN - Phoenix Park, Dinnington Resource Centre, 131 Laughton Road, Dinnington S25 2PP. Tel: (01909) 518555

From M1 J31, follow A57 Worksop Road East for 1 mile. At first traffic lights, turn left onto B6463 Todwick Road then Monks Bridge Road for 2 miles. At petrol station roundabout, take third exit signposted Dinnington and travel half-a-mile, then take first left at Morrell Tyres. Cross mini-roundabout at The Squirrel pub and travel on Laughton Road for 300 yards. Ground is on the left.

ECCLESHILL UNITED - The Smith Butler Stadium, Kingsway, Wrose, Bradford, BD2 1PN. Tel: (01274) 615739

M62 J26 onto M606, right onto Bradford Ring Road A6177, left on to A650 for Bradford at 2nd roundabout. A650 Bradford Inner Ring Road onto Canal Rd, branch right at Staples (Dixons Car showrooms on right), fork left after 30mph sign to junction with Wrose Road, across junction - continuation of Kings Rd, first left onto Kingsway. Ground is 200 yards on right.

GLASSHOUGHTON WELFARE - The Glasshoughton Centre, Leeds Rd, Glasshoughton, Castleford, WF10 4PF. Tel: (01977) 511234

Leave the M62 J32, signposted Castleford/Pontefract (A639). At the bottom of the slip road take the A656, taking carer to pick up the middle lane for Castleford. After approx. 1/4 mile, bear left at the first roundabout and, after a further 1/4 mile, left at the next roundabout on to Leeds Road. Ground is then 200 yards on the right.

GRIMSBY BOROUGH - Grimsby Community Stadium, Bradley Road, Grimsby, DN37 0AG

Head South East on the A180 to the Great Coates turn off come back over the A180 and follow for 1/2 mile to the roundabout, take first exit follow over one mini roundabout and through one set of traffic lights until you come to the Trawl Pub roundabout, take the second exit onto Littlecoates road and follow over one mini roundabout to the second roundabout and take the second exit onto Bradley Road. The ground is approx 800 yards on your left with car and coach parking facilities.

HALLAM - Sandygate, Sandygate Road, Crosspool, Sheffield, S10 5SE. Tel: (0114) 230 9484

A57 Sheffield to Glossop Rd, left at Crosspool shopping area signed Lodge Moor on to Sandygate Rd. Ground half mile on left opposite Plough Inn. 51 bus from Crucible Theatre.

HANDSWORTH - Handsworth Junior Sporting Club, Olivers Mount, Handsworth, Sheffield, S9 4PA

From M1 J33 or Sheffield City Centre: Take the A57/A630 Sheffield Parkway. Leave at the slip road showing the B6200 and follow the signs towards Darnall. This is Handsworth Road and should be followed until you pass the White Rose public house. Once through the pelican crossing just below the pub, turn right into Olivers Drive, go down the road and bear right up the hill which is Olivers Mount. The ground is at the top of Olivers Mount.

HEMSWORTH MINERS WELFARE - Fitzwilliam Stadium, Wakefield Road, Fitzwilliam, Pontefract, WF9 5AJ. Tel: (01977) 614997

From East/West: M62 to J32 towards Pontefract then follow A628 towards Hemsworth. At Ackworth roundabout (Stoneacre Suzuki Garage), take a right on to the A638 Wakefield Road. Travel half a mile to next roundabout then take first exit. Travel one mile to crossroads and turn left into Fitzwilliam. Pass a row of shops on your right and turn left after the bus shelter before an iron bridge. To ground.

From North: A1 South to M62 then follow above directions.

From South: A1(M) North to A638 Wakefield Road. Travel to Ackworth Roundabout (Stoneacre Suzuki Garage) and go straight across and follow the A638 to the next roundabout. Take first exit then to crossroads. Turn left into Fitzwilliam and pass row of shops on your right. Turn left after bus shelter before iron bridge and carry on to the ground. Alternative: M1 to J32 then take M18 to A1(M).

LOUTH TOWN - The Park Avenue Stadium, Park Avenue, Louth, LN11 8BY. Tel: 07891 965531

Enter Louth from the A16 onto North Home Road. Go 1/2 mile and follow the road as it bends to the right to become Newbridge Hill. At the junction, turn right onto Ramsgate. At the mini roundabout next to Morrisons, turn left onto Eastgate. Go 1/2 mile down Eastgate and turn right into Park Avenue just past the fire station.

PONTEFRACT COLLIERIES - Skinner Lane, Pontefract, WF8 4QE. Tel: (01977) 600818

M62 jct32 (Xscape) towards Pontefract. Left at lights after roundabout for park entrance and retail park. Traffic through town should follow racecourse signs through lights to roundabout and back to lights.

ROSSINGTON MAIN - Welfare Ground, Oxford Street, Rossington, Doncaster, DN11 0TE. Tel: (01302) 865524 (Matchdays only)

Enter Rossington and go over the railway crossings. Passing the Welfare Club, Oxford Street is the next road on the right. The ground is at the bottom of Oxford Street.

SHIREBROOK TOWN - Shirebrook Staff Sports and Social Club, Langwith Road, Shirebrook, Mansfield, Notts, NG20 8TF. Tel: (01623) 742535

Depart M1 at Junction 29, at roundabout take A617 towards Mansfield (for 3.5 miles), at next roundabout take 2nd Exit B6407 Common Lane towards Shirebrook (or 1.8 miles), go straight on at next roundabout (for 300 yards), at staggered crossroads turn right onto Main Street (for 1.1 miles), at T Junction turn right (for 100 yards), take the first road on your left (Langwith Road). The ground is 400 yards on the right.

TEVERSAL - Teversal Grange Sports and Social Centre, Carnarvon Street, Teversal, Sutton-in-Ashfield, NG17 3HJ. Tel: (07773) 922539

From North: Travel South on the M1 to junction 29 take the A6175 to Heath and Holmewood. Travel through Holmewood, and at the roundabout take the B6039 to Hardstaff and Tibshelf. At the T-junction in Tibshelf (pub on your left) turn left onto B6014 travelling over the motorway into Teversal. Follow the road round passing the Carnarvon Arms pub and under a bridge, take 2nd left onto Coppywood Close, travel to the top and following the road round with the ground at the top.

From South: From the M1 junction 28, take the A38 to Mansfield. Travel through a number of sets of traffic lights and after passing the Kings Mill Reservoir you will come to a major junction (King & Miller Pub and McDonalds on your left). Travel straight on taking the A6075 towards Mansfield Woodhouse, at the next set of traffic lights turn left onto the B6014 to Stanton Hill. You will come to a roundabout with a Kwik Save on your left, continue on the B6014 towards Tibshelf. Take the second right onto Coppywood Close, travel to the top and following the road round with the ground at the top.

WORKSOP PARRAMORE - The Windsor Foodservice Stadium, Sandy Land, Worksop S80 1TJ. Tel: 01909 479 955

From either the A1 or M1 J31, take the A57 towards Worksop. After approximately 7 miles, look out for the A60/Sandy Lane turnoff at the roundabout. Continue over two mini-roundabouts for ¾mile then turn left into the retail park and left again into the stadium car park.

WORSBOROUGH BRIDGE ATHLETIC - Park Road, Worsbrough Bridge, Barnsley, S70 5LJ. Tel: (01226) 284452

On the A61, Barnsley-Sheffield road two miles south of Barnsley, 2 miles from M1 J36 opposite Blackburns Bridge.

YORKSHIRE AMATEUR - Bracken Edge, Roxholme Road, Leeds, LS8 4DZ. Tel: (0113) 262 4093

From South - M1 to Leeds, then A58 to Wetherby Road to Fforde Green Hotel, left at lights and proceed to Sycamore Avenue (on right). From East - A1 to Boot & Shoe Inn then to Shaftesbury Hotel, turn right into Harehills Lane, then to Sycamore Avenue.

NORTHERN LEAGUE

Sponsored by: Skilltrainingltd
Founded: 1889
Recent Champions:
2006: Newcastle Blue Star
2007: Whitley Bay
2008: Durham City
2009: Newcastle Benfield
2010: Spennymoor Town
northernleague.org

DIVISION ONE	P	W	D	L	F	A	Pts
1 Spennymoor Town	42	33	4	5	116	31	103
2 Consett	42	29	6	7	103	51	93
3 Whitley Bay	42	28	9	5	73	32	93
4 Newcastle Benfield	42	27	6	9	94	53	87
5 Shildon	42	26	5	11	114	46	83
6 West Auckland Town	42	26	4	12	96	62	82
7 Dunston UTS	42	24	8	10	84	49	80
8 Ashington	42	21	5	16	83	65	68
9 Bedlington Terriers	42	20	7	15	94	62	67
10 Norton & Stockton Ancients	42	19	9	14	66	45	66
11 South Shields	42	17	7	18	61	66	58
12 Billingham Synthonia	42	16	9	17	63	65	57
13 Sunderland RCA	42	15	6	21	67	80	51
14 Bishop Auckland	42	15	6	21	75	93	51
15 Billingham Town	42	13	7	22	58	88	46
16 Stokesley	42	12	9	21	61	85	45
17 Penrith (-3)	42	12	10	20	65	76	43
18 Tow Law Town	42	12	7	23	49	77	43
19 Jarrow Roofing Boldon CA	42	10	9	23	50	98	39
20 West Allotment Celtic	42	9	5	28	51	82	32
21 Esh Winning	42	4	4	34	40	121	16
22 Ryton	42	2	2	38	34	170	8

BROOK MILESON MEMORIAL CUP

ROUND 1
Team Northumbria 2-1 Billingham Town
Esh Winning 1-2 Washington
Jarrow Roofing 4-0 Chester-le-Street Town
Morpeth Town 2-7 Bedlington Terriers
North Shields 5-2 Crook Town
Bishop Auckland 1-5 Stokesley (@ Stokesley)
Consett 5-0 Guisborough Town
Norton & Stockton Ancients 0-2 Dunston UTS
Brandon United 0-1 Newcastle Benfield
Whitehaven 5-0 Seaham Red Star

ROUND 2
Ashington 2-3 Shildon
Birtley Town 3-4 Sunderland RCA
Horden CW 1-4 West Allotment Celtic
Marske United 2-1 Gillford Park
North Shields 0-4 Spennymoor Town
South Shields 2-0 Whickham
Thornaby 0-7 Billingham Synthonia (@ Billingham Synthonia)
West Auckland Town 2-0 Washington
Whitehaven 2-4 Stokesley
Whitley Bay 1-4 Newton Aycliffe
Bedlington Terriers 4-1 Jarrow Roofing
Consett 4-0 Darlington Railway Athletic
Hebburn 2-3 Newcastle Benfield
Northallerton Town 3-1 Penrith
Tow Law Town 2-3 Team Northumbria
Dunston UTS 7-1 Ryton

ROUND 3
South Shields 1-2 Sunderland RCA
Bedlington Terriers 2-0 West Auckland Town
Consett 3-2 West Allotment Celtic
Shildon 2-1 Marske United
Newcastle Benfield 3-1 Northallerton Town
Stokesley 3-3 Billingham Synthonia
(Stokesley won 4-3 on penalties)
Spennmoor Town 5-1 Newton Aycliffe
Dunston UTS 1-0 Team Northumbria (@ Team Northumbria)

QUARTER FINALS
Sunderland RCA 4-1 Stokesley
Bedlington Terriers 0-2 Spennymoor Town
Consett 2-4 Newcastle Benfield
Shildon 2-2 Dunston UTS (Shildon won 4-2 on penalties)

SEMI-FINALS
Sunderland RCA 1-3 Spennymoor Town
Newcastle Benfield 3-1 Shildon

FINAL (@ Dunston UTS, 5/5/11)
Newcastle Benfield 3-1 Spennymoor Town

DIVISION ONE	1	2	3	4	5	6	7	8	9	10	11	12	13	14	15	16	17	18	19	20	21	22
1 Ashington		0-1	2-0	3-1	4-0	2-1	1-0	3-0	2-0	2-2	0-1	3-4	8-0	3-1	2-1	2-6	2-2	1-2	6-2	2-1	1-2	0-3
2 Bedlington Terriers	1-2		6-2	4-1	3-0	2-2	0-1	3-0	5-0	1-2	1-3	2-1	3-1	1-1	6-2	0-1	6-0	3-3	4-0	1-2	2-1	3-3
3 Billingham Synthonia	2-1	1-1		2-1	1-0	1-0	0-1	3-3	2-1	0-1	1-3	2-1	6-0	2-3	1-0	0-1	3-1	2-2	2-1	0-0	3-5	2-2
4 Billingham Town	3-2	1-0	0-3		3-2	0-2	2-4	2-0	2-2	0-4	0-2	1-1	5-2	1-0	1-2	0-5	0-0	0-1	3-0	3-2	2-2	4-1
5 Bishop Auckland	2-1	1-4	4-2	2-1		2-3	0-0	4-0	3-1	3-4	0-4	2-3	3-0	2-1	2-0	0-2	3-5	3-2	4-1	2-2	1-2	0-2
6 Consett	2-1	1-0	1-1	3-0	3-3		4-0	4-2	3-2	4-0	3-1	2-1	7-0	2-0	4-1	1-2	6-1	3-0	2-1	2-1	2-3	3-1
7 Dunston UTS	3-1	1-2	2-1	2-0	3-1	1-0		4-1	4-0	3-0	1-1	0-2	5-0	3-2	3-0	3-2	4-1	2-3	3-1	2-0	0-3	1-2
8 Esh Winning	1-2	0-3	0-3	0-2	0-2	2-5	1-1		3-3	1-3	0-1	3-1	7-0	0-4	1-2	0-4	0-2	0-1	0-4	0-3	0-3	1-5
9 Jarrow Roofing Boldon CA	0-5	4-0	0-3	2-1	1-2	1-3	3-3	1-0		0-2	2-2	3-0	1-0	2-2	0-1	0-5	2-1	1-0	1-1	0-4	1-4	0-0
10 Newcastle Benfield	0-3	3-2	1-1	3-0	4-2	5-1	2-1	7-0	4-0		2-1	2-0	6-0	1-4	1-0	0-3	1-2	5-0	5-0	2-1	0-0	0-3
11 Norton & Stockton Anc	0-3	2-2	0-1	3-0	3-0	1-1	1-2	2-0	6-0	1-2		1-1	2-0	1-2	1-1	0-1	4-0	1-0	1-2	1-0	2-4	0-2
12 Penrith	0-0	1-2	6-1	2-2	2-2	2-3	2-2	2-0	2-2	2-2	0-2		5-0	2-3	1-1	2-4	1-4	1-0	1-2	2-1	1-4	0-2
13 Ryton	0-1	0-3	5-3	2-2	3-5	1-3	1-5	4-5	0-3	2-5	0-2	2-3		0-7	1-3	0-2	0-5	0-4	1-1	0-2	2-5	0-2
14 Shildon	4-0	1-1	0-1	7-0	7-1	1-1	0-2	6-2	2-1	4-0	3-1	5-1	10-0		1-2	0-1	4-1	3-1	4-1	1-0	4-0	1-2
15 South Shields	0-1	2-4	2-1	0-1	1-1	0-2	0-1	4-2	5-2	0-1	2-2	3-1	5-0	1-2		0-3	0-2	3-2	4-1	3-0	3-1	0-3
16 Spennymoor Town	5-0	4-0	2-0	2-0	2-1	1-3	2-2	3-1	4-1	2-1	1-2	2-0	8-1	2-1	4-0		5-0	1-1	3-0	6-1	4-0	2-2
17 Stokesley	2-2	0-2	0-0	4-3	3-4	1-2	1-1	1-1	1-1	0-1	2-0	0-4	4-1	1-2	0-0	3-2		1-1	0-2	2-1	2-3	0-1
18 Sunderland Ryhope CA	3-2	2-0	2-0	4-3	0-3	1-1	0-5	7-0	4-1	1-4	1-3	3-0	1-2	1-2	1-2	0-2	3-2		1-2	1-1	3-2	0-2
19 Tow Law Town	1-2	3-2	1-1	3-2	3-0	1-2	0-0	2-1	0-1	2-2	0-0	0-0	3-1	1-3	0-1	0-2	0-2	3-4		2-0	0-1	0-1
20 West Allotment Celtic	2-2	1-5	0-2	1-2	1-1	2-3	3-0	1-2	2-3	1-3	1-0	0-1	2-1	0-4	2-3	1-2	3-1	2-0	0-2		2-7	0-2
21 West Auckland Town	4-1	3-2	2-1	0-1	4-1	1-2	1-2	3-0	3-1	0-1	1-1	0-3	5-0	1-2	1-1	2-1	3-1	4-1	2-0	1-0		0-3
22 Whitley Bay	0-2	3-1	1-0	2-2	2-1	2-1	2-1	1-0	2-0	0-0	0-1	1-0	3-1	0-0	0-0	0-0	1-0	2-0	2-0	3-2	2-3	

NORTHERN LEAGUE - STEP 5/6

DIVISION TWO	P	W	D	L	F	A	Pts
1 Newton Aycliffe	38	30	5	3	116	38	95
2 Guisborough Town	38	28	4	6	110	52	88
3 Marske United	38	25	7	6	95	41	82
4 North Shields	38	24	8	6	98	36	80
5 Team Northumbria	38	24	1	13	88	45	73
6 Whickham	38	21	5	12	70	51	68
7 Whitehaven	38	18	8	12	104	85	62
8 Chester-le-Street Town	38	18	5	15	78	63	59
9 Northallerton Town	38	17	7	14	80	58	58
10 Hebburn Town (-3)	38	17	5	16	76	72	53
11 Gillford Park	38	14	9	15	63	59	51
12 Crook Town	38	15	5	18	77	80	50
13 Birtley Town	38	13	10	15	70	89	49
14 Thornaby	38	12	6	20	53	84	42
15 Darlington Railway Athletic	38	12	3	23	54	92	39
16 Washington	38	9	7	22	46	95	34
17 Seaham Red Star	38	9	4	25	66	118	31
18 Horden Colliery Welfare	38	8	4	26	52	95	28
19 Brandon United	38	5	8	25	41	86	23
20 Morpeth Town	38	4	3	31	47	145	15

J.R. CLEATOR CUP
(League champions v League Cup winners)

(@ Spennymoor Town, 31/7/10)

Spennymoor Town 0-1 South Shields

ERNSET ARMSTRONG MEMORIAL CUP

ROUND 1

Crook Town 2-0 Horden CW
Guisborough Town 1-2 Morpeth Town
Seaham Red Star 3-4 Whickham
Brandon United 2-3 Washington

ROUND 2

North Shields 9-0 Morpeth Town
Chester-le-Street Town 4-3 Whitehaven
Hebburn Town 4-1 Washington
Darlington Railway Athletic 6-2 Birtley Town
Northallerton Town 1-2 Team Northumberia
Thornaby 2-5 Marske United
Gillford Park 3-4 Whitehaaven
Newton Aycliffe 3-1 Crook Town

QUARTER FINALS

Chester-le-Street Town 3-0 Hebburn Town
Marske United 4-0 Newton Aycliffe
Whickham 1-0 North Shields
Team Northumbria 3-0 Darlington Railway Athletic

SEMI-FINALS

Marske united 1-5 Team Northumbria
Whickham 0-1 Chester-le-Street Town

FINAL (@ Newcastle Benfield, 4/5/11)
Chester-le-Street Town 2-2 Team Nortumbria
(Team Northumbria won 3-0 on penalties)

DIVISION TWO	1	2	3	4	5	6	7	8	9	10	11	12	13	14	15	16	17	18	19	20
1 Birtley Town		1-3	2-1	4-7	1-1	2-2	3-3	3-2	4-2	1-1	5-3	1-6	0-0	2-0	4-2	0-6	1-0	2-4	0-2	2-1
2 Brandon United	0-1		0-2	1-2	1-3	0-2	0-2	1-1	1-1	1-2	1-1	1-4	1-3	2-2	2-4	0-1	3-2	1-0	2-4	1-2
3 Chester-le-Street Town	2-2	3-2		3-2	4-2	2-0	5-0	2-1	3-1	0-1	2-0	2-3	0-4	1-3	3-0	3-2	2-1	2-1	0-1	2-4
4 Crook Town	1-2	4-1	0-3		4-0	1-1	2-4	2-3	6-0	2-8	2-1	0-4	2-3	2-0	2-3	2-1	1-4	2-0	1-1	3-5
5 Darlington Railway Athletic	2-1	2-0	1-4	0-3		0-5	1-2	3-1	3-1	1-1	6-3	0-5	0-5	2-4	3-0	0-2	1-2	3-1	0-0	1-4
6 Gillford Park	3-2	2-2	1-5	0-1	3-1		1-4	0-1	1-3	0-2	4-0	0-2	1-1	0-1	4-0	2-1	2-2	4-0	3-1	1-1
7 Guisborough Town	2-2	4-0	4-1	5-2	4-0	4-3		1-4	5-1	1-2	9-1	2-2	1-3	1-0	3-2	1-0	1-0	8-1	1-1	5-2
8 Hebburn Town	4-0	2-1	2-1	2-2	0-1	1-2	0-3		4-2	1-3	5-0	1-5	1-6	4-1	2-1	2-3	3-1	1-1	2-3	2-4
9 Horden Colliery Welfare	0-1	1-2	2-1	2-4	2-0	1-2	1-3	0-2		0-2	6-0	1-3	0-2	1-4	0-3	0-3	4-1	1-3	1-2	3-3
10 Marske United	3-1	5-0	7-2	2-0	1-2	1-0	2-1	1-1	1-1		7-1	0-2	1-1	1-1	4-0	1-0	5-0	4-3	3-1	4-2
11 Morpeth Town	5-4	1-5	2-5	1-4	1-2	3-1	1-5	1-2	0-1	0-3		1-2	0-5	1-2	1-3	0-0	2-5	3-2	2-1	0-5
12 Newton Aycliffe	5-1	3-0	2-2	2-0	1-0	2-2	2-3	1-1	8-2	2-1	5-0		1-1	3-2	2-0	2-1	5-1	4-0	1-0	3-0
13 North Shields	2-2	4-0	2-1	0-1	4-1	1-0	0-1	1-4	2-0	4-1	4-1	0-3		1-1	4-0	1-0	3-0	7-1	1-0	0-1
14 Northallerton Town	0-0	3-0	2-1	3-0	2-0	0-1	1-2	8-3	1-3	1-3	9-0	0-2	2-2		5-2	1-3	0-1	5-0	2-3	5-3
15 Seaham Red Star	1-1	2-2	0-5	1-6	5-2	4-0	1-5	0-3	4-2	0-3	3-3	1-6	1-4	4-4		2-5	2-4	3-1	1-4	3-6
16 Team Northumbria	4-0	1-0	3-2	2-0	1-0	2-0	2-0	4-0	1-2	1-4	5-2	4-0	1-2	3-1	3-1		2-1	4-0	0-1	8-3
17 Thornaby	1-4	4-0	0-0	2-1	1-0	2-2	1-4	0-5	1-0	3-1	3-1	0-4	1-1	0-1	1-0	1-3		0-3	3-3	2-6
18 Washington	0-4	2-2	1-1	2-2	1-0	0-3	0-2	2-0	2-2	2-0	4-1	3-0	1-9	0-1	0-4	1-5	1-1		0-1	1-2
19 Whickham	3-0	1-0	2-0	3-0	3-5	1-3	1-2	1-3	3-0	1-3	2-0	2-5	4-1	0-1	4-1	2-1	3-1	1-1		2-0
20 Whitehaven	5-4	2-2	0-0	1-1	9-5	2-2	1-2	1-0	4-2	1-1	6-4	2-4	0-4	1-1	5-2	5-0	4-0	0-1	1-2	

ASHINGTON

Founded: 1883 Nickname: The Colliers

Secretary: Gavin Perry **(T)** 07870 824 922 **(E)** gav@monkseatonfc.com
Chairman: Ian Lavery **Manager:** **Prog Ed:** Gavin Perry
Ground: Woodhorn Lane, Ashington NE63 9HF **(T)** 01670 811 991
Capacity: **Seats:** **Covered:** **Midweek Matchday:** Tuesday **Clubhouse:** Yes **Shop:** Yes

Colours(change): Black & White stripes/black/black.
Previous Names:
Previous Leagues: Northern Alliance, Football League, N. Eastern, Midland, Northern Counties, Wearside, N.P.L.
Records: **Att:** 13,199 v Rochdale FA Cup 2nd round 1950
Senior Honours: Northern League Div.2 Champions 2000-01, 03-04.

10 YEAR RECORD

01-02	02-03	03-04	04-05	05-06	06-07	07-08	08-09	09-10	10-11
NL 1 19	NL 2 5	NL 2 1	NL 1 10	NL 1 16	NL 1 19	NL 1 17	NL 1 16	NL 1 6	NL 1 8

BEDLINGTON TERRIERS

Founded: 1949 Nickname: Terriers

Secretary: David Collop **(T)** 07958 664 536 **(E)** david.collop@bedlingtonterriersfc.co.uk
Chairman: David Holmes **Manager:** **Prog Ed:** Stewart Grimes
Ground: Dr. Pit Welfare Park, Park Road, Bedlington, NE22 5DA **(T)** 07853 052 450
Capacity: 3,000 **Seats:** 300 **Covered:** 500 **Midweek Matchday:** Wednesday **Clubhouse:** Yes **Shop:**

Colours(change): Red with white trim/red/red.
Previous Names: Bedlington Mechanics 1949-53 Bedlington United 1961-65
Previous Leagues: Northern Alliance
Records: **Att:** 2,400 v Colchester United FA Cup 1st round **Goalscorer:** John Milner
Senior Honours: Northern Lge Div 1: 97-98, 98-99, 99-00, 2000-01, 01-02. Northumberland Senior Cup 1996-97, 97-98, 2001-02,03-04.

10 YEAR RECORD

01-02	02-03	03-04	04-05	05-06	06-07	07-08	08-09	09-10	10-11
NL 1 1	NL 1 2	NL 1 3	NL 1 3	NL 1 2	NL 1 20	NL 1 15	NL 1 14	NL 1 7	NL 1 9

BILLINGHAM SYNTHONIA

Founded: 1923 Nickname: Synners

Secretary: Graham Craggs **(T)** 07702 530 335 **(E)** graham.craggs@gb.abb.com
Chairman: Stuart Coleby **Manager:** **Prog Ed:** Graeme Goodman
Ground: The Stadium, Central Ave, Billingham, Cleveland TS23 1LR **(T)** 01642 532 348
Capacity: 1,970 **Seats:** 370 **Covered:** 370 **Midweek Matchday:** Wednesday **Clubhouse:** Yes **Shop:** Yes

Colours(change): Green & white quarters/white/white
Previous Names: Billingham Synthonia Recreation
Previous Leagues: Teesside 1923-the war
Records: **Att:** 4,200 v Bishop Auckland 1958 **Goalscorer:** Tony Hetherington **App:** Andy Harbron
Senior Honours: Northern Lge 1956-57, 88-89, 89-90, 95-96. Div.2 86-87.

10 YEAR RECORD

01-02	02-03	03-04	04-05	05-06	06-07	07-08	08-09	09-10	10-11
NL 1 11	NL 1 4	NL 1 9	NL 1 2	NL 1 7	NL 1 14	NL 1 9	NL 1 15	NL 1 12	NL 1 12

BILLINGHAM TOWN

Founded: 1967 Nickname: Billy Town

Secretary: Glenn Youngman **(T)** 07984 258 608 **(E)** CFS_IFA@hotmail.com
Chairman: Tommy Donnelly **Manager:** **Prog Ed:** Peter Martin
Ground: Bedford Terrace, Billingham, Cleveland TS23 4AF **(T)** 01642 560 043
Capacity: 3,000 **Seats:** 176 **Covered:** 600 **Midweek Matchday:** Tuesday **Clubhouse:** Yes **Shop:** No

Colours(change): Blue/blue/white
Previous Names: Billingham Social Club
Previous Leagues: Stockton & District 1968-74 Teesside 1974-82
Records: **Att:** 1,500 v Man City FA Youth Cup 1985 **Goalscorer:** Paul Rowntree 396 **App:** Paul Rowntree 505
Senior Honours: Durham Cup 1976-77, 77-78, 2003-04

10 YEAR RECORD

01-02	02-03	03-04	04-05	05-06	06-07	07-08	08-09	09-10	10-11
NL 1 10	NL 1 3	NL 1 5	NL 1 7	NL 1 4	NL 1 2	NL 1 10	NL 1 17	NL 1 19	NL 1 15

BISHOP AUCKLAND

Founded: 1886 Nickname:

Secretary: Tony Duffy **(T)** 07974 286 812 **(E)** pauline@paulineduffy.wanadoo.co.uk
Chairman: Terry Jackson **Manager:** **Prog Ed:** Dave Strong
Ground: Heritage Park, Bishop Auckland, Co. Durham DL14 9AE **(T)** 01388 604 605
Capacity: **Seats:** **Covered:** **Midweek Matchday:** Wednesday **Clubhouse:** Yes **Shop:** No

Colours(change): Light & dark blue/blues/blues
Previous Names: Auckland Town 1889-1893
Previous Leagues: Northern Alliance 1890-91, Northern League 1893-1988, Northern Premier 1988-2006
Records: **Att:** 17,000 v Coventry City FA Cup 2nd round 1952 **App:** Bob Hardisty
Senior Honours: Post War: Nth Lge 1949-50, 50-51, 51-52, 53-54, 54-55, 55-56, 66-67, 84-85, 85-86 (18th Nth Lge title).

10 YEAR RECORD

01-02	02-03	03-04	04-05	05-06	06-07	07-08	08-09	09-10	10-11
NP P 21	NP 1 15	NP 1 13	NP P 19	NP 1 22	NL 1 16	NL 1 20	NL 1 18	NL 1 13	NL 1 14

CONSETT

Founded: 1899 Nickname: Steelman

Secretary: David Pyke **(T)** 07889 419 268 **(E)** david.pyke@phoenix.co.uk
Chairman: John Hurst **Manager:** Kenny Lindoe **Prog Ed:** Gary Welford
Ground: Belle Vue Park, Ashdale Road, Consett, DH8 6LZ **(T)** 01207 503 788
Capacity: 4,000 **Seats:** 400 **Covered:** 1000 **Midweek Matchday:** Wednesday **Clubhouse:** Yes **Shop:** No

Colours(change): All Red
Previous Names: None
Previous Leagues: N.All 1919-26, 35-37, N.E.C. 26-35, 37-58, 62-64, Midland 58-60, N.Co. 60-62, Wearside 64-70
Records: **Att:** 7000 v Sunderland Reserves, first match at Belle Vue 1950
Senior Honours: Norh Eastern Lg 39-40 Div 2 26-27, Northern Counties Lg 61-62, Northern Leageu Div.2 1988-89, 05-06.

10 YEAR RECORD

01-02	02-03	03-04	04-05	05-06	06-07	07-08	08-09	09-10	10-11
NL 1 17	NL 1 20	NL 2 3	NL 1 19	NL 2 1	NL 1 4	NL 1 2	NL 1 2	NL 1 10	NL 1 2

DUNSTON UTS

Founded: 1975 Nickname: The Fed

Secretary: Bill Montague **(T)** 07981 194 756 **(E)** w.montague@sky.com
Chairman: Malcolm James **Manager:** **Prog Ed:** Bill Montague
Ground: UTS Stadium, Wellington Rd, Dunston, Gateshead NE11 9LJ **(T)** 0191 493 2935
Capacity: 2,000 **Seats:** 120 **Covered:** 400 **Midweek Matchday:** Tuesday **Clubhouse:** Yes **Shop:** No

Colours(change): All Blue with white trim
Previous Names: Dunston Federation Brewery > 2007. Dunston Federation > 2009.
Previous Leagues: Northern Amateur & Wearside league
Records: **Att:** 1,550 v Sunderland Shipowners Cup Final 01.04.88 **Goalscorer:** Paul King **App:** Paul Dixon
Senior Honours: Wearside League 1988-89, 89-90. Northern League Div.2 92-93. Div.1 2003-04, 04-05.

10 YEAR RECORD

01-02	02-03	03-04	04-05	05-06	06-07	07-08	08-09	09-10	10-11
NL 1 3	NL 1 8	NL 1 1	NL 1 1	NL 1 3	NL 1 7	NL 1 6	NL 1 6	NL 1 4	NL 1 7

GUISBOROUGH TOWN

Founded: 1973 Nickname: Priorymen

Secretary: Keith Smeltzer **(T)** 07811 850 388 **(E)** keithsmeltzer@hotmail.co.uk
Chairman: Daniel Clark **Manager:** **Prog Ed:** Keith Smeltzer
Ground: King George V Ground, Howlbeck Road, Guisborough TS14 6LE **(T)** 01287 636 925
Capacity: **Seats:** **Covered:** **Midweek Matchday:** **Clubhouse:** **Shop:**

Colours(change): All red
Previous Names:
Previous Leagues: Northern Counties East 1982-85.
Records: **Att:** 3,112 v Hungerford FA Vase Semi-final. **Goalscorer:** Mark Davis 341. **Apps:** Mark Davis 587.
Senior Honours: Northern Alliance 1979-80. Northern League Cup 1987-88. Nth Riding Sen Cup 1989-90, 90-91, 91-92, 92-93, 94-95

10 YEAR RECORD

01-02	02-03	03-04	04-05	05-06	06-07	07-08	08-09	09-10	10-11
NL 1 9	NL 1 7	NL 1 14	NL 1 21	NL 1 19	NL 2 9	NL 2 12	NL 2 7	NL 2 5	NL 2 2

JARROW ROOFING BOLDON C.A. Founded: 1987 Nickname: Roofing

Secretary: Bryn Griffiths **(T)** 07889 279 647 **(E)** bgriffiths94@btinternet.com
Chairman: Richard McLoughlin **Manager:** **Prog Ed:** Bryn Griffiths
Ground: Boldon CA Sports Ground, New Road, Boldon Colliery NE35 9DZ **(T)** 07930 803 387
Capacity: 3,500 **Seats:** 150 **Covered:** 800 **Midweek Matchday:** Tuesday **Clubhouse:** Yes **Shop:** Yes

Colours(change): All blue with yellow trim
Previous Names:
Previous Leagues: S. Tyneside Senior 1987-88, Tyneside Am. 1988-91, Wearside 1991-96
Records: **Att:** 500 v South Shields **Goalscorer:** Mick Hales **App:** Paul Chow
Senior Honours:

10 YEAR RECORD

01-02	02-03	03-04	04-05	05-06	06-07	07-08	08-09	09-10	10-11
NL 1 12	NL 1 9	NL 1 6	NL 1 12	NL 1 15	NL 1 15	NL 1 22	NL 2 16	NL 2 3	NL 1 19

MARSKE UNITED Founded: 1956 Nickname: The Seasiders

Secretary: Les Holtby **(T)** 07804 150 880 **(E)** marskeunited@ntlworld.com
Chairman: Billy Park **Manager:** **Prog Ed:** Moss Holtby
Ground: GER Stad., Mount Pleasant Avenue, Marske by the Sea, Redcar TS11 7BW **(T)** 01642 471 091
Capacity: **Seats:** **Covered:** **Midweek Matchday:** **Clubhouse:** **Shop:**

Colours(change): Yellow/blue/blue
Previous Names: None
Previous Leagues: Wearside 1985-97.
Records: **Defeat:** 3-9. **Goalscorer:** Chris Morgan 169. **Apps:** Mike Kinnair 583.
Senior Honours: Teeside League 1980-81, 84-85. Wearside League 1995-96. North Riding Senior Cup 1994-95. North Riding County Cup 1980-81, 85-86.

10 YEAR RECORD

01-02	02-03	03-04	04-05	05-06	06-07	07-08	08-09	09-10	10-11
NL 1 4	NL 1 16	NL 1 20	NL 2 15	NL 2 10	NL 2 5	NL 2 8	NL 2 5	NL 2 4	NL 2 3

NEWCASTLE BENFIELD Founded: 1988 Nickname: The Lions

Secretary: Mark Hedley **(T)** 07973 699 506 **(E)** markhedley3@msn.com
Chairman: Jimmy Rowe **Manager:** **Prog Ed:** Jim Clark
Ground: Sam Smiths Park, Benfield Road, Walkergate NE6 4NU **(T)** 0191 265 9357
Capacity: 2,000 **Seats:** 150 **Covered:** 250 **Midweek Matchday:** Wednesday **Clubhouse:** Yes **Shop:** No

Colours(change): Blue & white hoops/blue/blue
Previous Names: Heaton Corner House. Newcastle Benfield Saints.
Previous Leagues: Northern Alliance 1988-2003
Records:
Senior Honours: Northern Alliance Div 2 Champions 1989-90, Div 1 1994-95, 2002-03. Northern League Cup 2006-07. Northern League Champions 2008-09.

10 YEAR RECORD

01-02	02-03	03-04	04-05	05-06	06-07	07-08	08-09	09-10	10-11
NAl P 3	NAl P 1	NL 2 2	NL 1 4	NL 1 9	NL 1 5	NL 1 4	NL 1 1	NL 1 5	NL 1 4

NEWTON AYCLIFFE Founded: 1965 Nickname: Aycliffe

Secretary: Stephen Cunliffe **(T)** 07872 985 501 **(E)** stecunliffe@aol.com
Chairman: Gary Farley **Manager:** **Prog Ed:** Paul McGeary
Ground: Moore Lane Park, Moore Lane, Newton Aycliffe, Co. Durham DL5 5AG **(T)** 01325 312 768
Capacity: **Seats:** Yes **Covered:** Yes **Midweek Matchday:** **Clubhouse:** Yes **Shop:**

Colours(change): All blue
Previous Names: None
Previous Leagues: Wearside 1984-94, 2008-09. Durham Alliance > 2008.
Records: **Att:** 520 v Teeside Athletic (Sunderland Shipwoners Final) 2008-09.
Senior Honours: Darlington & District Division 'A' 2004-05. Durham Alliance League 2007-08. Wearside League 2008-09. Northern League Division Two 2010-11.

10 YEAR RECORD

01-02	02-03	03-04	04-05	05-06	06-07	07-08	08-09	09-10	10-11
DaD'A'	DaD'A'	DaD'A'	DaD'A' 1			DuAl 1	Wear 1	NL 2 9	NL 2 1

NORTON & STOCKTON ANCIENTS

Founded: 1959 Nickname: Ancients

Secretary: Steven Lawson **(T)** 07871 206 474 **(E)** stevenlawson_16@hotmail.co.uk
Chairman: Michael Mulligan **Manager:** **Prog Ed:** Steven Lawson
Ground: Norton (Teesside) Sports Complex, Station Rd, Norton TS20 1PE **(T)** 01642 530 203
Capacity: 2,000 **Seats:** 200 **Covered:** yes **Midweek Matchday:** Wednesday **Clubhouse:** **Shop:**

Colours(change): Amber & black/black/black.
Previous Names: Norton & Stockton Cricket Club Trust
Previous Leagues: Teesside (pre-1982)
Records: **Att:** 1,430 v Middlesbrough, Friendly1988.
Senior Honours: Northern League Cup 1982-83.

10 YEAR RECORD

01-02	02-03	03-04	04-05	05-06	06-07	07-08	08-09	09-10	10-11
NL 2 12	NL 2 18	NL 2 18	NL 2 6	NL 2 7	NL 2 6	NL 2 10	NL 2 2	NL 1 8	NL 1 10

PENRITH

Founded: 1894 Nickname: Blues

Secretary: Ian White **(T)** 07960 958 367 **(E)** ianwhite77@hotmail.com
Chairman: Brian Williams **Manager:** **Prog Ed:** Brian Kirkbride
Ground: The Stadium, Frenchfield Park, Frenchfield, Penrith CA11 8UA **(T)** 01768 895 990
Capacity: 4,000 **Seats:** 200 **Covered:** 1,000 **Midweek Matchday:** Tuesday **Clubhouse:** Yes **Shop:** No

Colours(change): Blue/white/blue.
Previous Names: Penrith FC. Penrith Town.
Previous Leagues: Carlisle & Dist. Northern 1942-82, NWC 1982-87, 90-97. NPL 1987-90.
Records: 2,100 v Chester 1981
Senior Honours: Northern League Division 2 Champions 2002-03, 07-08.

10 YEAR RECORD

01-02	02-03	03-04	04-05	05-06	06-07	07-08	08-09	09-10	10-11
NL 2 4	NL 2 1	NL 1 21	NL 2 8	NL 2 4	NL 2 7	NL 2 1	NL 1 7	NL 1 14	NL 1 17

SHILDON

Founded: 1890 Nickname: Railwaymen

Secretary: Gareth Howe **(T)** 07976 822 453 **(E)** gareth.howe3@btopenworld.com
Chairman: Brian Burn **Manager:** **Prog Ed:** Anthony Webster
Ground: Dean Street, Shildon, Co. Durham DL4 1HA **(T)** 01388 773 877
Capacity: 4,000 **Seats:** 480 **Covered:** 1000 **Midweek Matchday:** Wednesday **Clubhouse:** Yes **Shop:** No

Colours(change): All red
Previous Names: Shildon Athletic > 1923.
Previous Leagues: Auckland & Dist 1892-86, Wear Valley 1896-97, Northern 1903-07, North Eastern 1907-32
Records: **Att:** 11,000 v Ferryhill Athletic, Durham Senior Cup 1922 **Goalscorer:** Jack Downing 61 (1936-7) **App:** Bryan Dale
Senior Honours: Durham Amateur Cup 1901-02, 02-03, Durham Challenge Cup 1907-08, 25-26, 71-72,
Northern League Champions 1933-34, 34-35, 35-36,36-37, 39-40, Div 2 2001-02.

10 YEAR RECORD

01-02	02-03	03-04	04-05	05-06	06-07	07-08	08-09	09-10	10-11
NL 2 1	NL 1 6	NL 1 4	NL 1 11	NL 1 18	NL 1 9	NL 1 5	NL 1 8	NL 1 2	NL 1 5

SOUTH SHIELDS

Founded: 1974 Nickname: Mariners

Secretary: Philip Reay **(T)** 07847 173 235 **(E)** philip@sheels.fsnet.co.uk
Chairman: Gary Crutwell **Manager:** **Prog Ed:** Philip Reay
Ground: Mariners Club, Filtrona Park, Shaftesbury Ave, Jarrow NE32 3UP **(T)** 0191 427 9839
Capacity: 2,500 **Seats:** 150 **Covered:** 400 **Midweek Matchday:** Tuesday **Clubhouse:** Yes **Shop:** Yes

Colours(change): Claret & blue/white/white
Previous Names: South Shields Mariners.
Previous Leagues: Northern Alliance 1974-76, Wearside 1976-95.
Records: **Att:**1,500 v Spennymoor, Durham Challenge Cup Final 1994-95.
Senior Honours: Northern Alliance 1974-75, 75-76, Wearside League 1976-77, 92-93, 94-95.
Monkwearmouth Charity Cup 1986-87.

10 YEAR RECORD

01-02	02-03	03-04	04-05	05-06	06-07	07-08	08-09	09-10	10-11
NL 2 8	NL 2 8	NL 2 12	NL 2 13	NL 2 18	NL 2 4	NL 2 2	NL 1 19	NL 1 11	NL 1 11

SPENNYMOOR TOWN

Founded: 1890 Nickname: Moors

Secretary: David Leitch **(T)** 07530 453 880 **(E)** leitchy1969@btinternet.com
Chairman: Bradley Groves **Manager:** **Prog Ed:** Mike Rowcroft
Ground: Brewery Field, Durham Road, Spennymoor DL16 6JN **(T)**
Capacity: 7,500 **Seats:** 300 **Covered:** 2,000 **Midweek Matchday:** Wednesday **Clubhouse:** Yes **Shop:** Yes

Colours(change): Black & white stripes/white/black
Previous Names: Amalgamation of Evenwood Town & Spennymoor Utd in 2005-06.
Previous Leagues: None
Records:
Senior Honours: Northern League Division Two 2006-07, Division One 2009-10, 2010-11.

10 YEAR RECORD

01-02	02-03	03-04	04-05	05-06	06-07	07-08	08-09	09-10	10-11
				NL 2 8	NL 2 1	NL 1 12	NL 1 4	NL 1 1	NL 1 1

STOKESLEY SPORTS CLUB

Founded: 1920 Nickname:

Secretary: Peter Grainge **(T)** 07712 883 874 **(E)** peterssc@hotmail.co.uk
Chairman: Eric Taylor **Manager:** **Prog Ed:** Tim Ellison
Ground: Stokesley Sports Club, Broughton Road, Stokesley TS9 5JQ **(T)** 01642 710 051
Capacity: **Seats:** **Covered:** **Midweek Matchday:** Wednesday **Clubhouse:** **Shop:**

Colours(change): Red & Black stripes/black/black
Previous Names: Stokesley Sports Club > 2009, Stokesley 2009-11.
Previous Leagues: Langbargh, South Bank, Stokesley & Dist., Teesside, Wearside.
Records:
Senior Honours: Stokesley & District League 1975-76. Northern League Division Two 2009-10.

10 YEAR RECORD

01-02	02-03	03-04	04-05	05-06	06-07	07-08	08-09	09-10	10-11
Wear 8	Wear 3	Wear 3	Wear 3	Wear 2	NL 2 8	NL 2 9	NL 2 13	NL 2 1	NL 1 16

SUNDERLAND RYHOPE C.A.

Founded: 1961 Nickname:

Secretary: Rob Jones **(T)** 07932 951 842 **(E)** Robert-jones10@live.co.uk
Chairman: Owen Haley **Manager:** Neil Hixon **Prog Ed:** Colin Wilson
Ground: Meadow Park, Beachbrooke, Stockton Rd, Ryhope, Sunderland SR2 0NZ **(T)** 0191 523 6555
Capacity: 2,000 **Seats:** 150 **Covered:** 200 **Midweek Matchday:** Wednesday **Clubhouse:** **Shop:**

Colours(change): Red & white halves/black/red
Previous Names: Ryhope Community Ass. FC
Previous Leagues: S.C. Vaux: Tyne & Wear, NorthEastern Am a Ryhope CA N Alliance.>82
Records: Not Known
Senior Honours: Northern Alliance League Cup 1981.

10 YEAR RECORD

01-02	02-03	03-04	04-05	05-06	06-07	07-08	08-09	09-10	10-11
NL 2 10	NL 2 11	NL 2 9	NL 2 16	NL 2 17	NL 2 19	NL 2 4	NL 2 4	NL 2 2	NL 1 13

TOW LAW TOWN

Founded: 1890 Nickname: Lawyers

Secretary: Steve Moralee **(T)** 07810 238 731 **(E)** stephen.moralee@btinternet.com
Chairman: Sandra Gordon **Manager:** **Prog Ed:** John Dixon
Ground: Ironworks Ground, Tow Law, Bishop Auckland DL13 4EQ **(T)** 01388 731 443
Capacity: 6,000 **Seats:** 200 **Covered:** 300 **Midweek Matchday:** Tuesday **Clubhouse:** Yes **Shop:** Yes

Colours(change): Black & white stripes/black/black
Previous Names: Tow Law.
Previous Leagues: Northern League 1894-1900, South Durham Alliance 1900-05, Crook & District 1905-12
Records: 5,500 v Mansfield Town FA Cup 1967.
Senior Honours: Northern League Champions 1923-24, 24-25, 94-95. League Cup 73-74.

10 YEAR RECORD

01-02	02-03	03-04	04-05	05-06	06-07	07-08	08-09	09-10	10-11
NL 1 2	NL 1 15	NL 1 16	NL 1 16	NL 1 12	NL 1 12	NL 1 7	NL 1 11	NL 1 9	NL 1 18

WEST AUCKLAND TOWN

Founded: 1893 | Nickname: West

Secretary: Allen Bayles **(T)** 07894 329 005 **(E)** allenbayles@hotmail.co.uk
Chairman: Jim Palfreyman **Manager:** **Prog Ed:** Michael Bainbridge
Ground: Darlington Road, West Auckland, Co. Durham DL14 9HU **(T)** 07800 796 630
Capacity: 3,000 **Seats:** 250 **Covered:** 250 **Midweek Matchday:** Tuesday **Clubhouse:** Yes **Shop:** No

Colours(change): All white
Previous Names: Auckland St Helens. St Helens. West Auckland.
Previous Leagues: Auck&D.,Wear Val,Sth D'ham All.Mid D'ham, Nth Lge 1919-20.Palantine 20-24.Sth D'ham 27-28.Gaunless Val 33-34
Records: **Att:** 6,000 v Dulwich Hamlet FA Amateur Cup 1958-59
Senior Honours: Sir Thomas Lipton Trophy 1909, 1911, Northern League 1959-60, 60-61. Div 2 1990-91. League Cup 1958-59, 62-63, Durham Challenge Cup 1964-65

10 YEAR RECORD

01-02	02-03	03-04	04-05	05-06	06-07	07-08	08-09	09-10	10-11
NL 1 7	NL 1 13	NL 1 13	NL 1 17	NL 1 5	NL 1 6	NL 1 16	NL 1 20	NL 1 16	NL 1 6

WHITLEY BAY

Founded: 1897 | Nickname: The Bay

Secretary: Derek Breakwell **(T)** 07889 888 187 **(E)** dbreakwell@hotmail.co.uk
Chairman: Paul McIlduff **Manager:** **Prog Ed:** Julian Tyley
Ground: Hillheads Park, Rink Way, Whitley Bay, NE25 8HR **(T)** 0191 291 3637
Capacity: 4,500 **Seats:** 450 **Covered:** 650 **Midweek Matchday:** Tuesday **Clubhouse:** Yes **Shop:** Yes

Colours(change): Blue & white stripes/blue/blue
Previous Names: Whitley Bay Athletic 1950-58
Previous Leagues: Tyneside 1909-10, Northern All. 1950-55, N. Eastern 1955-58, Northern 1958-88 N.P.L. 1988-00
Records: 7,301 v Hendon, FA Amateur Cup 1965.
Senior Honours: Northern Alliance 1952-53, 53-54. Northern League 1964-65, 65-66, 06-07. NPL Div 1 1990-91, FA Vase 2001-02, 08-09.

10 YEAR RECORD

01-02	02-03	03-04	04-05	05-06	06-07	07-08	08-09	09-10	10-11
NL 1 5	NL 1 10	NL 1 10	NL 1 5	NL 1 10	NL 1 1	NL 1 3	NL 1 3	NL 1 3	NL 1 3

NORTHERN COUNTIES EAST INS & OUTS

PREM - IN: Barton Town Old Boys (P), Retford (formerly Retford United) (R - Northern Premier League Premier Division), Staveley Miners Welfare (P).

OUT: Dinnington Town (R), Farsley (P - Northern Premier League Division One North), Hallam (R).

DIV ONE - IN: Albion Sports (P - West Riding County Amateur League Premier Division), Dinnington Town (R), Hallam (R), Worksop Parramore (formerly Sheffield Parramore) (P - Central Midlands League Supreme Division).

OUT: Barton Town Old Boys (P), Leeds Carnegie (F), Staveley Miners Welfare (P).

ALNWICK TOWN
Founded: 1879 Nickname:

Secretary: Cyril Cox **(T)** 07570 834 789 **(E)** uk2usa@hotmail.com
Chairman: Tommy McKie **Manager:** **Prog Ed:**
Ground: St. Jame's Park, Weavers Way, Alnwick, Northumberland NE66 1BG **(T)** 01665 603 612 **Capacity:**
Colours(change): Black & white stripes/black/black

ADDITIONAL INFORMATION: Previous Names: Alnwick Utd Services 1879-1900, Alnwick Utd Juniors 1900-1936.
Previous Lge: Northern Alliance 1935-82, 2007-11. Northern League 1982-2007.
Honours: Nothern Alliance title 9 times.

BIRTLEY TOWN
Founded: 1993 Nickname: The Hoops

Secretary: Trevor Armstrong **(T)** 07958 540 389 **(E)** trevellen1@sky.com
Chairman: John Heslington **Manager:** **Prog Ed:** Andrew Walker
Ground: Birtley Sports Complex, Durham Road, Birtley DH3 2TB **(T)** 07958 540 389 **Capacity:**
Colours(change): Green & white hoops/green/green

ADDITIONAL INFORMATION:
Previous League: Wearside 1993-2007.
Honours: Wearside League 2002-03, 06-07, Division 2 1994-95, League Cup 1998, 2002, 2006.

BRANDON UNITED
Founded: 1968 Nickname: United

Secretary: Barry Ross **(T)** 07717 673 090 **(E)** barryross430@btinternet.com
Chairman: Bill Fisher **Manager:** **Prog Ed:** Tommy Simm
Ground: Welfare Park, Rear Commercial Street, Brandon DH7 8PR **(T)** 07949 076 218 **Capacity:**
Colours(change): All red

ADDITIONAL INFORMATION: Previous League: Wearside 1981-83. **Record Att:** 2,500 F.A. Sunday Cup Seim-final.
Record: Goalscorer: Tommy Holden. **Apps:** Derek Charlton 1977-86. **Honours:** F.A. Sunday Cup 1975-76.
Northern Alliance Division 2 1977-78, 78-79. Northern League 2002-03, Division 2 1984-85, 99-2000.

CHESTER-LE-STREET TOWN
Founded: 1972 Nickname: Cestrians

Secretary: Lenny Lauchlan **(T)** 07749 924 318 **(E)** l.w.lauchlan@durham.ac.uk
Chairman: Joe Burlison **Manager:** **Prog Ed:** Keith Greener
Ground: Moor Park, Chester Moor, Chester-le-Street, Co.Durham DH2 3RW **(T)** 07972 419 275 **Capacity:**
Colours(change): Blue & white hoops/white/white

ADDITIONAL INFORMATION: Previous Name: Garden Farm 1972-78. **Previous League:** Wearside 1977-83.
Record Att: 893 v Fleetwood FA Vase 1985 **App:** Colin Wake 361.
Honours: Washington League 1975-6 Wearside League1980-81, Northern League Div 2 1983-84, 97-98.

CROOK TOWN
Founded: 1889 Nickname: Black & ambers

Secretary: Kieron Bennett **(T)** 07838 387 335 **(E)** k.bennett@leybourneurwinltd.co.uk
Chairman: Bill Penman **Manager:** **Prog Ed:** Kieron Bennett
Ground: The Sir Tom Cowie Millfield, West Road, Crook, Co.Durham DL15 9PW **(T)** 01388 762 959 **Capacity:**
Colours(change): Amber/black/amber

ADDITIONAL INFORMATION: Previous Name: Crook C.W. **Previous League:** Durham Central 1941-45.
Honours: FA Amateur Cup 1900-01, 53-54, 58-59, 61-62, 63-64. Northern League x5, League Cup x3.
Durham Challenge Cup x4. Durham Benefit Bowl x6. Ernest Armstrong Memorial Trophy 1997.

DARLINGTON R.A.
Founded: 1993 Nickname:

Secretary: Chris Griffin **(T)** 07837 447 662 **(E)** chris@cagms.co.uk
Chairman: Doug Hawman **Manager:** **Prog Ed:** Chris Griffin
Ground: Brinkburn Road, Darlington, Co. Durham DL3 9LF **(T)** 01325 468 125 **Capacity:**
Colours(change): All red

ADDITIONAL INFORMATION:
Previous League: Darlington & District 1993-99.
Honours: Auckland & District League 2000-01. Wearside League 2004-05.

EASINGTON COLLIERY
Founded: 1913 Nickname:

Secretary: Alan Purvis **(T)** 0191 489 6930 **(E)** saiger1267@sky.com
Chairman: Stephen Saiger **Manager:** Andy Collage **Prog Ed:**
Ground: Welfare Park, Easington Colliery SR8 3JJ **(T)** **Capacity:**
Colours(change): Green & white stripes/green/green

ADDITIONAL INFORMATION:
Previous Names: Easington Colliery Welfare 1913-64, 1973-80. Amalgamated with Easington Rangers in 1980 to form todays club.

ESH WINNING

Founded: 1885 Nickname: Stags

Secretary: David Thompson OBE (T) 07901 002 468 (E) thompsondr@sky.com
Chairman: Charles Ryan **Manager:** Adam Furness **Prog Ed:** Simon Bourne
Ground: West Terrace, Waterhouse, Durham DH7 9NQ (T) 0191 373 3872 **Capacity:** 3,500
Colours(change): Yellow/green/yellow

ADDITIONAL INFORMATION:
Record Att: 5,000 v Newcastle Utd Res. 1910 & Bishop Auckland 1921 **Goalscorer:** Alan Dodsworth 250+ **App:** Neil McLeary - 194 . **Honours:** Northern League Champions 1912-13.

GILLFORD PARK

Founded: 2005 Nickname:

Secretary: Michael Linden (T) 07717 103 666 (E) linden146@btinternet.com
Chairman: Donald Cameron **Manager:** **Prog Ed:** Sean Crilley
Ground: Gillford Park Railway Club, Off Pettrill Bank Rd, Carlisle, Cumbria CA1 3AF (T) 01228 526 449 **Capacity:**
Colours(change): All white

ADDITIONAL INFORMATION:
Previous Name: Gifford Park Spartans. **Previous League:** Northern Alliance 2005-09.
Honours: Northern Alliance Division 1 2006-07, Premier Division 2008-09, Challenge Cup 2008-09.

HEBBURN TOWN

Founded: 1912 Nickname: Hornets

Secretary: Tom Derrick (T) 07981 456 653 (E) tomderrick39@hotmail.com
Chairman: Bill Laffey **Manager:** **Prog Ed:** Richard Bainbridge
Ground: Hebburn Sports & Social, Victoria Rd West, Hebburn, Tyne&Wear NE31 1UN (T) 0191 483 5101 **Capacity:**
Colours(change): Yellow & navy stripes/navy/navy

ADDITIONAL INFORMATION: **Previous Names:** Reyrolles, Hebburn Reyrolles > 1988, Hebburn 1988-2000.
Previous League: Wearside 1960-89. **Record Att:** 503 v Darwen FA Cup Prelim replay 07/09/1991, **Win:** 10-1. **Defeat:** 3-10.
Honours: Tyneside League 1938-39, Northern Combination 1943-44, Wearside League 1966-67,

HORDEN C.W.

Founded: 1908 Nickname: Colliers

Secretary: John Stubbs (T) 07726 694 672 (E) johnstubbsuk@btinternet.com
Chairman: Norman Stephens **Manager:** **Prog Ed:** John Stubbs
Ground: Welfare Park, Seventh Street, Horden, Peterlee, Co. Durham SR8 4LX (T) **Capacity:**
Colours(change): Red/black/black

ADDITIONAL INFORMATION: **Previous Name:** Horden Athletic. **Previous League:** North Eastern 1962-64.
Record Att: 8,000 FA Cup 1937. **Honours:** Wearside League 1911-12, 12-13, 13-14, 33-34, 64-65, 67-68, 69-70, 70-71, 71-72, 72-73. Northern League Division 2 2008-09.

MORPETH TOWN

Founded: 1909 Nickname: Highwaymen

Secretary: David McMeekan (T) 07526 283 824 (E) drmcmeekan@yahoo.co.uk
Chairman: Jim Smith **Manager:** **Prog Ed:** Ken Waterhouse
Ground: Craik Park, Morpeth Common, Morpeth, Northumberland, NE61 2YX (T) 07526 283 824 **Capacity:**
Colours(change): Yellow & black stripes/black/black

ADDITIONAL INFORMATION:
Previous League: Northern Alliance > 1994.
Honours: Northern Alliance 1983-84, 93-94, Northern League Division 2 1995-96. Northumberland Senior Cup 2006-07.

NORTH SHIELDS

Founded: 1992 Nickname: Robins

Secretary: Kevin Larkham (T) 07976 569 006 (E) kevin7691@live.com
Chairman: Alan Matthews **Manager:** **Prog Ed:** Mark Scott
Ground: Ralph Gardner Park, West Percy Road, Chirton, North Shields (T) 07759 766 732 **Capacity:**
Colours(change): All red

ADDITIONAL INFORMATION:
Previous Names: Preston Colliery > 1928, North Shields Athletic 1995-99. **Previous League:** Wearside.
Honours: FA Amateur Cup 1968-69, N.C.E. Prem Div 91-92, Lge Cup 90-91. Wearside League 1998-99, 01-02, 03-04.

NORTHALLERTON TOWN

Founded: 1994 Nickname: Town

Secretary: Lesley Clark (T) 07891 595 267 (E) lesleyclark05@yahoo.co.uk
Chairman: Dave Watson **Manager:** **Prog Ed:** Ian Bolland
Ground: RGPS Stadium, Ainderby Road, Northallerton DL7 8HA (T) 01609 772 418 **Capacity:**
Colours(change): Black & white/black/black

ADDITIONAL INFORMATION: **Previous Name:** Northallerton FC 1994. **Previous League:** Harrogate & District.
Record Att: 695 v Farnborough Town FA Trophy 3rd Round 20/02/1993.
Honours: Northern League Division 2 1996-97, League Cup 1993-94.

RYTON & CRAWCROOK ALBION
Founded: 1970 Nickname:

Secretary: Ken Rodger **(T)** 07872 839 368 **(E)** kenneth@krodger.fsnet.co.uk
Chairman: Richard Hands **Manager:** **Prog Ed:** Chris Holt
Ground: Kingsley Park, Stannerford Road, Crawcrook NE40 3SN **(T)** 0191 413 4448 **Capacity:** 2,000
Colours(change): Blue & black stripes/black/blue

ADDITIONAL INFORMATION: Att: 1,100 v Newcastle United 1998
Northern Alliance Division 1 Champions 1996-97.

SEAHAM RED STAR
Founded: 1973 Nickname: The Star

Secretary: Kevin Turns **(T)** 0770 107 6848 **(E)** seahamredstarfc@aol.co.uk
Chairman: John McBeth **Manager:** **Prog Ed:** Sue Potts
Ground: Seaham Town Park, Stockton Road, Seaham. Co.Durham SR7 0HY **(T)** **Capacity:**
Colours(change): Red & white stripes/black/black

ADDITIONAL INFORMATION: Previous Name: Seaham Colliery Welfare Red Star 1978-87. **Previous League:** Wearside 1979-83.
Record Att: 1,500 v Guisborough. **App:** Michael Whitfield.
Honours: Durham Challenge Cup 1979-80, Wearside League & League Cup 1981-82, Norhtern League Cup 1992-93.

TEAM NORTHUMBRIA
Founded: 1999 Nickname:

Secretary: Gaz Lee **(T)** 07970 478 723 **(E)** gaz.lee@northumbria.ac.uk
Chairman: Ian Elvin **Manager:** **Prog Ed:** Gaz Lee
Ground: Coach Lane, Benton, Newcastle upon Tyne, NE7 7XA **(T)** 0191 215 6575 **Capacity:**
Colours(change): All red

ADDITIONAL INFORMATION:
Previous Name: Northumbria University > 2003. **Previous League:** Northern Alliance 1999-2006.
Honours: Northern Alliance Premier 2005-06.

THORNABY
Founded: 1980 Nickname:

Secretary: Trevor Wing **(T)** 07869 580 446 **(E)** trevor.wing10@btinternet.com
Chairman: Thomas Grant **Manager:** **Prog Ed:** Trevor Wing
Ground: Teesdale Park, Acklam Road, Thornaby, Stockton on Tees TS17 7JE **(T)** 07833 524 659 **Capacity:**
Colours(change): All blue

ADDITIONAL INFORMATION: Previous Names: Stockton Cricket Club 1965-1980, Stockton 1980-99 and Thornaby-on-Tees 1999-2000
Previous League: Wearside 1981-85. **Records Att:** 3,000 v Middlesborough friendly Aug 1986 **App:** Michael Watson
Honours: North Riding County Cup, 1985-86, Northern Lge Div 2 1987-88, 91-92

WASHINGTON
Founded: 1949 Nickname: Mechanics

Secretary: Barry Spendley **(T)** 07810 536 964 **(E)** Derek.Armstrong1@ntlworld.com
Chairman: Derek Armstrong **Manager:** **Prog Ed:** Bob Goodwin
Ground: Nissan Sports Complex, Washington Road Sunderland SR5 3NS **(T)** 07810 530 964 **Capacity:**
Colours(change): All red

ADDITIONAL INFORMATION:
Previous Names: Washington Mechanics, Washington Ikeda Hoover. **Previous League:** Wearside.
Record Att: 3,800 v Bradford Park Avenue FA Cup 1970.
Honours: Washington Amateur: 1956-57,57-58, 58-59,59-60,61-62,62-63, League Cup: 1955-56, 58-59, 60-61, 64-65.

WEST ALLOTMENT CELTIC
Founded: 1928 Nickname:

Secretary: Ted Ilderton **(T)** 07795 246 245 **(E)** tedilderton@o2.co.uk
Chairman: Roland Mather **Manager:** **Prog Ed:** David McMeekan
Ground: Whitley Park, Whitley Road, Benton NE12 9FA **(T)** 0191 270 0885 **Capacity:**
Colours(change): Green & white hoops/green/green & white.

ADDITIONAL INFORMATION: Att: 510 v Cray Wanderers FA Vase 2004
Northern Am. 1956-57, 57-58, 58-59, 59-60, 81-82, 82-83, Div 2: 38-39.
Northern Alliance: 1986-87, 90-91, 91-92, 97-98, 98-99, 99-2000, 01-02, 03-04. Northern League Div 2 2004-05

WHICKHAM
Founded: 1944 Nickname:

Secretary: Paul Nicholson **(T)** 07841 506 694 **(E)** paul-nicholson3@sky.com
Chairman: Brian McCartney **Manager:** **Prog Ed:** Michael Tucker
Ground: Glebe Sports Club, Rectory Lane, Whickham NE16 4NA **(T)** 0191 4200 186 **Capacity:**
Colours(change): Black & white stripes/black/black

ADDITIONAL INFORMATION: Record Att: 3,165 v Windsor & Eton FA Vase SF 1981.
Honours: FA Vase 1980-81, Wearside Lge 77-78, 87-88, Sunderland Shipowners Cup 77-78, 80-81,
Northern Comb 69-70, 72-73, 73-74 Lge Cup 60-61, 73-74

WHITEHAVEN		Founded: 1994	Nickname:
Secretary: W Robson	**(T)** 0759 5276 080	**(E)** whitehavenfc@aol.com	
Chairman: S Hocking	**Manager:**	**Prog Ed:** D J Moors	
Ground: Focus Scaffolding Sports Complex, Coach Road, Whitehaven, CA28 9DB		**(T)** 01946 692 211	**Capacity:**
Colours(change): Yellow/blue/yellow			

ADDITIONAL INFORMATION: Record Att: 207 v Workington Reds, Cumberland County Cup 13/12/2007.
Honours: Wearside League Division 2 1994-95, Wearside League 2005-06. Monkwearmouth Charity Cup 2006-07.

GROUND DIRECTIONS

ALNWICK TOWN - M1, at exit 32, take slip road left for M18 toward The North / Doncaster / Hull, at exit 2, take slip road left for A1(M) toward the North, keep straight onto A1 / Doncaster by Pass, keep straight onto A1(M), take slip road for A1(M) / Aberford by Pass, road name changes to A1 / Leeming Lane, keep straight onto A1(M), keep left onto A1, take slip road left for A1068 toward Alnwick / Alnmouth, at roundabout, take 1st exit onto Willowburn Avenue, turn left, and then immediately turn left onto St James Estate, ground is on the right.

ASHINGTON - Leave the A1 at the junction with the A19 north of Newcastle. Go along the A19 eastwards untio the next roundabout . Here take the second left (A189) signposted to Bedlington and Ashington. Continue along A189 until reach Woodhorn roundabout, turn left onto A197. Turn left at first roundabout. Just before the hospital car park entrance, turn right. Ground is on left.

BEDLINGTON TERRIERS - Take the A1068 from the south, and when in the town turn right onto the A193. Turn left at the Northumberland Arms on Front Street in Bedlington town centre. Continue along this road for approx .25 mile, then turn right into Park Road. The ground is 100 yards on right.

BILLINGHAM SYNTHONIA - Leave A19 onto A1027 sign posted towards Billingham. Continue straight ahead over a couple of roundabouts, and you will be on Central Avenue. The ground is on left opposite an empty office block.

BILLINGHAM TOWN - Leave A19 on A1027 signed Billingham. Turn left at third roundabout, into Cowpen Lane. Go over a railway bridge, then first left into Warwick Crescent, then first left again into Bedford Terrace (follow one-way signs) to the ground.

BIRTLEY TOWN - Leave A1(M) at Angel of the North and follow signs to Birtley (A167). Continue along main road through town. Go past Komatsu factory on right and then after approx 200 yards turn right into an unmarked side road. Ground is directly in front of you.

BISHOP AUCKLAND - NORTH: From junction 60 of the A1 follow the A689 to Bishop Auckland. Go straight across the next 2 roundabouts. At the 3rd roundabout turn left onto the A688 and straight across the next 2 roundabouts. At the following roundabout turn left at Aldi and then go straight across at the next roundabout. The stadium is 200 yards on your right. **SOUTH:** From junction 58 from the A1, take the A68 towards Bishop Auckland. At the West Auckland by-pass, turn right at the roundabout. Go straight across at the next roundabout and the stadium is located 500 yards on your left.

BRANDON UNITED - Leave A1 on A690, go through Durham and continue on A690. Once at 'Langley Moor' (you go under a railway bridge), turn right at the "Lord Boyne" pub. After 100 yards take the next left. Go up the road for approx half a mile, and turn right at the newsagents. Take the next left, and Brandon's ground is up a small track.

CHESTER LE STREET - Leave A1M at junction 63 and take the A167 towards Chester Le Street and Durtham. Keep going along this road for a couple of miles. You will go under a railway bridge, and as the road begins to climb, you will see the Chester Moor pub on your left. Turn into the pub and the ground is accessed along a track at the rear of the pub car park.

CONSETT - Take the A692 from the east into Consett. On the edge of the town, the A692 takes a left at a roundabout. Continue along the A692 for approx 100 yards, before turning right into Leadgate Road. Go along here for approx .25 mile, and turn right into Ashdale Road. There is a road sign for the Leisure Centre pointing into Ashdale Road. The ground is approx 200 yards along Ashdale Road on your right.

CROOK TOWN - Leave the A1 at Junction 62, and take the A690 towards Durham. Keep on this road through Durham, Meadowfield, Willington and Helmington Row. When you arrive in Crook town centre keep going straight ahead, as the A690 becomes the A689. The ground is situated on this road on your right, approximately 300 yards from the town centre.

DARLINGTON RAILWAY ATHLETIC - Leave A1(M) at junction 58 and follow the A68 into Darlington. Continue along the road until you see the Brown Trout public house on your right. Turn left at this point into Brinkburn Road, and the ground is 100 yards along on the left.

DUNSTON U.T.S. - From south take Dunston/Whickham exit off A1M. Turn right at top of slip road into Dunston Road and head down the bank. As the road veers left, the road becomes Wellington Road, and the ground is situated on your left.

ESH WINNING - Leave the A1 at Junction 62, and take the A690 towards Durham. Keep on this road through Durham. Once you start to head down a bank on the A690, you will come to a roundabout. Take the right turn onto the B6302, which will be signposted towards Ushaw Moor. Keep on this road though Ushaw Moor (there is a staggered crossroads to negotiate), and carry on the B6302 into Esh Winning. Keep on going as the ground is not in Esh Winning, but the next village along, Waterhouses. When the road takes a sharp left you will see a track continuing straight ahead. The ground is along this track.

EASINGTON COLLIERY - M1, at exit 32, take slip road left for M18 toward The North / Doncaster / Hull, at exit 2, take slip road left for A1(M) toward The North, keep straight onto A1 / Doncaster by Pass, keep straight onto A1(M), take slip road for A1(M) / Aberford by Pass, at exit Dishforth Interchange, take slip road left for A168 toward Teesside / Thirsk, road name changes to A19, take slip road left, at roundabout, take 1st exit onto A182 / Hall Walks, keep straight onto B1283 / Hall Walks, turn right onto Memorial Avenue.

GILLFORD PARK - Take junction 42 off the M6 and then the A6 into Carlisle. After 1.75 miles take left turn into Petterill Bank Road (junction is at traffic lights). After half a mile turn right onto track immediately before railway bridge. This leads you to the ground.

GUISBOROUGH TOWN - Turn off the A19 into the A174, then come off at the second junction, turning right onto the A172. Follow this round until roundabout with A1043, take left exit to join the A1043. Take right at next roundabout to join the A171. At second roundabout turn right into Middlesbrough Road (will be signposted towards Guisborough) then take left turning at traffic lights into Park Lane. Take first left into Howlbeck Road, and the ground is at the end of the road.

HEBBURN TOWN - Leave A1M on A194(M) (junction 65) and follow signs for Tyne Tunnel. Continue until fourth roundabout and turn left on to B1306 (Hebburn, Mill Lane). Right at traffic lights into Victoria Road. Ground 200 yards long this road on the left.

HORDEN C.W. - Take A19 to Peterlee turn off (B1320). Follow main road into Peterlee then through on the same road, following signs to Horden (B1320). At T-junction, turn left into Sunderland Road, at lights, (A1086) and then right into South Terrace. Ground is at bottom of South Terrace.

JARROW ROOFING - From south take A19 and follow signs for Tyne Tunnel. Turn right at junction marked Boldon Colliery (Testo Roundabout) on to the A184. Turn left at the next r'about, into the B1293, and head towards Asda. At second r'about, turn right at end of retail park. At the r'about at the entrance to Asda, take the "10 to" exit, and you will pass a large brick building on you right, known as The Shack. Turn right into the car park after this building, and at the far end of the car park there is a small lane that leads off left. Roofers ground is at the end of this track.
MARSKE UNITED - Leave A19 and join Parkway (A174) to Marske until Quarry Lane r'about. Take exit (A1085) into Marske. Take the next right after you pass under a railway, into Meadow Rd. Take the next left into Southfield Rd and the entrance is on your left shortly before a T-junc.
MORPETH TOWN - From south. Turn off the A1 onto A197, sign posted Morpeth. Turn left at sign pointing Belsay (B6524). Take right turn just before bridge under the A1. Ground is signposted and up a small track is on the right.
NEWCASTLE BENFIELD - Take the A1058 from either the Tyne Tunnel or central Newcastle. Turn off this road at the junction with Benfield Road. Turn south at this junction, and the Crosslings building will be on your left. Ground is around 400 metres on left, by taking the first turning after passing railway bridge. The ground is 100 yards along this road.
NEWTON AYCLIFFE - From North, leave the A1at junction 60, and travel west along the A689 towards Bishop Auckland. At the roundabout, turn left to join A167. Travel along here for a couple of miles, and at first traffic lights and turn right onto B6443 (Central Avenue). At first roundabout (Tesco's) turn left into Shafto Way then 3rd left into Gunn Way then right into Moore Lane.
NORTHALLERTON TOWN - Leave A1 at Leeming Bar (A684) and follow signs to Northallerton. Approaching the town take the left turn B1333, signed Romanby. Ground is on left after 50 yards in Romanby.
NORTH SHIELDS - Continue north on the A19 after Tyne Tunnel. Take right exit at roundabout onto the A1058. At next roundabout take third exit at Billy Mill, signed to North Shields. At roundabout with A193, turn right, then take second left into Silkey's Lane. Ground is 100 yards on left.
NORTON & STOCKTON ANCIENTS - Leave A19 at Stockton/Norton turn off (A1027) and follow signs to Norton. At the roundabout at the top of the bank take a right turn onto the B1274. Take the next right into Station Road. Ground entrance is on left of road in a large sports complex, the entrance to which is just before the railway crossing. The ground a 200 yards along this track.
PENRITH - Turn off M6 at junction 40 then onto dual carriageway to Appleby and Scotch Corner. Take the A686 (signposted Alston), for approximately half a mile. Then take a right turn (opposite Carleton Road), and follow the track running parallel with the A66. Turn left into the sports complex and follow the road to the far end.
RYTON & CRAWCROOK ALBION - Leave the A1 at the south side of the River Tyne (A694). At the roundabout take the A695 (sign posted Blaydon). At Blaydon take the B6317 through Ryton to reach Crawcrook. Turn right at the traffic lights (sign posted Ryton/Clara Vale). Kingsley Park is situated approximately 500 meters on the right.
SEAHAM RED STAR - Leave A19 on B1404 slip road. Follow signs to Seaham/Ryhope. Turn right at traffic lights on to the B1285. Then left at Red Star social club approximately 200 yards after the traffic lights. There is a car park at the next roundabout behid their social club The ground is a short walk at the top of the park.
SHILDON - Leave A1M at junction 58. Follow A68 signed Bishop Auckland, turn right at roundabout onto A6072. At Shildon turn right at second roundabout (onto B6282) , then left into Byerley Rd (still the B6282). Right at Timothy Hackworth pub into Main St., then at the top of the bank, left into Dean Street.
SOUTH SHIELDS - From A1 M take A194 (M) to South Shields. Follow signs for town centre. Turn left at traffic lights (TESCO supermarket) into Shaftesbury Avenue. Ground is at the far end of the road
SPENNYMOOR TOWN - Turn off A1M at J61. Onto A688 towards Spennymoor, turn right at small roundabout & straight on at Thinford roundabout (Still continuing on the A688). Straight over mini roundabout, and take fourth exit from large roundabout (B6288). Continue for approx. ? mile and take left into Durham Road. Ground is on Wood Vue, approx 300 yards on right just off Durham Rd.
STOKESLEY SPORTS CLUB - Turn off A19 onto A174 (Teesport/Redcar). Take third exit onto A172 (Whitby/Stokesley). Turn right and keep on A172 to Stokesley. In Stokesley bear left at first roundabout, still keeping on the A172. At next roundabout go straight across into Broughton Road (Second exit - B1257). Ground is 100 yards on left-hand side.
SUNDERLAND R.C.A. - From the A19, leave at the junction with the A690, but on that roundabout take the B1286 through Doxford Park. Continue along this road for some time (there are number of roundabouts), but there are signposts to Ryhope along this road. You will eventually come to a T-junction at the end of the B1286, and turn right onto the A1018. After 200 yards you will come to another roundabout, here take a right turn. Then take the next right into a new housing estate. There is a board at the entrance pointing you to Meadow Park, the home of R.C.A. The ground is at the far end of the estate.
TEAM NORTHUMBRIA - Take the A1058 from either the A19 or central Newcastle. Turn off this road at the junction with Benfield Road. Turn north at large Crosslings warehouse into Red Hall Drive, this then becomes Coach Lane. The ground is on the right just past Newcastle University halls of residence.
THORNABY - Turn off A19 onto A1130 and head towards Thornaby. Continue along Acklam Road for about half a mile. Ground is signposted from the main road - on the right up a track between houses after half a mile.
TOW LAW TOWN - Leave the A1 at junction 58 and turn on to A68. Follow signs for Tow Law/Corbridge. Ground is at far end of Tow Law on the left side. The ground is situated on Ironworks Road, which is the first left after a sharp left hand bend on the A68 in Tow Law.
WASHINGTON - Leave the A19 on slip road marked "Nissan Offices" as you pass Sunderland travelling north. This is the A1290. Continue to follow "Nissan Offices" signs. Left at traffic lights, then right at roundabout into complex. Ground is at far end of the plant.
WEST ALLOTMENT CELTIC - Continue on the A19 north after Tyne Tunnel until A191 exit. Take left exit marked Gosforth & Newcastle. A191 for three miles. The ground, The Blue Flames Sports Ground is on left.
WEST AUCKLAND TOWN - Leave A1 at junction 58 on to the A68. Follow signs to W. Auckland/Corbridge. On entering village, ground is behind factory on left side. Ground is up a track on the left side of road next to Oakley Grange Farm.
WHICKHAM - From A1M take the A692 junction, and travel in the direction signed to Consett. At top of the back the road forks left towards Consett, but you should take the right fork along the B6317 to Whickham. Follow this road for 1.5 miles, left turn into Rectory Lane (B6316). Take first right into Holme Avenue, and then first left. The ground is at top of lane. More car parking can be found further along Rectory Lane, take the next right. Walk past the cricket pitch to access the football club.
WHITEHAVEN - From the south, on A595, take the turning into Whitehaven at the top of Inkermann Terrace at traffic lights (A5094). Pass the Chase Hotel on left until reach set of traffic lights next to a garage. Turn left into Coach Lane and travel on until see an access to the left indicating a cycleway. Turn in and follow the path until meet the gates to the ground. From the north, it is easier to travel further down the A595, and follow instructions as above. This way you avoid the town centre.
WHITLEY BAY - Leave the A19 on the A191, and turn eastwards towards Whitely Bay. Continue along New York Road (A191) which then becomes Rake Lane (A191). Pass hospital on right & then into Shields Rd. and Hillheads Rd (both A191). Ground is to the right, floodlights can be seen from miles away! It is next to an ice rink.

SOUTH WEST PENINSULA LEAGUE

Sponsored by: Carlsberg

Founded: 2007

Recent Champions:

2008: Bodmin Town

2009: Bodmin Town

2010: Buckland Athletic

swpleague.co.uk

PREMIER DIVISION	P	W	D	L	F	A	Pts
1 Buckland Athletic	38	31	3	4	131	49	96
2 Bodmin Town	38	27	7	4	98	38	88
3 Plymouth Parkway	38	27	5	6	118	49	86
4 Torpoint Athletic	38	24	7	7	113	54	79
5 Falmouth Town	38	24	5	9	112	60	77
6 Saltash United	38	17	6	15	82	70	57
7 Ivybridge Town	38	17	5	16	98	77	56
8 St Blazey	38	16	8	14	83	72	56
9 Penzance	38	16	6	16	74	73	54
10 AFC St Austell	38	16	6	16	98	98	54
11 Launceston	38	15	8	15	76	84	53
12 Liskeard Athletic	38	13	8	17	59	69	47
13 Tavistock	38	13	6	19	58	79	45
14 Witheridge	38	11	9	18	66	86	42
15 Royal Marines	38	12	6	20	67	95	42
16 Cullompton Rangers	38	10	6	22	57	127	36
17 Bovey Tracey	38	8	9	21	58	104	33
18 Dartmouth	38	8	6	24	59	111	30
19 Elburton Villa	38	7	6	25	58	98	27
20 Wadebridge Town	38	5	4	29	44	116	19

THROGMORTON CUP

ROUND 1

AFC St Austell 2-1 Porthleven
Axminster Town 1-2 Bickleigh
Budleigh Salterton 6-0 Ottery St Mary
Camelford 5-1 Appledore
Cullompton Rangers 2-4 Royal Marines
Dartmouth 2-1 Liverton United
Elburton Villa 2-4 Bovey Tracey
Exeter Civil Service 5-5 Dobwalls
(Exeter Civil Service won 3-2 on penalties)
Exmouth Town 4-1 Crediton United
Foxhole Stars 1-1 Totnes & Dartington
Galmpton United 3-1 Newton Abbot Spurs
Hayle 1-2 Wadebridge Town
Holsworthy 0-3 Teignmouth
Newquay 0-3 Penryn Athletic
Perranporth 7-0 Mousehole
Plymstock United 4-5 Okehampton Argyle
Stoke Gabriel 4-0 Liskeard Athletic
Truro City reserves 0-5 Godolphin Atlantic
University of Exeter 4-4 Alphington
(University of Exeter won 4-2 on penalties)
Vospers Oak Villa 2-4 Callington Town

ROUND 2

AFC St Austell 0-1 Godolphin Atlantic
Bickleigh 0-2 Witheridge
Bodmin Town 7-0 Tavistock
Budleigh Salterton 1-2 Royal Marines
Callington Town 2-2 Stoke Gabriel
(Stoke Gabriel won 5-4 on penalties)
Camelford 2-1 Bovey Tracey
Dartmouth 2-0 Okehampton Argyle
Galmpton United 1-2 Teignmouth
Ivybridge Town 5-0 Exmouth Town
Penryn Athletic 5-4 Penzance
Perranporth 0-5 Falmouth Town
Saltash United 2-0 Launceston
St Blazey 3-0 Wadebridge Town
Torpoint Athletic 3-0 Exeter Civil Service
Totnes & Dartington 0-4 Plymouth Parkway
University of Exeter 2-5 Buckland Athletic

ROUND 3

Falmouth Town 1-3 Saltash United
Godolphin Atlantic 0-1 Plymouth Parkway
Ivybridge Town 5-3 Camelford
Penryn Athletic 1-5 Buckland Athletic
Royal Marines 2-1 Witheridge
Stoke Gabriel 0-3 Dartmouth
Teignmouth 2-3 St Blazey
Torpoint Athletic 2-3 Bodmin Town

PREMIER DIVISION	1	2	3	4	5	6	7	8	9	10	11	12	13	14	15	16	17	18	19	20
1 AFC St Austell		0-4	1-2	6-4	4-5	4-2	3-3	1-2	1-4	5-2	1-1	4-0	2-2	1-2	4-2	2-3	5-1	1-7	7-0	1-2
2 Bodmin Town	2-2		6-0	2-2	3-0	3-0	3-1	3-2	4-3	4-0	1-0	3-1	1-0	2-0	4-1	2-2	4-0	2-4	2-0	3-1
3 Bovey Tracey	3-4	0-3		1-4	6-2	1-1	4-1	2-4	1-5	1-1	0-3	0-0	0-7	1-3	0-1	1-3	1-1	3-4	3-2	3-1
4 Buckland Athletic	3-2	2-2	5-1		3-0	6-2	2-0	3-0	4-2	4-3	1-0	8-0	2-4	4-2	4-0	3-2	3-1	3-2	7-0	7-0
5 Cullompton Rangers	2-1	2-4	4-4	1-2		2-1	3-5	0-5	2-1	2-4	3-2	2-4	0-6	2-0	1-0	0-4	1-3	1-1	1-2	1-0
6 Dartmouth	2-6	0-4	0-4	0-4	5-3		4-3	2-2	0-3	0-2	2-3	0-3	1-3	3-5	5-3	1-3	3-1	0-5	3-1	2-2
7 Elburton Villa	1-5	1-2	5-0	1-2	1-2	0-1		1-6	2-4	4-3	2-2	2-2	2-4	4-2	1-2	0-1	2-1	0-2	1-4	1-5
8 Falmouth Town	6-1	2-1	4-2	3-2	6-1	3-1	1-1		3-4	1-1	2-1	2-1	6-1	3-0	6-2	4-0	3-0	1-1	3-0	2-1
9 Ivybridge Town	2-3	1-0	6-1	1-7	7-1	3-1	4-0	1-6		5-1	1-2	1-1	0-1	4-6	2-2	3-3	1-0	1-3	6-0	2-1
10 Launceston	1-2	4-4	3-2	1-2	3-1	4-0	2-2	3-1	2-1		1-1	3-0	1-4	0-3	1-3	1-1	3-2	0-4	3-1	7-1
11 Liskeard Athletic	1-4	1-3	0-0	1-3	2-2	4-4	2-4	2-4	1-0	0-1		0-2	1-2	0-1	3-0	3-1	2-1	1-3	3-3	3-2
12 Penzance	3-0	1-2	2-0	1-3	11-2	1-3	1-0	4-3	1-1	4-0	0-3		1-2	6-0	4-0	1-2	0-1	1-1	1-0	4-1
13 Plymouth Parkway	7-2	1-1	3-0	2-2	10-1	3-0	2-0	4-1	4-3	2-4	6-0	1-2		5-0	1-1	5-0	4-2	2-0	3-1	4-2
14 Royal Marines	3-3	0-5	1-3	0-1	3-0	1-5	3-2	4-2	1-1	3-1	2-3	1-3	2-2		1-2	1-3	2-2	1-5	3-0	1-0
15 Saltash United	6-1	0-1	1-1	5-1	8-0	4-0	4-1	0-1	2-1	1-2	0-1	1-1	0-2	4-3		4-2	1-0	1-2	4-1	4-1
16 St Blazey	4-0	1-2	3-3	0-1	2-2	4-1	5-0	2-2	2-1	3-3	0-0	5-0	3-4	4-0	2-4		0-1	1-5	2-1	4-2
17 Tavistock	2-2	0-3	2-0	0-1	2-2	0-0	1-0	2-4	4-1	3-1	0-3	2-6	1-0	3-2	2-2	1-0		4-2	4-3	0-3
18 Torpoint Athletic	1-4	0-1	6-1	0-2	1-1	4-1	2-1	4-2	1-4	5-1	3-1	9-1	2-0	1-1	5-2	2-1	5-1		4-0	1-1
19 Wadebridge Town	1-2	1-1	1-2	0-6	0-2	3-2	2-3	0-4	1-3	1-2	1-3	2-0	1-2	4-3	0-3	0-3	1-5	2-2		2-2
20 Witheridge	0-1	2-1	1-1	1-8	1-0	1-1	0-0	1-0	2-5	1-1	3-0	3-0	1-3	1-1	2-2	6-2	3-2	3-4	6-2	

DIVISION ONE	P	W	D	L	F	A	Pts
1 Liverton United	30	24	5	1	100	19	77
2 Budleigh Salterton	30	17	9	4	71	31	60
3 Stoke Gabriel	30	17	8	5	72	47	59
4 Teignmouth	30	16	5	9	68	46	53
5 Galmpton Gents	30	15	5	10	68	55	50
6 Appledore	30	14	7	9	48	37	49
7 Alphington	30	12	7	11	49	42	43
8 University of Exeter	30	12	6	12	60	54	42
9 Totnes & Dartington SC	30	13	2	15	55	69	41
10 Bickleigh	30	11	5	14	40	50	38
11 Exmouth Town	30	10	5	15	54	59	35
12 Exeter Civil Service	30	9	8	13	41	67	35
13 Ottery St Mary	30	9	2	19	40	82	29
14 Newton Abbot Spurs	30	6	8	16	41	64	26
15 Crediton United	30	6	4	20	40	73	22
16 Axminster Town	30	4	4	22	29	81	16

DIVISION ONE WEST	P	W	D	L	F	A	Pts
1 Camelford	30	20	8	2	85	27	68
2 Godolphin Atlantic	30	20	5	5	73	37	65
3 Callington Town	30	20	4	6	85	41	64
4 Vospers Oak Villa	30	16	8	6	72	40	56
5 Penryn Athletic	30	15	6	9	76	56	51
6 Porthleven	30	14	7	9	53	48	49
7 Plymstock United	30	14	6	10	63	48	48
8 Perranporth	30	14	6	10	54	40	48
9 Newquay	30	15	1	14	76	68	46
10 Holsworthy	30	10	5	15	40	67	35
11 Dobwalls	30	8	8	14	44	52	32
12 Truro City reserves	30	9	3	18	39	76	30
13 Foxhole Stars	30	7	4	19	41	79	25
14 Mousehole	30	5	6	19	39	84	21
15 Okehampton Argyle	30	5	5	20	47	81	20
16 Hayle	30	4	6	20	30	73	18

THROGMORTON CUP continued...

QUARTER FINALS

Buckland Athletic 2-3 Ivybridge Town

Dartmouth 0-4 Bodmin Town

Plymouth Parkway 3-0 Saltash United

Royal Marines 1-4 St Blazey

SEMI-FINALS

Ivybridge Town 0-3 Plymouth Parkway (@ Saltash United)

St Blazey 5-2 Bodmin Town (@ Liskeard Athletic)

FINAL (@ Newquay, 2/5/11)

Plymouth Parkway 6-4 St Blazey

CHARITY BOWL
(League champions v Throgmorton Cup winners)

FINAL (@ Tavistock, 1/8/10)

Bodmin Town 1-3 Buckland Atheletic

CHARITY VASE
(Division One East champions v Division One West)

FINAL (@ Tavistock, 1/8/10)

Royal Marines 2-0 Perranorth

DIVISION ONE EAST	1	2	3	4	5	6	7	8	9	10	11	12	13	14	15	16
1 Alphington		1-0	1-0	1-2	1-1	1-0	1-0	2-0	0-0	0-2	1-1	3-0	2-3	1-2	0-1	2-0
2 Appledore	3-0		1-1	3-2	0-3	2-0	4-0	2-1	2-5	2-3	1-0	0-1	2-2	1-1	1-2	0-0
3 Axminster Town	1-4	0-3		1-1	0-2	1-4	0-1	0-6	0-4	0-0	2-1	1-0	1-2	1-4	1-0	2-1
4 Bickleigh	1-1	1-1	2-1		0-2	0-1	0-1	1-2	0-2	2-6	3-2	2-2	1-3	4-1	0-1	1-0
5 Budleigh Salterton	1-0	0-0	3-2	4-3		3-1	6-0	1-1	1-1	1-1	7-1	6-1	0-0	2-0	4-2	4-1
6 Crediton United	2-1	1-3	5-4	0-4	2-2		2-1	2-3	0-3	0-3	2-2	5-1	1-3	0-1	2-3	2-4
7 Exeter Civil Service	2-2	2-1	2-0	0-0	1-1	4-4		2-2	3-2	1-3	3-2	1-2	2-2	2-0	3-3	2-2
8 Exmouth Town	1-4	1-2	2-0	0-3	0-1	5-0	3-0		2-3	1-1	1-1	4-1	3-4	2-3	4-1	0-1
9 Galmpton U & Torbay Gents	5-4	1-0	1-0	1-2	5-5	2-0	4-1	1-0		0-2	3-1	2-3	0-2	3-2	5-2	3-4
10 Liverton Unitedt	1-2	1-0	8-1	4-0	2-1	5-0	4-0	8-0	5-1		4-1	7-0	2-2	2-2	4-1	4-0
11 Newton Abbot Spurs	2-1	1-2	4-4	2-0	0-2	1-0	2-0	0-1	1-1	0-2		4-0	3-3	0-4	0-5	0-1
12 Ottery St Mary	1-4	1-3	1-0	1-2	1-0	3-1	0-3	3-4	4-2	0-5	2-0		2-2	1-4	2-3	0-4
13 Stoke Gabriel	2-2	0-1	5-2	2-0	3-0	1-0	7-0	4-3	4-1	1-4	1-1	3-2		2-3	2-0	0-5
14 Teignmouth	6-1	2-2	5-2	5-0	0-2	2-1	2-0	1-0	1-1	0-2	2-4	2-3	2-1		5-0	2-2
15 Totnes & Dartington S C	2-2	2-3	5-1	0-1	1-0	3-0	1-2	5-0	0-5	0-3	5-3	3-2	0-2	3-2		0-4
16 University Of Exeter	0-4	2-3	3-0	0-2	1-6	2-2	5-2	2-2	4-1	0-2	1-1	2-0	2-4	1-2	6-1	

DIVISION ONE EAST	1	2	3	4	5	6	7	8	9	10	11	12	13	14	15	16
1 Callington Town		1-1	2-0	0-1	3-1	8-0	5-0	7-0	6-3	3-1	5-2	1-1	4-3	3-4	1-0	1-2
2 Camelford	2-2		4-1	4-0	2-2	3-0	5-1	2-0	6-1	3-1	0-1	5-1	1-0	4-1	1-2	6-4
3 Dobwalls	1-3	1-1		2-3	3-2	0-1	3-0	1-1	0-3	2-0	0-3	1-3	2-1	3-0	0-2	2-4
4 Foxhole Stars	1-2	1-7	2-1		0-4	1-1	3-0	1-1	2-3	4-0	3-4	1-1	2-3	1-2	1-0	1-2
5 Godolphin Atlantic	2-1	2-2	3-1	5-1		4-0	2-2	3-1	3-0	2-1	4-0	1-1	4-1	3-0	2-2	0-2
6 Hayle	1-2	0-1	1-1	5-3	0-2		1-2	1-4	1-5	1-1	1-1	3-1	0-3	0-1	4-0	2-2
7 Holsworthy	1-2	0-4	1-1	5-0	1-2	3-2		4-2	1-0	3-2	2-2	1-4	2-1	1-3	0-3	2-1
8 Mousehole	2-5	0-2	1-2	1-3	1-4	3-1	2-2		3-2	1-1	1-2	0-3	1-1	2-3	2-1	2-2
9 Newquay	1-1	0-3	4-1	2-0	2-1	2-0	2-3	1-0		6-3	3-4	2-1	1-3	4-2	11-0	2-1
10 Okehampton Argyle	2-3	1-3	1-4	8-0	1-2	2-1	0-1	5-0	2-4		1-5	2-1	2-2	2-2	1-2	1-1
11 Penryn Athletic	1-4	0-3	1-1	1-1	1-4	5-1	2-1	10-3	7-3	3-0		2-0	0-1	0-1	6-0	2-2
12 Perranporth	0-2	1-1	1-1	1-0	1-2	1-0	2-0	4-1	3-0	2-1	4-2		1-2	2-1	0-2	2-1
13 Plymstock United	5-1	1-1	2-0	4-0	2-3	2-0	4-1	2-1	0-3	7-0	2-4	1-1		0-2	3-2	1-1
14 Porthleven	0-1	1-1	1-1	2-0	1-3	2-0	4-0	5-0	4-2	3-4	3-3	0-5	2-2		1-0	0-0
15 Truro City reserves	1-5	0-3	0-7	3-2	0-1	2-2	0-0	1-2	4-3	7-1	0-1	1-5	1-3	1-2		2-1
16 Vospers Oak Villa	2-1	1-4	1-1	5-3	4-0	6-0	3-0	3-1	3-1	3-0	2-1	3-1	5-1	0-0	5-0	

BODMIN TOWN
Founded: 1896 Nickname:

Secretary: Nick Giles **(T)** 01208 75794 **(E)**
Chairman: **Manager:** Darren Gilbert **Prog Ed:**
Ground: Priory Park, Bodmin, Cornwall PL31 2AE **(T)** 01208 78165 **Capacity:**
Colours(change): Yellow & black (All white)

ADDITIONAL INFORMATION:
Previous League: South Western.
Honours: South Western League 1990-91, 93-94, 2005-06. South West Peninsula Premier Division 2007-08, 08-09.

BOVEY TRACEY
Founded: 1950 Nickname: Moorlanders

Secretary: Steve Cooney **(T)** 07795 373 786 **(E)** c_moon@btinternet.com
Chairman: **Manager:** Steve Massey **Prog Ed:**
Ground: Western Counties Roofing (Mill Marsh Pk), Ashburton Rd, Bovey TQ13 9FF **(T)** 01626 832 780 **Capacity:**
Colours(change): All red (All green)

ADDITIONAL INFORMATION:
Previous League: South Devon.
Honours: Herald Cup 1960-61. South Devon League Premier Division 2007-08.

BUCKLAND ATHLETIC
Founded: 1977 Nickname: The Bucks

Secretary: Christine Holmes **(T)** 01626 369 345 **(E)**
Chairman: **Manager:** Anthony Lynch **Prog Ed:**
Ground: Homers Heath, South Quarry, Kingskerswell Road, Newton Abbot TQ12 5JU **(T)** 01626 361 020 **Capacity:**
Colours(change): All yellow (All blue)

ADDITIONAL INFORMATION:
Previous League: Devon County League 2000-07.
Honours: South West Peninsula League Premier Division 2009-10, 10-11. Throgmorton Cup 2009-10.

CAMELFORD
Founded: 1893 Nickname: Camels

Secretary: Hilary Kent **(T)** **(E)** hilarykent@camelfordfc.fsnet.co.uk
Chairman: **Manager:** Reg Hambly **Prog Ed:**
Ground: Trefew Park, PL32 9TS **(T)** **Capacity:**
Colours(change): White & blue (Blue & white)

ADDITIONAL INFORMATION:
Honours: South West Peninsula Division One West 2010-11.

CULLOMPTON RANGERS
Founded: 1945 Nickname: The Cully

Secretary: Marcus Scott **(T)** 07740 168 072 **(E)** scott.marcus@ukgateway.net
Chairman: **Manager:** Peter Buckingham & Richard Pears **Prog Ed:**
Ground: Speeds Meadow, Cullompton EX15 1DW **(T)** 01884 33090 **Capacity:**
Colours(change): Red & black (Yellow & blue)

ADDITIONAL INFORMATION:
Previous League: Devon County 1992-2007.

DARTMOUTH
Founded: 1908 Nickname: The Darts

Secretary: Kathy Greeno **(T)** 01803 832 720 **(E)** kathgreeno@hotmail.com
Chairman: **Manager:** Lance Worthington **Prog Ed:**
Ground: Longcross, Dartmouth TQ5 9LW **(T)** 01803 832 902 **Capacity:**
Colours(change): Red & black (All white)

ADDITIONAL INFORMATION:
Previous League: Devon County 1999-2007.
Honours: Devon County League 2001-02, 02-03, 06-07.

ELBURTON VILLA
Founded: 1982 Nickname: The Villa

Secretary: Duncan Hedges **(T)** **(E)** duncan@dhedges.fsworld.co.uk
Chairman: **Manager:** Simon Westlake **Prog Ed:**
Ground: Haye Road, Elburton, Plymouth PL9 8NS **(T)** 01752 480 025 **Capacity:**
Colours(change): Red & white stripes/black (White & red)

ADDITIONAL INFORMATION:
Previous League: Devon County 1992-2007.

FALMOUTH TOWN
Founded: 1950 Nickname: The Ambers

Secretary: Stephen Rose **(T)** 07968 515 525 **(E)** stephendrose@aol.com
Chairman: **Manager:** Alan Carey **Prog Ed:**
Ground: Bickland Park, Bickland Water Road, Falmouth TR11 4PB **(T)** 01326 375 156 **Capacity:**
Colours(change): Amber & black (Blue & white)

ADDITIONAL INFORMATION:
Honours: South Western League 1961-62, 65-66, 67-68, 70-71, 71-72, 72-73, 73-74, 85-86, 86-87, 88-89, 89-90, 91-92, 96-97, 99-2000. Western League 1974-75, 75-76, 76-77, 77-78. Cornwall Combination 1983-84.

IVYBRIDGE TOWN
Founded: 1925 Nickname: The Ivys

Secretary: Paul Cocks **(T)** 07967 736 952 **(E)** secretary@ivybridgefc.com
Chairman: **Manager:** Paul Edwards **Prog Ed:**
Ground: Erme Valley, Ermington Road, Ivybridge PL21 9ES **(T)** 01752 896 686 **Capacity:**
Colours(change): Green & black (Blue & white)

ADDITIONAL INFORMATION:
Previous League: Devon County.
Honours: Devon County League 2005-06.

LAUNCESTON
Founded: 1891 Nickname: The Clarets

Secretary: Keith Ellacott **(T)** 07966 497 453 **(E)** launcestonfc@aol.com
Chairman: **Manager:** Leigh Cooper **Prog Ed:**
Ground: Pennygillam Ind. Est., Launceston PL15 7ED **(T)** 01566 773 279 **Capacity:**
Colours(change): All claret (Sky blue & black)

ADDITIONAL INFORMATION:
Previous League: South Western.
Honours: South Western League 1995-96.

LISKEARD ATHLETIC
Founded: 1946 Nickname: The Blues

Secretary: Brian Olver **(T)** 01579 342 869 **(E)** brianolver25@yahoo.com
Chairman: **Manager:** Darren Edwards **Prog Ed:**
Ground: Lux Park Sport Association, Coldstyle Rd, Lux Park, Liskeard PL14 2HZ **(T)** 01566 773 279 **Capacity:**
Colours(change): All blue (All yellow)

ADDITIONAL INFORMATION:
Previous League: South Western 1995-2007.
Honours: South Western League 1976-77, 78-79. Western League Premier Division 1987-88.

PENZANCE
Founded: 1888 Nickname: The Magpies

Secretary: John Mead **(T)** 07952 312 906 **(E)** jamead@supanet.com
Chairman: **Manager:** Gary Marks & Wayne Quinn **Prog Ed:**
Ground: Penlee Park, Alexandra Place, Penzance TR18 4NE **(T)** 01736 361 964 **Capacity:**
Colours(change): White & black (Blue & white)

ADDITIONAL INFORMATION:
Honours: South Western League 1955-56, 56-57, 74-75. South West Peninsula Division 1 West 2008-09.
Cornwall Charity Cup 2008-09.

PLYMOUTH PARKWAY
Founded: 1988 Nickname: The Parkway

Secretary: Genny Turner **(T)** **(E)** genny.woolwell@btinternet.com
Chairman: **Manager:** Gez Baggott & Wayne Hillson **Prog Ed:**
Ground: Bolitho Park, St Peters Road, Manadon, Plymouth PL5 3OZ **(T)** **Capacity:**
Colours(change): Yellow & blue (Blue & white)

ADDITIONAL INFORMATION:
Previous Name: Ex-Air Flyers Plymouth.
Previous League: South Western 1998-2007.
Honours: Throgmorton Cup 2010-11.

ROYAL MARINES
Founded: 2008 Nickname: The Commandos

Secretary: Ian Mullholland **(T)** 07764 983 441 **(E)** rmfa-secretary@hotmail.co.uk
Chairman: **Manager:** Neil Middleditch **Prog Ed:**
Ground: Endurance Park, Heartbreak Lane, Lympstone EX8 5AR **(T)** 01392 414300 Ex 4038 **Capacity:**
Colours(change): All white (Green & white)

ADDITIONAL INFORMATION:
Honours: South West Peninsula League Division 1 East 2009-10.

SALTASH UNITED

Founded: 1945 | Nickname: The Ashes

Secretary: Luke Ranford **(T)** 07830 299 555 **(E)** luke.ranford@googlemail.com
Chairman: **Manager:** Kevin Hendy & Stuart Dudley **Prog Ed:**
Ground: Kimberley Stadium, Callington Road, Saltash PL12 6DX **(T)** 01752 845 746 **Capacity:**
Colours(change): Red & white stripes/black (Blue & white)

ADDITIONAL INFORMATION:
Previous League: South Western 2006-07.
Honours: South Western League 1953-54, 75-76. Western League Division 1 1976-77, Premier 1984-85, 86-87, 88-89.

ST. AUSTELL

Founded: 1890 | Nickname: The Lily Whites

Secretary: Peter Beard **(T)** 01726 64138 **(E)**
Chairman: **Manager:** Gary Penhaligon **Prog Ed:**
Ground: Poltair Park, Trevarthian Road, St Austell PL25 4LR **(T)** 01726 66099 **Capacity:**
Colours(change): White & black (Red & white)

ADDITIONAL INFORMATION:
Previous League: South Western 1951-2007.

ST. BLAZEY

Founded: 1896 | Nickname: The Green & Blacks

Secretary: George Allen **(T)** **(E)** geoallen.spurs@zen.co.uk
Chairman: **Manager:** Bobby Oaten **Prog Ed:**
Ground: Blaise Park, Station Road, St Blazey PL24 2ND **(T)** 01725 814 110 **Capacity:**
Colours(change): Green & black (Blue & white)

ADDITIONAL INFORMATION:
Previous League: South Western 1951-2007.
Honours: South Western Lge 1954-55, 57-58, 62-63, 63-64, 80-81, 82-83, 98-99, 2000-01, 01-02, 02-03, 03-04, 04-05, 06-07.

TAVISTOCK

Founded: 1888 | Nickname: The Lambs

Secretary: Phil Lowe **(T)** 01822 613 715 **(E)**
Chairman: **Manager:** Ian Southcott **Prog Ed:**
Ground: Langsford Park, Red & Black Club, Crowndale Road, Tavistock PL19 8DD **(T)** 01822 614 447 **Capacity:**
Colours(change): Red & black (All blue)

ADDITIONAL INFORMATION:
Previous League: South Western 1968-2007.

TORPOINT ATHLETIC

Founded: 1887 | Nickname: The Point

Secretary: Robbie Morris **(T)** **(E)** robbietafc81@live.co.uk
Chairman: **Manager:** Scott Bamford **Prog Ed:**
Ground: The Mill, Mill Lane, Carbeile Road, Torpoint PL11 2NA **(T)** 01752 812 889 **Capacity:**
Colours(change): Yellow & black (Red & white)

ADDITIONAL INFORMATION:
Previous League: South Western 1962-2007.
Honours: South Western League 1964-65, 66-67.

WITHERIDGE

Founded: 1920 | Nickname: The Withy

Secretary: Chris Cole **(T)** 07899 981 396 **(E)** chriscole128@hotmail.com
Chairman: **Manager:** Mike Taylor **Prog Ed:**
Ground: Edge Down Park, Fore Street, Witheridge EX16 8AH **(T)** 01884 861 511 **Capacity:**
Colours(change): Blue with orange trim (All claret)

ADDITIONAL INFORMATION:
Previous League: Devon County 2006-07.

SOUTH WEST PENINSULA INS & OUTS

PREM - IN: Camelford (P - Division One West)
OUT: Wadebridge Town (R - Division One West)
DIV ONE EAST - IN: Okehampton Argyle (S - Division One West),
Sidmouth Town (P - Devon & Exeter League Premier Division)
OUT: Bickleigh (F)
DIV ONE WEST - IN: Helston Athletic (P - Cornwall Combination),
St Dennis (P - East Cornwall League Premier Division), Wadebridge Town (R)
OUT: Camelford (P), Okehampton Argyle (S - Division One East)

DIVISION ONE EAST CONSTITUTION 2011-12

ALPHINGTON	The Chronicles, Church Road, Alphington, Exeter EX2 8SW	01392 279556
APPLEDORE	Marshford, Churchill Way, Appledore EX39 1PA	01237 475015
AXMINSTER TOWN	Sector Lane, Axminster EX13 5SD	01297 35161
BUDLEIGH SALTERTON	Greenway Lane, Budleigh Salterton EX9 6SG	01395 443850
CREDITON UNITED	Lords Meadow, Commercial Road, Crediton EX17 1ES	01363 774671
EXETER CIVIL SERVICE	Foxhayes, Exwick, Exeter EX4 2BQ	01392 273976
EXMOUTH TOWN	King George V Ground, Southern Road, Exmouth EX8 3EE	01395 263348
GALMPTON UNITED & TORBAY GENTS	War Memorial Playing Field, Greenway Road, Galmpton, Brixham TQ5 0LP	None
LIVERTON UNITED	Football & Sports Club, Halford, Liverton, Newton Abbot TQ12 6JF	None
NEWTON ABBOT SPURS	Recreation Ground, Marsh Road, Newton Abbot TQ12 2AR	01626 365343
OKEHAMPTON ARGYLE	Simmons Park, Mill Road, Okehampton EX20 1PR	01837 53997
OTTERY ST MARY	Washbrook Meadows, Butts Road, Ottery St Mary EX11 1EL	01404 812781
SIDMOUTH TOWN	Manstone Recreation Ground, Manstone Lane, Sidmouth EX10 9TF	01395 577087
STOKE GABRIEL	C J Churchward Mem. Ground, Broadley Lane, Stoke Gabriel, Totnes TQ9 6RR	01803 782223
TEIGNMOUTH	Coombe Valley, Coombe Lane, Teignmouth TQ14 9EX	01626 776688
TOTNES & DARTINGTON SC	Foxhole Sports Ground, Dartington TQ9 6EB	01803 868032
UNIVERSITY OF EXETER	University Sports Ground, Topsham Road, Topsham EX3 0LY	01392 879542

DIVISION ONE WEST CONSTITUTION 2011-12

CALLINGTON TOWN	Ginsters Marshfield Parc, Callington Community College, Launceston Rd, Callington PL17 7DR	01579 382647
DOBWALLS	Lantoom Park, Duloe Road, Dobwalls PL14 4LR	01626 776688
FOXHOLE STARS	Goverseth Park, Goverseth Terrace, Foxhole PL26 7UP	01726 824615
GODOLPHIN ATLANTIC	Godolphin Way, Newquay TR7 3BU	None
HAYLE	Trevassack Park, Viaduct Hill, Hayle TR27 5HT	01736 757157
HELSTON ATHLETIC	Kellaway Parc, Clodgy Lane, Helston TR13 8BN	01326 573742
HOLSWORTHY	Upcott Field, North Road, Holsworthy EX22 6HF	01409 254295
MOUSEHOLE	Trungle Parc, Paul, Penzance TR19 6XB	01736 731518
NEWQUAY	Mount Wise, Clevedon Road, Newquay TR7 2BU	01637 872935
PENRYN ATHLETIC	Kernick, Kernick Road, Penryn TR10 8QF	01326 375182
PERRANPORTH	Budnick Estate, Perranporth TR6 0DB	01872 575000
PLYMSTOCK UNITED	Dean Cross, Dean Cross Road, Plymstock PL9 7AZ	01752 406776
PORTHLEVEN	Gala Parc, Mill Lane, Porthleven TR13 9LQ	01326 574754
ST DENNIS	Boscawen Park, St Dennis PL26 8AP	01726 822635
TRURO CITY RESERVES	Treyew Road, Truro TR1 2TH	01872 225400 Fax: 01872 225402
VOSPERS OAK VILLA	The Mill, Ferndale Road, Weston Mill, Plymouth PL2 2EL	01752 363352
WADEBRIDGE TOWN	BODIEVE PARK, BODIEVE ROAD, WADEBRIDGE PL27 7AJ	01208 812537

GROUND DIRECTIONS - PREMIER DIVISION

BODMIN TOWN - Priory Park, Bodmin, Cornwall PL31 2AE. Tel: 01208 781 65.
Situated in Priory Park through main car park. Use football car park on Saturdays.

BOVEY TRACEY - Western Counties Roofing (Mill Marsh Park), Ashburton Road, Bovey Tracey TQ13 9FF. Tel: 01626 832 780.
Coming off the A38 East or Westbound at Drumbridges take the Bovey Tracey turn-off, straight through the lights at Heathfield. Next roundabout take 2nd exit, next roundabout take 3rd exit, then left, 35 yards, follow road to bottom of drive then enter through gate.

BUCKLAND ATHLETIC - Homers Heath, South Quarry, Kingskerswell Road, Newton Abbot TQ12 5JU. Tel: 01626 361 020.
From all areas head for Penn Inn roundabout then take the Newton Abbot turn-off. Keep in left-hand lane and filter left at first set of traffic lights. Go past Sainsbury's and follow road past the Keyberry Hotel. Carry straight on until you see the CLS Laundry then turn right into ground.

CAMELFORD - Trefrew Park PL32 9TS.
From the South drive into Camelford up Victoria Road for 300 yards, turn left into Oakwood Rise. Follow road around for approximately 300 yards. Entrance is on the right up the lane. From the North as you enter Camelford turn right into Oakwood Rise then as above.

CULLOMPTON RANGERS - Speeds Meadow, Cullompton EX15 1DW. Tel: 01884 33090.
Leave M5 at junction 28, left at Town Centre, at Meadow Lane turn left past Sports Centre, at end of road turn right, then in 100 yards turn left into ground at end of lane.

DARTMOUTH - Longross, Dartmouth TQ5 9LW. Tel: 01803 832 902.
From Totnes the ground is on the road into Dartmouth - on the right is a BP garage - take next right (Milton Lane) then first right into ground.

ELBURTON VILLA - Haye Road, Elburton, Plymouth PL9 8NS. Tel: 01752 480 025.
From Plymouth City Centre take A379 Kingsbridge Road. At third roundabout turn left into Haye Road (signposted Saltram House). Ground 50 yards on left.

FALMOUTH TOWN - Bickland Park, Bickland Water Road, Falmouth TR11 4PB. Tel: 01326 375 156.
Take Penryn by-pass from Asda roundabout. Leave by-pass at Hillhead roundabout, take first right and follow industrial estate signs. Ground 1/2 mile on the left.

IVYBRIDGE TOWN - Erme Valley, Ermington Road, Ivybridge. Tel: 01752 896 686.
From Plymouth - leave A38 at Ivybridge and follow signs towards Ermington. Ground is immediately next to South Devon Tennis Centre. From Exeter - leave A38 at Ivybridge. Ground is in front of you at the end of the slip road.

SOUTH WEST PENINSULA LEAGUE - STEP 6/7

LAUNCESTON - Pennygillam, Pennygillam Ind. Est., Launceston PL15 7ED. Tel: 01566 773 279.

Leave A30 onto Pennygillam roundabout, turn into Pennygillam Industrial Estate. Ground is 400 yards on the left.

LISKEARD ATHLETIC - Lux Park Sport Association, Coldstyle Road, Lux Park, Liskeard PL14 2HZ. Tel: 01579 342 665.

From the Parade (middle of town) turn left at the monument, then first right following signs for Leisure Centre at Lux Park.

PENZANCE - Penlee Park, Alexandra Place, Penzance TR18 4NE. Tel: 01736 361 964.

Follow road along harbour and promenade. Turn right at mini r'about into Alexandra Rd. Take either 1st (Mennaye Rd) 2nd (Alexandra Place) right.

PLYMOUTH PARKWAY - Bolitho Park, St Peters Road, Manadon, Plymouth PL5 3OZ.

From Cornwall/Exeter exit at the Manadon/Tavistock junction off the Plymouth Parkway (A38), off roundabout into St Peters Road. Entrance is one mile on the right.

ROYAL MARINES - Endurance Park, Heartbreak Lane EX8 5AR Tel: 01392 414 038

Take junction 30 off M5 and head towards Exmouth on A376. On approach to CTCRM turn left signposted Kings Squad Parking.

SALTASH UNITED - Ground: Kimberley Stadium, Callington Road, Saltash PL12 6DX. Tel: 01752 845 746.

At the top of Town Centre fork right at mini-roundabout. Ground is situated 400m ahead on the left-hand side next to Leisure Centre and Police Station.

ST AUSTELL - Poltair Park, Trevarthian Road, St Austell PL25 4LR Tel: 07966 130 158

Near Poltair School and St Austell Brewery (5 minutes from St Austell Rail Station).

ST BLAZEY - Blaise Park, Station Road, St Blazey PL24 2ND. Tel: 01725 814 110.

A390 from Lostwithiel to St Austell. At village of St Blazey turn left at traffic lights by Church/Cornish Arms pub into Station Road. Ground is 200 yards on the left.

TAVISTOCK - Langsford Park, Red & Black Club, Crowndale Road, Tavistock PL19 8DD. Tel: 01822 614 447.

From Launceston/Okehampton, stay on A386 trhough town signposted Plymouth, past Drake's statue. Over canal turn right, signposted football ground/recycle centre. Ground is 100 metres past Tavistock college. From Plymouth, stay on A386 pass Morrisons and Texaco garage, over River Tavy, turn left signposted football ground/ recycle centre. Then as above.

TORPOINT ATHLETIC - The Mill, Mill Lane, Carbeile Road, Torpoint PL11 2NA. Tel: 01752 812 889.

Take turning at Carbeile Inn onto Carbeille Road and first turning on the right into Mill Lane.

WITHERIDGE - Edge Down Park, Fore Street, Witheridge EX16 8AH. Tel: 01884 861 511.

B3137 Tiverton to Witheridge, on entering the village football pitch is on the right-hand side before the Fire Station and School.

SPARTAN SOUTH MIDLANDS LEAGUE

Sponsored by: Molten
Founded: 1998
Recent Champions:
2006: Oxford City
2007: Edgware Town
2008: Beaconsfield SYCOB
2009: Biggleswade Town
2110: Aylesbury United
ssmfl.org

PREMIER DIVISION	P	W	D	L	F	A	Pts
1 Chalfont St Peter	44	33	4	7	99	34	103
2 Tring Athletic	44	28	7	9	95	45	91
3 Royston Town	44	28	6	10	102	52	90
4 Leverstock Green	44	27	7	10	100	57	88
5 Colney Heath	44	28	4	12	93	70	88
6 Aylesbury United	44	23	8	13	94	71	77
7 Dunstable Town	44	22	4	18	82	75	70
8 Haringey Borough	44	19	10	15	80	67	67
9 Hertford Town	44	19	7	18	88	87	64
10 Broxbourne Borough	44	18	6	20	85	84	60
11 Hatfield Town	44	19	3	22	75	91	60
12 Kingsbury London Tigers	44	17	8	19	90	93	59
13 Stotfold	44	15	12	17	72	68	57
14 Hadley	44	16	9	19	58	66	57
15 Hanwell Town	44	16	8	20	77	79	56
16 Hillingdon Borough	44	15	10	19	84	80	55
17 Holmer Green	44	14	11	19	74	75	53
18 St Margaretsbury	44	15	6	23	53	65	51
19 Oxhey Jets	44	13	9	22	76	91	48
20 Biggleswade United	44	11	11	22	56	96	44
21 Harefield United	44	10	8	26	61	109	38
22 Kentish Town	44	7	8	29	51	117	29
23 Langford	44	7	6	31	53	126	27

PREMIER DIVISION CUP

ROUND 1
Haringey Borough 5-4 St Margaretsbury
Biggleswade United 1-2 Broxbourne Borough
Hanwell Town 1-2 Hillingdon Borough
Harefield United 4-6 Tring Athletic
Holmer Green 1-2 Leverstock Green
Hadley 1-4 Colney Heath
Kingsbury London Tigers 3-1 Royston Town

ROUND 2
Langford 5-2 Kentish Town
Kingsbury London Tigers 5-3 Hertford Town
Broxbourne Borough 1-2 Haringey Borough
Chalfont St Peter 1-2 Dunstable Town
Aylesbury United 1-3 Leverstock Green
Stotfold 4-0 Hatfield Town
Oxhey Jets 2-6 Colney Heath
Tring Athletic 1-3 Hillingdon Borough

QUARTER FINALS
Leverstock Green 2-1 Stotfold
Hillingdon Borough 4-1 Dunstable Town
Langford 1-5 Haringey Borough
Colney Heath 3-1 Kingsbury London Tigers

SEMI-FINALS
Leverstock Green 2-1 Haringey Borough
Colney Heath 5-1 Hillingdon Borough

FINAL (@ London Colney, 26/4/11)
Colney Heath 2-0 Leverstock Green

CHALLENGE TROPHY

ROUND 1
MK Wanderers 0-3 Bedford Town reserves
Hillingdon Borough 0-5 AFC Dunstable
Sport London e Benfica 1-3 Hertford Town
Aston Clinton v Chalfont St Peter
(tie awarded to Chalfont St Peter)
Harefield United 1-6 Padbury United
Welwyn Garden City 2-3 Wodson Park
Biggleswade United 1-0 Kentish Town
Winslow United 1-2 Tring Athletic
Kent Athletic 1-3 New Bradwell St Peter
Hanwell Town 7-0 Amersham Town
Oxhey Jets 2-0 Hadley
Brache Sparta Community 1-2 Cranfield United
Haringey Borough 5-1 Ampthill Town
Old Bradwell United 1-2 St Albans City reserves
Hoddesdon Town 1-3 Colney Heath

PREMIER DIVISION	1	2	3	4	5	6	7	8	9	10	11	12	13	14	15	16	17	18	19	20	21	22	23
1 Aylesbury United		3-3	1-3	2-2	2-0	5-2	2-2	3-1	3-1	0-3	1-3	2-2	1-0	2-0	6-1	5-1	2-0	2-2	4-0	0-2	2-0	1-1	1-0
2 Biggleswade United	2-2		2-1	1-4	2-4	2-3	2-0	2-1	2-1	0-0	1-1	3-3	1-3	1-2	4-1	3-4	2-0	0-4	0-0	0-5	3-1	0-1	1-3
3 Broxbourne Boro' V & E	2-0	5-1		2-0	0-1	1-2	1-1	1-1	1-2	0-1	2-0	2-4	1-4	1-0	0-1	3-1	4-0	5-3	0-1	1-5	4-4	4-1	1-2
4 Chalfont St Peter	5-1	4-1	1-0		5-1	2-0	2-0	0-0	1-0	4-2	2-1	2-1	1-0	2-0	2-0	1-2	3-0	3-2	4-0	1-2	3-0	0-0	1-0
5 Colney Heath	3-0	4-0	3-0	3-0		3-3	3-1	2-0	3-2	3-1	1-0	2-1	0-2	3-1	4-2	2-4	3-2	3-2	2-1	2-1	2-1	0-2	1-1
6 Dunstable Town	2-3	4-1	1-3	0-1	2-3		1-2	4-3	7-2	2-1	1-0	2-2	2-3	2-1	2-1	2-1	5-2	0-2	3-0	0-2	1-0	2-0	1-1
7 Hadley	5-1	1-1	2-0	0-1	1-2	1-2		1-1	2-1	1-0	0-2	2-2	0-4	1-1	6-1	0-1	1-1	2-3	2-1	2-3	2-0	1-1	3-2
8 Hanwell Town	2-3	1-2	4-0	1-3	2-1	1-0	1-2		2-0	5-1	5-1	2-3	0-3	0-2	2-1	0-3	2-1	0-1	4-3	1-1	0-1	1-3	1-3
9 Harefield United	0-5	0-0	2-6	1-4	1-3	4-2	2-1	1-6		0-0	1-2	8-2	2-0	1-1	1-0	0-3	1-1	1-3	2-2	0-5	1-0	2-5	1-2
10 Haringey Borough	1-3	1-0	2-3	1-0	0-0	2-3	3-0	1-4	3-0		6-1	1-3	3-3	0-1	5-1	2-2	2-1	1-0	2-2	2-1	2-1	0-2	1-2
11 Hatfield Town	0-4	4-0	1-4	1-3	3-3	1-2	4-0	0-0	1-3	1-5		3-0	2-3	5-1	2-1	3-1	5-2	0-4	2-1	3-2	3-2	4-3	0-3
12 Hertford Town	0-2	3-0	3-2	4-3	2-5	4-1	0-2	2-3	3-0	2-0	1-3		4-4	4-1	2-1	2-6	1-1	2-1	1-0	0-1	0-1	2-1	1-4
13 Hillingdon Borough	0-3	1-2	3-3	0-6	2-0	7-2	0-1	1-3	5-1	2-3	0-1	0-0		2-2	6-1	0-1	1-1	3-3	1-2	4-2	2-0	3-1	0-2
14 Holmer Green	0-3	4-1	3-1	1-2	1-3	2-1	3-0	2-2	0-2	1-2	3-1	1-3	1-1		2-0	3-3	8-0	2-2	0-0	1-3	5-1	0-2	3-0
15 Kentish Town	2-2	2-2	0-2	0-2	3-1	1-4	2-2	4-1	1-3	2-2	3-2	0-5	2-1	2-3		2-3	2-3	1-0	1-5	1-4	0-0	2-2	0-4
16 Kingsbury London Tigers	3-1	1-3	1-4	1-2	0-3	1-0	0-1	2-3	2-2	2-2	6-1	0-5	3-3	2-1	2-2		4-1	2-3	3-5	1-4	2-0	1-1	2-3
17 Langford	2-4	1-2	1-4	0-3	1-2	1-2	2-1	1-1	4-1	1-5	1-2	0-2	5-0	2-1	1-1	4-5		0-4	1-1	1-7	1-0	2-3	1-4
18 Leverstock Green	3-0	2-0	3-1	0-0	4-1	1-0	0-2	4-1	3-2	2-2	0-1	4-2	2-1	3-1	6-0	2-1	5-0		2-1	1-0	1-0	0-3	2-1
19 Oxhey Jets	2-0	3-3	2-2	1-6	0-2	0-1	0-3	4-5	2-2	1-3	2-1	3-2	0-1	2-2	3-0	3-4	6-0	2-3		1-2	1-2	4-2	2-1
20 Royston Town	0-2	1-1	7-1	0-5	4-0	0-2	2-0	2-3	3-0	2-0	1-0	4-1	1-1	3-4	3-1	1-0	2-1	3-3	3-2		1-0	2-0	1-0
21 St Margaretsbury	3-0	3-0	6-2	0-1	2-1	1-0	2-0	1-1	2-1	1-3	0-2	2-0	3-2	0-0	1-0	0-2	4-1	1-1	5-1	2-2		0-1	0-5
22 Stotfold	3-3	1-1	0-1	1-2	4-1	0-3	0-0	1-0	2-2	1-2	5-2	0-2	3-0	2-2	1-2	3-3	4-2	1-2	2-3	0-1	1-0		1-1
23 Tring Athletic	4-2	3-0	1-1	1-0	2-4	1-1	4-1	2-0	4-1	1-1	2-0	2-0	3-2	2-1	3-0	2-0	6-1	3-2	0-1	1-1	2-0	2-1	

DIVISION ONE	P	W	D	L	F	A	Pts
1 Berkhamsted	40	34	5	1	122	36	107
2 AFC Dunstable	40	29	5	6	118	48	92
3 Kings Langley	40	28	3	9	113	56	87
4 Crawley Green	40	27	5	8	95	44	86
5 London Colney	40	21	7	12	82	47	70
6 Bedford Town reserves	40	22	4	14	76	63	70
7 Harpenden Town	40	19	10	11	86	58	67
8 London Lions	40	19	7	14	94	71	64
9 Hoddesdon Town	40	16	12	12	75	62	60
10 New Bradwell St Peter	40	17	6	17	81	67	57
11 Sun Postal Sports	40	17	4	19	71	97	55
12 St Albans City reserves	40	14	10	16	74	76	52
13 Bedford	40	14	6	20	86	105	48
14 Wodson Park	40	12	10	18	71	78	46
15 Cockfosters	40	13	6	21	63	72	45
16 Ampthill Town	40	13	5	22	67	114	44
17 Welwyn Garden City	40	10	4	26	54	91	34
18 Buckingham Athletic	40	8	9	23	51	93	33
19 Cranfield United	40	7	11	22	51	92	32
20 Amersham Town	40	6	4	30	43	103	22
21 Stony Stratford Town	40	6	3	31	38	138	21

Sport London e Benfica - record expunged

DIVISION ONE CUP

ROUND 1
Kings Langley 8-1 Stony Stratford Town
Bedford Town reserves 2-1 Welwyn Garden City
Ampthill Town 1-2 AFC Dunstable
London Lions 6-1 Cranfield United
Sport London e Benfica 0-7 Wodson Park
ROUND 2
AFC Dunstable 5-2 Bedford
Crawley Green 2-1 Bedford Town reserves
Kings Langley 1-3 Sun Postal Sports
New Bradwell St Peter 1-2 Harpenden Town
Buckingham Athletic 5-2 Wodson Park
Hoddesdon Town 4-2 London Lions
London Colney 0-1 Berkhamsted
St Albans City reserves 4-3 Cockfosters
QUARTER FINALS
Harpenden Town 3-6 Berkhamsted
St Albans City reserves 5-2 Buckingham Athletic
Hoddesdon Town 6-1 Sun Postal Sports
Crawley Green 1-3 AFC Dunstable
SEMI-FINALS
St Albans City reserves 2-0 Hoddeson Town
AFC Dunstable 3-0 Berkhamsted
FINAL (@ Berkhamsted, 2/5/11)
AFC Dunstable 4-2 St Albans Town reserves

CHALLENGE TROPHY continued...

Hatfield Town 3-1 Tring Corinthians
Bucks Student Union 1-1 Buckingham Athletic
(Bucks Student Union won on penalties)
Totternhoe 4-0 Caddington
London Lions 1-2 Stotfold
Berkhamsted 2-3 Risborough Rangers
Dunstable Town 2-0 Pitstone & Ivinghoe
Cockfosters 0-4 St Margaretsbury
Kings Langley 6-7 Holmer Green
Mursley United 3-2 Stony Stratford Town
Crawley Green 3-2 Aylesbury United
Kingsbury London Tigers 1-2 Sun Postal Sports
London Colney 3-5 Langford
Bedford 5-2 Bletchley Town
Leverstock Green 2-1 Royston Town
ROUND 2
Risborough Rangers 2-1 St Margaretsbury
Sun Postal Sports 1-2 Cranfield United
Harpenden Town 2-3 Broxbourne Borough
Crawley Green 1-1 St Albans City reserves
(St Albans City reserves won on penalties)
Haringey Borough 2-2 Dunstable Town
(Dunstable Town won 4-3 on penalties)
Bedford Town reserves 1-2 Hatfield Town
Tring Athletic 0-2 Hanwell Town
Bucks Student Union scr-w/o Totternhoe
AFC Dunstable 3-1 Mursley United
Langford 0-2 Leverstock Green
Stotfold 4-0 New Bradwell St Peter
Colney Heath 1-0 Oxhey Jets
Holmer Green 3-1 Hertford Town
Padbury United 3-0 The 61 FC (Luton)
Biggleswade United 2-2 Chalfont St Peter
(Chalfont St Peter won 5-4 on penalties)
Bedford 2-3 Wodson Park
ROUND 3
Cranfield United 1-1 Hatfield Town
(Hatfield Town won 4-1 on penalties)
Risborough Rangers 3-2 Wodson Park
Leverstock Green 2-3 St Albans City reserves
Dunstable Town 2-1 Padbury United
Totternhoe 0-2 Stotfold
AFC Dunstable 0-4 Chalfont St Peter
Broxbourne Borough 1-4 Colney Heath
Holmer Green 3-2 Hanwell Town
QUARTER FINALS
Stotfold 1-2 Dunstable Town
Risborough Rangers 2-1 St Albans City reserves
Colney Heath 4-2 Hatfield Town
Holmer Green 1-2 Chalfont St Peter
SEMI-FINALS
Chalfont St Peter 2-0 Risborough Rangers
Colney Heath 0-1 Dunstable Town
FINAL (@ Harefield United, 3/5/11)
Chalfont St Peter 2-1 Dunstable Town

DIVISION ONE	1	2	3	4	5	6	7	8	9	10	11	12	13	14	15	16	17	18	19	20	21
1 AFC Dunstable		5-0	4-2	3-0	4-2	1-3	4-0	2-0	3-2	1-1	2-2	1-0	3-1	1-0	2-0	3-1	2-1	4-0	8-1	6-2	3-1
2 Amersham Town	2-0		1-1	1-4	0-1	0-2	0-2	1-4	1-4	2-2	0-2	0-2	0-3	0-5	1-2	1-4	1-2	3-1	2-3	2-1	3-1
3 Ampthill Town	0-5	2-1		0-4	0-3	4-4	3-2	1-2	2-1	3-2	1-1	2-2	0-7	2-1	3-6	3-0	2-1	3-2	1-6	3-1	2-5
4 Bedford	4-4	2-0	4-2		1-2	0-4	6-3	2-1	1-3	1-8	2-3	2-2	2-3	0-1	3-3	1-3	4-3	6-0	5-1	1-2	2-2
5 Bedford Town reserves	1-5	4-0	1-0	4-3		1-2	3-0	2-1	2-1	1-0	0-3	1-0	0-2	2-2	2-5	6-1	2-0	3-2	0-3	4-1	2-0
6 Berkhamsted	4-1	5-2	7-1	4-1	2-1		5-2	2-1	2-0	3-0	3-1	2-2	5-1	3-0	1-0	3-0	3-0	5-0	2-0	3-2	7-2
7 Buckingham Athletic	1-4	3-1	2-1	1-2	1-1	0-5		0-2	2-2	1-2	1-5	1-3	2-1	1-3	2-0	0-3	1-1	1-3	3-0	0-2	3-3
8 Cockfosters	0-2	4-1	3-1	7-0	1-8	0-2	1-1		3-0	2-2	0-0	2-1	0-2	0-2	1-3	0-1	2-3	5-0	2-3	1-2	3-2
9 Cranfield United	2-7	2-2	3-3	0-2	1-2	0-3	0-2	2-1		2-3	2-2	1-1	2-5	2-1	1-1	1-5	0-1	0-3	2-3	1-1	0-3
10 Crawley Green	0-2	2-0	1-0	3-2	2-2	0-3	4-2	2-1	6-0		4-0	1-0	2-1	0-2	5-4	2-0	5-0	3-1	7-0	3-1	1-0
11 Harpenden Town	4-1	4-1	1-2	1-0	2-3	0-2	3-0	1-1	4-0	0-1		1-2	1-3	1-1	2-2	3-2	3-3	5-1	1-3	6-1	1-1
12 Hoddesdon Town	1-2	3-2	4-1	1-0	3-1	1-3	4-4	0-0	3-0	0-2	2-4		2-3	4-3	5-0	2-1	3-1	4-2	1-1	2-2	0-2
13 King's Langley	0-2	2-1	5-3	7-3	2-1	5-0	3-0	5-1	2-2	1-3	3-1	2-2		1-2	3-1	3-1	4-3	7-0	2-0	3-2	4-0
14 London Colney	1-2	2-0	8-1	2-1	1-2	1-3	1-1	3-2	4-2	0-0	0-1	1-1	2-1		4-1	1-1	0-1	4-1	4-1	3-0	2-1
15 London Lions	1-2	3-1	3-1	7-0	3-2	1-1	2-0	5-1	0-1	2-5	0-2	1-1	0-0	1-4		4-1	3-2	1-3	6-0	4-1	3-2
16 New Bradwell St Peter	0-3	2-2	3-1	7-3	5-1	0-0	1-0	1-2	1-0	0-1	2-1	5-1	0-2	0-3	4-1		2-2	2-0	3-3	0-2	3-2
17 St Albans City reserves	2-2	3-1	4-0	2-2	2-1	3-4	1-1	1-2	1-1	0-3	2-2	1-2	0-1	2-2	0-4	0-5		2-2	2-1	2-0	6-2
18 Stony Stratford Town	1-9	0-2	0-4	2-4	0-1	0-5	1-4	1-1	1-3	1-0	1-4	2-1	1-4	2-1	1-6	0-8	0-5		1-3	0-3	1-3
19 Sun Postal Sports	3-2	2-1	2-1	2-4	0-0	0-2	4-0	3-0	0-2	1-0	1-3	1-4	1-5	0-3	0-0	3-2	0-1	4-0		6-3	4-2
20 Welwyn Garden City	2-1	2-4	1-3	0-1	0-1	1-2	1-1	0-2	2-2	1-4	2-3	0-2	4-1	0-1	0-2	1-0	0-5	4-0	3-0		1-4
21 Wodson Park	0-0	5-0	1-2	1-1	2-0	1-1	2-0	2-1	1-1	1-3	0-2	1-1	1-3	2-1	1-4	1-1	1-3	1-1	7-2	2-0	

DIVISION TWO	P	W	D	L	F	A	Pts
1 Padbury United	28	23	3	2	84	27	72
2 Totternhoe	28	17	9	2	82	38	60
3 Aston Clinton	28	18	3	7	80	30	57
4 Winslow United	28	17	4	7	76	34	55
5 Risborough Rangers	28	16	5	7	49	21	53
6 The 61 FC (Luton)	28	14	8	6	86	42	50
7 Tring Corinthians	28	13	4	11	61	50	43
8 Mursley United	28	12	6	10	53	47	42
9 Kent Athletic	28	11	7	10	71	56	40
10 Pitstone & Ivinghoe	28	8	5	15	47	63	29
11 Bletchley Town	28	7	5	16	53	81	26
12 Old Bradwell United	28	7	5	16	45	86	26
13 Caddington	28	5	4	19	40	86	19
14 Brache Sparta Community	28	4	3	21	37	95	15
15 MK Wanderers	28	0	5	23	24	132	5
Bucks Student Union - record expunged							

DIVISION TWO CUP

ROUND 1

Mursley United 1-3 Padbury United
Risborough Rangers 2-3 The 61 FC (Luton)
Old Bradwell United 1-2 Kent Athletic
Pitstone & Ivinghoe 4-0 Caddington
Totternhoe 1-2 Winslow United
Bletchley Town w/o-scr Bucks Student Union
MK Wanderers 1-2 Tring Corinthians
Brache Sparta Community 0-4 Aston Clinton

QUARTER FINALS

Bletchley Town 0-3 The 61 FC (Luton)
Kent Athletic 1-0 Tring Corinthians
Padbury United 7-0 Pitstone & Ivinghoe
Aston Clinton 1-3 Winslow United

SEMI-FINALS

Padbury United 0-2 Winslow United
Kent Athletic 1-2 The 61 FC (Luton)

FINAL (@ Ampthill Town, 4/5/11)

The 61 FC (Luton) 0-2 Winslow United

DIVISION TWO	1	2	3	4	5	6	7	8	9	10	11	12	13	14	15
1 Aston Clinton		3-0	4-1	7-1	6-1	7-0	8-0	1-1	1-3	3-0	1-0	1-4	1-1	1-0	2-0
2 Bletchley Town	2-8		2-1	1-3	1-4	7-0	0-1	2-1	2-3	1-3	1-4	0-8	5-5	2-2	2-1
3 Brache Sparta Community	0-2	4-1		1-6	1-8	1-1	2-5	2-1	1-4	1-1	1-4	2-3	1-3	2-7	1-0
4 Caddington	0-5	0-3	4-1		2-6	2-2	0-3	1-1	2-3	0-2	1-3	1-5	0-4	1-4	1-3
5 Kent Athletic	2-1	1-1	5-1	3-1		8-1	1-0	6-1	2-4	5-3	1-1	1-4	0-1	1-3	1-5
6 Milton Keynes Wanderers	0-1	2-3	1-6	2-3	1-8		1-1	1-3	0-5	1-6	0-0	0-4	0-8	1-2	1-5
7 Mursley United	2-4	5-2	3-0	0-0	0-0	1-1		6-1	0-2	2-1	0-1	4-0	1-2	2-1	2-2
8 Old Bradwell United	2-1	3-1	4-2	2-3	2-2	4-1	3-2		0-2	2-2	3-2	0-8	0-4	2-3	1-6
9 Padbury United	1-1	4-0	3-1	4-1	2-0	11-2	4-1	6-2		2-0	1-0	5-2	1-1	1-2	3-1
10 Pitstone & Ivinghoe	2-3	4-8	1-0	4-1	2-2	4-2	0-3	2-0	1-2		0-4	0-1	1-4	3-2	0-2
11 Risborough Rangers	0-3	2-0	8-1	2-1	1-1	3-0	3-0	3-1	0-2	3-0		1-0	0-1	0-0	0-1
12 The 61 F C	3-2	1-1	3-0	1-1	2-0	15-0	3-3	3-3	0-3	1-1	1-2		2-2	2-0	2-2
13 Totternhoe	2-1	3-2	3-3	5-1	2-1	6-2	1-3	3-1	4-1	1-1	0-0	2-2		6-1	1-3
14 Tring Corinthians	0-2	3-1	1-0	6-1	1-1	6-1	0-3	6-1	0-0	5-2	0-1	1-4	1-4		2-1
15 Winslow United	2-0	2-2	7-0	3-2	6-0	2-0	4-0	5-0	0-2	2-1	0-1	4-2	3-3	4-2	

RESERVE DIVISION ONE	P	W	D	L	F	A	Pts
1 Hadley reserves	30	18	6	6	86	50	60
2 Oxhey Jets reserves	30	18	5	7	72	42	59
3 St Margaretsbury reserves	30	17	3	10	70	52	54
4 Royston Town reserves	30	15	8	7	89	55	53
5 AFC Dunstable reserves	30	15	4	11	67	47	49
6 London Colney reserves	30	15	2	13	73	67	47
7 Holmer Green reserves	30	14	3	13	48	54	45
8 Kings Langley reserves	30	13	3	14	64	64	42
9 Wodson Park reserves	30	13	2	15	57	70	41
10 Stotfold reserves	30	9	13	8	61	58	40
11 Cockfosters reserves	30	12	3	15	36	51	39
12 Hatfield Town reserves	30	8	7	15	42	64	31
13 Hoddesdon Town reserves	30	9	4	17	37	61	31
14 Langford reserves (-3)	30	8	8	14	38	56	29
15 Ampthill Town reserves	30	8	5	17	49	84	29
16 Crawley Green reserves	30	8	4	18	52	66	28

RESERVE DIVISION TWO	P	W	D	L	F	A	Pts
1 The 61 FC (Luton) reserves	22	18	2	2	75	15	56
2 Risborough Rangers reserves	22	15	6	1	42	14	51
3 London Lions reserves	22	15	3	4	68	28	48
4 Buckingham Athletic reserves	22	11	4	7	52	38	37
5 Welwyn Garden City reserves	22	8	6	8	42	48	30
6 Kent Athletic reserves	22	8	3	11	36	36	27
7 Tring Corinthians reserves	22	7	4	11	32	50	25
8 Sun Postal Sports reserves	22	6	6	10	42	43	24
9 Totternhoe reserves	22	7	3	12	31	55	24
10 Old Bradwell United reserves	22	7	2	13	35	62	23
11 New Bradwell St Peter reserves	22	7	1	14	39	65	22
12 Stony Stratford Town reserves	22	2	2	18	22	62	8
Bletchley Town reserves - record expunged							

AFC DUNSTABLE

Founded: 1981 Nickname: Od's

Secretary: Craig Renfrew **(T)** 07976 192 530 **(E)** renfrewcraig@aol.com
Chairman: Simon Bullard **Manager:** Alex Butler **Prog Ed:** Craig Renfrew
Ground: Dunstable Town FC, Creasey Pk, Creasey Pk Dr, Brewers Hill Rd, LU6 1BB **(T)** TBC
Capacity: 3,500 **Seats:** 350 **Covered:** 1,000 **Midweek Matchday:** **Clubhouse:** Yes **Shop:** Yes

Colours(change): Blue/blue/white (Red & white/red/red)
Previous Names: Old Dunstablians 1981- 2004.
Previous Leagues:
Records:
Senior Honours: Spartan South Midlands Division Two 2003-04, 06-07.

10 YEAR RECORD

01-02	02-03	03-04	04-05	05-06	06-07	07-08	08-09	09-10	10-11
SSM2 4	SSM2 2	SSM2 1	SSM2 6	SSM2 2	SSM2 1	SSM2 4	SSM2 3	SSM1 5	SSM1 2

AYLESBURY UNITED

Founded: 1897 Nickname: The Ducks

Secretary: Steve Baker **(T)** 07768 353 265 **(E)** stevepb42@hotmail.com
Chairman: Graham Read **Manager:** Tony Joyce **Prog Ed:** Steve Baker
Ground: Leighton Town FC, Lake Street, Leighton Buzzard, Beds LU7 1RX **(T)** 01525 373311
Capacity: 2,800 **Seats:** 155 **Covered:** 300 **Midweek Matchday:** **Clubhouse:** Yes **Shop:** No

Colours(change): Green & white/green/white (Gold & black/black/black)
Previous Names: None
Previous Leagues: Post War: Spartan >1951, Delphian 51-63, Athenian 63-76, Southern 76-88, 2004-10, Conf. 88-89, Isthmian 89-2004
Records: **Att:** 6,000 v England 1988. **Goalscorer:** Cliff Hercules - 301. **Apps:** Cliff Hercules 651+18.
Senior Honours: Southern League 1987-88. Berks & Bucks Senior Cup x4. Isthmian Cup 1994-95.

10 YEAR RECORD

01-02	02-03	03-04	04-05	05-06	06-07	07-08	08-09	09-10	10-11
Isth1 3	Isth P 17	Isth P 24	SthP 10	SthP 21	SthM 6	SthM 8	SthM 10	SthM 22	SSM P 6

BERKHAMSTED

Founded: 2009 Nickname: Comrades

Secretary: Grant Hastie **(T)** 01799 584053 **(E)** gshastie@hotmail.com
Chairman: Steve Hawes **Manager:** Mick Vipond **Prog Ed:** Grant Hastie
Ground: Broadwater, Lower Kings Road, Berkhamsted HP4 2AL **(T)** 01442 865977
Capacity: 2,500 **Seats:** 170 **Covered:** 350 **Midweek Matchday:** **Clubhouse:** Yes **Shop:** Yes

Colours(change): Yellow/blue/blue (White/black/black)
Previous Names:
Previous Leagues:
Records:
Senior Honours: Spartan South Midlands League Division 1 2009-10, 10-11.

10 YEAR RECORD

01-02	02-03	03-04	04-05	05-06	06-07	07-08	08-09	09-10	10-11
								SSM1 1	SSM1 1

BIGGLESWADE UNITED

Founded: 1929 Nickname:

Secretary: Tracey James **(T)** 07714 661 827 **(E)** tracey.james10@ntlworld.com
Chairman: Steve Rowland **Manager:** Phil Childs **Prog Ed:** Tracey James
Ground: Second Meadow, Fairfield Rd, Biggleswade, Beds SG18 0BS **(T)** 01767 600 408
Capacity: 2,000 **Seats:** 30 **Covered:** 130 **Midweek Matchday:** Wednesday **Clubhouse:** Yes **Shop:** No

Colours(change): Red/navy/red (Yellow/royal blue/ royal blue)
Previous Names: None
Previous Leagues: Beds & District and Midland. Herts County.
Records: **Att:** 250 v Biggleswade Town
Senior Honours: Spartan South Midlands Division One 1996-97, Premier Division 2008-09. Hunts FA Premier Cup 1998-99.
Beds Senior Trophy 2003-04. Beds Senior Cup 2001-02.

10 YEAR RECORD

01-02	02-03	03-04	04-05	05-06	06-07	07-08	08-09	09-10	10-11
SSM1 4	SSM1 8	SSM1 8	SSM1 3	SSM P 9	SSM P 14	SSM P 18	SSM P 1	SSM P 20	SSM P 20

BROXBOURNE BOROUGH V & E

Founded: 1959 Nickname:

Secretary: John Venables **(T)** 07746 239 938 **(E)** venablesjohn@yahoo.co.uk
Chairman: Peter Harris **Manager:** Ashley Fisk **Prog Ed:** Peter Harris
Ground: Broxbourne Borougn V & E Club, Goffs Lane, Cheshunt, Herts EN7 5QN **(T)** 01992 624 281
Capacity: 500 **Seats:** 300 **Covered:** yes **Midweek Matchday:** Tuesday **Clubhouse:** Yes **Shop:** No

Colours(change): All Blue. (All Red)
Previous Names: Somerset Ambury V & E
Previous Leagues: Herts Senior
Records: **Att:** 120 **Goalscorer:** Wayne Morris **App:** Brian Boehmer
Senior Honours:

10 YEAR RECORD

01-02	02-03	03-04	04-05	05-06	06-07	07-08	08-09	09-10	10-11
SSM P 11	SSM P 13	SSM P 16	SSM P 9	SSM P 11	SSM P 8	SSM P 12	SSM P 4	SSM P 9	SSM P 10

COLNEY HEATH

Founded: 1907 Nickname: Magpies

Secretary: Martin Marlborough **(T)** 07960 155 463 **(E)** m.marlborough@stalbans.gov.uk
Chairman: Martin Marlborough **Manager:** Kevin Cooper & Glenn Draper **Prog Ed:** Martin Marlborough
Ground: The Recreation Ground, High St, Colney Heath, St Albans AL4 0NS **(T)** 01727 826 188
Capacity: **Seats:** **Covered:** **Midweek Matchday:** **Clubhouse:** Yes **Shop:**

Colours(change): Black & white stripes/black/black (All tangerine)
Previous Names:
Previous Leagues: Herts Senior County League 1953-2000
Records:
Senior Honours: Herts County League Div 2 Champions 1953-54 Div 1 A 55-56, Prem 58-99, 99-00, Div 1 88-89, Spartan South Midlands Div 1 2005-06 , SSML Cup 05-06

10 YEAR RECORD

01-02	02-03	03-04	04-05	05-06	06-07	07-08	08-09	09-10	10-11
SSM1 3	SSM1 5	SSM1 6	SSM1 5	SSM1 1	SSM P 16	SSM P 15	SSM P 12	SSM P 5	SSM P 5

DUNSTABLE TOWN

Founded: 1998 Nickname: The Blues

Secretary: Paul Harris **(T)** 07798 716 263 **(E)** hpaulharris@aol.com
Chairman: Roger Dance **Manager:** Darren Croft **Prog Ed:** Daniel Crooke
Ground: Creasey Park Stadium, Brewers Hill Rd, Dunstable LU6 1BB **(T)** 01582 667 555 / 07798 716 263
Capacity: 3,500 **Seats:** 350 **Covered:** 1000 **Midweek Matchday:** Tuesday **Clubhouse:** Yes **Shop:** Yes

Colours(change): All blue (All red)
Previous Names:
Previous Leagues: Spartan South Midlands 1998-2000. Isthmian 2003. Southern 2004-09.
Records:
Senior Honours: Spartan Sth. Midlands Div.1 1999-00. Premier 02-03. Bedfordshire Senior Cup 03-04, 08-09.

10 YEAR RECORD

01-02	02-03	03-04	04-05	05-06	06-07	07-08	08-09	09-10	10-11
SSM P 7	SSM P 1	Isth1N 5	SthP 20	SthW 21	SthM 11	SthM 13	SthM 21	SSM P 7	SSM P 7

HADLEY

Founded: 1882 Nickname:

Secretary: Bob Henderson **(T)** 07748 267 295 **(E)** gensecretary@hadleyfc.com
Chairman: Guy Slee **Manager:** Ian Gray **Prog Ed:** Steve Gray
Ground: Potters Bar Town FC, Watkins Rise (off The Walk), Potters Bar EN6 1QB **(T)** 01707 654 833
Capacity: 2,000 **Seats:** 150 **Covered:** 250 **Midweek Matchday:** **Clubhouse:** Yes **Shop:** Yes

Colours(change): Red/black/black (Blue/white/white)
Previous Names:
Previous Leagues: Barnet & Dist. 1922-57, Nth Suburban 57-70, Mid Herts 70-77, Herts Sen. 77-85, 99-2007, Sth Olym. 85-99, W Herts 2007-08.
Records:
Senior Honours: Hertfordshire Senior County League Division 3 1977-78, Division 1 2001-02, Premier 2003-04, 04-05. West Hertfordshire League 2007-08. Aubrey Cup 2005-06.

10 YEAR RECORD

01-02	02-03	03-04	04-05	05-06	06-07	07-08	08-09	09-10	10-11
Hert1 1	HertP 8	HertP 1	HertP 1	HertP 3	HertP 2	WHert 1	SSM2 2	SSM1 2	SSM P 14

HANWELL TOWN

Founded: 1948 Nickname: Magpies

Secretary: Bob Fisher **(T)** 07730 822 216 **(E)** bob.fisher@hanwelltfc.plus.com
Chairman: Bob Fisher **Manager:** Keith Rowlands **Prog Ed:** Bob Fisher
Ground: Reynolds Field, Preivale Lane, Perivale, Greenford, UB6 8TL **(T)** 0208 997 1801
Capacity: 1,250 **Seats:** 175 **Covered:** 600 **Midweek Matchday:** Tuesday **Clubhouse:** Yes **Shop:** No

Colours(change): Black & white stripes/black/black & white (Yellow/blue/white)
Previous Names:
Previous Leagues: Dauntless. Wembley & Dist. Middlesex. London Spartan. Southern.
Records: **Att:** 600 v Spurs **Goalscorer:** Keith Rowlands. **App:** Phil Player 617 (20 seasons)
Senior Honours: London Spartan Senior Div. 83-84. London Senior Cup 1991-92, 92-93.

10 YEAR RECORD

01-02	02-03	03-04	04-05	05-06	06-07	07-08	08-09	09-10	10-11
SSM P 3	SSM P 8	SSM P 6	SSM P 2	SSM P 3	SthS 21	SSM P 9	SSM P 7	SSM P 13	SSM P 15

HAREFIELD UNITED

Founded: 1868 Nickname: Hares

Secretary: Glenn Bellis **(T)** 07973 563 282 **(E)** glennbellis@btconnect.com
Chairman: Keith Ronald **Manager:** Darren Feighery **Prog Ed:** Keith Ronald
Ground: Preston Park, Breakespeare Road North, Harefield, UB9 6NE **(T)** 01895 824 287
Capacity: 1,200 **Seats:** 150 **Covered:** Yes **Midweek Matchday:** Tuesday **Clubhouse:** Yes **Shop:** No

Colours(change): Red/black/red. (White or orange/red or orange/black or orange)
Previous Names:
Previous Leagues: Uxbridge & District, Great Western Comb, Panthernon, Middlesex, Athenian & Isthmian.
Records: **Att:** 430 v Bashley FA Vase
Senior Honours: Middlesex Premier Cup 1985-86

10 YEAR RECORD

01-02	02-03	03-04	04-05	05-06	06-07	07-08	08-09	09-10	10-11
SSM1 2	SSM P 4	SSM P 5	SSM P 5	SSM P 4	SSM P 2	SSM P 5	SSM P 2	SSM P 6	SSM P 21

HARINGEY BOROUGH

Founded: 1907 Nickname: Borough

Secretary: John Bacon **(T)** 07979 050 190 **(E)** clubsecretary@haringeyboroughfc.com
Chairman: Aki Achillea **Manager:** Tom Loizu **Prog Ed:** John Bacon
Ground: Coles Park, White Hart Lane, Tottenham, London N17 7JP **(T)** 0208 889 1415 (Matchday)
Capacity: 2,500 **Seats:** 280 **Covered:** yes **Midweek Matchday:** **Clubhouse:** Yes **Shop:** No

Colours(change): Yellow/green/yellow (Green/yellow/green)
Previous Names: Tufnell Park 1907
Previous Leagues: London, Isthmian, Spartan, Delphian, Athenian
Records: **Att:** 400
Senior Honours: London Senior Cup 1912-13, 90-91, Athenian League 1913-14

10 YEAR RECORD

01-02	02-03	03-04	04-05	05-06	06-07	07-08	08-09	09-10	10-11
SSM P 12	SSM P 15	SSM P 18	SSM P 18	SSM P 19	SSM P 21	SSM1 2	SSM P 18	SSM P 15	SSM P 8

HATFIELD TOWN

Founded: 1886 Nickname:

Secretary: Joanne Gabbott **(T)** 07739 884 513 **(E)** joannegabbott@hatfieldtownfc.com
Chairman: Chris O'Connor **Manager:** Kevin Pearman **Prog Ed:** Tom Bailey
Ground: Gosling Sport Park, Stanborough Rd, Welwyn Garden City, Herts AL8 6XE **(T)** 01707 384 300
Capacity: 1,500 **Seats:** 40 **Covered:** 120 **Midweek Matchday:** **Clubhouse:** Yes **Shop:** Yes

Colours(change): All blue. (Orange/white/black).
Previous Names: Hatfield FC > 1906. Hatfield Utd > 1922. Hatfield Utd Ath. > 1948
Previous Leagues: Mid. Hertfordshire. Herts County. Parthenon. London. Metropolitan.
Records:
Senior Honours: Herts Senior Champions 2007-08

10 YEAR RECORD

01-02	02-03	03-04	04-05	05-06	06-07	07-08	08-09	09-10	10-11
HertP 14	Hert1 1	HertP 7	HertP 3	HertP 2	HertP 5	HertP 1	SSM1 3	SSM P 12	SSM P 11

HERTFORD TOWN

Founded: 1908 Nickname: The Blues

Secretary: Michael Persighetti **(T)** 07530 056 401 **(E)** m.persighetti@ntlworld.com
Chairman: Mike Varney **Manager:** Scott O'Donoghue **Prog Ed:** TBA
Ground: Hertingfordbury Park, West Street, Hertford, SG13 8EZ **(T)** 01992 583 716
Capacity: 6,500 **Seats:** 200 **Covered:** 1,500 **Midweek Matchday:** Tuesday **Clubhouse:** Yes **Shop:** Yes

Colours(change): All blue (Yellow/black/yellow)
Previous Names:
Previous Leagues: Herts Co. Spartan. Delphian 59-63. Athenian 63-72. Eastern Co 72-73.
Records: **Att:** 5,000 v Kingstonian FA Am Cup 2nd Round 55-56 **App:** Robbie Burns
Senior Honours: Herts Senior Cup 66-67 East Anglian Cup 62-63, 69-70

10 YEAR RECORD

01-02	02-03	03-04	04-05	05-06	06-07	07-08	08-09	09-10	10-11
Isth3 11	Isth1N 24	Isth2 3	Isth2 4	Isth2 13	SSM P 3	SSM P 4	SSM P 10	SSM P 16	SSM P 9

HILLINGDON BOROUGH

Founded: 19190 Nickname: Boro

Secretary: Graham Smith **(T)** 01895 673 181 **(E)** jackieandgraham@talktalk.net
Chairman: Michael Harris **Manager:** Jesse Smith **Prog Ed:** Oliver Chalk
Ground: Middlesex Stadium, Breakspear Rd, Ruislip HA4 7SB **(T)** 01895 639 544
Capacity: 1,500 **Seats:** 150 **Covered:** 150 **Midweek Matchday:** **Clubhouse:** Yes **Shop:**

Colours(change): White/royal blue/royal (White/royal blue/royal blue)
Previous Names: Yiewsley. Bromley Park Rangers.
Previous Leagues: Southern 1964-84, 2006-08. South Midlands 1990-2006. Isthmian 2008-09.
Records:
Senior Honours: South Midlands Cup 1996-97.

10 YEAR RECORD

01-02	02-03	03-04	04-05	05-06	06-07	07-08	08-09	09-10	10-11
SSM P 16	SSM P 12	SSM P 12	SSM P 6	SSM P 2	SthW 16	SthW 13	Isth1N 22	SSM P 18	SSM P 16

HOLMER GREEN

Founded: 1908 Nickname:

Secretary: John Ostinelli **(T)** 07900 081 814 **(E)** j.ostinelli@sky.com
Chairman: Rupert Perry **Manager:** Chris Allen **Prog Ed:** John Anderson
Ground: Airedale Park, Watchet Lane, Holmer Green, Bucks HP15 6UF **(T)** 01494 711 485
Capacity: 1,000 **Seats:** 25 **Covered:** yes **Midweek Matchday:** Tuesday **Clubhouse:** Yes **Shop:**

Colours(change): Green/white/green (Yellow/white/white)
Previous Names:
Previous Leagues: Chesham 1908-38, Wycombe Combination 1984-95, Chiltonian 1995-98.
Records:
Senior Honours: Spartan South Midlands Senior 1995-96, 98-99, Division 1 2009-10.

10 YEAR RECORD

01-02	02-03	03-04	04-05	05-06	06-07	07-08	08-09	09-10	10-11
SSM P 15	SSM P 19	SSM P 19	SSM P 13	SSM P 7	SSM P 19	SSM P 20	SSM P 20	SSM1 1	SSM P 17

LEVERSTOCK GREEN

Founded: 1895 Nickname: The Green

Secretary: Brian Barter **(T)** 07982 072 783 **(E)** b.barter@btopenworld.com
Chairman: Kate Binns **Manager:** Steve Heath **Prog Ed:** Brian Barter
Ground: Pancake Lane, Leverstock Green, Hemel Hempstead, Herts **(T)** 01442 246 280
Capacity: 1,500 **Seats:** 50 **Covered:** 100 **Midweek Matchday:** Tuesday **Clubhouse:** Yes **Shop:** No

Colours(change): White/green/green. (Yellow & blue/blue or Green & yellow/green/green)
Previous Names: None
Previous Leagues: West Herts (pre 1950) & Herts County 50-91
Records: **Att:** 1,000 **App:** Jonnie Wallace
Senior Honours: South Midlands Senior Division 1996-97.

10 YEAR RECORD

01-02	02-03	03-04	04-05	05-06	06-07	07-08	08-09	09-10	10-11
SSM1 8	SSM1 4	SSM P 9	SSM P 14	SSM P 6	SSM P 5	SSM P 7	SSM P 6	SSM P 10	SSM P 4

LONDON TIGERS

Founded: 2006 | Nickname: Tigers

Secretary: Jawar Ali **(T)** 07791 270 634 **(E)** info@londontigers.org
Chairman: Mesba Ahmed **Manager:** Goergij Minashvili **Prog Ed:** Sulthana Begum
Ground: Avenue Park, Western Avenue, Perivale, Greenford UB6 8GA **(T)** 020 7289 3395 (10am-6pm)
Capacity: **Seats:** **Covered:** **Midweek Matchday:** **Clubhouse:** **Shop:**

Colours(change): Orange/black/black (Yellow/blue/blue)
Previous Names: Kingsbury Town and London Tigers merged in 2006. Kingsbury London Tigers 2006-11.
Previous Leagues: None
Records:
Senior Honours:

10 YEAR RECORD

01-02	02-03	03-04	04-05	05-06	06-07	07-08	08-09	09-10	10-11
					SSM P 13	SSM P 14	SSM P 5	SSM P 8	SSM P 12

OXHEY JETS

Founded: | Nickname: Jets

Secretary: David Fuller **(T)** 07786 627 659 **(E)** d.g.fuller@ntlworld.com
Chairman: Phil Andrews **Manager:** Benny Higham **Prog Ed:** John Elliott
Ground: Boundary Stadium, Altham Way, South Oxhey, Watford WD19 6FW **(T)** 020 8421 6277
Capacity: 1,000 **Seats:** 100 **Covered:** 100 **Midweek Matchday:** Wednesday **Clubhouse:** Yes **Shop:** No

Colours(change): All royal blue (All yellow)
Previous Names:
Previous Leagues: Herts Senior County
Records: **Att:** 257 v Barnet Herts Senior Cup 05-06 **App:** Ian Holdon
Senior Honours: Herts Senior County Premier 2000-01, 01-02, 02-03. SSML Div 1 Champions 2004-2005, Herts Senior Centenary Trophy 2004-2005

10 YEAR RECORD

01-02	02-03	03-04	04-05	05-06	06-07	07-08	08-09	09-10	10-11
HertP 1	HertP 1	HertP 2	SSM1 1	SSM P 13	SSM P 7	SSM P 19	SSM P 13	SSM P 11	SSM P 19

ROYSTON TOWN

Founded: 1872 | Nickname: Crows

Secretary: Terry McKinnell **(T)** 07772 086 709 **(E)** terry.mckinnell@talktalk.net
Chairman: Steve Jackson **Manager:** Paul Attfield **Prog Ed:** Kelly Taylor
Ground: Garden Walk, Royston, Herts, SG8 7HP **(T)** 01763 241 204
Capacity: **Seats:** **Covered:** **Midweek Matchday:** **Clubhouse:** Yes **Shop:**

Colours(change): White/black/black (Red/white/red).
Previous Names: None
Previous Leagues: Cambridgeshire & Herts Co. Isthmian
Records: **Att:** 876 v Aldershot Town, 1993-94.
Senior Honours: Herts County Champions 1976-77. South Midlands Div.1 1978-79, 2008-09.

10 YEAR RECORD

01-02	02-03	03-04	04-05	05-06	06-07	07-08	08-09	09-10	10-11
SSM P 8	SSM P 16	SSM P 13	SSM P 16	SSM P 18	SSM P 20	SSM1 5	SSM1 1	SSM P 4	SSM P 3

ST MARGARETSBURY

Founded: 1894 | Nickname: Athletic

Secretary: Richard Palette **(T)** 07721 679 681 **(E)** richardpalette@aol.com
Chairman: Gary Stock **Manager:** Lee Judges **Prog Ed:** Gary Stock
Ground: Recreation Ground, Station Road, St Margarets SG12 8EW **(T)** 01920 870 473
Capacity: 1,000 **Seats:** 60 **Covered:** 60 **Midweek Matchday:** Tuesday **Clubhouse:** Yes **Shop:** No

Colours(change): Red & black stripes/black/black (Yellow/blue/yellow)
Previous Names: Stanstead Abbots > 1962
Previous Leagues: East Herts, Hertford & District, Waltham & District, 47-48 Herts Co. 48-92
Records: **Att:** 450 v Stafford Rangers FA Cup 2001-02
Senior Honours: Spartan Lg 95-96 Herts Senior Centenary Trophy 92-93, Herts Charity Shield 97-98

10 YEAR RECORD

01-02	02-03	03-04	04-05	05-06	06-07	07-08	08-09	09-10	10-11
SSM P 5	SSM P 5	SSM P 3	SSM P 7	SSM P 12	SSM P 15	SSM P 11	SSM P 14	SSM P 14	SSM P 18

STOTFOLD

Founded: 1946 Nickname: The Eagles

Secretary: Julie Longhurst **(T)** 07752 430 493 **(E)** julie.longhurst@btinternet.com

Chairman: Phil Pateman **Manager:** Gordon Bickerstaff **Prog Ed:** Phil Pateman

Ground: Roker Park, The Green, Stotfold, Hitchin, Herts SG5 4AN **(T)** 01462 730 765

Capacity: 5,000 **Seats:** 300 **Covered:** 300 **Midweek Matchday:** Tuesday **Clubhouse:** Yes **Shop:**

Colours(change): Amber/black/black. (Burgundy or blue & white hoops/burgundy or blue/burgundy or blue).

Previous Names:

Previous Leagues: Biggleswade & Dist, Norths Herts & South Midlands, United Counties >2010

Records: **Att:**1,000 **Goalscorer:** Roy Boon **Apps:** Roy Boon & Dave Chellew

Senior Honours: S. Midlands League 1980-81. Bedfordshire Senior Cup 1964-65, 93-94. Bedfordshire Premier Cup 1981-82, 98-99. United Counties League 2007-08.

10 YEAR RECORD

01-02	02-03	03-04	04-05	05-06	06-07	07-08	08-09	09-10	10-11
UCL P 9	UCL P 17	UCL P 10	UCL P 9	UCL P 11	UCL P 19	UCL P 1	UCL P 2	UCL P 7	SSM P 13

TRING ATHLETIC

Founded: 1958 Nickname: Athletic

Secretary: Bob Winter **(T)** 07979 816 528 **(E)** robert.winter2007@ntlworld.com

Chairman: Mick Eldridge **Manager:** Julian Robinson **Prog Ed:** Barry Simmons

Ground: Grass Roots Stadium, Pendley Sports Centre, Cow Lane, Tring HP23 5NT **(T)** 01442 891 144

Capacity: 1,233 **Seats:** 150 **Covered:** 100+ **Midweek Matchday:** Tuesday **Clubhouse:** Yes **Shop:** Yes

Colours(change): Red/black/black (Yellow/green/green)

Previous Names: None

Previous Leagues: West Herts 58-88

Records: **Goalscorer:** Andy Humphreys - 209 **App:** Mark Boniface - 642

Senior Honours: Spartan South Midlands Senior Division 1999-00

10 YEAR RECORD

01-02	02-03	03-04	04-05	05-06	06-07	07-08	08-09	09-10	10-11
SSM1 5	SSM1 3	SSM1 4	SSM P 4	SSM P 10	SSM P 11	SSM P 10	SSM P 8	SSM P 3	SSM P 2

SPARTAN SOUTH MIDLANDS INS & OUTS

PREM

IN: AFC Dunstable (P), Berkhamsted (P)

OUT: Chalfont St Peter (P - Southern League Division One Central), Kentish Town (R), Langford (R)

Kingsbury London Tigers become London Tigers

DIV ONE

IN: Chesham United Reserves (P - Suburban League Division One North), Kentish Town (R), Langford (R), Tokyngton Manor (N)

OUT: AFC Dunstable (P), Bedford Town Reserves (W), Berkhamsted (P), Sport London E Benfica (WS)

DIV TWO

IN: Hale Leys United (P - Aylesbury & District League Premier Division), Milton Keynes City (youth football)

OUT: Brache Sparta Community (F), Bucks Students Union (WS), Padbury United (W)

AMERSHAM TOWN

Founded: Nickname:

Secretary: Michael Gahagan **(T)** 07979 081827 **(E)** amgahagan@btinternet.com
Chairman: Lawrence Lipka **Manager:** Chris Martin & Paul Gray **Prog Ed:** Michael Gahagan
Ground: Spratleys Meadow, School Lane, Amersham, Bucks HP7 0EL **(T)** No telephone **Capacity:**
Colours(change): Black & white stripes/black/black (Yellow/yellow/yellow & black)

ADDITIONAL INFORMATION:

AMPTHILL TOWN

Founded: Nickname:

Secretary: Eric Turner **(T)** 07788 658 770 **(E)** ericturner789@btinternet.com
Chairman: Bernie Stuttard **Manager:** Steve Goodridge & Adam Dedman **Prog Ed:** Eric Turner
Ground: Ampthill Park, Woburn Street, Ampthill MK45 2HX **(T)** 01525 404440 **Capacity:**
Colours(change): Yellow/blue/blue (White & blue/black/black)

ADDITIONAL INFORMATION:

BEDFORD

Founded: 1957 Nickname:

Secretary: Paolo Riccio **(T)** 07868 370 464 **(E)** paolo.riccio@ntlworld.com
Chairman: Lui La Mura **Manager:** Luke Capon **Prog Ed:** Paul Warne
Ground: McMullen Park, Meadow Lane, Cardington, Bedford, MK44 3SB **(T)** 07831 594444 **Capacity:**
Colours(change): Black & white stripes/black/black (All blue)

ADDITIONAL INFORMATION:
Previous League: United Counties 1970-80.
Record Att: (at Fairhill) 1,500 v Bedford Town-South Mids Div 1 1992 **Apps:** Simon Fordham - 418

BUCKINGHAM ATHELTIC

Founded: Nickname:

Secretary: Colin Howkins **(T)** 07751 659 769 **(E)** colin@thehowkins.co.uk
Chairman: Stephen Orme **Manager:** Eddie Nix **Prog Ed:** Colin Howkins
Ground: Stratford Fields, Stratford Road, Buckingham MK18 1NY **(T)** 01280 816945 (MD) **Capacity:**
Colours(change): All navy blue (Yellow/black/black)

ADDITIONAL INFORMATION:

CHESHAM UNITED RESERVES

Founded: Nickname:

Secretary: Brian McCarthy **(T)** 07900 376 491 **(E)** brian_mccarthy@ntlworld.com
Chairman: Alan Calder **Manager:** Steve Benitez **Prog Ed:** David Jeffrey
Ground: The Meadow, Amy Lane, Chesham, Bucks HP5 1NE **(T)** 01494 783 964 **Capacity:**
Colours(change): All claret (Yellow/black/yellow)

ADDITIONAL INFORMATION:

COCKFOSTERS

Founded: 1921 Nickname: Fosters

Secretary: Graham Bint **(T)** 07729 709926 **(E)** graham.bint@ntlworld.com
Chairman: Roy Syrett **Manager:** Mark Adams **Prog Ed:** Alan Simmons
Ground: Cockfosters Sports Ground, Chalk Lane, Cockfosters, Herts EN4 9JG **(T)** 020 8449 5833 **Capacity:**
Colours(change): All red (White/navy/white)

ADDITIONAL INFORMATION:
Record Att: 408 v Saffron Walden.
Honours: London Interim Cup 1970-71, 89. Herts Sen Co Lge 78-79, 80-81. Aubrey Cup 78-79, 84-85. Herts Interm Cup 78-79

CRANFIELD UNITED

Founded: Nickname:

Secretary: Larry Corkrey **(T)** 07854 936405 **(E)** larrycor@btinternet.com
Chairman: Tony Beale **Manager:** Lee Bearman **Prog Ed:** Larry Corkrey
Ground: Crawley Road, Cranfield, Beds MK43 0AA **(T)** 01234 751444 **Capacity:**
Colours(change): Red & white/red/red (Sky blue/white/sky blue)

ADDITIONAL INFORMATION:

CRAWLEY GREEN

Founded: Nickname:

Secretary: Eddie Downey **(T)** 07956 107477 **(E)** eddied@thamesideltd.co.uk
Chairman: Alan Clark **Manager:** Darren Salton **Prog Ed:** Alan Clark
Ground: Barton Rovers FC, Sharpenhoe Road, Barton Le Cay, Beds MK45 4SD **(T)** 01582 882 398 **Capacity:**
Colours(change): All maroon (Sky blue/navy/sky blue)

ADDITIONAL INFORMATION:

HARPENDEN TOWN

Founded: 1891 Nickname: Town

Secretary: Les Crabtree **(T)** 07968 120032 **(E)** les-crabtree@lineone.net
Chairman: Les Crabtree **Manager:** Bob Fowler **Prog Ed:** Dennis Gibbs
Ground: Rothamstead Park, Amenbury Lane, Harpenden AL5 2EF **(T)** 07968 120032 **Capacity:**
Colours(change): Yellow/royal blue/royal blue (Red/red/black)

ADDITIONAL INFORMATION:
Previous Name: Harpenden FC 1891-1908. **Previous League:** Hertfordshire County.
Honours: South Midlands League x2. Hertfordshire Junior Cup x5.

HODDESDON TOWN

Founded: Formed: 1879 Nickname: Lilywhites

Secretary: Jane Sinden **(T)** 01767 631 297 & fax **(E)** janedsinden@fsmail.net
Chairman: Roger Merton **Manager:** Andy Crawford **Prog Ed:** Jane Sinden
Ground: The Stewart Edwards Stadium, Lowfield, Park View Hoddesdon EN11 8PX **(T)** 01992 463 133 **Capacity:**
Colours(change): White/black/black (All blue)

ADDITIONAL INFORMATION:
HONOURS (FA Comps & League): FA Vase 1974-75 (1st Winners).
Spartan League Champions 1970-71, Division 1 1935-36, Division 2 'B' 1927-28

KENTISH TOWN

Founded: 1994 Nickname: Townies

Secretary: Kevin Young **(T)** 07828 288 238 **(E)** kevin@young3493.freeserve.co.uk
Chairman: Catherine Dye **Manager:** John Creith **Prog Ed:** David Pohl
Ground: Barnet Copthall Stadium, Greenlands Lane, Hendon, London NW4 1RL **(T)** 0208 202 6478 **Capacity:**
Colours(change): Sky & navy/navy/blue (All red)

ADDITIONAL INFORMATION:

KINGS LANGLEY

Founded: Nickname:

Secretary: Andy Mackness **(T)** 07976 692801 **(E)** andymackness@yahoo.co.uk
Chairman: Derry Edgar **Manager:** Paul Hobbs **Prog Ed:** Roy Mitchard
Ground: Gaywood Park, Hempstead Road, Kings Langley Herts WD4 8BS **(T)** 07976 692801 **Capacity:**
Colours(change): Black & white stripes/black/black (Red & white stripes/blue/red)

ADDITIONAL INFORMATION:

LANGFORD

Founded: 1908 Nickname: Reds

Secretary: David Jenkins **(T)** 07530 138 934 **(E)** david_jenkinsj@hotmail.com
Chairman: Ian Chessum **Manager:** Wesley Byrne **Prog Ed:** Kerinda Boswell
Ground: Forde Park, Langford Road, Henlow, Beds SG16 6AG **(T)** 01462 816106 **Capacity:** 2,000
Colours(change): All red. (All blue).

ADDITIONAL INFORMATION: Att: 450 v QPR 75th Anniversary 1985

LONDON COLNEY

Founded: 1907 Nickname: Blueboys

Secretary: Dave Brock **(T)** 07508 035835 **(E)** davebrock42@hotmail.com
Chairman: Tony Clafton **Manager:** Ryan Thompson **Prog Ed:** Tony Clafton
Ground: Cotlandswick Playing Fields, London Colney, Herts AL2 1DW **(T)** 01727 822132 **Capacity:**
Colours(change): All royal blue (Red & black or black & white stripes/black/black)

ADDITIONAL INFORMATION:
Record Att: 300 v St Albans City Hertfordshire Senior Cup 1998-99.
Honours: Spartan South Midlands Premier Division 2001-02.

LONDON LIONS
Founded: Nickname:

Secretary: Basil Wein **(T)** 07970 661990 **(E)** basilw@londonlions.com
Chairman: Adam Solomons **Manager:** Tony Gold **Prog Ed:** Dan Jacobs
Ground: V & E Club, Goffs Lane, Cheshunt, Herts EN7 5QN **(T)** 01992 624281 **Capacity:**
Colours(change): All blue (All red or yellow/black/black)

ADDITIONAL INFORMATION:

NEW BRADWELL ST PETER
Founded: 1902 Nickname: Peters

Secretary: Ian Rollins **(T)** 07912 076473 **(E)** honsecretary@newbradwellstpeter.co.uk
Chairman: Scott Booden **Manager:** Gary Flinn **Prog Ed:** Ray Blackbrow
Ground: Recreation Ground, Bradwell Road, Bradville, Milton Keynes MK13 7AD **(T)** 01908 313835 **Capacity:**
Colours(change): All maroon (Yellow/blue/blue)

ADDITIONAL INFORMATION:
Honours: South Midlands Division 1 1976-77, 83-84, Senior Division 1997-98. Berks & Berks Senior Trophy 1999-2000.

ST ALBANS CITY RESERVES
Founded: Nickname: The Saints

Secretary: Steve Eames **(T)** 07805 769083 **(E)** steveeames@safc.co.uk
Chairman: Ian Ridley **Manager:** Franco Sidoli **Prog Ed:** Steve Eames
Ground: Clarence Park, York Road, St Albans, Herts AL1 4PL **(T)** 01727 848 914 **Capacity:**
Colours(change): Blue & yellow stripes/blue/yellow (All red)

ADDITIONAL INFORMATION:

STONY STRATFORD TOWN
Founded: 1898 Nickname:

Secretary: Steve Sartain **(T)** 07901 664000 **(E)** steve.sartain456@btinternet.com
Chairman: Robert Fisher **Manager:** Chris Miller **Prog Ed:** Annette Way
Ground: Ostlers Lane, Stony Stratford, Milton Keynes MK11 1AR **(T)** 07914 012709 **Capacity:**
Colours(change): Sky blue & navy/navy/navy (Yellow/black/black, yellow or white)

ADDITIONAL INFORMATION:
Previous League: Northampton Combination.
Record Att: 476 v Aston Villa U21 1996.

SUN POSTAL SPORTS
Founded: Nickname:

Secretary: Maurice Tibbles **(T)** 07895 066075 **(E)** tibbles.joe@live.com
Chairman: Jim Kempster **Manager:** Scott Patmore **Prog Ed:** Andrew Toon
Ground: Sun Postal Sports Club, Mountwood Avenue, Watford, Herts WD17 3BM **(T)** 01923 227453 **Capacity:**
Colours(change): Yellow/royal blue/royal blue (All Red)

ADDITIONAL INFORMATION:
Previous Names: Sun Postal Sports 2003. Sun Sports 2005.
Previous League: Hertfordshire Senior County > 2003.

TOKYNGTON MANOR
Founded: Nickname:

Secretary: Serine Deacon **(T)** 0208 903 9553 **(E)** hon.secretary@tokyngtonfc.co.uk
Chairman: Terry Springer **Manager:** Steven Sullivan **Prog Ed:** Tokyngton Community Ctr
Ground: Amersham Town FC, Spratleys Meadow, School Lane, Amersham HP7 0EL **(T)** No telephone **Capacity:**
Colours(change): Black & blue stripes/black/black (Yellow/blue/blue)

ADDITIONAL INFORMATION:

WELWYN GARDEN CITY
Founded: 1921 Nickname: Citizens

Secretary: Karen Browne **(T)** 07876 232 670 **(E)** kazzie.browne@gmail.com
Chairman: Gary Bevan **Manager:** Simon Braine **Prog Ed:** Karen Browne
Ground: Herns Way, Welwyn Garden City, Herts AL7 1TA **(T)** 01707 329358 **Capacity:**
Colours(change): Claret & sky blue/claret/sky blue (Orange/black/orange)

ADDITIONAL INFORMATION:
Previous League: Metropolitan & Greater London.
Honours: South Midlands League 1973-74, Division 1 1981-82.

WODSON PARK

Founded: Nickname:

Secretary: Sean Mynott (T) 07812 097 924 (E) seanmynott@aol.com
Chairman: Adam Phipps **Manager:** Kristian Munt **Prog Ed:** Sean Mynott
Ground: Ware FC, Wadesmill Road, Herts SG12 0UQ (T) 01920 463247 **Capacity:**
Colours(change): Green & black stripes/black/black (All amber)

ADDITIONAL INFORMATION:

SPARTAN SOUTH MIDLANDS DIVISION TWO CONSTITUTION 2011-12

ASTON CLINTON .... Aston Clinton Park, London Road, Aston Clinton, Bucks. HP22 5HL............................01296 631818
BLETCHLEY TOWN......................The Irish Centre, Manor Fields, Bletchley, Milton Keynes MK2 2HX 01908 375978
CADDINGTON ....Caddington Recreation Club, Manor Road, Caddington, Luton, Beds LU1 4HH 01582 450151
HALE LEYS UNITED .... Fairford Leys, Pitch 2, Andrews Way, Aylesbury, Bucks HP17 8QQ............................0777 244 0737
KENT ATHLETIC..Tenby Drive, Luton, LU4 9BN 01582 582723
MK WANDERERS.................Kents Hill Pavilion, Frithwood Crescent, Kents Hill, Milton Keynes MK7 6HQ........................ No telephone
MURSLEY UNITED................................ The Playing Field, Station Road, Mursley MK17 0SA.. No telephone
OLD BRADWELL UNITED.................. Abbey Road, Bradwell Village, Milton Keynes, MK13 9AR.......................................01908 312355
PITSTONE AND IVINGHOE ....Pitstone Recreation Ground, Vicarage Road, Pitstone LU7 9EY...........01296 661271 (match days)
RISBOROUGH RANGERS.......... " Windors" Horsenden Lane, Princes Risborough, Bucks HP27 9NE.............................07866 178822
THE 61 FC (LUTON)................................Kingsway Ground, Beverley Road, Luton LU4 8EU 07749 531492
TOTTERNHOE.............................. Recreation Ground, Dunstable Road, Totternhoe, Beds LU6 1QP...............................01582 606738
TRING CORINTHIANS .... Tring Corinthians FC, Icknield Way, Tring, Herts HP23 5HJ.....................................07886 528214
WINSLOW UNITED ....The Recreation Ground, Elmfields Gate, Winslow, Bucks MK18 3JG 01296 713057

GROUND DIRECTIONS - PREMIER & DIVISION ONE

AFC DUNSTABLE - Creasey Park Stadium, Creasey Park Drive, Brewers Hill Road, Dunstable, Beds LU6 1BB Tel 01582 667555
From the South: When travelling north on the A5, go straight across the lights in the centre of Dunstable. Turn left at the next main set of lights into Brewers Hill Road. You will immediately pass the Fire Station on your left. Carry on until you hit the first roundabout. Go over the roundabout and take the immediate right into Creasey Park Drive. *From North:* When travelling south on the A5, go through the chalk cutting and over the first set of traffic lights. At the next set of lights turn right into Brewers Hill Road. Go over the roundabout and take the immediate right into Creasey Park Drive. Public Transport: Creasey Park is well served by buses. Arriva and Centrebus services from Luton, Houghton Regis Leighton Buzzard and Aylesbury all stop at the bottom of Brewers Hill Road. Some 24 services stop directly opposite Creasey Park Drive in Weatherby.

AMERSHAM TOWN - Spratleys Meadow, School Lane, Amersham, Bucks HP7 No telephone
From London, take the A413 towards Aylesbury. At the first roundabout in Amersham where the A413 turns left, keep straight on. Then carry on straight over the next four roundabouts to Amersham Old Town. At the western end of the Old Town turn right into right into Mill Lane. At the top of Mill Lane turn left into School Lane. Ground is 100 yards on the left.

AMPTHILL TOWN - Ampthill Park, Woburn Street, Ampthill Tel: 01525 404440.
From the South, leave M1 at junction 12 Toddington. Turn right as signposted until you meet the junction with the Ampthill bypass. Go straight across until you meet a mini-roundabout at the town centre. Turn left into Woburn Street. The ground is about half a mile on the right, just past a lay-by. From the North, leave the M1 at J13 and turn left. At first set of traffic lights, turn right onto A507 Ridgmont bypass. Continue until you see the right-hand turning signposted for Ampthill. Ground is about a mile on the left, opposite the rugby ground.

AYLESBURY UNITED - Leighton Town FC, Lake Street, Leighton Buzzard, Beds LU7 1RX Tel 01525 373311
From Aylesbury: Take the A418 towards Leighton Buzzard and at the bypass turn right onto the A505. Go straight over the first two roundabouts; then turn left at the third onto the A4146. Stay on the A4146 at the next two roundabouts (second exit, first exit), then carry straight on at the next mini-roundabout. The entrance to the ground is about 50 yards after this mini-roundabout on the left. Car parking is on your left as you turn. Travel from the Midlands using the M1: Leave the M1 at junction 15 and take the A508 towards Milton Keynes. After 9 miles you will reach the A5 roundabout. Take the first exit and travel about 8 miles to the roundabout at the end of the dual carriageway. Take the second exit and follow the A5 towards Dunstable. After about 3 miles you will arrive at another roundabout (Flying Fox pub is on your left) take the third exit towards Heath & Reach and Leighton Buzzard. Follow this road for about 4 miles until you arrive at a large roundabout in Leighton Buzzard then take the first exit. At the next roundabout take the second exit, you will then go through 2 sets of lights. The ground and car park is on the right, immediately after the lights and opposite a petrol station.
From the South: Take the M1 to junction 8 (Hemel Hempstead) and head towards the town centre. As you go down the hill into Hemel you will reach a multi-directional roundabout. Turn right and follow the signs for Leighton Buzzard (A4146). Leighton Buzzard is about 16 miles northwest of Hemel Hempstead along this road.

BEDFORD FC - McMullen Park, Meadow Lane, Cardington, Bedford, MK44 3SB. Tel: 01234 831024
From the M1 Junction 13: take the A421 on to the Bedford Bypass, take the third exit onto the A603, the ground is 250 yards on the left. From the A1 at Sandy: take A603 to Bedford. The ground is on the right just before you reach the Bedford Bypass.

BERKHAMSTED - Broadwater, Lower Kings Road, Berkhamsted HP4 2AL Tel 01442 865977
Exit A41 onto A416. Go straight over the town centre traffic lights into Lower Kings Road. Go over the canal bridge and take first left into Broadwater. Follow the road to the left, going parallel to the canal. The ground is on the right hand side, sandwiched between the canal and the railway.

BIGGLESWADE UNITED - Second Meadow, Fairfield Road, Biggleswade SG18 0BS Tel 01767 316270
From A1 south take second roundabout (Sainsbury's NOT Homebase). Cross the river bridge and then take second left into Sun Street then take first left into Fairfield Road and travel to the very end and into lane. From A1 north, take first roundabout (Sainsbury's) and follow previous instructions.

BROXBOURNE BOROUGH V&E - V & E Club, Goffs Lane, Cheshunt, Herts EN7 5QN Tel & Fax 01992 624281
From M25 Junction 25 take A10 towards Cheshunt, at first roundabout turn left onto B198 (Cuffley and Goffs Oak). Go straight over next roundabout. At next roundabout at end of road, turn right into Goffs Lane. Clubhouse is on immediate right.

BUCKINGHAM ATHLETIC - Stratford Fields, Stratford Road, Buckingham MK18 1NY Tel: 01280 816945 (match days & opening hours only)
From Oxford, Aylesbury or Bletchley: take the Buckingham ring road to the roundabout where the A422 from Stony Stratford/Deanshanger meet - turn left, towards town centre. The ground is situated on the left behind fir trees at the bottom of the hill where 30mph begins (opposite a recently-built block of luxury apartments). From Milton Keynes: Up A5 then (A422) to Buckingham - straight across roundabout towards the town centre - ground location as above. From M1: come off at junction 13 and follow A421 straight through, turning right where it meets the Buckingham ring road – then follow as above, turning left at the next-but-one roundabout.

COLNEY HEATH - The Recreation Ground, High Street, Colney Heath, St Albans, Herts AL4 0NS Tel 01727 826188
From the A1, leave at junction 3 and follow A414 St. Albans. At long roundabout take the left into the village and ground is just past the school on left after 400 yards.
From the M25, leave at junction 22 and follow B556 Colney Heath. On entering the village turn left at Queens Head PH (roundabout) and follow High Street for 1/2 mile. The ground is on the right just before the school. From M1 going south; leave at junction 7. At Park Street roundabout follow A414 Hatfield. Continue on A414 past London Colney. Enter Colney Heath coming round the long roundabout and into village. The ground is past the school on the left after 400 yards.

CHESHAM UNITED RESERVES - The Meadow, Amy Lane, Chesham, Bucks HP5 1NE Tel 01494 783964
Take J20 off the M25 to the A41 Aylesbury/Hemel follow this road for about 7 miles, your turn off is after the Service Station, the turn off is for Berkhamsted/Chesham, take the right hand lane in the slip road to the A416 to Chesham. Follow this road through Ashley Green (being careful of the speed trap) past the college on your left, when you get to the bottom of the hill take a left turn at the mini roundabout. Follow the road for about 1.5 miles, go straight over the next two roundabouts, then get in to the left lane to take the first exit from the next roundabout, you will pass a pub called the Red Lion on your right shortly after this. Follow the road to a mini roundabout; take the right exit going past two petrol stations either side of the road. Ground is on the third exit off the next roundabout. See club website for other routes.

CRANFIELD UNITED - Crawley Road, Cranfield, Beds MK43 0AA Tel: 01234 751444.
upon entering the village, take the North Crawley/Newport Pagnell road. The ground is on the left hand side just before leaving the speed limit zone.

CRAWLEY GREEN - Barton Rovers FC, Sharpenhoe Road, Barton Le Cay, Beds MK45 4SD Tel 01582 882398
From M1 J12, turn right from South turn left from North, onto the A5120. After approximately 1.5 miles, take the second turning on the right signposted Harlington and Barton. Follow the road through Sharpenhoe to Barton. At mini-roundabout turn right and after about 400 yards, turn right into the ground. Ground entrance is in Luton Road.

DUNSTABLE TOWN - Creasey Park Drive, Brewers Hill Road, Dunstable, Beds LU6 1BB Tel 01582 667555
From the south: When travelling on the A5, go straight across the lights in the centre of Dunstable. Turn left at the next main set of lights into Brewers Hill Road. You will immediately pass the Fire Station on your left. Carry on until you hit the first roundabout, Go over the roundabout and take the immediate right into Creasey Park Drive. From the north: When travelling south on the A5, go through the chalk cutting and over the first set of traffic lights. At the next set of lights, turn right into Brewers Hill Road. Then proceed as above. From the East: Turn right at the traffic lights in the centre of Dunstable. Turn left at the next main set of traffic lights into Brewers Hill Road. Then proceed as above. From the east: When coming into Dunstable, go straight across the first roundabout you come to. Then turn left at the double mini-roundabout into Drovers Way. Follow this road for about 1/2 mile as it bears to the right and becomes Brewers Hill Road. Go over two mini-roundabouts and just before you hit the larger roundabout, turn left into Creasey Park Drive.
Public Transport: Creasey Park is well served by buses. Arriva and Centrebus services from Luton, Houghton Regis, Leighton Buzzard and Aylesbury all stop at the bottom of Brewers Hill Road. Some 24 services stop directly opposite Creasey Park Drive in Weatherby.

HADLEY - Potters Bar Town FC, Parkfield Stadium, Watkins Rise (off The Walk), Potters Bar EN6 1QB Tel 01707 654833
From M25, exit at junction 24 towards Potters Bar along Southgate Road A111. Turn right at first set of traffic lights into High Street A1000. After the petrol station on the left and pedestrian crossing, take the first left into The Walk. After 200 yards, turn right into Watkins Rise. The ground is at the end on the right. Nearest BR Station: Potters Bar.
PLEASE NOTE: do not park in the Mayfair Lodge Home car park opposite the ground. Offenders will be clamped.

HANWELL TOWN - Reynolds Field, Perivale Lane, Greenford, Middlesex UB6 8TL Tel 020 8998 1701
From West, junction 16 M25 and follow A40 (M) towards London. Go over the Greenford flyover and get into the nearside lane signposted Ealing & Perivale. Exit and turn right across the A40. The ground is immediately on the left. Turn left into Perivale Lane and the entrance is 200 yards on the left. Nearest railway station is Perivale (London Underground – Central Line).

HAREFIELD UNITED - Preston Park, Breakspear Road North, Harefield, Middlesex, UB9 6NE Tel: 01895 823474.
From the M25 at Junction 16 turn left. At the roundabout turn right towards Denham and at the next roundabout turn left then right at the end of the road. Turn left by the Pub and follow the road over the canal and into the village. Go straight across the roundabout into Breakspear Road and the ground is approximately 800 metres on the right.

HARINGEY BOROUGH - Coles Park, White Hart Lane, Tottenham, London N17 7JP Tel: 020 8889 1415
At junction 25 of the M25 or from the A406 (North Circular Road) turn south onto the A10 (Great Cambridge Road) towards Central London. At the junction of the A10 and White Hart Lane turn right (use slip road at traffic lights) into White Hart Lane and the ground is about 500 yards on the left, some 150 yards after a petrol station. PUBLIC TRANSPORT: Bus W3 from Finsbury Park station to Northumberland Park station via Alexandra Palace station and Wood Green underground station passes ground. In other direction W3 can be boarded at White Hart Lane station).

HARPENDEN TOWN - Rothamstead Park, Amenbury Lane, Harpenden AL5 2EF Tel: 07968 120032
Approaching Harpenden from St. Albans, turn left into Leyton Road at mini-roundabout by the Silver Cup and Fire Station. Coming from Luton, go through the town and as you leave (just past The George) turn right into Leyton Road. Turn left in Amenbury Lane and then left into car park after 300 yards. Entrance to the Club is up the pathway, diagonally across the car park in the far corner from the entrance. This is a pay-and-display car park up to 6.30pm.

HATFIELD TOWN - Gosling Sports Park, Stanborough Road, Welwyn Garden City, Herts AL8 6XE Tel 01707 384300
From A1 (M) junction 4, take A414 towards Hertford/Welwyn Garden City. At the roundabout take the 1st exit onto the A6129, heading to Stanborough/Wheathampstead. At the next roundabout take the 2nd exit onto the A6129 Stanborough Road. At the next roundabout take the 3rd exit into Gosling Sports Park.

HERTFORD TOWN - Hertingfordbury Park, West Street, Hertford, Herts SG13 8EZ Tel 01992 583716
From the A1 follow the A414 to Hertford until you see Gates Ford Dealership on the right. At next roundabout double back and immediately past Gates (now on your left) turn left into West Street. This is a narrow road and when it bears left, turn right and go down the hill and over a bridge to the ground. From the A10 follow the A414 until you see Gates.

HILLINGDON BOROUGH - Middlesex Stadium, Breakspear Road, Ruislip, Middlesex HA4 7SB Tel 01895 639544
From M40/A40 eastbound, leave the A40 at the Swakeleys roundabout, exit is sign-posted Ickenham & Ruislip and take the B467. At the second mini-roundabout turn left into Breakspear Road South. After approx 1 mile, turn right into Breakspear Road by the Breakspear Arms PH. The ground is a further 1/2 mile on the left-hand side.

HODDESDON TOWN - Stewart Edwards Stadium, Lowfield, Park View, Hoddesdon, Herts, EN11 8PU Tel: 01992 463133
For SatNav users, please key in EN11 8PX, which will take you to Park Road, directly opposite the ground
From the A10, take Hoddesdon turnoff (A1170). Follow the slip road to the roundabout at the bottom of the hill and then turn right into Amwell Street. Take the first right, at the church, into Pauls Lane. Follow the road round to left which becomes Taveners Way. At the mini-roundabout opposite the Iceland store, turn right into Brocket Road. At T junction turn left into Park View and the ground is 200 yards on the right.

HOLMER GREEN - Airedale Park, Watchet Lane, Holmer Green, Bucks HP15 6UF Tel 01494 711485
From Amersham on A404 High Wycombe Road. After approx 2 miles turn right into Sheepcote Dell Road. Continue until end of road at Bat & Ball pub. Turn right, then immediately left. Continue approx 1/2 mile until double mini-roundabouts. Turn left in front of the Mandarin Duck restaurant into Airedale Park 150 yards on the right

KENTISH TOWN - Barnet Copthall Stadium, Greenlands Lane, Hendon, London NW4 1RL Tel 020 8202 6478
From the North: take the M1, exiting at junction 4 (Edgware & Harrow.) onto the A41 towards Mill Hill, at the apex of the corner (junction with A1) go straight ahead on the A41. Go over a small roundabout and at the traffic lights (just before the M1 flyover) turn left into Page Street. Travel for about 1/2 mile and turn right into Champions Way. At mini-roundabout turn right into Greenlands Lane and the Stadium complex is on the left. From The South: Follow the A1/A41 towards Mill Hill. At the junction under the M1 flyover, turn right at the traffic lights into Page Street and follow the directions above. Nearest Tube Station is Mill Hill Broadway.
Please note that the service road by the stadium has several small posts which should be avoided.

KINGS LANGLEY - Gaywood Park, Hempstead Road, Kings Langley Herts WD4 8BS Tel: 07976 692801

From M25 leave at junction 20. Take A4251 to Kings Langley. Go through the village. The ground is approximately 1/2 mile on the right.

LANGFORD - Forde Park, Langford Road, Henlow, Beds SG16 6AG Tel: 01462 816106.

From West along A57 to Henlow then north on A6001. Ground at north end of Henlow

From North and East, leave A1 at Langford water tower then into Langford. Turn left at Boot Restaurant. Follow A6001 round to the left. Club is 1/2 mile away.

LEVERSTOCK GREEN - Pancake Lane, Leverstock Green, Hemel Hempstead, Herts Tel: 01442 246280.

From M1 at Junction 8, Follow A414 to second roundabout turn left along Leverstock Green Way. Pancake Lane is on the left 300 yards past the Leather Bottle Public House. Ground is 300 yards on left. All visitors are requested to park inside the ground.

LONDON COLNEY - Cotlandswick Playing Fields, London Colney, Herts AL2 1DW Tel: 01727 822132.

From M25 J22, follow the A1081 signposted to St Albans. At London Colney roundabout take A414, signposted Hemel Hempstead/Watford. There is a hidden turn into the ground after approximately 500 metres (just after lay-by) signposted Sports Ground and London Colney FC. Follow the ground around between the Rugby and Irish clubs to ground entrance.

LONDON LIONS - V & E Club, Goffs Lane, Cheshunt, Herts EN7 5QN Tel & Fax 01992 624281

From M25 Junction 25 take A10 towards Cheshunt, at first roundabout turn left onto B198 (Cuffley and Goffs Oak). Go straight over next roundabout. At next roundabout at end of road, turn right into Goffs Lane. Clubhouse is on immediate right.

LONDON TIGERS - Avenue Park, Western Avenue, Perivale, Greenford, Middlesex UB6 8GA Tel 020 7289 3395 (10am-6pm) – out of hours please call 07949 189191

Exit junction 16 of the M25 onto the A40 (M) towards London. After you pass the Target roundabout there will be a sharp left turn at the 200yard marker for the Greenford slip road from the A40 into Avenue Park, just past the overhead footbridge. If coming from Central London or Hangar Lane, drive up to the Target roundabout and do a U-turn onto the eastbound carriageway and turn left into Avenue Park after the footbridge. The nearest Tube station is Greenford on the Central Line, which is a 10-minute walk.

NEW BRADWELL ST PETER - Recreation Ground, Bradwell Road, Bradville, Milton Keynes MK13 7AD Tel: 01908 313835.

From M1 J14 go towards Newport Pagnell, turn left at first roundabout into H3 (A422 Monks Way). Go six roundabouts then turn right into V6 (Grafton Street). At first roundabout drive all the way around and then take the first left. At first mini-roundabout, turn left. Go 1/2 mile and straight across next mini-roundabout. Ground is then immediately on the left.

From Bushey Station, take Pinner Road (A4008) and continue along Oxhey Lane (towards Harrow). At the traffic lights turn right into Little Oxhey Lane. Altham Way is on left just after crossing Railway Bridge. Clubhouse is located next to swimming pool. Please park in the Pool/Jets overflow car park to avoid either blocking in cars, or being blocked in yourself.

ROYSTON TOWN - Garden Walk, Royston, Herts SG8 7HP. Tel: 01763 241204.

From A505 (town bypass), take A10 towards town centre. Go straight on at next roundabout. Garden Walk is the second turning on the left. Entrance to ground is approx. 200 metres on left.

ST ALBANS CITY RESERVES - Clarence Park, York Road, St Albans, Herts AL1 4PL Tel 01727 864296

From the North (M1): Take the M10 exit at junction 7 to St Albans. At the end of motorway take 2nd exit at roundabout onto A405. At next roundabout turn left onto A1081. Follow the road for approx 1 mile until mini-roundabout (GREAT NORTHERN PUB ON LEFT). Turn right into Alma Road. At traffic lights turn right into Victoria Street and continue to junction with Crown pub. Go straight across into Clarence Road, ground is first on left about 50 yards past junction or the next turning on the left into York Road, ground entrance is at the end of the road on the left.

From the North (A1M): Come off A1 (M) at junction 3 onto A414 to St Albans. At next major roundabout take A1081 exit to St Albans. Follow road for approx 1 mile until mini-roundabout (GREAT NORTHERN PUB ON LEFT). Then proceed as above.

From the West (A5183/A4147): At Batchwood Hall roundabout go straight on towards St Albans. At next mini-roundabout bear left past petrol station into Catherine Street. Follow road up to roundabout at top of St Peters Street in City centre. Go straight across into Hatfield Road, then straight over another mini-roundabout and over railway line to Crown pub junction. Turn left into Clarence Road, ground is about 50 yards past junction or take next turning on the left into York Road. Ground entrance is at the end of the road on the left.

From the M25 (clockwise): Exit M25 at junction 22 (A1081). Follow signs to St Albans from slip road. At London Colney roundabout (traffic light controlled) exit onto A1081. Follow road for approx 1 mile until mini-roundabout (GREAT NORTHERN PUB ON LEFT). Then proceed as above.

Parking: Ac small amount of parking is available at the Clarence Road entrance, if not, the station car park can be used or surrounding roads, but do not block driveways and be aware of local parking restrictions. Public Transport: St Albans City station is on the Thameslink service from Kings Cross Thameslink (20 minutes). Turn left out of the station into Station Way and cross Hatfield Road into Clarence Park. Follow the path round to the right of the ground until you reach the main entrance.

ST. MARGARETSBURY - Station Road, St. Margarets, Herts SG12 8EH Tel: 01920 870473

A10 to Cambridge. Exit at A414 Harlow & Chelmsford. Proceed 400 yards to Amwell roundabout and take 3rd exit (B181) to Stanstead Abbotts. Ground is 1/2 mile on the right-hand side.

STONY STRATFORD TOWN - Ostlers Lane, Stony Stratford, Milton Keynes MK11 1AR Tel: 07914 012709

From Dunstable on the A5 heading north: On approaching Bletchley continue on the main A5 trunk road signposted to Towcester & Hinckley. Continue to the very end of dual carriageway, where you will meet a main roundabout. This is where the main A5 intersects with the A508 to Northampton. At this roundabout take first exit, this is the old (single carriageway) A5. Follow the main road, straight through the traffic lights, over the river bridge and take the second turning right into Ostlers Lane. The ground is approx 200yds on the right.

From Buckingham on the A422: Continue on the A422, straight on at the first roundabout (pedestrian footbridge overhead). Continue on until you meet the next roundabout and take the last exit (the old single carriageway A5). Then proceed as above.

STOTFOLD - Roker Park, The Green, Stotfold, Hitchin, Herts SG5 4AN Tel 01462 730765

At A1 junction 10, take the A507 to Stotfold and right into town. Proceed along High Street and at traffic lights turn right (from Hitchin – straight over traffic lights) towards Astwick Turn right at the Crown pub into The Green. The ground is set back from The Green on the left.

SUN POSTAL SPORTS - Sun Postal Sports Club, Mountwood Avenue, Watford, Herts WD17 3BM Tel: 01923 227453

From Watford town centre take the A411 (Hempstead Road) away from the Town Hall towards Hemel Hempstead. At 2nd set of traffic lights turn left into Langley Way. At the next roundabout, where there is a parade of shops on the left and the "Essex Arms" on the right, take the third exit into Cassiobury Drive. Then take the first turn left into Bellmountwood Avenue then at the left hand bend turn right into the Club entrance.

TOKYNGTON MANOR - Amersham Town FC, Spratleys Meadow, School Lane, Amersham, Bucks HP7 0EL No telephone in clubhouse

From London take the A413 towards Aylesbury. At the far (western) end of Amersham Old Town turn right into Mill Lane. At the junction at the top of the Mill Lane, turn left into School Lane. The ground is 100 metres on the left.

TRING ATHLETIC - The Grass Roots Stadium, Pendley Sports Centre, Cow Lane, Tring, Herts HP23 5NT. Tel: 01442 891144

From M25 take A41 to Aylesbury. At roundabout at junction take last exit sign-posted Berkhamsted. Turn next left into Cow Lane. Stadium is on the right at end of Cow Lane.

WODSON PARK - Ware FC, Wadesmill Road, Herts SG12 0UQ Tel 01920 463247

From the South: leave the M25 at junction 25 and take the A10 north past Cheshunt and Hoddesdon. After crossing the Lea Valley with Ware below and to your right, leave the A10 at the junction for the A1170 (signposted for Wadesmill and Thundridge). The slip road comes off the A10 onto a roundabout. Turn left (first exit) onto Wadesmill Road (A1170) and come back over the A10 to a second roundabout. Go straight over and take the first turn on the left into Wodson Park Sports Centre. The football ground is on the far left of the car park. From the North: Leave the A10 at the Ware North turn off (A1170). The slip road takes you to a roundabout. Turn right (3rd exit) into Wadesmill Road and take the first left into Wodson Park Sports Centre.

SUSSEX COUNTY LEAGUE

Sponsored by: No sponsor
Founded: 1920
Recent Champions:
2006: Horsham YMCA
2007: Eastbourne Town
2008: Crowborough Athletic
2009: Eastbourne United Association
2110: Whitehawk
scfl.org.uk

DIVISION ONE	P	W	D	L	F	A	Pts
1 Crawley Down	38	28	7	3	100	35	91
2 Rye United	38	23	7	8	76	37	76
3 Peacehaven & Telscombe	38	22	10	6	74	38	76
4 Pagham	38	23	2	13	91	53	71
5 Three Bridges	38	23	1	14	69	49	70
6 Hassocks	38	19	11	8	64	38	68
7 East Grinstead Town	38	20	6	12	88	50	66
8 Redhill	38	16	8	14	77	68	56
9 Arundel	38	15	9	14	81	68	54
10 Ringmer	38	16	4	18	67	72	52
11 Lingfield	38	13	10	15	71	83	49
12 Crowborough Athletic	38	14	6	18	59	67	48
13 Sidley United	38	13	9	16	46	59	48
14 Chichester United (-3)	38	14	6	18	57	62	45
15 Wick	38	13	6	19	54	74	45
16 Hailsham Town	38	13	5	20	66	71	44
17 Selsey	38	13	5	20	49	78	44
18 Shoreham	38	8	7	23	46	89	31
19 St Francis Rangers	38	8	5	25	35	81	29
20 Eastbourne Utd Association	38	2	4	32	26	124	10

JOHN O'HARA CUP
(Division One & Division Two teams)

ROUND 1
Rye United 2-1 Chichester City
Selsey 1-0 Westfield
St Francis Rangers 3-2 Bexhill United
Worthing United 1-6 Arundel
Storrington 3-2 Littlehampton Town
Steyning Town 0-2 Lingfield

ROUND 2
AFC Uckfield 1-3 Peacehaven & Telscombe
Arundel 2-4 Redhill
East Grinstead Town 2-1 Ringmer
Eastbourne United 2-5 Crawley Down
Loxwood 1-3 Rustington
Midhurst 7 Easebourne 0-3 Pagham
Mile Oak 2-0 :Little Common
Rye United 2-0 Hassocks
Selsey 1-2 Lancing
Shoreham 5-2 Hailsham Town
Sidley United 0-1 Seaford Town
Southwick 2-1 St Francis Rangers
Storrington 4-0 Clymping
Wick 0-1 Crowborough Athletic
Oakwood 1-4 Three Bridges
Lingfield 1-3 East Preston

ROUND 3
Crowborough Athletic 1-2 Shoreham
East Grinstead 0-1 Crawley Down
East Preston 2-3 Mile Oak
Lancing 4-2 Storrington
Pagham 1-1 Rye United
Seaford Town 1-1 Rustington
Southwick 3-2 Peacehaven & Telscombe
Three Bridges 3-0 Redhill
Round 3 Replays
Rustington 4-3 Seaford Town
Rye United 3-2 Pagham

QUARTER FINALS
Shoreham 1-3 Three Bridges
Southwick 2-6 Crawley Down
Rye United 4-3 Mile Oak
Lancing 4-5 Rustington

SEMI-FINALS
Rustington 1-2 Rye United (@ Peacehaven & Telscombe)
Crawley Down 3-4 Three Bridges (@ East Grinstead Town)

FINAL (@ Lancing, 22/4/11)
Rye United 1-2 Three Bridges

DIVISION ONE	1	2	3	4	5	6	7	8	9	10	11	12	13	14	15	16	17	18	19	20
1 Arundel		0-2	1-1	2-3	0-0	3-2	2-3	1-1	0-2	2-4	3-3	2-4	1-1	3-3	2-0	4-2	2-0	4-2	1-2	6-2
2 Chichester City	1-5		2-2	2-0	1-3	3-0	1-0	1-2	2-0	1-2	0-1	3-2	2-0	0-2	3-4	2-2	1-2	2-1	1-0	8-0
3 Crawley Down	5-1	2-0		2-0	3-1	3-0	5-1	2-0	4-1	2-1	0-0	3-0	2-1	0-3	7-0	4-0	4-2	3-1	5-2	1-0
4 Crowborough Athletic	2-4	2-2	1-1		1-2	3-1	3-5	1-1	1-2	0-4	1-1	0-2	1-2	2-1	2-1	4-0	1-0	3-1	0-1	5-0
5 East Grinstead Town	2-1	5-0	1-1	3-1		4-1	3-3	0-1	6-2	0-2	1-0	3-0	3-4	2-3	2-0	10-2	2-1	3-0	0-1	1-0
6 Eastbourne United Assoc	2-5	2-4	1-5	2-1	0-4		0-2	0-2	1-2	1-8	1-0	1-1	0-1	0-2	0-0	2-4	0-2	2-3	1-6	0-0
7 Hailsham Town	4-0	2-0	2-6	0-1	0-0	1-0		0-2	0-2	2-3	1-2	2-6	1-2	0-0	1-1	1-4	2-0	2-0	1-2	1-0
8 Hassocks	1-1	1-0	0-2	1-3	0-3	2-1	2-4		1-1	4-2	1-1	2-1	5-0	1-1	2-1	2-0	5-0	3-0	0-1	3-0
9 Lingfield	1-3	3-3	2-3	0-3	3-2	3-0	2-2	1-0		2-0	2-2	2-2	3-1	3-3	2-3	2-5	2-2	1-0	4-1	2-3
10 Pagham	3-1	1-2	1-4	2-0	3-1	6-0	3-1	1-1	5-2		0-3	2-0	4-1	1-1	0-1	3-1	1-2	4-2	0-1	2-3
11 Peacehaven & Telscombe	2-0	2-0	2-2	3-0	2-0	9-1	4-3	1-1	6-3	1-0		4-3	3-1	1-0	2-0	0-1	0-2	3-1	1-0	4-1
12 Redhill	2-2	1-1	3-1	3-0	3-1	6-0	2-5	1-3	4-2	0-6	1-0		1-3	0-1	4-0	2-2	0-0	3-1	3-2	4-1
13 Ringmer	0-3	1-1	1-3	1-5	1-1	5-0	1-5	1-1	2-0	4-1	0-1	0-2		0-1	4-1	6-1	3-1	5-2	0-2	1-0
14 Rye United	2-1	1-0	0-2	4-1	5-2	5-0	1-0	1-2	2-2	1-3	1-2	0-1	2-1		0-1	1-0	5-0	4-0	4-0	1-0
15 Selsey	2-0	1-3	0-2	2-1	1-6	3-0	2-0	0-1	2-5	0-3	1-3	3-3	3-6	0-2		0-3	1-1	2-2	0-2	2-1
16 Shoreham	0-3	1-2	1-2	1-2	1-4	2-2	1-0	1-4	1-1	2-3	2-2	3-0	1-2	0-3	0-3		0-3	0-1	0-2	0-2
17 Sidley United	1-1	2-1	0-3	2-2	1-0	3-1	2-1	3-1	2-0	0-2	1-1	1-1	0-1	2-2	0-2	0-0		2-4	0-1	2-1
18 St Francis Rangers	0-6	2-0	1-2	1-1	0-3	1-0	0-4	0-0	0-3	1-3	0-1	1-3	1-0	0-1	2-1	0-0	0-1		1-2	2-1
19 Three Bridges	0-3	4-0	2-1	0-1	1-3	9-1	2-1	1-1	5-0	2-0	2-0	3-2	3-1	1-2	0-2	0-1	4-3	2-0		0-2
20 Wick	1-2	1-0	0-0	5-1	1-1	1-0	4-3	0-4	1-1	1-2	1-1	2-1	5-3	3-5	1-3	5-1	1-0	1-1	3-0	

DIVISION TWO	P	W	D	L	F	A	Pts
1 AFC Uckfield	34	24	7	3	107	47	79
2 Lancing	34	24	6	4	103	30	78
3 Worthing United	34	22	7	5	84	38	73
4 Bexhill United	34	17	9	8	71	47	60
5 Seaford Town	34	16	10	8	69	42	58
6 Loxwood	34	18	4	12	71	51	58
7 Mile Oak	34	18	4	12	71	52	58
8 Storrington	34	15	4	15	64	57	49
9 Rustington	34	14	7	13	51	46	49
10 Westfield	34	14	7	13	67	70	49
11 Littlehampton Town	34	12	9	13	71	72	45
12 Southwick	34	13	6	15	55	59	45
13 Little Common	34	12	7	15	55	61	43
14 East Preston	34	9	7	18	57	84	34
15 Midhurst & Easebourne	34	7	6	21	40	74	27
16 Steyning Town	34	6	7	21	52	103	25
17 Oakwood	34	3	7	24	42	100	16
18 Clymping	34	3	4	27	33	130	13

DIVISION TWO CUP

ROUND 1
Southwick 2-0 Worthing United
Loxwood 3-0 East Preston

ROUND 2
Littlehampton Town 3-4 Little Common
Midhurst & Easebourne 1-3 Storrington
Westfield 0-2 Bexhill United
Oakwood 1-7 AFC Uckfield
Rustington 4-0 Mile Oak
Steyning Town 1-3 Southwick
Lancing 1-0 Seaford Town
Clymping 6-3 Loxwood

QUARTER FINALS
Storrington 2-1 Southwick
Rustington 2-1 Bexhill United
Little Common 5-2 Clymping
AFC Uckfield 5-1 Lancing

SEMI-FINALS
Storrington 3-2 Rustington
Little Common 3-4 AFC Uckfield

FINAL (@ Lancing, 22/4/11)
Storrington 1-2 AFC Uckfield

DIVISION TWO	1	2	3	4	5	6	7	8	9	10	11	12	13	14	15	16	17	18
1 AFC Uckfield		4-2	10-0	2-2	0-0	7-1	4-3	4-1	3-1	2-0	4-0	2-0	0-0	4-2	7-2	4-2	1-2	1-1
2 Bexhill United	2-3		5-0	4-2	1-1	4-0	4-2	1-3	1-1	3-2	3-2	2-0	2-1	3-0	5-0	3-0	1-1	0-0
3 Clymping	2-2	1-3		2-2	1-3	1-2	0-0	1-6	0-2	1-6	3-2	2-3	0-4	0-5	1-5	0-9	1-4	1-7
4 East Preston	3-2	1-4	1-3		0-4	1-3	2-4	2-2	2-1	1-2	0-1	0-5	3-4	0-1	2-2	1-2	4-3	2-4
5 Lancing	2-0	2-2	7-1	3-0		3-2	4-3	3-0	8-1	2-0	8-0	2-0	4-1	2-2	9-0	2-0	3-2	1-2
6 Little Common Albion	2-7	4-0	1-2	2-2	1-5		0-1	2-2	1-0	0-0	4-0	2-1	0-2	3-1	3-2	0-0	2-3	0-1
7 Littlehampton Town	3-3	1-1	4-0	2-5	2-4	1-1		3-2	2-1	3-2	6-0	2-2	1-1	2-4	2-2	2-2	4-2	1-3
8 Loxwood	1-2	1-0	4-2	5-0	1-0	2-0	1-2		2-0	5-1	1-0	0-2	2-2	2-1	3-4	0-3	3-1	0-2
9 Midhurst & Easebourne	1-4	1-2	1-0	2-2	1-4	1-0	3-3	0-5		0-3	1-0	1-3	1-1	2-3	1-0	3-4	1-2	0-3
10 Mile Oak	2-3	4-2	4-0	1-2	1-4	2-1	1-2	2-3	2-1		1-1	2-1	2-3	4-2	1-0	1-0	1-1	1-1
11 Oakwood	2-6	2-3	1-1	2-6	2-2	2-6	1-2	0-2	3-3	0-2		1-3	2-3	1-2	4-4	1-2	4-2	1-3
12 Rustington	2-4	0-0	2-0	2-0	0-1	1-1	3-1	1-0	1-2	0-2	1-0		1-1	3-1	4-1	0-0	4-5	1-3
13 Seaford Town	2-3	1-1	3-1	0-1	1-0	2-1	2-0	1-1	0-1	1-2	6-1	4-0		1-1	2-1	1-2	4-2	1-2
14 Southwick	1-1	2-1	3-2	3-1	1-1	0-2	2-1	1-2	1-0	0-6	4-0	0-0	0-1		1-1	1-2	2-1	1-2
15 Steyning Town	0-1	2-2	4-1	3-4	0-4	3-3	1-2	0-5	1-0	3-2	2-1	1-2	0-4	0-4		1-4	2-3	0-3
16 Storrington	1-3	2-0	3-1	1-1	0-2	0-1	3-1	1-3	2-1	2-3	1-2	1-2	3-8	2-1	6-1		3-0	0-2
17 Westfield	2-3	0-1	5-1	2-0	2-1	0-3	2-0	2-0	3-3	1-3	1-1	2-1	1-1	1-0	4-4	2-0		1-6
18 Worthing United	0-1	1-3	7-1	1-2	0-2	2-1	4-3	5-1	3-2	1-3	2-2	0-0	0-0	5-2	3-0	3-1	2-2	

DIVISION THREE	P	W	D	L	F	A	Pts
1 Dorking Wanderers	30	24	2	4	93	35	74
2 Hurstpierpoint	30	18	4	8	61	37	58
3 Barnham	30	16	7	7	60	39	55
4 Bosham	30	17	4	9	73	55	55
5 Saltdean United	30	15	6	9	71	49	51
6 Broadbridge Heath	30	15	4	11	61	45	49
7 Newhaven	30	15	1	14	73	64	46
8 Haywards Heath Town	30	12	6	12	52	56	42
9 Pease Pottage Village	30	12	5	13	66	62	41
10 Rottingdean Village	30	11	6	13	41	49	39
11 TD Shipley	30	9	7	14	58	71	34
12 Ferring	30	9	6	15	56	67	33
13 Ifield Edwards	30	8	6	16	48	76	30
14 Uckfield Town	30	8	5	17	49	76	29
15 Forest	30	6	8	16	40	68	26
16 Sidlesham	30	4	5	21	39	92	17

DIVISION THREE CUP

ROUND 1
Forest 0-6 TD Shipley
Ifield Edwards 1-3 Hurstpierpoint
Pease Pottage Vilage 4-2 Dorking Wanderers
Sidlesham 1-0 Ferring
Uckfield Town 1-3 Rottingdean Village
Broadbridge Heath 2-1 Haywards Heath Town
Newhaven 1-2 Bosham
Barnham 0-3 Saltdean United

QUARTER FINALS
Bosham 3-2 Broadbridge Heath
Sidlesham 0-3 Saltdean United
TD Shipley 1-1 Rottingdean Village (Rottingdean Village won 6-5 on penalties)
Hurstpierpoint 0-4 Pease Pottage Village

SEMI-FINALS
Bosham 1-2 Rottingdean Village (@ Shoreham)
Saltdean United 2-0 Pease Pottage Village (@ Shoreham)

FINAL (@ Newhaven, 22/4/11)
Saltdean United 1-0 Rottingdean Village

DIVISION THREE	1	2	3	4	5	6	7	8	9	10	11	12	13	14	15	16
1 Barnham		3-3	2-1	2-3	1-0	1-1	3-1	0-2	2-1	0-1	3-5	1-0	2-0	1-1	5-0	4-1
2 Bosham	3-3		2-1	1-2	1-1	3-1	1-2	4-2	5-2	2-1	3-2	0-2	5-4	4-1	4-1	5-2
3 Broadbridge Heath	3-1	1-3		0-1	2-4	5-0	1-1	2-4	4-1	1-2	1-3	3-0	1-1	6-2	3-1	1-0
4 Dorking Wanderers	5-0	2-0	0-1		4-0	5-1	3-1	1-0	6-0	4-0	4-1	3-1	0-0	6-0	6-0	4-1
5 Ferring	0-2	1-4	1-2	3-4		1-1	2-0	1-1	4-1	6-3	3-2	1-1	1-4	4-0	1-2	1-1
6 Forest	1-1	1-2	3-2	2-3	0-1		0-3	2-5	3-3	2-1	1-1	1-2	3-3	5-0	2-1	1-2
7 Haywards Heath Town	1-4	2-1	1-1	2-4	2-1	0-1		1-2	1-1	2-2	3-4	2-2	2-1	1-0	1-0	4-0
8 Hurstpierpoint	0-0	1-0	0-3	3-1	3-1	4-1	2-1		2-3	1-0	4-3	4-0	2-4	1-0	1-1	3-0
9 Ifield Edwards	0-5	1-2	1-3	1-5	4-1	2-0	0-3	3-2		0-3	1-3	0-1	3-3	3-0	1-1	3-2
10 Newhaven	1-3	4-2	5-1	2-4	6-2	3-1	3-0	0-3	1-3		3-1	4-5	1-5	1-0	5-1	0-1
11 Pease Pottage Village	1-2	1-1	2-0	3-4	5-1	1-1	3-2	0-3	3-1	2-4		4-4	0-2	1-4	0-1	4-1
12 Rottingdean Village	0-2	5-2	0-1	1-0	2-1	1-0	1-2	0-2	2-0	2-3	0-1		2-1	2-0	1-1	1-1
13 Saltdean United	2-0	2-3	1-3	3-1	2-2	2-0	1-2	2-0	1-0	0-6	2-1	4-0		7-0	1-1	3-2
14 Sidlesham	0-3	0-2	2-3	1-1	3-5	2-2	2-2	0-0	2-3	3-2	1-4	1-0	3-5		3-4	4-2
15 T D Shipley	2-2	2-4	1-1	1-2	3-2	2-3	5-6	0-2	3-3	7-0	1-4	3-2	3-2	7-2		2-0
16 Uckfield Town	0-2	2-1	0-4	4-5	1-4	6-0	5-1	3-2	3-3	0-6	1-1	1-1	0-3	5-2	2-1	

RESERVE DIVISION PREMIER	P	W	D	L	F	A	Pts
1 Eastbourne Town res	22	20	1	1	74	15	61
2 Hassocks reserves	22	15	6	1	62	23	51
3 Pagham reserves	22	15	3	4	62	33	48
4 Mile Oak reserves	22	13	2	7	58	42	41
5 East Preston reserves	22	9	1	12	35	33	28
6 Eastbourne Utd Ass res	22	8	4	10	38	47	28
7 Hailsham Town reserves	22	7	5	10	26	50	26
8 Peacehaven & Tels res	22	6	4	12	30	44	22
9 St Francis Rangers res	22	5	6	11	45	55	21
10 Haywards Heath Tn res	22	6	3	13	39	64	21
11 Selsey reserves	22	6	3	13	29	58	21
12 Wick reserves	22	2	2	18	27	61	8

RESERVE DIVISION EAST	P	W	D	L	F	A	Pts
1 Sidley United reserves	22	17	2	3	63	20	53
2 Rye United reserves (-3)	22	16	3	3	62	34	48
3 Seaford Town reserves	22	13	3	6	43	33	42
4 AFC Uckfield reserves	22	11	5	6	60	35	38
5 Little Common reserves	22	11	1	10	60	50	34
6 Newhaven reserves	22	10	2	10	49	38	32
7 Bexhill United reserves	22	8	6	8	45	56	30
8 Ringmer reserves	22	8	4	10	38	40	28
9 Westfield reserves	22	6	6	10	38	62	24
10 Southwick reserves	22	4	4	14	31	47	16
11 Saltdean United reserves	22	4	3	15	28	64	15
12 Pease Pottage Village res	22	2	5	15	34	72	11

RESERVE DIVISION WEST	P	W	D	L	F	A	Pts
1 Lancing reserves	22	18	2	2	84	28	56
2 Dorking Wanderers res	22	17	1	4	76	31	52
3 Littlehampton Town res	22	15	4	3	67	28	49
4 Storrington reserves	22	13	2	7	58	33	41
5 Loxwood reserves	22	10	6	6	60	45	36
6 Chichester City reserves	22	10	3	9	50	39	33
7 Shoreham reserves	22	10	0	12	52	46	30
8 Bosham reserves	22	5	4	13	29	64	19
9 Steyning Town reserves	22	5	3	14	20	51	18
10 Rustington reserves	22	4	4	14	38	68	16
11 Broadbridge Heath rese	22	4	4	14	32	63	16
12 Midhurst & Easeb' res	22	3	3	16	33	103	12

NORMAN WINGATE TROPHY
(Division One champions v John O'Hara Cup holders)

FINAL (@ Peacehaven & Telscombe, 27/7/10)

Peacehaven & Telscombe 0-4 Whitehawk

DIVISION TWO CUP

ROUND 1

Haywards Heath Town reserves 1-2 Eastbourne Town reserves
Pease Pottage Village 2-6 Southwick reserves
Saltdean United reserves 0-6 Bexhill United reserves
Steyning Town reserves 1-2 Westfield reserves

ROUND 2

Hailsham Town reserves 3-4 Little Common reserves
AFC Uckfield reserves 5-3 Loxwood reserves
Newhaven reserves 2-3 Chichester City reserves
St Francis Rangers reserves 1-3 Lancing reserves
Broadbridge Heath reserves 0-3 Eastbourne United reserves
Selsey reserves 8-1 Midhurst & Easebourne reserves
Storrington reserves 6-0 Bosham reserves
Seaford Town reserves 4-1 Bexhill United reserves
Southwick reserves 3-2 Littlehampton Town reserves
Ringmer reserves 1-4 Rustington reserves
Rye United reserves 1-3 East Preston reserves
Sidley United reserves 5-2 Peacehaven & Telscombe reserves
Eastbourne Town reserves 0-1 Pagham reserves
Hassocks reserves 3-2 Wick reserves
Dorking Wanderers reserves 3-1 Westfield reserves
Shoreham reserves 1-4 Mile Oak reserves

ROUND 3

Southwick reserves 3-4 Little Common reserves
Seaford Town reserves 0-6 AFC Uckfield reserves
Hassocks reserves 7-0 Chichester City reserves
East Preston reserves 0-3 Storrington reserves
Rustington reserves 3-0 Eastbourne United reserves
Sidley United reserves 4-3 Lancing reserves
Pagham reserves 2-3 Mile Oak reserves
Selsey reserves 0-2 Dorking Wanderers reserves

QUARTER FINALS

Little Common reserves 4-2 Storrington reserves
Rustington reserves 0-1 Sidley United reserves
Dorking Wanderers reserves 1-3 Hassocks reserves
Mile Oak reserves 6-3 AFC Uckfield reserves

SEMI-FINALS

Little Common reserves 1-2 Mile Oak reserves (@ Ringmer)
Hassocks reserves 2-1 Sidley United reserves (@ Ringmer)

FINAL (@ Ringmer, 18/4/11)

Hassocks reserves 2-3 Mile Oak reserves

SUSSEX LEAGUE INS & OUTS

DIV ONE - IN: AFC Uckfield (P), Horsham YMCA (R - Isthmian League Division One South), Lancing (P), Worthing United (P) **OUT:** Crawley Down (P - Isthmian League Division One South), Eastbourne United Association (R), Hailsham Town (R), Wick (R)

DIV TWO - IN: Dorking Wanderers (P), Eastbourne United Association (R), Hailsham Town (R), Wick (R)
OUT: AFC Uckfield (P), Clymping (R), Lancing (P), Worthing United (P)

DIV THREE- IN: Clymping (R), Roffey (P - Mid-Sussex League Premier Division) **OUT:** Dorking Wanderers (P), Sidlesham (R - West Sussex League Premier Division)

A.F.C. UCKFIELD

Founded: 1988 Nickname:

Secretary: Derek York **(T)** 07847 453 767 **(E)** d-york1@sky.com
Chairman: Tom Parker **Manager:** Kevin Laundon **Prog Ed:** Anthony Harvey
Ground: The Oaks, Old Eastbourne Road, Uckfield TN22 5QL **(T)** 07847 662 337
Capacity: **Seats:** **Covered:** **Midweek Matchday:** **Clubhouse:** Yes **Shop:**

Colours(change): Sky & dark blue/dark blue/sky blue (All orange)
Previous Names: Wealden 1988-2010.
Previous Leagues:
Records:
Senior Honours: Sussex County League Division 2 League Cup 2004-05, Division Two 2010-11.

10 YEAR RECORD

01-02	02-03	03-04	04-05	05-06	06-07	07-08	08-09	09-10	10-11
SxC2 13	SxC2 7	SxC2 14	SxC2 5	SxC2 6	SxC2 4	SxC2 9	SxC2 15	SxC2 8	SxC2 1

ARUNDEL

Founded: 1889 Nickname: Mulletts

Secretary: Kathy Wilson **(T)** 07778 783 294 **(E)** kathy@kathy99.freeserve.co.uk
Chairman: Bob Marchant **Manager:** Simon Butler **Prog Ed:** Kathy Wilson
Ground: Mill Road, Arundel, W. Sussex BN18 9QQ **(T)** 01903 882 548
Capacity: 2,200 **Seats:** 100 **Covered:** 200 **Midweek Matchday:** Tuesday **Clubhouse:** Yes **Shop:** No

Colours(change): Red/white/red (All Blue)
Previous Names:
Previous Leagues: West Sussex
Records: **Att:** 2,200 v Chichester (League) 1967-68 **Goalscorer:** Paul J Bennett **App:** 537 Paul Bennett (Goalkeeper)
Senior Honours: Sussex County Champions 1957-58, 58-59, 86-87.

10 YEAR RECORD

01-02	02-03	03-04	04-05	05-06	06-07	07-08	08-09	09-10	10-11
SxC1 9	SxC1 17	SxC1 6	SxC1 9	SxC1 7	SxC1 3	SxC1 3	SxC1 2	SxC1 12	SxC1 9

CHICHESTER CITY

Founded: 2000 Nickname: Chi

Secretary: Michael Maiden **(T)** 07971 818 761 **(E)** michael.maiden@virgin.net
Chairman: Oliver Adnan **Manager:** Adrian Girdler **Prog Ed:** soccer@journalist.com
Ground: Oaklands Way, Chichester, W Sussex PO19 6AR **(T)** 01243 533 368
Capacity: 2,000 **Seats:** none **Covered:** 200 **Midweek Matchday:** Tuesday **Clubhouse:** Yes **Shop:** Yes

Colours(change): White/green/green.
Previous Names: Chichester FC (pre 1948), Chichester City 1948-2000. Merged with Portfield in 2000, Chicester City Utd 2000-08
Previous Leagues:
Records:
Senior Honours: Sussex County Division One 2003-04.

10 YEAR RECORD

01-02	02-03	03-04	04-05	05-06	06-07	07-08	08-09	09-10	10-11
SxC1 3	SxC1 4	SxC1 1	SxC1 16	SxC1 8	SxC1 11	SxC1 16	SxC1 7	SxC1 3	SxC1 14

CROWBOROUGH ATHLETIC

Founded: 1894 Nickname: The Crows

Secretary: Karen Scott **(T)** 07788 737 061 **(E)** kes7@talktalk.net
Chairman: Julian Head **Manager:** David Adams **Prog Ed:** Karen Scott
Ground: Crowborough Co. Stadium, Alderbrook Rec, Fermor Rd, TN6 3DJ **(T)** 01892 661 893
Capacity: 2,000 **Seats:** **Covered:** 150 **Midweek Matchday:** **Clubhouse:** **Shop:**

Colours(change): Sky blue & navy blue/navy/navy (All red).
Previous Names:
Previous Leagues: Sussex County 1974-2008. Isthmian 2008-09
Records:
Senior Honours: Sussex County Division One 2007-08. League Cup 2006-07.

10 YEAR RECORD

01-02	02-03	03-04	04-05	05-06	06-07	07-08	08-09	09-10	10-11
SxC3 4	SxC3 3	SxC3 1	SxC2 1	SxC1 6	SxC1 4	SxC1 1	Isth1S 22	SxC1 18	SxC1 12

EAST GRINSTEAD TOWN

Founded: 1890 Nickname: The Wasps

Secretary: Brian McCorquodale **(T)** 07802 528 513 **(E)** brian.mcc@egtfc.co.uk
Chairman: Richard Tramontin **Manager:** Tony Beckingham **Prog Ed:** Bruce Talbot
Ground: The GAC Stadium, East Court, College Lane, East Grinstead RH19 3LS **(T)** 01342 325 885
Capacity: 3,000 **Seats:** none **Covered:** 400 **Midweek Matchday:** **Clubhouse:** Yes **Shop:** No

Colours(change): Yellow & black/black/yellow & black (Blue & yellow/blue & yellow/royal blue)
Previous Names: East Grinstead > 1997.
Previous Leagues: Mid Sussex, Sussex County, Souhern Amateur
Records: **Att:** 2,006 v Lancing F A Am Cup **App:** Guy Hill
Senior Honours: Sussex County League Division Two 2007-08.

10 YEAR RECORD

01-02	02-03	03-04	04-05	05-06	06-07	07-08	08-09	09-10	10-11
SxC2 5	SxC2 3	SxC1 9	SxC1 18	SxC2 7	SxC2 11	SxC2 1	SxC1 17	SxC1 15	SxC1 7

HASSOCKS

Founded: 1902 Nickname: The Robins

Secretary: Dave Knight **(T)** 01273 842 023 **(E)** dw.knight45@googlemail.com
Chairman: Dave John **Manager:** Mickey Jewell **Prog Ed:** Paul Elphick
Ground: The Beacon, Brighton Road, Hassocks BN6 9NA **(T)** 01273 846 040
Capacity: 1,800 **Seats:** 270 **Covered:** 100 **Midweek Matchday:** Tuesday **Clubhouse:** Yes **Shop:** No

Colours(change): All Red. (Yellow/black/yellow)
Previous Names:
Previous Leagues: Mid Sussex, Brighton & Hove & Dist and Southern Counties Comb
Records: **Att:** 610 v Burgess Hill Town **Goalscorer:** Pat Harding 43
Senior Honours:

10 YEAR RECORD

01-02	02-03	03-04	04-05	05-06	06-07	07-08	08-09	09-10	10-11
SxC1 11	SxC1 8	SxC1 7	SxC1 8	SxC1 9	SxC1 5	SxC1 7	SxC1 16	SxC1 14	SxC1 6

HORSHAM YMCA

Founded: 1898 Nickname: YM's

Secretary: Andy Flack **(T)** 0777 585 7392 **(E)** andy.flack@horsham.gov.uk
Chairman: Mick Browning **Manager:** Sammy Donnelly **Prog Ed:** Alan Maguire
Ground: Gorings Mead, Horsham, West Sussex RH13 5BP **(T)** 01403 252 689
Capacity: 1,575 **Seats:** 150 **Covered:** 200 **Midweek Matchday:** **Clubhouse:** Yes **Shop:** No

Colours(change): White/black/red (Navy & sky blue quarters/navy/navy)
Previous Names:
Previous Leagues: Horsham & District, Brighton & Hove, Mid Sussex, Sussex County > 2006, Isthmian 2006-11.
Records: 950 v Chelmsford City - FA Cup 2000
Senior Honours: Sussex League 2004-05, 05-06.
John O'Hara Cup 2001-02.

10 YEAR RECORD

01-02	02-03	03-04	04-05	05-06	06-07	07-08	08-09	09-10	10-11
SxC1 10	SxC1 3	SxC1 13	SxC1 1	SxC1 1	Isth1S 9	Isth1S 21	SxC1 3	Isth1S 11	

LANCING

Founded: 1941 Nickname:

Secretary: John Rea **(T)** 07598 301 296 **(E)** john.rea62@yahoo.com
Chairman: Paul Blann **Manager:** Martin Gander **Prog Ed:** Clive Nutter
Ground: Culver Road, Lancing, West Sussex BN15 9AX **(T)** 01903 767 285
Capacity: **Seats:** **Covered:** **Midweek Matchday:** **Clubhouse:** Yes **Shop:**

Colours(change): Yellow/blue/yellow (All red)
Previous Names: Lancing Athletic
Previous Leagues: Brighton & Hove & District.
Records:
Senior Honours: Brighton League 1946-47, 47-48.

10 YEAR RECORD

01-02	02-03	03-04	04-05	05-06	06-07	07-08	08-09	09-10	10-11
SxC2 6	SxC2 9	SxC2 17	SxC2 13	SxC2 12	SxC2 14	SxC2 12	SxC2 9	SxC2 11	SxC2 2

LINGFIELD

Founded: 1893 Nickname:

Secretary: Pamela Tomsett **(T)** 07903 428 228 **(E)** pamtomsettlfc@hotmail.co.uk
Chairman: Bill Blenkin **Manager:** David Dean **Prog Ed:** TBC
Ground: Sports Pavillion, Godstone Road, Lingfield, Surrey RH7 6BT **(T)** 01342 834 269
Capacity: 1,000+ **Seats:** Yes **Covered:** Yes **Midweek Matchday:** Tuesday **Clubhouse:** Yes **Shop:** No

Colours(change): Red & Yellow stripes/black/yellow.(Blue & white stripes/blue/blue)
Previous Names: None.
Previous Leagues: Redhill. Surrey Intermediate. Combined Counties. Mid Sussex.
Records:
Senior Honours:

10 YEAR RECORD

01-02	02-03	03-04	04-05	05-06	06-07	07-08	08-09	09-10	10-11
SxC3 16	SxC3 9	SxC3 8	SxC3 3	SxC3 2	SxC2 10	SxC2 2	SxC1 8	SxC1 10	SxC1 11

PAGHAM

Founded: 1903 Nickname: The Lions

Secretary: Mark Warren **(T)** 07588 588 475 **(E)** marky216@hotmail.co.uk
Chairman: Brent Williams **Manager:** Carl Stabler **Prog Ed:** TBC
Ground: Nyetimber Lane, Pagham, W Sussex PO21 3JY **(T)** 01243 266 112
Capacity: 2,000 **Seats:** 200 **Covered:** 200 **Midweek Matchday:** **Clubhouse:** Yes **Shop:** No

Colours(change): White & black/black/white (All red)
Previous Names: None
Previous Leagues: Chichester 1903-50, West Sussex 50-69
Records: **Att:** 1,200 v Bognor 1971 **Goalscorer:** Dick De Luca **App:** Graham Peach
Senior Honours: Sussex County Division Two 1978-79, 86-87, 2006-07. Division One 80-81, 87-88, 88-89.

10 YEAR RECORD

01-02	02-03	03-04	04-05	05-06	06-07	07-08	08-09	09-10	10-11
SxC1 8	SxC1 9	SxC1 17	SxC1 19	SxC2 13	SxC2 1	SxC1 9	SxC1 11	SxC1 17	SxC1 4

PEACEHAVEN & TELSCOMBE

Founded: 1923 Nickname:

Secretary: Margaret Edwards **(T)** 07766 909 772 **(E)** mejim@edwards2412.fsworld.co.uk
Chairman: Jim Edwards **Manager:** Peter Edwards & Terry Hall **Prog Ed:** Phyllis Parris
Ground: The Sports Park, Piddinghoe Ave, Peacehaven, BN10 8RH **(T)** 01273 582 471
Capacity: **Seats:** **Covered:** **Midweek Matchday:** **Clubhouse:** **Shop:**

Colours(change): Black & white stripes/white & black/white & black (Luminous yellow/black/black)
Previous Names: Formed when Peacehaven Rangers and Telscombe Tye merged.
Previous Leagues:
Records:
Senior Honours: Sussex County Division Three 2005-06. Division Two 2008-09.

10 YEAR RECORD

01-02	02-03	03-04	04-05	05-06	06-07	07-08	08-09	09-10	10-11
SxC1 12	SxC1 18	SxC2 12	SxC2 17	SxC3 1	SxC2 5	SxC2 4	SxC2 1	SxC1 2	SxC1 3

REDHILL

Founded: 1894 Nickname: Reds/Lobsters

Secretary: Phil Whatling **(T)** 07929 742 081 **(E)** phil.whatling@ntlworld.com
Chairman: John Park **Manager:** Simon Colbran **Prog Ed:**
Ground: Kiln Brow, Three Arch Road, Redhill, Surrey RH1 5AE **(T)** 01737 762 129
Capacity: 2,000 **Seats:** 150 **Covered:** 150 **Midweek Matchday:** Tuesday **Clubhouse:** Yes **Shop:** Yes

Colours(change): Red & white stripes/red/red. (Yellow/blue/blue).
Previous Names:
Previous Leagues: E & W Surrey. Spartan. Southern Sub. London. Athenian.
Records: **Att:** 8,000 v Hastings U FA Cup 1956 **Goalscorer:** Steve Turner 119 **App:** Brian Medlicott 766
Senior Honours: Athenian League (2) Surrey Senior cup 28-29, 65-66.

10 YEAR RECORD

01-02	02-03	03-04	04-05	05-06	06-07	07-08	08-09	09-10	10-11
SxC1 15	SxC1 12	SxC1 11	SxC1 13	SxC1 18	SxC1 15	SxC1 8	SxC1 7	SxC1 5	SxC1 8

RINGMER

Founded: 1906 Nickname: Blues

Secretary: Sally Crouch **(T)** 07510 109 509 **(E)** sallycrouch@ringmerfc.co.uk
Chairman: Bob Munnery **Manager:** Bob Munnery **Prog Ed:** malcolm@ringmerfc.co.uk
Ground: Caburn Ground, Anchor Field, Ringmer BN8 5QN **(T)** 01273 812 738
Capacity: 1,000 **Seats:** 100 **Covered:** Yes **Midweek Matchday:** Tuesday **Clubhouse:** Yes **Shop:** Yes

Colours(change): Navy & light blue/navy/navy. (All orange).
Previous Names: None.
Previous Leagues: Brighton.
Records: 1,350 v Southwick, Sussex County League, 1970-71.
Senior Honours: Sussex County Division Two 1968-69. Division One 1970-71. Sussex Senior Cup 1972-73.

10 YEAR RECORD

01-02	02-03	03-04	04-05	05-06	06-07	07-08	08-09	09-10	10-11
SxC1 2	SxC1 7	SxC1 10	SxC1 6	SxC1 2	SxC1 9	SxC1 10	SxC1 9	SxC1 13	SxC1 10

RYE UNITED

Founded: Nickname: United

Secretary: Roger Bond **(T)** 07738 154 685 **(E)** e.r.bond@btinternet.com
Chairman: Clive Taylor **Manager:** Scott Price **Prog Ed:** Roger Bond
Ground: Rye Football & Cricket Salts, Fish Market Rd, Rye TN31 7LU **(T)** 07802 427 013
Capacity: 1,500 **Seats:** **Covered:** 100 **Midweek Matchday:** Tuesday **Clubhouse:** Yes **Shop:** No

Colours(change): Red & black/black/black (All blue).
Previous Names:
Previous Leagues: Sussex County & Kent County until 2000
Records: **Att:** 120 **App:**Scott Price
Senior Honours: Sussex County League Division Three 2000-01, Division Two 1955-56, 2001-02, 02-03, 09-10.

10 YEAR RECORD

01-02	02-03	03-04	04-05	05-06	06-07	07-08	08-09	09-10	10-11
SxC2 1	SxC2 1	SxC1 2	SxC1 2	SxC1 19	SxC1 19	SxC1 19	SxC2 6	SxC2 1	SxC1 2

SELSEY

Founded: 1903 Nickname: Blues

Secretary: Gordon Weller **(T)** 07852 954 042 **(E)** g.weller1@btinternet.com
Chairman: David Lee **Manager:** Ian Martin **Prog Ed:** Gordon Weller
Ground: High Street Ground, Selsey, Chichester, PO20 0QG **(T)** 01243 603 420
Capacity: 1,000 **Seats:** 25 **Covered:** 98 **Midweek Matchday:** Tuesday **Clubhouse:** Yes **Shop:** No

Colours(change): All blue (All yellow).
Previous Names:
Previous Leagues: Chichester & District, West Sussex.
Records: **Att:** 750-800 v Chichester or Portfield 1950's
Senior Honours: Sussex County Division Two 1963-64, 75-76.

10 YEAR RECORD

01-02	02-03	03-04	04-05	05-06	06-07	07-08	08-09	09-10	10-11
SxC1 4	SxC1 11	SxC1 18	SxC2 14	SxC2 2	SxC1 8	SxC1 15	SxC1 10	SxC1 11	SxC1 17

SHOREHAM

Founded: 1892 Nickname: Musselmen

Secretary: Gary Millis **(T)** 07801 477 979 **(E)** g.millis@sky.com
Chairman: Matthew Major **Manager:** Mark Burt & Kevin Keehan **Prog Ed:** Gary Millis
Ground: Middle Road, Shoreham-by-Sea, W Sussex, BN43 6LT **(T)** 01273 454 261
Capacity: 1,500 **Seats:** 150 **Covered:** 700 **Midweek Matchday:** **Clubhouse:** Yes **Shop:** No

Colours(change): All blue (All orange).
Previous Names: None.
Previous Leagues: West Sussex.
Records: **Att:** 1,342 v Wimbledon
Senior Honours: Sussex County Division One 1951-52, 52-53, 77-78. Division Two 61-62, 76-77, 93-94. John O'Hara League Cup 2007-08.

10 YEAR RECORD

01-02	02-03	03-04	04-05	05-06	06-07	07-08	08-09	09-10	10-11
SxC2 2	SxC1 16	SxC1 19	SxC2 3	SxC1 13	SxC1 13	SxC1 12	SxC1 6	SxC1 9	SxC1 18

SIDLEY UNITED

Founded: 1906 | Nickname: Blues

Secretary: Dane Martin **(T)** 07815 425 682 **(E)** dane.martin88@yahoo.co.uk
Chairman: Dicky Day **Manager:** John Lambert & Wayne Farrier **Prog Ed:** Dane Martin
Ground: Gullivers Sports Ground, Glovers Lane, Sidley Bexhill on Sea TN39 5BL **(T)** 01424 217 078
Capacity: 1,500 **Seats:** none **Covered:** 150 **Midweek Matchday:** **Clubhouse:** Yes **Shop:**

Colours(change): Navy blue & sky blue/navy/navy blue & sky blue (Yellow & black/black/yellow).
Previous Names:
Previous Leagues: East Sussex & Hastings & Dist
Records: **Att:** 1,300 in 1959 **App:** Jimmy Watson
Senior Honours: Sussex Division Two 1958-59, 64-65, 98-99, Division One 2000-01, Sussex Int Cup 1947-48, Sussex Jnr Cup 1924-25

10 YEAR RECORD

01-02	02-03	03-04	04-05	05-06	06-07	07-08	08-09	09-10	10-11
SxC1 5	SxC1 13	SxC1 16	SxC1 15	SxC1 11	SxC1 14	SxC1 20	SxC2 8	SxC2 3	SxC1 13

ST. FRANCIS RANGERS

Founded: 2002 | Nickname: Saints/Rangers

Secretary: John Goss **(T)** 07748 785 240 **(E)** j.goss462@btinternet.com
Chairman: John Goss **Manager:** Keiran Collins **Prog Ed:** John Goss
Ground: Princess Royal Hospital, Lewes Rd, Haywards Hth RH16 4EX **(T)** 01444 441 881
Capacity: 1,000 **Seats:** None **Covered:** 100 **Midweek Matchday:** Tuesday **Clubhouse:** Yes **Shop:** No

Colours(change): Black & white/black/black (Green & white/green/green)
Previous Names: Formed when Ansty Rangers & St Francis merged 2002.
Previous Leagues: None
Records:
Senior Honours:

10 YEAR RECORD

01-02	02-03	03-04	04-05	05-06	06-07	07-08	08-09	09-10	10-11
	SxC3 6	SxC3 2	SxC2 4	SxC2 3	SxC2 2	SxC1 14	SxC1 12	SxC1 16	SxC1 19

THREE BRIDGES

Founded: 1901 | Nickname: Bridges

Secretary: Martin Clarke **(T)** 07885 662 940 **(E)** m-clarke@blueyonder.co.uk
Chairman: Alan Bell **Manager:** Paul Falli **Prog Ed:** Alf Blackler
Ground: Jubilee Field, Three Bridges Rd, Crawley, RH10 1LQ **(T)** 01293 442 000
Capacity: 3,500 **Seats:** 120 **Covered:** 600 **Midweek Matchday:** **Clubhouse:** Yes **Shop:**

Colours(change): Amber & black stripes/black/black. (Blue & white stripes /blue/blue)
Previous Names: Three Bridges Worth 1936-52, Three Bridges Utd 53-64
Previous Leagues: Mid Sussex, E Grinstead, Redhill & Dist 36-52
Records: **Att;** 2,000 v Horsham 1948 **App:** John Malthouse
Senior Honours: Sussex RUR Cup 82-83

10 YEAR RECORD

01-02	02-03	03-04	04-05	05-06	06-07	07-08	08-09	09-10	10-11
SxC1 7	SxC1 14	SxC1 4	SxC1 7	SxC1 15	SxC1 12	SxC1 6	SxC1 5	SxC1 7	SxC1 5

WORTHING UNITED

Founded: 1952 | Nickname:

Secretary: Malcolm Gamlen **(T)** 07743 322 571 **(E)** helsnmark@aol.com
Chairman: Glen Houchen **Manager:** Dave Shearing & Tobi Hutchinson **Prog Ed:** helsnmark@aol.com
Ground: The Robert Albon Memorial Ground, Lyons Way BN14 9JF **(T)** 01903 234 466
Capacity: **Seats:** **Covered:** **Midweek Matchday:** **Clubhouse:** **Shop:**

Colours(change): Sky blue & whites stripes/navy blue/white (Red & white/red/red)
Previous Names: Wigmore Athletic 1952-88. Amalgamated with Southdown to form Worthing United in 1988.
Previous Leagues:
Records:
Senior Honours: Sussex County Division 2 1973-74, Division 3 1989-90.

10 YEAR RECORD

01-02	02-03	03-04	04-05	05-06	06-07	07-08	08-09	09-10	10-11
SxC2 9	SxC2 14	SxC2 2	SxC1 14	SxC1 16	SxC1 18	SxC1 17	SxC1 20	SxC2 2	SxC2 3

BEXHILL UNITED

Founded: Nickname:

Secretary: Mrs Tracy Aston **(T)** 07791 368 049 **(E)** tracyaston21@aol.com
Chairman: Robin Powell **Manager:** TBC **Prog Ed:** Mrs Tracy Aston
Ground: The Polegrove, Brockley Road, Bexhill on Sea TN39 3EX **(T)** 07791 368 049 **Capacity:**
Colours(change): White & black/black/black (Blue & yellow/royal blue/royal blue)

ADDITIONAL INFORMATION:

DORKING WANDERERS

Founded: Nickname:

Secretary: Dave Smith **(T)** 07799 881 849 **(E)** dorking.wanderersfc@hotmail.co.uk
Chairman: Marc White **Manager:** Marc White **Prog Ed:** Rob Cavallini
Ground: West Humble Playing Fields, London Road, Dorking, Surrey **(T)** 07841 671 825 **Capacity:**
Colours(change): Blue & black stripes/black/black (All yellow).

ADDITIONAL INFORMATION:
Honours: Sussex County Division Three 2010-11.

EAST PRESTON

Founded: 1966 Nickname:

Secretary: Keith Freeman **(T)** 07986 596913 **(E)** keweia@btinternet.com
Chairman: Andrew Kinchin **Manager:** Dominic Di Paola **Prog Ed:**
Ground: Roundstone Recreation Ground, Lashmar Road, East Preston BN16 1ES **(T)** 01903 776 026 **Capacity:**
Colours(change): White/black/black (All blue)

ADDITIONAL INFORMATION:

EASTBOURNE UNITED ASSOCIATION

Founded: 1894 Nickname: The U's

Secretary: Brian Dowling **(T)** 07507 225 450 **(E)** brian.dowling@btinternet.com
Chairman: Les Aisbitt **Manager:** Paul Daubeney **Prog Ed:** Brian Dowling
Ground: The Oval, Channel View Road, Eastbourne, BN22 7LN **(T)** 01323 726 989 **Capacity:** 3,000
Colours(change): White/black/white (Claret & blue/claret/claret).

ADDITIONAL INFORMATION: Att: 11,000 at Lynchmore

HAILSHAM TOWN

Founded: 1885 Nickname: The Stringers

Secretary: Sue Williams **(T)** 07719 590 268 **(E)** williams.susan8@sky.com
Chairman: Mervyn Walker **Manager:** Ken McCreadie **Prog Ed:** Alan Maur
Ground: The Beaconsfield, Western Road, Hailsham BN27 3JF **(T)** 01323 840 446 **Capacity:** 2,000
Colours(change): Yellow/green/green (All light blue)

ADDITIONAL INFORMATION: Att: 1350 v Hungerford T. FA Vase Feb 89 **Goalscorer:** Howard Stephens 51 **App:** Phil Comber 713

LITTLE COMMON

Founded: 1966 Nickname:

Secretary: Mrs Margaret Cherry **(T)** 01424 217 191 **(E)** danieleldridge11@btinternet.com
Chairman: Ken Cherry **Manager:** Mark Linch **Prog Ed:** Dan Eldridge
Ground: Little Common Recreation Ground, Green Lane, Bexhill on Sea TN39 4PH **(T)** 01424 845 861 **Capacity:**
Colours(change): Claret & blue/claret/claret (Yellow/navy/navy)

ADDITIONAL INFORMATION:
Previous Name: Albion United > 1986. **Previous League:** East Sussex 1994-2005.
Honours: East Sussex League 1975-76, 76-77, 2004-05.

LITTLEHAMPTON TOWN

Founded: 1896 Nickname:

Secretary: Alan Barnes **(T)** 07882 460 357 **(E)** truegritagb@aol.com
Chairman: Neil Taylor **Manager:** Mark Bennett **Prog Ed:** Dave Perrett
Ground: Sportsfield, St Flora's Road, Littlehampton BN17 6BD **(T)** 01903 716 390 **Capacity:**
Colours(change): Yellow/black/black (All white)

ADDITIONAL INFORMATION:
Lost in the F.A. Cup Preliminary Round v Tunbridge Wells 15-16 on penalties after 40 kicks had been taken - At the time a European record and only one short of the World record.

LOXWOOD

Founded: Nickname:

Secretary: George Read **(T)** 07791 766 857 **(E)** thomasread00@btinternet.com
Chairman: Derek Waterman **Manager:** Barry Hunter **Prog Ed:** George Read
Ground: Loxwood Sports Ass., Plaistow Road, Loxwood RH14 0RQ **(T)** 07791 766 857 **Capacity:**
Colours(change): Black & white/black/white (Red & white/white/red)

ADDITIONAL INFORMATION:
Previous League: West Sussex.
Honours: Sussex County League Division 3 2007-08.

MIDHURST & EASEBOURNE

Founded: Nickname:

Secretary: Ted Dummer MBE **(T)** 01730 813 887 **(E)** acs@harrisonrenwick.com
Chairman: Darren Chiverton **Manager:** Trever Waller **Prog Ed:** Ted Dummer MBE
Ground: Rotherfield, Dodsley Lane, Easebourne, Midhurst GU29 9BE **(T)** 01730 816 557 **Capacity:**
Colours(change): Royal blue with black trim/black/royal blue (Orange/royal blue/orange)

ADDITIONAL INFORMATION:
Previous League: West Sussex 1999-2002.
Honours: Sussex County League Division 2 Cup 1988-89, Division 3 Cup 2002-03.

MILE OAK

Founded: 1960 Nickname: The Oak

Secretary: Colin Brown **(T)** 07774 754 468 **(E)** colin.d.brown@ntlworld.com
Chairman: Leslie Hamilton **Manager:** Anthony Whittington **Prog Ed:** Colin Brown
Ground: Mile Oak Recreation Ground, Chalky Road, Portslade BN41 2YU **(T)** 01273 423 854 **Capacity:**
Colours(change): Tangerine & blacktrim/black/tangerine with black trim (All green)

ADDITIONAL INFORMATION:
Previous League: Brighton & Hove District.
Honours: Brighton & Hove District 1980-81. Sussex County League Division 2.

OAKWOOD

Founded: 1962 Nickname:

Secretary: Kelly Whittaker **(T)** 07973 752 761 **(E)** beccakel@hotmail.com
Chairman: Stuart Lovegrove **Manager:** TBC **Prog Ed:** Kelly Whittaker
Ground: Tinsley Lane, Three Bridges, Crawley RH10 8AJ **(T)** 01293 515 742 **Capacity:**
Colours(change): Red & black stripes/black/black (Blue/white/white)

ADDITIONAL INFORMATION:
Previous League: Southern Counties Combination 1980-84.
Honours: Sussex County Division 2 Cup 1989-90.

RUSTINGTON

Founded: Nickname:

Secretary: Paul Cox **(T)** 07771 623 224 **(E)** cox121@yahoo.com
Chairman: Frank Sumner **Manager:** Brett (Charlie) Torode **Prog Ed:** Paul Cox
Ground: Recreation Ground, Jubilee Avenue, Rustington BN16 3NB **(T)** 01903 770 495 **Capacity:**
Colours(change): All blue (Red & black/black/red)

ADDITIONAL INFORMATION:
Honours: Sussex County League Division 3 2006-07.

SEAFORD TOWN

Founded: Nickname:

Secretary: John Smith **(T)** 07919 993 751 **(E)** johnsmith@btinternet.com
Chairman: Bob Thomsett **Manager:** Tony Coade **Prog Ed:** Mick Webster
Ground: The Crouch, Bramber Road, Seaford BN25 1AG **(T)** 01323 892 221 **Capacity:**
Colours(change): All red (White/black/black)

ADDITIONAL INFORMATION:
Honours: Sussex County League Division 2 2005-06.

SOUTHWICK

Founded: 1882 Nickname:

Secretary: Paul Symes **(T)** 07908 289 758 **(E)** p.p.symes@btinternet.com
Chairman: Alan Petken **Manager:** Roger Feest & Lloyd Suanders **Prog Ed:** Paul Symes
Ground: Old Barn Way, Southwick BN42 4NT **(T)** 01273 701 010 **Capacity:**
Colours(change): Red & black/black/red (All grey)

ADDITIONAL INFORMATION:
Previous League: Isthmian 1985-92.
Honours: Sussex County League Division 1 x6. Sussex Senior Cup x10.

STEYNING TOWN

Founded: Nickname:

Secretary: David Kennett **(T)** 07585 601 213 **(E)** diddy.kennett1@btinternet.com
Chairman: Carol Swain **Manager:** Richard Whittington **Prog Ed:** David Kennett
Ground: The Shooting Field, Steyning, West Sussex BN44 3RQ **(T)** 01903 814 601 **Capacity:**
Colours(change): All red (Yellow/black/yellow)

ADDITIONAL INFORMATION:
Honours: Sussex County League Division 2 1977-78, Division 1 1984-85, 85-86, League Cup 1978-79, 83-84, 85-86.

STORRINGTON

Founded: 1920 Nickname:

Secretary: Keith Dalmon **(T)** 07889 367 956 **(E)** keithdalmon@btinternet.com
Chairman: Stan Rhodie **Manager:** James Baker **Prog Ed:**
Ground: Recreation Ground, Pulborough Road, Storrington RH20 4HJ **(T)** 01903 745 860 **Capacity:**
Colours(change): All blue (White/black/white)

ADDITIONAL INFORMATION:
Honours: Sussex County League Division 2 Cup 1979, Division 3 Cup 1998, Division 3 2005.
Vernon Wentworth Cup 1998, 2003.

WESTFIELD

Founded: 1927 Nickname:

Secretary: Gill Attewell **(T)** 07928 176 658 **(E)** gilljordan@rocketmail.com
Chairman: Graham Drinkwater **Manager:** Duncan Jones **Prog Ed:** Gill Attewell
Ground: The Parish Field, Main Road, Westfield TN35 4SB **(T)** 01424 751 011 **Capacity:**
Colours(change): Yellow/green/green (All blue)

ADDITIONAL INFORMATION:
Previous League: East Sussex 1971-97.
Honours: East Sussex 1977-78, League Cup 77-78. Hastings Senior Cup 2007-08.

WICK

Founded: 1892 Nickname: Wickers

Secretary: Steven Cox **(T)** 07880 608 090 **(E)** coxsteven1@aol.com
Chairman: Keith Croft **Manager:** Richard Towers **Prog Ed:** upfrontkc@hotmail.com
Ground: Coomes Way, Wick, Littlehampton, W Sussex BN17 7LS **(T)** 01903 713 535 **Capacity:** 1,000
Colours(change): Red & black flash/black with white flash/black with white flash (White/black/black).

ADDITIONAL INFORMATION: Att: 900
Sussex Senior Cup 92-93.

SUSSEX COUNTY DIVISION THREE CONSTITUTION 2011-12

BARNHAM	Mill Road, Slindon, Nr Arundel, West Sussex BN18 0LZ	07738 625 795
BOSHAM	Bosham Recreation Ground, Walton Lane, Bosham PO10 8QF	07542 283 247
BROADBRIDGE HEATH	Wickhurst Lane, Broadbridge Heath RH12 3YS	01403 211 311
CLYMPING	Clymping Village Hall, Clymping, Littlehampton BN17 5GW	07762 498 840
FERRING	The Glebelands, Ferring, West Sussex BN12 5JL	01903 243 618
FOREST	Roffey Sports & Social Club, Spooners Road, Roffey RH12 4DY	01403 210 223
HAYWARDS HEATH TOWN	Hanbury Park Stadium, Haywards Heath RH16 4GL	01444 412 837
HURSTPIERPOINT	Fairfield Recreation Ground, Cuckfield Road, Hurstpierpoint BN6 9SD	07985 126 432
IFIELD	Edwards Sports & Social Club, Ifield Green, Rusper Road, Crawley	01293 536 569
NEWHAVEN	Fort Road Recreation Ground, Newhaven BN9 9EE	01273 513 940
PEASE POTTAGE VILLAGE	Finches Field, Old Brighton Road, Pease Pottage RH11 9AH	01293 538 651
ROFFEY	Bartholomew Way, Horsham RH12 5JL	TBA
ROTTINGDEAN VILLAGE	Rottingdean Sports Centre, Falmer Road, Rottingdean BN2 7DA	01273 306 436
SALTDEAN UNITED	Hill Park, Coombe Vale, Saltdean, Brighton BN2 8HJ	07879 587 174
T D SHIPLEY	The Pavilion, Dragons Lane, Shipley RH13 8GB	07804 325 228
UCKFIELD TOWN	Victoria Pleasure Ground, Uckfield TN22 5DJ	01825 769 400 (Messages only)

AFC Uckfield. Photo: Alan Coomes.

Southwick FC. Photo: Alan Coomes.

GROUND DIRECTIONS

AFC UCKFIELD - The Oaks, Old Eastbourne Road, Uckfield, East Sussex TN22 5QL - 07847 662 337

Next to Rajdutt Restaurant on Old Eastbourne Road, south of Uckfield town centre.

ARUNDEL - Mill Road, Arundel, West Sussex BN18 9QQ - 01903 882 548

A27 from Worthing to Arundel over Railway Bridge to roundabout . Second exit into Queen Street to town centre and turn right over bridge. Car park leading to ground 100 yards on right.

CHICHESTER CITY - Oaklands Park, Oaklands Way, Chichester PO19 6AR - 07845 105 822

Half a mile north of the city centre, adjacent to festival theatre. Turn into Northgate car park and entrance to the ground is next to the Chichester Rackets Club.

CROWBOROUGH ATHLETIC - Crowborough Community Stadium, Alderbrook Recreation Ground, Fermor Road, TN6 3DJ

Entering Crowborough from the south on the A26, about half a mile past the Crow and Gate Pub, take the next right into Sheep Plain - This is also signposted for the Railway Station, which meanders into Hurtis Hill. At the mini-roundabout go straight into Fermor Road, take the second turning on the right and turn right immediately into Alderbrook Recreation Ground. The Stadium and parking is ahead of you.

EAST GRINSTEAD TOWN - East Court, East Grinstead RH19 3LS - 01342 325885

A264 Tunbridge Wells road (Moat Road) until mini roundabout at bottom of Blackwell Hollow ,turn immediately right by club sign then 1st left, ground 200 yards down lane past rifle club on right.

HASSOCKS - The Beacon, Brighton Rd., Hassocks BN6 9NA - 01273 846040

Off A273 Pyecombe Road to Burgess Hill. Ground is 300 yards south of Stonepound crossroads (B2116) to Hurstpeirpoint or Hassocks.

HORSHAM YMCA - Gorings Mead, Horsham, West Sussex RH13 5BP - 01403 252 689

From the east, take A281 (Brighton Road) and the ground is on the left and sign posted opposite Gorings Mead.

LANCING - Culver Road, Lancing, West Sussex BN15 9AX. - 01903 767 285.

From A27 turn south at Lancing Manor roundabout into Grinstead Lane, 3rd turning on right North Farm Rd. Turn left then immedlately. right into Culver Rd. From railway station take 3rd turning on left heading north.

LINGFIELD - Sports Pavilion, Godstone Road, Lingfield, Surrey RH7 6BT - 01342 834269

A22, 4 miles north of East Grinstead, to Mormon Temple roundabout, take exit Lingfield (B2028) Newchapel Road for 1 1/2 miles. Left at T junction into Godstone Road (B2029) and ground is 1/2 mile on left.

PAGHAM - Nyetimber Lane, Pagham, West Sussex PO21 3JY - 01243 266 112

Turn off A27 Chichester by-pass (signposted A259 Pagham). Ground in village of Nyetimber. Three miles from Bognor (BR). Buses 260 & 240

PEACEHAVEN & TELSCOMBE - The Sports Park, Piddinghoe Avenue, Peacehaven, E. Sussex BN10 8RJ - 01273 582471

From Brighton on A259, over roundabout & Piddinghoe Ave. is next left after 2nd set of lights - ground at end. From Newhaven, Piddinghoe Ave. is 1st right after 1st set of lights. 3 miles from Newhaven(BR). Peacehaven is served by Brighton to Newhaven & Eastbourne buses

REDHILL - Kiln Brow, Three Arch Road, Redhill, Surrey - 01737 762 129

On left hand side of A23 two and a half miles south of Redhill.

RINGMER - Caburn Ground, Anchor Field, Ringmer - 01273 812 738

From Lewes road turn right into Springett Avenue, opposite Ringmer village

RYE UNITED - Sydney Allnut Pavilion, Rye Football & Cricket Salts, Fishmarket Road, Rye TN31 7NU - 01797 223 855

Outskirts of Rye on the A268 joins A259 opposite Skinners Rover garage.

SELSEY - High Street Ground, Selsey, Chichester, West Sussex - 01243 603420

Through Selsey High Street to fire station. Take turning into car park alongside the station. Entrance is in the far corner. Regular buses from Chichester.

SHOREHAM - Middle Road, Shoreham-by-Sea, West Sussex BN43 6LT - 01273 454 261

From Shoreham (BR) go east over level crossing, up Dolphin Road. Ground is 150 yards on right.

SIDLEY UNITED - Gullivers Sports Ground, Glovers Lane, Sidley, Bexhill on Sea TN39 5BL - 01424 217 078

From Brighton: On A259 turn left at Little Common roundabout into Pear Tree Lane. Turn right into Turkey Road. Turn right onto A269 from Ninfield. Turn left at Glovers Lane and first left into North Road.

ST FRANCIS RANGERS - The Princess Royal Hospital, Lewes Road, Haywards Heath, RH16 4EX Tel No: 01444 474 021 and social club 01444 441 881

Enter through the main hospital entrance on the Lewes Road and follow signs to Sports Complex.

THREE BRIDGES - Jubilee Field, Jubilee Walk, Three Bridges Road, Crawley, West Sussex RH10 1LQ - 01293 442 000

From Three Bridges station turn left towards Crawley. Turn right at second lights into Three Bridges road. Take first left (opposite Plough Inn) into Jubilee Walk.

WORTHING UNITED - The Robert Albion Memorial Ground, Lyons Way, Worthing BN14 9JF. 01903 234 466.

From the West past Hill Barn roundabout to second set of traffic lights, turn left into Lyons Way. From East first set of traffic lights at end of Sompting bypass, turn right into Lyons Way.

DIVISION TWO

BEXHILL UNITED - The Polegrove, Brockley Road, Bexhill-on-Sea, East Sussex TN39 3EX - 07815 425 682.
A27 to Little Common then fourth exit off roundabout to Cooden Beach. Left and follow to end, turn right into Brockby Road. Ground at bottom of hill on the right.

DORKING WANDERERS - West Humble Playing Fields, London Road, Dorking.
Take A24 to Dorking at roundabout stay on A24 to Leatherhead. Go past Denbies Vineyard on left. At end of vineyard take 2nd turning on the left straight into the playing field.

EAST PRESTON - Roundstone Recreation Ground, Lashmar Road, East Preston, Sussex BN16 1ES - 01903 776 026
From Worthing proceed west for 6 miles on A259. At Roundstone Brewers Fayre pub turn south, over level crossing turn left for 50 yards then first right into Roundstone Drive.

EASTBOURNE UNITED AFC - The Oval, Channel View Ropad, Eastbourne, East Sussex BN22 7LN - 011323 726989
From A22 follow signs to Eastbourne East seafront. Turn left onto seafront and left again into Channel View Road at Princess Park & ground is first right.

HAILSHAM TOWN - The Beaconsfield, Western Road, Hailsham, East Sussex BN27 3DN - 01323 840446
A22 to Arlington Road, turn east, then left into South Road- left into Diplocks Way until Daltons. Four miles from Polegate BR (Brighton-Eastbourne line).

LITTLE COMMON - Little Common Spts Pavilion, Little Common Rec., Green Lane, Bexhill-on-Sea, TN39 4PH - 01424 845 861.
From the west take the A259, at Little Common roundabout take second exit into Peartree Lane and then left into Little Common Recreation Ground car park.

LITTLEHAMPTON TOWN - The Sportsfield, St Flora's Road, Littlehampton BN17 6BD - 01903 716 390
Leave A259 at Waterford Business Park and turn into Horsham Road. After Shell Garage turn left into St. Floras Road. Ground is at the end of road on the left.

LOXWOOD - Loxwood Sports Association, Plaistow Road, Loxwood RH14 0SX - 01404 753 185
Leave A272 between Billinghurst and Wisborough Green and join the B2133 for 3.4 miles. On entering Loxwood Village take 1st left into Plaistow Road, ground situated 100 yards on the left.

MIDHURST & EASEBOURNE - Rotherfield, Dodsley Lane, Easebourne, Midhurst, W. Sussex GU29 9BE - 01730 816 557.
Ground one mile out of Midhurst on London Road (A286) opposite Texaco Garage. Ample car parking.

MILE OAK - Mile Oak Recreation Ground, Chalky Road, Portslade - 01273 423 854.
From A27 (Brighton Bypass) leave at A293 exit. Right at first roundabout. Ground 1 mile on right. Parking in the Sports Centre opposite the ground (park) entrance.

OAKWOOD - Tinsley Lane, Three Bridges, Crawley RH10 8AJ - 01293 515 742.
From the South on M23, take junction 10 exit left onto A2011, next roundabout take fourth exit right, next roundabout second exit, take first right into Tinsley Lane. Ground entrance 100 metres on left.

RUSTINGTON - Recreation Ground, Jubilee Avenue, Rustington, West Sussex BN16 3NB - 01903 770 495.
From the East follow A259 past Sainsburys. Left at next roundabout on to B2187 over Windmill Bridge. Straight on at roundabout, first right, then first left into Woodlands Avenue. Car park is 80 yards on your right, next to the Village hall. From the West proceed to Watersmead roundabout with Bodyshop on your left. Take B2187 half a mile, past BP garage, take third right into Albert Road, then first right into Woodlands Avenue.

SEAFORD TOWN - The Crouch, Bramber Road, Seaford BN25 1AG - 01323 892 221.
A259 to Seaford. At mini roundabout by station, turn left (coming from Newhaven) or RIGHT (from Eastbourne). At end of Church Street, across junction, then left at end. After 500m turn left up Ashurst Road Bramber Road is at the top.

SOUTHWICK - Old Barn Way, off Manor Hall Way, Southwick, Brighton BN42 4NT - 01273 701 010
A27 from Brighton take first left after Southwick sign to Leisure Centre. Ground adjacent. Five minutes walk from Fishergate or Southwick stations.

STEYNING TOWN - The Shooting Field, Steyning, W. Sussex BN44 3RP. - 01903 812 228.
Entering Steyning from the west. Take 1st left in the High St (Tanyard Lane) Follow into Shooting Field estate, ground is 4th turn on the left. Entering Steyning from the east. From the High St., turn right into Church St.. Turn left by Church into Shooting Field estate. NB Coaches MUST park in Church Street Car Park.

STORRINGTON - Recreation Ground, Pulborough Road, Storrington RH20 4HJ - 01903 745 860.
A24 right at roundabout at Washington. Four miles to Storrington through village. Third exit at roundabout and second right into Spearbridge Road.

WESTFIELD - The Parish Field, Main Road, Westfield TN35 4SB - 01483 751 011.
From Hastings take the A21, turning right onto the A28 towards Ashford. Travel through Westfield, and the ground is located off Westfield Lane on the left.

WICK - Crabtree Park, Coomes Way, Wick, Littlehampton, West Sussex BN17 7LS Tel No: 01903 713 535
A27 to Crossbush.A284 towards Littlehampton. After one mile over level crossing left into Coomes Way next to Locomotive pub. Ground at end.

DIVISION THREE

BARNHAM - Mill Road, Slindon, Nr Arundel, West Sussex BN18 0LZ - 07738 625 795

On the A27 at Fontwell take the A29 to Slindon and at the Slindon crossroads the ground is on the right.

BOSHAM - Bosham Recreation Ground, Walton Lane, Bosham, Chichester PO18 8QF - 01243 574 011.

From Chichester take the A259 towards Portsmouth. On reaching Bosham turn left at the Swan P.H. roundabout. 1/2 mile to T junction, turn left & car park 50 yds on left.

BROADBRIDGE HEATH - Wickhurst Lane, Broadbridge Heath, Horsham RH12 3YS - 01403 211 311

Alongside A24, Horsham north/south bypass. From the A24 Horsham Bypass, at the large roundabout/underpass take the Broadbridge Heath Bypass towards Guildford and then at the first roundabout turn left into Wickhurst Lane.

CLYMPING - Clymping Village Hall, Clymping, Littelhampton BN17 5GW - 07951 196 784.

Follow A259 west of Littlehampton. Just over the Bridge, on the right hand side before the small roundabout.

FERRING - The Glebelands, Ferring, West Sussex BN12 5JL

To Ferring main shops, turn right into Greystoke Road.

FOREST - Roffey Sports & Social Club, Spooners Road, Roffey RH12 4DY - 01403 210 223.

Spooners Road. is off the main Crawley road, 100 yds from the `Star' PH, towards Crawley

HAYWARDS HEATH TOWN - Hanbury Park Stadium, Haywards Heath RH16 3PX - 01444 412 837.

A272 to Haywards Heath town centre. At Sussex roundabout, north on B2708 (Hazelgrove Road) take first right into New England Road, then the 4th right (Allen Road) leads to ground.

HURSTPIERPOINT - Fairfield Rec. Ground, Cuckfield Road, BN6 9SD - 01273 834 783.

At Hurstpierpoint crossroads, go north into Cuckfield Road (B2117) for 1km. Ground entrance between houses nos.158 & 160.

IFIELD EDWARDS - Edwards Sports & Social Club, Ifield Green, Rusper Road, Crawley. - 01293 420 598.

From A23 Crawley by-pass going north, left at roundabout signed Charlwood. Third left into Ifield Green, first right past Royal Oak (PH) into Rusper Road.

NEWHAVEN - Fort Road Recreation Ground, Newhaven, East Sussex BN9 9EE. - 01273 513 940.

A259, follow one-way system around town, left at Police Station into South Road, which becomes Fort Road.

PEASE POTTAGE VILLAGE - Finches Field, Old Brighton Road, Pease Pottage RH11 9AH - 01293 538 651

Off M23/A23 towards Brighton turn off at Pease Pottage. Past service station to roundabout, take 3rd exit over bridge sharp left, follow signs to Finches Field. Approx. 300 yards past Grapes Public House on the right.

ROFFEY - Bartholomew Way, Horsham RH12 5JL.

A24 heading South, turn left at Rusper roundabout. Take first left into Lemmington Way. Take left at T junction into Bartholomew Way.

ROTTINGDEAN VILLAGE - Rottingdean Sports Centre, Falmer Road, Rottingdean BN2 7DA. - 01273 306 436

After leaving the Rottingdean Village one way system go past Bazehill Road and the entrance to the ground is next on the right.

SALTDEAN UNITED - Hill Park, Coombe Vale, Saltdean, Brighton BN2 8HJ - 01273 309 898.

A259 coast road east from Brighton to Saltdean Lido, left into Arundel Drive West, and Saltdean Vale to bridle path at beginning of Combe Vale. Club 200yds along track.

TD SHIPLEY - The Pavilion, Dragons Lane, Shipley RH13 8GB - 07804 325 228.

Exit the A24 onto the A272 at the Buckbarn crossroads signposted Billinghurst. The ground is 1.5 miles on the right.

UCKFIELD TOWN - Victoria Pleasure Ground, Uckfield TN22 5DJ - 01825 769 400.

Take Eastbourne road (old A22) south of Uckfield town centre. Entrance to ground is 1/2 mile on the right (just after the Police station).

Eastbourne United Association - Photo: Roger Turner.

UNITED COUNTIES LEAGUE

Sponsored by: ChromaSport & Trophies
Founded: 1895
Recent Champions:
2006: Woodford United
2007: Deeping Rangers
2008: Stotfold
2009: Stewarts & Lloyds Corby
2010: Daventry Town
nwcfl.co.uk

PREMIER DIVISION	P	W	D	L	F	A	Pts
1 St Neots Town	40	33	6	1	160	33	105
2 Kings Lynn Town	40	33	4	3	135	39	103
3 Newport Pagnell Town	40	27	7	6	113	50	88
4 Long Buckby	40	24	7	9	84	42	79
5 Wellingborough Town 2004	40	22	7	11	83	59	73
6 Peterborough Northern Star	40	21	7	12	75	46	70
7 Boston Town	40	21	3	16	76	65	66
8 Stewart & Lloyds Corby	40	19	8	13	71	49	65
9 Blackstones	40	16	13	11	70	59	61
10 Irchester United	40	19	3	18	74	72	60
11 St Ives Town	40	16	8	16	60	64	56
12 Daventry United	40	18	1	21	76	81	55
13 Northampton Spencer	40	15	9	16	56	68	54
14 Deeping Rangers	40	14	3	23	74	94	45
15 Cogenhoe United	40	10	11	19	70	95	41
16 Yaxley	40	9	10	21	37	80	37
17 Holbeach United	40	10	6	24	54	90	36
18 Sleaford Town	40	9	8	23	40	87	35
19 Desborough Town	40	9	7	24	51	95	34
20 Raunds Town	40	5	2	33	45	126	17
21 Rothwell Corinthians	40	2	6	32	31	141	12

LEAGUE CUP

PRELIMINARY ROUND
Sleaford Town 3-2 Desborough Town
Holbeach United 6-3 Burton Park Wanderers
Thrapston Town 1-0 Rushden & Higham United
Huntingdon Town 1-0 Buckingham Town
Daventry United 3-0 Bourne Town
Northampton Spencer 0-1 Northampton Sileby Rangers

ROUND 1
Wellingborough Whitworth 1-2 Boston Town
Sleaford Town 1-5 irchester United
Olney town 0-2 Huntingdon Town
Eynesbury Rovers 0-6 St Neots Town
Rothwell Town 1-6 Northampton ON Chenecks
Yaxley 2-1 Rothwell Corinthians
Stewart & Lloyds Corby 1-0 Long Buckby
Northampton Sileby Rangers 2-3 Peterborough Northern Star
Wellngborough Town 2004 6-0 Potton United
St Ives Town 3-0 Harborough Town
Deeping Rangers 3-1 Raunds Town
Blackstones 2-3 Newport Pagnell Town
Kings Lynn Town 3-1 Daventry United
Thrapston Town 3-1 Wootton Blue Cross
Cogenhoe United 5-4 Bugbrooke St Michaels
AFC Kempston Rovers 3-2 Holbeach United

ROUND 2
Huntingdon Town 4-4 Peterborough Northern Star
(Peterborough Northern Star won 5-4 on penalties)
Thrapston Town 3-4 Cogenhoe United
Stewart & Lloyds Corby 1-2 Deeping Rangers
AFC Kempston Rovers 1-2 Boston Town
Newport Pagnell Town 4-2 Yaxley
Kings Lynn Town 4-1 Irchester United
St Ives Town 2-2 Wellingborough Town 2004
(St Ives Town won 3-2 on penalties)
St Neots Town 8-1 Northampton ON Chenecks

QUARTER FINALS
St Neots Town 2-1 Kings Lynn Town
(tie awarded to Kings Lynn Town)
St Ives Town 2-0 Deeping Rangers
Cogenhoe United 1-2 Boston Town
Newport Pagnell Town 2-3 Peterborough Northern Star

SEMI-FINALS
St Ives Town 1-0 Kings Lynn Town
Peterborough Northern Star 2-1 Boston Town

FINAL (@ Raunds Town, 7/5/11)
Peterborough Northern Star 2-0 St Ives Town

PREMIER DIVISION	1	2	3	4	5	6	7	8	9	10	11	12	13	14	15	16	17	18	19	20	21
1 Blackstones		1-3	1-3	2-0	4-1	1-2	0-0	4-0	1-1	4-1	0-3	1-2	2-0	2-1	3-0	5-0	1-1	0-6	1-1	2-1	1-0
2 Boston Town	4-3		2-1	3-2	2-0	3-2	1-2	1-0	0-1	2-3	1-1	1-2	1-0	3-2	6-2	0-3	0-2	0-5	2-2	1-2	2-0
3 Cogenhoe United	1-2	1-3		1-3	2-3	2-1	2-2	2-4	1-1	0-3	0-2	1-1	1-1	3-1	3-3	4-2	1-1	1-8	2-4	2-2	2-2
4 Daventry United	2-0	1-0	4-3		4-1	0-1	2-4	3-2	0-5	0-5	2-1	4-4	3-1	5-2	2-0	5-0	4-0	0-3	4-0	1-2	0-1
5 Deeping Rangers	1-3	2-3	3-2	2-4		2-0	4-3	1-5	2-1	3-2	2-2	0-2	1-6	3-0	7-1	5-1	2-3	0-1	0-5	2-2	1-2
6 Desborough Town	0-0	0-2	3-4	2-4	0-6		4-3	0-2	0-2	0-0	1-4	3-1	0-3	3-0	2-1	1-1	2-2	0-1	4-1	0-2	2-0
7 Holbeach United	2-2	0-1	2-3	1-0	1-2	3-2		2-1	1-3	0-0	1-5	0-1	1-3	0-3	3-1	2-1	0-1	0-3	2-3	1-4	0-1
8 Irchester United	0-0	2-1	3-2	3-0	3-1	4-0	0-2		0-5	1-2	2-3	2-1	3-1	3-2	6-0	1-0	2-4	1-5	0-2	3-1	3-0
9 King's Lynn Town	5-1	4-0	3-0	6-1	2-0	7-0	3-0	5-2		1-0	5-1	4-1	3-1	10-1	3-0	4-1	4-1	2-4	2-1	1-0	4-2
10 Long Buckby	1-1	1-2	3-1	3-2	0-1	1-0	1-0	3-1	3-0		2-3	3-1	2-1	5-1	5-1	3-1	2-0	1-1	1-3	1-1	2-0
11 Newport Pagnell Town	1-1	1-1	6-0	3-1	5-1	1-1	6-1	0-0	2-4	5-1		3-0	2-1	6-2	2-0	3-1	5-3	1-1	1-0	6-2	2-0
12 Northampton Spencer	1-1	3-2	1-3	1-3	0-2	2-0	1-1	0-3	3-4	0-2	0-1		0-3	3-0	4-1	0-0	1-0	1-3	2-1	1-1	1-1
13 Peterborough Northern Star	2-1	1-3	1-1	3-2	2-1	2-1	2-1	2-0	0-2	0-2	2-1	1-1		3-1	6-0	1-1	4-1	1-1	3-0	3-1	1-0
14 Raunds Town	1-3	4-3	0-3	0-2	0-2	5-2	0-1	4-4	0-3	0-4	0-5	1-4	0-2		1-3	1-3	2-1	0-6	1-2	1-5	0-1
15 Rothwell Corinthians	0-3	2-6	1-5	2-0	0-0	0-5	3-3	0-1	1-5	1-6	0-2	1-3	1-3	0-3		0-1	0-0	0-7	0-4	1-5	0-7
16 Sleaford Town	1-3	0-3	1-1	2-1	4-2	1-1	3-1	0-3	1-3	0-3	0-4	0-1	1-4	3-1	0-0		1-0	0-4	0-2	0-3	0-0
17 St Ives Town	1-1	2-1	1-2	3-0	3-2	4-3	6-3	5-0	2-2	0-2	0-2	1-1	1-0	3-0	2-0	0-3		1-2	1-0	1-0	0-0
18 St Neots Town	3-3	3-2	5-2	4-0	5-2	10-0	4-2	3-0	2-4	1-1	5-2	6-0	1-1	3-0	5-1	5-1	4-1		2-0	4-1	6-0
19 Stewart & Lloyds Corby	2-2	1-2	2-0	3-1	4-1	2-0	5-1	0-2	3-3	0-0	3-0	1-2	1-1	3-1	6-1	1-0	2-0	0-2		0-0	1-0
20 Wellingborough Town	3-0	1-0	3-1	0-3	4-3	4-1	2-0	3-1	0-2	3-2	1-4	2-1	1-0	5-2	3-3	5-1	3-0	1-3	2-0		0-0
21 Yaxley	2-4	0-3	1-1	2-1	1-0	2-2	1-2	2-1	0-6	0-2	2-6	1-2	0-3	1-1	3-0	1-1	0-2	0-13	0-0	1-2	

UNITED COUNTIES LEAGUE - STEP 5/6

DIVISION ONE	P	W	D	L	F	A	Pts
1 AFC Kempston Rovers	32	23	4	5	104	23	73
2 Thrapston Town	32	22	3	7	86	35	69
3 Bugbrooke St Michaels	32	21	2	9	81	48	65
4 Olney Town	32	15	5	12	58	51	50
5 Huntingdon Town	32	15	4	13	45	49	49
6 Eynesbury Rovers	32	14	5	13	58	55	47
7 Rothwell Town	32	13	8	11	56	53	47
8 Burton Park Wanderers	32	13	7	12	63	51	46
9 Northampton Sileby Rangers	32	12	5	15	51	60	41
10 Rushden & Higham United	32	11	6	15	40	64	39
11 Wootton Blue Cross	32	10	7	15	46	58	37
12 Bourne Town	32	11	4	17	41	63	37
13 Wellingborough Whitworth	32	9	9	14	51	62	36
14 Northampton ON Chenecks	32	11	3	18	45	75	36
15 Potton United	32	11	2	19	49	83	35
16 Buckingham Town	32	10	4	18	50	70	34
17 Harborough Town	32	9	6	17	31	55	33

RESERVE DIVISION ONE	P	W	D	L	F	A	Pts
1 Cogenhoe United reserves	28	19	7	2	81	30	64
2 AFC Kempston Rovers res	28	18	4	6	70	33	58
3 Blackstones reserves	28	19	1	8	76	41	58
4 St Neots Town reserves	28	17	5	6	74	41	56
5 Woodford United reserves	28	16	5	7	73	41	53
6 Peterbor' Northern Star res	28	13	3	12	86	57	42
7 North'ton Sileby Rangers res	28	12	5	11	57	49	41
8 Wellingborough Tn 2004 res	28	12	5	11	67	66	41
9 Stewart & Lloyds Corby res	28	12	4	12	54	58	40
10 Desborough Town reserves	28	10	3	15	53	83	33
11 Northampton Spencer res	28	9	4	15	53	71	31
12 North'pton ON Chenecks res	28	8	4	16	48	66	28
13 Huntingdon Town reserves	28	6	6	16	49	77	24
14 Welli'borough Whitworth res	28	4	7	17	40	73	19
15 Bourne Town reserves	28	2	3	23	24	119	9

RESERVE DIVISION TWO	P	W	D	L	F	A	Pts
1 Kings Lynn Town reserves	24	20	2	2	80	23	62
2 Thrapston Town reserves	24	16	2	6	68	45	50
3 Irchester United reserves	24	15	3	6	68	42	48
4 Raunds Town reserves	24	13	5	6	49	40	44
5 Bugbrooke St Michaels res	24	12	2	10	74	45	38
6 Olney Town reserves	24	12	1	11	56	52	37
7 Eynesbury Rovers reserves	24	9	3	12	45	49	30
8 Rothwell Corinthians res	24	8	4	12	44	59	28
9 Burton Park Wanderers rese	24	6	7	11	37	63	25
10 Harborough Town reserves	24	7	2	15	31	54	23
11 Rushden & Higham Utd res	24	6	4	14	25	59	22
12 St Ives Town reserves (-3)	24	6	5	13	31	54	20
13 Boston Town reserves	24	5	2	17	56	79	17

RESERVE LEAGUE CUP

FINAL (@ Peterborough Northern Star, 27/4/11)
Blackstones reserves 2-3 Thrapston Town reserves

RESERVE DIVISION TWO SUPPLEMENTARY CUP

FINAL (@ Eynesbury Rovers, 4/5/11)
Kings Lynn Town res. 2-4 Bugbrooke St Michaels res.

DIVISION TWO	1	2	3	4	5	6	7	8	9	10	11	12	13	14	15	16	17
1 AFC Kempston Rovers		3-0	6-1	1-1	5-1	5-2	4-0	1-2	4-0	1-3	5-0	5-0	1-1	7-0	2-1	6-1	1-0
2 Bourne Town	1-6		0-3	3-0	0-2	0-3	2-1	2-0	3-4	0-0	2-0	1-0	0-3	2-1	1-0	0-1	2-3
3 Buckingham Town	1-4	0-1		4-1	0-4	0-5	2-3	1-2	3-1	2-3	0-0	1-2	1-4	5-1	0-5	3-3	1-1
4 Bugbrooke St Michaels	1-0	6-0	2-0		3-1	5-1	6-1	3-2	1-2	3-1	1-0	5-3	8-2	2-3	4-2	4-2	0-0
5 Burton Park Wanderers	1-0	4-1	0-1	6-1		1-2	1-1	0-4	0-2	1-1	2-0	1-3	0-1	0-2	1-3	4-1	3-0
6 Eynesbury Rovers	0-0	2-0	0-2	1-2	2-2		1-0	1-4	3-1	2-1	2-2	6-0	1-2	1-0	0-3	1-1	2-4
7 Harborough Town	0-2	2-1	4-1	1-0	1-1	1-1		3-0	0-1	2-0	1-3	1-3	0-1	1-1	0-0	1-0	0-0
8 Huntingdon Town	1-3	2-1	1-0	0-1	1-1	4-1	2-0		0-0	2-1	0-3	2-0	2-1	0-1	1-3	1-3	1-2
9 Northampton ON Chenecks	0-7	2-2	3-2	0-2	1-3	1-2	2-0	1-2		1-2	0-1	1-2	4-3	3-2	0-5	3-5	2-3
10 Northampton Sileby Rangers	0-2	0-4	2-3	2-4	2-4	3-1	0-4	0-1	3-0		1-1	3-0	1-0	3-0	3-0	4-4	3-0
11 Olney Town	0-4	3-4	2-1	2-3	1-0	0-2	3-0	5-0	2-3	2-0		5-2	2-2	3-1	2-2	2-1	1-2
12 Potton United	1-2	0-0	3-1	3-2	1-6	1-4	3-0	3-5	0-1	0-1	1-5		1-2	0-1	2-7	2-1	4-2
13 Rothwell Town	0-0	5-2	2-3	1-2	4-4	2-1	3-1	0-1	0-0	2-1	3-1	1-2		2-1	0-2	1-0	2-2
14 Rushden & Higham United	0-7	1-1	0-3	2-5	2-2	0-3	0-1	5-0	2-5	2-2	0-1	2-0	2-1		2-1	2-1	0-0
15 Thrapston Town	3-2	3-1	3-2	1-0	2-1	3-1	5-1	1-0	6-0	7-1	3-0	6-2	4-2	0-1		2-0	2-3
16 Wellingborough Whitworth	1-6	3-0	1-1	0-3	2-3	3-1	3-0	1-1	2-0	3-0	1-3	2-2	1-1	1-1	0-0		1-3
17 Wootton Blue Cross	0-2	0-4	1-2	1-0	1-3	2-3	3-0	1-1	3-1	2-4	2-3	1-3	2-2	1-2	0-1	1-2	

AFC KEMPSTON ROVERS

Founded: 1884 Nickname: Walnut Boys

Secretary: Kevin Howlett **(T)** 07721 849 671 **(E)** howlett.home@btinternet.com
Chairman: Russell Shreeves **Manager:** Dave Randall **Prog Ed:** Mark Kennett
Ground: Hillgrounds Leisure, Hillgrounds Road, Kempston, Bedford MK42 8SZ **(T)** 01234 852 346
Capacity: 2,000 **Seats:** 100 **Covered:** 250 **Midweek Matchday:** Tuesday **Clubhouse:** Yes **Shop:**

Colours(change): Red & white stripes/black/black (Blue & black stripes/blue/blue)
Previous Names: Kempston Rovers > 2004.
Previous Leagues: South Midlands 1927-53
Records:
Senior Honours: U.C.L. Prem. 1973-74, Div 1 1957-58, 85-86, Div 2 1955-56, KO Cup 1955-56, 57-58, 59-60, 74-75, 76-77. UCL Division One 2010-11. Beds Senior Cup 1908-09, 37-38, 76-77, 91-92. Hinchingbrooke Cup 2010-11.

10 YEAR RECORD

01-02	02-03	03-04	04-05	05-06	06-07	07-08	08-09	09-10	10-11
UCL P 19	UCL P 21	UCL 1 16	UCL 1 16	UCL 1 4	UCL 1 3	UCL P 12	UCL 1 5	UCL 1 5	UCL 1 1

BLACKSTONES

Founded: 1920 Nickname: Stones

Secretary: Ian MacGillivray **(T)** 07749 620 825 **(E)** imacgilli@aol.com
Chairman: Kevin Boor **Manager:** Michael Goode & Darren Jarvis **Prog Ed:** Kevin Boor
Ground: Lincoln Road, Stamford, Lincs PE9 1SH **(T)** 01780 757 835
Capacity: 1,000 **Seats:** 100 **Covered:** yes **Midweek Matchday:** Wednesday **Clubhouse:** Yes **Shop:** No

Colours(change): Green/black/green. (Orange/black/orange)
Previous Names: Rutland Ironworks & Blackstone (until 1975)
Previous Leagues: Peterborough Works, Peterborough, Stamford & District
Records: **Att:** 700 v Glinton
Senior Honours: Lincolnshire Senior Cup A 1992-93, 2003-04. Lincolnshire Senior Trophy 2010-11.

10 YEAR RECORD

01-02	02-03	03-04	04-05	05-06	06-07	07-08	08-09	09-10	10-11
UCL P 12	UCL P 16	UCL P 11	UCL P 15	UCL P 10	UCL P 8	UCL P 4	UCL P 13	UCL P 13	UCL P 9

BOSTON TOWN

Founded: 1964 Nickname: Poachers

Secretary: Ron Bennett **(T)** 07985 471 691 **(E)** btfcsec@hotmail.co.uk
Chairman: Mick Vines **Manager:** Martyn Lakin **Prog Ed:** Pat Megginson
Ground: Tattershall Road, Boston, Lincs PE21 9LR **(T)** 01205 365 470
Capacity: 6,000 **Seats:** 450 **Covered:** 950 **Midweek Matchday:** Tuesday **Clubhouse:** Yes **Shop:**

Colours(change): Sky blue/navy blue/sky blue (Yellow/black/black)
Previous Names: Boston > 1994
Previous Leagues: Lincs, Central Alliance, Eastern co, Midland N. Co. E, C. Mids
Records: **Att:** 2,700 v Boston United FA Cup 1970. **Goalscorer:** Gary Bull 57 during 2006-07 season.
Senior Honours: Midland League 1974-75, 78-79, 80-81. Central Midlands 88-89. United Counties League 1994-95, 2000-01.

10 YEAR RECORD

01-02	02-03	03-04	04-05	05-06	06-07	07-08	08-09	09-10	10-11
UCL P 8	UCL P 8	UCL P 5	UCL P 11	UCL P 6	UCL P 2	UCL P 6	UCL P 5	UCL P 5	UCL P 7

COGENHOE UNITED

Founded: 1958 Nickname: Cooks

Secretary: Phil Wright **(T)** 07730 488 160 **(E)** secretary@cogenhoeunited.co.uk
Chairman: Derek Wright **Manager:** Andy Marks **Prog Ed:** Phil Wright
Ground: Compton Park, Brafield Road, Cogenhoe NN7 1ND **(T)** 01604 890 521
Capacity: 5,000 **Seats:** 100 **Covered:** 200 **Midweek Matchday:** Tuesday **Clubhouse:** Yes **Shop:** No

Colours(change): All Blue (White with black trim/black/black)
Previous Names:
Previous Leagues: Central Northants Comb, prem 67-84
Records: **Att:** 1,000 Charity game 90 **Goalscorer & Appearances:** Tony Smith
Senior Honours: United Counties League 2004-05. Buckingham Charity Cup 2010-11.

10 YEAR RECORD

01-02	02-03	03-04	04-05	05-06	06-07	07-08	08-09	09-10	10-11
UCL P 3	UCL P 9	UCL P 6	UCL P 1	UCL P 5	UCL P 5	UCL P 9	UCL P 9	UCL P 8	UCL P 15

DAVENTRY UNITED

Founded: 1968 Nickname: Motormen

Secretary: Nigel Foster **(T)** 07855 216 798 **(E)** dufcsecretary@btinternet.com
Chairman: Dave Hirons **Manager:** Darren Foster **Prog Ed:** Nigel Foster
Ground: Daventry Town FC, Communications Pk, Browns Rd, Daventry, NN11 4NS **(T)** 01327 311 239
Capacity: 2,000 **Seats:** 250 **Covered:** 250 **Midweek Matchday:** Wednesday **Clubhouse:** Yes **Shop:** No

Colours(change): Azure & Yellow/azure/azure (All purple & gold)
Previous Names: Ford Sports Daventry > 2007
Previous Leagues: Central Northants Combination 1968 - 1977.
Records:
Senior Honours: UCL Division One 1992-93, 95-96. Premier 1999-00, 01-02.

10 YEAR RECORD

01-02	02-03	03-04	04-05	05-06	06-07	07-08	08-09	09-10	10-11
UCL P 1	UCL P 11	UCL P 9	UCL P 6	UCL P 19	UCL P 20	UCL 1 5	UCL 1 2	UCL P 15	UCL P 12

DEEPING RANGERS

Founded: 1964 Nickname: Rangers

Secretary: Haydon Whitham **(T)** 07736 548 500 **(E)** roegroup@btconnect.com
Chairman: Kevin Davenport **Manager:** Tuncay Korkmaz **Prog Ed:** Robin Crowson
Ground: Deeping Sports Club, Outgang Road, Market Deeping, PE6 8LQ **(T)** 01778 344 701
Capacity: 1,000 **Seats:** 180 **Covered:** 250 **Midweek Matchday:** Tuesday **Clubhouse:** Yes **Shop:**

Colours(change): All claret & blue. (White/sky blue/sky blue)
Previous Names: None
Previous Leagues: Peterborough & District 1966 - 1999.
Records:
Senior Honours: Lincs Sen Cup, B Cup, Peterborough FA Cup (3). UCL Premier Champions 2006-07

10 YEAR RECORD

01-02	02-03	03-04	04-05	05-06	06-07	07-08	08-09	09-10	10-11
UCL P 10	UCL P 5	UCL P 17	UCL P 12	UCL P 20	UCL P 1	UCL P 7	UCL P 4	UCL P 4	UCL P 14

DESBOROUGH TOWN

Founded: 1896 Nickname: Ar Tam

Secretary: John Lee **(T)** 01536 760 002 **(E)** johnlee@froggerycottage85.fsnet.co.uk
Chairman: Ernie Parsons **Manager:** Martin McLeod **Prog Ed:** John Lee
Ground: Waterworks Field, Braybrooke Rd, Desborough NN14 2LJ **(T)** 01536 761 350
Capacity: 8,000 **Seats:** 250 **Covered:** 500 **Midweek Matchday:** Tuesday **Clubhouse:** Yes **Shop:**

Colours(change): All Blue (Yellow/yellow/black)
Previous Names: None
Previous Leagues: None
Records: **Att:** 8,000 v Kettering Town
Senior Honours: N'hants/Utd Co. Champs 1900-01, 01-02, 06-07, 20-21, 23-24, 24-25, 27-28, 48-49, 66-67. Lge C 77-78, 00-01, 07-08.
N'hants Sen C 1910-11, 13-14, 28-29, 51-52. Northants Senior Cup 1910-11, 13-14, 28-29, 51-52.

10 YEAR RECORD

01-02	02-03	03-04	04-05	05-06	06-07	07-08	08-09	09-10	10-11
UCL P 5	UCL P 18	UCL P 16	UCL P 10	UCL P 18	UCL P 14	UCL P 3	UCL P 11	UCL P 18	UCL P 19

HOLBEACH UNITED

Founded: 1929 Nickname: Tigers

Secretary: Karl Fawcett **(T)** 07955 947 606 **(E)** holbeachunitedfc@yahoo.co.uk
Chairman: Dave Dougill **Manager:** John Chand **Prog Ed:** Jamie Hiller
Ground: Carters Park, Park Road, Holbeach, Lincs PE12 7EE **(T)** 01406 424 761
Capacity: 4,000 **Seats:** 200 **Covered:** 450 **Midweek Matchday:** Tuesday **Clubhouse:** Yes **Shop:** No

Colours(change): Gold & black/black/gold & black.(Blue & white/blue/blue & white)
Previous Names:
Previous Leagues: Peterborough U Co L 46-55, Eastern 55-62, Midland Co 62-63
Records: **Att:** 4,094 v Wisbech 1954
Senior Honours: United Counties League 1989-90, 02-03. Lincs Sen A Cup (4), Senior Cup B 57-58

10 YEAR RECORD

01-02	02-03	03-04	04-05	05-06	06-07	07-08	08-09	09-10	10-11
UCL P 2	UCL P 1	UCL P 7	UCL P 3	UCL P 17	UCL P 11	UCL P 11	UCL P 16	UCL P 16	UCL P 17

IRCHESTER UNITED

Founded: 1883 Nickname:

Secretary: Glynn Cotter **(T)** 07802 728 736 **(E)** cotterg@visa.com
Chairman: Geoff Cotter **Manager:** Paul Hamblin **Prog Ed:** Geoff Cotter
Ground: Alfred Street, Irchester NN29 7DR **(T)** 01933 312877
Capacity: 1,000 **Seats:** none **Covered:** yes **Midweek Matchday:** **Clubhouse:** Yes **Shop:**

Colours(change): All blue (All red & black)
Previous Names: Irchester Eastfield 1980-90
Previous Leagues: Northamptonshire/United Counties 1896-97, 30-36, Rushden & District 1936-69
Records:
Senior Honours: Northants Lge Div 2 1930-31, 31-32, Rushden & District Lge (9), Northants Jnr Cup 1929-30, 33-34, 48-49, 75-76. United Counties League Division 1 2009-10.

10 YEAR RECORD

01-02	02-03	03-04	04-05	05-06	06-07	07-08	08-09	09-10	10-11
UCL 1 9	UCL 1 3	UCL 1 14	UCL 1 9	UCL 1 15	UCL 1 16	UCL 1 16	UCL 1 16	UCL 1 1	UCL P 10

KING'S LYNN TOWN

Founded: 1879 Nickname: Linnets

Secretary: Norman Cesar **(T)** 01553 631 336 **(E)** office@kltown.co.uknc@kltown.co.uk
Chairman: Keith Chapman **Manager:** Kevin Boon & Gary Setchell **Prog Ed:** Charlotte Rham
Ground: The Walks Stadium, Tennyson Road, King's Lynn PE30 5PB **(T)** 01553 760 060
Capacity: 8,200 **Seats:** 1,200 **Covered:** 5,000 **Midweek Matchday:** Tuesday **Clubhouse:** Yes **Shop:** Yes

Colours(change): Yellow & blue/blue/blue (Green & grey/grey/grey)
Previous Names: King's Lynn > 2010
Previous Leagues: N'folk & Suffolk, Eastern Co. 1935-39, 48-54, UCL 1946-48, Midland Co. 1954-58, NPL 1980-81, Southern, Conf
Records: **Att:** 12,937 v Exeter City FAC 1st Rnd 1950-51. **Goalscorer:** Malcolm Lindsey 321. **Apps:** Mick Wright 1,152 (British Record)
Senior Honours: Southern League Division 1 East 2003-04, Premier Division 2007-08, League Cup 2004-05.

10 YEAR RECORD

01-02	02-03	03-04	04-05	05-06	06-07	07-08	08-09	09-10	10-11
SthP 20	SthE 6	SthE 1	SthP 11	SthP 3	SthP 3	SthP 1	Conf N 17	NP P dnf	UCL P 2

LONG BUCKBY

Founded: 1937 Nickname: Bucks

Secretary: Eric Turvey **(T)** 07816 276 535 **(E)** ibafc01@gmail.com
Chairman: Guy Loveland **Manager:** Glenn Botterill **Prog Ed:** Eric Turvey
Ground: Station Road, Long Buckby NN6 7QA **(T)** 01327 842 682
Capacity: 1,000 **Seats:** 200 **Covered:** 200 **Midweek Matchday:** Tuesday **Clubhouse:** Yes **Shop:** No

Colours(change): Claret & white/claret & white/claret (White/black/black).
Previous Names: Long Buckby Nomads
Previous Leagues: Rugby & District Central, Northants Combination pre 68
Records: **Att:** 750 v Kettering Town
Senior Honours: United Counties League Div.2 1970-71, 71-72. Northants Senior Cup 2008-09. Munsell Cup 2009.

10 YEAR RECORD

01-02	02-03	03-04	04-05	05-06	06-07	07-08	08-09	09-10	10-11
UCL P 18	UCL P 20	UCL P 21	UCL P 8	UCL P 21	UCL P 12	UCL P 2	UCL P 8	UCL P 3	UCL P 4

NEWPORT PAGNELL TOWN

Founded: 1963 Nickname: Swans

Secretary: David Peters **(T)** 07980 236 772 **(E)** dp1211@live.co.uk
Chairman: Geoff Cardno **Manager:** Darren Lynch **Prog Ed:** Wayne Harmes
Ground: Willen Road, Newport Pagnell MK16 0DF **(T)** 01908 611 993
Capacity: 2,000 **Seats:** 100 **Covered:** 100 **Midweek Matchday:** Tuesday **Clubhouse:** Yes **Shop:** No

Colours(change): White & Green/black/green & black (All sky Blue)
Previous Names: Newport Pagnell Wanderers > 1972.
Previous Leagues: North Bucks 1963-71. South Midlands 1971-73.
Records:
Senior Honours: United Counties League Div.1 1981-82, 2001-02. Bucks & Berks Intermediate Cup 2001-02. Berks & Bucks Senior Trophy 2009-10, 10-11.

10 YEAR RECORD

01-02	02-03	03-04	04-05	05-06	06-07	07-08	08-09	09-10	10-11
UCL 1 1	UCL P 2	UCL P 13	UCL P 18	UCL P 15	UCL P 7	UCL P 15	UCL P 3	UCL P 6	UCL P 3

NORTHAMPTON SPENCER

Founded: 1936 Nickname: Millers

Secretary: Nick Hillery **(T)** 07894 150 853 **(E)**
Chairman: Graham Wrighting **Manager:** Andy Peaks **Prog Ed:** Andy Goldsmith
Ground: Kingsthorpe Mill, Studand Road, Northampton NN5 6NE **(T)** 01604 718 898
Capacity: 2,000 **Seats:** 100 **Covered:** 350 **Midweek Matchday:** Tuesday **Clubhouse:** Yes **Shop:** No

Colours(change): Green & yellow/green/green (All royal blue).
Previous Names: Spencer School Old Boys
Previous Leagues:
Records: **Att:** 800 v Nttm Forest 1993 **App;** P. Jelley 622 1984-2002
Senior Honours: United Counties League Division One 1984-85. Premier 1991-92. Northants Senior Cup Winners 2005-06.

10 YEAR RECORD

01-02	02-03	03-04	04-05	05-06	06-07	07-08	08-09	09-10	10-11
UCL P 17	UCL P 12	UCL P 18	UCL P 16	UCL P 3	UCL P 6	UCL P 13	UCL P 12	UCL P 14	UCL P 13

PETERBOROUGH NORTHERN STAR

Founded: 1900 Nickname:

Secretary: Glen Harper **(T)** 07884 288 756 **(E)** ghdjfc@hotmail.com
Chairman: Paul Arthur **Manager:** Chris Plummer **Prog Ed:** Rodney Payne
Ground: Chestnut Ave, Dogsthorpe, Eye, Peterborough, Cambs PE1 4PE **(T)** 01733 564 894
Capacity: 1,500 **Seats:** none **Covered:** yes **Midweek Matchday:** Wednesday **Clubhouse:** **Shop:**

Colours(change): Black & white stripes/black/black (Yellow/navy blue/yellow)
Previous Names: Eye Utd >2005
Previous Leagues: Peterborough Lge >2003
Records:
Senior Honours: Peterborough League 2002-03. Hinchingbrooke Cup 2009-10. United Counties League Division 1 2008-09. UCL Knock-out Cup 2010-11.

10 YEAR RECORD

01-02	02-03	03-04	04-05	05-06	06-07	07-08	08-09	09-10	10-11
		UCL 1 3	UCL 1 4	UCL 1 9	UCL 1 5	UCL 1 2	UCL 1 1	UCL 1 2	UCL P 6

SLEAFORD TOWN

Founded: 1968 Nickname: Town

Secretary: Jamie Shaw **(T)** 07870 271 751 **(E)** gotimhesgone@hotmail.com
Chairman: Mick Dwayne **Manager:** Brian Rowland **Prog Ed:** Steve Thomas
Ground: Estaforde Park, Boston Road, Sleaford, Lincs NG34 7GH **(T)** 01529 415 951
Capacity: **Seats:** 88 **Covered:** 88 **Midweek Matchday:** **Clubhouse:** Yes **Shop:**

Colours(change): Green/black/green (All red).
Previous Names:
Previous Leagues: Lincolnshire
Records:
Senior Honours: United Counties League Division One 2005-06.

10 YEAR RECORD

01-02	02-03	03-04	04-05	05-06	06-07	07-08	08-09	09-10	10-11
Lincs 5	Lincs 2	Lincs 1	UCL 1 6	UCL 1 1	UCL 1 2	UCL P 14	UCL P 15	UCL P 9	UCL P 18

SPALDING UNITED

Founded: 1921 Nickname: Tulips

Secretary: Audrey Fletcher **(T)** 07778 411 916 **(E)** tulips@uk2.net
Chairman: Chris Toynton **Manager:** Andy Stanhope **Prog Ed:** Ray Tucker
Ground: Sir Halley Stewart Playing Fields, Winfrey Avenue, Spalding PE11 1DA **(T)** 01775 712 047
Capacity: 2,700 **Seats:** 300 **Covered:** 500 **Midweek Matchday:** **Clubhouse:** Yes **Shop:** Yes

Colours(change): All royal blue (All orange & blue)
Previous Names: Not known
Previous Leagues: Peterborough, Utd Co.31-55,68-78,86-88,91-99,03-04, Ea. Co.55-60, Cen. All. 60-61, Midland Co.61-68, N.C.E.82-86, Sth.88-91, 99-03. NPL03-11.
Records: 6,972 v Peterborough - FA Cup 1982
Senior Honours: United Counties League 1954-55, 75-75, 87-88, 98-99, 2003-04. Northern Counties East 1983-84. Lincolnshire Senior Cup 1952-53.

10 YEAR RECORD

01-02	02-03	03-04	04-05	05-06	06-07	07-08	08-09	09-10	10-11
SthE 18	SthE 21	UCL P 1	NP 1 18	NP 1 20	SthM 19	NP 1 18	NP1S 17	NP1S 21	NP1S 22

ST. IVES TOWN
Founded: 1887 Nickname: Saints

Secretary: Simon Clark **(T)** 07884 398 770 **(E)** simon.clark@stivestownfc.co.uk
Chairman: Ashley Griffiths **Manager:** Warren Everdell & Jez Hall **Prog Ed:** Simon Clark
Ground: Westwood Road, St. Ives PE27 6WU **(T)** 01480 463 207
Capacity: **Seats:** Yes **Covered:** Yes **Midweek Matchday:** Tuesday **Clubhouse:** Yes **Shop:** No

Colours(change): White & black/black/black & white. (Red/white/white)
Previous Names: None
Previous Leagues: Cambs, Central Amateur, Hunts, Peterborough & District
Records:
Senior Honours: Hunts Senior Cup, Hunts Premier Cup, Hinchingbrooke Cup 2006-07. UCL Knockout Cup 2009-10.

10 YEAR RECORD

01-02	02-03	03-04	04-05	05-06	06-07	07-08	08-09	09-10	10-11
UCL 1 16	UCL 1 9	UCL 1 10	UCL 1 3	UCL P 9	UCL P 10	UCL P 5	UCL P 6	UCL P 10	UCL P 11

STEWARTS & LLOYDS CORBY
Founded: 1935 Nickname: The Foundrymen

Secretary: Kevin O'Brien **(T)** 07768 974 101 **(E)** kvnob@aol.com
Chairman: John Davies **Manager:** Daren Young & Lee Duffy **Prog Ed:** Kevin O'Brien
Ground: Recreation Ground, Occupation Road, Corby NN17 1EH **(T)** 01536 401 497
Capacity: 1,500 **Seats:** 100 **Covered:** 200 **Midweek Matchday:** Tuesday **Clubhouse:** Yes **Shop:** No

Colours(change): Maroon & amber/maroon/maroon. (All navy blue).
Previous Names: Hamlet S & L 1989-92.
Previous Leagues: Kettering Amateur
Records: **Goalscorer:** Joey Martin 46
Senior Honours: United Counties League Division One 1973-74, 74-75, Premier 85-86, 08-09.

10 YEAR RECORD

01-02	02-03	03-04	04-05	05-06	06-07	07-08	08-09	09-10	10-11
UCL P 14	UCL P 6	UCL P 19	UCL P 21	UCL P 16	UCL P 16	UCL P 12	UCL P 1	UCL P 12	UCL P 8

THRAPSTON TOWN
Founded: 1960 Nickname: Venturas

Secretary: Mark Brown **(T)** 07885 640 947 **(E)** mark@datsprint.co.uk
Chairman: Mark Brown **Manager:** Joe Smyth **Prog Ed:** Mrs Cathy Stevens
Ground: Chancery Lane, Thrapston, Northants NN14 4JL **(T)** 01832 732 470
Capacity: 1,000 **Seats:** Yes **Covered:** Yes **Midweek Matchday:** **Clubhouse:** Yes **Shop:**

Colours(change): All royal blue (Red/black/red)
Previous Names:
Previous Leagues: Kettering Amateur > 1978.
Records:
Senior Honours: Kettering Amateur League 1970-71, 72-73, 73-74, 77-78. Northants Junior Cup 1987-88, 98-99, 03-04.

10 YEAR RECORD

01-02	02-03	03-04	04-05	05-06	06-07	07-08	08-09	09-10	10-11
UCL 1 5	UCL 1 5	UCL 1 4	UCL 1 13	UCL 1 16	UCL 1 8	UCL 1 11	UCL 1 11	UCL 1 6	UCL 1 2

WELLINGBOROUGH TOWN 2004
Founded: 2004 Nickname: Doughboys

Secretary: Mick Walden **(T)** 07817 841 752 **(E)** mwalden@dsl.pipex.com
Chairman: Martin Potton **Manager:** Rob Gould **Prog Ed:** Mick Walden
Ground: The Dog & Duck, London Road, Wellingborough NN8 2DP **(T)** 01933 441 388
Capacity: **Seats:** Yes **Covered:** Yes **Midweek Matchday:** Tuesday **Clubhouse:** Yes **Shop:**

Colours(change): Yellow/royal blue/yellow. (All white)
Previous Names: Original team (Formed 1867) folded in 2002 reforming in 2004
Previous Leagues: Metropolitan. Southern.
Records:
Senior Honours: United Counties League 1964-65.

10 YEAR RECORD

01-02	02-03	03-04	04-05	05-06	06-07	07-08	08-09	09-10	10-11
UCL P 21				UCL 1 2	UCL P 3	UCL P 10	UCL P 18	UCL P 11	UCL P 5

YAXLEY

Founded: 1900 Nickname: The Cuckoos

Secretary: Mrs Sandra Cole **(T)** 07847 123 898 **(E)** sandracole22@ntlworld.com

Chairman: Alan Andrews **Manager:** Gary Clipston **Prog Ed:** Jeff Lenton

Ground: In2itive Park, Leading Drove, Holme Road, Yaxley, Peterborough PE7 3NA **(T)** 01733 244 928

Capacity: 1,000 **Seats:** 150 **Covered:** yes **Midweek Matchday:** Tuesday **Clubhouse:** Yes **Shop:** Yes

Colours(change): All blue (All red).
Previous Names: Yaxley Rovers.
Previous Leagues: Peterborough & Dist., Hunts & West Anglia
Records: **Goalscorer:** Ricky Hailstone 16
Senior Honours: United Counties League Division One 1996-97. Hunts Senior Cup (7), UCL Cup 2005-2006

10 YEAR RECORD

01-02	02-03	03-04	04-05	05-06	06-07	07-08	08-09	09-10	10-11
UCL P 11	UCL P 7	UCL P 8	UCL P 4	UCL P 7	UCL P 15	UCL P 16	UCL P 14	UCL P 19	UCL P 16

UNITED COUNTIES INS & OUTS

PREM

IN: AFC Kempston Rovers (P), Spalding United (R - Northern Premier Division One South), Thrapston Town (P)

OUT: Raunds Town (R), Rothwell Corinthians (R), St Neots Town (P - Southern League Division One Central)

DIV ONE:

IN: Raunds Town (R), Rothwell Corinthians (R)

OUT: AFC Kempston Rovers (P), Thrapston Town (P)

St Neots - Premier Division Champions - (Top) The squad celebrate their success. (Bottom Left) Skipper, Glen Fuff, resecives the trophy from league Vice-Chairman George Whiting. (Bottom Right) Will Fordham scores St Neots second in the 4-2 win over St Ives that sucured the title. Photos: Gordon Whittington.

DIVISION ONE

BOURNE TOWN
Founded: 1883 Nickname: Wakes

Secretary: Bob Lambert (T) 07514 804 404 (E) roblambert@btinternet.com
Chairman: TBC **Manager:** Darren Munton **Prog Ed:** Phil Jarman
Ground: Abbey Lawn, Abbey Road, Bourne, Lincs PE10 9EN (T) 01778 422 292 **Capacity:**
Colours(change): Claret & sky blue stripes/navy/navy (All yellow & green).

ADDITIONAL INFORMATION:
Record Att: FA Trophy 1970 **Goalscorer:** David Scotney.
U.C.L. Champions 1968-69, 69-70, 71-72, 90-91. Lincolnshire Senior A Cup 1971-72, 2005-06.

BUCKINGHAM TOWN
Founded: 1883 Nickname: Robins

Secretary: Darren Seaton (T) 07808 792 486 (E)
Chairman: Vince Hyde **Manager:** Dan Kingston **Prog Ed:** Carl Waine
Ground: The Winslow Centre, Ford Meadow, Ford Street, Buckingham MK18 1AG (T) 01280 816 257 **Capacity:**
Colours(change): All red (All white)

ADDITIONAL INFORMATION:
Paid: £7,000 to Wealdstone for Steve Jenkins 1992 Received: £1,000 from Kettering Town for Terry Shrieves.
Honours: Southern League Southern Division 1990-91. U.C.L. 1983-84, 85-86. Berks & Bucks Senior Cup 1983-84.

BUGBROOKE ST MICHAELS
Founded: 1929 Nickname: Badgers

Secretary: Debbie Preston (T) 07940 453 838 (E) billdebbiepreston@hotmail.com
Chairman: William Marriott **Manager:** Lee Herbert **Prog Ed:** Debbie Preston
Ground: Birds Close, Gayton Road, Bugbrooke NN7 3PH (T) 01604 830 707 **Capacity:**
Colours(change): Yellow & blue/royal blue/blue (Black & white stripes/black/black)

ADDITIONAL INFORMATION:
Record Att: 1,156. **Golascorer:** Vince Thomas. **Apps:** Jimmy Nord.
Honours: Northants Junior Cup 1989-90, Central Northants Comb. x6. U.C.L. Division 1 Champions 1998-99.

BURTON PARK WANDERERS
Founded: 1961 Nickname: The Wanderers

Secretary: Stewart Glendenning (T) 07795 368 731 (E) secretary@bpwfc.co.uk
Chairman: Stewart Glendenning **Manager:** Kevin Fox **Prog Ed:** Stewart Glendenning
Ground: Latimer Park, Polwell Lane, Burton Latimer, Northants NN15 5PS (T) 07980 013506 **Capacity:**
Colours(change): Azure/black/black (All red & black)

ADDITIONAL INFORMATION:
Record Att: 253 v Rothwell, May 1989.

EYNESBURY ROVERS
Founded: 1897 Nickname: Rovers

Secretary: Deryck Irons (T) 01234 268111 (E) deryckirons@aol.com
Chairman: Brian Abraham **Manager:** Matt Plumb & Paul Dodson **Prog Ed:** Graham Mills
Ground: Alfred Hall Memorial Ground, Hall Road, Eynesbury, St Neots PE19 2SF (T) 01480 477 449 **Capacity:**
Colours(change): Royal & white stripes/royal/royal (All yellow)

ADDITIONAL INFORMATION:
Record Att: 5,000 v Fulham 1953 (Stanley Matthews guested for Eynesbury). **Honours:** U.C.L. Division 1 1976-77.
Huntingdonshire Senior Cup x11. Huntingdonshire Premier Cup 1950-51, 90-91, 95-96.

HARBOROUGH TOWN
Founded: Formed: 1976 Nickname:

Secretary: Pauline Winston (T) 07708 404618 (E) p.winston2402@btinternet.com
Chairman: Andrew Winston **Manager:** Andrew Wilson **Prog Ed:** Tony Sansome
Ground: Bowden's Park, Northampton Road, Market Harborough, Leics. (T) 01858 467 339 **Capacity:**
Colours(change): Yellow and black (All green)

ADDITIONAL INFORMATION:
Previous League: Northants Combination.
Honours: Northants Combination 2009-10.

HUNTINGDON TOWN
Founded: 1995 Nickname:

Secretary: Russell Yezek (T) 07974 664818 (E) russell.yezek@ntlworld.com
Chairman: Paul Hunt **Manager:** Ricky Marheineke **Prog Ed:** Gemma Redgate
Ground: Jubilee Park, Kings Ripton Road,, Huntingdon, Cambridgeshire PE28 2NT (T) 07929 651 226 **Capacity:**
Colours(change): Red & black/red/red (All yellow & black)

ADDITIONAL INFORMATION:
Previous League: Cambridgeshire.
Honours: Cambridgeshire Div.1B 1999-2000. Hunts. Junior Cup 1999-00, 2000-01, 01-02. Hunts Scott Gatty Cup 2001-02.

NORTHAMPTON O.N. CHENECKS

Founded: 1946 Nickname:

Secretary: Trevor Cadden (T) 07894 425 823 (E) trevorcadden@btinternet.com
Chairman: Eddie Slinn **Manager:** Graham Cottle **Prog Ed:** Bryan Lewin
Ground: Old Northamptonians Sports Ground,Billing Road,Northampton NN1 5RX (T) 01604 634 045 **Capacity:**
Colours(change): White/navy/white (All red)

ADDITIONAL INFORMATION:
Honours: U.C.L. Div 1 1977-78, 79-80. Northants Junior Cup 2009-10.

NORTHAMPTON SILEBY RANGERS

Founded: 1968 Nickname: Sileby

Secretary: Dave Battams (T) 07913 909 068 (E) david@djbattams.f2s.com
Chairman: Robert Clarke **Manager:** Gary Petts **Prog Ed:** Dave Battams
Ground: Fernie Fields Sports Ground, Moulton, Northampton NN3 7BD (T) 01604 670366 **Capacity:**
Colours(change): All red (White/royal/white)

ADDITIONAL INFORMATION:
Record Att: 78.
Honours: Northampton Town Lg 1988-89 89-90. UCL Div 1 1993-94, 2002-03. Northants Jnr Cup 93-94, 96-97, 97-98, 2002-03

OLNEY TOWN

Founded: 1903 Nickname:

Secretary: Mrs Karen Keeping (T) 07808 776 715 (E) ikeeping@btinternet.com
Chairman: Paul Tough **Manager:** Neil Griffiths **Prog Ed:** Paul Tough
Ground: Recreation Ground, East Street, Olney, Bucks MK46 4DW (T) 01234 712 227 **Capacity:**
Colours(change): Green & white stripes/green/green (Yellow & green/yellow/yellow)

ADDITIONAL INFORMATION:
Previous League: Rushden & District.
Honours: U.C.L. Div 1 1972-73. Berks & Bucks Intermediate Cup 1992-93.

POTTON UNITED

Founded: 1943 Nickname: Royals

Secretary: Mrs Bev Strong (T) 07703 442 565 (E) bev.strong@tiscali.co.uk
Chairman: Alan Riley **Manager:** Glen Clark & Darren Staniforth **Prog Ed:** Mrs Bev Strong
Ground: The Hollow, Bigglewade Road, Potton, Beds SG19 2LU (T) 01767 261 100 **Capacity:**
Colours(change): All blue (Red/black/black)

ADDITIONAL INFORMATION:
Record Att: 470 v Hastings Town, FA Vase 1989.
Honours: U.C.L. 1986-87, 88-89, Div.1 2003-04. Beds Senior Cup x5. Huntingdonshire Premier Cup x4. E.Anglian Cup 1996-97

RAUNDS TOWN

Founded: 1946 Nickname: Shopmates

Secretary: Dave Jones (T) 07763 492 184 (E) david.jones180@ntlworld.com
Chairman: Pete Scanlon **Manager:** Stuart Brown **Prog Ed:** Dave Jones
Ground: Kiln Park, London Rd, Raunds, Northants NN9 6EQ (T) 01933 623 351 **Capacity:** 3,000
Colours(change): Red & black/black/black (White/red/red).

ADDITIONAL INFORMATION: Att: 1500 v Crystal Palace 1991 **Goalscorer:** Shaun Keeble. **App:** Martin Lewis - 355
Northants Senior Cup 1990-91.

ROTHWELL CORINTHIANS

Founded: 1934 Nickname: Corinthians

Secretary: Mark Budworth (T) 07730 416 960 (E) mbudworth@budworthhardcastle.com
Chairman: Mark Budworth **Manager:** Jason Thurland & Matt Clarke **Prog Ed:** Mark Budworth
Ground: Sergeants Lawn, Desborough Road, Rothwell, NN14 6JQ (T) 01536 418 688 **Capacity:**
Colours(change): Red/black/red. (All blue & black).

ADDITIONAL INFORMATION:

ROTHWELL TOWN

Founded: 1895 Nickname: The Bones

Secretary: Roger Barratt (T) 07702 311 792 (E) roger.barratt@eveden.com
Chairman: Ian Rice **Manager:** Dave Williams **Prog Ed:** Clair Martin
Ground: Home Close, Cecil Street, Rothwell, Northants NN14 2EZ (T) 01536 710 694 **Capacity:**
Colours(change): All white with blue trim (All blue & white)

ADDITIONAL INFORMATION:
Previous Grounds: Harrington Rd, Castle Hill. **Record Att:** 2,508 v Irthlingborough Diamonds, U.C.L. 1971.
Honours: U.C.L. 1992-93, 94-95. Northants Senior Cup 1899-1900, 1923-24, 59-60, 88-89, 96-96, 2001-02.

RUSHDEN & HIGHAM UNITED

Founded: Formed: 2007 Nickname:

Secretary: Chris Ruff (T) 01933 358 862 (E) chrisruff@talktalk.net
Chairman: Bill Perry **Manager:** Aidy Mann **Prog Ed:** Chris Ruff
Ground: Hayden Road, Rushden, Northants NN10 0HX (T) 01933 410 036 **Capacity:**
Colours(change): Orange/orange/black (All blue & white)

ADDITIONAL INFORMATION:
Club was formed after the merger of Rushden Rangers and Higham Town.

WELLINGBOROUGH WHITWORTH

Founded: Formed: 1973 Nickname: Flourmen

Secretary: Julian Souster (T) 07825 632 545 (E) julian.souster@yahoo.co.uk
Chairman: Brian Higgins **Manager:** M.Freeman, S.Medlin & S.Sargent **Prog Ed:** Julian Souster
Ground: London Road, Wellingborough, Northants NN8 2DP (T) 01933 227 324 **Capacity:**
Colours(change): Red/black/red (All blue & white)

ADDITIONAL INFORMATION:
Previous Name: Whitworths. **Previous League:** East Midlands Alliance > 1985.
Honours: Rushden & District League 1976-77. Northants Junior Cup 1996. U.C.L. Division One 2006-07.

WOOTTON BLUE CROSS

Founded: Nickname:

Secretary: Roy Leonard (T) 01234 306 313 (E)
Chairman: Eric Day **Manager:** Andy Arnold **Prog Ed:** Andy Arnold
Ground: Weston Park, Bedford Rd., Wootton MK43 9JT (T) 01234 767 662 **Capacity:**
Colours(change): Blue & white/blue/blue (Red & black stripes/black/red & black)

ADDITIONAL INFORMATION:
Previous Grounds: Recreation Ground, Fishers Field, Rose & Crown, Cockfield.
Record Att: 838 v Luton Beds Prem.Cup 1988. **Honours:** Beds Senior Cup 1970-71, 2001-02.

GROUND DIRECTIONS

AFC KEMPSTON ROVERS
Take A421 Bedford by pass turning as indicated to Kempston onto A5140 Woburn Road. At roundabout turn left into St John's Street then right into Bedford Road. After the shops and park on the left turn immediately left into Hillgrounds Road. Ground is past the swimming pool on right hand side.

BLACKSTONES FC
From Stamford Centre take A6121 towards Bourne. Turn left into Lincoln Road. Ground on the right hand side.
Go into town on A16 from Spalding. Turn left at roundabout into Liquor Pond Street becoming Queen Street over railway crossing along Sleaford Road. Turn right into Carlton Road then right at crossroads into Fydell Street. Over railway crossing and river take 2nd left (sharp turn) into Tattershall Road. Continue over railway crossing, ground on left.

BOURNE TOWN
From Town Centre turn east on A151 towards Spalding into Abbey Road. Ground approximately half a mile on right.

BUCKINGHAM TOWN
A421 ring road to Tesco roundabout. Turn right down hill towards town centre. Take slip road between Ford Garage and the Pub New Inn.

BUGBROOKE ST MICHAELS
At M1 Junction 16 take A45 to Northampton. At first roundabout follow signs to Bugbrooke. Go straight through village, ground entrance immediately past last house on the left.

BURTON PARK WANDERERS
From A14 take J10 towards Burton Latimer, at Alpro roundabout turn right, then straight over roundabout next to Versalift then right at Morrisions. Follow the round around the top of Morrisions continue until you are past the small Alumasc building on the left. Entrance to ground is next left.

COGENHOE UNITED
From A45 Northampton Ring Road turn as indicated to Billing/Cogenhoe. Go over River Nene and up hill ignoring first turning on left to Cogenhoe. Take next left and ground is on right hand side.

DAVENTRY UNITED
From Northampton or junction 16 of the M1 follow A45 westbound into Daventry, crossing the A5 on the way. At first roundabout bear left along A45 Daventry bypass. At next roundabout go straight over into Browns Road. The Club is at the top of this road

DEEPING RANGERS
From Town Centre head north on B1524 towards Bourne. Turn right onto Towngate East at Towngate Tavern Pub. Go straight over

mini roundabout onto Outgang Road. Ground 1/4 mile on left. From A16 by pass at roundabout with the A15 Bourne Road turn towards Deeping then left into Northfields Road, then left into Towngate/Outgang Road. Ground 1/4 mile on left.

DESBOROUGH TOWN

Take exit 3 marked Desborough off the A14 and follow bypass for 2 miles. At roundabout turn right and ground is 200 yards on the left hand side.

EYNESBURY ROVERS

From the A1 take the A428 towards Cambridge. Turn left at the Tesco roundabout and continue on Barford Road for half a mile going straight on at 4 roundabouts. Turn left into Hardwick Road and left into Hall Road. Ground at end of road

HARBOROUGH TOWN

Half a mile south of Market Harborough on the A508. 4 miles north of the A14 junction 2 towards Market Harborough turn left towards Leisure Centre, but keep left passed inflatable dome on the right, then through large car park, club house straight in front, with parking area.

HOLBEACH UNITED

Approaching Town Centre traffic lights from Spalding Direction take Second Left, or from Kings Lynn direction take sharp right, into Park Road. Ground is 300 yards on the left.

HUNTINGDON TOWN

At the A1 Brampton Hut roundabout, follow signs for A14 East until reaching the Spittals Interchange roundabout, Follow the A141 towards St Ives/March and go over 3 roundabouts. Take next left turn at traffic lights towards Kings Ripton and the ground is on the left.

IRCHESTER UNITED

From A509 Wellingborough/Newport Pagnell Road turn into Gidsy Lane to Irchester. Turn left into Wollaston Road B659. Alfred Street is on left hand side with the ground at the end.

KINGS LYNN TOWN

At A17/A47 roundabout, over River Ouse bridge to Hardwick roundabout, follow Town Centre sign over two sets of traffic lights. At Southgate roundabout take 4th exit, Vancouver Avenue. Continue over mini roundabout to Tennyson Road. Ground is on left

LONG BUCKBY AFC

From the Town Centre turn into Station Road. Ground on left hand side. Parking is available in South Close adjacent to the Rugby Club (do NOT park "half on half off" the pavement outside the ground)

NEWPORT PAGNELL TOWN

From the A422 Newport Pagnell by pass turn into Marsh End Road, then first right into Willen Road.

NORTHAMPTON ON CHENECKS

Leave A45 at exit marked Bedford A428 and Town Centre. Take exit into Rushmere Road marked Abington, Kingsthorpe and County Cricket. At first set of lights turn left into Billing Road, sports ground 250 yards on the right.

NORTHAMPTON SILEBY RANGERS

Approach from A43 (Kettering): From large roundabout with traffic lights, take the A5076 Talavera Way exit, signpostedto Market Harborough, Moulton Park and Kingsthorpe. The entrance to the ground is about a quarter of a mile on the left. Approach from A45: Take exit to A43 Ring Road / Kettering / Corby. Go straight over 1 roundabout to large roundabout with traffic lights. Then follow directions above.

NORTHAMPTON SPENCER

The ground is in Kingsthorpe area of Northampton on A508, Market Harborough road out of Town. Look for W Grose's garage (Vauxhall) and turn left at traffic lights into Thornton Rd, then first right into Studlands Rd. Follow to bottom of hill and onto track between allotments. Ground is after a right turn at end of track.

OLNEY TOWN

From the North enter via A509 Warrington Road then turn left into Midland Road and immediately right into East Street. Ground on left hand side after Fire Station.

PETERBOROUGH NORTHERN STAR

From A1 turn on to A1139 Fletton Parkway. Follow signs for A47 Wisbech. Exit at Junction 7 (near Perkins Engines Site). At top of slip road turn left into Eastfield Road. At Traffic lights turn right into Newark Avenue and then first right in to Eastern Avenue. Take 2nd left in to Chestnut Avenue and the club is on the right behind steel Palisade Fencing

POTTON UNITED

From Sandy, take B1042 into Potton. Head towards Potton Town Centre and take right turn towards Biggleswade (B1040). The ground is on left hand side at foot of hill

RAUNDS TOWN

From North, East or West, take A14 J13 and follow A45 signs to Raunds. Turn left at roundabout by BP garage. From South follow A45 towards Thrapston. Turn right at roundabout by BP garage. Ground on left.

ROTHWELL CORINTHIANS

A14 to Rothwell. Take B669 towards Desborough. Ground on right at rear of cricket field opposite last houses on the left. Parking on verge or in adjacent field if gate open. Access to ground via footpath.

ROTHWELL TOWN

Leave the A14 at Junction 4. At the roundabout, take the 2nd exit onto B576/Kettering Road. Go through 1 roundabout. At next roundabout turn right in to Bridge Street. Take third left in to Tresham Street. At top of road turn left in to ground.

RUSHDEN AND HIGHAM UNITED

From A6/A45 Junction take Higham/Rushden bypass. At third roundabout turn right, then turn right immediately after the school. From Bedford (A6) take bypass and turn left at first roundabout then turn right immediately after the school

SLEAFORD TOWN

A15 Sleaford By-pass, roundabout to A17 Holdingham Roundabout third exit towards Boston on A17 Take second exit of A17 towards Sleaford ground is 1 mile on right hand side before you enter Sleaford

SPALDING UNITED

From the North follow the A52 and pick up the A16 south, as you near Spalding follow A16 By-pass past the New Power Station (on right). Carry on the by-pass to Springfields Roundabout, (McDonalds is on the left) turn right. Follow signs to Spalding Town Centre over Fulney Bridge on the Holbeach Road and travel approx ¾ mile from by-pass. Turn right over second bridge forming the roundabout then straight over into West Elloe Avenue. Continue down to traffic lights (Approx 400 yards). Turn left into Pinchbeck Road. After approx 300 yards turn right at the traffic lights. Turn left at the next set of traffic lights into Winfrey Avenue. The Ground is on the left.

ST IVES TOWN

From A1123 Houghton Road rurn right at traffic lights into Ramsey Road. After Fire Station turn right into Westwood Road. Ground at end of road on right hand side immediately before St Ivo Recreation Centre Car Park

STEWARTS & LLOYDS CORBY

From the Oundle/Weldon Road turn at roundabout into A6086 Lloyds Road and continue to roundabout. Take second exit going over railway line along Rockingham Road. Continue over speed bumps then turn left into Occupation Road and first right into Cannock Road. Ground is beyond the British Steel Club and Rugby pitch.

THRAPSTON TOWN

Exit A14 at A605 roundabout, travel towards Peterborough till 1st roundabout (approx 700 metres).Take first exit into Thrapston. AT traffic lights turn into Oundle Road adjacent to Masons Arms Pub. Turn left into Devere Road and ground at bottom of hill

WELLINGBOROUGH TOWN 2004

Leave A.45 at Wellingborough turn-off, pass Tesco's Store on left-hand side, up to roundabout. Take first exit to town centre. Ground is 300 yards on right-hand side. Entry just past the Dog & Duck public house adjacent to entry to Whitworths ground

WELLINGBOROUGH WHITWORTH

Leave A45 by pass and go past Tescos etc. Turn left at roundabout then turn right immediately after Dog and Duck pub and go through 2nd gate down to the ground .

WOODFORD UNITED

A361 Daventry to Banbury Road. Turn left in Byfield. Follow road to Woodford Halse. Ground on left just past industrial estate.

WOOTTON BLUE CROSS

From A421 turn into Wootton as sign posted. Passing a garage on left hand side, turn right. Ground set back on right hand side behind post office and fish and chip shop.

YAXLEY

Leave A1 at Norman Cross and travel towards Peterborough. Turn off A15 at traffic lights. Bear immediately right and go past cemetery. At bottom of hill turn right into Main Street then left into Holme Road. After short distance go over small bridge and turn left between a bungalow and house into Leading Drove. Ground on left hand side.

A first minute goal from Aaron Baldwin gave AFC Kempston Rovers victory over Wootton Blue Cross - and won the Division One title for Rovers, thanks to Thrapston losing.
Photo: Gordon Whittington.

WESSEX LEAGUE

Sponsored by: Sydenhams
Founded: 1986
Recent Champions:
2006: Winchester City
2007: Gosport Borough
2008: AFC Totton
2009: Poole Town
2010: Poole Town
ncel.org.uk

PREMIER DIVISION	P	W	D	L	F	A	Pts
1 Poole Town	42	33	5	4	132	44	104
2 Bemerton Heath Harlequins	42	26	6	10	89	52	84
3 Winchester City	42	25	8	9	84	52	83
4 Brading Town	42	24	10	8	87	56	82
5 Bournemouth	42	23	11	8	100	43	80
6 Christchurch	42	21	12	9	86	60	75
7 Moneyfields	42	21	7	14	75	62	70
8 Fareham Town	42	19	10	13	76	69	67
9 Hamworthy United	42	19	9	14	88	70	66
10 Newport (IOW)	42	17	9	16	70	65	60
11 Lymington Town	42	18	5	19	77	79	59
12 Hamble ASSC	42	16	8	18	91	75	56
13 Alton Town	42	16	8	18	80	86	56
14 Blackfield & Langley	42	16	7	19	55	62	55
15 Alresford Town	42	13	6	23	82	84	45
16 Romsey Town	42	11	11	20	59	87	44
17 Laverstock & Ford	42	12	7	23	68	105	43
18 Totton & Eling	42	11	9	22	67	88	42
19 New Milton Town	42	10	7	25	56	104	37
20 Fawley	42	10	4	28	45	112	34
21 Hayling United	42	9	4	29	69	130	31
22 Brockenhurst	42	8	5	29	56	107	29

LEAGUE CUP

ROUND 2
Pewsey Vale 4-0 Stockbridge
Blackfield & Langley 2-0 Ringwood Town
Brockenhurst 0-1 Bemerton Heath Harlequins
Warminster Town 3-2 Shaftesbury
Bournemouth 2-0 Whitchurch United
Verwood Town 2-0 Andover New Street
Downton 8-1 Tadley Calleva
Christchurch 2-1 Hamworthy United
Hamble ASSC 5-0 Brading Town
United Services Portsmouth 2-3 Hayling United
Moneyfields 3-2 Fleet Spurs
Newport (IOW) 4-3 Alton Town
Lymington Town 4-0 Hythe & Dibden
Poole Town 3-1 Fareham Town
East Cowes Victoria 1-3 Winchester City
Totton & Eling 2-0 Petersfield Town

ROUND 3
Pewsey Vale 3-2 Blackfield & Langley
Bemerton Heath Harlequins 6-1 Warminster Town
Bournemouth 3-0 Verwood Town
Downton 1-0 Christchurch
Hamble ASSC 4-2 Hayling United
Moneyfields 5-2 Newport (IOW)
Lymington Town 2-1 Poole Town
Winchester City 4-2 Totton & Eling

QUARTER FINALS
Lymington Town 0-1 Winchester City
Pewsey Vale 1-4 Bemerton Heath Harlequins
Bournemouth 2-0 Downton
Hamble ASSC 4-1 Moneyfields

SEMI-FINALS
Bemerton Heath Harlequins 1-2 Bournemouth
Hamble ASSC 2-2 Winchester City
(Winchester City won 4-2 on penalties)

FINAL (@ AFC Totton, 7/5/11)
Bournemouth 1-0 Winchester City

PREMIER DIVISION	1	2	3	4	5	6	7	8	9	10	11	12	13	14	15	16	17	18	19	20	21	22
1 Alresford Town		4-3	1-3	2-4	0-3	2-2	1-2	2-2	0-3	4-0	1-1	3-2	3-0	2-6	0-0	3-0	3-1	4-0	0-2	0-1	2-1	0-3
2 Alton Town	2-3		1-1	0-1	0-6	2-2	1-0	1-2	2-2	5-0	1-5	2-2	3-3	2-1	0-3	3-3	1-3	2-1	1-4	1-1	5-3	3-2
3 Bemerton Heath Harlequins	4-1	1-3		3-1	4-1	2-0	2-2	1-2	2-0	2-0	2-3	4-0	4-0	1-1	2-0	3-1	2-1	2-1	0-3	0-0	3-1	1-2
4 Blackfield & Langley	3-2	0-1	1-1		2-1	0-3	2-1	1-2	0-1	1-2	1-0	0-1	5-2	3-1	1-3	2-1	3-3	0-2	3-1	2-0	2-1	0-6
5 Bournemouth	4-2	2-2	2-1	3-0		2-0	0-0	3-1	2-2	3-0	1-1	3-3	3-2	2-0	3-0	2-0	2-2	4-0	1-2	4-1	1-1	1-0
6 Brading Town	3-1	5-1	3-1	3-2	0-3		2-0	1-1	3-1	4-0	2-0	0-2	2-3	2-0	4-0	0-3	1-0	0-2	3-2	1-0	2-0	3-3
7 Brockenhurst	2-1	0-4	0-4	0-0	0-5	2-5		1-2	4-4	0-2	1-4	2-4	1-5	1-6	1-5	2-3	1-2	4-3	3-5	1-5	0-2	1-4
8 Christchurch	2-1	3-1	0-2	4-2	1-0	0-0	1-1		1-1	4-1	1-2	0-2	4-1	1-2	0-3	2-2	6-0	1-1	0-6	7-1	1-1	2-0
9 Fareham Town	2-1	4-3	3-0	0-0	1-3	2-2	0-4	3-0		4-1	2-1	2-1	3-0	0-0	2-0	2-3	2-1	0-1	3-2	1-1	4-1	1-0
10 Fawley	1-6	2-4	2-3	0-4	2-2	1-2	0-2	0-4	3-0		1-6	1-3	3-1	3-2	0-4	2-3	0-0	3-2	0-5	1-1	0-4	0-0
11 Hamble A S S C	3-3	0-2	2-6	1-0	0-3	1-3	3-0	2-2	5-1	5-0		1-2	2-0	4-4	0-1	3-3	1-2	2-3	1-3	1-4	3-0	1-3
12 Hamworthy United	0-0	1-3	0-1	2-2	0-2	1-3	1-0	2-2	1-2	3-2	0-1		3-1	5-2	1-1	1-1	3-1	0-2	4-1	4-2	3-0	0-2
13 Hayling United	0-7	2-6	2-5	1-0	2-7	0-2	2-1	0-1	2-3	2-1	0-5	1-6		4-4	4-2	0-2	3-4	0-2	1-3	4-4	1-2	2-3
14 Laverstock & Ford	3-2	0-2	1-2	2-1	0-3	1-2	1-7	1-4	0-6	2-0	0-6	1-1	0-3		2-0	2-1	2-3	1-4	1-7	2-3	1-0	2-1
15 Lymington Town	1-0	2-0	2-3	1-2	2-2	2-2	2-0	0-4	1-2	0-1	3-2	2-5	7-0	3-2		0-3	2-1	3-2	0-2	3-2	1-2	2-1
16 Moneyfields	1-0	2-1	0-1	1-0	1-0	2-3	0-1	3-1	3-1	2-3	2-0	3-2	2-1	1-1	5-1		1-0	0-2	0-3	2-1	0-3	1-1
17 New Milton Town	0-5	0-3	1-2	0-1	1-7	2-2	2-1	1-2	1-0	2-1	1-0	3-8	2-2	3-4	0-5	3-3		0-1	1-5	0-2	1-5	1-3
18 Newport (IOW)	4-3	0-1	0-1	1-0	1-0	1-1	1-0	1-3	1-1	4-1	2-2	2-2	6-0	1-1	3-3	1-3	2-0		1-3	0-1	3-2	1-2
19 Poole Town	2-0	4-0	3-0	1-0	1-1	4-1	4-1	5-5	5-0	3-0	3-3	4-0	3-1	2-0	4-0	3-2	3-1	2-2		2-2	2-0	1-0
20 Romsey Town	0-3	1-0	1-4	0-1	2-1	0-2	0-1	0-1	2-2	1-2	2-3	1-3	0-7	5-3	2-6	0-1	1-1	3-1	1-5		1-1	2-2
21 Totton & Eling	4-1	2-1	3-3	1-1	1-1	2-4	4-3	1-3	3-2	1-2	2-4	1-2	2-3	0-2	4-1	0-4	1-4	1-1	1-4	1-1		1-4
22 Winchester City	4-3	3-1	1-0	1-1	2-1	2-2	3-2	1-1	3-1	2-1	2-1	3-2	2-1	2-1	3-0	2-1	2-1	3-1	0-3	0-1	1-1	

DIVISION ONE	P	W	D	L	F	A	Pts
1 Downton	36	27	7	2	106	29	88
2 Horndean	36	25	4	7	104	53	79
3 AFC Portchester	36	20	9	7	85	52	69
4 Pewsey Vale	36	20	9	7	77	44	69
5 United Services Portsmouth	36	20	7	9	90	57	67
6 Ringwood Town	36	18	5	13	61	60	59
7 Whitchurch United	36	17	4	15	77	54	55
8 Cowes Sports (-1)	36	15	8	13	59	62	52
9 Verwood Town	36	13	11	12	70	66	50
10 Fleet Spurs	36	15	3	18	82	85	48
11 Petersfield Town	36	12	9	15	68	73	45
12 Warminster Town	36	13	6	17	72	79	45
13 Amesbury Town	36	14	3	19	62	90	45
14 Hythe & Dibden	36	9	9	18	60	72	36
15 East Cowes Victoria	36	9	9	18	52	77	36
16 Tadley Calleva	36	11	3	22	69	101	36
17 Andover New Street	36	10	6	20	60	93	36
18 Stockbridge	36	5	9	22	44	95	24
19 Shaftesbury	36	4	9	23	39	95	21

COMBINATION DIVISION	P	W	D	L	F	A	Pts
1 Sholing reserves	40	35	4	1	161	25	109
2 Christchurch reserves	40	29	2	9	142	69	89
3 Moneyfields reserves	40	26	4	10	112	58	82
4 AFC Totton reserves	40	25	5	10	134	49	80
5 Lymington Town reserves	40	24	5	11	92	69	77
6 Poole Town reserves	40	24	4	12	131	57	76
7 Horndean reserves	40	20	5	15	109	95	65
8 Alresford Town reserves	40	17	7	16	76	87	58
9 Hayling United reserves	40	18	4	18	84	115	58
10 Totton & Eling reserves	40	17	2	21	99	116	53
11 Hamble ASSC reserves	40	16	5	19	77	103	53
12 AFC Portchester reserves	40	15	6	19	95	96	51
13 Laverstock & Ford reserves	40	15	3	22	83	102	48
14 Bemerton Heath Harlequins res	40	13	5	22	88	129	44
15 Fawley reserves (-1)	40	13	5	22	67	111	43
16 Petersfield Town reserves	40	12	7	21	65	112	43
17 Alton Town reserves	40	12	6	22	88	112	42
18 Ringwood Town reserves	40	12	5	23	80	117	41
19 Romsey Town reserves	40	9	7	24	67	121	34
20 Brockenhurst reserves	40	9	6	25	63	104	33
21 Whitchurch United reserves	40	8	5	27	52	118	29

DIVISION ONE	1	2	3	4	5	6	7	8	9	10	11	12	13	14	15	16	17	18	19
1 AFC Portchester		4-0	2-0	6-1	1-5	2-1	1-1	1-2	2-1	2-2	0-3	3-1	3-3	2-1	3-2	4-0	2-3	3-2	2-0
2 Amesbury Town	1-2		4-1	0-4	0-4	5-4	3-1	2-3	3-1	3-7	1-1	1-5	5-0	0-4	2-9	1-4	1-0	6-2	2-1
3 Andover New Street	2-2	2-4		3-2	1-4	0-1	1-7	5-2	1-1	0-3	0-2	1-2	4-1	0-0	4-3	1-6	0-1	1-0	0-6
4 Cowes Sports	1-1	1-1	2-1		1-2	0-2	3-2	1-3	2-0	2-0	4-1	2-1	2-0	1-2	1-1	2-4	1-1	2-1	0-2
5 Downton	0-0	1-0	3-3	3-0		8-1	4-1	0-2	5-0	3-0	2-0	7-1	3-1	6-2	2-1	1-1	0-0	1-2	3-2
6 East Cowes Victoria Athletic	2-1	0-1	3-2	2-2	0-2		1-2	0-0	1-1	0-4	0-2	0-2	2-2	1-0	4-0	2-4	1-2	1-1	2-1
7 Fleet Spurs	2-3	5-1	1-2	1-2	2-5	2-4		2-8	3-0	1-2	0-4	5-1	3-1	2-2	2-1	1-4	2-7	2-3	2-0
8 Horndean	1-3	3-0	4-2	5-0	0-1	3-3	5-1		3-1	2-0	1-4	6-0	4-2	1-0	7-2	2-2	1-2	4-3	1-3
9 Hythe & Dibden	1-6	2-2	5-2	8-2	0-4	2-3	1-3	2-3		1-1	0-2	D-D	3-0	5-0	5-1	1-3	2-0	0-2	2-0
10 Petersfield Town	0-2	0-2	0-0	0-2	2-2	3-2	2-6	1-4	1-0		1-0	5-2	7-2	2-3	2-2	0-5	5-2	6-2	0-0
11 Pewsey Vale	1-1	4-0	0-2	1-1	0-0	3-0	4-1	2-2	3-2	2-1		0-0	2-1	7-0	4-3	4-4	2-3	2-1	3-0
12 Ringwood Town	1-0	3-2	2-1	1-0	0-3	2-1	0-0	0-1	4-0	3-0	5-2		2-1	0-1	2-1	5-1	2-1	2-3	3-2
13 Shaftesbury	0-4	1-2	0-4	0-2	0-4	1-0	0-2	2-1	3-1	1-1	0-2	1-1		1-1	3-0	0-3	3-6	1-3	0-2
14 Stockbridge	2-5	1-4	2-2	1-2	1-1	3-3	1-2	0-3	1-5	1-1	3-4	1-3	1-1		1-4	4-3	1-3	0-6	0-1
15 Tadley Calleva	1-3	2-0	4-2	2-6	1-5	3-0	1-4	1-3	0-1	0-3	2-0	0-3	2-2	3-2		4-3	3-1	5-2	1-8
16 United Services Portsmouth	3-3	3-0	7-2	0-2	0-1	3-1	0-2	0-2	1-1	3-2	1-1	2-0	3-0	1-0	3-1		1-1	5-2	3-1
17 Verwood Town	1-1	2-1	2-3	1-1	0-4	3-3	1-4	2-5	0-0	5-0	0-0	2-2	4-4	2-0	4-1	0-1		3-1	1-3
18 Warminster Town	1-5	1-2	0-4	1-1	2-3	1-1	3-2	0-3	2-2	5-3	1-3	3-0	5-0	1-1	4-1	3-1	1-1		2-0
19 Whitchurch United	4-0	2-0	5-1	2-1	1-4	4-0	4-3	3-4	3-3	1-1	1-2	1-0	1-1	7-1	0-1	0-2	4-3	2-0	

WESSEX LEAGUE INS & OUTS

PREM

IN: Downton (P), Horndean (P)

OUT: Brockenhurst (R), Poole Town (P - Southern League Division One South & West)

Hamble ASSC become GE Hamble

DIV ONE

IN: Brockenhurst (R), Team Solent (P - Hampshire Premier League)

OUT: Downton (P), Horndean (P), Shaftesbury (R - Dorset Premier League)

ALRESFORD TOWN

Founded: 1898 Nickname:

Secretary: Keith Curtis **(T)** 07703 346672 **(E)** secretary.alresfordtownfc@gmail.com
Chairman: Trevor Ingram **Manager:** Tim Cole **Prog Ed:** Gregory Boughton
Ground: Alresbury Park, The Avenue, Alresford, Hants SO24 9EP **(T)** 01962 735 100
Capacity: **Seats:** Yes **Covered:** Yes **Midweek Matchday:** Tuesday **Clubhouse:** Yes **Shop:**

Colours(change): Black & white stripes/black/black & white. (Yellow & blue/blue/yellow & blue)
Previous Names:
Previous Leagues: Winchester League, North Hants league, Hampshire League
Records:
Senior Honours: Winchester League Division Two & One

10 YEAR RECORD

01-02	02-03	03-04	04-05	05-06	06-07	07-08	08-09	09-10	10-11
Hant2 2	Hant1 11	Hant1 8	Wex2 10	Wex2 20	Wex1 2	WexP 21	WexP 18	WexP 17	WexP 15

ALTON TOWN

Founded: 1919 Nickname:

Secretary: Jim McKell **(T)** 07740 099 374 **(E)** jim@shadesoftime.net
Chairman: Jim McKell **Manager:** John Robson **Prog Ed:** Jim McKell
Ground: Alton (Bass) Sports Ground, Anstey Road, Alton, Hants GU34 2RL **(T)**
Capacity: 2,000 **Seats:** 200 **Covered:** 250 **Midweek Matchday:** Tuesday **Clubhouse:** Yes **Shop:** No

Colours(change): White/black/black (Yellow/green/yellow)
Previous Names: Present club formed in 1990 when Alton Town and Bass Alton merged.
Previous Leagues: Hampshire League >2002
Records:
Senior Honours: Hants Senior Cup 1958, 1969, 1972 & 1978. Hampshire Champions 2001-02.

10 YEAR RECORD

01-02	02-03	03-04	04-05	05-06	06-07	07-08	08-09	09-10	10-11
HantP 1	Wex1 17	Wex1 18	Wex1 19	Wex1 20	WexP 17	WexP 14	WexP 19	WexP 18	WexP 13

BEMERTON HEATH HARLEQUINS

Founded: 1989 Nickname: Quins

Secretary: Andy Hardwick **(T)** 07905 568007 **(E)** secretarybhhfc@hotmail.com
Chairman: Steve Slade **Manager:** **Prog Ed:** Steve Brooks
Ground: The Clubhouse, Western Way, Bemerton Heath Salisbury SP2 9DT **(T)** 01722 331925 (Club) 331218 (Office)
Capacity: 2,100 **Seats:** 250 **Covered:** 350 **Midweek Matchday:** Tuesday **Clubhouse:** Yes **Shop:** No

Colours(change): Black & white quarters/black/black & white (All orange)
Previous Names: Bemerton Athletic, Moon FC & Bemerton Boys merged in 1989
Previous Leagues: Salisbury & Wilts Comb, Salisbury & Andover Sunday
Records: **Att:**1,118 v Aldershot Town **App:** Keith Richardson
Senior Honours: Wiltshire Senior Cup 1992-93. Wessex League Cup 2009-10.

10 YEAR RECORD

01-02	02-03	03-04	04-05	05-06	06-07	07-08	08-09	09-10	10-11
Wex 11	Wex 18	Wex 12	Wex1 14	Wex1 14	WexP 11	WexP 13	WexP 12	WexP 3	WexP 2

BLACKFIELD & LANGLEY

Founded: 1935 Nickname:

Secretary: Andrew Hartmann **(T)** 07762 684 189 **(E)** andrewhartmann@aol.com
Chairman: Owen Lightfoot **Manager:** **Prog Ed:** Andrew Hartman
Ground: Gang Warily Rec., Newlands Rd, Southampton, SO45 1GA **(T)** 02380 893 603
Capacity: 2,500 **Seats:** 180 **Covered:** nil **Midweek Matchday:** Tuesday **Clubhouse:** Yes **Shop:**

Colours(change): White/green/green (Yellow/yellow/navy blue).
Previous Names:
Previous Leagues: Southampton Senior. Hampshire.
Records: **Att:** 240
Senior Honours: Hampshire League 1987-88, Division Two 1984-85, Southampton Senior Cup (4).

10 YEAR RECORD

01-02	02-03	03-04	04-05	05-06	06-07	07-08	08-09	09-10	10-11
Wex 17	Wex 21	Wex 21	Wex2 7	Wex2 14	Wex1 16	Wex1 10	Wex1 2	WexP 8	WexP 14

BOURNEMOUTH

Founded: 1875 Nickname: Poppies

Secretary: Mike Robins **(T)** 07947 687 808 **(E)** poppies1875@hotmail.co.uk
Chairman: Bob Corbin **Manager:** Ken Vaughan **Prog Ed:** Mike Robins
Ground: Victoria Park, Namu Road, Winton, Bournemouth, BH9 2RA **(T)** 01202 515 123
Capacity: 3,000 **Seats:** 205 **Covered:** 205 **Midweek Matchday:** Tuesday **Clubhouse:** Yes **Shop:** Yes

Colours(change): All Red (Yellow & blue/blue/blue)
Previous Names: Bournemouth Rovers, Bournemouth Wanderers, Bournemouth Dean Park
Previous Leagues: Hampshire
Records: Goalscorer (since 1990) DARREN McBRIDE 95 (111+26 games) Apps (since 1990) MARK DANCER 358 (318+40 games)
Senior Honours: Wessex League Cup Winners: 2011.

10 YEAR RECORD

01-02	02-03	03-04	04-05	05-06	06-07	07-08	08-09	09-10	10-11
Wex 18	Wex 14	Wex 20	Wex1 11	Wex1 7	WexP 5	WexP 5	WexP 15	WexP 4	WexP 5

BRADING TOWN

Founded: 1871 Nickname:

Secretary: Laurie Wallis **(T)** 07702 715 400 **(E)** bradingtown@hotmail.com
Chairman: Paul Morris **Manager:** Steve Brougham **Prog Ed:** Geoff Ruck
Ground: The Peter Henry Ground, Vicarage Lane, I.o.W. PO36 0AR **(T)** 01983 405 217
Capacity: **Seats:** **Covered:** **Midweek Matchday:** Tuesday **Clubhouse:** **Shop:**

Colours(change): White with red trim/red/red. (Blue/white/blue)
Previous Names:
Previous Leagues: Isle of Wight. Hampshire.
Records:
Senior Honours:

10 YEAR RECORD

01-02	02-03	03-04	04-05	05-06	06-07	07-08	08-09	09-10	10-11
HantP 8	HantP 17	HantP 18	Wex2 16	Wex2 3	WexP 10	WexP 15	WexP 14	WexP 14	WexP 4

CHRISTCHURCH

Founded: 1885 Nickname: Priory

Secretary: Ian Harley **(T)** 07900 133 954 **(E)** secretary@christchurchfc.co.uk
Chairman: Mark Duffy **Manager:** Graham Kemp **Prog Ed:** Fiona Kegg
Ground: Hurn Bridge S.C, Avon Causeway, Christchurch BH23 6DY **(T)** 01202 473 792
Capacity: 1,200 **Seats:** 215 **Covered:** 265 **Midweek Matchday:** Tuesday **Clubhouse:** Yes **Shop:**

Colours(change): All Blue (Red/black/black)
Previous Names:
Previous Leagues: Hampshire
Records: **App:** John Haynes
Senior Honours: Hants Jnr Cup (3), Hants Intermediate Cup 86-87, Bournemouth Senior Cup (5)

10 YEAR RECORD

01-02	02-03	03-04	04-05	05-06	06-07	07-08	08-09	09-10	10-11
Wex 15	Wex 13	Wex 11	Wex1 17	Wex1 10	WexP 14	WexP 16	WexP 7	WexP 5	WexP 6

DOWNTON

Founded: 1905 Nickname: The Robins

Secretary: Mike Turner **(T)** 07903 376 231 **(E)** therobins1@btinternet.com
Chairman: Mark Smith **Manager:** Jeff Softley **Prog Ed:** Mark Smith
Ground: Brian Whitehead Sports Ground Wick Lane Downton Wiltshire SP5 3NF **(T)** 01725 512162
Capacity: **Seats:** **Covered:** **Midweek Matchday:** Tuesday **Clubhouse:** **Shop:**

Colours(change): Red/white/red (Yellow/blue/yellow)
Previous Names:
Previous Leagues: Hampshire > 1993.
Records: **Att:** 55 v AFC Bournemouth - Friendly.
Senior Honours: Wiltshire Senior Cup 1979-80, 80-81. Wiltshire Junior Cup 1949-50. Wessex League Cup 1995-96. Wessex League Division One 2010-11.

10 YEAR RECORD

01-02	02-03	03-04	04-05	05-06	06-07	07-08	08-09	09-10	10-11
Wex 21	Wex 19	Wex 19	Wex1 22	Wex2 4	WexP 18	WexP 23	Wex1 17	Wex1 4	Wex1 1

FAREHAM TOWN

Founded: 1946 Nickname: The Robins

Secretary: Ian Tewson **(T)** 07930 853 235 **(E)** iantewson@aol.com
Chairman: Nick Ralls **Manager:** Paul Tanner **Prog Ed:** Paul Proctor
Ground: Cams Alders, Palmerston Drive, Fareham, Hants PO14 1BJ **(T)** 07930 853 235
Capacity: 2,000 **Seats:** 450 **Covered:** 500 **Midweek Matchday:** Wednesday **Clubhouse:** Yes **Shop:** Yes

Colours(change): Red/black/red (White/black/black or All blue)
Previous Names:
Previous Leagues: Portsmouth, Hampshire & Southern
Records: **Att:** 2,015 v Spurs (friendly 1985)
Senior Honours: Hampshire Senior Cup 1957, 1963, 1968, 1993. Hampshire League Champions.

10 YEAR RECORD

01-02	02-03	03-04	04-05	05-06	06-07	07-08	08-09	09-10	10-11
Wex 10	Wex 5	Wex 7	Wex1 16	Wex1 9	WexP 8	WexP 8	WexP 10	WexP 6	WexP 8

FAWLEY

Founded: 1923 Nickname:

Secretary: Richard Coxall **(T)** 07774 716 663 **(E)** fawleysecretary@hotmail.co.uk
Chairman: Kevin Mitchell **Manager:** **Prog Ed:** Jeff Moore
Ground: Waterside Spts & Soc. club, 179 Long Lane, Holbury, Soto, SO45 2QD **(T)** 02380 893750 (Club) 896621 (Office)
Capacity: **Seats:** **Covered:** **Midweek Matchday:** Wednesday **Clubhouse:** **Shop:**

Colours(change): All Blue (Red/white/red)
Previous Names: Esso Fawley > 2002
Previous Leagues: Hampshire Premier > 2004.
Records:
Senior Honours:

10 YEAR RECORD

01-02	02-03	03-04	04-05	05-06	06-07	07-08	08-09	09-10	10-11
HantP 19	HantP 18	HantP 16	Wex2 21	Wex2 7	Wex1 5	Wex1 6	Wex1 9	Wex1 2	WexP 20

GE HAMBLE

Founded: 1938 Nickname:

Secretary: Matthew Newbold **(T)** 07917 451 823 **(E)** hamble.assc@hotmail.co.uk
Chairman: Jennifer Headington **Manager:** **Prog Ed:** Ward Puddle
Ground: Folland Park, Kings Ave, Hamble, Southampton SO31 4NF **(T)** 02380 452 173
Capacity: 1,000 **Seats:** 150 **Covered:** 150 **Midweek Matchday:** Tuesday **Clubhouse:** Yes **Shop:** No

Colours(change): Sky blue & maroon/sky blue/sky blue (White/red/red)
Previous Names: Folland Sports (pre 1990), Aerostructures SSC 1990-97, Hamble ASSC 1997-2011.
Previous Leagues:
Records:
Senior Honours: Southampton Senior Cup 1984-85, 86-87, 91-92. Wessex League Division 1 2009-10.

10 YEAR RECORD

01-02	02-03	03-04	04-05	05-06	06-07	07-08	08-09	09-10	10-11
Wex 22	Wex 16	Wex 13	Wex1 21	Wex1 15	WexP 20	WexP 17	WexP 21	Wex1 1	WexP 12

HAMWORTHY UNITED

Founded: 1926 Nickname:

Secretary: Peter Gallop **(T)** 07897 959270 **(E)** sec-ham-utd-secretary@hotmail.co.uk
Chairman: Bruce Scammell **Manager:** Simon Browne **Prog Ed:** Jay Keating
Ground: The County Ground, Blandford Close, Hamworthy, Poole, BH15 4PR **(T)** 01202 674 974
Capacity: 2,000 **Seats:** **Covered:** **Midweek Matchday:** Tuesday **Clubhouse:** Yes **Shop:** No

Colours(change): Maroon & sky blue/sky blue/sky blue (Yellow & black/black/black)
Previous Names: Hamworthy St. Michael merged with Trinidad Old Boys 1926
Previous Leagues: Dorset Premier
Records:
Senior Honours: Dorset Premier League 2002-03, 03-04.

10 YEAR RECORD

01-02	02-03	03-04	04-05	05-06	06-07	07-08	08-09	09-10	10-11
Dor P 5	Dor P 1	Dor P 1	Wex1 15	Wex1 6	WexP 15	WexP 10	WexP 8	WexP 16	WexP 9

HAYLING UNITED

Founded: 1884 Nickname:

Secretary: Shirley Westfield **(T)** 07724 540 916 **(E)** shirley.westfield@ntlworld.com
Chairman: Argyll McLetchie **Manager:** Lee Paul **Prog Ed:** Mark Griffiths
Ground: Hayling College, Church Road, Hayling Island, Hampshire PO11 0NU **(T)** 02392 463 305
Capacity: **Seats:** **Covered:** **Midweek Matchday:** Tuesday **Clubhouse:** Yes **Shop:** No

Colours(change): Black & white/black/white (Yellow/yellow/white).
Previous Names:
Previous Leagues: Waterlooville & District > 1952 , Portsmouth 1952-91, Hampshire 1991-2004
Records:
Senior Honours: Hampshire League Division One 2002-03. Wessex Division One 2006-07.

10 YEAR RECORD

01-02	02-03	03-04	04-05	05-06	06-07	07-08	08-09	09-10	10-11
Hant1 3	Hant1 1	Hant1 5	Wex3 2	Wex2 2	Wex1 1	WexP 12	WexP 16	WexP 15	WexP 21

HORNDEAN

Founded: 1887 Nickname:

Secretary: Michael Austin **(T)** 07983 969644 **(E)** horndeanfc1887@yahoo.co.uk
Chairman: David Sagar **Manager:** Alan Knight **Prog Ed:** Ian Sheppard
Ground: Five Heads Park Five Heads Road Horndean Hampshire PO8 9NZ **(T)** 02392 591 363
Capacity: **Seats:** **Covered:** **Midweek Matchday:** Tuesday **Clubhouse:** **Shop:**

Colours(change): All red (All blue)
Previous Names:
Previous Leagues: Hampshire 1972-86, 1995-2004. Wessex 1986-95
Records: **Att:** 1,560 v Waterlooville, Victory Cup, April 1971. **Goalscorer:** Frank Bryson 348 (including 83 during the 1931-32 season)
Senior Honours:

10 YEAR RECORD

01-02	02-03	03-04	04-05	05-06	06-07	07-08	08-09	09-10	10-11
HantP 9	HantP 5	HantP 5	Wex2 9	Wex2 6	WexP 16	WexP 11	WexP 22	Wex1 12	Wex1 2

LAVERSTOCK & FORD

Founded: 1956 Nickname:

Secretary: Brian Ford **(T)** 07743 538 984 **(E)** sec.laverstockandfordfc@gmail.com
Chairman: Gino Nardiello **Manager:** Nev Beal **Prog Ed:** Michael Eyers
Ground: The Dell, Church Road, Laverstock, Salisbury, Wilts SP1 1QX **(T)** 01722 327 401
Capacity: **Seats:** **Covered:** **Midweek Matchday:** Tuesday **Clubhouse:** **Shop:**

Colours(change): Green & white hoops/green/green (Yellow/blue/white)
Previous Names:
Previous Leagues: Salisbury & District. Hampshire.
Records:
Senior Honours:

10 YEAR RECORD

01-02	02-03	03-04	04-05	05-06	06-07	07-08	08-09	09-10	10-11
Hant2 3	Hant2 1	Hant1 11	Wex3 11	Wex3 2	Wex1 12	Wex1 2	WexP 20	WexP 21	WexP 17

LYMINGTON TOWN

Founded: 1876 Nickname:

Secretary: Russell Young **(T)** 07922 065 803 **(E)** russellyoung626@hotmail.com
Chairman: George Shaw **Manager:** Stuart Hussey **Prog Ed:** Derek Webb
Ground: The Sports Ground, Southampton Road, Lymington SO41 9ZG **(T)** 01590 671 305
Capacity: 3,000 **Seats:** 200 **Covered:** 300 **Midweek Matchday:** Tuesday **Clubhouse:** **Shop:**

Colours(change): Red/white/black (Yellow/blue/yellow)
Previous Names:
Previous Leagues: Hampshire.
Records:
Senior Honours: Wessex League Cup 2006-07.

10 YEAR RECORD

01-02	02-03	03-04	04-05	05-06	06-07	07-08	08-09	09-10	10-11
HantP 14	HantP 15	HantP 7	Wex2 1	Wex1 17	WexP 12	WexP 20	WexP 18	WexP 20	WexP 11

MONEYFIELDS

Founded: 1987 Nickname: Moneys

Secretary: Wayne Dalton **(T)** 07766 411 346 **(E)** wayne.dalton@ntlworld.com
Chairman: Paul Gregory **Manager:** Miles Rutherford & Graeme Gee **Prog Ed:** David Hayter
Ground: Moneyfields Sports Ground, Moneyfield Ave, Copnor, P'mouth PO3 6LA **(T)** 02392 665 260
Capacity: 1,500 **Seats:** 150 **Covered:** 150 **Midweek Matchday:** Tuesday **Clubhouse:** Yes **Shop:** Yes

Colours(change): Yellow & navy blue/navy/yellow (White & blue/blue/white).
Previous Names: Portsmouth Civil Service
Previous Leagues: Portsmouth. Hampshire.
Records: **Att:** 250 v Fareham, WexD1 05-06 **Goalscorer:** Lee Mould 86 **App:** Matt Lafferty - 229 **Win:** 9-0v Blackfield & Langley 01-02.
Senior Honours: Portsmouth Premier Champions 1990-91, 91-92. Senior Cup 1990-91.
Hampshire Division Three 1991-92, Division Two 1992-93, Division One 1996-97.

10 YEAR RECORD

01-02	02-03	03-04	04-05	05-06	06-07	07-08	08-09	09-10	10-11
Wex 9	Wex 10	Wex 17	Wex1 10	Wex1 11	WexP 7	WexP 7	WexP 3	WexP 12	WexP 7

NEW MILTON TOWN

Founded: 2007 Nickname: The Linnets

Secretary: Richard Phippard **(T)** 07515 775 442 **(E)** secretary.newmilton@yahoo.co.uk
Chairman: John Breaker **Manager:** Darren Atkins & Steve May **Prog Ed:** Richard Phippard
Ground: Fawcett Fields, Christchurch Road, New Milton, BH25 6QB **(T)** 01425 628 191
Capacity: 3,000 **Seats:** 262 **Covered:** 262 **Midweek Matchday:** Tuesday **Clubhouse:** **Shop:**

Colours(change): All purple (All orange).
Previous Names: Lymington Town > 1988, AFC Lymington 1988-98, Lymington & New Milton 1998-07.
Previous Leagues: Isthmian. Southern.
Records:
Senior Honours: Wessex League 1998-99, 04-05.

10 YEAR RECORD

01-02	02-03	03-04	04-05	05-06	06-07	07-08	08-09	09-10	10-11
Wex 5	Wex 6	Wex 4	Wex1 1	Isth1 16	SthS 17	WexP 19	WexP 9	WexP 19	WexP 19

NEWPORT I.O.W.

Founded: 1888 Nickname: The Port

Secretary: John Simpkins **(T)** 07771 964 704 **(E)** simmo123@my-inbox.net
Chairman: Paul Phelps **Manager:** Derek Ohren **Prog Ed:** Sam Turner
Ground: St George's Park, St George's Way, Newport PO30 2QH **(T)** 01983 525 027
Capacity: 5,000 **Seats:** 300 **Covered:** 1,000 **Midweek Matchday:** Wednesday **Clubhouse:** Yes **Shop:** Yes

Colours(change): Yellow/blue/yellow. (Navy blue/navy/lime green)
Previous Names:
Previous Leagues: I.O.W. 1896-28. Hants 28-86. Wessex 86-90.
Records: **Att:** 2,270 v Portsmouth (friendly) 07.07.2001. **Goalscorer:** Roy Grilfillan - 220 1951-57. **Apps:** Jeff Austin - 540 1969-87.
Senior Honours: Southern League Eastern Division 2000-01. Hants Senior Cup (x8). I.O.W. Cup (34)

10 YEAR RECORD

01-02	02-03	03-04	04-05	05-06	06-07	07-08	08-09	09-10	10-11
SthP 19	SthE 16	SthE 19	Isth1 18	Isth1 22	SthS 20	SthS 22	WexP 6	WexP 9	WexP 10

ROMSEY TOWN

Founded: 1886 Nickname:

Secretary: Carolyn Mew **(T)** 0777 7072046 **(E)** waynemew@hotmail.co.uk
Chairman: Ken Jacobs **Manager:** **Prog Ed:** Cameron Melling
Ground: The Bypass Ground, South Front, Romsey, SO51 8GJ **(T)** 01794 513 685
Capacity: **Seats:** **Covered:** **Midweek Matchday:** Tuesday **Clubhouse:** Yes **Shop:**

Colours(change): White/black/black. (All blue).
Previous Names: None
Previous Leagues: Hampshire.
Records:
Senior Honours: Wessex League Champions 1989-90.

10 YEAR RECORD

01-02	02-03	03-04	04-05	05-06	06-07	07-08	08-09	09-10	10-11
Hant1 15	Hant2 13	Hant2 2	Wex2 4	Wex2 13	Wex1 3	WexP 18	WexP 11	WexP 10	WexP 16

TOTTON & ELING

Founded: 1925 Nickname:

Secretary: Mike Clarke **(T)** 07984 629051 **(E)** michael@clarke96.orangehome.co.uk
Chairman: Glen Donovan **Manager:** **Prog Ed:** Margaret Fiander
Ground: Totton & Eling Sports Club, Southern Gardens, Totton SO40 8RW **(T)** 02380 862 143
Capacity: **Seats:** Yes **Covered:** Yes **Midweek Matchday:** Tuesday **Clubhouse:** **Shop:**

Colours(change): Red/black/red (All yellow)
Previous Names: BAT Sports > 2007
Previous Leagues: Hampshire.
Records: 2,763 v AFC Wimbledon, FA Vase (game switched to AFC Wimbedon).
Senior Honours: Hampshire Champions 1987-88, 88-89. Wessex Division 1 2008-09.

10 YEAR RECORD

01-02		02-03		03-04		04-05		05-06		06-07		07-08		08-09		09-10		10-11	
Wex	19	Wex	11	Wex	15	Wex1	9	Wex1	18	Wex2	5	Wex1	5	Wex1	1	WexP	7	WexP	18

WINCHESTER CITY

Founded: Nickname:

Secretary: Bernadette McCarthy **(T)** 07884 225 611 **(E)** bernie.21@hotmail.com
Chairman: Bernadette McCarthy **Manager:** Paul McCarthy **Prog Ed:** Steve Woodgate
Ground: The City Ground, Hillier Way, Winchester SO23 7SR **(T)** 01962 810 200
Capacity: 2,500 **Seats:** 200 **Covered:** 275 **Midweek Matchday:** Tuesday **Clubhouse:** Yes **Shop:** Yes

Colours(change): Red with white trim/black/black (All white)
Previous Names: None
Previous Leagues: Hampshire 1898-71, 73-03. Southern 71-73, 06-09. Wessex 03-06.
Records: **Att:** 1,818 v Bideford, FA Vase Semi-final. **Goalscorer:** Andy Forbes. **Apps:** Ian Mancey.
Senior Honours: Hants Senior Cup 1932, 2005. Southampton Senior Cup 2000-01.
Hampshire Premier Division 2002-03. Wessex Division One 2003-04, 05-06. FA Vase 2004.

10 YEAR RECORD

01-02		02-03		03-04		04-05		05-06		06-07		07-08		08-09		09-10		10-11	
HantP	3	HantP	1	Wex	1	Wex1	2	Wex1	1	SthW	13	SthW	17	SthW	22	WexP	11	WexP	3

DIVISION ONE

AFC PORTCHESTER

Founded: Nickname:

Secretary: Colin Brans **(T)** 01329 311560 **(E)** colinbrans@yahoo.co.uk
Chairman: Mark Greenham **Manager:** Glen Bridgman **Prog Ed:** Peter Stiles
Ground: Wicor Recreation Ground Cranleigh Road Portchester Hampshire PO16 9DP **(T)** 07831 532 208 **Capacity:**
Colours(change): Tangerine/black/tangerine (Blue/white/blue)

ADDITIONAL INFORMATION:

AMESBURY TOWN

Founded: 1904 Nickname:

Secretary: Arthur Mundy **(T)** 07528 438103 **(E)** a.mundy094@virginmedia.com
Chairman: Jason Cameron **Manager:** Ian Jones **Prog Ed:** Mark Hilton
Ground: Bonnymead Park Recreation Road Amesbury SP4 7BB **(T)** 01980 623489 **Capacity:**
Colours(change): All blue (All yellow)

ADDITIONAL INFORMATION:
Previous Name: Amesbury FC. **Previous League:** Hampshire.
Record Att: 625 - 1997.

ANDOVER NEW STREET

Founded: 1895 Nickname:

Secretary: Mick Bugg **(T)** 07584 562 948 **(E)** andovernewstreetfc@hotmail.co.uk
Chairman: Martin Tobin **Manager:** **Prog Ed:** Jimmy Wilson
Ground: Foxcotte Park Charlton Andover Hampshire SP11 0HS **(T)** 01264 358358 **Capacity:**
Colours(change): Green & black/black/black (Yellow/white/white)

ADDITIONAL INFORMATION:
Record Att: 240.
Honours: Trophyman Cup 2003-04.

BROCKENHURST
Founded: 1898 Nickname: The Badgers

Secretary: Paul Christopher **(T)** 07837 587 657 **(E)** pc500@btinternet.com
Chairman: Dave Stansbridge **Manager:** John Pyatt **Prog Ed:** Paul Christopher
Ground: Grigg Lane, Brockenhurst, Hants SO42 7RE **(T)** 01590 623 544 **Capacity:** 2,000
Colours(change): Blue & white/blue/blue. (All green).

ADDITIONAL INFORMATION: Att: 1,104 v St Albans City
Hampshire League 1975-76.

COWES SPORTS
Founded: 1881 Nickname: Yachtsmen

Secretary: Glynn M Skinner **(T)** 07854 889446 **(E)** csfcsecretary@yahoo.com
Chairman: Ian Lee **Manager:** Steve Taylor **Prog Ed:** Peter Jeffery
Ground: Westwood Park Reynolds Close off Park Rd Cowes Isle of Wight PO31 7NT **(T)** 01983 293793 **Capacity:**
Colours(change): Blue & White stripes/black/blue (Red/white/white)

ADDITIONAL INFORMATION:
Previous League: Hampshire > 1994.
Honours: Hampshire League 1993-94.

EAST COWES VICTORIA ATHLETIC
Founded: Nickname:

Secretary: Darren Dyer **(T)** 07725 128701 **(E)** ecvics@live.co.uk
Chairman: Kenny Adams **Manager:** **Prog Ed:** Darren Dyer
Ground: Beatrice Avenue Whippingham East Cowes Isle of Wight PO32 6PA **(T)** 01983 297165 **Capacity:**
Colours(change): Red & white stripes/black/black (All green)

ADDITIONAL INFORMATION:

FLEET SPURS
Founded: Nickname:

Secretary: Paul Hampshire **(T)** 07850 810133 **(E)** secretary@fleetspursfc.co.uk
Chairman: Bryan Sheppard **Manager:** **Prog Ed:** Paul Hampshire
Ground: Kennels Lane Southwood Farnborough Hampshire, GU14 0ST **(T)** **Capacity:**
Colours(change): Blue with red trim/blue/blue (Yellow/black/yellow)

ADDITIONAL INFORMATION:

HYTHE & DIBDEN
Founded: Nickname:

Secretary: Nikki Oakley **(T)** 07769 951982 **(E)** hythedibdenfc@aol.com
Chairman: Robert J Parsons **Manager:** **Prog Ed:** Dee Harvey
Ground: Ewart Recreation Ground Jones Lane Hythe Southampton SO45 6AA **(T)** 02380 845264 (MD) **Capacity:**
Colours(change): Green & white/green/green (All blue)

ADDITIONAL INFORMATION:

PETERSFIELD TOWN
Founded: Nickname:

Secretary: Mark Nicoll **(T)** 07949 328240 **(E)** m.nicoll1@ntlworld.com
Chairman: Ian Essai **Manager:** Matt Short **Prog Ed:** Graeme Moir
Ground: Love Lane Petersfield Hampshire GU31 4BW **(T)** 01730 233416 **Capacity:**
Colours(change): Red & black stripes/black/black (All blue)

ADDITIONAL INFORMATION:
Previous Name: Petersfield United.
Previous League: Isthmian.

PEWSEY VALE
Founded: 1948 Nickname:

Secretary: Julie Wootton **(T)** 07789 168303 **(E)** secretary.pewseyvaleafc@hotmail.co.uk
Chairman: Alan Ritchie **Manager:** Adi Holcombe **Prog Ed:** Julie Wootton
Ground: Recreation Ground Kings Corner Ball Road Pewsey **(T)** 01672 562900 **Capacity:**
Colours(change): White/navy/navy (All yellow)

ADDITIONAL INFORMATION:
Previous League: Wiltshire.

RINGWOOD TOWN
Founded: 1879 Nickname:

Secretary: Aubrey Hodder **(T)** 07754 460501 **(E)** ringwoodtownfc@live.co.uk
Chairman: Steve Simpson **Manager:** Wayne Lockie **Prog Ed:** Ian Claxton
Ground: The Canotec Stadium Long Lane Ringwood Hampshire BH24 3BX **(T)** 01425 473448 **Capacity:**
Colours(change): All red (All blue)

ADDITIONAL INFORMATION:

STOCKBRIDGE
Founded: 1894 Nickname:

Secretary: Robin Smith **(T)** 01980 629781 **(E)** stockbridgefc@hotmail.co.uk
Chairman: Paul Barker **Manager:** Stuart Thompson **Prog Ed:** Mavis Savage
Ground: Stockbridge Recreation Ground High Street Stockbridge SP20 6EU **(T)** 07963 453162 **Capacity:**
Colours(change): All red (Blue & yellow/blue/blue & yellow)

ADDITIONAL INFORMATION:
Previous League: Hampshire.

TADLEY CALLEVA
Founded: Nickname:

Secretary: Steve Blackburn **(T)** 07787 501 028 **(E)** tadleycallevafc@sky.com
Chairman: Sandy Russell **Manager:** Danny Dolan **Prog Ed:** Steve Blackburn
Ground: Barlows Park Silchester Road Tadley Hampshire RG26 3PX **(T)** 07787 501 028 **Capacity:**
Colours(change): Yellow & black/black/yellow (Burgundy & blue/burgundy/blue)

ADDITIONAL INFORMATION:

TEAM SOLENT
Founded: Nickname:

Secretary: Claire Taylor **(T)** 07786 970 340 **(E)** claire.taylor@solent.ac.uk
Chairman: Phil Green **Manager:** **Prog Ed:** Peter Rosselli
Ground: Test Park, Lower Broomhill Road, Southampton SO16 9QZ **(T)** **Capacity:**
Colours(change): Red & black/red & black/red (Orange/orange/black).

ADDITIONAL INFORMATION:
Previous Lge: Hampshire > 2011.

UNITED SERVICES PORTSMOUTH
Founded: Nickname:

Secretary: Bob Brady **(T)** 07887 541782 **(E)** usportsmouthfc@hotmail.co.uk
Chairman: Richard Stephenson Lt. RN **Manager:** Bob Brady **Prog Ed:** Charlie Read
Ground: Victory Stadium HMS Temeraire Burnaby Road Portsmouth PO1 2HB **(T)** 02392 724 235 (Club) **Capacity:**
Colours(change): All royal blue (Red & white/red/red)

ADDITIONAL INFORMATION:
Previous Name: Portsmouth Royal Navy.

VERWOOD TOWN
Founded: 1920s Nickname:

Secretary: Roy Mortimer **(T)** 07801 713462 **(E)** secretary@vtfc.co.uk
Chairman: Michael Fry **Manager:** Adie Arnold **Prog Ed:** Dan Scott
Ground: Potterne Park Potterne Way Verwood Dorset BH21 6RS **(T)** 01202 814007 **Capacity:**
Colours(change): Red/black/black (Blue & white stripes/blue/yellow)

ADDITIONAL INFORMATION:
Previous League: Hampshire.

WARMINSTER TOWN
Founded: 1878 Nickname:

Secretary: Mr Jan Loftus **(T)** 07724 199 588 **(E)** janloftus@btinternet.com
Chairman: Peter Russell **Manager:** Tom O'Brien **Prog Ed:** Jan Loftus
Ground: 73 Weymouth Street Warminster Wiltshire BA12 9NS **(T)** 01985 217828 **Capacity:**
Colours(change): Red & black stripes/black/red (Light blue/dark blue/dark blue)

ADDITIONAL INFORMATION:
Previous League: Western

WHITCHURCH UNITED

Founded: 1903 Nickname:

Secretary: Paul Driver **(T)** 07921 548222 **(E)** driver999@btinternet.com
Chairman: Gary Shaughnessy **Manager:** Jim Macey **Prog Ed:** John Rutledge
Ground: Longmeadow Winchester Road Whitchurch Hampshire RG28 7RB **(T)** 01256 892493 **Capacity:**
Colours(change): Red & white stripes/black/red (All blue)

ADDITIONAL INFORMATION:

GROUND DIRECTIONS

AFC PORTCHESTER - Wicor Recreation Ground Cranleigh Road Portchester Hampshire PO16 9DP 07798 734678 (M)
Leave the M27 at Junction 11 and follow the signs to Portchester into Portchester Road. Carry on for approx 1 mile at the large roundabout, take the 3rd exit into Cornaway Lane and at the 'T' junction turn right in Cranleigh Road and follow the road to the end. Postcode for Satellite Navigation systems PO16 9DP

AFC TOTTON - Testwood Park Testwood Place Totton Southampton Hampshire SO40 3BE 02380 868981 (Club) 02380 263555 (Office)
Leave the M27 at Junction 3 and join the M271. At the roundabout take the second exit on to the slip road and join the A35 dual carriageway. Shortly after joining the carriageway take the next slip road on to the A36, which takes you under the bypass. Continue until you reach a roundabout; take the 3rd exit into Library Road. Follow this for approx 100 yards then turn left into Testwood Road, just after the Police Station. Testwood Place is the 2nd turning on the right with the ground entrance being 50 yards on the left. Postcode for Satellite Navigation systems SO40 3BE

ALRESFORD TOWN FC - Arlebury Park The Avenue Alresford Hampshire SO24 9EP 01962 735 100
Alresford is situated on the A31 between Winchester and Alton. Arlebury Park is on the main avenue into Alresford opposite Perins School.
Postcode for Satellite Navigation systems SO24 9EP

ALTON TOWN FC - Alton (Bass) Sports Ground Anstey Road Alton Hampshire GU34 2RL
Leave the A31 at the B3004 signposted to Alton. Follow the road round to the left passing Anstey Park on the right, the ground is then immediately on the left – opposite the turning into Anstey Lane. Postcode for Satellite Navigation systems GU34 2RL

AMESBURY TOWN FC - Bonnymead Park Recreation Road Amesbury SP4 7BB 01980 623489
From Salisbury take A345 to Amesbury, turn left just past the bus station and proceed through the one way system, when road splits with Friar Tuck Café and Lloyds Bank on left turn left and follow road over the river bridge and when road bears sharp right turn left into Recreation Road.
From A303 at Countess Roundabout go into Amesbury, straight over traffic lights, at mini-roundabout turn right into one way system and follow directions as above.
Postcode for Satellite Navigation systems SP4 7BB

ANDOVER NEW STREET FC - Foxcotte Park Charlton Andover Hampshire SP11 0HS 01264 358358 Weekends from Midday, Evenings from 1900 hrs
From Basingstoke follow the A303 to Weyhill roundabout. At roundabout turn right and 2nd roundabout turn left on to A342. Approx 1/2 mile turn right into Short Lane, continue into Harroway Lane to the 'T' junction at the top. Turn right into Foxcotte Lane and continue for about 3/4 mile then turn left, this still Foxcotte Lane, to the top some 3/4 mile to the roundabout straight across into Foxcotte Park. Postcode for Satellite Navigation systems SP11 0TA.

BEMERTON HEATH HARLEQUINS FC - The Clubhouse Western Way Bemerton Heath Salisbury Wiltshire SP2 9DT 01722 331925 (Club) 331218 (Office)
Turn off the A36 Salisbury to Bristol road at Skew Bridge (right turn if coming out of Salisbury), 1st left into Pembroke Road for 1/2 mile, 2nd left along Western Way – Ground is 1/4 mile at the end of the road. 40 minutes walk fro Salisbury railway station. Bus service 51 or 52 from the city centre.
Postcode for Satellite Navigation systems SP2 9DP

BLACKFIELD & LANGLEY FC - Gang Warily Community and Recreation Centre Newlands Road Fawley Southampton SO45 1GA 02380 893 603
Leave M27 at Junction 2 signposted A326 to Fawley. Head South along A326 through several roundabouts. Pass the Holbury P/H on your right at roundabout take the right fork signposted Lepe and Fawley.At the 1st set of traffic lights turn left then turn left into the ground, approx 200 yards. There is a sign at the traffic lights indicating Blackfield & Langley FC. Postcode for Satellite Navigation systems SO45 1GA

BOURNEMOUTH FC - Victoria Park Namu Road Winton Bournemouth Dorset BH9 2RA 01202 515 123
From the North and East – A338 from Ringwood. Take the 3rd exit signed A3060 Wimborne, going under the road you've just left. Stay on this road passing Castlepoint Shopping Centre (on your right), then the Broadway Hotel on your right, keep straight ahead passing the Horse & Jockey on your left, keep to the nearside lane. At roundabout take the 1st exit marked A347, pass Redhill Common on your right and the fire station on your left: continue on the A347 turning left at the filter with the pub – The Ensbury Park Hotel – immediately in front of you. 1st left into Victoria Avenue, and then third right into Namu Road, turning right at the end into the lane for the ground entrance.
From the West – A35 from Poole. Take the A3049 Dorset Way passing Tower Park (which is hidden from view) on your right, at the next roundabout take the second exit, and then the first exit at the next roundabout, taking up a position in the outside lane. At the next roundabout (with a pub called the Miller and Carter Steakhouse on your right) take the third exit, Wallisdown Road A3049. Go through the shopping area of Wallisdown across two roundabouts and at the third one take the first exit, you will see the ground on your right as you approach the pelican crossing. Turn right into Victoria Avenue, then third right into Namu Road, turning right at the end into the lane for the ground entrance. Postcode for Satellite Navigation systems BH9 2RA

BRADING TOWN FC - The Peter Henry Ground Vicarage Lane Brading Isle of Wight PO36 0AR 01983 405 217
Off the A3055 Ryde to Sandown Road. On entering Brading from Ryde take the first left off the mini roundabout – Vicarage Lane is adjacent to the main Brading car park. Postcode for Satellite Navigation systems PO36 0AR

BROCKENHURST FC - Grigg Lane Brockenhurst Hampshire SO42 7RE 01590 623544
Leave the M27 at Junction 1 and take the A337 to Lyndhurst. From Lyndhurst take the A337 signposted Brockenhurst, turn right at Careys Manor Hotel into Grigg Lane. Ground situated 200 yards on the right. Postcode for Satellite Navigation systems SO42 7RE

CHRISTCHURCH FC - Hurn Bridge Sports Club Avon Causeway Hurn Christchurc Dorset BH23 6DY 01202 473 792
A338 from Ringwood turn off at sign for Bournemouth International Airport (Hurn) on left. At T junction turn right, continue through traffic lights, at the small roundabout in Hurn turn right away from the Airport, exit signed Sopley and 100 yards on the right is Hurn Bridge Sports Ground. Postcode for Sat. Nav. systems BH23 6DY

COWES SPORTS FC - Westwood Park Reynolds Close off Park Road Cowes Isle of Wight PO31 7NT 01983 293 793

Turn left out of the Cowes pontoon, 1st right up Park Road approx 1/2 mile take the 4th right into Reynolds Close. Postcode for Sat. Nav. systems PO31 7NT

DOWNTON FC - Brian Whitehead Sports Ground Wick Lane Downton Wiltshire SP5 3NF 01725 512 162

The ground is situated 6 miles south of Salisbury on the A338 to Bournemouth. In the village – sign to the Leisure Centre (to west) – this is Wick Lane – football pitch and Club approx 1/4 mile on the left. Postcode for Satellite Navigation systems SP5 3NF

EAST COWES VICTORIA FC - Beatrice Avenue Whippingham East Cowes Isle of Wight PO32 6PA 01983 297 165

From East Cowes ferry terminal follow Well Road into York Avenue until reaching Prince of Wells PH, turn at the next right into Crossways Road then turn left into Beatrice Avenue, from Fishbourne follow signs to East Cowes and Whippingham Church, ground is 200 yards from the church on Beatrice Avenue.

Postcode for Satellite Navigation systems PO32 6PA

FAREHAM TOWN FC - Cams Alders Football Stadium Cams Alders Palmerston Drive Fareham Hampshire PO14 1BJ 07930 853 235 (Club)

Leave the M27 at Junction 11. Follow signs A32 Fareham – Gosport. Pass under the viaduct with Fareham Creek on your left, straight over at the roundabout then fork right – B3385 sign posted Lee-on-Solent. Over the railway bridge, Newgate Lane and turn immediately first right into Palmerston Business Park, follow the road to the ground. Postcode for Satellite Navigation systems PO14 1BJ

FAWLEY AFC - Waterside Sports and Social Club 179-182 Long Lane Holbury Southampton Hampshire SO45 2PA 02380 893750 (Club) 896621 (Office)

Leave the M27 at Junction 2 and follow the A326 to Fawley/Beaulieu. Head south for approx 7 miles. The Club is situated on the right hand side 2/3 mile after crossing the Hardley roundabout. The Club is positioned directly behind the service road on the right hand side. Postcode for Satellite Navigation systems SO45 2PA

FLEET SPURS FC - Kennels Lane Southwood Farnborough Hampshire, GU14 0ST

From the M3 Junction 4A take the A327 towards Farnborough/Cove. Left at the roundabout, over the railway line, left at the next roundabout Kennels Lane is on the right opposite the Nokia building, entrance is 100 yards on the left. Postcode for Satellite Navigation systems GU14 0ST

GE HAMBLE - Folland Park Kings Avenue Hamble-Le-Rice Southampton Hampshire SO31 4NF 02380 452 173

Leave the M27 at Junction 8 and take the turning for Southampton East At the Windhover roundabout take the exit for Hamble (B3397) Hamble Lane, proceed for 3 miles. Upon entering Hamble the ground is on the right via Kings Avenue, opposite the Harrier P/H. Postcode for Satellite Navigation systems SO31 4NF

GOSPORT BOROUGH FC - Privett Park Privett Road Gosport Hampshire PO12 3SX 02392 583 986 (Club) 02392 501 042 (Office)

Leave the M27 at Junction 11, take the A32 Fareham to Gosport Road, at the Brockhurst roundabout (after 3 miles) take the 3rd exit into Military Road past HMS Sultan, left into Privett Road at the next roundabout. Ground is 300 yards on the left. Postcode for Satellite Navigation systems PO12 3SX

HAMWORTHY UNITED FC - The County Ground Blandford Close Hamworthy Poole Dorset BH15 4BF 01202 674 974

From M27 to Cadnam – follow A31 to Ringwood – A347/A348 Ferndown - Bearcross – follow on this road until you pass the Mountbatten Arms on your left – turn right at next roundabout onto the A3049 and follow the signs to Dorchester and Poole. Continue on this dual carriageway over the flyover to the next roundabout – straight across and take the 2nd exit left off the dual carriageway to Upton / Hamworthy – go straight across 2 mini roundabouts and continue to Hamworthy passing the Co-op store on your left – then turn left at the 2nd set of traffic lights into Blandford Close. Postcode for Satellite Navigation systems BH15 4BF

HAYLING UNITED FC - College Ground The Hayling College Church Road Hayling Island,Hampshire PO11 0NU

From A27 take the Hayling Island exit, after crossing the Langstone Bridge continue past the Yew Tree P/H. After a mile turn left at the small roundabout into Church Road and after 1/2 mile turn left into Hayling College grounds.

NB All parking must be in front car park. Coaches to be parked in the lay-by outside the college. Postcode for Satellite Navigation systems PO11 0NU

HORNDEAN FC - Five Heads Park Five Heads Road Horndean Hampshire PO8 9NZ 02392 591 363

Leave A3(M) at Junction 2 and follow signs to Cowplain. Take the slip road passing Morrisons store on the right crossing over the mini roundabout then continue to the set of traffic lights ensuring you are in the right hand lane signed Horndean. Turn right at these traffic lights and continue on for approximately 400 yards until you reach the Colonial Bar on your left, next junction on your left after the Colonial Bar is Five Heads Road, turn left into Five Heads Road and the ground is approx 1/4 mile along this road. Postcode for Satellite Navigation systems PO8 9NZ

HYTHE & DIBDEN FC - Ewart Recreation Ground Jones Lane Hythe Southampton SO45 6AA 02380 845264 (Match days only) 07769 951982 (B)

Travel along the A326 then at the Dibden roundabout take the first left into Southampton Road. Continue for approx. 1 mile and then turn left into Jones Lane just before the Shell Filling Station and the ground is 200 yards on your left. Car parking is available in the Dibden Parish Hall car park at the bottom end of the ground. Postcode for Satellite Navigation systems SO45 6AA

LAVERSTOCK & FORD FC - The Dell Church Road Laverstock Salisbury Wiltshire SP1 1QX 01722 327 401

From Southampton – At the end of the carriageway from Southampton (A36) turn right at traffic lights for the Park & Ride by the Tesco store. Turn left at the traffic lights over the narrow bridge then take the next turning into Manor Farm Road. Take the next turning right into Laverstock Road, (do not turn left under the railway bridge). Keep left into Laverstock village, past the Church and the Club is situated on the left hand side directly opposite the Chinese takeaway and shop.

From Bournemouth – Follow the A36 to Southampton past Salisbury College and straight across the Tesco roundabout take left at traffic lights into the Park & Ride (take the corner slowly, the road goes back on itself) then follow directions as above. Postcode for Satellite Navigation systems SP1 1QX

LYMINGTON TOWN FC - The Sports Ground Southampton Road Lymington Hampshire SO41 9ZG 01590 671 305 (Club)

From the North & East – Leave the M27 at Junction 1 (Cadnam/New Forest) and proceed via Lyndhurst then Brockenhurst on the A337. On the outskirts of Lymington proceed through main set of traffic lights with Royal Quarter Housing Development and the Police Station on your right hand side. Continue for just another 250 metres and turn left immediately into St Thomas's Park with he ground in front of you.

Alternatively, turn left at the traffic lights into Avenue Road then first right, Oberland Court, with the Lymington Bowling Club facing you.

If travelling from the direction of Christchurch & New Milton using the A337 pass the White Hart P/H on the outskirts of Pennington and proceed down and up Stanford Hill. Passing the Waitrose Supermarket on your left hand side, the ground is situated immediately on your right hand side sign posted St Thomas Park.

Postcode for Satellite Navigation systems SO41 9ZG

MONEYFIELDS FC - Moneyfields Sports Ground Moneyfield Avenue Copnor Portsmouth Hampshire PO3 6LA 02392 665 260 (Club) 07766 250 812 (M)

Leave the A27 from the West and East at the Southsea turn off (A2030). Head down the Eastern Road and turn right into Tangiers Road at the fourth set of traffic lights – continue along this road until you pass the school and shops on your left and take the next right into Folkestone Road carrying on through to Martins Road and the Moneyfields Sports & Social Club is directly in front of you. Postcode for Satellite Navigation systems PO3 6LA

NEW MILTON TOWN FC - Fawcett Fields Christchurch Road New Milton Hampshire BH25 6QB 01425 628 191

Leave the M27 at Junction 2 and follow the signs to Lyndhurst. Carry on this road over four roundabouts and take the next slip road.At the traffic lights turn right to Lyndhurst. Go around the one way system and follow the signs to Christchurch (A35). After 10 miles at the Cat and Fiddle Public House turn left and continue towards the Chewton Glen Hotel. First exit at roundabout A337 to New Milton.The ground is one mile on the left. Postcode for Sat. Nav. systems BH25 6QB

NEWPORT (IOW) FC LTD. - St Georges Park St Georges Way Newport Isle of Wight PO30 2QH 01983 525 027 (Club)

From the Fishbourne Car Ferry Terminal take the A3054 towards Newport. At the large roundabout in the town centre take the A3020 towards Sandown, under the footbridge then 1st exit off the next roundabout. The ground is 200 yards on the left. Postcode for Satellite Navigation systems PO30 2QH

PETERSFIELD TOWN FC - Love Lane Petersfield Hampshire GU31 4BW 01730 233 416

Off circulatory one-way system in the town centre. Approx 10 minutes walk from Petersfield train station. Postcode for Satellite Navigation systems GU31 4BW

PEWSEY VALE FC - Recreation Ground Kings Corner Ball Road Pewsey 01672 562 900

From Pewsey's King Alfred statue, take the B3087 Burbage Road for 100 yards and then turn right into the Co-op car park, park in top right hand corner next to the bowls and tennis club and then walk through to the ground. Postcode for Satellite Navigation systems SN9 5BS

RINGWOOD TOWN FC - The Canotec Stadium Long Lane Ringwood Hampshire BH24 3BX 01425 473 448

Travel to Ringwood via the A31 (M27). From Ringwood town centre travel 1 mile on the B3347 towards Christchurch. At the Texaco petrol station turn into Moortown Lane and after 200 yards turn right into Long Lane. The ground is situated 250 yards on your left. Postcode for Satellite Navigation systems BH24 3BX

ROMSEY TOWN FC - The Bypass Ground South Front Romsey Hampshire SO51 8GJ

The ground is situated on the south of the town on the A27/A3090 roundabout (Romsey by pass), adjacent to the Romsey Rapids and Broadlands Estate.
Postcode for Satellite Navigation systems SO51 8GJ

SHOLING FC - VTFC Sports Ground Portsmouth Road Southampton SO19 9PW 02380 403 829

Leave the M27 at junction 8 and follow the signs to Hamble. As you drive up the dual carriageway, remain in the left hand lane. You come to the Windhover roundabout, take the 2nd exit getting into the lane marked "Hamble", take the right hand lane and go straight over at the small roundabout. After 200 yards bear right across the 2nd small roundabout (2nd exit). After 150 yards take the right hand lane and turn right into Portsmouth Road, sign posted Woolston. Continue for approx 1/2 mile until you see a large lay by on the left. The entrance to the VT Sports Ground is signposted opposite on your right next to the bus stop.
Postcode for Satellite Navigation systems SO19 9PW

STOCKBRIDGE FC - Stockbridge Recreation Ground High Street Stockbridge SP20 6EU 07963 453 162 (M)

From Stockbridge High Street turn right at BT Substation into ground. Postcode for Satellite Navigation systems SP20 6EU

TADLEY CALLEVA FC - Barlows Park Silchester Road Tadley Hampshire RG26 3PX

From M3 Basingstoke Junction 6 take the A340 to Tadley, travel through Tadley and at the main traffic lights turn right into Silchester Road, proceed for 0.5 mile then turn left into the car park. Postcode for Satellite Navigation systems RG26 3PX

TEAM SOLENT - Test Park, Lower Broomhill Road, Southampton SO16 9QZ

Leave the M27 at junction 3 for M271. Take the first slip road off the M271 and then first exit off the roundabout on to Lower Broomhill Road. Carry on to the next roundabout and take the last exit, (coming back on yourself) into Redbridge lane and the entrance to Test Park is approx. 500m on right.
From City centre take the Millbrook road to the M271, first slip road off on to roundabout, 3rd exit on to Lower Broomhill Way and then as above.
Postcode for Satellite Navigation systems SO16 9QZ

TOTTON & ELING FC - Totton & Eling Sports Club Southern Gardens Southampton SO40 8RW 02380 862 143

Enter Totton Central via the M271 and follow the signs for Ringwood & Cadnam. At the 1st roundabout take the 1st exit – Ringwood Road, 2nd roundabout, adjacent to Asda take the 2nd exit. Continue for approx 1/4 mile and enter Southern Gardens opposite Abbotswood School. Postcode for Sat. Nav. systems SO40 8RW

UNITED SERVICES PORTSMOUTH FC - Victory Stadium HMS Temeraire Burnaby Road Portsmouth Hampshire PO1 2HB
02392 724235 (Clubhouse) 02392 725315 (Office)

Leave the M27 at Junction 12 and join the M275 to Portsmouth. Follow the signs to Gunwharf, turn right at the traffic lights into Park Road then left at the next set of lights into Burnaby Road and the entrance is at the end of this road on the right.via HMS Temeraire.
NB Car parking in HMS Temeraire is for Senior Club and Match Officials only on the production of a current Sydenhams League (Wessex) pass. Free car parking for players and supporters is at the Portsmouth University Nuffield car park opposite the Registry Public House – follow Anglesea Road and signs for Southsea/Ferry Terminals, go under railway bridge past lights, keeping US Rogby Stadium on your right into Hampshire Terrace and keeping right, LOOP back into Anglesey Road, go through pedestrian lights and then immediately left into the car park. From car park turn right past pedestrian lights into Cambridge Road, then right into Burnaby Road. Postcode for Satellite Navigation systems PO1 2HB

VERWOOD TOWN FC - POTTERNE PARK POTTERNE WAY VERWOOD DORSET BH21 6RS 01202 814 007

Turn off the A31 at Verwood/Matchams junctions just West of Ringwood Town centre exit (immediately after garage if coming from the East) to join the B3081. Follow the B3081 through the forest for approximately 4 miles coming into Verwood itself. At the second set of traffic lights turn left into Black Hill. At the roundabout take the 1st exit left into Newtown Road. At the end of Newtown Road turn left and then 1st left into Potterne Way. Note: Along Black Hill on the left you will pass Bradfords Building Merchants and the entrance to the Verwood Sports & Social Club where post match refreshments are made available.
Postcode for Satellite Navigation systems BH21 6RS

WARMINSTER TOWN FC - 73 Weymouth Street Warminster Wiltshire BA12 9NS 01985 217 828

A36 from Salisbury, head for town centre, turn left at traffic lights in the town centre signposted A350 Shaftesbury. Club is situated approx.
400 yards on left hand side at top of Weymouth Street. Postcode for Satellite Navigation systems BA12 9HS

WHITCHURCH UNITED FC - Longmeadow Winchester Road Whitchurch Hampshire RG28 7RB 01256 892 493

From the South – take the A34 (North), 2 miles north of Bullington Cross take the Whitchurch exit. Head for Whitchurch Town Centre. The ground is 500 yards on your right. Postcode for Satellite Navigation systems RG28 7RB

WINCHESTER CITY FC - The City Ground Hillier Way Abbotts Barton Winchester Hampshire SO23 7SR 01962 810 200

From Junction 9 on the M3 take the A33/A34 for one mile then follow the A33 for a further mile. Take the first left into Kings Worthy and follow the road for about three miles. When you enter the 30 mph zone take the second left first right then left into Hillier Way. Ground is on the right.
Postcode for Satellite Navigation systems SO23 7SR

WEST MIDLANDS (REGIONAL) LEAGUE

Sponsored by: No sponsor

Founded: 1889

Recent Champions:

2006: Market Drayton Town

2007: Shifnal Town

2008: Bridgnorth Town

2009: AFC Wulfrunians

2010: Ellesmere Rangers

PREMIER DIVISION	P	W	D	L	F	A	Pts
1 Tividale	38	31	4	3	123	33	97
2 Gornal Athletic	38	27	5	6	106	43	86
3 AFC Wulfrunians	38	27	2	9	117	41	83
4 Wednesfield	38	24	8	6	87	38	80
5 Bustleholme	38	21	11	6	81	59	74
6 Bewdley Town	38	22	7	9	98	55	73
7 Bloxwich United	38	20	8	10	89	72	68
8 Cradley Town	38	17	7	14	90	71	58
9 Shifnal Town	38	16	6	16	79	67	54
10 Wellington	38	15	5	18	76	67	50
11 Lye Town	38	14	6	18	69	72	48
12 Wolverhampton Casuals (-3)	38	14	3	21	58	71	42
13 Dudley Town	38	12	5	21	53	106	41
14 Dudley Sports	38	13	0	25	47	88	39
15 Stafford Town	38	11	5	22	69	105	38
16 Darlaston Town	38	11	3	24	51	98	36
17 Shawbury United	38	10	5	23	48	96	35
18 W'ton Sporting Community	38	9	3	26	55	88	30
19 Goodrich	38	9	2	27	53	116	29
20 Bromyard Town	38	8	3	27	48	111	27

Heath Town Rangers changed their name to Wolverhampton Sporting Community during the season.

PREMIER CUP

ROUND 1

Bustleholme 3-1 Shawbury United
Bromyard Town 4-1 Dudley Town
Gornal Athletic 0-1 Wolverhampton Casuals
Tividale 2-1 Wednesfield

ROUND 2

AFC Wulfrunians 1-2 Cradley Town
Bewdley Town 3-4 Wellington
Wolverhampton Casuals 2-2 Darlaston Town
(Wolverhampton Casuals won 3-0 on penalties)
Shifnal Town 5-0 Bromyard Town
Stafford Town 2-4 Bloxwich United
Tividale 2-1 Dudley Sports
Wolverhampton SC 4-1 Goodrich
Bustleholme 4-1 Lye Town

QUARTER-FINALS

Cradley Town 3-7 Bustleholme
Wellington 1-2 Wolverhampton Casuals
Wolverhampton SC 1-6 Tividale
Bloxwich United 4-5 Shifnal Town

SEMI-FINALS (2 LEGS)

Tividale 0-1 Bustleholme
Bustleholme 1-3 Tividale
Tividale won 3-2 on aggregate
Wolverhampton Casuals 5-0 Shifnal Town
Shifnal Town 4-0 Wolverhampton Casuals
Wolverhampton Casuals won 5-4 on aggregate

FINAL (@ AFC Wulfrunians, 12/5/11)
Tividale 4-1 Wolverhampton Casuals

PREMIER DIVISION	1	2	3	4	5	6	7	8	9	10	11	12	13	14	15	16	17	18	19	20
1 A F C Wulfrunians		0-2	6-1	4-0	2-3	5-1	6-1	7-2	6-1	5-1	1-2	0-1	7-0	1-0	4-0	1-1	4-1	2-0	2-0	1-0
2 Bewdley Town	4-0		3-5	4-0	3-4	1-2	4-3	2-0	2-1	2-0	1-2	2-2	5-0	3-2	3-2	3-0	2-1	2-1	0-0	4-1
3 Bloxwich United	0-3	3-2		3-2	1-3	1-1	3-2	3-1	3-0	2-2	1-2	2-0	6-0	2-1	4-1	0-7	0-0	0-0	2-1	5-3
4 Bromyard Town	1-3	1-9	1-4		1-2	1-3	4-0	0-1	5-3	0-1	0-3	1-4	2-1	2-1	2-1	0-4	3-3	1-2	0-3	2-3
5 Bustleholme	3-2	0-5	1-1	4-1		2-3	2-1	4-2	3-2	3-1	1-1	3-3	3-0	2-1	1-1	2-3	3-3	3-0	2-2	2-1
6 Cradley Town	1-1	0-3	3-4	1-0	2-4		2-3	1-0	2-3	1-0	1-1	1-5	8-2	4-0	1-1	2-2	0-5	1-1	4-0	4-2
7 Darlaston Town	1-5	2-2	1-4	2-1	1-2	2-7		2-1	1-1	3-0	1-4	0-2	2-0	1-0	0-5	1-3	0-1	0-2	0-3	1-1
8 Dudley Sports	0-5	0-4	2-5	0-1	1-0	0-2	3-2		1-0	3-2	2-4	2-0	4-0	2-5	4-0	0-2	0-4	0-4	1-2	2-0
9 Dudley Town	0-4	2-2	3-1	3-4	2-2	0-7	2-1	1-0		4-1	2-4	1-3	0-1	0-2	0-3	0-6	0-5	1-6	2-0	4-3
10 Goodrich	1-3	1-2	0-5	2-2	1-2	1-5	0-1	3-1	2-3		1-7	1-4	2-1	1-3	6-3	2-1	0-6	4-7	1-3	1-0
11 Gornal Athletic	1-5	2-1	4-1	5-0	1-1	2-1	6-3	4-0	5-1	4-1		0-2	1-0	6-0	4-0	1-2	1-1	2-3	2-1	5-0
12 Lye Town	2-1	2-2	0-1	3-0	1-2	1-4	1-2	1-3	0-1	4-3	2-2		2-3	0-2	5-6	0-3	2-1	1-2	5-2	3-1
13 Shawbury United	0-5	3-1	1-2	2-2	0-3	2-1	2-3	4-2	3-3	0-1	0-2	2-2		3-0	3-5	0-0	1-3	3-2	2-1	0-3
14 Shifnal Town	4-2	0-1	2-1	3-0	1-1	3-3	4-0	5-0	2-2	5-1	0-1	3-4	2-2		3-0	0-2	2-2	4-4	4-3	1-0
15 Stafford Town	1-2	3-0	3-3	5-2	0-2	4-2	1-2	4-2	2-0	2-3	0-1	1-1	2-0	2-7		1-6	1-1	0-5	1-2	2-3
16 Tividale	1-0	0-3	3-1	6-1	4-1	2-0	5-1	3-1	9-0	5-2	3-1	5-0	2-0	3-0	8-1		1-1	2-1	2-1	2-1
17 Wednesfield	1-2	4-1	2-1	3-0	2-2	3-2	2-1	0-1	3-0	4-1	1-0	1-0	3-2	1-0	4-0	0-1		3-1	3-2	1-0
18 Wellington	1-3	2-2	2-2	4-1	1-2	0-1	5-1	0-1	0-1	1-2	0-4	2-1	1-2	0-2	6-1	3-6	0-2		2-1	0-1
19 Wolverhampton Casuals	1-4	1-3	2-2	4-1	1-0	0-3	2-0	2-1	1-2	4-1	3-5	2-0	2-1	3-1	0-2	0-3	0-3	1-2		2-1
20 Wolverhampton Sport Community	1-3	3-3	2-4	2-3	1-1	4-3	0-3	0-1	1-2	5-0	0-4	2-0	1-2	2-4	3-2	1-5	1-3	1-3	1-0	

WEST MIDLANDS LEAGUE - STEP 6/7

DIVISION ONE	P	W	D	L	F	A	Pts
1 Black Country Rangers	30	25	2	3	110	31	77
2 Wellington Amateurs	30	22	2	6	74	38	68
3 Sporting Khalsa	30	17	5	8	58	32	56
4 Wem Town (-3)	30	16	4	10	80	61	49
5 Hanwood United	30	14	6	10	52	45	48
6 Stone Old Alleynians	30	13	8	9	61	52	47
7 Warstone Wanderers	30	14	2	14	49	44	44
8 Blackheath Town	30	11	10	9	52	53	43
9 Bilston Town (2007)	30	10	12	8	68	59	42
10 Trysull	30	12	5	13	46	44	41
11 Penncroft	30	11	6	13	57	85	39
12 Wyrley	30	9	8	13	42	59	35
13 Shenstone Pathfinders	30	7	4	19	53	77	25
14 Bridgnorth Town reserves	30	6	3	21	43	81	21
15 AFC Wombourne United	30	4	8	18	41	75	20
16 Wolverhampton United	30	4	5	21	42	92	17

DIVISION ONE CUP

ROUND 1
Wyrley 2-0 Hanwood United
AFC Wombourne United 1-2 Blackheath Town
Bilston Town 0-1 Warstones Wanderers
Shenstone Pathfinder 0-5 Penn Croft (at Goodrich)
Stone Old Alleynians 0-1 Wem Town
Trysull 2-1 Black Country Rangers
Wolverhampton United 2-3 Bridgnorth Town Res.
Wellington Amateurs 1-0 Sporting Khalsa (at Sporting Khalsa)

QUARTER-FINALS
Blackheath Town 1-4 Wellington Amateurs
Warstones Wanderers 3-1 Bridgnorth Town Res.
Penn Croft 2-1 Wyrley
Trysull 1-2 Wem Town

SEMI-FINALS
Wem Town 0-1 Wellington Amateurs
Penn Croft 0-1 Warstones Wanderers (at Goodrich)

FINAL (@ at Wolverhampton Casuals, 10/5/11)
Wellington Amateurs 1-0 Warstones Wanderers

DIVISION ONE	1	2	3	4	5	6	7	8	9	10	11	12	13	14	15	16
1 A F C Wombourne United		2-2	0-5	1-3	3-1	0-2	2-4	5-1	1-3	1-1	0-1	0-4	1-3	4-4	1-2	5-1
2 Bilston Town	3-2		1-0	2-2	4-0	1-2	1-1	4-4	1-2	3-3	1-0	3-2	1-3	2-0	4-1	4-2
3 Black Country Rangers	3-0	4-3		1-1	3-1	2-1	8-1	2-1	2-1	1-0	5-3	2-1	2-1	7-1	8-2	4-1
4 Blackheath Town	4-1	4-4	0-6		1-1	0-0	2-2	5-0	0-0	1-1	1-0	0-3	2-4	0-3	4-1	0-1
5 Bridgnorth Town reserves	4-1	2-5	1-7	1-1		3-1	1-2	5-2	0-2	1-2	1-4	0-3	1-2	1-2	1-0	1-3
6 Hanwood United	1-3	1-1	1-1	5-2	3-1		5-0	1-0	1-1	1-2	5-0	1-0	0-0	4-4	2-1	1-0
7 Penncroft	1-1	2-2	1-11	1-4	2-5	5-0		5-0	1-5	4-2	2-5	1-4	4-2	5-2	2-1	2-2
8 Shenstone Pathfinder	2-2	3-2	2-4	4-1	5-2	0-2	4-0		2-3	2-2	1-2	1-2	2-3	1-2	0-2	2-0
9 Sporting Khalsa	4-0	4-2	0-2	1-0	0-1	2-0	2-3	3-0		6-1	0-2	1-2	0-3	1-2	4-1	3-0
10 Stone Old Alleynians	2-0	1-1	1-4	1-3	4-1	1-3	3-1	4-0	1-1		2-0	3-2	3-2	3-2	3-0	3-3
11 Trysull	0-0	1-0	1-4	2-3	3-1	3-1	0-1	1-1	0-1	1-1		0-0	2-3	1-2	2-2	0-1
12 Warstones Wanderers	2-1	1-3	1-0	0-0	5-1	0-3	1-3	3-2	0-1	0-2	0-2		0-3	1-0	1-0	3-0
13 Wellington Amateurs	2-0	3-1	2-1	0-2	3-0	3-0	1-0	5-3	0-0	2-0	1-3	3-1		2-0	4-3	1-0
14 Wem Town	7-1	3-3	2-4	1-4	3-1	5-0	7-1	3-2	1-2	2-1	2-0	2-4	3-1		4-1	4-2
15 Wolverhampton United	2-2	3-3	0-3	0-1	3-3	1-4	2-0	1-3	1-3	2-7	1-3	3-2	3-7	2-7		0-3
16 Wyrley Juniors	1-1	1-1	0-4	6-1	2-1	3-1	0-0	1-3	2-2	2-1	1-4	3-1	0-5	0-0	1-1	

DIVISION TWO	P	W	D	L	F	A	Pts
1 Malvern Rangers	24	18	3	3	89	33	57
2 St Martins	24	17	2	5	66	32	53
3 Leominster Town	24	15	4	5	72	33	49
4 AFC Smethwick	24	13	8	3	62	28	47
5 Penkridge Town	24	14	2	8	78	48	44
6 Wrens Nest	24	12	5	7	53	49	41
7 Tenbury United	24	12	3	9	53	46	39
8 Mahal	24	10	5	9	51	58	35
9 Team Dudley	24	10	1	13	37	47	31
10 Riverway	24	5	3	16	38	75	18
11 Bilston Town (2007) reserves	24	5	1	18	29	65	16
12 Ettingshall Park Farm	24	4	1	19	37	60	13
13 Wolv. Sporting Community res	24	2	0	22	18	109	6
Penn Colts - record expugned							
Warstones Wanderers reserves - record expunged							

DIVISION TWO CUP

ROUND 1
Bilston Town Res. 0-8 Malvern Rangers
Ettingshall Park Farm 2-0 Wolverhampton SC Res.
Mahal 1-3 Tenbury United
Penkridge Town 8-0 Warstones Wanderers Res.
Riverway 4-3 Penn Colts
St Martins 4-2 Wrens Nest
AFC Smethwick 3-1 Team Dudley

QUARTER-FINALS
AFC Smethwick 1-1 Ettingshall Park Farm
(AFC Smethwick won 5-4 on penalties)
Leominster Town 4-5 St Martins
Malvern Rangers 5-2 Penkridge Town
Riverway 2-2 Tenbury United
(Tenbury United won 5-3 on penalties)

SEMI-FINALS (2 LEGS)
AFC Smethwick 5-2 St Martins
St Martins 3-3 AFC Smethwick
AFC Smethwick won 8-5 on aggregate
Malvern Rangers 1-1 Tenbury United
Tenbury United 2-0 Malvern Rangers
Tenbury United won 3-1 on aggregate

FINAL (@ at Tividale, 10/5/11)
AFC Smethwick 2-1 Tenbury United

WEST MIDLANDS INS & OUTS

PREM- IN: Black Country Rangers (P), Malvern Town (R - Midland Alliance), Pegasus Juniors (S - Hellenic League Premier Division), Sporting Khalsa (P) **OUT:** Bloxwich United (S - Midland Combination Premier Division), Tividale (P - Midland Alliance)
DIV ONE - IN: AFC Smethwick (P), Leominster Town (P) **OUT:** Black Country Rangers (P), Sporting Khalsa (P)
DIV TWO - IN: Haughmond (P - Shropshire County League Premier Division), Hereford Lads Club (P - Herefordshire League Premier Division), Red Star Alma (P - Wolverhampton Combination), Sikh Hunters (P - Wolverhampton Combination)
OUT: AFC Smethwick (P), Bilston Town Reserves (W), Leominster Town (P), Malvern Rangers (W), Penn Colts (WS), Warstones Wanderers Reserves (WS)

DIVISION TWO	1	2	3	4	5	6	7	8	9	10	11	12	13
1 A F C Smethwick		0-2	0-0	0-0	4-0	2-2	5-3	0-1	2-4	2-2	4-1	1-0	1-1
2 Bilston Town reserves	1-6		0-4	2-4	0-6	0-5	0-3	3-3	0-2	2-1	2-4	1-2	0-2
3 Ettingshall Park Farm	0-1	1-3		0-2	3-4	1-3	1-4	3-0	1-4	0-1	1-4	4-1	2-3
4 Leominster Town	1-1	4-0	3-1		6-2	6-1	4-1	6-0	1-2	5-1	1-2	7-0	3-0
5 Mahal	0-5	3-2	2-1	6-0		2-1	1-1	4-1	0-9	0-3	1-2	2-1	1-1
6 Malvern Rangers	2-2	2-0	3-1	1-1	6-1		2-1	8-0	4-1	3-1	4-0	7-0	3-2
7 Penkridge Town	3-4	3-1	6-2	2-1	5-3	0-4		5-0	4-2	3-1	2-2	11-0	2-5
8 Riverway	0-5	1-6	5-1	1-1	2-2	2-4	2-3		0-2	1-2	1-3	4-0	6-3
9 St Martins	2-2	3-0	2-0	2-4	2-2	1-2	3-2	3-1		3-1	1-3	3-0	7-1
10 Team Dudley	0-4	2-0	2-0	1-4	0-3	1-4	1-3	3-0	0-1		2-1	3-0	1-3
11 Tenbury United	0-3	1-0	4-1	1-2	2-0	4-5	1-3	5-0	1-2	0-3		6-3	3-3
12 Wolverhampton Sptg Com reserves	2-3	0-4	1-9	2-5	0-5	0-11	0-6	1-6	1-3	0-3	1-2		1-3
13 Wrens Nest	1-5	3-0	2-0	4-1	1-1	4-2	3-2	2-1	0-2	5-2	1-1	0-2	

PREMIER DIVISION

A.F.C. WULFRUNIANS

Founded: 2005 Nickname:

Secretary: Ian Davies **(T)** 07989 953 738 **(E)** jaki.davies1512@btinternet.com
Chairman: Jason Scott **Manager:** **Prog Ed:**
Ground: Castlecroft Stadium, Castlecroft Road, Wolverhampton WV3 8NA **(T)** 01902 761410 **Capacity:**
Colours(change): Red & white/black/red

ADDITIONAL INFORMATION:
Honours: West Midlands (Regional) League Premier Division 2008-09.

BEWDLEY TOWN

Founded: 1978 Nickname:

Secretary: Steve Godfrey **(T)** 07739 626 169 **(E)** steve_g09@fsmail.net
Chairman: Geoff Edwards **Manager:** **Prog Ed:**
Ground: Ribbesford Meadows, Ribbesford, Bewdley, Worcs DY12 2TJ **(T)** 07739 626 169 **Capacity:**
Colours(change): Blue with yellow trim/blue/blue

ADDITIONAL INFORMATION:

BLACK COUNTRY RANGERS

Founded: 1996 Nickname:

Secretary: Paul Garner **(T)** 07510 957 447 **(E)** paulgarnertransport@hotmail.com
Chairman: Paul Garner **Manager:** **Prog Ed:**
Ground: Tividale FC, The Beeches, Packwood Road, Tividale B69 1UL **(T)** 01384 211 743 **Capacity:**
Colours(change): All red.

ADDITIONAL INFORMATION:
Honours: West Midlands (Regional) Division One 2010-11.

BROMYARD TOWN

Founded: 1893 Nickname:

Secretary: Richard Haverfield **(T)** 07885 849 948 **(E)** tony.haverfield@virgin.net
Chairman: Richard Greenhall **Manager:** **Prog Ed:**
Ground: Delahay Meadow, Stourport Road, Bromyard HR7 4NT **(T)** 01885 483 974 **Capacity:**
Colours(change): All blue

ADDITIONAL INFORMATION:

BUSTLEHOLME

Founded: 1975 Nickname:

Secretary: Angela Bowden (T) 07921 167 173 (E) bowdenfoster@aol.com
Chairman: Geoff Benbow **Manager:** **Prog Ed:**
Ground: Tipton Town F C, Wednesbury Oak Road, Tipton, West Mid. DY4 0BS (T) 0121 502 5534 **Capacity:**
Colours(change): Yellow/green/green

ADDITIONAL INFORMATION:

CRADLEY TOWN

Founded: 1948 Nickname:

Secretary: David Attwood (T) 07708 659 636 (E) d.attwood@sky.com
Chairman: Trevor Thomas **Manager:** **Prog Ed:**
Ground: The Beeches, Beeches View Avenue, Cradley, Halesowen B63 2HB (T) 07799 363 467 **Capacity:**
Colours(change): Red & white/red/red

ADDITIONAL INFORMATION:

DARLASTON TOWN

Founded: 1874 Nickname:

Secretary: Steven Poole (T) 07988 189 378 (E) steven.poole@sandwell.ac.uk
Chairman: Paul Tonks **Manager:** **Prog Ed:**
Ground: City Ground, Waverley Road, Darlaston, West Mids WS10 8ED (T) **Capacity:**
Colours(change): Blue & white/blue/blue

ADDITIONAL INFORMATION:

DUDLEY SPORTS

Founded: 1978 Nickname:

Secretary: John Lewis (T) 07737 099 385 (E) kath-john.lewis@blueyonder.co.uk
Chairman: Ashley Forrest **Manager:** **Prog Ed:**
Ground: Hillcrest Avenue, Brierley Hill, West Mids DY5 3QH (T) 01384 826 420 **Capacity:**
Colours(change): Green & black/green/green & white

ADDITIONAL INFORMATION:

DUDLEY TOWN

Founded: 1893 Nickname:

Secretary: David Ferrier (T) 07986 549 675 (E) davef.dtfc@blueyonder.co.uk
Chairman: Stephen Austin **Manager:** **Prog Ed:**
Ground: The Dell Stadium, Bryce Road, Brierley Hill, West Mids DY5 4NE (T) 01384 812 943 **Capacity:**
Colours(change): Red/black/black

ADDITIONAL INFORMATION:

GOODRICH

Founded: 1995 Nickname:

Secretary: Graham Turvey (T) 07813 467 220 (E) graham.turvey@goodrich.com
Chairman: Graham Turvey **Manager:** **Prog Ed:**
Ground: Stafford Road, Fordhouses, Wolverhampton WV10 7EH (T) **Capacity:**
Colours(change): All red

ADDITIONAL INFORMATION:

GORNAL ATHLETIC

Founded: 1945 Nickname:

Secretary: Kevin Williams (T) 07762 585 149 (E) k.williams880@btinternet.com
Chairman: Mat Danks **Manager:** **Prog Ed:**
Ground: Garden Walk Stadium, Garden Walk, Lower Gornal, Dudley DY3 2NR (T) 01384 358 398 **Capacity:**
Colours(change): All royal blue

ADDITIONAL INFORMATION:

LYE TOWN
Founded: 1930 Nickname:

Secretary: Yvonne Bignell **(T)** 07921 662 837 **(E)**
Chairman: Brian Blakemore **Manager:** **Prog Ed:**
Ground: Sports Ground, Stourbridge Road, Lye, Stourbridge, West Mids DY9 7DH **(T)** 01384 422 672 **Capacity:**
Colours(change): All blue

ADDITIONAL INFORMATION:

MALVERN TOWN
Founded: 1947 Nickname:

Secretary: Margaret Scott **(T)** 07944 110 402 **(E)** margscott55@hotmail.com
Chairman: Stanford Cullen **Manager:** **Prog Ed:**
Ground: Langland Stadium, Lamgland Avenue, Malvern WR14 2QE **(T)** 01684 574 068 **Capacity:** 2,500
Colours(change): Claret/sky blue/claret

ADDITIONAL INFORMATION: Att: 1,221 v Worcester City FA Cup. **Goals:** Graham Buffery. **Apps:** Nick Clayton.
Honours: Worcestershire Senior Urn (x7). Midland Combination Division One 1955-56.

PEGASUS JUNIORS
Founded: 1955 Nickname: The Redmen

Secretary: Chris Wells **(T)** 07980 465 995 **(E)** cwells@freenetname.co.uk
Chairman: Roger Hesten **Manager:** **Prog Ed:**
Ground: Old School Lane, Hereford HR1 1EX **(T)** 07980 465 995 **Capacity:** 1,000
Colours(change): All red.

ADDITIONAL INFORMATION: Att: 1,400 v Newport AFC, 1989-90.
Honours: Worcestershire Senior Urn 85-86. Hellenic Div.1 Champions 84-85, 98-99.
Previous Lge: Hellenic > 2011.

SHAWBURY UNITED
Founded: 1992 Nickname:

Secretary: Tracie Howells **(T)** 07950 740 089 **(E)** traciehowells72@yahoo.co.uk
Chairman: Wayne Price **Manager:** **Prog Ed:**
Ground: Wem Sports & Social Club, Bowensfield, Wem, Shrewsbury SY4 5AP **(T)** 01939 233 287 **Capacity:**
Colours(change): All blue

ADDITIONAL INFORMATION:

SHIFNAL TOWN
Founded: 1964 Nickname:

Secretary: Derek Groucott **(T)** 07910 120 512 **(E)** carolderek2@blueyonder.co.uk
Chairman: Glyn Davies **Manager:** **Prog Ed:**
Ground: Phoenix Park, Coppice Green Lane, Shifnal, Shrops TF11 8PB **(T)** 01952 463 257 **Capacity:**
Colours(change): Red & white stripes/black/red

ADDITIONAL INFORMATION:
Honours: West Midlands (Regional) League Premier Division 2006-07.

SPORTING KHALSA
Founded: 1991 Nickname:

Secretary: Parmjit Singh Gill **(T)** 07976 606 132 **(E)** parm@sportingkhlsa.com
Chairman: Rajinder Singh Gill **Manager:** **Prog Ed:**
Ground: Aspray Arena, Noose Lane, Willenhall WV13 3BB **(T)** 01902 219 208 **Capacity:**
Colours(change): Yellow/blue/blue.

ADDITIONAL INFORMATION:

STAFFORD TOWN
Founded: 1976 Nickname:

Secretary: David Howard **(T)** 07789 110 923 **(E)** staffordtown@hotmail.co.uk
Chairman: Gordon Evans **Manager:** **Prog Ed:**
Ground: Evans Park, Riverway, Stafford ST16 3TH **(T)** **Capacity:**
Colours(change): All red

ADDITIONAL INFORMATION:

WEDNESFIELD

Founded: 1961 Nickname:

Secretary: Ronald Brown (T) 07528 589 508 (E) rbwedfc@gmail.com
Chairman: David Hough **Manager:** **Prog Ed:**
Ground: Cottage Ground, Amos Lane, Wednesfield WV11 1ND (T) **Capacity:**
Colours(change): Red/black/black

ADDITIONAL INFORMATION:

WELLINGTON

Founded: 1968 Nickname:

Secretary: Michael Perkins (T) 07842 186 643 (E) perkins@haworth13.freeserve.co.uk
Chairman: Phillip Smith **Manager:** Colin Bowcott & Anthony Stokes **Prog Ed:**
Ground: Wellington Playing Field, Wellington, Hereford HR4 8AZ (T) **Capacity:**
Colours(change): Orange/orange/orange & white

ADDITIONAL INFORMATION:

WOLVERHAMPTON CASUALS

Founded: 1899 Nickname:

Secretary: Barry Austin (T) 01902 831 519 (E) judy_barry@blueyonder.co.uk
Chairman: Garth Deacon **Manager:** **Prog Ed:**
Ground: Brinsford Stadium, Brinsford Lane, Wolverhampton WS10 7PR (T) 01902 783 214 **Capacity:**
Colours(change): All green

ADDITIONAL INFORMATION:

WOLVERHAMPTON SPORTING COMMUNITY

Founded: 2001 Nickname:

Secretary: Mark Hopson (T) 07966 505 425 (E) wolvessporting@yahoo.co.uk
Chairman: John Quarry **Manager:** **Prog Ed:**
Ground: Wednesfield F C, Cottage Ground, Amos Lane, Wednesfield. WV11 1ND (T) 01902-735506 **Capacity:**
Colours(change): Blue & black/black/blue

ADDITIONAL INFORMATION:
Previous Name: Heath Town Rangers 2001-10.

WEST MIDLANDS (REGIONAL) LEAGUE DIVISION ONE CONSTITUTION 2011-12

A F C SMETHWICK ....York Road Social and Sports Club, York Road, Oldbury, West Mids. B65 0RR 0121-559-5563

A F C WOMBOURNE UNITED ....AFC Wulfrunians, Castlecroft Road, Wolverhampton. WV3 3NA 01902-761410

BILSTON TOWN ....Queen Street, Bilston WV14 7EX ....No number

BLACKHEATH TOWN.............Halesowen Town FC, The Grove, Old Hawne Lane, Halesowen. B63 3TB 0121-661-9392

BRIDGNORTH TOWN RESERVES.........Crown Meadow, Innage Lane, Bridgnorth WV16 4HS 01746-763001

HANWOOD UNITED.................................Hanwood Recreation Ground, Hanwood SY5 8JN ....No number

LEOMINSTER TOWN ....Bridge Street Park, Bridge Street, Leominster HR6 8EA 01568-611172

PENNCROFT ....Aldersley Leisure Village, Aldersley Road, Wolverhampton WV6 9NW 01902-556200

SHENSTONE PATHFINDER...... Shenston PF Pavilion Club, Birmingham Road, Shenstone WS14 0LR 01543-481658

STONE OLD ALLEYNIANS.........................Motiva Park, Yarnfield Lane, Yarnfield ST15 0NF 01785-761891

TRYSULL......................Wolverhampton Casuals FC, Brinsford Road, Coven Heath, Wolverhampton WV10 7PR 01902-783214

WARSTONES WANDERERS .... Cradley Town FC, Beeches View Avenue, Cradley B63 2HB ....No number

WELLINGTON AMATEURS ....School Grove, Oakengates TF2 6BQ ....No number

WEM TOWN...Butler Sports Centre, Bowens Field, Wem SY4 5AP 01939-233287

WOLVERHAMPTON UNITED..................... Prestwood Road West, Wednesfield WV11 1HL...01902-730881

WYRLEY JUNIORS.....................Long Lane Park, Long Lane, Essington, Wolverhampton. WV11 2AA..............................01922-406604

WEST MIDLANDS (REGIONAL) LEAGUE DIVISION TWO CONSTITUTION 2011-12

ETTINGSHALL PARK FARM .... Pendeford Lane, off Wobaston Road, Wolverhampton. WV9 5HQ................................01902-396666

HAUGHMOND.............................. Shrewsbury Sports Village, Sundorne Road, Shrewsbury. SY1 4RG.............................01743-256260

HEREFORD LADS..................County Ground, Widemarsh Common, Grandstand Road, Hereford. HR4 ....No number

MAHAL ....Hadley Stadium, Wilson Road, Smethwick B68 9JW.. 0121-434-4848

MALVERN TOWN RESERVES...........Langland Stadium, Langland Avenue, Malvern. WR14 2QE....................................01684-574068

PENKRIDGE TOWN ....Monkton Recreation Centre, Pinfold Lane, Penkridge ST19 5QP ....No number

RED STAR ALMA..............................Bentley Youth FC, Bentley Road South, Darlaston. WV10 8LN...No number

RIVERWAY..........................Beaconside Sports Centre, Staffordshire Uni, Weston Road, Stafford ST18 0AD...................01785 353286

SIKH HUNTERS......................... Bloxwich United AFC, Somerfield Road, Bloxwich, Walsall. WS3 2EJ.....................Tel: 01902-405835

ST MARTINS................................. The Venue, Burma Road, Parkhall, Oswestry, Shrops. SY11 8AS..............................01691-684840

TEAM DUDLEY..The Dell Stadium, Bryce Road, Brierley Hill DY5 4NE..01384 812943

TENBURY UNITED................................Palmers Meadow, Burford, Tenbury Wells WR15 8AP ....No number

WOLVERHAMPTON SPORTING COM. RES Pendeford Lane, Wolverhampton WV9 5HQ...No number

WRENS NEST.....................................Handrahan Sports Stadium, Mile Flat, Wallheath DY6 0AX ....No number

GROUND DIRECTIONS - PREMIER DIVISION

AFC WULFRUNIANS - Castlecroft Stadium, Castlecroft Road, Wolverhampton WV3 8NA. Tel: 01902-761410
From Wolverhampton, depart on Darlington Street. At the roundabout, take the second exit onto Chapel Ash A41. Bear left onto Merridale Road. Turn right onto Merridale Lane. Turn left onto Compton Road A454. Bear right onto Bridgnorth Road A454. At the roundabout, take the first exit onto Bridgnorth Road A454 Turn left onto Windmill Lane. Turn right onto Castlecroft Avenue. Turn right onto Castlecroft Road.
Ground is on left hand side.

BEWDLEY TOWN - Ribbesford Meadows, Ribbesford, Bewdley, Worcs. DY12 2TJ Tel: 07739-626169
From Kidderminster follow signs to Bewdley on A456 past West Midlands Safari Park and follow signs to Town Centre at next Island. Go over River Bridge into Town and turn left at side of Church (High Street). Stay on this road for 1 ½ miles. Entrance to ground is on left.

BLACK COUNTRY RANGERS - Tividale F C, The Beeches, Packwood Road, Tividale, West Mids. B69 1UL Tel: 01384-211743
Leave M5 at Junction 2. Follow signs to Dudley A4123. Approximately 1 mile past school and playing fields on right, go under Pedestrian walkway to traffic lights. Turn left into Regent Road. Turn left into Elm Terrace. First left into Birch Crescent, second left into Packwood Road. Ground is at the end of the Cul-de-sac.

BROMYARD TOWN - Delahay Meadow, Stourport Road, Bromyard. HR7 4NT Tel: 01885-483974
From M5, leave motorway at Junction 7 for Worcester (South) and follow A4440 Southern Link through to last roundabout, and then take A44 signposted Bromyard. Pass through Broadwas and over Bringsty Common to Bromyard. After passing narrow stone bridge on the perimeter of town, turn first right into Sherwood Street and follow signs for Stourport and Kidderminster (B4203).
Keep straight on into Church Street, passing Post Office on your right and St Peters Church on your left. Ground is approximately ½ mile on right hand sided through a wide entrance and steel gates, immediately before cottages, next to The Holly Tree Inn.
From Stourport, follow B4203 from Great Witley, up and over Downs, and ground is at bottom of hill, on left, 100 yards after passing the Holly Tree Inn. From Leominster, keep on A44 down by-pass and turn first left after "Ford" garage into Sherwood Street, then as above.

BUSTLEHOLME - Tipton Town F C, Wednesbury Oak Road, Tipton, West Mids. DY4 0BS Tel: 0121-502-5534
From M6 Junction 9, take A461 through Wednesbury Town Centre to Ocker Hill island. Follow signpost here taking a full right turn towards Bilston A4098 for half mile, turning left at traffic lights A4037. Ground is 50 yards on left. From M5 junction 2, take A4123 for about three miles until you reach Burnt Tree island. Take 2nd Exit towards Wolverhampton and continue to next set of traffic lights. Turn right onto A4037 and follow this road for about three miles. After passing Asda on your right, ground is down hill, 200 yards on right.

CRADLEY TOWN - The Beeches, Beeches View Avenue, Cradley, Halesowen, West Mids. B63 2HB Tel: 07799-363467
From M5 junction 3 take A456 Manor Way (signposted to Kidderminster) Turn right at second island into Hagley Road pass Foxhunt Inn on left and turn third left into Rosemary Road. Straight on into Landsdowne Road/Dunstall Road and turn left at T Junction into Huntingtree Road/Lutley Mill Road. Left again at next T junction into Stourbridge Road and immediately left again into Beecher Road East, first left into Abbey Road straight up to the end and turn right into Beeches View Avenue. The entrance to ground is 20 yards on the left between houses 50 and 48.

DARLASTON TOWN - City Ground, Waverley Road, Darlaston, West Mids. WS10 8ED
Leave M6 at Junction 10. Take the A454 towards Willenhall. Turn left at the traffic lights, outside the Lane Arms Public House into Bentley Road North. Follow this road down the hill, over the railway and canal bridges to the traffic lights. Cross over the lights into Richards Street and along into Victoria Road. Take the first right into Slater Street and the ground is on the left. Entrance next left in Waverley Road.

DUDLEY SPORTS - Hillcrest Avenue, Brierley Hill, West Mids. DY5 3QH Tel: 01384-826420
The Ground is situated in Brierley Hill, just off A461. It can be approached from Stourbridge off the Ring Road to Amblecote, turning right at third set of traffic lights or from Dudley passing through Brierley Hill Town centre. A – Z ref, 4H, page 67.

DUDLEY TOWN - The Dell Stadium, Bryce Road, Brierley Hill, West Mids. DY5 4NE Tel: 01384-812943
From M5 Junction 4 follow signs for Stourbridge.
From the Ring Road, take A491 sign posted Wolverhampton.
At the second set of lights, turn right onto Brettle Lane A461. After approx 6 miles you will approach Brierley Hill High Street. Turn left at lights onto bank Street. You will see Civic hall and Police Station. Carry on over small bridge and at next set of traffic lights you will see Bryce Road and Stadium is on your left. A-Z Birmingham 5F 93 A-Z West Midlands 5B 88

GOODRICH - Stafford Road, Fordhouses, Wolverhampton. WV10 7EH

Turn onto M54 off M6 Northbound and leave at Junction 2.

Turn left onto A449 to Wolverhampton. Go to 2nd set of traffic lights and turn right into slip road. Entrance to Sports ground is 50 yards on the left.

GORNAL ATHLETIC - Garden Walk Stadium, Garden Walk, Lower Gornal, Dudley. DY3 2NR Tel: 01384-358398

From Dudley, take A459 to Sedgley, past the Fire Station. Turn left at the Green Dragon Public House, on the B4175 (Jews Lane). Follow the road until you come to the Old Bull's Head Pub, turn left into Redhall Road. Take the second left to Garden Walk.

From Wolverhampton, use A449 past Wombourne. Turn left at Himley House lights. (B4176) Over next set of major traffic lights at Bull Street. Second left into Central Drive. Left into Bank Road. Follow road round to the Ground.

LYE TOWN - Sports Ground, Stourbridge Road, Lye, Stourbridge, West Mids. DY9 7DH Tel: 01384-422672

Situated on A458 Birmingham to Stourbridge Road.

From M5 Junction 3, take road marked Kidderminster, as far as lights at the bottom of Hagley Hill. Turn right, then take the third turning off the first island. Carry straight on at the next island. Turn left at Lights/Crossroads, onto the A458. Ground approximately 400 yards on the left hand side.

MALVERN TOWN - Langland Stadium, Langland Avenue, Malvern. WR14 2QE Tel: 01684-574068

Leave M5 at Junction 7 and turn towards Worcester. Turn left at next roundabout onto A4440 towards Malvern. Straight over next two roundabouts and take left slip road onto A449 at next roundabout. When approaching Malvern, turn left onto B4208 signposted Welland. Straight over three roundabouts and then take the third left into Orford Way. Take the third left into Langland Avenue. Ground is 300 yards on left.

PEGASUS JUNIORS - Old School Lane, Hereford. HR1 1EX Tel: 07980-465995

Approach City on A4103 from Worcester. At roundabout on outskirts take 2nd exit (A4103) over railway bridge, traffic light controlled. Take 2nd turning on left into Old School Lane. Ground entrance 150 metres on left.

Approach City on A49 from Leominster. On City outskirts take 1st exit at roundabout – Roman Road. First turning on right is Old School Lane. Ground entrance 150 metres on left.

SHAWBURY UNITED - Butler Sports Ground, Bowensfield, Wem, Shrewsbury. SY4 5AP Tel: 01939-233287

From the A5 Shrewsbury by-pass, take the A49 heading towards Whitchurch. Go through the villages of Hadnall & Preston Brockhurst and then take a left turn at crossroads onto the B5063 sign posted Wem. At next junction turn right under Railway Bridge on to the B5476 into Mill Street. At next Junction by Church turn right into High Street, take the next left after pedestrian crossing into New Street and then next left by the Public House into Pyms Road. Take the 2nd left into Bowens Field and ground is 100 yards straight ahead.

SHIFNAL TOWN - Phoenix Park, Coppice Green Lane, Shifnal, Shrops. TF11 8PB Tel: 01952-463257

From M54 junction 3, take A41 towards Newport and Whitchurch. Take first left signposted Shifnal. As you enter Shifnal, take first turning on right signposted football stadium. The ground is approximately 500 yards on left past Idsall School.

If travelling along A464 Wolverhampton Road to Shifnal. On entering Shifnal, just under the railway bridge and before the traffic lights turn right and sharp right again along Aston Street. Continue along this street until sharp right hand bend. Take left turn and then sharp right along Coppice Green Lane. Ground is approximately 500 yards on left past Idsall School.

SPORTING KHALSA - Aspray Arena, Noose Lane, Willenhall. WV13 3BB Tel: 09102-219208

From M6 junction 10, take 2nd exit onto A454 to Wolverhampton/Dudley A463. Take the A454 exit towards Wolverhampton. At Keyway junction take 2nd exit onto the Keyway A454 and continue on A454 going through one roundabout. At next traffic lights make a u turn at Nechells Lane. Turn left into Noose Lane and over roundabout. Ground is located on your left.

STAFFORD TOWN - Evans Park, Riverway, Stafford. ST16 3TH

From M6 Junction 13, take A449 to Stafford for 1.5 miles until reaching traffic lights by Esso petrol station. Turn right at lights into Rickerscote Road and follow road round over railway bridge to mini island. Bear left into Silkmore Lane. At next mini island take second exit and carry on to large island. Take second exit towards Stafford Town Centre (A34 Lichfield Road) go over railway bridge with Alstom factory on left hand side. Straight on at first set of traffic lights then bear left at next lights at 20 metres (A518 Uttoxeter) and follow road round with B & Q and Argos on your left hand side. At roundabout take 2nd exit A518 Uttoxeter and follow to traffic lights. Go straight over lights into Riverway, ground entrance is on right hand side approximately 80 metres. Follow driveway round behind cricket pavilion to Stadium entrance and car park.

WEDNESFIELD - Cottage Ground, Amos Lane, Wednesfield. WV11 1ND

Going south, leave M6 at Junction 11 onto A460 towards Wolverhampton. After approx. 3 miles turn left at the Millhouse Public House into Pear Tree Lane. Continue on across mini-island into Knowle Lane. At Red Lion Public House continue across mini-island into Long Knowle Lane. Continue across mini-island into Amos Lane. Ground is about ½ mile along on left hand side.

Going north, leave M6 at Junction 10A onto M54. Leave M54 at Junction 1 onto A460 towards Wolverhampton. Turn left at Millhouse Public House and continue as above.

WELLINGTON - Wellington Playing Field, Wellington, Hereford. HR4 8AZ

The Ground is situated in Wellington, behind School and opposite the Church. Wellington is 8 miles South of Leominster or 6 miles North of Hereford on the A49. At the Hereford end of the dual carriageway take the turn for Wellington.

WOLVERHAMPTON CASUALS - Brinsford Stadium, Brinsford Lane, Wolverhampton. WV10 7PR Tel: 01902-783214

Turn onto M54 off M6 Northbound. Take Junction 2 and turn right onto A449 to Stafford. Go to next island and come back on yourself towards M54. Brinsford Lane is approximately ½ mile from island on left.

Ground is 200 yards on left in Brinsford Lane.

WOLVERHAMPTON SPORTING C. - Wednesfield F C, Cottage Ground, Amos Lane, Wednesfield. WV11 1ND Tel: 01902-735506

Going south, leave M6 at Junction 11 onto A460 towards Wolverhampton. After approx. 3 miles turn left at the Millhouse Public House into Pear Tree Lane. Continue on across mini-island into Knowle Lane. At Red Lion Public House continue across mini-island into Long Knowle Lane. Continue across mini-island into Amos Lane. Ground is about ½ mile along on left hand side.

Going north, leave M6 at Junction 10A onto M54. Leave M54 at Junction 1 onto A460 towards Wolverhampton. Turn left at Millhouse Public House and continue as above.

WESTERN LEAGUE

Sponsored by: Toolstation
Founded: 1892
Recent Champions:
2006: Bideford
2007: Corsham Town
2008: Truro City
2009: Bitton
2010: Bideford
toolstationleague.com

PREMIER DIVISION	P	W	D	L	F	A	Pts
1 Larkhall Athletic	36	25	4	7	83	46	79
2 Bitton	36	21	7	8	71	37	70
3 Ilfracombe Town	36	20	7	9	59	37	67
4 Willand Rovers	36	18	11	7	69	40	65
5 Bishop Sutton	36	18	9	9	66	38	63
6 Dawlish Town	36	17	10	9	78	65	61
7 Bristol Manor Farm	36	18	7	11	73	63	61
8 Odd Down (Bath)	36	17	8	11	60	47	59
9 Wells City	36	16	7	13	67	55	55
10 Corsham Town	36	14	9	13	48	49	51
11 Barnstaple Town	36	15	6	15	65	74	51
12 Radstock Town	36	15	3	18	59	56	48
13 Street	36	12	9	15	50	61	45
14 Sherborne Town	36	13	4	19	58	70	43
15 Brislington	36	9	11	16	36	56	38
16 Hallen	36	10	6	20	56	79	36
17 Longwell Green Sports	36	7	5	24	35	79	26
18 Wellington	36	5	6	25	48	87	21
19 Welton Rovers	36	4	7	25	38	80	19

LES PHILLIPS CUP

PRELIMINARY ROUND
Brislington 3-0 Sherborne Town
Dawlish Town 4-2 Gillingham Town
Hallen 6-1 Roman Glass St George
Longwell Green Sports 0-1 Shrewton United
Melksham Town 5-4 Welton Rovers
Portishead Town 1-2 Westbury United

ROUND 1
Almondsbury UWE 2-1 Melksham Town
Barnstaple Town 0-1 Hallen
Bishop Sutton 3-1 Wells City
Bradford Town 1-2 Bristol Manor Farm
Calne Town 3-0 Bitton
Corsham Town 2-3 Ilfracombe Town
Dawlish Town 0-1 Street
Devizes Town 5-1 Hengrove Athletic
Keynsham Town 2-0 Bridport
Larkhall Athletic 6-1 Chard Town
Oldland Abbotonians 1-2 Cadbury Heath
Radstock Town 2-1 Wellington
Shepton Mallet 0-2 Odd Down
Shrewton United 2-2 Brislington
(Brislington won 4-3 on penalties)
Westbury United 5-1 Elmore
Willand Rovers 4-0 Merthyr Town

ROUND 2
Almondsbury UWE 0-2 Cadbury Heath
Bristol Manor Farm 4-0 Calne Town
Dawlish Town 1-3 Willand Rovers
Hallen 2-3 Brislington
Keynsham Town 1-0 Bishop Sutton
Odd Down 1-0 Devizes Town
Radstock Town 0-2 Larkhall Athletic
Westbury United 0-4 Ilfracombe Town

QUARTER FINALS
Brislington 0-1 Odd Down
Bristol Manor Farm 4-0 Keynsham Town
Cadbury Heath 4-1 Willand Rovers
Ilfracombe Town 1-0 Larkhall Athletic

SEMI-FINALS
Cadbury Heath 3-1 Odd Down
Ilfracombe Town 1-1 Bristol Manor Farm
(Ilfracombe Town won 3-2 on penalties)

FINAL (@ Wells City, 7/5/11)
Ilfracombe Town 3-1 Cadbury Heath

PREMIER DIVISION	1	2	3	4	5	6	7	8	9	10	11	12	13	14	15	16	17	18	19
1 Barnstaple Town		4-2	0-4	1-0	2-3	2-2	1-4	2-1	0-0	0-4	4-0	2-4	2-6	2-4	3-0	3-2	1-2	5-1	0-1
2 Bishop Sutton	4-0		1-1	1-0	3-3	0-0	0-1	4-2	1-1	3-0	1-0	4-1	0-0	2-3	2-1	0-2	3-0	2-1	0-3
3 Bitton	5-1	2-1		0-0	1-2	1-1	4-5	1-0	0-1	1-1	1-1	1-0	4-2	0-1	1-0	5-2	3-3	3-2	1-3
4 Brislington	1-1	0-3	0-3		0-0	3-1	0-2	2-0	1-2	0-4	0-1	1-2	2-2	0-3	0-0	2-1	2-2	1-0	2-2
5 Bristol Manor Farm	3-1	0-2	1-2	1-2		0-4	3-3	3-0	1-2	1-2	3-0	3-1	2-1	4-2	0-0	3-2	0-2	1-1	1-4
6 Corsham Town	1-0	0-1	0-2	2-2	2-1		2-1	2-0	2-1	0-2	1-0	1-2	3-1	3-1	2-2	1-1	1-2	2-0	0-2
7 Dawlish Town	1-1	0-3	1-0	1-3	2-2	3-3		6-1	3-3	3-0	3-2	1-0	3-0	2-3	2-0	1-1	2-0	4-3	0-4
8 Hallen	0-2	3-4	1-2	2-2	5-6	1-2	4-3		0-1	0-6	3-1	4-2	1-2	2-1	4-1	4-0	2-6	1-1	1-1
9 Ilfracombe Town	0-4	2-2	2-0	3-0	0-1	3-0	1-1	1-0		6-0	3-1	0-1	1-0	5-2	3-1	2-1	1-0	3-1	0-1
10 Larkhall Athletic	5-2	2-1	3-0	2-0	3-4	2-0	5-1	1-1	1-0		2-0	0-1	2-1	4-0	5-1	3-2	0-5	1-0	3-1
11 Longwell Green Sports	2-4	0-5	0-3	4-0	0-4	0-2	2-5	1-1	0-1	1-1		5-2	0-2	1-3	0-1	2-1	4-2	2-0	0-4
12 Odd Down	4-1	0-0	1-2	2-1	1-0	0-1	3-3	0-1	3-0	2-2	1-1		4-0	4-0	2-2	2-1	2-2	1-0	1-1
13 Radstock Town	2-3	2-0	0-2	4-0	0-1	1-2	2-3	1-2	1-2	1-2	4-3	2-0		2-1	3-0	3-1	0-1	2-1	0-1
14 Sherborne Town	0-1	2-1	0-4	0-1	6-1	0-0	0-0	1-5	2-2	2-3	2-0	0-1	2-3		2-2	3-0	0-1	2-0	1-0
15 Street	1-3	0-3	0-2	0-1	2-3	2-1	2-1	1-1	1-1	0-6	4-0	3-1	2-1	2-0		7-1	1-1	2-0	0-6
16 Wellington	1-2	1-1	0-2	0-6	1-4	3-1	3-1	1-2	2-3	2-3	0-1	2-2	1-2	2-3	0-1		2-3	2-2	1-1
17 Wells City	0-1	0-2	0-2	1-1	2-4	3-1	1-2	2-1	2-1	3-0	4-0	0-2	0-1	4-2	0-0	3-0		4-2	3-4
18 Welton Rovers	3-3	0-3	0-5	0-0	1-3	3-1	1-2	3-0	1-2	0-1	2-0	0-3	1-1	2-1	0-3	2-5	3-3		1-4
19 Willand Rovers	1-1	1-1	1-1	3-0	1-1	1-1	2-2	4-0	1-0	1-2	0-0	0-2	1-4	4-3	0-5	1-2	2-0	2-0	

DIVISION ONE	P	W	D	L	F	A	Pts
1 Merthyr Town	36	29	3	4	118	33	90
2 Oldland Abbotonians	36	22	10	4	93	46	76
3 Bridport	36	23	3	10	74	44	72
4 Cadbury Heath (-1)	36	20	9	7	88	49	68
5 Devizes Town	36	21	2	13	63	65	65
6 Bradford Town	36	18	7	11	84	62	61
7 Gillingham Town	36	18	6	12	73	57	60
8 Melksham Town	36	14	13	9	63	51	55
9 Shrewton United	36	15	6	15	71	79	51
10 Hengrove Athletic	36	13	7	16	52	58	46
11 Calne Town (-4)	36	14	6	16	72	56	44
12 Almondsbury UWE	36	11	11	14	55	64	44
13 Chard Town	36	11	8	17	57	68	41
14 Shepton Mallet	36	11	5	20	47	76	38
15 Roman Glass St George	36	10	6	20	43	76	36
16 Keynsham Town	36	9	8	19	45	61	35
17 Westbury United	36	9	3	24	45	82	30
18 Portishead Town	36	6	11	19	48	84	29
19 Elmore	36	5	2	29	47	127	17

DIVISION ONE	1	2	3	4	5	6	7	8	9	10	11	12	13	14	15	16	17	18	19
1 Almondsbury U W E		1-1	2-0	0-2	1-1	1-1	4-1	1-2	1-3	1-1	2-1	1-1	2-2	2-2	3-1	0-0	1-3	2-1	2-1
2 Bradford Town	3-1		1-0	1-2	3-1	3-2	0-1	10-2	1-2	3-1	2-0	1-2	0-4	1-3	2-2	5-3	0-0	2-1	4-2
3 Bridport	1-3	2-0		1-3	2-1	0-3	2-0	9-1	1-2	4-2	0-1	1-0	0-3	2-1	4-1	3-1	1-0	5-1	2-0
4 Cadbury Heath	1-4	6-1	0-0		0-2	3-1	9-2	3-2	1-3	1-1	1-1	2-1	3-1	3-3	5-1	1-1	4-2	2-1	1-0
5 Calne Town	4-0	1-3	1-2	3-1		2-3	7-0	2-1	0-0	2-0	2-2	0-1	0-4	1-3	2-2	1-2	0-0	3-0	0-1
6 Chard Town	1-1	2-1	2-0	0-4	0-3		4-1	3-0	2-2	1-2	2-2	0-0	1-7	1-3	5-1	3-1	2-3	2-4	2-1
7 Devizes Town	1-0	0-2	1-0	4-1	3-0	1-0		3-1	3-2	2-0	2-1	0-1	0-5	5-2	3-2	1-2	3-1	1-1	3-0
8 Elmore	6-3	1-5	1-2	2-2	0-4	1-3	1-3		0-8	0-2	0-2	2-2	0-3	0-5	2-1	1-2	5-3	3-5	1-4
9 Gillingham Town	1-3	3-3	2-4	0-1	3-3	2-1	3-1	5-1		0-1	5-1	4-4	2-3	1-2	0-2	2-0	2-0	2-1	1-0
10 Hengrove Athletic	2-0	2-2	0-0	0-4	1-0	1-1	0-2	3-2	0-1		3-0	1-2	0-3	0-3	1-1	4-0	3-0	2-3	1-2
11 Keynsham Town	3-0	4-1	0-3	1-4	3-4	3-1	0-1	4-0	0-3	2-3		1-2	0-1	1-2	0-0	1-1	0-2	2-2	0-0
12 Melksham Town	3-1	2-2	2-3	1-1	0-5	1-1	2-1	5-0	2-2	1-2	2-4		1-0	0-0	1-1	5-0	4-1	4-2	0-1
13 Merthyr Town	1-0	2-4	2-2	4-3	2-1	4-1	3-0	3-1	5-1	4-2	3-0	4-1		2-2	5-1	3-0	4-0	3-0	4-0
14 Oldland Abbotonians	1-1	2-2	1-3	1-0	4-3	1-0	1-1	5-1	3-0	1-1	5-2	0-0	2-1		2-1	4-1	3-1	2-3	4-1
15 Portishead Town	1-3	2-1	2-3	1-5	3-2	2-1	1-2	0-4	0-1	4-2	0-0	1-2	1-4	3-3		1-1	1-1	1-3	3-4
16 Roman Glass St George	4-1	2-4	0-2	1-1	3-0	1-2	2-4	2-0	1-2	0-4	1-0	2-1	0-4	1-6	0-0		1-2	1-2	1-0
17 Shepton Mallet	1-2	0-3	3-5	0-4	1-2	2-0	3-1	2-1	1-2	2-1	0-1	1-4	1-5	1-4	1-1	1-0		2-3	3-1
18 Shrewton United	3-3	0-2	0-1	0-0	1-5	2-1	1-2	6-1	2-0	3-1	1-0	2-2	1-8	0-3	6-1	4-2	1-1		2-5
19 Westbury United	3-2	1-5	1-4	2-4	1-4	2-2	1-4	2-1	3-1	1-2	0-2	1-1	0-2	0-4	0-2	1-3	1-2	2-3	

WESTERN LEAGUE INS & OUTS

PREM

IN: Bridport (P), Merthyr Town (P)

OUT: Dawlish Town (F), Wellington Town (R), Welton Rovers (R)

DIV ONE

IN: Wellington Town (R), Welton Rovers (R)

OUT: Bridport (P), Merthyr Town (P)

BARNSTAPLE TOWN

Founded: 1906 Nickname: Barum

Secretary: David Cooke **(T)** 07939 217 084 **(E)** dcooke81@yahoo.com
Chairman: Steve James **Manager:** Owen Pickard **Prog Ed:**
Ground: Mill Road, Barnstaple, North Devon EX31 1JQ **(T)** 01271 343 469
Capacity: 5,000 **Seats:** 250 **Covered:** 1,000 **Midweek Matchday:** Tuesday **Clubhouse:** Yes **Shop:** Yes

Colours(change): All red. (All blue)
Previous Names: Pilton Yeo Vale
Previous Leagues: North Devon, Devon & Exeter, South Western
Records: **Att:** 6,200 v Bournemouth FA Cup 1st Round 51-52 **App:** Ian Pope
Senior Honours: Western Champions 1952-53, 79-80, Devon Pro Cup (12), Devon Senior Cup 1992-93. Western League Division One 1993-94.

10 YEAR RECORD

01-02	02-03	03-04	04-05	05-06	06-07	07-08	08-09	09-10	10-11
WestP 12	WestP 15	WestP 10	WestP 12	WestP 13	WestP 7	WestP 12	WestP 18	WestP 15	WestP 11

BISHOP SUTTON

Founded: 1977 Nickname: Bishops

Secretary: Steve Hillier **(T)** 07713 681 235 **(E)** steve@bishopsuttonafc.com
Chairman: George Williams **Manager:** Lee Lashenko **Prog Ed:**
Ground: Lakeview, Wick Road, Bishops Sutton, Bristol BS39 5XN. **(T)** 01275 333 097
Capacity: 1,500 **Seats:** 100 **Covered:** 200 **Midweek Matchday:** Wednesday **Clubhouse:** Yes **Shop:** No

Colours(change): All Blue (All yellow)
Previous Names:
Previous Leagues: Weston & District (youth), Bristol & Avon, Somerset Senior >1991
Records: **Att:** 400 v Bristol City
Senior Honours: Somerset Junior Cup 1980-81. Western League Division One 1997-98.

10 YEAR RECORD

01-02	02-03	03-04	04-05	05-06	06-07	07-08	08-09	09-10	10-11
WestP 15	WestP 12	WestP 16	WestP 18	WestP 16	WestP 21	WestP 19	WestP 15	WestP 4	WestP 5

BITTON

Founded: 1922 Nickname: The Ton

Secretary: Mrs Becky Jones **(T)** 0797 164 1834 **(E)** rebeccalangdon@btconnect.com
Chairman: John Langdon **Manager:** Rich Fey **Prog Ed:**
Ground: Recreation Ground, Bath Road, Bitton, Bristol BS30 6HX. **(T)** 0117 932 3222
Capacity: 1,000 **Seats:** 48 **Covered:** 200 **Midweek Matchday:** Wednesday **Clubhouse:** Yes **Shop:** No

Colours(change): Red & white/black/black (Yellow/green/yellow)
Previous Names:
Previous Leagues: Avon Premier Combination, Gloucestershire County
Records: **Goalscorer:** A. Cole
Senior Honours: Somerset Senior Cup 1992-93. Les Phillips Cup 2007-08. Western League Premier Division 2008-09.

10 YEAR RECORD

01-02	02-03	03-04	04-05	05-06	06-07	07-08	08-09	09-10	10-11
West1 6	West1 8	West1 2	WestP 8	WestP 8	WestP 8	WestP 7	WestP 1	WestP 8	WestP 2

BRIDPORT

Founded: 1885 Nickname: Bees

Secretary: Chris Tozer **(T)** 07500 064 317 **(E)** sevie@tiscali.co.uk
Chairman: Adrian Scadding **Manager:** Trevor Senior **Prog Ed:**
Ground: St Mary's Field, Bridport, Dorset DT6 5LN **(T)** 01308 423 834
Capacity: **Seats:** **Covered:** **Midweek Matchday:** Tuesday **Clubhouse:** **Shop:**

Colours(change): Red & black/black/black (All blue)
Previous Names:
Previous Leagues: Dorset Combination 1984-89.
Records: **Att:** 1,150 v Exeter City 1981.
Senior Honours: Dorset Senior Cup x8. Dorset Senior Amateur Cup x6.

10 YEAR RECORD

01-02	02-03	03-04	04-05	05-06	06-07	07-08	08-09	09-10	10-11
WestP 17	WestP 14	WestP 12	WestP 19	West1 6	West1 11	West1 18	West1 13	West1 10	West1 3

BRISLINGTON

Founded: 1956 Nickname: Bris

Secretary: Kevin Jacobs **(T)** 07976 724 202 **(E)** kevinjacobs919@btinternet.com
Chairman: Fred Hardwell **Manager:** Jeff Meacham **Prog Ed:**
Ground: Ironmould Lane, Brislington, Bristol BS4 4TZ **(T)** 0117 977 4030
Capacity: 2,000 **Seats:** 144 **Covered:** 1,500 **Midweek Matchday:** Tuesday **Clubhouse:** Yes **Shop:** No

Colours(change): Red & black/black/red. (All yellow)
Previous Names:
Previous Leagues: Somerset Senior until 1991
Records:
Senior Honours: Somerset Senior League 1988-89. Somerset Premier Cup 1992-93. Western League Division One 1994-95.

10 YEAR RECORD

01-02	02-03	03-04	04-05	05-06	06-07	07-08	08-09	09-10	10-11
WestP 3	WestP 2	WestP 7	WestP 10	WestP 10	WestP 17	WestP 13	WestP 10	WestP 9	WestP 15

BRISTOL MANOR FARM

Founded: 1964 Nickname: The Farm

Secretary: Andy Radford **(T)** 07747 038 423 **(E)** andy@bristolmanorfarm.com
Chairman: Geoff Sellek **Manager:** John Black **Prog Ed:**
Ground: The Creek, Portway, Sea Mills, Bristol BS9 2HS **(T)** 0117 968 3571
Capacity: 2,000 **Seats:** 98 **Covered:** 350 **Midweek Matchday:** Tuesday **Clubhouse:** Yes **Shop:** No

Colours(change): Red/black/black (All yellow)
Previous Names:
Previous Leagues: Bristol Suburban 64-69, Somerset Senior 69-77
Records: **Att;** 500 v Portway **App:** M. Baird
Senior Honours: Glos Trophy 1987-88, Glos Am. Cup 1989-90. Western League Division One 1982-83.

10 YEAR RECORD

01-02	02-03	03-04	04-05	05-06	06-07	07-08	08-09	09-10	10-11
WestP 19	WestP 11	WestP 3	WestP 7	WestP 3	WestP 12	WestP 16	WestP 5	WestP 7	WestP 7

CORSHAM TOWN

Founded: 1884 Nickname:

Secretary: Richard Taylor **(T)** 07944 183 973 **(E)** richtaylor_ctfc@hotmail.com
Chairman: Ken Baldwin **Manager:** Mel Gingell **Prog Ed:**
Ground: Southbank Ground, Lacock Road, Corsham SN13 0EX **(T)** 07963 030 652
Capacity: 1,500 **Seats:** no **Covered:** yes **Midweek Matchday:** Wednesday **Clubhouse:** Yes **Shop:** Yes

Colours(change): Red & white/red/red (Yellow & blue/blue/blue)
Previous Names: None.
Previous Leagues: Wiltshire County
Records: **Att:** 550 v Newport Co. FA Cup **App:** Craig Chaplin
Senior Honours: Wiltshire Senior Cup 1975-76, 96-97, 04-05. Western Premier Division 2006-07.

10 YEAR RECORD

01-02	02-03	03-04	04-05	05-06	06-07	07-08	08-09	09-10	10-11
West1 9	West1 6	West1 5	WestP 2	WestP 2	WestP 1	WestP 5	WestP 19	WestP 17	WestP 10

HALLEN

Founded: 1949 Nickname:

Secretary: Richard Stokes **(T)** 07791 492 640 **(E)** sinbad88@hotmail.co.uk
Chairman: Barrie Phillips **Manager:** Paul Owen **Prog Ed:**
Ground: Hallen Centre, Moorhouse Lane, Hallen Bristol BS10 7RU **(T)** 0117 950 5559
Capacity: 2,000 **Seats:** 200 **Covered:** 200 **Midweek Matchday:** Monday **Clubhouse:** Yes **Shop:**

Colours(change): Blue & black/black/blue (Red & white/red/red)
Previous Names: Lawrence Weston Ath, Lawrence Weston Hallen
Previous Leagues: Gloucestershire County, Hellenic
Records: **Att:** 803 v Bristol Rovers 1997
Senior Honours: Gloucestershire Co. Lge 1988-89, 92-93. Western Division One 2003-04.

10 YEAR RECORD

01-02	02-03	03-04	04-05	05-06	06-07	07-08	08-09	09-10	10-11
West1 10	West1 4	West1 1	WestP 4	WestP 9	WestP 9	WestP 15	WestP 9	WestP 12	WestP 16

ILFRACOMBE TOWN

Founded: 1902 Nickname: Bluebirds

Secretary: Tony Alcock **(T)** 07973 469 673 **(E)** afalcock@aol.com
Chairman: Allan Day **Manager:** Barry Yeo **Prog Ed:**
Ground: Marlborough Park, Ilfracombe, Devon EX34 8PD **(T)** 01271 865 939
Capacity: 2,000 **Seats:** 60 **Covered:** 450 **Midweek Matchday:** Tuesday **Clubhouse:** Yes **Shop:**

Colours(change): All blue (Yellow/red/red)
Previous Names:
Previous Leagues: North Devon, East Devon Premier, Exeter & District, Western,
Records: **Att:** 3,000 v Bristol City **Goalscorer:** Kevin Squire **App:** Bob Hancock 459
Senior Honours: East Devon Premier League, North Devon Senior League, North Devon Premier League.

10 YEAR RECORD

01-02	02-03	03-04	04-05	05-06	06-07	07-08	08-09	09-10	10-11
West1 14	West1 18	West1 16	West1 8	West1 4	West1 3	WestP 8	WestP 14	WestP 3	WestP 3

LARKHALL ATHLETIC

Founded: 1914 Nickname: Larks

Secretary: Garry Davy **(T)** 07942 445 498 **(E)** garrydvy@aol.com
Chairman: Jim McClay **Manager:** Lee Collier **Prog Ed:**
Ground: Plain Ham, Charlcombe Lane, Larkhall, Bath BA1 8DJ **(T)** 01225 334 952
Capacity: 1,000 **Seats:** Yes **Covered:** 50 **Midweek Matchday:** Wednesday **Clubhouse:** Yes **Shop:**

Colours(change): All blue - day, White/white/blue - evening (All red)
Previous Names: None
Previous Leagues: Somerset Senior
Records:
Senior Honours: Somerset Senior Cup 1975-76, Somerset Senior Champions. Western Division One 1988-89, 93-94, 94-95, 08-09. Western Premier Division 2010-11.

10 YEAR RECORD

01-02	02-03	03-04	04-05	05-06	06-07	07-08	08-09	09-10	10-11
West1 12	West1 13	West1 8	West1 5	West1 7	West1 5	West1 3	West1 1	WestP 14	WestP 1

LONGWELL GREEN SPORTS

Founded: 1966 Nickname: The Green

Secretary: David Heal **(T)** 07917 778 463 **(E)** dave@monaghannorthern.co.uk
Chairman: Chris Wyrill **Manager:** Matthew Hale **Prog Ed:**
Ground: Longwell Green Com. Centre, Shellards Road BS30 9DW **(T)** 01179 323 722
Capacity: 1,000 **Seats:** Yes **Covered:** 100 **Midweek Matchday:** Tuesday **Clubhouse:** Yes **Shop:** Yes

Colours(change): Blue & white/black/black (All green)
Previous Names: None
Previous Leagues: Gloucestershire County.
Records: **Att:** 500 v Mangotsfield 2005
Senior Honours:

10 YEAR RECORD

01-02	02-03	03-04	04-05	05-06	06-07	07-08	08-09	09-10	10-11
			GlCo 2	West1 12	West1 8	West1 8	West1 2	WestP 11	WestP 17

MERTHYR TOWN

Founded: 2010 Nickname: Martyrs

Secretary: Jamie Mack **(T)** 07823 776 422 **(E)** merthysec@gmail.com
Chairman: John Strand **Manager:** Garry Shephard **Prog Ed:**
Ground: Penydarren Park, Park Terrance, Merthyr Tydfil CF47 8RF **(T)** 07980 363 675
Capacity: **Seats:** **Covered:** **Midweek Matchday:** Tuesday **Clubhouse:** **Shop:**

Colours(change): White/black/black & white (All red)
Previous Names: None
Previous Leagues: None
Records:
Senior Honours: Western Division One 2010-11.

10 YEAR RECORD

01-02	02-03	03-04	04-05	05-06	06-07	07-08	08-09	09-10	10-11
									West1 1

ODD DOWN (BATH)

Founded: 1901 Nickname: The Down

Secretary: Lorraine Brown **(T)** 07734 924 435 **(E)** lorainebrown@btinternet.com
Chairman: Dave Loxton **Manager:** Lee Burns **Prog Ed:**
Ground: Lew Hill Memorial Ground, Combe Hay Lane, Odd Down BA2 8AP **(T)** 01225 832 491
Capacity: 1,000 **Seats:** 160 **Covered:** 250 **Midweek Matchday:** Tuesday **Clubhouse:** Yes **Shop:** No

Colours(change): Blue & black/black/black (All yellow)
Previous Names:
Previous Leagues: Wilts Premier, Bath & District & Somerset Senior
Records: **App:** Steve Fuller 475 **Goalscorer:** Joe Matano 104
Senior Honours:

10 YEAR RECORD

01-02	02-03	03-04	04-05	05-06	06-07	07-08	08-09	09-10	10-11
WestP 11	WestP 9	WestP 9	WestP 13	WestP 15	WestP 11	WestP 21	West1 19	West1 2	WestP 8

RADSTOCK TOWN

Founded: 1895 Nickname:

Secretary: Simon Wilkinson **(T)** 07557 276 619 **(E)** rtfc@hotmail.co.uk
Chairman: Dave Wilkinson **Manager:** Terry Moore **Prog Ed:**
Ground: Southfields Recreation Ground, Southfields, Radstock BA3 2NZ **(T)** 01761 435 004
Capacity: 1,500 **Seats:** 80 **Covered:** yes **Midweek Matchday:** Tuesday **Clubhouse:** Yes **Shop:** No

Colours(change): Red/black/black (All Yellow)
Previous Names: Radstock.
Previous Leagues: Somerset Senior League.
Records:
Senior Honours:

10 YEAR RECORD

01-02	02-03	03-04	04-05	05-06	06-07	07-08	08-09	09-10	10-11
SomP 7	SomP 10	SomP 3	West1 3	WestP 12	WestP 16	WestP 17	WestP 17	WestP 16	WestP 12

SHERBORNE TOWN

Founded: 1894 Nickname:

Secretary: Colin Goodland **(T)** 07929 090 612 **(E)** goody@cgoodland.freeserve.co.uk
Chairman: Steve Paradise **Manager:** Mickey Spencer **Prog Ed:** Gavin Dodge
Ground: Raleigh Grove, Terrace Playing Field, Sherborne DT9 5NS **(T)** 01935 816 110
Capacity: **Seats:** Yes **Covered:** Yes **Midweek Matchday:** Wednesday **Clubhouse:** Yes **Shop:**

Colours(change): Black & white/black/black (All yellow).
Previous Names:
Previous Leagues: Dorset Premier
Records: **Att:** 1,000 v Eastleigh, Andy Shephard Memorial match 27.07.03.
Senior Honours: Dorset Premier League 1981-82, Dorset Senior Cup 2003-04.

10 YEAR RECORD

01-02	02-03	03-04	04-05	05-06	06-07	07-08	08-09	09-10	10-11
Dor P 2	Dor P 6	Dor P 5	Dor P 6	Dor P 2	West1 4	West1 2	WestP 12	WestP 18	WestP 14

STREET

Founded: 1880 Nickname: The Cobblers

Secretary: Dave Green **(T)** 01458 442 188 **(E)** daveg55@hotmail.co.uk
Chairman: Phil Norton-Ashley **Manager:** Dave Pople **Prog Ed:** Phil Norton-Ashley
Ground: The Tannery Ground, Middlebrooks, Street BA16 0TA **(T)** 01458 445 987
Capacity: 2,000 **Seats:** 120 **Covered:** 25 **Midweek Matchday:** Tuesday **Clubhouse:** Yes **Shop:**

Colours(change): White/green/white (Red & white/red/red)
Previous Names: None
Previous Leagues: Somerset Senior.
Records: **Att;** 4,300 v Yeovil Town FA Cup 47
Senior Honours: Somerset Senior League 1996-97.

10 YEAR RECORD

01-02	02-03	03-04	04-05	05-06	06-07	07-08	08-09	09-10	10-11
West1 8	West1 15	West1 12	West1 7	West1 3	WLaP 19	WestP 18	WestP 13	WestP 6	WestP 13

WELLS CITY

Founded: 1890 Nickname:

Secretary: Stephen Vowles **(T)** 07727 091 317 **(E)** stevievowles@aol.com
Chairman: Steve Loxton **Manager:** Tim Moxey **Prog Ed:**
Ground: Athletic Ground, Rowdens Road, Wells, Somerset BA5 1TU **(T)** 01749 679 971
Capacity: **Seats:** **Covered:** **Midweek Matchday:** Tuesday **Clubhouse:** **Shop:**

Colours(change): Blue/blue/white (All yellow)
Previous Names:
Previous Leagues: Somerset County.
Records:
Senior Honours: Western League Division One 2009-10.

10 YEAR RECORD

01-02	02-03	03-04	04-05	05-06	06-07	07-08	08-09	09-10	10-11
SomP 3	SomP 15	SomP 14	SomP 9	SomP 5	SomP 5	SomP 2	West1 10	West1 1	WestP 9

WILLAND ROVERS

Founded: 1946 Nickname: Rovers

Secretary: Tony Baker **(T)** 07887 587 811 **(E)** tonybaker@burnrew.gotadsl.co.uk
Chairman: Mike Mitchell **Manager:** Clive Jones **Prog Ed:**
Ground: Silver Street, Willand, Collumpton, Devon EX15 2RG **(T)** 01884 33885
Capacity: 2,000 **Seats:** 75 **Covered:** 150 **Midweek Matchday:** Tuesday **Clubhouse:** Yes **Shop:**

Colours(change): All White (Yellow/blue/yellow)
Previous Names: None.
Previous Leagues: Devon County.
Records: **Att:** 650 v Newton Abbot 1992-3 **Goalscorer:** Paul Foreman
Senior Honours: Devon County League 1998-99, 00-01, Western League Division One 2004-05, Les Phillips Cup 2006-07.

10 YEAR RECORD

01-02	02-03	03-04	04-05	05-06	06-07	07-08	08-09	09-10	10-11
West1 15	West1 7	West1 6	West1 1	WestP 6	WestP 6	WestP 3	WestP 3	WestP 2	WestP 4

WELCH HIRE
Competitive Rates
Unlimited Mileage
24 Hour Service
Contact
Andy
WELCH
01823 490 776
Mobile:
07860 291 798
WELCH MOTOR REPAIRS
Repairs, Servicing, Engine Tuning, M.O.T. Preparation

ALMONDSBURY U.W.E.

Founded: Nickname:

Secretary: Douglas Coles **(T)** 07748 655 399 **(E)** doug2004.coles@blueyonder.co.uk
Chairman: Mike Blessing **Manager:** David Hillier **Prog Ed:**
Ground: The Field, Almondsbury, Bristol BS34 4AA **(T)** 01454 612 240 **Capacity:**
Colours(change): White & green/green/green (All yellow)

ADDITIONAL INFORMATION:

BRADFORD TOWN

Founded: 1992 Nickname:

Secretary: Nikki Akers **(T)** 07866 693 167 **(E)** nikki.akers@3disp.co.uk
Chairman: Les Stevens **Manager:** Paul Shanley **Prog Ed:**
Ground: Bradford Sports & Social Club, Trowbridge Rd, Bradford on Avon BA15 1EE **(T)** 01225 866 649 **Capacity:**
Colours(change): Navy & white/navy/navy (Yellow/black/yellow)

ADDITIONAL INFORMATION:
Previous League: Wiltshire Senior.

CADBURY HEATH

Founded: Nickname:

Secretary: Martin Painter **(T)** 07971 399 268 **(E)** martinbristol1955@hotmail.com
Chairman: Steve Plenty **Manager:** Andy Black **Prog Ed:**
Ground: Springfield, Cadbury Heath Road, Bristol BS30 8BX **(T)** 0117 9675731(social cl) **Capacity:**
Colours(change): Red & white/red/red (Yellow/blue/blue)

ADDITIONAL INFORMATION:
Previous League: Gloucestershire County.
Honours: Gloucestershire County League 1998-99.

CALNE TOWN

Founded: 1886 Nickname: Lilywhites

Secretary: Shaun Smith **(T)** 07817 476 898 **(E)** s_k_smith@hotmail.com
Chairman: Acting - John Rumming **Manager:** Jeff Roberts **Prog Ed:**
Ground: Bremhill View, Calne, Wiltshire SN11 9EE **(T)** 07920 864 879 **Capacity:**
Colours(change): White/black/black (All blue)

ADDITIONAL INFORMATION:
Record Att: 1,100 v Swindon, friendly 1987. **Goalscorer:** Robbie Lardner. **Apps:** Gary Swallow - 259.
Honours: Wiltshire Senior Cup x3.

CHARD TOWN

Founded: Nickname: The Robins

Secretary: Michael Hawes **(T)** 07906 904 138 **(E)** michael.hawes2@virgin.net
Chairman: Willie Whitelaw **Manager:** **Prog Ed:**
Ground: Denning Sports Field, Zembard Lane, Chard, Somerset TA20 1JL **(T)** 01460 61402 **Capacity:**
Colours(change): All red (All blue)

ADDITIONAL INFORMATION:
Honours: Somerset Senior League 1949-50, 53-54, 59-60, 67-68, 69-70. Somerset Senior Cup 1952-53, 66-67.
South West Counties Cup 1988-89.

DEVIZES TOWN

Founded: 1885 Nickname:

Secretary: Neil Fautley **(T)** 07891 341 344 **(E)** neil@hallmarkflooring.co.uk
Chairman: Shaun Moffat **Manager:** Mark Love **Prog Ed:**
Ground: Nursteed Road, Devizes, Wiltshire SN10 3DX **(T)** 01380 722 817 **Capacity:**
Colours(change): Red & white/black/red (All blue)

ADDITIONAL INFORMATION:
Honours: Western League Division One 1999-2000. Wiltshire Senior Cup x14.

ELMORE

Founded: 1947 Nickname: Eagles

Secretary: Neville Crocker **(T)** 07814 923 708 **(E)** neville.crocker@googlemail.com
Chairman: Julian (Jed) Hewitt **Manager:** Chris Vinnicombe **Prog Ed:**
Ground: Horsdon Park, Heathcoat Way, Tiverton, Devon EX16 4DB **(T)** 01884 252 341 **Capacity:**
Colours(change): All green (Red & white/red/red)

ADDITIONAL INFORMATION:
Record Att: 1,713 v Tiverton Town Friday April 14th 1995. **Apps:** P Webber. **Win:** 17-0. **Defeat:** 2-7.
Honours: East Devon Senior Cup 1972-73, 75-76. Devon Senior Cup 1987-88.

GILLINGHAM TOWN

Founded: Nickname:

Secretary: Terry Lucas **(T)** 07873 587 455 **(E)** terrylucas@sky.com
Chairman: Dave Graham **Manager:** Adrian Foster **Prog Ed:**
Ground: Hardings Lane, Gillingham, Dorset SP8 4HX **(T)** 01747 823 673 **Capacity:**
Colours(change): Tangerine/black/tangerine (Navy & sky/navy/sky)

ADDITIONAL INFORMATION:
Previous League: Dorset Premier.

HENGROVE ATHLETIC

Founded: 1948 Nickname:

Secretary: Lee Watts **(T)** 07747 791 245 **(E)** leewatts65@hotmail.co.uk
Chairman: Nigel Gray **Manager:** Jamie Hillman **Prog Ed:**
Ground: Norton Lane, Whitchurch, Bristol BS14 0BT **(T)** 01275 832 894 **Capacity:**
Colours(change): All green (All red)

ADDITIONAL INFORMATION:
Previous League: Somerset County 1974-2006.
Honours: Somerset County League Premier Division 2005-06. Somerset Senior Cup 1979-80.

KEYNSHAM TOWN

Founded: 1895 Nickname: K's

Secretary: John Peake **(T)** 07704 340 170 **(E)** helejohn@btinternet.com
Chairman: Nigel Kay **Manager:** Steve Cains **Prog Ed:**
Ground: Crown Field, Bristol Road, Keynsham BS31 2BE **(T)** 0117 986 5876 **Capacity:**
Colours(change): Gold/black/gold (All white)

ADDITIONAL INFORMATION:
Previous League: Somerset Senior.
Honours: Somerset Senior Cup 1951-52, 57-58, 2002-03.

MELKSHAM TOWN

Founded: 1876 Nickname:

Secretary: Mark Jeffery **(T)** 07739 905 575 **(E)** markmtfc@virginmedia.com
Chairman: Dave Wiltshire **Manager:** Adam Young **Prog Ed:**
Ground: The Conigre, Market Place, Melksham, Wiltshire SN12 6ES **(T)** 01225 702 843 **Capacity:**
Colours(change): Yellow/black/yellow (All red)

ADDITIONAL INFORMATION:
Record Att: 2,821 v Trowbridge Town, FA Cup 1957-58.
Honours: Western League Division 1 1979-80, 96-97. Wiltshire Shield x6. Wiltshire Senior Cup x4.

OLDLAND ABBOTONIANS

Founded: 1910 Nickname: The O's

Secretary: Derek Jones **(T)** 07836 648 327 **(E)** avontruckandvan@btconnect.com
Chairman: Robert Clarke **Manager:** Paul Bitton **Prog Ed:**
Ground: Aitchison Playing Field, Castle Road, Oldland Common, Bristol BS30 9PP **(T)** 0117 932 8263 **Capacity:**
Colours(change): Blue & white/blue/blue (All yellow)

ADDITIONAL INFORMATION:
Previous League: Somerset County.
Honours: Les Phillips Cup 2008-09.

PORTISHEAD TOWN

Founded: 1910 Nickname: Posset

Secretary: Brian Hobbs **(T)** 07791 412 724 **(E)** hobbs.posset@hotmail.co.uk
Chairman: John Shaddick **Manager:** Ray Johnstone **Prog Ed:**
Ground: Bristol Road, Portishead, Bristol BS20 6QG **(T)** 01275 817 600 **Capacity:**
Colours(change): White/black/black (All blue)

ADDITIONAL INFORMATION:
Previous League: Somerset County.
Honours: Somerset County League 2004-05.

ROMAN GLASS ST GEORGE

Founded: Nickname:

Secretary: Emily Baldwin **(T)** 07708 277 592 **(E)** emilyjaynebaldwin@blueyonder.co.uk
Chairman: Roger Hudd **Manager:** Roger Hudd **Prog Ed:**
Ground: Oaklands Park, Gloucester Road, Alomndsbury BS32 4AG **(T)** 07708 277 592 **Capacity:**
Colours(change): White/black/white (All red)

ADDITIONAL INFORMATION:
Previous League: Gloucestershire County.
Honours: Gloucestershire County League 2006-07.

SHEPTON MALLET

Founded: 1986 Nickname:

Secretary: Gary Banfield **(T)** 07762 880 705 **(E)** gkrkb@tiscali.co.uk
Chairman: John Hugill **Manager:** Glynn Shaw **Prog Ed:**
Ground: Playing Fields, Old Wells Road, West Shepton, Shepton Mallet BA4 5XN **(T)** 01749 344 609 **Capacity:**
Colours(change): Black & white/black/black (Claret/yellow/grey)

ADDITIONAL INFORMATION:
Record Att: 274 v Chippenham Town FA Cup 2000-01.
Honours: Somerset Senior League 2000-01.

SHREWTON UNITED

Founded: Nickname:

Secretary: Paul Robinson **(T)** 07786 802 688 **(E)** paul@shrewtonunitedfc.net
Chairman: Gemma Foot **Manager:** Steve Chalk **Prog Ed:**
Ground: Recreation Ground, Mill Lane, Shrewton, Wilts SP3 4JY **(T)** 07786 802 688 **Capacity:**
Colours(change): Marron & sky blue/sky blue/sky blue (Yellow/royal/royal)

ADDITIONAL INFORMATION:
Previous League: Wiltshire > 2003.
Honours: Wiltshire League Premier Division 2001-02, 02-03, Senior Cup 2001-02, 02-03.

WELLINGTON TOWN

Founded: 1892 Nickname: Wellie

Secretary: Ken Pearson **(T)** 07789 055 942 **(E)** ken_pearson@btinternet.com
Chairman: Ken Bird **Manager:** Colin Merrick **Prog Ed:**
Ground: Wellington Playing Field, North St, Wellington TA21 8NA **(T)** 01823 664 810 **Capacity:** 3,000
Colours(change): All tangerine (All blue)

ADDITIONAL INFORMATION: Goalscorer: Ken Jones

WELTON ROVERS

Founded: 1887 Nickname: Rovers

Secretary: Malcolm Price **(T)** 07970 791 644 **(E)** malcolm@weltonr.plus.com
Chairman: Maurice Down **Manager:** Nick Beaverstock **Prog Ed:**
Ground: West Clewes, North Road, Midsomer Norton BA3 2QD **(T)** 01761 412 097 **Capacity:** 2,400
Colours(change): Green & white/green/green (Yellow/blue/yellow).

ADDITIONAL INFORMATION: Att: 2,000 v Bromley FA Am Cup 1963 **Goalscorer:** Ian Henderson 51
Somerset Senior Cup (10). Somerset Premier Cup 2009-10.

WESTBURY UNITED

Founded: 1921 Nickname: White Horsemen

Secretary: Roger Arnold **(T)** 07919 380 911 **(E)** rogerarnold33@hotmail.com
Chairman: Philip Alford **Manager:** Steve Seals **Prog Ed:**
Ground: Meadow Lane, Westbury, Wiltshire BA13 3AF **(T)** 01373 823 409 **Capacity:**
Colours(change): Green & white/green/green (Blue & gold/blue/blue)

ADDITIONAL INFORMATION:
Record Att: 4,000 v Llanelli FA Cup 1st Round 1937 & v Walthamstow Avenue FA Cup 1937.
Honours: Wiltshire League 1934-35, 37-38, 38-39, 49-50, 50-51, 55-56. Western League Div.1 1991-92. Wilts Senior Cup x4.

GROUND DIRECTIONS

BARNSTAPLE TOWN - Mill Road, Barnstaple, North Devon EX31 1JQ 01271 343469
From M5 South, exit junction 27, take A361 to Barnstaple, in town take A361 for Ilfracombe, then first left over bridge is Mill Road.

BISHOP SUTTON - Lakeview, Wick Road, Bishop Sutton BS39 5XN 01275 333097
On main A368 Bath to Weston-Super-Mare road at rear of Butchers Arms Public House.

BITTON - Recreation Ground, Bath Road, Bitton, Bristol BS30 6HX 0117 932 3222
From M4 leave at Junction 18. Take A46 towards Bath, at first roundabout take A420 for Wick / Bridgeyate. On approach to Bridgeyate turn left at mini-roundabout onto A4175 and follow for 2.2 miles, then turn left for Bath on A431. The ground is 100 yards on the right.
From Bath take A431, go through Kelston and Bitton village. Ground is on the left.
From Chippenham take A420 to Bristol and turn left at mini-roundabout onto A4175 and follow as above.

BRIDPORT - St Marys Field, Bridport, Dorset DT6 5LN 01308 423 834
Follow Bridport by-pass in any direction to the Crown Inn roundabout. Take exit to town centre, at first set of traffic lights (Morrisons) turn left. Ground is 200 yards on the right.

BRISLINGTON - Ironmould Lane, Brislington, Bristol BS4 4TZ 0117 977 4030
On A4 Bristol to Bath road, about 500 yards on Bath side of Park & Ride. Opposite the Wyevale Garden Centre.

BRISTOL MANOR FARM - The Creek, Portway, Sea Mills, Bristol BS9 2HS 0117 968 3571
Leaving M5 at Junction 18, take A4 marked Bristol. U-turn on dual carriageway by Bristol and West Sports Ground and then ground is half-mile on left hand side

CORSHAM TOWN - Southbank, Lacock Road, Corsham, Wiltshire SN13 9HS 01249 715609
A4 into Corsham, at Hare and Hounds Roundabout take the Melksham Road B3353 until the War Memorial, then Lacock Road. Ground a half a mile on the right side.

HALLEN - Hallen Centre, Moorhouse Lane, Hallen, Bristol BS10 7RU 0117 950 5559
From Junction 17 M5 follow A4018 towards Bristol. At third roundabout turn right into Crow Lane. Proceed to T junction - turn right and right again at mini roundabout by Henbury Lodge Hotel. At next mini roundabout turn left into Avonmouth Way. Continue for 1.5 miles into Hallen village. At crossroads turn left into Moorhouse Lane

ILFRACOMBE TOWN - Marlborough Park, Ilfracombe, Devon EX34 8PD 01271 865 939
Take A361 for Ilfracombe and in town take first right after traffic lights. Follow Marlborough Road to top and ground is on the left.

LARKHALL ATHLETIC - Plain Ham, Charlcombe Lane, Larkhall, Bath BA1 8DJ 01225 334 952
Take A4 east from Bath city centre. After approximately 1 mile fork left into St Saviours Road. In Larkhall Square take left exit and turn right at T Junction. Road bears left into Charlcombe Lane where ground is on right as road narrows.

LONGWELL GREEN SPORTS - Longwell Green Community Centre, Shellards Road, Longwell Green BS30 9DW 0117 932 3722
Leave Junction 1 M32 follow signs for Ring Road (A4174). At Kingsfield roundabout turn into Marsham Way. At first set of traffic lights turn left into Woodward Drive. Continue to min roundabout and turn right into Parkway Road and continue to Shellards Road. Ground is situated to the rear of the Community Centre.

MERTHYR TOWN - Penydarren Park, Park Terrance, Merthyr Tydfil CF47 8RF 07980 363675
Leave the M4 at Junction 32 and join the A470 to Merthyr Tydfil. After approx 22 miles at the fourth roundabout take 3rd exit. At next roundabout go straight on and go straight on through two sets of traffic lights. At third set turn left (ground signposted Merthyr Tydfil FC from here). After 50 yards take first right, then first right just after Catholic Church into Park Terrace. The ground is at the end of the road approx. 200 yards on.

ODD DOWN - Lew Hill, Memorial Ground, Combe Hay Lane, Odd Down, Bath BA2 8AP 01225 832 491
Situated behind Odd Down Park & Ride on main A367 Bath to Exeter road.

RADSTOCK TOWN - Southfields Recreation Ground, Southfields, Radstock BA3 2NZ 01761 435 004
The town of Radstock is situated 15 miles south east of Bristol and 8 miles southwest of Bath on the A367. At the double roundabout in Radstock town centre take the A362 towards Frome. The ground is on the right hand bend, third turning. Turn right into Southfield, ground is 200 yards ahead.

SHERBORNE TOWN - Raleigh Grove, The Terrace Playing Field, Sherborne, Dorset DT9 5NS 01935 816 110
From Yeovil take A30 - marked Sherborne. On entering town turn right at traffic lights, over next traffic lights and at the next junction turn right. Go over bridge, take second left marked 'Terrace Pling Fields'. Turn into car park, football club car park is situated in the far right-hand corner.

STREET - The Tannery Field, Middlebrooks, Street, Somerset BA16 0TA 01458 445 987
Ground is signposted from both ends of A39 and B3151.

WELLS CITY - Athletic Ground, Rowdens Road, Wells, Somerset BA5 1TU 01749 679 971
From North & Southwest - Follow A39 to Strawberry Way to roundabout, follow A371 East Somerset Way and take right turn into Rowdens Road. Ground is on left. From East - Follow A371 from Shepton Mallet. After approximately 5 miles on East Somerset Way take left turn into Rowdens Road. Ground is on left.

WILLAND ROVERS - Silver Street, Willand, Cullompton, Devon EX15 2RG 01884 33885
Leave M5 Junction 27 and take first left at roundabout. Follow signs to Willand. After passing Halfway House pub on right, go straight over mini-roundabout (signposted to Cullompton) ground is 400 metres on left hand side.

DIVISION ONE

ALMONDSBURY UWE - The Field, Almondsbury, Bristol BS34 4AA 01454 612 240
Exit M5 at Junction 16. Arriving from the south take the left exit lane. Turn left at lights and ground is 150m on right hand side. Arriving from east take right hand lane on slip road. Take 3rd exit and ground is 150m on right hand side.

BRADFORD TOWN - Bradford Sports & Social Club, Trowbridge Road, Bradford on Avon, Wiltshire BA15 1EW 01225 866 649
From Bath or Melksham on entering Bradford on Avon follow the signs for A363 to Trowbridge. The ground is after a mini roundabout and behind a stone wall on the right hand side. From Trowbridge, follow A363 to Bradford-on-Avon. The ground is just past shop on right, behind stone wall on left.

WESTERN LEAGUE - STEP 5/6

CADBURY HEATH - Springfield, Cadbury Heath Road, Bristol BS30 8BX 0117 967 5731 (social club)
M5-M4-M32 Exit 1 follow signs for ring road, exit roundabout for Cadbury Heath left, 100m mini roundabout straight across, 400m mini roundabout turn right into Tower Road North, 150m turn right into Cadbury Heath Road, ground 50m on right via Cadbury Heath Social Club car park.

CALNE TOWN - Bremhill View, Calne, Wiltshire SN11 9EE
Take A4 to Calne from Chippenham, on approaching Calne turn left at the first roundabout on to A3102 Calne bypass. At the next roundabout turn right, next left and then right and right again.

CHARD TOWN - Dening Sports Field, Zembard Lane, Chard, Somerset TA20 1JL 01460 61402
From A30 High Street, follow Swimming Pool/Sports Centre signs via Helliers road. Turn right into Crimchard, turn left into Zembard Lane. Ground is on right hand side.

DEVIZES TOWN - Nursteed Road, Devizes, Wiltshire SN10 3DX 01380 722 817
Leave Devizes on A342 for Andover. Ground is on the right hand side opposite Eastleigh Road.

ELMORE - Horsdon Park, Heathcoat Way, Tiverton, Devon EX16 4DB 01884 252 341
Leave M5 at Junction 27. Follow A373 towards Tiverton, dual-carriageway, for approximately 7 miles. Follow signpost Tiverton and Industrial Estate, ground is 320 metres on right.

GILLINGHAM TOWN - Hardings Lane, Gillingham, Dorset SP8 4HX 01747 823 673
Proceed to middle of town to the High Street. Hardings Lane is a turning off of the High Street, at the Shaftesbury or Southern end of the High Street.

HENGROVE ATHLETIC - Norton Lane, Whitchurch, Bristol BS14 0BT 01275 832 894
Take A37 from Bristol through Whitchurch village past Maes Knoll pub, over hump bridge taking next turning on right, which is Norton Lane. Ground is immediately after Garden Centre.

KEYNSHAM TOWN - Crown Field, Bristol Road, Keynsham BS31 2DZ 0117 986 5876
On A4175 off the Bristol to Bath A4. On left immediately after 30mph sign.

MELKSHAM TOWN - The Conigre, Market Place, Melksham, Wiltshire SN12 6ES 01225 702 843
Turn into Market Place car park and then left into grounds of Cooper Avon Tyres Sports & Social Club (Melksham House) Ground situated at end of drive.

OLDLAND ABBOTONIANS - Aitchison Playing Field, Castle Road, Oldland Common, Bristol BS30 9PP 0117 932 8263
Exit M4 at Jct19 to M32. Exit M32 at Jct 1after 400 yds and take 1st exit from roundabout for A4174. Straight over traffic lights to next roundabout continuing on A4174. Go over five roundabouts for approximately 4.8 miles. At next roundabout take 1st exit to Deanery Road (A420) and continue for 0.9 miles to Griffin Public house and turn right into Bath Road (A4175) . Continue for 1.3 miles to Oldland Common High Street and look for Dolphin Public House. Turning for Castle Street is next left between Chinese Chip Shop and Post Office. Ground is at the end of Castle Road.

PORTISHEAD - Bristol Road, Portishead, Bristol BS20 6QG 01275 817 600
Leave M5 at Junction 19 and take road to Portishead. At outskirts of town take 1st exit from small roundabout signposted Clevedon and Police H.Q. Ground is 150 yds along road on left by bus stop.

ROMAN GLASS ST GEORGE - Oaklands Park, Gloucester Road, Almondsbury BS32 4AG 07708 277592
Exit M5 at Junction 16. Arriving from the south take the left exit lane. Turn left at lights and ground is 100m on left hand side. Arriving from east take right hand lane on slip road. Take 3rd exit nd ground is 100m on left hand side.

SHEPTON MALLET - Playing Fields, Old Wells Road, West Shepton, Shepton Mallet BA4 5XN 01749 344 609
From the town take B3136 (Glastonbury Road) for approximately 1/2 mile. Turn right at junction of Old Wells Road near King William Public House. Approximately 300 yards up the Old Wells Road turn left into the playing fields.

SHREWTON UNITED - Recreation Ground, Mill Lane, Shrewton, Wilts SP3 4JY 07786 802 688
At the mini roundabout in the village turn into High Street and then turn left at the George Inn. Follow signs to the football club, approximately 200 metres on right hand side.

WELLINGTON - The Playing Field, North Street, Wellington, Somerset TA21 8NA 01749 679 971
Leave the M5 motorway at Junction 26 and follow directions to Wellington. At town centre traffic lights take turning into North Street. Take the next left adjacent to the Fire Station and signposted 'Car Park'. The ground is in the corner of the car park.

WELTON ROVERS - West Clewes, North Road, Midsomer Norton BA3 2QD 01761 412 097
The ground is on the main A362 in Midsomer Norton.

WESTBURY UNITED - Meadow Lane, Westbury, Wiltshire BA13 3AF 01373 823 409
From town centre proceed along Station Road towards rail station. At double mini roundabout turn right. Ground is 300 metres on left hand side opposite Fire Station.

ANGLIAN COMBINATION LEAGUE

Sponsored by: Gleave & Associates
Founded: 1964
Recent Champions:
2006: Cromer Town
2007: Blofield United
2008: Wroxham Reserves
2009: Kirby Muxloe SC
2010: Blofield United
angliancombination.org.uk

PREMIER DIVISION	P	W	D	L	F	A	Pts
1 Cromer Town	30	23	3	4	83	37	72
2 Blofield United	30	18	4	8	72	37	58
3 Mattishall	30	17	3	10	58	36	54
4 Norwich St Johns	30	17	3	10	69	51	54
5 Acle United	30	17	2	11	75	41	53
6 Beccles Town	30	14	7	9	56	55	49
7 St Andrews	30	13	9	8	52	39	48
8 Wroxham reserves	30	13	8	9	64	37	47
9 Hempnall	30	13	6	11	44	39	45
10 Sheringham	30	11	6	13	47	57	39
11 Spixworth	30	10	6	14	43	42	36
12 Kirkley & Pakefield reserves	30	8	7	15	42	62	31
13 Loddon United	30	9	4	17	45	69	31
14 North Walsham Town	30	8	5	17	42	57	29
15 Dersingham Rovers	30	6	4	20	42	79	22
16 Brandon Town (-1)	30	3	3	24	34	130	11

DON FROST CUP

(Premier Division champions v Mummery Cup holders)

Blofield United 4-1 Mattishall

MUMMERY CUP
(Premier and Division One Clubs)

ROUND 1
Norwich United 1-0 Loddon United
Acle United 0-0 Dersingham Rovers
(Acle United won 5-4 on penalties)
Beccles Town 1-0 Horsford United
Blofield United 2-0 Reepham Town
Brandon Town 0-6 Bradenham Wanderers
Caister 1-4 Sheringham
Corton 4-0 Hindringham
Cromer Town 2-0 Wymondham Town
Holt United 1-1 Kirkley & Pakefield reserves
(Kirkley & Pakefield won 4-2 on penalties)
Poringland Wanderers 3-2 Wroxham reserves
Spixworth 7-1 Watton United
Sprowston Athletic 0-1 Hempnall
St Andrews 0-1 Stalham Town
Wells Town 4-4 Long Stratton
(Wells Town won 4-2 on penalties)
Bungay Town 2-6 Mattishall

ROUND 2
Kirkley & Pakefield reserves 0-0 Mattishall
(Kirkley & Pakefield won 4-3 on penalties)
Stalham Town 1-5 Hempnall
Sheringham 2-0 North Walsham Town
Poringland Wanderers 4-2 Cromer Town
Bradenham Wanderers 1-3 Spixworth
Beccles Town 1-0 Norwich St Johns
Acle United 4-2 Wells Town
Blofield United 5-0 Corton

QUARTER FINALS
Blolfield United 3-0 Beccles Town
Acle United 2-0 Hempnall
Sheringham 3-1 Poringland Wanderers
Kirkley & Pakefield reserves 0-2 Spixworth

SEMI-FINALS
Sheringham 1-4 Acle United
Spixworth 0-0 Blofield United (Spixworth won 3-1 on penalties)

FINAL (@ Wroxham, 2/5/11)
Acle United 2-2 Spixworth (Spixworth won 4-3 on penalties)

PREMIER DIVISION	1	2	3	4	5	6	7	8	9	10	11	12	13	14	15	16
1 Acle United		5-0	1-1	3-0	3-4	8-2	1-2	0-2	8-0	0-1	4-0	3-0	0-1	2-1	0-1	3-2
2 Beccles Town	3-2		1-1	3-0	1-5	2-0	2-2	2-4	2-0	2-1	2-1	2-4	1-2	0-2	2-0	3-3
3 Blofield United	2-3	1-3		5-2	2-2	3-0	4-0	3-0	2-3	1-0	1-3	4-0	6-1	2-1	2-0	3-2
4 Brandon Town	2-4	3-7	0-3		2-7	0-7	1-4	2-2	4-3	0-2	1-1	0-10	4-8	0-6	1-1	0-7
5 Cromer Town	4-0	3-3	2-0	W-L		3-2	3-0	3-1	2-0	1-3	2-1	4-1	3-0	1-2	3-1	3-2
6 Dersingham Rovers	0-5	0-1	1-7	3-1	2-3		0-2	1-2	2-1	1-1	1-5	2-3	2-1	2-0	2-2	0-4
7 Hempnall	1-2	0-0	0-2	2-0	0-2	2-0		0-0	4-0	0-1	6-0	0-1	1-1	1-1	3-1	1-5
8 Kirkley & Pakefield reserves	1-0	1-3	1-3	1-2	1-4	2-0	2-1		3-3	0-4	3-0	1-3	2-2	1-2	1-4	2-1
9 Loddon United	0-2	0-0	3-2	6-2	2-2	4-2	2-3	3-0		3-1	1-3	1-2	1-3	1-0	0-3	1-2
10 Mattishall	0-1	0-3	3-0	7-1	2-4	4-2	0-1	2-2	3-1		2-1	4-2	3-1	2-0	0-2	2-0
11 North Walsham Town	0-2	5-0	0-3	5-1	2-4	0-2	0-1	2-1	0-0	1-1		2-3	1-3	1-2	0-1	0-0
12 Norwich St Johns	5-3	0-0	3-1	5-0	0-3	2-1	0-2	3-1	5-1	0-1	3-1		5-1	1-0	2-2	0-3
13 Sheringham	0-4	2-3	0-3	2-3	0-2	1-1	3-4	1-0	0-2	1-0	1-2	4-2		2-0	3-0	0-0
14 Spixworth	2-3	1-3	0-1	5-2	0-3	2-2	0-0	4-1	3-0	3-1	3-1	2-2	0-1		0-0	1-3
15 St Andrews	3-2	5-1	2-2	3-0	2-1	3-0	2-1	2-2	3-1	0-2	3-3	1-2	1-1	3-0		1-1
16 Wroxham reserves	1-1	2-1	0-2	8-0	2-0	5-2	3-0	2-2	1-2	2-5	0-1	1-0	1-1	0-0	1-0	

ANGLIAN COMBINATION PREMIER DIVISION CONSTITUTION 2011-12

ACLE UNITED	Bridewell Lane, Acle, Norwich NR13 3RA	01493 752989
BECCLES TOWN	College Meadow, Common Lane, Beccles NR34 7FA	07729 782817
BLOFIELD UNITED	Old Yarmouth Road, Blofield, Norwich NR13 4LE	07748 863203
CROMER TOWN	Cabbell Park, Mill Road, Cromer NR27 0AD	07940 092131
HEMPNALL	Bungay Road, Hempnall, Norwich NR15 2NG	01508 498086
KIRKLEY & PAKEFIELD RESERVES	Kirkley & Pakefield Comm Cnte, Walmer Road, Lowestoft NR33 7LE	01502 513549
LODDON UNITED	George Lane Playing Field, Loddon, Norwich NR14 6NB	01508 528497
MATTISHALL	Mattishall Playing Fields, South Green, Mattishall, Norwich NR20 3JY	01362 850246
NORTH WALSHAM TOWN	Sports Centre, Greens Road, North Walsham NR28 0HW	01692 406888
NORWICH ST JOHNS	Cringleford Recreation Ground, Oakfields Road, Cringleford NR4 6XE	None
SHERINGHAM	Recreation Ground, Weybourne Road, Sheringham NR26 8WD	01263 824804
SPIXWORTH	Spixworth Village Hall, Crostick Lane, Spixworth, Norwich NR10 3NQ	01603 898092
ST ANDREWS	Thorpe Recreation Ground, Laundry Lane, Thorpe St Andrew, Norwich NR7 0XQ	01603 300316
WELLS TOWN	Beach Road, Wells-next-the-Sea NR23 1DR	01328 710907
WROXHAM RESERVES	Trafford Park, Skinners Lane, Wroxham NR12 8SJ	01603 783538
WYMONDHAM TOWN	Kings Head Meadow, Back Lane, Wymondham NR18 0LB	01953 607326

IN: *Wells Town (P), Wymondham Town (P)*
OUT: *Brandon Town (R), Wymondham Town (R)*

DIVISION ONE	P	W	D	L	F	A	Pts
1 Wells Town	28	24	1	3	83	34	73
2 Wymondham Town	28	20	4	4	79	33	64
3 Bradenham Wanderers	28	16	3	9	55	39	51
4 Horsford United	28	15	3	10	51	40	48
5 Reepham Town	28	13	7	8	56	50	46
6 Holt United	28	14	1	13	58	52	43
7 Stalham Town	28	11	7	10	44	45	40
8 Long Stratton	28	12	3	13	45	55	39
9 Watton United	28	12	1	15	61	67	37
10 Sprowston Athletic	28	11	3	14	48	58	36
11 Caister	28	11	2	15	59	70	35
12 Hindringham	28	10	4	14	44	60	34
13 Corton	28	8	7	13	42	49	31
14 Poringland Wanderers	28	4	3	21	43	78	15
15 Bungay Town	28	2	5	21	35	73	11

DIVISION TWO	P	W	D	L	F	A	Pts
1 Norwich CEYMS	30	23	4	3	87	36	73
2 Hellesdon	30	22	4	4	109	31	70
3 Foulsham	30	23	1	6	118	52	70
4 Mundford	30	17	7	6	82	39	58
5 Attleborough Town	30	15	5	10	77	56	50
6 Thetford Rovers	30	15	4	11	88	44	49
7 Hempnall reserves	30	13	9	8	69	46	48
8 Wortwell (-1)	30	15	3	12	69	45	47
9 Acle United reserves	30	13	6	11	49	51	45
10 Scole United	30	9	6	15	38	49	33
11 Beccles Caxton	30	7	5	18	52	79	26
12 Sprowston Wanderers (-1)	30	8	3	19	35	94	26
13 Downham Town reserves	30	8	1	21	37	93	25
14 Thorpe Village	30	6	5	19	43	84	23
15 Southwold Town (-1)	30	7	3	20	43	97	23
16 Sprowston Athletic reserves	30	4	4	22	37	137	16

CYRIL BALLYN TROPHY
(Division Two, Three, Four, Five and Six first teams and external league reserve sides)

ROUND 1
Harleston Town 5-3 Newton Flotman
Hempnall reserves 1-1 Acle United
(Acle United won on penalties)
Mundford 3-1 Scole United
Redgrave Rovers 3-1 Southwold Town
Saham Toney 2-4 Downham Town reserves
Waveney 2-3 Buxton

ROUND 2
Fakenham Town reserves 1-4 Easton
Anglian Windows 3-1 Norwich CEYMS
Buxton 1-13 Attleborough Town
CNSOBU 1-6 Beccles Caxton
Foulsham 5-1 Downham Town reserves
Harleston Town 2-0 Acle United reserves
Hemsby 2-1 Freethorpe
Hoveton Wherrymen 2-5 Aylsham
Marlingford 6-2 Thorpe Village
Mulbarton Wanderers 3-3 Thetford Rovers
(Thetford Rovers won 4-2 on penalties)
Sprowston Athletic reserves 2-3 South Walsham
Sprowston Wanderers 1-10 Mundford
Swaffham Town reserves 3-3 Hellesdon
(Swaffham Town reserves won 5-4 on penalties)
Thorpe Rovers 1-1 Martham (Martham won 5-3 on penalties)
UEA 4-3 East Harling
Wortwell 3-2 Redgrave Rovers

ROUND 3
Marlingford 1-2 Beccles Caxton
Mundford 3-2 Harleston Town
South Walsham 3-1 Attleborough Town
Anglian Windows 3-2 Hemsby
Swaffham Town reserves 1-2 Aylsham
Thetford Rovers 1-2 Martham
UEA 0-1 Easton
Wortwell 5-1 Foulsham

QUARTER FINALS
Anglian Windows 3-0 Mundford
Easton 1-1 Aylsham (Aylsham won 3-1 on penalties)
South Walsham 1-2 Beccles Caxton
Wortwell 3-1 Martham

SEMI-FINALS
Anglian Windows 1-3 Aylsham
Wortwell 4-3 Beccles Caxton

Final (@ Watton United, 11/5/11)
Aylsham 0-0 Wortwell (Aylsham won 4-3 on penalties)

DIVISION ONE	1	2	3	4	5	6	7	8	9	10	11	12	13	14	15
1 Bradenham Wanderers		5-1	2-4	3-2	0-2	4-0	3-0	1-0	2-0	1-3	1-0	1-1	3-1	1-2	0-1
2 Bungay Town	1-3		0-4	0-2	0-2	2-2	2-1	1-2	1-2	1-2	1-1	0-1	6-2	3-4	2-3
3 Caister	2-4	4-3		3-3	3-2	3-1	1-3	0-2	5-3	5-1	1-3	2-2	1-3	1-3	1-4
4 Corton	1-2	1-0	1-2		1-0	1-3	1-5	4-1	2-0	3-3	1-1	2-0	0-1	1-2	1-4
5 Hindringham	0-3	0-0	6-1	2-2		0-2	1-4	1-1	3-2	1-4	3-0	1-2	4-3	1-5	2-1
6 Holt United	3-2	5-0	3-0	2-1	4-1		1-2	0-1	5-0	0-3	4-2	4-1	1-2	0-1	2-5
7 Horsford United	0-2	2-1	3-2	1-1	1-0	2-1		1-2	1-1	0-0	5-1	2-1	3-2	0-3	0-1
8 Long Stratton	1-4	2-2	2-1	1-2	5-1	3-4	1-0		5-0	0-1	2-1	0-2	3-0	1-4	1-4
9 Poringland Wanderers	1-2	3-0	1-2	0-1	2-6	0-2	1-3	2-0		3-3	6-1	1-3	4-5	3-3	1-3
10 Reepham Town	2-3	5-2	2-0	3-3	1-0	2-1	2-3	4-1	2-1		0-1	3-3	1-4	0-5	2-2
11 Sprowston Athletic	1-0	2-1	3-0	2-1	2-3	0-1	1-5	1-1	4-2	2-5		2-4	4-1	3-0	0-3
12 Stalham Town	1-1	2-0	0-4	2-0	1-1	3-0	4-2	0-3	3-1	0-0	2-1		1-2	0-3	2-2
13 Watton United	2-1	2-2	2-5	3-2	0-1	2-3	0-2	8-0	6-2	1-2	2-5	1-0		1-2	1-4
14 Wells Town	7-1	4-2	3-2	2-1	3-0	4-2	3-0	5-1	2-1	2-0	3-2	2-1	1-2		4-0
15 Wymondham Town	0-0	5-1	5-0	1-1	7-0	5-2	1-0	1-3	3-0	2-0	0-2	4-2	4-2	4-1	

ANGLIAN COMBINATION DIVISION ONE CONSTITUTION 2011-12

BRADENHAM WANDERERS	Hale Road, Bradenham, Thetford IP25 7RA	None
BRANDON TOWN	Remembrance Playing Field, Church Road, Brandon IP27 0JB	01842 813177
CAISTER	Caister Playing Fields, off Allendale Road, Caister-on-Sea NR30 5ES	None
CORTON	The Street, Corton, Lowestoft NR32 5HE	None
DERSINGHAM ROVERS	Behind Feathers Hotel, Manor Road, Dersingham, King's Lynn PE31 6LN	01485 542707
HELLESDON	Hellesdon Community Centre, Wood View Road, Hellesdon, Norwich NR6 5QB	01603 427675
HINDRINGHAM	Sports & Social Club, Wells Rd, Hindringham, Fakenham NR21 0PN	01328 878608
HOLT UNITED	Sports Centre, Kelling Road, Holt NR25 7DU	01263 711217
HORSFORD UNITED	Village Hall, Holt Road, Horsford NR10 3DN	01603 893317
LONG STRATTON	Manor Road Playing Fields, Long Stratton, Norwich NR15 2XR	None
NORWICH CEYMS	Hilltops Sports Centre, Main Road, Swardeston, Norwich NR14 8DU	01508 578826
PORINGLAND WANDERERS	Poringland Memorial Field, The Footpath, Poringland, Norwich NR14 7RF	01508 495198
REEPHAM TOWN	Stimpson's Piece Rec Ground, Bartle Court, Reepham, Norwich NR10 4LL	None
SPROWSTON ATHLETIC	Sprowston Sports & Social Club, Blue Boar Lane, Sprowston, Norwich NR7 8RJ	01603 427688
STALHAM TOWN	Rivers Park, Stepping Stone Lane, Stalham, Norwich NR12 9EP	None
WATTON UNITED	Watton Playing Field, Dereham Road, Watton, Thetford IP25 6EZ	01953 881281

IN: *Brandon Town (R), Hellesdon (P), Norwich CEYMS (P), Wymondham Town (R)*
OUT: *Bungay Town (R), Wells Town (P), Wymondham Town (P)*

DIVISION TWO	1	2	3	4	5	6	7	8	9	10	11	12	13	14	15	16
1 Acle United reserves		0-1	2-1	4-1	0-2	1-3	3-2	2-2	2-4	2-0	8-1	1-1	W-L	0-3	2-2	0-2
2 Attleborough Town	7-0		2-2	7-1	2-3	0-0	2-6	1-3	1-3	2-2	7-2	7-1	5-0	0-3	6-1	0-3
3 Beccles Caxton	1-1	2-3		4-0	0-3	3-6	1-3	1-9	2-3	3-1	3-1	4-5	5-0	1-2	1-2	1-0
4 Downham Town reserves	0-6	0-0	3-2		3-1	0-4	1-3	1-2	4-1	0-1	W-L	5-0	2-4	2-4	3-1	0-3
5 Foulsham	7-1	1-2	4-2	4-2		5-3	3-2	1-0	5-0	5-1	5-1	9-0	10-1	3-1	5-1	3-2
6 Hellesdon	2-1	5-1	5-1	7-0	3-0		5-1	2-1	0-1	1-1	4-1	11-1	7-0	2-0	8-1	3-1
7 Hempnall reserves	0-1	3-1	1-1	2-0	3-2	2-3		0-0	1-1	2-1	4-1	6-0	3-3	4-0	5-1	2-2
8 Mundford	1-1	0-1	6-2	2-0	2-2	1-0	4-2		1-1	2-0	3-0	3-1	9-2	1-5	2-2	3-1
9 Norwich C E Y M S	2-0	2-1	5-0	7-0	6-3	1-1	1-1	3-1		1-3	6-2	4-0	3-0	1-0	5-0	5-0
10 Scole United	1-2	0-2	0-2	1-2	3-1	0-3	0-0	2-1	0-3		5-1	6-0	0-2	0-0	0-2	0-2
11 Southwold Town	1-2	2-5	2-1	2-1	2-6	0-3	0-2	2-2	2-4	2-2		3-1	3-0	1-0	1-1	0-2
12 Sprowston Athletic reserves	2-3	3-4	2-2	2-3	0-8	0-5	2-2	1-7	2-6	0-3	5-0		1-1	1-11	2-0	2-4
13 Sprowston Wanderers	0-2	1-2	1-1	2-0	1-5	0-6	2-1	0-5	2-3	0-3	3-4	0-1		2-1	4-3	0-4
14 Thetford Rovers	0-0	5-1	4-0	7-0	4-5	0-2	3-3	0-2	2-3	1-2	8-2	7-0	4-0		6-1	3-2
15 Thorpe Village	1-2	0-2	2-1	3-1	3-5	2-2	0-2	1-4	0-2	0-0	1-3	6-1	0-2	2-3		1-3
16 Wortwell	1-0	2-2	1-2	7-2	1-2	5-3	2-1	2-3	L-W	5-0	3-1	6-0	1-2	1-1	1-3	

ANGLIAN COMBINATION DIVISION TWO CONSTITUTION 2011-12

ACLE UNITED RESERVES	Bridewell Lane, Acle, Norwich NR13 3RA	01493 752989
ATTLEBOROUGH TOWN	Recreation Ground, Station Road, Attleborough NR17 2AS	01953 455365
AYLSHAM	Sir Williams Lane, Aylsham, Norwich NR11 6AN	None
BECCLES CAXTON	Caxton Meadow, Adj. Beccles Station, Beccles NR34 9QH	01502 712829
BUNGAY TOWN	Maltings Meadow, Ditchingham, Bungay NR35 2RU	01986 894028
DOWNHAM TOWN RESERVES	Memorial Playing Field, Lynn Road, Downham Market PE38 9QE	01366 388424
EAST HARLING	Memorial Fields, Church Street, East Harling NR16 2NA	01953 718251
FOULSHAM	Playing Field, Guist Road, Foulsham, Dereham NR20 5RZ	None
HARLESTON TOWN	Rec & Memorial Leisure Centre, Wilderness Lane, Harleston IP20 9DD	01379 854519
HEMPNALL RESERVES	Bungay Road, Hempnall, Norwich NR15 2NG	01508 498086
MUNDFORD	The Glebe, Mundford, Thetford IP26 5EJ	None
SCOLE UNITED	Ransome Avenue Playing Field, Scole, Diss IP21 4EA	01379 741204
SPROWSTON WANDERERS	Sprowston Cricket Club, Barkers Lane, Sprowston, Norwich NR7 8QZ	01603 404042
THETFORD ROVERS	Euston Park, Euston, Thetford IP24 2QP	None
THORPE VILLAGE	Thorpe Recreation Ground, Laundry Lane, Thorpe St Andrew, Norwich NR7 0XQ	01603 300316

***IN:** Aylsham (P), Bungay Town (R), East Harling (P), Harleston Town (P)*

***OUT:** Hellesdon (P), Norwich CEYMS (P), Southwold Town (R), Sprowston Athletic Reserves (R), Wortwell (W)*

DIVISION THREE	P	W	D	L	F	A	Pts
1 Harleston Town	30	25	1	4	105	41	76
2 Aylsham	30	19	5	6	71	34	62
3 East Harling	30	16	4	10	79	52	52
4 Loddon United reserves	30	16	3	11	57	52	51
5 Easton	30	14	6	10	54	46	48
6 Martham	30	14	4	12	65	59	46
7 Swaffham Town reserves	30	12	9	9	67	54	45
8 Cromer Town reserves	30	12	9	9	64	55	45
9 Blofield United reserves	30	12	6	12	65	68	42
10 Freethorpe	30	11	7	12	67	56	40
11 Marlingford	30	11	6	13	63	68	39
12 Anglian Windows	30	11	6	13	43	58	39
13 Wymondham Town res (-1)	30	10	6	14	58	66	35
14 North Walsham Town reserves	30	8	5	17	56	76	29
15 Newton Flotman	30	7	2	21	46	84	23
16 Beccles Town reserves	30	2	1	27	31	122	7

DIVISION FOUR	P	W	D	L	F	A	Pts
1 UEA	28	24	2	2	90	30	74
2 Hemsby	28	18	6	4	67	24	60
3 Waveney	28	18	5	5	85	25	59
4 Hoveton Wherrymen	28	18	2	8	100	48	56
5 Sheringham reserves	28	17	5	6	86	55	56
6 South Walsham	28	12	7	9	57	53	43
7 St Andrews reserves	28	13	2	13	58	56	41
8 Mattishall reserves	28	10	6	12	58	57	36
9 Bungay Town reserves	28	10	4	14	61	87	34
10 Fakenham Town reserves (-2)	28	9	4	15	44	67	29
11 Thorpe Rovers	28	8	3	17	34	76	27
12 Caister reserves	28	5	7	16	53	90	22
13 Long Stratton reserves (-1)	28	7	1	20	42	85	21
14 Spixworth reserves	28	5	5	18	35	83	20
15 Watton United reserves	28	5	3	20	44	78	18

DIVISION FIVE	P	W	D	L	F	A	Pts
1 Mulbarton Wanderers	26	20	3	3	92	33	63
2 Redgrave Rangers	26	20	1	5	93	35	61
3 Norwich CEYMS reserves	26	15	6	5	59	37	51
4 Corton reserves	26	14	3	9	52	47	45
5 Reepham Town reserves	26	13	4	9	63	50	43
6 Poringland Wanderers res.	26	13	1	12	53	52	40
7 Buxton (-1)	26	12	2	12	76	60	37
8 Saham Toney (-3)	26	11	4	11	56	47	34
9 Hindringham reserves	26	11	1	14	70	71	34
10 Attleborough Town reserves	26	8	2	16	40	85	26
11 Mundford reserves	26	7	4	15	37	76	25
12 Wells Town reserves (-1)	26	7	2	17	41	61	22
13 Brandon Town reserves (-1)	26	7	2	17	47	100	22
14 Stalham Town reserves	26	5	3	18	39	64	18

DIVISION SIX	P	W	D	L	F	A	Pts
1 Bradenham Wanderers res.	24	17	2	5	82	40	53
2 Aylsham reserves	24	16	3	5	70	37	51
3 Holt United reserves	24	15	4	5	72	34	49
4 Foulsham reserves	24	14	3	7	76	48	45
5 Scole United reserves (-1)	24	13	1	10	53	42	39
6 East Harling reserves	24	11	4	9	68	44	37
7 Hemsby reserves	24	11	4	9	44	51	37
8 Easton reserves	24	11	2	11	66	58	35
9 Horsford United reserves	24	8	3	13	41	73	27
10 Thorpe Village reserves (-1)	24	6	7	11	34	61	24
11 Freethorpe reserves	24	4	5	15	45	67	17
12 Martham reserves	24	5	2	17	49	96	17
13 CNSOBU (-1)	24	5	0	19	37	86	14

Hellesdeon reserves - record expunged

CS MORLEY CUP
(Anglian Combination reserve teams)

Final (@ Wroxham, 9/5/11)
Aylsham reserves 2-2 St Andrews reserves
(Aylsham reserves won 4-3 on penalties)

DIVISION THREE	1	2	3	4	5	6	7	8	9	10	11	12	13	14	15	16
1 Anglian Windows		0-0	5-0	2-2	2-2	2-3	0-2	4-1	0-1	2-1	1-1	2-1	1-0	3-0	0-4	3-2
2 Aylsham	6-1		4-1	1-2	2-1	0-2	4-1	4-3	2-0	3-1	1-0	4-3	6-1	2-0	1-1	4-0
3 Beccles Town reserves	1-3	1-5		5-3	3-2	0-2	1-3	1-10	0-1	0-1	2-2	0-3	1-2	2-7	0-1	1-7
4 Blofield United reserves	0-0	1-3	2-1		2-2	1-0	1-3	2-1	2-3	3-2	2-3	1-2	2-2	2-1	0-0	3-2
5 Cromer Town reserves	2-1	1-1	2-0	3-3		1-6	2-1	2-0	1-3	4-0	2-2	1-0	7-2	4-3	2-2	2-2
6 East Harling	5-1	2-4	10-3	2-5	1-0		1-1	1-1	1-2	5-1	1-2	2-3	5-4	1-2	3-1	6-1
7 Easton	4-0	3-1	3-1	0-2	1-1	0-4		0-1	1-0	2-0	1-2	2-2	2-1	3-1	2-2	3-1
8 Freethorpe	1-3	0-1	6-1	2-3	1-3	1-1	2-2		4-1	2-2	1-2	2-5	3-0	3-1	3-1	2-0
9 Harleston Town	4-0	4-2	12-1	7-2	7-1	2-1	4-1	4-1		4-2	8-2	3-1	4-1	1-4	5-2	2-1
10 Loddon United reserves	2-1	1-0	3-0	2-1	2-0	1-3	4-0	1-4	0-1		2-2	3-2	1-0	7-2	2-1	2-5
11 Marlingford	1-2	2-1	4-3	3-1	0-2	3-0	3-5	2-2	1-4	1-3		2-3	7-0	1-1	1-2	1-2
12 Martham	5-2	0-3	2-0	4-3	0-6	1-2	3-1	2-2	2-2	2-2	3-1		4-1	1-0	1-3	2-1
13 Newton Flotman	0-1	0-1	5-1	1-4	2-0	1-2	1-3	1-2	1-3	1-2	2-5	2-1		6-1	3-2	4-1
14 North Walsham Town reserves	3-0	2-2	3-1	6-3	1-1	3-4	0-4	2-4	1-5	1-2	4-0	0-3	3-0		0-0	2-6
15 Swaffham Town reserves	1-1	0-0	7-0	3-2	1-6	3-1	1-0	3-1	3-8	0-1	3-4	4-3	7-0	2-2		6-1
16 Wymondham Town reserves	3-0	0-3	2-0	2-5	4-1	2-2	0-0	1-1	L-W	0-4	4-3	2-1	2-2	3-0	1-1	

ANGLIAN COMBINATION DIVISION THREE CONSTITUTION 2011-12

ANGLIAN WINDOWS	Horsford Manor, Cromer Road, Norwich NR5 8AP	01603 404723
BLOFIELD UNITED RESERVES	Old Yarmouth Road, Blofield, Norwich NR13 4LE	07748 863203
CROMER TOWN RESERVES	Cabbell Park, Mill Road, Cromer NR27 0AD	07940 092131
EASTON	Easton College, Bawburgh Road, Norwich NR9 5DX	01603 731208
FREETHORPE	School Road, Freethorpe, Norwich NR13 3NZ	01493 701533
HEMSBY	Walters Lane, Hemsby NR29 4LE	01493 733543
LODDON UNITED RESERVES	George Lane Playing Field, Loddon, Norwich NR14 6NB	01508 528497
MARLINGFORD	Bayer Social Club, Marlpit Lane, Norwich NR5 8YT	01603 787661
MARTHAM	Coronation Recreation Ground, Rollesby Road, Martham, Great Yarmouth NR29 4SP	01493 740252
NORTH WALSHAM TOWN RESERVES	Sports Centre, Greens Road, North Walsham NR28 0HW	01692 406888
SOUTHWOLD TOWN	Reydon High School, Wangford Road, Reydon, Southwold IP18 6QA	None
SPROWSTON ATHLETIC RESERVES	Sprowston Sports & Social Club, Blue Boar Lane, Sprowston, Norwich NR7 8RJ	01603 427688
SWAFFHAM TOWN RESERVES	Shoemakers Lane, off Cley Road, Swaffham PE37 7NT	01760 722700
UEA	UEA Sports Ground, Colney Lane, Norwich NR4 7RG	None
WYMONDHAM TOWN RESERVES	Kings Head Meadow, Back Lane, Wymondham NR18 0LB	01953 607326

IN: *Hemsby (P), Southwold Town (R), Sprowston Athletic Reserves (R), UEA (P)*
OUT: *Aylsham (P), Beccles Town Reserves (R), East Harling (P), Harleston Town (P), Newton Flotman (R)*

DIVISION FOUR	1	2	3	4	5	6	7	8	9	10	11	12	13	14	15
1 Bungay Town reserves		6-2	4-2	0-2	3-2	2-1	1-0	0-3	1-3	1-1	7-4	5-0	1-3	4-2	1-11
2 Caister reserves	4-4		2-3	0-3	1-4	3-2	4-3	1-4	0-2	2-2	3-2	0-1	0-2	3-8	1-3
3 Fakenham Town reserves	6-1	2-2		0-1	1-4	2-1	1-1	2-2	2-3	2-0	5-1	5-3	0-2	0-1	2-8
4 Hemsby	1-1	6-1	4-0		2-1	W-L	2-0	2-2	2-2	5-0	0-1	4-2	1-2	2-0	0-0
5 Hoveton Wherrymen	7-1	6-2	2-0	1-3		9-1	2-2	2-4	2-2	1-2	3-1	4-0	2-6	8-2	0-2
6 Long Stratton reserves	2-2	2-1	W-L	0-4	4-5		0-4	5-3	3-1	3-2	3-2	2-3	1-4	1-3	0-4
7 Mattishall reserves	6-1	3-3	0-0	1-2	0-8	2-1		2-2	3-2	5-1	2-1	3-1	0-7	1-0	1-4
8 Sheringham reserves	7-1	5-1	2-4	3-2	1-4	3-1	2-1		1-2	4-0	3-1	4-1	2-0	7-2	1-0
9 South Walsham	3-2	2-3	1-2	1-1	1-5	4-2	2-1	3-3		3-1	2-3	3-1	1-1	2-1	2-2
10 Spixworth reserves	1-2	2-2	3-0	1-2	1-4	5-1	1-9	3-4	0-0		0-1	3-1	1-1	1-0	0-3
11 St Andrews reserves	3-0	1-1	4-0	1-3	0-4	4-1	1-0	2-6	3-2	6-0		6-0	4-3	2-1	1-0
12 Thorpe Rovers reserves	4-3	0-8	W-L	0-5	0-3	2-1	1-1	1-2	0-4	5-0	1-0		1-2	3-0	1-1
13 UEA	5-3	4-0	8-0	2-1	5-3	5-1	4-2	4-1	3-1	4-1	2-1	3-1		3-0	2-1
14 Watton United reserves	0-3	3-3	1-3	1-6	0-2	1-3	0-5	6-3	2-3	5-1	1-1	1-1	0-2		2-3
15 Waveney	2-1	5-0	6-0	1-1	1-2	5-0	3-0	2-2	3-0	7-2	3-1	3-0	0-1	2-1	

ANGLIAN COMBINATION DIVISION FOUR CONSTITUTION 2011-12

BECCLES TOWN RESERVES	College Meadow, Common Lane, Beccles NR34 7FA	07729 782817
BUNGAY TOWN RESERVES	Maltings Meadow, Ditchingham, Bungay NR35 2RU	01986 894028
CAISTER RESERVES	Caister Playing Fields, off Allendale Road, Caister-on-Sea NR30 5ES	None
FAKENHAM TOWN RESERVES	Clipbush Park, Clipbush Lane, Fakenham NR21 8SW	01328 855445 Club:01328 855859
HOVETON WHERRYMEN	Playing Field, Stalham Road, Hoveton, Wroxham NR12 8DG	None
LONG STRATTON	Manor Road Playing Fields, Long Stratton, Norwich NR15 2XR	None
MATTISHALL RESERVES	Mattishall Playing Fields, South Green, Mattishall, Norwich NR20 3JY	01362 850246
MULBARTON WANDERERS	Mulberry Park, Mulbarton NR14 8AE	None
NEWTON FLOTMAN	Newton Flotman Village Centre, Grove Way, Newton Flotman, Norwich NR15 1PU	None
REDGRAVE RANGERS	Redgrave Sports Field, Church Way, Redgrave, Diss IP22 1RL	None
SHERINGHAM RESERVES	Recreation Ground, Weybourne Road, Sheringham NR26 8WD	01263 824804
SOUTH WALSHAM	The Playing Field, South Walsham	None
ST ANDREWS RESERVES	Thorpe Recreation Ground, Laundry Lane, Thorpe St Andrew, Norwich NR7 0XQ	01603 300316
THORPE ROVERS	Dussindale Park, Pound Lane, Thorpe, Norwich NR7 0SR	None
WAVENEY	Denes Community Centre, Yarmouth Road, Lowestoft NR32 4AH	None

IN: *Beccles Town Reserves (R), Redgrave Rangers (P), Mulbarton Wanderers (P), Newton Flotman (R)*
OUT: *Hemsby (P), UEA (P), Spixworth Reserves (R), Watton United Reserves (R)*

BEDFORDSHIRE COUNTY LEAGUE

Sponsored by: No sponsor
Founded: 1904
Recent Champions:
2006: Caldecote
2007: Westoning Recreation Club
2008: Campton
2009: Caldecote
2010: Blunham
bedfordshirefootballleague.co.uk

PREMIER DIVISION	P	W	D	L	F	A	Pts
1 Blunham	24	18	3	3	92	35	57
2 Shefford Town & Campton	24	17	5	2	66	35	56
3 Wilshamstead	24	14	4	6	76	54	46
4 Renhold United	24	14	4	6	56	37	46
5 Caldecote	24	13	2	9	62	50	41
6 Leighton United	24	10	6	8	56	47	36
7 Flitwick Town	24	9	4	11	39	50	31
8 Dunton	24	9	4	11	32	45	31
9 Oakley Sports	24	7	4	13	34	54	25
10 Sharnbrook	24	7	3	14	43	54	24
11 Woburn	24	5	4	15	37	67	19
12 AFC Kempston Town	24	4	7	13	32	63	19
13 Arlesey Town reserves	24	2	4	18	37	71	10

Biggleswade United reserves - record expunged
Ickwell & Old Warden - record expunged
Southill Alexander - record expunged

DIVISION ONE	P	W	D	L	F	A	Pts
1 Blunham	24	18	3	3	92	35	57
2 Shefford Town & Campton	24	17	5	2	66	35	56
3 Wilshamstead	24	14	4	6	76	54	46
4 Renhold United	24	14	4	6	56	37	46
5 Caldecote	24	13	2	9	62	50	41
6 Leighton United	24	10	6	8	56	47	36
7 Flitwick Town	24	9	4	11	39	50	31
8 Dunton	24	9	4	11	32	45	31
9 Oakley Sports	24	7	4	13	34	54	25
10 Sharnbrook	24	7	3	14	43	54	24
11 Woburn	24	5	4	15	37	67	19
12 AFC Kempston Town	24	4	7	13	32	63	19
13 Arlesey Town reserves	24	2	4	18	37	71	10

Biggleswade United reserves - record expunged
Ickwell & Old Warden - record expunged
Southill Alexander - record expunged

BRITANNIA CUP

ROUND 1
Caldecote 3-2 Arlesey Town reserves
Leighton United 2-0 Flitwick Town
Renhold United 3-1 Blunham
Sharnbrook 1-3 Oakley Sports
Wilshamsted 2-2 Shefford Town & Campton
(Shefford Town & Campton won 5-4 on penalties)
Woburn 1-5 Dunton
Biggleswade United reserves scr-w/o AFC Kempston Town
Southill Alexander - Bye

QUARTER FINALS
AFC Kempston Town 0-3 Renhold United
Dunton 2-2 Leighton United (Leighton United won 4-3 on penalties)
Oakley Sports 1-3 Shefford Town & Campton
Caldecote w/o-scr Southill Alexander

SEMI-FINALS
Renhold United 0-6 Shefford Town & Campton (@ AFC Kempston Rovers)
Leighton United 1-0 Caldecote (@ Biggleswade United)

FINAL (@ Biggleswade United, 7/5/11)
Shefford Town & Campton 3-1 Leighton United

DIVISION TWO	P	W	D	L	F	A	Pts
1 Lea Sports PSG	26	21	3	2	91	23	66
2 Westoning Recreation Club	26	16	4	6	65	42	52
3 Kings AFC	26	17	0	9	70	50	51
4 Lidlington United Sports	26	15	4	7	60	41	49
5 Bromham United	26	13	3	10	51	46	42
6 Elstow Abbey 06	26	12	2	12	56	24	38
7 Queens Park Crescents	26	12	2	12	51	47	38
8 Clifton	26	11	4	11	46	49	37
9 Shefford Town & Campton res.	26	9	5	12	45	54	32
10 Marabese Ceramics	26	9	2	15	28	39	29
11 Great Barford	26	9	2	15	31	74	29
12 Stopsley Park	26	7	6	13	61	63	27
13 Stevington	26	7	2	17	46	68	23
14 Kempston Hammers Sports	26	4	1	21	21	102	13

Arlesey Social Galacticos - record expunged
Harpur - record expunged

PREMIER DIVISION	1	2	3	4	5	6	7	8	9	10	11	12	13
1 AFC Kempston Town		2-2	0-7	1-3	0-1	3-1	2-2	2-2	2-4	1-2	1-3	1-4	2-2
2 Arlesey Town reserves	9-0		1-2	3-5	0-1	1-2	1-2	5-0	1-5	0-1	0-1	1-7	2-2
3 Blunham	3-0	4-0		5-3	9-3	3-0	3-0	7-0	2-2	4-2	3-1	4-0	8-2
4 Caldecote	1-1	3-1	4-5		2-0	6-2	4-2	3-5	0-1	3-1	3-1	2-5	6-1
5 Dunton	1-2	1-0	2-0	2-1		0-0	1-2	1-0	3-3	1-2	1-3	1-2	1-0
6 Flitwick Town	3-0	3-1	3-1	1-4	4-1		2-2	3-1	1-3	3-2	2-3	0-2	2-1
7 Leighton United	1-1	7-0	3-3	1-3	0-1	2-2		2-0	W-L	3-2	1-1	6-2	3-1
8 Oakley Sports	1-0	3-0	1-3	1-1	1-1	0-3	0-2		1-2	5-3	0-0	2-1	L-W
9 Renhold United	2-1	5-1	0-2	1-2	2-1	2-0	2-8	5-1		2-0	1-3	8-2	3-1
10 Sharnbrook	2-2	2-1	1-4	7-0	1-1	1-1	3-1	1-2	0-2		4-5	2-3	0-3
11 Shefford Town & Campton	4-2	8-2	2-1	2-0	7-2	4-1	3-1	3-2	0-0	2-1		3-3	1-1
12 Wilshamstead	1-2	2-2	4-4	W-L	4-1	5-0	7-3	4-2	1-1	4-1	3-4		3-2
13 Woburn	2-4	3-3	1-5	1-3	0-4	2-0	3-2	2-4	4-0	1-2	0-2	2-7	

BEDFORDSHIRE COUNTY PREMIER DIVISION CONSTITUTION 2011-12

Club	Ground	Telephone
AFC KEMPSTON & BEDFORD COLL.	Hillgrounds Road, Kempston, Bedford MK42 8SZ	01234 852346
ARLESEY TOWN RESERVES	Hitchin Road, Arlesey SG15 6RS	01462 734504
		Boardroom: 01462 734512
BEDFORD HATTERS	Meltis Sports & Social Club, 12 Miller Road, Bedford MK42 9NY	01234 352872
BLUNHAM	The Playing Fields, Blunham Road, Moggerhanger, Sandy MK44 3RG	None
CALDECOTE	Harvey Close, Upper Caldecote, Biggleswade SG18 9BQ	01767 600236
DUNTON	Horseshoe Close, Dunton SG18 8RY	None
FLITWICK TOWN	Flitwick Leisure Centre, Flitwick, Bedford MK45 1TH	01462 611575
LEIGHTON UNITED	Stanbridge Road, Tilsworth LU7 9PL	01525 211792
OAKLEY SPORTS	Oakley Village Sports Centre, Oakley, Bedford MK43 7RG	None
POTTON WANDERERS	Potton Recreation Ground, Mill Lane, Potton SG19 2PG	None
RENHOLD UNITED	Renhold Playing Fields, Renhold, Bedford MK41 0LR	None
SHARNBROOK	Playing Fields, Lodge Road, Sharnbrook MK44 1JP	None
SHEFFORD TOWN & CAMPTON	STMA Digswell, Hitchin Road, Shefford SG17 5JA	01462 813377
WILSHAMSTEAD	Jubilee Playing Fields, Bedford Road, Wilshamstead MK45 3HN	None
WOBURN	Crawley Road, Woburn MK17 9QD	None

IN: *Bedford Hatters (P), Potton Wanderers (P)*
OUT: *Biggleswade United Reserves (WS), Ickwell & Old Warden (WS), Southill Alexander (WS)*
AFC Kempston Town become AFC Kempston & Bedford College

DIVISION ONE	1	2	3	4	5	6	7	8	9	10	11	12	13
1 AFC Kempston Town reserves		0-4	L-W	2-1	1-0	1-2	3-2	1-3	0-4	0-6	1-2	0-11	1-4
2 Bedford Hatters	4-0		3-1	W-L	3-1	5-0	2-1	3-0	5-0	1-0	5-1	2-1	4-0
3 Bedford SA	6-0	5-3		4-0	3-4	2-2	7-3	1-1	4-0	2-5	5-2	0-3	3-2
4 Blunham reserves	2-2	L-W	L-W		L-W	2-2	2-0	2-1	3-1	2-3	1-2	W-L	2-2
5 Caldecote reserves	2-1	2-4	2-0	1-2		1-3	0-1	2-2	4-0	0-2	4-2	1-3	5-1
6 F C Meppershall	4-3	2-1	4-3	10-1	3-4		2-3	3-2	7-1	2-7	0-2	W-L	2-4
7 Henlow	5-0	0-6	4-4	2-1	3-3	W-L		3-3	1-2	1-1	1-3	0-6	2-3
8 Ickwell & Old Warden reserves	2-1	0-3	2-4	2-2	1-2	2-2	2-0		3-1	1-2	2-0	W-L	0-2
9 Luton Old Boys	3-4	0-9	3-1	2-1	W-L	1-2	3-3	3-2		1-1	2-0	2-6	1-4
10 Marston Shelton Rovers	2-1	1-0	0-1	6-1	4-1	2-1	4-2	0-3	2-1		1-0	0-2	1-0
11 Meltis Albion	6-0	1-4	3-0	4-0	3-2	2-1	0-3	1-0	5-0	1-2		1-3	2-2
12 Potton Wanderers	4-0	1-3	7-2	W-L	3-1	4-3	3-0	4-0	5-1	4-2	3-0		5-1
13 Sandy	2-3	2-2	5-4	1-1	3-1	2-0	1-5	0-2	2-1	3-2	6-4	1-4	

DIVISION THREE	P	W	D	L	F	A	Pts
1 Sharnbrook reserves	28	22	1	5	89	40	67
2 M & DH Oakley	28	19	3	6	78	42	60
3 Pavenham	28	18	5	5	92	36	59
4 Sundon Park Rangers	28	16	7	5	102	46	55
5 Co-op Sports	28	17	4	7	91	45	55
6 Cranfield United reserves	28	15	4	9	52	38	49
7 Renhold Village	28	13	6	9	84	52	45
8 Royal Oak Kempston	28	10	5	13	50	67	35
9 Westoning Recreation Club res.	28	10	3	15	69	75	33
10 Wilshamstead reserves	28	10	3	15	54	85	33
11 Dunton reserves	28	10	1	17	38	74	31
12 Riseley Sports	28	8	5	15	54	66	29
13 Flitwick Town reserves	28	6	4	18	36	93	22
14 Shefford Town & Campton "A"	28	4	5	19	26	89	17
15 Caldecote "A"	28	4	0	24	35	102	12

DIVISION FOUR	P	W	D	L	F	A	Pts
1 AFC Turvey	26	26	0	0	139	23	78
2 Goldington	26	21	1	4	113	36	64
3 Potton Town	26	18	2	6	66	39	56
4 Eastcotts	26	16	3	7	80	37	51
5 Thurleigh	26	16	1	9	68	40	49
6 Dinamo Flitwick	26	15	3	8	68	54	48
7 Stewartby Village	26	10	3	13	49	73	33
8 Clifton reserves	26	9	2	15	67	87	29
9 Sandy reserves	26	9	1	16	47	68	28
10 Lea Sports PSG reserves	26	7	4	15	34	63	25
11 Goldington Hammers	26	8	0	18	48	105	24
12 Bedford Park Rangers	26	6	2	18	54	83	20
13 Kempston Athletic	26	5	2	19	47	105	17
14 Wootton Village	26	3	2	21	33	100	11

CENTENARY CUP

Final (@ Biggleswade United, 6/5/11)
Bedford Hatters 1-0 Bedford SA

JUBILEE CUP

Final (@ Biggleswade United, 29/4/11)
Westoning Recreation Club 4-0 Kings

WATSON SHIELD

Final (@ Biggleswade United, 12/5/11)
Co-Op Sports 5- 3 Royal Oak Kempston

CAMBRIDGESHIRE COUNTY LEAGUE

Sponsored by: Kershaw and BIS
Founded: 1891
Recent Champions:
2006: Sawston United
2007: Great Shelford
2008: Waterbeach
2009: Fulbourn Institute
2010: Fulbourn Institute

PREMIER DIVISION	P	W	D	L	F	A	Pts
1 Lakenheath	32	24	6	2	103	23	78
2 Over Sports	32	19	8	5	69	29	65
3 Fulbourn Institute	32	19	7	6	80	37	64
4 Littleport Town	32	17	12	3	63	35	63
5 Great Shelford	32	19	5	8	72	39	62
6 Hardwick	32	17	5	10	74	44	56
7 Chatteris Town (-1)	32	14	12	6	69	50	51
8 Foxton	32	13	7	12	60	57	46
9 West Wratting	32	12	5	15	54	62	41
10 Eaton Socon	32	11	5	16	47	63	38
11 Whittlesford United	32	10	7	15	55	66	37
12 Ely City reserves	32	8	7	17	45	56	31
13 Cottenham United	32	8	7	17	40	86	31
14 Newmarket Town reserves (-3)	32	9	5	18	51	75	29
15 Waterbeach	32	6	7	19	44	78	25
16 Somersham Town	32	5	7	20	37	81	22
17 Hundon	32	3	4	25	20	102	13

PREMIER DIVISION CUP

ROUND 1
West Wratting 1-4 Whittlesford United
Chatteris Town 1-2 Littleport Town

ROUND 2
Hundon 1-2 Newmarket Town reserves
Over Sports 3-1 Cottenham United
Foxton 1-2 Somersham Town
Fulbourn Institute 0-1 Great Shelford
Whittlesford United 2-1 Littleport Town
Eaton Socon 0-2 Ely City reserves
Lakenheath 4-0 Hardwick
Waterbeach w/o-scr Histon "A"

QUARTER FINALS
Newmarket Town reserves 2-4 Over Sports
Somersham Town 0-2 Great Shelford
Whittlesford United 2-1 Ely City reserves
Lakenheath 3-0 Waterbeach

SEMI-FINALS
Over Sports 1-3 Great Shelford
Whittlesford United 1-4 Lakenheath

FINAL (@ Histon, 2/5/10)
Great Shelford 4-3 Lakenheath

PREMIER DIVISION	1	2	3	4	5	6	7	8	9	10	11	12	13	14	15	16	17
1 Chatteris Town		5-3	1-1	1-1	3-2	5-4	2-1	1-2	6-1	1-1	1-1	3-2	1-0	1-1	6-1	4-3	0-2
2 Cottenham United	1-0		2-0	0-6	2-10	3-3	2-4	0-3	2-1	0-3	1-3	1-3	0-6	2-1	2-1	2-3	1-1
3 Eaton Socon	4-3	2-1		2-1	2-1	0-3	1-3	0-1	3-0	1-3	0-1	0-2	0-3	3-1	2-2	4-1	2-4
4 Ely City reserves	1-1	1-2	0-0		0-1	2-1	1-4	3-2	0-1	0-3	0-1	1-2	2-3	1-2	1-2	3-0	3-1
5 Foxton	2-2	5-2	4-2	0-1		3-6	1-1	1-4	3-1	0-7	1-2	1-0	3-2	0-0	1-0	2-1	2-2
6 Fulbourn Institute	1-2	6-0	0-0	3-1	2-1		2-0	3-0	1-0	3-2	0-0	5-1	2-2	3-0	2-2	1-0	1-2
7 Great Shelford	2-1	2-1	4-0	3-4	0-0	1-2		5-0	3-2	0-2	2-5	5-0	4-0	2-0	3-1	1-1	3-1
8 Hardwick	1-1	4-0	4-3	0-0	1-3	0-4	2-1		7-0	2-1	0-1	9-1	1-3	4-1	3-0	2-1	2-2
9 Hundon	1-5	0-0	0-4	2-1	0-3	0-7	0-3	0-6		1-2	0-3	1-1	1-2	0-0	1-3	0-3	3-0
10 Lakenheath	5-1	4-0	5-1	0-0	4-0	1-1	3-2	1-1	8-0		1-1	3-1	1-1	4-0	3-0	5-1	4-0
11 Littleport Town	0-0	3-3	1-1	4-1	2-1	1-1	1-2	2-0	6-0	0-5		2-0	1-0	2-0	1-1	3-3	2-0
12 Newmarket Town reserves	1-2	2-1	1-2	3-3	1-1	2-3	0-1	0-3	3-0	2-3	2-2		0-3	4-3	2-1	1-1	2-6
13 Over Sports	0-0	1-1	2-0	1-1	1-0	4-1	0-0	3-2	3-0	0-3	3-0	2-1		4-0	3-0	4-0	2-0
14 Somersham Town	1-3	1-1	3-0	2-4	2-2	0-2	0-2	0-3	4-1	0-8	3-3	0-6	0-0		6-2	3-0	0-2
15 Waterbeach	3-3	1-1	2-1	3-0	1-3	1-5	2-4	1-4	1-1	2-3	1-1	2-0	0-4	4-1		1-4	1-2
16 West Wratting	0-3	0-1	1-2	3-0	3-1	1-0	2-2	2-1	3-1	1-3	2-3	2-1	1-4	4-0	2-1		4-2
17 Whittlesford United	1-1	1-2	3-4	3-2	0-2	0-2	0-2	0-0	6-1	0-2	0-5	3-4	3-3	4-2	3-1	1-1	

CAMBRIDGESHIRE COUNTY PREMIER DIVISION CONSTITUTION 2011-12

BRAMPTON	Thrapston Road Playing Fields, Brampton, Huntingdon PE28 4TB	None
CHATTERIS TOWN	West Street, Chatteris PE16 6HW	01354 692139
COTTENHAM UNITED	King George V Playing Field, Lamb Lane, Cottenham, Cambridge CB4 8TB	01954 250873
EATON SOCON	River Road, Eaton Ford, St Neots PE19 3AU	None
ELY CITY RESERVES	The Unwin Ground, Downham Road, Ely CB6 2SH	01353 662035
FOXTON	Hardman Road, off High Street, Foxton CB22 6RP	None
FULBOURN INSTITUTE	Fulbourn Recreation, Home End, Fulbourn CB1 5BS	None
GREAT SHELFORD	Recreation Ground, Woollards Lane, Great Shelford CB2 5LZ	01223 842590
HARDWICK	Egremont Road, Hardwick, Cambridge CB3 7XR	None
LAKENHEATH	The Nest, Wings Road, Lakenheath IP27 9HW	None
LINTON GRANTA	Recreation Ground, Meadow Lane, Linton, Cambridge CB21 6HX	None
LITTLEPORT TOWN	Sports Centre, Camel Road, Littleport, Ely CB6 1PU	01353 860600
NEWMARKET TOWN RESERVES	Sherbourn Stadium, Tow Ground, Cricket Field Rd, off New Cheveley Rd, Newmarket CB8 8BT	01638 663637
OVER SPORTS	Over Recreation Ground, The Dole, Over, Cambridge CB4 5NW	None
SOMERSHAM TOWN	West End Ground, St Ives Road, Somersham, Huntingdon PE27 3EN	01487 843384
WATERBEACH	Waterbeach Reacreation Ground, Cambridge Road, Waterbeach CB5 9NJ	None
WEST WRATTING	Recreation Ground, Bull Lane, West Wratting CB1 5NJ	None
WHITTLESFORD UNITED	The Lawn, Whittlesford CB2 4NG	None

***IN:** Brampton (P), Linton Granta (P)*
***OUT:** Histon Reserves (WN), Hundon (R)*

SENIOR DIVISION A	P	W	D	L	F	A	Pts
1 Linton Granta	26	21	1	4	111	25	64
2 Brampton	26	15	7	4	64	40	52
3 Milton	26	15	5	6	73	42	50
4 Soham Town Rangers reserves	26	13	6	7	65	40	45
5 Wisbech Town reserves	26	13	4	9	64	47	43
6 Hemingfords United	26	12	5	9	61	57	41
7 Sawston United	26	11	6	9	65	60	39
8 Cherry Hinton	26	9	6	11	54	53	33
9 Castle Camps	26	9	4	13	69	69	31
10 Girton United	26	8	7	11	57	61	31
11 Needingworth United	26	6	6	14	34	59	24
12 Soham United	26	6	5	15	46	79	23
13 Wimblington	26	6	5	15	34	74	23
14 Mildenhall Town reserves (-6)	26	2	5	19	40	131	5

Fordham - record expunged

WILLIAM COCKELL CUP

ROUND 1

Brampton 4-1 Soham Town Rangers reserves

Castle Camps 9-1 Needingworth United

Cherry Hinton 3-4 Soham United

Fordham reserves 2-4 Sawston United

Girton United 4-2 Hemingfords United

Wimblington 0-5 Milton

Wisbech Town reserves 4-0 Mildenhall Town reserves

QUARTER FINALS

Girton United 2-2 Sawston United

(Sawston United won 3-1 on penalties)

Linton Granta 4-1 Brampton

Milton 3-1 Castle Camps

Soham United 1-3 Wisbech Town reserves

SEMI-FINALS

Sawston United 1-3 Linton Granta

Wisbech Town reserves 2-4 Milton

FINAL (@ Histon, 2/5/11)

Linton Granta 1-1 Milton (Linton Granta won 10-9 on penalties)

SENIOR 'A' DIVISION	1	2	3	4	5	6	7	8	9	10	11	12	13	14
1 Brampton		4-0	1-3	2-1	4-2	1-1	3-3	1-1	2-1	3-0	2-0	1-1	3-0	3-2
2 Castle Camps	1-1		3-4	1-4	2-1	2-1	18-0	0-3	1-1	1-7	3-2	4-2	0-1	2-3
3 Cherry Hinton	2-5	3-5		0-2	3-5	0-5	4-0	1-2	4-0	0-0	3-0	2-3	2-3	2-1
4 Girton United	1-1	2-2	6-0		4-2	1-6	8-4	0-2	0-3	2-2	0-4	3-0	3-3	3-0
5 Hemingfords United	1-5	4-1	3-3	2-1		2-4	4-2	3-3	0-0	4-2	0-5	4-2	2-2	1-0
6 Linton Granta	5-0	6-2	3-0	7-2	6-0		12-0	2-1	5-1	6-1	4-1	6-0	8-0	0-1
7 Mildenhall Town reserves	0-4	3-8	0-6	1-1	1-7	4-5		0-5	1-1	2-6	2-2	0-0	3-1	4-5
8 Milton	1-2	3-2	2-2	4-1	2-0	3-0	2-3		3-1	3-3	2-4	8-3	6-1	2-0
9 Needingworth United	0-0	4-1	1-1	4-2	0-4	0-2	4-1	2-3		3-3	0-3	3-2	2-3	0-6
10 Sawston United	3-5	1-4	0-1	2-2	2-1	0-7	5-1	4-1	4-0		2-3	5-1	1-1	2-1
11 Soham Town Rangers reserves	4-1	2-2	1-0	3-1	1-1	1-0	5-1	5-1	4-0	0-1		0-0	6-0	4-4
12 Soham United	2-3	1-2	1-1	3-3	2-5	0-3	5-3	0-5	2-1	3-5	2-1		2-3	4-3
13 Wimblington	1-5	2-1	0-6	0-2	0-2	1-4	5-1	0-3	1-2	1-3	3-3	0-1		0-1
14 Wisbech Town reserves	4-2	4-1	1-1	3-2	0-1	1-3	5-0	2-2	1-0	4-1	5-1	5-4	2-2	

CAMBRIDGESHIRE COUNTY SENIOR 'A' DIVISION CONSTITUTION 2011-12

CAMBRIDGE CITY RESERVES	The City Ground , Milton Road , Cambridge CB4 1UY	01223 357973 Fax: 01223 351582
CASTLE CAMPS	Recreation Ground, Bumpstead Road, Castle Camps, Cambridge CB1 6SN	None
CHERRY HINTON	Recreation Ground, High Street, Cherry Hinton, Cambridge CB1 9HX	None
DEBDEN	Recreation Ground, High Street, Debden, Saffron Walden CB11 3LB	None
GIRTON UNITED	Girton Recreation Ground, Cambridge Road, Girton CB3 0FH	None
GREAT PAXTON	Recreation Ground, High Street, Great Paxton, St Neots PE19 6RG	None
HEMINGFORDS UNITED	Peace Memorial Playing Fields, Manor Road, Hemingford Grey, Huntingdon PE28 9BX	None
HUNDON	Upper North Street, Hundon CO10 8EE	None
MILTON	Milton Recreation Ground, The Sycamores, Milton, Cambridge CB4 6ZN	None
NEEDINGWORTH UNITED	Mill Field, Holywell Road, Needingworth PE27 8TE	None
SAWSTON UNITED	Spicers Sports Ground, New Road, Sawston CB2 4BW	None
SOHAM TOWN RANGERS RESERVES	Julius Martin Lane, Soham, Ely CB7 5EQ	01353 720732/722139 Fax: 01353 722139 Club: 01353 722139
SOHAM UNITED	Qua Fen Common, Soham, Ely CB7 5DQ	None
WIMBLINGTON	Parkfield Sports & Social Club, Chapel Lane, Wimblington, March PE15 0QX	01354 741555
WISBECH ST MARY	Station Road, Wisbech St Mary, Wisbech PE13 4RT	None
WISBECH TOWN RESERVES	Tom Woods Beer Fenland Stadium, Lynn Road, Wisbech PE14 7AL	None

***IN:** Cambridge City Reserves (P), Debden (P), Great Paxton (P), Hundon (R), Wisbech St Mary (P)*

***OUT:** Brampton (P), Fordham (WS), Linton Granta (P), Mildenhall Town Reserves (R)*

CAMBRIDGESHIRE COUNTY LEAGUE - STEP 7

SENIOR DIVISION B	P	W	D	L	F	A	Pts
1 Wisbech St Mary	30	21	4	5	95	31	67
2 Great Paxton	30	20	4	6	85	35	64
3 Debden	30	20	4	6	77	38	64
4 Cambridge City reserves	30	19	4	7	84	44	61
5 West Row Gunners	30	16	7	7	76	64	55
6 Longstanton	30	16	6	8	91	58	54
7 Comberton United	30	14	4	12	70	61	46
8 Melbourn	30	12	8	10	76	66	44
9 Fulbourn Institute reserves	30	12	6	12	59	68	42
10 West Wratting reserves	30	8	10	12	51	68	34
11 Saffron Crocus (-6)	30	9	5	16	47	80	26
12 Ely City "A"	30	7	3	20	56	87	24
13 Lakenheath reserves (-3)	30	8	2	20	59	75	23
14 Swavesey Institute	30	6	5	19	45	87	23
15 Outwell Swifts	30	7	2	21	46	99	23
16 Fowlmere	30	6	4	20	34	90	22

PERCY OLDHAM CUP

ROUND 1
Outwell Swifts scr-w/o West Row Gunners
Comberton United 4-6 Longstanton
Debden 3-3 Melbourn (Debden won 6-5 on penalties)
Ely City "A" 2-4 West Wratting reserves
Fowlmere 0-3 Saffron Crocus
West Row Gunners 4-1 Swavesey Institute
Wisbech St Mary 4-2 Lakenheath reserves
Cambridge City reserves 8-4 Fulbourn Institute reserves

QUARTER FINALS
Longstanton 0-3 Great Paxton
Wisbech St Mary 3-0 Cambridge City reserves
West Row Gunners 3-1 Saffron Crocus
West Wratting reserves 0-2 Debden

SEMI-FINALS
Debden 2-5 Wisbech St Mary
West Row Gunners 1-2 Great Paxton

FINAL (@ Histon, 4/5/11))
Great Paxton 3-2 Wisbech St Mary

CREAKE CHARITY SHIELD FINAL (@ Histon, 3/5/11)
Dullingham 0-1 Steeple Bumpstead
JOHN ABLETT CUP FINAL (@ Cambridge City, 5/5/11)
Bar Hill Sports & Social 1-3 Orwell
HAIGH & PECK CUP FINAL (@ Chatteris Town, 12/5/11)
Wisbech St Mary "B" 0-3 Glemsford & Cavendish Utd reserves

SENIOR 'B' DIVISION	1	2	3	4	5	6	7	8	9	10	11	12	13	14	15	16
1 Cambridge City reserves	2-1	2-0	4-2	6-0	2-2	1-1	5-0	2-2	7-0	4-2	3-2	1-0	6-1	5-0	0-5	
2 Comberton United	5-2		0-2	3-1	0-2	1-2	4-5	3-0	1-1	1-3	4-2	5-1	3-2	4-1	2-1	0-2
3 Debden	2-0	3-2		6-1	3-1	2-1	0-3	4-1	3-2	2-2	3-0	1-0	9-1	2-3	1-1	1-1
4 Ely City "A"	0-1	1-6	1-4		2-2	2-5	1-1	3-2	3-4	7-1	0-1	6-1	2-2	4-3	3-2	0-2
5 Fowlmere	2-3	2-1	0-4	3-2		0-1	1-0	2-2	0-6	1-5	2-3	2-4	4-3	2-4	1-1	0-3
6 Fulbourn Institute reserves	1-3	2-4	0-1	3-1	1-0		1-3	1-0	3-5	4-2	2-2	1-2	2-1	3-1	1-1	4-4
7 Great Paxton	1-1	1-2	0-4	5-0	8-1	6-1		2-4	2-1	0-0	3-2	4-1	4-1	6-0	3-1	1-0
8 Lakenheath reserves	3-1	5-6	0-3	3-1	3-0	5-2	0-3		1-2	0-1	0-1	2-3	5-1	1-2	1-4	1-4
9 Longstanton	3-0	1-1	3-2	4-1	4-0	1-2	1-4	3-0		5-5	8-0	8-2	3-2	3-5	6-2	0-5
10 Melbourn	1-2	3-0	1-2	6-1	2-2	2-2	1-3	4-2	2-1		4-1	1-1	8-3	3-3	1-2	4-3
11 Outwell Swifts	1-4	1-4	2-5	1-0	3-0	0-4	2-4	5-4	1-3	0-5		1-1	0-1	2-7	5-3	1-2
12 Saffron Crocus	1-6	0-2	1-4	0-4	2-0	3-0	0-6	0-6	3-3	0-2	5-0		1-2	1-1	2-3	1-0
13 Swavesey Institute	1-4	2-2	2-1	2-3	0-3	0-3	0-1	3-0	1-1	4-3	4-3	1-5		1-3	1-1	2-4
14 West Row Gunners	1-5	1-1	0-0	5-1	4-1	8-3	1-0	2-1	3-1	2-1	3-2	1-1	4-1		2-2	3-2
15 West Wratting reserves	3-2	2-1	0-3	3-2	4-0	2-2	1-5	1-4	1-3	1-1	4-1	2-3	1-1	1-1		0-4
16 Wisbech St Mary	1-0	8-1	7-0	2-1	6-0	4-0	2-0	3-3	1-3	4-2	6-1	3-0	3-0	3-1	1-1	

CAMBRIDGESHIRE COUNTY SENIOR 'B' DIVISION CONSTITUTION 2011-12

CAMBRIDGE UNIVERSITY PRESS RES.	CUP Sports Ground , Shaftesbury Road , Cambridge CB2 2BS	None
COMBERTON UNITED	Recreation Ground, Hines Lane, Comberton CB3 7BZ	None
DUXFORD UNITED	Duxford Recreation Ground, Hunts Road, Duxford, Cambridge CB22 4RE	None
ELY CITY A	The Unwin Ground, Downham Road, Ely CB6 2SH	01353 662035
FENSTANTON	Hall Green Lane, Fenstanton, Huntingdon PE28 9JH	None
FULBOURN INSTITUTE RESERVES	Fulbourn Recreation, Home End, Fulbourn CB1 5BS	None
LAKENHEATH RESERVES	The Nest, Wings Road, Lakenheath IP27 9HW	None
LONGSTANTON	Longstanton Recreation Ground, Over Road, Longstanton CB24 5DW	None
MELBOURN	The Recreation Ground, The Moor, Melbourn, Royston SG8 6EF	None
MILDENHALL TOWN RESERVES	Recreation Way, Mildenhall, Bury St Edmunds IP28 7HG	01638 713449
OUTWELL SWIFTS	The Nest, Wisbech Road, Outwell, Wisbech PE14 8PA	None
SAFFRON CROCUS	Ickleton Recreation Ground, Frogge Street, Ickleton CB10 1NS	None
ST IVES RANGERS	California Road, St Ives, Huntingdon PE27 6SJ	None
SWAVESEY INSTITUTE	The Green, High Street, Swavesey CB24 4QU	None
WEST ROW GUNNERS	Beeches Road, West Row, Bury St Edmunds IP28 8NY	None
WEST WRATTING RESERVES	Recreation Ground, Bull Lane, West Wratting CB1 5NJ	None

***IN:** Cambridge University Press Reserves (P), Fenstanton (P), Mildenhall Town Reserves (R), St Ives Rangers (P)*
***OUT:** Cambridge City Reserves (P), Debden (P), Fowlmere (R), Great Paxton (P), Wisbech St Mary (P)*

DIVISION ONE A	P	W	D	L	F	A	Pts
1 Cambr Univ Press res	24	21	1	2	81	17	64
2 Duxford United	24	14	5	5	43	29	47
3 Dullingham	24	13	3	8	59	36	42
4 Saffron Walden T res	24	13	3	8	44	28	42
5 Gamlingay United	24	11	4	9	54	44	37
6 Hardwick reserves	24	11	2	11	42	34	35
7 Bottisham Sports	24	9	7	8	35	31	34
8 Sawston Rovers	24	10	4	10	45	54	34
9 Steeple Bumpstead	24	8	6	10	44	50	30
10 Eaton Socon reserves	24	9	2	13	39	53	29
11 Barrington	24	8	4	12	38	47	28
12 Whittlesf'd U res (-3)	24	5	3	16	30	50	15
13 Girton United res	24	1	2	21	26	107	5

Camden United - record expunged

DIVISION ONE B	P	W	D	L	F	A	Pts
1 Fenstanton	24	17	5	2	76	28	56
2 St Ives Rangers	24	16	4	4	51	28	52
3 Elsworth Sports	24	15	3	6	72	39	48
4 March Town Utd res	24	14	2	8	62	40	44
5 Littleport Town res	24	11	7	6	53	41	40
6 Somersham Town res	24	10	6	8	35	33	36
7 Huntingdon Utd RGE	24	9	7	8	60	43	34
8 Haddenham Rovers	24	9	3	12	36	49	30
9 Hemingfords Utd res	24	7	4	13	42	58	25
10 Buckden	24	6	5	13	45	72	23
11 Waterbeach reserves	24	6	2	16	37	64	20
12 Cottenham United res	24	4	4	16	37	74	16
13 Bluntisham Rangers	24	3	6	15	31	68	15

DIVISION ONE PLAY-OFF (@ Fenstanton, 11/5/11)
Fenstanton 0-1 Cambridge University Press

DIVISION TWO A	P	W	D	L	F	A	Pts
1 Royston Town "A"	24	19	3	2	82	25	60
2 RHS United	24	19	1	4	73	29	58
3 Fulbourn Sports & Social Club	24	16	1	7	89	36	49
4 Great Chishill	24	14	4	6	66	53	46
5 Great Shelford reserves	24	11	4	9	84	62	37
6 City Life	24	10	2	12	49	61	32
7 Bassingbourn	24	8	7	9	37	46	31
8 Papworth	24	8	4	12	45	54	28
9 Cambourne Rovers	24	7	5	12	37	65	26
10 Ashdon Villa	24	7	4	13	39	50	25
11 Cambridge Univ. Press "A" (-6)	24	8	3	13	44	49	21
12 Thaxted Rangers	24	7	0	17	49	80	21
13 Wilbraham	24	3	0	21	25	109	9

Newmarket Town "A" - record expunged

DIVISION TWO B	P	W	D	L	F	A	Pts
1 Chatteris Town reserves	26	20	1	5	74	32	61
2 Earith United	26	19	3	4	87	35	60
3 Burwell Swifts	26	18	3	5	74	38	57
4 Doddington United	26	15	4	7	48	37	49
5 Witchford 96	26	14	5	7	57	33	47
6 Godmanchester Rovers res	26	11	2	13	62	53	35
7 Manea United	26	9	8	9	51	54	35
8 Wisbech St Mary reserves	26	11	2	13	58	69	35
9 March Rangers	26	10	3	13	45	51	33
10 Over Sports reserves	26	9	2	15	54	63	29
11 Sutton United	26	8	4	14	66	72	28
12 Milton reserves	26	8	3	15	41	66	27
13 The Vine	26	4	4	18	35	76	16
14 Barton Mills	26	3	2	21	22	95	11

DIVISION TWO PLAY-OFF (@ Chatteris Town, 16/5/11)
Chatteris Town reserves 2-3 Royston Town "A"

DIVISION THREE A	P	W	D	L	F	A	Pts
1 Glemsford & Cavendish United	26	22	3	1	91	14	69
2 Sawston United reserves	26	21	3	2	104	23	66
3 Great Chesterford	26	14	7	5	73	50	49
4 Figleaves	26	12	6	8	65	45	42
5 Balsham	26	11	6	9	58	41	39
6 Lode	26	12	2	12	74	72	38
7 Steeple Morden	26	11	4	11	58	82	37
8 Eaton Socon "A"	26	10	4	12	54	50	34
9 Hardwick "A"	26	9	3	14	49	53	30
10 Comberton United reserves	26	8	6	12	52	79	30
11 Abington United	26	10	0	16	55	83	30
12 Hundon reserves	26	8	2	16	42	76	26
13 Fulbourn Institute "A"	26	6	1	19	43	69	19
14 Duxford United reserves	26	4	1	21	31	112	13

DIVISION THREE B	P	W	D	L	F	A	Pts
1 Isleham United	26	19	4	3	70	27	61
2 Bluntisham Rangers reserves	26	17	4	5	81	41	55
3 Tydd United	26	17	2	7	85	39	53
4 Mepal Sports	26	15	6	5	54	28	51
5 Estover Park	26	13	5	8	69	48	44
6 Stretham Hotspurs	26	11	6	9	70	63	39
7 Little Downham Swifts	26	10	7	9	70	59	37
8 Exning Athletic	26	11	2	13	50	82	35
9 Brampton reserves	26	9	4	13	55	56	31
10 Fordham	26	9	2	15	54	66	29
11 Wimblington reserves	26	7	4	15	36	56	25
12 Hemingfords United "A"	26	7	1	18	35	97	22
13 Ely Crusaders	26	6	3	17	39	68	21
14 Fenstanton reserves	26	6	0	20	40	78	18

DIVISION THREE PLAY-OFF (@ Mildenhall Town, 13/5/11)
Isleham united 2-0 Glemsford & Cavendish United

DIVISION FOUR A	P	W	D	L	F	A	Pts
1 Orwell	28	19	7	2	87	34	64
2 Linton Granta reserves	28	19	2	7	87	28	59
3 Saffron Walden Town "A"	28	16	8	4	69	38	56
4 Foxton reserves	28	15	3	10	69	71	48
5 Debden reserves	28	13	5	10	60	64	44
6 Saffron Rangers	28	12	5	11	70	59	41
7 Meldreth	28	12	5	11	61	51	41
8 Great Paxton reserves	28	12	2	14	61	70	38
9 Fowlmere reserves	28	10	5	13	69	78	35
10 Litlington Athletic	28	10	4	14	61	78	34
11 Cherry Hinton reserves	28	10	4	14	78	97	34
12 City of Cambridge Crusaders	28	10	3	15	45	68	33
13 West Wratting "A" (-3)	28	10	2	16	58	77	29
14 Thurlow	28	6	7	15	71	77	25
15 Sawston Rovers reserves	28	4	2	22	50	106	14

DIVISION FOUR B	P	W	D	L	F	A	Pts
1 Bar Hill	24	22	1	1	122	18	67
2 West Row Gunners reserves	24	18	3	3	55	23	57
3 Wisbech St Mary "A"	24	17	3	4	80	28	54
4 Longstanton reserves	24	17	1	6	64	39	52
5 Gransden	24	13	3	8	75	34	42
6 Wicken Amateurs	24	13	2	9	80	55	41
7 Soham United reserves	24	8	5	11	53	60	29
8 Milton "A"	24	7	4	13	29	63	25
9 Haddenham Rovers reserves	24	8	0	16	46	94	24
10 Chatteris Town "A"	24	4	4	16	43	91	16
11 Cottenham United "A"	24	5	1	18	32	108	16
12 Murrow Bell (-6)	24	6	1	17	47	72	13
13 Burwell Swifts reserves	24	2	4	18	28	69	10

Wisbech Fen Stars - record expunged

DIVISION FOUR PLAY-OFF (@ Bar Hill Sports & Social, 12/5/11)
Bar Hill Sports & Social 6-1 Orwell

DIVISION FIVE A	P	W	D	L	F	A	Pts
1 Haverhill Athletic	24	19	4	1	107	31	61
2 Dalehead United	24	18	4	2	106	28	58
3 Castle Camps res	24	16	5	3	76	32	53
4 Glemsford & CU res	24	13	6	5	79	37	45
5 Studlands Park	24	14	3	7	85	54	45
6 Steeple Bumpst'd res	24	12	2	10	84	63	38
7 Saffron Dynamos	24	10	4	10	68	44	34
8 Sawston United "A"	24	9	4	11	48	58	31
9 Saffron Crocus res	24	9	2	13	44	71	29
10 Lode reserves	24	5	2	17	41	96	17
11 Hundon "A"	24	3	4	17	39	118	13
12 Newport Veterans	24	2	3	19	12	116	9
13 Dullingham res (-6)	24	3	3	18	33	74	6

DIVISION FIVE B	P	W	D	L	F	A	Pts
1 Camb. Ambassadors	24	20	1	3	70	28	61
2 Elsworth Sports res	24	16	5	3	88	37	53
3 Buckden reserves	24	15	1	8	71	47	46
4 City Life reserves	24	12	4	8	62	38	40
5 Melbourn reserves	24	12	2	10	71	61	38
6 Papworth reserves	24	11	3	10	62	44	36
7 Cambourne Rov ress	24	10	3	11	53	56	33
8 Therfield & Kelshall	24	9	5	10	71	55	32
9 Mott MacDonald	24	8	6	10	63	68	30
10 Barrington reserves	24	9	2	13	48	62	29
11 Haslingfield	24	5	4	15	40	92	19
12 Steeple Mord. res (-6)	24	6	2	16	25	71	14
13 Great Chishill res	24	3	2	19	22	87	11

DIVISION FIVE C	P	W	D	L	F	A	Pts
1 Willingham Wolves	22	20	0	2	97	11	60
2 Girton United "A"	22	18	4	0	78	15	58
3 Swavesey Inst. res	22	17	2	3	96	29	53
4 Waterbeach "A"	22	12	2	8	46	31	38
5 Witchford 96 res	22	11	2	9	51	54	35
6 Earith United res	22	9	2	11	49	51	29
7 St Ives Rangers res	22	8	2	12	55	40	26
8 Barton Mills res (-3)	22	8	3	11	36	43	24
9 Isleham United res	22	5	4	13	34	39	19
10 Sutton United res (-3)	22	5	4	13	39	66	16
11 Burwell Swifts "A"	22	4	1	17	34	123	13
12 Little Dow. S res (-3)	22	1	2	19	34	147	2

DIVISION FIVE D	P	W	D	L	F	A	Pts
1 Wisbech St Mary "B"	22	19	1	2	76	26	58
2 Benwick Athletic	22	16	2	4	83	37	50
3 March Rangers res	22	15	3	4	69	24	48
4 Coldham United	22	14	0	8	55	44	42
5 Mepal Sports res	22	11	4	7	54	41	37
6 Wimblington "A"	22	9	4	9	55	41	31
7 Estover Park reserves	22	10	0	12	42	58	30
8 Chatteris Fen Tigers	22	8	3	11	56	62	27
9 Manea United res	22	7	3	12	47	58	24
10 Doddington Utd res	22	7	3	12	38	55	24
11 Walsoken United	22	2	1	19	26	80	7
12 Upwell Town	22	1	2	19	19	94	5

Outwell Swifts reserves - record expunged

DIVISION FIVE PLAY-OFFS
Semi-Finals
Wisbech st Mary "B" 3-2 Willingham Wolves
Cambridge Ambassadors 3-2 Haverhill Athletic
Final (@ Wisbech St Mary, 18/5/11)
Wisbech St Mary "B" 1-0 Cambridge Ambassadors

CENTRAL MIDLANDS LEAGUE

Sponsored by: Abacus Lighting
Founded: 1971
Recent Champions:
2006: Barton Town Old Boys
2007: Bottesford Town
2008: Askern Welfare
2009: Radcliffe Olympic
2010: Louth Town

SUPREME DIVISION	P	W	D	L	F	A	Pts
1 Sheffield Parramore	34	27	4	3	107	31	85
2 Blidworth Welfare	34	27	1	6	119	36	82
3 Pinxton	34	24	3	7	97	52	75
4 Kinsley Boys	34	21	4	9	88	46	67
5 Kirkby Town	34	19	7	8	82	56	64
6 Westella & Willerby	34	18	4	12	88	59	58
7 Dronfield Town	34	17	7	10	87	59	58
8 Newark Town	34	17	5	12	69	46	56
9 Clipstone Welfare	34	16	1	17	63	82	49
10 Parkhouse	34	15	2	17	72	72	47
11 Harworth C I	34	14	3	17	63	59	45
12 Southwell City	34	13	6	15	53	60	45
13 Ollerton Town	34	9	8	17	56	76	35
14 Nettleham	34	10	4	20	57	82	34
15 Church Warsop S & SC	34	7	7	20	46	100	28
16 Sutton Town	34	6	2	26	35	128	20
17 Calverton MW	34	5	4	25	40	81	19
18 Kimberley Town	34	4	2	28	28	125	14

PREMIER DIVISION	P	W	D	L	F	A	Pts
1 Yorkshire Main	28	23	2	3	133	28	71
2 Bentley Colliery	28	21	4	3	117	31	67
3 South Normanton Athletic	28	20	4	4	110	47	64
4 AFC Hucknall	28	15	3	10	82	52	48
5 Thoresby CW	28	13	6	9	59	49	45
6 Kiveton Park	28	13	3	12	72	66	42
7 Thorne Colliery (-3)	28	14	2	12	69	73	41
8 Easington United	28	11	7	10	60	57	40
9 Hutton Cranswick United (-3)	28	12	6	10	44	49	39
10 Phoenix	28	9	5	14	40	59	32
11 Bulwell Town	28	9	4	15	55	60	31
12 Whatton United	28	9	1	18	46	76	28
13 FC 05 Bilsthorpe	28	6	6	16	53	85	24
14 Nottingham United	28	4	2	22	36	100	14
15 Welbeck Welfare	28	3	1	24	17	161	10

FC Brimington - record expunged
Moorland Railway - record expunged

LEAGUE CHALLENGE CUP

PRELIMINARY ROUND
Kimberley Town 0-9 Yorkshire Main
Kiveton Park 3-5 South Normanton Athletic
Phoenix 3-5 Blidworth Welfare

ROUND 1
AFC Hucknall 4-2 Harworth C I
Bentley Colliery 3-2 FC 05 Bilsthorpe
Bulwell Town 2-1 Nettleham
Clipstone Welfare 4-3 Whatton United
Dronfield Town 5-0 Southwell City
FC Brimington 3-0 Newark Town
Hutton Cranswick United 3-6 Kirkby Town
Kinsley Boys 3-2 Sheffield Parramore
Parkhouse 2-2 Easington United
Pinxton 8-0 Church Warsop S & S C
South Normanton Athletic 2-4 Sutton Town
Thoresby Colliery Welfare 2-2 Blidworth Welfare
Thorne Coliery 2-6 Yorkshire Main
Welbeck Welfare 1-6 Ollerton Town
Westella & Willerby 4-1 Nottingham United
Calverton Miners Welfare scr-w/o Moorland Railway

Round 1 Replays
Blidworth Welfare 3-2 Thoresby Colliery Welfare
Easington United 1-0 Parkhouse

ROUND 2
A F C Hucknall 0-3 Clipstone Welfare
Bulwell Town 0-3 Dronfield Town
Calverton Miners Welfare 0-3 Kirkby Town
Easington United 2-4 Bentley Colliery
Kinsley Boys 4-2 Blidworth Welfare
Westella & Willerby 2-0 Ollerton Town
Sutton Town scr-w/o Yorkshire Main
Pinxton w/o-scr FC Brimington

QUARTER FINALS
Clipstone Welfare 1-10 Yorkshire Main
Dronfield Town 2-2 Kirkby Town
Pinxton 4-1 Bentley Colliery
Westella & Willerby 1-2 Kinsley Boys

QUARTER FINAL REPLAY
Kirkby Town 2-1 Dronfield Town

SEMI-FINALS
Kirkby Town 2-6 Kinsley Boys (@ South Normanton Athletic)
Pinxton 0-2 Yorkshire Main (@ Harworth CI)

FINAL (@ Alfreton Town, 8/5/11)
Yorkshire Maine 2-2 Kirkby Town
(Yorkshire Main won 3-2 on penalties)

SUPREME DIVISION	1	2	3	4	5	6	7	8	9	10	11	12	13	14	15	16	17	18
1 Blidworth Welfare	4-1	7-0	4-2	4-0	2-1	3-1	5-1	1-2	2-1	4-0	2-2	1-2	6-1	1-2	5-2	7-1	3-0	
2 Calverton Miners Welfare	0-1		3-4	2-3	1-2	1-4	4-1	0-1	2-2	0-3	0-1	1-2	1-3	1-2	0-5	1-1	0-4	2-1
3 Church Warsop S & S	1-10	2-1		3-3	2-1	1-6	4-1	0-4	1-2	3-3	2-3	1-2	0-3	1-0	0-4	1-4	2-3	0-2
4 Clipstone Welfare	1-3	3-1	4-0		1-3	2-0	2-0	0-5	4-1	3-1	0-7	3-2	4-1	1-6	0-3	4-1	3-0	0-6
5 Dronfield Town	4-3	1-1	0-0	3-2		1-3	7-1	2-0	3-2	5-2	2-2	6-2	1-2	1-0	3-5	2-0	4-2	0-1
6 Harworth Colliery Institute	0-4	1-0	3-0	0-1	2-4		4-0	2-2	4-2	1-0	0-1	0-2	1-1	1-2	0-2	1-2	2-3	0-3
7 Kimberley Town	0-5	0-5	2-1	0-2	1-5	0-6		1-7	0-3	4-2	1-2	0-2	0-1	1-2	0-6	2-2	0-3	1-1
8 Kinsley Boys	1-0	4-1	5-2	3-1	3-3	1-0	6-0		0-1	6-2	2-1	6-1	3-1	1-0	0-2	1-2	0-0	2-3
9 Kirkby Town	0-2	3-1	2-2	2-3	3-1	3-1	3-0	3-3		3-0	4-3	4-1	3-2	2-2	1-1	1-0	9-0	1-5
10 Nettleham	1-4	2-1	1-0	4-0	1-1	0-3	4-1	0-3	1-3		2-1	2-2	1-3	3-4	2-3	2-0	5-1	0-3
11 Newark Town	2-5	2-1	0-0	4-0	1-1	3-1	2-0	1-2	3-0	2-0		1-0	1-2	0-1	1-0	2-2	4-2	1-3
12 Ollerton Town	0-2	2-2	3-3	5-1	1-3	2-2	1-2	0-3	2-2	1-2	1-0		2-3	2-5	0-0	0-4	1-2	1-1
13 Parkhouse	0-6	1-2	2-3	2-1	1-3	3-3	9-1	0-5	2-3	7-0	0-3	2-1		2-3	1-2	1-1	5-0	6-3
14 Pinxton	2-3	8-1	7-1	4-2	3-1	4-2	5-1	3-1	0-0	3-2	3-3	4-0	4-1		1-0	2-0	9-1	0-2
15 Sheffield Parramore	2-1	2-0	6-1	0-3	2-2	5-2	4-1	3-1	4-3	2-1	2-1	3-1	4-0	7-1		5-0	9-0	1-1
16 Southwell City	0-2	0-3	1-1	3-0	2-1	1-2	6-1	1-2	1-3	2-3	2-1	0-5	2-1	0-1	1-2		2-1	1-0
17 Sutton Town 2002	1-4	1-0	0-4	0-2	1-4	0-2	1-3	0-1	1-4	1-1	0-5	3-5	1-2	1-3	0-5	1-3		2-3
18 Westella & Willerby	2-3	5-0	2-0	3-2	0-7	2-3	5-1	5-3	0-2	4-3	1-5	1-2	3-1	1-2	1-4	0-0	15-0	

PREMIER DIVISION	1	2	3	4	5	6	7	8	9	10	11	12	13	14	15
1 A F C Hucknall		0-4	4-1	1-3	4-1	6-0	8-0	5-1	3-1	7-2	3-1	0-2	1-0	1-2	0-4
2 Bentley Colliery	0-3		4-1	4-1	7-2	3-0	3-1	4-0	9-0	2-1	4-1	3-1	13-0	3-1	2-0
3 Bulwell Town	3-1	1-3		2-2	0-4	0-2	2-3	3-0	0-0	2-2	1-3	6-1	6-0	1-0	0-1
4 Easington United	3-4	0-0	3-1		1-1	0-2	3-0	6-1	1-1	0-3	1-2	4-2	W-L	10-1	1-0
5 F C 05 Bilsthorpe	0-0	1-8	1-3	2-2		4-1	1-5	5-1	1-1	0-6	1-2	2-4	1-2	1-2	0-8
6 Hutton Cranswick United	3-1	1-2	0-1	2-1	0-0		2-2	2-0	1-3	2-2	2-1	3-1	6-0	1-0	2-2
7 Kiveton Park	3-4	2-2	4-1	0-2	4-2	2-1		5-0	1-4	3-4	0-2	2-0	6-1	2-1	0-4
8 Nottingham United	3-0	0-8	1-4	3-3	1-1	0-1	0-3		0-1	2-4	1-3	3-7	8-0	2-1	0-8
9 Phoenix	0-3	0-2	3-2	2-3	3-6	0-0	0-0	1-2		0-3	1-3	2-1	4-0	4-2	0-2
10 South Normanton Athletic	8-2	2-2	2-0	7-0	6-1	6-0	7-3	9-3	1-0		3-2	3-3	10-0	2-1	3-5
11 Thoresby Colliery Welfare	1-1	3-3	2-2	2-2	3-2	1-1	2-3	3-2	2-0	0-1		3-2	5-1	4-0	2-2
12 Thorne Colliery	2-7	2-7	5-2	6-2	1-0	3-0	4-3	2-1	2-1	2-4	1-0		5-0	2-0	4-2
13 Welbeck Colliery Welfare	0-10	0-12	0-4	3-4	1-6	1-5	2-11	1-0	0-5	0-4	2-1	2-2		0-7	1-9
14 Whatton United	3-3	3-0	4-3	2-1	2-5	3-4	2-3	2-1	0-3	1-4	1-4	3-2	1-0		0-5
15 Yorkshire Main	1-0	4-3	5-3	3-1	7-2	4-0	2-1	8-0	9-0	4-1	6-1	8-0	15-0	5-1	

CENTRAL MIDLANDS NORTHERN DIVISION (NEW DIVISION) CONSTITUTION 2011-12

BENTLEY COLLIERY	Bentley Miners Welfare , The Avenue, Bentley , Doncaster DN5 0PN	01302 874420
DRONFIELD TOWN	Stonelow Playing Fields, Stonelow Road, Dronfield S18 2DA	None
EASINGTON UNITED	Low Farm, Beak Street, Easington, Hull HU12 0TT	None
FC05 BILSTHORPE	Bilsthorpe Sports Field, Eakring Road, Bilsthorpe, Newark NG22 8SX	None
HARWORTH COLLIERY INSTITUTE	Recreation Ground, Scrooby Road, Bircotes, Doncaster DN11 8JT	01302 750614
HUTTON CRANSWICK UNITED	Rotsea Lane, Hutton Cranswick, Driffield YO25 9QG	None
KINSLEY BOYS	Kinsley Playing Fields, Wakefield Road, Kinsley WF9 5EH	07883 373232
KIVETON PARK	Kiveton Park MW, Hard Lane, Kiveton Park, Sheffield S26 6NB	07763 467979
NOTTINGHAM UNITED	Gresham Park Road, Wilford Lane, West Bridgford, Nottingham NG2 7YE	None
OLLERTON TOWN	The Lane, Walesby Lane, New Ollerton, Newark NG22 9UX	None
PARKHOUSE	Mill Lane Ground, Mill Lane, Clay Cross, Chesterfield S42 6AE	07816 758778
PHOENIX SPORTS & SOCIAL	Phoenix Sports Complex, Bawtry Road, Brinsworth, Rotherham S60 5PA	01709 363864
THORESBY COLLIERY WELFARE	Thoresby Colliery Spts Ground, Fourth Avenue, Edwinstowe NG21 9NS	07802 417987
THORNE COLLIERY	Moorends Welfare, Grange Road, Moorends, Thorne, Doncaster DN8 4LU	07855 545221
WELBECK WELFARE	Colliery Ground, Elkesley Road, Meden Vale, Warsop, Mansfield NG20 9PS	07863 568576
		Welfare:01623 842267
WESTELLA & WILLERBY	Blackburn Leisure Social Club, Prescott Avenue, Brough HU15 1BB	01482 667353
YORKSHIRE MAIN	Edlington Lane, Edlington, Doncaster DN12 2DA	07775 714558

IN: *Bentley Colliery (S-Premier Division), Dronfield Town (S-Supreme Division), Easington United (S-Premier Division), FC 05 Bilsthorpe (S-Premier Division), Harworth Colliery Institute (S-Supreme Division), Hutton Cranswick United (S-Premier Division), Kinsley Boys (S-Supreme Division), Kiveton Park (S-Premier Division), Nottingham United (S-Premier Division), Ollerton Town (S-Supreme Division), Parkhouse (S-Supreme Division), Phoenix Sports & Social (S-Premier Division), Thoresby Colliery Welfare (S-Premier Division), Thorne Colliery (S-Premier Division), Welbeck Welfare (S-Premier Division), Westella & Wellaby (S-Supreme Division), Yorkshire Main (S-Premier Division)*

CENTRAL MIDLANDS SOUTHERN DIVISION (NEW DIVISION) CONSTITUTION 2011-12

AFC HUCKNALL	Watnall Road, Hucknall NG15 6EY 0115 963 0206 Fax: 0115 963 0716	Club: 0115 956 1253
BASFORD UNITED	Greenwich Avenue, Bagnall Road, Basford, Nottingham NG6 0LE	01949 839412
BELPER UNITED	Alton Manor, Nailers Way, Belper DE56 0HT	None
BILBOROUGH PELICAN	Brian Wakefield Sports Ground, Trentside Lane,Old Lenton Lane, Nottingham NG7 2SA	0115 929 4728
BLIDWORTH WELFARE	Blidworth Welfare Miners SC, Mansfield Road, Blidworth, Mansfield NG21 0LR	01623 793361
BULWELL TOWN	Goosedale Sports Ground, Goosedale Lane, Moor Road, Bestwood Village NG15 8FG	0115 963 0180
CALVERTON MINERS WELFARE	Calverton Miners Welfare, Hollinwood Lane, Calverton NG14 6NR	0115 965 4390
CLIFTON	Green Lane, Clifton, Nottingham NG11 9AY	0115 921 5401
CLIPSTONE WELFARE	Lido Ground, Clipstone Road East, Clipstone, Mansfield NG21 5AZ	01623 477978
KIMBERLEY TOWN	The Stag Ground, Nottingham Road, Kimberley NG16 2ND	0115 938 2788
KIRKBY TOWN	Summit Centre, Lowmoor Road, Kirkby-in-Ashfield NG17 7LL	01623 751822
NEWARK TOWN	Collingham FC, Station Road, Collingham NG23 7RA	01636 892303
NOTTINGHAMSHIRE POLICE	Bestwood Workshops, Park Road, Bestwood Village, Nottingham NG6 8TQ	0115 967 0999
PINXTON	Welfare Ground, Wharf Road, Pinxton NG16 6LG	07989 324249
REAL UNITED	Grove Farm, Lenton Lane, Nottingham NG7 2SA	None
SOUTH NORMANTON ATHLETIC	ExChem Sports Ground, Lees Lane, South Normanton, Alfreton DE55 2AD	01773 581491
SOUTHWELL CITY	War Memorial Recreation Ground, Bishop's Drive, Southwell NG25 0JP	01636 814386
SUTTON TOWN	The Fieldings, Huthwaite Road, Sutton-in-Ashfield NG17 2HB	01623 552376
WHATTON UNITED	Spa Lane, Orston NG13 9NX None	

IN: *AFC Hucknall (S-Premier Division), Basford United (P-Notts Senior League Senior Division), Belper United (P-Midland Regional Alliance Premier Division), Bilborough Pelican (P-Notts Senior League Senior Division), Blidworth Welfare (S-Supreme Division), Bulwell Town (S-Premier Division), Calverton Miners Welfare (P-Supreme Division), Clifton (P-Notts Senior League Senior Division), Clipstone Welfare (S-Supreme Division), Kimberley Town (S-Supreme Division), Kirkby Town (S-Supreme Division), Newark Town (S-Supreme Division), Notts Police (P-Notts Senior League Senior Division), Pinxton (S-Supreme Division), Real United (P-Notts Amateur Alliance Premier Division), South Normanton (S-Premier Division), Southwell City (S-Supreme Division), Sutton Town (S-Supreme Division), Whatton United (S-Premier Division)*

CHESHIRE LEAGUE

Sponsored by: No sponsor
Founded: 1919
Recent Champions:
2006: Middlewich Town
2007: Middlewich Town
2008: Styal
2009: Woodley
2010: Club AZ

DIVISION ONE	P	W	D	L	F	A	Pts
1 Greenalls Padgate St Oswalds	30	17	8	5	67	34	59
2 Pilkington	30	18	5	7	68	44	59
3 Eagle Sports	30	18	1	11	73	40	55
4 Middlewich Town	30	15	7	8	57	37	52
5 Gamesley	30	14	6	10	61	61	48
6 Lostock Gralam	30	14	3	13	60	57	45
7 Rylands	30	11	11	8	54	41	44
8 Knutsford	30	12	7	11	56	51	43
9 Styal (-3)	30	12	4	14	56	73	37
10 Northwich Villa	30	10	6	14	55	60	36
11 Garswood United	30	10	6	14	37	47	36
12 Golborne Sports	30	10	6	14	48	64	36
13 Club AZ	30	10	5	15	40	45	35
14 Billinge FC	30	9	8	13	45	58	35
15 Tarporley Victoria	30	8	6	16	39	77	30
16 Linotype & Cheadle Heath N.	30	4	7	19	45	72	19

DIVISION TWO	P	W	D	L	F	A	Pts
1 Denton Town	26	18	5	3	76	30	59
2 Grappenhall Sports	26	17	4	5	84	42	55
3 Whitchurch Alport	26	17	4	5	56	38	55
4 Crewe	26	12	9	5	55	35	45
5 Rudheath Social	26	14	3	9	58	42	45
6 Moore United	26	12	4	10	53	45	40
7 Runcorn Town reserves (-3)	26	11	3	12	54	60	33
8 Poynton	26	9	4	13	42	63	31
9 Monk (-6)	26	10	5	11	52	48	29
10 Daten	26	7	5	14	42	56	26
11 Congleton Town reserves	26	8	2	16	49	66	26
12 Malpas	26	6	7	13	46	63	25
13 Barnton	26	6	4	16	35	70	22
14 Maine Road reserves	26	4	3	19	45	89	15

DIVISION ONE CUP

ROUND 1
Linotype/Cheadle Heath Nomads 2-4 Club AZ
Tarporley Victoria 6-2 Pilkington Recreation
Garswood United 2-1 Golborne Sports
Northwich Villa 0-1 Billinge
Styal 3-5 Eagle Sports
Gamesley 1-2 Middlewich Town
Lostock Gralam 0-6 Knutsford
Rylands 0-6 Greenalls Padgate St Oswalds
QUARTER FINALS
Club AZ 3-1 Tarporley Victoria
Garswood United 2-0 Billinge
Eagle Sports 2-2 Middlewich Town
(Middlewich Town won 5-4 on penalties)
Knutsford 1-2 Greenalls Padgate St Oswalds
SEMI-FINALS
Club AZ 0-4 Garswood United (@ Egerton Boys Club)
Middlewich Town 3-2 Greenalls Padgate St Oswalds
FINAL (@ Trafford, 20/4/11)
Garswood United 0-1 Middlewich Town

DIVISION TWO CHALLENGE CUP

ROUND 1
Denton 1-2 Maine Road reserves
Runcorn Town reserves 2-1 Poynton
Daten 1-2 Malpas
Congleton Town reserves 1-4 Rudheath Social
Barnton 0-2 Moore United
Grappenhall Sports 2-1 Monk
QUARTER FINALS
Maine Road reserves 1-2 Whichurch Alport
Runcorn Town reserves 4-1 Malpas
Crewe 2-1 Rudheath Social
Moore United 3-2 Grappenhall Sports
SEMI-FINALS
Whitchurch Alport 4-0 Runcorn Town reserves
Crewe 1-0 Moore United
FINAL (@ Northwich Victoria, 16/3/11)
Whitchurch Alport 3-1 Crewe

RESERVES CHALLENGE CUP

FINAL (@ Trafford, 30/3/11)
Rylands reserves 0-3 Pilkington Recreation reserves

DIVISION ONE	1	2	3	4	5	6	7	8	9	10	11	12	13	14	15	16
1 Billinge		0-4	2-1	0-2	1-2	2-2	0-2	1-2	2-0	4-3	1-2	2-0	1-3	2-2	2-0	4-1
2 Club A Z	2-0		1-2	0-0	2-1	3-2	1-1	2-0	1-0	0-2	1-2	1-1	0-1	1-4	2-1	1-1
3 Eagle Sports	2-3	0-1		2-0	2-3	2-2	0-1	4-0	2-1	5-2	5-4	3-2	4-2	0-1	4-0	5-1
4 Gamesley	6-0	5-2	1-0		2-2	1-0	1-1	2-0	4-2	2-3	1-1	2-0	1-4	2-1	1-6	1-0
5 Garswood United	2-0	0-1	2-1	1-3		0-1	2-1	1-3	3-2	1-2	1-2	3-1	0-0	1-0	1-1	4-2
6 Golborne Sports	3-2	2-0	3-1	2-3	0-2		2-1	3-3	2-0	1-3	3-2	3-4	0-1	2-1	4-3	1-2
7 Greenalls Padgate St Oswalds	0-0	1-0	3-2	1-6	1-0	9-0		3-0	1-1	2-0	2-3	1-4	4-0	3-0	7-1	1-1
8 Knutsford	2-2	2-1	0-2	4-1	3-0	1-1	1-2		1-1	1-1	0-0	2-2	2-1	3-1	0-3	6-1
9 Linotype & Cheadle Heath Nomads	3-3	3-2	0-4	4-4	1-1	4-1	2-3	1-5		2-3	1-2	1-2	0-1	2-4	1-4	1-2
10 Lostock Gralam	1-2	2-1	0-5	6-0	3-0	3-1	1-1	1-4	1-2		1-1	2-0	0-4	1-2	2-3	4-0
11 Middlewich Town	1-1	3-1	0-2	2-2	3-1	1-0	0-1	0-1	1-2	1-2		1-0	1-3	1-1	6-1	3-3
12 Northwich Villa	2-2	2-1	1-0	5-1	1-0	1-2	1-5	6-4	3-3	2-1	0-3		2-3	0-1	2-3	0-1
13 Pilkington Recreation	2-1	3-1	3-4	4-1	1-1	5-3	2-2	3-1	3-0	3-1	0-3	1-1		2-2	3-1	5-1
14 Rylands	1-1	1-1	1-2	3-0	2-2	2-2	1-2	1-0	2-2	2-1	0-2	3-3	3-0		1-1	5-0
15 Styal	2-4	2-1	0-4	3-5	1-0	2-0	1-1	2-1	3-2	3-4	0-4	3-2	3-1	1-5		1-1
16 Tarporley Victoria	3-0	1-5	0-3	2-1	4-0	0-0	1-4	2-4	2-1	2-4	0-2	2-5	0-4	1-1	2-1	

CHESHIRE LEAGUE DIVISION ONE CONSTITUTION 2011-12

Club	Ground	Tel
BILLINGE	Billinge Comm. Spts/Soccer Cte , Carrmill Road , Billinge WN5 7TX	01744 893533
DENTON TOWN	Whittles Park, Heather Lea, Denton M34 6EJ	None
EAGLE SPORTS	Eagle Sports Club, Thornton Road, Great Sankey, Warrington WA5 2SZ	01925 632926
GAMESLEY	Melandra Park, Melandra Castle Road, Gamesley, Glossop SK13 0JR	None
GARSWOOD UNITED	The Wooders, Simms Lane End, Garswood Road, Garswood, Ashton-in-Makerfield WN4 0XH	01744 893968
GOLBORNE SPORTS	Simpson Playing Fields, Stone Cross Road, Lowton WA3 2SL	01942 510161
GRAPPENHALL SPORTS	Grappenhall Sports Club, Stockton Lane, Grappenhall, Warrington WA4 3HQ	01925 600899
GREENALLS PADGATE ST OSWALDS	Carlsberg Tetley Social Club, Long Lane, Warrington WA2 8PU	01925 634904
KNUTSFORD	Manchester Road, Knutsford WA16 0GU	None
LINOTYPE & CHEADLE HN	The Heath, Norbreck Avenue, Cheadle, Stockport SK8 2ET	0161 282 6574
LOSTOCK GRALAM	The Park Stadium, Manchester Road, Lostock Gralam CW9 7PJ	01606 42148
MIDDLEWICH TOWN	Seddon Street, Middlewich CW10 9DT	01606 835842
PILKINGTON	Ruskin Drive, Dentons Green, St Helens WA10 6RP	01744 22893
RYLANDS	Rylands Recreation Club, Gorsey Lane, Warrington WA2 7RZ	01925 625700
STYAL	Altrincham Road, Styal, Wilmslow SK9 4JE	01625 529303
TARPORLEY VICTORIA	Tattenhall Recreation Club, Field Lane, Tattenhall CH3 9QF	01829 770710

IN: *Denton Town (P), Grappenhall Sports (P)*
OUT: *Club AZ (W), Northwich Villa (P-North West Counties League Division One)*

DIVISION TWO	1	2	3	4	5	6	7	8	9	10	11	12	13	14
1 Barnton		4-2	0-6	2-1	1-1	0-3	5-1	0-1	1-3	2-2	1-1	1-3	2-4	0-1
2 Congleton Town reserves	2-0		0-7	2-0	1-2	1-2	5-0	1-2	3-3	4-3	4-1	0-1	0-3	1-4
3 Crewe	2-0	3-1		2-1	1-1	3-3	4-1	2-0	1-0	2-0	3-3	1-1	3-3	0-1
4 Daten	4-2	3-2	4-2		0-6	1-1	7-1	2-1	0-4	1-1	2-3	3-1	1-2	2-2
5 Denton Town	5-1	3-0	2-2	4-1		4-2	2-1	1-0	0-0	4-1	7-0	2-5	5-2	1-1
6 Grappenhall Sports	7-0	3-2	3-0	4-0	2-1		6-2	4-2	5-1	3-1	2-2	2-1	3-0	7-2
7 Maine Road reserves	2-2	1-2	0-0	3-1	1-4	2-6		4-4	6-0	3-5	2-4	2-0	1-2	2-1
8 Malpas	1-3	2-2	2-2	2-1	2-6	2-3	4-3		2-2	1-1	2-3	1-3	1-3	2-2
9 Monk	6-0	5-0	0-0	0-0	2-4	3-2	4-2	4-3		4-5	4-0	0-2	2-0	2-3
10 Moore United	1-2	2-0	1-2	2-3	0-2	4-3	2-1	0-0	2-0		4-2	3-0	4-0	3-0
11 Poynton	3-1	2-3	0-1	1-0	1-3	2-2	3-2	4-1	W-L	1-2		1-3	2-1	0-1
12 Rudheath Social	1-2	2-5	1-0	2-1	1-4	2-1	8-0	4-5	4-0	3-2	5-1		2-0	1-1
13 Runcorn Town reserves	4-3	5-4	5-2	1-1	2-1	3-5	4-1	0-3	1-2	0-2	4-1	1-1		1-2
14 Whitchurch Alport	3-0	3-2	2-4	3-2	0-1	1-0	4-1	3-0	2-1	2-0	3-1	3-1	6-3	

CHESHIRE LEAGUE DIVISION TWO CONSTITUTION 2011-12

Club	Ground	Tel
BARNTON	Townfield, Townfield Lane, Barnton, Northwich CW8 4LH	None
CONGLETON TOWN RESERVES	Booth Street Ground, off Crescent Road, Congleton CW12 4DG	01260 274460 Fax:01260 274460
CREWE	Cumberland Arena, Thomas Street, Crewe CW1 2BD	01270 537150
DATEN	Culcheth Sports Club, Charnock Road, Culcheth, Warrington WA3 5SH	01925 763096
MAINE ROAD RESERVES	Manchester Co. FA Ground, Branthingham Rd, Chorlton-cum-Hardy M21 0TT	0161 604 7620
MALPAS	Malpas & District Sports Club, Oxheys, Wrexham Road, Malpas SY14 7EJ	01948 860662
MOORE UNITED	Carlsberg Tetley Club, Long Lane, Warrington WA2 8PU	01925 634904
POYNTON	London Road North (A523), Poynton, Stockport SK12 1AG	01625 875765
RUDHEATH SOCIAL	Moss Farm Leisure Complex, Winnington, Northwich CW8 4BG	01606 783835
RUNCORN TOWN RESERVES	Pavilions Club, Sandy Lane, Weston Point, Runcorn WA7 4EX	01928 590508
SANDBACH UNITED	Winsford United FC, The Barton Stadium, Wharton Road, Winsford CW7 3AE	01606 558447
WHALEY BRIDGE	Park Road, Whaley Bridge, High Peak SK23 7DJ	None
WHITCHURCH ALPORT	Yockings Park, Blackpark Road, Whitchurch SY13 1PG	01948 667415

IN: *Sandbach United (S-Staffs County Senior League Premier Division), Whaley Bridge (P-Hope Valley League)*
OUT: *Denton Town (P), Grappenhall Sports (P), Monk Sports (W)*

RESERVE DIVISION	P	W	D	L	F	A	Pts
1 Pilkington reserves	30	22	2	6	102	39	68
2 Eagle Sports reserves	30	20	6	4	69	47	66
3 Rylands reserves	30	18	3	9	72	42	57
4 Greenalls Padgate St Os. res.	30	16	4	10	77	42	52
5 Linotype & Cheadle Hth N res.	30	15	2	13	74	61	47
6 Golborne Sports reserves	30	14	4	12	67	66	46
7 Crewe reserves	30	12	5	13	50	64	41
8 Denton Town reserves	30	12	4	14	70	76	40
9 Gamesley reserves	30	11	5	14	64	65	38
10 Styal reserves	30	12	2	16	54	69	38
11 Poynton reserves	30	11	3	16	50	81	36
12 Middlewich Town reserves	30	10	5	15	51	57	35
13 Billinge reserves	30	9	7	14	54	69	34
14 Grappenhall Sports res. (-3)	30	9	6	15	38	58	30
15 Garswood United reserves	30	7	7	16	41	61	28
16 Daten reserves	30	7	5	18	43	79	26

DORSET PREMIER LEAGUE

Sponsored by: Magna
Founded: 1957
Recent Champions:
2006: Holt United
2007: Westland Sports
2008: Portland United
2009: Portland United
2010: Hamworthy Recreation

		P	W	D	L	F	A	Pts
1	Hamworthy Recreation	34	26	5	3	107	25	83
2	Weymouth reserves	34	25	6	3	104	31	81
3	Westland Sports	34	25	4	5	97	33	79
4	Portland United	34	21	7	6	102	35	70
5	Sturminster Marshall	34	17	7	10	73	56	58
6	Holt United	34	18	3	13	84	61	57
7	Wincanton Town	34	18	3	13	64	53	57
8	Sherborne Town reserves	34	15	8	11	71	71	53
9	Bridport reserves	34	16	1	17	72	75	49
10	Parley Sports	34	12	8	14	47	59	44
11	Poole Borough (-3)	34	11	7	16	62	73	37
12	Merley Cobham Sports (-3)	34	12	4	18	55	66	37
13	Blandford United	34	11	4	19	59	82	37
14	Chickerell United	34	11	4	19	47	77	37
15	Hamworthy United res (-3)	34	8	2	24	46	112	23
16	Swanage Tn & Herston (-3)	34	6	7	21	48	105	22
17	Cranborne (-3)	34	5	7	22	44	94	19
18	Sturminster Newton	34	4	3	27	29	103	15

LEAGUE CUP

PRELIMINARY ROUND
Hamworthy Recreation 2-1 Swanage Town & Herston
Sturminster Newton United 1-0 Hamworthy United reserves

ROUND 1
Blandford United 1-2 Holt United
Bridport reserves 1-3 Portland United
Merley Cobham Sports 2-0 Sturminster Newton United
Parley Sports 1-2 Hamworthy Recreation
Sherborne Town reserves 6-1 Cranborne
Sturminster Marshall 3-3 Poole Borough
(Poole Borough won 5-4 on penalties)
Westland Sports 2-1 Chickerell United
Weymouth reserves 5-1 Wincanton Town

ROUND 2
Holt United 1-2 Sherborne Town reserves
Hamworthy Recreation 0-3 Westland Sports
Poole Borough 1-1 Merley Cobham Sports
(Merley Cobham Sports won 5-3 on penalties)
Weymouth reserves 2-1 Portland United

SEMI FINALS
Weymouth reserves 2-3 Sherborne Town reserves
Westland Sports 6-0 Merley Cobham Sports

FINAL (@ Dorchester Town, 27/4/11)
Merley Cobham Sports 1-2 Weymouth reserves

		1	2	3	4	5	6	7	8	9	10	11	12	13	14	15	16	17	18
1	Blandford United		0-4	3-2	0-1	1-3	4-2	3-4	2-0	3-2	0-3	1-8	2-3	1-2	4-1	2-1	1-2	2-2	0-4
2	Bridport reserves	3-4		1-0	4-1	2-3	7-1	1-2	1-3	1-3	6-3	0-10	4-1	0-3	3-1	2-1	0-4	2-3	3-1
3	Chickerell United	2-1	0-1		2-3	1-2	2-2	1-6	3-4	2-1	3-1	0-2	2-2	0-4	4-2	3-1	1-2	0-3	2-1
4	Cranborne	0-4	3-1	2-2		1-9	1-2	3-6	3-1	2-3	0-2	0-6	4-4	2-0	1-2	3-5	0-2	2-2	0-0
5	Hamworthy Recreation	2-0	5-0	6-0	0-0		3-0	4-1	1-0	6-0	7-1	5-0	3-1	2-1	1-1	0-0	1-0	1-0	3-2
6	Hamworthy United reserves	0-3	0-5	1-3	3-2	0-6		0-3	0-5	2-0	1-5	2-5	1-3	2-1	1-0	6-2	0-2	0-2	1-3
7	Holt United	3-1	1-3	3-0	2-0	0-2	2-2		0-0	2-2	3-1	1-2	2-4	2-3	1-2	3-1	5-2	1-3	1-2
8	Merley Cobham Sports	1-3	1-2	1-2	4-1	0-0	1-2	2-1		0-1	1-2	2-0	2-2	1-4	5-2	0-1	0-5	0-4	3-2
9	Parley Sports	2-0	2-1	1-0	0-0	1-5	2-1	1-2	1-2		0-0	0-2	2-0	2-3	3-0	2-2	1-4	2-1	0-1
10	Poole Borough	2-2	0-1	1-2	2-0	0-2	5-1	2-7	0-2	1-1		1-1	3-1	3-3	3-1	2-2	1-4	2-2	0-1
11	Portland United	2-0	3-1	4-0	3-2	2-2	9-0	0-2	5-0	2-2	5-0		2-0	4-0	5-1	4-0	2-2	0-0	3-1
12	Sherborne Town reserves	3-2	1-0	0-2	2-1	0-3	6-3	4-3	1-5	3-1	5-4	1-1		1-1	2-0	2-0	4-1	0-1	3-0
13	Sturminster Marshall	2-2	2-2	1-1	1-0	1-0	5-2	2-4	1-2	3-0	0-1	2-0	3-3		4-2	4-1	3-2	1-2	3-2
14	Sturminster Newton	0-2	1-3	1-3	5-3	1-8	0-1	0-2	1-0	1-1	0-7	0-4	1-1	1-2		1-4	0-5	1-3	0-2
15	Swanage Town & Herston	2-2	2-8	2-1	1-1	1-2	3-2	1-6	3-3	3-4	0-3	0-2	3-3	0-4	2-0		0-7	2-4	1-3
16	Westland Sports	7-1	5-0	5-1	5-1	3-2	4-1	3-0	4-1	2-2	W-L	2-1	2-1	1-1	2-0	4-0		0-0	1-0
17	Weymouth reserves	4-1	4-0	4-0	5-0	2-1	4-2	3-1	4-2	1-2	6-0	3-1	5-1	5-1	7-0	10-1	2-0		1-1
18	Wincanton Town	3-2	1-0	3-0	4-1	2-7	4-2	1-2	2-1	1-0	3-1	2-2	2-3	3-2	4-0	2-0	0-3	1-2	

DORSET PREMIER LEAGUE CONSTITUTION 2011-12

BLANDFORD UNITED	Recreation Ground, Park Road, Blandford Forum DT11 7BX	None
BRIDPORT RESERVES	St Marys Field, Skilling Hill Road, Bridport DT6 5LN	01308 423834
CHICKERELL UNITED	Weymouth College, Cranford Avenue, Weymouth DT4 7LQ	01305 208892
COBHAM SPORTS	Cobham Sports & Social Club, Merley House Lane, Wimborne BH21 3AA	01202 885773
CRANBORNE	Recreation Ground, Penny's Lane, Cranborne, Wimborne BH21 5QE	01725 517440
HAMWORTHY RECREATION	Hamworthy Rec. Club, Magna Road, Canford Magna, Wimborne BH21 3AP	01202 881922
HAMWORTHY UNITED RESERVES	The County Ground, Blandford Close, Hamworthy, Poole BH15 4BF	01202 674974
HOLT UNITED	Gaunts Common, Holt, Wimborne BH21 4JR	01258 840379
PARLEY SPORTS	Parley Sports Club, Christchurch Road, West Parley BH22 8SQ	01202 573345
POOLE BOROUGH	Turlin Moor Recreation Ground, Blandford Moor, Hamworthy, Poole BH21 5XX	None Club Office: 01202 674973
PORTLAND UNITED	New Grove Corner, Grove Road, Portland DT5 1DP	01305 861489
SHAFTESBURY	Cockrams, Coppice Street, Shaftesbury SP7 8PF	01747 853990
SHERBORNE TOWN RESERVES	Raleigh Grove, The Terrace Playing Fields, Sherborne DT9 5NS	01935 816110
STURMINSTER MARSHALL	Churchill Close, Sturminster Marshall BH21 4BQ	None
SWANAGE TOWN & HERSTON	Day's Park, off De Moulham Road, Swanage BH19 2JW	01929 424673
TINTINHULL	Montacute Road, Tintinhull, Yeovil BA22 8QD	None
WESTLAND SPORTS	Alvington Lane, Yeovil BA22 8UX	None
WEYMOUTH RESERVES	Wessex Stadium, Radipole Lane, Weymouth DT4 9XJ	01305 785558 Fax: 01305 766658
WINCANTON TOWN	Wincanton Sports Ground, Moor Lane, Wincanton BA9 9EJ	01963 31815

IN: *Shaftesbury (Wessex League Division One), Tintinhull (P-Dorset League Senior Division)*
OUT: *Sturminster Newton United (R-Dorset League Senior Division)*

ESSEX & SUFFOLK BORDER LEAGUE

Sponsored by: Kent Blaxill
Founded: 1911
Recent Champions:
2006: Gas Recreation
2007: Gas Recreation
2008: Gas Recreation
2009: West Bergholt
2010: Gas Recreation

PREMIER DIVISION	P	W	D	L	F	A	Pts
1 Brightlingsea Regent	34	31	2	1	111	20	95
2 Gas Recreation	34	28	5	1	131	35	89
3 West Bergholt	34	24	5	5	91	29	77
4 Rowhedge	34	22	1	11	98	66	67
5 Holland	34	16	6	12	63	61	54
6 University of Essex	34	14	8	12	71	56	50
7 Sudbury Athletic	34	16	2	16	79	67	50
8 Wormingford Wanderers	34	14	6	14	64	66	48
9 Dedham Old Boys	34	13	5	16	72	67	44
10 Great Bentley	34	13	4	17	54	75	43
11 Alresford Colne Rangers	34	12	5	17	58	75	41
12 Harwich & Parkeston	34	11	5	18	47	75	38
13 Little Oakley	34	11	3	20	59	66	36
14 Hatfield Peverel	34	9	7	18	47	72	34
15 Hedinghams United	34	9	7	18	50	91	34
16 White Notley	34	9	5	20	55	87	32
17 Earls Colne	34	7	4	23	42	77	25
18 Tiptree Jobserve	34	5	4	25	35	142	19

LEAGUE CUP

PRELIMINARY ROUND
Coggeshall Town 1-0 Sudbury Athletic
Brightlingsea Regent 6-0 Boxted Lodgers
Wormingford Wanderers 3-0 St Osyth
Hedinghams United 3-4 Tiptree Jobserve

ROUND 1
Bradfield Rovers 4-5 Kirby United
Tiptree Jobserve w/o-scr Bures United
West Bergholt w/o-scr Weeley Athletic
Gas Recreation 3-1 White Notley
Foxash Social 4-2 West Clacton
Bell United 2-6 Alresford Colne Rangers
Rowhedge 0-2 Lawford Lads
Dedham Old Boys 0-1 Holland
Little Oakley 1-1 Mersea Island
(Mersea Island won 4-3 on penalties)
Gosfield United 1-3 Harwich & Parkeston
Great Bentley 1-3 University of Essex
Earls Colne 3-0 Clare Town
Hatfield Peverel 5-2 Newbury Forest
Coggeshall Town 1-2 Barnston
Clacton United 6-0 Rayne
Brightlingsea Regent 1-1 Wormingford Wanderers
(Brightlingsea Regent won 4-1 on penalties)

PREMIER DIVISION	1	2	3	4	5	6	7	8	9	10	11	12	13	14	15	16	17	18
1 Alresford Colne Rangers		0-4	4-3	0-0	0-1	3-1	2-1	3-0	3-0	1-3	2-3	0-5	4-4	2-2	1-1	2-3	3-0	6-0
2 Brightlingsea Regent	3-0		4-1	4-0	2-2	3-0	11-0	4-0	5-0	1-0	4-1	4-1	3-1	5-0	5-1	1-1	5-0	2-1
3 Dedham Old Boys	2-1	1-4		4-2	1-4	1-2	3-0	1-1	1-2	0-1	1-1	7-3	0-1	9-1	2-2	5-4	6-1	0-2
4 Earls Colne	0-3	0-2	1-3		2-4	3-0	0-2	1-2	3-1	0-2	1-0	1-3	2-2	9-1	2-1	1-5	3-2	0-2
5 Gas Recreation	5-2	4-1	2-1	4-1		5-1	5-0	6-1	8-1	4-0	3-2	6-0	2-0	4-1	4-0	3-3	6-1	2-1
6 Great Bentley	1-0	0-3	0-0	3-0	0-8		1-3	2-3	2-2	0-3	3-1	1-3	3-2	4-0	1-0	4-1	3-1	2-2
7 Harwich & Parkeston	3-0	0-2	0-3	1-0	0-5	2-1		1-1	2-5	7-2	0-0	3-5	1-3	4-1	1-5	L-W	4-1	0-1
8 Hatfield Peverel	2-3	0-4	2-0	0-2	0-3	2-0	1-3		6-1	0-4	1-0	2-0	1-3	4-1	1-2	0-0	0-1	1-2
9 Hedinghams United	0-0	3-5	4-4	2-1	2-6	1-0	1-4	0-3		0-2	4-3	0-4	0-3	3-2	0-1	1-1	3-0	2-2
10 Holland	3-0	0-1	2-1	5-2	0-0	3-1	1-2	2-2	1-1		0-2	3-2	0-3	3-1	1-1	0-4	2-2	2-2
11 Little Oakley	1-2	1-2	1-0	1-0	2-6	1-0	1-0	3-1	5-0	1-2		2-3	1-4	9-0	5-3	1-1	0-1	3-0
12 Rowhedge	2-5	0-1	6-1	3-0	3-2	4-2	4-1	3-3	2-1	4-3	2-1		4-0	12-2	0-3	0-1	3-0	5-1
13 Sudbury Athletic	1-2	1-2	2-3	2-0	1-2	2-4	3-0	3-2	2-3	7-1	3-1	2-3		3-2	1-3	0-4	3-1	0-4
14 Tiptree Jobserve	3-1	0-3	1-0	2-0	1-6	1-4	1-1	4-1	2-2	2-6	2-0	0-2	0-5		0-9	0-5	0-3	0-11
15 University of Essex	6-1	0-5	0-1	2-0	2-2	1-1	1-1	1-1	0-2	3-1	1-0	5-2	5-2	7-1		0-3	2-0	1-3
16 West Bergholt	5-2	0-1	1-2	4-0	0-2	7-0	3-0	3-0	W-L	2-0	7-1	3-1	2-1	3-0	2-1		5-0	5-0
17 White Notley	5-0	0-3	2-4	2-2	1-3	3-5	0-0	2-2	4-1	2-3	4-3	0-2	2-5	1-1	3-0	0-2		4-1
18 Wormingford Wanderers	2-0	1-2	3-1	3-3	2-2	1-2	2-0	4-1	4-2	0-2	3-2	0-2	0-4	1-0	1-1	0-1	2-6	

ESSEX & SUFFOLK BORDER LEAGUE PREMIER DIVISION CONSTITUTION 2011-12

ALRESFORD COLNE RANGERS	Ford Lane, Alresford, Colchester CO7 8AU	07796 036467
DEDHAM OLD BOYS	Old Grammar School Ground, The Drift, Dedham, Colchester CO7 6AH	None
GAS RECREATION	Bromley Road, Colchester CO4 3JE	01206 860383
GREAT BENTLEY	The Green, Heckfords Road, Great Bentley, Colchester CO7 8LY	01206 251532
HARWICH & PARKESTON	The Royal Oak, Main Road, Dovercourt, Harwich CO12 4AA	01255 503643
HATFIELD PEVEREL	Strutt Memorial Field, Maldon Road, Hatfield Peverel CM3 2HT	None
HEDINGHAMS UNITED	Lawn Meadow, Yeldham Road, Sible Hedingham, Halstead CO9 3QH	None
HOLLAND	Eastcliff Sports Ground, Dulwich Road, Holland-on-Sea CO15 5HP	01255 814874
LAWFORD LADS	School Lane, Lawford, Manningtree CO11 2JA	01206 397211
LITTLE OAKLEY	War Memorial Club Ground, Harwich Road, Little Oakley, Harwich CO12 5ED	01255 880370
NEWBURY FOREST	London Marathon Sports Ground, Forest Road, Hainault, Ilford IG6 3HJ	020 8500 3486
ROWHEDGE	Rectory Road, Rowhedge CO5 7HR	01206 728022
SUDBURY ATHLETIC	Delphi Sports Club, Alexandra Road, Sudbury CO10 2XH	01787 372331
UNIVERSITY OF ESSEX	University Essex Sports Centre, Wivenhoe Park, Colchester CO4 3SQ	01206 873250
WEST BERGHOLT	Lorkin Daniel Field, Lexden Road, West Bergholt, Colchester CO6 3BW	01206 241525
WHITE NOTLEY	Oak Farm, Faulkbourne, Witham CM8 1SF	01376 519864
WORMINGFORD WANDERERS	Wormingford Playing Field, Main Road, Wormingford, Colchester CO6 3AF	None

IN: *Lawford Lads (P), Newbury Forest (P)*
OUT: *Brightlingsea Regent (P-Eastern Counties League Division One), Earls Colne (R), Tiptree Jobserve (R)*

DIVISION ONE	P	W	D	L	F	A	Pts
1 Lawford Lads	32	27	3	2	124	42	84
2 Newbury Forest (-3)	32	25	4	3	152	38	76
3 West Clacton	32	22	1	9	116	43	67
4 Clacton United (+3)	32	20	1	11	85	49	64
5 Coggeshall Town	32	19	5	8	76	35	62
6 St. Osyth (+3)	32	16	2	14	84	75	53
7 Kirby Athletic	32	15	7	10	61	46	52
8 Barnston (-1)	32	14	5	13	83	70	46
9 Clare Town (-1)	32	12	9	11	80	62	44
10 Rayne	32	12	5	15	76	79	41
11 Gosfield United	32	13	2	17	61	80	41
12 Boxted Lodgers	32	9	7	16	53	75	34
13 Bradfield Rovers (+2)	32	7	9	16	67	99	32
14 Mersea Island (-4)	32	9	7	16	42	73	30
15 Foxash Social	32	8	4	20	53	90	28
16 Weeley Athletic	32	5	3	24	28	102	18
17 Bell United (+3)	32	0	4	28	30	213	7

RESERVE KNOCKOUT CUP

FINAL (@ Stanway Rovers , 20/4/11)

Brightlingsea Regent Res. 2-4 Rowhedge Res.

TOMMY THOMPSON KNOCK-OUT CUP

FINAL (@ Lawford Lads, 2/5/11)

Rowhedge Res. 7-1 Boxted Lodgers

AV LEE MEMORIAL TROPHY

(League winners v League Cup holders, @ Gas Recreation, 30/8/10)

Gas Recreation 2-1 West Bergholt

LEAGUE CUP continued...

ROUND 2

Brightlingsea United 3-0 Mersea Island

Kirby Athletic 1-1 Harwich & Parkeston

(Kirby Athletic won 5-4 on penalties)

Barnston 0-6 University of Essex

West Bergholt 3-1 Gas Recreation

Clacton United 3-1 Tiptree Jobserve

Holland 3-0 Earls Colne

Lawfords Lads 5-1 Hatfield Peverel

Foxash Social 1-5 Alresford Colne Rangers

QUARTER-FINALS

Lawford Lads 3-1 Clacton United

Alresford Colne Rangers 2-0 Kirby Athletic

Holland 2-3 West Bergholt

University of Essex 1-4 Brightlingsea Regent

SEMI-FINALS

Brightlingsea Regent 5-3 Lawford Lads

(Brightlingsea Regent expelled)

Alresford Colne Rangers 1-1 West Bergholt

(West Bergholt won 4-3 on penalties)

FINAL (@ AFC Sudbury, 20/4/11)

West Bergholt 2-0 Lawford Lads

DIVISION ONE	1	2	3	4	5	6	7	8	9	10	11	12	13	14	15	16	17
1 Barnston		20-1	2-1	0-2	2-3	5-3	0-1	1-0	0-1	1-1	0-3	3-1	1-2	4-2	3-3	4-1	2-4
2 Bell United	3-3		3-3	1-5	0-10	0-7	1-5	1-2	0-5	2-2	1-7	2-2	0-4	1-6	3-9	0-3	0-9
3 Boxted Lodgers	0-2	3-1		3-3	1-5	0-1	0-3	2-2	3-2	4-3	1-4	1-1	3-3	3-2	1-2	5-1	3-1
4 Bradfield Rovers	5-2	13-3	2-5		2-2	2-2	0-2	0-4	4-4	0-0	1-11	1-1	0-6	4-0	3-4	0-0	2-3
5 Clacton United	3-2	10-0	1-3	9-2		W-L	3-4	2-1	2-0	0-1	2-1	7-0	4-2	4-0	0-2	1-0	1-0
6 Clare Town	1-1	13-0	8-0	1-4	1-0		1-1	2-1	1-2	3-3	0-1	2-2	4-4	4-4	2-1	6-1	2-1
7 Coggeshall Town	0-0	8-0	1-0	0-0	4-1	2-0		3-0	2-3	0-1	3-4	1-1	0-2	3-1	5-1	4-0	3-1
8 Foxash Social	2-3	10-1	0-0	3-2	1-2	3-1	1-5		2-1	2-2	0-1	1-2	1-5	2-4	1-3	0-1	0-1
9 Gosfield United	2-4	W-L	1-0	2-2	0-1	0-2	2-4	7-0		4-1	0-4	2-3	0-7	1-3	0-4	2-0	2-4
10 Kirby Athletic	1-2	W-L	3-0	2-0	6-2	2-3	1-0	2-2	6-2		1-2	0-1	2-1	2-1	3-0	5-0	2-3
11 Lawford Lads	3-1	9-0	3-2	3-1	5-1	4-3	1-0	7-3	3-1	3-2		4-2	3-3	3-1	4-0	7-0	3-1
12 Mersea Island	0-3	W-L	1-0	3-0	0-1	0-1	0-3	1-0	2-5	1-3	0-1		2-4	1-1	3-0	2-0	4-5
13 Newbury Forest	9-0	17-0	7-1	9-1	2-0	6-0	3-1	12-1	6-1	2-0	3-3	5-0		W-L	4-2	10-1	W-L
14 Rayne	3-1	6-3	4-0	5-2	3-1	3-3	3-4	2-3	1-2	1-2	4-4	5-5	0-3		2-3	W-L	2-1
15 St Osyth	5-6	10-0	2-1	4-2	2-0	2-1	0-3	8-2	0-4	0-0	1-3	3-0	1-4	2-3		4-1	2-3
16 Weeley Athletic	2-1	4-3	0-3	1-2	1-5	1-1	1-1	1-3	1-2	1-2	1-9	2-1	2-4	0-4	0-3		1-5
17 West Clacton	2-4	8-0	1-1	4-0	1-2	6-1	3-0	5-0	8-1	3-0	3-1	7-0	4-3	8-0	8-1	3-0	

ESSEX & SUFFOLK BORDER LEAGUE DIVISION ONE CONSTITUTION 2011-12

BARNSTON	High Easter Road , Barnston , Dunmow CM6 1LZ	07712 129459
BOXTED LODGERS	The Playing Field, Cage Lane, Boxted, Colchester CO4 5RE	01206 271969
BRADFIELD ROVERS	The Playing Field, The Street, Bradfield, Manningtree CO11 2UU	None
CLACTON UNITED	Vista Road Recreation Ground, Vista Road, Clacton-on-Sea CO15 6DB	01255 429647
COGGESHALL TOWN	The Crops, West Street, Coggeshall CO6 1NS	01376 562843
COLNE ENGAINE & BELL UNITED	Kynaston Road, Panfield, Braintree CM7 1WX	None
EARLS COLNE	Green Farm Meadow, Halstead Road, Earls Colne, Colchester CO6 2NG	01787 223584
FOXASH SOCIAL	Foxash Playing Field, Harwich Road, Lawford, Manningtree CO11 2LP	01206 231309
GOSFIELD UNITED	The Playing Field, Church Lane, Gosfield, Halstead CO9 1UB	None
HAVERHILL SPORTS ASSOCIATION	The New Croft, Chalkerstone Way, Haverhill CB9 0LD	01440 702137
KIRBY ATHLETIC	Kirby Playing Field, Halstead Road, Kirby Cross CO13 0LS	None
MALDON ST MARYS	Tiptree Sports Centre, Maypole Road, Tiptree, Colchester CO5 0EJ	01621 817499
MERSEA ISLAND	The Glebe, Colchester Road, West Mersea CO5 8RS	01206 385216
RAYNE	Rayne Village Hall, Oak Meadow, Gore Road, Rayne, Braintree CM77 6TX	01376 349408
ST OSYTH	Cowley Park, Mill Street, St Osyth, Clacton-on-Sea CO16 8EJ	None
TIPTREE JOBSERVE	Warriors Rest, Maypole Road, Tiptree CO5 0EN	None

IN: *Earls Colne (R), Haverhill Sports Association (N), Maldon St Marys (S-Essex Olympian League Division Two), Tiptree Jobserve (R)*

OUT: *Clare Town (S-Cambs County League Div One A), Lawford Lads (P), Newbury Forest (P), Weeley Athletic (W), West Clacton(W)*

Bell United have merged with Colchester & East Essex club Colne Engaine to become Colne Engaine & Bell United

ESSEX OLYMPIAN LEAGUE

Sponsored by: Pro Kit UK
Founded: 1966
Recent Champions:
2006: Harold Wood Athletic
2007: White Ensign
2008: White Ensign
2009: Harold Wood Athletic
2010: Harold Wood Athletic

PREMIER DIVISION	P	W	D	L	F	A	Pts
1 Kelvedon Hatch	26	19	3	4	49	20	60
2 Harold Wood Athletic (+3)	26	18	3	5	58	31	60
3 Frenford Senior	26	15	4	7	53	35	49
4 Rayleigh Town	26	14	2	10	64	56	44
5 Manford Way	26	13	4	9	50	30	43
6 M & B Club (+3)	26	12	4	10	56	45	43
7 Buckhurst Hill	26	12	5	9	53	41	41
8 Ongar Town	26	11	4	11	44	48	37
9 Westhamians (-3)	26	10	8	8	46	47	35
10 Mountnessing (-3)	26	8	7	11	28	37	28
11 Canning Town	26	7	4	15	34	50	25
12 White Ensign	26	6	5	15	38	57	23
13 Galleywood	26	4	5	17	28	61	17
14 Epping	26	3	2	21	34	77	11

SENIOR CUP

ROUND 1

Newham United 1-2 Debden Sports
Roydon 4-1 Benfleet
Maldon St Marys 1-0 Leigh Ramblers
Manford Way 9-0 Waltham Abbey Res.
Catholic United 5-0 Takeley Res.
Kelvedon Hatch 3-1 Old Chelmsfordians
Writtle 1-2 M & B Club
Broomfield 1-2 Leytonstone United
Thurrock Res. 0-1 Burnham Ramblers Res.
Southminster St Leonards 4-2 Bowers & Pitsea Res.
Hutton 2-1 Sungate
Runwell Hospital 3-2 Sawbridgeworth Town Res.
Basildon Town 0-4 Westhamians
Harold Wood Athletic 5-2 Aldborough Athletic
Forest Glade 4-1 Ramsden
Lakeside 3-3 Upminster (Lakeside won 3-1 on penalties)
Galleywood 3-5 Bishop's Stortford Swifts
Shenfield Association 3-2 Ryan
Herongate Athletic 1-1 Hannakins Farm
(Hannakins Farm won 4-3 on penalties)
Old Southendian 3-4 Rayleigh Town

PREMIER DIVISION	1	2	3	4	5	6	7	8	9	10	11	12	13	14
1 Buckhurst Hill		2-1	6-2	1-2	5-0	1-4	1-0	3-0	2-2	2-0	1-3	2-4	0-3	2-1
2 Canning Town	1-1		2-1	2-2	3-1	0-3	1-3	3-5	0-1	0-1	4-1	1-3	1-1	0-0
3 Epping	2-2	2-3		2-3	0-3	1-2	0-5	0-4	0-1	0-1	2-4	3-5	1-1	1-5
4 Frenford Senior	2-1	4-1	4-1		1-0	1-2	1-2	0-1	2-1	0-0	1-4	5-2	2-2	3-0
5 Galleywood	0-0	1-2	2-1	1-5		0-3	0-3	0-3	1-2	2-1	1-1	3-4	1-1	5-1
6 Harold Wood Athletic	2-1	0-2	W-L	3-0	5-1		3-3	3-2	4-3	0-1	2-0	2-1	5-2	3-1
7 Kelvedon Hatch	0-2	3-0	2-1	2-0	2-1	1-0		2-1	2-0	2-1	2-2	2-1	0-0	W-L
8 M & B Club	0-2	2-0	4-1	4-3	3-0	4-4	1-2		3-2	1-1	0-2	1-3	1-2	0-0
9 Manford Way	3-1	4-0	3-0	1-2	3-0	1-0	0-1	5-1		0-0	2-2	1-2	1-0	6-0
10 Mountnessing	1-3	W-L	1-2	1-3	0-0	0-0	2-1	1-6	0-1		0-1	3-1	4-3	5-2
11 Ongar Town	2-5	2-1	2-3	0-4	2-1	0-1	1-0	2-5	1-3	1-1		3-2	1-3	4-0
12 Rayleigh Town	3-5	4-1	4-0	0-1	5-1	3-1	1-3	1-1	4-3	2-1	2-0		0-3	1-5
13 Westhamians	2-1	1-4	2-5	1-2	3-3	1-4	0-3	2-1	1-1	2-0	W-L	3-3		2-1
14 White Ensign	1-1	2-1	6-3	0-0	2-0	1-2	0-3	1-2	1-0	2-2	2-3	2-3	2-5	

ESSEX OLYMPIAN LEAGUE PREMIER DIVISION CONSTITUTION 2011-12

BUCKHURST HILL	Roding Lane, Buckhurst Hill IG9 6BJ	020 8504 1189
CANNING TOWN	Terence McMillan Stadium, Newham Leisure Centre, 281 Prince Regents Lane, London E13 8SD	020 7511 4477
FRENFORD SENIOR	Oakfields Sports Ground, Forest Road, Barkingside IG6 2JL	020 8500 1998
GALLEYWOOD	Clarkes Field, Slades Lane, Galleywood, Chelmsford CM2 8RW	01245 352975
HANNAKINS FARM	Hannakins Farm Community Centre, Rosebay Avenue, Billericay CM12 0SY	01277 630851
HAROLD HILL	Brentwood Town FC, The Arena, The Brentwood Centre, Doddinghurst Road, Brentwood CM15 9NN	07776 232071
HAROLD WOOD ATHLETIC	Harold Wood Recreation Park, Harold View, Harold Wood RM3 0LX	01708 375698
HUTTON	Shenfield Match Day Centre, Shenfield School, Alexander Lane, Shenfield CM15 8RY	None
KELVEDON HATCH	New Hall, School Road, Kelvedon Hatch, Brentwood CM15 0DH	None
M & B CLUB	Sanofi-Aventis Spts/Soc. Club, Dagenham Road, Dagenham RM7 0QX	020 8919 2156
MANFORD WAY	London Marathon Sports Ground, Forest Road, Hainault IG6 3HJ	020 8500 3486
RAYLEIGH TOWN	Rayleigh Town Sports/Soc. Club, London Road, Rayleigh SS6 9DT	01268 784001
WESTHAMIANS	Fairlop Oak Playing Field, Forest Road, Hainault IG6 3HJ	None
WHITE ENSIGN	Borough Football Comb. HQ, Eastwoodbury Lane, Southend-on-Sea SS2 6XG	01702 520482

IN: *Hannakins Farm (P), Hutton (P)*
OUT: *Epping (R), Ongar Town (R)*
Mountnessing become Harold Hill

SENIOR CHALLENGE CUP
(Premier Champions v Senior Cup Holders)

@Harold Wod Athletic, 21/8/10)
Harold Wood Athletic 2-1 Westhamians

DIVISION ONE	P	W	D	L	F	A	Pts
1 Hutton	24	18	2	4	74	39	56
2 Hannakins Farm (+3)	24	15	4	5	62	38	52
3 Runwell Hospital	24	14	5	5	44	25	47
4 Sandon Royals	24	13	6	5	55	36	45
5 Benfleet	24	12	3	9	50	41	39
6 S'ster St. Leonards	24	12	1	11	60	47	37
7 Old Chelmsfordians	24	11	4	9	44	40	37
8 Aldborough Athletic	24	9	5	10	45	46	32
9 Thurrock reserves	24	10	2	12	39	45	32
10 Bishops Stort. Swifts	24	9	3	12	43	50	30
11 Lakeside	24	5	2	17	26	58	17
12 Sungate (-3)	24	3	9	12	36	72	15
13 Ryan	24	1	2	21	32	73	5

SENIOR CUP continued...

ROUND 2

M & B Club 2-3 Manford Way
Rayleigh Town 3-1 Maldon St Marys
Westhamians 8-2 Forest Glade
Catholic United 2-5 Wadham Lodge
Bishop's Stortford Swifts 2-3 Kelvedon Hatch
Stansted Res. 2-1 Castle United
Springfield 5-3 Roydon
Burnham Ramblers Res. 3-2 Lakeside
Hutton 0-1 Harold Wood Athletic
Shenfield Association 0-2 Frenford Senior
White Ensign 4-1 Southminster St Leonards
Ongar Town 5-3 Hannakins Farm
Mountnessing 2-0 Sandon Royals
Runwell Hospital 2-0 Epping
Canning Town 4-1 Leytonstone United
Buckhurst Hill 3-0 Debden Sports

ROUND 3

Canning Town 1-0 White Ensign
Stansted Res. 0-1 Runwell Hospital
Springfield 3-3 Rayleigh Town
(Rayleigh Town won 4-3 on penalties)
Wadham Lodge 1-2 Harold Wood Athletic
Westhamians 1-2 Burnham Ramblers Res.
Ongar Town 6-5 Manford Way
Buckhurst Hill 1-2 Frenford Senior
Mountnessing 1-2 Kelvedon Hatch

DIVISION ONE	1	2	3	4	5	6	7	8	9	10	11	12	13
1 Aldborough Athletic		1-1	4-1	1-1	0-2	2-1	1-0	1-2	3-0	0-1	2-4	2-2	0-3
2 Benfleet	5-1		6-4	0-3	1-0	1-1	1-0	0-1	4-0	2-3	2-1	2-4	1-2
3 Bishop's Stortford Swifts	3-1	0-1		0-1	4-3	1-1	1-2	1-0	6-3	0-2	4-2	3-0	4-3
4 Hannakins Farm	5-3	2-0	3-1		2-4	1-0	1-1	1-2	3-2	4-5	2-1	8-2	5-2
5 Hutton	3-2	2-0	7-2	2-0		4-0	4-1	2-1	3-2	3-3	3-2	2-2	5-1
6 Lakeside	0-2	2-6	L-W	0-4	1-2		1-3	2-3	2-0	2-9	1-3	2-0	1-4
7 Old Chelmsfordians	4-2	1-2	3-2	1-2	2-5	3-1		3-1	1-0	1-0	2-0	2-2	1-1
8 Runwell Hospital	1-1	2-1	1-1	0-0	3-0	3-0	4-3		2-0	1-2	4-2	0-0	W-L
9 Ryan	1-6	2-3	2-3	1-2	3-5	2-1	0-1	1-5		0-3	3-4	1-1	0-2
10 Sandon Royals	3-3	2-3	2-1	3-3	1-3	0-1	0-0	2-2	3-1		0-1	2-2	1-0
11 Southminster St Leon's	1-2	2-2	1-0	1-3	5-1	2-3	5-3	0-1	2-1	2-3		6-1	4-1
12 Sungate	2-3	2-5	1-1	5-3	0-6	0-1	0-4	1-5	4-4	1-3	2-6		1-0
13 Thurrock reserves	0-2	3-1	1-0	1-3	1-3	3-2	4-2	1-0	4-3	0-2	1-3	1-1	

ESSEX OLYMPIAN LEAGUE DIVISION ONE CONSTITUTION 2011-12

ALDBOROUGH ATHLETIC	Fairlop Oak Playing Fields, Forest Road, Hainault IG6 3HJ	020 8500 3777
BENFLEET	The Club House, Woodside Extension, Manor Rd, Benfleet, Rayleigh SS7 4BG	01268 743957
BISHOP'S STORTFORD SWIFTS	Silver Leys, Hadham Road (A1250), Bishop's Stortford CM23 2QE	01279 658941
EPPING	Stonards Hill Rec Ground, Tidy's Lane, Epping CM16 6SP	None
HERONGATE ATHLETIC	Adjacent to 77 Billericay Road, Herongate, Brentwood CM13 3PU	01277 810717
LAKESIDE	Lakeside Pitches, Lakeside Retail Park, Thurrock RM20 2ZL	01375 379352
OLD CHELMSFORDIANS	Lawford Lane, Roxwell Road, Chelmsford CM1 2NS	01245 420442
ONGAR TOWN	Sports Ground, Love Lane, High Street, Ongar CM5 9BL	01277 363838
RUNWELL HOSPITAL	Runwell Hospital, Runwell Chase, Wickford SS11 7QA	None
SANDON ROYALS	Sandon Sports Club, Woodhill Road, Sandon, Chelmsford CM2 7AQ	01245 476626
SOUTHMINSTER ST LEONARDS	King George V Playing Fields, Station Road, Southminster CM0 7EW	07718 869883
THURROCK RESERVES	Ship Lane, Grays RM19 1YN	01708 865492
		Fax: 01708 868863 Club: 01708 865492
WADHAM LODGE	Wadham Lodge Sports Ground, Kitchener Road, Walthamstow E17 4JP	020 8527 2444

IN: *Epping (R), Herongate Athletic (P), Ongar Town (R), Wadham Lodge (P)*

OUT: *Hannakins Farm (P), Hutton (P), Ryan (R), Sungate (R)IN: Hannakins Farm (P), Hutton (P)*

DIVISION TWO	P	W	D	L	F	A	Pts
1 Wadham Lodge	24	20	3	1	91	25	63
2 Herongate Athletic	24	18	2	4	53	25	56
3 Forest Glade	24	14	3	7	59	44	45
4 Broomfield	24	11	5	8	44	45	38
5 Stansted reserves	24	9	6	9	46	37	33
6 Maldon St Marys	24	9	6	9	44	44	33
7 Burnham Rambl. res	24	10	3	11	43	43	33
8 Upminster (+3)	24	8	5	11	49	50	32
9 Takeley reserves	24	8	2	14	45	45	26
10 Leigh Ramblers	24	7	4	13	41	67	25
11 Leytonstone Utd (+3)	24	5	5	14	29	67	23
12 Roydon	24	6	2	16	32	67	20
13 Waltham Ab. res (-6)	24	6	4	14	37	54	16

SENIOR CUP continued...

QUARTER-FINALS

Rayleigh Town 3-1 Ongar Town
Frenford Senior 1-0 Canning Town
Kelvedon Hatch 0-3 Harold Wood Athletic
Runwell Hospital 4-2 Burnham Ramblers Res.

SEMI-FINALS

Rayleigh Town 3-3 Harold Wood Athletic
(Rayleigh Town won 4-3 on penalties)
Runwell Hospital 1-1 Frenford Senior
(Runwell Hospital won 3-1 on penalties)

FINAL (@ AFC Hornchurch, 10/5/11)
Rayleigh Town 2-1 Runwell Hospital

DENNY KING MEMORIAL CUP
(Senior Cup first and second round losers)

ROUND 1

Sungate 3-2 Old Southendian
Hannakins Farm 2-3 Thurrock Res.
Roydon 4-1 Maldon St Marys
Hutton 6-1 Broomfield

ROUND 2

Castle United 6-2 Lakeside
Thurrock Res. 3-1 Leytonstone United
Benfleet 3-1 Debden Sports
Galleywood 2-1 Waltham Abbey Res.
Basildon Town 6-0 Ramsden
Upminster 2-1 Writtle
Sandon Royals 1-0 Aldborough Athletic
Bishop's Stortford Swifts 3-2 Ryan
Leigh Ramblers 1-3 Herongate Athletic
Newham United 6-2 Old Chelmsfordians

DIVISION TWO	1	2	3	4	5	6	7	8	9	10	11	12	13
1 Broomfield		2-1	4-3	0-1	6-1	1-1	1-0	0-0	2-1	1-0	5-2	2-5	1-1
2 Burnham Ramblers res	2-0		3-1	0-2	1-1	0-0	1-2	2-0	0-1	3-1	2-4	0-5	3-1
3 Forest Glade	3-1	3-1		4-3	2-4	4-4	2-2	3-0	2-0	4-2	3-1	2-5	W-L
4 Herongate Athletic	2-1	2-1	1-2		4-0	2-0	2-2	5-0	2-0	4-1	1-0	1-0	3-1
5 Leigh Ramblers	2-3	2-6	1-6	1-2		4-0	0-0	3-1	3-6	1-5	4-2	1-5	W-L
6 Leytonstone United	0-4	1-2	2-1	1-4	3-2		1-1	1-3	0-0	2-3	3-1	1-2	0-1
7 Maldon St Mary's	2-3	2-0	0-3	1-1	3-1	4-0		2-4	5-2	0-2	3-2	1-6	7-0
8 Roydon	3-0	1-5	0-2	0-2	3-3	0-2	2-0		1-3	2-1	2-4	0-2	3-2
9 Stansted reserves	2-2	1-4	1-1	1-3	4-2	8-0	1-2	4-1		2-0	1-1	1-2	1-1
10 Takeley reserves	1-1	1-3	2-5	0-1	0-1	5-2	5-1	5-1	1-2		0-2	0-1	2-1
11 Upminster	4-1	0-0	1-0	6-2	0-1	8-0	1-1	3-2	0-0	2-8		0-3	3-5
12 Wadham Lodge	6-0	5-0	5-1	3-2	1-1	6-2	4-2	7-1	2-1	3-0	2-2		8-1
13 Waltham Abbey reserves	2-3	5-3	1-2	0-1	4-2	1-3	0-1	6-2	0-3	0-0	1-0	3-3	

ESSEX OLYMPIAN LEAGUE DIVISION TWO CONSTITUTION 2011-12

BROOMFIELD	The Angel Meadow, Main Road, Broomfield, Chelmsford CM1 7AH	01245 443819
BURNHAM RAMBLERS RESERVES	Leslie Field, Springfield Road, Burnham-on-Crouch CM0 8TE	01621 784383
CASTLE UNITED	Town Mead Leisure Centre, Brooker Road, Waltham Abbey EN9 1JH	01992 714949
FOREST GLADE	The Springhouse, Springhouse Road, Corringham SS17 7QT	01375 673100
LEIGH RAMBLERS	Belfairs Park, Eastwood Road North, Leigh-on-Sea SS9 4LR	01702 421077
LEYTONSTONE UNITED	Ilford Wanderers RFC, Forest Road, Hainault IG6 3HJ	020 8500 4622
OLD SOUTHENDIAN	Warner's Bridge Park, Chandlers Way, Southend-on-Sea SS2 5RR	01702 549000
ROYDON	Roydon Playing Fields, Harlow Road, Roydon, Harlow CM19 5HE	None
RYAN	Town Mead Leisure Park, Brooker Road, Waltham Abbey EN9 1JH	01992 714949
SPRINGFIELD	Springfield Hall Park, Arun Close, Springfield, Chelmsford CM1 7QE	01245 492441
SUNGATE	Ford Sports & Social Club, Aldborough Rd South, Newbury Pk, Ilford IG3 8HG	020 8590 3797
UPMINSTER	Hall Lane Playing Fields, Hall Lane, Upminster, Romford RM14 1AU	01708 220320

IN: *Castle United (P), Old Southendian (P), Ryan (R), Springfield (P), Sungate (R)*

OUT: *Herongate Athletic (P), Maldon St Marys (S - Essex & Suffolk Border League Division One), Stansted Reserves (S-Essex Senior League Reserve Division), Takeley Reserves (S-Essex Senior League Reserve Division), Wadham Lodge (P), Waltham Abbey Reserves (S-Essex Senior League Reserve Division*

ESSEX OLYMPIAN LEAGUE - STEP 7

DIVISION THREE	P	W	D	L	F	A	Pts
1 Springfield	22	18	2	2	89	28	56
2 Castle United (+2)	22	16	4	2	97	33	54
3 Old Southendian	22	15	2	5	61	42	47
4 Basildon Town	22	13	2	7	52	36	41
5 Catholic United (+3)	22	11	0	11	44	45	36
6 Newham United	22	10	2	10	49	42	32
7 Bowers & Pitsea reserves	22	7	3	12	60	71	24
8 Debden Sports (-1)	22	7	4	11	40	56	24
9 Shenfield	22	7	2	13	40	56	23
10 Ramsden	22	6	2	14	29	68	20
11 Writtle	22	4	3	15	39	81	15
12 Sawbridgewth T res (-3)	22	4	2	16	33	75	11

DENNING CUP continued...

Shenfield Association 0-4 Forest Glade
Sawbridgeworth Town Res. 1-3 Bowers & Pitsea Res.
Sungate 3-4 Southminster St Leonards
Hutton 0-1 Takeley Res.
M & B Club 3-1 Epping
Roydon 2-3 Catholic United

ROUND 3

M & B Club 3-2 Bishop's Stortford Swifts
Benfleet 2-0 Bowers & Pitsea Res.
Newham United 3-4 Castle United
Galleywood 0-1 Southminster St Leonards
Sandon Royals 1-0 Upminster
Catholic United 2-4 Basildon Town
Thurrock Res. 3-0 Herongate Athletic
Takeley Res. 4-2 Forest Glade

QUARTER-FINALS

Basildon Town 1-2 Southminster St Leonards
M & B Club 4-0 Takeley Res.
Benfleet 2-4 Castle United
Thurrock Res. 2-1 Sandon Royals

SEMI-FINALS

Castle United 6-1 Thurrock Res.
M & B Club 2-0 Southminster St Leonards

FINAL (@ AFC Hornchurch, 19/5/11)
Castle United 4-3 M & B Club

RESERVE DIVISION LEAGUE CUP

FINAL (@ AFC Hornchurch, 17/5/11)
Harold Wood Athletic Res. 3-0 Mountnessing Res.

DIVISION THREE	1	2	3	4	5	6	7	8	9	10	11	12
1 Basildon Town		3-3	0-5	2-0	4-1	2-0	2-3	6-0	4-2	2-0	0-2	1-1
2 Bowers & Pitsea reserves	2-4		2-7	1-2	3-3	3-1	2-4	3-1	4-5	2-3	2-6	4-0
3 Castle United	2-4	3-3		6-1	6-0	3-1	1-1	W-L	8-0	4-3	1-4	14-1
4 Catholic United	0-2	4-2	1-2		2-1	1-3	1-3	3-0	3-1	1-4	0-2	7-3
5 Debden Sports	1-0	2-6	1-1	1-2		3-2	0-2	1-5	4-2	1-2	4-2	6-2
6 Newham United	2-1	4-2	2-3	2-0	5-1		2-3	1-1	4-2	1-1	2-3	4-2
7 Old Southendian	3-2	4-1	3-4	1-4	4-3	2-1		4-0	4-0	4-2	1-5	2-1
8 Ramsden	1-4	2-5	1-7	1-3	1-0	0-2	2-5		2-1	2-1	1-9	1-0
9 Sawbridgeworth Tn res	1-2	1-3	1-4	1-0	2-2	2-3	2-4	1-5		3-0	0-5	3-1
10 Shenfield Association	2-3	3-2	1-5	3-5	0-1	0-3	1-1	8-0	2-0		0-5	0-6
11 Springfield	4-2	7-1	2-2	4-1	0-1	4-2	3-1	2-2	9-1	3-1		4-2
12 Writtle	1-2	2-4	1-9	0-3	3-3	3-2	3-2	2-1	2-2	2-3	1-4	

ESSEX OLYMPIAN LEAGUE DIVISION THREE CONSTITUTION 2011-12

BASILDON TOWN	Selex Sports Ground , Gardiners Lane South , Gardiners Way, Basildon SS14 3AP	01268 883128
CATHOLIC UNITED	SE Essex College Spts Ground, Wellstead Gardens, Westcliff-on-Sea SS0 0AY	01702 348786
CHINGFORD ATHLETIC	Wadham Lodge Sports Ground, Kitchener Road, Walthamstow E17 4JP	020 8527 2444
DEBDEN SPORTS	Chigwell Lane, Loughton, Ilford IG10 3TP	020 8508 9392
NEWHAM UNITED	Cave Road, Plaistow E13 9DX	07939 788048
OLD BARKABBEYANS	Barking Abbey Comprehensive, South Park Drive, Ilford IG11 8UF	None
RAMSDEN	Nursery Sports Ground, Downham Road, Ramsden Heath, Billericay CM11 1PU	01268 711502
SHENFIELD ASSOCIATION	The Drive, Warley, Brentwood CM13 3BH	01277 226816
STAMBRIDGE UNITED	Stambridge Recreation Ground, Rochford Road, Gt Stambridge, Rochford SS4 2AX	01702 258988
TOBY	Fairlop Oak Playing Field, Forest Road, Hainault IG6 3HJ	None
WRITTLE	Paradise Road Playing Fields, Writtle, Chelmsford CM1 3HW	01245 420332

IN: *Chingford Athletic (P), Old Barkabbeyans (P-Essex Business Houses League Premier Division), Stambridge United (P), Toby (P-Essex Business Houses League Premier Division)*

OUT: *Bowers & Pitsea Reserves (S-Essex Senior League Reserve Division), Castle United (P), Old Southendian (P), Sawbridgeworth Town Reserves (S-Essex Senior League Reserve Division), Springfield (P)*

GLOUCESTERSHIRE COUNTY LEAGUE

Sponsored by: Surridge
Founded: 1968
Recent Champions:
2006: Lydney Town
2007: Roman Glass St George
2008: Hardwicke
2009: Slimbridge
2010: Thornbury Town
kentcountyfootballleague.co.uk

		P	W	D	L	F	A	Pts
1	Brimscombe and Thrupp	32	24	4	4	75	30	76
2	AXA	32	17	9	6	46	35	60
3	Chipping Sodbury Town	32	16	10	6	64	35	58
4	Yate Town reserves	32	17	7	8	74	48	58
5	Patchway Town	32	15	7	10	57	46	52
6	Tuffley Rovers	32	15	4	13	55	55	49
7	Henbury	32	13	7	12	51	44	46
8	Kings Stanley	32	14	4	14	60	62	46
9	DRG Stapleton	32	11	10	11	49	52	43
10	Taverners	32	10	10	12	52	51	40
11	Berkeley Town	32	11	6	15	45	60	39
12	Rockleaze Rangers	32	9	9	14	47	55	36
13	Thornbury Town	32	9	8	15	48	56	35
14	Bishops Cleeve reserves (-1)	32	8	8	16	30	45	31
15	Ellwood	32	9	4	19	31	59	31
16	Kingswood	32	7	8	17	50	66	29
17	Hanham Athletic (-3)	32	7	5	20	46	81	23

LES JAMES LEAGUE CUP

ROUND 1
Berkeley Town 1-3 Yate Town reserves
AXA 5-2 Rockleaze Rangers

ROUND 2
Henbury 3-0 Chipping Sodbury Town
Bishops Cleeve reserves 0-2 Ellwood
Patchway Town 0-6 Brimscombe & Thrupp
Tuffley Rovers 1-2 Yate Town reserves
Hanham Athletic 0-1 AXA
Thornbury Town - Bye
DRG 0-2 Taverners
Kingswood 3-1 Kings Stanley

QUARTER FINALS
Brimscombe & Thrupp 2-0 Yate Town reserves
AXA 1-4 Thornbury Town
Henwood 1-0 Ellwood
Taverners 3-2 Kingswood

SEMI-FINALS
Henbury 3-1 Brimscombe & Thrupp
Thornbury Town 1-0 Taverners

FINAL (@ Kingswood, 15/5/11)
Henbury 2-2 Thornbury Town (Henbury won 3-1 on penalties)

		1	2	3	4	5	6	7	8	9	10	11	12	13	14	15	16	17
1	AXA		2-1	2-0	1-3	2-0	1-0	1-0	1-2	2-1	0-3	2-2	1-3	1-0	2-0	2-1	0-2	0-0
2	Berkeley Town	1-2		0-0	0-4	2-1	0-2	2-2	1-3	2-1	1-3	3-1	1-0	3-3	1-1	0-1	0-6	3-2
3	Bishops Cleeve reserves	1-1	0-0		0-1	1-2	1-2	0-1	3-2	1-0	1-2	2-1	1-1	0-3	2-3	2-2	1-2	2-1
4	Brimscombe & Thrupp	0-0	0-1	2-1		1-1	2-0	2-0	4-1	4-0	6-1	5-1	2-1	2-0	2-1	3-2	3-1	2-2
5	Chipping Sodbury Town	0-1	3-5	1-0	4-1		6-0	5-2	4-2	1-0	2-3	2-2	0-0	2-0	2-2	1-0	4-0	1-0
6	DRG Stapleton	3-3	3-1	0-0	2-3	2-1		0-0	2-1	1-3	2-2	4-3	1-1	0-1	2-2	2-1	0-0	1-2
7	Ellwood	1-2	2-4	1-0	1-3	1-3	3-2		2-0	0-1	1-3	1-2	2-0	1-0	0-4	0-1	0-3	2-2
8	Hanham Athletic	1-2	2-1	1-1	0-3	0-6	2-2	0-1		0-0	2-3	1-6	1-3	2-1	2-2	1-8	0-2	1-1
9	Henbury	2-2	4-1	0-2	0-2	1-1	1-4	3-1	2-0		1-1	2-0	2-3	3-2	2-2	2-2	0-1	6-2
10	Kings Stanley	3-5	2-3	1-0	4-2	2-4	1-1	0-1	4-2	0-2		2-2	1-2	2-1	0-3	0-3	2-3	1-2
11	Kingswood	1-3	1-1	2-2	0-3	0-0	1-3	2-1	1-2	0-1	0-3		1-3	1-2	0-1	5-1	6-3	0-5
12	Patchway Town	2-3	2-1	0-1	1-1	0-1	1-0	1-2	2-0	2-0	1-2	3-0		4-1	2-1	4-1	3-3	2-2
13	Rockleaze Rangers	0-0	2-1	6-0	1-5	0-0	1-1	3-0	1-3	1-3	1-0	0-4	2-2		1-0	1-1	1-0	2-3
14	Taverners	1-0	1-2	1-2	0-1	1-1	2-3	2-0	1-5	2-2	1-2	1-1	4-3	2-2		4-0	1-0	4-2
15	Thornbury Town	0-0	1-0	1-2	0-1	1-2	2-1	2-2	3-2	0-3	4-3	1-1	0-1	3-3	1-1		1-4	0-1
16	Tuffley Rovers	0-1	1-0	1-0	3-1	1-1	0-3	3-0	4-3	0-3	0-2	2-3	1-4	2-2	2-1	2-1		1-3
17	Yate Town reserves	1-1	2-3	2-1	0-1	2-2	4-0	3-0	4-2	2-0	3-2	1-0	7-0	4-3	4-0	0-3	5-2	

GLOUCESTERSHIRE COUNTY LEAGUE CONSTITUTION 2011-12

BERKELEY TOWN	Station Road, Berkeley GL13 9AJ	07831 232100
BISHOPS CLEEVE RESERVES	Kayte Lane, Southam, Cheltenham GL52 3PD	01242 676166
BRISTOL ACADEMY	Filton College WISE Campus, New Road, Stoke Gifford, Bristol BS34 8LP	0117 919 2601
CHIPPING SODBURY TOWN	The Ridings, Wickwar Road, Chipping Sodbury, Bristol BS37 6BQ	07787 522100
CRIBBS FRIENDS LIFE	AXA Sports Ground, Station Road, Henbury, Bristol BS10 7TB	0117 950 2303
DRG STAPLETON	Frenchay Park Road, Frenchay, Bristol BS16 1LG	07954 132819
ELLWOOD	Bromley Road, Ellwood, Coleford GL16 7LY	01594 832967
HANHAM ATHLETIC	The Playing Fields Pavilion, 16 Vicarage Road, Hanham, Bristol BS15 3AH	07840 660527
HENBURY	Arnell Drive Playing Field, Lorain Walk, Henbury, Bristol BS10 7AS	0117 959 0475
KINGS STANLEY	Marling Close, Broad Street, Kings Stanley, Stonehouse GL10 3PN	01453 828975
KINGSWOOD	Kingswood PF, Wickwar Road, Kingswood, Wotton-under-Edge GL12 8RF	07971 682091
LONGLEVENS	The Pavilion, Longlevens PF, Longford Lane, Longlevens, Gloucester GL2 9EU	01452 530388
PATCHWAY TOWN	Scott Park, Coniston Road, Patchway, Bristol BS34 5JR	0117 949 3952
ROCKLEAZE RANGERS	Coombe Dingle Sport Complex, Coombe Dingle, Bristol BS9 2BJ	0117 962 6718
TAVERNERS	Nailsworth Primary School, Forest Green, Nailsworth, Stroud GL6 0ET	07826 8419700
THORNBURY TOWN	Mundy Playing Fields, Kington Lane, Thornbury BS35 1NA	01454 413645
TUFFLEY ROVERS	Glevum Park, Lower Tuffley Lane, Gloucester GL2 6DT	01452 423402
YATE TOWN RESERVES	Lodge Road, Yate, Bristol BS37 7LE	Club: 01454 228103

IN: *Bristol Academy (N), Longlevens (P-Glos Northern Senior League Division One)*
OUT: *Brimscombe & Thrupp (P-Division One West)* *AXA become Cribbs Friends Life*

BRIMSCOMBE & THRUPP
Back Row L.R: Phil Baker, Paul Webster, Neil Long, Ian Probert, James Tubbs, Jack Cannon, Oliver Roberts, Mike Beckingham, John Davies, John Dalton, Louise Purse, Adam Thomas, Martin McDermott, Gary Probert.
Front Row: Peter Smith, Kris Murray, Chris Underwood, Ben Jones, Mathew Blythe.

HENBURY
Back Row, L to R: Jo Love, Ed Wright, Aaron Anglin, Vinny Coote, Jack Bebbington, James Loud, Aaron Rosser, Ben Sandle, Phil O'Connell.
Front Row: Adam Rosser, Ross Johnson, Kris Sage, Eddie Howell, Billy George, George Watts.

HAMPSHIRE PREMIER LEAGUE

Sponsored by: Puma Engineering
Founded: 2007
Recent Champions:
2008: AFC Stoneham
2009: Colden Common
2010: Colden Common
bedfordshirefootballleague.co.uk

SENIOR DIVISION	P	W	D	L	F	A	Pts
1 Liphook United	32	25	4	3	118	41	79
2 Team Solent	32	22	2	8	88	47	68
3 University of Portsmouth	32	20	3	9	104	47	63
4 QK Southampton	32	18	5	9	94	58	59
5 Winchester Castle	32	17	5	10	59	39	56
6 Paulsgrove	32	17	3	12	88	54	54
7 Colden Common	32	15	7	10	64	49	52
8 AFC Stoneham	32	15	5	12	64	63	50
9 Otterbourne	32	14	6	12	73	65	48
10 Fleetlands	32	13	7	12	88	66	46
11 Clanfield	32	14	3	15	58	80	45
12 Locks Heath	32	12	7	13	71	68	43
13 Overton United	32	11	2	19	55	85	35
14 Sporting Bishops Waltham	32	9	6	17	49	75	33
15 AFC Aldermaston	32	7	5	20	41	87	26
16 Hamble Club	32	4	2	26	38	119	14
17 Liss Athletic	32	3	0	29	40	149	9
Lyndhurst - record expunged							

SENIOR CUP

ROUND 1
Paulsgrove 1-0 Clanfield
University of Portsmouth 2-3 Lyndhurst

ROUND 2
AFC Stoneham 1-3 Lyndhurst
Fleetlands 2-2 QK Southampton
(Fleetlands won 4-3 on penalties)
Hamble Club 1-2 Team Solent
Liss Athletic 3-2 AFC Aldermaston
Liphook United 4-2 Locks Heath
Overton United 1-4 Colden Common
Paulsgrove 1-2 Otterbourne
Winchester Castle 2-1 Sporting Bishops Waltham

QUARTER FINALS
Fleetlands 5-4 Otterbourne
Liss Athletic 0-2 Colden Common
Team Solent w/o-scr Lyndhurst
Winchester Castle 1-3 Liphook United

SEMI-FINALS
Fleetlands 4-1 Liphook United
Team Solent 3-2 Colden Common

FINAL (@ Gosport Borough, 2/5/11)
Fleetlands 1-1 Team Solent
(Team Solent won 4-2 on penalties)

COMBINATION CUP

FINAL (@ Gosport Borough, 2/5/11)
Liphook United res. 1-4 Sporting Bishops Waltham res.

SENIOR DIVISION	1	2	3	4	5	6	7	8	9	10	11	12	13	14	15	16	17
1 AFC Aldermaston		1-3	2-1	1-3	0-3	1-3	0-5	4-2	1-2	1-1	2-0	1-5	3-1	1-1	0-1	1-5	1-4
2 AFC Stoneham	2-2		1-2	1-4	2-0	2-0	3-7	2-1	2-2	2-1	2-1	4-3	2-0	5-0	0-1	2-4	1-2
3 Clanfield	3-1	1-5		0-1	1-1	7-1	2-1	0-6	5-2	7-2	0-1	3-2	4-1	1-1	1-5	2-1	0-3
4 Colden Common	6-1	1-1	2-2		2-2	3-2	1-2	3-1	3-3	1-4	2-1	1-1	2-3	3-1	0-2	2-0	0-1
5 Fleetlands	3-1	2-2	7-0	0-4		3-1	3-3	6-1	1-2	2-5	1-5	2-2	3-5	1-2	1-4	1-2	2-3
6 Hamble Club	1-1	2-3	1-2	0-2	1-5		0-7	6-2	0-3	0-1	2-5	1-4	1-4	2-4	0-2	2-6	1-4
7 Liphook United	8-3	2-0	8-1	5-1	4-4	2-0		2-1	1-0	6-1	7-2	3-1	3-1	4-0	1-1	5-3	1-3
8 Liss Athletic	1-4	1-3	2-0	1-3	0-5	1-4	1-5		2-9	2-8	0-9	1-7	0-3	0-9	1-4	0-5	0-6
9 Locks Heath	8-0	2-2	1-2	1-0	1-6	7-1	2-2	4-2		2-2	3-1	0-1	2-2	1-2	3-3	1-4	0-3
10 Otterbourne	4-0	4-2	4-0	1-0	1-1	9-0	1-5	3-0	1-0		5-0	0-3	4-4	3-1	0-3	2-2	1-1
11 Overton United	2-1	1-3	1-2	1-2	2-7	2-2	1-3	4-2	3-1	1-0		0-3	0-4	3-2	0-3	0-5	3-2
12 Paulsgrove	3-0	3-0	2-3	2-1	1-2	4-1	2-4	11-0	2-3	2-0	7-1		2-3	3-0	3-2	0-1	2-0
13 QK Southampton	1-2	4-0	1-0	5-1	2-5	9-0	1-0	3-1	6-2	4-0	2-3	3-3		3-3	2-1	3-0	5-1
14 Sporting Bishops Waltham	0-3	0-3	1-3	2-2	2-1	0-1	0-3	3-1	2-0	2-4	4-1	1-3	2-5		0-8	2-3	1-1
15 Team Solent	2-0	1-3	5-3	0-5	2-6	6-2	1-3	1-6	4-0	4-0	4-0	4-1	1-0	3-0		2-5	3-0
16 University of Portsmouth	1-0	6-1	5-0	1-1	3-1	6-0	1-3	11-0	2-3	5-0	2-1	6-0	3-3	0-1	1-4		3-1
17 Winchester Castle	2-2	2-0	3-0	1-2	0-1	2-0	0-3	2-1	0-1	2-1	0-0	3-0	4-1	0-0	0-1	3-2	

HAMPSHIRE PREMIER LEAGUE SENIOR DIVISION CONSTITUTION 2011-12

AFC ALDERMASTON	AWE Recreational Society, Aldermaston, Reading RG7 4PR	0118 982 7614/4544
AFC STONEHAM	Pirelli Sports Ground, Chestnut Avenue, Eastleigh, Southampton SO50 9PF	07765 046429
BOURNEMOUTH SPORTS	Bournemouth Sports Club, Chapel Gate, East Parley, Christchurch BH23 6BD	01202 581933
CLANFIELD	Peel Park, Chalton Lane, Clanfield, Waterlooville PO8 0PR	07765 238231
COLDEN COMMON	Colden Common Rec., Main Road, Colden Common, Winchester SO21 1RP	01962 712365
FLEETLANDS	DARA Fleetlands, Lederle Lane, Gosport PO13 0AA	023 9223 9723
HAMBLE CLUB	Shell Mex Ground, Hamble Lane, Hamble-le-Rice, Southampton SO31 4TS	07818 204400
HEDGE END RANGERS	Norman Rodaway Rec Ground, Heathouse Lane, Hedge End, Southampton SO30 0LE	None
LIPHOOK UNITED	Recreation Ground, London Road, Liphook GU30 7AN	07974 983114
LISS ATHLETIC	Newman Collard Ground, Hill Brow Road, Liss GU33 7LH	07980 424834
LOCKS HEATH	Locksheath Rec, 419 Warsash Rd, Titchfield Common, Fareham PO14 4JX	01489 600932
OTTERBOURNE	Oakwood Park, Oakwood Avenue, Otterbourne SO21 2ED	01962 714681
OVERTON UNITED	Overton Recreation Centre, Bridge Street, Overton RG25 3LZ	01256 770561
PAULSGROVE	Paulsgrove Social Club, Marsden Road, Paulsgrove, Portsmouth PO6 4JB	02392 324102
QK SOUTHAMPTON	Lordshill Recreation Centre, Redbridge Lane, Lordshill, Southampton SO16 0XN	07801 550337
SPORTING BISHOPS WALTHAM	Priory Park, Elizabeth Way, Bishop Waltham, Southampton SO32 1SQ	07740 506777
UNIVERSITY OF PORTSMOUTH	Langston Campus, Furze Lane, Milton, Portsmouth PO4 8LW	023 9284 4526
WINCHESTER CASTLE	Hants Co. Council Spts Ground, Petersfield Rd (A31),Chilcombe, Winchester SO23 8ZB	01962 866989

IN: *Bournemouth Sports (P-Bournemouth League), Hedge End Rangers (P-Hampshire League 2004)*
OUT: *Lyndhurst STJs (WS), Team Solent (P-Wessex League Division One)*

HERTS SENIOR COUNTY LEAGUE

Sponsored by: No sponsor
Founded: 1898
Recent Champions:
2006: Whitewebbs
2007: Whitewebbs
2008: Hatfield Town
2009: Metropolitan Police Bushey
2010: London Lions

PREMIER DIVISION	P	W	D	L	F	A	Pts
1 Hinton	28	20	2	6	66	29	62
2 Letchworth Garden City Eagles	28	18	5	5	87	39	59
3 Metropolitan Police Bushey	28	16	8	4	82	35	56
4 Baldock Town Letchworth	28	16	5	7	63	29	53
5 Codicote	28	14	6	8	63	54	48
6 Sandridge Rovers	28	12	7	9	53	40	43
7 Wormley Rovers	28	12	7	9	53	54	43
8 Cuffley	28	10	8	10	56	51	38
9 Sarratt	28	11	3	14	49	55	36
10 Harpenden Rovers	28	8	11	9	39	47	35
11 Bovingdon	28	8	5	15	42	74	29
12 Chipperfield Corinthians (-7)	28	8	8	12	42	51	25
13 Standon & Puckeridge	28	7	4	17	52	81	25
14 Croxley Guild	28	3	5	20	34	79	14
15 Lemsford	28	3	4	21	29	92	13

AUBERY CUP

ROUND 1
Croxley Guild 0-1 Mill End Sports

ROUND 2
Harpenden Rovers 4-1 Lemsford
Cuffley 3-2 Bovingdon
Bedmond S & S 1-2 Chipperfield Corinthians
Hinton 4-1 Wormley Rovers
AFC Hatfield Town 3-2 Standon & Puckeridge
Evergreen v Letchworth Garden City Eagles (tie awarded to Letchworth Garden City Eagles)
Allenbury's Sports v Mill End Sports (tie awarded to Mill End Sports)
AFC Hertford 0-2 St Peters
London Colney Blues v Bushey Rangers (tie awarded to London Colney Blues)
Codicote 3-4 Eight Bells Old Hatfield
Hertford Heath 5-3 Knebwotrh
Metropolitan Police Bushey 4-0 Belstone
Baldock Town Letchworth 2-1 Sandridge Rovers
Old Parmiterians 3-4 Sarratt
Kimpton Rovers 1-6 Buntingford Town
Goffs Oak 1-0 Whitwell

PREMIER DIVISION	1	2	3	4	5	6	7	8	9	10	11	12	13	14	15
1 AFC Hatfield Town		6-2	5-4	2-1	1-5	6-2	3-4	3-3	4-2	4-5	1-2	1-3	4-0	1-1	3-2
2 AFC Hertford	4-0		0-0	2-2	1-2	1-1	1-1	4-1	1-1	2-1	0-1	1-2	2-2	3-4	1-1
3 Bedmond Sports & Social	2-1	1-3		1-2	1-5	4-1	2-8	2-5	2-1	3-2	1-3	3-2	0-1	2-0	2-1
4 Belstone	3-4	2-2	2-1		2-2	5-0	4-0	3-1	6-0	3-0	0-2	2-3	3-1	4-0	1-2
5 Buntingford Town	7-0	2-6	1-1	2-3		15-0	1-5	4-0	5-0	6-3	6-2	0-7	2-0	0-1	6-0
6 Bushey Rangers	7-1	1-3	3-0	2-2	0-6		1-7	6-1	1-4	3-1	2-4	0-5	3-3	1-2	3-0
7 Goffs Oak	2-1	4-1	3-0	1-3	0-0	W-L		5-2	5-0	1-1	4-0	4-2	5-1	1-2	1-0
8 Hertford Heath	2-3	3-2	4-2	4-1	2-2	3-4	3-2		9-3	3-0	5-0	2-2	3-0	0-5	2-1
9 Kimpton Rovers	2-3	1-1	0-1	0-2	0-3	2-2	0-4	1-6		0-5	0-5	1-6	0-8	1-2	0-5
10 Knebworth	3-1	3-1	0-3	0-0	3-2	2-0	2-2	5-1	2-0		3-1	1-1	0-1	3-0	0-1
11 London Colney Blues	1-0	0-4	2-1	0-4	1-5	3-0	1-5	1-3	3-0	2-1		1-1	2-3	1-2	0-2
12 Mill End Sports	W-L	1-0	3-0	3-1	3-1	8-2	1-5	2-3	6-1	1-1	4-2		5-2	6-2	2-2
13 Old Parmiterians	5-2	4-2	3-0	1-5	2-9	3-3	0-3	2-3	1-1	3-1	1-2	2-4		1-2	0-1
14 St Peter's	2-2	2-2	5-1	1-0	1-5	2-0	1-5	2-1	5-1	6-1	1-1	1-1	1-0		2-1
15 Whitwell Village	2-1	4-1	2-0	3-1	0-3	3-0	0-0	1-5	2-0	4-2	1-3	4-5	2-0	3-2	

HERTS SENIOR COUNTY PREMIER DIVISION CONSTITUTION 2011-12

BALDOCK TOWN	North Herts Arena, Norton Road, Baldock SG6 2EN	01462 892288
BOVINGDON	Green Lane, Bovingdon, Hemel Hempstead HP3 0LA	01442 832628
BUNTINGFORD TOWN	Sainsburys Distribution Centre, London Road, Buntingford SG9 9JR	01763 271522
CHIPPERFIELD CORINTHIANS	Queens Street, Chipperfield, Kings Langley WD4 9BT	07958 744441
CODICOTE	Gosling Sports Park, Stanborough Road, Welwyn Garden City AL8 6XE	01707 331056
CUFFLEY	King George's Playing Fields, Northaw Road East, Cuffley EN6 4LU	07815 174434
GOFFS OAK	Goffs Oak Pavillion, Goffs Oak, Waltham Cross EN7 5ET	None
HINTON	Holtwhites Sports & Social, Kirkland Drive, Enfield EN2 0RU	020 8363 4449
LETCHWORTH GARDEN CITY EAGLES	Pixmore Playing Fields, Ledgers Lane, Baldock Road, Letchworth SG6 2EN	None
METROPOLITAN POLICE BUSHEY	Aldenham Road, Bushey, Watford WD2 3TR	01923 243947 Fax:01923 245963
MILL END SPORTS	King George V Playing Fields, Penn Road, Mill End, Rickmansworth WD3 8QX	01923 776392
SANDRIDGE ROVERS	Spencer Recreation Ground, Sandridge, St Albans AL4 9DD	01727 835506
SARRATT	King George V Playing Fields, George V Way, Sarratt WD3 6AU	None
ST PETERS	Colney Heath FC, Rec Ground, High Street, Colney Heath AL4 0NS	01727 826188
STANDON & PUCKERIDGE	Station Road, Standon, Ware SG11 1QT	01920 823460
WORMLEY ROVERS	Wormley Sports Club, Church Lane, Wormley EN10 7QF	01992 460650

IN: *Buntingford Town (P), Goffs Oak (P), Mill End Sports (P), St Peters (P)*
OUT: *Croxley Guild (R), Harpenden Rovers (W), Lemsford (R)*
Baldock Town Letchworth become Baldock Town

DIVISION ONE		P	W	D	L	F	A	Pts
1	Goffs Oak	28	19	5	4	87	33	62
2	Mill End Sports	28	18	6	4	89	45	60
3	Buntingford Town	28	17	4	7	107	45	55
4	St Peters	28	16	5	7	57	48	53
5	Hertford Heath	28	15	3	10	80	68	48
6	Belstone	28	14	5	9	67	40	47
7	Whitwell	28	14	3	11	50	46	45
8	London Colney Blues	28	13	2	13	46	60	41
9	Knebworth	28	10	5	13	51	55	35
10	AFC Hatfield Town	28	10	3	15	63	78	33
11	AFC Hertford	28	7	10	11	53	53	31
12	Bedmond S & S Club	28	9	2	17	40	68	29
13	Old Parmiterians	28	8	4	16	50	70	28
14	Bushey Rangers	28	6	5	17	48	96	23
15	Kimpton Rovers	28	1	4	23	22	105	7
	Allenbury's Sports - record expunged							
	Eight Bells Old Hatfield - record expunged							

RESERVE DIVISION ONE		P	W	D	L	F	A	Pts
1	Baldock Town L'wth res	18	12	3	3	59	27	39
2	Hinton reserves	18	12	2	4	54	27	38
3	Cuffley reserves	18	10	4	4	43	29	34
4	Ch'field Corinthians res	18	10	2	6	44	30	32
5	Codicote reserves	18	9	2	7	43	39	29
6	Bovingdon reserves	18	7	3	8	31	43	24
7	Sarratt reserves	18	7	1	10	34	51	22
8	Wormley Rovers res	18	5	3	10	35	47	18
9	Met Police Bushey res	18	3	3	12	32	55	12
10	Croxley Guild reserves	18	3	1	14	21	48	10
	Evergreen reserves - record expunged							

RESERVE DIVISION TWO		P	W	D	L	F	A	Pts
1	Letchworth G C Eagl res	18	14	3	1	68	25	45
2	Sandridge Rovers res	18	12	2	4	40	28	38
3	Harpenden Rovers res	18	11	2	5	76	26	35
4	Buntingford Town res	18	11	2	5	41	32	35
5	Knebworth reserves	18	8	1	9	53	36	25
6	Bedmond S & S Club res	18	7	4	7	50	47	25
7	Lemsford reserves	18	6	5	7	43	42	23
8	Mill End Sports reserves	18	6	3	9	36	49	21
9	Old Parmiterians res	18	2	2	14	25	64	8
10	Bushey Rangers reserves	18	1	0	17	17	100	3

AUBERY CUP continued...

ROUND 3

Buntingford Town 3-1 St Peters

Sarratt 6-2 AFC Hatfield Town

Goffs Oak 0-2 Metropolitan Police Bushey

Letchworth Garden City Eagles 5-1 Chipperfield Corinthians

Hinton 2-0 Cuffley

Eight Bells Old Hatfield 0-3 Mill End Sports

Baldock Town Letchworth v Bushey Rangers (tie awarded to Baldock Town Letchworth)

QUARTER FINALS

Buntingford Town 1-4 Baldock Town Letchworth

Letchworth Garden City Eagles 4-0 Sarratt

Harpenden Rovers 3-1 Hinton

Mill End Sports 1-2 Metropolitan Police Bushey

SEMI-FINALS

Harpenden Rovers 2-1 Metropolitan Police Bushey

Baldock Town Letchworth 0-3 Letchworth Garden City Eagles

FINAL (@ Herts County FA Ground, 2/5/11)

Harpenden Rovers 1-4 Letchworth Garden City Eagles

RESERVES CUP

FINAL (@ Herts County FA Ground, 2/5/11)

Harpenden Rovers reserves 1-4 Codicote reserves

DIVISION ONE	1	2	3	4	5	6	7	8	9	10	11	12	13	14	15
1 AFC Hatfield Town		6-2	5-4	2-1	1-5	6-2	3-4	3-3	4-2	4-5	1-2	1-3	4-0	1-1	3-2
2 AFC Hertford	4-0		0-0	2-2	1-2	1-1	1-1	4-1	1-1	2-1	0-1	1-2	2-2	3-4	1-1
3 Bedmond Sports & Social	2-1	1-3		1-2	1-5	4-1	2-8	2-5	2-1	3-2	1-3	3-2	0-1	2-0	2-1
4 Belstone	3-4	2-2	2-1		2-2	5-0	4-0	3-1	6-0	3-0	0-2	2-3	3-1	4-0	1-2
5 Buntingford Town	7-0	2-6	1-1	2-3		15-0	1-5	4-0	5-0	6-3	6-2	0-7	2-0	0-1	6-0
6 Bushey Rangers	7-1	1-3	3-0	2-2	0-6		1-7	6-1	1-4	3-1	2-4	0-5	3-3	1-2	3-0
7 Goffs Oak	2-1	4-1	3-0	1-3	0-0	W-L		5-2	5-0	1-1	4-0	4-2	5-1	1-2	1-0
8 Hertford Heath	2-3	3-2	4-2	4-1	2-2	3-4	3-2		9-3	3-0	5-0	2-2	3-0	0-5	2-1
9 Kimpton Rovers	2-3	1-1	0-1	0-2	0-3	2-2	0-4	1-6		0-5	0-5	1-6	0-8	1-2	0-5
10 Knebworth	3-1	3-1	0-3	0-0	3-2	2-0	2-2	5-1	2-0		3-1	1-1	0-1	3-0	0-1
11 London Colney Blues	1-0	0-4	2-1	0-4	1-5	3-0	1-5	1-3	3-0	2-1		1-1	2-3	1-2	0-2
12 Mill End Sports	W-L	1-0	3-0	3-1	3-1	8-2	1-5	2-3	6-1	1-1	4-2		5-2	6-2	2-2
13 Old Parmiterians	5-2	4-2	3-0	1-5	2-9	3-3	0-3	2-3	1-1	3-1	1-2	2-4		1-2	0-1
14 St Peter's	2-2	2-2	5-1	1-0	1-5	2-0	1-5	2-1	5-1	6-1	1-1	1-1	1-0		2-1
15 Whitwell Village	2-1	4-1	2-0	3-1	0-3	3-0	0-0	1-5	2-0	4-2	1-3	4-5	2-0	3-2	

HERTS ENIOR COUNTY DIVISION ONE CONSTITUTION 2011-12

AFC HATFIELD TOWN	Birchwood Leisure Centre, Birchwood, Longmead, Hatfield AL10 0AN	01707 270772
BEDMOND SPORTS & SOCIAL	Toms Lane Recreation Ground, Toms Lane, Bedmond, Abbots Langley WD5 0RB	01923 267991
BELSTONE	The Medburn Ground, Watling Street, Radlett WD6 3AB	020 8207 2395
BUSHEY RANGERS	Moatfield, Bournehall Lane, Bushey WD23 3JU	020 8386 1875
CROXLEY GUILD	Croxley Guild of Sport, The Green, Croxley Green, Watford WD3 3JX	01923 770534
EVERGREEN	South Way, Abbotts Langley WD4 8PN	01923 267812
HERTFORD HEATH	The Playing Field, Trinity Road, Hertford Heath SG13 7QS	None
HERTFORD TOWN	Hertingfordbury Park, West Street, Hertford SG13 8EZ	01992 583716
KIMPTON ROVERS	Kimpton Recreation Ground, High Street, Kimpton, Hitchin SG4 8RA	None
KNEBWORTH	The Recreation Ground, Watton Road, Knebworth, Stevenage SG3 6AH	None
LEMSFORD	Welwyn Playing Fields, Ottway Walk, Welwyn AL6 9AT	None
LONDON COLNEY BLUES	Morris Playing Field, White Horse Lane, London Colney AL2 1JP	None
OLD PARMITERIANS	Thomas Parmiter Sports Centre, Garston, Watford WD25 0JU	01923 682805
PANSHANGER	Moneyhole Lane Playing Fields, Sylvan Way, Welwyn Garden City AL7 2RT	None
WARE TRINITY	Fanhams Hall Road, Ware SG12 7NN	None
WHITWELL VILLAGE	King George V Recreation Grnd, Bradway, Whitwell SG4 8BE	None

IN: *Croxley Guild (R), Evergreen (P), Lemsford (R), Panshanger (P), Ware Trinity (P)*

OUT: *Allenburys Sports (WS), Buntingford Town (P), Eight Bells Old Hatfield (WS), Goffs Oak (P), Mill End Sports (P), St Peters (P)*

KENT COUNTY LEAGUE

Sponsored by: Haart
Founded: 1922
Recent Champions:
2006: Lewisham Borough (Community)
2007: Holmesdale
2008: Norton Sports
2009: Hollands & Blair
2010: Stansfield O & B Club

PREMIER DIVISION	P	W	D	L	F	A	Pts
1 Hollands & Blair	30	22	6	2	76	24	72
2 Canterbury City	30	17	4	9	69	54	55
3 Cray Valley (PM)	30	15	7	8	73	39	52
4 Bridon Ropes	30	15	7	8	55	40	52
5 Phoenix Sports	30	14	5	11	55	50	47
6 Bearsted	30	12	10	8	49	51	46
7 Lewisham Borough (Community)	30	13	5	12	50	41	44
9 Charlton Athletic Community	30	12	8	10	58	59	44
10 Woodstock Park	30	10	7	13	36	54	37
11 Sutton Athletic (-1)	30	10	6	14	54	53	35
12 Fleet Leisure	30	10	5	15	44	67	35
13 Stansfeld O&B Club	30	9	7	14	48	58	34
14 Rusthall	30	9	4	17	41	52	31
15 Bly Spartans	30	6	7	17	45	60	25
16 Tonbridge Invicta (-1)	29	5	5	20	31	64	19

DIVISION ONE EAST	P	W	D	L	F	A	Pts
1 Bromley Green	24	19	4	1	84	26	61
2 APM	24	18	5	1	81	22	59
3 Bredhurst Juniors (-1)	24	16	5	3	60	32	52
4 Staplehurst & Mon U	24	11	5	8	58	48	38
5 Sheerness East	24	10	4	10	37	39	34
6 Otford United	24	8	6	10	31	44	30
7 Milton & Fuls. U (-1)	24	8	5	11	47	56	28
8 Univ. of Kent (-4)	24	9	3	12	58	49	26
9 New Romney	24	6	6	12	39	55	24
10 Kennington	24	6	5	13	35	72	23
11 Sheppey United (-1)	24	6	6	12	34	74	23
12 Premier	24	6	3	15	47	58	21
13 Larkfield & NH W	24	1	7	16	31	67	10

DIVISION ONE WEST	P	W	D	L	F	A	Pts
1 Farnborough OB Gld	22	13	5	4	46	24	44
2 Eltham Palace	22	13	5	4	40	23	44
3 Tudor Sports	22	13	2	7	36	30	41
4 Orpington	22	10	2	10	33	33	32
5 Greenways	22	8	6	8	41	28	30
6 Metrogas	22	8	5	9	43	33	29
7 Chipstead	22	8	4	10	41	41	28
8 Coney Hall	22	8	4	10	34	37	28
9 Forest Hill Park	22	7	4	11	42	49	25
10 AFC Sevenoaks	22	7	4	11	31	56	25
11 Belvedere	22	6	6	10	29	40	24
12 Crockenhill	22	4	7	11	21	43	19

Wickham Park - record expunged

BILL MANLOW INTER REGIONAL CHALLENGE CUP

ROUND 1 EAST
APM 0-3 Bredhurst Juniors
Bromley Green 1-3 Sheppey United
Larkfield & New Hythe Wanderers 2-3 Kennington

ROUND 2 EAST
Milton & Fulston United w/o-scr Premier
Otford United 1-1 Sheerness East
(Otford United won 7-6 on penalties)
Kennington 1-3 Bly Spartans
Hollands & Blair 3-2 Woodstock Park
University of Kent 0-4 Bearsted
Snodland 3-2 Canterbury City
Sheppey United 2-4 Staplehurst & Monarchs United
New Romney 3-2 Bredhurst Juniors

ROUND 3 EAST
Staplehurst & Monarchs United 0-3 Bearsted
Bly Spartans 5-1 New Romney
Milton & Fulston United 2-6 Hollands & Blair
Otford United 2-3 Snotland

ROUND 1 WEST
Eltham Palace 0-4 Phoenix Sports
Orpington 4-2 Greenways
Belvedere 0-3 Tudor Sports
Coney Hall 3-0 Chipstead
Wickham Park 1-5 AFC Sevenoaks
Metrogas 2-1 Forest Hall Park
Farnborough Old Boys Guild 3-1 Crockenhill

ROUND 2 WEST
Farnborough OBG 3-0 Coney Hall
Stansfeld O & B Club 0-4 Sutton Athletic
Phoenix Sports 0-2 Orpington
Cray Valley (PM) 2-2 Charlton Athletic Community
(Cray Valley (PM) won 6-5 on penalties)
Metrogas 0-2 Tonbridge Invicta
Fleet Leisure 1-0 Bridon Ropes
AFC Sevenoaks 2-1 Lewisham Borough (Community)
Rusthall 1-3 Tudor Sports

ROUND 3 WEST
Sutton Athletic 2-1 Fleet Leisure
Orpington 4-1 AFC Sevenoaks
Farnborough OBG 1-0 Tonbridge Invicta
Tudor Sports 0-1 Cray Valley (PM)

QUARTER FINALS
Bearsted 2-4 Cray Valley (PM)
Snodland 1-2 Bly Spartans
Farnborough OBG 2-3 Sutton Athletic
Orpington 2-1 Hollands & Blair

SEMI-FINALS
Cray Valley (PM) 2-1 Orpington
Bly Spartans 0-2 Sutton Athletic

FINAL (@ Chatham Town, 5/5/11)
Cray Valley (PM) 1-3 Sutton Athletic

PREMIER DIVISION	1	2	3	4	5	6	7	8	9	10	11	12	13	14	15	16
1 Bearsted		4-1	2-3	1-2	2-2	0-7	1-6	1-1	1-1	3-3	1-0	1-1	0-3	1-0	W-L	0-2
2 Bly Spartans	0-1		1-2	1-3	0-0	1-1	1-2	1-1	1-2	1-2	3-1	2-4	1-3	0-4	0-1	4-2
3 Bridon Ropes	2-2	3-0		1-1	3-1	3-2	0-1	0-1	2-0	0-1	1-0	2-2	0-0	2-1	2-0	3-0
4 Canterbury City	0-3	4-3	2-1		4-2	3-2	5-1	0-2	2-0	3-1	3-1	6-1	5-4	3-3	1-3	1-1
5 Charlton Athletic Community	2-2	1-1	0-2	2-2		1-1	3-1	1-3	1-0	0-2	2-1	2-3	2-2	3-1	1-0	2-2
6 Cray Valley P M	3-1	2-1	0-1	3-1	1-5		4-1	1-2	0-1	2-0	0-0	9-0	5-1	2-1	3-3	0-0
7 Fleet Leisure	0-5	3-3	2-1	0-1	1-4	1-2		0-5	1-2	1-2	3-0	1-1	3-2	1-0	2-0	0-1
8 Hollands & Blair	1-1	2-0	2-0	2-0	2-1	2-1	6-0		1-2	1-0	5-1	3-0	1-1	2-0	9-1	2-0
9 Lewisham Borough (Community)	0-1	0-3	2-2	2-1	5-1	2-4	2-1	3-3		3-1	0-1	1-1	0-2	2-0	3-1	1-2
10 Phoenix Sports	1-3	3-2	2-5	2-1	6-0	1-1	5-5	2-3	0-2		2-1	1-1	3-1	1-2	2-0	2-3
11 Rusthall	1-1	1-1	2-4	3-2	2-3	0-3	4-0	2-4	3-1	1-2		2-3	4-1	3-0	0-2	2-0
12 Snodland	1-2	2-4	1-2	0-1	3-2	0-3	0-0	2-4	0-5	1-2	1-0		3-0	1-0	3-0	1-1
14 Stansfeld O & B Club	1-2	1-2	4-2	2-4	2-3	0-3	3-3	0-0	2-1	1-0	1-2	0-1		1-1	4-3	1-0
15 Sutton Athletic	3-2	0-3	3-3	5-4	3-4	3-3	4-1	0-2	2-1	2-3	1-0	0-0	1-1		3-0	6-1
16 Tonbridge Invicta	2-2	2-2	3-3	2-3	2-5	2-4	0-1	0-2	0-0	1-3	0-1	0-1	1-3	1-0		1-0
17 Woodstock Park	2-3	3-2	2-0	0-1	0-2	2-1	0-2	3-2	1-6	0-0	2-2	1-1	2-1	2-5	1-0	

KENT COUNTY LEAGUE PREMIER DIVISION CONSTITUTION 2011-12

APM CONTRAST Cobdown Sports & Social Club, Ditton Corner, Station Road, Aylesford ME20 6AU 01622 717771
BREDHURST JUNIORS Sheppey Sports Club, Holm Place, Halfway, Sheerness ME12 3DG 01795 668054
BROMLEY GREEN Waterside, Turner Close, Newton Rd, South Willesborough, Ashford TN24 0BB 01233 645982
CHARLTON ATHLETIC COMMUNITY Eltham Town FC, Starbuck Close, Eltham SE9 2TD 07932 913817
ELTHAM PALACE Green Court Sports Ground, Green Court Road, Crockenhill, Swanley BR8 8HE 01322 666442
FARNBOROUGH OLD BOYS GUILD Farnborough (Kent) Sports Club, High Street, Farnborough BR6 7BA 01689 862949
FLEET LEISURE Fleet Leisure Sports Club, Nelson Road, Northfleet DA11 7EE 01474 359222
GREENWAYS Fleet Leisure Sports Club, Nelson Road, Northfleet DA11 7EE 01474 359222
SHEERNESS EAST Sheerness East WMC, 47 Queensborough Road, Halfway, Sheerness ME12 3BZ 01795 662049
SNODLAND Potyn's Field, Paddlesworth Road, Snodland ME6 5DL 01634 241946
STANSFELD O & B CLUB Metrogas Sports Grd, Marathon PF, Forty Foot Way, Avery Hill Rd, New Eltham SE9 2EX 020 8859 1579
STAPLEHURST & MONARCHS UNITED Jubilee Sports Ground, Headcorn Road, Staplehurst TN12 0DS 07703 288622
TONBRIDGE INVICTA Swanmead Sports Ground, Swanwead Way, off Cannon Lane, Tonbridge TN9 1PP 01732 350473
TUDOR SPORTS STC Sports Ground, Ivor Grove, New Eltham SE9 2AJ 020 8850 2057

***IN:** APM Contrast (formerly APM), (P-Division One East), Bredhurst Juniors (P-Division One East), Bromley Green (P-Division One East), Eltham Palace (P-Division One West), Farnborough Old Boys Guild (P-Division One West), Greenways (P-Division One West), Sheerness East (P-Division One East), Staplehurst & Monarchs United (P-Division One East), Tudor Sports (P-Division One West)*

***OUT:** Bearsted (P-Kent Invicta League), Bly Spartans (P-Kent Invicta League), Bridon Ropes (P-Kent Invicta League), Canterbury City (P-Kent League Premier Division), Cray Valley Paper Mills (P-Kent League Premier Division), Crockenhill (P-Kent Invicta League), Hollands & Blair (P-Kent Invicta League), Lewisham Borough (Community) (P-Kent Invicta League), Lydd Town (P-Kent Invicta League), Meridian Sports (P-Kent Invicta League), Orpington (P-Kent Invicta League), Phoenix Sports (P-Kent Invicta League), Rusthall (P-Kent Invicta League), Sutton Athletic (P-Kent Invicta League), Woodstock Park (P-Kent Invicta League)*

DIVISION ONE EAST	1	2	3	4	5	6	7	8	9	10	11	12	13
1 APM		2-2	3-3	8-1	4-0	3-0	2-0	5-0	4-2	2-1	10-1	1-0	4-0
2 Bredhurst Juniors	0-0		2-2	2-0	2-0	2-1	1-0	2-1	W-L	4-2	7-1	4-5	5-2
3 Bromley Green	3-2	0-0		8-1	2-1	7-0	3-0	3-2	W-L	3-1	13-0	4-0	3-2
4 Kennington	0-1	2-1	1-3		4-1	2-1	1-4	1-1	4-4	0-0	1-3	1-4	4-3
5 Larkfield & New HW	0-4	3-4	3-3	2-2		1-1	4-1	1-1	1-4	2-3	2-3	2-3	1-9
6 Milton & Fulston United	3-9	1-4	2-1	5-1	3-0		3-3	2-2	5-1	1-4	4-0	2-3	2-0
7 New Romney	0-3	3-1	1-8	1-2	1-1	0-0		1-2	2-4	1-2	3-3	1-0	2-2
8 Otford United	0-4	1-3	0-4	3-1	2-0	0-2	1-3		1-0	2-1	2-2	2-2	2-1
9 Premier	L-W	1-3	L-W	5-2	3-2	4-4	4-3	1-3		L-W	4-1	4-4	2-7
10 Sheerness East	1-2	1-3	0-2	1-1	0-0	4-3	3-1	0-2	W-L		2-1	2-0	2-3
11 Sheppey United	2-5	1-1	2-4	1-2	1-1	0-2	1-1	1-0	3-2	2-0		2-1	1-4
12 Staplehurst & Mon Utd	2-2	1-4	1-2	6-1	3-1	4-0	3-4	1-1	5-1	4-4	2-1		2-1
13 University of Kent	1-1	2-3	2-3	4-0	4-2	1-0	1-3	3-0	4-1	0-3	1-1	1-2	

DIVISION ONE WEST	1	2	3	4	5	6	7	8	9	10	11	12
1 AFC Sevenoaks		4-2	0-2	1-2	2-2	2-5	1-2	1-0	0-0	2-1	2-2	0-2
2 Belvedere	0-3		0-0	0-1	2-0	0-2	0-0	3-5	2-1	2-0	2-3	0-1
3 Chipstead	7-0	2-2		1-2	2-2	1-3	2-5	5-3	0-0	1-0	1-2	4-1
4 Coney Hall	0-2	3-1	0-4		4-1	2-2	2-2	5-2	0-0	2-2	1-2	0-1
5 Crockenhill	0-4	0-0	3-2	1-0		0-0	0-1	2-0	1-1	1-5	1-3	0-2
6 Eltham Palace	1-2	2-2	1-0	2-0	2-2		2-1	2-0	2-3	2-1	0-1	1-1
7 Farnborough O B Guild	1-1	4-0	4-0	3-2	3-0	0-1		5-1	0-5	1-1	2-0	3-1
8 Forest Hill Park	5-2	1-1	5-1	3-5	0-1	2-3	2-2		2-1	2-2	2-0	2-4
9 Greenways	9-0	2-4	3-0	3-1	2-2	1-2	0-2	0-0		2-0	0-1	1-0
10 Metrogas	4-2	1-2	2-1	1-2	4-1	0-2	0-1	3-0	6-2		4-1	1-1
11 Orpington	5-0	1-2	1-2	2-0	3-1	1-3	0-3	0-1	0-3	2-2		3-0
12 Tudor Sports	4-0	4-2	2-3	1-0	1-0	1-0	3-1	1-4	3-2	1-3	1-0	

KENT COUNTY LEAGUE DIVISION ONE (MERGER OF ONE EAST & WEST) CONSTITUTION 2011-12

AFC SEVENOAKS Waller Park, Wood Lane, Darenth, Dartford DA2 7LR 01322 221006
BELVEDERE War Memorial Sports Ground, 101a Woolwich Road, Abbey Wood SE2 0DY 01322 436724
CHIPSTEAD Chipstead Rec, Chevening Road, Chipstead, Sevenoaks TN13 2SA 07753 603944
CONEY HALL Tiepigs Lane, Coney Hall, Bromley BR4 9BT 020 8462 9103
FLEETDOWN UNITED Heath Lane Open Space, Heath Lane (Lower), Dartford DA1 2QE 01322 273848
FOREST HILL PARK Ladywell Arena, Doggett Road, Catford SE6 4QX 020 8314 1986
HILDENBOROUGH ATHLETIC Racecourse Sports Ground, The Slade, Tonbridge TN9 1DS 07595 386657
KENNINGTON Kennington Cricket Club, Ulley Road, Kennington, Ashford TN24 9HY 07887 995219
METROGAS Marathon Playing Fields, Forty Foot Way, Avery Hill Road, New Eltham SE9 2EX 020 8859 1579
MILTON & FULSTON UNITED UK Paper Sports Ground, Gore Court Road, Sittingbourne ME10 1QN 01795 477047
NEW ROMNEY The Maud Pavilion, Station Road, New Romney TN28 8LQ 07710 077702
OTFORD UNITED Otford Recreation Ground, High Street, Otford, Sevenoaks TN14 5PG 07802 736279
SAGA SPORTS & SOCIAL South Road, Hythe CT21 6AR 07772 108324
SHEPPEY UNITED Holm Place, Queensborough Road, Sheerness ME12 3DD 07729 290351
UNIVERSITY OF KENT The Oast House, Park Wood Road, Giles Lane, University of Kent, Canterbury CT2 7SY 01227 827430

***IN:** Fleetdown United (P-Division Two West), Hildenborough Athletic (P-Division Two West), Saga Sports & Social (P-Division Two East)*

EASTERN SECTION LES LECKIE CUP

ROUND 1
Sheerness East 3-0 Larkfield & New Hythe Wanderers
Lydd Town 0-3 APM
Tenterden Town 4-1 Saint Nicholas
Saga Sports & Social 1-0 Platt United
NK Aces 0-3 Bredhurst Juniors
Chartham Sports scr-w/o New Romney
Guru Nanak 1-3 Swale United
Premier 1-7 Otford United
Sheppey United 1-3 University of Kent
Broadstairs 1-0 Kennington

ROUND 2
Staplehurst & Monarchs United 5-3 Hawkenbury
Malgo 2-4 Saga Sports & Social
New Romney 2-3 Otford United
Swale United 2-1 Borden Village
Bromley Green 3-0 Broadstairs
University of Kent 3-1 Tenterden Town
Bredhurst Juniors 2-1 APM
Milton & Fulston United 1-2 Sheerness East

QUARTER FINALS
Staplehurst & Monarchs United 1-2 Bredhurst Juniors
Sheerness East 0-2 Bromley Green
University of Kent 1-2 Saga Sports & Social
Swale United 1-1 Otford United
(Swale United won 7-6 on penalties)

SEMI-FINALS
Swale United 1-3 Bromley Green
Bredhurst Juniors 1-1 Saga Sports & Social
(Saga Sports & Social won 5-4 on penalties)

FINAL (@ Faversham Town, 26/4/11)
Bromley Green 0-1 Saga Sports & Social

BARRY BUNDOCK WEST KENT SHIELD

ROUND 1
Bexlians 2-5 Metrogas
Belvedere 4-1 Seven Acre Sports
Hildenborough Athletic 4-0 Bexley
Westerham 2-3 Tudor Sports
Farnborough Old Boys Guild 3-0 AFC Sevenoaks
Bexley Borough 2-2 Fleetdown United
(Fleetdown United won on penalties)
Forest Hall Park 4-1 Crofton Albion (@ Crofton Albion)
Meridian 0-3 Blackheath United
Wickham Park 1-3 Coney Hall
Halls 0-2 Orpington

ROUND 2
Blackheath United 1-2 Lanes End
Belvedere 1-1 Greenways (Belvedere won 5-4 on penalties)
Metrogas 1-2 Tudor Sports
Fleetdown United 2-3 Erith 147 Sports
Hildenborough Athletic 1-0 Chipstead
Coney Hall 1-3 Forest Hall Park
Farnborough Old Boys Guild 1-0 Crockenhill
Orpington 3-2 Eltham Palace

QUARTER FINALS
Hildenborough Athletic 3-2 Belvedere
Farnborough Old Boys Guild 1-3 Erith 147 Sports
Forest Hall Park 3-0 Lanes End
Tudor Sports 1-0 Orpington

SEMI-FINALS
Erith 147 Sports 2-3 Forest Hall Park
Hildenborough Athletic 3-2 Tudor Sports

FINAL (@ Sevenoaks Town, 11/5/11)
Forest Hill Park 1-0 Hildenborough Athletic

DIVISION TWO EAST	P	W	D	L	F	A	Pts
1 Saga Sports & Social	20	15	3	2	54	21	48
2 Lydd Town	20	14	5	1	71	21	47
3 Swale United	20	13	3	4	47	23	42
4 Platt United	20	10	3	7	50	38	33
5 N K Aces	20	10	3	7	40	39	33
6 Malgo	20	6	6	8	49	42	24
7 Guru Nanak	20	7	1	12	39	59	22
8 Hawkenbury	20	6	2	12	36	46	20
9 Borden Village	20	6	1	13	33	55	19
10 Broadstairs (-1)	20	4	4	12	35	55	15
11 Tenterden Town	20	3	1	16	25	80	10
St Nicholas - record expunged							

DIVISION TWO WEST	P	W	D	L	F	A	Pts
1 Hildenborough Ath	24	20	1	3	90	29	61
2 Fleetdown United	24	15	3	6	53	26	48
3 Erith 147	24	13	7	4	54	30	46
4 Seven Acre Sports	24	14	3	7	63	44	45
5 Bexley	24	12	7	5	51	33	43
6 Bexlians	24	10	7	7	61	46	37
7 Blackheath Utd (-1)	24	11	5	8	38	40	37
8 Halls	24	7	6	11	38	48	27
9 Crofton Albion	24	7	5	12	41	46	26
10 Bexley Borough	24	6	4	14	23	52	22
11 Lanes End	24	6	2	16	38	58	20
12 Meridian (-1)	24	4	4	16	32	73	15
13 Westerham (-1)	24	3	2	19	23	80	10

DIVISION ONE EAST	1	2	3	4	5	6	7	8	9	10	11
1 Borden Village		3-1	1-4	5-0	2-1	2-7	0-1	1-7	4-1	0-1	4-2
2 Broadstairs	0-0		2-0	2-3	2-5	3-1	0-2	0-0	0-6	2-4	7-2
3 Guru Nanak	4-2	2-1		1-3	1-2	4-3	3-1	2-4	1-4	2-5	4-1
4 Hawkenbury	4-3	3-4	1-1		0-1	1-4	3-1	7-1	1-2	0-3	4-2
5 Lydd Town	5-1	6-2	10-2	4-0		1-1	8-1	2-0	0-0	3-2	4-0
6 Malgo	4-1	1-1	4-3	2-2	1-4		1-1	2-4	1-2	2-2	4-1
7 N K Aces	3-2	3-2	3-0	2-1	0-4	3-2		6-2	0-1	2-3	3-0
8 Platt United	2-0	4-1	5-0	2-1	2-2	3-3	3-2		2-3	0-1	7-1
9 Saga Sports & Social	5-0	2-0	5-3	2-1	2-2	3-2	1-1	1-0		3-1	10-1
10 Swale United	2-0	2-2	0-1	3-1	1-1	1-0	1-3	2-0	1-0		5-0
11 Tenterden Town	1-2	6-3	2-1	1-0	1-6	0-4	2-2	1-2	0-1	1-7	

DIVISION TWO WEST	1	2	3	4	5	6	7	8	9	10	11	12	13
1 Bexley		5-0	2-2	2-2	1-0	1-3	2-1	1-1	3-3	3-2	2-1	3-1	5-0
2 Bexley Borough	0-3		0-2	1-0	2-2	0-2	1-4	1-3	0-3	2-1	3-0	0-5	2-0
3 Bexlians	1-1	2-2		2-2	0-1	2-3	3-2	2-1	0-3	5-2	3-1	0-3	5-3
4 Blackheath United	2-1	2-0	0-3		2-1	0-5	1-3	2-1	2-1	2-0	3-2	6-2	2-0
5 Crofton Albion	2-2	3-0	3-0	1-1		0-2	1-3	0-0	3-6	2-1	6-0	2-2	4-2
6 Erith 147	2-0	2-0	3-3	1-1	2-3		1-1	1-1	0-2	3-1	7-1	3-2	3-3
7 Fleetdown United	0-2	0-0	2-2	1-0	3-1	3-0		1-0	0-1	5-0	4-0	2-1	4-2
8 Halls	2-2	0-1	0-4	1-3	2-1	0-0	1-2		1-7	2-1	2-5	1-2	9-0
9 Hildenborough Athletic	1-2	4-1	4-3	3-0	6-1	3-2	3-2	8-0		2-1	4-1	2-4	5-0
10 Lanes End	1-4	2-1	3-3	2-3	2-1	1-4	2-0	1-2	1-4		2-1	1-2	4-1
11 Meridian S & S	2-3	1-1	0-6	3-2	2-0	1-1	0-5	1-4	0-2	2-2		0-3	1-3
12 Seven Acre Sports	3-1	6-4	4-3	4-0	3-2	1-2	1-2	2-2	2-3	4-2	2-2		2-1
13 Westerham	1-0	0-1	1-5	0-0	2-1	0-2	1-3	0-2	0-10	0-3	3-5	0-2	

KENT COUNTY LEAGUE DIVISION TWO EAST CONSTITUTION 2011-12

BORDEN VILLAGE	Borden Playstool, Wises Lane, Borden, Sittingbourne ME9 8LP	07921 912209
BROADSTAIRS	Jackey Bakers Sports Groud, Highfield Road, Ramsgate CT12 6QX	01843 592166
DEAL TOWN RANGERS	Castle Community College, Mill Road, Deal CT14 9HH	01304 373363
GREENHILL	Bridge Road Recreation Ground, Bridge, Canterbury CT4 5BL	07804 822533
GURU NANAK	Guru Nanak Sports Ground, Khalsa Avenue, Gravesend DA12 1LV	07956 514264
HADLOW EVOLUTION	Hadlow College, Hadlow TN11 0EH	07973 489377
HAWKENBURY	Hawkenbury Recreation Ground, Hawkenbury Road, Tunbridge Wells TN2 5BJ	07899 806170
LARKFIELD & NEW HYTHE WANDERERS	Larkfield & NH Sports Club, New Hythe Lane, Larkfield, Maidstone ME20 6PU	07724 050971
MALGO	The Old County Ground, Norman Road, West Malling ME19 6RL	07850 751795
NK ACES	Istead Rise Community Centre, Worcester Close, Gravesend DA13 9LB	01474 833903
PLATT UNITED	Stonehouse Field, Longmill Lane, St Marys Platt, Sevenoaks TN15 8ND	07702 634344
SEVENOAKS	Greatness Park, Seal Road (on main A25), Sevenoaks TN14 5BL	01732 741987
SWALE UNITED	UK Paper Sports Ground, Gore Court Road, Sittingbourne ME10 1QN	01795 564213
TENTERDEN TOWN	Recreation Ground Road, High Street, Tenterden TN30 6RB	07720 785001

IN: *Deal Town Rangers (youth football), Greenhill (N), Larkfield & New Hythe Wanderers (R), Sevenoaks (N)*
OUT: *Premier (W), Saga Sports & Social (P), St Nicholas (WS)*

KENT COUNTY LEAGUE DIVISION TWO WEST CONSTITUTION 2011-12

AFC MOTTINGHAM	Coldharbour Leisure Centre, Chapel Farm Road, New Eltham SE9 3LX	020 8851 8692
BEXLEIANS	Footscray Sports Club, 239 Footscray Road, London SE9 2EL	020 8850 4698
BEXLEY	St Marys Recreation Ground, Lesley Close, Bourne Road, Bexley DA5 1LX	07944 552763
BEXLEY BOROUGH	Apex Arena, Danson Yth Centre, Brampton Road, Bexleyheath DA7 4EZ	020 8303 6052
BLACKHEATH UNITED	Segas Sports Ground, Worsley Bridge Road, Beckenham BR3 1RL	07773 716607
CROFTON ALBION	Crofton Albion Sports & Social, Weigall Road, Lee SE12 8HF	020 8856 8385
DULWICH VILLAGE	Dulwich Sports Ground, Tierney Road, Dulwich SE21 7JH	020 7733 7671
ERITH '147 SPORTS	STC Sports Ground, Ivor Grove, New Eltham SE9 2AJ	020 8858 2057
HALLS	Stone Recreation Ground, London Road, Greenhithe DA9 9DQ	01322 224246
HALSTEAD	Halstead Recreation Ground, Station Road, Halstead TN14 7DH	07884 428658
HOLLAND SPORTS	Holland Sports & Social Club, The Pavilion, Mill Lane, Hurst Green RH8 9DF	01883 716529
LANES END	Waller Park, Wood Lane, Darenth, Dartford DA2 7LR	01322 221006
PARKWOOD RANGERS	Bexley Park Sports & Social Club, Calvert Drive, Bexley DA2 3QW	01322 521093
PHOENIX ACADEMY	Phoenix Sports Club, Mayplace Road East, Barnehurst DA7 6JT	01322 526159

IN: *AFC Mottingham (P-South London Alliance Division One), Dulwich Magic (youth football), Halstead United (P-Sevenoaks & District League Premier Division), Holland Sports (P-Redhill & District League Premier Division), Parkwood Rangers (P-South London Alliance Division Four), Phoenix Academy (N)*
OUT: *Fleetdown United (P), Hildenborough Athletic (P), Seven Acre Sports (P-Kent Invicta League), Westerham (W)*

	RESERVE DIVISION EAST	P	W	D	L	F	A	Pts
1	Bromley Green res	22	14	3	5	48	28	45
2	Canterbury City res	22	12	6	4	62	33	42
3	Bly Spartans res (-3)	22	13	3	6	48	31	39
4	Bearsted reserves	22	12	3	7	44	32	39
5	APM reserves	22	10	6	6	40	36	36
6	Otford United res	22	9	4	9	37	35	31
7	Kennington reserves	22	8	5	9	38	43	29
8	Sheerness East res	22	9	2	11	38	47	29
9	New Romney rese	22	7	6	9	29	34	27
10	Staplehurst & MU res	22	6	5	11	37	52	23
11	Platt United reserves	22	4	4	14	31	51	16
12	Lar'd&NHW res (-1)	22	4	1	17	28	58	12
	Borden Village reserves - record expunged							

	RESERVE DIVISION WEST	P	W	D	L	F	A	PTS
1	Hildenborough Ath	24	20	1	3	90	29	61
2	Fleetdown United	24	15	3	6	53	26	48
3	Erith 147	24	13	7	4	54	30	46
4	Seven Acre Sports	24	14	3	7	63	44	45
5	Bexley	24	12	7	5	51	33	43
6	Bexlians	24	10	7	7	61	46	37
7	Blackheath Utd (-1)	24	11	5	8	38	40	37
8	Halls	24	7	6	11	38	48	27
9	Crofton Albion	24	7	5	12	41	46	26
10	Bexley Borough	24	6	4	14	23	52	22
11	Lanes End	24	6	2	16	38	58	20
12	Meridian (-1)	24	4	4	16	32	73	15
13	Westerham (-1)	24	3	2	19	23	80	10

RESERVES CUP

ROUND 1
Platt United reserves 3-0 Borden Village reserves
Bearsted reserves 2-0 Staplehurst & Monarchs United reserves
Kennington reserves 1-5 Otford United
Canterbury City reserves 5-1 Sheerness East reserves
Bly Spartans reserves 0-2 Bromley Green reserves
Fleet Leisure reserves 0-1 Sutton Athletic reserves
Coney Hall reserves 5-2 Rusthall reserves
Crockenhill reserves 0-6 Phoenix Sports reserves
Stansfeld O & B Club reserves 3-1 Belvedere reserves
Greenways reserves 6-1 Bexley Borough reserves
Westerham reserves scr-w/o Fleetdown United reserves

ROUND 2
Larkfield & New Hythe Wanderers reserves 3-6 APM reserves
Platt United reserves 2-2 New Romney reserves
(New Romney reserves won 4-2 on penalties)
Bearsted reserves 5-0 Bromley Green reserves
Canterbury City reserves 3-3 Otford United reserves
(Canterbury City reserves won 5-4 on penalties)
Chipstead reserves 3-1 Orpington reserves
Coney Hall reserves 1-2 Sutton Athletic reserves
Fleetdown United reserves 1-0 Greenways reserves
Phoenix Sports reserves 2-1 Stansfeld O & B Club reserves

QUARTER FINALS
New Romney reserves 3-2 Phoenix Sports reserves
APM reserves 0-1 Fleetdown United reserves
Chipstead reserves 3-4 Sutton Athletic reserves
Canterbury City reserves 1-2 Bearsted reserves

SEMI-FINALS
Fleetdown United reserves 5-0 New Romney reserves
Bearsted reserves 1-2 Sutton Athletic reserves

FINAL (@ Faversham Town, 4/5/11)
Sutton Athletic reserves 2-1 Fleetdown United reserves

haart of kent county league

Cyril Windiate - League Chairman - receives Football Association 50 Years Long Service Award from Barry Bright and Philip Smith.

Scott Fletcher, Spicerhaart Ltd and Cyril Windiate sign three year sponsorship contract.

Aford Awards Manager of the Year
Paul Piggott - Hollands & Blair FC

Sutton Athletic FC
Bill Manklow Inter Regional Challemge Cup Winners

Hollands & Blair FC
Premier Division Winners
Kent Intermediate Challenge Shield Winners

Saga Sports & Social FC
Les Leckie Cup Winners
Division Two East Winners

Farborough Old Boys Guild FC
Division One West Winners

Forest Hill Park FC
Barry Bundock West Kent Challenge Shield
Winners

Sutton Athletic Reserves FC
Reserve Division Cup Winners

Hildenborough Athletic FC
Division Two West Winners

Referee of the Year
Martin Staveley
with Barry Bright and Stephen Kendall

New Romney FC
Fair Play Trophy Winners
with John Moules

LEICESTERSHIRE SENIOR LEAGUE

Sponsored by: Everards Brewery
Founded: 1919
Recent Champions:
2006: Friar Lane & Epworth
2007: Stapenhill
2008: Kirby Muxloe SC
2009: Anstey Nomads
2010: Thurmaston Town

PREMIER DIVISION	P	W	D	L	F	A	Pts
1 Ashby Ivanhoe	30	23	2	5	109	57	71
2 FC Dynamo	30	20	2	8	104	50	62
3 Blaby & Whetstone Athletic	30	19	3	8	75	29	60
4 Stapenhill	30	16	8	6	64	34	56
5 Rothley Imperial	30	16	7	7	67	50	55
6 Lutterworth Athletic	30	17	3	10	70	41	54
7 Thurmaston Town	30	16	4	10	85	44	52
8 Aylestone Park	30	13	8	9	70	49	47
9 Birstall United	30	13	8	9	72	56	47
10 Kirby Muxloe reserves	30	12	4	14	45	61	40
11 Saffron Dynamo	30	11	5	14	50	58	38
12 Sileby Town	30	11	5	14	46	58	38
13 Highfield Rangers	30	10	1	19	50	70	31
14 Cottesmore Amateurs	30	5	7	18	38	79	22
15 Ratby Sports	30	2	3	25	32	104	9
16 Asfordby Amateurs (-3)	30	0	2	28	18	155	-1

DIVISION ONE	P	W	D	L	F	A	Pts
1 Desford	28	18	8	2	64	25	62
2 Dunton & Broughton Rang.	28	15	11	2	50	23	56
3 Barlestone St Giles	28	13	10	5	54	24	49
4 Earl Shilton Albion	28	13	9	6	79	47	48
5 Caterpillar (-3)	28	14	6	8	67	42	45
6 Friar Lane & Epworth res	28	12	6	10	52	51	42
7 Belgrave	28	13	1	14	71	79	40
8 Coalville Town reserves	28	12	3	13	53	60	39
9 Newhall United	28	10	5	13	42	54	35
10 Narborough & Littlethorpe	28	10	3	15	55	62	33
11 Hathern	28	9	6	13	44	53	33
12 Melton Mowbray	28	9	4	15	57	71	31
13 Shepshed Dynamo reserves	28	9	3	16	43	62	30
14 FC Khalsa & Evington	28	6	5	17	44	79	23
15 Lutterworth Town	28	6	2	20	31	74	20

BEACON BITTER CUP

ROUND 1
Sileby Town 0-2 Rothley Imperial
Shepshed Dynamo reserves 6-1 FC Khalsa & Evington
Ratby Sports 0-5 Saffron Dynamo
Melton Mowbray 1-5 Barlestone St Giles
Lutterworth Athletic 0-0 Thurmaston Town
(Lutterworth Athletic won 5-4 on penalties)
Highfield Rangers 1-1 FC Dynamo
(Highfield Rangers won 4-3 on penalties)
Hathern 1-1 Earl Shilton Albion (Hathern won 4-2 on penalties)
Dunton & Broughton Rangers 2-2 Coalville Town reserves
(Dunton & Broughton Rangers won 3-2 on penalties)
Desford 2-0 Narborough & Littlethorpe
Caterpillar 1-1 Friar Lane & Epworth reserves
Blaby & Whetstone Athletic 1-1 Stapenhill (Blaby & Whetstone Athletic won 4-3 on penalties)
Birstall United 2-1 Cottesmore Amateurs
Belgrave 1-2 Lutterworth Town
Ashby Ivanhoe 8-0 Asfordby Amateurs
Aylestone Park 0-0 Kirby Muxloe reserves

ROUND 2
Rothley Imperial 2-0 Birstall United
Shepshed Dynamo reserves 3-1 Newhall United
Lutterworth Town 2-0 Hathern
Lutterworth Athletic 3-0 Ashby Ivanhoe
Dunton & Broughton Rangers 2-4 Desford
Barlestone St Giles 5-2 Friar Lane & Epworth reserves
Saffron Dynamo 5-1 Highfield Rangers
Aylestone Park 0-5 Blaby & Whetstone Athletic

QUARTER FINALS
Lutterworth Athletic 4-2 Desford
Shepshed Dynamo reserves 1-6 Barlestone St Giles
Saffron Dynamo 4-1 Lutterworth Town
Rothley Imperial w/o-scr Blaby & Whetstone Athletic

SEMI-FINALS
Lutterworth Athletic 1-0 Saffron Dynamo
Barlestone St Giles 2-1 Rothley Imperial

FINAL (@ Barow Town, 17/5/11)
Barlestone St Giles 1-2 Lutterworth Athletic

PREMIER DIVISION	1	2	3	4	5	6	7	8	9	10	11	12	13	14	15	16
1 Asfordby Amateurs		1-5	0-6	0-8	0-5	2-4	0-5	0-4	1-1	0-9	1-3	2-4	0-8	2-3	1-3	1-7
2 Ashby Ivanhoe	15-1		6-1	3-2	1-4	2-0	4-3	6-2	6-2	3-1	5-1	1-2	3-1	4-3	3-0	2-1
3 Aylestone Park	2-0	2-4		1-1	0-0	4-0	2-1	3-1	3-1	2-0	1-1	3-3	4-1	6-0	2-2	3-6
4 Birstall United	8-0	2-2	3-3		0-2	2-1	0-4	3-1	2-4	2-2	4-1	4-1	4-1	1-1	2-1	1-5
5 Blaby & Whetstone Athletic	4-0	3-1	4-1	5-2		3-1	3-1	2-0	3-0	0-2	3-1	2-3	3-0	1-3	1-2	0-3
6 Cottesmore Amateurs	1-0	0-3	1-0	0-1	1-1		2-7	4-2	1-2	1-4	1-1	1-3	0-4	0-2	2-2	1-3
7 Highfield Rangers	7-0	4-2	1-1	3-1	2-1	7-1		2-1	7-1	2-5	4-0	3-2	4-1	5-2	3-4	3-4
8 Leicestershire Constabulary	4-1	1-2	3-2	4-1	1-4	2-2	0-4		1-3	2-3	2-0	0-2	2-3	2-5	0-4	2-0
9 Lutterworth Athletic	3-0	1-3	0-1	1-1	0-3	2-2	2-1	0-2		0-4	3-0	1-1	3-0	0-2	0-1	0-3
10 Ratby Sports	7-0	2-4	0-1	0-2	0-2	2-2	1-2	2-1	1-2		3-1	0-1	5-3	1-0	1-0	3-0
11 Rothley Imperial	2-2	1-2	1-13	1-2	0-5	5-1	1-8	1-3	1-2	1-3		2-3	1-3	1-3	0-4	0-6
12 Saffron Dynamo	9-1	3-4	2-1	3-2	2-1	1-3	3-3	3-2	1-2	1-1	3-2		2-1	2-1	1-1	2-2
13 Sileby Town	2-0	1-5	0-0	1-5	0-2	3-1	1-3	3-0	3-2	4-1	2-1	0-0		0-0	0-2	3-2
14 Stapenhill	2-0	3-4	0-1	1-1	0-7	1-1	1-2	0-1	1-2	1-4	2-0	1-4	3-1		1-0	4-1
15 Thurmaston Town	5-1	2-2	5-1	1-1	1-1	3-1	0-2	4-1	4-2	1-2	5-2	1-0	0-0	4-0		0-0
16 Thurnby Nirvana	9-1	7-2	2-0	3-4	1-0	5-2	4-1	1-3	2-3	0-1	5-0	2-0	0-0	0-0	1-2	

LEICESTERSHIRE SENIOR LEAGUE PREMIER DIVISION CONSTITUTION 2011-12

ASHBY IVANHOE	Hood Park, North Street, Ashby-de-la-Zouch LE65 1HU	01530 412181
AYLESTONE PARK	Dorset Avenue, Wigston, Leicester LE18 4WB	0116 277 5307
BIRSTALL UNITED	Meadow Lane, Birstall LE4 4FN	0116 267 1230
COTTESMORE AMATEURS	Rogues Park, Main Street, Cottesmore, Oakham LE15 4DH	01572 813486
DESFORD	Sport in Desford, Peckleton Lane, Desford, Leicester LE9 9JU	01455 828786
DUNTON & BROUGHTON RANGERS	Station Road, Dunton Bassett LE17 5LF	07780 957479
FC DYNAMO	Nanpantan Sports Ground, Nanpantan Road, Loughborough LE11 3YD	01509 237148
HIGHFIELD RANGERS	443 Gleneagles Avenue, Rushey Mead, Leicester LE4 7YJ	0116 266 0009
KIRBY MUXLOE SC RESERVES	Ratby Lane, Kirby Muxloe, Leicester LE9 9AQ	0116 239 3201
LUTTERWORTH ATHLETIC	Dunley Way, Lutterworth LE17 4NP	07837 668392
RATBY SPORTS	Desford Lane, Ratby, Leicester LE6 0LE	0116 239 2474
ROTHLEY IMPERIAL	Loughborough Road, Mountsorrell, Leicester LE7 7NH	0116 292 0538
SAFFRON DYNAMO	Cambridge Road, Whetstone LE8 3LG	07957 151630
SILEBY TOWN	Memorial Park, Seagrave Road, Sileby, Loughborough LE12 7TP	07708 231563/07860
842046		
STAPENHILL	Maple Grove, Stapenhill, Burton-on-Trent DE15 1RW	01283 533133
THURMASTON TOWN	Elizabeth Park, Checkland Road, Thurmaston, Leicester LE4 8FN	0116 260 2519

IN: *Desford (P), Dunton & Broughton Rangers (P)*

OUT: *Asfordby Amateurs (R), Blaby & Whetstone Athletic (P-East Midlands League)*

DIVISION ONE	1	2	3	4	5	6	7	8	9	10	11	12	13	14	15
1 Barlestone St Giles		3-0	3-1	4-0	0-1	2-0	1-1	4-2	0-0	1-1	2-1	3-0	2-2	6-0	4-1
2 Belgrave	2-2		2-5	1-3	0-4	0-6	4-5	4-1	5-3	1-6	6-2	6-3	2-1	5-1	5-3
3 Caterpillar	0-0	3-0		5-1	2-2	2-2	1-5	1-1	0-0	1-2	7-0	3-0	3-2	3-6	2-1
4 Coalville Town reserves	4-2	2-1	2-0		2-2	2-4	3-2	2-5	0-2	4-0	4-2	1-1	4-2	2-1	1-3
5 Desford	0-0	6-2	1-0	2-2		1-1	1-1	3-0	3-2	5-1	1-0	5-1	6-1	2-1	3-0
6 Dunton & Broughton Rangers	2-0	4-0	1-1	1-0	0-0		2-2	1-1	2-2	1-1	2-1	2-1	0-2	3-1	1-0
7 Earl Shilton Albion	2-2	5-3	1-4	1-0	0-1	1-1		3-3	4-0	1-1	5-3	1-1	9-0	2-3	2-1
8 FC Khalsa & Evington	0-1	2-3	2-1	1-3	0-5	0-2	2-6		2-6	1-1	2-2	5-3	0-4	0-2	1-2
9 Friar Lane & Epworth reserves	1-1	0-2	1-3	0-3	1-2	0-0	1-9	4-0		3-2	3-0	3-2	4-1	2-0	0-1
10 Hathern	0-3	3-2	0-5	3-1	1-0	1-2	0-2	5-2	1-2		3-0	3-5	4-0	0-3	0-1
11 Lutterworth Town	0-4	0-3	0-6	4-0	0-1	0-1	2-0	1-2	0-2	1-0		4-3	2-1	0-2	0-2
12 Melton Mowbray	0-3	2-5	1-2	4-3	4-1	1-2	1-1	5-3	0-1	3-1	1-2		0-6	3-1	0-0
13 Narborough & Littlethorpe	0-0	3-1	5-1	3-1	2-2	0-3	3-0	1-3	2-0	1-2	5-0	1-3		4-0	0-4
14 Newhall United	1-0	0-4	0-3	3-1	1-2	0-0	1-3	3-0	3-3	1-1	3-3	0-1	2-0		2-0
15 Shepshed Dynamo reserves	2-1	1-2	1-2	1-2	0-2	1-4	2-5	1-3	3-6	1-1	3-1	3-8	4-3	1-1	

LEICESTERSHIRE SENIOR LEAGUE DIVISION ONE CONSTITUTION 2011-12

ASFORDBY AMATEURS	*Hoby Road Sports Ground, Hoby Road, Asfordby, Melton Mowbray LE14 3TL*	*01664 434545*
BARLESTONE ST GILES	*Barton Road, Barlestone CV13 0EP*	*01455 291392*
BELGRAVE	*Co-Op Sports & Social Club, Birstall Road, Birstall, Leicester LE4 4DE*	*0116 267 4059*
CASTLE DONINGTON TOWN	*Moira Dale Playing Fields, Castle Donington, Derby DE74 2BJ*	
CATERPILLAR SPORTS	*Peckleton Lane, Desford, Leicester LE9 9JT*	*07856 179485*
EARL SHILTON ALBION	*Stoneycroft Park, New Street, Earl Shilton LE9 7FR*	*01455 844277*
FC KHALSA & EVINGTON	*Judge Meadow Community College, Marydene Drive, Evington, Leicester LE5 6HP*	*0116 2417580*
FRIAR LANE & EPWORTH	*Knighton Lane East, Aylestone Park, Leicester LE2 6FT*	*0116 283 3629*
HATHERN	*Pasture Lane, Hathern, Loughborough LE12 5LJ*	*07952 113090*
LUTTERWORTH TOWN	*Hall Lane, Bitteswell, Lutterworth LE17 4LN*	*01455 554046*
MELTON MOWBRAY	*All England Sports Ground, Saxby Road, Melton Mowbray LE13 1BP*	*07977 266729*
NARBOROUGH & LITTLETHORPE	*Leicester Road, Narborough LE19 2DG*	*0116 275 1855*
NEWHALL UNITED	*The Hadfields, St Johns Drive, Newhall, Swadlincote DE11 0SU*	*01283 551029*
SHEPSHED DYNAMO RESERVES	*The Dovecote, Butt Hole Lane, Shepshed, Loughborough LE12 9BN*	*01509 650992*
SILEBY SAINTS	*Platts Lane, Cossington, Leicester LE7*	*None*

IN: *Asfordby Amateurs (R), Castle Donington Town (P-Midland Regional Alliance Premier Division), Sileby Saints (P-North Leics League Premier Division)*

OUT: *Coalville Town Reserves (S-Midland Combination Reserve Division One), Desford (P), Dunton & Broughton Rangers (P)*
Friar Lane & Epworth Reserves become Friar Lane & Epworth

LIVERPOOL COUNTY PREMIER LEAGUE

Sponsored by: No sponsor
Founded: 2006
Recent Champions:
2007: Waterloo Dock
2008: Waterloo Dock
2009: Waterloo Dock
2010: Waterloo Dock

PREMIER DIVISION	P	W	D	L	F	A	Pts
1 Waterloo Dock	30	22	7	1	101	39	73
2 Old Xaverians	30	15	7	8	66	45	52
3 Ford Motors	30	15	7	8	50	37	52
4 East Villa	30	15	6	9	64	47	51
5 St Aloysius	30	14	9	7	66	53	51
6 Red Rum	30	14	7	9	65	43	49
7 Aigburth Peoples Hall	30	15	3	12	71	53	48
8 Sacre Coeur Former Pupils	30	13	6	11	54	50	45
9 Essemmay Old Boys	30	10	9	11	50	51	39
10 South Sefton Borough	30	11	6	13	43	54	39
11 Cheshire Lines	30	9	9	12	52	58	36
12 Page Celtic	30	9	7	14	40	56	34
13 REMYCA United	30	9	7	14	52	70	34
14 South Liverpool	30	8	8	14	50	56	32
15 Stoneycroft	30	5	4	21	41	93	19
16 Lucas Sports	30	3	4	23	35	95	13

GEORGE MAHON CUP

ROUND 1
Alder 1-3 Croxteth
Eli Lilly 2-3 Halewood Town
Walton Players 2-5 Liobians
ROMA 2-4 Collegiate Old Boys
West Everton Xaviers 5-4 Edge Hill BCOB
Blueline 3-0 Redgate Rovers
Old Holts 3-2 Liverpool North
Waterloo Grammar 5-2 NELTC

ROUND 2
Halewood Town 1-2 South Sefton Boough
Lucas Sports 1-6 West Everton Xaviers
Waterloo Dock 5-1 Collegiate Old Boys
Alumni 0-1 St Aloysius
Cheshire Lines 4-3 Copperas Hill
Essemmay Old Boys 1-4 Aigburth Peoples Hall
Old Xaverians 2-4 East Villa
Page Celtic 2-3 Stoneycroft
Pinewoods 2-1 BRNESC
REMYCA United 2-1 Liobians
Red Rum 0-1 Sacre Coeur
Ford Motors 7-0 Blueline
Waterloo Grammar 0-2 Leyfield
Croxteth 3-0 Old Holts

PREMIER DIVISION	1	2	3	4	5	6	7	8	9	10	11	12	13	14	15	16
1 Aigburth People's Hall		0-1	3-1	1-3	0-0	4-2	2-1	0-1	2-1	8-2	0-2	3-1	4-1	1-3	3-1	3-3
2 Cheshire Lines	2-3		3-3	1-0	0-0	6-1	1-2	3-3	2-2	2-1	2-3	3-3	3-0	0-2	3-0	2-2
3 East Villa	0-3	3-2		2-3	1-2	6-1	3-1	3-1	2-0	0-0	2-2	3-0	1-3	3-1	3-1	3-3
4 Essemmay Old Boys	0-5	2-2	1-1		2-2	4-0	0-1	2-2	5-2	0-3	1-0	1-5	5-1	1-1	2-2	1-3
5 Ford Motors	3-4	2-2	0-4	2-0		3-1	1-1	2-0	4-0	1-0	4-2	2-2	2-1	1-2	3-0	1-3
6 Lucas Sports	2-8	0-1	L-W	1-3	1-2		2-3	2-0	2-0	2-7	0-0	0-2	1-2	0-2	1-2	3-7
7 Old Xaverians	2-3	2-1	2-2	0-1	1-0	3-3		2-0	4-2	3-1	2-4	4-1	1-1	6-0	6-0	2-2
8 Page Celtic	2-5	3-1	1-3	1-1	1-0	W-L	0-2		3-3	1-1	3-0	2-1	0-1	4-5	2-0	0-4
9 REMYCA United	3-2	3-0	1-2	2-1	0-3	3-3	3-0	2-2		3-2	0-0	2-1	0-1	4-3	5-1	1-3
10 Red Rum	4-0	1-1	2-1	3-2	2-3	4-0	0-0	1-0	1-1		1-2	2-0	1-2	3-1	5-1	2-5
11 Sacre Coeur Former Pupils	2-0	2-1	3-1	1-2	2-3	5-0	2-2	0-1	3-2	0-4		2-2	2-2	0-1	3-2	1-2
12 South Liverpool	2-0	0-2	0-1	2-0	0-1	1-1	3-1	2-0	3-4	1-2	3-0		2-2	1-1	2-2	3-4
13 South Sefton Borough	1-4	1-0	0-2	2-1	0-1	4-1	1-4	0-0	5-0	2-2	1-3	3-2		0-2	1-2	0-1
14 St Aloysius	1-1	5-1	3-0	2-2	2-1	5-0	2-4	6-3	3-2	0-0	1-3	2-2	0-0		1-1	1-1
15 Stoneycroft	4-2	2-3	0-5	0-3	2-0	3-4	2-3	2-3	1-1	0-6	3-4	2-3	1-5	2-6		2-4
16 Waterloo Dock	2-0	7-1	5-3	1-1	1-1	5-1	2-1	2-1	6-0	1-2	2-0	4-0	6-0	6-2	4-1	

LIVERPOOL COUNTY PREMIER LEAGUE PREMIER DIVISION CONSTITUTION 2011-12

AIGBURTH PEOPLE'S HALL	Cheshire Lines FC, Southmead Road, Allerton, Liverpool L19 5NB	0151 427 7176
CHESHIRE LINES	Southmead Road, Allerton, Liverpool L19 5NB	0151 427 7176
CROXTETH	MYA, Long Lane, Aintree, Liverpool L9 7AA	None
EAST VILLA	Litherland Sports Park, Boundary Road, Litherland, Liverpool L21 7NW	0151 288 6338
ESSEMMAY OLD BOYS	Heron Eccles Playing Field, Abbottshey Avenue, Liverpool L18 7JT	0151 724 4796
FORD MOTORS	Ford Sports & Social Club, Cronton Lane, Widnes WA8 5AJ	0151 424 7078
OLD XAVERIANS	St Francis Xaviers College, Beconsfield Road, Liverpool L25 6EG	0151 288 1000
PAGE CELTIC	Huyton Arts & Sports Centre, Seel Road, Huyton, Liverpool L36 6DG	0151 477 8860
REMYCA UNITED	Playfootball.com, Drummond Road, Thornton L20 6DX	None
RED RUM	Croxteth Comm. Comp. School, Parkstile Lane, Liverpool L11 0PB	0151 546 4168
ROMA	Kirkby Sports Centre, Valley Road, Kirkby L20 9PQ	0151 443 4404
SACRE COEUR FORMER PUPILS	Scargreen Playing Fields, Scargreen Avenue, Norris Green, Liverpool L11 3BE	None
SOUTH SEFTON BOROUGH	Mill Dam Park, Bridges Lane, Sefton Village L29 7WA	None
ST ALOYSIUS	King George V Sports Complex, Long View Lane, Huyton, Liverpool L36 7UN	0151 443 5712
WARBRECK	Playfootball.com, Drummond Road, Thornton L20 6DX	None
WATERLOO DOCK	Edinburgh Park, Townsend Lane, Liverpool L6 0BB	0151 263 5267

IN: *Croxteth (P), Roma (P), Warbreck (P)*
OUT: *Lucas Sports (R), South Liverpool (S-West Cheshire League Division Three), Stoneycroft (R)*

DIVISION ONE	P	W	D	L	F	A	Pts
1 Croxteth	28	20	5	3	82	32	65
2 Warbreck	28	18	4	6	84	54	58
3 Roma	28	17	5	6	86	61	56
4 Pinewoods	28	16	4	8	68	42	52
5 Edge Hill BCOB	28	15	7	6	73	55	52
6 BRNESC	28	14	4	10	69	61	46
7 Leyfield	28	13	5	10	66	49	44
8 Halewood Town	28	11	4	13	79	79	37
9 Alumni	28	8	6	14	53	67	30
10 South Liverpool reserves	28	8	5	15	57	80	29
11 Copperas Hill	28	8	4	16	56	76	28
12 Old Holts	28	7	7	14	61	86	28
13 NELTC	28	8	3	17	47	65	27
14 Collegiate Old Boys	28	6	7	15	47	66	25
15 Kingsley United	28	5	2	21	44	99	17
Angus Village - record expunged							

DIVISION TWO	P	W	D	L	F	A	Pts
1 Liverpool North	20	16	1	3	85	33	49
2 Waterloo Grammar	20	15	2	3	59	29	44
3 West Everton Xaviers	20	14	2	4	61	33	44
4 Liobians	20	10	3	7	47	40	33
5 Warbreck reserves	20	10	2	8	59	53	32
6 Eli Lilly	20	9	2	9	33	40	29
7 Collegiate Old B res	20	7	4	9	50	57	28
8 Walton Players	20	8	2	10	49	46	26
9 Alder	20	6	4	10	49	54	22
10 Blueline	20	2	2	16	38	81	8
11 Redgate Rovers	20	1	0	19	19	83	3
Clubmoor Farmers - record expunged							
Liverpool Hope University - record expunged							

GEORGE MAHON CUP continued...

ROUND 3

Pinewood s 0-1 Stoneycroft
South Sefton Borough 2-1 REMYCA United
Aigburth Peoples Hall 3-4 Waterloo Dock
East Villa 3-0 West Everton Xaviers
St Aloysius 0-1 Ford Morots
Cheshire Lines 6-5 Leyfield
Kingsley United 0-4 Croxteth

QUARTER FINALS

Cheshire Lines 2-1 South Sefton Borough
Ford Motors 1-2 East Villa
Stoneycroft 0-2 Sacre Couer
Croxteth 2-3 Waterloo Dock

SEMI-FINALS

East Villa 3-1 Cheshire Lines
Waterloo Dock 4-3 Sacre Coeur

FINAL (@ LCFA, Wavertree, 24/5/11)

East Villa 4-1 Waterloo Dock

PREMIER CUP

South Liverpool 1-0 Waterloo Dock

ROY WADE DIVISION ONE CUP

Copperas Hill 0-2 Croxteth

LORD WAVERTREE DIVISION TWO CUP

Alder 4-0 Collegiate Old Boyss reserves

JOHN GREGSON MEMORIAL CUP

Alder 0-3 Liverpool North

LIVERPOOL COUNTY PREMIER LEAGUE DIVISION ONE CONSTITUTION 2011-12

ALUMNI	Jericho Lane , Aigburth , Liverpool L17 5AR	None
BRNESC	Melling Road, Aintree, Liverpool L9 0LQ	None
COLLEGIATE OLD BOYS	Alder Road Sports Club, Alder Road, West Derby, Liverpool L12 2BA	None
COPPERAS HILL	Breckside Park, Liverpool L6 4DJ	None
EDGE HILL BCOB	William Collins Mem. Ground, Commercial Road, Liverpool L5 7QY	None
HALEWOOD TOWN	Hollies Road Playing Fields, Hollies Road, Halewood, Liverpool L26 0TH	None
LEYFIELD	Thomas Lane Playing Fields, Thomas Lane, Liverpool L14 5NR	None
LIVERPOOL NORTH	Playfootball.com, Drummond Road, Thornton L20 6DX	None
LUCAS SPORTS	William Collins Mem. Ground, Commercial Road, Liverpool L5 7QY	None
NELTC	Edinburgh Park, Townsend Lane, Liverpool L6 0BB	None
OLD HOLTS	Simpson Ground, Hillfoot Road, Liverpool L25 0ND	0151 486 3166
PINEWOODS	Carr Lane Playing Fields, Carr Lane, Ainsdale, Southport PR8 3EE	None
STONEYCROFT	Maiden Lane Playing Fields, Maiden Lane, Liverpool L13 9AN	None
WATERLOO GSOB	Moss Lane, Litherland, Liverpool L21 7NW	None
WEST EVERTON XAVERIANS	St Francis Xavier College, Beconsfield Road, Liverpool L25 6EQ	0151 288 1000

***IN:** Liverpool North (P), Lucas Sports (R), Stoneycroft (R), Waterloo GSOB (P), West Everton Xaverians (P)*

***OUT:** Angus Village (WS), Croxteth (P), Kingsley United (R), Roma (P), Warbreck (P)*

LIVERPOOL COUNTY PREMIER LEAGUE DIVISION TWO CONSTITUTION 2011-12

AFC LIVERPOOL RESERVES	Formby FC, Alcar Road, Formby L37 8DL	01704 833505
ALDER	Alder Road Sports Club, Alder Road, West Derby, Liverpool L12 2BA	None
ALLERTON	t.b.a.	
BLUNDELL ELECTRICS	Buckley Hill Playing Fields, Buckley Hill Lane, Netherton, Bootle L29 1YB	None
COLLEGIATE OLD BOYS RESERVES	Alder Road Sports Club, Alder Road, West Derby, Liverpool L12 2BA	None
ELI LILLY	Thomas Lane Playing Fields, Thomas Lane, Liverpool L14 5NR	None
KCFC	Breckside Park, Liverpool L6 4ES	None
KINGSLEY UNITED	Quarry Bank School Playing Fds, Greenhill Road, Allerton, Liverpool L18 6HF	None
LIOBIANS	Mersey Road, Aigburth, Liverpool L17 6AG	None
PARK BROW	t.b.a.	
QUARRY BANK OLD BOYS	Calderstone Playing Field, Greenhill Road, Liverpool L18 6JJ	None
REDGATE ROVERS	Clarence House School, West Lane, Freshfield, Formby, Liverpool L37 7AZ	01704 82151
ROBY COLLEGE OLD BOYS	Jericho Lane, Aigburth, Liverpool L17 5AR	None
WARBRECK RESERVES	Playfootball.com, Drummond Road, Thornton L20 6DX	None

***IN:** AFC Liverpool (N), Allerton (P-Sunday football), Blundell Electrics (N), Halewood Town Reserves (N), KCFC (formerly King Charles) (P-Liverpool CMS League Premier Division), Kingsley United (R), Park Brow (P-I Zingari Combination), Quarry Bank Old Boys (Liverpool Old Boys League), Roby College Old Boys (P-Liverpool Old Boys League)*

***OUT:** Blueline (W), Clubmoor Farmers (WS), Liverpool Hope University (WS), Liverpool North (P), Walton Players (W), Waterloo GSOB (P), West Everton Xaverians (P*

MANCHESTER LEAGUE

Sponsored by: Bridgewater Office Supplies
Founded: 1893
Recent Champions:
2006: Prestwich Heys
2007: Prestwich Hays
2008: Wigan Robin Park
2009: Gregorians
2010: AVRO

PREMIER DIVISION	P	W	D	L	F	A	Pts
1 AVRO	30	19	4	7	81	42	61
2 Manchester Gregorians	30	19	3	8	61	35	60
3 Stockport Georgians	30	17	7	6	49	25	58
4 Walshaw Sports	30	17	5	8	76	46	56
5 Hindsford	30	15	5	10	71	47	50
6 East Manchester	30	14	6	10	55	50	48
7 Bury Amateurs	30	13	8	9	52	40	47
8 Wythenshawe Amateurs (-1)	30	14	4	12	46	50	45
9 Dukinfield Town	30	11	7	12	75	63	40
10 Old Alts	30	11	4	15	60	68	37
11 Springhead	30	10	4	16	62	68	34
12 Prestwich Heys	30	8	7	15	51	68	31
13 Royton Town (-6)	30	10	6	14	47	60	30
14 Leigh Athletic	30	7	9	14	66	83	30
15 Atherton Town	30	6	5	19	56	86	23
16 Hollinwood	30	7	0	23	54	131	21

GILGRYST CUP

ROUND 1

Hollinwood 3-1 Prestwich Heys
Manchester Gregorians 0-2 East Manchester
Hindsford 1-2 Dukinfield Town
Leigh Athletic 1-3 Wythenshawe Amateurs
Royton Town 2-2 Stockport Georgians
(Royton Town won 5-4 on penalties)
Springhead 2-0 Bury Amateurs
Walshaw Sports 3-1 Avro
Old Alts 3-1 Atherton Town

QUARTER FINALS

Dukinfield Town 0-10 Royton Town
Hollinwood 3-1 Springhead
Walshaw Sports 3-2 East Manchester
Wythenshawe Amateurs 3-1 Atherton Town

SEMI-FINALS

Hollinwood 1-5 Walshaw Sports
Royton Town 2-1 Wythenshawe Amateurs

FINAL (@ Hyde United, 9/5/11)

Royton Town 3-4 Walshaw Sports

PREMIER DIVISION	1	2	3	4	5	6	7	8	9	10	11	12	13	14	15	16
1 Atherton Town		2-5	2-5	4-3	0-3	1-1	2-4	2-2	0-1	2-3	0-1	2-2	2-3	2-3	1-5	1-2
2 Avro	6-1		1-2	4-1	1-0	3-1	1-2	3-2	1-0	4-2	0-0	6-0	3-1	0-2	1-0	4-2
3 Bury Amateurs	0-1	2-1		0-1	1-1	0-1	6-1	0-0	0-2	5-1	1-1	2-2	4-2	0-0	3-0	2-0
4 Dukinfield Town	3-4	3-3	1-1		0-2	3-3	5-3	4-1	0-1	1-2	9-1	2-1	3-3	2-1	2-2	2-1
5 East Manchester	4-3	0-0	0-2	3-2		2-4	3-1	1-1	3-3	2-4	3-1	0-1	0-3	2-3	3-1	2-1
6 Hindsford	5-0	3-1	0-1	2-0	0-1		8-1	6-2	0-2	2-1	3-2	2-1	2-1	1-1	2-3	1-2
7 Hollinwood	3-9	2-7	3-5	2-6	3-2	3-6		1-2	5-3	1-6	6-5	0-1	2-4	0-1	3-2	1-4
8 Leigh Athletic	2-1	3-4	3-3	4-7	2-2	1-4	9-1		3-2	3-3	4-4	2-2	3-4	0-1	0-2	6-1
9 Manchester Gregorians	3-0	1-2	3-1	3-2	5-0	1-0	6-0	1-2		3-2	3-0	2-0	2-1	1-1	2-0	2-3
10 Old Altrinchamians	2-1	3-3	2-0	1-4	0-1	3-1	9-1	3-1	0-2		3-1	1-2	2-4	0-0	1-3	0-2
11 Prestwich Heys	3-2	2-1	1-1	0-3	0-4	2-4	3-0	2-2	1-2	3-3		3-2	3-0	1-1	1-2	2-0
12 Royton Town	5-1	0-4	1-2	2-2	0-3	0-2	1-3	1-2	2-3	4-0	3-1		2-2	2-1	1-5	2-0
13 Springhead	0-2	3-5	1-2	1-1	3-4	1-1	3-1	7-2	3-0	2-3	2-1	1-3		0-3	3-2	0-1
14 Stockport Georgians	2-3	1-0	2-0	3-0	0-2	1-1	4-0	1-0	0-2	3-0	2-1	4-1	3-2		3-0	1-0
15 Walshaw Sports	3-3	1-3	5-1	3-2	2-2	2-1	6-0	7-1	3-0	5-0	2-1	1-1	4-2	1-0		2-1
16 Wythenshawe Amateurs	2-2	0-4	1-0	2-1	3-0	5-4	2-1	3-1	0-0	2-0	0-4	1-2	2-0	1-1	2-2	

MANCHESTER LEAGUE PREMIER DIVISION CONSTITUTION 2011-12

AFC BURY	Cams Lane, Radcliffe M26 3SW	
AFC MONTON	Granary Lane, Worsley M28 4PH	None
AVRO	Lancaster Club, Broadway, Failsworth, Oldham M35 0DX	0161 681 3083
DUKINFIELD TOWN	Woodhams Park, Birch Lane, Dukinfield SK16 5AP	0161 343 4529
EAST MANCHESTER	Wright Robinson Sports College, Abbey Hey Lane, Gorton M18 8RL	0161 370 5121
HEYWOOD ST JAMES	Phoenix Ground, Shepherd Street, Heywood OL10 1JW	None
HINDSFORD	Squires Lane, Tyldesley M29 8JF	None
MANCHESTER GREGORIANS	MCFC, Platt Lane Complex, Yew Tree Road, Fallowfield M14 7UU	None
OLD ALTRINCHAMIANS	Crossford Bridge Sports Ground, Danefield Road, Sale M33 7WR	0161 767 9233
PRESTWICH HEYS	Sandgate Road, Whitefield M45 6WG	0161 773 8888
ROYTON TOWN	Crompton Cricket Club Complex, Christine Street, Shaw, Oldham OL2 7SF	01706 847421
SPRINGHEAD	Ashfield Crescent PF, St John Street, Lees, Oldham OL4 4DG	0161 627 0260
STOCKPORT GEORGIANS	Cromley Road, Woodsmoor, Stockport SK2 7DT	0161 483 6581
WALSHAW SPORTS CLUB	Walshaw Sports Club, Sycamore Road, Tottington, Bury BL8 3EG	01204 882448
WEST DIDSBURY & CHORLTON	Brookburn Road, Chorlton-cum-Hardy M21 8EH	None
WYTHENSHAWE AMATEUR	Longley Lane, Northenden, Wythenshawe M22 4LA	0161 998 7268

***IN:** AFC Monton (formerly Monton Amateurs) (P), Heywood St James (P), West Didsbury & Chorlton (P)*
***OUT:** Atherton Town (R), Hollinwood (R), Leigh Athletic (R)*

DIVISION ONE	P	W	D	L	F	A	Pts
1 West Didsbury & Chorlton	24	21	2	1	60	17	65
2 Heywood St James	24	18	2	4	89	36	56
3 Monton Amateurs	24	17	2	5	84	36	53
4 Wythenshawe Town	24	17	1	6	76	45	52
5 Beechfield United	24	13	4	7	61	47	43
6 Chapel Town	24	12	6	6	46	35	42
7 Wilmslow Albion	24	7	5	12	48	56	26
8 Rochdale Sacr. Heart	24	6	4	14	54	74	22
9 Pennington	24	5	3	16	35	64	18
10 Breightmet United	24	5	3	16	36	68	18
11 Salford Victoria	24	5	3	16	53	98	18
12 Fives Athletic	24	5	2	17	42	75	17
13 Elton Vale	24	4	5	15	35	68	17

PREMIER DIVISION INVITATION CUP (@ AVRO, 7/8/10)
AVRO 6-1 Walshaw Sports

DIVISION ONE INVITATION CUP (@ BURY AMATEURS, 10/8/10)
Bury Amateurs 3-1 Monton Amateurs

MILES N KENYON CUP (@ Bury, 3/5/11)
Walshaw Sports reserves 1-1 Bury Amateurs
(Bury Amateurs won 6-5 on penalties)

OPEN TROPHY (@ Wythenshawe Town, 2/5/11)
Avro reserves 2-1 Fives Athletic reserves

LEAGUE CUP (@ Wythenshawe Town, 2/5/11)
West Didsbury & Chorlton reserves 0-1 Wythenshawe Amateurs reserves

MURRAY SHIELD

ROUND 1

Wilmslow Albion 2-4 Wythenshawe Town

Salford Victoria 3-4 Elton Vale

Pennington 2-3 Heywood St James

Chapel Town 3-2 Beechfield United

Breightmet United 1-3 West Didsbury & Chorlton

QUARTER FINAL

Rochdale Sacred Heart 1-0 Wythenshawe Town

Elton Vale 0-2 West Didsbury & Chorlton

Monton Amateurs 8-0 Fives Athletic

Chapel Town 2-5 Heywood St James

SEMI-FINALS

Heywood St James 2-0 West Didsbury & Chorlton

Rochdale Sacred Heart 2-1 Monton Amateurs

FINAL (@ Hyde United, 28/4/11)

Heywood St James 3-4 Rochdale Sacred Heart

DIVISION ONE	1	2	3	4	5	6	7	8	9	10	11	12	13
1 Beechfield United		2-3	1-1	4-2	1-0	1-5	3-5	1-1	4-2	3-3	1-3	4-3	3-1
2 Breightmet United	2-3		0-3	3-3	0-1	1-3	2-3	2-1	1-2	2-2	0-2	2-2	3-2
3 Chapel Town	2-2	3-0		1-0	H-W	0-1	0-0	3-2	3-2	6-2	0-2	1-0	2-5
4 Elton Vale	0-3	2-1	0-1		4-3	0-7	1-11	4-2	0-1	2-2	1-2	1-2	0-7
5 Fives Athletic	0-4	6-2	2-3	2-2		2-6	1-4	2-3	3-2	2-1	2-4	1-2	2-3
6 Heywood St James	5-2	4-2	2-4	4-2	5-1		1-2	5-0	2-2	10-1	2-1	3-2	1-3
7 Monton Amateurs	0-1	5-1	3-2	2-1	5-1	2-6		3-0	4-2	6-1	1-2	1-1	0-1
8 Pennington	0-4	1-2	4-2	1-1	1-3	0-2	2-4		1-1	3-2	0-1	4-2	3-4
9 Rochdale Sacred Heart	1-3	2-1	2-2	3-2	3-3	2-4	3-6	5-2		5-4	1-4	1-3	5-6
10 Salford Victoria	1-4	4-1	2-5	1-4	10-4	2-5	0-4	3-0	7-4		0-3	2-9	0-8
11 W Didsbury & Chorlton	2-1	5-0	1-1	1-0	4-1	1-1	1-0	2-0	4-1	3-0		3-2	3-1
12 Wilmslow Albion	4-3	3-5	0-0	2-2	2-0	0-3	1-5	0-3	4-2	1-2	0-3		3-3
13 Wythenshawe Town	1-3	4-0	2-1	2-1	4-0	3-2	2-8	6-1	1-0	4-1	1-3	2-0	

MANCHESTER LEAGUE DIVISION ONE CONSTITUTION 2011-12

ATHERTON TOWN	Eckersley Fold Lane, Leigh Road, Atherton M46 0QQ	01942 884882
BEECHFIELD UNITED	Salford Sports Village, Littleton Road, Salford M7 3NQ	0161 604 7600
BREIGHTMET UNITED	Moss Park, Bury Road, Breightmet, Bolton BL2 6NY	01204 533930
CHAPEL TOWN	Rowton Park, Willow Drive, Chapel-en-le-Frith, High Peak SK23 0ND	None
ELTON VALE	Elton Sports Club, Elton Vale Road, Bury BL8 2RZ	0161 762 0666
FIVES ATHLETIC	Harriet Street, Walkden, Worsley M28 3QA	None
HOLLINWOOD	Chapel Road Playing Fields, Grammar School Rd, Hollinwood, Oldham OL8 4QY	0161 911 5017
LEIGH ATHLETIC	Leigh Sports Village, Madley Park, Charles Street, Leigh WN7 4GX	01942 673500
PENNINGTON	Jubilee Park, Leigh Road, Atherton M46 0PJ	None
ROCHDALE SACRED HEART	Fox Park, Belfield Mill Lane, Rochdale OL16 2UB	None
SALFORD VICTORIA	Salford Sports Village, Lower Kersal, Littleton Road, Salford M7 3NQ	0161 604 7600
WILMSLOW ALBION	Oakwood Farm, Styal Road, Wilmslow SK9 4HP	01625 535823
WOODLEY SPORTS RESERVES	Lambeth Grove Stadium, Lambeth Grove, Woodley, Stockport SK6 1QX	0161 406 6896 Club: 0161 494 6429
WYTHENSHAWE TOWN	Ericstan Park, Timpson Road, Baguley M23 9RT	0161 998 5076

IN: *Atherton Town (R), Hollinwood (R), Leigh Athletic (R), Woodley Sports Reserves (N)*

OUT: *Heywood St James (P), Monton Amateurs (now AFC Monton) (P), West Didsbury & Chorlton (P)*

MIDDLESEX COUNTY LEAGUE

Sponsored by: Cherry Red Books
Founded: 1984
Recent Champions:
2006: Battersea Ironsides
2007: Sport London E Benfica
2008: Indian Gymkhana
2009: Bethnal Green United
2010: Interwood

PREMIER DIVISION	P	W	D	L	F	A	Pts
1 Willesden Constantine	26	21	2	3	84	34	65
2 Stedfast United	26	17	3	6	64	39	54
3 Indian Gymkhana (SSH) (-3)	26	16	2	8	52	40	47
4 Singh Sabha Slough	26	13	5	8	43	36	44
5 Broadfields United	26	12	6	8	56	44	42
6 Interwood (-3)	26	12	5	9	55	41	38
7 FC Deportivo Galicia (-3)	26	11	5	10	42	52	35
8 Southall	26	8	6	12	41	53	30
9 Sporting Hackney (-3)	26	7	9	10	40	41	27
10 Kodak (Harrow)	26	7	6	13	44	61	27
11 Sloane	26	6	7	13	29	40	25
12 Hounslow Wanderers	26	7	4	15	44	63	25
13 Springfield	26	5	8	13	35	52	23
14 Stonewall	26	4	4	18	44	77	16

ALEC SMITH PREMIER DIVISION CUP

ROUND 1
Willesden Constantine 4-0 FC Deportivo Galicia
Sloane 0-1 Stedfast United
Singh Sabha Slough 0-2 Southall
Sporting Hackney 3-2 Stonewall
Hounslow Wanderers 0-3 Indian Gymkhana (SSH)
Kodak (Harrow) 2-1 Springfield

QUARTER FINALS
Interwood 5-0 Southall
Sporting Hackney 5-2 Indian Gymkhana (SSH)
Broadfields United 2-4 Stedfast United
Willesden Constantine 5-1 Kodak (Harrow)

SEMI-FINALS
Interwood 0-0 Willesden Constantine
(Interwood won 4-2 on penalties)
Sporting Hackney 1-3 Stedfast United

FINAL (@ Harrow Borough, 23/4/11)
Interwood 2-1 Stedfast United

PREMIER DIVISION	1	2	3	4	5	6	7	8	9	10	11	12	13	14
1 Broadfields United		4-4	2-0	0-1	3-5	1-0	1-2	1-0	2-2	0-1	1-1	6-0	4-2	2-3
2 FC Deportivo Galicia	2-6		3-0	W-L	W-L	1-4	1-3	1-0	1-2	1-1	3-2	0-1	3-2	1-1
3 Hounslow Wanderers	4-1	3-1		0-3	2-3	3-2	1-2	0-0	4-4	1-0	4-2	2-3	3-5	1-6
4 Indian Gymkhana	2-3	2-1	3-1		2-1	4-2	3-1	2-1	1-2	1-3	4-0	1-0	2-1	1-2
5 Interwood	0-0	0-1	1-0	3-4		1-1	2-0	3-0	3-3	1-1	0-0	1-2	4-1	4-1
6 Kodak (Harrow)	3-3	2-3	3-1	1-3	1-2		1-1	2-0	2-2	2-1	2-2	0-5	3-0	0-3
7 Singh Sabha Slough	1-1	3-0	1-0	0-1	0-1	1-1		0-2	5-1	1-1	1-0	0-3	3-0	1-3
8 Sloane	3-0	1-1	5-2	0-3	0-4	6-1	0-1		1-0	2-2	0-0	1-1	2-2	1-3
9 Southall	1-3	3-2	2-3	1-2	1-4	4-1	0-4	2-0		3-0	1-1	0-3	0-3	L-W
10 Sporting Hackney	2-3	1-3	1-1	2-2	4-1	3-2	2-2	2-1	1-3		3-0	0-2	3-0	3-3
11 Springfield	0-1	2-5	1-2	4-0	2-0	3-4	1-5	1-1	0-1	2-2		0-0	2-0	2-3
12 Stedfast United	5-1	2-2	2-1	4-0	1-7	3-0	7-0	3-0	3-0	3-1	1-3		2-0	2-3
13 Stonewall	0-4	1-2	3-3	3-3	7-3	2-4	1-2	0-2	2-2	1-0	2-3	4-5		2-7
14 Willesden Constantine	0-3	6-0	4-2	4-2	4-1	3-0	2-3	3-0	2-1	W-L	6-1	6-1	6-0	

MIDDLESEX COUNTY LEAGUE PREMIER DIVISION CONSTITUTION 2011-12

BROADFIELDS UNITED	The Hive, Camrose Avenue, Edgware HA8 6DQ	020 8238 5920
FC DEPORTIVO GALICIA	Osterley Sports Club, Tentelow Lane, Osterley, Southall UB2 4LW	020 8574 7055
HILLINGDON	Hillingdon Athletics Stadium, Gatting Way, Park Road, Uxbridge UB8 1ES	0845 130 7324
HOUNSLOW WANDERERS	Rosedale College, Wood End Green Road, Hayes UB3 2SE	020 8573 2097
INDIAN GYMKHANA	Indian Gymkhana Club, Thornbury Avenue, Osterley TW7 4NQ	020 8568 4009
INTERWOOD	Leyton Stadium, 282 Lea Bridge Road, Leyton E10 7LD	020 8988 7642
KODAK (HARROW)	Zoom Leisure Centre, Kodak Sports Ground, Harrow View, Harrow HA2 6QQ	020 8427 1957
NORTH KENSINGTON	Vale Farm Sports Ground, Sudbury Court, East Lane, Wembley HA0 4UR	020 8904 8169/8908 5461
SINGH SABHA SLOUGH	Eton Wick FC, Haywards Mead, Eton Wick, Windsor SL4 6JN	None
SLOANE	King's Sports Ground, Windsor Avenue, New Malden KT3 5HA	None
SOUTHALL	Northolt Rugby Club, Cayton Road, Greenford UB2 4LW	020 8813 1701
SPORTING HACKNEY	Haggerston Park, Hackney E2 8NH	None
SPRINGFIELD	Frederick Knight Sports Ground, 80 Willoughby Lane, Tottenham N17 0SL	020 8801 8233
STEDFAST UNITED	Stockley Park, Chestnut Avenue, Yiewsley UB7 8BU	None
WEST ESSEX	Rolls Sports Ground, Hickmans Avenue, Hickmans Park E4 9JG	020 8527 3889
WILLESDEN CONSTANTINE	Alperton Playing Fields, Alperton Lane, Wembley HA0 1JH	020 8997 9909

IN: *Hillingdon (P-Division One West), North Kensington (P-Division One West), West Essex (P-Division One Central & East)*
OUT: *Stonewall (R)*

DIVISION ONE CENTRAL & EAST	P	W	D	L	F	A	Pts
1 West Essex	20	14	2	4	66	28	44
2 FC Romania	20	14	2	4	64	35	44
3 Bethnal Green Utd "A"	20	13	1	6	50	28	40
4 St Johns Arsenal Deaf	20	12	2	6	63	46	38
5 Vallance	20	10	2	8	45	40	32
6 Hendon "A"	20	10	1	9	53	50	31
7 St Lawrence	20	8	3	9	48	47	27
8 Regents Park (-6)	20	6	3	11	29	50	15
9 The Wilberforce Wands	20	4	3	13	37	65	15
10 Greens United	20	4	2	14	36	65	14
11 N Lon F'ball Acad. (-3)	20	2	5	13	32	69	8
FC Team - record expunged							

DIVISION ONE WEST	P	W	D	L	F	A	Pts
1 North Kensington	18	12	3	3	55	29	39
2 Hillingdon	18	10	5	3	43	20	35
3 Sandgate	18	11	2	5	38	32	35
4 Chiswick Homefields	18	10	2	6	58	30	32
5 Grosvenor House	18	7	5	6	30	26	26
6 Imperial College Old B	18	7	4	7	33	43	25
7 Kensington Dragons	18	5	4	9	34	42	19
8 Brentham	18	6	1	11	36	53	19
9 LPOSSA	18	3	6	9	29	39	15
10 FC Assyria	18	2	2	14	22	64	8
Al Amal All Stars - record expunged							
Hanworth Villa "A" - record expunged							

DIVISION TWO	P	W	D	L	F	A	Pts
1 Pitshanger Dynamo	22	16	4	2	66	22	52
2 Feltham "A"	22	16	1	5	66	31	49
3 Kilburn	22	14	1	7	72	45	43
4 Christchurch Roxeth (-3)	22	14	2	6	71	43	41
5 Elite Youth	22	9	5	8	41	47	32
6 Horseed (-3)	22	9	7	6	40	25	31
7 East Fulham	22	7	5	10	51	72	26
8 CB Hounslow U Soc (-3)	22	8	4	10	41	47	25
9 W London Saracens (-3)	22	8	2	12	36	44	23
10 Hanworth Sports (-3)	22	6	4	12	28	49	19
11 Warren	22	4	2	16	27	71	14
12 Eutectic (-3)	22	2	1	19	25	68	4
Junior All Stars - record expunged							
Uxbridge Town - record expunged							

SENIOR OPEN CUP

ROUND 1

Southall 3-1 The Wilberforce Wanderers
Kensington Dragons 3-2 FC Romania
Kodak (Harrow) 2-1 North London Football Academy
Hillingdon 3-2 St Lawrence
Hanworth Villa "A" w/o-scr Tokyngton Manor
Bethnal Green United "A" 2-3 St Johns Arsenal Deaf
Imperial College Old Boys 3-1 Al Amal All Stars

ROUND 2

Hendon "A" 0-3 Vallance
Sporting Hackney 3-1 North Kensington
Sandgate 1-0 Imperial College Old Boys
Southall 0-3 Broadfields United
Stonewall 2-1 FC Assyria
Indian Gymkhana (SSH) 4-2 Chiswick Homefields
Greens United 4-2 Kodak (Harrow)
(tie awarded to Kodak (Harrow))
Singh Sabha Slough 6-1 FC Deportivo Galicia
West Essex 2-4 Willesden Constantine
Springfield 3-2 Sloane
LPOSSA 0-4 Kensington Dragons
Grosvenor House 0-1 Hounslow Wanderers
Regents Park 5-3 Hanworth Villa "A"
Brentham 0-2 FC Team
St Johns Arsenal Deaf 2-5 Interwood
Stedfast United 8-0 Hillingdon

ROUND 3

Indian Gymkhana (SSH) 1-0 Sporting Hackney
Stonewall 0-3 Kodak (Harrow)
Broadfields United 4-0 Regents Park
Singh Sabha Slough 3-2 Hounslow Wanderers
Stedfast United 3-2 Springfield
Kensington Dragons 0-1 Interwood
Vallance 1-7 Willesden Constantine
Sandgate w/o-scr FC Team

QUARTER FINALS

Interwood 3-5 Sandgate
Singh Sabha Slough 3-0 Indian Gymkhana (SSH)
Kodak (Harrow) 3-4 Broadfields United
Stedfast United 1-5 Willesden Constantine

SEMI-FINALS

Willesden Constantine 2-1 Singh Sabha Slough
Sandgate 2-1 Broadfields United

FINAL (@ Harrow Borough, 7/5/11)
Willesden Constantine 2-2 Sandgate
(Willesden Constantine won 5-4 on penalties)

JUNIOR OPEN CUP

FINAL (@ Harrow Borough, 30/4/11)
Elite Youth 0-2 Pitshanger Dynamo

JIM ROGERS PRESIDENT'S DIVISION ONE CUP

FINAL (@ Harrow Borough, 16/4/11)
Sandgate 1-0 Bethnal Green United "A"

DIVISIONTWO CUP (H & D)

FINAL (@ Harrow Borough, 9/4/11)
Pitshanger Dynamo 3-1 Horseed

PD MARDON DIVISION 3 CUP

FINAL (@ Harrow Borough, 2/4/11)
Apna Southall 8-1 AFC Heathrow

JEFF NARDIN RESERVE DIVISION CUP

FINAL (@ Harorw Borough, 26/3/11)
Sandgate reserves 1-3 Hillingdon reserves

NORTH BERKSHIRE LEAGUE

Sponsored by: No sponsor
Founded: 1909
Recent Champions:
2006: Lambourn Sports
2007: Ardington & Lockinge
2008: Lambourn Sports
2009: Saxton Rovers
2010: Saxton Rovers
nbfl.co.uk

DIVISION ONE		P	W	D	L	F	A	Pts
1	Lambourn Sports	22	17	3	2	67	19	54
2	Didcot Casuals	22	15	3	4	51	36	48
3	Saxton Rovers	21	14	3	4	57	23	45
4	AFC Wallingford	21	12	4	5	66	22	40
5	Wootton & Dry Sandford	21	12	4	5	38	28	40
6	Childrey United	21	8	6	7	46	51	30
7	Faringdon Town	22	9	1	12	38	46	28
8	Harwell International	22	5	7	10	32	44	22
9	Harwell Village	22	5	4	13	25	46	19
10	Crowmarsh Gifford	22	5	4	13	30	61	19
11	Kintbury Rangers	22	4	5	13	21	47	17
12	Drayton	22	1	2	19	23	71	5

NORTH BERKS CUP

ROUND 1
Didcot Casuals 1-0 Long Wittenham Athletic
Ardington & Lockinge 4-5 Stanford-in-the-Vle
Bampton Town 1-4 Sutton Courtenay
Benson Lions 0-2 AFC Wallingford
Botley United 3-4 Wootton & Dry Sandford
Challow United 3-6 Hanney United
Coleshill United 6-0 Uffington United
Faringdon Town 1-4 Saxton Rovers
Harwell Interntional 1-4 Childrey United
Kintbury Rangers 2-3 Benson
Lambourn Sports 2-5 East Hendred
Marcham 1-3 Hagbourne United
Radley United 2-3 Berinsfield
Steventon 0-3 Harwell Village

ROUND 2
Appleton Stars 1-5 Hagbourne United
Berinsfield 4-2 Harwell Village
Childrey United 6-3 East Hendred
Saxton Rovers 3-0 Crowmarsh Gifford
Sutton Courtenay 3-3 Benson (Benson won 4-3 on penalties)
Wootton & Dry Sandford 6-1 Stanford-in-the-Vale
Coleshill United w/o-scr AFC Wallingford
Hanney United 0-5 Didcot Casuals

QUARTER FINALS
Hagbourne United 2-5 Berinsfield
Saxton Rovers 1-1 Wootton & Dry Sandford
Benson 4-0 Coleshill United
Didcot Casuals 1-0 Childrey United

SEMI-FINALS
Berinsfield 3-1 Didcot Casuals
Saxton Rovers 2-4 Benson

FINAL (@ Abingdon United, 7/5/11)
Benson 0-3 Berinsfield

DIVISION ONE	1	2	3	4	5	6	7	8	9	10	11	12
1 AFC Wallingford		0-0	L-W	8-0	5-1	4-0	3-0	4-0	4-2	1-2	2-2	
2 Childrey United	1-9		2-2	2-3	1-1	4-2	3-3	6-3	5-1	2-8		0-1
3 Crowmarsh Gifford	0-4	0-3		3-4	4-1	1-4	2-2	0-3	2-2	0-5	1-7	1-2
4 Didcot Casuals	2-2	1-1	2-2		2-0	2-0	4-3	1-0	3-1	2-1	2-4	0-1
5 Drayton	1-5	1-3	1-4	2-4		0-6	2-4	1-3	2-3	1-4	1-2	1-4
6 Faringdon Town	1-5	0-3	3-0	1-3	3-1		2-1	2-1	3-0	0-2	1-4	1-3
7 Harwell International	2-3	3-3	5-1	1-4	2-1	0-1		1-0	1-1	0-3	3-1	0-0
8 Harwell Village	W-L	1-4	0-4	2-4	0-2	4-2	0-0		2-1	1-3	1-1	1-2
9 Kintbury Rangers	0-3	1-2	0-1	0-1	1-1	2-1	0-0	2-2		0-3	0-1	1-0
10 Lambourn Sports	1-1	6-0	5-0	2-1	3-1	3-1	3-0	1-0	6-1		1-1	2-2
11 Saxton Rovers	3-2	3-0	2-0	0-4	5-0	1-2	4-0	4-0	4-0	1-2		5-1
12 Wootton & Dry Sandford	4-1	2-1	4-2	0-2	3-1	2-2	3-1	1-1	0-2	3-1	0-2	

NORTH BERKSHIRE LEAGUE DIVISION ONE CONSTITUTION 2011-12

AFC WALLINGFORD	Wallingford Sports Park , Hithercroft Road , Wallingford OX10 9RB	01491 835044
BENSON	Benson Recreation Ground, Benson	None
CHILDREY UNITED	Childrey Playing Field, Sparsholt Road, Childrey, Wantage OX12 9PN	None
CROWMARSH GIFFORD	Crowmarsh Recreation Ground, Crowmarsh Gifford, Wallingford OX10 8EB	07951 959090
DIDCOT CASUALS	Didcot Town Training Pitch, Ladygrove, Didcot OX11 7GA	None
DRAYTON	Recreation Ground, Lockway, Drayton, Abingdon OX14 4LF	None
EAST HENDRED	Hendred Sports & Social Club, Mill Lane, East Hendred OX12 8JS	01235 821008
FARINGDON TOWN	Tucker Park, Park Road, Faringdon SN7 7DP	01367 241759
HARWELL INTERNATIONAL	Main Gate, Harwell International Bus. Cte, Didcot OX11 0RA	01235 820220
HARWELL VILLAGE	Westfields Recreation Ground, Harwell, Didcot OX11 0LG	None
KINTBURY RANGERS	Inkpen Road, Kintbury, Hungerford RG17 9TY	01488 657001
LONG WITTENHAM ATHLETIC	Bodkins Sports Field, East End of Village, Long Wittenham	None
SAXTON ROVERS	Recreation Ground, Caldecott Road, Abingdon OX14 5HR	None
WOOTTON & DRY SANDFORD	Community Centre, Besseleigh Road, Wootton OX13 6DN	None

IN: *Benson (P), East Hendred (P), Long Wittenham Athletic (P)*
OUT: *Lambourn Sports (P-Hellenic League Division One East)*

DIVISION TWO	P	W	D	L	F	A	Pts
1 Benson	18	14	3	1	65	18	45
2 East Hendred	18	11	3	4	51	25	36
3 Long Wittenham Athletic	18	11	3	4	33	27	36
4 Botley United	18	10	3	5	57	36	33
5 Marcham	18	8	2	8	23	33	26
6 Benson Lions	18	8	0	10	27	39	24
7 Steventon	18	6	5	7	34	39	23
8 Hanney United	18	6	1	11	23	51	19
9 Bampton Town	18	3	1	14	23	34	10
10 Saxton Rovers reserves	18	2	1	15	23	57	7

DIVISION THREE	P	W	D	L	F	A	Pts
1 Sutton Courtenay	22	19	3	0	62	18	60
2 Ardington & Lockinge	22	16	1	5	97	31	49
3 Lambourn Sports res	22	16	1	5	78	33	49
4 Benson reserves	22	13	2	7	55	45	41
5 Coleshill United	22	13	1	8	54	45	40
6 Faringdon Town reserves	22	11	3	8	60	48	36
7 Stanford-in-the-Vale	22	10	1	11	67	58	31
8 Shrivenham "A"	22	7	4	11	47	62	25
9 Kintbury Rangers res	22	8	0	14	33	66	24
10 Drayton reserves	22	5	2	15	45	78	17
11 Wootton & Dry Sand res	22	3	1	18	29	83	10
12 Uffington United	22	0	3	19	37	97	3

DIVISION FOUR	P	W	D	L	F	A	Pts
1 Berinsfield	24	20	3	1	108	35	63
2 Hagbourne United	24	14	5	5	55	26	47
3 Wantage Town "A"	24	14	5	5	53	46	47
4 Didcot Casuals res	24	14	2	8	76	61	44
5 East Hendred res	24	12	6	6	57	47	42
6 Radley United	24	10	4	10	56	59	34
7 Harwell Intern'l res	24	10	2	12	52	63	32
8 Harwell Village res	24	9	4	11	68	55	31
9 Long Wittenham res	24	8	4	12	47	63	28
10 Faringdon Town "A"	24	8	2	14	44	58	26
11 Steventon reserves	24	7	2	15	44	68	23
12 Coleshill United res	24	5	3	16	27	66	18
13 Challow United	24	4	0	20	43	83	12

DIVISION FIVE	P	W	D	L	F	A	Pts
1 Marcham reserves	20	16	3	1	75	23	51
2 Didcot Casuals "A"	20	13	3	4	77	30	42
3 Sutton Courtenay res	20	12	3	5	56	30	39
4 Hagbourne United res	20	10	3	7	47	40	33
5 Benson Lions reserves	20	11	0	9	31	24	33
6 Bampton Town reserves	20	8	1	11	56	35	25
7 Faringdon Town "B"	20	8	1	11	45	47	25
8 Ardington & Lockin. res	20	8	0	12	53	59	24
9 Hanney United reserves	20	7	0	13	35	77	21
10 Stanford-in-the-Vale res	20	6	2	12	48	62	20
11 Appleton Stars	20	3	0	17	22	118	9

Uffington United reserves - record expunged

NORTH BERKS CHARITY SHIELD

ROUND 1

Appleton Stars 0-14 Drayton
Bampton Town 2-3 East Hendred
Benson 1-3 Kintbury Rangers
Botley United 2-3 Harwell Village
Childrey United 2-3 Sutton Courtenay
Coleshill United 8-1 Challow United
Hagbourne united 0-1 Wootton & Dry Sandford
Harwell International 0-2 Didcot Casuals
Long Wittenham Athletic 2-0 Hanney United
Marcham 4-1 Steventon
Stanford-in-the-Vale 2-4 Lambourn Sports
Uffington United 2-4 Berinsfield
Saxton Rovers 4-1 Crowmarsh Gifford
Radley United 1-3 AFC Wallingford
Benson Lions 3-3 Faringdon Town
(Faringdon Town won 4-3 on penalties)

ROUND 2

Ardington & Lockinge 7-0 Marcham
Drayton 1-5 Saxton Rovers
East Hendred 2-4 AFC Wallingford
Kintbury Rangers 1-3 Lambourn Sports
Sutton Courtenay 3-7 Coleshill United
Wootton & Dry Sandford 2-0 Long Wittenham Athletic
Faringdon Town 5-0 Berinsfield
Harwell Villge 1-4 Didcot Casuals

QUARTER FINALS

Ardington & Lockinge 1-2 Lambourn Sports
Faringdon Town 2-0 Coleshill United
Saxton Rovers 1-4 Didcot Casuals
Wootton & Dry Sandford 1-2 AFC Wallingford

SEMI-FINALS

Faringdon Town 1-3 Lambourn Sports
Didcot Casuals 2-0 AFC Wallingford

FINAL @ Abingdon United, 30/4/11)
Didcot Casuals 0-3 Lambourn Sports

AG KINGHAM CUP

FINAL (@ Abingdon United, 7/5/11)
Benson reserves 2-0 Faringdon Town reserves

NAIRNE PAUL TROPHY

FINAL (@ Abingdon United, 30/4/11)
Drayton reserves 3-2 Benson reserves

LEAGUE CUP

FINAL (@ AFC Wallingford, 16/4/11)
Marcham reserves 1-2 Faringdon Town "A"

WAR MEMORIAL TROPHY

FINAL (@ Wantage Town, 15/4/11)
Berinsfield 0-2 Long Wittenham Athletic

NORTHAMPTONSHIRE COMBINATION

Sponsored by: MDH Teamwear
Founded: N/K
Recent Champions:
2006: Corby Hellenic Fisher
2007: Harpole
2008: Harpole
2009: Harpole
2010: Harborough Town
northantscombination.co.uk

PREMIER DIVISION	P	W	D	L	F	A	Pts
1 Brixworth All Saints	22	17	3	2	68	22	54
2 Weldon United	22	17	2	3	58	21	53
3 Harpole	22	12	8	2	49	32	44
4 Welford Victoria	22	13	3	6	57	30	42
5 Corby Pegasus	22	10	3	9	42	40	33
6 Medbourne	22	7	4	11	42	50	25
7 Heyford Athletic	22	7	4	11	29	42	25
8 Moulton	22	6	5	11	33	42	23
9 Kislingbury	22	6	5	11	31	49	23
10 Roade	22	6	3	13	36	53	21
11 Milton	22	4	4	14	32	51	16
12 Corby Khalsa	22	2	6	14	28	73	12

Whitefield Norpol - record expunged

PREMIER DIVISION CUP (RUSSELL ROOFING)

ROUND 1

Corby Khalsa 0-4 Brixworth All Saints
Harpole 3-4 Roade
Heyford Athletic 6-2 Whitefield Norpol
Moulton 2-0 Milton
Weldon United 0-2 Corby Pegasus

QUARTER-FINALS

Medbourne 3-2 Corby Pegasus
Brixworth All Saints 2-0 Moulton
Kislingbury 2-6 Roade
Heyford Athletic 0-2 Welford Victoria

SEMI-FINALS

Brixworth All Saints 3-2 Roade
Welford Victoria 1-0 Medbourne

FINAL (@ Northampton Town, 10/5/11)
Brixworth All Saints 0-1 Welford Victoria

PREMIER DIVISION	1	2	3	4	5	6	7	8	9	10	11	12
1 Brixworth All Saints		2-0	4-2	6-1	2-1	4-2	3-0	1-1	4-0	5-2	2-2	1-0
2 Corby Khalsa	0-5		4-4	0-2	2-2	1-4	2-2	3-1	1-5	1-2	0-6	1-6
3 Corby Pegasus	1-5	1-1		1-2	0-2	4-1	1-0	2-1	3-0	2-3	3-1	1-2
4 Harpole	1-3	5-1	2-1		4-0	1-1	3-3	2-1	1-1	3-1	1-1	1-1
5 Heyford Athletic	0-3	4-0	2-1	1-1		1-1	3-1	2-0	2-0	5-3	1-3	0-5
6 Kislingbury	0-3	1-1	2-3	0-2	4-1		1-0	0-2	0-4	0-2	0-4	1-1
7 Medbourne	2-2	6-3	0-2	0-4	4-0	4-1		4-3	4-1	1-4	1-3	3-2
8 Milton	2-4	1-5	1-1	2-3	0-0	3-4	0-4		3-1	1-1	1-2	0-2
9 Moulton	2-1	0-0	1-3	2-2	2-1	1-1	4-2	2-3		1-1	0-1	1-2
10 Roade	0-5	3-0	1-3	2-3	1-0	1-3	2-2	2-4	1-3		0-2	1-2
11 Weldon United	3-1	4-1	0-3	1-2	3-0	5-1	1-0	3-1	5-0	4-1		2-1
12 Welford Victoria	0-2	7-1	5-0	3-3	2-1	1-3	5-1	3-1	3-2	3-2	1-2	

NORTHANTS COMBINATION PREMIER DIVISION CONSTITUTION 2011-12

BRIXWORTH ALL SAINTS	St Davids Close, off Froxhill Crescent, Brixworth NN6 9EA	01604 880073
CORBY KHALSA	Corby Rugby Club, Rockingham Road, Corby NN17 1AE	01536 204466
CORBY PEGASUS	West Glebe South Pavilion, Cottingham Road, Corby NN17 1EL	01536 402041
GRETTON	Kirby Road, Gretton, Corby NN17 3DB	None
HARPOLE	Playing Field, Larkhall Lane, Harpole NN7 4DP	None
HEYFORD ATHLETIC	Nether Heyford Playing Field, Nether Heyford NN7 3LL	None
KISLINGBURY	Playing Fields, Beech Lane, Kislingbury, Northampton NN7 4AL	01604 831225
MEDBOURNE	Medbourne Sports & Social Club, Hallaton Road, Medbourne LE16 8DR	None
MILTON	Collingtree Road, Milton Malsor, Northampton NN7 3AU	None
MOULTON	Brunting Road, Moulton, Northampton NN3 7QF	01604 492675
RINGSTEAD RANGERS	Gladstone Street, Ringstead NN14 4DE	None
ROADE	Connolly Way, Hyde Road, Roade NN7 2LU	01604 862814
WELDON UNITED	Oundle Road, Weldon NN17 3JT	None
WELFORD VICTORIA	Welford Sports Field, Newlands Road, Welford NN6 6HR	None

IN: *Gretton (P), Ringstead Rangers (P)*
OUT: *Queen Eleanor Great Houghton (R), Whitefield Norpol (WS)*

DIVISION ONE	P	W	D	L	F	A	Pts
1 Ringstead Rangers	22	19	3	0	59	16	60
2 Corby Morton Vikings	22	13	4	5	65	44	43
3 Gretton (-3)	22	10	6	6	65	37	33
4 Earls Barton United	22	8	7	7	33	40	31
5 Stanion United	22	9	4	9	43	56	31
6 Dav.Drayton Grange (-6)	22	9	4	9	47	53	25
7 Wootton St George	22	7	4	11	36	48	25
8 James King Bliswth (-6)	22	9	1	12	35	22	22
9 Kettering Nomads	22	6	4	12	44	57	22
10 Spratton	22	6	4	12	25	55	22
11 Stanwick Rovers	22	5	6	11	35	34	21
12 Finedon Volta	22	4	7	11	22	47	19

DIVISION TWO	P	W	D	L	F	A	Pts
1 Wellingboro' Ranelagh	22	17	2	3	82	37	53
2 Burton United	22	14	1	7	63	38	43
3 Corby Everards	22	13	3	6	61	46	42
4 Kettering Orchard Park	22	11	6	5	58	42	39
5 W'boro Old Gram (-6)	22	12	6	4	51	33	36
6 Wollaston Victoria	22	11	1	10	47	45	34
7 Wellingboro' Rising Sun	22	8	3	11	48	51	27
8 Cold Ashby Rovers	22	7	3	12	42	62	24
9 Corby Strip Mills	22	8	0	14	33	54	24
10 Clipston	22	6	3	13	40	53	21
11 Great Doddington	22	6	3	13	40	64	21
12 Islip United	22	3	1	18	36	76	10

DIVISION THREE	P	W	D	L	F	A	Pts
1 Corby Locomotives	20	16	3	1	87	33	51
2 Wellingborough Saxons	20	15	2	3	79	44	47
3 Kettering Ise Lodge (-6)	20	14	2	4	71	36	38
4 Weedon	20	11	2	7	71	50	35
5 Corby Eagles	20	11	1	8	63	43	34
6 Wilby	20	10	1	9	72	65	31
7 West Haddon	20	9	1	10	43	54	28
8 Hillmorton (-3)	20	6	2	12	44	62	17
9 Wilbarston	20	4	1	15	33	75	13
10 Ristee Towers	20	4	1	15	26	73	13
11 Corby Talisman	20	2	0	18	52	106	6
Wellingborough WMC - record expunged							

DIVISION FOUR	P	W	D	L	F	A	Pts
1 Dainite Sports	18	15	1	2	110	38	46
2 Corby Redstar	18	14	2	2	84	24	44
3 CSV United	18	12	1	5	55	42	37
4 Ferrers	18	9	0	9	63	52	27
5 F.C.Higham	18	9	0	9	52	55	27
6 Walgrave Amber	18	8	1	9	57	53	25
7 Corby Kingswood	18	7	2	9	39	54	23
8 Kettering Orchard Pk U	18	3	3	12	37	79	12
9 Kettering Park Rovers	18	3	2	13	32	81	11
10 Yardley United	18	3	2	13	49	100	11

RESERVE PREMIER DIVISION	P	W	D	L	F	A	Pts
1 Weldon United reserves	24	19	4	1	75	27	61
2 Brixworth All Saints reserves	24	17	2	5	70	33	53
3 Moulton reserves	24	15	5	4	61	32	50
4 Harpole reserves	24	13	3	8	67	50	42
5 Gretton reserves	24	12	2	10	48	49	38
6 Corby Khalsa reserves	24	11	2	11	62	58	35
7 Kettering Nomads reserves	24	9	5	10	55	40	32
8 ON Chenecks "A"	24	7	5	12	31	49	26
9 Milton reserves	24	8	2	14	44	74	26
10 James King Blisworth res	24	6	5	13	44	55	23
11 Roade reserves	24	7	2	15	48	70	23
12 Kislingbury reserves	24	7	1	16	40	76	22
13 Kettering Orch. Park res (-6)	24	4	4	16	34	66	10
Whitefield Norpol reserves - record expunged							

RESERVE DIVISION ONE	P	W	D	L	F	A	Pts
1 Corby Pegasus reserves	24	18	3	3	65	25	57
2 Wootton St George reserves	24	17	4	3	84	29	55
3 Heyford Athletic reserves	24	13	6	5	59	35	45
4 Weedon reserves	24	12	5	7	58	42	41
5 Medbourne reserves	24	10	6	8	61	47	36
6 Earls Barton United reserves	24	10	6	8	50	49	36
7 Bugbrooke St.Mich. "A" (-3)	24	11	2	11	56	60	32
8 Ringstead Rangers reserves	24	9	3	12	55	67	30
9 Weldon United "A" (-6)	24	9	4	11	51	52	25
10 Finedon Volta reserves (-3)	24	8	2	14	39	63	23
11 Stanion United reserves	24	4	5	15	51	81	17
12 Wollaston Victoria res (-3)	24	4	6	14	45	79	15
13 Corby Locomotives reserves	24	3	4	17	31	76	13

RESERVE DIVISION TWO	P	W	D	L	F	A	Pts
1 Daventry Drayton Grange res	26	23	2	1	112	30	71
2 W'borough Old Gramm. res	26	22	1	3	116	42	67
3 Corby Everards reserves	26	18	2	6	78	45	56
4 Welford Victoria reserves	26	15	2	9	67	39	47
5 Bugbr. St Michaels "B" (-3)	26	15	2	9	69	57	44
6 Spratton reserves	26	13	2	11	57	62	41
7 Wilby reserves	26	12	2	12	69	78	38
8 Corby Strip Mills reserves	26	10	4	12	58	71	34
9 West Haddon "A"	26	8	5	13	60	76	29
10 Stanwick Rovers reserves	26	8	3	15	50	76	27
11 Islip United reserves	26	7	4	15	42	69	25
12 Dainite Sports reserves	26	5	4	17	57	80	19
13 CSV United reserves	26	3	4	19	49	84	13

DIVISION ONE CUP

FINAL (@ Northampton Sileby Rangers, 26/4/11)
Ringstead Rangers 3-1 Kettering Nomads

DIVISION TWO CUP

FINAL (@ Northampton Sileby Rangers, 14/4/11)
Great Doddington 0-0 Wellingborough Old Grammarians
(Wellingborough Old Grammarians won 4-3 on penalties)

DIVISION THREE CUP

FINAL (@ Raunds Town, 7/4/11)
Corby Eagles 3-1 Corby Locomotives

DIVISION FOUR CUP

FINAL (@ Cogenhoe United, 21/4/11)
Corby Red Star 2-0 Dainite Sports

NORTHERN ALLIANCE

Sponsored by: No sponsor
Founded: 1890
Recent Champions:
2006: Team Northumbria
2007: Harraby Catholic Club
2008: Walker Central
2009: Walker Central
2010: Harraby Catholic Club

PREMIER DIVISION	P	W	D	L	F	A	Pts
1 Ponteland United	32	22	5	5	72	31	71
2 Alnwick Town	32	21	7	4	74	39	70
3 Harraby Catholic Club	32	19	8	5	76	36	65
4 Seaton Delaval Amateurs	32	20	5	7	71	45	65
5 Heaton Stannington	32	15	9	8	67	54	54
6 Carlisle City	32	15	5	12	57	54	50
7 Shankhouse	32	14	6	12	68	64	48
8 Percy Main Amateurs	32	13	7	12	59	48	46
9 Blyth Town	32	13	6	13	73	58	45
10 Ashington Colliers (-3)	32	13	8	11	59	50	44
11 Killingworth Sporting	32	12	4	16	51	66	40
12 Walker Central	32	11	4	17	51	70	37
13 Stocksfield	32	9	4	19	55	77	31
14 Gateshead Rutherford (-4)	32	7	9	16	44	67	26
15 Murton	32	6	6	20	38	66	24
16 Wark	32	5	6	21	48	92	21
17 Cramlington Town (-3)	32	7	1	24	45	91	19

CHALLENGE CUP (KICKS LEISURE)

PRELIMINARY ROUND
Ponteland United 1-2 Percy Main Amateurs
ROUND 1
Alnwick Town 3-2 Harraby Catholic Club
Ashington Colliers 1-6 Murton
Gateshead Rutherford 1-2 Blyth Town
Heaton Stannington 1-2 Shankhouse
Killingworth Sporting 3-2 Stocksfield
Percy Main Amateurs 3-1 Carlisle City
Seaton Delaval Amateurs 2-1 Wark
Walker Central 4-3 Cramlington Town
QUARTER FINALS
Blyth Town 2-1 Walker Central
Killingworth Sporting 2-4 Percy Main Amateurs
Seaton Delaval Amateurs 2-1 Shankhouse
Murton 3-4 Alnwick Town
SEMI-FINALS
Alnwick Town v Blyth Town (tie awarded to Blyth Town)
Seaton Delaval Amateurs 1-1 Percy Main Amateurs (Seaton Delaval Amateurs won 4-3 on penalties)
FINAL (@ Ashington, 8/4/11)
Blyth Town 2-3 Seaton Delaval Amateurs

PREMIER DIVISION	1	2	3	4	5	6	7	8	9	10	11	12	13	14	15	16	17
1 Alnwick Town		0-1	1-0	2-2	4-2	6-2	1-1	1-2	4-0	3-0	5-3	2-2	0-1	3-1	4-1	2-1	2-0
2 Ashington Colliers	1-2		5-2	2-1	3-0	2-1	0-1	1-1	0-2	1-1	1-2	0-2	1-2	1-4	5-2	5-0	7-3
3 Blyth Town	0-1	5-0		2-3	4-2	2-3	2-1	7-3	1-2	4-1	2-0	1-2	1-2	1-1	6-2	2-1	6-1
4 Carlisle City	2-3	1-1	0-3		1-0	3-2	1-1	3-4	0-2	4-0	0-1	3-1	2-1	1-3	3-2	1-2	4-0
5 Cramlington Town	1-4	1-2	4-1	1-2		1-2	0-4	0-3	0-4	2-1	3-2	1-2	1-4	5-4	2-5	0-4	2-1
6 Gateshead Rutherford	1-2	2-2	0-0	0-0	3-0		0-1	3-2	0-3	1-1	0-1	1-1	2-2	1-1	2-3	0-2	2-2
7 Harraby Catholic Club	0-1	3-1	5-1	2-2	4-2	2-1		1-1	5-0	5-2	3-1	3-1	1-4	2-2	2-1	8-1	3-0
8 Heaton Stannington	3-3	1-2	1-2	2-3	3-0	3-0	2-0		0-1	2-1	2-1	3-1	1-4	3-1	3-1	2-2	4-1
9 Killingworth Sporting	4-4	2-2	2-5	3-1	2-0	0-1	1-5	1-3		1-4	1-1	0-3	1-4	1-2	5-0	2-4	3-0
10 Murton	1-3	0-0	0-0	0-1	5-0	2-1	1-3	0-0	1-4		2-1	3-4	0-1	0-2	3-2	2-0	1-2
11 Percy Main Amateurs	0-1	2-2	0-0	3-0	2-1	9-0	0-0	1-2	1-1	3-0		0-2	0-2	2-1	1-1	4-1	3-2
12 Ponteland United	2-2	2-0	3-2	1-2	4-1	3-0	1-1	0-0	4-0	4-1	3-1		2-1	2-0	4-0	3-1	2-0
13 Seaton Delaval Amateurs	1-2	2-2	0-3	3-1	2-0	0-4	3-0	4-4	4-0	2-1	2-2	1-0		2-4	2-2	2-1	5-1
14 Shankhouse	2-2	1-0	3-2	2-3	4-2	1-4	0-2	2-2	4-1	3-1	4-6	0-4	1-2		2-1	2-1	1-4
15 Stocksfield	1-2	0-3	5-2	4-1	1-6	2-2	1-4	2-2	2-0	3-1	1-3	0-1	0-2	0-2		4-0	2-0
16 Walker Central	1-0	1-3	1-1	0-2	2-3	5-2	0-1	3-0	1-0	1-1	1-0	0-3	3-1	1-6	0-3		7-2
17 Wark	0-2	1-3	3-3	1-4	2-2	3-1	2-2	2-3	0-2	3-1	2-3	1-3	2-3	2-2	2-1	3-3	

NORTHERN ALLIANCE PREMIER DIVISION CONSTITUTION 2011-12

ASHINGTON COLLIERS	Ashington FC, Hirst Welfare, Alexandra Road, Ashington NE63 9HF	07517 764653
BLYTH TOWN	South Newsham Playing Fields, Blyth NE24 3PP	None
CARLISLE CITY	Sheepmount Sports Complex, Sheepmount, Carlisle CA3 8XL	01228 625599
GATESHEAD RUTHERFORD	Farnacres, Beggarswood Park, Coach Lane, Lobley Hill, Gateshead NE11 8HJ	None
HARRABY CATHOLIC CLUB	Harraby Community Centre, Edgehill Road, Carlisle CA1 3SL	None
HEATON STANNINGTON	Grounsell Park, Newton Road, High Heaton, Newcastle-upon-Tyne NE7 7HP	None
HEBBURN REYROLLE	Hebburn Sports Ground, 16 South Drive, Hebburn NE31 1UN	0191 483 5101
KILLINGWORTH SPORTING	Amberley Park, Garth 21, Killingworth, Newcastle-upon-Tyne NE6 4YA	None
MURTON	Recreation Park, Church Lane, Murton, Seaham SR7 9RD	None
PERCY MAIN AMATEURS	Purvis Park, St John's Green, Percy Main, North Shields NE29 6HE	0191 257 4831
PONTELAND UNITED	The Leisure Centre Ground, Callerton Lane, Ponteland, Newcastle-upon-Tyne NE20 9EG	01661 825441
SEATON DELAVAL AMATEURS	Wheatridge Park, Seaton Delaval, Whitley Bay NE25 0QH	None
SHANKHOUSE	Northburn Sports Complex, Crawhall Lane, Cramlington NE23 3YP	01670 714154
STOCKSFIELD	Stocksfield Sports Ground, Main Road, Stocksfield NE43 7NN	None
WALKER CENTRAL	Monkchester Green, Walker, Newcastle-upon-Tyne NE6 5LJ	0191 265 7270
WHITLEY BAY A	Hillheads Park, Rink Way, off Hillheads Road, Whitley Bay NE25 8HR	0191 291 3637

IN: *Hebburn Reyrolle (P), Whitley Bay A (P)*
OUT: *Alnwick Town (P-Northern League Division Two), Cramlington Town (R), Wark (R)*

DIVISION ONE	P	W	D	L	F	A	Pts
1 Hebburn Reyrolle	30	26	2	2	110	31	80
2 Whitley Bay "A"	30	24	5	1	78	33	77
3 Amble United	30	19	4	7	72	39	61
4 Newcastle University	30	15	6	9	53	40	51
5 South Shields United (-1)	30	14	6	9	78	47	47
6 Heddon	30	15	2	13	64	55	47
7 Wallington	30	14	3	13	68	58	45
8 Cullercoats	30	12	6	12	57	43	42
9 Gosforth Bohemians	30	9	9	12	36	55	36
10 Newcastle East End	30	11	2	17	57	78	35
11 Morpeth Sporting Club (-3)	30	10	2	18	52	76	29
12 Peterlee Town	30	7	8	15	53	80	29
13 Berwick United Ultras	30	7	7	16	53	86	28
14 Stobswood Welfare	30	8	2	21	54	84	26
15 Forest Hall	30	8	1	21	51	67	25
16 North Shields Athletic	30	7	3	20	33	97	24

Chopwell Officials Club - record expunged

COMBINATION CUP (PIN POINT RECRUITMENT)

PRELIMINARY ROUND

Gosforth Bohemians 2-0 Berwick United Ultras

ROUND 1

Hebburn Reyrolle 3-0 Morpeth Sporting Club
Amble United 4-0 South Shields United
Chopwell Officials Club 0-8 Cullercoats
Forest Hall 3-1 North Shields Athletic
Newcastle East End 0-2 Whitley Bay "A"
Peterlee Town 0-2 Wallington
Newcastle University 2-1 Gosforth Bohemians
Stobswood Welfare 2-5 Heddon

QUARTER FINALS

Amble United 1-2 Hebburn Reyrolle
Newcastle University 3-0 Forest Hall
Heddon 2-1 Cullercoats
Whitley Bay "A" 2-1 Wallington

SEMI-FINALS

Hebburn Reyrolle 2-0 Whitley Bay "A"
Newcastle University 1-0 Heddon

FINAL (@ Percy Main Amateurs, 2/5/11)

Hebburn Reyrolle 2-0 Newcastle University

GEORGE DOBBIN LEAGUE CUP (KICKS LEISURE)

ROUND 1

Alnwick Town 10-0 Chopwell Officials Club
Amble United 4-2 Seaton Burn
Carlisle City 3-6 Ashington Colliers
Cramlington Town 2-0 Morpeth Sporting Club
Cramlington United 2-3 Gateshead Rutherford
Gosforth Bohemians 0-6 Whitley Bay "A"
Harraby Catholic Club 4-1 Swalwell
Hexham 1-0 Killingworth Sporting
Newcastle British Telecom 2-6 Hebburn Reyrolle
North Shields Athletic 0-2 Walker Central
Northbank Carlisle 3-2 Berwick United Ultras
Peterlee Town 5-1 Simonside S C
Ponteland United 7-0 Cullercoats Custom Planet
Red House Farm 2-0 Stobswood Welfare
Seaton Delaval Amateurs 6-2 Forest Hall
Wallsend Boys Club 3-4 Shankhouse
Wallsend Town 4-1 Stocksfield
Whitley Bay Town 0-5 Cullercoats
Willington Quay Saints 4-1 South Shields United

ROUND 2

Hebburn Reyrolle 3-2 Seaton Delaval Amateurs
Alnwick Town 7-0 Red House Farm
Amble United 3-1 Wallington
Ashington Colliers 4-0 Amble
Cramlington Town 0-4 Walker Central
Cullercoats 2-2 Ponteland United
(Cullercoats won 4-3 on penalties)
Harraby Catholic Club 4-2 Tynemouth United
Hexham 1-4 Whitley Bay "A"
Murton 4-1 Wallsend Town
Newcastle Chemfica (Independent) 0-5 Shankhouse
Newcastle East End 4-6 Heaton Stannington
Newcastle University 3-2 Berwick United Ultras
Percy Main Amateurs 4-0 Peterlee Town
Wark 2-0 Gateshead Rutherford
Wideopen & District 2-3 Heddon
Willington Quay Saints 4-6 Blyth Town

DIVISION ONE	1	2	3	4	5	6	7	8	9	10	11	12	13	14	15	16
1 Amble United		5-0	0-3	2-0	1-1	1-2	2-0	5-0	6-0	2-1	3-0	4-1	1-0	3-1	3-2	1-2
2 Berwick United Ultras	1-1		3-1	2-3	1-0	0-4	1-6	3-0	3-3	2-2	3-3	4-3	0-4	2-4	2-0	1-3
3 Cullercoats	1-3	1-0		1-2	2-2	0-1	1-3	1-0	0-2	0-0	4-1	2-0	3-0	6-1	2-2	2-3
4 Forest Hall	0-2	6-1	0-3		3-1	1-3	2-3	2-3	1-2	2-3	8-0	3-4	1-4	2-2	1-3	2-3
5 Gosforth Bohemians	2-2	3-2	2-1	0-2		0-2	1-1	2-1	0-3	0-1	1-1	1-1	0-0	5-2	0-2	0-5
6 Hebburn Reyrolle	7-2	2-2	3-0	3-0	3-0		1-0	2-1	5-0	2-3	4-1	4-2	1-1	3-1	3-2	8-1
7 Heddon	1-2	5-1	2-1	1-2	3-0	1-3		2-2	4-2	2-1	4-1	2-0	1-3	3-1	1-5	1-2
8 Morpeth Sporting Club	2-0	0-1	3-5	2-1	0-1	2-8	4-1		7-2	2-0	2-3	1-1	3-5	2-1	1-4	0-5
9 Newcastle East End Railway	3-2	4-2	2-7	4-3	0-1	1-3	1-3	2-0		1-3	6-0	2-3	4-3	3-0	3-4	1-2
10 Newcastle University	4-0	2-2	1-3	1-0	0-2	1-5	3-2	1-3	1-1		2-0	1-1	4-2	2-1	4-0	0-2
11 North Shields Athletic	0-7	2-1	1-1	1-0	2-3	2-6	0-4	2-4	1-2	1-5		1-2	2-8	2-0	0-3	0-1
12 Peterlee Town	1-6	2-2	1-1	2-1	1-1	1-7	1-3	0-3	5-0	0-3	1-3		2-2	4-0	4-0	2-3
13 South Shields United	L-W	6-4	2-2	0-1	6-0	0-2	3-1	3-1	2-1	0-2	6-0	8-2		1-2	2-1	1-1
14 Stobswood Welfare	2-3	4-7	0-2	3-1	4-3	2-6	1-2	7-0	2-0	2-1	1-2	2-2	2-4		2-4	1-2
15 Wallington	1-2	3-0	2-1	5-1	2-3	0-5	2-1	3-2	2-0	0-1	0-1	8-3	2-2	2-3		2-3
16 Whitley Bay "A"	1-1	4-0	1-0	3-0	1-1	3-2	6-1	3-1	3-2	0-0	5-0	2-1	1-0	5-0	2-2	

NORTHERN ALLIANCE DIVISION ONE CONSTITUTION 2011-12

AMBLE UNITED	Running Track Pitch, Coquet High School, Acklington Road , Amble NE65 0NG	01665 710636
CRAMLINGTON TOWN	Sporting Club of Cramlington, Highburn, Cramlington NE23 6YB	01670 591970
CULLERCOATS	Links Avenue, Farringdon Road, Cullercoats NE30 3EY	None
FOREST HALL	East Palmersville Sports, Great Lime Road, Forest Hall NE12 9HW	None
GOSFORTH BOHEMIANS	Benson Park, Gosforth, Newcastle-upon-Tyne NE3 2EJ	None
HEDDON	Walbottle Campus, Hexham Road, Newcastle-upon-TYne NE15 9TP	0191 229 3307
MORPETH SPORTING CLUB	Morpeth Town FC, Craik Park, Morpeth Common, Morpeth NE61 2YX	01670 513785
NEWCASTLE CHEMFICA	Heaton Sports Ground, Heaton, Newcastle-upon-Tyne NE6 5NY	None
NEWCASTLE EAST END	Miller's Dene Sports Ground, Fossway, Walkergate, Newcastle-upon-Tyne NE6 4YA	None
NEWCASTLE UNIVERSITY	Cochrane Park, Etherstone Avenue, Newcastle-upon-Tyne NE7 7JX	None
WALLINGTON	Oakford Park, Scots Gap, Morpeth NE61 4EJ	None
WALLSEND TOWN	Langdale School Ground, Mitford Gardens, Wallsend NE28 0HG	None
WARK	Wark Sports Club, Wark, Hexham NE48 3NP	01434 230259

IN: *Cramlington Town (R), Newcastle Chemfica (P), Wallsend Town (P), Wark (R)*

OUT: *Berwick United Ultras (W), Chopwell Officials Club (WS), Hebburn Reyrolle (P), North Shields Athletic (R), Peterlee Town (S-Wearside League), South Shields United (W), Stobswood Welfare (W), Whitley Bay A (P)*

DIVISION TWO	P	W	D	L	F	A	Pts
1 Newcastle Chemfica (Independenr)	26	22	0	4	87	38	66
2 Wallsend Town	26	20	2	4	101	42	62
3 Simonside SC	26	17	4	5	84	64	55
4 Tynemouth United	26	14	2	10	75	59	44
5 Swalwell	26	12	5	9	58	56	41
6 Wallsend Boys Club	26	12	4	10	54	40	40
7 Willington Quay Saints	26	13	1	12	69	78	40
8 Northbank Carlisle	26	11	5	10	51	43	38
9 Seaton Burn	26	12	1	13	45	54	37
10 Red House Farm	26	11	2	13	60	54	35
11 Hexham	26	7	6	13	42	47	27
12 Whitley Bay Town	26	6	2	18	34	71	20
13 Cramlington United	26	2	4	20	31	86	10
14 Wideopen & District	26	2	4	20	27	86	10

Amble - record expunged
Cullercoates Custom Planet - record expunged
Newcastle BT - record expunged

AMATEUR CUP (PIN POINT RECRUITMENT)

PRELIMINARY ROUND
Wallsend Town 1-0 Amble
ROUND 1
Cramlington United 0-2 Swalwell
Cullercoats Custom Planet 0-7 Northbank Carlisle
Newcastle British Telecom 2-5 Seaton Burn
Newcastle Chemfica (Independent) 2-3 Wallsend Boys Club
Simonside SC 2-5 Wallsend Town
Tynemouth United 6-0 Red House Farm
Wideopen & District 1-0 Hexham
Willington Quay Saints 2-3 Whitley Bay Town
QUARTER FINALS
Wallsend Boys Club 0-1 Wallsend Town
Wideopen & District 1-6 Swalwell
Northbank Carlisle 1-1 Seaton Burn
(Northbank Carlisle won 4-2 on penalties)
Whitley Bay Town 2-1 Tynemouth United
SEMI-FINALS
Wallsend Town 3-2 Northbank Carlisle
Swalwell 4-1 Whitley Bay Town
FINAL (@ Blyth Town, 25/4/11)
Swalwell 2-2 Wallsend Town (Swalwell won 4-3 on penalties)

GEORGE DOBBIN LEAGUE CUP continued...

ROUND 3
Harraby Catholic Club 0-1 Whitley Bay "A"
Amble United 2-3 Percy Main Amateurs
Ashington Colliers 3-1 Newcastle University
Shankhouse 1-3 Walker Central
Alnwick Town 3-0 Heddon
Blyth Town 1-1 Cullecoats (Blyth Town won 4-2 on penalties)
Heaton Stannington 1-0 Murton
Wark 2-1 Hebburn Reyrolle
QUARTER FINALS
Heaton Stannington 3-1 Percy Main Amateurs
Whitley Bay "A" 2-2 Alnwick Town (Whitley Bay "A" won 8-7 on penalties)
Blyth Town 4-1 Walker Central
Ashington Colliers 7-4 Wark
SEMI-FINALS
Heaton Stannington 2-2 Whitley Bay "A" (Heaton Stannington won 4-2 on penalties)
Blyth Town 1-3 Ashington Colliers
FINAL (@ Killingworth Sporting, 25/5/11)
Heaton Stannington 1-0 Ashington Colliers 0

CHARITY CUP (PIN POINT RECRUITMENT)

QUARTER FINALS
Forest Hall 1-4 Simonside SC
Gosforth Bohemians 4-0 Swalwell
Stocksfield 4-0 Cullercoats Custom Planet
Northbank Carlisle 0-2 South Shields United
SEMI-FINALS
South Shields United 3-0 Gosforth Bohemians
Stocksfield 3-0 Simonside SC
FINAL (@ Swalwell, 12/5/11)
South Shields United 2-3 Stocksfield

DIVISION TWO	1	2	3	4	5	6	7	8	9	10	11	12	13	14
1 Cramlington United		2-1	1-3	0-0	0-0	0-2	4-6	2-3	2-2	1-3	3-7	5-4	2-3	1-3
2 Hexham	6-0		0-1	1-1	2-1	2-0	2-2	0-2	2-0	1-2	1-2	1-1	3-0	1-4
3 Newcastle Chemfica (Independent)	8-0	3-2		2-1	3-4	6-2	3-5	6-2	4-1	1-0	4-2	2-1	5-0	1-3
4 Northbank Carlisle	3-1	2-4	0-2		3-0	0-1	2-2	3-2	3-1	1-0	3-3	3-0	6-0	2-4
5 Red House Farm	4-1	4-0	0-1	1-1		0-1	1-3	1-2	5-2	2-3	1-3	2-3	5-1	5-2
6 Seaton Burn	3-0	2-1	1-2	1-2	3-1		3-4	2-0	1-2	1-3	0-7	1-2	1-1	1-0
7 Simonside Social Club	3-0	2-1	1-4	3-2	2-1	3-2		1-1	5-3	1-8	3-2	3-0	6-1	5-4
8 Swalwell	3-0	2-2	2-4	2-1	3-2	2-1	2-2		4-1	0-1	1-2	0-0	5-1	3-5
9 Tynemouth United	6-2	4-0	2-4	4-0	1-4	4-1	5-4	3-1		5-1	2-3	3-5	2-1	6-2
10 Wallsend B C	2-0	3-3	1-3	3-0	2-3	4-1	5-3	2-2	1-3		1-3	0-1	0-0	0-1
11 Wallsend Town	5-1	3-2	2-1	3-1	4-1	2-3	6-1	7-1	2-2	3-2		5-0	3-1	9-2
12 Whitley Bay Town	1-0	1-2	1-5	1-3	2-3	3-5	1-5	1-3	2-5	0-1	0-5		1-0	2-4
13 Wideopen & District	2-2	1-1	2-3	1-2	3-4	2-3	0-5	2-3	0-3	0-5	0-5	3-1		0-5
14 Willington Quay Saints	3-1	2-1	2-6	1-6	3-5	1-3	1-4	4-7	0-3	1-1	5-3	2-0	5-2	

NORTHERN ALLIANCE DIVISION TWO CONSTITUTION 2011-12

ALNWICK TOWN RESERVES	*St James's Park , Weavers Way , Alnwick NE66 1BG*	*01665 603162*
ALSTON MOOR SC	*Tyne Willows Playing Field, Station Road, Alston CA9 3HZ*	*None*
BEDLINGTON TERRIERS RESERVES	*Welfare Park, Park Road, Bedlington NE22 5DA*	*01670 825485*
CRAMLINGTON UNITED	*Shankhouse FC, Northburn Sports Complex, Crawhall Lane, Cramlington NE23 3YP*	*01670 714154*
HARTON & WESTOE CW	*Harton & Westoe Sports, Low Lane, South Shields NE34 0NA*	*None*
HEXHAM	*Wentworth Leisure Centre, Wentworth Park, Hexham NE46 3PD*	*01434 607080*
NEW FORDLEY	*John Willie Sams Centre, Cramlington NE23 7HS*	*None*
NORTH SHIELDS ATHLETIC	*John Spence Community School, Preston Road, North Shields NE29 9PU*	*0191 200 5220*
NORTHBANK CARLISLE	*Sheepmount Sports Complex, Sheepmount, Carlisle CA3 8XL*	*01228 625599*
RED HOUSE FARM	*Kingston Park Road, Newcastle-upon-Tyne NE3 2HY*	*0191 285 2181*
SEATON BURN	*Seaton Burn Welfare, Seaton Burn, Newcastle-upon-Tyne NE13 6BW*	*None*
SWALWELL	*Spa-Well Road, Derwenthaugh, Blaydon-on-Tyne NE21 6JA*	*None*
WALLSEND BOYS CLUB	*Rheydt Avenue, Wallsend NE28 7LQ*	*None*
WHICKHAM LANG JACKS	*Whickham FC, The Glebe, Rectory Lane, Whickham NE16 4PF*	*0191 420 0186*
WIDEOPEN & DISTRICT	*Lockey Park, Great North Road, Wideopen, Newcastle-upon-Tyne NE13 6LN*	*None*
WILLINGTON QUAY SAINTS	*Wallsend Rising Sun Ground, King's North Road, Wallsend NE28 9JJ*	*None*

IN: Alnwick Town Reserves (N), Alston Moor SC (P-Westmorland League Division Two), Bedlington Terriers Reserves (N), New Fordley (P-Sunday football), North Shields Athletic (R), Whickham Lang Jacks (P-Tyneside Amateur League). OUT: Amble (WS), Cullercoats Custom Planet (WS), Newcastle British Telecom (WS), Newcastle Chemfica (P), Tynemouth United (W), Wallsend Town (P), Whitley Bay Town (W). Simonside Social Club become Harton & Westoe CW

OXFORDSHIRE SENIOR LEAGUE

Sponsored by: No sponsor
Founded: N/K
Recent Champions:
2006: Oxford University Press
2007: Garsington
2008: Rover Cowley
2009: Garsington
2010: Adderbury Park

PREMIER DIVISION	P	W	D	L	F	A	Pts
1 Hinksey	24	20	1	3	85	30	61
2 Mansfield Road	24	15	3	6	78	41	48
3 Adderbury Park	24	15	3	6	60	44	48
4 Garsington	24	15	2	7	70	38	47
5 Bletchingdon	24	12	6	6	66	54	42
6 Marston Saints	24	12	4	8	60	46	40
7 Freeland	24	11	3	10	55	52	36
8 Oxford University Press	24	10	3	11	48	59	33
9 Kennington United	24	8	6	10	43	43	30
10 Stonesfield Sports	24	6	2	16	36	63	20
11 Horspath	24	5	4	15	30	67	19
12 Enstone Sports	24	3	3	18	28	74	12
13 Eynsham Association	24	3	2	19	30	78	11

Rover Cowley - record expunged

PRESIDENTS CUP

ROUND 1
Bletchingdon 2-2 Stonesfield
(Stonesfield won 4-3 on penalties)
Hinksey 7-1 Broughton & NN
Oxford Irish 3-1 Northway
Horspath 5-2 Rover Cowley
Freeland 3-2 Mansfield Road
Marston Saints 6-1 Kidlington OB
Enstone 1-2 Garsington
North Oxford 1-2 Watlington
Middleton Cheney 3-3 Oakley (Oakley won 4-2 on penalties)
OUP 1-2 Slade Farm
Kennington 3-2 Adderbury Park
Yarnton 2-1 Eynsham
ROUND 2
Oxford Irish 0-0 Slade Farm (Slade Farm won 3-1 on penalties)
Hinksey 8-1 Watlington
Freeland 4-5 Garsington
Kennington 4-3 Yarnton
Oakley 3-3 Horpsath (Horspath won 3-1 on penalties)
Stonesfield 2-2 Marston Saints
(Stonesfield won 6-5 on penalties)
Charlton 4-0 Long Crendon
Quarry 09 1-0 Chadlington
QUARTER FINALS
Stonesfield w/o-scr Quarry 09
Kennington 0-1 Charlton
Horspath 1-5 Hinksey
Garsington 2-0 Slade Farm
SEMI-FINALS
Garsington 2-1 Charlton
Hinksey 7-0 Stonesfield
FINAL (@ Kidlington, 2/5/11)
Garsington 0-1 Hinksey

PREMIER DIVISION	1	2	3	4	5	6	7	8	9	10	11	12	13
1 Adderbury Park		4-4	3-0	4-1	4-2	4-3	2-0	6-1	2-1	2-2	4-1	4-1	6-1
2 Bletchingdon	3-0		2-1	5-0	2-1	0-5	2-4	2-1	2-2	5-5	3-2	5-2	8-0
3 Enstone Sports	0-2	2-3		1-1	2-3	2-4	1-7	1-2	3-0	0-3	3-1	0-0	1-2
4 Eynsham Association	1-2	1-4	2-1		2-5	1-2	1-2	1-3	1-3	1-6	2-3	1-2	3-3
5 Freeland	0-0	6-4	4-0	2-3		4-2	1-1	6-3	3-2	0-5	2-2	1-3	2-0
6 Garsington	5-1	4-1	8-1	1-0	3-2		0-3	5-0	6-1	W-L	1-2	3-1	1-5
7 Hinksey	6-1	5-1	5-1	6-1	3-0	W-L		4-1	3-1	3-0	5-4	9-0	W-L
8 Horspath	2-1	1-1	2-2	1-3	2-1	0-1	1-5		1-1	2-5	0-5	1-3	1-2
9 Kennington United	0-1	4-1	0-4	4-0	1-2	2-2	4-2	0-1		2-3	2-2	1-1	3-0
10 Mansfield Road	3-0	2-2	3-1	3-1	3-1	3-5	3-2	7-1	0-2		1-4	4-0	4-2
11 Marston Sports	0-3	1-1	4-1	7-1	2-1	3-1	3-4	2-1	2-2	3-2		1-2	2-0
12 Oxford University Press	7-3	1-3	4-0	6-1	1-2	2-2	2-4	2-1	1-2	1-6	2-1		3-2
13 Stonesfield Sports	0-1	0-2	9-0	2-1	2-4	0-6	0-2	1-1	0-3	1-5	2-3	2-1	

OXFORDSHIRE SENIOR LEAGUE PREMIER DIVISION CONSTITUTION 2011-12

ADDERBURY PARK	Lucy Plackett Playing Field, Round Close Road, Adderbury, Banbury OX17 3EE	None
BLETCHINGTON	Rover Cowley Sports Ground, Romanway, Cowley, Oxford OX4 6NL	None
FREELAND	The Simon Hole Memorial Ground, Wroslyn Road, Freeland, Witney OX29 8HL	None
GARSINGTON	Garsington Sports Club, Denton Lane, Garsington, Oxford OX44 9EL	01865 361720
HINKSEY	Brasenose College Sports Ground, Abingdon Road, Oxford OX1 4PN	01865 243478
HORSPATH	Rover Cowley Sports Ground, Romanway, Cowley, Oxford OX4 6NL	None
KENNINGTON UNITED	Playfield Road, Kennington, Oxford OX1 5RS	None
LAUNTON SPORTS	The Playing Field, Bicester Road, Bicester OX26 5DP	01869 242007
MANSFIELD ROAD	The University Club, Mansfield Road, Oxford OX1 3SZ	01865 271044
MARSTON SAINTS	Boults Lane, Old Marston, Oxford OX3 0PW	01865 203970
OXFORD IRISH	Rover Cowley Sports Ground, Romanway, Cowley, Oxford OX4 6NL	None
OXFORD UNIVERSITY PRESS	Jordan Hill, Banbury Road, Oxford OX2 8EF	None
SLADE FARM UNITED	Bicester Community College, Queens Avenue, Bicester OX26 2NS	01869 243331
STONESFIELD SPORTS	Stonesfield Playing Field, Field Close, Longmore, Stonesfield OX29 8HA	None

IN: *Launton Sports (P-Hellenic League Division One West), Oxford Irish (P), Slade Farm United (P)*
OUT: *Enstone Sports (R), Eynsham Association (R), Rover Cowley (WS)*

OXFORDSHIRE SENIOR LEAGUE - STEP 7

DIVISION ONE	P	W	D	L	F	A	Pts
1 Slade Farm	24	18	6	0	72	12	60
2 Oxford Irish	24	17	3	4	60	33	54
3 Kidlington OB	24	14	4	6	65	40	46
4 Northway	24	13	5	6	72	43	44
5 Broughton & Nth Newington	24	13	3	8	76	46	42
6 Charlton	24	12	3	9	47	38	39
7 Middleton Cheney	24	10	3	11	44	55	33
8 Yarnton	24	9	5	10	58	49	32
9 Oakley	24	7	5	12	42	55	26
10 Watlington	24	6	5	13	23	49	23
11 North Oxford	24	6	5	13	33	70	23
12 Chadlington	24	2	5	17	19	61	11
13 Long Crendon	24	2	2	20	24	84	8

Quarry 09 - record expunged

IVOR GUBBINS CUP

QUARTER FINALS
Broughton & NN reserves 4-3 Enstone reserves
Charlton reserves 3-4 Eynsham reserves
Garsington reserves 3-1 Yarnton reserves
Stonesfield reserves 0-5 Slade Farm reserves
SEMI-FINALS
Eynsham reserves 2-5 Slade Farm reserves
Broughton & NN reserves 4-5 Garsington reserves
FINAL (@ OUP, 25/4/11)
Garsington reserves 3-4 Slade Farm reserves

BEN TURNER CUP

ROUND 1
North Oxford 0-3 Adderbury Park
Middleton Cheney 2-1 Eynsham
Northway 0-1 Enstone
Broughton & NN 7-1 Long Crendon
Mansfield Road 3-5 OUP
QUARTER FINALS
Bletchingdon 2-1 Enstone
OUP 1-1 Broughton &NN (OUP won 5-4 on penalties)
Middleton Cheney 2-1 Chadlington
Adderbury Park 0-2 Kidlington OB
SEMI-FINALS
Middleton Cheney 2-5 Bletchingdon
OUP 3-4 Kidlington OB
FINAL (@ OUP, 25/4/11)
Bletchingdon 5-3 Kidlington OB

CLARENDON CUP

ROUND 1
Eynsham reserves 1-1 Horspath reserves
(Horspath reserves won on penalties)
Oakley reserves 3-1 Enstone reserves
Stonesfield reserves 2-2 OUP reserves
(OUP reserves won on penalties)
Bletchingdon reserves 6-2 Broughton & NN reserves
Freeland reserves 8-2 Charlton reserves
Kidlington OB reserves 5-3 Slade Farm reserves
Marston Saints reserves 4-2 Garsington reserves
Adderbury Park reserves 6-3 Yarnton reserves
QUARTER FINALS
OUP reserves 2-5 Horspath reserves
Freeland reserves 4-2 Adderbury Park reserves
Bletchingdon reserves 10-2 Oakley reserves
Kidlington OB reserves 9-1 Marston Saints reserves
SEMI-FINALS
Kidlington OB reserves 1-4 Freeland reserves
Bletchingdon reserves 9-0 Horspath reserves
FINAL (@ Kidlington, 2/5/11)
Bletchingdon reserves 2-2 Freeland reserves
(Bletchingdon reserves won 4-3 on penalties)

DIVISION ONE	1	2	3	4	5	6	7	8	9	10	11	12	13
1 Broughton & North Newington		4-0	4-0	1-2	6-0	2-3	5-0	2-2	4-0	1-3	0-0	5-2	5-3
2 Chadlington	1-5		0-3	0-2	3-1	1-2	1-2	0-6	2-2	0-2	1-1	L-W	0-5
3 Charlton	1-3	1-1		0-1	2-0	4-1	1-2	5-3	0-0	1-2	0-2	6-1	2-1
4 Kidlington OB	4-2	3-1	2-3		3-1	2-5	3-3	2-2	5-0	4-0	2-3	5-0	0-3
5 Long Crendon	1-7	3-4	1-2	0-7		2-3	1-3	2-5	2-2	0-3	0-6	1-0	1-9
6 Middleton Cheney	2-1	4-0	2-4	2-3	3-2		1-1	1-4	4-2	0-2	0-7	0-2	1-3
7 North Oxford	2-8	1-0	1-4	1-4	4-1	0-0		0-4	0-2	2-3	0-4	2-2	1-1
8 Northway	6-0	5-1	3-1	4-4	2-0	3-0	5-2		4-0	4-2	0-3	W-L	4-4
9 Oakley	1-2	5-1	4-3	1-3	2-0	0-6	0-3	6-2		1-3	1-2	1-2	6-1
10 Oxford Irish	2-2	1-1	2-0	3-1	3-1	3-0	8-1	3-1	5-4		1-2	3-2	1-3
11 Slade Farm	4-1	W-L	1-1	3-0	3-0	6-1	7-1	0-0	1-1	1-1		4-0	4-0
12 Watlington	0-3	1-1	0-1	1-2	1-1	1-1	2-1	1-0	0-1	0-2	0-5		3-3
13 Yarnton	7-3	2-0	1-2	1-1	1-3	0-2	3-0	4-3	0-0	1-2	1-3	1-2	

OXFORDSHIRE SENIOR LEAGUE DIVISION ONE CONSTITUTION 2011-12

BROUGHTON & NORTH NEWINGTON	*Shutford Road, North Newington, Banbury OX16 9AT*	*None*
CHADLINGTON	*Chadlington Sports & Social, Chapel Road, Chadlington, Chipping Norton OX7 3NX*	*01608 676723*
CHARLTON UNITED	*Charlton PF, Oddington Road, Charlton-on-Otmoor, Kidlington OX5 2TJ*	*None*
ENSTONE SPORTS	*Charlbury Road, Enstone OX2 6UT*	*01608 677823*
EYNSHAM ASSOCIATION	*Oxford Road, Eynsham, Witney OX29 4DA*	*None*
KIDLINGTON OLD BOYS	*Exeter Close, Crown Road, Kidlington OX5 1AP*	*None*
LONG CRENDON	*Rec Ground, Chearsley Road, Long Crendon, Aylesbury HP18 9AP*	*None*
MIDDLETON CHENEY	*Astrip Road, Middleton Cheney, Banbury OX17 2PG*	*None*
NORTH OXFORD	*Rover Cowley Cricket Ground, Romanway, Cowley, Oxford OX4 6NL*	*None*
NORTHWAY	*Northway Sports Centre, Maltfield Road, New Marston, Oxford OX3 9RG*	*01865 742048*
OAKLEY UNITED	*Playfield Fields, Oxford Road, Oakley, Aylesbury HP18 9RE*	*None*
RIVERSIDE	*Quarry Recreation Ground, Margaret Road, Headington, Oxford OX3 8AJ*	*None*
WATLINGTON TOWN	*Shirburn Road, Watlington OX49 5BZ*	*None*
YARNTON	*Green Lane, Yarnton OX5 1TE*	*01865 842037*

IN: Enstone Sports (R), Eynsham Association (R), Riverside (formerly Crown & Thistle) (P-Oxford City League Premier Division)
OUT: Oxford Irish (P), Quarry (WS), Slade Farm United (P)

PETERBOROUGH & DISTRICT LEAGUE

Sponsored by: ChromaSport
Founded: 1902
Recent Champions:
2006: Ortonians
2007: Peterborough Sports
2008: Perkins Sports
2009: Ramsey Town
2010: Rutland Rangers

PETERBOROUGH SENIOR CUP

FINAL (@Peterborough United, 2/5/11)

Moulton Harrox 2-0 Ramsey Town 0

PREMIER DIVISION	P	W	D	L	F	A	Pts
1 Ramsey Town	30	23	3	4	94	25	72
2 Pinchbeck United	30	21	3	6	91	37	66
3 Moulton Harrox (+2)	30	17	6	7	91	55	59
4 Uppingham Town	30	18	4	8	64	39	58
5 Netherton United	30	17	6	7	66	36	57
6 Eye Sports	30	16	4	10	59	44	52
7 Whittlesey United (+3)	30	12	5	13	48	50	44
8 Coates Athletic	30	12	7	11	60	50	43
9 Crowland Town	30	13	3	14	47	58	42
10 Deeping Sports	30	12	2	16	53	58	38
11 Oundle Town (-2)	30	11	4	15	48	67	35
12 Parson Drove	30	9	4	17	47	57	31
13 Rutland Rangers	30	8	4	18	51	93	28
14 Leverington Sports (-3)	30	8	6	16	34	61	27
15 Alconbury	30	5	4	21	33	92	19
16 Stamford Belvedere	30	4	3	23	34	98	15

DIVISION ONE	P	W	D	L	F	A	Pts
1 Kings Cliffe United	20	17	2	1	89	23	53
2 Peterborough Sports	20	15	2	3	90	27	47
3 Langtoft United (-4)	20	16	1	3	53	17	45
4 Powerleague	20	14	1	5	75	29	43
5 Stilton United (+3)	20	10	3	7	58	34	36
6 FC Inter	20	9	1	10	55	55	28
7 Sawtry	20	6	3	11	39	52	21
8 Ketton	20	6	2	12	32	40	20
9 Long Sutton Athletic	20	6	2	12	45	64	20
10 Thorney	20	1	1	18	21	109	4
11 Warboys Town	20	1	0	19	19	126	3

PREMIER DIVISION	1	2	3	4	5	6	7	8	9	10	11	12	13	14	15	16
1 Alconbury		0-4	2-3	1-7	0-4	1-1	2-1	1-3	2-1	1-3	1-3	2-5	1-1	2-1	0-2	0-5
2 Coates Athletic	2-2		3-0	3-1	0-1	1-1	1-2	0-0	2-2	2-2	1-1	1-2	2-3	3-0	4-2	2-3
3 Crowland Town	5-2	2-0		1-4	2-3	2-1	1-7	0-5	7-0	0-4	0-1	0-4	3-1	2-3	2-2	0-1
4 Deeping Sports	4-1	2-0	0-3		0-1	3-0	3-1	0-3	1-2	2-2	1-3	2-3	4-1	4-1	0-3	2-1
5 Eye Sports & Social	3-0	4-2	0-0	0-0		1-2	2-8	0-2	5-0	3-0	4-3	0-2	4-0	4-1	2-2	2-0
6 Leverington Sports	1-1	2-3	0-2	0-1	0-3		1-1	2-3	1-2	2-0	0-4	1-4	1-1	3-2	2-1	1-1
7 Moulton Harrox	7-0	3-1	3-0	6-2	4-2	2-3		1-1	0-0	0-0	1-4	0-2	5-0	6-0	4-4	4-2
8 Netherton United	4-1	3-1	1-1	3-0	3-2	2-0	3-4		1-4	1-1	4-4	0-2	6-0	4-3	0-2	0-1
9 Oundle Town	2-1	3-4	0-1	1-0	1-0	2-1	1-5	0-1		1-2	1-4	1-2	4-2	5-1	0-1	2-2
10 Parson Drove	0-1	2-3	0-2	1-3	1-2	0-1	2-3	0-1	6-3		2-1	0-1	2-3	3-1	1-2	2-3
11 Pinchbeck United	5-1	0-1	2-0	6-0	5-0	3-0	1-3	2-1	6-2	7-1		2-1	5-2	2-1	0-3	2-0
12 Ramsey Town	5-1	0-0	5-0	2-0	2-1	5-0	7-0	1-1	1-2	1-0	3-2		5-1	7-0	2-3	4-0
13 Rutland Rangers	2-1	1-6	1-5	4-3	1-2	6-1	3-3	1-4	1-3	1-2	2-5	1-5		2-1	1-0	2-2
14 Stamford Belvedere	1-2	2-5	0-2	1-0	1-1	2-1	3-4	0-3	2-2	2-6	0-4	0-9	1-6		0-2	1-1
15 Uppingham Town	5-3	3-1	3-0	4-0	1-0	2-3	1-2	0-2	2-1	4-1	0-3	1-1	2-1	0-1		4-1
16 Whittlesey United	2-0	1-2	0-1	0-4	1-3	0-2	3-1	2-1	3-0	0-1	1-1	3-1	5-0	3-2	1-3	

PETERBOROUGH & DISTRICT LEAGUE PREMIER DIVISION CONSTITUTION 2011-12

ALCONBURY	Great North Road, Alconbury, Huntingdon PE28 4EX	01480 891313
COATES ATHLETIC	Manor Leisure Centre, Station Road, Whittesey, Peterborough PE17 1UA	01733 202298
CROWLAND TOWN	Snowden Field, Thorney Road, Crowland PE6 0AL	01733 211548
DEEPING RANGERS RESERVES	Outgang Road, Towngate East, Market Deeping PE6 8LQ	01778 344701
EYE SPORTS & SOCIAL	Lindisfarne Road, Eye, Peterborough PE6 7ED	None
KINGS CLIFFE UNITED	Kings Cliffe Sports Centre, Kings Cliffe, Peterborough	None
LEVERINGTON SPORTS	Church Road, Leverington, Wisbech PE12 5ED	01945 465082
MOULTON HARROX	Broad Lane, Moulton, Spalding PE12 6PN	01406 371991
NETHERTON UNITED	The Grange, Mayors Walk, Peterborough PE3 6EU	None
OAKHAM UNITED	Greetham Community Centre, Great Lane, Greetham, Oakham LE15 7NG	01572 813117
OUNDLE TOWN	Station Road, Oundle, Peterborough PE8 4BZ	07950 964205
PARSON DROVE	Main Road, Parson Drove, Wisbech PE13 4LA	None
PETERBOROUGH SPORTS PARKWAY	Peterborough Sports & Leisure, Lincoln Road, Peterborough PE1 3HA	01733 567835
PINCHBECK UNITED	Glebe Playing Fields, Knight Street, Pinchbeck, Spalding PE11 3RB	07966 303275
RAMSEY TOWN	Cricketfield Lane, Ramsey, Huntingdon PE26 1BG	01487 814218
ST NEOTS TOWN RESERVES	Rowley Park, Kester Way, St Neots PE19 6SN	01480 470012
UPPINGHAM TOWN	North Street East, Uppingham LE15 9QL	01572 821446
WHITTLESEY UNITED	Manor Leisure Centre, Station Road, Whittlesey, Peterborough PE7 1UA	01733 202298

IN: *Kings Cliffe United (P), Peterborough Sports Parkway (P), St Neots Town Reserves (P-United Counties League Reserve Div. One)*
OUT: *Stamford Belvedere (R)*
Deeping Sports become Deeping Rangers Reserves, Rutland Rangers become Oakham United

DIVISION TWO	P	W	D	L	F	A	Pts
1 Whittlesey Blue Star	24	21	2	1	108	23	65
2 Hampton Sports	24	19	2	3	118	38	59
3 Riverside Rovers	24	14	6	4	73	37	48
4 Castor & Ailsworth	24	13	5	6	62	52	44
5 Peterborough Rovers (+3)	24	13	3	8	61	52	41
6 Farcet United	24	11	2	11	48	61	35
7 Ryhall United	24	8	8	8	47	47	32
8 Hartford Sun	24	10	1	13	55	63	31
9 Werrington Town	24	8	3	13	56	84	27
10 Parkside (+3)	24	6	4	14	52	85	25
11 Gedney Hill	24	4	6	14	44	74	18
12 Woodston (+3)	24	3	0	21	34	99	12
13 Guyhirn (-11)	24	3	4	17	38	81	2

COMBINATION DIVISION ONE	P	W	D	L	F	A	Pts
1 Holbeach reserves (+2)	20	13	3	4	70	34	44
2 Netherton United res (+4)	20	11	6	3	52	26	41
3 Moulton Harrox reserves (+2)	20	11	4	5	56	25	39
4 Pinchbeck Utd reserves	20	11	3	6	45	29	36
5 Eye Sports & Social res (-4)	20	9	4	7	39	37	27
6 Langtoft United reserves	20	8	3	9	39	45	27
7 Deeping Sports reserves (-2)	20	6	8	6	39	37	24
8 Ramsey Town reserves (-4)	20	7	4	9	39	45	21
9 Long Sutton Athletic res (+2)	20	4	5	11	24	44	19
10 Alconbury reserves (+2)	20	4	2	14	24	62	16
11 Whittlesey United reserves	20	2	6	12	17	60	12

COMBINATION DIVISION TWO	P	W	D	L	F	A	Pts
1 Crowland Town reserves	16	9	5	2	40	23	32
2 Uppingham Town reserves	16	9	2	5	44	24	29
3 Leverington Sports reserves	16	7	4	5	33	29	25
4 Coates Athletic reserves	16	7	3	6	36	30	24
5 Kings Cliffe United res (+3)	16	6	2	8	23	32	23
6 Netherton United "A"	16	5	7	4	36	34	22
7 Peterborough Rovers reserves	16	5	4	7	36	43	19
8 Ketton reserves	16	5	2	9	31	42	17
9 Stamford Belvedere res (-4)	16	3	3	10	21	43	8

COMBINATION DIVISION THREE	P	W	D	L	F	A	Pts
1 Oundle Town reserves (+4)	18	11	6	1	62	23	43
2 FC Inter reserves (+3)	18	12	3	3	57	25	42
3 Ramsey Town "A" (-5)	18	12	3	3	60	26	34
4 Powerleague reserves (-2)	18	10	4	4	55	38	32
5 Stilton United reserves (-9)	18	11	3	4	49	29	27
6 Sawtry reserves (+5)	18	5	2	11	30	51	22
7 Thorney reserves	18	6	2	10	44	53	20
8 Warboys Town reserves (+1)	18	3	2	13	33	60	12
9 Ryhall United reserves	18	3	0	15	25	80	9
10 Leverington Sports "A" (-3)	18	2	5	11	23	53	8

READING LEAGUE

Sponsored by: No sponsor
Founded: 1989
Recent Champions:
2006: Cookham Dean
2007: Ascot United
2008: Westwood United
2009: Woodley Town
2010: Reading YMCA

SENIOR DIVISION	P	W	D	L	F	A	Pts
1 Highmoor Ibis	22	16	3	3	66	28	51
2 Woodcote Stoke R (+3)	22	12	4	6	50	40	43
3 Sandhurst Devels	22	12	4	6	51	25	40
4 Reading YMCA	22	12	3	7	52	31	39
5 Unity	22	11	4	7	39	29	37
6 Westwood United (-3)	22	11	4	7	56	30	34
7 Cookham Dean	22	8	8	6	39	38	32
8 Theale	22	8	2	12	36	38	26
9 Wokingham & Emm res	22	8	2	12	32	41	26
10 Frilsham & Yattendon	22	5	5	12	28	53	20
11 Taplow United	22	4	4	14	25	67	16
12 Mortimer	22	2	3	17	22	76	9

SENIOR CUP (BERKSHIRE TROPHY CENTRE)

ROUND 1
Woodley Town reserves 1-2 Wokingham & Emmbrook res.
West Reading 4-0 Newtown Henley
South Reading 4-1 Taplow United
Mortimer 1-4 Reading YMCA
Marlow United 1-2 Westwood United

ROUND 2
Woodcote Stoke Row 3-3 Sandhurst Devels
(Woodcote Stoke Row won 4-2 on penalties)
Wokingham & Emmbrook reserves 4-3 Cookham Dean
Westwood United 1-3 Theale
West Reading 0-1 Unity
REME Arborfield 1-0 Park United
Frilsham & Yattendon 0-3 Highmoor Ibis
Ashridge Park scr-w/o South Reading
Berks County Sports 4-0 Reading YMCA

QUARTER FINALS
Unity 1-0 Wokingham & Emmbrook reserves
REME Arborfield 2-1 Theale
Highmoor Ibis 2-3 Woodcote Stoke Row
Berks County Sports 1-4 South Reading

SEMI-FINALS
Woodcote Stoke Row 1-0 Unity
REME Arborfield 3-2 South Reading

FINAL (@ Reading, 19/5/11)
Woodcote Stoke Row 4-2 REME Arborfield

SENIOR DIVISION	1	2	3	4	5	6	7	8	9	10	11	12
1 Cookham Dean		0-0	1-1	7-0	2-0	0-0	6-0	3-2	1-1	0-5	4-1	1-3
2 Frilsham & Yattendon	1-3		2-4	4-2	2-1	1-3	2-2	0-5	0-0	2-2	1-3	5-1
3 Highmoor & Ibis	8-0	4-1		2-0	4-0	0-0	2-0	3-2	4-2	5-3	3-1	4-5
4 Mortimer	2-3	1-3	0-0		0-6	0-4	2-2	4-2	0-1	0-4	0-2	1-4
5 Reading Y M C A	5-0	6-0	1-5	5-0		1-0	3-1	2-1	1-2	2-1	3-2	4-4
6 Sandhurst Devels	2-2	5-1	0-1	3-3	0-2		7-1	4-2	2-1	2-1	3-0	2-0
7 Taplow United	1-1	2-1	3-2	1-3	1-2	1-6		3-1	1-3	0-9	1-0	2-4
8 Theale	1-0	1-0	2-3	5-0	0-4	1-0	2-0		0-1	2-0	2-1	1-4
9 Unity	3-1	2-0	3-1	4-0	0-0	1-2	4-3	0-0		3-0	1-2	0-1
10 Westwood United	1-1	5-0	0-2	6-1	3-2	2-4	0-0	2-1	4-1		3-0	1-1
11 Wokingham & Emm reserves	1-3	0-0	0-2	7-3	2-2	2-1	3-0	3-2	2-0	0-1		0-3
12 Woodcote & Stoke Row	0-0	1-2	2-6	1-0	1-0	2-1	4-0	1-1	4-6	1-3	3-0	

READING LEAGUE SENIOR DIVISION CONSTITUTION 2011-12

COOKHAM DEAN	Alfred Major Rec Ground, Hillcrest Avenue, Cookham Rise , Maidenhead SL6 9NB	01628 819423
FRILSHAM & YATTENDON	Frilsham Playing Field, Frilsham Common, Frilsham, near Hermitage	01635 201847
HIGHMOOR-IBIS RESERVES	Prudential IBIS Sports Club, Scours Lane, Reading RG3 6AY	0118 942 4130
MARLOW UNITED	Gossmore Park, Gossmore Lane, Marlow SL7 1QF	None
MORTIMER	Alfred Palmer Memorial PF, West End Road, Mortimer, Reading RG7 3TW	None
PARK UNITED	Bishopswood Sports Ground, Horsepond Road, Sonning Common, Reading RG4 9BT	None
READING YMCA	Reading Town FC, Scours Lane, Tilehurst, Reading RG30 6AY	0118 945 3555
SANDHURST DEVELS	Sandhurst Memorial Ground, York Town Road, Sandhurst GU47 9BJ	None
SOUTH READING	Lower Whitley Rec Ground, Basingstoke Road, Reading RG2 0JA	None
TAPLOW UNITED	Stanley Jones Field, Berry Hill, Taplow SL6 0DA	01628 621745
THEALE	Theale Recreation Ground, Englefield Road, Theale, Reading RG7 5AS	None
UNITY	Cintra Park, Cintra Avenue, Reading RG2 7AU	0118 954 7275
WESTWOOD UNITED	Cotswold Sports Centre, Downs Way, Tilehurst, Reading RG31 6LS	0118 941 4690
WOODCOTE & STOKE ROW	Woodcote Recreation Ground, Woodcote, Reading RG8 0QY	None

IN: *Highmoor-IBIS Reserves (P), Marlow United (P), Park United (P), South Reading (P)*
OUT: *Highmoor-IBIS (P-Division One East), Wokingham & Emmbrook Reserves (W)*

READING LEAGUE - STEP 7

PREMIER DIVISION	P	W	D	L	F	A	Pts
1 South Reading	18	16	1	1	74	20	49
2 R.E.M.E Arborfield	18	11	4	3	45	29	37
3 Park United	18	9	5	4	32	25	32
4 Marlow United	18	7	3	8	38	34	24
5 Woodley Town reserves	18	7	2	9	31	35	23
6 Berks County Sports	18	5	7	6	36	28	22
7 West Reading	18	6	4	8	25	31	22
8 Ashridge Park	18	5	4	9	31	48	19
9 Highmoor Ibis reserves	18	5	2	11	42	58	17
10 Westwood United res	18	2	2	14	15	61	8
Newtown Henley - record expunged							

DIVISION ONE	P	W	D	L	F	A	Pts
1 SRCC	21	17	3	1	59	16	54
2 Barton Rovers (-1)	22	17	2	3	66	24	53
3 W'ham & Emmbr'k "A"	22	14	2	6	48	26	44
4 Reading YMCA Rapids	22	11	4	7	51	40	37
5 Sonning (+3)	22	9	4	9	41	50	34
6 Sandhurst Devels res	22	9	5	8	42	43	32
7 Goring United	22	7	3	12	35	56	24
8 AFC Corinthians	22	7	2	13	34	52	23
9 Hurst	22	6	3	13	27	49	21
10 Wr'tchoice CSA Yth (-3)	21	6	3	12	45	51	18
11 Theale reserves	22	5	3	14	34	53	18
12 Berks County Sports res	22	5	2	15	29	51	17

DIVISION TWO	P	W	D	L	F	A	Pts
1 Highmoor Ibis "A"	22	16	4	2	69	30	52
2 Woodley Town "A"	22	13	5	4	55	29	44
3 Wargrave	22	11	9	2	64	38	42
4 Woodcote Stoke Row res	22	11	2	9	45	51	35
5 Twyford & Ruscombe	22	8	9	5	34	32	33
6 Radstock	22	9	5	8	54	52	32
7 Winnershe Rangers	22	8	5	9	48	50	29
8 Hurst reserves	22	8	1	13	48	54	25
9 Turnpike Sports	22	7	3	12	46	46	24
10 Taplow United reserves	22	6	3	13	32	49	21
11 AFC Corinthians res (+3)	22	4	2	16	27	75	17
12 Mortimer reserves (-3)	22	5	4	13	37	53	16

INTERMEDIATE CUP (BERKSHIRE TROPHY CENTRE)

ROUND 1

Barton Rovers 4-1 Mortimer reserves
Berks County Sports reserves 0-4 Sonning
Goring United 4-3 Hurst
Radstock 1-2 Taplow United reserves
Sandhurst Devels reserves 4-3 Highmoor Ibis reserves
Theale 5-1 Woodcote Stoke Row reserves
Winnershe Rangers 3-1 Reading YMCA Rapids

ROUND 2

Westwood United reserves 3-1 Winnershe Rangers
Barton Rovers 3-4 Wokingham & Emmbrook "A"
SRCC scr-w/o Wrightchoice CSA Youth
Sonning 4-4 Turnpike Sports (Sonning won 5-4 on penalties)
Taplow United reserves 0-3 AFC Corinthians
Theale reserves 1-4 Wargrave
Twyford & Ruscombe 0-3 Sandhurst Devels reserves
Woodley Town "A" 2-2 Goring United
(Woodley Town "A" won 4-3 on penalties)

QUARTER FINALS

Wokingham & Emmbrook "A" 4-1 Wrightchoice CSA Youth
Wargrave 2-0 Westwood United reserves
Sandhurst Devels 7-6 AFC Corinthians
Woodley Town "A" 3-1 Sonning

SEMI-FINALS

Wokingham & Emmbrook "A" 0-3 Sandhurst Devels reserves
Wargrave 1-0 Woodley Town "A"

FINAL (@ Reading Town, 21/5/11)

Wargrave 0-4 Sandhurst Devels reserves

DIVISION THREE (TOP THREE)	P	W	D	L	F	A	Pts
1 Royal Albion	18	13	3	2	62	24	42
2 Frilsham & Yatt'don res	18	11	6	1	62	25	39
3 Park United reserves	18	11	3	4	47	25	36

DIVISION FOUR (TOP THREE)	P	W	D	L	F	A	Pts
1 Woodley Town "B"	22	18	3	1	81	24	57
2 Wood. Hammers (-3)	22	17	2	3	111	37	50
3 Pinewood	22	15	0	7	62	39	45

PREMIER DIVISION	1	2	3	4	5	6	7	8	9	10	11	12
1 AFC Corinthians		0-4	2-3	0-2	5-2	1-0	1-2	3-3	4-1	0-5	1-4	3-2
2 Barton Rovers	4-2		3-2	5-2	3-0	5-0	3-2	5-2	7-0	1-0	2-0	2-4
3 Berkshire County Sp res	1-3	0-2		1-2	1-3	0-6	0-3	0-4	3-1	3-0	2-2	3-0
4 Goring United	0-1	1-5	W-L		0-0	3-3	0-2	4-2	2-2	2-1	1-4	6-4
5 Hurst	1-1	2-0	0-2	2-1		0-3	0-4	0-3	1-2	3-0	0-4	4-1
6 Reading YMCA Rapids	3-1	2-2	3-1	2-1	2-4		1-5	1-2	1-2	4-3	1-2	3-0
7 S Reading Cricket Club	1-0	2-0	3-1	4-1	3-2	1-1		3-0	4-1	3-0	2-2	
8 Sandhurst Devels res	3-2	1-2	1-0	4-0	4-0	3-3	0-5		1-0	3-3	0-4	3-2
9 Sonning	3-1	2-2	4-2	5-3	3-1	1-2	1-4	1-1		6-2	0-1	3-3
10 Theale reserves	0-2	0-5	1-1	1-2	2-2	2-3	1-3	1-0	4-1		2-0	1-5
11 Wok & Emmbrook "A"	3-0	0-4	2-1	5-0	2-0	1-4	0-2	3-1	L-W	2-1		5-1
12 Wrightchoice CSA Yth	5-1	L-W	6-2	3-2	3-0	0-3	1-1	1-1	1-2	2-4	1-2	
South Reading Cricket Club v Wrightchoice CSA Youth was declared void and left unplayed.												

READING LEAGUE SENIOR DIVISION CONSTITUTION 2011-12

ASHRIDGE PARK	Cantley Park , Twyford Road , Wokingham RG40 5QT	None
BARTON ROVERS	Turnhams Farm, Little Heath Road, Tilehurst, Reading RG31 5TX	None
BERKS COUNTY SPORTS	Berks Co. Sports & Social Club, Sonning Lane, Sonning, Reading RG4 6ST	None
REME ARBORFIELD	Sports Pavilion, Biggs Lane, Hazelbrook Barracks,Arborfield, Reading RG2 9NH	None
READING YMCA RAPIDS	Reading Town FC, Scours Lane, Tilehurst, Reading RG30 6AY	0118 945 3555
SRCC	Lower Whitley Rec Ground, Basingstoke Road, Reading t.b.a.	None
SANDHURST DEVELS RESERVES	Sandhurst Memorial Ground, York Town Road, Sandhurst GU47 9BJ	None
WEST READING	Victoria Recreation Ground, Kentwood Hill, Tilehurst, Reading RG31 6HH	None
WESTWOOD UNITED RESERVES	Cotswold Sports Centre, Downs Way, Tilehurst, Reading RG31 6LS	0118 941 4690
WOODLEY TOWN RESERVES	East Park Farm, Park Lane, Charvil, Reading RG10 9QP	None

IN: *Barton Rovers (P), Reading YMCA Rapids (P), SRCC (P), Sandhurst Devels Reserves (P)*

OUT: *Highmoor-IBIS Reserves (P), Marlow United (P), Newtown Henley (WS), Park United (P), South Reading (P)*

SOMERSET COUNTY LEAGUE

Sponsored by: Errea
Founded: 1890
Recent Champions:
2006: Hengrove Athletic
2007: Burnham United
2008: Nailsea United
2009: Bridgwater Town Reserves
2010: Bridgwater Town Reserves

PREMIER DIVISION	P	W	D	L	F	A	Pts
1 Shirehampton	34	23	7	4	118	46	76
2 Watchet Town	34	20	8	6	81	38	68
3 Nailsea United	34	20	8	6	77	46	68
4 Cheddar	34	19	6	9	92	49	63
5 Cutters Friday	34	18	5	11	74	55	59
6 Clevedon United	34	17	7	10	54	54	58
7 Ashton & Backwell Utd (-7)	34	19	4	11	55	48	54
8 Langford Rovers 2000	34	17	3	14	89	83	54
9 Stockwood Green	34	12	11	11	48	40	47
10 Taunton Blackbrook (-3)	34	14	7	13	52	48	46
11 Minehead	34	13	7	14	59	68	46
12 Bishops Lydeard	34	13	3	18	53	73	42
13 St George Easton in Gordano	34	11	6	17	59	75	39
14 Bridgwater Town reserves	34	9	6	19	52	84	33
15 Glastonbury Town	34	8	7	19	46	74	31
16 Brislington reserves (-4)	34	8	5	21	41	76	25
17 Castle Cary	34	4	8	22	38	86	20
18 Winscombe (-1)	34	6	2	26	43	88	19

Mangotsfield United reserves - record expunged

LES JAMES LEAGUE CUP

ROUND 1
Clevedon United 2-1 Castle Cary
Timsbury Athletic 0-8 Ashton & Backwell United
Langford Rovers 2000 5-1 Portishead Town reserves
Weston St Johns 4-0 Salford

ROUND 2
Shirehampton 4-2 Odd Down reserves
Mangotsfield United reserves 2-2 Cleeve West Town (Cleeve West Town won 5-4 on penalties)
Bishop Sutton reserves 2-3 Berrow
Watchet Town 4-0 Winscombe
Street reserves 0-3 Fry Club
Stockwood Green 3-2 Bridgwater Town reserves
St George Easton in Gordano 6-3 Taunton Blackbrook
Nailsea Town 2-1 Brislington reserves
Ilminster town 1-0 Minehead
Glastonbury Town 0-4 Purnell Sports
Frome Collegians 2-4 Nailsea United
Clevedon United 4-3 Weston St Johns
Cheddar 1-2 Keynsham Town reserves
Burnham United 5-0 Bishops Lydeard
Ashton & Backwell United 3-1 Langford Rovers 2000
Larkhall Athletic reserves 2-0 Cutters Friday

PREMIER DIVISION	1	2	3	4	5	6	7	8	9	10	11	12	13	14	15	16	17	18
1 Ashton & Backwell United		3-0	2-4	2-0	2-0	3-0	2-1	3-2	2-1	2-0	2-0	0-3	0-3	5-2	0-0	0-2	1-4	1-0
2 Bishop's Lydeard	4-0		4-3	1-1	3-1	2-1	2-1	1-2	3-1	5-2	1-5	0-1	1-4	0-4	1-2	0-0	2-2	5-2
3 Bridgwater Town reserves	3-0	2-4		1-1	1-0	0-6	0-2	2-1	0-1	2-4	4-0	3-4	3-3	1-4	1-1	0-1	0-2	3-1
4 Brislington reserves	0-1	1-0	0-1		1-1	2-3	1-1	1-2	2-0	1-3	2-5	0-5	0-3	2-1	4-3	1-1	1-4	3-1
5 Castle Cary	0-2	1-2	0-3	0-1		0-3	1-1	1-2	3-2	1-1	3-3	0-4	1-7	1-5	3-2	1-2	1-1	3-6
6 Cheddar	3-0	2-1	7-2	5-0	4-2		1-2	4-2	6-3	5-1	3-0	2-1	1-1	5-1	2-2	4-0	1-2	3-0
7 Clevedon United	2-1	3-1	4-1	1-0	3-2	2-0		3-2	0-0	3-2	4-0	0-1	0-8	1-1	1-1	1-0	0-4	2-0
8 Cutters Friday	5-2	2-1	7-1	2-1	2-0	2-1	3-1		1-1	5-3	3-0	1-2	4-1	4-3	2-0	3-1	0-0	2-0
9 Glastonbury Town	2-1	0-1	2-2	2-1	3-3	1-1	4-1	1-1		3-2	1-3	1-2	2-4	4-1	0-4	0-3	3-0	0-5
10 Langford Rovers	2-6	5-2	2-0	4-1	3-2	3-7	2-4	4-1	3-2		4-3	6-2	1-5	1-0	2-0	3-2	3-2	7-3
11 Minehead Town	0-1	3-0	2-0	8-4	2-1	1-1	0-3	2-1	2-0	1-4		1-3	2-6	2-0	2-2	0-5	3-0	2-2
12 Nailsea United	0-1	6-0	0-1	2-1	1-1	3-2	2-2	3-2	1-1	1-1	1-0		1-2	2-2	1-0	3-3	0-4	7-1
13 Shirehampton	0-2	1-2	3-0	4-0	7-0	5-2	2-2	2-2	7-1	2-1	4-1	2-2		6-3	1-1	3-1	2-2	3-0
14 St George Easton-In-Gordano	2-2	2-1	3-0	1-5	2-0	3-3	0-1	3-1	1-0	2-2	1-2	1-3	2-5		0-0	3-1	1-4	3-2
15 Stockwood Green	1-2	3-0	3-3	1-0	3-1	1-0	3-0	0-0	4-1	2-1	0-0	1-2	1-3	1-0		1-2	1-0	3-1
16 Taunton Blackbrook	0-0	1-0	4-1	3-2	0-0	0-2	2-0	2-1	1-2	2-0	1-3	0-0	0-3	5-1	1-1		1-3	3-0
17 Watchet Town	1-1	4-0	2-2	4-0	1-2	0-0	5-1	5-2	2-1	4-3	0-0	3-4	4-1	3-0	2-0	2-0		4-1
18 Winscombe	1-3	2-3	4-2	0-1	1-2	1-2	0-1	0-2	1-0	0-4	1-1	1-4	1-5	0-1	1-0	4-2	0-1	

SOMERSET COUNTY LEAGUE PREMIER DIVISION CONSTITUTION 2011-12

ASHTON & BACKWELL UNITED	The Playing Fields, West Town Road, Backwell, Bristol BS48 3HG	01275 462612
BERROW	Red Road Playing Fields, Berrow, Burnham-on-Sea TA8 2LY	None
BISHOPS LYDEARD	Darby Way, Bishops Lydeard TA4 3BE	None
BRIDGWATER TOWN RESEVES	Fairfax Park, College Way, Bath Road, Bridgwater TA6 4TZ	01278 446899
CHEDDAR	Bowdens Park, Draycott Road, Cheddar BS27 3RL	01934 743736
CLEVEDON UNITED	Coleridge Vale Playing Flds, Southley Road, Clevedon BS21 6PF	01275 871878
CUTTERS FRIDAY	The Cutters Club, Stockwood Lane, Stockwood, Bristol BS14 8SJ	01275 839830
GLASTONBURY TOWN	Abbey Moor Stadium, Godney Road, Glastonbury BA6 9AF	01458 831460
LANGFORD ROVERS	Westland United FC, Winterstoke Road, Weston-super-Mare BS24 9AA	01934 632037
MINEHEAD	Recreation Ground, Irnham Road, Minehead TA24 5DP	01643 704989
NAILSEA TOWN	Fryth Way, Pound Lane, Nailsea BS48 2AS	None
NAILSEA UNITED	Grove Sports Ground, Old Church, Nailsea BS48 4ND	01275 856892
ODD DOWN RESERVES	Lew Hill Memorial Ground, Combe Hay Lane, Odd Down, Bath BA2 8PH	01225 832491
SHIREHAMPTON	Recreation Ground, Penpole Lane, Shirehampton, Bristol BS11 0EA	0117 923 5461
ST GEORGE EASTON-IN-GORDANO	Court Hay, Easton-in-Gordano, Bristol BS20 0PY	01275 374235
STOCKWOOD GREEN	Hursley Lane, Woolard Lane, Whitchurch, Bristol BS14 0QY	01275 891300
TAUNTON BLACKBROOK	Taunton Town FC, Wordsworth Drive, Taunton TA1 2HG	01823 278191 Fax: 01823 322975
WATCHET TOWN	Memorial Ground, Doniford Road, Watchet TA23 0TG	01984 631041

IN: *Berrow (P), Nailsea Town (P), Odd Down Reserves (P)*
OUT: *Brislington Reserves (R), Castle Cary (R), Mangotsfield United Reserves (WS), Winscombe (R)*

SOMERSET COUNTY LEAGUE - STEP 7

DIVISION ONE	P	W	D	L	F	A	Pts
1 Berrow	34	23	6	5	87	46	75
2 Nailsea Town	34	20	11	3	69	29	71
3 Odd Down reserves	34	21	4	9	66	46	67
4 Weston St Johns	34	19	6	9	84	53	63
5 Ilminster Town	34	18	8	8	57	43	62
6 Frome Collegians	34	16	7	11	66	48	55
7 Burnham United	34	12	12	10	74	49	48
8 Bishop Sutton reerves	34	13	8	13	87	67	47
9 Fry Club	34	12	11	11	48	45	47
10 Larkhall Athletic reserves	34	12	10	12	56	50	46
11 Purnells Sport	34	11	13	10	50	46	46
12 Cleeve West Town (-4)	34	13	7	14	47	51	42
13 Saltford	34	10	9	15	42	57	39
14 Street reserves (-1)	34	12	4	18	59	75	39
15 Portishead Town reserves	34	7	8	19	48	92	29
16 Nailsea United reserves	34	7	6	21	58	79	27
17 Keynsham Town reserves	34	6	7	21	48	90	25
18 Timsbury Athletic	34	2	7	25	34	114	13

LES JAMES LEAGUE CUP continued...

ROUND 3

Nailsea Town 2-4 Burnham United

Ashton & Backwell United 2-0 Clevedon United

Berrow 5-1 Larkhall Athletic reserves

Fry Club 1-0 Ilminster Town

Nailsea United 6-2 Cleeve West Town

Purnell Sports 1-1 Watchet Town

(Purnell Sports won 5-4 on penalties)

St George Easton in Gordano 1-3 Shirehampton

Stockwood Green 0-1 Keynsham Town reserves

QUARTER FINALS

Purnell Sports 1-6 Shirehampton

Berrow 3-1 Fry Club

Burnham United 1-0 Keynsham Town reserves

Ashton & Backwell United 3-1 Nailsea United

SEMI-FINALS

Shirehampton 6-4 Berrow

Ashton & Backwell United 3-1 Burnham United

FINAL (@ Portishead Town, 19/5/11)

Ashton & Backwell United 0-1 Shirehampton

DIVISION ONE	1	2	3	4	5	6	7	8	9	10	11	12	13	14	15	16	17	18
1 Berrow		3-2	2-2	1-1	3-2	5-0	1-2	5-0	3-0	0-2	1-0	5-2	7-1	3-1	3-0	4-1	3-2	1-1
2 Bishop Sutton reserves	1-3		2-3	1-4	2-2	3-1	2-2	4-1	2-1	1-0	8-1	0-3	5-1	4-0	1-2	5-2	8-0	1-5
3 Burnham United	1-2	3-1		2-0	2-0	0-0	2-2	4-1	4-0	1-3	0-0	1-2	6-2	2-1	0-2	1-2	6-0	2-2
4 Cleeve West Town	1-2	1-1	0-5		2-2	0-1	0-0	3-2	2-0	1-1	4-3	0-2	5-1	0-0	3-1	0-1	1-0	3-2
5 Frome Collegians	0-0	3-2	3-3	1-2		1-1	1-0	2-2	3-1	1-3	4-3	0-1	2-4	1-0	4-1	7-1	2-0	4-1
6 Fry Club	2-5	1-1	1-1	2-0	1-1		0-0	8-1	1-1	1-1	3-1	0-1	1-4	0-0	0-1	1-1	5-2	1-2
7 Ilminster Town	2-1	1-4	3-3	2-0	0-2	2-1		2-0	0-2	1-1	2-1	2-0	3-1	2-1	2-1	1-0	3-1	2-4
8 Keynsham Town reserves	1-2	5-5	2-1	1-3	1-4	0-1	0-2		2-2	0-1	1-4	1-4	0-2	1-1	2-1	4-0	2-3	0-4
9 Larkhall Athletic reserves	2-2	2-5	2-1	1-1	1-0	2-2	1-2	2-0		0-2	5-0	0-1	3-3	1-0	3-0	2-1	8-1	1-2
10 Nailsea Town	2-3	2-1	1-0	2-1	1-0	1-0	2-2	3-1	0-0		2-0	3-2	1-2	2-2	1-1	1-0	6-0	0-0
11 Nailsea United reserves	1-3	2-0	2-2	2-0	1-3	1-2	2-3	2-2	1-1	0-3		2-3	4-0	3-3	1-2	5-1	5-0	1-4
12 Odd Down reserves	0-2	2-2	3-1	3-1	1-2	4-0	2-1	2-0	1-0	1-2	2-1		3-0	2-3	4-0	1-6	2-1	2-1
13 Portishead Town reserves	3-7	0-6	2-3	0-3	4-1	0-1	1-0	1-3	3-3	2-2	2-1	0-0		0-0	0-0	2-3	0-0	2-5
14 Purnell Sports	0-0	3-1	1-1	3-0	0-2	0-2	1-1	4-1	1-2	2-2	4-0	2-2	1-0		3-3	2-0	1-0	1-1
15 Saltford	0-1	1-1	2-2	3-1	0-2	1-2	0-3	0-0	1-0	1-1	1-1	0-1	3-1	2-1		4-3	3-1	2-3
16 Street reserves	4-0	4-1	1-0	1-2	1-0	0-2	0-2	3-5	1-1	1-4	4-0	4-2	3-0	2-3	3-2		2-2	1-5
17 Timsbury Athletic	0-4	1-1	2-2	1-0	0-3	0-4	3-4	4-5	1-3	0-8	2-6	0-2	2-2	2-3	1-1	2-2		0-6
18 Weston St John	7-0	2-3	0-7	1-2	3-1	2-0	2-1	1-1	1-3	1-3	2-1	3-3	5-2	1-2	2-0	2-0	1-0	

SOMERSET COUNTY LEAGUE DIVISION ONE CONSTITUTION 2011-12

BISHOP SUTTON RESERVES	Lake View, Wick Road, Bishop Sutton, Bristol BS39 5XP	01275 333097
BRISLINGTON RESERVES	Ironmould Lane, Brislington, Bristol BS4 5SA	0117 977 4030
BURNHAM UNITED	Burnham Road Playing Fields, Cassis Close, Burnham-on-Sea TA8 1NN	01278 794615
CASTLE CARY	Donald Pither Memorial PF, Catherines Close, Castle Cary BA7 7HP	01963 351538
CLEEVE WEST TOWN	King George V Playing Fields, Meeting House Lane, Cleeve BS49 4PD	01934 832173
CLUTTON	Warwick Fields, Upper Bristol Road, Clutton, Bristol BS39 5TA	None
CONGRESBURY	Broadstones Playing Fields, Stonewell Lane, Congresbury BS49 5DL	01934 832150
FROME COLLEGIANS	Selwood School, Berkley Road, Frome BA11 2EF	None
FRY CLUB	Fry Club, Somerdale, Keynsham, Bristol BS31 2AU	0117 937 6500/6501
ILMINSTER TOWN	Recreation Ground, Ilminster TA19 0EF	None
LARKHALL ATHLETIC RESERVES	Plain Ham, Charlcombe Lane, Larkhall, Bath BA1 8DJ	01225 334952
PURNELL SPORTS	Paulton Rovers FC, Athletic Ground, Winterfield Road, Paulton BS39 7RF	01761 412907
SALTFORD	Playing Fields, Norman Road, Saltford BS31 0BQ	01225 873725
SHEPTON MALLET RESERVES	West Shepton Playing Fields, Old Wells Road, Shepton Mallet BA4 5XN	01749 344609
STREET RESERVES	The Tannery Ground, Middlebrooks, Street BA16 0TA	01458 445987
WESTON ST JOHNS	Coleridge Road, Bournville Estate, Weston-super-Mare BS23 3UP	01934 612862
WINSCOMBE	Recreation Ground, The Lynch, Winscombe BS25 1AP	01934 842720(cricket club)
YATTON ATHLETIC	Hangstones Playing Fields, Stowey Road, Yatton BS49 4HY	None

IN: *Brislington Reserves (R), Castle Cary (R), Clutton (P-Division One East), Congresbury (P-Division One West), Winscombe (R), Shepton Mallet Reserves (P-Division One East), Yatton Athletic (P-Division One West)*

OUT: *Berrow (P), Keynsham Town Reserves (R-Division One East), Nailsea Town (P), Nailsea United Reserves (R-Division One West), Portishead Town Reserves (R-Division One West), Odd Down Reserves (P), Timsbury Athletic (R-Division One East)*

DIVISION TWO EAST	P	W	D	L	F	A	Pts
1 Clutton	28	21	5	2	82	27	68
2 Shepton Mallet reserves	28	17	6	5	63	33	57
3 Welton Rovers reserves (-4)	28	17	5	6	71	36	52
4 Peasedown Athletic	28	14	6	8	65	41	48
5 Tunley Athletic	28	15	3	10	54	39	48
6 Radstock Town reserves	28	12	7	9	53	42	43
7 Westfield	28	11	7	10	80	52	40
8 Cutters Friday reserves	28	10	6	12	42	49	36
9 Fry Club reserves	28	10	5	13	50	51	35
10 Imperial	28	10	3	15	51	64	33
11 Stockwood Green reserves	28	9	5	14	51	53	32
12 Purnells Sports reserves	28	7	7	14	48	70	28
13 Hengrove Athletic res (-17)	28	10	7	11	48	63	20
14 Dundry Athletic (-7)	28	5	7	16	40	57	16
15 Timsbury Athletic res (-3)	28	2	1	25	21	142	4

DIVISION TWO WEST	P	W	D	L	F	A	Pts
1 Congresbury (-7)	26	20	5	1	67	18	58
2 Yatton Athletic	26	17	5	4	85	43	56
3 Combe St Nicholas	26	15	6	5	52	36	51
4 Ashton&Backwell U res (-1)	26	14	5	7	59	38	46
5 Westland United	26	12	5	9	42	38	41
6 Churchill Club 70	26	9	8	9	54	56	35
7 Creech St Michael (-4)	26	12	2	12	55	48	34
8 Wells City reserves	26	9	6	11	43	47	33
9 Long Ashton (-1)	26	8	4	14	52	55	27
10 Cheddar reserves	26	7	6	13	44	59	27
11 Banwell (-7)	26	9	4	13	38	56	24
12 Burnham United reserves	26	6	6	14	33	60	24
13 Worle	26	5	7	14	32	57	22
14 Wrington Redhill	26	2	5	19	29	74	11

DIVISION TWO CUP (ERREA)

ROUND 1

Churchill Club 70 4-2 Peasedown Athletic
Creech St Michael 0-2 Purnell Sports reserves
Fry Club reserves 0-2 Radstock Town reserves
Imperial 3-2 Clutton
Timsbury Athletic reserves 0-5 Shepton Mallet reserves
Tunley Athletic 1-2 Ashton & Backwell United reserves
Westfield 9-1 Hengrove Athletic reserves
Wrington Redhill 2-3 Welton Rovers reserves
Wells City reserves 2-1 Yatton Athletic
Burnham United reserves 0-2 Westland United
Cheddar reserves 1-2 Long Ashton
Stockwood Green reserves 2-4 Congresbury

ROUND 2

Long Ashton 4-2 Churchill Club 70
Imperial 1-0 Dundry Athletic
Radstock Town reserves 4-1 Ashton & Backwell United res.
Shepton Mallet reserves 1-0 Combe St Nicholas
Westland United 0-3 Congresbury
Worle 4-1 Banwell
Wells City reserves 0-2 Purnell Sports reserves
Westfield 2-4 Welton Rovers reserves

QUARTER FINALS

Welton Rovers reserves 2-1 Long Ashton
(tie awarded to Long Ashton)
Imperial 0-2 Worle
Purnell Sports reserves 1-0 Congresbury
Shepton Mallet reserves 2-1 Radstock Town reserves

SEMI-FINALS

Purnell Sports reserves 1-3 Long Ashton
Shepton Mallet reserves 1-2 Worle

FINAL (@ Wells City, 17/5/11)

Long Ashton 2-0 Worle

DIVISION TWO EAST	1	2	3	4	5	6	7	8	9	10	11	12	13	14	15
1 Clutton		2-1	1-1	1-0	8-0	6-1	3-0	5-2	1-0	6-1	4-2	8-0	1-1	6-2	5-4
2 Cutters Friday reserves	1-2		1-0	4-0	1-1	3-1	1-0	2-1	0-1	2-5	2-0	0-2	2-1	2-2	3-0
3 Dundry Athletic	2-2	2-4		3-1	1-3	2-6	1-2	2-3	0-4	0-1	2-2	3-0	0-1	1-2	1-1
4 Fry Club reserves	0-1	4-1	3-0		3-3	1-2	3-1	0-0	2-3	1-1	1-0	9-1	0-1	0-1	3-1
5 Hengrove Athletic reserves	1-3	1-1	0-0	4-2		1-2	4-2	2-2	3-0	1-5	3-1	3-2	0-0	0-4	1-0
6 Imperial	0-0	5-0	2-5	1-3	5-1		1-2	3-1	2-0	1-3	3-3	4-1	0-1	2-4	2-1
7 Peasedown Athletic	1-0	3-1	4-1	4-1	4-0	4-0		1-1	0-2	0-4	2-0	8-0	0-2	2-2	2-2
8 Purnell Sports reserves	1-3	0-2	0-4	1-1	1-2	3-1	1-3		0-5	2-3	2-0	6-2	3-2	1-6	0-4
9 Radstock Town reserves	1-1	1-1	2-1	3-0	4-3	2-2	1-1	2-2		0-1	1-1	6-2	1-4	0-1	4-2
10 Shepton Mallet reserves	0-1	1-0	1-0	3-3	2-1	5-0	3-3	1-1	1-0		2-3	6-0	1-0	2-1	2-3
11 Stockwood Green reserves	0-3	3-1	0-0	4-1	1-2	2-0	2-5	4-1	0-1	2-1		7-0	2-3	1-3	0-4
12 Timsbury Athletic reserves	0-3	1-1	2-5	0-3	0-2	0-4	0-6	2-6	2-4	1-3	1-7		1-0	1-8	0-4
13 Tunley Athletic	4-0	3-1	3-1	2-3	2-1	2-0	2-3	3-1	2-2	0-4	0-1	10-0		2-1	1-6
14 Welton Rovers reserves	1-3	1-1	4-0	4-0	5-3	2-1	1-0	2-2	3-1	0-0	2-0	6-0	0-1		0-2
15 Westfield	0-3	6-3	2-2	1-2	2-2	6-0	2-2	3-4	4-2	1-1	3-3	10-0	4-1	2-3	

DIVISION TWO WEST	1	2	3	4	5	6	7	8	9	10	11	12	13	14
1 Ashton & Backwell United reserves		1-2	5-1	3-2	1-1	4-0	0-0	1-2	3-0	0-2	3-0	4-0	1-1	2-1
2 Banwell	4-1		0-2	0-2	0-4	1-2	2-6	4-1	4-2	3-2	0-5	0-0	2-1	0-5
3 Burnham United reserves	2-1	1-2		1-0	1-4	1-3	0-1	1-1	1-2	1-5	0-0	1-2	3-3	2-7
4 Cheddar reserves	2-2	4-0	2-2		4-2	2-2	0-2	1-2	1-1	1-1	2-1	2-2	3-1	1-5
5 Churchill Club 70	2-5	1-1	4-0	3-1		1-1	0-6	4-0	2-1	1-1	0-0	4-0	3-2	2-6
6 Combe St Nicholas	0-1	2-1	2-1	5-2	2-0		1-1	1-0	2-2	1-1	0-4	2-0	5-0	1-1
7 Congresbury	1-0	2-1	1-0	4-0	3-1	1-0		2-0	3-1	4-0	2-1	2-0	0-3	2-2
8 Creech St Michael	2-3	1-0	3-1	5-1	4-1	6-1	1-2		2-4	4-1	1-2	3-2	6-0	3-3
9 Long Ashton	2-4	1-2	1-2	6-0	3-3	3-4	1-4	2-0		2-2	0-1	4-1	2-0	1-3
10 Wells City reserves	0-2	1-0	3-3	2-0	3-2	0-1	1-1	0-2	4-1		0-2	1-4	4-2	0-2
11 Westland United	1-1	1-2	3-3	2-1	2-2	1-2	0-6	3-1	4-2	3-1		1-0	1-0	0-1
12 Worle	1-3	2-2	0-1	1-4	5-2	1-3	1-1	3-2	0-5	1-4	1-0		1-1	2-2
13 Wrington & Redhill	4-6	2-2	0-1	0-4	2-3	1-6	0-6	1-2	0-1	1-2	2-3	0-0		2-1
14 Yatton Athletic	5-2	4-3	5-1	4-2	2-2	0-3	2-4	4-1	3-2	3-2	5-1	3-2	6-0	

SOMERSET COUNTY LEAGUE DIVISION TWO EAST CONSTITUTION 2011-12

CUTTERS FRIDAY RESERVES	The Cutters Club , Stockwood Lane, Stockwood , Bristol BS14 8SJ	01275 839830
DUNDRY ATHLETIC	Dundry Playing Field, Crabtree Lane, Dundry, Bristol BS41 8LN	0117 964 5536
FARRINGTON GURNEY	Farrington Recreation Ground, Farrington Gurney	
FRY CLUB RESERVES	Fry Club, Somerdale, Keynsham, Bristol BS31 2AU	0117 937 6500/6501
HENGROVE ATHLETIC RESERVES	Norton Lane, Whitchurch, Bristol BS14 0BT	01275 832894
IMPERIAL	Bristol Imperial Sports Club, West Town Lane, Whitchurch, Brislington BS4 5DT	01275 546000
KEYNSHAM TOWN RESERVES	Crown Field, Bristol Road, Keynsham, Bristol BS31 2BE	0117 986 5876
PEASEDOWN ATHLETIC	Miners Welfare Park, Church Road, Peasedown St John, Bath BA2 8AF	01761 437319
PURNELL SPORTS RESERVES	Greyfield Sports & Social Club, Bristol Road, Paulton BS39 7NX	01761 412809
RADSTOCK TOWN RESERVES	Southfield Recreation Ground, Frome Hill, Radstock BA3 3NZ	01761 435004
STOCKWOOD GREEN RESERVES	Hursley Lane, Woolard Lane, Whitchurch, Bristol BS14 0QY	01275 891300
TIMSBURY ATHLETIC	Recreation Ground, North Road, Timsbury, Bath BA2 0JH	01761 472523
TUNLEY ATHLETIC	The Recreation Centre, Bath Road, Tunley BA2 0EB	None
WELTON ROVERS RESERVES	West Clewes, North Road, Midsomer Norton BA3 2QD	01761 412097
WESTFIELD	Fosseway Playing Fields, Charlton Lane, Midsomer Norton BA3 4BD	None

IN: *Keynsham Town Reserves (R), Farrington Gurney (P-Mid-Somerset League Premier Division), Timsbury Athletic (R)*

OUT: *Clutton (P), Shepton Mallet Reserves (P), Timsbury Athletic Reserves (R-Mid-Somerset League Premier Division)*

SOMERSET COUNTY LEAGUE DIVISION TWO WEST CONSTITUTION 2011-12

ASHTON & BACKWELL UNITED RES.	The Playing Fields , West Town Road, Backwell , Bristol BS48 3HG	01275 462612
BANWELL	Riverside Ground, Riverside, Banwell BS29 6EE	01934 820773
BURNHAM UNITED RESERVES	Burnham Road Playing Fields, Cassis Close, Burnham-on-Sea TA8 1NN	01278 794615
CHEDDAR RESERVES	Bowdens Park, Draycott Road, Cheddar BS27 3RL	01934 743736
CHURCHILL CLUB	Ladymead Lane, Churchill, Winscombe BS25 5NH	01934 852739
COMBE ST NICHOLAS	Slades Cross, Combe St Nicholas TA20 3HQ	01460 234743
CREECH ST MICHAEL	Creech St Michael Rec, Hyde Lane, Creech St Michael, Taunton TA3 5QJ	None
LONG ASHTON	Long Ashton Rec., Keedwell Hill, Long Ashton BS41 9DP	None
NAILSEA UNITED RESERVES	Grove Sports Ground, Old Church, Nailsea BS48 4ND	01275 856892
PORTISHEAD TOWN RESERVES	Bristol Road Playing Fields, Portishead, Bristol BS20 6QB	01275 847136
WELLS CITY RESERVES	The Athletic Ground, Rowdens Road, Wells BA5 1TU	01749 679971
WESTLAND UNITED	Westland Sports Club, Winterstoke Road, Weston-super-Mare BS24 9AA	01934 632037
WORLE	Worle Recreation Ground, Station Road, Worle, Weston-super-Mare BS22 6AU	None
WRINGTON-REDHILL	Recreation Ground, Silver Street, Wrington BS40 5QE	None

IN: *Nailsea United Reserves (R), Portishead Town Reserves (R)*

OUT: *Congresbury (P), Yatton Athletic (P)*

STAFFORDSHIRE COUNTY SENIOR LEAGUE

Sponsored by: No sponsor
Founded: 1957
Recent Champions:
2006: Hanley Town
2007: Wolstanton United
2008: Wolstanton United
2009: Foley
2010: Stretton Eagles

PREMIER DIVISION	P	W	D	L	F	A	Pts
1 Ball Haye Green	30	23	6	1	79	22	75
2 Hanley Town	30	23	2	5	90	31	71
3 Newcastle Town reserves	30	22	4	4	90	35	70
4 Wolstanton United	30	18	6	6	85	45	60
5 Abbey Hulton United	30	17	6	7	64	38	57
6 Congleton Vale	30	14	8	8	56	43	50
7 Goldenhill Wanderers	30	14	4	12	61	61	46
8 Florence	30	13	4	13	51	51	43
9 Redgate Clayton	30	11	6	13	70	62	39
10 Eccleshall AFC	30	9	7	14	42	58	34
11 Stone Dominoes reserves	30	10	3	17	38	51	33
12 Sandbach United	30	9	4	17	54	53	31
13 Kidsgrove Athletic reserves	30	9	4	17	47	78	31
14 Norton	30	7	5	18	50	75	26
15 Manor Inne	30	2	5	23	24	100	11
16 Foley	30	2	0	28	25	123	6

LEAGUE CUP

ROUND 1
Stone Dominoes reserves 1-4 Sandbach United
Longton Harriers 2-4 Hanley Town reserves
Hanley Town 4-1 Congleton Vale
Florence 3-1 Eccleshall AFC
Congleton Athletic 3-2 Kidsgrove Athletic reserves
Barton United 3-2 Wolstanton United
Abbey Hulton United 0-2 Manor Inne
Redgate Clayton reserves 3-2 Newcastle Town reserves
Norton 1-4 Cheadle Town
Northwood Town 2-2 Wolstanton United reserves (Wolstanton reserves won 7-8 on penalties)
Holt JCB 0-4 Redgate Clayton
Chesterton 4-0 Foley
Audley 1-0 Alsager Town reserves
Ashbourne 4-2 Talbot Athletic
Goldenhill Wanderers 2-3 Stretton Eagles

ROUND 2
Wolstanton United reserves 3-2 Congleton Athletic
Sandbach United 1-2 Hanley Town
Ball Haye Green 3-1 Stretton Eagles
Ashbourne 2-6 Redgate Clayton
Hanley Town reserves 3-1 Manor Inne
Chesterton 0-4 Florence
Audley 2-1 Barton Rovers
Redgate Clayton reserves 0-3 Cheadle Town

PREMIER DIVISION	1	2	3	4	5	6	7	8	9	10	11	12	13	14	15	16
1 Abbey Hulton United		1-2	2-1	1-1	0-1	2-1	2-0	5-3	5-0	4-0	1-1	2-1	1-1	4-2	2-1	1-1
2 Ball Haye Green	4-1		3-3	3-0	3-0	8-0	4-1	1-1	1-1	2-1	5-0	4-1	1-0	3-0	3-1	1-0
3 Congleton Vale	1-1	2-2		1-1	3-1	4-1	2-1	1-3	1-0	0-1	2-2	2-1	2-0	1-0	5-2	2-2
4 Eccleshall	2-1	0-2	2-2		0-1	1-0	0-3	0-2	1-1	3-2	0-4	3-0	1-3	1-4	0-1	2-6
5 Florence	0-2	0-1	0-3	0-1		1-2	0-2	4-2	4-1	1-0	0-2	4-1	3-3	2-1	3-1	0-4
6 Foley	0-5	0-5	0-2	0-7	1-4		1-2	0-4	1-3	2-4	2-6	2-6	0-7	0-5	3-4	1-2
7 Goldenhill Wanderers	0-4	1-1	3-1	5-0	0-5	2-1		1-4	3-5	3-0	3-1	5-0	2-2	0-2	3-1	3-5
8 Hanley Town	0-2	2-0	3-0	2-3	5-1	4-0	5-0		5-2	5-0	0-1	2-0	3-1	2-0	1-0	1-1
9 Kidsgrove Athletic reserves	2-1	0-3	1-3	1-2	0-0	4-2	0-7	0-4		4-1	3-7	1-0	0-4	1-4	2-3	5-3
10 Manor Inne	0-2	0-2	0-3	1-4	0-2	0-2	1-1	2-5	1-1		0-10	1-1	1-4	1-1	0-3	0-2
11 Newcastle Town reserves	4-0	1-1	1-0	2-1	6-1	2-0	2-1	1-2	2-0	8-0		1-0	1-1	3-2	2-0	3-1
12 Norton	1-3	2-5	3-4	1-1	4-6	6-2	1-2	2-6	0-5	2-2	2-1		3-4	3-0	1-0	1-1
13 Redgate Clayton	2-3	1-3	0-0	1-1	0-5	4-0	1-3	2-3	6-2	8-2	3-5	1-2		3-1	1-0	0-5
14 Sandbach United	2-1	1-3	2-3	3-0	1-1	4-0	2-2	0-4	0-1	7-1	2-4	1-2	2-3		0-1	0-0
15 Stone Dominoes reserves	2-3	0-1	3-1	2-2	1-1	3-0	0-1	0-4	2-1	4-1	0-2	1-1	2-1	0-3		0-1
16 Wolstanton United	2-2	1-2	2-1	3-2	1-0	12-1	8-1	1-3	2-0	4-1	2-5	3-2	5-3	3-2	2-0	

STAFFS COUNTY SENIOR LEAGUE PREMIER DIVISION CONSTITUTION 2011-12

ABBEY HULTON UNITED	Birches Head Road, Abbey Hulton, Stoke-on-Trent ST2 8DD	01782 544232
AUDLEY & DISTRICT	Town Fields, Old Road, Bignall, Stoke-on-Trent ST7 8QH	01782 723482
BALL HAYE GREEN	Ball Haye Green WMC, Ball Haye Green, Leek ST13 6BH	01538 371926
BIDDULPH TOWN	Knypersley Sports & Social, Tunstall Road, Knypersley, Stoke-on-Trent ST8 7AQ	01782 522737
CONGLETON VALE ROVERS	Knypersley Sports & Social, Tunstall Road, Knypersley, Stoke-on-Trent ST8 7AQ	01782 522737
ECCLESHALL AFC	Pershall Park, Chester Road, Eccleshall ST21 6NE	01785 851351
FLORENCE	Florence Sports & Social, Lightwood Road, Longton, Stoke-on-Trent ST3 4JS	01782 312881 Fax: 01782 313468
HANLEY TOWN	Abbey Lane, Abbey Hulton, Bucknall, Stoke-on-Trent ST2 8AU	01782 267234
KEELE UNIVERSITY	Sports Centre, Keele University, Keele ST5 5BG	01782 733368
KIDSGROVE ATHLETIC RESERVES	The Seddon Stadium, Hollinwood Road, Kidsgrove, Stoke-on-Trent ST7 1DH	01782 782412
NEWCASTLE TOWN RESERVES	Lyme Valley Parkway Stadium, Buckmaster Avenue, Clayton, Newcastle-under-Lyme ST5 3BF	01782 662351 Club: 01782 622350
NORTON	Norton CC & MW Institute, Community Drive, Smallthorne, Stoke-on-Trent ST6 1QF	01782 838290
REDGATE CLAYTON	Northwood Lane, Clayton, Newcastle-under-Lyme ST5 4BN	01782 717409
STONE DOMINOES RESERVES	Motiva Park, Yarnfield Lane, Yarnfield, Stone ST15 0NF	01782 761891
STRETTON	Shobnall Sports & Social Club, Shobnall Road, Burton-on-Trent DE14 2BB	01283 567991
WOLSTANTON UNITED	Bradwell Community Centre, Riceyman Road, Bradwell, Newcastle-under-Lyme ST5 8LF	01782 660818

__IN:__ Audley & District (P), Biddulph Town (formerly Biddulph Victoria) (R-Midland Alliance), Keele University (P), Stretton (formerly Stretton Eagles Reserves) (P). __OUT:__ Foley (R), Goldenhill Wanderers (W), Manor Inne (W), Sandbach United (S-Cheshire League Division Two). Congleton Vale become Congleton Vale Rovers.

STAFFORDSHIRE COUNTY SENIOR LEAGUE - STEP 7

DIVISION ONE	P	W	D	L	F	A	Pts
1 Audley	30	22	7	1	69	18	73
2 Barton United	30	21	6	3	83	30	69
3 Keele University	30	17	9	4	68	31	60
4 Stretton Eagles reserves	30	18	2	10	62	42	56
5 Wolstanton United reserves	30	15	8	7	50	38	53
6 Hanley Town reserves	30	16	4	10	75	62	52
7 Cheadle Town Old Boys	30	13	9	8	84	48	48
8 Congleton Athletic	30	13	7	10	67	55	46
9 Redgate Clayton reserves	30	12	4	14	57	62	40
10 Alsager Town reserves	30	10	7	13	42	57	37
11 Ashbourne	30	9	3	18	56	73	30
12 Northwood Town	30	9	2	19	64	78	29
13 Chesterton	30	6	5	19	36	73	23
14 Talbot Athletic	30	5	7	18	45	78	22
15 Holt JCB	30	3	10	17	47	72	19
16 Longton Harriers	30	5	2	23	32	120	17

LEAGUE CUP continued...

QUARTER FINALS

Ball Haye Green 3-0 Wolstanton United

Hanley Town reserves 0-1 Redgate Clayton

Audley 1-3 Florence

Cheadle Town 2-3 Hanley Town

SEMI-FINALS

Hanley Town 3-1 Ball Haye Green

Redgate Clayton 4-3 Florence

FINAL (@ Norton United, 4/4/11)

Hanley Town 0-1 Redgate Clayton

PRESIDENT'S TROPHY

EXTRA PRELIMINARY ROUND

Wolstanton United reserves 0-1 Redgate Clayton reserves
Hawkins Sports 1-2 Audley reserves
Cheadle Town reserves 6-1 Longton Harriers
Cheadle Town 4-1 Sandbach United reserves

ROUND 1

Stretton Eagles 1-2 Barton United
Talbot Athletic 3-1 Rugeley Rangers
Stone Old Alleynians 0-3 Alsager Town
Longton Harriers 3-1 Hanley Town reserves
Lea Hall 2-4 Redgate Clayton reserves
Holt JCB 0-1 Audley reserves
Hawkins Sports 5-3 Abbey Hulton United reserves
Congleton Athletic 4-1 Talbot Athletic reserves
Chesterton 4-3 Northwood Town
Cheadle SMU 4-0 Kidsgrove Athletic Youth
Bradwell 1-3 Cheadle Town reserves
Audley 0-1 Wolstanton United reserves

ROUND 2

Ashbourne 1-4 Cheadle Town
Florence reserves 10-0 Tunstall Town
Congleton Athletic 5-1 Cheadle SMU
Chesterton 1-1 Alsager Town reserves (Alsager Town reserves won 5-4 on penalties)
Talbot Athletic 0-1 Barton United

ROUND 3

Barton United 2-1 Cheadle Town
Alsager Town reserves 2-1 Florence reerves
Congleton Athletic 2-3 Audley reserves
Cheadle Town reserves 1-4 Redgate Clayton reserves

DIVISION ONE	1	2	3	4	5	6	7	8	9	10	11	12	13	14	15	16
1 Alsager Town reserves		1-0	1-1	1-1	1-1	1-1	2-1	0-5	2-1	1-2	1-2	5-4	4-0	1-1	2-3	1-2
2 Ashbourne	2-1		0-1	1-3	3-7	2-1	2-2	2-4	2-2	1-2	8-1	3-1	1-3	0-5	3-1	1-4
3 Audley	2-0	1-0		0-0	5-2	0-0	2-1	3-0	2-1	1-0	4-1	2-0	2-1	2-0	3-1	5-0
4 Barton United	6-1	4-0	2-1		4-4	7-0	1-0	8-2	2-0	2-2	2-0	1-0	2-2	1-2	3-1	1-0
5 Cheadle Town Old Boys	4-0	5-2	2-2	2-3		4-0	1-1	4-1	2-2	1-1	10-0	2-1	6-0	0-2	6-1	2-2
6 Chesterton	0-1	2-3	1-2	1-3	3-1		2-1	3-5	3-4	4-4	4-2	1-0	0-2	0-2	1-5	1-0
7 Congleton Athletic	2-0	1-1	0-3	1-2	2-0	2-1		2-5	6-0	2-2	7-0	4-2	3-2	3-1	2-2	1-2
8 Hanley Town reserves	0-1	3-2	0-1	1-2	1-3	4-0	3-4		5-5	1-0	4-2	4-1	2-1	1-3	6-2	2-1
9 Holt JCB	1-2	0-3	1-1	1-4	1-1	4-1	3-3	1-1		0-3	8-0	3-4	1-2	0-5	2-2	0-1
10 Keele University	3-1	1-0	0-3	1-2	3-2	0-0	7-2	1-1	1-1		1-0	4-1	3-1	2-1	2-1	2-0
11 Longton Harriers	2-5	1-3	0-10	0-9	1-5	2-1	1-2	1-4	3-2	0-4		0-3	3-4	3-0	1-0	0-5
12 Northwood Town	4-0	7-1	0-2	2-2	2-3	1-2	3-4	0-1	2-0	0-10	3-2		4-1	1-2	3-3	4-2
13 Redgate Clayton reserves	3-4	3-1	1-1	1-2	2-1	1-1	2-2	2-4	3-0	0-2	6-1	4-2		0-3	2-1	1-2
14 Stretton Eagles reserves	1-0	3-2	2-4	1-0	2-1	5-1	0-2	5-2	3-1	0-0	3-1	1-6	4-2		0-2	1-2
15 Talbot Athletic	1-1	0-5	0-2	1-4	0-2	3-0	2-4	1-2	1-1	1-4	2-2	3-1	0-3	1-4		3-3
16 Wolstanton United reserves	1-1	3-2	1-1	1-0	0-0	2-1	1-0	1-1	2-1	1-1	0-0	6-2	0-2	1-0	4-1	

STAFFS COUNTY SENIOR LEAGUE DIVISION ONE CONSTITUTION 2011-12

ABBEY HULTON UNITED RESERVES	Birches Head Road, Abbey Hulton, Stoke-on-Trent ST2 8DD	01782 544232
ALSAGER TOWN RESERVES	The Town Ground, Woodland Court, Alsager ST7 2DP	01270 882336
ASHBOURNE	Cockayne Avenue, Ashbourne DE6 1NF	None
BRADELEY TOWN	Bradeley Sports Centre, Chell Heath Road, Bradeley ST6 7LH	None
CHEADLE TOWN OLD BOYS	South Moorlands Leisure Centre, Allen Street, Cheadle ST10 1SA	01538 753883
CHESTERTON	Red Street Community Centre, Talke Road, Chesterton, Newcastle-under-Lyme ST5 7AH	None
CONGLETON ATHLETIC	Back Lane Playing Fields, Back Lane, Congleton CW12 4RB	None
FOLEY	Whitcombe Road, Meir, Stoke-on-Trent ST3 6NU	01782 595274
HANLEY TOWN RESERVES	Abbey Lane, Abbey Hulton, Bucknall, Stoke-on-Trent ST2 8AU	01782 267234
LEA HALL	Lea Hall WMC, Sandy Lane, Rugeley WS15 2LB	None
LONGTON HARRIERS	Malthouse, Leek Road, Cellarhead ST3 5BF	None
MMU CHESHIRE	Alsager Campus, Hassall Road, Alsager ST7 2HL	None
REDGATE CLAYTON RESERVES	Northwood Lane, Clayton, Newcastle-under-Lyme ST5 4BN	01782 717409
RUGELEY RANGERS	Red Lion Ground, Armitage Lane, Brereton, Rugeley WS15 1ED	01889 585526
SANDBACH UNITED RESERVES	Bentley FC, Sunny Bank Road, Crewe CW2 8WD	01270 656868
WOLSTANTON UNITED RESERVES	Bradwell Community Centre, Riceyman Road, Bradwell, Newcastle-under-Lyme ST5 8LF	01782 660818

IN: *Abbey Hulton United Reserves (P), Foley (R), Lea Hall (P), MMU Cheshire (P), Rugeley Rangers (P), Sandbach United Res. (P)*
OUT: *Audley & District (P), Barton United (S-Midland Combination Division Two), Keele University (P), Northwood Town (W), Stretton Eagles Reserves (now Stretton) (P).*
Talbot Athletic are now Bradeley Town

DIVISION TWO	P	W	D	L	F	A	Pts
1 MMU Cheshire	28	23	1	4	134	21	70
2 Lea Hall	28	22	3	3	120	35	69
3 Abbey Hulton United reserves	28	20	3	5	81	41	63
4 Sandbach United reserves	28	19	5	4	94	43	62
5 Rugeley Rangers	28	17	4	7	74	33	55
6 Audley reserves	28	13	4	11	77	44	43
7 Hawkins Sports	28	14	0	14	63	62	42
8 Stone Old Alleynians reserves	28	12	3	13	81	56	39
9 Cheadle SMU	28	11	3	14	57	46	36
10 Bradwell	28	11	3	14	66	70	36
11 Kidsgrove Athletic Youth	28	9	3	16	64	73	30
12 Florence reserves	28	7	3	18	53	72	24
13 Cheadle Town Old Boys res	28	6	3	19	53	97	21
14 Talbot Athletic reserves	28	5	4	19	54	108	19
15 Tunstall Town	28	0	0	28	5	275	0

DIVISION TWO CUP

ROUND 1

Bradwell 2-4 Abbey Hulton United Res.
Lea Hall 2-3 Cheadle Town Old Boys Res.
Rugeley Rangers 5-0 Tunstall Town
Sandbach United Res. 1-2 Kidsgrove Athletic Youth
Stone Old Alleynians Res. 7-2 Florence Res.
Talbot Athletic Res. 1-6 Audley Res.

QUARTER-FINALS

Cheadle South Moorlands United 1-0 Cheadle Town O B Res.
Hawkins Sports 0-4 Audley Res.
Kidsgrove Athletic Youth 0-6 Rugeley Rangers
Stone Old Alleynians Res 0-1 Abbey Hulton United Res.

SEMI-FINALS

Audley Res. 2-2 Cheadle South Moorlands United (Audley reserves won 3-1 on penalties)
Rugeley Rangers 4-1 Abbey Hulton United Res.

FINAL (@ Norton United, 30/3/11)
Audley Res. 1-3 Rugeley Rangers

PRESIDENT'S TROPHY continued...

SEMI-FINALS

Barton United 4-1 Redgate Clayton reserves
Audley reserves 2-2 Alsager Town reserves
(Alsager Town reserves won 3-1 on penalties)

FINAL (@ Norton United, 6/4/11)
Alsager Town reserves 1-1 Barton United
(Barton United won 3-0 on penalties)

LEEK & MOORLAND CUP

ROUND 1

Chesterton 3-3 Talbot Athletic (Talbot Athletic won 5-4 on pens)

ROUND 2

Audley 0-1 Congleton Vale
Ball Haye Green 2-1 Eccleshall AFC
Talbot Athletic 0-9 Wolstanton United
Florence 7-2 Norton
Hanley Town 2-1 Newcastle Town Res.
Northwood Town 2-1 Manor Inne
Redgate Clayton 4-2 Cheadle Town Old Boys
Stone Dominoes Res. 4-0 Abbey Hulton United

QUARTER-FINALS

Ball Haye Green 2-1 Congleton Vale
Wolstanton United 1-1 Hanley Town
(Hanley Town won 6-5 on penalties)
Florence 1-0 Northwood Town
Stone Dominoes Res. 2-3 Redgate Clayton

SEMI-FINALS

Hanley Town 4-0 Redgate Clayton
Florence 2-1 Ball Haye Green

FINAL (@ Ball Haye Green, 25/3/11)
Hanley Town 2-1 Florence (at Ball Haye Green)

DIVISION TWO	1	2	3	4	5	6	7	8	9	10	11	12	13	14	15
1 Abbey Hulton United reserves		2-2	4-1	3-2	1-0	2-0	4-1	1-2	1-0	0-5	3-1	1-3	4-3	2-0	15-0
2 Audley reserves	0-2		0-0	3-1	11-0	3-0	7-2	3-2	0-1	1-4	2-3	1-2	2-1	2-0	12-0
3 Bradwell	2-4	1-3		1-3	3-1	3-1	1-3	4-0	1-4	1-3	1-4	0-2	2-1	5-1	5-1
4 Cheadle SMU	0-1	2-0	2-0		1-0	3-1	0-3	2-1	0-3	2-2	2-1	1-2	0-2	5-0	8-0
5 Cheadle Town Old Boys res	2-2	3-7	4-2	4-1		2-1	2-3	1-1	0-11	0-5	0-2	1-6	1-1	1-6	9-0
6 Florence reserves	0-4	1-3	2-5	5-1	5-4		2-4	2-2	1-3	1-6	0-5	0-2	3-1	8-2	10-0
7 Hawkins Sports	2-4	1-0	0-1	3-0	0-1	2-0		3-1	0-7	0-3	0-4	2-0	2-3	1-3	4-0
8 Kidsgrove Athletic Youth	0-5	1-0	3-4	1-0	4-2	0-1	0-5		0-9	1-4	1-1	1-5	1-0	4-3	14-1
9 Lea Hall	2-2	0-0	5-1	3-2	5-1	3-1	5-0	6-2		4-1	2-0	4-1	2-4	6-2	6-0
10 MMU Cheshire	5-0	7-1	5-1	1-0	4-0	3-0	3-0	2-1	6-1		4-0	1-2	5-0	2-0	19-0
11 Rugeley Rangers	1-3	2-0	5-1	1-2	3-1	4-0	5-1	2-0	4-4	1-0		2-2	1-1	2-1	8-0
12 Sandbach United reserves	2-4	3-2	3-3	2-2	8-1	2-2	3-1	5-2	2-3	3-1	2-0		4-1	4-2	12-0
13 Stone Old Alleynians reserves	4-2	0-6	1-2	1-0	3-0	1-0	1-2	2-1	2-6	1-5	0-2	3-3		6-0	19-0
14 Talbot Athletic reserves	0-2	3-3	5-5	2-2	1-0	2-2	2-8	0-5	1-10	0-12	0-3	2-5	0-1		9-2
15 Tunstall Town	1-3	0-3	0-10	0-13	0-12	0-4	0-10	0-13	0-5	0-16	0-7	0-4	0-18	0-7	

STAFFS COUNTY SENIOR LEAGUE DIVISION TWO CONSTITUTION 2011-12

AFC MILTON	Northwood Stadium, Keeling Road, Hanley, Stoke-on-Trent ST1 6PA	01782 234400
AUDLEY & DISTRICT RESERVES	Town Fields, Old Road, Bignall, Stoke-on-Trent ST7 8QH	01782 723482
BRADWELL	Tricketts Lane, Willaston, Nantwich CW5 6PX	None
CHEADLE SOUTH MOORLANDS UtD	South Moorlands Leisure Centre, Thorley Drive, Cheadle ST10 1SA	01538 753883
CHEADLE TOWN OLD BOYS RES.	South Moorlands Leisure Centre, Allen Street, Cheadle ST10 1SA	01538 753883
CONGLETON VALE ROVERS RES.	Congleton High School, Box Lane, Congleton CW12 4NS	01260 387000
HAWKINS SPORTS	Hawkins Sports Club, Coppice Lane, Cheslyn Hay, Walsall WS6 7EY	01922 417286
HILTON HARRIERS ATHLETIC	Main Street, Church Broughton DE65 5AS	None
KIDSGROVE ATHLETIC YOUTH	The Seddon Stadium, Hollinwood Road, Kidsgrove, Stoke-on-Trent ST7 1DH	01782 782412
NORTON RESERVES	Norton CC & MW Institute, Community Drive, Smallthorne, Stoke-on-Trent ST6 1QF	01782 838290
STONE DOMINOES YOUTH	Motiva Park, Yarnfield Lane, Yarnfield, Stone ST15 0NF	01782 761891
STONE OLD ALLEYNIANS RESERVES	Motiva Park, Yarnfield Road, Yarnfield, Stone ST15 0NF	01785 761891
TUNSTALL TOWN	Alsager Leisure Club, Hassal Road, Alsager ST7 2HP	01270 529501
VODAFONE STOKE	Milton Youth & Adult Centre, Leek Road, Stoke-on-Trent ST2 7AF	None
WHITTINGTON	Whittington Barracks, Lichfield WS14 9PY	None

IN: *AFC Milton (N), Congleton Vale Rovers Reserves (N), Hilton Harriers Athletic (N), Norton Reserves (N), Stone Dominoes Youth (N), Vodafone Stoke (N), Whittington (youth football)*

OUT: *Abbey Hulton United Reserves (P), Florences Reserves (W), Lea Hall (P), MMU Cheshire (P), Rugeley Rangers (P), Sandbach United Reserves (P), Talbot Athletic Reserves (W)*

SUFFOLK & IPSWICH LEAGUE

Sponsored by: Kingsley Healthcare
Founded: 1896
Recent Champions:
2006: East Bergholt United
2007: Grundisburgh
2008: Brantham Athletic
2009: Grundisburgh
2010: Old Newton United

SENIOR DIVISION	P	W	D	L	F	A	Pts
1 Grundisburgh	30	20	6	4	80	32	66
2 Achilles	30	18	6	6	68	42	60
3 Ipswich Athletic	30	18	4	8	58	46	58
4 Ransomes Sports	30	16	6	8	69	44	54
5 Felixstowe United	30	16	5	9	63	38	53
6 Capel Plough	30	13	6	11	44	43	45
7 East Bergholt United	30	12	7	11	54	45	43
8 Woodbridge Athletic	30	11	9	10	61	48	42
9 Melton St Audrys	30	12	5	13	44	46	41
10 Framlingham Town	30	9	11	10	53	61	38
11 Crane Sports	30	11	3	16	50	70	36
12 Haughley United	30	8	9	13	42	57	33
13 Old Newton United	30	9	4	17	53	67	31
14 Stanton	30	8	5	17	46	72	29
15 Coplestonians	30	5	8	17	46	66	23
16 Westerfield United	30	5	4	21	37	91	19

OMNICO CUP

ROUND 1
AFC Brickmakers 1-2 Great Blakenham
AFC Crowley 2-0 Henley Athletic
Aldeburgh Town 4-3 Felixstowe Harpers
Bacton United 4-1 Benhall St Mary
Bramford Road Old Boys 4-1 Tacket Street BBOB
Cedars Park 6-1 Willis
Claydon 8-1 Ufford Sports
Coddenham 6-4 Salvation Army
Dennington United scr-w/o Bramford United
Elmswell 2-9 Bildeston Rangers
FC Adhara 2-2 Stradbroke United
(Stradbroke United won 3-2 on penalties)
Kesgrave Kestrels 6-2 AFC Titans
Parkside United 7-2 St Clements Hospital
Shotley 9-3 Woolverstone United
Sizewell Associates 1-5 Sproughton Sports
Sporting '87 4-3 Waterside
Sproughton United 0-4 AFC Hoxne
Tattingstone United 2-6 Somersham
Walsham-le-Willows A 4-2 Ipswich Exiles
ROUND 2
AFC Crowley 3-2 Leiston St Margaret's
Bramford Road Old Boys 4-2 Bramford United

SENIOR DIVISION	1	2	3	4	5	6	7	8	9	10	11	12	13	14	15	16
1 Achilles		2-2	2-1	2-1	2-1	1-3	2-2	0-0	1-1	3-1	3-2	2-0	1-2	2-1	4-0	2-1
2 Capel Plough	1-0		3-1	1-0	3-0	0-3	2-2	3-1	0-1	0-2	0-1	1-1	2-0	3-1	2-0	1-5
3 Coplestonians	2-5	2-0		0-1	2-2	1-3	2-3	1-2	2-2	2-3	0-2	1-0	0-1	3-2	2-1	2-2
4 Crane Sports	2-3	0-2	5-1		2-4	0-0	2-1	0-5	2-1	1-4	3-0	3-0	2-4	4-3	0-2	1-2
5 East Bergholt United	2-3	2-1	1-1	0-1		0-2	6-2	3-1	0-2	1-1	1-3	3-2	1-1	5-1	5-3	4-0
6 Felixstowe United	6-1	1-2	2-1	5-1	2-3		2-3	1-3	3-1	0-2	0-1	1-0	4-3	2-0	2-2	1-1
7 Framlingham Town	3-2	0-0	3-3	4-1	1-1	0-0		2-4	0-0	2-3	4-1	3-2	0-8	3-0	1-1	0-4
8 Grundisburgh	2-0	0-0	3-3	5-1	2-0	0-1	2-1		3-1	4-0	3-2	6-1	1-1	5-1	7-1	1-0
9 Haughley United	0-6	3-0	2-1	2-3	0-2	1-1	4-3	1-5		1-2	0-2	2-2	2-1	0-2	2-3	1-1
10 Ipswich Athletic	1-3	3-2	1-0	4-0	2-1	3-0	1-1	1-4	3-0		1-1	1-1	1-0	0-3	5-2	3-2
11 Melton St Audrys	2-4	1-1	1-0	2-3	1-1	2-1	2-2	1-3	1-1	0-2		1-3	1-2	4-1	2-1	0-1
12 Old Newton United	1-2	5-4	2-3	3-0	1-2	1-0	1-4	3-2	3-6	6-1	0-2		1-2	0-1	4-0	3-3
13 Ransomes Sports	2-2	4-2	2-2	3-0	1-3	1-2	2-0	0-0	1-0	0-3	2-0	6-1		3-0	5-2	4-3
14 Stanton	0-4	1-2	2-1	5-5	1-0	2-6	1-1	0-2	2-2	1-2	0-4	5-0	1-1		3-2	3-2
15 Westerfield United	0-4	1-2	2-2	0-4	1-0	0-4	0-2	2-2	1-2	3-2	1-2	0-5	2-5	3-2		1-6
16 Woodbridge Athletic	0-0	0-2	6-4	2-2	0-0	2-5	2-0	1-2	1-1	2-1	2-0	0-1	5-2	1-1	4-0	

SUFFOLK & IPSWICH LEAGUE SENIOR DIVISION CONSTITUTION 2011-12

ACHILLES	Pauls Social Club, Salmet Close, Ipswich IP2 9BA	01473 604874
CAPEL PLOUGH	Friars, Capel St Mary, Ipswich IP9 2XS	None
CRANE SPORTS	Gresham Sports & Social Club, Tuddenham Road, Ipswich IP4 3QJ	01473 250816
EAST BERGHOLT UNITED	Gandish Road, East Bergholt, Colchester CO7 6TP	01473 728581
FELIXSTOWE UNITED	Trimley Sports & Social Club, High Road, Trimley St Martin, Felixstowe IP11 0RJ	01394 275240
FRAMLINGHAM TOWN	Sports Field, Badlingham Road, Framlingham, Woodbridge IP13 9HS	01728 724038
GRUNDISBURGH	The Playing Field, Ipswich Road, Grundisburgh, Woodbridge IP13 6TJ	07974 047221
HAUGHLEY UNITED	King George V Playing Field, Green Road, Haughley IP14 3RA	01449 673460
IPSWICH ATHLETIC	Bourne Vale Social Ground, Halifax Road, Ipswich IP2 8RE	01473 687685
LEISTON ST MARGARETS	Junction Meadow, Abbey Road, Leiston IP16 4RD	01728 831239
MELTON ST AUDRYS	St Audrys Sports & Social Club, Lodge Farm Lane, Melton, Woodbridge IP12 1LX	None
OLD NEWTON UNITED	Church Road, Old Newton, Stowmarket IP14 4ED	01449 770035
RANSOMES SPORTS	Ransomes Sports & Social Club, Sidegate Avenue, Ipswich IP4 4JJ	01473 726134
STANTON	Stanton Recreation Ground, Old Bury Road, Stanton, Bury St Edmunds IP31 2BX	None
WICKHAM MARKET	The Playing Field, Wickham Market IP13 0HE	01728 747303
WOODBRIDGE ATHLETIC	RAF Woodbridge, Rock Barracks, Otley Road, Sutton Heath Estate, Woodbridge IP2 3LU	None

***IN:** Leiston St Margarets (P), Wickham Market (P)*
***OUT:** Coplestonians (R), Westerfield United (R)*

DIVISION ONE	P	W	D	L	F	A	Pts
1 Leiston St Margarets	26	22	2	2	82	26	68
2 Wickham Market	26	19	2	5	92	35	59
3 Ipswich Exiles	26	16	5	5	64	37	53
4 Wenhaston United	26	15	5	6	80	39	50
5 BT Trimley	26	15	1	10	48	39	46
6 Trimley Red Devils	26	14	3	9	70	44	45
7 Saxmundham Sports	26	12	6	8	50	41	42
8 Stonham Aspal	26	10	4	12	47	57	34
9 Mendlesham	26	10	2	14	48	57	32
10 St Johns (-6)	26	10	2	14	44	55	26
11 Thurston	26	7	4	15	58	74	25
12 Cockfield United (-3)	26	5	5	16	25	67	17
13 Halesworth Town (-6)	26	3	5	18	24	82	8
14 Stowupland Falcons	26	0	2	24	17	96	2

INTERMEDIATE DIVISION A	P	W	D	L	F	A	Pts
1 Ipswich Athletic reserves	24	18	3	3	73	42	57
2 Woodbridge Athletic reserves	24	17	5	2	97	39	55
3 Grundisburgh reserves	24	15	4	5	72	39	49
4 Coplestonians reserves	24	13	4	7	58	33	43
5 Westerfield United reserves	24	9	4	11	56	54	31
6 Achilles reserves	24	8	4	12	58	63	28
7 Old Newton United reserves	24	8	4	12	54	76	28
8 Crane Sports reserves	24	7	6	11	49	60	27
9 Melton St Audrys reserves	24	6	7	11	50	58	25
10 Felixstowe United reserves	24	6	7	11	38	59	25
11 Ransomes Sports rese (-4)	24	7	7	10	47	47	24
12 Framlingham Town res (-2)	24	7	5	12	33	56	24
13 Saxmundham Sports res (-1)	24	3	4	17	25	84	12

St John's reserves - record expunged

INTERMEDIATE DIVISION B	P	W	D	L	F	A	Pts
1 East Bergholt United reserves	26	20	3	3	101	28	63
2 Capel Plough reserves	26	18	4	4	75	29	58
3 Stanton reserves	26	19	0	7	79	35	57
4 Stonham Aspal reserves	26	18	3	5	72	30	57
5 Wickham Market reserves	26	18	3	5	63	24	57
6 Leiston St Margarets reserves	26	16	4	6	75	36	52
7 Wenhaston United reserves	26	9	5	12	42	46	32
8 Haughley United res (-6)	26	11	3	12	43	51	30
9 Mendlesham reserves (-1)	26	8	4	14	48	50	27
10 Ipswich Exiles reserves (-1)	26	7	5	14	39	63	25
11 Thurston reserves	26	5	2	19	31	86	17
12 Cockfield United res (-3)	26	5	3	18	39	86	15
13 BT Trimley reserves (-2)	25	4	2	19	32	82	12
14 Stowupland Falcons res (-1)	25	1	3	21	19	112	5

BT Trimley reserves v Stowupland Falcons reserves remained unplayed

DIVISION TWO	P	W	D	L	F	A	Pts
1 Henley Athletic	26	16	5	5	68	32	53
2 Bramford United	26	16	1	9	91	49	49
3 Benhall St Mary	26	16	1	9	66	39	49
4 Sporting 87	26	14	7	5	46	34	49
5 Claydon	26	14	3	9	74	55	45
6 Bacton United 89	26	12	4	10	76	57	40
7 Bramford Road Old Boys	26	12	4	10	73	61	40
8 Somersham	26	10	4	12	47	42	34
9 AFC Crowley	26	10	4	12	54	64	34
10 Parkside United	26	10	2	14	48	67	32
11 Salvation Army	26	8	8	10	42	64	32
12 Great Blakenham	26	8	2	16	44	73	26
13 AFC Hoxne (-3)	26	7	4	15	41	88	22
14 Elmswell	26	3	3	20	31	76	12

DIVISION THREE	P	W	D	L	F	A	Pts
1 Bildeston Rangers	24	15	5	4	97	41	50
2 Sproughton Sports	24	14	6	4	65	38	48
3 Coplestonians "A" (-3)	24	13	7	4	69	36	43
4 Bacton United 89 reserves	24	12	1	11	58	50	37
5 Tacket Street BBOB	24	11	3	10	59	60	36
6 St Clements Hospital	24	10	4	10	52	64	34
7 Waterside (-3)	23	10	5	8	50	61	32
8 Tattingstone United	24	8	6	10	57	66	30
9 Willis	24	9	3	12	47	60	30
10 Walsham-le-Willows "A"	24	8	4	12	51	51	28
11 Woolverstone United	24	8	4	12	53	65	28
12 Ufford Sports	24	6	4	14	37	71	22
13 Stradbroke United	23	3	4	16	39	71	13

Stradbroke United v Waterside remained unplayed

OMNICO CUP continued...

Cedars Park 3-2 Walsham-le-Willows A
Claydon 2-6 Wickham Market
Cockfield United 3-2 Aldeburgh Town
Great Blakenham scr-w/o Trimley Red Devils
Saxmundham Sports 4-0 Bacton United
Shotley 2-4 Mendlesham
Sproughton Sports 2-3 Sporting '87
St Johns 4-1 Stowupland Falcons
Stradbroke United 4-2 Halesworth Town
Thurston 6-1 Kesgrave Kestrels
Wenhaston United 6-0 Parkside United
Bildeston Rangers 8-1 AFC Hoxne
Stonham Aspal 2-0 BT Trimley
Coddenham 5-1 Somersham Town

ROUND 3

Achilles 3-0 Coplestonians
AFC Crowley 0-2 Westerfield United
Bramford Road Old Boys 2-0 Trimley Red Devils
East Bergholt United 2-3 Sporting '87
Felixstowe United 2-1 Ipswich Athletic
Framlingham Town 6-0 Cedars Park
Grundisburgh 2-1 Stanton
Haughley United 2-0 Capel Plough
Melton St Audrys 1-0 Old Newton United
Ransomes Sports 4-2 Mendlesham
Saxmundham Sports 3-1 Cockfield United
St Johns 3-4 Crane Sports
Stradbroke United 3-5 Coddenham
Woodbridge Athletic 7-0 Thurston
Stonham Aspal 2-4 Wickham Market
Bildeston Rangers 3-1 Wenhaston United

ROUND 4

Felixstowe United 0-2 Wickham Market
Crane Sports 1-0 Melton St Audrys
Bramford Road Old Boys 1-0 Haughley United
Framlingham Town 6-1 Westerfield United
Sporting '87 1-4 Achilles
Woodbridge Athletic 4-0 Saxmundham Sports
Coddenham 1-3 Ransomes Sports
Grundisburgh 3-1 Bildeston Rangers

QUARTER-FINALS

Crane Sports 2-1 Grundisburgh
Wickham Market 8-1 Bramford Road Old Blues
Ransomes Sports 1-2 Achilles
Woodbridge Athletic 2-1 Framlingham Town

SEMI-FINALS

Wickham Market 4-3 Achilles
Woodbridge Athletic 1-2 Crane Sports

FINAL (@ Woodbridge Town, 11/5/11)
Crane Sports 3-2 Wickham Market

TOUCHLINE SPORTS INTERMEDIATE CUP

FINAL (@ Walsham-le-Willows, 6/5/11)
Ransomes Sports Res. 2-1 Grundisburgh Res.

CLUB COLOURS JUNIOR CUP

FINAL (@ Framlingham Town, 28/4/11)
Coplestonians A 4-0 St Clements Hospital Res.

SURREY ELITE INTERMEDIATE LEAGUE

Sponsored by: No Sponsor

Founded: 2008

Recent Champions:

2009: Eversley

2010: Epsom Eagles

INTERMEDIATE DIVISION	P	W	D	L	F	A	Pts
1 Spelthorne Sports (+2)	30	22	4	4	90	22	72
2 Epsom Athletic	30	20	2	8	111	55	62
3 Battersea Ironsides	30	17	5	8	51	39	56
4 Ripley Village	30	16	5	9	58	47	53
5 Bletchingley (-3)	30	14	9	7	49	43	48
6 Virginia Water (+3)	30	13	5	12	65	52	47
7 Hersham Elm Grove (-3)	30	13	7	10	50	47	43
8 Oxted & District (+3)	30	11	5	14	48	53	41
9 Tongham	30	12	3	15	73	84	39
10 Horsley	30	10	6	14	38	73	36
11 Reigate Priory	30	10	4	16	45	59	34
12 Coulsdon United	30	10	3	17	60	65	33
13 Crescent Rovers (+3)	30	8	6	16	69	88	33
14 Burpham (-1)	30	8	9	13	48	65	32
15 Tooting Bec (-3)	30	8	8	14	41	56	29
16 Croydon Greenside	30	7	1	22	38	86	22

INTERMEDIATE LEAGUE CHALLENGE CUP

ROUND 1

Bletchingley 4-2 Hersham Elm Grove

Burpham 1-3 Virginia Water

Crescent Rovers 2-1 Croydon Geenside

Epsom Athletic 4-2 Reigate Priory

Horsley 0-3 Tooting Bec (tie awarded to Horsley)

Oxted & District 6-0 Coulsdon United

Ripley Village 2-0 Battersea Ironsides

Tongham 2-7 Spelthorne Sports

QUARTER FINALS

Oxted & District 6-1 Crescent Rovers

Ripley Village 4-3 Virginia Water

Spelthorne Sports 3-0 Bletchingley

Horsley 2-2 Epsom Athletic (Horsley won 4-3 on penalties)

SEMI-FINALS

Spelthorne Sports 1-0 Horsley (@ Raynes Park Vale)

Ripley Village 2-2 Oxted & District

(Ripley Village won 4-3 on penalties) @t Redhill)

FINAL (@Carshalton Athletic, 11/5/11)

Ripley Village 1-2 Spelthorne Sports

INTERMEDIATE DIVISION	1	2	3	4	5	6	7	8	9	10	11	12	13	14	15	16
1 Battersea Ironsides		0-1	4-1	1-1	2-1	2-4	2-1	3-1	3-4	3-2	1-0	1-0	1-0	3-0	W-L	2-0
2 Bletchingley	0-0		W-L	1-2	2-1	3-0	3-3	2-2	W-L	2-0	3-2	2-0	0-0	4-3	2-2	3-0
3 Burpham	0-3	1-1		3-2	4-4	2-0	2-4	1-3	4-3	1-2	1-0	1-1	1-3	2-5	4-0	2-2
4 Coulsdon United	0-5	1-1	2-2		1-5	6-1	1-2	2-1	11-0	2-1	1-2	1-3	0-4	1-3	3-0	0-3
5 Crescent Rovers	2-5	5-2	1-1	4-3		5-0	2-3	0-1	1-1	1-3	4-1	2-3	1-7	3-2	3-3	2-2
6 Croydon Greenside	0-1	3-4	2-0	0-2	5-6		1-4	0-0	1-2	0-1	2-0	1-3	0-8	2-5	2-1	1-2
7 Epsom Athletic	2-0	3-1	2-6	4-1	5-2	5-3		8-0	6-0	6-2	5-1	3-3	2-3	2-4	5-0	6-1
8 Hersham Elm Grove	1-1	1-1	4-0	4-1	4-1	2-0	0-3		3-0	2-0	2-0	1-2	1-4	4-1	1-1	1-1
9 Horsley	1-1	2-1	1-1	2-0	2-1	0-1	4-1	1-2		1-1	4-3	1-4	0-5	1-2	1-1	0-4
10 Oxted & District	2-0	3-1	1-1	0-3	4-4	2-3	1-5	1-3	5-0		0-1	1-0	0-1	4-0	1-1	2-1
11 Reigate Priory	1-2	1-2	3-0	0-5	5-1	5-0	0-4	0-0	1-0	3-0		2-1	0-2	1-1	1-5	3-7
12 Ripley Village	1-3	1-1	2-1	2-1	1-2	3-2	4-3	3-2	0-1	2-0	0-0		2-2	2-0	0-2	3-2
13 Spelthorne Sports	4-0	4-1	1-1	3-0	5-1	4-0	3-2	4-0	6-0	0-1	1-2	2-1		5-1	1-0	1-3
14 Tongham	4-0	1-3	7-0	6-4	4-2	4-2	1-6	3-1	2-2	4-4	0-3	3-4	1-6		0-3	2-3
15 Tooting Bec	2-2	2-1	1-3	0-2	2-1	1-2	3-2	2-1	1-2	1-4	0-0	2-4	0-1	1-4		3-2
16 Virginia Water	3-0	0-1	1-2	2-1	5-1	3-0	1-4	1-2	1-2	1-0	5-4	2-3	0-0	6-0	1-1	

SURREY ELITE INTERMEDIATE LEAGUE INTERMEDIATE DIVISION CONSTITUTION 2011-12

AFC CUBO	Barn Elms Sports Ground, Queen Elizabeth Walk, Barnes SW13 0DG	None
ABBEY RANGERS	Addlestone Moor, Addlestone Moor Road, Addlestone KT15 2QH	01932 442962
BATTERSEA IRONSIDES	Battersea Ironsides S&S Club, Burntwood Lane, Earlsfield SW17 0AW	020 8874 9913
BLETCHINGLEY	Grange Meadow, High Street, Bletchingley RH1 4PE	01883 742844
COULSDON TOWN	Woodplace Lane, Coulsdon CR5 1NF	01737 557509
CRESCENT ROVERS	Wallington Sports/Social Club, Mollison Drive, Wallington SM6 9BY	020 8647 2558
EPSOM ATHLETIC	Chessington & Hook United FC, Chalky Lane, Chessington KT9 2NF	01372 745777
FARNBOROUGH NORTH END	Rushmoor Community FC, Grasmere Road, Farnborough GU14 0LE	None
HORSLEY	Toms Field, Long Reach, West Horsley KT24 6NE	01483 282516
OLD FARNBORONIANS	Cody S&S Club, Armstrong Way, The Fairway, Farnborough GU14 0LP	01252 543009
OXTED & DISTRICT	Master Park, Church Lane, Oxted RH8 9LD	01883 716001
REIGATE PRIORY	Reigate Priory Cricket Club, off Park Lane, Reigate RH2 8JX	01737 240872
RIPLEY VILLAGE	The Green, Ripley, Woking GU23 6AN	01483 225484
TOOTING BEC	Raynes Park Vale FC, Princes Georges PF,Grand Drive, Raynes Park SW20 9DZ	020 8540 8843
VIRGINIA WATER	The Timbers, Crown Road, Virginia Water GU25 4HS	01344 843811
WESTON GREEN SPORTS	Weston Green Sports Ground, Longmead Road, Thames Ditton KT7 0JF	None

IN: *AFC Cubo (P-Surrey South Eastern Combination Division One), Abbey Rangers (P-Surrey Intermediate League (West) Premier Division), Farnborough North End (R-Combined Counties League Division One), Old Farnboronians (P-Aldershot & District League Premier Division), Weston Green Sports (P-Surrey South Eastern Combination Division One).* ***OUT:*** *Burpham (R-Guildford & Woking Alliance), Croydon Greenside (R-Surrey South Eastern Combination), Hersham Elm Grove (F), Spelthorne Sports Club (P-Combined Counties League Division One), Tongham (R-Surrey Intermediate League (West). Coulsdon United become Coulsdon Town.*

WEARSIDE LEAGUE

Sponsored by: No Sponsor
Founded: 1892
Recent Champions:
2006: Whitehaven Amateurs
2007: Birtley Town
2008: New Marske Sports Club
2009: Newton Aycliffe
2010: Ryhope Colliery Welfare

		P	W	D	L	F	A	Pts
1	Ryhope Colliery Welfare	38	28	5	5	104	29	89
2	Easington Colliery	38	26	5	7	99	39	83
3	New Marske	38	24	5	9	96	59	77
4	Redcar Athletic	38	22	8	8	78	34	74
5	Jarrow	38	22	6	10	97	52	72
6	Kirkbymoorside	38	23	2	13	92	65	71
7	Windscale	38	18	11	9	85	44	65
8	Hartlepool	38	18	9	11	70	52	63
9	Darlington Cleveland Bridge	38	18	4	16	62	70	58
10	Stockton Town	38	16	8	14	59	56	56
11	Ashbrooke Belford House	38	17	5	16	59	64	56
12	Annfield Plain	38	16	6	16	61	74	54
13	Wolviston	38	16	5	17	66	65	53
14	Willington	38	14	2	22	49	78	44
15	Cleator Moor Celtic	38	10	7	21	56	78	37
16	Boldon Community Assoc	38	11	3	24	74	98	36
17	Silksworth	38	9	6	23	51	83	33
18	Prudhoe Town	38	6	5	27	50	114	23
19	Houghton Town	38	7	2	29	37	127	23
20	Coxhoe Athletic	38	5	4	29	39	103	19

LEAGUE CUP

PRELIMINARY ROUND
Boldon CA 3-4 Stockton Town
Hartlepool 1-4 Cleator Moor Celtic
Jarrow 2-1 Ashbrooke Belford House
Willington 3-2 Darlington Cleveland Bridge

ROUND 1
Cleator Moor Celtic 2-3 Jarrow
Coxhoe Athletic 1-2 New Marske
Prudhoe Town 1-2 Annfield Plain
Ryhope CW 3-1 Kirkbymoorside
Silksworth 1-2 Willington
Stockton Town 0-3 Easington Colliery
Wolviston 2-3 Redcar Athletic

QUARTER FINALS
Jarrow 3-2 Windscale
New Marske 2-1 Easington Colliery
Ryhope CW 3-2 Annfield Plain
Willington 2-0 Redcar Athletic

SEMI-FINALS
New Marske 1-2 Ryhope CW
Willington 2-1 Jarrow

FINAL (@ Willington, 21/5/11)
Willington 0-0 Ryhope CW (Ryhope CW won 4-2 penalties)

	1	2	3	4	5	6	7	8	9	10	11	12	13	14	15	16	17	18	19	20
1 Annfield Plain		1-1	3-2	2-0	2-1	0-2	1-3	1-1	4-1	2-1	2-1	1-3	3-2	1-2	1-2	3-1	0-0	0-1	4-3	2-0
2 Ashbrooke Belford House	1-2		1-3	2-0	2-1	5-1	0-3	1-1	2-0	0-4	3-0	0-3	6-2	3-2	0-3	0-3	2-0	2-4	0-1	4-1
3 Boldon Community Assoc	4-0	0-2		4-4	5-0	0-1	2-3	1-3	6-1	0-5	1-3	2-4	2-0	0-1	0-5	0-3	0-2	0-1	2-2	6-1
4 Cleator Moor Celtic	6-1	2-1	2-6		1-0	4-1	1-3	2-1	3-4	2-2	1-0	0-1	1-3	1-4	0-3	2-0	1-1	1-4	0-2	2-1
5 Coxhoe Athletic	2-4	0-0	7-0	1-1		0-1	0-4	1-2	0-1	1-3	1-1	0-6	2-2	0-3	1-6	0-5	0-1	2-3	0-3	0-1
6 Darlington Cleveland Bridge	2-0	2-0	1-1	4-2	3-0		3-3	1-2	2-3	1-2	2-3	0-1	4-2	0-3	0-5	1-2	1-2	4-1	0-4	1-3
7 Easington Colliery	3-1	3-1	2-0	4-3	6-0	1-2		2-0	6-0	1-0	4-1	7-0	7-0	2-1	1-1	2-0	2-2	4-0	1-1	0-3
8 Hartlepool	2-2	1-3	4-2	3-2	3-1	1-2	0-1		1-0	2-2	1-0	1-1	0-0	0-0	2-3	2-1	0-1	2-0	1-2	1-1
9 Houghton Town	1-3	0-2	0-5	2-2	4-1	1-2	1-4	0-5		1-4	1-0	0-3	3-1	2-5	0-3	0-3	0-2	1-2	1-11	1-5
10 Jarrow	6-4	5-0	2-3	4-0	3-1	2-3	3-2	1-3	8-0		4-2	3-0	3-0	1-2	0-2	4-1	2-5	2-0	0-0	2-1
11 Kirkbymoorside	1-5	6-0	4-2	3-1	4-3	1-0	0-2	3-2	6-1	2-2		3-2	10-1	2-1	0-1	2-0	1-0	3-2	3-1	0-1
12 New Marske S C	4-1	1-2	3-1	1-0	1-2	2-2	1-2	1-4	4-1	5-0	4-3		2-1	1-3	1-1	2-0	0-0	4-0	2-1	6-2
13 Prudhoe Town	1-1	0-1	2-4	1-0	0-1	1-2	3-1	1-3	2-0	1-5	3-4	5-7		1-5	0-3	1-1	1-3	4-1	1-2	0-3
14 Redcar Athletic	2-0	2-2	1-2	1-0	6-2	2-0	1-0	2-2	1-0	1-2	0-2	3-0	6-0		2-2	1-1	1-0	0-1	1-1	3-0
15 Ryhope Colliery Welfare	2-0	0-2	3-0	1-0	2-1	6-0	3-1	0-1	9-0	0-1	5-1	2-4	5-0	1-1		6-0	1-0	2-0	1-2	2-1
16 Silksworth	0-1	1-3	4-2	3-3	0-2	1-2	0-4	3-4	1-1	1-3	0-3	1-3	3-1	0-4	3-3		0-1	3-2	0-0	1-0
17 Stockton Town	4-1	2-0	4-2	1-2	4-1	1-2	1-1	4-3	2-1	0-4	1-5	2-2	2-1	0-2	1-2	5-2		1-1	0-1	1-3
18 Willington	1-2	0-3	4-3	0-2	1-4	0-3	2-0	0-1	0-1	1-0	1-3	0-4	2-2	0-2	1-2	3-2	1-0		1-4	3-1
19 Windscale	0-0	2-0	6-1	2-2	7-0	1-2	0-1	2-2	4-2	0-0	3-4	2-4	2-2	0-0	0-3	4-0	4-0	3-2		2-0
20 Wolviston	5-0	2-2	4-0	1-0	2-0	2-2	1-3	2-0	3-1	2-2	1-2	1-3	1-2	2-1	1-3	3-1	3-3	1-3	1-0	

WEARSIDE LEAGUE CONSTITUTION 2011-12

ANNFIELD PLAIN	Derwent Park , West Road , Annfield Plain DH9 8PZ	None
ASHBROOKE BELFORD HOUSE	Silksworth Park, Blind Lane, Silksworth, Sunderland SR3 1AX	None
BOLDON COMMUNITY ASSOCIATION	Boldon Welfare, New Road, Boldon Colliery NE35 9DS	0191 536 4180 (Cricket Club)
CLEATOR MOOR CELTIC	Celtic Club, Birks Road, Cleator Moor CA25 5HR	01946 812476
COXHOE ATHLETIC	Beechfield Park, Coxhoe DH6 4SD	None
DARLINGTON CLEVELAND BRIDGE	Eastbourne Sports Complex, Bourne Avenue, Darlington DL1 1LJ	01325 243177/243188
GATESHEAD LEAM RANGERS	Dawdon Welfare Park, Green Drive, Dawdon, Seaham SR7 7XL	None
HARTLEPOOL	Grayfields Enclose, Jesmond Gardens, Hartlepool TS24 8QS	None
JARROW	Perth Green Community Assoc., Inverness Road, Jarrow NE32 4AQ	0191 489 3743
KIRKBYMOORSIDE	Kirkby Mills, Kirkbymoorside, York YO62 6NS	None
PETERLEE TOWN	Eden Lane Playing Fields, Peterlee SR8 5DS	0191 586 3004
PRUDHOE TOWN	Kimberley Park, Broomhouse Road, Prudhoe NE42 5EH	01661 835900
REDCAR ATHLETIC	Green Lane, Redcar TS10 3RW	None
RYHOPE COLLIERY WELFARE	Ryhope Recreation Park, Ryhope Street, Ryhope, Sunderland SR2 0AB	0191 521 2843
SILKSWORTH	Silksworth Park, Blind Lane, Silksworth, Sunderland SR3 1AX	None
STOCKTON TOWN	Bishopton Road West, Stockton-on-Tees TS19 0QD	None
SUNDERLAND WEST END	Ford Quarry, Keelmans Lane, Pennywell, Sunderland	
WILLINGTON	Hall Lane Ground, Hall Lane Estate, Willington DL15 0QF	01388 746221
WOLVISTON	Metcalfe Park, Wynyard Road, Wolviston, Billingham TS22 5NE	07768 321651

IN: Gateshead Leam Rangers (P-Durham Alliance), Peterlee Town (S-Northern Alliance Division One)
OUT: Easington Colliery (P-Northern League Division Two), New Marske (W), Windscale (W)
Houghton Town have merged with Wearside Combination club Sunderland West End, Silksworth have merged with Herrington Grindon Rangers to become Silksworth Rangers

MONKWEARMOUTH CHARITY CUP

PRELIMINARY ROUND
New Marske 5-1 Prudhoe Town
Easington Colliery 1-0 Darlington Cleveland Bridge
Ashbrooke Belford House 2-3 Redcar Athletic
Hartlepool 3-1 Houghton Town

ROUND 1
New Marske 4-0 Coxhoe Athletic
Windscale 1-1 Cleator Moor Celtic
(Windscale won 4-3 penalties)
Jarrow 3-0 Wolviston
Willington 0-6 Ryhope Colliery Welfare
Kirkbymoorside 3-2 Annfield Plain
Silksworth 1-4 Easington Colliery
Hartlepool 4-0 Boldon Community Association
Stockton Town 0-1 Redcar Athletic

QUARTER-FINALS
Kirkbymoorside 0-0 Easington Colliery
(Kirkbymoorside won 7-6 penalties)
Redcar Athletic 2-0 Jarrow
Hartlepool 1-2 New Marske
Ryhope Colliery Welfare 2-1 Windscale

SEMI-FINALS
Redcar Athletic 1-2 Ryhope Colliery Welfare
New Marske 1-2 Kirkbymoorside

FINAL (@ Kirkbymoorside, 25/4/11)
Kirkbymoorside 0-1 Ryhope Colliery Welfare

SUNDERLAND SHIPOWNERS CUP

PRELIMINARY ROUND
Prudhoe Town 2-3 Wolviston
Willington 5-1 Coxhoe Athletic
Hartlepool 4-3 Boldon Community Association
Kirkbymoorside 3-2 Ashbrooke Belford House

ROUND 1
Hartlepool 1-3 Easington Colliery
Kirkbymoorside 1-0 New Marske
Silksworth 1-4 Redcar Athletic
Stockton Town 3-1 Darlington Cleveland Bridge
Cleator Moor Celtic 4-1 Wolviston
Annfield Plain 3-1 Windscale
Ryhope Colliery Welfare 6-0 Willington
Jarrow 6-0 Houghton Town

QUARTER-FINALS
Stockton Town 0-2 Easington Colliery
Jarrow 0-2 Ryhope Colliery Welfare (@ Ryhope Colliery Welfare)
Redcar Athletic 0-2 Cleator Moor Celtic
Kirkbymoorside 2-0 Annfield Plain

SEMI-FINALS
Ryhope Colliery Welfare 2-1 Kirkbymoorside
Easington Colliery 4-2 Cleator Moor Celtic

FINAL (@ Ryhope Colliery Welfare, 2/5/11)
Ryhope Colliery Welfare 3-2 Easington Colliery

WEST CHESHIRE LEAGUE

Sponsored by: Carlsberg
Founded: 1892
Recent Champions:
2006: Poulton Victoria
2007: West Kirby
2008: West Kirby
2009: West Kirby
2010: Cammell Laird Reserves

DIVISION ONE	P	W	D	L	F	A	Pts
1 West Kirby	28	23	2	3	76	35	71
2 Maghull	28	22	1	5	81	25	67
3 Heswall	28	18	3	7	60	32	57
4 Helsby	28	17	6	5	60	35	57
5 Southport Trinity	28	16	4	8	54	40	52
6 Newton	28	14	4	10	55	40	46
7 Vauxhall Motors reserves	28	10	8	10	40	37	38
8 Marshalls	28	10	6	12	70	54	36
9 Marine reserves	28	11	3	14	46	51	36
10 Ellesmere Port	28	10	4	14	39	48	34
11 Upton Athletic Association	28	7	7	14	36	56	28
12 Christleton	28	6	8	14	34	56	26
13 Willaston	28	8	1	19	31	71	25
14 Cammell Laird reserves	28	5	5	18	34	59	20
15 Blacon Youth Club	28	1	2	25	17	94	5
Groves Social - record expunged							

PYKE CUP

ROUND 1
Vauxhall Motors reserves 0-1 Newton
Southoprt Trinity 3-3 West Kirkby
(Southport Trinity won 3-1 on penalties)
Marine reserves 0-1 Heswall
Maghull 2-0 Blacon Youth Club
Helsby 1-3 Upton Athletic Association
Ellesmere Port 3-1 Marshalls
Christleton 2-1 Cammell Laird reserves

QUARTER FINALS
Southport Trinity 1-3 Willaston
Newton 4-3 Upton Athletic Association
Ellesmere Port 2-1 Heswall
Maghull 3-0 Christleton

SEMI-FINALS
Maghull 2-1 Ellesmere Port
Willaston 0-2 Newton

FINAL (@ Vauxhall Motors, 6/5/11)
Maghull 3-0 Newton

DIVISION ONE	1	2	3	4	5	6	7	8	9	10	11	12	13	14	15
1 Blacon Youth Club		1-4	0-4	1-3	0-2	1-6	1-4	0-1	0-3	0-5	2-3	0-2	1-4	2-4	1-2
2 Cammell Laird reserves	1-1		1-1	1-3	0-2	0-1	1-4	2-3	3-2	2-1	2-3	2-1	1-0	2-3	0-3
3 Christleton	1-0	2-0		3-3	0-2	0-4	1-4	1-1	0-4	1-1	2-4	1-1	1-1	2-2	1-4
4 Ellesmere Port	2-2	2-1	2-0		1-2	2-3	1-2	1-0	2-0	0-1	1-0	1-2	2-2	1-3	2-1
5 Helsby	5-0	3-1	3-0	3-2		0-0	2-1	2-2	5-2	3-1	3-2	1-1	4-1	1-2	3-0
6 Heswall	4-1	1-1	3-2	0-1	2-1		2-1	2-0	2-2	0-2	2-1	4-0	0-2	0-2	6-1
7 Maghull	5-0	5-0	4-0	2-0	3-1	2-0		4-0	3-2	2-1	3-2	4-1	1-1	1-2	4-0
8 Marine reserves	5-1	4-3	1-0	2-1	4-0	0-1	1-3		3-3	2-3	2-0	1-2	5-0	1-4	2-1
9 Marshalls	8-0	2-2	2-3	4-0	1-1	1-4	0-2	3-1		1-2	3-3	4-0	2-1	1-5	5-0
10 Newton	3-0	2-2	1-0	3-1	0-2	1-2	0-4	4-1	3-3		0-1	2-1	2-0	1-3	1-2
11 Southport Trinity	2-0	2-0	3-1	2-1	3-1	3-1	2-1	3-1	2-1	0-1		4-2	0-0	2-3	2-1
12 Upton Athletic Association	1-2	2-1	1-3	1-1	2-2	1-3	1-2	2-0	3-1	2-2	1-1		0-2	1-5	2-2
13 Vauxhall Motors reserves	6-0	1-0	1-1	0-1	1-1	0-2	1-0	0-1	3-1	2-5	1-1	2-1		0-2	5-1
14 West Kirby	2-0	2-0	2-1	3-2	2-3	4-2	2-4	3-1	1-4	3-2	4-0	2-0	1-1		1-0
15 Willaston	2-0	2-1	1-2	4-0	1-2	0-3	0-6	2-1	0-5	0-5	0-3	1-2	0-2	0-4	

WEST CHESHIRE LEAGUE DIVISION ONE CONSTITUTION 2011-12

ASHVILLE	Villa Park, Cross Lane, Wallasey Village, Wallasey CH45 8RH	0151 638 2127
BLACON YOUTH CLUB	Cairns Crescent Playing Fields, Blacon, Chester CH1 5JF	None
CAMMELL LAIRD RESERVES	Kirklands, St Peters Road, Rock Ferry, Birkenhead CH42 1PY	0151 645 3121
CHESTER NOMADS	Garrison Ground, Eaton Road, Chester CH4 7ER	None
CHRISTLETON	Little Heath Road, Christleton, Chester CH3 7AH	01244 336589
ELLESMERE PORT	Whitby Sports & Social Club, Chester Road, Whitby, Ellesmere Port CH66 2NX	0151 200 7080/7050
HESWALL	Gayton Park, Brimstage Road, Heswall CH60 1XG	0151 342 8172
MAGHULL	Old Hall Field, Hall Lane, Maghull L31 7BB	0151 526 7320
MARINE RESERVES	Arriva Stadium, College Road, Crosby, Liverpool L23 3AS	0151 924 1743
	Fax: 0151 924 1743 Club:	0151 924 4046
MARSHALLS	IM Marsh Campus, Barkhill Road, Aigburth, Liverpool L17 6BD	0151 231 5233
NEWTON	Millcroft, Frankby Road, Greasby CH47 0NB	0151 677 8282
SOUTHPORT TRINITY	Rookery Sports Ground, Roe Lane, Southport PR9 7HR	01704 225841
UPTON ATHLETIC ASSOCIATION	Cheshire County S & S Club, Plas Newton Lane, Chester CH2 1PR	01244 318167
VAUXHALL MOTORS RESERVES	Vauxhall Sports Ground, Rivacre Road, Hooton, Ellesmere Port CH66 1NJ	0151 328 1114
	Fax: 0151 328 1114 Club:	0151 327 2294
WEST KIRBY	Marine Park, Greenbank Road, West Kirby CH48 5HL	None
WILLASTON	Johnston Recreation Ground, Neston Road, Willaston CH64 2TL	None

IN: *Ashville (P), Chester Nomads (P)*
OUT: *Groves (WS), Helsby (R-Division Three)*

WEST CHESHIRE LEAGUE - STEP 7

DIVISION TWO	P	W	D	L	F	A	Pts
1 Ashville	26	21	3	2	82	23	66
2 Chester Nomads	26	18	5	3	62	31	59
3 Mossley Hill Athletic	26	17	2	7	54	31	53
4 New Brighton	26	15	5	6	60	41	50
5 Richmond Raith Rovers	26	14	4	8	58	52	46
6 Heswall reserves	26	10	3	13	40	47	33
7 Hale (-3)	26	9	7	10	50	56	31
8 AFC Bebington Athletic	26	9	4	13	37	49	31
9 West Kirby reserves	26	8	5	13	42	51	29
10 Prescot Cables reserves	26	8	5	13	46	58	29
11 Maghull reserves	26	7	6	13	48	60	27
12 Capenhurst Villa	26	5	10	11	38	47	25
13 Mallaby	26	6	3	17	36	68	21
14 Bronze Social	26	3	2	21	28	67	11

WEST CHESHIRE BOWL (HAWORTH & GALLAGHER)

ROUND 1

West Kirby reserves 0-2 AFC Bebington Athletic
New Brighton 4-1 Hale
Chester Nomads 2-0 Richmond Raith Rovers
Capenhurst Villa 3-2 Maghull reserves
Ashville 2-1 Mallaby
Heswall reserves 2-1 Mossley Hill Athletic

QUARTER FINALS

Chester Nomads 5-7 Heswall reserves
Capenhurst Villa 3-2 Bronze Social
Prescot Cables reserves 1-7 Ashville
New Brighton 2-1 AFC Bebington Athletic

SEMI-FINALS

Heswall reserves 0-1 Capenhurst Villa
Ashville 4-0 New Brighton

FINAL (@ Capenhurst Villa, 4/5/11)

Capenhurst Villa 1-6 Ashville

DIVISION TWO	1	2	3	4	5	6	7	8	9	10	11	12	13	14
1 AFC Bebington Athletic		2-0	3-1	0-0	1-3	4-4	4-3	3-1	0-1	0-3	2-1	1-1	0-1	2-0
2 Ashville	4-0		3-0	3-1	0-0	6-1	3-1	4-1	7-2	2-1	2-0	4-2	4-0	2-1
3 Bronze Social	1-3	0-6		3-0	1-2	1-3	1-3	1-3	2-3	0-3	1-0	2-2	4-5	0-2
4 Capenhurst Villa	1-0	2-2	0-0		2-3	1-1	0-0	1-1	1-0	1-5	1-2	3-4	0-2	2-3
5 Chester Nomads	1-0	2-2	3-0	2-2		2-2	3-1	3-1	4-0	3-2	3-2	3-0	5-1	1-0
6 Hale	2-3	1-3	2-1	2-3	0-2		3-1	2-4	3-3	2-1	4-3	3-0	2-2	2-1
7 Heswall reserves	4-0	0-3	1-0	1-3	0-3	3-0		2-0	1-0	1-2	0-1	1-0	0-2	2-2
8 Maghull reserves	3-3	1-3	1-3	2-2	1-3	2-2	1-1		4-2	1-4	2-3	1-0	1-4	2-1
9 Mallaby	1-3	1-5	4-1	1-0	1-1	1-4	1-5	4-2		0-2	0-3	0-2	2-4	1-2
10 Mossley Hill Athletic	2-1	2-1	2-1	2-1	1-0	0-1	7-2	1-0	2-1		0-0	4-3	2-0	3-0
11 New Brighton	3-1	0-4	3-0	4-4	5-3	3-1	4-0	3-2	1-1	2-1		4-1	3-2	3-2
12 Prescot Cables reserves	4-0	1-3	4-2	0-4	1-4	1-1	1-4	0-2	4-1	3-0	2-2		3-2	4-3
13 Richmond Raith Rovers	2-1	0-2	3-1	2-1	4-0	4-2	2-3	3-3	2-1	2-2	1-4	3-2		2-1
14 West Kirby reserves	2-0	1-4	3-1	2-2	1-3	1-0	1-0	2-6	3-4	3-0	1-1	1-1	3-3	

WEST CHESHIRE LEAGUE DIVISION TWO CONSTITUTION 2011-12

AFC BEBINGTON ATHLETIC	Unilever Sports Ground , , Bromborough CH62 3PU	None
ASHVILLE RESERVES	Villa Park, Cross Lane, Wallasey Village, Wallasey CH45 8RH	0151 638 2127
BRONZE SOCIAL	Unilever Sports Ground, Bromborough CH62 3PU	None
CAPENHURST VILLA	Capenhurst Sports Ground, Capenhurst Lane, Capenhurst CH1 6ER	None
HALE	Hale Park, The High Street, Hale Village, Liverpool L24 4AF	None
HESWALL RESERVES	Gayton Park, Brimstage Road, Heswall CH60 1XG	0151 342 8172
MAGHULL RESERVES	Old Hall Field, Hall Lane, Maghull L31 7BB	0151 526 7320
MALLABY	Unilever Sports Ground, Bromborough CH62 3PU	None
MANOR ATHLETIC	OC Sports & Leisure Club, 28 Bridle Road, Bromborough CH62 6AR	0151 356 6159
MARSHALLS RESERVES	IM Marsh Campus, Barkhill Road, Aigburth, Liverpool L17 6BD	0151 231 5233
MOSSLEY HILL ATHLETIC	Mossley Hill Athletic Club, Mossley Hill Road, Liverpool L18 8DX	0151 724 4377
NEW BRIGHTON	Harrison Drive, Wallasey Village, Wallasey CH45 3HL	None
PRESCOT CABLES RESERVES	St Helens Sports College, Elton Head Road, Lea Green, St Helens WA9 5AU	01744 678859
RICHMOND RAITH ROVERS	Childwall Sports College, Queens Drive, Fiveways L15 6XZ	0151 722 1561
RUNCORN LINNETS RESERVES	Millbank Linnets Stadium, Murdishaw Avenue, Runcorn WA7 6HP	07050 801733
WEST KIRBY RESERVES	Marine Park, Greenbank Road, West Kirby CH48 5HL	None

IN: *Ashville Reserves (P), Manor Athletic (P), Marshalls Reserves (P), Runcorn Linnets Reserves (P)*
OUT: *Ashville (P), Chester Nomads (P)*

DIVISION THREE	P	W	D	L	F	A	Pts
1 Runcorn Linnets reserves	28	24	1	3	90	35	73
2 Manor Athletic	28	21	2	5	72	27	65
3 Ashville reserves	28	18	2	8	93	54	56
4 Marshalls reserves	28	16	5	7	57	38	53
5 Helsby reserves	28	14	4	10	61	56	46
6 Mossley Hill Athletic reserves	28	12	6	10	57	49	42
7 New Brighton reserves	28	12	4	12	66	59	40
8 Merseyside Police	28	12	2	14	60	75	38
9 Christleton reserves	28	9	5	14	64	80	32
10 Ellesmere Port reserves	28	10	2	16	49	80	32
11 Mersey Royal	28	8	6	14	50	60	30
12 Capenhurst Villa reserves	28	8	4	16	44	70	28
13 Upton Athletic Association res.	28	7	6	15	60	78	27
14 AFC Bebington Athletic reserves	28	7	3	18	50	72	24
15 Hale reserves	28	5	2	21	48	88	17
Blacon Youth Club reserves - record expunged							

W H WEIGHT MEMORIAL CUP
(Divisional Champions and Pyke Cup Winners)

SEMI-FINALS

West Kirby 2-3 Hale

Cammell Laird reserves 0-0 Southport Trinity

(Southport Trinity won 5-4 on penalties)

FINAL (@ Vauxhall Motors 14/9/10)

Hale 0-0 Southport Trinity

(Southport Trinity won 4-3 on penalties)

WEST CHESHIRE SHIELD (COMPLETE FOCUS)

ROUND 1

Capenhurst Villa reserves 2-1 Mossley Hill Athletic reserves

New Brighton reserves w/o-scr Blacon Youth Club reserves

Ellesmere Port reserves 1-3 AFC Bebington Athletic

Helsby 2-3 Marshalls reserves

Manor Athletic 6-0 Mersey Royal

Merseyside Police 4-4 Hale reserves

(Hale reserves won 3-1 on penalties)

Runcorn Linnets reserves 4-2 Christleton reserves

Upton Athletic Association reserves 0-10 Ashville reserves

QUARTER FINALS

Hale reserves 5-3 Capenhurst Villa reserves

New Brighton reserves 6-4 Marshalls reserves

Runcorn Linnets reserves 4-3 AFC Bebington Athletic

Manor Athletic 1-0 Ashville reserves

SEMI-FINALS

Hale reserves 0-4 Manor Athletic

New Brighton reserves 1-5 Runcorn Linnets reserves

FINAL (@ Vauxhall Motors, 3/5/11)

Manor Athleic 0-1 Runcorn Linnets reserves

DIVISION THREE	1	2	3	4	5	6	7	8	9	10	11	12	13	14	15
1 AFC Bebington Athletic reserves		2-3	1-2	0-1	2-0	2-4	2-5	0-0	1-0	2-0	3-0	2-3	2-1	0-3	2-2
2 Ashville reserves	5-3		3-1	2-4	9-2	5-1	5-2	0-3	2-1	1-1	6-1	2-3	2-1	2-4	4-0
3 Capenhurst Villa reserves	2-0	0-6		3-1	3-1	3-2	0-1	0-1	0-4	1-3	2-2	2-2	1-2	0-3	5-5
4 Christleton reserves	0-4	2-3	2-1		2-1	5-2	4-3	0-3	1-4	2-2	5-3	2-2	2-3	1-3	4-3
5 Ellesmere Port reserves	4-1	2-5	3-1	3-2		3-1	1-4	2-1	2-0	1-0	1-2	1-3	1-1	0-7	0-1
6 Hale reserves	1-6	0-3	1-3	2-1	4-2		1-2	0-4	0-0	4-3	2-3	1-5	3-4	0-2	1-1
7 Helsby reserves	3-1	1-2	0-4	1-1	7-3	3-2		0-1	1-3	2-2	6-1	2-0	2-2	1-6	3-2
8 Manor Athletic	4-1	2-1	7-0	3-3	5-2	2-1	2-1		0-1	4-2	4-1	1-2	4-1	5-1	1-0
9 Marshalls reserves	4-2	3-4	2-1	2-2	3-3	3-0	0-1	1-0		5-3	3-1	3-2	1-1	1-4	2-0
10 Mersey Royal	4-2	4-3	1-0	2-1	3-1	1-2	1-2	1-3	2-3		0-2	1-1	1-3	2-2	3-5
11 Merseyside Police	3-3	3-2	3-2	5-2	2-3	6-1	6-1	0-2	1-2	2-1		2-1	2-5	1-6	3-1
12 Mossley Hill Athletic reserves	5-2	2-2	3-1	3-6	1-2	3-2	2-1	1-2	1-0	1-1	1-2		0-0	1-2	4-1
13 New Brighton reserves	2-0	0-6	2-4	9-2	5-1	5-4	0-4	1-2	1-2	0-1	5-0	0-5		0-1	7-1
14 Runcorn Linnets reserves	5-3	4-2	7-0	5-4	2-1	1-0	4-1	2-0	1-3	3-2	1-0	2-0	3-2		5-0
15 Upton Athletic Association reserves	6-1	2-3	2-2	3-2	2-3	4-4	1-2	2-6	1-1	2-3	4-3	4-0	2-3	3-1	

WEST CHESHIRE LEAGUE DIVISION THREE CONSTITUTION 2011-12

AFC BEBINGTON ATHLETIC RES.	Unilever Sports Ground , , Bromborough CH62 3PU	None
BELFRY	Hillside School, Breeze Hill, Bootle L20 9NU	
CAPENHURST VILLA RESERVES	Capenhurst Sports Ground, Capenhurst Lane, Capenhurst CH1 6ER	None
CHESTER NOMADS RESERVES	Garrison Ground, Eaton Road, Chester CH4 7ER	None
CHRISTLETON RESERVES	Little Heath Road, Christleton, Chester CH3 7AH	01244 336589
ELLESMERE PORT RESERVES	Whitby Sports & Social Club, Chester Road, Whitby, Ellesmere Port CH66 2NX	0151 200 7080/7050
HALE RESERVES	Hale Park, The High Street, Hale Village, Liverpool L24 4AF	None
HELSBY	Helsby Community Sports Club, Chester Road, Helsby WA6 0DL	01928 722267
MANOR ATHLETIC RESERVES	OC Sports & Leisure Club, 28 Bridle Road, Bromborough CH62 6AR	0151 356 6159
MERSEY ROYAL	Unilever Sports Ground, Bromborough CH62 3PU	None
MERSEYSIDE POLICE	Riversdale Road, Aigburth, Liverpool L19 3QN	0151 724 5214
MOSSLEY HILL ATHLETIC RESERVES	Mossley Hill Athletic Club, Mossley Hill Road, Liverpool L18 8DX	0151 724 4377
NESTON NOMADS	Neston Recreation Centre, Neston CH64 9NQ	None
NEW BRIGHTON RESERVES	Harrison Drive, Wallasey Village, Wallasey CH45 3HL	None
SOUTH LIVERPOOL RESERVES	Jericho Lane, Aigburth, Liverpool L17 5AR	None
UPTON ATHLETIC ASSOCIATION RES.	Cheshire County S & S Club, Plas Newton Lane, Chester CH2 1PR	01244 318167

IN: *Belfry (N), Chester Nomads Reserves (N), Helsby (R-Premier Division), Manor Athletic Reserves (N), Neston Nomads (N), South Liverpool (S-Liverpool County Premier League Division One)*

OUT: *Ashville Reserves (P), Blacon Youth Club Reserves (WS), Manor Athletic (P), Marshalls Reserves (P), Runcorn Linnets Reserves (P), Southport Trinity Reserves (WN)*

WEST LANCASHIRE LEAGUE

Sponsored by: Sports 360
Founded: 1904
Recent Champions:
2006: Kirkham & Wesham
2007: Kirkham & Wesham
2008: Garstang
2009: Charnock Richard
2010: Blackpool Wren Rovers

PREMIER DIVISION	P	W	D	L	F	A	Pts
1 Blackpool Wren Rovers	30	24	3	3	98	29	75
2 Charnock Richard	30	22	4	4	87	31	70
3 Euxton Villa	30	15	10	5	68	35	55
4 Thornton Cleveleys (-4)	30	16	9	5	64	43	53
5 Eagley	30	13	7	10	58	46	46
6 Fulwood Amateurs	30	11	12	7	62	53	45
7 Vickerstown CCFC	30	12	8	10	51	49	44
8 Freckleton (-6)	30	15	4	11	49	48	43
9 Coppull United (-6)	30	13	8	9	47	49	41
10 Fleetwood Hesketh	30	10	7	13	44	48	37
11 Poulton Town	30	8	4	18	42	72	28
12 Stoneclough	30	7	5	18	37	60	26
13 Garstang	30	7	4	19	35	55	25
14 Lostock St. Gerards	30	7	4	19	45	73	25
15 Tempest United	30	4	8	18	43	92	20
16 Dalton United	30	4	7	19	26	73	19

RICHARDSON CUP

ROUND 1
Charnock Richard 4-0 Blackpool Wren Rovers
Coppull United 0-2 Vickerstown CC
Eagley 1-2 Dalton United
Garstang 1-2 Fulwood Amateurs
Lostock St Gerards 3-2 Freckleton
Stoneclough 0-1 Fleetwood Hesketh
Tempest United 0-1 Euxton Villa
Thornton Cleveleys 4-2 Poulton Town

QUARTER-FINALS
Dalton United 3-1 Fleetwood Hesketh
Fulwood Amateurs 0-2 Charnock Richard
Thornton Cleveleys 1-2 Lostock St Gerards
Vickerstown CC 2-4 Euxton Villa

SEMI-FINALS
Euxton Villa 1-0 Dalton United (@ Blackpool Wren Rovers)
Lostock St Gerards 2-2 Charnock Richard (Lostock Gralam won 4-2 on penalties) (@ Blackpool Wren Rovers)

FINAL (@ LCFA, Leyland, 21/4/11)
Lostock St Gerards 1-0 Euxton Villa

WILF CARR MEMORIAL TROPHY
(@ Blackpool Wren Rovers, 14/9/10)
Blackpool Wren Rovers 4-2 Fulwood Amateurs

PREMIER DIVISION	1	2	3	4	5	6	7	8	9	10	11	12	13	14	15	16
1 Blackpool Wren Rovers		3-1	5-2	3-0	3-1	3-2	4-1	7-0	6-1	4-1	1-1	5-1	2-0	7-1	1-3	6-0
2 Charnock Richard	0-2		1-1	5-0	4-1	3-1	4-0	2-0	2-1	2-1	8-1	0-3	3-1	1-0	2-1	2-0
3 Coppull United	1-3	2-2		3-0	0-2	0-3	2-1	0-1	2-2	1-0	2-0	3-2	3-2	3-0	3-1	0-4
4 Dalton United	2-6	0-7	1-2		3-3	0-2	2-0	0-2	2-2	0-3	1-2	0-0	3-0	2-2	1-3	1-1
5 Eagley	1-2	1-5	0-1	1-1		2-2	2-0	3-2	2-2	2-0	0-0	1-1	2-0	3-1	1-2	6-2
6 Euxton Villa	3-1	1-1	2-2	5-0	1-1		1-1	2-1	1-1	2-0	2-0	8-2	3-0	3-1	2-0	3-2
7 Fleetwood Hesketh	1-1	2-1	2-0	1-1	2-1	0-3		1-2	0-2	1-1	6-3	1-3	2-0	1-1	0-2	1-3
8 Freckleton	0-5	1-3	4-0	2-1	0-1	3-1	0-1		0-3	3-2	2-1	1-2	3-1	4-0	2-2	1-0
9 Fulwood Amateurs	0-1	3-3	0-0	3-0	6-3	1-1	1-1	2-2		2-0	1-5	1-0	1-3	9-2	2-2	0-0
10 Garstang	3-2	0-3	1-3	1-0	0-2	1-1	0-3	1-2	0-2		3-0	3-2	0-1	2-0	0-2	2-3
11 Lostock St Gerards	1-2	0-3	2-3	0-2	0-2	2-4	3-2	0-3	2-2	2-0		3-2	1-1	5-1	0-3	1-2
12 Poulton Town	0-2	0-2	1-0	0-1	1-3	3-3	0-4	0-1	2-5	0-4	3-0		1-0	2-1	0-3	0-2
13 Stoneclough	0-2	2-4	2-2	4-1	1-3	2-0	0-3	1-1	1-2	2-1	5-3	1-3		1-1	1-2	3-2
14 Tempest United	0-6	0-4	1-2	6-0	0-7	1-6	1-4	2-2	1-2	3-3	1-3	6-3	2-0		2-2	1-0
15 Thornton Cleveleys	1-1	2-4	3-3	1-0	2-0	1-0	2-2	1-3	5-2	4-1	4-3	2-2	3-1	3-3		1-1
16 Vickerstown CCFC	1-2	1-5	1-1	3-1	2-1	0-0	2-0	3-1	4-1	1-1	2-1	6-3	1-1	2-2	0-1	

WEST LANCASHIRE LEAGUE PREMIER DIVISION CONSTITUTION 2011-12

BLACKPOOL WREN ROVERS	Bruce Park, School Road, Marton, Blackpool FY4 5DX	01253 349853
BURNLEY UNITED	Barden Sports Ground, Barden Lane, Burnley BB10 1JQ	01282 437943
CHARNOCK RICHARD	Mossie Park, Charter Lane, Charnock Richard, Chorley PR7 5LZ	01257 794288
COPPULL UNITED	Springfield Road, Coppull PR7 5EJ	01257 795190
EAGLEY	Eagley Sports Complex, Dunscar Bridge, Bolton BL7 9PQ	01204 306830
EUXTON VILLA	Jim Fowler Memorial Ground, Runshaw Hall Lane, Euxton, Chorley PR7 6HH	None
FLEETWOOD HESKETH	Fylde Road, Southport PR9 9XH	01704 227968
FULWOOD AMATEURS	Lightfoot Lane, Fulwood, Preston PR2 3LP	01772 861827
GARSTANG	The Riverside, High Street, Garstang PR3 1EB	01995 601586
LOSTOCK ST GERARDS	Wateringpool Lane, Lostock Hall, Preston PR5 5UA	None
POULTON TOWN	Cottam Hall Playing Fields, Blackpool Old Road, Poulton-le-Fylde FY6 7RH	01253 896150
SLYNE-WITH-HEST	Bottomdale Road, Slyne, Lancaster LA2 6BG	None
STONECLOUGH	Brook Street, opposite Europa Business Park, Stoneclough, Kearsley, Bolton M26 1HE	None
TEMPEST UNITED	Tempest Road, Chew Moor Village, Lostock, Bolton BL6 4HP	01942 811938
THORNTON CLEVELEYS	Bourne Road, Cleveleys, Thornton Cleveleys FY5 4QA	01253 869666
VICKERSTOWN CC	Park Vale, Mill Lane, Walney, Barrow-in-Furness LA14 3NB	None

IN: *Burnley United (P), Slyne-with-Hest (P)*
OUT: *Dalton United (R), Freckleton (W)*

DIVISION ONE	P	W	D	L	F	A	Pts
1 Burnley United	26	18	6	2	76	30	60
2 Slyne with Hest	26	18	5	3	61	26	59
3 Hawcoat Park	26	15	4	7	73	39	49
4 Longridge Town	26	13	8	5	76	41	47
5 Norcross & Warbreck	26	14	3	9	51	36	45
6 BAC/EE Springfield	26	13	5	8	64	47	44
7 Crooklands Casuals	26	12	7	7	64	51	43
8 Haslingden St.Mary`s	26	9	7	10	57	52	34
9 Mill Hill St. Peters	26	8	10	8	46	48	34
10 Wyre Villa	26	8	6	12	53	61	30
11 Millom	26	7	0	19	56	96	21
12 Turton (-3)	26	5	5	16	40	67	17
13 Hesketh Bank	26	4	2	20	43	95	14
14 Croston Sports	26	3	2	21	33	104	11

PRESIDENTS SHIELD

ROUND 1

Crooklands Casuals 3-1 Wyre Villa

Hawcoat Park 3-1 BAC/EE Springfields

Millom 2-1 Longridge Town

Burnley United 4-1 Mill Hill St Peters

Turton 3-2 Slyne-with-Hest

Croston Sports 0-1 Haslingden St Mary's

QUARTER-FINALS

Burnley United 3-0 Turton

Crooklands Casuals 3-1 Haslingden St Mary's

Millom 2-3 Hesketh Bank

Norcross & Warbreck 2-1 Hawcoat Park

SEMI-FINALS

Crooklands Casuals 2-4 Norcross & Warbreck

Hesketh Bank 0-1 Burnley United

FINAL (@ Lancaster City, 3/5/11)

Burnley United 0-3 Norcross & Warbreck

DIVISION ONE	1	2	3	4	5	6	7	8	9	10	11	12	13	14
1 BAC / EE Springfield		4-6	4-1	3-2	2-0	1-2	3-1	3-4	2-1	2-1	1-4	1-2	4-4	3-3
2 Burnley United	0-0		3-3	3-1	3-1	3-1	3-0	5-2	2-0	8-1	1-0	1-0	2-0	3-2
3 Crooklands Casuals	2-2	2-0		4-0	3-3	1-3	2-1	2-2	5-0	2-4	2-3	1-4	7-0	3-2
4 Croston Sports Club	0-6	2-7	1-3		3-3	1-11	2-3	0-1	3-2	1-4	2-5	0-4	0-4	2-4
5 Haslingden St Mary's	1-2	0-4	2-3	4-1		1-4	3-2	1-1	3-3	5-0	2-3	4-3	8-1	3-0
6 Hawcoat Park	0-4	3-3	7-0	4-1	3-1		10-2	0-3	0-0	4-1	5-0	1-3	3-1	0-2
7 Hesketh Bank	1-3	2-3	2-2	4-4	1-3	1-2		1-5	4-1	1-2	1-3	1-3	0-4	2-4
8 Longridge Town	0-3	1-3	1-1	4-0	4-2	4-0	7-2		3-3	6-2	0-1	0-0	2-2	0-0
9 Mill Hill St Peter's	2-1	2-2	0-2	7-1	2-0	1-1	4-1	1-5		3-2	1-0	1-1	1-1	1-1
10 Millom	4-3	0-3	2-5	6-2	0-2	0-3	13-4	0-6	3-4		3-4	0-6	3-2	2-3
11 Norcross & Warbreck	0-1	1-1	0-2	3-0	1-2	1-1	0-2	2-2	2-1	6-0		1-2	2-0	1-0
12 Slyne with Hest	2-2	1-0	2-0	3-0	0-0	2-1	3-1	4-3	1-1	5-2	1-2		2-1	1-0
13 Turton	1-3	0-0	0-3	1-2	1-1	1-2	1-3	2-5	1-3	2-0	2-1	0-3		8-3
14 Wyre Villa	3-1	1-7	3-3	1-2	2-2	1-2	5-0	1-5	1-1	4-1	1-5	2-3	4-0	

WEST LANCASHIRE LEAGUE DIVISION ONE CONSTITUTION 2011-12

BAC/EE SPRINGFIELD	BAC Sports Ground, South Meadow Lane, Preston PR1 8JP	01772 464351
CROOKLANDS CASUALS	Longlands Park, Greystone Lane, Dalton-in-Furness LA15 8JF	01229 465010
DALTON UNITED	Railway Meadow, Beckside Road, Dalton-in-Furness LA15 8DP	None
FURNESS ROVERS	Wilkie Road, Barrow-in-Furness LA14 5UG	None
HASLINGDEN ST MARY'S	South Shore Street, Haslingden, Rossendale BB4 5DX	01706 221814
HAWCOAT PARK	Hawcoat Park Sports Ground, Hawcoat Lane, Barrow-in-Furness LA14 4HF	01229 825296
HESKETH BANK	Centenary Sports Ground, Station Road, Hesketh Bank PR4 6SR	None
LONGRIDGE TOWN	Inglewhite Road, Longridge, Preston PR3 2NA	None
LYTHAM TOWN	Lytham Academy, Ballam Road, Lytham St Annes FY8 4LE	01253 733873
MILL HILL ST PETERS	Queen Victoria Street, Mill Hill, Blackburn BB2 2RZ	None
MILLOM	Millom RL Club, Devonshire Road, Millom LA18 4PG	01229 772030
NORCROSS & WARBRECK	Anchorsholme Lane, Thornton Cleveleys, Blackpool FY5 3DA	01253 859836
TURTON	Thomasson Fold, Turton, Edgworth, Bolton BL7 0PD	None
WYRE VILLA	Hallgate Park, Stalmine Village, Poulton-le-Fylde FY6 0LB	01253 701468

IN: *Dalton United (R), Furness Rovers (P), Lytham Town (P)*

OUT: *Burnley United (P), Croston Sports (R), Slyne-with-Hest (P)*

WEST LANCASHIRE LEAGUE - STEP 7

DIVISION TWO	P	W	D	L	F	A	Pts
1 Lytham Town	24	19	2	3	86	24	59
2 Furness Rovers	24	16	6	2	59	24	54
3 Ambleside United	24	15	3	6	89	42	48
4 Kendal County	24	13	5	6	61	45	44
5 Whinney Hill	24	12	1	11	50	51	37
6 Todmorden Borough	24	10	5	9	46	38	35
7 Furness Cavaliers	24	10	3	11	38	60	33
8 Milnthorpe Corinthians	24	10	2	12	41	50	32
9 Bolton County	24	8	5	11	55	60	29
10 GSK Ulverston Rangers	24	8	5	11	49	61	29
11 Askam United	24	7	5	12	45	64	26
12 Walney Island	24	3	2	19	28	79	11
13 Ladybridge	24	1	4	19	33	82	7

Lancashire Constabulary - record expunged

THE CHALLENGE CUP

ROUND 1

Ambleside United 2-1 Kendal County

Bolton County 1-5 Todmorden Borough

Ladybridge 0-4 Furness Rovers

Lytham Town 6-1 GSK Ulverston Rangers

Whinney Hill 3-1 Walney Island

QUARTER-FINALS

Furness Rovers 3-0 Askam United

Lytham Town 4-1 Ambleside United

Milnthorpe Corinthians wo-scr Furness Cavaliers

Whinney Hill 0-2 Todmorden Borough

SEMI-FINALS

Milnthorpe Corinthians 0-2 Lytham Town

Todmorden Borough 2-1 Furness Rovers

FINAL (@ Squires Gate, 26/4/11)

Lytham Town 1-2 Todmorden Borough

DIVISION TWO	1	2	3	4	5	6	7	8	9	10	11	12	13
1 Ambleside United		4-1	7-0	4-1	2-5	2-2	2-4	12-5	1-1	4-2	5-0	9-0	2-0
2 Askam United	3-3		2-1	4-0	1-3	3-3	3-2	1-4	2-4	2-1	3-3	1-0	5-1
3 Bolton County	2-3	5-0		8-2	1-1	2-5	3-3	4-2	1-6	3-1	1-1	3-1	1-0
4 Furness Cavaliers	1-4	2-1	1-3		1-2	3-2	0-5	3-2	5-3	1-0	2-1	3-3	2-2
5 Furness Rovers	2-1	2-2	3-1	0-0		2-1	2-0	5-0	1-1	5-0	2-1	0-1	2-3
6 G S K Ulverston Rangers	1-4	4-2	2-2	2-4	0-5		0-5	4-0	0-3	0-1	0-0	4-1	1-0
7 Kendal County	2-0	4-4	3-1	1-0	1-2	1-1		2-2	0-3	4-2	4-1	3-1	5-4
8 Ladybridge	0-4	0-1	2-2	1-2	1-3	2-4	1-3		0-6	2-3	0-4	1-1	2-4
9 Lytham Town	5-0	3-0	3-0	3-0	0-2	6-0	4-5	7-2		3-0	3-1	3-1	5-2
10 Milnthorpe Corinthians	0-2	5-1	4-3	5-0	2-2	1-5	0-0	2-1	0-3		2-0	4-1	1-3
11 Todmorden Borough	4-0	5-1	2-1	0-2	2-2	6-3	2-1	2-2	0-1	0-2		4-0	1-0
12 Walney Island	1-5	3-2	2-5	1-2	1-2	3-4	1-2	2-1	0-8	2-3	0-4		1-3
13 Whinney Hill	0-9	2-0	4-2	3-1	1-4	3-1	6-1	1-0	1-2	3-0	1-2	3-1	

WEST LANCASHIRE LEAGUE DIVISION TWO CONSTITUTION 2011-12

AMBLESIDE UNITED	Hillard Park, Vicarage Road, Ambleside LA22 0EE	None
ASKAM UNITED	Duddon Road, James Street, Askam-in-Furness LA16 7AH	01229 464576
BOLTON COUNTY	Radcliffe Road, Darcy Lever, Bolton BL3 1AN	None
BURSCOUGH RICHMOND	Richmond Park, Junction Lane, Burscough L40 5SN	None
CROSTON SPORTS	Old Emmanuel School, Westhead Road, Croston, Leyland PR26 9RR	01772 600261
FURNESS CAVALIERS	Rampside Road, Barrow-in-Furness LA13 0HN	None
GSK ULVERSTON RANGERS	off North Lonsdale Road, Ulverston LA12 9DZ	01229 582261
KENDAL COUNTY	Netherfield Cricket Club, Parkside Road, Kendal LA9 7BL	01539 724051
LADYBRIDGE	Tempest Road, Lostock, Bolton BL6 4EP	None
MILNTHORPE CORINTHIANS	Strands Lane, Milnthorpe LA7 7AE	01539 562135
TODMORDEN BOROUGH	Bellholme, Warland, Rochdale Road, Todmorden OL14 6UH	None
WALNEY ISLAND	Tummerhill Play Flos, Ocean Road, Walney, Barrow-in-Furness LA14 3HN	None
WHINNEY HILL	Burnley Road, Clayton-le-Moors, Accrington BB5 5NF	None

IN: *Burscough Richmond (P-Preston & District League Premier Division), Croston Sports (R)*

OUT: *Furness Rovers (P), Lancashire Constabulary (WN), Lytham Town (P)*

WILTSHIRE LEAGUE

Sponsored by: Plaister Auto Services
Founded: 1976
Recent Champions:
2006: Corsham Town Reserves
2007: Corsham Town Reserves
2008: Wroughton
2009: New College Swindon
2010: New College Swindon

PREMIER DIVISION	P	W	D	L	F	A	Pts
1 Corsham Town reserves	32	27	3	2	115	29	84
2 FC Chippenham Youth	32	20	5	7	80	36	65
3 New College Swindon	32	19	2	11	106	59	59
4 AFC Bradford Town (-1)	32	18	5	9	66	33	58
5 Wilts Calne Town	32	16	10	6	73	49	58
6 Chalke Valley	32	18	3	11	88	53	57
7 SKS Blyskawica	32	17	4	11	60	48	55
8 Southbrook	32	16	3	13	61	55	51
9 Moredon Cheney	32	14	5	13	71	72	47
10 RGV Shrewton	32	14	3	15	63	81	45
11 Devizes Town (-1)	32	13	3	16	59	72	41
12 Purton Redhouse (-4)	32	12	7	13	59	69	39
13 Vale of Pewsey	32	10	3	19	50	74	33
14 Marlborough Town	32	8	3	21	38	73	27
15 AFC Amesbury Town (-1)	32	7	3	22	44	95	23
16 Wroughton (-5)	32	6	2	24	41	93	15
17 Wilton Town (-1)	32	4	2	26	37	120	13

AFC Npower - record expunged
KC Club - record expunged

SENIOR KO CUP (CORSHAM PRINT)

ROUND 1
AFC Amesbury Town 0-6 Chalke Valley
Southbrook 2-2 New College Swindon
(New College Swindon won 4-1 on penalties)
Devizes Town Res. 4-1 AFC NPower

ROUND 2
Wroughton w/o-scr KC Club
Marlborough Town 1-5 SKS Blyskawica
Corsham Town Res. w/o-scr RGV Shrewton
Devizes Town Res. 1-2 New College Swindon
Vale of Pewsey 1-2 Purton Redhouse
AFC Bradford Town 1-0 Wilts Calne
Moredon Cheney 0-3 FC Chippenham Youth
Wilton Town 1-4 Chalke Valley

QUARTER-FINALS
Chalke Valley 3-3 FC Chippenham Youth
(FC Chippenham Youth won 6-5 on penalties)
AFC Bradford Town 4-2 Purton Redhouse
New College Swindon 2-1 Corsham Town Res.
SKS Blyskawica 3-1 Wroughton

SEMI-FINALS
New College Swindon 4-1 SKS Blyskawica
FC Chippenham Youth 2-2 AFC Bradford Town

FINAL (@ Corsham Town, 30/4/11)
FC Chippenham Youth 2-2 New College Swindon Youth
(FC Chippenham Youth won 4-3 on penalties)

PREMIER DIVISION	1	2	3	4	5	6	7	8	9	10	11	12	13	14	15	16	17
1 AFC Amesbury Town		0-2	3-0	2-6	1-3	1-3	1-0	3-4	0-8	2-2	0-1	0-2	1-4	0-2	3-0	2-2	4-2
2 AFC Bradford Town	6-1		2-0	1-2	4-0	1-3	5-0	1-1	3-1	3-0	1-3	0-1	3-1	4-0	5-0	0-0	W-L
3 Chalke Valley	3-2	1-1		2-3	6-3	1-1	7-1	3-2	1-0	11-0	0-1	1-2	4-3	8-0	0-3	0-2	W-L
4 Corsham Town reserves	4-0	6-3	2-0		5-1	1-1	4-0	7-0	1-0	1-2	3-1	4-2	3-1	2-2	9-0	3-0	5-2
5 Devizes Town reserves	2-0	1-4	0-2	0-3		0-2	2-0	0-2	1-2	2-2	6-2	5-2	1-0	4-3	0-1	1-1	9-2
6 FC Chippenham Youth	6-0	2-0	4-5	1-0	1-2		2-0	6-1	3-0	6-0	5-0	0-1	1-3	3-7	1-0	1-2	6-1
7 Marlborough Town	3-1	0-2	1-2	1-4	2-0	1-2		4-3	0-3	1-2	1-2	2-3	2-3	2-0	2-0	0-2	0-2
8 Moredon Cheney	6-0	3-1	3-2	1-7	0-2	1-1	3-3		5-4	3-2	3-1	0-3	1-1	7-0	2-1	0-1	4-1
9 New College Swindon	4-0	2-2	1-4	2-3	3-2	1-3	7-2	5-1		1-0	2-1	5-1	4-0	4-0	14-0	6-4	3-1
10 Purton Redhouse	3-1	0-1	1-2	1-2	3-0	1-0	2-2	1-0	2-1		3-3	1-3	1-0	1-1	7-2	0-3	4-0
11 R G V Shrewton	2-3	2-1	3-4	0-5	2-3	1-5	1-0	1-4	3-2	3-2		1-5	3-2	2-0	4-1	2-5	2-2
12 S K S Blyskawica	1-2	2-0	1-2	2-2	1-1	0-3	1-0	3-2	1-3	1-3	0-0		1-3	5-1	3-1	0-3	3-0
13 Southbrook	3-2	0-2	3-2	0-1	6-0	1-1	0-1	3-2	3-5	1-1	2-0	1-0		4-2	3-0	2-1	1-0
14 Vale of Pewsey	0-3	0-3	2-1	1-3	1-3	0-1	3-1	1-1	5-0	4-1	1-3	1-3	5-0		2-0	1-0	3-0
15 Wilton Town	6-2	0-2	1-5	0-7	2-3	2-2	2-3	1-4	2-7	0-3	2-7	0-4	2-3	2-1		1-1	2-3
16 Wilts Calne	4-4	0-0	2-2	0-3	3-1	1-2	2-2	3-0	2-2	5-4	7-4	1-1	2-0	1-0	4-2		2-1
17 Wroughton	1-0	1-3	0-7	0-4	4-1	1-2	0-1	0-2	3-4	4-4	1-2	0-2	1-4	2-1	4-1	2-7	

WILTSHIRE LEAGUE PREMIER DIVISION CONSTITUTION 2011-12

AFC AMESBURY TOWN	Bonnymead Park, Recreation Road, Amesbury SP4 7BB	01980 623489
AFC BRADFORD TOWN	Avon Sports Ground, Trowbridge Road, Bradford-on-Avon BA15 1EE	01225 866649
CORSHAM TOWN RESERVES	Southbank Ground, Lacock Road, Corsham SN13 9HS	01249 715609
DEVIZES TOWN RESERVES	Nursteed Road, Devizes SN10 3EJ	01380 722817
FC CHIPPENHAM YOUTH	Stanley Park Sports Ground, Stanley Lane, London Road, Chippenham SN15 3RR	01249 463905
FC SANFORD	Hunts Copse, South Marston, Swindon	None
LUDGERSHALL SPORTS	Astor Crescent, Ludgershall, Andover SP11 9RG	01264 398200
MARLBOROUGH TOWN	Elcot Lane, Marlborough SN8 2BG	01672 513340
MOREDON CHENEY	County Ground Extension, County Road, Swindon SN1 2ED	None
PURTON RESERVES	The Red House, Church Street, Purton SN5 4DY	01793 770262
RGV SHREWTON	Recreation Ground, Mill Lane, Shrewton, Salisbury SP3 4JU	07796 098122
SKS BLYSKAWICA	Southbrook Recreation Ground, Pinehurst Road, Swindon SN2 1RJ	None
SOUTHBROOK	Southbrook Recreation Ground, Pinehurst Road, Swindon SN2 1RJ	None
VALE OF PEWSEY	Recreation Ground, Kings Corner, Ball Road, Pewsey SN9 5BS	01672 562990
WILTS CALNE TOWN	Lickhill Road, Bremhill View, Calne SN11 8AE	01249 819186
WROUGHTON	The Weir Field, Wroughton WMC, Devizes Road, Wroughton SN4 0SA	01793 812319

IN: *FC Sanford (P), Ludgershall Sports (P)*
OUT: *AFC NPower (WS), Chalke Valley (W-Salisbury & District League), New College Swindon (P-Hellenic League Division One West), Wilton Town (R)*
Purton Redhouse become Purton Reserves

WILTSHIRE LEAGUE - STEP 7

DIVISION ONE	P	W	D	L	F	A	Pts
1 FC Sanford	30	28	0	2	110	28	84
2 Ludgershall Sports	30	21	5	4	106	45	68
3 Marshfield	30	21	2	7	98	45	65
4 Ashton Keynes	30	20	1	9	104	66	61
5 Madames	30	15	7	8	98	60	52
6 Old Town Wanderers	30	16	2	12	87	58	50
7 Intel	30	15	3	12	67	55	48
8 Pembroke	30	14	4	12	97	81	46
9 Byrons Wanderers (-2)	30	14	4	12	94	84	44
10 Ramsbury	30	12	4	14	43	80	40
11 Lower Stratton	30	9	6	15	56	79	33
12 Swindon NALGO	30	7	3	20	69	83	24
13 Swindon Irons	30	5	8	17	68	87	23
14 Moredon Cheney reserves	30	7	2	21	58	116	23
15 FC Chippenham Youth res (-6)	30	6	3	21	65	122	15
16 Marlborough Town res (-2)	30	2	2	26	25	156	6

Malmesbury Victoria reserves - record expugned

JUNIOR KO CUP (FOUNTAIN TROPHIES)

ROUND 1

FINAL (@ Corsham Town, 30/4/11)

Intel 3 Ludgershall Sports 0

DIVISION ONE	1	2	3	4	5	6	7	8	9	10	11	12	13	14	15	16
1 Ashton Keynes		6-4	4-1	0-1	2-1	5-1	0-1	5-1	11-0	3-2	2-2	2-1	3-2	7-0	5-1	5-2
2 Byrons Wanderers	1-3		3-1	3-4	1-5	4-2	0-3	1-2	9-3	3-1	2-3	1-8	0-4	5-0	8-2	3-2
3 FC Chippenham Youth reserves	2-4	1-4		3-6	1-4	2-3	1-14	0-5	8-4	2-3	2-9	0-5	5-3	3-4	2-1	2-6
4 FC Sanford	5-0	6-3	3-0		4-0	1-2	4-0	2-1	5-0	4-0	6-1	1-3	3-2	4-0	2-1	2-0
5 Intel	6-2	2-5	2-2	1-3		2-1	0-1	1-1	4-1	1-0	2-1	1-0	3-1	1-3	5-2	2-0
6 Lower Stratton	4-1	1-1	3-1	1-3	0-1		3-3	3-1	3-0	1-4	1-2	3-5	8-3	1-2	2-2	2-7
7 Ludgershall Sports	4-2	2-1	3-3	1-4	1-0	9-1		2-1	5-0	1-3	7-2	2-1	7-0	5-0	0-0	3-1
8 Madames	6-1	2-6	3-3	1-3	3-2	2-1	6-0		5-0	1-2	7-1	4-1	1-1	1-1	7-3	3-2
9 Marlborough Town reserves	0-8	0-7	1-4	1-6	0-4	1-1	1-3	2-10		0-9	0-1	0-10	1-7	0-2	0-3	3-3
10 Marshfield	1-2	6-6	6-1	1-2	6-2	4-0	0-0	1-3	5-0		5-2	3-1	3-0	6-1	1-0	2-1
11 Moredon Cheney reserves	1-2	2-2	5-4	0-6	2-3	1-2	0-4	3-7	2-3	2-5		2-5	3-8	1-2	3-2	2-11
12 Old Town Wanderers	3-4	2-3	2-1	0-2	4-2	6-1	2-5	1-1	5-0	1-4	4-0		3-6	2-1	2-1	0-2
13 Pembroke	4-5	1-1	4-1	1-7	3-2	3-1	1-3	4-0	5-1	2-4	5-2	0-2		6-0	3-3	5-2
14 Ramsbury	3-2	6-1	2-1	0-4	0-4	2-2	2-3	0-5	1-0	0-3	2-0	3-3	3-3		0-3	2-1
15 Swindon Irons	3-1	2-3	4-5	0-2	4-4	0-0	5-5	5-5	8-0	2-5	2-3	3-4	2-6	0-1		2-2
16 Swindon NALGO	3-7	2-3	2-3	2-5	1-0	1-2	1-9	3-3	2-3	1-3	3-0	0-1	2-4	3-0	1-2	

WILTSHIRE LEAGUE DIVISION ONE CONSTITUTION 2011-12

AFC WROUGHTON	Maunsell Way, Wroughton SN4 9JE	None
ASHTON KEYNES	Rixon Gate, Ashton Keynes, Swindon SN6 6PH	None
BOX ROVERS	Recreation Ground, Box	
BYRONS WANDERERS	Ridgeway School, Inverary Road, Wroughton SN4 9DJ	01793 846100
FC CHIPPENHAM YOUTH RES.	Stanley Park Sports Ground, Stanley Lane, London Road, Chippenham SN15 3RR	01249 463905
FC SANFORD RESERVES	Hunts Copse, South Marston, Swindon	None
INTEL	Commonweal School, The Mall, Swindon SN1 4JE	01793 612727
LOWER STRATTON	Grange Drive Community Centre, Stratton, Swindon SN3 4JY	None
MADAMES	Shrewsbury Road, Walcot, Swindon SN3 3AH	None
MALMESBURY VICTORIA RESERVES	Flying Monk Ground, Gloucester Road, Malmesbury SN16 0AJ	01666 822141
MARLBOROUGH TOWN RESERVES	Elcot Lane, Marlborough SN8 2BG	01672 513340
MARSHIELD	Withymead Road, Marshfield, Chippenham SN14 8PB	None
MOREDON CHENEY RESERVES	Penhill Recreation Ground, Crossways Avenue, Swindon	None
OLD TOWN WANDERERS	Shrewsbury Roaf, Walcot, Swindon SN3 3AH	None
PEMBROKE	Pembroke Gardens, Abbey View Road, Moredon, Swindon SN25 3EG	None
RAMSBURY	Ramsbury Rec, Hilldrop Lane, Ramsbury, Marlborough SN8 2HZ	None
WILTON TOWN	Castle Meadow, Castle Lane, North Street, Wilton SP2 0HG	None

IN: *AFC Wroughton (N), Box Rovers (N), FC Sanford Reserves (N), Wilton Town (R)*

OUT: *FC Sanford (P), Ludgershall Sports (P), Swindon NALGO (W), Swindon Irons (W*

CORNWALL COMBINATION

Sponsored by: Jollys
Founded: 1959
Recent Champions:
2006: Truro City Reserves
2007: Illogan RBL
2008: Truro City Reserves
2009: Perranporth
2010: Illogan RBL
cmboleaguearchive.athost.net

		P	W	D	L	F	A	Pts
1	Helston Athletic	38	33	2	3	150	37	101
2	Perranwell	38	29	5	4	125	34	92
3	Illogan RBL	38	28	6	4	118	25	90
4	Penryn Athletic reserves	38	27	2	9	115	43	83
5	Pendeen Rovers	38	26	4	8	143	53	82
6	St Just	38	24	7	7	107	56	79
7	St Agnes	38	23	5	10	116	54	74
8	Falmouth Town reserves	38	21	6	11	131	60	69
9	RNAS Culdrose	38	15	6	17	90	88	51
10	Wendron United	38	16	3	19	87	107	51
11	Troon	38	14	6	18	73	86	48
12	Mullion	38	11	7	20	81	104	40
13	St Ives Town	38	14	0	24	64	87	39
14	St Day	38	11	5	22	69	114	38
15	Porthleven reserves (-3)	38	11	7	20	67	103	37
16	Newquay reserves	38	9	5	24	59	95	32
17	Hayle reserves (-1pt, 2goals)	38	9	5	24	53	105	31
18	Penzance reserves	38	8	3	27	39	123	27
19	Holman SC	38	7	2	29	53	122	23
20	Ludgvan	38	0	2	36	18	267	2

SUPPLEMENTARY CUP

(Combination Cup Preliminary and First Round Losers)

SEMI-FINALS

Illogan RBL 0-2 Wendron United (@ Helston Athletic)
Hayle Res. 1-1 St Agnes
(Hayle reserves won 4-1 on penalties) (@ Illogan RBL)

FINAL (@ Penryn Athletic, 22/5/11)

Hayle reserves 2-1 Wendron United

LEAGUE CUP

PRELIMINARY ROUND

Falmouth Town reserves 3-2 Wendron United
Penzance reserves 2-0 Ludgvan
Newquay reserves 0-3 St Just
Illogan RBL 3-3 Penryn Athletic reserves
Preliminary Round Replay
Penryn Athletic 1-0 Illogan RBL

ROUND 1

Falmouth Town reserves 1-3 Pendeen Rovers
Penryn Athletic reserves 4-1 St Agnes
Hayle reserves 1-2 St Day
Helston Athletic 7-1 Troon
Holman Sports Club 1-8 St Just
Perranwell 4-0 St Ives Town
Porthleven reserves 3-3 Penzance reserves
RNAS Culdrose 5-4 Mullion
Round 1 Replay
Penzance reserves 2-2 Porthleven reserves
(Penzance won 5-4 on penalties)

QUARTER FINALS

Penryn Athletic reserves 1-2 Perranwell
Penzance reserves 0-4 St Just
RNAS Culdrose 3-6 Helston Athletic
St Day 0-5 Pendeen Rovers

SEMI-FINALS

Perranwell 6-1 St Just (@ Hayle)
Helston Athletic 1-2 Pendeen Rovers (@ Ludgvan)

FINAL (@ Porthleven, 23/4/11)

Perranwell 3-1 Pendeen Rovers
(Perranwell won 3-1 on penalties)

EVELY CUP

(Combination League Cup winners v East Cornwall League Cup winners, @ Helston Athletic, 29/5/11)

Perranwell 2-1 St Dennis

		1	2	3	4	5	6	7	8	9	10	11	12	13	14	15	16	17	18	19	20
1	Falmouth Town reserves		2-2	0-2	6-1	0-2	19-0	5-2	0-3	0-3	3-1	2-0	2-1	6-0	5-3	2-2	6-0	1-3	4-0	3-2	4-1
2	Hayle reserves	1-7		0-6	0-3	1-1	7-0	0-2	2-1	1-5	1-4	1-0	0-3	2-4	3-1	1-2	0-4	2-3	3-0	1-2	4-1
3	Helston Athletic	2-0	4-1		4-1	2-2	2-1	2-1	3-0	7-0	1-4	2-0	3-2	4-1	3-1	2-1	10-1	4-1	3-2	4-1	6-0
4	Holman S C	0-2	1-4	0-4		2-0	4-0	1-7	3-1	2-3	0-5	5-0	1-7	0-2	0-5	0-3	2-3	3-2	1-2	0-0	0-0
5	Illogan R B L	1-4	7-0	1-2	4-0		8-0	4-0	2-0	2-0	1-1	4-0	0-3	3-1	3-2	3-1	8-0	1-0	2-0	3-0	4-1
6	Ludgvan	0-14	2-2	0-12	0-6	0-14		2-7	0-7	0-9	0-6	1-6	0-7	2-2	2-5	0-5	2-6	0-8	0-2	2-6	0-7
7	Mullion	4-4	1-3	0-6	7-4	0-4	7-0		1-1	0-3	0-3	2-1	1-1	1-0	2-2	3-3	0-6	1-3	2-2	5-2	2-5
8	Newquay reserves	2-0	3-1	1-4	1-0	1-2	2-0	3-1		1-4	0-1	5-3	1-2	1-1	2-3	0-3	1-1	1-3	1-5	3-2	2-6
9	Pendeen Rovers	2-1	6-1	2-3	6-2	1-1	19-0	4-1	5-1		1-3	7-0	2-2	2-0	2-2	4-0	1-0	1-2	3-0	3-1	9-0
10	Penryn Athletic reserves	2-0	5-0	1-4	6-0	0-2	13-2	2-0	3-1	0-2		6-0	0-1	9-1	3-1	0-2	2-0	3-0	2-0	3-3	3-2
11	Penzance reserves	5-3	0-2	0-11	1-0	0-4	3-0	1-3	3-3	1-7	2-5		1-0	1-5	1-0	1-5	1-7	0-1	3-1	0-3	0-3
12	Perranwell	2-2	3-1	5-3	8-1	1-0	16-0	3-0	1-0	5-1	2-0	1-0		4-3	6-2	0-1	1-0	3-0	2-1	4-2	9-2
13	Porthleven reserves	2-2	1-1	1-4	2-1	1-2	4-0	1-1	4-1	1-9	1-2	0-0	L-W		5-2	2-7	3-1	1-0	0-2	0-2	2-6
14	R N A S Culdrose	1-3	6-1	1-7	3-1	0-2	4-0	1-0	3-1	3-4	0-1	7-1	0-0	3-1		3-1	6-0	3-2	3-3	3-1	2-4
15	St Agnes	5-3	1-0	2-5	7-1	1-1	6-0	4-2	7-0	3-2	2-3	7-0	0-1	7-1	3-1		0-0	1-0	1-2	1-3	5-1
16	St Day	0-3	1-1	0-1	4-1	0-5	2-1	0-4	3-1	3-3	2-6	0-3	0-7	4-3	4-4	1-6		7-1	1-3	2-1	1-3
17	St Ives Town	0-4	3-0	0-4	1-3	1-2	3-0	3-4	4-3	0-2	1-2	2-0	2-5	0-2	3-1	0-2	4-0		2-5	1-6	1-2
18	St Just	1-1	4-0	2-1	2-1	1-1	6-1	8-4	2-2	3-1	3-0	6-0	1-1	7-3	7-0	3-2	3-1	3-1		2-2	3-2
19	Troon	0-1	3-1	0-2	3-2	0-5	3-0	3-2	5-1	0-3	0-5	1-1	0-4	2-4	1-1	1-1	5-3	2-1	1-4		4-1
20	Wendron United	3-6	0-7	1-1	4-2	0-4	8-0	4-1	2-1	1-2	2-0	1-0	1-2	2-2	0-2	2-6	2-1	3-5	1-3	3-1	

DEVON & EXETER LEAGUE

Sponsored by: Fresha
Founded: 1900
Recent Champions:
2006: Heavitree Social United
2007: Axminster Town
2008: University of Exeter Reserves
2009: St. Martins
2010: Thorverton
defleague.co.uk

PREMIER DIVISION	P	W	D	L	F	A	Pts
1 Sidmouth Town	30	19	9	2	76	26	66
2 Seaton Town	30	20	3	7	86	51	63
3 Newtown	30	16	6	8	84	55	54
4 Clyst Valley	30	16	6	8	62	47	54
5 Topsham Town (-4)	30	15	7	8	62	44	48
6 St Martins	30	14	4	12	65	62	46
7 Thorverton	30	12	3	15	55	70	39
8 Heavitree Social United	30	10	6	14	55	61	36
9 Beer Albion	30	10	6	14	38	49	36
10 University of Exeter reserves	30	9	8	13	62	68	35
11 Hatherleigh Town	30	10	5	15	56	73	35
12 Budleigh Salterton reserves	30	9	7	14	43	61	34
13 Alphington reserves	30	9	5	16	56	70	32
14 Willand Rovers reserves	30	7	10	13	46	66	31
15 Exmouth Amateurs	30	9	3	18	44	60	30
16 Wellington Town	30	7	8	15	50	77	29

EAST DEVON SENIOR CUP

ROUND 1
Beer Albion 3-2 Witheridge Res.
Bow AAC 2-0 Chagford
Clyst Valley 1-2 Alphington Res.
Exmouth Amateurs 1-3 Budleigh Salterton Res (@ Budleigh Salterton)
East Budleigh 5-3 Elmore Res.
Feniton 4-7 Newtown
Hatherleigh Town 2-5 Heavitree Social United
Morchard Bishop 6-0 Willand Rovers Res.
Seaton Town 3-2 Tipton St John
Thorverton 5-1 Wellington Town Res.
Topsham Town 6-1 Cullompton Rangers Res.

ROUND 2
Halwill 3-3 Honiton Town 5 4
St Martins 1-0 Sidbury United
Beer Albion 0-3 Alphington
Bow AAC 2-0 Morchard Bishop
East Budleigh 1-3 Thorverton
Newtown 5-3 Topsham Town
Seaton Town 1-2 Budleigh Salterton Res.
Sidmouth Town 5-1 Heavitee Social United

QUARTER FINALS
Halwill 0-1 Budleigh Salterton Res. (@ Budleigh Salterton)
Newtown 2-3 Alphington Res.
St Martins 0-3 Bow AAC
Thorverton 0-2 Sidmouth Town

SEMI-FINALS
Bow AAC 3-1 Alphington Res.
Sidmouth Town 1-0 Budleigh Salterton Res.

FINAL (@ Topsham Town, 28/5/11)
Sidmouth Town 1-0 Bow AAC

PREMIER DIVISION	1	2	3	4	5	6	7	8	9	10	11	12	13	14	15	16
1 Alphington reserves		0-1	1-1	1-4	1-3	1-1	3-1	1-4	4-2	2-0	1-4	3-0	1-1	5-3	0-2	1-0
2 Beer Albion	4-2		1-0	1-2	3-2	3-1	1-1	3-3	0-4	0-0	1-3	1-0	4-1	1-1	1-2	1-2
3 Budleigh Salterton reserves	3-3	1-0		0-2	2-1	2-3	2-2	1-3	1-1	1-1	3-2	0-3	2-2	2-1	3-0	0-4
4 Clyst Valley	4-1	2-1	1-2		2-0	3-0	3-1	2-2	1-3	0-4	4-3	2-1	3-1	1-2	6-1	0-0
5 Exmouth Amateurs	1-3	1-3	2-1	1-2		5-1	4-1	1-2	0-1	0-1	1-5	3-1	1-0	1-5	2-1	2-2
6 Hatherleigh Town	0-2	0-1	2-0	1-0	4-1		3-1	3-3	1-6	0-3	2-3	3-3	3-2	7-1	1-6	3-3
7 Heavitree Social United	0-4	1-1	2-3	2-2	1-1	0-4		3-5	3-1	2-5	4-1	1-2	1-1	2-0	4-1	3-0
8 Newtown	5-1	5-0	2-0	3-0	1-4	5-2	0-4		7-2	1-1	0-2	1-2	4-1	2-2	2-2	3-0
9 Seaton Town	3-2	0-0	3-1	3-3	2-1	2-1	5-3	2-1		0-1	6-3	3-2	2-1	2-1	3-0	5-2
10 Sidmouth Town	3-2	4-0	6-0	1-2	4-1	5-2	3-0	3-1	2-1		1-1	3-1	2-0	2-2	4-1	2-0
11 St Martins	3-2	2-0	3-2	1-2	3-0	4-0	1-3	2-3	1-7	1-4		4-0	1-3	2-1	2-3	0-5
12 Thorverton	3-1	3-1	1-1	3-1	2-0	0-1	2-1	6-1	3-2	0-6	1-2		0-4	1-7	3-4	2-2
13 Topsham Town	4-2	2-0	4-2	3-3	2-1	3-1	1-0	4-3	2-0	1-1	0-3	2-0		1-1	1-1	7-0
14 University of Exeter reserves	4-1	0-4	1-3	1-3	1-1	4-1	1-2	0-5	4-5	1-1	1-1	3-1	0-3		6-3	4-2
15 Wellington Town	2-2	3-1	1-3	3-1	0-3	1-1	1-3	0-3	0-6	2-2	0-0	4-5	2-4	1-2		0-0
16 Willand Rovers reserves	4-3	1-0	3-1	1-1	3-0	0-4	0-3	1-4	0-4	1-1	2-2	3-4	0-1	2-2	3-3	

DIVISION ONE	P	W	D	L	F	A	Pts
1 Barstaple Town reserves	28	21	3	4	75	24	66
2 Morchard Bishop	28	20	5	3	73	27	65
3 East Budleigh	28	17	5	6	69	34	56
4 Bow AAC	28	16	4	8	55	40	52
5 University of Exeter "A"	28	14	3	11	58	55	45
6 Cullompton Rangers reserve	28	12	6	10	52	53	42
7 Tipton St John	28	13	2	13	56	56	41
8 Witheridge reserves	28	11	6	11	46	49	39
9 Chagford	28	10	4	14	56	59	34
10 Heavitree Social United res	28	10	3	15	69	81	33
11 Feniton	28	9	5	14	42	59	32
12 Sidbury United	28	8	6	14	48	48	30
13 Hointon Town	28	7	8	13	51	66	29
14 Elmore reserves	28	5	3	20	29	84	18
15 Halwill	28	3	5	20	31	75	14

DIVISION TWO	P	W	D	L	F	A	Pts
1 Phoenix Club	26	20	4	2	101	31	64
2 Exeter Civil Service	26	17	3	6	72	39	54
3 Beacon Knights	26	16	3	7	59	37	51
4 Culm United	26	14	6	6	73	36	48
5 University of Exeter "B"	26	13	3	10	68	56	42
6 Uplowman Athletic	26	12	6	8	49	56	42
7 Westexe Rovers	25	9	7	9	54	40	34
8 Colyton	25	10	4	11	46	54	34
9 Broadclyst	26	9	6	11	55	59	33
10 Sidlmouth Town reserves	26	8	8	10	55	50	32
11 Clyst Valley reserves	26	8	3	15	55	61	27
12 Newtown reserves	26	7	5	14	44	78	26
13 North Tawton (-1)	26	5	3	18	48	95	17
14 Axminster Town reserves (-2)	26	1	3	22	18	105	4
Royal Marines reserves - record expunged							

DIVISION THREE	P	W	D	L	F	A	Pts
1 Topsham Town reserves	28	20	4	4	112	43	64
2 Chard Town reserves	28	20	4	4	84	30	64
3 Pinhoe	28	17	6	5	103	46	57
4 Offwell Rangers (-1)	28	18	2	8	75	45	55
5 Sansford (-3)	28	15	5	8	90	70	48
6 Upottery	28	12	6	10	60	47	42
7 Dawlish United	28	12	5	11	62	41	41
8 Lympstone	28	12	5	11	54	57	41
9 South Zeal United (-1)	28	11	5	12	51	51	37
10 Winkleigh	28	11	2	15	64	67	35
11 Crescent	28	11	2	15	65	101	35
12 Dawlish Town reserves (-3)	28	8	5	15	62	81	26
13 Bampton	28	6	4	18	35	69	22
14 Countess Wear Dynamoes	28	6	3	19	42	85	21
15 Exmouth Amateurs reserves (-1)	28	2	0	26	22	148	5

DIVISION FOUR	P	W	D	L	F	A	Pts
1 Bickleigh reserves	26	17	5	4	86	45	56
2 Colaton Raleigh	26	17	4	5	79	51	55
3 Crediton United reserves	26	14	5	7	66	35	47
4 Tedburn St Mary	26	13	5	8	75	53	44
5 Seaton Town reserves	26	13	3	10	53	47	42
6 Kentisbeare	26	12	4	10	70	72	40
7 Thorverton reserves	25	11	6	8	50	42	39
8 Hemyock	26	10	2	14	60	51	32
9 Okehampton Argyle reserves	25	10	1	14	58	72	31
10 Newton St Cyres	26	7	9	10	54	60	30
11 Lapford	26	8	6	12	38	52	30
12 Sidbury United reserves	26	7	6	13	49	74	27
13 Newtown "A" (-1)	26	6	6	14	35	72	23
14 St Martins reserves (-2)	26	3	4	19	39	86	11

DIVISION FIVE	P	W	D	L	F	A	Pts
1 Dolphin	28	26	1	1	116	24	79
2 University of Exeter "C"	28	22	3	3	107	47	69
3 Whipton & Pinhoe	28	20	3	5	96	47	63
4 Heavitree Social United "A"	28	19	3	6	92	56	60
5 Woodbury	28	16	2	10	91	53	50
6 AFC Sidford	28	14	3	11	77	82	45
7 Sampford Peverrell (-1)	28	13	2	13	73	72	40
8 Alphington reserves	28	11	1	16	63	77	34
9 Lord's XI	28	9	6	13	61	67	33
10 Cullompton Rangers "A"	28	10	2	16	43	64	31
11 Beer Albion reserves	28	9	3	16	48	73	30
12 Dunkeswell Rovers	28	7	4	17	54	87	25
13 Westexe Rovers reserves	28	6	6	16	44	79	24
14 Feniton reserves	28	5	2	21	44	101	17
15 Broadclyst reserve	28	2	1	25	38	118	7

DIVISION SIX	P	W	D	L	F	A	Pts
1 Exmouth Town reserves	28	23	3	2	133	28	72
2 Hatherleigh Town reserves	28	19	3	6	102	50	60
3 Axmouth United	28	19	1	8	88	51	58
4 Culm United reserves	28	17	4	7	92	54	55
5 Clyst Valley "A"	28	14	2	12	95	60	44
6 Chagford reserves	28	12	4	12	61	58	40
7 UAU Exeter	28	13	1	14	72	75	40
8 Awliscombe United	28	12	4	12	54	65	40
9 East Budleigh reserves (-3)	28	12	4	12	66	61	39
10 Priory	28	10	6	12	67	85	36
11 Cheriton Fitzpaine (-1)	28	10	5	13	65	75	34
12 Uplowman Athletic reserves (-1)	28	9	5	14	79	86	31
13 Honiton Town reserves (-1)	28	5	6	17	40	85	20
14 Silverton (-1)	28	5	3	20	45	164	17
15 Bapton reserves	28	4	1	23	37	99	13

DIVISION SEVEN	P	W	D	L	F	A	Pts
1 Chulmleigh	28	22	3	3	148	37	69
2 Topsham Town "A"	28	21	4	3	113	39	67
3 Bow AAC reserves	28	20	7	1	80	31	67
4 Dawlish United reserves	28	19	0	9	97	53	57
5 Amory Park Rangers	28	15	3	10	98	52	48
6 Langdon (-1)	28	12	6	10	71	55	41
7 Amory Argyle (-1)	28	13	3	12	81	79	41
8 Sandford reserves (-4)	28	13	4	11	63	60	39
9 Hemyock reserves	28	10	3	15	48	69	33
10 Bradninch	28	10	3	15	56	96	33
11 North Tawton reserves	28	7	4	17	61	95	25
12 Halwill reserves	28	6	5	17	51	80	23
13 Newton St Cyres reserves (-5)	28	9	1	18	52	115	23
14 Folly Gate & Inwardleigh	28	4	3	21	42	140	15
15 Countess Wear Dynamoes R.	28	2	5	21	31	91	11
Five Star Security - record expunged							

DIVISION EIGHT	P	W	D	L	F	A	Pts
1 Morchard Bishop reserves	28	23	4	1	126	31	73
2 Okehampton Argyle "A"	28	23	0	5	107	44	69
3 Topsham Town "B"	28	20	4	4	107	38	64
4 Tipton St John reservs	28	17	4	7	73	43	55
5 Feniton "A"	28	16	5	7	103	61	53
6 Lympstone reserves	28	16	4	8	90	49	52
7 Offwell Rangers reserves	28	13	3	12	96	74	42
8 Met Office	28	12	3	13	46	63	39
9 Otterton	28	10	4	14	45	68	34
10 Colyton reserves	28	9	4	15	60	65	31
11 Tedburn St Mary reserves	28	7	4	17	36	120	25
12 Cheriton Fitzpaine reserves	28	5	4	19	38	81	19
13 Winkleigh reserves	28	6	1	21	46	109	19
14 Lapford reserves	28	5	3	20	46	102	18
15 Langdon reserve	28	2	5	21	47	118	11

DORSET COUNTY LEAGUE

Sponsored by: No sponsor
Founded: N/K
Recent Champions:
2006: Sturminster Marshall
2007: Wincanton Town
2008: Chickerell United
2009: Parley Sports
2010: Easton United

	SENIOR DIVISION	P	W	D	L	F	A	Pts
1	Tintinhull	26	15	8	3	56	30	53
2	Okeford United	26	15	6	5	49	32	51
3	Kingston Lacy	26	14	5	7	57	48	47
4	Portland United reserves	26	13	4	9	51	37	43
5	Witchampton United	26	12	5	9	48	36	41
6	Bishops Caundle	26	12	5	9	41	31	41
7	Wareham Rangers	26	11	7	8	55	35	40
8	Weymouth Sports	26	12	4	10	54	42	40
9	Upwey and Broadwey	26	11	6	9	59	43	39
10	Gillingham Town res (+3)	26	9	4	13	48	58	34
11	Stourpaine	26	10	3	13	45	61	33
12	Chickerell United reserves	26	7	5	14	37	52	26
13	Poole Borough reserves	26	5	4	17	24	71	19
14	Swanage T & Herston res (-3)	26	2	2	22	27	75	5

	DIVISION ONE	Pld	W	D	L	F	A	Pts
1	Piddletrenthide United	20	14	4	2	65	27	46
2	Blandford United res	20	11	4	5	57	35	37
3	Bere Regis	20	10	4	6	61	42	34
4	Poundbury Rovers	20	9	6	5	57	34	33
5	Dorchester Borough	20	9	5	6	56	45	32
6	Shaftesbury reserves	20	9	4	7	53	41	31
7	Kangaroos	20	9	4	7	53	47	31
8	Wincanton Town res	20	9	2	9	43	43	29
9	Wool RBL	20	5	3	12	41	51	18
10	Sturminster Newton res	20	3	2	15	27	86	11
11	Wareham Rangers res	20	3	0	17	26	88	9
	AC Matravers - record expunged							

	DIVISION TWO	Pld	W	D	L	F	A	Pts
1	Mere Town	22	16	4	2	89	28	52
2	Granby Rovers	22	14	3	5	67	40	45
3	The Balti House	22	14	3	5	70	48	45
4	Bridport "A" (-3)	22	13	5	4	65	30	41
5	Milborne Sports	22	10	3	9	68	51	33
6	Sturminster Marshall res	22	10	2	10	73	55	32
7	Dorchester Sports	22	9	2	11	50	60	29
8	Weymouth Spartans	22	8	3	11	51	61	27
9	Lytchett Red Triangle	22	8	3	11	39	63	27
10	Corfe Castle	22	7	5	10	54	73	26
11	Child Okeford	22	3	3	16	51	92	12
12	Portesham United	22	0	4	18	22	98	4

	DIVISION THREE	Pld	W	D	L	F	A	Pts
1	Corfe Mullen United	24	21	2	1	107	28	65
2	Wyke Regis Social Cl	24	15	4	5	68	35	49
3	Gillingham Tn "A"	24	14	6	4	54	27	48
4	Donhead United	24	15	2	7	90	42	47
5	Stickland United	24	12	4	8	72	44	40
6	Maiden N & C'stock	24	10	8	6	60	53	38
7	Cranborne reserves	24	8	3	13	46	64	27
8	Piddlehinton United	24	8	2	14	43	60	26
9	Witchampton Utd res	24	8	2	14	37	64	26
10	Okeford United res	24	7	3	14	51	76	24
11	Swanage T & H "A"	24	5	6	13	35	81	21
12	Puddletown	24	3	7	14	26	66	16
13	Stalbridge	24	2	7	15	27	76	13

	DIVISON FOUR	Pld	W	D	L	F	A	Pts
1	Poole Link	18	15	3	0	52	20	48
2	Galaxy Windows	18	11	4	3	60	28	37
3	Soccer	18	9	3	6	40	24	30
4	Flight Refuelling	18	9	3	6	43	35	30
5	Shaftesbury "A"	18	8	2	8	39	31	26
6	Dorchester Castle	18	7	4	7	40	46	25
7	Bishops Caundle res	18	5	4	9	41	56	19
8	Owermoigne	18	5	1	12	27	43	16
9	Handley Sports	18	4	1	13	30	70	13
10	Poundbury Rovers res	18	3	3	12	29	48	12
	F C Windowman - record expunged							

	DIVISION FIVE	Pld	W	D	L	F	A	Pts
1	Cerne Abbas	18	18	0	0	117	15	54
2	Littlemoor	18	13	1	4	84	52	40
3	Galaxy Windows res	18	11	3	4	60	40	36
4	AFC Blandford	18	9	3	6	58	36	30
5	Pimperne Sports	18	8	2	8	43	56	26
6	M N & Cattistock res	18	7	1	10	45	70	22
7	Wyke Workies (-3)	18	7	2	9	43	42	20
8	Milborne Sports res (+3)	18	4	2	12	34	56	17
9	Donhead Utd reserves	18	5	0	13	49	73	15
10	Dor Community Church	18	1	0	17	19	112	3

SENIOR DIVISION	1	2	3	4	5	6	7	8	9	10	11	12	13	14
1 Bishops Caundle		2-1	1-2	1-1	1-2	0-0	5-0	0-1	2-0	2-2	1-2	1-2	4-2	2-1
2 Chickerell United reserves	1-2		0-1	2-3	1-1	3-4	2-1	1-3	6-2	0-3	1-1	1-5	1-0	1-2
3 Gillingham Town reserves	2-6	8-2		2-3	1-1	2-0	4-2	2-0	W-L	2-2	2-4	2-3	1-2	0-2
4 Kingston Lacy	4-1	3-1	3-1		3-3	3-1	2-1	4-3	4-3	3-1	1-0	1-1	5-4	1-0
5 Okeford United	0-1	2-0	2-6	2-0		1-0	1-0	3-1	6-0	0-1	2-1	4-2	2-2	1-0
6 Poole Borough reserves	0-2	2-2	1-1	1-0	1-4		0-1	2-5	1-0	1-1	1-7	0-6	1-2	0-6
7 Portland United reserves	2-0	0-0	2-0	2-1	1-1	9-0		4-3	5-1	3-0	3-1	3-1	1-0	2-0
8 Stourpaine	1-1	0-1	2-1	3-2	1-2	2-0	0-5		2-1	1-1	2-4	0-3	4-3	2-7
9 Swanage Town & Herston reserves	0-1	2-3	1-5	1-4	1-2	1-2	2-1	0-3		1-2	2-4	1-1	1-1	0-1
10 Tintinhull	3-2	2-1	1-1	3-1	1-1	3-2	6-1	3-0	3-1		2-3	4-1	1-1	1-0
11 Upwey & Broadwey	0-1	1-1	7-0	4-2	1-2	3-0	1-1	4-2	2-1	0-3		2-3	1-2	2-2
12 Wareham Rangers	0-1	1-4	2-0	2-2	0-1	1-0	4-0	1-1	9-0	1-1	1-1		1-3	4-0
13 Weymouth Sports	1-0	0-1	3-0	4-0	3-2	6-2	1-0	1-2	2-3	1-4	2-2	2-0		2-3
14 Witchampton United	1-1	1-0	6-2	1-1	3-1	0-2	1-1	5-1	3-2	0-2	3-1	0-0	0-4	

EAST CORNWALL LEAGUE

Sponsored by: Cornish Guardian
Founded: 1960
Recent Champions:
2006: Saltash United Reserves
2007: Foxhole Stars
2008: Torpoint Athletic Reserves
2009: Torpoint Athletic Reserves
2010: Torpoint Athletic Reserves

PREMIER DIVISION	P	W	D	L	F	A	Pts
1 St Dennis	30	25	1	4	108	38	76
2 Torpoint Athletic reserves	30	24	3	3	105	27	75
3 Sticker	30	21	3	6	91	39	66
4 Plymouth Parkway reserves	30	18	3	9	101	51	57
5 Saltash United reserves	30	18	3	9	85	49	57
6 Bere Alston United	30	16	1	13	68	56	49
7 Bude Town	30	14	4	12	77	59	46
8 Launceston reserves	30	12	8	10	70	56	44
9 Probus	30	13	4	13	62	59	43
10 Tavistock reserves	30	10	7	13	62	70	37
11 St Stephens Borough	30	12	1	17	66	76	37
12 Lanreath	30	9	5	16	49	71	32
13 Wadebridge Town reserves	30	8	3	19	39	80	27
14 Bodmin Town reserves (-3)	30	9	1	20	52	98	25
15 Morwenstow	30	5	4	21	42	83	19
16 Biscovey	30	0	1	29	20	185	1

LEAGUE CUP

ROUND 1
Callington Town Res. 2-1 Wadebridge Town Res.
Bude Town 2-3 Torpoint Athletic Res.
Camelford Res. 1-3 Launceston Res.
Kilkhampton 3-7 Plymouth Parkway Res.
Liskeard Athletic Res. 4-0 St Dominick
Roche 0-2 Millbrook
Saltash United Res. 4-2 St Stephens Borough
St Dennis 4-0 Lanreath
St Stephen 3-2 Edgcumbe
Sticker 7-0 Probus
Tavistock Res. 4-0 Nanpean Rovers
Elburton Villa Res. 8-0 St Blazey Res.
St Teath 7-0 Holsworthy Res.
Polperro 2-3 Plymstock United Res.
Biscovey 0-7 Bodmin Town Res.
Morwenstow 1-3 Bere Alston United

ROUND 2
Bere Alston United 2-2 Tavistock Res. (Bere Alston United won 4-2 on penalties)
Bodmin Town Res. 2-0 Callington Town Res.
Millbrook Res. 4-1 Launceston Res.
Plymouth Parkway Res. 1-2 Liskeard Athletic Res.
St Dennis 3-1 Saltash United Res.
St Stephen 1-4 Torpoint Athletic Res.
Sticker 6-0 Elburton Villa Res.
Plymstock United Res. 2-4 St Teath

QUARTER-FINALS
Bere Alston United 1-3 St Dennis
Bodmin Town Res. 2-5 Liskeard Athletic Res.
St Teath 1-1 Sticker (St Teath won 5-4 on penalties)
Millbrook 1-3 Torpoint Athletic Res.

PREMIER DIVISION	1	2	3	4	5	6	7	8	9	10	11	12	13	14	15	16
1 Bere Alston United		1-0	3-4	3-1	3-2	3-4	1-0	2-3	2-0	2-3	1-4	1-3	0-1	1-0	1-3	4-0
2 Biscovey	1-12		1-6	1-6	1-7	0-1	1-1	0-5	1-9	0-2	1-5	0-4	2-5	1-5	1-6	1-7
3 Bodmin Town reserves	1-2	2-0		0-5	5-2	2-1	1-2	1-7	3-1	1-5	0-3	0-4	2-4	0-2	0-3	4-0
4 Bude Town	2-3	9-0	3-1		3-2	2-2	6-1	1-1	5-1	2-0	1-5	3-1	1-3	4-2	2-2	1-0
5 Lanreath	2-0	2-1	3-4	2-2		2-4	2-2	2-0	4-1	0-3	0-2	1-0	1-0	1-1	1-5	0-0
6 Launceston reserves	1-2	11-0	1-1	2-1	2-0		2-1	6-4	1-1	2-2	2-3	0-1	2-2	1-1	0-2	2-0
7 Morwenstow	1-2	4-1	5-3	1-3	4-2	3-1		1-3	1-5	1-4	2-5	0-6	0-1	2-2	0-6	2-2
8 Plymouth Parkway reserves	4-3	10-1	12-0	2-1	6-0	4-1	2-1		1-3	4-0	2-3	3-0	3-1	2-2	0-5	6-0
9 Probus	1-4	4-1	3-0	2-1	1-3	3-3	1-0	0-2		2-2	0-1	2-3	2-3	2-8	3-1	2-0
10 Saltash United reserves	3-0	13-0	4-3	6-1	2-0	3-0	5-3	5-4	0-1		1-3	3-2	0-3	2-1	4-3	5-0
11 St Dennis	5-2	14-1	2-3	0-1	4-1	5-3	2-0	2-2	3-1	2-0		6-1	3-0	5-1	1-2	5-1
12 St Stephens Borough	2-2	7-1	7-2	4-3	3-0	1-3	3-2	2-3	0-1	0-2	1-6		2-3	1-3	1-4	3-2
13 Sticker	2-1	7-0	6-1	5-1	5-1	3-0	3-0	1-3	0-0	4-3	3-4	6-1		5-1	1-2	5-0
14 Tavistock reserves	1-2	9-1	W-L	0-4	2-2	2-5	3-0	3-1	1-7	0-0	0-4	7-1	0-3		0-4	3-2
15 Torpoint Athletic reserves	1-2	10-1	3-2	5-1	5-0	1-1	3-1	2-1	3-0	2-1	5-0	3-0	1-1	6-1		5-0
16 Wadebridge Town reserves	1-3	1-0	4-0	2-1	0-4	1-6	2-1	2-1	2-3	3-2	0-1	4-2	2-5	1-1	0-2	

LEAGUE CUP continued...

SEMI-FINALS (2 LEGS)

Torpoint Athletic Res. 1-1 St Dennis
St Dennis 4-3 Torpoint Athletic Res.
St Dennis won 5-4 on penalties
St Teath 3-0 Liskeard Athletic Res.
Liskeard Athletic Res. 1-1 St Teath
St Teath won 4-1 on penalties

FINAL (@ St Dennis, 24/4/11)
St Dennis 3-2 St Teath

DIVISION ONE	P	W	D	L	F	A	Pts
1 St Dominick	30	20	5	5	82	38	65
2 Elburton Villa reserves	30	19	4	7	63	28	64
3 Liskeard Athletic reserves	30	19	3	8	81	40	60
4 Polperro	30	16	7	7	84	49	55
5 Millbrook	30	16	6	8	71	41	54
6 St Teath	30	16	6	8	85	56	54
7 Plymstock United	30	17	1	12	66	51	52
8 Roche	30	16	4	10	48	48	52
9 Edgcumbe	30	12	6	12	66	57	42
10 St Stephen	30	11	5	14	64	66	38
11 St Blazey reserves (-3)	30	9	7	14	55	49	31
12 Camelford reserves	30	7	7	16	41	76	28
13 Kilkhampton	30	7	5	18	41	92	26
14 Holsworthy reserves	30	7	2	21	30	78	23
15 Callington Town reserves	30	6	4	20	39	58	22
16 Nanpean Rovers (-3)	30	5	2	23	36	125	14

SUPPLEMENTARY CUP

ROUND 1

Camelford Res. 0-3 Polperro
Lanreath 2-0 Holsworthy Res.
Morwenstow 5-1 Biscovey
Nanpean Rovers 4-2 Kilkhampton
Roche 1-0 St Dominick
St Stephens Borough 4-2 Probus
Bude Town 6-1 Wadebridge Town Res.
St Blazey Res. 1-2 Edgcumbe

QUARTER-FINALS

Bude Town 4-1 Morwenstow
Roche 2-3 St Stephens Borough
Edgcumbe 14-0 Nanpean Rovers
Lanreath 0-6 Polperro

SEMI-FINALS

Polperro 1-0 St Stephens Borough
Edgcumbe 1-2 Bude Town

FINAL (@ Camelford, 15/5/11)
Polperro 3-1 Bude Town

EAST CORNWALL DIVISION ONE	1	2	3	4	5	6	7	8	9	10	11	12	13	14	15	16
1 Callington Town reserves		1-2	1-1	0-3	1-2	2-0	2-3	0-2	4-5	1-3	0-2	0-1	1-1	0-2	2-1	1-2
2 Camelford reserves	0-0		1-4	2-0	3-0	1-0	1-3	2-3	0-0	3-7	4-2	2-3	1-4	0-3	0-0	1-4
3 Edgcumbe	0-2	0-0		4-2	3-1	3-1	3-0	0-2	10-0	3-0	2-2	0-1	3-1	1-2	4-4	3-4
4 Elburton Villa reserves	3-0	3-2	2-0		2-0	2-1	0-1	1-2	1-2	4-0	2-2	3-0	W-L	3-1	4-1	7-0
5 Holsworthy reserves	0-5	4-0	0-0	0-1		2-5	0-6	2-6	1-0	1-5	0-3	2-1	1-0	1-4	0-1	0-7
6 Kilkhampton	3-2	3-3	5-1	2-1	1-0		1-6	1-6	1-1	1-1	1-7	0-2	0-4	2-2	3-1	2-1
7 Liskeard Athletic reserves	2-1	5-1	1-1	3-1	0-2	11-0		5-2	4-2	3-1	2-3	2-1	1-2	1-3	3-4	2-0
8 Millbrook	2-2	4-1	3-0	1-4	1-1	5-1	1-1		9-0	0-2	1-1	1-2	3-2	1-0	0-2	2-2
9 Nanpean Rovers	1-3	0-4	1-6	0-1	3-4	3-2	0-4	1-6		1-7	6-7	0-5	3-2	1-2	1-5	0-11
10 Plymstock United reserves	3-1	3-1	3-0	1-2	6-2	1-0	3-2	1-2	W-L		2-1	1-4	3-1	2-0	4-1	1-2
11 Polperro	3-0	0-0	6-1	0-3	2-1	6-1	1-3	0-2	6-0	3-1		2-2	3-4	1-1	5-1	4-3
12 Roche	2-1	3-0	0-3	1-1	2-1	2-0	0-0	1-0	2-0	2-0	0-3		3-1	0-1	2-1	1-3
13 St Blazey reserves	1-2	1-1	0-2	1-1	3-0	2-2	0-1	L-W	4-1	2-0	1-0	2-2		2-4	7-1	1-3
14 St Dominick	2-1	7-0	2-1	0-4	2-1	6-1	0-2	2-1	9-0	2-1	2-2	7-1	4-3		2-0	1-1
15 St Stephen	3-1	9-1	8-2	1-2	1-0	5-0	0-2	2-1	0-3	0-3	1-3	4-2	2-2	4-4		0-0
16 St Teath	3-2	0-4	2-5	0-0	4-1	3-1	4-2	2-2	5-1	6-1	2-4	7-0	1-1	0-5	3-1	

GLOUCESTERSHIRE NORTHERN SENIOR LEAGUE

Sponsored by: Errea
Founded: 1922
Recent Champions:
2006: Berkeley Town
2007: Tuffley Rovers
2008: Slimbridge
2009: Longlevens
2010: Sharpness

DIVISION ONE	P	W	D	L	F	A	Pts
1 Brockworth Albion	30	21	6	3	76	40	69
2 Broadwell Amateurs	30	19	6	5	70	33	63
3 Shortwood United reserves	30	18	6	6	61	42	60
4 Longlevens	30	16	9	5	71	37	57
5 Stonehouse Town	30	12	11	7	53	36	47
6 Leonard Stanley	30	11	13	6	44	36	46
7 Star	30	13	6	11	53	46	45
8 Ramblers	30	12	7	11	61	50	43
9 Smiths Athletic	30	13	4	13	51	55	43
10 Gala Wilton	30	10	6	14	54	65	36
11 Sharpness	30	8	9	13	54	62	33
12 Lydbrook Athletic	30	8	6	16	34	57	30
13 Dursley Town	30	7	7	16	34	53	28
14 Stroud	30	7	5	18	49	67	26
15 Tetbury Town	30	6	4	20	29	73	22
16 Barnwood United	30	4	5	21	37	83	17

DIVISION TWO	P	W	D	L	F	A	Pts
1 Frampton United	26	19	5	2	91	23	62
2 Harrow Hill	26	20	2	4	68	38	62
3 Winchcombe Town	26	17	4	5	60	29	55
4 Moreton Rangers	26	15	3	8	91	39	48
5 Soudley	26	15	3	8	56	42	48
6 Cam Bulldogs	26	15	2	9	69	45	47
7 Cheltenham Civil Service	26	10	7	9	63	45	37
8 Bredon	26	10	5	11	48	43	35
9 FC Barometrics	26	10	3	13	56	53	33
10 Chalford	26	10	2	14	40	65	32
11 Bourton Rovers	26	7	2	17	48	92	23
12 Viney St Swithins	26	4	6	16	33	61	18
13 Wotton Rovers (-3)	26	5	4	17	35	69	16
14 Longford	26	0	2	24	19	134	2

Hatherley Rangers - record expunged

REG DAVID MEMORIAL CUP

ROUND 1
Hatherley Rangers 1-4 FC Barometrics
Leonard Stanley 1-3 Shortwood United reserves
Moreton Rangers 1-0 Stonehouse Town (@ Stonehouse Town)
Frampton United 4-1 Chalford
Bredon 3-4 Winchcombe Town
Sharpness 0-2 Dursley Town
Broadwell Amateurs 2-0 Ramblers
Lydbrook Athletic 0-2 Harrow Hill
Star 0-3 Longlevens
Smiths Athletic 0-0 Viney St Swithins (Smiths Athletic won on penalties)
Gala Wilton w/o-scr Aylburton Rovers
Brockworth Albion 2-0 Cheltenham Civil Service
Tetbury Town 1-1 Wotton Rovers (Tetbury Town won on penalties)
Longford 1-2 Soudley
Stroud 0-2 Barnwood United
Bourton Rovers 3-3 Cam Bulldogs (@ Longlevens. Bourton Rovers won 5-4 on penalties)

ROUND 2
Shortwood United reserves 0-2 Tetbury Town
Dursley Town 1-1 Smiths Athletic (Smiths Athletic won on penalties)
FC Barometrics 2-0 Winchcombe Town
Harrow Hill 1-4 Moreton Rangers
Frampton United 4-1 Bourton Rovers
Gala Wilton 1-6 Brockworth Albion (tie awarded to Gala Wilton)
Longlevens 1-0 Soudley
Broadwell Amateurs 2-3 Barnwood United

QUARTER FINALS
Frampton United 4-3 Barnwood United
Tetbury Town 0-2 Moreton Rangers
Smiths Athletic 1-2 FC Barometrics
Gala Wilton 1-4 Longlevens

SEMI-FINALS
FC Barometrics 3-1 Frampton United
Longlevens 2-1 Moreton Rangers

FINAL (@ Tuffley Rovers, 6/10/10)
FC Barometrics 2-3 Longlevens

DIVISION ONE	1	2	3	4	5	6	7	8	9	10	11	12	13	14	15	16
1 Barnwood United		1-4	2-4	2-2	1-2	1-2	1-3	1-2	3-3	0-0	2-2	1-4	1-0	1-4	5-2	3-2
2 Broadwell Amateurs	6-0		1-0	2-0	4-0	4-1	3-2	2-0	3-0	1-3	2-1	2-0	7-3	0-0	1-0	2-1
3 Brockworth Albion	6-2	0-0		1-0	5-2	3-1	2-2	1-0	3-2	6-3	3-4	3-1	4-2	1-0	1-0	5-2
4 Dursley Town	2-1	2-1	0-0		2-2	0-2	0-3	2-1	3-2	1-2	0-2	2-3	1-0	0-1	2-4	0-0
5 Gala Wilton	1-3	4-2	1-5	2-1		2-4	1-1	1-1	0-3	2-5	3-4	3-0	2-0	1-1	2-0	4-0
6 Leonard Stanley	0-0	2-2	2-4	0-3	4-2		0-0	4-0	1-1	1-1	1-2	1-0	1-0	1-1	2-0	3-1
7 Longlevens	3-0	2-2	1-2	1-1	2-1	2-1		3-0	4-1	3-0	3-2	2-4	1-0	2-4	3-1	5-0
8 Lydbrook Athletic	2-1	0-2	2-2	2-2	1-0	1-1	0-2		4-2	2-1	0-1	3-2	0-2	0-3	0-1	0-2
9 Stroud	5-0	3-2	0-0	1-1	3-5	1-1	1-1	2-1		0-1	5-0	1-2	2-3	2-0	2-1	3-0
10 Ramblers	3-2	2-2	3-4	1-2	2-4	2-2	1-1	1-2	3-3		0-3	3-4	1-2	2-0	1-3	5-1
11 Sharpness	2-0	1-2	3-0	2-0	1-0	0-0	0-5	2-2	4-2	2-2		1-0	2-0	4-1	5-1	3-1
12 Shortwood United reserves	4-3	1-2	0-2	2-1	2-2	1-1	1-3	2-0	1-0	3-0	2-4		0-3	0-3	3-2	3-1
13 Smiths Athletic	2-1	0-0	1-2	1-0	2-1	1-1	2-2	5-0	0-3	2-2	3-1	3-2		2-1	2-2	4-0
14 Star	3-1	2-1	2-2	6-3	4-0	1-1	2-1	1-1	1-2	0-0	2-2	1-1	3-2		0-0	4-0
15 Stonehouse Town	5-2	1-3	0-3	4-1	0-2	0-2	3-3	4-6	2-4	1-3	0-1	2-2	3-3	2-1		1-2
16 Tetbury Town	3-0	1-5	1-2	2-0	2-2	0-1	1-5	2-1	0-2	3-1	0-0	0-1	0-3	1-1	0-4	

HEREFORDSHIRE LEAGUE

Sponsored by: Hereford Times
Founded: N/K
Recent Champions:
2006: Ewyas Harold
2007: Wellington Rangers
2008: Woofferton
2009: Westfields Reserves
2010: Leominster Town

PREMIER DIVISION	P	W	D	L	F	A	Pts
1 Westfields reserves	24	17	0	7	77	28	51
2 Lads Club	24	15	4	5	46	26	49
3 Hinton	24	14	1	9	52	34	43
4 Ledbury Town	24	13	3	8	61	51	42
5 Kington Town	24	13	2	9	70	53	41
6 Ewyas Harold	24	11	7	6	37	27	40
7 Wellington reserves	24	12	1	11	57	58	37
8 Bartestree	24	10	4	10	53	44	34
9 Hay St Mary's reserves (-3)	24	9	2	13	53	52	26
10 Bromyard Town res (-3)	24	8	2	14	49	60	23
11 Holme Lacy	24	4	6	14	33	67	18
12 Pegasus Juniors res (-6)	24	6	4	14	39	76	16
13 Fownhope	24	3	6	15	21	72	15

DIVISION ONE	P	W	D	L	F	A	Pts
1 Mercia Athletic	20	18	0	2	100	20	54
2 Ewyas Harold reserves	20	17	1	2	73	30	52
3 Wellington Colts	20	11	3	6	62	32	36
4 Shobdon	20	9	2	9	45	49	29
5 Weobley	20	8	3	9	36	42	27
6 Kingstone Rovers	20	8	3	9	46	69	27
7 Bucknell United	20	7	4	9	35	56	25
8 Hinton reserves	20	6	2	12	39	51	20
9 Woofferton	20	6	1	13	40	46	19
10 Stoke Prior (-9)	20	7	6	7	36	42	18
11 Orcop Juniors	20	0	1	19	21	96	1

DIVISION TWO	P	W	D	L	F	A	Pts
1 Ledbury Town "A"	20	14	3	3	88	29	45
2 Orleton Colts	20	13	3	4	70	36	42
3 Lads Club Colts	20	12	5	3	62	34	41
4 Dore Valley	20	11	3	6	53	39	36
5 Bartestree reserves	20	10	4	6	51	38	34
6 Holmer	20	9	5	6	63	47	32
7 Kington Town reserves	20	7	3	10	55	56	24
8 Holme Lacy reserves	20	7	3	10	47	55	24
9 Burghill	20	4	3	13	29	56	15
10 Fownhope reserves	20	3	2	15	21	92	11
11 Toros	20	2	2	16	24	81	8
Ledbury Colts - record expunged							

SENIOR CUP (STRONGBOW)

ROUND 1
Hinton 3-1 Ewyas Harold
Holme Lacy 5-1 Kington Town
Lads Club 1-0 Fownhope
Leominster Town reserves scr-w/o Hay St Mary's
Westfields reseres 3-0 Ledbury Town
Bromyard Town reserves 5-3 Pegasus reserves

QUARTER FINALS
Bromyard Town reserves 3-0 Hay St Mary's
Lads Club 1-4 Westfields reserves
Holme Lacy 1-6 Hinton
Wellington reserves 2-1 Batestree

SEMI-FINALS
Bromyard Town reserves 0-2 Wellington reserves
Hinton 5-2 Westfields reserves

FINAL (@ Holmer Sports, 2/5/11)
Hinton 2-0 Wellington reserves

JOURNAL TROPHY

ROUND 1
Leominster Town reserves scr-w/o Kington town
Ewyas Harold 3-2 Westfields reserves
Lads Club 3-4 Ledbury Town
Bartrestree 1-3 Wellington reserves
Holme Lacy 1-4 Bromyard Town reserves
Hinton 3-2 Hay St Mary's

QUARTER FINALS
Kington Town 4-3 Ewyas Harold
Ledbury Town 5-2 Wellington reserves
Bromyard Town reserves 4-2 Hinton
Fownhope 1-4 Pegasus reserves

SEMI-FINALS
Kington Town 1-4 Ledbury Town
Bromyard Town reserves 7-8 Pegasus reserves

FINAL (@ Westfields, 27/4/11)
Ledbury Town 1-4 Pegasus reserves

DIVISION TWO	P	W	D	L	F	A	Pts
1 Sinkum	20	18	1	1	116	18	55
2 Woofferton Colts (-3)	20	16	1	3	87	37	46
3 Pencombe	20	13	0	7	68	40	39
4 Leominster Town Colts	20	10	2	8	75	50	32
5 Civil Service	20	10	2	8	57	57	32
6 Wolseley (-1)	20	10	1	9	52	49	30
7 Kingstone Harriers	20	8	2	10	46	49	26
8 Weston	20	7	2	11	42	38	23
9 Tenbury Town	20	6	3	11	37	69	21
10 Orleton Colts reserves	20	2	4	14	34	83	10
11 Relentless (-3)	20	0	2	18	19	143	-1
Bartestree "A" - record expunged							

PREMIER DIVISION	1	2	3	4	5	6	7	8	9	10	11	12	13
1 Bartestree		2-1	0-2	0-0	0-0	0-4	5-1	4-2	0-2	2-2	2-1	4-3	1-0
2 Bromyard Town reserves	3-1		2-0	2-2	0-3	2-5	1-2	3-5	2-3	3-5	3-7	1-3	3-1
3 Ewyas Harold	1-0	0-0		3-1	1-1	1-2	1-1	1-1	0-0	6-1	0-0	3-1	3-0
4 Fownhope	0-6	1-2	0-0		0-6	1-4	1-1	1-5	0-3	0-4	4-2	0-3	0-8
5 Hay St Mary's reserves	2-5	3-5	1-2	0-1		1-2	4-3	3-2	3-4	3-4	5-1	1-4	1-2
6 Hereford Lads Club	3-2	2-0	0-1	5-0	1-2		2-1	3-4	1-2	0-1	2-1	3-1	1-2
7 Hinton	3-2	1-5	1-4	1-1	2-1	0-3		2-3	0-0	0-0	2-2	1-4	0-2
8 Holme Lacy	2-3	2-1	2-1	7-1	5-3	4-2	6-0		0-2	1-0	6-1	2-3	4-1
9 Kington Town	0-0	2-0	4-0	2-0	0-1	2-1	4-2	2-0		2-3	3-1	5-2	2-4
10 Ledbury Town	2-0	1-4	4-3	2-2	2-4	4-1	7-0	3-1	1-0		2-3	6-2	1-6
11 Pegasus Juniors reserves	2-13	3-2	0-1	1-4	0-3	0-2	2-6	3-3	0-0	2-1		3-0	1-6
12 Wellington reserves	1-0	5-2	4-1	2-1	4-2	2-2	2-1	5-3	0-2	3-5	1-2		2-6
13 Westfields reserves	7-1	1-2	1-2	3-0	2-0	0-1	5-2	5-0	5-0	3-0	5-1	2-0	

HUMBER PREMIER LEAGUE

Sponsored by: No sponsor
Founded: 2000
Recent Champions:
2006: Reckitts
2007: Sculcoates Amateurs
2008: Sculcoates Amateurs
2009: Chalk Lane
2010: Reckitts

PREMIER DIVISION	P	W	D	L	F	A	Pts
1 Sculcoates Amateurs	30	23	3	4	97	33	72
2 Reckitts	30	20	4	6	81	32	64
3 Chalk Lane	30	14	7	9	58	35	49
4 North Ferriby United reserves	30	15	4	11	67	53	49
5 Beverley Town	30	13	7	10	56	48	46
6 Crown	30	12	9	9	45	45	45
7 Pocklington Town	30	10	11	9	47	53	41
8 Hessle Rangers	30	12	5	13	51	64	41
9 Hall Road Rangers reserves	30	12	4	14	56	55	40
10 Bridlington Sports Club	30	13	1	16	64	71	40
11 Hornsea Town	30	11	5	14	57	66	38
12 St Andrews	30	11	1	18	44	70	34
13 Hedon Rangers	30	9	5	16	45	75	32
14 Westella & Willerby reserves	30	9	4	17	49	77	31
15 Malet Lambert YC	30	7	9	14	56	74	30
16 Hessle Sporting Club	30	7	5	18	40	62	26

DIVISION ONE	P	W	D	L	F	A	Pts
1 Hodgsons	22	19	2	1	94	33	59
2 North Cave	22	18	2	2	79	22	56
3 Brandesburton	22	14	1	7	68	44	43
4 North Ferriby Athletic	22	10	4	8	70	65	34
5 Bransholme Athletic	22	9	5	8	61	64	32
6 Scarborough Athletic res	22	9	4	9	66	45	31
7 Howden	22	7	5	10	69	75	26
8 Kingburn Athletic	22	7	5	10	33	39	26
9 Withernsea	22	8	1	13	50	79	25
10 East Riding Rangers	22	5	4	13	37	50	19
11 Long Riston	22	5	2	15	37	81	17
12 Inter Charter	22	3	1	18	34	101	10

GRAYS CUP

ROUND 1

Bridlington Sports Club 3-3 Scarborough Athletic res.
(Scarborough Athletic reserves won 4-3 on penalties)
Withernsea 3-2 St Andrew
Westella & Willerby reserves 0-3 North Cave
Pocklington Town 0-1 Beverley Town
North Ferriby United reserves 2-0 Hessle Rangers
Malet Lambert YC 5-1 Long RIston
Crown 3-0 Bransholme Athletic
Sculcoates Amateurs 5-1 North Ferriby Athletic
Reckitts 3-3 Chalk Lane
(Reckitts won 4-3 on penalties)

ROUND 2

Kingburn 4-3 Howden
Hessle Sporting Club 3-3 Malet Lambert YC
Crown 2-0 Withernsea
Hodgsons 2-5 North Cave
East Riding Rangers 1-4 Bransholme
Sculcoates Amateurs 4-3 Hornsea Town
Reckitts 2-1 North Ferriby United reserves
Hall Road Rangers res. 4-0 Scarborough Athletic res.

QUARTER FINALS

North Cave 2-0 Beverley Town
Crown 2-3 Brandesburton
Reckitts 1-3 Sculcoates Amateurs
Hessle Sporting Club 2-4 Hall Road Rangers reserves

SEMI-FINALS

North Cave 2-7 Brandesburton
Sculcoates Amateurs 2-3 Hall Road Rangers reserves

FINAL (@ North Ferriby United, 6/5/11)

Brandesburton 2-3 Hall Road Rangers reserves

PREMIER DIVISION	1	2	3	4	5	6	7	8	9	10	11	12	13	14	15	16
1 Beverley Town		4-1	3-2	0-0	1-1	3-0	2-0	2-0	4-2	4-4	3-2	1-1	0-4	0-2	2-1	1-1
2 Bridlington Sports Club	0-1		2-3	4-0	1-4	2-1	2-3	3-2	3-2	8-2	4-1	3-3	3-7	1-3	3-0	5-0
3 Chalk Lane	1-1	2-1		4-0	4-0	0-1	5-1	1-0	0-2	4-2	1-2	4-1	1-1	1-4	3-1	5-1
4 Crown	1-2	2-0	1-1		2-0	3-1	2-0	1-1	1-3	2-2	2-2	0-1	1-8	1-4	2-3	5-1
5 Hall Road Rangers reserves	3-2	2-1	1-1	1-1		2-1	1-2	0-5	3-4	2-5	3-1	3-0	0-1	1-2	4-0	1-2
6 Hedon Rangers	4-2	2-3	0-4	1-4	2-1		1-4	2-1	0-5	0-0	3-4	0-6	3-2	2-6	1-2	2-2
7 Hessle Rangers	0-5	4-0	0-0	0-2	2-4	2-2		1-0	4-3	2-1	3-0	2-2	0-2	0-7	5-1	4-2
8 Hessle Sporting Club	1-0	1-2	1-3	1-2	1-6	1-1	0-1		0-0	3-3	3-1	2-4	0-1	0-0	1-4	1-5
9 Hornsea Town	4-2	4-5	1-0	1-1	1-0	1-3	1-0	1-3		1-3	0-5	1-2	2-3	1-4	4-3	1-5
10 Malet Lambert Y C	3-0	4-2	0-3	0-1	1-3	1-2	1-1	1-2	2-3		1-5	2-2	4-3	2-1	0-2	2-3
11 North Ferriby United reserves	1-0	1-2	2-1	0-2	4-2	5-2	7-3	2-0	1-1	2-3		4-1	2-1	0-1	1-1	3-2
12 Pocklington Town	1-1	0-1	1-1	1-1	2-1	0-3	2-2	1-3	2-2	2-2	0-0		1-3	2-3	2-1	1-0
13 Reckitts	2-0	3-1	0-0	0-0	2-2	2-3	4-2	4-1	2-1	5-0	2-0	1-2		4-0	4-0	4-1
14 Sculcoates Amateurs	3-2	2-0	1-2	3-0	2-0	4-0	3-1	7-1	3-3	1-1	3-2	4-0	0-3		6-0	8-3
15 St Andrews	3-5	3-0	2-1	0-1	1-3	1-0	1-2	2-1	2-0	3-2	3-5	1-2	0-3	0-3		0-2
16 Westella & Willerby reserves	0-3	5-1	2-0	0-4	1-2	2-2	1-0	1-4	0-2	2-2	0-2	1-2	2-0	0-7	2-3	

LINCOLNSHIRE LEAGUE

Sponsored by: Sills & Betteridge
Founded: 1948
Recent Champions:
2006: Hykeham Town
2007: Skegness Town
2008: Skegness Town
2009: CGB Humbertherm
2010: Hykeham Town

PREMIER DIVISION	P	W	D	L	F	A	Pts
1 Boston United reserves	26	20	2	4	85	19	62
2 Lincoln United reserves	26	15	4	7	75	40	49
3 Cleethorpes Town	26	14	7	5	70	43	49
4 Swineshead Institute	26	14	4	8	75	46	46
5 Skegness Town	26	13	6	7	56	46	45
6 Horncastle Town	26	13	5	8	74	45	44
7 Hykeham Town	26	13	5	8	58	36	44
8 Heckington United	26	13	2	11	52	54	41
9 CGB Humbertherm	26	12	4	10	64	67	40
10 Skellingthorpe PFC	26	9	4	13	49	68	31
11 Louth Town reserves	26	9	3	14	51	62	30
12 Ruston Sports	26	5	3	18	27	86	18
13 Grimsby Borough reserves	26	2	5	19	29	86	11
14 Sleaford Town reserves	26	2	2	22	26	93	8

CHALLENGE CUP

ROUND 1
Sleaford Town reserves scr-w/o Skegness Town
Lincoln United reserves 3-1 Heckington United
Swineshead Institute 5-4 Louth Town reserves
Skellingthorpe PFC 0-5 Hykeham Town
Grimsby Borough reserves 1-6 CGB Humbertherm
Cleethorpes 2-3 Ruston Sports

QUARTER FINALS
Lincoln United reserves 6-1 swineshead Institute
Ruston Sports 0-2 Horncastle Town
Boston United reserves 4-3 Skegness Town
CGB Humbertherm 2-5 Hykeham Town

SEMI-FINALS
Luncoln United reserves 2-2 Hykeham Town (Lincoln United reserves won 6-5 on penalties)
Boston United reserves 0-1 Horncastle Town

FINAL (@ Lincoln City, 30/4/11)
Horncastle Town 1-2 Lincoln United reserves

SUPPLEMENTARY CUP

ROUND 1
Heckington United 5-2 Grimsby Borough reserves
CGB Humbertherm 0-2 Ruston Sports

QUARTER FINALS
Ruston Sports 2-5 Heckington United
Cleethorpes Town 4-0 Skegness Town
Sleaford Town reserves 1-3 Swineshead Intitute
Louth Town reserves 6-1 Skellingthorpe PFC

SEMI-FINALS
Cleethorpes Town 3-1 Swineshead Institute
Louth Town 1-3 Heckington United

FINAL (@ Lincoln City, 30/4/11)
Cleethopes Town 5-1 Heckington United

PREMIER DIVISION	1	2	3	4	5	6	7	8	9	10	11	12	13	14
1 Boston United reserves		6-2	1-1	7-0	5-0	5-1	1-0	1-0	3-0	5-0	7-0	1-2	5-0	2-0
2 C G B Humbertherm	1-6		1-1	10-0	2-2	3-9	3-1	1-4	6-1	4-3	0-1	3-0	3-0	4-2
3 Cleethorpes Town	1-1	2-3		2-0	6-4	4-3	5-2	3-1	2-0	5-0	0-2	4-0	7-1	3-3
4 Grimsby Borough reserves	1-2	3-3	0-1		L-W	2-4	0-4	0-2	3-1	L-W	1-4	2-2	3-1	3-11
5 Heckington United	0-5	6-0	1-2	W-L		0-2	3-0	6-3	3-2	2-1	3-3	4-1	2-0	0-3
6 Horncastle Town	1-0	6-1	3-3	1-1	3-1		0-2	1-2	8-0	8-1	1-0	1-1	0-0	1-4
7 Hykeham Town	0-2	4-0	3-3	4-0	2-0	1-0		2-2	2-2	5-0	1-1	6-2	6-1	4-0
8 Lincoln United reserves	1-2	0-1	2-2	9-0	0-1	4-4	0-1		2-1	3-2	3-0	4-1	7-4	1-1
9 Louth Town reserves	1-2	0-1	2-1	4-2	5-4	3-0	5-1	1-4		1-1	2-2	5-1	4-0	2-0
10 Ruston Sports	0-4	2-7	0-5	W-L	0-2	0-3	0-4	1-7	4-3		0-0	0-6	4-1	3-3
11 Skegness Town	4-2	3-2	4-0	3-3	2-3	2-4	2-1	1-3	0-2	1-0		3-2	9-1	3-1
12 Skellingthorpe P F C	0-6	1-1	1-0	2-2	2-1	0-3	2-0	0-6	7-3	5-3	2-3		7-0	0-4
13 Sleaford Town reserves	0-2	0-2	2-3	4-2	2-4	0-4	L-W	2-3	W-L	0-2	2-2	1-2		1-6
14 Swineshead Institute	3-2	4-0	3-4	5-1	3-0	5-3	2-2	1-2	3-1	2-0	0-1	2-0	4-3	

NORTH DEVON LEAGUE

Sponsored by: North Devon Gazette
Founded: 1904
Recent Champions:
2006: Morwenstow
2007: Boca Seniors
2008: Boca Seniors
2009: Boca Seniors
2010: Shamwickshire Rovers

PREMIER DIVISION	P	W	D	L	F	A	Pts
1 Boca Seniors	28	27	0	1	125	33	81
2 Braunton	28	19	1	8	76	47	58
3 Appledore reserves	28	16	8	4	75	48	56
4 Shamwickshire Rovers	28	16	4	8	69	50	52
5 North Molton Sports Cl (-3)	28	14	2	12	69	53	41
6 Torridgeside	28	11	8	9	62	54	41
7 Georgeham & Croyde	28	11	6	11	63	56	39
8 Torrington	28	9	5	14	66	80	32
9 Combe Martin	28	8	7	13	43	72	31
10 Ilfracombe Town reserves	28	9	3	16	44	64	30
11 Dolton	28	7	7	14	40	67	28
12 Barnstaple AAC	28	7	6	15	51	78	27
13 Bradworthy United	28	7	5	16	42	70	26
14 Putford	28	7	4	17	44	61	25
15 Bideford reserves (-3)	28	8	2	18	36	72	23

SENIOR DIVISION	P	W	D	L	F	A	Pts
1 Pilton Academicals	30	25	3	2	127	25	78
2 Bratton Fleming	30	24	2	4	123	37	74
3 Shebbear United	30	23	2	5	117	50	71
4 Northam Lions	30	20	2	8	114	54	62
5 Woolsery	30	18	4	8	90	51	58
6 Chittlehampton	30	17	5	8	76	57	56
7 Shamwickshire Rovers res	30	15	5	10	67	52	50
8 Braunton reserves	30	12	4	14	85	63	40
9 Bude Town reserves (-3)	30	11	5	14	64	88	35
10 Barnstaple AAC reserves	30	10	4	16	82	90	34
11 South Molton	30	9	3	18	57	94	30
12 North Molton Spts Cl res (-3)	30	6	7	17	62	105	22
13 Torrington reserves	30	6	4	20	53	103	22
14 Park United (-3)	30	7	1	22	68	126	19
15 Combe Martin reserves (-6)	30	6	4	20	42	101	16
16 Hartland	30	3	1	26	29	160	10

COMBE MARTIN CUP - FINAL (@ Combe Martin, 23/4/11)
Shebbear United 0-4 Braunton Fleming

ARLINGTON CUP - FINAL (@ Ilfracombe Town, 30/4/11)
Wrey Arms 1-3 Woolacombe & Mortehoe

NORTH DEVON JOURNAL CUP - FINAL @ Torrington, 16/4/11)
Fremington 1-3 Torridgeside reserves

BRAYFORD CUP

ROUND 1
Shamwickshire Rovers 3-2 Torrington
Ilfracombe Town res. 0-6 North Molton Sports Club
Combe Martin 4-3 Bideford reserves
Boca Seniors 9-1 Georgeham & Croyde
Barnstaple AAC 2-5 Dolton
Appledore reserves 1-0 Torridgeside
Putford 0-1 Braunton

QUARTER FINALS
Appledore reserves 0-1 Braunton
Boca Seniors 3-0 Shamwickshire Rovers
Bradworthy United 4-1 Combe Martin
North Molton Sports Club 6-2 Dolton

SEMI-FINALS
Boca Seniors 3-3 Braunton
(Boca Seniors won 4-3 on penalties)
Bradworthy United 2-1 North Molton Sports Club

FINAL (@ Appledore, 7/5/11)
Bradworthy United 1-2 Boca Seniors

DIVISION ONE	P	W	D	L	F	A	Pts
1 Wrey Arms	30	25	2	3	99	37	77
2 Lynton & Lynmouth	30	20	6	4	86	41	66
3 Ilfracombe Town "A"	30	19	5	6	105	58	62
4 Merton	30	14	8	8	82	56	50
5 Woolacombe & Mortehoe	30	15	4	11	103	75	49
6 Sporting Barum	30	15	4	11	75	73	49
7 Equalizers	30	14	5	11	97	85	47
8 Clovelly (-3)	30	14	2	14	68	90	41
9 Northam Lions reserves	30	12	3	15	73	79	39
10 Woolsery Reserves	30	9	7	14	60	72	34
11 High Bickington	30	10	2	18	72	95	32
12 AFC Anchor	30	8	5	17	64	83	29
13 Braunton "A"	30	9	2	19	57	86	29
14 Landkey Town (-3)	30	9	4	17	68	87	28
15 Putford reserves	30	8	2	20	46	93	26
16 Buckland Brewer	30	6	5	19	36	81	23

DIVISION TWO	P	W	D	L	F	A	Pts
1 Northside Atlantic	28	25	1	2	113	23	76
2 Fremington	28	22	0	6	137	35	66
3 Barnstaple	28	20	3	5	135	45	63
4 Anchor Chiefs	28	16	3	9	65	52	51
5 Bradworthy reserves	28	15	3	10	74	72	48
6 Torridgeside reserves	28	14	3	11	82	64	45
7 Pilton Academicals reserves	28	12	6	10	70	62	42
8 Braunton "B"	28	11	5	12	81	73	38
9 Bratton Fleming reserves	28	10	6	12	75	93	36
10 Northam Lions "A"	28	9	7	12	51	68	34
11 South Molton reserves (-3)	28	9	4	15	61	100	28
12 Hartland reserves	28	7	6	15	50	87	27
13 AFC Anchor reserves (-3)	28	4	5	19	48	108	14
14 Chittlehampton reserves (-3)	28	4	4	20	55	106	13
15 North Molton Sports Cl "A"	28	3	2	23	34	143	11

PREMIER DIVISION	1	2	3	4	5	6	7	8	9	10	11	12	13	14	15
1 Appledore reserves		8-1	3-2	1-3	2-1	4-1	4-1	2-0	3-1	2-1	3-3	3-2	0-0	2-2	4-2
2 Barnstaple A A C	1-3		1-2	4-1	1-1	1-3	2-2	0-6	2-5	3-1	3-2	1-3	2-1	0-1	2-2
3 Bideford reserves	1-6	3-0		0-3	2-1	0-1	2-2	2-4	3-2	0-4	2-3	0-1	2-1	0-3	1-4
4 Boca Seniors	6-0	5-2	8-1		8-0	5-2	10-0	3-0	5-3	3-1	6-2	4-1	5-1	3-1	3-2
5 Bradworthy United	2-2	1-3	5-1	0-3		1-2	0-2	5-2	2-0	1-0	3-1	1-3	1-1	2-2	2-0
6 Braunton	2-1	6-1	3-0	4-6	4-0		7-3	2-1	0-3	2-2	4-1	3-0	5-2	1-0	4-2
7 Combe Martin	2-2	3-2	W-L	0-1	4-1	0-1		1-1	1-1	4-0	0-2	1-0	1-2	2-6	2-2
8 Dolton	1-1	2-1	4-1	0-2	3-2	0-3	2-2		1-1	2-1	0-2	1-0	2-2	1-1	1-2
9 Georgeham & Croyde	1-2	1-1	4-2	1-5	2-2	2-1	3-0	6-1		1-0	4-1	0-0	1-3	5-4	5-1
10 Ilfracombe Town reserves	1-2	2-10	1-2	1-2	2-1	3-0	3-2	1-0	2-3		0-8	2-0	5-0	1-2	2-2
11 North Molton Sports Club	2-4	1-1	4-2	1-2	5-2	L-W	3-0	7-0	3-2	4-1		3-0	1-4	2-3	2-1
12 Putford	1-5	3-4	0-2	2-3	1-2	4-2	5-1	1-1	2-1	3-3	0-2		0-2	2-2	2-3
13 Shamwickshire Rovers	4-2	4-0	0-1	0-7	7-2	2-0	6-0	6-1	4-1	0-1	W-L	4-3		4-3	3-0
14 Torridgeside	1-1	1-1	2-2	0-5	4-1	2-5	0-2	3-1	2-1	5-1	6-1	1-2	1-1		0-3
15 Torrington	3-3	5-1	2-0	3-8	3-0	1-8	4-5	7-2	3-3	0-2	0-3	4-3	3-5	2-4	

NOTTS SENIOR LEAGUE

Sponsored by: Precision Training
Founded: 2004
Recent Champions:
2006: Wollaton
2007: Cotgrave
2008: Caribbean Cavaliers
2009: Bilborough Pelican
2010: Clifton

SENIOR DIVISION	P	W	D	L	F	A	Pts
1 Boots Athletic	30	20	6	4	80	32	66
2 Basford United	30	17	7	6	63	33	58
3 Clifton	30	17	6	7	76	44	57
4 Wollaton	30	17	6	7	72	41	57
5 Gedling Southbank	30	16	5	9	83	63	53
6 Attenborough	30	15	7	8	68	54	52
7 Bilborough Pelican	30	13	7	10	67	54	46
8 Hucknall Rolls Leisure	30	13	6	11	71	64	45
9 Kimberley Miners Welfare	30	12	4	14	48	42	40
10 Awsworth Villa	30	11	6	13	59	67	39
11 FC Cavaliers	30	9	9	12	45	51	36
12 Cotgrave Welfare	30	11	3	16	35	55	36
13 Bulwell	30	9	6	15	47	59	33
14 Keyworth United	30	8	8	14	45	58	32
15 Notts Police	30	6	1	23	37	96	19
16 Linby Colliery Welfare	30	2	1	27	26	109	7

Forest Town - record expunged

DIVISION ONE	P	W	D	L	F	A	Pts
1 Ruddington Village	30	25	1	4	93	40	76
2 Clifton reserves	30	22	7	1	96	46	73
3 Boots Athletic reserves	30	18	5	7	78	56	59
4 Vernon Villa	30	17	4	9	54	37	55
5 Wollaton reserves	30	16	4	10	55	40	52
6 Keyworth United reserves	30	11	8	11	61	58	41
7 Radcliffe Olympic reserves	30	11	5	14	55	72	38
8 Cotgrave Welfare reserves	30	9	9	12	54	59	36
9 Magdala Amateurs	30	10	6	14	57	64	36
10 Hucknall Rolls Leisure res	30	10	6	14	49	65	33
11 Basford United reserves	30	9	7	14	44	60	34
12 Southwell City reserves	30	8	8	14	54	61	32
13 Arnold Town reserves	30	8	7	15	56	72	31
14 Sandhurst	30	9	2	19	45	76	29
15 Netherfield Albion	30	6	7	17	58	64	25
16 Gedling Southbank reserves	30	8	0	22	40	79	24

Bilborough Pelican reserves - record expunged
Matrixgrade - record expunged

SENIOR SECTION LEAGUE CUP

ROUND 1
Basford United 7-1 Nottinghamshire
Clifton 1-6 Southwell St Mary's
Cotgrave Welfare 1-2 FC Cavaliers
Forest Town 1-0 Attenborough
Gedling Southbank 3-3 Bilborough Pelican (Gedling Southbank won 5-4 on penalties)
Hucknall Rolls Leisure 7-0 Notts Police
Keyworth United 1-0 Magdala Amateurs
Netherfield Albion 5-6 Chilwell Town
Ruddington Village 5-1 Linby CW
Vernon Villa 4-2 Beeston
Wollaton 6-1 Kimberley MW

ROUND 2
Sandhurst 2-1 Ruddington Village
Bulwell 1-2 Vernon Villa
Chilwell Town 0-2 FC Cavaliers
Gedling Southbank 1-0 Basford United
Hucknall Rolls Leisure 3-0 Keyworth United
Underwood Villa 2-0 Awsworth Villa
Wollaton 3-0 Forest Town
Boots Athletic 4-0 Southwell St Mary's

QUARTER FINALS
Boots Athletic 2-0 Underwood Villa
Gedling Southbank 2-3 Wollaton
Hucknall Rolls Leisure 5-1 Sandhurst
Vernon Villa 0-3 FC Cavaliers

SEMI-FINALS
Wollaton 2-3 Boots Athletic
Hucknall Rolls Leisure 3-2 FC Cavaliers

FINAL (@ Arnold Town, 17/5/11)
Boots Athletic 3-1 Hucknall Rolls Leisure

DIVISION TWO	P	W	D	L	F	A	Pts
1 Southwell St Marys	28	21	4	3	91	38	67
2 Chilwell Town	28	20	3	5	113	54	63
3 Nottinghamshire	28	16	7	5	88	45	55
4 Carlton Town Academy	28	15	3	10	79	58	48
5 Underwood Villa	28	12	7	9	85	53	43
6 Hucknall Town reserves	28	12	6	10	58	49	42
7 Awsworth Villa reserves	28	11	6	11	62	69	39
8 Calverton MW Academy	28	10	8	10	64	60	38
9 Kimberley MW reserves	28	10	4	14	57	62	34
10 FC Cavaliers reserves	28	9	6	13	47	80	33
11 Linby CW reserves	28	9	5	14	48	79	32
12 Magdala Amateurs reserves	28	6	10	12	49	59	28
13 Bulwell reserves	28	8	4	16	70	93	28
14 Beeston (-3)	28	7	6	15	56	67	24
15 Sandhurst reserves	28	3	3	22	34	135	12

Forest Town reserves - record expunged
Newark Flowserve -record expunged

SENIOR DIVISION	1	2	3	4	5	6	7	8	9	10	11	12	13	14	15	16
1 Attenborough		3-0	0-1	0-6	2-3	2-0	3-5	3-0	2-2	1-0	3-3	1-1	2-2	6-0	5-1	0-0
2 Awsworth Villa	4-2		0-1	4-1	1-3	0-2	1-4	0-1	0-2	4-1	0-4	2-8	1-3	4-2	4-3	4-4
3 Basford United	6-1	3-3		0-0	1-0	1-1	0-3	1-0	1-0	2-2	3-2	0-1	1-0	6-0	5-0	3-1
4 Bilborough Pelican	1-2	1-1	3-1		1-1	0-3	4-2	5-0	2-2	4-2	1-3	8-0	1-1	5-3	4-3	2-4
5 Boots Athletic	3-1	4-1	1-1	5-0		4-0	1-1	0-2	3-1	1-0	2-4	2-1	2-2	3-0	4-0	2-1
6 Bulwell	2-3	0-3	0-3	2-2	3-3		1-3	2-0	0-1	4-4	4-2	3-1	1-0	3-0	4-1	1-4
7 Clifton	6-0	2-3	0-2	3-1	1-1	2-1		3-0	1-1	1-2	1-1	6-3	3-0	2-2	2-1	2-1
8 Cotgrave Welfare	0-0	2-1	2-4	0-1	2-1	3-1	1-0		2-0	0-2	0-2	2-1	0-1	1-0	3-0	1-1
9 FC Cavaliers	2-3	1-1	1-2	1-4	0-4	1-1	4-2	3-1		3-3	4-1	0-0	1-0	6-0	1-2	1-4
10 Gedling Southbank	2-2	5-2	1-6	1-2	4-8	2-0	5-3	5-1	3-1		4-2	2-0	3-1	3-2	5-3	3-1
11 Hucknall Rolls Leisure	1-2	2-2	1-1	4-2	0-4	1-2	3-3	5-1	2-2	1-5		4-0	1-5	8-1	3-1	0-2
12 Keyworth United	1-3	0-1	3-2	1-4	1-1	1-1	0-4	1-1	2-3	0-2	0-1		2-0	3-0	1-2	1-1
13 Kimberley Miners Welfare	2-5	1-2	2-1	1-1	1-2	2-1	1-2	5-0	4-0	2-1	1-3	0-0		4-1	2-0	2-3
14 Linby Colliery Welfare	0-3	0-7	0-3	0-1	0-2	2-1	1-2	0-5	0-1	1-7	2-3	2-7	0-2		4-2	1-4
15 Notts Police	0-7	1-2	1-1	1-0	0-7	3-1	0-3	2-4	1-0	2-5	1-2	0-2	1-3	3-1		2-0
16 Wollaton	0-1	1-1	4-1	3-0	3-1	5-2	0-4	3-2	0-0	2-0	5-2	0-1	2-0	2-1	2-0	

SHEFFIELD & HALLAMSHIRE SENIOR LEAGUE

Sponsored by: Windsor Food Services
Founded: N/K
Recent Champions:
2006: Mexborough Main Street
2007: Athersley Recreation
2008: Wombwell Main
2009: Athersley Recreation
2010: Sheffield Reserves

PREMIER DIVISION	P	W	D	L	F	A	Pts
1 Swallownest Miners Welfare	26	19	7	0	69	30	64
2 Athersley Recreation (-3)	26	18	5	3	84	28	56
3 Penistone Church	26	13	6	7	43	30	45
4 Millmoor Juniors	26	15	0	11	62	60	45
5 Stocksbridge Park Steels res	26	13	4	9	44	39	43
6 South Kirkby Colliery	26	12	5	9	60	34	41
7 High Green Villa	26	11	5	10	44	42	38
8 Sheffield reserves	26	9	7	10	56	58	34
9 Ecclesfield Red Rose	26	9	5	12	44	54	32
10 Davy	26	6	10	10	38	51	28
11 Wombwell Main	26	6	8	12	49	53	26
12 Oughtibridge WMSC	26	6	5	15	35	51	23
13 Dinnington Town res (-3)	26	6	4	16	28	47	19
14 Caribbean Sports (-1)	26	1	5	20	24	103	7

DIVISION ONE	P	W	D	L	F	A	Pts
1 Handsworth res (-3)	24	21	2	1	89	35	62
2 Penistone Church res	24	16	3	5	54	34	51
3 Everest	24	14	6	4	55	28	48
4 Hallam reserves (-3)	24	15	4	5	55	30	46
5 Sheffield Athletic	24	13	1	10	54	48	40
6 Frickley Colliery	24	11	2	11	47	51	35
7 Frecheville CA	24	10	4	10	55	61	34
8 Wickersley	24	8	4	12	44	53	28
9 Worsbro' Common	24	7	5	12	42	49	26
10 Bramley Sunnyside J	24	6	4	14	40	43	22
11 Wors. Bridge Ath res	24	7	1	16	56	82	22
12 Thorpe Hesley	24	6	2	16	29	53	20
13 Silkstone United	24	2	2	20	21	74	8

LEAGUE CUP (from 2nd Round)

ROUND 2
Athersley Recreation reserves 3-0 Thorncliffe
Sheffield Athletic 0-1 High Green Villa
Clowne Villa 1-2 Worsbrough Bridge Athletic reserves
De La Salle Old Boys 4-2 Everest
Frecheville CA 1-3 Frickley Colliery
Houghton Main 2-1 Silkstone United
Millmoor Juniors reserves 0-2 Davy
Oughtibridge WMSC 1-2 Caribbean Sports
Penisstone Church 1-2 Athersley Recreation
Sheffield Bankers 0-1 Ecclesfield Red Rose
Sheffield Lane Top 0-4 Dinnington Town reserves
Sheffield Parramore reserves 3-4 South Kirby Colliery
Swallownest Miners Welfare 3-2 Millmoor Juniors
Wickersley 3-1 Hallam reserves
Worsbrough Common 8-3 Handsworth reserves

ROUND 3
Athersley Recreation 2-1 Worsbrough Common
Frickley Colliery 1-2 Dinnington Town reserves
Houghton Main 1-1 Athersley Recreation reserves
(Houghton Main won on penalties)
South Kirby Colliery 1-3 Sheffield reserves
Swallownest Miners Welfare 2-3 High Green Villa
Wickersley 1-3 De La Salle Old Boys
Worsbrough Bridge Athletic reserves 3-1 Davy
Caribbean Sports 4-8 Ecclesfield Red Rose

QUARTER FINALS
High Green Villa 5-1 Worsbrough Bridge Athletic reserves
Houghton Main 3-1 De La Salle Old Boys
Dinnington Town reserves 0-1 Sheffield reserves
Ecclesfield Red Rose 3-3 Athersley Recreation (Athersley Recreation won on penalties)

SEMI-FINALS
Athersley Recreation 3-1 Houghton Main
High Green Villa 1-4 Sheffield reserves

FINAL (@ Stocksbridge Park Steels, 14/4/110
Athersley Recreation 1-0 Sheffield reserves

DIVISION TWO	P	W	D	L	F	A	Pts
1 Houghton Main	26	20	2	4	111	27	62
2 Swinton Station Athletic	26	17	5	4	84	31	56
3 Sheffield Parramore res (-1)	26	17	5	4	96	46	55
4 Clowne Villa (-3)	26	18	2	6	65	37	53
5 Athersley Recreation res (-3)	26	13	8	5	72	25	44
6 Millmoor Juniors reserves	26	13	2	11	49	41	41
7 De La Salle Old Boys	26	11	4	11	50	53	37
8 Sheffield Lane Top	26	10	6	10	50	45	36
9 Thorncliffe	26	10	4	12	41	59	34
10 Boynton Sports	26	8	5	13	49	59	29
11 Sheffield Bankers	26	7	3	16	40	68	24
12 Clowne Wanderers	26	4	2	20	28	131	14
13 New Bohemians (-3)	26	3	6	17	28	81	12
14 Sheffield City Frecheville	26	4	0	22	28	88	12

PREMIER DIVISION	1	2	3	4	5	6	7	8	9	10	11	12	13	14
1 Athersley Recreation		8-0	6-1	4-0	8-0	3-0	2-0	3-1	2-1	6-2	1-3	3-0	2-2	3-1
2 Caribbean Sports	1-4		1-3	0-5	0-3	2-8	3-5	0-2	0-1	0-6	0-3	0-2	1-3	2-2
3 Davy	2-2	1-1		1-0	3-0	4-2	0-2	3-3	1-1	2-2	3-3	2-2	0-0	3-0
4 Dinnington Town reserves	1-3	0-1	1-0		1-1	1-3	0-1	4-1	0-3	2-1	0-4	0-1	0-1	0-0
5 Ecclesfield Red Rose	2-2	2-0	3-1	3-3		2-1	1-3	3-2	2-3	4-5	1-1	1-2	0-1	1-0
6 High Green Villa	2-1	1-1	0-0	4-1	1-1		1-5	1-0	0-2	3-1	3-2	2-0	1-1	2-1
7 Millmoor Juniors	0-4	7-1	2-1	0-1	2-6	3-2		4-0	2-1	3-1	1-0	2-3	3-5	4-2
8 Oughtibridge W M S C	1-1	8-2	1-2	3-1	1-0	2-0	0-3		1-2	1-1	0-0	1-2	1-4	1-1
9 Penistone Church	0-1	1-1	1-0	3-1	4-1	1-0	6-2	1-0		2-0	1-3	0-1	2-4	2-2
10 Sheffield reserves	2-6	3-1	3-1	2-1	3-2	1-2	5-1	2-1	2-2		0-4	1-1	2-2	5-1
11 South Kirkby Colliery	0-1	10-1	4-2	3-0	3-1	2-1	1-4	6-0	0-1	1-1		0-2	1-2	3-0
12 Stocksbridge Park Steels reserves	1-5	7-1	1-1	0-2	0-2	1-3	4-2	2-0	1-1	3-1	3-0		1-4	3-2
13 Swallownest Miners Welfare	2-2	3-3	5-0	3-3	3-0	3-0	2-0	2-0	2-0	4-2	3-1	1-0		5-4
14 Wombwell Main	3-1	5-1	5-1	1-0	1-2	1-1	8-1	1-4	1-1	2-2	2-2	2-1	1-2	

SHROPSHIRE COUNTY LEAGUE

Sponsored by: Sportsjamkits.com
Founded: 1950
Recent Champions:
2006: Hanwood United
2007: Hanwood United
2008: Hanwood United
2009: Wem Town
2010: St Martins

PREMIER DIVISION	P	W	D	L	F	A	Pts
1 Haughmond	22	17	2	3	61	19	53
2 Ellesmere Rangers res	22	15	4	3	66	24	49
3 Ludlow Town	22	14	2	6	94	32	44
4 Newport Town	22	12	5	5	54	29	41
5 FC Hodnet	22	11	6	5	48	26	39
6 Shifnal United 97	22	10	4	8	29	33	34
7 Ketley Bank United	22	7	8	7	27	44	29
8 Broseley Juniors	22	6	5	11	26	45	23
9 Impact Utd (Leegomery)	22	4	5	13	34	58	17
10 Telford Juniors	22	4	4	14	35	64	16
11 Morda United	22	5	1	16	22	58	16
12 Dawley Villa	22	1	6	15	25	89	9

DIVISION ONE	P	W	D	L	F	A	Pts
1 Wellington Amateurs res	20	13	6	1	64	25	45
2 Church Stretton	20	12	1	7	51	28	37
3 Whitchurch Alport res	20	9	5	6	40	39	32
4 Wroxeter Rovers	20	9	4	7	54	35	31
5 Atlas	20	9	4	7	52	49	31
6 Oakengates Athletic	20	8	6	6	48	35	30
7 Bishops Castle Town	20	8	6	6	35	34	30
8 Hanwood United res	20	5	9	6	45	52	24
9 Brown Clee	20	7	3	10	37	48	24
10 Meole Brace	20	4	2	14	28	71	14
11 Clee Hill	20	1	4	15	27	65	7

RON JONES MEMORIAL CUP (INSIGHT)

ROUND 1
Church Stretton 3-2 Impact United (Leegomery)
Atlas 4-2 Brown Clee
Clee Hill 0-3 Wellington Amateurs reserves
FC Hodnet 6-1 Dawley Villa
Ketley Bank United 3-2 Hanwood United reserves
Shifnal United 97 3-4 Ellesmere Rangers reserves
Telford Juniors 5-2 Meole Brace

ROUND 2
Church Stretton 2-1 Telford Juniors
Haughmond 3-1 Wellington Amateurs
Atlas 1-1 Broseley Juniors
(Broseley Juniors won 4-3 on penalties)
Bishops Castle Town 1-3 Newport Town
FC Hodnet 6-1 Morda United
Ketley Bank United 3-4 Wroxeter Rovers
Ludlow Town 4-4 Ellesmere Rangers reserves
(Ellesmere Rangers reserves won 3-1 on penalties)
Oakengates Athletic 4-0 Whitchurch Alport reserves

QUARTER FINALS
Haughmond 2-0 Church Stretton
Broseley Juniors 1-2 Ellesmere Rangers reserves
Newport Town 2-1 Wroxeter Rovers
Oakengates Athletic 4-1 FC Hodnet

SEMI-FINALS
Ellesmere Rangers 1-3 Oakengates Athletic
Haughmond 2-1 Newport Town

FINAL (@ Ellesmere Rangers, 12/5/11)
Oakengates Athletic 1-4 Haughmond

PREMIER DIVISION CUP - FINAL (@ Ellesmere Rangers, 21/5/11)
Haughmond 0-2 FC Hodnet

DIVISION ONE CUP - FINAL (@ Ellesmere Rangers, 5/5/11)
Bishops Castle Town 1-2 Wellington Amateurs reserves

COMMANDER ETHELSTON CHARITY CUP - FINAL
(@ Whitchurch Alport, 14/5/11)
FC Hodnet 0-2 Wellington Amateurs reserves

PREMIER DIVISION	1	2	3	4	5	6	7	8	9	10	11	12
1 Broseley Juniors		3-0	1-0	1-1	0-2	1-1	0-0	4-1	3-1	1-3	1-2	2-3
2 Dawley Villa	0-0		0-6	1-4	0-2	2-8	2-2	3-1	2-3	1-5	0-5	2-5
3 Ellesmere Rangers res	5-1	6-0		0-0	3-0	5-2	1-1	5-2	4-2	2-1	3-0	6-2
4 FC Hodnet	0-1	2-2	2-0		1-1	3-2	1-1	3-1	2-0	0-4	0-1	9-1
5 Haughmond	3-0	7-0	3-2	3-1		5-1	5-0	0-2	4-0	3-1	4-2	2-1
6 Impact Utd (Leegomery)	3-0	3-3	1-3	0-3	1-6		1-1	0-4	0-1	1-4	L-W	3-0
7 Ketley Bank United	2-1	2-1	0-4	0-5	1-3	6-0		1-4	3-1	0-0	2-0	1-0
8 Ludlow Town	7-0	14-1	2-2	2-4	1-1	6-1	8-0		8-0	5-1	4-0	8-0
9 Morda United	2-3	3-1	0-3	0-1	1-3	1-3	0-2	1-4		2-1	1-1	1-0
10 Newport Town	5-1	2-2	1-2	3-3	1-0	1-1	6-1	2-1	1-0		3-0	2-2
11 Shifnal United	2-0	2-2	3-3	2-0	0-2	1-0	0-0	0-5	3-0	0-1		3-1
12 Telford Juniors	2-2	4-0	0-1	0-3	0-2	2-2	1-1	3-4	6-2	1-6	1-2	

SURREY INTERMEDIATE LEAGUE (WESTERN)

Sponsored by: No sponsor
Founded: 1891
Recent Champions:
2006: Old Rustlishians
2007: Knaphill
2008: Horsley
2009: Ripley Village
2010: Burpham

PREMIER DIVISION	P	W	D	L	F	A	Pts
1 Wrecclesham	26	21	1	4	77	43	64
2 Abbey Rangers	26	16	2	8	63	35	50
3 Milford & Witley	26	15	5	6	49	21	50
4 Yateley Green	26	13	2	11	54	45	41
5 Yateley	26	12	2	12	54	42	38
6 Chiddingfold	26	10	5	11	43	53	35
7 AFC Bourne	26	11	1	14	59	57	34
8 Royal Holloway Old Boys	26	10	4	12	50	50	34
9 University of Surrey	26	10	2	14	47	58	32
10 Merrow (-6)	26	11	4	11	47	47	31
11 Shottermill & Haslemere	26	8	7	11	40	49	31
12 Worplesdon Phoenix	26	9	1	16	36	62	28
13 Pyrford	26	8	3	15	39	73	27
14 Guildford C Weysiders (-4)	26	5	7	14	33	56	18

DIVISION ONE	P	W	D	L	F	A	Pts
1 Cranleigh	24	15	3	6	52	37	48
2 Abbey (-18)	24	21	2	1	88	19	47
3 Unis Old Boys	24	15	1	8	59	35	46
4 Woking & Horsell	24	14	4	6	57	35	46
5 AFC Spelthorne Spts	24	14	1	9	71	45	43
6 Lightwater United	24	12	5	7	46	40	41
7 Shalford	24	11	1	12	55	53	34
8 Old Salesians (-3)	24	10	4	10	46	45	31
9 Godalming & Farn A	24	8	5	11	42	42	29
10 AFC Bedfont Green	24	6	5	13	56	66	23
11 Ewhurst	24	4	4	16	35	67	16
12 Burymead	24	4	1	19	34	100	13
13 Hammer United	24	3	2	19	33	90	11

RESERVE PREMIER DIVISION	P	W	D	L	F	A	Pts
1 Yateley Green reserves	26	20	4	2	76	22	64
2 University of Surrey reserves	26	17	4	5	81	30	55
3 Wrecclesham reserves	26	17	2	7	75	31	53
4 Milford & Witley res (-3)	26	17	2	7	52	28	50
5 Abbey Rangers reserves	26	15	1	10	49	38	46
6 Yateley reserves	26	13	3	10	55	45	42
7 Chiddingfold reserves	26	11	5	10	49	58	38
8 Merrow reserves	26	8	7	11	39	46	31
9 Pyrford reserves	26	9	3	14	39	40	30
10 Shottermill & Haslemere res	26	8	4	14	41	60	28
11 Worplesdon Phoenix reserves	26	7	7	12	41	66	28
12 Royal Holloway OB res (-1)	26	7	3	16	39	73	23
13 AFC Bourne reserves	26	7	1	18	41	75	22
14 Guildford City Weysiders res	26	1	4	21	18	83	7

PREMIER CHALLENGE CUP

ROUND 1
Yateley Green 1-4 AFC Bourne
University of Surrey 2-1 Royal Holloway Old Boys (at Royal Holloway Old Boys)
Merrow 1-2 Wrecclesham
Chiddingfold 3-0 Unis Old Boys
Milford & Witley 3-0 AFC Bedfont Green
Shalford 1-0 Worplesdon Phoenix
Ewhurst 1-2 Abbey Rangers
Abbey 2-1 Lightwater United
Cranleigh 4-2 Pyrford
Burymead 1-3 Old Salesians
Guildford City Weysiders 4-0 Spelthorne Sports

ROUND 2
Shottermill & Haslemere 3-5 Old Salesians
Shalford 1-4 Abbey Rangers
Chiddingfold 1-0 Yateley
AFC Bourne 2-5 University of Surrey
Godalming & Farncombe Athletic 5-1 Cranleigh
Milford & Witley 1-3 Wrecclesham
Abbey 1-2 Woking & Horsell
Hammer United 2-4 Guildford City Weysiders

QUARTER-FINALS
Wrecclesham 5-2 Godalming & Farncombe Athletic
University of Surrey 3-2 Abbey Rangers
Guildford City Weysiders 0-3 Woking & Horsell
Old Salesians 3-2 Chiddingfold

SEMI-FINALS
Old Salesians 1-1 Woking & Horsell (Woking & Horsell won 4-3 on penalties)
Wrecclesham 4-2 University of Surrey

FINAL (@Godalming Town, 5/5/11)
Wrecclesham 1-0 Woking & Horsell

RESERVE DIVISION ONE	P	W	D	L	F	A	Pts
1 Unis Old Boys res	24	18	3	3	60	21	57
2 AFC Bedfont Grn res	24	17	3	4	77	40	54
3 AFC Spelthorne S res	24	17	2	5	83	42	53
4 Cranleigh reserves	24	15	4	5	68	30	49
5 Lightwater U res (-3)	24	15	5	4	100	34	47
6 Shalford reserves	24	10	2	12	60	60	32
7 Woking & Horsell res	24	9	3	12	51	54	30
8 Godalming & F A res	24	8	5	11	50	52	29
9 Burymead reserves	24	7	2	15	31	66	23
10 Abbey reserves	24	7	1	16	38	74	22
11 Old Salesians res	24	6	3	15	44	78	21
12 Ewhurst reserves	24	6	1	17	45	80	19
13 Hammer United res	24	4	0	20	25	101	12

RESERVES CHALLENGE CUP - FINAL (@Godalming Town, 20/4/11)
University of Surrey Res. 2-1 Chiddingfold Res.

PREMIER DIVISION	1	2	3	4	5	6	7	8	9	10	11	12	13	14
1 AFC Bourne		5-0	2-0	1-0	4-6	0-1	2-1	7-1	2-1	5-1	4-0	4-0	1-2	2-2
2 Abbey Rangers	2-4		4-0	3-1	2-2	L-W	6-0	3-0	0-3	5-1	1-2	1-2	0-3	1-3
3 Chiddingfold	2-4	4-5		2-1	0-2	0-0	2-1	1-1	3-0	2-1	2-3	1-3	3-1	3-2
4 Guildford City Weysiders	2-1	2-0	1-1		0-3	2-2	1-1	0-1	0-0	4-2	0-1	0-5	5-5	1-3
5 Merrow	0-2	3-2	2-2	3-2		0-2	3-0	0-3	1-1	2-0	2-1	1-3	1-3	2-3
6 Milford & Witley	1-2	5-0	6-0	3-0	2-1		1-2	1-0	4-1	3-1	1-1	4-1	3-0	1-2
7 Pyrford	4-3	2-1	2-4	5-1	1-3	1-0		2-2	4-1	4-2	0-1	1-8	0-1	3-3
8 Royal Holloway Old Boys	3-2	3-4	1-2	0-1	2-2	1-1	1-0		1-2	2-5	1-2	2-3	3-2	3-0
9 Shottermill & Haslemere	2-1	3-1	1-1	3-3	1-3	0-0	1-2	1-4		3-1	2-1	2-3	3-2	1-3
10 University of Surrey	0-1	1-5	1-2	2-2	1-0	2-1	6-0	0-3	1-1		2-1	1-2	3-2	2-1
11 Worplesdon Phoenix	0-2	1-6	0-4	1-4	2-0	3-1	3-2	1-3	2-3	0-3		3-4	1-2	2-5
12 Wrecclesham	4-1	2-4	2-0	W-L	4-3	1-3	6-0	1-0	2-2	5-3	5-2		2-1	3-1
13 Yateley	0-0	4-1	4-2	3-0	3-0	0-1	5-0	5-3	2-1	1-2	1-2	2-3		0-1
14 Yateley Green	0-1	1-2	3-0	5-0	1-2	0-2	6-1	2-6	2-1	1-3	2-0	1-3	1-0	

TEESIDE LEAGUE

Sponsored by: Jack Hatfield Sports
Founded: 1891
Recent Champions:
2006: Carlin How WMC
2007: Carlin How WMC
2008: BEADS
2009: BEADS
2010: BEADS

DIVISION ONE	P	W	D	L	F	A	Pts
1 Grangetown Boys Club (-3)	22	17	4	1	84	29	52
2 Richmond Town	22	16	4	2	77	27	52
3 Acklam Steelworks	22	14	2	6	61	39	44
4 Nunthorpe Athletic	22	13	5	4	55	35	44
5 Thornaby Dubliners	22	11	3	8	55	39	36
6 BEADS	22	8	5	9	39	40	29
7 Richmond Mavericks (-3)	22	9	4	9	49	43	28
8 North Ormesby Sports	22	8	2	12	39	40	26
9 Fishburn Park	22	5	4	13	23	52	19
10 Norton WMC (-3)	22	4	5	13	32	65	14
11 Stokesley reserves	22	3	4	15	26	63	13
12 Darlington Grammar Sch RA	22	2	2	18	25	80	8

DIVISION TWO	P	W	D	L	F	A	Pts
1 Whinney Banks YCC	26	22	1	3	142	32	67
2 Cargo Fleet (-9)	26	23	1	2	119	34	61
3 Great Ayton United	26	16	3	7	85	41	51
4 Grangetown YCC	26	14	3	9	91	59	45
5 Guisborough Town reserves	26	13	4	9	66	49	43
6 Darlington Rugby	26	14	1	11	83	68	43
7 Stockton Town	26	13	4	9	75	63	43
8 Redcar Rugby	26	10	6	10	69	58	36
9 Redcar Athletic	26	9	6	11	42	53	33
10 Stockton West End	26	9	6	11	49	95	33
11 Redcar Newmarket	26	5	4	17	38	80	19
12 Norton & Stockton A res (-3)	26	6	2	18	44	84	17
13 St Mary's College (-3)	26	4	2	20	27	82	11
14 Billingham Tn Intermediates	26	1	3	22	39	171	6

MCMILLAN BOWL

ROUND 1
Redcar Nemarket 1-5 Great Ayton United
Norton WMC 3-1 Fishburn Park
Grangetown YCC 3-3 Acklam Steelworks
St Mary's College 0-1 Norton & Stockton Ancients res.
Redcar Rugby Club 2-1 Guisborough Town reserves
Billingham Town Intermediates 4-11 Nunthorpe Ath.
Stockton Town 4-2 Stokesley reserves
Richmond Mavericks 1-3 Thornaby Dubliners
Darlington Grammar School RA 4-1 Redcar Athletic

ROUND 2
Norton & Stockton Ancients res. 1-3 North Ormesby
Darlington Grammar School RA 0-3 Cargo Fleet
Whinney Banks YCC 4-0 Stockton Town
Thornaby Dubliners 5-1 Redcar Rugby Club
Richmond Town 3-2 Grangetown BC
Nunthorpe Athletic 5-1 Stockton West End
Great Ayton United 1-0 Norton WMC
Grangetown YCC 5-4 BEADS

QUARTER FINALS
Nunthorpe Athletic 2-1 Thornaby Dubliners
Cargo Fleet 3-4 North Ormesby
Grangetown YCC 4-4 Richmond Town (Grangetown YCC won 5-4 on penalties)
Great Ayton United 5-4 Whinney Banks YCC

SEMI-FINALS
Grangetown YCC 5-2 North Ormesby
Nunthorpe Athletic 0-1 Great Ayton United

FINAL (@ Guisborough Town, 11/5/11)
Grangetown YCC 2-1 Great Ayton United

RT RAINE TROPHY - FINAL (@ Guisborough Town, 25/4/11)
Guisborough Town reserves 1-2 Richmond Mavericks

LOU MOORE SHIELD - FINAL (@ Grangetown, 4/5/11)
Grangetown BC 1-2 Richmond Mavericks

ALEX BURNESS PLATE - FINAL (@ Grangetown, 2/5/11)
Grangetown YCC 4-5 St Mary's College

JV MADDEN TROPHY (@ BEADS, 7/8/11)
BEADS 3 North Ormesby Sports 0

DIVISION ONE	1	2	3	4	5	6	7	8	9	10	11	12
1 Acklam Steelworks		1-2	6-2	3-3	2-4	3-1	5-1	0-0	2-1	1-5	6-1	2-1
2 BEADS	0-1		3-3	0-1	1-1	2-2	2-5	0-1	0-0	2-1	1-2	3-1
3 Darlington Grammar School RA	0-5	0-3		4-2	2-4	0-2	2-2	0-3	2-4	2-7	1-2	1-4
4 Fishburn Park	1-0	2-5	3-0		0-2	0-1	0-3	0-5	1-0	0-4	2-2	0-1
5 Grangetown Boys Club	2-0	4-2	5-0	6-1		6-0	2-2	3-2	7-1	2-2	4-2	4-1
6 North Ormesby Sports	3-4	1-2	3-2	3-1	2-5		5-1	2-4	3-0	1-4	2-0	3-3
7 Norton WMC	0-2	2-4	1-2	0-1	0-8	2-1		1-2	3-3	1-6	2-2	2-2
8 Nunthorpe Athletic	6-7	1-4	6-0	1-0	2-2	1-0	3-2		2-3	2-2	3-2	1-1
9 Richmond Mavericks	0-4	4-0	1-0	2-2	2-3	3-0	7-0	0-1		2-5	3-1	3-0
10 Richmond Town	3-0	4-2	1-0	6-0	4-2	2-0	4-0	3-3	1-1		4-0	3-2
11 Stokesley reserves	0-3	1-1	4-0	0-0	1-6	1-2	1-2	2-4	1-4	1-6		0-1
12 Thornaby Dubliners	3-4	2-0	9-2	4-3	0-2	5-0	2-0	1-2	3-2	3-2	6-0	

WEST RIDING COUNTY AMATEUR LEAGUE

Sponsored by: No sponsor
Founded: 1922
Recent Champions:
2006: Bay Athletic
2007: Wibsey 2008: Bay Athletic
2009: Bay Athletic 2010: Bay Athletic

PREMIER DIVISION	P	W	D	L	F	A	Pts
1 Bay Athletic	30	27	2	1	109	29	83
2 Albion Sports	30	24	2	4	101	33	74
3 Campion	30	18	5	7	80	50	59
4 Kirkburton	30	17	6	7	74	52	57
5 Marsden	30	16	5	9	60	60	53
6 Storthes Hall	30	13	8	9	77	70	47
7 Steeton	30	13	6	11	73	66	45
8 Tyersal	30	13	4	13	72	61	43
9 Ovenden West Riding	30	11	5	14	79	64	38
10 Lower Hopton	30	10	8	12	59	67	38
11 Brighouse Town reserves	30	11	4	15	64	66	37
12 Golcar United	30	9	7	14	64	81	34
13 Wibsey	30	6	4	20	63	100	22
14 Hall Green United	30	5	7	18	52	93	22
15 Hunsworth	30	3	5	22	36	103	14
16 Tingley Athletic	30	2	6	22	42	110	12

DIVISION ONE	P	W	D	L	F	A	Pts
1 Littletown	26	18	4	4	82	26	58
2 Bay Athletic reserves	26	18	4	4	78	33	58
3 AFC Emley reserves	26	17	3	6	80	43	54
4 Ventus/Yeadon Celtic	26	16	3	7	77	53	51
5 Salts	26	16	1	9	77	38	49
6 Halifax Irish	26	9	4	13	46	54	31
7 Wakefield City	26	8	6	12	57	73	30
8 Westbrook YMCA	26	8	5	13	51	55	29
9 Dudley Hill Rangers	26	7	8	11	53	80	29
10 Heckmondwike Town	26	7	7	12	59	75	28
11 Bronte Wanderers	26	8	4	14	38	57	28
12 Overthorpe Sports Club	26	7	5	14	43	88	26
13 Tyersal reserves	26	6	5	15	55	89	23
14 Eastmoor	26	6	3	17	50	82	21

DIVISION TWO	P	W	D	L	F	A	Pts
1 Lepton Highlanders	26	21	2	3	115	31	65
2 Storthes Hall reserves	26	19	4	3	65	29	61
3 Campion reserves	26	17	3	6	72	33	54
4 West Horton	26	12	10	4	71	38	46
5 Kirkburton reserves	26	13	3	10	53	44	42
6 Rawdon Old Boys	26	12	5	9	39	40	41
7 Long Lee	26	12	4	10	55	48	40
8 Huddersfield YMCA	26	10	7	9	51	39	37
9 Steeton reserves	26	12	1	13	47	60	37
10 Ovenden West Riding res	26	11	2	13	60	55	35
11 Golcar United reserves	26	10	4	12	42	54	34
12 Morley Town	26	4	1	21	30	59	13
13 Crag Road United	26	3	1	22	34	114	10
14 Tingley Athletic reserves	26	2	1	23	25	115	7

PREMIER DIVISION CUP

ROUND 1
Brighouse Town Reserves 1-4 Tyersal
Tingley Athletic 6-2 Hall Green United
Storthes Hall 3-3 Ovenden West Riding (Ovenden West Riding won 6-5 on penalties)
Wibsey 0-4 Bay Athletic
Marsden 4-3 Golcar United
Campion 0-2 Albion Sports
Lower Hopton 0-3 Kirkburton
Steeton 4-1 Hunsworth

QUARTER-FINALS
Steeton 0-2 Kirkburton
Albion Sports 4-3 Bay Athletic (@ Bradford Park Avenue)
Tyersal 2-0 Tingley Athletic
Ovenden West Riding 6-1 Marsden

SEMI-FINALS
Albion Sports 0-2 Tyersal (@ Brighouse Town)
Kirkburton 0-2 Ovenden West Riding (@ Brighouse Town)

FINAL (@ Brighouse Town, 2/5/11)
Tyersal 1-0 Ovenden West Riding

DIVISION ONE CUP - FINAL (@ Lower Hopton, 20/5/11)
Overthorpe Sports Club 0-5 Bay Athletic reserves

DIVISION TWO CUP - FINAL (@ Ovenden West Riding, 23/5/11)
Lepton Highlanders 1-1 Long Lee Juniors
(Long Lee Juniors won 5-4 on penalties)

DIVISION THREE CUP - FINAL (@ Littletown, 14/5/11)
Albion Sports reserves 4-1 Lower Hopton reserves

DIVISION THREE	P	W	D	L	F	A	Pts
1 Albion Sports reserves	18	14	2	2	87	33	44
2 Marsden reserves	18	11	2	5	52	35	35
3 Littletown reserves	18	11	1	6	52	37	34
4 Salts reserves	18	9	4	5	32	33	31
5 Hunsworth reserves	18	9	1	8	38	44	28
6 Hall Green United res	18	7	3	8	40	34	24
7 Lower Hopton reserves	18	7	1	10	39	53	22
8 Ventus/Yeadon Celtic res	18	6	2	10	46	54	20
9 Bronte Wanderers res	18	3	2	13	28	55	11
10 Long Lee Juniors res	18	1	6	11	26	62	9

PREMIER DIVISION	1	2	3	4	5	6	7	8	9	10	11	12	13	14	15	16
1 Albion Sports		0-2	4-1	3-0	8-1	2-0	3-1	1-1	5-2	3-1	2-1	3-3	4-2	4-1	5-0	W-L
2 Bay Athletic	3-1		2-1	0-3	5-1	11-2	6-0	2-0	3-2	4-1	3-0	6-1	2-0	5-1	4-2	8-0
3 Brighouse Town reserves	0-6	1-2		0-1	2-4	5-1	2-3	1-4	3-3	3-0	4-3	0-1	0-4	1-1	4-2	5-2
4 Campion	0-1	0-4	4-4		5-0	5-2	4-1	1-2	4-3	2-2	2-0	3-1	1-1	5-2	4-1	1-3
5 Golcar United	2-5	0-5	2-2	2-4		3-3	3-2	1-2	3-1	1-2	3-1	0-1	3-1	4-1	1-1	3-6
6 Hall Green United	1-4	2-4	0-1	0-2	5-1		1-1	1-3	3-5	2-3	1-3	3-0	2-2	3-3	0-4	2-1
7 Hunsworth	0-2	0-2	1-2	2-3	1-5	2-2		0-3	1-1	1-2	1-1	1-4	2-2	1-6	1-6	3-7
8 Kirkburton	2-1	3-4	3-2	0-0	1-0	6-2	6-0		0-2	2-3	3-0	2-1	3-3	2-3	2-2	1-0
9 Lower Hopton	0-7	1-2	4-1	1-4	1-1	1-1	4-2	1-2		0-1	1-5	3-2	1-1	2-1	1-2	7-2
10 Marsden	W-L	0-2	2-1	5-0	2-2	3-1	5-0	5-2	1-1		1-1	1-3	1-2	4-0	2-1	2-1
11 Ovenden West Riding	4-6	0-2	0-2	1-5	3-3	3-1	5-0	3-4	1-3	6-0		2-3	1-3	9-0	3-3	3-1
12 Steeton	0-4	1-4	3-1	2-5	2-2	1-3	5-0	2-2	0-0	7-1	1-1		1-0	8-0	1-6	3-3
13 Storthes Hall	2-6	2-2	2-1	1-3	3-2	3-1	5-1	3-5	1-2	4-4	2-7	5-3		6-3	1-0	7-2
14 Tingley Athletic	0-3	2-2	0-7	1-6	2-3	2-2	1-2	3-3	0-1	1-2	2-4	0-6	3-4		0-5	0-2
15 Tyersal	1-2	2-4	0-1	2-0	2-0	2-3	5-3	3-2	5-2	2-3	1-5	2-3	2-2	1-0		3-0
16 Wibsey	1-3	0-4	2-6	3-3	2-8	7-2	0-3	2-3	3-3	2-0	1-3	3-4	2-3	3-3	2-4	

WEST YORKSHIRE LEAGUE

Sponsored by: No sponsor
Founded: 1928
Recent Champions:
2006: Leeds Met Carnegie
2007: Bardsey 2008: Carlton Athletic
2009: Knaresborough Town 2010: Bardsey

PREMIER DIVISION	P	W	D	L	F	A	Pts
1 Bardsey	30	21	7	2	80	25	70
2 Knaresborough Town	30	18	4	8	80	46	58
3 Leeds City	30	18	4	8	65	47	58
4 Carlton Athletic	30	14	8	8	69	56	50
5 East End Park	30	14	7	9	69	63	49
6 Beeston St Anthony's	30	13	8	9	78	54	47
7 Otley Town	30	14	4	12	59	51	46
8 Boroughbridge	30	13	4	13	59	59	43
9 Pool	30	12	5	13	43	54	41
10 Fields	30	10	5	15	51	60	35
11 Sherburn White Rose	30	10	5	15	34	54	35
12 Ripon City	30	10	4	16	43	74	34
13 Whitkirk Wanderers	30	8	9	13	60	62	33
14 Altofts	30	9	6	15	54	65	33
15 Rothwell Athletic	30	5	6	19	28	55	21
16 Kellingley Welfare (-3)	30	7	2	21	31	78	20

DIVISION ONE	P	W	D	L	F	A	Pts
1 Oxenhope Recreation	30	22	4	4	87	34	70
2 Wetherby Athletic	30	21	6	3	80	32	69
3 Robin Hood Athletic	30	18	7	5	88	32	61
4 Old Centralians	30	19	3	8	62	34	60
5 Brighouse Old Boys	30	19	2	9	82	33	59
6 Wyke Wanderers	30	16	4	10	62	46	52
7 Kippax	30	16	4	10	61	60	52
8 Horbury Town	30	13	7	10	48	42	46
9 Baildon Trinity Athletic	30	7	10	13	52	61	31
10 Mount St. Mary's	30	8	5	17	51	82	29
11 Swillington Saints	30	9	2	19	53	88	29
12 Ilkley Town	30	6	10	14	45	59	28
13 Aberford Albion (-4)	30	9	4	17	47	62	27
14 Ossett Common Rovers	30	7	2	21	41	77	23
15 Hartshead	30	4	8	18	29	85	20
16 Nostell Miners Welfare	30	5	4	21	46	107	19

DIVISION TWO	P	W	D	L	F	A	Pts
1 Rothwell Juniors	26	21	4	1	78	24	67
2 Old Headingley	26	20	2	4	95	30	62
3 UK Richmond (-3)	26	17	6	3	91	36	54
4 Stanley United	26	15	4	7	78	55	49
5 Rothwell Town	26	14	3	9	65	54	45
6 Glasshoughton Welfare res.	26	11	7	8	74	59	40
7 Barwick	26	11	6	9	72	69	39
8 Featherstone Colliery	26	10	4	12	74	63	34
9 Hunslet	26	7	4	15	43	85	25
10 Great Preston	26	6	6	14	55	80	24
11 Woodhouse Hill WMC	26	5	6	15	46	71	21
12 Garforth Rangers (-3)	26	5	7	14	47	68	19
13 Howden Clough	26	4	4	18	40	82	16
14 South Milford	26	3	3	20	35	117	12

LEAGUE CUP

ROUND 1
Horbury Town 1-3 Beeston St Anthony's
Old Centralians 2-0 Altofts
Stanley United 2-5 Bardsey
Old Headingley 2-3 Ilkley Town
Ripon City 2-2 Kippax (Ripon City won 4-1 on penalties)
South Milford 0-3 Rothwell Town
Wetherby Athletic 6-0 Barwick
Swillington Saints 1-2 Baildon Trinity Athletic
Whitkirk Wanderers 2-0 Glasshoughton Welfare reserves
Leeds City 2-1 Brighouse Old Boys
Howden Clough 0-5 Otley Town
Featherstone Colliery 6-2 Garforth Rangers
Ossett Common Rovers 2-5 Oxenhope Recreation
Field Sports & Social 5-5 Aberford Albion
(Aberford Albion won 9-8 on penalties)

ROUND 2
Bardsey 1-2 Otley Town
Sherburn White Rose 1-2 Ilkley Town
Rothwell Town 0-4 Carlton Athletic
Wetherby Athletic 4-3 Aberford Albion
Boroughbridge 2-2 Baildon Trinity Athletic
(Boroughbridge won 4-3 on penalties)
Robin Hood Athletic 0-1 Rothwell Athletic
Leeds City 1-0 Whitkirk Wanderers
Ripon City 4-4 Beeston St Anthony's
(Ripon City won 4-3 on penalties)
Featherstone Colliery 5-7 East End Park WMC
Kellingley Welfare 1-1 Oxenhope Recreation
(Oxenhope Recreation won 4-3 on penalties)
Nostell Miners Welfare reserves 3-3 Woodhouse Park WMC
(Nostell Miners Welfare reserves won 3-1 on penalties)
Mount St Mary's 0-4 Pool
UK Richmond 0-1 Knaresborough Town
Great Preston 2-6 Rothwell Juniors
Hartshead 0-2 Wyke Wanderers
Hunslet 0-5 Old Centralians

ROUND 3
Leeds City 1-0 Oxenhope Recreation
Nostell Miners Welfare reserves 3-1 Wetherby Athletic
(@ Wetherby Athletic)
Wyke Wanderers 4-0 Ripon City
Otley Town 1-1 Ilkley Town (Otley Town won 5-3 on penalties)
East End Park WMC 0-3 Boroughbridge
Old Centralians 2-1 Knaresborough Town
Rothwell Athletic 2-3 Carlton Athletic
Rothwell Juniors 1-2 Pool

QUARTER-FINALS
Boroughbridge 3-1 Old Centralians
Leeds City w/o-scr Nostell Miners Welfare reserves
Wyke Wanderers 0-1 Ilkley Town
Carlton Athletic 1-1 Pool (Pool won 3-1 on penalties)

SEMI-FINALS
Leeds City 1-2 Otley Town (@ Glasshoughton Welfare)
Boroughbridge 2-1 Pool (@ Glasshoughton Welfare)

FINAL (@ Wakefield, 5/5/11)
Boroughbridge 2-1 Otley Town

LEAGUE TROPHY - FINAL(@ Altofts, 19/5/11)
Carlton Athletic reserves 1-4 Knaresborough Town reserves

PREMIER DIVISION	1	2	3	4	5	6	7	8	9	10	11	12	13	14	15	16
1 Altofts		2-5	2-5	3-2	3-3	2-2	1-2	0-1	2-1	5-0	4-3	1-2	1-2	1-0	3-0	1-2
2 Bardsey	2-2		3-0	1-1	2-2	4-2	4-1	5-0	1-1	1-0	0-0	3-0	3-0	1-0	6-0	4-2
3 Beeston St Anthony's	5-1	2-0		3-1	4-0	2-2	3-2	9-0	0-7	4-4	2-2	3-3	3-4	2-0	1-2	4-2
4 Boroughbridge	3-1	0-0	0-5		0-2	5-0	4-2	5-3	2-4	1-2	3-1	0-2	3-1	0-2	3-0	3-1
5 Carlton Athletic	2-2	0-2	0-1	1-3		2-2	5-3	2-0	3-2	1-1	4-0	5-0	2-1	4-2	5-1	4-1
6 East End Park	4-1	1-3	3-2	5-3	1-0		3-1	2-0	3-1	3-4	5-1	3-2	6-1	2-1	0-0	2-2
7 Field Sports & Social	2-3	0-2	2-0	2-2	4-1	2-3		2-0	1-1	0-4	0-3	1-2	4-1	1-1	2-2	1-3
8 Kellingley Welfare	1-1	2-5	4-2	0-3	1-2	2-1	1-2		1-3	1-3	2-0	0-3	3-4	2-1	2-1	1-4
9 Knaresborough Town	3-2	1-2	2-2	3-4	5-4	3-0	2-1	2-1		1-2	3-0	2-1	6-0	4-2	0-1	4-2
10 Leeds City	2-1	3-2	1-2	0-0	5-0	4-5	1-4	2-1	0-2		3-1	4-0	5-2	1-0	3-0	1-0
11 Otley Town	6-1	0-3	0-7	3-2	2-2	4-1	4-0	5-0	1-2	5-1		2-0	4-0	3-1	2-0	2-0
12 Pool	1-0	1-2	2-1	2-1	2-2	0-0	0-2	4-0	0-3	1-0	1-2		3-5	3-4	3-2	1-0
13 Ripon City	0-2	0-3	1-0	2-3	1-1	3-1	0-0	3-0	2-2	1-4	2-1	1-2		3-1	0-3	2-1
14 Rothwell Athletic	1-0	0-4	1-1	0-2	1-4	2-2	0-1	0-1	2-1	1-2	0-0	0-0	1-1		2-1	2-5
15 Sherburn White Rose	2-5	1-6	1-1	1-0	0-1	1-2	3-0	2-1	2-3	1-2	1-0	3-0	1-0	1-0		0-0
16 Whitkirk Wanderers	1-1	1-1	2-2	7-0	4-5	5-3	1-6	0-0	2-6	1-1	1-2	2-2	5-0	2-0	1-1	

OTHER LEAGUES 2010-11

ACCRINGTON COMBINATION

Division One	P	W	D	L	F	A	Pts
Park	15	13	0	2	65	15	39
Crown Rovers	15	11	3	1	59	26	36
Hapton	15	6	3	6	38	44	21
Os'twistle St M A -6	15	6	2	7	36	39	14
Whinney Hill	15	2	1	12	27	56	7
Church Town -3	15	2	1	12	21	66	4

Church Kirk, Lounge United - records expunged.

Division Two	P	W	D	L	F	A	Pts
Park Rangers	21	19	1	1	104	25	58
St Mary's College OB	21	17	3	1	99	36	54
Globe Bullough Park	21	9	4	8	60	72	31
Sydney Street WMC	21	8	3	10	44	54	27
Calderstones United	21	7	4	10	61	71	25
Burnley Rd Bowling	21	4	5	12	43	64	17
Accrington Town -3	21	5	2	14	50	75	14
AFC.Burnley -6	21	2	4	15	27	91	4

ALDERSHOT & DISTRICT LEAGUE

Senior	P	W	D	L	F	A	Pts
Headley United	22	19	1	2	91	24	58
Old Farnboronians	22	19	0	3	101	25	57
Bagshot	21	14	2	5	65	28	44
Hale Rovers	22	12	2	8	63	48	38
West Meon & Warnford	22	11	1	10	53	46	34
Frimley Select	22	10	4	8	46	51	34
Fleet Spurs Reserves	22	9	0	13	41	52	27
Aldershot Spartans	22	6	5	11	51	63	23
Hindhead Athletic	21	6	3	12	42	78	21
South Farnborough	22	5	2	15	36	76	17
Farnborough Nth End Res.	22	3	6	13	31	67	15
Sandhurst Sports	22	3	2	17	27	89	11

Division One	P	W	D	L	F	A	Pts
Alton Athletic	20	18	0	2	102	13	54
Shalford Social	20	16	1	3	79	25	49
Old Farnboronians Res.	20	15	2	3	73	34	47
Aldershot Rangers	20	9	3	8	48	55	30
Eversley "A"	20	6	7	7	40	47	25
Fleet Spurs "A"	20	7	3	10	26	43	24
Letef Select	20	6	3	11	32	58	21
Wey Valley	20	5	4	11	34	43	19
AFC Froyle	20	6	1	13	34	66	19
Headley United Reserves	20	5	0	15	26	74	15
Hartley Wintney "A"	20	4	2	14	44	80	14

Division Two	P	W	D	L	F	A	Pts
Frogmore Rangers	19	16	2	1	68	20	50
Farnham United	20	14	0	6	62	40	42
West End Village	20	12	4	4	58	27	40
Alton United	20	9	7	4	52	37	34
Courtmoor	20	8	3	9	44	50	27
Hindhead Athletic Res.	19	8	2	9	32	39	26
Four Marks Reserves	20	6	3	11	26	47	21
Normandy	20	5	4	11	42	61	19
Duke of York	20	5	3	12	44	63	18
Lindford	20	4	5	11	33	49	17
Ropley	20	4	3	13	37	65	15

Game between Frogmore Rangers and Hindhead Athletic Reserves remained unplayed.

Division Three	P	W	D	L	F	A	Pts
Wrecclesham "A"	20	13	2	5	79	33	41
Shalford Social Reserves	20	13	2	5	57	31	41
BOSC United	20	11	4	5	55	29	37
Normandy Reserves	20	11	2	7	46	46	35
Yateley "A"	20	10	2	8	55	45	32
Yateley Green "A"	20	8	7	5	46	31	31
Rushmoor Community	20	9	4	7	41	34	31
Fleet Spurs Vet	20	6	4	10	45	54	22
West End Village Res.	20	6	2	12	36	53	20
Frogmore Rangers Res.	20	5	2	13	54	83	17
South Farnborough Res.	20	1	3	16	26	101	6

Lindford Reserves - record expunged.

AMATEUR COMBINATION

Premier	P	W	D	L	F	A	Pts
Old Meadonians	18	10	4	4	44	27	34
Bealonians	18	9	3	6	33	27	30
Old Parmiterians	18	8	3	7	28	25	27
Old Minchendenians	18	6	8	4	38	32	26
Hon. Artillery Co.	18	7	5	6	29	26	26
Parkfield	18	7	4	7	31	38	25
Old Hamptonians	18	7	2	9	32	33	23
Albanian	18	7	2	9	34	38	23
Old Suttonians	18	5	7	6	22	24	22
Old Belgravians	18	3	4	11	28	49	13

Senior One	P	W	D	L	F	A	Pts
UCL Academicals	18	12	2	4	42	17	38
Old Salvatorians	18	10	5	3	46	26	35
Old Uffingtonians	18	11	2	5	52	40	35
Old Aloysians	18	10	2	6	52	37	32
Hale End Athletic	18	5	6	7	39	42	21
Old Ignatians	18	4	9	5	33	37	21
Wood Green Old B.	18	6	3	9	36	59	21
Southgate County	18	5	4	9	33	42	19
Sinjuns Grammarians	18	6	0	12	38	50	18
Clapham Old Xavs	18	3	3	12	22	43	12

OTHER LEAGUES

Senior Two	P	W	D	L	F	A	Pts
Enfield Old Gramms	22	15	2	5	56	36	47
Economicals	22	14	3	5	50	27	45
Leyton County OB	22	12	2	8	53	37	38
Old Thorntonians	22	10	5	7	46	39	35
Pegasus	22	10	5	7	38	34	35
Shene Old Gramms	22	11	2	9	43	40	35
Hon. Artillery Co. Res.	22	9	3	10	44	39	30
O. Hamptonians Res.	22	7	5	10	34	48	26
Old Pauline	22	8	1	13	41	50	25
Bealonians Res.	22	6	6	10	38	49	24
Old Danes	22	6	1	15	40	66	19
Old Kolsassians	22	5	3	14	34	52	18

Senior Three North	P	W	D	L	F	A	Pts
Old Woodhouseians	18	13	2	3	60	21	41
UCL Academicals Res.	18	13	2	3	44	28	41
Latymer Old Boys	18	13	1	4	64	31	40
Globe Rangers	18	10	2	6	51	39	32
Old Parmiterians Res.	18	7	1	10	31	55	22
Albanian Reserves	18	6	3	9	44	44	21
Birkbeck College	18	6	3	9	41	52	21
Old Challoners (-3)	18	7	1	10	51	50	19
Old Vaughanians	18	5	3	10	50	49	18
Parkfield Reserves	18	1	0	17	13	80	3

William Fitt - record expunged.

Senior Three South	P	W	D	L	F	A	Pts
Dorkinians	18	15	2	1	50	23	47
Old Tenisonians	18	11	4	3	63	30	37
Old Bromleians (-3)	18	11	2	5	45	30	32
Chertsey Old Salesians	18	9	2	7	49	33	29
Fulham Compton Old B	18	7	4	7	40	39	25
Old Isleworthians	18	6	6	6	34	41	24
Old Meadonians Reserves	18	5	5	8	37	39	20
Clapham Old Xav's Res.	18	4	3	11	36	55	15
Old Hamptonians "A"	18	4	2	12	25	58	14
Old Sedcopians	18	3	0	15	28	59	9

Old Josephians - record expunged.

Intermediate North	P	W	D	L	F	A	Pts
Old Minchendenians Res.	14	9	2	3	43	29	29
Old Salvatorians Reserves	14	7	4	3	43	26	25
Enfield Old Gramm Res.	14	8	0	6	33	29	24
Old Tollingtonians	14	6	3	5	34	29	21
Old Aloysians Reserves	14	6	0	8	23	27	18
Lea Valley	14	5	2	7	32	40	17
UCL Academicals "A"	14	5	1	8	25	36	16
Hale End Athletic Res.	14	3	2	9	22	39	11

Old Edmontonians - record expunged.

William Fitt Reserves - record expunged.

Intermediate West	P	W	D	L	F	A	Pts
Old Salvatorians "A"	18	13	1	4	52	27	40
Old Manorians	18	13	1	4	51	30	40
Old Magdalenians	18	12	2	4	49	24	38
Old Vaughanians Res.	18	9	2	7	56	42	29
Brent	18	9	1	8	49	31	28
Old Danes Reserves	18	9	0	9	49	50	27
Old Meadonians "B"	18	8	2	8	37	34	26
Fitzwilliam Old Boys	18	6	1	11	33	47	19
Birkbeck College Res.	18	6	0	12	38	60	18
Old Uffingtonians Res.	18	0	0	18	21	90	0

Intermediate South	P	W	D	L	F	A	Pts
Kings Old Boys	18	12	4	2	75	32	40
Old Meadonians "A"	18	8	4	6	33	39	28
Old Pauline Reserves	18	7	6	5	33	35	27
Old Suttonians Reserves	18	6	8	4	39	32	26
Old St Marys	18	8	2	8	42	41	26
Hampstead Heathens	18	6	6	6	30	26	24
Old Tiffinians	18	6	4	8	30	36	22
Royal Bank of Scotland	18	6	3	9	41	39	21
Old Guildfordians	18	5	5	8	27	38	20
Wandsworth Borough	18	4	2	12	31	63	14

Old Wokingians - record expunged.

Division One North	P	W	D	L	F	A	Pts
Mayfield Athletic	18	14	3	1	82	33	45
Albanian "A"	18	12	3	3	59	32	39
Old Buckwellians	18	11	2	5	55	35	35
Old Ignatians Reserves	18	9	6	3	41	33	33
Queen Mary College OB	18	7	3	8	42	38	24
Bealonians "A"	18	6	2	10	45	41	20
Univ. of Hertfordshire	18	6	0	12	36	53	18
Southgate County Res.	18	4	4	10	31	49	16
Old Aloysians "A"	18	3	5	10	21	53	14
Egbertian	18	2	4	12	23	68	10

Division One South	P	W	D	L	F	A	Pts
Economicals Reserves	18	14	0	4	59	22	42
Old Wokingians Reserves	18	12	2	4	45	28	38
Witan	18	10	2	6	46	35	32
Nat'l Westminster Bank	18	8	4	6	40	36	28
John Fisher Old Boys	18	8	3	7	49	45	27
Mickleham Old Boxhill's	18	8	2	8	40	44	26
Sinjuns Gramm's res (-1)	18	6	2	10	39	42	19
Glyn Old Boys Reserves	18	5	3	10	35	43	18
Clapham Old Xav "A"	18	5	3	10	29	53	18
City of London	18	2	3	13	30	64	9

Division Two North	P	W	D	L	F	A	Pts
Old Parmiterians "A"	18	17	1	0	57	22	52
Oakhill Tigers	18	10	4	4	60	35	34
Globe Rangers Reserves	18	10	2	6	62	34	32
Royal Brit Leg Loughton	18	9	3	6	45	40	30
Hale End Athletic "A"	18	7	3	8	31	31	24
Latymer Old Boys Res.	18	7	2	9	38	42	23
Mill Hill County Old B	18	6	4	8	39	40	22
Leyton County Old B Res.	18	6	2	10	39	36	20
Old Aloysians "B"	18	4	5	9	30	49	17
Egbertian Reserves	18	0	2	16	23	95	2

Division Two West	P	W	D	L	F	A	Pts
Old Manorians "A"	20	15	2	3	56	28	47
Old Magdalenians Res.	20	13	3	4	53	24	42
Cardinal Manning OldB	20	11	0	9	45	43	33
Parkfield "B"	20	10	2	8	41	37	32
Teddington	20	10	2	8	52	49	32
Phoenix Old Boys	20	8	6	6	38	35	30
Old Vaughan's "A" (-3)	20	10	2	8	51	41	29
Old Salvatorians "C"	20	9	2	9	42	41	29
Heathrow Seniors	20	6	1	13	43	52	19
Old Kingsburians Res.	20	4	2	14	37	57	14
Old Isleworth's "A" (-3)	20	2	2	16	28	79	5

Division Two South	P	W	D	L	F	A	Pts
Old Tenisonians Reserves	20	18	2	0	76	16	56
Dorkinians Reserves	20	14	2	4	61	30	44
Reigatians	20	13	3	4	74	36	42
Ryl Bank of Scotland Res.	20	10	5	5	57	38	35
Old Suttonians "A"	20	5	7	8	23	39	22
Economicals "A"	20	5	5	10	36	52	20
Old Meadonians "C"	20	3	7	10	43	69	16
Nat West Bank res (-11)	20	7	5	8	40	42	15
Sinjuns Grammar's "A"	20	2	8	10	36	57	14
Shene Old Gramma's Res.	20	2	8	10	25	49	14
Tilburg Regents	20	1	8	11	33	76	11

Division Three North	P	W	D	L	F	A	Pts
Albanian "B"	16	11	4	1	46	26	37
Old Parmiterians "B"	16	10	4	2	59	23	34
Wood Green Old B Res.	16	9	4	3	52	35	31
Old Edmontonians Res.	16	8	1	7	40	27	25
Enfield Old Gram's "A"	16	7	1	8	33	33	22
Egbertian "A" (-3)	16	6	3	7	24	38	18
Old Ignatians "A"	16	3	5	8	25	49	14
Queen Mary Col. OB Res.	16	2	4	10	26	47	10
Bealonians "B"	16	2	2	12	37	64	8

Old Aloysians "C" - record expunged.

Division Three West	P	W	D	L	F	A	Pts
Old Manorians "B"	20	15	2	3	101	35	47
Phoenix Old Boys Res.	20	13	5	2	72	30	44
Old Kolsassians Reserves	20	13	3	4	50	30	42
Somerville Old Boys	20	11	1	8	58	37	34
Hampstead Heathens Res.	20	8	3	9	49	47	27
Parkfield "C"	20	6	5	9	38	58	23
Old Uxonians	20	6	3	11	45	65	21
Old Uffingtonians "A"	20	5	5	10	44	58	20
Ealing Association	20	6	1	13	37	67	19
Brent Reserves	20	4	6	10	38	64	18
Old Vaughanians "B"	20	5	2	13	47	88	17

Division Three South	P	W	D	L	F	A	Pts
Old Bromleians Reserves	20	14	2	4	74	40	44
Citigroup	20	12	4	4	69	29	40
Old Whitgiftian	20	12	3	5	66	55	39
Standard Chartered Bank	20	9	7	4	65	46	34
Royal Sun Alliance	20	10	2	8	53	52	32
Reigatians Reserves	20	8	1	11	34	51	25
Cl'm Old Xaverians "B"	20	6	5	9	35	41	23
Old Crosbeians	20	6	5	9	35	44	23
Nat West Bank "A" (-4)	20	6	3	11	39	46	17
Glyn Old Boys "A"	20	4	5	11	38	56	17
Old Tenisonians "A"	20	4	1	15	25	73	13

Division Four North	P	W	D	L	F	A	Pts
Latymer Old Boys "A"	18	12	3	3	61	26	39
Old Minchendenians "A"	18	10	4	4	62	41	34
Leyton County OB "A"	18	9	3	6	42	30	30
Old Woodhouseians Res.	18	8	4	6	44	38	28
Wood Green Old B "A"	18	9	1	8	44	44	28
Old Buckwellians Res.	18	6	5	7	34	34	23
UCL Academicals "B"	18	4	7	7	41	42	19
London Hospital Old B	18	4	5	9	41	56	17
Hale End Athletic "B"	18	4	5	9	47	74	17
Bealonians "C"	18	3	5	10	30	61	14

Division Four West	P	W	D	L	F	A	Pts
Old Salvatorians "D"	12	7	3	2	30	15	24
Old Manorians "C"	12	8	0	4	38	24	24
London Welsh Reserves	12	7	2	3	44	18	23
Phoenix Old Boys "A"	12	5	1	6	31	28	16
Ealing Association Res.	12	4	2	6	25	36	14
Old Isleworthians "B"	12	4	0	8	27	63	12
Brent "A"	12	3	0	9	23	34	9

Old Challoners "A - record expunged.

Old Uffingtonians "A" - record expunged.

OTHER LEAGUES

Division Four South	P	W	D	L	F	A	Pts
Economicals "B"	18	14	1	3	52	16	43
Old Thorntonians Res.	18	13	1	4	67	33	40
Old Sedcopians Reserves	18	11	3	4	57	35	36
Old Wokingians "A"	18	8	2	8	36	40	26
Wandsworth Borough Res.	18	6	5	7	36	54	23
Old St Marys Reserves	18	6	4	8	30	37	22
Witan Reserves	18	6	2	10	39	36	20
Kings Old Boys Reserves	18	6	2	10	34	55	20
The Comets	18	3	7	8	25	40	16
Old Suttonians "B"	18	2	3	13	24	54	9

Temple Bar - record expunged.

Division Five North	P	W	D	L	F	A	Pts
Lea Valley Reserves	18	17	0	1	105	15	51
Old Parmiterians "C"	18	15	1	2	84	29	46
Ravenscroft Old Boys	18	10	3	5	70	40	33
Albanian "C"	18	11	0	7	66	40	33
Old Camdenians	18	5	3	10	39	69	18
Old Tollingtonians Res.	18	5	3	10	34	73	18
Egbertian "B"	18	5	2	11	36	76	17
Southgate County "A"	18	4	3	11	34	62	15
Goffs Old Boys	18	4	3	11	34	65	15
Old Buckwellians "A"	18	4	2	12	40	73	14

Division Five South	P	W	D	L	F	A	Pts
Old Grantonians	18	14	0	4	61	22	42
Glyn Old Boys "B"	18	11	4	3	57	33	37
City of London Reserves	18	11	0	7	37	37	33
Old Meadonians "D"	18	10	2	6	39	23	32
Fulham Compton OB Res.	18	7	2	9	36	38	23
Old Wokingians "B"	18	7	2	9	43	51	23
Old Tiffinians Reserves	18	6	2	10	37	52	20
Dorkinians "A"	18	6	1	11	42	48	19
Clapham Old Xav's "C"	18	5	3	10	25	48	18
Old Suttonians "C"	18	4	2	12	29	54	14

Division Six North	P	W	D	L	F	A	Pts
Old Minchendenians "B"	18	14	2	2	79	25	44
Old Parmiterians "D"	18	12	2	4	48	21	38
Oakhill Tigers Reserves	18	10	7	1	64	22	37
UCL Academicals "C"	18	10	1	7	54	35	31
Leyton County OB "B"	18	9	2	7	57	49	29
Old Edmontonians "A"	18	8	3	7	83	45	27
Old Woodhouseians "A"	18	6	3	9	38	55	21
Old Aloysians "D"	18	4	0	14	34	136	12
Mill Hill County OB Res.	18	3	1	14	33	65	10
Latymer Old Boys "B"	18	3	1	14	42	79	10

Division Six South	P	W	D	L	F	A	Pts
Old Suttonians "D"	18	15	1	2	69	25	46
Economicals "C"	18	13	3	2	72	21	42
Old Thorntonians "A"	18	12	3	3	58	40	39
Fulham Comp. OB "A"	18	10	3	5	38	38	33
John Fisher Old Boys Res.	18	9	3	6	55	44	30
Old Meadonians "E"	18	5	3	10	35	41	18
Reigatians "A"	18	3	5	10	34	46	14
Old Sedcopians "A"	18	4	2	12	22	47	14
Shene Old Gramm's "A"	18	2	6	10	30	59	12
Old Josephians Reserves	18	0	5	13	31	83	5

Division Seven North	P	W	D	L	F	A	Pts
Mayfield Athletic Res.	20	13	4	3	72	33	43
Old Parmiterians "E"	20	12	3	5	72	43	39
Ravenscroft Old B Res.	20	11	3	6	64	49	36
Old Edmontonians "B"	20	11	2	7	55	42	35
Enfield Old Gramms "B"	20	11	0	9	75	52	33
Old Ignatians "B"	20	9	4	7	82	68	31
Albanian "C"	20	9	2	9	49	63	29
Bealonians "D"	20	7	4	9	48	63	25
Q Mary College OB "A"	20	6	3	11	57	82	21
Wood Green Old B " B"	20	6	1	13	47	69	19
Davenant Wands OB (-6)	20	1	2	17	42	99	-1

Division Seven South	P	W	D	L	F	A	Pts
Old Bromleians "A"	20	15	1	4	73	29	46
Glyn Old Boys "C"	20	12	3	5	53	43	39
John Fisher Old B "A"	20	11	5	4	45	25	38
Old Pauline "A"	20	10	3	7	52	46	33
Fulham C OB "B" (-3)	20	10	4	6	50	34	31
Old Guildfordians Res.	20	8	3	9	36	32	27
Old Wokingians "C"	20	6	5	9	41	50	23
Old Tenisonians "B" (-3)	20	7	3	10	35	45	21
Old Sedcopians "B"	20	4	6	10	42	53	18
Reigatians "B"	20	4	5	11	29	55	17
Old Suttonians "E"	20	1	6	13	26	70	9

Division Eight North	P	W	D	L	F	A	Pts
Lea Valley "A"	20	16	2	2	90	25	50
Old Camdenians Reserves	20	13	3	4	66	40	42
UCL Academicals "D"	20	12	2	6	60	38	38
Old Parmiterians "F"	20	9	3	8	32	39	30
Old Woodhouseians "B"	20	9	2	9	55	51	29
Mill Hill Village	20	9	2	9	54	53	29
Southgate County "B"	20	8	4	8	49	49	28
Leyton County OB "C"	20	7	0	13	37	48	21
Latymer Old Boys "C"	20	5	5	10	32	64	20
Old Kingsburians "A"	20	4	4	12	29	54	16
Old Ignatians "C"	20	3	3	14	29	72	12

Division Eight South	P	W	D	L	F	A	Pts
Fulh. Compton OB "C"	20	15	2	3	70	36	47
John Fisher Old B "B"	20	14	3	3	79	48	45
Old Guildfordians "A"	20	11	6	3	59	28	39
Glyn Old Boys "D"	20	11	2	7	56	38	35
Old Tiffinians "A"	20	10	1	9	48	44	31
Old Whitgiftian Reserves	20	9	2	9	59	52	29
Old Wokingians "D"	20	5	6	9	36	50	21
City of London "A	20	6	0	14	28	55	18
Old Bromleians "B"	20	5	2	13	33	48	17
Clapham Old Xav's "D"	20	5	2	13	32	70	17
Mickleham Old Box. Res.	20	4	4	12	35	66	16

Division Nine North	P	W	D	L	F	A	Pts
Ravenscroft Old B "A"	18	15	1	2	74	26	46
Mill Hill Village Reserves	18	12	1	5	63	37	37
Old Edmontonians "C"	18	11	3	4	74	43	36
Old Kingsburians "B"	18	10	1	7	53	39	31
Old Parmiterians "G"	18	10	0	8	42	50	30
Enfield Old Gramms "C"	18	7	3	8	33	46	24
Old Minchendenians "C"	18	6	2	10	56	73	20
Mayfield Athletic "A"	18	6	1	11	36	47	19
Goffs Old Boys Reserves	18	3	2	13	43	76	11
Bealonians "E"	18	2	2	14	30	67	8

Division Nine South	P	W	D	L	F	A	Pts
Old St Marys "A"	20	14	3	3	63	29	45
Old Suttonians "F"	20	14	1	5	58	29	43
Wandsworth Boro "A"	20	12	3	5	49	33	39
Old Wokingians "E"	20	9	6	5	53	44	33
Old Guildfordians "B"	20	8	5	7	48	43	29
Dorkinians "B"	20	8	4	8	49	51	28
Shene Old Gram "B" (-1)	20	9	0	11	49	64	26
Reigatians "C"	20	7	3	10	49	51	24
Old Sedcopians "C"	20	6	2	12	40	57	20
Sinjuns Gramms "B"	20	5	1	14	32	59	16
Old Pauline "B"	20	3	2	15	29	59	11

Division Ten South	Pld	W	D	L	F	A	Pts
Old Thorntonians "B"	20	14	4	2	73	31	46
Wandsworth Boro "B"	20	12	4	4	62	38	40
Old Grantonians Reserves	20	10	6	4	64	33	36
Old Suttonians "G"	20	10	2	8	45	44	32
Reigatians "D"	20	9	4	7	50	35	31
Old St Marys "B"	20	8	6	6	58	43	30
Old Guildfordians "C"	20	8	3	9	39	50	27
Old Meadonians "F" (-3)	20	8	2	10	44	49	23
Tilburg Regents Reserves	20	7	1	12	23	48	22
Old Wokingians "F"	20	5	1	14	26	65	16
Old Sedcopians "D"	20	1	3	16	20	68	6

ANDOVER & DISTRICT LEAGUE

	P	W	D	L	F	A	Pts
ABC United -3	20	18	1	1	106	24	52
Wolversdene Sports	20	16	1	3	83	18	49
AFC Andover	20	13	2	5	107	31	41
Downton Sports	20	12	1	7	69	45	37
Whitchurch United A	20	11	3	6	44	27	36
Sutton Scotney	20	10	2	8	68	41	32
King's Somborne	20	8	5	7	56	33	29
Test Valley Lions	20	4	2	14	23	123	14
Hayward Gunners	20	4	0	16	25	82	12
Sparten	20	3	2	15	26	95	11
Wykeham Warr. Gerri.	20	1	1	18	18	106	4

AFC Star, Inkpen Sports, Southampton Arms Sports - records expunged.

ARTHURIAN ALLIANCE

Premier	P	W	D	L	F	A	Pts
Old Carthusians	18	15	2	1	67	16	47
Old Etonians	18	10	4	4	32	22	34
Lancing Old Boys	18	8	6	4	39	23	30
Old Harrovians	18	9	3	6	44	40	30
Old Foresters	18	8	5	5	33	33	29
Old Brentwoods -6	18	9	2	7	36	27	23
Old Chigwellians	18	5	4	9	26	34	19
Old Cholmeleians	18	4	3	11	18	41	15
Old King's (Wimbledon)	18	4	2	12	24	46	14
Old Salopians	18	1	3	14	25	62	6

Division One	P	W	D	L	F	A	Pts
Old Haileyburians	16	10	2	4	44	26	32
Old Wykehamists	16	9	3	4	39	26	30
Old Malvernians	16	7	6	3	44	35	27
Old Aldenhamians -6	16	8	6	2	36	23	24
Old Radleians	16	7	2	7	42	40	23
Old Westminsters	16	6	3	7	41	34	21
Old Tonbridgians	16	5	4	7	35	35	19
Old King's Scholars	16	3	3	10	24	51	12
Old Reptonians	16	1	3	12	25	60	6

Division Two	P	W	D	L	F	A	Pts
Old Carthusians Res.	16	8	6	2	34	18	30
Old Carthusians A	16	8	5	3	38	25	29
Old Bradfieldians	16	9	2	5	35	27	29
Old Chigwellians Res.	16	7	3	6	25	25	24
Old Foresters Res.	16	6	4	6	32	35	22
Old Oundelians	16	6	2	8	38	43	20
Old Haberdashers	16	5	3	8	33	37	18
Old Etonians Res.	16	5	2	9	24	36	17
Old Brentwoods Res.	16	4	1	11	16	29	13

Division Three	P	W	D	L	F	A	Pts
Old Wellingtonians	16	10	2	4	47	26	32
Lancing Old B. Res.	16	10	2	4	31	22	32
Old Harrovians Res.	16	8	2	6	37	28	26
Old Salopians Res.	16	7	2	7	32	35	23
Old Aldenh's Res -3	16	7	3	6	33	37	21
Old Amplefordians	16	6	2	8	38	35	20
Old Westminsters Res.	16	5	5	6	26	43	20
Old Brentwoods A	16	4	2	10	17	23	14
Old Eastbournians	16	3	4	9	26	38	13

Division Four	P	W	D	L	F	A	Pts
Old Cholmelians A	14	10	2	2	50	27	32
Old King's (Wim.) Res.	14	6	4	4	32	24	22
Old Marlburians	14	6	4	4	29	23	22
Old Chigwellians A	14	6	3	5	28	26	21
Old Cholmeleians Res.	14	6	1	7	25	27	19
Old Foresters A	14	5	1	8	24	35	16
Old Berkhamstedians	14	4	3	7	23	34	15
Old Foresters B	14	3	2	9	20	35	11

OTHER LEAGUES

Division Five	P	W	D	L	F	A	Pts
Old Epsomians	14	9	4	1	57	29	31
Old Wykehamists Res.	14	9	2	3	39	22	29
Old Malvernians Res.	14	7	3	4	45	21	24
Old Citizens	14	7	1	6	39	52	22
Old Harrovians A	14	6	2	6	31	37	20
Old Chigwellians B	14	3	3	8	20	28	12
Old Brentwoods B	14	3	2	9	25	41	11
Old Cholmeleio B	14	3	1	10	27	53	10

AYLESBURY & DISTRICT LEAGUE

Premier	P	W	D	L	F	A	Pts
Bierton	22	18	1	3	72	26	55
Thame Town	22	17	3	2	72	23	54
Walton Court Wdrs	22	14	4	4	78	44	46
Aylesbury Dynamos	22	11	0	11	59	60	33
P & IC United	22	10	2	10	62	49	32
Aston Park	22	9	3	10	55	60	30
Downley Albion	22	8	5	9	48	48	29
Berkhamsted Sports	22	7	4	11	45	53	25
Elmhurst	22	7	2	13	57	53	23
St Johns	22	7	0	15	35	61	21
Wendover	22	6	0	16	38	104	18
Aston Clinton Res.	22	4	4	14	30	70	16

Division One	P	W	D	L	F	A	Pts
Bedgrove United	20	18	2	0	67	9	56
Bucks CC	20	13	4	3	70	41	43
Britannia	20	12	2	6	89	34	38
Bedgrove Dynamos	20	10	2	8	44	44	32
FC Spandits	20	8	2	10	48	54	26
Wingrave	20	7	3	10	33	49	24
Haddenham United	20	6	5	9	40	45	23
Long Marston	20	6	3	11	36	57	21
Bierton Res.	20	6	1	13	34	60	19
Quarrendon Royals	20	5	4	11	26	72	19
P & IC United Res.	20	5	0	15	27	49	15

Division Two	P	W	D	L	F	A	Pts
FC Bedgrove	28	22	3	3	92	44	69
Thame Town Res.	28	21	4	3	116	41	67
Cheddington	28	18	5	5	76	37	59
Haydon United	28	16	8	4	80	38	56
Mandeville	28	16	3	9	73	54	51
Long Marston Res.	28	14	3	11	64	63	45
Ludgershall	28	13	4	11	70	62	43
Fairford Leys	28	11	8	9	53	46	41
Great Milton	28	12	0	16	65	79	36
Aston Clinton A.	28	9	6	13	42	55	33
Keltic Colts	28	10	2	16	53	68	32
St Johns Res.	28	6	4	18	31	83	22
Quainton	28	5	4	19	36	89	19
Wendover Res.	28	3	4	21	44	78	13
Brill United	28	2	6	20	26	84	12

BANBURY & LORD JERSEY FA

Premier Division	P	W	D	L	F	A	Pts
Sinclair United	20	16	1	3	49	18	49
Bodicote Sports	20	11	4	5	62	27	37
Woodford United "A"	20	10	7	3	60	39	37
Bishops Itchington	20	11	3	6	67	40	36
Deddington Town	20	10	1	9	44	32	31
Highfield Old Boys	20	9	3	8	69	53	30
KEA	20	9	2	9	42	46	29
Steeple Aston	20	7	4	9	37	53	25
Cropredy	20	6	2	12	52	62	20
The Bell Sports	20	4	3	13	43	94	15
Hornton	20	1	2	17	17	78	5

Division One	P	W	D	L	F	A	Pts
Heyford Athletic	20	15	3	2	75	21	48
Bardwell	20	11	5	4	62	42	38
Sporting Hethe	20	12	2	6	53	44	38
FC Naranja	20	10	4	6	42	30	34
Glory Farm	20	9	4	7	34	36	31
Kings Sutton	20	10	1	9	44	49	31
Bloxham	20	8	1	11	42	48	25
Oxon Shamrock	20	6	3	11	42	37	21
Heyford United	20	6	1	13	47	57	19
Hardwick Old Boys	20	6	0	14	38	80	18
Bishops Itchington Res.	20	4	2	14	32	67	14

Division Two	P	W	D	L	F	A	Pts
Abba Athletic	20	17	1	2	91	35	52
Priors United	20	14	2	4	88	39	44
Sinclair United Reserves	20	14	2	4	51	25	44
Pepperpot United	20	12	3	5	67	50	39
Middleton Cheney	20	9	5	6	53	42	32
Wroxton Sports	20	7	3	10	42	60	24
Kings Sutton Reserves	20	7	1	12	34	67	22
FC Langford	20	6	1	13	45	55	19
Deddington Town Res.	20	5	3	12	38	52	18
Swis	20	4	3	13	29	64	15
Paragon United	20	3	0	17	37	86	9

Division Three	P	W	D	L	F	A	Pts
Fenny Compton	22	20	2	0	113	16	62
Highfield Old Boys Res.	22	15	2	5	71	52	47
The Bell Sports Reserves	22	15	1	6	78	49	46
Bodicote Sports Reserves	22	13	2	7	71	45	41
Banbury Town	22	11	2	9	70	61	35
Heyford Athletic Res.	22	9	4	9	56	49	31
Souldern	22	8	2	12	40	54	26
Merton	22	7	3	12	48	87	24
Finmere	22	7	1	14	46	54	22
Banbury Galaxy	22	5	2	15	39	85	17
Steeple Aston Reserves	22	5	2	15	30	76	17
KEA Reserves	22	5	1	16	29	63	16

BASINGSTOKE & DISTRICT LEAGUE

Premier Division	P	W	D	L	F	A	Pts
R & B Sports	20	16	1	3	56	17	49
FC CenSo	20	11	5	4	42	22	38
Welly Old Boys	20	11	5	4	45	30	38
Tadley Calleva Reserves	20	12	2	6	42	43	38
Hook	20	11	4	5	45	28	37
Headley Athletic	20	10	1	9	42	52	31
Bramley United	20	7	2	11	32	46	23
Kingsclere	20	7	1	12	37	45	22
Silchester United	20	5	3	12	36	46	18
AXA Winterthur	20	3	3	14	29	52	12
Sherfield	20	3	1	16	34	59	10

Oakley Sports - record expunged.

Division One	P	W	D	L	F	A	Pts
Basingstoke Rangers	16	13	1	2	64	30	40
Sherborne St.John	16	11	1	4	47	19	34
Old Basing	16	10	3	3	43	30	33
Tron	16	9	2	5	36	25	29
Welly Old Boys Reserves	16	6	2	8	29	38	20
Bounty United	16	5	2	9	32	46	17
Baughurst	16	4	1	11	18	39	13
FC Burghclere	16	3	2	11	39	48	11
AFC Berg	16	3	2	11	27	60	11

Pure Lounge Bar - record expunged.

Division Two	P	W	D	L	F	A	Pts
Heathpark	20	16	3	1	71	27	51
Chineham Albion	20	15	1	4	69	31	46
Headley Athletic Reserves	20	12	0	8	46	39	36
Herriard Sports	20	10	2	8	51	39	32
AFC Aldermaston "A"	20	10	1	9	49	50	31
Kingsclere Reserves	20	9	2	9	69	51	29
Platforms	20	8	2	10	58	61	26
Basingstoke Labour Club	20	8	0	12	44	65	24
Sherborne St John Reserves	20	7	1	12	38	47	22
Tron Reserves	20	4	2	14	29	64	14
Overton United "A"	20	2	4	14	29	79	10

AFC Berg Reserves - record expunged.

Sherfield Reserves - record expunged.

BATH & DISTRICT LEAGUE

Division One	P	W	D	L	F	A	Pts
Odd Down A	14	10	1	3	37	23	31
Trowbridge House	14	9	4	1	28	18	31
AFC Durbin United	14	5	6	3	27	24	21
University of Bath	14	5	3	6	30	26	18
Bath Arsenal	14	5	3	6	24	28	18
Saltford Res.	14	5	3	6	23	28	18
Great Western	14	4	3	7	27	27	15
Fry Club Old Boys	14	0	3	11	15	37	3

BECKETT LEAGUE

Division One	P	W	D	L	F	A	Pts
Kirkbymoorside Reserves	20	18	2	0	80	8	56
Gillamoor	20	12	4	4	54	35	40
Sinnington	20	10	5	5	43	34	35
Bagby & Balk	20	11	1	8	45	34	34
Thornton Dale	20	11	1	8	39	30	34
Union Rovers	20	10	0	10	41	46	30
Rosedale	20	8	3	9	37	35	27
Kirkdale United	20	7	1	12	32	44	22
Pro Pak	20	7	1	12	29	41	22
Slingsby	20	5	0	15	24	73	15
Aislaby United	20	2	0	18	19	63	6

Old Malton St Mary's "A" - record expunged.

BIRKENHEAD & WIRRAL LEAGUE

Division One	P	W	D	L	F	A	Pts
Birkenhead	18	16	0	2	90	38	32
McGinty's	18	15	0	3	77	30	30
Fender	18	10	1	7	58	54	21
Myrtle	17	8	1	8	44	51	17
Claughton Hotel	17	7	1	9	42	43	15
Queens Arms	18	4	1	13	31	60	9
Bird FC	18	0	0	18	24	90	0

(one match unplayed)

Division Two	P	W	D	L	F	A	Pts
Bromborough Rake	18	16	2	0	76	22	34
AFC Stadium	18	13	2	3	57	32	28
Ridgewood Rangers	18	7	3	8	33	37	17
Parkfield BA	18	7	2	9	40	54	16
FC Wirral	18	6	1	11	35	43	13
Bronze Social Res.	18	3	3	12	32	56	9
Neston Legion	18	3	3	12	30	59	9

Greenbank - record expunged.

BIRMINGHAM AFA

Premier	P	W	D	L	F	A	Pts
Sutton United	26	20	4	2	59	20	64
Village	26	16	4	6	59	29	52
Shirley Athletic	26	15	4	7	62	39	49
St Francis	26	13	7	6	58	33	46
Handsworth GSOB	26	14	3	9	57	51	45
Inter Vaughans	26	12	3	11	52	50	39
Wake Green Amats	26	11	4	11	43	38	37
Boldmere Spts/Soc.	26	9	7	10	38	41	34
Old Wulfrunians	26	9	4	13	44	50	31
AFC Somers	26	9	2	15	37	55	29
Silhill	26	6	7	13	29	44	25
Harborne Town	26	5	8	13	34	63	23
Walsall Phoenix	26	6	4	16	38	64	22
Flamengo	26	6	1	19	34	67	19

Division One	P	W	D	L	F	A	Pts
St Georges Warriors	22	17	3	2	64	25	54
Cresconians	22	16	5	1	73	27	53
Sutton United	22	15	4	3	54	30	49
St Pauls	22	11	2	9	57	45	35
Village	22	11	1	10	43	40	34
Crusaders	22	10	2	10	45	63	32
Athletic Sparkhill	22	9	4	9	52	49	31
Handsworth GSOB Res.	22	10	0	12	44	42	30
CPA Holy Name -3	22	8	1	13	53	63	22
Parkfield Amateurs	22	5	3	14	34	51	18
Old Wulfrunians Res.	22	3	2	17	34	72	11
Wake Green A. Res.	22	2	3	17	18	64	9

Ajax CV JKS, Balsallona - record expunged.

OTHER LEAGUES

Division Two	P	W	D	L	F	A	Pts
St Georges War. Res.	24	15	7	2	58	25	52
Desi	24	16	2	6	73	44	50
Shirley Athletic Res.	24	15	4	5	70	35	49
Shere Punjab	24	14	6	4	63	32	48
West Hagley	24	13	3	8	66	47	42
Village A	24	10	4	10	47	47	34
Malremo Rangers	24	9	5	10	53	45	32
AFC Hayes Harriers	24	9	4	11	51	48	31
Britannia Old Boys	24	8	4	12	58	77	28
Sutton United A -3	24	9	3	12	37	48	27
Bearwood Athletic	24	8	2	14	62	74	26
Silhill Res.	24	3	6	15	37	82	15
Great Barr	24	1	2	21	17	88	5

Erdington Albion - record expunged.

Division Three	P	W	D	L	F	A	Pts
Woodbourne Sports	24	20	2	2	85	27	62
Old Hill	24	17	2	5	66	28	53
Smithswood Colts	24	14	3	7	51	42	45
Easy Reds -3	24	15	2	7	68	47	44
Silhill A	24	13	4	7	71	44	43
Cresconians Res.	24	13	2	9	63	58	41
JE Yardley	24	9	4	11	55	47	31
Wednesbury Athletic	24	7	3	14	33	64	24
Wake Green Amats A	24	7	2	15	40	60	23
Walsall Phoenix Res.	24	6	3	15	39	50	21
Urban Athletic	24	5	6	13	39	71	21
Northfield Village	24	4	6	14	39	66	18
BTFC	24	5	3	16	32	77	18

Division Four	P	W	D	L	F	A	Pts
Aston Res.	18	13	5	0	66	27	44
Handsworth United	18	14	0	4	63	29	42
Bentley Heath United	18	11	3	4	40	23	36
AG Wythall	18	8	2	8	53	50	26
Pathfinder	18	7	3	8	39	45	24
Village B	18	7	3	8	31	40	24
Meriden Athletic	18	7	2	9	34	54	23
Sportsco	18	3	6	9	22	35	15
Old Wulfrunians A	18	4	2	12	35	52	14
Wood Wanderers	18	1	4	13	20	48	7

Birch Coppice Bullets, Crusaders Res., Sheldon Royal Seniors - record expunged.

Division Five	P	W	D	L	F	A	Pts
Castle Vale United	24	17	2	5	119	48	53
St Georges Warr. A	24	16	4	4	84	48	52
Aston A	24	14	5	5	76	47	47
Dosthill Cosmopolis	24	14	4	6	71	37	46
Shirley Athletic A	24	12	5	7	74	64	41
Boldmere S & S Res.	24	11	5	8	47	36	38
Cosmopolitans	24	10	4	10	54	59	34
Parkfield Amats Res.	24	10	4	10	53	72	34
Bourneville Colts	24	7	4	13	50	59	25
Silhill B	24	8	0	16	51	96	24
Sutton United B	24	7	2	15	58	81	23
Coton Green A	24	4	3	17	40	75	15
Birmingham Citadel	24	2	6	16	36	91	12

Division Six	P	W	D	L	F	A	Pts
White Hart CCCs	22	16	3	3	84	25	51
Premier FC 2008	22	13	7	2	41	18	46
Real Riverside	22	13	5	4	51	30	44
Old Wulfrunians B	22	14	1	7	70	42	43
Wake Green Ams B	22	13	2	7	56	42	41
Dosthill Colts A	22	9	4	9	53	51	31
Sutton United C	22	7	7	8	45	45	28
Desi Res.	22	8	2	12	47	51	26
Harborne Athletic	22	7	3	12	33	41	24
Village C	22	7	2	13	32	53	23
Walsall Phoenix A	22	3	4	15	22	71	13
Handsworth GSOB A	22	1	2	19	26	91	5

Division Seven	P	W	D	L	F	A	Pts
Quinton Dynamos	26	19	5	2	97	40	62
Coldlands	26	18	4	4	79	30	58
Maypole	26	18	3	5	100	37	57
St Georges Warr. B	26	18	1	7	90	40	55
Sporting Aztecs	26	17	3	6	74	28	54
Kingshurst -3	26	13	2	11	94	61	38
Edgbaston Untied	26	11	1	14	52	74	34
AFC Hayes H. Res.	26	9	5	12	57	70	32
Coldfield Rangers	26	8	7	11	51	56	31
Premier FC 2008 Res.	26	8	2	16	58	65	26
Maple Leaf Rovers	26	5	6	15	29	95	21
Selly Oak Legend	26	6	2	18	37	88	20
Manchester Warriors	26	4	7	15	38	92	19
Handsworth GSOB B	26	2	4	20	25	105	10

Division Eight	P	W	D	L	F	A	Pts
Amanah -3	24	19	2	3	91	31	56
Olympia 808	24	17	3	4	87	49	54
Garden House Rgrs	24	16	1	7	85	46	49
Dosthill Boys Club	24	13	5	6	76	51	44
Dosthill Cos. Res.	24	12	5	7	66	51	41
Mahal Warriors -6	24	11	4	9	68	54	31
Real Birmingham -3	24	10	3	11	68	68	30
Village D	24	8	4	12	60	80	28
Sutton United D -3	24	9	2	13	56	59	26
Red Star Galaxy	24	7	5	12	64	70	26
Wake Green Ams C	24	6	3	15	46	80	21
Real Riverside Res.	24	5	4	15	50	75	19
Steelhouse Lane	24	2	1	21	33	136	7

Bournville Colts Res. - record expunged.

BISHOP'S STORTFORD, STANSTED & DISTRICT LEAGUE

Premier	P	W	D	L	F	A	Pts
North Weald	21	17	2	2	48	20	36
Alemite Athletic	21	16	1	4	69	26	33
Old Street	21	13	3	5	65	36	29
Heath Rovers	21	13	0	8	51	30	26
Sheering	21	8	2	11	33	44	18
Avondale Rangers	21	4	5	12	28	46	13
Birchanger	21	3	2	16	24	52	8
Hatfield Heath	21	2	1	18	18	82	5

Division One	P	W	D	L	F	A	Pts
Alemite Athletic Reserves	21	16	3	2	62	24	35
North Weald Reserves	21	10	3	8	46	50	23
Albury	21	9	4	8	45	45	22
Hertfordshire Rangers	21	9	3	9	49	45	21
Hatfield Heath Reserves	21	9	3	9	47	49	21
Frontiers	21	9	2	10	60	53	20
Thorley Park	21	5	4	12	34	46	14
Sheering Reserves	21	5	2	14	31	62	12

Pelly House - record expunged.

Division Two	P	W	D	L	F	A	Pts
Langley Rangers	21	17	0	4	79	33	34
Heath Rovers Reserves	21	13	3	5	57	31	29
Avondale Rangers Reserves	21	11	2	8	62	49	24
Potter Street	21	10	4	7	50	48	24
Dunmow Rhodes	21	9	2	10	63	62	20
Lower Street	21	7	4	10	47	57	18
Thaxted Rangers Reserves	21	7	3	11	43	46	17
Frontiers Reserves	21	1	0	20	25	100	2

BLACKBURN & DISTRICT COMBINATION

Premier	P	W	D	L	F	A	Pts
Knuzden	24	16	5	3	74	29	53
The Ivy Hotel	24	15	5	4	69	33	50
Blackburn United	24	15	3	6	56	41	48
Mill Hill Hotel	24	11	5	8	67	60	38
Bank Top	24	10	4	10	47	57	34
Blue Star	24	8	3	13	68	75	27
The Manxman	24	7	2	15	65	83	23
Rishton United	24	6	4	14	49	74	22
Blackburn Olympic	24	4	1	19	46	89	13

Division Two	P	W	D	L	F	A	Pts
Islington	24	16	4	4	67	38	52
Feildens Arms	24	13	6	5	61	43	45
Clifton	24	11	8	5	69	46	41
Blackburn Utd Res.	24	11	6	7	57	40	39
Fallons Ales	24	9	7	8	50	36	34
Hindle Arms	24	10	4	10	48	55	34
Fenis. & Pleas. Res.	24	8	4	12	62	63	28
Rishton United Res.	24	7	2	15	54	65	23
Worth Avenue	24	2	1	21	28	110	7

Division Three	P	W	D	L	F	A	Pts
Langho A	27	16	5	6	79	52	53
The Lion	27	14	6	7	64	53	48
Rhoden Inn	27	13	5	9	70	50	44
Hole I'The Wall	27	13	5	9	65	70	44
Whalley Range	27	12	7	8	87	66	43
Navigation	27	10	6	11	58	68	36
Knowles Arms	27	9	5	13	53	54	32
Vauxhall Inn	27	9	5	13	58	63	32
Rishton United A	27	10	1	16	46	69	31
Pendle Youth	27	6	1	20	33	68	19

BOSTON & DISTRICT LEAGUE

Premier	P	W	D	L	F	A	Pts
Wyberton	22	16	4	2	62	23	52
Pointon	22	14	4	4	58	39	46
Old Leake	22	13	4	5	52	35	43
Spilsby Town	22	12	4	6	51	27	40
Kirton Town	22	11	3	8	52	37	36
Freiston (+3)	22	10	3	9	55	58	36
Skegness Town res (+5)	22	9	3	10	44	42	35
Old Doningtonians	22	8	2	12	54	57	26
Billinghay Athletic (-6)	22	10	1	11	44	48	25
Woodhall Spa United	22	5	2	15	38	57	17
Swineshead Inst. res (-1)	22	4	2	16	21	63	13
Coningsby (-1)	22	1	6	15	31	76	8

Division One	P	W	D	L	F	A	Pts
Tavern Colts	20	13	4	3	84	33	43
Boston Town Old Boys	20	12	4	4	51	25	40
Fishtoft	20	11	4	5	52	37	37
Spalding Harriers	20	11	3	6	52	33	36
Wainfleet United	20	10	3	7	55	39	33
Sutterton	20	9	0	11	50	57	27
Spalding Town	20	7	4	9	54	50	25
Wyberton Reserves	20	8	1	11	38	63	25
Billinghay Athletic Res.	20	5	3	12	38	64	18
Holbeach Bank	20	4	4	12	36	74	16
Westside Rangers	20	3	4	13	31	66	13

Division Two	P	W	D	L	F	A	Pts
Benington (-3)	22	19	1	2	84	27	55
Boston Utd Community	22	17	2	3	96	36	53
Mareham United	22	14	5	3	59	32	47
Tydd St Mary	22	10	4	8	66	46	34
Fishtoft Reserves (+3)	22	8	3	11	43	54	30
Kirton Leisure	22	10	0	12	55	71	30
Fosdyke	22	7	7	8	41	41	28
Coningsby Reserves	22	8	3	11	43	56	27
Pointon Reserves	22	7	5	10	43	54	26
Spalding Town res (-3)	22	6	3	13	44	80	18
Skegness Town "A"	22	4	4	14	48	71	16
Friskney	22	3	1	18	22	76	10

Division Three	P	W	D	L	F	A	Pts
Mareham United Res.	18	14	2	2	81	33	44
Freiston Reserves	18	12	4	2	73	36	40
F.C. Kirton	17	11	3	3	58	33	36
Park United	18	11	1	6	49	35	34
Spalding Harriers Res.	17	8	3	6	43	32	27
Kirton Town Reserves	18	7	4	7	47	49	25
Woodhall Spa United Res.	18	7	0	11	35	48	21
Old Doningtonians Res.	18	4	3	11	37	67	15
Holbeach Bank Reserves	18	2	2	14	29	72	8
F.C. Hammers	18	2	0	16	20	67	6

Spalding Harriers Reserves v FC Kirton was declared void and was not replayed.

BOURNEMOUTH LEAGUE

Premier	P	W	D	L	F	A	Pts
Westover Bournemouth	20	14	5	1	51	16	47
Bournemouth Electric	20	15	2	3	52	25	47
Bournemouth Sports	20	10	5	5	42	24	35
Portcastrian	20	9	3	8	50	38	30
Old Oakmeadians	20	9	3	8	40	34	30
Trinidad	20	9	1	10	30	45	28
Redlynch & Woodfalls	20	8	2	10	34	35	26
Parley Sports Res.	20	8	2	10	24	35	26
Sway -1	20	5	3	12	25	41	17
Hamworthy Rec. Res.	20	5	2	13	33	51	17
Mudeford Mens Club	20	3	2	15	22	59	11

Suttoners Civil - record expunged.

OTHER LEAGUES

Division One	P	W	D	L	F	A	Pts
B'mouth Electric Res.	22	16	4	2	80	39	52
Allendale	22	13	2	7	71	39	41
Holt United Res.	22	12	3	7	47	42	39
Twynham Rangers	22	11	4	7	49	47	37
Tuakana	22	11	2	9	57	38	35
Harrington United	22	10	2	10	49	50	32
Fern. T. Greenfields	22	9	5	8	37	42	32
Alderholt	22	8	7	7	46	45	31
Verwood Town Res.	22	6	6	10	50	53	24
Bournemouth Res.	22	7	2	13	44	58	23
St Marys	22	5	3	14	29	62	18
Fencing Centre	22	3	2	17	24	68	11

Division Two	P	W	D	L	F	A	Pts
Bisterne United	20	13	3	4	53	21	42
Ferndown Sports	20	12	4	4	54	39	40
Galleon	20	10	3	7	40	26	33
Mploy	20	8	5	7	49	41	29
Sway Res.	20	8	4	8	41	40	28
Westover B'mth Res.	20	7	4	9	36	39	25
New Milton Linnets	20	7	4	9	39	46	25
Seyward Windows	20	7	4	9	39	47	25
Merley Cobham Res.	20	7	4	9	33	48	25
Fordingbridge Turks	20	5	4	11	37	53	19
Redhill Rangers	20	5	3	12	40	61	18

Suttoners Civil Res. - record expunged.

Division Three	P	W	D	L	F	A	Pts
Richmond Pk Cons	22	19	2	1	108	21	59
S Coast Demolition -3	22	15	3	4	89	33	45
Queens Park Athletic	22	13	4	5	74	48	43
Parkside Wanderers	22	13	3	6	76	47	42
Parley Sports A -3	22	11	1	10	49	50	31
AFC Burton	22	8	5	9	51	64	29
Stourvale	22	7	3	12	41	55	24
Wallisdown Con	22	7	3	12	42	71	24
Seabournes	22	5	5	12	24	63	20
O Oakm ians Res -6	22	8	1	13	41	63	19
Red. & Woodfalls Res.	22	4	4	14	33	70	16
Ferndown Sports Res.	22	3	4	15	24	67	13

Bournemouth Town - record expunged.

Division Four	P	W	D	L	F	A	Pts
Bournemth Electric A	20	15	3	2	52	18	48
FC Athletico	20	12	3	5	62	37	39
Bisterne Rangers	20	13	0	7	48	32	39
AFC Pennington	20	9	6	5	48	35	33
New Milton Eagles	20	8	6	6	53	50	30
BU Staff	20	8	5	7	34	37	29
Fifa Standards	20	7	2	11	33	41	23
Magpies	20	7	2	11	37	62	23
AFC Highcliffe	20	6	2	12	41	48	20
Burley	20	4	3	13	25	55	15
Albany Athletic	20	3	4	13	33	51	13

Branksome Celtic - record expunged.

Division Five	P	W	D	L	F	A	Pts
Mudeford Mens Res.	22	19	2	1	90	23	59
Walker Scott	22	16	4	2	52	25	52
Red. & Woodfalls U A	22	15	1	6	75	36	46
Twynham Rgrs Res.	22	14	2	6	66	27	44
Screw It Carpentry	22	11	4	7	64	43	37
Allendale Res.	22	10	1	11	52	54	31
Bournemouth A	22	8	3	11	48	51	27
Shamrock	22	7	4	11	46	61	25
Rockbourne	22	6	4	12	25	55	22
Hurn Jets	22	5	4	13	34	67	19
Bransgore United	22	4	4	14	48	76	16
Fernheath CFC	22	0	1	21	14	96	1

Branksome Celtic Res. - record expunged.

Division Six	P	W	D	L	F	A	Pts
Queens Pk Ath Res.	24	21	3	0	140	17	66
AFC Bransgore	24	21	2	1	117	22	65
Alderholt Res.	24	14	2	8	57	43	44
Ferndown TG Res.	24	12	2	10	59	49	38
B'rnemouth Hospital	24	11	3	10	51	52	36
Townsend Spartans	24	9	7	8	61	52	34
Portcastrian Res.	24	10	3	11	52	61	33
Lymington Argyle	24	9	4	11	61	84	31
Lower Parksone CFC	24	8	5	11	62	77	29
AFC Burton Res.	24	7	3	14	49	78	24
F'bridge Turks Res.	24	5	2	17	39	93	17
Bransgore Utd Res.	24	3	7	14	42	88	16
Ringwood Athletic	24	4	1	19	38	112	13

BRIGHTON, HOVE & DISTRICT LEAGUE

Premier	P	W	D	L	F	A	Pts
Montpelier Villa	22	16	4	2	68	23	52
Brighton North End	22	16	2	4	68	27	50
Amptio	22	13	3	6	62	37	42
AFC Falmer Falcons	22	12	3	7	59	44	39
AFC Stanley	22	11	4	7	48	37	37
Brighton Electricity	22	9	3	10	54	48	30
O & G United	22	9	1	12	55	42	28
CCK	22	8	3	11	46	43	27
Portslade Athletic	22	7	6	9	31	38	27
American Express	22	5	6	11	31	63	21
Ovingdean	22	5	3	14	45	81	18
Southern Rgrs OB	22	1	2	19	25	109	5

Division One	P	W	D	L	F	A	Pts
Hair Razors	12	9	1	2	34	10	28
Rottingdean Vill. Res.	12	7	2	3	19	18	23
White Hart Revolution	12	7	1	4	35	20	22
Montpelier Villa Res.	12	4	2	6	20	27	14
Montpelier View	12	4	1	7	14	24	13
BSM08	12	4	0	8	26	35	12
Constant Service	12	2	3	7	15	29	9

Orb 360, Whitehawk United, The White Schooner - records expunged.

Division Two	P	W	D	L	F	A	Pts
Chailey -3	18	15	1	2	67	11	43
PHS United	18	12	1	5	51	32	37
AFC Brigh & Hove +3	18	10	2	6	56	41	35
Vista	18	7	5	6	43	41	26
Millhouse	18	8	1	9	48	45	25
Royal Hove +2	18	6	4	8	52	38	24
R'dean Village A -1	18	7	4	7	56	60	24
Saltdean Sharks	18	7	2	9	31	46	23
Boys Brigade OB	18	6	3	9	50	62	21
Deans Dynamos	18	0	1	17	22	100	1

Division Three	P	W	D	L	F	A	Pts
Midway	18	15	2	1	87	30	47
AFC B on/Hove Res.	18	14	3	1	124	39	45
Montreal Arms	18	12	1	5	78	42	37
Portslade Ath. Res.	18	10	1	7	55	54	31
Montpelier Villa A	18	9	3	6	45	37	30
Southwick Rangers	18	6	2	10	50	64	20
Boys Brigade Res.	18	6	2	10	41	65	20
CCK Res.	18	3	3	12	29	75	12
Hove Park Tavern	18	3	2	13	31	76	11
FC Shepherds	18	2	1	15	20	78	7

BRISTOL & AVON FOOTBALL LEAGUE

	P	W	D	L	F	A	Pts
FC Bristol	26	22	2	2	137	31	68
AFC Hartcliffe	26	21	3	2	164	42	66
Carmell United	26	20	3	3	123	36	63
Cutters Friday A	26	18	4	4	103	31	58
Imperial Res.	26	16	2	8	58	33	50
De Veys Res.	26	13	1	12	102	44	40
Amana SYC	26	12	3	11	64	51	39
Real St George	26	12	3	11	66	83	39
Iron Acton A	26	9	4	13	46	68	31
Wanderers Res.	26	8	2	16	51	77	26
Greyfriars Athletic B	26	5	3	18	28	99	18
Golden Hill Sports A	26	4	3	19	27	121	15
Bradley Stoke Town A	26	3	2	21	30	145	11
Wessex Wanderers A	26	1	1	24	24	162	4

BRISTOL & DISTRICT LEAGUE

Senior	P	W	D	L	F	A	Pts
Old Sodbury	26	19	2	5	73	37	59
Hanham Ath. Res.	26	15	4	7	47	29	49
Shirehampton Res.	26	15	3	8	58	43	48
Brislington Cricketers	26	13	4	9	69	49	43
AXA Res.	26	12	5	9	62	50	41
Chipping Sodbury Res.	26	12	3	11	57	52	39
Wick Reserves	26	10	5	11	57	57	35
Longwell Green S. A	26	10	5	11	51	63	35
Nicholas Wdrs Res.	26	10	3	13	37	54	33
Coalpit Heath	26	8	5	13	50	63	29
Hallen A	26	8	5	13	44	67	29
Roman Glass SG A	26	7	6	13	49	54	27
Seymour United Res.	26	6	5	15	49	65	23
St Pancras -3	26	7	5	14	54	74	23

Division One	P	W	D	L	F	A	Pts
Eden Grove	26	20	3	3	88	34	63
Sea Mills Park	26	20	2	4	69	29	62
Warmley Saints	26	18	6	2	70	23	60
Iron Acton	26	17	2	7	78	44	53
Hambrook	26	14	4	8	61	39	46
Rangeworthy	26	11	4	11	61	57	37
Talbot Knowle Res.	26	10	3	13	53	60	33
Bitton A	26	9	3	14	59	62	30
Crosscourt United	26	8	4	14	55	80	28
AEK Boco Res.	26	7	2	17	43	59	23
Miners Rangers	26	7	2	17	39	92	23
Patchway Town A	26	6	4	16	42	79	22
Bendix	26	5	6	15	54	81	21
Pucklechurch Res.	26	6	3	17	45	78	21

Division Two	P	W	D	L	F	A	Pts
DRG Res.	26	20	4	2	86	23	64
Mendip United Res.	26	17	4	5	79	42	55
Stockwood Wdrrs	26	15	4	7	60	38	49
BBS Plumb.co.uk	26	15	2	9	90	62	47
Bradley Stoke Town	26	14	3	9	63	44	45
Shireway Sports	26	10	5	11	48	51	35
South Bristol Central	26	10	4	12	44	65	34
AFC Stanton	26	10	3	13	56	57	33
Nicholas Wdrs A	26	9	4	13	53	64	31
Fry Club A	26	8	7	11	52	75	31
Chipping Sodbury A	26	9	1	16	50	77	28
Winterbourne U. A	26	8	3	15	44	52	27
Hanham Athletic A	26	6	9	11	49	72	27
Hartcliffe Res.	26	3	3	20	37	89	12

BRISTOL DOWNS LEAGUE

Division One	P	W	D	L	F	A	Pts
Sneyd Park	26	19	2	5	64	27	59
Torpedo	26	15	8	3	60	26	53
Ashley	26	15	4	7	58	42	49
Lawes Juniors	26	13	7	6	49	22	46
Sporting Greyhound	26	12	7	7	49	35	43
Clifton St Vincents	26	13	4	9	63	52	43
Cotswool	26	12	3	11	39	45	39
Bristol Barcelona	26	10	3	13	36	35	33
Saints Old Boys	26	9	4	13	54	58	31
Jamaica Bell	26	9	2	15	40	47	29
Portland Old Boys	26	7	7	12	38	55	28
Retainers	26	8	4	14	39	62	28
AFC Bohemia -3	26	5	5	16	49	76	17
Lion	26	3	4	19	36	92	13

Division Two	P	W	D	L	F	A	Pts
Sneyd Park Res.	26	18	5	3	72	33	59
Torpedo Res.	26	14	9	3	49	22	51
Bristol Barcelona Res.	26	14	6	6	43	43	48
Clifton Rockets	26	13	8	5	66	36	47
Evergreen	26	11	5	10	49	39	38
Easton Cowboys	26	11	2	13	63	51	35
Hare on the Hill	26	10	5	11	54	59	35
Stoke Bishop	26	8	8	10	41	55	32
Clifton St Vin. Res.	26	7	9	10	51	50	30
Cotswool Res.	26	8	6	12	53	79	30
Tebby	26	6	8	12	56	55	26
Cabot Asset Finance	26	7	5	14	38	53	26
Ashley Res.	26	6	7	13	50	61	25
St Andrews	26	5	5	16	35	84	20

Division Three	P	W	D	L	F	A	Pts
Jersey Rangers	26	16	6	4	83	37	54
Sporting Grey. Res.	26	16	5	5	71	34	53
Beachcroft LLP	26	15	3	8	94	58	48
Clifton Rockets Res.	26	12	6	8	69	56	42
Portland Old B. Res.	26	12	4	10	53	68	40
Retainers Res.	26	11	5	10	59	57	38
Wellington Wanderers	26	9	8	9	53	46	35
Torpedo A	26	9	7	10	60	57	34
Durdham Down AS	26	10	4	12	51	71	34
Clifton St Vincents A	26	9	6	11	43	65	33
Easton Cowboys Res.	26	8	5	13	43	69	29
LA Cricketers	26	8	3	15	52	77	27
Sneyd Park A -3	26	8	5	13	61	59	26
Luccombe Garage	26	1	9	16	35	73	12

Division Four	P	W	D	L	F	A	Pts
Saints Old Boys Res.	26	18	4	4	88	42	58
Corinthians	26	15	7	4	47	22	52
Bengal Tigers	26	15	3	8	60	36	48
West Town United	26	14	5	7	58	39	47
Helios	26	14	4	8	58	46	46
Cotham Old Boys	26	11	7	8	60	35	40
Clifton St Vincents B	26	13	1	12	51	56	40
Lion Res.	26	10	5	11	52	59	35
Sneyd Park B	26	9	5	12	41	46	32
Torpedo B	26	7	6	13	56	58	27
Retainers A	26	6	7	13	39	58	25
Tebby Res.	26	6	5	15	35	51	23
NCSF United	26	5	7	14	45	81	22
Conham Rangers	26	5	2	19	27	88	17

BRISTOL PREMIER COMBINATION

Premier	P	W	D	L	F	A	Pts
Mendip United	26	20	3	3	80	30	63
Longwell Green Res.	26	16	3	7	75	39	51
Bitton Res.	26	12	7	7	55	39	43
Wick	26	12	7	7	53	42	43
Hartcliffe	26	10	8	8	45	44	38
Lawrence Rovers	26	11	5	10	45	50	38
Talbot Knowle Utd	26	9	7	10	45	52	34
Lebeq	26	9	6	11	52	53	33
Nicholas Wanderers	26	9	5	12	56	46	32
RG St George Res.	26	7	8	11	54	58	29
Hallen Res.	26	8	5	13	46	66	29
Pucklechurch Spts	26	8	4	14	37	62	28
Seymour United -3	26	7	6	13	45	60	24
AEK Boco -3	26	5	4	17	36	83	16

Division One	P	W	D	L	F	A	Pts
Totterdown United	24	15	2	7	58	33	47
Winterbourne U. Res.	24	14	4	6	75	49	46
Patchway Res. -3	24	14	6	4	60	22	45
Henbury Res.	24	13	4	7	62	47	43
Shaftesbury Crusade	24	12	5	7	57	42	41
Olveston United	24	10	5	9	43	40	35
Made For Ever	24	10	4	10	56	49	34
Oldland Abbs Res.	24	10	4	10	50	57	34
Frampton Athletic	24	9	4	11	40	43	31
Highridge United	24	9	3	12	48	61	30
Fishponds Athletic	24	6	3	15	41	71	21
Greyfriars Athletic	24	6	2	16	49	78	20
Brimsham Green	24	3	4	17	30	77	13

BRISTOL & SUBURBAN LEAGUE

Premier One	P	W	D	L	F	A	Pts
Bristol Telephones	28	22	3	3	95	41	69
Southmead CS Ath.	28	21	4	3	73	37	67
Cadbury Heath Res.	28	19	2	7	80	43	59
Avonmouth +3	28	14	3	11	61	48	48
CTK Southside	28	14	2	12	64	57	44
Broad Plain House	28	12	4	12	60	58	40
Ashton United	28	12	3	13	62	61	39
Sth Glos (Hambrook)	28	11	4	13	66	62	37
Almondsbury T. Res.	28	10	5	13	42	51	35
Old Georgians	28	10	4	14	50	53	34
St Aldhelms	28	10	3	15	53	79	33
Winford PH	28	9	4	15	46	79	31
Fishponds Old Boys	28	7	6	15	46	69	27
Almonsbury UWE Res.	28	6	4	18	59	95	22
Bristol Athletic	28	5	5	18	45	69	20

Premier Two	P	W	D	L	F	A	Pts
Little Stoke	26	23	0	3	109	34	69
Lawrence Weston	26	19	4	3	85	47	61
Easton Cowboys Sub	26	19	3	4	83	31	60
Stoke Gifford United	26	15	2	9	77	47	47
Severn Beach	26	10	6	10	52	57	36
Ridings High	26	11	3	12	56	70	36
Glenside 5 Old Boys	26	9	6	11	48	51	33
Whitchurch	26	9	5	12	52	71	32
St Aldhelms Res.	26	8	7	11	54	59	31
Lockleaze	26	7	5	14	45	63	26
Tytherington Res.	26	7	4	15	41	63	25
Avonmouth Res. -3	26	8	2	16	43	75	23
Brislington A	26	7	1	18	37	84	22
Wessex Wanderers	26	4	4	18	35	65	16

Division Two	P	W	D	L	F	A	Pts
Southmead CS Res.	26	21	2	3	87	28	65
Shield Sports	26	20	2	4	95	29	62
Filton Athletic	26	16	5	5	72	32	53
Ingleside	26	15	4	7	68	38	49
Rockleaze Res.	26	13	5	8	52	46	44
Ashton Back. Colts	26	12	6	8	57	39	42
Ridings High Res.	26	11	3	12	72	66	36
Old Cothamians	26	10	4	12	51	57	34
Thrissell Nomads	26	10	3	13	61	70	33
Totterdown POB	26	8	4	14	60	83	28
Broad Plain Hse Res.	26	7	3	16	39	79	24
Fishponds OB Res.	26	8	0	18	43	84	24
Hengrove Athletic	26	7	2	17	48	69	23
Keynsham Town A	26	2	1	23	27	112	7

CAPITAL LEAGUE

Central	P	W	D	L	F	A	Pts
Aveley Res.	18	10	5	3	47	29	35
Harlow Town Res.	18	10	4	4	52	30	34
Colney Heath Res.	18	9	5	4	38	23	32
AFC Hornchurch Res.	18	8	5	5	34	36	29
Thurrock Res.	18	8	4	6	33	31	28
Enfield Town Res.	18	8	2	8	41	40	26
Cheshunt Res.	18	5	4	9	30	41	19
Redbridge Res.	18	5	3	10	34	49	18
Potters Bar Town Res.	18	4	4	10	21	42	16
Enfield 1893 Res.	18	3	4	11	23	32	13

East	P	W	D	L	F	A	Pts
Braintree Town A	18	12	1	5	54	39	37
Brentwood Town Res.	18	10	4	4	43	30	34
Ebbsfleet United Res.	18	10	3	5	48	35	33
Chelmsford City Res.	18	10	2	6	47	37	32
Great Wakering Res.	18	7	1	10	33	54	22
Witham Town A	18	6	3	9	51	49	21
Bishop's Stortford Res.	18	6	3	9	42	47	21
Billericay Town Res.	18	6	3	9	40	45	21
Bromley Res.	18	6	3	9	30	37	21
Canvey Island Res.	18	4	3	11	31	46	15

East	P	W	D	L	F	A	Pts
Hayes & Yeading Res.	14	11	3	0	50	14	36
Harrow Borough	14	10	2	2	48	17	32
Wealdstone Res.	14	6	4	4	34	29	22
Staines Town Res.	14	5	2	7	35	37	17
Hitchin Town Res.	14	4	3	7	31	39	15
Ashford (Middx) Res.	14	3	4	7	22	35	13
Burnham Res.	14	4	0	10	24	49	12
Biggleswade Town	14	3	2	9	21	45	11

Windsor & Eton Res. - record expunged.

CENTRAL & SOUTH NORFOLK LEAGUE

Division One	P	W	D	L	F	A	Pts
Bridgham United	26	20	2	4	84	32	62
Thetford Rovers Res.	26	19	3	4	127	42	60
Dereham Town A	26	18	4	4	86	38	58
Gressenhall	26	15	6	5	57	27	51
Hingham Athletic	26	15	5	6	73	53	50
Shipdham	26	16	2	8	53	38	50
Tacolneston	26	14	0	12	77	57	42
Swaffham Town A	26	11	4	11	75	64	37
Bunwell	26	11	2	13	81	76	35
Narborough	26	10	2	14	46	57	32
Rockland United	26	5	5	16	24	65	20
Great Ryburgh	26	4	3	19	32	96	15
Cranworth	26	4	1	21	31	91	13
Cockers	26	0	1	25	30	140	1

Division Two	P	W	D	L	F	A	Pts
Feltwell United	26	21	3	2	90	24	66
Northwold S&SC	26	20	5	1	92	39	65
Morley Village	26	16	5	5	100	48	53
Shropham United	26	15	7	4	100	43	52
Castle Acre Swifts	26	13	7	6	72	32	46
Nostro	26	12	6	8	81	54	42
Hethersett Athletic	26	12	4	10	57	49	40
Saham Toney Res.	26	9	6	11	75	73	33
Yaxham	26	9	6	11	61	72	33
Necton	26	9	3	14	63	67	30
Sporle	26	7	3	16	70	88	24
Wymondham Town A	26	6	4	16	43	85	22
West End	26	3	1	22	31	114	10
Hingham Ath. Res.	26	0	0	26	25	172	0

Division Three	P	W	D	L	F	A	Pts
Thurton & Ashby	26	22	0	4	125	33	66
North Elmham	26	20	2	4	99	34	62
Breckland Wanderers	26	16	6	4	103	50	54
Methwold Rovers	26	17	2	7	100	56	53
Gressenhall Res.	26	15	4	7	92	56	49
Bawdeswell	26	14	3	9	86	62	45
Wendling	26	14	2	10	90	54	44
Marham Wanderers	26	12	5	9	80	54	41
Stoke Ferry	26	8	3	15	64	84	27
Narborough Res.	26	7	3	16	45	65	24
Splitz United	26	6	3	17	41	95	21
Great Cressingham	26	7	0	19	38	111	21
Rockland Utd Res.	26	5	1	20	31	125	16
Shipdham Res.	26	2	0	24	29	144	6

Division Four	P	W	D	L	F	A	Pts
Diss Town A	26	24	1	1	189	25	73
Mulbarton Wanderers	26	21	3	2	114	24	66
Tugas United	26	15	4	7	96	30	49
Rampant Horse	26	14	7	5	93	54	49
Scarning	26	15	0	11	100	68	45
Mattishall A	26	12	3	11	73	58	39
Colkirk	26	12	1	13	87	60	37
Beetley United	26	10	4	12	60	69	34
Nostro Res.	26	9	2	15	63	99	29
Weasenham Wdrs	26	8	2	16	68	96	26
Tacolneston Res.	26	7	5	14	50	78	26
North Elmham Res.	26	7	5	14	72	105	26
Shropham Utd Res.	26	7	3	16	73	129	24
Dereham Cockers U.	26	1	0	25	17	260	3

CHELTENHAM ASSOCIATION LEAGUE

Division One	P	W	D	L	F	A	Pts
Real Whaddon	24	21	1	2	92	25	64
Whaddon United	24	16	5	3	63	29	53
Broadway United -3	24	13	5	6	62	46	41
AC Olympia	24	12	1	11	46	44	37
Siddington -3	24	12	2	10	54	41	35
Endsleigh	24	8	7	9	53	52	31
Kings	24	8	6	10	38	43	30
Finlay Rovers	24	7	7	10	54	58	28
Newton	24	7	6	11	44	54	27
Star Res.	24	7	6	11	42	64	27
Apperley & Tewk Dyn	24	6	3	15	36	63	21
Bishops Cleeve A	24	5	4	15	24	58	19
Winchcombe T. Res.	24	3	9	12	35	66	18

Woodmancote - record expunged.

Division Two	P	W	D	L	F	A	Pts
Falcons	24	17	2	5	89	39	53
Charlton Rovers	24	17	2	5	92	49	53
Gloucester Elmleaze	24	13	2	9	59	45	41
Northway	24	12	3	9	79	68	39
Northleach Town -3	24	13	2	9	56	48	38
Dowty Dynamos	24	11	3	10	57	60	36
Butlers	24	11	1	12	65	54	34
Gala Wilton Res.	24	10	4	10	47	48	34
Bredon Res.	24	10	3	11	62	59	33
Brockworth A. Res.	24	9	5	10	33	44	32
Prestbury Rovers -3	24	8	2	14	54	78	23
Barometrics Res. -1	24	7	3	14	57	83	23
Andoversford	24	2	0	22	33	108	6

Cinderford Town Res. - record expunged.

Division Three	P	W	D	L	F	A	Pts
Smiths Athletic Res.	24	16	2	6	68	39	50
Tewkesbury Town	24	15	2	7	88	50	47
Upton Town	24	14	4	6	63	32	46
Hanley Swan	24	14	4	6	64	41	46
Belmore	24	12	6	6	57	43	42
C & G	24	11	4	9	51	52	37
Charlton Rov. Res.	24	10	6	8	67	57	36
Chelt Civil S. Res.	24	10	4	10	42	44	34
Churchdown Panthers	24	9	5	10	52	54	32
Southside -9	24	10	4	10	46	35	25
Chelt. Saracens A -3	24	7	2	15	55	91	19
Bourton Rovers Res.	24	2	3	19	42	98	9
Elmbridge OB	24	1	4	19	27	86	7

Division Four	P	W	D	L	F	A	Pts
RSG	24	22	1	1	91	25	67
Tivoli Rovers	24	18	1	5	78	38	55
Whaddon Utd Res.	24	15	4	5	83	43	49
Falcons Res.	24	14	0	10	58	47	42
Hatherley R. Res -3	24	13	2	9	56	47	38
Star A	24	11	4	9	53	38	37
Cheltenham CS A	24	11	1	12	50	67	34
Cheltenham Sara. B -3	24	10	3	11	61	67	30
Phoenix United -3	24	10	2	12	47	57	29
Kings Res.	24	6	2	16	37	53	20
Bredon A	24	6	1	17	35	77	19
66 Star United -14	24	8	2	14	56	66	12
Smiths Athletic A -3	24	0	1	23	20	105	-2

Finlay - record expunged.

OTHER LEAGUES

Division Five	P	W	D	L	F	A	Pts
FC Lakeside	24	22	2	0	147	23	68
WMK	24	17	3	4	97	47	54
Leckhampton Rovers	24	16	3	5	70	37	51
Montpellier	24	15	2	7	73	42	47
AC Olympia Res.	24	13	2	9	55	53	41
Gala Wilton A	24	11	6	7	56	45	39
Fintan	24	10	5	9	64	48	35
FC Baromet. A -8	24	9	7	8	59	56	26
Apperley & T D Res.	24	6	4	14	52	78	22
Sherborne Harriers	24	6	4	14	61	93	22
Tewkesbury T. Res.	24	5	3	16	36	78	18
Andoversford Res -3	24	2	4	18	35	107	7
Chelt. Civ Service B	24	0	3	21	15	113	3

Division Six	P	W	D	L	F	A	Pts
Cheltonians	24	21	0	3	99	32	63
Priors	24	17	2	5	118	55	53
Dowty Dynamos Res.	24	15	1	8	87	43	46
Winchcombe Tn A	24	13	3	8	54	46	42
Chelt. Saracens C	24	12	1	11	73	73	37
Southside Res.	24	10	6	8	59	42	36
Hesters Way Utd -3	24	12	2	10	67	47	35
Charlton Rovers A -3	24	10	3	11	53	59	30
Northleach Town Res.	24	9	2	13	47	69	29
Pittville United -4	24	9	5	10	56	51	28
Charlton Kings	24	5	1	18	26	117	16
Fintan Res.	24	3	4	17	33	82	13
App/Tewk. Dyn. A -3	24	4	2	18	42	98	11

CHESTERFIELD & DIST. AMATEUR LEAGUE

	P	W	D	L	F	A	Pts
All Inn	22	19	3	0	117	15	60
Hopflower	22	17	3	2	80	28	54
Renishaw Social Club	22	15	1	6	81	38	46
Nags Head	22	12	3	7	51	47	39
Holmefield Arms	22	12	2	8	55	40	38
Tibshelf	22	9	4	9	43	50	31
Shirebrook Rangers	22	8	4	10	39	51	28
Chesterfield Town	22	7	5	10	52	51	26
New Houghton Villa	22	7	0	15	43	89	21
Holmewood & Heath	22	5	2	15	48	92	17
Middle	22	3	2	17	32	99	11
Clowne Villa Res.	22	2	3	17	28	69	9

Wheatsheaf, Duckmanton Community - records expunged.

CIRENCESTER & DISTRICT LEAGUE

Division One	P	W	D	L	F	A	Pts
Bibury	18	17	1	0	90	13	52
Avonvale United	18	13	0	5	44	35	39
CHQ United	18	11	2	5	47	33	35
Oaksey	18	9	4	5	40	26	31
South Cerney	18	8	2	8	36	46	26
The Beeches	18	6	4	8	29	34	22
Kingshill Sports	18	5	1	12	34	53	16
Real Fairford	18	4	3	11	34	41	15
Stratton United	18	4	1	13	25	62	13
Tetbury Town A	18	3	2	13	22	58	11

Division Two	P	W	D	L	F	A	Pts
Down Ampney	18	16	0	2	96	33	48
Lechlade '87	18	9	5	4	47	43	32
Avonvale Utd Res -6	18	11	4	3	62	30	31
Ashton Keynes Res -3	18	9	4	5	63	36	28
Poulton	18	7	5	6	35	28	26
Minety	18	7	4	7	34	49	25
Bibury Res.	18	6	6	6	41	40	24
The Beeches Res.	18	4	3	11	31	46	15
Corinium Sports -3	18	3	4	11	21	53	10
Chalford A -3	18	0	1	17	16	88	-2

Division Three	P	W	D	L	F	A	Pts
South Cerney Res.	16	10	1	5	53	26	31
Down Ampney Res.	16	10	1	5	42	25	31
CHQ United Res.	16	9	1	6	49	38	28
Stroud Res. -6	16	10	3	3	40	25	27
Oaksey Res.	16	7	3	6	44	35	24
Stratton United Res.	16	5	2	9	30	45	17
Kingshill Sports Res.	16	5	1	10	31	51	16
Sherston Res.	16	4	2	10	42	62	14
Poulton Res.	16	3	4	9	34	58	13

COLCHESTER & EAST ESSEX LEAGUE

Premier Division	P	W	D	L	F	A	Pts
Tollesbury	24	22	1	1	109	19	67
Colne Engaine	24	18	2	4	88	31	56
Harwich & P'ton Res.	24	18	2	4	89	40	56
Univ. of Essex "A"	24	14	2	8	60	35	44
Castle	24	10	4	10	48	69	34
Cinque Port	24	10	3	11	50	63	33
Oyster	24	9	2	13	41	59	29
Colchester Hotspurs	24	8	3	13	44	54	27
Wimpole 2000	24	8	3	13	71	86	27
Stoke-by-Nayland	24	8	1	15	44	101	25
Colchester Athletic	24	6	4	14	42	49	22
Brigh'sea Regent "A"	24	7	1	16	66	91	22
AXA	24	3	2	19	34	89	11

COVENTRY ALLIANCE

Premier Division	P	W	D	L	F	A	Pts
Christ The King	28	23	5	0	110	25	74
Alvis	28	21	1	6	82	25	64
Highway Coundon Court	28	21	1	6	82	44	64
Stockton	28	16	3	9	81	41	51
Bedworth Ex Service	28	11	7	10	53	48	40
Ambleside Sports	28	10	7	11	47	56	37
Folly Lane	28	12	4	12	54	45	36
Hawkesmill Sports	28	10	5	13	54	59	35
Bulkington SS	28	10	5	13	42	55	35
Peugeot	28	10	3	15	53	66	33
Woodlands WMC	28	9	5	14	41	61	32
The Bell (AEI) Rugby	28	8	3	17	45	80	27
Triumph Athletic	28	7	5	16	55	81	26
Collycroft Sports	28	9	5	14	54	70	23
Dunlop	28	3	1	24	27	124	7

Division One	P	W	D	L	F	A	Pts
Stock'ford AA Pavilion	22	18	1	3	96	31	55
Copsewood (Coventry)	22	16	4	2	64	24	52
Alvis Reserves	22	15	2	5	62	46	44
Christ The King Reserves	22	12	1	9	57	43	37
Stockton Reserves	22	11	2	9	52	43	35
Fillongley	22	9	2	11	54	65	29
Coventry University	22	10	1	11	51	55	28
Brooklands/Jaguar	22	7	6	9	47	48	27
Coventry Colliery	22	7	5	10	52	59	26
Potters Green	22	8	2	12	51	62	26
Bourton Frankton	22	1	5	16	22	86	8
Nuneaton Griff & Coton	22	1	3	18	14	60	5

CRAVEN & DISTRICT LEAGUE

Premier Division	P	W	D	L	F	A	Pts
Skipton LMS	20	15	3	2	74	34	48
Cowling	20	14	3	3	72	30	45
Ighton Leigh	20	12	2	6	63	45	38
Grindleton	20	12	2	6	52	51	38
Grassington United	20	10	4	6	48	45	34
Embsay	20	9	3	8	39	44	30
WFC Clitheroe	20	6	6	8	42	47	24
Rolls (-3)	20	7	4	9	45	43	22
Pendle Athletic	20	5	2	13	32	55	17
Gargrave	20	3	1	16	39	67	10
Waddington	20	1	2	17	31	76	5

Division One	P	W	D	L	F	A	Pts
Carleton	20	15	0	5	66	40	45
Settle United	20	12	6	2	64	33	42
Trawden Celtic	20	11	3	6	59	42	36
Bingley Town	20	9	5	6	63	50	32
Chatburn	20	9	2	9	57	50	29
Cononley Sports	20	8	4	8	51	50	28
Wilsden Juniors	20	7	6	7	58	45	27
Oxenhope Recreation	20	8	3	9	55	48	27
Silsden Whitestar	20	7	4	9	66	62	25
Oakworth	20	5	2	13	46	68	17
Skipton LMS Reserves	20	1	1	18	12	109	4

Division Two	P	W	D	L	F	A	Pts
Cross Hills	20	15	2	3	68	32	47
Earby Town	20	14	1	5	63	28	43
Pendle Renegades	20	11	5	4	61	38	38
Ighton Leigh Reserves	20	12	1	7	73	57	37
Hellifield Sports	20	9	4	7	59	45	31
Embsay Reserves	20	8	3	9	40	38	27
AFC Padiham	20	5	7	8	48	54	22
Rolls Reserves	20	5	6	9	39	51	21
Bradley	20	6	3	11	31	57	21
Skipton Town	20	3	4	13	33	71	13
Gargrave Reserves	20	3	2	15	18	62	11

Long Preston - record expunged.

CREWE & DISTRICT LEAGUE

	P	W	D	L	F	A	Pts
Cuddington	24	18	2	4	91	30	56
Tarporley Victoria Reserves	24	16	4	4	64	25	52
MMU Cheshire Reserves	24	13	5	6	79	48	44
Malpas Reserves	24	13	3	8	77	48	42
MMU Cheshire "A"	24	12	4	8	46	51	40
Sandbach Town	24	10	6	8	68	60	36
Bentley	24	10	4	10	82	67	34
Curshaws	24	10	2	12	51	44	32
Barnton Wanderers (-1)	24	8	4	12	58	65	27
Winnington Avenue Yth C.	24	7	3	14	51	68	24
Barnton Reserves	24	7	1	16	49	84	22
Lostock Gralam Reserves	24	6	3	15	52	99	21
Barnton Wanderers res.	24	4	3	17	46	125	15

CROOK & DISTRICT LEAGUE

Division One	P	W	D	L	F	A	Pts
B Auck Masons Moor	18	14	3	1	79	26	45
Roddymoor	18	14	2	2	74	29	44
Evenwood White Swan	18	10	3	5	50	27	33
Shildon Elm Rd WMC	18	8	4	6	42	29	28
M'stone Moor Mas.	18	7	5	6	35	33	26
Willington WMC	18	7	2	9	34	44	23
How.-le-Wear Aust'n	18	4	4	10	32	57	16
Framwellgate M. Salutation	18	4	4	10	35	66	16
Stanhope Tn S&S C.	18	3	4	11	29	64	13
Wearhead United	18	2	3	13	24	59	9

Division Two	P	W	D	L	F	A	Pts
Bowes	18	15	1	2	101	24	46
DSRM Social Club	18	13	0	5	73	24	39
Heighington	18	11	2	5	72	37	35
Deepdale	18	11	2	5	69	34	35
Etherley Welfare	18	10	3	5	64	33	33
Crook Town Wdrs	18	8	4	6	50	40	28
D'ton Hole In The Wall	18	6	1	11	29	58	19
Middleton Rangers	18	5	2	11	31	71	14
Darl. Shuttle & Loom	18	2	1	15	24	91	7
Ck Coach/Horses -3	18	0	2	16	16	117	-1

CUMBERLAND COUNTY LEAGUE

Premier Division	P	W	D	L	F	A	Pts
Netherhall	18	16	0	2	71	17	48
Longtown	18	15	0	3	73	27	45
Aspatria	18	12	1	5	66	33	37
FC 32	18	9	1	8	44	47	28
Cockermouth	18	8	3	7	46	46	27
Mirehouse	18	8	2	8	58	49	26
Wigton Harriers	18	5	3	10	50	45	18
Frizington Whitestar	18	4	3	11	27	83	15
Carlisle AFC (-6)	18	3	3	12	34	54	6
Bransty Rangers	18	1	2	15	33	101	5

Division One	P	W	D	L	F	A	Pts
Carlisle City Reserves	22	16	4	2	81	23	52
Borough	22	15	3	4	52	23	48
Warwick Wanderers	22	14	4	4	62	20	46
Harraby Cath. C res (-3)	22	14	3	5	56	27	42
Silloth	22	13	3	6	52	29	42
Whitehaven Reserves	22	10	3	9	51	49	33
Cleator Moor Celtic Res.	22	9	0	13	48	76	27
Windscale Reserves	22	7	1	14	39	53	22
Wigton Athletic	22	5	4	13	33	52	19
Parton United (-3)	22	6	3	13	32	75	18
Whitehaven Miners	22	4	2	16	36	78	14
St Bees	22	3	2	17	51	88	11

South Workington - record expunged.

DONCASTER & DISTRICT SENIOR LEAGUE

Premier	P	W	D	L	F	A	Pts
AFC Sportsman Rovers	26	19	3	4	86	33	60
Sutton Rovers	26	15	6	5	65	36	51
Maltby MW JFC	26	15	3	8	67	53	48
Kinsley Boys Reserves	26	14	4	8	62	49	46
Swinton Station Athletic	26	14	2	10	54	56	44
Rossington Main Reserves	26	13	3	10	67	48	42
South Kirkby Colliery "A"	26	11	4	11	55	53	37
Edlington Town	26	10	5	11	71	63	35
South Elmsall Utd Services	26	9	6	11	55	68	33
Retford Town	26	10	2	14	53	57	32
Adwick Park Rangers	26	10	2	14	49	57	32
Doncaster Deaf	26	7	3	16	36	73	24
Bawtry Town	26	6	4	16	52	82	22
Yorkshire Main Reserves	26	5	1	20	29	73	16

FC Thorne Town - record expunged.
Hemsworth Town - record expunged.

Division One	P	W	D	L	F	A	Pts
Carcroft Village	28	19	5	4	95	50	62
Bramley Sunnyside	28	17	3	8	104	46	54
Hatfield Main	28	16	4	8	118	46	52
FC Tavern	28	15	5	8	97	62	50
Hemsworth Town Reserves	28	14	6	8	84	73	48
Travellers	28	15	2	11	97	68	47
Ackworth United	28	13	6	9	64	58	45
Hemsworth MW Reserves	28	12	6	10	91	67	42
Upton Brookside	28	11	5	12	89	83	38
ISG Doncaster	28	10	6	12	61	79	36
Woodlands Rhinos	28	10	4	14	76	82	34
South Kirkby Colliery "B"	28	8	2	18	63	115	26
Bawtry Town Reserves	28	7	3	18	46	114	24
Edlington Rangers	28	6	3	19	55	117	21
Adwick Park Rangers Res.	28	7	0	21	50	130	21

Doncaster Athletic - record expunged.

DUCHY LEAGUE

Premier	P	W	D	L	F	A	Pts
Torpoint Athletic A	24	19	1	4	82	35	58
Fowey United	24	15	4	5	89	33	49
St Mawgan	24	16	1	7	64	46	49
Altarnun	24	12	3	9	42	34	39
Mevagissey	24	11	5	8	62	47	38
Lamerton	24	11	4	9	58	46	37
Saltash United A	24	11	4	9	53	44	37
Probus Res.	24	11	3	10	50	53	36
Gunnislake	24	10	4	10	46	45	34
Bodmin Saints	24	9	2	13	63	71	29
St.Cleer	24	7	2	15	54	66	23
Foxhole Stars Res -3	24	6	2	16	33	66	17
St.Columb Major -9	24	0	1	23	24	134	-8

Division One	P	W	D	L	F	A	Pts
Calstock	24	19	4	1	84	25	61
St Newlyn East	24	17	4	3	91	43	55
Polperro Res.	24	14	5	5	55	42	47
St Dominick Res.	24	13	1	10	61	44	40
Week St.Mary	24	10	3	11	48	56	33
Godolphin A Res. -3	24	10	4	10	47	43	31
Grampound	24	10	1	13	55	68	31
Bere Alston Res -3	24	9	3	12	45	61	27
Pelynt	24	7	5	12	68	76	26
Boscastle	24	8	2	14	52	66	26
Looe Town	24	6	5	13	37	56	23
Lanreath Res.	24	5	6	13	40	68	21
Pensilva	24	5	3	16	38	73	18

Division Two	P	W	D	L	F	A	Pts
St Austell Res.	20	16	2	2	67	20	50
St Dennis Res.	20	13	4	3	56	24	43
Premier Sixes	20	13	3	4	65	28	42
Lostwithiel	20	11	2	7	46	30	35
Maker with Rame	20	10	2	8	51	53	32
Holywell B/Cubert A	20	10	0	10	53	59	30
St Breward	20	7	2	11	36	52	23
Queens Rangers	20	5	2	13	37	58	17
St Stephen Res.	20	5	2	13	29	55	17
Gunnislake Res.	20	4	3	13	31	51	15
AFC Bodmin -3	20	5	0	15	24	65	12

Looe Town Res. - record expunged.

Division Three	P	W	D	L	F	A	Pts
Sticker Res.	24	18	3	3	83	28	57
Biscovey Res.	24	17	3	4	119	42	54
Lewdown Rov. Res.	24	16	4	4	80	30	52
Gerrans & St Mawes	24	14	5	5	72	31	47
Roche Res.	24	13	2	9	82	56	41
Callington Town A -3	24	11	5	8	63	53	35
St.Minver	24	11	2	11	51	55	35
Tintagel	24	9	2	13	57	61	29
Stratton United	24	7	5	12	67	70	26
Delabole United -3	24	7	2	15	48	79	20
Nanpean Rov. Res -3	24	6	4	14	42	55	19
Wadebridge Town A	24	5	3	16	37	73	18
Camelford A	24	2	0	22	21	189	6

Division Four	P	W	D	L	F	A	Pts
North Petherwin	22	16	2	4	99	34	50
Mount Charles	22	14	3	5	92	46	45
Tregony	22	13	6	3	61	43	45
Padstow United	22	14	2	6	62	38	44
Charlestown Saints	22	11	3	8	62	48	36
Gorran	22	8	2	12	45	66	26
Altarnun Res.	22	7	3	12	57	53	24
Pelynt Res.	22	7	3	12	30	62	24
Pensilva Res.	22	6	4	12	34	71	22
St Teath Res.	22	6	3	13	32	61	21
Southgate Seniors -3	22	7	1	14	48	71	19
Mevagissey Res. -3	22	7	0	15	44	73	18

Division Five	P	W	D	L	F	A	Pts
Lanivet Inn	22	20	0	2	88	20	60
LC Phoenix	22	19	2	1	130	25	59
Stoke Climsland	22	13	4	5	72	36	43
St Mawgan Res.	22	12	4	6	67	56	40
Calstock Res.	22	12	3	7	51	39	39
Torpoint Comrades	22	9	5	8	54	45	32
St Newlyn E. Res -3	22	8	2	12	62	75	23
North Hill	22	6	2	14	37	70	20
Grampound Res.	22	6	1	15	44	66	19
Boscastle Res.	22	6	1	15	33	71	19
Delabole United Res.	22	6	0	16	41	100	18
Duke of Cornwall	22	2	2	18	24	100	8

DURHAM FOOTBALL ALLIANCE

	P	W	D	L	F	A	Pts
Cornforth United	32	26	4	2	104	43	82
Coundon/Leeholme	32	25	5	2	120	30	80
Brandon Brit. Legion	32	24	2	6	118	55	74
Hartlepool Town	32	23	2	7	113	51	71
Birtley St Josephs	32	19	3	10	101	67	60
Leam Rangers	32	19	3	10	98	80	60
Whitehill -3	32	14	7	11	77	61	46
Wheatley Hill WMC	32	12	4	16	75	92	40
Shildon Railway	32	11	3	18	73	91	36
Washington Town	32	9	8	15	60	72	35
Durham Gardn Hse	32	9	7	16	65	94	34
Ebchester	32	9	7	16	58	92	34
Hartlepool St Francis -3	32	11	1	20	63	88	31
Washington CC	32	8	3	21	51	91	27
Brandon United Res.	32	6	6	20	53	90	24
Hebburn Town Jnrs	32	6	4	22	43	115	22
Coxhoe United	32	3	7	22	47	107	16

Nissan Sunderland - record expunged.

EAST BERKSHIRE LEAGUE

Premier	P	W	D	L	F	A	Pts
Eton Wick	20	16	2	2	66	24	50
Slough Laurencians	20	12	5	3	50	28	41
FC Beaconsfield	20	9	5	6	40	36	32
Stoke Green	20	9	4	7	39	30	31
Orchard Park Rangers	20	9	2	9	28	28	29
Slough Heating	20	7	8	5	36	39	29
Wraysbury	20	8	3	9	39	33	27
Burnham Beeches	20	6	4	10	31	48	22
Waltham	20	6	3	11	40	45	21
Chalvey Sports	20	5	3	12	39	44	18
Windsor Great Park	20	2	3	15	18	71	9

Iver Heath Rovers - record expunged.

Division One	P	W	D	L	F	A	Pts
Britwell	20	18	1	1	63	21	55
Bracknell Forest	20	12	4	4	46	14	40
Alpha Arms Academi's	20	12	2	6	46	38	38
Iver	20	10	4	6	44	29	34
North Hillingdon FC	20	8	5	7	42	39	29
Datchet	20	6	6	8	36	31	24
Falcons	20	7	3	10	37	44	24
Slough Irish Society	20	6	3	11	27	40	21
New Hanford	20	5	5	10	34	50	20
Delaford	20	4	4	12	34	60	16
Maidenhead Town	20	3	1	16	39	82	10

Burnham United - record expunged.

Division Two	P	W	D	L	F	A	Pts
Old Windsor	18	13	1	4	44	26	40
KS Gryf	18	11	3	4	48	21	36
Slough Heating Reserves	18	10	4	4	63	39	34
Cippenham Sports	18	10	2	6	65	45	32
Stoke Road Legion	18	7	3	8	42	51	24
Burnham Swan	18	6	2	10	32	53	20
Stoke Poges	18	5	4	9	36	39	19
Richings Park	18	5	4	9	28	43	19
Upton Lea	18	4	4	10	36	53	16
Beaconsfield Town	18	4	3	11	24	48	15

Alpha Arms Academicals Reserves - record expunged.

Division Three	P	W	D	L	F	A	Pts
Berkshire United	20	17	2	1	76	41	53
Slough Laurencians Res.	20	13	2	5	83	43	41
Braybrooke	20	12	1	7	63	48	37
Frontline	20	11	3	6	36	35	36
Black Horse	20	8	4	8	52	47	28
AFC Ascot	20	8	4	8	59	55	28
Campion United	20	6	5	9	52	57	23
Willow Wanderers	20	5	6	9	46	62	21
Stoke Green Reserves	20	6	3	11	39	63	21
Windsor Great Park Res.	20	4	4	12	54	76	16
Boyne Hill	20	2	2	16	33	66	8

EAST CHESHIRE LEAGUE

	P	W	D	L	F	A	Pts
Boarhound FC	22	18	0	4	101	49	54
Club AZ Reserves	22	16	2	4	82	45	50
High Lane	22	15	2	5	77	48	47
Poynton Kings	22	13	1	8	64	55	40
Cheadle Hulme	22	12	1	9	55	40	37
Handforth (-3)	22	11	4	7	57	44	34
Poynton Nomads	22	9	3	10	44	48	30
Mary Dendy	22	8	3	11	61	56	27
Old Alts East	22	7	2	13	41	68	23
Old Alts "B"	22	5	2	15	32	69	17
Wilmslow Sports Res.	22	3	3	16	37	71	12
Poynton Village	22	2	3	17	37	95	9

Juno United - record expunged.

EAST LANCASHIRE LEAGUE

Division One	P	W	D	L	F	A	Pts
Rimington	24	19	4	1	95	33	61
Mill Hill	24	16	2	6	79	40	50
Hurst Green	24	13	3	8	87	50	42
Canberra	24	12	6	6	61	44	42
Pendle Forest	24	12	5	7	61	40	41
Worsthorne	24	11	8	5	63	50	41
Langho	24	10	3	11	57	41	33
Oswaldtwistle St M	24	8	5	11	40	52	29
Burnley GSOB	24	7	7	10	55	70	28
Stacksteads St Jos.	24	6	8	10	54	67	26
Read United	24	4	5	15	43	88	17
Colne United	24	3	6	15	47	90	15
Enfield	24	3	2	19	32	109	11

Division Two	P	W	D	L	F	A	Pts
Edenfield	24	20	2	2	105	26	62
Feniscowles & Pl'ton	24	17	4	3	91	34	55
Churchtown	24	15	4	5	77	46	49
Rock Rovers	24	15	2	7	77	35	47
Burnley Belvedere	24	14	4	6	74	44	46
Barrowford Celtic	24	13	3	8	68	44	42
Padiham "A"	24	10	6	8	64	34	36
Clitheroe RBL	24	9	4	11	58	58	31
Borrowdale United	24	9	4	11	61	65	31
Bacup CC	24	6	3	15	56	75	21
Calder Vale	24	4	2	18	37	79	14
Peel Park	24	3	2	19	27	109	11
Daneshouse	24	1	0	23	28	174	3

EAST RIDING AMATEUR LEAGUE

Premier	P	W	D	L	F	A	Pts
Quaddy Rangers	22	19	2	1	89	32	59
Pinefleet Wolfreton	22	14	7	1	77	30	49
AFC Hull	22	11	5	6	80	59	38
AFC Preston	22	11	4	7	62	43	37
East Hull Ship AWS	22	11	2	9	65	53	35
Rapid Solicitors	22	11	2	9	59	53	35
Eddie Beedle	22	9	7	6	56	51	33
Bev Road Rangers	22	7	4	11	46	52	25
Kingburn Athletic Res.	22	6	6	10	43	53	24
Swiss Cottage	22	6	1	15	45	79	19
Goodwin	22	3	1	18	39	117	10
St Andrews Res.	22	2	3	17	35	74	9

Division One	P	W	D	L	F	A	Pts
Queens County	22	19	1	2	82	37	58
AFC Salth'e Tavern	22	17	2	3	60	27	53
Pinefleet Wolfreton Res.	22	17	0	5	71	36	51
West Hull United	22	10	6	6	59	49	36
Cavalier Wanderers	22	9	5	8	42	46	32
SC Electrical	22	7	8	7	46	53	29
Anlaby Park	22	6	8	8	54	68	26
AFC Malt Shovel	22	8	1	13	38	54	25
Cross Keys Cottingham	22	6	4	12	41	48	22
AFC Piper	22	5	5	12	54	62	20
AFC Orchard	22	4	4	14	34	66	16
Willerby Hol. Homes	22	2	0	20	17	52	6

EAST RIDING COUNTY LEAGUE

Premier	P	W	D	L	F	A	Pts
Driffield Evening Inst.	22	17	4	1	63	24	55
Wawne Ferry	22	17	1	4	76	34	52
Viking Raiders	22	13	4	5	51	28	43
Woodlands	22	12	5	5	58	41	41
South Cave United	22	11	2	9	51	42	35
Forum	22	9	5	8	26	25	32
AFC Rovers	22	7	6	9	38	40	27
Park Athletic	22	7	3	12	38	40	24
Easington United Res.	22	6	3	13	29	57	21
Beverley Town Reserves	22	5	5	12	30	44	20
Holme Rovers	22	3	6	13	38	71	15
North Cave Reserves	22	1	4	17	21	73	7

Division One	P	W	D	L	F	A	Pts
Little Weighton	22	17	4	1	63	23	55
Sculcoates Amateurs Res.	22	15	4	3	57	18	49
Reckitts Reserves	22	15	2	5	70	37	47
Barrel Walkington	22	13	3	6	47	29	42
St George's	22	12	2	8	57	45	38
Beverley Town Beavers	22	8	3	11	33	46	27
Hedon Rangers Reserves	22	7	3	12	38	47	24
Mill Lane United	22	7	2	13	34	62	23
Westella & Willerby Jun.	22	6	3	13	46	49	21
Haltemprice	22	5	4	13	35	63	19
Gilberdyke	22	5	3	14	45	67	18
Leven Members Club	22	4	3	15	32	71	15

Division Two	P	W	D	L	F	A	Pts
Wawne Ferry Reserves	22	18	1	3	65	26	55
Hodgsons Reserves	22	15	5	2	68	29	50
Molescroft Rangers	22	15	2	5	57	26	47
West Hull Amateurs	22	14	0	8	62	44	42
Hornsea Town Reserves	22	13	2	7	74	40	41
Withernsea Reserves	22	9	3	10	51	64	30
Howden Reserves	22	10	0	12	40	67	30
Skidby Millers	22	8	3	11	44	54	27
Aldborough United	22	6	7	9	42	43	25
Long Riston Reserves	22	4	3	15	35	74	15
FC Ridings	22	4	1	17	25	58	13
Brandesburton Reserves	22	2	1	19	18	56	7

Division Three	P	W	D	L	F	A	Pts
Haltemprice Rangers	22	14	6	2	66	34	48
Skirlaugh	22	14	3	5	64	39	45
Eastella Rangers	22	13	3	6	55	40	42
Shiptonthorpe United	22	12	5	5	58	52	41
Full Measure	22	11	3	8	51	41	36
South Cave United Res.	22	11	1	10	48	43	34
Old Zoological	22	10	3	9	69	51	33
Roos	22	7	4	11	54	66	25
Viking Raiders Reserves	22	4	8	10	39	50	20
Eastrington Village	22	6	2	14	46	65	20
Woodlands Reserves	22	5	4	13	61	76	19
Market Weighton United	22	3	2	17	36	90	11

Division Four	P	W	D	L	F	A	Pts
Market Weighton Utd Res.	22	19	1	2	86	22	58
Priory Athletic	22	16	2	4	79	35	50
Eastern Raiders	22	16	0	6	94	38	48
Real Ruscador	22	13	2	7	56	47	41
Marist Rovers	22	12	1	9	80	58	37
Holme Rovers Reserves	22	9	3	10	50	55	30
East Riding Rangers Res.	22	9	1	12	33	71	28
Molescroft Rangers Res.	22	7	4	11	43	65	25
Leven Members Club Res.	22	7	2	13	47	78	23
Gilberdyke Reserves	22	7	1	14	57	64	22
Hedon Rangers Juniors	22	6	3	13	36	68	21
Howden "A"	22	1	0	21	19	79	3

Division Five	P	W	D	L	F	A	Pts
Long Riston "A"	20	15	2	3	65	33	47
Hornsea Town "A"	20	14	0	6	55	38	42
Skirlaugh Reserves	20	12	3	5	47	32	39
Shiptonthorpe United Res.	20	11	5	4	70	53	38
Thorngumbald Trinity	20	12	1	7	75	44	37
Easington Utd Casuals	20	9	2	9	38	41	29
South Cave United "A"	20	8	4	8	39	40	28
Haltemprice Reserves	20	5	5	10	38	45	20
Withernsea "A"	20	5	3	12	39	70	18
Brandesburton Academy	20	4	1	15	38	62	13
Eastrington Village Res.	20	1	2	17	22	68	5

EAST SUSSEX LEAGUE

Premier Division	P	W	D	L	F	A	Pts
St Leonards Social (-3)	20	16	1	3	60	28	46
Hollington United	20	12	4	4	60	38	40
Rock A Nore	20	12	3	5	53	27	39
Peche Hill Select	20	11	2	7	54	44	35
Polegate Town	20	10	4	6	49	34	34
Wadhurst United	20	9	5	6	43	28	32
Sedlescombe Rang. (+3)	20	7	2	11	47	66	26
Robertsbridge United	20	5	6	9	46	52	21
Peasmarsh & Iden	20	5	3	12	45	70	18
Punnetts Town	20	4	4	12	35	58	16
Hooe Sports	20	1	2	17	24	71	5

Hospital Social - record expunged.

The JC Tackleway - record expunged.

Division One	P	W	D	L	F	A	Pts
White Knight	16	10	3	3	33	22	33
Old Town Athletic	16	8	5	3	45	25	29
Ninfield United	16	8	4	4	29	21	28
Bexhill AAC	16	8	3	5	30	25	27
Hollington United Res.	16	8	3	5	34	30	27
Eastbourne Town "A"	16	7	2	7	27	30	23
Catsfield	16	5	2	9	32	37	17
Mountfield United	16	4	1	11	18	32	13
Wheatsheaf Willingdon	16	2	1	13	16	42	7

Peasmarsh & Iden Reserves - record expunged.

Division Two	P	W	D	L	F	A	Pts
Eastbourne Galaxy	18	13	3	2	52	16	42
Ticehurst	18	12	2	4	54	26	38
Sandhurst	18	10	3	5	52	32	33
Crowhurst	18	8	2	8	47	48	26
Eastbourne Dynamos	18	7	3	8	40	36	24
Hastings Rangers	18	7	0	11	44	53	21
Cinque Ports	18	6	3	9	33	52	21
Icklesham Casuals	18	6	2	10	35	48	20
Northiam 75	18	6	1	11	35	58	19
Hurst	18	4	3	11	37	60	15

Division Three	P	W	D	L	F	A	Pts
St Helens	18	13	1	4	46	27	40
E'bourne Fishermen (-1)	18	13	1	4	61	29	39
Battle Baptists	18	12	2	4	58	26	38
Magham Down	18	12	0	6	47	34	36
Battle Rangers	18	10	0	8	58	51	30
Hawkhurst United	18	8	0	10	45	41	24
Cranbrook Town (+2)	18	6	2	10	33	29	22
Herstmonceux	18	6	4	8	39	49	22
Hollington United "A"	18	3	2	13	15	52	11
Beulah Baptists	18	1	0	17	20	84	3

Division Four	P	W	D	L	F	A	Pts
Orington	18	15	1	2	103	27	46
Peche Hill Select Res.	18	14	2	2	56	19	44
Pebsham Sibex	18	13	1	4	37	26	40
The J.C. Tackleway Res.	18	11	1	6	47	32	34
Peasmarsh & Iden "A"	18	7	1	10	49	47	22
Travaux	18	6	4	8	37	67	22
Mayfield	18	6	1	11	34	44	19
Punnetts Town Reserves	18	5	2	11	34	52	17
Victoria Baptists	18	3	2	13	34	67	11
Icklesham Casuals Res.	18	2	1	15	23	73	7

Division Five	P	W	D	L	F	A	Pts
Burwash	18	12	4	2	43	34	40
Sedlescombe Rangers Res.	18	11	3	4	41	27	36
Ninfield United reseRes.	18	10	3	5	38	30	33
Hastings Elite	18	10	2	6	53	34	32
Eastbourne Athletic	18	8	4	6	39	34	28
Guestling	18	8	1	9	35	36	25
Kurdistan United	18	6	3	9	34	39	21
Wadhurst United rese	18	6	3	9	19	34	21
Bexhill AAC Reserves	18	5	2	11	26	40	17
HG Aerospace	18	1	1	16	22	42	4

Division Six	P	W	D	L	F	A	Pts
Sidley (+3)	20	17	0	3	75	20	54
Catsfield Reserves (+2)	20	15	2	3	65	39	49
E'bourne Fishermen Res.	20	15	1	4	71	33	46
Polegate Town res (-3)	20	14	3	3	72	31	42
Eastbourne Royals	20	9	1	10	61	52	28
West Hill United	20	8	2	10	42	57	26
Westfield "A"	20	7	2	11	50	56	23
The J.C. Tackleway "A"	20	5	1	14	33	59	16
Parkfield	20	5	1	14	39	73	16
Northiam 75 Reserves	20	4	3	13	45	72	15
Magham Down res (-1)	20	1	4	15	33	94	6

Division Seven	P	W	D	L	F	A	Pts
Eastbourne Rangers	18	12	3	3	52	15	39
Herstmonceux Reserves	18	10	4	4	48	28	34
Guestling Reserves	18	9	4	5	38	25	31
Robertsbridge United Res.	18	9	4	5	26	24	31
Winkney Seniors	18	8	4	6	39	27	28
Hampden Park United	18	8	1	9	30	35	25
Battle Baptists Reserves	18	5	5	8	22	29	20
Sandhurst Reserves	18	6	2	10	30	38	20
Orington Reserves	18	5	4	9	31	32	19
Hawkhurst United Res.	18	0	5	13	12	75	5

ENFIELD ALLIANCE

	P	W	D	L	F	A	Pts
Brimsdown Rovers A	16	14	1	1	47	12	43
Persian	16	13	0	3	64	23	39
Broadwater United	16	11	2	3	44	28	35
Renegades	16	6	3	7	38	31	21
Crescent Rangers	16	6	3	7	35	34	21
Riverside	16	4	4	8	36	55	16
Origin	16	4	3	9	27	28	15
PERME	16	4	0	12	30	71	12
Lea Valley United	16	1	2	13	20	59	5

Chingford Town - record expunged.

ESKVALE & CLEVELAND LEAGUE

	P	W	D	L	F	A	Pts
Lingdale	24	23	1	0	115	19	70
Boosbeck United	24	18	5	1	86	31	59
Lingdale United	24	15	3	6	87	45	48
Loftus Athletic	24	14	2	8	66	47	44
Lealholm	24	14	2	8	61	44	44
Staithes Athletic	24	13	1	10	65	49	40
Stokesley SC	24	10	3	11	69	66	33
Goldsborough Utd	24	7	5	12	43	76	26
Hollybush United	24	6	5	13	50	90	23
N. Skelton Bulls Hd	24	6	4	14	40	67	22
Great Ayton Res.	24	5	3	16	31	87	18
Brotton Railway Arms	24	4	5	15	40	71	17
Carlin How WMC	24	0	3	21	21	82	3

ESSEX BUSINESS HOUSES LEAGUE

Premier	P	W	D	L	F	A	Pts
Brampton Park	18	12	1	5	41	30	37
RWMC	18	11	2	5	51	29	35
Toby	18	9	3	6	49	31	30
Flanders	18	9	3	6	42	33	30
Bancroft	18	9	3	6	38	36	30
Clapton Res.	18	8	4	6	40	44	28
West Green	18	8	2	8	48	43	26
Ford Basildon	18	7	1	10	24	25	22
Barking Boro. Seniors	18	3	3	12	20	39	12
Loass	18	2	2	14	29	72	8

FALMOUTH & HELSTON LEAGUE

Division One	P	W	D	L	F	A	Pts
Falmouth Athletic DC	26	24	0	2	112	23	72
St Agnes Reserves	26	18	3	5	70	26	57
Falmouth Albion	26	15	4	7	68	42	49
Mawnan	26	14	3	9	65	49	45
Penryn Athletic	26	13	6	7	65	50	45
Mousehole Reserves	26	13	4	9	46	50	43
Carharrack (+6)	26	10	3	13	54	72	39
St Keverne	26	8	6	12	45	60	30
Perranwell Reserves (-3)	26	10	3	13	44	61	30
Constantine	26	9	2	15	60	68	29
Chacewater	26	8	3	15	47	62	27
Portreath (-1)	26	6	5	15	52	79	22
Perranporth Reserves (-1)	26	7	2	17	33	70	22
Mullion Reserves	26	4	2	20	33	82	14

Camborne Park - record expunged.

Division Two	P	W	D	L	F	A	Pts
St Day Reserves	30	27	1	2	119	22	82
Lizard Argyle	30	21	3	6	114	42	66
Helston Athletic Reserves	30	20	4	6	92	45	64
Stithians	30	20	2	8	110	54	62
Rosudgeon-Kenneggy (-4)	30	20	1	9	107	54	57
Trispen (+3)	30	15	1	14	78	81	49
Cury	30	16	0	14	104	67	48
Wendron United res (+2)	30	12	5	13	82	82	43
RNAS Culdrose Reserves	30	14	1	15	59	69	43
Penryn Athletic "B"	30	13	1	16	76	73	40
Frogpool and Cusgarne (+3)	30	11	1	18	61	88	37
Lanner	30	10	6	14	60	99	36
Holman Sports Club res.	30	11	0	19	57	111	33
Pendeen Rovers res. (-3)	30	9	1	20	48	74	25
Constantine Reserves	30	3	3	24	34	109	12
Troon Reserves	30	2	2	26	35	166	8

Division Three	P	W	D	L	F	A	Pts
Falmouth Ath. DC res (+2)	28	23	3	2	141	34	74
Mawnan Reserves	28	18	4	6	92	41	58
St Day "A" (-1)	28	18	3	7	90	40	56
Wendron United "A" (+3)	28	13	5	10	81	51	47
Porthleven Rangers (-6)	28	16	3	9	80	40	45
Ruan Minor	28	13	6	9	78	52	45
West Cornwall Reserves	28	13	6	9	64	50	45
Mullion "A"	28	13	3	12	67	65	42
Hayle "A"	28	11	4	13	48	65	37
Frogpool & Cusgarne res.	28	11	4	13	62	85	37
Carharrack Reserves	28	10	3	15	62	89	33
Lizard Argyle Reserves	28	8	6	14	38	63	30
Stithians Reserves	28	7	2	19	50	89	23
Marazion Blues (+3)	28	4	4	20	53	104	19
Troon "A"	28	3	2	23	28	166	11

FURNESS PREMIER LEAGUE

Premier	P	W	D	L	F	A	Pts
Barrow Wanderers	22	13	7	2	85	38	46
Bootle	22	13	5	4	63	36	44
Vickerstown CC Res.	22	13	4	5	56	35	43
Kirkby United	22	11	4	7	71	45	37
Furness Rovers Res.	22	8	7	7	47	44	31
Holker Old Boys Res.	22	8	7	7	52	56	31
Hawcoat Park Res.	22	7	8	7	58	54	29
Haverigg United	22	8	4	10	54	36	28
Barrow Celtic	22	8	4	10	55	69	28
Millom Res.	22	7	4	11	44	61	25
Dalton United Res.	22	5	2	15	34	77	17
Furness Cav. Res.	22	2	2	18	25	93	8

Division One	P	W	D	L	F	A	Pts
Crooklands Cas. Res.	18	16	0	2	94	15	48
Barrow Athletic	18	13	1	4	62	29	40
Barrow Island	18	10	3	5	87	45	33
Askam United Res.	18	10	2	6	41	23	32
Barrow Wdrs Res.	18	10	1	7	69	52	31
Millom A	18	6	1	11	32	77	19
Vickerstown CC A	18	6	0	12	27	65	18
SDO -3	18	5	3	10	27	49	15
Dalton United A	18	4	1	13	14	65	13
Walney Island Res.	18	3	2	13	35	68	11

Division Two	P	W	D	L	F	A	Pts
Britannia	20	16	1	3	92	17	49
Holker Old Boys A	20	14	2	4	69	26	44
Swarthmoor S. Res.	20	12	4	4	59	38	40
Haverigg United Res.	20	12	2	6	44	40	38
GSK Ulverston Res.	20	9	2	9	54	45	29
Furness Rovers A	20	7	4	9	43	50	25
Kirkby United Res.	20	5	6	9	34	64	21
Barrow Celtic Res.	20	6	2	12	44	71	20
Walney Island A	20	4	3	13	37	76	15
Hawcoat Park A -6	20	6	2	12	49	60	14
Askam United A	20	4	2	14	39	77	14

GAINSBOROUGH & DISTRICT LEAGUE

	P	W	D	L	F	A	Pts
Goro. Town Canute	22	20	2	0	100	17	62
AFC Ropery	22	15	2	5	104	43	47
Bridon	22	13	3	6	76	47	42
BFC Birches	22	11	5	6	65	41	38
Harworth Colliery	22	10	6	6	61	45	36
Mattersey	22	9	6	7	49	40	33
East Drayton	22	7	4	11	32	58	25
Haxey	22	7	1	14	39	63	22
Marshalls Sports	22	6	4	12	43	77	22
Fox/Hounds Willingham	22	7	0	15	46	91	21
Retford Town Res.	22	4	5	13	37	84	17
Wroot	22	3	2	17	27	73	11

GRANTHAM & DISTRICT LEAGUE

Premier	P	W	D	L	F	A	Pts
Beehive United	18	16	2	0	71	7	50
Ruskington Rovers	18	14	2	2	62	24	44
Buckminster United	18	10	2	6	57	27	32
Greyhounders	18	10	1	7	47	31	31
Ancaster Rovers	18	10	1	7	35	32	31
Barrowby	18	8	1	9	37	28	25
Bottesford	18	6	0	12	33	66	18
Granth. Squash Club	18	5	2	11	29	62	17
Barkston & Syston	18	4	1	13	36	66	13
Croxton	18	1	0	17	21	85	3

RHP Newark - record expunged.

GRAVESEND LEAGUE

Division One	P	W	D	L	F	A	Pts
NK Aces Res.	20	20	0	0	66	20	60
Lullingstone Castle	20	15	2	3	96	19	47
Fleetdown United B	20	14	0	6	51	38	42
Viewpoint Res.	20	13	0	7	74	49	39
Culverstone United	20	7	5	8	43	37	26
Meopham	20	8	2	10	44	62	26
Kent Celts	20	6	2	12	43	71	20
Ash Green	20	6	2	12	33	65	20
AZ 82	20	4	4	12	43	73	16
Earl Grey	20	2	5	13	21	48	11
Swan Valley	20	2	4	14	32	64	10

Guru Nanak Res. - record expunged.

GREAT YARMOUTH & DISTRICT LEAGUE

Division One	P	W	D	L	F	A	Pts
Catfield	18	17	1	0	119	12	52
MK United	18	13	2	3	125	37	41
Albion	18	13	2	3	79	24	41
Norfolk & Chance	18	10	0	8	59	54	30
Bohemians	18	8	3	7	42	28	27
Grt Y International -6	18	9	1	8	51	48	22
Great Yarmouth Utd	18	7	1	10	41	52	22
Gt Yarmouth Peelers	18	3	2	13	60	78	11
Feathers	18	3	1	14	33	104	10
Caister United A -3	18	0	1	17	15	187	-2

Division Two	P	W	D	L	F	A	Pts
Belton	18	13	3	2	59	18	42
Caister Com. Cent. -3	18	14	1	3	66	22	40
MK United Res.	18	9	5	4	38	26	32
Prostar Windows	18	9	1	8	46	33	28
Arches	18	8	4	6	48	36	28
Carpathians	18	7	3	8	49	44	24
South Yarmouth	18	8	0	10	48	54	24
Caister Youth	18	7	2	9	50	59	23
Wellington	18	4	3	11	37	68	15
Martham A	18	0	0	18	20	101	0

GRIMSBY & DISTRICT LEAGUE

Division One	P	W	D	L	F	A	Pts
Harvest -1	12	10	1	1	51	19	30
Number One Pub	12	7	3	2	43	16	24
Immingham Bluestone	12	5	3	4	39	24	18
Buddies	12	5	1	6	26	26	16
FC So Thai	12	4	2	6	27	44	14
Caistor Tennyson	12	4	1	7	23	48	13
Imm. Blossom Way	12	1	1	10	15	47	4

Division Two	P	W	D	L	F	A	Pts
D M S	21	17	0	4	88	27	51
Everyone Active	21	16	1	4	94	47	49
Car Services	21	16	0	5	85	33	48
Mitchells	21	9	3	9	80	67	30
Holten Wanderers	21	7	1	13	54	81	22
N E L C	21	7	1	13	51	79	22
FC Sentiments	21	4	2	15	26	80	14
Grimsby Plates	21	4	0	17	33	97	12

GUERNSEY LEAGUE

Division One	P	W	D	L	F	A	Pts
St Martins	18	16	1	1	77	17	49
Belgrave Wanderers	18	10	3	5	38	27	33
Northerners	18	9	2	7	46	35	29
Vale Recreation	18	7	4	7	23	34	25
Rangers	18	6	2	10	47	56	20
Rovers	18	6	1	11	30	47	19
Sylvans	18	2	1	15	21	66	7

Athletics - record expunged.

Division Two	P	W	D	L	F	A	Pts
Guernsey Rgrs Res.	24	20	2	2	92	34	62
Belgrave Wanderers	24	16	3	5	78	35	51
Vale Recreation Res.	24	14	2	8	72	49	44
St Martins Res.	24	12	3	9	77	46	39
Northerners Res.	24	12	3	9	58	61	39
Sylvans Res.	24	8	2	14	45	88	26
Centrals	24	7	2	15	49	86	23
Bavaria Nomads	24	6	1	17	30	55	19
Rovers Res.	24	3	2	19	28	75	11

GUILDFORD & WOKING ALLIANCE

Premier	P	W	D	L	F	A	Pts
Hambledon	20	14	3	3	56	18	45
AFC Walton/Hersham	20	14	3	3	64	31	45
Millmead	20	13	1	6	75	36	40
Knaphill Athletic	20	12	3	5	56	34	39
Shepperton FB	20	10	3	7	50	45	33
New Haw Wanderers	20	10	2	8	46	47	32
Pirbright Sports	20	7	2	11	31	38	23
Windlesham	20	7	2	11	34	59	23
Holmbury St Mary	20	6	3	11	43	51	21
Ockham	20	5	2	13	39	58	17
Milford & Witley A	20	0	0	20	12	89	0

OTHER LEAGUES

Division One	P	W	D	L	F	A	Pts
Oatlands	18	16	0	2	105	26	48
Puttenham United	18	14	0	4	70	37	42
AFC Woburn Arms	18	10	2	6	57	45	32
West Byfleet Albion	18	9	1	8	43	40	28
Guild. C Weysiders A	18	8	1	9	42	44	25
Knaphill Athletic Res.	18	8	1	9	34	44	25
NLU	18	7	3	8	36	35	24
University of Surrey A	18	7	0	11	45	50	21
Hersham Elm Grove A	18	3	2	13	28	80	11
Cresent & Star	18	3	0	15	37	96	9

Robin Hood Allstars - record expunged.

Division Two	P	W	D	L	F	A	Pts
FC Shepperton	20	17	2	1	117	24	53
Staines Lammas A	20	15	2	3	93	27	47
Keens Park Rangers	20	12	5	3	64	33	41
Mytchett Rangers	20	12	2	6	63	52	38
Elstead	20	8	5	7	44	42	29
Weybrook Wanderers	20	7	5	8	32	46	26
Dunsfold	20	8	1	11	50	64	25
Windlesham Res.	20	5	1	14	35	84	16
Worplesdon Pho. A	20	4	3	13	47	82	15
Guildford Park	20	3	4	13	42	85	13
AFC Gomshall	20	3	2	15	40	88	11

Division Three	P	W	D	L	F	A	Pts
Merrow A	20	18	1	1	74	10	55
Guildford Rail. Club	20	15	3	2	81	23	48
AFC Crown & Anchor	20	14	3	3	80	25	45
Guildford Rangers	20	13	2	5	59	33	41
Holmbury St M. Res.	20	12	3	5	50	19	39
Ripley Village A	20	6	3	11	31	43	21
NLU Res.	20	7	0	13	29	58	21
Hambledon Res.	20	5	1	14	36	72	16
Worplesdon Pho. B	20	5	0	15	39	69	15
Ockham Res.	20	5	0	15	26	74	15
Shalford Youth	20	2	0	18	27	106	6

Division Four North	P	W	D	L	F	A	Pts
AFC Bedfont Green A	20	13	3	4	59	33	42
Staines Lammas B	20	13	3	4	52	29	42
Freedom Spart. Ath.	20	11	5	4	61	35	38
Christian C. Woking	20	11	4	5	50	33	37
AFC Guildford Res.	20	10	5	5	43	23	35
Surrey Athletic	20	8	4	8	59	59	28
Knaphill Athletic A	20	8	3	9	35	43	27
Allianz	20	8	2	10	52	53	26
Woking Tigers	20	8	2	10	51	73	26
AFC Woburn A. Res.	20	2	1	17	31	71	7
Byfleet	20	1	2	17	34	75	5

Division Four South	P	W	D	L	F	A	Pts
AFC Bedfont Green B	20	15	2	3	73	45	47
Burpham A	20	13	4	3	81	34	43
AFC Guildford	20	11	5	4	69	39	38
Guildford Park Res.	20	12	1	7	58	42	37
Elstead Res.	20	10	3	7	55	44	33
Astolat Athletic	20	10	2	8	58	54	32
Guildford Rail Res.	20	8	3	9	49	55	27
Dunsfold Res.	20	8	1	11	53	45	25
Milford & Witley B	20	7	3	10	55	65	24
Millmead Res.	20	3	0	17	38	74	9
Shalford Youth Res.	20	1	0	19	26	118	3

HALIFAX & DISTRICT LEAGUE

Premier	P	W	D	L	F	A	Pts
Hebden Royd Red Star	22	20	1	1	76	24	61
Elland United	22	14	2	6	71	38	44
Greetland	22	11	4	7	61	45	37
Holmfield	22	11	4	7	59	45	37
Sowerby United	22	11	2	9	55	46	35
Stump Cross	22	10	4	8	37	35	34
Shelf United	22	8	6	8	57	48	30
Warley Rangers	22	9	2	11	49	44	29
Ryburn United	22	9	1	12	44	49	28
Calder 76	22	8	2	12	55	60	26
Midgley United	22	5	4	13	39	68	19
Halifax Irish Centre	22	0	0	22	19	120	0

Division One	P	W	D	L	F	A	Pts
Stainland United	18	15	3	0	83	32	48
AFC Crossleys	18	11	5	2	72	37	38
Sowerby Bridge	18	10	2	6	73	52	32
Northowram	18	9	2	7	57	46	29
Hebden Royd Red St Res.	18	8	4	6	48	47	28
Volunteer Arms	18	8	2	8	60	60	26
Denholme United	18	5	2	11	57	65	17
Mixenden United	18	5	1	12	36	62	16
Salem	18	5	1	12	39	70	16
Brighouse Old B "A"	18	2	2	14	25	79	8

Division Two	P	W	D	L	F	A	Pts
Copley United	16	13	1	2	80	29	40
Ryburn United Reserves	16	13	1	2	48	14	40
Greetland Reserves	16	8	2	6	33	38	26
Shelf United Reserves	16	8	2	6	34	52	26
Sowerby Bridge Reserves	16	7	2	7	37	34	23
Halifax Athletic	16	7	1	8	36	37	22
Elland Allstars	16	6	1	9	44	41	19
Halifax Irish Centre Res.	16	2	2	12	28	65	8
Warley Rangers Reserves	16	2	0	14	15	45	6

Division Three	P	W	D	L	F	A	Pts
Wadsworth United	20	17	1	2	74	21	52
Elland United Reserves	20	13	4	3	75	41	43
Sowerby United Reserves	20	11	3	6	60	36	36
Stainland United Reserves	20	10	6	4	61	42	36
AFC Crossleys Reserves	20	10	3	7	72	58	33
Volunteer Arms Reserves	20	8	3	9	48	51	27
Midgley United Reserves	20	8	2	10	52	53	26
Calder 76 Reserves	20	7	4	9	41	41	25
Denholme United Res.	20	7	1	12	51	68	22
Elland Allstars Reserves	20	5	1	14	38	81	16
Salem Reserves	20	0	0	20	24	104	0

HALSTEAD & DISTRICT LEAGUE

Premier	P	W	D	L	F	A	Pts
Glemsford Gladiators	18	12	3	3	58	34	39
Pebmarsh	17	10	2	5	48	40	35
Sporting 77	18	10	1	7	42	35	28
Acton Crown	18	7	6	5	42	32	27
Kedingto	18	8	3	7	35	26	27
Essex Arms	17	7	5	5	47	41	26
Clare Reserves	18	6	6	6	46	34	24
Belchamps	18	7	3	8	43	48	24
Punch 68	18	5	4	9	45	48	19
Toppesfield	18	0	1	17	19	87	4

Pembarsh v Essex Arms was postponed and not re-arranged.

HARROGATE & DISTRICT LEAGUE

Premier	P	W	D	L	F	A	Pts
Thirsk Falcons	20	14	3	3	79	21	45
Harrogate RA A	20	14	3	3	54	27	45
Bedale Town	20	10	3	7	55	36	33
Harlow Hill	20	9	5	6	36	24	32
Kirk Deighton Rgrs	20	8	7	5	38	33	31
Otley Town A	20	9	2	9	44	46	29
Bramham	20	7	5	8	33	39	26
Otley Rovers	20	7	2	11	41	51	23
Pateley Bridge	20	6	2	12	35	60	20
Kirkby Malzeard	20	5	2	13	37	58	17
Burley Trojans	20	2	4	14	26	83	10

Harold Styans, Knaresborough Celtic - records expunged.

Division One	P	W	D	L	F	A	Pts
Beckwithshaw Saints	20	17	2	1	48	18	53
Kirk Deighton R. Res.	20	13	2	5	58	34	41
Pannal Sports	20	10	7	3	51	36	37
Wigton Moor	20	11	3	6	51	36	36
Thirsk Falcons Res.	20	8	6	6	51	46	30
Pool Res.	20	8	1	11	54	54	25
Killinghall Nomads	20	6	5	9	41	46	23
Boston Spartans	20	6	3	11	43	46	21
Clifford	20	4	5	11	36	53	17
Westbrook YMCA Res.	20	5	2	13	26	53	17
Bramhope	20	2	4	14	20	57	10

Harold Styans Res. - record expunged.

Division Two	P	W	D	L	F	A	Pts
Bedale Town Res.	24	18	2	4	69	28	56
Ripon Red Arrows	24	15	4	5	98	52	49
Harlow Hill Res.	24	16	1	7	57	31	49
Kirkby Malzeard Res.	24	13	4	7	52	31	43
Wetherby Athletic A	24	13	4	7	74	57	43
Beckwithshaw Res.	24	12	4	8	72	50	40
Boroughbridge A	24	11	1	12	69	57	34
Burley Trojans Res.	24	10	2	12	75	62	32
Pannal Sports Res.	24	9	5	10	42	47	32
Brafferton Rangers	24	8	4	12	43	75	28
Dalton Athletic	24	7	1	16	33	86	22
Addingham	24	6	1	17	48	87	19
Pool A	24	0	3	21	34	103	3

Division Three	P	W	D	L	F	A	Pts
Wigton Moor Res.	20	15	3	2	76	41	48
Pateley Bridge Res.	20	11	5	4	54	35	38
Hampsthwaite United	20	11	3	6	53	35	36
Bramham Res.	20	11	3	6	48	43	36
Catterick Village	20	9	5	6	49	45	32
Hampsthwaite Rvns	20	9	2	9	43	47	29
Ilkley Town A	20	8	2	10	49	51	26
Kirkby Malzeard A	20	5	3	12	30	46	18
Pannal Sports A	20	5	3	12	43	65	18
Helperby United	20	4	5	11	41	59	17
Thirsk Falcons A	20	3	4	13	27	46	13

Boston Spartans Res. - record expunged.

HERTFORD & DISTRICT LEAGUE

Premier	P	W	D	L	F	A	Pts
Greenbury United	18	11	6	1	46	22	28
Baldock Cannon	18	11	1	6	47	38	23
Waltham Abbey "A"	18	10	3	5	23	17	23
Bengeo Trinity	18	7	7	4	40	31	21
Hertford County	18	7	5	6	44	27	19
Harlow Link	18	7	5	6	45	32	19
Broxbourne Badgers	18	5	3	10	27	39	13
Hertford Heath Reserves	18	3	6	9	25	44	12
Cheshunt "A"	18	4	4	10	30	54	12
Westmill	18	3	4	11	21	44	10

Division One	P	W	D	L	F	A	Pts
Waltham Abbey "B"	20	15	1	4	67	32	31
Bury Rangers	20	12	4	4	45	23	28
Oracle Components	20	12	2	6	54	36	26
Elizabeth Allen Old B	20	11	3	6	48	34	25
Watton at Stone	20	9	4	7	54	46	22
Baldock Cannon Reserves	20	7	3	10	32	42	17
Wodson Park "A"	20	6	5	9	46	57	17
Broxbourne Badgers Res.	20	7	3	10	34	49	17
Inter	20	6	3	11	35	52	15
Cottered	20	5	3	12	34	51	13
Buntingford Wanderers	20	3	3	14	21	48	9

Division Two	P	W	D	L	F	A	Pts
Nazeing	24	18	5	1	62	27	41
Ware Lions Re-Utd	24	15	4	5	59	36	34
Roydon Spartans	24	13	5	6	62	37	31
Braughing	24	14	3	7	50	32	31
Thundridge	24	11	5	8	53	48	27
El'beth Allen OB Res.	24	11	4	9	56	40	26
Much Hadham	24	11	4	9	51	59	26
Hertford Celtic	24	9	2	13	51	55	20
County Hall Rangers	24	7	5	12	37	46	19
Broxb' Badgers "A"	24	7	3	14	55	70	17
Bengeo Trinity Res.	24	7	2	15	50	58	16
Westmill Reserves	24	6	2	16	45	68	14
Mangrove	24	5	0	19	42	97	10

Division Three	P	W	D	L	F	A	Pts
Mangrove Reserves	22	21	1	0	98	23	43
Ware Lions Old Boys	22	17	1	4	97	29	35
Braughing Reserves	22	13	2	7	64	62	28
Hertford County Reserves	22	12	2	8	65	42	26
Nazeing Reserves	22	10	3	9	43	49	23
Deaconsfield	22	9	2	11	70	57	20
Buntingford Wands Res.	22	9	2	11	54	47	20
Cottered Reserves	22	10	0	12	69	69	20
Watton at Stone Reserves	22	7	2	13	34	80	16
Elizabeth Allen OB "A"	22	7	0	15	57	82	14
Thundridge Reserves	22	6	1	15	49	56	13
Westwell	22	3	0	19	31	135	6

HOPE VALLEY AMATEUR LEAGUE

Premier	P	W	D	L	F	A	Pts
Whaley Bridge	22	19	1	2	86	13	58
Buxton Town	22	16	1	5	73	31	49
Harpur Hill	22	13	1	8	64	33	40
Dronfield Woodhse	22	12	4	6	50	40	40
Dove Holes	22	11	5	6	63	43	38
Tintwistle Villa	22	11	4	7	43	50	37
Dronfield Town "A"	22	8	5	9	45	41	29
Grindleford	22	6	4	12	34	39	22
Brampton	22	7	1	14	39	63	22
Furness Vale	22	6	2	14	36	77	20
Bakewell Town	22	5	1	16	26	75	16
Totley Sports	22	2	3	17	26	80	9

Hayfield - record expunged.

A Division	P	W	D	L	F	A	Pts
Holmesfield	26	20	3	3	101	33	63
Bradwell	26	16	6	4	71	41	51
Hathersage	26	14	6	6	65	47	48
Hunters Bar	26	13	5	8	64	51	44
Whaley Bridge Reserves	26	12	6	8	64	54	42
Buxton Christians	26	13	2	11	86	68	41
Dronfield Woodhouse res.	26	12	5	9	60	50	41
Tideswell United	26	10	6	10	54	61	36
Blazing Rag	26	8	11	7	60	58	35
Dove Holes Reserves	26	11	4	11	63	67	34
Peak Dale	26	9	4	13	60	56	31
Dronfield Town "B"	26	5	2	19	43	84	17
Edale	26	4	5	17	35	87	17
Grindleford Reserves	26	0	5	21	22	91	5

B Division	P	W	D	L	F	A	Pts
Youlgrave United	26	20	3	3	77	21	63
Buxworth	26	19	2	5	89	41	59
Red Lion	26	17	5	4	84	34	56
Calver	26	16	4	6	77	51	52
FC United of Tideswell	26	15	5	6	92	49	50
Bamford	26	13	6	7	73	41	45
Tideswell United Blue Star	26	13	3	10	74	49	42
Eyam	26	9	5	12	57	52	32
Stoney Middleton	26	7	6	13	47	66	27
Bakewell Town Reserves	26	7	5	14	43	63	26
Baslow	26	8	1	17	45	85	22
Wheatsheaf	26	5	3	18	43	83	18
Furness Vale Reserves	26	7	1	18	47	96	13
Winster Wasps	26	1	1	24	20	137	4

HUDDERSFIELD & DISTRICT LEAGUE

Division One	P	W	D	L	F	A	Pts
Hepworth United	22	17	2	3	68	25	53
Newsome	22	15	2	5	58	36	47
Netherton	22	12	2	8	57	44	38
Uppermill	22	11	3	8	50	32	36
Britannia Sports	22	11	3	8	56	50	36
Moldgreen	22	9	6	7	39	50	33
Diggle	22	10	1	11	47	44	31
Shepley	22	7	4	11	39	47	25
Berry Brow	22	7	4	11	35	45	25
Lepton Highlanders Res.	22	7	2	13	29	48	23
Cumberworth	22	3	6	13	29	51	15
Meltham Athletic	22	4	3	15	33	68	15

Division Two	P	W	D	L	F	A	Pts
Slaithwaite United	20	13	5	2	55	29	44
Holmbridge	20	12	6	2	37	16	42
Scholes	20	12	4	4	52	31	40
Skelmanthorpe	20	10	6	4	60	31	36
Westend	20	7	6	7	48	54	27
Kirkheaton Rovers	20	7	3	10	41	44	24
Scissett	20	7	2	11	38	41	23
Royal Dolphins	20	6	4	10	47	62	22
Heywood Irish Centre	20	5	6	9	33	54	21
Honley	20	5	1	14	43	61	16
Wooldale Wanderers	20	1	7	12	28	59	10

Lamb Inn - record expunged.

Division Three	P	W	D	L	F	A	Pts
Shelley	22	20	0	2	97	25	60
Heyside	22	16	1	5	65	29	49
Dalton Crusaders	22	15	0	7	72	47	45
KKS Sun Inn	22	11	2	9	55	41	35
Grange Moor	22	11	2	9	69	63	35
Brook Motors	22	11	1	10	52	59	34
YMCA	22	10	1	11	43	58	31
Upperthong SC	22	8	4	10	43	49	28
Savile Town	22	9	0	13	48	73	27
New Mill 94	22	7	4	11	52	62	25
HV.Academicals	22	4	1	17	36	71	13
Paddock Rangers	22	0	4	18	18	73	4

Division Four	P	W	D	L	F	A	Pts
AFC Waterloo	22	18	2	2	104	29	56
Linthwaite Athletic	22	18	1	3	115	40	55
Holmfirth Town	22	17	2	3	99	32	53
Moldgreen Con	22	14	4	4	87	44	46
Hade Edge	22	12	3	7	64	51	39
Cartworth Moor	22	7	5	10	51	62	26
Fenay Bridge	22	8	0	14	34	70	24
Mount	22	7	2	13	44	88	23
Spotted Cow	22	6	2	14	52	59	20
Flockton	22	5	5	12	46	73	20
AFC Lindley	22	3	1	18	38	96	10
AFC Black Horse	22	3	1	18	27	117	10

HUDDERSFIELD & DISTRICT WORKS & COMBINATION LEAGUE

Division One	P	W	D	L	F	A	Pts
Coach & Horses	21	15	1	5	67	37	46
Lindley Liberal Club	21	13	5	3	54	37	44
Sovereign Sports	21	11	2	8	31	40	35
Moldgreen Reserves	21	9	1	10	60	47	28
Hepworth United Reserves	21	7	4	10	35	62	25
Aimbry	21	7	2	12	40	46	23
Lepton Highlanders "A"	21	7	2	12	52	61	23
Bay Athletic "A"	21	3	5	13	30	39	14

Division Two	P	W	D	L	F	A	Pts
Golcar United "A"	18	14	0	4	70	44	42
Kirkheaton Rovers "B"	18	12	2	4	48	33	38
Ireti Athletic	18	11	4	3	69	41	37
Uppermill "C"	18	9	3	6	53	33	30
Moldgreen Con Reserves	18	8	2	8	53	60	26
Shelley "A"	18	7	0	11	43	52	21
Marsden "A"	18	5	5	8	70	64	20
Clothiers Arms	18	4	4	10	41	59	16
Grange Moor Reserves	18	3	6	9	44	56	15
Lindley Liberal Club Res.	18	3	2	13	36	85	11

I ZINGARI COMBINATION

Division One	P	W	D	L	F	A	Pts
Old Xaverians Reserves	22	19	1	2	68	23	58
Park Brow	22	18	2	2	69	20	56
BRNESC Reserves	22	11	4	7	57	36	37
Essemmay Old Boys Res.	22	10	5	7	51	38	35
Manweb	22	8	8	6	41	46	32
Alder Reserves	22	8	6	8	47	53	30
Aintree Villa	22	9	2	11	48	68	29
Sacre Coeur FP Reserves	22	8	4	10	47	37	28
Liverpool Cavaliers	22	6	3	13	39	66	21
Leyfield Reserves	22	4	5	13	29	51	17
Stoneycroft Reserves	22	4	4	14	37	71	16
Liobians Reserves	22	3	4	15	40	64	13

Edge Hill BC Old Boys Reserves - record expunged.

Division Two	P	W	D	L	F	A	Pts
AFC Tuebrook	22	20	0	2	110	20	60
Storrsdale	22	19	1	2	83	18	58
Liver Academy	22	14	4	4	73	35	46
Adlam Park	22	14	2	6	84	34	44
Walton CTC -	22	11	2	9	57	47	35
St Lukes	22	9	1	12	51	53	28
Mackets Grenadier	22	8	4	10	49	52	28
Rockville (Wallasey)	22	8	1	13	58	72	25
Old English	22	6	6	10	44	56	24
Barrluca	22	5	2	15	39	70	17
Mexoc (-3)	22	6	1	15	41	75	16
Flames	22	0	0	22	15	172	0

Cedar - record expunged.

Riverside - record expunged.

ISLE OF MAN SENIOR LEAGUE

Premier League	P	W	D	L	F	A	Pts
St Georges	24	22	2	0	126	10	68
DHSOB	24	19	3	2	79	23	60
Peel	24	17	3	4	113	36	54
Laxey	24	15	3	6	79	40	48
St Marys	24	13	2	9	74	36	41
Rushen	24	13	2	9	54	53	41
Ramsey	24	9	6	9	52	55	33
Corinthians	24	7	5	12	47	69	26
Ayre United	24	6	5	13	44	81	23
Castletown	24	4	6	14	35	73	18
Gymnasium	24	5	1	18	47	94	16
Michael United	24	4	1	19	28	98	13
Douglas Royal	24	2	1	21	29	139	7

Division Two	Pld	W	D	L	F	A	Pts
St Johns	24	24	0	0	194	17	72
RYCOB	24	17	1	6	71	42	52
Union Mills	24	16	1	7	77	37	49
Colby	24	14	1	9	75	54	43
Pulrose United	24	13	4	7	59	46	43
Police	24	12	4	8	72	80	40
Braddan	24	11	2	11	71	74	35
Onchan	24	10	3	11	56	46	33
Marown	24	9	2	13	62	72	29
Douglas & District	24	6	1	17	46	87	19
Foxdale	24	5	2	17	41	80	17
Malew	24	5	2	17	38	132	17
Ronaldsway	24	2	1	21	27	122	7

Combination One	P	W	D	L	F	A	Pts
Peel Reserves	24	23	1	0	130	8	70
St Georges Reserves	24	19	3	2	90	18	60
Ramsey Reserves	24	18	1	5	85	40	55
DHSOB Reserves	24	17	1	6	96	38	52
Laxey Reserves (-3)	24	15	1	8	108	51	43
Rushen Reserves	24	13	3	8	84	69	42
St Marys Reserves	24	11	1	12	67	61	34
Corinthians Reserves	24	7	4	13	41	73	25
Ayre United Reserves	24	6	3	15	46	95	21
Castletown Reserves	24	3	5	16	43	94	14
Michael Utd Reserves	24	3	4	17	28	114	13
Douglas Roy res (-3)	24	4	1	19	38	114	10
Gymnasium Reserves	24	2	2	20	36	117	8

Combination Two	P	W	D	L	F	A	Pts
Union Mills Reserves	24	19	3	2	76	27	60
St Johns Reserves	24	18	4	2	116	39	58
Marown Reserves	24	16	1	7	91	52	49
Colby Reserves	24	15	3	6	70	39	48
Onchan Reserves	24	15	3	6	71	47	48
Foxdale Reserves	24	13	3	8	66	53	42
RYCOB Reserves	24	10	4	10	80	55	34
Braddan Reserves	24	9	4	11	54	62	31
Pulrose Reserves	24	8	3	13	62	58	27
Police Reserves	24	4	4	16	42	90	16
Malew Reserves (-3)	24	6	0	18	55	116	15
Ronaldsway Reserves	24	4	1	19	37	99	13
Douglas & Dist Res.	24	2	1	21	26	109	7

ISLE OF WIGHT LEAGUE

Division One	P	W	D	L	F	A	Pts
West Wight	26	21	3	2	80	21	66
Northwood St Johns	26	18	3	5	74	22	57
Brading Town Reserves	26	17	6	3	72	23	57
Shanklin	26	16	5	5	66	32	53
Cowes Sports Reserves	26	13	5	8	51	39	44
Newport IOW Reserves	26	13	2	11	55	60	41
GKN	26	13	4	9	69	55	43
Oakfield	26	12	2	12	54	52	38
Ventnor	26	10	7	9	46	41	37
Binstead & COB	26	8	3	15	61	68	27
Newchurch	26	6	3	17	49	66	21
Carisbrooke United	26	2	8	16	36	92	14
St Helens Blue Star	26	2	4	20	34	89	10
Brighstone	26	3	1	22	30	115	10

Division Two	P	W	D	L	F	A	Pts
Ryde Saints	21	13	4	4	77	24	43
Niton	21	13	4	4	60	32	43
Shanklin VYCC	21	12	5	4	71	25	41
W & B Sports	21	12	4	5	74	36	40
Osborne Coburg	21	12	4	5	67	30	40
Pan Sports	21	11	4	6	85	45	37
Sandown	21	10	6	5	67	25	36
E Cowes Victoria Athletic R.	21	10	2	9	60	32	32

Division Three	P	W	D	L	F	A	Pts
Seaview	20	12	2	6	90	40	38
Wroxall	20	8	1	11	55	53	25
Yarmouth & Calbourne	20	7	1	12	53	52	22
Wakes	20	7	0	13	37	69	21
East Cowes Youth	20	3	2	15	39	65	11
Kyngs Towne	20	3	2	15	25	84	11
Rookley	20	0	1	19	12	214	1

JERSEY FOOTBALL COMBINATION

Premiership	P	W	D	L	F	A	Pts
St Paul's	16	14	2	0	56	7	44
Jersey Wanderers	16	9	2	5	41	28	29
Grouville	16	6	4	6	29	29	22
St Peter	16	6	4	6	24	24	22
Trinity	16	7	1	8	28	40	22
Jersey Scottish	16	6	3	7	29	27	21
St Ouen	16	6	1	9	28	33	19
Portuguese	16	5	4	7	20	31	19
St Clement	16	2	1	13	20	56	7

Championship	P	W	D	L	F	A	Pts
First Tower United	18	14	3	1	47	14	45
Rozel Rovers	18	13	3	2	59	18	42
St Brelade	18	10	2	6	47	30	32
Sporting Academics	18	7	4	7	37	41	25
St Martin/SCF	18	7	4	7	40	56	25
St Lawrence	18	7	3	8	28	30	24
Beeches OB	18	7	2	9	31	44	23
Jersey Nomads	18	5	4	9	35	36	19
Magpies	18	3	2	13	22	56	11
St John	18	2	3	13	27	48	9

Division One	P	W	D	L	F	A	Pts
Jersey Wanderers Reserves	16	12	1	3	55	23	37
Grouville Reserves	16	10	3	3	42	17	33
St Ouen Reserves	16	8	3	5	54	39	27
St Paul's Reserves	16	8	3	5	49	34	27
Jersey Scottish res (-3)	16	7	1	8	19	40	19
First Tower Utd Reserves	16	5	1	10	34	51	16
Rozel Rovers Reserves	16	4	2	10	23	39	14
Portuguese Reserves	16	3	5	8	23	37	14
Trinity Reserves (-1)	16	4	3	9	27	46	14

Division Two	P	W	D	L	F	A	Pts
St Peter Reserves	18	17	0	1	97	18	51
St Clement Reserves	18	14	1	3	68	34	43
St Brelade Reserves	18	10	1	7	47	32	31
St Lawrence Reserves	18	10	1	7	54	40	31
St John Reserves	18	9	1	8	48	47	28
Jersey Nomads rese (-3)	18	7	3	8	50	66	21
Sprtg Academics res (-1)	18	6	2	10	36	56	19
St Martin/SCF Reserves	18	4	4	10	29	46	16
Magpies Reserves	18	5	1	12	40	63	16
Beeches OB Reserves	18	1	0	17	22	89	3

Division Three	P	W	D	L	F	A	Pts
St Peter "A"	18	14	3	1	39	17	45
Jersey Wanderers "A"	18	13	2	3	79	17	41
Grouville "A" (-3)	18	14	2	2	54	15	41
St Ouen "A"	18	10	1	7	53	31	31
Rozel Rovers "A"	18	7	4	7	38	39	25
St Clement "A" (-3)	18	8	3	7	42	42	24
Magpies "A"	18	2	6	10	18	35	12
Sporting Academics "A"	18	3	3	12	32	68	12
St Martin/SCF "A"	18	3	1	14	25	96	10
St John "A" (-1)	18	3	1	14	34	54	9

KIDDERMINSTER & DISTRICT LEAGUE

Premier Division	P	W	D	L	F	A	Pts
Birch Coppice	24	15	3	6	62	48	48
Wyre Forest	24	14	5	5	77	44	47
KS Athletic	24	13	5	6	56	31	44
Kings Heath Old Boys	24	13	5	6	69	49	44
Netherton Athletic	24	13	5	6	62	45	44
Areley Kings	24	13	5	6	59	44	44
Lodge Farm	24	12	7	5	70	45	43
Two Gates	24	11	5	8	54	41	38
Kinver	24	7	3	14	49	66	24
Dudley Wood Athletic	24	5	5	14	45	75	20
Oldswinford Harriers (-1)	24	6	2	16	27	52	19
Cookley	24	3	3	18	33	82	12
Burlish Olympic	24	2	5	17	30	71	11

Division One	P	W	D	L	F	A	Pts
Dudley Villa	21	16	3	2	86	23	51
Orton Vale	21	15	1	5	63	30	46
Lodgefield Park	21	10	7	4	47	28	37
Claverley	21	9	4	8	53	45	31
Claverley Colts	21	8	3	10	48	43	27
Netherton Wanderers	21	7	5	9	45	45	26
Blackheath Liberals	21	5	3	13	33	54	18
Three Crowns United	21	1	0	20	14	121	3

KINGSTON & DISTRICT LEAGUE

Premier Division	P	W	D	L	F	A	Pts
AFC Molesey	16	13	2	1	39	11	41
Chessington KC	16	10	1	5	54	25	31
AFC Watermans	16	8	2	6	54	29	26
Maori Park	16	7	3	6	23	33	24
Old Rutlishians Reserves	16	6	2	8	19	27	20
Summerstown	16	6	1	9	25	28	19
AC.Malden	16	4	5	7	22	37	17
Kingston Albion	16	4	3	9	24	45	15
LM United	16	4	1	11	19	44	13

Division One	P	W	D	L	F	A	Pts
SHFC London	18	14	0	4	47	27	42
Robin Hood	18	11	4	3	59	31	37
Parkside	18	11	2	5	49	25	35
Darkside	18	10	4	4	45	31	34
AFC West End	18	7	4	7	32	34	25
Repton	18	7	1	10	31	53	22
Old Roehamptonians	18	6	3	9	35	45	21
Esher United	18	6	2	10	29	42	20
Maori Park Reserves	18	2	5	11	26	43	11
Oxshott Royals	18	3	1	14	22	44	10

Division Two	P	W	D	L	F	A	Pts
NPL "A"	16	10	1	5	41	20	31
Richmond & Kingstn OB	16	9	3	4	48	28	30
Wandle	16	9	3	4	52	35	30
Sunbury Galaxy	16	8	4	4	41	25	28
Esher	16	7	0	9	37	36	21
Thornton Heath	16	6	2	8	45	58	20
Old Rutlishians "A"	16	5	4	7	18	33	19
Red Star	16	5	3	8	27	43	18
Twickenham Athletic	16	3	0	13	28	59	9

Division Three	P	W	D	L	F	A	Pts
Chessington KC Reserves	16	13	2	1	65	18	41
Banstead Town	16	11	1	4	53	25	34
Lower Green	16	9	1	6	48	24	28
St Martins	16	9	1	6	50	36	28
Surbiton Eagles	16	9	1	6	49	41	28
Surrey Fire	16	6	4	6	28	34	22
Epsom Casuals	16	4	3	9	19	53	15
Westside "A"	16	2	2	12	15	51	8
AFC Hampton	16	1	1	14	21	66	4

Division Four	P	W	D	L	F	A	Pts
AFC Molesey Reserves	18	13	4	1	48	21	43
NPL "B"	18	13	1	4	49	25	40
Claygate & Ditton Res.	18	11	2	5	58	25	35
Dynamo Kingston	18	9	2	7	45	41	29
Barnslake	18	7	2	9	39	45	23
Merton Social	18	7	2	9	38	45	23
Parkside Reserves	18	6	4	8	37	43	22
Hook Venturers	18	6	2	10	31	39	20
Skylarks	18	3	4	11	29	44	13
Lower Green Reserves	18	3	1	14	24	70	10

Division Five	P	W	D	L	F	A	Pts
FC Carlisle	16	11	3	2	37	15	36
AFC Watermans Reserves	16	11	2	3	42	19	35
Darkside Reserves	16	10	3	3	48	23	33
St Martins Reserves	16	7	1	8	36	46	22
AFC Kingston	16	6	3	7	24	37	21
Barnes Common	16	6	1	9	32	14	19
Chessington KC "A"	16	5	4	7	27	26	19
Red Star Reserves	16	4	1	11	27	38	13
Merton Social Reserves	16	2	2	12	10	65	8

LANCASHIRE & CHESHIRE LEAGUE

Premier Division	P	W	D	L	F	A	Pts
Whalley Range	26	21	3	2	78	20	66
Cheadle Hulme Villa	26	16	2	8	59	39	50
Mellor	26	14	5	7	70	50	47
Rochdalians	26	14	4	8	50	32	46
Old Trafford	26	14	2	10	72	62	44
Spurley Hey	26	13	4	9	55	43	43
Old Ashtonians	26	13	4	9	63	55	43
Old Stretfordians	26	11	4	11	46	47	37
Bedians	26	10	4	12	52	50	34
Hazel Grove	26	7	7	12	34	53	28
South Manchester	26	6	7	13	37	56	25
Hooley Bridge Celtic	26	7	1	18	47	88	22
Govan Athletic	26	5	3	18	33	62	18
Stoconians	26	4	4	18	38	77	16

Division One	P	W	D	L	F	A	Pts
Chorltonians	26	18	6	2	78	43	60
AFC Oldham 2005	26	15	8	3	91	55	53
Deans	26	15	3	8	100	60	48
Irlam Steel	26	14	4	8	86	65	46
Alkrington Dynamoes	26	12	5	9	65	63	41
Heaton Mersey	26	11	4	11	60	63	37
Parrswood Celtic	26	9	8	9	65	68	35
Newton	26	9	7	10	61	61	34
Burnage Metro	26	10	4	12	67	82	34
Milton	26	10	3	13	58	70	33
Abacus Media	26	9	5	12	80	72	32
Newton Heath	26	8	5	13	42	55	29
Moston Brook	26	5	3	18	54	83	18
Eagle (-6)	26	2	5	19	47	114	5

OTHER LEAGUES

Division Two	P	W	D	L	F	A	Pts
Bedians Reserves	24	19	3	2	75	21	60
Tintwistle Athletic	24	15	4	5	71	39	49
Santos	24	15	2	7	76	42	47
Mellor Reserves	24	14	3	7	70	46	45
Gorse Hill Athletic	24	11	5	8	92	61	38
Rochdalians Reserves	24	11	2	11	58	62	35
Droylsden Amateurs	24	9	5	10	71	64	32
Gatley	24	9	4	11	66	67	31
Hollingworth OB	24	8	6	10	53	60	30
Moorside Rangers	24	8	5	11	53	54	29
Aldermere	24	8	3	13	53	71	27
VIP	24	2	5	17	36	101	11
Oldham Victoria	24	3	1	20	36	122	10

Division Three	P	W	D	L	F	A	Pts
Fletcher Moss Rangers	18	18	0	0	115	15	54
Ardwick	18	14	0	4	88	41	42
Inter Macc	18	12	1	5	64	23	37
Urmston Town	18	11	1	6	64	32	34
Whalley Range Reserves	18	10	2	6	56	44	32
Trafford United	18	10	0	8	55	44	30
Hazel Grove Reserves	18	4	2	12	28	58	14
Chorltonians Reserves (-3)	18	5	0	13	36	51	12
Old Bartonians	18	1	0	17	23	109	3
Harpurhey United (-3)	18	2	0	16	11	123	3

Bar Hill - record expunged.

Marauders - record expunged.

Division A	P	W	D	L	F	A	Pts
Deans Reserves	22	15	5	2	55	26	50
Burnage Metro Reserves	22	13	2	7	49	42	41
Whitworth Park Reserves	22	12	3	7	68	53	39
Cheadle Hulme Villa Res.	22	9	5	8	63	46	32
Old Trafford Reserves	22	9	4	9	60	53	31
Old Ashtonians Reserves	22	7	8	7	46	49	29
Old Stretfordians Res.	22	6	8	8	42	44	26
Manchester Rovers	22	6	6	10	51	66	24
Spurley Hey Reserves	22	6	5	11	42	63	23
Moston Brook Reserves	22	7	2	13	41	62	23
South Manchester Res.	22	5	7	10	51	50	22
Newton Heath res (-3)	22	5	9	8	47	61	21

Division B	Pld	W	D	L	F	A	Pts
Hooley Bridge Celtic Res.	22	15	4	3	63	31	49
Gorse Hill Athletic Res.	22	12	5	5	70	38	41
Irlam Steel Reserves	22	12	4	6	80	49	40
Moorside Rangers Res.	22	12	3	7	65	42	39
Eagle Reserves	22	11	1	10	67	56	34
Chorltonians “A”	22	10	3	9	68	69	33
Abacus Media Reserves	22	8	6	8	54	50	30
West End Reserves	22	8	5	9	64	68	29
Stoconians Reserves	22	7	3	12	34	61	24
Milton Reserves	22	6	3	13	55	87	21
Newton Reserves	22	6	2	14	39	75	20
Whalley Range “A”	22	4	3	15	43	76	15

Division C	P	W	D	L	F	A	Pts
Parrswood Celtic Res.	20	15	1	4	48	25	46
Staly Lions	20	14	2	4	79	36	44
Mellor “A”	20	14	0	6	63	35	42
Bedians “A”	20	12	2	6	57	33	38
Old Stretfordians “A”	20	10	3	7	43	39	33
Droylsden Amats res (-3)	20	10	1	9	67	57	28
Chorltonians “B”	20	8	4	8	45	54	28
Santos FC Reserves	20	8	2	10	54	52	26
Govan Athletic Reserves	20	5	0	15	30	72	15
Aldermere Reserves	20	1	7	12	40	67	10
Milton “A”	20	1	2	17	33	89	5

Oldham Victoria Reserves - record expunged.

Division D	P	W	D	L	F	A	Pts
Fletcher Moss Reserves	18	13	4	1	70	20	43
Irlam Steel “A”	18	9	5	4	63	43	32
Old Ashtonians “A”	18	8	5	5	48	47	29
Stoconians “A”	18	7	8	3	35	34	29
Hooley Bridge Celt. “A”	18	8	3	7	46	43	27
Staly Lions FC Reserves	18	7	6	5	33	32	27
AFC Oldham 2005 Res.	18	7	3	8	39	41	24
Mellor “B”	18	6	2	10	33	47	20
Old Stretfordians “B”	18	2	4	12	26	43	10
Chorltonians “C”	18	3	0	15	37	80	9

Division E	P	W	D	L	F	A	Pts
Ardwick Reserves	22	17	1	4	108	31	52
Burnage Metro “A”	22	13	3	6	45	32	42
Stoconians “B”	22	12	1	9	69	56	37
Inter Macc Reserves (-3)	22	12	3	7	65	43	36
Alkrington Dynam. Res.	22	10	1	11	58	53	31
Hillgate Reserves	22	9	4	9	56	57	31
Heaton Mersey Reserves	22	9	4	9	34	41	31
Trafford United Reserves	22	9	2	11	49	66	29
Moorside Rang. “A” (-3)	22	10	1	11	52	54	28
AFC Oldham 2005 “A”	22	8	3	11	50	67	27
Gorse Hill Ath. “A” (-3)	22	5	5	12	51	65	17
Spurley Hey “A”	22	2	4	16	39	111	10

Division F	P	W	D	L	F	A	Pts
Bedians “B”	18	16	0	2	88	27	48
Stoconians “C”	18	11	3	4	70	30	36
Moston Brook “A”	18	12	0	6	65	33	36
Whalley Range “B”	18	10	0	8	43	59	30
Aldermere “A” (-3)	18	8	4	6	37	50	25
Old Stretford’s “C” (-3)	18	7	2	9	32	39	20
AFC Oldham 2005 “B”	18	4	5	9	31	50	17
Spurley Hey “B” (-3)	18	4	6	8	21	26	15
Staly Lions “A”	18	3	3	12	20	49	12
Burnage Metro “B”	18	2	3	13	23	67	9

Cheadle Hulme Village “A” - record expunged.

LANCASHIRE AMATEUR LEAGUE

Premier Division	P	W	D	L	F	A	Pts
Failsworth Dynamos	26	19	3	4	85	30	60
Bury GSOB	26	18	5	3	57	28	59
Old Boltonians	26	15	3	8	68	35	48
Rossendale Amateurs	26	12	4	10	52	49	40
Howe Bridge Mills	26	12	4	10	49	61	40
Chaddertonians	26	11	6	9	57	50	39
Chew Moor Brook	26	12	3	11	55	52	39
Old Mancunians	26	10	4	12	51	52	34
Castle Hill (-2)	26	10	5	11	55	57	33
Little Lever	26	8	7	11	56	58	31
Horwich Victoria (-4)	26	9	5	12	59	63	28
Rochdale St.Clements	26	8	3	15	40	53	27
Old Blackburnians	26	8	3	15	45	82	27
Radcliffe Town	26	2	1	23	27	86	7

Division One	P	W	D	L	F	A	Pts
Prestwich	26	19	5	2	82	23	62
Hesketh Casuals	26	17	5	4	67	42	56
Bolton Wyresdale	26	13	9	4	43	36	48
Prairie United	26	13	5	8	72	52	44
Rossendale Amateurs Res.	26	12	3	11	48	39	39
Hindley Juniors	26	11	5	10	54	45	38
Old Blackburnians Reserves	26	10	4	12	55	63	34
Broughton Amateurs	26	10	3	13	45	56	33
Horwich RMI	26	10	2	14	41	45	32
Mostonians	26	8	5	13	50	55	29
Thornleigh	26	9	1	16	42	60	28
Tyldesley United (-4)	26	8	7	11	53	60	27
Ainsworth	26	6	4	16	40	71	22
Little Lever SC Reserves	26	6	2	18	38	83	20

Division Two	P	W	D	L	F	A	Pts
Rochdale St Clements res.	26	21	2	3	76	36	65
Roach Dynamos	26	19	2	5	90	52	59
Old Standians	26	17	4	5	74	42	55
Old Boltonians Reserves	26	14	5	7	82	58	47
Chaddertonians Reserves	26	14	4	8	69	51	46
Accrington Amateurs	26	13	4	9	74	51	43
Bolton Ambassadors	26	14	1	11	68	60	43
Radcliffe Boys	26	12	3	11	89	75	39
Oldham Hulmeians	26	10	6	10	58	59	36
Chadderton Reserves	26	8	4	14	64	61	28
Old Mancunians Reserves	26	5	7	14	47	90	22
Bury GSOB Reserves	26	5	4	17	43	71	19
Lymm	26	2	5	19	27	92	11
Bolton Lads Club	26	2	1	23	39	102	7

Division Three	P	W	D	L	F	A	Pts
North Walkden	24	22	1	1	124	20	67
Ashtonians	24	16	1	7	70	43	49
Radcliffe Town Res.	24	12	5	7	58	50	41
Failsworth Dyn Res.	24	12	4	8	53	43	40
Bacup United	24	11	4	9	62	59	37
Castle Hill Reserves	24	11	2	11	46	53	35
Tottington United	24	10	3	11	55	62	33
Chaddertonians "A"	24	9	2	13	55	64	29
Rossendale Am "A"	24	7	6	11	51	67	27
Mostonians Reserves	24	6	5	13	56	70	23
Broughton Amat Res.	24	7	2	15	46	71	23
Astley Bridge (-4)	24	7	3	14	54	87	20
Bolton Wyresdale Res.	24	5	4	15	43	84	19

Division Four	P	W	D	L	F	A	Pts
Old Boltonians "A"	22	18	2	2	87	37	56
Hesketh Casuals Reserves	22	15	1	6	65	35	46
Rossendale Amats "B"	22	12	3	7	62	43	39
Horwich Victoria Res.	22	11	3	8	68	53	36
Horwich RMI Reserves	22	9	6	7	46	41	33
Old Blackburnians 'A'	22	10	1	11	71	53	31
Accrington Amateurs Res.	22	9	4	9	46	48	31
Rochdale St Clem "A"	22	9	4	9	37	49	31
Old Standians Reserves	22	9	1	12	44	52	28
Old Mancunians "A"	22	7	3	12	51	57	24
Radcliffe Boys Reserves	22	5	3	14	41	63	18
Lymm Reserves	22	2	1	19	37	124	7

Division Five	P	W	D	L	F	A	Pts
Prestwich Reserves	22	19	2	1	103	25	59
Oldham Hulmeians Res.	22	17	2	3	87	27	53
Ainsworth Reserves	22	15	1	6	82	31	46
Roach Dynamos Reserves	22	14	1	7	85	65	43
Thornleigh Reserves	22	12	3	7	84	47	39
Howe Bridge Mills Res.	22	11	2	9	59	41	35
Bolton Ambassadors Res.	22	9	1	12	59	85	28
Hesketh Casuals "A"	22	6	2	14	44	87	20
Rochdale St Clem "B"	22	5	4	13	29	63	19
Bury GSOB "A"	22	6	1	15	35	92	19
Old Boltonians 'B'	22	3	3	16	33	62	12
Mostonians "A"	22	3	2	17	33	108	11

Division Six North	P	W	D	L	F	A	Pts
Rossendale Amats "C"	20	14	3	3	69	35	45
Prestwich "A"	20	14	2	4	72	35	44
Thornleigh "A"	20	12	3	5	67	35	39
Broughton Amateurs "A"	20	12	2	6	63	44	38
Old Blackburnians "B"	20	12	1	7	73	54	37
Tottington United Res.	20	8	4	8	56	66	28
Hesketh Casuals "B"	20	7	5	8	47	60	26
Broughton Amateurs "B"	20	7	4	9	51	59	25
Rossendale Amats "D"	20	4	2	14	35	74	14
Horwich RMI "A"	20	2	4	14	35	67	10
Bolton Wyresdale "B"	20	1	4	15	26	65	7

Division Six South	P	W	D	L	F	A	Pts
Ashtonians Reserves	20	16	3	1	61	24	51
Radcliffe Town "A"	20	16	1	3	83	40	49
Oldham Hulmeians "A"	20	11	0	9	54	58	33
Radcliffe Town "B"	20	10	1	9	61	60	31
Lymm "A"	20	9	3	8	62	48	30
Old Mancunians "B"	20	8	4	8	44	49	28
Bury GSOB "B"	20	8	2	10	41	48	26
Bolton Wyresdale "A"	20	7	3	10	50	64	24
Chaddertonians "B" (-4)	20	7	2	11	51	56	19
Thornleigh "B"	20	5	4	11	36	55	19
Oldham Hulm's "B" (-4)	20	0	3	17	25	66	-1

LANCASHIRE LEAGUE

East	P	W	D	L	F	A	Pts
Bradford Pk Ave. Res.	20	14	4	2	67	20	46
Thackley Res.	20	14	2	4	53	19	44
Farsley Res.	20	11	5	4	39	26	38
Ossett Albion Res.	20	11	4	5	47	33	37
Wakefield Res.	20	8	6	4	31	31	30
Guiseley Res.	20	8	3	9	47	41	27
Harrogate Rail A. Res.	20	7	5	8	37	42	26
Tadcaster Albion Res.	20	7	4	9	34	45	25
Ossett Town Res.	20	6	3	11	36	53	21
Silsden Res.	20	3	2	15	22	58	11
Eccleshill United Res.	20	1	2	17	22	67	5

(ontefract Collieries Res. - record expunged.

West	P	W	D	L	F	A	Pts
Bamber Bridge Res.	20	14	2	4	56	36	44
Fleetwood Town Res.	20	11	3	6	57	33	36
Mossley Res.	20	11	3	6	46	33	36
Lancaster City Res.	20	10	3	7	39	30	33
Stalybridge Celtic Res.	20	10	1	9	33	33	31
Workington Res.	20	9	2	9	44	55	29
Curzon Ashton Res.	20	7	7	6	34	30	28
Witton Albion Res.	20	6	4	10	32	48	22
Formby Res.	20	6	1	13	43	56	19
Colne Res.	20	6	1	13	41	55	19
AFC Fylde Res.	20	5	3	12	35	50	18

Woodley Sports Res. - record expunged.

LEEDS RED TRIANLE LEAGUE

Premier Division	P	W	D	L	F	A	Pts
Wortley Reserves	18	15	3	0	60	26	48
Halton Moor	18	12	2	4	43	30	38
Churwell	18	10	2	6	52	24	32
Halfway House Morley	18	8	5	5	47	42	29
Crossgates	18	8	2	8	35	40	26
Beeston St Anthonys "A"	18	6	3	9	22	29	21
Red Star Harehills	18	6	2	10	37	40	20
Seacroft WMC	18	6	1	11	43	65	19
Yorkshire Amateur U19	18	4	3	11	26	38	15
Middleton Park	18	3	1	14	42	73	10

Division One	P	W	D	L	F	A	Pts
CFYDC	20	16	3	1	58	22	51
Wortley "A"	20	14	4	2	53	29	46
Sporting Armley	20	12	1	7	62	53	37
Drighlington Adwalton	20	10	2	8	42	36	32
Drighl'ton Malt Shovel	20	10	1	9	40	44	31
Dudley Hill Rangers Res.	20	9	1	10	44	43	28
Amarnath	20	6	1	13	29	35	19
Prince of Wales Bradford	20	6	1	13	42	53	19
Leodis	20	5	4	11	30	47	19
Belle Isle WMC	20	5	3	12	37	52	18
Merlins	20	4	5	11	30	53	17

Division Two	P	W	D	L	F	A	Pts
Pudsey Britannia	20	16	4	0	120	30	52
Kirkstall Crusaders OB	20	17	1	2	84	23	52
FC Headingley Reserves	20	15	1	4	82	26	46
Cricketers Arms	20	14	2	4	80	35	44
South Leeds Saints PA	20	11	0	9	58	62	33
Churwell Reserves	20	9	2	9	66	56	29
Leeds Deaf	20	6	2	12	41	83	20
Swillington Reserves	20	5	3	12	55	91	18
Middleton Park Reserves	20	5	2	13	34	74	17
Travellers Stanningley	20	3	0	17	34	88	9
Cross Keys	20	0	1	19	27	113	1

New Farnley CC - record expugned

LEICESTER & DISTRICT LEAGUE

Premier Division	P	W	D	L	F	A	Pts
Blaby United	20	13	5	2	48	20	44
Guru Nanak Gurdwar	20	13	4	3	56	34	43
Houghton Rangers	20	13	3	4	49	26	42
Glenfield Town	20	11	1	8	48	43	34
Birstall RBL (-3)	20	11	3	6	60	42	33
County Hall	20	9	2	9	36	39	29
Mountsorrel Amateurs	20	6	5	9	48	46	23
Kirkland	20	6	2	12	43	59	20
Oadby Boys Club 93	20	5	3	12	35	45	18
Magna 73	20	5	3	12	30	54	18
Cosby United	20	2	1	17	25	70	7

Kingway Rangers - record expunged.

Midland Syston St Peters - record expunged.

Division One	P	W	D	L	F	A	Pts
Thurnby United	22	18	2	2	88	28	56
Kibworth Town	22	15	3	4	86	43	48
Leicester Tile 08	22	15	3	4	57	26	48
Glen Villa	22	11	4	7	44	48	37
Queniborough	22	10	5	7	57	47	35
Birstall Social	22	9	1	12	49	52	28
Huncote	22	8	3	11	36	44	27
Ashby Road	22	7	3	12	40	53	24
St Patricks	22	7	0	15	34	66	21
Burbage Old Boys	22	5	5	12	34	51	20
North Kilworth	22	6	1	15	31	67	19
Welby Lane United	22	4	4	14	30	61	16

Newbold Verdon - record expunged.

Division Two	P	W	D	L	F	A	Pts
Allexton and New Parks	26	26	0	0	138	13	78
Kingsway Celtic	26	17	3	6	97	50	54
Fleckney Athletic	26	16	3	7	64	41	51
Oakham Imperial	26	13	7	6	75	55	46
Thurlaston Magpies	26	14	3	9	69	61	45
Desford "A"	26	14	2	10	58	50	44
Sporting Sapcote (-3)	26	12	4	10	71	60	37
Aylestone Lounge	26	12	1	13	69	69	37
Rafters	26	11	2	13	58	59	35
Braunstone Trinity	26	9	0	17	62	72	27
Barlestone St Giles	26	8	3	15	49	72	27
Broughton Astley	26	6	3	17	27	88	21
Belgrave "A"	26	5	3	18	40	104	18
NKF United	26	1	2	23	14	97	5

Reserve Premier Div	P	W	D	L	F	A	Pts
Cosby United Reserves	22	17	0	5	71	37	51
Glenfield Town Reserves	22	14	2	6	64	52	44
Kirkland Reserves	22	11	5	6	65	45	38
Houghton Rangers Res.	22	11	4	7	53	37	37
North Kilworth Reserves	22	9	6	7	61	48	33
Birstall RBL Reserves	22	9	5	8	53	43	32
Mountsorrel Amats Res.	22	9	5	8	56	54	32
County Hall Reserves	22	8	7	7	66	68	31
Guru Nanak Gurdwar Res.	22	7	7	8	39	48	28
Magna 73 Reserves	22	8	3	11	47	54	27
St Patricks Reserves	22	3	1	18	38	83	10
Glen Villa Reserves	22	2	3	17	33	77	9
Reserve Division One	**P**	**W**	**D**	**L**	**F**	**A**	**Pts**
Allexton & NewP Res.	24	20	1	3	116	33	61
Oadby Boys Cl 93 Res.	24	16	4	4	69	36	52
Blaby United Res.	24	14	5	5	83	48	47
Cosby United "A"	24	13	4	7	89	69	43
Queniborough Res.	24	12	6	6	76	58	42
Thurnby United Res.	24	12	3	9	71	57	39
Sporting Sapcote Res.	24	12	0	12	61	65	36
Kibworth Town Res.	24	9	6	9	62	51	33
Midland Sys. St P Res.	24	9	3	12	68	71	30
Huncote Reserves	24	8	4	12	52	69	28
Birstall Social Res.	24	3	4	17	32	81	13
Oakham Imperial Res.	24	3	3	18	39	105	12
Thurlaston Magpies Res.	24	3	1	20	29	104	10

LEICESTER CITY LEAGUE

	P	W	D	L	F	A	Pts
Braders	14	14	0	0	81	14	42
Saffron Lounge Bar	14	12	0	2	63	30	36
Aylestone United 2009	14	6	2	6	43	39	20
FC Cricks	14	6	1	7	36	44	19
FC Rowlatts	14	5	2	7	33	46	17
FC Braunstone	14	4	3	7	35	43	15
Park End 74	14	3	1	10	26	51	10
Shakha	14	1	1	12	15	65	4

LINCOLN & DISTRICT LEAGUE

	P	W	D	L	F	A	Pts
Ivy Tavern CSA	20	17	2	1	68	24	53
Market Rasen Town	20	13	3	4	44	27	42
Washingborough	20	13	2	5	56	28	41
Waddington United	20	13	2	5	51	30	41
Nettleham Reserves	20	12	2	6	38	26	38
RM Imps	20	9	2	9	50	49	29
Metheringham	20	6	2	12	35	49	20
Ruston Sports	20	5	2	13	29	61	17
Middle Rasen	20	3	5	12	29	57	13
Fulbeck United	20	2	5	13	29	50	11
Horncastle Town Res.	20	3	1	16	45	73	10

Cherry Knights - record expunged.

LINCOLNSHIRE LEAGUE

	P	W	D	L	F	A	Pts
Boston United Res.	26	20	2	4	85	19	62
Lincoln United Res.	26	15	4	7	75	40	49
Cleethorpes Town	26	14	7	5	70	43	49
Swineshead Institute	26	14	4	8	75	46	46
Skegness Town	26	13	6	7	57	47	45
Horncastle Town	26	13	5	8	74	45	44
Hykeham Town	26	13	5	8	58	36	44
Heckington United	26	13	2	11	52	54	41
CGB Humbertherm	26	12	4	10	65	69	40
Skellingthorpe PFC	26	9	4	13	50	68	31
Louth Town Res.	26	9	3	14	51	62	30
Ruston Sports	26	5	3	18	27	86	18
Grimsby Boro. Res.	26	2	5	19	29	86	11
Sleaford Town Res.	26	2	2	22	26	93	8

LIVERPOOL CMS LEAGUE

Premier Division	P	W	D	L	F	A	Pts
Vale Madrid	24	17	5	2	92	44	56
Lord Warden	24	17	4	3	69	31	55
King Charles	24	17	3	4	76	33	54
Western Spee	24	14	6	4	85	38	48
FC Nou Camp	24	12	3	9	68	57	39
FC Stadium	24	12	0	12	77	63	36
South Hope	24	10	4	10	52	53	34
Mersey Harps	24	9	3	12	38	58	30
Polonia Camps	24	7	5	12	48	50	26
Dunnies RCU	24	7	4	13	57	97	25
Mosslane	24	7	2	15	47	86	23
Glasshouse	24	6	2	16	28	70	20
Everton Foundation	24	0	1	23	13	70	1
Division One	**P**	**W**	**D**	**L**	**F**	**A**	**Pts**
Fountains Abbey	26	20	2	4	100	40	62
Parkway	26	19	3	4	72	20	60
Mere Bank	26	16	7	3	92	43	55
The Clock	26	17	3	6	85	34	54
FC Nou Camp Reserves	26	16	3	7	87	32	51
Elmoore	26	13	6	7	70	43	45
The Claremont	26	13	2	11	65	53	41
Wavertree Ash	26	12	5	9	58	56	41
Lowerhouse	26	11	1	14	58	64	34
Irish Swifts	26	9	0	17	40	74	27
Engineers	26	8	0	18	30	67	24
Liverpool 8	26	5	3	18	28	110	18
Ashburn Reserves	26	3	3	20	42	124	12
Hope Re'United	26	1	0	25	5	72	3

LIVERPOOL OLD BOYS LEAGUE

Division One	P	W	D	L	F	A	Pts
Roby College OB	18	16	1	1	71	24	49
Old Cathinians	18	12	4	2	50	19	40
Bankfield OB	18	10	4	4	45	28	34
Quarry Bank OB	18	9	3	6	37	37	30
Old Xaverians "A"	18	9	2	7	39	26	29
Cardinal Newman	18	7	5	6	30	23	26
F.C. Salle	18	6	0	12	32	51	18
Oaks Institute OB	18	4	2	12	23	41	14
Old Holts	18	2	3	13	23	61	9
Wavertree WDOB	18	2	2	14	24	64	8

Heygreen OB - record expunged.

Division Two	P	W	D	L	F	A	Pts
Quarry Bank OB Reserves	20	16	1	3	71	30	49
Old Xaverians "B"	20	13	4	3	48	30	43
Old Bootleians	20	10	4	6	41	34	34
De La Salle OB	20	10	3	7	50	46	33
Cardinal Newman Reserves	20	9	5	6	43	37	32
Liverpool Medics	20	7	2	11	39	42	23
Ercanil OB	20	6	4	10	36	38	22
Alsop OB	20	5	7	8	44	51	22
Waterloo GSOB (-3)	20	7	2	11	36	41	20
Convocation	20	4	3	13	36	69	18
Sacre Coeur FP "A"	20	5	1	14	26	52	16

Mossley Hill - record expunged.

LONDON COMMERCIAL LEAGUE

Division One	P	W	D	L	F	A	Pts
Roxeth	18	15	1	2	66	29	46
British Airways	18	14	1	3	58	16	43
HFC	18	12	2	4	83	38	38
Shebu (Shep. Bush)	18	11	0	7	63	38	33
Sporting Duet	18	8	3	7	38	38	27
Fulham Dynamo Spts	18	6	3	9	36	45	21
Manor House	18	5	2	11	31	60	17
West End Rangers	18	5	0	13	21	60	15
Travaux Saints	18	4	2	12	32	70	14
Charing Cross Assoc.	18	2	2	14	25	59	8

Division Two	P	W	D	L	F	A	Pts
Nth Greenford Utd A	14	10	2	2	50	19	32
Northwood A	14	9	1	4	40	23	28
British Airways Res.	14	9	0	5	40	17	27
Southall Rangers	14	8	3	3	33	21	27
Sudbury Court	14	8	0	6	31	33	24
New Hanford	14	4	2	8	39	39	14
Abbey National S&S	14	3	0	11	20	53	9
Old Alpertonians	14	1	0	13	21	69	3

Stars United - record expunged.

Division Three	P	W	D	L	F	A	Pts
British Airways A	16	13	0	3	77	24	39
AFC Ruislip	16	12	1	3	55	22	37
Sandgate Old Boys	16	10	1	5	45	27	31
Fulham Dyn. Sp. Res.	16	10	1	5	34	37	31
Greenwood	16	7	2	7	44	41	23
Hillingdon A	16	4	2	10	28	47	14
LPOSSA Res.	16	3	5	8	31	61	14
Barnet Municipal Off.	16	3	1	12	27	53	10
Ealing Old Boys	16	3	1	12	23	52	10

Division Four	P	W	D	L	F	A	Pts
Viking Sports	16	13	1	2	60	35	40
Old Alpertonians Res.	16	11	1	4	42	30	34
Hounslow Wdrs Res.	16	10	1	5	68	27	31
Brentford Athletic	16	7	2	7	46	47	23
Chis. Homefields Res.	16	7	1	8	49	46	22
St Gabriels	16	6	1	9	27	56	19
Lampton Park	15	6	0	9	34	51	18
Harrow Lyons	15	4	1	10	27	56	13
Oriel Allstars	16	2	2	12	28	33	8

LOWESTOFT & DISTRICT LEAGUE

Division One	P	W	D	L	F	A	Pts
Oxford Arms	22	18	2	2	72	16	56
Hearts of Oak	22	13	4	5	71	31	43
Norton Athletic	22	13	2	7	70	53	41
Waveney Reserves	22	11	4	7	69	44	37
Spexhall	22	10	5	7	65	37	35
Pot Black	22	8	6	8	39	45	30
Blundeston Magpies	22	8	5	9	47	50	29
Barsham	22	8	3	11	37	59	27
Pakefield Re-United (-3)	22	8	3	11	67	62	24
Kirkley & Pakefield "A"	22	5	6	11	43	58	21
G Yarmouth Tn Hall (-3)	22	5	7	10	48	61	19
Corton Wh Horse Seltic	22	1	1	20	20	132	4

Division Two	P	W	D	L	F	A	Pts
DK Consultants (-3)	26	23	3	0	123	29	69
Hopton	26	21	4	1	115	30	67
Mutford & Wrentham	26	14	7	5	76	41	49
Waveney Gunners	26	16	1	9	69	49	49
Spexhall Reserves	26	13	2	11	65	52	41
Bungay Town "A"	26	12	5	9	57	66	41
Crusaders	26	10	7	9	78	65	37
Earsham	26	10	7	9	37	40	37
Lowestoft International	26	8	5	13	42	50	29
Norton Athletic Reserves	26	9	2	15	54	76	29
Waveney "A"	26	8	1	17	63	99	25
Beccles Caxton Reserves	26	7	0	19	44	86	21
Telecom Rovers	26	6	2	18	41	90	20
Ellingham	26	0	4	22	23	114	4

Division Three	P	W	D	L	F	A	Pts
FC Eastport	24	20	2	2	132	38	62
Corton Wh Horse Seltic Res.	24	20	2	2	109	26	62
Mutford & Wrentham Res.	24	18	0	6	94	40	54
Kirkley & Pakefield "B"	24	11	6	7	67	39	39
Royal Oak	24	12	2	10	73	58	38
Harleston Town res. (-6)	24	13	3	8	101	48	36
Factory Arms	24	10	4	10	69	62	34
Carlton Rangers	24	9	2	13	53	62	29
Blundeston Magpies res.	24	8	3	13	69	72	27
Westhall	24	5	6	13	59	74	21
Oxford Arms Reserves	24	5	5	14	62	78	20
Southwold Town res (-6)	24	7	1	16	44	101	16
Lowestoft Albion (-3)	24	0	0	24	11	245	-3

Marquis of Lorne - record expunged.

LUTON DISTRICT & SOUTH BEDS LEAGUE

Premier	P	W	D	L	F	A	Pts
Real F'n'E	18	13	5	0	57	25	44
Stopsley Common	18	11	4	3	61	39	37
Farley Boys	18	10	3	5	58	27	33
Lewsey Park	18	10	2	6	38	27	32
Offley Social	18	9	3	6	66	48	30
Christians in Sport	18	9	2	7	55	37	29
Ewe & Lamb	18	4	5	9	30	46	17
St Josephs	18	4	2	12	21	61	14
USL Saturday	18	3	4	11	37	61	13
Luton Leagrave	18	2	0	16	22	74	6

Division One	P	W	D	L	F	A	Pts
FourModel	16	13	2	1	51	16	41
St Josephs Reserves	16	11	2	3	51	23	35
Square	16	10	0	6	42	24	30
Christians in Sport Res.	16	9	3	4	44	30	30
The 61FC "A"	16	8	2	6	31	36	26
Farley Boys Reserves	16	8	1	7	40	30	25
Caddington Reserves	16	5	2	9	42	50	17
Blue Line Aces	16	1	1	14	20	35	4
North Sundon Wanderers	16	0	1	15	16	93	1

Co-Op Sports Reserves - record expunged.

MAIDSTONE & DISTRICT LEAGUE

Premier	P	W	D	L	F	A	Pts
Leeds SV	12	7	3	2	41	14	24
Downswood	12	7	2	3	24	20	23
Castle Colts	12	6	4	2	26	13	22
Eccles	12	5	3	4	27	22	18
Headcorn	12	5	1	6	32	36	16
East Malling	12	3	0	9	14	38	9
AFC Biddenden	12	1	3	8	17	38	6

Addington, Shepway United, Smarden - records expunged.

Division One	P	W	D	L	F	A	Pts
Trisports	16	14	0	2	69	27	42
Lenham Wanderers	16	11	1	4	51	26	34
Larkfield	16	10	1	5	45	32	31
Hunton	16	7	3	6	32	34	24
Cobdown United	16	7	2	7	36	39	23
West Farleigh	16	6	1	9	34	48	19
Aylesford	16	6	0	10	47	50	18
Three Suttons	16	4	2	10	30	49	14
Malgo Res.	16	2	0	14	26	65	6

Division Two	P	W	D	L	F	A	Pts
Saxon Chief	20	16	0	4	97	26	48
Addington Res.	20	13	4	3	65	39	43
RKP United	20	12	5	3	61	31	41
Malgo A	20	11	2	7	84	48	35
Eccles Res.	20	10	3	7	54	64	33
Aylesford Res.	20	6	9	5	56	49	27
Leybourne Athletic	20	8	2	10	62	70	26
Parkwood Jupitors	20	5	3	12	42	61	18
Walnut Tree (Loose)	20	4	3	13	20	72	15
Hunton Res.	20	4	1	15	32	78	13
Maidstone Athletic	20	2	6	12	35	70	12

Division Three	P	W	D	L	F	A	Pts
Hollingbourne	20	16	1	3	91	27	49
Wateringbury Colts	20	15	4	1	71	25	49
Headcorn Res.	20	12	3	5	49	37	39
Lenham Wdrs Res.	20	10	3	7	49	39	33
Kingshill SpitfiRes.	20	10	2	8	48	37	32
West Farleigh Res.	20	9	3	8	43	54	30
Thurnham United	20	6	3	11	29	52	21
Wheatsheaf Celtic	20	6	2	12	33	53	20
Sutton Saints	20	5	1	14	45	82	16
RKP United Res.	20	4	3	13	35	47	15
Phoenix United	20	4	1	15	35	75	13

MATLOCK & DISTRICT LEAGUE

	P	W	D	L	F	A	Pts
Kings Arms	26	19	1	6	88	47	58
Hilcote United	26	18	3	5	117	49	57
Laburnum Saints	26	17	2	7	78	60	53
Darley Dale Lions	26	16	4	6	68	60	52
Riddings Rovers	26	15	3	8	87	63	48
Woodthorpe Rovers	26	14	2	10	75	47	44
Wirksworth Albion	26	12	7	7	75	69	43
Shirland Miners Welfare	26	12	6	8	79	57	42
Matlock Town Youth	26	10	5	11	54	58	35
AFC Lea Holloway	26	9	3	14	61	69	30
Tibshelf	26	6	3	17	49	80	21
Tansley	26	5	3	18	44	86	18
Black Hippo	26	5	2	19	54	102	17
Harveys Bar	26	1	2	23	32	114	5

MID-ESSEX LEAGUE

Premier	P	W	D	L	F	A	Pts
Scotia Billericay	22	18	2	2	63	17	56
Braintree/Bocking U.	22	16	2	4	77	26	50
Great Baddow	22	11	5	6	45	23	38
St Clere's	22	11	4	7	57	41	37
Silver End United +3	22	10	3	9	42	42	36
Utd Ch'ford Churches	22	9	5	8	47	45	32
Little Waltham	22	9	5	8	43	43	32
Beacon Hill Rovers	22	8	7	7	38	41	31
Byfleet Rayleigh -4	22	9	3	10	41	38	26
Harold Wood Ath A	22	4	4	14	36	63	16
Springfield Rouge	22	3	2	17	25	75	11
Focus Ferrers	22	1	4	17	18	78	7

Division One	P	W	D	L	F	A	Pts
Scotia Billericay Res.	24	23	0	1	75	11	69
Rhodesia United	24	17	3	4	76	25	54
Ferrers Athletic	24	17	2	5	88	28	53
Writtle Manor	24	15	2	7	76	35	47
Frenford Senior A	24	12	4	8	44	46	40
Stags Head	24	10	3	11	50	57	33
Sparta Basildon	24	9	4	11	40	49	31
Shenfield Hollands	24	8	5	11	34	29	29
Swan Mead	24	8	2	14	27	31	26
Bradwell United	24	8	2	14	39	75	26
Mundon Victoria	24	4	7	13	27	70	19
Old Chelmfdns A +3	24	3	1	20	18	82	13
Manford Way A -4	24	4	1	19	27	83	9

Division Two	P	W	D	L	F	A	Pts
Manford Way B	24	20	3	1	60	24	63
Broomfield Res.	24	14	4	6	81	43	46
Hutton A	24	13	5	6	54	39	44
Battlesbridge	24	12	6	6	60	45	42
Brendans +3	24	12	1	11	55	47	40
Sprtg Brentwood -1	24	12	1	11	69	50	36
St Margarets	24	11	0	13	47	53	33
Rayleigh -3	24	10	4	10	50	52	31
Boreham	24	8	6	10	45	50	30
Sungate A	24	7	5	12	26	42	26
Little Waltham Res.	24	7	4	13	39	56	25
Harold Wood Ath B	24	6	1	17	35	66	19
Shelley Royals	24	2	4	18	26	80	10

MID-SOMERSET LEAGUE

Premier Division	P	W	D	L	F	A	Pts
Meadow Rangers	18	14	1	3	58	23	43
Farrington Gurney	18	11	3	4	47	36	36
Mells & Vobster United	18	9	5	4	41	28	32
Chew Magna	18	9	4	5	36	35	31
Westfield Reserves	18	8	3	7	48	35	27
Coleford Athletic	18	8	1	9	56	47	25
Chilcompton Sports	18	8	1	9	38	35	25
Pilton United	18	5	3	10	44	44	18
Belrose	18	6	0	12	30	51	18
Evercreech Rovers	18	1	1	16	22	86	4
Wookey - record epunged							

Division One	P	W	D	L	F	A	Pts
Welton Arsenal	20	16	3	1	83	25	51
Oakhill	20	13	3	4	53	23	42
Wells City "A"	20	12	4	4	52	24	40
Frome Collegians Res.	20	12	2	6	50	30	38
Temple Cloud	20	10	3	7	63	49	33
Meadow Rangers Res.	20	7	2	11	56	74	23
Glastonbury Town Res.	20	6	4	10	36	48	22
Stoke Rovers,	20	5	6	9	39	40	21
Frome Town Sports Res.	20	5	3	12	39	63	18
Tunley Athletic Reserves	20	5	2	13	29	74	17
Chilcompton Sp res (-14)	20	3	0	17	30	80	-5

Division Two	P	W	D	L	F	A	Pts
Interhound	20	16	2	2	88	27	50
FC Sun Sports	20	15	1	4	78	36	46
Shepton Mallet Tn "A"	20	14	4	2	50	14	46
Coleford Athletic Res.	20	11	2	7	76	46	35
Mells & Vobster Utd Res.	20	10	3	7	75	51	33
Clutton Reserves	20	10	2	8	47	48	32
Purnells Sports "A"	20	9	1	10	41	41	28
Westfield "A" (-1)	20	7	3	10	41	55	23
Farrington Gurney Res.	20	4	1	15	45	78	13
Chilcompton United	20	3	0	17	33	100	9
Belrose Reserves	20	1	1	18	26	104	4

Division Three	P	W	D	L	F	A	Pts
Camerton Athletic	22	18	3	1	95	27	57
Pensford	22	17	2	3	113	20	53
Radstock Town "A"	22	16	2	4	83	42	50
High Littleton	22	12	7	3	53	30	43
Tor Leisure	22	10	2	10	60	61	32
Temple Cloud Reserves	22	8	6	8	47	55	30
Westhill Sports	22	9	2	11	48	53	29
Stoke Rovers Reserves	22	8	1	13	46	97	25
Purnells Sports "B"	22	6	4	12	39	60	22
Cheddar "B"	22	4	2	16	42	82	14
Pilton United Reserves	22	4	2	16	42	90	14
Evercreech Rovers Res.	22	3	1	18	35	86	10

MID-SUSSEX LEAGUE

Premier Division	P	W	D	L	F	A	Pts
Maresfield Village	26	17	3	6	75	34	54
Roffey	26	16	5	5	65	35	53
Jarvis Brook	26	13	6	7	60	36	45
Hassocks A	26	13	3	10	57	56	42
Wisdom Sports	26	13	3	10	56	61	42
Balcombe	26	10	7	9	53	49	37
Lindfield	26	10	7	9	51	51	37
East Grinstead U. +2	26	9	7	10	43	54	36
O Varndeanians -3	26	11	4	11	58	42	34
Crawley Down A	26	8	9	9	45	61	33
Cuckfield Town +3	26	5	9	12	42	54	27
Willingdon Athletic	26	6	9	11	33	50	27
Rotherfield	26	6	8	12	30	40	26
Forest Row -4	26	4	2	20	21	66	10

Division One	P	W	D	L	F	A	Pts
AFC Grinstead	20	17	2	1	73	27	53
Burgess Hill Albion	20	15	2	3	51	18	47
Cuckfield Rangers	20	14	2	4	57	20	44
Felbridge	20	9	3	8	46	39	30
Lindfield Res.	20	7	7	6	35	35	28
Sporting Crawley	20	7	5	8	46	51	26
Framfield/Blackboys	20	6	4	10	38	35	22
St Francis Rangers A	20	7	1	12	32	53	22
Ardingly -3	20	7	0	13	37	49	18
Hartfield	20	4	4	12	29	48	16
Wisdom S. Res. +3	20	1	2	17	17	86	8

Division Two	P	W	D	L	F	A	Pts
Keymer & Hassocks	18	13	2	3	45	25	41
Peacehaven United	18	12	1	5	54	20	37
Newick -3	18	10	3	5	37	29	30
Ashurst Wood	18	8	2	8	44	42	26
Hurstpierpoint Res.	18	8	2	8	36	34	26
East Grinstead T. A	18	6	5	7	38	35	23
Barcombe	18	7	2	9	31	40	23
West Hoathly	18	6	3	9	26	35	21
East Court +3	18	3	3	12	35	59	15
Furnace Green Rov.	18	4	3	11	25	52	15

Division Three	P	W	D	L	F	A	Pts
Copthorne	18	16	1	1	65	19	49
Village of Ditchling	18	10	5	3	56	28	35
Real Hydraquip	18	8	5	5	50	34	29
Sporting Lindfield	18	8	2	8	47	48	26
Cuckfield Town Res.	18	7	4	7	41	37	25
Maresfield Vill. Res.	18	6	6	6	32	37	24
Willingdon Ath. Res.	18	6	3	9	34	58	21
Wingspan	18	6	0	12	43	57	18
Scaynes Hill	18	4	4	10	39	60	16
Fletching	18	3	2	13	30	59	11

Division Four	P	W	D	L	F	A	Pts
Roffey Res.	22	19	1	2	92	29	58
Ansty Sports & S. +2	22	15	2	5	70	42	49
Plumpton Athletic +1	22	12	4	6	70	42	41
Turners Hill Res.	22	13	2	7	64	36	41
Burg. Hill Alb. Res. +3	22	10	1	11	37	51	34
Dormansland Res. -3	22	9	4	9	47	39	28
Old Varndeanians A	22	7	5	10	40	57	26
Balcombe Res.	22	7	1	14	43	61	22
Phoenix Utd Res. -1	22	7	1	14	50	73	21
East Grin. Utd Res.	22	6	3	13	42	67	21
East Grinstead Wdrs	22	6	3	13	37	62	21
Horsted Keynes	22	6	3	13	37	70	21

Division Five	P	W	D	L	F	A	Pts
Fairwarp	18	12	5	1	50	29	41
Copthorne Res.	18	10	4	4	51	25	34
Wivelsfield Green	18	10	2	6	59	31	32
Furn. Green Gal. Res.	18	9	3	6	35	26	30
Handcross Village	18	9	2	7	43	36	29
Danehill	18	9	2	7	48	45	29
Ifield Edwards A	18	6	3	9	41	43	21
Buxted Res.	18	5	3	10	27	38	18
Horley Wanderers	18	3	6	9	34	48	15
Newick Res.	18	1	2	15	18	85	5

Division Six	P	W	D	L	F	A	Pts
Halsford Lions	20	16	3	1	78	29	51
Jarvis Brook Res.	20	16	2	2	55	13	50
Lindfield A	20	12	3	5	54	32	39
Sporting Crawley Res.	20	11	1	8	52	48	34
Rott. Village Veterans	20	9	3	8	56	43	30
Ardingly Res.	20	9	1	10	54	44	28
Forest Row Res.	20	7	1	12	42	46	22
Rotherfield Res.	20	7	1	12	36	61	22
Copthorne Rovers	20	7	0	13	34	61	21
Bolney Rovers	20	4	1	15	31	69	13
Nutley	20	3	2	15	27	73	11

Division Seven	P	W	D	L	F	A	Pts
United Services	20	17	2	1	87	21	53
East Grin. Mavericks	20	15	2	3	57	17	47
Maresfield Village A	20	11	2	7	51	31	35
Ashurst Wood Res.	20	9	5	6	34	39	32
Felbridge Res.	20	10	1	9	57	49	31
Real Hydraquip Res.	20	9	4	7	42	42	31
Peacehaven U. Res.	20	9	3	8	42	32	30
Pilgrims	20	6	2	12	34	60	20
Franklands Vill. Res.	20	5	4	11	34	55	19
Fletching Res.	20	3	1	16	31	69	10
Hartfield Res.	20	3	0	17	25	79	9

Division Eight	P	W	D	L	F	A	Pts
Cuckfield Town A	18	15	2	1	51	16	47
Fairwarp Res.	18	12	3	3	46	21	39
Cherry Lane	18	12	0	6	60	28	36
Willingdon Athletic A	18	8	5	5	51	44	29
East Grinstead T. B	18	8	4	6	38	30	28
West Hoathly Res.	18	8	3	7	44	43	27
Ansty Spts & S. Res.	18	6	3	9	26	39	21
Fairfield	18	4	1	13	20	45	13
Stones	18	3	1	14	21	63	10
Barcombe Res.	18	2	2	14	27	55	8

Division Nine	P	W	D	L	F	A	Pts
Copthorne A	20	16	2	2	80	29	50
Plumpton Ath Res.	20	13	4	3	72	37	43
Framfield & BU Res.	20	13	1	6	60	39	40
Cuckfield Rgrs Res.	20	12	2	6	40	46	38
Wivelsfield G. Res.	20	9	4	7	50	43	31
Keymer & Hass. Res.	20	9	1	10	56	42	28
Handcross Vill. Res.	20	9	1	10	47	62	28
Danehill Res.	20	7	2	11	48	67	23
Lindfield B	20	5	3	12	36	52	18
Maresfield Village B	20	3	4	13	31	63	13
Burgess Hill Albion A	20	2	0	18	24	64	6

Division Ten	P	W	D	L	F	A	Pts
Ardingly A	21	15	5	1	58	18	50
Copthorne Rv Res. -1	21	13	3	5	88	38	41
Sporting Devils +2	21	9	5	7	51	39	34
Buxted A	21	10	3	8	57	58	33
Lindfield V	21	9	0	12	39	50	27
Scaynes Hill Res.	21	5	5	11	46	93	20
Heath Rangers	21	4	7	10	35	55	19
Rotherfield A	21	3	4	14	39	62	13

Division Eleven	P	W	D	L	F	A	Pts
Wingspan Res.	18	14	0	4	86	40	42
Roffey A	18	11	1	6	59	24	34
Cherry Lane Res.	18	10	1	7	42	49	31
Ridgewood	18	8	1	9	57	41	25
AFC Haywards -3	18	9	1	8	37	33	25
Pease Pottage Vill. A	18	8	0	10	33	45	24
Scaynes Hill A +3	18	1	0	17	11	93	6

MIDLAND AMATEUR ALLIANCE

Premier Division	P	W	D	L	F	A	Pts
Coronation	26	21	1	4	99	43	64
Ilkeston Rutland	26	18	4	4	96	44	58
Brunts Old Boys	26	16	7	3	78	39	55
Woodborough United	26	14	5	7	60	44	47
Southwell St Marys res.	26	13	3	10	62	69	42
Team DNF	26	11	4	11	45	55	37
Old Elizabethans	26	10	6	10	64	56	36
Trent Vineyard	26	11	3	12	61	62	36
Radcliffe Olympic "A"	26	10	4	12	78	65	34
Beeston Reserves	26	9	2	15	58	76	29
Wollaton "A"	26	7	4	15	62	80	25
Beeston Old Boys Assoc	26	6	4	16	44	73	22
Steelers	26	5	4	17	38	84	19
Nottinghamshire Reserves	26	4	3	19	43	98	15

Division One	P	W	D	L	F	A	Pts
Sherwood Colliery	22	16	3	3	86	28	51
Nuthall Athletic	22	15	3	4	87	36	48
Wollaton "B"	22	13	2	7	68	65	41
Bassingfield	22	12	3	7	61	42	39
FC Interski	22	10	4	8	61	43	34
Tibshelf Community	22	10	4	8	62	55	34
EMTEC	22	10	3	9	67	46	33
Nottingham United Reserves	22	9	3	10	54	49	30
Broadmeadows	22	10	0	12	45	68	30
Lady Bay	22	6	2	14	48	72	20
FC 05 Bilsthorpe Reserves	22	4	1	17	34	101	13
Nottinghamshire "A"	22	2	2	18	36	104	8

Division Two	P	W	D	L	F	A	Pts
Rainworth Rangers	28	24	1	3	136	35	73
Eaton Hall College	28	21	1	6	114	42	64
A S Plant	28	19	4	5	97	44	61
Pinxton Rangers Old Boys	28	18	2	8	107	67	56
Tibshelf Community Reserves	28	18	1	9	101	72	55
Southwell St Marys "A"	28	17	2	9	69	47	53
Sherwood Colliery Reserves	28	16	4	8	82	47	52
Nottingham United "A"	28	11	6	11	85	68	39
Town Mill	28	10	3	15	65	83	33
Old Bemrosians	28	9	3	16	54	84	30
Chilwell Villa	28	9	2	17	49	97	29
Ravenshead	28	8	3	17	50	100	27
Cambridge Knights	28	6	1	21	31	106	19
Nottinghamshire "B"	28	4	4	20	53	110	16
Gedling Town United	28	1	1	26	28	119	4

Derybshire Amateurs Reserves - record expunged.

MIDLAND REGIONAL ALLIANCE

Premier Division	P	W	D	L	F	A	Pts
Allenton United	30	25	2	3	111	41	77
Willington	30	20	2	8	83	60	62
Melbourne Dynamo	30	16	7	7	73	50	55
Rowsley	30	16	5	9	73	46	53
Wirksworth Town	30	14	9	7	65	39	51
Swanwick Pent. Res.	30	12	7	11	61	53	43
Cromford	30	13	3	14	79	74	42
Long Eaton Utd Res.	30	12	6	12	50	48	42
Derby Rolls R. Leis.	30	11	6	13	56	60	39
Belper United	30	11	6	13	57	65	39
Newmount	30	11	4	15	61	71	37
Ashover	30	9	3	18	55	85	30
Cas. Donington T. -4	30	9	6	15	54	68	29
Holbrook St Mich. -3	30	9	5	16	49	73	29
Sandiacre Town	30	7	3	20	62	96	24
Chellaston	30	7	2	21	46	106	23

Division One	P	W	D	L	F	A	Pts
Mickleover RBL	28	24	2	2	84	14	74
Derby Royals	28	19	4	5	88	31	61
Matlock Sports	28	19	3	6	78	34	60
Punjab United	28	14	3	11	73	37	45
Selston	28	13	5	10	77	45	44
Belper United Res.	28	11	10	7	75	53	43
Derby Rolls R. Res.	28	11	3	14	44	53	36
Little Eaton	28	9	7	12	46	67	34
Allestree -4	28	10	7	11	58	68	33
Derbyshire Amats -3	28	9	7	12	45	62	31
Ripley Town -3	28	8	7	13	43	72	30
PastuRes.	28	7	7	14	44	75	28
Findern	28	8	3	17	37	80	27
Bargate Rovers	28	7	2	19	43	88	23
Holbrook SM Res.	28	4	4	20	34	90	16

Shirland Athletic - record expunged.

Division Two	P	W	D	L	F	A	Pts
Rowsley Res.	30	23	1	6	105	37	70
Derby Singh Brothers	30	22	4	4	98	36	70
Woolley Moor United	30	22	3	5	100	43	69
Sandiacre Town Res.	30	14	11	5	75	41	53
Mickleover RBL Res.	30	17	1	12	69	50	52
Swanwick PR Res.	30	14	7	9	97	58	49
Melbourne Dyn. Res.	30	14	4	12	66	55	46
Selston Res. -3	30	15	3	12	62	48	45
Wirksworth Town Res.	30	12	6	12	55	61	42
Wirksworth Ivanhoe	30	12	4	14	63	61	40
Ambergate -3	30	10	5	15	65	86	32
Punjab United Res.	30	10	2	18	53	89	32
Pastures Res.	30	8	3	19	43	91	27
Roe Farm	30	6	5	19	46	108	23
Hilton Harriers	30	4	4	22	45	109	16
Bargate Rovers Res.	30	4	3	23	31	100	15

Castle Donnington T. Res. - record expunged.

MINING LEAGUE

Division One	P	W	D	L	F	A	Pts
Illogan RBL Reserves	28	26	1	1	200	21	79
St Buryan	28	23	2	3	145	47	71
Threemilestone	28	19	4	5	133	50	61
Goonhavern Athletic	28	19	3	6	142	50	60
Gwinear Churchtown	28	16	1	11	141	69	49
Robartes Arms	28	15	1	12	92	60	46
Gulval	28	15	0	13	90	68	45
Halsetown (-3)	28	11	5	12	87	55	35
Redruth United	28	10	5	13	93	73	35
Camborne Sch. of Mines (-3)	28	12	2	14	95	93	35
Newlyn Non-Athletico (-3)	28	10	3	15	56	92	30
Trevenson United (-6)	28	8	4	16	77	96	22
Sennen	28	6	2	20	56	122	20
Storm (-6)	28	3	1	24	35	151	4
Madron	28	0	0	28	12	407	0

Division Two	P	W	D	L	F	A	Pts
Carbis Bay United	28	22	1	5	106	35	67
Titans	28	20	3	5	111	37	63
West Cornwall (-3)	28	20	5	3	110	33	62
Praze-An-Beeble	28	19	5	4	89	48	62
Illogan RBL "A"	28	17	3	8	73	38	54
St Just "A"	28	15	4	9	94	73	49
St Ives Town Reserves (-3)	28	14	4	10	91	56	43
Threemilestone Reserves	28	12	2	14	58	67	38
St Agnes "A" (-6)	28	12	4	12	86	71	34
Trispen Reserves (-3)	28	11	4	13	84	104	34
Mousehole "A"	28	6	0	22	52	111	18
Halsetown Reserves (-6)	28	7	2	19	54	88	17
Mount Ambrose	28	5	2	21	65	152	17
Chacewater Reserves (-3)	28	5	4	19	48	115	16
Gulval Reserves (-6)	28	2	3	23	46	139	3

Storm Reserves resigned prior to the start of the season.

Division Three	P	W	D	L	F	A	Pts
Hayle "B"	28	20	5	3	121	45	65
Goonhavern Athletic res.	28	19	5	4	107	42	62
Cornish New Boys	28	18	5	5	128	63	59
St Buryan Reserves	28	18	4	6	112	43	58
Wendron United "B" (-1)	28	18	4	6	83	49	57
Redruth United Reserves	28	17	3	8	107	60	54
Rosudgeon-Kenneggy res.	28	14	9	5	102	38	51
Madron Reserves	28	16	3	9	96	57	51
Newquay "A"	28	12	1	15	74	90	37
Praze-An-Beeble Reserves	28	10	3	15	54	83	33
Newlyn Non-Athletico res.	28	7	1	20	60	118	22
Ludgvan Reserves (-3)	28	7	0	21	52	89	18
Trevenson United Reserves	28	5	1	22	36	147	16
Perranporth "A" (-3)	28	3	3	22	31	102	9
St Ives Mariners	28	2	1	25	34	171	7

NORTH & MID-HERTS LEAGUE

	P	W	D	L	F	A	Pts
Probuild	24	21	2	1	84	23	65
Potters Bar Crusaders	24	19	2	3	99	22	59
City Hearts (+2)	24	14	3	7	75	62	47
Wodson Park Seniors	24	13	5	6	52	34	44
Global	24	14	2	8	38	35	44
Inn on the Green	24	11	3	10	51	62	36
Asia	24	9	4	11	52	59	31
London Colney "A"	24	7	5	12	39	91	26
Warriors XI (-4)	24	8	4	12	37	58	24
St Ippolyts	24	6	5	13	40	72	23
FC Letchworth (+3)	24	5	4	15	38	54	22
St Albans Wanderers	24	4	5	15	36	51	17
Shephall Centre	24	2	2	20	22	40	8

Redbourn - record expunged.

NORTH BUCKS & DISTRICT LEAGUE

Senior Division	P	W	D	L	F	A	Pts
Minsterworth	30	27	3	0	134	31	84
Brackley Sports	24	16	3	5	85	40	51
Hale Leys United	24	16	3	5	71	41	51
Stewkley	24	14	6	4	85	47	48
Southcott Village RA	24	15	3	6	58	46	48
Potterspury	24	13	2	9	63	62	41
Loughton Manor	24	11	4	9	48	45	37
Grendon Rangers	24	10	6	8	54	51	36
Silverstone	24	10	4	10	49	46	34
Thornborough Athletic	24	8	4	12	43	46	28
Wolverton Town	24	7	3	14	53	77	24
Yardley Gobion	24	6	2	16	40	59	20
Deanshanger Athletic	24	4	6	14	35	76	18
MK Titans	24	2	2	20	40	88	8

Castlethorpe - record expunged.

Intermediate Division	P	W	D	L	F	A	Pts
MK Wanderers	24	16	4	4	70	29	52
Denbigh Sports & Social	24	14	4	6	67	41	46
Stoke Hammond	24	13	6	5	74	50	45
Brackley Sports Reserves	24	13	6	5	45	29	45
Great Linford	24	14	2	8	55	42	44
Syresham	24	10	8	6	49	44	38
Heath Panthers United	24	10	7	7	63	46	37
AFC Santander	24	10	3	11	70	61	33
Great Horwood	24	7	5	12	49	51	26
Winslow United Reserves	24	8	1	15	46	57	25
Wicken Sports	24	5	7	12	57	77	22
MK Titans Reserves	24	5	9	14	34	70	20
Twyford United	24	1	2	21	28	110	5

E & H - record expunged.

Division One	P	W	D	L	F	A	Pts
Celtic MK	28	24	3	1	143	27	75
Stoke Hammond Reserves	28	19	4	5	84	52	61
Steeple Claydon	28	19	2	7	76	49	59
Hanslope	28	17	5	6	116	65	56
Southcott Village RA Res.	28	16	2	10	71	58	50
Grendon Rangers Reserves	28	16	2	10	76	68	50
Charlton	28	12	4	12	72	83	40
Bletchley Bridge	28	10	7	11	55	61	37
Old Stratford	28	10	3	15	65	76	33
Potterspury Reserves	28	9	5	14	61	67	32
Marsh Gibbon	28	9	2	17	49	80	29
Sherington	28	6	4	18	39	87	22
Stewkley Reserves	28	7	0	21	42	83	21
Deashanger Athletic res.	28	6	3	19	39	90	21
Woughton	28	4	6	18	44	86	18

Castlethorpe Reserves - record expunged.

Division Two	P	W	D	L	F	A	Pts
Olney Town Colts	30	25	1	4	107	31	76
City Colts	30	24	2	4	135	41	74
Heath Panthers United Res.	30	21	5	4	109	58	68
Westbury	30	19	4	7	96	60	61
United MK	30	18	2	10	115	67	56
Syresham Reserves	30	13	4	13	61	68	43
Twyford United Reserves	30	11	8	11	75	80	41
Wicken Sports Reserves	30	12	3	15	61	80	39
Wing Village Reserves	30	11	4	15	75	91	37
Hanslope Reserves	30	11	2	17	69	83	35
Yardley Gobion Reserves	30	10	4	16	62	84	34
Marsh Gibbon Reserves	30	10	2	18	52	92	32
Great Horwood Reserves	30	9	3	18	55	101	30
Great Linford Reserves	30	7	7	16	53	78	28
LB Galaxy	30	7	1	22	55	98	22
Silverstone Reserves	30	2	8	20	32	100	14

NORTH EAST NORFOLK LEAGUE

Division One	P	W	D	L	F	A	Pts
Gimingham	22	15	4	3	80	32	49
Coltishall	22	13	4	5	89	42	43
Runton	22	13	1	8	73	49	40
Ludham	22	11	3	8	58	49	36
East Ruston	22	10	5	7	78	52	35
North Walsham Tn "A"	22	10	4	8	53	49	34
Aldborough Lions	22	10	3	9	53	54	33
Horning	22	9	4	9	51	49	31
Corpusty & Saxthorpe	22	7	5	10	40	44	26
Briston (-2)	22	6	4	12	41	67	20
North Walsham Old B	22	5	2	15	35	106	17
Hickling	22	2	3	17	45	103	9

Division Two	P	W	D	L	F	A	Pts
Haisboro Athetlic	20	17	3	0	73	21	54
Worstead	20	14	3	3	85	41	45
Lyng	20	11	3	6	68	45	36
Aylsham "A"	20	10	4	6	68	37	34
Mundesley	20	10	3	7	57	47	33
Holt "A"	20	6	7	7	55	61	25
Cromer Youth Old Boys	20	6	6	8	44	41	24
Buxton Reserves	20	6	5	9	33	49	23
Erpingham	20	5	3	12	32	73	18
Corpusty & Saxth'pe Res.	20	4	2	14	35	62	14
Felmingham	20	0	3	17	20	93	3

Division Three	P	W	D	L	F	A	Pts
Blakeney	18	17	1	0	130	19	52
Cawston	18	12	1	5	54	17	37
Aldborough Lions Res.	18	11	0	7	56	36	33
Gimingham Reserves	18	10	1	7	56	49	31
Sutton Rangers	18	8	4	6	46	40	28
Glaven Valley	18	8	1	9	51	47	25
Mundesley Reserves (-1)	18	7	2	9	32	39	22
Holt Colts	18	5	3	10	35	60	18
East Ruston Reserves	18	4	1	13	29	94	13
Erpingham Reserves	18	0	2	16	19	107	2

Briston Reserves - record expunged.

NORTH GLOSCESTERSHIRE LEAGUE

Premier Division	P	W	D	L	F	A	Pts
Minsterworth	30	27	3	0	134	31	84
Staunton & Corse	30	19	5	6	68	38	62
Milkwall	30	20	2	8	87	59	62
Ruardean Hill Rgrs	30	19	4	7	57	33	61
Mitcheldean	30	17	3	10	59	40	54
Newent Town	30	16	3	11	78	50	51
English Bicknor	30	13	2	15	54	42	41
Woolaston	30	12	5	13	39	44	41
Newnham United	30	11	5	14	71	75	38
Westbury United	30	11	4	15	53	74	37
Lydney Town Res.	30	10	6	14	58	68	36
Broadwell Amats Res.	30	10	5	15	57	64	35
Mushet & Coalway	30	9	3	18	45	75	30
Tidenham	30	9	1	20	41	78	28
Huntley -6	30	7	5	18	64	74	20
Coleford United	30	0	4	26	14	134	4

OTHER LEAGUES

Division One	P	W	D	L	F	A	Pts
Whitecroft	24	21	3	0	66	17	66
Sedbury United	24	16	5	3	84	38	53
Bream Amateurs	24	15	5	4	75	34	50
Newent Town Res.	24	12	3	9	62	57	39
Lydbrook Athletic Res.	24	12	2	10	57	47	38
Redbrook Rovers	24	11	4	9	60	57	37
Ruardean Hill Res.	24	10	2	12	45	65	32
Aylburton Rov. Res.	24	8	3	13	52	51	27
Yorkley	24	6	6	12	38	59	24
Mitcheldean Res.	24	6	5	13	41	56	23
Ellwood Res.	24	6	4	14	44	62	22
Blakeney	24	5	2	17	35	68	17
Rank Outsiders	24	5	2	17	37	85	17

Division Two	P	W	D	L	F	A	Pts
St Briavels	22	17	4	1	75	22	55
Puma	22	14	5	3	59	31	47
Howle Hill	22	9	7	6	62	49	34
Harrow Hill Res.	22	8	7	7	34	44	31
Soudley Res.	22	8	5	9	45	35	29
Whitecroft Res.	22	7	8	7	32	35	29
Staunton/Corse Res.	22	9	2	11	41	50	29
White Horse	22	7	4	11	48	51	25
Lydney Town A	22	8	1	13	45	59	25
Westbury United Res.	22	6	5	11	48	54	23
Lydbrook Athletic A	22	5	8	9	32	58	23
Woolaston Res.	22	4	4	14	38	71	16

Division Three	P	W	D	L	F	A	Pts
Weston Athletic	24	20	4	0	131	18	64
Worrall Hill	24	18	3	3	75	26	57
Redmarley	24	14	4	6	55	36	46
Sling United	24	13	3	8	76	42	42
Milkwall Res.	24	11	3	10	60	54	36
Mushet & Coal Res.	24	10	4	10	53	54	34
English Bicknor Res.	24	11	1	12	51	60	34
Blakeney Res.	24	9	3	12	59	89	30
Puma Res.	24	9	2	13	56	87	29
Minsterworth Res.	24	8	3	13	46	69	27
Redbrook Rovers Res.	24	5	4	15	47	93	19
Rank Outsiders Res.	24	4	4	16	29	68	16
Tidenham Res.	24	5	0	19	35	77	15

Division Four	P	W	D	L	F	A	Pts
Ruardean United	24	20	1	3	82	29	61
Viney St Swithins Res.	24	19	3	2	108	31	60
Chepstow Rifles	24	18	3	3	115	34	57
United Longhope	24	16	3	5	103	35	51
Bream Amateurs Res.	24	12	8	4	85	43	44
Hardwicke A	24	11	5	8	81	43	38
Whitecroft A	24	8	3	13	28	70	27
Puma A	24	7	2	15	43	94	23
Yorkley Res.	24	6	4	14	51	75	22
Littledean	24	6	4	14	46	102	22
St Briavels Res.	24	5	2	17	31	73	17
Mitcheldean A	24	4	5	15	36	92	17
Sling United Res.	24	1	3	20	25	113	6

NORTH LANCS & DISTRICT LEAGUE

Premier Division	P	W	D	L	F	A	Pts
Highgrove	26	19	4	3	82	27	61
Bowerham Furness	26	15	3	8	43	38	48
Morecambe Royals	26	11	9	6	40	28	42
Storeys	26	12	6	8	41	41	42
Carnforth Rangers	26	12	5	9	51	38	41
Slyne with Hest Res.	26	11	8	7	40	29	41
Marsh United	26	12	4	10	52	40	40
Cartmel & District	26	10	6	10	43	42	36
Swarthmoor Social	26	11	2	13	33	50	35
Ingleton	26	8	7	11	39	45	31
Bentham	26	8	5	13	52	58	29
Galgate	26	5	10	11	40	52	25
TIC.Dynamos	26	6	4	16	21	50	22
Freehold	26	4	3	19	28	67	15

Division One	P	W	D	L	F	A	Pts
Arnside	24	17	4	3	92	34	55
Caton United	24	16	3	5	80	39	51
College	24	16	1	7	60	30	49
Trimpell	24	14	5	5	71	36	47
Millhead	24	10	5	9	56	69	35
Kirkby Lonsdale	24	10	4	10	62	59	34
Cartmel & Dist. Res.	24	10	4	10	32	39	34
More. Royals Res.	24	9	6	9	57	62	33
Marsh United Res.	24	8	5	11	47	60	29
Boys Club	24	8	3	13	47	59	27
Bolton Le Sands	24	5	6	13	30	56	21
Storeys Res.	24	5	1	18	38	89	16
Ingleton Res.	24	3	3	18	38	78	12

Division Two	P	W	D	L	F	A	Pts
Grange	22	18	4	0	73	22	58
Heysham	22	12	7	3	63	43	43
Highgrove Res. -9	22	13	3	6	72	39	33
Westgate Wanderers	22	9	5	8	48	41	32
Overton/Middleton	22	8	4	10	60	57	28
Carnforth R Res -9	22	11	1	10	57	43	25
Torrisholme -9	22	10	4	8	53	39	25
Bentham Res.	22	7	3	12	49	71	24
Galgate Res. -3	22	7	5	10	39	49	23
Slyne with Hest A	22	4	7	11	32	58	19
Allithwaite Rangers	22	3	5	14	29	64	14
Kirkby L'ale Res -3	22	5	2	15	35	84	14

Division Three	P	W	D	L	F	A	Pts
Morecambe Gold	22	14	6	2	53	25	48
Boys Club Res.	22	14	3	5	49	27	45
Moghuls	22	13	5	4	55	41	44
Villa Royale	22	13	4	5	66	42	43
Gregson	22	10	2	10	45	42	32
Burton Thistle	22	8	5	9	63	51	29
Caton United Res.	22	9	2	11	38	45	29
Pilling -3	22	8	5	9	64	67	26
Trimpell Res.	22	8	2	12	49	57	26
AFC Moorlands	22	5	2	15	33	66	17
O'ton/Mid'ton Res -7	22	6	5	11	43	60	16
Carnforth Rgrs A -9	22	2	3	17	25	60	0

Division Four	P	W	D	L	F	A	Pts
Moor Lane	18	15	3	0	62	16	48
Lancaster Rovers	18	13	3	2	77	22	42
Freehold Res.	18	13	2	3	52	24	41
Millhead Res. -3	18	8	4	6	58	43	25
Arnside Res.	18	8	1	9	33	35	25
Burton Thistle Res -3	18	9	1	8	38	43	25
Gregson Res.	18	5	3	10	27	56	18
Bolton Le Sands Res.	18	3	2	13	28	65	11
Heysham Res.	18	2	3	13	34	69	9
College Res. -3	18	2	2	14	26	62	5

Ingleton A - record expunged.

NORTH LEICS LEAGUE

Premier Division	P	W	D	L	F	A	Pts
Sileby Saints	26	21	2	3	80	31	65
Genesis	26	16	4	6	80	41	52
Anstey Town	26	15	5	6	74	58	50
Falcons	26	14	6	6	69	35	48
Markfield	26	15	3	8	80	47	48
Loughborough Town	26	11	5	10	63	59	38
Ingles	26	11	7	7	44	45	37
Asfordby Village -1	26	8	7	11	45	63	30
Shepshed Amateurs	26	9	3	14	41	60	30
Sileby Victoria	26	8	5	13	53	66	29
Birstall Old Boys	26	9	2	15	47	63	29
Whitwick Wanderers	26	6	5	15	31	59	23
Anstey Crown	26	6	3	17	54	84	21
Loughborough -6	26	3	3	20	38	88	6

Division One	P	W	D	L	F	A	Pts
East Leake Athletic	20	16	1	3	60	23	49
Kegworth Imperial	20	14	3	3	111	25	45
Butler Court -3	20	15	1	4	72	31	43
Marlborough Rovers	20	12	4	4	62	40	40
Sutton Bonington	20	9	3	8	59	41	30
Ingles Res. -1	20	8	5	7	67	56	28
Woodhouse Imperial	20	7	2	11	44	57	23
Bagworth Colliery	20	6	3	11	55	55	21
Loughborough Ath.	20	4	3	13	37	66	15
Belton Villa -1	20	2	1	17	42	108	6
Loughboro. Res. -9	20	2	2	16	25	132	-1

Division Two	P	W	D	L	F	A	Pts
Greenhill YC	20	15	4	1	103	23	49
Sut. Bonington Acad	20	16	1	3	83	27	49
Whitwick Wdrs Res.	20	13	4	3	65	26	43
The Railway EWM	20	12	2	6	42	32	38
Thringstone MW	20	7	4	9	56	47	25
Markfield Res.	20	7	3	10	43	43	24
East Leake Ath. Res.	20	7	1	12	59	55	22
Castle Donington	20	6	2	12	43	76	20
ATI Garryson -3	20	6	1	13	45	90	16
Thurmaston Rangers	20	3	4	13	37	79	13
Moira United	20	3	4	13	41	119	13

Loughborough A - record expunged.

Division Three	P	W	D	L	F	A	Pts
Coalville Labour Club	20	16	2	2	69	27	50
Markfield A -3	20	15	2	3	95	50	46
Sileby Saints Res.	20	13	2	5	70	36	41
Measham Imperial	20	9	2	9	42	51	29
Sileby Victoria Res.	20	9	1	10	52	55	28
Victoria	20	9	1	10	56	59	28
L'boro. Emmanuel -1	20	7	4	9	55	51	24
Ferrari	20	7	1	12	49	59	22
Loughborough Utd	20	6	3	11	45	62	21
Woodhouse Imp. Res.	20	6	1	13	36	62	19
Mountsorrel	20	2	3	15	23	80	9

Long Clawson - record expunged.

Division Four	P	W	D	L	F	A	Pts
Shepshed Ams Res.	22	16	2	4	79	35	50
Genesis Res.	22	14	5	3	81	34	47
Loughboro. Galaxy	22	14	2	6	54	27	44
Anstey Crown Res.	22	13	3	6	66	40	42
Greenhill YC Res.	22	12	2	8	66	37	38
Kegworth Imp. Res.	22	12	2	8	52	36	38
Sutton Bonington Res.	22	11	2	9	62	51	35
Cas. Donington Res.	22	7	6	9	54	65	27
Birstall OB Res -1	22	6	4	12	40	62	21
Loughboro. Uth Res.	22	5	2	15	37	74	17
Loughboro. Ath. Res.	22	4	3	15	37	77	15
ATI Garryson Res. -1	22	1	1	20	29	121	3

NORTH NORTHUMBERLAND LEAGUE

Division One	P	W	D	L	F	A	Pts
Alnwick Town Reserves	14	13	1	0	67	12	40
Bedlington Terriers Reserves	14	11	1	2	41	14	34
Lynemouth Institute	14	6	2	6	42	40	20
Shilbottle CW	14	5	4	5	31	27	19
Springhill	14	4	4	6	31	40	16
Tweedmouth Harrow	14	3	3	8	27	49	12
Longhoughton Rangers	14	2	3	9	23	45	9
Rothbury	14	2	2	10	19	54	8

Acklington Athletic - record expunged.

Division Two	P	W	D	L	F	A	Pts
Wooler	20	17	2	1	92	14	53
Berwick United res (-3)	20	16	0	4	67	30	45
Embleton WR	20	13	4	3	60	33	43
Belford	20	11	3	6	63	39	36
Bamburgh Castle	20	8	5	7	52	51	29
Shilbottle CW res (-3)	20	8	2	10	42	48	23
Alnmouth United	20	5	6	9	49	49	21
Craster Rovers	20	6	2	12	32	53	20
Tweedmouth Rangers	20	5	3	12	49	71	18
Longhoughton Rang. Res.	20	3	3	14	29	77	12
Hedgeley Rovers	20	1	4	15	24	94	7

NORTH WEST NORFOLK LEAGUE

Division One	P	W	D	L	F	A	Pts
Reffley Royals	22	18	2	2	95	26	56
Lynn North End	22	15	4	3	87	42	49
Gayton United	22	13	3	6	58	35	42
Terrington	22	12	3	7	44	33	39
Lynn Discovery	22	11	4	7	65	46	37
Sutton Bridge	22	10	4	8	53	59	34
Heacham	22	9	3	10	49	43	30
Docking -3	22	7	6	9	54	67	24
West Winch	22	7	2	13	38	66	23
Lynn Napier -1	22	4	4	14	34	76	15
Ingoldisthorpe	22	2	4	16	41	86	10
Sandringham -10	22	2	5	15	42	81	1

Division Two	P	W	D	L	F	A	Pts
Redgate Rangers	24	22	1	1	139	21	67
Great Massingham	24	17	4	3	86	29	55
William Burt	24	18	1	5	79	25	55
South Creake	24	15	3	6	76	40	48
Watlington	24	13	4	7	65	32	43
Lynn Docklands -6	24	11	4	9	44	51	31
Ingold'thorpe Res -3	24	10	2	12	45	83	29
Denver -3	24	9	2	13	42	56	26
Hunstanton	24	7	2	15	34	58	23
Dersingham Res.	24	7	1	16	39	80	22
Downham Town A	24	6	2	16	51	89	20
Terrington Res.	24	6	1	17	35	74	19
Gaywood -3	24	1	1	22	17	114	1

Division Three	P	W	D	L	F	A	Pts
Sedgeford	22	18	2	2	95	24	56
Discovery Royals	22	17	0	5	77	35	51
Wiggenhall	22	12	4	6	64	53	40
Birchwood	22	12	2	8	64	63	38
Snettisham -3	22	10	4	8	55	46	31
Smithdon	22	9	3	10	56	63	30
Riverside	22	7	6	9	42	41	27
Castle Rising	22	7	4	11	50	74	25
West Winch Res. -3	22	8	2	12	37	46	23
Heacham Res. -3	22	7	4	11	42	60	22
Walsingham	22	3	3	16	36	81	12
Gayton Utd Res -3	22	3	4	15	33	65	10

Burnham Market - record expunged.

Division Four	P	W	D	L	F	A	Pts
Emneth Spartans	22	19	3	0	133	26	60
Springwood	22	15	3	4	63	40	48
Tilney All Saints -3	22	15	4	3	62	32	46
Greyfriars	22	11	4	7	58	46	37
Lynn Williams -3	22	9	3	10	48	49	27
Lynn Napier Res.	22	7	4	11	40	68	25
Sutton Bridge Res.	22	6	4	12	55	54	22
Watlington Res -3	22	8	1	13	50	85	22
The Woottons	22	5	4	13	32	54	19
Dersingham R. A -6	22	8	1	13	38	64	19
Pentney -3	22	6	1	15	39	78	16
Heacham A -6	22	6	2	14	44	66	14

Snettisham Res. - record expunged.

NORTHAMPTON TOWN LEAGUE

Premier Division	P	W	D	L	F	A	Pts
Northampton Harlequins	16	14	1	1	53	12	43
Delapre Old Boys	16	10	2	4	43	17	32
Denton	16	9	2	5	50	32	29
AFC Wombles	16	9	2	5	44	32	29
Rosebery	16	6	6	4	37	28	24
FC Crispin (-3)	16	6	3	7	46	37	18
Hometech	16	5	0	11	27	49	15
SPA	16	2	2	12	20	69	8
Thorplands United	16	1	2	13	13	57	5

Liberty Stars - record expunged.

NSDF Rainbow Club - record expunged.

University of Northampton - record expunged.

Division One	P	W	D	L	F	A	Pts
Mereway United	18	16	1	1	82	23	49
Northampton H'quins Res.	18	11	4	3	74	36	37
Harborough Town "A"	18	9	3	6	33	38	30
Spinney Hill 2010	18	9	1	8	44	44	28
Obelisk United	18	8	3	7	41	39	27
Ja King Blisworth "A"	18	8	1	9	47	62	25
West Haddon Reserves	18	7	2	9	33	47	23
Thorplands Club 81	18	6	4	8	57	45	22
Kett. Orchard Park U Res.	18	5	2	11	38	63	17
Northants Police (-6)	18	0	1	17	10	62	-5

Cripps - record expunged.

SPA Reserves - record expunged.

NORWICH & DISTRICT BUSINESS HOUSES LEAGUE

Division One	P	W	D	L	F	A	Pts
Drayton	22	16	2	4	80	40	50
UEA Res.	22	15	4	3	58	21	49
Yelverton	22	13	5	4	74	27	44
Jubilee Rangers	22	13	4	5	77	35	43
Marlborough OB	22	10	4	8	52	52	34
Costessey Crown	22	9	4	9	59	62	31
Salhouse Rovers	22	9	3	10	54	56	30
Mousehold Athletic	22	7	3	12	36	53	24
Norwich Medics -5	22	7	6	9	43	43	22
Lingwood Cavaners	22	5	3	14	44	69	18
Loddon United A	22	4	5	13	36	60	17
Homecare United	22	1	3	18	34	129	6

Division Two	P	W	D	L	F	A	Pts
UEA A	20	17	0	3	85	23	51
Sprowston Beehive	20	14	1	5	63	33	43
Blofield United A	20	10	3	7	50	53	33
Costessey C. Res -7	20	13	0	7	60	38	32
Jarrolds	20	10	2	8	64	48	32
South Walsham Res.	20	9	4	7	56	48	31
Dyers Arms	20	8	5	7	58	47	29
Horsford United A	20	7	3	10	37	55	24
Yelverton Res.	20	5	2	13	41	64	17
Wensum Albion	20	3	3	14	28	60	12
Mousehold A. Res -3	20	2	1	17	23	96	5

Division Three	P	W	D	L	F	A	Pts
Circle Anglia	20	17	0	3	70	28	51
Hockering	20	16	1	3	74	33	49
Newton Flotman Res.	20	13	1	6	62	30	40
Drayton Res.	20	10	3	7	73	53	33
Horsford United B	20	8	4	8	39	45	28
Old Catton Rovers -2	20	8	3	9	47	38	25
Taverham	20	6	5	9	48	45	23
Worstead Res.	20	5	5	10	48	54	20
Ketts Tavern Toucans	20	5	4	11	34	59	19
Hempnall A	20	5	3	12	41	74	18
Thorpe Village A	20	1	3	16	15	92	6

Reepham Town A - record expunged.

NOTTS AMATEUR ALLIANCE

Premier Division	P	W	D	L	F	A	Pts
Burton Joyce	22	16	3	3	85	42	51
Coopers Arms	22	13	2	7	71	56	41
Santos	22	11	3	8	51	49	36
Kashmir	22	11	2	9	60	57	35
Real United	22	11	2	9	46	56	35
Headstocks	22	10	4	8	64	54	34
Kirton Brickworks	22	8	4	10	50	50	28
Trident	22	8	4	10	52	63	28
Ashland Rovers	22	8	3	11	40	45	27
Nuthall	22	7	4	11	50	55	25
FC Samba	22	5	6	11	41	50	21
Gedling Southbank A	22	4	3	15	33	66	15

Aspley Beacon, East Valley United - records expunged.

Division One	P	W	D	L	F	A	Pts
Durham Ox	22	15	3	4	74	48	48
Nottingham Sikh Lions	22	13	5	4	73	44	44
Kimberley MW A	22	13	5	4	68	44	44
Premium	22	14	1	7	73	55	43
Clifton Wanderers	22	13	2	7	68	49	41
Calverton Miners W A	22	11	4	7	59	46	37
AFC Bridgford	22	11	2	9	86	46	35
FC Banter	22	8	4	10	41	58	28
Bingham Town	22	8	2	12	67	68	26
Vernon Villa Res.	22	6	4	12	44	54	22
St Helens	22	2	2	18	31	112	8
Clifton Academy	22	1	0	21	27	87	3

Notts Metropolis - record expunged.

Division Two	P	W	D	L	F	A	Pts
Bilborough United	28	27	1	0	136	30	82
FC Gunthorpe	28	19	2	7	117	46	59
FC Dynamo	28	16	5	7	99	54	53
Strelley Rose	28	15	3	10	94	75	48
Kirk Hallam	28	14	5	9	85	56	47
Heath Hill	28	15	2	11	73	59	47
Boots Athletic A	28	14	2	12	60	75	44
Ali Islam	28	12	5	11	95	87	41
Robin Hood Colts	28	12	3	13	69	61	39
Wilford Rangers	28	10	8	10	55	63	38
Sherwood Club	28	10	1	17	64	83	31
Premium Res.	28	9	3	16	65	79	30
AFC Bridgford Res.	28	9	1	18	40	90	28
West 8	28	4	2	22	40	121	14
Ged. Southbank Colts	28	2	1	25	36	149	7

Division Three	P	W	D	L	F	A	Pts
Netherfield Alb. Res.	28	22	2	4	115	37	68
Beeston Rovers	28	20	5	3	101	47	65
Kimberley MW Acad.	28	19	5	4	82	49	62
Red Heart	28	19	5	4	65	37	62
FC Geordie	28	16	6	6	83	46	54
Netherfield Town	28	16	1	11	91	79	49
Bestwood	28	14	3	11	74	63	45
Clifton Tigers	28	12	4	12	83	73	40
Globo Gym	28	8	5	15	58	70	29
Netherfield Seniors	28	7	8	13	64	88	29
Aspley Villa	28	8	3	17	83	102	27
Beeston Rylands	28	7	2	19	56	93	23
Bingham Town Res.	28	7	2	19	51	95	23
Kashmir A	28	3	6	19	39	97	15
FC Samba Res.	28	2	3	23	30	99	9

PERRY STREET & DISTRICT LEAGUE

Premier Division	P	W	D	L	F	A	Pts
South Petherton	20	18	1	1	98	18	55
Lyme Regis	20	15	3	2	75	20	48
Beaminster	20	14	3	3	57	21	45
Merriott Rovers	20	10	2	8	50	47	32
Farway United	20	8	3	9	53	45	27
Ilminster Town Res.	20	9	0	11	34	58	27
West/Mid Chinnock	20	6	3	11	37	64	21
Perry Street & YH	20	5	3	12	41	45	18
Combe St Nich. Res.	20	5	2	13	34	58	17
Barrington	20	4	4	12	38	71	16
Misterton	20	2	4	14	31	101	10

Division One	P	W	D	L	F	A	Pts
Crewkerne Town	20	17	2	1	95	25	53
Winsham	20	16	0	4	77	24	48
Millwey Rise	20	15	2	3	94	31	47
Netherbury	20	12	2	6	51	38	38
Forton Rangers	20	10	2	8	49	51	32
Lyme Regis Res.	20	8	3	9	38	43	27
Perry Street Res. -1	20	6	1	13	32	75	18
Iminster Town Colts	20	5	1	14	37	70	16
Norton Athletic	20	5	1	14	31	71	16
Thorncombe	20	4	1	15	28	63	13
Charmouth	20	4	1	15	32	73	13

Division Two	P	W	D	L	F	A	Pts
Beaminster Res.	20	16	3	1	91	29	51
Shepton Beauchamp	20	13	6	1	64	24	45
Dowlish & Donyatt	20	12	2	6	60	34	38
Hinton St George	20	9	3	8	49	49	30
Pymore	20	8	5	7	47	55	29
S. Petherton Res. -1	20	8	3	9	46	46	26
Uplyme	20	7	4	9	66	56	25
Chard Rangers	20	5	4	11	41	67	19
Crewkerne Rangers	20	5	4	11	42	70	19
Hawkchurch	20	5	3	12	47	70	18
Forton Rangers Res.	20	2	3	15	29	82	9

Division Three	P	W	D	L	F	A	Pts
Misterton Res.	18	15	2	1	81	28	47
Crewkerne Town Res.	18	12	2	4	71	35	38
Luso-Chard	18	9	3	6	68	36	30
Chard United	18	9	2	7	49	36	29
Combe St Nicholas A	18	8	2	8	46	46	26
Winsham Res.	18	7	4	7	63	64	25
Millwey Rise Res.	18	6	3	9	45	50	21
Drimpton	18	4	3	11	30	77	15
Farway Utd Res. -4	18	4	3	11	27	83	11
Lyme Bantams -1	18	3	2	13	28	53	10

Division Four	P	W	D	L	F	A	Pts
W & M Chinnock Res.	20	16	1	3	118	34	49
Hinton St George Res.	20	15	3	2	71	28	48
Waytown Hounds	20	13	1	6	61	38	40
Shepton B. Res. -1	20	11	1	8	54	56	33
Combe St Nicholas B	20	9	3	8	54	54	30
Chard United Res.	20	9	2	9	48	47	29
Ilminster Town A -1	20	9	0	11	58	68	26
Barrington Res. -2	20	7	3	10	51	54	22
Thorncombe Res.	20	5	3	12	26	53	18
Hawkchurch Res.	20	3	3	14	29	86	12
Chard Rangers Res.	20	2	2	16	25	77	8

PLYMOUTH & WEST DEVON COMB.

Division One	Pld	W	D	L	F	A	Pts
Mount Gould	22	17	5	0	80	21	56
Roborough (-6)	22	15	3	4	69	29	42
United Services Mermaid	22	10	4	8	50	58	34
Ordulph Arms	22	10	3	9	52	50	33
Ivybridge Town Reserves	22	9	5	8	55	44	32
Wessex Rangers	22	10	1	11	77	62	31
FC Manadon	22	10	1	11	57	60	31
W Mortgage Services	22	9	2	11	54	50	29
Horrabridge Rangers SA	22	9	2	11	50	61	29
Univ of Plymouth (-14)	22	10	4	8	72	46	20
Lee Moor	22	6	2	14	54	88	20
Staddiscombe Colts	22	1	0	21	30	131	3

Division Two	P	W	D	L	F	A	Pts
Chaddlewood Miners	22	18	2	2	72	28	56
Plymouth Marjon	22	14	2	6	68	41	44
Chard United	22	13	4	5	79	58	43
Shakespeare	22	14	0	8	79	45	42
Windsor Car Sales	22	9	3	10	64	63	30
Yealm Old Boys	22	9	2	11	45	58	29
Caf Roma	22	8	3	11	71	76	27
Yelverton	22	7	4	11	50	51	25
University Plym. Res.	22	9	4	9	59	62	22
Plympton	22	4	7	11	41	75	19
Roborough Res.	22	4	3	15	42	77	12
Morley Rangers	22	4	4	14	33	69	12

Division Three	P	W	D	L	F	A	Pts
Vospers Oak V. Res.	18	17	1	0	87	15	52
Wembury Rovers	18	11	4	3	55	22	37
The Railway Club	18	9	1	8	46	42	28
Cofely	18	9	6	3	44	30	27
Morley Rangers Res.	18	7	3	8	50	37	24
Chad'wd Miners Res.	18	6	3	9	33	52	21
Stonehouse Glass	18	6	2	10	50	70	20
University of Plym A	18	7	3	8	40	45	15
Hooe Rovers	18	3	1	14	23	58	10
Plymouth Hope	18	2	2	14	24	81	8

All Nations - record expunged.

PORTSMOUTH LEAGUE

Premier Division	P	W	D	L	F	A	Pts
Waterlooville Social Cl	16	12	2	2	68	21	38
St Helena Bobs	16	11	2	3	69	31	35
Shearer United	16	10	1	5	43	25	31
Wymering	16	8	1	7	35	38	25
Meon United	16	8	1	7	40	53	25
Prospect	16	3	5	8	33	51	14
Portsmouth Kurdish Utd	16	3	4	9	27	42	13
Farefield Sports	16	4	1	11	34	52	13
CD Galaxy	16	3	3	10	29	65	12
Division One	**P**	**W**	**D**	**L**	**F**	**A**	**Pts**
NAP Construction	16	12	0	4	58	31	36
Southside	16	9	3	4	40	32	30
AFC Ventora	16	9	2	5	50	42	29
Voyers	16	8	4	4	41	38	28
Mead End	16	7	0	9	30	31	21
Horndean United Res.	16	6	1	9	40	46	19
Rovers Reunited	16	5	3	8	38	42	18
Newcome Arms	16	5	3	8	36	56	18
AFC Hilsea	16	2	2	12	18	33	8
Division Two	**P**	**W**	**D**	**L**	**F**	**A**	**Pts**
St Helena Bobs res (-3)	16	14	0	2	71	22	39
AFC Hereford	16	11	2	3	62	28	35
FC Southsea	16	9	1	6	60	41	28
Portchester	16	7	3	6	33	43	24
Segensworth	16	6	3	7	41	41	21
Carberry	16	4	5	7	40	42	17
Compass Rose	16	3	5	8	37	50	14
Century	16	2	5	9	25	48	11
Valley	16	3	2	11	28	83	11
Division Three	**P**	**W**	**D**	**L**	**F**	**A**	**Pts**
Horndean Hawks	18	14	3	1	77	12	45
AFC Stella	18	12	3	3	74	31	39
The Unit	18	10	4	4	81	31	34
Cosham Pk Rangers (-3)	18	11	3	4	72	26	33
Uplands United	18	10	2	6	37	35	32
Castle Rovers	18	8	2	8	56	54	26
Queens Park Grovers	18	7	2	9	59	36	23
Westover	18	5	0	13	35	87	15
DCP United	18	2	0	16	36	109	6
Tempest Crusaders	18	1	1	16	18	124	4

PRESTON & DISTRICT LEAGUE

Premier Division	P	W	D	L	F	A	Pts
Burscough Richmond	22	17	3	2	76	22	54
Leyland	22	17	2	3	74	29	53
Leyland Red Rose	22	15	2	5	73	43	47
Preston Wanderers	22	14	4	4	72	39	46
Southport Amateurs	22	11	4	7	63	39	37
Town Green	22	10	4	8	60	48	34
Hoole United	22	9	3	10	61	53	30
Eccleston & Heskin	22	5	3	14	40	68	18
Baxters	22	5	3	14	42	82	18
Appley Bridge	22	4	5	13	35	69	14
Charnock Richard "A"	22	3	4	15	31	75	13
New Longton Rovers	22	3	1	18	28	88	10
Division One	**P**	**W**	**D**	**L**	**F**	**A**	**Pts**
Blessed Sacrement	20	15	4	1	85	31	49
Preston GSA	20	12	4	4	59	27	40
Penwortham Town	20	11	4	5	54	37	37
Mawdesley	20	10	2	8	55	43	32
Deepdale	20	10	2	8	56	51	32
Southport Trinity Res.	20	9	5	6	47	45	32
Highcross	20	7	4	9	44	48	25
Birkdale United	20	6	6	8	43	49	21
Tarleton Corinthians	20	7	0	13	35	67	21
Southport Amateurs Res.	20	5	3	12	30	59	15
Walton Le Dale	20	0	2	18	17	68	2
Plungington Celtic - resigned, record expunged.							
Division Two	**P**	**W**	**D**	**L**	**F**	**A**	**Pts**
Penwortham St Teresas	20	18	0	2	86	27	54
Eccleston & Heskin Res.	20	13	1	6	61	40	40
Hoghton West End	20	12	2	6	58	41	38
Walmer Bridge	20	11	3	6	44	37	36
Adelphi	20	10	2	8	80	49	32
Skelmersdale Athletic	20	10	0	10	63	54	30
Newman College	20	8	1	11	35	60	25
Burscough Bridge	20	7	3	10	55	57	24
Wyre	20	6	2	12	44	72	20
Chipping	20	5	2	13	34	64	17
Leyland Red Rose Res.	20	2	0	18	25	84	6
Division Three	**P**	**W**	**D**	**L**	**F**	**A**	**Pts**
Bolton United	22	18	2	2	86	26	56
Leyland Reserves	22	17	1	4	114	36	52
Burscough Richmond Res.	22	14	3	5	83	39	45
Ribbleton Rovers	22	12	3	7	85	45	39
Muldoons	22	12	1	9	69	62	37
Leyland Athletic	22	9	2	11	56	65	29
Ribchester	22	10	1	11	55	62	28
Farington Villa	22	8	1	13	49	61	25
Walmer Bridge Reserves	22	7	3	12	36	59	24
New Longton Rovers Res.	22	5	3	14	44	89	18
Hoole United Reserves	22	4	3	15	36	80	15
Hesketh Bank "A"	22	3	3	16	38	127	6

Division Four	P	W	D	L	F	A	Pts
Cadley	20	16	2	2	103	27	50
Wilbraham	20	16	2	2	104	40	50
Goosnargh	20	12	4	4	74	42	40
Preston Academicals	20	12	2	6	65	44	38
Greenlands	20	9	1	10	62	59	28
AFC Preston	20	8	1	11	57	62	25
Eccleston & Heskin "A"	20	6	4	10	44	68	22
RAOB	20	6	1	13	45	82	16
New Longton Rov. "A"	20	5	3	12	37	93	15
Clayton Brook	20	3	3	14	32	67	12
East Lancs United	20	4	3	13	27	66	12

Tarleton Corinthians Reserves - record expunged.

REDHILL & DISTRICT LEAGUE

Division One	P	W	D	L	F	A	Pts
Racing Epsom	16	13	1	2	51	16	40
South Park A	16	10	1	5	40	20	31
Merstham A	16	9	3	4	39	23	30
Warlingham A	16	8	3	5	37	22	27
Reigate Sala	16	6	6	4	29	32	24
Woodmansterne Hyde	16	5	4	7	28	37	19
Horley Town A	16	4	3	9	24	33	15
Reed	16	1	5	10	20	49	8
Leigh Res.	16	1	4	11	24	60	7

Division Two	P	W	D	L	F	A	Pts
Caterham Old Boys	16	13	1	2	73	17	40
Heath Old Boys	16	12	2	2	63	22	38
Monotype	16	10	2	4	32	16	32
Merstham Newton Res.	16	9	1	6	37	34	28
RH123 Athletic Res.	16	8	1	7	50	44	25
Smallfield Res.	16	6	1	9	30	38	19
South Godstone Res.	16	4	1	11	30	50	13
Charlwood Res.	16	2	2	12	23	57	8
Nutfield Res.	16	2	1	13	24	84	7

Division Three	P	W	D	L	F	A	Pts
Warlingham B	18	14	1	3	61	19	43
Reigate Hill Res.	18	12	2	4	82	45	38
Heath Old Boys	18	12	2	4	70	33	38
Alliance	18	11	1	6	75	47	34
Overton Athletic	18	9	2	7	29	27	29
Holland Sports Res.	18	8	2	8	38	44	26
Limpsfield Blues Res.	18	7	1	10	42	46	22
Reigate Priory A	18	4	3	11	39	55	15
Oxted & District A	18	3	0	15	17	76	9
Brockham Res.	18	3	0	15	14	75	9

Division Four	P	W	D	L	F	A	Pts
Wallington	20	17	2	1	91	29	53
W'mansterne H. Res.	20	13	3	4	60	36	42
RH123 Athletic A	20	12	2	6	47	42	38
Netherne Falcons	20	11	2	7	39	34	35
The Plough Ifield	20	10	3	7	54	39	33
Port Louis Starlite	20	9	2	9	39	45	29
Westcott 35 Res.	20	9	0	11	45	50	27
Merstham B	20	8	1	11	53	61	25
AFC Redhill	20	4	3	13	31	60	15
Walton Heath Res.	20	4	3	13	34	71	15
Park Lane	20	2	1	17	23	49	7

Division Five	P	W	D	L	F	A	Pts
South Park B	18	14	2	2	72	22	44
RH123 Athletic B	18	11	5	2	60	35	38
Alpine Lane	18	11	4	3	62	18	37
AFC Redhill Res.	18	9	1	8	52	43	28
Nutfield A	18	8	0	10	60	46	24
Horley Res.	18	7	3	8	38	50	24
Frenches Athletic Res.	18	7	2	9	39	58	23
Walton Heath A	18	7	2	9	56	87	23
Reigate Priory B	18	4	1	13	26	56	13
Merstham C	18	1	2	15	22	72	5

Westcott 35 A - record expunged.

ROMFORD & DISTRICT SENIOR LEAGUE

Senior Division	Pld	W	D	L	F	A	Pts
Old Barkabbeyans	16	13	2	1	47	7	41
Heath Park	16	11	2	3	49	26	35
Upney Royal Oak	16	11	2	3	46	23	35
Millhouse	16	9	2	5	44	35	29
Stifford Clays Soc Club	16	8	2	6	54	41	26
Duckwood	16	6	0	10	40	45	18
Brabazon Sports	16	4	2	10	29	40	14
East Ham WMC	16	2	0	14	24	57	6
Newbury Forest Reserves	16	2	0	14	23	83	6

Premier Division	P	W	D	L	F	A	Pts
Iona	22	19	2	1	59	13	59
Clack United	22	17	2	3	79	35	53
Rush Green	22	14	3	6	51	44	45
Old Barkabbeyans Res.	22	13	4	5	53	30	43
Dagenham United	22	10	7	5	36	19	37
Liberty	22	8	6	8	31	26	30
Mansard Rovers	22	9	1	12	46	52	28
Allied Rec	22	8	2	12	27	51	26
Euro Dagenham	22	7	3	12	40	38	24
May & Baker	22	3	5	14	21	49	14
OG United	22	3	4	15	20	51	13
Phoenix	22	1	2	19	12	64	4

Division One	P	W	D	L	F	A	Pts
Spartan Athletic	18	11	3	4	46	28	36
AFC Stanford	18	9	4	5	56	24	31
Emeronians	18	9	3	6	37	29	30
Harold Wood Hospital	18	9	2	7	42	34	29
Old Barkabbeyans A	18	8	4	6	38	36	28
Northend	18	7	5	6	32	29	26
Verona	18	6	6	6	43	37	24
Cromer Park	18	7	2	9	29	29	23
Mayfair Athletic	18	5	2	11	26	53	17
Canning Town A	18	2	1	15	15	65	7

Upminster A - record expunged.

Division Two	P	W	D	L	F	A	Pts
Ferns Seniors	22	17	2	3	71	30	53
Coryton Athletic	22	14	5	3	71	42	47
Oakwood Sports	22	14	2	6	51	34	44
East Ham WMC Res.	22	11	4	7	65	46	37
Cedars	22	11	4	7	52	38	37
Aveley Northend Res.	22	11	3	8	63	45	36
Northend Res.	22	10	3	9	50	46	33
Old Barkabbeyans B	22	9	4	9	50	36	31
Clockwork	22	8	2	12	40	43	26
Merit	22	4	4	14	49	93	16
Brentwood United	22	3	2	17	26	74	11
Fleet Hill	22	1	3	18	22	82	6

OTHER LEAGUES

Division Three	P	W	D	L	F	A	Pts
Eastside Rovers	22	17	1	4	66	27	52
Haver Town	22	16	3	3	88	25	51
Oakwood Sports Res.	22	16	2	4	72	27	50
Aveley Northend A	22	10	6	6	61	45	36
Real Dagenham	22	10	3	9	53	48	33
Northend A	22	9	3	10	48	47	30
Elmhurst	22	8	5	9	37	55	29
Lionside United	22	9	2	11	46	66	29
Coryton Athletic Res.	22	9	2	11	47	69	29
Co-Op United	22	3	6	13	33	55	15
Markyate	22	4	3	14	39	75	14
Upminster B	22	2	3	17	27	78	9

SALISBURY & DISTRICT LEAGUE

Premier Division	P	W	D	L	F	A	Pts
Alderbury	20	13	5	2	90	30	44
Durrington Dynamoes	20	12	7	1	70	17	43
Stockton & Codford	19	10	5	4	51	19	35
Sth Newton & Wishford	20	10	4	6	62	31	34
Friends Provident	20	9	5	6	41	39	32
Tisbury United	20	9	4	7	53	39	31
Porton Sports	20	7	7	6	53	44	28
Boscombe Down	20	6	3	11	40	44	21
Nomansland & Landford	20	5	3	12	44	65	18
Durrington WMC	19	4	4	11	34	53	16
Enford	20	0	1	19	20	177	1

Chalke Valley Reserves - record expunged.

Division One	P	W	D	L	F	A	Pts
The Coach & Horses	14	11	0	3	57	21	33
West Harnham	14	9	2	3	52	34	29
Whiteparish	14	6	5	3	41	29	23
Tisbury United Reserves	14	6	3	5	36	35	21
Figheldean Rangers	14	6	1	7	51	38	19
Winterslow	14	5	4	5	41	32	19
George & Dragon	14	2	4	8	15	40	10
Alderbury Reserves	14	1	1	12	14	78	4

Alderholt "A" - record expunged.

The Coach & Horses - record expunged.

Division Two	Pl	W	D	L	F	A	Pts
Victoria Hotel	20	18	2	0	93	14	56
Devizes Inn	20	13	2	5	59	42	41
S Newton &Wishford Res.	20	12	3	5	57	42	39
Stockton & Codford Res.	20	10	4	6	50	44	34
Burgess Trees	20	9	5	6	61	40	32
Huntsman Tavern	20	8	7	5	51	47	31
Boscombe Down Rec Cl	20	7	5	8	60	53	26
Value Cars	20	6	3	11	35	52	21
West Harnham Reserves	20	4	3	13	39	63	15
Langford United	20	2	3	15	28	80	9
Winterslow Reserves	20	2	1	17	21	77	7

SCARBOROUGH & DIST. LEAGUE

Division One	P	W	D	L	F	A	Pts
Ryedale SC	22	20	1	1	96	26	61
Edgehill Res.	22	17	3	2	84	33	54
Eastfield St J. Res.	22	14	0	8	71	47	42
Fishburn Park Res.	22	14	2	6	58	28	44
Seamer Sports	22	10	4	8	56	40	34
FC Rosette	22	10	2	10	56	53	32
Rillington Athletic	22	7	4	11	30	46	25
West Pier Res.	22	7	3	12	36	68	24
Filey Town Res. -3	22	8	1	13	39	62	22
Newlands Pk Res -3	22	6	5	11	42	59	20
Snainton	22	2	3	17	26	79	9
Cayton Corries Res.	22	2	2	18	29	82	8

Division Two	P	W	D	L	F	A	Pts
Whitby Fishermans S.	20	19	1	0	144	21	58
Riskers United	20	14	4	2	79	42	46
Whitby RUFC	20	14	1	5	91	34	43
Heslerton-SD	20	11	6	3	75	48	39
FC Filey	20	10	3	7	77	45	33
Westover Wasps Res.	20	8	3	9	69	57	27
Seamer Sports Res.	20	6	4	10	45	81	22
Scalby Res. -3	20	5	2	13	38	85	14
Ayton Res.	20	3	5	12	39	87	14
Falsgrave Pirates	20	4	0	16	41	95	12
Ganton	20	1	1	18	14	117	4

SCUNTHORPE & DISTRICT LEAGUE

Division One	P	W	D	L	F	A	Pts
Limestone Rangers	20	13	3	4	44	22	42
Epworth Town	20	10	6	4	39	24	36
Swinefleet Juniors	20	11	3	6	40	41	36
AFC Brumby	20	10	4	6	40	41	34
Barton Town Old B Res.	20	8	5	7	47	40	29
College Wanderers	20	7	7	6	43	35	28
BBM	20	6	8	6	48	36	26
Crowle Town Colts	20	7	3	10	39	46	24
Scotter United	20	6	5	9	40	44	23
Scunthonians	20	4	3	13	28	46	15
Crosby Colts	20	3	3	14	26	59	12

Division Two	P	W	D	L	F	A	Pts
Crosby Colts Reserves	14	9	3	2	61	35	30
Barton Tn OB Colts (-3)	14	10	0	4	43	29	27
SJJ Fusion	14	8	2	4	52	19	26
Barnetby United	14	8	1	5	55	29	25
Epworth Town Reserves	14	5	3	6	40	37	18
New Holland Villa (-3)	14	6	1	7	29	34	16
Scotter United res (+6)	14	2	0	12	15	77	12
Barrow Wanderers	14	3	0	11	25	60	9

Luddington - record expunged.

Middlehouse - record expunged.

Revision - record expunged.

Division Three	P	W	D	L	F	A	Pts
Butchers Arms	20	16	1	3	83	26	49
Sherpa (-3)	20	15	2	3	95	29	44
AFC Winterton (-3)	20	12	2	6	66	51	35
Briggensians (+3)	20	10	2	8	57	54	35
Scunthonians Reserves	20	10	3	7	63	53	33
Crowle Tn Colts Reserves	20	9	2	9	55	37	29
Crosby Colts Juniors	20	8	1	11	65	63	25
New Holland Rangers	20	8	1	11	33	60	25
Limestone Rangers Res.	20	5	4	11	31	52	19
College Wand. res (+3)	20	4	3	13	30	51	18
Santon	20	2	1	17	35	137	7

SELBY & DISTRICT LEAGUE

Division One	P	W	D	L	F	A	Pts
Pontefract SSC	20	18	1	1	111	27	55
Pontefract Amateurs (-2)	20	18	2	0	72	22	54
Garfotrth Rangers "A"	20	12	7	1	56	48	37
Rock Inn (-5)	20	11	7	2	51	49	35
Moorends	20	8	7	5	43	36	29
CAS Celtics	20	9	11	0	66	66	27
Ferrybridge Amateurs	20	7	8	5	41	42	26
Pontefract Town	20	5	13	2	38	55	17
Knottingley Albion	20	5	13	2	33	51	17
Pontefract	20	3	13	4	35	77	13
Sherburn White Rose "A"	20	2	16	2	28	104	8

Division Two	P	W	D	L	F	A	Pts
Inter Crown	20	15	3	2	78	39	47
Kippax A	20	14	3	3	67	36	45
Chequerfield United	20	13	5	2	77	44	41
Fairburn United	20	12	5	3	59	33	39
Kellington	20	8	7	5	69	76	29
Wetherby	20	8	8	4	44	48	28
Drax SSC	20	8	12	0	48	67	24
Hensall Athletic	20	5	13	2	48	64	17
Rock Inn reerves	20	4	12	4	38	52	16
Swillington	20	4	13	3	42	84	15
Great Preston Res.	20	3	13	4	33	58	13

SEVENOAKS & DISTRICT LEAGUE

Premier Division	P	W	D	L	F	A	Pts
Kemsing	22	19	2	1	84	30	59
Halstead	22	14	6	2	49	19	48
Eynsford	22	15	1	6	74	35	46
Nomads	22	12	4	6	80	38	40
Borough Green Utd	22	12	2	8	68	45	38
Ightham	22	9	6	7	64	56	33
St Lawrence	22	9	4	9	61	60	31
Tonbdge Bapt. Ch'ch	22	6	6	10	47	54	24
Ide Hill	22	7	1	14	46	85	22
Chipstead A	22	5	3	14	34	70	18
Kingsdown Racers	22	4	2	16	40	101	14
Dunton Green	22	1	1	20	20	74	4

Division One	P	W	D	L	F	A	Pts
Old Boars	20	14	3	3	54	37	45
Wilderpark	20	13	3	4	51	29	42
Potters	20	13	2	5	43	26	41
Seal	20	12	4	4	51	24	40
Hildenborough A. Res.	20	10	1	9	61	43	31
Fleetdown United A	20	8	5	7	40	33	29
Sevenoaks Weald	20	6	4	10	36	36	22
Eynsford Res.	20	6	4	10	33	42	22
Halls Res.	20	6	1	13	45	64	19
St Lawrence Res.	20	5	1	14	24	69	16
Westerham A	20	3	0	17	34	68	9

(subject to an appeal by Potters)

Division Two	P	W	D	L	F	A	Pts
Kingsdown Rac. Res.	18	14	2	2	80	28	44
Borough Green Res.	18	12	2	4	67	31	38
Halstead Res.	18	11	4	3	52	26	37
Kemsing Res.	18	10	2	6	75	43	32
Swanley Oaks	18	9	1	8	84	52	28
Otford United A	18	9	1	8	36	41	28
Seal Res.	18	7	1	10	49	50	22
Hildenborough A. A	18	5	1	12	34	58	16
Nomads A	18	4	2	12	28	62	14
Wilderpark Res.	18	1	0	17	16	131	3

Division Three	P	W	D	L	F	A	Pts
Nomads B	18	13	2	3	51	21	41
Real Mayo	18	13	1	4	73	30	40
Chipstead B	18	13	0	5	60	22	39
AW London	18	9	4	5	37	33	31
Ton. Bap. Church Res.	18	9	1	8	37	42	28
Borough Green	18	7	0	11	33	55	21
Radius	18	6	2	10	38	46	20
Sevenoaks Weald Res.	18	4	3	11	19	40	15
Ide Hill Res.	18	3	4	11	20	60	13
Ightham Res.	18	2	5	11	17	36	11

Dunton Green Res. - record expunged.

SHROPSHIRE ALLIANCE

	P	W	D	L	F	A	Pts
Rock Rovers	14	11	1	2	44	23	34
Oswestry Boys Club	14	9	1	4	42	27	28
Weston Rhyn	14	8	2	4	37	27	26
Oswestry Tn Lions	14	5	2	7	32	28	17
Prees United	14	4	4	6	25	28	16
Ludlow Town Colts	14	5	0	9	26	41	15
Hopesgate United	14	2	6	6	24	33	12
Bayston Hill	14	3	2	9	24	47	11

SOUTH DEVON LEAGUE

Premier Division	P	W	D	L	F	A	Pts
Upton Athletic	26	22	3	1	113	32	69
Watts Blake Bearne	26	20	4	2	90	29	64
Buckland Ath. Res.	26	18	2	6	76	33	56
Brixham United -6	26	18	3	5	98	42	51
Abbotskerswell	26	15	2	9	81	48	47
Kingskerswell & Chel.	26	13	2	11	72	59	41
Brixham Villa	26	13	2	11	63	61	41
Staverton & Landscove	26	12	2	12	54	51	38
Ipplepen Athletic	26	10	1	15	53	69	31
East Allington United	26	8	2	16	44	78	26
Galmpton Res. +3	26	6	2	18	42	100	23
Totnes & Dartington Res.	26	7	1	18	43	92	22
Ashburton	26	4	2	20	40	103	14
Waldon Athletic	26	2	0	24	25	97	6

Division One	P	W	D	L	F	A	Pts
Loddiswell Athletic	24	17	5	2	73	36	56
Stoke Gabriel Res.	24	14	6	4	76	35	48
Kingskerwell/C. Res.	24	13	4	7	50	42	43
Dartmouth Res.	24	13	3	8	48	46	42
N. Abbot Spurs Res.	24	12	4	8	58	38	40
Buckfastleigh Rgrs	24	10	4	10	61	47	34
Kingsteignton Athletic	24	9	5	10	42	40	32
Riviera Spurs	24	8	6	10	50	58	30
Chudleigh Athletic	24	8	5	11	49	58	29
Brixham Villa Res.	24	9	1	14	47	67	28
Paignton Villa	24	8	3	13	46	61	27
Hele Rovers	24	4	5	15	48	79	17
Harbertonford -3	24	3	5	16	34	75	11

Galmpton & TG Res. - record expunged.

Division Two	P	W	D	L	F	A	Pts
Stoke Fleming	26	21	2	3	111	36	65
Teignmouth Res.	26	19	5	2	112	31	62
Newton Abbot 66	26	19	3	4	116	29	60
Langdon	26	15	6	5	88	33	51
Hookhills United	26	15	5	6	96	50	50
Teign Village	26	15	3	8	75	50	48
Beesands Rovers	26	13	4	9	52	44	43
Newton United	26	12	2	12	59	65	38
Upton Ath. Res. -6	26	9	4	13	53	71	25
Paignton Saints	26	7	4	15	53	79	25
Brixham United Res.	26	6	4	16	58	93	22
Hele Rovers Res. -3	26	5	1	20	27	118	13
Kingsteignton Res. -3	26	4	1	21	29	85	10
East Allington Res. -3	26	0	0	26	13	158	-3

Division Three	P	W	D	L	F	A	Pts
Watcombe Wdrs	26	23	2	1	122	22	71
Broadhempston U.	26	16	6	4	67	50	54
Buckland Ath. A -3	26	17	4	5	102	33	52
Watts Blake B. Res.	26	12	7	7	54	33	43
Bovey Tracey Res. -3	26	12	8	6	54	40	41
Staverton & L. Res.	26	12	4	10	70	60	40
Liverton Utd Res. -3	26	13	3	10	71	58	39
South Brent	26	10	8	8	53	56	38
Meadowbrook Ath.	26	7	8	11	57	64	29
Waldon Athletic Res.	26	7	5	14	53	80	26
Dartmouth A -3	26	6	5	15	56	78	20
Moretonhampston -3	26	6	4	16	44	92	19
Denbury Athletic -3	26	4	3	19	46	85	12
Totnes/Dartington A	26	3	1	22	28	126	10

Division Four	P	W	D	L	F	A	Pts
Abbotskerswell Res.	26	18	4	4	86	42	58
Brixham Town	26	20	1	5	98	35	55
N. Abbot Spurs A	26	18	0	8	81	54	54
Kingskerwell/C. A -3	26	17	1	8	65	48	49
Babbacombe Cor.	26	14	5	7	62	39	47
Stoke Gabriel A	26	14	4	8	69	38	46
Ipplepen Athletic Res.	26	14	2	10	65	53	44
Ilsington Villa	26	11	3	12	66	71	36
Torbay Christians	26	10	4	12	40	54	34
Foxhole United	26	10	3	13	58	62	33
Brixham Villa A -3	26	6	4	16	40	71	19
Loddiswell Ath. Res. -6	26	5	5	16	35	63	14
Malborough Utd -6	26	4	2	20	41	103	8
Stoke Fleming Res.	26	1	2	23	30	103	5

Division Five	P	W	D	L	F	A	Pts
Bishopsteignton Utd	26	21	2	3	121	35	65
Marldon	26	18	4	4	90	43	58
Watts Blake Bearne A	26	17	5	4	78	50	56
South Brent Res.	26	13	5	8	94	75	44
Paignton V. Res. -3	26	15	2	9	87	75	44
Harbertonford Res. -3	26	14	2	10	83	77	41
Buckfastleigh Res.	26	10	5	11	64	73	35
Chudleigh A. Res. -3	26	11	3	12	62	71	33
Babbacombe Res.	26	7	3	16	61	83	24
Paignton Sts Res. -3	26	6	7	13	55	76	22
Newton United Res.	26	6	4	16	55	81	22
Ashburton Res. -3	26	6	6	14	61	86	21
Bovey Tracey A	26	7	0	19	51	91	21
Riviera Spurs Res. -3	26	4	6	16	41	87	15

Division Six	P	W	D	L	F	A	Pts
Buckland & M. Res.	20	15	1	4	58	20	46
Newton Abb. 66 Res.	20	14	1	5	58	33	43
Dittisham United	20	13	2	5	65	43	41
Watcombe W. Res.	20	10	2	8	58	38	32
Kingsbridge/Kellaton	20	9	5	6	53	38	32
Broadhempston Res.	20	7	7	6	52	53	28
Teign Village Res.	20	7	4	9	50	69	25
Riviera United	20	7	2	11	43	53	23
Salcombe Town	20	7	1	12	42	56	22
Chelston -3	20	3	4	13	34	58	10
Ipplepen Athletic A	20	3	1	16	37	89	10

Denbury Athletic Res. - record expunged.

SOUTH LONDON ALLIANCE

Division One	P	W	D	L	F	A	Pts
AFC Mottingham	22	19	2	1	102	27	59
Bridon Ropes A	22	14	3	5	56	42	45
Old Roan	22	14	1	7	88	46	43
Long Lane	22	13	4	5	60	30	43
Wickham Park Res.	22	12	3	7	56	36	39
Thames Borough	22	10	2	10	52	44	32
Farnboro' OBG Res.	22	9	4	9	36	45	31
Bexlians Res.	22	5	7	10	27	52	22
Eltham Town	22	6	1	15	37	60	19
Beaverwood	22	6	1	15	33	81	19
Tudor Sports A	22	4	2	16	34	61	14
Seven Acre Sp. Res.	22	4	2	16	20	77	14

Old Colfeians - record expunged.

Division Two	P	W	D	L	F	A	Pts
Blackheath Wdrs	24	19	4	1	63	26	61
Red Velvet	24	19	1	4	76	32	58
Old Roan Res.	24	15	2	7	77	41	47
Chislehurst Sports	24	15	1	8	94	62	46
Crofton Albion Res.	24	10	5	9	60	55	35
Knights Old B. Res.	24	10	3	11	55	55	33
Shirley Seniors	24	10	3	11	46	55	33
Avery Hill College	24	9	3	12	43	55	30
Johnson & Phil. Res.	24	9	2	13	33	54	29
Longlands Athletic	24	7	3	14	50	56	24
West Bromley Albion	24	7	3	14	51	67	24
West Hill	24	5	3	16	35	100	18
FC Delavaran	24	3	3	18	30	55	12

Division Three	P	W	D	L	F	A	Pts
Old Roan A	20	15	2	3	68	45	47
Lewisham Athletic	20	12	3	5	71	42	39
Seven Acre Sports A	20	12	2	6	59	49	38
New Park Res. (-3)	20	12	2	6	42	28	35
Heathfield	20	9	3	8	53	40	30
Elite	20	9	3	8	43	43	30
Eltham Town Res.	20	9	1	10	41	35	28
Old Colfeians Res.	20	7	2	11	43	55	23
AFC Wickham	20	5	3	12	41	61	18
Bexley Res.	20	6	0	14	25	58	18
Foresters	20	2	3	15	27	57	9

Cray Wdrs Development - record expunged.

Division Four	P	W	D	L	F	A	Pts
Thames Borough Res.	24	18	3	3	105	33	57
Long Lane Reserves	24	16	4	4	74	24	52
Parkwood Rangers	24	16	3	5	69	34	51
Southmere	24	16	0	8	102	38	48
Oldsmiths	24	15	3	6	67	33	48
Iron Tugboat City	24	13	7	4	63	37	46
Our Lady Seniors	24	11	3	10	46	49	36
Cam	24	11	0	13	66	45	33
Farnboro' OBG "A"	24	9	1	14	60	58	28
Meridian S & S Club	24	8	2	14	55	65	26
Crayford Arrows	24	6	2	16	47	80	20
Junior Reds-S SabRes.	24	1	1	22	21	143	4
West Hill Reserves	24	1	1	22	21	157	4

SOUTH YORKSHIRE AMATEUR LEAGUE

Premier Division	P	W	D	L	F	A	Pts
Gleadless	16	14	0	2	87	23	42
Jubilee Sports	16	12	2	2	75	27	38
Manor Castle	16	12	0	4	69	33	36
Sheffield Medics	16	8	1	7	47	41	25
Sheffield West End	16	5	4	7	47	42	19
Noah's Ark	16	5	3	8	35	61	18
Dale Dynamos	16	4	3	9	21	56	15
Swallownest MW Res.	16	2	3	11	24	74	9
Sheffield Bankers Res.	16	1	2	13	15	63	5

Burngreave - record expunged.

Division One	P	W	D	L	F	A	Pts
Royston	12	10	2	0	40	16	32
Shafton Villa	12	10	0	2	59	17	30
Byron House 2010	12	6	2	4	35	30	20
British Oak	12	4	4	4	32	29	16
Thurgoland Welfare	12	3	4	5	28	31	13
Beighton Albion	12	1	1	10	23	50	4
Barnsley International	12	1	1	10	15	59	4

Oxspring United - record expunged.

SOUTHAMPTON LEAGUE

Premier Division	P	W	D	L	F	A	Pts
Bush Hill	18	14	2	2	63	18	44
Nursling	18	12	1	5	53	28	37
London Airways	18	10	4	4	42	36	34
AFC Redbridge	18	9	3	6	42	30	30
BTC Southampton	18	9	1	8	32	35	28
Cutbush Athletic	18	7	4	7	29	37	25
AFC Hiltingbury	18	7	0	11	45	50	21
Northend United	18	3	5	10	28	55	14
Solent WTL	18	4	1	13	35	57	13
Bishopstoke WMC	18	3	3	12	23	46	12

Brendon - record expunged.

Senior One	P	W	D	L	F	A	Pts
Netley Central S. Res.	20	17	2	1	87	18	53
Allbrook FC	20	16	2	2	82	29	50
Forest Town NFC	20	13	4	3	75	24	43
Burridge AFC	20	11	6	3	52	26	39
Hythe Aztecs	20	9	3	8	40	44	30
Michelmersh/T. Res.	20	9	1	10	34	55	28
Hare & Hounds	20	8	3	9	47	37	27
BTC Southampton Res.	20	5	3	12	27	78	18
Durley Res.	20	5	1	14	22	67	16
Sholing Sports	20	2	0	18	24	50	6
Wellow	20	1	3	16	21	83	6

Junior One	P	W	D	L	F	A	Pts
Warren Social	16	14	1	1	78	21	43
Cadnam United	16	13	0	3	65	22	39
Hedge End Town	16	10	2	4	53	25	32
BTC Southampton A	16	9	3	4	39	30	30
Veracity Vipers	16	6	1	9	27	30	19
Yacht Sports	16	5	2	9	38	72	17
Braishfield	16	5	0	11	31	65	15
Otterbourne A	16	4	1	11	31	50	13
Inmar	16	0	2	14	14	61	2

Junior Two	P	W	D	L	F	A	Pts
Thornhill Health Kicks	18	11	4	3	52	30	37
Southampton Energy	18	11	2	5	64	54	35
Wombles FC	18	11	1	6	46	38	34
AFC Grains	18	10	3	5	56	36	33
Compton	18	8	3	7	39	32	27
Solent Saints	18	7	4	7	47	41	25
AFC Chandlers Ford	18	7	3	8	41	42	24
Langley Manor	18	5	5	8	47	52	20
Hedge End Rgrs Res.	18	5	2	11	33	45	17
Lowford	18	1	1	16	20	75	4

Junior Three	P	W	D	L	F	A	Pts
East Boldre	20	18	1	1	79	19	55
Park Sports	20	16	2	2	86	29	50
QK Southampton A	20	13	3	4	58	33	42
Hamble Utd	20	10	4	6	49	43	34
Infinity Res.	20	8	4	8	55	52	28
Warsash Wasps Res.	20	7	6	7	44	51	27
Compton Res.	20	7	2	11	34	47	23
Freemantle	20	6	3	11	29	52	21
AFC Hiltingbury Res.	20	4	2	14	27	55	14
Cricketers Academy	20	3	3	14	32	60	12
Priory Rovers	20	2	2	16	25	77	8

Junior Four	P	W	D	L	F	A	Pts
Polygon	16	13	2	1	56	21	41
Banjo's	16	11	1	4	49	25	34
AFC Aldermoor	16	8	3	5	33	23	27
Capital	16	8	1	7	30	27	25
Southside Sports	16	6	3	7	38	41	21
New Forest	16	5	3	8	34	35	18
Good Companions	16	4	4	8	29	36	16
Brigadier Gerard	16	5	1	10	37	48	16
Upham Res.	16	3	0	13	23	73	9

Junior Five	P	W	D	L	F	A	Pts
Riverside Reds	20	16	1	3	74	28	49
FC Wellington	20	14	3	3	51	23	45
Allbrook Res.	20	13	4	3	76	30	43
West Totton	20	13	2	5	61	31	41
Botley Village Res.	20	11	1	8	62	46	34
Inter Northam	20	7	3	10	39	64	24
Athletico Romsey	20	7	2	11	33	45	23
Bitterne Park	20	6	2	12	44	31	20
Horton Heath	20	6	2	12	43	73	20
Stanton	20	3	3	14	30	56	12
Braishfield Res.	20	2	1	17	15	101	7

Junior Six	P	W	D	L	F	A	Pts
Forest Town NFC Res.	18	14	2	2	73	23	44
Exford Arms	18	14	1	3	68	22	43
Chandlers Ford	18	13	1	4	57	34	40
Hamble United Res.	18	12	1	5	64	39	37
London Airways Res.	18	7	3	8	46	54	24
Burridge Village	18	7	2	9	39	45	23
AFC Station	18	5	4	9	30	54	19
Sporting Wessex	18	5	1	12	26	54	16
Ampthill Athletic	18	4	2	12	42	71	14
Michelmersh & Tim. A	18	0	1	17	31	80	1

SOUTHEND BOROUGH COMBINATION

Premier Division	Pld	W	D	L	F	A	Pts
Rochford Town	18	15	2	1	62	20	32
Stambridge United	18	16	0	2	56	17	32
Sthch Hall Old Scholars	18	10	2	6	55	42	22
Shoebury Town	18	10	1	7	45	42	21
Borough Rovers	18	9	0	9	40	49	18
Leigh Town	18	7	3	8	42	38	17
Corinthians	18	7	2	9	34	49	16
All Claims	18	6	0	12	32	41	12
Ensign	18	2	2	14	30	61	6
Weir Sports	18	1	2	15	25	62	4

SOUTHEND & DISTRICT LEAGUE

	P	W	D	L	F	A	Pts
AFC Horndon	18	14	1	3	47	24	43
Club Sirrus	18	13	1	4	48	24	40
Thundersley Rovers	18	10	4	4	30	26	34
Pethetico Madrid	18	10	1	7	51	22	31
Hockley Spartans	18	9	2	7	32	23	29
Signet United	18	9	0	9	40	37	27
Rayleigh Town "A"	18	7	1	10	42	41	22
Sparco	18	6	1	11	34	46	19
Wickford Rangers	18	4	1	13	24	64	13
Chalkwell Park	18	2	0	16	10	51	6

SOUTHERN AMATEUR LEAGUE

Senior Division One	P	W	D	L	F	A	Pts
Nottsborough	20	15	2	3	52	23	47
Old Owens	20	12	2	6	47	28	38
Old Wilsonians	20	10	6	4	51	23	36
Winchmore Hill	20	10	6	4	42	23	36
West Wickham	20	10	5	5	30	23	35
Old Salesians	20	9	4	7	35	30	31
Polytechnic	20	9	2	9	33	35	29
East Barnet Old Gramm	20	7	1	12	36	42	22
Broomfield	20	6	1	13	23	53	19
Carshalton	20	4	0	16	20	53	12
Old Actonians Assoc.	20	3	1	16	23	59	10

Senior Division Two	P	W	D	L	F	A	Pts
Norsemen	20	15	4	1	54	25	49
Old Parkonians	20	13	3	4	52	26	42
Civil Service	20	11	2	7	45	27	35
BB Eagles	20	9	5	6	33	32	32
Weirside Rangers	20	9	3	8	39	28	30
Crouch End VampiRes.	20	9	3	8	33	38	30
Old Esthameians	20	6	7	7	43	38	25
Alleyn Old Boys	20	7	3	10	40	50	24
Old Finchleians	20	5	4	11	32	35	19
Alexandra Park	20	3	4	13	24	53	13
HSBC	20	2	4	14	23	66	10

Senior Division Three	P	W	D	L	F	A	Pts
Old W'minster Citizens	20	16	3	1	66	32	51
Merton	20	13	6	1	47	19	45
Bank of England	20	12	1	7	53	46	37
Lloyds TSB Bank	20	8	2	10	54	51	26
Old Stationers	20	7	4	9	42	46	25
Old Latymerians	20	7	3	10	38	39	24
Ibis	20	6	6	8	33	35	24
South Bank Cuaco	20	7	1	12	39	49	22
Old Lyonians	20	5	7	8	28	42	22
Southgate Olympic	20	3	6	11	27	47	15
Kew Association (-3)	20	5	3	12	35	56	15

Intermediate Division One	Pld	W	D	L	F	A	Pts
Old Owens Reserves	20	14	2	4	61	33	44
Nottsborough Reserves	20	12	6	2	49	19	42
Civil Service Reserves	20	11	2	7	42	31	35
Norsemen Reserves	20	8	4	8	39	42	28
Carshalton Reserves	20	8	3	9	41	56	27
Winchmore Hill Reserves	20	7	5	8	26	29	26
Old Actonians Assoc Res.	20	8	2	10	41	48	26
Alleyn Old Boys Res.	20	6	7	7	43	40	25
East Barnet Old Gr. Res.	20	7	2	11	41	49	23
West Wickham Reserves	20	4	9	7	27	40	21
Merton Reserves	20	0	8	12	18	41	8

Intermediate Division Two	P	W	D	L	F	A	Pts
Polytechnic Reserves	20	14	3	3	50	17	45
Old Salesians Reserves	20	12	3	5	53	47	39
Old Esthameians res (-1)	20	13	2	5	70	39	38
Old Wilsonians Reserves	20	12	2	6	49	38	38
Old Parkonians Reserves	20	12	1	7	62	25	37
BB Eagles Reserves	20	8	5	7	45	33	29
Alexandra Park Reserves	20	7	4	9	24	40	25
Weirside Rangers Res.	20	6	2	12	31	45	20
Old Finchleians Reserves	20	5	3	12	27	62	18
Old Westminster C. Res.	20	5	1	14	33	55	16
HSBC Reserves	20	2	2	16	27	70	8

Intermediate Div. Three	P	W	D	L	F	A	Pts
Old Stationers Reserves	20	15	4	1	77	22	49
Lloyds TSB Bank Res.	20	11	5	4	52	32	38
Kew Association Res.	20	11	5	4	41	26	38
Ibis Reserves	20	11	3	6	48	31	36
Crouch E Vampires Res.	20	11	0	9	47	46	33
Bank of England Res.	20	9	4	7	42	36	31
Broomfield Reserves	20	7	5	8	48	47	26
South Bank Cuaco Res.	20	7	2	11	38	53	23
Old Lyonians Reserves	20	7	1	12	42	66	22
Southgate Olympic Res.	20	2	5	13	28	62	11
Old Latymerians res (-3)	20	1	2	17	18	60	2

Junior Division One	P	W	D	L	F	A	Pts
Old Owens "A"	20	15	3	2	59	18	48
Winchmore Hill "A"	20	14	2	4	61	34	44
Nottsborough "A"	20	13	3	4	41	18	42
West Wickham "A"	20	12	4	4	46	17	40
Old Actonians A. "A"	20	10	2	8	47	33	32
East Barnet O.G. "A"	20	9	4	7	48	35	31
Weirside Rangers "A"	20	7	4	9	32	37	25
Alleyn Old Boys "A"	20	7	2	11	32	35	23
O Esthameians "A" (-4)	20	4	2	14	27	67	10
Carshalton "A"	20	3	0	17	27	80	9
Old Westminster C. "A"	20	2	2	16	24	70	8

Junior Division Two	Pld	W	D	L	F	A	Pts
Civil Service "A"	18	15	2	1	64	28	47
Polytechnic "A"	18	15	1	2	71	18	46
Norsemen "A"	18	10	3	5	58	32	33
Old Parkonians "A"	18	8	1	9	33	40	25
Old Salesians "A" (-3)	18	7	6	5	41	33	24
Old Wilsonians "A"	18	7	3	8	40	46	24
Broomfield "A"	18	7	2	9	35	28	23
BB Eagles "A"	18	4	4	10	30	43	16
Kew Association "A"	18	3	2	13	23	67	11
Crouch End Vamps "A"	18	1	2	15	22	82	5

Old Stationers "A" - record expunged.

Junior Division Three	P	W	D	L	F	A	Pts
Merton "A"	20	14	3	3	68	25	45
Old Finchleians "A"	20	13	4	3	54	31	43
South Bank Cuaco "A"	20	12	4	4	51	38	40
Alexandra Park "A"	20	11	2	7	45	27	35
Ibis "A"	20	8	4	8	48	42	28
HSBC "A"	20	7	3	10	37	42	24
Old Latymer's "A" (-6)	20	8	5	7	37	40	23
Bank of England "A"	20	6	5	9	33	54	23
Lloyds TSB Bank "A"	20	5	3	12	34	39	18
Old Lyonians "A" (-3)	20	6	1	13	30	55	16
Southgate Olympic "A"	20	1	4	15	26	70	7

Minor Division One	P	W	D	L	F	A	Pts
Winchmore Hill "B"	20	14	4	2	81	37	46
Old Actonians Assoc "B"	20	13	3	4	51	25	42
Civil Service "B"	20	10	5	5	59	40	35
Old Owens "B"	20	8	5	7	53	47	29
Nottsborough "B"	20	9	2	9	48	47	29
Old Parkonians "B"	20	8	2	10	45	61	26
Civil Service "C"	20	7	3	10	40	46	24
Old Actonians Assoc "C"	20	7	3	10	35	43	24
Polytechnic "B"	20	7	2	11	54	51	23
Alexandra Park "B"	20	7	0	13	36	56	21
Carshalton "B"	20	5	1	14	36	85	16

Minor Division Two North	P	W	D	L	F	A	Pts
Norsemen "B"	20	17	0	3	121	41	51
Old Stationers "B"	20	13	3	4	68	35	42
Crou. End Vampires "B"	20	12	3	5	54	37	39
Winchmore Hill "C"	20	11	2	7	75	52	35
Old Finchleians "B"	20	11	2	7	57	48	35
Norsemen "C"	20	11	2	7	48	50	35
Old Owens "C"	20	7	2	11	61	73	23
Winchmore Hill "D"	20	6	3	11	41	68	21
East Barnet O.G. "B"	20	5	4	11	58	69	19
Old Owens "D"	20	5	1	14	46	74	16
Southgate Olympic "B"	20	1	0	19	29	111	3

Minor Division Two South	P	W	D	L	F	A	Pts
BB Eagles "B"	20	15	3	2	66	25	48
Carshalton "C"	20	10	2	8	60	44	32
Polytechnic "C"	20	9	5	6	52	46	32
Polytechnic "D"	20	8	6	6	32	36	30
HSBC "B"	20	8	5	7	53	50	29
BB Eagles "C"	20	7	5	8	64	57	26
Kew Association "B"	20	8	2	10	47	45	26
Weirside Rangers "B"	20	6	7	7	34	48	25
West Wickham "B"	20	7	3	10	32	39	24
Old Actonians Ass. "D"	20	5	5	10	45	60	20
Civil Service "D"	20	5	1	14	27	62	16

Minor Div. Three North	P	W	D	L	F	A	Pts
Old Finchleians "C"	20	16	1	3	73	25	49
East Barnet O.G. "C"	20	15	0	5	74	37	45
Broomfield "B"	20	13	1	6	71	53	40
Old Finchleians "D"	20	13	1	6	51	44	40
Old Parkonians "C"	20	10	0	10	65	66	30
Norsemen "D"	20	9	1	10	61	58	28
Alexandra Park "C"	20	7	3	10	45	40	24
Broomfield "C"	20	7	0	13	42	74	21
O Esthameians "B" (-3)	20	5	4	11	40	52	16
Winchmore Hill "E"	20	4	3	13	43	70	15
Crouch E Vampires "C"	20	2	4	14	36	82	10

Minor Div. Three South	P	W	D	L	F	A	Pts
Old Wilsonians "B"	18	13	2	3	56	25	41
Old Westminster C. "B"	18	12	2	4	54	25	38
Old Wilsonians "C"	18	9	7	2	52	29	34
Carshalton "D"	18	10	2	6	54	29	32
Alleyn Old Boys "B"	18	9	2	7	34	32	29
Alleyn Old Boys "C"	18	7	1	10	33	51	22
Ibis "B"	18	6	3	9	29	37	21
Kew Association "C"	18	5	3	10	33	52	18
Old Westminster C. "C"	18	3	3	12	32	57	12
West Wickham "C"	18	2	3	13	24	64	9

Carshalton "E" - record expunged.

Minor Division Four North	P	W	D	L	F	A	Pts
Old Parkonians "E"	18	13	2	3	54	22	41
Winchmore Hill "F"	18	13	0	5	55	28	39
Southgate Olympic "C"	18	11	2	5	76	44	35
Old Parkonians "D"	18	9	4	5	43	37	31
East Barnet O.G. "D"	18	9	1	8	49	33	28
Norsemen "E"	18	9	1	8	54	59	28
Norsemen "F"	18	5	1	12	41	66	16
Alexandra Park "D"	18	4	3	11	33	57	15
Crouch End Vamps "D"	18	4	2	12	27	52	14
Winchmore Hill "G"	18	4	2	12	24	58	14

Southgate Olympic "D" - record expunged.

OTHER LEAGUES

Minor Division Four South	P	W	D	L	F	A	Pts
Old Actonians A. "E"	20	16	4	0	104	29	52
HSBC "C"	20	14	4	2	54	23	46
Polytechnic "E"	20	11	2	7	60	30	35
South Bank Cuaco "B"	20	10	3	7	54	40	33
HSBC "D"	20	9	2	9	39	44	29
Lloyds TSB Bank "B"	20	9	2	9	36	47	29
Old Actonians A. "F"	20	8	2	10	48	61	26
Old Salesians "B"	20	6	5	9	41	48	23
Merton "B"	20	7	1	12	33	58	22
Kew Association "D"	20	4	4	12	33	65	16
Old Lyonians "B"	20	1	1	18	24	81	4

Minor Division Five North	P	W	D	L	F	A	Pts
Old Finchleians "F"	20	14	3	3	89	48	45
Old Owens "E"	20	13	4	3	100	44	43
Old Finchleians "E"	20	11	5	4	72	34	38
Old Parkonians "G"	20	11	3	6	55	38	36
Old Stationers "C"	20	10	1	9	53	46	31
Old Parkonians "F"	20	9	3	8	61	58	30
Broomfield "D"	20	9	3	8	59	59	30
East Barnet O.G. "E"	20	7	4	9	51	68	25
Alexandra Park "E"	20	7	3	10	46	53	24
East Barnet O.G. "F"	20	2	2	16	30	90	8
Alexandra Park "F"	20	1	1	18	17	95	4

Minor Division Five South	Pld	W	D	L	F	A	Pts
South Bank Cuaco "D"	20	16	4	0	104	21	52
South Bank Cuaco "C"	20	14	3	3	82	34	45
Old Wilsonians "E" (-3)	20	12	2	6	56	32	35
HSBC "E"	20	9	1	10	52	64	28
West Wickham "D"	20	8	4	8	53	66	28
Merton "C"	20	7	3	10	39	61	24
Lloyds TSB Bank "C"	20	6	5	9	50	51	23
Old Wilsonians "D"	20	4	9	7	39	50	21
Old Actonians Ass. "G"	20	4	4	12	41	69	16
Polytechnic "F" (-3)	20	6	1	13	40	73	16
Bank of England "B"	20	3	6	11	36	71	15

Kew Assocation "E" - record expunged.

Minor Division Six South	P	W	D	L	F	A	Pts
Weirside Rangers "C"	18	14	4	0	56	18	46
Old Salesians "C"	18	12	3	3	54	19	39
Old Latymerians "B"	18	12	2	4	77	29	38
BB Eagles "D"	18	10	4	4	55	30	34
Polytechnic "G"	18	9	0	9	47	56	27
Old Westminster C. "D"	18	8	0	10	44	54	24
HSBC "F"	18	6	0	12	29	49	18
Civil Service "E"	18	5	2	11	41	58	17
Lloyds TSB Bank "D"	18	5	1	12	44	70	16
Lloyds TSB Bk "E" (-3)	18	0	2	16	26	90	-1

Kew Association "F" - record expunged.

Minor Div. Seven South	P	W	D	L	F	A	Pts
BB Eagles "E"	18	13	3	2	80	24	42
South Bank Cuaco "E"	18	13	2	3	76	31	41
Alleyn Old Boys "D"	18	13	1	4	66	35	40
Bank of England "C"	18	8	2	8	43	53	26
Civil Service "F"	18	7	3	8	43	41	24
Old Actonians Ass. "H"	18	7	2	9	39	52	23
Merton "D"	18	6	3	9	39	42	21
Old Wilsonians "F"	18	6	2	10	43	59	20
Old Wilsonians "G"	18	4	2	12	41	77	14
Lloyds TSB Bank "F"	18	2	2	14	31	87	8

SOUTHPORT & DISTRICT LEAGUE

	P	W	D	L	F	A	Pts
Formby Athletic	24	18	3	3	93	37	57
Christ the King OB	24	16	5	3	88	52	53
Redgate Rovers Reserves	24	16	2	6	71	37	53
Sandy Lane	24	15	2	7	70	49	47
Pinewoods Reserves	24	14	1	9	65	50	43
Poulton Wanderers	24	11	1	12	53	50	34
St Pauls	24	10	6	8	75	61	33
Trojan Security	24	9	4	11	63	57	31
Devonshire	24	8	4	12	60	63	28
Formby Dons	24	9	1	14	52	75	28
Imperial	24	6	2	16	43	89	20
Banks Saturday	24	5	4	15	43	76	19
Birkdale Crown	24	1	1	22	30	110	4

SPEN VALLEY & DISTRICT LEAGUE

Premier Division	P	W	D	L	F	A	Pts
Oakwell	16	13	2	1	78	25	41
TVR United	16	9	4	3	53	37	31
Wellington	16	9	3	4	62	34	30
Youth 2000	16	8	3	5	56	51	27
Ravensthorpe Rangers	16	6	6	4	53	31	24
Bradford	16	6	4	6	43	39	22
Thornhill United	16	5	1	10	45	52	16
Quarry	16	3	1	12	36	67	10
George Healey	16	1	0	15	24	114	3

Bosnia - record expunged.

Division One	P	W	D	L	F	A	Pts
W Brad. Spartans (-3)	20	18	0	2	77	50	51
Park	20	15	2	3	135	37	47
Fairbank United	20	15	2	3	82	25	47
BD3 United	20	14	2	4	70	30	44
Marsh	20	9	1	10	47	52	28
Inter Batley	20	8	3	9	50	63	27
Oakwell Reserves (-1)	20	8	1	11	63	87	24
Norfolk	20	4	3	13	45	73	15
ALC	20	5	0	15	30	72	15
Howden Cl. "A" (-2)	20	4	1	15	33	90	11
Stithy	20	1	3	16	40	93	6

Park - record expunged.

Ring O'Bells - record expunged.

ST EDMUNDSBURY LEAGUE

Division One	P	W	D	L	F	A	Pts
St Edmunds 1965	20	16	2	2	68	35	50
Priors	20	15	4	1	92	23	49
Bartons	20	16	0	4	88	30	48
Bushel	20	13	2	5	68	32	41
Barrow	20	11	3	6	56	29	36
Ixworth Pykkerell	20	8	1	11	49	48	25
Westbury United	20	8	1	11	47	53	25
Mildenhall United	20	7	1	12	49	67	22
Lawshall Swan	20	4	2	14	43	73	14
RF Saints	20	2	0	18	25	77	6
Elephant & Castle	20	2	0	18	20	138	6

STRATFORD ALLIANCE

Division One	Pld	W	D	L	F	A	Pts
Bidford Boys Club	22	17	4	1	67	27	55
South Redditch Athletic	22	17	2	3	75	24	53
Alcester Town	22	14	4	4	75	31	46
Shipston Excelsior	22	11	2	9	49	41	35
Studley Swan (-3)	22	10	1	11	75	59	28
Stoneleigh	22	8	4	10	54	61	28
Kenilworth Town KH Res.	22	7	5	10	39	61	26
Quinton	22	7	3	12	42	61	24
FISSC (-3)	22	7	5	10	36	51	23
Cubbington Albion (-6)	22	8	3	11	43	45	21
Henley Forest Reserves	22	6	2	14	24	50	20
Stratford Town Reserves	22	2	1	19	25	93	7

Division Two	P	W	D	L	F	A	Pts
Badsey Rangers	26	21	1	4	72	34	64
Moreton Rangers	26	17	4	5	91	34	55
Alcester Town Res.	26	17	2	7	93	46	53
Washford Lions	26	14	4	8	73	46	46
Snitterfield Snipers	26	14	2	10	73	67	44
Coventry Ams Res -3	26	16	3	7	98	60	42
RS Sports	26	13	2	11	63	49	41
Coventry SpiRes.	26	10	7	9	57	49	37
Blockley Sports	26	9	6	11	70	78	33
Ilmington Revolution	26	8	2	16	51	80	26
Shipston Excel. Res.	26	5	9	12	49	69	24
Henley Forest A -3	26	5	3	18	35	101	15
International	26	3	6	17	41	113	15
Claverdon -3	26	2	5	19	33	73	8

Division Three	P	W	D	L	F	A	Pts
The Badgers	26	21	2	3	91	40	65
Tysoe United	26	19	4	3	96	39	61
Quinton Res.	26	15	3	8	69	51	48
Badsey United	26	15	1	10	76	65	46
Inkberrow Res. -3	26	15	3	8	71	39	45
Kenilw□h Town KH A	26	11	8	7	67	67	41
Moreton Rg. Colts -3	26	12	5	9	79	48	38
FISSC Res.	26	11	5	10	61	53	38
Bidford Boys Res.	26	10	4	12	51	64	34
RS Sports Res. -3	26	6	10	10	60	72	25
Littleton Rovers	26	7	2	17	43	71	23
Red Alert -3	26	6	5	15	51	65	20
Shipston Excel. Colts	26	3	5	18	30	81	14
Wickham Warriors -3	26	2	1	23	38	128	4

STROUD & DISTRICT LEAGUE

Division Two	P	W	D	L	F	A	Pts
Gloucester Civil Serv.	24	19	2	3	67	21	59
Slimbridge Res.	24	19	1	4	87	25	58
Quedgeley Wdrs	24	15	4	5	68	24	49
Dursley Town Res.	24	13	3	8	55	33	42
Tibberton United	24	10	3	11	43	46	33
Kingswood Res.	24	10	3	11	33	44	33
Cashes Green	24	9	4	11	41	55	31
AC Royals	24	10	0	14	58	68	30
Ramblers Res.	24	9	3	12	34	44	30
Thornbury Town Res.	24	7	7	10	31	49	28
Uley	24	7	5	12	35	53	26
Shurdington Rovers	24	7	3	14	50	65	24
Ebley -3	24	0	4	20	35	110	1

Division Three	P	W	D	L	F	A	Pts
Upton St Leonards	24	19	3	2	74	19	60
Taverners Res.	24	17	5	2	62	31	56
Eastcombe	24	11	7	6	44	41	40
Frampton United Res.	24	11	5	8	42	38	38
Abbeymead Rov. Res.	24	11	4	9	56	48	37
Cam Bulldogs Res.	24	11	2	11	47	48	35
Wotton Rovers Res.	24	9	5	10	55	50	32
Berkeley Town Res.	24	9	5	10	45	48	32
Sharpness Res.	24	9	4	11	57	46	31
Matchplay -3	24	8	8	8	47	50	29
Barnwood U. Res -3	24	5	4	15	50	69	16
Coaley Rovers	24	2	6	16	22	70	12
Minch'n/RDS Res -3	24	4	2	18	34	77	11

Division Four	P	W	D	L	F	A	Pts
Didmarton	24	18	5	1	62	26	59
AFC Pheonix	24	18	3	3	43	20	57
Brimscombe/T. Res.	24	14	7	3	58	27	49
Chalford Res.	24	15	3	6	66	28	48
Quedgeley W. Res.	24	12	6	6	58	32	42
Wickwar Wanderers	24	11	3	10	61	37	36
Arlingham	24	9	2	13	55	69	29
Longlevens A	24	7	6	11	53	47	27
Whitminster Res.	24	6	5	13	43	58	23
Stonehouse Town A	24	5	5	14	40	67	20
Ramblers A -3	24	7	2	15	34	72	20
Gloucester CS Res.	24	3	4	17	24	71	13
Longford Res -6	24	4	3	17	33	76	9

Division Five	P	W	D	L	F	A	Pts
Stroud Imperial	22	16	4	2	90	35	52
Leonard Stanley Res.	22	16	2	4	89	38	50
Tredworth Tigers -6	22	17	0	5	81	36	45
Whitminster A	22	13	2	7	55	57	41
Nympsfield	22	9	3	10	61	45	30
Randwick Res.	22	8	5	9	45	43	29
Glevum United	22	8	5	9	60	79	29
Alkerton Rangers	22	8	4	10	61	91	28
Dursley Town A	22	8	3	11	54	51	27
Charfield Res.	22	4	4	14	26	81	16
Chipping Sodbury B	22	3	4	15	31	69	13
Uley Res.	22	4	0	18	45	73	12

Ebley Res. - record expunged.

Division Six	P	W	D	L	F	A	Pts
Bush	20	16	2	2	89	22	50
Hardwicke Res.	20	16	0	4	90	31	48
Sherston	20	13	2	5	69	53	41
Stroud Harriers	20	11	4	5	77	45	37
Brockworth Alb. A	20	10	1	9	30	38	31
Upton St Leon. Res.	20	9	3	8	58	46	30
Eastcombe Res.	20	7	0	13	40	68	21
Wotton Rovers A	20	6	1	13	40	82	19
Cashes Green Res.	20	6	0	14	42	71	18
Horsley Utd Res -6	20	5	1	14	46	85	10
North Nibley -3	20	3	2	15	31	71	8

Division Seven	P	W	D	L	F	A	Pts
McCadam	22	17	3	2	75	20	54
Quedgeley Wdrs A	22	13	8	1	61	27	47
Berkeley Town A	22	11	6	5	51	30	39
Coaley Rovers Res.	22	10	7	5	48	47	37
Sharpness A -3	22	9	5	8	45	46	29
Woodchester	22	7	4	11	56	64	25
Avonvale United A	22	7	4	11	41	49	25
Longlevens B	22	7	3	12	36	57	24
Uley A -3	22	7	4	11	51	66	22
Cam Bulldogs A -3	22	7	4	11	47	63	22
Matchplay Res.	22	5	6	11	46	58	21
Randwick A	22	1	8	13	26	56	11

OTHER LEAGUES

Division Eight	P	W	D	L	F	A	Pts
Kingsholm	26	20	3	3	125	42	63
Golden Heart	26	20	1	5	144	45	61
St Nicholas Old Boys	26	19	1	6	119	55	58
Cotswold Rangers	26	19	1	6	94	46	58
Wickwar Wdrs Res.	26	17	1	8	98	64	52
Linden Snakes	26	10	2	14	69	89	32
Stroud Imperial Res.	26	8	7	11	77	83	31
Stonehouse Town B	26	9	4	13	64	81	31
Gloucester CS A	26	8	5	13	39	46	29
Hawkesbury Stallions -3	26	10	2	14	55	81	29
Stratford Wanderers	26	8	0	18	61	103	24
GL United -9	26	9	4	13	69	99	22
Shurdington Res.	26	4	4	18	47	95	16
Alkerton Rgrs Res. -3	26	3	1	22	52	185	7

SUBURBAN LEAGUE

Premier Division	P	W	D	L	F	A	Pts
AFC Wimbledon Res.	30	21	7	2	80	31	70
Met Police Res.	30	18	4	8	72	51	58
Hampton & RB Res.	30	15	9	6	67	39	54
Tonbridge Ang. Res.	30	14	8	8	54	46	50
Eastbourne B. Res.	30	14	6	10	73	51	48
Uxbridge Res.	30	12	5	13	53	58	41
Carshalton Ath. Res.	30	12	5	13	58	64	41
Woking Res.	30	11	7	12	58	61	40
Leatherhead Res.	30	10	9	11	60	57	39
Tooting & MU Res.	30	12	3	15	54	66	39
Hemel Hempstead Res.	30	11	4	15	55	68	37
Sutton United Res.	30	9	9	12	48	43	36
Three Bridges Res.	30	9	8	13	44	71	35
Eastleigh Res.	30	8	8	14	46	55	32
Beaconsfield Res.	30	8	5	17	45	62	29
Northwood Res.	30	4	7	19	35	79	19

South	P	W	D	L	F	A	Pts
Banstead Ath. Res.	34	26	2	6	105	41	80
Corinthian-Cas. Res.	34	24	4	6	97	41	76
Chipstead Res.	34	21	7	6	107	48	70
East Grinstead T. Res.	34	21	4	9	91	35	67
Merstham Res.	34	19	7	8	97	50	64
Crawley Down Res.	34	16	11	7	75	45	59
Corinthan Res.	34	18	5	11	75	55	59
Colliers Wood Res.	34	17	6	11	71	56	57
Crowborough A. Res.	34	15	4	15	77	83	49
South Park Res.	34	12	7	15	68	71	43
Cobham Res.	34	12	4	18	53	76	40
Epsom & Ewell Res.	34	12	3	19	55	77	39
Redhill Res.	34	11	5	18	55	77	38
Lingfield Res.	34	11	3	20	75	92	36
Molesey Res.	34	9	4	21	52	78	31
Chessington/H. Res.	34	9	4	21	48	107	31
Horley Town Res.	34	4	6	24	34	119	18
Oakwood Res.	34	3	6	25	44	128	15

Whitehawk Res. - record expunged.

SURREY SOUTH EASTERN COMB.

Intermediate Division One	P	W	D	L	F	A	Pts
AFC Cubo	26	20	5	1	75	19	65
Weston Green Sports	26	19	4	3	86	30	61
Westminster Casuals	26	14	7	5	49	34	49
Puretown	26	14	6	6	59	38	48
Battersea	26	12	7	7	48	36	43
Old Rutlishians	26	11	5	10	52	44	38
Old Plymouthians	26	11	2	13	52	58	35
St Andrews -3	26	11	3	12	49	66	33
Sporting Kitz	26	9	5	12	28	25	32
N P L	26	9	5	12	62	70	32
RH123 Athletic	26	10	1	15	31	55	31
Sutton High	26	6	4	16	21	44	22
Thornton Hth R. +3	26	3	3	20	26	76	15
South Godstone	26	3	3	20	24	67	12

Intermediate Division One	P	W	D	L	F	A	Pts
Real Holmesdale	22	16	2	4	64	29	50
Claygate & Ditton	22	15	5	2	53	20	50
Cheam Village W. +3	22	14	2	6	42	34	47
Fulham Deaf	22	13	6	3	81	44	45
Merton Abbey -3	22	12	5	5	53	38	38
Brockham	22	9	4	9	47	41	31
Tolworth Athletic	22	9	3	10	47	47	30
Merstham Newton	22	7	5	10	41	49	26
Croygas Phoenix	22	7	4	11	45	65	25
Westside	22	4	4	14	30	50	16
Ashtead	22	3	2	17	37	97	11
Sporting Bahia -3	22	2	0	20	19	45	3

Junior Division One	P	W	D	L	F	A	Pts
Project Clapham	18	15	1	2	64	19	46
Trinity	18	13	2	3	69	28	41
Kerria Knights	18	9	2	7	45	34	29
Norton	18	9	1	8	50	35	28
Wilf Kroucher +3	18	6	3	9	50	56	24
Shaftesbury Town	18	6	3	9	28	40	21
Epsom Eagles	18	5	5	8	26	36	20
Worcester Park A	18	5	2	11	33	57	17
Supercala	18	5	2	11	37	63	17
St Andrews Res. -3	18	5	3	10	35	69	15

Junior Division Two	P	W	D	L	F	A	Pts
Old Boys Clapham	20	13	2	5	72	37	41
Pilgrims Well -3	20	13	3	4	47	31	39
Park Boys	20	11	5	4	57	41	38
N P L Res. -3	20	11	3	6	48	29	33
Westside Res.	20	10	3	7	48	48	33
Battersea Res.	20	7	6	7	46	40	27
Battersea Ironsides A	20	7	2	11	24	45	23
Crescent Rov. A +3	20	5	2	13	35	62	20
Croydon Greenside u-23	20	5	4	11	28	22	19
O. Plymouthians Res.	20	5	4	11	31	43	19
Ashtead Res.	20	5	2	13	26	64	17

Junior Division Three	P	W	D	L	F	A	Pts
Shirley Town -3	20	15	3	2	59	25	45
Tooting Bec Res.	20	12	4	4	48	36	40
Epsom Athletic A -3	20	12	2	6	58	45	35
Surbiton Town +2	20	10	2	8	57	46	34
Oakhill Pugbats	20	10	4	6	55	48	34
Trinity Res. +2	20	9	3	8	52	42	32
Epsom Eag. Res. +6	20	5	6	9	39	48	27
Destiny Academy -4	20	8	6	6	51	46	26
Weston G. S. Res. +2	20	4	4	12	35	59	18
Cheam Village W. Res.	20	5	2	13	45	62	17
Sutton High Res.	20	1	2	17	30	72	5

Junior Division Four	P	W	D	L	F	A	Pts
Thornton Hth Res. -3	20	14	3	3	59	22	42
Shirley Town Res.	20	13	2	5	55	34	41
Old Plymouthians A	20	12	1	7	42	32	37
Croydon Greenside B -3	20	12	1	7	50	25	34
Old Town -3	20	10	4	6	61	31	31
Addington Athletic	20	9	4	7	42	35	31
Rollers Athletic +3	20	6	2	12	39	57	26
Crescent Rovers B	20	7	4	9	51	37	25
Epsom Athletic B +3	20	8	1	11	40	52	25
Cheam Vill. W. A +2	20	3	5	12	24	67	16
Fulham Deaf Res. +2	20	2	1	17	20	91	9

SUSSEX LEAGUE

Prem	P	W	D	L	F	A	Pts
St Leonards Soc. -3	20	16	1	3	60	28	46
Hollington United	20	12	4	4	60	38	40
Rock-a-Nore	20	12	3	5	53	27	39
Peche Hill Select	20	11	2	7	54	44	35
Polegate Town	20	10	4	6	49	34	34
Wadhurst United	20	9	5	6	43	28	32
Sedlescombe R. +3	20	7	2	11	47	66	26
Robertsbridge Utd	20	5	6	9	46	52	21
Peasmarsh & Iden	20	5	3	12	45	70	18
Punnetts Town	20	4	4	12	35	58	16
Hooe Sports	20	1	2	17	24	71	5

Hospital Social, Junior Club Tackleway - records expunged.

Division One	P	W	D	L	F	A	Pts
White Knight	16	10	3	3	33	22	33
Old Town Athletic	16	8	5	3	45	25	29
Ninfield United	16	8	4	4	29	21	28
Bexhill A.A.C.	16	8	3	5	30	25	27
Hollington Utd Res.	16	8	3	5	34	30	27
Eastbourne Town A	16	7	2	7	27	30	23
Catsfield	16	5	2	9	32	37	17
Mountfield United	16	4	1	11	18	32	13
Wheatsheaf Willingdon	16	2	1	13	16	42	7

Division Two	P	W	D	L	F	A	Pts
Eastbourne Galaxy	18	13	3	2	52	16	42
Ticehurst	18	12	2	4	54	26	38
Sandhurst	18	10	3	5	52	32	33
Crowhurst	18	8	2	8	47	48	26
Eastbourne Dynamos	18	7	3	8	40	36	24
Hastings Rangers	18	7	0	11	44	53	21
Cinque Ports	18	6	3	9	33	52	21
Icklesham Casuals	18	6	2	10	35	48	20
Northiam 75	18	6	1	11	35	58	19
Hurst	18	4	3	11	37	60	15

Division Three	P	W	D	L	F	A	Pts
St Helens	18	13	1	4	46	27	40
Eastbourne Fishermen -1	18	13	1	4	61	29	39
Battle Baptists	18	12	2	4	58	26	38
Magham Down	18	12	0	6	47	34	36
Battle Rangers	18	10	0	8	58	51	30
Hawkhurst United	18	8	0	10	45	41	24
Cranbrook Town +2	18	6	2	10	33	29	22
Herstmonceux	18	6	4	8	39	49	22
Hollington United A	18	3	2	13	15	52	11
Beulah Baptists	18	1	0	17	20	84	3

Division Four	P	W	D	L	F	A	Pts
Orington	18	15	1	2	103	27	46
Peche Hill Select Res.	18	14	2	2	56	19	44
Pebsham Sibex	18	13	1	4	37	26	40
JC Tackleway Res.	18	11	1	6	47	32	34
Peasmarsh & Iden A	18	7	1	10	49	47	22
Travaux	18	6	4	8	37	67	22
Mayfield	18	6	1	11	34	44	19
Punnetts Town Res.	18	5	2	11	34	52	17
Victoria Baptists	18	3	2	13	34	67	11
Icklesham Cas. Res.	18	2	1	15	23	73	7

Division Five	P	W	D	L	F	A	Pts
Burwash	18	12	4	2	43	34	40
Sedlescombe Res.	18	11	3	4	41	27	36
Ninfield United Res.	18	10	3	5	38	30	33
Hastings Elite	18	10	2	6	53	34	32
Eastbourne Athletic	18	8	4	6	39	34	28
Guestling	18	8	1	9	35	36	25
Kurdistan United	18	6	3	9	34	39	21
Wadhurst United Res.	18	6	3	9	19	34	21
Bexhill AAC Res.	18	5	2	11	26	40	17
HG Aerospace	18	1	1	16	22	42	4

Division Six	P	W	D	L	F	A	Pts
Sidley +3	20	17	0	3	75	20	54
Catsfield Res. +2	20	15	2	3	65	39	49
Eastbourne Fishermen Res.	20	15	1	4	71	33	46
Polegate T. Res. -3	20	14	3	3	72	31	42
Eastbourne Royals	20	9	1	10	61	52	28
West Hill United	20	8	2	10	42	57	26
Westfield A	20	7	2	11	50	56	23
The JC Tackleway A	20	5	1	14	33	59	16
Parkfield	20	5	1	14	39	73	16
Northiam 75 Res.	20	4	3	13	45	72	15
Magham D. Res. -1	20	1	4	15	33	94	6

Division Sevon	P	W	D	L	F	A	Pts
Eastbourne Rangers	18	12	3	3	52	15	39
Herstmonceux Res.	18	10	4	4	48	28	34
Guestling Res.	18	9	4	5	38	25	31
Robertsbridge Res.	18	9	4	5	26	24	31
Winkney Seniors	18	8	4	6	39	27	28
Hampden Park Utd	18	8	1	9	30	35	25
Battle Baptists Res.	18	5	5	8	22	29	20
Sandhurst Res.	18	6	2	10	30	38	20
Orington Res.	18	5	4	9	31	32	19
Hawkhurst Utd Res.	18	0	5	13	12	75	5

SWINDON & DISTRICT LEAGUE

	P	W	D	L	F	A	Pts
Queensfield United	24	21	2	1	145	23	65
DJC Marlborough	24	18	5	1	62	21	59
Fratellos	24	17	2	5	90	29	53
VBA Rangers	24	15	1	8	95	50	46
Queenstown	24	15	1	8	82	40	46
Swindon Auto Engine Tune	24	14	2	8	75	41	44
Citifaith	24	10	4	10	69	64	34
Ramsbury	24	9	1	14	47	52	28
Pembroke Reserves	24	8	2	14	37	75	26
Lower Stratton Reserves	24	6	4	14	46	68	22
Spectrum	24	5	5	14	38	95	20
Chiseldon Reserves	24	2	1	21	37	139	7
Citifaith Ajax	24	0	2	22	22	148	2

The Globe - record expunged.

TAUNTON & DISTRICT LEAGUE

Division One	Pld	W	D	L	F	A	Pts
Porlock	20	14	2	4	55	30	44
Locomotives	20	11	5	4	46	22	38
Middlezoy Rovers	20	9	6	5	47	38	33
Predators	20	8	7	5	52	45	31
Bridgwater Sports	20	8	4	8	41	43	28
Staplegrove	20	7	5	8	37	47	26
Bishops Lydeard Res.	20	5	7	8	40	44	22
Alcombe Rovers	20	6	4	10	40	47	22
Highbridge Town	20	5	6	9	39	47	21
Cannington Colts (-3)	20	5	5	10	43	54	17
Dulverton Town	20	3	7	10	25	48	16

Division Two	P	W	D	L	F	A	Pts
Civil Service	20	14	4	2	39	21	46
North Petherton	20	12	2	6	76	45	38
Sampford Blues	20	11	5	4	56	34	38
Nether Stowey	20	10	4	6	63	40	34
Wyvern Rangers	20	8	4	8	49	44	28
Staplegrove Res.	20	8	4	8	46	56	28
Westonzoyland	20	6	5	9	35	46	23
Watchet Town Res.	20	4	8	7	30	36	20
Bridgwater Spts Res.	20	4	6	10	31	47	18
Minehead Town Res.	20	4	5	11	38	55	17
Appletree	20	4	3	13	31	70	15

Division Three	P	W	D	L	F	A	Pts
Wembdon Saints	22	21	1	0	79	16	64
Middlezoy Rov. Res.	22	16	0	6	71	33	48
Stogursey Greyh ds	22	11	4	7	54	39	37
Wembdon -3	22	11	4	7	46	42	34
Williton	22	10	3	9	29	44	33
Redgate	22	9	4	9	43	50	31
Highbridge T. Res.	22	9	2	11	51	51	29
Sydenham Rangers	22	8	2	12	46	50	26
Norton Fitzwarren	22	8	0	14	40	63	24
Old Inn All Stars	22	7	0	15	57	81	21
Porlock Res. -3	22	6	2	14	45	66	17
B'water Sports Colts	22	2	6	14	37	63	12

Division Four	P	W	D	L	F	A	Pts
Hamilton Hawks	20	19	1	0	100	21	58
Bish. Lydeard Colts	20	14	3	3	87	29	45
Alcombe Rovers Res.	20	12	5	3	54	33	41
Rhode Lane Wdrs	20	8	5	7	48	43	29
Milverton Rgrs -3	20	9	3	8	43	52	27
Staplegrove Colts	20	7	2	11	53	67	23
Dulverton Town Res.	20	6	5	9	39	58	23
Norton Fitzwarren Res.	20	6	3	11	46	68	21
Westonzoyland Res.	20	5	5	10	37	66	20
Exmoor Rangers	20	3	3	14	35	50	12
Nether Stowey Res.	20	2	3	15	40	95	9

Division Five	P	W	D	L	F	A	Pts
Blagdon Hill	18	16	1	1	127	27	49
Merry Monk	18	16	0	2	111	17	48
Gallery	18	12	1	5	64	35	37
North Petherton Reserves	18	8	3	7	47	53	27
Sampford Blues Reserves	18	6	6	6	55	56	24
Tone Youth	18	6	4	8	47	58	22
Halcon	18	5	3	10	38	84	18
Galmington Dragons	18	3	3	12	32	74	12
Wembdon Saints Res.	18	3	3	12	35	84	12
Bridgwater Grasshoppers	18	2	2	14	21	89	8

THANET & DISTRICT LEAGUE

	P	W	D	L	F	A	Pts
Brenlam Flooring	22	16	2	4	128	46	50
AFC Margate	22	16	2	4	100	27	50
Racing Greyhound	22	16	1	5	115	35	49
Barnaby Rudge	22	16	1	5	88	46	49
Westcliff United	22	13	2	7	75	48	41
Orb City	22	10	5	7	73	50	35
SLT United	22	11	1	10	76	76	34
Pfizer	22	8	3	11	91	65	27
Minster	22	7	1	14	50	62	22
Sportsman Inn	22	6	4	12	72	98	22
Hugin Viking United	22	2	0	20	47	176	6
Weston Athletic	22	0	0	22	15	201	0

Oddfellows - record expunged.

TONBRIDGE & DISTRICT LEAGUE

Premier Division	P	W	D	L	F	A	Pts
Southborough	20	19	1	0	96	17	58
Hadlow Evolution	20	15	2	3	58	16	47
East Peckham Juniors	20	12	4	4	46	28	40
High Brooms Cas. (-3)	20	12	0	8	57	44	33
Blackham & Ashurst	20	10	0	10	54	39	30
Tonbridge Invicta Res.	20	7	3	10	39	50	24
Pembury (+3)	20	6	2	12	31	40	23
Woodlands	20	6	2	12	55	82	20
AFC Valour	20	5	4	11	39	50	19
Hadlow Harrow	20	4	3	13	31	55	15
Hawkenbury Reserves	20	2	3	15	27	112	9

Division One	P	W	D	L	F	A	Pts
Penshurst Park	20	15	1	4	64	28	46
Southborough Reserves	20	14	4	2	59	25	46
Swan (Edenbridge)	20	14	2	4	79	30	44
High Brooms Casuals Res.	20	13	4	3	98	35	43
Paddock Wood	20	10	1	9	50	54	31
Capel Sports and Social	20	8	4	8	46	49	28
Roselands	20	8	2	10	63	55	26
Dowgate	20	5	5	10	26	37	20
Pembury Reserves (-1)	20	4	4	12	31	63	15
Rusthall "A"	20	4	2	14	58	82	14
Leigh (+2)	20	0	1	19	19	135	3

Division Two	Pld	W	D	L	F	A	Pts
Tonbridge I "A" (+4)	24	15	6	3	73	41	55
Hawkenbury "A" (-2)	24	15	3	6	93	43	46
AFC Valour Reserves	24	14	4	6	61	39	46
Ashton Prime	24	13	3	8	64	44	42
Rusthall "B"	24	11	6	7	97	59	39
Staplehurst&MU "A"	24	11	4	9	64	43	37
Brenchley Wanderers	24	12	1	11	59	61	37
East Peckham Jun Res.	24	12	1	11	41	52	37
Woodlands res (-1)	23	9	5	9	58	43	31
FC Revolution	24	9	1	14	62	79	28
Frant	23	8	2	13	50	60	26
Roselands Reserves	24	3	2	19	45	111	11
Paddock Wood Res.	24	3	2	19	33	125	11

TROWBRIDGE & DISTRICT LEAGUE

Division One	P	W	D	L	F	A	Pts
Foresters	22	14	2	6	74	41	44
Freshford United	22	13	4	5	46	26	43
Seend United	22	12	5	5	41	34	41
Westbury United Res.	22	12	4	6	60	35	40
Broughton Gifford	22	11	7	4	53	33	40
The Deverills	22	10	6	6	49	43	36
Trowbridge Wanderers	22	8	5	9	51	46	29
Blue Circle	22	8	2	12	50	64	26
Semington Magpies (-4)	22	7	5	10	48	56	22
Steeple Ashton	22	5	5	12	53	70	20
Frome Town Sports	22	5	1	16	44	74	16
Bradford United	22	2	4	16	35	82	10

Division Two	Pld	W	D	L	F	A	Pts
Melksham Town Res.	20	18	0	2	98	16	54
Castle Combe	20	11	7	2	58	21	40
Bratton (-2)	20	12	2	6	45	42	36
T'bridge Wands Res.	20	10	3	7	71	60	33
Worton & Cheverell	20	10	3	7	56	46	33
North Bradley (-3)	20	9	1	10	57	69	25
Calne Eagles	20	8	1	11	39	55	25
FC Northbridge (-2)	20	8	1	11	44	52	23
Warminster T res (-3)	20	7	4	9	34	48	22
Heytesbury (-1)	20	3	2	15	27	57	10
Westwood S Cl (-2)	20	2	0	18	36	99	4

Bromham - record expunged.

Chippenham Old Boys - record expunged.

Division Three	P	W	D	L	F	A	Pts
Boomsbury	18	18	0	0	127	10	54
Holt	18	11	3	4	59	30	36
Trowbridge Tn res (-3)	18	11	2	5	67	31	32
United	18	9	3	6	55	43	30
Westbury Town (-3)	18	8	3	7	44	48	24
Bratton Reserves (-1)	18	6	4	8	42	61	21
Bradford United Reserves	18	6	1	11	38	59	19
FC Calne (-4)	18	6	2	10	30	74	16
The Lamb	18	3	1	14	21	72	10
The Stiffs	18	2	1	15	29	84	7

Taylor Davis - record expunged.

TYNESIDE AMATEUR LEAGUE

Division One	P	W	D	L	F	A	Pts
Whickham Lang Jacks	24	18	3	3	86	43	57
Red Star Benwell	24	15	5	4	71	29	50
Rutherford (Gateshead) Res.	24	15	5	4	66	31	50
New York	24	13	1	10	64	57	40
Walker Central Reserves	24	11	4	9	68	51	37
Grainger Park Boys Club	24	11	3	10	73	57	36
West Jesmond	24	12	0	12	48	52	36
Blyth Spartans "A" (-3)	24	10	5	9	48	48	35
Bellingham (-3)	24	8	4	12	37	55	25
High Howdon Social Club	24	7	1	16	57	81	22
Blyth Town Reserves	24	8	1	15	35	64	22
Gosforth Bohemians res.	24	7	0	17	44	79	21
Lindisfarne Athletic	24	4	2	18	55	105	14

Division Two	P	W	D	L	F	A	Pts
Blyth Isabella	26	21	2	3	112	24	65
Cullercoats Reserves	26	17	4	5	85	47	55
Newcastle Diggers United	26	16	5	5	83	41	53
Newcastle Medicals	26	13	4	9	67	66	43
Blaydon Huntsman	26	11	6	9	75	64	39
Cramlington Town "A"	26	11	6	9	59	62	39
Swalwell Amateur	26	10	8	8	45	41	38
Heaton Rifles	26	12	2	12	73	77	38
Killingworth Plough (-3)	26	10	2	14	68	83	29
Newcastle RVI Lochside	26	9	2	15	55	70	29
Longbenton	26	7	4	15	50	78	25
Newcastle Chemfica Ind "A"	26	7	3	16	48	71	24
Gosforth Bohemians "A"	26	6	5	15	40	78	23
Wardley	26	3	5	18	37	95	14

WAKEFIELD & DISTRICT LEAGUE

Premier Division	P	W	D	L	F	A	Pts
Dodworth Miners Welf	20	15	3	2	75	28	48
Thornhill	20	16	0	4	83	53	48
Rose & Crown (Darton)	20	14	1	5	71	53	43
Gate	20	10	2	8	62	48	32
Woodman	20	10	2	8	58	61	32
Kingstone United WMC	20	7	3	10	45	58	24
Wilton	20	6	2	12	53	64	20
Dewsbury Rangers OB	20	5	4	11	51	64	19
Battyeford FC Wasps	20	5	4	11	31	57	19
Crofton Sports	20	5	2	13	44	69	17
AFC Shepherds Arms	20	3	5	12	30	48	14

Outwood Victoria - record expunged.

Division One	P	W	D	L	F	A	Pts
Garforth WMC	22	19	2	1	76	22	59
AFC Grimethorpe	22	12	3	7	66	37	39
Walton	22	12	3	7	53	46	39
Pontefract	22	10	5	7	66	44	35
Morley C & SC	22	9	5	8	62	38	32
Wortley	22	9	4	9	36	46	31
Prince of Wales	22	7	5	10	58	64	26
Ossett Two Brewers	22	7	3	12	46	68	24
AFC Two Brewers	22	8	0	14	45	70	24
Snydale Athletic	22	6	5	11	28	43	23
Eastmoor	22	6	4	12	49	78	22
Woodhse Hill WMC Res.	22	6	3	13	42	71	21

Division Two	P	W	D	L	F	A	Pts
Fieldhead Hospital	22	17	2	3	80	25	53
Hopetown	22	16	3	3	84	39	51
Thornes	22	15	4	3	57	25	49
Inns of Court	22	14	3	5	48	26	45
Old Bank WMC	22	10	3	9	52	51	33
Nostell Miners Welf "A"	22	7	7	8	43	47	28
Garforth Rangers Res.	22	8	4	10	40	45	28
Scissett Reserves	22	7	2	13	48	70	23
Horbury Town "A"	22	6	2	14	49	73	20
Wrenthorpe	22	5	3	14	41	80	18
Prostar	22	5	1	16	46	75	16
Featherstone Col. res (-1)	22	3	4	15	34	66	12

Division Three	P	W	D	L	F	A	Pts
White Hart	22	16	4	2	84	26	52
Plough	22	14	4	4	94	47	46
College	22	13	3	6	61	49	42
Wagon (-1)	22	11	7	4	59	25	39
Garforth WMC Reserves	22	11	5	6	64	48	38
Waterloo	22	10	2	10	68	44	32
AFC Foresters	22	9	3	10	49	51	30
Horbury Athletic (-3)	22	10	1	11	50	70	28
Crofton Sports Reserves	22	7	5	10	37	58	26
Blue Light S&S (Sat)	22	6	6	10	49	58	24
Snydale Athletic Reserves	22	2	3	17	22	78	9
Dewsbury R OB res (-1)	22	1	1	20	27	110	3

WEARSIDE COMBINATION

Premier Division	P	W	D	L	F	A	Pts
Sunderland Hendon	24	19	3	2	110	35	60
Sunderland West End	24	19	3	2	98	25	60
Sunderland Redhouse	24	17	2	5	97	41	53
S'land Hall Farm Blakeneys	24	13	3	8	66	50	42
Sun'land The Colliery Tavern	24	12	2	10	88	67	38
Sunderland Chesters Ath.	24	11	3	10	66	53	36
Sunderland Hendon Grange	24	11	3	10	60	67	36
Sunderland Aquatic Sports	24	12	0	12	71	79	36
S'land Hylton Coll Juns (-3)	24	12	1	11	84	56	34
Sunderland Hylton Coll Welf	24	6	2	16	47	71	20
Shiney Row Trav. Rest (-6)	24	6	4	14	58	92	16
Sunderland The Cambridge	24	3	1	20	36	105	10
Sunderland Usworth (-3)	24	1	1	22	23	163	1

Sunderland Sassco.co.uk - record expunged.

Division One	P	W	D	L	F	A	Pts
Sund'land Thorney Close Inn	26	23	3	0	159	32	72
Sunderland Oddfellows	26	17	4	5	104	46	55
Silksworth Golden Fleece	26	15	1	10	95	71	46
East Durham Spartans	26	14	3	9	98	80	45
Seaham Harkers Bar	26	11	5	10	74	64	38
Shiney Row Country Pk Inn	26	10	6	10	74	61	36
Sunderland FC Chesters	26	10	6	10	71	70	36
Sunderland Dray and Horses	26	10	6	10	59	66	36
Sunderland The Times Inn	26	10	5	11	56	81	35
Sunderland Victoria Gardens	26	8	4	14	70	91	28
Sunderland Park View	26	8	1	17	53	91	25
Sunderland Hollycarrside	26	7	4	15	54	108	25
FC Whitburn	26	7	3	16	62	117	24
Sunderland The Saltgrass	26	6	1	19	58	109	19

WENSLEYDALE LEAGUE

	P	W	D	L	F	A	Pts
Colburn Town	24	22	0	2	114	16	66
Richmond Academy	24	20	2	2	127	25	62
Leyburn United	24	15	3	6	95	39	48
Buck Inn Old Boys (-3)	24	14	1	9	95	55	40
Richmond Mavericks res.	24	12	3	9	76	57	39
Unicorn	24	11	2	11	71	74	35
Buck Inn Broncos	24	11	1	12	89	65	34
Spennithorne & Harmby	24	10	2	12	70	69	32
Hawes United	24	10	1	13	73	64	31
Carperby Rovers	24	10	0	14	57	75	30
Reeth & District Ath. Club	24	6	3	15	57	73	21
Askrigg United	24	5	2	17	43	97	17
Hawes "B"	24	0	0	24	6	264	0

WEST END LEAGUE

Premier Division	P	W	D	L	F	A	Pts
Arian	16	11	0	5	40	25	33
Primrose Hill	16	9	3	4	43	35	30
Earlsberg Eagles	16	7	5	4	33	21	26
Racing Chiswick	16	7	3	6	29	25	24
Clissold Park Rangers	16	6	6	4	26	31	24
Bishops Park	16	6	4	6	26	25	22
Mavericks	16	5	5	6	38	37	20
Inter Markfield	16	3	3	10	32	52	12
Sevenths	16	3	1	12	23	39	10

Division One	P	W	D	L	F	A	Pts
North Acton	14	10	2	2	35	19	32
Hub Athletic	14	9	2	3	44	26	29
Northern Town	13	8	4	1	33	19	28
Atholl 1965	14	7	1	6	28	27	22
West End	13	5	2	6	24	32	17
Olympic Waterloo	14	4	3	7	22	19	15
Iranian Association	14	2	1	11	25	51	7
Milton Rovers	14	1	3	10	23	41	6

Division Two	P	W	D	L	F	A	Pts
Cambridge Heath	18	15	1	2	48	22	46
BUOB	18	14	2	2	74	33	44
Primrose Hill "A"	18	9	2	7	44	40	29
Viva Capri	18	9	2	7	39	37	29
Rac.Chiswick Legends	18	4	3	11	39	41	15
Clissold Park Rang "A"	18	2	4	12	20	44	10
Hub Athletic "A"	18	3	0	15	29	76	9

WEST SUSSEX LEAGUE

Premier Division	P	W	D	L	F	A	Pts
Angmering	20	15	3	2	60	19	48
Newtown Villa	20	13	4	3	50	22	43
Cowfold	20	11	6	3	49	16	39
University of Chichester	20	10	4	6	47	42	34
Upper Beeding	20	9	4	7	37	33	31
Billingshurst	20	9	3	8	55	39	30
West Chiltington	20	7	4	9	40	37	25
Clymping Reserves	20	7	1	12	31	50	22
Lancing United	20	6	2	12	30	60	20
East Dean	20	4	1	15	26	63	13
Southwater	20	3	0	17	22	66	9

Division One	P	W	D	L	F	A	Pts
Hunston CC	20	17	2	1	83	23	53
Watersfield	20	13	3	4	49	18	42
Holbrook	20	13	2	5	49	20	41
Barnham Reserves	20	11	4	5	47	34	37
Lavant	20	10	3	7	54	47	33
Faygate United	20	7	6	7	39	36	27
Newtown Villa Reserves	20	6	7	7	44	28	24
Petworth	20	6	4	10	35	46	22
Stedham United	20	5	1	14	35	80	16
Capel	20	3	3	14	21	67	12
Ashington Rovers	20	0	3	17	13	70	3

Division Two North	P	W	D	L	F	A	Pts
Cowfold Reserves	22	13	7	2	58	31	46
Barns Green	22	13	5	4	47	23	44
Henfield	22	13	4	5	57	34	43
Alfold	22	11	5	6	42	33	38
Billingshurst Reserves	22	10	6	6	52	30	36
AFC Roffey	22	9	3	10	51	57	30
Pulborough	22	8	4	10	50	45	28
Wisborough Green	22	5	7	10	36	42	22
Newdigate	22	6	4	12	32	54	22
Rudgwick	22	6	3	13	36	50	21
Partridge Green	22	6	3	13	30	67	21
Horsham Trinity	22	5	3	14	39	64	18

Division Two South	P	W	D	L	F	A	Pts
Yapton	20	16	2	2	73	27	50
Hunston CC Reserves	20	13	2	5	48	36	41
Wittering United	20	11	3	6	62	41	36
Newtown Villa "A"	20	10	2	8	68	35	32
Worthing BCOB	20	9	3	8	46	57	30
Lodsworth	20	8	5	7	45	38	29
Boxgrove	20	9	2	9	50	51	29
Barnham "A"	20	6	5	9	43	46	23
Fernhurst	20	5	5	10	41	55	20
The Vardar VIP	20	4	2	14	41	76	14
Lancing United Reserves	20	2	3	15	25	80	9

Division Three North	P	W	D	L	F	A	Pts
Fittleworth	20	16	2	2	72	23	50
Ashington Rovers Reserves	20	16	2	2	78	33	50
Upper Beeding Reserves	20	15	2	3	91	23	47
Holbrook Reserves	20	13	1	6	104	42	40
Horsham Olympic	20	10	1	9	47	41	31
T D Shipley Reserves	20	9	2	9	45	36	29
Henfield Reserves	20	5	3	12	42	55	18
Pulborough Reserves	20	6	0	14	28	94	18
Southwater Reserves	20	5	2	13	27	58	17
Forest Reserves	20	3	2	15	26	111	11
Slinfold	20	3	1	16	29	73	10

Division Three South	P	W	D	L	F	A	Pts
Selsey "A"	18	14	2	2	57	17	44
Predators	18	13	3	2	47	21	42
Lavant Reserves	18	12	1	5	71	35	37
Angmering Reserves	18	11	0	7	54	41	33
The Ship	18	9	0	9	29	33	27
Tangmere	18	8	2	8	49	45	26
Harting	18	7	0	11	30	43	21
Rustington Park Seniors	18	4	2	12	15	46	14
Square Deal	18	3	2	13	28	53	11
Sportsman	18	2	2	14	26	72	8

Division Four North	P	W	D	L	F	A	Pts
Faygate United Reserves	20	14	4	2	57	28	46
Cowfold "A"	20	12	4	4	59	26	40
Rusper	20	11	6	3	51	27	39
Ockley	20	11	3	6	63	43	36
Horsham Trinity Reserves	20	10	4	6	50	48	34
Horsham Crusaders	20	9	3	8	45	36	30
Henfield "A"	20	7	6	7	41	44	27
Holbrook "A"	20	7	2	11	44	59	23
West Chiltington Reserves	20	5	3	12	29	44	18
Horsham Baptists	20	3	3	14	25	64	12
Barns Green Reserves	20	1	2	17	18	63	5

Division Four South	P	W	D	L	F	A	Pts
Whyke United	16	14	1	1	58	19	43
Rogate 08	16	13	1	2	58	24	40
Graffham	16	12	0	4	94	30	36
Yapton Reserves	16	9	1	6	54	43	28
Watersfield Reserves	16	7	0	9	35	41	18
Rustington Park Seniors R.	16	5	1	10	41	66	16
Chapel	16	5	0	11	37	60	15
Coal Exchange	16	4	0	12	34	66	12
Stedham United Reserves	16	1	0	15	23	85	3

Division Five Central	P	W	D	L	F	A	Pts
Rudgwick Reserves	16	11	1	4	57	25	34
Alfold Reserves	16	10	3	3	55	27	33
Billingshurst "A"	16	10	2	4	54	24	32
Cowfold "B"	16	9	3	4	47	32	30
Plaistow	16	8	1	7	50	29	25
Fittleworth Reserves	16	7	4	5	39	46	25
Wisborough Green Reserves	16	5	3	8	26	28	18
Slinfold Reserves	16	2	1	13	21	75	7
Southwater "A"	16	1	0	15	13	76	3

Division Five North	P	W	D	L	F	A	Pts
Ockley Reserves	18	13	3	2	61	25	42
Border Wanderers	18	11	3	4	75	41	36
Chapel Reserves	18	11	2	5	53	33	35
Rowfant Village	18	9	3	6	43	40	30
Newdigate Reserves	18	6	4	8	39	47	22
Holbrook "B"	18	6	3	9	41	49	21
Horsham Baptists Reserves	18	6	3	9	29	55	21
Billingshurst Athletic	18	4	5	9	37	57	17
Horsham Olympic Reserves	18	5	1	12	49	56	16
Horsham Trinity "A"	18	4	3	11	34	58	15

Division Five South	P	W	D	L	F	A	Pts
Predators Reserves	16	12	3	1	59	22	39
Wittering United Reserves	16	11	2	3	54	13	35
Ambassadors	16	9	4	3	47	24	31
Regis Veterans	16	7	5	4	32	27	26
Whyke United Reserves	16	7	4	5	39	36	25
Milland	16	5	4	7	23	33	19
Tangmere Reserves	16	4	4	8	23	39	16
Vapours	16	2	2	12	28	61	8
Lodsworth Reserves	16	0	2	14	15	65	2

Fernhurst Sport Reserves - record expunged.

WESTON-SUPER-MARE & DISTRICT LEAGUE

Division One	P	W	D	L	F	A	Pts
East Worle	20	13	5	2	58	28	44
Weston St J Sportsbar	20	13	1	6	49	29	40
Nailsea United "A"	20	12	2	6	61	45	38
Clevedon United Res.	20	11	3	6	51	24	36
Hutton	20	9	1	10	49	43	28
Nailsea Town Reserves	20	8	4	8	43	41	28
Selkirk United	20	8	3	9	40	48	27
Draycott	20	7	2	11	41	54	23
Kewstoke Lions	20	5	5	10	31	45	20
Portishead T "A" (-4)	20	7	2	11	35	63	19
Cleeve West Town Res.	20	3	0	17	18	56	9

Division Two	P	W	D	L	F	A	Pts
Weston St Johns Reserves	18	15	3	0	79	26	48
St George (EIG) res (-4)	18	12	4	2	54	33	36
Winscombe Reserves (-3)	18	10	2	6	45	30	29
Churchill Club 70 Res.	18	7	3	8	49	42	24
Locking Park	18	7	3	8	36	42	24
Axbridge Town	18	6	3	9	44	49	21
Nailsea United "B"	18	5	5	8	38	49	20
Westland United res (-6)	18	6	3	9	49	49	15
Portishead WMC (-3)	18	5	3	10	40	54	15
Bournville Rovers	18	2	1	15	34	94	7

Division Three	P	W	D	L	F	A	Pts
Burnham United "A"	18	14	0	4	63	25	42
Berrow Reserves	18	13	1	4	66	27	40
Congresbury Reserves	18	13	0	5	55	33	39
Clevedon Dons	18	8	4	6	44	38	28
Wedmore	18	8	2	8	44	33	26
Portishead Town "B"	18	8	1	9	57	48	25
Yatton Athletic Reserves	18	7	2	9	44	43	23
Cleeve West Tn "A" (-3)	18	5	3	10	35	65	15
Kewstoke Lions Reserves	18	3	3	12	24	63	12
Worle Reserves	18	2	2	14	20	77	8

Division Four	P	W	D	L	F	A	Pts
Cheddar "A"	18	15	2	1	66	20	47
Tickenham United	18	13	2	3	61	21	41
Clevedon United "A"	18	11	1	6	45	41	34
Westend	18	10	2	6	56	42	32
King Alfred SC	18	9	3	6	58	38	30
Shipham	18	7	1	10	44	49	22
Winscombe "A"	18	6	2	10	38	69	20
Nailsea United Colts	18	3	5	10	39	60	14
Wrington Redhill Res.	18	3	2	13	25	56	11
Hutton Reserves	18	2	2	14	33	69	8

Division Five	P	W	D	L	F	A	Pts
Weston Super Seagulls	20	17	0	3	75	43	51
Sporting Weston (-6)	20	16	1	3	89	30	43
Selkirk United Reserves	20	11	2	7	50	32	35
AFC Nailsea	20	10	1	9	38	40	31
St George (EIG) "A"	20	9	3	8	70	59	30
Banwell Reserves	20	10	0	10	52	61	30
East Worle Reserves	20	9	0	11	47	51	27
Portishead Town Colts	20	8	1	11	45	49	25
Dolphin Athletic (-3)	20	6	1	13	32	51	16
South Park Rangers	20	5	1	14	32	70	16
Draycott Reserves (-1)	20	3	2	15	29	73	10

Division Six	P	W	D	L	F	A	Pts
Weston Players	16	15	0	1	74	22	45
St George (EIG) "B"	16	13	0	3	50	26	39
Wedmore Reserves	16	8	0	8	35	42	24
Worle Rangers	16	7	1	8	46	39	22
Shipham Reserves (-3)	16	7	2	7	39	43	20
KVFC	16	4	3	9	32	39	15
AFC Nailsea Reserves	16	4	3	9	22	44	15
Axbridge Town Reserves	16	4	3	9	34	59	15
Yatton Athletic "A"	16	3	2	11	41	59	11

WIGAN & DISTRICT AMATEUR LEAGUE

Premier Division	P	W	D	L	F	A	Pts
Winstanley St Aidans	26	19	5	2	81	34	62
Standish St Wilfrid's	26	13	6	7	57	45	45
AFC Scholes	26	13	2	11	54	55	41
Hindley Town	26	10	7	9	57	49	37
Digmoor	26	10	6	10	61	49	36
Newburgh United	25	9	9	7	49	39	36
Highfield	26	10	6	10	49	74	36
Bickerstaffe	26	10	5	11	55	53	35
Downall Green United	26	10	5	11	51	55	35
Fir Tree Rangers	26	8	8	10	74	56	32
Pemberton	26	9	4	13	52	61	31
Gidlow Athletic	26	7	8	11	41	56	29
Shevington	26	7	7	12	44	53	28
Leigh Phoenix	25	6	2	17	35	81	20

One game was abandoned and was not replayed.

Division One	P	W	D	L	F	A	Pts
Ince	24	19	1	4	80	47	58
Ince Central	24	17	5	2	69	25	56
Winstanley St A. Res.	24	17	4	3	56	22	55
Farnworth Town	24	12	5	7	59	45	41
Atherton Royal	24	12	4	8	63	54	40
UpHolland	24	12	4	8	61	56	40
Goose Green United	24	6	10	8	53	58	28
Atherton Town	24	6	7	11	47	54	25
St.Judes	24	6	7	11	30	45	25
AFC Tyldesley	24	7	4	13	52	69	25
Shevington Reserves	24	6	5	13	36	58	23
Ormskirk	24	5	3	16	53	71	18
Wigan Rovers	24	1	1	22	24	79	4

Division Two	P	W	D	L	F	A	Pts
Orrell	22	15	5	2	86	31	50
Standish St.Wilf. Res.	22	14	6	2	64	28	48
Foundry	22	14	5	3	65	33	47
Leigh Legion	22	15	1	6	86	40	46
Fir Tree Rangers Res.	22	9	5	8	51	58	32
Bickerstaffe Reserves	22	9	4	9	43	40	31
Hindley Celtic	22	9	3	10	69	76	30
Hindley Town Res.	22	7	5	10	48	64	26
Farnworth Town Res.	22	7	3	12	47	64	24
Boars Head	22	4	6	12	40	65	18
Wigan Rovers Res.	22	3	2	17	30	88	11
Springfield	22	1	5	16	26	68	8

Lowton Church Inn - record expunged.

Division Three	P	W	D	L	F	A	Pts
Holy Family	24	23	0	1	125	22	69
Aspull (-3)	24	17	3	4	72	26	51
Atherton Hag Fold	24	15	1	8	88	50	46
Hindley Celtic Reserves (-3)	24	15	3	6	77	56	45
Orrell Res.	24	13	4	7	69	54	43
Lowton Rams	24	12	3	9	70	63	39
Billinge Community	24	9	3	12	47	67	30
Winstanley Warriors	24	7	3	14	45	72	24
Wigan Celtic	24	6	4	14	41	80	22
Cart and Horses	24	4	8	12	39	57	20
Litten Tree (-3)	24	5	7	12	34	63	19
Ashton Villa	24	4	6	14	28	71	18
Edna Road	24	1	5	18	32	86	8

FC Culcheth Sports - record expunged.

WIMBLEDON & DISTRICT LEAGUE

Premier Division	P	W	D	L	F	A	Pts
South East London	20	16	4	0	50	15	52
Claremont	20	11	2	7	39	29	35
Goldfingers	20	10	5	5	40	32	35
Brentnal	20	10	2	8	42	32	32
Union	20	8	5	7	31	34	29
Partizan Wandsworth	20	7	7	6	38	32	28
PWCA (Wimbledon)	20	8	3	9	47	45	27
Croydon Red Star	20	7	3	10	34	51	24
AFC Battersea	20	5	4	11	32	41	19
AFC Cubo Reserves	20	3	5	12	22	41	14
Real Phoenix	20	2	6	12	25	48	12

WITNEY & DISTRICT LEAGUE

Premier Division	P	W	D	L	F	A	Pts
Hanborough	20	16	3	1	48	17	51
Ducklington	20	14	2	4	43	27	44
Spartan Rangers	20	12	2	6	51	22	38
Charlbury Town	20	11	2	7	54	45	35
Combe	20	10	2	8	38	36	32
Witney Royals	20	8	5	7	45	29	29
Wychwood Forest	20	8	3	9	41	43	27
Hailey	20	6	5	9	50	45	23
Kingham All Blacks	20	6	2	12	38	50	20
AC Finstock	20	3	3	14	25	69	12
Minster Lovell	20	0	3	17	29	79	3

Division One	P	W	D	L	F	A	Pts
North Leigh "A"	22	15	4	3	66	27	49
FC Chequers	22	15	4	3	54	21	49
Chad Park	22	15	1	6	45	33	46
Brize Norton	22	13	3	6	54	32	42
Chipping Nor. T Swifts	22	12	0	10	37	32	36
FC Nomads	22	9	3	10	32	45	30
West Witney	22	9	2	11	56	41	29
Aston FC	22	7	5	10	38	43	26
Ducklington Reserves	22	5	6	11	39	49	21
FC Mills	22	6	2	14	37	59	20
Hanborough Reserves	22	5	3	14	26	53	18
Witney Wanderers	22	3	3	16	22	71	12

Division Two	P	W	D	L	F	A	Pts
Stanton Harcourt	22	16	3	3	71	29	51
Witney Royals Reserves	22	12	3	7	46	37	39
Ducklington "A"	22	10	6	6	57	45	36
Two Rivers	22	10	6	6	56	45	36
Southrop	22	10	5	7	49	38	35
Brize Norton Reserves	22	9	6	7	51	52	33
Middle Barton	22	9	6	7	47	49	33
Hailey Reserves	22	9	2	11	46	44	29
Charlbury Town Reserves	22	6	4	12	31	34	22
Wootton Sports	22	6	3	13	38	54	21
Milton under Wychwood	22	6	2	14	34	69	20
Spartan Rangers Reserves	22	6	0	16	38	68	18

Division Three	P	W	D	L	F	A	Pts
Freeland "A"	22	15	3	4	118	35	48
FC Chequers Reserves	22	15	1	6	57	36	46
West Witney Reserves	22	13	6	3	73	33	45
North Leigh "B"	22	12	3	7	61	39	39
Eynsham Sports & S Cl	22	11	4	7	70	52	37
Kingham All Blacks Res.	22	8	6	8	41	46	30
Witney Royals "A"	22	9	2	11	45	57	29
Aston Reserves	22	8	3	11	39	42	27
Chipping Norton TS Res.	22	7	5	10	33	53	26
Minster Lovell Reserves	22	5	8	9	46	48	23
Tackley (+3)	22	5	5	12	34	59	23
FC Mills Reserves (-3)	22	1	0	21	22	139	0

Division Four	P	W	D	L	F	A	Pts
Carterton Pumas	20	19	1	0	81	9	58
FC Hollybush	20	16	1	3	90	27	49
AFC Marlborough	20	15	3	2	66	26	48
Wychwood Forest Res.	20	13	2	5	73	38	41
Eynsham	20	7	3	10	63	56	24
Corinthians	20	6	2	12	34	70	20
Freeland "B"	20	6	1	13	36	46	19
Combe Reserves	20	5	4	11	20	45	19
Spartan Rangers "A"	20	5	3	12	30	48	18
Ducklington "B"	20	4	6	10	26	64	18
Eynsham S & S Club Res.	20	0	2	18	28	118	2

WORCESTER & DISTRICT LEAGUE

	P	W	D	L	F	A	Pts
Powick	26	23	2	1	158	24	71
VBL Sports	26	23	0	3	163	34	69
Hallow	26	18	2	6	87	30	56
Newtown Sports	26	17	0	9	107	51	51
Worcester Raiders	26	16	3	7	106	59	51
University of Worcester	26	16	3	7	101	57	51
Malvern Town Reserves	26	13	1	12	79	72	40
Northway	26	11	2	13	57	80	35
GDL Athletic	26	9	2	15	61	116	29
Malvern Rangers res (-3)	26	9	2	15	73	80	26
West Malvern TC	26	8	2	16	73	99	26
Perrywood Reserves	26	4	1	21	42	83	13
YM Rangers (-3)	26	3	2	21	44	139	8
Worcester Anchors	26	1	0	25	15	242	3

WORTHING & DISTRICT LEAGUE

Premier Division	P	W	D	L	F	A	Pts
Worthing Leisure	22	19	2	1	70	14	59
L & S Athletic	22	16	4	2	92	23	52
Shoreham RBL	22	14	3	5	75	50	45
Sompting	22	13	4	5	69	30	43
GSK Sports	22	12	4	6	67	30	40
Ferring Reserves	22	8	3	11	51	57	27
Goring St Theresa's	22	8	2	12	34	56	26
FC Sporting	22	7	3	12	28	51	24
Highdown Rovers	22	7	1	14	32	69	22
Durrington RAFA	22	6	3	13	32	69	21
Northbrook	22	6	0	16	39	66	18
Worthing Albion	22	0	3	19	20	94	3

WYCOMBE & DISTRICT LEAGUE

Senior Division	P	W	D	L	F	A	Pts
Wycombe Community U	18	15	3	0	81	23	48
AFC Spartans	18	13	3	2	71	22	42
Hambleden	18	9	3	6	41	46	30
Wycombe Judo	18	8	4	6	31	34	28
AC Marlow	18	6	4	8	41	53	22
Prestwood	18	6	2	10	29	32	20
Great Missenden	18	5	4	9	39	49	19
Penn & Tylers Grn "A"	18	4	4	10	31	71	16
Winchmore Hill	18	3	5	10	27	43	14
FC Titans	18	3	4	11	38	56	13

AFC Castlefield - record expunged.

Premier Division	P	W	D	L	F	A	Pts
Bucks Students Un Res.	22	16	1	5	73	45	49
Hazlemere Sports	22	14	3	5	59	40	45
Stokenchurch	22	12	4	6	86	57	40
Wooburn Athletic	22	10	4	8	47	46	34
Kings Chur. (Amersham)	22	7	9	6	48	40	30
Wycombe Athletic	22	8	5	9	48	53	29
Lane End	22	9	1	12	47	56	28
AC Marlow Reserves	22	8	4	10	49	60	28
Winchmore Hill Reserves	22	8	2	12	52	59	26
AFC Amersham	22	7	3	12	49	61	24
Chinnor "A"	22	7	1	14	43	68	22
FC Leisure	22	4	7	11	40	56	19

Division One	P	W	D	L	F	A	Pts
Corinthians	16	14	1	1	72	20	43
The Wizards	16	13	1	2	52	15	40
Bucks Students Un "A"	16	12	1	3	62	21	37
Holmer Green "A"	16	7	2	7	44	35	23
Hambleden Reserves	16	5	4	7	47	39	19
Wycombe Judo Reserves	16	5	2	9	40	51	17
Lane End Reserves	16	5	2	9	29	40	17
Chinnor "B"	16	3	2	11	29	64	11
AFC Wycombe	16	0	1	15	10	100	1

Prestwood Reserves - record expunged.

YEOVIL & DISTRICT LEAGUE

Premier Division	P	W	D	L	F	A	Pts
Henstridge	20	17	1	2	78	27	52
Westland Sports Reserves	20	15	3	2	80	32	48
Normalair	20	13	1	6	91	48	40
Keinton Mandeville	20	10	2	8	47	42	32
Milborne Port	20	9	2	9	47	44	29
Victoria Sports	20	8	3	9	59	51	27
Barwick & Stoford	20	8	3	9	41	44	27
Templecombe Rovers	20	7	0	13	46	67	21
Baltonsborough	20	7	0	13	47	82	21
Castle Cary Reserves	20	4	3	13	38	53	15
Stoke	20	2	2	16	29	113	8

Division One	P	W	D	L	GD		Pts
Mermaid United	20	18	1	1	56	19	55
Ilchester	20	14	1	5	63	25	43
Tor	20	13	3	4	72	33	42
Butleigh Dynamos	20	11	6	3	61	39	39
Somerton Sports	20	11	3	6	53	34	36
Martock United	20	9	2	9	44	42	29
Normalair Reserves	20	7	2	11	41	44	23
Odcombe	20	7	1	12	48	56	22
AFC Wessex (-1)	20	5	3	12	57	63	17
Castle Cary "A"	20	2	2	16	30	79	8
Pen Mill	20	1	0	19	26	117	3

Arrow - record expunged.

Division Two	P	W	D	L	GD		Pts
Aller Park	18	16	1	1	77	22	49
Clifton Sports	18	16	1	1	62	19	49
Somerton Sports Reserves	18	11	2	5	69	24	35
Barwick & Stoford Res.	18	9	1	8	43	43	28
Abbey Moor	18	8	2	8	41	33	26
Milborne Port Reserves	18	7	3	8	53	45	24
Bradford Abbas	18	7	3	8	48	60	24
Tor Sports	18	4	1	13	31	70	13
Keinton M'ville res (-3)	18	2	1	15	27	66	4
Bruton United (-3)	18	2	1	15	29	98	4

Castle Cary Colts - record expunged.

Division Three	P	W	D	L	GD		Pts
Brhoden	20	18	1	1	114	23	55
Ilchester Reserves	20	17	1	2	109	15	52
Wincanton Town	20	10	6	4	80	47	36
Martock United Reserves	20	10	3	7	43	32	33
Victoria Sports Reserves	20	10	1	9	51	47	31
Odcombe Reserves	20	10	1	9	50	62	31
Zeal Development	20	7	0	13	45	57	21
Templecombe Rovers Res.	20	6	2	12	52	88	20
Baltonsborough res (-7)	20	6	4	10	54	61	15
Huish Langport	20	4	1	15	34	88	13
Mudford	20	1	2	17	15	127	5

YORK LEAGUE

Premier Division	P	W	D	L	F	A	Pts
Dringhouses	26	22	0	4	89	38	66
Dunnington	26	19	0	7	78	33	57
Old Malton St Marys	26	16	2	8	62	38	50
York Railway Institute	26	16	1	9	85	58	49
Copmanthorpe	26	15	4	7	70	49	49
Huntington Rovers	26	15	2	9	68	51	47
Riccall United (-3)	26	13	2	11	56	53	38
Haxby United	26	11	4	11	72	61	37
Tadcaster Albion "A"	26	7	5	14	41	67	26
Poppleton United	26	7	5	14	31	59	26
Wilberfoss	26	7	4	15	47	69	25
Hamilton Panthers	26	4	6	16	34	76	18
York St John University	26	5	2	19	53	88	17
Easingwold Town	26	4	5	17	35	81	17

Kartiers (Selby) - record expunged.

Division One	P	W	D	L	F	A	Pts
Wigginton Grasshoppers	20	16	3	1	78	23	51
Nestlé Rowntree	20	13	2	5	57	32	41
Malton & Norton	20	13	2	5	38	27	41
Selby RSSC (-3)	20	12	1	7	44	25	34
St Clements	20	10	3	7	55	37	33
Pocklington Town Res.	20	10	1	9	33	27	31
Hemingbrough United	20	9	1	10	39	42	28
Tockwith	20	8	2	10	46	45	26
Bishopthorpe United	20	4	2	14	28	43	14
Post Office (-3)	20	4	4	12	23	61	13
Thorpe United	20	0	1	19	13	92	1

Division Two	P	W	D	L	F	A	Pts
Terrington Glory	20	15	2	3	64	30	47
Amotherby & Swinton	20	12	3	5	57	32	39
Heworth	20	11	4	5	61	33	37
Strensall	20	11	3	6	56	38	36
Heslington	20	10	3	7	45	33	33
Ch Fenton White Horse	20	9	3	8	37	36	30
Crayke	20	7	5	8	40	47	26
Huby United	20	5	3	12	29	55	18
Rawcliffe (-6)	20	7	1	12	32	43	16
Stamford Bridge	20	4	2	14	33	71	14
Ouseburn United	20	4	1	15	27	63	13

Division Three	Pld	W	D	L	F	A	Pts
Cliffe	20	12	6	2	60	30	42
Aviva	20	11	7	2	54	31	40
Osbaldwick	20	12	3	5	66	38	39
Fulford FC United	20	11	5	4	55	19	38
Civil Service	20	10	4	6	49	46	34
F1 Racing	20	10	3	7	57	30	33
Elvington Harriers (-3)	20	7	3	10	48	48	21
Wheldrake	20	5	5	10	26	44	20
Rufforth United	20	4	2	14	26	64	14
Stillington	20	3	4	13	39	83	13
Barmby Moor	20	3	2	15	27	74	11

Division Four	P	W	D	L	F	A	Pts
Tadcaster Magnets	18	18	0	0	126	10	54
Selby Olympia	18	14	2	2	77	38	44
Sporting Knavesmire	18	9	2	7	56	39	29
KS Polonia/St Clements	18	8	2	8	48	42	26
LNER Builders	18	6	8	4	48	47	26
Melbourne	18	8	2	8	35	50	26
Bubwith	18	7	3	8	37	51	24
Bishop Wilton	18	4	2	12	31	55	14
Fox	18	2	4	12	31	88	10
Moor Lane	18	1	1	16	40	109	4

Reserve Division A	P	W	D	L	F	A	Pts
Dunnington Reserves	18	16	0	2	68	16	48
Copmanthorpe Reserves	18	10	3	5	39	32	33
York St John Univ. Res.	18	10	2	6	51	41	32
Huntington Rovers Res.	18	10	0	8	51	44	30
Wigginton G'hoppers Res.	18	7	2	9	43	46	23
Old Malton St Marys Res.	18	7	2	9	39	44	23
Haxby United Reserves	18	6	4	8	39	52	22
Easingwold Town Res.	18	6	3	9	24	35	21
Aviva Reserves	18	4	3	11	27	46	15
Bishopthorpe United Res.	18	4	1	13	28	53	13

Reserve Division B	P	W	D	L	F	A	Pts
Dringhouses Reserves	16	14	1	1	64	15	43
Riccall United Reserves	16	12	2	2	63	26	38
Amotherby&Swinton Res.	16	9	1	6	44	36	28
Pocklington Town Res.	16	8	3	5	41	33	27
Hamilton Panthers Res.	16	6	2	8	45	42	20
Heslington Reserves	16	5	2	9	31	58	17
Ch Fent White H res (-3)	16	4	4	8	32	55	13
Wilberfoss Reserves	16	3	3	10	29	45	12
Thorpe United res (-6)	16	1	2	13	21	60	-1

Kartiers (Selby) Reserves - record expunged.

Reserve Division C	P	W	D	L	F	A	Pts
York R'way Institute Res.	18	15	1	2	87	30	46
Malton & Norton Res.	18	12	3	3	44	16	39
Fulford FC United Res.	18	9	1	8	35	43	28
St Clements Reserves	18	7	3	8	37	48	24
Nestlé Rowntree Reserves	18	6	5	7	56	64	23
Poppleton United res (-3)	18	8	1	9	45	38	22
Tockwith Reserves (-3)	18	7	3	8	36	39	21
Crayke Reserves	18	6	3	9	32	45	21
Hemingbrough Utd Res.	18	5	3	10	26	44	18
Stamford Bridge Reserves	18	2	3	13	27	58	9

OTHER LEAGUES

Reserve Division D	P	W	D	L	F	A	Pts
Cliffe Reserves	21	15	3	3	65	23	48
Tadcaster Magnets Res.	21	15	1	5	74	27	46
Strensall Reserves	21	11	5	5	60	22	38
Civil Service Reserves	21	11	5	5	54	37	38
Selby RSSC Reserves	21	9	3	9	45	43	30
Huby United Reserves	21	7	3	11	45	54	24
F1 Racing Reserves	21	5	1	15	31	79	16
Bishop Wilton Reserves	21	0	1	20	25	114	1

YORKSHIRE OLD BOYS LEAGUE

Senior A	P	W	D	L	F	A	Pts
Stanningley OB	20	15	4	1	67	29	49
Alwoodley OB	20	14	3	3	70	20	45
Old Modernians	20	13	5	2	61	28	44
Gild'some Spurs OB (-3)	20	13	2	5	72	33	38
FC Headingley	20	11	1	8	48	37	34
Leeds Medics & Dentists	20	7	5	8	35	31	26
Huddersfield Amateur	20	7	2	11	46	54	23
Ealandians	20	6	0	14	48	81	18
Shire Academics	20	5	2	13	28	50	17
Trinity &All Saints COB	20	3	5	12	34	62	14
St Nicholas	20	1	1	18	21	105	4

Senior B	P	W	D	L	F	A	Pts
Bainbridge	18	16	2	0	65	10	50
Leeds Med & D res (-3)	18	11	3	4	70	30	33
Gildersome Spurs OB Res.	18	9	4	5	45	35	31
Old Thornesians	18	8	5	5	51	43	29
Bramley Juniors OB (-3)	18	9	4	5	49	32	28
Calverley	18	5	5	8	28	38	20
Old Batelians	18	5	2	11	36	66	17
St Bedes OB	18	5	2	11	36	66	17
Collingham Juniors OB	18	4	4	10	35	58	16
Old Centralians	18	1	3	14	22	59	6

Division One	P	W	D	L	F	A	Pts
Grangefield OB	22	16	3	3	99	37	51
Old Modernians Reserves	22	15	2	5	74	43	47
Sandal Athletic	22	13	6	3	63	38	45
Leeds Med & Dent "A"	22	13	4	5	63	40	43
Beeston OB	22	13	3	6	72	39	42
East Ardsley Wanderers	22	9	3	10	52	77	30
Bramley Juniors OB Res.	22	8	3	11	43	44	27
East Leeds Trinity OB	22	8	3	11	52	56	27
Western Juniors OB	22	8	2	12	47	62	26
Old Collegians	22	4	5	13	44	65	17
Huddersfield Amat. Res.	22	5	1	16	30	81	16
Shadwell	22	1	3	18	23	80	6

Division Two	P	W	D	L	F	A	Pts
North East Leeds	22	19	1	2	105	25	58
Stanningley OB Reserves	22	17	5	0	72	16	56
Alwoodley OB Reserves	22	13	1	8	65	40	40
Collingham Jun. OB Res.	22	10	2	10	45	57	32
Shire Academics Res.	22	9	2	11	37	58	29
Colton	22	7	6	9	49	48	27
Leeds Medics & Den "B"	22	8	3	11	39	45	27
Farnley Sports	22	7	5	10	36	55	26
Gild'some Spurs OB "A"	22	7	5	10	42	65	26
W'hse Moor Methodists	22	6	5	11	44	57	23
Calverley Reserves	22	5	2	15	29	68	17
Trin & All Sts COB Res.	22	4	3	15	41	70	15

Division Three	P	W	D	L	F	A	Pts
St Bedes OB Reserves	24	17	2	5	50	25	53
Leeds Independent	24	17	1	6	66	29	52
Bramley JOB "A"(-3)	24	16	4	4	65	20	49
Sandal Wanderers	24	14	5	5	65	58	47
Ealandians Reserves	24	11	5	8	73	52	38
Old Modernians "A"	24	11	5	8	62	42	38
Leeds City OB	24	12	2	10	60	62	38
Grangefield OB Res.	24	10	3	11	50	53	33
Heckm'wike GSOB	24	10	0	14	62	52	30
Old Batelians Res.	24	8	2	14	60	97	26
Old Centralians Res.	24	7	1	16	46	73	22
Colton Reserves	24	4	0	20	38	90	12
O Collegians res (-1)	24	3	2	19	28	72	10

Division Four	P	W	D	L	F	A	Pts
Colton "A"	22	18	1	3	84	39	55
Almondburians	22	18	0	4	122	30	54
Norristhorpe	22	15	2	5	100	39	47
Old Thornesians Reserves	22	14	2	6	77	44	44
Huddersfield Amat "A"	22	11	2	9	46	42	35
Leeds City OB Reserves	22	10	1	11	40	57	31
Old Modernians "B"	22	9	3	10	58	60	30
Old Batelians "A"	22	7	3	12	74	90	24
Sandal Athletic Reserves	22	5	5	12	47	76	20
Old Centralians "A"	22	6	2	14	41	89	20
E Ardsley Wanderers Res.	22	6	1	15	31	82	19
Shadwell Reserves	22	2	0	20	30	102	6

Division Five	P	W	D	L	F	A	Pts
Beeston OB Reserves	20	19	1	0	90	24	58
Leeds City OB "A"	20	16	1	3	84	28	49
St Bedes OB "A"	20	13	2	5	52	33	41
Bramley Jun OB "B"	20	12	2	6	52	36	38
Alwoodley OB "A"	20	8	3	9	44	53	27
H'field Amateur "B"	20	6	2	12	36	66	20
Ealandians "A"	20	5	4	11	46	60	19
Old Centr's "B" (-1)	20	6	2	12	34	61	19
Old Thorn's "A" (-1)	20	5	4	11	37	56	18
Old Modernians "C"	20	4	2	14	28	54	14
Wheelwright OB	20	4	1	15	33	65	13

Old Collegians "A" - record expunged.
Shadwell "A" - record expunged.

WELSH TABLES 2010-11

WELSH PREMIER

	P	W	D	L	F	A	Pts
Bangor City	32	22	4	6	80	44	70
The New Saints	32	20	8	4	87	34	68
Neath	32	16	10	6	62	41	58
Llanelli	32	15	8	9	58	41	53
Aberystwyth Town	32	11	9	12	42	54	42
Airbus UK Broughton	32	11	8	13	53	52	41
Prestatyn Town	32	10	10	12	44	46	40
Port Talbot Town	32	8	12	12	37	48	36
Newtown	32	8	11	13	40	55	35
Carmarthen Town	32	10	5	17	39	64	35
Bala Town	32	10	3	19	41	57	33
Haverfordwest County	32	5	4	23	30	77	19

The table split after each team played each other twice. The top 6 teams then met another twice each to determine the Championship, while the bottom 6 teams met to determine relegation.

CYMRU ALLIANCE

	P	W	D	L	F	A	Pts
Gap Connahs Quay	30	23	2	5	89	33	71
Rhyl	30	19	5	6	73	32	62
Cefn Druids	30	18	6	6	60	29	60
Rhos Aelwyd	30	15	6	9	68	64	51
Caersws	30	15	5	10	59	49	50
Llandudno	30	13	10	7	50	35	49
Flint Town United	30	13	7	10	64	55	46
Porthmadog	30	14	4	12	59	53	46
Buckley Town	30	13	6	11	46	48	45
Llangefni Town	30	11	4	15	67	64	37
Penrhyncoch	30	9	10	11	49	56	37
Ruthin Town	30	11	4	15	39	58	37
Guilsfield	30	8	6	16	43	56	30
Rhydymwyn	30	4	6	20	27	82	18
Rhayader Town	30	4	3	23	34	76	15
Technogroup Welshpool (-18)	30	5	6	19	39	76	3

WELSH LEAGUE

Division One	P	W	D	L	F	A	Pts
Bryntirion Athletic	30	23	1	6	76	27	70
Afan Lido	30	20	5	5	63	28	65
Cambrian & Clydach	30	17	6	7	68	37	57
Pontardawe Town	30	15	6	9	54	44	51
Caerau (Ely)	30	15	4	11	66	52	49
Bridgend Town	30	14	5	11	60	47	47
West End	30	13	6	11	57	47	45
Cardiff Corinthians	30	12	4	14	58	52	40
Taffs Well	30	12	3	15	47	57	39
Aberaman Athletic	30	12	3	15	58	74	39
Goytre United	30	10	8	12	47	53	38
Cwmbran Celtic	30	10	7	13	45	50	37
Barry Town	30	9	8	13	39	55	35
Caldicot Town	30	8	3	19	37	48	27
Garden Village	30	6	7	17	41	75	25
Penrhiwceiber Rangers	30	4	4	22	27	97	16

Division Two	P	W	D	L	F	A	Pts
Ton Pentre	30	22	8	0	98	34	74
Cwmaman Institute	30	19	4	7	70	37	61
AFC Porth	30	16	7	7	49	35	55
Croesyceiliog	30	15	9	6	73	46	54
Aberbargoed Buds	30	13	7	10	64	52	46
Ely Rangers	30	12	9	9	56	50	45
Dinas Powys	30	12	8	10	47	42	44
Caerleon	30	12	7	11	44	37	43
Newport YMCA	30	12	6	12	55	49	42
Bettws	30	12	5	13	38	49	41
Newcastle Emlyn	30	10	8	12	54	58	38
Ammanford	30	10	6	14	40	50	36
Treharris Athletic Western	30	9	6	15	49	55	33
Abertillery Bluebirds	30	9	5	16	58	74	32
AFC Llwydcoed	30	3	8	19	30	65	17
Llangeinor	30	1	3	26	20	112	6

Division Three	P	W	D	L	F	A	Pts
Monmouth Town	34	19	9	6	96	64	66
Corus Steel	34	18	10	6	64	40	64
Caerau	34	18	9	7	83	51	63
Goytre	34	19	6	9	82	53	63
Pontypridd Town	34	19	6	9	73	50	63
Newport Civil Service	34	17	6	11	78	54	57
Briton Ferry Llansawel	34	17	5	12	68	54	56
Risca United	34	16	4	14	74	61	52
UWIC	34	14	7	13	59	48	49
Treowen Stars	34	13	6	15	48	68	45
Cardiff Grange Harlequins	34	10	11	13	57	58	41
Pontyclun	34	12	3	19	62	72	39
Llanwern	34	9	10	15	56	65	37
Tredegar Town	34	9	9	16	46	65	36
Cwmamman United	34	10	6	18	51	88	36
South Gower	34	8	10	16	52	77	34
Cwmbran Town	34	7	11	16	38	59	32
Porthcawl Town Athletic	34	4	6	24	31	91	18

Reserve Division Central	P	W	D	L	F	A	Pts
Cardiff Corinthians reserves	22	17	3	2	79	33	54
Ely Rangers reserves	22	16	1	5	64	36	49
Bettws reserves	22	13	4	5	74	36	43
Cambrian & Clydach res	22	13	3	6	67	47	42
Bryntirion Athletic reserves	22	12	4	6	80	35	40
AFC Porth reserves	22	9	2	11	50	53	29
Dinas Powys reserves	22	7	4	11	46	68	25
Treharris Ath. Western res	22	8	0	14	48	55	24
UWIC reserves (-4)	22	8	4	10	33	44	24
AFC Llwydcoed reserves	22	6	1	15	35	84	19
Pontyclun reserves	22	4	2	16	29	66	14
Porthcawl Town Athletic res	22	4	2	16	31	79	14

WELSH LEAGUES

Reserve Division East	P	W	D	L	F	A	Pts
Cwmbran Celtic reserves	24	20	3	1	89	27	63
Caerleon reserves	24	14	6	4	70	40	48
Croesyceiliog reserves	24	14	3	7	62	31	45
Newport YMCA reserves	24	12	6	6	70	56	42
Caldicot Town reserves	24	13	3	8	50	40	42
Treowen Stars reserves	24	12	4	8	65	47	40
Aberbargoed Buds reserves	24	12	3	9	60	44	39
Abertillery Bluebirds res	24	7	6	11	43	52	27
Newport Civil Service res	24	6	6	12	49	58	24
Risca United reserves	24	7	3	14	45	67	24
Goytre reserves (-6)	24	8	2	14	48	66	20
Monmouth Town reserves	24	3	3	18	35	87	12
Cwmbran Town reserves	24	3	2	19	25	96	11

Reserve Division West	P	W	D	L	F	A	Pts
Afan Lido reserves	14	13	1	0	49	10	40
Pontardawe Town reserves	14	8	3	3	44	19	27
West End reserves	14	8	0	6	53	36	24
Neath reserves	14	7	1	6	42	27	22
Garden Village reserves	14	6	0	8	37	33	18
Briton Ferry Llansawel res	14	6	0	8	22	43	18
Newcastle Emlyn reserves	14	3	3	8	21	46	12
Ammanford reserves (-3)	14	0	2	12	12	66	-1

WELSH ALLIANCE

Division One	P	W	D	L	F	A	Pts
Conwy Utd	30	25	2	3	89	30	77
Holyhead Hotspur	30	20	6	4	82	36	66
Holywell Town	30	17	3	10	68	40	54
Denbigh Town	30	13	7	10	53	53	46
Caernarfon Town	30	13	4	13	58	59	43
Llanfairpwll	30	12	6	12	55	52	42
Gwalchmai	30	10	10	10	47	45	40
Nefyn Utd	30	10	7	13	40	54	37
Bethesda Athletic	30	10	7	13	57	82	37
Glan Conwy	30	10	6	14	47	50	36
Pwllheli (-3)	30	10	9	11	42	46	36
Llanrwst Utd	30	9	8	13	50	60	35
Llanrug Utd	30	11	2	17	62	75	35
Barmouth & Dyffryn Utd	30	10	5	15	59	77	35
Llandudno Junction	30	8	10	12	54	65	34
Llanberis	30	4	4	22	42	81	16

Division Two	P	W	D	L	F	A	Pts
Caernarfon Wanderers	20	15	1	4	63	29	46
Bodedern	20	14	3	3	55	25	45
Connahs Quay Town	20	13	2	5	49	26	41
Llandyrnog Utd	20	12	1	7	54	28	37
Amlwch Town	20	8	4	8	43	49	28
Greenfield	20	7	5	8	42	38	26
Penmaenmawr Phoenix	20	6	3	11	43	48	21
Nantlle Vale	20	6	1	13	23	55	19
Halkyn Utd	20	5	3	12	30	51	18
Blaenau Ffestiniog	20	5	2	13	32	61	17
Gaerwen (-3)	20	5	3	12	40	64	15

CLYWD LEAGUE

Premier Division	P	W	D	L	F	A	Pts
Abergele Rovers	22	19	2	1	103	20	59
Sychdyn	22	14	4	4	52	34	46
Mochre Sports	22	12	2	8	58	45	38
Meliden	22	11	3	8	45	35	36
Llansannan	22	11	1	10	42	48	34
Rhos United	22	9	5	8	46	49	32
Rhuddlan Town	22	10	1	11	53	43	31
St Asaph	22	9	3	10	67	48	30
Caerwys	22	7	3	12	41	6	24
Brynford United	22	7	3	12	40	63	24
Shotton Steel	22	4	4	14	30	76	16
Aston Park Rangers	22	3	1	18	25	77	10

Division One	P	W	D	L	F	A	Pts
FC Nomads	24	23	1	0	104	25	70
Point of Ayr	24	18	2	4	113	37	56
Prestatyn Rovers	24	17	4	3	109	31	55
Y Glannau	24	14	2	8	56	45	44
Abergele Dragons	24	11	4	9	57	55	37
Mostyn Dragons	24	11	3	10	68	56	36
Connah's Quay Tigers	24	10	5	9	52	55	35
Rhyl Athletic	24	11	2	11	55	73	35
Llannefydd	24	6	6	12	55	70	24
Betws-yn-Rhos	24	7	3	14	40	67	24
Cerrigydrudion	24	4	2	18	32	88	14
Flint Mountain	24	3	2	19	28	99	11
Bro Cernyw	24	2	2	20	28	96	8

Reserve Division	P	W	D	L	F	A	Pts
Holywell Town reserves	16	13	1	2	72	29	40
Shotton Steel reserves	16	12	1	3	67	22	37
Flint Town United Youth	16	10	3	3	59	32	33
Llanrwst United reserves	16	8	3	5	48	41	27
Abergele Dragons reserves	16	6	3	7	39	38	21
Rhuddlan Town reserves	16	6	0	10	42	46	18
Aston Park Rangers reserves	16	5	1	10	34	51	16
Prestatyn Rovers reserves	16	4	2	10	36	66	14
Caerwys reserves	16	1	0	15	15	87	3

GWENT COUNTY LEAGUE

Division One	P	W	D	L	F	A	Pts
Undy Athletic	28	19	5	4	92	36	62
Albion Rovers	28	18	8	2	76	32	62
Lliswerry	28	16	6	6	64	38	54
PILCS	28	16	5	7	70	40	53
Chepstow Town	28	14	10	4	66	43	52
AC Pontymister	28	16	1	11	68	61	49
Govilon	28	13	2	13	72	62	41
Clydach Wasps	28	11	7	10	68	54	40
Pentwynmawr Athletic	28	9	8	11	46	54	35
Abercarn United	28	10	3	15	58	77	33
Abertillery Excelsiors	28	8	8	12	59	65	32
Coed Eva Athletic	28	9	3	16	52	67	30
Blaenavon Blues	28	7	4	17	44	75	25
Spencer Youth & Boys	28	7	2	19	50	85	23
Cwmffrwdoer Sports	28	0	2	26	30	126	2

Division Two	P	W	D	L	F	A	Pts
Fleur-De-Lys Welfare	26	21	5	0	90	20	68
Fairfield United	26	21	2	3	110	38	65
Trethomas Bluebirds	26	16	3	7	78	46	51
Newport Corinthians	26	15	4	7	70	39	49
Panteg	26	12	8	6	76	42	44
Malpas United	26	13	5	8	59	50	44
Cromwell	26	12	3	11	62	63	39
RTB Ebbw Vale	26	12	0	14	60	56	36
Cefn Forest	26	7	5	14	55	73	26
Tranch	26	8	2	16	48	100	26
Llanhilleth Athletic	26	7	3	16	41	63	24
Sudbrook Cricket Club	26	5	6	15	33	58	21
Mardy	26	4	4	18	38	93	16
Rogerstone	26	3	2	21	45	124	11

Division Three	P	W	D	L	F	A	Pts
Pill	26	17	3	6	96	47	54
Lucas Cwmbran	26	16	6	4	90	52	54
Rockfield Rovers	26	16	3	7	73	49	51
Rhymney	26	15	4	7	68	47	49
Whiteheads	26	14	4	8	88	61	46
Marshfield	26	13	6	7	82	60	45
Trinant	26	13	3	10	66	83	42
Caldicot Castle	26	12	2	12	53	52	38
New Inn	26	12	1	13	67	84	37
Sebastopol	26	11	2	13	51	58	35
Trevethin (-3)	26	8	3	15	86	97	24
Abergavenny Thursdays	26	5	2	19	47	84	17
Underwood Athletic SC	26	5	1	20	46	90	16
Race	26	4	2	20	40	89	14

GWENT CENTRAL LEAGUE

Premier Division	P	W	D	L	F	A	Pts
Llanarth	21	17	0	4	100	38	51
Pontypool Town	21	14	1	6	91	61	43
Pandy	21	11	1	9	70	56	34
Raglan (-3)	21	11	3	7	70	69	33
Usk Town	21	10	2	9	65	58	32
Gilwern & District	21	6	3	12	57	89	21
Crickhowell	21	4	3	14	51	65	15
Llanfoist (-3)	21	4	1	16	33	101	10

Division One	P	W	D	L	F	A	Pts
Govilon	22	18	2	2	93	19	56
Clydach Wasps	22	16	2	4	87	33	50
Blaenavon Blues	22	15	2	5	65	30	47
PILCS	22	15	1	6	72	40	46
Tranch (-3)	22	10	4	8	56	55	31
Fairfield United	22	8	4	10	51	41	28
Panteg (-6)	21	10	3	8	53	55	27
Mardy	22	7	3	12	51	74	24
Cwmffrwdoer (-6)	22	6	5	11	62	76	17
New Inn (-3)	21	6	2	13	42	63	17
Sebastopol	22	3	4	15	36	81	13
Race (-3)	21	0	2	19	21	120	-1

Trevethin - record expunge.

GWYNEDD LEAGUE

	P	W	D	L	F	A	Pts
Bro Goronwy	18	13	2	3	77	30	41
Glantraeth	18	13	1	4	57	28	40
Beaumaris	18	11	4	3	57	26	37
Holyhead Hotspur	18	10	4	4	40	26	34
Llanfairfechan	18	7	4	7	43	34	25
Bangor University	18	5	7	6	34	36	22
Bethel	18	7	0	11	42	55	21
Llanystumdwy	18	6	3	9	41	57	21
Bangor City	18	2	4	12	28	58	10
Bontnewydd	18	0	3	15	17	86	3

MID WALES LEAGUE

Division One	P	W	D	L	F	A	Pts
Llanrhaeadr	28	23	1	4	75	23	70
Berriew	28	21	5	2	97	29	68
Llanidloes Town	28	18	3	7	62	31	57
Carno	28	18	3	7	66	37	57
Llansantffraid Village	28	15	2	11	64	47	47
Tywyn Bryncrug	28	13	3	12	58	48	42
Bow Street	28	11	4	13	66	65	37
Newbridge	28	10	3	15	51	88	33
Dolgellau	28	10	2	16	57	66	32
Waterloo	28	8	8	12	52	61	32
Aberystwyth University (-3)	28	10	4	14	41	53	31
Builth Wells	28	9	4	15	41	58	31
Penparcau	28	7	6	15	59	87	27
Dyffryn Banw	28	5	5	18	39	70	20
Presteigne St Andrews	28	4	3	21	39	104	15

WELSH LEAGUES

Division Two	P	W	D	L	F	A	Pts
Montgomery	24	18	5	1	101	23	59
Rhosgoch	24	15	3	6	74	35	48
Tregaron	24	14	4	6	48	42	46
Bont	24	10	6	8	45	45	36
Kerry	24	10	5	9	43	51	35
Llanfair United	24	10	4	10	47	41	34
Four Crosses	24	9	7	8	41	50	34
Llandrindod Wells	24	8	8	8	48	44	32
Aberaeron	24	7	7	10	30	35	28
Abermule	24	7	5	12	38	49	26
Talgarth	24	6	7	11	36	55	25
Llanfyllin Town	24	7	3	14	54	76	24
Meifod (-3)	24	2	2	20	23	82	5

SOUTH WALES AMATEUR LEAGUE

Division One	P	W	D	L	F	A	Pts
Kenfig Hill	30	20	3	7	71	36	63
Carnetown	30	19	2	9	76	34	59
Ton & Gelli BC	30	19	2	9	63	52	59
Trefelin BGC	30	17	6	7	63	39	57
Llantwit Major (-3)	30	17	6	7	74	41	54
Treforest	30	15	6	9	64	48	51
Splott Albion	30	14	7	9	67	48	49
Aber Valley YMCA	30	15	3	12	70	55	48
Rhoose	30	13	8	9	58	57	47
Troedyrhiw	30	12	4	14	57	67	40
Llantwit Fardre	30	9	4	17	49	65	31
Blaenrhondda	30	9	3	18	60	81	30
Cardiff Draconians	30	7	4	19	46	99	25
Baglan Dragons	30	5	9	16	36	62	24
Llanharry	30	5	6	19	50	86	21
Rhydyfelin	30	4	7	19	46	80	19

Division Two	P	W	D	L	F	A	Pts
STM Sports	28	23	1	4	98	35	70
Caerau BC	28	20	6	2	91	42	66
Graig	28	20	5	3	99	47	65
Penygraig	28	16	5	7	103	42	53
Merthyr Saints	28	16	4	8	90	59	52
Llangynwyd Rangers	28	14	2	12	79	57	44
Hirwaun/Mackworth	28	13	4	11	74	62	43
AFC Bargoed Red'z	28	12	3	13	62	76	39
Trelewis Welfare (-3)	28	11	1	16	54	83	31
Ynysddu Crusaders	28	9	4	15	53	89	31
Ferndale BC	28	8	5	15	58	73	29
Pencoed Athletic	28	7	5	16	52	76	26
Brynna	28	5	5	18	45	81	20
FC Abercwmboi (-6)	28	5	4	19	44	88	13
Cwm Ni	28	3	2	23	37	125	8

Penyrheol – record expunged.

SOUTH WALES SENIOR LEAGUE

Division One	P	W	D	L	F	A	Pts
Bridgend Street	30	22	5	3	108	32	71
Sully Sports	30	19	3	8	94	47	60
Grange Albion	30	16	8	6	83	44	56
Cwm Welfare	30	14	9	7	74	69	51
Tonypandy Albion	30	15	5	10	63	53	50
Cwmbach Royal Stars	30	14	4	12	84	78	49
AFC Butetown	30	14	4	12	58	61	46
Tonyrefail BGC	30	14	3	13	51	55	45
Lewistown	30	12	5	13	77	70	41
Cogan Coronation	30	10	11	9	43	48	41
Llanrumney United	30	12	4	14	70	60	40
Pentwyn Dynamos	30	10	7	13	74	88	37
Penydarren BGC	30	9	4	17	46	80	28
AFC Caerphilly	30	5	9	16	49	81	24
Cadoxton Barry	30	3	8	19	43	92	17
Garw SGBC	30	3	7	20	37	100	16

Division Two	P	W	D	L	F	A	Pts
Lisvane/Llanishen	30	21	6	3	85	32	69
Brecon Corries	30	20	5	5	87	34	64
Penrhiwceiber Cons Ath	30	20	3	7	91	55	63
Ynyshir Albion	30	19	5	6	99	59	62
St Albans	30	15	7	8	63	53	51
Fochriw	30	15	4	11	97	73	49
Llwynypia BGC	30	13	3	14	55	66	45
St Josephs	30	12	5	13	73	70	41
AFC Whitchurch	30	12	5	13	63	60	41
Ynyshir/Wattstown BYC	30	11	5	14	70	74	41
Fairwater	30	12	3	15	60	73	36
Penrhiwfer	30	10	2	18	59	78	32
Tongwynlais	30	8	5	17	57	86	32
Stanleytown	30	7	8	15	41	85	29
St Athan	30	5	5	20	35	94	13
Nelson Cavaliers	30	1	7	22	31	89	12

CEREDIGION LEAGUE

Division One	P	W	D	L	F	A	Pts
New Quay	22	19	2	1	87	17	59
Cardigan	22	18	1	3	70	16	55
Lampeter	22	14	0	8	70	35	42
St Dogmaels	22	10	4	8	72	45	34
Pencader	22	10	3	9	54	52	33
Maesglas	22	9	4	9	47	47	31
Crannog	22	8	6	8	34	37	30
Felinfach	22	8	2	12	47	69	26
Llanboidy	22	7	3	12	47	59	24
Aberporth	22	6	6	10	37	54	24
Dewi Stars	22	5	3	14	26	58	18
Ffostrasol	22	0	2	20	8	110	2

Division Two	P	W	D	L	F	A	Pts
Aberaeron reserves	22	20	2	0	102	23	62
Llanybydder	22	18	3	1	95	18	57
Newcastle Emlyn "A"	22	16	1	5	57	42	49
Bargod Rangers	22	15	3	4	68	26	48
Llandysul	22	12	0	10	59	55	36
Lampeter reserves (-6)	22	10	2	10	68	43	26
Saron	22	7	2	13	61	79	23
St Dogmaels reserves	22	7	2	13	46	79	23
Cardigan reserves (-6)	22	6	6	10	62	74	18
New Quay reserves (-3)	22	4	3	15	47	74	12
Maeglas reserves	22	1	3	18	26	122	6
SDUC (-3)	22	2	1	19	24	80	4

Reserve Division	P	W	D	L	F	A	Pts
Llanybydder reserves	16	14	1	1	96	28	43
Bargod reserves (-3)	16	11	0	5	49	25	30
Llanboidy reserves	16	7	5	4	48	31	26
Crannog reserves	16	6	5	5	43	26	23
Felinfach reserves	16	6	5	5	38	23	23
Pencader reserves (-6)	16	7	3	6	41	38	18
Aberporth reserves (-9)	16	5	1	10	26	68	7
SDUC reserves (-3)	16	2	3	11	19	55	6
Ffostrasol reserves (-3)	16	2	1	13	17	83	4

Reserve Division Play-offs

Semi-Finals

Bargod reserves 3-4 Llanboidy reserves

Llanybydder reserves 5-4 Crannog reserves

Final (@ Saron, 24/5/11)

Llanboidy reserves 1-3 Llanybydder reserves

MID WALES (SOUTH) LEAGUE

Division One	P	W	D	L	F	A	Pts
Rhayader Town reserves	28	26	1	1	124	19	79
Newcastle	28	20	6	2	121	24	66
Knighton Town	28	21	3	4	97	26	66
Presteigne St Andrews res.	28	16	5	7	66	43	53
Builth Wells reserves	28	16	3	9	113	46	51
Talgarth Town reserves	28	14	3	11	61	46	45
Penybont	28	14	1	13	65	53	43
Newbridge reserves	28	12	4	12	81	59	40
Llandrindod Wells reserves	28	10	8	10	68	51	38
Hay St Mary's	28	12	2	14	74	76	38
Radnor Valley	28	8	1	19	37	100	25
Knighton Victoria	28	6	6	16	53	88	24
St Harmon	28	5	0	23	21	145	15
Bronllys	28	2	5	21	17	98	11
Sennybridge	28	3	2	23	29	153	11

NEATH & DISTRICT LEAGUE

Premier Division	P	W	D	L	F	A	Pts
Giants Grave	22	18	3	1	108	33	57
Ystradgynlais	22	15	3	4	83	31	47
Seven Sisters	22	11	3	8	46	36	36
AFC Pontardawe	22	11	2	9	49	61	35
Bryn Rovers	22	9	3	10	51	48	30
Cwm Wanderers	22	9	3	10	30	42	30
Park Travellers	22	8	2	12	45	68	26
Sunnybank WMC	22	6	7	9	34	45	25
Lonlas	22	7	3	12	50	77	24
Coelbren Athletic	22	7	1	14	40	53	22
AFC Caewern	22	6	4	12	28	46	22
FC Clydach	22	6	4	12	33	57	22

Division One	P	W	D	L	F	A	Pts
St Ives	18	16	2	0	70	19	50
Ynysymeudwy Athletic	18	11	2	5	42	26	35
Briton Ferry Llansawel	18	8	6	4	46	33	30
Ynysygerwen	18	8	2	8	42	39	26
Cilfrew Rovers	18	8	2	8	47	46	26
Glynneath Town	18	7	3	8	43	46	24
Resolven	18	6	4	8	35	45	22
Rhos	18	6	3	9	39	46	21
Clydach Sports	18	3	5	10	33	50	14
Tonna	18	2	1	15	30	77	7

Division Two	P	W	D	L	F	A	Pts
Pontardawe Town	20	16	2	2	116	26	50
Cimla FSC	20	15	4	1	104	36	49
Harp Rovers	20	14	1	5	83	40	43
INCO Vale	20	13	3	4	93	37	42
Longford	20	10	2	8	61	51	32
Cwmamman United	20	9	3	8	53	49	30
Godregraig Athletic	20	9	0	11	49	57	27
FC Nedd	20	5	4	11	35	60	19
Borough	20	6	1	13	42	73	19
Bear	20	1	2	17	26	121	5
Bryncoch	20	0	2	18	10	122	2

Reserve Division One	P	W	D	L	F	A	Pts
Giants Grave reserves	16	11	3	2	67	22	36
AFC Pontardawe reserves	16	7	5	4	62	47	26
Bryn Rovers reserves	16	8	2	6	46	39	26
Glynneath Town reserves	16	7	4	5	43	43	25
Briton Ferry Llansawel res	16	7	2	7	39	51	23
Resolven reserves	16	6	3	7	45	57	21
Sunnybank WMC reserves	16	6	1	9	38	52	19
Rhos FC reserves	16	6	0	10	56	68	18
Ynysygerwen reserves	16	3	2	11	25	42	11

WELSH LEAGUES

Reserve Division Two	P	W	D	L	F	A	Pts
AFC Caewern reserves	18	11	5	2	51	26	38
Cilfrew Rovers reserves	18	9	6	3	58	34	33
Cwm Wanderers reserves	18	9	5	4	63	38	32
Ynysymeudwy Ath reserves	18	8	3	7	42	33	27
Harp Rovers reserves	18	9	0	9	43	53	27
Tonna reserves	18	6	6	6	35	36	24
FC Clydach reserves	18	5	7	6	38	42	22
Clydach Sports reserves	18	5	4	9	34	49	19
Park Travellers reserves	18	5	3	10	48	67	18
INCO Vale reserves	18	3	1	14	23	57	10

Reserve Division Three	P	W	D	L	F	A	Pts
Cimla FSC reserves	16	13	0	3	71	32	39
Ystradgynlais reserves	16	11	1	4	73	30	34
Glynneath Town "A"	16	10	2	4	59	29	32
Seven Sisters reserves	16	8	3	5	55	42	27
Longford reserves	16	8	1	7	64	40	25
Bryn Rovers "A"	16	5	3	8	34	56	18
Godregraig Athletic reserves	16	4	1	11	36	60	13
Harp Rovers "A"	16	4	1	11	34	63	13
INCO Vale "A"	16	2	2	12	31	105	8

NEWPORT & DISTRICT LEAGUE

Premier X Division	P	W	D	L	F	A	Pts
K-2	26	21	3	2	131	28	66
Llanwern RTB	26	19	4	3	119	34	61
Villa Dino Christchurch	26	18	2	6	117	57	56
St Julians	26	17	2	7	79	39	53
Ponthir	26	16	3	7	126	57	51
Graig-Y-Rhacca	26	16	2	8	98	61	50
Cwmcarn Athletic	26	13	4	9	86	59	43
Pontnewydd United	26	12	3	11	94	52	39
Docks Cons	26	8	5	13	57	83	29
Glan-Yr-Afon	26	8	2	16	60	125	26
Pill Hibernians	26	7	3	16	66	118	24
CCYP	26	3	4	19	47	135	13
Henllys Rangers	26	4	0	22	50	132	12
Caerleon Town	26	1	1	24	23	173	4

Premier Y Division	P	W	D	L	F	A	Pts
Cwmbran Celtic	26	22	2	2	108	22	68
AC Pontymister	26	21	3	2	94	24	66
Albion Rovers	26	18	3	5	84	44	57
Pill26	15	3	8	92	55	48	
Lliswerry	26	13	3	10	67	59	42
Malpas United	26	11	4	11	54	61	37
Coed Eva Athletic	26	9	6	11	74	82	33
Cromwell Youth	26	9	5	12	59	72	32
Lucas Cwmbran	26	8	6	12	62	84	30
Newport Corinthians	26	8	5	13	69	85	29
Spencer Y & B Club	26	8	3	15	57	81	27
Marshfield	26	7	2	17	46	87	23
Trethomas Bluebirds	26	4	3	19	50	97	15
Rogerstone	26	5	0	21	42	105	15

Division One	P	W	D	L	F	A	Pts
AC Pontymister	22	18	2	2	107	31	56
MS Dynamo	22	16	2	4	87	39	50
Oakfield Inn	22	13	5	4	93	42	44
Lliswerry	22	12	1	9	60	59	37
K-2	22	10	3	9	72	64	33
Graig-Y-Rhacca	22	9	3	10	69	55	30
Albion Rovers	22	10	0	12	62	68	30
Shaftesbury Youth	22	8	2	12	38	75	26
Sporting Baneswell Social	22	7	4	11	65	75	25
Villa Dino Christchurch	22	6	1	15	46	79	19
Ty-Sign	22	6	1	15	52	87	19
Pontnewydd United	22	5	0	17	41	118	15

Bettws Social Club - record expunged.

Marshfield - record expunged.

Division Two	P	W	D	L	F	A	Pts
Newport Corinthians	20	15	2	3	87	38	47
Newport Eagles	20	14	2	4	95	42	44
Gaer Park Rangers	20	13	3	4	80	57	42
Machen	20	13	0	7	85	55	39
Cromwell Youth	20	12	1	7	73	55	37
Llanyrafon	20	10	1	9	66	64	31
Racing Club Newport	20	7	1	12	40	61	22
Cwmcarn Athletic	20	6	3	11	45	56	21
Cwmbran Celtic	20	6	1	13	48	68	19
Caerleon Town	20	4	0	16	30	84	12
Rogerstone	20	2	2	16	20	89	8

Bettws Social Club - record expunged.

Lliswerry - record expunged.

Pill Hibernians - record expunged.

Division Three	P	W	D	L	F	A	Pts
Bettws Socialdad	26	25	1	0	171	21	76
Racing Club Newport	26	20	2	4	87	31	62
Riverside Tavern	26	18	2	6	126	59	56
Lucas Cwmbran	26	14	6	6	93	53	48
Pill26	14	2	10	72	60	44	
Ferns	26	13	2	11	72	71	41
FC Pockets	26	12	3	11	70	75	39
AC Pontymister	26	12	1	13	70	64	37
Ponthir	26	9	1	16	43	83	28
CCYP	26	7	3	16	56	102	24
Risca Athletic	26	6	4	16	69	97	22
Albion Rovers	26	6	4	16	66	131	22
Coed Eva Athletic	26	4	5	17	55	129	17
Newport Eagles	26	4	0	22	40	114	12

PEMBROKESHIRE LEAGUE

Division One	P	W	D	L	F	A	Pts
Hakin United (-1)	26	22	2	2	107	43	67
Tenby	26	19	4	3	100	24	61
Goodwick United	26	19	3	4	90	45	60
Merlins Bridge (-1)	26	17	5	4	92	41	55
Haverfordwest County	26	15	4	7	85	45	49
Pennar Robins	26	12	4	10	66	52	40
Neyland	26	11	3	12	49	59	36
Johnston	26	8	7	11	43	58	31
Solva	26	7	5	14	59	78	26
Clarbeston Road	26	8	1	17	49	98	25
Hundleton	26	7	3	16	49	80	24
Narberth	26	6	3	17	56	85	21
Herbrandston	26	5	4	17	47	84	19
Kilgetty	26	1	2	23	28	128	5

Division Two	P	W	D	L	F	A	Pts
Monkton Swifts	26	21	2	3	113	44	65
Milford United	26	18	7	1	81	27	61
St Ishmaels	26	15	7	4	70	38	52
Carew	26	16	4	6	57	31	52
Goodwick United II	26	13	5	8	55	44	44
Milford Athletic	26	11	3	12	54	48	36
Lamphey	26	10	4	12	55	59	34
Saundersfoot Sports	26	9	6	11	54	59	33
Prendergast Villa	26	9	5	12	32	43	32
Letterston	26	8	6	12	37	65	30
Angle	26	7	3	16	44	70	24
Camrose	26	7	3	16	39	66	24
Pendine (-3)	26	5	4	17	41	92	16
St Clears (-3)	26	1	5	20	27	73	5

Division Three	P	W	D	L	F	A	Pts
Hakin United II	26	19	5	2	88	33	62
West Dragons	26	20	1	5	95	34	61
Broad Haven	26	16	5	5	88	43	53
Lawrenny	26	15	2	9	66	47	47
Tenby II	26	15	1	10	89	59	46
Merlins Bridge II (-4)	26	14	4	8	110	68	42
Pennar Robins II	26	11	4	11	71	65	37
Narberth II	26	10	3	13	68	86	33
Haverfordwest Cricket Club	26	9	5	12	60	58	32
Hubberston (-3)	26	10	2	14	64	93	29
Manorbier United	26	7	5	14	52	83	26
Pembroke Boro	26	4	6	16	52	78	18
Solva II (-3)	26	4	4	18	38	121	13
Herbrandston II	26	3	3	20	31	104	12

Division Four	P	W	D	L	F	A	Pts
Johnston II	26	19	5	2	87	32	62
Clarbeston Road II	26	19	4	3	101	55	61
Monkton Swifts II	26	17	3	6	109	43	54
St Florence	26	15	3	8	73	61	48
Fishguard Sports	26	14	0	12	81	72	42
Milford United II (-1)	26	11	2	13	58	57	34
St Ishmaels II	26	10	3	13	69	79	33
Milford Athletic II	26	10	2	14	64	69	32
Carew II	26	9	4	13	57	75	31
Camrose II	26	10	1	15	59	83	31
Saundersfoot Sports II (-1)	26	10	1	15	74	92	30
Prendergast Villa II	26	9	1	16	55	70	28
Kilgetty II	26	8	3	15	52	100	27
Hundleton II	26	4	2	20	44	95	14

Division Five	P	W	D	L	F	A	Pts
Cosheston Cougars	18	17	0	1	101	24	51
Pennar Robins III	18	13	0	5	78	26	39
Neyland II	18	11	0	7	45	32	33
West Dragons II	18	9	1	8	60	62	28
Haverfordwest Cricket Cl. II	18	8	2	8	44	50	26
Lawrenny II	18	7	2	9	34	55	23
Letterston II	18	6	3	9	31	58	21
Fishguard Sports II	18	4	2	12	25	62	14
St Clears II (-3)	18	5	1	12	33	55	13
Pembroke Boro II	18	3	3	12	35	62	12

WELSH NATIONAL LEAGUE (WREXHAM) AREA)

Premier	P	W	D	L	F	A	Pts
Penycae	30	21	2	7	85	36	65
Venture	30	19	6	5	83	38	63
Coedpoeth United	30	18	6	6	84	56	60
Chirk AAA	30	18	4	8	60	38	58
FC Cefn	30	16	7	7	92	65	55
Corwen	30	15	6	9	56	41	51
Hawarden Rangers	30	15	5	10	73	55	50
Overton	30	11	8	11	60	57	41
Llangollen Town	30	11	7	12	66	73	40
Mold Alexandra	30	11	6	13	53	62	39
Llay Welfare	30	11	4	15	51	65	37
Johnstown Youth	30	8	7	15	43	81	31
Gresford Athletic	30	7	6	17	40	61	27
Brymbo	30	5	7	18	43	78	22
Brickfield Rangers	30	5	4	21	44	85	19
Lex X1	30	4	5	21	41	83	17

WELSH LEAGUES

Division One	P	W	D	L	F	A	Pts
Penyffordd	24	18	3	3	84	31	57
Borras Park Albion	24	17	5	2	77	28	56
Saltney Town	24	15	4	5	73	45	49
New Brighton	24	14	4	6	58	37	46
Castell Alun Colts	24	12	3	9	52	54	39
Buckley United	24	11	3	10	51	38	36
Acrefair Youth (-3)	24	11	4	9	65	57	34
Garden Village	24	8	6	10	47	52	30
Llanuwchllyn	24	8	5	11	57	48	29
Penley (-3)	24	8	4	12	59	59	25
Mold Juniors	24	4	4	16	33	67	16
Hawkesbury Villa	24	3	4	17	23	75	13
Glyn Ceiriog	24	1	3	20	19	107	6

Reserve Division	P	W	D	L	F	A	Pts
Rhos Aelwyd reserves	28	23	3	2	114	35	72
Ruthin Town reserves	28	22	1	5	80	32	67
Airbus UK reserves (-3)	28	18	6	4	77	32	57
Bala Town reserves	28	16	2	10	74	43	50
Chirk AAA reerves	28	14	7	7	72	46	49
Penycae reserves (-3)	28	15	1	12	94	61	43
Cefn Druids reserves	28	12	5	11	75	66	41
Coedpoeth United res.	28	11	5	12	47	56	38
Borras Park Albion res.	28	12	2	14	47	57	38
Corwen reserves	28	11	4	13	51	61	37
Hawarden Rangers res.	28	10	2	16	54	67	32
Llay Welfare reserves	28	7	4	17	42	76	25
Castell Alun Colts res.	28	5	5	18	45	88	20
Gresford Athletic res.	28	3	5	20	28	101	14
Lex XI reserves	28	1	8	19	36	115	11

Reserve & Colts Division	P	W	D	L	F	A	Pts
Airbus UK Colts	30	20	3	7	92	42	63
Venture reserves	30	18	3	9	82	70	57
Rhos Aelwyd Colts	30	16	8	6	76	38	56
Overton reserves	30	15	8	7	68	46	53
New Brighton reserves	30	15	6	9	83	61	51
Ruthin Town Colts	30	15	4	11	75	54	49
FC Cefn reserves	30	12	9	9	75	65	45
Penyffordd reserves	30	12	8	10	84	81	44
Johnstown Youth reserves	30	11	8	11	80	77	41
Acrefair Youth reserves (-3)	30	14	0	16	82	90	39
Saltney Town reserves	30	11	5	14	60	71	38
Brymbo reserves	30	9	9	12	63	60	36
Penley reserves	30	9	5	16	69	109	32
Borras Park Albion Colts	30	7	5	18	63	88	26
Brickfield Rangers reserves	30	6	5	19	44	102	23
Garden Village reserves (-3)	30	6	2	22	52	94	17

WELSH CUP

FIRST QUALIFYING ROUND

Fleur de Lys 5-0 Talgarth Town (@ Talgarth Town)
STM Sports 3-0 Llantwit Fardre
Llanwern 2-1 Tredegar Town
Baglan Dragons 1-2 Fochriw (@ Fochriw)
Ferndale & District 0-3 Bridgend Street
South Gower 2-0 Cadoxton Barry
Treowen Stars 6-0 Cornelly United
Pontyclun 3-1 Rhydyfelin
Penrhiwceiber Constitutional 1-1 RTB Ebbw Vale
(RTB Ebbw Vale won 4-3 on penalties)
Cardiff Hibernian 3-4 Cwmbran Town
Brecon Corinthians 0-5 Monmouth Town
Newport Civil Service 2-3 Goytre
Corus Steel 1-0 Cwmamman United
Trethomas Bluebirds 2-1 Llandrindod Wells
Risca United 0-1 Pontypridd Town
Penclawdd scr-w/o Seven Sisters
Troedyrhiw 3-3 Nelson Cavaliers
(Nelson Cavaliers won 4-3 on penalties)
Penmaenmawr Phoenix 4-1 Glantraeth
Halkyn United 2-3 Amlwch Town
Aberaeron 0-7 Bodedern Athletic
Greenfield 5-3 Machynlleth
Connah's Quay Town 10-3 Llanfair United
Y Felinhelli 2-1 Blaenau Ffestiniog
Tregaron Turfs 2-3 Montgomery Town
Treaddur Bay United 1-0 Brynford United
Caernarfon Wanderers 2-7 Bro Goronwy
Llandyrnog United 1-1 Llanystumdwy
(Llandyrnog United won 4-2 on penalties)
Bethel 0-2 FC Nomads of Connah's Quay
Meifod 1-2 Gaerwen
Llanllyfni 3-2 Borras Park Albion
(Borras Park Albion won 4-2 on penalties)

Second Qualifying Round

Cardiff Bay Harlequins 2-1 Llanwern
Briton Ferry Llansawel 1-2 Pontypridd Town
Abertillery Bluebirds 1-2 Pontyclun
Bridgend Street 11-1 Fochriw
Corus Steel 3-2 AFC Llwydcoed
Ammanford 3-0 Presteigne St Andrews
Hay St Marys 1-5 AFC Porth
Cwmaman Institute 1-0 Aberbargoed Buds
Ton Pentre 0-1 Bettws
Treowen Stars 2-3 Treharris Athletic Western
Nelson Cavaliers 2-4 Monmouth Town

UWIC 2-1 Cwmbran Town
Goytre 5-4 Llangenior
Ely Rangers 3-2 Caerleon
Caerau 4-1 Newport YMCA
Newbridge on Wye 3-5 South Gower
STM Sports 4-3 Trethomas Bluebirds
Seven Sisters 0-1 Croesyceiliog
RTB Ebbw Vale 1-4 Fleur de Lys
Newcastle Emlyn 2-1 Dinas Powys
Pwllheli 5-1 Bodedern Athletic
Borras Park Albion 7-3 Glan Conwy
Llandyrnog United 4-2 Llangollen Town
Llanidloes Town 2-1 Llansantffraid Village
Gwalchmai 4-0 Dyffryn Banw
Barmouth & Dyffryn United 3-2 Hawarden Rangers
Dyffryn Nantle Vale 0-1 Llanrhaeadr ym Mochnant
Penycae 3-1 Llanrug United
Tywyn Bryncrug 3-2 Berriew
Llanberis 0-4 Brickfield Rangers
Venture Community 2-3 Johnstown Youth
Bro Goronwy 2-4 Connah's Quay Town
Conwy United 2-1 Denbigh Town
Brymbo 0-4 Waterloo Rovers
Corwen 0-1 Dolgellau A A
Gaerwen 1-3 Greenfield
Montgomery Town 1-2 Penmaenmawr Phoenix
Gresford Athletic 0-4 Penparcau (@ Penparcau)
Llandudno Junction 2-4 Holyhead Hotspurs
Llay Welfare 2-4 Bow Street
Y Felinhelli 3-5 Bethesda Athletic
Amlwch Town 1-3 Coedpoeth United
Lex XI 3-2 FC Nomads of Connah's Quay
Carno 4-3 Chirk AAA
Caernarfon Town 5-1 Holywell Town
Treaddur Bay United 3-0 Mold Alexandra
Overton Recreational 1-3 Llanfairpwll
Llanrwst United 1-2 Nefyn United (@ Nefyn United)

ROUND 1

Barry Town 3-0 STM Sports
Bettws 0-3 Aberaman Athletic
Bridgend Town 5-3 Monmouth Town
Bryntirion Athletic 0-0 Cwmbran Celtic (Bryntirion Athletic won 4-2 on penalties)
Caerau 1-3 Afan Lido
Cardiff Grange Harlequins 4-2 Bridgend Street
Corus Steel 5-2 Cardiff Corinthians
Croesyceiliog 0-2 Garden Village
Cwmaman Institute 1-2 Taffs Well
Fleur de Lys 1-0 Ely Rangers
Goytre 3-1 Caerau Ely
Goytre United 5-3 Ammanford
Newcastle Emlyn 4-0 South Gower
Penrhiwceiber Rangers 0-2 Cambrian & Clydach Vale
Pontypridd Town 2-0 Pontardawe Town
Treharris Athletic Western 2-1 Pontyclun
UWIC 2-0 Caldicot Town
West End 1-2 AFC Porth
Borras Park Albion 0-8 Rhos Alewyd
Bow Street 2-1 Lex XI
Brickfield Rangers 3-4 Bethesda Athletic
Caersws 4-0 Rhayader Town
Carno 1-5 Porthmadog (@ Porthmadog)
Cefn Druids 6-4 Penycae
Coedpoeth United 4-3 Greenfield
Connah's Quay Town 6-1 Johnstown Youth
Conwy United 4-1 Waterloo Rovers
CPD Gwalchmai 4-0 Barmouth & Dyffryn United
Dolgellau A A 1-2 Llandudno Town (@ Llandudno Town)
Holyhead Hotspurs 4-1 Technogroup Welshpool
Llandyrnog United 1-5 Flint Town United
Llangefni Town 3-2 Llanfairpwll
Llanidloes Town 1-0 Ruthin Town
Llanrhaedr ym Mochnant 0-5 Rhyl
Nefyn United 3-2 Tywyn & Bryncrug
Penmaenmawr Phoenix 3-5 Caernarfon Town
Penrhyncoch 2-2 Guilsfield (Guilsfield won 6-4 on penalties)
Pwllheli 1-5 Gap Connah's Quay
Rhydymwyn 1-4 Buckley Town
Trearddur Bay United 7-3 Penparcau

ROUND 2

Goytre United 3-1 Fleur de Lys
Pontypridd Town 1-2 Bryntirion Athletic
Afan Lido 1-2 Cambrian & Clydach Vale
A F C Porth 2-0 Goytre
Barry Town 1-2 Corus Steel
Garden Village 1-6 Aberaman Athletic
Taffs Well 2-4 Bridgend Town
Newcastle Emlyn 1-4 U W I C
Cardiff Grange Harlequins 3-0 Treharris Atheltic Western
Flint Town United 3-4 Llanidloes Town
Nefyn United 1-3 Caersws
Gap Connah's Quay 6-1 Bethesda Athletic
Holyhead Hotspurs 1-0 Llangefni Town
Caernarfon Town 1-2 Guilsfield
Trearddur Bay United 0-7 Cefn Druids
Connah's Quay Town 1-2 Bow Street
Rhos Aelwyd 2-1 Coedpoeth United
Gwalchmai 2-2 Buckley Town
(Gwalchmai won 4-2 on penalties)
Rhyl 2-1 Llandudno Town
Conwy United 1-4 Porthmadog

ROUND 3

Cous Steel 0-2 Cardiff Grange Harlequins

Airbus U K Broughton 2-3 The New Saints

Newtown 1-2 Bridgend Town

Llanelli 1-0 Aberystwyth Town

Bow Street 2-2 U W I C (U W I C won 6-5 on penalties)

Guilsfield 1-2 Rhos Aelwyd

Haverfordwest County 3-2 Holyhead Hotspurs

Porthmadog 0-1 Bala Town

Gwalchmai 1-4 Port Talbot Town

Goytre United 2-3 Carmarthen Town

Aberaman Athletic 0-4 Cefn Druids

Cambrian & Clydach Vale 2-3 Prestatyn Town

Caersws 4-2 Llanidloes Town

Gap Connah's Quay 5-3 A F C Porth

Bangor City 2-1 Bryntirion Athletic

Neath 1-1 Rhyl (Rhyl won 7-6 on penalties)

ROUND 4

Bangor City 5-3 Haverfordwest County

Cardiff Grange Harlequins 1-0 Bridgend Town

Carmarthen Town 2-3 Gap Connah's Quay

Cefn Druids 1-4 Llaenlli

Port Talbot Town 3-0 Caersws

Rhos Aelwyd 1-6 Prestatyn Town

Rhyl 1-7 The New Saints

U W I C 4-1 Bala Town

QUARTER FINALS

Gap Connah's Quay 4-0 U W I C

Port Talbot Town 0-3 Bangor City

The New Saints 2-0 Cardiff Grange Harlequins

Llanelli 1-0 Prestatyn Town

SEMI-FINALS

Bangor City 1-0 Gap Connah's Quay (@ Rhyl)

The New Saints 0-1 Llanelli (@ Aberystwyth Town)

FINAL (@ Parc y Scarlets, Llanelli, 8/5/11)

Bangor City 1-4 Llanelli

WELSH TROPHY

ROUND 1

Aberaeron 3-1 CPD Llansannan

Acrefair Youth 6-5 Tywyn & Bryncrug

Barmouth & Dyffryn United 4-1 Johnstown Youth

Berriew 2-0 Bow Street

Bethesda Athletic 4-1 Corwen

Bodedern Athletic 3-2 Llanrhaedr ym Mochnant

Brickfield Rangers 3-4 Glantraeth

Brymbo 3-4 Mold Alexandra

Caernarfon Town 3-2 Abergele Rovers

Caernarfon Wanderers 0-4 Llandudno Junction

Carno 1-1 Bont (@ Bont. Bont won 8-7 on penalties)

Connah's Quay Town 1-3 Penmaenmawr Phoenix

CPD Dyffryn Nantlle 1-2 Coedpoeth United

CPD Llanberis 2-3 Nefyn United

CPD Llanuwchllyn 1-5 Penycae

CPD Y Felinheli 3-3 Llangollen Town
(Llangollen Town won 5-4 on penalties)

FC Nomads of Connah's Quay 3-1 Brynford United
(@ Brynford United)

Gaerwen 0-4 Glan Conwy

Holywell Town 0-4 Chirk AAA

Llandyrnog United 5-1 Llanllyfni

Llanfairpwll 6-1 CPD Bethel

Llanidloes Town 1-0 Borras Park Albion

Llanrug United 3-4 Conwy United

Llanrwst United 2-0 Amlwch Town (@ Amlwch Town)

Llanystumdwy 2-4 Montgomery Town

Llay Welfare 2-4 Llansantffraid Village

Machynlleth 2-1 Caerwys

Meliden 2-1 Denbigh Town

Mountain Rangers scr-w/o Blaenau Ffestiniog

Overton Recreational 3-0 Tregaron Turfs

Rhosgoch Rangers 1-7 Gresford Athletic

Venture Community 2-4 Pwllheli

Baglan Dragons 1-3 Llangynwydd Rangers

Baili Glas 0-11 Newport YMCA

Bonymaen Colts 2-3 Panteg

Carnetown BGC 1-0 STM Sports

Cefn Forest 6-2 Graig y Rhacca

Coed Eva Athletic 1-1 Lisvane/Llanishen
(Lisvane/Llanishen won 4-2 on penalties)

Cogan Coronation 1-2 Abercarn United

Creigiau 2-0 Cathays Tennants

Cwmbach Royal Stars 5-2 Cornelly United

Cwmfelin Press 0-5 Perthcelyn United

Fleur de Lys 6-3 Tongwynlais

Gors 1-3 Cardiff Hibernian
Kenfig Hill 2-3 Abertillery Excelsiors
Llandrindod Wells 1-0 Cadoxton Barry
Margam Youth Centre 1-4 Splott Albion
New Inn 3-2 Villa Dino Christchurch
Newbridge on Wye 2-4 Llanharry
Newport Civil Service 4-1 Pengelli United
Pennar Robins 6-2 Presteigne St Andrews
Pentwynmawr Welfare 2-1 Clydach Wasps
Pontnewydd United 1-3 Graig
Pontyclun 6-1 Nelson Cavaliers
Race 1-2 CRC Rangers
Rhydyfelin 4-6 Lucas Cwmbran
Risca United 9-0 Waunarllwydd
RTB Ebbw Vale 4-3 Bryn Rovers
Seaside w/o-scr AC Central
Sully Sports 4-0 Penrhiwceiber Constitutional Athletic
Swansea Dockers 6-2 Ferndale Boys Club
The VNU 0-5 Ragged School
Ton & Gelli B C 5-1 S P Construction
Ynystawe Athletic 4-1 Garw SBGC

ROUND 2

Aberaeron 0-2 Holywell Town
Blaenau Ffestiniog 2-0 Montgomery Town
Caernarfon Town 8-5 Nefyn United
Coedpoeth United 5-1 Bont
Glan Conwy 3-2 Berriew
Gresford Athletic 5-1 Acrefair Youth
Llandudno Junction 2-1 Llanrwst United
Llangollen Town 3-1 Barmouth & Dyffryn United
Llanidloes Town 2-1 F C Nomads Of Connah's Quay
Machynlleth 3-6 Conwy United
Meliden 0-2 Bethesda Athletic
Mold Alexandra 0-6 Llansantffraid Village
Overton Recreational 1-4 Llanfairpwll
Penmaenmawr Phoenix 1-2 Glantraeth
Penycae 0-1 Bodedern Athletic
Pwllheli 2-1 Llandyrnog United
Abercarn United 3-0 Creigiau
Abertillery Bluebirds 3-3 Sully Sports
(Abertillery Bluebirds won 7-6 on penalties)
Cardiff Hibernian 2-0 Perthlcelyn United
Carnetown B G C 4-1 Seaside
Graig 1-3 Ragged School
Llandrindod Wells 1-3 Pentwynmawr Welfare
Llangynwyd Rangers 1-1 Ynystawe Athletic
(Llangynwyd Rangers won 4-3 on penalties)
Llanharry 1-3 Splott Albion
Lucas Cwmbran 2-8 C R C Rangers
New Inn 6-3 Fleur de Lys Welfare
Panteg 5-1 Lisvane/Llanishen
Pennar Robins 1-2 Ton & Gelli B C
Pontyclun 6-4 Cefn Fforest
Risca United 6-1 Cwmbach Royal Stars
R T B Ebbw Vale 2-3 Newport Y M C A
Swansea Dockers 3-1 Newport Civil Service

ROUND 3

Bethesda Athletic 2-3 Conwy United
Blaenau Ffestiniog 0-5 Llanfairpwll
Glan Conwy 2-0 Caernarfon Town
Glantraeth 2-1 Bodedern Athletic
Gresford Athletic 3-2 Llansantffraid Village
Holywell Town 11-1 Llangollen Town
Llanidloes Town 1-3 Coedpoeth United
Pwllheli 3-1 Llandudno Junction
Cardiff Hibernian 4-1 Pentwynmawr Welfare
Carnetown B G C 5-0 C R C Rangers
Llangynwyd Rangers 1-2 Swansea Dockers
New Inn 4-3 Abercarn United
Pontyclun 4-2 Panteg
Ragged School 3-2 Newport Y M C A
Risca United 1-0 Abertillery Excelsiors
Splott Albion 1-4 Ton & Gelli B C

ROUND 4

Coedpoeth United 3-4 Glan Conwy (@ Glan Conwy)
Glantraeth 3-4 Conwy United
Holywell Town 3-1 Gresford Athletic
Pwllheli 1-2 Llanfairpwll
New Inn 1-4 Carnetown B G C
Pontyclun 0-1 Ton & Gelli B C (@ Ton & Gelli B C)
Ragged School 2-1 Cardiff Hibernian
Risca United 2-5 Swansea Dockers

QUARTER FINALS

Conwy United 2-1 Swansea Dockers
Glan Conwy 3-2 Ragged School
Holywell Town 3-2 Carnetown
Llanfairpwll 2-2 Ton & Gelli B C
(Ton & Gelli B C won 5-3 on penalties)

SEMI-FINALS

Glan Conwy 1-2 Conwy United (@ Llandudno)
Ton & Gelli B C 1-3 Holywell Town (@ Llanidloes Town)

FINAL (@ Rhyl, 16/4/11)

SCOTTISH TABLES 2010-11

EAST OF SCOTLAND LEAGUE

Premier Division	P	W	D	L	F	A	Pts
Spartans	22	17	4	1	62	18	55
Stirling University	22	12	5	5	57	28	41
Lothian Thistle	22	10	4	8	40	36	34
Whitehill Welfare	22	9	5	8	32	29	32
Edinburgh University	22	8	8	6	27	26	32
Edinburgh City	22	6	13	3	32	30	31
Vale of Leithen	22	7	9	6	30	29	30
Civil Service Strollers	22	8	5	9	29	37	29
Tynecastle	22	6	6	10	32	34	24
Selkirk	22	4	5	13	31	54	17
Preston Athletic	22	4	5	13	30	61	17
Heriot-Watt University	22	3	7	12	27	47	16

Division One	P	W	D	L	F	A	Pts
Gretna 2008	22	19	1	2	85	18	58
Leith Athletic	22	18	2	2	79	24	56
Eyemouth United	22	12	4	6	62	49	40
Gala Fairydean	22	11	4	7	54	49	37
Easthouses Lily	22	10	5	7	45	33	35
Craigroyston	22	8	6	8	42	36	30
Peebles Rovers	22	9	3	10	36	58	30
Berwick Rangers res	22	8	2	12	43	50	26
Coldstream	22	7	2	13	34	48	23
Kelso United	22	4	8	10	40	52	20
Ormiston	22	2	7	13	25	49	13
Hawick Royal Albert	22	1	2	19	17	96	5

HIGHLAND LEAGUE

	P	W	D	L	F	A	Pts
Buckie Thistle	34	24	5	5	84	42	77
Deveronvale	34	23	3	8	100	45	72
Cove Rangers	34	22	5	7	100	43	71
Keith	34	22	4	8	93	54	70
Nairn County	34	18	9	7	86	49	63
Forres Mechanics	34	19	6	9	72	56	63
Inverurie Loco Works	34	19	5	10	81	50	62
Turriff United	34	15	8	11	89	60	53
Formartine United	34	15	3	16	71	68	48
Huntly	34	13	6	15	63	72	45
Brora Rangers	34	13	6	15	51	64	45
Lossiemouth	34	12	8	14	52	63	44
Fraserburgh	34	11	9	14	69	65	42
Wick Academy	34	12	3	19	75	78	39
Clachnacuddin	34	9	7	18	68	89	34
Rothes	34	6	4	24	43	92	22
Strathspey Thistle	34	2	4	28	36	131	10
Fort William	34	2	3	29	36	148	9

SOUTH OF SCOTLAND LEAGUE

	P	W	D	L	F	A	Pts
Threave Rovers	24	20	2	2	100	36	62
Dalbeattie Star	24	19	3	2	73	21	60
St Cuthbert Wand.	24	19	2	3	83	32	59
Stranraer “A”	24	12	4	8	61	40	40
Crichton	24	9	6	9	63	63	33
Newton Stewart	24	8	6	10	53	58	30
Mid-Annandale	24	8	5	11	45	53	29
Heston Rovers	24	7	5	12	42	59	26
Creetown	24	8	2	14	40	61	26
Wigtown	24	6	6	12	31	53	24
Fleet Star	24	6	3	15	31	65	21
Nithsdale Wanderers	24	7	0	17	36	75	21
Abbey Vale	24	4	2	18	30	72	14

SJFA EAST REGION

Superleague	P	W	D	L	F	A	Pts
Boness United	22	12	6	4	38	26	42
Hill of Beath Hawthorn	22	10	9	3	33	22	39
Linlithgow Rose	22	12	3	7	46	37	39
Bonnyrigg Rose	22	11	4	7	33	31	37
Lochee United	22	10	5	7	37	30	35
Forfar West End	22	8	6	8	34	31	30
Musselburgh Athletic	22	8	3	11	36	46	27
Bathgate Thistle	22	6	8	8	33	40	26
Kelty Hearts	22	7	3	12	26	35	24
Camelon Juniors	22	6	6	10	32	43	24
Tayport	22	6	4	12	30	33	22
Newtongrange Star	22	6	3	13	33	37	21

Premier League	P	W	D	L	F	A	Pts
St Andrews United	22	17	3	2	51	21	54
Carnoustie Panmure	22	12	6	4	48	32	42
Broxburn Athletic	22	13	2	7	58	35	41
Glenrothes	22	11	3	8	56	39	36
Penicuik Athletic	22	9	5	8	39	35	32
Ballingry Rovers	22	9	4	9	40	49	31
Armadale Thistle	22	7	7	8	34	33	28
Broughty Athletic	22	7	7	8	44	49	28
Arniston Rangers	22	8	3	11	27	41	27
Kinnoull	22	7	2	13	32	48	23
Whitburn Juniors	22	5	3	14	29	48	18
Thornton Hibs	22	2	5	15	32	60	11

Central Division	P	W	D	L	F	A	Pts
Oakley United	24	19	2	3	85	15	59
Dundonald Bluebell	24	17	2	5	70	36	53
Kirkcaldy YM	24	15	4	5	67	39	49
Jeanfield Swifts	24	15	2	7	60	36	47
Lochgelly Albert	24	14	3	7	55	37	45
Bankfoot	24	11	4	9	49	38	37
Lochore Welfare	24	11	3	10	49	46	36
Steelend Vics	24	10	4	10	58	53	34
Crossgates Primrose	24	8	5	11	39	44	29
Scone Thistle	24	7	2	15	43	76	23
Newburgh	24	5	4	15	40	61	19
Rosyth	24	5	3	16	47	62	18
Luncarty	24	0	0	24	19	138	0

North Division	P	W	D	L	F	A	Pts
Downfield	24	16	4	4	55	26	52
Dundee North End	24	16	4	4	59	32	52
Dundee Violet	24	14	4	6	67	34	46
Montrose Roselea	24	13	5	6	41	25	44
Arbroath Vics	24	12	5	7	57	40	41
Arbroath SC	24	11	5	8	47	31	38
Kirriemuir Thistle	24	10	8	6	63	49	38
Blairgowrie	24	11	4	9	58	52	37
Brechin Vics	24	7	4	13	36	54	25
Lochee Harp	24	5	6	13	29	45	21
East Craigie	24	5	5	14	35	58	20
Forfar Albion	24	3	6	15	32	67	15
Coupar Angus	24	2	2	20	22	88	8

South Division	P	W	D	L	F	A	Pts
Sauchie Juniors	26	18	6	2	87	24	60
Fauldhouse United	26	17	2	7	65	44	53
Livingston United	26	15	5	6	57	33	50
Haddington Athletic	26	15	4	7	68	39	49
Tranent Juniors	26	14	3	9	63	41	45
Stoneyburn Juniors	26	13	5	8	44	39	44
Blackburn United	26	13	3	10	43	33	42
Edinburgh United	26	10	4	12	61	59	34
Spartans	26	10	2	14	59	58	32
Dunbar United	26	8	5	13	36	55	29
West Calder United	26	8	4	14	42	65	28
Dalkeith Thistle	26	7	6	13	43	59	27
Pumpherston Juniors	26	4	3	19	34	66	15
Harthill Royal	26	2	4	20	21	108	10

SJFA NORTH REGION

Superleague	P	W	D	L	F	A	Pts
Culter	26	19	3	4	92	34	60
Hall Russell United	26	15	3	8	71	35	48
Hermes	26	13	2	11	56	51	41
Banks O'Dee	26	13	1	12	53	41	40
Dyce Juniors	26	12	4	10	53	43	40
Sunnybank	26	12	3	11	55	56	39
Banchory St Ternan	26	12	3	11	53	57	39
Lewis United	26	11	5	10	57	65	38
Maud	26	11	3	12	49	56	36
Stonehaven	26	11	2	12	56	61	35
Ellon United	26	8	9	9	33	45	33
FC Stoneywood	26	10	2	14	37	65	32
Longside	26	7	4	15	36	35	25
Fraserburgh United	26	3	6	17	38	68	15

Division One	P	W	D	L	F	A	Pts
Inverness City	26	21	1	4	89	25	64
Forres Thistle	26	17	3	6	64	36	54
Glentanar	26	16	3	7	60	35	51
New Elgin	26	16	2	8	61	43	50
Islavale	26	14	5	7	52	43	47
Buchanhaven Hearts	26	14	4	8	54	53	46
Lossiemouth United	26	10	3	13	50	60	33
Hillhead	26	9	5	12	46	45	32
Deveronside	26	9	4	13	51	56	31
East End	26	8	3	15	53	60	27
Burghead Thistle	26	7	3	16	38	54	24
Dufftown	26	7	3	16	35	59	24
Buckie Rovers	26	5	5	16	40	80	20
Bishopmill United	26	5	3	18	38	75	18

SCOTTISH AMATEUR FA LEAGUES

ABERDEENSHIRE AMATEUR FOOTBALL ASSOCIATION

Premier Division	P	W	D	L	F	A	Pts
Kincorth	26	18	5	3	80	40	59
University	26	16	6	4	74	31	54
Cowie Thistle	26	16	0	10	64	46	48
Sportsmans Club	26	13	4	9	66	56	43
Woodside	26	13	4	9	49	42	43
Echt	26	10	7	9	53	51	37
Westdyke	26	10	4	12	48	49	34
Dyce ITC Hydraulics	26	10	4	12	56	62	34
Kintore	26	9	6	11	54	80	33
Bon-Accord City	26	9	5	12	49	46	32
Tarves	26	8	4	14	51	57	28
Old Aberdonians	26	7	6	13	41	55	27
Beacon Rangers (-7)	26	7	5	14	55	84	19
AC Mill Inn	26	4	4	18	37	78	16

SCOTTISH FOOTBALL

Division One North	P	W	D	L	F	A	Pts
Mearns United	24	17	2	5	80	39	53
Great Western United	24	15	2	7	60	43	47
Insch	24	12	4	8	56	46	40
MS United	24	12	3	9	57	53	39
Rattrays XI	24	11	6	7	63	52	39
Lads Club Amateurs	24	8	9	7	49	39	33
West End	24	9	4	11	46	56	31
Banchory	24	8	7	9	37	45	31
Nicolls Amateurs	24	8	6	10	62	64	30
Stonehaven Athletic	24	8	4	12	52	63	28
Ellon Thistle	24	7	7	10	39	55	28
Hazlehead United	24	8	3	13	51	60	27
Bervie Caledonian	24	2	5	17	26	63	11

FC Geldie - record expunged.

Division Two East	P	W	D	L	F	A	Pts
Rothie Rovers	26	18	4	4	85	36	58
Westhill	26	15	7	4	72	43	52
Johnshaven Athletic	26	14	7	5	86	45	49
Burghmuir	26	15	3	8	62	47	48
Feughside	26	14	4	8	74	57	46
Kemnay Youth	26	10	7	9	53	55	37
FC Polska	26	10	4	12	68	72	34
McTeagle	26	10	3	13	47	56	33
Mintlaw	26	9	2	15	44	75	29
Mugiemoss Youth (-7)	26	10	5	11	63	76	28
University Colts	26	7	3	16	49	68	24
Highland Hotel	26	5	3	18	33	84	18
Huntly Amateurs	26	3	4	19	28	67	13
Ferryhill (-42)	26	12	4	10	73	56	-2

Division Three	P	W	D	L	F	A	Pts
JS XI	26	21	1	4	100	45	64
St Laurence	26	16	4	6	95	56	52
Alford	26	17	0	9	97	59	51
West End Electrical	26	15	2	9	71	56	47
Cammachmore	26	14	3	9	78	59	45
Torphins	26	12	6	8	89	68	42
Northern United	26	13	2	11	62	56	41
Glentanar Reflex	26	12	3	11	59	65	39
Northern Hotspurs	26	12	3	11	61	73	39
Auchnagatt Barons	26	8	4	14	53	78	28
BSFC	26	7	6	13	41	57	27
Monymusk	26	6	2	18	35	93	20
Parkway Thistle	26	5	1	20	29	68	16
Fintray Thistle	26	3	5	18	36	73	14

Cruden Bay - record expunged.

BORDER AMATEUR LEAGUE

A League	P	W	D	L	F	A	Pts
Duns Ams	22	20	2	0	78	17	62
Leithen Rovers	22	17	2	3	74	41	53
Pencaitland	22	14	4	4	66	33	46
West Barns Star	22	12	0	10	70	51	36
Gala Rovers	22	10	4	8	34	40	34
Chirnside (-3)	22	9	4	9	44	44	28
Gordon	22	8	4	10	39	54	28
Newtown	22	7	1	14	41	68	22
Hawick Wav'ley	22	5	6	11	50	69	21
Hawick Legion	22	6	0	16	36	61	18
Jed Legion	22	5	3	14	28	61	18
Greenlaw	22	4	0	18	37	58	12

B League	P	W	D	L	F	A	Pts
Tweeddale R.	22	18	1	3	80	20	55
Langholm L.	22	17	3	2	52	23	54
Linton H.	22	13	0	9	75	47	39
Eyemouth	22	11	6	5	46	38	39
Stow	22	11	3	8	61	48	36
Ancrum	22	9	4	9	49	46	31
Tweedm'th A.	22	9	4	9	56	54	31
Chirnside C.	22	9	3	10	60	54	30
Coldstream A.	22	7	6	9	43	56	27
Hawick United (-3)	22	5	4	13	49	66	16
Earlston R.	22	3	2	17	38	83	11
Gala United (-6)	22	1	2	19	27	101	-1

C League	P	W	D	L	F	A	Pts
Selkirk Victoria	20	17	3	0	78	24	54
Hearts of L'dale	20	14	2	4	80	32	44
Gala Hotspur	20	11	3	6	71	52	36
Lauder (-3)	20	10	5	5	40	24	32
CFC Bowholm (-3)	20	8	4	8	49	41	25
Peebles RR	20	6	7	7	44	45	25
Hawick LR	20	5	6	9	34	62	21
St Boswells	20	6	1	13	28	71	19
Yetholm (-6)	20	6	5	9	39	55	17
Tweedm'th AC	20	4	2	14	28	42	14
Kelso Thistle (-9)	20	3	2	15	28	71	2

CALADONIAN LEAGUE

Premier Division	P	W	D	L	F	A	Pts
Bannockburn	22	15	5	2	59	28	50
Glasgow Harp	22	13	6	3	61	43	45
Cambusbarron Rovers	22	13	3	6	53	45	42
Milton	22	9	7	6	48	39	34
Strathclyde University	22	8	5	9	49	47	29
Giffnock North	22	8	4	10	44	42	28
Glasgow University	22	7	7	8	44	42	28
Dumbarton	22	6	8	8	42	46	26
St Mungo	22	7	4	11	41	46	25
Westerlands	22	5	8	9	32	41	23
Doune Castle	22	6	3	13	39	62	21
Balmore	22	4	2	16	43	74	14

DUMFRIES & DISTRICT AMATEUR LEAGUE

	P	W	D	L	F	A	Pts
Lochar Thistle	14	13	1	0	74	17	40
Lochmaben	14	10	1	3	51	20	31
Upper Annandale	14	9	2	3	56	24	29
Morton Thistle	14	7	1	6	32	40	22
Dynamo Star	14	6	1	7	41	46	19
Maxwelltown Thistle	14	5	1	8	41	33	16
YMCA	14	2	1	11	23	70	7
Terregles Athletic	14	0	0	14	14	82	0

SCOTTISH JUNIOR CUP

ROUND 1

Oakley United 1-2 Beith Juniors
Burghead Thistle 1-6 Vale of Leven
Bishopmill United 0-2 St Anthony's (@ Elgin City)
F C Stoneywood 2-2 Cumbernauld United
Dundee North End 0-2 Vale of Clyde
Auchinleck Talbot 4-1 Kirkcaldy Y M
Irvine Meadow XI 9-0 Buchanhaven Hearts
Sauchie Juniors 9-0 Nairn St Ninian
Spartans 3-3 Ballingry Rovers
Maybole Juniors 0-2 Shettleston
Lanark United 3-1 Inverness City
New Elgin 0-4 Port Glasgow Juniors
Islavale 2-1 West Calder United
Hurlford United 4-1 Hillhead Juniors
Wishaw Juniors 1-4 Annbank United
Bo'ness United 1-0 Dundee Violet
Kelty Hearts 0-1 Glenrothes Juniors
Larkhall Thistle 3-0 Fauldhouse United
Blairgowrie Juniors 2-0 Maud
Whitburn Juniors 6-0 R A F Lossiemouth
Dundee East Craigie 2-1 Crossgates Primrose
Hall Russell United 0-6 Armadale Thistle
Steelend Victoria 1-3 Ardrossan Winton Rovers
Blantyre Victoria 8-1 Irvine Victoria
Cumnock Juniors 1-1 Benburb
Parkvale 2-3 Lesmahagow Juniors
Ashfield 6-4 Carluke Rovers
Kilbirnie Ladeside 4-0 Newmachar United
Kilwinning Rangers 1-1 Penicuik Athletic
Camelon Juniors 1-2 Pollok
Buckie Rovers 0-2 Yoker Athletic
Kirriemuir Thistle 1-2 Stoneyburn
East Kilbride Thistle 2-2 Kirkintilloch Rob Roy
Largs Thistle 2-0 Royal Albert

ROUND 1 REPLAYS

Cumbernauld United 3-0 F C Stoneywood
Ballingry Rovers 0-0 Spartans (Ballingry Rovers won 4-2 on penalties)
Benburb 1-3 Cumnock Juniors
Penicuik Athletic 0-1 Kilwinning Rangers
Kirkintilloch Rob Roy 4-1 East Kilbride Thistle

ROUND 2

Aberdeen East End 3-3 Bankfoot Athletic
Pollok 0-1 Neilston Juniors
Thorniewood United 2-3 Lochee Harp (@ Bellshill Athletic)
St Anthony's 0-3 Shettleston
Longside 0-2 Ardrossan Winton Rovers
Kinnoull 2-2 Bo'ness United
Whitburn Juniors 3-6 Cumnock Juniors
Banchory St Ternan 1-1 Newburgh
Dufftown 0-5 Haddington Athletic
Luncarty 0-3 Lochee United
Kello Rovers 3-5 Banks O'Dee
Dyce Juniors 0-0 Stoneyburn
Forth Wanderers 1-2 Greenock Juniors
Blairgowrie Juniors 4-0 Deveronside
Newtongrange Star 6-1 Fraserburgh United
Glenafton Athletic 1-4 Bellshill Athletic
Kilbirnie Ladeside 5-4 Newmains United
Larkhall Thistle 3-2 Annbank United
Yoker Athletic 1-1 Saltcoats Victoria
Lugar Boswell Thistle 0-0 Lochgelly Albert
Dundee Downfield 2-3 Rosyth Recreation
Port Glasgow Juniors 0-0 Troon
Harthill Royal 0-9 Tayport
Livingston United 1-2 Hill of Beath Hawthorn
Whitehills 3-1 Fochabers
Dunipace 1-3 Lochore Welfare
Lanark United 2-1 Ballingry Rovers
Cruden Bay 0-8 Rutherglen Glencairn
Irvine Meadow XI 3-1 Bathgate Thistle

Blantyre Victoria 2-2 Ashfield

Bonnyrigg Rose Athletic 4-2 Johnstone Burgh

Dundee East Craigie 2-2 Stonehaven

Thornton Hibs 1-3 Kilsyth Rangers

Petershill 3-1 Dalkeith Thistle

Dundonald Bluebell 0-5 Auchinleck Talbot

Shotts Bon Accord 2-0 Lesmahagow Juniors

Jeanfield Swifts 1-4 Tranent Juniors

Broughty Athletic 2-0 Stonehouse Violet

Coupar Angus 1-4 Glasgow Perthshire

Edinburgh United 4-6 Girvan

Brechin Victoria 2-3 Dunbar United

Forres Thistle 0-6 Musselburgh Athletic

Carnoustie Panmure 1-2 Sauchie Juniors

Forfar Albion 1-3 Culter

Maryhill 4-0 Glentanar

Renfrew 2-1 Largs Thistle

Lossiemouth United 1-4 Forfar West End

Arbroath Sporting Club 1-2 Kirkintilloch Rob Roy

Dalry Thistle 7-1 St Roch's

Arniston Rangers 0-3 Arthurlie

Vale of Clyde 1-0 Kilwinning Rangers

Craigmark Burntonians 4-9 Sunnybank

Cambuslang Rangers 3-0 Montrose Roselea

Linlithgow Rose 1-0 Clydebank

Beith Juniors 5-1 Hurlford United

Darvel Juniors 4-1 Hermes

Cumbernauld United 0-2 Vale of Leven

Blackburn United 1-2 Pumpherston

Glenrothes Juniors 2-1 Scone Thistle

Islavale 1-0 Lewis United

Arbroath Victoria 1-4 St Andrews United

Ardeer Thistle 1-2 Broxburn Athletic

Whitletts Victoria 5-0 Ellon United

Muirkirk Juniors 2-0 Armadale Thistle

(@ Lugar Boswell Thistle)

ROUND 2 REPLAYS

Bankfoot Athletic 4-0 Aberdeen East End

Bo'ness United 4-0 Kinnoull

Newburgh 0-2 Banchory St Ternan

Stoneyburn 3-2 Dyce Juniors

Saltcoats Victoria 0-1 Yoker Athletic

Lochgelly Albert 3-3 Lugar Boswell Thistle (Lugar Boswell Thistle won 3-1 on penalties)

Troon 0-4 Port Glasgow Juniors

Ashfield 1-1 Blantyre Victoria (Blantyre Victoria won 4-3 on penalties)

Stonehaven 1-2 Dundee East Craigie

ROUND 3

Tayport 0-0 Petershill

Lanark United 0-1 Whitletts Victoria

Maryhill 5-0 Muirkirk Juniors

Forfar West End 1-3 Hill of Beath Hawthorn

Stoneyburn 1-5 Musselburgh Athletic

Haddington Athletic 2-1 Rosyth Recreation

Lochore Welfare 0-3 Cumnock Juniors

Neilston Juniors 1-0 Vale of Clyde

Larkhall Thistle 1-2 Greenock Juniors

Edinburgh United 2-5 Arthurlie

St Andrews United 1-2 Ardrossan Winton Rovers

Sunnybank 2-1 Glasgow Perthshire

Sauchie Juniors 4-1 Cambuslang Rangers

Banchory St Ternan 0-2 Vale of Leven

Glenrothes Juniors 3-0 Tranent Juniors

Kirkintilloch Rob Roy 5-2 Banks O'Dee

Blantyre Victoria 1-2 Broughty Athletic

(@ Ravenscraig Sports Complex)

Yoker Athletic 1-4 Bo'ness United

Shotts Bon Accord 0-1 Bellshill Athletic

Darvel Juniors 1-2 Kilsyth Rangers

Linlithgow Rose 2-2 Auchinleck Talbot

Shettleston 3-1 Port Glasgow Juniors

Newtongrange Star 1-1 Beith Juniors

Kilbirnie Ladeside 8-0 Blairgowrie Juniors

Dalry Thistle 2-1 Rutherglen Glencairn

Culter 0-0 Broxburn Athletic (@ Montrose)

Renfrew 2-2 Lochee United

Lochee Harp 0-1 Lugar Boswell Thistle

Irvine Meadow XI 9-0 Dundee East Craigie

Whitehills 1-2 Dunbar United

Bonnyrigg Rose Athletic 4-0 Pumpherston

Islavale 2-2 Bankfoot Athletic

ROUND 3 REPLAYS

Petershill 0-0 Tayport (Petershill won 5-4 on penalties)

Auchinleck Talbot 2-1 Linlithgow Rose

Beith Juniors 6-2 Newtongrange Star

Broxburn Athletic 3-3 Culter (Culter won 5-3 on penalties)

Lochee United 2-3 Renfrew

Bankfoot Athletic 2-2 Islavale

(Bankfoot Athletic won 3-2 on penalties)

ROUND 4

Bellshill Athletic 1-2 Bo'ness United
Kilsyth Rangers 1-3 Irvine Meadow XI
Whitletts Victoria 1-1 Kilbirnie Ladeside
Lugar Boswell Thistle 2-3 Haddington Athletic
Glenrothes Juniors 2-1 Arthurlie
Dalry Thistle 5-1 Neilston Juniors
Sunnybank 2-2 Sauchie Juniors
Hill of Beath Hawthorn 1-1 Kirkintilloch Rob Roy
Renfrew 1-0 Bankfoot Athletic
Cumnock Juniors 0-3 Auchinleck Talbot
Bonnyrigg Rose Athletic 4-0 Vale of Leven
Maryhill 3-3 Shettleston
Dunbar United 1-1 Petershill
Greenock Juniors 2-2 Beith Juniors
Broughty Athletic 0-3 Musselburgh Athletic
Ardrossan Winton Rovers 3-2 Culter

FOURTH ROUND REPLAYS

Kilbirnie Ladeside 2-1 Whitletts Victoria
Sauchie Juniors 3-0 Sunnybank (@ Alloa Athletic)
Kirkintilloch Rob Roy 2-1 Hill of Beath Hawthorn
Shettleston 2-0 Maryhill
Petershill 1-1 Dunbar United
(Petershill won 5-3 on penalties)
Beith Juniors 5-1 Greenock Juniors

FIFTH ROUND

Auchinleck Talbot 4-1 Sauchie Juniors
Petershill 0-1 Bo'ness United
Shettleston 0-4 Irvine Meadow XI
Kilbirnie Ladeside 3-3 Beith Juniors
Glenrothes Juniors 1-2 Kirkintilloch Rob Roy
Dalry Thistle 2-1 Haddington Athletic
Musselburgh Athletic 5-0 Renfrew
Ardrossan Winton Rovers 2-6 Bonnyrigg Rose Athletic

ROUND 5 REPLAY

Beith Juniors 0-1 Kilbirnie Ladeside

QUARTER FINALS

Irvine Meadow XI 1-3 Auchinleck Talbot
Dalry Thistle 3-1 Kirkintilloch Rob Roy
Bo'ness United 4-0 Bonnyrigg Rose Athletic
Musselburgh Athletic 2-0 Kilbirnie Ladeside

SEMI-FINALS (2 LEGS)

Auchinleck Talbot 2-0 Bo'ness United
Bo'ness United 1-3 Auchinleck Talbot
Auchinleck Talbot won 5-1 on aggregate
Musselburgh Athletic 1-0 Dalry Thistle
Dalry Thistle 1-1 Musselburgh Athletic
Musselburgh Athletic won 2-1 on aggregate

FINAL (@ Kilmarnock, 28/5/11)

Auchinleck Talbot 2-1 Musselburgh Athletic

All final tables, league and cup results and news from each Junior region and the three Senior Leagues for 2010/2011 Season

24th Annual Edition

£3

2010/11 EDITION AVAILABLE NOW (£3 plus 65p postage)

The Review of 2010/2011 is the twenty fourth in the series and like the previous editions includes all the league tables, in addition to all league results and cup results from each of the three Junior regions and the Highland, East and South of Scotland Leagues. There are also ten pages of amateur details and tables in addition to details of all the regional senior county cup competitions.

Stewart Davidson
12 Windsor Road, Renfrew PA 4 0SS
Payment for the review should be by cheque or postal order.

For further details and information on more of Stewart's publications
log on to: www.snlr.co.uk

NO Respect
Referee
Game

One match in three is played without a referee because of abuse from players.

Isn't it time to show some Respect?

TheFA.com/Respect

TheFA
Respect

the
FOOTBALL ASSOCIATION COMPETITIONS

ENGLAND C

The England C movement is gaining in reputation throughout Europe with many countries electing to use their full Under 21 and 23 teams to play against us either in the International Challenge Trophy or in friendly games. This is a testament to how the organisation has grown. It is now totally different from my first game against Belgium on 11th February 2003 in Ostend. The approach is so professional and whilst we have lost the Four Nations Tournament we have gained the ICT which has exposed the players and coaches to different styles of play and tactics used by the opposition countries. The ICT has moved forward to the point that we now have neutral match officials who are monitored by UEFA for bigger competitions; a sort of taster for their aspiring officials.

Season 2010-11 began in September with a fixture against Wales held in Newtown. The September date is now used to look at new, emerging players in time for the ICT fixtures which are now played in what is known as International week. These are the same dates used for all of Europe including England's first team. These dates have been agreed with The Blue Square Bet Conference board who are fully supportive of England C. The team is ever changing simply because we lose players to the professional game each transfer window. It can be frustrating but also a great challenge and opportunity for the new lads. The game against Wales ended in a 2-2 draw. Having gone into a 2-0 lead we made numerous changes that affected our momentum. Wales's spirited second half performance saw them pull back two goals. We had several opportunities to close the game but lacked composure at the vital moment. The game provided an insight of the new arrivals to the scene.

Having overcome Ireland at the end of the previous it was off to Estonia to play our next group members. The group travelled to Tallinn in early October and even at that time it was rather cold to say the least. I'd had an opportunity to travel to Estonia prior to the game to see them play Ireland and thought I'd got a handle on their team. However, having lost to Ireland, they viewed the game against us differently. Only three players remained in the squad. They played five players with full international experience and gave opportunities to others. The game was played in freezing conditions on a good surface with us winning 1-0. Whilst the score line suggested it was tight, we won quite comfortably. The game saw the emergence of the likes of Sam Hatton, Aiden Flint, Charlie Henry and Jake Howells.

Winning in Tallinn meant we had won our group and had qualified for the semi finals. Belgium, who had beaten us in the previous final, had come through their group so we knew their strength and their ability. The game was played at Luton Town in February. The Belgium FA have a system and structure that allows groups of gifted players to move forward together through the years. The Belgium squad were the official U'20 squad who they saw as the future of Belgium football. Players came from leading clubs; Boyata of Manchester City was pulled from the squad a couple of days before the game. Again we were able to watch their previous game and noted that they played exactly the same system as the one we faced in my first game in 2003. Throughout the years Belgium have played 4-2-1-3. They play with exceptional width and always deploy a "number 10" behind the sole striker. In a terrifically hard fought game a Matthew Barnes-Homer goal was enough to gain us a place in the Final. It was great to welcome back Josh Simpson to the squad who had signed for Crawley Town from Peterborough United. There were new caps for Jamie Day, Rob Atkinson, Andy Mangan, Paul Bignot and Jack Byrne.

Due to severe restrictions, mainly imposed upon us by Portugal, we were forced to play the final against them in a period that clashed with the Blue Square Bet Conference play-offs. It meant that eight of the squad who had played in the semi-final were unavailable. The game was staged at Northampton Town in May. Portugal who were new to the competition had been fielding very strong teams in previous game and they were not going to make an exception now! There were a couple of players valued at £7m and £8m. The final provided opportunities for eight new players and whilst we have always dealt with the sided changing personnel on a regular basis, on this occasion it proved to be too many. Portugal for all their stars could only manage a solitary goal but alas it proved to be enough for them to lift the trophy. The positives for us are the fact that we have made the last three final; winning one and losing the last two by a solitary goal.

The Football Association and The Blue Square Bet Conference can be proud of the manner in which our young players conduct themselves when on International duty. They never fail to give me enjoyment and always make me smile; which after all (apart from winning) is what it should be about.

Paul Fairclough
England C - Manager

ENGLAND C

RESULTS 2010-11

No.	Date	Comp	H/A	Opponents	Att:	Result	Goalscorers
1	Sept 14	F	A	Wales		D 2-2	McFadzean, Rodman
2	Oct 12	ICT GB	A	Estonia		**W** 1-0	Howells 52
3	Feb 9	ICT SF	H	Belgium	2,315	**W** 1-0	Barnes-Homer 7
4	May 19	ICT F	H	Portugal	1,517	L 0-1	

ICT - International Challenge Trophy (GB - Group B). F - Friendly

THE PLAYERS

NAME		CLUB	2010-11 CAPS	10-11 GOALS	TOTAL CAPS	TOTAL GOALS
Atkinson	Robert	Grimsby Town	2	0	2	0
Barnes-Homer	Matthew	Luton Town	3	1	5	2
Bignot	Paul	Newport County	1	0	1	0
Blair	Matthew	Kidderminster Harriers	1	0	1	0
Brown	Seb	AFC Wimbledon	3	0	3	0
Byrne	Jack	Kidderminster Harriers	1	0	1	0
Clancy	Sean	Fleetwood Town	1	0	1	0
Coulson	Josh	Cambridge United	1	0	1	0
Day	Jamie	Rushden & Diamonds	1	0	1	0
Donnelly	George	Fleetwood Town	1	0	1	0
Edwards	Preston	Ebbsfleet United	1	0	1	0
Flint	Aden	Alfreton Town	2	0	2	0
Franklin	Connor	Alfreton Town	1	0	1	0
Gash	Michael	York City	1	0	1	0
Gregory	Steven	AFC Wimbledon	3	0	4	0
Hatton	Sam	AFC Wimbledon	3	0	3	0
Henry	Charlie	Newport County	2	0	2	0
Howells	Jake	Luton Town	3	1	4	1
Mangan	Andy	Wrexham	2	0	2	0
McFadzean	Kyle	Crawley Town	1	1	3	1
Morgan-Smith	Amari	Luton Town	1	0	2	0
Newton	Shaun	AFC Telford Utd	1	0	5	0
Nix	Kyle	Mansfield Town	1	0	2	0
Porter	Max	Rushden & Diamonds	4	0	6	1
Roberts	Dale	Rushden & Diamonds	1	0	5	0
Rodman	Alex	Tamworth	2	1	3	1
Rose	Danny	Newport County	2	0	2	0
Saah	Brian	Cambridge United	1	0	1	0
Simpson	Josh	Crawley Town	2	0	3	0
Styche	Reece	Forest Green Rovers	1	0	1	0
Taylor	Greg	Kettering Town	1	0	1	0
Vaughan	Lee	AFC Telford United	1	0	2	0
Wright	Ben	Kidderminster Harries	2	0	2	0
Wylde	Michael	Tamworth	3	0	3	0

England 2010 Back Row Rodman, Taylor, Roberts, Brown, Flint, Wright, Barnes-Homer, McFadzean, Hatton, Saah Front Row Henry, Howells, Gregory, Porter, Rose, Gash.

England C v Wales

Wright gets his shot in under pressure from Johnston.

Above Gash shoots for goal.

Right: Dale Roberts manages to get in a block to clear the danger.

Photos: Keith Clayton.

ENGLAND'S RESULTS 1979 - 2011

BARBADOS

02.06.08	Bridgetown	2 - 0

BELGIUM

11.02.03	KV Ostend	1 - 3
04.11.03	Darlington	2 - 2
15.11.05	FC Racing Jets	2 - 0
19.05.09	Oxford United	0 - 1
09.02.11	Luton Town	1 - 0

BOSNIA & HERZEGOVINA

16.09.08	Grbavia Stadium	2 - 6

ESTONIA

12.10.10		1 - 0

FINLAND UNDER-21

14.04.93	Woking	1 - 3
30.05.94	Aanekoski	0 - 2
01.06.07	FC Hakka	1 - 0
15.11.07	Helsinki	2 - 0

GIBRALTAR

27.04.82	Gibraltar	3 - 2
31.05.95	Gibraltar	3 - 2
21.05.08	Colwyn Bay	1 - 0

GRENADA

31.05.08	St. George's	1 - 1

HOLLAND

03.06.79	Stafford	1 - 0
07.06.80	Zeist	2 - 1
09.06.81	Lucca	2 - 0
03.06.82	Aberdeen	1 - 0
02.06.83	Scarborough	6 - 0
05.06.84	Palma	3 - 3
13.06.85	Vleuten	3 - 0
20.05.87	Kirkaldy	4 - 0
11.04.95	Aalsmeer	0 - 0
02.04.96	Irthlingborough	3 - 1
18.04.97	Appingedam	0 - 0
03.03.98	Crawley	2 - 1
30.03.99	Genemuiden	1 - 1
21.03.00	Northwich	1 - 0
22.03.01	Wihemina FC	3 - 0
24.04.02	Yeovil Town	1 - 0
25.03.03	BV Sparta 25	0 - 0
16.02.05	Woking	3 - 0
29.11.06	Burton Albion	4 - 1

HUNGARY

15.09.09	Szekesfehervar	1 - 1

IRAQ

27.05.04	Macclesfield	1 - 5

IRISH PREMIER LEAGUE XI

13.02.07	Glenavon FC	1 - 3

ITALY

03.06.80	Zeist	2 - 0
13.06.81	Montecatini	1 - 1
01.06.82	Aberdeen	0 - 0
31.05.83	Scarborough	2 - 0
09.06.84	Reggio Emilia	0 - 1
11.06.85	Houten	2 - 2
18.05.87	Dunfermline	1 - 2
29.01.89	La Spezia	1 - 1
25.02.90	Solerno	0 - 2
05.03.91	Kettering	0 - 0
01.03.99	Hayes	4 - 1
01.03.00	Padova	1 - 1
20.11.02	AC Cremonese	3 - 2
11.02.04	Shrewsbury	1 - 4
10.11.04	US Ivrea FC	1 - 0
15.02.06	Cambridge United	3 - 1
12.11.08	Benevento	2 - 2

MALTA UNDER-21

17.02.09	Malta	4 - 0

NORWAY UNDER-21

01.06.94	Slemmestad	1 - 2

POLAND

17.11.09	Gradiszk Wielpolski	2 - 1

PORTUGAL

19.05.11	Sixfields Stadium	0 - 1

REPUBLIC OF IRELAND

24.05.86	Kidderminster	2 - 1
26.05.86	Nuneaton	2 - 1
25.05.90	Dublin	2 - 1
27.05.90	Cork	3 - 0
27.02.96	Kidderminster	4 - 0
25.02.97	Dublin	0 - 2
16.05.02	Boston	1 - 2
20.05.03	Merthyr Tydfil	4 - 0
18.05.04	Deverondale	2 - 3
24.05.05	Cork	1 - 0
23.05.06	Eastbourne Boro'	2 - 0
22.05.07	Clachnacuddin	5 - 0
26.05.10	Waterford United	2 - 1

SCOTLAND

31.05.79	Stafford	5 - 1
05.06.80	Zeist	2 - 4
11.06.81	Empoli	0 - 0
05.06.82	Aberdeen	1 - 1
04.06.83	Scarborough	2 - 1
07.06.84	Modena	2 - 0
15.06.85	Harderwijk	1 - 3
23.05.87	Dunfermline	2 - 1
18.05.02	Kettering	2 - 0
24.05.03	Carmarthen Town	0 - 0
23.05.04	Deverondale	3 - 1
28.05.05	Cork	3 - 2
27.05.06	Eastbourne Boro'	2 - 0
25.05.07	Ross County	3 - 0
22.05.08	Colwyn Bay	1 - 0

USA

20.03.02	Stevenage Boro.	2 - 1
09.06.04	Charleston USA	0 - 0

WALES

27.03.84	Newtown	1 - 2
26.03.85	Telford	1 - 0
18.03.86	Merthyr Tydfil	1 - 3
17.03.87	Gloucester	2 - 2
15.03.88	Rhyl	2 - 0
21.03.89	Kidderminster	2 - 0
06.03.90	Merthyr Tydfil	0 - 0
17.05.91	Stafford	1 - 2
03.03.92	Aberystwyth	1 - 0
02.03.93	Cheltenham	2 - 1
22.02.94	Bangor	2 - 1
28.02.95	Yeovil Town	1 - 0
23.05.99	St Albans	2 - 1
16.05.00	Llanelli	1 - 1
13.02.01	Rushden & Dia.	0 - 0
14.05.02	Boston	1 - 1
22.05.03	Merthyr Tydfil	2 - 0
20.05.04	Keith FC	0 - 2
26.05.05	Cork	1 - 0
25.05.06	Eastbourne Boro'	1 - 1
27.05.07	Clachnacuddin	3 - 0
21.02.08	Exeter City	2 - 1
24.05.08	Rhyl	3 - 0
15.09.10	Newtown FC	2 - 2

RESULTS SUMMARY 1979 - 2011

	P	W	D	L	F	A
Barbados	1	1	0	0	2	0
Belgium	5	2	1	2	6	6
Bosnia & Herzegovina	1	0	0	1	2	6
Finland Under-21	4	2	0	2	4	5
Estonia	1	1	0	0	1	0
Grenada	1	0	1	0	1	1
Gibraltar	3	3	0	0	7	4
Holland	19	14	5	0	40	8
Hungary	1	0	1	0	1	1
Iraq	1	0	0	1	1	5
Irish Premier League XI	1	0	0	1	1	3
Italy	17	5	7	4	23	21
Malta	1	1	0	0	4	0
Norway Under-21	1	0	0	1	1	2
Poland	1	1	0	0	2	1
Portugal	1	0	0	1	0	1
Republic of Ireland	13	10	0	3	30	11
Scotland	15	10	3	2	30	15
USA	2	1	1	0	2	1
Wales	24	13	7	4	34	20
TOTALS	**113**	**64**	**26**	**22**	**192**	**111**

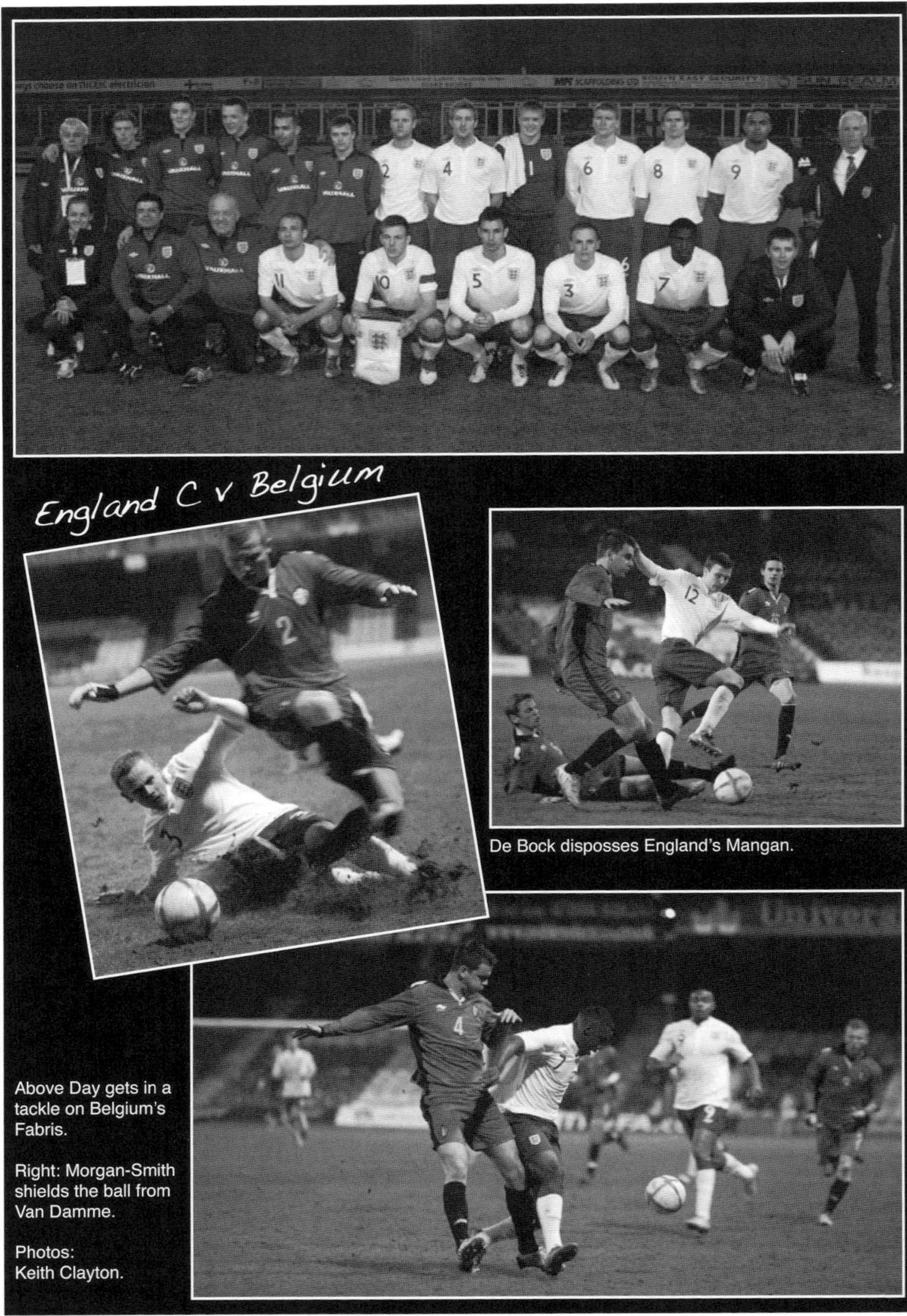

De Bock disposses England's Mangan.

Above Day gets in a tackle on Belgium's Fabris.

Right: Morgan-Smith shields the ball from Van Damme.

Photos:
Keith Clayton.

GOALSCORERS 1979 - 2011

13 GOALS...
Carter, Mark

7 GOALS...
Cole, Mitchell

6 GOALS...
Ashford, Noel

5 GOALS...
Davison, Jon
Williams, Colin

4 GOALS...
Culpin, Paul
D'Sane, Roscoe
Johnson, Jeff
Mackhail-Smith, Craig

3 GOALS...
Adamson, David
Guinan, Steve
Grayson,Neil
Hatch, Liam
Kirk, Jackson
Morison, Steve
Morrison, Michael
Opponents
Watkins, Dale

2 GOALS...
Alford, Carl
Barnes-Homer, Matthew
Barrett, Keith
Bishop, Andrew
Burgess, Andrew
Casey, Kim
Cordice, Neil
Elding, Anthony
Hayles, Barry
Hill, Kenny
Howell, David
Mutrie, Les
Patmore, Warren
Richards, Justin
Seddon, Gareth
Southam, Glen
Watson, John
Weatherstone, Simon
Whitbread, Barry

1 GOAL...
Agana, Tony
Anderson, Dale
Ashton, John
Benson, Paul
Blackburn, Chris
Boardman, Jon
Bolton, Jimmy
Boyd, George
Bradshaw, Mark
Briscoe, Louis
Brown, Paul
Browne, Corey
Carey-Bertram, Daniel
Carr, Michael
Cavell, Paul
Charles, Lee
Charley, Ken
Charnock, Kieran
Constable, James
Crittenden, Nick
Davies, Paul
Day, Matt
Densmore, Shaun
Drummond, Stewart
Fleming, Andrew
Furlong, Paul
Grant, John
Harrad, Shaun
Hine, Mark
Holroyd, Chris
Humphreys, Delwyn
Howells, Jake
Kennedy, John
Kerr, Scott
Kimmins,Ged
King, Simon
Leworthy, David
McDougald, Junior
McFadzean, Kyle
Mayes, Bobby
Moore, Neil
Moore, Luke
Newton, Sean
O'Keefe, Eamon
Oli, Dennis
Penn, Russell
Pitcher, Geoff
Porter, Max
Ricketts, Sam
Robbins, Terry
Robinson, Mark
Roddis,Nick
Rodgers, Luke
Rodman, Alex
Rogers, Paul
Ryan, Tim
Sellars, Neil
Shaw, John
Sheldon, Gareth
Simpson, Josh
Sinclair, Dean
Smith, Ian
Smith, Ossie
Stansfield, Adam
Stephens,Mickey
Stott, Steve
Taylor, Steve
Thurgood, Stuart
Tubbs, Matthew
Venables, David
Way, Darren
Webb, Paul
Wilcox, Russ

MANAGERS 1979 - 2011

		P	W	D	L	F	A	*Win%
1979	Howard Wilkinson	2	2	0	0	6	1	-
1980 - 1984	Keith Wright	17	9	5	3	30	16	53
1985 - 1988	Kevin Verity	12	7	2	3	23	15	58
1989 - 1996	Tony Jennings	19	10	4	5	27	18	53
1997	Ron Reid	2	0	1	1	0	2	-
1998 - 2002	John Owens	14	8	5	1	22	10	57
2002 -	Paul Fairclough	47	28	9	10	84	49	60

*Calculated for those who managed for 10 games or more.

ENGLAND SEMI-PROFESSIONALS, NATIONAL GAME XI AND ENGLAND 'C' CAPS 1979 - 2011

KEY TO COUNTRY CODES:

Ba - Barbados B - Belgium BH - Bosnia & Herzegovina
E - Eire Es - Estonia F - Finland G - Gibraltar Gr - Granada H - Holland Hu - Hungary
I - Italy IP - Irish Premier Lge IQ - Iraq M - Malta N - Norway P - Poland Por - Portugal
S - Scotland W - Wales US - U.S.A.

2010-11 DEBUTANTS	
Robert Atkinson (Grimsby Town) **11** v B, Por.	2
Paul Bignot (Newport County) **11** v B.	1
Matthew Blair (Kidderminster Harriers) **11** v Por.	1
Seb Brown (AFC Wimbledon) **11** v W, Es, B.	3
Jack Byrne (Kidderminster Harriers) **11** v Por.	1
Sean Clancy (Fleetwood Town) **11** v Por.	1
Josh Coulson (Cambridge United) **11** v Por.	1
Jamie Day (Rushden & Diamonds) **11** v B.	1
George Donnelly (Fleetwood Town) **11** v Por.	1
Preston Edwards (Ebbsfleet United) **11** v Por.	1
Aden Flint (Alfreton Town) **11** v W, Es.	2
Connor Franklin (Alfreton Town) **11** v Por.	1
Michael Gash (York City) **11** v W.	1
Sam Hatton (AFC Wimbledon) **11** v W, Es, B.	3
Charlie Henry (Newport County) **11** v W, Es.	2
Andy Mangan (Wrexham) **11** v B, Por.	2
Danny Rose (Newport County) **11** v W, Por.	2
Brian Saah (Cambridge United) **11** v W.	1
Reece Styche (Forest Green Rovers) **11** v Por.	1
Greg Taylor (Kettering Town) **11** v W.	1
Nick Wright (Tamworth) **11** v Es.	0
Ben Wright (Kidderminster Harriers) **11** v W.	2
Michael Wylde (Tamworth) **11** v Es, B, Por.	3

Gary Abbott (Welling) **87** v I(s), S(s), 92 W(s)	3
David Adamson (Boston Utd) **79 v** S, H **80** v I,S, H	5
Les Afful (Forest Green Rovers) **07** v H, IP	2
Tony Agana (Weymouth) **86** v E	1
Junior Agogo (Barnet) **03** v H, i (s), S	3
Danny Alcock (Stafford Rangers) **07** v IP	1
Carl Alford (Kettering T. & Rushden & Ds) **96** v E,H	2
Dale Anderson (Burton Albion) **02** v H **03** v I	2
Mark Angel (Boston United) **02** v W(s), E, S	3
Ian Arnold (Kettering Town) **95** v W(s), H	2
Jim Arnold (Stafford Rangers) **79** v S, H	2
Nathan Arnold (Mansfield Town) **09** v BH	1
Steve Arnold (Grays Athletic) **09** v M	1
Nick Ashby (Kettering & Rushden & Diamonds)	5
94 v F, N, **95** v G **96** v E, H	
Noel Ashford (Enfield & Redbridge Forest.)	21
82 v G,H,S. **83 v** I,H,S, **84** W,H,S,I, **85** W,I(s), **86** E,E,	
87 W(s), I,H,S. **90** v W,E **91** I(s)	
John Ashton (Rushden & Diamonds) **07** v E, S, W, F	4
John Askey (Macclesfield) **90** v W	1
Ryan Austin (Burton Albion) **06** v I. **07** v H.	2
Danny Bacon (Hucknall Town) **04** v IQ	1
Carl Baker (Southport) **06** v I. **07** v F.	2
Matt Baker (Hereford United) **03** v I, S, **04** E,S,IQ,US	6
Nicky Bailey (Barnet) **05** v H, E, S, W.	4
Stephen Bailey (Grays Athletic) **09** v BH	1
Paul Bancroft (Kidderminster H.) **89** v I,W **90** I,W.E, **91** v W	6
Chris Banks (Cheltenham T.) **98** v H, 99 W	2
Matthew Barnes-Homer (Luton Town) **10** v P, E. **11** v W, Es, B.	5
Keith Barrett (Enfield) **81** v H,S,I **82 v** G,I,H,S **83** v I,H,S	
84 v W(s), H, S **85** I,H,S	16
Adam Bartlett (Blyth Spartans) **07** v F. **08** v G,W,Ba. **09** v I,B	6
Laurence Batty (Woking) **93** v F(s), **95** v W,H,G	4
Mark Beeney (Maidstone) **89** v I(s)	1
Paul Beesley (Chester C.) **01** v H(s)	1
Dean Bennett (Kidderminster H) **00** v W(s)	1
Paul Benson (Dagenham & Redbridge) **07** v IP.	1
Graham Benstead (Kettering) **94** v W,F,N(s)	3
Kevin Betsy (Woking) **98** v H(s)	1
Marcus Bignot (Kidderminster H) **97** v H	1
Andy Bishop (York City) **05** v I,H. **06** v B,I.	4
Neil Bishop (York City) **07** v E, W.	2
James Bittner (Exeter City) **04** v B,I	2
Chris Blackburn (Chester C. & Morecambe) **03** v I. **05** v I,H. **06** v I.	4
Shane Blackett (Dagenham & Red). **06** v E,S.	2
Greg Blundell (Northwich Victoria) **03** v H	1
Jon Boardman (Woking) **03** v I, S. **04** I,W,US	5
Jimmy Bolton (Kingstonian) **95** v G	1
Steve Book (Cheltenham Town) **99 v** I,H,W	3
Michael Bostwick (Stevenage Borough) **09** v I	1
George Boyd (Stevenage Boro') **06** v B,I,E,W,S. **07** v H.	6
Adam Boyes (York City) **09** v M	1
Lee Boylan (Canvey Island) **04** v US	1
Gary Brabin (Runcorn) **94 v** W,F,N	3
Mark Bradshaw (Halifax T.) **98** v H	1
Leon Braithwaite (Margate) **02** v US	1
John Brayford (Burton Albion) **08** v F,W,G,S,W,Gr,Ba.	7
Paul Brayson (Northwich Victoria) **07** v S.	1
Colin Brazier (Kidderminster) **87** v W	1
David Bridges (Cambridge Utd) **06** v I	1
Stewart Brighton (Bromsgrove) **94** v W	1
Louis Briscoe (Mansfield Town) **10** v Hu.	1
Richard Brodie (York City) **09** v BH. **10** v P	2
Steve Brooks (Cheltenham) **88** v W(s) **90** v W,E	3
Derek Brown (Woking) **94 v** F(s),N	2
Kevan Brown (Woking) **95** v W,H,G **96** v H **97** v E	5

ENGLAND C

Paul Brown (Barrow) **09** v M 1

Wayne Brown (Chester C.) **01** v W, H(s), **02** v US, H(s),W,S. **03** v H 7

Corey Browne (Dover) **94** v F(s),N(s), **95** v H(s) 3

Liam Brownhill (Witton Albion) **08** v F,W. 2

David Buchanan (Blyth) **86** v E(s),E 2

Nicki Bull (Aldershot Town) **03** v B. **04** v I, H, E. 4

Andrew Burgess (Oxford United/Rushden & Dia.) **07** v E,S,W. **08** v G,S,W,Gr,Ba. 8

Brian Butler (Northwich) **93** v F 1

Steve Butler (Maidstone) **88** v W, **89 v** I,W 3

Gary Butterworth (Rushden & Diamonds) **97** v E,H **98 v** H **99** v I,H,W **00** v I 7

Chris Byrne (Macclesfield T.) **97** v H 1

Joel Byrom (Northwich Victoria) **09** v B 1

Michael Byron (Droylsden) **09** v M 1

Tom Cadmore (Hayes & Yeading United) **10** v H, E 2

DJ Campbell (Yeading) **05** v E, S. 2

Paul Carden (Burton Albion) **07** v E,W. 2

Daniel Carey-Bertram (Hereford Utd) **06** v B 1

Danny Carlton (Morecambe) **04** v IQ 1

Michael Carr (Northwich) **06** v B,I,E,W,S. **07** v H.IP. 7

Mark Carter (Runcorn & Barnet) v **87 v** W,I,H,S **88** v W, **89 v** I,W, **90** v I,E, **91** v I,W(s) 11

Kim Casey (Kidderminster) **86** v W,E,E(s), **87 v** W,I 5

Paul Cavell (Redbridge) **92** v W **93** v F 2

Peter Cavanagh (Accrington) **04** v B,I,E 3

Jon Challinor (Aldershot Town) **04** v B,I 2

Lewis Chalmers (Altrincham/Aldershot) **07** v H,E,S,F. **08** v F,W,G,W,Gr,Ba. 10

Darius Charles (Ebbsfleet United) **09** v B. **10** v P 2

Lee Charles (Hayes) **99** v I(s), H(s), W(s) 3

Anthony Charles (Aldershot/Farnborough) **04** v B,I 2

Kevin Charlton (Telford) **85** v W,I 2

Ken Charlery (Boston U) **01** v H(s) 1

Kieran Charnock (Northwich) **05** v E,W. **06** v B,I,E,W,S. **07** v H,IP,E,W. 11

Andrew Clarke (Barnet) **90** v E,E 2

David Clarke (Blyth Spartans) **80** v I,S(s),H, **81** v H,S,I **82** v I,H,S **83** v H,S **84** v H,S,I 14

Gary Clayton (Burton) **86** v E 1

Paul Clayton (Alfreton Town) **09** v M,B 2

Robert Codner (Barnet) **88** v W 1

Mitchell Cole (Stevenage Borough) **07** v E,S,W,F. **08** v W,G,S,W,Gr,Ba. **09** v BH,I. 12

John Coleman (Morecambe) **93** v F(s) 1

Darren Collins (Enfield) **93** v F(s), **94** v W,F,N 4

Matt Collins (Nuneaton Borough) **04** v I 1

Andy Comyn (Hednesford T.) **98 v** H(s), **99 v** I(s),H(s),W(s) 4

Steve Conner (Dartford, Redbridge & Dagenham & R) **90** v I **91** v I,W **92** v W **93** v F. 5

James Constable (Kidderminster & Oxford Utd) **08** v F. **09** I,B 3

David Constantine (Altrincham) **85** v I,H,S **86 v** W 4

Robbie Cooke (Kettering) **89** v W(s), **90** v I 2

Scott Cooksey (Hednesford T.) **97** v E, **98** vH(s) **01** v W(s),H 4

Alan Cordice(Wealdstone)**83** v I,H,S **84** vW,S(s), I(s),**85** I,H,S 9

Rob Cousins (Yeovil Town) **00 I** v I(s),H,W 3

Gavin Cowan (Canvey Island) **04** v B,IQ 2

Ken Cramman (Gateshead & Rushden & Diamonds) **96** v E **97** v E,H 3

Ian Craney (Altrincham & Accrington) **03** v B. **04** US. **05** I. **06** v B,I,E,W. 7

Nick Crittendon (Yeovil Town) **02** v US (s) 1

Lance Cronin (Ebbsfleet United) **07** v H,E,W,F. **08** v F,W. **09** vBH 7

Paul Cuddy (Altrincham) **87** v I,H,S 3

Paul Culpin (Nuneaton B) **84** v W, **85** v W(s) ,I,H,S 5

Jonathan D'Laryea (Mansfield Town) **09** v Bh,I. 2

Michael Danzey (Woking) **99** v I,H 2

Paul Davies (Kidderminster H.) **86** v W, **87 v** W,I,S, **88 v** W **89** v W 6

John Davison (Altrincham) **79** v S,H **80** v I,S, **81 v** H,S ,I. **82 v** G,I,H,S **83** I,H,S. **84** W,H,I,S **85 v** I,H,S 86 **v** W,E,E. 24

Matt Day (Oxford United) **09** v BH 1

Sam Deering (Oxford United) **10** v E 1

John Denham (Northwich Victoria) **80** v H 1

Peter Densmore (Runcorn) **88** v W **89** v I 2

Shaun Densmore (Altrincham) **09** v M,B. **10** v P,E. 4

Phil Derbyshire (Mossley) **83** v H(s) S(s) 2

Scott Doe (Weymouth) **09** v M. 1

Mick Doherty (Weymouth) **86** v W(s) 1

Neil Doherty (Kidderminster H.) **97** v E 1

Clayton Donaldson (York City) **07** v H,IP. 2

Stuart Drummond (Morecambe) **00** v I(s),H ,W **01 v** W ,H **02** v US, W,E(s), S **03** v H, I, W, S (s) 13

Roscoe D'Sane (Aldershot Town) **03** v B(s),H(s),E,W,S. **04** B,I 7

Chris Duffy (Canvey Island) **03** v B 1

Neil Durkin (Leigh RMI) **02** v H(s) 1

Lee Elam (Morecambe) **03** v H,E,W,S)s) 4

Anthony Elding (Stevenage Borough) **04** v B. **05** v I,H,E,W,S. 6

Paul Ellender (Scarborough) **01** v W(s) 1

Lee Endersby (Harrow Bor.) **96 v** H 1

Mick Farrelly (Altrincham) **87 v** I,H,S 3

Steve Farrelly (Macclesfield & Kingstonian) **95** v H(s),G(s), **00** v I,H,W(s) 5

Trevor Finnegan (Weymouth) **81** v H,S 2

Murray Fishlock (Yeovil Town) **99** v H(s) 1

Andrew Fleming (Wrexham) **09** v B. **10** v E. 2

Richard Forsyth (Kidderminster) **95** v W,H,G 3

Danny Foster (Dagenham & Redbridge) **07** v E,S,F. 3

Ian Foster (Kidderminster H) **00** v W(s) 1

Luke Foster (Oxford United) **09** v BH. 1

Amos Foyewa (Woking) **04** v E,W,S 3

Barry Fuller (Stevenage Borough) **07** v IP. 1

Paul Furlong (Enfield) **90 v** I,E,E **91** v I,W 5

Mark Gardiner (Macclesfield T.) **97** v E 1

Scott Garner **10** v Hu 1

Exodus Geohaghon (Kettering Town) **09** v I,B. 2

Jerry Gill (Yeovil T.) **97** v E 1

Matt Glennon (Carlisle Utd) **05** v W,S. 2

Dan Gleeson (Cambridge Utd) **08** v F,W,G,S,Gr,Ba. **09** v I. 7

John Glover (Maidstone Utd) **85** v W,I,H,S 4

Mark Golley (Sutton Utd.) **87** v H(s),S, **88** v W, **89** v I,W, **92** v W 6

Jason Goodliffe (Hayes) **00** v I, H,W, **01** W **02** US, W,E,S. 8

Paul Gothard (Dagenham & Redb.) **97** v E(s), **99** v I(s),W(s) 3

Jeff Goulding (Fisher Athletic) **08** v W. 1

Mark Gower (Barnet) **02** v H, W, E, S(s) 4

Simon Grand (Carlisle) **05** v H. 1

John Grant (Aldershot Town) **07** v E,S,W,F. 4

Neil Grayson (Cheltenham T.) **98** v H **99** v I,H,W 4

Matt Green **10** v Hu 1

Steven Gregory (AFC Wimbledon) **10** v E. **11** v W, Es, B. 4

Phil Gridelet (Hendon & Barnet) **89** v I,W, **90** v W,E,E 5

Scott Griffiths (Dagenham & Redbridge) **07** v H,IP. 2

Steve Guinan (Hereford) **04** v E,W,S,US 4

Steve Guppy (Wycombe W.) **93** v W 1

Scott Guyett (Southport) **01** v H, **03** v H,I,W,S. 5

Ryan Hall (Bromley) **10** v E 1

Tim Hambley (Havant & Waterlooville) **02** v H 1

Steve Hanlon (Macclesfield) **90** v W 1

Ben Harding (Aldershot) **08** v W,G,W. 3

David Harlow (Farnborough T.) **97** v E(s),H 2

Shaun Harrad (Burton Albion) **07** v F. **08** v F,W,G,S,W,Gr,Ba. **09** v BH,I. 8

Stephen Haslam (Halifax) **05** v E,W,S. 3

Liam Hatch (Barnet) **04** v E,W,S,IQ,US. **05** H. 6

Wayne Hatswell (Chester City/Cambridge Utd) **03** v E(s),W(s). **08** v S,W,Gr,Ba. 6

Karl Hawley (Carlisle Utd) **05** v I,H. 2

Barry Hayles (Stevenage Bor.) **96** v E,H 2

Greg Heald (Barnet) **02** v H 1

Brian Healy (Morecambe) **98** v H 1

Liam Hearn (Alfreton Town) **09** v B. 1

John Hedge (FC Halifax Town) **10** v P 1

Ronnie Henry (Stevenage Boro) **06** v S. **07** v IP. **08** v F,W. 4

Tony Hemmings (Northwich) **93** v F 1

Andy Hessenthaler (Dartford) **90** v I 1

Kenny Hill (Maidstone Utd) **80** v I,S,H 3

Mark Hine (Gateshead) **95** v W(s),H 2

Simeon Hodson (Kidderminster) **94** v W,F,N 3

Lewis Hogg (Barnet) **04** v B 1

Colin Hogarth (Guiseley) **95 v** W,H 2

Steven Holden (Kettering) **94** v W,F,N(s) **95** v H,G 5

Ricky Holmes (Chelmsford City) **08** v W. 1

Chris Holroyd (Cambridge United) **10** v H, P 2

Mark Hone (Welling United) **90** v I **93** v F, **94** vW(s),F(s),N 5

Gary Hooley (Frickley) **85** v W 1

Dean Hooper (Kingstonian) **98** v H 1

Keith Houghton (Blyth Spartans) **79** v S 1

Barry Howard (Altrincham) **81** v H,S,I **82** v G,I,H,S 7

Neil Howarth (Macclesfield) **95** v H(s) **97** v E 2

David Howell (Enfield) **85** v H(s),S(s) **86** v W,E **87** v W,I,H,S **88** v W, **89** v I,W **90** v I,E,E 14

Jake Howells (Luton Town) **10** v P. **11** v W, Es, B. 4

Lee Howells (Cheltenham T.) **98** v H **99 v** W 2

Lee Hughes (Kidderminster Harriers) **96** v E,H **97** v E,H 4

Delwyn Humphreys (Kidderminster H.) **91** v W(s) **92** v W **94** v W,F,N **95** v W,H 7

Steve Humphries (Barnet) **87** v H(s) 1

Nicky Ironton (Enfield) **83** H(s) **84** v W 2

Jimmy Jackson (Gravesend & Northfleet) 03 v H(s) 1

Simon Jackson (Woking) **05** v I. 1

Justin Jackson (Morecambe & Rushden & Diamonds) **00** v W **01** v W 2

Kirk Jackson (Stevenage Borough) **02** v US, E,S,(Yeovil Town) **03** v E,W,S(s) 6

Shwan Jalal (Woking) **05** v H. **06** v I,E,W,S. 5

Mark Janney (Dagenham & Redbridge) **03** v H 1

Rossi Jarvis (Luton Town) **10** v H, P, E 3

Tony Jennings (Enfield) **79** v S,H **80** v I,S,H **81 v** H,S,I **82** v G,I,H,S 12

Jeff Johnson (Altrincham) **81** v S,I **82** v G,I,H,S **83** v I,H,S **84 v** H,S,I **84 v** I,H,S **86** v W(s),E,E 18

Lee Johnson (Yeovil Town) **03** v I, H(s), E, W, S 5

Paul Jones (Exeter City) **06** v I 1

Steve Jones (Leigh RMI) **01** v H 1

Tom Jones (Weymouth) **87** v W 1

Tom Jordan (Tamworth) **04** v B 1

Antone Joseph(Telford U. & Kidderm'terH.)**84** v S(s), **85** v W,I, H,S **86** v W(s), **87** W,I(s),H, **88** v W **89** v I,W **90 v** I,E,E 15

John Keeling (Purfleet) **03** v B(s) 1

Marcus Kelly (Rushden & Diamonds) **07** v IP. 1

Darran Kempson (Morecambe) **06** v E,W. 2

John Kennedy (Canvey Island) **03** v I, B, H, E, W, S. **04** IQ,US 8

Jon Kennedy (Accrington) **04** v I,IQ,US 3

Andy Kerr (Wycombe) **93** v W 1

Scott Kerr (Scarborough) **04** v E,W,S,IQ. **05** v I,H,E,W,S 9

Lance Key (Kingstonian) 03 v B 1

Ged Kimmins (Hyde Utd.) **96** v E(s),H(s) **97 v** E(s) 3

Simon King (Barnet) **05** v I,H,S. 3

Natt Knight-Percival **10** v Hu 1

Scott Laird (Stevenage Borough) **09** v B. 1

Mike Lake (Macclesfield) **89** v I 1

Martin Lancaster (Chester City) **03** vI (s)

Andy Lee (Telford U. & Witton A.) **89** I(s), **91** v I,W 3

Arran Lee-Barrett (Weymouth) **07** v H. 1

Stuart Lewis (Stevenage Borough) **08** v F. 1

David Leworthy (Farnborough & Rushden & Diamonds) **93 v** W, **94** v W **97** v E,H 4

Adam Lockwood (Yeovil Town) **02** v E **03** v I 2

Stacey Long (Gravesend & Northfleet) **07** v IP. 1

Kenny Lowe (Barnet) **91 v** I,W 2

Junior MacDougald (Dagenham & Redbridge) **01** v H(s) **02** W, E(s), S(s) 4

Craig McAllister (Basingstoke Town) **03** v B 1

Martin McDonald (Macclesfield) **95** v G(s) 1

Danny McDonnell (Worcester City) **04** v W 1

Kyle McFadzean (Alfreton Town) **10** v H, E. **11** v 3

Mark McGregor (Forest Green Rovers & Nuneaton Borough) **00** v I(s),H(s) **01** v W(s) 3

Kevin McIntyre (Doncaster Rovers) **00 v** H(s)W, **01 v** W(s)H 4

John McKenna (Boston Utd) **88 v** W(s), **90** v I,E,E. **91 v** I,W, **92** vW 7

Aaron McLean (Aldershot & Grays) **04** v B,I. **06** v E,W,S. 5

Lewis McMahon (Gainsborough Trinity) **09** v M. 1

David McNiven (Leigh RMI) **04** v W,S,IQ,US 4

Chris McPhee (Ebbsfleet Utd) **08** v G,S,W. 3

Craig Mackhail-Smith (Dag. & Red.) **05** v W,S. **06** v I,E,W,S. **07** v H. 7

Tamika Mkandawire (Hereford Utd) **06** v B,I. 2

Fiston Manuella (Aylesbury United) **03** v B 1

John Margerrison (Barnet) **87 v** W 1

Player	Caps
Simon Marples (Doncaster Rovers) **00 v** I,H	2
John Martin (Stevenage Borough) **08** v G,S,W.	3
Leroy May (Stafford R.) **95 v** G(s)	1
Bobby Mayes (Redbridge) **92 v** W	
Paul Mayman (Northwich Vic) **80 v** I,S	2
Stewart Mell (Burton) **85v** W	1
Neil Merrick (Weymouth) **80** v I(s),S	2
Adam Miller (Aldershot Town) **04** v I	1
Russell Milton (Dover) 94 v F,N	2
Mark Molesley (Aldershot Town) **07** v E,S,W,F.	4
Luke Moore (Ebbsfleet United) **09** v BH.	1
Neil Moore (Telford United) **02** v US (s),H, W, E,S	5
Steve Morison (Stevenage Borough) **07** v H,IP,F. **08** v G,S,W,Gr,Ba.	8
Amari Morgan-Smith (Ilkeston Town) **10** v E. **11** v B.	2
Trevor Morley (Nuneaton) **84 v** W,H,S,I **85 v** W,S(s)	6
Michael Morrison (Cambridge Utd) **07** v H. **08** v F,W,G,S,W,Gr,Ba.	8
Dean Moxey (Exeter City) **05** v H. **08** v W,S.	3
Chris Murphy (Telford United) **04** v B	1
Karl Murrphy (Woking) **04** v B,I	2
Tarkan Mustafa (Rushden & Diamonds) **01** v W,H	2
Les Mutrie (Blyth Spartans) **79 v** S,H, **80** v I,S,H	5
Mark Newson (Maidstone U) **84 v** W,H,S,I, **85 v** W	5
Doug Newton (Burton) **85** v W,H,S	3
Shaun Newton (Droylsden) **09** v M,B. **10** v P,E. **11** v Es.	5
Paul Nicol (Kettering T) **91 v** I,W, **92** v W	3
Kevin Nicholson (Forest Green Rovers/Torquay Utd) **07** v E.S.W. **08** v G,S,W,Gr,Ba.	8
Kyle Nix (Mansfield Town) **10** v Hu. **11** v Es.	2
Richard Norris (Northwich Victoria) **03** v H, S,	2
Steve Norris (Telford) **88** v W(s)	1
John Nutter (Grays) **06** v E,W,S.	3
Curtis Obeng (Wrexham) **10** v E	1
Joe O'Connor (Hednesford T.) **97 v** E,H(s)	2
Eamon O'Keefe (Mossley) **79 v** S,H	2
Erkan Okay (Histon) **08** v F.	1
Dennis Oli (Grays) **06** v B,E,W,S. **07** v H.	5
Luke Oliver (Woking) **05** v H.	1
Frank Ovard (Maidstone) **81** v H(s),S(s),I(s)	3
Andy Pape (Harrow Bor. & Enfield) **85** v W(s,)H,S. **86** v W(s),E, **87** v W,I,H,S **88** v W, **89** IW, **90** I,W,E	15
Brian Parker (Yeovil Town) **80 v** S	1
Warren Patmore (Yeovil Town) **99** v I,H,W, **00 v** I,H, **01** W,H	7
Gary Patterson (Kingstonian) **99** v I,H, **00** v H,W, **01 v** W,H	7
Steve Payne (Macclesfield T.) **97 v** H	1
Trevor Peake (Nuneaton Bor) **79 v** S,H	2
David Pearce (Harrow Bor) **84 v** I(s)	1
Russell Penn (Kidderminster) **08** v F,W,G,W,Gr,Ba. **09** v I,B.	8
David Perkins (Morecambe) **04** v B,I,E,S,IQ,US. **05** v I. **06** v B,I.	9
Warren Peyton (Nuneaton Borough) **02** v H(s) **03** v I	2
Brendan Phillips (Nuneaton Bor. & Kettering T.), **79 v** S,H, **80 v** S(s),H.	4
Gary Philips (Barnet) **82 v** G	1
Owen Pickard (Yeovil T.) **98** v H(s)	1
Geoff Pitcher (Kingstonian) **99 v** W, **00 v** I,H,W, **01** v W,H	6
Jon-Paul Pitman (Crawley Town) **09** v I.	1

Player	Caps
Max Porter (Rushden & Diamonds) **10** v P, E. **11** v W,Es,B,Por.	6
Phil Power (Macclesfield T.) **96** v E(s),H(s)	2
Ryan Price (Stafford R. & Macclesfield) **92** v W(s) **93** v W,F. **96** v E,H **97** v H.	6
Steve Prindiville **98 v** H(s)	1
Andy Proctor (Accrington Stanley) **04** v IQ	1
Marc Pullan (Crawley Town) **03** v B	1
Robert Purdie (Hereford United) **04** v I. **05** v I.	2
Wayne Purser (Barnet) **03** v I	1
Mark Quayle (Telford United) **02** v H	1
Adam Quinn (Halifax Town) **07** v H,IP,E,S,W,F.	6
Simon Read (Farnborough) **92** v W(s)	1
Jai Reason (Cambridge United) **10** v P	1
Matt Redmile (Barnet) **04** v E,W,S	3
Andy Reid (Altrincham) **95 v** W	1
Sam Rents **10** v Hu	1
Callum Reynolds (Luton Town) **10** v Hu	1
Martin Rice (Exeter City) **07** v IP.	1
Carl Richards (Enfield) **86 v** E	1
Justin Richards (Woking) **06** v E,W,S.	3
Derek Richardson (Maidstone U) **83 v** I, **84 v** W, **86** v E	4
Ian Richardson (Dagenham & Red) **95 v** G	1
Kevin Richardson (Bromsgrove) **94** v W,F,N	3
Paul Richardson (Redbridge) **92** v W, **93 v** W, F	3
Scott Rickards (Tamworth) **03** v B. **04** B	2
Sam Ricketts (Telford) **04** v B,E,W,S	4
Adriano Rigoglioso (Morecambe) **03** v H(s)	1
Martin Riley (Kidderminster Harriers) **09** v M.	1
Anthony Rivierre (Welling United) **03** v B	1
Terry Robbins (Welling) **92 v** W, **93** v W,F, **94** v W,F,N	6
Dale Roberts (Rushden & Diamonds) **09** v M. **10** v H,P,E. **11** v W.	5
Gary Roberts (Accrington) **06** v I,E,W,S.	4
Anton Robinson (Weymouth) **09** v BH,I.	2
Mark Robinson (Hereford) **05** v E,W,S.	3
Peter Robinson (Blyth S) **83 v** I,H,S **84** W,I 85 v W	6
Ryan Robinson (Morecambe) **06** v B.	1
Nick Roddis (Woking) **01 v** H **02** US,H,W,E(s),S	6
Luke Rodgers (Shrewsbury) **04** v B,I.	2
Alex Rodman (Oxford United) **10** v E. **11** v W, Es.	3
John Rogers (Altrincham) **81 v** H,S,I **82 v** I(s),S	5
Paul Rogers (Sutton) **89** v W, **90** v I, E(2), **91** I,W	6
Colin Rose (Witton Alb.) **96 v** E(s), H	2
Kevin Rose (Kidderminster) **94 v** F(s),N	2
Michael Rose (Hereford United) **03** v I, H, E, S	4
Brian Ross (Marine) **93 v** W(s),F(s), **94** v W(s) **95 v** W,H	5
Carl Ruffer (Chester City) **01** v H(s)	1
Tim Ryan (Southport & Doncaster Rovers) **98 v** H. **99 v** I,H,W, **00 v** I,H,W **01** v W,H **02** v US,H,W,I,S	14
Gareth Seddon (Hyde United) **07** v E.W.	2
Jake Sedgemore (Shrewsbury) **04** v E,W,S,IQ,US.	5
Neil Sellars (Scarboro) **81** v H,S,I **82** v G,H(s),S, **83 v** I,H,S	9
Mark Shail (Yeovil T.) **93** v W	1
John Shaw (Halifax Town) **08** v G,S,W,Gr,Ba.	5
Jon Shaw (Burton Albion) **06** v I.	1
Simon Shaw (Doncaster Rovers) **99** v I,H	2
Tom Shaw (Tamworth) **09** v M. **10** v P.	2
Peter Shearer (Cheltenham) **89 v** I(s)	1
Gareth Sheldon (Exeter) **04** v I,E,W,S,IQ,US.	6

Paul Shirtliff (Frickley A. & Boston U.) **86** vE,E **87** v W,I,H. **88** v W **89 v** I, W, **90 v** I,W,E,E, **92 v** W **93** v W,F	15
Paul Showler (Altrincham) **91** v I(s),W	2
Tim Sills (Kingstonian) **03** v B	1
Gordon Simmonite (Boston United) **79** v S(s,)H(s), **80** v I,S,H.	5
Gary Simpson (Stafford R.) **86** v E,E, **87** v I,H,S,**90** v I,W,E,E.	9
Josh Simpson (Histon) **09** v I. **10** v Hu. **11** v B, Por.	4
Wayne Simpson (Stafford) **94** v F,N(s)	2
Dean Sinclair (Barnet) **05** v I,H,E,W,S.	5
Terry Skiverton (Yeovil Town) **01 v** W **02 v** US **03** v 1,W,	4
Glenn Skivington (Barrow) **90** v I,W,E **91** v I,W	5
Jamie Slabber (Grays) **06** v B.	1
Adrian Smith (Kidderminster H) **00** v I(s),H(s),W	3
Alan Smith (Alvechurch) **82** v G,I,S	3
Ian Smith (Mossley) **80** v I,S,H(s)	3
James Smith (Ebbsfleet Utd) **08** v Gr,Ba. **09** v BH,I.	4
Mark Smith (Stevenage Bor.) **96** v E,H **98** v H **99** v I,H,W. **00** v I,H,W(s).	9
Ossie Smith (Runcorn) **84** v W	1
Phil Smith (Margate) **04** v B	1
Tim Smithers (Nuneaton) **85** v W(s),I **86** v W	3
Guiseppe Sole (Woking) **07** v H,IP,F.	3
Adam Sollitt (Kettering Town) **00** v I(s),H(s),W	3
Leon Solomon (Welling United) **07** v F.	1
Glen Southam (Bishop's Stort' & Dag & R.) **04** v E,W,S,IQ,US. **05** v W,S. **06** v S. **07** v E,S,W,F.	12
Craig Stanley (Hereford & Morecambe) **05** v E,W. **07** v H,IP.	4
Adam Stansfield (Yeovil Town & Hereford) **02** v W (s), I, S **05** v E,S.	5
Simon Stapleton (Wycombe) **93** v W	1
Mickey Stephens (Sutton), **82** v G,S(s) **86 v** W,E,E(s)	5
Jamie Stevens (Crawley Town) **09** v BH.	1
Billy Stewart (Southport) **98** v H	1
Mark Stimson (Canvey Islland) **02** v US	1
Bob Stockley (Nuneaton Borough) **80** v H	1
David Stockdale (York) **05** v I.	1
Darren Stride (Burton Albion) **02** v H	1
Steve Stott (Kettering T., Rushden & Ds & Yeovil T.) **95** v W,H(s),G **96** v E,H **99** v H,W(s)	7
Ryan Sugden (Chester City) 03 v I	1
Ben Surey (Gravesend & Nflt.) **05** v I.	1
Andy Taylor (Exeter City) **05** v E,W,S.	3
James Taylor (Havant & Waterlooville) **02** v H,W, E(s),S(s)	4
Peter Taylor (Maidstone) **84** v HSI	3
Steve Taylor (Bromsgrove R.) **95** v G	1
Shaun Teale (Weymouth) **88** v W	1
Paul Terry (Dagenham & Redbridge) **03** vE (s), W(s), S	3
Stuart Terry (Altrincham) **95** v W	1
Brian Thompson(Yeovil & Maidstone) **79** v S,H **81** v H,S,I. **82** v I,H,S **83 v** I,H,S **84** v W,H,S,I	15
Neil Thompson (Scarborough) **87** v W,I,H,S	4
Garry Thompson (Morecambe) **03** v I. **04** v E,W,IQ,US	5
Steve Thompson (Wycombe) **93** v W	1
Stuart Thurgood (Grays Ath.) **05** v I,H. **06** v E,W,S.	5
Kevin Todd (Berwick Rangers) **91** v W	1
Lee Tomlin (Rushden & Diamonds) **09** v M,B.	2
Mike Tomlinson (Runcorn F.C.Halton) **03** v B (s)	1
Anthony Tonkin (Yeovil Town) **02** v US	1

Simon Travis (Forest Green R & Hereford) **02 v** US, H. **05** v E. **06** v E,W,S.	6
Carl Tremarco (Wrexham) **09** v I.	1
Andy Tretton (Hereford) **04** v E,W,S,US	4
Matthew Tubbs (Salisbury City) **07** v E. **08** v F.	2
Mark Tucker (Woking) **96** v E	1
Tony Turner (Telford) **85 v** W	1
Scott Tynan (Rushden & Diamonds) **07** v S,W. **08** v S,Gr.	4
Paul Underwood (Rushden & D) **99** v I,H **00 v** I**01** v W	4
Lee Vaughan (AFC Telford Utd) **10** v Hu. **11** v Por.	1
David Venables(Stevenage B)**94 v** W(s)**95 v** H,G**96 v** E,H(s)	5
Jamie Victory (Cheltenham T.) **98** vH(s)	1
Ashley Vickers (Dagenham & Redbridge) **04** v IQ	1
David Waite (Enfield) **82** v G	1
Steve Wales (Yeading) **06** v B.	1
Jason Walker (Barrow) **09** v M.	1
Paul Walker (Blyth) **86 v** W,E,E(s), **87 v** S(s)	4
Steve Walters (Northwich Victoria) **97** v H	1
Mark Ward (Northwich Victoria) **83** v S(s)	1
Steve Ward (Canvey Island) **03** v B	1
Dale Watkins (Cheltenham T.) **98** v H **99** v I(s), **00** v I,H,W	5
John Watson (Wealdstone, Scarborough & Maidstone) **79** v S(s),H **80** v I,S,H **81** v H,S,I **82** v I,H,S **83** v I,H,S **84** v W(s),H,S,I	18
Steve Watson (Farnborough Town) **02** v US(s), W(s), S	3
Liam Watson (Marine) **95** v W,H(s)	2
Paul Watts (Redbridge Forest) **89** v W **90** v I,E,E **91** v I **92** v W **93** v W,F	8
Darren Way (Yeovil Town) **03** vI (s), E, W	3
Chris Weale (Yeovil Town) **03** v I (s), H (s), E, W.	4
Simon Weatherstone (Boston United) **02** v W(s),E,S(s)	3
Paul Webb (Bromsgrove R & Kidderminster H) **93** v F **94** v W,F,N(s) **95** v W,H,G **96** v E,H **97** v E,H	11
Aaron Webster (Burton Albion) **02 v** H(s),W,S(s) **03** v I	3
Joe Welch **10** v Hu	1
Ishmael Welsh (Grays Athletic) **09** v M,B.	2
Mark West (Wycombe W) **91** v W	1
Steve West (Woking) **01** v W(s)	1
Barry Whitbread (Runcorn & Altrincham) **79 v** S,H **80** v I,S,H, **81 v** I	6
Tristram Whitman (Doncaster Rovers) **03** v W(s), S	2
Russ Wilcox (Frickley) **86** v W,E	2
Adam Wilde (Worcester City) **03** v B	1
Barry Williams (Nuneaton Borough) **99** v H(s),W	2
Colin Williams (Scarborough & Telford Utd.) **81** v H,S. **82** v I,H,S. **84** v H,S,I. **85** v I,H,S.	12
Roger Willis (Barnet) **91** v I(s)	1
Paul Wilson (Frickley Athletic) **86** v W	1
Martyn Woolford (York City) **08** v Gr,Ba.	2
Andy Woods (Scarborough) **02** v US,H(s),W,S.	4
Simon Wormull (Dover Athletic) **99** v I(s),W **02 v** W,E,S.	5
Mark Wright (Thurrock) **09** v BH.	1
Jake Wright (Tamworth) **09** v I.	1
Nick Wright (Tamworth) **10** v H,P.	2
Nicky Wroe (Torquay United) **09** v M,B.	2
Adam Yates (Morecambe) **07** v H,S,W.	3
Mark Yates (Cheltenham Town) **99** v I, W	2
Ismail Yakubu (Barnet) **04** v I,US. **05** v I,E,W,S.	6

THE FA CUP

2010-11

The Harrow Borough fans enjoyed a run to the First Round Proper during the 2010-11 campaign. Photo: Bill Wheatcroft.

EXTRA PRELIMINARY ROUND

Many small clubs are still welcoming players back from the summer holidays and getting to know their new signings when they prepare for their first F.A. Cup tie. Some did get caught out with very one sided matches and high scoring opening cup games last season included:
New Mills 10 Alsager 2 (with both clubs from The North West Counties, Premier Division)
Hassocks 7 Eastbourne United 1 (Both Sussex County Division One).
In this round the away clubs enjoyed a particularly good day with Congleton leading the way:
Daisy Hill 0 Congleton Town 8 (N.W Counties Premier club beating a Division One club) with Bartley Green (Midland Combination Premier) beating Willenhall (Midland Alliance) 6-0 and Laverstock & Ford (Wessex Premier) winning 6-1 at Hook Norton (Hellenic Div.1 West). Seven more clubs registered five goal away triumphs and twenty two more scored four on their travels. Five of the thirty five replayed cup ties were decided by penalties four by a 4-3 scoreline and St Helens Town (N.W. Counties Premier) went all the way with a 5-4 total.
Having won the F.A.Vase with just about the last kick of the previous season, Whitley Bay were obviously well prepared to start the new campaign and came back from Liversedge (N.Counties Premier) with a 3-0 victory.

AFC Uckfield's Owen Hill (centre) just gets a touch to clear against VCD Athletic in the Extra Preliminary Round. Photo: Alan Coomes.

Above: South Park's Daniel Guscott clears from Greenwich Borough's Peter Afolayan in the Preliminary Round. Photo: Alan Coomes

Mark Bunker's penalty gives AFC Kempston Rovers the lead against Godmanchester Rovers during Kempston's 4-0 Extra Preliminary tie win. Photo: Gordon Whittington.

EXTRA PRELIMINARY ROUND

SATURDAY 14 AUGUST 2010 - WINNING CLUBS TO RECEIVE £750

1	Ryton	v	Scarborough Athletic	0-1	177
2	Liversedge	v	Whitley Bay	0-3	219
3	Brandon United	v	Chester-Le-Street Town	1-2	74
4	Shildon	v	Sunderland RCA	4-3	104
5	Pickering Town	v	South Shields (15/8)	1-4	210
6	Ashington	v	Billingham Town	4-1	198
7	Tow Law Town	v	Jarrow Roofing Boldon CA	0-2	61
8	West Auckland Town	v	Whickham	2-1	58
9	West Allotment Celtic	v	Tadcaster Albion	1-2	75
10	Norton & Stockton Ancients	v	Penrith	2-1	105
11	Guisborough Town	v	Armthorpe Welfare	0-3	90
12	Bishop Auckland	v	Consett (15/8)	3-3	200
	Consett	v	Bishop Auckland (18/8)	2-3	202
13	Brighouse Town	v	Dunston UTS	1-2	200
14	Hebburn Town	v	Marske United	1-1	87
	Marske United	v	Hebburn Town (18/8)	2-0	121
15	Whitehaven	v	Team Northumbria	4-1	
16	Esh Winning	v	Northallerton Town	0-4	71
17	Pontefract Collieries	v	Selby Town	0-2	160
18	Silsden	v	Crook Town	2-2	228
	Crook Town	v	Silsden (18/8)	1-0	190
19	Hall Road Rangers	v	Newcastle Benfield	2-2	72
	Newcastle Benfield	v	Hall Road Rangers (18/8)	3-1	84
20	Bridlington Town	v	Horden CW	5-1	167
21	Stokesley	v	Thackley	1-1	70
	Thackley	v	Stokesley (17/8)	2-1	92
22	Leeds Carnegie	v	Billingham Synthonia	0-0	23
	Billingham Synthonia	v	Leeds Carnegie (18/8)	3-1	134
23	Spennymoor Town	v	Bedlington Terriers	1-0	262
24	Morpeth Town	v	AFC Emley (17/8)	1-2	85
25	Seaham Red Star	v	North Shields	0-1	51
26	Irlam	v	Chadderton	1-2	56
27	Rossendale United	v	Formby	3-1	71
28	Ashton Athletic	v	Parkgate	0-2	35
29	Hallam	v	Atherton Collieries (15/8)	2-3	195
30	Ramsbottom United	v	Winsford United	4-1	147
31	Leek CSOB	v	Bootle	1-1	42
	Bootle	v	Leek CSOB (17/8)	6-0	124
32	New Mills	v	Alsager Town	10-2	125
33	Holker Old Boys	v	Abbey Hey	1-1	46
	Abbey Hey	v	Holker Old Boys (17/8)	0-1	40
34	Daisy Hill	v	Congleton Town	0-8	54
35	Glossop North End	v	Wigan Robin Park	2-2	210
	Wigan Robin Park	v	Glossop North End (17/8)	0-1	115
36	Runcorn Linnets	v	Maine Road	1-1	453
	Maine Road	v	Runcorn Linnets (17/8)	3-4	140
37	Nelson	v	Atherton LR		
	(walkover for Atherton LR – Nelson removed)				
38	Staveley MW	v	Padiham	5-0	90
39	Flixton	v	Bacup Borough	0-3	45
40	Nostell MW	v	St Helens Town	1-1	67
	St Helens Town	v	Nostell MW (17/8)	2-2aet	74
	(St Helens Town won 5-4 on kicks from the penalty mark)				
41	Colne	v	Ashton Town	2-0	83
42	Cheadle Town	v	Squires Gate	3-0	45
43	Hemsworth MW	v	AFC Liverpool	4-1	252
44	Willenhall Town	v	Bartley Green	0-6	75
45	Coalville Town	v	Stone Dominoes	1-1	94
	Stone Dominoes	v	Coalville Town (17/8)	0-3	77
46	Loughborough University	v	Stratford Town	1-4	84
47	Boldmere St Michaels	v	Westfields	0-1	42
48	Coventry Sphinx	v	Castle Vale	3-0	69
49	Pegasus Juniors	v	Heather St Johns	1-1	68
	Heather St Johns	v	Pegasus Juniors (17/8)	5-1	86
50	Causeway United	v	Ellesmere Rangers (15/8)	2-1	86
	(at Boldmere St Michaels FC)				
51	Rocester	v	Pilkington XXX	1-2	79
52	Eccleshall	v	Southam United	3-0	56
53	Cradley Town	v	Malvern Town	3-4	52
54	Shifnal Town	v	Dudley Town	1-1	63
	Dudley Town	v	Shifnal Town (18/8)	2-0	87
55	Kirby Muxloe	v	Walsall Wood	4-2	92
56	Alvechurch	v	Tipton Town	0-5	59
57	Bardon Hill Sports	v	Bewdley Town	2-5	51
58	Tividale	v	Oadby Town	1-2	40
59	Pelsall Villa	v	Dosthill Colts	0-2	56
60	Bridgnorth Town	v	Highgate United	4-0	90
61	Ledbury Town	v	Castle Vale JKS		
	(walkover for Castle Vale JKS – Ledbury Town removed)				
62	AFC Wulfrunians	v	Heath Hayes	1-3	83
63	Brocton	v	Coleshill Town	4-4	57
	Coleshill Town	v	Brocton (17/8)	2-1	59
64	Nuneaton Griff	v	Studley	2-1	61
65	Norton United	v	Hinckley	1-0	22
66	Biddulph Victoria	v	Wellington (15/8)	1-1	79
	Wellington	v	Biddulph Victoria (17/8)	1-1aet	76
	(Biddulph Victoria won 4-3 on kicks from the penalty mark)				
67	Wednesfield	v	Bolehall Swifts	2-0	52
68	Gedling Town	v	Boston Town	2-4	74
69	Blackstones	v	Maltby Main	1-1	70
	Maltby Main	v	Blackstones (18/8)	0-0aet	110
	(Maltby Main won 4-3 on kicks from the penalty mark)				
70	Heanor Town	v	Borrowash Victoria	0-0	133
	Borrowash Victoria	v	Heanor Town (17/8)	2-1	117
71	Long Eaton United	v	Barton Town Old Boys	1-1	68
	Barton Town Old Boys	v	Long Eaton United (17/8)	1-0	115
72	Holbeach United	v	Radcliffe Olympic	0-1	124
73	Wisbech Town	v	St Andrews	5-0	663
74	Rossington Main	v	Shirebrook Town	0-3	75
75	Greenwood Meadows	v	Winterton Rangers	3-4	36
76	Teversal	v	Bottesford Town	0-0	68
	Bottesford Town	v	Teversal (18/8)	3-1	85
77	Barrow Town	v	Arnold Town	2-1	90
78	Dunkirk	v	Dinnington Town	4-3	72
79	Gedling MW	v	Holwell Sports	2-2	68
	Holwell Sports	v	Gedling MW (17/8)	3-4	149
80	Holbrook Sports	v	Sleaford Town	4-0	61
81	Lincoln Moorlands Railway	v	Friar Lane & Epworth	3-1	61
82	Deeping Rangers	v	Gresley	0-2	139
83	Haverhill Rovers	v	Hadleigh United	2-1	178
84	Diss Town	v	Daventry United	1-2	111
85	Brantham Athletic	v	Woodbridge Town	4-2	81
86	St Neots Town	v	Dereham Town	2-0	299
87	Potton United	v	Stewarts&Lloyds Corby (13/8)	1-2	81
88	Newmarket Town	v	Yaxley	3-0	73
89	Whitton United	v	Thetford Town	1-1	64
	Thetford Town	v	Whitton United (17/8)	0-2	68
90	Northampton Spencer	v	Leiston	0-2	93
91	Wellingborough Town	v	Kirkley & Pakefield	3-0	85
92	Walsham Le Willows	v	Long Buckby	1-4	65
93	Team Bury	v	Ampthill Town	2-1	110
94	Ely City	v	Raunds Town	4-0	82
95	Wroxham	v	Rothwell Corinthians	5-1	95
96	Felixstowe & Walton Utd	v	Mildenhall Town	4-1	91
97	Great Yarmouth Town	v	Norwich United	0-4	120
98	March Town United	v	Gorleston	1-0	85
99	St Ives Town	v	Cogenhoe United	2-3	97
100	Rothwell Town	v	Desborough Town	3-4	243
101	Godmanchester Rovers	v	AFC Kempston Rovers	1-1	84
	AFC Kempston Rovers	v	Godmanchester Rovers (17/8)	4-0	68
102	St Margaretsbury	v	Welwyn Garden City	2-1	148
	(at Welwyn Garden City FC)				
103	Biggleswade United	v	Newport Pagnell Town	1-4	52
104	Saffron Walden Town	v	Mauritius Sports Association	3-2	126
105	Hadley	v	Barking (15/8)	0-0	146
	Barking	v	Hadley (18/8)	1-0	105
106	Kentish Town	v	Stansted (15/8)	1-0	35
	(at Kingsbury London Tigers FC)				
107	Chalfont St Peter	v	Stotfold	1-0	66
108	Clapton	v	Stanway Rovers	0-4	78
109	Burnham Ramblers	v	Hoddesdon Town	2-1	83
110	Oxhey Jets	v	Hatfield Town	3-2	62
111	Bethnal Green United	v	Basildon United	4-0	76
112	Bowers & Pitsea	v	Dunstable Town	4-1	63

Alim Sesay, Dulwich Hamlet, fires in a shot which is saved by Tunbridge Wells 'keeper Czanner in the Preliminary Round. Photo: Roger Turner. Above a second goal from Kempston Rovers' Kofi Schultz makes it 2-2 against Norwich United. Schultz went on to win the tie with a last minute strike. Photo: Gordon Whittington.

Team Bury's Danny Hitchins clears from under the bar whilst Felixstowe and Walton's Dan Davis (5) watches on. Photo: Alan Coomes.

Above: Tom Potter nets Hitchin Town's winner against Ware in the Preliminary Round. Photo: Gordon Whittington.

Suliaman Bangura, Dulwich Hamlet's No.2, has his flying header saved by the Tunbridge Wells goalkeeper during this Preliminary Round tie. Photo: Roger Turner.

EXTRA PRELIMINARY ROUND

SATURDAY 14 AUGUST 2010 - WINNING CLUBS TO RECEIVE £750

113	Takeley	v	Hertford Town	0-4	185
114	Cockfosters	v	Hullbridge Sports	2-1	65
115	Kingsbury London Tigers	v	FC Clacton	1-2	31
	(at Aveley FC)				
116	Witham Town	v	Wembley	3-0	76
117	Colney Heath	v	Broxbourne Borough V&E	3-0	76
118	Langford	v	Aylesbury United	1-3	68
119	Tring Athletic	v	Enfield 1893	2-0	126
120	Leverstock Green	v	Harefield United	1-2	56
121	Haringey Borough	v	Hillingdon Borough	3-0	62
122	London APSA	v	Halstead Town	3-3	48
	Halstead Town	v	London APSA (17/8)	2-0	84
123	Hanwell Town	v	London Colney	1-3	61
124	Royston Town	v	Crawley Green	1-2	130
125	Eton Manor	v	Bedford	3-0	35
126	Barkingside	v	Southend Manor	0-2	105
127	Cobham	v	Wick	2-0	55
128	Hassocks	v	Eastbourne United	7-1	72
129	Farnham Town	v	Badshot Lea	2-1	75
130	Molesey	v	Hartley Wintney	0-2	62
131	Croydon	v	Crowborough Athletic	5-2	87
132	Chessington & Hook Utd	v	Raynes Park Vale	1-2	63
133	Alresford Town	v	Herne Bay	5-2	72
134	St Francis Rangers	v	Banstead Athletic (15/8)	1-3	152
135	Sidley United	v	Lancing (15/8)	0-3	73
	(at Hailsham Town FC)				
136	Binfield	v	Crawley Down	3-2	90
137	Horley Town	v	Ash United	4-1	67
138	East Grinstead Town	v	Holyport	2-0	103
139	Camberley Town	v	Petersfield Town	2-1	60
140	Cove	v	Three Bridges	1-1	50
	Three Bridges	v	Cove (17/8)	4-1	58
141	Alton Town	v	Chichester City	4-1	75
142	Erith Town	v	Colliers Wood United	2-1	42
143	Arundel	v	Hailsham Town	4-1	76
144	Greenwich Borough	v	South Park (15/8)	1-2	134
145	Epsom & Ewell	v	Shoreham	3-0	91
146	Holmesdale	v	Erith & Belvedere	0-2	97
147	Mile Oak	v	Tunbridge Wells	0-1	77
148	Egham Town	v	Guildford City	1-3	70
149	Littlehampton Town	v	Beckenham Town (15/8)	1-1	71
	(at Worthing FC)				
	Beckenham Town	v	Littlehampton Town (17/8)	3-0	71
150	Hythe Town	v	Bookham	4-0	169
151	Selsey	v	Worthing United	1-4	128
152	Lordswood	v	Pagham	1-5	67
153	Norton Sports	v	Redhill	2-0	63
154	Flackwell Heath	v	Oakwood	2-1	58
155	Deal Town	v	Sandhurst Town	3-0	94
156	Frimley Green	v	Peacehaven & Telscombe	0-4	63
157	Lingfield	v	Sevenoaks Town (15/8)	1-0	101
	(at East Grinstead Town FC)				
158	Dorking	v	Bracknell Town	0-5	113
159	Mole Valley SCR	v	Chertsey Town (13/8)	0-5	167
160	VCD Athletic	v	AFC Uckfield	3-1	71
161	East Preston	v	Ringmer	1-4	82
162	Brading Town	v	Romsey Town	1-1	72
	Romsey Town	v	Brading Town (17/8)	0-4	58
163	Bradford Town	v	Wootton Bassett Town	1-1	70
	Wootton Bassett Town	v	Bradford Town (17/8)	3-3aet	82
	(Wootton Bassett Town won 4-3 on kicks from the penalty mark)				
164	Fairford Town	v	Lydney Town	0-0	49
	Lydney Town	v	Fairford Town (17/8)	3-1	101
165	Christchurch	v	Hamble ASSC	0-1	55
166	Ringwood Town	v	Cowes Sports (13/8)	5-0	118
167	Thame United	v	Shrivenham	3-0	24
168	Hayling United	v	Blackfield & Langley	1-2	74
169	Lymington Town	v	Moneyfields (15/8)	1-3	100
	(at Brockenhurst FC)				
170	Highworth Town	v	Melksham Town (15/8)	2-1	129
171	Bournemouth	v	Abingdon Town	1-0	71
172	Totton & Eling	v	Bemerton H. H. (13/8)	2-0	126
173	Wantage Town	v	Shortwood United	2-3	67
174	Downton	v	Bitton	0-2	64
175	Hallen	v	Winchester City	4-1	154
176	Milton United	v	Witney United	0-2	115
177	Bristol Manor Farm	v	Ardley United	5-3	41
178	Calne Town	v	Corsham Town	2-1	122
	(tie awarded to Corsham Town – Calne Town removed)				
179	Amesbury Town	v	Almondsbury UWE	0-5	77
180	Newport (IW)	v	Kidlington	1-0	172
181	New Milton Town	v	Longwell Green Sports	1-1	37
	Longwell Green Sports	v	New Milton Town (17/8)	3-2	58
182	Bicester Town	v	Westbury United	0-2	46
183	Warminster Town	v	Reading Town	1-2	159
184	Fareham Town	v	Clanfield 85	3-1	89
185	Hook Norton	v	Laverstock & Ford	1-6	35
	(at Laverstock & Ford FC)				
186	Brockenhurst	v	Old Woodstock Town	0-1	90
187	Larkhall Athletic	v	Gillingham Town	5-1	78
188	Bridport	v	Welton Rovers	3-0	128
189	Launceston	v	Bodmin Town	0-3	104
190	Willand Rovers	v	Merthyr Town	2-0	144
191	Sherborne Town	v	Portishead Town	2-1	85
192	Elmore	v	Hamworthy United	1-5	247
193	St Blazey	v	Torpoint Athletic	1-1	143
	Torpoint Athletic	v	St Blazey (17/8)	5-1	222
194	Odd Down	v	Verwood Town	1-1	46
	Verwood Town	v	Odd Down (18/8)	1-4	106
195	Street	v	Barnstaple Town	4-1	92
196	Buckland Athletic	v	Radstock Town	4-4	145
	Radstock Town	v	Buckland Athletic (17/8)	3-2	130
197	Brislington	v	Wellington	0-1	45
198	Keynsham Town	v	Tavistock	0-2	61
199	Saltash United	v	Bishop Sutton	1-1	78
	Bishop Sutton	v	Saltash United (17/8)	4-4aet	84
	(Bishop Sutton won 4-3 on kicks from the penalty mark)				
200	Poole Town	v	Dawlish Town	3-0	202
201	Ilfracombe Town	v	Falmouth Town	4-4	108
	Falmouth Town	v	Ilfracombe Town (18/8)	1-2	175

PRELIMINARY ROUND

For the older football fans in the North East, Spennymoor Town (who used to be United) achieved a 2-0 victory over Crook Town and Bishop Auckland's 2-2 draw with Whitley Bay will be a reminder of the great Amateur Cup days in the area. Goalscoring settled down a bit in this Round as the very weak clubs had probably been eliminated, but The Metropolitan Police (Isthmian Div 1 South) enjoyed themselves with a 6-0 victory at Horley Town (Combined Counties Premier), Clevedon Town (Southern Division One South) won by the same score at Bridport (Western Division One) and Lincoln Moorlands Railway (N.Co East Premier) won 6-0 at Glapwell (NPL Div 1 South)

The home clubs also managed to register some resounding victories with Bedworth United (Southern Div 1 Central) winning 6-1 v Dudley Town (West Midlands Premier) and Brigg Town (NPL Div 1 South) beat Rainworth Miners Welfare from the same division, 6-2. In the South, Worthing (Isthmian Div 1 South) put local rivals Arundel (Sussex Div One) in their place with a 6-0 beating and Old Woodstock Town (Hellenic Premier) provided a relatively new name to F.A. Cup headlines by beating Laverstock and Ford 6-3 after the Wessex club had scored six themselves in the previous round!

Little clubs who had got their squads together in the summer and prepared for the two August F.A. Cup ties successfully, would now find themselves nearly £2,000 richer - what a lovely way for a little club to start the season!

First Qualifying Round action between Cinderford Town and Ringwood Town - here the Ringwood player gets a shot away. Photo: Peter Barnes.

The first of Brett Donnelly's two goals for the Waders in this 3-3 draw between Biggleswade and Stamford. Stamford won the First Qualifying Replay 3-0. Photo: Gordon Whittington.

PRELIMINARY ROUND

SATURDAY 28 AUGUST 2010 - WINNERS RECEIVE £1,500

1	Spennymoor Town	v	Crook Town	2-0	209
2	Selby Town	v	Ossett Albion	0-4	113
3	Chester-Le-Street Town	v	Scarborough Athletic	2-1	203
4	South Shields	v	Dunston UTS	1-1	160
	Dunston UTS	v	South Shields (31/8)	3-0	201
5	Newcastle Benfield	v	North Shields	3-3	83
	North Shileds	v	Newcastle Benfield (31/8)	0-1	211
6	Armthorpe Welfare	v	Marske United	2-4	74
7	Wakefield	v	Ashington	2-3	141
8	AFC Emley	v	Northallerton Town (29/8)	0-1	141
9	Garforth Town	v	Tadcaster Albion	0-1	94
10	Jarrow Roofing Boldon CA	v	Durham City	1-2	190
11	Thackley	v	Harrogate RA	5-0	146
12	Billingham Synthonia	v	West Auckland Town	0-3	91
13	Shildon	v	Bridlington Town	1-0	151
14	Whitehaven	v	Norton & Stockton Ancients	1-5	41
15	Bishop Auckland	v	Whitley Bay	2-2	292
	Whitley Bay	v	Bishop Auckland (31/8)	3-1	385
16	Radcliffe Borough	v	Lancaster City	2-1	128
17	Hemsworth MW	v	Bamber Bridge	0-0	135
	Bamber Bridge	v	Hemsworth MW (31/8)	4-1	166
18	Holker Old Boys	v	Trafford	0-2	77
19	Curzon Ashton	v	Congleton Town	0-0	107
	Congleton Town	v	Curzon Ashton (31/8)	1-2aet	186
20	Cheadle Town	v	Ramsbottom United	1-3	66
21	Skelmersdale United	v	AFC Fylde	3-1	167
22	New Mills	v	Chadderton	3-1	127
23	Bacup Borough	v	Clitheroe	5-3	130
24	Staveley MW	v	Parkgate	1-3	110
25	Bootle	v	Warrington Town	1-2	223
26	Atherton Collieries	v	Prescot Cables	2-2	70
	Prescot Cables	v	Atherton Collieries (31/8)	2-0	104
27	St Helens Town	v	Glossop North End	1-1	113
	Glossop North End	v	St Helens Town (1/9)	3-1aet	229
28	Sheffield	v	Colne	3-1	199
29	Leigh Genesis	v	Runcorn Linnets	1-0	173
30	Salford City	v	Chorley	2-1	236
31	Atherton LR	v	Woodley Sports (27/8)	0-0	134
	Woodley Sports	v	Atherton LR (31/8)	3-0	77
	(at Cheadle Town FC)				
32	Rossendale United	v	Cammell Laird	5-2	91
33	Mossley	v	Witton Albion	2-0	221
34	Rugby Town	v	Atherstone Town	1-1	332
	Atherstone Town	v	Rugby Town (31/8)	0-3	222
35	Castle Vale JKS	v	Wednesfield	3-3	72
	Wednesfield	v	Castle Vale JKS (31/8)	6-0	68
36	Pilkington XXX	v	Bromsgrove Rovers		
	(walkover for Pilkington XXX - Bromsgrove Rovers removed)				
37	Leek Town	v	Eccleshall	0-1	210
38	Bridgnorth Town	v	Coventry Sphinx	1-1	85
	Coventry Sphinx	v	Bridgnorth Town (31/8)	1-0	113
39	Kidsgrove Athletic	v	Biddulph Victoria	0-0	168
	Biddulph Victoria	v	Kidsgrove Athletic (31/8)	0-4	162
40	Causeway United	v	Bartley Green	2-2	54
	(at Boldmere St Michaels FC)				
	Bartley Green	v	Causeway United (31/8)	4-2aet	107
41	Bewdley Town	v	Sutton Coldfield Town	2-3	107
42	Tipton Town	v	Stratford Town	3-1	84
43	Heather St Johns	v	Coleshill Town	2-3	48
44	Westfields	v	Market Drayton Town	0-2	90
45	Oadby Town	v	Malvern Town	2-0	65
46	Stourport Swifts	v	Dosthill Colts	3-3	79
	Dosthill Colts	v	Stourport Swifts (1/9)	1-0	85
47	Bedworth United	v	Dudley Town	6-1	146
48	Rushall Olympic	v	Romulus	0-0	83
	Romulus	v	Rushall Olympic (31/8)	4-2	103
49	Kirby Muxloe	v	Norton United	1-3	53
50	Coalville Town	v	Heath Hays	5-1	86
51	Newcastle Town	v	Nuneaton Griff	5-0	73
52	Lincoln United	v	Boston Town	2-2	83
	Boston Town	v	Lincoln United (31/8)	2-4	126
53	Bottesford Town	v	Barrow Town	2-1	76
54	Loughborough Dynamo	v	Shepshed Dynamo	1-1	191
	Shepshed Dynamo	v	Loughborough Dynamo (31/8)	2-3	299
55	Gresley	v	Quorn	4-0	203
56	Barton Town Old Boys	v	Shirebrook Town	1-4	83
57	Dunkirk	v	Grantham Town	2-2	123
	Grantham Town	v	Dunkirk (31/8)	2-3aet	190
58	Spalding United	v	Goole	1-0	101
59	Brigg Town	v	Rainworth MW	6-2	108
60	Maltby Main	v	Winterton Rangers	0-1	45
61	Glapwell	v	Lincoln Moorlands R. (29/8)	0-6	107
62	Carlton Town	v	Borrowash Victoria	2-1	75
63	Gedling MW	v	Barwell	0-1	75
64	Radcliffe Olympic	v	Wisbech Town	1-0	166
65	Belper Town	v	Holbrook Sports	1-3	173
66	Long Buckby	v	Daventry United	4-1	80
67	Norwich United	v	AFC Kempston Rovers	2-2	86
	AFC Kempston Rovers	v	Norwich United (31/8)	3-2	88
68	Wellingborough Town	v	Haverhill Rovers	1-1	82
	Haverhill Rovers	v	Wellingborough Town (31/8)	1-3	201
69	Daventry Town	v	Needham Market	2-3	102
70	Whitton United	v	Woodford United	0-3	34
71	Stewart & Lloyds Corby	v	Soham Town Rangers	2-1	59
72	AFC Sudbury	v	Stamford	2-2	260
	Stamford	v	AFC Sudbury (31/8)	2-1	227
73	March Town United	v	Desborough Town	1-2	106
74	Felixstowe & Walton Utd	v	Team Bury	2-1	158
75	Wroxham	v	Ely City	2-2	88
	Ely City	v	Wroxham (31/8)	1-1aet	133
	(Ely City won 4-3 on kicks from the penalty mark)				
76	Cogenhoe United	v	Leiston	0-3	89
77	Newmarket Town	v	Biggleswade Town	1-5	83
78	Brantham Athletic	v	St Neots Town	1-2	143
79	North Greenford United	v	Bowers & Pitsea	4-2	56
80	Arlesey Town	v	Aylesbury	1-1	135
	Aylesbury	v	Arlesey Town (31/8)	1-2	138
81	Witham Town	v	Ilford	0-0	80
	Ilford	v	Witham Town (1/9)	0-0aet	
	(Ilford won 3-2 on kicks from the penalty mark)				
82	Kentish Town	v	Bethnal Green United (29/8)	1-3	70
	(at Kingsbury London Tigers FC)				
83	Crawley Green	v	Harefield United	2-0	47
84	Barking	v	Redbridge	0-1	106
85	Waltham Forest	v	Enfield Town	0-3	119
86	Hitchin Town	v	Ware	2-1	234
87	Halstead Town	v	Stanway Rovers	1-2	153
88	Burnham Ramblers	v	Haringey Borough	5-1	34
89	Oxhey Jets	v	St Margeretsbury	4-1	51
90	Burnham	v	Chalfont St Peter	2-1	86

This Ringwood Town player keeps the ball under close control whilst under pressure from the Cinderford Town player behind. Photo: Peter Barnes.

Sonny Miles of Tonbridge out jumps Simon Cooper, Guldford (stripes), but puts his header wide in the First Qualifying Round. Photo: Alan Coomes.

Second Qualifying Round action between Chelmsford and Chertsey - here Chelmsford's Sam Higgins gets in a shot despite a desperate lunge by Simon Cox. Photo: Alan Coomes.

PRELIMINARY ROUND

SATURDAY 28 AUGUST 2010 - WINNERS RECEIVE £1,500

91	Marlow	v	London Colney	1-2	98
92	Uxbridge	v	Tilbury	0-1	50
93	Tring Athletic	v	AFC Hayes	3-2	126
94	Southend Manor	v	Brentwood Town	0-4	82
95	Newport Pagnell Town	v	Potters Bar Town	3-2	130
96	Colney Heath	v	FC Clacton	0-0	87
	FC Clacton	v	Colney Heath (31/8)	1-5	108
97	Harlow Town	v	Barton Rovers	1-0	183
98	Aylesbury United	v	Eton Manor (29/8)	3-2	117
99	Maldon & Tiptree	v	Hertford Town	4-2	63
100	Romford	v	Beaconsfield SYCOB (29/8)	3-1	120
101	Leighton Town	v	Heybridge Swifts	2-2	110
	Heybridge Swifts	v	Leighton Town (30/8)	0-1	155
102	East Thurrock United	v	Waltham Abbey	3-0	100
103	Cheshunt	v	Cockfosters	2-2	156
	Cockfosters	v	Cheshunt (31/8)	1-2	138
104	Saffron Walden Town	v	Great Wakering Rovers	1-1	155
	Great Wakering Rovers	v	Saffron Walden Town (31/8)	3-1	101
105	Wingate & Finchley	v	Northwood	0-0	116
	Northwood	v	Wingate & Finchley (31/8)	3-1	137
106	Thamesmead Town	v	Beckenham Town	2-3	59
107	Binfield	v	Camberley Town	5-1	164
108	AFC Totton	v	Sholing	1-2	254
109	Norton Sports	v	Banstead Athletic	2-0	57
110	Hartley Wintney	v	Whitehawk	2-2	110
	Whitehawk	v	Hartley Wintney (30/8)	4-0	120
111	Fleet Town	v	Bedfont Town	4-0	67
112	Lingfield	v	Corinthian Casuals	0-2	60
	(at Corinthian Casuals FC)				
113	Epsom & Ewell	v	Flackwell Heath	3-2	59
114	Deal Town	v	Hythe Town	2-4	189
115	Whitstable Town	v	Croydon	3-0	168
116	Cobham	v	Alresford Town	2-2	40
	Alresford Town	v	Cobham (31/8)	0-4	76
117	Leatherhead	v	Burgess Hill Town	0-2	131
118	Peacehaven & Telscombe	v	Ashford Town (Middx)	1-2	75
119	Chipstead	v	Whyteleafe	4-3	184
120	Guildford City	v	Three Bridges	2-1	69
121	Ramsgate	v	Godalming Town	1-1	171
	Godalming Town	v	Ramsgate (31/8)	3-0	137
122	Walton & Hersham	v	Bracknell Town	3-0	95
123	Ashford Town	v	Erith Town		
	(walkover for Erith Town – Ashford Town removed)				
124	Faversham Town	v	Pagham	2-0	122
125	Chertsey Town	v	Chatham Town	2-1	152
126	Alton Town	v	Merstham	2-1	95
127	Raynes Park Vale	v	East Grinstead Town	1-4	62
128	VCD Athletic	v	Eastbourne Town	1-1	90
	Eastbourne Town	v	VCD Athletic (1/9)	2-1aet	141
129	Walton Casuals	v	Worthing United	3-0	75

130	Horley Town	v	Metropolitan Police	0-6	92
131	Sittingbourne	v	Andover	0-2	108
132	Tunbridge Wells	v	Dulwich Hamlet	3-3	172
	Dulwich Hamlet	v	Tunbridge Wells (31/8)	0-1	189
133	Lancing	v	Slough Town	1-4	212
134	Hassocks	v	Farnham Town	3-2	90
135	Bognor Regis Town	v	Ringmer	1-0	244
136	Worthing	v	Arundel	6-0	313
137	South Park	v	Horsham YMCA	4-0	251
138	Gosport Borough	v	Erith & Belvedere	0-0	131
	Erith & Belvedere	v	Gosport Borough (31/8)	2-1	125
139	Old Woodstock Town	v	Laverstock & Ford	6-3	32
140	Bitton	v	Fareham Town	2-0	113
141	Reading Town	v	Newport (IW)	1-4	50
	(at Newbury FC)				
142	Almondsbury UWE	v	Wootton Bassett Town	0-1	62
143	Blackfield & Langley	v	Almondsbury Town	0-2	48
144	Bournemouth	v	Highworth Town	0-2	71
145	Cinderford Town	v	North Leigh	2-1	89
146	Hallen	v	Bristol Manor Farm	3-4	89
147	Hungerford Town	v	Moneyfields	2-1	85
148	Corsham Town	v	Brading Town	0-1	85
149	Bishop's Cleeve	v	Westbury United	4-0	74
150	Thatcham Town	v	Witney United	2-2	115
	Witney United	v	Thatcham Town (31/8)	2-4	139
151	Thame United	v	Lydney Town	2-1	27
152	Ringwood Town	v	Yate Town	4-1	98
153	Mangotsfield United	v	Abingdon United	5-0	158
154	Totton & Eling	v	Shortwood United (27/8)	0-0	162
	Shortwood United	v	Totton & Eling (31/8)	1-3aet	135
155	Longwell Green Sports	v	Hamble ASSC	0-3	61
156	Bridgwater Town	v	Street	1-0	204
157	Frome Town	v	Ilfracombe Town	1-0	179
158	Bideford	v	Wimborne Town	1-2	205
159	Willand Rovers	v	Radstock Town	1-0	107
160	Paulton Rovers	v	Larkhall Athletic	4-1	169
161	Bridport	v	Clevedon Town	0-6	187
162	Wellington	v	Bodmin Town (29/8)	0-3	116
	(at Elmore FC)				
163	Torpoint Athletic	v	Odd Down	1-1	148
	Odd Down	v	Torpoint Athletic (31/8)	0-1	84
164	Poole Town	v	Bishop Sutton	3-0	194
165	Hamworthy United	v	Sherborne Town	2-2	122
	Sherborne Town	v	Hamworth United (1/9)	3-0	154
166	Tavistock	v	Taunton Town	1-2	98

FIRST QUALIFYING ROUND

Clubs from the Evo-Stik, Ryman and Zamaretto Premier Divisions enter the fray in this Round which gives those clubs who have worked their way through the Preliminary Rounds a chance to take on senior opposition.

Best Victories

Home	Lowestoft Town (Ryman Premier)	7	Desborough Town (Utd Co Premier)	1
	Wealdstone (Ryman Premier)	7	Tring Athletic (S.Midlands Premier)	1
	AFC Hornchurch (Ryman Premier)	8	Oxhey Jets (S.Midlands Premier)	2
	Truro City (Zamaretto Premier)	8	Bridgwater T (Zamaretto Div 1SW)	2
Away:	Retford United (Evo-Stik Premier)	1	Mickleover Sports (Evo-Stik Premier)	5

Best Attendances

FC United v Radcliffe Borough 1144; FC Halifax Town v Whitby Town 976;
Salisbury City v Highworth Town 596; Lowestoft Town v Desborough Town 566
Leamington v Brackley Town 532

Hat Trick Marksman

Danny Burnell *(Wealdstone) 4 v Tring Athletic; Danny Carter (Coleshill Town) v Evesham United (a)
Danny Curd (Burgess Hill Town) v Eastboune Town; Joe Flack (AFC Hornchurch) v Oxhey Jets
Chrs Henderson (Bury Town) v Woodford United (a): Stewart Yetton (Truro City) v Bridgwater Town
* came on as a substitute after 33 minutes

Second Qualifying Round action - this Gloucester City player gets the better of the Weston-Super-Mare player. Photo: Peter Barnes.

Brackley's No.9 shapes up to take on the Buxton defender during their 2nd Qualifying Round tie. Photo: Peter Barnes.

FIRST QUALIFYING ROUND

SATURDAY 11 SEPTEMBER 2010 - WINNERS RECEIVE £3,000

1	Tadcsater Albion	v	Shildon	1-1	191
	Shildon	v	Tadcaster Albion (15/9)	4-2aet	194
2	Ossett Albion	v	Whitley Bay	1-2	172
3	Durham City	v	Dunston UTS (12/9)	1-3	145
	(at Esh Winning FC)				
4	North Ferriby United	v	Ossett Town	2-1	112
5	Ashington	v	Northallerton Town	3-1	230
6	Norton & Stockton Ancients	v	Chester-Le-Street Town	2-1	89
7	West Auckland Town	v	Bradford (Park Avenue)	3-1	180
8	Newcastle Benfield	v	Spennymoor Town	1-0	139
9	Thackley	v	Marske United	3-1	201
10	FC Halifax Town	v	Whitby Town	2-0	976
11	FC United of Manchester	v	Radcliffe Borough	3-0	1144
12	Parkgate	v	Warrington Town	1-3	122
13	Nantwich Town	v	Burscough	4-0	247
14	Salford City	v	Northwich Victoria	0-1	220
15	Curzon Ashton	v	New Mills	1-1	184
	New Mills	v	Curzon Ashton (13/9)	3-2	220
16	Prescot Cables	v	Ashton United	2-2	142
	Ashton United	v	Prescot Cables (13/9)	4-0	109
17	Frickley Athletic	v	Kendal Town	3-2	185
18	Marine	v	Colwyn Bay	1-1	312
	Colwyn Bay	v	Marine (14/9)	2-0	234
19	Bamber Bridge	v	Bacup Borough	2-0	152
20	Rossendale United	v	Leigh Genesis	3-4	84
21	Stocksbridge Park Steels	v	Trafford	4-2	120
22	Glossop North End	v	Mossley	0-4	354
23	Ramsbottom United	v	Skelmersdale United	0-2	164
24	Woodley Sports	v	Sheffield (12/9)	2-2	100
	(at Cheadle Town FC)				
	Sheffield	v	Woodley Sports (14/9)	3-1	
25	Wednesfield	v	Rugby Town	5-1	149
26	Stourbridge	v	Romulus	2-0	244
27	Evesham United	v	Coleshill Town	1-3	89
28	Leamington	v	Brackley Town	2-2	525
	Brackley Town	v	Leamington (14/9)	2-0	306
29	Pilkington XXX	v	Market Drayton Town	0-2	91
30	Oadby Town	v	Dosthill Colts	2-1	65
31	Coventry Sphinx	v	Sutton Coldfield Town	1-0	110
32	Tipton Town	v	Norton United	1-0	56
33	Kidsgrove Athletic	v	Chasetown	3-0	233
34	Coalville Town	v	Eccleshall	5-0	138
35	Bartley Green	v	Bedworth United	1-1	111
	Bedworth United	v	Bartley Green (14/9)	4-0	129
36	Hednesford Town	v	Newcastle Town	1-2	305
37	Winterton Rangers	v	Radcliffe Olympic	2-2	85
	Radcliffe Olympic	v	Winterton Rangers (14/9)	2-0	156
38	Bottesford Town	v	Buxton	0-3	135
39	Lincoln Moorlands Railway	v	Gresley	2-2	147
	Gresley	v	Lincoln Moorlands R. (14/9)	1-2	247
40	Matlock Town	v	Worksop Town	3-1	428
41	Spalding United	v	Brigg Town	2-2	103
	Brigg Town	v	Spalding United (14/9)	4-0	105
42	Holbrook Sports	v	Loughborough Dynamo	1-3	121
43	Barwell	v	Hucknall Town	2-0	163
44	Shirebrook Town	v	Lincoln United	1-3	119
45	Carlton Town	v	Dunkirk	1-1	148
	Dunkirk	v	Carlton Town (14/9)	1-2aet	105
46	Retford United	v	Mickleover Sports	0-5	144
47	Cambridge City	v	Long Buckby	3-0	270
48	Lowestoft Town	v	Desborough Town	7-1	566
49	Ely City	v	Stewart & Lloyds Corby	0-1	102
50	Woodford United	v	Bury Town	1-3	84
51	Felixstowe & Walton United	v	Wellingborough Town	2-1	191
52	Needham Market	v	AFC Kempston Rovers	6-1	204
53	Leiston	v	St Neots Town	3-2	236
54	Biggleswade Town	v	Stamford	3-3	160
	Stamford	v	Biggleswade Town (14/9)	3-0	199
55	Great Wakering Rovers	v	Harrow Borough	2-4	95
56	Brentwood Town	v	Aylesbury United	4-0	142
57	Wealdstone	v	Tring Athletic	7-0	196
58	Hemel Hempstead Town	v	Concord Rangers	1-2	184
59	Burnham	v	Colney Heath	2-1	109
60	Romford	v	Crawley Green	1-1	93
	Crawley Green	v	Romford (15/9)	1-2	127
61	North Greenford United	v	Northwood	2-1	134
62	Ilford	v	Maldon & Tiptree	0-1	66
63	AFC Hornchurch	v	Oxhey Jets	8-2	171
64	Canvey Island	v	Newport Pagnell Town	4-1	266
65	Redbridge	v	London Colney	2-0	72
66	Grays Athletic	v	Windsor & Eton (12/9)	1-0	314
	(at East Thurrock United FC)				
67	Stanway Rovers	v	Bedford Town	1-1	128
	Bedford Town	v	Stanway Rovers (14/9)	2-0	221
68	Arlesley Town	v	Enfield Town	0-2	186
69	Billericay Town	v	Tilbury	1-0	329
70	East Thurrock United	v	Leighton Town	2-1	110
71	Hendon	v	Cheshunt (12/9)	4-1	182
72	Hitchin Town	v	Aveley	2-1	224
73	Harlow Town	v	Bethnal Green United	1-1	214
	Bethnal Green United	v	Harlow Town (13/9)	0-4	173
74	Burnham Ramblers	v	Chesham United	0-3	115
75	Hythe Town	v	Epsom & Ewell	2-0	182
76	Sholing	v	Hassocks	5-0	85
77	Corinthian Casuals	v	Erith & Belvedere	1-2	75
78	Cobham	v	Chipstead	0-1	50
79	Sutton United	v	Alton Town	1-2	298
80	Carshalton Athletic	v	Tunbridge Wells	2-1	250
81	Tonbridge Angels	v	Guildford City	0-1	385
82	Tooting & Mitcham United	v	Walton Casuals	4-1	212
83	Godalming Town	v	Metropolitan Police	1-2	142
84	Erith Town	v	Slough Town	1-0	104
85	Beckenham Town	v	Norton Sports	3-2	71
86	Burgess Hill Town	v	Eastbourne Town	3-2	165
87	Fleet Town	v	Faversham Town	3-1	124
88	Folkestone Invicta	v	Horsham	4-2	327
89	Kingstonian	v	Croydon Athletic		
	(walkover for Kingstonian – Croydon Athletic withdrawn)				
90	Whitstable Town	v	East Grinstead Town	1-0	199
91	Ashford Town (Middx)	v	Worthing	1-1	133
	Worthing	v	Ashford lTown (Middx) (14/9)	5-1	173
92	Whitehawk	v	Maidstone United	3-1	115
93	Cray Wanderers	v	South Park (12/9)	1-0	217
94	Binfield	v	Margate	0-3	394
95	Bognor Regis Town	v	Hastings United	3-2	374
96	Walton & Hersham	v	Bashley	1-4	110
97	Andover	v	Chertsey Town	0-4	81
	(at Whitchurch United FC)				
98	Bitton	v	Old Woodstock Town	2-3	94
99	Oxford City	v	Mangotsfield United	0-1	155
100	Swindon Supermarine	v	Brading Town	4-0	82
101	Banbury United	v	Chippenham Town	1-2	277
102	Newport (IW)	v	Bishop's Cleeve	0-3	178
103	Thatcham Town	v	Thame United	0-1	112
104	Almondsbury Town	v	Bristol Manor Farm	1-1	100
	Bristol Manor Farm	v	Almondsbury Town (14/9)	2-2aet	
	(Bristol Manor Farm won 3-1 on kicks from the penalty mark)				
105	Hungerford Town	v	Totton & Eling	6-2	81
106	Highworth Town	v	Salisbury City	1-1	422
	Salisbury City	v	Highworth Town (14/9)	5-0	596
107	Hamble ASSC	v	Wootton Bassett Town	1-1	94
	Wootton Bassett Town	v	Hamble ASSC (14/9)	0-2	
86					
108	Cinderford Town	v	Ringwood Town	5-0	78
109	Cirencester Town	v	Didcot Town	0-0	125
	Didcot Town	v	Cirencester Town (14/9)	3-1	136
110	Tiverton Town	v	Paulton Rovers	1-1	296
	Paulton Rovers	v	Tiverton Town (13/9)	2-0	299
111	Truro City	v	Bridgwater Town	8-2	325
112	Torpoint Athletic	v	Clevedon Town	2-4	258
113	Wimborne Town	v	Sherborne Town	1-3	226
114	Bodmin Town	v	Poole Town	1-4	131
115	Taunton Town	v	Weymouth	1-2	288
116	Frome Town	v	Willand Rovers	1-0	176

SECOND QUALIFYING ROUND

The prize money is mounting and it's getting exciting, especially for the little clubs who were wondering just how far they could go in the famous competition.

BEST VICTORIES

Home	Lowestoft Town (Ryman Premier)	7	Desborough Town (Utd Co Premier)	1
	Chelmsford City	7	Chertsey Town	0
	Coleshill Town	5	Lincoln United	1
	Vauxhall Motors	5	Blyth Spartans	1
	Salisbury City	5	Sholing	1
	AFC Telford United	5	Stourbridge	2
	North Ferriby United	5	Stocksbridge Park Steels	2
	Mewcastle Town	5	Wednesfield	3
Away	Burnham	2	Whitehawk	6
	Erith Town	1	Dover Athletic	5
	Grays Athletic	1	Bury Town	4
	Mangotsfield T	1	Dorcester Town	4
	Romford	0	Hampton & Richmond B	4
	Tooting & Mitcham Utd	1	Staines Town	4

LARGEST ATTENDANCES

1447 - AFC Telford United v Stourbridge
1037 - F.C.United v Gainsborough Trinity
1352 - Boston United v Worcester City
1024 - Dartford v Lowestoft Town

HAT TRICK HEROES

Sam Higgins (Chelmsford City) 4 v Chertsey Town
Karl Espley(Newcastle Ton) 3 v Wednesfield
Byron Harrison (Carshalton Athletic) 3 v East Thurrock
Dan Carter (Coleshill Town) 3 v Lincoln United
Joe Gatting (Whitehawk) 3 v Burnham (a)
Jake Reed (Salisbury City) 3 v Sholing

More Second Qualifying Round action from the tie between Brackley Town and Buxton. Left, Buxton score one of their three, whilst below left we see a Brackley player firing towards goal. Photos: Peter Barnes.

Gloucester City's No.9 manages to hold off the challange from an unseen Weston player. Photo: Peter Barnes.

SECOND QUALIFYING ROUND

SATURDAY 25 SEPTEMBER 2010 - WINNERS RECEIVE £4,500

1	Frickley Athletic	v	Newcastle Benfield	2-1	217
2	Bamber Bridge	v	Warrington Town	1-1	223
	Warrington Town	v	Bamber Bridge (28/9)	4-2	236
3	Norton & Stockton Ancients	v	Leigh Genesis	2-1	127
4	New Mills	v	Harrogate Town	0-2	309
5	Vauxhall Motors	v	Blyth Spartans	5-1	216
6	North Ferriby United	v	Stocksbridge Park Steels	5-2	196
7	Dunston UTS	v	Mossley	1-2	248
8	Ashington	v	Thackley	1-0	336
9	Colwyn Bay	v	Guiseley	1-1	457
	Guiseley	v	Colwyn Bay (28/9)	3-0	256
10	Nantwich Town	v	Whitley Bay	2-3	344
11	FC United Of Manchester	v	Gainsborough Trinity	2-1	1037
12	Hyde	v	Droylsden	0-0	375
	Droylsden	v	Hyde (27/9)	3-1	354
13	Ashton United	v	FC Halifax Town	1-2	525
14	Stalybridge Celtic	v	Alfreton Town	1-1	373
	Alfreton Town	v	Stalybridge Celtic (28/9)	1-2aet	387
15	Shildon	v	Skelmersdale United	2-0	234
16	Sheffield	v	Northwich Victoria	2-2	422
	Northwich Victoria	v	Sheffield (28/9)	1-2	429
17	Workington	v	West Auckland Town	2-1	413
18	Boston United	v	Worcester City	2-3	1352
19	Ilkeston Town	v	Lincoln Moorlands Railway		
	(walkover for Lincoln Moorlands Railway – Ilkeston Town removed)				
20	Tipton Town	v	Market Drayton Town	2-0	82
21	Eastwood Town	v	Stafford Rangers	1-1	347
	Stafford Rangers	v	Eastwood Town (28/9)	1-3	429
22	Brigg Town	v	Nuneaton Town	3-3	276
	Nuneaton Town	v	Brigg Town (28/9)	2-0	545
23	Coleshill Town	v	Lincoln United	5-1	76
24	Hinckley United	v	Coventry Sphinx	2-0	301
25	Oadby Town	v	Radcliffe Olympic	1-3	135
26	Barwell	v	Coalville Town	3-2	307
27	Loughborough Dynamo	v	Redditch United	0-2	185
28	Stewarts & Lloyds Corby	v	Mickleover Sports	2-2	102
	Mickleover Sports	v	Stewarts & Lloyds C. (29/9)	3-2aet	120
29	Brackley Town	v	Buxton	1-3	306
30	Carlton Town	v	Matlock Town	0-1	199
31	Bedworth United	v	Corby Town	0-1	241
32	Newcastle Town	v	Wednesfield	5-3	146
33	Solihull Moors	v	Kidsgrove Athletic	2-0	233
34	AFC Telford United	v	Stourbridge	5-2	1447
35	Hythe Town	v	Erith & Belvedere	4-1	230
36	Erith Town	v	Dover Athletic	1-5	282
37	Bury Town	v	Grays Athletic	2-2	582
	Grays Athletic	v	Bury Town (29/9)	1-4	268
38	Chesham United	v	Wealdstone	2-2	565
	Wealdstone	v	Chesham United (27/9)	4-1	366
39	Braintree Town	v	Welling United	2-0	434

40	Tooting & Mitcham United	v	Staines Town	1-4	378
41	Bishop's Stortford	v	Bromley	2-2	257
	Bromley	v	Bishop's Stortford (28/9)	2-1	347
42	Cambridge City	v	Hitchin Town	2-2	388
	Hitchin Town	v	Cambridge City (28/9)	0-2	324
43	Billericay Town	v	Concord Rangers	1-1	301
	Concord Rangers	v	Billericay Town (28/9)	1-0aet	283
44	Folkestone Invicta	v	Leiston	1-1	280
	Leiston	v	Folkestone Invicta (28/9)	2-1	307
45	Lewes	v	Harlow Town	2-0	785
46	AFC Hornchurch	v	Brentwood Town	0-0	279
	Brentwood Town	v	AFC Hornchurch (28/9)	1-0	212
47	East Thurrock United	v	Carshalton Athletic	1-1	163
	Carshalton Athletic	v	East Thurrock United (28/9)	3-2	188
48	Hendon	v	Maldon & Tiptree (26/9)	2-1	166
49	Enfield Town	v	Worthing (26/9)	1-0	304
50	North Greenford United	v	Felixstowe & Walton United	1-1	118
	Felixstowe & Walton Utd	v	North Greenford United (28/9)	0-3	305
51	Needham Market	v	Chipstead	0-0	231
	Chipstead	v	Needham Market (28/9)	0-2	139
52	Romford	v	Hampton & Richmond Boro'	0-4	193
53	Canvey Island	v	Whitstable Town	1-0	271
54	Redbridge	v	Harrow Borough	1-2	82
55	Burnham	v	Whitehawk	2-6	103
56	Bedford Town	v	Boreham Wood	0-2	361
57	Thurrock	v	Stamford	3-1	122
58	Cray Wanderers	v	Ebbsfleet United	2-2	408
	Ebbsfleet United	v	Cray Wanderers (28/9)	4-2	530
59	St Albans City	v	Beckenham Town	3-1	303
60	Metropolitan Police	v	Burgess Hill Town	2-1	102
61	Margate	v	Kingstonian	1-1	438
	Kingstonian	v	Margate (27/9)	1-1aet	312
	(Kingstonian won 3-2 on kicks from the penalty mark)				
62	Dartford	v	Lowestoft Town	2-1	1024
63	Chelmsford City	v	Chertsey Town	7-0	623
64	Hamble ASSC	v	Old Woodstock Town	2-1	115
65	Eastleigh	v	Bognor Regis Town	2-0	477
66	Sholing	v	Salisbury City	2-2	360
	Salisbury City	v	Sholing (28/9)	5-1	604
67	Chippenham Town	v	Farnborough	0-1	486
68	Havant & Waterlooville	v	Frome Town	1-0	448
69	Mangotsfield United	v	Dorchester Town	1-4	265
70	Paulton Rovers	v	Didcot Town	0-1	279
71	Bristol Manor Farm	v	Basingstoke Town	2-2	183
	Basingstoke Town	v	Bristol Manor Farm (27/9)	1-0	223
72	Sherborne Town	v	Hungerford Town	1-2	138
73	Bashley	v	Fleet Town	2-2	195
	Fleet Town	v	Bashley (28/9)	0-2	146
74	Poole Town	v	Thame United	1-1	315
	Thame United	v	Poole Town (28/9)	0-1aet	126
75	Guildford City	v	Clevedon Town	1-2	150
76	Bishop's Cleeve	v	Woking	1-2	252
77	Gloucester City	v	Weston Super Mare (26/9)	0-2	380
78	Swindon Supermarine	v	Weymouth	3-0	185
79	Maidenhead United	v	Truro City	1-0	237
80	Alton Town	v	Cinderford Town	2-2	233
	Cinderford Town	v	Alton Town (28/9)	2-1aet	129

THIRD QUALIFYING ROUND

Four clubs with comparatively new identity are attracting the bggest Cup attendances so far, and once again in the last round before the Blue Square Premier clubs join in, F.C Halifax , F.C.United of Manchester, AFC Telford United and Nuneaton Town scored sixteen goals between them and attracted three of the best attendances. The winners of the Concord Rangers v Hythe Town and Radcliffe Olympic v Tipton Town matches will be really looking forward to the final qualifying round draw and Byron Harrison will be particularly happy with the F.A. Cup having registered his second hat-trick in the last two rounds.

BEST VICTORIES

Home	Nuneaton Town	6	Coleshill Town	0
	Clevedon Town	0	Eastleigh	5
	Leiston	5	North Greenford	0
Away	Norton & Stockton	2	F.C.United	5
	Ossett Town	0	Ashton United	5

BEST ATTENDANCES

1835	F.C.Halifax v Harrogate Town
1526	Norton & Stockton v F.C.United
1122	AFC Telford United v Buxton
1011	Chelmsford City v Bromley
965	Nuneaton Town v Coleshill Town
918	Bury Town v Staines Town

HAT TRICK HEROS

Aaron Burns Ashton United v Ossett Town (a)
Byron Harrison Carshalton Athletic v Braintree Town
Gareth Heath Leiston v North Greenford
Nick Stanley Swindon Supermarine v Hungerford T

Midfield action from the 3rd Qualifying tie between Cinderford Town (stripes) and Maidenhead United. Photo: Peter Barnes.

FOURTH QUALIFYING ROUND

Senior clubs from the Blue Square Premier will probably consider qualification for the competition proper imperative for their season's budget forcast to be fulfilled. Clubs involved in this round from The Blue Square North and South will have prayed for a home draw and of course the little clubs who have battled through the qualifying rounds will just be thrilled to be involved and will desperately hope their luck can run for at least one more round.

Harrow Borough had been drawn away from home three times in four rounds but it appeared to be their year and a n excellent 4-2 away victory at Eastbourne Borough was highlighted by a hat trick from Troy Hewitt. Histon's defeat at Havant & Waterlooville wasn't a surprise as the Premier division club was really struggling to find form and two local derbys attracted good crowds with 2,792 watching Rushden & Diamonds winning at Kettering Town and 4,144 saw Luton Town put St Albans City firmly in their place with a 4-0 victory.

BEST VICTORIES

Home	Dover Athletic	5	Farnborough	0*
	Luton Town	4	St Albans City	0
Away	Mossley	2	Darlington	6

SURPRISING VICTORIES

Eastbourne Borough	2	Harrow Borough	4
Hythe Town	2	Staines Town	0
Bath City	3	Swindon Supermarine	4*
F.C.United	1	Barrow	0*

BEST ATTENDANCES

4,144 Luton Town v St Albans City
2,986 F.C.Halifax Town v Mansfield Town
2,247 Newport County v Crawley Town
3,263* F.C.United v Barrow
2,792 Kettering Town v Rushden & Diamonds
2,052 Wrexham v Southport

HAT TRICK HEROES

Adam Birchall (Dover Athletic) 3* v Farnborough
Lee Brown (Hayes &Yeading) 3 v Poole Town (a)
Troy Hewitt(Harrow Borough) 3 v Eastbourne Borough (a)
Amari Morgan-Smith (Luton Town) 3 v St Albans City

THIRD QUALIFYING ROUND

SATURDAY 9 OCTOBER 2010 - WINNERS RECEIVE £7,500

1	FC Halifax Town	v	Harrogate Town	4-0	1385
2	Sheffield	v	Frickley Athletic	1-1	632
	Frickley Athletic	v	Sheffield (12/10)	1-2	322
3	Guiseley	v	Whitley Bay	3-0	704
4	Norton & Stockton Ancients	v	FC United Of Manchester	2-5	1536
5	Workington	v	Shildon	2-1	513
6	North Ferriby United	v	Vauxhall Motors	2-2	369
	Vauxhall Motors	v	North Ferriby United (12/10)	1-1aet	202
	(Vauxhall Motors won 4-3 on kicks from the penalty mark)				
7	Warrington Town	v	Stalybridge Celtic	1-3	429
8	Lincoln Moorlands Railway	v	Mossley	1-1	216
	Mossley	v	Lincoln Moorlands Railway (12/10)	4-1	
180					
9	Ashington	v	Droylsden	1-4	543
10	Solihull Moors	v	Barwell	1-1	387
	Barwell	v	Solihull Moors (12/10)	3-1	343
11	Mickleover Sports	v	Newcastle Town	1-2	562
12	Buxton	v	AFC Telford United	1-1	836
	AFC Telford United	v	Buxton (12/10)	2-2aet	1122
	(Buxton won 5-4 on kicks from the penalty mark)				
13	Redditch United	v	Hinckley United	1-0	563
14	Corby Town	v	Worcester City	2-1	520
15	Matlock Town	v	Eastwood Town	0-3	655
16	Nuneaton Town	v	Coleshill Town	6-0	695
17	Radcliffe Olympic	v	Tipton Town	3-3	516
	Tipton Town	v	Radcliffe Olympic (13/10)	2-0	495
18	Chelmsford City	v	Bromley	2-2	1011
	Bromley	v	Chelmsford City (12/10)	0-3	619
19	Leiston	v	North Greenford United	5-0	315
20	Brentwood Town	v	Woking	1-1	748
	Woking	v	Brentwood Town (12/10)	1-0	460
21	Harrow Borough	v	Hampton & Richmond Borough	2-1	342
22	St Albans City	v	Kingstonian	0-0	484
	Kingstonian	v	St Albans City (11/10)	1-2	367
23	Metropolitan Police	v	Wealdstone	1-1	390
	Wealdstone	v	Metropolitan Police (11/10)	1-2aet	303
24	Lewes	v	Thurrock	2-1	854
25	Needham Market	v	Ebbsfleet United	0-1	573
26	Whitehawk	v	Hendon	1-2	196
27	Boreham Wood	v	Enfield Town	3-1	361
28	Carshalton Athletic	v	Braintree Town	4-1	490
29	Concord Rangers	v	Hythe Town	0-1	163
30	Dover Athletic	v	Cambridge City	3-1	820
31	Bury Town	v	Staines Town	2-2	918
	Staines Town	v	Bury Town (12/10)	2-0	274
32	Canvey Island	v	Dartford	2-2	715
	Dartford	v	Canvey Island (12/10)	3-3aet	665
	(Dartford won 9-8 on kicks from the penalty mark)				
33	Swindon Supermarine	v	Hungerford Town	4-0	365
34	Salisbury City	v	Weston Super Mare	1-0	871
35	Didcot Town	v	Basingstoke Town	0-4	401
36	Havant & Waterlooville	v	Dorchester Town	4-1	708
37	Farnborough	v	Hamble ASSC	2-0	503
38	Poole Town	v	Bashley	1-0	837
39	Clevedon Town	v	Eastleigh	0-5	313
40	Cinderford Town	v	Maidenhead United	0-4	235

FOURTH QUALIFYING ROUND

SATURDAY 23 OCTOBER 2010 - WINNERS RECEIVE £12,500

1	Mossley	v	Darlington	2-6	619
2	Sheffield	v	Tipton Town	2-2	1026
	Tipton Town	v	Sheffield (27/10)	2-0	1429
3	Guiseley	v	Redditch United	2-1	808
4	Fleetwood Town	v	Buxton	2-1	1181
5	Altrincham	v	Gateshead	0-2	797
6	Vauxhall Motors	v	Newcastle Town	1-0	323
7	FC United of Manchester	v	Barrow (24/10)	1-0	3263
8	Workington	v	Nuneaton Town	1-1	520
	Nuneaton Town	v	Workington (26/10)	1-0	943
9	Tamworth	v	Grimsby Town	1-1	928
	Grimsby Town	v	Tamworth (26/10)	0-1	1612
10	Kidderminster Harriers	v	York City	0-2	1123 11
	FC Halifax Town	v	Mansfield Town	0-1	2986
12	Wrexham	v	Southport	1-2	2052
13	Stalybridge Celtic	v	Eastwood Town	1-2	659
14	Droylsden	v	Barwell	3-0	411
15	Woking	v	Eastleigh	3-2	1048
16	Hythe Town	v	Staines Town	2-0	808
17	Eastbourne Borough	v	Harrow Borough	2-4	681
18	Cambridge United	v	Lewes	3-0	1626
19	Corby Town	v	Salisbury City	3-0	957
20	Newport County	v	Crawley Town	0-1	2247
21	Luton Town	v	St Albans City	4-0	4144
22	Farnborough	v	Dover Athletic	1-1	845
	Dover Athletic	v	Farnborough (26/10)	5-0	1044
23	Kettering Town	v	Rushden & Diamonds	1-2	2792
24	Carshalton Athletic	v	Chelmsford City	1-1	1024
	Chelmsford City	v	Carshalton Athletic (25/10)	3-2	1069
25	Hendon	v	Metropolitan Police	0-0	269
	Metropolitan Police	v	Hendon (27/10)	0-2	302
26	Leiston	v	Dartford	0-0	832
	Dartford	v	Leiston (26/10)	3-2	1074
27	Basingstoke Town	v	AFC Wimbledon	0-1	1750
28	Swindon Supermarine	v	Bath City	0-0	551
	Bath City	v	Swindon Supermarine (26/10)	3-4	665
29	Havant & Waterlooville	v	Histon	2-0	905
30	Forest Green Rovers	v	Maidenhead United	1-0	580
31	Poole Town	v	Hayes & Yeading United	1-3	1219
32	Ebbsfleet United	v	Boreham Wood	3-0	1005

FIRST ROUND PROPER

The Blue Square Premier clubs had entered the competition in the Fourth Qualifying Round and fifteen survived their first challenge:-

Home Winners (5): Cambridge United, Ebbsfleet United, Fleetwood Town, Forest Green Rovers, Luton Town,
Away Winners (10): AFC Wimbledon, Crawley Town, Darlington,Gateshead, Hayes & Yeading, Mansfield Town, Rushden & Diamonds, Southport,Tamworth (after a replay) and York City.

Blue Square North and South teams had to come through two qualifying rounds and between them had supplied 11 clubs for the First Round

Blue Square North:
Home Winners (5): Corby Town, Droylsden, Guiseley, Nuneaton Town (after a replay) and Vauxhall Motors.
Away Winners (1): Eastwood Town

Blue Square South:
Home Winners (5): Chelmsford City, Dartford (after a replay), Dover Athletic (after a replay), Havant & Waterlooville and Woking
Away Winners (0):

The two clubs who started out on Saturday 28th August in the Preliminary Round were Hythe Town and Tipton Town

Hythe Town.

Preliminary Round	4-2	v Deal Town (away)
First Qualifying Round	4-1	v Erith & Belvedere
Second Qualifying Round	2-0	v Epsom & Ewell
Third Qualifying Round	1-0	v Concord Rangers (away)
Fourth Qualifying Round	2-0	v Staines Town

Tipton Town

Preliminary Round	2-1	v Stratford Town
First Qualifying Round	1-0	v Norton United
Second Qualifying Round	2-0	v Market Drayton
Third Qualifying Round	3-3	v Radcliffe Olympic
Third Qualifying Round Replay	2-0	v Radcliffe Olympic
Fourth Qualifying Round	2-2	v Sheffield F.C. (away)
Fourth Qualifying Round Replay	2-0	v Sheffield F.C.

Six clubs who had survived at least three rounds to give their supporters the thrill of a place in The First Round Proper draw with the First and Second Division clubs were:

Harrow Borough (Ryman Premier)	0-2	Chesterfield (Leaders in League Two)
Chelmsford City (Blue Square South)	3-2	**Hendon (Ryman Premier)**
Hereford United (League Two)	5-1	**Hythe Town (Kent League)**
Carlisle United (League One)	6-0	**Tipton Town (Midland Football Alliance)**
Swindon Supermarine (Zamaretto Premier)	2-1	Eastwood Town (Blue Square North)
Rochdale (League One)	2-3	**F.C. United of Manchester (Evo-Stik Premier)**

The two clubs who had entered the competition on 28th August, Tipton Town and Hythe Town enjoyed the thrill of a visit to a Football League ground but were well beaten. No one will be particularly unhappy however, as both clubs will have banked £29,250 prize money and everyone involved will remember this F.A. Cup campaign for the rest of their lives.

F.C. United enjoyed themselves again with a fine away victory over Rochdale, who had been playing well in Division One and were featured on television. Four all non-league ties enabled AFC Wimbledon, Crawley Town, Droylsden and Luton Town to move on but the headlines were dominated by Dover Athletic who achieved a very special 2-0 victory over Kent neighbours Gillingham, Tamworth beat Crewe Alexandra 2-1 and Darlington won by the same score at home to Bristol Rovers. The most resounding victory however, was achieved by York City who beat Rotherham United 3-0 at home in a replay. Woking also impressed on television against a very confident Brighton & Hove side before losing on penalties after a thrilling replay and Cambridge United only lost to two injury time winners in a replay at Huddersfield Town, another confident Division One club.

Top Ten- Best Attendances at Non-League Club in First Round

4,490 - Southport v Sheffield Wednesday
3,679 - Dartford v Port Vale
3,127 - Cambridge United v Huddersfield Town
2,644* - York City v Rotherham United
2,319 - Fleetwood Town v Walsall
4.193* - Woking v Brighton & Hove Albion
3,219 - AFC Wimbledon v Ebbsfleet United
3,050 - Luton Town v Corby Town
2,406 - Vauxhall Motors v Hartlepool United
2.306 - Ebbsfleet United v AFC Wimbledon

FIRST ROUND PROPER

SATURDAY 6 NOVEMBER 2010 - WINNERS RECEIVE £18,000

1	Colchester United	v	Bradford City	4-3	2736
2	Corby Town	v	Luton Town	1-1	1750
	Luton Town	v	Corby Town (17/11)	4-2	3050
3	Harrow Borough	v	Chesterfield	0-2	1050
4	Notts County	v	Gateshead	2-0	3235
5	Stevenage	v	Milton Keynes Dons	0-0	2956
	Milton Keynes Dons	v	Stevenage (16/11)	1-1aet	3977
	(Stevenage won 7-6 on kicks from the penalty mark)				
6	Southport	v	Sheffield Wednesday (7/11)	2-5	4490
7	Rotherham United	v	York City	0-0	3227
	York City	v	Rotherham United (17/11)	3-0	2644
8	Havant & Waterlooville	v	Droylsden	0-2	1102
9	Bury	v	Exeter City	2-0	2359
10	Cheltenham Town	v	Morecambe	1-0	2066
11	Hayes & Yeading United	v	Wycombe Wanderers	1-2	1426
12	Dagenham & Redbridge	v	Leyton Orient	1-1	3378
	Leyton Orient	v	Dagenham & Redbridge (16/11)	3-2	2901
13	AFC Wimbledon	v	Ebbsfleet United	0-0	3219
	Ebbsfleet United	v	AFC Wimbledon (18/11)	2-3aet	2306
14	Lincoln City	v	Nuneaton Town	1-03084 15	
15	Mansfield Town	v	Torquay United	0-1	2179
16	Hereford United	v	Hythe Town	5-1	2217
17	AFC Bournemouth	v	Tranmere Rovers	5-3	3951
18	Chelmsford City	v	Hendon	3-2	1685
19	Swindon Supermarine	v	Eastwood Town	2-1	1159
20	Rushden & Diamonds	v	Yeovil Town	0-1	1666
21	Southampton	v	Shrewsbury Town	2-0	10410
22	Cambridge United	v	Huddersfield Town	0-0	3127
	Huddersfield Town	v	Cambridge United (16/11)	2-1	3766
23	Burton Albion	v	Oxford United (7/11)	1-0	2483
24	Gillingham	v	Dover Athletic	0-2	7475
25	Tamworth	v	Crewe Alexandra	2-1	1776
26	Darlington	v	Bristol Rovers	2-1	1602
27	Guiseley	v	Crawley Town	0-5	1609
28	Brighton & Hove Albion	v	Woking	0-0	5868
	Woking	v	Brighton & Hove Albion (16/11)	2-2aet	4193
	(Brighton & Hove Albion won 3-0 on kicks from the penalty mark)				
29	Macclesfield Town	v	Southend United	2-2	1582
	Southend United	v	Macclesfield Town (16/11)	2-2aet	2730
	(Macclesfield Town won 5-3 on kicks from the penalty mark)				
30	Rochdale	v	FC United of Manchester (5/11)	2-3	7048
31	Carlisle United	v	Tipton Town	6-0	4241
32	Dartford	v	Port Vale	1-1	3679
	Port Vale	v	Dartford (16/11)	4-0	3590
33	Forest Green Rovers	v	Northampton Town	0-3	1479
34	Fleetwood Town	v	Walsall	1-1	2319
	Walsall	v	Fleetwood Town (16/11)	2-0	2056
35	Barnet	v	Charlton Athletic	0-0	2684
	Charlton Athletic	v	Barnet (16/11)	1-0	4803
36	Plymouth Argyle	v	Swindon Town	0-4	5226
37	Accrington Stanley	v	Oldham Athletic	3-2	2779
38	Hartlepool United	v	Vauxhall Motors	0-0	2381
	Vauxhall Motors	v	Hartlepool United (16/11)	0-1	1109
39	Stockport County	v	Peterborough United	1-1	2001
	Peterborough United	v	Stockport County (16/11)	4-1	2312
40	Brentford	v	Aldershot Town	1-1	4090
	Aldershot Town	v	Brentford (16/11)	1-0	3627

SECOND ROUND PROPER

SATURDAY 27 NOVEMBER 2010 - WINNERS RECEIVE £27,000

1	Sheffield Wednesday	v	Northampton Town	3-2	8932
2	Burton Albion	v	Chesterfield	3-1	3801
3	Huddersfield Town	v	Macclesfield Town	6-0	4924
4	AFC Wimbledon	v	Stevenage	0-2	3633
5	Hartlepool United	v	Yeovil Town (14/12)	4-2	1914
6	Bury	v	Peterborough United	1-2	2514
7	Notts County	v	AFC Bournemouth (14/12)	3-1	2881
8	Droylsden	v	Leyton Orient (29/11)	1-1	1762
	Leyton Orient	v	Droylsden (7/12)	8-2aet	1345
9	Crawley Town	v	Swindon Town (26/11)	1-1	3895
	Swindon Town	v	Crawley Town (7/12)	2-3aet	2955
10	Brighton & Hove Albion	v	FC United of Manchester	1-1	5362
	FC United of Manchester	v	Brighton & Hove Albion (8/12)	0-4	7000
11	Southampton	v	Cheltenham Town	3-0	9276
12	Torquay United	v	Walsall	1-0	2334
13	Charlton Athletic	v	Luton Town	2-2	8682
	Luton Town	v	Charlton Athletic (9/12)	1-3	5914
14	Colchester United	v	Swindon Supermarine	1-0	2932
15	Hereford United	v	Lincoln City	2-2	1803
	Lincoln City	v	Hereford United (8/1)	3-4	1794
16	Port Vale	v	Accrington Stanley (26/11)	1-0	4016
17	Wycombe Wanderers	v	Chelmsford City	3-1	3205
18	Carlisle United	v	Tamworth	3-2	3599
19	Dover Athletic	v	Aldershot Town	2-0	4123
20	Darlington	v	York City	0-2	3481

THIRD ROUND PROPER

SATURDAY 8 JANUARY 2011 - WINNERS RECEIVE £67,500

1	Burnley	v	Port Vale	4-2	9442
2	Coventry City	v	Crystal Palace	2-1	8162
3	Bristol City	v	Sheffield Wednesday	0-3	11376
4	Fulham	v	Peterborough United	6-2	15936
5	Doncaster Rovers	v	Wolverhampton Wanderers	2-2	8616
	Wolverhampton Wanderers	v	Doncaster Rovers (18/1)	5-0	10031
6	Brighton & Hove Albion	v	Portsmouth	3-1	7792
7	Huddersfield Town	v	Dover Athletic	2-0	7894
8	Crawley Town	v	Derby County (10/1)	2-1	4125
9	West Ham United	v	Barnsley	2-0	24881
10	Reading	v	West Bromwich Albion	1-0	13605
11	Arsenal	v	Leeds United	1-1	59520
	Leeds United	v	Arsenal (19/1)	1-3	38232
12	Sheffield United	v	Aston Villa	1-3	16888
13	Leicester City	v	Manchester City	2-2	31200
	Manchester City	v	Leicester City (18/1)	4-2	27755
14	Bolton Wanderers	v	York City	2-0	13120
15	Blackburn Rovers	v	Queens Park Rangers	1-0	10284
16	Swansea City	v	Colchester United	4-0	7005
17	Wycombe Wanderers	v	Hereford United	0-1	2353
18	Stevenage	v	Newcastle United	3-1	6644
19	Burton Albion	v	Middlesbrough	2-1	5296
20	Millwall	v	Birmingham City	1-4	9841
21	Southampton	v	Blackpool	2-0	21464
22	Watford	v	Hartlepool United	4-1	8950
23	Chelsea	v	Ipswich Town	7-0	41654
24	Sunderland	v	Notts County	1-2	17582
25	Scunthorpe United	v	Everton	1-5	7028
26	Manchester United	v	Liverpool	1-0	74727
27	Hull City	v	Wigan Athletic	2-3	10433
28	Stoke City	v	Cardiff City	1-1	18629
	Cardiff City	v	Stoke City (18/1)	0-2aet	13671
29	Tottenham Hotspur	v	Charlton Athletic	3-0	35698
30	Preston North End	v	Nottingham Forest	1-2	9636
31	Norwich City	v	Leyton Orient	0-1	18087
32	Torquay United	v	Carlisle United	1-0	3005

SECOND ROUND PROPER

Non-League Clubs drawn at Home: AFC Wimbledon, Crawley Town, Darlington, Dover Athletic, Droylsden and Away: F.C. United, Tamworth, Luton Town, Swindon Supermarine, Chelmsford City, York City.

Zamaretto Premier club Swindon Supermarine were playing their seventh F.A. Cup tie of the season having joined the competition for the 1st Qualifying Round on 11th September and they did extremely well to hold Colchester United away to just a single goal. F.C. United who had joined at the same stage were the second Non-League club to draw at Brighton in the Cup this season, but they lost in a replay which was also their seventh cup tie of the campaign. Tamworth and Chelmsford City lost at Carlisle United and Wycombe Wanderers respectively, but Luton Town achieved an uplifting 2-2 draw at Charlton Athletic before losing the home replay. Over 14,000 spectators had seen these two ties but just one non-league club drawn away from home had managed to survive the Round and that was York City who beat fellow Blue Square club Darlington.

The home clubs obviously hoped for better luck and with larger than normal attendances, famous victories were possible. Crawley Town equalized late in the game to force a replay with Swindon Town, where they achieved a famous televised victory, but AFC Wimbledon lost to Blue Square Premier 'old boys' Stevenage Borough, York had beaten Darlington and Droylsden after holding Leyton Orient to a 1-1 draw lost heavily away and this left Dover Athletic who had already beaten one League Club. Adam Birchall who had scored eight F.A. Cup goals for Dover before reaching the competition proper, had registered once against Gillingham and scored two more to eliminate Aldershot Town 2-0.

So Non-League football would be represented by Crawley Town, Dover Athletic and York City in the last 64, including the Premier League clubs who would all be contesting The FA Challenge Cup.

4th Qualifying Round action between Corby Town and Salisbury City - here we see Nathan Jarman scoring his second goal to wrap up the Steelmen's victory. Photo: Gordon Whittington.

Action from the First Round tie between Forest Green Rovers and Northampton Town. Photo: Peter Barnes.

An inch perfect tackle by Crewe's Ada denies Tamworth's Rodman in the 1st Round. Photo: Keith Clayton

FOURTH ROUND PROPER

SATURDAY 29 JANUARY 2011 - WINNERS RECEIVE £90,000

1	Torquay United	v	Crawley Town	0-1	5055
2	Watford	v	Brighton & Hove Albion	0-1	14519
3	Bolton Wanderers	v	Wigan Athletic	0-0	14950
	Wigan Athletic	v	Bolton Wanderers (16/2)	0-1	7515
4	Arsenal	v	Huddersfield Town (30/1)	2-1	59375
5	Fulham	v	Tottenham Hotspur (30/1)	4-0	21829
6	Everton	v	Chelsea	1-1	28376
	Chelsea	v	Everton (19/2)	1-1aet	41113
7	Southampton	v	Manchester United	1-2	28792
8	Swansea City	v	Leyton Orient	1-2	6281
9	Burnley	v	Burton Albion	3-1	11664
10	Birmingham City	v	Coventry City	3-2	16669
11	Wolverhampton Wanderers	v	Stoke City (30/1)	0-1	11967
12	Notts County	v	Manchester City (30/1)	1-1	16587
	Manchester City	v	Notts County (20/2)	5-0	27276
13	Stevenage	v	Reading	1-2	6614
14	Aston Villa	v	Blackburn Rovers	3-1	26067
15	West Ham United	v	Nottingham Forest (30/1)	3-2	29287
16	Sheffield Wednesday	v	Hereford United	4-1	16578

FIFTH ROUND PROPER

SATURDAY 19 FEBRUARY 2011 - WINNERS RECEIVE £180,000

1	West Ham United	v	Burnley (21/2)	5-1	24488
2	Manchester City	v	Aston Villa (2/3)	3-0	25470
3	Stoke City	v	Brighton & Hove Albion	3-0	21312
4	Birmingham City	v	Sheffield Wednesday	3-0	14607
5	Leyton Orient	v	Arsenal (20/2)	1-1	9136
	Arsenal	v	Leyton Orient (2/3)	5-0	59361
6	Everton	v	Reading (1/3)	0-1	29976
7	Manchester United	v	Crawley Town	1-0	74778
8	Fulham	v	Bolton Wanderers (20/2)	0-1	19871

SIXTH ROUND PROPER

SATURDAY 12 MARCH 2011 - WINNERS RECEIVE £360,000

1	Stoke City	v	West Ham United (13/3)	2-1	24550
2	Manchester City	v	Reading (13/3)	1-0	41550
3	Birmingham City	v	Bolton Wanderers	2-3	23699
4	Manchester United	v	Arsenal	2-0	74693

SEMI FINALS

WINNERS RECEIVE £900,000 RUNNERS-UP £450,000

SATURDAY 16 APRIL 2011 - at Wembley Stadium

1	Manchester City	v	Manchester United	1-0	86549

SUNDAY 17 APRIL 2011 - at Wembley Stadium

2	Bolton Wanderers	v	Stoke City	0-5	75064

THE FINAL

SATURDAY 14 MAY 2011 - at Wembley Stadium WINNERS RECEIVE £1.8m RUNNERS-UP £900,000

MANCHESTER CITY	1	0	STOKE CITY	88643

Harrow's Kenta Nakashima tries a spectacular shot but Chesterfield's Mark Allot manages to clear, during their 1st Round match which Chesterfield won 2-0. Photo: Bill Wheatcroft.

THIRD ROUND PROPER

All three of our representatives were drawn away, but at this stage, as complete underdogs home or away, its probably best to enjoy the thrill of visiting a League club and always hoping the day could provide one of those famous cup upsets.

York City crossed the Pennines and visited Bolton Wanderers, where 13,120 saw York City hold on until the last ten minutes before the famous Premier club scored twice to ease into the Fourth Round. Dover Athletic were faced with an equally tough away trip to the high riding Huddersfield Town club and although the home team raced into a 2-0 lead within ten minutes, no more goals were scored and a happy cup run came to an end with Adam Birchall favourite to finish as top scorer in the competition with eleven goals.

THIRD ROUND PROPER

Crawley Town were drawn against Derby County and a televised thriller saw the Blue Square Premier club deservedly through to the Fourth Round by a 2-1 margin and then two of the most junior clubs in the Round draw were paired together and Crawley Town travelled to Torquay United where they won 1-0

Crawley Town's dream tie in the 5th Round was a trip to Manchester United where they enjoyed the wonderful publicity, faced, and held, a very strong looking United line-up and just failed to equal Burton Albion and Exeter City's comparatively recent achievements of taking United to a replay.

CRAWLEY TOWN F.A. CUP 2010-2011

4th Q. Round	A	Newport County (BS Premier)	1-0	McAllister	2,247
1st Round	A	Guiseley (Evo Stick P)	5-0	Tubbs,Neilson, Hall, Brodie, Torres	5,609
2nd Round	H	Swindon Town (League One)	1-1	Tubbs	3,895
Replay	A	Swindon Town	3-2*	B.Smith 2, P.Smith (og)	2,955
3rd Round	H	Derby County (Championship)	2-1	McAllister, Torres	4,145
4th Round	A	Torquay United (League Two)	1-0	Tubbs	5,065
5th Round	A	Manchester United (Premiership)	0-1		74,778

The Non-League F.A. Cup season was over and once again there were some wonderful matches and great memories that will last lifetimes. Whether your club enters the competition in August and wins fabulous prize money by competing in five F.A. Cup rounds, or perhaps your little club beats two League clubs, your main striker scores eleven F.A. Cup goals, perhaps your club has just played in the competition for the first time, or, of course, you might have taken on Manchester United on equal terms. Whatever your experiences in the famous competition, the F.A. Challenge Cup is still very special indeed to 98% of the English football world and by the time you read this, the next competition will probably be well under way!

Nick Jupp, in the Harrow goal, makes a great save against Chesterfield in the First Round. Photo: Bill Wheatcroft.

Tamworth's Rodman turns Crewe's Ada during the BS Premier side's 2-1 victory of their Football League counterparts. Photo: Keith Clayton.

THE FA TROPHY

2010-11

Chris Senior (right) scores in the last minute of extra-time to win Darlington the FA Trophy. Photo: Roger Turner.

Preliminary Round action between Cinderford Town and Mangotsfield United which, after a 1-1 draw, saw Cinderford winning the replay 1-2 to progress to the 1st Qualifying Round.

Photos: Peter Barnes.

Sheffield's Mark Hales saves David Graham's (16 - Rainworth MW) shot during their Preliminary Round match. Photo: Bill Wheatcroft.

PRELIMINARY ROUND

SATURDAY 2 OCTOBER 2010 - WINNERS RECEIVE £2,000

1	Newcastle Town	v	Goole	2-2	100
	Goole	v	Newcastle Town (5/10)	1-2	119
2	Loughborough Dynamo	v	Romulus	2-4	113
3	Shepshed Dynamo	v	Warrington Town	2-1	123
4	Woodley Sports	v	Lancaster City	1-1	87
	Lancaster City	v	Woodley Sports (5/10)	7-1	122
5	Atherstone Town	v	Stamford	2-4	187
6	Witton Albion	v	Sutton Coldfield Town	1-0	210
7	Brigg Town	v	Bedworth United	1-3	113
8	Leigh Genesis	v	Garforth Town	0-5	60
9	AFC Fylde	v	Market Drayton Town	1-2	163
10	Lincoln United	v	Barwell	3-2	110
11	Ossett Albion	v	Salford City	4-1	109
12	Skelmersdale United	v	Wakefield	5-1	136
13	Clitheroe	v	Leek Town	5-0	242
14	Glapwell	v	Spalding United	3-0	68
15	Belper Town	v	Harrogate Railway Athletic	0-1	139
16	Rainworth MW	v	Sheffield	1-1	109
	Sheffield	v	Rainworth MW (5/10)	3-1aet	135
17	Grantham Town	v	Carlton Town	0-2	164
18	Mossley	v	Kidsgrove Athletic	1-1	136
	Kidsgrove Athletic	v	Mossley (5/10)	1-4	116
19	Rushall Olympic	v	Trafford	1-0	85
20	Brentwood Town	v	East Thurrock United	4-3	98
21	Barton Rovers	v	Maldon & Tiptree	3-1	62
22	Waltham Abbey	v	Soham Town Rangers	0-2	54
23	Eastbourne Town	v	Walton Casuals	1-2	80
24	Needham Market	v	Hitchin Town	4-2	216
25	Ilford	v	Whitstable Town	2-0	62
26	Ware	v	Whitehawk	1-2	85
27	Fleet Town	v	Tilbury	3-1	65
28	Wingate & Finchley	v	Horsham YMCA	4-1	155
29	Thamesmead Town	v	Heybridge Swifts	0-0	62
	Heybridge Swifts	v	Thamesmead Town (5/10)	1-2aet	76
30	Chipstead	v	Godalming Town	1-2	71
31	Walton & Hersham	v	Faversham Town	1-2	82
32	Ashford Town	v	Ramsgate		
	(walkover for Ramsgate – Ashford Town removed)				
33	Merstham	v	AFC Sudbury	4-6	101
34	Corinthian Casuals	v	Potters Bar Town	0-3	44
35	Leatherhead	v	Enfield Town	1-3	186
36	Arlesey Town	v	Sittingbourne	2-0	107
37	Metropolitan Police	v	Biggleswade Town	1-1	82
	Biggleswade Town	v	Metropolitan Police (5/10)	2-0	85
38	Bognor Regis Town	v	Whyteleafe	0-0	252
	Whyteleafe	v	Bognor Regis Town (5/10)	1-6	126
39	Cheshunt	v	Great Wakering Rovers	0-2	109
40	Redbridge	v	Chatham Town	2-1	57
41	Burnham	v	Northwood	1-1	77
	Northwood	v	Burnham (5/10)	1-2	72
42	Andover	v	Bideford	2-3	66
	(at Winchester City FC)				
43	Slough Town	v	Marlow	2-2	221
	Marlow	v	Slough Town (5/10)	0-3	223
44	Leighton Town	v	Rugby Town	0-1	137
45	Bromsgrove Rovers	v	Frome Town		
	(walkover for Frome Town - Bromsgrove Rovers removed)				
46	Wimborne Town	v	Gosport Borough	2-1	279
47	AFC Totton	v	Yate Town	3-0	192
48	Cinderford Town	v	Mangotsfield United	1-1	85
	Mangotsfield United	v	Cinderford Town (4/10)	1-2	183
49	Bedfont Town	v	Uxbridge	0-2	71
50	Clevedon Town	v	Bishop's Cleeve	0-1	135
51	North Greenford United	v	Thatcham Town	2-1	63
52	Stourport Swifts	v	Bridgwater Town	0-1	87
53	North Leigh	v	Sholing	3-2	58
54	Taunton Town	v	Hungerford Town	2-2	131
	Hungerford Town	v	Taunton Town (5/10)	1-0	101

PRELIMINARY ROUND

To be realistic, not many clubs playing in the Preliminary round really imagine they will be challenging for a place in the Wembley Final, but reaching the competition proper by surviving the qualifying rounds would be considered a fine achievement. For clubs involved for the first time, having graduated from The F.A. Vase, it is also a big challenge.

Indeed, some clubs who made their names through F.A. Vase Finals such as , A.F.C. Sudbury , Arlesey Town, Rugby Town, Stamford and Wimborne Town will remember Wembley with pride and although losing in the Final, Barton Rovers, Clitheroe, Rainworth Miners Welfare, Sheffield and Warrington Town will have enjoyed the days when they were amongst the competition favourites. Taunton Town had experienced losing at Wembley but winning the F.A. Vase at Villa Park, but last season all these clubs started out in the very first F.A. Trophy week-end.

Looking back even further, the old F.A. Amateur Cup used to attract huge attendances to the Wembley Finals and once again some of those little clubs now feature in the F.A. Trophy Preliminary Round such as Corinthian-Casuals, Leatherhead , Enfield, Slough Town, Skelmersdale United and Walton & Hersham.

The largest attendance of 279 was attracted by Wimborne Town to see their 2-1 victory in their local 'derby' against Gosport Borough. Witton Albion, a past F.A. Trophy Winner, edged through 1-0 at home to Sutton Coldfield and Hungerford Town's first ever game in the competition, having competed in the F.A. Vase since it was introduced in 1974-1975, was an away draw at Taunton. Impressive victories were enjoyed by Needham Market 4-1 at home to Hitchin Town and Bishop's Cleeve 1-0 away to Clevedon Town, but this was just the beginning.

Action from the 2nd Qualifying Round between Cirencester Town (in the stripes) and Weymouth. Photo: Peter Barnes.

Action from the same match between Cirencester and Weymouth which the hosts went on to win 2-1. Photo: Peter Barnes.

Craig Hammond celebrates the first of his two goals which gave Cambridge City a 2-1 win over Daventry Town in the 2nd Qualifying Round. Photo: Gordon Whittington.

FIRST QUALIFYING ROUND

SATURDAY 16 OCTOBER 2010 - WINNERS RECEIVE £2,200

1	Marine	v	Ashton United	2-2	216
	Ashton United	v	Marine (18/10)	1-3	130
2	Matlock Town	v	Bedworth United	10-0	266
3	Nantwich Town	v	Prescot Cables	6-2	274
4	Hednesford Town	v	Whitby Town	1-2	313
5	Cammell Laird	v	Witton Albion	1-2	140
6	Lancaster City	v	Ossett Town	4-2	178
7	North Ferriby United	v	Bamber Bridge	0-2	179
8	Sheffield	v	Chasetown	1-1	240
	Chasetown	v	Sheffield (19/10)	3-1	316
9	Harrogate RA	v	Ossett Albion	2-1	119
10	Carlton Town	v	Rushall Olympic	1-1	87
	Rushall Olympic	v	Carlton Town (19/10)	4-1	77
11	Colwyn Bay	v	Bradford (Park Avenue)	2-0	337
12	Chorley	v	Quorn	1-0	734
13	Retford United	v	Romulus	2-2	131
	Romulus	v	Retford United (19/10)	2-1	73
14	Curzon Ashton	v	Skelmersdale United	3-1	169
15	FC United Of Manchester	v	Newcastle Town	5-0	1035
16	Burscough	v	Clitheroe	0-2	201
17	Buxton	v	Stocksbridge Park Steels	1-2	321
18	Shepshed Dynamo	v	Mossley	1-4	137
19	Radcliffe Borough	v	Garforth Town	1-1	104
	Garforth Town	v	Radcliffe Borough (19/10)	1-2	78
20	Mickleover Sports	v	Hucknall Town	2-1	186
21	Glapwell	v	Stamford	2-0	134
22	Kendal Town	v	Frickley Athletic	3-0	182
23	Northwich Victoria	v	Lincoln United	0-0	357
	Lincoln United	v	Northwich Victoria (19/10)	2-3	101
24	Durham City	v	FC Halifax Town	0-2	282
25	Market Drayton Town	v	Worksop Town	1-1	147
	Worksop Town	v	Market Drayton Town (20/10)	1-0	159
26	Wealdstone	v	Potters Bar Town	2-2	201
	Potters Bar Town	v	Wealdstone (19/10)	1-3	137
27	Bury Town	v	Barton Rovers	2-0	353
28	Bognor Regis Town	v	Croydon Athletic	1-0	283
29	Harrow Borough	v	Hendon	0-1	174
30	Canvey Island	v	AFC Sudbury	1-2	293
31	Arlesey Town	v	Ramsgate	0-0	96
	Ramsgate	v	Arlesey Town (19/10)	2-3aet	105
32	Enfield Town	v	Walton Casuals	2-1	220
33	Great Wakering Rovers	v	Thamesmead Town	1-2	76
34	Dulwich Hamlet	v	Hastings United	2-2	216
	Hastings United	v	Dulwich Hamlet (19/10)	1-2	243
35	Sutton United	v	Tooting & Mitcham United	3-1	448
36	Cray Wanderers	v	Wingate & Finchley	2-1	98
37	Maidstone United	v	Burgess Hill Town	2-0	232
38	Soham Town Rangers	v	Grays Athletic	1-2	164
39	Needham Market	v	Lowestoft Town	2-2	381
	Lowestoft Town	v	Needham Market (19/10)	6-2	546
40	Waltham Forest	v	Romford	0-2	72
41	Tonbridge Angels	v	Concord Rangers	3-2	384
42	Cambridge City	v	Aveley	1-0	243
43	Faversham Town	v	Kingstonian	1-2	230
44	Fleet Town	v	Godalming Town	0-2	122
45	AFC Hornchurch	v	Brentwood Town	2-1	214
46	Harlow Town	v	Bedford Town	3-2	256
47	Carshalton Athletic	v	Ilford	2-0	216
48	Margate	v	Whitehawk	5-1	227
49	Biggleswade Town	v	Billericay Town	0-1	166
50	Folkestone Invicta	v	Worthing	4-2	236
51	Horsham	v	Redbridge	3-0	188
52	Swindon Supermarine	v	Beaconsfield SYCOB	4-2	111
53	Uxbridge	v	Abingdon United	4-1	56
54	Truro City	v	Bishop's Cleeve	1-0	330
55	Woodford United	v	Leamington	1-3	398
56	Windsor & Eton	v	Aylesbury	1-1	156
	Aylesbury	v	Windsor & Eton (19/10)	1-2	107
57	Almondsbury Town	v	Didcot Town	1-0	85
58	Weymouth	v	Bashley	2-1	363
59	Cinderford Town	v	Hungerford Town	2-2	72
	Hungerford Town	v	Cinderford Town (19/10)	1-2aet	75
60	Bridgwater Town	v	Stourbridge	1-3	201
61	Ashford Town (Middx)	v	North Greenford United	6-2	78
62	Burnham	v	Brackley Town	0-0	102
	Brackley Town	v	Burnham (19/10)	4-0	106
63	Banbury United	v	Wimborne Town	1-1	239
	Wimborne Town	v	Banbury United (19/10)	1-3aet	236
64	Slough Town	v	Chippenham Town	1-1	251
	Chippenham Town	v	Slough Town (19/10)	4-1	244
65	Cirencester Town	v	Halesowen Town	3-0	112
66	Evesham United	v	Frome Town	1-0	107
67	Paulton Rovers	v	North Leigh	3-3	182
	North Leigh	v	Paulton Rovers (19/10)	1-2	71
68	Bideford	v	Tiverton Town	4-2	268
69	Chesham United	v	Salisbury City	1-1	297
	Salisbury City	v	Chesham United (19/10)	2-1	463
70	Hemel Hempstead Town	v	Rugby Town	2-3	167
71	AFC Totton	v	AFC Hayes	5-0	219
72	Oxford City	v	Daventry Town	1-4	152

FIRST QUALIFYING ROUND

The Ryman, Evo-Stik and Zamaretto clubs were all involved in this round and the headlines were most definitely featuring Matlock Town, who destroyed Bedworth United with a 10-0 victory and an incredible seven goals for Ross Hannah, who went on to enjoy a great season finishing with 44 goals and a move into the Football League with Bradford City.

The biggest attendance of 1,035 watched F.C. United score five against Newcastle Town and other impressive crowds turned out at Chorley, where 734 saw a 1-0 victory over Quorn and 446 at Sutton United to see them win their local 'derby' 3-0 against Tooting & Mitcham United.

Although Hednesford Town were fancied to do well, they lost 1-2 at home to Whitby Town, but there were very few real upsets although some high scoring victories were enjoyed by Ashford Town (Midx) 6-2 v North Greenford, Nantwich Town 6-2 v Prescot Cables (with Michael Lennon scoring four) and Lowestoft Town 6-2 v Needham Market in a replay watched by 652.

At this stage of the competition results aren't every exciting, but they are extremely important for raising extra prize money and of course bringing clubs nearer to glamour ties against the Blue Square Premier clubs in later rounds.

SECOND QUALIFYING ROUND

A victory in this round provides a place in the next draw and a chance of taking on Blue Square clubs in the last qualifying round. The very first tie in alphabetical order, brought a superb result for A.F.C. Sudbury who had started out in the Preliminary Round. They beat Hendon 5-1 and two other clubs celebrating with five goals were Chasetown, who were to experience a record breaking Trophy season, and won 5-2 at Mickleover Sports, and in 'the match of the day' Swindon Supermarine. The Wiltshire club travelled to Paulton Rovers, for whom Matt Cooper scored a hat trick in his side's four goals, but the visitors won a thriller 5-4 with the winner coming three minutes from time.

This round brought some exciting ties such as Bideford entertaining the famous ex amateur club Dulwich Hamlet and winning 1-0, the glamorous F.C. United, at home again, and once more attracting the top attendance of 1,259 to see their victory over Colwyn Bay. It was not surprising to see that Ross Hannah and Michael Lennon, were both on target for their clubs, with Matlock earning a replay at Kendal Town and Nantwich Town winning 2-1 at Mossley.

Maidstone United featured a thrilling game which finished in spectacular fashion, when they were trailing to near neighbours Cray Wanderers by a single goal on ninety minutes, but scored two goals for victory in injury time. The next draw would be an exciting one, especially for A.F.C. Sudbury, Bideford, Bognor Regis Town, Harrogate RA, Uxbridge and Witton Albion who all featured in the Preliminary Round and would already have won £ 7,200 in prize money.

3rd Qualifying Round action between Cirencester Town and Grays Athletic. This original tie ended in a 2-2 draw with Cirencester winning the replay 0-1. Photos: Peter Barnes.

THIRD QUALIFYING ROUND

With the introduction of the Blue Square North and South clubs, at least the early qualifiers had a chance to be drawn against some new opposition. Bideford lost 0-3 at home to A.F.C. Hornchurch, Harrogate RA lost 3-4 at home to Nantwich Town, for whom Michael Lennon scored two to bring his Trophy total to seven and Witton Albion and Bognor Regis Town lost in replays to Harrogate Town and Hampton & Richmond Borough respectively. So it was left to A.F.C. Sudbury and Uxbridge to keep the flag flying for the Preliminary Round clubs, Sudbury winning 2-1 at Truro City and Uxbridge winning a thriller 4-3 at Maidenhead United.

Attendances naturally improved and three ties attracted crowds of over a thousand; for the third time F.C. United made the most of another home draw by attracting 1,249 but lost to the odd goal in three to Hinckley United. Boston United's 2-1 victory over neighbours Gainsborough Trinity was watched by 1,136 and A.F.C. Telford United who attracted over a thousand for very home game of the season, had 1,028 spectators for their 2-1 victory over Corby Town.

Boreham Wood won 3-0 at home to Romford and benefitted from two 'own goals' from their opponents and the only hat trick of the round was scored by Andy Forbes in Sutton United's 4-2 home victory over Billericay Town. Excellent away victories were achieved by Woking at Dover Athletic and Worcester City at Nuneaton Town but all the winners could celebrate the fact that they had qualified for the competition proper, extra prize money and a chance to take on a Blue Square Premier Club in the next round.

SECOND QUALIFYING ROUND

SATURDAY 30 OCTOBER 2010 - WINNERS RECEIVE £3,000

1	Curzon Ashton	v	FC Halifax Town	2-1	392
2	Leamington	v	Bamber Bridge	3-0	510
3	Romulus	v	Harrogate RA	1-2	107
4	Kendal Town	v	Matlock Town	1-1	245
	Matlock Town	v	Kendal Town (2/11)	1-2	242
5	Worksop Town	v	Lancaster City	2-1	262
6	Rushall Olympic	v	Stourbridge	0-1	241
7	Mossley	v	Nantwich Town	2-3	194
8	Mickleover Sports	v	Chasetown	2-5	250
9	FC United Of Manchester	v	Colwyn Bay	2-1	1259
10	Radcliffe Borough	v	Witton Albion	1-1	193
	Witton Albion	v	Radcliffe Borough (3/11)	3-1	188
11	Chorley	v	Marine	3-1	834
12	Whitby Town	v	Clitheroe	3-1	265
13	Northwich Victoria	v	Glapwell	4-0	323
14	Stocksbridge Park Steels	v	Rugby Town	3-2	152
15	Kingstonian	v	Wealdstone	3-5	428
16	Salisbury City	v	Almondsbury Town	2-1	577
17	Cirencester Town	v	Weymouth	2-1	95
18	Margate	v	AFC Hornchurch	1-2	325
19	Tonbridge Angels	v	Enfield Town	2-0	517
20	Billericay Town	v	Banbury United	2-1	285
21	AFC Sudbury	v	Hendon	5-1	289
22	Brackley Town	v	Windsor & Eton	4-0	187
23	Arlesey Town	v	Uxbridge	2-2	102
	Uxbridge	v	Arlesey Town (2/11)	4-2	74
24	Daventry Town	v	Cambridge City	1-2	311
25	Paulton Rovers	v	Swindon Supermarine	4-5	159
26	Grays Athletic	v	Cinderford Town	2-1	198
27	Truro City	v	Horsham	2-0	361
28	Folkestone Invicta	v	Thamesmead Town	0-0	232
	Thamesmead Town	v	Folkestone Invicta (2/11)	1-3	87
29	Bognor Regis Town	v	Godalming Town	1-1	298
	Godalming Town	v	Bognor Regis Town (2/11)	2-5	161
30	Evesham United	v	Sutton United	0-1	188
31	Harlow Town	v	Carshalton Athletic	2-0	306
32	Ashford Town (Middx)	v	Bury Town	2-1	100
33	Cray Wanderers	v	Maidstone United	1-2	224
34	Bideford	v	Dulwich Hamlet	1-0	246
35	Chippenham Town	v	Lowestoft Town	1-1	383
	Lowestoft Town	v	Chippenham Town (2/11)	3-1aet	577
36	AFC Totton	v	Romford	1-3	284

THIRD QUALIFYING ROUND

SATURDAY 20 NOVEMBER 2010 - WINNERS RECEIVE £4,000

1	Alfreton Town	v	Kendal Town	4-0	399
2	Vauxhall Motors	v	Stalybridge Celtic	1-3	280
3	Blyth Spartans	v	Stafford Rangers	1-0	391
4	Whitby Town	v	Northwich Victoria	2-2	247
	Northwich Victoria	v	Whitby Town (23/11)	1-0	260
5	AFC Telford United	v	Corby Town	2-1	1028
6	Curzon Ashton	v	Solihull Moors	2-1	162
7	Leamington	v	Hyde	1-2	522
8	FC United Of Manchester	v	Hinckley United	1-2	1249
9	Worksop Town	v	Stocksbridge Park Steels	4-1	290
10	Boston United	v	Gainsborough Trinity	2-1	1136
11	Droylsden	v	Stourbridge	3-2	246
12	Eastwood Town	v	Cambridge City	2-0	246
13	Chorley	v	Guiseley	0-1	890
14	Harrogate Town	v	Witton Albion	1-1	243
	Witton Albion	v	Harrogate Town (24/11)	1-2	175
15	Harrogate Railway Athletic	v	Nantwich Town	3-4	142
16	Workington	v	Chasetown	0-0	305
	Chasetown	v	Workington (23/11)	4-0	334
17	Nuneaton Town	v	Worcester City	1-2	582
18	Dover Athletic	v	Woking	1-2	818
19	Braintree Town	v	Farnborough	2-0	255
20	Lewes	v	Salisbury City	1-3	598
21	Maidenhead United	v	Uxbridge	2-4	211
22	Weston Super Mare	v	Dorchester Town	1-3	184
23	Basingstoke Town	v	Havant & Waterlooville	2-2	301
	Havant & Waterlooville	v	Basingstoke Town (22/11)	1-2	353
24	Eastleigh	v	Folkestone Invicta	2-1	253
25	Cirencester Town	v	Grays Athletic	2-2	157
	Grays Athletic	v	Cirencester Town (23/11)	0-1	153
26	Sutton United	v	Billericay Town	4-2	329
27	Ebbsfleet United	v	Bromley (23/11)	4-0	611
28	Thurrock	v	Dartford	0-2	405
29	Boreham Wood	v	Romford	3-0	103
30	Welling United	v	Tonbridge Angels	1-0	431
31	St Albans City	v	Staines Town	3-1	249
32	Truro City	v	AFC Sudbury	1-2	349
33	Bishop's Stortford	v	Ashford Town (Middx)	1-2	226
34	Brackley Town	v	Wealdstone	0-1	302
35	Lowestoft Town	v	Swindon Supermarine	2-1	622
36	Bideford	v	AFC Hornchurch	0-3	265
37	Harlow Town	v	Maidstone United	3-0	294
38	Bognor Regis Town	v	Hampton & Richmond Borough	2-2	376
	Hampton & Richmond B.	v	Bognor Regis Town (23/11)	2-0	188
39	Gloucester City	v	Chelmsford City	1-0	316

Bye:- Redditch United

FIRST ROUND PROPER

The importance of doing well in the F.A. Challenge Trophy is questioned to-day by the pressure put on managers of the senior clubs to gain promotion into The Football League. They copy the quite unbalanced attitudes to the F.A. Cup by many senior Premier League clubs thinking they should copy the attitude with reference to the Trophy and its effect on injuries, tiredness and their chase for financial rewards. Ask the players and most would still give a great deal to play at Wembley, and do four or five extra cup ties really disrupt their season if they are properly trained and fit.
A.F.C. Sudbury lost 1-4 at home to Hampton & Richmond Borough so Uxbridge became the last of the original Preliminary Round clubs to survive in the competition by winning 3-2 at Lowestoft Town when the score was 1-1 with just six minutes to play.
The only defeats for Blue Square Premier clubs from lower ranked opposition on First Round Saturday were Barrow who lost 2-3 at home to Guiseley, Hayes & Yeading who were beaten 3-1 by Ebbsfleet United and Boston United won 1-0 away at York City. In replays Kettering Town lost at home 1-2 to Chasetown after extra time and their near neighbours Rushden & Diamonds lost away at Eastwood Town 3-4.
The round was ruined by the weather which delayed many ties and so it was difficult for the competition to make its usual impact as the senior clubs only joined in as the weather allowed.

SECOND ROUND PROPER

This was a real cup week-end with some terrific ties. A 'local derby', bringing back memories of their old Isthmian League clashes in their amateur days, was fought out in front of 2,365 as Woking beat A.F.C. Wimbledon 3-2 at Kingston. Cambridge United drew a thrilling tie, 3-3 at Alfreton Town in front of 929 and Eastbourne Borough drew by the same scoreline away at Dorchester Town. While six more goals were scored as Mansfield Town beat Newport County 4-2 at Field Mill Stadium.
Blyth Spartans revived memories of great knockout results with a 2-1 victory over Altrincham and little Chasetown beat Grimsby Town 2-1 at home watched by 1,012. Salisbury City beat Wrexham 1-0, but Gateshead upheld the honour of the Premier clubs with a 6-0 thrashing of Hampton & Richmond Borough.
There were just three draws all finishing 3-3 and when the dust settled after 16 ties and three replays, 73 goals had been scored, highlighted by an amazing 3-6 scoreline in Alfreton Town's favour after extra time in the replay away to Cambridge United!
Finally, it was good bye and well done to Uxbridge, whose magical F.A. Trophy run had finally come to an end Luton Town, where 'The Hatters' won 4-0 watched by 1.958. Of the last sixteen clubs, only five were from The B.S. Premier League- were they taking the competition seriously?

THIRD ROUND PROPER

Six Blue Square North clubs featured in this round but the only winners were Blyth Spartans, with an impressive 4-0 replay victory away to league colleagues Droylsden and Guiseley, who drew 1-1 at Premier club Eastbourne Borough before winning the replay 2-1 with a late goal. The two North Eastern representatives, Darlington and Gateshead, put junior opposition from A.F.C. Telford United and Dartford in their place with 3-0 victories, but Luton Town and Mansfield Town won tough battles with Alfreton Town and Gloucester City.
To the outside observer, Luton Town's interest in the F.A. Trophy was doubtful as they were well and truly committed to chasing promotion, but Mansfield Town seemed committed and challenges from the North East could never be taken lightly. Meanwhile two great Trophy runs were being enjoyed by Chasetown, who won 3-1 away at Eastleigh and Salisbury City, whose 2-1 victory at Woking was certainly impressive at the home of a club with a great Trophy pedigree.

FOURTH ROUND PROPER

The thrill of an appearance at Wembley Stadium still appeals apparently. All four quarter final Trophy ties were won by Blue Square Premier clubs. Granted, only Luton Town were still involved with the promotion race but quality certainly won the day, as Gateshead triumphed away in the North Eastern 'derby' at Blyth with two first half goals. A second triumph for area saw Darlington beat a plucky Salisbury City 2-1, with the visitors only scoring their goal in injury time. Mansfield Town's difficult tie against the giant killers of Chasetown was postponed, but a storming cup tie in front of 2.000 produced a late equalizer for the Evo-Stik club and the 2-2 result forced a replay in which 'The Stags' managed to 'pull rank' and won 3-1 watched by 2,295.

SEMI-FINALS

The two first legs of the Semi-Finals produced magnificent battles. The two North Eastern clubs fought out a five goal thriller in front of 4,243, with home advantage just giving Darlington a 3-2 lead after Gateshead had been two goals up at half time. In the other match, played on the Sunday, the only goal of the game, scored midway through the second half, also gave Mansfield a lead to take to Luton. Once the winning clubs face up to defending their lead in the second legs of these ties, supporters cannot expect the same attacking football that may have thrilled them in the first meetings. The importance of a Wembley appearance for players at this level also brings pressure as the second legs are fought out, and in this case, both winning clubs held on to their single goal advantage. Darlington by completing a 0-0 draw claimed the first place in the Final and at Luton, a goal early in the second half from Lloyd Owusu forced extra time but with two minutes left Louis Briscoe scored a memorable winner to take Mansfield Town to Wembley.
So a Darlington v Mansfield Town F.A. Trophy Final would give the clubs and their supporters the wonderful experience of a Wembley Stadium Final and of course there was also the prize money of £25,000 for the runners-up and £50,000 for the Winners to bring the season to a very special end for all concerned.

FIRST ROUND PROPER

SATURDAY 11 DECEMBER 2010 - WINNERS RECEIVE £5,000

	Home		Away	Score	Att
1	Wrexham	v	Kidderminster Harriers	2-0	1122
2	Rushden & Diamonds	v	Eastwood Town	1-1	657
	Eastwood Town	v	Rushden & Diamonds	4-3aet	314
3	Worksop Town	v	Mansfield Town (14/12)	0-5	682
	(at New Manor Ground, Ilkeston)				
4	Droylsden	v	Hinckley United	4-3	175
5	Curzon Ashton	v	Altrincham (14/12)	0-2	268
	(11/12, tie abandoned after 45 mins due to power failure, 2-1)				
6	Darlington	v	Tamworth (14/12)	3-2	432
7	Harrogate Town	v	AFC Telford United	0-3	247
8	Chasetown	v	Kettering Town	3-3	444
	Kettering Town	v	Chasetown (14/12)	1-2aet	581
9	Stalybridge Celtic	v	Nantwich Town	2-1	321
10	York City	v	Boston United	0-1	1318
11	Blyth Spartans	v	Fleetwood Town (14/12)	2-0	354
12	Alfreton Town	v	Hyde (14/12)	3-0	254
13	Worcester City	v	Northwich Victoria	1-0	577
14	Grimsby Town	v	Redditch United	3-0	1116
15	Barrow	v	Guiseley	2-3	923
16	Gateshead	v	Southport (14/12)	2-2	223
	Southport	v	Gateshead	0-1	302
17	Dorchester Town	v	St Albans City	3-0	333
18	Histon	v	Bath City	2-3	263
19	Luton Town	v	Welling United (12/12)	0-0	1639
	Welling United	v	Luton Town (14/12)	1-2	404
20	Eastleigh	v	Sutton United	1-1	388
	Sutton United	v	Eastleigh (14/12)	0-4	237
21	Harlow Town	v	Woking	0-2	364
22	Ashford Town (Middx)	v	AFC Hornchurch	1-0	161
23	Cirencester Town	v	Gloucester City	1-1	406
	Gloucester City	v	Cirencester Town (15/12)	3-0	222
24	Eastbourne Borough	v	Boreham Wood	3-1	422
25	Ebbsfleet United	v	Hayes & Yeading United	3-1	614
26	Cambridge United	v	Forest Green Rovers	2-1	1045
27	Crawley Town	v	Dartford	3-3	1033
	Dartford	v	Crawley Town (14/12)	1-0	605
28	AFC Sudbury	v	Hampton & Richmond Borough	1-4	279
29	Lowestoft Town	v	Uxbridge	2-3	609
30	Newport County	v	Wealdstone	0-0	1047
	Wealdstone	v	Newport County (13/12)	0-1aet	324
31	AFC Wimbledon	v	Braintree Town	3-0	1201
32	Basingstoke Town	v	Salisbury City	0-2	475

SECOND ROUND PROPER

SATURDAY 15 JANUARY 2011 - WINNERS RECEIVE £6,000

	Home		Away	Score	Att
1	Gateshead	v	Hampton & Richmond Borough	6-0	336
2	Boston United	v	Gloucester City	0-1	1110
3	AFC Wimbledon	v	Woking	2-3	2259
4	Droylsden	v	Ebbsfleet United	1-0	336
5	Chasetown	v	Grimsby Town	2-1	1012
6	Alfreton Town	v	Cambridge United	3-3	929
	Cambridge United	v	Alfreton Town (18/1)	3-6aet	1098
7	Ashford Town (Middx)	v	Dartford	0-1	474
8	Luton Town	v	Uxbridge	4-0	1958
9	AFC Telford United	v	Eastwood Town	1-0	1159
10	Darlington	v	Bath City	4-1	956
11	Mansfield Town	v	Newport County	4-2	1137
12	Blyth Spartans	v	Altrincham	2-1	620
13	Dorchester Town	v	Eastbourne Borough	3-3	402
	Eastbourne Borough	v	Dorchester Town (18/1)	1-0	487
14	Guiseley	v	Stalybridge Celtic	2-1	417
15	Eastleigh	v	Worcester City	3-3	407
	Worcester City	v	Eastleigh (17/1)	1-4	564
16	Salisbury City	v	Wrexham	1-0	1032

THIRD ROUND PROPER

SATURDAY 5 FEBRUARY 2011 - WINNERS RECEIVE £7,000

	Home		Away	Score	Att
1	Eastbourne Borough	v	Guiseley	1-1	471
	Guiseley	v	Eastbourne Borough (8/2)	2-1	446
2	Mansfield Town	v	Alfreton Town	1-1	3408
	Alfreton Town	v	Mansfield Town (8/2)	1-2	2131
3	Blyth Spartans	v	Droylsden	2-2	708
	Droylsden	v	Blyth Spartans (7/2)	0-4	229
4	Luton Town	v	Gloucester City (4/2)	1-0	2212
5	AFC Telford United	v	Darlington	0-3	1505
6	Woking	v	Salisbury City	0-2	1551
7	Eastleigh	v	Chasetown	1-3	562
8	Gateshead	v	Dartford	3-0	501

FOURTH ROUND PROPER

SATURDAY 26 FEBRUARY 2011 - WINNERS RECEIVE £8,000

	Home		Away	Score	Att
1	Blyth Spartans	v	Gateshead	0-2	2719
2	Guiseley	v	Luton Town	0-1	1152
3	Darlington	v	Salisbury City	2-1	1864
4	Chasetown	v	Mansfield Town (1/3)	2-2	2000
	Mansfield Town	v	Chasetown (8/3)	3-1	2295

SEMI FINALS

WINNERS RECEIVE £16,000

	Home		Away	Score	Att
	1ST LEG – SATURDAY 12 MARCH 2011				
2	Darlington	v	Gateshead	3-2	4243
	2ND LEG – SATURDAY 19 MARCH 2011				
2	Gateshead	v	Darlington	0-0	5156
	1ST LEG – SUNDAY 13 MARCH 2011				
1	Mansfield Town	v	Luton Town	1-0	3208
	2ND LEG – SATURDAY 19 MARCH 2011				
1	Luton Town	v	Mansfield Town	1-1aet	6133

Brett Solkhon (19) gives Kettering a 1-0 lead v Chasetown in the 1st Round. Photos: Bill Wheatcroft.

Danny Smith puts the ball over Matthews and into the net 2-1 Chasetown v Eastleigh in the 3rd Round.

Richard Whyte of Cray Wanderers beats Maidstone 'keeper, Andy Walker, but puts his shot wide in the 2nd Round. Photo: Alan Coomes.

Action from the 4th Round tie between Manfield Town and Chasetown which the eventual finalists won 3-1. Photo: Bill Wheatcroft.

Luton's Barnes-Homer fires in a shot against Mansfield Town in the first leg of their Semi-Final.

Louis Briscoe scores the only goal of the Semi-Final first leg against Luton Town.

The Final...

For both these teams reaching Wembley was a much appreciated honour after their many struggles with finance, stadium problems and the inevitable drop in support which comes with fairly recent departure from the Football League. Indeed Mansfield could only declare four subs such was the state of their depleted squad. Sad to report the tension of the occasion showed, both sides displaying more caution than adventure, so that the match itself was a fairly drab affair, enlivened only sporadically by a very few near misses. As the majority of these were from Darlington attackers then there was some sort of justice in the final result although the one score, coming as it did in the last few seconds of extra time, was extremely painful for the Stags supporters who outnumbered their Quaker rivals by pretty well two to one. However both sets of fans were, at appropriate moments, very vocal in their partisanship but it is pleasing to report that there was absolutely no unpleasantness. Commendably the same sporting behaviour was forthcoming from both managements and their players. The pitch too, which has been much criticised, presented no problems. In fact it looked pristine under the pleasant sunshine although it has to be said that it did not look like real grass.

The first player to stand out was the energetic Mansfield captain, Adam Murray, whose threatening surge saw Sam Russell rushing from his goal to boot clear. Next second, in a repeat clearance, Russell kicked over the trickling ball but was fortunately able to retrieve his error before true disaster could occur. Opposition keeper Alan Marriott then had to punch away Aaron Brown's corner before plucking a threatening cross from Chris Moore out of the air. Tommy Wright shot over and Gary Smith lost a shooting chance as he tried to dribble round one too many an opponent. In a Mansfield attack Paul Connor was halted by a fine tackle from Ian Miller before the half drew to a close with Russell rushing out to prevent Connor making anything of a pass which had set him clear. These were the highlights of a disappointing first half.

The second half was a slight improvement, punctuated as it was with a series of half chances. Jamie Chandler's influence in the Quakers' midfield lifted the spirits of their supporters but Mansfield's supporters grew edgier as their ineffectiveness in front of goal became more apparent, despite Louis Briscoe moving forward further than in his first half anonymity.

Coming on as sub for Darlington, Chris Senior neatly jinked down the left and shot on target but straight into Marriott's arms. The main threat of a score came when another Quaker sub, Aman Verma, burst from his own penalty area only to be stopped by Tyrone Thompson's tackle. Unfortunately for Thompson the referee saw this as a foul. Up stepped Marc Bridge-Wilkinson to smack his shot into Marriott's right hand post from where it rebounded to safety. This was the nearest either side had come to opening their account. What minute was this excitement?- the last minute of normal time, minute 90, which stresses the dearth of goalmouth action yet in the second minute of added time Darlington spurned another opportunity, Tommy Wright glancing Bridge-Wilkinson's cross wide.

As we awaited extra time we pondered on what we had seen so far. Had fear of losing, or just the venue, the crowd, or the occasion proved too much? Why had so many players not seemed able to judge the pace of the ball? Why was the killer ball missing? Would the tedium be lifted? We were not hopeful and visualised the spot kick lottery.

The action in the first fifteen minutes of extra time resulted in the first booking of the match, Wright of Darlington, and little else of note. Not losing seemed the evident aim of both sides as they stretched their tiring limbs. 108 th minute and Stags' Connor just failed to get his head to a bouncing cross from the right. In the other goalmouth Wright headed a corner against the foot of a post, the rebound being hacked gratefully away. Both sets of supporters raised the decibel level yet again as their sides, like exhausted, lumbering elephants, struggled desperately to dredge up one last gasp of energy with which to lunge forward before the dreaded penalties came to define the winner. Just as the spot kicks became inevitable a lob into the Mansfield penalty area was headed on to the crossbar and all Marriott could do with the consequent follow up from Senior was to parry it into the roof of his net. Darlington manager, Mark Cooper, having run on to the pitch to join his players' celebrations, had to be sent speedily back to his technical area but he was only there for seconds before Mr Attwell's whistle underlined that right at the death fortune had gone Darlington's way. The black and white shirted fans celebrated while many in blue and yellow snaked for the exits, their understandable disappointment evident for all to see. And so the Quakers triumphed over the Stags at the end of what had been a sadly unexciting encounter.

Arthur Evans

DARLINGTON (Senior 120) 1
MANSFIELD TOWN 0

Wembley Stadium

Attendance: 24,668

Photo: Eric Marsh

Below: Liam Hatch, Darlington, holds off two Mansfield Town defenders. Photo: Roger Turner.

Chris Senior's expression says it all. Photo: Keith Clayton.

Darlington: Sam Russell, Paul Arnison, Ian Miller, Liam Hatch, Aaron Brown, Jamie Chandler*, Chris Moore, Marc Bridge-Wilkinson (sub Paul Terry 100th min), Gary Smith (sub Arman Verma 38th min), John Campbell (sub Chris Senior 75th min), Tommy Wright.
Subs not used – Danzelle St Louis-Hamilton (gk) and Phil Gray. * - Man of the Match

Mansfield Town: Alan Marriott, Gary Silk, Stephen Foster, Tom Naylor, Dan Spence, Louis Briscoe, Tyrone Thompson, Kyle Nix, Adam Smith (sub Ashley Cain 95th min), Adam Murray (sub Danny Mitchley 108th min), Paul Connor
Subs not used – Paul Stonehouse and Neil Collett (gk)

Referee Stuart Atwell assisted by Simon Long and Andrew Madley. Fourth official – Craig Pawson.

An early Darlington corner is cleared in the Final. Photo: Graham Brown.

Action from the 4th Round tie between Manfield Town and Chasetown which the eventual finalists won 3-1. Photo: Bill Wheatcroft.

Action from the 4th Round tie between Manfield Town and Chasetown which the eventual finalists won 3-1. Photo: Bill Wheatcroft.

PAST FINALS

1970 MACCLESFIELD TOWN 2 (Lyons, B Fidler) — **TELFORD UNITED 0** — **Att: 28,000**
Northern Premier League — *Southern League*
Macclesfield: Cooke, Sievwright, Bennett, Beaumont, Collins, Roberts, Lyons, B Fidler,Young, Corfield, D Fidler.
Telford: Irvine, Harris, Croft, Flowers, Coton, Ray,Fudge, Hart, Bentley, Murray, Jagger. Ref: K Walker

1971 TELFORD UTD 3 (Owen, Bentley, Fudge) — **HILLINGDON BORO. 2 (Reeve, Bishop)** — **Att: 29,500**
Southern League — *Southern League*
Telford: Irvine, Harris, Croft, Ray, Coton, Carr, Fudge, Owen, Bentley, Jagger ,Murray.
Hillingdon B.: Lowe, Batt, Langley, Higginson, Newcombe, Moore, Fairchild,Bishop, Reeve, Carter, Knox. Ref: D Smith

1972 STAFFORD RANGERS 3 (Williams 2, Cullerton) — **BARNET 0** — **Att: 24,000**
Northern Premier League — *Southern League*
Stafford R.: Aleksic, Chadwick, Clayton, Sargeant, Aston, Machin, Cullerton, Chapman,Williams, Bayley, Jones.
Barnet: McClelland, Lye, Jenkins, Ward, Embrey, King, Powell, Ferry, Flatt, Easton, Plume . Ref: P Partridge

1973 SCARBOROUGH 2 (Leask, Thompson) — **WIGAN ATHLETIC 1 (Rogers) aet** — **Att:23,000**
Northern Premier League — *Northern Premier League*
Scarborough: Garrow, Appleton, Shoulder, Dunn, Siddle, Fagan, Donoghue, Franks,Leask (Barmby), Thompson, Hewitt.
Wigan: Reeves, Morris, Sutherland, Taylor,Jackson, Gillibrand, Clements, Oats (McCunnell), Rogers, King, Worswick. Ref: H Hackney

1974 MORECAMBE 2 (Richmond, Sutton) — **DARTFORD 1 (Cunningham)** — **Att: 19,000**
Northern Premier League — *Southern League*
Morecambe: Coates, Pearson, Bennett, Sutton, Street, Baldwin, Done, Webber,Roberts (Galley), Kershaw, Richmond.
Dartford: Morton, Read, Payne, Carr, Burns,Binks, Light, Glozier, Robinson (Hearne), Cunningham, Halleday. Ref: B Homewood

1975(1) MATLOCK TOWN 4 (Oxley, Dawson, T Fenoughty, N Fenoughy) — **SCARBOROUGH 0** — **Att: 21,000**
Northern Premier League — *Northern Premier League*
Matlock: Fell, McKay, Smith, Stuart, Dawson, Swan, Oxley, N Fenoughy, Scott, T Fenoughty, M Fenoughty.
Scarborough: Williams, Hewitt, Rettitt, Dunn, Marshall, Todd, Houghton, Woodall, Davidson, Barnby, Aveyard. Ref: K Styles

1976 SCARBOROUGH 3 (Woodall, Abbey, Marshall(p)) — **STAFFORD R. 2 (Jones 2) aet** — **Att: 21,000**
Northern Premier League — *Northern Premier League*
Scarborough: Barnard, Jackson, Marshall, H Dunn, Ayre (Donoghue), HA Dunn, Dale,Barmby, Woodall, Abbey, Hilley.
Stafford: Arnold, Ritchie, Richards, Sargeant,Seddon, Morris, Chapman, Lowe, Jones, Hutchinson, Chadwick. Ref: R Challis

1977 SCARBOROUGH 2 (Dunn(p), Abbey) — **DAGENHAM 1 (Harris)** — **Att: 21,500**
Northern Premier League — *Isthmian League*
Scarborough: Chapman, Smith, Marshall (Barmby), Dunn, Ayre, Deere, Aveyard,Donoghue, Woodall, Abbey, Dunn.
Dagenham: Hutley, Wellman, P Currie, Dunwell,Moore, W Currie, Harkins, Saul, Fox, Harris, Holder. Ref: G Courtney

1978 ALTRINCHAM 3 (King, Johnson, Rogers) — **LEATHERHEAD 1 (Cook)** — **Att: 20,000**
Northern Premier League — *Isthmian League*
Altrincham: Eales, Allan, Crossley, Bailey, Owens, King, Morris, Heathcote,Johnson, Rogers, Davidson (Flaherty).
Leatherhead: Swannell, Cooper, Eaton, Davies,Reid, Malley, Cook, Salkeld, Baker, Boyle (Bailey). Ref: A Grey

1979 STAFFORD RANGERS 2 (A Wood 2) — **KETTERING TOWN 0** — **Att: 32,000**
Northern Premier League — *Southern League*
Stafford: Arnold, F Wood, Willis, Sargeant, Seddon, Ritchie, Secker, Chapman, A Wood, Cullerton, Chadwick (Jones).
Kettering: Lane, Ashby, Lee, Eastell, Dixey,Suddards, Flannagan, Kellock, Phipps, Clayton, Evans (Hughes). Ref: D Richardson

1980(2) DAGENHAM 2 (Duck, Maycock) — **MOSSLEY 1 (Smith)** — **Att: 26,000**
Isthmian League — *Northern Premier League*
Dagenham: Huttley, Wellman, Scales, Dunwell, Moore, Durrell, Maycock, Horan,Duck, Kidd, Jones (Holder).
Mossley: Fitton, Brown, Vaughan, Gorman, Salter, Polliot, Smith, Moore, Skeete, O'Connor, Keelan (Wilson). Ref: K Baker

1981(3) BISHOP'S STORTFORD 1 (Sullivan) — **SUTTON UNITED 0** — **Att: 22,578**
Isthmian League — *Isthmian League*
Bishop's Stortford: Moore, Blackman, Brame, Smith (Worrell), Bradford, Abery, Sullivan,Knapman, Radford, Simmonds, Mitchell.
Sutton Utd.: Collyer, Rogers, Green, J Rains,T Rains, Stephens (Sunnucks), Waldon, Pritchard, Cornwell, Parsons, Dennis. Ref: J Worrall

1982 ENFIELD 1 (Taylor) — **ALTRINCHAM 0** — **Att: 18,678**
Alliance Premier League — *Alliance Premier League*
Enfield: Jacobs, Barrett, Tone, Jennings, Waite, Ironton, Ashford, Taylor,Holmes, Oliver (Flint), King. Ref: B Stevens
Altrincham: Connaughton, Crossley, Davison, Bailey, Cuddy, King (Whitbread), Allan, Heathcote, Johnson, Rogers, Howard.

Notes:
1 The only occasion three members of the same family played in the same FA Trophy Final team.
2 The first of the Amateurs from the Isthmian League to win the FA Trophy.
3 Goalkeeper Terry Moore had also won an Amateur Cup Winners Medal with Bishop's Stortford in 1974.
All games played at Wembley (old & new) unless stated.

1983 TELFORD UTD 2 (Mather 2) — **NORTHWICH VICTORIA 1 (Bennett)** — **Att: 22,071**
Alliance Premier League — *Alliance Premier League*
Telford: Charlton, Lewis, Turner, Mayman (Joseph), Walker, Easton, Barnett,Williams, Mather, Hogan, Alcock.
Northwich: Ryan, Fretwell, Murphy, Jones, Forshaw, Ward, Anderson, Abel (Bennett), Reid, Chesters, Wilson. Ref: B Hill

1984 NORTHWICH VICTORIA 1 (Chester) — **BANGOR CITY 1 (Whelan)** — **Att: 14,200**
Replay NORTHWICH VICTORIA 2 (Chesters(p), Anderson) — **BANGOR CITY 1 (Lunn)** — **Att: 5,805 (at Stoke)**
Alliance Premier League — *Alliance Premier League*
Northwich: Ryan, Fretwell, Dean, Jones, Forshaw (Power 65), Bennett, Anderson,Abel, Reid, Chesters, Wilson. Ref: J Martin
Bangor: Letheren, Cavanagh, Gray, Whelan, Banks,Lunn, Urqhart, Morris, Carter, Howat, Sutcliffe (Westwood 105) . Same in replay.

1985 WEALDSTONE 2 (Graham, Holmes) — **BOSTON UNITED 1 (Cook)** — **Att: 20,775**
Alliance Premier League — *Alliance Premier League*
Wealdstone: Iles, Perkins, Bowgett, Byatt, Davies, Greenaway, Holmes, Wainwright,Donnellan, Graham (N Cordice 89), A Cordice.
Boston: Blackwell, Casey, Ladd,Creane, O'Brien, Thommson, Laverick (Mallender 78), Simpsom, Gilbert, Lee, Cook. Ref: J Bray

1986 ALTRINCHAM 1 (Farrelly) — **RUNCORN 0** — **Att: 15,700**
Gola League — *Gola League*
Altrincham: Wealands, Gardner, Densmore, Johnson, Farrelly, Conning, Cuddy,Davison, Reid, Ellis, Anderson. Sub: Newton.
Runcorn: McBride, Lee, Roberts,Jones, Fraser, Smith, S Crompton (A Crompton), Imrie, Carter, Mather, Carrodus. Ref: A Ward

1987 KIDDERMINSTER HARRIERS 0 — **BURTON ALBION 0** — **Att: 23,617**
Replay KIDDERMINSTER HARRIERS 2 (Davies 2) — **BURTON ALBION 1 (Groves)** — **Att: 15,685 (at West Brom)**
Conference — *Southern League*
Kidderminster: Arnold, Barton, Boxall, Brazier (sub Hazlewood in rep), Collins (sub Pearson 90 at Wembley), Woodall, McKenzie, O'Dowd, Tuohy, Casey, Davies. sub:Jones.
Burton: New, Essex, Kamara, Vaughan, Simms, Groves, Bancroft, Land, Dorsett, Redfern, (sub Wood in replay), Gauden.
Sub: Patterson. Ref: D Shaw

1988 ENFIELD 0 — **TELFORD UNITED 0** — **Att: 20,161**
Replay ENFIELD 3 (Furlong 2, Howell) — **TELFORD 2 (Biggins, Norris(p))** — **Att: 6,912 (at W Brom)**
Conference — *Conference*
Enfield: Pape, Cottington, Howell, Keen (sub Edmonds in rep), Sparrow (sub Hayzleden at Wembley), Lewis (sub Edmonds at Wembley), Harding, Cooper, King,Furlong, Francis.
Telford: Charlton, McGinty, Storton, Nelson, Wiggins, Mayman (sub Cunningham in rep (sub Hancock)), Sankey, Joseph, Stringer (sub Griffiths at Wembley, Griffiths in replay), Biggins, Norris. Ref: L Dilkes

1989 TELFORD UNITED 1 (Crawley) — **MACCLESFIELD TOWN 0** — **Att: 18,102**
Conference — *Conference*
Telford: Charlton, Lee, Brindley, Hancock, Wiggins, Mayman, Grainger, Joseph, Nelson, Lloyd, Stringer. Subs: Crawley, Griffiths.
Macclesfield: Zelem, Roberts, Tobin, Edwards, Hardman, Askey, Lake, Hanton, Imrie, Burr, Timmons. Subs: Devonshire, Kendall.

1990 BARROW 3 (Gordon 2, Cowperthwaite) — **LEEK TOWN 0** — **Att: 19,011**
Conference — *Northern Premier League*
Barrow: McDonnell, Higgins, Chilton, Skivington, Gordon, Proctor, Doherty (Burgess), Farrell (Gilmore), Cowperthwaite, Lowe, Ferris.
Leek: Simpson, Elsby (Smith), Pearce, McMullen, Clowes, Coleman (Russell),Mellor, Somerville, Sutton, Millington, Norris Ref: T Simpson

1991 WYCOMBE W. 2 (Scott, West) — **KIDDERMINSTER HARRIERS 1 (Hadley)** — **Att: 34,842**
Conference — *Conference*
Wycombe: Granville, Crossley, Cash, Kerr, Creaser, Carroll, Ryan, Stapleton,West, Scott, Guppy (Hutchinson). Ref: J Watson
Kidderminster: Jones, Kurila, McGrath, Weir, Barnett, Forsyth, Joseph (Wilcox), Howell (Whitehouse), Hadley, Lilwall, Humphries

1992 COLCHESTER UTD* 3 (Masters, Smith, McGavin) — **WITTON ALBION 1 (Lutkevitch)** — **Att: 27,806**
Conference — *Conference*
Colchester: Barrett, Donald, Roberts, Knsella, English, Martin, Cook, Masters,McDonough (Bennett 65), McGavin, Smith. Ref: K P Barratt
Witton: Mason, Halliday, Coathup, McNeilis, Jim Connor, Anderson, Thomas, Rose, Alford, Grimshaw (Joe Connor), Lutkevitch (McCluskie)

1993 WYCOMBE W*. 4 (Cousins, Kerr, Thompson, Carroll) — **RUNCORN 1 (Shaughnessy)**
Att: 32,968
Conference — *Conference*
Wycombe: Hyde, Cousins, Cooper, Kerr, Crossley, Thompson (Hayrettin 65),Carroll, Ryan, Hutchinson, Scott, Guppy. Sub: Casey.
Runcorn: Williams, Bates, Robertson, Hill, Harold (Connor 62), Anderson, Brady (Parker 72), Brown, Shaughnessy, McKenna, Brabin

1994 WOKING 2 (D Brown, Hay) — **RUNCORN 1 (Shaw (pen))** — **Att: 15,818**
Conference — *Conference*
Woking: Batty, Tucker, L Wye, Berry, Brown, Clement, Brown (Rattray 32), Fielder, Steele, Hay (Puckett 46), Walker. Ref: Paul Durkin
Runcorn: Williams, Bates, Robertson, Shaw, Lee, Anderson, Thomas, Connor, McInerney (Hill 71), McKenna, Brabin. Sub: Parker

1995 WOKING 2 (Steele, Fielder) — **KIDDERMINSTER HARRIERS 1 aet (Davies)** — **Att: 17,815**
Conference — *Conference*
Woking: Batty, Tucker, L Wye, Fielder, Brown, Crumplin (Rattray 42), S Wye, Ellis, Steele, Hay (Newberry 112), Walker. (Sub: Read(gk)
Kidderminster: Rose, Hodson, Bancroft, Webb, Brindley (Cartwright 94), Forsyth, Deakin, Yates, Humphreys (Hughes 105), Davies, Purdie. Sub: Dearlove (gk) Ref: D J Gallagher

THE FA TROPHY

1996 MACCLESFIELD TOWN 3 (Payne, OG, Hemmings) *Conference* **NORTHWICH VICTORIA 1 (Williams)** *Conference* **Att: 8,672**

Macclesfield: Price, Edey, Gardiner, Payne, Howarth(C), Sorvel, Lyons, Wood (Hulme 83), Coates, Power, Hemmings (Cavell 88).
Northwich: Greygoose, Ward, Duffy, Burgess (Simpson 87), Abel (Steele), Walters, Williams, Butler (C), Cooke, Humphries, Vicary.
Ref: M Reed

1997 WOKING 1 (Hay 112) *Conference* **DAGENHAM & REDBRIDGE 0** *Isthmian League* **Att: 24,376**

Woking: Batty, Brown, Howard, Foster, Taylor, S Wye, Thompson (sub Jones 115), Ellis, Steele (L Wye 108), Walker, Jackson (Hay 77).
Dagenham: Gothard, Culverhouse, Connor, Creaser, Jacques (sub Double 75), Davidson, Pratt (Naylor 81), Parratt, Broom, Rogers, Stimson (John 65).
Ref: J Winter

1998 CHELTENHAM TOWN 1 (Eaton 74) *Conference* **SOUTHPORT 0** *Conference* **Att: 26,387**

Cheltenham: Book, Duff, Freeman, Banks, Victory, Knight (Smith 78), Howells, Bloomer, Walker (sub Milton 78), Eaton, Watkins. Sub: Wright.
Southport: Stewart, Horner, Futcher, Ryan, Farley, Kielty, Butler, Gamble, Formby (sub Whittaker 80), Thompson (sub Bollard 88), Ross. Sub: Mitten.
Ref: G S Willard

1999 KINGSTONIAN 1 (Mustafa 49) *Conference* **FOREST GREEN ROVERS 0** *Conference* **Att: 20,037**

Kingstonian: Farrelly, Mustafa, Luckett, Crossley, Stewart, Harris, Patterson, Pitcher, Rattray, Leworthy (Francis 87), Akuamoah. Subs (not used): John, Corbett, Brown, Tranter
Forest Green Rovers: Shuttlewood, Hedges, Forbes, Bailey (Smart 76), Kilgour, Wigg (Cook 58), Honor (Winter 58), Drysdale, McGregor, Mehew, Sykes. Subs (not used): Perrin, Coupe
Ref: A B Wilkie

2000 KINGSTONIAN 3 (Akuamoah 40, 69, Simba 75) *Conference* **KETTERING TOWN 2 (Vowden 55, Norman 64p)** *Conference* **Att: 20,034**

Kingstonian: Farelly, Mustafa, Luckett, Crossley, Stewart (Saunders 77), Harris, Kadi (Leworthy 83), Pitcher, Green (Basford 86), Smiba, Akuamoah. Subs (not used): Hurst, Allan
Kettering Town: Sollit, McNamara, Adams, Perkins, Vowden, Norman (Duik 76), Fisher, Brown, Shutt, Watkins (Hudson 46), Setchell (Hopkins 81). Subs (not used): Ridgway, Wilson
Ref: S W Dunn

2001 CANVEY ISLAND 1 (Chenery) *Isthmian League* **FOREST GREEN ROVERS 0** *Conference* **Att: 10,007 at Villa Park**

Forest Green Rovers: Perrin, Cousins, Lockwood, Foster, Clark, Burns, Daley, Drysdale (Bennett 46), Foster (Hunt 75), Meecham, Slater. Subs (not used): Hedges, Prince, Ghent
Canvey Island: Harrison, Duffy, Chenery, Bodley, Ward, Tilson, Stimson (Tanner 83), Gregory, Vaughan (Jones 76), Parmenter. Subs (not used): Bennett, Miller, Thompson.
Ref: A G Wiley

2002 YEOVIL TOWN 2 (Alford, Stansfield) *Conference* **STEVENAGE BOROUGH 0** *Conference* **Att: 18,809 at Villa Park**

Yeovil Town: Weale, Lockwood, Tonkin, Skiverton, Pluck (White 51), Way, Stansfield, Johnson, Alford (Giles 86), Crittenden (Lindegaard 83), McIndoe. Subs (not used): O'Brien, Sheffield
Stevenage Borough: Wilkerson, Hamsher, Goodliffe, Trott, Fraser, Fisher, Wormull (Stirling 71), Evers (Williams 56), Jackson, Sigere (Campbell 74), Clarke. Subs (not used): Campbell, Greygoose
Ref: N S Barry

2003 BURSCOUGH 2 (Martindale 25, 55) *Northern Premier* **TAMWORTH 1 (Cooper 78)** *Southern Premier* **Att: 14,265 at Villa Park**

Burscough: Taylor, Teale, Taylor, Macauley (White 77), Lawless, Bowen, Wright, Norman, Martindale (McHale 80), Byrne (Bluck 84), Burns. Subs (not used): McGuire (g/k) Molyneux.
Tamworth: Acton, Warner, Follett, Robinson, Walsh, Cooper, Colley, Evans (Turner 64), Rickards (Hatton 88), McGorry, Sale (Hallam 54). Subs (not used): Grocutt, Barnes (g/k).
Ref: U D Rennie

2004 HEDNESFORD TOWN 3 (Maguire 28, Hines 53, Brindley 87) *Southern Premier* **CANVEY ISLAND 2 (Boylan 46, Brindley 48 og)** *Isthmian Premier Champions* **Att: 6,635 at Villa Park**

Hednesford Town: Young, Simkin, Hines, King, Brindley, Ryder (Barrow 59), Palmer, Anthrobus, Danks (Piearce 78), Maguire, Charie (Evans 55). Subs (not used): Evans (g/k) McGhee.
Canvey Island: Potter, Kennedy, Duffy, Chenery, Cowan, Gooden (Dobinson 89), Minton, Gregory (McDougald 80), Boylan, Midgley (Berquez 73), Ward. Subs (not used): Theobald, Harrison (g/k).
Ref: M L Dean

2005 GRAYS ATHLETIC 1 (Martin 65) Pens: 6 *Conference South* **HUCKNALL TOWN 1 (Ricketts 75) Pens: 5** *Conference North* **Att: 8,116 at Villa Park**

Grays Athletic: Bayes, Brennan, Nutter, Stuart, Matthews, Thurgood, Oli (Powell 80), Hopper (Carthy 120), Battersby (sub West 61), Martin, Cole. Subs (not used): Emberson, Bruce..
Hucknall Town: Smith, Asher, Barrick (Plummer 30), Hunter, Timons, Cooke, Smith (Ward 120), Palmer (Heathcote 94), Ricketts, Bacon, Todd. Subs (not used): Winder, Lindley.
Ref: P Dowd

2006 GRAYS ATHLETIC 2 (Oli, Poole) *Conference* **WOKING 0** *Conference* **Att: 13,997 at Upton Park**

Grays Athletic: Bayes, Sambrook, Nutter, Stuart, Hanson, Kightly (Williamson 90), Thurgood, Martin, Poole, Oli, McLean. Subs (not used): Eyre (g/k), Hooper, Olayinka, Mawer.
Woking: Jalal, Jackson, MacDonald, Nethercott (Watson 60), Hutchinson, Murray, Smith (Cockerill 60), Evans (Blackman 85), Ferguson, McAllister, Justin Richards. Subs (not used): Davis (g/k), El-Salahi.
Ref: Howard Webb (Sheffield)

2007 KIDDERMINSTER HARRIERS 2 (Constable 2) *Conference* — **STEVENAGE BOROUGH 3 (Cole, Dobson, Morrison)** *Conference* — **Att: 53,262 (New Trophy record)**

Kidderminster Harriers: Bevan, Kenna, Hurren, Creighton, Whitehead, Blackwood, Russell, Penn, Smikle (Reynolds 90), Christie (White 75) , Constable.
Subs not used: Taylor, Sedgemore, McGrath.
Stevenage Borough: Julian, Fuller, Nutter, Oliver, Gaia, Miller, Cole, Morrison, Guppy (Dobson 63), Henry, Beard.
Subs not used: Potter, Slabber, Nurse, McMahon. Ref: Chris Foy (Merseyside)

2008 EBBSFLEET UNITED 1 (McPhee) *Blue Square Premier* — **TORQUAY UNITED 0** *Blue Square Premier* — **Att: 40,186**

Ebbsfleet United: Cronin, Hawkins, McCarthy, Smith, Opinel, McPhee, Barrett, Bostwick, Long (MacDonald 84), Moore, Akinde.
Subs not used: Eribenne, Purcell, Ricketts, Mott.
Torquay United: Rice, Mansell, Todd, Woods, Nicholson, D'Sane (Benyon 66), Hargreaves, Adams, Zebroski, Sills (Hill 88), Phillips (Stevens 46). Subs not used: Hockley and Robertson. Ref: Martin Atkinson (West Riding)

2009 STEVENAGE BOROUGH 2 (Morison, Boylan) *Blue Square Premier* — **YORK CITY 0** *Blue Square Premier* — **Att: 27,102**

Stevenage Borough: Day, Henry, Bostwick, Roberts, Wilson, Mills, Murphy, Drury, Vincenti (Anaclet 86), Boylan, Morison.
Subs not used: Bayes, Albrighton, Maamria and Willock.
York City:Ingham, Purkiss, McGurk, Parslow, Pejic, Mackin, Greaves(McWilliams 74), Rusk (Russell 80), Brodie, McBreen (Sodje 60), Boyes. Subs not used – Mimms and Robinson. Referee: Michael Jones.

2010 BARROW 2 (McEvilly 79, Walker 117) *Blue Square Premier* — **STEVENAGE BOROUGH 1 (Drury 10)** *Blue Square Premier* — **Att: 21,223**

Barrow: Stuart Tomlinson, Simon Spender, Paul Jones, Phil Bolland, Paul Edwards, Simon Wiles (sub Carlos Logan 63rd min), Robin Hulbert, Andy Bond, Paul Rutherford (sub Mark Boyd 109th min), Jason Walker, Gregg Blundell (sub Lee McEvilly 73rd min).
Subs not used – Tim Deasy and Mike Pearson.
Stevenage Borough: Chris Day (sub Ashley Bayes 90th min), Ronnie Henry, Jon Ashton, Mark Roberts, Scott Laird, Joel Byrom (sub Lawrie Wilson 58th min), David Bridges, Michael Bostwick, Andy Drury, Chris Beardsley (sub Charlie Griffin 64th min), Yemi Odubade. Subs not used – Stacey Long and Peter Vincenti.
Man of the match – Paul Rutherford. Referee Lee Probert.

Ashley Stott heads home for Witton Albion against Sutton Coldfield, the only goal of this Preliminary Round fixture. Photo: Keith Clayton.

THE FA VASE

2010-11

Photo: Roger Turner.

Clubs competing in Step Five downwards with acceptable facilities, can compete in The F.A. Challenge Vase, a national knock out competition that last season attracted a massive entry of 549 clubs. By the 18th March the first and second qualifying rounds had involved 319 ties from which of course half the clubs would no longer be involved in The First Round Proper. Clubs winning both their qualifying ties would have received £750 + £800 in prize money, which is extremely helpful for the little clubs battling at this level.

It is very important for managers to ensure their playing squads realize the importance of a Vase run. Prize money, morale boosting, and the chance to play more senior opposition in different parts of the country, add up to a club's all round development with players building experience and the teams developing a winning habit.
The first challenge for a club playing in the qualifying rounds is to ensure they will still be involved in the First Round draw.

When you realize that 421 clubs had already been knocked out of the F.A. Vase by the first week of October, it is easy to understand why so many clubs fail to appreciate the possibilities of the competition, but gradually the competition enables clubs to be matched with clubs outside their 'geographical safety net' and the real challenge begins. Which regional leagues are really the strongest? Who takes the competition seriously and will always be difficult to beat?

The senior clubs who have been exempt enter the competition and after the early season rush, the F.A. Vase settles down to one Round each Month. The Third Round was still basically drawn in two sections, North and South, but was completely ruined by the weather and it took three weeks to complete the thirty two games.

Regional favourites were now emerging and of course, Whitley Bay the holders for the past two years, had made it known that their ambition was a famous hat-trick of Wembley victories. The North East are traditionally strong in this competition and Spennymoor Town and Billingham Synthonia joined 'The Bay' in the Fifth Round draw. Other fancied clubs included Kings Lynn Town in a new life, having dropped out of senior football after financial troubles, Poole Town who were making a name for themselves in the Wessex League and
Coalville Town who were enjoying their best ever season in The Midland Alliance.

The fun of the long distance cup tie was really appreciated in the Fifth Round, as Billingham travelled all the way down to Cornwall to lose by the only goal of the game at Torpoint Athletic, while neighbours Spennymoor lost by the odd goal in five at Poole Town. Whitley Bay made the most of the holders luck with a home draw and beat Dunstable with an emphatic 5-1 victory. Conversely Kings Lynn played host to near neighbours St Neots Town and won 2-1. With Coalville beating Holbrook Sports 3-1 at home, the favourites had all been given home advantage and all four had qualified for the last eight.

A situation that all except the holders enjoyed again in The Quarter Finals. This is always the round when your home supporters, pitch, atmosphere and lack of travelling are all really important. Although, perhaps the stars of Whitley Bay could cope away from home with their experience of the competition, and sure enough they came back from a goal at half time to win 2-1 at Dunstable UTS. Meanwhile Coalville Town beat visitors Leiston 1-0, and Poole Town after conceding a second minute lead to visitors Torpoint were in the lead by half time and played out a goalless second half. This left King Lynn, who, having attracted a splendid crowd of 1,657 were taken to extra time by Rye United, but eventually sent the fans home happy with a 3-1victory.

Semi-Finals are traditionally two legged affairs with most clubs hoping to be at home in the second game. But Coalville gave themselves every chance to progress, by crashing three goals past Kings Lynn in the first leg roared on by 1,800 fans. The second meeting was killed off early with Coalville adding two more goals but Kings Lynn didn't lie down in front of an excellent 2,354 attendance, and eventually only lost by 2-3 on the day but emphatically 2-6 over the two legs. Whitley Bay also made sure there were no mistakes with two victories 2-1 at Poole (1,562) and 3-1 at home (2,842) so they were back at Wembley for the third consecutive year and would face Coalville Town who would be making wonderful history for their club. T.W.

Erith Town's Ben Payne slips the ball under Badshot Lea 'keeper Lee Allen but sees his shot hit the post in this 1st Qyalifying Round encounter. Photo: Alan Coomes.

Above: Southwick 'keeper Piers Walsh and defender Sol Bowra keep out Peter Huggins of Lordswood in this 2nd Qualfying Round tie. Photo: Alan Coomes

Scott Curly scores from a corner to give Clipstone Welfare the lead against Kimberley Town in the 2nd Qyalifying Round. Photo: Gordon Whittington.

FIRST QUALIFYING ROUND

SATURDAY 4 SEPTEMBER 2010 - WINNERS RECEIVE £750

1	Easington Colliery	v	Hall Road Rangers	5-4	38
2	Tadcaster Albion	v	Prudhoe Town	5-0	63
3	Thornaby	v	Newcastle Benfield	0-3	52
4	Crook Town	v	Team Northumbria	4-2	82
5	Darlington Railway Athletic	v	Liversedge	2-4	60
6	Ashington	v	Whickham	4-0	219
7	Seaham Red Star	v	Scarborough Athletic	0-3	164
8	Selby Town	v	Sunderland RCA	3-2	106
9	South Shields	v	North Shields	2-0	261
10	Eccleshill United	v	Gillford Park	2-1	22
11	Willington	v	Bishop Auckland	0-3	127
12	Silsden	v	Tow Law Town	1-2	124
13	West Allotment Celtic	v	Newton Aycliffe	5-1	101
14	Glasshoughton Welfare	v	Brighouse Town	0-2	65
15	AFC Emley	v	Hemsworth MW (3/9)	4-2	135
16	Cheadle Town	v	Worsborough Bridge Athletic	1-2	61
17	Penrith	v	FC Brimington	4-1	70
18	Nelson	v	Abbey Hey		
	(walkover for Abbey Hey – Nelson removed)				
19	Chadderton	v	Holker Old Boys	1-2	31
20	Maltby Main	v	Ashton Town	2-2aet	20
	Ashton Town	v	Maltby Main (7/9)	2-1	16
21	Dinnington Town	v	Wigan Robin Park	2-0	72
22	St Helens Town	v	Brodsworth Welfare	8-1	34
	(at Atherton Collieries FC)				
23	Bacup Borough	v	Nostell MW	3-1aet	75
24	Daisy Hill	v	Whitehaven	2-3aet	53
25	Parkgate	v	Congleton Town	4-2	80
26	Hinckley	v	Walsall Wood	0-5	43
27	Pershore Town	v	Leek CSOB	2-1	44
28	Biddulph Victoria	v	Stafford Town (5/9)	2-1aet	80
	(at Norton United FC)				
29	Ellistown	v	Highgate United	0-5	38
30	Bromyard Town	v	Continental Star	2-6	24
31	Dudley Town	v	Warstones Wanderers	4-2	51
32	Boldmere St Michaels	v	Lutterworth Athletic	4-1	63
33	Castle Vale JKS	v	Anstey Nomads	1-1aet	76
	(at Anstey Nomads FC)				
	Anstey Monads	v	Castle Vale JKS (8/9)	3-2	111
34	Pelsall Villa	v	Bardon Hill Sports	1-0	50
35	Goodrich	v	Nuneaton Griff	2-0	28
36	Cradley Town	v	Malvern Town	1-3	44
37	Shifnal Town	v	Cadbury Athletic	2-0aet	44
38	Ellesmere Rangers	v	Kirby Muxloe	2-0	70
39	Rocester	v	Loughborough University	0-1	97
40	Pilkington XXX	v	Coleshill Town	3-1	83
41	Tividale	v	Oadby Town	8-1	67
42	Alvechurch	v	Ibstock United	5-0	65
43	Shawbury United	v	Bridgnorth Town	0-2	73
	(at Bridgnorth Town FC)				
44	Dosthill Colts	v	Studley	1-8	46
45	Racing Club Warwick	v	Thurnby Nirvana	1-6	83
46	Sporting Khalsa	v	AFC Wulfrunians	0-3	30
47	Barrow Town	v	Heather St Johns	1-2aet	94
48	Dudley Sports	v	Ashby Ivanhoe	3-4	61
49	Castle Vale	v	Stone Dominoes	0-1	31
50	Bewdley Town	v	Wellington	2-1	52
51	Winterton Rangers	v	Long Eaton United	2-0	76
52	Greenwood Meadows	v	Ollerton Town	2-1	27
53	Forest Town	v	Radford	7-0	62
54	Blackstones	v	Shirebrook Town	2-0	83
55	Pinxton	v	Bottesford Town	2-1	107
56	Sleaford Town	v	Holbrook Sports	2-3	84
57	Newark Town	v	Arnold Town	0-1	71
58	Grimsby Borough	v	Radcliffe Olympic	1-0	59
	(at Radcliffe Olympic FC)				
59	Blackwell MW	v	Borrowash Victoria	1-5	50
60	Teversal	v	Blidworth Welfare	1-2	80
61	Walsham Le Willows	v	Cornard United	5-0	48
62	Rothwell Town	v	Cogenhoe United	2-3aet	93
63	Whitton United	v	Rushden & Higham United	3-0	59
64	Stewarts & Lloyds Corby	v	Wisbech Town	0-4	45
65	Gorleston	v	Ely City	1-1aet	75
	Ely City	v	Gorleston (7/9)	0-1aet	72
66	Newmarket Town	v	Diss Town	3-0	92
67	Irchester United	v	Ipswich Wanderers (5/9)	0-3	132
68	Huntingdon Town	v	Mildenhall Town	2-1aet	73
69	March Town United	v	Daventry United	0-1	63
70	Thetford Town	v	Rothwell Corinthians	2-2aet	54
	Rothwell Corinthians	v	Thetford Town (7/9)	0-5	48
71	Dereham Town	v	Kings Lynn Town	1-2aet	689
72	Brantham Athletic	v	Stowmarket Town	1-2	48
73	Hadleigh United	v	Yaxley	1-0	118
74	Long Melford	v	Fakenham Town	0-0aet	56
	Fakenham Town	v	Long Melford (7/9)	1-3	92
75	Haverhill Rovers	v	Northampton Spencer	4-0	199
76	Codicote	v	Hanworth Villa	1-4	37
77	Tokyngton Manor	v	Haringey Borough		
	(walkover for Haringey Borough – Tokyngton Manor removed)				
78	Wodson Park	v	Feltham	4-1	49
79	Baldock Town Letchworth	v	Milton United	2-1	40
80	Eton Manor	v	Southill Alexander	3-0	26
81	Bucks Student Union	v	Harefield United	2-3	55
82	Bedford	v	Hoddesdon Town	3-1	32
83	Langford	v	Mountnessing	1-1aet	37
	Mountnessing	v	Langford (9/9)	2-3	27
84	Kingsbury London Tigers	v	Southend Manor	0-1	37
85	Holmer Green	v	Newport Pagnell Town	1-1aet	118
	(Newport Pagnell Town won 5-4 on kicks from the penalty mark)				
	(at Newport Pagnell Town FC)				
86	Ascot United	v	Staines Lammas	3-0	197
87	Welwyn Garden City	v	Crawley Green	1-0	33
88	Sawbridgeworth Town	v	Hatfield Town	3-1	61
89	Hertford Town	v	Mauritius Sports Association UK	3-0	96
90	Shrivenham	v	Potton United	5-1	98
91	Basildon United	v	Kings Langley	5-3	91
92	AFC Kempston Rovers	v	Hadley	0-1	46
93	St Margaretsbury	v	Oxhey Jets	1-2	40
94	Buckingham Athletic	v	Barkingside	2-2aet	72
	Barkingside	v	Buckingham Athletic (6/9)	7-0	79
95	Wantage Town	v	London Colney	4-2	55
96	Bedfont Sports	v	AFC Dunstable	0-5	56
97	Stanway Rovers	v	Broxbourne Borough V&E	2-1aet	80
98	Buckingham Town	v	Saffron Walden Town	0-1	90
99	Dunstable Town	v	Hanwell Town	4-2aet	49
100	Mile Oak	v	United Services Portsmouth	4-2	55
101	Hayling United	v	Shoreham	1-3	70
102	Greenwich Borough	v	Newhaven	5-2	34
103	Deal Town	v	Crawley Down	0-4	95
104	Three Bridges	v	Littlehampton Town	5-1	71
105	Hamble ASSC	v	Totton & Eling	2-0	43
106	Molesey	v	Dorking (3/9)	2-1	95
107	Chessington & Hook Utd	v	South Park	1-3aet	80
108	Sidley United	v	Corinthian (5/9)	0-1	94
	(at Hailsham Town FC)				

Action from the 2nd Qualifying Round between Lydney Town and Corsham.
Photo: Peter Barnes.

Callum Cutler of Chichester City holds off Erith & Belvederes Danny Tipple in the 1st Round Proper.
Photo: Alan Coomes.

Godmanchester's Hayden Beasley and Eynesbury's Craig Lanham challenge for the ball during their 2nd Qualifying Round match. Photo: Bill Wheatcroft.

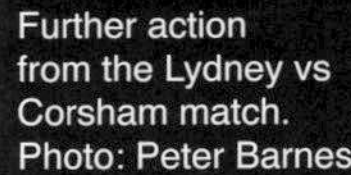

Further action from the Lydney vs Corsham match.
Photo: Peter Barnes.

FIRST QUALIFYING ROUND

SATURDAY 4 SEPTEMBER 2010 - WINNERS RECEIVE £750

109	Fisher	v	Ringwood Town (5/9)	2-1aet	160
110	Mole Valley SCR	v	Banstead Athletic (3/9)	2-3	75
111	Selsey	v	Lordswood	0-1	99
112	Alresford Town	v	Cove	0-4	56
113	Raynes Park Vale	v	Westfield	3-0	33
114	Horndean	v	Horley Town	1-3	50
115	Tunbridge Wells	v	Hailsham Town	3-0	101
116	Fleet Spurs	v	Petersfield Town	6-1	13
117	Brockenhurst	v	Crowborough Athletic	4-1	93
118	Winchester City	v	Holmesdale	1-0	107
119	Norton Sports	v	New Milton Town	3-2	46
120	Blackfield & Langley	v	Hassocks	3-2	50
121	Moneyfields	v	Farnborough North End	5-2	58
122	Guildford City	v	Sevenoaks Town	5-0	61
123	Newport (IW)	v	Whitchurch United	4-1	131
124	Lancing	v	AFC Uckfield	3-2	106
125	Cobham	v	Rye United	1-2	55
126	Andover New Street	v	East Cowes Victoria Athletic	1-3	41
127	Erith Town	v	Badshot Lea	3-1	41
128	Hartley Wintney	v	Brading Town	0-1	45
129	Worthing United	v	Lingfield	2-1	48
130	Oakwood	v	East Preston	3-4	24
131	Cheltenham Saracens	v	Hallen	1-2	43
132	Devizes Town	v	Amesbury Town	2-1aet	28
133	Old Woodstock Town	v	Shrewton United	3-1	34
134	Thame United	v	Slimbridge	2-1	22
135	Highworth Town	v	Bradford Town	1-2	74
136	Hook Norton	v	Laverstock & Ford	0-4	42
	(at Laverstock & Ford FC)				
137	Bicester Town	v	Cadbury Heath	1-2	56
138	Kidlington	v	Malmesbury Victoria	5-0	92
139	Westbury United	v	Ardley United	0-3	75
140	Corsham Town	v	Oxford City Nomads	1-1aet	72
	Oxford City Nomads	v	Corsham Town (8/9)	1-3	55
141	Almondsbury UWE	v	Pewsey Vale	4-2	40
142	Crediton United	v	Cullompton Rangers (3/9)	3-3aet	109
	Cullompton Rangers	v	Crediton United (7/9)	2-0	68
143	Elmore	v	Porthleven	2-3	49
144	Odd Down	v	Wells City	2-0	46
145	Keynsham Town	v	Swanage Town & Herston	2-1	61
146	Larkhall Athletic	v	Hamworthy United	0-3	110
147	Falmouth Town	v	Saltash United	2-2aet	126
	Saltash united	v	Falmouth Town (7/9)	3-1	99
148	Brislington	v	Witheridge	1-0	52
149	Hengrove Athletic	v	Gillingham Town	1-0	55
150	Welton Rovers	v	Verwood Town	0-3	66
151	St Blazey	v	Dartmouth	3-2aet	105

SECOND QUALIFYING ROUND

SATURDAY 18 SEPTEMBER 2010 - WINNERS RECEIVE £800

1	Consett	v	Washington	1-3	120
2	Ryton	v	South Shields	0-8	73
3	Birtley Town	v	Esh Winning	3-3aet	50
	Esh Winning	v	Birtley Town (21/9)	3-4	46
4	Hebburn Town	v	Easington Colliery	3-4	59
5	Bedlington Terriers	v	West Allotment Celtic	3-1	104
6	Northallerton Town	v	Jarrow Roofing Boldon CA	4-3	95
7	Askern Villa	v	Tadcaster Albion	1-2	72
8	West Auckland Town	v	Selby Town	3-3aet	93
	Sellby Town	v	West Auckland Town (21/9)	0-3	119
9	Tow Law Town	v	Pontefract Collieries	3-2	100
10	Billingham Synthonia	v	Newcastle Benfield	2-1	81
11	Brandon United	v	Stokesley	1-3	42
12	Horden CW	v	Leeds Carnegie	0-1	31
13	Brighouse Town	v	Yorkshire Amateur	3-1	85
14	Liversedge	v	Eccleshill United	0-0aet	54
	Eccleshill United	v	Liversedge (21/9)	2-1	48
15	Morpeth Town	v	Ashington	0-5	51
16	Bishop Auckland	v	Chester-Le-Street Town (19/9)	1-0	102
17	Scarborough Athletic	v	Crook Town	3-2	462
18	Guisborough Town	v	Billingham Town	1-3	113
19	Formby	v	Alsager Town	2-1	37
20	Holker Old Boys	v	Colne	0-2	61
21	St Helens Town	v	Worsborough Bridge Athletic	4-0	34
22	Atherton LR	v	Ashton Athletic	3-2	41
23	Staveley MW	v	Atherton Collieries	4-0	80
24	Hallam	v	Penrith	6-2	65
25	Padiham	v	Bacup Borough	1-1aet	144
	Bacup Borough	v	Padiham (22/9)	3-1aet	80
26	Maine Road	v	Barnoldswick Town	1-0	71
27	AFC Emley	v	Rossington Main (19/9)	3-0	111
28	Runcorn Linnets	v	Whitehaven	1-0aet	290
29	Parkgate	v	Runcorn Town	1-3	56
30	AFC Liverpool	v	Dinnington Town	1-0	116
31	AFC Blackpool	v	Squires Gate	3-2	90
32	Flixton	v	Ashton Town	2-1aet	20
33	Abbey Hey	v	Oldham Boro	0-0aet	50
	Oldham Boro	v	Abbey Hey (21/9)	3-2aet	58
	(at Abbey Hey FC)				
34	Winsford United	v	Irlam	1-2	74
35	Dudley Town	v	Coventry Copsewood	3-3aet	42
	Coventry Copsewood	v	Dudley Town (21/9)	4-1	30
36	Bewdley Town	v	Blaby & Whetstone Athletic	1-3	54
37	Bustleholme	v	Darlaston Town	5-0	108
38	Westfields	v	Lye Town	4-0	103
39	Oldbury Athletic	v	Anstey Nomads		
	(walkover for Anstey Nomads – Oldbury Athletic removed)				
40	Boldmere St Michaels	v	Norton United	3-1	30
41	Walsall Wood	v	Heather St Johns	0-1	54
42	Malvern Town	v	Loughborough University	1-0	44
43	Ellesmere Rangers	v	Pilkington XXX	1-2aet	88
44	Wolverhampton Casuals	v	Pegasus Juniors	4-2	42
45	AFC Wulfrunians	v	Studley	2-3	58
46	Bridgnorth Town	v	Pershore Town	2-1	60
47	Goodrich	v	Heath Hayes	1-2	42
48	St Andrews	v	Shifnal Town	1-2	24
49	Tividale	v	Highgate United	4-1	45
50	Eccleshall	v	Biddulph Victoria	5-3	66
51	Friar Lane & Epworth	v	Continental Star	1-1aet	24
	Continental Star	v	Friar Lane & Epworth (22/9)	2-1	45
52	Bartley Green	v	Bloxwich United	0-3	39
53	Holwell Sports	v	Alvechurch	2-1	82
54	Coventry Sphinx	v	Brocton	1-0	66
55	Wednesfield	v	Ashby Ivanhoe	5-1	59
56	Stone Dominoes	v	Bolehall Swifts	4-2	40

Adam Sargent, Eastbourne United's 'keeper, cuts out a Warlingham cross in teh 2nd Qualifying Round. Photo: Roger Turner.

Left: Action from the 4th Round tie between Cadbury and Spennymoor Town.
Photo: Peter Barnes.

More action from the Cadbury vs Spennymoor Town tie which saw the latter progress to the 5th Round courtesy of a 1-5 victory. Photo: Peter Barnes.

SECOND QUALIFYING ROUND

SATURDAY 18 SEPTEMBER 2010 - WINNERS RECEIVE £800

57	Heath Town Rangers	v	Ledbury Town		
	(walkover for Heath Town Rangers – Ledbury Town removed)				
58	Gornal Athletic	v	Pelsall Villa	7-0	50
59	Southam United	v	Thurnby Nirvana	1-1aet	59
	Thurnby Nirvana	v	Southam United (21/9)	3-0	57
60	Dunkirk	v	Appleby Frodingham	4-1	41
61	Clipstone Welfare	v	Kimberley Town	2-1	45
62	Graham St Prims	v	Gedling Town	1-2	45
63	Boston Town	v	Forest Town	1-3	73
64	Blackstones	v	Glossop North End	0-0aet	103
	Glossop North End	v	Blackstones (22/9)	3-1aet	160
65	Greenwood Meadows	v	Borrowash Victoria	3-0	30
66	Heanor Town	v	Sutton Town	4-2	95
67	Grimsby Borough	v	Winterton Rangers	0-3	86
	(at Winterton Rangers FC)				
68	Calverton MW	v	Arnold Town	2-4	74
69	Barton Town Old Boys	v	Pinxton	3-0	92
70	Gedling MW	v	Holbrook Sports	0-1	31
71	Holbeach United	v	Blidworth Welfare	3-6aet	66
72	Lincoln Moorlands Railway	v	Louth Town	1-2	111
73	Ipswich Wanderers	v	Raunds Town	4-1	73
74	Bugbrooke St Michaels	v	Wellingborough Town	0-1	74
75	Thrapston Town	v	Team Bury (17/9	2-1	90
76	Gorleston	v	Daventry United	3-2	88
77	Huntingdon Town	v	Felixstowe & Walton United	1-3	60
78	Cogenhoe United	v	Long Melford	3-0	62
79	Haverhill Rovers	v	Debenham LC	3-0	146
80	Godmanchester Rovers	v	Eynesbury Rovers	2-1	85
81	Woodbridge Town	v	Whitton United	0-2	59
82	Norwich United	v	Desborough Town	3-0	74
83	Swaffham Town	v	Hadleigh United	0-3	74
84	Newmarket Town	v	Wisbech Town	2-3	103
85	Stowmarket Town	v	Framlingham Town	1-2	87
86	Thetford Town	v	Walsham Le Willows	0-1	75
87	Kings Lynn Town	v	Great Yarmouth Town	4-3	865
88	Harefield United	v	AFC Wallingford	1-2	55
89	Ampthill Town	v	Takeley	1-2	61
90	Abingdon Town	v	Holyport	0-1	32
91	London APSA	v	Sandhurst Town	3-1aet	23
92	Wokingham & Emmbrook	v	Langford	1-2	83
93	Bedford	v	Kentish Town	1-3	20
94	Hanworth Villa	v	Stanway Rovers	1-3	238
95	Ascot United	v	Hertford Town	0-1	143
96	Sawbridgeworth Town	v	Shrivenham	2-3	44
97	Hayes Gate	v	Hullbridge Sports	0-2	33
	(at Hullbridge Sports FC)				
98	AFC Dunstable	v	Barkingside	6-2	104
99	Oxhey Jets	v	Haringey Borough	2-5	41
100	Newport Pagnell Town	v	Clapton	4-0	103
101	Leverstock Green	v	Welwyn Garden City	6-0	45
102	Basildon United	v	Baldock Town Letchworth	1-3	52
103	Canning Town	v	Wodson Park (19/9)	2-3	81
104	Berkhamsted	v	Eton Manor	2-3	126
105	Biggleswade United	v	Barking	0-3	54
106	Colney Heath	v	Hadley	4-1aet	74
107	Binfield	v	Bethnal Green United	2-0	71
108	FC Clacton	v	Saffron Walden Town	4-0	122
109	Dunstable Town	v	Cranfield United	2-1	63
110	Cockfosters	v	Halstead Town	4-1	61
111	Newbury	v	Southend Manor	3-1	65
112	Bowers & Pitsea	v	Wantage Town	0-1	51
113	Hillingdon Borough	v	Wembley	1-0	45
114	Romsey Town	v	Horley Town	2-3	28
115	Blackfield & Langley	v	Fareham Town	3-2	62
116	Moneyfields	v	AFC Portchester	2-1	95
117	Winchester City	v	Hamble ASSC	0-2	101
118	Mile Oak	v	St Francis Rangers	1-2	46
119	Eastbourne United	v	Warlingham	1-2aet	61
120	South Park	v	Guildford City	0-1	75
121	Fisher	v	Norton Sports (19/9)	3-0	75
122	Shoreham	v	East Cowes Victoria Athletic	7-3	72
123	Redhill	v	Colliers Wood United	2-5	63
124	Molesey	v	Brockenhurst	4-1	51
125	Worthing United	v	Christchurch	1-2	58
126	Croydon	v	Hythe & Dibden	3-1	42
127	Raynes Park Vale	v	Erith Town	1-0	38
128	Fleet Spurs	v	Rye United	1-2	18
129	Lordswood	v	Southwick	3-0	59
130	Ash United	v	Corinthian	1-5	52
131	Pagham	v	Brading Town	2-3	55
132	Banstead Athletic	v	Lancing	2-4	61
133	Ringmer	v	Cove	0-2	61
134	Arundel	v	Three Bridges	2-5	60
135	Tunbridge Wells	v	East Preston	6-2	103
136	Cowes Sports	v	Lymington Town	0-1aet	90
137	Alton Town	v	Greenwich Borough	2-3aet	71
138	Crawley Down	v	Farnham Town	2-0	46
139	Erith & Belvedere	v	Saltdean United (19/9)	2-0	98
140	East Grinstead Town	v	Newport (IW)	2-3	135
141	Frimley Green	v	Bookham	1-2aet	22
142	Bradford Town	v	Melksham Town	0-1	139
143	Bitton	v	Thame United	3-2	70
144	Cadbury Heath	v	Ardley United	3-0	62
145	Kidlington	v	Old Woodstock Town	1-0	95
146	Laverstock & Ford	v	Almondsbury UWE	4-0	45
147	Calne Town	v	Longwell Green Sports	1-0aet	50
148	Downton	v	Hallen	2-2aet	53
	Hallen	v	Downton (20/9)	1-6	73
149	Clanfield 85	v	Warminster Town	2-1	32
150	Lydney Town	v	Corsham Town	1-0	87
151	Devizes Town	v	Wootton Bassett Town	0-4	26
152	Fairford Town	v	Highridge United		
	(walkover for Fairford Town – Highridge United removed)				
153	Brislington	v	Shaftesbury	2-1aet	62
154	Tavistock	v	Chard Town	4-3	62
155	Sherborne Town	v	Shepton Mallet	3-0	86
156	Hamworthy United	v	Verwood Town	2-3aet	117
157	Hengrove Athletic	v	Portishead Town	2-0	50
158	Porthleven	v	Newquay	1-4	135
159	Minehead	v	Keynsham Town	0-1	41
160	Wadebridge Town	v	Torpoint Athletic	0-3	59
161	Street	v	Odd Down	0-1	79
162	Buckland Athletic	v	Bridport	1-2	103
163	Budleigh Salterton	v	Liskeard Athletic	3-0	60
164	Saltash United	v	Penzance	3-1	82
165	Barnstaple Town	v	Radstock Town	2-3	109
166	St Blazey	v	Cullompton Rangers	5-2	117
167	Bodmin Town	v	Launceston	5-2	63
168	Wellington	v	Merthyr Town	2-1	104

FIRST ROUND PROPER

SATURDAY 2 OCTOBER 2010 - WINNERS RECEIVE £900

1	Bedlington Terriers	v	Spennymoor Town	0-1	230
2	Leeds Carnegie	v	Easington Colliery	4-0	36
3	Tadcaster Albion	v	Tow Law Town	2-0	132
4	West Auckland Town	v	Birtley Town	6-0	59
5	Northallerton Town	v	Stokesley	3-4	142
6	Billingham Town	v	Ashington	3-4aet	147
7	Dunston UTS	v	Washington	2-1	138
8	Scarborough Athletic	v	Bridlington Town	2-2aet	777
	Bridlington Town	v	Scarborough Athletic (5/10)	1-3	727
9	Bishop Auckland	v	Billingham Synthonia (3/10)	3-4aet	102
10	South Shields	v	Thackley	0-2	136
11	Brighouse Town	v	Eccleshill United	3-3aet	111
	Eccleshill United	v	Brighouse Town (5/10)	2-1	80
12	AFC Liverpool	v	Hallam	3-0	150
13	Atherton LR	v	Runcorn Town (1/10)	2-3	98
14	Formby	v	Flixton	2-0	34
15	Rossendale United	v	Bacup Borough	0-2	141
16	Irlam	v	Colne	2-0	63
17	St Helens Town	v	Oldham Boro	2-1	37
	(at Ashton Town FC)				
18	AFC Emley	v	Runcorn Linnets	3-1	163
19	Ramsbottom United	v	Staveley MW	0-1	101
20	Maine Road	v	AFC Blackpool	2-2aet	72
	AFC Blackpool	v	Maine Road (5/10)	2-1	55
21	Blaby & Whetstone Athletic	v	Westfields	2-5	82
22	Coalville Town	v	Stratford Town	2-1	95
23	Coventry Sphinx	v	Anstey Nomads	4-3	86
24	Malvern Town	v	Heather St Johns	2-6	70
25	Wednesfield	v	Studley	4-3	80
26	Holwell Sports	v	Tividale	4-3	131
27	Coventry Copsewood	v	Heath Town Rangers	2-1	21
28	Wolverhampton Casuals	v	Bustleholme	1-3	65
29	Stone Dominoes	v	Heath Hayes	1-4	50
30	Willenhall Town	v	Gornal Athletic	0-2	43
31	Boldmere St Michaels	v	Continental Star	1-0	47
32	Eccleshall	v	Bridgnorth Town	2-4	53
33	Bloxwich United	v	Pilkington XXX	5-0	55
34	Thurnby Nirvana	v	Shifnal Town	1-2	64
35	Gedling Town	v	Glossop North End	2-1	87
36	Holbrook Sports	v	Arnold Town	4-4aet	49
	Arnold Town	v	Holbrook Sports (5/10)	1-3	87
37	Forest Town	v	Greenwood Meadows	3-1	50
38	Dunkirk	v	Blidworth Welfare	2-0	63
39	Louth Town	v	Barton Town Old Boys	3-3	123
	Barton Town Old Boys	v	Louth Town (12/10)	1-0aet	142
	(5/10 – tie abandoned at half time due to floodlight fire, 1-2)				
40	Winterton Rangers	v	Deeping Rangers	3-1	63
41	Heanor Town	v	Clipstone Welfare	6-2	124
42	Wisbech Town	v	Cogenhoe United	5-1	362
43	Gorleston	v	Hadleigh United	1-0	125
44	Ipswich Wanderers	v	Walsham Le Willows	1-2	106
45	Leiston	v	Haverhill Rovers	3-2aet	139
46	Cambridge Regional College	v	Wellingborough Town (3/10)	4-0	123
47	Thrapston Town	v	Kings Lynn Town	2-4	410
48	Whitton United	v	Norwich United	2-0	37
49	St Neots Town	v	Felixstowe & Walton United	11-0	282
50	Godmanchester Rovers	v	Framlingham Town	4-0	74
51	Binfield	v	Hillingdon Borough	3-2	101
52	Wantage Town	v	Shrivenham	2-1	68
53	Eton Manor	v	FC Clacton (3/10)	4-2	42
54	Dunstable Town	v	AFC Wallingford	5-0	70
55	Reading Town	v	Newport Pagnell Town	4-2	56
56	Chalfont St Peter	v	Newbury	6-0	66
57	Stansted	v	Takeley	2-0	62
58	Aylesbury United	v	Hertford Town (3/10)	4-3aet	128
59	Haringey Borough	v	Tring Athletic	1-3	41
60	Baldock Town Letchworth	v	Holyport	0-1	74
61	Barking	v	Flackwell Heath	1-2	50
62	Cockfosters	v	Witham Town	0-3	53
63	Leverstock Green	v	Enfield 1893	5-4	79
64	Langford	v	Hullbridge Sports	1-3	53
65	Burnham Ramblers	v	Kentish Town	2-0aet	44
66	AFC Dunstable	v	Colney Heath (1/10)	3-1	126
67	Stanway Rovers	v	London APSA	4-0	62
68	Bracknell Town	v	Wodson Park	2-0	67
69	Guildford City	v	Horley Town	3-2aet	58
70	Wick	v	VCD Athletic	0-2aet	46
71	Corinthian	v	Tunbridge Wells	0-4	56
72	Fisher	v	Warlingham	1-3	113
73	Peacehaven & Telscombe	v	Hamble ASSC	1-0	61
74	Newport (IW)	v	Shoreham	3-0	150
75	Crawley Down	v	Rye United+	0-1	68
76	Croydon	v	Beckenham Town	3-7	64
77	Lancing	v	Christchurch	1-1aet	126
	Christchurch	v	Lancing (5/10)	0-1	64
78	Moneyfields	v	Greenwich Borough	1-0	40
79	Lymington Town	v	Bournemouth	1-2	84
80	Raynes Park Vale	v	Hythe Town	0-3	62
81	Colliers Wood United	v	Cove	5-2	40
82	Egham Town	v	Molesey	2-0	74
83	Bookham	v	Herne Bay	0-4	31
84	Lordswood	v	Three Bridges	1-2	67
85	Camberley Town	v	Blackfield & Langley	2-1	60
86	Brading Town	v	St Francis Rangers	4-2	69
87	Erith & Belvedere	v	Chichester City	2-1aet	85
88	Bemerton Heath H.	v	Lydney Town	5-2aet	164
89	Cadbury Heath	v	Wootton Bassett Town+	2-1	54
90	Calne Town	v	Downton	1-2	70
91	Kidlington	v	Bitton	0-1	74
92	Clanfield 85	v	Fairford Town	2-1	59
93	Melksham Town	v	Laverstock & Ford	3-1	94
94	Saltash United	v	Newquay	9-1	85
95	Verwood Town	v	Budleigh Salterton	1-0aet	70
96	Brislington	v	St Blazey	0-1	82
97	Bishop Sutton	v	Keynsham Town	2-2aet	48
	Keynsham Town	v	Bishop Sutton (5/10)	1-0	105
98	Wellington	v	Tavistock	5-0	49
99	Sherborne Town	v	Bodmin Town	2-2aet	100
	Bodmin Town	v	Sherborne Town (6/10)	1-0	88
100	Odd Down	v	Bridport	7-0	69
101	Ilfracombe Town	v	Hengrove Athletic	1-2	77
102	Torpoint Athletic	v	Radstock Town	4-1	104

SECOND ROUND PROPER

SATURDAY 13 NOVEMBER 2010 - WINNERS RECEIVE £1,000

1	Leeds Carnegie	v	Marske United	4-3aet	136
2	Billingham Synthonia	v	Stokesley	3-1	108
3	Eccleshill United	v	Runcorn Town (16/11)	0-2	40
4	Bootle	v	Shildon	1-3	209
5	Thackley	v	Whitley Bay	0-1	273
6	Formby	v	Bacup Borough (16/11)	1-0	51
7	AFC Blackpool	v	AFC Liverpool	0-2	135
8	New Mills	v	Ashington	2-4	204
9	Forest Town	v	Tadcaster Albion	0-4	110
10	Dunston UTS	v	AFC Emley	4-0	188
11	Winterton Rangers	v	St Helens Town	0-2	79
12	West Auckland Town	v	Spennymoor Town	1-3	320
13	Norton & Stockton Ancients	v	Irlam	4-3	125
14	Staveley MW	v	Pickering Town	1-0aet	115
15	Scarborough Athletic	v	Armthorpe Welfare	2-2aet	464
	Armthorpe Welfare	v	Scarborough Athletic (16/11)	2-3	167
16	Coventry Sphinx	v	Dunkirk	0-3	66
17	Gresley	v	Heanor Town	2-0	289
18	Bridgnorth Town	v	Coalville Town	2-4	57
19	Boldmere St Michales	v	Gornal Athletic	1-2	44
20	Holbrook Sports	v	Holwell Sports	7-0	66
21	Causeway United	v	Gedling Town	2-0	50
22	Shifnal Town	v	Bloxwich United	2-2aet	79
	Bloxwich United	v	Shifnal Town (16/11)	5-3	49
23	Wednesfield	v	Heather St Johns	1-3aet	68
24	Westfields	v	Coventry Copsewood	3-0	78
25	Bustleholme	v	Barton Town Old Boys	2-0	100
26	Heath Hayes	v	Tipton Town	2-1	57
27	Kings Lynn Town	v	Gorleston	4-0	806
28	St Neots Town	v	Burnham Ramblers	6-1	451
29	Hullbridge Sports	v	Leverstock Green	1-5	47
30	AFC Dunstable	v	Tring Athletic	1-2	204
31	Dunstable Town	v	Cambridge Regional College	2-1	106
32	Witham Town	v	Walsham Le Willows	3-1	114
33	Stotfold	v	Whitton United	2-1	106
34	Kirkley & Pakefield	v	Long Buckby	0-1	134
35	St Ives Town	v	Aylesbury United	2-1	205
36	Stansted	v	Eton Manor	3-1	72
37	Wroxham	v	Wisbech Town	4-0	160
38	Royston Town	v	Leiston	2-2aet	196
	Leiston	v	Royston Town (16/11)	1-0	200
39	Godmanchester Rovers	v	Stanway Rovers	0-1	97
40	Egham Town	v	Newport (IW)	1-2	71
41	Chertsey Town	v	Moneyfields	1-2	201
42	Epsom & Ewell	v	Bracknell Town	4-0	123
43	Wantage Town	v	Binfield	3-1	82
44	Erith & Belvedere	v	Lancing	0-2	96
45	VCD Athletic	v	Hythe Town	1-5	118
46	Reading Town	v	Warlingham	1-0	110
47	Flackwell Heath	v	Three Bridges	1-2	62
48	Herne Bay	v	Camberley Town	3-0	180
49	Tunbridge Wells	v	Holyport	8-0	129
50	Rye United (at Sussex FA, Lancing)	v	Chalfont St Peter	4-4aet	106
	Chalfont St Peter	v	Rye United (16/11)	1-2	115
51	Beckenham Town	v	Peacehaven & Telscombe	2-1aet	78
52	Colliers Wood United (at Croydon FC)	v	Witney United (20/11)	1-0	52
53	Guildford City	v	Brading Town	5-2	87
54	Dawlish Town	v	Bodmin Town	0-2	81
55	Clanfield 85	v	Bemerton Heath Harlequins	0-3	74
56	Plymouth Parkway	v	Melksham Town	6-1	193
57	St Blazey	v	Hengrove Athletic	1-1aet	123
	Hengrove Athletic	v	St Blazey (16/11)	0-2	145
58	Poole Town	v	Wellington	4-3	198
59	Downton	v	Cadbury Heath	2-3	119
60	Bristol Manor Farm	v	Torpoint Athletic	3-7	55
61	Bitton	v	Shortwood United	2-1	157
62	Verwood Town	v	Keynsham Town	2-1	85
63	Bournemouth	v	Odd Down	5-0	60
64	Willand Rovers	v	Saltash United	2-1	104

Rye 'keeper, Josh Pelling, claims this Staveley corner during this 4th Round match.
Photo: Bill Wheatcroft.

5th Round action between Poole Town and Spennymoor Town - here we see Kallum Griffiths (left) challenging Poole's Carl Preston.

During the same match, Moors' 'keeper Craig Turns just beats Poole's Dave Sturgess to the ball.

Brading Town's Josh Appell vies for the ball with former FA Trophy winner Geoff Pitcher now of St Francis Rangers in the 1st Round.

All Photos: Graham Brown.

THIRD ROUND PROPER

SATURDAY 4 DECEMBER 2010 - WINNERS RECEIVE £1,100

1	Westfields	v	Billingham Synthonia (9/1)	1-2aet	104
2	Dunkirk	v	Ashington (8/1)	1-2	131
3	Leeds Carnegie	v	Staveley MW (11/12)	1-4	
4	Shildon	v	Coalville Town (8/1)	0-2	235
5	Formby	v	Tadcaster Albion (11/12)	2-3	73
6	Whitley Bay	v	AFC Liverpoool (8/1)	7-1	738
7	Scarborough Athletic	v	Spennymoor Town (14/12)	0-3	383
8	Heath Hayes	v	Bloxwich United (14/12)	1-3	53
9	Dunston UTS	v	Heather St Johns (15/1)	2-0	227
10	Gresley	v	Bustleholme (14/12)	4-2	183
11	Holbrook Sports	v	St Helens Town (15/12)	4-0	80
12	Causeway United	v	Norton & Stockton A. (12/12)	0-3	89
13	Gornal Athletic	v	Runcorn Town (9/1)	0-3	90
14	Tring Athletic	v	Dunstable Town (11/12)	1-6	148
15	Lancing	v	Witham Town (11/12)	4-2aet	
16	Wroxham	v	St Ives Town (11/12)	0-1aet	109
17	Stotfold	v	Long Buckby (4/12)	0-3	141
18	Epsom & Ewell	v	St Neots Town (14/12)	1-2	86
19	Beckenham Town	v	Kings Lynn Town (8/1)	1-2	178
20	Leverstock Green	v	Tunbridge Wells (11/12)	3-1	127
21	Stanway Rovers	v	Stansted (11/12)	0-1	72
22	Leiston	v	Hythe Town (11/12)	3-1	191
23	Three Bridges	v	Rye United (11/12)	1-3aet	91
24	Herne Bay	v	Colliers Wood United (11/12)	2-0	213
25	Cadbury Heath	v	Reading Town (15/12)	4-1	82
26	Guildford City	v	Moneyfields (11/12)	4-3	94
27	Willand Rovers	v	Bournemouth (11/12)	2-1	105
28	Bitton	v	Newport (IW) (8/1)	4-1	203
29	Poole Town	v	Wantage Town (11/12)	3-2	204
30	St Blazey	v	Bemerton Heath Harlequins (8/1)	1-2	149
31	Verwood Town	v	Torpoint Athletic (15/12)	2-5	92
32	Plymouth Parkway	v	Bodmin Town (11/12)	1-3aet	176

FOURTH ROUND PROPER

SATURDAY 22 JANUARY 2011 - WINNERS RECEIVE £1,200

1	Dunstable Town	v	Willand Rovers	2-0	158
2	Bloxwich United	v	Torpoint Athletic	2-3	110
3	Leverstock Green	v	Bemerton Heath Harlequins	4-1	224
4	Gresley	v	St Neots Town (29/1)	1-3	407
5	Norton & Stockton A.	v	Kings Lynn Town	0-1	249
6	Holbrook Sports	v	Lancing (29/1)	2-1	182
7	Poole Town	v	St Ives Town	3-2	380
8	Bitton	v	Coalville Town	2-3	293
9	Bodmin Town	v	Stansted	1-4	164
10	Long Buckby	v	Ashington	3-2	167
11	Herne Bay	v	Whitley Bay	1-2	655
12	Guildford City	v	Leiston	2-6aet	189
13	Cadbury Heath	v	Spennymoor Town	1-5	362
14	Staveley MW	v	Rye United	0-3	232
15	Runcorn Town	v	Dunston UTS	1-3	185
16	Billingham Synthonia	v	Tadcaster Albion	2-1	159

FIFTH ROUND PROPER

SATURDAY 12 FEBRUARY 2011 - WINNERS RECEIVE £1,300

1	Whitley Bay	v	Dunstable Town	5-1	1110
2	Coalville Town	v	Holbrook Sports	3-1aet	321
3	Torpoint Athletic	v	Billingham Synthonia	1-0	449
4	Poole Town	v	Spennymoor Town	3-2	688
5	Leverstock Green	v	Rye United	1-2	377
6	Leiston	v	Long Buckby	2-1	363
7	Kings Lynn Town	v	St Neots Town	2-1	1612
8	Stansted	v	Dunston UTS	0-2	430

SIXTH ROUND PROPER

SATURDAY 5 MARCH 2011 - WINNERS RECEIVE £1,500

1	Poole Town	v	Torpoint Athletic	2-1	924
2	Coalville Town	v	Leiston	1-0	558
3	King's Lynn Town	v	Rye United	3-1aet	1657
4	Dunston UTS	v	Whitley Bay	1-2	1496

SEMI FINALS

WINNERS RECEIVE £3,000

1ST LEG – SATURDAY 26 MARCH 2011

1	Coalville Town	v	King's Lynn Town	3-0	1690
2	Poole Town	v	Whitley Bay	1-2	1652

2ND LEG – SATURDAY 2 APRIL 2011

1	King's Lynn Town	v	Coalville Town	2-3	2354
2	Whitley Bay	v	Poole Town	3-1	2842

The Final...

I have a distinct preference for the Vase over the Trophy, generally finding ties more open and chancy with players not unnecessarily constrained by systems but freer to express themselves and, while conforming to the requirement to operate as part of a team, still given the chance to display their own talents and gifts. This tie was a fine example of that, with moments of drama and theatre which gloriously outshone the plodding, unexciting performance of the previous day's Trophy final. As the cliché goes "it was a shame either side had to lose". However there was no shame or disgrace for the Leicestershire runners up who, on the balance of play and chances created and missed, probably deserved the victory. That was not the result and so, for the third consecutive year and the fourth time overall, Whitley Bay took the Vase back to the North East. They were certainly given a much stiffer task than the previous year, showing great resilience in making the most of the chances that came their way. Goals win games and from far fewer opportunities their success rate exceeded Coalville's and presented them with the victory.

Without counting I deduced, as the teams lined up, that Coalville's support exceeded that of the Seahorses by a narrow margin, reflective perhaps of the distances from Wembley and Bay's fans many previous opportunities to visit the national stadium. I do wonder how impressed attendees were by the loudspeakered blarings, which I refuse to describe as music. Do they really add to the buzz of the occasion? Drum rolls, such as you hear at the cinema as gladiators enter the arena during a Roman epic, surely don't impact on the senses of normal supporters with anything other than a feeling that this is over hype, even mockery, especially when accompanied by that screaming dervish of an announcer working himself into such a false lather of euphoria. It almost makes one want to head for the exit and the real world, while still sane.

I am glad I didn't on this occasion as we witnessed a gloriously refreshingly open contest in which I particularly enjoyed the forward play of Matt Moore and Jerome Murdock up front for the Ravens. As for the opposition defenders can never rest when Paul Chow is around and Lee Kerr was as busy as ever although I was not endeared one iota by the excremental colouring of his footwear. (Is there such a word as excremental? There is now. In either case hopefully you will still visualise the disastrous orangey colour. How did his mates let him on the field in those?)

Coalville were very much the dominant attackers, three corners to them, the first of which required heading off the line, before Bay gained one. Cameron Stuart landed a lob on the Northerners' net, a Moore shot rebounded from keeper Terry Burke's grasp with no one near to take advantage and Murdock just failed to get his head to Moore's cross. At this stage it was not would Chow score to achieve a goal for him in each round of the 2011 Vase but would Chow actually touch the ball. No sooner had the thought arisen when Craig McFarlane raced away on the right, centred while the Coalville defence stood mesmerised, and who should be on the spot four yards from goal but Mr Chow. He misses few, especially not from there. 28 minutes gone and the Sea horses one up. Three minutes later Coalville thought they had equalised but an assistant's flag indicated the ball had previously gone out so a goal kick was the result. Murdock missed the target with a very reasonable heading chance and Burke stopped Moore's shot at the second attempt. Ryan Robbins' shot flew just past and Chow's lob nearly sent Bay in two up.

Burke again turned over a Murdock shot but in the 58th minute Coalville deservedly equalised, Moore heading in from close range with just sufficient force to beat Burke. Three minutes later and, despite those boots, Kerr was able to nudge a header past Sam Bowles to restore his team's lead. Moore responded with a header smacking into the bar and Murdock brought an acrobatic save and another tip over from the busy Burke. 'Ville were not to be denied and Anthony Carney's corner was gleefully headed home by Adam Goodby as the Bay defence stood flat footed.

That was it. Ten minutes for Coalville to emphasise their superiority and take the lead but the Sea horses had other ideas. Recognising possible defeat they roused themselves. Paul Robinson went close and then, as Craig McFarlane raced down the left, previous hero Goodby brought him down. Kerr's free kick hit the bar; the ball bounced down right on to Chow's toe. Whether he knew anything about it or not as he was perched on the goal line there was no chance of a clearance. 3-2 to Bay. In the four added minutes Burke punched away just before Moore could knock in and Lee Miveld's effort went inches over but there was no further way back. The experienced Northern Leaguers had once again shown their resilience. Who's to say they won't return in 2012 for another Wembley appearance? If it produces an engaging spectacle like this then bring them on.

Arthur Evans

COALVILLE TOWN (Moore 58, Goodby 80) 2
WHITLEY BAY (Chow 28,90, Kerr 61) 3

Wembley Stadium **Attendance: 8,778**

Above: Paul Chow scores Whitley Bay's winning goal in the 2010-11 FA Vase final. Photo: Gordon Whittington.

Right: Scorer of Coalville Town's first goal, Matt Moore, shields the ball from a Whitley defender. Photo: Roger Turner.

Coalville Town: Sean Bowles, Ashley Brown (sub Matthew Gardner 88th min), Cameron Stuart, Adam Goodby, Zach Costello, Lee Miveld, Callum Woodward, Anthony Carney (sub Craig Attwood 90th min), Ryan Robbins (sub Ashley Wells 66th min), Matt Moore, Jerome Murdock.
Subs not used – Richard Williams (gk) and James Dodd.

Whitley Bay: Terry Burke, Craig McFarlane (sub Steve Gibson 90th min), Callum Anderson, Darren Timmons, Gareth Williams (sub David Coulson 68th min), Damon Robson, Lee Kerr, Paul Chow, Paul Robinson, David Pounder (sub Brian Smith 68th min), Gary Ormston.
Subs not used – Kyle Hayes (gk) and Brian Rowe.

Referee – Scott Mathieson, assistants Darren Bond and Darren England.
Fourth official, Robert Madley.

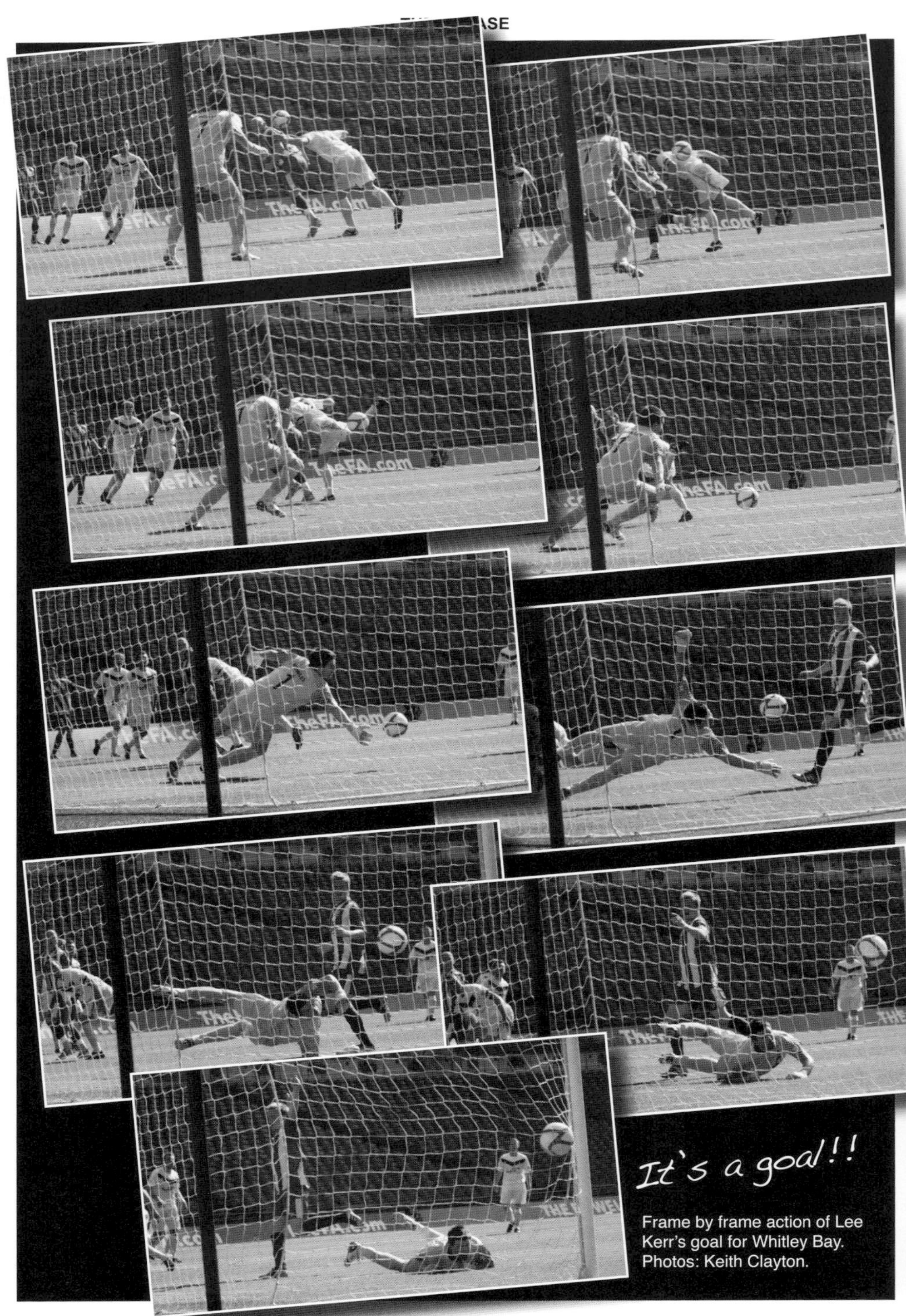

It's a goal!!

Frame by frame action of Lee Kerr's goal for Whitley Bay. Photos: Keith Clayton.

PAST FINALS

1975 HODDESDON TOWN 2 ***(South Midlands)*** **EPSOM & EWELL 1** ***(Surrey Senior)*** **Att: 9,500**
Sedgwick 2 **Wales** **Ref: Mr R Toseland**
Hoddesdon: Galvin, Green, Hickey, Maybury, Stevenson, Wilson, Bishop, Picking, Sedgwick, Nathan, Schofield
Epsom & Ewell: Page, Bennett, Webb, Wales, Worby, Jones, O'Connell, Walker, Tuite, Eales, Lee

1976 BILLERICAY TOWN 1 ***(Essex Senior)*** **STAMFORD 0 (aet)** ***(United Counties)*** **Att: 11,848**
Aslett **Ref: Mr A Robinson**
Billericay: Griffiths, Payne, Foreman, Pullin, Bone, Coughlan, Geddes, Aslett, Clayden, Scott, Smith
Stamford: Johnson, Kwiatowski, Marchant, Crawford, Downs, Hird, Barnes, Walpole, Smith, Russell, Broadbent

1977 BILLERICAY TOWN 1 ***(Essex Senior)*** **SHEFFIELD 1 (aet)** ***(Yorkshire)*** **Att: 14,000**
Clayden **Coughlan og** **Ref: Mr J Worrall**
Billericay: Griffiths, Payne, Bone, Coughlan, Pullin, Scott, Wakefield, Aslett, Clayden,Woodhouse, McQueen. Sub: Whettell
Sheffield: Wing, Gilbody, Lodge, Hardisty, Watts, Skelton, Kay, Travis, Pugh, Thornhill,Haynes. Sub: Strutt
Replay BILLERICAY TOWN 2 **SHEFFIELD 1** **Att: 3,482**
Aslett, Woodhouse **Thornhill** **at Nottingham Forest**
Billericay: Griffiths, Payne, Pullin, Whettell, Bone, McQueen, Woodhouse, Aslett, Clayden, Scott, Wakefield
Sheffield: Wing, Gilbody, Lodge, Strutt, Watts, Skelton, Kay, Travis, Pugh, Thornhill, Haynes

1978 NEWCASTLE BLUE STAR 2 ***(Wearside)*** **BARTON ROVERS 1** ***(South Midlands)*** **Att: 16,858**
Dunn, Crumplin **Smith** **Ref: Mr T Morris**
Newcastle: Halbert, Feenan, Thompson, Davidson, S Dixon, Beynon, Storey, P Dixon, Crumplin, Callaghan, Dunn. Sub: Diamond
Barton Rovers: Blackwell, Stephens, Crossley, Evans, Harris, Dollimore, Dunn, Harnaman, Fossey, Turner, Smith. Sub: Cox

1979 BILLERICAY TOWN 4 ***(Athenian)*** **ALMONDSBURY GREENWAY 1** ***(Glos. Co)*** **Att: 17,500**
Young 3, Clayden **Price** **Ref: Mr C Steel**
Billericay: Norris, Blackaller, Bingham, Whettell, Bone, Reeves, Pullin, Scott, Clayden,Young, Groom. Sub: Carrigan
Almondsbury: Hamilton, Bowers, Scarrett, Sulllivan, Tudor, Wookey, Bowers, Shehean, Kerr, Butt, Price. Sub: Kilbaine

1980 STAMFORD 2 ***(United Counties)*** **GUISBOROUGH TOWN 0** ***(Northern Alliance)*** **Att: 11,500**
Alexander, McGowan **Ref: Neil Midgeley**
Stamford: Johnson, Kwiatkowski, Ladd, McGowan, Bliszczak I, Mackin, Broadhurst, Hall,Czarnecki, Potter, Alexander. Sub: Bliszczak S
Guisborough: Cutter, Scott, Thornton, Angus, Maltby, Percy, Skelton, Coleman, McElvaney,Sills, Dilworth. Sub: Harrison

1981 WHICKHAM 3 ***(Wearside)*** **WILLENHALL 2 (aet)** ***(West Midlands)*** **Att: 12,000**
Scott, Williamson, Peck og **Smith, Stringer** **Ref: Mr R Lewis**
Whickham: Thompson, Scott, Knox, Williamson, Cook, Ward, Carroll, Diamond, Cawthra,Robertson, Turnbull. Sub: Alton
Willenhall: Newton, White, Darris, Woodall, Heath, Fox, Peck, Price, Matthews, Smith,Stringer. Sub: Trevor

1982 FOREST GREEN ROVERS 3 ***(Hellenic)*** **RAINWORTH M.W 0** ***(Notts Alliance)*** **Att: 12,500**
Leitch 2, Norman **Ref: Mr K Walmsey**
Forest Green: Moss, Norman, Day, Turner, Higgins, Jenkins, Guest, Burns, Millard, Leitch, Doughty. Sub: Dangerfield
Rainworth M.W: Watson, Hallam, Hodgson, Slater, Sterland, Oliver, Knowles, Raine, Radzi, Reah, Comerford. Sub: Robinson

1983 V.S. RUGBY 1 ***(West Midlands)*** **HALESOWEN TOWN 0** ***(West Midlands)*** **Att: 13,700**
Crawley **Ref: Mr B Daniels**
VS Rugby: Burton, McGinty, Harrison, Preston, Knox, Evans, ingram, Setchell, Owen,Beecham, Crawley. Sub: Haskins
Halesowen Town: Coldicott, Penn, Edmonds, Lacey, Randall, Shilvock, Hazelwood, Moss, Woodhouse,P Joinson, L Joinson. Sub: Smith

1984 STANSTED 3 ***(Essex Senior)*** **STAMFORD 2** ***(United Counties)*** **Att: 8,125**
Holt, Gillard, Reading **Waddicore, Allen** **Ref: Mr T Bune**
Stanstead: Coe, Williams, Hilton, Simpson, Cooper, Reading, Callanan, Holt, Reevs,Doyle, Gillard. Sub: Williams
Stamford: Parslow, Smitheringate, Blades, McIlwain, Lyon, Mackin, Genovese, Waddicore,Allen, Robson, Beech. Sub: Chapman

1985 HALESOWEN TOWN 3 ***(West Midlands)*** **FLEETWOOD TOWN 1** ***(N W Counties)*** **Att: 16,715**
L Joinson 2, Moss **Moran** **Ref: Mr C Downey**
Halesowen: Coldicott, Penn, Sherwood, Warner, Randle, Heath, Hazlewood, Moss (Smith),Woodhouse, P Joinson, L Joinson
Fleetwood Town: Dobson, Moran, Hadgraft, Strachan, Robinson, Milligan, Hall, Trainor, Taylor(Whitehouse), Cain, Kennerley

1986 HALESOWEN TOWN 3 ***(West Midlands)*** **SOUTHALL 0** ***(Isthmian 2 South)*** **Att: 18,340**
Moss 2, L Joinson **Ref: Mr D Scott**
Halesowen: Pemberton, Moore, Lacey, Randle (Rhodes), Sherwood, Heath, Penn, Woodhouse, PJoinson, L Joinson, Moss
Southall: Mackenzie, James, McGovern, Croad, Holland, Powell (Richmond), Pierre,Richardson, Sweales, Ferdinand, Rowe

THE FA VASE

1987 ST. HELENS 3 ***(N W Counties)*** — **WARRINGTON TOWN 2** ***(N W Counties)*** — **Att: 4,254**
Layhe 2, Rigby — **Reid, Cook** — **Ref: Mr T Mills**
St Helens: Johnson, Benson, Lowe, Bendon, Wilson, McComb, Collins (Gledhill), O'Neill,Cummins, Lay, Rigby. Sub: Deakin
Warrington: O'Brien. Copeland, Hunter, Gratton, Whalley, Reid, Brownville (Woodyer), Cook,Kinsey, Looker (Hill), Hughes

1988 COLNE DYNAMOES 1 ***(N W Counties)*** — **EMLEY 0** ***(Northern Counties East)*** — **Att: 15,000**
Anderson — **Ref: Mr A Seville**
Colne Dynamoes: Mason, McFafyen, Westwell, Bentley, Dunn, Roscoe, Rodaway, Whitehead (Burke),Diamond, Anderson, Wood (Coates)
Emley: Dennis, Fielding, Mellor, Codd, Hirst (Burrows), Gartland (Cook), Carmody,Green, Bramald, Devine, Francis

1989 TAMWORTH 1 ***(West Midlands)*** — **SUDBURY TOWN 1 (aet)** ***(Eastern)*** — **Att: 26,487**
Devaney — **Hubbick** — **Ref: Mr C Downey**
Tamworth: Bedford, Lockett, Atkins, Cartwright, McCormack, Myers, Finn, Devaney, Moores,Gordon, Stanton. Subs: Rathbone, Heaton
Sudbury Town: Garnham, Henry, G Barker, Boyland, Thorpe, Klug, D Barker, Barton, Oldfield,Smith, Hubbick. Subs: Money, Hunt
Replay TAMWORTH 3 — **SUDBURY TOWN 0** — **Att: 11,201**
Stanton 2, Moores — **at Peterborough**
Tamworth: Bedford, Lockett, Atkins, Cartwright, Finn, Myers, George, Devaney, Moores,Gordon, Stanton. Sub: Heaton
Sudbury Town: Garnham, Henry, G Barker, Boyland, Thorpe, Klug, D Barker, Barton, Oldfield,Smith, Hubbick. Subs: Money, Hunt

1990 YEADING 0 ***(Isthmian 2 South)*** — **BRIDLINGTON TOWN 0 (aet)** ***(N Co East)*** — **Att: 7,932**
Ref: Mr R Groves
Yeading: Mackenzie, Wickens, Turner, Whiskey (McCarthy), Croad, Denton, Matthews, James(Charles), Sweates, Impey, Cordery
Bridlington: Taylor, Pugh, Freeman, McNeill, Warburton, Brentano, Wilkes (Hall), Noteman,Gauden, Whiteman, Brattan (Brown)

Replay YEADING 1 — **BRIDLINGTON TOWN 0** — **Att: 5,000**
Sweales — **at Leeds Utd FC**
Yeading: Mackenzie, Wickens, Turner, Whiskey, Croad (McCarthy), Schwartz, Matthews,James, Sweates, Impey (Welsh), Cordery
Bridlington: Taylor, Pugh, Freeman, McNeill, Warburton, Brentano, Wilkes (Brown), Noteman,Gauden (Downing), Whiteman, Brattan

1991 GRESLEY ROVERS 4 ***(West Midlands)*** — **GUISELEY 4 (aet)** ***(Northern Co East)*** — **Att: 11,314**
Rathbone, Smith 2, Stokes — **Tennison 2, Walling, A Roberts** — **Ref: Mr C Trussell**
Gresley: Aston, Barry, Elliott (Adcock), Denby, Land, Astley, Stokes, K Smith, Acklam,Rathbone, Lovell (Weston)
Guiseley: Maxted, Bottomley, Hogarth, Tetley, Morgan, McKenzie, Atkinson (Annan),Tennison, Walling, A Roberts, B Roberts

Replay GUISELEY 3 — **GRESLEY ROVERS 1** — **Att: 7,585**
Tennison, Walling, Atkinson — **Astley** — **at Bramall Lane**
Guiseley: Maxted, Annan, Hogarth, Tetley, Morgan, McKenzie (Bottomley), Atkinson,Tennison (Noteman), Walling, A Roberts, B Roberts
Gresley: Aston, Barry, Elliott, Denby, Land, Astley, Stokes (Weston), K Smith, Acklam, Rathbone, Lovell (Adcock)

1992 WIMBORNE TOWN 5 ***(Wessex)*** — **GUISELEY 3** ***(Northern Premier Div 1)*** — **Att: 10,772**
Richardson, Sturgess 2, Killick 2 — **Noteman 2, Colville** — **Ref: Mr M J Bodenham**
Wimborne: Leonard, Langdown, Wilkins, Beacham, Allan, Taplin, Ames, Richardson, Bridle,Killick, Sturgess (Lovell), Lynn
Guiseley: Maxted, Atkinson, Hogarth, Tetley (Wilson), Morgan, Brockie, A Roberts,Tennison, Noteman (Colville), Annan, W Roberts

1993 BRIDLINGTON TOWN 1 ***(NPL Div 1)*** — **TIVERTON TOWN 0** ***(Western)*** — **Att: 9,061**
Radford — **Ref: Mr R A Hart**
Bridlington: Taylor, Brentano, McKenzie, Harvey, Bottomley, Woodcock, Grocock, A Roberts, Jones, Radford (Tyrell), Parkinson. Sub: Swailes
Tiverton Town: Nott, J Smith, N Saunders, M Saunders, Short (Scott), Steele, Annunziata, KSmith, Everett, Daly, Hynds (Rogers)

1994 DISS TOWN 2 ***(Eastern)*** — **TAUNTON TOWN 1** ***(Western)*** — **Att: 13,450**
Gibbs (p), Mendham — **Fowler** — **Ref: Mr K. Morton**
Diss Town: Woodcock, Carter, Wolsey (Musgrave), Casey (Bugg), Hartle, Smith, Barth, Mendham, Miles, Warne, Gibbs
Taunton Town: Maloy, Morris, Walsh, Ewens, Graddon, Palfrey, West (Hendry), Fowler, Durham, Perrett (Ward), Jarvis

1995 ARLESEY TOWN 2 ***(South Midlands)*** — **OXFORD CITY 1** ***(Ryman 2)*** — **Att: 13,670**
Palma, Gyalog — **S Fontaine** — **Ref: Mr G S Willard**
Arlesey: Young, Cardines, Bambrick, Palma (Ward), Hull, Gonsalves, Gyalog, Cox, Kane,O'Keefe, Marshall (Nicholls). Sub: Dodwell
Oxford: Fleet, Brown (Fisher), Hume, Shepherd, Muttock, Hamilton (Kemp), Thomas, Spittle, Sherwood, S Fontaine, C Fontaine. Sub: Torres

1996 BRIGG TOWN 3 ***(N Co East)*** — **CLITHEROE 0** ***(N W Counties)*** — **Att: 7,340**
Stead 2, Roach — **Ref: Mr S J Lodge**
Brigg: Gawthorpe, Thompson, Rogers, Greaves (Clay), Buckley (Mail), Elston, C Stead, McLean, N Stead (McNally), Flounders, Roach
Clitheroe: Nash, Lampkin, Rowbotham (Otley), Baron, Westwell, Rovine, Butcher, Taylor (Smith), Grimshaw, Darbyshire, Hill (Dunn)

1997 WHITBY TOWN 3 ***(Northern)*** — **NORTH FERRIBY UTD. 0** ***(N Co East)*** — **Att: 11,098**
Williams, Logan, Toman — **Ref: Graham Poll**
North Ferriby: Sharp, Deacey, Smith, Brentano, Walmsley, M Smith, Harrison (Horne), Phillips (Milner), France (Newman), Flounders, Tennison
Whitby Town: Campbell, Williams, Logan, Goodchild, Pearson, Cook, Goodrick (Borthwick), Hodgson, Robinson, Toman (Pyle), Pitman (Hall)

1998 TIVERTON TOWN 1 *(Western)* — **TOW LAW TOWN 0 *(Northern)*** — **Att: 13,139**
Varley — **Ref: M A Riley**

Tiverton: Edwards, Felton, Saunders, Tatterton, Smith J, Conning, Nancekivell (Rogers), Smith K (Varley), Everett, Daly, Leonard (Waters)
Tow Law: Dawson, Pickering, Darwent, Bailey, Hague, Moan, Johnson, Nelson, Suddick, Laidler (Bennett), Robinson.

1999 TIVERTON TOWN 1 *(Western)* — **BEDLINGTON TERRIERS 0 *(Northern)*** — **Att: 13, 878**
Rogers 88 — **Ref: W. C. Burns**

Bedlington Terriers: O'Connor, Bowes, Pike, Boon (Renforth), Melrose, Teasdale, Cross, Middleton (Ludlow), Gibb, Milner, Bond. Subs: Pearson, Cameron, Gowans
Tiverton Town: Edwards, Fallon, Saunders, Tatterton, Tallon, Conning (Rogers), Nancekivell (Pears), Varley, Everett, Daly, Leonard. Subs: Tucker, Hynds, Grimshaw

2000 DEAL TOWN 1 *(Kent)* — **CHIPPENHAM TOWN 0 *(Western)*** — **Att: 20,000**
Graham 87 — **Ref: E. K. Wolstenholme**

Deal Town: Tucker, Kempster, Best, Ash, Martin, Seager, Monteith, Graham, Lovell, Marshall, Ribbens. Subs: Roberts, Warden, Turner
Chippenham Town: Jones, James, Andrews, Murphy, Burns, Woods, Brown, Charity, Tweddle, Collier, Godley. Subs: Tiley, Cutler

2001 TAUNTON TOWN 2 *(Western)* — **BERKHAMPSTED TOWN 1 *(Isthmian 2)*** — **(at Villa Park) Att: 8,439**
Fields 41, Laight 45 — **Lowe 71** — **Ref: E. K. Wolstenholme**

Taunton Town: Draper, Down, Chapman, West, Hawkings, Kelly, Fields (Groves), Laight, Cann (Tallon), Bastow, Lynch (Hapgood). Subs: Ayres, Parker
Berkhampsted Town: O'Connor, Mullins, Lowe, Aldridge, Coleman, Brockett, Yates, Adebowale, Richardson, Smith, Nightingale. Subs: Ringsell, Hall, Knight, Franklin, Osborne

2002 WHITLEY BAY 1 *(Northern)* — **TIPTREE UNITED 0 *(Eastern)*** — **(at Villa Park) Att: 4742**
Chandler 97 — **Ref: A Kaye**

Whitley Bay: Caffrey, Sunderland, Walmsley, Dixon (Neil), Anderson, Locker, Middleton, Bowes (Carr), Chandler, Walton, Fenwick (Cuggy). Subs: Cook, Livermore
Tiptree United: Haygreen, Battell, Wall, Houghton, Fish, Streetley (Gillespie), Wareham (Snow), Daly, Barefield, Aransibia (Parnell), Brady. Subs: Powell, Ford.

2003 A.F.C SUDBURY 1 *(Eastern Counties)* — **BRIGG TOWN 2 *(Northern Co.East)*** — **(at Upton Park) Att: 6,634**
Raynor 30 — **Housham 2, Carter 68** — **Ref: M Fletcher**

AFC Sudbury:- Greygoose, Head (Norfolk 63), Spearing, Tracey, Bishop, Anderson (Owen 73), Rayner, Gardiner (Banya 79), Bennett, Claydon, Betson. Subs (not used) Taylor, Hyde.
Brigg Town:- Steer, Raspin, Rowland, Thompson, Blanchard, Stones, Stead (Thompson 41), Housham, Borman (Drayton 87), Roach, Carter. Subs (not used) Nevis, Gawthorpe.

2004 A.F.C SUDBURY 0 *(Eastern Counties)* — **WINCHESTER CITY 2 *(Wessex)*** — **(at St Andrews) Att: 5,080**
Forbes 19, Smith 73 (pen) — **Ref: P Crossley**

AFC Sudbury:- Greygoose, Head, Wardley, Girling, Tracey, Norfolk, Owen (Banya 62), Hyde (Calver 57), Bennett, Claydon, Betson (Francis 73n). Subs (not used) - Rayner, Nower.
Winchester City:- Arthur, Dyke (Tate 83), Bicknell, Redwood, Goss, Blake, Webber, Green, Mancey, Forbes (Rogers 70), Smith (Green 90). Subs (not used) - Lang and Rastall.

2005 A.F.C SUDBURY 2 *(Eastern Counties)* — **DIDCOT TOWN 3 *(Hellenic)*** — **(at White Hart Lane) Att: 8,662**
Wardley, Calver (pen) — **Beavon (2), Wardley (og)** — **Ref: R Beeeby**

AFC Sudbury:- Greygoose, Girling, Wardley, Bennett, Hyde (Hayes 78), Owen (Norfolk 65), Claydon (Banya 59), Head, Calver, Betson, Terry Rayner. Subs (not used) – Howlett, Nower.
Didcot Town:- Webb, Goodall, Heapy, Campbell, Green, Parrott, Hannigan, Ward, Concannon (Jones 88), Beavon (Bianchini 90), Powell. Subs (not used) – Cooper, Allen, Spurrett.

2006 HILLINGDON BOROUGH 1 *(Spartan S.Mids P.)* — **NANTWICH TOWN 3 *(NWC 1)*** — **(at St Andrews) Att: 3,286**
Nelson — **Kinsey (2), Scheuber**

Hillingdon Borough:- Brown, Rundell (Fenton 80),Kidson, Phillips, Croft, Lawrence, Duncan (Nelson 46), Tilbury, Hibbs, Wharton (Lyons 38). Subs (not used): O'Grady, White.
Nantwich Town:- Hackney, A.Taylor, T.Taylor, Smith, Davis, Donnelly, Beasley, Scheuber (Parkinson 69), Kinsey (Marrow 69), Blake (Scarlett 86) and Griggs. Subs (not used): O'Connor and Read.

2007 AFC TOTTON 1 *(Wessex Division 1)* — **TRURO 3 *(Western Division 1)*** — **Att: 27,754 (New Vase record)**
Potter — **Wills (2), Broad** — **Ref: P Joslin**

AFC Totton: Brunnschweiler, Reacord, Troon (Stevens 60), Potter (Gregory 82), Bottomley, Austen, Roden, Gosney, Hamodu (Goss 89), Osman, Byres. Subs not used: Zammit, McCormack.
Truro City: Stevenson, Ash, Power, Smith, Martin (Pope 84), Broad, Wills, Gosling, Yetton, Watkins, Walker (Ludlam 90). Subs not used: Butcher, Routledge, Reski.

2008 **KIRKHAM & WESHAM 2** ***(North West Co. Div.2)*** **Walwyn (2)** — **LOWESTOFT TOWN 1** ***(Eastern Co. Premier)*** **Thompson (og)** — **Att: 19,537** **Ref: A D'Urso**

Kirkham and Wesham: Summerfield, Jackson (Walwyn 79), Keefe (Allen 55), Thompson, Shaw, Eastwood, Clark, Blackwell, Wane, Paterson (Sheppard 90), Smith. Subs not used: Moffat and Abbott

Lowestoft Town: Reynolds, Poppy, Potter, Woodrow, Saunders, Plaskett (McGee 79), Godbold, Darren Cockrill (Dale Cockrill 46), Stock, Hough, King (Hunn 55). Subs not used: McKenna and Rix.

2009 **GLOSSOP NORTH END 0** ***(North West Co. Prem)*** — **WHITLEY BAY 2** ***(Northern Division One)*** **Kerr, Chow** — **Att: 12,212** **Ref: K Friend**

Glossop North End: Cooper, Young, Kay, Lugsden, Yates, Gorton, Bailey (Hind 57), Morris, Allen (Balfe 65), Hamilton (Bailey 72), Hodges. Subs not used: Whelan and Parker.

Whitley Bay: Burke, Taylor, Picton, McFarlane (Fawcett 60), Coulson, Ryan, Moore, Robson, Kerr, Chow (Robinson 73), Johnston (Bell 60). Subs not used: McLean and Reay.

2010 **WHITLEY BAY 6** ***(Northern Division One)*** **Chow 21(sec), Easthaugh 16 (og), Kerr, Johnston, Robinson, Gillies** — **WROXHAM 1** ***(Eastern Counties Premier Division)*** **Cook 12** — **Att: 8,920** **Ref: A Taylor**

Whitley Bay: Terry Burke, Craig McFarlane, Callum Anderson, Richard Hodgson, (sub Lee Picton 69th min), Darren Timmons, Leon Ryan, Adam Johnston (sub Joshua Gillies 77th min), Damon Robson, Lee Kerr, Paul Chow (sub Phillip Bell 61st min), Paul Robinson.
Subs not used – Tom Kindley and Chris Reid.

Wroxham: Scott Howie, Gavin Pauling (sub Ross Durrant 57th min), Shaun Howes, Graham Challen, Martin McNeil (sub Josh Carus 46th min), Andy Easthaugh (sub Owen Paynter 69th min), Steve Spriggs, Gavin Lemmon, Paul Cook, Danny White, Gary Gilmore.
Subs not used – Danny Self and Gareth Simpson.

All Finals at Wembley unless otherwise stated.

Coalville Town's Adam Goodby (No.4) heads the ball back across the six yard box against Whitley Bay in the final.
Photo: Roger Turner.

PRELIMINARY ROUND

1	Chester Le Street Town	v	Gateshead (9/9)	4-2aet	154
2	York City	v	Sunderland RCA		
	(walkover for York City – Sunderland RCA withdrawn)				
3	Ryton	v	Workington		
	(walkover for Ryton – Workington withdrawn)				
4	Congleton Town	v	Formby (8/9)	2-6	107
5	Stalybridge Celtic	v	Vauxhall Motors (8/9)	0-4	88
6	Prescot Cables	v	Fleetwood Town (6/9)	1-3aet	102
7	AFC Fylde	v	Altrincham (8/9)	4-2	126
8	AFC Liverpool	v	Wrexham (9/9)	0-2	131
9	Marine	v	Lancaster City (9/9)	2-3	74
10	Nostell MW	v	Hallam (9/9)	0-2	41
11	Thackley	v	Sheffield (8/9)	0-8	62
12	Maltby Main	v	Pontefract Collieries (8/9)	4-2aet	50
13	Teversal	v	Barton Town Old Boys		
	(walkover for Teversal – Barton Town Old Boys withdrawn)				
14	Deeping Rangers	v	Grimsby Town (8/9)	0-11	108
15	Spalding United	v	Blaby & Whetstone Athletic (8/9)	2-7	14
16	Ilkeston Town	v	New Mills (8/9)	6-3	185
17	Mickleover Sports	v	Gresley (9/9)	3-1	68
18	Lincoln United	v	Retford United (8/9)	1-0	30
19	Glossop North End	v	Oadby Town (9/9)	4-4aet	90
	(Glossop North End won 3-1 on kicks from the penalty mark)				
20	Stamford	v	Carlton Town (9/9)	2-3	67
21	Worcester City	v	Rugby Town (6/9)	4-2	70
22	Bromyard Town	v	Stone Dominoes (6/9)	0-7	46
23	Nuneaton Town	v	Bedworth United (8/9)	0-0aet	105
	(Bedworth United won 6-5 on kicks from the penalty mark)				
24	Rocester	v	Ellesmere Rangers (7/9)	1-4	12
25	Highgate United	v	Nuneaton Griff (8/9)	3-0	30
26	Wolverhampton Casuals	v	Solihull Moors (8/9)	1-2	35
27	Stourbridge	v	Chasetown (6/9)	3-2	101
28	Bewdley Town	v	Pegasus Juniors (9/9)	6-1	58
29	Malvern Town	v	Wellington (9/9)	3-0	24
30	Newcastle Town	v	Romulus (9/9)	1-2	59
31	Bromsgrove Rovers	v	Kidsgrove Athletic		
	(walkover for Kidsgrove Athletic - Bromsgrove Rovers removed)				
32	AFC Telford United	v	Sutton Coldfield Town (6/9)	3-1	75
33	Fakenham Town	v	Brantham Athletic (9/9)	0-1	38
34	Walsham Le Willows	v	Norwich United (9/9)	0-5	43
35	Thetford Town	v	Wroxham (6/9)	3-1aet	70
36	Gorleston	v	Ipswich Wanderers (8/9)	4-0	64
37	Histon	v	Hadleigh United (9/9)	5-1	90
38	Lowestoft Town	v	Dereham Town (8/9)	3-0	66
39	Diss Town	v	Needham Market (9/9)	0-6	70
40	Stowmarket Town	v	Woodbridge Town (9/9)	2-5	34
41	Wellingborough Town	v	AFC Kempston Rovers (6/9)	2-3	61
42	Rothwell Corinthians	v	Dunstable Town		
	(walkover for Rothwell Corinthians – Dunstable Town withdrawn)				
43	Rushden & Higham United	v	Corby Town (9/9)	2-3	43
44	Stotfold	v	Raunds Town (9/9)	4-1	38
45	Brackley Town	v	Daventry Town (8/9)	8-0	37
46	Thrapston Town	v	Kettering Town (7/9)	6-2	20
47	Ware	v	Halstead Town (9/9)	1-0	52
48	Stansted	v	Hitchin Town (8/9)	3-1aet	45
49	Chelmsford City	v	AFC Hornchurch (8/9)	2-1	79
50	Hemel Hempstead Town	v	Witham Town (9/9)	3-4	72
51	Burnham Ramblers	v	Concord Rangers (8/9)	1-3	47
52	Leverstock Green	v	Harlow Town		
	(walkover for Leverstock Green – Harlow Town withdrawn)				
53	Hullbridge Sports	v	Bishop's Stortford (9/9)	1-3	52
54	London Colney	v	Stanway Rovers (8/9)	0-1	25
55	St Albans City	v	Thurrock (8/9)	3-4	71
56	Codicote	v	Grays Athletic (14/10)	1-2	58
	(9/9 - tie abandoned after 82 mins, 3-1)				
57	Oxhey Jets	v	Cheshunt (8/9)	3-5	56
58	Waltham Abbey	v	Romford (8/9)	7-2	103
59	Uxbridge	v	Wealdstone (8/9)	2-4aet	83
60	Thamesmead Town	v	Wingate & Finchley (1/9)	5-2	29
61	Enfield Town	v	Hampton & Richmond B.(6/9)	0-2	43
62	North Greenford United	v	Northwood (8/9)	0-5	57
63	Hayes & Yeading United	v	Harrow Borough (6/9)	3-2	82
64	Barking	v	Staines Town (8/9)	3-2	106
65	Hanwell Town	v	Corinthian Casuals		
	(walkover for Hanwell Town – Corinthian Casuals withdrawn)				
66	Harefield United	v	Kingsbury London Tigers (8/9)	4-0	34
67	Dulwich Hamlet	v	Croydon Athletic (8/9)	4-1	44
68	Bromley	v	Chatham Town (7/9)	3-0	109
69	Redhill	v	Eastbourne Town (8/9)	1-0aet	72
70	Oakwood	v	Merstham (9/9)	1-3	47
71	Welling United	v	Sutton United (8/9)	0-3	112
72	Mile Oak	v	Whyteleafe (8/9)	0-1	49
73	Lingfield	v	Maidstone United (9/9)	0-3	50
	(at Tunbridge Wells FC)				
74	Ramsgate	v	Lewes (9/9)	2-1	72
75	Crowborough Athletic	v	Saltdean United		
	(walkover for Crowborough Athletic – Saltdean United withdrawn)				
76	Crawley Down	v	Carshalton Athletic (9/9)	0-9	92
77	South Park	v	Cray Wanderers (9/9)	2-2aet	48
	(Cray Wanderers won 4-2 on kicks from the penalty mark)				
78	East Grinstead Town	v	Margate (9/9)	2-0	45
79	Folkestone Invicta	v	Dover Athletic (8/9)	1-2	105
80	Three Bridges	v	Whitstable Town (8/9)	1-0	38
81	VCD Athletic	v	Sevenoaks Town (9/9)	3-1	
82	Molesey	v	Kingstonian (8/9)	3-2	83
83	Tunbridge Wells	v	Eastbourne Borough (7/9)	1-0	68
84	Dartford	v	Erith & Belvedere (7/9)	4-1	96
85	Horsham YMCA	v	Whitehawk (9/9)	1-3	65
86	Dorking	v	Wick		
	(walkover for Dorking – Wick withdrawn)				
87	Burgess Hill Town	v	Westfield (6/9)	5-1	56
88	Epsom & Ewell	v	Chichester City (6/9)	2-1aet	29
89	Cobham	v	Shoreham (6/9)	6-2	62
90	Horsham	v	Chertsey Town (1/9)	4-1	72
91	Walton & Hersham	v	Worthing (8/9)	2-5aet	48
92	Thatcham Town	v	AFC Wallingford (8/9)	0-7	47
93	Sandhurst Town	v	Chalfont St Peter (8/9)	1-3	25
94	Chesham United	v	North Leigh		
	(walkover for Chesham United – North Leigh withdrawn)				
95	Basingstoke Town	v	Alton Town (8/9)	2-1	124
96	Aylesbury	v	Marlow (9/9)	2-3	65
97	Bracknell Town	v	Banbury United (8/9)	2-0	40
98	Newport Pagnell Town	v	Buckingham Town (9/9)	6-3aet	94
99	Cove	v	Witney United (8/9)	1-2	32
100	Reading Town	v	Binfield (8/9)	4-1	72
101	Sherborne Town	v	Pewsey Vale (8/9)	5-0	50
102	Eastleigh	v	Bournemouth (8/9)	7-0	96
103	Petersfield Town	v	Andover (9/9)	1-0	65
104	Dorchester Town	v	Christchurch (7/9)	2-4	42
105	Bristol Manor Farm	v	Mangotsfield United (8/9)	2-0	72
106	Merthyr Town	v	Forest Green Rovers (6/9)	1-2	30
107	Gloucester City	v	Lydney Town (7/9)	4-3	42
	(at Harrow Hill FC)				
108	Cheltenham Saracens	v	Chard Town (9/9)	2-3aet	42
109	Tiverton Town	v	Brislington (9/9)	0-1	42
	(tie awarded to Tiverton Town – Brislington removed)				
110	Paulton Rovers	v	Bishop's Cleeve (8/9)	2-4aet	54
111	Bitton	v	Portishead Town (6/9)	4-1	62
112	Weston Super Mare	v	Newport County (6/9)	0-0aet	85
	(Newport County won 5-4 on kicks from the penalty mark)				

FIRST ROUND QUALIFYING

1	Chester Le Street Town	v	Whitley Bay (23/9)	0-1	116
2	Ryton	v	Ashington (22/9)	3-4	54
3	Dunston UTS	v	Darlington		
	(walkover for Darlington – Dunston UTS withdrawn)				
4	Bedlington Terriers	v	York City (20/9)	2-3	140
5	AFC Fylde	v	Curzon Ashton (23/9)	2-1aet	88
6	Bootle	v	Burscough (23/9)	2-1	97
7	Daisy Hill	v	Nantwich Town (21/9)	0-7	40
8	Ashton Athletic	v	Woodley Sports (23/9)	2-1aet	34
9	Colne	v	Fleetwood Town		
	(walkover for Fleetwood Town – Colne withdrawn)				
10	Southport	v	Vauxhall Motors (23/9)	0-2	60
11	Warrington Town	v	Salford City		
	(walkover for Warrington Town – Salford City withdrawn)				
12	Wrexham	v	Ashton Town (23/9)	9-0	75
13	Northwich Victoria	v	Mossley (23/9)	0-2	106
14	Lancaster City	v	Formby (24/9)	1-0	46
15	Staveley MW	v	North Ferriby United (21/9)	2-1	40
16	Harrogate RA	v	Yorkshire Amateur (20/9)	4-1	106
17	Hallam	v	Stocksbridge Park Steels (22/9)	4-2aet	50
18	Liversedge	v	Maltby Main (23/9)	1-3	52
19	Hemsworth MW	v	Sheffield (23/9)	3-3aet	65
	(Sheffield won 5-4 on kicks from the penalty mark)				
20	Goole	v	Wakefield (23/9)	1-4	58
	(at Wakefield FC)				
21	Brighouse Town	v	Ossett Town (22/9)	3-4	40
22	Ossett Albion	v	Garforth Town (23/9)	1-4	43
23	Ilkeston Town	v	Arnold Town		
	(walkover for Arnold Town – Ilkeston Town removed)				
24	Boston United	v	Bottesford Town (22/9)	6-1	146
25	Holwell Sports	v	Glossop North End (22/9)	1-0	60
26	Barwell	v	Matlock Town (22/9)	5-1	62
27	Hinckley United	v	Blaby & Whetstone Athletic (20/9)	6-1	78
28	Loughborough Dynamo	v	Grimsby Town (23/9)	0-4	105
29	Long Eaton United	v	Radford (23/9)	2-3aet	12
30	Mickleover Sports	v	St Andrews (23/9)	3-1	52
31	Carlton Town	v	Mansfield Town		
	(walkover for Carlton Town – Mansfield Town withdrawn)				
32	Lincoln United	v	Teversal (22/9)	6-0	45
33	Ellesmere Rangers	v	Eccleshall (23/9)	2-2aet	40
	(Eccleshall won 5-4 on kicks from the penalty mark)				
34	Redditch United	v	Coventry Sphinx (22/9)	0-2	31
35	Gornal Athletic	v	Stone Dominoes (23/9)	0-4	50
36	Malvern Town	v	Stratford Town (21/9)	0-3	50
37	Kidsgrove Athletic	v	Worcester City (20/9)	2-5	50
38	Bolehall Swifts	v	Boldmere St Michaels (21/9)	2-1	68
39	Wednesfield	v	Stourbridge (20/9)	0-3	56
40	Walsall Wood	v	AFC Telford United (22/9)	3-1	53
41	Highgate United	v	Solihull Moors (20/9)	4-5	60
42	Kidderminster Harriers	v	Bewdley Town (22/9)	3-0	131
43	Romulus	v	Stourport Swifts (23/9)	3-1aet	52
44	Dosthill Colts	v	Bedworth United (23/9)	0-2	26
45	Lowestoft Town	v	Gorleston (22/9)	4-3	103
46	Great Yarmouth Town	v	Newmarket Town (22/9)	1-4	18
47	Brantham Athletic	v	Needham Market (29/9)	1-5	31
	(at Needham Market FC)				
48	Bury Town	v	Thetford Town (27/9)	11-1	70
49	Histon	v	Norwich United (23/9)	2-0	133
50	Soham Town Rangers	v	Leiston (22/9)	0-1	45
51	Woodbridge Town	v	Felixstowe & Walton Utd (23/9)	2-3	32
52	Cornard United	v	Cambridge United (22/9)	0-4	37
53	Brackley Town	v	Corby Town (20/9)	3-0	29
54	Luton Town	v	Cogenhoe United (22/9)	11-2	155
55	AFC Kempston Rovers	v	Thrapston Town (23/9)	0-1	58
56	St Ives Town	v	Rushden & Diamonds (23/9)	0-7	152
57	Stotfold	v	Rothwell Corinthians (23/9)	4-0	36
58	Leighton Town	v	Bugbrooke St Michaels (20/9)	6-0	78
59	Arlesey Town	v	Yaxley (22/9)	2-4	34
60	St Neots Town	v	Bedford Town (23/9)	2-3	87
61	Witham Town	v	Boreham Wood (23/9)	0-5	81
62	East Thurrock United	v	Bowers & Pitsea (22/9)	4-0	79
63	Brentwood Town	v	Stansted (23/9)	1-2	43
64	Thurrock	v	Ilford (21/9)	3-0	96
65	Cheshunt	v	Ware (22/9)	2-2aet	115
	(Cheshunt won 5-4 on kicks from the penalty mark)				
66	Billericay Town	v	Aveley (22/9)	2-3aet	63
67	Southend Manor	v	Bishop's Stortford (22/9)	1-0	20
68	Hoddesdon Town	v	Waltham Abbey (22/9)	1-3	61
69	Concord Rangers	v	Leverstock Green (21/9)	3-2	30
70	Royston Town	v	Stanway Rovers (22/9)	0-1	63
71	Grays Athletic	v	St Margaretsbury (19/10)	3-2aet	42
	(at St Margaretsbury FC)				
72	Braintree Town	v	Chelmsford City		
	(walkover for Chelmsford City – Braintree Town withdrawn)				
73	Barking	v	Northwood (22/9)	2-4aet	85
74	Clapton	v	Tokyngton Manor		
	(walkover for Clapton – Tokyngton Manor removed)				
75	Wealdstone	v	Hanwell Town (22/9)	4-1	64
76	Kentish Town	v	Hampton & Richmond B. (20/9)	2-6	21
77	Hayes & Yeading United	v	Thamesmead Town (23/9)	1-3	63
78	AFC Wimbledon	v	Hendon		
	(walkover for AFC Wimbledon – Hendon withdrawn)				
79	Harefield United	v	Ashford Town (Middx) (22/9)	1-0aet	75
80	Metropolitan Police	v	Dulwich Hamlet (23/9)	2-6	51
81	Molesey	v	Carshalton Athletic (22/9)	0-5	
82	VCD Athletic	v	Sutton United (23/9)	1-0	41
83	Peacehaven & Telscombe	v	Hastings United (23/9)	4-3	73
84	Dartford	v	Deal Town (21/9)	2-0	61
85	Ramsgate	v	Colliers Wood United (23/9)	5-2	86
86	St Francis Rangers	v	Redhill (23/9)	1-2	25
87	Tonbridge Angels	v	Tunbridge Wells (20/9)	3-1	209
88	Chipstead	v	Ashford Town		
	(walkover for Chipstead – Ashford Town removed)				
89	Whyteleafe	v	Tooting & Mitcham United (23/9)	1-2	78
90	Merstham	v	Three Bridges (23/9)	2-1	56
91	Crowborough Athletic	v	Crawley Town (23/9)	0-2	81
92	East Grinstead Town	v	Erith Town (23/9)	0-2	55
93	Maidstone United	v	Croydon (23/9)	5-1	39
	(at Tunbridge Wells FC)				
94	Cray Wanderers	v	Ebbsfleet United (22/9)	1-3	130
	(at Ebbsfleet United FC)				
95	Horley Town	v	Faversham Town (22/9)	4-2	40
96	Bromley	v	Dover Athletic (21/9)	3-1	106
97	Woking	v	Cobham (21/9)	4-1	194
98	Pagham	v	Burgess Hill Town (20/9)	1-3	59
99	Leatherhead	v	Whitehawk (22/9)	3-1	30
100	Worthing	v	Dorking (20/9)	6-1	126
101	Epsom & Ewell	v	Lancing (20/9)	0-5	
102	Horsham	v	Camberley Town (22/9)	1-6	63
	(at Three Bridges FC)				
103	Basingstoke Town	v	Fleet Town (20/9)	5-4	135
104	Slough Town	v	Farnborough (21/9)	1-3	105
105	Didcot Town	v	Bracknell Town (23/9)	2-3	68
106	Abingdon United	v	Reading Town (23/9)	2-1	39
107	Burnham	v	Chesham United (22/9)	1-5	28
108	Flackwell Heath	v	Chalfont St Peter (23/9)	3-2	60
109	Witney United	v	Oxford City (20/9)	1-2aet	60
110	Beaconsfield SYCOB	v	Maidenhead United (16/9)	0-6	32
111	Newport Pagnell Town	v	Kidlington (23/9)	7-1	37
112	Marlow	v	AFC Wallingford (20/9)	2-3	71
113	Gosport Borough	v	Christchurch (21/9)	2-0	74
114	Poole Town	v	Swindon Supermarine		
	(walkover for Poole Town – Swindon Supermarine withdrawn)				
115	Sherborne Town	v	Havant & Waterlooville (20/9)	0-3	70
116	Shaftesbury	v	Petersfield Town (22/9)	5-0	40
117	AFC Totton	v	Eastleigh (21/9)	2-0aet	205
118	Sholing	v	Salisbury City (23/9)	0-3	109
119	Moneyfields	v	Calne Town		
	(walkover for Moneyfields – Calne Town withdrawn)				
120	Weymouth	v	Ringwood Town (20/9)	4-1	82
121	Bishop's Cleeve	v	Chard Town (20/9)	5-2	26
122	Cirencester Town	v	Radstock Town (20/9)	10-1	60
123	Bristol Manor Farm	v	Bitton (22/9)	1-5	82
124	Yate Town	v	Gloucester City (21/9)	1-5	72
125	Tiverton Town	v	Forest Green Rovers (23/9)	2-5aet	25
126	Almondsbury UWE	v	Clevedon Town (22/9)	1-2	28
127	Newport County	v	Bishop Sutton (20/9)	6-0	155
128	Bath City	v	Elmore (20/9)	4-2	40

SECOND ROUND QUALIFYING

1	York City	v	Darlington (6/10)	0-4	183
2	Whitley Bay	v	Ashington (7/10)	5-0	79
3	Ashton Athletic	v	Nantwich Town (6/10)0-2		40
4	AFC Fylde	v	Bootle (4/10)	3-0	54
5	Wrexham	v	Warrington Town (11/10)	9-0	123
6	Fleetwood Town	v	Vauxhall Motors (4/10)	6-1	137
7	Harrogate RA	v	Staveley MW (4/10)	1-2	81
8	Mossley	v	Lancaster City (5/10)	5-1	35
9	Wakefield	v	Sheffield (6/10)	2-0	53
10	Hallam	v	Maltby Main (7/10)	2-1	50
11	Boston United	v	Arnold Town (6/10)	3-2	165
12	Ossett Town	v	Garforth Town (7/10)	1-2aet	53
13	Grimsby Town	v	Hinckley United (9/10)	3-0	
14	Holwell Sports	v	Barwell (6/10)	2-2aet	59
	(Barwell won 6-5 on kicks from the penalty mark)				
15	Lincoln United	v	Carlton Town (5/10)	5-4aet	50
16	Radford	v	Mickleover Sports (7/10)	2-3	29
17	Stratford Town	v	Stone Dominoes (6/10)	2-0	76
18	Eccleshall	v	Coventry Sphinx (5/10)	0-5	33
19	Walsall Wood	v	Stourbridge (6/10)	0-2	68
20	Worcester City	v	Bolehall Swifts (4/10)	1-2	100
21	Bedworth United	v	Romulus (6/10)	1-2	67
22	Solihull Moors	v	Kidderminster Harriers (6/10)	0-3	60
23	Bury Town	v	Needham Market (7/10)	3-2aet	56
24	Lowestoft Town	v	Newmarket Town (6/10)	1-4	81
25	Cambridge United	v	Felixstowe & Walton Utd (7/10)	14-0	78
26	Histon	v	Leiston (7/10)	3-0	98
27	Rushden&Diamonds	v	Thrapston Town (6/10)	8-0	114
28	Brackley Town	v	Luton Town (4/10)	1-5	52
29	Bedford Town	v	Yaxley (4/10)	1-2	62
30	Stotfold	v	Leighton Town (14/10)	4-0	56
31	Thurrock	v	Stansted (5/10)	2-1aet	90
32	Boreham Wood	v	East Thurrock United (6/10)	3-3aet	81
	(Boreham Wood won 5-4 on kicks from the penalty mark)				
33	Waltham Abbey	v	Southend Manor (6/10)	4-0	37
34	Cheshunt	v	Aveley (6/10)	4-2aet	85
35	Chelmsford City	v	Grays Athletic (27/10)	4-2	87
36	Concord Rangers	v	Stanway Rovers (6/10)	3-1	38
37	Hampton & Richmond Boro'	v	Wealdstone (11/10)	2-3	303
38	Northwood	v	Clapton (7/10)	1-0	32
39	Dulwich Hamlet	v	Harefield United (6/10)	3-1	48
40	Thamesmead Town	v	AFC Wimbledon (7/10)	0-1	108
41	Dartford	v	Peacehaven & Telscombe (6/10)	2-0	86
42	Carshalton Athletic	v	VCD Athletic (6/10)	3-1aet	64
43	Chipstead	v	Tonbridge Angels (6/10)	2-2aet	43
	(Tonbridge Angels won 5-4 on kicks from the penalty mark)				
44	Ramsgate	v	Redhill (7/10)	2-3	112
45	Erith Town	v	Crawley Town (4/10)	1-2	75
46	Tooting & Mitcham United	v	Merstham (6/10)	3-3aet	61
	(Tooting & Mitcham United won 5-4 on kicks from the penalty mark)				
47	Bromley	v	Horley Town (4/10)	6-0	96
48	Maidstone United	v	Ebbsfleet United (7/10)	2-4	71
	(at Tunbridge Wells FC)				
49	Worthing	v	Leatherhead (4/10)	3-3aet	116
	(Leatherhead won 5-3 on kicks from the penalty mark)				
50	Woking	v	Burgess Hill Town (4/10)	4-1	108
51	Farnborough	v	Basingstoke Town (6/10)	4-4aet	225
	(Farnborough won 3-2 on kicks from the penalty mark)				
52	Lancing	v	Camberley Town (7/10)	2-5	59
53	Flackwell Heath	v	Chesham United (7/10)	0-2	60
54	Bracknell Town	v	Abingdon United (6/10)	1-0	50
55	AFC Wallingford	v	Newport Pagnell Town (4/10)	3-2	39
56	Oxford City	v	Maidenhead United (4/10)	1-4	48
57	Shaftesbury	v	Havant & Waterlooville (7/10)	1-3	70
58	Gosport Borough	v	Poole Town (5/10)	5-1	70
59	Weymouth	v	Moneyfields (4/10)	1-0	65
60	AFC Totton	v	Salisbury City (7/10)	0-3	151
61	Gloucester City	v	Bitton (5/10)	3-2aet	22
	(at Harrow Hill FC)				
62	Bishop's Cleeve	v	Cirencester Town (4/10)	3-5	59
63	Bath City	v	Newport County (4/10)	1-6	82
64	Forest Green Rovers	v	Clevedon Town (4/10)	2-1	78

THIRD ROUND QUALIFYING

1	Nantwich Town	v	Fleetwood Town (25/10)	2-3	110
2	Wakefield	v	AFC Fylde (20/10)	1-4	53
3	Whitley Bay	v	Staveley MW (21/10)	3-0	82
4	Hallam	v	Wrexham (25/10)	1-2	95
5	Darlington	v	Mossley (27/10)	3-0	139
6	Barwell	v	Boston United (20/10)	0-3	88
7	Stourbridge	v	Garforth Town (18/10)	4-2	113
8	Bolehall Swifts	v	Romulus (21/10)	2-2aet	70
	(Bolehall Swifts won 5-4 on kicks from the penalty mark)				
9	Grimsby Town	v	Kidderminster Harriers (19/10)	5-1	191
10	Coventry Sphinx	v	Mickleover Sports (20/10)	2-1	76
11	Lincoln United	v	Stratford Town (20/10)	0-1	40
12	Histon	v	Yaxley (21/10)	2-1aet	133
13	Waltham Abbey	v	Luton Town (20/10)	2-3	113
14	Boreham Wood	v	Cambridge United (20/10)	0-4	57
15	Cheshunt	v	Concord Rangers (21/10)	2-3	126
16	Bury Town	v	Chelmsford City (3/11)	3-2aet	88
17	Stotfold	v	Thurrock (21/10)	0-3	45
18	Newmarket Town	v	Rushden & Diamonds (21/10)	1-4	200
19	Crawley Town	v	Tooting & Mitcham United (18/10)	2-1	222
20	Carshalton Athletic	v	Chesham United (20/10)	4-3	64
21	AFC Wallingford	v	Dulwich Hamlet (18/10)	1-2	47
22	Maidenhead United	v	Dartford (20/10)	0-1	22
23	Camberley Town	v	Northwood (18/10)	0-3	58
24	AFC Wimbledon	v	Wealdstone (20/10)	1-0	172
25	Bromley	v	Tonbridge Angels (19/10)	1-0	127
26	Ebbsfleet United	v	Redhill (20/10)	5-1	95
27	Woking	v	Leatherhead (19/10)	4-0	175
28	Havant & Waterlooville	v	Gosport Borough (18/10)	4-1	148
29	Weymouth	v	Cirencester Town (18/10)	0-4	65
30	Forest Green Rovers	v	Salisbury City (18/10)	2-0	83
31	Gloucester City	v	Newport County (19/10)	2-4aet	63
	(at Harrow Hill FC)				
32	Bracknell Town	v	Farnborough (20/10)	2-0	87

FIRST ROUND PROPER

1	Crewe Alexandra	v	AFC Fylde (27/10)	4-0	395
2	Bradford City	v	Rochdale (3/11)	4-2	144
3	Hartlepool United	v	Whitley Bay (27/10)	3-1	112
4	Carlisle United	v	Wrexham (16/11)	3-1aet	207
5	Stockport County	v	Tranmere Rovers (1/11)	1-4aet	211
6	Macclesfield Town	v	Fleetwood Town (3/11)	4-1	107
7	Accrington Stanley	v	Darlington (6/11)	1-2	48
	(at Clitheroe FC)				
8	Bury	v	Oldham Athletic (18/10)	2-5	261
9	Rotherham United	v	Sheffield Wednesday (3/11)	2-3aet	215
10	Huddersfield Town	v	Morecambe (3/11)	5-1	159
11	Histon	v	Notts County (2/11)	0-3	395
12	Bolehall Swifts	v	Northampton Town (1/11)	1-0	100
13	Chesterfield	v	Port Vale (27/10)	1-3	700
14	Grimsby Town	v	Stourbridge (3/11)	3-0	
15	Burton Albion	v	Stratford Town (9/11)	0-2	165
16	Lincoln City	v	Peterborough United (26/10)	2-4	200
17	Shrewsbury Town	v	Boston United (3/11)	5-1	
18	Milton Keynes Dons	v	Walsall (26/10)	0-1	404
19	Coventry Sphinx	v	Hereford United (2/11)	2-1	111
20	Thurrock	v	Leyton Orient (4/11)	1-0	240
21	Barnet	v	Wycombe Wanderers (26/10)	2-3	328
22	Northwood	v	Dulwich Hamlet (4/11)	1-3	92
23	Bury Town	v	Bromley (11/11)	5-4	68
24	Brighton & Hove Albion	v	Ebbsfleet United (3/11)	3-0	73
	(at Bognor Regis Town FC)				
25	Dagenham & Redbridge	v	Stevenage (1/11)	2-2aet	480
	(Dagenham & Redbridge won 3-2 on kicks from the penalty mark)				
26	Colchester United	v	Woking (30/10)	3-5	189
27	Southend United	v	Luton Town (3/11)	3-1aet	230
28	Charlton Athletic	v	Crawley Town (3/11)	2-0	226
29	Concord Rangers	v	Brentford (3/11)	0-5	102
30	Rushden & Diamonds	v	Carshalton Athletic (3/11)	1-0	124
31	Gillingham	v	Cambridge United (28/10)	1-2aet	299
32	Dartford	v	AFC Wimbledon (3/11)	1-2	127
33	Newport County	v	Bristol Rovers (1/11)	1-2aet	289
34	Forest Green Rovers	v	Swindon Town (1/11)	1-2aet	191
35	Torquay United	v	Bracknell Town (3/11)	4-0	139
36	Havant & Waterlooville	v	Yeovil Town (3/11)	0-2	112

First Round Proper continued....

No	Home		Away	Score	Att
37	Cheltenham Town	v	Oxford United (9/11)	2-2aet	216
	(Cheltenham Town won 4-1 on kicks from the penalty mark)				
38	Plymouth Argyle	v	Southampton (27/10)	1-3	229
39	Cirencester Town	v	Aldershot Town (3/11)	2-3	90
40	AFC Bournemouth	v	Exeter City (3/11)	1-1aet	269
	(Exeter City won 3-2 on kicks from the penalty mark)				

SECOND ROUND PROPER

No	Home		Away	Score	Att
1	Huddersfield Town	v	Darlington (17/11)	0-4	126
2	Peterborough United	v	Stratford Town (17/11)	5-0	329
3	Notts County	v	Shrewsbury Town (15/11)	2-0	369
4	Port Vale	v	Grimsby Town (22/11)	1-1aet	212
	(Grimsby Town won 5-4 on kicks from the penalty mark)				
5	Carlisle United	v	Walsall (15/12)	0-2	119
6	Bolehall Swifts	v	Bradford City (11/11)	0-4	103
7	Oldham Athletic	v	Sheffield Wednesday (16/11)	3-2	240
8	Macclesfield Town	v	Hartlepool United (16/11)	0-2	94
9	Tranmere Rovers	v	Crewe Alexandra (17/11)	1-2	322
10	Dagenham & Redbridge	v	Bristol Rovers (10/11)	2-2aet	173
	(Bristol Rovers won 4-2 on kicks from the penalty mark)				
11	AFC Wimbledon	v	Aldershot Town (17/11)	0-3	187
12	Woking	v	Cheltenham Town (18/11)	2-4	215
13	Dulwich Hamlet	v	Yeovil Town (17/11)	3-2aet	86
14	Southampton	v	Thurrock (9/11)	2-0	367
15	Brighton & Hove Albion	v	Torquay United (17/11)	6-0	50
	(at Bognor Regis Town FC)				
16	Cambridge United	v	Exeter City (17/11)	1-2	119
17	Rushden & Diamonds	v	Wycombe Wanderers (16/11)	1-0	187
18	Southend United	v	Brentford (22/11)	3-0	234
19	Swindon Town	v	Coventry Sphinx (16/11)	6-1	268
20	Charlton Athletic	v	Bury Town (24/11)	4-0	153
	(at Welling United FC)				

THIRD ROUND PROPER

No	Home		Away	Score	Att
1	West Ham United	v	Aldershot Town (7/12)	5-0	414
2	Blackburn Rovers	v	Reading (9/12)	3-2aet	454
3	Doncaster Rovers	v	Middlesbrough (12/1)	2-4aet	277
4	Dulwich Hamlet	v	Newcastle United (6/1)	2-6	439
5	Grimsby Town	v	Burnley (15/12)	3-2	
6	Watford	v	Swindon Town (9/12)	2-0	315
7	Leicester City	v	Hartlepool United (7/12)	2-1	
8	Sunderland	v	Chelsea	0-2	
9	Arsenal	v	Darlington (14/12)	6-1	217
	(at Barnet FC)				
10	Oldham Athletic	v	Manchester City (15/12)	5-6	405
11	Brighton & Hove Albion	v	Derby County (14/12)	0-3	67
	(at Bognor Regis Town FC)				
12	Notts County	v	Liverpool (15/12)	0-4	508
13	Barnsley	v	Tottenham Hotspur (14/12)	3-1	810
14	Bristol City	v	Birmingham City (13/12)	0-2	613
15	Bristol Rovers	v	Aston Villa (19/1)	0-1	434
16	Wigan Athletic	v	Stoke City (7/12)	3-0	186
17	Millwall	v	Walsall	3-1	279
18	Queens Park Rangers	v	Nottingham Forest (7/12)	2-2aet	306
	(Nottingham Forest won 5-3 on kicks from the penalty mark)				
19	Bolton Wanderers	v	Crewe Alexandra (30/11)	1-2	537
20	Fulham	v	West Bromwich Albion (1/12)	6-4aet	254
21	Leeds United	v	Scunthorpe United (7/12)	3-0	248
22	Norwich City	v	Charlton Athletic (7/12)	1-0	306
23	Hull City	v	Rushden & Diamonds (20/1)	2-3	152
	(at North Ferriby United FC)				
24	Southend United	v	Coventry City (12/1)	3-1	259
25	Everton	v	Wolverhampton W'derers (12/1)	2-1	482
	(at Stobart Stadium, Halton)				
26	Blackpool	v	Exeter City (15/12)	5-1	204
27	Preston North End	v	Swansea City (16/12)	2-1	
88					
28	Cardiff City	v	Crystal Palace (14/12)	0-3	406
29	Cheltenham Town	v	Sheffield United (12/1)	1-4	179
30	Bradford City	v	Southampton (14/12)	1-1aet	209
	(Bradford City won 9-8 on kicks from the penalty mark)				
31	Manchester United	v	Portsmouth (10/1)	3-2	414
	(at Altrincham FC)				
32	Ipswich Town	v	Peterborough United (25/11)	2-3	287

FOURTH ROUND PROPER

No	Home		Away	Score	Att
1	Barnsley	v	Rushden & Diamonds (26/1)	4-0	710
2	Nottingham Forest	v	Manchester City (12/1)	2-1	564
3	Crewe Alexandra	v	Leeds United (19/1)	0-0aet	1031
	(Leeds United won 3-2 on kicks from the penalty mark)				
4	Watford	v	Wigan Athletic (19/1)	3-2	322
5	Peterborough United	v	Aston Villa (26/1)	1-3aet	665
6	Middlesbrough	v	Everton (24/1)	1-0	529
7	Leicester City	v	Blackburn Rovers (31/1)	3-1	490
8	West Ham United	v	Manchester United (19/1)	0-1	1405
9	Blackpool	v	Birmingham City (19/1)	4-3	281
10	Sheffield United	v	Millwall (18/1)	3-0	523
11	Derby County	v	Southend United (26/1)	1-3	462
12	Newcastle United	v	Grimsby Town (27/1)	2-1aet	1043
13	Liverpool	v	Crystal Palace (8/1)	3-1aet	1197
14	Fulham	v	Norwich City (14/1)	3-0	645
15	Preston North End	v	Bradford City (19/1)	1-1aet	630
	(Preston North End won 4-2 on kicks from the penalty mark)				
16	Chelsea	v	Arsenal (20/1)	2-1	4383

FIFTH ROUND PROPER

No	Home		Away	Score	Att
1	Leicester City	v	Preston North End (23/2)	4-3aet	395
2	Leeds United	v	Aston Villa (15/2)	0-2	604
3	Manchester United	v	Newcastle United (16/2)	1-0	657
	(at Altrincham FC)				
4	Fulham	v	Watford (4/12)	0-2	698
5	Liverpool	v	Southend United (14/2)	9-0	1716
6	Sheffield United	v	Blackpool (26/1)	3-1aet	828
7	Chelsea	v	Barnsley (11/2)	2-1	2282
8	Nottingham Forest	v	Middlesbrough (2/2)	0-1	562

SIXTH ROUND PROPER

No	Home		Away	Score	Att
1	Liverpool	v	Manchester United (13/3)	2-3	10199
2	Aston Villa	v	Middlesbrough (6/3)	3-1	820
3	Leicester City	v	Sheffield United (9/3)	1-2	521
4	Chelsea	v	Watford (2/3)	2-1	2160

SEMI FINALS 1ST LEG

No	Home		Away	Score	Att
1	Chelsea	v	Manchester United (10/4)	3-2	5518
2	Aston Villa	v	Sheffield United (16/3)	0-1	1541

SEMI FINALS 2ND LEG

No	Home		Away	Score	Att
1	Manchester United	v	Chelsea (20/4)	4-0	9124
2	Sheffield United	v	Aston Villa (6/4)	2-0	4016

THE FINAL 1ST LEG

Home		Away	Score	Att
SHEFFIELD UNITED	v	MANCHESTER UNITED	2-2	29977

THE FINAL 2ND LEG

Home		Away	Score	Att
MANCHESTER UNITED	v	SHEFFIELD UNITED	4-1	24916

PREVIOUS TEN FINALS

Year	Winner		Runner-up	Aggregate Score
2010	Chelsea	v	Aston Villa	3-2
2009	Arsenal	v	Liverpool	6-2
2008	Manchester City	v	Chelsea	4-2
2007	Liverpool	v	Manchester Utd	2-2* 4-3p
2006	Liverpool	v	Manchester City	3-2
2005	Ipswich Town	v	Southampton	3-2
2004	Middlesbrough	v	Aston Villa	4-0
2003	Manchester Utd	v	Middlesbrough	3-1
2002	Aston Villa	v	Everton	4-2
2001	Arsenal	v	Blackburn Rovers	6-3

FIRST ROUND

1	Shropshire	v	Staffordshire (16/10)	2-3
2	Nottinghamshire	v	Isle Of Man (10/10)	1-2
3	Northumberland	v	Cheshire (16/10)	2-1
4	West Riding	v	North Riding (16/10)	3-1
5	Leicestershire & Rutland	v	Birmingham (16/10)	1-5
6	Herefordshire	v	Devon (16/10)	1-1aet
	(Herefordshire won 4-2 on kicks from the penalty mark)			
7	Sussex	v	Somerset (16/10)	2-5
8	Essex	v	Huntingdonshire (16/10)	3-1
9	Oxfordshire	v	Surrey (9/10)	0-1
10	Wiltshire	v	Cambridgeshire (9/10)	5-0
11	Suffolk	v	London (16/10)	4-1
12	Gloucestershire	v	Berks & Bucks (2/10)	4-6
13	Dorset	v	Norfolk (16/10)	1-2

SECOND ROUND

1	Liverpool	v	Staffordshire (6/11)	1-2
2	Lincolnshire	v	Manchester (13/11)	1-4
3	Cumberland	v	Durham (30/10)	0-4
4	Northumberland	v	Isle Of Man (13/11)	6-2
5	Westmorland	v	East Riding (9/10)	0-4
6	West Riding	v	Sheffield & Hallamshire (6/11)	1-2
7	Lancashire	v	Birmingham (6/11)	1-2
8	Middlesex	v	Suffolk (6/11)	5-2
9	Cornwall	v	Northamptonshire (30/10)	3-7
10	Kent	v	Berks & Bucks (13/11)	0-2
11	Hertfordshire	v	Essex (7/11)	1-0aet
12	Norfolk	v	Surrey (6/11)	3-0
13	Guernsey	v	Wiltshire (13/11)	2-6
14	Bedfordshire	v	Worcestershire (23/10)	6-2aet
15	Herefordshire	v	Jersey (6/11)	2-3aet
16	Amateur Football Alliance	v	Somerset (13/11)	1-2

THIRD ROUND

1	Northumberland	v	Birmingham (8/1)	1-2
2	Northamptonshire	v	Jersey (11/12)	5-3aet
3	Sheffield & Hallamshire	v	Bedfordshire (9/1)	3-1
4	Hertfordshire	v	Norfolk (8/1)	0-4
5	Manchester	v	Durham (15/1)	5-0
6	Wiltshire	v	East Riding (15/1)	1-0
7	Somerset	v	Staffordshire (15/1)	0-2
8	Berks & Bucks	v	Middlesex (11/12)	1-5

FOURTH ROUND

1	Wiltshire	v	Norfolk (5/12)	0-1
2	Sheffield & Hallamshire	v	Northamptonshire (29/1)	2-1
3	Staffordshire	v	Manchester (5/12)	2-1
4	Birmingham	v	Middlesex (29/1)	0-0aet
	(Birmingham won 4-2 on kicks from the penalty mark)			

SEMI FINALS

1	Sheffield & Hallamshire	v	Staffordshire (19/2)	0-2
2	Birmingham	v	Norfolk (12/3)	0-1

THE FINAL

SATURDAY 30 APRIL 2011 – 2.00pm

STAFFORDSHIRE	v	NORFOLK	2-4	580

AT STOKE CITY FC

PREVIOUS TEN FINALS

2010	Kent FA	v	Sheffield & Hallamshire	1-0
2009	Birmingham FA	v	Kent FA	2-1
2008	Suffolk FA	v	Cambridgeshire FA	2-1
2007	West Riding FA	v	Suffolk FA	1-1*, 4-3p
2006	Bedfordshire FA	v	Durham FA	3-2
2005	Suffolk FA	v	Hampshire FA	2-1
2004	Durham FA	v	North Riding FA	4-0
2003	Northumberland FA	v	Liverpool FA	1-0
2002	Birmingham FA	v	Durham FA	2-1
2001	Northamptonshire FA	v	Birmingham FA	3-0

FIRST ROUND

1	Swanfield	v	Sunderland RCA Barnes	0-1
2	West Lee	v	Kelloe WMC	
	(walkover for Kelloe WMC – West Lee withdrawn)			
3	AFC Blackburn Leisure	v	Dawdon Colliery Welfare	1-2aet
4	Witton Park Rose & Crown	v	Shankhouse United	6-1
5	Hartlepool Lion Hillcarter	v	Hessle Rangers	5-1
6	Derby Lane Gym	v	Salford Celtic	3-1
7	Paddock	v	Ford Motors	6-1
8	Frizington Whitestar	v	Eden Vale	1-2
9	Poulton Royal	v	Thirly	2-0
10	Malt Shovel	v	West Bowling	1-2
11	Woodchurch	v	Oyster Martyrs	1-4
12	Silsden (Sunday)	v	Alder	
	(walkover for Alder – Silsden (Sunday) withdrawn)			
13	Salisbury Athletic	v	Oak Tree Pub	4-2
14	Chapeltown Brazil	v	Mariners	0-2
15	Tower	v	Dengo United	4-2
16	Allerton	v	Lobster	2-4
17	Queens Park	v	BRNESC	2-1
18	Huddersfield Irish Centre	v	St Sebastians	3-2
19	Obiter	v	Sandstone	1-4
20	Nicosia	v	Home & Bargain	
	(walkover for Home & Bargain – Nicosia withdrawn)			
21	Red Lion	v	Fforde Grene	2-3
22	St Bees Village	v	Brow	2-3
23	Towngate	v	JOB	1-2
24	Belt Road	v	Wisbech St Mary	
	(walkover for Belt Road – Wisbech St Mary withdrawn)			
25	Loughborough Falcons	v	Bartley Green Sunday	4-2
26	Advance Couriers	v	Britannia Revolution	5-1
27	Loughborough Saints	v	Station Gates	10-0
28	Barwell Sports Bar	v	Hundred Acre	1-7
29	Warstones Wanderers (Sunday)	v	Birstall Stamford	
	(walkover for Birstall Stamford – Warstones Wanderers (Sunday) withdrawn)			
30	Brereton Town	v	Clumber	0-7
31	The Blue Mugge	v	R.H.P Sports & Social	5-2
32	Kingshurst Sporting Club	v	Thatch	8-2aet
33	Coventry Colliery	v	Travellers	0-8
34	Club Lewsey	v	Dee Road Rangers	5-3
35	St Josephs (Luton)	v	Northampton Duke Of York	1-2
36	Britannia United	v	Houghton Town (Sunday)	1-0aet
37	Rumours	v	Celtic SC (Luton)	1-1aet
	(Rumours won 5-4 on kicks from the penalty mark)			
38	Wrightchoice Comm Spts A.	v	Stanbridge & Tilsworth	2-0
39	AC Sportsman & R.	v	Standens Barn	2-0
40	Gamlingay United Sunday	v	FC Houghton Centre	5-6
41	Wycombe Town	v	Silsoe Park Rangers	
	(walkover for Silsoe Park Rangers – Wycombe Town withdrawn)			
42	AFC Donsville	v	Sandy (Sunday)	
	(walkover for AFC Donsville – Sandy (Sunday) withdrawn)			
43	St Margarets	v	Crawley Green (Sunday)	3-0
44	Comets Sports Club	v	Hammer	3-3aet
	(Comet Spts won 5-4 on kicks from the penalty mark)			
45	Nicolas Wybacks	v	Bungay Town	
	(tie awarded to Nicolas Wybacks – Bungay Town removed for failure to fulfil fixture)			
46	Belstone	v	Gossoms End	7-2
47	Offley Moat	v	Royal Falcons	2-1
48	Torrun United	v	Nirankari Stevenage	1-3
49	FC Tripimeni-Aris	v	AFC Harrow	4-0
50	Broadfields United	v	Greengate	1-4
51	CB Hounslow (Sunday)	v	North West Neasden	1-2aet
52	London Maccabi Lions	v	Enfield Rangers	1-5
53	Bedfont Sunday	v	AFC Kumazi Strikers	3-0
54	Knighton Arms	v	Goring Rangers	
	(tie awarded to Knighton Arms – Goring Rangers removed for failure to fulfil fixture)			
55	Baldon Sports	v	The Lounge	2-4
56	Ajax LA	v	Golden Lion	2-6
57	Lebeqs Tavern Courage	v	Lakeside Athletic	0-2
58	Windmill	v	Downend	3-0
59	Sporting Bristol	v	Wonford United	1-2
60	Springers	v	C.K.	4-0
61	Ashton	v	Bluebird United	3-6
62	Applebys	v	Hanham Sunday	1-11

Clubs exempt to 2nd Rd
Hetton Lyons Cricket Club
Magnet Tavern

SECOND ROUND

1	West Bowling	v	Mariners	2-5
2	Sunderland RCA Barnes	v	Derby Lane Gym	2-0
3	Dawdon Colliery Welfare	v	Paddock	0-3
4	Kelloe WMC	v	Oyster Martyrs	2-3
5	Alder	v	Tower	4-2
6	Salisbury Athletic	v	Poulton Royal	0-0aet
	(Salisbury Athletic won 4-2 on kicks from the penalty mark)			
7	Huddersfield Irish Centre	v	Hartlepool Lion Hillcarter	4-0
8	Hetton Lyons Cricket Club	v	Brow	4-1
9	Witton Park Rose & Crown	v	Queens Park (12/12)	0-2
	(tie reversed)			
10	JOB	v	Lobster	1-3
11	Fforde Grene	v	Sandstone	0-2
12	Home & Bargain	v	Eden Vale	2-2aet
	(Eden Vale won 4-3 on kicks from the penalty mark)			
13	Hundred Acre	v	The Blue Mugge	6-4
14	Loughborough Saints	v	Travellers	0-3
15	Belt Road	v	Birstall Stamford	2-3
16	AC Sportsman & R.	v	Loughborough Falcons	2-1
17	Clumber	v	Magnet Tavern	2-1
18	Kingshurst Sporting Club	v	Advance Couriers	2-0
19	FC Houghton Centre	v	Rumours	3-1
20	Club Lewsey	v	St Margarets	2-0
21	Silsoe Park Rangers	v	Northampton Duke Of York	0-4
22	AFC Donsville	v	The Lounge	2-3
23	Nicholas Wybacks	v	Golden Lion	1-3
24	North West Neasden	v	Comets Sports Club	1-4
25	Greengate	v	Bedfont Sunday	3-4
26	FC Tripimeni-Aris	v	Enfield Rangers	4-1
27	Belstone	v	Nirankari Stevenage	2-0
28	Offley Moat	v	Britannia United	1-4
29	Hanham Sunday	v	Lakeside Athletic	4-2
30	Springers	v	Wonford United	0-3
31	Windmill	v	Knighton Arms (28/11)	3-4
32	Bluebird United	v	Wrightchoice Comm Spts Ass	4-2

THIRD ROUND

1	Mariners	v	Alder (20/1)	4-0
	(tie reversed)			
2	Huddersfield Irish Centre	v	Oyster Martyrs (9/1)	3-5
	(tie reversed)			
3	Sunderland RCA Barnes	v	Sandstone (9/1)	2-0
	(tie reversed)			
4	Hetton Lyons CC	v	Paddock (9/1)	2-3
	(tie reversed)			
5	Eden Vale	v	Queens Park (9/1)	2-3aet
6	Lobster	v	Salisbury Athletic (23/1)	0-4
	(tie reversed)			
7	FC Houghton Centre	v	Travellers	1-5aet
8	Comets SC	v	Clumber	4-4aet

(Comets SC won 4-3 on kicks from the penalty mark)

9	The Lounge	v	Britannia United	0-3
10	Belstone	v	Birstall Stamford	2-0
11	Hundred Acre	v	Kingshurst Sporting Club (9/1)	2-3aet
12	Golden Lion	v	Club Lewsey	2-8
13	Bedfont Sunday	v	AC Sportsman & Ravensborough	2-0aet
14	FC Tripimeni-Aris	v	Northampton Duke of York	0-1
15	Knighton Arms	v	Hanham Sunday	2-1
16	Wonford United	v	Bluebird United (9/1)	3-1

FOURTH ROUND

1	Salisbury Athletic	v	Mariners (13/2)	2-3
2	Oyster Martyrs	v	Sunderland RCA Barnes	7-1
3	Queens Park	v	Paddock	1-2
4	Northampton Duke Of York	v	Travellers	2-1
5	Comets SC	v	Belstone	3-1
6	Club Lewsey	v	Kingshurst Sporting Club	3-1
7	Bedfont Sunday	v	Wonford United	2-1
8	Britannia United	v	Knighton Arms	0-4

FIFTH ROUND

1	Oyster Martyrs	v	Club Lewsey	1-0
2	Mariners	v	Northampton Duke Of York	1-2
3	Knighton Arms	v	Paddock	1-4
4	Bedfont Sunday	v	Comets SC	1-2

SEMI FINALS

1	Paddock (Liverpool & District)	v	Comets SC (Berkhamsted)	4-1	346
	At Marine FC, The Arriva Stadium				
2	Northampton Duke Of York (Northamptonshire Sunday Combination)	v	Oyster Martyrs (Liverpool & District)	0-3	384
	At Rushden & Diamonds FC, Nene Park				

THE FINAL

SUNDAY 1 MAY 2011 – 2.00pm

OYSTER MARTYRS	v	PADDOCK	1-0	1105

AT TRANMERE ROVERS FC

NATIONAL LEAGUE SYSTEMS CUP

PRELIMINARY ROUND

Gloucestershire County League	v	Mid Sussex League	4-0
Liverpool County FA Premier Lge	v	Teesside League	2-1
Sussex County League (Div 3)	v	Brighton Hove & District League	5-0
Manchester League	v	Wearside League	2-1
Amateur Football Combination	v	Surrey Elite Intermediate League	1 - 2
Northern Football Alliance	v	Lancashire & Cheshire Am Lge	2 - 2
Northern Football Alliance won 3-1 on kicks from the penalty mark			
Middlesex County League	v	Herts Senior County League	3-3
Herts Senior County League won 5-4 on kicks from the penalty mark			
Reading League	v	Kent County League	1-1
Reading League won 6-5 on kicks from the penalty mark			
Lancashire Amateur League	v	Isle of Man League	1-3
Northamptonshire Combination	v	Cambridgeshire County League	1-2
Anglian Combination	v	Nottinghamshire Senior League	
walkover for Anglian Combination - Nottinghamshire Senior League withdrawn			
Suffolk & Ipswich League	v	Bedfordshire County League	4-0
Peterborough & District League	v	Lincolnshire League	1-2
Worthing & District League	v	Somerset County League	3-4
Birmingham & District AFA	v	West Riding County Amateur Lge	0-2
Dorset Premier League	v	Hampshire Premier League	2-2
Dorset Premier League won 5-4 on kicks from the penalty mark			

FIRST ROUND

SATURDAY 15TH OCTOBER 2011

1	Manchester League	v	Cheshire League
2	Cumberland County Lge	v	Liverpool County FA Premier League
3	Northern Football Alliance	v	Yorkshire Amateur League
4	West Cheshire League	v	Isle of Man League
5	Northampton Town Lge	v	Cambridgeshire County League
6	Lincolnshire League	v	Anglian Combination
7	West Yorkshire League	v	Humber Premier League
8	West Riding County Am.	v	Midland Football Combination (Div 1)
9	Jersey Football Comb.	v	Gloucestershire County League
10	Somerset County League	v	Dorset Premier League
11	Devon & Exeter League	v	Guernsey Senior County League
12	Sussex County Lge (Div 3)	v	Wiltshire League
13	Spartan South Mid. (Div 2)	v	Southern Amateur League
14	Surrey Elite Intermediate	v	Essex & Suffolk Border League
15	Suffolk & Ipswich League	v	Reading League
16	Essex Olympian League	v	Herts Senior County League

UEFA REGIONS CUP GROUP A

Croatia (Dalmatian Region)	v	England (Guernsey Co. Sen Lge)	1-1
England	v	Wales (Gwent County League)	3-0
England	v	Turkey (Ankara)	0-3

FINAL TABLE	P	W	D	L	F	A	PTS	GD
Turkey (Ankara)	3	2	1	0	7	1	7	3
Croatia (Dalmacija)	3	1	2	0	7	3	4	4
ENGLAND (Guernsey)	**3**	**1**	**1**	**1**	**4**	**4**	**4**	**0**
Wales (Gwent County)	3	0	0	3	3	13	0	-10

FIRST QUALIFYING ROUND

1	Rutherford Ravens	v	Gateshead Cleveland Hall (10/10)	2-5
2	Seaton Carew JFC	v	Forest Hall Women's YPC (10/10)	0-1
3	California Ladies	v	Ashington CFC Ladies (10/10)	2-1
4	Prudhoe Youth Club	v	Percy Main Ladies	1-6
5	North Shields Ladies	v	York City	0-11
6	Lumley Ladies	v	Walker Central	
	(walkover for Lumley Ladies – Walker Central removed)			
7	Norton & Stockton Ancients	v	Birtley Town Ladies (10/10)	2-1
8	St Francis 2000 Ladies	v	Tynedale Ladies (10/10)	2-2aet
	(Tynedale Ladies won 5-4 on kicks from the penalty mark)			
9	Accrington Girls & Ladies	v	Chester City (10/10)	1-3
10	Kendal Town	v	Morecambe Ladies	1-9
11	Middleton Athletic	v	Crown Newlaithes (10/10)	9-0
12	Abbeytown Women's	v	Dalton Girls & Ladies	1-3
13	Kirklees	v	Bradford Park Avenue (10/10)	6-1
14	Hemsworth MW	v	Steel City Wanderers (10/10)	0-3
	(at Hemsworth MW FC)			
15	Asfordby Amateurs Ladies	v	Friar Lane & Epworth	0-5
16	Market Warsop	v	Retford United	3-0
17	Huntingdon Town Ladies	v	Mansfield Town	0-4
18	Tipton Town Ladies	v	Rugby Town	1-1aet
	(Rugby Town won 4-1 on kicks from the penalty mark)			
19	Crusaders Ladies	v	AFC Telford United Ladies	5-0
20	Redditch United Women's	v	Silverdale (10/10)	4-5
21	Stalham Town Ladies	v	Bungay Town	0-5
22	Rothwell Town	v	Leighton United Vixens	2-0
23	AFC Trinity Ladies	v	Brackley Sports	6-3
24	Thorplands United	v	Brandon Ladies	2-7
25	Stevenage Borough	v	Whitwell Ladies	4-0
26	Leverstock Green	v	Hemel Hempstead Town	1-2
27	C&K Basildon	v	Colchester Town	1-2
28	Runwell Hospital	v	Barking	0-4
29	Tring Athletic	v	Brentwood Town	0-1
30	Billericay Town	v	Hoddesdon Owls	2-0
31	Hannakins Ladies	v	St Albans City Ladies	3-2
32	Hampstead	v	Leyton Ladies	5-1
33	Wandgas	v	Haringey Borough (10/10)	3-3aet
	(Haringey Borough won 4-2 on kicks from the penalty mark)			
34	AFC Wimbledon Ladies	v	Victoire Ladies	8-0
35	Seahaven Harriers Ladies & Girls	v	Rottingdean Village	5-2
36	Christchurch	v	New Forest Ladies (10/10)	2-4
37	University Of Portsmouth	v	Crawley Wasps	5-2aet
38	Boscombe Albion	v	Andover New Street	0-11
39	Henley Town	v	Maidenhead United Ladies (10/10)	0-2
40	Bitton Ladies	v	Reading Girls	
	(walkover for Bitton Ladies – Reading Girls withdrawn)			
41	Marlow Ladies	v	Reading Town	0-7
42	Forest Of Dean	v	Stony Stratford Town (10/10)	1-2
43	Swindon Spitfires	v	Swindon Supermarine Ladies	2-2aet
	(Swindon Spitfires won 5-4 on kicks from the penalty mark)			
44	Ilminster Town	v	Launceston	2-1
45	Exeter City	v	Keynsham Town Development (10/10)	1-2
	(at Exeter City FC)			
46	Weymouth Ladies	v	Winscombe	
	(walkover for Weymouth Ladies – Winscombe withdrawn)			
47	Purbeck Ladies	v	Marine Academy Plymouth	2-6

SECOND QUALIFYING ROUND

1	Peterlee Town	v	Brandon United	5-1
2	Lumley Ladies	v	Redcar Athletic	5-1
3	Percy Main Ladies	v	Forest Hall Women's YPC	4-2
4	Teesside Sport	v	Gateshead Cleveland Hall	4-2
5	Norton & Stockton Ancients	v	Tynedale Ladies	2-1
6	York City	v	Whitley Bay Women	2-6
7	Durham City	v	California Ladies	6-2
8	Whitehaven Ladies	v	Birkenhead Ladies	2-4
9	Dalton Girls&Ladies	v	Middleton Athletic	3-5aet
10	Warrington Town	v	Blackpool Wren Rovers	1-4
11	Morecambe Ladies	v	Bolton Wanderers	8-0
12	Crewe Alexandra	v	Chester City	1-0
13	Penrith Ladies	v	Blackpool Girls & Ladies	3-2
14	Huddersfield Town	v	Hull City	5-4aet
15	Barnsley	v	Steel City Wanderers	2-0
16	Sheffield Utd Community	v	Kirklees	6-0
17	Guiseley Ladies	v	Ossett Albion	2-1aet
18	Oadby & Wigston Girls & Ladies	v	Sandiacre Town	
	(walkover for Sandiacre Town – Oadby & Wigston Girls & Ladies withdrawn)			
19	Long Eaton United	v	Mansfield Town	1-1aet
	(Mansfield Town won 5-4 on kicks from the penalty mark)			
20	Peterborough	v	Hucknall Town	
	(walkover for Peterborough – Hucknall Town withdrawn)			
21	Market Warsop	v	West Bridgford	2-1
22	Peterborough Azure	v	Friar Lane & Epworth	
	(walkover for Friar Lane & Epworth – Peterborough Azure failed to fulfil fixture)			
23	Loughborough Foxes	v	Shepshed Dynamo	1-0
24	Hereford Pegasus	v	Cottage Farm Rangers	0-2
25	Bedworth United	v	Silverdale	4-3
26	Southam United	v	Stafford Town Ladies	1-3
27	Crusaders Ladies	v	Walsall	2-3
28	Solihull Ladies	v	Rugby Town	11-0
29	Stratford Town	v	Lichfield Diamonds	2-0
30	Hethersett Athletic	v	Cambridge University	4-4aet
	(Cambridge University won 4-3 on kicks from the penalty mark)			
31	Fakenham Town	v	Arlesey Town Ladies	1-2aet
32	Thorpe United	v	Bungay Town	5-1
33	Haverhill Rovers	v	Woodbridge Town	1-5
34	Daventry Town	v	Brandon Ladies	8-2
35	Corby S&L	v	AFC Trinity Ladies (31/10)	4-2
36	Kingsthorpe Ladies & Girls	v	Rothwell Town	1-8
37	Raunds Town	v	Kettering Town	1-8
38	Hutton Ladies	v	Brentwood Town	2-3
39	Barking	v	Colchester Town	3-2
40	Hannakins Ladies	v	Sawbridgeworth Town	2-1
41	Hemel Hempstead Town	v	Boreham Wood Ladies	2-1
42	Billericay Town	v	Stevenage Borough	1-1aet
	(Billericay Town won 3-1 on kicks from the penalty mark)			
43	Chelmsford City	v	Royston Town	
	(walkover for Chelmsford City – Royston Town failed to fulfil fixture)			
44	Panthers	v	AFC Wimbledon Ladies	6-1
45	MSA Ladies	v	Haringey Borough	2-0
46	Denham United	v	Hampstead	5-0
47	Westfield Ladies	v	Dorking	9-1
48	Ramsgate	v	London Corinthians	1-4
49	Milton & Falston United	v	Maidstone Town	1-5

50	Bexhill United	v	Seahaven Harriers Ladies & Girls	1-4
51	Eastbourne Borough	v	Eastbourne Town	1-7
52	Shanklin	v	Andover New Street	1-3
53	Aldershot Town	v	University Of Portsmouth	1-1aet
	(Aldershot Town won 3-1 on kicks from the penalty mark)			
54	Chichester City	v	New Forest Ladies	3-0
55	East Preston & Littleh. L	v	Haywards Heath Town	5-2
56	Banbury United	v	Cheltenham Town Ladies	0-4
57	Beaconsfield SYCOB	v	Launton	3-4
58	Stony Stratford Town	v	Bitton Ladies	
	(walkover for Bitton – Stony Strartford Town withdrawn)			
59	Oxford United	v	Maidenhead United Ladies	1-2
60	Bracknell Town	v	Newbury Ladies	5-0
61	Swindon Spitfires	v	Salisbury City	3-4aet
62	Stoke Lane Athletic	v	Reading Town	5-0
63	Keynsham Town Dev.	v	Falmouth Town Ladies	5-1
64	Ilminster Town	v	Poole Town	3-1
65	Marjon Old Suttonians	v	Marine Academy Plymouth	0-2aet
66	Larkhall Athletic	v	Taunton Town	5-1
67	Frome Town	v	Weymouth Ladies	1-3

THIRD QUALIFYING ROUND

1	Birkenhead Ladies	v	Salford Ladies	1-2
2	Middleton Athletic	v	Teesside Sport	3-1
3	Blackpool Wren Rovers	v	Durham City (21/11)	4-1
	(at Blackpool Wren Rovers FC)			
4	South Durham Railway Ath.	v	Crewe Alexandra	2-2aet
	(South Durham RA won 4-3 on kicks from the penalty mark)			
5	Percy Main Ladies	v	Liverpool Feds	0-7
6	Middlesbrough	v	Lumley Ladies	5-1aet
7	Whitley Bay Women	v	Tranmere Rovers	2-1
8	Stockport County	v	Norton & Stockton Ancients	4-0
9	Mossley Hill	v	Peterlee Town	4-3
10	Morecambe Ladies	v	Penrith Ladies	4-3
11	Sheffield Ladies	v	Bradford City	2-0
12	Rotherham United	v	Wakefield Ladies	3-1
13	Guiseley Ladies	v	Sheffield United Community	1-3
14	Barnsley	v	Scunthorpe United	3-2
15	Huddersfield Town	v	Sheffield Wednesday Women	1-5
16	Sporting Club Albion	v	Market Warsop	12-0
17	Loughborough Foxes	v	Leafield Athletic	2-4
18	Solihull Ladies	v	Walsall	6-1
19	MK Dons	v	Wolverhampton Wanderers	2-2aet
	(Wolverhampton Wanderers won 5-3 on kicks from the penalty mark)			
20	Stratford Town	v	Sandiacre Town	6-3
21	Leicester City Ladies	v	TNS Ladies	5-0
22	Stafford Town Ladies	v	Stoke City	1-8
23	Radcliffe Olympic	v	Mansfield Town	2-1
24	Peterborough	v	Bedworth United	3-1
25	Cottage Farm Rangers	v	Copsewood (Coventry)	0-8
26	Friar Lane & Epworth	v	Loughborough Students	1-7
27	Cambridge Women's	v	Braintree Town	4-0
28	Luton Town Ladies	v	Rothwell Town (21/11)	7-0
	(at Stockwood Park Athletics Stadium, Luton)			
29	Thorpe United	v	Cambridge University	0-3
30	Kettering Town	v	Woodbridge Town	0-1
31	Daventry Town	v	Corby S&L	3-2aet
32	Northampton Town	v	Ipswich Town	3-3aet
	(Ipswich Town won 5-4 on kicks from the penalty mark)			
33	Norwich City Ladies	v	Arlesey Town Ladies	5-1
34	Chelmsford City	v	Barking	2-2aet
	(Chelmsford City won 6-5 on kicks from the penalty mark)			
35	Brentwood Town	v	Tottenham Hotspur	1-4
36	Billericay Town	v	Enfield Town	1-5
37	Panthers	v	MSA Ladies	5-1
38	Hannakins Ladies	v	Denham United	0-4
39	Old Actonians	v	Hemel Hempstead Town	1-2
40	East Preston & L. L.	v	Westfield Ladies (21/11)	2-1
	(at East Preston FC)			
41	Seahaven Harriers L.G.	v	Ebbsfleet United (21/11)	1-4
	(at Seaford FC)			
	(14/11 tie abandoned after 5 mins due to waterlogged pitch, 0-0)			
42	London Corinthians	v	Crystal Palace	0-1
43	Lewes	v	Chichester City	5-1
44	Aldershot Town	v	Havant & Waterlooville	0-8
45	Maidstone Town	v	Eastbourne Town	3-1
46	Bracknell Town	v	Cheltenham Town Ladies	2-0
47	Forest Green Rovers	v	Swindon Town	7-2
48	Salisbury City	v	Andover New Street	3-5
49	Maidenhead United Ladies	v	Oxford City	3-4
50	Chesham United	v	Launton	8-0
51	Southampton Saints	v	Gloucester City	3-1
52	Plymouth Argyle	v	Bitton Ladies	6-0
53	Cullompton Ladies	v	Marine Academy Plymouth (21/11)	4-1
	(at Cummompton Rangers FC)			
54	Newquay Ladies	v	Ilminster Town	
	(walkover for Newquay Ladies – Ilminster Town failed to fulfil fixture)			
55	Stoke Lane Athletic	v	Weymouth Ladies	0-1
56	Keynsham Town Dev.	v	Larkhall Athletic	1-2

FIRST ROUND

1	Blackpool Wren Rovers	v	Salford Ladies (9/1)	2-1
	(tie reversed)			
2	Middleton Athletic	v	Whitley Bay Women (2/1)	1-2
	(tie reversed)			
3	Middlesbrough	v	Stockport County (2/1)	2-0
	(tie reversed)			
4	Mossley Hill	v	South Durham Railway Athletic	2-0
5	Liverpool Feds	v	Morecambe Ladies (2/1)	4-3
	(tie reversed)			
6	Loughborough Students	v	Leafield Athletic	5-2
7	Barnsley	v	Sheffield Ladies (16/1)	0-2
	(tie reversed – at Sheffield FC)			
8	Sheffield Utd Community	v	Stoke City (2/1)	3-4
	(tie reversed)			
9	Wolverhampton Wanderers	v	Solihull Ladies (2/1)	4-0
10	Stratford Town	v	Sheffield Wednesday Women	1-2
11	Radcliffe Olympic	v	Sporting Club Albion (2/1)	0-3
12	Daventry Town	v	Rotherham United (2/1)	1-11
	(tie reversed)			
13	Copsewood (Coventry)	v	Leicester City Ladies	0-2
14	Ipswich Town	v	Cambridge Women's	1-2
15	Peterborough	v	Hemel Hempstead Town	2-3
16	Norwich City Ladies	v	Cambridge University (2/1)	6-1
	(tie reversed)			
17	Tottenham Hotspur	v	Chelmsford City	5-0
18	Luton Town Ladies	v	Woodbridge Town	4-1

First Round continued....

19	Crystal Palace	v	Panthers (2/1)	6-0
	(tie reversed)			
20	Ebbsfleet United	v	Maidstone Town (2/1)	3-0
	(tie reversed)			
21	Enfield Town	v	Lewes	2-1
22	Chesham United	v	Denham United	1-2
23	East Preston & L.L	v	Havant & Waterlooville	0-5
24	Newquay Ladies	v	Weymouth Ladies	4-2
25	Oxford City	v	Plymouth Argyle	1-3
26	Forest Green Rovers	v	Andover New Street	5-5aet
	(Andover New Street won 3-2 on kicks from the penalty mark)			
27	Larkhall Athletic	v	Southampton Saints (2/1)	1-3
	(tie reversed)			
28	Cullompton Ladies	v	Bracknell Town	4-2

SECOND ROUND

1	Blackpool Wren Rovers	v	Sheffield Wednesday Women (23/1)	0-6
	(at Blackpool Rovers FC)			
2	Manchester City	v	Mossley Hill	2-3aet
3	Rochdale AFC Ladies	v	Preston North End (23/1)	3-1
	(tie reversed – at Uclan Sports Arena, Preston)			
4	Newcastle United	v	Liverpool Feds (16/1)	2-0
5	Whitley Bay Women	v	Leeds City Vixens	1-2
6	Curzon Ashton	v	Middlesbrough	4-1
7	Stoke City	v	Cambridge Women's	3-3aet
	(Cambridge Women won 4-3 on kicks from the penalty mark)			
8	Derby County	v	Rotherham United	4-2
9	Sheffield Ladies	v	Loughborough Students (23/1)	1-2
10	Leicester City	v	Leicester City Ladies	5-1
11	Wolverhampton W.	v	Coventry City	2-3aet
12	Aston Villa	v	Sporting Club Albion	0-2
13	Tottenham Hotspur	v	Colchester United (16/1)	1-2
14	Ebbsfleet United	v	Gillingham	0-6
15	Havant & Waterlooville	v	Enfield Town	1-2aet
16	Portsmouth	v	Crystal Palace	6-1
17	West Ham United	v	Norwich City Ladies	4-1
18	Hemel Hempstead Town	v	Brighton & Hove Albion	3-3aet
	(Brighton&Hove Albion won 3-1 on kicks from the penalty mark)			
19	Denham United	v	Charlton Athletic	0-8
20	Luton Town Ladies	v	Queens Park Rangers	2-1aet
21	Southampton Saints	v	Keynsham Town	1-0
22	Yeovil Town	v	Cardiff City	0-1
23	Newquay Ladies	v	Plymouth Argyle	2-1
	(tie awarded to Plymouth Argyle – Newquay Ladies removed)			
24	Cullompton Rangers L.	v	Andover New Street (23/1)	1-6
	(tie reversed - at Andover New Street FC)			
32	Bluebird United	v	Wrightchoice Comm Spts Ass	4-2

THIRD ROUND

1	Sporting Club Albion	v	Millwall Lionesses	0-4
2	Coventry City	v	Rochdale AFC Ladies	1-2
3	Nottingham Forest	v	Leicester City	4-2
4	Curzon Ashton	v	Charlton Athletic	1-3
5	Gillingham	v	Reading FC Women	3-5
6	Derby County	v	Plymouth Argyle	2-0
7	Leeds United Ladies	v	Blackburn Rovers	0-0aet
	(Blackburn Rovers won 5-4 on kicks from the penalty mark)			
8	Colchester United	v	Newcastle United	2-1
9	Sunderland	v	Portsmouth	7-2
10	Andover New Street	v	Watford	2-3
11	Cardiff City	v	Sheffield Wednesday Women	1-2
12	Loughborough Students	v	Barnet FC Ladies	0-4
13	West Ham United	v	Brighton & Hove Albion	1-0
14	Cambridge Women's	v	Leeds City Vixens	0-3
15	Southampton Saints	v	Enfield Town	0-1
16	Mossley Hill	v	Luton Town Ladies	3-2

FOURTH ROUND

1	Enfield Town	v	Mossley Hill	4-2
2	Blackburn Rovers	v	Millwall Lionesses	0-3
3	Derby County	v	Sunderland (6/3)	0-0aet
	(Sunderland won 4-2 on kicks from the penalty mark)			
4	Reading FC Women	v	Charlton Athletic	2-2aet
	(Charlton Athletic won 5-4 on kicks from the penalty mark)			
5	Leeds City Vixens	v	Barnet FC Ladies	0-1
6	Nottingham Forest	v	Watford (6/3)	3-3aet
	(Watford won 4-3 on kicks from the penalty mark)			
7	West Ham United	v	Colchester United (6/3)	4-2
8	Rochdale FC Ladies	v	Sheffield Wednesday Women	1-3

FIFTH ROUND

1	Enfield Town	v	West Ham United	0-1
2	Sheffield Wednesday W.	v	Bristol Academy	0-8
3	Liverpool	v	Charlton Athletic	5-0
4	Birmingham City	v	Barnet FC Ladies	1-2
5	Everton	v	Arsenal	0-2
6	Chelsea	v	Doncaster Rovers Belles	0-1
7	Sunderland	v	Lincoln Ladies	1-0
8	Millwall Lionesses	v	Watford	5-0

SIXTH ROUND

1	Sunderland	v	Arsenal	2-3aet
2	Millwall Lionesses	v	Bristol Academy	1-2
3	Liverpool	v	Doncaster Rovers Belles	3-0
4	Barnet FC Ladies	v	West Ham United	3-2aet

SEMI FINALS

SUNDAY 17 APRIL 2011

1	Liverpool	v	Bristol Academy	0-3	224
	At Southport FC				

SUNDAY 24 APRIL 2010

2	Barnet FC Ladies	v	Arsenal	0-5	502
	At Uxbridge FC				

THE FINAL

SATURDAY 21 MAY 2011

ARSENAL	v	BRISTOL ACADEMY	2-0	13885

AT RICOH ARENA, COVENTRY

THE FINALS

MEN'S COMPITITION

GROUP A	P	W	D	L	F	A	PTS	GD
1 Sheffield Futsal Club	3	3	0	0	17	4	9	13
2 Passlona	3	2	0	1	15	10	6	5
3 Futsal Club Enfield	3	1	0	2	9	18	3	-9
4 Team Bath	3	0	0	3	7	16	0	-9

GROUP B	P	W	D	L	F	A	PTS	GD
1 Team United Birmingham	3	3	0	0	11	2	9	9
2 Kickers FC	3	2	0	1	19	5	6	14
3 Loughborough University	3	1	0	2	5	6	3	-1
4 Stoke on Trent College	3	0	0	3	2	24	0	-22

GROUP C	P	W	D	L	F	A	PTS	GD
1 Helvecia FC	3	3	0	0	16	7	9	9
2 Leeds Futsal Club	3	2	0	1	7	5	6	2
3 Futsal 5	3	1	0	2	6	8	3	-2
4 Liverpool Futsal Club	3	0	0	3	2	11	0	-9

GROUP D	P	W	D	L	F	A	PTS	GD
1 Manchester Futsal Club	3	2	1	0	24	2	7	22
2 FC Baltic	3	2	1	0	13	4	7	9
3 London United Futsal Club	3	1	0	0	9	10	3	-1
4 Team Northumbria	3	0	0	3	5	35	0	-30

QUARTER-FINALS

1	Sheffield Futsal Club	v	FC Baltic	0-1
2	Team United Birmingham	v	Leeds Futsal Club	3-5
3	Helvecia FC	v	Kickers FC	7-1
4	Manchester Futsal Club	v	Passiona	2-1

SEMI-FINALS

1	Helvecia FC	v	Manchester Futsal Club	0-1
2	FC Baltic	v	Leeds Futsal Club	1-1*, 5-4p

THE FINAL

FC Baltic	v	Manchester Futsal Club	2-5

GOLDEN BOOT

Daniel Haralambous Manchester Futsal Club	9
Jose De Souza Leeds Futsal Club	8
Emmanuel Gueyes Team United Birmingham	6
Robert Ursell Helvecia	6

PREVIOUS WINNERS

2003 – Sheffield & Hallamshire
2004 – Team USSR
2005 – Doncaster College for the Deaf
2006 – London White Bear
2007 – Ipswich Wolves FC
2008 – Helvecia
2009 – Helvecia
2010 – Helvecia

WOMEN'S COMPITITION

GROUP A	P	W	D	L	F	A	PTS	GD
1 Team Bath Ladies	3	3	0	0	14	1	9	13
2 Midland Mix	3	2	0	1	14	8	6	6
3 Hereford Futsal Club Ladies	3	1	0	0	13	14	3	-1
4 Pro5 Ladies	3	0	0	3	5	23	0	-18

GROUP B	P	W	D	L	F	A	PTS	GD
1 Team Utd Birmingham Ladies	3	3	0	0	23	2	9	21
2 Reading Futsal Club	3	2	0	1	23	4	6	19
3 Westside	3	1	0	2	6	15	3	-9
4 FC Enfield Ladies	3	0	0	3	3	34	0	-31

GROUP C	P	W	D	L	F	A	PTS	GD
1 City Utd Ladies Futsal Club	3	3	0	0	24	8	9	16
2 Cardiff City FC	3	2	0	1	13	9	6	4
3 Haringey Ladies FC	3	1	0	2	8	18	3	-10
4 Brazil Ladies	3	0	0	3	10	20	0	-10

QUARTER-FINALS

1	Cardiff City FC	v	Team Bath Ladies	1-2
2	Team Utd Birmingham L.	v	Hereford Futsal Club Ladies	3-1
3	City United Ladies FC	v	Westside	5-2
4	Reading Futsal Club	v	Midland Mix	

SEMI-FINALS

1	Team Utd Birmingham L.	v	Team Bath Ladies	2-0
2	City United Ladies	v	Reading Futsal Club	0-7

THE FINAL

Reading Futsal Club	v	Team United Birmingham Ladies	5-3

GOLDEN BOOT

Nikki Watts Reading Futsal Club	15
Jemma Connor - Iommi Team United Birmingham	11
Amy Wathan Cardiff City FC	10
Christina Torkildsen City United Ladies	9

PREVIOUS WINNERS

2007 – Watford Ladies
2008 – Doncaster Rovers Belles
2009 – Watford Ladies
2010 – Team Bath Ladies

ENGLAND FUTSAL RESULTS 2010-11

F	Macedonia	v	England	L	4-0
F	Macedonia	v	Enlgand	L	5-1
F	England	v	Andorra	**W**	3-1
F	England	v	Andorra	**W**	5-0
EC	Macedonia	v	England	L	3-1
EC	England	v	Georgia	L	0-4
EC	Estonia	v	England	**W**	2-3
F	Enlgand	v	Montenegro	L	2-4
F	Enlgand	v	Montenegro	**W**	2-1
F	England	v	Greece	D	1-1
F	Enlgand	v	Greece	L	1-6

F - Friendly. EC - European Championship - Preliminary Qualifying Rounds.

THE FINALS - at WEMBLEY STADIUM

MEN'S COMPITITION

GROUP C		PTS	GD
1	Halifax	12	5
2	Wanted	7	3
3	Pro Evo	7	2
4	Corinthians	3	-3
5	Lucky Break	0	-7

GROUP D		PTS	GD
1	MDU	10	6
2	Raj United	7	8
3	St Thomas Spartans	5	-1
4	Allstarz	3	-3
5	Quilligans Café Bar	3	-10

GROUP E		PTS	GD
1	Top Draw	12	10
2	Team SMG	9	4
3	James King FC	6	1
4	FIFA 11	3	-7
5	2 Jugs	0	-8

GROUP F		PTS	GD
1	International	10	5
2	Thanks for Coming	7	3
3	Real Fox	4	-1
4	AC Warriors	4	-3
5	Deepdale La Coruna	3	-4

QUARTER-FINALS

1	Halifax	v	Thanks for Coming	4-2*
2	MDU	v	Team SMG	5-2
3	Top Draw	v	Raj United	6-3
4	International	v	Wanted	3-0

SEMI-FINALS

1	Halifax	v	MDU	0-2
2	Top Draw	v	International	4-0

THE FINAL

MDU v Top Draw 4-2*

LUCKY 8'S FINAL

Scouting for Goals v Mevan 6-0

CORPORATE CUP FINAL

PlayFootball v Goals 7-1

Action from the finals played at Wembley Stadium, here we see Bideford and Loddiswell Athletic's Nick Barker (stripes) being challenged for the ball.

WOMEN'S COMPITITION

GROUP A		PTS	GD
1	Adelaide City	12	8
2	The Poly	9	13
3	Cheltenham Town	6	-8
4	Pro 5	3	-7
5	Tiny Tempers	0	-6

GROUP B		PTS	GD
1	Newcastle Utd Blues	7	6
2	Hardly Athletic	5	1
3	Kukri Birmingham	4	-2
4	Jan FC	0	-5

SEMI-FINALS

1	Adelaide City	v	Hardly Athletic	0-1
2	Newcastle United Blues	v	The Poly	3-1

THE FINAL

Hardly Athletic v Newcastle United Blues 0-1

CORPORATE CHALLENGE FINAL

FA Ladies beat Umbro Ladies

COUNTY FOOTBALL ASSOCIATIONS

BEDFORDSHIRE F.A.

Tel: 01582 565 111 Fax: 01582 565 222

Email: info@bedfordshirefa.com

Century House, Skimpot Road,

Dunstable, Bedfordshire LU5 4JU

Chief Executive: Peter D Brown.

BERKS & BUCKS F.A.

Tel: 01367 242 099 Fax: 01367 242 158

Email: info@berks-bucksfa.com

15a London Street, Faringdon,

Oxon SN7 7HD

Chief Executive: Brian Moore

BIRMINGHAM COUNTY F.A.

Tel: 0121 357 4278 Fax: 0121 358 1661

Email: info@birminghamfa.com

Ray Hall Lane, Great Barr, Birmingham

B43 6JF

Chief Executive: Mike Pennick

CAMBRIDGESHIRE F.A.

Tel: 01223 209 020 Fax: 01223 209 030

Email: info@cambridgeshirefa.com

Bridge Road, Impington, Cambridgeshire

CB24 9PH

Chief Executive: Chris Pringle

CHESHIRE F.A.

Tel: 01606 871 166 Fax: 01606 871 292

Email: info@cheshirefa.com

Hartford House, Hartford Moss Rec. Centre,

Winnington, Northwich CW8 4BG

Chief Executive: Ms Maureen Dunford

CORNWALL F.A.

Tel: 01208 269 010 Fax: 01208 892 665

Email: secretary@cornwallfa.com

Kernow House, 15 Callywith Gate

Launceston Road, Bodmin

Cornwall PL31 2RQ

Secretary: Barry Cudmore

CUMBERLAND F.A.

Tel: 01900 872 310 Fax: 01900 616 470

Email: secretary@cumberlandfa.com

17 Oxford Street, Workington, Cumbria,

CA14 2AL

Chief Executive: Geoff Turrell.

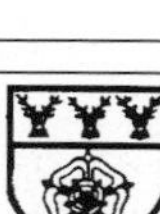

DERBYSHIRE F.A.

Tel: 01332 361 422 Fax: 01332 360 130

Email: info@derbyshirefa.com

Units 8-9 Stadium Business Court,

Millennium Way, Pride Park, Derby DE24 8HP

Chief Executive: Miss Dawn Heron.

DEVON F.A.

Tel: 01626 332 077 Fax: 01626 336 814

Email: info@devonfa.com

County Headquarters, Coach Road,

Newton Abbot, Devon TQ12 1EJ

Chief Executive: Paul Morrison.

DORSET F.A.

Tel: 01202 682 375 Fax: 01202 666 577

Email: sue.hough@dorsetfa.com

County Ground, Blandford Close,

Hamworthy, Poole BH15 4BF

Chief Executive: Sue Hough.

DURHAM F.A.

Tel: 0191 387 2929

Email: info@durhamfa.com

'Codeslaw', Riverside South,

Chester le Street, Co.Durham DH3 3SJ

Secretary: John Topping.

EAST RIDING F.A.

Tel: 01482 221 158 Fax: 01482 221 169

Email: info@eastridingfa.com

Roy West Centre, 220 Inglemire Lane,

Hull HU6 7TS

Chief Executive: Adam Lowthorpe.

ESSEX F.A.

Tel: 01245 465 271 Fax: 01245 393 089

Email: info@essexfa.com

The County Office, Springfield Lyons Approach,

Springfield, Chelmsford CM2 5LB

Chief Executive: Phil Sammons.

GLOUCESTERSHIRE F.A.

Tel: 01454 615 888 Fax: 01454 618 088

Email: info@gloucestershirefa.com

Oaklands Park, Almondsbury, Bristol

BS32 4AG

Chief Executive: David Neale.

HAMPSHIRE F.A.

Tel: 01256 853 000 Fax: 01256 357 973

Email: info@hampshirefa.com

Winklebury Football Complex,

Winklebury Way, Basingstoke RG23 8BF

Chief Executive: Neil Cassar.

HEREFORDSHIRE F.A.

Tel: 01432 342 179 Fax: 01432 279 265

Email: info@herefordshirefa.com

County Ground Offices,

Widemarsh Common, Hereford HR4 9NA

Chief Executive: Jim Lambert.

HERTFORDSHIRE F.A.

Tel: 01462 677 622 Fax: 01462 677 624

Email: info@hertfordshirefa.com

County Ground, Baldock Road, Letchworth,

Herts SG6 2EN

Chief Executive: Nick Perchard.

HUNTINGDONSHIRE F.A.

Tel: 01480 414 422 Fax: 01480 447 489

Email: info@huntsfa.com

Cromwell Chambers, 8 St Johns Street,

Huntingdon, Cambs PE29 3DD

Secretary: Mark Frost.

KENT F.A.

Tel: 01622 791 850 Fax: 01622 790 658

Email: info@kentfa.com

Invicta House, Cobdown Park,

London Road, Ditton, Nr Aylesford,

Kent ME20 6DQ

Chief Executive: Paul Dolan.

LANCASHIRE F.A.

Tel: 01772 624 000 Fax: 01772 624 700

Email: secretary@lancashirefa.com

The County Ground, Thurston Road, Leyland

PR25 2LF

Chief Executive: David Burgess.

LEICESTERSHIRE & RUTLAND F.A.

Tel: 0116 286 7828 Fax: 0116 286 4858

Email: info@leicestershirefa.com

Holmes Park, Dog & Gun Lane, Whetstone

LE8 6FA

Chief Executive: Laurence Jones.

LINCOLNSHIRE F.A.

Tel: 01522 524 917 Fax: 01522 528 859

Email: secretary@lincolnshirefa.com

Deepdale Enterprise Park, Deepdale Lane,

Nettleham, Lincs LN2 2LL

Secretary: John Griffin.

LIVERPOOL F.A.

Tel: 0151 523 4488 Fax: 0151 523 4477

Email: info@liverpoolfa.com

Liverpool Soccer Centre, Walton Hall Park,

Walton Hall Avenue, Liverpool L4 9XP

Secretary: David Pugh.

LONDON F.A.

Tel: 08707 743 010 Fax: 0207 610 8370

Email: info@londonfa.com

11 Hurlingham Business Park, Sulivan Road,

Fulham, London SW6 3DU

Chief Executive: David Fowkes.

MANCHESTER F.A.

Tel: 0161 604 7620 Fax: 0161 604 7622

Email: info@manchesterfa.com

Salford Sports Village, Littleton Road,

Lower Kersal, Salford, Manchester M7 3NQ

Chief Executive: Colin Bridgford

MIDDLESEX F.A.

Tel: 020 8515 1919 Fax: 020 8515 1910

Email: info@middlesexfa.com

39 Roxborough Road, Harrow, Middlesex

HA1 1NS

Chief Executive: Peter Clayton.

NORFOLK F.A.

Tel: 01603 704 050 Fax: 01603 704 059

Email: info@norfolkfa.com

11 Meridian Way, Thorpe St Andrew, Norwich

NR7 0TA

Chief Executive: Shaun Turner.

NORTH RIDING F.A.

Tel: 01642 717 770 Fax: 01642 717 776

Email: info@northridingfa.com

Broughton Road, Stokesley, Middlesbrough

TS9 5NY

Chief Executive: Tom Radigan.

NORTHAMPTONSHIRE F.A.

Tel: 01604 670 741 Fax: 01604 670 742

Email: info@northamptonshirefa.com

9 Duncan Close, Red House Square,

Moulton Park, Northampton NN3 6WL

Chief Executive: Kevin Shoemake.

NORTHUMBERLAND FOOTBALL ASSOCIATION

NORTHUMBERLAND F.A.

Tel/Fax: 0191 270 0700

Email: rowland.maughan@northumberlandfa.com

Whitley Park, Whitley Road,

Newcastle upon Tyne NE12 9FA

Chief Executive: Rowland E Maughan.

NOTTINGHAMSHIRE F.A.

Tel: 0115 983 7400 Fax: 0115 946 1977

Email: info@nottnghamshirefa.com

Unit 6b, Chetwynd Business Park,

Chilwell, Nottinghamshire NG9 6RZ

Chief Executive: Elaine Oram.

OXFORDSHIRE F.A.

Tel: 01993 894 400 Fax: 01993 772 191

Email: info@oxfordshirefa.com

Unit 3, Witan Park, Avenue 2, Station Lane,

Witney, Oxon OX28 4FH

Secretary: Ian Mason.

SHEFFIELD & HALLAMSHIRE F.A.

Tel: 0114 241 4999 Fax: 0114 241 4990

Email: info@sheffieldfa.com

Clegg House, 69 Cornish Place, Cornish St.,

Sheffield S6 3AF

Chief Executive: James Hope-Gill.

SHROPSHIRE F.A.

Tel: 01743 362 769 Fax: 01743 270 494

Email: secretary@shropshirefa.com

The New Stadium, Oteley Road,

Shrewsbury, Shropshire SY2 6ST

Chief Executive: David Rowe.

SOMERSET F.A.

Tel: 01458 832 359 Fax: 01458 835 588
Email: info@somersetfa.com
Charles Lewin House,
Unit 10 Landmark House,
Wirral Bus. Park, Glastonbury, Somerset
BA6 9FR
Chief Executive: Jon Pike.

STAFFORDSHIRE F.A.

Tel: 01785 256 994 Fax: 01785 279 837

Email: secretary@staffordshirefa.com

Dyson Court, Staffordshire Technology Park,

Beaconside, Stafford ST18 0LQ

Chief Executive: Brian Adshead.

SUFFOLK F.A.

Tel: 01449 616 606 Fax: 01449 616 607

Email: info@suffolkfa.com

The Buntings, Cedars Park, Stowmarket,

Suffolk IP14 5GZ

Chief Executive: Phil Knight.

SURREY F.A.

Tel: 01372 373 543 Fax: 01372 361 310

Email: info@surreyfa.com

Connaught House, 36 Bridge Street,

Leatherhead, Surrey KT22 8BZ

Secretary: Ray Ward.

SUSSEX F.A.

Tel: 01903 753 547 Fax: 01903 761 608

Email: info@sussexfa.com

Culver Road, Lancing, West Sussex

BN15 9AX

Chief Executive: Ken Benham.

WEST RIDING F.A.

Tel: 01132 821 222 Fax: 01132 821 525

Email: info@wrcfa.com

Fleet Lane, Woodlesford, Leeds

LS26 8NX

Chief Executive: Roy Carter.

WESTMORLAND F.A.

Tel: 01539 730 946 Fax: 01539 740 567

Email: info@westmorlandfa.com

Unit 1, Riverside Business Park, Natland Rd,

Kendal, Cumbria LA9 7SX

Chief Executive: Peter Ducksbury.

WILTSHIRE F.A.

Tel: 01793 486 047 Fax: 01793 692 699

Email: mike.benson@wiltshirefa.com

Units 2/3 Dorcan Business Village, Dorcan,

Swindon, Wiltshire SN3 5HY

Secretary: Mike Benson.

WORCESTERSHIRE F.A.

Tel: 01905 827 137 Fax: 01905 798 963

Email: info@worcestershirefa.com

Craftsman House, De Salis Drive,

Hampton Lovett Ind.Est., Droitwich WR9 0QE

Secretary: Mervyn Leggett.

ADDITIONAL FOOTBALL ASSOCIATIONS

AMATEUR FOOTBALL ALLIANCE
CEO: Mike Brown
Address: Unit 3, 7 Wenlock Road, London, N1 7SL Tel: 020 8733 2613 Fax: 020 7250 1338
Email: info@amateur-fa.com

ARMY FA
Secretary: Major Billy Thomson
Address: Ministry of Defence (ASCB), Clayton Barracks, Thornhill Road, Aldershot, Hampshire, GU11 2BG
Tel: 01252 348 571/4 Fax: 01252 348 630/b Email: info@armyfa.com

GUERNSEY FA
County Secretary: Mike Kinder
Address: GFA Headquarters, Corbet Field, Grand Fort Road, St Sampsons, Guernsey, GY2 4FG Tel: 01481 200 443
Fax: 01481 200 451 Email: info@guernseyfa.com

ISLE OF MAN FA
CEO: Frank Stennet
Address: Cromwell Chambers, 8 St John's Street, Huntingdon, PE29 3DD Tel: 01624 615 576 Fax: 01624 615 578
Email: ann.garrett@isleofmanfa.com

JERSEY FA
CEO: Paul Creeden
Address: Springfield Stadium, St Helier, Jersey, JE2 4LF Tel: 01534 449 765 Fax: 01534 500 029
Email: paul.creeden@jerseyfa.com

RAF FA
Secretary: Vince Williams
Address: RAF FA, RAF Brize Norton, Carterton, Oxfordshire, OX18 3LX Tel: 01993 895 559 Fax: 01993 897 752
Email: info@royalairforcefa.com

ROYAL NAVY FA
CEO: Lt Cdr Steve Vasey
Address: HMS Temeraire, Burnaby Road, Portsmouth, Hampshire, PO1 2HB Tel: 02392 722 671 Fax: 02932 724 923
Email: secretary@navyfa.com

Crawley Green after their Bedfordshire Senior Trophy success over Potton United.
Photo: Gordon Whittington.

Newport Pagnell Town of the United Counties League and Berks & Bucks Senior Trophy winners.
Photo: Gordon Whittington.

SENIOR COUNTY CUPS

A.F.A. SENIOR CUP

ROUND 1

Old Guildfordians 1-2 Old Esthameians
Sinjuns Grammarians 7-4 Old Actonians Association
Wandsworth Borough 1-4 Lancing Old Boys
Parkfield 6-1 Old Malvernian
Old Uffingtonians 2-1 Old Stationers
Old Paulines 1-0 Lloyds TSB Bank
Bealonians 2-0 Alleyn Old Boys
Latymer Old Boys 1-7 Old Carthusian
Old Vaughanians 1-2 Carshalton
B B Eagles 11-4 Old Bromleians
Old Finchleians 1-6 Wood Green Old Boys
Merton 5-4 Old Kolsassians

ROUND 2

Polytechnic 1-0 Old Suttonians
Civil Service 4-0 Alexandra Park
Old Parkonians 2-0 West Wickham
Merton 1-2 Old Salesians
East Barnet Old Grammarians 6-2 Leyton County O. B.
Old Isleworthians 1-4 Old Parmiterians
Albanian 2-1 Old Ignatians
Southgate County 2-3 Old Minchendenians
HSBC 3-6 Old Thorntonians
Old Chigwellians 0-3 Honourable Artillery Company
Old Hamptonians 4-1 Broomfield
Kew Association 2-3 Chertsey Old Salesians
Crouch End Vampires 2-1 Bank of England
Economicals 1-0 Ibis
Norsemen 3-1 Hale End Athletic
Bealonians 2-1 Weirside Rangers
Old Foresters 0-4 Nottsborough
Lancing Old Boys 1-3 Old Aloysians
Old Salvatorians 0-1 Old Cholmeleians
Old Edmontonians 1-4 Wake Green Amateur
Old Westminster Citizens 2-1 B B Eagles
Winchmore Hill 8-1 Old Latymerians
Sinjuns Grammarians 1-0 Old Lyonian
Old Meadonians 5-2 Enfield Old Grammarians
Old Owens 1-3 Old Carthusian
Old Wilsonians 4-1 South Bank Cuaco
Southgate Olympic 5-0 Old Woodhouseians
Pegasus 0-5 Parkfield
Old Belgravians 1-3 Old Uffingtonians
FC Romania v Carshalton (tie awarded to Carshalton)
UCL Academicals 3-1 Old Paulines
Old Esthameians 3-5 Wood Green Old Boys

ROUND 3

Southgate Olympic 2-8 Old Parmiterians
U C L Academicals 1-1 Old Aloysians (UCL Academicals won 5-4 on penalties)
Old Meadonians 3-1 Wake Green Amateur
Albanian 2-0 Polytechnic
Economicals 1-3 East Barnet Old Grammarians
Old Thorntonians 2-7 Nottsborough
Old Carthusian 3-1 Old Hamptonians
Old Salesians 4-0 Old Westminster Citizens
Old Wilsonians 2-1 Crouch End Vampires
Bealonians 4-1 Norsemen
Sinjuns Grammarians 2-3 Old Parkonians
Old Uffingtonians 1-0 Carshalton
Honourable Artillery Company 2-1 Chertsey O Salesians
Parkfield 3-4 Old Minchendenians
Winchmore Hill 5-1 Wood Green Old Boys
Old Cholmelians 1-4 Civil Service

ROUND 4

Albanian 0-1 Civil Service
Old Salesians 2-2 Old Uffingtonians (Old Salesians won 3-1 on penalties)
Old Carthusian 4-1 Old Parmiterians
U C L Academicals 1-1 Bealonians (Bealonians won 4-3 on penalties)
Old Wilsonians 0-1 Old Minchendenians
East Barnet Old Grammarians 2-5 Old Meadonians
Winchmore Hill 1-0 Nottsborough
Honourable Artillery Company 3-2 Old Parkonians

QUARTER FINALS

Old Minchendenians 1-4 Bealonians
Old Salesians 1-0 Honourable Artillery Company
Old Meadonians 2-4 Old Carthusian
Winchmore Hill 1-2 Civil Service

SEMI-FINALS

Old Salesians 3-0 Bealonians (@ HSBC)
Civil Service 0-1 Old Carthusian (@ HSBC)

FINAL (@ Winchmore Hill, 9/4/11)
Old Carthusian 2-3 Old Salesian

BEDFORDSHIRE PREMIER CUP

FINAL (@ Arlesey Town, 10/8/10)
Arlesey Town 1-3 Luton Town

BEDFORDSHIRE SENIOR CUP

ROUND 1

Stotfold 0-2 Leighton Town
Bedford Town 1-0 Dunstable Town

QUARTER FINALS

Bedford Town 0-1 Arlesey Town
Barton Rovers 3-0 Luton Town
Biggleswade Town 7-0 Biggleswade United
Leighton Town 6-1 Langford

SEMI-FINALS

Arlesey Town 2-0 Barton Rovers
Biggleswade Town 3-1 Leighton Town

FINAL (@ Luton Town, 12/5/11)
Arlesey Town 3-0 Biggleswade Town

BERKS & BUCKS SENIOR CUP

ROUND 2

Aylesbury 0-1 Chesham United
Thatcham Town 1-3 Hungerford Town
Burnham 1-0 Windsor & Eton
Abingdon United 0-1 Didcot Town
Marlow 3-2 Slough Town

QUARTER FINALS

Chesham United 3-1 Beaconsfield SYCOB
Wycombe Wanderers 4-0 Burnham
Marlow 1-5 Maidenhead United
Hungerford Town 1-1 Didcot Town (Didcot Town won 5-4 on penalties)

SEMI-FINALS

Maidenhead United 2-0 Didcot Town
Wycombe Wanderers 4-1 Chesham United

FINAL (@ Burnham, 2/5/11)
Maidenhead United 2-3 Wycombe Wanderers

BIRMINGHAM SENIOR CUP

ROUND 1

Coventry Sphinx 2-0 Banbury United
Tipton Town 2-1 Walsall
Solihull Moors 2-0 Studley
Atherstone Town 0-5 Sutton Coldfield Town
Tamworth 0-4 Birmingham City
Romulus 0-1 Rugby Town
Boldmere St Michaels 0-1 Hednesford Town
Alvechurch 1-2 Chasetown
Coleshill Town 3-1 Halesowen Town
Willenhall Town 1-4 West Bromwich Albion
Bedworth United 4-2 Burton Albion
Rushall Olympic 5-2 Redditch United
Highgate United 1-0 Causeway United
Stourbridge 3-1 Wolverhampton Wanderers
Stratford Town 2-0 Leamington

ROUND 2

Chasetown 0-2 Rushall Olympic
Rugby Town 3-4 Highgate United
Stratford Town 1-2 Nuneaton Town
Solihull Moors 4-2 Coventry Sphinx
Stourbridge 4-1 West Bromwich Albion
Sutton Coldfield Town 4-1 Tipton Town
Coleshill Town 1-5 Birmingham City
Hednesford Town 0-1 Bedworth United

QUARTER FINALS

Nuneaton Town 3-0 Stourbridge
Solihull Moors 0-1 Sutton Coldfield Town
Bedworth United 1-0 Rushall Olympic
Highgate United 1-2 Birmingham City

SEMI-FINALS

Birmingham City 2-3 Sutton Coldfield Town
Bedworth United 0-1 Nuneaton Town

FINAL (@ Tamworth, 10/5/11)
Sutton Coldfield Town 2-3 Nuneaton Town

CAMBRIDGESHIRE PROFESSIONAL CUP

FINAL (@ Histon, 31/7/10)
Histon 0-1 Cambridge City

CAMBRIDGESHIRE INVITATION CUP

ROUND 1

Cambridge City 3-2 Wisbech Town
Ely City 2-5 Fulbourn Institute
Godmanchester Rovers 2-3 Great Shelford
Haverhill Rovers 3-0 Whittlesey United
Mildenhall Town 3-1 Cambridge University Press
Newmarket Town 1-4 C R C
Royston Town 2-2 March Town United (March Town United won 5-4 on penalties)
Soham Town Rangers 1-1 Histon reserves (Histon reserves won 4-1 on penalties)

QUARTER FINALS

Cambridge City 4-5 C R C
March Town United 3-1 Fulbourn Institute
Mildenhall Town 3-0 Great Shelford
Haverhill Rovers 5-3 Histon reserves

SEMI-FINALS

Mildenhall Town 1-0 C R C
Haverhill Rovers 2-0 March Town United

FINAL (@ Cambridge United, 12/4/11)
Mildenhall Town 2-0 Haverhill Rovers

CHESHIRE PREMIER CUP

SEMI-FINALS

Crewe Alexandra 2-1 Macclesfield Town
Stockport County 2-0 Tranmere Rovers

FINAL (@ Stockport County, 12/4/11)
Stockport County 0-0 Crewe Alexandra (Stockport County won 4-2 on penalties)

CHESHIRE SENIOR CUP

ROUND 1

Alsager Town 3-1 Vauxhall Motors
Altrincham 3-2 Hyde United
Chester 2-3 Congleton Town
Nantwich Town 3-2 Cammell Laird
Northwich Victoria 3-0 Cheadle Town
Runcorn Town 1-1 Warrington Town (Warrington Town won 4-2 on penalties)
Winsford United 1-2 Runcorn Linnets
Woodley Sports 5-1 Witton Albion

QUARTER FINALS

Alsager Town 3-1 Woodley Sports (@ Woodley Sports)
Northwich Victoria 5-2 Nantwich Town
Runcorn Linnets 3-4 Altrincham
Warrington Town 2-0 Congleton Town

SEMI-FINALS

Northwich Victoria 2-1 Warrington Town
Altrincham 12-1 Alsager Town

FINAL (@ Nantwich Town, 5/4/11)
Northwich Victoria 2-0 Altrincham

CORNWALL SENIOR CUP

PRELIMINARY ROUND

Holman S C 1-6 Edgcumbe
Ludgvan 1-3 Kilkhampton (tie awarded to Ludgvan)
Morwenstow 5-2 St Ives Town
Mullion 1-4 R N A S Culdrose
Perranwell 2-1 Nanpean Rovers
Roche 2-1 Bude Town
St Dennis 3-1 St Agnes
St Dominick 6-1 Wendron United
St Stephens Borough 2-1 Lanreath
St Teath 6-3 St Just
Troon 0-6 Probus

ROUND 1

St Dominick 0-1 St Stephens Borough
Morwenstow 1-5 Perranwell
Edgcumbe 8-1 Ludgvan
Helston Athletic 4-2 Illogan R B L
St Dennis 5-3 Probus
R N A S Culdrose 1-3 St Teath
Millbrook 1-3 Polperro
Biscovey 0-4 St Day
Sticker 5-2 Roche
Pendeen Rovers 5-1 St Stephen

ROUND 2

Callington Town 2-0 Truro City
Dobwalls 0-1 Liskeard Athletic
Falmouth Town 6-2 St Dennis
Hayle 0-2 Saltash United
Mousehole 1-7 Camelford
Newquay 4-1 St Day
Penzance 0-0 Launceston
Perranporth 2-1 St Stephens Borough
Porthleven 2-1 Foxhole Stars
St Blazey 0-2 A F C St Austell
Torpoint Athletic 1-1 Bodmin Town
Perranwell 1-2 Penryn Athletic
Edgcumbe 1-3 Polperro (@ Polperro)
Helston Athletic 3-1 Wadebridge Town
St Teath 3-4 Godolphin Atlantic
Pendeen Rovers 1-2 Sticker

ROUND 2 REPLAYS

Launceston 1-1 Penzance
(Penzance won 4-3 on penalties)
Bodmin Town 2-1 Torpoint Athletic

ROUND 3

Porthleven 3-4 Liskeard Athletic
Bodmin Town 2-0 Perranporth
Camelford 0-3 A F C St Austell
Penzance 2-1 Newquay
Callington Town 1-4 Falmouth Town
Polperro 3-5 Penryn Athletic
Helston Athletic 1-3 Saltash United
Godophin Atlantic 3-2 Sticker

QUARTER FINALS

Bodmin Town 2-1 Penryn Athletic
A F C St Austell 2-0 Liskeard Athletic
Godolphin Atlantic 1-2 Penzance
Saltash United 3-1 Falmouth Town

SEMI-FINALS

Bodmin Town 3-2 Penzance (@ Newquay)
Saltash United 1-3 A F C St Austell (@ Liskeard Athletic)

FINAL (@ Hayle, 25/4/11)
Bodmin Town 3-2 A F C St Austell

CUMBERLAND SENIOR CUP

ROUND 1

Warwick Wanderers 1-2 Harraby Catholic Club
Frizington White Star 2-3 South Workington
Windscale 6-1 Borough
Penrith Saints - Penrith Rangers
(tie awarded to Penrith Saints)
Carlisle City 8-0 Parton United
Cockermouth 2-3 Kirkoswald

ROUND 2

Carlisle United 9-1 Aspatria
Gillford Park 2-0 Cleator Moor Celtic
Greystoke 1-6 Keswick
Mirehouse - Alston Moor Sports Club
(tie awarded to Mirehouse)
Langwathby United 2-3 Netherall
Carlisle 3-4 Eden Thistle
Whitehaven Miners Social 0-10 Northbank
Workington 1-3 Penrith
St Bees 0-5 Silloth
Longtown 4-2 Wetheriggs United
Whitehaven scr-w/o Carlisle City
South Workington 5-2 Bransty Rangers
Wigton Athletic 0-2 Wigton
Kirkoswald 5-2 Braithwaite
Penrith Saints 1-3 F C 32
Windscale 2-2 Harraby Catholic Club
(Harraby Catholic Club won 3-2 on penalties)

ROUND 3

Wigton 2-2 Carlisle City (Wigton won 4-2 on penalties)
F C 32 1-4 Netherall
Carlisle United 2-0 Penrith
Kirkoswald 7-0 South Workington
Northbank 2-1 Silloth
Mirehouse 2-5 Longtown
Gillford Park 8-0 Keswick
Eden Thistle 3-2 Harraby Catholic Club

QUARTER FINALS

Kirkoswald 1-4 Netherall
Northbank 3-0 Eden Thistle
Gillford Park 1-0 Longtown
Carlisle United 7-0 Wigton

SEMI-FINALS

Northbank 0-2 Netherall
Carlisle United 4-1 Gillford Park

FINAL (@ Carlisle United, 27/4/11)
Netherall 0-2 Carlisle United

DERBYSHIRE SENIOR CUP

ROUND 1

Long Eaton United 3-0 Pinxton

ROUND 2

Glossop North End 5-0 Stapenhill
Dronfield Town 2-3 South Normanton Athletic
Gresley 9-0 Blackwell Miners Welfare
Newhall United 1-3 Shirebrook Town
New Mills 11-0 Parkhouse
Heanor Town 1-3 Long Eaton United
Graham Street Prims 1-7 Gamesley
Borrowash Victoria 3-1 Holbrook Sports

ROUND 3

Derby County 14-1 Shirebrook Town (@ Belper Town)
Matlock Town 3-0 Glapwell
Glossop North End 3-0 Grelsey
New Mills 1-4 Belper Town
Gamesley 2-3 Borrowash Victoria
Buxton 3-0 Long Eaton United
Mickleover Sports 0-4 Chesterfield (@ Chesterfield)
Alfreton Town 6-1 South Normanton Athletic

QUARTER FINALS

Glossop North End 1-2 Borrowash Victoria
Buxton 2-0 Belper Town
Alfreton Town 0-1 Glapwell
Derby County 3-3 Chesterfield (@ Chesterfield. Derby County won 4-2 on penalties)

SEMI-FINALS

Glapwell 0-2 Derby County
Buxton 2-1 Borrowash Victoria

FINAL (@ Chesterfield, 20/4/11)
Buxton 0-5 Derby County

DEVON ST LUKES CUP

Sponsored by Westinsure

ROUND 1

Buckland Athletic 2-1 Elburton Villa
Barnstaple Town 2-4 Royal Marines
Plymouth Parkway 1-0 Dartmouth
Cullompton Rangers 4-8 Bideford

ROUND 2

Plymouth Parkway 1-3 Plymouth Argyle
Dawlish Town 5-8 Ivybridge Town
Elmore 1-7 Buckland Athletic
Tavistock 1-6 Torquay United
Royal Marines 0-3 Tiverton Town
Witheridge 2-5 Bideford
Ilfracombe Town 3-0 Bovey Tracey
Willand Rovers 1-4 Exeter City

QUARTER FINALS

Bideford 2-2 Plymouth Argyle
(Plymouth Argyle win 4-1 on penalties)
Buckland Athletic 2-1 Torquay United
Ivybridge Town 0-1 Tiverton Town (@ Tiverton Town)
Ilfracombe Town 2-4 Exeter City

SEMI-FINALS

Plymouth Argyle 2-2 Buckland Athletic (Buckland Athletic won 5-4 on penalties)
Tiverton Town 2-0 Exeter City

FINAL (@ Tiverton Town, 28/4/11)
Tiverton Town 2-2 Buckland Athletic (Buckland Athletic won 3-2 on penalties)

DEVON SENIOR CUP

FINAL (@ Coach Road, Newton Abbot 10/05/11)
Loddiswell Athletic 3-2 Barnstaple Town Reserves

DORSET SENIOR CUP

ROUND 1

Sturminster Marshall 0-1 Swanage Town & Herston
Parley Sports 1-2 Verwood Town
Sturminster Newtown United 2-3 Bridport
Hamworthy Recreation 2-3 Poole Borough
Cranborne 2-4 Merley Cobham Sports
Gillingham Town 6-1 Blandford United
Shaftesbury w/o-scr Guernsey Athletics

ROUND 2

Portland United 1-2 Hamworthy United
Bridport 3-0 Swanage Town & Herston
Sherborne United 3-1 Chickerell United
Verwood Town 1-3 Poole Borough
Dorchester Town 5-1 Gillingham Town
Shaftesbury 1-3 Poole Town
Holt United 1-2 Wimborne Town
Weymouth 9-3 Merley Cobham Sports

QUARTER FINALS

Dorchester Town 2-0 Poole Borough
Hamworthy United 0-4 Weymouth
Wimborne Town 1-2 Bridport
Sherborne Town 1-2 Poole Town

SEMI-FINALS

Weymouth 3-1 Bridport (@ Dorchester Town)
Dorchester Town 3-1 Poole Town (@ Hamworthy United)

FINAL (@ Weymouth, 12/4/11)
Weymouth 2-6 Dorchester Town

DURHAM SENIOR CHALLENGE CUP

PRELIMINARY ROUND

Esh Winning 0-1 Darlington Railway Athletic
Whickham 5-2 Sunderland Silksworth
Jarrow 2-1 Seaham Red Star
Washington 3-2 Easington Colliery
Annfield Plain 2-5 Wolviston
Sunderland R C A 1-0 Coxhoe Athletic
Peterlee Town 3-4 Hartlepool
Darlington 3-1 Willington
Stockton Town 0-5 Ryhope Colliery Welfare
Spennymoor Town 6-0 Hebburn Town
Gateshead 11-0 Brandon United
Bishop Auckland 3-0 Darlington Cleveland Bridge
Sunderland Belford House 1-3 Houghton Town

ROUND 1
Gateshead 3-2 Ryhope Colliery Welfare
Tow Law Town 0-5 Spennymoor Town
Shildon 0-5 Bishop Auckland
Crook Town 2-1 Washington
Billingham Town 2-2 Darlington Railway Athletic
(Billingham Town won 4-3 on penalties)
Wolviston 4-2 Hartlepool
Billingham Synthonia 2-0 Jarrow
Boldon C A 2-3 Hartlepool United
Norton & Stockton Ancients 2-1 Darlington
Newton Aycliffe 1-1 Consett
(Newton Aycliffe won 4-2 on penalties)
Horden Colliery Welfare 1-2 West Auckland Town
Dunston U T S 9-1 Houghton Town
Chester-le-Street Town 2-1 South Shields
Jarrow Roofing Boldon C A 2-3 Durham City
Sunderland R C A 6-0 Ryton
Whickham 3-0 Birtley Town

ROUND 2
Whickham 0-1 Norton & Stockton Ancients
Billingham Synthonia 3-1 Hartlepool United
West Auckland Town 0-2 Spennymoor Town
Durham City 2-0 Newton Aycliffe
Billingham Town 2-4 Gateshead
Dunston U T S 2-0 Bishop Auckland
Wolviston 0-1 Crook Town
Sunderland R C A 2-1 Chester-le-Street Town

QUARTER FINALS
Durham City 2-3 Dunston U T S
Gateshead 5-4 Sunderland R C A
Norton & Stockton Ancients 3-1 Crook Town
Spennymoor Town 4-1 Billingham Synthonia

SEMI-FINALS
Dunston U T S1-1 Spennymoor Town (Dunston UTS won 3-2 on penalties)
Gateshead 2-0 Norton & Stockton Ancients

FINAL (@ Eppleton CW, 22/4/11)
Gateshead 2-0 Dunston UTS

EAST RIDING SENIOR CUP

ROUND 1
Hall Road Rangers 1-2 Westella & Willerby
Pocklington Town 0-2 Hessle Sporting Club
Hodgsons 0-1 Beverley Town
A F C Hull 4-3 St Andrews
Crown 2-3 Hedon Rangers
Easington United 1-2 Malet Lambert Y C
Sculcoates Amateurs 3-0 Chalk Lane

ROUND 2
Hessle Rangers 2-6 Hull City
Sculcoates Amateurs 3-2 Hedon Rangers
Hutton Cranswick United 2-2 Beverley Town (Hutton Cranswick United won 4-2 on penalties)
Hall Road Rangers 3-2 Westella & Willerby
Bridlington Town 3-1 Reckitts
North Ferriby United 8-0 Hessle Sporting Club
Hornsea Town 4-0 Bridlington Sports Club
A F C Hull 2-5 Malet Lambert Y C

QUARTER FINALS
North Ferriby United 7-0 Malet Lambert Y C
Hornsea Town 3-8 Hull City
Bridlington Town 3-1 Sculcoates Amateurs
Hall Road Rangers 3-0 Hutton Cranswick United

SEMI-FINALS (both at Roy West Centre)
Hall Road Rangers 2-1 Bridlington Town
Hull City 2-3 North Ferriby United

FINAL (@ Hull City, 10/5/11)
Hall Road Rangers 1-3 North Ferriby United

ESSEX SENIOR CUP

Sponsored by BBC Radio Essex

ROUND 1
Halstead Town 1-2 Hullbridge Sports

ROUND 2
Stansted 3-1 Stanway Rovers
London A P S A 3-3 Basildon United
(London A P S A won 3-1 on penalties)
Hullbridge Sports 4-3 F C Clacton
Barking 4-0 Takeley
Southend Manor 2-2 Eton Manor
(Eton Manor won 4-3 on penalties)
Burnham Ramblers 2-3 Witham Town
Wivenhoe Town 3-1 Saffron Walden Town
Bowers & Pitsea 2-0 Barkingside

ROUND 3
Romford 2-4 Stansted
Heybridge Swifts 3-1 Maldon & Tiptree
Wivenhoe Town 0-2 Grays Athletic
Chelmsford City 2-1 Witham Town
Canvey Island 4-1 Harlow Town
Southend United 4-1 Barking
Bowers & Pitsea 0-2 Brentwood Town
Tilbury 2-5 Aveley
Hullbridge Sports 2-1 Redbridge
London A P S A 0-1 Billericay Town
Eton Manor 1-6 A F C Hornchurch
East Thurrock United 3-2 Waltham Abbey
Great Wakering Rovers 3-1 Waltham Forest
Concord Rangers 3-1 Thurrock
Dagenham & Redbridge 3-2 Colchester United
Braintree Town 2-0 Ilford

ROUND 4
Brentwood Town 0-2 Great Wakering Rovers
Chelmsford City 1-1 Southend United
(Southend United won 2-0 on penalties)
Aveley 2-0 Braintree Town
Billericay Town 3-0 East Thurrock United
Concord Rangers 2-3 A F C Hornchurch
Stansted 1-2 Grays Athletic
Hullbridge Sports 0-2 Heybridge Swifts
Dagenham & Redbridge 2-3 Canvey Island

QUARTER FINALS
Heybridge Swifts 2-0 A F C Hornchurch
Billericay Town 2-0 Great Wakering Rovers
Canvey Island 2-3 Aveley
Grays Athletic 1-2 Southend United

SEMI-FINALS
Aveley 2-1 Southend United
Billericay Town 3-2 Heybridge Swifts

FINAL (@ Thurrock, 11/4/11)
Aveley 0-2 Billericay Town

GLOUCESTERSHIRE SENIOR CHALLENGE CUP

ROUND 1
Forest Green Rovers 2-1 Cirencester Town
Mangotsfield United 0-2 Gloucester City
Yate Town 1-3 Cinderford Town
(tie awarded to Yate Town)

QUARTER FINALS
Forest Green Rovers 3-3 Bristol City
(Bristol City won 13-12 on penalties)
Bishops Cleeve 0-2 Yate Town
Almondsbury Town 1-2 Bristol Rovers
Gloucester City 2-5 Cheltenham Town

SEMI-FINALS
Bristol Rovers 0-4 Cheltenham Town
Yate Town 2-1 Bristol City

FINAL (@ Yate Town, 4/5/11)
Cheltenham Town 2-3 Yate Town

HAMPSHIRE SENIOR CUP

Sponsored by BSA-Regal Group

ROUND 1
Cowes Sports 2-2 Horndean
(Horndean won 4-3 on penalties)
Brading Town 7-2 Fawley
Ringwood Town 3-0 Whitchurch United
Farnborough North End 2-4 Bournemouth
Hartley Wintney 1-0 Blackfield & Langley
East Cowes Victoria Athletic 4-2 Petersfield Town
Alton Town 1-3 Brockenhurst
Newport I O W w/o-scr Fleet Spurs
Lymington Town 6-1 Eversley
New Milton Town 2-3 A F C Portchester
Winchester City 5-0 Moneyfields
Belgrave Wanderers 3-5 Hythe & Dibden
Andover New Street 0-6 Tadley Calleva
Fareham Town 4-2 Cove
Guernsey Rangers 4-2 Hamble A S S C
Romsey Town 3-2 Stockbridge

ROUND 2
Alresford Town 3-2 East Cowes Victoria Athletic
Havant & Waterlooville 4-1 Guernsey Rangers
A F C Totton 4-1 Romsey Town
Basingstoke Town 3-0 Ringwood Town
Fleet Town 3-0 Aldershot Town
Eastleigh 2-0 United Services Portsmouth
Newport I O W 4-1 A F C Portchester
Lymington Town 2-3 Sholing
Gosport Borough 1-2 Andover
Hartley Wintney 1-0 Christchurch
Fareham Town 4-5 Farnborough
Bashley 1-1 Horndean (Horndean won 4-2 on penalties)
Tadley Calleva 1-14 Bournemouth
Brading Town 0-3 Totton & Eling
Winchester City 5-1 Hayling United
Brockenhurst 4-0 Hythe & Dibden

ROUND 3
Havant & Waterlooville 5-1 Eastleigh
Sholing 4-1 Newport I O W
Brockenhurst 4-0 Alresford Town
Farnborough 5-0 Totton & Eling
Bournemouth 2-0 Horndean
Hartley Wintney 1-7 Basingstoke Town
A F C Totton 5-0 Andover
Winchester City 3-1 Fleet Town

QUARTER FINALS
Basingstoke Town 2-4 Farnborough
Havant & Waterlooville 0-1 Winchester City
Brockenhurst 2-3 Sholing
A F C Totton 1-0 Bournemouth

SEMI-FINALS
Winchester City 1-3 A F C Totton
Farnborough 1-3 Sholing

FINAL (@ Southampton, 25/5/11)
A F C Totton 3-1 Sholing

HEREFORDSHIRE CHALLENGE CUP

ROUND 1
Holme Lacy 0-5 Wellington
Pegasus Juniors 2-0 Bromyard Town
Bartrestree 2-3 Kington Town
Fownhope 0-7 Ewyas Harold
Westfields 3-2 Leominster Town

QUARTER FINALS
Kington Town 0-8 Westfields
Hereford Lads Club 0-1 Ewyas Harold
Wellington 3-2 Pegasus Juniors
Ledbury Town 3-2 Hinton

SEMI-FINALS
Westfields 5-0 Ewyas Harold
Ledbury Town 0-1 Wellington

FINAL (@ Hereford United, 25/4/11)
Westfields 3-1 Wellington

HERTS SENIOR CHALLENGE CUP

ROUND 1
Hemel Hempstead Town 1-0 Oxhey Jets
Stevenage 2-0 Watford
Hadley 3-1 Tring Athletic
Royston Town 2-3 St Margaretsbury
Hitchin Town 3-4 Ware
St Albans City 1-4 Hatfield Town

ROUND 2
Ware 3-1 Colney Heath
St Margaretsbury 2-0 Leverstock Green
Hatfield Town 2-3 Sawbridgeworth Town
Cheshunt 2-1 Bishop's Stortford

Broxbourne Borough V & E 3-2 Potters Bar Town
Hertford Town 2-1 Boreham Wood
Hadley 1-4 Barnet
Hemel Hempstead Town 0-4 Stevenage

QUARTER FINALS
Cheshunt 2-1 Hertford Town
Sawbridgeworth Town 0-6 Stevenage
Ware 2-1 St Margaretsbury
Barnet 6-2 Broxbourne Borough V & E

SEMI-FINALS
Cheshunt 0-1 Barnet
Ware 3-4 Stevenage

FINAL (@ Barnet, 12/4/11)
Barnet 2-1 Stevenage

HUNTINGDONSHIRE SENIOR CUP

ROUND 1
Somersham Town 1-2 Ramsey Town
Godmanchester Rovers w/o-scr A F C Fletton
Alconbury 2-5 Eaton Socon

QUARTER FINALS
St Ives Town 2-1 Ramsey Town
Eaton Socon 0-0 Yaxley
(Eaton Socon won 5-4 on penalties)
St Neots Town 11-2 Eynesbury Rovers
Huntingdon Town 2-1 Godmanchester Rovers

SEMI-FINALS
St Ives Town 2-1 Huntingdon Town
Eaton Socon 0-3 St Neots Town

FINAL (@ Huntingdon Town, 2/5/11)
St Ives Town 0-2 St Neots Town

KENT SENIOR CUP

ROUND 1
Faversham Town 0-2 Thamesmead Town
Ramsgate 3-1 Chatham Town
Whitstable Town 3-0 Welling United
Maidstone United 2-3 Ebbsfleet United
Dartford 2-0 Tonbridge Angels
Folkestone Invicta 0-2 Sittingbourne
Cray Wanderers 3-1 Dover Atheltic
Margate 0-2 Bromley

QUARTER FINALS
Dartford 6-1 Whitstable Town
Ramsgate 1-0 Thamesmead Town
Bromley 2-0 Ebbsfleet United
Cray Wanderers 2-1 Sittingbourne

SEMI-FINALS
Cray Wanderers 2-3 Bromley
Ramsgate 0-3 Dartford

FINAL (@ Dartford, 2/5/11)
Bromley 1-4 Dartford

LANCASHIRE SENIOR TROPHY

Sponsored by Co-Operative

ROUND 1
Bacup Borough 1-1 A F C Fylde
(A F C Fylde won 5-4 on penalties)
Leigh Genesis 1-2 Atherton Collieries
A F C Darwen 1-3 Chorley (@ Chorley)
Squires Gate 2-1 Rossendale United
Rochdale Town 1-2 Radcliffe Borough
Padiham 0-2 Wigan Robin Park
Burscough 2-3 Marine
Bamber Bridge 2-1 A F C Blackpool
Colne 0-1 Lancaster City
Ashton Athletic 2-3 Daisy Hill
Ramsbottom United 3-3 Holker Old Boys
(Ramsbottom United won 5-4 on penalties)

ROUND 2
Fleetwood Town 3-0 Atherton Collieries
Bamber Bridge 2-0 Squires Gate
Marine 2-2 Chorley (Chorley won 5-4 on penalties)
Southport 2-0 Barrow
Daisy Hill 0-3 Radcliffe Borouygh
Kendal Town 2-3 Chorley
Wigan Robin Park 1-1 Lancaster City
(Wigan Robin Park won 6-5 on penalties)
Ramsbotttom United 1-1 A F C Fylde
(A F C Fylde won 3-1 on penalties)

QUARTER FINALS
Fleetwood Town 1-3 A F C Fylde
Clitheroe 2-4 Bamber Bridge
Radcliffe Borough 3-2 Wigan Robin Park
Southport 0-4 Chorley

SEMI-FINALS
Bamber Bridge 3-1 Radcliffe Borough
(@ Lancs FA Ground, Leyland)
Chorley 0-2 A F C Fylde (@ Lancs FA Ground, Leyland)

FINAL (@ Bolton Wanderers, 14/3/11)
Bamber Bridge 0-1 A F C Fylde

LEICESTERSHIRE CHALLENGE CUP

Sponsored by Westerby Homes

ROUND 1
Shepshed Dynamo 2-3 Hinckley
Kirby Muxloe 0-2 Friar Lane & Epworth
Bardon Hill Sports 0-5 Quorn
Hinckley United 4-1 Loughborough University

QUARTER FINALS
Hinckley 1-0 Loughborough Dynamo
Oadby Town 1-0 Friar Lane & Epworth
Hinckley United 3-0 Coalville Town
Quorn 3-2 Barwell

SEMI-FINALS
Hinckley 0-1 Quorn
Oadby Town 3-5 Hinckley United

FINAL (@ Barlestone St Giless, 10/5/11)
Hinckley United 4-5 Quorn

LINCOLNSHIRE SENIOR CUP

SEMI-FINALS

Scunthorpe United 1-1 Grimsby Town
(Scunthorpe United won 4-3 on penalties)

FINAL (@ Grimsby Town, 30/7/10)
Grimsby Town 4-2 Lincoln City

LINCOLNSHIRE SENIOR SHIELD

QUARTER FINALS

Boston United 4-0 Grantham Towm
Stamford 0-0 Lincon United
(Stamford won 5-3 on penalties)
Brigg Town 0-0 Gainsborough Trinity
(Gainsborough Trinity won 6-5 on penalties)

SEMI-FINALS

Stamford 5-0 Spalding United
Gainborough Trinity 1-2 Boston United

FINAL (@ Boston United, 19/4/11)
Stamford 0-0 Boston United
(Stamford won 4-3 on penalties)

LIVERPOOL SENIOR CUP

ROUND 1

Cammell Laird 4-1 A F C Liverpool
Warrington Town 2-2 Skelmersdale United
(Skelmersdale United won 3-0 on penalties)
Burscough 0-1 Marine

ROUND 2

St Helens Town 3-1 Skelmersdale United
Bootle 0-2 Cammell Laird
Prescot Cables 2-1 Formby
Marine 1-0 Ashton Town

QUARTER FINALS

Prescot Cables 1-2 Liverpool
St Helens Town 2-4 Tranmere Rovers (@ Ashton Town)
Marine 0-1 Everton
Southport 3-0 Cammell Laird

SEMI-FINALS

Tranmere Rovers 0-2 Southport
Liverpool 1-4 Everton (@ The Academy, Kirkby)

FINAL (@ Southport, 23/7/11)
Southport 2-0 Everton

LONDON SENIOR CUP

ROUND 1

Mauritius Sports Association UK 0-2 Erith Town
Cockfosters 4-1 Lewisham Borough (Community)
Clapton 0-2 Fisher
Kingsbury London Tigers 2-1 South Kilburn

ROUND 2

Redbridge 2-0 Leyton
Dulwich Hamlet 1-0 Erith Town
Corinthian-Casuals 2-4 Beckenham Town
Croydon 0-2 Erith & Belvedere
Thamesmead Town 3-1 Hanwell Town
Haringey Borough 2-1 Cockfosters
Barking 4-1 Fisher
Wingate & Finchley 3-0 Kingsbury London Tigers

ROUND 3

Croydon Athletic 1-2 Erith & Belvedere
Redbridge 1-3 Tooting & Mitcham United
Barking 0-2 Beckenham Town
Thamesmead Town 4-1 Welling United
Hendon 3-1 Metropolitan Police (@ Metropolitan Police)
Cray Wanderers 3-0 Haringey Borough
Harrow Borough 1-1 Wingate & Finchley
(Wingate & Finchley won 3-1 on penalties)
Dulwich Hamlet 2-3 A F C Wimbledon

QUARTER FINALS

Thamesmead Town 0-2 Hendon
Beckenham Town 3-4 A F C Wimbledon
Erith & Belvedere 1-2 Wingate & Finchley
Tooting & Mitcham United 2-0 Cray Wanderers

SEMI-FINALS

Wingate & Finchley 3-0 Tooting & Mitcham United
A F C Wimbledon 2-3 Hendon

FINAL @ Tooting & Mitcham United, 10/5/11)
Wingate & Finchley 3-1 Hendon

MANCHESTER SENIOR CUP

FINAL (@ Mancheter United, 16/5/11)
Bolton Wanderers 1-3 Manchester United

MANCHESTER PREMIER CUP

ROUND 1

Mossley 2-3 Curzon Ashton
Maine Road 1-2 Ashton United
Chadderton 2-0 New Mills
Salford City 0-0 Irlam (Irlam won 6-5 on penalties)
Hyde 4-0 Oldham Boro
Glossop North End 3-1 Radcliffe Borough
Trafford 2-1 Abbey Hey

QUARTER FINALS

Droylsden 3-1 Hyde United
Ashton United 7-0 Irlam
Chadderton 3-3 Curzon Ashton (Chadderton won 4-3 on penalties)
Trafford 3-1 Glossop North End

SEMI-FINALS

Chadderton 1-4 Ashton United
Droylsden 2-0 Trafford

FINAL (@ Hyde, 28/3/11)
Ashton United 3-4 Droylsden

MIDDLESEX SENIOR CUP

ROUND 1

Hillingdon Borough 2-5 Hayes & Yeading United
Hendon 3-2 Enfield Town
Enfield 1893 2-1 North Greenford United
A F C Hayes 3-4 Hanworth Villa
Hampton & Richmond Borough 2-1 Harefield United

ROUND 2
Ashford Town (Middlesex) 1-3 Harrow Borough
Bedfont Town 2-1 Hanworth Villa
Wingate & Finchley 2-3 Hendon
Wealdstone 1-0 Northwood
Tokyngton Manor scr-w/o Hayes & Yeading United
Enfield 0-1 Hampton & Richmond Borough
Staines Town 6-2 Uxbridge
Hanwell Town 1-2 Wembley

QUARTER FINALS
Hampton & Richmond Borough 0-1 Hendon
Harrow Borough 2-5 Hayes & Yeading United
Bedfont Town 2-1 Wembley
Wealdstone 3-3 Staines Town
(Staines Town won 3-2 on penalties)

SEMI-FINALS
Staines Town 4-1 Hendon
Hayes & Yeading United 1-0 Bedfont Town

FINAL (@ Harrow Borough, 25/4/11)
Staines Town 3-2 Hayes & Yeading United

NORFOLK SENIOR CUP

ROUND 1
Poringland Wanderers 2-1 Reepham Town
Wymondham Town 6-1 Hindringham
Horsford United 1-0 Long Stratton

ROUND 2
Sprowston Athletic 4-1 Stalham Town
Sheringham 2-1 Wells Town
Dersingham Rovers 4-1 Wymondham Town
Loddon United 3-0 Caister
Watton United 1-3 Bradenham Wanderers
Poringland Wanderers 1-4 Norwich St John's
Horsford United 1-4 Holt United
Spixworth 2-3 St Andrew's

ROUND 3
Gorleston 3-1 Holt United
Dersingham Rovers 3-3 Blofield United
Thetford Town 2-1 Swaffham Town
Sheringham 1-2 Fakenham Town
Norwich St John's 3-0 Bradenham Wanderers
Mattishall 0-1 Hempnall
Sprowston Athletic 1-4 North Walsham Town
Downham Town 0-3 St Andrew's
Cromer Town 1-0 Acle United
Loddon United 0-2 Diss Town

ROUND 3 REPLAY
Blofield United 5-0 Dersingham Rovers

ROUND 4
Gorleston 0-2 Dereham Town
Fakenham Town 0-3 Norwich City reserves
North Walsham Town 1-2 Norwich United
Norwich St John's 0-5 Diss Town
Great Yarmouth Town 1-5 King's Lynn Town
St Andrew's 1-2 Blofield United
Thetford Town 1-0 Hempnall
Wroxham 5-1 Cromer Town

QUARTER FINALS
Blofield United 2-3 Dereham Town
Wroxham 0-2 King's Lynn Town
Diss Town 1-3 Thetford Town
Norwich City reserves 1-0 Norwich United

SEMI-FINALS
King's Lynn Town 5-1 Thetford Town
Norwich City reserves 1-2 Dereham Town

FINAL (@ Norwich City, 13/5/11)
King's Lynn Town 1-4 Dereham Town

NORTH RIDING SENIOR CUP

Sponsored by YSL-Errea

ROUND 1
Scarborough Athletic 2-3 Stokesley
Thornaby 5-9 Guisborough Town(@ Guisborough Town)
Northallerton Town 2-2 Marske United
(Marske United won 4-1 on penalties)
Grangetown Boys Club 3-1 Fishburn Park
Kirkbymoorside 2-2 Nunthorpe Athletic
(Kirkbymoorside won 4-3 on penalties)
Redcar Athletic 0-1 Pickering Town

QUARTER FINALS
York City 2-3 Pickering Town
Stokesley 2-1 Kirkbymoorside
Guisborough Town 1-0 Middlesbrough
Marske United 1-1 Grangetown Boys Club (Marske United won 4-2 on penalties)

SEMI-FINALS
Stokesley 1-1 Guisborough Town (Guisborough Town won 4-1 on penalties)
Pickering Town 2-3 Marske United

FINAL (@ Stokesley, 30/3/11)
Guisborough Town 1-0 Marske United

NORTHANTS MAUNSELL CUP

FINAL (@ Corby Town, 1/8/10)
Corby Town 1-0 Peterborough United

NORTHANTS HILLIER SENIOR CUP

ROUND 1
Irchester United 2-3 Peterborough Northern Star

ROUND 2
Brackley Town 3-1 Woodford United
Cogenhoe United 2-1 Corby Town
Corby Stewart & Lloyds 3-0 Raunds Town
Rushden & Diamonds 8-0 Daventry United
Northampton Spencer 2-0 Desborough Town
Rothwell Corinthians 1-2 Kettering Town
Long Buckby 4-1 Wellingborough Town
Daventry Town 4-1 Peterborough Northern Star

QUARTER FINALS
Kettering Town 0-4 Corby Stewart & Lloyds
Northampton Spencer 2-1 Long Buckby
Daventry Town 2-2 Cogenhoe United
(Cogenhoe United won 4-2 on penalties)
Rushden & Diamonds 0-2 Brackley Town

SEMI-FINALS
Brackley Town 5-2 Cogenhoe United
Northampton Spencer 0-1 Corby Stewart & Lloyds

FINAL (@ Northampton Town, 12/4/11)
Brackley Town 1-0 Corby Stewart & Lloyds

NORTHUMBERLAND SENIOR CUP

ROUND 1
North Shields 3-0 Morpeth Town
West Allotment Celtic 3-2 Team Northumbria

QUARTER FINALS
Whitley Bay 1-2 Ashington
Blyth Spartans 4-0 North Shields
Newcastle Benfield 3-2 West Allotment Celtic
Newcastle United reserves 2-0 Bedlington Terriers

SEMI-FINALS
Newcastle Benfield 0-2 Blyth Spartans
Newcastle United reserves 2-0 Ashington

FINAL (@ Newcastle United, 11/5/11)
Newcastle United reserves 4-0 Blyth Spartans

NOTTINGHAMSHIRE SENIOR CUP

ROUND 1
Gedling Town 4-3 Radcliffe Olympic
(tie awarded to Radcliffe Olympic)
Kimberley Miners Welfare 3-2 Bulwell
Clifton 0-3 Newark Town
Basford United 0-1 Boots Athletic
Hucknall Rolls Leisure 5-2 Retford Town
Calverton Miners Welfare 4-2 Cotgrave Welfare
Teversal 0-6 Arnold Town
Kimberley Town 1-3 Greenwood Meadows
Sutton Town scr-w/o Clipstone Welfre
Ollerton Town 5-1 Bilborough Pelican
F C Cavaliers 0-3 Blidworth Welfare
Radford 1-3 Wollaton

ROUND 2
Kimberley Miners Welfare 0-3 Boots Athletic
Calverton Miners Welfare 2-4 Ollerton Town
Blidworth Welfare 2-1 Clipstone Welfare
Wollaton 4-3 Hucknall Rolls
Arnold Town 2-0 Newark Town
Radcliffe Olympic 1-2 Greenwood Meadows

ROUND 3
Southwell City 1-4 Ollerton Town
Dunkirk 3-0 Boots Athletic
Retford United 0-4 Eastwood Town
Wollaton w/o-scr Forest Town
Gedling Miners Welfare 2-2 Rainworth Miners Welfare
(Rainworth Miners Welfare won 4-2 on penalties, tie later awarded to Gedling Miners Welfare)
Blidworth Welfare 1-2 Hucknall Town
Kirkby Town 1-2 Arnold Town
Ollerton Town 1-1 Greenwood Meadows
(Greenwood Meadows won 5-4 on penalties)

QUARTER FINALS
Hucknall Town 4-1 Greenwood Meadows
Dunkirk 3-1 Wollaton
Gedling Miners Welfare 0-4 Eastwood Town
Carlton Town 2-0 Arnold Town

SEMI-FINALS
Dunkirk 0-1 Eastwood Town
Carlton Town 3-2 Hucknall Town

FINAL (@ Mansfield Town, 3/5/11)
Carlton Town 1-6 Eastwood Town

OXFORDSHIRE SENIOR CUP

ROUND 1
Easington Sports 4-1 Garsington
Henley Town 0-2 Ardley United
Marston Saints 2-1 Bletchingdon
Freeland 1-3 Clanfield
Launton Sports 0-8 Old Woodstock Town
Headington Amateurs 2-5 Kidlington
Bicester Town 1-1 Chinnor
(Bicester Town won 4-3 on penalties)
Thame United 3-1 Woodcote/Stoke Row
Mansfield Road 3-0 Rover (Cowley)
Oxford City Nomads 8-0 Hook Norton
A F C Hinksey 5-0 Eynsham Association
Stonesfield Sports 2-3 Adderbury Park
Carterton 7-0 Oxford University Press

ROUND 2
Kidlington 3-1 Ardley United
Witney United 6-0 Marston Saints
Carterton 5-2 A F C Hinksey
Thame United 4-0 Clanfield
Adderbury Park 3-1 Mansfield Road
Bicester Town 6-0 Enstone Sports
Old Woodstock Town 4-0 Horspath
Oxford City Nomads 3-0 Easington Sports

ROUND 3
Kidlington 2-0 Thame United
Old Woodstock Town 0-1 Oxford City Nomads
Carterton 1-0 Adderbury Park
Witney United 1-2 Bicester Town

QUARTER FINALS
Oxford United 9-3 North Leigh (@ Thame United)
Kidlington 2-2 Oxford City Nomads
(Kidlington won 5-4 on penalties)
Banbury United 1-0 Bicester Town
Carterton 1-2 Oxford City (tie awarded to Carterton)

SEMI-FINALS
Carterton 0-2 Kidlington
Banbury United 0-2 Oxford United

FINAL (@ Oxford United, 12/4/11)
Kidlington 0-4 Oxford United

SHEFFIELD & HALLAMSHIRE SENIOR CUP

ROUND 1

Dinnington Town 2-1 A F C Sportsman Rovers
Harworth Colliery Institute 1-3 Bentley Colliery
Athersley Recreation 3-0 F C Brimington
Staveley Miners Welfare 8-1 Frecheville C A
Penistone Church 2-1 Rossington Main
Maltby Main 8-1 Frickley Colliery
Nostell Miners Welfare 3-3 Hallam
(Hallam won 4-2 on penalties)
Worsbrough Bridge Athletic 3-2 Handsworth
A F C Emley 2-0 Yorkshire Main
Sheffield 1-0 Houghton Main
Hemsworth Miners Welfare 1-3 Kinlsey Boys
Parkgate 6-1 Phoenix
South Kirkby Colliery 6-1 Sheffield Parramore
Brodsworth Welfare 0-7 Worksop Town

ROUND 2

Frickley Athletic 4-0 Maltby Main
Penistone Church 1-5 Stocksbridge Park Steels
A F C Emley 1-8 Sheffield
South Kirkby Colliery 6-1 Bentley Colliery
Parkgate 3-2 Dinnington Town
Kinsley Boys 1-2 Athersley Recreation
Worbrough Bridge Athletic 2-4 Worksop Town
Staveley Miners Welfare 6-2 Hallam

QUARTER FINALS

South Kirkby Colliery 0-2 Stocksbridge Park Steels
Parkgate 3-1 Staveley Miners Welfare
Frickley Athletic 0-3 Sheffield
Worksop Town 1-0 Athersley Recreation

SEMI-FINALS

Parkgate 4-3 Sheffield
Worksop Town 1-2 Stocksbridge Park Steels

FINAL (@ Sheffield Wednesday, 3/5/11)
Parkgate 0-3 Stocksbridge Park Steels

SHROPSHIRE SENIOR CUP

FINAL (@ Shrewsbury Town, 27/4/11)
A F C Telford United 0-1 Shrewsbury Town

SHROPSHIRE CHALLENGE CUP

ROUND 1

Dawley Villa 1-4 Telford Juniors
F C Hodnet 0-1 Wellington Amateurs
Bridgnorth Town 4-2 Newport Town
St Martins 2-1 Shifnal Town
Impact United 4-0 Shifnal United 97

ROUND 2

Whitchurch Alport 4-1 Broseley Juniors
Morda United 2-4 Shawbury United
Ketley Bank United 0-4 Wellington Amateurs
Haughmond 3-4 Ellesmere Rangers
Wem Town 3-2 Ludlow Town
Hanwood United 5-1 Impact United
St Martins 2-1 Telford Juniors
Bridgnorth Town 1-2 Market Drayton Town

QUARTER FINALS

Market Drayton Town 1-4 Whitchurch Alport
Wellington Amateurs 3-0 Ellesmere Rangers
Wem Town 3-0 Shawbury United
St Martins 1-5 Hanwood United

SEMI-FINALS

Market Drayton Town 2-0 Hanwood United
Wem Town 2-0 Wellington Amateurs

FINAL (@ Shrewsbury Town, 11/4/11)
Market Drayton Town 1-0 Wem Town

SOMERSET PREMIER CUP

ROUND 1

Radstock Town 2-2 Bath City
(Radstock Town won 4-3 on penalties)
Larkhall Athletic 4-0 Welton Rovers
Shepton Mallet 0-1 Bishop Sutton
Frome Town 3-0 Brislington
Portishead Town 1-3 Bridgwater Town
Chard Town 1-1 Taunton Town
(Taunton Town won 4-1 on penalties)
Wellington 6-3 Wells City

ROUND 2

Paulton Rovers 4-1 Keynsham Town
Yeovil Town 6-0 Odd Down
Clevedon Town 4-1 Bridgwater Town
Bristol Manor Farm 2-3 Frome Town
Bishop Sutton 1-4 Weston super Mare
Wellington 1-4 Taunton Town
Radstock Town 2-0 Street
Hengrove Athletic 2-1 Larkhall Athletic

QUARTER FINALS

Taunton Town 1-2 Weston super Mare
Paulton Rovers 1-2 Clevedon Town
Frome Town 3-3 Radstock Town
(Radstock Town won 4-2 on penalties)
Hengrove Athletic 0-1 Yeovil Town

SEMI-FINALS

Clevedon Town 1-3 Yeovil Town
Weston super Mare 2-1 Radstock Town

FINAL (@ Yeovil Town, 3/5/11)
Yeovil Town 0-1 Weston super Mare

STAFFORDSHIRE SENIOR CUP

ROUND 1

Kidsgrove Athletic 3-0 Stone Dominoes
Rocester 1-4 Biddulph Victoria
Chasetown 2-5 Hednesford Town
Heath Hayes 0-1 Port Vale
Leek Town 1-3 Rushall Olympic
Market Drayton Town 1-4 Stafford Rangers

QUARTER FINALS

Newcastle Town 0-1 Kidsgrove Athletic
Port Vale 0-4 Stoke City
Stafford Rangers 4-2 Hednesford Town
Rushall Olympic 0-1 Biddulph Victoria

SEMI-FINALS
Biddulph Victoria 0-1 Stoke City
Stafford Town 0-2 Kidsgrove Athletic

FINAL (@ Leek Town, 20/4/11)
Stoke City 0-1 Kidsgrove Athletic

SUFFOLK PREMIER CUP

(Sponsored by LB Group)

ROUND 1
Woodbridge Town 3-2 Haverhill Rovers
Walsham-le-Willows 1-2 Felixstowe & Walton United
Hadleigh United 2-1 Debenham L C
Leiston 0-2 Lowestoft Town
Newmarket Town 1-0 Mildenhall Town
Brantham Athletic 0-4 Needham Market
A F C Sudbury 3-5 Bury Town

QUARTER FINALS
Hadleigh United 1-3 Needham Market
Felixstowe & Walton United 0-2 Bury Town
Lowestoft Town 5-0 Newmarket Town
Woodbridge Town 1-3 Kirkley & Pakefield

SEMI-FINALS
Kirkley & Pakefield 0-2 Needham Market
Bury Town 3-0 Lowestoft Town

FINAL (@ Ipswich Town, 15/4/11)
Needham Market 0-2 Bury Town

SURREY SATURDAY SENIOR CUP

ROUND 1
Banstead Athletic 1-3 Whyteleafe
Lingfield 1-2 Colliers Wood United
Molesey 2-0 Camberley Town
Dorking 2-3 Bookham
Walton & Hersham 1-2 Merstham

ROUND 2
Chertsey Town 3-4 Tooting & Mitcham United
Colliers Wood United 2-1 A F C Wimbledon
Walton Casuals 1-2 Guildford City
Bookham 1-2 Croydon
Ashford Town (Middx) 0-1 Chipstead
Raynes Park Vale 3-2 Horley Town
Ash United 2-1 Crystal Palace
Redhill 1-4 Carshalton Athletic
Chessington & Hook United 0-3 Corinthian-Casuals
Mole Valley S C R 1-3 Egham Town
Epsom & Ewell 2-3 Beckenham Town
Merstham 1-2 Godalming Town
Leatherhead 1-0 Kingstonian
Molesey 1-0 Sutton United
Whyteleafe 3-1 Woking
Badshot Lea 2-4 Metropolitan Police

ROUND 3
Leatherhead 1-0 Egham Town
Raynes Park Vale 4-2 Guildford City
Carshalton Athletic 3-1 Croydon
Colliers Wood United 1-0 Chipstead
Tooting & Mitcham United 1-0 Godalming Town
Corinthian-Casuals 3-2 Whyteleafe
Molesey 2-1 Ash United
Beckenham Town 0-2 Metropolitan Police

QUARTER FINALS
Leatherhead 4-1 Tooting & Mitcham United
Carshalton Athletic 0-2 Molesey
Raynes Park Vale 1-2 Metropolitan Police
Corinthian-Casuals 3-2 Colliers Wood United

SEMI-FINALS
Metropolitan Police 1-2 Corinthian-Casuals
Leatherhead 1-0 Molesey

FINAL (@ Sutton United, 10/5/11)
Corinthian-Casuals 2-0 Leatherhead

SUSSEX SENIOR CUP

ROUND 1
Crowborough Athletic 4-5 Shoreham
Littlehampton Town 0-2 Lancing
Arundel 4-0 East Preston
Ringmer 0-3 East Grinstead Town
Seaford Town 4-2 Westfield
Oakwood 0-2 Sidley United
Selsey 0-1 Rye United
Three Bridges 1-4 A F C Uckfield
Midhurst & Easebourne 1-3 Loxwood
Bexhill United 0-2 Hailsham Town
Crawley Down 4-0 St Francis Rangers
Pagham 4-1 Worthing United
Steyning Town 1-1 Hassocks
Mile Oak 2-1 Little Common
Storrington 2-1 Southwick
Clymping 2-6 Rustington

ROUND 1 REPLAY
Hassocks 5-1 Steyning Town

ROUND 2
Mile Oak 0-5 Eastbourne Borough
Burgess Hill Town 5-0 Loxwood
Horsham 2-0 Crawley Town
Lancing 2-4 Crawley Down
Eastbourne Town 4-0 Eastbourne United Association
Shoreham 1-3 Lewes
Steyning Town 2-1 Whitehawk
Hastings United 2-3 A F C Uckfield
Brighton & Hove Albion reserves 6-2 Horsham Y M C A
Rye United 2-1 Pagham
Peacehaven & Telscombe 0-0 Rustington
Bognor Regis Town 6-0 Seaford Town
Storrington 1-3 Hailsham Town
Sidley United 4-2 Arundel
Chichester City 1-1 East Grinstead Town
Wick 0-2 Worthing

ROUND 2 REPLAYS
East Grinstead Town 3-0 Chichester City
Rustington 0-0 Peacehaven & Telscombe (Rustington won 5-4 on penalties)

ROUND 3
Hassocks 2-4 Horsham
Lewes 1-0 Bognor Regis Town
Eastbourne Borough 3-0 Rustington
Eastbourne Town 0-2 Burgess Hill Town
Sidley United 0-3 Brighton & Hove Albion reserves
Crawley Down 1-1 A F C Uckfield
Hailsham Town 1-3 East Grinstead Town
Worthing 2-3 Rye United

ROUND 3 REPLAY
A F C Uckfield 2-8 Crawley Down

QUARTER FINALS
Crawley Down 1-0 East Grinstead Town
Brighton & Hove Albion reserves 1-0 Lewes
Eastbourne Borough 3-0 Rye United
Burgess Hill Town 1-1 Horsham

QUARTER FINAL REPLAY
Horsham 3-1 Burgess Hill Town

SEMI-FINALS
Horsham 0-2 Brighton & Hove Albion reserves
Eastbourne Borough 5-2 Crawley Down

FINAL (@ New Brighton & Hove Albion, 16/7/11)
Brighton & Hove Albion reserves 2-0 Eastbourne Borough

WEST RIDING COUNTY CUP

ROUND 1
Goole 2-1 Silsden
Selby Town 1-2 Askern Villa
Pontefract Collieries 1-0 Glasshoughton Welfare
Harrogate Railway Athletic 4-0 Wakefield
Eccleshill United 1-3 Bradford Park Avenue
(tie awarded to Eccleshill United)
Tadcaster Albion 1-4 Thackley
Armthorpe Welfare 2-3 Farsley
Ossett Town 0-5 F C Halifax Town
Leeds Carnegie 4-3 Yorkshire Amateur

ROUND 2
Askern Villa 1-0 Leeds Carnegie
Harrogate Railway Athletic 4-1 Farsley
Garforth Town 3-2 Ossett Albion
Goole 2-0 Harrogate Town
Liversedge 1-2 Pontefract Collieries
Barnoldswick Town 0-5 F C Halifax Town
Guiseley 1-0 Brighouse Town
Ecceshill United 1-3 Thackley

QUARTER FINALS
Thackley 2-1 Garforth Town
Goole 4-3 Askern Villa
Harrogate Railway Athletic 2-3 F C Halifax Town
Pontefract Collieries 1-2 Guiseley

SEMI-FINALS
F C Halifax Town 1-3 Guiseley
Goole 1-4 Thackley

FINAL (@ Bradford City, 13/4/11)
Guiseley 4-2 Thackley

WESTMORLAND SENIOR CUP

ROUND 1
Burton Thistle 1-7 Appleby
Esthwaite Vale United 1-9 Wetheriggs United
Corinthians 4-2 Ambleside United
Kendal Celtic 4-3 Eden Thistle
Burneside 7-4 Coniston
Kirkby Lonsdale 4-1 Braithwaite
Carvetii United 6-4 Penrith Rangers
Lunesdale United 3-0 Langwathby United
Keswick 5-0 Windermere S C
Endmoor K G R 2-5 Kendal County
Ibis 2-1 Sedbergh Wanderers

ROUND 2
Kirkoswald 5-1 Keswick County
Lunesdale United 1-2 Shap
Staveley United 4-1 Keswick
Appleby 3-4 Kendal United
Penrith Saints 1-7 Burneside
Ibis 1-6 Wertheriggs United
Kendal Celtic 4-1 Carvetii United
Corinthians 4-3 Kirkby Lonsdale

QUARTER FINALS
Burneside 1-8 Corinthians
Kirkoswald 4-2 Kendal United
Wetheriggs United 4-1 Kendal Celtic
Staveley United 5-2 Shap

SEMI-FINALS
Corinthians 1-0 Staveley United
Kirkoswald 2-2 Wetheriggs United (Kirkoswald won 4-3 on penalties)

FINAL (@ Kendal Town, 16/4/11)
Corinthians 0-2 Kirkoswald

WILTSHIRE PREMIER SHIELD

SEMI-FINALS (2 LEGS)
Chippenham Town 1-0 Swindon Supermarine
Swindon Supermarine 1-1 Chippenham Town
Chippenham Town won 2-1 on aggregate

Salisbury City 0-3 Swindon Town
Played as a single game due to fixture congestion

FINAL (@ Chippenham Town, 18/4/11)
Chippenham Town 1-0 Swindon Town

WILTSHIRE SENIOR CUP

ROUND 1
Amesbury Town 2-0 Shrewton United
Bradford Town 7-1 Chalke Valley
Devizes Town 0-1 F C Chippenham Youth
Pewsey Vale 0-2 Corsham Town
Warminster Town 3-0 New College Swindon
Westbury United 4-3 Wootton Bassett Town
Wroughton 0-4 Purton

ROUND 2

Bemerton Heath Harlequins 2-0 Warminster Town
Calne Town 1-4 Downton
Corsham Town 1-1 Laverstock & Ford
(Laverstock & Ford won 5-4 on penalties)
Cricklade Town 1-4 Purton
Highworth Town 3-0 Amesbury Town
Malmesbury Victoria 0-7 Bradford Town
Melksham Town 3-0 Westbury United
Trowbridge Town 2-1 F C Chippenham Youth

QUARTER FINALS

Bradford Town 3-1 Trowbridge Town
Bemerton Heath Harlequins 5-3 Purton
Downton 4-1 Melksham Town
Highworth Town 4-1 Laverstock & Ford

SEMI-FINALS

Bradford Town 3-2 Downton
Bemerton Heath Harlequins 3-0 Highworth Town

FINAL (@ Swindon Supermarine, 3/5/11)
Bemerton Heath Harlequins 2-0 Bradford Town

WORCESTERSHIRE SENIOR CUP

QUARTER FINALS

Bromsgrove Rovers scr-w/o Redditch United

Evesham United 1-2 Stourbridge

Kidderminster Harriers 1-3 Worcester City

Halesowen Town 2-1 Stourport Swifts

SEMI-FINALS

Redditch United 0-4 Stourbridge

Halesowen Town 1-2 Worcester City

FINAL (@ Kidderminster Harriers, 27/4/11)

Stourbridge 2-0 Worcester City

ARTHURIAN LEAGUE CUPS 2010-11

ARTHUR DUNN CUP

ROUND 1

Old Eastbournians 0-8 Old Westminsters
Old King's Scholars 0-4 Old Etonians
Old Radleians 4-2 Old Aldenhamians
Old Bradfieldians 0-6 Lancing Old Boys
Old Oundelians 1-2 Old Malvernians
Old Wellingtonians 1-2 Old King's Wimbledon
Old Wykehamists 0-5 Old Brentwoods
Old Haberdashers 0-9 Old Carthusians
Old Amplefordians 2-3 Old Reptonians
Old Forersters 14-0 Old Wellingburnians

ROUND 2

Old Radleians 3-1 Old Harrovians
Lancing Old Boys 3-0 Old King's Wimbledon
Old Foresters 3-1 Old Chigwellians
Old Etonians 1-0 Old Westminsters
Old Malvernians 0-1 Old Brentwoods
Old Cholmelians 4-0 Old Tonbridgians
Old Salopians 9-1 Old Reptonians
Old Berkhamstedians scr-w/o Old Carthusians

QUARTER FINALS

Lancing Old Boys 2-0 Old Cholmelians
Old Carthusians 2-1 Old Salopians
Old Etonians 2-1 Old Foresters
Old Radleians 2-4 Old Brentwoods

SEMI-FINALS

Old Carthusians 2-1 Lancing Old Boys
Old Brentwoods 1-3 Old Etonians

FINAL (@ Imperial University Sports Ground, 11/4/11)
Old Carthusians 3-3 Old Etonians
(Old Carthusians won on penalties)

JUNIOR LEAGUE CUP

PRELIMINARY ROUND

Old Epsomians 4-3 Old Chigwellians "B"
Old Malvernians reserves 3-0 Old Brentwoods "B"

ROUND 1

Old Westminsters reserves 8-1 Old Cholmelians "B"
Old Carthusians reserves 10-0 Old Aldenhamians res.
Old Eastbournians 1-5 Old Cholmelians reserves
Old Epsomians 4-3 Old Carthusians "A"
Lancing Old Boys reserves 3-5 Old Cholmelians "A"
Old Marlburnians 4-2 Old Etonians reserves
Old Wykehamists reserves 1-4 Old Berkhamstedians
Old Chigwellians "A" 0-0 Old Brentwoods reserves (Old Brentwoods reserves won 3-2 on penalties)
Old Citizens 2-4 Old Harrovians reserves
Old Foresters "A" 0-4 Old Chigwellians reserves
Old Haberdashers 8-1 Old Foresters "B"
Old Kings Wimbledon reserves 2-0 Old Brentwoods "A"
Old Wellingtonians 4-2 Old Oundelians

ROUND 2

Old Epsomians 5-3 Old Westminsters reserves
Old Cholmelians reserves 4-2 Old Chigwellians reserves
Old Cholmelians "A" 2-3 Old Bradfieldians
Old Berkhamstedians 3-6 Old Haberdashers
Old Harrovians reserves 3-2 Old Malvernians reserves
Old Kings Wimbledon reserves 5-2 Old Foresters res.
Old Marlburnians 1-4 Old Cathusians reserves
Old Wellingtonians 0-3 Old Brentwoods reserves

QUARTER FINALS

Old Epsomians 1-7 Old Carthusians reserves
Old Haberdashers 1-4 Old Cholmelians
Old Brentwoods reserves 2-0 Old Bradfieldians
Old Harrovians 6-2 Old Kings Wimbledon

SEMI-FINALS

Old Harrovians II 6-1 Old Cholmeleians II
Old Brentwoods II 2-3 Old Carthusians II

FINAL

Old Carthusians II 2-3 Old Harrovians II

3rd York Regiment celebrate their **ARMY CHALLENGE CUP** win over 9th Regiment AAC. The final finished 1-1 after extra time with 3rd York team winning 4-3 on penalties. Photo: Eric Marsh.

MASSEY TROPHY - FINAL TABLES

DIVISION ONE	P	W	D	L	F	A	Pts
RSIGNALS	12	6	4	2	25	14	22
RLC	12	7	2	3	27	21	23
REME	12	5	4	3	20	16	19
RE	12	5	2	5	31	22	17
AGC	12	2	5	5	16	25	11
RAPTC	12	3	4	5	21	25	13
INFANTRY	12	2	3	7	13	33	7

DIVISION TWO	P	W	D	L	F	A	Pts
RA	8	6	1	1	25	8	19
INT	8	6		2	14	16	18
RAC	8	3	1	4	19	17	10
AAC	8	2	2	4	16	19	8
AMS	8	1		7	7	21	3

ROYAL NAVY FA CUP/PLATE

SEMI FINAL

HMS Seahawk 6 - 0 HMS Heron

HM Naval Base Portsmouth 1 - 2 HMS Ark Royal

FINAL - 05/05/11

HMS Ark Royal 1 - 3 HMS Seahawk

ROYAL AIR FORCE FA CHALLENGE CUP

SEMI-FINALS (played on neutral grounds)

CUP

RAF Cosford 0-2 RAF Brize Norton (@ RAF Halton)

RAF Wittering 2-1 RAF Waddington
(@ RAF Brize Norton)

PLATE

RAF Coningsby 1-0 RAF Marham (@ RAF Cosford)

RAF Leuchars 0-2 RAF Benson (@ RAF Cranwell)

FINALS (played at RAF Cranwell)

CUP

RAF Brize Norton 1-3 RAF Wittering

PLATE

RAF Coningsby 1-5 RAF Benson

BRITISH UNIVERSITIES CUP RESULTS 2010-11

All 1st Teams unless stated.

MEN'S CHAMPIONSHIP

SEMI-FINALS

Edinburgh University 2-2 Bournemouth University
(Edinburgh won on penalties)

UWE Hartpury 2-1 Loughborough University

FINAL (@ Sheffield United, 11/5/11)
Edinburgh University 2-4 UWE Hartpury

MEN'S TROPHY

SEMI FINAL

University of Lincoln 5-2 York St John
Loughborough University 2nd 2-3 Uni. of Portsmouth

FINAL (Don Valley Stadium, Sheffield 17/3/11
University of Lincoln 3-7 University of Portsmouth

MEN'S NORTHERN CONFERENCE CUP

PRELIMINARY ROUND

SEMI FINAL

Newcastle University 1-2 Leeds Met. Carnegie 2nd
Liverpool John Moores University 2-1 MMU Cheshire

FINAL (23.3.11)
Leeds Met. Carnegie 2nd 0-4 Liverpool John Moores U.

MEN'S MIDLANDS CONFERENCE CUP

SEMI FINAL

Nottingham Trent Uni. 3rd 2-1 Uni. of Cambridge
Birmingham City University 1-2 Coventry University

FINAL (23.3.11)
Nottingham Trent Uni. 3rd 3-1 Coventry University

MEN'S WESTERN CONFERENCE CUP

SEMI FINAL

UWE Hartpury 2nd 4-1 UWIC Men's 3rd
Uni. of Winchester 1-2 College of St Mark & St John

FINAL (23.3.11)
UWE Hartpury 2nd 3-0 College of St Mark & St John

MEN'S SOUTH EASTERN CONFERENCE CUP

SEMI-FINALS

Queen Mary, Uni of London 3-1 Uni of Chichester 2nd
University of East London 4-2 Uni. of Portsmouth 3rd

FINAL (@ Surrey Sports Park 23.3.11)
Queen Mary, Uni. of London 1-1 Uni. of East London
(Queen Mary won 6-5 on penalties)

MEN'S SCOTTISH CONFERENCE CUP

SEMI FINAL

Aberdeen University 1-2 Glasgow Caledonian University
Edinburgh Napier University 1-0 Uni. of Stirling 2nd

FINAL (@ Riverside Playing Fields 23.3.11)
Glasgow Caledonian Uni. 1-3 Edinburgh Napier Uni.

MEN'S SCOTTISH CONFERENCE PLATE

SEMI-FINALS

West of Scotland Uni 3rd 0-1 Edinburgh Napier Uni. 2nd
University of Dundee 2nd 4-2 Uni. of Strathclyde 3rd

FINAL (@ Riverside Playing Fields 23.3.11)
University of Dundee 2nd 0-0 Edinburgh Napier Uni. 2nd
(Dundee won 4-3 on penalties)

MEN'S PREMIER LEAGUE FINAL TABLES

NORTH	P	W	D	L	F	A	Pts
1 Stirling	10	6	4	0	21	11	22
2 Birmingham	10	6	3	1	28	12	21
3 Loughborough	10	4	2	4	15	16	14
4 Northumbria	10	3	1	6	20	21	10
5 Leeds	10	2	2	6	15	32	8
6 Leeds Met. Carnegie	10	2	2	6	13	20	8

SOUTH	P	W	D	L	F	A	Pts
1 UWE Hartpury	10	9	1	0	39	8	28
2 Bournemouth	10	7	1	2	31	14	22
3 Bath	10	5	2	3	27	17	17
4 Brighton	10	3	1	6	15	30	10
5 Cardiff	10	1	2	7	11	30	5
6 Brunel West London	10	1	1	8	12	36	4

NORTHERN CONFERENCE CHAMPIONS	P	W	D	L	F	A	Pts
1 Manchester	10	9	1	0	40	14	28

MIDLANDS CONFERENCE CHAMPIONS	P	W	D	L	F	A	Pts
1 Loughborough 2nd	10	7	1	2	25	11	22

WESTERN CONFERENCE CHAMPIONS	P	W	D	L	F	A	Pts
1 Glamorgan	8	6	0	2	24	10	18

SOUTH EASTERN CONFERENCE CHAMPIONS	P	W	D	L	F	A	Pts
1 St Mary's	10	9	1	0	22	10	28

ENGLISH SCHOOLS' FOOTBALL ASSOCIATION

4, Parker Court, Staffordshire Technology Park, Beaconside, Stafford ST 18 0WP

Tel: 01785 785970; website: www.esfa.co.uk

Chief Executive: John Read (john.read@schoolsfa.com)

Competitions Manager: Mike Spinks (mike.spinks@schoolsfa.com)

Non-League Directory Contributor: Mike Simmonds (m.simmonds31@btinternet.com)

(0115 9313299)

Photos: RWT Photogrpahy

Website: www.rwt.photography.co.uk

THE INTERNATIONAL SEASON

Back Row (l to r): Alex Meaney (Lancs); Fabio Goncalves-Abreu (Gtr.Manchester); Josh White (Somerset); Ed Baldy (Wilts); Jack Wood (Glos); Josh Hart (Merseyside); Jordan Ayris (Oxon); Jack Vallis (Wilts); Jamie Summers (Surrey)

Middle Row: Shaun Hemming (GK Coach); Arthur Tabor (Doctor); Jack Sherratt (Staffs); Josh Glover (Staffs); Jonathan Barden(Middlesex); Cliff oyo (Staffs); Scott Cheetham (Gtr.Manchester); Tom Hurley (Somerset); Thomas Boakye (Glos); Dave Burns (Physio); Andy Buckingham (Asst. Team Manager).

Front Row: Jonathon Evans (Durham); Nigel Brown; Mike Coyne (Chairman); John Read (CEO); Andy Williams (Team Manager); Connor Thompson (Glos)

THE UNDER 18 CENTENARY SHIELD

FINAL TABLE 210-2011	**P**	**W**	**D**	**L**	**F**	**A**	**P**
Northern Ireland	4	2	2	0	6	2	8
Scotland	4	2	2	0	6	3	8
England	4	2	0	2	4	5	6
Republic of Ireland	4	0	2	2	5	8	2
Wales	4	0	2	2	2	5	2

Northern Ireland and Scotland were joint winners as positions ar calculated on points only.

ENGLAND RESULTS

v. Northern Ireland	0-2	(AFC Telford); v. Wales 1-0 (Jordan Ayris) (Yeovil Town);
v. Scotland	0-1	(Inverness Caledonian Thistle);
v. Republic of Ireland	3-2	(Shamrock Rovers FC) (Goncalves-Abreu 2, Jack Wood);
v. Poland (Katowice)	1-4	(Goncalves-Abreu)

HIGHLIGHTS OF THE SEASON

The Under 18 international side had a generally disappointing season, never really recovering from a poor performance against Northern Ireland in their first match, but there were two particular highlights. The first came when they defeated Wales at Huish Park (Yeovil Town) in front of one of the biggest crowds for a provincial international for many years, 6,157. The game was settled by a delightful chip from Jonathan Ayris which was the only goal of a game which England should have won in a canter.

The second was the first ever England Schools' visit to Poland where they met a side which although a year younger, consisted entirely of young players from clubs in the Polish, German and Italian leagues. England led at the interval thanks to a goal by Fabio Goncalves-Abreu but in the second half, the superior fitness of the opposition and the fact that England used their full bench of substitutes saw Poland took full control to win 4-1.

Also on the international scene, there was another 'first' for the Association. when an England Schools Girls' international team was fielded for the first time. They met Scotland at Under 15 level at the Toryglen Indoor Arena next to Hampden Park on a full sized 3G pitch which is sometimes used in bad weather by Scottish League clubs. A fine attacking display brought England a 3-1 win thanks to two goals by Millie Fowler and a penalty by Jodie Brett

.

Once again, there were large entries for most of the national competitions now organised by the English Schools' F.A. with the small-sided events at Primary level attracting nearly 3,000 school teams and most of the Secondary competitions around 600 at each age group. Three of the highlights here were the performances of Malet Lambert School from Kingston-upon Hull in the Under 16 Boys' Cup. Not only did they defeat Broadlands (Bath and North East Somerset) 5-0 in the final but they played ten fixtures to win the trophy, scoring 51 goals and conceding only six. Moreover, at least six of their squad represented Humberside in the Under 16 boys inter-county competition which the Yorkshire county won 4-1 and remarkably, two of their players, Tom Dungworth and Danny Chambers scored in both finals. Other close fought games were the Inter-Association Under 15 final between two small Associations, Mid-Oxfordshire and Dacorum (Hertfordshire) which the latter won 2-1 after extra time and the F.A. Premier League Under 14 final which produced seven goals with Richard Challoner School winning 4-3. Four matches had to be settled by penalties after extra time had failed to separate the sides.

U18 GIRLS SCHOOLS TROPHY FINAL
WEDNESDAY 16 MARCH 2011
CARROW ROAD, NORWICH CITY FC

THURSTABLE (COLCHESTER & N.E. ESSEX SFA	1	BALBY CARR (DONCASTER SFA)	0

Referee: Stuart Reeve (Norfolk)
Goalscorers: Maegan Doyle (Thurstable)

U18 GIRLS COLLEGES TROPHY FINAL
MONDAY 21 MARCH 2011
KEEPMOAT STADIUM, DONCASTER ROVERS FC

GATESHEAD (GATESHEAD SFA)	2	FILTON COLLEGE (BRISTOL & SOUTH GLOUCESTERSHIRE SFA)	2 a.e.t.,1-1 at full-time

Filton College won 4-3 on penalties
Referee: Martin Dexter (Leicestershire)
Goalscorers: Gabby Bird (Filton), Charlotte Jones (Filton), Keira Ramshaw (2, Gateshead)

U16 GIRLS INTER COUNTY TROPHY FINAL
WEDNESDAY 23 MARCH 2011
CITY GROUND, NOTTINGHAM FOREST FC

DURHAM CSFA	3	KENT CSFA	2

Referee: Declan Bourne (Nottinghamshire)
Goalscorers: Zoe Ness (2, Durham), Charlotte Wilson (Durham), Charlottle Wilson (og, Kent), Courtenay Gibson (Kent)

U16 BOYS INTER COUNTY TROPHY FINAL
THURSDAY 31 MARCH 2011
THE LONDON BOROUGH OF BARKING AND DAGENHAM STADIUM,
DAGENHAM AND REDBRIDGE FC

HUMBERSIDE CSFA	4	SURREY CSFA	1

Referee: Alec Berry (Essex)
Goalscorers: Tom Davy, Tom Dungworth, Sam Topliss and Danny Chambers (Humberside), Arran Nurse (Surrey)

U16 GIRLS INTER SCHOOLS CUP FINAL
WEDNESDAY 6 APRIL 2011
PIRELLI STADIUM, BURTON ALBION FC

WESTLANDS (SWALE SFA)	1	SOUTH HOLDERNESS (EAST RIDING SFA)	4

Referee: Adam Lenton (West Midlands)
Goalscorers: Hope Knight (2, South Holderness), Natalie Gray (2, South Holderness), Kit Graham (Westlands)

U16 BOYS INTER SCHOOLS CUP FINAL
WEDNESDAY 6 APRIL 2011
PIRELLI STADIUM, BURTON ALBION FC

BROADLANDS (BATH & N.E.SOMERSET SFA)	0	MALET LAMBERT (KINGSTON-UPON-HULL SFA)	5

Referee: Roy Burton (Staffordshire)
Goalscorers: Danny Chambers (2, Malet Lambert), Tom Dungworth (Malet Lambert), Kieran King (Malet Lambert), Jack Varney (Malet Lambert)

U18 BOYS INTER SCHOOLS CUP FINAL
THURSDAY 7 APRIL 2011
HILLSBOROUGH, SHEFFIELD WEDNESDAY FC

MONKSEATON HIGH)NORTH TYNESIDE SFA)	0	BARKING ABBEY (BARKING & DAGENHAM SFA)	2

Referee: Des Coulson (North Yorkshire)
Goalscorers: Daniel Jones (2, Barking Abbey)

U18 BOYS INTER COUNTY TROPHY FINAL
THURSDAY 7 APRIL 2011
HILLSBOROUGH, SHEFFIELD WEDNESDAY FC
LANCASHIRE CSFA 1 HERTFORDSHIRE CSFA 1 (AET, 1-1 at full-time)
Lancashire won 5-4 on penalties
Referee: Howard Webb (South Yorkshire)
Goalscorers: Tom Kilifin (Lancashire), Steve O'Connor (Hertfordshire)
It was very good to have the 2010 World Cup Final referee officiating at this game. He then spoke to everyone in the post-match reception. It's not every day that a World Cup Final referee officiates at an ESFA game.

U18 BOYS COLLEGES TROPHY FINAL
MONDAY 11 APRIL 2011
EDGAR STREET, HEREFORD UNITED FC
QUEENS 0 GATESHEAD COLLEGE 2
(WATFORD SFA) (GATESHEAD SFA)
Referee: Steve Hames (South Wales)
Goalscorers: Michael Dodds, Josh Allen (Gateshead)

U15 GIRLS SCHOOLS CUP FINAL
WEDNESDAY 4 MAY 2011
VALE PARK, PORT VALE FC
SOUTH HUNSLEY 4 HABERDASHERS'ASKE'S 1
(EAST RIDING SFA) (BLACKHEATH SFA)
Referee: Mark Warren (Staffordshire)
Goalscorers: Nelly Rawson (2, South Hunsley), Liberty Bott (2, South Hunsley), Dominique Harris (Haberdashers)

U14 BOYS INTER COUNTY TROPHY FINAL
TUESDAY 10 MAY 2011
GRIFFIN PARK, BRENTFORD FC
SURREY CSFA 2 OXFORDSHIRE CSFA 2 (AET, 2-2 at full-time)
Surrey won 4-3 on penalties
Referee: Daniel Wyatt (London)
Goalscorers: Andrew Mills (2, Surrey CSFA), Scott Gee (Oxfordshire CSFA), Jack Alexander (Oxfordshire CSFA)

U14 BOYS SCHOOLS CUP FINAL
SPONSORED BY PREMIER LEAGUE
WEDNESDAY 11 MAY 2011
CITY OF MANCHESTER STADIUM, MANCHESTER CITY FC
WRIGHT ROBINSON 3 RICHARD CHALLONER 4
(MANCHESTER SFA) (KINGSTON SFA)
Referee: Rob Lewis (Shropshire)
Goalscorers: Kean Bryan (3, Wright Robinson), Jack Watret (2, Richard Challoner), Jeremie Boga (Richard Challoner), Ryan Sweeney (Richard Challoner)

U13 GIRLS SCHOOLS CUP FINAL
WEDNESDAY 11 MAY 2011
THE MEMORIAL GROUND, BRISTOL ROVERS FC
BRIMSHAM GREEN 0 ST BEDE'S 1
(BRISTOL & SOUTH GLOUCS SFA) (BLACKBURN & DARWEN SFA)
Referee: Mandy Kerfoot (Gloucestershire)
Goalscorers: Gabrielle Taylor (St Bede's)

U12 BOYS SCHOOLS CUP FINAL
SPONSORED BY DANONE NATIONS UK
WEDNESDAY 11 MAY 2011
CRAVEN COTTAGE, FULHAM FC
CARDINAL HEENAN 4 WHITGIFT 1
(LIVERPOOL SFA) (CROYDON SFA)
Referee: Dermot Gallagher (Oxfordshire)
Goalscorers: Kevin Cringle (Cardinal Heenan), Luke Carroll-Burgess (Cardinal Heenan), Callum Lacy (Cardinal Heenan), Tom Grivosti (Cardinal Heenan)

U15 INTER ASSOCIATION TROPHY FINAL
THURSDAY 19 MAY 2011
KASSAM STADIUM, OXFORD UNITED FC
MID OXFORDSHIRE SFA 1 DACORUM SFA 2 a.e.t., 1-1 at full-time
Referee: John Busby (Oxfordshire)
Goalscorers: Jacob Hughes (Mid Oxfordshire), Kai Lewis (2, Dacorum)

U15 BOYS SCHOOLS CUP FINAL
FRIDAY 20 MAY 2011
BRAMALL LANE, SHEFFIELD UNITED FC
NORTHAMPTON (NORTHAMPTON SFA) 0 LANCASTER (LEICESTER SFA) 1
Referee: Steve Rushton (Staffordshire)
Goalscorers: Eric Agyei-Bekoe (Lancaster)

U13 INTER ASSOCIATION TROPHY FINAL
MONDAY 23 MAY 2011
STADIUM MK, MILTON KEYNES DONS FC
SOUTHAMPTON SFA 0 YORK & DISTRICT SFA 2
Referee: Dermot Gallagher (Oxfordshire)
Goalscorers: Ben Hirst (York), Joe McCormick (York)

U13 BOYS SCHOOLS CUP FINAL
WEDNESDAY 25 MAY 2011
WESTON HOMES COMMUNITY STADIUM, COLCHESTER UNITED FC
EASTBURY (BARKING & DAGENHAM SFA) 1 CARDINAL HEENAN (LIVERPOOL SFA) 1 (AET, 1-1 at full-time)
Cardinal Heenan won 4-3 on penalties
Referee: Steve Moore (Essex)
Goalscorers: John Massala (Eastbury), Lee Jones (Cardinal Heenan)

UNDER 12 BOYS INDOOR 5-A-SIDE CUP FINAL- SPONSORED BY MUNICH TROPHIES
MONDAY, MARCH 7TH 2011
DERBY POWER LEAGUE SOCCER CENTRE
SANDWELL (WEST BROMWICH SFA) 1 PRIESTNELL (STOCKPORT SFA) 0

UNDER 12 GIRLS INDOOR 5-A-SIDE CUP FINAL-SPONSORED BY MUNICH TROPHIES
MONDAY, MARCH 7TH
DERBY POWER LEAGUE SOCCER CENTRE
ALDER (TAMESIDE SFA) 3 CHENEY (OXFORD CITY SFA) 4 (AET)

PRIMARY COMPETITIONS

U11 BOYS 7-A-SIDE CUP
SATURDAY 21 MAY 2011
UNIVERSITY COLLEGE LONDON, WATFORD FC TRAINING GROUND
MELTHAM CE PRIMARY SCHOOL (HUDDERSFIELD SFA) Winners
WARREN PARK PRIMARY SCHOOL (HAVANT SFA) Runners-up

U11 GIRLS 7-A-SIDE CUP
SATURDAY 21 MAY 2011
UNIVERSITY COLLEGE LONDON, WATFORD FC TRAINING GROUND
MURRAYFIELD PRIMARY SCHOOL (IPSWICH & SOUTH SUFFOLK SFA) Winners
WOLD PRIMARY SCHOOL (KINGSTON UPON HULL SFA) Runners-up

U11 SMALL SCHOOLS SOCCER SEVENS
SATURDAY 21 MAY 2011
UNIVERSITY COLLEGE LONDON, WATFORD FC TRAINING GROUND
CHETWYNDE SCHOOL (BARROW IN FURNESS SFA) Winners
ST AIDAN'S CATHOLIC PRIMARY SCHOOL (HUYTON SFA) Runners-up

U11 INTER ASSOCIATION 7-A-SIDE TROPHY
SATURDAY 21 MAY 2011
UNIVERSITY COLLEGE LONDON, WATFORD FC TRAINING GROUND
LIVERPOOL SFA Winners
KINGSTON UPON HULL SFA Runners-up

Barking Abbey School, winners of the ESFA Under 18 Schools' Cup.

Action from the Under 15 Girls' Final at Vale Park between South Hunsley and Haberdasher's Aske which the former won 4-1.

Durham County Schools' F.A winners of the Under 16 Girls County Championship at Nottingham Forest F.C.

(Above) Malet Lambert School (Kingston -upon-Hull) Under 16s, winners of the ESFA Under 16 Boys' Cup; one of the strongest ever school teams ?

(Left) Cardinal Heenan School, winners of the ESFA Danone Nations UK Cup.

Aston Villa LFC
v
Leicester City WFC

Photos by Jonathan Holloway

FA PREMIER LEAGUE TABLES 2010-11

NATIONAL DIVISION

		P	W	D	L	F	A	GD	Pts
1	Sunderland WFC	14	9	3	2	30	16	14	30
2	Nottingham Forest LFC	14	6	5	3	19	16	3	23
3	Reading FC Women	14	6	2	6	24	21	3	20
4	Leeds United LFC	14	5	3	6	17	17	0	18
5	Barnet FC Ladies	14	4	4	6	20	22	-2	16
6	Watford LFC	14	3	7	4	21	26	-5	16
7	**Blackburn Rovers LFC**	**14**	**4**	**4**	**6**	**18**	**24**	**-6**	**16**
8	**Millwall Lionesses LFC**	**14**	**3**	**4**	**7**	**22**	**29**	**-7**	**13**

NORTHERN DIVISION

		P	W	D	L	F	A	GD	Pts
1	**Aston Villa LFC**	**18**	**14**	**0**	**4**	**40**	**18**	**22**	**42**
2	Coventry City LFC	18	13	2	3	45	22	23	41
3	Leicester City WFC	18	12	1	5	59	20	39	37
4	Manchester City LFC	18	12	1	5	37	18	19	37
5	Derby County LFC	18	8	3	7	27	28	-1	27
6	Leeds City Vixens LFC	18	5	2	11	31	46	-15	17
7	Rochdale AFC Ladies	18	5	1	12	36	57	-21	16
8	Preston North End WFC	18	4	3	11	22	46	-24	15
9	Newcastle United WFC	18	4	3	11	22	48	-26	15
10	Curzon Ashton LFC	18	3	4	11	22	38	-16	13

SOUTHERN DIVISION

		P	W	D	L	F	A	GD	Pts
1	**Charlton Athletic WFC**	**18**	**11**	**3**	**4**	**30**	**12**	**18**	**36**
2	Cardiff City LFC	18	11	3	4	26	19	7	36
3	West Ham United LFC	18	10	3	5	29	17	12	33
4	Portsmouth FC Ladies	18	10	1	7	33	30	3	31
5	Keynsham Town LFC	18	9	3	6	26	22	4	30
6	Colchester United FC	18	6	3	9	22	23	-1	21
7	Brighton & Hove Albion WFC	18	5	4	9	25	35	-10	19
8	Queens Park Rangers LFC	18	5	3	10	16	26	-10	18
9	Gillingham LFC	18	5	2	11	17	27	-10	17
10	Yeovil Town LFC	18	3	5	10	18	31	-13	14

FA PREMIER LEAGUE CUP FINAL (@ Adams Park, Wycombe 24/3/11)
Barnet FC Ladies 0 - 0 Nottingham Forest
(Barnet won 4-3 on penalties after extra time)

ENGLAND SENIOR TEAM 2010-11

	Date	Opponents	H/A	Comp.	Result	Goalscorers
1	Sept 12	Switzerland	H	World Cup Regional Stages	**W** 2-0	Williams 44, K.Smith 45*
2	16	Switzerland	A	World Cup Regional Stages	**W** 3-2	K.Smith 32, Aluko 34, Williams 50 (pen)
3	Oct 19	South Korea	A	Peace Cup	D 0-0	
4	21	New Zealand	N	Peace Cup	D 0-0	
5	Mar 2	Italy	N	Cyprus Cup	**W** 2-0	E.White 3, K.Smith 38 (pen)
6	4	Scotland	N	Cyprus Cup	L 0-2	
7	7	Canada	N	Cyprus Cup	L 0-2	
8	9	South Korea	N	Cyprus Cup	**W** 2-0	S.Smith 16,80
9	April 2	USA	H	Friendly	**W** 2-1	Clarke 8, Yankey 36
10	May 17	England	H	Friendly	**W** 2-0	J.Scott 46, Carney 70 (pen)
11	Jun 27	Mexico	N	World Cup Finals Grp B	D 1-1	Williams 21
12	July 1	New Zealand	N	World Cup Finals Grp B	**W** 2-1	J.Scott 63, Clarke 81
13	7	Japan	N	World Cup Finals Grp B	**W** 2-0	E.White 15, Yankey 66
14	9	France	N	World Cup Finals QF	D 1-1	J.Scott 59 (Lost 3-4 on penalties)

*This was Kelly Smith's 41st goal for England, a tally that saw her become the all-time leading goalscorer for the Women's National side.

ENGLAND'S SQUAD

(As at 09/07/2011)

	Club	Caps	Goals
GOALKEEPERS			
Karen Bardsley	New Jersey Sky Blue	17	0
Rachel Brown	Everton	73	0
Siobhan Chamberlain	Bristol Academy	18	0
DEFENDERS			
Sophie Bradley	Lincoln Ladies	8	0
Claire Rafferty	Chelsea	5	0
Alex Scott	Boston Breakers	81	12
Casey Stoney	Lincoln Ladies	92	4
Dunia Susi	Birmingham City	13	0
Rachel Unitt	Everton	93	7
Faye White	Arsenal	90	11
MIDFIELDERS			
Anita Asante	New Jersey Sky Blue	51	1
Laura Bassett	Birmingham City	20	0
Jess Clarke	Lincoln Ladies	27	7
Steph Houghton	Arsenal	17	1
Jill Scott	Everton	49	8
Fara Williams	Everton	95	35
Rachel Yankey	Arsenal	113	15
FORWARDS			
Eniola Aluko	New Jersey Sky Blue	58	11
Karen Carney	Birmingham City	64	11
Kelly Smith	Boston Breakers	108	43
Ellen White	Arsenal	18	6

NON-LEAGUE PUBLICATIONS

'Non-League Football' is a term that describes all of our national winter sport played beneath Divisions One and Two of the Football League.
It can justifiably claim to be representing 95% of English football and deserves the excellent Sunday newspaper that covers all aspects of
the competitions involved. We hope that our 'Directory' also serves this level of the game by supplying a creditable annual of its own and as you
can see below, the non-league game is well served by some excellent publications.

The Non-League Paper is about to publish its 600th edition and gives a wonderful coverage of the week's non-league football every Sunday for £1.50. Editor : David Emery
e-mail: nlp@greenwaysmedia.co.uk
web: www.non-leaguefootballpaper.com

The wonderful quarterly magazine **'Groundtastic'** (80 pages) gives a comprehensive review of all grounds old and new.
(email: editors@groundtastic.co.uk and website: www.groundtastic.co.uk).
Editors: Vince Taylor & Paul Claydon

'Non League Digest' (60 pages) gives a very thorough monthly round-up of features including all aspects of the game that interest groundhoppers.
(email: steveking@nonleaguedigest.com and website: www.nonleaguedigest.com).
Editor: Steve King.

'Non League Retrospect' The National Game History magazine (46 pages) is packed with fascinating historical facts and features.
(email: enquiries@3 books.co.uk and website: www.3 books.com)
Editors: Fred Hawthorn and Ronald Price.

The Football Traveller is a weekly publication giving you up to date details of fixtures from over a hundred competitions plus news and features on programmes and travel around the country.
(email: berrytft@googlemail.com and website: www.thefootballtraveller.co.uk)
Editor: Bill Berry.

Soccer History Magazine (56 pages) is a quarterly publication covering all aspects of the history of the game. Website: www.soccer-history.co.uk

The Football Trader and Collector Magazine (38 pages).
Monthly Magazine. Editor: Rob Budd (07871 539661) Website: www.thefootballtrader.co.uk

A New magazine to look out for, covering the north-east's non-league scene, is **Spirit of the North** the brainchild of Peter Mann and Neil Thaler.
They are hoping to have the magazine ready for launch very soon and will cover Gateshead, Darlington and York City in the Blue Square Premier, Blyth Spartans in the Blue Square North, Whitby Town in the Evo-Stik Premier and Durham City in the Evo-Stik North. There will also be coverage of the Northern League, Northern Alliance and Wearside Leagues, and much more. Throughout the season the magazine aims to include interviews, match reports, quality photos, statistics and historical articles from a wide range of writers both old and new.
To get a taster log on to: https://sites.google.com/site/nonleague1/

CLUB INDEX

CLUB INDEX

CLUB INDEX

CLUB INDEX

F

CLUB INDEX

CLUB INDEX

CLUB INDEX

CLUB INDEX

CLUB INDEX

CLUB INDEX